1 MONTH OF
FREE
READING

at
www.ForgottenBooks.com

By purchasing this book you are eligible for one month membership to ForgottenBooks.com, giving you unlimited access to our entire collection of over 1,000,000 titles via our web site and mobile apps.

To claim your free month visit:
www.forgottenbooks.com/free973472

ISBN 978-0-260-81865-2
PIBN 10973472

This is a Key-Numbered Volume

Each syllabus paragraph in this volume is marked with the topic and Key-Number section ⟵ under which the point will eventually appear in the American Digest System.

The lawyer is thus led from that syllabus to the exact place in the Digests where we, as digest makers, have placed the other cases on the same point—*This is the Key-Number Annotation.*

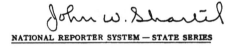

NATIONAL REPORTER SYSTEM — STATE SERIES

THE

SOUTHWESTERN REPORTER

VOLUME 231

PERMANENT EDITION

COMPRISING ALL THE CURRENT DECISIONS OF THE

SUPREME AND APPELLATE COURTS OF ARKANSAS
KENTUCKY, MISSOURI, TENNESSEE
AND TEXAS

WITH KEY-NUMBER ANNOTATIONS

JULY 6 — AUGUST 10, 1921

ST. PAUL
WEST PUBLISHING CO.
1921

JUDGES

OF THE COURTS REPORTED DURING THE PERIOD COVERED BY THIS VOLUME

ARKANSAS

Supreme Court

CHIEF JUSTICE
EDGAR A. McCULLOCH

ASSOCIATE JUSTICES
CARROLL D. WOOD
JESSE C. HART
FRANK G. SMITH
THOMAS H. HUMPHREYS

KENTUCKY

Court of Appeals

CHIEF JUSTICE
ROLLIN HURT

ASSOCIATE JUSTICES
ERNEST S. CLARKE
GUS THOMAS
FLEM D. SAMPSON
WARNER E. SETTLE
HUSTON QUIN
WILLIAM ROGERS CLAY

COMMISSIONER OF APPEALS
C. C. TURNER

MISSOURI

Supreme Court

CHIEF JUSTICE
ROBERT F. WALKER [1]
JAMES T. BLAIR [2]

Division No. 1.

PRESIDING JUDGE
ARCHELAUS M. WOODSON

ASSOCIATE JUDGES
JAMES T. BLAIR [2]
WALLER W. GRAVES
CONWAY ELDER

SUPREME COURT COMMISSIONERS
STEPHEN S. BROWN
WILLIAM T. RAGLAND
CHARLES E. SMALL

Division No. 2

PRESIDING JUDGE
EDWARD HIGBEE

ASSOCIATE JUDGES
ROBERT F. WALKER
DAVID E. BLAIR

SUPREME COURT COMMISSIONERS
ROBERT T. RAILEY
JOHN TURNER WHITE
NORMAN A. MOZLEY [3]
ALBERT L. REEVES [4]

St. Louis Court of Appeals

PRESIDING JUDGE
WILLIAM H. ALLEN

ASSOCIATE JUDGES
WM. DEE BECKER
CHARLES H. DAUES

MISSOURI (Continued)

St. Louis Court of Appeals (C't'd)

COURT OF APPEALS COMMISSIONERS
DAVIS BIGGS
SIMON G. NIPPER
THEODORE C. BRUERE

Kansas City Court of Appeals

PRESIDING JUDGE
FRANCIS H. TRIMBLE

ASSOCIATE JUDGES
EWING C. BLAND
HENRY L. ARNOLD

Springfield Court of Appeals

PRESIDING JUDGE
ARGUS COX

ASSOCIATE JUDGES
JOHN S. FARRINGTON
JOHN H. BRADLEY

TENNESSEE

Supreme Court

CHIEF JUSTICE
DAVID L. LANSDEN

ASSOCIATE JUSTICES
GRAFTON GREEN
COLIN P. McKINNEY
FRANK P. HALL
NATHAN L. BACHMAN

TEXAS

Supreme Court

CHIEF JUSTICE
NELSON PHILLIPS

ASSOCIATE JUSTICES
THOMAS B. GREENWOOD
WILLIAM PIERSON

Commission of Appeals

Section A

PRESIDING JUDGE
WILLIAM M. TAYLOR

JUDGES
FRENCH SPENCER
JESSE N. GALLAGHER

Section B

PRESIDING JUDGE
JAMES W. McCLENDON

JUDGES
NORMAN G. KITTRELL, SR.
BEN H. POWELL

Court of Criminal Appeals

PRESIDING JUDGE
WRIGHT C. MORROW

JUDGES
OFFA S. LATTIMORE
FRANK LEE HAWKINS

TEXAS (Continued)

Courts of Civil Appeals

First District

CHIEF JUSTICE
ROBERT A. PLEASANTS

ASSOCIATE JUSTICES
CHARLES E. LANE
GEORGE W. GRAVES

Second District

CHIEF JUSTICE
TRUMAN H. CONNER

ASSOCIATE JUSTICES
IRBY DUNKLIN
RAYMOND H. BUCK

Third District

CHIEF JUSTICE
WILLIAM M. KEY

ASSOCIATE JUSTICES
CHARLES H. JENKINS
JOHN W. BRADY

Fourth District

CHIEF JUSTICE
WILLIAM S. FLY

ASSOCIATE JUSTICES
THOMAS D. COBBS
EDWARD W. SMITH

Fifth District

CHIEF JUSTICE
ANSON RAINEY

ASSOCIATE JUSTICES
JAMES M. TALBOT [5]
DEXTER HAMILTON

Sixth District

CHIEF JUSTICE
SAMUEL P. WILLSON

ASSOCIATE JUSTICES
RICHARD B. LEVY
WILLIAM HODGES

Seventh District

CHIEF JUSTICE
STERLING P. HUFF

ASSOCIATE JUSTICES
ROBERT W. HALL
WILLIAM BOYCE

Eighth District

CHIEF JUSTICE
JAMES R. HARPER

ASSOCIATE JUSTICES
ERASTUS F. HIGGINS
ANDERSON M. WALTHALL

Ninth District

PRESIDING JUDGE
LEWIS B. HIGHTOWER, JR.

ASSOCIATE JUSTICES
WILLIAM B. O'QUINN
DANIEL WALKER

[1] Term as Chief Justice expired June 7, 1921.
[2] Elected Chief Justice to take effect June 7, 1921.
[3] Resigned April 19, 1921.
[4] Elected to take effect July 1, 1921.
[5] Died July 25, 1921.

CASES REPORTED

See End of Index for Tables of Southwestern Cases in State Reports

THE

SOUTHWESTERN REPORTER

VOLUME 231

TOWNSEND v. STATE. (No. 333.)

(Supreme Court of Arkansas. May 16, 1921.
Rehearing Denied June 6, 1921.)

1. Criminal law ⬤⟲511(6) — Evidence of defendant's possession of property offered for sale held sufficient to corroborate accomplice witnesses.

In a prosecution for burglary and larceny of meat, evidence as to defendant, who was not in the meat business, having smoked meat for sale or trade, in view of the circumstances, *held* sufficient corroboration of the testimony of defendant's accomplices to satisfy the requirements of Crawford & Moses' Dig. § 3181, that accomplice's testimony be corroborated as to identifying defendant with the crime.

2. Burglary ⬤⟲41(1) — Larceny ⬤⟲55 — In a prosecution for burglary and larceny, evidence held sufficient to sustain conviction.

In a prosecution for burglary and grand larceny of meat from a box car in the nighttime, evidence *held* sufficient to sustain conviction.

Appeal from Circuit Court, Chicot County; Turner Butler, Judge.

Leroy Townsend was convicted of burglary and grand larceny. From judgments of conviction, he appeals. Affirmed.

N. B. Scott, of Lake Village, for appellant.
J. S. Utley, Atty. Gen., and Elbert Godwin and W. T. Hammock, Asst. Attys. Gen., for the State.

HUMPHREYS, J. Appellant was indicted, tried, and convicted in the Chicot circuit court for the crimes of burglary and grand larceny, committed by breaking and entering a box car in the nighttime, and taking from the possession of the Missouri Pacific Railroad Company meat of the value of $150, and his punishment was assessed for the former at five years in the penitentiary, and for the latter at two years. From the judgments of conviction, an appeal has been duly prosecuted to this court.

The convictions were procured on the testimony of St. Clair Crane and Sam Lynch, accomplices in the alleged crimes, Fred Morris and C. W. Tillman, agent and clerk, respectively, of the Missouri Pacific Railroad Company, Tom Baker, and Harry Donaldson.

The evidence disclosed that, on the night of December 5, 1920, four cases of wrapped bacon, weighing about 500 pounds, manufactured by the Independence Packing Company of Kansas City, Mo., of the value of 20 cents per pound, were stolen from a sealed car at Eudora, Ark., same being in the possession of the Missouri Pacific Railroad Company. The accomplices testified, in substance, that they, in connection with Clarence Snell and appellant, broke the seal of a box car at Eudora, Chicot county, Ark., on the night of December 5, 1920, and stole meat of the value of about $100.

Tom Baker testified that, in the month of December, appellant tried to sell him some meat; and Harry Donaldson, in the same month appellant tried to swap him some smoked meat for meal. The evidence disclosed that appellant was not a dealer in meats.

[1, 2] Appellant contends that the evidence of the accomplices in the crimes is not sufficiently corroborated to warrant the conviction, under Crawford & Moses' Digest, § 3181, which is as follows:

"A conviction cannot be had in any case of felony upon the testimony of an accomplice, unless corroborated by other evidence tending to connect the defendant with the commission of the offense; and the corroboration is not sufficient if it merely shows that the offense was committed, and the circumstances thereof. Provided, in misdemeanor cases a conviction may be had upon the testimony of an accomplice."

This court said, in the case of Vaughan v. State, 58 Ark. 353, 24 S. W. 885, in construing the statute in relation to felonies, that the corroborating evidence "must relate to material facts which go to the identity of defendant in connection with the crime." The corroborating evidence in the instant case is to the effect that, near about the time the offenses were committed, appellant was attempting to sell or trade smoked meat. Appellant was not engaged in the meat business. It was too early in the season for farmers, or others who had killed hogs in the fall, to have smoked meat for sale. It is a matter of common knowledge that wrapped bacon, put up by manufacturing houses, has been smoked, and, at that season of the year, is the only kind of smoked meat on the market. We think the corroborating evidence was of a substantial character, independent of the statement of the accomplices, tending to connect the defendant with the commission of the crimes. The evidence in the whole case was therefore sufficient to sustain the conviction.

No error appearing, the judgment is affirmed.

ROBINSON v. STATE. (No. 11.)

(Supreme Court of Arkansas. May 23, 1921.)

1. **Criminal law** ⬅️407(2), 419, 420(11), 1169(12)—**Conversation between mother of prosecutrix in rape case inadmissible as hearsay, not effecting an admission by silence.**

In a prosecution for rape on a stepdaughter, resulting in a conviction of assault with intent, where prosecutrix after the offense informed her mother she was going to leave home, and her mother replied, "You are no better than your other sister," such statement made by the mother to the prosecutrix, near enough for the jury to find that defendant heard it, was not competent as an admission of defendant that he had been guilty of improper conduct with the other sister, not having called for denial by him, and was hearsay and incompetent, and its admission constituted error prejudicial to defendant.

2. **Criminal law** ⬅️789(12)—**Instruction defining reasonable doubt as one on which person would be willing to act in everyday walks of life erroneous.**

In a prosecution for rape, resulting in conviction of assault with intent, instruction defining reasonable doubt as one on which the jury would be willing to act in any manner confronting them in the everyday walks of life was erroneous, as the definition was broad enough to include the trivial affairs of life; it should have been limited to the important or grave affairs of life.

3. **Criminal law** ⬅️844(2)—**General objection reaches inherent defect, as improper definition of reasonable doubt.**

A general objection to an instruction will reach an inherent defect therein, as an improper definition of reasonable doubt.

Appeal from Circuit Court, Clay County; R. E. L. Johnson, Judge.

Oscar Robinson was convicted of assault with intent to commit rape, and he appeals. Judgment reversed, and cause remanded.

Oliver & Oliver, of Corning, for appellant. J. S. Utley, Atty. Gen., and Elbert Godwin and W. T. Hammock, Asst. Attys. Gen., for the State.

HUMPHREYS, J. Appellant was indicted and tried for rape at the January, 1921, term of the Clay circuit court, Western district, Second division, and convicted for an assault with intent to commit rape, his punishment being fixed at imprisonment in the state penitentiary for five years. From that judgment is this appeal.

[1] The prosecuting witness is a stepdaughter of appellant, and resided in his home, near Corning, at the time it is alleged the offense was committed. She testified that, on the morning of July 11, 1920, while her mother was milking at the water gap, about 100 yards from the house, appellant forcibly obtained carnal knowledge of her; that when her mother returned to the house she was in the kitchen, and appellant in the adjoining room fumbling with a trunk; that there was no door between the two rooms; that her mother asked why the house had not been cleaned, and she answered by saying, "You ought to make your man leave me alone;" that she then informed her mother she was going to leave home, and her mother replied, "You are no better than your other sister." The statement made by Mrs. Robinson to her daughter, near enough for the jury to have found that appellant heard it, was admitted in evidence, over the proper objection and exception of appellant, and appellant now insists that the court committed reversible error in allowing the statement to go to the jury. The statement, standing alone, and disconnected from evidence subsequently adduced, did not imply a charge against appellant that he had been guilty of similar conduct toward the other sister. Appellant was not called upon, therefore, to make a denial, even if he heard the statement. The statement was not, therefore, competent evidence as an admission of appellant that he had been guilty of conduct with the other sister similar to that now charged against him. The statement, however, was purely hearsay evidence, and clearly incompetent on that ground. The admission of it constituted reversible error, if prejudicial to the cause of appellant. We think it clearly prejudicial when considered in connection with the evidence introduced later, tending to show a sexual intimacy between appellant and the other sister.

[2] Appellant also contends that the court erred in giving instruction No. 12, upon reasonable doubt, which is as follows:

"The burden is upon the state to establish its case to your satisfaction beyond a reasonable doubt. This is a wise and sane provision of our law, which is designed in no case to enable any guilty person to escape just punishment, but, on the contrary, to shield and protect the innocent from unjust conviction. It means simply that if, after a consideration of all the facts and circumstances adduced in

---

proof in the case, there naturally arises in your minds a substantial doubt as to the guilt of the defendant, then it will be your duty to acquit him. It is not a far-fetched or chimerical doubt to be conjured up for the purpose of enabling a guilty man to escape just punishment, but a reasonable doubt means a doubt that is reasonable, and one upon which you yourselves would be willing to act in any matter with which you might be confronted in the everyday walks of life."

A reasonable doubt is defined in this instruction as one upon which a person would be willing to act in a matter confronting him in the everyday walks of life. This definition is broad enough to include the trivial affairs of life, and for that reason is inherently wrong. It should have been limited to the important or grave affairs of life. In trivial affairs of life, one would act upon a high degree of probability; whereas, in important or grave affairs, he would want to know to a moral certainty before acting. In the case of Byrd v. State, 69 Ark. 537, 64 S. W. 270, this court condemned an instruction which told the jury that "A moral certainty signifies only a high degree of probability;" and further said that—

"A high degree of probability is not sufficient; for the jury might think there was a high degree of probability that the defendant is guilty, and yet think there is a reasonable doubt as to his guilt from the evidence in the case."

[3] The objection to the instruction was general, but a general objection will reach an inherent defect, such as we find here. The court committed reversible error in thus defining reasonable doubt.

Other assignments of error are insisted upon for reversal, but we deem it unnecessary to discuss them, as some are not well taken and others will not likely recur upon a new trial.

For the errors indicated, the judgment is reversed, and the cause remanded for a new trial.

PORTER v. VAIL. (No. 10.)

(Supreme Court of Arkansas. May 23, 1921.)

Landlord and tenant ⇐=326(1)—Rent agreement held not to include volunteer hay crop, but only cultivated grains.

A written contract renting land construed as not including a volunteer hay crop, but only cultivated grain crops which were to have been divided in the proportion of two-thirds to tenant and one-third to landlord and for which the parties were to furnish the seed in the same proportion.

Appeal from Circuit Court, Woodruff County; J. M. Jackson, Judge.

Actions by M. A. Porter against Frank M. Vail in unlawful detainer and in replevin. Judgments for defendant, and plaintiff appealed. The appeals were considered together. Judgment in each case reversed and remanded, with directions to enter judgment in each case for the appellant.

Jonas F. Dyson, of Cotton Plant, for appellant.

Ross Mathis, of Cotton Plant, for appellee.

HUMPHREYS, J. The appeals are briefed separately, but the issue involved on each appeal is between the same parties, and dependent upon a construction of the same contract, so one opinion will suffice in the two cases.

No. 6721 is an action of unlawful detainer for the possession of a farm, and No. 6722 a suit in replevin for 266 bales of hay cut and removed from the farm.

The issues joined in the first action are whether appellee was unlawfully evicted from the premises, and, if so, the extent of the damages sustained by him on account of the loss of the volunteer hay crop upon the farm, resulting from the eviction.

The issue joined in the second action involved the title to 266 bales of hay which appellee cut and removed from the premises to a barn in the nearby town of Hunter, before the eviction.

The causes were submitted upon the pleadings and evidence, at the conclusion of which both appellant and appellee asked for a peremptory instruction in the first case, which resulted in a directed verdict and judgment in that case for appellee for damages to the amount of $500; and, in the second case, a directed verdict on the court's own motion in favor of appellee for the hay, or its value, $266.

From the judgment in each case, an appeal has been duly prosecuted to this court.

The evidence in the two cases is, in substance, as follows: In January, 1919, appellant verbally leased appellee the farm in question for the year, to raise rice, cotton, corn, and peanuts, for a stipulated rental of one-third of the crops. Appellee failed to comply with the verbal contract, and, on the 1st day of June, 1920, the following written contract was entered into between the parties, to wit:

"Contract by M. A. Porter, first party, and F. M. Vail, second party.

"I, M. A. Porter, party of the first part, agree to lease all farming land in section 20, township 5 north, range 1 west, not in cultivation in rice in the past year, 1919, A. D., to be farmed in corn, peanuts and all grain and crops, and party of the first part agrees to furnish one-third of all seed planted on said land.

"Party of the second part, F. M. Vail, hereby agrees to furnish two-thirds of all seed planted, also plant, cultivate, harvest and deliver in barn or wareroom one-third all crops grown on said land.

"Party of the second part, F. M. Vail, also agrees to vacate residence on said land at any time with ten days' notice from party of the first part, M. A. Porter.

"M. A. Porter.
"Frank M. Vail.

"Hunter, Arkansas, June 1, 1919."

Appellee did not plant or cultivate the land leased. He remained in possession, however, and in August harvested about 25 acres of wild grass which grew on the land that should have been cultivated. He baled and removed 266 bales of the hay to a barn in Hunter, and, according to the evidence of appellee hauled one load of the third left in shocks upon the ground to the baler, when he was told by appellant not to touch any more of the hay. Appellee left the rest of the hay upon the ground, and, in obedience to the written notice from appellant and the writ issued in the unlawful detainer action, moved off of the premises. There was an estimate of 1,500 bales of hay, cut and standing, left upon the ground. It would have cost $500 to harvest it, and its value in the bale would have been about $1,500.

The sole question presented by this appeal is whether the court erred in construing the contract to include the volunteer hay crop. Appellee's contention is that the contract had relation to all crops grown on the leased land, whether volunteer or cultivated crops. We think the contract entirely unambiguous and that such crops as were to be harvested and divided in the proportion of two-thirds to one-third were crops to be planted and cultivated by appellee. It was specified in the contract that the landlord should furnish one-third and the tenant two-thirds of the seed to be planted, and the only kinds of crops mentioned were peanut, corn, and other grain crops. Reading the contract as an entirety, it is apparent that the parties had in contemplation crops to be planted and cultivated, not volunteer crops. The contract did not embrace uncultivated grass grown on lands which should have been cultivated. Under the undisputed facts, the court should have directed a verdict in each case for appellant.

For the error indicated, the judgment in each case is reversed and remanded, with directions to enter a judgment in each case for appellant.

BERGER v. JONESBORO MOTOR CO. (No. 5.)

(Supreme Court of Arkansas. May 23, 1921.)

Sales ⊄⊃77(2)—Buyer of automobile held not obligated to pay costs of transporting car to city of purchase.

Where the contract for the purchase of an automobile read that the car was sold f. o. b. the city of purchase, and there was an understanding between the buyer and seller that if there was an advance in price at the factory, and the car cost the seller more money, the buyer would have to pay it, the parties did not have in mind that there might be an increase in the cost of the car on account of transportation charges, and the buyer was not liable for the cost of bringing the car from the factory to the city of purchase.

Appeal from Circuit Court, Craighead County; R. H. Dudley, Judge.

Action by the Jonesboro Motor Company against J. M. Berger. From judgment for plaintiff, defendant appeals. Reversed, and cause dismissed.

Sloan & Sloan, of Jonesboro, for appellant. Lamb & Frierson, of Jonesboro, for appellee.

WOOD, J. This suit was instituted by the appellee against the appellant to recover the possession of a certain automobile which is described in the complaint and affidavit for replevin. The appellee alleged that it was the owner and entitled to the immediate possession of the automobile. The complaint and the affidavit contained the usual allegations in replevin. The appellant answered denying all the material allegations of the complaint and set up that he purchased the car of the appellee for the sum of $1,650; that he made tender of payment as contemplated by the contract, and that the appellee demanded of appellant $100 in excess of the contract price; that it was the understanding that if the Buick Automobile Company raised the factory price of the car in controversy $100 before the same could be delivered to the appellant, then the appellant was to pay this additional sum, but the appellant alleged that the appellee procured the car from the factory at the market price existing on the day of appellant's purchase.

J. R. Lane testified that he was the manager of the appellee on March 29, 1920. He exhibited the contract between appellant and the appellee under which the car was purchased, which contained, among others, the following provision:

"In case this car costs the Jonesboro Motor Company $100.00 more, J. M. Berger will pay same."

Witness testified:

"We signed up this contract and I told him that it would cost more money; that the factory would raise the price the first of April and he said that would be all right, and he signed up the contract like I wrote it. He saw me write this (the above provision) in the contract."

Witness further testified substantially that the above provision meant in case the car cost appellee $100 more to get the car to Jonesboro, which witness said it did, as follows: He and three others went to Flint, Mich., and drove the cars from there to Lima, Ohio, a distance of 200 miles, and witness paid the expenses, which made it cost appellee more than $100 to get the car to Jonesboro. Witness had in mind in entering into the contract two prices—the delivered price and the cost to witness. The delivered price was the price to the man who bought. The cost provision in the contract meant that the delivered price would have been less than $1,700. The testimony of witness showed that the appellant had complied with the contract, except that appellant was only willing to pay $1,650 for the car at Jonesboro, whereas the appellee was unwilling to accept less than $1,750.

Another witness testified that he heard the discussion between Lane and the appellant at the time of the execution of the contract regarding the $100, and that the agreement between them was that if the car cost the appellee $100 more than the factory price, appellant was to pay that additional amount.

The appellant testified in substance that the provision in the contract above quoted meant the advanced price of the car and the price was supposed to advance about April 1st. Lane told appellant that there would be an advance at that time. He said he had several cars bought at the old price, and if this car cost him more money, appellant would have to pay it. There was nothing said at the time the deal was made about some fellows being sent up to Flint to drive the car back. Witness told Lane that he did not want his car driven at all. Witness wanted the car shipped from the factory to Jonesboro. When the car arrived Lane did not say a word with reference to the increase in the factory price. When witness went to settle with Lane, Lane said witness would have to pay him $100 more. Witness asked Lane if it cost him more, and he said, "No"; that he got it at the old price, but it cost him $100 more on the car to get it to Jonesboro, and he was charging appellant that much more. Witness told Lane that such was not the contract. Witness bought the car f. o. b. Jonesboro.

The above are substantially the facts upon which the appellant asked the court to instruct the jury to return a verdict in his favor, which the court refused. The court, instead, instructed the jury in effect that if the provision in the contract was intended by the parties to cover either an advance in the cost of the car or expense incurred by the appellee in procuring and delivering the car, they should return a verdict in favor of the appellee and fix the value of the car at $1,750. On the other hand, if the parties intended the above provision to cover only the advance, if any, in the price of the car, then

the jury would fix the value of the car at $1,650. The jury returned a verdict in favor of the appellee fixing the value of the car at $1,750, and judgment was rendered in favor of appellee, from which is this appeal.

The court erred in refusing to instruct the jury to return a verdict in favor of the appellant. The undisputed evidence showed that the price of the automobile was f. o. b. Jonesboro; that it was the custom of automobile factories to quote the price of their automobiles f. o. b. city of purchase. The testimony of Lane, the manager of the appellee at Jonesboro, as well as the testimony of the appellant, shows that when this contract was entered into the parties had in mind that there would be an advance in the factory price of cars about the first of April. This was clearly the meaning of Lane's language when he said:

"I told him that it would cost more money; that the factory would raise the price the first of April."

Berger also said:

"Russell told me there would be an advance in the price of the car the first of April. He said he had several cars bought at the old price, and if this car cost him more money, I would have to pay it."

When the provision of the contract quoted is construed in the light of this undisputed evidence of the intention of the parties, it is absolutely unambiguous, and the court erred in submitting it to the jury for construction, but should have construed it to mean that the appellant was to pay an additional $100 to the contract price of $1,650 in case the factory advanced the price to the appellee; that is, in the event appellee had to pay the factory $100 more, then the appellant should pay the advanced price to the extent of $100. The price of the car was fixed f. o. b. Jonesboro and showed that the parties did not have in mind at the time the contract was entered into that there might be any increase in the cost of the car to appellee on account of transportation charges. The provision under review was clearly intended to cover the advance price of $100, which the parties contemplated at the time the appellee might have to pay the factory. It was not intended to cover any additional cost or expense that appellee might have to incur in order to deliver the car f. o. b. Jonesboro.

"Where the terms of a written contract are unambiguous in the light of the undisputed evidence, it is the duty of the court to construe it." Capitol Food Co. v. Mode & Clayton, 112 Ark. 165, 165 S. W. 637; Starnes v. Boyle, 101 Ark. 469, 142 S. W. 1143; and other cases cited in 2 Crawford's Digest, Contract, § 81.

Now, the undisputed evidence shows that the factory price of the car in controversy at the time of its purchase was $1,595 with war tax added. The factory did not advance the price, and the undisputed evidence shows that the appellee did not have to ·pay $100 more on account of the advance in factory price to it. On the contrary, Lane testified that the car cost him $1,650 counting in his profit. He added the $100 because it cost him more than that to get it to Jonesboro.

For the error in refusing to give the appellant's instruction No. 1, the judgment is reversed, and the cause is dismissed.

JOHNSON et al. v. HAMLEN et al. (No. 8.)

(Supreme Court of Arkansas. May 23, 1921.)

1. Municipal corporations ⟐323(3)—Demurrer to answer in action attacking organization of improvement districts held properly overruled.

In an action wherein it was claimed that an improvement district for the purpose of grading, curbing, and guttering certain streets and another improvement district for the purpose of paving the same streets, boundaries of which were identical and coterminus, were created for but one improvement, court did not err in overruling a demurrer to answer of members of the board of improvement wherein they denied that the improvements were in their nature essentially a single improvement and alleged that the streets could be graded, drained, curbed, and guttered, and it would be one complete improvement, and that the second district providing for the paving was in itself a complete improvement, and that either could be done without the other, and that the cost of neither would exceed 20 per cent. of the value of the land in the district.

2. Municipal corporations ⟐450(2)—Mistake in description of boundaries of improvement district in notice held unimportant.

Mistake in last call in description of boundaries of improvement district in notice in newspaper, reading "thence north north fifty-one degrees west 50 feet to point of beginning," instead of "thence north forty-one degrees west 50 feet to point of beginning," such call being from one known point to another known point and a line drawn between such two points completing the district, was immaterial.

Appeal from Pulaski Chancery Court; Jno. E. Martineau, Chancellor.

Action by Willis W. Johnson and others against J. R. Hamlen and others, constituting the Board of Improvement for Street Improvement Districts Nos. 274 and 275 of Little Rock. Demurrer to answer overruled, and plaintiffs appeal. Affirmed.

S. L. White, of Little Rock, for appellants. Wallace Townsend, of Little Rock, for appellees.

SMITH, J. The complaint in this cause contained the following allegations: That appellees constituted the board of improvement for street improvement districts Nos. 274 and 275 of Little Rock, and that appellants, who were the plaintiffs below, are owners of real property within the boundaries of each of said districts; that said district No. 274 was created for the purpose of grading, draining, curbing, and guttering certain streets, more particularly described in the ordinance creating same; that district No. 275 was established on the same day for the purpose of paving the same streets; that the petitions for the two districts were circulated at the same time, were signed by the same petitioners, and were a part of the same movement for the improvement; that the boundaries of the districts were identical and coterminous, and that the streets to be graded, drained, curbed, and guttered in district 274 were the identical streets to be paved in district 275, and that both districts were created for but one improvement, the grading, etc., being a portion of the street and an essential part of the paving; that the paving could not be done except without the grading, draining, curbing, and guttering; that the organization of the two districts for the one improvement was in violation of the law; that the cost of the improvement would be in excess of 20 per cent. of the value of the real estate within the boundaries of the district.

It was further alleged that the ordinance creating district 275, as passed by the city council, correctly described a portion of the district as "thence north forty-one degrees west fifty feet to point of beginning," but in the publication of the ordinance in the newspaper said portion of the district is erroneously described in the preamble to section 1 as "thence north north fifty-one degrees west fifty feet to point of beginning," and was erroneously described in section 1 of the ordinance as "thence north fifty-one degrees west fifty feet to point of beginning."

The complaint further alleged that the law required the city clerk to publish the ordinance in some newspaper within 20 days; but the notice published was no notice, as one could not ascertain the boundaries of the district on account of the error in description set out above.

The commissioners answered, and denied that the improvements contemplated were in their nature essentially a single improvement. They alleged that the streets could ·be graded, drained, curbed, and guttered, and it would be one complete improvement; that the second district provided for the paving, which was in itself a complete improvement; and that either improvement could be done without the other, and that the cost of neither district would exceed 20 per cent. of the value of the land in the district.

⟐For other cases see same topic and KEY-NUMBER in all Key-Numbered Digests and Indexes

A demurrer to this answer was overruled, and the plaintiffs have appealed.

[1] On the question of the identity of the improvement, the case is controlled by the case of Bottrell v. Hollipeter, 135 Ark. 315, 204 S. W. 843. The question here raised was there decided, and the question arose in that case, as in this, on demurrer.

It was contended in the case of Bottrell v. Hollipeter, supra, that the opinion of this court in the case of Board of Improvement v. Brun, 105 Ark. 65, 150 S. W. 154, was controlling, and that therefore the separate districts petitioned for could not be organized. But the court distinguished the cases on the facts and said:

"Appellant cites and relies upon the case of Improvement District v. Brun, supra, as authority for his contention, that the districts herein challenged were created to complete what was in fact but a single improvement. The case does not support appellant's contention. There was no allegation that the underground drainage was unnecessary and not incident to the work of paving. But here the allegations of fact in the answer are that 'the storm-sewers are not an essential part of the pavement but are entirely separate.' That 'the pavement could be made without the storm-sewer.' * * * That 'the curbing is no part of the paving, * * * nor is the gutter an essential part of the pavement.' These allegations were properly pleaded and the demurrer to the answer admitted the truth of them. * * *

"The petition of the property owners for, and the ordinance pursuant thereto creating the two districts, are at least prima facie evidence that the petitioners and the town council considered that the improvements provided for did not constitute a 'single' improvement, as designated in the statute. The facts stated in the answer and admitted by the demurrer of appellant to be true show that they were not essentially one improvement."

[2] The objection to the description is not well taken. The description complained of began at a fixed known point, and was given to another known point, which was 50 feet from the point of beginning. This last call in the description—the one complained of—should have read, "Thence north forty-one degrees west fifty feet to point of beginning." Instead, it read, "thence north north forty-one degrees west fifty feet to point of beginning." This discrepancy is unimportant. As we have said, the last call was from one known point to another known point, and a line drawn between those two points completed the boundary. This last boundary line was only 50 feet in length, and any discrepancy in the notice as published as to the number of degrees west of north which this line would run in connecting the two fixed points is immaterial, as both course and distance yield to fixed monuments in land surveying. Doe v. Porter, 3 Ark. 18, 36 Am. Dec. 448; Harrell v. Hill, 19 Ark. 102, 68

Am. Dec. 202; Brown v. Hardin, 21 Ark. 324; Chapman & Dewey Lbr. Co. v. Levee Dist., 100 Ark. 94, 139 S. W. 625; Scott v. Dunkle Box & Lbr. Co., 106 Ark. 83, 152 S. W. 1025; Paschal v. Swepston, 120 Ark. 230, 179 S. W. 339.

Decree affirmed.

FARMERS' BANK & TRUST CO. v. FARMERS' STATE BANK OF BROOKPORT. (No. 4.)

(Supreme Court of Arkansas. May 23, 1921.)

Banks and banking ⟨⟩149 — Bank drawing cashier's check on which payee's indorsement was forged entitled to recover from other bank which paid on such indorsement.

Where plaintiff bank issued its cashier's check, payable to its customer moving to another point, and put it in the mail properly addressed to him at such other point, but it never reached him, and was presented to defendant bank by a negro, who forged the payee's indorsement and received part of the funds called for, leaving the rest on deposit, and defendant bank indorsed the check on the back with a guaranty of all prior indorsements, and transmitted it to plaintiff bank for payment, which was made, plaintiff bank, after discovery of the forgery, could recover from defendant bank the amount paid.

Appeal from Circuit Court, Mississippi County; R. H. Dudley, Judge.

Action by the Farmers' State Bank of Brookport against the Farmers' Bank & Trust Company. From judgment for plaintiff, defendant appeals. Affirmed.

Davis, Costen & Harrison, of Blytheville, for appellant.

W. D. Gravette, of Blytheville, for appellee.

WOOD, J. This cause was submitted to the trial court, sitting as a jury upon an agreed statement of facts, as follows:

On or about December 1, 1919, J. W. Neely, a former citizen and resident of Brookport, Ill., and a patron of the Farmers' State Bank, the plaintiff herein, emigrated to Arkansas, and located near Blytheville, his correct post office address being "Blytheville, Ark., R. F. D. No. 1." Before leaving Illinois, he had disposed of some property there, and on the 4th day of December, 1919, the plaintiff bank issued its cashier's check, payable to J. W. Neely, for the sum of $540.85, which was put in the mail properly addressed to him at Blytheville, Ark., R. F. D. No. 1. The check never reached the person for whom it was intended, but was presented to defendant bank between the 4th and 13th of December, 1919, by a person, a negro, who represented himself to be J. W. Neely, and who indorsed the name "J. W. Neely" upon said check, without the consent or authority of the person for whom said check was intended. That the person presenting said check received from the defendant bank the sum of $140.85 in cash, and left the balance of $400 on deposit in said bank to the credit of J. W. Neely. That after receiving said check as above, the defendant bank indorsed said check on the back, as follows:

"Pay to the order of any bank, banker, or trust company, all prior indorsements guaranteed. Farmers' Bank & Trust Company, Blytheville, Arkansas, H. E. Barnett, Cashier."

Defendant bank then transmitted same to plaintiff bank for payment, which was made on December 13, 1919. Upon learning that said check had not reached the hands for which it was intended, the defendant bank paid over the $400 left on deposit to plaintiff bank, but refused to pay over the sum of $140.85, the amount paid upon presentation of said check; and this suit is by plaintiff bank to recover that sum.

It is further agreed that, upon receipt of information that the party for whom the said check was intended had never received same, plaintiff bank immediately wrote defendant bank, advising it that said indorsement was a forgery, but that said letter was not received by defendant bank, and that plaintiff bank had paid to the person who purchased said cashier's check the amount represented thereby.

The finding and judgment of the court was in favor of the appellee, from which is this appeal.

Learned counsel for appellant rely upon the case of State Bank v. Cumberland Savings & Trust Co., 168 N. C. 605, 85 S. E. 5, L. R. A. 1915D, 1138; Bank of St. Albans v. Farmers' & Mechanics' Bank, 10 Vt. 141, 33 Am. Dec. 188.

The first of the above cases is comparatively recent, the opinion having been rendered by the Supreme Court of North Carolina in 1915. The facts and the law announced as applicable thereto, reported in the syllabus to that case in 168 N. C. 605, 85 S. E. 5, L. R. A. 1915D, 1138, are as follows:

"Plaintiff bank, which, in the course of business, received through another bank a check purporting to be drawn on it, and indorsed by a third person, whose signatures were both forged, and which had been cashed by defendant bank, in reliance upon the indorsement, 'All prior indorsements guaranteed,' and the custom to take such checks relying upon the exercise of due diligence on the part of the bank first cashing it, could not recover the amount paid on the forged check, as it should know the signature of the drawer, its own depositor."

This doctrine has no application to the facts of this record. Here its cashier's check made the appellee both the drawer and the drawee. In this case the drawee was not required to know the signatures of the indorsers. To apply the doctrine of State Bank v. Cumberland Savings & Trust Co., supra, to the facts of this record would be to ignore a wholesome principle of natural justice and equity which has also been thoroughly established as a rule of law, to wit: That, as between two innocent parties to a transaction which must result in financial loss, the loss must fall upon that one whose acts contributed most to produce it. The principle is well expressed in the case of Danvers Bank v. Salem Bank, 151 Mass. 280, 24 N. E. 44, 21 Am. St. Rep. 450, as follows:

"Where a loss which must be borne by one of two parties alike innocent of the forgery can be traced to the neglect or fault of either, it is reasonable that it should be borne by him, even if innocent of any intentional fraud, through whose means it has succeeded. * * * To entitle the holder to retain money obtained by a forgery, he should be able to maintain that the whole responsibility of determining the validity of the signature was placed upon the drawee, and that the vigilance of the drawee was not lessened, and that he was not lulled into a false security by any disregard of duty on his own part, or by the failure of any precautions which, from his implied assertion in presenting the check as a sufficient voucher, the drawee had a right to believe he had taken. * * * When this check was forwarded by the defendant for redemption, the plaintiff was without the means it would have had if it had been presented at its own counter of ascertaining the character of the person offering it. It had a right to believe that the defendant, in cashing a check purporting to be drawn by one not its own customer, or entitled to draw upon it, had by the usual and proper investigation satisfied itself of its authenticity. The indorsement, which was not necessary to the transfer of the check, was a guaranty of the signature of the drawer, and the plaintiff had a right to believe that the indorser was known to the defendant by proper inquiry."

See, also, People's Bank v. Franklin Bank, 88 Tenn. 299, 12 S. W. 716, 6 L. R. A. 724, 17 Am. St. Rep. 884; Farmers' National Bank of Augusta v. Farmers' & Traders' Bank of Maysville, 159 Ky. 141, 166 S. W. 986, L. R. A. 1915A, 77; Cureton v. Farmers' State Bank, 227 S. W. 423.

The rule invoked by appellant is an exception to the rule that money which has been paid through a mistake can generally be recovered. This exception is mentioned by Judge Riddick, speaking for the court in LaFayette v. Merchants' Bank, 73 Ark. 561, 566, 84 S. W. 700, 68 L. R. A. 231, 108 Am. St. Rep. 71. This exceptional rule, however, as held in the case of Farmers' National Bank of Augusta v. Farmers' & Traders' Bank of Maysville, supra, does not—

"require the drawee bank to know the signature of an indorser; that burden is upon the holder, who is bound to know that the previous indorsements, including that of the payee, are in the handwriting of the parties whose names appear upon the check, or were duly authorized by them."

In First 'National Bank v. Northwestern National Bank, 152 Ill. 296, 38 N. E. 739, 26 L. R. A. 289, 43 Am. St. Rep. 247, it is held (quoting syllabus):

"A bank indorsing and collecting a check warrants the genuineness of all the pre-existing indorsements thereon, including the indorsement of the respective payees named in such check, and is answerable for moneys received by it if any of such indorsements are forgeries."

In the case of Schaap v. First National Bank of Ft. Smith, 137 Ark. 251, 208 S. W. 309, we said:

"In other words, the true owner of a check with a forged or unauthorized indorsement may ratify the act of a bank in receiving it in that condition, and collecting the proceeds or paying them out without authority, and yet not ratify the forged or unauthorized indorsement. In such cases, the bank cannot avoid liability by showing that its conduct was governed by good faith, and the payee is entitled to recover unless he has been guilty of fraud or negligence in the matter."

The facts of this record show that the appellee was not guilty of any fraud, and if it could be said to be in the least negligent, its negligence in a measure was superinduced by the indorsement of the appellant, which was calculated to lull the appellee into a sense of security in reliance upon such indorsement, and thereby lessened the diligence which it doubtless otherwise would have exercised.

It follows that the rulings of the circuit court are in all things correct, and its judgment is therefore affirmed.

GEORGE v. STATE. (No. 9.)

(Supreme Court of Arkansas. May 23, 1921.)

1. Criminal law ⇔450—Testimony of witness as to what certain fact indicated properly excluded.

Where one accused of murder and his victim met on a stairway, and a witness, who did not see the parties at the time and had no personal knowledge of their relative positions, was asked what the appearance of a freshly scraped place on the third step indicated, the court properly sustained an objection, and confined the witness' testimony to what he saw, since the inference called for was for the jury.

2. Homicide ⇔300(8) — Instruction accused could not plead self-defense, if aggressor, held not abstract.

Where the testimony in a prosecution for murder warranted a finding that defendant was the aggressor, instructions that if he was the aggressor he could not plead self-defense were not objectionable as being abstract.

3. Criminal law ⇔805(1)—Separate instructions on different phases of cases not prejudicial, where both correct.

Where one instruction, in a prosecution for murder, correctly instructed the jury that one may not kill another, even in self-defense, except as a last resort, and when he has done all in his power consistent with his safety to avoid the danger, and another correctly declared the law in respect to the appearance of danger as defendant saw it, defendant was not prejudiced by the court's dealing with different phases of the case in separate instructions.

Appeal from Circuit Court, White County; J. M. Jackson, Judge.

Lee George was convicted of murder in the second degree, and he appeals. Affirmed.

J. N. Rachels, of Searcy, and G. G. McKay, of Bald Knob, for appellant.

J. S. Utley, Atty. Gen., and Elbert Godwin and W. T. Hammock, Asst. Attys. Gen., for the State.

SMITH, J. Appellant was convicted of murder in the second degree for killing Bliss Chatman. He admits the testimony is legally sufficient to support the verdict, but insists that error was committed in excluding testimony, and in giving and in refusing instructions.

According to appellant, he and deceased were good friends prior to the time of the killing, and spent much of their time together. Appellant testified that some money and a razor and some other personal effects were stolen from a dresser in his room, and he had reason to suspect the deceased had taken them. He further testified that Chatman had made an insulting proposition to his wife; but that fact had not been communicated to him by her at the time of the killing. He went to see Chatman about the lost articles, and upon meeting him inquired, "Bliss, what do you mean —?" But the question was not completed, as deceased immediately assaulted him. It is the theory of the defense that Chatman supposed appellant was inquiring about the insult to his wife, and, believing he was about to be assaulted, if not killed, he made such a vigorous assault on appellant as that appellant was compelled to shoot in his necessary self-defense, when, in fact, appellant had no purpose of provoking a difficulty, and intended by his question only to inquire about the lost articles.

The testimony on the part of the state is to the effect that appellant armed himself and went in search of Chatman, and assaulted him as soon as he found him, and killed him by shooting him.

10   231 SOUTHWESTERN REPORTER   (Ark.

[1] The men met on a stairway, and a witness, Foster, was asked about a freshly scraped place on the third step from the bottom. Foster was asked what the appearance of the place indicated, and the court sustained an objection to that question, and in doing so said: "Let the witness state what he saw." The court was correct in this ruling. The witness did not see the parties at the time of the difficulty, and had no personal knowledge of their relative positions on the stairway, and his testimony was properly confined to a statement of what he saw. The inferences deducible from the appearance of the scraped place on the step were for the jury, and not for the witness, to make.

[2] Over appellant's objection the court gave the following instruction:

"You are further instructed that if you find from the evidence in this case that the defendant, Lee George, was the aggressor in the difficulty or that he mutually engaged in the difficulty, he cannot plead self-defense in justification of his act in shooting and killing the deceased, Bliss Chatman."

This was an oral instruction. In addition, there were written instructions numbered 1 and 2 which deal with the same phase of the case. These instructions told the jury also that if appellant was the aggressor, he would have had no right to kill the deceased; but the written instructions contained this qualification:

"Unless he in good faith withdrew from the conflict as far as he could, and did all in his power consistent with his safety to avoid the danger and avert the necessity of killing the deceased."

The court would, no doubt, have qualified the oral instruction to conform to the written instructions had that point been made. But the absence of this qualification from the oral instruction does not appear to have been the ground of the objection to it. The objection is that the instructions on that phase of the case were abstract, in that there was no testimony that appellant was the aggressor. Counsel is mistaken in this contention. According to appellant's own testimony he was hemmed in by deceased on the stairway and viciously assaulted; but the jury did not accept that version of the difficulty as the truth. As has been said, the testimony fully warranted a finding that appellant was the aggressor throughout.

[3] Over appellant's objection the court gave an instruction numbered 3, which reads as follows:

"No. 3. You are instructed that the law has such regard for the sanctity of human life that one person may not kill another, even in his necessary self-defense, except as a last resort, and when he has done all in his power consistent with his safety to avoid the danger and avert the necessity of the killing; so, in this case, if you find from the evidence and circumstances, beyond a reasonable doubt, that the defendant could have reasonably avoided the danger to himself and averted the necessity of killing the deceased, it was his duty to have done so."

The objection to this instruction is that it leaves out of account the appearance of danger as appellant saw it. The instruction is a correct declaration of the phase of the case with which it dealt, and another instruction dealt with the appearance of danger as the appellant saw it, and correctly declared the law in that respect.

No instruction could declare the whole law in the case, and appellant was not prejudiced by the action of the court in dealing with different phases of the case in separate instructions, inasmuch as each instruction correctly declared the law applicable to the phase of the case with which it dealt.

Appellant asked a number of instructions, which were refused. But these instructions, in so far as they correctly declared the law applicable to the issues raised, were covered by other instructions which were given.

No error appearing, the judgment is affirmed.

FARMERS' BANK & TRUST CO. v. BOSHEARS. (No. 2.)

(Supreme Court of Arkansas. May 23, 1921.)

1. Banks and banking ⬤⟞121—Bank, receiving deposits after hours, cannot escape liability for deposit.

Where it was the custom of employees of a bank to receive deposits after the usual banking hours to accommodate belated customers, the bank cannot escape liability for a deposit so received on account of the time of the deposit.

2. Banks and banking ⬤⟞154(9) — Whether objection by customer to statement not showing deposit made within reasonable time a jury question.

In an action against a bank by its customer to recover a deposit claimed to have been made by him, but denied by the bank, whether or not the objection, made by plaintiff customer to the statement of his account rendered by the bank, not showing the deposit was within a reasonable time, held a question for the jury under the evidence.

3. Banks and banking ⬤⟞154(8) — Evidence held to warrant inference customer was diligent in protesting failure of bank to show deposit on statement rendered.

In an action against a bank by its customer to recover a deposit claimed to have been made by him, but denied by the bank, evidence held to warrant the jury in drawing the inference that plaintiff customer proceeded with proper diligence in presenting his protest to the bank when he received a statement not showing the deposit, and that such protest was made within reasonable time in view of the circumstances.

⬤⟞For other cases see same topic and KEY-NUMBER in all Key-Numbered Digests and Indexes

4. Banks and banking ⬤⟳154(8) — Evidence held to warrant finding deposit made.

In an action against a bank by its customer to recover a deposit claimed to have been made by him, but denied by the bank, evidence *held* sufficient to warrant the jury in finding that plaintiff customer deposited the sum mentioned in the manner which he described in his testimony.

Appeal from Circuit Court, Mississippi County; R. H. Dudley, Judge.

Action by B. Boshears against the Farmers' Bank & Trust Company. From judgment for plaintiff, defendant appeals. Affirmed.

Davis, Costen & Harrison, of Blytheville, for appellant.

A. G. Little, of Blytheville, and Arthur L. Adams, of Jonesboro, for appellee.

McCULLOCH, C. J. Appellant is a banking corporation engaged in business in the city of Blytheville, in this state, and during the autumn of the year 1919, appellee, a farmer living 8 or 10 miles out in the country from Blytheville, was one of its depositors. He claimed that he made a deposit of $250 on October 17, 1919, which does not appear to his credit, and on the refusal of the bank to place it to his credit he instituted this action to recover that sum.

The issues in the case are whether the amount was deposited by appellee, as claimed by him; whether the deposit was received by an employee of the bank, if at all, at such time as they were authorized to receive deposits; and whether appellee is precluded from recovery of the sum by his failure within apt time to make objection to the account rendered him by the bank.

Appellee was a tenant on the farm of a Mr. Gay, who was formerly the president of appellant bank, and at the time of the transaction in controversy was one of its directors. According to appellee's testimony he brought cotton to Blytheville on October 17, 1919, and after selling it he and Mr. Gay had a settlement of their accounts, and he paid Mr. Gay a small balance due him, and that, having the sum of $250 left out of the proceeds of the cotton, he deposited it in appellant bank. He described the method of deposit, as follows: That he counted out the money to Mr. Gay, who made out a deposit slip and handed it to Mr. Cheatham, the assistant cashier, who accepted the money and placed the letters O. K. on the deposit slip, with his initials attached. This was after the usual closing time of the bank, but the assistant cashier was in the bank at the time, and received this deposit. Appellee testified further that he was accustomed to making deposits in this way after the usual banking hours, for the reason that he came a long distance with his cotton, and did not usually sell it until after the bank closed. There was other testimony tending to show that it was the custom of the bank to receive deposits after the usual banking hours.

The testimony adduced by appellant tended to show that the money was never received by the bank or any of its employees. Cheatham testified that he had no recollection of the deposit, and it is shown by his testimony and that of other employees that the deposit had never been entered on the books of the bank, and that the amount of funds in the bank did not indicate that they exceeded the amount entered on the books. Mr. Cheatham also testified that the initials on the deposit slip held by appellee was not in his handwriting.

On October 21st appellant sent to appellee, by mail, a statement of his account, which did not show this deposit. The statement concluded with the following notice:

"This statement is furnished you instead of balancing your passbook. It saves you the trouble of bringing your passbook to the bank and waiting for it to be balanced. These statements will be found very convenient to check up and file. All items are credited subject to final payment. Use your passbook only as a receipt book when making deposits."

Another such statement was furnished in like manner on December 15, 1919. There is a conflict in the testimony as to when appellee made objection to the bank that his account was not correctly set forth in the statement furnished to him. He testified that he made the discovery in three or four days after he received the statement by checking up the account with his deposit slips at home; that because of the fact that Mr. Gay was one of the directors of the bank he had made the deposit through the latter, and waited to see him before making his protest to the bank, and that it was several weeks before he could find Mr. Gay in town. He testified that at the first opportunity he presented the matter to Mr. Gay, and that they went to see the cashier of the bank, and presented the deposit slip, showing the deposit of this amount on the date mentioned.

The issues were properly submitted to the jury, and the court, among other instructions, gave the following:

"Even though you may believe from the evidence that the deposit in question was received by the officers of the bank, if you further find and believe from the evidence that thereafter the plaintiff, Boshears, received a statement or statements from the bank, showing the amount of the deposits made by him and the charges against his account, as shown by the vouchers, and upon receiving such statement or statements he did not in a reasonable time thereafter notify the bank of the errors here complained of, and that such failure upon his part to so notify the bank occasioned injury to the bank, you will find for the defendant."

[1, 2] The contention of appellant's counsel is that the court should have given a peremp-

tory instruction for the reason that the undisputed evidence shows that the money was received by the bank's employees, if at all, after banking hours, when there was no officer to receive such deposit and also the fact that the undisputed evidence shows that appellant waited an unreasonable length of time before he made objection to the statement sent to him, omitting this deposit. We think the contention of counsel in both respects is unfounded. There is testimony tending to show that it was the custom of the employees of the bank to receive deposits in the bank after the usual banking hours for the purpose of accommodating belated customers. The testimony also warranted a submission of the issue as to whether or not the objection made by appellee to the statement of his account was within a reasonable time. The rule approved by this court in several cases was stated by the Supreme Court of the United States in Leather Manufacturers' National Bank v. Morgan, 117 U. S. 96, 6 Sup. Ct. 657, 29 L. Ed. 811, as follows:

"While no rule can be laid down that will cover every transaction between a bank and its depositor, it is sufficient to say that the latter's duty is discharged when he exercises such diligence as is required by the circumstances of the particular case, including the relations of the parties, and the established or known usages of banking business." Citizens' Bank & Trust Co. v. Hinkle, 126 Ark. 266, 189 S. W. 679; Bank of Black Rock v. B. Johnson & Son Tie Co., 229 S. W. 1.

[3] Considering the circumstances under which the alleged deposit was made and the circumstances under which appellee was placed when he received the notice omitting this deposit, we think that the trial jury was warranted in drawing the inference that appellant proceeded with proper diligence in presenting his protest to the bank, and that it was made within a reasonable time, considering all those circumstances.

[4] The testimony was conflicting as to whether or not the deposit was actually made, but there was sufficient evidence to warrant the jury in finding that appellee deposited the sum mentioned in the manner which he described in his testimony.

Judgment is therefore affirmed.

MEYER et al. v. BOARD OF IMP. PAVING DIST. NO. 3. (No. 7.)

(Supreme Court of Arkansas. May 23, 1921.)

1. Municipal corporations ☞513(5) — After expiration of time to question validity of improvement assessments, third persons cannot be made parties.

After expiration of the 30-day period limited by Crawford & Moses' Dig. § 5668, to at-

tack improvement ordinances, third persons who are not parties to actions previously instituted cannot become party plaintiffs, and by adopting the pleadings of the original parties attack the validity of the assessment.

2. Municipal corporations ☞488, 489(3) — Signing of petition for improvement district does not estop petitioners from attacking ordinance on the ground that they exceeded the law.

Petitioners for creation of municipal improvement districts may attack the validity of ordinances creating the districts on the ground that the law was not followed, for the petitions conferred no authority beyond the statute.

3. Municipal corporations ☞488, 489(1) — Property owners may estop themselves to attack validity of improvement districts.

Where property owners know that the commissioners of improvement district are exceeding their authority, they may by affirmative act estop themselves from thereafter questioning the legality of the commissioners' action.

4. Municipal corporations ☞450(2)—Boundaries of improvement district sufficient.

Boundaries of an improvement district which was described as along B. street, thence to the point of beginning, is not open to attack because B. street did not extend to the point of beginning, another street intervening; for the line between two fixed points is definite, and both course and distance yields to fixed monuments.

5. Boundaries ☞3(3) — Course and distance yield to fixed monuments.

Both course and distance yield to fixed monuments in land survey.

6. Municipal corporations ☞463—Assessment for street improvements open to attack as exceeding 20 per cent. limit.

Where the report of commissioners of an improvement district included an item for unforeseen expenses, and the estimated cost including that item exceeded the 20 per cent. limit fixed by statute, the assessment cannot be upheld on the theory that the item might not be needed.

7. Municipal corporations ☞440—That property in improvement district abutted on streets already paved should be considered.

In determining benefits from street improvements, the fact that some property abutted on streets already paved, which gave the owners access, should be considered.

8. Municipal corporations ☞440 — Construction of improvements by owners should be considered by commissioners of improvement districts.

Under Crawford & Moses' Dig. § 5672, the commissioners of an improvement district should, where owners of property therein had previously constructed individual improvements, determine whether they are of value, so as to warrant allowance therefor on account of the assessment, and the rejection of all claim for allowance is error.

☞For other cases see same topic and KEY-NUMBER in all Key-Numbered Digests and Indexes

9. Municipal corporations ⟐══439 — That betterments assessed equal to the estimated cost of improvement no ground for objection.

Property owners cannot object that the betterments assessed exactly equal the cost of improvements, for the assessing officers, if acting honestly and impartially, may conclude that the betterment will exceed the cost, and they may proportionately reduce their estimate of betterments, so that the total betterments assessed shall not exceed the known estimates of cost, although in no event can the cost exceed the betterments.

10. Municipal corporations ⟐══484(3) — Testimony that separate improvements could be constructed as one will not overcome presumption in favor of legality of separate districts.

Where separate districts for paving and guttering streets were attacked on the ground that the work was in reality a single improvement, and that the estimated cost exceeded the 20 per cent. tax limit, testimony by a contractor that such work was essentially one improvement is inadmissible, for it does not rebut the prima facie presumption arising from the petition of property owners for and the ordinances establishing such districts, and it is necessary to show that it would be impracticable to make one improvement without the other.

Appeal from Crawford Chancery Court; J. V. Bourland, Chancellor.

Consolidated suits by H. F. Meyer and others against the Board of Improvement of Paving District No. 3. From a decree dismissing the suits, plaintiffs appeal. Reversed and remanded.

Starbird & Starbird, of Alma, and Joseph R. Brown, of Ft. Smith, for appellants.

E. L. Matlock, of Van Buren, for appellee.

SMITH, J. On September 9, 1919, an ordinance was passed by the council of the city of Van Buren creating paving district No. 3 for the purpose of paving certain streets therein designated. On the same day the council passed an ordinance creating curb and gutter district No. 1 for the purpose of curbing, guttering, and draining the streets which were to be paved by paving district No. 3.

Within the time limited by law, J. L. Rea, J. H. Butler, and H. F. Meyer filed suits attacking the two districts on numerous grounds. About the same time M. L. Garrett and W. J. Martin filed suits for the same purpose. All these plaintiffs had signed the petitions for both improvements. The causes were consolidated and tried together, and from a decree dismissing these suits for want of equity is this appeal.

The districts are attacked on the following grounds:

(1) That the boundaries of the districts have not been designated with the certainty required by statute.

(2) That the commissioners of the district and the city council have assessed and levied more than 20 per centum of the value of the real estate according to the last county assessment.

(3) That the assessors specifically refused to consider the present condition of appellants' lands in the districts by reason of their paving needs being wholly or partly supplied by public and private pavements and improvements already built.

(4) The fact that the assessments are an expense spread upon the districts, and are not special benefits enjoyed by appellants' lands fairly assessed against them.

(5) That the improvements proposed as separate improvements constitute in fact a single improvement, the cost of which very largely exceeds 20 per cent. of the value of the real estate lying in the district.

In answer to these objections it is first contended on behalf of the districts that the plaintiffs are estopped to raise these questions for the reason that they had signed the petitions for the creation of the districts. The court below appeared to have had this view, and permitted other property owners who had not signed the petitions to become parties plaintiff to the suits, and the trial proceeded in the name of these new parties to a final decree.

[1] We think the court should not have permitted the new parties to be made plaintiffs. Several months had then expired since the publication of the notices of the ordinances creating the districts; and the effect of the court's action was to permit these persons, by adopting the pleadings of the persons whose names are set out above, to prosecute litigation which the statute required them to begin within 30 days.

Section 5668, C. & M. Digest, prescribes the period of limitation for the institution of suits to test the validity of these ordinances, and is as follows:

"Sec. 5668. Within thirty days after the passage of the ordinance mentioned above, the recorder or city clerk shall publish a copy of it in some newspaper published in such town or city for one time. And all persons who shall fail to begin legal proceedings within thirty days after such publication for the purpose of correcting or invalidating such assessment shall be forever barred and precluded."

[2] We think, however, the court was in error in dismissing the plaintiffs' complaint because they had signed the petitions for the districts. The petitioners, in signing the petitions, consented only that the law be followed, and the petitions themselves conferred no authority beyond the statute. Rayder v. Warrick, 133 Ark. 491, 202 S. W. 831; Nunes v. Coyle, 230 S. W. 11.

[3] Of course, where property owners know that the commissioners have exceeded their

authority, they may do some affirmative act which will estop them from thereafter questioning the legality of the commissioners' action, as was done in the case of Harnwell v. White, 115 Ark. 88, 171 S. W. 108. But these plaintiffs took no such action. They merely petitioned in conformity with the statute for the creation of the districts.

[4, 5] We think the boundaries of the districts were sufficiently described. The objection to the boundary is that, after reaching Bois d'Arc street, the boundary is described as thence northwesterly along Bois d'Arc street to the place of beginning. Bois d'Arc street does not extend to the place of beginning. Second street intervenes between the end of Bois d'Arc street and Main street, the place of beginning, and the distance is three blocks. But Second street is an extension of Bois d'Arc street. A line to the point of beginning from Bois d'Arc street is a straight one, and this part of the boundary line—a line between two fixed points—is therefore definite and certain, as both course and distance yield to fixed monuments in land surveying. Johnson v. Hamlen, 231 S. W. 6; Doe v. Porter, 3 Ark. 18, 36 Am. Dec. 448; Harrell v. Hill, 19 Ark. 102, 68 Am. Dec. 202; Brown v. Hardin, 21 Ark. 324; Chapman & Dewey Lbr. Co. v. Levee Dist., 100 Ark. 94, 139 S. W. 625; Scott v. Dunkel Box & Lbr. Co., 106 Ark. 83, 152 S. W. 1025; Paschal v. Swepston, 120 Ark. 230, 179 S. W. 339.

[6] We think the second objection is well taken in so far as it applies to paving district No. 3. The valuation of the real estate in the district, as shown by the last county assessment, was $418,420. The 20 per cent. limitation fixed by statute would limit the cost of any improvement in that district to $83,684. The estimated cost of the paving is, we think, $84,000, which is, of course, in excess of the 20 per cent.

On behalf of the district it is insisted that the estimated cost of the improvement is only $78,000. The controversy about the estimated cost arises over an item of $6,764, which is designated as "unforeseen" in the report of the board of commissioners of paving district No. 3 which was filed in open council meeting March 1, 1920. The court below excluded this item of $6,764 in determining the estimated cost; and that action is defended on the ground that no showing is made that its expenditure will be necessary to complete the improvement, and that the cost of the known and necessary expenditures is only $77,236. Such, however, is not the case. The expenditure of this item of $6,764 is sufficiently probable to cause its insertion in the estimate of cost contained in the commissioners' report to the council, and the ordinance creating the paving district, which was passed April 12, 1920, contains a recital that "the estimated cost of said improvement is $125,000." While this last-named sum appears to include interest—a

thing permitted by the statute—it appears also to include the estimated construction cost of $84,000.

[7] We think the third objection is also well taken. It was shown that, before the organization of paving district No. 3, lots in this district 3 belonging to certain of the plaintiffs herein, fronting on Main street, had been paved and curbed upon that front at great expense, and that such paving and curbing was in good repair, and was in daily use, and was sufficient for the needs of all the property so fronting on Main street. But the assessors, in making the assessment, refused to take into consideration the condition of said property by reason of said former pavement, which had been built by paving district No. 1, and that certain other plaintiffs had, privately and at their own expense, paved portions of their own property, and had built curbs and gutters, and the assessors had also refused to take that paving and curbing and guttering into account in assessing the betterments.

These improvements should have been taken into account. In assessing benefits to accrue to property by reason of an improvement, it is the duty of the assessors to take into consideration the peculiar situation of each and every piece of property to be assessed.

It is true district No. 3 did not propose to repave streets which an older district had paved; but this older district had paved streets on which lots in district No. 3 fronted, and it would have been proper, therefore, to consider that the lots which would be in two districts had access to pavements already constructed in determining what additional enhancement in value would result from the construction of other pavements. This, of course, is a question of fact, and we do not undertake to say what finding the commissioners should have made. We only hold that those conditions should have been taken into account in determining what betterment would result from the construction of the proposed improvements.

[8] Section 5672, C. & M. Digest, applicable to this phase of the case, reads as follows:

"Sec. 5672. If in the construction of sidewalks or making other improvements any owner of taxable property in the district shall be found to have improved his own property in such manner that his improvement may be profitably made a part of the general improvement of the kind in the district, being also as good as that required by the system determined upon by said board, the board of improvement shall appraise the value of the improvement made by the owner, and shall allow its value as a set-off against the assessments against his property. And, in case the owner who has made such improvements shall be found to have failed to come up to the required standard, the board may allow him the value of the materials thereof, so far as the same may be profitably used in perfecting the system aforesaid, as a set-off against his property thus improved. In such cases the board shall issue to the owner a certificate showing the amount of set-off allowed, which certificate shall be received by the collector in lieu of money for the amount named therein charged against said property."

The commissioners should have taken into account the contention of the property owners in regard to their curbing and guttering. Their curbs and gutters might, or might not, have possessed value as defined in section 5672, C. & M. Digest, supra. But the property owners' contention in this respect should have received sufficient attention at the hands of the commissioners for them to have determined that fact. The assessment of betterments by the assessors is not influenced by the value to the district of the curbing and guttering, but when the curbs and gutters have value to the district that value should be ascertained by the commissioners as provided in section 5672, C. & M. Digest, and certificates issued by the commissioners showing what that value is, to the end that the certificate may be paid to "the collector in lieu of money for the amount named therein charged against said property."

[9] We do not think the fourth objection is well taken. It does appear that the betterments assessed exactly equal the total estimated cost. No attempt was made to show that the assessment was otherwise improper than the failure of the assessors to take into account certain existing improvements, which failure we have already discussed. It is not shown that excessive betterments have been assessed. The showing is that total estimated betterments equal total estimated cost. This, of itself, is not a fatal defect. The cost of the improvement can, of course, never exceed the betterments. But where the betterments are fairly and uniformly determined, and that finding is not the result of a purpose to raise sufficient revenue to construct the improvement, whether the betterments equal the cost of the improvement or not, there is no legal or constitutional requirement that the full betterment be assessed. No betterment can be assessed unless an honest and impartial finding is made that an enhancement of value results from the proposed improvement, and the amount of this betterment can never exceed the estimated enhancement in value resulting from the improvement. But if, acting honestly and impartially, the assessing officers conclude the betterment will exceed cost, and they decide to proportionately reduce their estimate of betterments so that the total betterments assessed shall not exceed the known estimates of cost, we think they have not transcended their authority, nor have they acted in contravention of the Constitution or the statutes of the state.

[10] We think the court did not err in the ruling made excluding the testimony of a witness named Foos in regard to the identity of the improvements. In the case of Bottrell v. Hollipeter, 135 Ark. 315, 204 S. W. 843, we said:

"The petition of the property owners for, and the ordinance pursuant thereto creating, the two districts, are at least prima facie evidence that the petitioners and the town council considered that the improvements provided for did not constitute a 'single' improvement, as designated in the statute. The facts stated in the answer and admitted by the demurrer of appellant to be true show that they were not essentially one improvement."

The witness was a contractor, and had never seen the plans for the proposed improvement. He would have testified—had he been permitted to do so—that such improvements were considered by the engineering profession as constituting a single improvement. He did not offer to testify, however, that the improvements could not be separately and successfully constructed. He would have testified that they were usually constructed together, and therefore regarded by the engineering profession as a single improvement. But that testimony would not have shown that they were essentially one improvement.

To overcome the prima facie presumption arising out of the petition of the property owners and the ordinance of the council, something more is required than a mere showing that paving and curbing and guttering are ordinarily constructed as a single improvement.

The presumption would not be overcome unless there was an affirmative showing that it was not practicable to construct one without constructing the other, or the showing made that one might not be first constructed as a complete improvement and the other subsequently constructed as another separate and complete improvement.

There are cases cited in appellants' brief which hold that the question of the identity of these improvements is judicial, and not one of fact. But this court held otherwise in the case of Bottrell v. Hollipeter, supra, and we now hold that the testimony excluded by the court was not sufficient to overcome the prima facie presumption arising out of the enactment of the ordinances creating the districts.

Other objections to the districts are urged in the briefs, but they are questions which we think do not require discussion here. These were certain questions of fact in regard to the assessed values of property within the districts, and it does not appear that the finding of the court thereon was clearly against the preponderance of the evidence.

Decree reversed and cause remanded.

HINES, Director General of Railroads, v. PARTRIDGE.

(Supreme Court of Tennessee. March 25, 1921.)

1. Municipal corporations ⚌111(1) — Ordinance requiring flagman at crossing not void for failing to prescribe penalties.

A provision of an ordinance, relating to the keeping of a flagman on duty at a railroad crossing, was not void because it failed to prescribe a penalty, and failure of railroad to observe it was negligence per se, even though the municipality could not enforce it by a criminal proceeding, the ordinance in question being designed for the protection of individuals, and not the municipality itself.

2. Railroads ⚌236 — Ordinance limiting speed to 4 miles per hour not unreasonable.

An ordinance cannot be held unreasonable simply because it limits the speed of trains to 4 miles an hour at a crossing within the city, since to justify courts in declaring void an ordinance limiting the speed of railroad trains within a city, its unreasonableness or want of necessity as a police regulation must be clear, manifest, and undoubted.

3. Railroads ⚌350(5, 11) — Negligent in backing train at unlawful speed over crossing without flagman held for jury.

In action for damages arising from a collision between an automobile and defendant railroad's train at a crossing in a city, held that court did not err in not directing a verdict in favor of defendant upon a count of the declaration, alleging that the train was being backed over the crossing at a rate of speed in excess of that prescribed by an ordinance of the city, and without having flagman present, as required by such ordinance.

4. Trial ⚌143 — No direction of verdict where material evidence conflicting.

There can be no constitutional exercise of the power to direct a verdict in any case, where there is a dispute as to any material evidence, or any legal doubt as to the conclusion to be drawn from the whole evidence on the issues to be tried, but the case must go to the jury.

5. Trial ⚌178 — On motion for directed verdict for defendant, view of evidence most favorable to plaintiff to be taken.

In considering defendant's motion for a directed verdict. that view of the evidence most favorable to plaintiff's case must be taken by the court; and, if there is any doubt as to the conclusion to be drawn from the whole evidence, the motion must be denied.

6. Appeal and error ⚌1002 — Finding of jury on disputed questions of fact binding on Supreme Court.

Finding of jury upon disputed questions of fact are binding on the Supreme Court.

7. Railroads ⚌350(13) — Automobilist's negligence held for jury.

In an action for damages arising from collision between automobile and defendant's train

at railroad crossing in city, whether plaintiff was guilty of contributory negligence held for the jury.

8. Negligence ⚌136(26) — Contributory negligence question for jury.

Where there is a controversy in respect of facts, upon which the defense of contributory negligence is predicated, the question should be submitted to the jury.

9. Death ⚌24 — Beneficiary not prejudiced by contributory negligence of cobeneficiary.

Contributory negligence of husband could not prejudice in any way minor children who were not at fault in an action to recover damages for wrongful death of wife and mother under Shan. Code, §§ 4029a1, 4029a2.

10. Death ⚌58(1) — Burden of proving contributory negligence on defendant.

In an action by husband to recover damages for wrongful death of wife, under Shan. Code, §§ 4029a1, 4029a2, the burden of proof on the issue of contributory negligence of the husband is upon the defendant.

11. Railroads ⚌324(3) — Automobilist's violation of statute does not affect right to recover damages.

Acts 1917, c. 36, making it a misdemeanor for drivers of automobiles not to come to a full stop before crossing railroad tracks, cannot be construed as bearing on or in any way affecting the common-law right of recovery of litigants in damage suits, and court did not err in refusing to charge in a damage suit against a railroad that failure to stop constituted contributory negligence.

12. Death ⚌104(6) — Instruction on damages for death of wife held not prejudicial error.

In action for wrongful death of wife under Shan. Code, §§ 4029a1, 4029a2, an instruction, "If you find in favor of the plaintiff, it will be your duty to fix the amount of his recovery. The measure of the recovery would be reasonable compensation for the life of the deceased. In determining that, take into consideration her age, the state of her health, her expectancy of life, of a person of her state of health and age, and let your verdict be for reasonable compensation," held not prejudicially erroneous, although the court should have charged the jury that the measure of damages was the pecuniary value of the life of deceased, and not any sentimental value which the jury might place on the deceased's life, and that it should be taken into consideration that at best the duration of life is uncertain.

13. Death ⚌99(4) — $10,000 not excessive for death of wife.

A verdict of $10,000 for the wrongful death of a wife and mother, 34 years of age, and in good health, was not the result of sentiment, nor excessive.

Appeal from Circuit Court, Hamilton County; Oscar Yarnell, Judge.

Action by H. W. Partridge against Walker D. Hines, Director General of Railroads. From a judgment for plaintiff, defendant appealed to the Court of Civil Appeals, and from action of the circuit court judge in peremptorily instructing the jury to return verdict for defendant as to certain counts of the declaration, plaintiff appealed to such court, and, the Court of Civil Appeals having affirmed the action of the circuit judge in peremptorily directing a verdict·for defendant as to certain counts and reversing such action as to one count, both parties bring certiorari. Judgment of Court of Civil Appeals reversed, and judgment of circuit court affirmed.

W. H. Watkins and Brown, Spurlock & Brown, all of Chattanooga, for Walker D. Hines.

Whitaker & Foust, of Chattanooga, for H. W. Partridge.

HALL, J. This is an action of damages brought by H. W. Partridge, who will hereinafter be referred to as the plaintiff, against W. D. Hines, Director General of Railroads, who will hereinafter be referred to as the defendant, to recover for the alleged wrongful and negligent killing of his wife, Mrs. Dove Partridge, on February 21, 1919, in the city of Chattanooga, Tenn., in a collision between the plaintiff's automobile and one of the trains controlled and operated by the defendant, at Market street in said city.

A trial of the case in the court below before the court and jury resulted in verdict and judgment in favor of the plaintiff for the sum of $10,000 from which judgment the defendant appealed to the Court of Civil Appeals. The plaintiff also appealed to that court from the action of the circuit judge in peremptorily instructing the jury to return a verdict for the defendant as to the first, second, and fourth counts of the declaration; the case being submitted to the jury alone on the third count.

The Court of Civil Appeals affirmed the action of the circuit judge in peremptorily directing a verdict in favor of the defendant as to the second and fourth counts of the declaration, but reversed his action as to the first count, holding that the case should have been submitted to the jury as to this count also. That court, however, reversed the judgment rendered upon the third count for the reasons to be hereinafter stated, and remanded the case for a new trial.

Both the plaintiff and the defendant have filed petitions for writs of certiorari, and the case is now before this court for review.

The plaintiff, by his assignments of error, challenges the action of the Court of Civil Appeals in reversing the verdict and judgment rendered on the third count of his declaration, as well as its action in affirming the judgment of the circuit judge directing a verdict in favor of the defendant as to the second and fourth counts of his declaration.

The defendant, in his petition, challenges the action of the Court of Civil Appeals in refusing to hold that the circuit judge erred in not directing a verdict in his favor as to the third count of the declaration on his motion made at the conclusion of all the evidence, and in pretermitting certain of his assignments of error made in that court presenting certain questions of law, which will be hereinafter referred to.

Mrs. Dove Partridge, the wife of the plaintiff, was killed by a collision between an automobile, in which she was riding with plaintiff, and a backing train of the Central of Georgia Railway Company, moving at the time over the tracks of the Nashville, Chattanooga & St. Louis Railway Company; both of said corporations being under the control and management of the defendant, and were being operated by him at the time of the accident resulting in the death of Mrs. Partridge. No one was in the automobile at the time of the collision except the plaintiff and his wife, whom the proof shows was then 34 years of age. The accident occurred at a grade crossing where Market street crosses the tracks of the Nashville, Chattanooga & St. Louis Railway Company at about the hour of 12:20 a. m. Plaintiff and his wife were going from their home in Highland Park to the Terminal Station, which is located a half mile south of the the place where the accident occurred, for the purpose of meeting a relative of the plaintiff's wife. The train, which collided with plaintiff's automobile, consisted of a switch engine, tender, one coal car, and three box cars. The engine was in front of the cars, and was pushing them backwards in a westerly direction. The coal car was next to the tender, and the box cars were moving in front. The general direction of Market street is north and south, and the railroad tracks cross Market street, at the point where the accident occurred, diagonally. There are six railroad tracks at said crossing. They run approximately parallel to each other, but they widen out somewhat in a fan shape as they extend westward across Market street. Plaintiff was traveling south on Market street at the time of the collision. He had crossed five of said tracks, and the collision occurred on the sixth or southernmost track.

Plaintiff offered testimony tending to show that as he approached the crossing, and while crossing the tracks north of the last one, he looked and listened for a train, but did not see or hear one until his automobile was within about five feet of the train which collided with his car; that no bell on the train was being sounded at the time, and there was no signal of any character given indicating that a train was about to cross Market street; that his wife first saw the train and screamed, and at that time he saw it also, but his automobile was too close to it to stop and prevent the collision; that as he went across the other tracks and approached the southernmost track his automobile was running at a speed

231 S.W.—2

of between 8 and 10 miles an hour; that there were no lights on the train, and it was running at a speed of from 10 to 12 miles an hour; that the front box car struck the automobile on the left-hand side near the wind shield and fender, and knocked or pushed it along the track westward about 60 feet before the train was brought to a stop; that the automobile was totally wrecked, and the impact of the train against it threw him and his wife out upon the track, and his wife was killed and he was seriously injured; that at the time of the collision his automobile was being operated along the right hand or west side of the street car track, which crosses the railroad tracks at said crossing, and runs north and south in the center of Market street, and that the left wheels of his automobile were running along on the plank that runs along the west rail of the street car track, and immediately outside of it.

The third count of the plaintiff's declaration averred that the defendant was negligent in the operation of its train, in that it was being pushed or backed over said crossing at Market street at a rate of speed in excess of that prescribed by an ordinance of the city of Chattanooga, which is incorporated in section 397 of the Code of said city, and which ordinance was in force at the time of the collision. This ordinance provides:

"It shall be the duty of the railroad companies using the tracks across Market street, Cowart, and Montgomery avenue, to place and keep one flagman on Hook, one flagman on Cowart, two flagmen on Market at Central Depot, two flagmen at Nashville crossing, one flagman on King, one flagman on Montgomery or Alabama Great Southern, one flagman on Montgomery for Chattanooga, Rome, and Columbus, one flagman on Montgomery for Belt, one flagman on Rossville avenue. All trains shall be preceded by a flagman walking in front of cars or engines while crossing or backing, whose duty it shall be to prevent all railroad trains passing said tracks, from going at a greater rate of speed than four miles an hour; and further to protect the lives of persons passing along the streets at the points mentioned. All railroad engineers or firemen who drive or run an engine or train, across said Market, Cowart, Montgomery avenue, Boyce, East End avenue, and King streets, in said city, at a greater rate of speed than four miles an hour, shall be deemed guilty of a violation of this ordinance, and upon conviction thereof before the recorder, shall be punished by a fine of not less than ten ($10.00) dollars, for each offense."

In the third count it was further averred that the defendant was negligent in failing to have, at the time of the collision, any flagman at the Market street crossing on duty, and negligently failed to have said train preceded by a flagman walking in front thereof while it was crossing said street, and that such negligence was the direct and proximate cause of the death of plaintiff's wife.

The trial judge gave this ordinance in charge to the jury, stating to them as follows:

"The defendants, gentlemen of the jury, had a right to operate their train over this crossing, but it was incumbent upon them to observe the provisions of this ordinance. It was their duty in backing ·their train at this time and place to run it at a speed not to exceed 4 miles per hour; it was also their duty to have on hand two flagmen, and to have one of them preceding the train, to walk out in front of it so as to give warning to the traffic. If they failed to do this, then they were guilty of negligence per se, that is, negligence as a matter of law, and if the negligent violation of the provision of this ordinance resulted in the death of the plaintiff's wife here, then the plaintiff is entitled to recover."

The Court of Civil Appeals was of the opinion that the first provision of said ordinance, which required the defendant to keep two flagmen on duty at the crossing where the collision occurred, one of whom should precede trains across the same by walking in front of them, for the purposes stated in said ordinance was invalid because it did not prescribe any penalty for its violation either by the defendant, or the flagmen stationed or kept at said crossing, and that therefore the defendant was not bound to regard it. The Court of Civil Appeals was further of the opinion that the trial judge committed error in giving that provision of the ordinance in charge to the jury, and reversed the judgment of the court below for that reason.

It may be remarked here that the defendant, neither in the court below nor in the Court of Civil Appeals, challenged the validity of said ordinance upon the ground that it failed to prescribe any penalty for its violation, but this question was raised by the Court of Civil Appeals of its own motion. The defendant did challenge the validity of the ordinance upon the ground that it was unreasonable, in that it limited the speed of trains to 4 miles an hour at said crossing. This contention, however, was overruled by the Court of Civil Appeals.

[1] We do not think it can be said that the provision of the ordinance relating to the keeping of flagmen on duty at said crossing is void because it fails to prescribe a penalty. We think that, notwithstanding the ordinance prescribes no penalty for its violation in this regard, it is one the defendant was bound to observe, and its failure to observe it was negligence per se. The ordinance is in the nature of a police regulation, it is true, and while the municipality could not enforce it by a criminal proceeding, or a proceeding in its nature criminal, it prescribed a rule of conduct which the defendant was bound to observe in the operation of its trains, for the safety of persons using the highway. The very object of the ordinance was to protect persons using Market street against injury

from the operation of the defendant's trains at said crossing. The defendant had previously recognized and accepted this ordinance by keeping two flagmen at this crossing for the purpose of performing the duties imposed by said ordinance, and it was insisted by the defendant that said flagmen were in the performance of their duties at the time of the accident, though, as before stated, the jury found this contention against the defendant. In Chicago, etc., R. R. Co. v. Hines, 82 Ill. App. 488, it was held that a statutory prohibition is equally efficacious, and the illegality of a breach of the statute is the same, whether a thing be prohibited absolutely, or only under a penalty. That was a suit brought by the plaintiff, Hines, to recover of the railroad company for personal injuries resulting to him from the negligence of the railroad company in violating a speed ordinance of the city of Chicago, in the operation of one of its trains. The court, in passing on the validity of the ordinance said:

"Neither do we think the ordinance ineffective because it does not appear that a penalty is prescribed for its violation. The section is expressly prohibitive in terms, and is certified by the clerk to be a true copy of section 1830 of the Municipal Code of the city passed by the city council, etc. Blackstone defines municipal law as 'A rule of civil conduct prescribed by the supreme power in a state, commanding what is right and prohibiting what is wrong.' 1 Cooley's Bl. marg. p. 44. A statute may be expressly prohibitory, or it may be prohibitory by implication, as by prescribing a penalty. Sedgwick on Con. of Statutes (2d Ed.) p. 71; 1 Kent's Com. (12th Ed.) 467." '

The latter author says:

"'The principle is now settled that the statutory prohibition is equally efficacious, and the illegality of a breach of the statute is the same whether a thing be prohibited absolutely or only under a penalty."

To the same effect is the rule announced in the case of De Scheppers v. Railroad, 179 Ill. App. 298.

The Court of Civil Appeals, in its opinion, cites cases from New Jersey, Vermont, and Kansas to support its holding that the ordinance in question, in so far as it imposed the duty on the defendant to keep flagmen at the crossing where the accident occurred, is void, because it does not prescribe a penalty for its violation in this particular; but when those cases are examined it is found that in each case the ordinance involved prescribed some duty for the protection of the municipality itself, and not for the protection of individuals composing the municipality. There is a marked distinction between the two classes of ordinances. The former can be enforced only by means of a penalty, while as to the latter the violator may be called to answer in a civil action by the individual who suffers injury by reason of its violation. McQuillin on Municipal Corporations, vol. 2, §§ 673, 674.

[2] We do not understand that counsel for the defendant controvert the general and well-established rule to the effect that the violation of such an ordinance, if it be valid, is negligence per se; but it is insisted that the ordinance in question is unreasonable because it limits the speed of trains to 4 miles an hour at said crossing. We cannot assent to this contention. To justify the courts in declaring void an ordinance limiting the speed of railroad trains within the limits of a city, its unreasonableness, or want of necessity, as a police regulation, must be clear, manifest, and undoubted. Central R. & Bkg. Co. v. Brunswick, 87 Ga. 386, 13 S. E. 520; Gratiot v. Railroad, 116 Mo. 450, 21 S. W. 1094, 16 L. R. A. 189; Louisville & W. R. Co. v. Webb, 90 Ala. 185, 8 South. 518, 11 L. R. A. 674.

In this last case it was held that an ordinance limiting the rate of speed of locomotives moving within the city to 4 miles an hour was a reasonable police regulation.

Numerous cases could be cited holding similar ordinances reasonable, and especially is this true of ordinances applying to trains and locomotives being operated within and through populous sections of cities, and over muchly traveled streets. The evidence shows that Market street, in the city of Chattanooga is the principal street of the city, and is extensively traveled.

[3] We do not think, in view of the evidence offered by the plaintiff, that it can be held that the trial judge committed error in not directing a verdict in favor of the defendant upon the third count of the plaintiff's declaration. The plaintiff expressly testified that there was no flagman or watchman on duty at the crossing at the time of the collision; that no agent or servant of the company gave any signal or warning of the approach of the train whatever. He also offered evidence tending to show that the train was moving at the time of the collision, at a speed in excess of that prescribed by the ordinance. Several witnesses testified that the train was moving at the rate of from 10 to 12 miles an hour at the time it collided with the plaintiff's automobile. In view of this evidence, it is manifest that the trial judge acted properly in not directing a verdict in favor of the defendant.

[4] There can be no constitutional exercise of the power to direct a verdict in any case where there is a dispute as to any material evidence, or any legal doubt as to the conclusion to be drawn from the whole evidence upon the issues to be tried, but the case must go to the jury. Tennessee Central R. R. Co. v. Morgan, 132 Tenn. 1, 175 S. W. 1148; Norman v. Southern R. Co., 119 Tenn. 401, 104 S. W. 1088; Kinney v. Y. & M. V. R. R. Co., 116 Tenn. 450, 92 S. W. 1116.

[5] In considering defendant's motion for

a directed verdict, that view of the evidence most favorable to the plaintiff's case must be taken by the court, and, if there is any doubt as to the conclusion to be drawn from the whole evidence, the motion must be denied. Nashville v. Reese, 138 Tenn. 471, 197 S. W. 492, L. R. A. 1918B, 349.

[6] It is true that there was a conflict in the evidence. The defendant offered evidence tending to show that it had two flagmen on duty at the crossing at the time of the collision, and that one of these flagmen was preceding the train across at the time, and as required by the ordinance herein referred to; that when the front car had reached a point near the west side of the crossing the plaintiff, who was operating his automobile at a high rate of speed, to wit, 25 or 30 miles an hour, attempted to cross immediately in front of the train by swerving his car to the right, and in so doing his automobile was struck by the front box car. The jury have resolved this disputed question of fact in favor of the plaintiff's contention, and its finding is binding upon this court.

[7] Nor do we think the defendant's contention is well taken that the plaintiff was guilty of contributory negligence, and that the Court of Civil Appeals should therefore have held that the trial judge erred in not directing a verdict in his favor on this ground.

We think this was a question properly determinable by the jury under proper instructions from the court. The court instructed the jury on this question as follows:

"Now, it was the duty of the plaintiff here to exercise ordinary care for his own safety, that is such care as you would expect from an ordinarily prudent person situated as he was there at that time and place, operating an automobile as he was. It was his duty on approaching that railroad track to use his senses of sight and hearing, and if he saw that train approaching or upon the crossing, or if he could have seen it by the exercise of ordinary care and tried to run around it, to run in front of it, when an ordinarily prudent man would not have done it, then he would be guilty of contributory negligence, and if that proximately contributed to bring about the death of his wife, he cannot recover."

Again, in a subsequent part of his charge, the trial judge instructed the jury as follows:

"On the other hand the defendants, insist that in operating their train they were complying with the terms of this ordinance; that it was not running its train over there at a greater rate of speed than 4 or 5 miles an hour; that its watchmen were there, and that one of the trainmen, one of the switching crew, and one of the watchmen preceded the train across the crossing, and that, after the train became an obstruction at the crossing, over the crossing, the plaintiff in his automobile approached, running at a negligent and rapid rate of speed, at an unlawful rate of speed, and undertook to run around the train, and ran over where the curb was in order to get around, and that while he was trying to get around he was struck by the train and pushed down the track, and his wife was killed. Now, gentlemen of the jury, if you believe from the evidence that the defendants' contention is true, or if the plaintiff by the greater weight of the evidence has failed to show you that it is not true, then the plaintiff, is not entitled to recover, and your verdict should be in favor of the defendants. How the facts are is for you to determine. You are the exclusive judges of the facts, the weight of the evidence, and the credibility of the witnesses. You will take the law as given you in charge by the court."

[8] Where there is a controversy in respect of the facts upon which the defense of contributing negligence is predicated, the question should be submitted to the jury. La Follette, etc., R. Co. v. Minton, 117 Tenn. 415, 101 S. W. 178, 11 L. R. A. (N. S.) 478; Railroad v. Bohan, 116 Tenn. 271, 94 S. W. 84; Knoxville v. Cox, 103 Tenn. 368, 53 S. W. 734; Robertson v. Cayard, 111 Tenn. 356, 77 S. W. 1056.

[9] We think the charge very fully presented the defendant's contention of contributory negligence to the jury; in fact, the charge on this question was more favorable to the defendant that the law warranted. The declaration avers, and the evidence shows, that, in addition to the plaintiff (her husband) Mrs. Partridge left surviving her three minor children, and under chapter 86 of the Acts of 1897, carried into Shannon's New Code at sections 4029a1 and 4029a2, the damages recoverable go to the plaintiff and said children equally. The children of the deceased were in no way at fault in the matter of their mother's death, and the fault of the plaintiff could not prejudice their rights. Only the beneficiary, whose negligence proximately contributed to the accident, is barred. Z. E. Anderson, Administrator v. Memphis Street Railway Co., 227 S. W. 39, decided at the present term of the court. Opinion for publication.

[10] Furthermore, the trial judge, in his second instruction on the question of the plaintiff's contributory negligence hereinbefore set out, placed the burden of proof upon the plaintiff to show by the greater weight of the evidence that he was not guilty of contributory negligence in crossing the track of the defendant upon which its train was moving. This was error against the plaintiff. The burden of proof was on the defendant to show such negligence.

[11] By chapter 36 of the Acts of 1917, the drivers of automobiles, crossing a railroad track at grade on public roads, are required to come to a full stop at a distance of not less than 10 nor more than 50 feet from the nearest rail of said track before crossing, and their failure to do so is made a misdemeanor.

The trial judge was requested by the defendant to charge the jury that if they should find from the evidence that the crossing at which the accident occurred was at grade, and that there was no flagman or watchman protecting the crossing, it was the duty of the plaintiff to have stopped his automobile at a distance of not less than 10 nor more than 50 feet from the nearest rail of the railroad track which he was approaching, and upon which the train was being operated, and if he failed to do so before undertaking to cross the track, he was guilty of negligence per se, or negligence as a matter of law, and that if this negligence on his part contributed proximately to the accident in any degree, the plaintiff could not recover.

We do not think that chapter 36 of the Acts of 1917 has any bearing on the plaintiff's right to recover. The act expressly provides that none of its provisions "shall be construed as abridging or in any way affecting the common-law right of recovery of litigants in damage suits that may be pending or hereafter brought against any railroad company or other common carrier."

We think this provision of the statute cuts off the right of the defendant to rely on its violation by the plaintiff as negligence which could in any manner affect his right to recover.

It is next urged by the defendant that the Court of Civil Appeals erred in not holding that the trial judge should have submitted in charge to the jury a number of other special requests offered by the defendant bearing upon the question of the plaintiff's contributory negligence.

There are nine of these requests, and we have considered each of them, and are of the opinion that it was not error to refuse them. We think the court fully instructed the jury upon the question of the plaintiff's contributory negligence, and, as before stated, the charge upon that question was more favorable to the defendant than he was entitled to.

[12, 13] It is next insisted that the trial judge committed error in instructing the jury on the measure of damages. The jury was instructed on this point as follows:

"If you find in favor of the plaintiff, it will be your duty to fix the amount of his recovery. The measure of the recovery would be reasonable compensation for the life of the deceased. In determining that, take into consideration her age, the state of her health. her expectancy of life, of a person of her state of health and age, and let your verdict be for reasonable compensation. If you find for the defendant, you will so state, without more."

It is said that the trial court should have charged the jury that the measure of damages was the pecuniary value of the life of the deceased, and not any sentimental value which the jury might place on the deceased's life, and, further, in arriving at the value of the life, it should be taken into consideration that at best the duration of life is uncertain.

We are of the opinion that while this instruction was not strictly accurate, in that it failed to tell the jury that the plaintiff could only recover for the pecuniary value of the deceased's life, still we cannot see wherein the defendant was prejudiced. We do not think that the verdict is in any sense sentimental. It is not for more than the reasonable pecuniary value of the deceased's life when her age and state of health are taken into consideration. It is true that her life expectancy was not shown, but it was shown that she was only 34 years of age, and was in good health. Therefore she necessarily had a long life expectancy, and, in view of the proof, we do not think it can be said that the verdict was in any sense the result of sentiment, nor do we think it is excessive.

The judgment of the Court of Civil Appeals will therefore be reversed, and the judgment of the circuit court will be affirmed, with costs.

BRIDGFORD v. STEWART DRY GOODS CO.

(Court of Appeals of Kentucky. May 20, 1921.)

1. Negligence ⟷32(1)—Reasonable care required as to customer.

A shopkeeper owes those who enter its premises by invitation the duty of using reasonable or ordinary care to keep the premises in a safe condition, but is not an insurer of a customer's safety.

2. Negligence ⟷51—Shopkeeper may allow customers on wet floor.

Where its basement was flooded through no negligence of shopkeeper, it is not bound, the place being well lighted, to erect barriers in order to exclude customers.

3. Negligence ⟷66(2)—Customer knowingly going on wet floor assumes risk.

Where plaintiff a customer in a store knew that the wooden floor of the basement was wet as a result of an unusual rainstorm, plaintiff assumed the risk of injury in going on the floor, which was well lighted, and cannot recover for injuries resulting from a fall, even if the storekeeper be otherwise deemed guilty of negligence.

Appeal from Circuit Court, Jefferson County, Common Pleas Branch, Third Division.

Action by Nancy Bridgford against the Stewart Dry Goods Company. From a judgment for defendant, plaintiff appeals. Affirmed.

Edwards, Ogden & Peak, of Louisville, for appellant.

Humphrey, Crawford, Middleton & Humphrey, of Louisville, for appellee.

CLARKE, J. The defendant, now appellee, conducts a department store in Louisville and maintains on the basement floor a checkroom or counter for use of its patrons. About 3 o'clock in the afternoon of July 29, 1919, plaintiff went to this checkroom for her grip, and in walking back to the stairway fell and received serious, if not permanent, injuries. Just a few minutes before this the floor of the basement had been covered about an inch deep with water, as a result of an unusual rainstorm. It is conceded by counsel for plaintiff that the flooding of the floor was not caused by any negligence upon the part of defendant, but it is alleged that as a result thereof the floor of the basement was wet, slick, and in an "unsafe and dangerous condition for persons to walk upon and over, and this condition was known to the defendant, its agents, servants, and employés, or could have been known by it and them by the exercise of ordinary care, and was unknown to this plaintiff; that the defendant negligently failed to warn or notify plaintiff of

the unsafe and dangerous condition of said floor and negligently failed to place barricades at the entrance to said basement, or otherwise prevent plaintiff from using said floor." These allegations of the petition were denied by the answer, and upon a trial at the conclusion of the plaintiff's testimony the court gave a peremtory instruction in favor of the defendant. From the judgment entered thereon the plaintiff has prosecuted this appeal.

[1] The evidence of plaintiff shows that she was upon the premises by invitation of the defendant, and as a consequence the defendant owed her the duty of using reasonable or ordinary care to keep the premises in a safe condition, but was not an insurer of her safety. Anderson & Nelson Distilleries Co. v. Hair, 103 Ky. 196, 44 S. W. 658, 19 Ky. Law Rep. 1822; Branham's Adm'r v. Buckley et al., 158 Ky. 848, 166 S. W. 618, Ann. Cas. 1915D, 861; 29 Cyc. 454.

[2, 3] The evidence shows that immediately upon the flooding of the floor and before plaintiff entered the basement some planks were taken up at one end of same to allow the water to run through, and janitors were put to work mopping up the floor where it was wet; that the basement was well lighted; that there were no barriers erected to prevent plaintiff from going on the floor, and that no one warned or notified her not to do so. Plaintiff testified that she was caused to slip and fall by the wet or damp condition of the floor. Upon cross-examination she was asked and answered the following questions:

"Q. You say when you came down the steps you found the room well lighted? A. It was well lighted; yes.

"Q. The floor was perfectly level and in good condition as far as you could see? A. As far as I could see.

"Q. What was there on the floor that could cause anybody to slip? A. From where they had been mopping.

"Q. That is all? A. That is all I could see.

"Q. Just a little dampness on the floor where they had just finished mopping, evidently? A. It was water, from the condition of my clothes.

"Q. Did you notice this dampness as you walked toward the counter for your grip? A. No, sir; not until I stood there waiting for my grip; I noticed them mopping just beyond the checkroom, past me.

"Q. Then you noticed the floor all around you was slightly moist? A. Yes.

"Q. And that it was in that condition between the check counter and the steps that you were going to? A. Yes.

"Q. So when you walked across that floor you knew it was moist? A. Yes."

Upon this testimony it is plain that the plaintiff, while she was waiting at the counter for her grip, saw the porters mopping up the floor, and that the floor was moist between the check counter and the steps. Hence she knew of the very condition which she claims rendered the floor unsafe, and her accident was not the result of defendant's failure to give her notice or warning, even if it be conceded that ordinary care required notice that an ordinary wood floor in a well-lighted room was moist or damp, which is at least doubtful. See American Tobacco Co. v. Adams, 187 Ky. 414, 125 S. W. 1067. Certain it is that the mere fact the floor was moist or damp did not render it so dangerous as to require of defendant, in the exercise of ordinary care for the safety of its customers, that it should place barricades across the entrance to the basement and prevent its use altogether until the floor was entirely dried out. We are inclined to the opinion that proof simply that an ordinary wood floor in a well-lighted room is moist or damp is no evidence that it is not in a reasonably safe condition for use, but, if mistaken in that, we are quite sure that one who uses such a floor with full knowledge of its condition assumes any and all risks incident to its use. We are therefore of the opinion that the trial court did not err in directing a verdict in favor of the defendant. Wherefore the judgment is affirmed.

HINES, Director General of Railroads, v. WILSON'S ADM'X.

(Court of Appeals of Kentucky. May 20, 1921.)

1. Appeal and error ⟝1003—Verdict unsupported by evidence cannot be allowed to stand.

Under Civ. Code Prac. § 340, subsec. 6, a verdict not supported by the evidence will be set aside and the cause remanded, even though the evidence was not such as to warrant direction of verdict for defendant.

2. Railroads ⟝369(3)—Lookout and signals required where tracks are used by public.

Where the public generally, with the knowledge and acquiescence of a railroad company, have continually used its tracks as a footpath for a long period of time, the presence of persons on the tracks must be anticipated, and it is the company's duty to give warning of the approach of trains and to operate them at a reasonable rate of speed, maintaining proper lookout, and, unless signals are given, an engineer has no right to assume that a person with his back to the train knows of its approach.

3. Railroads ⟝356(1)—Habitual use of tracks determines right to go thereon.

It is the habitual use by the public rather than the location of tracks which determines whether one walking thereon is a trespasser or licensee.

4. Railroads ⟝400(2)—License to use tracks held question for jury.

In an action for the death of plaintiff's intestate, who, while walking on the railroad tracks, was struck by a train, the question whether decedent was a trespasser or licensee *held* for the jury.

5. Railroads ⟝377—Injury to pedestrian who steps directly in front of train not actionable.

If a train is operated at a reasonable speed, and due warning of its approach given, and lookout maintained, while passing over tracks habitually used by the public as a footpath, the railroad is not liable for injuring one so using the tracks, if he leaves a place of safety and steps in front of the engine when the distance is so short that it is impossible for the engineer in the use of means at his command to avoid injury.

Appeal from Circuit Court, Muhlenburg County.

Action by Lucien Wilson's administratrix against Walker D. Hines, Director General of Railroads. From a judgment for plaintiff, defendant appeals. Reversed for further proceedings.

Taylor, Eaves & Sparks, of Greenville, and Benjamin D. Warfield, of Louisville, for appellant.

John C. Duffy, of Hopkinsville, and Hubert Meredith, of Greenville, for appellee.

QUIN, J. The Wickliffe mines are located about one-half mile north of Browder, a town of approximately 200 people. These mines had been in operation for a period of several months prior to July 9, 1918, on which date appellee's intestate was killed while going from Browder to the mines. The accident happened about 6:30 in the morning.

The railroad depot is located near the south side of the town. The coal company's commissary to the north of the depot fronts on the railroad, as do a number of residences in the town. To the north of the depot is a road crossing. About one-fourth mile south of the depot is a signal post. From this point for about one-half mile north the track is straight and level. Some 15 to 30 miners daily used this track at that time in the morning on their way to the mines. In addition to the miners the track is used by other persons in the neighborhood. As is to be expected, the witnesses are not in accord as to the number of persons so using the track. Practically all the witnesses for both parties agree that a north-bound coal train which reached Browder at that time whistled when south of the depot. The trainmen say the bell was ringing, but several say they did not hear the bell ring. Decedent was walking in the same direction in which the train was going, and when the engine got within about 30 feet of him it gave several shrill blasts of the whistle. Decedent turned his head slightly, and as he did so he was struck and instantly killed. The accident happened about 200 yards north of the commissary.

For the defendant the enginemen testify that in addition to the signal for the depot they whistled for the crossing, and that the bell was ringing. They saw people walking alongside the track, but no one was on the track until decedent stepped onto the track when the train got within approximately 30 feet of him. As soon as he was seen to leave a point of safety the whistle was blown, but too late to avoid the accident. Plaintiff's witnesses, with one exception, corroborate defendant's testimony. Only one of them claims to have seen decedent on the track at a greater distance than 30 feet from the train. The one exception is a miner by the name of Wherry, who says he was 100 yards ahead of decedent when the train struck him. He heard the train whistle for the depot, but, like most of the witnesses, heard no more whistles until the distress signal was given.

From the testimony of this witness it is impossible to tell just how long decedent had been on the main track before he was struck by the engine.

In answer to a question as to how far decedent had been walking down the track, he answers:

"I suppose he was walking down the track 50 yards."

When asked whether people ever traveled up and down the track, he said:

"No; not on the track; I suppose not."

This witness further testified as follows:

"Q. After Mr. Wilson got on the track in front of the engine, between the rails on the main track, I will get you to state whether or not the engineer could have stopped that train in time to have prevented the injury; you say it was just 30 feet away?" A. You mean after the man got on the main track?

"Q. Yes. A. I don't think he could have stopped the train at all after the train gave the distress signal."

This last answer is in exact agreement with the testimony of all the witnesses to the accident. At the time the distress signals were given the train was so close to decedent it was impossible for him to have gotten out of its way. The trainmen say the distress signals were sounded as soon as decedent started toward the main track. There is no contrariety in the proof on this point. It is not surprising the witnesses do not agree in their estimate of the distance of the train from Wilson when the whistle was blown. According to Wherry's supposition, Wilson had been on the track for 50 yards. No other witness fixes the distance exceeding 30 feet. No one testifies the distress signal was not given as soon as Wilson got on the track or attempted to do so. Whether, therefore, it

was 50 yards or 30 feet, all agree the train could not have been stopped in time to have prevented the accident. Nor, according to the weight of the evidence, was the train moving at an excessive rate of speed at the time.

Wherry says he was 100 yards ahead of Wilson when the train hit him, and that there was a bunch of men along there at the time on their way to work. He does not state when he first turned around, but whether it was when the distress whistle was heard by him, or before, it is quite possible from his position looking straght backward, and considering the presence of men on the track, he could have been mistaken in his estimate of the distance between the train and Wilson when he saw the latter on the track.

[1] Considering the record from any viewpoint, it presents, at most, a case cognizable under Civil Code, § 340, subsec. 6, which authorizes a new trial when the verdict or decision is not sustained by sufficient evidence. As said in L. & N. R. R. Co. v. Baker's Adm'r, 183 Ky. 795, 210 S. W. 674, under this section a verdict will not be set aside unless it is flagrantly against the evidence, but when such is the case it is not only the right, but the duty, of the court to reverse and remand for a new trial. This must be the order here.

[2] It is urged by defendant that it was entitled to a directed verdict, but with this conclusion we cannot agree.

There were two tracks at Browder, the main track and the siding. Their use is variously stated by the witnesses as being from 40 to 300 persons daily. Where the public generally, with the knowledge and acquiescence of the railroad company, have continuously used its tracks for a long period of time, the presence of persons on the track at the point where it is so used must be anticipated by the company in the running of its trains thereon, and it is the company's duty in the movement of cars at such places, whether in the daytime or at night, to give warning of the approach of its trains, and to operate same at a reasonable rate of speed and to maintain a proper lookout. Unless signals are given, the engineer has no right to assume that a person with his back to the train knows of its approach.

[3-5] It is the habitual use rather than the location of the tracks that determines the question whether one is a trespasser or licensee. Whether there was such use in the present instance was for the jury, and if the tracks between Browder and the mines were habitually used at the time of morning when decedent was killed by such large numbers of persons as to impose upon the company the exercise of the duties above mentioned, the company would be liable if it failed on the occasion mentioned to perform these duties. There is no question of lookout in this case, because the engineer admits he saw the peo-

ple on the track. If, however, the train was being operated at a reasonable rate of speed, and due warning of its approach was given and lookout maintained, the company would not be liable if decedent left a place of safety and got on the track in front of the engine at a time when the distance between decedent and the engine was so short that it was impossible for the engineer of said train, in the use of the means at his command, to stop or check the train in time to avoid the injury.

These, and these only, are the issues triable upon the next calling of the case; the evidence being substantially the same as upon the first trial.

The conclusions reached render unnecessary reference to other points raised by defendant's counsel; e. g. alleged error of the court in refusing to grant a continuance on the ground of an absent witness. Nor do we find it necessary to discuss the question of instructions. Upon a new trial the court should instruct the jury in accordance with the views herein expressed.

Wherefore the judgment is reversed for further proceedings consistent herewith.

COMMONWEALTH v. FARMERS' BANK OF KENTUCKY et al.

(Court of Appeals of Kentucky. May 20, 1921.)

1. **Depositaries** ⇐=10—**Commonwealth can recover from depository only balance above payments from defaulter's surety.**

Where a bank in which the funds of the commonwealth had been deposited had paid out sums on checks fraudulently indorsed by an assistant auditor, the commonwealth cannot recover from the depository more than the difference between the amount of the checks so paid and the amount which the commonwealth had received from the assistant auditor's surety, since the bank was under no obligation to reimburse the surety.

2. **Depositaries** ⇐=13—**Surety of defaulting employee held real party in interest to suit in name of commonwealth.**

In a suit brought in the name of a commonwealth against a state depository to recover the amount paid by the depository on checks fraudulently indorsed by the assistant auditor, where it was stipulated between the commonwealth and the surety of the officer that from any recovery in that suit the surety was first to be paid the amount it had paid to the commonwealth and an attorney's fee, and the amount payable to the surety exceeded the amount which could have been recovered from the bank, the surety was the real party in interest within Civ. Code Prac. § 18, so that the suit by the commonwealth must be dismissed.

Appeal from Circuit Court, Franklin County.

Suit by the Commonwealth of Kentucky against the Farmers' Bank of Kentucky and others. From a judgment dismissing the petition, plaintiff appeals. Affirmed.

Eli H. Brown, Jr., of Louisville, Chas. H. Morris, of Frankfort, Lewis A. Nuckols, of Roanoke, Va., Brown & Nuckols, of Frankfort, and Chas. I. Dawson, Atty. Gen., for the Commonwealth.

Guy H. Briggs, Elwood Hamilton, J. C. W. Beckham, and Hamilton & Polsgrove, all of Frankfort, for appellees.

QUIN, J. Charles E. Booe was connected with the office of Auditor of Public Accounts of the State of Kentucky for several years, and during the incumbency of Auditor S. W. Hager acted as clerk and also Assistant Auditor. Following the expiration of Hager's term of office it was discovered that through the manipulations and fraudulent indorsements of Booe there had been paid out on checks issued and signed by the State Treasurer the sum of over $30,000.

Under Ky. Stats. § 4692, the Treasurer is directed to designate in writing to the Governor not less than three solvent banks as state depositories, and under this designation the appellee on January 15, 1904, was selected as one of the state depositories, and continued as such during the period involved in this litigation. As required by law, appellee executed bond, with approved surety, covenanting with the commonwealth that it would pay over when demanded all money deposited with it by the Treasurer and comply with all the requirements of law relating to it as a depository. During the years named appellee paid the sum of $31,414.88 on 326 checks fraudulently indorsed by Booe. Of this sum about $22,000, the proceeds of 141 checks, was paid by appellee direct to Booe, mostly upon checks upon which he had indorsed the name of the payee, usually a fictitious person, followed by his own indorsement, and on the remaining 185 checks appellee paid the sum of about $9,000 to different persons, including local merchants from whom Booe had procured the money on similar fraudulent indorsements. Of the total amount thus paid Booe repaid $1,481.82, leaving a balance of $29,933.06, for which sum recovery is sought in this action.

The Title, Guaranty & Surety Company of Scranton, Pa., as surety upon a bond executed to Hager by Booe for the faithful performance of the latter's duty as clerk and Assistant Auditor.

In a suit instituted by the commonwealth against Hager and his surety, the United States Fidelity & Guaranty Company, seeking to recover the amount of this defalcation,

Hager filed a cross-petition against Booe's surety asking that it be required to pay to Hager such sums as might be recovered against him by the state. During the pendency of that suit a stipulation was signed by the parties wherein for the consideration of $17,500 paid by the Title, Guaranty & Surety Company to the commonwealth, and the settlement of the costs of that action, the commonwealth agreed: (a) To dismiss without prejudice the pending suit against Hager and his surety; (b) not to insist any further upon the payment of said claim by Hager or his surety; (c) to institute suit or suits against the various state depositories and their sureties for the recovery of said claim. It was further stipulated that the Attorney General was to appear as counsel for the state in said proceedings and co-operate with counsel employed by Booe's surety; such counsel to be authorized to represent the state in such proceedings without cost or expense to the state, the surety company to assume the cost incident to such litigation. It was further provided in said agreement that:

"In the event a recovery from said depositories on their sureties is had on such claim, out of such recovery the Title, Guaranty & Surety Company is to be repaid the said sum of $17,500, together with the costs and expenses incurred by it, including a reasonable attorney's fee, such fee in no event to exceed $2,000, and the excess, if any, of such recovery over and above the amount to be repaid to said company, as above indicated, is to belong to the state of Kentucky."

After the dismissal of that action the present suit was instituted by the commonwealth against appellee and its sureties seeking to recover the sum so paid out by appellee on the checks aforesaid, less the amount returned by Booe. Upon final hearing the petition was dismissed, and an appeal has been prosecuted by the commonwealth.

Having reached the conclusion the lower court correctly ordered a dismissal of the petition, we find it unnecessary to discuss many of the points raised by respective counsel.

[1] The commonwealth, which sues in its own name, has been paid the sum of $17,500, so, at most, it is not entitled to a recovery exceeding the difference between that sum and the net amount of the defalcation, or $12,433.06, and this sum is subject, under the stipulation aforesaid, to a further deduction of $2,000 as the agreed fee to special counsel. While the commonwealth appears as the nominal and only plaintiff, it is obvious that the real party in interest is none other than the Title, Guaranty & Surety Company.

The brief is from the pen of counsel for the surety company; the suit is being prosecuted without cost or expense to the commonwealth. From any recovery had in this action it is provided the said surety company shall first be reimbursed for the amount it has heretofore paid the commonwealth, next its counsel is to receive $2,000, and then, if there is any excess after the payment of these two sums, it is payable to the commonwealth.

We can perceive of no circumstances under which the Title, Guaranty & Surety Company might be entitled to reimbursement from appellee for the amount paid by the surety company to the commonwealth. It follows, therefore, that the amount recoverable in the present action cannot exceed the net amount the state is out by reason of Booe's defalcation, to wit, $12,433.06.

[2] The stipulation hereinbefore referred to is set out in full in appellant's reply, and it is alleged that said writing constitutes the entire agreement between the commonwealth and the Title, Guaranty & Surety Company. In effect, this pleading is an admission on the part of the commonwealth that, in the event there should be a recovery in this action, out of the proceeds of said judgment Booe's surety is to receive the amount it has heretofore paid the state, and is to have its counsel fees settled before the commonwealth receives anything. Inasmuch as the maximum sum recoverable in this action is several thousand dollars less than the amount the commonwealth has stipulated and concedes is payable to the surety company, it necessarily results that in so far as the commonwealth is concerned this is a moot case, it has no interest whatever in this proceeding, and can have no share in any judgment that might be rendered.

In Civil Code, § 18, it is provided:

"Every action must be prosecuted in the name of real party in interest, except as is provided in section 21."

The provisions of section 21 have no application to this action.

Within the meaning of the Code provision supra, the real party in interest is the one entitled to the benefits of the action upon the successful termination thereof, and this, in the present instance, could mean none other than the Title, Guaranty & Surety Company. The real party in interest is the one who is actually and substantially interested in the subject-matter as distinguished from one who has only a nominal interest therein. The test is: Does the plaintiff satisfy the call of the person who has the right to control and receive the fruits of the litigation? Application of this test to the present proceeding would necessarily produce a negative answer. The authorities on this question are collated in the case of Taylor, etc., v. Hurst, Trustee, etc., 186 Ky. 71, 216 S. W. 95.

It is impossible to read the contract between the commonwealth and Booe's surety without reaching the conclusion that this action is prosecuted solely in the interest and for the benefit of said surety. This being true, and the commonwealth being without right to maintain the action, the judgment must be, and is accordingly, affirmed.

———

KRIEGER, County Judge, et al. v. STANDARD PRINTING CO.

(Court of Appeals of Kentucky. May 20, 1921.)

I. Counties ⬧⬧⬧116—County clerk may contract for ballots without competitive bidding.

Under Ky. St. Supp. 1918, § 1465, making it the duty of the county clerk to furnish ballots, etc., the fiscal court is bound by his contract just as it is bound in case of a contract by the sheriff to provide election booths under section 1465, and competitive bidding is unnecessary,' Const. § 247, requiring the letting of public printing of the state on competitive bidding, having no application, and hence, in an action by a printer to recover for the printing of ballots, etc., an instruction requiring the contract to have been let on competitive bidding placed an unwarranted burden on the printer.

2. Appeal and error ⬧⬧⬧1033(5) — Defendant cannot complain of instruction placing undue burden on plaintiff.

Defendant cannot complain of instruction placing undue burden on plaintiff.

3. Counties ⬧⬧⬧125 ᴸ—Where contract is unenforceable, but services and work are accepted by agency empowered to contract therefor, recovery may be had on quantum meruit.

Where the contract declared on is unenforceable, quantum meruit recovery may be had if a government agency has accepted the services or work and had power to make the valid contract therefor; hence in an action to recover for printing ballots for the county clerk an instruction allowing a recovery on the quantum meruit if the contract was unenforceable was proper.

4. Counties ⬧⬧⬧114—County clerk may make binding contract for printing ballots.

Under Ky. St. Supp. 1918, § 1465, the county clerk may make a binding contract for the printing of ballots for an election, and, where he acts within his powers without fraud, the fiscal court cannot repudiate his contract.

5. Trial ⬧⬧⬧337—Judgment reversed where jury disregards instructions, whether right or wrong.

Instructions, whether right or wrong, are binding on the jury, and a reversal will be ordered if the jury disregards the same.

6. Counties ⬧⬧⬧129—Verdict in favor of printer against fiscal court not contrary to instructions.

Under the instructions which allowed printer who furnished ballots under contract with the county clerk to recover full amount of his claim if the work was let on competitive bidding, etc., held, that evidence warranted the verdict rendered in favor of the printer, and that it was not open to attack as contrary to the instructions.

Appeal from Circuit Court, Jefferson County, Common Pleas Branch, Third Division.

Action by the Standard Printing Company against William Krieger, County Judge, and others, composing the Fiscal Court of Jefferson County. From a judgment for plaintiff, defendants appeal. Affirmed.

John B. Baskin and J. Matt Chilton, both of Louisville, for appellants.

Burnett, Batson & Cary, of Louisville, for appellee.

CLARKE, J. This is an appeal by the members of the fiscal court of Jefferson county, to whom we shall refer as defendants, from a verdict and judgment against them for $2,169 in favor of the Standard Printing Company, called plaintiff herein.

The judgment is the full amount of plaintiff's bill for supplying to the county clerk of Jefferson county all of the supplies for the November, 1919, election, which by section 1465, vol. 3, Kentucky Statutes, he was required to provide. When the county clerk, having approved the bill, presented it to the fiscal court for payment, that body objected to the amount charged for printing each of the two kinds of ballots furnished, and reduced the amounts charged therefor a total of $750, allowing only $1,419 in satisfaction of the bill. This the plaintiff refused to accept and appealed to the circuit court, where it filed a petition in which it alleged that the several items of the bill were furnished to the county clerk upon a contract and at the prices set out in the bill. The defendants filed an answer admitting that the county was indebted to the plaintiff in the sum of $1,419, and they did not deny the alleged contract; but they averred that the charges were excessive and fraudulent to the extent of $615 for the large ballots, and to the extent of $135 for the small ballots; that either the clerk was unfamiliar with the value of such work, and plaintiff had practiced a fraud upon and deceived him as to the real value of same, or else the clerk and plaintiff had fraudulently colluded to defraud the county out of the said sums aggregating $750; that one or the other, but defendants did not know which, of these state of facts was true. A reply traversing the affirmative allegations of the answer completed the issues.

Plaintiff offered evidence to prove that the county clerk had awarded it a contract within the time required by law and upon competitive bidding for printing and binding the regular or large ballots which contained the names of all candidates for the sum of $1,250; that the small or constitutional amendment ballots were furnished upon order of the county clerk and without bids; that there was no fraud or collusion; and that the sums charged, $1,250 for the large ballots and $375.50 for the small ballots, were customary and reasonable.

Defendant's evidence tends to prove that the contract for printing the larger ballots was awarded to plaintiff by the county clerk collusively and without competitive bidding; that the printing and binding of the large ballots was reasonably worth only from about $600 to $685 and of the small ballots from $240 to $250.

At the conclusion of the evidence the court overruled motions of both parties for a directed verdict, and, over the objections of each party, gave to the jury a single instruction which for convenience we have divided into two parts as follows:

"(1) If the jury shall believe from the evidence that the county clerk gave reasonable notice to persons and corporations engaged in the printing trade in the city of Louisville, who had the requisite facilities for doing the work required, of his requirements of election paraphernalia for the November election, 1919, and of the time within which bids for said work would be received, and thereafter, at the time fixed, he opened said bids and awarded the work to the lowest and best bidder, and that the Standard Printing Company was the lowest and best bidder, and was awarded the contract at and for the price of $2,169, then the law is for the plaintiff, and the jury should find for the Standard Printing Company in said sum of $2,169, with interest from December 24, 1919."

"(2) But, unless you so believe from the evidence, or if you believe from the evidence that the plaintiff and the said clerk colluded for the purpose of enabling the plaintiff to charge said county an unreasonable price for said articles and work, and that in pursuance of said collusion, if they did so collude, the plaintiff charged said county unreasonable prices for the articles and services mentioned, or any part thereof, then in either of said state of events you can only find for the plaintiff the fair and reasonable market value of the work and services performed by the plaintiff at the time delivery was required of it, to wit, October 4, 1919, with or without interest in the discretion of the jury, from December 24, 1919, the award, however, not to be less than the sum of $1,419, which sum the defendant admits as owing to the plaintiff."

For reversal defendants insist: (1) That the instructions given are prejudicially erroneous; and (2) that the jury disregarded the instructions.

[1] The first part of the instruction assumes, it will be noticed, that the law required that the contract for printing the ballots must be let by the county clerk after due notice to the lowest and best bidder, and whether or not this is true is the principal question at issue upon this appeal.

Section 1465 of the Statutes makes it the duty of the county clerk to furnish the ballots, tally sheets, and certain other utensils required in holding an election, just as section 1467 makes it the duty of the sheriff to provide the election booths. With reference to these sections of the statutes, we said in Fiscal Court of Jefferson County v. Louisville Tent & Awning Co., 185 Ky. 466, 215 S. W. 88:

"The above duties are intrusted to the named officers, who are necessarily authorized to contract for the printing and supplies, and the fiscal courts are bound by their contracts, without any previous orders by that court authorizing the officers to make the contracts, * * * and the fiscal court is bound to allow, and direct to be paid, the costs of booths provided by the sheriff and used in the elections, in the county, when the contract for the booths was not the result of fraud and practiced by the vendor upon the sheriff, nor of fraudulent collusion between the sheriff and the vendor."

Section 1467 does not require that the sheriff shall let the contract for furnishing the booths by competitive bidding, nor is there any provision in section 1465 or elsewhere in the Statutes requiring the county clerk to let the contract by competitive bidding for the ballots and other utensils he is required to provide for an election. It is quite universally held that, in the absence of a constitutional or statutory mandate, competitive bids are not necessary. Braaten v. Olson, County Treasurer, 28 N. D. 235, 148 N. W. 829; State v. Supervisors of Dixon County, 24 Neb. 106, 37 N. W. 936; State v. Lincoln County, 35 Neb. 346, 53 N. W. 147; Henry County v. Gillies, 138 Ind. 667, 38 N. E. 40; Riverside County v. Yawman, etc., Co., 3 Cal. App. 691, 86 Pac. 900; 15 C. J. 549.

Counsel for defendants concede there is no such statutory mandate, but insist that section 247 of the Constitution, which requires that contracts for "the printing, and binding of the laws, journals, department reports and all other public printing and binding" shall be given to the lowest responsible bidder, is applicable here. This contract, however, is for county printing, and that section of the Constitution refers only to the public printing of the state, as is clearly shown by the provision therein that all such contracts as are referred to to shall be subject to the approval of the Governor.

[2, 3] We are therefore of the opinion, there being neither constitutional nor statutory provision requiring the county clerk to purchase by competitive bidding the election supplies he must buy under section 1465 of the Statutes, that such contracts as he may make therefor are binding upon the fiscal court, just as are the contracts of sheriffs for election booths, except where the contract is the result of fraud upon the part of the vendor or fraudulent collusion between the vendor and the county clerk. It therefore re-

sults that the first instruction given is erroneous and placed upon the plaintiff a more onerous burden of proof than the law authorized, but of this the defendants, of course, cannot complain. Neither can they complain of the second instruction, which is in substantial accord with the only instruction they asked the court to give, and is besides correct in substance if not in form, since we have held more than once that, even where the contract declared upon is unenforceable, a quantum meruit recovery may be had if a governmental agency has accepted the services or work and had the power to make a valid contract therefor. Nicholasville Water Co. v. Board of Councilmen, 36 S. W. 546, 38 S. W. 430, 18 Ky. Law Rep. 592; City of Providence v. Providence Electric Light Co., 122 Ky. 237, 91 S. W. 664, 28 Ky. Law Rep. 1015.

[4] Counsel for defendants are quite insistent this principle is not applicable here upon the theory that the fiscal court, and not the county clerk, is the only agency empowered thus to bind the county. But, as we have already seen from the Fiscal Court v. Louisville Tent & Awning Co., supra, section 1465 of the Statutes empowers the county clerk, instead of the fiscal court, to purchase and receive for the county such election supplies as are here involved; hence it is to his acts, and not the fiscal court's, we must look to ascertain whether there is a binding contract or an acceptance with resultant obligation of any kind upon the county. There is therefore no merit in defendants' first contention.

Their second contention, that the judgment must be reversed because the jury disregarded the court's instructions, is likewise untenable.

[5] There are numerous cases to sustain the contention that the instructions given, whether right or wrong, are binding upon a jury, and that a reversal will be ordered if the jury disregards the court's instructions. Lynch v. Snead Iron Works, 182 Ky. 247, 116 S. W. 693; St. Paul Fire & Marine Insurance Co. v. Kendle, 163 Ky. 146, 173 S. W. 373; Yellow Poplar Lumber Co. v. Bartley, 164 Ky. 763, 176 S. W. 201.

[6] But counsel for defendants are mistaken as to the facts. A verdict for plaintiff for the full amount of its claim was authorized under the first instruction if the jury believed from the evidence the contract was let in the manner therein specified or under the second instruction if the jury believed from the evidence the work was worth the amount charged therefor. There was, as counsel contends, no evidence to sustain the verdict under the first instruction, but there was evidence that the work was worth the amount charged therefor, and the verdict is therefore sustained by the evidence under

one of the two instructions given by the court. Hence it cannot be said that the jury disregarded the court's instructions.

Wherefore the judgment is affirmed.

NATIONAL COUNCIL KNIGHTS AND LADIES OF SECURITY v. DEAN.

(Court of Appeals of Kentucky. May 24, 1921.)

1. Appeal and error ⟷928(5)—Omission in instruction presumed to have been cured by other instructions.

Where the insurer alleged misrepresentation by insured which was both fraudulent and false and material, either of which will avoid a policy under Ky. St. § 639, an instruction, which submitted only the defense of fraudulent misrepresentation, does not require reversal of the judgment against insurer, where the other instructions were not embraced in the bill of exceptions or made part of the record by order of the court, since it will be presumed that they correctly presented the defense that the statement was false and material.

2. Appeal and error ⟷301—Sufficiency of evidence to sustain verdict not reviewable without motion for new trial on that ground.

The objection that the verdict was not sustained by sufficient evidence is not reviewable, where appellant did not ask a new trial on that ground.

Appeal from Circuit Court, Hickman County.

Action by John C. Dean against the National Council Knights and Ladies of Security. Judgment for plaintiff, and defendant appeals. Affirmed.

J. D. Via, of Clinton, for appellant.
Bennett, Robbins & Robbins, of Clinton, for appellee.

CLAY, J. John C. Dean, the beneficiary, brought suit against the National Council of Knights and Ladies of Security, a fraternal insurance company, to recover on a policy insuring the life of his daughter, Susie E. Dean. The company pleaded in substance that Susie E. Dean stated in her application that her mother died of "change of life," when, as a matter of fact, she died of tuberculosis, and that Susie E. Dean knew that the answer was false, and made the statement for the fraudulent purpose of deceiving the company and procuring insurance. It further pleaded that if the truth had been known, it would not have issued the policy. On the first trial there was a directed verdict for the plaintiff, but the judgment was reversed on the ground that the evidence of Susie E. Dean's knowledge of the falsity of the statement was sufficient to take the case to the jury. National Council of Knights and Ladies of Security v. Dean, 183 Ky. 43, 207 S. W. 702. On the next trial the case was submitted to a jury, which returned a verdict in favor of plaintiff. Defendant appeals.

The only grounds relied on for a new trial were: (1) Admission of incompetent evidence; (2) rejection of competent evidence; and (3) error in instruction No. 3.

Our attention has not been called to the improper admission or rejection of evidence, and our examination of the record convinces us that the trial was free from error in these respects.

[1] Instruction No. 3 is as follows:

"The court instructs the jury that if you believe that the answer given by the assured, Susie E. Dean, to the question set up in instruction No. 2 was untrue, and was known by her at the time of making of the application, or the receipt of said policy, to be untrue, and was made by her for the purpose of deceiving the defendant, insurance company, and procuring the policy thereby, and the defendant insurance company was deceived by issuing said policy by such untrue statement, which was known by her to be untrue, the law is for the defendant, and the jury should so find."

It is insisted that a representation, if false and material, will defeat the policy, even though the applicant had no knowledge of its falsity, and that the above instruction is erroneous in requiring the jury to believe that the false statement was knowingly made. It is true that our statute provides in effect that a misrepresentation, which is either material or fraudulent, will avoid a policy. Section 639, Kentucky Statutes; Security Life Insurance Co. of America v. Black's Adm'r., 190 Ky. 23, 226 S. W. 355. Conceding that the answer presented two defenses, one that the statement was false and material, and the other that it was false and fraudulent, it was not necessary for both defenses to be presented in the same instruction. Instruction No. 3 presented the defense of fraud, and was correct as far as it went. The other instructions are not embraced in the bill of exceptions or made a part of the record by order of court, and it will be presumed that they correctly presented the defense that the statement was false and material.

[2] Counsel for the company devotes the greater portion of his brief to a discussion of the facts in an effort to show that the verdict was not correct. It appears, however, that the company did not ask a new trial on the ground that the verdict was not sustained by sufficient evidence, and that being true, the matter is not subject to review. Hartsfield v. Pace, 189 Ky. 93, 224 S. W. 647.

Judgment affirmed.

HILL et al. v. BRIDGES et al.

(Court of Appeals of Kentucky. May 24, 1921.)

1. **Wills 545(4)—Limitation over on death of child held to relate to death in the lifetime of the life tenant.**

Under a will providing testator's wife should have his personalty and the full use of his realty, and absolutely his personal estate, and, should she marry, that she should have her distributable part of the land, and the balance be equally divided between the children, and if any of the children should marry, and have any child or children, that such child or children should have equally their father's or mother's portion of the estate, where the children survived the widow, who never remarried, they took the fee-simple title in the land, in view of another clause in the will providing that, if any of testator's children died without issue and unmarried, the interest of such deceased child shall pass to the other living children and their representatives, as the provision for limitation over to grandchildren was applicable only in case of the death of a child of testator in the lifetime of the wife, the life tenant.

2. **Wills 439—Intention controls other rules of construction.**

Testator's intention, when ascertainable, controls the interpretation to be put on the will, and supersedes all other rules of construction.

Appeal from Circuit Court, Montgomery County.

Suit by M. W. Bridges and others against T. B. Hill and others. From judgment for plaintiffs, defendants appeal. Affirmed.

R. G. Kern, of Mt. Sterling, for appellants.
W. B. White, of Mt. Sterling, for appellees.

SAMPSON, J. The second clause of the probated will of Willis D. M. Bridges, who died domiciled in Montgomery county in 1871, and which will gave rise to this lawsuit, reads as follows:

"It is my will and desire that my beloved wife Sarah Bridges shall have my personal estate and the full use of my real estate and absolutely my personal estate and should she marry, it is my will that my said wife shall have her distributable part of my land and the balance to be equally divided between my children, and if any one of my children should marry, and have any child or children, it is my will that such child or children shall have equally their fathers or mothers portion of my estate."

The testator owned about 125 acres of land at the time of his death. His widow, who never married, lived until 1907, and left surviving them their four children.

This action seeks two things: (1) A construction of the will of Bridges; (2) the specific performance of an executory contract for the sale of a tract of 240 acres of land, of which 57 acres descended from Willis D. M. Bridges aforesaid, and which, it is contended by appellant Hill, gave a life estate to the widow of Bridges and at her death or marriage, to the testator's children for life with the remainder to his children's children, if they should marry and have a child or children.

Because of this question as to the sufficiency of the title Hill, the purchaser of the land, refused to accept the deed of M. W. Bridges or pay the purchase price.

The lower court construed the will to pass a fee-simple title to the land to the children of testator, of whom appellee M. W. Bridges is one, adjudged the title good, and directed the purchaser Hill, to accept the deed of M. W. Bridges. Hill, the purchaser, appeals.

The clause of the will above quoted is so unskillfully and awkwardly worded that it is difficult to arrive at and certainly know the real intention and purpose of the testator. Evidently the draftsman of the will was not experienced in such work, nor was he a lawyer, if we may judge from the phraseology of the instrument.

The third clause of the will may throw some light on the question, and we copy it here:

"It is my will and desire that if either of my children shall die without children or issue, not having a living husband or wife alive, then it is my will that my other living children and their representatives shall have equally said estate of such deceased child—and should the wife or husband of such child survive them it is my will that said wife or husband have a life estate in said child's portion, provided that said child shall die without leaving child or children as before stated."

[1] Undoubtedly the testator by the second clause of the will intended to and did give all his personal estate to his wife absolutely, but only gave her the "full use" of his lands during her life if she did not marry. In event of her marriage she was not to have the use of the whole of his lands, but only such share as the statute gives the widow, the balance of his landed estate to pass to and vest immediately upon the death or marriage of the widow in his children, share and share alike. He also provided in case of death of one or more of his children after the estate became vested in them by the happening of one of the contingencies above mentioned that the share or shares of such child or children should go to and vest in equal portion in the other children of testator.

In arriving at the foregoing construction of the will we have had resort to certain well-known rules of construction of such instruments, one of such rules is that, where an estate is devised to one for life with remainder to another, and if the remainderman die

without child or issue then to another person, the provision regarding the death of the remainderman without issue relates to his death during the existence of the life estate, and not after its termination. Spacy v. Close, 184 Ky. 523, 212 S. W. 127.

If we apply this rule to the facts of this case, the will giving the widow a life estate with remainder to the children of testator, the children all surviving the widow, we must hold that the grandchildren of testator do not take under the will but that testator's children took the whole estate.

[2] But, putting aside all such arbitrary rules of construction, we think that a reading of the whole testamentary instrument shows with reasonable certainty that the testator intended to give his wife a life estate with remainder to his four children, who are parties to this action. His intention, when ascertainable, controls the interpretation to be put upon the will and supersedes all other rules of construction.

Holding this to be the correct construction of the will, it follows that M. W. Bridges is the owner of the land, the title to which appellant Hill rejected, and the lower court correctly so held, and decreed a specific performance of the contract of sale of the land.

Judgment affirmed.

JONES v. COMMONWEALTH.

(Court of Appeals of Kentucky. May 13, 1921.)

1. **Criminal law ☞706—Laying foundation for impeachment of witness without introducing impeaching statement held improper.**

Cross-examination of witness as to whether she had not made statements to named persons inconsistent with her testimony without subsequently calling such named persons to impeach the witness, notwithstanding foundation so laid, and notwithstanding the presence of such persons in the courtroom, if purpose of counsel was to damage credibility of witness without the intention of impeaching her testimony, was highly improper.

2. **Homicide ☞158(2, 3) — Testimony as to defendant's threat held too indefinite and remote.**

In a homicide prosecution, testimony that some two months before the killing defendant stated to witness that "he didn't know how mean he was and never would know until he killed some d——d s—— of a b——; said he was going to kill the first one that fooled with him, and if he couldn't get him to fool with him he would kill him one anyhow," offered as evidence of a threat held incompetent; the threats being too indefinite and remote.

3. Homicide ⇐⇒338(4)—Withdrawal of testimony from jury before submission of case cured error in introduction.

In a homicide prosecution, error in introduction of incompetent testimony as to indefinite and remote threat *held* cured by withdrawal of testimony from the jury before the case was submitted to it.

4. Criminal law ⇐⇒706—Action of prosecuting attorney in insisting upon introduction of testimony knowing it to be incompetent held improper.

Action of commonwealth's attorney in insisting upon the introduction of testimony known by him to be incompetent for the purpose of getting it before the jury with the thought that it would influence jurors, even though it should be thereafter withdrawn, *held* improper.

5. Homicide ⇐⇒190(7) — Uncommunicated threats admissible.

In homicide prosecution, in which defendant claimed to have acted in self-defense, testimony as to threats made by deceased *held* admissible, though uncommunicated to defendant.

6. Criminal law ⇐⇒1186(4), 1189—Misconduct of counsel and newly discovered evidence held ground for reversal and new trial.

In a homicide prosecution, in which the commonwealth's attorney laid a foundation for impeachment of defendant's witness without introduction of impeaching testimony, and insisted on the introduction of incompetent testimony, where there was evidence that he knew the testimony to be incompetent, but sought to have it introduced for its effect upon the jury, even though it should be subsequently withdrawn, and in which there was newly discovered evidence for defendant, which could not have been discovered before the trial, the court's refusal to grant a new trial under Cr. Code, § 271, subsec. 7, entitling defendant who has not received a fair and impartial trial to a new trial, was error prejudicial to defendant's substantial rights, authorizing the Court of Appeals to reverse the judgment of conviction with direction to grant a new trial, under section 340.

Appeal from Circuit Court, Whitley County.

Russ Jones was convicted of voluntary manslaughter, and he appeals. Reversed, with directions.

Stephens & Steely and Tye & Siler, all of Williamsburg, for appellant.

Chas. I. Dawson, Atty. Gen., and Thos. B. Mc Gregor, Asst. Atty. Gen., for the Commonwealth.

THOMAS, J. Upon his trial under an indictment for voluntary manslaughter wherein he was accused of killing Dewey Smith, the appellant, Russ Jones, was convicted, and his punishment fixed at a term of five years' confinement in the penitentiary, upon which judgment was pronounced. Defendant's motion for a new trial, which contained about 15 reasons why it should be granted, was overruled, and he prosecutes this appeal. Many of the specified reasons in the motion are extremely technical, and, we think, wholly immaterial, and in the course of this opinion we shall refer to and consider only those which we deem worthy of notice.

The facts of the case are comparatively short, and there exists but little, if any, material contradiction in the testimony of the witnesses. The killing occurred between 9 and 10 o'clock on the night of October 2, 1920, on a public road in Whitley county. There was a bright moonlight, but the place of the killing was in the shadow of a tree, thus preventing some of the witnesses, except those immediately present at the place of the shooting, from seeing exactly what occurred. Hence the only witnesses who saw or pretended to testify as to what happened at the time of the shooting were the defendant and Grace Worley, a young lady between 15 or 16 years of age. There had been a box or pie party at Thomps White's schoolhouse in the earlier part of the evening, but it was over with by about 9 o'clock, and the attendants started for their respective homes. Defendant and one or two others went to that party traveling horseback or muleback and accompanied by no lady companion, and the same was true as to the deceased, Dewey Smith. Miss Worley and another young lady went to the party unaccompanied by any gentlemen, and they rode the horse of the father of the former. When the party broke up and the people started home, the latter rode behind defendant on the animal he was riding, while her companion rode behind another young gentleman who had gone to the party with defendant, and another young man rode the horse that was ridden by Miss Worley in going to the party. A short distance from the schoolhouse the deceased passed defendant and Miss Worley, and he and others stopped in front of the barn of Doc Smith, who was the father of deceased, and were engaged in a discussion as to whether they would make up a dance to be held at a neighbor's house to furnish entertainment for a portion of the rest of the night. This discussion was going on when defendant and Miss Worley and the other couple accompanying them overtook the crowd in front of the barn, and during the conversation deceased asked Miss Worley if she would attend the dance if it was gotten up, when she answered in substance that she had promised her father to come home direct from the box party, and that she felt like she could not attend the contemplated dance; and some of the witnesses say that she stated in that connection that she had always gone with him anywhere he wanted her to. After a little while she got upon the horse that she had ridden to the party, and, in company with defendant, started down the road in the direction of their homes with others following them a short distance behind. In some 10 or 15 minutes the deceased and his crowd concluded to get up the dance, and he started in a gallop down the road in the direction traveled by Miss Worley and defendant, and what occurred when he overtook them is thus told by her:

"He came on down the road and galloped in between us and caught hold of my horse's bridle and said to wait, and we stopped and Dewey said to me that Aswald Dail told him to bring me back to the crowd where we left them, and I told I couldn't go back, and Jones said, 'What do you think you are celebrating?' and he said, 'God damn you, I don't think I am celebrating a damn thing.' Jones said, 'I didn't aim to make you mad;' and Dewey said, 'Shut your mouth you s—— of a b——, or I will kill you;' and Jones said, 'You will kill the best friend you have got when you do that;' and Dewey cursed Jones two or three times and told him twice again he would shoot him, and Jones said to me to 'Let's go;' and Dewey said, 'No; by God you will not go, you God damned hairy necked s—— of a b—— I will shoot you.' "

Some of the witnesses say that the deceased, when he asked Miss Worley if she would attend the dance and upon her answer that she could not because she had promised her father to return home, said, "We will attend to your damned father," and that when she and defendant started away deceased said, "Take him and go to h——l with him, God damn him." Following the above testimony the witness stated that at the time of the shooting deceased had his back to her, and that she could not see what was going on in front of him, but she saw his elbow raised and his right hand lifted, but could not see what he was doing with it.

The testimony of the defendant as to what occurred just before he and Miss Worley left the crowd in front of the barn and as to what happened at the time of the killing, as shown by the record, is that when he and Miss Worley overtook the crowd in front of the Smith barn deceased said to her, "Where in the hell are you going?" and his testimony continued:

"She said, 'I am started home;' and he said, 'By God, you are going to the dance;' and she said, 'No; my father is at home, and said for me to bring this mare back;' and he said, 'God damn your father; we will get by him all right;' and she got on her mare and rode up to me and said to 'let's go,' and when we started off and go out about 10 steps he said, 'Go to hell, God damn both of you.' And we rode on and got down the road between Nattie Smith's and Aunt Emily Steely's place, and he came on and overtook us and ran between our horses and grabbed my mule by the bridle and turned his mule loose and grabbed her horse's bridle, and I said, 'What do you think you are celebrating;' and he said, 'You thought you were running away with me;' and I said that I wasn't, that I didn't think that; and he said I needn't tell no God damned lie, and said he would kill me;

231 S.W.—3

and I said, 'You will kill the best friend you have;' and he said, 'God damn you, I will kill you;' and she said, 'Dewey, I never saw you do this way before in my life.' He was cursing her, and in a few minutes I said to her to 'let's go,' and he said, 'God damn you, Grace, you are not going, for Aswald Dail said to bring you back, and I will kill you, you God damned hairy necked s—— of a b——,' and I shot him."

He subsequently stated that deceased ran his right hand in his bosom as if to draw a weapon, and that he thought deceased was going to shoot him or inflict upon him great bodily harm, and that he shot deceased in what he believed was his necessary self-defense. The testimony of these two witnesses is not materially contradicted by any other witnesses, although it is shown that the deceased, who was shot in the head and fell dead in the road, had no pistol, though he had a knife in the pocket of his pantaloons. It appears from the testimony that deceased had been paying attentions to Miss Worley for something like three years, while defendant had been in her company only two or three times before the fatal occasion.

[1] One of the grounds urged for a new trial is misconduct of counsel hired to assist the prosecution, which misconduct consisted in asking Miss Worley on cross-examination, highly improper questions, and in introducing as a witness in behalf of the commonwealth Jack Stephens. One of the questions asked Miss Worley about which complaint is made is this one:

"Did you not go to the grave of the deceased one time and there state in the presence of Mary Smith, Nellie Huddleston, Dora Smith, and Jesse Huddleston and say this in words or substance, 'Poor Dewey; I didn't tell the truth about how it took place or how come him to be killed by Jones, but when it comes time I will tell the truth about it'?"

She answered that she made no such statement. Other questions purporting to lay the foundation for impeaching the witness were also asked with like answers. These supposed impeaching witnesses who were named in the question were present at the trial, and none of them were introduced or offered to be introduced to prove the impeaching statement, and the record is silent as to the reason, if any, why they were not introduced. If counsel was deceived by them as to what they would testify, he made no effort to manifest that fact by anything appearing in the record. This furnishes grounds for the suspicion that the purpose of the question was to damage the credibility of Miss Worley and to weaken her testimony in the minds of the jury by means of this wholly unwarranted "smoke screen," under the belief that they would conclude that "Where there was smoke there must be some fire." If such was the purpose of counsel, his conduct was, to mildly put it, most highly improper, a fact which we believe will be universally admitted. The chief purpose in the conduct of trials is, or should be, to see that justice, as near as may be, shall prevail. This can never be accomplished by the injection of misleading matters into the record, either directly or indirectly; for the temple of justice has for its sole foundation, and is built upon, truth, and it is upon this alone that all the law of the country, both civil and criminal, is erected. Attorneys are officers of the court and constitute as much a part of its machinery for administering right and justice in the conduct of trials as does his honor upon the bench, and it would certainly be an unheard-of proceeding for the latter to engage in an effort to create a false impression upon the minds of that part of the judicial machinery whose duty it is to pass upon the facts. Cases are not wanting where similar conduct of counsel has been held prejudicial, even to the extent of authorizing a reversal of the judgment. L. & N. R. R. Co. v. Payne, 133 Ky. 539, 118 S. W. 352, 19 Ann. Cas. 294; Shields, Adm'r, v. Rowland, 151 Ky. 136, 152 S. W. 943, and Baker v. Commonwealth, 184 Ky. 207, 211 S. W. 566.

[2] The witness Stephens said that he was at a school fair some two months before the killing, and while there he met defendant, whom he scarcely knew, and with whom he had never conversed before, and that defendant took the witness to one side, when this occurred:

"He said he didn't know how mean he was and never would know until he killed some d——d s—— of a b——; said he was going to kill the first one that fooled with him, and if he couldn't get him to fool with him he would kill him one anyhow."

The testimony was objected to, but the objection was overruled, and it was admitted. At the close of all the evidence, however, the court withdrew the testimony of that witness from the jury and directed them not to consider it. That the alleged indefinite and remote threat testified to by that witness was incompetent there can be no question. 21 Cyc. 922; Johnson v. Commonwealth, 9 Bush, 224; Hollingsworth v. Warnock, 112 Ky. 96, 65 S. W. 163, 23 Ky. Law Rep. 1395; Whittaker v. Commonwealth, 17 S. W. 358, 13 Ky. Law Rep. 504; Commonwealth v. Hoskins, 35 S. W. 285, 18 Ky. Law Rep. 59; and Cardwell v. Commonwealth, 46 S. W. 705, 20 Ky. Law Rep. 496.

[3, 4] Since, however, this testimony was withdrawn from the jury before the case was submitted to it, under the doctrine announced in the recent case of Welch v. Commonwealth, 189 Ky. 579, 225 S. W. 470, and cases referred to therein, the error in its introduction was no doubt cured, and a reversal will not be ordered therefor; but it appears in this case, from a preponderance of the evidence heard, that the same employed prosecuting counsel, contrary to the suggestion of the commonwealth's attorney, insisted upon the introduc-

tion of this testimony and stated that he thought it was incompetent, but, if he could get it before the jury, it would have its effect, notwithstanding it might afterwards be withdrawn. And it is of this conduct on the part of the attorney that the chief complaint concerning this testimony is made. Our opinion concerning this is fully expressed above, and we will not attempt to enlarge upon it.

[5] One of the grounds for a new trial was newly discovered evidence since the trial of which the defendant had no knowledge, nor could have discovered it by ordinary care before the trial. In support of that ground he filed the affidavits of William Goins and John Goins. William Goins stated in his affidavit that about the last of July, 1920, he had a conversation with deceased, Dewey Smith, in which he said:

That "if he [Smith] ever caught Jones [defendant] with his girl across the river, he would fix him; that it would do him good to kill him."

John Goins stated in his affidavit that upon another occasion he met the deceased in Williamsburg where deceased said to him:

"That Russ Jones had been going with his girl; that she had been attending meeting over at the place, and asked me if I had ever heard Russ Jones say anything about him. Affiant told him that he had not, and he then said that if he ever caught him with his girl again that he would use this on him, showing him [affiant] a pistol which he [deceased] had in his front pants pocket."

It is shown that these witnesses never communicated those threats to defendant or his attorneys, and he knew nothing of them until after the trial. That they were relevant and pertinent under the facts of this record there can be no doubt. In the case of Newton v. Commonwealth, 102 S. W. 264, 31 Ky. Law Rep. 327, similar uncommunicated threats made by the deceased are declared to be admissible, the court saying:

"Threats, though uncommunicated, may be admitted to prove the ill feeling of the person making them toward the person threatened, or, where the matter is in issue, to show who began a conflict resulting in homicide. Miller v. Commonwealth, 10 Ky. Law Rep. 672, 89 Ky. 653; Wheeler v. Commonwealth, 27 Ky. Law Rep. 1090, 120 Ky. 697."

See, also, Marshall v. Glover, 190 Ky. 113, 226 S. W. 398.

It furthermore appears that, after the case had been submitted and the jury had been placed in the hands of the sheriff to be kept together until a verdict was rendered, W. T. Smith, a cousin of the deceased, and who took an active part in the prosecution, mixed with the members, while the jury was upon the sidewalk and the sheriff was in the streets, and created some commotion and was talking to some of them and patted some of them upon the shoulder. It is not shown that he said anything to any of them concerning the trial. It may be that this relative of the deceased had no ulterior motive in his conduct, but, to say the least of it, it cannot be said that in conversing and in coming in contact with the jury at that time his actions were void of criticism. He certainly had an opportunity to whisper a word or to create the impression with some member of the jury that he desired the conviction of the defendant. His conduct created strong grounds for suspicion, and the commonwealth did not successfully explain it away. Defendant knew nothing of the above matter till after the verdict. Our criticism of this conduct is based upon the same grounds hereinbefore expressed concerning the conduct of counsel in the trial of the case. Defendant in this case may be guilty, i. e., he may have shot the deceased without justifiable excuse; but, whether so or not, he is entitled to a fair and impartial trial of that issue. The commonwealth does not desire, nor does the law permit it, through either elected or employed counsel, to persecute the accused, but only to prosecute him. While, possibly, none of the errors hereinbefore recited, standing alone, would be sufficient to authorize a reversal of the judgment of conviction if defendant's guilt was clearly proven, we have often held that a number of them, each of which approaches close to the line of being sufficiently prejudicial, will combined authorize a reversal, unless guilt is convincingly established. Subsection 7 of section 271 of the Criminal Code of Practice authorizes the granting of a new trial if "from any other cause the court be of opinion that the defendant has not received a fair and impartial trial"; while section 340 of the same Code authorizes this court to reverse a judgment of conviction when, "upon consideration of the whole case, the court is satisfied that the substantial rights of the defendant have been prejudiced thereby."

[8] Considering the errors referred to all together, we have concluded that the defendant has not had a fair and impartial trial within the intent and purpose of the law, and because thereof the judgment is reversed, with directions to grant a new trial and for proceedings consistent with this opinion.

COMMONWEALTH v. BOWMAN.

(Court of Appeals of Kentucky. May 24, 1921.)

1. **Constitutional law ⬌35 — Provisions of Constitution mandatory.**

All the provisions of the Constitution are mandatory.

2. **Statutes ⬌141(1)—Amendatory act as to carrying concealed weapons, invalid because not setting out any of amended act.**

Acts 1918, c. 84 (now Ky. St. Supp. 1918, § 1309a) entitled "An act to amend * * * Ky. St. § 1309, * * * relating to carrying concealed deadly weapons," then merely declaring all judges to "have penal jurisdiction of the first offense herein described," but describing none, and that the penalties and fines for same shall be enforced and collected as in other cases in their final jurisdiction, but providing that an inferior court judge on entering such penal judgment shall transmit a copy thereof to the circuit court, the judge of which shall thereupon adjudge its operation to be to disfranchise the defendant for two years, is invalid as contravening Const. § 51, providing that no law shall be amended by reference to its title only, but so much as remains in force shall be set out.

Appeal from Circuit Court, Barren County.

Colston Bowman was convicted in police court of carrying a concealed deadly weapon, but on transmission of a copy thereof to the circuit court, the latter court refused to render a judgment disfranchising defendant, and the Commonwealth appeals. Affirmed.

Chas. I. Dawson, Atty. Gen., and J. Lewis Williams, Commonwealth's Atty., of Glasgow, for the Commonwealth.

Basil Richardson, of Glasgow, for appellee.

HURT, C. J. This appeal involves the validity of an act of the General Assembly which was enacted at the legislative session of 1918, and is now section 1309a, 3 Ky. Stats., and is, including its title, as follows:

"An act to amend an act, section 1309 of Kentucky Statutes Carroll's 1915 Edition, relating to carrying concealed deadly weapons.

"Be it enacted by the General Assembly of the commonwealth of Kentucky:

"Sec. 2. All judges, justices of the peace and police judges shall have penal jurisdiction for the first offense herein described, the penalties and fines for same to be enforced and collected as in other cases in their final jurisdiction, but it shall be the duty of each justice of the peace, police judge and county judge entering such penal judgment to forthwith transmit to the clerk of the circuit court of the county in which such judgment is rendered a copy thereof, whereupon such clerk shall place the case upon the criminal docket of the circuit court and upon call of the docket a judgment shall be entered by the circuit court adjudging that the operation of the judgment is to disfranchise the defendant named therein, and to deprive him of the right of suffrage for a period of two years from the date thereof."

The question regarding the validity of the above enactment was raised by the appellee, who had been convicted in the police court in the city of Glasgow, a city of the fifth class, of the offense of carrying concealed upon or about his person a deadly weapon other than an ordinary pocketknife, and his punishment fixed at a fine of $100 and imprisonment for 10 days, and the judge of the police court, in obedience to the quoted statute, transmitted to the clerk of the circuit court a copy of the judgment. The judgment was filed in the circuit court, and the style of the cause placed upon the docket, but when it came to be considered the court declined to render a judgment disfranchising the appellee, and dismissed the proceeding. From the judgment the commonwealth's attorney has prayed an appeal, as authorized by section 337 of the Criminal Code.

Section 1309, Ky. Stats., to which the quoted statute, section 1309a, is an amendment, in its present form, was enacted in 1914, and by its provisions the carrying concealed upon or about the person of a deadly weapon other than an ordinary pocketknife was made a high misdemeanor, the punishment for which was fixed at a fine of not less than $50 nor in excess of $100, imprisonment in the county jail for not less than 10 nor more than 40 days, and disfranchisement for the period of 2 years from the date of the judgment. A conviction of such an offense, committed after a former conviction for the same offense, was declared to be a felony, and punishable by confinement for a term in the penitentiary.

The circuit court, being a court of general jurisdiction, was invested with·authority to finally try one charged ,with the offense of carrying concealed upon or about his person a deadly weapon other than an ordinary pocketknife, and to inflict upon one adjudged therein to be guilty the penalties prescribed by the statute, but, previous to the attempted amendment of section 1309 by the enactment of section 1309a, there could be no pretense that the circuit court ,was authorized to adjudge that an offender should be disfranchised, basing its judgment upon a copy of a judgment of conviction of such an offense rendered by an inferior court, which had imposed upon the offender the fine and imprisonment provided. Neither could there be any pretense that there was any authority for a police judge, county judge, or justice of the peace filing a judgment of conviction of such an offender in the circuit court, in fact there was no authority of any kind for the proceeding in the circuit court provided for by section 1309a until the enactment of that statute. The proceeding in the circuit court provided for by section 1309a, after a conviction before a county or police judge, or a justice of the peace, has none of the essential elements of an appeal, as the statute makes no provision for a retrial of the action after the filing of the judgment, and does not even provide for notice of the proceeding to the convict, nor does it provide for the filing of any part of the record of the action in the inferior court, except the judgment, upon which the circuit court must necessarily base its judgment of disfranchisement, without further investigation or opportunity for defense. Hence the proceeding in the circuit court being based entirely upon the authority of section 1309a, if such amendment is for any reason invalid, the court was without authority to render a judgment, disfranchising the appellee, upon the faith of the judgment of conviction rendered by the police judge, and was not in error in refusing to render a judgment thereon and dismissing the proceeding.

[1, 2] Thus it becomes necessary to determine the validity of the amendment, section 1309a, and it is needless to say that this court always approaches the subject of holding an act of the General Assembly to be void with hesitation, but the uniform decisions of this court for a century past have made it the accepted law of the Commonwealth that this court is invested not only with the authority, but the duty is imposed upon it to determine and declare when any department of the government has exceeded the authority to which it is limited by the Constitution, and to protect the covenants made by the people with each other in the adoption of the Constitution from infringement. It is also needless to say that with the wisdom or propriety of the constitutional requirements ,we have no concern, as all the provisions of that instrument are mandatory, and have been so considered by a uniform and consistent line of adjudications of this court. Varney v. Justice, 86 Ky. 596, 6 S. W. 457, 9 Ky. Law Rep. 743; McCreary, Governor, v. Speer, 156 Ky. 783, 162 S. W. 99; Board of Penitentiary Commissioners v. Spencer, 159 Ky. 260, 166 S. W. 1017. It is insisted that the amendatory act, section 1309a, was enacted in violation of section 51 of the Constitution, and for that reason is of no effect. So much of section 51 of the Constitution as is applicable to the present controversy is as follows:

"And no law shall be revised, amended, or the provisions thereof extended or conferred by reference to its title only, but so much thereof as is revised, amended, extended or conferred shall be re-enacted and published at length."

The act embraced by section 1309, supra, consisted of one section only, and the amendment embraced in section 1309a does not repeal any portion of the former act, but leaves all of its provisions in full force. Neither the title of section 1309a nor the body of the act refers to section 1309, which it proposes to amend, except by its title only. The amendment, not repealing any portion of the original act, nor striking out any portion of it, nor substituting anything for any portion of it, has the effect of amending the entire act embraced in section 1309. Section 1309a does not set out in full the provisions of section 1309 which it proposes to amend, nor does it re-enact any of the provisions of section 1309, which are left in full force and effect. Section 51 of the Constitution expressly provides, as it will be observed, that when the Legislature proposes to amend an act it must set it out at length in the amendatory act, and republish the portion of the original act which is amended, and which is left in force, and re-enact the same. This, as before said was not attempted or pretended to be done in the attempted enactment of section 1309a. The enactment of section 1309a was thus attempted in a manner strictly and expressly contrary to a mandatory provision of the Constitution. Board of Penitentiary Commissioners v. Spencer, supra. As said in Varney v. Justice, supra, with reference to the mandatory character of the provisions of the Constitution:

"Whenever the language gives a direction as to the manner of exercising a power, it was intended that the power should be exercised in the manner directed, and in no other manner."

One of the reasons which has been assigned why it was that the provisions of the Constitution require the Legislature in amending an act, or a portion of the act, to set out at length the act, or a portion of it which is amended, and which is still left in force in the amendatory act, and to re-enact the same, was that the members of the General Assembly should have before them the entire act which would be in force when it was amended, and would thus be enabled to more intelligently consider it, and to more intelligently vote for or against its enactment. It is a matter of common knowledge that the failure to observe this procedure in legislation was the source of great abuses under the former Constitutions. Other reasons have been assigned, which are not necessary to be here adverted to, as we must either hold that the amendment attempted by section 1309a was enacted in a manner contrary to the express provisions of the Constitution, and therefore invalid, or else section 51 of the Constitution is without force or meaning. In Purnell v. Mann, 105 Ky. 95, 48 S. W. 407, 49 S. W. 346, 50 S. W. 264, 20 Ky. Law Rep. 1146, 20 Ky. Law Rep. 1396, 21 Ky. Law Rep. 1129, in considering the requirement of section 51 of the Constitution with relation to the manner of the enactment of an amendatory act, the court said:

"We think the manifest intention was that the provision should apply only to so much of the law as after passage of the new act remains in force amended."

Thus it has been held, in accordance with the express provision of section 51, that in amending an act the provisions of the act amended, or the portion of an act amended which remain in force, must be set out in the amendatory act, and those provisions must be re-enacted.

The conclusion above arrived at is without considering the fact that section 1309a consists of only one section, and that section is numbered "2," which indicates strongly that it is incomplete as published, and its enactment resulted from a misunderstanding upon the part of the members of the General Assembly arising from the failure to conform, in the exercise of its powers, to the requirements of section 51 of the Constitution. The amendatory act as it now appears upon the statute books proposes to confer jurisdiction upon all judges, justices of the peace, and police judge of what it describes as the "first offense herein described," although the act, as it appears, does not describe any offense whatever, and the offense to which it refers can be conjectured only by a reference to section 1309, which the amendatory act refers to by its title only.

The judgment is therefore affirmed, and this opinion ordered to be certified.

=====

WILSON v. PIONEER COAL CO.

(Court of Appeals of Kentucky. May 6, 1921.)

1. **Quieting title ⟷10(4)—Title by adverse possession supports action.**

Title by adverse possession will support an action to quiet title.

2. **Deeds ⟷38(1)—Deeds held to have covered tract involved in action to quiet title.**

Deeds to plaintiff's father and those under whom he claimed held to have covered the tract of land involved in plaintiff's action to quiet title.

3. **Dedication ⟷44—Evidence insufficient to show dedication for burial purposes.**

Evidence held insufficient to sustain contention that the land had been dedicated to the public for burial purposes.

4. **Dedication ⟷31, 41—Dedication presumed from public use; acceptance necessary to make road a public highway.**

Where the former owners of land now owned by plaintiff and defendant for at least 40 years suffered the public to use a roadway, knowing it was claimed as a matter of right, the law presumes a dedication to the public, but such a dedication by the owners to public use is not alone sufficient to make the road a public highway; acceptance by the public being necessary.

5. **Dedication ⟷35(3)—Accepted by public user and official action.**

Where the public used a road for a long time, some 40 years, and the proper officials took charge of the road and worked it as a part of the public road system of the county, the dedication of the road as a highway was accepted by such public user and official action.

Appeal from Circuit Court, Bell county.

Action by Annie Wilson against the Pioneer Coal Company. From judgment for defendant, plaintiff appeals. Judgment reversed, with directions to dismiss defendant's counterclaim, and quiet plaintiff's title.

J. G. Rollins, of Pineville, for appellant.
James H. Jeffries, of Pineville, for appellee.

CLARKE, J. Alleging that she was the owner and in possession of a described tract of land containing less than half an acre, and that the defendant was interfering with her enjoyment and possession of same and had built a fence across the public road thereto, the plaintiff, Annie Wilson, now appellant, instituted this action in equity to quiet her title, and also to enjoin the defendant from interfering with her possession of the land and from obstructing the road leading thereto.

The defendant filed an answer and counterclaim of six paragraphs, the first of which is a traverse of the allegations of the petition and contains an admission that the defendant has no title to or interest in the land involved except as stated in succeeding paragraphs. In the second paragraph it is pleaded that the land claimed by plaintiff, together with a small adjoining parcel, was dedicated more than 30 years before the institution of this suit, by the then owners of same, to the general public living in the neighborhood, for burial and graveyard purposes. In the third paragraph it is alleged that when plaintiff procured her deed to the land same was in the actual adverse possession of the persons buried thereon, and that her deed was therefore champertous and void. In the fourth paragraph it is alleged that all of the land claimed by plaintiff is covered by a patent for 50,000 acres issued to Abraham Moorehouse in 1799, and that same is elder and superior to plaintiff's title. In the fifth paragraph it is alleged that plaintiff and her brothers, by the terms of their deed in conveying a large adjoining tract of land on Kettle Island creek to A. J. Asher in October, 1900, recognized and confirmed the former dedication of the tract and themselves dedicated same to defendant and the public for graveyard purposes. In the sixth paragraph defendant alleged that plaintiff's claim of title to the small tract and the right to use the road or passway to same over its land is a cloud upon its title to lands adjoining that claimed by plaintiff.

The prayer is that plaintiff's petition be dismissed, and that the court adjudge that the tract of land claimed by plaintiff had been dedicated to the public as a graveyard and for burial purposes, and that it cannot be used by plaintiff or others for secular or business purposes.

The affirmative allegations of the answer and counterclaim having been traversed by reply, the proof was heard and transcribed in open court by agreement. This appeal is from the chancellor's judgment dismissing the petition and granting defendant the affirmative relief sought by its counterclaim.

The land claimed by plaintiff lies on the left-hand side of the crest and at the end of the ridge which forms the watershed between the left-hand and right-hand forks of Kettle Island creek, and includes a small piece of bottom land, formed about 1876 by a change in the course of the left-hand fork of the creek. The tract which defendant claims has been dedicated to the public as a graveyard, and which we shall refer to as the graveyard tract, is the whole of the tract claimed by plaintiff and a small tract adjoining same and lying on the right-hand side and at the tip end of the crest of the dividing ridge.

There is practically no conflict in the evidence, and the pertinent facts are these. Plaintiff was in the actual possession of the land claimed by her when she instituted this action, and her tenant was conducting a store in a building he had constructed on same in competition with defendant's commissary. Defendant owns all of the land on Kettle Island creek and its two forks within a mile of the forks, except this graveyard tract, which it had inclosed by a fence, but which it admits it did not own or have in possession. Defendant acquired the land surrounding the graveyard tract in 1911 by one deed from the Edgemont Coal Company, which likewise acquired it by a single deed from A. J. Asher in 1907, but in both of these deeds the lands on the two forks of the creek are described separately, just as in separate deeds to Asher from the Wilsons for the land on the one fork and from Abraham Lock on the other. Neither of these deeds to Asher covered any portion of the graveyard tract, although each referred to same as "the graveyard" in describing the lines where same adjoined the lands conveyed.

[1] In 1870, which is as far back as the titles are traced, Thomas M. Lock lived upon and claimed to own the lands on the left-hand fork of the creek, and Abraham Lock lived upon and claimed to own the lands on the right-hand fork. Thomas M. Lock conveyed his land in 1875 by deed to Jas. W. Ward, who took possession of, lived upon, and claimed to own same, until he sold and conveyed it to J. D. Asher on November 16, 1877. Ward remained upon the land as Asher's tenant until the latter sold and conveyed same in 1880 to W. F. M. Wilson, who took possession and lived upon the land until his death intestate about 1889. His children, plaintiff and her two brothers, were in possession of the land by tenants until 1900, when they conveyed all of same to A. J. Asher, except the small tract involved here, which her brothers later conveyed to plaintiff. Hence plaintiff has proven that she and her brothers

and those under whom they claimed were in the actual, adverse possession of all the land covered by their deeds continuously from 1870 until 1900, or for 30 years. Therefore, if these deeds cover the tract in controversy, plaintiff and her brothers had a perfect title to same by adverse possession for more than the statutory period, when in 1900 they made the deed to Asher for the other lands admittedly covered by those deeds, unless, as claimed by defendant, same had been dedicated as a graveyard theretofore, or was so dedicated by that deed. Since, as this court has frequently held, title by adverse possession will support an action to quiet title, it is obvious there is no merit in appellee's first two contentions that the dismissal of plaintiff's petition was proper because of her failure to trace her title back to the commonwealth, and because of the fact the land she now claims is covered by the old patent for 60,000 acres issued to Abraham Moorehouse in 1799. Le Moyne v. Hays, 145 Ky. 415, 140 S. W. 552; Williams v. Lowe, 175 Ky. 369, 194 S. W. 342.

The questions upon which her title depends are, as we have seen: (1) Do the deeds to her father and those under whom he claimed, cover the tract here involved? and (2) If so, has same been dedicated to the public for burial purposes?

[2] The two lines involved are described in substantially the same way in each of the deeds under which plaintiff claims, and also in the deeds prior to 1900 conveying the adjoining lands on the right-hand fork of the creek. These two lines which we have italicized and the lines preceding and following them are thus described in the deed to appellant's father:

"Thence with said Rice's line crossing the head of the hollow to the top of the fork ridge which divides the right and left hand fork of Kettle Island branch; *thence with the top of the ridge down to the graveyard; thence with the left-hand fork of said branch to its junction;* thence with the main branch to Straight creek."

The evidence shows conclusively and without contradiction that the "graveyard" there referred to is the small portion of the Abraham Lock land adjoining the crest of the ridge on the right-hand side thereof, since it was not until long after appellant's father acquired the lands on the left-hand side of this ridge that any persons were buried on his side of the ridge, whereas for many years the Locks had permitted any one that desired to do so to bury their relatives upon their lands at this place. There were about 40 graves on the Lock side, and not a single one on the Wilson side, when this deed was made in 1880.

Since the upper part of the graveyard is on the crest of the dividing ridge, and the next call is "thence with the left-hand fork of said branch to its junction," it is insisted

there is a connecting line omitted that must be supplied. Admitting this to be true, it could have been supplied easily by extending the line down the ridge about 20 feet to the creek, since it is only that distance between the upper end of the graveyard as it then existed and the old channel of the left-hand fork of the creek, which was evidently referred to in all these old deeds employing this description. By so doing all of the tract now claimed by plaintiff was covered by the deeds of her father and those under whom he claimed. We do not, however, have to rest the decision of this point alone upon a reasonable application of the calls of the deed to the objects called for a ridge and a creek, since this was done, and any uncertainty in the description in the deed was settled by the interested parties, as is shown by the fact that since from as far back as any of the witnesses can remember until rather recently there was a fence from above the upper end of the old Lock graveyard, running with the crest of the ridge to the end of same and thence down the left-hand fork of the creek. This fence was built by Lock, and was recognized by him and all parties who ever owned the land on either side of this dividing ridge as on his side and near the dividing line between their lands.

Not only does all of the evidence show that plaintiff and her brothers had title to this tract of land when they made deed to A. J. Asher in 1900 for the rest of the land inherited from their father, but the very contention of defendant that by that deed plaintiff and her brothers dedicated this tract to the public as a graveyard is necessarily an admission that they had the necessary title therefor.

[3] Coming now to the question of a dedication, there is absolutely no proof whatever to sustain such a contention prior to the time appellant's father acquired the land, since, as already pointed out, it had never been so used by any one, and the reference to a graveyard in his and prior deeds was to the Lock graveyard. Nor is the fact that he buried his wife and two children on the hillside at the upper end of this small tract, and that plaintiff and her brothers buried him beside his wife when he died and have since permitted one other child to be buried there, and that one other person has been buried there without their knowledge or consent, any evidence of a dedication of even that portion of the tract on the hillside adjoining the old Lock graveyard, much less the piece of bottom land, upon which plaintiff is conducting a store in competition with defendant's commissary and about which the parties are really concerned.

To sustain the contention that by their deed to Asher plaintiff and her brothers so dedicated this land to use as a graveyard that it cannot now be used by them for secular or business purposes, counsel for defendant rely upon the cases of Johnson et al. v. Elkhorn Gas Coal Mining Co., 176 Ky. 676, 197 S. W. 409; Damron v. Justice, 162 Ky. 101, 172 S. W. 120, and Brown v. Anderson, 88 Ky. 578, 11 S. W. 607, 11 Ky. Law Rep. 107, but there is absolutely no analogy or resemblance between those cases and this one. In those cases the tract of land conveyed included a small tract used for burial purposes and which by the deed was reserved to the grantor for burial purposes alone, and he did not therefore have any other rights therein and could not use same for secular or business purposes. In the instant case the land involved was not a part of the land conveyed, and there is no reservation or stipulation of any kind with reference to it. It was not involved in any way in the transaction between the parties, and it was not mentioned in the deed except in describing the lines around it where it adjoins the land conveyed. That deed therefore contains no element of a dedication or parting with title or commitment of any kind by the grantors with reference to this tract of land.

It therefore results the chancellor erred in refusing to quiet plaintiff's title and in granting defendant the affirmative relief asked by way of counterclaim.

This leaves for consideration plaintiff's right to an injunction requiring defendant to remove the obstructions it has placed in the road leading through its lands to plaintiff's land. Plaintiff alleges and defendant denies that this road is a public road.

The proof shows that since 1860 or earlier there has been an open road up Kettle Island creek to its forks and up each fork for some distance; that it follows the creek, is clearly defined, and has been used continuously as matter of right by the people who have lived on the creek and its forks and the public generally as the only means of ingress and egress by wagon or vehicle; that for some years there was a gristmill up the left-hand fork beyond the Wilson lands, and that for some years, while this mill was being operated, overseers were appointed by the county court, who caused the road up as far as the mill to be worked by the residents of the neighborhood, required by law to work the public roads of the county; that Sol Baker was the overseer and worked the road in 1876 and 1877, beginning about 200 yards below the forks and working up the creek past plaintiff's land; that it was then a "public wagon road," to employ the language of one witness; but there is no evidence that it has been worked by county officials as a public road later than some 16 or 17 years ago, although it has continued to be used as such. The gates were placed across the road by the Edgemont Coal Company in 1907, and defendant locked same against plaintiff's tenant shortly before the suit was filed, and for

the purpose, as stated by defendant's manager, of keeping delivery wagons from driving up through its mining camp, which contains more than 100 miners' houses and a government post office, besides tipples, commissary, etc.

[4] It is therefore shown that the former owners of the lands now owned by both plaintiff and defendant, for at least 40 years, suffered, not only those owning or living upon land on the waters of the main creek and up the left-hand fork as far as the old gristmill, but the public as well, to use this roadway, knowing it was claimed as a matter of right, from which the law presumes a dedication to the public. But a dedication by the owners to public use is not alone sufficient to make the road a public highway; an acceptance by the public is necessary. Just what would constitute an acceptance by the public was formerly in much doubt in this jurisdiction, but in Riley v. Buchanan, 116 Ky. 625, 76 S. W. 527, 25 Ky. Law Rep. 863, 63 L. R. A. 642, 3 Ann. Cas. 788, after an exhaustive review of the authorities, the court stated its conclusions as follows:

"We feel constrained by reason and authority to hold that, while an acceptance by the public is essential to a complete dedication of a public highway or passway, the acceptance may be either by formal ratification by the proper official board of the municipality; or by implication by it, where it takes charge of the road by directing improvements on behalf of the public, or otherwise by overt act recognizing it as a public road; or it may be by the public by such protracted and continued use as to clearly indicate its acceptance, when the road dedicated is a benefit to the public and not a burden. In the last-named state of case, a formal acceptance by the proper legal authority will be conclusively presumed to have taken place. Should the road become a burden to the public, it may be discontinued in the method pointed out by the statutes.".

These principles have been adhered to and reaffirmed by this court in many cases; the most recent being Rockcastle County v. Norton, 189 Ky. 690, 225 S. W. 1079.

[5] It is therefore established that this road was not only dedicated by the owners of the land as a public highway but was accepted as such by the long period of time it was so used by the public and by the proper officials taking charge of same and working it as a part of the public road system of the county. And as stated in 13 R. C. L. 62;

"The rule relative to the discontinuance of highways is 'once a highway, always a highway,' unless it is abandoned or vacated in due course of law; and the burden of showing a discontinuance, vacation, or abandonment is on the party who asserts it."

There is no proof of a discontinuance by legal proceedings, and the only evidence of abandonment is proof that it has not been worked as a public road by the county officials for 16 or 17 years. But this is not sufficient. The mere failure of public officials to perform their duties or exercise their rights with reference to working a public highway, however long continued, could not possibly work an abandonment so as to defeat the public's right to use the road; and especially is this true where, as here, the public continued to use the road without let or hindrance from any one until defendant's predecessor, the Edgemont Coal Company, without right, so far as the record discloses, placed gates across it in 1907; and there is no evidence that even since then any one has ever been denied its use until just before this action was filed, when defendant locked the gates against plaintiff's tenant. In fact counsel for defendant concedes there is now a public road from the forks down Kettle Island creek to Straight creek, and contends only that the portion of same leading up the left-hand fork to plaintiff's land has been abandoned, but there is no more or different proof of an abandonment of this portion of the road than of the other; the only difference in the proof being that the one has been more extensively used than the other, which was always the case.

Hence the court also erred in denying plaintiff's prayer for an injunction requiring defendant to remove the gates from the road.

Wherefore the judgment is reversed, with directions to dismiss defendant's counterclaim, quiet plaintiff's title to the land described in the petition, and enjoin defendant from obstructing the road thereto.

COMMONWEALTH v. ALLEN.

(Court of Appeals of Kentucky. May 24, 1921.)

1. Indictment and information ⇐110(5)—Indictment for abortion need not follow language of statute.

Indictment for abortion under Ky. St. § 1219a, though not attempting to follow the language of the statute, *held* sufficient under Cr. Code Prac. §§ 122, 124, as to what an indictment must contain, and in what respects be direct and certain.

2. Witnesses ⇐61(1)—Wife may testify to abortion on her.

The wife is competent to testify to commission of abortion on her by her husband against her will, under the exception at common law, also implied in Civ. Code Prac. § 606, of an offense on or against her person.

Appeal from Circuit Court, Logan County.

John H. Allen was acquitted on a charge of abortion, and the Commonwealth appeals. Error.

Chas. I. Dawson, Atty. Gen., Thos. B. McGregor, Asst. Atty. Gen., James R. Mallory, of Elkton, and Coleman Taylor, of Russellville, for the Commonwealth.

S. R. Crewdson, of Russellville, and Selden Y. Trimble, of Hopkinsville, for appellee.

SETTLE, J. The grand jury of Logan county found and returned in the circuit court of that county an indictment against the appellee, John H. Allen, accusing him of the crime of abortion. Omitting the merely formal parts of the indictment, its description of the acts constituting the crime charged is as follows:

"The said Allen * * * did unlawfully, willfully, and feloniously use a metal instrument, a spoon or sound, a more particular description of which is to the grand jury unknown, upon the body and person of his wife, Sallie Mildred Allen, who was at the time pregnant, during the period of gestation, which was well known to him, by forcing, thrusting, and inserting the said instrument into the body, private parts, and womb of the said Mrs. Allen, with the intent thereby to procure the miscarriage of said woman, all of which was over her protest, against her will, and not necessary to preserve her life, and, as a result of said acts so done with the intent and in the manner aforesaid, the miscarriage of the said Mrs. Allen was procured, the death of two unborn children was caused, and the said Mrs. Allen did miscarry. * * *"

The trial of appellee under the indictment resulted in his acquittal by the verdict of the jury, complaining of which, the ruling of the trial court in excluding certain evidence offered in its behalf, and of its refusal to grant it a new trial, the commonwealth has appealed.

The crime of abortion is defined and made a felony by Kentucky Statutes, § 1219a, subsecs. 1–4; the penalty prescribed by subsection 1 being applicable where the conviction of the accused results from his committing, with the intent to procure a miscarriage, when not necessary to preserve the woman's life, the acts by which, as defined by the section, it may be effected, but without actually causing it. The penalty prescribed by subsection 2 applies where the conviction of the accused occurs by reason of his committing, with the intent to procure a miscarriage, when not necessary to preserve the woman's life, the acts prescribed in subsection 1 and the miscarriage actually results from such acts; and, in addition, causes the death of the unborn child, whether before or after quickening time. If, however, the woman upon whom the acts described in subsection 1 are committed with the intent to procure the miscarriage, when not necessary to preserve her life, should by reason thereof die, subsection 3 of the statute provides that the person offending, if convicted, "shall be punished as now prescribed by law for the offense of murder or manslaughter, as the facts may justify." By subsection 4 it is provided that the consent of the woman to the means employed to procure the abortion shall be no defense; that she shall be a competent witness in any prosecution under the statute, and for that purpose shall not be considered an accomplice.

It is apparent from the language of subsections 1, 2, and 3 of the statute, supra, that the offense denounced by each is a felony, and manifest from that of the indictment in the instant case that the acts alleged therein to have been committed by the appellee constitute the offense as defined in subsections 1 and 2, for which, if found guilty by the jury, he would have been amenable to the punishment, by way of confinement in the penitentiary, prescribed by subsection 3.

[1] Without raising the question in the court below, or seriously arguing it here, counsel for the commonwealth contends that the indictment is not sufficient to sustain a conviction; hence the appellee was not placed in jeopardy by his trial thereunder, for which reason the judgment appealed from should be reversed, and the case remanded, with direction to the court below to set it aside and refer the case to the grand jury for the return of another and sufficient indictment against appellee. Without consuming time in discussing this contention, it is deemed only necessary to say that the indictment in form and substance sufficiently complies with the provisions of Criminal Code, § 122, subsecs. 1, 2, and section 124, subsecs. 1 to 4, inclusive, in that it is direct and certain as regards: (1) The party charged; (2) the offense charged; (3) the county in which it was committed; (4) "a statement of the acts constituting the offense, in ordinary and concise language, and in such manner as to enable a person of common understanding to know what is intended; and with such degree of certainty as to enable the court to pronounce judgment, on conviction, according to the right of the case." While the indictment does not attempt to follow the language of the statute, it omits no allegation of fact or circumstance necessary to constitute the offense therein named. Therefore it is 'clear that the appellee was placed in jeopardy by his trial thereunder in the court below, and that this court is powerless to reverse the judgment of that court based upon the verdict of the jury acquitting him of the crime charged. So our authority is confined to a review of such of the rulings of the circuit court on the trial as are assigned as error on the appeal and to declaring the law regarding same.

[2] The remaining important question presented for decision by the appeal, and respecting which counsel for the appellant are most insistent, is: Was the wife of the appellee, the party injured by his alleged acts constituting the crime charged in the indictment, a competent witness for the commonwealth on his trial under the indictment? It appears from the record that the only evidence introduced on the trial of appellee in the court below was in behalf of the commonwealth, and, while it was sufficient to prove that appellee's wife suffered a miscarriage as charged in the indictment, resulting in the premature birth of two children (twins) without life, and that such miscarriage was caused by some sort of force or violence employed upon the person of Mrs. Allen, with the exception of one witness who testified as to a statement of appellee that his wife was pregnant, and, in substance, that he intended to cause her to have a miscarriage, there was little, if anything, in the evidence tending to connect him with the procurement of the abortion, which doubtless led the jury to entertain such doubt of his guilt as to cause the verdict of acquittal returned by them. It was to supply this lack of evidence, therefore, that the wife of appellee, who better than all others knew the facts regarding his guilt or innocence, was offered as a witness by the commonwealth. She was, however, excluded upon appellee's objection as a witness, and her offered testimony rejected by the trial court, to which ruling counsel for the commonwealth at the time took an exception, and thereupon entered of record an avowal that the witness Mrs. Allen, "if permitted to testify, would state that her husband [appellee], over her protest and against her will, forcibly inserted a metal instrument into her private parts, person, and body for the purpose of causing a miscarriage of her unborn child [or children], and the result of same was a miscarriage."

The antiquity of the common-law rule that neither the husband nor wife shall testify for nor against the other is so great as to render even the century of its origin well-nigh undiscoverable. It was mainly founded upon two reasons: (1) The danger of causing dissension and· of disturbing the peace of families; (2) the natural repugnance in all fair-minded persons to compelling the husband or wife to be the means of the other's condemnation. It may therefore be said that the rule in question was' bottomed upon a humane public policy intended to protect the sanctity of the home and happiness of the family. But the rule, like practically all others, has its salutary exceptions, one of which is that the wife may testify against the husband in a criminal or penal prosecution for an offense or attempted offense against her person.

In Comlth. v. Sapp, 90 Ky. 580, 14 S. W. 834, 12 Ky. Law Rep. 484, 29 Am. St. Rep. 405, we had occasion to pass directly on this question. Sapp was indicted for attempting to poison his wife, and upon his trial the wife was offered by the commonwealth as a witness against him; its counsel avowing that she would state that she saw the husband sprinkle a substance upon a piece of watermelon intended for her, which substance was shown by other testimony on the trial to be arsenic, a deadly poison. The trial court refused to permit her to testify, holding that she could not be a witness for any purpose. But on the appeal of the case we held that her rejection as a witness was error. The opinion, following a review of the common-law and numerous judicial decisions on the subject, declares that section 606, Civil Code of Practice, is "but declaratory of the common law," and that, notwithstanding its emphatic provisions to the effect that neither a husband nor his wife shall testify for or against each other, this rule "is subject necessarily to some exceptions, one of which is where the husband commits or attempts to commit a crime against the person of his wife."

Although in the case supra the wife had been divorced from the husband before she was offered as a witness, this fact the court held of no consequence, saying in the opinion:

"The policy upon which the rule that the husband and wife cannot testify for or against each other is based is so far overcome as to create the exception by that superior policy which dictates the punishment of crime, and which, without the exception to the rule, would very likely go unpunished. It is of necessity. If it be said that our statute forbids the introduction of the husband or wife as a witness against the other, we reply, and so did the common law; and yet the exception named existed, and so it should, is our opinion, under our statute. The necessity of the case requires such a construction, and, as already said, the statute forbidding husband or wife to testify against each other is but declaratory of the common law. As the divorced wife would have been a competent witness if she had still been the wife of the accused at the time of the trial as to the alleged attempted felony upon her, it follows a fortiori that being divorced did not disqualify her."

In Wharton's Criminal Law, vol. 1, § 762, it is said:

"Where, however, violence has been committed on the person of the wife by the husband, she is competent to prove such violence."

See Roscoe's Crim. Evidence, 150; Stein v. Bowman, etc., 13 Pet. 221, 10 L. Ed. 129.

In the very recent case of Commonwealth v. Wilson, 190 Ky. 813, 229 S. W. 60, the right of the wife to testify against the husband in such a state of case as is here presented is recognized. In approving in that case the decision holding the wife a competent witness against the husband reached in Comth. v. Sapp, supra, we said of the exception, both to the common-law

and Code provisions, upon which her right to testify was therein rested:

"But the exception was created and is allowed from the necessities of the case, in order to subserve the larger policy of the state, that the guilty should be punished, which would in many cases be defeated if the mouth of the wife was closed and she was not permitted to testify to the facts constituting the offense against her person."

In Commonwealth v. Wilson, supra, we held that the wife was a competent witness against the husband under an indictment accusing him of obtaining by false pretenses upon her check, fraudulent, made out by his procurement for an unauthorized amount, money belonging to the wife. The question decided, therefore, was whether the wife was a competent witness against the husband where the offense charged was one affecting her property, instead of her person, as in the Sapp Case. But the opinion, in responding to the insistence of counsel for the commonwealth that the superior policy of the state constituting the exception to the rule of the common-law and Code provisions under which the competency of the wife's testimony was declared in the Sapp Case made the wife a competent witness where as in the Wilson Case, the crime of the husband caused the loss to her of her property, while admitting the force of this contention and the support given it by the weight of authority in other states, held the decision of the question unnecessary, as the competency of Wilson's wife as a witness against him was put beyond doubt by the amendment to section 606, Civil Code, made by act of the Legislature of February 23, 1898, providing:

"And except that when a husband or wife is acting as agent for his or her consort, either of them may testify as to any matter connected with such an agency."

So, while it is true, as claimed by counsel for appellee, that the court did not have before it in Comth. v. Wilson the precise question passed on in Comth. v. Sapp, its approval of the conclusion regarding the wife's competency as a witness against the husband expressed in the opinion of the latter case, and of the reasons supporting the conclusion, persuasively indicate it to be the intention of the court to be understood as adhering to the rule as to the wife's right to testify against the husband where, as in the Sapp Case and the instant case, the crime of the latter was committed or attempted to be committed on the person of the wife.

In Barclay v. Commonwealth, 116 Ky. 275, 76 S. W. 4, we reaffirmed the rule of necessity with respect to the right of the wife to testify against the husband announced in Commonwealth v. Sapp, supra. Barclay was indicted for unlawfully and feloniously hiring and procuring a man unknown to the grand jury and without authority to solemnize a marriage to conduct and solemnize, under pretense of having such authority, a marriage between him (Barclay) and Adeline Chandler. On the trial of Barclay under the indictment Adeline Chandler, over his objection, was permitted by the court to testify against him as to the mock marriage, which, according to her testimony, she supposed had been legally solemnized by one having authority to act in performing such a rite. After the pretended. marriage Barclay took her to Tennessee and there lived with her a week as his wife, she believing all the while that they had been legally married.

Section 2110, Ky. Statutes, makes it a felony, punishable by confinement in the penitentiary not exceeding three years, for any person not authorized to solemnize a marriage to do so under pretense of having such authority, Barclay, as an accessory to the false marriage and before the fact, was liable under section 1128, Ky. Statutes, to the same punishment as the person by whom the illegal marriage was pretended to be solemnized. Section 2097, Ky. Statutes, declares a marriage void when not solemnized or contracted in the presence of an authorized person or society. It is, however, provided by section 2102 that—

"No marriage solemnized before any person professing to have authority therefor shall be invalid for the want of such authority, if it is consummated with the belief of the parties or either of them, that he had authority and that they have been lawfully married."

On the appeal of the case it was insisted for the appellant, Barclay, that, as the marriage had been consummated with the belief on the part of Adeline Chandler that she and appellant had been lawfully married, it was by the terms of the statute not invalid for want of authority in the person solemnizing it, for which reason she could not testify against him. But in overruling this contention we in the opinion said:

"We cannot concur in this conclusion. The case falls within one of the well-settled exceptions to the rule that a wife cannot testify against her husband. In 1 Greenleaf on Evidence, § 343, it is said: 'To this general rule excluding the husband and wife as witnesses there are some exceptions, which are allowed from the necessity of the case, partly for the protection of the wife in her life and liberty, and partly for the sake of public justice. But the necessity which calls for this exception for the wife's security is described to mean, 'not a general necessity, as where no other witnesses can be had, but a particular necessity, as where, for instance, the wife would otherwise be exposed, without remedy, to personal injury.' Thus a woman is a competent witness against a man indicted for forcible abduction and marriage, if the force were continuing upon her until the marriage, of which fact she is also a

competent witness, and this by the weight of the authorities, notwithstanding her subsequent assent and voluntary cohabitation, for otherwise the offender would take advantage of his wrong."

"Other authorities might be cited, but the principle is so well settled that we deem it unnecessary. If the rule were otherwise, it would be in the power of the defendant by consummating the marriage, and thus adding another wrong to the crime he had already committed in procuring the mock marriage, to protect himself from punishment for the crime."

Under the ruling in Commonwealth v. Sapp and Barclay v. Commonwealth, supra, it may be said to be a well-settled rule of law in this jurisdiction that the wife is a competent witness against the husband in a prosecution of the latter for a criminal offense alleged to have been committed upon or against the person of the former.

In the majority of the states the courts recognize the right of the wife to testify against the husband in a criminal prosecution against the latter for an offense involving actual or threatened injury to her person; and in many of them the doctrine that the wife may testify against him in any criminal prosecution charging him with injury to her property is also given recognition. Williamson v. Morton, 2 Md. Ch. 94; Miller v. State, 78 Neb. 645, 111 N. W. 637; Murray v. State, 48 Tex. Cr. R. 141, 86 S. W. 1024, 122 Am. St. Rep. 737; People v. Northrup, 50 Barb. (N. Y.) 147; Comth. v. Spink, 137 Pa. 255, 20 Atl. 680; Dill v. People, 19 Colo. 469, 36 Pac. 229, 41 Am. St. Rep. 254; Davis v. Commonwealth, 99 Va. 838, 38 S. E. 191; Comth. v. Kreuger, 17 Pa. Co. Ct. R. 181.

A well-considered case, among the many of other jurisdictions on the question under consideration, is that of State v. Dyer, 59 Me. 303. An indictment against the husband and another charged them with using an instrument upon the wife by forcing and inserting it into her womb for the purpose of procuring a miscarriage. The question for decision was whether the wife was a competent witness against the husband. It was held that she could testify: (1) Because the charge was gross personal violence on the person of the wife; (2) that the wife acted under the coercion of the husband; (3) that the intent was to procure the miscarriage of the woman. These facts were sufficient, as held by the court, to bring the case within the exception to the rule of the common law excluding husband and wife as witnesses for or against each other. In discussing the reasons for the exception the court, in part, said:

"The object and purpose of the exception measures the extent of it. In a given case the inquiry must be: What is the nature of the offense charged, and is it one implying personal violence to the wife? If so, she may be a witness, not only to obtain security for herself, but also when he is charged, by indictment, with an assault upon her. * * * The rule of exclusion, it is well known, is based upon the unity in view of the law of husband and wife, and the 'idea that her testimony would tend to destroy domestic peace, and introduce dis-cord, animosity, and confusion.' The excep-tions which necessity soon forced upon the courts are based primarily on the idea that the protection of the person of the wife from ac-tual violence and assault or cruel treatment by the husband is of more practical importance than the legal assumption of unity, or the the-oretical fears of domestic discord."

We fully indorse the reasons advanced by the Supreme Court of Maine in the case, supra, in support of the right of the wife to testify against the husband when it is sought in a criminal or penal prosecution to bring him to account for an injury wantonly in-flicted or threatened, to her person, for we believe them in full accord with a salutory public policy, the enforcement of which will have beneficent effect in protecting the sanc-tity of the home and happiness of the fam-ily. Indeed, any other view of the matter would be contrary to reason and repugnant to the demands of justice.

We do not find that the authorities relied on by counsel for appellee militate against the view we entertain of the law. None of the cases cited in their brief is precisely analogous to the case at bar, in point of fact or as regards the conclusion reached. That of Comth. v. Winfrey, 169 Ky. 650, 184 S. W. 1121, strongly relied on, though apparently similar in some of its features of fact, did not require a decision of the question of the wife's right to testify. The only questions decided in the case on the appeal was as to the right of the common-wealth's attorney, denied by the trial court, to dismiss by motion an indictment under section 243, Criminal Code, over the defend-ant's objection, and whether a writ of pro-hibition would lie to control the action of that court upon such motion. It was held by us that the writ of prohibition did not lie, but, as the commonwealth had taken an appeal from the order of the trial court overruling the motion of its attorney to dis-miss the indictment, its action thereon was reviewable on the appeal, and further that such action of the trial court in overruling the motion of the commonwealth's attorney to dismiss the indictment was error; hence for that reason, and no other, the judgment was reversed.

While comment is made in the opinion upon the claim of counsel that the marriage of the defendant to the prosecutrix after his indictment for procuring an abortion upon her had rendered her incompetent to testify against him, it can hardly be claimed that the court by what was said admitted the disqualification of the wife as a witness

by her marriage to the defendant. Fairly construed, the language used means that, if it were true such disqualification of the witness resulted from the marriage, as claimed, that fact could not be urged by the defendant as a ground for defeating the right of the commonwealth to renew the prosecution against him under another in-dictment, if the parties should thereafter be divorced. We think it manifest that the court did not intend, by the language re-ferred to, to make the opinion conflict with those of Comth. v. Sapp and Barclay v. Comth., supra. At most, what was said in Comth. v. Winfrey was unnecessary to the decision of the question upon which the judgment appealed from was reversed; and, this being true, it is to be regarded obiter dictum.

It follows from the conclusions we have expressed that the ruling of the circuit court excluding the testimony of the wife of the appellee as a witness in the instant case was error. Hence it is so declared, and this opinion certified to that court as the law of the case.

CRENSHAW v. WILLIAMS.

(Court of Appeals of Kentucky. May 20, 1921.)

1. Vendor and purchaser ⬤=351(8)—Purchaser not entitled to damages for loss of bargain on inability of vendor, who acted in good faith, to convey good title.

Where vendor in making contract to convey land acts in good faith, and is guilty of no posi-tive or actual fraud in the transaction, but is unable to perform because of inability to con-vey a good title to the land, the purchaser cannot recover as damages the difference be-tween the market value of the land and the con-tract price; that is, damages for the loss of his bargain.

2. Vendor and purchaser ⬤=351(8)—Vendor's failure to disclose condition of title to pur-chaser held not fraud entitling purchaser to damages for loss of bargain.

Where land had been devised to named dev-isee during her life and after her death to her children, vendor's failure to disclose to pur-chaser the condition of the title, to refer pur-chaser to the will by which land had been de-vised, which was of record, and to inform pur-chaser that the court had held that there was yet a possibility of the devisee bearing children, held not such fraud as to entitle purchaser, on vendor's breach of contract, to convey because of inability to give good title, to recover dam-ages for loss of his bargain.

Appeal from Circuit Court, Scott County.

Action by J. W. Crenshaw against D. W. Williams. Judgment of dismissal, and plain-tiff appeals. Affirmed.

Ford & Ford, of Georgetown, for appellant.

Bradley & Bradley and James Bradley, all of Georgetown, for appellee.

THOMAS, J. On January 19, 1920, appellee and defendant below, D. W. Williams, signed a contract, agreeing to convey to the appellant and plaintiff below, J. W. Crenshaw, on March 1 thereafter, a tract of land in Scott county containing 398½ acres, the consideration being $400 per acre, amounting in the aggregate to $159,400. Ten per cent. of the purchase price, or $15,940, was paid at the time, and 40 per cent. of the consideration was to be paid at the date of the deed, and the balance was to be divided into two equal payments, evidenced by notes of plaintiff, and payable in one and two years thereafter, with interest from date and a lien upon the land. On the appointed day for the execution of the deed, or perhaps before that time, it was discovered by plaintiff that defendant could not convey a perfect title, and the executory contract for the sale of the land was not performed according to its terms.

This suit was brought by plaintiff against defendant on April 22, 1920, seeking to recover damages for the failure of the latter to make the conveyance, which consisted of interest on the 10 per cent. payment at the time of the contract, and $310, alleged expenses incurred by plaintiff in surveying the land and in examining the title thereto. In the third paragraph of the petition it was alleged that the land at the time of the contract, as well as at the stipulated day for its performance, was reasonably worth on the market $179,400, and that plaintiff had sustained damage because of the "loss of his bargain" in the sum of $20,000. Besides alleging defendant's failure to convey, it is also averred in the petition (but in paragraphs other than the third) that defendant "fraudulently failed to disclose to this plaintiff at the time of the execution of said contract" his inability to convey a perfect fee-simple title to the land. Afterwards an amended petition was filed, setting up the defect in defendant's title, which was that the title to the land of defendant and his wife, emanated from the will of J. B. Graves, her father, and in which he devised the property involved to Mrs. Williams during her life and after her death to her children. The answer averred, inter alia, that plaintiff knew of the condition of the title before and at the time of the execution of the contract sued on; that Mrs. Williams was at an age where in the ordinary course of nature she would bear no more children, and that she was the mother of two children, one of whom died without descendants, and that she inherited his interest, and therefore became the owner of a one-half undivided interest in remainder to the land in question

after the expiration of her life estate, and that her only other child (a daughter) had joined with herself and husband in a deed to plaintiff, which he declined to accept, and that defendant had returned to plaintiff the 10 per cent. cash payment, made by him at the date of contract, with interest thereon, and by mutual agreement of the parties the contract was rescinded. The demurrer filed to the answer was sustained, but the one filed to the petition as amended was overruled as to the first and second paragraphs, but it was sustained as to the third paragraph, seeking to recover damages for the loss of plaintiff's bargain, and, plaintiff declining to amend that paragraph, it was dismissed, to which he excepted and prayed, and has prosecuted an appeal to this court. Plaintiff dismissed his action, seeking a recovery of the interest on the 10 per cent. cash payment (since it had been paid), and the court gave judgment in his favor for a part of the other damages claimed. Defendant has not appealed therefrom, nor has he appealed or moved for a cross-appeal from the judgment of the court sustaining a demurrer to his answer, and none of the questions involved therein are before us.

[1] It will thus be seen that the sole question for determination is whether plaintiff may recover substantial damages under the facts presented for what is known in the law as "the loss of his bargain"; i. e., the excess market value of the land above what he agreed to pay for it. If this question had been submitted to us without investigation, we should have unhesitatingly said that plaintiff was entitled to recover such damages; but our investigation has shown that the courts generally, including this one, deny such recovery in the sale of real estate where the vendor acts in good faith, and is guilty of no positive or active fraud in the transaction.

Approaching the question in somewhat reverse order, and addressing ourselves for the moment to what we term an exactly analogous question, it may be confidently stated that this court, from its beginning, has uniformly held that the measure of damages upon a breach of warranty of title contained in a deed is the value of the land at the time of the conveyance, if the entire title failed, or the proportionate part of that value which the acreage of the land lost on account of the breach bore to the entire acreage of the tract, and other items of expense resulting proximately from the breach; and that, in the absence of some showing to the contrary, the value of the land entering into the measure of the damages in such cases was the consideration paid or agreed to be paid. In no case has this court permitted the recovery in such cases of any increase in the market value of the land above that which was agreed to be and was actually paid. New Domain Oil & Gas Co. v. McKinney, 188 Ky. 183, 221 S. W. 245 (and cases therein referred to) ; Helton v. Asher, 135 Ky. 751, 123 S. W. 285; Sullivan v. Hill, 112 S. W. 564, 33 Ky. Law Rep. 962, and Robertson v. Lemon, 2 Bush, 301. If no other value may be taken into consideration in estimating the damages to the covenantee in a suit by him upon the breach of a warranty actually made than that agreed upon by the parties as a consideration for the conveyance of the land, it is difficult to perceive the reason for the application of a different rule where the obligation sued on, instead of being an executed warranty, is only an agreement to execute one. It is the absence of any semblance of logical distinction between the two cases that influenced the English courts in an early day, and the courts of most of the states of the Union, including this one, to adopt the rule first above stated, i. e., denying substantial damages because of increased market value of the land in a suit for the breach of a contract to convey it where the vendee was guiltless of active fraud and acted in good faith. The earliest English case coming under our observation so holding is Flureau v. Thornhill, 2 W. Bl. 1078. That case has since been followed by those of Pounsett v. Fuller, 17 C. B. 660; Walker v. Moore, 10 Barn. & C. 416; Sikes v. Wild, 1 Best & S. 587; s. c., 4 Best & S. 421; Bain v. Fothergill, L. R. 6 Exch. 59; s. c., L. R. 7 H. L. 158; Engell v. Fitch, L. R. 4 Q. B. 659, 10 B. & S. 738, and Jones v. Gardner, 1 Ch. 191, 71 L. J. Ch. 93, 86 L. T. Rep. N. S. 74. In support of the above rule and for a list of cases, both English and American, supporting it, we refer to the note to case of Beck v. Staats, 16 L. R. A. (N. S.) on page 771; 39 Cyc. pp. 2105–2111, inclusive, and 27 R. C. L. 633–634. In the last work cited, in stating the general rule, the text says:

"A distinction is usually made as regards the general damages recoverable between cases where the vendor acts in good faith in entering into the contract and cases where good faith is wanting. In the former case it is held that the measure of damages is the amount of the purchase money paid with interest, thereby denying to the purchaser any recovery for the loss of his bargain. This is the rule laid down in the early English case of Flureau v. Thornhill (2 W. Black, 1078) decided in 1775 and subsequently followed in that country, and has been adopted in most jurisdictions in this country, and in Canada."

See, also, note to the case of Ontario Asphalt Block Co. v. Montreuil, Ann. Cas. 1917B, 852, on page 860. The above authorities, in addition to containing references to cases from the courts of various states of the Union, England and Canada, also show that some of the states have adopted the rule by statute.

Coming now to the opinions in our court the first case directly in point seems to be

that of Allen v. Anderson, 2 Bibb, 415, which was a suit on a contract similar in all respects to the one now under consideration. After referring to the case of Cox's Heirs v. Strode, 2 Bibb, 276, 5 Am. Dec. 603, which was a suit for breach of warranty of title, and in which it was first held that the value as fixed by the consideration agreed to be paid should measure the criterion of damages, the opinion says:

"On a covenant to convey, where the vendor is without fraud incapable of making a title, the rule should be the same. In either case, the real damage the party has sustained is the purchase money, with interest from the time it was paid. In reason there exists no distinction between the two cases; a purchaser before the seller completes his engagement is not entitled to compensation for the fancied goodness of his bargain, which he may suppose he has lost, more than he is after it is completed. As to the damages that ought to be recovered on a covenant to convey, see the case of Flureau v. Thornhill, 2 Black, Rep. 1078."

The next case directly in point is that of Rutledge v. Lawrence, 1 A. K. Marsh. 396, which was also a suit exactly similar to the one here, and we insert this excerpt from the opinion:

"It has been settled by a current of decisions in this court that where one contracts to convey land, and is without fraud, unable to make a title, the measure of damages, to which the vendee is entitled, is the value of the land at the time of the sale, to be ascertained by the consideration fixed, or other evidence. Where the inability of the vendor has been produced by fraud on his part, a different rule has prevailed; but a failure to convey has never been adjudged to be evidence of a fraudulent inability, and we think ought not to be so adjudged. For an inability to convey may, and frequently does, happen without fraud, and fraud is odious in law, and ought never to be presumed."

Other cases in point are Kelly's Heirs v. Bradford, 3 Bibb, 317, 6 Am. Dec. 656; Goff v. Hawks, 5 J. J. Marsh. 341; Combs v. Tarlton's Adm'rs, 2 Dana, 464; Herndon v. Venable, 7 Dana, 371; Triplett v. Gill, 7 J. J. Marsh. 438; Rankin v. Maxwell, 2 A. K. Marsh. 488, 12 Am. Dec. 431; Booker's Adm'r v. Bell's Ex'rs, 3 Bibb, 173, 6 Am. Dec. 641; and Grundy v. Edwards, 7 J. J. Marsh. 368, 23 Am. Dec. 409. In the Goff Case, supra, which was also one on all fours with this one, the opinion says:

"Since the decision in the case of Cox's Heirs v. Strode, 2 Bibb, 276, the criterion of damages upon a covenant to convey land, which has been violated, but without fraud on the part of the covenantor, is the purchase money and interest thereon, or in the language of the case of Rutledge v. Lawrence, 1 A. K. Marsh. 397, it is the 'value of the land at the time of the sale, to be ascertained by the consideration fixed or other evidence.' If, however, the covenantor has been guilty of fraud, a different rule may govern the case. Then he would be responsible for the increased value of the land, at the time his covenant should have been performed."

We deem it unnecessary to fortify this thoroughly established rule by reference to other authorities or cases, except to say that in the case of Freeman v. Falconer, 201 Fed. 785, 120 C. C. A. 32, the federal Circuit Court of Appeals for the Sixth Circuit had before it for determination the exact question here presented, and which arose out of an agreement to sell land situated in Kentucky. The court applied the above rule (usually denominated the "good faith rule"), and in doing so said:

"We understand the rule in Kentucky to be that in contracts for the sale of land situated in that state, and in cases not involving his fraud or bad faith, the vendor, in the event of his failure to convey, is liable to the vendee on the basis of the value of the land at the date of making the contract, rather than such value at some later date contemplated for conveyance, and is liable, also, for such expense as the vendee may reasonably and properly incur under the contract."

At the time that opinion was rendered this court had apparently held to the contrary in the case of Whitworth v. Pool, 96 S. W. 880, 29 Ky. Law Rep. 1104 (a case relied on by appellant), but in rejecting the opinion in that case as an authority against the well-settled rule in this commonwealth, and distinguishing it, that court said:

"But the case of Whitworth v. Pool is, we think, clearly distinguishable from the instant case. There the land in question was owned by R. J. Whitworth and his wife, Mary Whitworth, each owning an undivided one-half interest, and they arbitrarily (and so, necessarily, in bad faith) refused to convey it."

Necessarily an arbitrary refusal to convey, or putting it out of the power of the covenantor to convey, between the date of the contract and the time for conveyance, are each acts of bad faith and in and of themselves remove the case from the application of the rule under consideration, and the federal Circuit Court of Appeals in the case referred to correctly held that the Whitworth Case was not an authority in conflict with prior Kentucky decisions.

Fortifying the reason for the rule, and as illustrating the views of this court upon the question involved, we refer to the unbroken line of cases decided by this court holding that, in a suit for a deficit in the quantity of land agreed to be conveyed, the plaintiff, where he is allowed to recover it all, must do so on the basis of the value of the shortage as of the date of conveyance, which is that fixed by the parties as a consideration therefor. There has been no departure from that rule in those cases, some of the later ones of which are, Moreland v. Henry, 156 Ky. 712, 161 S. W. 1105, Hunter v. Keightley, 184 Ky. 835, 213 S. W. 201, and Harts-

field v. Wray, 181 Ky. 836, 205 S. W. 965. So that we not only find that this court has heretofore held (with one exception hereafter to be noticed) that on the precise facts we have here (conceding there was no fraud, this question hereafter to be noticed) substantial damages for the loss of the bargain are not recoverable, a doctrine also followed by the great majority of foreign courts, but the same rule is also applied in the two analogous cases referred to, viz. in actions for a breach of warranty contained in a deed, and in cases to recover damages for a deficit in the amount of land conveyed.

The exception referred to and relied on by counsel for appellant is the case of Jenkins v. Hamilton, 153 Ky. 163, 154 S. W. 937; and it must be conceded that the opinion in that case, although the facts are somewhat different from those here involved, constitutes a departure from the long line of cases preceding it. It may be that in that case the court concluded that defendant was guilty of bad faith disentitling him to the benefits of the "good faith rule," above discussed, since he did not pretend to have any title at all, or any interest whatever in the premises which he contracted to convey; but whether so or not, it does appear that the question hereinbefore dealt with was not referred to or discussed in the opinion, nor was there any reference made to any of the numerous cases from this court, or elsewhere, applying the above rule. The foreign cases discussed in that opinion bear only upon the question as to whether the knowledge of the plaintiff concerning the condition of the title, and the defendant's inability to convey, are sufficient to constitute a defense to the suit. None of them referred to the measurement of damages, but only to the question as to whether the suit was maintainable. It may be, so far as we are capable of judging from the opinion, that the question was not made or argued in that case; but, be that as it may, we are convinced that the brief statement contained in it, announcing a different rule for the measurement of damages in cases like this, is so much out of harmony with the great preponderance of the law, as we have herein shown, that the abstract announcement therein made should no longer be followed, and that it is our duty to return to the plainly marked and well-beaten path theretofore traveled by us.

It has been wisely said, in substance, that it is not so material as to what the law is as that it be certain. It is, of course, the intent of the law, and the desire of the courts, that abstract justice should prevail in every case, and that judicial declarations should harmonize with logic and reason as inspirations for them; but in the multiplicity of complicated facts found in almost every case, which control its final destiny, such a coveted result cannot always be obtained by fallible humanity. There can be, however, in the same jurisdiction approximate certainty as to the law applicable to the same state of facts, and courts of last resort should strive for the consummation of that end. Thus guided, and remembering the stare decisis doctrine, we are constrained to hold that the doctrine of the cases hereinbefore referred to (except the Jenkins Case) is the one which we should adopt in this case.

If it should be asked why there should be a different rule, governing the measurement of damages for failure to comply with a contract relating to real estate, than the one applying to a contract for the sale of personalty, we might find it difficult to give a satisfactory answer. The English courts put the distinction upon the ground of the intricate involvement of titles to real estate growing out of the variously worded deeds, wills, and other muniments of title, so that a vendor might innocently believe that he could convey a good title when a learned attorney or a court might determine otherwise. Another reason suggesting itself to us is that real property is the only character of property absolutely essential to human existence, and that it is the policy of the law for it to remain in the hands of homebuilders and home maintainers, and not to encourage speculative or chance bargaining in it, but to adjust the rights of the parties concerning its transfer, in the absence of fraud or bad faith, by placing them in statu quo, which, in the absence of a contrary showing, will be presumed to have been in their contemplation. Furthermore, land values oscillate, because of rapidly occurring events which the parties at the time of making the contract could not possibly contemplate; illustrations of which are, the discovery of minerals in the land or in the neighborhood of it, the existence of which were wholly unknown at the time of the contract, and perhaps other equally unanticipated developments. But, whatever the reason may be, it is our duty to administer the law as it is, and not as we might have written it at the beginning.

[2] But it is insisted that plaintiff's pleading brings this case within the exception to the rule discussed, and shows that defendant was guilty of fraud, such as to deprive him of the benefit of the rule, and to permit plaintiff to recover damages for the loss of his bargain. We do not so construe the language of the petition. It nowhere charges any active fraudulent act on the part of defendant. The only fact which plaintiff alleged as constituting the fraud upon which he relies is that defendant did not disclose to him the condition of the title, i. e., did not refer him to the will of J. B. Graves (which was of record), and did not inform him that this court had held that there was yet a possibility of Mrs. Williams bearing

children. We do not think that such silence on the part of defendant constituted that character of fraud referred to in the authorities supra as being sufficient to change the rule.

Of course, each case must be governed by its own peculiar facts, and, looking to them as they appear in this case, we have concluded that the court properly determined the case, and its judgment is affirmed.

ISAACS et al. v. MAUPIN.

(Court of Appeals of Kentucky. May 17, 1921.)

1. Covenants ⬅102(2) — Grantee failing to obtain possession in ejectment suit may sue his covenantor as though evicted.

A judgment against a grantee in an ejectment suit brought by him to obtain possession is equivalent to eviction.

2. Covenants ⬅121(2)—Purchaser suing for possession without calling on covenantors, if unsuccessful, may show judgment to show eviction, but must prove adversary's paramount title.

If a grantee seeking to recover possession of premises from adverse claimants wants to avoid the necessity of proving the eviction by paramount title, he must give his vendor or covenantor timely notice and call on him to make good his warranty, and if he fails to defend, or does so unsuccessfully, he is nevertheless bound by the judgment of eviction and cannot thereafter call it in question except for fraud or collusion, but, if notice is not given and the grantee is unsuccessful, he cannot rely upon the judgment of an eviction alone to establish his right against a grantor or covenantor, for such judgment is only evidence of the eviction, and grantee must show that the eviction was by paramount title in the hands of adverse claimant.

3. Descent and distribution ⬅128—Purchaser may recover from vendor's heirs for failure of title, where they have inherited property sufficient to cover loss.

Though grantee gave no notice to his grantor's heirs of the pendency of suits to obtain possession from adverse claimants, he nevertheless had the right to recover on the warranty of the ancestor of the defendant heirs by showing that the title was subservient to those holding adverse claims and that the heirs received estate from grantors sufficient to cover the loss.

4. Ejectment ⬅12—Party in actual possession has superior title to one unable to prove complete paper title from commonwealth.

One in actual possession of lands with no other title has superior title to all other persons who are unable to prove complete paper title, and such a possessory title is paramount to a paper title, which cannot be traced to the commonwealth.

5. Covenants ☞101—Title which must prevail over other title held "paramount" and "superior."

That title is "superior" and "paramount" which will prevail over that which is asserted against it, so that the title of adverse claimants in possession of land of which purchasers sought possession having prevailed in that action, must be considered paramount in purchaser's action against the heirs of his vendor.

[Ed. Note.—For other definitions, see Words and Phrases, Paramount Title.]

6. Covenants ☞130(3) — Purchaser compromising with grantee's heirs can recover from them only the damages for breach of covenant.

Where purchaser's grantee's heirs were evicted because of superior adverse title existing before purchaser bought, it was proper for purchaser to compromise with them, but he could not, because of such settlement, recover from his grantors more than he was entitled to have for the breach of the covenant.

Appeal from Circuit Court, Estill County.

Suit by C. H. Maupin against Margaret Isaacs and others. Judgment for the plaintiff, and the defendants appeal. Affirmed.

Kelly Kash, of Lexington, for appellants. Hugh Riddell, of Irvine, and Grant E. Lilly, of Lexington, for appellee.

SAMPSON, J. Isaacs and Maupin exchanged lands in 1902, each making the other a deed of general warranty. The land which Isaacs conveyed to Maupin was in two tracts, containing in all 212 acres, and lay in Jackson county, while that which Maupin conveyed Isaacs was situated in Estill county. As the Jackson county lands were unimproved wild land, Isaacs gave two acres of it for one acre of the Maupin lands in Estill county and agreed and covenanted in the deed to Maupin that, if the title to the lands in Jackson county should fail in whole or in part, Maupin should have a lien on the lands in Estill county, conveyed by him to the extent of such loss, if any. Maupin very soon thereafter, and without seeing the said lands, sold and conveyed by deed of general warranty all the Jackson county lands to Capt. Thomas of Ford, Ky., at the price of $5 per acre. Both Isaacs and Thomas died leaving heirs.

Finding that the Jackson county lands were in the possession of third parties who asserted ownership thereof and were taking and removing the timber which constituted its chief value, the Thomas heirs brought two ejectment suits in the Jackson circuit court against the several claimants of the Jackson county lands, and notified and called upon Maupin, the vendor and warrantor of Thomas, to appear and make good his covenant of quiet enjoyment. Maupin claims to have given, by letter, a similar notice to the heirs

of Isaacs; but this is not sustained by satisfactory evidence.

The two suits in the Jackson circuit court were duly prepared and tried, one before a jury and the other by the court; the defendants defeating the Thomas heirs in each case. Judgments were entered against the Thomas heirs adjudging them not the owners of all but a small portion of the Jackson county lands, the part which they saved not being claimed by the defendants. In those actions the Thomas heirs claimed title through Maupin and Isaacs to a certain Ambrose patent which they asserted covered and included the lands in controversy. This the defendants denied by answer, and in a second paragraph asserted title to the lands by adverse possession. The plaintiffs were unable to show that the lands which they claimed, but lost in those suits, were embraced in the Ambrose patent. After judgments had been entered in those cases against the Thomas heirs, they demanded of Maupin that he make good the loss in acreage according to his covenant, and were about to file suit against him when he paid the Thomas heirs $1,100 in settlement. He thereupon demanded of the heirs of Isaacs a similar sum in fulfillment of their ancestors' warranty, but the Isaacs heirs denied liability, and this suit was instituted by Maupin against them in the Estill circuit court to recover $1,100 with interest and certain costs, and he prayed that he be adjudged a lien on the Estill county lands which he had given Isaacs in exchange for the lands in Jackson county, from which his grantee had been ousted by judgments of court. On a trial Maupin was awarded the sum of $856.75 and interest against the Isaacs heirs, being $5 an acre for the number of acres lost by Maupin and his grantee, and this sum was adjudged a lien against the Estill county lands.

In prosecuting this appeal the Isaacs heirs assert that the trial court erred to their prejudice in two respects: (1) In holding that Maupin was entitled to recover against them, who were not parties to the action, nor notified of its pendency without showing that his vendee had been evicted from the lands by one holding a paramount title; (2) in allowing a recovery against them without a showing that Maupin was compelled to pay the amount of the loss to the Thomas heirs, it being admitted that he compromised with them before suit was filed.

We will consider these questions in the order stated:

[1] 1. It is a general rule that a grantee who has been evicted by paramount title may sue his immediate grantor or any one or more prior covenantors in the chain of title and recoup his loss. Even one who holds under a special warranty deed may sue a remote covenantor on his warranty.

Thomas v. Bland, 91 Ky. 1, 14 S. W. 955, 11 L. R. A. 240.

If the vendee, as in this case, never obtains actual possession of the premises, because in the possession of the adverse claimant, a judgment against him in an ejectment suit commenced by him to obtain possession is equivalent to an eviction. In such case the title fails from the beginning and the grantee has a right of action as though evicted after entry. 7 R. C. ·L. 1153; ˙ Cummins v. Kennedy, 3 Litt. 118, 14 Am. Dec. 45; Pryse v. McGuire, 81 Ky. 610.

[2] But if he wants to avoid the necessity of proving the eviction by paramount title, he must give his vendor or covenantor timely notice of the litigation and call on him to make good his warranty, thus giving him a chance to vindicate his covenant of title. If he fails to defend or does so unsuccessfully, he is nevertheless bound by the judgment of eviction and cannot thereafter call it in question except for fraud or collusion. Graham v. Dyer, 29 S. W. 346, 16 Ky. Law Rep. 543; 7 R. C. L. 1197. If no notice is given by the grantee to the grantor of the litigation and the grantee undertakes to defend but is unsuccessful, he cannot rely upon the judgment of eviction alone to establish his right to recover against his grantor, for such judgment is only evidence of the eviction, not that it was by paramount title in the hands of the adversary claimant, and the vendee is obliged to aver and prove that the eviction was by paramount title. 7 R. C. L. 1148; Huff v. Cumberland Valley Land Co., 30 S. W. 660, 17 Ky. Law Rep. 213; Hubbard v. Stanaford, 100 S. W. 232, 30 Ky. Law Rep. 1044.

"It has become customary in most of the states of this country, whenever an action is brought upon a paramount claim against any person entitled to the benefit of the covenant of warranty of title, that he should give proper notice to such warrantor of the pendency of the suit, requiring him to come in and defend it, and by so doing he relieves himself from the burden of proving in · an action for breach of the covenant, the validity of the alleged paramount claim. The doctrine is well established that a judgment against a warrantee, in an action of which the warrantor had proper notice, is conclusive against the warrantor, in the absence of fraud or collusion." 7 R. C. L. 1197, 1198.

Failure to give notice of the pendency of such litigation to the covenantor, however, does not take away the right of the evicted vendee to have a recovery, but only puts upon him the additional burden of proving that the title which the vendor warranted to him was at the time of the conveyance subordinate to the title under which the adversary claimant of the lands evicted him.

[3-6] Though Maupin gave no notice to the Isaacs heirs of the pendency of the two suits in the Jackson circuit court, he nevertheless had the right to recover on the warranty of the ancestor of the appellants by showing that the title which he warranted to Maupin was subservient to those who held and claimed the lands which his said deed purported to convey and that the heirs of Isaacs received estate from him sufficient to cover the loss. The judgments were sufficient to prove the eviction—nothing more. Other evidence in the record proves that the Thomas heirs' title failed because there were persons in the actual possession of the lands at the time and long before the conveyance of Isaacs to Maupin, claiming the lands under a different title, which title was paramount to any title ·which the Thomas heirs were able to prove rested in them. One in the actual possession of lands with no other right has a superior title to all other persons who are unable to prove complete paper title, and such a possessory title is paramount to a paper title which cannot be traced to the commonwealth. It being admitted that the defendants in the Jackson county suits were in the actual adverse possession of the lands claiming it as their own, and denying the title of the Thomas heirs under the Isaacs and Maupin chain of title, the burden was on the Thomas heirs who brought the suits to sustain their claim of title. That title is superior and paramount which will prevail over that which is asserted against it, and the title of the claimants in possession of the Jáckson county lands must be held paramount to that of the Thomas heirs.

"When lands are exchanged, and the title of one of the tracts, which in the exchange between the parties was conveyed with general warranty, fails, a recovery may be had against the grantor for the value of the lands, with interest and costs, and the value fixed and agreed upon at the time of the exchange will be taken to be the true measure of the damages recoverable." 7 R. C. L. 1172.

[8] 2. It is insisted that Maupin had no right to compromise with the Thomas heirs after their eviction, and that such a compromise is not binding on the Isaacs heirs. It may be conceded that the compromise agreement is not binding on the Isaacs heirs, although Maupin had a right to make the best bargain he could after it was manifest .that he was liable to the Thomas heirs for a loss of a great number of acres of the Jackson county land. The law does not require one to do a vain and useless thing, or to litigate a perfectly obvious claim, but it rather discourages such litigation and favors compromises and settlements out of court. If, however, in the compromise Maupin paid more than the law would have exacted, he cannot recover the excess, but only so much as he was legally bound to pay. He was bound on his warranty to make good the loss sustained by the Thomas heirs by the eviction, and it would have served no useful purpose for Maupin to have denied

so obvious a liability and put the Thomas heirs to the expense and necessity of instituting a suit, and the courts to the trouble of deciding a case which it is admitted could have had but one conclusion. Had there been no eviction, there could have been no compromise or settlement that would have entitled Maupin to recover for an eviction must precede every recovery on a covenant of general warranty. Huff v. Cumberland Valley Land Co., 30 S. W. 660, 17 Ky. Law Rep. 213.

The amount recovered by Maupin is no more than he is entitled to have, but much less than the sum expended by him in defending two suits and satisfying the compromise agreement.

No error appearing to the prejudice of appellant, the judgment is affirmed.

PETTY'S HEIRS v. PETTY.

(Court of Appeals of Kentucky. May 10, 1921. Rehearing Denied June 7, 1921.)

1. Evidence ☞67(1)—Presumption is that possession of deed to wife continued in husband.

When deed to husband and wife is once shown to have been in the possession of the husband, the presumption is that it continued so.

2. Evidence ☞78—Defendant's failure to produce deed executed by him and in his possession held strong evidence against him.

When the execution and existence of deed from defendant husband to his first wife, under whom plaintiff, suing to quiet title, claims, were proven, and the deed was shown to have been in defendant husband's possession and control when it was last seen, it was defendant husband's duty to produce the deed or account for its loss if he proposed to rely upon it, having conveyed less than a fee to his first wife, and his failure to produce the deed is a strong circumstance tending to support plaintiff's contention that the deed conveyed a fee, and not a lesser estate.

3. Quieting title ☞44(4)—Evidence held to warrant finding of delivery of deed by defendant husband to first wife, plaintiff's ancestor, etc.

In action to quiet title brought by a grandson claiming through his grandmother, the grandfather's first wife, against his grandfather, evidence *held* to warrant the chancellor's finding as a fact the existence and delivery of the deed by the grandfather to his first wife, its recording, that it covered and included the lands in controversy, and conveyed to the first wife a fee-simple title.

Appeal from Circuit Court, Grayson County.

Action by L. L. Petty against Garten Petty, which, defendant having died, was revived

against his heirs. From judgment for plaintiff, defendants appeal. Affirmed.

Allen P. Cubbage, of Leitchfield, for appellants.

G. W. Stone, of Leitchfield, for appellee.

SAMPSON, J. This action was brought by L. L. Petty against his grandfather, Garten Petty, to quiet title to a tract of about 265 acres of land in Grayson county which it is alleged was once owned by Garten Petty, conveyed by him in 1876 to his wife, Sarah G. Petty, who died in 1895 intestate, leaving appellee, L. L. Petty as her only lineal descendant and heir, he being a grandson.

The appellee, L. L. Petty, plaintiff below, relies upon a lost deed alleged to have been made by his grandfather, Garten Petty, to appellee's grandmother, Sarah G. Petty, to sustain his claim to a remainder interest in the lands described and in which he admits his grandfather held a life estate by curtesy at the time this action was commenced.

The lower court adjudged the plaintiff the owner of the lands in remainder and quieted his title thereto as against the grandfather, who denied the execution or existence of the alleged lost deed.

On this appeal the grandfather being now dead, his heirs insist that the judgment should be reversed for the reasons: (1) That the existence and contents of the lost deed were not sufficiently proven; (2) the alleged lost deed, having admittedly been made in fraud of creditors of the grantor in which both grantor and grantee participated, is not enforceable in equity; (3) defendants' plea of adverse possession of the lands in question was fully established; and (4) the court erred in holding one spouse cannot acquire title by adverse possession of the lands of the other spouse after the death of the first spouse.

Garten Petty was twice married. Sarah G. Petty was his first wife. To them was born one son and one daughter, but the daughter died in infancy. The son married and became the father of appellee, L. L. Petty, but died before the commencement of this litigation. By his second wife Garten Petty had two children, and they are now parties by revivor to this litigation.

It is admitted that appellee, L. L. Petty, is the sole heir of Sarah G. Petty, from whom it is claimed he inherited the tract of land which is the subject of this controversy. It is also admitted that Garten Petty was once the owner of the lands, and that he continued to be the owner thereof until his death if he did not convey the same to his wife Sarah G. Petty about the year 1876; in other words, appellee, L. L. Petty, claims under a deed which he avers was made by his grandfather, Garten Petty, to appellee's grandmother, Sarah G. Petty, about 1876. The original deed, he avers, is concealed, lost, or destroyed through the wrongful act of his grandfather, who was the original and only defendant in this action, and ;the record thereof in the office of the clerk of the Grayson county court was destroyed in a fire which burned the courthouse several years before this action was commenced. While this suit was pending in the lower court and before judgment, Garten Petty died leaving a widow and two children, and this action was revived against them.

About the year 1875 Garten Petty became involved in a fight in a store near his home, and during the encounter inflicted an injury to the person of an innocent bystander named Miss Pickrell, who shortly sued Garten Petty for damages and recovered a verdict and judgment for an amount stated to have been $1,-000. Admittedly Garten Petty was the owner of the land at the time of the happening of the tort to Miss Pickrell, and perhaps at the time of the recovery of the judgment, but appellee contends that about that time, and in order to avoid the payment of the Pickrell judgment, Garten Petty conveyed the whole of his land then consisting of about 700 acres to his wife Sarah G. Petty, and that she took, and ever afterwards to her death held and claimed, said land as her sole property. The exact date of the deed is not known, but it is proven in the record that before 1876 all conveyances of parts of the land were made by Garten Petty, and he received the consideration therefor, but that after that date Sarah G. Petty sold and conveyed two or three small portions of the land, her husband joining with her, but she receiving all the consideration. It is also shown that before the date of the alleged deed Garten Petty's name always appeared first in the body of each deed of conveyance as the real owner, and his name was first subscribed to the deeds, and his wife's name came second, but after the said date all deeds ran in the name of Sarah G. Petty as first party and owner "and her husband, Garten Petty," and the notes for deferred payments of the purchase price were made to Sarah G. Petty, and actually paid to her, and not to her husband Garten Petty.

Several witnesses testified to having seen or read the deed from Garten Petty to Sarah G. Petty for the lands in controversy, but none undertook to tell in detail the exact date of the deed or its contents further than that it was a conveyance of the lands of Petty to his wife, but there are a number of facts and circumstances shown in evidence which aid in determining the contents and nature of the deed and on which appellee, L. L. Petty, relies to show the contents and effect of the operative clauses of the alleged deed.

It may be conceded that Garten Petty made a deed for the tract of land in question to his wife Sarah G. Petty about the year 1876, for this is fairly established by the evidence, but the question arises: What was the nature and contents of said deed? The rule is that,

where one relies upon a lost deed to sustain his title to real estate, he must establish the original existence of the deed, its loss, and the material parts thereof by clear and satisfactory evidence, and this rule is invoked by appellants to defeat appellee's claim to the land under the deed, for it is insisted that, if secondary evidence is to be substituted for primary evidence, the oral testimony must be substantially as complete as the writing itself, with proof of the contents of the writing. Lipps et al. v. Turner, 164 Ky. 626, 176 S. W. 42; Mould v. Rohm, 274 Ill. 547, 113 N. E. 991; Garland v. Foster County Bank, 11 N. D. 374, 92 N. W. 452; Gilmore v. Fitzgerald, 26 Ohio St. 171.

According to the testimony of some of the witnesses, Garten Petty stated on various and divers occasions and in the presence of different persons after 1876 and before the death of his wife Sarah G. Petty that he had conveyed the lands to his wife Sarah G. Petty, and that she was the sole owner thereof. In fact, he practically admits in his testimony in this case he made and delivered the deed to her, but he was not asked to its contents. If it be conceded that Petty made the deed to his wife in 1876, then it must be further conceded that he did so for the purpose of defeating the collection of the judgment against him, for the evidence is abundant on this point, and there was no other consideration shown or reason given for the conveyance.

If this was the purpose of the conveyance, as is admitted, nothing less than a deed for the fee would have availed. So the estate conveyed by the deed of 1876 must have been in fee. Aside from this, the presumption is, after great lapse of time, and, in the absence of a contrary showing, that the deed was an absolute conveyance of the entire estate in the lands conveyed, and not an estate of less degree.

Both Garten Petty and his wife Sarah. G. Petty fraudulently entered into the execution and delivery of the deed to Sarah G. Petty, asserted that the latter was the owner of the lands under the deed, and she exercised complete control over it. Moreover, when portions of the lands were conveyed, she made the deeds and received the money therefor, which is wholly and entirely inconsistent with the conduct of one who held and owned an estate less than fee. When Sarah G. Petty died she had the deed in her possession, lodged in a box in a bureau drawer among her belongings and personal effects. It had been duly acknowledged and recorded. It was seen among her personal belongings by at least two witnesses after her death. Garten Petty took charge of her effects, including the deed, after the death of Sarah G. Petty, and the deed has not since been seen.

[1, 2] When the deed was once shown to be in the possession of the husband, the presumption is that it continued so. 10 R. C. L. 872.

It was against the interest of Garten Petty to produce the deed if it was one in fee, and he did not do so on the trial, although it was shown to have been in his possession and control the last time it was seen by a witness, and that he took possession of her belongings after her death, and did not attempt to account for its whereabouts or its loss. When the execution and existence of the deed was proven and it was shown to have been in his possession and control when last seen, it was Garten Petty's duty to have produced the deed or to have accounted for its loss if he proposed to rely upon it conveying less than a fee, and his failure so to produce the deed is a strong circumstance tending to support the contention that the deed in question conveyed a fee, and not a lesser estate. It has been held by some courts that nonproduction of such a document shown to be in the possession of a party who denies its existence or alleged contents is a circumstance which may be considered by a court. It has further been held that slight evidence of the contents of a paper should be deemed sufficient against a party who has the power to remove all doubts as to the contents thereof by producing the paper itself, but fails or refuses to do so when the matter is fairly put in issue. Tobin v. Shaw, 45 Me. 331, 71 Am. Dec. 547; Eastman v. Amaskeag, 44 N. H. 143, 82 Am. Dec. 201; 10 R. C. L. 922.

[3] We therefore conclude that the chancellor was fully warranted in finding as a fact the existence and delivery of the deed by Garten Petty to Sarah G. Petty, its recording, that it covered and included the lands in controversy and conveyed the grantee a fee-simple title.

Judgment affirmed.

CITY OF NEWPORT et al. v. SCHMIT.

(Court of Appeals of Kentucky. May 20, 1921.)

1. Municipal corporations ⏾821(6)—Whether a tiled portion of sidewalk laid by an abutting owner was unsafe question for the jury.

In an action for injuries suffered when plaintiff fell on the tiled portion of a sidewalk which was constructed by the operator of a theater as a continuation of its lobby for advertising purposes, the question whether the tiles by reason of their hard, slick surface were unsafe for use by ordinarily shod pedestrians held, under the evidence, for the jury.

2. Appeal and error ⏾1001(2)—That the appellate court might have found differently immaterial.

Where the evidence was conflicting, and so was for the jury, the fact that the appellate court might have found differently on the evidence is immaterial.

3. Municipal corporations ⏾817(1)—Consent of municipality to replacing sidewalk with tiles inferable.

Where the operator of a theater removed a portion of the sidewalk and replaced it with tiles similar to that used in its lobby, the consent of municipality may be inferred where the work was done under the supervision of its inspector.

4. Municipal corporations ⏾764(3)—Municipality liable for failure to maintain entire width of sidewalk in reasonably safe condition if sufficient time has elapsed to give notice.

It is the duty of a municipality to keep and maintain the entire width of its sidewalks in a reasonably safe condition for public travel, and a failure on the part of the municipality to use ordinary care in that respect after notice of a sidewalk's unsafe condition or when by the exercise of ordinary care it could have had knowledge of the defective condition of the walk will render the municipality liable if sufficient time has elapsed after notice, etc., for the municipality to have remedied the condition.

5. Municipal corporations ⏾771—Municipality not guarantor of safety of pedestrians, and not liable for slippery sidewalk caused by rain.

A municipality is not a guarantor of the safety of person on its sidewalks or streets, and one does not have a cause of action merely because he may slip and fall when the result is not caused by an inherently dangerous or unsafe condition of the sidewalk, as where rain makes it slippery.

6. Municipal corporations ⏾809(1)—Both creator and maintainer of a nuisance liable.

If tiling laid in place of a sidewalk in front of a theater was by reason of its slippery condition a public nuisance when laid, both the creator and the maintainer of such nuisance are liable for damages resulting to persons thereby.

7. Municipal corporations ⏾808(1)—Subsequent owner or lessee liable for injuries resulting from defective sidewalks which amounted to nuisance.

Where a tiled portion of a sidewalk was an extension of theater lobby, etc., was not a nuisance when laid, but became such by failure to maintain it in a reasonably safe condition for public travel, a subsequent owner or lessee who appropriated the same to his own use in connection with the business and building is liable to one injured by a fall on the slick tiling, where such subsequent owner or lessee admitted its liability to maintain the walk, and it had opportunity before the accident to have abated the nuisance.

8. Municipal corporations ⏾808(1, 4)—Occupant not liable for defects in sidewalks which he did not create.

An occupant of abutting property whether the owner or lessee is not liable for defects in a sidewalk which he did not create nor for a failure to repair a sidewalk if he did not cause the necessity therefor.

⏾For other cases see same topic and KEY-NUMBER in all Key-Numbered Digests and Indexes

9. Municipal corporations ☜808(1)—Abutting owner who imposes "servitude" on sidewalk is liable if he allows it to become a nuisance and dangerous.

Where an abutting owner creates a servitude upon a sidewalk which is an addition to the general use the public may make of the sidewalk, as for example the placing of a door or coalhole in the walk, he is bound to maintain the servitude so that it will not become a nuisance, and if he fails he is liable to persons injured as a result of the defect, and so an abutting owner who continued a tiled portion of a sidewalk placed by his predecessor to advertise the theater business is liable where it became dangerous and slick.

10. Municipal corporations ☜808(1) — Nuisance ☜42, 76—Subsequent owner or lessee not liable for nuisance by predecessor until request for abatement.

In case of private nuisance a subsequent owner or lessee is not liable for a nuisance which the former owner or landlord created until he has been requested to abate it, but this rule is not applicable where the nuisance is a public one as the creation of a slippery zone in the sidewalk by laying ornamental tiles for advertising, etc., for the nuisance is a public one, and only the municipality could enforce abatement.

11. Damages ☜132(7)—$5,000 award to injured woman not excessive.

Where as a result of a fall a woman who was earning $10 to $14 per week was incapacitated for a year, at the end of which time she could earn only $10 to $12 a month, though wages had increased and she had to have assistance at her toilet because her right arm was permanently disabled so that it could not be elevated, and she was unable to stand for any length of time or rest on her knee, the cap of which had been broken, an award of $5,000 was not excessive.

Appeal from Circuit Court, Campbell County.

Action by Margaret E. Schmit against the City of Newport and another. From a judgment for plaintiff, defendants appeal. Affirmed.

William A. Burkamp and Brent Spence, both of Newport, for appellants.

P. J. Ryan and George Herold, both of Newport, for appellee.

HURT, C. J. This action by the appellee, Margaret E. Schmit, against the appellants, city of Newport and the Frankel Amusement Company, had for its purpose the recovery of damages which she avers that she sustained on account of personal injuries received when she slipped and fell upon the sidewalk in front of the theater owned, conducted, and controlled by the Frankel Amusement Company, and which bore the name of the "Hippodrome." The sidewalk, at the point where the appellee's feet slipped from under her and she fell upon it, is about 12½

feet in width, and all of it is constructed of cement, except a strip 27 feet in length and 3 feet in width, which immediately adjoins the property line in front of the entrance to the theater, and extends into the sidewalk to the distance of 3 feet, and this strip is made of tiles. The entrance into the theater from the sidewalk is through a lobby, which is also paved with tiles, and the portion of the sidewalk made of tiles is a continuation of the floor of the lobby. The basis of the claim for recovery, as alleged in the petition as amended, is that the sidewalk upon which the appellee fell and was injured was a sidewalk in the city, under its management and control through its officers, whose duty it was to maintain it in a reasonably safe condition for travel by pedestrians, and, though under such duty, the city permitted the Hippodrome Amusement Company, which in April, 1915, erected the building in which the theater is conducted, to remove the cement sidewalk in front of the building and adjoining its property line to a width of 3 feet and a length of 27 feet, and to substitute for the removed cement a surface made of smooth, glazed, and slippery tiles, with a grade from the property line to the cement of one-half inch to the foot, and that the portion of the sidewalk thus constructed of tiles was rendered dangerous and unsafe for travel by pedestrians, ordinarily shod, by reason of the glazed, slippery, and slick condition of the surface of the tiles, and the slanting surface given to it by the grade upon which it was constructed from the house line to where it joined the cement portion of the sidewalk, and it was this dangerous and unsafe condition which caused the appellee to slip and fall and injure herself. The tiled portion of the sidewalk, which was formed by permitting the Hippodrome Amusement Company to extend the floor of its lobby into the sidewalk to a distance of 3 feet, with the grade as above stated, was the portion upon which the appellee was walking at the time her feet slipped from under her and she fell. The tiles composing the strip were white in color, except in the center of the strip, and immediately in front of the lobby, the word "Hippodrome" was constructed of tiles of a different color. The tiled portion of the sidewalk and the name of the theater inserted in it were for the special benefit of the owner of the theater building and the business conducted in it in the way of an advertisement of the building and its business. On the 20th day of June, 1916, the appellant Frankel Amusement Company became or assumed to be the owner of the building, conducted and conducted its business in it until March 16, 1917, when appellee received the injuries complained of. There was some evidence to the effect that the tiled portion of the sidewalk was in the same condition when appellee fell upon it as when it was first constructed, except that from use it had become more slick, and therefore more unsafe and dangerous. It was averred that the city and its officers at all times knew of the dangerous and unsafe condition of the sidewalk, caused by the tiled portion of it, or by the exercise of ordinary care would have known of it, and negligently failed to remedy, or cause to be remedied, the defects in it so as to render it reasonably safe for travel, and the Frankel Amusement Company knew of its injurious character at all times previous to the incurrence of the injuries, but maintained and used the tiled portion of it for its own special benefit, and negligently failed to remove the tiles from the sidewalk, or to otherwise take precautions to render that portion of the sidewalk reasonably safe for pedestrians, and negligence of the city and the amusement company, as before stated, was the proximate cause of the injuries which the appellee received. The foregoing contentions of appellee were denied by the answers of the appellants, and the trial resulted in a verdict by the jury in favor of appellee against the city for the sum of $1,000 in damages, and against the Frankel Amusement Company for the sum of $4,000, and each have appealed.

[1, 2] (a) At the conclusion of the evidence for the plaintiff, and at the conclusion of all the evidence, each of the defendants moved the court for a directed verdict in its favor, and, these motions being overruled, each of them now insists, as a common ground for the reversal of the judgment, that the court erred in thus disposing of their motions. It is not contended nor insisted for either of the defendants that the time which had expired from the construction of the tiled portion of the sidewalk to the time of the injury or from the time the theater came under the control of the Frankel Amusement Company to the time of the injury was insufficient to charge the defendants with notice of its unsafe and dangerous condition, and to have enabled them, with the exercise of ordinary diligence, to have remedied the alleged unsafe condition, but it is insisted for each that the evidence was insufficient upon the issue as to the unsafe condition for travel of the sidewalk to require a submission to the jury. It may be confessed that, if there were no contradictions in the evidence upon that subject, and all of the evidence conduced to prove the conclusions drawn from it by counsel for defendants, they were eminently right in their contention, but when the evidence as to the character of the tiled portion of the sidewalk, with regard to its condition of safety for travel, is examined, it is apparent that the evidence upon that subject is very contradictory, and made necessary a submission to the jury of that issue, and the fact that we would arrive from the evidence at a conclusion different from that at which the jury arrived is aside from the subject, nor will a conclusion upon our part, if we had been the triers upon the facts, that the verdict should have been upon the issue for the defendants, warrant a conclusion that the issue ought not to have been submitted.

[3, 4] While it is not expressly proven that the city authorized the owner of the theater to extend the tile floor of the lobby out into the sidewalk to the distance above stated, such may be inferred from the fact that the work was done under the supervision of an inspector for the city, but whether the city was or was not consulted in the matter is immaterial, since the duty of a municipality to keep and maintain its sidewalks in a reasonably safe condition for public travel applies to the entire width of a sidewalk, and for a failure upon the part of the municipality to exercise ordinary care to keep and maintain its sidewalks in a reasonably safe condition for travel by pedestrians, after notice of its unsafe condition, or when by the exercise of ordinary care to attend to its duties in that respect it would have had knowledge of the defective condition of the sidewalk, it will be liable for injuries sustained by persons on account of such unsafe condition, if sufficient time has elapsed after notice, or after it is chargeable with notice, within which to have reasonably enabled it to have remedied the conditions. Eagan v. Covington, 166 Ky. 825, 179 S. W. 1026; Louisville v. Hough, 157 Ky. 643, 163 S. W. 1101; Covington v. Belser, 123 S. W. 249; Gnau v. Ackerman, 166 Ky. 258, 179 S. W. 217; Dayton v. Lory, 169 Ky. 94, 183 S. W. 252; West Ky. Telephone Co. v. Pharis, 78 S. W. 917, 25 Ky. Law Rep. 1838.

[5] It is true that municipalities are not guarantors of the safety of persons upon their sidewalks and streets, nor does one have a cause of action because he may slip and fall upon a sidewalk, when such result is not caused by an inherent dangerous or unsafe condition of the sidewalk, nor are defects in a sidewalk sufficient to support a cause of action, if in spite of the defects, in the opinion of reasonable men the sidewalk is reasonably safe for public travel, nor does the fact that a fall of rain or snow upon an otherwise safe sidewalk makes it slippery give a cause of action to one slipping down upon it. Many cases supporting these doctrines are cited by the appellants, and of the results in those cases we have no controversy, but the instant case does not seem to come within the principles applicable to the facts of either of the cases cited. There were witnesses who deposed that the tiled surface of the strip of the lobby floor, which extended out into the sidewalk, was as "slick as glass," that it was "intensely slick," and that it was "slippery, very slippery." There was evidence tending to prove that the tiles had a hard, very smooth and glazed surface which rendered them inherently slick, and made one

ordinarily shod unable to retain the footing upon it necessary to enable him to escape falling. It was proven that four or five other persons had slipped down upon it previous to the mishap of the plaintiff. A witness deposed that its slickness was similar to a piece of tile brought up in the record, and this piece is very hard, glazed, and slick. From this inherent condition of the tiles, taken in connection with the fact that the surface was slanting to the extent that it was 1½ inches lower where it joined the cement than at the house line, which was a distance of only 3 feet, it cannot be said that as a matter of law it was reasonably safe for public travel. There was other evidence which tended to prove that the tiles of which the strip upon the sidewalk was constructed were not too slick to enable a pedestrian, shod in the ordinary way, to pass safely over it, and there was other evidence which tended to prove that the tiles did not have the glazed, slick condition contended for by the plaintiff. There was also evidence which tended to prove that the use of the sidewalk had rendered the tiled portion of it very much slicker than it originally was, and that this condition had existed for a long period before the mishap to the plaintiff. Under this state of evidence, the issue as to the reasonable safety of the sidewalk at that point for travel by pedestrians was an issue for the jury, and which the court could not take away from it, as the defendants insisted that it should, without entirely ignoring a very considerable portion, and probably a preponderating portion of the evidence. City of Lebanon v. Graves, 178 Ky. 749, 199 S. W. 1064, L. R. A. 1918B, 1016; City of Dayton v. Lory, supra. The liability of the Frankel Amusement Company as an abutting property owner for the unsafe condition of the sidewalk in front of its property will be hereafter considered.

[6, 7] (b) In addition to the foregoing ground it is insisted for the Frankel Amusement Company that a verdict should have been directed in its favor, because of a failure of the evidence touching its connection with the property. The petition alleged that the Hippodrome Company, when the owner of the building extended the floor of the lobby into the sidewalk, as heretofore stated, and the Frankel Amusement Company thereafter assumed the ownership, occupancy, and control of the building, and appropriated the use of the tiled portion of the sidewalk for its own special use and benefit, and that of its business, and maintained the tiled portion of the sidewalk in its dangerous and unsafe condition for travel. If that portion of the sidewalk was in the condition contended for by appellee, it was a public nuisance, and both the creator and the maintainer of such nuisance is liable for the damages resulting to persons therefrom, if it was a nuisance when created; but, if not a nuisance when

created, if it thereafter became such by failure and neglect to maintain it in a reasonably safe condition for public travel, a subsequent owner or lessee who appropriates it for his own use is liable for the injuries caused by it. Hence, although in the former opinion of this court in this case, in 184 Ky. 342, 212 S. W. 113, it inadvertently treated the Frankel Amusement Company as both creator and maintainer of the alleged nuisance, the inadvertent statement is immaterial, since the evidence shows, without contradiction, that the latter company was either owner or lessee of the building, and in control of it at the time of the mishap to appellee, and there is no pretense that it was unable for any reason to abate the nuisance, nor any claim made that it was absolved from liability by reason of no notice or request to it to abate the nuisance before the incurrence of the injury. In fact, it offered upon the trial an instruction in substance advising the jury that it was the duty of the Frankel Amusement Company to maintain the tiled strip in a reasonably safe condition for public travel. Under the facts of this case, the Frankel Amusement Company would not be liable for an injury on account of the alleged nuisance, unless it continued and maintained it for its own special use and benefit, or that of its building and business, and negligently failed to maintain it in a reasonably safe condition for travel by pedestrians.

[8] Of course, it will be conceded that an occupant of abutting property, whether the owner or lessee, is not liable for defects in the sidewalk which he did not create, nor for a failure to repair a sidewalk if he did not cause the necessity therefor. Webster v. C. & O. Ry. Co., 105 S. W. 945, 32 Ky. Law Rep. 404.

[9] If, however, one creates a nuisance upon a sidewalk, he will be liable for the consequences in the way of injuries to individuals caused by the nuisance. Hence, if an abutting property owner creates a nuisance upon the sidewalk in front of his premises, he will be liable for the injuries caused by it, and further, if he creates a servitude upon the sidewalk, which is in addition to the general use the public may make of the sidewalk, and which is for the exclusive benefit of himself or of his property, he is under a duty to so maintain it that it will not become a nuisance, and, if he fails to do so, he will be liable in damages to one of the public who suffers injuries because of his failure to maintain it in a way which will make it in a reasonably safe condition for the travel of the public who use the sidewalk. Louisville v. Metropolitan Realty Co., 168 Ky. 204, 182 S. W. 172; Hippodrome Amusement Co. v. Carius, 175 Ky. 783, 195 S. W. 113, L. R. A. 1918E, 377; Stephens' Adm'r v. Deickman, 158 Ky. 337, 164 S. W. 931, 51 L. R. A. (N. S.) 309; Covington, etc., Co. v. Drex-

ilus, 120 Ky. 493, 87 S. W. 266, 27 Ky. Law Rep. 903, 117 Am. St. Rep. 593; Varney v. Covington, 155 Ky. 662, 160 S. W. 173; Harrodsburg v. Vanarsdall, 148 Ky. 507, 147 S. W. 1. A familiar example of such servitudes and the consequent liability of the abutting owner who creates them is where a cellar door, or coalhole, or section of the sidewalk is composed of glass, or other transparency for the benefit of the property of the abutting owner, or a covered gutter across the sidewalk to carry away the water from the house of an abutting owner. But the liability of a subsequent owner of property or a tenant or lesseee of property for a nuisance upon or attached to the property which was created by the original owner, or in case of a tenant or lessee by the owner previous to its occupancy by the lessee, is a subject of wide divergence of opinion in the different jurisdictions. In some jurisdictions it is held that no liability attaches to a tenant, lessee, or subsequent owner for a nuisance existing when he takes possession or control of the property, except such as arises from his negligence in the use of the subject of·the nuisance. In others it is held that a subsequent owner, lessee, or tenant is liable for continuing a nuisance which existed when his occupancy began, if he has knowledge of its injurious tendencies, and such knowledge is sufficient to fix a liability upon him without further notice or request to abate it. Southern R. Co. v. Plott, 131 Ala. 812, 31 South. 33; Willitts v. Chicago, etc., Co., 88 Iowa, 281, 55 N. W. 313, 21 L. R. A. 608; Union Trust Co. v. Cuppy, 26 Kan. 754; Pinney v. Berry, 61 Mo. 359; Dickson v. Chicago, etc., Co., 71 Mo. 575; Nicket v. St. Louis, etc., Co., 135 Mo. App. 661, 116 S. W. 477; Ahern v. Steele, 115 N. Y. 203, 22 N. E. 193, 5 L. R. A. 449, 12 Am. St. Rep. 778.

[10] In other jurisdictions it is held that a subsequent owner or lessee is not liable for a nuisance which the former owner or landlord created until he has been requested to abate it, and such has been the general rule adhered to by this court, but the facts in neither of the adjudicated cases bear any similarity to the facts of this case. West Bros. v. I. C. & L. R. R. Co., 8 Bush, 405; Gleason v. Schneider, 7 Ky. Law Rep. 834; Ray v. Sellers, 1 Duv. 255; Glenn v. Crescent Coal Co., 145 Ky. 137, 140 S. W. 43, 37 L. R. A. (N. S.) 197; Ireland v. Bowman, 114 S. W. 338; Central Consumers' Co. v. Pinkert, 122 Ky. 729, 92 S. W. 957, 13 Ann. Cas. 105. It will be observed that the nuisance complained of in each of the foregoing cases was either a purely private one, or one where the circumstances were such as good faith required a request for an abatement and an opportunity on the part of the complainant to do so. In the latter cited case it was said:

"The doctrine is also recognized that the continuer of the nuisance is liable without a request to remove it, if by some positive act he adopts it, or the nuisance results from the use, rather than from the erection itself."

In line with that decision are the cases which hold that no notice is necessary to a subsequent owner or lessee of the existence of a nuisance created by the former owner or landlord where the subsequent owner or lessee appropriates the nuisance to his own use and continues and maintains it for his own purposes, or where the continued use of it is in itself a nuisance. Whitenack v. Philadelphia, etc., Co. (C. C.) 57 Fed. 901; Walter v. Wicomico County Com'rs, 35 Md. 385. This is aside from the doctrine of those cases which hold that a tenant or occupant of premises, who has the control of them, is, so far as third persons are concerned, to be regarded as the owner, and is therefore prima facie liable for all nuisances upon the premises injurious to the adjacent owners, and for all injuries which arise from defects of repairs in the premises or their approaches. Chicago v. O'Brennan, 65 Ill. 160; Oakham v. Holbrook, 11 Cush. (Mass.) 302; Fisher v. Thirkell, 21 Mich. 1, 4 Am. Rep. 422; Tate v. Mo., etc., R. Co., 64 Mo. 149; Clancy v. Bryne, 56 N. Y. 129, 15 Am. Rep. 391.

The rule which applies to the liability of a subsequent owner or a lessee of premises on account of a private nuisance does not seem to be applicable in a case presenting facts similar to the instant one, where the nuisance is a public one, and is in a public street and sidewalk of a city, and where only the municipality could enforce an abatement, and where a private individual would have no cause of action on account of the nuisance, except by reason of some special injury received by him. In Leahan v. Cochran, 178 Mass. 566, 60 N. E. 382, 53 L. R. A. 891, 86 Am. St. Rep. 506, it is expressly held that a subsequent owner of property does not have to have notice nor request to abate a nuisance which is attached to the property, to create a liability for the consequences of it if the nuisance is a public one, and this doctrine is sustained, at least in principle, in Davie v. Levy, 39 La. Ann. 551, 2 South. 395, 4 Am. St. Rep. 225, and Vaughan v. Buffalo, etc., Ry. Co., 72 Hun, 471, 25 N. Y. Supp. 246. This seems to be the just rule where the subsequent owner or lessee has knowledge of the hurtful character of the nuisance. There could be no question that the tiled extension of the lobby floor in the sidewalk, in front of the entrance to the theater, with the name of the theater constructed therein, in the instant case was a servitude imposed upon the sidewalk for the special and exclusive benefit of the theater and of the owner or lessee thereof, and the occupant of the building who was in control of it, and who received the benefits of the additional servitude upon the sidewalk, was necessarily under obligation to use ordinary care at least to maintain the servitude in the manner so as not to render the sidewalk dangerous and unsafe for travel, and the location of the object imposing the servitude is such as to dispel any contention as to who was maintaining it, and for whose benefit it existed. There could be no doubt of the appropriation of it by the occupant of the building in the conduct of its business as a theater, as there was no conflict in the evidence upon that subject, and, if it should be insisted that it composed a portion of the sidewalk, that the occupant of the building could not abate the nuisance without the consent of the city, yet there were other practical means of rendering it harmless and reasonably safe for travel, and which could have been made use of by the occupant of the property without the consent of any one. No complaint is made of the instruction which fixed the liability of the Frankel Amusement Company, and, as before said, an instruction offered by it was substantially the same as that given as to its liability on account of the alleged nuisance.

[11] (c) The appellee, as the consequences of the injury, was unable to do any work for more than a year. The evidence for her proves that her right arm is permanently disabled, her right kneecap was fractured by the fall, and a considerable unnatural growth has come upon it, which renders the injury to it a permanent one. She suffered and has continued to suffer a great deal of pain. At the time of the injury her avocation rewarded her with $12 to $14 per week, and after a year of total inability to work she is now unable to earn more than $10 to $12 per month, and at a much higher rate of wages than existed at the time of the injuries. She has to have assistance in dressing her hair and bathing her person, on account of the injury to her right arm, which she cannot elevate from her side. The injury to her knee renders her unable to stand for any considerable length of time, or to rest upon her knee. Hence we cannot say that the damages allowed were excessive.

The judgment is therefore affirmed, with damages.

BONFILS v. MARTIN'S FOOD SERVICE CO. (No. 22446.)

(Supreme Court of Missouri, in Banc. April 1, 1921. Rehearing Denied May 24, 1921.)

Landlord and tenant ⬤➩290(2)—Lessee who holds over with knowledge that lease cannot be renewed guilty of unlawful detainer.

Lessee, who remained in possession after expiration of lease with knowledge that prior to expiration thereof lessor had leased the premises to third persons, could not defend unlawful detainer on ground that he relied upon lessor's promises to renew lease, and that the holding over was, by virtue of the oral permission of lessor, and not willfully or unlawfully, under Rev. St. 1909, § 7657, providing that a tenant, who willfully and without force holds over, shall be deemed guilty of an unlawful detainer.

Appeal from Circuit Court, Jackson County; W. O. Thomas, Judge.

Suit by F. G. Bonfils against Martin's Food Service Company. Judgment was rendered for plaintiff in the justice court, but was reversed, and judgment rendered for defendant in the circuit court, and plaintiff appeals. Judgment of circuit court reversed, and cause remanded.

This is an unlawful detainer suit, instituted by the plaintiff against the defendant for the possession of the premises described in the complaint, located in Kansas City, Mo. The suit was instituted before Casimir J. Welch, justice of the peace, within and for the Sixth district, in Kaw township, Jackson county, in which the property is situated.

The complaint alleges that the plaintiff was the owner of the property and that on January 1, 1915, by written lease he leased the premises to the defendant for a period of five years, from and including January 1, 1915, to and including December 31, 1919, at a rental of $258.33 per month. The complaint also charged that the defendant's lease had expired by limitations, and that he willfully and unlawfully retained the possession of the premises after said expiration of the lease, and refused to restore the possession thereof to the plaintiff, as required by the terms of said lease, and prayed judgment for the restoration of the premises, and $5,000 damages, rents, etc.

The cause was tried in the justice court, and a judgment was rendered for the plaintiff and defendant attempted to appeal the case to the circuit court, which was denied by the justice, and after some time, and through many legal proceedings, the cause finally reached the circuit court, which upon trial there resulted in a judgment for the defendant, and the plaintiff duly appealed the case to this court.

The cause had a checkered career in both

the justice court and in the circuit court, which presents many legal propositions for determination to this court, but from the view we take of the case there is but one of them which we deem worthy of consideration, as it fully disposes of the case, all the others relate only to matters of practice in the justice court and the circuit court, which are governed by statutory provisions; but none of them touch the merits of the case, excepting the one to be considered.

The evidence for the defendant practically concedes the foregoing facts, probably, more accurately speaking, it does not tend to deny any of those facts, but seeks to evade the legal effect of the same, by introducing testimony tending to show that some time prior to September, 1919, the president of the defendant company had a talk with plaintiff, looking toward a renewal of the lease, but nothing came of that, because the latter was not in Kansas City any more, until the early part of November, 1919, but during the latter month they did meet and talked over the matter of renewing the lease, and the president of the defendant company testified that they practically agreed orally upon the terms of the renewal, which was denied by the plaintiff. But at all events no actual renewal was executed. The defendant's testimony tended to show that while the terms of the negotiations for the renewal of the lease were still pending, the plaintiff, on November 15, 1919, executed to Charles H. and Dora C. Surber a written lease for the premises for a period of five years at $350 per month, from and after the expiration of the defendant's lease, which was December 31, 1919.

The defendant's evidence also tended to show that it had a very expensive plant installed in the plaintiff's building, and that he had one or two other opportunities to lease another building for his business, and would have done so, had it not been for the fact that he was led to believe that he was going to procure a renewal of the plaintiff's lease, also that defendant had an offer on November 1, 1919, to sell his business as established in the plaintiff's building for a profit of $3,000 bonus for the good will of the defendant, but that offer fell through because the plaintiff failed to renew the lease, etc.

I think this is a favorable statement of the case for both parties as the record warrants, although the record covers about 180 pages.

There is but a single legal proposition presented by this record which demands our consideration, as all the other questions are subordinate to and must give way to its legal effect.

Frank M. Lowe and Kenneth McC. De Weese, both of Kansas City, for appellant.

Wilkinson & Wilkinson and Cook & Gossett, all of Kansas City, for respondent.

WOODSON, J. (after stating the facts as above). I. This case is controlled by section 7657, R. S. 1909, and, in so far as it is here material, reads as follows:

"When any person shall willfully and without force hold over any lands, tenements or other possessions, after the termination of the time for which they were demised or let to him, or the person under whom he claims, * * * shall refuse or neglect to quit such possession, such person shall be deemed guilty of an unlawful detainer."

There is no doubt but what this case falls squarely within the provisions of this statute, and the attempt of defendant to show that he had had some negotiations with the plaintiff looking to a renewal of the lease does not take the case from the operation of the statute. There is no pretense made that a renewal was in fact made, nor that the negotiations had between the parties were sufficient in legal effect to justify a court of equity to specifically enforce that agreement, had it been made.

But we do not understand that counsel for defendant are really insisting upon that right, and, if they did, it would be unavailing, because no such issue is made by the pleading, nor did the justice of the peace have jurisdiction to pass upon that question, had the same been presented. But the real contention of counsel for defendant, as I understand it to be, is that the negotiations had between the plaintiff and defendant looking to a renewal of the lease so misled the defendant as to cause him to hold over, and therefore the holding over was not willful or unlawful.

There is no merit in this contention, for the record shows that as early as November 1, 1919, the defendant tried to sell its business, but could not effectuate the sale because the plaintiff would not renew the lease, and that 15 days thereafter, November 15, 1919, the plaintiff actually leased the premises to Chas. H. and Dora C. Surber for $350 per month, for a period of five years, which facts were well known to the defendant.

The facts in this case are so radically different from those in the case of Ish v. Chilton, 26 Mo. 256, cited and so confidently relied upon by counsel for the respondent, that the most casual reading of it will show that it has no application whatever to this case.

Upon those facts it cannot be seriously contended that the defendant held over after the expiration of the time of its lease, because it believed and relied upon the plaintiff's oral promises to renew the lease, and therefore it was holding over by virtue of the oral permission, and not willfully or unlawfully.

After the defendant knew the plaintiff would not renew the lease to it, it had about two months to vacate the property, according to the plain terms of the lease, had it been proper to have done so.

II. In oral argument some question was raised as to the jurisdiction of this court of this cause because of the amount involved, but after an examination of the record we find that this question is destitute of all merit, for the reason that the damages asked for in the complaint are $5,000, and under section 7674, if the plaintiff recovers, that sum will have to be doubled, and in addition thereto the rents amounted to several thousand dollars, making the amount involved considerably over the amount which confers jurisdiction upon this court.

III. It might also be proper to state in this connection that it is contended by counsel that the justice of the peace of Kaw township had no jurisdiction of this cause, but they in no way present any facts showing that such charge is true.

For the reasons stated the judgment of the circuit court is reversed, and the cause remanded for a new trial in conformity to the views herein expressed.

All concur.

GEYER v. DENHAM et al. (No. 13842.)

(Kansas City Court of Appeals. Missouri. March 7, 1921. Rehearing Denied May 23, 1921.)

1. **Landlord and tenant** ⇙1—**Relation may arise from privity of contract or privity of estate.**

(Lessee's liability to lessor may arise by privity of contract from his express covenant, or by privity of estate on an implied obligation.)

2. **Landlord and tenant** ⇙208(2)—**Lessee's assignee liable for rent regardless of his actual entry.**

(Lessor's acceptance of lessee's assignment to third person made third person liable to lessor for rent under the lease without regard to whether there was an actual entry by assignee under the assignment, the acceptance of the assignment and the assignee's legal possession implied by ownership being sufficient.)

3. **Landlord and tenant** ⇙208(4)—**Lessee's assignee, who reassigned lease to lessee, liable for rent for period subsequent to reassignment.**

(Where lease was assigned with lessor's consent subject to all the covenants in the lease, and assignee subsequently reassigned lease to lessee, the assignee was liable for the rent for the period subsequent to reassignment, since the covenant to pay rent assumed by original assignment remained an obligation, notwithstanding reassignment.)

Appeal from Circuit Court, Jackson County; Daniel E. Bird, Judge.

"Not to be officially published."

Action by Elizabeth Geyer against Clarence E. Denham and another. Judgment for plaintiff, and defendants appeal. Affirmed.

Smart & Strother, of Kansas City, for appellants.

H. H. McCluer and Omar E. Robinson, both of Kansas City, for respondent.

ARNOLD, J. Plaintiff, on September 2, 1909, leased to Clarence E. Denham the east 65 feet of lots 7 and 8, block 7, Vineyard's addition to Kansas City, Mo., for a period of 99 years, beginning October 1, 1909, and ending September 30, 2008.

The lessee undertook and agreed to pay $600 rent each year for the period beginning October 1, 1909, and ending September 30, 1914, and $900 per year for each year for the period beginning October 1, 1914, and ending September 30, 1919, and $1,200 per year for the period beginning October 1, 1919, and ending September 30, 2008, payable quarterly. Lessee also covenanted to pay all taxes both general and special and in default thereof plaintiff might, at her option, pay said taxes, general or special, and any other charge or claim against the property, and that lessee should be bound to refund to lessor all such advancements or payments so made, together with 8 per cent. interest per annum from the date of such payments. The lease further provided the lessee might, at any time, subject to the provisions of said lease, sell, assign, incumber, sublet, or otherwise dispose of same. On December 31, 1909, lessee assigned said lease to the Ozark Investment Company, a corporation; the consideration therefor specified in the assignment being $2,000.

By the terms of said assignment, the assignee accepted the same subject to all the terms and conditions contained in said lease to be performed by the lessee therein, and the assignee expressly covenanted and agreed to observe and comply with all the terms of said lease remaining to be complied with by lessee.

November 6, 1916, the Ozark Investment Company assigned the lease to Clarence E. Denham, in which said assignment the following clause appears:

"The said Clarence E. Denham having assigned the above-mentioned lease to Ozark Investment Company on December 31, 1909, for the purpose of holding the title for the convenience of said Clarence E. Denham, this instrument is made for the purpose of reconveying said title to said Clarence E. Denham."

The suit was filed against Clarence E. Denham and Ozark Investment Company to recover alleged unpaid rentals, taxes paid by plaintiff in the sum of $2,558.45, and interest thereon. The suit was filed March 29, 1917, and resulted in a verdict and judgment for plaintiff and against both defendants in the sum of $2,558.45 and interest, $441.55, amounting in total to the sum of $3,000.

Defendant Ozark Investment Company appeals.

The answer of the Ozark Investment Company to plaintiff's petition is a general denial; and a special defense admits the assignment of the lease from Clarence E. Denham to the company on December 31, 1909, but alleges that said assignment was executed and delivered to said company without consideration; that it was made merely for the convenience of the assignor for the purpose of having defendant company hold the title for said assignor; and that defendant company never entered into possession of the premises.

A jury was waived and the cause heard by the court, and judgment was rendered upon special findings of law and fact.

There is no dispute as to the facts in the case. The lease, the assignment to the defendant company by Denham, and by the company back to Denham, were all introduced in evidence. Defendant company makes no denial that the rent and taxes are not paid, but contends that as the company was merely holding the lease in its name by assignment for the accommodation of Denham, the company is not liable for the rents and other charges under the lease.

[1] As stated in Whetstone v. McCartney, 32 Mo. App. loc. cit. 434:

"There are two ways in which a lessee may be liable to his lessor; one arises from his express covenant to pay whereby he is held in privity of contract; the other arises, in the absence of an express covenant to pay rent, on an implied obligation, whereby he is held in privity of estate. * * * The assignee is likewise liable to the original lessor for the term he occupies, not by reason of a promise, but by reason of the privity of estate. And the lessor may pursue one, or both, at the same time, though he will be entitled to but a single satisfaction."

[2] Section 7 of the lease provides that—

"Lessee may at any time, subject to the provisions of this lease, sell, assign, incumber, sublet or otherwise dispose of this lease," etc.

On the 31st of December, 1909, lessee, Denham, for a stipulated consideration of $2,000, "did sell, assign, transfer and convey to" the defendant company herein, "its successors and assigns, all the right, title and interest of the grantor herein." The defendant company thereby became the purchaser, acquiring all the estate and interest that Denham had in the lease. The acceptance of the assignment by the defendant company creates the liability, and the legal possession which ownership implies is all that is required. Smith v. Brinker, 17 Mo. 148, 157 Am. Dec. 265.

It is our opinion that an actual entry under an assignment is not necessary to render the assignee liable for rent. As stated above, the acceptance of the assignment creates the liability, and the legal possession which the ownership implies is all that is required. St. Louis Pub. Schools v. Insurance Co., 5 Mo. App. 91. The actual possession is immaterial; the possession in law by the assignment of title which passed the right of possession is sufficient. Walker v. Reeves, 2 Doug. 461; Schools v. Insurance Co., supra. If the assignee allowed the assignor to remain in possession, it was his own voluntary act. Smith v. Brinker, supra. The lessor is entitled to pursue one or both for the rent. There was an absolute assignment of the lease.

We recognize a distinction between the case at bar and McKee v. Angelrodt, 16 Mo. 283. In the latter there was not an absolute assignment of the lease, but a mortgage of it. That was a mere security, and before a mortgagee of a lease becomes, in such a case, liable for rent, he must have possession. The assignee having the right of possession, although he may not be in actual, physical possession, is liable for the rent. Schools v. Insurance Co., supra.

We fail to see, in this connection, the application of the doctrine that the assignee is the trustee of the legal title, as enunciated in Hall v. Bank, 145 Mo. 418, 46 S. W. 1000. The fact that plaintiff never heard of the assignment until after this suit was brought (though we find no direct evidence in the record that she did not know of it, but that, rather, her brother and agent did) has no bearing on the merits of the case. And in this view of the case, Kazee v. Insurance Co., 217 S. W. 389, and Guthrie v. Holmes, 272 Mo. 215, 198 S. W. 854, Ann. Cas. 1918D, 1123, do not apply. If notice were necessary (which we do not conclude), the recording of the assignment was constructive notice and is binding on all.

The case was tried by plaintiff and the trial court upon the theory above set out, and we think correctly, and the trial court committed no error in striking out the evidence that appellant never took actual possession of the property, nor paid rents or taxes, nor exercised ownership or control of the property. The same may be said of the trial court's action in refusing to give defendant's declarations of law numbered 1, 2, and 4. We also conclude, therefore, that there is no conflict with plaintiff's theory of the case in the action of the trial court in giving declarations of law numbered 3 and 5. The conclusions of the court on these declarations of the law were proper.

[3] The only question remaining for determination is whether the defendant company is liable for all of the rent in arrears; that is to say, after the assignment of the lease on November 6, 1916, by the company to

Clarence E. Denham. This question has been decided in Lindsley v. Schnaide Brewing Co., 59, Mo. App. 271, wherein it was held:

"An agreement between a lessor and an assignee of the lease, by which the former assents to the assignment subject to all of the covenants in the lease, and the latter accepts the assignment with all its responsibilities, amounts to an assumption by the assignee of the covenants of the lessee, and therefore obligates him to perform those covenants after the termination of all privity of estate between the lessor and himself."

It follows that the covenant still remains an obligation, even though the assignee has assigned its right, title, and interest in the lease. It cannot throw off its obligation by thus assigning its interest. Whetstone v. McCartney, 32 Mo. App. loc. cit. 434; Springer v. De Wolf, 194 Ill. 218, 62 N. E. 542, 56 L. R. A. 465, 88 Am. St. Rep. 155; Consumers' Ice Co. v. Bixler, 84 Md. 437, 35 A'tl. 1086. The reason is clear. If the liability of the assignee were for the use and occupation of the land, it would be liable for the reasonable value of such use and occupation, independently of the lease. The liability of defendant in the present case arises out of its relation to, not for its use of, the land. And defendant cannot relieve itself of liability under the covenant by assignment. To hold otherwise would be to say that an assignee could relieve himself from the obligation to pay rent at any time by assigning his rights to an irresponsible person. In the present case defendant company is not sued for use and occupation, but is sued for the amount which is payable by the terms of the lease.

For the reasons above stated, the judgment is affirmed.

All concur.

THOMAS v. CITY OF ST. JOSEPH.
(No. 13725.)

(Kansas City Court of Appeals, Missouri.
May 23, 1921.)

1. Municipal corporations ⬅️812(2) — Notice to city condition precedent to maintaining action for injuries from defective streets or sidewalks.

Under Rev. St. 1919, § 7955, the giving of notice within 60 days, to the mayor of a city of the first class, of accidents as the result of defective streets or sidewalks, is a condition precedent to recovery.

2. Sunday ⬅️30(3) — Notice of injury sufficient, though received by mayor on Sunday.

Notice to the mayor of a city of the first class of an accident on a defective sidewalk is not in any sense legal process, under Rev. St. 1919, § 1211, declaring that the service of every such writ on Sunday shall be void; hence, where such notice was received on Sunday, but the 60-day period within which notice was required to be given by Rev. St. 1919, § 7955, did not expire with Sunday, but there yet remained several secular days, the notice is in time and should be considered, for the mayor had it on the following Monday.

3. Damages ⊂⟐132(2) — Award of $1,000 in favor of girl whose kneecap was dislocated and probably permanently affected held not excessive.

An award of $1,000 in favor of a girl of 14 years, whose kneecap was dislocated as the result of a fall, so that her leg was bruised and swollen and she suffered much pain, cannot be deemed excessive, where her physician testified that the kneecap had a tendency to slip out of place, thus weakening the knee, and that this tendency would probably continue throughout life.

Appeal from Circuit Court, Buchanan County; Thos. B. Allen, Judge.

"Not to be officially published."

Action by Truetta Thomas, by next friend, against the City of St. Joseph. From a judgment for plaintiff, defendant appeals. Affirmed.

Alva F. Lindsay, O. W. Meyer, and A. G. Hamm, all of St. Joseph, for appellant. Mytton & Parkinson, of St. Joseph, for respondent.

ARNOLD, J. This is a suit for personal injuries sustained by plaintiff in stepping into a hole in a sidewalk. Plaintiff, a girl about 14 years of age, was injured on a defective sidewalk at or near Eighth and Hickory streets, in the city of St. Joseph, at about 5 o'clock on April 19, 1919. She testified that she was walking westward on the south side of Hickory street, and when she reached a point of about five feet east of the Rock Island track she stepped into a hole in the board walk and was thereby thrown to the ground and her knee injured.

The petition charges negligence on the part of the city, the Director General of Railroads, and the Chicago, Rock Island & Pacific Railroad Company, in that they carelessly and negligently permitted the sidewalk at the point where the injury occurred to be and become in a dangerous and not reasonably safe condition, and that the injury resulted from such negligence. The answer of defendant city is a general denial and a plea of contributory negligence. Before the trial, the court sustained a motion to dismiss as to the railroad company, and at the close of plaintiff's case the Director General of Railroads went out on a demurrer to the evidence, thus leaving the city of St. Joseph as the sole defendant. Verdict was for plaintiff in the sum of $1,000, and defendant city appeals.

[1, 2] Persons having claims against cities of the first class arising on account of injuries received in defective sidewalks, etc., are required by statute, as a condition precedent to maintaining an action therefor, to notify the mayor in writing within 60 days of the occurrence, "stating the place where, the time when such injury was received, and the character and circumstances of the injury, and that the person so injured will claim damages therefor." Rev. Stat. 1919, § 7955.

Defendant urges, first, that the statutory notice in this case, having been given on Sunday, June 15, 1919, is null and void. There is no complaint that the required notice was not given within 60 days from the date of the alleged injury, but defendant confines his objections to the one question of the same being void because given on Sunday, and bases his contention on section 1211, Rev. Stat. 1919:

"No person, on Sunday or any other day declared and established a public holiday by any statute of this state, shall serve or execute any writ, process, warrant, order or judgment, except in criminal cases; * * * and the service of every such writ, process, warrant, order or judgment shall be void, and the person serving or executing the same shall be as liable to the suit of the party aggrieved as if he had done the same without any writ, process, warrant, order or judgment." Section 1785, R. S. 1909.

If the notice was given into the hands of the mayor on the 15th day of June, he had it on the 16th (Monday), and it was yet three days within the statutory limit. In Jacobs v. City of St. Joseph, 127 Mo. App. loc. cit. 671, 106 S. W. 1073, it is said:

"Since an action might be brought at any time within the period of limitations, the object of the statute is to give the city opportunity to investigate the case while conditions are fresh and thus protect itself against actions which may be brought long after the occurrence" (citing Harris v. Newbury, 128 Mass. 321).

The statute relied on by defendant to support his contention that the notice was void because given on Sunday refers to the service on Sunday of any "writ, process, warrant, order or judgment," and it cannot be contended seriously that the notice in this case is in any sense a legal process within the meaning of the statute, and we so hold.

Defendant, during the progress of the trial, objected to the sufficiency of the notice, but the contention seems to have been abandoned on appeal.

The remaining assignment of error is that of excessive verdict.

[3] This court is loath to interfere with the conclusions of a jury where there is proof to sustain the same. The proof shows that plaintiff, a girl 14 years of age, as a result of the injury, had her kneecap dislocated,

her leg at and above the knee was swollen, bruised, and discolored, and she suffered much pain. Her physician testified that the kneecap had a tendency to slip out of place, thus weakening her knee, and that this tendency would probably continue for the rest of her life. We think this proof is sufficient to sustain the amount of the verdict.

For the reasons above stated, we conclude the judgment should be affirmed. It is so ordered.

All concur.

WALKER v. CITY OF ST. JOSEPH.
(No. 13726.)

(Kansas City Court of Appeals. Missouri. May 23, 1921.)

Municipal corporations ⬤322(1)—Trial ⬤194(16)—Instruction that fact of fall was no evidence of negligence improper.

In an action against a municipality for injury suffered by plaintiff who stepped in a hole in the sidewalk space and fell, an instruction, that the mere fact plaintiff was injured by falling was no evidence that the city was negligent, was improper, where it omitted the words "of itself," despite the fact that plaintiff fall does not warrant a recovery, since the question whether the defect was likely to cause an accident was one of the matters to be considered by the jury in determining whether the place was reasonably safe.

Appeal from Circuit Court, Buchanan County; Thos. B. Allen, Judge.

"Not to be officially published."

Action by Orva Earl Walker against the City of St. Joseph. There was a verdict and judgment for defendant, and plaintiff moved for a new trial. The motion was sustained, and defendant appeals. Affirmed.

Alva F. Lindsay, C. W. Meyer, and A. G. Hamm, all of St. Joseph, for appellant.

O. E. Shultz, of St. Joseph, for respondent.

TRIMBLE, P. J. Plaintiff brought this action for damages alleged to have been caused by the negligence of the city in permitting a hole to exist in the sidewalk space of a public street and immediately against the edge of a narrow board sidewalk thereon upon which plaintiff was walking in the nighttime and, while doing so, stepped into said hole and fell and injured his arm.

There was a verdict and judgment for the defendant city, and the court sustained plaintiff's motion for a new trial, assigning, as a reason therefor, error in giving defendant's instruction No. 1, which, abstractly and not in connection with any other point or matter in the case, told the jury that the mere fact plaintiff was injured by falling in the street at the point in question

was no evidence that the city was negligent. The instruction does not come up to the standard of the instruction approved in Coffey v. City of Carthage, 186 Mo. 573, 585, 85 S. W. 532, and similar cases, since it omitted the words "of itself." It is true the rule of law is that the mere fact that plaintiff fell does not warrant a recovery against the city. Carvin v. City of St. Louis, 151 Mo. 334, 345, 52 S. W. 210; Lee v. Jones, 181 Mo. 291, 79 S. W. 927, 103 Am. St. Rep. 596. But it is a very different thing to tell the jury that the mere fact that plaintiff was injured by falling in the street is no evidence of negligence, since the question of whether the defect in the street was likely to cause such an accident is one of the matters to be considered by the jury in determining whether or not the street at that point was or was not reasonably safe. Orris v. Chicago, etc., R. Co., 279 Mo. 1, 214 S. W. 124, 126, 127; Walker v. Quincy, Omaha, etc., R. Co. (Sup.) 178 S. W. 108, 110. The trial court, therefore, correctly ruled that the giving of such instruction was error, and the action in sustaining the motion for new trial cannot be disapproved.

The contention that there is no substantial evidence entitling plaintiff to go to the jury is without merit. It is pre-eminently a case for the jury and one in which the evidence would support a verdict either way.

The judgment is affirmed.

All concur.

SWIFT & CO. v. McFARLAND. (No. 13961.)

(Kansas City Court of Appeals. Missouri. May 23, 1921.)

1. Bills and notes ⬤359—Indorsee of note for which maker received nothing held a "holder in due course" for value.

Where the maker of a note delivered it to the payee under an agreement that the payee would increase its capital stock and sell agricultural implements to the maker at a reduction, but the stock was not increased, and the maker received nothing for the note, which was indorsed to a third party in payment of an indebtedness of the payee, the indorsee having no knowledge of the circumstances, held, that the indorsee was a holder in due course under Rev. St. 1919, §§ 838 and 843, and had executed the note for value under sections 812 and 814.

[Ed. Note.—For other definitions, see Words and Phrases, First and Second Series, Holder in Due Course.]

2. Bills and notes ⬤497(3)—Indorsement and delivery of note raises presumption of transfer for value.

Indorsement and delivery of a note by a payee to a third person raises a presumption that it was for value.

3. Bills and notes ⬩497(2)—Burden on defendant to show purchaser before maturity not holder in due course.

Defendant, having admitted the execution and delivery of the note, and the indorsement and delivery thereof before maturity to plaintiff, had the burden of showing that plaintiff was not a holder in due course.

Appeal from Circuit Court, Cooper County; John G. Slate, Judge.

"Not to be officially published."

Action by Swift & Co. against E. McFarland. Judgment for defendant, and plaintiff appeals. Reversed and remanded, with directions.

L. O. Schaumburg, of Boonville, for appellant.

John Cosgrove, of Kansas City, for respondent.

TRIMBLE, P. J. This is an action upon a negotiable promissory note for $200 executed and delivered by the defendant to the Hawkins Hardware Company and by it indorsed and transferred for value, before maturity and without notice, to the plaintiff herein. The case was tried before the court without a jury, and judgment was rendered for defendant, whereupon plaintiff appealed.

No brief or appearance of any kind has been made by the respondent, so we are not enlightened as to the theory on which the court found for him. The case was submitted upon an agreed statement of facts to the effect that defendant executed and delivered the note in question to the Hawkins Hardware Company under an agreement between an officer and stockholder thereof with defendant that the hardware company was about to increase its capital stock and was going to deal in agricultural implements and would sell to its stockholders goods at cost plus 10 per cent., which was considerably less than to persons not stockholders; that said capital stock was never increased, and defendant received nothing for said note; that the Hawkins Hardware Company was indebted to plaintiff for as much or more than the said note, and before the maturity of the note the payee therein indorsed and delivered the note to plaintiff and received credit on payee's debt to plaintiff in the full amount of said note; but that plaintiff had no knowledge of the facts and circumstances under which said note was executed by defendant, but was told by the hardware company, and did believe the fact to be, that the note was given in payment for fertilizer bought by defendant of the hardware company.

[1-3] The note is in the ordinary form of a negotiable promissory note. Plaintiff was a "holder in due course." Section 838, R. S. 1919. The maker of a negotiable promissory note cannot raise a defense, which he

had as between himself and the payee, against an indorsee who is a holder in due course. Section 843, R. S. 1919. Under the agreed facts, the Hawkins Hardware Company's indorsement and delivery of the note was in payment of a debt it owed the plaintiff. This brought the transfer of the note within the statutory definition of "for value." Sections 812, 814, R. S. 1919; State Bank of Freeport v. Cape Girardeau, etc., R. Co., 172 Mo. App. 662, 675, 155 S. W. 1111. The law does not presume a gift, and hence the indorsement and delivery of the note by the payee to plaintiff raises the presumption that it was for value—i. e., in payment of a debt. In re U. S. Hair Co., 289 Fed. 703, 706, 152 C. C. A. 537. There was no countervailing testimony, and after the admitted execution and delivery of the note, and the indorsement and delivery thereof before maturity to plaintiff, the burden was on defendant to show that plaintiff was not the holder in due course. Bank of Polk v. Wood, 189 Mo. App. 62, 173 S. W. 1093.

In view of the foregoing, we must hold that the court erred in rendering judgment for defendant. Wherefore the judgment is reversed, and the cause is remanded, with directions to render judgment for plaintiff for the full amount of the note sued on with interest and costs.

All concur.

ALEXANDER v. KANSAS CITY RYS. CO.
(No. 13867.)

(Kansas City Court of Appeals. Missouri. April 4, 1921. Rehearing Denied May 23, 1921.)

1. Husband and wife ⬩209(3)—In case of injury to married woman two causes of action arise, one to the wife for pain and suffering, and the other to the husband for his marital injury.

When a married woman, without fault on her part, is personally injured by the negligence of another, two causes of action arise, one to the wife for her pain and suffering, and the other to the husband in his own favor, for his expenses and injury to his marital rights, consequently, in an action by husband for injuries to his wife, an instruction, allowing recovery without any proof of injury to the husband, is improper; for, unless his right to the services, comfort, and society of his wife were invaded, he is not injured.

2. Trial ⬩296(1)—Omission in instruction to plaintiff purporting to cover entire case, not cured by defendant's instructions.

An omission in an instruction for plaintiff, purporting to cover the whole case of a hypothetical fact which must be found in favor of plaintiff to warrant recovery, cannot be cured by an instruction given for defendant, for the two will conflict, and hence such omission necessitates reversal.

Appeal from Circuit Court, Jackson County; Allen C. Southern, Judge.

"Not to be officially published."

Action by Fay Alexander against the Kansas City Railways Company. From judgment for plaintiff, defendant appealed and on plaintiff's death pending appeal, Dollie M. Alexander, as administratrix, was substituted as respondent. Reversed and remanded.

R. J. Higgins, of Kansas City, Kan., and Gabriel & Conkling, of Kansas City, Mo., for appellant.

Strother & Campbell, Guthrie, Conrad & Durham, and Hale Houts, all of Kansas City, Mo., for respondent.

ARNOLD, J. This is an action instituted by a husband for loss of companionship, society, and services of his wife and expenses incurred by him by reason of negligent injury to her in a collision while she was a passenger on one of defendant's street cars in Kansas City. Fay Alexander, the husband, died pending appeal, and Dollie M. Alexander, administratrix of his estate, has been substituted in this court as respondent. On November 15, 1917, Dollie M. Alexander, the wife of Fay Alexander, was a passenger on a Prospect avenue car of the defendant company, bound eastward on Fifteenth street. After crossing the Paseo the car in which Mrs. Alexander was a passenger collided with and struck the rear end of another car of defendant with such force as to throw passengers into the aisles and against the seats. Mrs. Alexander was seated on one of the longitudinal seats in the rear of the car, and was facing towards the southwest. By reason of the collision she was thrown against the back of the last cross seat, and injured in the back and shoulder, the region of the groin and lower abdomen; the flesh was discolored and bruised, and internal injuries developed. She was in bed a few days, suffered severe pain, and about December 6, 1917, was operated upon, and one ovary and the uterus removed.

Mrs. Alexander was not sound in health prior to the injury complained of, and had undergone an operation in February, 1916, wherein uterine fixation was performed and one ovary was removed.

Plaintiff's amended petition alleges the facts set out above, upon which he bases his suit, and states that—

"On account of said injuries to his wife, * * * occasioned by the carelessness and negligence of defendant, * * * he has been compelled to and has paid out for medicines, hospital, physicians, and nursing of the reasonable value of $600; that he will be compelled to pay out large sums of money on account of the injuries to his said wife hereafter; that the injuries received by his said wife are permanent, * * * and that the services of his said wife have been entirely lost to him, and will be lost to him for a long time hereafter; that plaintiff has been deprived, and will be hereafter depriv-

ed, of the comfort, society, and association of his said wife, to his damage in the sum of $7,500."

The issues were made by a general denial. The trial resulted in a verdict and judgment for plaintiff in the sum of $1,200. Defendant appealed.

[1] Defendant complains that the court erred in giving instruction numbered 1 for plaintiff, in that it permitted plaintiff to recover for personal injuries sustained by his wife, and argues that the cause of action for those injuries was and is the exclusive property right of the wife.

"When a married woman, without fault on her part, is personally injured by the negligence of another, two causes of action arise; one for the wife for the pain and suffering and the expenses she has herself paid, and the other by the husband, in his own favor for what he has actually lost." Thompson v. Street Ry., 135 Mo. 217, 36 S. W. 625.

The instruction complained of charges the jury:

"That if you find and believe from the evidence that on the 15th day of November, 1917, plaintiff's wife was a passenger on a car operated by the defendant, its servants and agents as a common carrier for hire, and that while she was being carried as such passenger, if you so find, * * * said car was caused and permitted by said agents and servants of defendant to collide with and strike another car on the tracks of defendant, and that by reason of said collision, if any, plaintiff's wife was thrown upon and against the seat in front of her and thereby injured, then your verdict shall be for the plaintiff, unless you find and believe from the evidence that said collision, if any, was not caused by negligence on the part of the defendant."

It will be noted that this instruction, as contended by defendant, does not charge the jury that before they may find for plaintiff they must first find that plaintiff was damaged by reason of the alleged injury to his wife. The instruction is good as far as it goes, but it omits a very necessary element of plaintiff's cause of action, to wit, damage to plaintiff. The instruction complained of purports to cover plaintiff's entire case and directs a verdict.

It is fundamental law that the husband may not recover in an action brought by him for the pain or injury suffered by his wife. It must be conceded that the husband's right to recover is primarily bottomed on the damages to his wife. The husband possesses a legal right to the services, comfort, and society of his wife, and the law is well settled that where a legal right has been invaded plaintiff is entitled to damages. Also it must be conceded that before the husband can recover for negligent injury to his wife he must also show that he was damaged in his own rights, and such injury must be proved, and an instruction on this point is necessary. The instruction complained of does not properly cover this element.

"Plaintiff was not entitled to recover in this action for the pain and suffering his wife endured, but he was entitled to the services of his wife, of which such pain and suffering deprived him, and he was entitled, too, to the companionship and society of his wife, free of such pain and suffering as defendant's negligent act entailed upon her." Reeves v. Lutz, 179 Mo. App. loc. cit. 83, 162 S. W. 280, 286.

[2] The conclusion is inevitable that instruction numbered 1, given for plaintiff, does not contain all the elements necessary to a finding for plaintiff. The instruction authorizes recovery by plaintiff for personal injuries sustained by the wife, and fails to require the jury to find that the husband was damaged in his own rights. This error was not cured by other instructions given.

In State ex rel. Lusk v. Ellison et al., 271 Mo. 463, 196 S. W. 1088, the court correctly declared the rule that where an instruction for plaintiff purports to cover the whole case, and omits a hypothetical fact which must be found in favor of plaintiff, the omission cannot be cured by an instruction given for defendant, because the two would conflict. See cases therein cited on this point. Also see Kelley v. City of St. Joseph, 170 Mo. App. 358, 156 S. W. 804; Graf & Case Realty Co. v. Lovell, 180 Mo. App. 706, 163 S. W. 877; Beggs v. Shelton, 173 Mo. App. 127, 155 S. W. 885; Riegel v. Biscuit Co., 169 Mo. App. 513, 155 S. W. 59.

It is therefore concluded, for the reasons above stated, that instruction numbered 1, as given for plaintiff, was erroneous and prejudicial. As the case must be remanded, other points raised need not herein be determined.

The judgment is reversed, and the cause remanded.

All concur.

CLAYTON et al. v. KANSAS CITY RYS. CO. (No. 14046.)

(Kansas City Court of Appeals. Missouri. May 23, 1921.)

1. Appeal and error ⬆️1140(3)—Where verdict for damages is excessive and the amount of excess admitted, it may be remitted.

In action against street railway for damages resulting from collision between its car and plaintiff's motortruck, where the verdict is excessive and the amount of the excess admitted, plaintiff should be allowed to remit the excess, and the judgment may be affirmed for the amount of verdict less such excess.

2. Street railroads ⬆️117(29)—Driving on track without looking back held not contributory negligence as matter of law.

Where the driver of a motortruck towing another truck, struck by defendant's street car, drove along the track for several blocks in the nighttime without looking back for street cars, though there was room to have driven between tracks and curb, but the street was so wet and slippery that he was afraid the tow would strike the curb, his failure to look back after he drove on the track was not contributory negligence as a matter of law, there being no evidence that conditions were such that he would not have heard a warning signal if one had been sounded by the motorman.

3. Street railroads ⬆️117(27)—Motortruck driver held not negligent as a matter of law in not clearing track.

Where motortrucks going 20 miles per hour were struck by a street car heard by the driver when it was closer to his trailing truck than 50 feet, it cannot be said as a matter of law that he had time to drive truck and tow off the track in time to avoid collision, especially where the speed of the street car is not given.

Appeal from Circuit Court, Jackson County; Thomas B. Buckner, Judge.

"Not to be officially published."

Action by Pauline Clayton and William E. Clayton, partners, doing business as the Acme Motor Transfer Company, against the Kansas City Railways Company. Verdict and judgment for plaintiffs, and the defendant appeals. Affirmed for amount of verdict, less excess admitted.

Chas. N. Sadler, John E. Connors, and Ed. C. Hyde, all of Kansas City, for appellant.

Denny Simrall, of Kansas City, for respondents.

BLAND, J. This is a suit to recover damages to two motortrucks owned by plaintiffs. There was a verdict and judgment in favor of plaintiffs in the sum of $500, and defendant appealed.

The case originated in a justice court, and the statement upon which the case was tried in the circuit court alleged general negligence on the part of the defendant. No evidence was introduced by defendant except as to the situation of lights in the vicinity of the accident. The facts show that about 2 a. m. of October 19, 1918, William E. Clayton, one of the plaintiffs herein, was in charge of and driving a Ford motortruck belonging to plaintiffs. Said truck was towing another truck of plaintiffs being guided by one Rutter. The trucks entered McGee street at Eighteenth street in Kansas City, Mo., and proceeded north to a point 50 or 100 feet north of Twelfth street when the rear truck was struck from behind by one of defendant's north-bound street cars, causing said truck to run against the front truck, breaking the connection between the two trucks. The rear truck then ran into a fire plug at the curb, and the street car struck the front truck. Both trucks were damaged. The two trucks were tied together with a rope and were 10 feet apart before the collision.

There were no street car tracks on McGee street south of Fifteenth street, though they entered McGee street at that point. No gong was sounded or warning signal given by the street car before the collision. The street car did not stop at Twelfth street, and the first notice that said plaintiff and Rutter had of its approach was on hearing it cross the tracks at said street. The trucks were going at a rate of speed of from 15 to 20 miles per hour. The street was brightly lighted at and in the vicinity of the scene of the accident. There was a headlight on the car, and a tail light was burning on the rear truck. There was a space of 10 feet between the tracks and the curb, and no automobile was parked along McGee street, leaving ample room for said plaintiff to have driven along the east side of McGee without going upon the street car track. Said plaintiff, who was driving astride the east rail of the north-bound track, when asked if there was any reason why he could not have used the portion of the street between the curb and the tracks, testified that—

"The car was tied on the back. I kept it away, the back car would naturally slide into the curb, that was the reason I was staying away from it."

It appeared that it had been raining shortly before the accident. When said plaintiff heard the rumbling of the street car 50 to 100 feet, or less, to his rear he made a turn to the right toward the curbstone, trying to get away from the street car, but, as he testified, "It was too close to me; I could not get away."

[1] There was evidence that the repair bill was $273.99, and that the value of the use of the trucks was $15 per day. No other loss was shown. One truck was out of service for nine days, and the other seven days, so defendant contends the two trucks were out of use on an average of eight days at $15 a day, making a loss on this account of $120; that the two items would amount to $393.99; that the verdict for $500 is excessive; and that the case must be remanded for a new trial, for the reason that there is no way of fixing the amount that plaintiffs should remit. Plaintiffs' damages were $393.99, and it would be necessary to remit $106.01 to bring the judgment within the proof. We think there is no question but that plaintiffs should be allowed to remit the latter amount from the judgment, for the reason that the amount of the verdict in excess of the amount of loss shown in evidence is exactly calculable from the evidence, and both defendant and plaintiffs have been able to make such calculation and agree as to the amount, the latter agreeing

to remit to $393.99. Brown v. Planing Mill Co., 217 S. W. 332, 335; Crawford v. Doppler, 120 Mo. 362, 25 S. W. 93; State ex rel. v. Hope, 121 Mo. 34, 42, 25 S. W. 893; Smoot v. Kansas City, 194 Mo. 513, 523, 92 S. W. 363.

[2] It is insisted that the court erred in refusing to give defendant's instruction in the nature of a demurrer to the evidence for the reason that plaintiff William E. Clayton was guilty of contributory negligence as a matter of law. Defendant says that said plaintiff was negligent in two respects: First, by driving along the car tracks for several blocks in the nighttime without looking back for street cars when there was ample room for him to have driven on the right side of the street and clear of the street car track; and, second, that after he saw or heard the car cross Twelfth street he had sufficient time to have gotten off the track before the injury, and that he failed to do so. Said plaintiff explained why he was driving in the middle of the street. It was raining, and the inference is that the street was slick. He was afraid of tow would run into the curb if he drove on the right side of the street. We think there is no question but that said plaintiff was not guilty of contributory negligence as a matter of law in not looking again after he drove onto the track. There is no evidence that the conditions were such that said plaintiff and Rutter would not have heard a warning signal if one had been sounded. Said plaintiff had a right to rely upon the sounding of the gong to give him timely warning to get off the track, and the failure of said plaintiff to look back was not such negligence as to make him guilty of contributory negligence as a matter of law. Conrad Grocery Co. v. Rd., 89 Mo. App. 391; Kennayde v. Pac. R. R. Co., 45 Mo. 255, 262. Of course, we do not mean to hold that said plaintiff would have been guilty of contributory negligence as a matter of law if there had been no reason for his driving on the street car track save for his own convenience.

[3] There was evidence that the collision happened as close to Twelfth street as 50 feet. The trucks were going 20 miles per hour, so there is an inference that when plaintiff William E. Clayton heard the car it was closer to the rear truck than 50 feet. We cannot say as a matter of law that said plaintiff had time under the conditions present to have driven his truck and tow off of defendant's tracks and out of the path of danger while the street car was going 50 feet or less, and he was proceeding at the rate of 20 miles per hour, especially in view of the fact that the speed of the street car is not given. Said Clayton testified in reference to the amount of time that elapsed after he first heard the car cross Twelfth street, as follows:

"I don't know the exact seconds, I didn't count them; but I heard the noise; then an impulse come to me it might be back of me. I turned around; the other truck was in back of me, and just as I turned around it seemed to hit that truck that was back of me; as it hit the other truck, I turned my truck to the right. It tore the other truck loose, and then hit me before I could get my car off the track."

The judgment is affirmed in the sum of $393.99.

All concur.

POSHEK v. MARCELINE COAL & MINING CO. (No. 12178.)

(Kansas City Court of Appeals. Missouri. May 23, 1921.)

1. Appeal and error ⊗═586(1)—"Abstract" of record, containing nothing but copy of petition and answer, held insufficient.

An abstract of record, containing nothing but a copy of the petition and answer, and which fails to show the filing of a motion for new trial or in arrest of judgment, with the action of the court thereon, that time was granted in which to file a bill of exceptions, and that the bill was filed, or that an appeal was allowed, is insufficient; the term "abstract," as applied to a record, meaning a complete history in short, abbreviated form of the case as found in the record, complete enough to show that the questions presented for review have been properly reserved.

[Ed. Note.—For other definitions, see Words and Phrases, First and Second Series, Abstract.]

2. Appeal and error ⊗═581(3)—Abstract held insufficient, as not complying with court rule.

An abstract of record failing to show that "the record entries evidencing his leave to file, or filing of a bill of exceptions," and to "state that the bill of exceptions was duly filed," as required by rule 26 of this court (169 S. W. xv), is insufficient.

Appeal from Circuit Court, Linn County; Fred Lamb, Judge.

"Not to be officially published."

Action by Joseph Poshek against the Marceline Coal & Mining Company. Judgment for plaintiff, and defendant appeals. Affirmed.

C. M. Kendrick, of Marceline, for appellant.

L. R. Owen, of Marceline, and Davis & Ashby and J. D. Allen, all of Chillicothe, for respondent.

ARNOLD, J. This is a suit in damages for personal injury. The case was tried in the circuit court of Linn county.

The answer to the petition of plaintiff was, first, a general denial, and as a further de-

fense pleads contributory negligence. Judgment was for plaintiff in the sum of $400, and defendant appeals.

[1] Defendant has filed in this court what it calls an abstract of record, and also a brief and argument discussing the merits of the case in full. Plaintiff, in his brief and argument, urges the insufficiency of the abstract of record filed herein, and charges that the record proper fails to show: (a) The filing of a motion for a new trial; (b) the action of the trial court thereupon; (c) the filing of a motion in arrest of judgment; (d) the action of the court thereon; (e) that time was granted in which to file a bill of exceptions; (f) that the bill of exceptions was filed; or (g) that an appeal was allowed.

All of these objections are well taken. An examination of the record shows that it contains nothing but a copy of the petition and answer. In Harding v. Bedoll et al., 202 Mo. 625, 100 S. W. 638, the Supreme Court through Graves, J., in discussing that case, decided all of the questions covered by the objections of plaintiff to the abstract of record herein; and an extended discussion of the principles therein treated needs not be entered into in extenso here. However, we may quote therefrom briefly with profit (202 Mo. loc. cit. 630, 100 S. W. 639):

"What is an abstract of the record, and what should it contain under our rules? Speaking generally, it is said: 'As a noun, the word "abstract" denotes a less quantity containing the virtue and force of a greater quantity.' 1 Cyc. 211. As applied to a record, it would mean a complete history in short abbreviated form of the case as found in the record. It would have to be complete enough to show that the questions presented for review have been properly preserved in the case. As to the record proper, it would not mean that the whole pleadings should be set out, unless some question urged required it. It would mean, however, that there should be a showing to the effect that pleadings had been filed in some lower court at some particular times, and the character of such pleadings, so that the issues raised could be easily ascertained. It would likewise mean that there should be a concise statement of the judgment and the date of its rendition, and also of the fact that a motion for new trial or in arrest of judgment had been filed, and the time thereof, so that this court can see that it is filed within the four days prescribed by the statute. * * * So also should be the showing as to the overruling of such motion, the leave to file bill of exceptions, filing of bill of exceptions, the affidavit for appeal, and the order granting the appeal."

In the instant case the abstract meets none of these necessary requirements excepting to set out the petition and answer.

[2] Plaintiff further contends that the abstract of record in this case does not meet the requirements of rule 26 (169 S. W. xv) of this court. Rule 26 referred to was adopt-

ed January 6, 1913, and abrogates any rule to the contrary:

"Hereafter an appellant, filing here a certified copy of the order granting an appeal, need not abstract the record entries showing the steps taken below to perfect such appeal. If the abstract state the appeal was duly taken, then, absent a record showing to the contrary by respondent, it will be presumed the proper steps were taken at the proper time and term.

"Hereafter no appellant need abstract record entries evidencing his leave to file, or filing of, a bill of exceptions. It shall be sufficient if his abstract state the bill of exceptions was duly filed. The burden is then on respondent to produce here the record showing the contrary to be true, if he makes the point."

In the case at bar the purported abstract fails to show that the "record entries evidencing his leave to file, or. filing of, a bill of exceptions" and it also fails to "state that the bill of exceptions was duly filed," as required by said rule 26.

For the reasons herein stated, the judgment should be affirmed, and it is so ordered.

All concur

———

CALIFORNIA SPECIAL ROAD DIST. v. BUEKER. (No. 13963.)

(Kansas City Court of Appeals. Missouri. May 23, 1921.)

Courts ⬥⇒231(6)—Where constitutional question is raised, Supreme Court alone has jurisdiction.

In an action by a road district for the statutory penalty for failure to remove obstructions, where defendant asserted that Rev. St. 1919, § 10720, on which the action was based, was in violation of Const. art. 2, §§ 12, 20, 21, the Court of Appeals has no jurisdiction over an appeal by the road district from an adverse judgment, and the cause must be transferred to the Supreme Court, notwithstanding defendant, respondent on appeal, moved to dismiss for failure of appellant's brief to comply with Rev. St. 1919, §§ 1511, 2421, and the rules of the Court of Appeals.

Appeal from Circuit Court, Moniteau County; J. G. Slate, Judge.

"Not to be officially published."

Action by the California Special Road District against Louis Bueker. From a judg-

ment for defendant, plaintiff appeals. Cause transferred to Supreme Court.

S. C. Gill and Embry & Embry, all of California, Mo., for appellant.

J. B. Gallagher, of California, Mo., and Irwin & Haley, of Jefferson City, for respondent.

PER CURIAM. Plaintiff, a special road district organized under the provisions of article 7, chapter 98, R. S. 1919, brought this action based on section 10720, R. S. 1919, for the statutory penalty of $5 per day, from and after ten days from the date defendant was notified to remove an obstruction which it is charged he willfully and knowingly maintained in a certain road and has refused to remove. Upon a trial, the jury returned a verdict for defendant, and the plaintiff has appealed. No briefs have been filed by respondent, save a manuscript brief in support of a motion to dismiss the appeal on the ground that appellant's brief does not comply with sections 1511 and 2421, R. S. 1919, and our rules 15, 16, and 17 (169 S. W. ix, x).

The reason for respondent filing no brief becomes apparent when, upon examining the record, it is seen that at the very outset defendant's answer invokes the constitutional provisions of sections 20 and 21 of article 2 of the Missouri Constitution, and of section 12 of article 2 of said Constitution, claiming that the section on which the action is based is a violation of said provisions and is not therefore enforceable.

The raising of these constitutional questions places the jurisdiction of this appeal in the Supreme Court. This court has no cognizance of constitutional questions, "not even for the purpose of determining its considering the question of its own jurisdiction, whether such questions are fairly debatable." State ex rel. Campbell v. St. Louis Court of Appeals, 97 Mo. 276; State v. Dinnisse, 41 Mo. App. 23." Bennitt v. Missouri Pac. R. Co., 44 Mo. App. 372, 374.

If the jurisdiction of the appeal is in the Supreme Court, of course that tribunal is also the proper one to pass upon the question of whether the appellant's brief is or is not vulnerable to the attack made upon it by respondent's motion to dismiss. Accordingly, the case is transferred to the Supreme Court.

YARBROUGH v. HAMMOND PACKING CO.
(No. 13730.)

(Kansas City Court of Appeals. Missouri.
May 23, 1921.)

1. Negligence ⬅️119(1)—Specific charge must be established.

Where a plaintiff makes a general charge of negligence, and follows by pleading a specific act, in order to sustain a finding for plaintiff, the proof must clearly establish the specific act pleaded.

2. Negligence ⬅️119(1)—Proof of one of specific acts charged sufficient.

If several specific acts of negligence are pleaded, and there is substantial proof to support one of them, it is sufficient to support a verdict.

3. Master and servant ⬅️285(2)—Evidence of cause of escape of illuminating gas held to demand a peremptory instruction.

In a servant's action, where the petition charged general and specific acts of negligence, causing injuries by asphyxiation from inhaling illuminating gas in defendant's packing plant, held, that defendant was entitled to a peremptory instruction in the nature of a demurrer to the evidence, which showed that the proximate cause of the injury was escaping gas from an open valve, the cause of its position being a matter of conjecture, and not from gas escaping when the valves were in a position designed to stop the flow of said gas, as specifically alleged.

4. Master and servant ⬅️101, 102(2)—Master not an insurer of safety.

While the duty of a master is to exercise ordinary care to furnish his servant a reasonably safe place and reasonably safe tools and appliances in which and with which to do his work, he is not an insurer of the safety of the place or tools and appliances.

Appeal from Circuit Court, Buchanan County; Lawrence A. Vories, Judge.

"Not to be officially published."

Action by William Yarbrough against the Hammond Packing Company. Judgment for plaintiff, and defendant appeals. Reversed and remanded.

Robert A. Brown and Richard L. Douglas, both of St. Joseph, for appellant.

Mytton & Parkinson, of St. Joseph, for respondent.

ARNOLD, J. This is a personal injury suit, instituted by a servant against the master. Plaintiff was injured October 9, 1919, by being asphyxiated from inhaling illuminating gas in the packing plant of defendant, the Hammond Packing Company, at St. Joseph, Mo. The defendant in its plant uses illuminating gas for heating branding irons used for branding certain of its products with the United States Inspector's seal. Part of this branding is done in a room of house

No. 3 on the fourth floor of defendant's plant, known as the pickle cellar. This room is approximately 200 by 300 feet in size. The branding iron involved in this suit was located on a post near the south end of said room, and near the center thereof from east to west, and connected with a gas pipe attached to said post. The brander is used at intervals during working hours, from 7 a. m. to 3:30 p. m.

The plaintiff, a man 63 years of age at the time in question, was employed as janitor or clean-up man, with duties pertaining particularly to the room above referred to. His working hours were from 9 a. m. to 5:30 p. m., so as to clean up after the business of the day in said room was over and the other employés had left. Plaintiff had spent practically all of his life on a farm, and had little or no experience in the use of gas. He testified: That for about two weeks prior to his injury, and while in the performance of his duties about the post where the brander was located, he had detected a strong odor of gas, after the use of the branding iron was ended for the day. That two weeks prior to the injury he had called the attention of the superintendent in charge to this fact, and that the latter had advised him that the situation was not dangerous and for him to continue at work. That the gas odor continued daily, and two or three days prior to the injury plaintiff again called the attention of the superintendent in charge to the gas odor, and again had been informed that he could work there in safety, and that the leak, or defect, would be repaired. With this assurance plaintiff continued to work there, but plaintiff testified that he knew of no leak.

On October 9, 1919, plaintiff went to the said room about 4 p. m. to clean up as was his duty, and again smelled gas in the vicinity of the brander in question, but strongest near the post from which the same was supplied with gas. While in the exercise of his duties, washing tables, he became so dizzy that he fell three times, but was able to reach a door opening on a hallway, where he got some fresh air. Again he tried to work, then became unconscious, and fell to the floor. He was found shortly after in an unconscious condition by a fellow employé and taken to the plant hospital, where he was given some treatment by the use of a pulmotor and medicine. He was revived, taken to his home in St. Joseph, and for some weeks was confined to his bed, and has continued to suffer from the effects of the asphyxiation.

The amended petition charges that "for a long time prior to the 9th of October, 1919, the defendant carelessly and negligently kept its pickle cellar and the gas pipes and fixtures and appliances and the ventilating system therein in a dangerous, unsafe, and not reasonably safe condition for plaintiff and other employés to work in and about the performance of their duties," and then pleads a specific charge of negligence as follows:

"That the gas pipes and systems and valves or shut-off cocks therein in said pickle cellar would permit said illuminating gas to escape into said pickle cellar in large quantities, and accumulate therein when said valves or shut-off cocks were in a position designed to stop the flow of said gas; that said gas would leak and escape from said gas pipes and the valves and cocks thereof when said gas was not being used for any purpose in said room."

The answer was a general denial. Trial to a jury resulted in a verdict in favor of plaintiff for $2,000. Defendant appeals.

Defendant charges, among other assignments of error, that the trial court erred in refusing to give the peremptory instruction in the nature of a demurrer to the evidence, requested by defendant at the close of plaintiff's case, and again at the close of all the testimony, and assigns as reason therefor that plaintiff sought to recover upon specific acts of negligence alleged in the petition, and that there was a total failure of proof as to any act of negligence.

[1, 2] The rule is fundamental that, where a plaintiff makes a general charge of negligence and follows by pleading a specific act, in order to sustain a finding for plaintiff, the proof must clearly establish the specific act pleaded; and if several specific acts of negligence are pleaded, if there is substantial proof to support one of them, it is sufficient to support a verdict. Troutman v. Cotton Oil Co., 224 S. W. 1014; Gibler v. Railroad, 129 Mo. App. 93, 107 S. W. 1021; Jackson v. Railroad, 171 Mo. App. 481, 156 S. W. 1005. In the case at bar plaintiff pleaded several specific acts of negligence, but during the progress of the trial all were abandoned, save the one set out above. We shall, therefore, confine our consideration to this one point.

The specific charge is that the "gas pipe and systems and valves or shut-off cocks * * * would permit illuminating gas to escape * * * in large quantities * * * when said valves or shut-off cocks were in a position intended to stop the flow of said gas." Plaintiff's testimony was to the effect that the odor of gas was present in the room in question each day for a period of two weeks before the accident complained of, but in this statement he was corroborated by no one. Further, he testified that on two occasions prior to the accident he had notified the superintendent of the fact. He is contradicted in this statement by the superintendent, Mr. Lord. The testimony tends to show that on the day of the accident the gas was turned off at the brander in question at 3:25 p. m. by defendant's assistant foreman, C. W. Riesenmy, who testified that he had

nothing to do with locking up the brander; "but I was in charge of turning off the gas. Q. Tell the jury whether or not you did turn off the gas? A. Yes, sir; I turned off the gas at 25 minutes after 3."

As stated, the testimony shows that plaintiff went to work that day at about 4 o'clock in the afternoon. Charles Sive, general foreman in defendant's hog-killing department, testified that he was on the fifth floor of the building in question, starting downstairs with Mr. Roberts, general superintendent, when they smelled gas, and that he got off at the fourth floor to investigate, while Mr. Roberts went to the floor below. In the pickle room Sive found the gas valve at the north side of the room closed, and then turned his attention to the valve on the post at the middle of the south side of the room. He was asked, "In what condition did you find that valve?" and answered, "The valve was open. Q. Was the gas escaping? A. Yes, sir."

[3] Thus we find that the valve which was closed at 3:25 p. m. was found open and emitting gas at the time plaintiff was found asphyxiated. From what cause the valve was opened after having been closed at 3:25 p. m. the record fails to enlighten us, nor can we safely enter the realm of speculation to determine it. Taking into consideration all the facts and circumstances of the case, we must conclude that the proximate cause of plaintiff's injury was the escaping gas from the open valve, and not from gas escaping "when said valves or shut-off cocks were in a position designed to stop the flow of said gas," nor from gas which had leaked or escaped "from said gas pipes and the valves and cocks thereof when said gas was not being used for any purpose in said room."

[4] The duty of the master is to exercise ordinary care to furnish his servant a reasonably safe place and reasonably safe tools and appliances in which and with which to do his work. The master, however, is not an insurer of the safety of the place or tools and appliances.

"It is, therefore, a rule of universal law that in suits of this character it is necessary for the plaintiff to allege and prove a causal connection between the injury and the negligence of the master. The corollary of this rule is that, if the accident might have resulted from more than one cause, for one of which the master is liable and for the other he is not liable, it is necessary for the plaintiff to prove, in the first instance, that the injury arose from the cause for which the master is liable, for it is not the province of a court or jury to speculate or guess from which cause the accident happened." Rogers v. Packing Co., 167 Mo. App. loc. cit. 56, 150 S. W. 558; Goransson v. Mfg. Co., 186 Mo. loc. cit. 307, 85 S. W. 338, and cases therein cited.

The testimony fails to show any causal connection between the injury and the negligence charged in the petition. The conclusion is, therefore, that plaintiff failed to support his pleaded cause by any substantial evidence, and that defendant's demurrer at the close of the testimony should have been sustained.

The judgment is reversed, but, inasmuch as plaintiff may be able to plead and prove a cause of action on a new trial, the cause is remanded.

All concur.

CLARK v. FIDELITY–PHENIX FIRE INS. CO. OF NEW YORK. (No. 13556.)

(Kansas City Court of Appeals. Missouri. May 2, 1921. Rehearing Denied May 23, 1921.)

1. Insurance ⟜232—No cancellation of policy where agents promised to cancel but neglected to do so before loss.

Where the local agents of a fire insurance company promised an insured to cancel so much of his policy as covered certain household goods, but neglected to do so, and, after a fire in which the goods were destroyed, informed the insured of their neglect and that he had "some loss" under the policy, and thereafter defendant's special agent credited the insured's premium note for the amount of the premium oh the household goods there was no cancellation; the mere agreement to cancel being insufficient.

2. Insurance ⟜388(3)—Where insured procured other insurance in belief induced by agents of company that policy was canceled, company estopped to assert defense.

Where, because of the promise of local agents of a fire insurance company to cancel insured's policy covering certain household goods, insured procured other insurance, and the local agents failed to make the promised cancellation, but, after a fire destroying the goods, informed the insured that he had "some loss" under the policy, the company was estopped to assert as a defense that the insured had procured other insurance, the company issuing the other policy having paid only one-half the amount thereof, on the ground of the existence of the insurance sued for.

Appeal from Circuit Court, Sullivan County; Fred Lamb, Judge.

"Not to be officially published."

Action by C. G. Clark against the Fidelity-Phenix Fire Insurance Company of New York. Judgment for plaintiff, and defendant appeals. Affirmed.

John W. Clapp, of Milan, and Fyke, Snider & Hume, of Kansas City, for appellant.

R. E. Ash, of Green City, and D. M. Wilson, of Milan, for respondent.

TRIMBLE, P. J. Plaintiff brought suit on that feature of defendant's policy of fire insurance which covered plaintiff's household goods, the object of the suit being to recover one-half of the amount of the loss sustained by a fire, the other one-half having been paid by another company having insurance thereon. There was no dispute as to the fire or the amount of the loss. The defenses set up were: (1) That the policy sued on was, as to the household goods, canceled by a mutual agreement, which, in law, effected a cancellation even though no formal act of cancellation was in fact done; (2) that, under a provision of the policy sued on, the taking out of other insurance on the property without the consent of the defendant insurer, rendered the policy herein sued on null and void.

To these defenses plaintiff replied that the insurance never had been in fact canceled, and that the company was estopped from setting up the defense of other insurance.

A jury was waived and the cause was tried by the court. No instructions or declarations of law were asked or given, and at the close of all the evidence, the case was submitted without a demurrer. The trial court rendered judgment in plaintiff's favor for one-half of the loss alleged and sued for, and defendant has appealed.

It seems that plaintiff's mother owned 40 acres with a house and barn thereon, and with insurance on same, including household goods, in the other company. After plaintiff bought the property, he applied for and obtained the policy in suit on the house, barn, and personal property, and executed and delivered to defendant his note for the premium. Shortly thereafter he discovered that he could secure the insurance on the personalty by having the insurance thereon held by his mother assigned to him. He therefore went to the local agents of the defendant, who had countersigned the policy herein sued on, and told them he wanted to drop the insurance he had taken out on the personalty, as he was taking the insurance his mother had thereon, by having it assigned to him, which he was having done. They promised to take steps to have the policy canceled, but neglected to do so. The mother's insurance was assigned to plaintiff three days after the local agents had countersigned and issued the policy to plaintiff which is herein sued on.

About 30 days after the mother's insurance had been assigned to plaintiff, the fire occurred and the goods were destroyed. After the fire, and before the plaintiff settled with the other insurance company, the agents of the defendant informed plaintiff that they had forgotten to write in to the company and have the policy canceled. Up to that time plaintiff supposed the insurance had been canceled, but was then informed by defendant's agents that it was not and that plaintiff had "some loss" under the policy.

When plaintiff went to settle with the other company, it, knowing that the policy in the defendant company had not been canceled, paid only its proportionate part of the loss, namely, one-half thereof. It is for the other one-half of the loss that the present suit is brought.

The provision in the policy in reference to cancellation is as follows:

"This policy shall be canceled at any time at the request of the insured; or by the company by giving five days notice of such cancellation. If this policy shall be canceled as herein before provided, or becomes void, or cease, the premium having been actually paid, the unearned portion shall be returned on surrender of this policy or last renewal, this company retaining the customary short rate; except that when this policy is canceled by this company by giving notice it shall retain only the pro rata premium."

The provision as to additional insurance is as follows:

"This entire policy unless otherwise provided by agreement indorsed hereon or added hereto, shall be void if the insured now has or shall hereafter make or procure any other contract of insurance, whether valid or not, on property covered in whole or in part by this policy."

[1, 2] The evidence as disclosed in the record is such as to be amply sufficient to justify the trial court in finding that nothing was in fact done in the way of canceling the insurance, although plaintiff asked the agents to do so and thought for a time that it had been done, and, acting upon that supposition, took the other insurance; also, that the alleged credit on plaintiff's premium note for the proportionate part thereof represented by the premium on the personalty insured was not entered on the note until after the fire had occurred, when the credit was then placed on said note by the defendant's special agent who was sent there to investigate matters. This, however, was not only after the loss, but also after both plaintiff and the defendant's agents recognized, and the former was led to believe by the latter, that, although they had intended a cancellation of the insurance on the goods, yet no cancellation was in fact done, and the insurance was still in force. Under this situation and state of facts, the other insurance company paid only the part it could be compelled to pay in view of the existence of the insurance herein sued for. In other words, while it was agreed that the insurance on the personalty was to be canceled, yet in fact the same was never done, but was afterwards recognized as being still in force, and plaintiff was not only led into the situation of procuring other insurance, but could receive from the other company only its proportionate share of the loss and then look to the defendant for the other half. These circumstances render the situation entirely different from that in the authorities cited by defendant in support of its contention that the mere agreement between the plaintiff and the agents that the policy would be canceled, of itself and without anything more, effected a cancellation. There was no move made to cancel the policy, and, on the other hand, it was treated as a subsisting contract. The proposed cancellation was never carried into effect, and the fact of other insurance was not only waived, but the defendant is estopped to assert it as a defense. Hayward v. National Ins. Co., 52 Mo. 181, 14 Am. Rep. 400; Rogers v. Home Ins. Co., 155 Mo. App. 276, 136 S. W. 743; Polk v. Western Assurance Co., 114 Mo. App. 514, 90 S. W. 397; Nute v. Hartford Fire Ins. Co., 109 Mo. App. 585, 83 S. W. 83.

The judgment is affirmed.

All concur.

On Motion for Rehearing.

Appellant's sole reason urged as ground for a rehearing is that the opinion erred in saying no demurrer to the evidence was offered. The opinion does not say no demurrer was ever filed, but that, "at the close of all the evidence, the case was submitted without a demurrer," and this language was used advisedly.

Appellant did offer a demurrer which was overruled, but after it was overruled the case was reopened, and other evidence was heard, and then the case was submitted without any demurrer being offered. So that it is strictly true that at the close of all the evidence the case was submitted without a demurrer. However, if one had been submitted and had been overruled, we cannot see in what way it would have affected the result.

The motion for rehearing is overruled.

All concur.

ANDERSON v. MUTUAL BENEFIT HEALTH & ACCIDENT ASS'N. (No. 13934.)

(Kansas City Court of Appeals. Missouri.
May 2, 1921. Rehearing Denied
May 23, 1921.)

1. Insurance ⬅=668(11)—Evidence held sufficient to take to the jury the question whether disease resulted from accidental injury.

In an action for disability benefits under an accident insurance policy, where the insurance company admitted insured had received an accidental injury to his finger resulting in blood poisoning, testimony by a physician that the diabetes from which insured was suffering and which was still disabling him might have been, and in the physician's opinion was, caused by the injury, is sufficient to take to the jury the question whether the disability from the disease resulted from the accidental injury.

2. Insurance ☞466—Disease resulting from accidental injury within accident policy.

If diabetes was an effect of insured's accidental injury, a mere link in the chain between the accident and its effect, the condition of insured would be attributable to the accidental injury, and not the disease.

3. Insurance ☞669(10)—Instruction on accidental injury as proximate cause of disease held correct.

In an action on an accident insurance policy for disability benefits during the time plaintiff was disabled by disease, the evidence showed could have resulted from the accident, an instruction that, if the jury found plaintiff was injured by accidental means and further found that as a direct result of his bodily injury he had been continuously and wholly disabled since the date thereof, he could recover, was correct.

4. Insurance ☞668(14)—Fraud by agent in securing release from insured is question for jury.

In an action for disability benefits under an accident insurance policy, where the dependent pleaded a release by insured, which the plaintiff in reply alleged was procured by fraud of the agent of insured, the question of the agent's fraud was one for the jury where there was evidence to support a finding of fraud.

5. Insurance ☞668(1) — Evidence adjuster canceled policy and threatened to sue insured held to raise question of vexatious refusal to pay.

In an action on an accident insurance policy, evidence that, after the insurance company had made certain payments to plaintiff, its adjuster had taken the policy from plaintiff and canceled it and had threatened to sue plaintiff for accepting payments to which he was not entitled, *held* sufficient to take to the jury the question whether the refusal of the company to pay disability benefits while insured was disabled by disease resulting from the injury was vexatious.

Appeal from Circuit Court, Clinton County; A. D. Burnes, Judge.

"Not to be officially published."

Action by Charles Anderson against the Mutual Benefit Health & Accident Association. Judgment for the plaintiff, and defendant appeals, after which appeal John H. Anderson, as administrator of the plaintiff, was substituted as party plaintiff. Judgment affirmed.

F. B. Ellis, of Plattsburg, for appellant.
W. S. Herndon and R. H. Musser, both of Plattsburg, for respondent.

ARNOLD, J. This is an action to recover benefits under the terms of a health and accident policy of insurance.

On May 1, 1919, plaintiff purchased from defendant an insurance policy which specified benefits payable under the terms thereof for sickness or injury. On June 7, 1919,

plaintiff was accidentally injured by mashing the third finger of his right hand in turning a wagon, while laboring at concrete construction. Following the injury plaintiff attempted to work for two or three days, but was unable to do so. On the 10th day of June, 1919, Dr. P. M. Steckman lanced the injured finger and removed a great deal of pus therefrom, and thereafter plaintiff suffered from blood poisoning. In September, 1919, the attending physician discovered that plaintiff was afflicted with diabetes.

Defendant company paid plaintiff the sum of $200 under the policy for damages beginning August 16, 1919, and ending May 13, 1920, in payments of $50 each.

The petition alleges that under the provisions of the policy defendant was to pay plaintiff as accident benefits for total disability $20 per week for one day or more, and not exceeding 104 consecutive weeks, for loss of time resulting from bodily injury received through accidental means, which shall independently of all other causes immediately, continuously, and wholly disable the insured, that from June 7, 1919, until September 18, 1920, plaintiff was totally disabled as a result of the injured finger, independently of all other causes, and that defendant wrongfully and willfully refuses to pay the balance due and vexatiously requires plaintiff to litigate the same. Plaintiff asks judgment for $1,140 balance due, 10 per cent. statutory penalty for vexatious delay, and for reasonable attorney's fee with interest and costs.

The first amended answer is a general denial, and, further answering, defendant admits the injury and resulting disability, also the payments made as above stated, and states that on June 12, 1920, plaintiff in writing fully released defendant from all other obligations under its certificate of membership for or on account of the injury received about June 6, 1919, and sets out said release.

Replying, plaintiff alleges that on June 2, 1920, defendant's attorney wrongfully, falsely, and fraudulently deceived plaintiff as to his rights and benefits under the policy, and secured from plaintiff the surrender of said policy and the cancellation thereof by the payment by defendant of $50 and $1.50 unearned premium, that said pretended release and settlement is null and void, and that the check for $51.50 was never cashed and was returned to defendant.

The case was submitted to the court and jury upon the pleadings thus made. Verdict was for plaintiff in the sum of $1,340, less the sum of $200 already paid, or $1,140; for vexatious refusal to pay same, $————; for attorney's fee, $200—total amount of verdict, $1,340. Defendant appeals.

Since the trial of this cause in the circuit

court, Charles Anderson has died, and John H. Anderson, administrator of his estate, has been substituted as party plaintiff.

The simple basis of this suit is that defendant refuses to accept the theory that the diabetes from which plaintiff admittedly suffered was the direct result of the injury to the finger received on June 7, 1919. Supplemental thereto is the question of the validity of the written release executed June 12, 1920. Upon these two questions rests the determination of this appeal.

Plaintiff predicates his action upon the accident clause in the policy, and not upon the health clause, and defendant argues with much ability that the company already paid plaintiff more than was due him for the injury to the finger, and claims that the disability after the mashed finger had healed was due solely to diabetes, for which plaintiff could not recover under the injury clause of the policy.

Defendant first complains that the court erred in overruling defendant's instruction in the nature of a demurrer to the evidence.

It was admitted in the answer that plaintiff received the injury alleged, and by paying benefits therefor defendant admitted the damage. Testimony of the physician who attended plaintiff tended to show that the diabetes from which plaintiff suffered might have been, and in his opinion was, the direct result of the injury to the finger, and this testimony is not refuted. There was also substantial evidence that the release pleaded in defendant's answer was invalid. Further the testimony tended to show that plaintiff was totally disabled from work from the date of the injury until September 21, 1920.

[1] We can arrive at no other conclusion from a consideration of the evidence than that the court properly overruled defendant's demurrer to the evidence. And this conclusion is supported by the rulings in Powell v. Trav. Protective Ass'n, 160 Mo. App. 571, 140 S. W. 939, and in that case the court was guided by Jamison v. Casualty Co., 104 Mo. App. 306, 78 S. W. 812; Meadows v. Ins. Co., 129 Mo. 76, 31 S. W. 578, 50 Am. St. Rep. 427; Fetter v. Fidelity & Casualty Co., 174 Mo. 256, 73 S. W. 592, 61 L. R. A. 459, 97 Am. St. Rep. 560; Powell v. St. L. & S. F. R. R., 229 Mo. 246, 129 S. W. 963. If the diabetes from which plaintiff admittedly suffered was the direct result of the injury to the finger alleged in the petition and admitted by defendant, then defendant was liable under the terms of the policy, about which there is no dispute.

It is said by Johnson, J., in Driskell v. Insurance Co., 117 Mo. App. loc. cit. 370, 93 S. W. 882:

"When evidence is introduced that points to the injury as the sole active force that brings into operation death-producing agencies, the issue of proximate cause is one of fact for the jury, and not of law for the court. * * * Whether the insured was wholly or partially disabled at once by the accident was a matter that concerned the indemnity to be paid him for loss of time, and is not at all determinative of the right to recover upon a death claim. The intervening results of the injury are facts that should be received in evidence as bearing upon the solution of the principal issue of fact—the proximate cause of death—but, aside from this, they have no other importance."

[2] Applying the principles thus enunciated to the case at bar, in the light of the testimony of the attending physician to the effect that diabetes might have been, and in his opinion was, the direct result of the injury to the finger and the resulting blood poisoning (which testimony was undisputed), it was a case for the wise consideration of the jury. If the diabetes is an effect of the accidental injury, a mere link in the chain between the accident and its effect, the condition of plaintiff would be attributable to the accidental injury, and not to the disease. Western Commercial Trav. v. Smith, 85 Fed. 401, 29 C. C. A. 223, 40 L. R. A. 653; Trav. Ins. Co. v. Melick, 65 Fed. 178, 12 C. C. A. 544, 27 L. R. A. 629; Railway v. Kellogg, 94 U. S. 469, 24 L. Ed. 256.

Defendant further complains that the trial court erred in giving instructions numbered 1 and 2 on behalf of plaintiff.

[3] Instruction No. 1 properly submitted to the jury the question hereinabove discussed in the following language:

"That is, the jury therefore find and believe from the evidence that plaintiff, Charles Anderson, on the 7th day of June, 1919, received bodily injury, if any, and that such bodily injury, if any, was received by accidental means, and further find and believe from the evidence that as direct and proximate result of said bodily injury he has been immediately, continuously, and wholly disabled since said date, and has suffered loss of time in his occupation and labor, then the plaintiff is entitled to recover, and your verdict should be for the plaintiff."

Instruction No. 2, as to the amount properly recoverable if the jury found the facts included in instruction No. 1, logically follows the same, and is not error.

[4] Instruction No. 3 properly informs the jury as to the law applicable to the charge of fraud in procuring the written release. The question of fraud and unfair dealing on the part of defendant's agent was a question of fact for the determination of the jury under the law as defined by the court, and its submission to the jury was not error.

[5] Defendant complains finally that error was committed by the court in giving instruction No. 4 for plaintiff, on the ground that there was no evidence, either direct or inferential, that the refusal to pay plaintiff

was without reasonable grounds, or was vexatious.

The language of the instruction is that—

"If you shall believe from the evidence that the defendant * * * refused to pay the plaintiff the amount due him under the policy of insurance in this case, and that the same was done prior to the institution of this action, and still further find from all the facts and circumstances shown by the evidence that his refusal to pay was vexatious—that is, without reasonable cause—then you may allow plaintiff, in addition to the amount of your verdict, if any, on the policy, a sum not exceeding 10 per cent. in addition to your verdict on the policy, and a reasonable attorney's fee, and you should return a verdict for the aggregate sum if you find the issues for the plaintiff herein."

The plaintiff testified that when defendant's adjuster called upon him, at the time the final release was secured, the said adjuster took his policy, canceled it, and informed plaintiff that the company could sue him for having accepted payments to which he was not entitled. The adjuster denied this, but it raised the question of fair dealing on the part of the adjuster. We think this fact, with all the other facts and circumstances in the case, authorized the submission of this question to the jury. The arbitrary action of the adjuster in taking up and canceling the policy, coupled with his implied threat to sue, would be a fact tending to show the willful refusal of defendant to pay the amount recoverable under the policy, while it may not be any evidence of the right to recover. The fact that defendant refused to pay the amount demanded by plaintiff, and elected to submit the matter to 'a determination by a lawsuit, might justly be considered an element in the question of vexatious delay, the solution of which would naturally follow the final determination of the suit on its merits; and defendant took its chances along with plaintiff relative thereto.

In accordance with the views above expressed, and finding no reversible error in the record, the judgment is affirmed.

All concur.

TAYLOR v. WESTERN UNION TELEGRAPH CO. (No. 13552.)

(Kansas City Court of Appeals. Missouri. May 28, 1921.)

1. Evidence ⟐34, 46—Judicial notice of acts of Congress and proclamations of President thereunder taken.

The courts will take judicial notice of acts of Congress and of the proclamations of the President pursuant thereto.

2. Evidence ⟐23(1)—Judicial notice of cessation of control by federal government of telegraph companies taken.

The courts will take judicial notice of the fact that the control of telegraph companies by the federal government ceased on a certain date by virtue of a repealing act of Congress.

3. Telegraphs and telephones ⟐26¼. New, vol. 7A Key-No. Series—Not liable for delay during federal control.

In an action against a telegraph company to recover the penalty provided by Rev. St. 1909, § 3330 (now Rev. St. 1919, § 10136), for delay in delivering a telegram, where it appeared that at the time telegraph companies were under federal control, held, that a demurrer to plaintiff's evidence should have been sustained.

Appeal from Circuit Court, Chariton County; Fred Lamb, Judge.

Action by John D. Taylor against the Western Union Telegraph Company. Judgment for plaintiff, and defendant appeals. Reversed.

Francis R. Stark, of New York City, New, Miller, Camack & Winge, of Kansas City, and Mahan, Smith & Mahan, of Hannibal, for appellant.

John D. Taylor, of Keytesville, for respondent.

TRIMBLE, P. J. This suit was instituted June 3, 1919, to recover the $300 statutory penalty provided by section 3330, R. S. 1909 (now section 10136, R. S. 1919), for failure to promptly deliver a telegram alleged to have been sent by plaintiff from St. Louis, Mo., to Keytesville, Mo., on the 6th day of April, 1919. The answer was a general denial, and it further set up as a defense that at the time the telegram was filed for transmission defendant was not in control and operation of its telegraph system, but that the same had been taken over, and was being operated, by the United States government under a resolution of Congress of July 16, 1918, a proclamation of the President, dated July 22, 1918, and an order of the Postmaster General, dated August 1, 1918, and that the business of receiving, transmitting, and delivering telegrams was under the direction, control, and operation of the United States, through its Postmaster General, and that the defendant did not undertake to receive, transmit, or deliver the telegram filed by plaintiff. The defendant demurred at the close of plaintiff's evidence, and again at the close of all the evidence, but was overruled, and judgment was rendered in the sum of $300, the statutory penalty, and from this judgment the defendant has appealed.

There is no contention made by respondent over the proposition that if, as a matter of fact, the defendant's telegraph system was in the hands of, and being operated by, the United States government on April 6, 1919, when the telegram was filed for transmission, then this suit, being against the defendant company itself, cannot be maintained. Respondent's position is that the blanks on which the telegram was sent had nothing on them to show that the government was in control or that any one other than the defendant itself was undertaking to contract in reference to the message, and that the defendant contented itself merely with showing that, under the joint resolution of Congress of July 16, 1918 (40 U. S. Stats. at Large, 904), the President's proclamation of July 22, 1918 (40 U. S. Stats. at Large, 1807), and the Postmaster General's announcement of August 1, 1918, the defendant's lines were taken charge of by, and were under control of, the United States government, its officers and agents, on and from midnight of July 31, 1918, but that there was no showing that such control continued and was in existence down to and on April 6, 1919, the date the telegram was filed for transmission. This contention concedes, in effect, that it was shown at the trial that government control was assumed on July 31, 1918, but it asserts that the burden was on defendant to show that such possession and control was in existence at the time the message was filed. It may be well to here observe that, as a matter of fact, such governmental possession and control continued until midnight of July 31, 1919, as shown by the Act of Congress of July 11, 1919, c. 10, 41 Stat. 157, repealing the joint resolution, which date of cessation of control was nearly four months after the filing of the message for transmission.

[1] It would seem that, governmental control having been once shown to exist, that condition is presumed to have existed until the contrary is shown by the party disputing the continuance of the condition. Lawson on Presump. Evid. 211–240; 22 C. J. 86; 22 Am. & Eng. Ency. of Law (2d Ed.) 1238. However, if the fact that the telegram blanks made no mention of government control would ordinarily be a sufficient circumstance to rebut that presumption, yet it is not so in this instance, since the courts will take judicial knowledge of the acts of Congress and of the proclamations of the President pursuant thereto and thereunder. Pipes v. Missouri Pacific R., 267 Mo. 385, 393, 184 S. W. 79; Armstrong v. United States, 13 Wall. 154, 20 L. Ed. 614; Jenkins v. Collard, 145 U. S. 546, 561, 12 Sup. Ct. 868, 36 L. Ed. 812. Practically the same contention made by plaintiff herein was made in Dessery v. Western Union, 107 Kan. 526, 528, 192 Pac. 728, 729, but in answer thereto the Supreme Court of Kansas said:

"That may be true, but the court is compelled to take judicial notice of the fact that the company was not then operating its telegraph lines, and evidence could not be properly received to disprove that fact."

That the courts will take judicial notice of the acts of Congress and presidential proclamations thereunder is further clearly supported by the following authorities: Western Union, etc., Co. v. Glover (Ala. App.) 86 South. 154; McFeena's Adm'r v. Paris Home Telephone, etc., Co., 190 Ky. 299, 227 S. W. 450; Western Union, etc., Co. v. Leslie (Ala. App.) 84 South. 864, 865; Western Union, etc., Co. v. Robinson (Tex. Civ. App.) 225 S. W. 877; Western Union, etc., Co. v. Davis, 142 Ark. 304, 218 S. W. 833; Western Union, etc., Co. v. Conditt (Tex. Civ. App.) 223 S. W. 234.

[2] Likewise the courts take judicial notice of the fact that the control ceased on a certain date by virtue of a repealing act of Congress. Crenshaw v. Corbitt (C. C. A.) 264 Fed. 962. As to nonliability of defendant for delay or failure in transmission of telegrams during the period of that control, see, also, Foster v. Western Union, etc., Co., 219 S. W. 107; Amerson v. Western Union, etc., Co. (D. C.) 265 Fed. 909; Mitchell v. Cumberland, etc., Co., 188 Ky. 263, 221 S. W. 547, 10 A. L. R. 946; Spring v. American T. & T. Co. (W. Va.) 103 S. E. 206, 10 A. L. R. 951; Western Union, etc., Co. v. Johnson (Tex. Civ. App.) 224 S. W. 203.

[3] It follows, therefore, that the defendant cannot be held liable for the failure to promptly send the telegram in question, and that the demurrer to the evidence should have been sustained.

Consequently the judgment must be, and the same is, reversed.

The other Judges concur.

———

EVANS v. CLAPP et al. (No. 13919.)

(Kansas City Court of Appeals. Missouri. April 4, 1921. Rehearing Denied May 23, 1921.)

1. **Appeal and error ⬤=927(5)—In reviewing denial of demurrer to evidence, only evidence supporting verdict can be considered.**

Where defendant assigned as error the overruling of its demurrer to the evidence, the appellate court must accept as true all the evidence supporting plaintiff's case, unless it is wholly opposed to well-known physical laws or is contrary to the common experience of mankind, while defendant's evidence must be treated as untrue.

2. **Appeal and error ⬤=927(5)—In reviewing denial of demurrer to evidence, plaintiff entitled to every reasonable inference.**

In reviewing the denial of a demurrer to the evidence, plaintiff is entitled to every reasonable inference which the jury could draw in support of the verdict from any evidence in the case, including that offered by defendant.

3. Appeal and error ⚫997(2)—Overruling demurrer to evidence sustained, unless no evidence to support verdict.

It is only where there is no substantial evidence to support the verdict that an appellate court can set it aside on the ground that a demurrer to the evidence should have been sustained.

4. Physicians and surgeons ⚫18(8) — Evidence held to warrant finding that plaintiff was burned by defendant's negligent use of X-ray machine.

In an action against a physician for injuries claimed to result from negligent operation of an X-ray machine, evidence *held* to warrant finding that the burns resulted from exposure to X-ray negligently administered by defendant.

5. Physicians and surgeons ⚫15 — Where X-ray was used merely for diagnosis, and patient was burned, physician cannot defeat recovery on the ground of honest mistake in treatment.

Where X-ray was used merely for diagnosis and the trouble discovered in the first examination, but the physician caused other examinations to be made for his own purposes and the patient was burned, he cannot, in an action for malpractice, defeat recovery on any theory of honest mistake in the careful application of the treatment intended to be applied.

6. Physicians and surgeons ⚫18(7) — That X-ray examinations do not, when carefully used, produce burns, might be considered on question of care.

Where plaintiff, as the result of defendant's X-ray examinations, was severely burned, the fact that such examinations, when carefully and properly made, do not produce burns, might be considered as showing that the degree of care and skill ordinarily exercised by persons of the medical profession using such agencies was not exercised by defendant.

7. Physicians and surgeons ⚫15—In action for X-ray burns, the rules governing the liability of physicians and surgeons are applicable.

The rules governing the duty and liability of physicians and surgeons are applicable to them in the use and manipulation of an X-ray machine and in an action for burns.

8. Physicians and surgeons ⚫14(1)—Degree of care required by physicians using X-ray machines stated.

A physician in operating an X-ray machine must use such reasonable and ordinary care, skill, and diligence as is ordinarily possessed by others in the same line of practice in similar localities, and the term "similar localities" in that connection must have a general and relative meaning so as to include other users who possessed the ordinary proficiency in and acquaintance with the use of that agency which obtains in the same section of the country, and the distinction made between urban and rural practitioners should not prevail.

9. Physicians and surgeons ⚫18(10) — Instruction on the care required of a physician not erroneous.

·In an action by patient burned by X-ray, an instruction that by using the phrase "reasonable skill, care, and prudence," was meant that degree of skill, care and prudence that an ordinarily capable doctor would use in the same or like situation, is not improper as imposing an excessive requirement, for the definition amounted to no more than requiring defendant to use the ordinary skill, care, and prudence used by average members of the profession, which is less than is required.

10. Appeal and error ⚫1033(5) — Defendant cannot complain of an instruction unduly favorable to it.

Where an instruction, in a malpractice action, as to the degree of care required by the defendant physician, required less care than that imposed by law, the physician cannot complain; the instruction being unduly favorable to him.

11. Damages ⚫50—Mental anguish and physical pain are proper elements of damage.

Mental anguish and physical pain arising from bodily injuries are proper elements of damage, where such bodily injuries accrued and defendant's liability is established.

12. Damages ⚫161—Physical pain and mental anguish may be recovered, though not stated.

Physical pain and mental anguish may be considered as elements of damage for bodily injuries, though not stated in the petition.

13. Damages ⚫216(10)—Instruction not objectionable as allowing recovery for mental anguish unaccompanied by injury.

In a malpractice action against a physician who burned plaintiff in the operation of an X-ray, an instruction that the jury should take into consideration the mental pain which the injuries had caused and which they would cause in the future, if any, is not objectionable as allowing recovery for mental anguish, regardless of any physical suffering, where it appeared that X-ray burns are likely to break out any time in the future and there was evidence that as a result of the burn the skin on plaintiff's back had adhered to fibrous covering over the bone which would cause continual discomfort.

14. Damages ⚫216(1)—Instruction not objectionable as tending to improper recovery.

In a malpractice action based on X-ray burns, an instruction that the jury should award plaintiff such damages as would adequately compensate for her injury is not objectionable because of the word "adequately," particularly in view of the fact that the verdict was only for $5,000 and that plaintiff had spent large sums of money and undergone two years of suffering.

Appeal from Circuit Court, Macon County; Vernon L. Drain, Judge.

"Not to be officially published."

Action by Bess Evans against C. B. Clapp and another. From judgment for plaintiff, defendants appeal. Affirmed.

John R. Hughes, Dan R. Hughes, and Otho F. Matthews, all of Macon, and Hunter & Chamier, of Moberly, for appellants.

Harris & Price, of Columbia, and Walter C. Goodson, of Macon, for respondent.

TRIMBLE, P. J. Defendant Clapp is a physician at Moberly, Mo., in charge of and practicing in the private hospital of the Woodland Hospital Company, codefendant herein and a corporation all the shares of which, except one, are owned by defendant Clapp and his wife. The plaintiff was a patient in said hospital and brought this suit for negligent malpractice based upon her claim that she was severely burned by defendant Clapp's application to her of the wonderful and mysterious, yet dangerous, X-ray. There was a verdict and judgment of $5,000 in plaintiff's favor, and from this defendants have appealed.

[1-3] As appellants' principal contention is that their instructions in the nature of demurrers to the evidence should have been given, it is necessary to state the facts with some degree of particularity. In doing this, however, inasmuch as the verdict of the jury is in plaintiff's favor, we set forth only that evidence which tends to support the verdict, disregarding all of defendants' evidence contradictory of plaintiff's theory. For the rule appellate courts must follow, in dealing with the propriety of a demurrer to the evidence in a law case, is that all of the evidence supporting plaintiff's case must be accepted as true, unless it is wholly opposed to well-known physical laws or is contrary to the common experience of mankind; and the defendant's evidence which contradicts that of plaintiff must be treated as untrue, 'since the jury have shown, by their verdict, that they did not accept it. In such case, the plaintiff is also entitled to the benefit of every reasonable inference which the jury could rightfully draw, in support of the verdict, from any evidence in the case, including that offered in defendants' behalf; and it is only where there is no substantial evidence to support the verdict that an appellate court can set it aside on the ground that a demurrer to the evidence should have been sustained. Only a few of the many authorities are here cited in support of the foregoing: Fink v. Kansas City Southern R. Co., 161 Mo. App. 314, 143 S. W. 568; Peak v. Taubman, 251 Mo. 390, 158 S. W. 656; Lawler v. Montgomery, 217 S. W. 856; Crawford v. Kansas City Stock Yards Co., 215 Mo. 394, 409, 114 S. W. 1057; Beckermann v. Kortkamp Jewelry Co., 175 Mo. App. 279, 157 S. W. 855; Steffens v. Fisher, 161 Mo. App. 386, 143 S. W. 1101; Behncke v. Mitchell Clay Mining Co., 189 Mo. App. 639, 175 S. W. 271. Indeed, the foregoing is so

well established that it would seem almost unnecessary to say anything about it, but a mention or restatement thereof may perhaps be useful in alleviating, in some degree, the amazement and dismay experienced by a defeated litigant when, on reading an appellate court opinion in his case, he finds that the evidence he relied upon most confidently as a defense is given little attention, or, perhaps, is not mentioned at all.

With the foregoing in mind, the record contains ample evidence to support the following as the facts in the case:

Plaintiff, a widow living in Centralia, able to do her work and apparently in ordinary health, except that she suffered with attacks of severe sick headache, went to Dr. Clapp at Moberly and consulted him as to their cause. He advised her to come to his hospital, where he would give her the "bismuth meal" and tell her what caused the headaches.

Accordingly, on Saturday, September 1, 1917, plaintiff went to Dr. Clapp, and he placed her in his hospital, and on the following Monday began the work of examining her with his X-ray machine to ascertain the cause of her trouble.

It is conceded that this powerful agency was not used upon her at any time for purposes of treatment, but the sole object in having her to subject herself to the ray was merely to discover the cause of her headaches. Nor were any X-ray pictures or negatives taken at any time, but merely fluoroscopic views were had by causing the X-rays to penetrate the patient's body and cast upon a fluorescent screen a view of her bodily internal arrangements, which the radiographer, or person operating the machine, could see and observe so long as the rays were being generated and allowed to be directed against the plaintiff's body.

It seems that while the X-ray will pass through many otherwise opaque substances, lead is largely impervious to it, and therefore the point at which this agency is generated is inclosed in a lead box having an opening in one side through which the X-rays are allowed to pass to the object at which they are desired to be directed, which opening is controlled by an adjustable shutter which the operator can easily open or close, thereby allowing the ray to pass through the opening or not as he desires, and which shutter is so arranged as to make the opening, through which the rays pass, large or small as the operator desires, according as he wants the field of vision to be large or small. The current of electricity by which the X-rays are produced can also be turned off and on at the will of the operator. A sheet of aluminum, called the aluminum filter, is placed immediately in front of the exit of the rays from the tube, the purpose of which is to filter or take out what are called the "soft rays" which

231 S.W.—6

have an immediate and harmful burning effect on the skin and tissues. But even with this filter, if the X-rays are allowed to penetrate the bodily tissues for a longer time than they should, they will produce a burn of the tissues underneath the skin which will manifest itself afterward by working from the burned tissues outward to the skin, and not fróm the skin inward as ordinary burns, from contact with a hot substance, will do. Such X-ray burns are therefore deep-seated and exceedingly painful, and very difficult, almost if not entirely impossible, to cure. Often they will apparently heal over on the outside only to break out again in sores with a running therefrom of blood and serum.

In making a fluoroscopic examination the patient is required to stand, with his back against the aluminum filter, facing the radiographer, and between him and the patient is the fluorescent screen on which the rays, after passing through the patient's body, cast a shadow or view of the patient's internal bodily arrangements as heretofore stated. As the fleshly organs are not opaque to the X-rays, they pass readily through and cast no shadow of such organs on the fluorescent screen. Consequently, it is necessary to introduce some substance which is opaque to the rays and which at the same time is harmless to the patient. Barium sulphate is such a substance, and it is commonly administered by having the patient, at the time of examination, drink buttermilk with which is mixed the barium sulphate. This was done at the times the plaintiff was examined. As the buttermilk with the barium sulphate passes along the esophagus and into the stomach, the operator can see the outline thereof on the screen and can see the shadow of the barium sulphate where it rests thereafter. In this way he can ascertain, not only the shape and position of the organs through which it passes or into which it goes, but can note any rough places, ulcers, contractions, displacements, etc., which may exist therein.

According to plaintiff's evidence, she was subjected to 20 exposures to the X-ray within a period of 8 days, beginning on Tuesday, September 4, 1917, and ending on Tuesday, September 11th. In her deposition, taken before the trial, she seems to have said there were 22 exposures; and her evidence at the trial and in her deposition seems to differ slightly as to the number of exposures on Wednesday and Thursday, but she explained these by saying she made a memorandum of the exposures, but, though she had it with her when her deposition was taken, she did not refer to it but testified solely from her memory. At any rate, she testified on the trial that there were 20 exposures, and particularly enumerated 16 of these. She says that when Dr. Clapp attempted an X-ray examination of her on Monday, September 3d, the doctor was un-

able to get the machine to work, but finally said: "I can't operate the machine, it won't work to-day."

On Tuesday, plaintiff was again placed before the machine, and this time it worked. Plaintiff swallowed the buttermilk, and the doctor watched its progress as depicted on the screen, and finally he called the nurse's attention, and said: "I have discovered the cause of her headaches. She has a fallen stomach."

Thereafter, on the same day, plaintiff was again placed before the machine, and again about 5 o'clock that afternoon she was placed before it, the rays being turned on each time, and on each occasion the fallen stomach was revealed.

On Wednesday morning, the machine was again turned on her; at noon of that day this was repeated, and it was again done Wednesday evening. Plaintiff says, if she remembers correctly, there were four taken that day.

On Thursday morning, she was again placed before the machine, but it would not work. Dr. Clapp tried and tried to make it work, but could not, and finally said:

"I can't do anything with it. Dr. Streeter is gone, my man that handles this for me, and I can't fix it."

He tried throughout the day on Thursday, and plaintiff was in the fluoroscopic room two or three times that day, but no fluoroscopic results were obtained. Plaintiff was called to the fluoroscopic room several times on Friday, but at none of these times would the machine work.

On Saturday morning, she was again called to the fluoroscopic room, and this time the machine worked and the X-ray was applied. About 11 o'clock a. m. of that day, plaintiff was again called to the fluoroscopic room and found several ladies assembled there; among them, the doctor's wife. The doctor said to plaintiff, "I want to show these ladies your fallen stomach." Plaintiff was thereupon placed before the machine and the X-ray turned on, and the doctor's sister, his wife, and the nurse, stood back of him watching the screen. The wife said, "I can't see anything," and the doctor said to his wife, "Dolly, try to see," whereupon the wife moved to her husband's other side and, looking over his shoulder, said, "Oh, yes! I think I do," and then laughingly said to plaintiff, "You have an interesting anatomy."

About 1 o'clock in the afternoon of the same day, plaintiff was again called to the fluoroscopic room, and Dr. Clapp told plaintiff that a young doctor from another hospital was there, and that he (Dr. Clapp) wanted "him to see this." Thereupon the X-ray was again applied, during which Dr. Clapp called the young doctor's attention to what was shown on the screen, and, while the machine was in operation, Dr. Clapp told the young doctor the patient had a fallen stomach, and the two doctors discussed the condition that produced headaches and autointoxication.

On Sunday, about 3 o'clock in the afternoon, plaintiff was again taken to the fluoroscopic room, the doctor taking plaintiff's sister with them, and there the X-ray was again turned on plaintiff, and the doctor with a pencil traced on the screen, for the sister's benefit, the outline of plaintiff's stomach, the sister standing in a stooped position by his side in front of the screen. In the course of this examination, the doctor told plaintiff's sister that plaintiff had a low-lying stomach and that that was all that was wrong. This examination occupied so long a time that the sister, tiring of the stooped position she was in, got upon her knees, and when the doctor asked why she did this, she told him, and he then inquired of the plaintiff if she were tired. Plaintiff testified there were three other examinations that day, Sunday, and on Monday following three others were had, and on Tuesday, the 11th, two others were had, after which defendant Clapp told plaintiff to go to a physician in Kansas City for the trouble he had found.

Agreeable to Dr. Clapp's advice, plaintiff went to Kansas City and consulted the physician recommended. According to her evidence, she told the Kansas City physician, who was a stomach specialist, that Dr. Clapp had discovered, by the use of the X-ray, that she had a fallen stomach. The Kansas City physician placed her under the X-ray for a total period of from 1 to 1½ minutes in order to see for himself the fallen stomach. The X-ray was administered in this instance by an expert who devoted his entire time to that kind of work, and plaintiff says the X-ray was turned on and then turned off very quickly, and then as the fallen condition of the stomach was disclosed, she was put to bed and merely a rest cure, with a fitted surgical apparatus that holds the stomach up, together with some medicine, was all that was done. Plaintiff went to Kansas City on the 12th of September, and on the 22d or 23d of that month a burn developed on her back, the skin getting red at first and then getting darker from day to day, and the patient began suffering therefrom, and it grew worse and worse until a skin specialist was called on the 29th of September.

The evidence of this expert is to the effect that plaintiff had on her back a large area, about six inches square at least, that on the outer edge thereof it was a light red, a darker red a little further in, and in the center, a place about four inches square, was a collection of blisters with blisters shooting off from the sides thereof, and these blisters

were bluish-colored and filled with blood. In about two weeks the burn began to manifest to the expert unmistakable signs of being an X-ray burn, and in a month he became certain that it was. He began inquiries and learned that she had had a number of X-ray exposures. He treated her until the 12th of the following March, when he was called to the army.

The evidence is that such a burn is extremely painful and that plaintiff suffered torture from it, escaping pain only in the sleep of exhaustion. In June, plaintiff left Kansas City, and in July, went to Colorado, where she was treated for the burn. October 6, she returned to her sister's in Kansas City. From that time until November 16, 1919, the burn was dressed by others, and at the time of the trial in December, 1919, the burn appeared as if healed over, but it had healed over a good many times previously and then had broken out again. The evidence is that the burn was a "third degree burn," that is, one that goes through the true skin and into the tissues beneath; that the burn extended to the bone, being in a place where there was little thickness of tissue between the skin and the bone, and that the skin at the time of the trial was adhered to the fibrous tissue covering the bone, and if the place does not break out again, the adherence would always cause discomfort in walking; that the only method of curing an X-ray burn is by skin grafting, but that would not be likely to relieve the adherent condition in her case, and that in the expert's opinion the injury was permanent.

The evidence is that the X-ray penetrating the body produces no sensation, and a patient does not know he is being burned at the time; that when a burn has been received it will not manifest itself for some three weeks afterward; that the effect of various successive exposures to the X-ray, for a period of about three weeks, is cumulative, that is, that the effect of one continued exposure to the ray for a certain number of minutes is not essentially different from the effect of a number of exposures, aggregating the same number of minutes, but given within a period of three weeks.

The evidence also discloses that there is a definite dosage or method of measuring the X-ray the same as any drug to be administered; and that there are well-settled, definite rules commonly known, and ordinarily used by those administering this agency, as to how much exposure to the X-ray can be safely given to a patient without injury, and how much will produce bad results or be likely to prove injurious. This dosage, or length of time to which a person may be safely exposed to the ray, is dependent upon several factors, namely, the distance of the patient's skin from the X-ray tube, the amount of electrical current going through the machine, the width of the spark gap, and the filter used; that the standard unit of measurement is the "milliampere minute," which is obtained by multiplying the number of minutes a person is exposed by the number of milliamperes of electric current going through the machine. Thus an exposure of one minute in time to a three milliampere current will give a dose of three milliampere minutes, designated by the symbol MM.

It is conceded that the current defendants used was one of three milliamperes; and according to defendant Clapp's deposition, taken about a month before the trial (but not signed by him until about three weeks after it was taken), he used a three-milliampere current, a 6-inch spark gap, an aluminum filter the thickness of which he did not know, with the patient's skin "about eight inches" from the anode or point of the ray. In this deposition, and also at the trial, he testified that he only gave plaintiff eight exposures. In the deposition, he specified the exposures as being three on Monday, September 3d, the first of 3½, the second of 2, and the third of 1½ minutes respectively; two on Thursday, September 6th, of 3 and 2 minutes each; one on Saturday of 1½ minutes; one on Sunday, September 9th, of 1 minute; and one on Monday, September 10, of 1 minute; all of which aggregate a total of 15½ time minutes and would make, with the factors given, a dose of 46½ MM within a period of eight days.

After defendant had thus testified in his deposition, plaintiff took the deposition of an expert in Kansas City, who testified that, with a 3-milliampere current and a 12-inch distance, a dose of 20 milliampere minutes is considered safe; that at 8 inches the same dose would produce a reddening of the skin; that at a distance of 8 inches with an 8-inch spark, a dose of 12 milliampere minutes could be given safely; that a dose of 30 MM might cause an actual burning, and 40 MM would cause an ulcer or sore; that 45 MM would make a bad sore and would be very dangerous; that the longer the exposure the deeper the burn, and that with an 8-inch distance an exposure of 46½ MM, with only a 6-inch spark, would produce a burn and could be justified only in an emergency where the ray was used for treatment to save a patient's life. He also testified that a filter of 1 millimeter in thickness would make a difference of 5 MM, and that in his experience there was little difference in the effects between an 8-inch and a 6-inch spark.

After this testimony was thus given in a deposition taken in plaintiff's behalf as heretofore stated, defendant, before signing the deposition he had given prior thereto, insisted upon interlining the words "off and on" after each number of minutes he had said he applied the ray to plaintiff, and also the words "but I never measured it" after the words "about 8 inches" used in stating the distance of the anode or X-ray tube from the patient's skin, though conceding at the trial that when his deposition was taken he did not use the words afterward inserted. At the trial defendant testified that his machine was so constructed that the anode, or point where the X-ray was generated, could not be placed closer than 12 inches to the patient's body, that the aluminum screen was one millimeter thick, and that during his examination of plaintiff the current was turned on and off at intervals, so that the time the ray was actually penetrating her body was about half the 15½ minutes of time his records showed the exposures were, consequently his evidence tended to show that the amount of exposure he gave plaintiff was only from 22¼ to 24 MM at a distance of 12 inches, or about one-fourth of what 46½ MM would be at 8 inches. Defendant offered expert witnesses, one of whom stated that with a 1-milliampere machine, a spark of 6 inches and a distance of 12 inches from the anode, a dose of 60 MM would be considered safe, while another said a dose of 80 MM would be safe, and they both said that at 12 inches it would take 2¼ times as long to give the same dose as at 8 inches.

Since the defendant's evidence shows that the apparatus he has is the latest, most up-to-date and approved appliance, and since the evidence all shows that X-ray work is frequently, if not ordinarily, done at 8 inches, the jury could well form its own opinion as to whether the latest and most improved machine was so made that work at 8 inches could not be done, and whether it would accept the doctor's evidence as to distance and time, changed as the former was from the deposition given, and changed, as the latter was, even from the time given by his own records of the 8 exposures he claims. Whether there were 8 exposures as he claims, or 20 as plaintiff claims, and whether the 8 exposures lasted 15½ minutes of time as the hospital records show, or whether the 20 lasted the time plaintiff claims they did, are matters solely for the jury to determine; and their conclusion thereon cannot be disturbed by us unless there is no substantial evidence to support plaintiff's claim, or unless it conclusively appears to be as defendants contend, neither of which exists in this case.

Defendants seem to think that plaintiff could give no substantial evidence as to the length of time the X-ray was in actual operation upon her. It is true the penetration of the ray into her body produced no sensation at the time, but plaintiff's evidence is that the machine made a noise as the spark was generated and she could hear that, and although there may have been, as defendant says, a shutter which could be opened or closed at the operator's will, yet there is evidence from which the jury could find that it was not closed during the examinations of plaintiff, especially when the outlines of her organs were being traced upon the screen and shown to others having difficulty in seeing it owing to their unfamiliarity with its use. Again, the evidence of defendant is that before the ray is turned on, the room in which the examination takes place is made as absolutely dark as possible; and manifestly, therefore, the light falling upon the screen, if sufficient to show the operator and those present the internal arrangements of plaintiff's anatomy, would be at least sufficient to be cognizable by plaintiff who faced the radiographer, and the screen was between the two, or, in other words, was in front of her. Be this as it may, however, she says the time the ray was actually upon her varied, on the many and different occasions she was subjected to it, from 1 to 15 minutes. She frankly said she had no means of measuring accurately these times, but gave as her best judgment that the first time was certainly as long as 1 minute and afterwards the exposures were not over 2 minutes at times when others were not present to view the sight; but that on four occasions, when others were there and being shown the outlines on the screen, the exposure must have been 10 minutes each time. If this be true, then the jury could reasonably find that she was exposed to the ray for a total of from 68 to 71 minutes of time in the 8 days, which would equal 204 MM or 213 MM in that length of time; and this, even under the evidence given by defendants' expert witnesses, would be far beyond a safe dose and would be reasonably certain to produce a severe burn.

Again, it is urged that the location of the burn conclusively shows that defendants' ray did not produce it. But this rests upon defendants' evidence that the ray was not directed that low on plaintiff's anatomy. The evidence in plaintiff's behalf was that the burn was from the Gluteal Fold for a distance of six inches up the back, the center of the burn being a little below the top of the pelvic bones and the top of it reached above them. (There was some evidence that the burn went up the back for a distance of seven inches.) Plaintiff was a slight woman, short of stature, and the evidence is she had a fallen or low-lying stomach, and the X-ray was directed toward the lower portion thereof to observe the pyloric orifice. The evidence that the ray was not directed as low as the burn came from defendant Clapp, who indicated on a chart or diagram, not shown in the record, where he said the plaintiff's stomach came to; and defendants' expert witnesses said that whether the plaintiff's stomach would be on a line with the burn would, of course, depend on where her stomach lay, and, while they did not know where it lay in

plaintiff's case, they did not think it could lie as low as the scar they saw, which was the place of the alleged burn.

But, however this may be, we cannot say that it is conclusively shown that defendants' X-ray did not produce the burn. The burn is there, and plaintiff's evidence amply tends to show that it came from the defendants' X-ray. While there is evidence that other things than the X-ray, such as a hot iron, falling against a hot stove, prolonged pressure, irritating substances, radiant energy, a hot water bottle, a dry burn, a wet burn, scald, or an adhesive plaster with ichthyol on it, could produce the scar manifest at the trial, yet there is no evidence that between the time the defendants' X-ray was administered and the time the burn appeared, any of these things occurred or were used, to cause such a condition. Plaintiff went immediately from defendants' hospital to the Kansas City physician, and the burn developed in the time ordinarily required for such things to manifest themselves, and during this time plaintiff was in hospitals and under the care of others.

Nor can we say that the 1½ minute exposure to the X-ray by the Kansas City physician caused the burn, or that it is as likely to have come from that as from defendants' exposures. The evidence is that the exposure given by the Kansas City physician was so slight and of such duration as to produce no appreciable effect even when added to what had already been given. There is therefore no room for the application, against plaintiff, of the rule that where the result complained of may as well have arisen from a cause for which defendants are not liable, as from a cause for which they are liable, the plaintiff must fail.

[4, 5] It is manifest from the foregoing that it cannot be said the jury could not reasonably find that plaintiff received an X-ray burn at the hands of the defendants, and that it was negligently administered. It is a dangerous agency, exceedingly capable of producing serious injury unless administered with care and caution. State v. Lester, 127 Minn. 282, 149 N. W. 297, L. R. A. 1915D, 201. As hereinbefore stated, the X-ray was not applied in this case for purposes of treatment, but merely to ascertain the cause of plaintiff's headaches, and this was disclosed at the first examination. There is no room, therefore, for the application of any theory of mere honest mistake in the careful application of a treatment intended to be applied in the accomplishment of a result similar to the one produced but not to the extent thereof.

[6-8] On the contrary, the X-ray was to be used only to discover a condition which was at once shown, and the many other exposures were not made in the interest of the patient but for other purposes. Examinations, when

carefully and properly made, do not produce burns; hence when a burn is produced, this fact is of itself some evidence from which the jury may find that the degree of care and skill ordinarily exercised by persons of like profession and using such agencies was not exercised in that particular case. George v. Shannon, 92 Kan. 801, 806, 142 Pac. 967, Ann. Cas. 1916B, 338; Shockley v. Tucker, 127 Iowa, 456, 103 N. W. 360. Of course the rules governing the duty and liability of physicians and surgeons in the performance of professional services are applicable to them in the use and manipulation of an X-ray machine. 21 R. C. L. 386. And in applying this dangerous agency they must use such reasonable and ordinary care, skill, and diligence as is ordinarily possessed by others in the same line of practice and work in similar localities. It would seem that the ordinary care required in the use of the X-ray agency (a dangerous thing if not properly used) would not be quite subject to the distinction usually made between ordinary medical practice in a rural and in a city community, for the standard of care in the use of X-ray machines must be derived from among the users thereof, and the term "similar localities" must, in this connection, have a somewhat general and relative meaning so as to include other users of such machines who possess the ordinary proficiency in, and acquaintanceship with, the use of that agency which obtains in similar localities or in the same section of country. These observations, however, are not made with reference to any contention that any improper standard elsewhere was used in the trial, for no such contention arises, both sides obtaining their expert evidence as to the proper use of such machines from Kansas City.

[8, 10] The idea here expressed does, however, have a bearing upon the contention defendants make with reference to that part of plaintiff's instruction No. 2 which said that—

"By the phrase 'reasonable skill, care, and prudence' is meant that degree of skill, care, and prudence that an ordinarily capable doctor would use in the same or like situation and condition of circumstances."

We cannot see how this instruction could have harmed the defendants. It stated the degree of care and skill which has been approved. Gore v. Brockman, 138 Mo. App. 231, 237, 119 S. W. 1082; Wheeler v. Bowles, 163 Mo. 398, 63 S. W. 675. We fail to see any material distinction between the skill, care, and prudence of "an ordinarily capable doctor," and the "ordinary skill, care, and prudence used by the average members of the profession," and this last was approved in West v. Martin, 31 Mo. 375, 80 Am. Dec. 107; Krinard v. Westerman, 279 Mo. 680, 692, 216 S. W. 938. In fact, if anything, the instruction would appear to require a lesser degree of skill of the defendant, since it required

only the skill of an ordinarily capable doctor. If so, the defendants cannot complain. Krinard v. Westerman, supra, 279 Mo. loc. cit. 694, 216 S. W. 938. But, of course, the jury could not have failed to understand that it meant an ordinarily capable doctor, ordinarily skilled in the use of such a machine.

[11-14] Plaintiff's instruction in the measure of damages told the jury that if they found for the plaintiff they could take into consideration the pain and suffering she underwent, if any, the expense, if any, she incurred by reason of her injuries, and the permanency thereof, if they found them to be permanent, and then added:

"You should also take into consideration the mental pain, anguish, and worry which the injuries have caused the plaintiff, if any, and which they will cause her in the future, if any, and after a consideration of these matters the jury should award the plaintiff such damages as will adequately compensate the plaintiff for her injuries, if any, etc."

Mental anguish and physical pain arising from bodily injuries are proper elements of damages, and where such bodily injuries are proved, and defendant's liability therefor is established, physical pain and mental anguish can be considered as elements of damages even though not stated in the petition. Brown v. Hannibal, etc., R. Co., 99 Mo. 310, 319, 12 S. W. 655; Chilton v. St. Joseph, 143 Mo. 192, 199, 44 S. W. 766; Wingate v. Bunton, 193 Mo. App. 470, 477, 186 S. W. 32; Hall v. Mfgrs. Coal & Coke Co., 260 Mo. 351, 370, 168 S. W. 927, Ann. Cas. 1916C, 375. We do not think the jury could have been misled as to any future mental anguish or pain in the absence of any future breaking forth of the burn. No reasonable man would think of one having physical pain or mental anguish in the future from the place, located as it was, unless it gave trouble in some way by being tender to the touch, as the evidence showed it would, or would break out again as it had often done and was reasonably likely to do again. Besides, this objection ignores the testimony that the adherence of the skin to the fibrous covering of the bone would cause discomfort in walking. Nor do we perceive reversible error in the use of the word "adequate" as applied to the compensation she was entitled to receive. The size of the verdict does not indicate that the jury were led astray, in view of the large amount shown to have been expended by plaintiff in the endeavor to cure the burn and the more than two years of severe suffering she had endured therefrom up to the time of the trial.

Having considered the points urged by appellants, and finding no reason for upholding them or warrant for disturbing the verdict, we must affirm the judgment. It is so ordered.

All concur.

GOTTSCHALL v. GEIGER.   (No. 13731.)

(Kansas City Court of Appeals. Missouri.
May 2, 1921. Rehearing Denied
May 23, 1921.)

1. **Witnesses ⬤══52(1, 2)—Husband competent
witness in wife's lawsuit only where made so
by statute.**

Husband's testimony is competent in wife's
lawsuit only where made so by Rev. St. 1919,
§ 5415, making the husband a competent witness when the action is based upon, rose out of,
or is connected with, a transaction conducted by him as the wife's agent, and perhaps in
a few other limited instances; such testimony
being incompetent at common law.

2. **Witnesses ⬤══56(3)—Husband's testimony
held incompetent in wife's action against physician for malpractice.**

In a wife's action against a physician for
negligence in diagnosing her condition and in
deciding to operate for a tumor, where in fact
the wife was merely pregnant and did not have
a tumor, the mere fact that the husband was
present at the time of the operation did not
render his testimony competent under Rev.
St. 1919, § 5415, making husband's testimony
competent, where the action is connected with
or grew out of a transaction conducted by husband as wife's agent, since the action in such
case was based upon the negligent diagnosis,
and not upon the manner in which operation
was performed.

3. **Physicians and surgeons ⬤══15—Physician's
mistake in diagnosis, to be actionable, must
have been negligent.**

A patient, suing physician for negligence
in making diagnosis and in advising an operation where in fact none was necessary, must
prove, not only that the physician made a mistake, but must show in addition that the mistake was a negligent mistake, and that the
operation was so palpably unnecessary that a
surgeon of ordinary care and prudence would
not have advised nor undertaken it.

4. **Physicians and surgeons ⬤══15—Negligence
in advising an operation must be determined
in light of conditions existing before operation.**

Whether a physician was negligent in making a diagnosis and in advising an operation
where in fact no operation was necessary must
be determined in the light of conditions as they
existed before the operation was performed.

5. **Evidence ⬤══481(1)—Whether surgeon's decision to operate was negligence should be determined from testimony of experts.**

If there were conditions existing prior to
performance of operation such as to raise a
question of whether an operation was advisable
or proper, the question of whether the physician's decision to operate was negligence should
be gathered from the opinions and testimony
of those who have special knowledge of such
matters.

6. **Physicians and surgeons ⬤══18(9)—Whether physician was negligent in advising unnecessary operation held for jury.**

In action by a married woman against a
physician for malpractice, the question of
whether the physician was negligent in making
diagnosis and in advising an operation for tumor, where in fact no operation was necessary
and where plaintiff's condition was merely that
of pregnancy, *held* a question for the jury.

Appeal from Circuit Court, Buchanan
County; Lawrence A. Vories, Judge.

Action by Elsie Gottschall against Jacob
Geiger. Judgment for plaintiff, and defendant appeals. Reversed and remanded.

Robert A. Brown, Richard L. Douglas,
Strop & Mayer, and William E. Stringfellow,
all of St. Joseph, for appellant.

Randolph & Randolph, of St. Joseph, for
respondent.

TRIMBLE, P. J. This is an action for
damages on account of alleged negligent malpractice. The plaintiff is a farmer's wife,
about 33 years of age, living in De Kalb
county. Defendant is a physician and surgeon, of 51 years' practice, in St. Joseph, Mo.,
who formerly held the chair of surgery in
Ensworth Medical College and in St. Louis
University, and who is now dean of the first-
named institution. He is unquestionably of
high repute and standing in his profession,
and there is no charge of a lack of the requisite qualifications of knowledge, skill, training or experience on his part. The gist of
the cause of action submitted is that defendant was negligent in diagnosing plaintiff's
condition and in advising and deciding upon
a surgical operation which he undertook to
perform on plaintiff but, upon opening her
abdomen, found that pregnancy, and not a
tumor, was the cause of her trouble. There
was no charge or complaint of any negligence
in the manner of performing the operation.
A trial was had, resulting in a verdict and
judgment for plaintiff in the sum of $3,000,
from which defendant has appealed.

In April, 1918, plaintiff was the mother of
two children, one 10 and the other 2½ years
old, and up to the last day of May in that
year she was strong and well, able to do the
work of a housewife and of assisting her husband in certain of the farm work. On the
last-named date, however, she became sick
and, upon examination by her family physician, Dr. Clark, he said she had "some involvement of gall bladder." Plaintiff about
the last of July went to defendant in St. Joseph, where he diagnosed her trouble as appendicitis, and where he, on August 1, 1918,
performed an operation on her for that disease, and also, he says, for ovarian trouble,
which he says he suspected. According to
defendant's testimony (and there is no evi-

dence to the contrary), when he performed this operation he found a long, large, highly inflamed appendix. He further found that the right tube, broad ligament, and ovary and all parts lying in close proximity thereto were inflamed, that the omentum, or apron that lies over the bowels, was grown fast to the inflamed mass in the right side; that he loosened this, removed the appendix, the right tube, right ovary, and broad ligament, because they were all diseased and highly inflamed. The left ovary was also cystic, and he says he removed about seven-eighths of it, leaving a small healthy portion of that ovary. (The evidence of all the medical experts is that the common and proper practice, in removing the ovaries, is to leave a small portion of one ovary, if possible, since that will help to hinder or prevent nervousness and other untoward effects which will be certain to arise if the whole of both ovaries is removed.) Defendant testified that he also, in this operation of August 1, 1918, found a double tear of the womb produced by her former confinements, and that he sewed up these rents and scraped the womb.

It is agreed on all sides that from this operation plaintiff rapidly recovered, leaving the hospital and going home on the 11th of August, 1918; and plaintiff says that thereafter she was as well and strong as she ever was.

While some vague complaint of this operation seems to be made in the petition, yet, as submitted, the case does not rest upon any cause of action growing out of this operation, but upon the defendant's advising and deciding upon a second operation, performed in May, 1919, as the matters hereinafter stated will more fully disclose.

According to plaintiff's evidence, the defendant told her after the first operation that, owing to the removal of her ovaries, she could never bear children; that it would be an impossibility. However, along in December, 1918, she says she began to think she was pregnant, and about January 1, 1919, she sent her husband to the defendant, telling him of her symptons, and the defendant sent back word that if she did not get better she had better come in and let him see her. On April 26, 1919, she did so. She says he asked her what the trouble was, and she told him it was in her stomach; that he placed her on the examining table and pressed across her abdomen and said she was in the "family way"; that she replied she thought she was, but that he had told her when she was operated on in August that she could not get that way; that he then asked what the operation was, and said he had so many he could not remember them unless he looked up his records. He referred to his records, and said she could not be in a family way; his records showed he had removed her ovaries. Plaintiff says he then "pressed

across the abdomen quite a little bit, and said it was a tumorous growth," that she would have to have it removed right away, as they grew very rapidly. Plaintiff told him, so she says, that she thought she was in the family way, and that it could not be anything else, and upon defendant asking her why she thought that, she told him "the movement was so strong," and she had every symptom she had before with her other two children; that defendant thereupon said it was not that—it could not be—and that if plaintiff could not stay at that time to have an operation, she must come back right away and have it done; she must not wait over two weeks, as they (the tumorous growth) grew very rapidly. She also says he told her he could not "determine just where the tumor was," and would have an X-ray examination to find out.

Plaintiff says she waited three weeks, however, and came back on May 19, 1919, for the operation; that defendant examined her again in the same manner, and told her to go to the hospital that evening; that it was a tumor, that they grew rapidly and it must be removed right away. She says that after the examination, her husband asked defendant if he were not going to use the X-ray, and defendant replied no, that it would cost her $15, and he did not think he could tell. Plaintiff says she told defendant she still thought she was pregnant, but that defendant said no, it was not that; it could not be that, and to dismiss it from her mind.

The next morning, May 20, 1919, she was placed on the operating table, an anæsthetic was administered, and an incision about 6 inches long was made in the abdomen about on, or a little to the right of, the median line and below the navel. The doctor put his hand into the opening, felt around, and found that plaintiff was pregnant. (The doctor says he found the womb bound down by adhesions, which he removed, restoring the womb to its normal position.) Plaintiff was then sewed up, and on the 8th day thereafter left the hospital and went to the home of a relative in the city, where she stayed three days and then went to her home. On the 19th day of July thereafter she gave birth to a 9-pound healthy baby boy, fully developed, and, according to Dr. Clark, the physician who attended her, one that had gone the full nine-month period. It was in good health and thriving at the time of the trial.

Plaintiff claims that as a result of her second operation she has become nervous and weak. She does not have any pain whatever, but feels extremely weak, nervous, and has spells of severe headache. These nervous spells come on about every week or ten days; when she tries to do her work they will come on in an instant, and she has to go to bed. She had to wear a bandage about her abdomen after the second operation until her baby was born; and during that period she suffered pain from the incision that was made, but the incision healed up about a week before the child was born. All that plaintiff complained of at the time of the trial was that she was extremely weak and nervous and possibly the attacks of headache above mentioned. During the time between the second operation and the birth of the child, she worried over the latter, fearing the effects of the incision that had been made in her abdomen.

According to the evidence of Mr. and Mrs. Brink, neighbors of plaintiff, they were at the hospital in June after the operation and before the baby was born and talked to defendant, and, according to them, Mrs. Brink asked defendant if it would have been necessary to operate if he had used the X-ray, and he replied: "No; I probably made a mistake; in fact I know I made a mistake." Mrs. Brink did not understand him to say he made a mistake in not using the X-ray, but supposed he meant he made a mistake in operating. Mr. Brink says defendant said, "Probably not," when asked, Would it have been necessary to operate if he had used the X-ray? and that he also said, "I probably made a mistake; in fact I know I did;" and that he further said, "I only know of one other case like it."

The defendant testified that after the first operation, the plaintiff came to him in April, 1919, complaining that she was not getting along well, that her stomach pained her, that she was nervous and constipated, had a dragging down feeling in her abdomen, and said there was a lump there. Defendant says he looked up the record of her previous operation and made a bimanual examination, having one hand on the abdomen and the other in the vagina; he found a mass to the right of the median line, the principal part of which was immovable, but the lower part was not; that the neck of the womb was turned to the left high up; that he could not make out what the mass was and told her he did not know what it was—it might be a tumor—that there was something growing there, and that she might have to have an X-ray examination. Defendant says he told her maybe they had better wait a couple of months, and at the end of that time he could tell better what it was; that in three or four weeks she came back, saying she could not get along any more, the pulling, dragging, and burning in her stomach and her nervousness was so great that something had to be done. The doctor says he again examined her, and told her he did not know what it was; it acted more like a tumor than anything else; and that—

"Nothing short of an exploratory operation, nothing short of an operation, is going to relieve you, and I advise you to go to the hospital and let us find out what is the matter and try to relieve you."

He says he had in mind, at that time, three things, one of which might be the matter with her, namely, first, an intermural fibroid tumor, which sometimes grows very rapidly; second, a sarcoma of the womb; or, third, possibly pregnancy. The defendant says he did not wholly exclude pregnancy as one of the possible conditions, but that he placed it last in the scale of possibilities, because it was very unusual for a woman, with only a small portion of one ovary left, to become pregnant; but the main thing was her complaining and the fact that the womb was turned to one side and immovable, not entirely so, but it was fastened down and was tender; that he knew there was some pathological or abnormal condition there, but just what it was he did not know further than this, that as a result of what was done at the former operation there necessarily would be some "adhesions" (i. e., places where different parts lying against each other, where they were raw or inflamed, had, upon healing, grown together); that the position of the womb in turning to one side, instead of rising up in the abdomen along the median line, indicated that it was held down by adhesions; that he could have inserted a "sound," a metallic instrument, into the womb and determined its depth thereby, since the womb is deeper and longer if it contains a fibroid tumor, but if he had inserted a sound and the patient was pregnant it would almost invariably have produced an abortion; that where there is a tumor and no adhesions you can move the mass, a pregnant womb is also more freely movable, unless it is bound down, but a womb with a tumor in it, and having adhesions, becomes immovable. Defendant further testified that whenever the womb of a pregnant woman is bound down by adhesions, the womb cannot develop to the full extent, and pain follows and vomiting, indigestion, etc., and abortion or premature delivery may take place at any time. He further testified as to the difficulty in determining whether pregnancy or some other condition existed; that so-called "kicking" or movements felt in the body were unreliable as indications of pregnancy, there being so many movements in the belly, for instance, peristalsis of the intestines, which, in case of constipation as the plaintiff had, would cause great muscular movement in the abdomen; that these movements had often been felt by women who it afterward turned out had never been pregnant; that there was no way by which he could absolutely and positively have told whether plaintiff was pregnant, except by introducing the sound, which, as stated, would have brought on an abortion if pregnancy did exist.

Defendant further testified that, owing to the condition and position he found the womb in and the other symptoms heretofore referred to, the proper course was to open the abdomen, and, if the mass was a tumor, to remove it, but if only pregnancy existed, then remove the adhesions so the womb could resume its natural position and develop properly as the child grew, and thus not only remove the condition giving rise to the unpleasant symptoms, but also avoid the danger of abortion or premature delivery, and perhaps save the life of the mother as well as that of the child itself.

Defendant says that for this purpose, and with this end in view, he made an outside cut in the outer wall of the abdomen somewhat larger than the one in the inside wall or through the muscles and the peritoneum, the latter cut being about 2½ inches in length, and through this opening he found, on examination that the womb was firmly bound down on the right side to the pelvic fascia, or the lining on the inside of the hip, which gave rise to plaintiff's pain, sick stomach, and constipation; that the womb was lying, not transversely, but very obliquely, so that it could not rise up in the abdomen without pulling and giving rise to disturbances. The omentum was found to be again adhered and bound down. Defendant says he put in his fingers and loosened the adhesions as far as he could, and, finding some so large and tough that he could not separate them with his fingers, he inserted a pair of scissors and snipped them loose, allowing the womb to resume its natural position. He says the womb was not large, and he thought the child therein was some four or five months along. He says that the plaintiff might possibly have gone on and had the child without the operation of loosening these adhesions, but not in his judgment; that if it had not been done it is his opinion that she would ultimately have had an abortion and lost her child; that had he known at the time she was pregnant he would have done just what he did do; that in addition to the womb lying obliquely and being bound down on the right side, the neck thereof was turned almost to the left, that such position of the womb made childbirth very difficult; that in his opinion the second operation benefited plaintiff, and probably saved the child's life, and there was nothing about the operation which could have produced the condition of weakness and nervousness of which plaintiff complained at the trial. The defendant admitted talking to Mr. and Mrs. Brink about the case, but denied answering in the way they said he did; that he did say he did not know what the trouble was, and that it was a very unusual case, but that he never said he made a mistake in performing the second operation; that he did not say such was a mistake, because he did not know fully the condition, and it was not a normal pregnancy, and could not be, after the big operation she had had in August before; and that he made no mistake in determining upon the second operation.

The records of the hospital showed that after the operation complained of the patient slept well every night, rested well every day, and on May 28, 1919, was discharged from the hospital in good condition.

The only medical witness plaintiff offered was her family physician, Dr. Clark, of Maysville, who testified that at the trial plaintiff "seems very nervous and irritable, and seems to have lost considerable weight," but that she was not nervous and irritable during the years he knew her before defendant operated on her. Whether he meant the first or second operation does not appear. When he was asked by plaintiff's counsel whether pregnancy at seven months (the stage plaintiff claims the pregnancy had reached at the time of the second operation) was a difficult thing to determine in an examination, Dr. Clark replied:

"That is a very difficult question to answer; it depends on who it is and the conditions and the patient."

He said, however, that ordinarily it is not. Plaintiff then asked her medical expert the hypothetical question, assuming that plaintiff was seven months along in pregnancy and was given an anæsthetic and her abdomen opened, under the supposition that she had a tumor, by a surgeon, who then found she was pregnant, and she was then sewed up and had to wear a bandage for the remaining period of her pregnancy, whether or not the anæsthetic, the wounding, and the subsequent condition that followed it "would account for her present condition." The doctor attempted to reply and said, "That is beyond my—" when plaintiff's counsel broke in with another question, and the following took place:

"Q. Would that probably account for it? A. I wouldn't attempt to answer that question.

"Q. What do you say is the cause of her present condition? A. I don't know.

"Q. Would such a wound and the anæsthetic, under the circumstances I have mentioned, be likely or probable to produce a nervous condition of that kind? A. Well, now, I would say that the accompanying distress and worry she has gone through with it would.

"Q. That it would with the accompanying distress? A. Yes, sir.

"Q. Do you know any other cause for her condition except that? A. No.

"Q. You know of no other cause? A. No."

Plaintiff's medical witness further testified that, in an operation for appendicitis and for removal of the ovaries, adhesions will always follow if there has been infection; that adhesions resulted from infection or irritation; that adhesions all around in the region of the infected place and of the appendix might involve the ovaries; that whether a woman could carry a child to seven months with the womb adhered to the walls of the abdomen would all depend on the extent and cause of the adhesions; that in his opinion, if the womb adhered to the walls of the abdomen and was held down by them, the fetus would not grow, and in that event probably an abortion would take place; that the womb enlarges as pregnancy advances and rises higher, but the adhesions might become elastic and follow the womb, in which case they would cause pain; that even if the adhesions became elastic and gave or stretched as the womb enlarged, they might cause a miscarriage, depending upon the amount of binding on the womb and the irritation thereto caused thereby; in other words, adhesions might cause an abortion in one case and not in another, depending on the extent thereof; that if the movement of the womb was limited and restricted or bound down in some way, there was some pathological condition; that if there were adhesions arising from the infection and former operation, they would cause pain and unusual nausea, and an operation relieving the adhesions might be a proper thing to do, depending greatly on the woman's personal knowledge or appearance, and the surgeon who has the case in charge is the better judge of what should be done. He also said that a very small portion of the ovary, a piece as large as a bean, if left, could function so as to produce the ovum, resulting in pregnancy if impregnated by the male germ.

On behalf of the defendant, the following witnesses testified: Miss Bailey, the nurse who was present at the second operation, says the plaintiff, when brought in to be operated on, "seemed real sick to me"; she was vomiting and seemed to be very sore and tender in the abdomen whenever they moved her, and she had to be lifted onto the operating table; that before the operation the defendant said he did not know what he was going to find—he had a mass of some sort; he did not know what it was— that he thought it was a tumor, but he did not know; that the doctor, after opening the plaintiff's abdomen, said she was pregnant; that witness saw him pull loose adhesions and use his scissors in cutting other of the adhesions loose; and that the operation was completed promptly without the doctor leaving the patient or the room; and that the patient progressed very nicely after that.

Dr. Bergher, a physician who happened to be at the hospital at the time, but who was not connected with it or the defendant, came into the operating room just as the operation was about to begin. He says he asked the defendant what he had—i. e., what was the trouble with the patient—and the defendant said, "That is what I am trying to find out." Witness also said he saw the defendant make the incision and open the abdomen; that he put in his hand and said, "This woman is pregnant," and then loosened the adhesions with his fingers and cut others with his scissors; that the defendant did not to his knowledge go out of the room

during the course of the operation, though the witness did not remain in the room until the patient was removed.

In support of the correctness of the defendant's theory and the surgical course he pursued in plaintiff's case, the defendant introduced nine physicians and surgeons of thorough knowledge and long experience in surgery and obstetrics. Of these, Dr. Thompson, a practitioner of medicine, surgery, and obstetrics for 32 years, during which time he had had experience with over 1,800 obstetrical cases, testified that it was a very rare occurrence for a woman with only one-eighth of an ovary to become pregnant, that under the conditions specified in this case he would not have expected to find pregnancy; that the conditions found at the first operation always result in adhesions being formed; that adhesions to any part of the womb at any time during pregnancy will interfere with it; that the chances are that, with the womb bound by adhesions as stated, the child would not have lived, and both mother and child would have run a greater risk of death if the operation had not been performed; that it is not always possible to positively diagnose pregnancy at seven months, sometimes it cannot be done; he had seen the best experts in America fail on it; that in this case it would not have been possible to definitely diagnose this case as one of pregnancy; that in pregnancy the enlargement is on the median line and when the mass is aside from the median line the strong indications are that it is a tumor; that where the womb is bound by adhesions the experiment known as "ballottement" will not disclose pregnancy; that under the conditions the second operation was one which a physician and surgeon of reasonable care and skill in similar communities would have performed, even if the condition of pregnancy were absolutely known; that the pregnancy in this case was not a normal one.

The testimony of the other experts were to the same effect, namely, that under the conditions named, pregnancy is very difficult to positively diagnose; that it is very rare for a woman, with only a fragment of one ovary, to have children, and pregnancy would be considered very improbable under such circumstances; that vomiting after the third or fourth month indicates a toxic or poisoned condition of some kind; that they would not have diagnosed plaintiff's case as pregnancy; that adhesions follow an infection and operation such as plaintiff had the first time; that they interfere with pregnancy, and any abnormal pregnancy is difficult to diagnose; that the X-ray is not commonly used to diagnose pregnancy; it will not disclose the fetus at seven months, and is not reliable even at eight months; that the use of the stethoscope will not always reveal the heartbeat of the fetus; that the second operation was a proper one, such as an ordinarily skillful and careful surgeon of that community would have performed; that if it had not been performed, plaintiff's condition would probably have resulted in the loss of the child.

One of these experts, Dr. Byrne, testified that abnormal pregnancy is one of the most difficult conditions to diagnose physicians have to meet, that he had seen Dr. Murphy of Chicago, one of the world's greatest surgeons, open a woman's abdomen, exposing a large womb, and, after examining it carefully, was still unable to say whether she was pregnant or not; that he had seen Dr. Andrews, another surgeon of wide reputation, open a woman's abdomen and remain uncertain whether she was pregnant or not, though he decided to act on the assumption that she was about six months along.

The medical testimony of these experts was also to the effect that there is no reason why the second operation should have affected the plaintiff's general health and produce the symptoms complained of by her at the time of the trial, that the use of an anæsthetic does not injure a pregnant woman, that women are sometimes nervous wrecks following a childbirth which is apparently normal; that nervousness always results from the removal of the ovaries. Dr. C. R. Woodson testified that the operation was justifiable and proper under the circumstances named in defendant's hypothetical question, since if the adhesions had not been removed, the chances are that the plaintiff would have miscarried, or the womb bound down so as to prevent the child from turning, and thereby make delivery very difficult, resulting in the death of the child; that so far from the second operation producing great nervousness and extreme weakness ten months or a year after the operation, it should have prevented nervousness, and would benefit the patient, and evidently did so, as she gave birth to a healthy normal child.

In setting forth the evidence offered by plaintiff in support of her case, we have heretofore purposely omitted the testimony of her husband, which was introduced over the objections of defendant. We have done this because, in our view, the husband's testimony was not admissible, and therefore the question of whether plaintiff had sufficient evidence to go to the jury should be determined from all the evidence and lawful inferences in her favor, without regard to the husband's testimony. The admission of the husband's evidence came about in this way:

Plaintiff testified in her first direct examination that her husband was present in the operating room at the first operation at her request, because, she says, "I wanted him to see what was done." Later on she was asked by her counsel, "When the second operation was performed, state whether or not you requested and directed that any person be present to *represent you at that operation.*" (Italics ours.) She answered, "Yes, sir; I asked my husband to." And again, in reply to the question of her counsel relative to the second operation, "At the time the anæsthetic was administered, was your husband there present at your request?" she said, "When I left the room, I requested him to go with me, and he was right at my side when they gave the medicine."

Thereafter the husband was introduced as a witness, but the court would not let him testify concerning either the first or second operation, but did allow him to testify as to the message defendant sent back to plaintiff when she first sent her husband to see the doctor in January, as has been heretofore stated. Thereafter plaintiff was recalled, and was asked:

"Q. When your husband came with you to this first operation, did you—for what purpose did you have him there—did you give him any directions what to do or anything?"

And she replied:

"A. I asked him to go to the operating room and stay through the operation and see what was done.

"Q. Was that all you said to him? A. Yes, I think it was."

And as to the second operation, she said:

"I asked him to go along and see what was done.

"Q. That was all there was to it? A. Yes."

After the defense had closed in chief, and after plaintiff had put in her rebuttal, the plaintiff's husband was again placed upon the stand, and was asked if he was in the operating room at the time of the first operation. The defendant objected, not only upon the ground that the husband was an incompetent witness, but also on the ground that the wife had already testified fully as to agency, and, as the principal having done so, the agent could not enlarge it, and also on the further ground that there was no question or pretense that anything was wrong in the first operation. The objections were overruled by the trial court on the theory that, if the wife requested the husband to be present in the operating room for the purpose of witnessing the operation, and the husband acted for her in any capacity there, in any consultation that took place about what was going on or ought to go on, the two things together, in the court's view, constituted the husband the agent of the wife for that purpose. Thereupon the husband testified he was present at the first operation at his wife's request, and that he was there "for the purpose of seeing what was done." Thereafter, over the objections and exceptions of defendant, the husband was allowed to testify that during the course of the first operation he (the husband) stepped to the door to get fresh air, and was called back by defendant who told him his wife's ovaries were in bad shape, one practically dead and the other badly diseased and ought to be removed, and asked the husband what about it. The latter told the doctor to use his own judgment, as he (the husband) would not know how they were. To this the doctor replied:

"I say remove them, but you understand, if they are removed, she can't bear any more children."

The husband testified that thereupon the doctor took out all of one ovary and all but about probably one-fourth of the other one, giving as his reason for leaving a portion that her passions would not be destroyed; that the doctor took out nothing else that he saw at all, except the ovaries and the appendix. Over the objections and exceptions of defendant, the husband was then asked if he were present at the second operation, and said he was, at his wife's request, and that the purpose was "to see just what was done at the operation." Then, over the objections and exceptions of the defendant, the husband testified that, at the second operation, after his wife went under the anæsthetic, defendant approached him and said:

"If I cut in and find a cancer, there's no doing anything for her, but if it's a tumor—well, it's a little different."

The husband asked him:

"Doctor, you figure this a very serious operation?".

To which the doctor replied:

"Very, very, but the rapid condition this is growing, she can't live long under that condition."

The husband testified that the doctor made a 6 or 7 inch incision, put his hand in and felt around, then turned about and said, "This woman is undoubtedly pregnant, but it can't be possible; I removed both ovaries;" that the doctor put his hand back into the opening, felt around again, pulled it out and left the room, pulling at one of his gloves like he was going to take it off. He was gone about a minute and returning, said to the nurse, "Loosen her limbs; I am going to examine her." He then made an examination through the vagina and said, "That's all ails this woman; let's sew her up." He then walked out of the room again, and in a minute or a minute and a half or two minutes he returned, saying, "There's a few adhesions; I'll loosen them." He then hooked his fingers, reached in, and gave a couple of pulls, and then sewed her up without using any scissors. After unsuccessful efforts to have the testimony stricken out, the husband was cross-examined, and testified that at the first op-

eration the doctor took out something he said was the ovary; the witness did not know an ovary from any other part; that he (the husband) was not caring anything about whether she would have children, but about the condition of her health, and he consented that the ovaries be taken out, and left the decision of that matter to the physician; that witness thought the doctor left about one-fourth of one of the ovaries, left a part, something around a fourth; knew it was a piece of it; a small piece was all he knew about it; that at the second operation, when the doctor inserted his hand, he said, "Undoubtedly this woman is pregnant, but it is impossible; I removed her ovaries;" and was excited. The defendant denied he made the statement attributed to him, or that he left the room and acted as the husband says he did, and his version of what took place at the second operation was corroborated by Dr. Bergher and the nurse, both of whom were present.

Before passing on the question of whether plaintiff has sufficient evidence to entitle her to go to the jury, we deem it proper to first consider the question of the admissibility of the husband's testimony, since, if that was not admissible, the question of the demurrer to the evidence must be decided with the husband's testimony left out of consideration.

[1] At common law, the husband was not a competent witness in his wife's lawsuit. Joice v. Branson, 73 Mo. 28; Tockstein v. Bimmerle, 150 Mo. App. 491, 131 S. W. 126. And he cannot be a competent witness for her except where the statute (section 5415, R. S. 1919), has modified the common-law rule, and, perhaps, in a few other limited instances which have been judicially determined to be exceptions to the rule upon one ground or another, which will shortly be stated. The statute removes the disqualification of the husband to testify as a witness in his wife's suit "when such suit or proceeding is based upon, grows out of, or is connected with, any matter of business or business transaction, where the transaction or business was had with or was conducted by such married man as the agent of his wife." The qualification permitted by the statute is a limited one. The suit must be based upon, grow out of, or be connected with, the particular business transaction had with or conducted by the husband as the agent of the wife. White v. Chaney, 20 Mo. App. 389, 394; First Nat. Bank of Leavenworth v. Wright, 104 Mo. App. 242, 78 S. W. 686; Gardner v. St. Louis, etc., R. Co., 124 Mo. App. 461, 101 S. W. 684; Fishback v. Harrison, 137 Mo. App. 664, 119 S. W. 465; Senaca Co. v. Ellison, 208 S. W. 103; Taylor v. George, 176 Mo. App. 215, 161 S. W. 1187; Baird v. First Nat. Bank, 149 Mo. App. 367, 129 S. W. 961; Connecticut Fire Ins. Co. v. Chester, etc., R. Co., 171 Mo. App. 70, 153 S. W. 544.

So far as the record shows, the husband

nowhere acted as the wife's agent, except when he was sent by her in January to tell the doctor of her symptoms, and in what is here said we are not dealing with the evidence as to that interview. Later, plaintiff herself went to the defendant and had him examine her. The doctor told her to go home and wait, which she did; at least she did go home. She returned later for further examination, and, so far as the record shows, she made these visits and arranged for the second operation herself.

It is true the husband testified that during the first operation the doctor asked him about removing the ovaries, but there is no evidence that the husband was requested by the wife to be in there for any purpose of deciding how far the operation shoul§ go. The wife at the trial said she "didn't care anything about whether they [the ovaries] were removed out or not," and the only dissatisfaction at all on her part over the first operation seems to have been because the doctor had told her she could not have children, as he had removed her ovaries, whereas he had left a small piece of one ovary there, and she afterwards had become pregnant. So clear was it that no complaint of negligence was made in regard to the first operation that the court in its instructions excluded from the consideration of the jury any issue of negligence connected with, or growing out of, the first operation, either in the manner or the fact of its performance. So that the fact that the husband was consulted by the doctor with reference to the ovaries at the first operation could not constitute him her agent and make him competent to testify as to the second operation. At this second operation the husband was merely a silent spectator; so far as the record shows it was performed pursuant to arrangements made by plaintiff herself, and without question or suggestion on the part of the husband. The contract of employment between plaintiff and defendant was, in legal effect, that he was to use his best judgment, carefully exercised, in determining what should be done for her and in treating her professionally. There was no business to be transacted between the doctor and the husband while the doctor was operating or after the plaintiff was put under the anæsthetic. Plaintiff did not testify that, if during the operation some question arose as to what the nature or extent of it should be, she wanted her husband to decide it for her, nor did any question of the kind arise. She testified merely that at the first operation, she requested her husband to go with her, stay through the operation, and see what was done; and at the second operation she asked him to go along and see what was done. If one spouse can, by saying to the other, "I want you to be present and witness what is done," thereby make such spouse a competent witness on the

ground of agency, then it would seem to be all easy matter to avoid the common-law rule and the express limitation of the statute.

[2] But the plaintiff, being under an anæsthetic, was unconscious, and this would be the same as if she were not there, and hence, it may be urged that plaintiff thereby had the right to have an agent present to see and act for her. No doubt she would have the right to appoint her husband her agent to represent and act for her in any matter of business or business transaction where she was unconscious or absent or even present and conscious, but before the husband could testify as a witness, the transaction constituting the basis of the action must be one that is "had with or conducted by" the husband as her agent. And in this case it was nothing of the sort. In fact, the basis of the suit is not with regard to the manner of performance of the operation or the extent thereof. The action is for negligently diagnosing plaintiff's condition and in deciding to perform an operation. If the charge is true, the negligence was complete before the operation began, the operation itself being merely the result of that negligence, giving rise to the damage claimed, and there is no denial but that the operation itself was performed. The case is not, therefore, one where the husband's testimony is admissible under some exception to the common-law rule, or where it is admissible rei necessitate rei, on the grounds of public policy, as in the case of a criminal abortion performed on the wife, or a fraud or an assault perpetrated on her by her husband, or by others through the husband's agency. Such, for example, are the cases cited by plaintiff, to wit, Turner v. Overall, 172 Mo. 271, 72 S. W. 644, Henry v. Sneed, 99 Mo. 407, 12 S. W. 663, 17 Am. St. Rep. 580, Moeckel v. Heim, 134 Mo. 576, 36 S. W. 226, and Cramer v. Hurt, 154 Mo. 112, 117, 120, 55 S. W. 258, 77 Am. St. Rep. 752. In Orchard v. Collier, 171 Mo. 390, 399, 71 S. W. 677, the Supreme Court held that, while it was proper to prove by the husband certain things he did, he having been shown to be the wife's agent, yet that it was error to permit him to testify to things not done by him as the agent for his wife, as the disqualification existing at common law "was not removed by that or any other statute." It would seem that such holding is applicable to this case, since clearly the basis of the suit is not in reference to the way in which the second operation was performed, nor was either the decision to operate or the operation itself a matter of business or business transaction had with or conducted by the husband as the agent of his wife. For the foregoing reasons, we entertain the view that the testimony of the husband was erroneously admitted, and the judgment should on this account be reversed, and the cause remanded for a new trial if there is sufficient evidence

remaining in the case to justify its submission to a jury.

[3-5] Should the defendant's demurrer to the evidence have been sustained? The burden is on plaintiff to show, not only that defendant made a mistake in diagnosing her condition and in deciding upon and advising the second operation, but she must also show that such was a negligent mistake, and that the operation was so palpably unnecessary that a surgeon of ordinary care and prudence would not have advised nor undertaken it. Vanhooser v. Berghoff, 90 Mo. 487, 3 S. W. 72; Fausette v. Grim, 193 Mo. App. 585, 186 S. W. 1177; Nevinger v. Haun, 197 Mo. App. 416, 196 S. W. 39; Spain v. Burch, 169 Mo. App. 94, 154 S. W. 172. And the question of whether defendant was negligent in making the diagnosis and in deciding upon the operation must be determined in the light of the conditions as they existed before the operation was performed. In other words, if conditions were such as to load a surgeon of ordinary care and skill to think that plaintiff was not pregnant, or even that as a remote possibility she might be, and yet an operation was necessary, and defendant in the honest exercise of his best judgment thought an operation was proper, then defendant would not be liable, even though it afterward turned out that defendant was mistaken in diagnosing plaintiff's condition. Fausette v. Grim, supra; Langford v. Jones, 18 Or. 307, 322, 22 Pac. 1064; 21 R. C. L. 388; Staloch v. Holm, 100 Minn. 276, 111 N. W. 264, 9 L. R. A. (N. S.) 712. And it is also true, if there were conditions existing such as to raise a question whether an operation was advisable or proper, then the question of whether the defendant's decision to operate was negligent or not should be gathered from the opinions and testimony of those who have special knowledge and are qualified to speak on such matters. Moore v. St. Louis Transit Co., 226 Mo. 689, 705, 126 S. W. 1013; Farrell v. Haze, 157 Mich. 374, 380-392, 122 N. W. 197; McGraw v. Kerr, 23 Colo. App. 163, 128 Pac. 870, 873; Adolay v. Miller, 60 Ind. App. 656, 111 N. E. 313, 315; Getchell v. Hill, 21 Minn. 464, 465; Pettigrew v. Lewis, 46 Kan. 78, 81, 26 Pac. 458; Ball v. Skinner, 134 Iowa, 298, 308, 111 N. W. 1022; Spaulding v. Bliss, 83 Mich. 311, 47 N. W. 210; Ewing v. Goode (C. C.) 78 Fed. 442.

But in the case at bar there is a dispute over the following matters: Whether there were any such existing, untoward, and abnormal conditions; whether the defendant made as full and as exhaustive an examination as he should have done before deciding upon what should be done; whether he did not carelessly assume that plaintiff was not pregnant merely because he had removed her ovaries, when he knew he had left a small portion of one of them, and knew, or should have known, as a medical man, that it was not impossible for her to become pregnant.

According to plaintiff's testimony, the doctor, upon placing his hand upon her abdomen, at once announced that she was pregnant, but when he learned he had removed her ovaries he, with no examination other than pressing upon her abdomen, said she had a tumor, and advised an operation. She further says that he could move her womb freely, although not so far as ordinarily, on account of its size; that all he did was to press his hands upon her abdomen; that her symptoms were the same as in the case of her other pregnancies, and that she told him so; that she had no pains, except that she had a pain in the pit of her stomach when she had the "flu" in January; that her nerves did not bother her; that she told him repeatedly she thought she was pregnant, and says she would not have worried about the growth in her womb had not the doctor told her it could not be pregnancy; that she had nothing in the way of adhesions tying her womb down, but had perfect freedom of movement, and the evidence was that a few days before going to the hospital she assisted in papering her house, including the ceiling, and experienced no difficulty in getting her arms up to do so; that the doctor told her it was a tumor, and not pregnancy; that he said nothing about adhesions or about making a merely exploratory operation to learn what was the matter.

Dr. Clark, her family physician, gave testimony tending to show that when he examined her before the first operation he found her ovaries free in the abdomen, not enlarged and not tender; that the child, born July 19, was a fully developed nine-months child; consequently she was 7 months along when the defendant finally examined and operated on her. The substance of his testimony is that, while adhesions could cause an abortion or premature birth, it would all depend on the extent thereof, and that adhesions to such an extent as to cause that would prevent the fetus from growing, and a woman "certainly would not" be able thus to carry a child to a period of seven months; that although adhesions arise from infected conditions and follow an operation, the tendency is for nature to eliminate them, and frequently they disappear in a short time. In other words, there is sufficient evidence in the record to make it an issue of fact as to whether plaintiff's pregnancy was anything other than a normal pregnancy, unaccompanied by adhesions which bound the womb down to such an extent as to prevent pregnancy from being discovered had a careful investigation been made, or to cause plaintiff to be in such a condition as to reasonably give rise to the thought that the second operation should be had. The mere fact that plaintiff became pregnant notwithstanding she had only a small portion of one ovary left does not, of itself, show that her pregnancy was abnormal, i. e., that abnormal conditions existed with that pregnancy, for the expert evidence is that a woman with only a small piece of ovary may become pregnant, and if a small piece of the ovary is left it will function, and if it does, and the same is impregnated with the male germ, pregnancy will result. Knowledge of this fact would not justify a physician in, at once, and without careful examination, jumping to the premature conclusion that plaintiff had a tumor.

There was evidence, even from the expert witnesses offered by defendant, that if at the time plaintiff was operated on the second time she had perfect freedom of movement in every way and her symptoms and condition were no different from those of her other pregnancies, and she told the doctor she had been pregnant and had borne children twice before and thought she was pregnant again and the doctor, only two months before the birth of a fully developed full-period child, merely pressed his hand across her abdomen and decided she had a tumor, then such was not a sufficient and careful examination. There was also evidence that "ballottement" was one of the tests proper to be used, and that the beating of the fetal heart could be determined by the use of the stethoscope. The defendant says he did not use the stethoscope, and, if plaintiff's evidence is true, he did not use the ballottement. There was also expert evidence to the effect that if at seven months the uterus and its contents could be manipulated freely from side to side and there was no pain, no catching or holding on the inside and no hindrance to the freedom of movement the diagnosis would be that there were no adhesions—at least, no adhesions dense enough to interfere with pregnancy or childbirth and a woman could go through the latter all right.

[6] So that the question of whether there was evidence of negligence on the part of defendant comes down at last to whether the facts and conditions were as claimed by plaintiff, or whether they were as asserted to be by defendant. If they were as plaintiff says they were, then there was evidence from which the jury could find that proper care and precaution was not taken. After a careful study of the record, we have come to the conclusion that, aside from the husband's testimony, plaintiff had sufficient evidence to go to the jury, though this conclusion has been reached not without considerable diffi-

culty, at least in the mind and on the part of the author hereof. There are some things which may appear to cast doubt upon the extent to which plaintiff goes in asserting her facts, but these are matters for the jury to pass upon in deciding the question of her credibility; they do not destroy her testimony altogether.

Neither are we able to say that there is no evidence whatever tending to show that plaintiff has suffered no ill effects from the second operation. Of course she did suffer pain and worry as a result of it. Whether her present weak and nervous condition is a result thereof or not we cannot say. Dr. Clark, however, undoubtedly says that it, in connection with the worry produced thereby, could produce such a condition. We note that the record discloses that the plaintiff had the "flu" in January preceding the second operation. Just how much of her present condition may be traceable to that we do not know, nor is any mention of that fact made by either side. No doubt the second operation, if unnecessary, did not add to her recuperative powers. We cannot say, however, that plaintiff has suffered no ill effects from the second operation, and the contention that her present weak and nervous condition is not the result of the operation would, if established, go only to the extent of her recovery; it would not necessarily entitle defendant to have his demurrer to the evidence sustained.

A number of criticisms are made of the instructions which need not be noticed. Those submitting the question whether defendant was negligent in diagnosing plaintiff's condition "and advising and performing the surgical operation" of May 20 could perhaps have been more accurately drawn if they had been so worded as to clearly set forth that the negligence as to the last-named matter was in deciding to perform the operation, or in undertaking it at all, rather than in the performing of it, i. e., the manner of its performance. However, there was no claim, and no evidence, of any negligence in the manner of its performance, and hence it is not reasonable to suppose that the jury could have been misled by the expression used. But it would doubtless be better to avoid any possible ambiguity in this regard.

The judgment is reversed and the cause remanded for a new trial.

All concur.

GULLY v. GULLY. (No. 2941.)

(Supreme Court of Texas. May 18, 1921.)

Divorce ⟺324—Father's liability to maintain child not lost by divorce decree awarding custody to mother without provision for support.

A father, owning an adequate estate, could be required to pay the value of necessaries for his minor children when furnished by the mother, from her own adequate estate, after divorce decree awarding the custody of the children to the mother and failing to provide for their maintenance; the father not being relieved of his primary duty to support the children by a divorce decree which is either silent as to their custody and maintenance or awards their custody to the mother.

Error to Court of Civil Appeals of Sixth Supreme Judicial District.

Action by M. E. Gully against T. R. Gully. From a judgment for plaintiff, the defendant appealed to the Court of Civil Appeals, which reformed and affirmed the judgment (184 S. W. 555), and the defendant brings error. Judgment of the Court of Civil Appeals affirmed.

H. N. Nelson, of Carthage, for plaintiff in error.

Young & Young, of Marshall, for defendant in error.

GREENWOOD, J. By decree of the district court of Panola county, entered in 1912, defendant in error, Mrs. M. E. Gully, was granted a divorce from plaintiff in error, T. R. Gully, and the custody of their seven minor children. The decree ordered partition of the community property, including 968.90 acres of land, a sawmill, stocks of lumber and merchandise, 50 bales of cotton, etc., and set aside the homestead of 6.37 acres of land and certain appurtenant personalty for the use of defendant in error and her minor children so long as any one of them was under age or was an unmarried daughter. The decree adjudged 567½ acres of land, to plaintiff in error as his separate estate. By appropriate recital the court reserved jurisdiction to make provision for the maintenance of the minors.

In 1913 the court rendered a final judgment partitioning the community property, in accordance with its previous decree, and at the same time the court fixed $100 per month as an allowance for the support, maintenance, and education of the minors, and adjudged that same be paid one-half by defendant in error and one-half by plaintiff in error.

Upon the refusal of plaintiff in error to pay one-half of the minors' monthly allowance, defendant in error applied for and obtained an order of the court directing the sale, in satisfaction of same, of a portion of the community property which had been partitioned to plaintiff in error. On appeal the order was reversed; the provision for the monthly allowances to the minors being held inoperative and void. Gully v. Gully, (Civ. App.) 173 S. W. 1178.

Afterwards this suit was brought to recover of plaintiff in error the amount expended by defendant in error subsequent to the decree of divorce for necessaries for the children. In the trial court defendant in error recovered a judgment for such expenditures as were found to have been reasonable and necessary for the support of the children. On appeal the Texarkana Court of Civil Appeals reversed this judgment and rendered judgment for defendant in error for one-half the amount recovered in the court below, one of the justices dissenting on the ground that defendant in error ought to have been denied any recovery whatever. Gully v. Gully, 184 S. W. 555.

The judges of the Court of Civil Appeals concurred in the view that the duty rested primarily on the father, during the marriage, to support the minor children. A majority of the judges concluded that, when the marriage relation was terminated by the decree of divorce with an award of the custody of the children to the mother, then, the duty to provide necessary support for the children rested equally on the father and mother. The minority judge considered that the duty to support followed the custody and passed to the mother alone.

The assignments here urge that the judgments in the divorce suit dissolving the bonds of matrimony between the husband and wife, awarding the custody of the minor children to the wife, and settling the property rights of the husband and wife, had the legal effect to absolve the husband from any obligation to support the children, or to make his obligation secondary to that of the wife, or had the legal effect to at least absolve the husband from any obligation for the children's support which could be enforced otherwise than by further proceedings in the divorce suit.

The judgments in the divorce suit, together with the adjudication of the invalidity of the order for stipulated monthly allowances, had the same effect, in so far as this controversy is concerned, as if the court had simply decreed the divorce and awarded the custody of the children to the mother. Apart from the provision of a homestead and its furnishings, for which no compensation was sought in this action, there is nothing in the judgments not in every judgment of divorce awarding the children to the mother's custody, which could impair the obligation of either parent to support the children, except the order for monthly allowances, which was adjudged void.

The truly important question to be decided is whether the father, owning an adequate estate, can be required to pay the value of necessaries for his minor children, when furnished by the mother, from her own adequate estate, after the mother has been divorced from the father, and after the custody of the children has been adjudged to the wife; the decree of divorce failing to provide for the children's maintenance.

The decisions in Texas uniformly recognize and declare that both parents are charged with a natural and legal duty to support their children during minority.

Perhaps the parent's natural duty has no-,where been better stated than by the court, speaking through Judge Brown, in State v. Deaton, 93 Tex. 247, 54 S. W. 903, when he said:

"God, in his wisdom, has placed upon the father and mother the obligation to nurture, educate, protect, and guide their offspring, and has qualified them to discharge these important duties by writing in their hearts sentiments of affection and establishing between them and their children ties which cannot exist between the children and any other persons."

A succinct statement of the parent's legal duty was made in Judge Stayton's opinion in G. H. & H. Ry. Co. v. Moore, 59 Tex. 68, 46 Am. Rep. 265, as follows:

"The parent is under a legal obligation to educate and maintain the child, and it has no legal claim upon others to perform that duty."

Our statutes define a "neglected child" as one who has not proper parental care, and make it a misdemeanor for "any parent" to willfully or without justification neglect or refuse to provide for the support and maintenance of his or her child under the age of 16 years in destitute or necessitous circumstances. Article 2184, R. S.; chapter 101, Acts 33d Leg. (Vernon's Ann. Pen. Code 1916, art. 640a); White's Penal Code, p. 1828.

The court is enjoined, in decreeing a divorce, to respect the rights of the children, in disposing of the estates of both parents. Article 4634, R. S. In order to provide revenues for the maintenance of the children, the interest of each parent in the community property and the separate property of both parents may be utilized, subject alone to the statutory limitation that neither parent be divested of title to realty. Fitts v. Fitts, 14 Tex. 454; Rice v. Rice, 21 Tex. 58. Thus the law regards the right of minor children to maintenance as paramount to the rights of the parents to the use of any and all property belonging to them.

A duty could not be more plainly defined as legal than by providing means for its enforcement in both civil and criminal courts; and there can be no question about it resting on those against whom it is expressly made enforceable.

Though both parents are under the duty, legal as well as moral, to support and educate their children during minority, the duty rests primarily in this state, without doubt, upon the father.

The court said in Magee v. White, 23 Tex. 192:

"We are of opinion that the law imposes upon the husband the obligation to support his wife and children. If he have separate property, and there is no common property, it cannot for a moment be pretended that his separate property cannot be charged for necessaries for the support of his family. The law recognizes him as the head of his family. It declares that he shall support his children, because every man is under obligation to provide for those descended from his loins. Blackstone."

The doctrine of Magee v. White is reaffirmed as settled law in Hutchinson v. Underwood, 27 Tex. 256.

The father's primary obligation was the necessary foundation of the court's declaration by Chief Justice Hemphill in Rice v. Rice, 21 Tex. 68, that where on divorce the minors were intrusted to the mother, the funds for their support must be furnished by the father, but, where the minors were intrusted to the father, he was bound for their maintenance.

On no other theory than that the legal duty of the father is both primary and continuing can be upheld the settled doctrine in this state that a recovery of damages by a child on account of the death of his father may be sustained for the entire cost of his support until he becomes of age, though the child is in the custody of his mother, by whom he is supported, and though he has no expectation of any voluntary contribution to his support from the father. I. & G. N. R. R. Co. v. Culpepper, 19 Tex. Civ. App. 182, 46 S. W. 923, 925; Taylor v. S. A. Gas & Elec. Co. (Civ. App.) 93 S. W. 675; G., C. & S. F. Ry. Co. v. Delaney, 22 Tex. Civ. App. 427, 55 S. W. 538; G., C. & S. F. Ry. Co. v. Anderson (Civ. App.) 126 S. W. 930; S. A. & A. P. v. Boyed, 201 S. W. 220.

We do not think that a decree of divorce which is either silent as to the children's custody and maintenance or which awards their custody to the mother relieves the father of his primary duty to support the children.

The duty to support a minor child is imposed primarily on the father in the interest of the child. The chief concern of the state is the child's welfare. It is best for the child to impose the duty in the first instance on the father, because human experience demonstrates that he is best able to perform the duty. It is as much to the advantage of the child that the primary obligation of the father continue after as before the divorce. Being blameless with respect to the fault occasioning the divorce, the child certainly ought not to be thereby deprived of a right of real and continuing value.

We do not feel warranted in adopting the conclusion on which Judge Levy's majority opinion largely rests, that there was no reason save the disability of the mother during coverture for making her duty to support the children secondary at common law. Other weighty reasons may be found in natural differences between the sexes and in the necessity to equalize parental burdens. Who can say that the average mother, inspired by sacrificial love, contributes less to the good of the family than the father, though he performs every paternal duty, including the support of the family, during the marriage, as well as the support of the children, during minority, irrespective of divorce?

The mother's obligation ought not to be made more onerous because the custody of the child is confided to her in promotion of his highest interest; and in no other mode than is plainly indicated by explicit statutes ought important parental duties be subject to change.

The cases upholding the doctrine that a decree of divorce awarding the custody of a child to the mother shifts the duty to maintain the child from the father to the mother appear to be mainly grounded on the view that the right to the custody and services of the child and the duty to support and educate are reciprocal, so that discharge of the duty necessarily follows deprivation of the right.

In order for this view to be sound, the father's duty to the child must rest on advantage to the father, which is the opposite of what we deem the true conception. The real design of the duty is to develop the child as perfectly as possible, physically, mentally, and spiritually. It is to attain the same result that the father is deprived of the child's custody. In the eye of the law the attainment of this result justifies whatever deprivation the father must suffer.

The father's duty is all the more imperative where the child, on account of youth or affliction, renders no services. That is conclusive against the duty being grounded on material benefit to the parent instead of on the need of the child.

In Dunbar v. Dunbar, 190 U. S. 351, 23 Sup. Ct. 757, 47 L. Ed. 1084, it was held

that the father's common-law obligation to support his children continued throughout their minority and was enforceable despite the father's discharge in bankruptcy, subsequent to a decree of divorce awarding the custody of the children to the mother.

Most of the reported cases, especially the later cases, sustain the conclusion that a decree of divorce ,which awards the custody of the child to the mother and makes no provision for the child's support does not terminate the father's duty of maintenance. Evans v. Evans, 125 Tenn. 112, 140 S. W. 745, Ann. Cas. 1913C, 295, and note page 296; note Ann. Cas. 1915D, 813; 19 C. J. 354.

The case of Hall v. Fields, 81 Tex. 558, 17 S. W. 82, presented the question as to whether a constituent of his family survived the father so that his residence homestead was exempt from administration for the payment of the debts against his estate, where the father resided alone on the homestead after being divorced by a decree awarding the custody of his minor children to their mother, who thereafter held the children in her actual custody. It was determined that the minors were nevertheless constituents of the father's family, the court saying that the award of the custody of the children to the mother, made no difference in their right to the exemption, for the reason that—

"Their father was still legally bound for their support, and it would be a double misfortune to them to be deprived, on account of the unhappy termination of the marriage of their father and mother, both of their right to the society and protection of the father. * * * They have no home; they are the minor children of a father, the head of a family, who has died leaving a homestead."

It was determined in Speer v. Sykes, 102 Tex. 451, 119 S. W. 86, 152 Am. St. Rep. 896, that the residence of the father continued exempt from execution after the rendition of a decree of divorce, with award of his children to the custody of the wife. In Judge Brown's opinion it is said:

"The fact that the court awarded the custody of the minor children to the wife did not deprive Sykes of his paternal interest in them, nor did it discharge him from his legal and moral obligation to care for and support them. They were still his offspring and a part of his family."

These cases are conclusive that the obligation of the father is not discharged by the loss of the custody of his children. As the head of the family he is primarily responsible for the children's support prior to divorce. Continuing the head of a family, of which the children remain a part, subsequent to the divorce and the loss of their custody, his primary liability continues.

In determining the duty of the husband to supply necessaries to his children, before or after divorce, it is to be borne in mind that his duty corresponds to his financial ability, having due regard to all his lawful obligations, which may include those assumed to another wife and to other children, and in no event is he liable for food, clothing, attention, or education other than such as is suitable to his and their circumstances in life. Moreover, since we treat his duty as a continuing primary one, the father should not be held liable when he has actually supplied his children with their reasonable necessaries. In a suit to recover the value of necessaries furnished minor children the burden to prove that he has supplied the children with necessaries is on the father. Parsons v. Keyes, 43 Tex. 559.

Again, circumstances may exist under which the father would be entitled to be relieved of his primary obligation, just as the court has already determined that the mother may be entitled to be relieved of her obligation, on adequate equitable considerations. Freybe v. Tiernan, 76 Tex. 290, 13 S. W. 370; Rivers v. Rivers (Civ. App.) 133 S. W. 526.

In pronouncing a decree of divorce, it is within the power of the court to make suitable provision for the maintenance of the children by means of the property of both parents. Where the court has provided for the children's support and education in the decree of divorce, such provision excludes liability therefor otherwise than as ordered by the court rendering the decree.

It is now settled that the power of the court granting a divorce to make suitable provision for the children out of the revenue of the property of the parents is a continuing one, so that complete justice may be done in the light of the varying conditions of the children and of the parents, and the court's continuing authority may be invoked to safeguard the rights of the parents as well as those of the children. Bemus v. Bemus, 63 Tex. Civ. App. 148, 133 S. W. 503; Plummer v. Plummer (Civ. App.) 154 S. W. 598.

Here the court decreeing the divorce did not undertake to provide for the support of the children save in a manner decreed to be void. As the judgment of the Court of Civil Appeals does no more than to partially enforce an obligation resting primarily on plaintiff in error and from which he had not been absolved, and as plaintiff in error alone complains of that judgment, it follows that the judgment should be affirmed; and it is so ordered.

MISSOURI, K. & T. RY. CO. OF TEXAS v. PLANO MILLING CO. et al.

(No. 238–3425.)

(Commission of Appeals of Texas, Section A. June 1, 1921.)

1. **Commerce ☞33—Shipment held interstate.**

Where grain was shipped from Missouri to a point in Texas, and the Texas purchaser, on paying the draft with bill of lading attached, sold the grain to a purchaser in another part of Texas, and defendant railroad company before arrival of the shipment issued a bill of lading for transportation to the new destination, that shipment was interstate.

2. **Carriers ☞177(4)—Connecting carrier issuing bill of lading for shipment held liable for damages, though it did not have possession.**

A car of grain shipped from St. Joseph, Mo., to Sherman, Tex., was originally routed over the defendant connecting carrier's line, but after bill of lading was issued the routing was changed on request of the shipper. The bill of lading with draft attached was forwarded to the purchaser, who paid the draft, and, receiving the bill of lading, presented the same to the agent of the defendant with request that the car be forwarded to another point in Texas. The agent accepted it and issued a new bill of lading, though the car had not arrived. A month after the car arrived in Sherman, and was forwarded by defendant to the new destination, where the grain was found to be in a damaged condition and sold at a loss. *Held,* that defendant was liable notwithstanding the car was transported to Sherman by an agency other than defendant due to the change in the routing; for on notice to defendant that the car was in Sherman it was its duty to transport the same in a reasonable time.

Appeal from Court of Civil Appeals of Sixth Supreme Judicial District.

Suit by the Plano Milling Company against the Missouri, Kansas & Texas Railway Company of Texas and others, in which J. G. Puterbaugh intervened. From a judgment for the intervener, the named defendant and another appealed to the Court of Civil Appeals, where judgment was affirmed in part and in part reversed and rendered (214 S. W. 833), and the named defendant brings error. Judgment of Court of Civil Appeals affirmed.

Dinsmore, McMahan & Dinsmore, of Greenville, and Wallace Hughston, of McKinney, for appellant.

J. E. Whitehead, of Oklahoma City, Okl., and G. P. Brown, of McKinney, for appellee Plano Milling Co.

Lee & Lomax, of Fort Worth, and Head, Dillard, Smith, Maxey & Head, of Sherman, for appellee Houston & T. C. Ry. Co.

Slay, Simon & Smith, of Fort Worth, for appellee Walker Grain Co.

SPENCER, J. On February 24, 1912, the Burke Grain Company delivered to the Chicago & Great Western Railway Company at St. Joseph, Mo., a car of corn which the grain company had sold to the Walker Grain Company of Fort Worth. The railway company issued a bill of lading showing the shipment to have been consigned to the order of the Burke Grain Company notify the Walker Grain Company. The car was routed, according to the bill of lading, over the line of the initial carrier to Kansas City, and thence over the Missouri, Kansas & Texas Railway to Sherman, Tex. At the request of the shipper, made February 27th, the railway company changed the routing, and the shipment moved in accordance with this change from Kansas City to Sherman over the lines of the Atchison, Topeka & Sante Fé Railway, the Gulf, Colorado & Sante Fé Railway, and the Houston & Texas Central Railway Company. The shipper attached the bill of lading, which did not show the changed routing, to a draft drawn on the Walker Grain Company. Upon presentation Walker Grain Company paid the draft and thus procured the bill of lading.

On February 29, the Walker Grain Company, presented this bill of lading to the agent of the Missouri, Kansas & Texas Railway Company of Texas, with request that the car be forwarded to Plano, Tex. In compliance with the request, the agent accepted the bill of lading and issued in lieu thereof its bill of lading calling for a delivery of the car at Plano, Tex., to the order of Walker Grain Company, notify Plano Milling Company, Plano, Tex.

The Walker Grain Company attached the latter bill of lading to a draft on the Plano Milling Company for the purchase price of the car, which draft was paid upon presentation.

Immediately upon arrival of the car at Sherman March 12, 1912, the agent of the Houston & Texas Central Railway Company notified the Walker Grain Company of its arrival, and the grain company in turn notified plaintiff in error and requested it to have the car forwarded to Plano.

As soon as the agent at Sherman learned that the car was intended for delivery at Plano, it was forwarded there. The record does not reveal the exact delay at Sherman, but it must have been considerable, as demurrage had accrued, and the car did not reach Plano until April 13, 1912. Upon inspection at Plano, the car was found to be in a greatly damaged condition and was sold at a loss.

This suit was instituted by the Plano Milling Company against the Atchison, Topeka & Santa Fé Railway Company, the Gulf, Colorado & Santa Fé Railway Company, the Missouri, Kansas & Texas Railway Company, the Houston & Texas Central Railway Company, the Missouri, Kansas & Texas Railway Company of Texas, the Chicago & Great Western Railway Company, and the Walker Grain Company to recover the loss sustained. J. G. Puterbaugh, having purchased of the milling company the claim upon which the suit is based, intervened to assert his right. Judgment of dismissal was rendered as to the grain company and the first four mentioned railway companies, and no appeal was taken from this judgment.

Judgment was also rendered that the milling company take nothing by its suit, and that intervener recover against the Chicago & Great Western Railway Company and the Missouri, Kansas & Texas Railway Company of Texas in the sum of $1,292.35. Upon appeal the Court of Civil Appeals reversed and rendered the judgment as to the Chicago & Great Western Railway Company, and affirmed the judgment as to the Missouri, Kansas & Texas Railway Company of Texas, 214 S. W. 833. The Missouri, Kansas & Texas Railway Company of Texas alone appeals.

The defendant in error predicates its cause of action against plaintiff in error upon the theory that it in good faith purchased the order bill of lading issued by plaintiff in error, paying value therefor and relying upon the recitals contained therein that the car was in its possession and under its control.

[1] It is admitted by the parties to this appeal that the shipment was interstate. That the shipment was interstate is in accord with the holding by the Supreme Court of the United States in A., T. & S. F. Ry. Co. v. Harold, 241 U. S. 371, 36 Sup. Ct. 665, 60 L. Ed. 1050.

[2] Plaintiff in error insists that, as the court found that it had never received the car in question, it was not bound by the recitals in the bill of lading as to the receipt of the goods, but that it could show, even as against an innocent holder of the bill of lading, that it did not in fact receive the goods, and that therefore there was no valid contract to carry or deliver them. In support of this contention it relies upon Friedlander v. Texas & P. Ry. Co., 130 U. S. 424, 9 Sup. Ct. 570, 32 L. Ed. 994, and The Carlos F. Roses, 177 U. S. 665, 20 Sup. Ct. 803, 44 L. Ed. 933 which hold in effect that the agent of a carrier has no authority to sign a bill of lading for goods not actually received, and if he does so his act does not bind the carrier, even in favor of an innocent purchaser of the bill for value.

The rule announced in those cases is inapplicable here. In all of those cases the goods called for by the bills of lading were never at any time in the actual or constructive possession of the carriers sought to be charged; while in this case the carrier had constructive, if not actual, possession of the goods. Plaintiff in error did not deny the authority of its agent to issue the bill of lading in lieu of the original one. Had the shipment not been diverted, it would have reached the Texas state line, where the Missouri, Kansas & Texas Railway Company connects with the Missouri, Kansas & Texas Railway Company of Texas, over the Missouri, Kansas & Texas Railway Company, and thereafter carried by the Missouri, Kansas & Texas Railway Company of Texas to Sherman, and had it thereafter moved, as contemplated by the bill of lading issued by plaintiff in error, the latter would have delivered it to the Houston & Texas Central Railway Company for transportation to Plano.

The possession of the original bill of lading by plaintiff in error and the execution of the bill of lading by it imposed the duty upon it to demand and receive the car from the Missouri, Kansas & Texas Railway Company, and upon receipt thereof to deliver the same to the Houston & Texas Central Railway Company to be transported to Plano. The terms of the bill of lading bound plaintiff in error to transport the car from Sherman to Plano. It is not to be excused from a performance of its duty to deliver the car at Plano merely because the car was found in possession of the Houston & Texas Central Railway Company—the agency selected by it to complete the haul. Its duty to have the haul completed in accordance with the contract arose simultaneously with the notice to it that the car was in possession of the Houston & Texas Central Railway Company. The bill of lading became operative from the date of such notice. The situation here is somewhat analogous to that where a bill of lading is prematurely issued and the goods called for by the bill are subsequently delivered. In such cases the rule, as announced by the Supreme Court of the United States, is:

"It is not only the utterance of common honesty, but the declaration of judicial tribunals, that a delivery of goods to a ship corresponding in substance with a bill of lading given previously, if intended and received to meet the bill of lading, makes the bill operative from the time of such delivery. At that instant it becomes evidence of the ownership of the goods. Thus in Rowley v. Bigelow, 12 Pick. 307, it is said, a bill of lading operates by way of estoppel against the master, and also against the shipper and indorser. 'The bill acknowledges the goods to be on board before the bill of lading is signed. But if, through inadvertence or otherwise, the bill of lading is signed before the goods are on board, upon the faith and assurance that they are at hand, as if they are received on the wharf ready to be shipped, or in the shipper's own warehouse, * * * and afterwards they are placed on board, as and for the goods embraced in the bill of lading, as against the shipper and master the bill will operate on those goods by way of relation and estoppel.'" The Idaho, 93 U. S. 575, 23 L. Ed. 978.

Plaintiff in error, having declined, upon being notified that the shipment was in the hands of the Houston & Texas Central Railway Company, to take any steps toward having the haul completed, thereby breached its contract, and is therefore liable for the damages suffered as a result of the breach.

We recommend, therefore, that the judgment of the Court of Civil Appeals be affirmed.

PHILLIPS, C. J. The judgment recommended in the report of the Commission of Appeals is adopted, and will be entered as the judgment of the Supreme Court.

———

ELDER, DEMPSTER & CO., Limited, v. WELD-NEVILLE COTTON CO., Inc.*
(No. 186-3230.)

(Commission of Appeals of Texas, Section B. June 1, 1921.)

1. **Trial ⟵404(1)—Findings should be given construction which supports judgment.**

The entire findings of the trial court should be read together and construed as a whole, and when they permit of more than one reasonable construction, that construction should be adopted which will support the judgment.

2. **Shipping ⟵108—Finding against general custom fixing density of cotton held not to conflict with finding of density after proper baling.**

In an action for breach of a contract for the shipment of high density Webb cotton, a finding by the trial court that there was no general custom fixing the weight of a bale of such cotton is not in conflict with a finding that a bale of cotton properly compressed by the Webb process would weigh more than the average weight of the bales furnished for shipment, and that plaintiff thereby breached his contract.

3. **Shipping ⟵108—Contract for shipment of compressed cotton implies it is to be compressed in workmanlike manner.**

A contract for the shipment of a specified number of bales of high density Webb cotton implies that the cotton is to be compressed by the Webb process in a workmanlike manner.

4. **Pleading ⟵433(3)—Pleadings not specially excepted to held to support judgment on finding cotton was not compressed in workmanlike manner.**

A petition for damages for breach of contract to ship a specified number of bales of high density Webb compressed cotton, which disclosed that the theory of recovery was that the specified cotton should have a higher density than that furnished for shipment, so that the cotton shipped occupied more space than the same weight of properly compressed cotton should have, is sufficient, in the absence of a special exception, to support recovery on the finding that the cotton was not compressed in a workmanlike manner, as impliedly required by the contract.

5. Shipping ⟺108 — Provisions relating to standard cotton held applicable to high density cotton, except as to weight.

Where a contract for the shipment of high density cotton was upon a printed form for the shipment of standard cotton, a provision on the back of the form covering the payment of additional freight if the cotton did not conform to the weight stated for standard cotton is applicable to the shipment of high density cotton, except as to the provision stating the weight.

6. Shipping ⟺108—Proof additional cargo was available unnecessary to recovery for shipment of cotton not properly compressed.

In an action for breach of a contract for shipment of high density Webb compressed cotton. where the breach alleged was the shipment of cotton less dense than the minimum density of the specified cotton properly compressed, so that the cargo occupied more space than was paid for at the rate per 100 pounds established for cotton of that grade properly compressed, the shipowner can recover for the additional space occupied without proof that other cargo was available for the ship, which would be necessary to recover for a shortage in the quantity of cargo furnished.

Error to Court of Civil Appeals of First Supreme Judicial District.

Action by Elder Dempster & Co., Limited, against Weld-Neville Cotton Company, Incorporated, to recover damages for breach of two contracts. A judgment for plaintiff was reversed by the Court of Civil Appeals, and the cause remanded for retrial (204 S. W. 678), and plaintiff brings error. Judgment of the Court of Civil Appeals reversed, and that of the district court affirmed.

Edward F. Harris and Harris & Harris, all of Galveston, for plaintiff in error.

C. C. McRae and Baker, Botts, Parker & Garwood, all of Houston, for defendant in error.

McCLENDON, P. J. Elder Dempster Steamship Company, Limited, brought this action against Weld-Neville Cotton Company, Incorporated, to recover damages for alleged breach of two contracts by which the latter agreed to deliver to the former two 1,000-bale consignments of "high density Webb" compressed cotton, to be transported by the steamship company from Galveston, Tex., to Havre, France, at the rate of $2.95 per hundred weight. The alleged breach of contract consisted in the contention that the cotton actually delivered had a less minimum density than it should have had, in order to constitute compliance with the contract; whereby it occupied, to the extent of its lack of density below the required minimum, proportionately greater volume of ship space. The case was tried before the trial judge,

without a jury, and judgment was rendered for plaintiff, based upon the findings that the actual density of the cotton delivered was 31 pounds per cubic foot, when it should have had a minimum density of 32 pounds per cubic foot; recovery being awarded for the additional ship space at the rate arrived at by applying the contract rate per hundred weight to the required minimum density. The judgment was reversed by the Court of Civil Appeals (204 S. W. 678), and the cause remanded for retrial.

The question of leading importance, and the one upon which the reversal was predicated, is whether the trial court's findings of fact will support recovery. So much of those findings as bear upon this issue are as follows:

"4. There was in January, 1916, no trade usage at Houston, Galveston, or Texas City fixing a specific number of pounds to the cubic foot as the minimum 'density' of the cotton contracted for. The trade usages, as far as affect the controversy at the three points were the same. Webb high density cotton presses were only established at Houston and Galveston in 1913–14. The shipment of such cotton was increased largely since the beginning of the European war, on account of the demand for tonnage and the higher prices for cubic space on ocean carrying vessels.

"5· The ship agents had endeavored to fix a minimum density of 34 pounds, but did not live up to it themselves, and the attempt even was not generally known to cotton exporters, such as the defendant in this case, who had neither knowledge or notice of it. Exporters generally at the time regarded any cotton turned out by Webb high density presses in shipshape, or in workmanlike manner, as compliance with contracts such as sued on, and knew of no different contention.

"6· Ship agents, more or less generally, stipulated in contracts such as those sued on the minimum density required in the particular transaction, varying from 32 to 34 pounds. Some would have accepted cotton as low as 30 pounds density, as in compliance with such contracts.

"7· My conclusion is that cotton turned out by a Webb high density press in a workmanlike manner should have had a minimum average density of 32 pounds to the cubic foot.

"8· The cotton furnished by the defendant had gone through a Webb high density press, but it had not all been compressed in a workmanlike manner. Its average density was 31 pounds.

"Law.

"In the absence of a usage of trade as to what constituted Webb high density cotton at the time of the making of these contracts, the true measure of plaintiff's right and ·of the defendant's liability is for cotton turned out by Webb high density presses in a workmanlike manner."

As found by the Court of Civil Appeals, these findings are amply supported by pleading and proof. The conclusion reached by 'that court, as given in the syllabus of the published opinion, follows:

"Where steamship owners sued cotton shippers because cotton shipped was not 'Webb high density cotton' as agreed, and took up too much room, they could not recover when court found that cotton turned out by Webb high density presses in workmanlike manner, without reference to density, was generally regarded as compliance with contract calling for such cotton, notwithstanding further finding that such cotton should have specified average minimum density."

[1] It is a general rule that applies to findings of the trial court that the entire findings should be read together and construed as a whole, and that when they permit of more than one reasonable construction that construction should be adopted which will support the action of the court as expressed in the judgment rendered upon the findings.

[2] Applying this rule, we see no irreconcilable conflict in the several findings. The seventh and eighth findings are clearly to the effect that the cotton contracted for, "high density Webb," when compressed in a workmanlike manner, should have a minimum density of 32 pounds per cubic foot; that the cotton delivered was not compressed in a workmanlike manner, and had a density of only 31 pounds per cubic foot. These findings we think sufficient to support the alleged breach of contract.

[3] In the absence of any pertinent stipulation in the contract, the law would imply that cotton compressed in a workmanlike manner was intended. A failure to furnish cotton so compressed would constitute a breach of the contract. The fact that there was no generally recognized trade custom requiring any specified minimum density for "high density Webb" cotton does not militate against this conclusion. The contract rate was based upon weight, and the evidence showed that ocean freight rates are based upon volume of ship space. Under these circumstances the contract warranted the implication, even in the absence of such custom, that the cotton should have the minimum density of "high density Webb" cotton compressed in a workmanlike manner.

[4] It is urged that this theory of recovery is not supported by the pleadings, in that the latter—

"did not apprise appellant of a claim to be made that the cotton was not pressed in a workmanlike manner; but of a claim that, regardless of care in pressing it, the cotton should have been of a density of not less than 34 pounds to the cubic foot; and, as it was upon the former ground, and not the latter, that the judgment was rendered, it is erroneous."

. The pleadings clearly show that the entire theory of recovery was that "High Density Webb" cotton should have a minimum density greater than that of the cotton delivered. In the absence of a special exception calling for more specific allegation, it was not requisite that the pleadings should show by what particular defect, or from what particular cause, the cotton fell short in the density which the term used in the contract was alleged to imply.

Error is also assigned upon rendering judgment for plaintiff upon the ground that no damage for breach of contract in the particular alleged was proved. This assignment is predicated upon the proposition that the only proper measure of damages was the amount of freight plaintiff would have received by filling the excess space occupied by the cotton, and since there was no showing that plaintiff, but for the breach of contract, could have filled this space with other cargo, no damage was shown.

[5] Plaintiff contends, on the other hand, that, by express stipulation, the contracts provide for the measure of recovery applied by the trial court. The contracts were identical, and were upon regular printed forms for shipment of "standard" compressed cotton. On the face of the contracts, the word "standard" was erased, and "high density Webb" substituted. Upon the back of the contracts was the following stipulation:

"Every compressed bale shall contain a minimum density of 22½ pounds per cubic foot when delivered at vessel's loading berth, and any bale containing less density shall be rejected; but the ship agent may, at his option, accept any bales containing less density than 22½ pounds, in which event the ship agent shall (provided such can be done without delay to the steamer and the required minimum density be secured) compress for shipper's account, at a cost not exceeding the price any available compress in Texas City will compress the bale for, or accept it in the condition tendered, *charging the shipper extra freight proportionately for the additional space occupied*, but not less than fifty cents (50¢) per bale. The certificate of the Texas City Maritime Exchange as to density shall be conclusive proof, and govern under this rule, and copy thereof shall be sent to the shipper." (Italics ours).

Under the uncontradicted evidence, the minimum density provided for in this stipulation applied only to "standard" compressed cotton, and could have no application to "high density" cotton, the density of which was invariably from 9 to 12 or more pounds greater than that of "standard." The relative contentions of the parties with reference to this stipulation are these: Defendant contends that, as no interlineation was made therein, either the entire stipulation must be rejected as having reference only to "standard," and not "high density" cotton, or the minimum density therein given for "standard" cotton must be applied. Plaintiff contends that only those portions of the stipulation which are clearly not applicable to "high density" cotton should be rejected, leaving intact that portion of the stipulation in italics. We are inclined to accede to the correctness of the latter interpretation, especially in view of the fact that the evidence supports the allegations of the petition that ocean freight rates on cotton, by whatever method compressed, were based upon density —the greater the density, the lower the rate.

[6] But, independently of this stipulation, we do not think the court applied an improper method of computing the damage. The general rule is that, where the contract affords a means of computing damages for its breach, it is not improper to apply the measure of compensation thus provided. Had there been a failure to furnish the amount of freight provided in the contract, the rule contended for by the defendant might apply. But here there was a greater amount of freight tendered and carried than contracted for; that is, the freight tendered, by reason of its lack of density below the required minimum, occupied more space in the ship than if it had been of the minimum required density. We see no objection to requiring defendant to pay for this additional space at the contract rate for the smallest amount of cotton by weight of the required minimum density necessary to fill it.

The other errors assigned are, we think, without merit, and not of sufficient importance to require discussion.

We conclude that the judgment of the Court of Civil Appeals should be reversed, and that of the district court affirmed.

PHILLIPS, C. J. The judgment recommended in the report of the Commission of Appeals is adopted, and will be entered as the judgment of the Supreme Court.

CAMPBELL v. STATE. (No. 6279.)

(Court of Criminal Appeals of Texas. May 11, 1921.)

Criminal law ⚖=1025—Jurisdiction on appeal defeated by defendant's escape and failure to return.

Escape of defendant, after perfecting appeal from a judgment of conviction, and failure to return to custody within the time allowed by law, defeats the jurisdiction of the Court of Criminal Appeals to pass on the merits of the case.

Appeal from District Court, Hunt County; A. P. Dohoney, Judge.

Shorty Campbell was convicted of robbery, and appeals. Stricken from docket.

R. H. Hamilton, Asst. Atty. Gen., for the State.

MORROW, P. J. Appellant was convicted of robbery; punishment fixed at confinement in the penitentiary for five years.

After perfecting the appeal, appellant, on the 5th day of March, 1921, escaped, and since that time has been at large. This is made known by the affidavit of the sheriff of Hunt county, which accompanies the state's motion to dismiss the appeal. The escape and failure to return to custody with, in the time allowed by law operates to defeat the jurisdiction of this court to pass on the merits of the case.

It is therefore ordered stricken from the docket.

CHANDLER v. STATE. (No. 6260.)

(Court of Criminal Appeals of Texas. May 11, 1921.)

1. Criminal law ⚖=507(1)—A purchaser of liquor is an "accomplice."

One who purchases liquor is an "accomplice," and so, in a prosecution based on his testimony, the refusal of a charge on accomplice testimony necessitates reversal.

[Ed. Note.—For other definitions, see Words and Phrases, First and Second Series, Accomplice.]

2. Criminal law ⚖=780(2)—Charge on accomplice testimony necessary.

Where the state relied on the testimony of a purchaser of liquor who was an accomplice, a charge on accomplice testimony is necessary.

3. Intoxicating liquors ⚖=168—One who advised purchaser as to procuring liquor is not a principal.

Where the prosecuting witness and another, discovering that defendant was not at home, found him in another place, and defendant, in response to an inquiry as to where the prosecuting witness could procure whisky, stated that he had a cotton picker who could furnish liquor, etc., but defendant was not present at the sale, he is not guilty as a principal, for he was not present, he did not keep, watch, he did not assist in the unlawful act, he did not endeavor to secure the safety or concealment of the sellers, he did not employ an innocent agent, and he did not advise or agree to the commission of the offense.

Appeal from District Court, Kaufman County; Joel R. Bond, Judge.

John Chandler was convicted of selling intoxicating liquor, and he appeals. Reversed, and cause remanded.

Wynne & Wynne, of Kaufman, Miller & Miller, of Athens, and Huffmaster & Huffmaster, of Kaufman, for appellant.

R. H. Hamilton, Asst. Atty. Gen., for the State.

HAWKINS, J. Appellant was convicted for selling intoxicating liquor to one S. L,

Holley, and his punishment assessed at confinement in the penitentiary for one year.

Holley, in company with Sam Jenkins, went to appellant's house, and found he was away from home, at Mr. Haynie's. They went to Haynie's, and found appellant; and Holley inquired of him if he knew where he could get a quart of whisky. Appellant told him there was a cotton picker at his (appellant's) house by the name of Slim, and told him to go call Clyde Chandler, appellant's son, and that he (Clyde) would get Slim to sell him the whisky. The witness Jenkins heard none of the conversation between appellant and Holley. They left appellant and went back to his house, and Holley communicated to Clyde Chandler what his father, this appellant, had told him. Clyde, Slim, and Holley then went in the house, and Holley got a quart of whisky, throwing $10 down on the floor as he left. The witness Jenkins does not seem to have heard either the conversation with appellant at Mr. Haynie's or the conversation with Clyde Chandler and Slim after they had returned to appellant's house. He saw the three parties go to the well, and saw them go into the house, and knows that after they left the house Holley had some corn whisky; disclaims having anything to do with the purchase of the whisky, and did not know what Holley was going for at the time he went to Chandler. The first he knew of Holley having any whisky was after they had started away from appellant's house in the buggy; and claims he does not know where Holley got the whisky. The statement of facts is very brief, and the foregoing is a condensed statement of all the evidence in the case.

[1, 2] Appellant requested a charge on accomplice testimony, and also a charge directing the jury to return a verdict of "not guilty," because of the insufficiency of the evidence. Both of these charges were refused by the court. There is no question but that Holley was an accomplice, and without his testimony the state would have had no semblance of a case; Jenkins disclaims knowing anything about the selling or purchase of the whisky. The case must be reversed for the failure of the court to charge on accomplice testimony, under the authority of the cases: Robert v. State, 228 S. W. 230; Franklin v. State, 227 S. W. 486, and many cases following them.

[3] We have serious doubts as to whether a case would have been made out against the appellant, John Chandler, even had there been sufficient corroborating testimony. He was charged as a principal with the sale of the whisky to Holley. He was not present at the time the sale was made. A party may be a principal, under certain circumstances, although not present at the time of the commission of the offense, but we doubt if the facts in this case bring appellant within any of the rules where a party, in his absence

from the place of the commission of the crime, may be a principal. In Middleton v. State, 86 Tex. Cr. R. 307, 217 S. W. 1046, this court undertook to clear up the confusion which had existed with reference to principals, and laid down six ways in which a party might occupy that relation to a crime. These will be found referred to in Kolb v. State, 228 S. W. 210:

(1) "When A. actually commits the offense, knowing the unlawful intent, and aids by acts or encourages by words." Appellant was not present; therefore the first subdivision has no application.

(2) "When A. actually commits the offense, but B. keeps watch, so as to prevent the interruption of A." Clyde Chandler seems to have made the sale, or he, together with Slim made it; and there is no evidence that appellant was keeping watch at the time to prevent their interruption.

(3) "When A. is actually executing the unlawful act, and B. is engaged in procuring aid, arms, or means of any kind to assist while A. executes said unlawful act." There is no evidence that appellant was engaged in procuring any aid, arms, or means of any kind to assist Clyde Chandler or Slim at the time they were executing the unlawful act; to wit, the sale.

(4) "When A. actually commits the offense, but B., at the time of such commission, is endeavoring to secure the safety or concealment of A., or of A. and B." There is no evidence that appellant, at the time Clyde Chandler and Slim committed the offense, was endeavoring to secure the safety or concealment of them, or of them and himself.

(5) "When A. employs an innocent agent, or by indirect means causes the injury, or brings about the commission of the offense." There is no evidence which would place appellant in that attitude with reference to the sale of the liquor.

(6) "When A. advises or agrees to the commission of the offense, and is present when the same is committed, whether he aid or not." There is evidence which would indicate that appellant agreed, and perhaps advised, the sale of the intoxicating liquor, but he was not present when the sale was made, and therefore he did not come under the terms of the sixth subdivision.

In fact, the evidence in this case discloses only that Holley and Jenkins went to appellant, and that Holley inquired where he could likely secure some whisky; that appellant gave the information and directions as hereinbefore set out in this opinion; and he seems to have had no other connection with the transaction at all. The record does not disclose what he was doing at Haynie's at the time Holley and Jenkins went there and had the conversation with him, but they seem to have left him where they found him, presumably engaged in doing what he was at the time they approached him. We have made the foregoing observations in view of another trial, for the consideration of the court and the prosecuting officers.

For the error suggested, the judgment of the trial court must be reversed, and the cause remanded.

CHANDLER v. STATE.   (No. 6262.)

(Court of Criminal Appeals of Texas.   May 11, 1921.)

Appeal from District Court, Kaufman County; Joel R. Bond, Judge.

John Chandler was convicted of selling intoxicating liquor, such sale not being for medicinal, mechanical, scientific, or sacramental purposes, and he appeals.   Reversed and remanded.

Ross Huffmaster, of Kaufman, Miller & Miller, of Athens, and Wynne & Wynne, of Kaufman, for appellant.
R. H. Hamilton, Asst. Atty. Gen., for the State.

LATTIMORE, J.   Appellant was convicted in the district court of Kaufman county of selling intoxicating liquor, such sale not being for medicinal, mechanical, scientific, or sacramental purposes, and his punishment fixed at confinement in the penitentiary for a period of one year.

An examination of the record discloses that the conviction of appellant rested upon the uncorroborated testimony of the purchasers. It is admitted by the Assistant Attorney General that there is no testimony in the record sufficient to support the conviction, and that the judgment is erroneous.   Being of opinion that this position is correct, the judgment is reversed, and the cause remanded.

CHANDLER v. STATE.   (No. 6263.)

(Court of Criminal Appeals of Texas.   May 11, 1921.)

1. Criminal law ⟺507(1)—Purchaser of liquor will be deemed an "accomplice" if prosecution is for unlawful possession.

In a prosecution for possession of intoxicating liquor not for medicinal, mechanical, scientific, or sacramental purposes, a purchaser of liquor will, under the Dean Law, be deemed an "accomplice," and a conviction cannot be had on his uncorroborated testimony, for the term "accomplice," as used in Vernon's Ann. Code Cr. Proc. 1916, art. 801, is used in a different sense from the term as used in Pen. Code 1911, art. 79, and includes any person connected with the crime by unlawful act or omission transpiring either before, at, or after

the commission of the offense, and under such definition purchaser is an accomplice.

[Ed. Note.—For other definitions, see Words and Phrases, First and Second Series, Accomplice.]

2. Criminal law ⟺507(1)—For evidential purposes, an accomplice is any one connected with the offense.

For evidential purposes, within Vernon's Ann. Code Cr. Proc. 1916, art. 801, any person connected with the crime by unlawful act or omission either before, at, or after the offense is an accomplice, the term including principals and accessories alike.

3. Criminal law ⟺507(5)—Purchaser of stolen goods is an accomplice.

One who receives or conceals property theretofore stolen by another, knowing it to have been so acquired, is an accomplice, within Vernon's Ann. Code Cr. Proc. 1916, art. 801, though the offense was complete before the guilty connection of the receiver began.

Appeal from District Court, Kaufman County; Joel R. Bond, Judge.

John Chandler was convicted of having in his possession intoxicating liquor not for medicinal, mechanical, scientific, or sacramental purposes, and he appeals.   Reversed and remanded.

Wynne & Wynne, of Kaufman, Miller & Miller, of Athens, and Ross Huffmaster, of Kaufman, for appellant.
R. H. Hamilton, Asst. Atty. Gen., for the State.

LATTIMORE, J.   Appellant was convicted in the district court of Kaufman county of having in his possession intoxicating liquor, not for medicinal, mechanical, scientific, or sacramental purposes, and his punishment fixed at confinement in the penitentiary for a period of one year.

[1, 2] The conviction rested upon the testimony of two witnesses who bought liquor from the appellant in Kaufman county at or about the time alleged in the indictment, and the testimony of a man who helped appellant make and manufacture whisky about that time. Appellant contends that the judgment is without support, because based entirely upon the uncorroborated testimony of accomplices. It is well settled that, under the provisions of what is known as the Dean Law, forbidding the manufacture, possession, sale, etc., of intoxicating liquor (Acts Second Called Session, Thirty-Sixth Legislature, p. 228), that the purchaser of intoxicating liquor is an accomplice to the sale. It is insisted, however, in this case by the state, that, inasmuch as the possession of such liquor is complete and severable from its sale, therefore the purchaser of such liquor is not,

'in law, an accomplice to the fact of possession, and that a conviction resting upon the uncorroborated testimony of a purchaser may therefore be legally sustained. We regret that we cannot agree with this contention of the state. Without discussing the proposition that a conviction cannot be sustained when had upon the uncorroborated testimony of an accomplice, or any number of accomplices, we refer to pages 732 et seq., Vernon's C. C. P., and observe that authorities almost without number are cited in support of the proposition that the word "accomplice," as used in article 801 of said Code of Criminal Procedure, is used in a different sense from the technical meaning given to the word "accomplice" in article 79 of the Penal Code, and that, as used, referring to one who is a witness, or to the evidence of such person, it includes principals and accessories, and all persons who are particeps criminis. It means a person who either, as principal, engaged in the actual commission of the offense, or who, prior to the actual commission of the offense, does those acts which would make him an accomplice, or to a person who, after the actual commission of an offense, is so connected therewith as to make him an accessory. So that, in an evidential sense the expression "accomplice" includes all persons who are connected with the crime by unlawful act or omission, transpiring either before, at the time of, or after the commission of the offense, whether such person be participating in the actual commission of the offense or not.

We do not need to review these authorities to show their application to the instant case. It would not be necessary to argue that if one who came upon the scene where a murder had just been committed, after the death of the injured party, and who connected himself with the transaction in a guilty manner by assisting in the flight or escape of the murderer, would be an accomplice to the crime, and that his testimony would need to be corroborated before a conviction could be sustained. In the instant case, the entire connection of the purchasers with said intoxicating liquor was one which is made penal under our statute, and we are unable to escape the conclusion that they were accomplices within the meaning of our law.

[3] It is well settled that one who receives or conceals property theretofore stolen by another, knowing it to have been so acquired, is an accomplice, though the offense of the taker is complete before the guilty connection of the receiver begins. We do not think the proposition needs further argument. See article 801, Vernon's C. C. P., and authorities collated thereunder.

For the reason that the judgment in this case is supported only by the uncorroborated testimony of accomplices, it must be reversed and remanded; and it is so ordered.

CHANDLER v. STATE. (No. 6264.)

(Court of Criminal Appeals of Texas. May 11, 1921.)

Criminal law ⟨⟩507(1), 510—Purchaser of liquor is accomplice, whose testimony is alone insufficient to sustain conviction.

In a prosecution for the unlawful sale of intoxicating liquors, the alleged purchaser was an accomplice whose testimony is insufficient to sustain the conviction in the absence of any corroborating facts.

Appeal from District Court, Kaufman County; Joel R. Bond, Judge.

John Chandler was convicted of the unlawful sale of intoxicating liquors, and he appeals. Reversed and remanded.

Wynne & Wynne, of Kaufman, Miller & Miller, of Athens, and Ross Huffmaster, of Kaufman, for appellant.

R. H. Hamilton, Asst. Atty. Gen., for the State.

MORROW, P. J. Appellant was convicted of the unlawful sale of intoxicating liquors. The state relied solely upon the testimony of the alleged purchaser of the liquor. He was an accomplice, and, in the absence of any corroborating facts, the evidence is insufficient. Franklin v. State, 227 S. W. 486.

The judgment is reversed, and the cause remanded.

CHANDLER v. STATE. (No. 6265.)

(Court of Criminal Appeals of Texas. May 11, 1921.)

1. Criminal law ⟨⟩200(4)—Conviction of unlawful sale of liquor will not preclude conviction of unlawful possession.

The conviction of the unlawful sale of intoxicating liquors will not preclude a conviction for unlawful possession of such liquors, and this is so notwithstanding the two prosecutions were based on the same transaction.

2. Criminal law ⟨⟩507(1)—Purchaser of liquor is an "accomplice."

A purchaser of intoxicating liquors is an accomplice with the seller, even though the prosecution against the seller is for unlawful possession.

[Ed. Note.—For other definitions, see Words and Phrases, First and Second Series, Accomplice.]

3. Intoxicating liquors ⟨⟩236(6½)—Evidence insufficient to sustain a conviction of unlawful possession.

In prosecution for unlawful possession of intoxicating liquors, evidence insufficient to sustain a conviction.

Appeal from District Court, Kaufman County; Joel R. Bond, Judge.

John Chandler was convicted of the unlawful possession of intoxicating liquors, and he appeals. Reversed and remanded.

Wynne & Wynne, of Kaufman, Miller & Miller, of Athens, and Huffmaster, & Huffmaster, of Kaufman, for appellant.

R. H. Hamilton, Asst. Atty. Gen., for the State.

MORROW, P. J. Conviction is for the unlawful possession of intoxicating liquors. The questions presented in the motion to quash the indictment are the same heretofore ruled upon in the case of Ves Banks v. State, 227 S. W. 670, recently decided, and Ex parte Gilmore, 228 S. W. 199.

[1] We think the contention of appellant that his conviction in another case of the offense of the unlawful sale of intoxicating liquors would preclude his conviction for the possession of such liquors is not sound. Ordinarily, it is conceived that one unlawfully possessing a quantity of intoxicating liquors for sale, and thereby committing the offense of unlawful possession of such liquors, could not plead a conviction of such offense in bar of a prosecution for the unlawful sale of such liquors, or a part thereof, and so the sale of the liquors unlawfully would not bar a conviction for the unlawful possession. The offenses are not the same, nor do they consist in the same act. No facts are found in the record from which we can conclude that the identity of the transaction would prevent the carving of two offenses. Todd v. State, 229 S. W. 515.

[2, 3] The evidence relied on is the statement of the witness Holley to the effect that, on the 3d of October, he, in company with one Jenkins, went to the home of John Chandler. They, failing to find him there, sought him elsewhere, and made inquiry whether he knew where they could buy whisky. He replied that there was a cottonpicker on his premises named Slim, who would sell them whisky, and that, if they would call Clyde Chandler, he would communicate with Slim. The witness left the appellant, and saw Clyde and Slim, and discussed the purchase of the whisky. Slim went to the house. Later, Clyde called the witness, who went into a room and found whisky in fruit jars. The witness took some of the whisky, and left the money to pay for it.

Jenkins testified that he and Holley went to the home of appellant. Failing to find him, they went to the house of one Haynie, where they found him. Holley talked to Chandler, but Jenkins did not hear the conversation. They returned to Chandler's house, and Holley, Clyde Chandler, and Slim went to a well, he thought, and then back to

the house. After leaving, Holley had some whisky. Jenkins' testimony does not, we think, tend to connect appellant with the possession of the whisky. Appellant was not at the place where the whisky was obtained. Jenkins heard him make no statements concerning it. The full measure of his testimony is that, while he and Holley were together, they saw the appellant and Holley converse; that appellant was not at his home; that after Holley conversed with appellant, Jenkins and Holley went to appellant's home; that Holley was there in company with Clyde Chandler and Slim, and later was in possession of some whisky. Aside from the testimony of the accomplice Holley, the record fails to disclose any fact which, in our judgment, tends, in a legal sense, to connect the appellant with the possession of the liquor. Holley purchased the liquor, according to his testimony, from Clyde and Slim. In making the purchase, he committed an offense himself, and aided them in doing so. His status as an accomplice witness, we think, could not be made the subject of controversy. Franklin v. State, 227 S. W. 486. Even if it were not so, we think it is more than questionable whether his testimony shows that the appellant was guilty of the offense charged. The evidence is not, in our opinion, sufficient.

The judgment is reversed, and the cause remanded.

CHANDLER v. STATE. (No. 6259.)

(Court of Criminal Appeals of Texas.
May 19, 1921.)

1. Criminal law ⟝200(4)—Conviction of unlawful sale of liquor will not preclude conviction of having possession.

The conviction of the unlawful sale of intoxicating liquors will not preclude a conviction for unlawful possession of the same liquor, and this is so notwithstanding the two prosecutions were based on the same transaction.

2. Criminal law ⟝507(1), 510—Purchaser of liquor is an accomplice, and testimony must be corroborated.

A purchaser of intoxicating liquor is an accomplice and a conviction against defendant who delivered the liquor cannot be based solely on his testimony, even though the sale was made by defendant's son, defendant delivering the liquor.

Appeal from District Court, Kaufman County; Joel R. Bond, Judge.

John Chandler was convicted of being in possession of intoxicating liquor not for medicinal, sacramental, scientific, or mechanical purposes, and he appeals. Reversed and remanded.

Wynne & Wynne, of Kaufman, Miller & Miller, of Athens, and Ross Huffmaster, of Kaufman, for appellant.

R. H. Hamilton, Asst. Atty. Gen., for the State.

HAWKINS, J. Appellant was convicted of being in the possession of intoxicating liquor, not for medicinal, sacramental, scientific, or mechanical purposes.

Only one witness testified upon the trial, and his evidence is here copied in full:

"My name is Beverly Jones. I live down near Kemp, on the farm. I am 20 years of age. I remember having some transaction with Clyde Chandler and John Chandler along about the 15th day of September, or somewhere about that time. I bought the whisky from Clyde in Kemp, and paid him the money, and went out and got the whisky. I bought a gallon, and paid him $7.50. He did not deliver the whisky. I went out to John Chandler's; I went out and told him (Mr. Chandler) that he said give me the whisky. Mr. Chandler said all right, and went and got the whisky, and brought it to me. He gave me a gallon. He got it back in the barn somewhere. I drank some of it, and it had a 'kick.' If I had drunk enough, it would have made me drunk."

[1] Appellant raises the question of former conviction, and urges that, because he was convicted for the sale of this identical liquor to Beverly Jones, he cannot also be convicted for having possession of the same liquor. This contention has been decided adversely to appellant in cause No. 6265, John Chandler v. State, 231 S. W. 108, in an opinion delivered May 11, 1921. The exact question was there presented, and Presiding Judge Morrow uses the following terse statement: "The offenses are not the same, nor do they consist in the same act."

[2] The court was requested to charge the jury to return a verdict of "not guilty," because of insufficient evidence. Jones purchased the whisky from Clyde Chandler, but took delivery of it from appellant. The purchaser became an accomplice, as held in Franklin v. State, 227 S. W. 486, and Robert v. State, 228 S. W. 230. When the taint of accomplice attaches, it remains during the dealing with the property, the purchase of which produced the taint. It must indeed have been an unsatisfactory sale to Jones until it was consummated by the delivery of the whisky by appellant; and, although appellant was charged in this case with "possession," and not the "sale," Jones was none the less an accomplice. No. 6263, John Chandler v. State, 231 S. W. 107, decided May 11, 1921, in an opinion by Judge Lattimore, expressly settles the question.

There being no testimony other than of Jones, an accomplice, the refusal of the court to give the requested peremptory charge was error.

The judgment of the trial court is reversed, and the cause remanded.

WILLIAMS v. STATE. (No. 6168.)

(Court of Criminal Appeals of Texas. May 11, 1921.)

1. **Criminal law ⇐1166½(12) — Remarks of judge to jury not reversible error in view of instructions, and where rights of accused not prejudiced.**

Remarks of the judge to the jury before the trial of one accused of robbery that they should pay close attention to the testimony, and thereby avoid controversy among themselves and reach a verdict more speedily and satisfactorily, were not reversible error, where the court on objection instructed the jury not to consider his statement as evidence, or as tending to show guilt or innocence, and the remarks were not calculated to prejudice the rights of the accused.

2. **Criminal law ⇐406(5)—Oral statement of accused, leading to finding of pistol with which offense committed, admissible.**

Under Code Cr. Proc. 1911, art. 810, excluding oral statements made by the accused while under arrest unless they conduce to establish his guilt, such as finding the instrument with which the offense was committed, a statement so made by one accused of robbery, which led to the finding of the pistol claimed to have been used, was admissible.

3. **Criminal law ⇐409—Accused may prove exculpatory statements made in connection with inculpatory statements proved by state.**

Under Code Cr. Proc. 1911, art. 811, declaring that when part of an act, declaration, or conversation is given in evidence by one party, the whole on the subject may be introduced by the other, and that an act or declaration necessary to make fully understood or to explain the same may be given by the opposing party, one accused of robbery could prove that, in connection with certain inculpatory statements proved by the state, he made other exculpatory statements.

4. **Criminal law ⇐1120(3)—Exclusion of evidence not reviewable, where matter excluded is not shown by bill of exceptions.**

The weight of a ruling, denying defendant the right to prove exculpatory statements made by him in connection with inculpatory statements brought out by the state, cannot be appraised on appeal, when the bill of exceptions does not show what declarations were excluded.

5. **Criminal law ⇐404(4)—Exhibition to jury of articles found on scene of robbery not erroneous.**

In a prosecution for robbery, the exhibition to the jury of a pocketbook belonging to the injured party and a pistol and certain playing cards found on the scene of the robbery was not erroneous; they being circumstances available to the state in connection with testimony showing their relation to the transactions.

6. Criminal law ⬤══409—Accused may testify as to acts and declarations explanatory of admission, though not part of res gestæ.

Under Code Cr. Proc. 1911, art. 811, providing that when a detailed act, declaration, conversation, or writing is given in evidence any other act, declaration, or writing necessary to make it fully understood may be given in evidence, one accused of robbery may testify, in explanation of his admission of having thrown away the pistol and playing cards found on the scene of the robbery, that he told the arresting officer immediately after he was arrested that he won the money gambling, and, believing he was to be arrested for gambling, fled and threw away his pistol and the playing cards, and that he told the names of the others in the game and where they were, and requested the officer to go get them; the statute not being restricted to declarations that are part of the res gestæ, but embracing explanatory acts and declarations by the accused after his arrest.

7. Criminal law ⬤══409—Accused may introduce in evidence statement explanatory of statement used to incriminate him, though latter claimed exculpatory.

Where the state, in a prosecution for robbery, used defendant's admission of having thrown away the pistol found at the scene of the robbery to incriminate him, defendant's right to introduce evidence explanatory of the admission could not be nullified by the state's claim that the part of the transaction and conversation introduced by it was exculpatory.

8. Criminal law ⬤══1091(5)—Where excluded evidence relevant and material, bill of exceptions need not so state.

Where it appeared from the bill of exceptions that excluded evidence proffered by defendant was both relevant and material, it was not necessary that the bill expressly so state; a reasonable and substantial compliance with the law concerning bills of exceptions being sufficient.

Appeal from Criminal District Court, Tarrant County; George E. Hosey, Judge.

J. M. Williams was convicted of robbery, and he appeals. Reversed.

Callaway & Shead, of Fort Worth, for appellant.

Jesse M. Brown, Cr. Dist. Atty., and W. R. Parker, Asst. Cr. Dist. Atty., both of Fort Worth, and R. H. Hamilton, Asst. Atty. Gen., for the State.

MORROW, P. J. Conviction is for robbery; punishment fixed at confinement in the penitentiary for seven years.

Blackwell, the alleged injured party, gave direct testimony to the fact that the appellant and one Patterson committed the robbery, each presenting a pistol.

[1] After the jury was impaneled, and before otherwise proceeding with the trial, the trial judge instructed the jury that they should pay close attention to the testimony, thereby avoid controversy among themselves touching the statements of the witnesses, and that by thus proceeding a verdict might be reached more speedily and more satisfactorily. Appellant made objection to this statement, whereupon the court instructed the jury that the statement should not be considered as evidence or tending in any manner to show the guilt or innocence of the accused. The practice of lecturing the jury is always fraught with the danger that either the language or the motive of the court may be misconstrued. It does not in all cases necessarily result in a reversal. Such result ensues when the remarks are calculated to prejudice the rights of the accused. Wilson v. State, 28 S. W. 200; Dow v. State, 31 Tex. Cr. R. 278, 20 S. W. 583. In the instant case, it is, in our judgment, not of this class. Hammett v. State, 84 Tex. Cr. R. 638, 209 S. W. 661, 4 A. L. R. 347.

[2] Bill No. 5 refers to a statement made by the appellant, while under arrest, concerning a pistol which the state claimed was used in perpetrating the robbery. It is stated in the bill "that the information elicited from the appellant led to the finding of the pistol." We fail to discern anything in the bill which would render this testimony inadmissible. It would seem to be within the purview of article 810, Code of Criminal Procedure, in which statements made by the accused while under arrest, which are not in writing, are excluded unless in connection therewith he made statements of facts or circumstances that are found to be true, which conduce to establish his guilt, such as finding the instrument with which the offense was committed. See Garcia v. State, 228 S. W. 938. The court withdrew the testimony complained of.

[3, 4] In bill No. 6 complaint is made of the refusal of the court to permit the appellant, upon cross-examination of the officer who arrested him and by whom the state proved certain inculpatory statements were made, to prove that in connection therewith the appellant made other statements of fact which he desired to introduce as exculpatory. As we understand the bill, this testimony was admissible under article 811, Code of Criminal Procedure, in which it is declared that when part of an act, declaration, or conversation is given in evidence by one party, the whole on the subject may be introduced by the other, and where an act or declaration, which is necessary to make fully understood or to explain the same, may also be given by the opposing party. We do not think that the construction of the statute would be correct which would permit the state to prove that the appellant made declarations which

led to the finding of the pistol with which the offense was committed, and exclude other declarations made in the same connection which would tend to be exculpatory. The bill, however, as prepared, does not enlighten us as to what declarations were excluded. We would therefore be unable to appraise the weight of the ruling complained of.

[5] The exhibition to the jury of a pocketbook which belonged to the injured party, a pistol which was found upon the scene of the robbery, and certain playing cards that were also found there, was not erroneous, but in connection with the testimony showing their relation to the transactions they were circumstances available to the state on the issues involved.

[6] Appellant's theory, as developed from his testimony, was, in substance, that while in a game of cards with the Blackwell brothers, and while two other persons were present, the Blackwells were the losers; that, incensed at the loss, they threatened to cause the arrest of the appellant and his companion Patterson; that, believing he was to be arrested for gambling, he fled and threw away his pistol and the cards with which they had been playing. The fact that the pistol and the cards were found was proved by the state, as was also the declaration of the appellant to the officer who arrested him that he had thrown away his pistol. Appellant offered to testify to other declarations which he claimed to have made to the officer at the same time that he made the declarations about throwing away the pistol. From the bill we take the following quotation:

" 'Now, tell the jury what you said with reference to those two fellows that was there watching the game,' said statement having been made immediately after the arrest of the defendants, and at the time the Officer Averitt inquired as to the statement with reference to the pistol, the objection of the assistant district attorney being that said statement would be a statement made after the commission of the offense, after the defendant was under arrest, and would be a self-serving declaration. Said witness would have stated, if permitted, that he told the officer immediately after he was arrested that at the time he was first put under arrest he did not get the money from the witness Blackwell, but that he won the same in a gambling game, and that there were two other persons present, and that they had run away, and that if the officer would pursue them and bring them back from the cut on the railroad where they were hiding they would straighten the whole matter up, and exonerate both of the defendants from the charge of robbery, and that he, the said Williams, told the officers where these parties were, and that he requested the officers to go get them."

The court, in our judgment, was not warranted in excluding this testimony.

The statement of facts shows that the officer who arrested the appellant gave testimony to the fact that he chased him quite a distance before he succeeded in arresting him,

that he searched him and found no pistol, but that appellant declared he had thrown his pistol away, and described the pistol. The state, by other testimony, showed that the pistol was found, also the cards.

We quote our statute:

"When part of an act, declaration or conversation or writing is given in evidence by one party, the whole on the same subject may be inquired into by the other, as, when a letter is read, all other letters on the same subject between the same parties may be given. And when a detailed act, declaration, conversation or writing is given in evidence any other act, declaration or writing which is necessary to make it fully understood or to explain the same may also be given in evidence." C. C. P. art. 811.

The construction of this statute which would support the ruling of the court is, in our judgment, at variance with the interpretation of it heretofore made. In the Greene Case, 17 Tex. App. 405, the court, after quoting the statute, says:

"This article expands the common-law rule with reference to such evidence. At common law, when a confession or admission is introduced in evidence against a party, such party is entitled to prove the whole of what he said on the subject at the time of making such confession or admission. 1 Greenl. Ev. §§ 201–218; Whart. Cr. Ev. § 688. But the above-quoted article does not restrict the explanatory act, declaration, conversation, or writing to the time when the act, declaration, conversation, or writing sought to be explained occurred, but extends the rule so as to render such acts or statements admissible, if necessary to a full understanding of, or to explain the acts or statements introduced in evidence by the adverse party, although the same may have transpired at a different time, and at a time so remote even as to not be admissible as res gestæ.

"This article of the Code has not heretofore been considered and construed with direct reference to the question we are now discussing. In the case of Shrivers v. State, 7 Tex. Ct. App. 450, the question was presented and discussed, but without reference to this article of the Code. In that case the statements made by the defendant, explanatory of the statements proved against him by the state, were held admissible as res gestæ, and the court said: To render such after declarations or statements admissible as explanations, it must appear that they were made recently after the former, and it must also be obvious from the circumstances that they are not obnoxious to, but come within the exceptions to, the general rule that a party cannot make evidence for himself either by his acts or his declarations.' The rule thus stated would be correct when applied to declarations of the defendant offered in his own behalf as original evidence, and not in explanation of statements or confessions proved against him by the prosecution. Davis v. State, 3 Tex. Ct. App. 91, and authorities there cited.

"But, in a case like this, where the statements offered are offered only in explanation of defendant's statements introduced in evidence against him by the state, we can find no warrant in the statute for thus limiting their admissibility. In so far as the language used in the opinion in Shrivers' Case conflicts with the construction we now give to the article quoted, the same is overruled. We are of the opinion that under this article the statement of the defendant made before the inquest, if it be necessary to make his confession fully understood, or to explain the same, was admissible."

This interpretation of the statute has not been questioned so far as we are aware, but, on the contrary, has received frequent and express sanction. Pratt v. State, 53 Tex. Cr. R. 285, 109 S. W. 138; Smith v. State, 46 Tex. Cr. R. 283, 81 S. W. 936, 108 Am. St. Rep. 991; Harrison v. State, 20 Tex. App. 399, 54 Am. Rep. 529; Rainey v. State, 20 Tex. App. 470; Gaither v. State, 21 Tex. App. 540, 1 S. W. 456; Rogers v. State, 26 Tex. App. 431, 9 S. W. 762; Spearman v. State, 34 Tex. Cr. R. 281, 30 S. W. 229; Potts v. State, 56 Tex. Cr. R. 47, 118 S. W. 535.

The citation of the authorities illustrating the rule that the operation of the statute is not restricted to declarations that are part of the res gestæ, and would not, in the instant case, be confined simply to declarations concerning the possession of the pistol, but would embrace explanatory acts and declarations such as the appellant sought to introduce, as disclosed by the bill of exceptions. He was by his acts, proved by the state, put upon explanation of the possession of his pistol, his flight, his throwing the pistol away, the presence of the cards, his association with the injured parties, and declarations made by him at the times set out in the bill of exceptions were such as he was entitled to have before the jury. Branch's Ann. Tex. Penal Code, § 92.

[7] The state assumes the position that the right of appellant under the statute to introduce other declarations explanatory of those proved by the state did not accrue, for the reason that those in evidence were exculpatory. With this view we are unable to concur either as to the facts or the law. The exculpatory character of the proof of flight and possession and disposal of the pistol is not apparent, but if this were questionable it was used to incriminate him, and his right to introduce legitimate evidence explanatory of it could not be nullified by the claim of the state that the part of the transaction and conversation introduced by it was exculpatory. Bailey v. State, 40 Tex. Cr. R. 150, 49 S. W. 102; Dover v. State, 81 Tex. Cr. R. 553, 197 S. W. 192, and authorities there cited.

[8] The criticism of the bill of exceptions that the relevancy and the materiality of the proffered testimony is not thereby disclosed, we think, is not tenable. It is required that the relevancy and the materiality must appear, but it is not demanded that, in every instance, the bill must so state in terms. Stanton v. State, 42 Tex. Cr. R. 271, 59 S. W.

271; Farrar v. State, 29 Tex. App. 253, 15 S. W. 719. From the bill before us, it is made plain that the officer who arrested appellant, testified for the state that appellant had made inculpatory declarations; and it also appears from the bill that appellant sought to make proof that the same declarations were accompanied by others made by the appellant at the time, which were explanatory and tended to obviate the injurious effect of those proved by the state. Viewing the bill in the light of the parts of the record which this court is bound to examine, it becomes clear that the evidence excluded was both relevant and material. This, thus appearing to disregard the bill, would place an arbitrarily restrictive construction upon the law concerning bills of exceptions above a reasonable and substantial compliance therewith. Rules of procedure are made to facilitate, not to obstruct, the administration of justice, and it has been the practice of the courts of this state, in deciding questions as to the sufficiency of bills of exceptions, to bear in mind and apply this principle. Railway v. Pemberton, 106 Tex. 466, 161 S. W. 2, 168 S. W. 126; Farrar v. State, supra; Jenkins v. State, 34 Tex. Cr. R. 202, 29 S. W. 1078; Stanton v. State, supra; Robinson v. State, 70 Tex. Cr. R. 81, 156 S. W. 212; Plummer v. State, 86 Tex. Cr. R. 498, 218 S. W. 499. In rejecting the testimony referred to in the bill, the court, in our opinion, fell into substantial error, calculated to prejudice the appellant's case.

A reversal of the judgment is ordered.

LEWIS v. STATE. (No. 6233.)

(Court of Criminal Appeals of Texas. May 19, 1921.)

1. Homicide ⬥⇒309(4)—Charge on manslaughter proper, where there is evidence from which jury may deduce finding.

    If there is evidence which, however weak or inconclusive it may seem to the court, tends to prove facts from which the jury may deduce a finding of manslaughter, it is error to fail to charge on it.

2. Homicide ⬥⇒309(6) — Special charge on manslaughter, requested by defendant, incorrect.

    In a prosecution for murder, special charge requested by defendant on manslaughter *held* incorrect; it embracing a clause telling the jury that insulting words of the person killed toward a female relative was "adequate cause," while there was no testimony justifying such a charge, etc.

3. Homicide ⬥⇒49—Epithet "son of a bitch" does not support a charge on manslaughter.

    The language used by deceased in calling defendant a "son of a bitch" will not support a charge on manslaughter that insulting words as to a female relative was adequate cause.

4. Homicide ⟐⟐309(1)—Proper charge on manslaughter outlined.

In a prosecution for homicide, *held*, the jury should have been charged that if the conduct and language of deceased, or deceased and his son, either alone or in connection with any previous abuse or assault by deceased, on defendant, aroused in defendant's mind such a degree of anger, rage, resentment, or terror as rendered him incapable of cool reflection, and the facts and circumstances were sufficient to have produced such state of mind in a person of ordinary temper, there was adequate cause, and, if the killing occurred under such circumstances, defendant was guilty of manslaughter, unless he was acting in self-defense.

5. Homicide ⟐⟐309(2)—Issue of manslaughter becomes pertinent, where it is claimed killing resulted from fight.

If the case is one either of murder or perfect self-defense, it is not error to fail to charge on manslaughter; but where the case becomes involved from the issues raised, and it is claimed the killing resulted from a fight, and the facts of its inception or progress become controverted issues raising the question of self-defense, the issue of manslaughter almost universally becomes pertinent.

6. Homicide ⟐⟐300(2)—Instruction on appearance of danger to defendant erroneous.

In a prosecution for murder, special charge requested by defendant on the matter of the appearance of danger as viewed from defendant's standpoint *held* improper, as tending to convey the idea that the whole transaction, the whole case, should be viewed from defendant's standpoint; it is only the question of the appearance of danger that must be viewed from defendant's standpoint.

7. Homicide ⟐⟐116(1)—Defendant had right to act on appearances in own defense.

If it appeared to defendant charged with murder, viewing it from his standpoint, from the acts or words coupled with the acts of deceased and defendant's other assailants, that his (defendant's) life was in danger, he had a right to act on such appearances in his own defense.

8. Criminal law ⟐⟐789(3)—Instruction erroneous as omitting element of conviction of jury beyond reasonable doubt.

In a prosecution for murder, charge that, if jury found from the evidence that defendant unlawfully and with malice aforethought killed deceased, to find him guilty of murder, *held* erroneous, as not telling the jury that they must so find from the evidence beyond a reasonable doubt.

9. Homicide ⟐⟐308(1)—Elements of offense of murder stated; may be embraced in charge.

Where manslaughter and self-defense are issues, the jury must find three things beyond a reasonable doubt before they are warranted in convicting for murder: First, that accused acted with malice aforethought; second, that the killing did not occur under circumstances

reducing the offense to manslaughter; and, third, that accused was not acting in self-defense, and such matters may be embraced in the clause of the charge submitting murder.

10. Criminal law ⟐⟐762(5) — Instruction against verdict by lot not erroneous, as conveying impression court was of opinion defendant would be convicted.

In a prosecution for murder, instruction that the question of defendant's guilt must not be determined by lot or chance, and, in case of conviction, the punishment must not be determined in any such manner, *held* not error as conveying the impression the court was of the opinion defendant would be convicted.

11. Criminal law ⟐⟐448(8)—Testimony as to condition of scene of killing inadmissible as conclusion.

In a prosecution for murder, testimony of witnesses for defendant, after describing the appearance of the surroundings at the scene of the killing, as to what, in their opinion, the tracks, heel prints, and tearing down of the corn stalks indicated, was inadmissible as an opinion and conclusion, not coming under the classification of a shorthand rendering of the facts.

Appeal from District Court, Guadalupe County; M. Kennon, Judge.

Monroe Lewis was convicted of murder, and he appeals. Judgment reversed, and cause remanded.

Wurzbach & Wirtz, B. S. Terrell, and Dibrell & Mosheim, all of Seguin, for appellant. R. H. Hamilton, Asst. Atty. Gen., for State.

HAWKINS, J. Appellant was convicted of the murder of Clarence Mathews, and his punishment assessed at 40 years' confinement in the penitentiary.

The court declined to charge on manslaughter. Timely objections were urged because of this omission, and a special charge on the subject presented, which was refused.

[1] All the parties to this homicide were negroes. The trouble resulting in the killing arose over a dispute between appellant, on the one hand, and the deceased, Clarence Mathews, and his son, Ewart, on the other, over the manner in which the Mathewses were gathering corn. Cleveland Williams was assisting in gathering corn. He was in sight of the parties, and testified about the killing, but claims not to have heard what was said between them. Ewart Mathews was the main state's witness. His and Williams' testimony make a case of unprovoked murder, with no semblance of either manslaughter or self-defense, in which Clarence Mathews was killed, and Ewart Mathews shot and severely wounded by appellant. Appellant was dependent almost wholly on his own testimony for the contention that the issue of manslaughter

was in the case. If any evidence raised the issue, the determination of it passed from the court to the jury, under appropriate instructions. "In a doubtful case the charge on manslaughter should be given." Pickens v. State, 86 Tex. Cr. R. 662, 218 S. W. 755; McLaughlin v. State, 10 Tex. App. 359; Arnwine v. State, 49 Tex. Cr. R. 6, 90 S. W. 39. "After all the evidence is in, if it is questionable in the court's mind as to whether the issue of manslaughter is raised, it should be resolved in the defendant's favor, and the matter passed to the jury." Steen v. State, 225 S. W. 531.

The substance of appellant's testimony is:

"That on the morning of the killing, the deceased, his son, and Williams were in one part of defendant's cornfield, gathering corn for defendant's landlord. That previously there had been an agreement between defendant and the deceased as to the manner of dividing the corn. That a few days before the killing deceased and his son, in gathering another portion of the corn, made a mistake in dividing the rows. That on the morning of the killing defendant had prepared to haul a wagon loan of watermelons from his home to San Marcos, and had hitched his mules to the wagon, and directed his boy and a woman by the name of Tinie Saffold to drive the wagon along the turning road through the field, toward the premises of Mr. Scheibe, where he had engaged to deliver some watermelons en route to San Marcos. That he went in a different direction by a potato patch to get his pistol that he had dropped there the night previous, and went from that place to the northwest corner of the cornfield to examine where the corn had been gathered, to ascertain if it had been gathered according to the previous agreement. He was a distance of about 150 yards from deceased and his son, inspecting the rows, and did not invite deceased and his son to assist him in making the inspection, but that deceased's son first came to where he was and inquired of him what the trouble was. That defendant informed deceased's son that a mistake had been made there, as had been made in the other field, but no angry words passed between them, and that in a few minutes the deceased voluntarily got from the wagon which he was driving and came over to the place where defendant and deceased's son were examining the rows that had been gathered and those that had been left ungathered, and in an insulting way addressed defendant. That one word led on to another, and that deceased cursed defendant and called him a black son of a bitch, and attempted to strike defendant with his fist. That thereupon a difficulty ensued between defendant, deceased, and deceased's son, and that defendant was assaulted by both deceased and his son, was struck with an ax handle by the son of deceased, and at the very time the deceased was shot both deceased and his son were attempting to commit a battery upon defendant." That while the assaults were being made on him he was trying to get his pistol out, but deceased fired at appellant before he succeeded in getting his pistol, and that when he did secure it he shot both deceased and his son.

Evidence was introduced tending to show that at the place where the difficulty started there were indications that a struggle or scuffle had occurred, corn and weeds being mashed down, and footprints all about. The state combated this by showing that many parties had been walking about the place before the observations were made. Appellant also testified that on a prior occasion, about cotton chopping time, deceased had charged him with not carrying out his contract about the crop, had cursed him, and threatened an assault upon him with a monkey wrench, if he did not get the money and pay a small amount he owed deceased by Saturday; that appellant got the money, paid deceased, and that matters moved along fairly well until the trouble came up about the corn.

We have given more in detail the evidence of appellant than of the state, because it is to the former we must look to determine whether manslaughter should have been submitted. The court does not determine the weight of the testimony, nor whether it is true or false, in concluding whether to submit manslaughter. His only duty is to ascertain if any evidence raises the issue, regardless of what he may think of its cogency.

"If there is evidence which, however weak or inconclusive it may seem to the court, tends to prove facts from which the jury may deduce a finding of manslaughter, it is error to fail to charge on it." Branch's Criminal Law, § 504, and a collation of authorities supporting the text quoted.

As was tersely stated by Judge Lattimore in the Steen Case, supra:

"The causes named in our statute as adequate to reduce a homicide to manslaughter are well understood to be instances, and not limitations."

The jury had the right, and it was their province, to believe any part of the testimony of appellant or any other witness, which to them seemed reasonable, and, on the other hand, to reject all or any part to which they did not give credence. The jury evidently rejected appellant's testimony, in which he claims that deceased shot at him before he killed deceased. Having found against appellant on the issue of self-defense, they still had a right to believe that deceased and his son made an assault on appellant, and that the three of them became engaged in a fight and struggle, and from this alone, or in connection with previous abuse and assault with the monkey wrench, appellant's mind became so inflamed from anger, rage, resentment, or terror as to render him incapable of cool reflection, and that the facts and circumstances were sufficient to produce such a state of mind in a person of ordinary temper. If they should have reached such a conclusion from the evidence, no rule is given them in the charge directing them what to do under such a finding.

[2-4] We do not believe the special charge requested by appellant on manslaughter was correct. It embraced a clause telling the jury that "insulting words of the person killed towards a female relative," etc., was "adequate cause." We find in the record no testimony justifying such a charge. If it was predicated on the evidence that deceased called appellant a "son of a bitch," it was not the law. It has been held such language, however obnoxious it may be, will not support such a charge. Authorities collated under section 505, Branch's Criminal Law. But such language, in connection with other things, might be "adequate cause" under article 1130, P. C., providing:

"By the expression 'adequate cause' is meant such as would commonly produce a degree of anger, rage, resentment or terror in a person of ordinary temper sufficient to render the mind incapable of cool reflection."

If the evidence raises an issue of fact as to something which article 1132, P. C., expressly makes "adequate cause," such as a blow causing pain, the jury ought to be told, if they find it did occur, it would be adequate cause; and where the facts are involved it is always proper to submit a general charge in addition thereto. We believe in the instant case the jury ought to have been told, in some appropriate way, that if the conduct and language of deceased, or deceased and his son, either alone or in connection with any previous abuse or assault by deceased upon appellant, aroused in his mind such a degree of anger, rage, resentment, or terror as rendered him incapable of cool reflection, and they believe the facts and circumstances were sufficient to have produced such state of mind in a person of ordinary temper, then the same would be "adequate cause," and if the killing occurred under such circumstances the appellant would be guilty of manslaughter, unless he was acting in self-defense.

[5] "If the case is either murder or perfect self-defense, it is not error to fail to charge on manslaughter" (Branch's Crim. Law, § 505, and collated authorities) but where the case becomes involved from the issues raised, and it is claimed the killing resulted from a fight, and the facts of its inception or progress, become controverted issues raising the question of self-defense, it is a rare instance where the issue of manslaughter does not also become pertinent. Steen v. State, 225 S. W. 529; Washington v. State, 68 Tex. Cr. R. 589, 151 S. W. 819; Menefee v. State, 67 Tex. Cr. R. 201, 149 S. W. 138; Pickens v. State, 86 Tex. Cr. R. 662, 218 S. W. 755; Arnwine v. State, 49 Tex. Cr. R. 6, 90 S. W. 39.

Upon the issue of self-defense the court charged that if deceased had shot at appellant with a pistol, or if deceased's son was striking, or was in the act of striking appellant with an ax handle, he should be acquitted. Exception was reserved to this charge

as being too restrictive, in that it singled out certain things under which the jury might acquit, but failed to enumerate all the facts and circumstances shown by the evidence, or which the evidence tended to show, as authorizing the appellant to act in self-defense.

The court did not charge on appearance of danger as viewed from appellant's standpoint, and a special charge was requested on that subject as follows:

"In this case the court, at defendant's request, instructs the jury as follows: In considering the action of the defendant at the time of the killing, you will consider the same in the light of facts and circumstances, as you believe from the evidence, they appeared to the defendant at the time of the killing, and to the defendant alone, and not from any other standpoint, and determine from the evidence what were the appearances to the defendant and what the standpoint of the defendant was, and in what light he in fact did view the facts and circumstances at the time. And if you believe from the evidence the defendant, so viewing the facts and circumstances believed his life in danger, or his person in danger of serious bodily injury from deceased, or from any other person present and acting with deceased, shot and killed the deceased, you will acquit the defendant."

The court refused to give the charge, and exception was reserved. The two assignments last above mentioned may be treated together. The writer, from experience, knows that where a case is developed by witnesses of the character relied on by the state and defendant in this case, the issues are often not clearly drawn; the trial court has much difficulty in determining what issues are raised, and the jury in finding which are established; much testimony may be rejected by the jury, because not comporting with human experience generally; therefore the frequent necessity of the trial judge resorting to a general submission of the various issues. The jury had a right to, and from the verdict evidently did, disregard appellant's testimony that deceased shot at him, and that his (deceased's) son struck, or was striking, appellant with an ax handle, because they were told if the killing occurred under those circumstances they should acquit. The jury found that appellant was in no actual danger of suffering death or serious bodily injury. If no other issue than actual attack and danger was in the case, there was no error in the charge given on the one refused. While the jury evidently disbelieved appellant's theory of the attack upon him with a pistol and ax handle, yet there was evidence from which they could have found that deceased had previously ill-treated, cursed, assaulted, and threatened appellant. They could have found that a struggle and fight occurred at the time of the killing; that both deceased and his son were engaged in it as against appellant; that he was contending against more than one assailant, though perhaps they were not armed,

(221 S.W.)

as he claimed. If so, he had a right to act upon the hostile demonstration of either or both.

If it did happen in such wise, how did it look to appellant at the time? His theory was that deceased and his son had failed to gather one field of corn according to agreement, and had promised to correct it when they gathered the field where the killing occurred; that upon going to where they were at work, and checking up the rows, he found they not only had not corrected the other error, but were further violating their contract, and made a joint assault upon him when he remonstrated with them, and threatened to go to law about their differences. The affair may not have happened that way, and the jury may have so found; but they should have been told what the law was in event they did adopt even a part of appellant's theory. Under article 1105, subd. 1, P. C., we believe, under the facts of this case, the jury should have been told, if from the acts of deceased and his son, or from the acts of either or both of them, or if from the words of either or both of them, coupled with the acts of either or both, it reasonably appeared to appellant as viewed from his standpoint at the time from all the facts and circumstances within his knowledge, that he was in danger of losing his life, or suffering serious bodily injury at the hands of either or both of them, and he killed deceased under such circumstances, he should be acquitted.

[6, 7] We cannot give our unqualified indorsement to the special requested charge copied above. It may not have been so designed, but it rather tends to convey the idea that the whole transaction, the whole case, should be viewed from the standpoint of the defendant. There are expressions in some of the opinions which would authorize such a conclusion; but it is our understanding of the law that it is the question of the appearance of danger that must be viewed from the defendant's standpoint. If it appeared to appellant, viewing it from his standpoint, from the acts, or words coupled with the acts of his assailants, that his life was in danger, he had a right to act on these appearances. Swain v. State, 48 Tex. Cr. R. 103, 86 S. W. 335.

[8, 9] In the fifth paragraph of the court's charge the jury were told, in substance, if they found from the evidence that defendant unlawfully and with malice aforethought killed Clarence Mathews, to find him guilty of murder. The charge is attacked because it does not tell the jury they must so find from the evidence "beyond a reasonable doubt." The criticism is well taken. The error was doubtless the result of an oversight. In view of another trial we would suggest that where manslaughter and self-defense are issues the jury must find three things beyond a reasonable doubt before they are warranted in convicting for murder: (a) That the accused acted with malice aforethought; (b) that the killing did not occur under circumstances which would reduce the offense to manslaughter; (c) and that accused was not acting in self-defense. It is always proper to embrace them in the clause submitting murder, substantially telling the jury, if they find from the evidence beyond a reasonable doubt that accused, with malice aforethought killed deceased, and that he was not acting under the influence of sudden passion aroused from an adequate cause, and that he was not acting in self-defense, they would find him guilty of murder.

[10] The court charged the jury:

"You are further instructed that the question of the guilt of the defendant must not be determined by lot, or in any manner by chance; and in case of conviction the punishment to be assessed must not be determined in any such manner."

Exception was reserved to the foregoing charge on the ground that it conveyed to the jury the impression that the court was of the opinion that defendant would be convicted, and in what manner the punishment shall be determined. We cannot agree that the charge is subject to such construction. We must assume that the jurors were ordinarily intelligent citizens; otherwise they ought not to have been on the jury. They knew from the beginning of the trial to its close that the main issue was to determine whether accused was guilty; that was the question around which all the evidence revolved, and the court told them that question must not be determined by chance or lot, and then in effect said, "If you find he is guilty, you must not determine the punishment in that manner." The jury knew beforehand that conviction must be followed by punishment, and the court properly admonished them with avoid in fixing it.

[11] An issue was joined between the state and accused as to whether the condition of the ground and vegetation at the place of the killing was the result of a scuffle during the difficulty, or was caused by people tramping around there after the killing. Witnesses for appellant after describing the appearance of the surroundings, were asked, "What, in your opinion, did the tracks, heel prints, and tearing down of the corn stalks indicate?" The state objected because it was calling for an opinion and conclusion of the witnesses. The objection was sustained. If permitted they would have answered that it indicated a scuffle there on the ground. We hardly think this would come under a "shorthand" rendering of the facts. In most cases where that rule has been invoked the witness, in an effort to describe a thing or condition, used the expression complained of to describe it. Here the very issue for the jury was, "What caused the conditions?" and, after having otherwise

described it, it is sought to have the witness express his opinion and draw his conclusion as to what caused it. We think it was going further than the rule authorizes, and would have been permitting the substitution of the witness' conclusion for that of the jury. A correct rule of evidence should work for or against the state and accused alike. If the accused could properly have elicited such an answer, then with equal propriety a state's witness could have testified that he observed the conditions, and in his opinion they were caused by people walking about the place after the killing. The jury would have been called upon to determine which witness' opinion was entitled to most weight, instead of reaching their own conclusion from the description given.

The other questions raised by bills of exceptions will not likely occur on another trial, and are not discussed.

For the errors pointed out, the judgment must be reversed, and the cause remanded.

RAINEY v. STATE. (No. 5926.)

(Court of Criminal Appeals of Texas. May 11, 1921. Rehearing Denied June 1, 1921.)

1. **Indictment and information ⊂⟹110(31)—Indictment for possessing intoxicants sufficient, though not using expression "had in his possession."**

An indictment, charging that defendant "did possess" intoxicating liquor not for mechanical, etc., purposes, in violation of the Dean Act, was sufficient, though not using the expression "had in his possession."

2. **Criminal law ⊂⟹696(2)—Answer of witness in liquor prosecution held to have required motion to strike rather than objection.**

In a prosecution for having in possession intoxicating liquor not for medical, etc., purposes, where the state's attorney asked a witness, "What first attracted your attention to the defendant?" and the witness answered, "I was standing at the fountain, watching for him," etc., if such answer was objectionable, the proper procedure would have required motion to strike it out as unresponsive, and objection to the question asked was not well taken.

3. **Criminal law ⊂⟹1170½(1)—Witnesses ⊂⟹240(4)—Question held not leading or harmful to defendant.**

In a prosecution for having in possession intoxicating liquor not for medical, etc., purposes, question, "Did any liquor come into your hands by anybody?" was not leading, and did not contain matter harmful to defendant.

4. **Criminal law ⊂⟹1169(1)—Testimony held not prejudicial as conveying impression defendant engaged in selling liquor found in possession.**

In a prosecution for having in possession intoxicating liquors not for medical, etc., pur-

poses, in violation of the Dean Act, where state's counsel exhibited to a witness two bottles, a funnel, and a glass jug, and asked him what was the size of the bottle at the mouth, and the witness answered, "Just a little bit larger than the little end of the funnel," such answer was not prejudicial, as conveying the impression that defendant was selling the liquor found in his possession; it being necessary that the possession of the accused be for some purpose other than that excepted by statute.

5. **Criminal law ⊂⟹459—Testimony of witnesses that defendant had whisky admissible.**

In a prosecution for having in possession intoxicating liquors not for medical, etc., purposes, in violation of the Dean Act, testimony of a state witness, who said he was acquainted with the smell of whisky and had smelled lots of it, that the bottles taken from defendant's car, from their odor, contained whisky, and testimony of another witness, who said he had not much experience with whisky, but that in his judgment that shown him was whisky, was also admissible.

6. **Criminal law ⊂⟹1091(10)—Bill of exceptions to admission of evidence must show meritorious ground of objections.**

When objections are made to evidence, the bill setting them forth must show affirmatively not only the grounds of objections stated, but enough facts to make it reasonably apparent that such objections are meritorious.

7. **Criminal law ⊂⟹406(7)—Statement of defendant bootlegger to sheriff admissible to show intent.**

In a prosecution for having in possession intoxicating liquor not for medical, etc., purposes, in violation of the Dean Act, testimony as to defendant's conversation with the sheriff after his arrest, and defendant's making bond, in which defendant stated, in response to what was said by the sheriff, that he did not deny having liquor in his possession, but made his mistake by being caught with it, held admissible as bearing on the question that the liquor was possessed for an unlawful purpose, as was his statement that he drank too much.

8. **Criminal law ⊂⟹459—Testimony of witness that bottles contained homemade whisky admissible.**

In a prosecution for having in possession intoxicating liquors not for medical, etc., purposes, in violation of the Dean Act, testimony of a witness that from his experience in manufacturing, drinking, and handling whisky, he could tell that the bottle shown him contained homemade whisky, and that it was intoxicating, held admissible.

9. **Criminal law ⊂⟹1037(2)—Argument of state's counsel in prosecution of bootlegger not reversible error, in absence of request for corrective instruction.**

In a prosecution for having in possession intoxicating liquor not for medical, etc., purposes, in violation of the Dean Law, argument of state's counsel, when he had before him three bottles, two containing the liquor in question and one empty, also a funnel, "Look at that stuff, put a pistol beside it, then you would

⊂⟹For other cases see same topic and KEY-NUMBER in all Key-Numbered Digests and Indexes have a picture of unlawful weapons," *held* not so materially injurious to defendant as to require reversal in the absence of request for instruction that the jury do not consider it.

Appeal from District Court, Van Zandt County; Joel R. Bond, Judge.

Jim Polk Rainey was convicted of having in his possession intoxicating liquors not for mechanical or other authorized purposes, in violation of the Dean Act, and he appeals. Affirmed.

Stanford & Sanders, of Canton, for appellant.

Alvin M. Owsley, Asst. Atty. Gen., for the State.

LATTIMORE, J. Appellant was convicted in the district court of Van Zandt county of having in his possession intoxicating liquor, not for mechanical, scientific, medicinal, or sacramental purposes in violation of what is termed the Dean Act (acts 2d called Sess. 36th Leg. c. 78), and his punishment fixed at one year in the penitentiary.

There are 14 bills of exception in this record, the contentions in which will be noticed without mention of the formal objections made.

[1, 2] A motion to quash the indictment for its failure to use the expression "had in his possession" the liquor in question, was properly overruled as it appears that the indictment charged the accused "did possess" such liquor, and we see no substantial variance. That the law under which the prosecution was had is unconstitutional, etc., has been fully decided in Ex parte Gilmore, 228 S. W. 199. That the state's attorney asked a witness, "What first attracted your attention to the defendant?" did not appear to call for the answer given, which was "I was standing at the fountain watching for him, expecting him; I had been called—well I was watching for him." It would seem that if this answer was objectionable the proper procedure would have required a motion to strike out same as not being responsive, and that an objection to the question asked would not seem to be well taken.

[3] The question, "Did any liquor come into your hands, by anybody?" does not seem to be open to the objection that it was leading, or contained matter hurtful to appellant.

[4] State's counsel exhibited to a witness two bottles, a funnel, and a glass jug, and asked him what was the size of the bottle at the mouth, and the witness answered, "Just a little bit larger than the little end of the funnel." No objection was made to this as not being responsive, but it was objected to as having a tendency to convey to the jury the impression that appellant was engaged in selling the liquor found in his possession, and that the effect of this was

prejudicial. We do not agree to this proposition, for it is a necessary part of the proof in a case such as the instant case that it be shown that the possession of the accused was for some purpose other than those excepted by statute, and if the proof showed that he had the liquor in question for sale, it would be pertinent as establishing the kind of possession made punishable by statute.

[5] Appellant objected to a state witness, who said he was acquainted with the smell of whisky and "had smelled lots of it," being permitted to testify that the bottles taken from appellant's car, from their odor, contained whisky, because not qualified. We are unable to see any sufficient reason why one who knows the smell, taste, or appearance of a given substance may not testify from such examination his conclusion as to what the substance so examined is. The objection would seem to refer more to the weight than to the admissibility of the testimony. This is true of the objection to the testimony of the witness Osborne, who said he had not much experience with whisky, but that in his judgment that shown him was whisky.

[6] This witness also testified that a jug shown him had the same smell as "it had that night." The bill sets out various grounds of objection to this testimony which does not seem to us to be of much materiality, but no statement of the surrounding facts, relating to the matter objected to, is made in the bill of exceptions from which we may determine whether the objections made are tenable. This condition also obtains in appellant's bill of exceptions No. 9, which sets out certain objections to testimony to the effect that the contents of certain bottles, by taste and smell, appeared to be sorry corn whisky in the judgment of the witness. The objection seems to be that the witness was not qualified, and that there was no identification of the liquor exhibited to him, as that found in appellant's possession. When objections are made the bill setting same forth must show affirmatively, not only the grounds of objections stated, but enough facts to make it reasonably apparent that such objections are meritorious.

[7] Bill of exceptions No. 10 sets forth a conversation had between appellant and the sheriff after the arrest of appellant and he had made bond. The bill is not clear, but the court below approved same with a reference to the statement of facts, from which we gather that appellant went to the sheriff on said occasion and asked his opinion as to the best course to pursue, and the officer told him what he thought, and in response to what was said by the officer appellant stated he did not deny having the liquor in question, but had made his mistake by being caught with it. The statement of appellant, and that which was part of the same con-

versation and which elicited his statement and shed light upon it, was admissible. In this same conversation appellant said that he drank too much. This was admissible as bearing upon the question that the liquor was possessed for an unlawful purpose.

[8] The witness Kellis was permitted to state that from his experience in manufacturing, drinking, and handling whisky, he could tell that the bottle shown him contained homemade whisky, and that it was intoxicating. This does not appear to be erroneous. The liquor involved was tasted, examined, and smelled by a number of witnesses, each of whom testified to its character, and the record is practically bare of any serious contention on that question.

A witness testified, without apparent objection, that appellant had a pistol in his car when arrested. The record also shows that upon motion of appellant this testimony was excluded.

[9] By his fourteenth bill of exceptions appellant complains that during the argument state's counsel had before him three bottles, two containing the liquor in question, and one empty; also a funnel, and that he said to the jury, "Look at that stuff, put a pistol beside it, then you would have a picture of unlawful weapons." The bill of exceptions states that this was objected to, and the court asked to instruct the jury not to consider same, but we are unable to find in the record any written request to the jury asking them not to consider such argument. The only question thus presented to us is whether such argument was of that character as to make it so materially injurious to the rights of appellant as to require a reversal, in the absence of any requested instruction such as just mentioned. We do not think so. It was not the statement of any fact dehors the record, which was likely to produce substantial injury to the accused, but would appear to be more in the nature of an attempted pleasantry on the part of counsel for the state. Appellant was not charged with making an assault upon anybody by the use or carriage of unlawful weapons, and a statement that putting three whisky bottles and a pistol together would make a picture of unlawful weapons would not appear to us to produce any serious injury to the rights of appellant.

We have given careful attention to each of the matters presented by appellant, and, finding no reversible error in the record, an affirmance is ordered.

On Motion for Rehearing.

HAWKINS, J. Since the motion for rehearing has been filed, we have again examined the statement of facts, in order to consider the bills of exceptions in the light of the entire record. Having done so patiently and carefully, we find no reason for changing our former opinion.

Believing the case was properly disposed of, the motion for rehearing is overruled.

STANCHEL v. STATE.   (No. 6269.)

(Court of Criminal Appeals of Texas.
May 19, 1921.)

1. Criminal law ⊂⊃369(15), 371(8), 372(1)— That accused had automatic pistol at time of arrest the night after robbery not admissible where accused not charged with use of firearms.

In a prosecution for robbery, where defendant was not charged with robbery by firearms, testimony of the arresting officer that defendant was armed with an automatic pistol at the time of arrest the night after the robbery was inadmissible, as it did not tend to connect defendant with the offense charged, shed no light on his intent or identity in connection therewith, and had no bearing on showing system.

2. Criminal law ⊂⊃351(2)—Offer of bribe to arresting officer to release accused held inadmissible.

In a prosecution for robbery, testimony of an arresting officer that defendant offered to pay him to release him was inadmissible, under Code Cr. Proc. 1911, art. 810, restricting the circumstances under which a confession while under arrest may be received in evidence, the offer, if not a confession of guilt, laying the foundation for argument equally harmful, and being offered as an inculpatory fact.

3. Criminal law ⊂⊃721½(2)—Statements in argument as to why defendant's witness was not put on stand held harmful error in absence of evidence justifying same.

Where one accused of robbery claimed to have been at home asleep at the hour the same was committed, as his father and others in the house knew, and his father was not used as a witness by either party, though summoned by the defense and present in court, argument by the district attorney that defendant's father was not put on the stand because he had told the arresting officer, before he knew his son was arrested, that defendant did not get home until 10 o'clock the night of the robbery, and because he was already "sewed up," was harmful error, though the court reprimanded the attorney and verbally instructed the jury not to consider the argument, no evidence having been introduced that any such conversation occurred between defendant's father and the officer.

Appeal from Criminal District Court, Dallas County; Robert B. Seay, Judge.

Henry Stanchel was convicted of robbery, and he appeals. Reversed and remanded.

Rosser Thomas, of Dallas, for appellant.
R. H. Hamilton, Asst. Atty. Gen., for the State.

HAWKINS, J. Appellant was convicted of robbery, his punishment being fixed at 15 years in the penitentiary.

It will not be necessary to set out the evidence, in order to discuss the legal questions raised, further than it may be referred to incidentally.

[1] It is urged that error was committed in permitting, over objection, the officer who arrested appellant to testify that he was armed with an automatic pistol at the time of arrest, which was the next night after the alleged robbery. The trial judge admitted the testimony on the ground that it was "admissible on the subject of resistance, and escape from arrest." Appellant was not charged with robbery by firearms, and Mrs. Cheatham, the lady robbed, does not claim the party doing the robbing had or used, or that she saw, a pistol of any kind. The officer said appellant had his hand in his pocket when arrested, but took it out when told to do so, and expressly states that appellant did not try to use the pistol, and that he made no resistance. No overt act is shown by the evidence of any attempt to escape. Under the authority of Riggins v. State, 42 Tex. Cr. R. 472, 60 S. W. 877, and Watson v. State, 225 S. W. 753, this testimony was clearly inadmissible. It proved a separate and distinct offense, which did not tend to connect appellant with the offense for which he was on trial, shed no light on his intent or identity in connection with that charge, and had no bearing on showing system.

[2] S. C. Martindale, one of the officers who made the arrest, testified, over objection, that, while the other officer had gone to make some inquiries, appellant offered him $15 to turn him loose, and that after he had been taken into the presence of Mrs. Cheatham, he offered $50 and his pistol to be released. Exception was reserved to this evidence, because it was in the nature of a confession made while under arrest, and without the formalities required by article 810, C. C. P. This evidence was elicited for the evident basis of an argument that appellant's consciousness of guilt impelled the offer to secure his release. It may appear to be anomalous that, if one under arrest, by some overt act, such as flight, or resistance, seeks to effect his release, it may be shown, while an offer to bribe the officer to effect the same purpose cannot; but our statute on confessions makes it necessary to so hold. The history of legislation in this state on the subject of confessions, and the reasons behind it, would be interesting to recount, but that is not necessary. The Legislature, by amendments, instead of making the rule more lax, has from time to time, by changes, made it more restrictive. The case of Nolen v. State, 14 Tex. App. 474, 46 Am. Rep. 247, construes the law as it existed then as follows:

"Where the confessions of a defendant under arrest are inadmissible against him because made while uncautioned, his acts, if tantamount to such a confession, and done under similar circumstances, are likewise inadmissible."

There are apparently some exceptions to this rule, such as permitting footprints or finger prints for comparison to be made, though accused be under arrest; but they are not here involved.

The offer of one under arrest to pay the officer for his release, if not tantamount to a confession of guilt, lays the foundation for argument which would be equally cogent and harmful to the accused as a direct confession. The Nolen Case was cited and approved by Judge White in Fulcher v. State, 28 Tex. App. 465, 13 S. W. 750, wherein he says: "Since the rule was announced in the Nolen Case it has been followed and recognized in this State." In Hankins v. State, 75 S. W. 787, it was held that the testimony of a confederate to the effect that the defendant, while both were in jail, had offered to pay a part of the witness' fine if he would take the blame for the offense and exculpate defendant, was inadmissible.

"The purpose and effect of this statute [article 810, C. C. P.] is to prevent the prosecution from using against accused the testimony of the officer having him under arrest to a verbal statement made by accused which the state seeks to use to prove his guilt." Dover v. State, 81 Tex. Cr. R. 553, 197 S. W. 196.

And in the case last above cited we approved the rule laid down in the Hernan Case, 42 Tex. Cr. R. 464, 60 S. W. 766, as correct, viz.:

"Any fact or circumstance involved in a statement by defendant while in jail or under arrest, and when he has not been cautioned, which may be used by the state as a criminative or inculpatory fact against him, comes within the statutory rule as to confession, although the same may not be technically a confession or admission."

In the instant case, the state could have offered the objectionable evidence for no purpose save that of proving or tending to prove appellant's guilt; it was a criminative and inculpatory fact against him. The state was evidently not impressed with the idea that it was in appellant's favor, or its introduction over objection would not have been insisted on.

[3] Appellant's defense was alibi. He claimed to have been at home asleep at the hour Mrs. Cheatham says she was robbed, and that his father, Jim Stanchel, and others were at the house, and knew this. For some reason appellant's father was not used as a witness by either party. During his argument the district attorney made use of the following language:

"Why did not the defendant have his father, Jim Stanchel, on the stand? He was summoned as a defense witness, and was present here in court. The reason is that Jim Stanchel, this negro's father, had already been seen and talked with by the officer before he knew Henry was arrested, and told the officer that Henry did not get home until 10 o'clock on the night of the robbery."

There was no evidence before the jury that any such conversation occurred between the elder Stanchel and the officer. The court reprimanded the district attorney, and verbally instructed the jury not to consider the argument. Later in his argument, he again said:

"Why has not Jim Stanchel, the defendant's father, testified in this case? He was already sewed up; that's why."

He was again reprimanded, and the jury also verbally told to disregard the last statement. It was perfectly legitimate for counsel to criticize the failure to produce available evidence, and deduce a conclusion that, if offered, it would not be favorable. But the district attorney in his zeal went further than this court can sanction. We understand that in the heat of debate attorneys for both the state and defendant are likely to violate the rules of argument; but here counsel passed from the domain of argument and conclusion, and entered the realm in which a witness only is entitled to move. It was a damaging statement against appellant, and we cannot hold the same to have been harmless, in view of the penalty inflicted. Brookreson v. State, 225 S. W. 375; McIntosh v. State, 85 Tex. Cr. R. 417, 213 S. W. 659; Coleman v. State, 49 Tex. Cr. R. 82, 90 S. W. 501.

For the errors pointed out, the judgment of the trial court is reversed, and the cause remanded.

JONES v. STATE.   (No. 6221.)

(Court of Criminal Appeals of Texas. April 27, 1921. Rehearing Granted May 19, 1921.)

1. **Criminal law ⬅️1081—Notice of appeal essential to jurisdiction.**

Without notice of appeal, the Court of Criminal Appeals has no jurisdiction under provision of Vernon's Ann. Code Cr. Proc. 1916, art. 915.

On Motion for Rehearing.

2. **Criminal law ⬅️195(2)—Where defendant fires at one and wounds another, state may charge assault on both or either, but judgment in one case bars prosecution in other.**

Where defendant fired at one person and wounded another, it was within the discretion of the state to charge an assault on both or either of them; but conviction or acquittal in one case would bar prosecution in the other.

3. **Homicide ⬅️89(2)—Fact shot fired at one with intent to murder him wounded another no excuse.**

Where defendant fired a shot at one person, with malice, intending to kill him, the fact that it wounded another, whom he did not intend to kill, would not excuse him from liability for assault with intent to murder.

4. **Assault and battery ⬅️75—Indictment for assault with intent to commit another offense need not give elements of offense intended to be committed.**

Under Const. art. 1, § 10, guaranteeing accused the right to demand the nature and cause of the accusation, in charging an assault with intent to commit another offense, it is necessary only to allege such matters as bring the offense within the definition of an assault coupled with an intention to commit such other offense, naming it, without giving the constituent elements of the offense intended to be committed.

5. **Indictment and information ⬅️174—Principal offender may be convicted under indictment charging him directly with offense.**

A principal offender, by reason of the part performed by him in the commission of an offense, may be convicted under an indictment charging him directly with its commission.

6. **Indictment and information ⬅️125(44)—Indictment may charge murder of two or more by same act in single count.**

An indictment for murder may, in a single count, charge the murder of two or more persons by the same act.

7. **Homicide ⬅️142(10)—Under charge of assault to murder one, proof of intent to murder another is admissible.**

Under an indictment charging an assault upon M. with the intent to murder him, the state could prove that the shot which wounded him was fired at E. with intent to murder E.; the fact that M. was the victim rendering it no less an assault with intent to murder.

8. **Homicide ⬅️319—No error in overruling motion for new trial, where testimony of absent witness is contradictory.**

It was not error to overrule a motion for a new trial on the ground of newly discovered evidence, where the testimony of an absent witness as to an uncommunicated threat against defendant, made by one at whom he shot with intent to murder, was so contradictory that the court was justified in disregarding it.

9. **Homicide ⬅️319—New trial for newly discovered evidence properly denied, where defendant knew of same before trial.**

It was not error to overrule a motion for a new trial on the ground of newly discovered evidence, where an absent witness would have testified to threats against defendant by one at whom he shot with intent to murder, which were communicated to defendant; defendant having known of them before the trial.

Appeal from District Court, Marion County; J. A. Ward, Judge.

Mike Jones was convicted of assault with intent to murder, and he appeals. Affirmed.

T. D. Rowell, of Jefferson, for appellant.

R. H. Hamilton, Asst. Atty. Gen., for the State.

MORROW, P. J. The conviction is for assault with intent to murder; punishment fixed at confinement in the penitentiary for a period of 10 years.

[1] We find it necessary to sustain the motion made by the state to dismiss the appeal because of the absence of any notice of appeal. Without notice of appeal, this court has no jurisdiction. Article 915, Vernon's Texas Criminal Statutes, vol. 2, p. 877, and cases there listed.

On Motion for Rehearing.

Appellant is convicted for assault with intent to murder; punishment fixed at confinement in the penitentiary for 10 years. The omissions in the record having been supplied, the motion for rehearing is granted, and the dismissal set aside.

The indictment charges that the appellant did "make an assault in and upon Jud Mathis, with the intent then and there to murder the said Jud Mathis." Upon the facts, the theory was presented that the shot fired by the appellant, which injured Mathis, was not fired at him, but was fired at Marion Elliott. The court instructed the jury that if they believed from the evidence, beyond a reasonable doubt, that the appellant, with malice aforethought, fired the shot that injured Mathis with the specific intent to kill Elliott, he would be guilty of an assault with intent to murder Mathis. The correctness of the treatment of the matter is challenged upon the ground that, the indictment having charged an assault upon Mathis, under this pleading there could be no conviction upon proof showing that the shot was fired at Elliott, against whom there was malice, and by accident striking Mathis, against whom no ill will was entertained. Apparently the law upon the subject is stated in the opinion of the court in Mathis v. State, 39 Tex. Cr. R. 552, 47 S. W. 464, thus:

"The assault is only required to be with intent to murder; that is, to murder some one. And we hold that if A. shoots at B. with intent of his malice aforethought to kill and murder B., but accidentally shoots C. and inflicts a wound upon him, that the malice is carried over to C., and that this is an assault with implied malice to murder C."

The legal proposition thus stated finds support in several cases, among them being Richards v. State, 35 Tex. Cr. R. 43, 30 S. W. 805; Smith v. State, 95 S. W. 1058. See, also, State v. Thomas, 127 La. 576, 53 South. 868, 37 L. R. A. (N. S.) 172, Ann. Cas. 1912A, 1059; Spannell v. State, 83 Tex. Cr. R. 418, 203 S. W. 357, 2 A. L. R. 593.

The evidence goes to show that while Mathis and Elliott were walking together in the nighttime a shot was fired, taking effect upon Mathis; that Elliott fled, and two other shots were fired. Other evidence connects the appellant with the assault. The state proved his admission that he fired the shot, and by the same witness, on cross-examination, it was shown that at the same time he said that the shot was fired at Elliott, and not at Mathis. Both Elliott and Mathis testified that they had had no difficulty with the appellant. Shortly before the shooting, all the parties were at the home of a negro woman of unchaste character. Appellant and a companion left first, and the shooting occurred soon after Mathis and Elliott took their departure.

[2, 3] The theory of an accidental shooting of Mathis was developed by the appellant. Assuming that the appellant fired at Elliott and wounded Mathis, it was within the discretion of the state to charge an assault upon both Elliott and Mathis, or upon either of them; but the conviction or acquittal in one case would bar the prosecution in the other. Spannell v. State, 83 Tex. Cr. R. 423, 203 S. W. 357, 2 A. L. R. 593. If the appellant fired the shot at Elliott with malice, intending to kill him, the fact that it wounded Mathis, whom he did not intend to kill, would not excuse him.

[4] Appellant does not controvert the proposition last stated, but insists that, in writing the indictment, it is essential that it should contain averments setting out all facts which it is necessary that the state prove in order to sustain a conviction, referring to 22 Cyc. pp. 285–295, Hewitt v. State, 25 Tex. 722, Williams v. State, 12 Tex. App. 395, and other cases. There is a distinction between the facts that must be proved and those that may be proved under an indictment. A statement in the indictment of the facts necessary to make certain, specific, and complete description of the offense is required by the Constitution. Huntsman v. State, 12 Tex. App. 619; Hewitt v. State, 25 Tex. 722; Harris' Texas Constitution, p. 85. It is not necessary, however, to allege matters in the nature of evidence. 22 Cyc. p. 285. An indictment for murder, charging that the accused did "then and there unlawfully and with express malice aforethought kill the deceased (naming him) by shooting him with a gun" was held in an opinion embracing a complete review of the principles and precedents, a sufficient averment in an indictment for murder. Caldwell v. State, 28 Tex. App. 576, 14 S. W. 122; Rose's Notes, vol. 5, p. 789. In charging an assault with intent to commit another offense, it is necessary only to allege such matters as bring the offense within the definition of an assault, coupled with an intention to commit such other offense, naming it, without giving the

constituent elements of the offense intended to be committed. Morris v. State, 13 Tex. App. 72.

[5, 6] If one be a principal offender by reason of the part performed by him in the commission of the offense, he may be convicted under an indictment charging him directly with its commission. Tuller v. State, 8 Tex. App. 506. This principle has been given general application. Branch's Ann. Penal Code, § 676; Dodd v. State, 83 Tex. Cr. R. 164, 201 S. W. 1014. It has often been held that an indictment for murder may, in a single count, charge one with the murder of two or more persons by the same act. Rucker v. State, 7 Tex. App. 549; Chivarrio v. State, 15 Tex. App. 334.

[7] In the case before us, it was necessary to establish, by evidence, that the appellant made an assault upon Mathis with the intent to murder him. These constituted the elements of the offense which were set out in the indictment. To establish them it was competent that the state prove that the shot which wounded Mathis was fired by the appellant at Elliott, because by proving that the shot was fired with intent to murder Elliott the offense would be complete. Though the shot struck, not Elliott, but Mathis, it was intended to murder; it was an assault. That Mathis was the victim of it rendered it no less an assault with intent to murder.

[8, 9] There was no error in overruling that phase of the motion for a new trial referring to newly discovered evidence. One of the absent witnesses would have given testimony of an uncommunicated threat made by Elliott against the appellant. Her testimony was contradictory to a degree that the court was justified in disregarding it. The other witness would have testified to threats communicated to the appellant. All this appellant manifestly knew before the trial, and in fact the absence of knowledge on his part of all the alleged newly discovered evidence is not made clear.

The record reveals no error, and the affirmance of the judgment must result.

GULF PRODUCTION CO. et al. v. STATE et al. (No. 6532.)

(Court of Civil Appeals of Texas. San Antonio. April 30, 1921. Rehearing Denied May 26, 1921.)

1. Evidence ⊂⊃83(3)—State lands presumed to have been appraised and notice given.

In state's action to cancel sale of public land sold as dry agricultural land for $1.50 an acre, upon the ground that land was legally appraised at $2 an acre at the time of the sale, and that the Commissioner of the General Land Office had not notified the county clerk of

county in which land was situated of classification of land and the appraisement thereof at $1.50 an acre, under Act of 1897, c. 129 (10 Gammel's Laws, p. 1238), it will be presumed that the Commissioner in awarding land to the purchaser had classified the land as agricultural and had appraised it at $1.50 an acre, and that the county clerk had been notified of such classification and appraisement in the manner prescribed by the statutes in force at such time, the burden of proof being upon the state to rebut such presumption by direct and affirmative evidence.

2. Public lands ⊂⊃173(4)—Evidence held to prove land appraised at figure at which it was sold.

In state's action to cancel sale of public land sold as dry agricultural land for $1.50 an acre upon the ground that land was legally appraised at $2 an acre at the time of the sale, and that the commissioner of the General Land Office had not notified the county clerk of county in which land was situated of classification of land and the appraisement thereof at $1.50 an acre, under Act of 1897, c. 129 (10 Gammel's Laws, p. 1238) evidence *held* to prove that the land had been duly appraised at $1.50 an acre, and that notice thereof had been sent to and received and recorded by the county clerk at the time of the sale.

3. Public lands ⊂⊃173(22)—Purchaser's right to reinstatement on same terms as original purchase not affected by Land Commissioner's subsequent reclassification of land.

Purchaser of public land classified at time of purchase as agricultural land, who defaulted in payment of interest, was entitled to reinstatement of sale with all rights received at time of original purchase, on payment of amount due, where no rights of third persons had intervened, under Rev. St. art. 5423, providing that land forfeiture of land for nonpayment of interest "be resold under the provisions of this act or any future law," but that purchaser be reinstated on payment of amount due if no rights of third persons have intervened, notwithstanding reclassification of purchased land, during an interval between purchase and forfeiture, as mineral land under article 5433, providing for sale of such land with reservation of minerals to the state, where article 5423, giving purchaser the right to reinstatement, was in existence at time of purchaser, and was therefore a right which the Land Commissioner's subsequent reclassification of the land could not operate to destroy.

4. Public lands ⊂⊃173(22)—Forfeitures not favored.

Forfeitures by statute or contract are not favored, and must be scrutinized, while statutes or contracts designed to give relief from the rigors of forfeiture are liberally construed so as to afford the maximum relief.

5. Public lands ⊂⊃173(22) — Purchaser after forfeiture of previous sale, who voluntarily abandoned land, had no intervening rights barring reinstatement of original purchaser.

Purchaser's right to reinstatement under Rev. St. art. 5423, providing for reinstatement where no rights of third persons have intervened, following forfeiture for nonpayment of interest, was not affected by the fact that during interval between forfeiture and reinstatement third person made application to purchase the land, where such person did not complete his purchase by actually settling on the land, but voluntarily abandoned it.

6. Public lands ⟪⇒⟫173(22)—Right to reinstatement not affected by fact that cancellation of abandoned sale to third person had not been formally entered on Land Office books.

Where third person, who had made an application to purchase land after forfeiture for previous sale for nonpayment of interest under Rev. St. art. 5423, did not complete purchase, but voluntarily abandoned it without acquiring any substantial right, purchaser or his vendee, by payment of amount due, under such statute, were entitled to reinstatement, even though cancellation of sale to third person had not been formally entered on the Land Office books.

7. Deeds ⟪⇒⟫121—Quitclaim deed conveys no more than present interest of grantor.

A quit claim deed conveys no more than the present interest of the grantor in the land described, and does not extend to an interest subsequently accruing.

8. Public lands ⟪⇒⟫173(22)—Quitclaim deed, executed after forfeiture, entitled grantee to reinstatement under statute.

A quitclaim deed, executed by purchaser's successor in interest after forfeiture of sale for nonpayment of interest under Rev. St. art. 5423, entitled grantee to reinstatement on payment of amount due, if rights of third parties have not intervened, under such statute; the grantor having enjoyed such a right and having conveyed by quitclaim deed the interest held by him at time of the execution of the deed.

9. Public lands ⟪⇒⟫173(22)—Right to reinstatement not affected by false representations to Land Commissioner.

The right to reinstatement of successor in interest of purchaser of public land under Rev. St. art. 5423, after forfeiture for nonpayment of interest, was a vested right, where no rights of third parties intervened, which could not be affected by any false representations to Land Commissioner by successor in interest.

Cobbs, J., dissenting on motion for rehearing.

Appeal from District Court, Travis County; George Calhoun, Judge.

Suit by the State of Texas and another against the Gulf Production Company and others. Judgment for plaintiffs, and defendants appeal. Reversed and rendered.

D. Edward Greer, of Houston, Brooks, Hart & Woodward, of Austin, John G. Gregg, of Fort Worth, Kay, Akin & Kenley, of Wichita Falls, White, Cartledge & Wilcox, of Austin, W. P. McLean, of Fort Worth, and Black & Smedley, of Austin, for appellants. Williams & Williams, T. J. Conway, John

Maxwell, and J. N. Gallagher, all of Waco, and E. R. Pedigo, C. M. Cureton, and E. F. Smith, all of Austin, for appellees.

SMITH, J. The land in dispute is valued in the pleadings at $8,000,000. Up to the 1st day of June, 1920, the last day to which an accounting is shown in the record, petroleum oil of the cash value, including interest to said date, of $737,479.04, had been produced from the land. The expense incurred in producing the oil was $420,068.36, which was deducted in the judgment from the gross proceeds. The state of Texas obtained judgment for $92,184.88, and P. K. Shuler for $225,225.80, being the net balance after deducting the cost of production, and for improvements, placed on the land by the company producing the oil, of the value of $114,599.88. The land was originally offered by the state at $1 an acre, without a taker. Subsequently, the price was raised to $2, then sold, in 1899, at $1.50 an acre. The transcript of the record in the case comprises 311 pages, and the statement of facts, 208 pages, while counsel have kindly favored us with 446 pages of briefs. There lies before us, then, the grand total, and prodigious task, of 960 pages. But the properties in controversy are of commanding value, the questions raised in the record are serious and far-reaching, and in their briefs counsel have very ably and very frankly presented these questions to the obvious end that a just result may be ultimately reached in the litigation.

The litigation grows out of a dispute over the title to 160 acres of public land in Stephens county, described as the northeast quarter of section 22, in block 6, Texas & Pacific Railway Company surveys, and was classified as "dry agricultural," up to some time in 1916, when it was reclassified as "mineral." On October 30, 1899, J. M. Kidd made application through the General Land Office to purchase the land as dry agricultural, at $1.50 an acre, and the application, as well as the first payment on the basis of $1.50 an acre, was accepted by the Land Commissioner, and in pursuance thereof the land was sold and awarded to Kidd on January 22, 1900. Each year thereafter, on the 1st day of November, the time fixed by law, Kidd and his successors in title regularly paid to the state the annual interest on the purchase price, on the basis of $1.50 an acre, until November 1, 1915. There was default, however, in the interest payment due on that date, and the following month the sale was forfeited by the Commissioner because of such default. On June 14, 1916, while the sale to Kidd was in suspense, the land was awarded to one V. Griffin, but upon his failure to settle thereon within 90 days, as required by law, this sale was, on February 9, 1917, canceled, and in that way Griffin dropped out of the title. On the same day, upon payment to the state of the past-due interest, the Kidd sale was reinstated, as provided by the statute. In pursuance of an opinion of the Attorney General, that the reinstatement of the Kidd sale was invalid, and because of the receipt of that opinion, the Land Commissioner, on September 2, 1919, canceled the sale to Kidd, and on the same day issued to P. K. Shuler a permit to prospect for oil and gas on the land in dispute, and this suit was instituted by the state of Texas to enforce the cancellation of the Kidd sale and establish the validity of the Shuler permit, and for this purpose was joined by Shuler as a party plaintiff. Those holding under the Kidd title, by transfer or by lease, were made defendants.

The cause was tried by a jury upon special issues, and upon the answers of the jury to these special issues judgment was rendered in favor of plaintiffs and against defendants in the court below for the title to and possession of the land, and in favor of the state of Texas for $92,184.88, being the value of one-eighth of the oil taken from the land up to June 20, 1920, and in favor of Shuler for $225,225.80, the net balance of the value of said oil after deducting $420,068.36 covering the expense of production thereof, and for the title to and possession of improvements placed on the land by the Gulf Production Company and used by it in the development of the land for oil purposes, of the value of $114,599.78. All defendants have appealed.

The basis of the litigation is the sale of the land to J. M. Kidd in 1899. ·The state of Texas and its coplaintiff, Shuler, attack the validity of that sale as being void upon the ground that at the time it was made the land was legally appraised at $2 an acre, whereas Kidd applied to purchase it, and it was sold to him, at the price of $1.50 an acre. It was upon this ground that appellees recovered, although they sought recovery upon other grounds as well, to be adverted to hereafter. In response to the only two special issues submitted to them the jury found (a) that the Commissioner of the General Land Office did not, after August 20, 1897 (on which date the minimum value of the land was reduced by statute from $2 to $1.50 an acre) reduce the valuation of the land from $2 to $1.50 an acre, and (b) that the Commissioner did not notify in writing the county clerk of Stephens county of such reduction prior to the sale to Kidd, and that the said clerk did not receive such notice prior to that time. Before undertaking to set out the facts disclosed by the record, it is well to consider the statutes bearing upon the questions raised:

Under the Acts of 1879 (section 1, c. 28, 9 Gammel's, 55) the public free school lands of the state were put on the market, it being provided (Id. § 2) that such lands should be classified and their value appraised by the respective county surveyors, subject to approval and correction by the county commissioners' courts, but that in no case should such value be fixed at less than $1 an acre. This act seems to have been superseded by the Acts of 1883, which provided (section 2, c. 88, 9 Gammel's, 391) for the creation of the State Land Board, consisting of the Governor, Attorney General, Comptroller, Treasurer, and Commissioner of the General Land Office, which should (Id. § 3) cause the public lands to be classified as agricultural, pasture, or timber, and further providing (Id. § 4) that such lands should not be sold for less than $2 for lands not watered or timbered, $3 for watered lands, and $5 for timbered lands. In 1895 (section 3, c. 47, 10 Gammel's, 793) it was provided that the Commissioner of the General Land Office should cause the public lands to be classified or appraised, or classify and appraise them himself, into (Id. § 4) agricultural, pasture, or timber lands; that (Id. § 6)—

"It shall be the duty of the Commissioner of the General Land Office to notify in writing the county clerk of each county of the valuation fixed upon each section of land in his county, and in each county attached to it for judicial purposes, which he offers for sale, which notification shall be kept by the clerk in his office and recorded in a well-bound book, which shall be open to public inspection."

This article has not been amended, and is still in force. It was further provided by this act (Id. § 7) that the lands should not be sold at less than $2 an acre, except pasture lands, which should not be sold for less than $1 an acre, and timber lands, which should not be sold for less than $5 an acre. By the act of 1897 (chapter 129, 10 Gammel's, 1238) the authority of the Land Commissioner to classify and appraise the lands was continued, but the minimum price at which agricultural lands should be sold was fixed at $1.50 an acre, and grazing lands at $1 an acre. These minimum prices were in effect at the time of the application of and sale to Kidd.

So it will be seen that, according to a strict construction of the statutes then in force, the land was not subject to the sale to Kidd unless it had theretofore been appraised at $1.50 an acre, and notice of such appraisement sent to and received by the county clerk of Stephens county.

We have made the most painstaking examination of the record, and have reached the conclusion that the evidence conclusively shows that the land in controversy was in fact appraised by the Commissioner of the General Land Office at the price of $1.50 an acre, and that notice thereof had been given to and received by the county clerk at the time Kidd applied to purchase the land. Practically all the material evidence in the case consisted of records solemnly made, some of them long years ago, while the transactions were actually transpiring, and others at intervals thereafter. And there was no conflict in the parol evidence, which was explanatory of, and fortified the effect of, the documentary evidence, thus in effect eliminating all issues of fact, so that the only questions arising in the case are questions of law to be applied to undisputed facts.

[1] In the first place, then, the act of the Commissioner of the General Land Office in awarding the land to Kidd created the definite presumption that the Commissioner had classified the land as agricultural and appraised it at $1.50, and the county clerk of Stephens county had been notified of such classification and appraisement, each in the manner prescribed by the statutes then in force. And while appellees in attacking the validity of the sale and award had the right to rebut that presumption, the burden of proof was upon them to do so, and by direct and affirmative evidence. Corrigan v. Fitzsimmons, 97 Tex. 595, 80 S. W. 989; Smithers v. Lowrance, 100 Tex. 77, 93 S. W. 1064; Holt v. Cave, 38 Tex. Civ. App. 64, 85 S. W. 309; Hood v. Pursley, 39 Tex. Civ. App. 477, 87 S. W. 870; Stolley v. Lilwall, 38 Tex. Civ. App. 49, 84 S. W. 689. In Corrigan v. Fitzsimmons, supra, Chief Justice Gaines said that "under the present law, it is the duty of the Commissioner of the General Land Office to cause the lands to be classified and appraised, and to notify the clerk of the county court of the county in which they are situate and thus put them upon the market. It is also his duty to know that this has been done before he awards a sale," and that when he makes the award the law presumes that these things have been done, that "the fact that he awarded the lands under the application is evidence of the existence of the facts necessary to give him authority to sell." Even if that presumption in this case had stood alone, and without any support in the testimony, we think the evidence introduced to overcome the presumption was wholly insufficient for that purpose. All such evidence was of a purely negative nature. None of it was direct, or affirmative. On the other hand, the evidence introduced in support of the facts presumed was overwhelming, and in our opinion conclusively establishes the facts without the aid of the presumption. We will set out some of this evidence:

Kidd did not himself undertake to make out his application to purchase the land. At his request the county clerk of Stephens county made it out for him, although he was not charged by law with that duty. When Kidd made the request of him, the clerk withdrew to another room in his office, presumably to get from his records the necessary data upon which to base the application. Kidd so testified upon direct examination, although upon cross-examination he said he did not see just what the clerk did while in the other room. In the very nature of the circumstances, however, it may be assumed, although such is not necessary to the finding on any material issue here, that the clerk went into the other room to inform himself from his records as to the status—the description, classification, appraisement, etc.—of this tract of land, since it would be absurd to assume that he would have all this information tabulated in his mind ready at all times for instant use. But whether his retirement to another room was for this purpose or not, the clerk on this or some prior occasion obtained this information from his records, or from some other source of information satisfactory to himself as county clerk, charged by law with the duty of keeping records of such official information since it is a fact that upon his return to where Kidd was awaiting him he wrote out the application, filling in all the blanks, including description, classification, appraisement, and such other matters as were necessary to put the paper in a form acceptable to the Commissioner of the General Land Office. He showed the classification to be "dry agricultural," and the appraisement to be "$1.50," which later checked with the records of the land office and was there "O. K.'d." He figured out for Kidd, the applicant, the amount of the first payment, on the basis of $1.50 an acre, which was later accepted as correct by the Land Commissioner. Kidd did nothing in the premises but sign and swear to the application, execute the obligation, and furnish the remittance for the first payment. The clerk then forwarded the application and payment to the General Land Office, where it was received and filed on October 30, 1899. It appears that it was not taken up for consideration in the General Land Office until after December 9, 1899, when, in the usual course, it was referred to the head sales clerk, who in turn referred it to the examining clerk. At that time it bore on its back the indorsements, among others, "classification, dry agricultural," and "appraisement, $1.50." The examining clerk took it to the records in the office and compared it with such records to ascertain if the land had been applied for by Kidd at the correct classification and appraisement. This clerk, after running the records, entered his "O. K." on the back of the application opposite each of the indorsements, "classification, dry agricultural," and "appraisement, $1.50," which meant that he had found from the records that the land was in fact classified as dry agricultural and appraised at $1.50 an acre. Upon this showing, and finding the application in due form in all other respects, the head sales clerk indorsed thereon the word, "accept," which meant that it had come to him, showing the land to be dry agricultural and appraised at $1.50, and that there was no conflict, and that the land was to be awarded as applied for. The award was actually made on January 22, 1900, and official notice thereof was given to the county clerk by the Commissioner on February 1, 1900. While the Kidd application was pending, however, and before it had been reached for consideration in the Land Office, one J. M. Cook wrote the

Commissioner that he desired to apply to purchase the land in dispute, and asked as to the existing status thereof, and was officially advised by the Commissioner, on December 9, that the land was classified as dry agricultural, and "the price is $1.50 an acre." And again: On September 22, 1899, this same man, Cook, made application to the Land Office to purchase the land in controversy as dry grazing and at $1 an acre. This application took the same course in the Land Office as the Kidd application did later on. The head sales clerk gave it to the examining clerk, who took it and ran the records for verification. The indorsements on the back of the paper showed "dry grazing" and "appraisement, $1," instead of "dry agricultural," and "appraisement, $1.50," as in the Kidd application. And, when the clerk checked those indorsements with the records, instead of writing "O. K." opposite them, as he did on the Kidd application, he wrote "dry agricultural" and "appraisement, $1.50," thus asserting that he had found from an examination of the records that the land was classified as dry agricultural and appraised at $1.50 an acre, at which it was subsequently sold to Kidd. And, instead of indorsing the Cook application "accept," as he did the Kidd application later on, the head sales clerk indorsed it "reject and refund," and the Cook application was thus rejected because the examination of the records by the clerk charged with that duty disclosed that the land was classified as dry agricultural and not dry grazing, and appraised at $1.50 and not $1. This rejection occurred November 27, 1899, after the Kidd application was filed, but before it had been reached for examination in the Land Office. Thus, in each of these three groups of circumstances the Commissioner of the General Land Office, through his authorized subordinates, officially ascertained and determined from the records of his office, and declared, the land in controversy to be appraised at $1.50 an acre. And this all occurred while Kidd's application was on file and before the award was actually made to him. As a matter of fact Cook subsequently, in May, 1900, purchased the quarter section adjoining the Kidd quarter section on the south, as dry agricultural, and at the price of $1.50 an acre, the same as the Kidd classification and appraisement.

These further facts were shown: Prior to 1897, while the minimum price of this and similar lands was fixed by law at $2 an acre, the Land Commissioner had prepared in his office what was designated as "daily work book No. 6," in which the classification and appraisement of the public lands were shown for the guidance of the Commissioner and his subordinates in carrying on the work of the office in the sale and lease of those lands. In this work book 6, the land in dispute was shown to be appraised at $2 an acre, the then minimum, and at which price the land had theretofore been formally appraised. In 1897 the Legislature reduced the minimum price of this and like classified lands to $1.50 an acre. The Commissioner had theretofore adopted the minimum price of lands, as fixed by the statute, as the appraised and selling value of such lands, and this was the fixed policy of the office, under definite instructions of the Commissioner to his subordinates, and the various county clerks, including the Stephens county clerk, had been so advised, and it was so generally understood by the public. This policy was in effect in 1897, when the minimum was reduced on this land to $1.50. Shortly after this reduction, the Commissioner had prepared daily work book No. 5, and because of the adoption of the minimum as the appraised and selling value of the lands, the clerks preparing the book 5 were directed by the Commissioner to omit the appraised value from its appropriate column in the book, "and consider the lands on the market at the minimum." This was done, and in this way there was no showing of such appraisements in this book 5. When this book was completed, about 1898, it was put in use in the place of book 6, above described, the active use of which was thereupon discarded. So, the appraised value of the land in dispute, as well as of hundreds of other tracts, was not shown in work book 5, which continued in use until 1902, when it was superseded by book 30, which showed this land to have been classified as dry agricultural and appraised at $1.50, and sold to Kidd. This work book 30 is still in use. In 1902, also, the Commissioner mailed out to the Stephens county clerk a list of lands in that county, showing this tract to be classified as dry agricultural and appraised at $1.50 and sold to Kidd. The bookkeeping account with Kidd, as kept in the Land Office, showed the annual interest payments as they accrued for 18 years, always paid and accepted on the basis of $1.50 an acre. So far as we are able to find, every reference to the appraised value of this land in the records of the Land Office and in the Stephens county clerk's office, made since 1895, when the land was formally appraised at $2 and notice given to and recorded by the clerk, shows such appraisement to be $1.50 an acre. And, finally, in March, 1918, more than 18 years after the sale to Kidd occurred, we find the Commissioner of the General Land Office definitely reiterating that at the time Kidd purchased it the land was classified as dry agricultural and appraised at $1.50 an acre, as will be seen from the following significant correspondence:

"Joseph L. Mayfield, Oil Producer.

"Wichita Falls, Texas, March 19, 1918.
"Hon. J. T. Robison, Land Commissioner, Austin, Texas—Dear Sir: I am desirous of learning the classification on the N. E. ¼. Sec.

22, Blk. 6, T. & P. Ry. Co., Certificate 2/845, in Stephens county, Texas.

"I think this land was originally purchased by a Mr. Kid, transferred a number of times and finally forfeited for the nonpayment of interest, sold, reforfeited and finally reinstated to a Mr. Jno. F. Lewis under the original purchase.

"Am desirous of knowing the original classification, also if there was any reclassification under the reinstatement.

"Please send bill.

"Yours very truly,	Joseph L. Mayfield.
"Received Mar 20, 1918.
"Referred to Old Title."

"March 21, 1918.

"Mr. Joseph L. Mayfield, Wichita Falls, Texas—Dear Sir: Replying to yours of the 19th instant, beg to advise that the N. E. ¼ of section 22, block 6, Cert. 2/845, T. & P. Ry. Co., 160 acres in Stephens county, was classified as dry agricultural land and appraised at $1.50 per acre under the act of 1895, amended by act of May 19, 1897, and awarded J. M. Kidd as an actual settler January 22, 1900, on his application filed October 30, 1899, on said classification and appraisement. J. M. Kidd made proof of three years' occupancy and the required improvements of said land, November 7, 1905, and filed the same in this office November 9, 1905. Said land was forfeited for nonpayment of interest December 30, 1915, and subsequently awarded V. Griffin as his home tract June 14, 1916, on his application filed May 2, 1916, as mineral and agricultural land at $6.00 per acre. The sale to Griffin, however, was canceled February 9, 1917, on account of his failure to file his affidavit of settlement on said land within the required time and the J. M. Kidd purchase was reinstated on the records of this office February 9, 1917. It is now in good standing in his name and the annual interest is paid on said account to November 1, 1917.

"There is no transfer to Jno. F. Lewis of this land on file and classification and appraisement of said land under the J. M. Kidd stands as the correct classification and appraisement thereof. It was subsequently reclassified as mineral and agricultural after the forfeiture of the Kidd purchase, but the sale to Kidd having been reinstated, the former classification and appraisement governs. Fee 50 cents for this information.

"Yours very truly,
"J. T. Robison, Commissioner."

The present Commissioner of the General Land Office, who was a clerk in that office at the time the sale to Kidd was made, and whose long and honorable service in this office as such clerk and as Commissioner excites great respect and admiration, testified that while he signed the Mayfield letter, it was in fact dictated by C. M. Calloway, the "old title" clerk in the office, and that he did not "think that letter shows the true record facts of my office," but he did not undertake to point out the particulars in which there were errors in the letter. The record shows, too, that Mr. Calloway, who dictated the Mayfield letter, has been a clerk in the Land Office for over 50 years, and we are induced

by this fact to look with much respect upon his solemn declarations concerning the contents and effects of the records of that office.

Now, to overcome the presumption of law, and the force of the facts hereinabove set out, appellees introduced and call our attention to this additional evidence: On June 11, 1895, the Land Commissioner classified the whole of section 22 (of which the land in dispute is the northeast quarter) as dry agricultural, and appraised it at $2 an acre, and this classification and appraisement was sent to, received and recorded by, the Stephens county clerk. This classification and appraisement was shown in work book No. 6, heretofore referred to, and which was in use from 1895 to the latter part of 1897 or early part of 1898, shortly after the minimum price of this land was reduced by the Legislature from $2 to $1.50. The northwest quarter of section 22 was sold at $2 an acre, in February, 1897, before the minimum price was reduced to $1.50. The southwest quarter was sold in 1900 as dry grazing land, at $1 an acre, the minimum price for that class of land. The southeast quarter was sold to Cook, in May, 1900, as dry agricultural, at $1.50, the then minimum price. The Land Commissioner and the county clerk of Stephens county testified that they had before the trial searched their respective offices, and were unable to find any record of where the land had been formally appraised at $1.50 an acre, or at any other price than $2. The present Commissioner also testified that in investigating matters arising with reference to this land after its sale to Kidd, and involving the classification and appraisement, clerks would first refer to the record of the sale; if upon such reference there was anything on the face of the record indicating any inaccuracy or importing irregularity in the classification or appraisement, the searchers would go on back to the sources of original information, but in the absence of such indications he would assume the record of the sale showed the true facts and go no further. Appellees contend that this method of investigation neutralizes the probative effect of the fact that all the records and other documentary evidence created since 1895 show the appraisement of the land at $1.50. But we are unable to agree with that view, or to give such vital effect to such conjecture. And in no event would the rule apply to the reasons shown for the rejection of the application of Cook on November 27, 1899, nor to the declaration of the Commissioner in his letter to Cook of December 9, 1899, that the land was classified as dry agricultural and appraised at $1.50 an acre, because it affirmatively appears from the letter to Cook that at that time the Kidd application had not been reached for examination in the Land Office, nor the sale to Kidd consummated.

In the letter to Cook, obviously referring to Kidd's application, the Commissioner, in an official communication signed by his chief clerk, advises Cook:

"There is an application on file in the office for the N. E. ¼ of this section (22), but I do not know whether it will be accepted or not, as it has not yet been reached."

It was not reached, or at least was not acted on, until January 22, 1900, six weeks later. So, in correcting the indorsement on the Cook application on November 27, 1899, so as to show the appraisement to be $1.50, instead of $1 as applied for, and in writing Cook on December 9, 1899, that this land was appraised at $1.50, the searchers were compelled to go to the sources of original information in order to ascertain, in each instance, what the true appraisement was. They could not have had recourse to the sale to Kidd, which not only had not been made, but the application for which had not yet been reached even.

[2] Now, we have gone into the facts in the case at great length, of course, and no doubt with tedious particularity, but the whole appeal pivots about the question of fact discussed, which is entitled to the greatest consideration. And upon such consideration we hold that these facts conclusively show that the land, at the time of the sale, had been duly appraised at $1.50 an acre. It is true, of course, that some of the facts we have set out do not apply to or bear upon the question of whether or not notice of this appraisement was sent to and received by the county clerk of Stephens county. As has been shown, the act of awarding the land to Kidd created a presumption that such notice was given, received, and recorded by the clerk. In addition to that is the fact that when the clerk undertook to make out Kidd's application he obviously consulted his records to ascertain the appraisement. As for that, it does not matter whether he consulted these records at the moment, or the day before, or at any other particular time, since the reference, whensoever made, disclosed the true appraisement. Obviously he did not consult or rely on the 1895 appraisement, because that showed $2; whereas, he wrote in the application the true appraisement of $1.50. We think the circumstances make conclusive the presumption of law, and neither those facts nor the presumption are shaken by the mere testimony of the present county clerk that, after 20 years, he has not been able, after search at this time, to locate in his office any formal appraisement at $1.50 an acre.

We hold, then, that the sale to Kidd of the land in controversy was regularly made, and is valid, and not subject to the attack made upon it by appellees.

[3] Appellees present a number of cross-assignments of error, and it is appropriate that they be now considered. It appears that prior to the reinstatement of the Kidd sale the land in dispute, theretofore classified as dry agricultural, was reclassified as mineral, and under the act of 1907 (now article 5433, R. S.) it was provided by statute that land theretofore or thereafter so classified might be sold for agricultural or grazing purposes, but that such sales should be upon the express condition that the minerals in such lands should be reserved to the state, and that such reservation should be stated in all applications to purchase. Appellees make the contention that because of such reclassification and of that statutory provision, the reinstatement of the Kidd sale was forever barred, in view of the provision in the Acts of 1895 and 1897 (now article 5423, R. S.) that forfeited lands should revert to the state and be resold under the provisions of those acts or of any future law. This contention of appellees was covered by allegations in their trial petition, which were stricken out upon the exception that the act of 1907, even if applicable, and the reclassification by the Land Commissioner subsequent to Kidd's purchase of the land, could not operate to destroy the right, given Kidd by statutes in force at the time he purchased, to reinstate the sale.

The logical effect of appellees' contention is that when he permitted a forfeiture of his sale Kidd had no more rights in the land in dispute than did any other person anywhere; that the act of the Land Commissioner in reclassifying the land forever cut off Kidd from the previous right which existed at the time he purchased, to reinstate his purchase by making the payment provided by the statute in force at the time he purchased; that the only right he really had was the right, enjoyed by every one, to apply for and purchase the land under the new classification, and in accordance with the provisions of the act of 1907 (article 5433).

It is true, as appellees urge in support of their cross-assignments, that when Kidd permitted the forfeiture the land reverted "to the particular fund to which it originally belonged," and was thereupon subject to be "resold under the provisions" of the law then existing or subsequently enacted, as provided by the forfeiture statute (article 5423). It would have been absurd, of course, for the Legislature to provide for the forfeiture without also providing for the resale of the land so returned to the state. Otherwise purchasers could cause the state's lands to lie idle until doomsday by the simple device of defaulting in payments, thereby inducing the forfeitures provided for. But having provided for the forfeiture and resale of the lands, the Legislature sought to relieve the harshness of the forfeiture by providing for the reinstatement of the forfeited sales, under certain named conditions.

[4] The primary object of the state in placing its public domain upon the market was the securing of actual settlers on these lands. The revenues to be derived from sales was but a secondary consideration, a mere incident to the greater purpose of supplying homes to those who sought and lived in them in good faith. The wisdom of this policy of our forefathers has never been seriously questioned, and the provision for the reinstatement of sales forfeited was an expression of the spirit of that policy. It was right and just that those who had settled upon and improved the state's lands in response to the invitation of the state, and who had endured the hardships incident to such settlement, and the privations incident to such improvement, should be given an opportunity to retrieve their lands when forfeited by reason of temporary misfortunes and the consequent inability to meet their payments in strict compliance with their obligations. Forfeitures by statute or contract are not favored. They must be viewed with a cold and literal scrutiny, that the injury wrought may be held to the minimum. On the other hand, statutes or contracts designed to relieve from the rigors of forfeiture are looked upon warmly and construed liberally, so as to afford the maximum relief. And this reciprocal rule applies as well to the great state of Texas as to its humblest citizen. So, the provisions of the statute for the forfeiture of sales, and for the reinstatement of such sales, should be tested by the rule in question. The provision for reinstatement will be quoted:

" * * * In any cases where lands have been forfeited to the state for the nonpayment of interest, the purchasers, or their vendees, may have their claims reinstated on their written request, by paying into the treasury the full amount of interest due on such claim up to the date of reinstatement, provided that no rights of third persons may have intervened. In all such cases, the original obligations and penalties shall thereby become as binding as if no forfeiture had occurred. * * *"

It will be observed that there are two conditions upon which reinstatement may be had: First, the payment of the full amount of interest due by the purchaser up to the date of reinstatement; and, second, the absence of intervening rights of third persons. Appellees seek to inject here a third condition, to wit, that the classification of the land has not been changed since the original purchase was made. And under this third condition appellees seek to defeat the reinstatement of the Kidd sale by simply showing that when Kidd applied for and purchased the land it was classified as dry agricultural, and priced at $1.50 an acre, whereas, at the time of the reinstatement it was classified as mineral, and appraised at another value; that this reclassification and reappraisement after the award to Kidd and be-

fore the reinstatement of his purchase was an absolute bar to the reinstatement. But we cannot subscribe to this theory. To do so would require us to write into the reinstatement provision a condition not therein created, and wholly foreign to such provision—a condition that would entirely defeat the very purpose of the act. If the Legislature had intended to provide that the reinstatement must be subject to or defeated by an arbitrary change by the Land Commissioner of the classification and appraisement of the land, it should and would have affirmatively and definitely said so in terms. The provisions for reinstatement were in effect when Kidd purchased the land, and were embraced in the contract between the state and Kidd when the latter purchased, and neither Kidd nor the state could thereafter arbitrarily and without the consent of the other write into the contract any provision or condition varying, restricting, or enlarging the terms thereof. If the state could by act of its Legislature ingraft this onerous condition onto the contract, then by the same license it could by like means increase the original purchase price of the land, or the rate of interest or terms of payment thereon. The payment of the back interest was the only condition, so far as the state was concerned, required of Kidd in procuring the reinstatement of his purchase, and the subsequent act of the Commissioner in reclassifying and reappraising the land could not serve to create an additional condition. Anderson v. Neighbors, 94 Tex. 240, 59 S. W. 543; Hooks v. Kirby, 58 Tex. Civ. App. 335, 124 S. W. 156 (writ of error denied); Wing v. Dunn, 60 Tex. Civ. App. 16, 127 S. W. 1101 (writ of error denied [Sup.] 128 S. W. 108); Jumbo Co. v. Bacon, 79 Tex. 5, 14 S. W. 840; Bates v. Bratton, 96 Tex. 279, 72 S. W. 157; Houston Oil Co. v. McGrew, 107 Tex. 220, 176 S. W. 45. In Hooks v. Kirby, supra, this principle is well stated in the following:

"The law under which the timber was purchased from the state gave the absolute right to the purchaser to buy the land at any time within five years from the date of the sale of the timber to him, or at least until all the timber is removed. This right formed a part of the consideration paid for the timber, and entered into the contract as much as did the cash consideration of the $5 per acre which he paid. When he paid the cash and took a deed to the timber, the law wrote into the contract that he was also thereby granted the right to buy the land within a certain time for a certain further consideration, and this right became vested and cannot be impaired by subsequent legislation."

Appellees contend that the act of 1895 (article 5423), providing that forfeited lands should revert and "be resold under the provisions of this act or any future law," subjected the resale of such lands to the provision of the act of 1907 (article 5433), that "the land which is now or may hereafter be reclassed as mineral may be sold for agricultural or grazing purposes, but all sales of such land shall be upon the express condition that the minerals shall be and are reserved to the fund to which the land belongs," and that as the land in dispute had been reclassified as mineral at the time Kidd's vendee undertook to have his purchase reinstated, the status of the land was so altered as to prevent the reinstatement; that the act of 1907 was a "future law" as contemplated by the act of 1895. The most obvious fallacy in this contention is that both the provisions relied on relate exclusively to the resale of the lands. They do not purport, directly or indirectly to relate to the reinstatement of forfeited sales. This is so obvious from the plain language of these provisions that appellees' contention approaches the frivolous. The provision in article 5423 is a part of the forfeiture clause, relates solely to resale, and is wholly disconnected from and does not in any respect whatever refer, or purport to refer, to the provision for reinstatement. The forfeiture clause in article 5423 provides for three steps, (a) forfeiture, (b) reversion to the school fund, and (c) resale. The clause for reinstatement, which is separate and apart from the forfeiture clause, prescribes two conditions upon which the reinstatement may be had, (a) payment of all back interest, and (b) absence of intervening rights of third parties. There is no condition there that the reinstatement cannot occur in the face of a reclassification or reappraisement of the land. Moreover, the clause affirmatively provides that "in all such cases" of reinstatement "the original obligations and penalties shall thereby become as binding as if no forfeiture had ever occurred." This provision relates alike, of course, to the state and to the purchaser. And article 5433, upon which appellees rely as prohibiting the reinstatement of the Kidd sale, has no reference to reinstatement, either directly or by implication. That article simply provides that lands thereafter classed as "mineral may be sold, * * * but all sales of such land shall be upon the express condition that the minerals shall be and are reserved to the fund to which the land belongs, and such reservation shall be stated in all applications to purchase." It will be seen from its language that by no stretch of construction can this provision be made to refer to the reinstatement of forfeited sales. Appellees cite the case of Lawless v. Wright, 39 Tex. Civ. App. 26, 86 S. W. 1039, decided by this court, in support of their contention here. We adhere to every phase of the opinion in that case, but that decision defeats, .rather than supports, appellees' contention here. It was there held, simply, that in case of forfeiture, title to the land reverted to the state, and that during the period in which the sale was in suspense, between the date of forfeiture and date of reinstatement, the purchaser's possession was interrupted for

limitation purposes; that is to say, that the forfeiture broke the continuity of the purchaser's adverse possession against third persons for limitation purposes. In that case, as here, the land had been reclassified and reappraised, but the sale was reinstated, and the validity of the reinstatement was incidentally recognized by this court,, which stated that:

"In this case, after the forfeiture, the state exercised its right to again sell the land, and had it not been for the voluntary relinquishment of his title by D. Lawless [an intervening purchaser], the purchase made by Fancher [the original purchaser] could never have been reinstated. The forfeiture destroyed his claim to the land completely, and the privilege given to him to have it restored on certain payments and on the rights of others not intervening."

[5] Appellees contend, also, that the right of Kidd to reinstate his purchase was lost to him by reason of the fact that after the forfeiture, and before the reinstatement, one V. Griffin purchased the land in question; that although Griffin did not complete his purchase by actually settling on the land, and voluntarily abandoned the land, the sale to Kidd, nevertheless, could not lawfully be reinstated, since Griffin's purchase was such an intervening right of a third person as would bar the reinstatement. The facts showed that after the Kidd forfeiture Griffin applied to purchase the land as mineral land, at $6 an acre; that the application was accepted and the land awarded to Griffin. At that time the applicant was required by the statute (articles 5408, 5410) to actually settle on the land within 90 days from the date of the application, and within 30 days after the expiration of the 90-day period file in the Land Office an affidavit showing such settlement, and that forfeiture should follow the failure either to settle or to file the affidavit. Griffin, however, instead of settling on the land, abandoned it, made no settlement thereon, filed no affidavit of settlement, and subsequently wrote the Commissioner, advising that he had found the land to be "worthless," and that the sale to him could be marked forfeited, which was done, whereupon, upon request, and the payment of back due interest, the Kidd sale was reinstated. Appellees contend that the Griffin transaction was such intervening right of a third person as absolutely destroyed the right of Kidd to reinstate. The provision in the statute for reinstatement is that such reinstatement may be made, "provided that no rights of third parties may have intervened," and appellees contend that this phrase contemplates any right that accrued at any time while the original sale was in suspense, even though such right was but momentary and had ceased to exist, and was unenforceable at the time reinstatement was sought; that it did not contemplate only such rights of third parties as were existing and enforceable at

the time the reinstatement of the original sale was sought. But we think this construction of the statute is strained and unreasonable, and was not in contemplation of the Legislature which enacted it. We think, rather, that the Legislature had in mind such rights of third parties as constituted a present existing bar to reinstatement—an existing, vested right, enforceable at the time by the party owning such right. This provision was not inserted for the benefit of the state of Texas, but for the benefit of third parties in whose favor such intervening rights existed; and, when there are no third parties who can lawfully complain of the reinstatement, the state cannot be heard to do so. In this instance Griffin is not complaining; he could not do so, if so disposed, since whatever rights he had at one time had long since ceased to exist in law. In fact, he never had any substantial rights, because, by the very terms of the act under which he sought to purchase he could not transfer the rights he acquired, and had he attempted to do so he would have thereby automatically forfeited all of his rights to purchase. Article 5416, R. S.; Good v. Terrell, 100 Tex. 275, 98 S. W. 641. But we do not think the meagerness of his rights material. If he had the strongest of rights, they were entirely lost and destroyed at the time the Kidd sale was reinstated, and were no longer a bar to such reinstatement. Appellees cite no authority in support of their contention, while on the other hand the conclusion we have reached is supported by abundant authorities, among them being Mound Oil Co. v. Terrell, 99 Tex. 625, 92 S. W. 451; Wyerts v. Terrell, 100 Tex. 409, 100 S. W. 133; Lawless v. Wright, 39 Tex. Civ. App. 26, 86 S. W. 1039; Anderson v. Neighbors, supra; Lee v. Green, 24 Tex. Civ. App. 109, 58 S. W. 196, 847; Davis v. Yates, 63 Tex. Civ. App. 6, 133 S. W. 281; Good v. Terrell, 100 Tex. 275, 98 S. W. 641.

[6, 7] Appellees alleged, in support of a further contention, that on February 3, 1917, six days prior to the reinstatement of the Kidd sale, appellant J. F. Lewis secured from W. J. Bellamy (a remote vendee of Kidd) a quitclaim deed to the land in dispute, but that this instrument conveyed no rights whatever, because at that time Bellamy had no interest in the land; that at that time the land belonged to Griffin and stood in Griffin's name on the Land Office records, and the sale to Griffin was not canceled until February 9, six days after the conveyance of the Kidd title by quitclaim; that Bellamy having no right, title, or interest in the land at the time of the quitclaim, any after-acquired title would not inure to the benefit of Lewis. Exceptions were sustained to these allegations, and appellees complain thereat. It has been shown that Griffin had at this time completely lost all his right to purchase the land. In fact, he had never completely acquired any

substantial right, or any right that he could even transfer. He had simply made an attempt to purchase the land, but failed to follow up such attempt, and voluntarily and very deliberately abandoned it. This removed him as a possible impediment to the reinstatement of the Kidd sale, which, so far as Griffin was concerned, could have been enforced by mandamus at the time of the transfer from Bellamy to Lewis. The fact that the cancellation of the Griffin sale had not been formally entered on the Land Office books could not affect the right of Kidd's vendee to a reinstatement. So appellees' contention that the Griffin transaction was in any way an obstacle to the projection of the Kidd title is, in our opinion, quite clearly untenable and without any force at all. But the proposition that at the time of the Bellamy to Lewis quitclaim the former had no interest to convey, and by reason thereof the latter secured no right, title, or interest in the land, is a more serious one. If at that time Bellamy had no interest in or claim upon the land, then his quitclaim to Lewis was a nullity. All that a quitclaim deed could convey to Lewis was such interest as Bellamy at that time had in the title to the land, and if Bellamy had no interest in the title, then of course none passed to Lewis. The question is most interesting. Appellants cite no authorities except Bedford v. Rayner, 13 Tex. Civ. App. 618, 35 S. W. 931, which merely determines that the deed involved in that case was not a quitclaim in effect. That question is not involved here, since we are here to determine the sufficiency of allegations as to the effect of a quitclaim deed, the language of which is not set out, under the particular facts alleged. Appellees cite only one Texas case, Rodgers v. Burchard, 34 Tex. 441, 7 Am. St. Rep. 283, which decides only that a quitclaim deed conveys no more than the present interest of the grantor in the land described, and does not extend to an interest subsequently accruing. This is elemental, as we understand it. Neither party cites the case of Bates v. Bacon, 66 Tex. 348, 1 S. W. 256. In that case a void patent was issued to one Russell, the land was sold and conveyed by the sheriff, under a judgment against Russell, to Bacon; later on the Legislature validated the patent, and Bacon claimed the title created by the act validating the patent under which he purchased. The sheriff's deed may be likened, for the purpose of this inquiry, unto a quitclaim deed. We quote from the opinion in the case cited:

"The plaintiff below admitted that the patent, through which he claimed, was the same held by this court to be void in the case of Bacon & Bates v. Russell, 57 Tex. 409. He insists, however that the grant was validated by the act of March 31, 1883, and that his title was thereby perfected. His claim to the benefits of that act is through an execution sale against Russell, the patentee, made on June 5, 1877. At that time Russell had no interest in the land. The title was in the state, and there remained until by the cited act the patent was vitalized as a grant. A sheriff's deed conveys only the right, title, and interest of the defendant in execution; if it was the act of the defendant, it contains no recital, stipulation, or covenant that could estop him from disputing the title of the purchaser upon any subsequently acquired or accruing right in himself. Freeman on Ex. § 335. The plaintiff acquired, by the sheriff's deed, only the title Russell then had—and he had none—and not what he afterwards acquired by the state's bounty.

"It was in the power of the Legislature in confirming the void grants embraced in the act of March 31, 1883, to pass its benefits to the assigns of the grantees, but this was not done, although the act passed was doubtless suggested by the opinion in the case of Bacon & Bates v. Russell. It was probably considered that the title would pass to the assignee by estoppel without legislation in all instances in which it was wise that it should pass. It certainly was not politic to pass to the purchaser at execution sale any claim the defendant in execution may have had upon the charity or liberality of the sovereign."

[8] The language of that opinion affords much food for thought when considered in connection with the provision in the statute that when a sale is forfeited, as here, the land reverts to the particular fund to which it originally belonged, and when further considered in connection with article 5423 and the holding by this court in Lawless v. Wright, supra, that the forfeiture reinvests the title in the state. But upon reflection we conclude that neither the statute nor the decisions mentioned operate to cut off Lewis as vendee from the right to enforce reinstatement of the Kidd sale. It is true that a quitclaim deed conveys no more interest than the grantor has at the time, and that it conveys no interest in an after-acquired title—that the quitclaim deed from Bellamy to Lewis conveyed no interest to the latter, unless the former at that time had such interest. It is true, also, as held in Lawless v. Wright, that the state of Texas at that time was invested with the title to the land, and the right to resell the land, subject, however, and always, to the right of Kidd or his vendees to reinstate the original sale at any time in the absence of intervening rights of third parties. And just there is precisely the interest that Bellamy owned at the time of the transfer to Lewis. And that was a vested right which no statute or act of the Land Commissioner could take away from him. Moreover, the statute (article 5423) expressly gives that right to "the original purchasers or their vendees." This right may be momentarily obscured by a shadow, such as the Griffin transaction; or entirely obliterated by a complete and permanent resale, but it is there, nevertheless, and is written in clear and express language into the contract

between the state and the original purchaser. It is just as clear and definite and tangible as is the right, given in the same contract, to continue the title in force by paying the interest on the 1st of November each year. Now, in the Bates v. Bacon Case, supra, the patent was held to be absolutely void. This holding made the patentee as a complete stranger to the title, divesting him of every relation thereto and claim thereon. The state was under no further legal obligation whatever to him. And while in this attitude the patentee's title was conveyed by the sheriff to Bacon, as if the patentee had done so by quitclaim deed. Subsequently the Legislature validated the patent, and the Supreme Court held that the title revitalized by this act did not inure to the benefit of the assignee of the grantee in the patent, in the absence of an express provision for that purpose; that the assignee did not acquire a title afterwards acquired "by the state's bounty" or any claim upon the "charity or liberality of the sovereign." These considerations clearly distinguish that case from this. The rights conveyed by Bellamy to Lewis were not based on any claim to the state's "bounty," or dependent upon the "charity or liberality of the sovereign," but were clear and definite rights, expressly vested in Kidd and his vendees by the terms of the original contract between the sovereign and one of its citizens. So we hold that the quitclaim deed from Bellamy to Lewis conveyed the right to reinstate the Kidd purchase.

[9] Appellees alleged, also, that the procuring of the quitclaim deed by Lewis from Bellamy was a fraud upon the state of Texas, in that, in December, 1916, Lewis represented to the Land Commissioner that he had no interest in the land in dispute, and in January, 1917, represented to the Commissioner that he owned the land, when as a matter of fact he had no interest therein; that Lewis was seeking to procure title to and possession of the land, knowing it to be near oil production and valuable, and yet knowing, also, that the Commissioner was unaware of this peculiar value; that later on Lewis procured the quitclaim deed from Bellamy and had the sale reinstated for his own use and benefit and with the intention of depriving the state of the value of the land. These allegations were stricken out upon exception that no showing of fraud was made by the allegations, which were mere conclusions of the pleader. We are quite clear that the allegations were subject to the exception, which was properly sustained. The right to reinstate the Kidd sale was a vested right, and could be defeated only by a failure to pay the accrued interest on the land, or by enforceable intervening rights of third parties. No representations of Lewis, whether true or false, could affect that right. He was, or was not, entitled to the reinstatement, and nothing he could say

would enlarge or lessen the authority of the Land Commissioner.

The conclusions we have written dispose of all material matters raised. We sustain appellants' first assignment of error, complaining of the refusal of the trial court to direct a verdict for the defendants therein. This renders immaterial appellants' remaining assignments of error, which will not be discussed. We overrule all of appellees' cross-assignments. The judgment of the district court must be reversed, and as the facts were very fully developed in the court below, judgment will be here rendered in favor of appellants.

Reversed and rendered.

On Rehearing.

PER CURIAM. Rehearing denied.

COBBS, J. (dissenting). I cannot agree with the majority of the court in respect to the disposition made of this case on appeal. It is unnecessary to extend my reasons to any great length. When the state offers her lands for sale on a credit and requires certain necessary precedent things to be done, every single requirement must be strictly met. In such cases, to acquire her title, the burden of proof is on the purchaser to establish the antecedent equities, rights, and the requirements step by step until it is finally merged in a final patent.

In this case, J. M. Kidd applied to purchase this land, alleging it was classified as agriculture land and valued at $1.50 per acre, at which price he purchased. The state denied this, and introduced some evidence to show the land had by the proper authority at the time of the alleged purchase been valued at the sum of $2 per acre, not $1.50. This issue of fact was fairly submitted to the jury, who found against the Kidd contention, that is, the land was not valued at $1.50 per acre, but at $2. Accepting their finding as we must, then Kidd acquired no right against the state. This court, in its majority opinion, found facts and reasons to set aside the finding of the jury, and substituted therefor the court's findings and conclusions in lieu thereof, which cannot be done. I understand it is well settled, it is true, that there is always a presumption of law that officers do their duty, but I do not understand any rule of law that will justify the indulgence of inferences to overcome that presumption in the face of some evidence to support the jury's finding, however slight, supporting the official action. The state will not be, in such cases, estopped or bound by illegal acts of her officers.

Another reason for this dissent is because Kidd did not complete his purchase, and all his rights became forfeited to the state by reason of the very facts stated at length in the majority opinion. The Commissioner of the General Land Office ascertained that this land which had been erroneously classified as dry agricultural land was in fact very valuable mineral land, and thereupon reclassified it as mineral land, and changed the value from $2 to $5 per acre. But this classification was not had until after Kidd's default in his purchase requiring a forfeiture to the state. Thereafter, on the 2d day of May, 1896, V. Griffin filed his application to purchase the land, whereupon the land was legally awarded to him, and the cash payment properly applied, and the obligation of $936 deferred payment retained by the Commissioner. Here was the "intervening right" the statute speaks of, the third party that cut off the right of Kidd ever afterwards to come in on his original purchase. The state, under its right secured to it by Kidd's forefeiture, had ascertained the land Kidd had claimed to purchase as dry agricultural land, at $1.50 per acre, was not dry agricultural land at all, but immensely valuable mineral land, whereupon a new classification was placed thereon representing its true and real condition reclassified at a time when the state had the power to make such reclassification and revaluation of her own land which Kidd had forfeited and abandoned to her. Surely the state had this right and dominion over her own property, for there had arisen this intervening right, and the intervening right of a third party, too. As the state sold this land, and thereby whatever right, if any, Kidd may at any time have had, was by these proceedings lost to him and passed to the intervening purchaser. Griffin failing to comply with the law respecting settlement, lost his right to complete his purchase, and he was canceled out. Now, where did the title go? It did not go up in thin air. It did not go back to Kidd or his assignees. Something had to be done again to secure the original status of purchase, if Kidd was to be reinstated. I cannot believe any supposed equity had been left in Kidd after Griffin's purchase under the law to obliterate everything done between Kidd's supposed purchase and permit his assignee to secure from the state this vastly valuable mineral land, which was, through the mistake of her officers, improperly classified, illegally sold, and valued, at the mistaken value placed thereupon at the time of his alleged purchase.

On the 3d day of February, 1917, appellant J. F. Lewis secured from W. J. Bellamy and wife a quitclaim deed to the land, but no right passed by that instrument at that time, because Griffin was then the intervening purchaser, whose purchase was not canceled out until the 9th day of February, 1917.

I cannot agree with my Associates that Kidd or his assignee had any vested right of reinstatement whatever, for the statute itself contained an express prohibition against it. That right became lost and annulled the very minute of Griffin's purchase, and there is no word or suggestion that such a privilege was conferred upon him after the intervening right of a third person had come in, that survived beyond the intervening purchaser's right for reinstatement. My construction of the statute is that up to such time as the land was unsold to another, he might do so. It was not passed to protect the right of a third person, because such right was protected by the Constitution and all law. Obviously, it was intended as a period of limitation, and after that one intervening right the statute itself is silent. To give it any other construction would be to extend that right ad infinitum; it would make no difference how many other sales became forfeited and canceled out. Such statutes must be given strict construction.

There is in my mind another very serious objection to reversing and rendering this judgment. The land was, in the first place, erroneously and illegally classified as dry agricultural land. So, when sold and purchased there was both a mutual mistake as to its classification and as to its real value. This was discovered by the officers of the state whose duty it was to classify lands after the land had reverted to the state under the forfeiture of all of Kidd's rights. In this condition of the land, and upon its proper classification and value, it was sold to Griffin. When Kidd's assignee makes this discovery after the cancellation of Griffin's rights, ignoring its real and true valuation, they attempt a reinstatement of the former purchase of land they knew had been erroneously classified and valued. I do not think they should be allowed to profit by the mistake of the state's officer, and in a case like this be reinstated. It was a mutual mistake at most that should call for a reformation of the contract if they be allowed a reinstatement. The state should not be bound by that mistake, under the circumstances of his abandonment and the intervening rights, to allow a defaulted purchaser to enforce an inequitable, defaulted, and abandoned contract, whicu, when supposed bad, he forfeited, and when found so good as to enrich him, ask specific performance.

For the foregoing and many other reasons I cannot concur in the opinion or the disposition of this case. It is my judgment that the motions for rehearing should be granted and the opinion withdrawn, a new one written in lieu thereof, and the judgment be in all things affirmed.

SMITH et al. v. FLEMING et ux.   (No. 1214.)*

(Court of Civil Appeals of Texas. El Paso.
May 12, 1921.)

1. Witnesses ⬦⬦150(2)—Fraudulent declarations of lessee since deceased held admissible in action against assignees to cancel lease.

In action against assignees of oil and gas lease to cancel lease, plaintiff lessor was not prohibited by reason of Rev. St. 1911, art. 3690, relating to testimony as to declarations by a decedent from testifying as to fraudulent declarations by lessee, since deceased and against whom the suit had been dismissed, made at the time of the execution of the lease in reference to the term for which the lease was taken and as to the amount of rentals agreed to be paid; the lessee having prepared the lease.

2. Evidence ⬦⬦434(6)—Testimony held not to vary written instrument.

In action to cancel an oil and gas lease, it would not be varying the instrument by parol testimony to permit lessor to testify that lessee prepared the lease to run for a period of six months, and after the delivery of the lease struck out the words "six months" and inserted the words "ten years."

3. Evidence ⬦⬦135(1)—No error in refusing evidence of other fraudulent transactions.

In action to cancel oil and gas lease on ground of alterations in instrument after delivery, court did not err in refusing to permit defendant assignees to give evidence of other leases taken by lessee with other parties in the same vicinity; the purpose being to show that the same erasures and interlineations appear in them as in the lease in question.

4. Appeal and error ⬦⬦1066 — Reversible error to submit issue without evidence to support it.

In action to cancel oil and gas lease on ground that alterations were made after delivery, it was reversible error to submit to the jury issue as to whether interlineations were made before or after the execution and delivery of the lease by striking out a six-months term and inserting a ten-year term, the fact clearly appearing, from the instrument itself, that there was no six-month term in the lease except as to the payment of rentals, and such term was not erased and no term inserted instead, the issue being without evidence to support it.

5. Mines and minerals ⬦⬦59—Issue submitted held without basis in pleading in suit to cancel lease.

An issue whether lessee represented to lessor that lease was only for a period of six months was without basis in the pleading, and should not have been submitted in an action to cancel the lease, where petition alleged the agreement was that the term of the lease was to be for only six months, and that lessee assured lessor that the lease had been so prepared; there being no allegation that lessee represented to lessor that the lease was only for a period of six months.

⬦⬦For other cases see same topic and KEY-NUMBER in all Key-Numbered Digests and Indexes
*Motion for leave to file motion for rehearing denied 231 S. W. 1117.

6. Mines and minerals ⟐⇒58—Fraudulent statement as to term ground for avoiding lease.

Where lessee drew up an oil and gas lease, and lessors relied on his statement as to the time the lease would run, and believed that the lease was written for only six months instead of ten years, and, to induce that belief, lessee pointed out a six months' clause in the lease as the term for which it was to run and remarked, "I will make it for six months so you will understand it," and lessors believed the six months' time had reference to the time that lease was to run and acted upon it, but in truth it had reference instead to the payment of rentals, and not to the time the lease was to run, and though lessor might have ascertained by the exercise of ordinary care the application of the six months' clause, such representation would be sufficient ground if promptly acted upon to avoid the lease.

7. Mines and minerals ⟐⇒58—Lessor estopped to deny validity of lease fraudulently obtained.

Lessor under oil lease was estopped to set up fraud of lessee in obtaining the lease by telling him that it was for six months instead of ten years, where he accepted rentals after the expiration of the six months knowing that the lease had been assigned, and such was true even though the lease was altered after execution and delivery, changing the term.

Appeal from District Court, Eastland County; E. A. Hill, Judge.

Action by S. A. Fleming and wife against C. P. Smith and others. Judgment for plaintiffs, and certain defendants appeal. Reversed and rendered.

Scott, Brelsford & Smith, of Cisco, for appellants.

W. O. Morton, of Breckenridge, and Burkett, Anderson & Orr, of Eastland, for appellees.

WALTHALL, J. S. A. Fleming and wife brought this suit on the 14th day of June, 1919, against J. F. Colt, C. P. Smith, and R. N. Dorsey to cancel an oil and gas lease on 181 acres of land in Eastland county, executed and delivered by them to J. F. Colt on the 26th day of November, 1917.

The oil and gas lease recites that the lessors, for the consideration of $181 paid and the covenants and agreements therein contained, grant, bargain, and sell all the oil and gas in and under the land described, and grant, demise, lease, and let said land itself unto the lessee for the sole and only purpose of operating for and producing oil and gas thereon and therefrom, with rights of way, etc., and to have and to hold said lands and all rights and privileges granted hereunder to and unto the lessee, his heirs and assigns, for the term of ten years from the date hereof, and as much longer as oil and gas is produced from said land in paying quantities. The lease provides that in consid-

eration of the premises the lessee should deliver to the lessor an eighth part of the oil produced and saved from the leased premises as a royalty, or to pay the market price therefor. The term of the lease as printed in the instrument was five years. The printed word "five" is erased and the word "ten" is written in red ink instead wherever the words "five years" occurs in the instrument, thus making the term of years for which the lease was to run to read ten years instead of five years.

The instrument provides:

"If operations for the drilling of a well are not commenced on said land on or before the 1st day of June, 1918, this lease shall terminate as to both parties, unless the lessee, on or before that date, shall pay or tender the lessor the sum of forty-five ($45.25) and 25/100 dollars in the manner hereinafter provided, which payment or tender shall operate as a rental for six months from and after the date last above stated."

In stating the rental period in the above quotation the space for the number of months is left vacant in the printing, and the word "six" is written therein, thus making the instrument to read as above quoted.

Without stating the verbiage of the petition, plaintiffs alleged that it was never understood or agreed that the terms of said lease should extend for a longer period than six months from its date, unless drilling for a well should be sooner begun, in which event it was to remain in full force as long as oil and gas might be produced in paying quantities; that Colt undertook to reduce said agreement to writing; that plaintiffs were inexperienced, and for that reason relied upon him to incorporate in the instrument the meaning of the contract and agreement which had been made between them; that Colt had with him a form of printed lease contract containing blank spaces for the insertion of dates, term of years, consideration, description of land, etc.; that in filling out the lease Colt inserted words therein which made it appear that the lease was to run for a period of six months, but fraudulently and without plaintiff's knowledge or consent, and after the delivery of the lease, changed said period from six months to ten years in the printed portion, which Colt had assured plaintiffs provided for only a period of six months; that in filling out the consideration in said lease as paid Colt falsely inserted the sum of $181 when same was not the true consideration, and true consideration being 25 cents per acre, or $45.25.

Plaintiffs allege that after the lease contract was written Colt submitted it to plaintiffs, but they did not read all of the lease, and only glanced over it, and, seeing that same provided for only six months in one place, relied upon what Colt said, that it was for only six months; that after the lease was executed and delivered Colt changed the lease by altering and erasing the words "six months" and inserting in lieu thereof the words and figures "ten years." Plaintiffs further allege that Colt, in taking the lease, was acting for himself and as the agent and representative of O. P. Smith and R. N. Dorsey, and that they were charged with notice of said act; that on December 10, 1917, Colt assigned the lease to O. P. Smith, and Smith assigned one-eighth to R. N. Dorsey, and that Smith and Dorsey were each well aware of the changes and alterations made by Colt in the lease after its execution; plaintiffs did not discover the alterations in the lease until the latter part of July, 1918; that plaintiffs consulted an attorney who advised that the lease could not be canceled, and that thereafter he consulted another attorney who advised that the lease could be canceled; that after that date plaintiffs refused to accept any further rentals, and treated the lease as canceled.

Plaintiffs pleaded in the alternative that, if plaintiffs did not agree to drill a well within any definite time, then they pleaded that the contract was unilateral.

Pending the suit, and before trial, Colt died, and the suit was dismissed as to him.

Smith and Dorsey answered by general demurrer, special exceptions, general denial, special denial that Colt was their agent in taking the lease; denied any knowledge of the circumstances attending the execution of the lease; that Colt was not acting for or on behalf of either of them; that they purchased the lease for a valuable consideration and without any notice of any vice in its execution, and knew nothing of the attending circumstances surrounding the same, and that they were innocent purchasers for valuable consideration paid and without notice; that they are legal and equitable holders and owners of the lease by assignment, and have paid all the rental payments due under the terms of the lease, and have complied with the terms of the lease. They pleaded estoppel of plaintiffs to deny the legality of the lease by reason of having accepted the annual rental on said lease.

The cause was tried with a jury, and the case submitted on special issues, resulting in a judgment in favor of plaintiffs canceling the lease.

The jury found:

(1) The interlineations in red ink upon the lease were made after Fleming and wife signed the lease.

The jury made no answers to questions 2 and 3.

(4) At the time the lease was executed by Fleming and wife, Colt represented to them that the lease was only for a period of six months.

(5) Fleming and wife relied solely upon the representation made by Colt that the lease ran for a period of only six months.

(6) Smith, when he purchased the lease from Colt, when he noticed interlineations upon said instrument, did not use such ordinary care and reasonable diligence as an ordinarily prudent man would have used under like or similar cicumstances to ascertain the status of the real or apparent irregularity appearing on the face of said instrument.

(7) Dorsey purchased an interest in said lease for a valuable consideration without notice of the circumstances attending the execution of said lease.

(8) Dorsey in the purchase of the interest in the lease claimed by him did not exercise "reasonable care" as that term is hereinbefore set out.

[1] It was not error, as submitted in the first assignment, to permit Fleming to testify, over objections of Smith and Dorsey, in the suit against them, by reason of article 3690, Revised Statutes, as to declaration made by Colt at the time of the execution of the lease in reference to the term for which the lease was taken, and as to the amount of rentals agreed to be paid.

[2] It would not be varying the original instrument by parol testimony as insisted under the second proposition under the first assignment to permit Fleming to testify that Colt prepared the lease to run for a period of six months, and after the delivery of the lease struck out the words "six months" and inserted the words "ten years." It would be more a question of the weight of the evidence to sustain the allegation that the original lease was changed, and not one as to the admission of the evidence offered. But the original lease was introduced in evidence, and is found in the record, and shows on its face that the clause referred to by the witness, viz. "which payment or tender shall operate as a rental for six months from and after the date last above stated," has not been erased, nor the words "ten years" written in their stead. The six months' clause does not appear to be erased.

[3] The court was not in error, we think, as claimed by appellants in the second assignment, in refusing to permit the introduction in evidence in connection with the evidence of witness Willis of other leases taken by Colt with other parties in the same vicinity; the purpose being to show that the same erasures and interlineations appear in them as in the Fleming lease. This was a special contract with Fleming, and we think it would not be proper to turn aside and try out other transactions on the ground that, in some respects, there appears to be a similarity of conditions, as to interlineations with red ink, as would appear on the face of the instruments offered. Willis did not know anything about the interlineations on

this or the offered instruments; said he did not see Colt make the interlineations on the lease in question; he did not see the interlineations; did not know this lease or other leases were interlined; would not say it was interlined before Fleming signed it; he did not know whether the Fleming lease was drawn for a five-year or a ten-year lease, but thinks it was a ten-year lease. Had Colt been a witness and had himself testified to the times this and other leases were interlined, the probative force of the interlineations on leases other than the instant lease would have been no more than an inference, and, we think, self-serving.

In view of the disposition we make of the case, we deem it unnecessary to discuss assignments 4, 9, and 13, complaining of the refusal of the court to submit requested special instructions.

[4] Was it reversible error, as submitted in the fifth assignment, to submit to the jury issue No. 1, as to whether the interlineations were made before or after the execution and delivery of the lease, by striking out the six-month term and inserting the ten-year term? The fact clearly appears from the instrument itself that there was no six-month term in the lease except as to the payment of the rentals, and such term was not erased, and no term inserted instead, as we construe the allegation in the pleading. The issue, as pleaded, and as submitted, is without evidence to support it.

[5] Appellants' seventh assignment is directed to the submission of the fourth issue: "Did J. F. Colt represent to them [Fleming and wife] that said lease was only for a period of six months?" The jury answered "Yes." As we construe the petition, it does not allege that Colt represented to Fleming and wife that the lease as prepared by him was for a period of only six months. The petition alleges the agreement was that the term of the lease was to be for only six months, and that Colt assured Fleming and wife that the lease had been so prepared, but there is no allegation that Colt represented to them that said lease was only for a period of six months. The issue submitted is without basis in the pleading and should not have been submitted.

The eighth assignment complains of the submission of the fifth issue, on the ground that under the evidence Fleming and wife were bound by the terms of the lease as finally written, they having read the lease, and testified that it was originally written for six months, and thereafter changed to ten years.

The fifth issue did not submit the question of the change in the writing, but the issue submitted was: Did Fleming and wife rely solely upon the representation by Colt that the lease (as written) would run for six months only?

The petition alleged that the agreement was that the lease when written was to be for a period not exceeding six months from its date unless the drilling of a well for oil should begin prior to the expiration of that time, or a new agreement entered into extending the term of the lease; that they were not familiar with or skilled in the forms, reading, or interpretation of such instruments, and that Colt was, and for that reason they relied upon him to write into the instrument before it was signed the intent and meaning of the agreement as had been made between them; that in filling out the blank form of the lease in the blank space for inserting the period for which the lease was to run Colt inserted words which made it appear that the lease was to run for six months, and led plaintiffs to believe that the lease was for six months, but fraudulently and after the lease was delivered Colt changed the time in the printed portion of the lease from six months to ten years. The lease provides, and without any interlineations as to that provision, that—

"If operations for the drilling of a well are not commenced on the said land on or before the 1st day of June, 1918, this lease shall terminate, unless the lessee, on or before that date shall pay the lessor the sum of $45.25 in the manner hereinafter provided."

It seems to us that the pleading is somewhat confused in its statements as to what Fleming and wife were led to believe the writing was to be when written, and what it was when written, and the fraud in the change made as to the time for which the lease was made to run. The issue submitted was as to the representations made by Colt to Fleming and wife, that the lease as written would run for only six months. The assignment embraces issues pleaded, but not submitted in the fifth issue.

[6] Was it reversible error to submit the issue whether Fleming and wife relied solely upon the representation (the pleading reads assurance) of Colt that the lease (necessarily, as written) would run for six months only? We think that the well-established rule might be applied to the facts presented to the effect that, where representations were of a character to induce Fleming and wife to rely upon what Colt said as to the time the lease would run, and they believed that the lease was written for only six months, and to induce that belief Colt pointed out a six months' clause in the lease as the term for which it was to run and remarked, "I will make it for six months so you will understand it," and Fleming believed the six months' time had reference to the time the lease was to run, and acted upon it, but in truth it had reference instead to the payment of rentals, and not to the time the lease was to run, and although Fleming might have ascertained by the exercise of ordinary

care the application of the six months' clause, such representation would be sufficient ground, if promptly acted upon, to avoid the lease. Labbe v. Corbett, 69 Tex. 503, 6 S. W. 808; Griffeth v. Hanks, 46 Tex. 217; Holstein v. Adams, 72 Tex. 485, 10 S. W. 560; Wright v. United States Mortg. Co., 42 S. W. 789; International, etc., R. Co. v. Harris, 65 S. W. 885, affirmed in 95 Tex. 346, 67 S. W. 315. See, also, Hall v. Grayson County Nat. Bank, 36 Tex. Civ. App. 317, 81 S. W. 762, stating the rule to be that one induced by reliance on false representations to enter into a contract is not precluded from defeating its enforcement by the fact that by ordinary diligence he could have discovered their falsity before acting upon them. Fleming testified that the parol contract that was to be expressed in the lease‑was for a six months' time; that he relied upon what Colt said the lease contained, and that, while Colt submitted the lease to them to read, they did not read all of it, but only glanced over it, and, seeing the six months' clause in one place, they relied upon what Colt said, that the lease was only for six months.

Under the tenth assignment it is insisted that the findings of the jury on the special issues submitted are insufficient to sustain the judgment canceling the lease.

We might concede the correctness of the proposition but for the matter discussed under the eighth assignment. It seems clear to us that Fleming and wife had in mind no period of time other than for six months.

It is quite evident that Fleming was mistaken as to the erasure of the six months' clause in the lease, but the jury found in answer to the fifth issue that Colt represented to them that said lease was for only six months, a very pertinent and distinct fact, and that Fleming and wife relied solely upon the representation made by Colt as to the fact expressing, as Fleming understood it, the period of time for which the lease was to run. If we are not in error in our conclusion that such finding constitutes a cause for the cancellation of the lease, the judgment should be sustained, if not defeated by other and subsequent matters discussed under another assignment.

What we have said in discussing other assignments sufficiently indicates our views on the matters complained of in the eleventh and twelfth assignments.

This brings us to the fourteenth assignment.

[7] Defendants pleaded an estoppel on the part of Fleming and wife in that they received and accepted two rentals falling due under the terms of the lease as written, one falling due on May 26, 1918, and one falling due on November 26, 1918. Now, whatever Fleming might have been led by Colt to believe as to the period of time for which the lease was

to run, he knew that he was accepting rentals long after the lease had expired by its own terms, as he was led to believe. Fleming knew that neither Colt nor Smith and Dorsey had commenced to drill a well upon the land in controversy at the end of the six months' period. Fleming knew at the end of the eighteen months' period, when he accepted the third payment, that a well had not been drilled on the land. Fleming knew that on the 10th day of December, 1917, Colt assigned the lease to Smith, and that on the 11th day of December, 1917, Smith had assigned an interest in the lease to Dorsey, both assignments having been duly recorded in 1917. Fleming had actual knowledge of the interlineations in the lease changing the printed period of time from five to ten years in July, 1918.

The above facts are not controverted. Whatever might be said primarily of the deception or fraud of Colt in leading Fleming and wife to believe that the lease extended for a period of six months only, he was undeceived at the end of the six months' period, and other periods when additional rentals, as above, were accepted by him, and by accepting the rentals reaffirmed the lease.

We have concluded that as a matter of law, by reason of the facts, he is now estopped from having a cancellation of his lease by reason of the fraud of Colt in inducing the belief that the period of the lease was for six months only, and his sole reliance upon what Colt led him to believe.

For the reason stated, the cause is reversed, and, the facts having been fully developed, judgment is here rendered for appellants.

Reversed and rendered.

CITY SERVICE CO. v. BROWN et ux.
(No. 1232.)

(Court of Civil Appeals of Texas. El Paso. May 12, 1921. Rehearing Denied June 2, 1921.)

1. **Master and servant** ⟜330(1)—Burden is on person injured to shew servant acted within scope of employment.

The burden is on plaintiff, seeking to hold the master for an injury inflicted by the servant, to show that the servant did the wrong while acting within the scope of his employment, and the act must be done in furtherance of the master's business and for the accomplishment of the object for which the servant was employed.

2. **Master and servant** ⟜330(1)—Automobile driver presumed acting within scope of employment.

Evidence that defendant owned the car causing injury, that the driver was in its employment, that after the accident the driver

---

telephoned the employer about the occurrence, and that it sent a physician, *held* to raise the presumption that the driver was acting in the employer's business, in the absence of affirmative proof to the contrary.

3. Master and servant ⚖330(3)—Evidence insufficient to show driver of automobile acted within scope of employment.

In an action for personal injuries through being struck by defendant's automobile operated by its driver, evidence as to whether the driver was acting within the scope of his employment *held* insufficient to support a verdict for plaintiffs.

Appeal from District Court, El Paso County; P. R. Price, Judge.

Action by F. O. Brown and wife against the City Service Company. Judgment for plaintiffs, and defendant appeals. Reversed and rendered.

Beall, Kemp & Nagle and H. Potash, all of El Paso, for appellant.

Joseph McGill, of El Paso, for appellees.

HARPER, C. J. Appellees, F. O. Brown and Sarah Brown, sued appellant, City Service Company, in the district court of El Paso county, Tex., for personal injuries alleged to have been sustained by them on the evening of the 8th of July, 1920, at about half past 10 o'clock. Appellees alleged that while they were standing at a point on Alameda avenue, in the city of El Paso, Tex., waiting to board a street car they (appellees) were struck by an automobile owned by appellant and were knocked down and injured; that the said automobile was being operated by one of appellant's employees in a negligent, careless, and reckless manner.

Appellant, defendant in the court below, answered by general demurrer, general denial and denial that if plaintiffs were injured they were injured by an automobile operated by the City Service Company, or by any employee of the defendant acting within the scope of his authority or upon the defendant's business, and averred that if plaintiffs were struck by the said automobile the driver of said automobile was not engaged in any service for the defendant. The case was submitted to the jury on special issues.

[1] The appellant has raised but one question, i. e., that the evidence is not sufficient to support the verdict; the jury having found that the appellees were injured by being knocked down by an automobile negligently driven by an employee of appellant at the time acting within the scope of his employment. The evidence upon every question except the latter is unquestionably sufficient, so the only question for our determination is: Is there any evidence of probative value to support the finding that the driver of the car

was acting for the appellant and within the scope of his authority, or was he engaged in the business of the defendant, so as to make it liable for his negligence? In the case of Van Cleave v. Walker, 210 S. W. 767, it is said:

"The liability of the master in cases of this kind is to be determined by the application of the general principles of the law of master and servant. In such cases the burden is upon the plaintiff seeking to hold the master for an injury inflicted by the servant to 'show that the servant did the wrong while acting within the scope of his employment,' and the act (of driving the automobile in this instance) 'must be done in furtherance of the master's business and for the accomplishment of the object for which the servant is employed.'" I. & G. N. Ry. Co. v. Anderson, 82 Tex. 516, 17 S. W. 1039, 27 Am. St. Rep. 902.

There is an expression seemingly in conflict with this ho'ding in the case of Studebaker B. Co. v. Kitts, 152 S. W. 464, as to where the burden of proof lies, cited by appellees, but it is not supported by any Texas case.

[2] Appellee insists that the following facts and circumstances show a prima facie case for appellee. Appellant owned the car. The driver was at the time of the accident in its employment; that soon after the accident, after the appellees had been taken into a nearby house, the driver of the car telephoned the company about the occurrence and that it sent out a physician, and that physicians at the instance of appellant attended to the injuries several times later. We think these matters sufficient to raise the presumption that the driver was acting in the master's business, in the absence of affirmative proof to the contrary; but presumptions are not evidence (1 Jones on Evidence, § 9), and they "disappear when confronted with facts in the form of unimpeached positive evidence." Paxton v. Boyce, 1 Tex. 317; Moore v. Supreme Assembly, 42 Tex. Civ. App. 366, 93 S. W. 1077; Largen v. State, 76 Tex. 323, 13 S. W. 161.

The driver of the car testified:

"That none of the officials of the City Service Company knew that he had taken the car from the garage; that he simply cranked it up and went out at the side door; and that, the office being in the front, no one saw him. I was driving the car on my own hook." That he was on an errand of his own, and not performing any service for the defendant company; that he was not checked out and for that reason no record was kept of the car; that he picked up a passenger down town, whose name he refused to divulge, and that she was in the car when the accident occurred.

The manager of the defendant company testified that his company owned the car, and that the driver was in its employ. Witness further testified as to the manner in which the business is conducted in the garage on West San Antonio street; that when a call comes into the garage for an automobile the chauffeurs are called to the desk and that the deskman assigns a chauffeur to a particular call; that a proper record is made of the hour at which the call comes in, of the time when the chauffeur departs, and the place to which the automobile is directed; and a record is also kept of the amount of money collected by the chauffeur and the hour at which he returns to the garage.

Witness further testified in detail as to the manner in which a record is kept as to the movement of all cars and chauffeurs; that it is impossible to keep chauffeurs from having free access to the entire garage; that no chauffeur is permitted, nor was permitted at that time, to take a car out except under orders of the deskman or superintendent in charge of the business; that it was possible for a chauffeur to get into the garage, crank up a car, and go out one of the other doors without the knowledge of the manager or of the officers immediately in charge of the business.

Witness further testified that he was present himself on the night in question at the desk and that he had no knowledge of the chauffeur Greathouse going out on the night in question. Witness further testified that the chauffeur Greathouse was not checked out on the night in question and no record of his leaving the garage on any business of the company or on any service to be performed for the company were made.

[3] In the face of these undisputed facts, the circumstances relied on by appellees are not sufficiently tangible to form the basis of a verdict. Van Cleave v. Walker, 210 S. W. 767; Christensen v. Christiansen, 155 S. W. 995.

The cause is therefore reversed and rendered.

═══════

ANDERSON et al. v. SMITH. (No. 1175.)

(Court of Civil Appeals of Texas. El Paso. April 14, 1921. Rehearing Denied June 2, 1921.)

1. Appeal and error ⟨⇒931(1)—Viewed in aspect most favorable to appellee.

Evidence must be viewed in its aspect most favorable to appellee.

2. Statutes ⟨⇒117(8) — Amendatory statute making natural person liable for death caused by agent, invalid.

Acts 33d Leg. (1913) c. 143 (Vernon's Sayles' Ann. Civ. St. 1914, art. 4694), amending Rev. St. 1911, art. 4694, is invalid in so far as it undertakes to make a natural person liable in damages for a wrongful death caused by his agent or servant; the change not being

within the scope of the caption of the amending act.

3. Death ⟨⇒33—Joint tort-feasors liable.

Liability for wrongful death under Rev. St. 1911, art. 4694, is not limited to person whose hand inflicted the death wound, but extends to his joint tort-feasor.

4. Torts ⟨⇒22—Joint tort-feasors jointly and severally liable.

Joint tort-feasors are jointly and severally responsible for the consequences of their wrongful act.

5. Torts ⟨⇒22—"Joint tort-feasors" defined.

When two or more persons participate in concerted action to commit a common tort and accomplish their purpose, they become "tort-feasors."

[Ed. Note.—For other definitions, see Words and Phrases, First and Second Series, Joint Tort-Feasors.]

6. Death ⟨⇒75—Evidence held to show concerted killing.

In an action against father and son for death of plaintiff's husband shot by son, evidence held to show concerted action between father and son to wrongfully kill the husband.

7. Death ⟨⇒33—Father held liable as "joint tort-feasor" with son who shot deceased.

Where son shot deceased after there had been concerted action between father and son to wrongfully kill deceased, the father was a "joint tort-feasor" and was equally liable in damages for decedent's death under Rev. St. 1911, art. 4694.

Appeal from District Court, Jones County; W. R. Chapman, Judge.

Suit by Mrs. E. O. Smith against F. W. Anderson and another. Judgment for plaintiff, and defendants appeal. Affirmed.

W. S. Pope, of Anson, and Stinson, Chambers & Brooks, of Abilene, for appellants. Jno. B. Thomas, of Anson, and Joe O. Randel, of Hamlin, for appellee.

HIGGINS, J. This suit was brought by the appellee for herself and as next friend of her minor children against appellants, F. W. Anderson and his son, Ray Anderson, to recover damages for the wrongful killing of Otto Smith, her husband and the father of her children. The case was tried without a jury and judgment rendered in favor of plaintiff against both defendants, jointly and severally, for the sum of $8,000. Findings of fact and conclusions of law were not filed by the trial court. Both defendants appeal, but no assignment of error is presented questioning the correctness of the judgment against Ray Anderson. All of the assignments relate to the judgment against F. W. Anderson.

There is evidence to the following effect: The deceased, Otto Smith, was a tenant upon the farm of F. W. Anderson. On Friday afternoon, August 2, 1918, the deceased was in his field cutting cane. His brother, Will Smith, was present. F. W. Anderson came into the field where they were at work, and a quarrel arose between Anderson and deceased. No blows passed, however. The Smiths resumed their work, and Anderson left, saying to the deceased: "Ha, Ha, this ain't settled yet! I'll get you!"

The next morning deceased, his brother, Will Smith, and a cousin, Tom Smith, started to town in an open-top one-seated buggy. The public road leading to town passed the home of F. W. Anderson. As they approached the Anderson home and got in about 200 yards thereof, F. W. and Ray Anderson appeared in the road; the latter armed with a gun and the former carrying a club. F. W. Anderson stood in the middle of the road, and Ray Anderson over next to the fence. The Smiths stopped and turned back. As they did so, deceased said to the Andersons: "If that's your game, we'll go back." To which F. W. Anderson replied: "I'll get you sons a bitches," or, "You sons a bitches, we'll get you," and the deceased said, "Look out, old man, I know too much on you." The Smiths went back home, and thence to town by another road avoiding the Anderson home. The Smiths remained in town until afternoon, when they started back to the home of Otto Smith. While in town, Will and Tom Smith saw F. W. Anderson, and he saw them. Going back home, the Smiths traveled the direct public road which led by the Anderson home. They first went to the home of John Smith, where the deceased procured a loaded shotgun. From the home of John Smith they continued their journey, deceased carrying the shotgun with them. They passed the home of Anderson and came to the home of John Gooding, which was on the public road and between the Anderson and Otto Smith homes. The road at Gooding's house was in a lane. The Smiths stopped their buggy in the lane in front of the Gooding house. The buggy did not stop in the middle of the lane, but was drawn over next to the wire fence between the road and the house. All three remained in the buggy seated on its one seat. Gooding came out and approached the buggy, and the four engaged in conversation. When they had been thus engaged for a few minutes, an automobile was seen approaching at a rapid speed down the public road, coming in the direction of the Gooding house, Anderson's house, and town. As it neared the party, the Smiths recognized the occupants of the car as F. W. and Ray Anderson. F. W. Anderson was driving. The car passed the Smiths at a rapid rate and continued on its way. As the car passed the Smiths, Ray Anderson, without warning and without justification, suddenly raised a gun and fired at the Smiths, wounding Otto Smith so severely that he died in a few minutes. Will Smith testified:

"About the time they passed the buggy, Ray just come over with the gun and shot. The car looked to be about even with the buggy at that time, almost even with the buggy. He just come over with the gun and shot when he passed. We were on the west side of the road. Looked like the car was in three or four or five feet of the buggy. It looked like he pulled in towards us; I couldn't say that he did, but it looked that way."

[1] We do not undertake to detail all of the evidence. It must be viewed in its aspect most favorable to the appellee, and the statement made is from that viewpoint. [2] Under the first assignment it is asserted that the judgment against F. W. Anderson is unsupported by the evidence because the death of Otto Smith was caused by the wrongful act of Ray Anderson, who fired the fatal shot, and it is not shown that in so doing Ray Anderson acted as the agent or servant of F. W. Anderson. If the judgment were dependent upon the establishment of such a relationship, it could not be sustained in view of the recent ruling in Rodgers v. Tobias, 225 S. W. 804, and in which a writ of error has been refused. In that case it was held that the amendment of 1913 (Acts 33d Leg. Reg. Sess. p. 288 [Vernon's Sayles' Ann. Civ. St. 1914, art. 4694]) to section 2 of article 4694, R. S., is invalid in so far as it undertakes to make a natural person liable in damages for a wrongful death caused by his agent or servant; the ruling being predicated upon the fact that such a change in the law was not within the scope of the caption to the amending act.

In view of this ruling, the law remains as it was before the amendment. Article 4694, R. S. 1911, provides that—

"An action for actual damages on account of injuries, causing the death of any person may be brought in the following cases: * * * (2) When the death of any person is caused by the wrongful act, negligence, unskillfulness, or default of another."

Our statutes upon the subject are based upon Lord Campbell's Act passed in England in 1846. The English act was speedily followed in this country by the passage of laws in the several states having in view the same general purpose. Though these laws have been in effect for many years, there seem to be very few decisions involving the right of recovery for death intentionally and wrongfully inflicted against one whose own immediate act was not the cause of the death.

[3] In the instant case the fatal shot was fired by Ray Anderson. It was his immediate act that caused the death of Otto Smith. But in our opinion liability under the statute is not necessarily limited to the one whose hand inflicted the death wound.

[4] It is a familiar rule that joint tort-feasors are jointly and severally responsible for the consequences of their wrongful act. "Wrongs may be committed either by one person or by several. When several participate, they may do so in different ways, at different times, and in very unequal proportions. One may plan, another may procure the men to execute, others may be the actual instruments in accomplishing the mischief, but the legal blame will rest upon all as joint actors." 1 Cooley on Torts (3d Ed.) 213.

[5] So when two or more persons participate in concerted action to commit a common tort and accomplish their purpose, they become joint tort-feasors. Wolf v. Perryman, 82 Tex. 112, 17 S. W. 772.

[6, 7] In our opinion the evidence is sufficient to show concerted action between F. W. and Ray Anderson to wrongfully kill Otto Smith. If this view of the evidence be correct, F. W. Anderson became a joint tort-feasor and equally liable in damages under the statute with Ray Anderson, who fired the shot which caused Smith's death. McCue v. Klein, 60 Tex. 168, 48 Am. Rep. 260;

Gray v. McDonald, 104 Mo. 303, 16 S. W. 398; Benson v. Ross, 143 Mich. 452, 106 N. W. 1120, 114 A. S. R. 675.

Briefly, the facts which show concert of action between the Andersons are: The threat made by F. W. Anderson against deceased the afternoon preceding the killing; the action of the Andersons on the morning of the killing when they confronted the Smiths in the road both armed and with the evident common purpose at that time of committing an assault with a deadly weapon; the threat then made by F. W. Anderson; direct and active participation by F. W. Anderson as the driver of the car in which Ray Anderson rode to the scene of the homicide and which rapidly carried him away and out of danger; the evidence of Will Smith to the effect that as the car passed the buggy in which they were seated it seemed to have been pulled in towards them. From Smith's testimony it may be inferred that F. W. Anderson swerved the car near the buggy so that Ray Anderson might more surely shoot.

What has been said disposes of all assignments except the third which complains of rulings upon evidence. For various reasons this latter assignment is regarded as presenting no error; in any event, no error sufficient to require a reversal.

Affirmed.

HILL v. BRADY.　(No. 2419.)

(Court of Civil Appeals of Texas. Texarkana. May 13, 1921. Rehearing Denied June 2, 1921.)

1. **Appeal and error ⇐=870(3) — Defendant waived right to review action of trial court on plea of privilege when he failed to appeal from order.**

In view of Vernon's Ann. Civ. St. Supp. 1918, art. 1903, giving right of appeal from orders sustaining or overruling plea of privilege, defendant waived the right to have the action of the trial court in overruling his plea reviewed when he failed to prosecute an appeal from the order overruling the plea.

On Appellant's Motion for Rehearing.

2. **Appeal and error ⇐=2—Statute giving right of appeal from order on plea of privilege not unconstitutional.**

Act April 2, 1917 (Laws 1917, c. 176 [Vernon's Ann. Civ. St. Supp. 1918, art. 1903]) amending Rev. St. 1911, art. 1903, to give right of appeal from orders sustaining or overruling plea of privilege, is not unconstitutional.

Appeal from Hopkins County Court; Homer L. Pharr, Judge.

Suit by A. M. Brady against John D. Hill. Judgment for plaintiff and defendant appeals. Affirmed.

Alleging that appellant promised in writing to pay him in Hopkins county sums aggregating $395 and had failed to do so, appellee sued appellant in the county court of said county. The latter by a sufficient plea filed at a proper time asserted a right he claimed to have the cause transferred to Cameron county, where he resided, for trial. The plea was controverted by appellee and overruled by the court by an order made January 4, 1921. Appellant did not, as he might, prosecute an appeal from that order. The cause was tried on its merits January 8, 1921, and on findings made by a jury on special issues submitted to them judgment was rendered in appellee's favor against appellant for the amount sued for. The appeal is from that judgment.

Dial, Melson & Brim, of Sulphur Springs, for appellant.

T. J. Flewharty and H. C. Connor, both of Sulphur Springs, for appellee.

WILLSON, C. J. (after stating the facts as above). [1] The contention, and only contention, presented by the assignments in appellant's brief is that the court below erred when he overruled appellant's "plea of privilege," and refused to transfer the cause to Cameron county for trial. We are of opinion appellant waived the right he had to have the action of the trial court in that respect reviewed when he failed to prosecute an appeal from the order overruling said plea.

Evidently the purpose of the Legislature in enacting the statute giving a right of appeal from an order sustaining or overruling such a plea (article 1903, Vernon's Statutes, 1918 Supplement) was to have the question as to venue finally determined before the cause was tried on its merits, and so avoid useless expense to the parties, as well as waste of their time and the court's, which often resulted under the practice prevailing when the statute was enacted of trying a cause on its merits before the question as to venue was settled; for under that practice, if it was determined on an appeal of the cause that the question as to venue had been wrongly decided by the trial court, a reversal of the judgment followed as a matter of course. If that, as we think, was the purpose of the Legislature, it would not be accomplished if the statute should be construed as entitling a party who might have appealed from the order, but did not have a judgment on the merits reversed because of error in the ruling of the trial court on the plea.

The judgment is affirmed.

On Appellant's Motion for Rehearing.

[2] The attack on the constitutionality of the act of April 2, 1917 (General Laws, p. 388, [Vernon's Ann. Civ. St. Supp. 1918, art. 1903]) amending article 1903, Revised Statutes 1911, seems to be without merit. See Womack v. Gardner, 10 Tex. Civ. App. 367, 30 S. W. 589; Womack v. Garner (Tex. Sup.) 31 S. W. 358; Gunter v. Tex. Land & Mortg. Co., 82 Tex. 498, 17 S. W. 840; 25 R. C. L. 871.

The court is still of the opinion the question as to the meaning of the act was correctly determined, and therefore think the motion should be overruled.

═══════

MAIER v. LANGERHANS.　(No. 6566.)

(Court of Civil Appeals of Texas. San Antonio. May 4, 1921. Rehearing Denied June 1, 1921.)

1. **Appeal and error ⇐=930(1) — Everything sustained by testimony deemed found in support of judgment.**

Where defendant did not request the submission of any issue, everything that the testimony will sustain will be deemed by the Court of Civil Appeals to be found in support of judgment adverse to defendant.

2. **Brokers ⇐=85(1) — Whether broker who procured exchange praised property immaterial.**

In a suit for commission on procuring an exchange of defendant's store for a ranch, whether plaintiff praised defendant's property and commended the price fixed on it was immaterial; plaintiff having procured the exchange

3. Evidence ⚷=471(2) — Irrelevant conclusion properly rejected.

In a suit for commission on procuring an exchange of defendant's store for a ranch, testimony sought to be elicited by defendant store owner from himself, constituting merely a conclusion or opinion of defendant, and irrelevant, was properly rejected.

4. Brokers ⚷=85(1)—Whether plaintiff broker put forth effort to get abstract of title immaterial.

In a suit for commission on procuring an exchange of defendant's store for a ranch, it was immaterial whether plaintiff broker put forth any efforts to get an abstract of title or not; there being no question of the title to the property, and it not devolving on plaintiff to procure an abstract.

Appeal from District Court, Gillespie County; N. T. Stubbs, Judge.

Action by F. J. Maler against Fritz Langerhans. From judgment for plaintiff, defendant appeals. Affirmed.

A. P. C. Petsch, of Fredericksburg, and Taliaferro, Cunningham & Moursund, of San Antonio, for appellant.

Sagebiel & Usener, of Fredericksburg, for appellee.

FLY, C. J. Appellee recovered a judgment against appellant for $423.65, based on the responses of a jury to three special issues submitted by the trial court. The amount was alleged to be due as commissions on an exchange of properties procured by appellee at the instance and request of appellant, and for which he agreed to pay a commission of 2½ per cent. on a valuation of $16,000 on the property of appellant.

The jury found that on or about April 1, 1919, appellant requested appellee to procure a person who would exchange a ranch for appellant's "Daylight Store" in Fredericksburg, Tex., and agreed to pay him for his services a commission of 2½ per cent. on a valuation of $16,000 for said store. Appellee procured a party willing to exchange a ranch for the town property, and the exchange was made. Appellant refused to pay the commission.

[1] The first assignment of error is overruled. The evidence showed that appellee was the procuring cause of an exchange of the properties, and when Rogers offered a trade appellant wanted $18,000 for his store. There was no question about the store being taken at a valuation of $16,000, but Rogers wanted $2,000 difference between the two properties, but got only $1,000. Appellant did not request the submission of any issue. Everything that the testimony will sustain will be deemed by this court to have been found in support of the judgment. Whatever value may have been received by appellant for his store in the exchange would not matter, because the evidence showed that the value of $16,000, was fixed by appellant as a basis for the amount he would pay appellee for his services.

[2] The evidence whose rejection is complained of in the second assignment of error had no bearing whatever on the issues in the case, and was properly rejected. Whether appellee praised the property of appellant and commended the price fixed on it or not could have had no weight in the case, as the fact remained that an exchange was procured, and appellee must have procured it, as he alone represented appellant. Schneider swore that he was representing Rogers and not appellant. The same can be said in regard to the testimony, rejection of which is complained of in the third assignment of error, and it is overruled.

[3] The testimony sought to be elicited by appellant from himself, and rejection of which is assailed in the fourth assignment, was merely a conclusion or opinion of appellant, was utterly irrelevant, and was properly rejected.

[4] The fifth assignment of error is overruled. It was immaterial as to whether appellee put forth any efforts to get an abstract of title or not. There was no question about the title to the property, and it did not devolve upon appellee to procure an abstract of title.

The judgment is affirmed.

HOLDEN v. EVANS. (No. 6546.)

(Court of Civil Appeals of Texas. San Antonio. April 13, 1921. Rehearing Denied May 11, 1921.)

1. Pleading ⚷=236(3)—Permitting plaintiff to file trial amendment discretionary with court.

Permitting plaintiff to file trial amendment to petition is within discretion of the trial court, subject to correction for any abuse thereof.

2. Trial ⚷=351(5)—Refusal of requested special issue held proper, in view of special issue submitted.

Refusal of requested special issue, "At the time defendant entered into the contract to sell to plaintiff the rooming house and property in question, did defendant have authority from the owners of said property to sell the same?" held proper, in view of submitted special issue as to "whether defendant had authority from the owners to sell upon the particular terms of the contract made by him with E. (plaintiff)."

3. Appeal and error ⚷=704(1)—No review of refusal of special issue without record showing issues submitted.

Assignments of error complaining of refusal to submit requested special issue will not be considered, where no record references are given in the statement under the assignment, either as to the issues given or the issues tendered, and where the appellate court is unable to determine from the brief whether or not the issue tendered was embraced in the special issues actually given.

4. Appeal and error ⏍725(2), 742(3), 743(1)—Assignments of error complaining of overruling of exceptions held insufficient for consideration.

Assignments of error complaining of action of court in overruling special exceptions, without a statement thereunder and without the special exceptions being set out, in substance or otherwise, and without record references being given or a showing made as to action taken on the exceptions, will not be considered.

5. Appeal and error ⏍742(5)—Assignment of error submitted as a proposition held too general for consideration.

Assignment of error submitted as a proposition, without being followed by a specific proposition, that "it was error for the court to submit the charge to the jury at failed and refused to instruct the jury upon whom rested the burden of proof" without record references, and without setting out the charge given by the court, held too general for consideration.

6. Trial ⏍255(3)—Failure to instruct on burden of proof not error, in absence of request therefor.

Failure to charge jury as to burden of proof held not error, in absence of a request for an instruction covering the omission.

Error from District Court, Tarrant County.

Action by E. J. Evans against C. W. Holden. Judgment for plaintiff, and defendant brings error. Affirmed.

Graves & Houtchens, of Fort Worth, for plaintiff in error.

Simpson & Moore, of Fort Worth, for defendant in error.

SMITH, J. Writ of error from a judgment in favor of E. J. Evans against C. W. Holden, growing out of a deal by which the latter, as a real estate dealer and agent of the owner, agreed to sell and deliver to Evans the furniture in a Fort Worth hotel. Defendant in error has filed no briefs, and we are unable to clearly ascertain from plaintiff in error's brief just what the trouble is. The cause was submitted on special issues, but these special issues are not shown in the briefs, nor are the answers of the jury thereto. The judgment of the lower court is not set out in full or in substance in the briefs, and just what that judgment was, or for what amount, is not shown.

The first assignment of error complains of the overruling of the general demurrer, but the statement thereunder is not sufficient to enable this court to determine to its own satisfaction whether or not the petition of plaintiff below was good as against a general demurrer. However, we have examined the petition set out in the transcript, and have concluded that it states a cause of action. The first assignment of error is accordingly overruled.

[1] The second assignment of error is overruled. In that assignment plaintiff in error complains of the action of the court in permitting plaintiff below to file a trial amendment. Such matters are within the discretion of the trial court, subject, of course, to correction for any abuse thereof. We do not think the court in this instance abused that discretion; it is not shown that any injury resulted to plaintiff in error by reason of the exercise of that discretion.

In his third assignment of error plaintiff in error complains of the refusal of the court below to give the following requested special issue:

"At the time defendant entered into the contract to sell to plaintiff the rooming house and property in question did defendant have authority from the owners of said property to sell the same?"

[2] It does not appear in the statement under the assignment whether the matter embraced in this issue was included in any of the issues submitted to and answered by the jury, these issues not being shown in the brief, but in the argument under that assignment it appears that the matter was submitted by the court in a special issue, "whether defendant had authority from the owners to sell upon the particular terms of the contract made by him with Evans"; this quotation being from said argument. Given no more light than shines from plaintiff in error's brief upon this particular transaction, we are not prepared to hold that the court erred in refusing to give this requested special issue; on the contrary, it seems to us that the issue as given was the better way to submit the matter.

[3] We overrule the fourth assignment of error, in which complaint is made of the refusal of the court below to submit to the jury plaintiff in error's requested special issue No. 2. We are unable to determine from the brief whether or not the issue thereto tendered was embraced in the special issues actually given, and which are not shown in the brief. No record references are given in the statement under this assignment, either as to the issues given or the issue tendered.

For obvious reasons we also overrule the fifth assignment of error, which we quote:

"The court erred in failing and refusing to submit to the jury defendant's bill of exception No. 4."

[4] The sixth to the ninth assignments of error complain of the alleged action of the court in overruling certain special exceptions of plaintiff in error. No statement is given

under either of these assignments. The special exceptions are not set out, in substance or otherwise; it is not shown what action was taken on them; no record references are given. The assignments therefore will not be considered.

The tenth assignment of error, submitted as a proposition and followed by no specific proposition, is as follows:

"It was error for the court to submit the charge to the jury as failed and refused to instruct the jury upon whom rested the burden of proof."

[5, 6] The statement under this assignment gives no record references, nor does it purport to set out the charge given by the court, and is too general to invite consideration. However, it appears that plaintiff in error requested no special charge covering the alleged omission, and the assignment is accordingly overruled.

The eleventh assignment of error complains of the overruling of plaintiff in error's "objections and in submitting to the jury special issue No. 8."

The statement under this assignment does not set out special issue No. 8, or the substance thereof, or the objections thereto, and the assignment will therefore be disregarded.

The judgment is affirmed.

───────

LANCASTER et al. v. ALLEN.   (No. 2417.)

(Court of Civil Appeals of Texas. Texarkana. May 24, 1921. Rehearing Denied June 2, 1921.)

1. Trial ⬥⇒352(1)—Special issue of railroad's violation of federal rule as to safety of locomotive wheel held proper.

In an action under the federal law for the death of a fireman when the locomotive became derailed, a special question whether the flange on a wheel had a flat vertical surface, when tested by the rule prescribed by the Interstate Commerce Commission, required the jury to find that the measurement of the flange was made by the metal gauge required by the rule of the commission, and was not erroneous as permitting recovery based on opinions of witnesses notwithstanding the wheel conformed to the standard.

2. Master and servant ⬥⇒286(12)—Railroad's negligence in violating federal rule as to safety of locomotive wheel held for jury.

In an action under the federal law for the death of a locomotive fireman when the engine was derailed, evidence on behalf of plaintiff that the flange of the wheel was defective, and that a plaster cast of the wheel when measured by the gauge prescribed by the Interstate Commerce Commission rule showed it to be defective, held to raise the issue of defendant's negligence in using a wheel which was defec-

tive when tested by the gauge, notwithstanding evidence of defendant's witnesses to the contrary.

3. Witnesses ⬥⇒252 — Plaster cast of wheel held sufficiently identified to be used as basis of measurement.

A plaster cast is sufficiently identified as that of the locomotive wheel alleged to have caused the derailing of an engine and the death of a fireman by testimony of a witness that he saw the plaster cast taken off of the wheel in controversy, to make it the basis of testimony by the witness that the wheel was defective as shown by a gauge measurement of the cast.

4. Master and servant ⬥⇒297(4)—Special findings held to show railroad's negligence under federal safety rules as to locomotive trucks.

In an action under the federal law for the death of a locomotive fireman, an answer to the special question, stating that the reason for the flange on a locomotive wheel being worn was that the truck was out of tram, is a finding that the truck was out of tram, which, when sustained by the evidence, is sufficient to show the master's negligence, under the rule of the Interstate Commerce Commission, requiring trucks to be maintained in a safe and suitable condition for service.

5. Death ⬥⇒67 — Evidence of deceased fireman's chance of promotion admissible.

In an action for the death of a locomotive fireman, brought under the federal law, evidence that deceased was in line of promotion from fireman to engineer is admissible on the issue of damages.

Appeal from District Court, Harrison County; P. O. Beard, Judge.

Action by Mrs. Clara Allen, administratrix, against Lancaster and Wallace, Receivers of the Texas & Pacific Railway. Judgment for plaintiff, and defendants appeal. Affirmed.

T. O. Allen was a locomotive fireman in the employ of the receivers of the Texas & Pacific Railway, and while operating a passenger train was killed by the derailment of the engine, occurring near the station of Texarkana on September 5, 1917. The railway, as an admitted fact, was operated as an interstate carrier, and the passenger train was a through train, and was engaged in interstate commerce at the time T. O. Allen, operating it, was killed. The appellee, his widow, was appointed administratrix, and brought the suit for damages resulting to her and the children by reason of the death of T. O. Allen. The negligence proximately causing the death as alleged was (1) that the switch points or switch rails at the place of derailment were out of line, worn, old, and broken; (2) that the flange of the right-hand lead wheel of the truck in the front of the engine was worn to a flat vertical or sharp surface one inch or more from the tread of the wheel, causing the wheel to climb the rail of the track and derail the engine; that the use of the wheel in this condition was in violation of the rules and regulations established and promulgated by the Interstate Commerce Commission as a standard of safety of locomotives and their appurtenances engaged in interstate commerce under authority of the Safety Appliance Act approved February 17, 1911 (U. S. Comp. St. §§ 8630–8639), and as amended by Act approved March 4, 1915 (U. S. Comp. St. §§ 8639a–8639d), and (3) that the front truck of the engine, and the wheels of the truck, were "out of tram," or not squarely or properly adjusted, to the extent of causing the front wheel to press and grind the flange against the rail, proximately causing it to climb the rail at the switch, or curve, and derail the engine.

The defendant specially denied (1) any negligence, and (2) that the track caused the derailment by being out of line and not in good condition, and (3) that the truck or the wheels were worn or out of tram, and (4) that the flange on the wheel of the truck of the engine was worn so as to be defective and not in compliance with the standard and the orders of the Interstate Commerce Commission and the federal statute.

The controversy arising in the evidence was (1) whether or not the flange in the wheel was in compliance with the rules and instructions for inspection and testing locomotives and their appurtenances established and fixed by order of the Interstate Commerce Commission in conformity with the acts of Congress, and (2) whether or not the circumstances went to show that the front truck of the engine and the wheels of the truck were "out of tram," or not squarely or properly adjusted, to the extent of causing the front right-hand wheel to grind and press against the rail, proximately causing it to climb the rail at the switch, or curve, and derail the engine.

The following rules, as adopted by the Interstate Commerce Commission, were offered in evidence:

"Rule 146. Forged Steel or Steel-Tired Wheels.

"(a) Forged steel or steel-tired wheels with any of the following defects shall not be continued in service:

"(b) Loose wheels; loose, broken or defective retaining rings or tires; broken or cracked hubs, plates or bolts.

"(c) Slide flat spot 2½ inches or longer; or if there are two or more adjoining spots, each 2 inches or longer.

"(d) Defective tread on account of cracks or shelled out spots 2½ inches or longer, or so numerous as to endanger the safety of the wheel.

"(e) Broken flange.

"(f) Flange worn to fifteen-sixteenths inch above the tread, or having flat vertical surface one inch or more from tread; tread worn five-sixteenths inch; flange more than one and one-half inches from tread to top of flange or thickness of tires or rims less than shown in figures 4, 5, 6, and 7.

"(g) Wheels out of gauge.

"Note. The determination of flat spots and worn flanges shall be made by a gauge as shown in figure 8."

In this connection it was shown that there was a prescribed metal gauge adopted and used in measuring the wheel and the flange in order to determine whether or not the wheel and the flange met the requirements of the several subdivisions of the rule. The wheel in question was shown to be a steel wheel. Subsection "f" is the section that is in question in the case.

"Rule 143. (a) Trucks, leading and trailing. Trucks shall be maintained in safe and suitable condition for service. Center places shall fit properly, and the male center place shall extend into the female center place not less than three-fourths inch. All centering devices shall be properly maintained.

"(b) A suitable safety chain shall be provided at each front corner of all four-wheel engine trucks.

"(c) All parts of trucks shall have sufficient clearance to prevent them from seriously interfering with any other part of the locomotive."

The special issues submitted by the court and the answers of the jury thereto are as follows:

"Question 1. Did the flange on the right-hand lead truck wheel have a flat vertical surface one inch or more from the tread of the wheel when tested by the rule prescribed by the Interstate Commerce Commission? Answer: Yes.

"Question 2. If you answer question No. 1 'Yes,' then answer this question: Was the condition of the flange the proximate cause, or one of the proximate causes, of the derailment? Answer: Yes.

"Question No. 3. Was the flange of the wheel worn sharp or vertical? Answer: Yes.

"Question No. 4. If you answer question No. 3 'Yes,' then state the reason for the flange being worn or vertical. Answer: Truck out of tram; too much pressure on right lead wheel.

"Question No. 5. If you answer question No. 3 'Yes,' then answer this question: Was the sharp or vertical condition of the flange, if it was sharp or vertical, one of the proximate causes of the derailment? Answer: Yes.

"Question No. 6. Was the switch point in the track in a reasonably safe condition for use? Answer: Yes."

The amount awarded was apportioned by the jury to the widow and five of the children, but any recovery was denied the three adult children.

The engine of the passenger train was suddenly derailed and turned over, according to the evidence, at a point about 700 feet west of the Union Depot in the city of Texarkana; and T. O. Allen, the fireman, was scalded and bruised to the extent that he died within a few hours afterwards. The train was running at about 10 or 12 miles an hour. The switch had been set for the train to go down track 22 to the station. As the engine, at the point of the switch, headed up track 22 the front right-hand wheels of the pony truck of the engine suddenly got off the rail; and the rear wheels, on hitting the frog of the switch, left the rail, and the engine then turned over on its side. Appellant's yard switchman testified:

"I had the switches set before the train was due. When the engine got in sight I gave the signal to come ahead. It passed me before it was derailed. I noticed fire from the grinding of the wheel on the rail under the truck of the engine. I knew it was unusual. I tried to catch the engineer's eye to give him a signal to stop, but he failed to look back. The engine ran about three engine lengths after I saw the fire flying under it, before it turned over. The engine turned over between track 21 and 22, and on its left side. * * * The engine was derailed about 12 or 14 inches from the points of the switch, headed up track 22, where I first found any marks. * * * There was no obstruction on the track where the engine was derailed. The switches were all properly lined up, and there was no cause there for the derailment."

It appears that the cause of the derailment was looked into about "twenty minutes after the engine turned over." The evidence strongly goes to show that "the right front pony truck wheel was the first wheel to get off the rail." Physical marks on the ball of the rail showed "kind of a cutting mark" that the flange of the wheel made on the top of the rail. The flange on this wheel showed "a worn flange, or vertical, sharp flange is the common term." And, as further said, "the bevel had worn off and it had become vertical, which would cause it to run off the track, as it did," and "the flange was worn just about to the center of the flange, half of it worn away, or nearly half." "A vertical flange" is, as shown, when "the flange becomes right-angle to the tread of the wheel." It was testified that "the flange on the other wheel was not bright." "The bright part is the part we call vertical." The witness Holloway testified:

"I was" for about seven years "clerk in the locomotive and car departments and storekeeper and wheel inspector. * * * A vertical or straight flange will not keep the wheel on the rail. Beveled flanges cause the wheels to move laterally around curves, whereas, if vertical, flanges have tendency to climb any defect on the rail and get off. In going around sharp curves, won't hardly stay on; they get off. I looked at the wheel at the time. I thought it had been worn out; thought it was a bad wheel. To my mind it was not a good wheel. In my judgment I did not think it was a good wheel to be a lead wheel under a locomotive, because the bevel had worn off and it had become vertical, which would cause it to run off the track, as it did. * * * I thought that was a condemnable wheel. * * * The flange

was worn just about to the center of the flange; half of it was worn away, or nearly half. * * * I think the flange of this wheel was worn practically to the center line. That means half of the throat side worn away. The portion that was left was straight down, perpendicular to the tread of the wheel. * * * It should not wear to that center line; would be dangerous when it wears to center line, I would say. * * * I was present when the Master Car Builders' gauge was applied to the flange on that wheel. It lacked a very small fraction of coming down to the tread of the wheel. It was a very small fraction. It lacked about one-eighth of an inch of coming down to the tread of the wheel. The gauge did not go down completely. I did not measure how far it went down. It was approximately one-eighth of an inch until it got to the throat of the flange. I think it came up to the standard rules, according to all that discussion we had with the railway officials."

The witness Neville testified that he had experience "as a locomotive fireman, and run a switch engine and an engine on the road also." The witness further said he examined the wheel. He said:

"I examined a part of the flange of that wheel he showed me. I suppose I examined about eight inches of the flange—part of the circle of the wheel. The flange was worn. It was what I would call a sharp flange. I mean by a sharp flange, not one worn clear to the tip. I mean a flange where the bevel is worn in the throat. I mean a flange worn to a straight edge going up to where the flange comes down to tread of the wheel; the bevel practically worn off. * * * I never tested a flange with one of those gauges. I would consider a gauge more reliable than testing with the eye alone."

The witness Mayes testified:

"I went to Texarkana with Mr. Casey to examine the wheel. While I was there I saw a metal gauge for gauging wheel flanges applied to the wheel, just like the one you have in your hand. When the 'U' part of the gauge was applied to the flange it went over the flange. While I was there Mr. Casey made a plaster cast of the wheel. I was not right at the spot when he made the cast, because I was looking for an engine to come back around the 'Y.' I saw the plaster cast taken off; saw it applied to the wheel. The cast you hold in your hand is the plaster cast referred to. In applying the plaster to the wheel it extended over to the edge of the flange to the inside edge."

The plaster cast was before the witness at the time this testimony was given. The witness McKiernan, a division foreman, testified:

"You have what appears to be a plaster cast in your hand. If it is a correct cast of the flange there, it would be a condemnable wheel, and I would order it taken out if under my observation."

The witness McDermott, foreman of the shops, testified:

"The pattern, as shown by the plaster cast, shows a bad wheel. The pattern you have here shows a straight flange."

The evidence on the part of appellant strongly went to show that when the gauge was applied to the wheel itself it disclosed that the flange of the wheel was not condemnable under the rule.

There is evidence to show by circumstances that the front truck of the engine was, and had for some time been, out of tram, or not squarely or properly adjusted, to the extent of causing the front wheel to press and grind against the rail, and to cause the wheel in its worn condition to climb the rail at the switch or curve and derail the engine. The witness Faulkner, a wheel inspector and general foreman, testified:

"With the lead wheel flange wearing away to the extent it was, almost vertical down to the throat, if not quite so, and the other flange not grinding away, that truck would not be in good condition to operate. The two wheels ought to wear something about alike. If they did not it would show something wrong. With the wheel binding against the rail from any cause so as to wear the flange away, that binding would have a tendency, if it got to a worn switch point or chipped out or broken switch point, to climb the rail. If it come to any defect in the rail, it would be liable to climb it, and that would wreck the train."

The witness McDermott, foreman of the mechanical department, testified:

"The flange on the left front wheel was not worn as straight as the one on the right-hand side. Some of the things that make the flange wear straight is because they would not be in tram; that is, exactly square. That causes considerable pressure of the wheel against the rail. If the flange got worn bad enough it would cause it to climb the rail. Some of the things that make the flange on one end of the axle wear straight while the other would not, is because not in tram."

The witness Dogenhart, switchman, testified:

"I had the switches set before the train was due. * * * I noticed fire from the wheels grinding on the rails or trucks or something under the engine; that is the first thing I noticed of anything unusual. I merely saw fire flying from something unusual. The engine was derailed about 12 or 14 inches from the points of the switch. I noticed all the wheels. The flange on the right-hand front truck wheel was worn some, but, not being an expert, I could not tell whether it was worn to unsafety or not. It was worn so that it was not beveled like the wheel on the other side. * * * If the rails were too close together, that could have caused the derailment. If the lead truck of the engine had been improperly lined, this fact might have caused the derailment. I have never formed a conclusion of what caused the derailment."

There is evidence, we conclude, to warrant the findings of the jury and to support the judgment of the court.

Prendergast & Prendergast, of Marshall, for appellant.

S. P. Jones, of Marshall, for appellee.

LEVY, J. (after stating the facts as above).

[1] The court submitted to the jury, and appellant predicates error on the following question for answer:

"Did the flange on the right-hand lead truck wheel have a flat vertical surface one inch or more from the tread of the wheel when tested by the rule prescribed by the Interstate Commerce Commission?"

Rule 146, § f, being "the rule" referred to in the instruction, provided that "steel-tired wheels," like the one in controversy, "shall not be continued in service" with "any of the following defects:" of "flange," as claimed in this case, "having flat vertical service one inch or more from tread." And the question required the jury to determine from the evidence whether or not "the flange on the right-hand truck wheel" was, in point of fact, in a prohibited condition for use in the service, "when tested by the rule prescribed by the Interstate Commerce Commission." The rule was in evidence before the jury, as was also the regulation requiring that the determination of worn flanges shall be made by a prescribed metal gauge or measurement; and the metal gauge was introduced in evidence, and witnesses testified respecting whether or not the flange of the wheel in controversy was defective when the metal gauge was applied to it. The language of the question permitted, and the jury could reasonably understand, that it required them to consider all the evidence respecting metal gauge and the measurement of the flange of the wheel by the metal gauge in determining whether or not the condition of the flange violated the plain provision of the rule. It did not exclude from the consideration of the jury, as contended by appellant, the measurement of the flange by the metal gauge. The term "when tested by the rule," as used, includes and refers to the method of measurement adopted and required, and was intended to have that restrictive meaning. It is believed there was no reversible error in the charge, and assignments Nos. 2 and 4 are overruled. Lancaster v. Allen, 110 Tex. 213, 217 S. W. 1032.

[2] The appellant requested and complains of the refusal of the court to give the following special charge:

"In this case it appears without contradiction that the flange of the wheel on the engine in question complied with the standard established by the Interstate Commerce Commission under the act of Congress, and therefore the jury cannot find that the railroad company was negligent in that regard."

The evidence raises the issue, we conclude, of the flange of the wheel in evidence being in a condition prohibited by the rule established by the Interstate Commerce Commission. Appellant showed by several witnesses that the flange of the wheel, when the metal gauge or measurement was applied, met and was within the requirement of the rule. Appellee, though, showed by several witnesses that in their opinion, from an actual observation and examination of the wheel, though not tested by the metal gauge, the wheel was condemnable under the rule. And the appellee, following this testimony, then showed by the evidence of the witness Mayes that a plaster cast was taken of the wheel. The witness said: "I saw the plaster cast taken off; saw it applied to the wheel. The cast you hold in your hand is the plaster cast referred to." And then appellee offered several witnesses, who testified that the plaster cast, when the metal gauge is applied to it, shows a flange condemnable and prohibited by the rule.

[3] The plaster cast was sufficiently proven to make it the basis of having the witnesses testify that it showed by measurement of the metal gauge that the wheel of which it was a cast showed a condition prohibited by the rule. Assignments Nos. 1 and 3 are overruled.

[4] The appellant challenges questions and answers Nos. 3 and 4. In view of the pleading and evidence, the effect, we think, of these answers and the real meaning to be given, is a finding by the jury that the "truck" of the engine was "out of tram," making "too much pressure on the right lead wheel" to the extent and degree, in point of fact of wearing the flanges of the wheel "sharp or vertical," proximately causing the derailment. It was alleged, and the circumstances of the case went strongly to show, that the front truck of the engine was "out of tram," or not properly adjusted, and by reason thereof had caused the front wheel to grind against the rail long enough to wear the flange to the extent that it would easily climb, as it did, the rail on a sharp curve, as in evidence, causing derailment. When the engine passed the yard switchman, just before derailment, he saw "fire from the grinding of the wheel on the rail." And this finding of fact would, of itself, support the judgment in this case. Rule 143 of the Commission provided that "trucks shall be maintained in safe and suitable condition for service." The wheel being worn is merely a result of the "truck being out of tram," as found by the jury; and the liability, in this phase of the case, would arise, not upon the condition of the wheel, but upon "the truck" being in a condition not authorized by the rule of the Commission, and thus proximately causing the derailment. Assignments of error Nos. 5, 6, and 8 are overruled.

[5] The tenth assignment of error predicates error upon allowing appellee to prove, over objection, that the deceased was in line of promotion from fireman to engineer. The proposition is:

"The chance of a locomotive fireman 45 years old to a promotion to a position with a better salary is too speculative, remote, and uncertain to be the basis for increasing the damages to be found by the jury caused by his death."

The evidence shows that deceased was in line of promotion. This evidence has been permitted under the rule in Texas, and no reason is perceived why it should not apply simply because the instant case is a cause of action arising under the law of Congress. The assignment is overruled.

We have considered each of the remaining assignments, and concluded that they should be overruled. Assignments numbered 7 and 11 to 17 inclusive are overruled.

The judgment is affirmed.

ADAMS et al. v. HENRY et al. (No. 1807.)

(Court of Civil Appeals of Texas. Amarillo. May 4, 1921.)

1. Wills ⟷665—Right of devisee not affected by his statement before testatrix's death nor by subsequent belief of one entitled to benefit under condition of will.

One to whom a will devised land with provision that his sisters were to have a home there when needed, and that if he did not comply with the condition, but refused to give them a home when sick or out of employment, the land should be divided equally between them, having after death of testatrix accepted under the will, his interest in the land was not affected either by any statement of his before testatrix's death, when his rights were not fixed, that his sisters should not have a home there, nor by the fact that after such death one of them, who would have had a right to go there for a home, did not seek it, believing from what he had so previously said that it would be refused.

2. Wills ⟷658 — Devise held to vest fee on condition subsequent.

A will, which gave land to testatrix's nephew "H. (with express understanding that his sisters are to have a home there whenever they need one, I put this in so my brother's children will all have a home to go to should misfortune come to them), to have and to hold his heirs and assigns forever provided he comply with the conditions herein mentioned, but if he refuses to give them a home (I do not mean he is to support them, but a home free of charge when sick or out of employment) it shall be divided equally between them," held not to create a condition precedent, but to vest the fee in the nephew, on a condition subsequent, a defeasance in case of a refusal of a home when needed and requested; Rev. St. art. 1106, providing that an estate devised shall be deemed in fee simple if a lesser be not limited by express words or does not appear by construction or operation of law, and the words in parentheses being part of the defeasance clause.

3. Wills ⊜665 — Word "refuse" in condition of will cannot be construed as "fail."

As words can be changed in a will only when it will effectuate a clearly apparent intent of testator, the word "refuse" in a devise with provision that, if devisee refuse a home to his sisters when sick or out of employment, the land shall be divided equally between them, cannot be changed to "fail."

Appeal from District Court, Grayson County; Silas Hare, Judge.

Suit by Lula Adams and others against Lizzie Henry and another. Judgment for defendants, and plaintiffs appeal. Affirmed.

Webb, Cantrell & Webb and Wood, Jones & Hassell, all of Sherman, for appellants.

J. H. Randell, of Denison, and McReynolds & Hay, of Sherman, for appellees.

HUFF, C. J. We adopt the statement of the trial court in his findings of fact and conclusions of law:

"I. Suit instituted December 8, 1915, by Lula Adams and husband, Ava Throckmorton and husband, Katie Parsons and husband, and Bert Mitchell, as plaintiffs, against Lizzie Henry and Frankie B. Henry, defendants, in trespass to try title and partition 160 acres of land in Grayson county. By amendment plaintiffs asked that the will of Mrs. Mary McCloy be construed by the court and in the alternative that judgment be entered decreeing plaintiffs the right of a home on said land. Defendants duly entered a general denial, plea of not guilty, and specially replied to the allegations in plaintiff's petition.

"II. Mary McCloy was the owner of the land described in plaintiffs' petition, by deed from Isaac Linley, of date December 1, 1882, recorded in Volume 55, p. 307, deed records of Grayson county.

"III. On September 17, 1894, Mary McCloy made the will which is under consideration in this case.

"IV. Mary McCloy died October 9, 1904, and said will was duly probated in the state of Michigan, and is recorded in Volume 236, p. 67, Grayson county deed records, whereby she disposed of the land in controversy in this suit, and the following portion of the will germane to this inquiry reads as follows: 'I give and bequeath to my brother's wife, Jane Henry, all of my real estate situated in the state of Texas, consisting of 160 acres of land in Grayson county, Texas, being all of the quarter No. 4 and being the S. E. quarter of section 2, University League No. 12, to have and to hold during her lifetime. At her death to her son, Frank Henry (with express understanding that his sisters are to have a home there whenever they need one, his sister, Jessie Mitchell's three children included. I put this in so my brother's children will all have a home to go to should misfortune come to them in life's journey). To have and to hold his heirs and assigns forever

provided he comply with the conditions herein mentioned, but if he refuses to give them a home (I do not mean he is to support them, but a home free of charge when sick or out of employment) it shall be divided equally between them.'

"V. The parties referred to in the foregoing extract from the will of Mrs. McCloy are Jane Henry (wife of the brother of said Mary McCloy); Frank Henry (son of Jane Henry); Ada Throckmorton (daughter of Jane Henry and sister of Frank Henry); Lula Adams (daughter of Jane Henry and sister of Frank Henry); Kate Mitchell Parsons (granddaughter of Jane Henry and daughter of Jessie Mitchell); H. B. Mitchell (grandson of Jane Henry and son of Jessie Mitchell). There were other children of Jane Henry, also of Jessie Mitchell, but they died without issue, and their sole heirs are parties to this suit.

"VI. Jessie Mitchell died June 4, 1895.

"VII. Jane Henry died August 3, 1913.

"VIII. Frank Henry died July 21, 1917, leaving as his sole surviving heirs a wife, Lizzie Henry, and a child, Frankie B. Henry. This child was born after the death of said Frank Henry.

"IX. Frank Henry and his wife were occupying the land in controversy as a homestead at the time of his death, and the surviving wife, Lizzie Henry, and child, Frankie B. Henry, are now and ever since his death have been occupying it as a home.

"X. Bert Mitchell testified that his mother made application for a home on this property when she was sick in Sherman. This was before the death of Mrs. McCloy. Bert Mitchell further testified that at the time of his mother's death his sister made application for a home on this property. Furthermore, that at this time he has no home of his own. Mrs. Ada Throckmorton testified that she is 63 years old; owns a piece of land in Oklahoma that is heavily mortgaged, and that she never made application to Frank Henry for a home on this property. Mrs. Lula Adams testified that she never lived on this property after Mrs. McCloy's death; used to go there every year and sometimes oftener; that she has no property; that she has no home and could use this property; that she has a husband who supports her; that she knew about the will ever since it was made. Her mother had a copy of it in her trunk, and witness had heard her mother read the will to Frank Henry, and Frank Henry knew of the will before Mrs. McCloy's death. Mrs. Kate Parsons testified that she is the daughter of Jessie Mitchell; that her mother had been sick about two months when she died in Sherman; that since Mrs. McCloy's death witness had needed a home altogether about two or three years; that the reason she did not go on the place and make application for a home there was that Frank Henry told her to leave and never come back; that Frank Henry had refused witness and the mother of witness and the sister of witness the right to occupy this place as a home; these refusals were all before the death of Mrs. McCloy; that no application had been made to Frank Henry by witness for permission to live on the place since the death of Mrs. McCloy for the reason that the witness knew from previous conduct and statements of Frank Henry that such application would be refused; that witness had no property and is in need of this property as a home. Mrs. Lizzie Henry testified that she is the surviving wife of Frank Henry. They married December 8, 1914, and he died July 21, 1915. The child was born August 19, 1915; that the defendant Frankie B. Henry is the only living child of the deceased Frank Henry.

"XI. None of the plaintiffs herein have ever made application to Frank Henry for a home upon said premises since the death of Mrs. Mc-Cloy. There is no evidence to the effect that either of · the plaintiffs are sick or out of employment, nor is there any evidence that they have ever been sick or out of employment and as a consequence made application to Frank Henry for a home on said premises. There is nothing in this record tending to show that Frank Henry, since the death of Mrs. McCloy, refused to give either of plaintiffs herein a home on this property, free of charge when they were sick or out of employment.

"Conclusions of Law.

"1. The clear interpretation of the will of Mrs. McCloy is:

"(a) A life estate to Jane Henry.

"(b) The right of plaintiffs herein to have a home on said premises when they needed it, and this need is defined to be when they are sick or out of employment, and this right of occupancy extends to each of the plaintiffs during their life and is not restricted to the life of Frank Henry.

"(c) Fee-simple title to Frank Henry, conditioned that he permit the plaintiffs herein to have a home upon said premises free of charge when they are sick or out of employment.

"2· Frank Henry never refused to give plaintiffs a home on said property free of charge when they were sick or out of employment since the death of Mrs. McCloy, and, Frank Henry now being dead, a forfeiture under the terms of the will becomes impossible. The acts and statements of Frank Henry before the death of Mrs. McCloy and before her will became effective cannot be taken as evidence of what his attitude would be after the will became effective. In order for him to be subjected to the forfeiture clause of the will, he must have been called upon to act after the will became effective and when he was in position to act with authority. Declarations of his before the death of Mrs. McCloy before he had any authority to permit or deny them the occupancy of the premises has no probative force on the question of what his attitude or conduct would be after the will was given vitality and he was vested with the power to act.

"3· Fee-simple title to this land is vested in the child, Frankie B. Henry, subject to the life estate of the widow, Lizzie Henry.

"4· The plaintiffs herein are not entitled to any of the relief prayed for, for the reason that the conditions set forth in the will which would give them the right of occupancy of the place as a home are not shown to have ever arisen. Should the plaintiffs herein ever need a home on the premises, they are entitled to it free of charge when they are sick or out of employment, but only so long as they are sick or out of employment. This is a right, however, that is personal to them and cannot pass to their heirs or assigns. The said rights of plaintiffs are a charge against the land in controversy, but is not to interfere with the homestead right of the defendant Lizzie Henry.

"5· Therefore the judgment of the court is that the plaintiffs take nothing by their suit and that they be adjudged to pay the costs; that the defendant Frankie B. Henry be vested with the title in fee simple to the land in controversy, subject to the life estate of the defendant Lizzie Henry."

[1] Assignments from 1 to 4, inclusive, present as error the action of the court in sustaining objections to the evidence of Bert Mitchell, to the effect that Frank Henry told Jessie Mitchell, that she nor her children should ever come on the premises in controversy, and his further testimony that he knew of his mother and sister making application to Frank Henry for a home on the premises, and that he refused them and told them they should never have a home on the premises; and rejected the testimony of Mrs. Kate Parsons that her mother with three small children owned no home at the time and made application to Frank Henry for one and he refused them and that they should never come there; also, her testimony to the effect that she had been in need of a home, but did not go on the place and make application because of the previous conduct of Frank Henry towards her mother and her and the sister. The objections made and sustained to the refusal by Henry to permit the parties on the premises was that it occurred at a time when he was living with his mother, Jane Henry, and under the express provisions of the will he was not given the use and occupancy of the place and had no right to grant or refuse the parties a home thereon at that time. That at that time the will was not in force and effect. Mrs. McCloy was then alive and no action had been taken on the will or could have been taken at that time. One of the parties, Mrs. Lula Adams, had testified that Frank Henry knew of the will and its terms and that her mother had a copy of Mrs. McCloy's will in her trunk and she had heard her read it to Frank Henry. The evidence shows that Mrs. Jessie Mitchell was one of the beneficiaries under the will and was sick at the time at which it was proposed to show the refusal by Henry had been made to give her a home. The evidence shows at the time of the several requests above offered Mrs. McCloy was then living. It will be observed, however, from the court's finding, that he sets out in substance the testimony which appellant contends was rejected, and the statement of facts shows it was admitted. However, it seems to be the contention of appellant that his then refusal was sufficient to show that he had not complied with the con-

ditions of the will, and we will therefore notice the assignments at this time.

So long as Mrs. McCloy was living there was no disposition of the land under the will. The will was necessarily ambulatory and revocable during life. There was no estate then vested by the will in Frank Henry, burdened with the condition that Mrs. Mitchell and her children should have a home thereon, when he made such purported declarations. The rights of the parties became fixed upon probate of the will and it evidenced no title until it was probated. Robertson v. Dubose, 76 Tex. 1, 13 S. W. 303, column 2; Miler v. Sims, 171 S. W. 784 (5). A will speaks from the death of the testator. Connely v. Putnam, 51 Tex. Civ. App. 233, 111 S. W. 164. When the declarations were made there could have been no election to either give Mrs. Mitchell or her children a home on the land or take the land subject to the partition. By such declarations there was no abandonment of the estate in the land for the sufficient reason there was no estate vested, and there was nothing to abandon. At most, the statement that she or her children should never have a home thereon was but a declared purpose to renounce the right to hold the land burdened with the conditional home for them when the contingency should arise which should vest the title. After the death of Mrs. McCloy, Frank Henry seems to have accepted under the will and hence took the title thereto, subject to the burden imposed. Smith v. Butler, 85 Tex. 126, 19 S. W. 1083; Torno v. Torno, 43 Tex. Civ. App. 117, 95 S. W. 762. A declared intention before such title vested at some future time to abandon it, however positively made, would not operate to terminate it, because after her death by his acceptance he in a more emphatic manner affirmed the existence of his title so burdened and manifested the right under the terms of the will. The mere fact that one of the parties who would have had the right to go there for a home did not seek it because she thought or believed from what Henry said before he was clothed with or assumed the duty of giving such home, that he would refuse, it in no way proved or tended to prove a refusal on his part. The witness' thought or belief did not put Henry in default. The question is not here presented that he did actually refuse when he could act so as to fix the rights of the parties to the land. It may be, had the testimony shown an actual refusal had been made when the will operated, that his pre-declarations could be looked to for the purpose of ascertaining his intent and perhaps as fixing the estate in the land. That question is not here now involved or necessary to decide. We think the court correctly sustained the objections.

[2] We will not discuss the assignments in the order made, but believe we may properly dispose of the issues by giving our construction of the will. The findings of fact by the trial court are assailed. We believe the evidence supports the findings. The eleventh finding of fact is especially excepted to because Frank Henry did refuse to give the appellants a home. This, we take it, is based on the testimony heretofore discussed, and for the reasons given we think there is no error shown in the finding. Error is urged to the holding of the trial court to the effect that the will vested in Frank Henry a fee-simple title, conditioned that the appellants have a home free of charge when they are sick or out of employment. It is asserted Henry to choose between taking all the land charged with the condition named in the will or to take a proportional part thereof charged with no condition. It is also insisted that the word "refuse" should be read "fail" in the clause, "but if he refuse to give them a home." We may assume that the appellants' contention is correct that the intention of the testatrix was to permit Henry to choose whether he took with or without the conditions. The real question is, When was he to make the choice? Or, when was he required to choose? We do not think the will created a condition precedent. There was to be no choice until the appellants requested a home thereon, when they needed one. It was that condition which gave them a home, and not until then. There was no defeasance of the estate devised until Henry refused to comply with the request. Courts do not favor holding estates in abeyance, but are inclined to that construction that will give the devisee a vested estate. A fair construction of the will, we think, vested in Frank Henry and his heirs at the time of the death of his mother the fee to the entire tract of land, with a condition in the nature of a defeasance. Every estate in lands devised shall be deemed in fee simple if a lesser be not limited by express words or does not appear devised by construction or by operation of law. Article 1106, R. C. S.

"The general rule is that every part of an instrument must be given effect, if possible, but this rule is subordinate to the rule that an habendum should not be construed so as to contradict or defeat the estate granted by the premises, and that a devise of an estate shall be deemed a fee simple, unless limited by express words. This construction of the will gives effect to the intention of the testator as shown by the whole instrument, and this is the ultimate test of the proper interpretation of wills." Winfree v. Winfree, 139 S. W. 36; Weller v. Weller, 22 Tex. Civ. App. 247, 54 S. W. 652.

We do not believe the parenthetical clause was intended as part of the premises of the will or, as for that matter, of the habendum, but was simply thrown in and intended to be part of the proviso or defeasance clause, which when so construed would read:

"At her death to her son, Frank C. Henry, to have and to hold, his heirs and assigns forever, provided, he comply with the conditions herein mentioned, with the express understanding that his sisters are to have a home whenever they need one, his sister, Jessie Mitchell's three children included. I put this in so my brother's children will all have a home to go to should misfortune come to them in life's journey; but if he refuse to give them a home it shall be divided equally between them. I do not mean he is to support them but a home, free of charge when sick or out of employment."

So understood, it vested Henry with the fee at his mother's death, with the charge thereon in the nature of a condition subsequent operating as a defeasance.

"If the act to be done does not necessarily precede the vesting of the estate, but may accompany it or follow it, if this is to be collected from the whole will, the condition is subsequent. Finlay v. King, 3 Pet. 346, 7 L. Ed. 701; Bowden v. Walker, 4 Baxt. (63 Tenn.) 600." "Directions for the payment of a legacy or charge on a gift which implies possession of a fund are commonly not treated as conditions precedent; and where it appears from the language of the will and the circumstances that the enjoyment of the property is necessary to enable a devisee to perform the condition, the indication is that the condition is not precedent. A provision that the devise shall be void on nonperformance tends to show that the condition is not precedent, since, if it were, such provision would be unnecessary." Brannon v. Mercer, 138 Tenn. 415, 196 S. W. 253.

Applying these rules, the trial court correctly held the remainder in the fee vested in Frank Henry upon the death of his mother, upon a condition subsequent.

We think the intent of the will is, as expressed, that Frank Henry must have refused to give appellants a home on the land when they go to him, when misfortune overtakes them. This misfortune is particularly defined in the will as part of the defeasance clause, which is, "when sick or out of employment." The home was to be free of charge. It was not meant that he should support them, and does not express that they should receive support from the land, further than a home thereon. If the appellants were in such circumstances as entitled them under the will to go to the land for a home, they were free to do so, or to remain away. They could call upon Henry to permit them that privilege or they could decline to do so. The clause was for their benefit, and it was for them to make the proper demand, or they could waive it. If they waived the right, or did not exercise it no forfeiture resulted, however much they may have needed a home. Bryant's Adm'r v. Dungan, 92 Ky. 627, 18 S.

W. 636, 36 Am. St. Rep. 618; Lynch v. Melton, 150 N. C. 595, 64 S. E. 497, 27 L. R. A. (N. S.) 684. "Forfeitures are never favored, and, since she failed to claim a defeasance of the estate for the breach of the condition, the title remained with the grantees, subject to the payment of the installment which had matured." Berryman v. Schumaker, 67 Tex. 312, 3 S. W. 46. If appellants went to a home of their own selection, or one furnished by some one else, they were not entitled to a division of the land. That is a state of case not anticipated and provided for in the will. There is no failure to comply when Henry could have done so, hence no defeasance is shown entitling appellants to a partition. We think the case cited by appellants, Lynn v. Busby, 46 Tex. at page 604, supports the trial court in his interpretation.

[3] We do not think we would be justified in changing the word "refuse" to "fail." This would be to change the meaning of the testatrix as gathered from the context of the entire clause of the will. She evidently intended a forfeiture of the estate could be had only upon refusal by Henry when applications for a home were made to him and when the circumstances of the appellants were such as would entitle them to the home. Such change might require the devisee to establish a home for the appellants when there was no necessity or in anticipation of a necessity. Words may be changed when it will effectuate the intent of the testator when that intention is clearly apparent. The change cannot be made to carry out a conjecture or hypothesis. 40 Cyc. 1399–1402. There is no assignment which requires at our hands a determination as to whether the estate in the land inherited by the child of Frank Henry is subject to the defeasance for a noncompliance with the conditions of the will. The trial court, by his judgment, has fixed a charge on the fee in the interest of appellants under the terms of the will. Whether the rule in Haring v. Shelton, 103 Tex. 10, 122 S. W. 13, will apply after the death of Frank Henry, we do not undertake to say at this time. It may be the condition should not be treated as a mere covenant, to be performed by Frankie Henry and her mother, Lizzie Henry. We take it the purpose of the judgment was to leave the rights of the parties to be determined under future conditions and to hold there was no forfeiture by Frank Henry under the conditions of the will before his death, and that none could be so declared for any of his acts or conduct during his life, after his death.

We believe the judgment of the trial court should be affirmed.

GREAT SOUTHERN OIL & REFINING ASS'N v. COOPER et al. (No. 8527.)

(Court of Civil Appeals of Texas. Dallas. April 23, 1921. Rehearing Denied May 28, 1921.)

1. Appeal and error ⬥⟿1051(1) — Evidence harmless where fact otherwise shown.

The admission of an unsigned resolution of a corporation was harmless where all the evidence tended to show there was in fact such a resolution.

2. Evidence ⬥⟿471(25)—Testimony of secretary he performed duties not a conclusion.

In an action for salary by the secretary of an association, testimony of plaintiff that during the time the salary sued for was accruing he performed all the duties of secretary he was called upon to perform was not inadmissible as a conclusion.

3. Appeal and error ⬥⟿1050(1) — Evidence harmless where same testimony given without objection.

In suit for salary as secretary of an association, error in the admission of plaintiff secretary's testimony that he performed all the duties he was called upon to perform was harmless to defendant association, where the same testimony was given by another witness without objection.

4. Appeal and error ⬥⟿1056(2)—Error in exclusion of testimony immaterial.

In suit by the secretary of an association for his salary, there was no material error in excluding testimony as to what disposition was made of the draft alleged to have been drawn in favor of the president of the association; such testimony bearing solely on the issues made by the cross-action.

5. Contracts ⬥⟿152 — Words to be taken in common sense.

In construing a contract, words are always to be taken in the common sense in which they are used.

6. Evidence ⬥⟿461(1) — Parol evidence inadmissible to show intent of parties to unambiguous written contract.

Where the language employed in a contract is unmistakable and certain, resort may not be had to parol evidence to show that the intention of the parties was other than that clearly expressed.

7. Evidence ⬥⟿450(5)—Contract held not ambiguous to admit parol evidence.

Provision in a contract between an association and an individual providing that the individual should pay the salaries of officers of the association was not ambiguous or uncertain to admit parol evidence as to the intention of the parties.

8. Frauds, statute of ⬥⟿33(2)—Where purpose of promisor is to subserve own purpose, promise not within statute.

The general rule is that, wherever the main purpose and object of the promisor is not to answer for another, but to subserve some purpose of his own, his promise is not within the statute, though it may be in form a promise to pay the debt of another, and though performance of it may incidentally have the effect of extinguishing the liability of another.

9. Frauds, statute of ⬥⟿33(2) — Promise of members of association made for own benefit to pay salary of secretary not within statute.

Where the promise of members to a joint-stock association through its president to pay the salary of its secretary was not to guarantee or secure for the benefit of the secretary the debt he held against the association, but was to subserve their own purposes and promote their financial interests or gain by keeping the association from being abandoned by its president, a man of influence and ability, the promises of the members of the association to pay the debt were not within the statute, and they are estopped from setting up such defense.

Error from Dallas County Court; W. L. Thornton, Judge.

Action by Paul Cooper against the Great Southern Oil Refining Association and others. To review judgment for plaintiff, defendant Association brings error. Affirmed in part; reversed and remanded in part.

J. L. Goggans and B. O. Baker, both of Dallas, for plaintiff in error.

Cockrell, Gray, McBride & O'Donnell, H. P. Edwards, and Read, Lowrance & Bates, all of Dallas, for defendants in error.

TALBOT, J. Paul Cooper, plaintiff, brought this suit in the justice court of precinct No. 1, Dallas county, against Great Southern Oil & Refining Association, a joint-stock company, operating under a trust agreement, A. E. Shahan, L. S. Grant, O. McGaffey, M. M. Lee, O. B. Colquitt, C. U. Connellee, H. A. Wroe, L. S. Brotherton, Thomas W. Duncan, and M. E. Florence, to recover the sum of $200, alleged to be due as salary for services rendered as secretary of the defendant Great Southern Oil & Refining Association. From a judgment rendered in the justice court in favor of the plaintiff against all defendants except Florence an appeal was taken to the county court. In the county court the defendants Great Southern Oil & Refining Association, O. E. Colquitt, C. U. Connellee, H. A. Wroe, L. S. Brotherton, and Thomas Duncan by an amended answer, in addition to a general demurrer, a general denial, and special answer which we deem unnecessary to state, pleaded by way of cross-bill against their codefendant, A. E. Shahan, and R. D. Lindley, who was made a party defendant, that by virtue of the terms of a certain contract executed on June 12, 1918, the said Shahan, for himself and the said Lindley, expressly promised and agreed to pay, among other outstanding obligations of the Great

Southern Oil & Refining Association, the claim sued on by the plaintiff, and prayed that, in the event any judgment was rendered in favor of the plaintiff against defendants or either of them, they have judgment for a like amount over against the said A. E. Shahan and R. D. Lindley. Said defendants further alleged that subsequent to the execution and delivery of the written contract by the defendant A. E. Shahan above referred to, and on or about June 21, 1918, the said Shahan and Lindley verbally promised and agreed to pay the salaries of the officers of the Great Southern Oil & Refining Association, and that, by reason of the facts alleged, said Shahan and Lindley were estopped to deny the force and effect of such agreement. Said defendants further alleged that, if the written contracts set up in their pleadings did not provide for the payment of the salaries of officers, including the claim of the plaintiff, the same was omitted through accident and mutual mistake, and prayed that the contracts be reformed accordingly. When the introduction of the evidence was concluded, the court instructed the jury to return a verdict for the plaintiff, Paul Cooper, against the defendant Great Southern Oil & Refining Association and the sureties on its appeal bond from the justice court, Edgar L. Pike and I. L. Kramer, in the sum of $218.16, and against the plaintiff, Cooper, and in favor of the other defendants and against the Great Southern Oil & Refining Association and other defendants, and in favor of the defendants A. E. Shahan and R. D. Lindley on their cross-action. The plaintiff, Cooper, filed a remittitur of $18.16, and final judgment was entered decreeing that he recover from the Great Southern Oil & Refining Association the sum of $200, with interest thereon at the rate of 6 per cent., that the plaintiff take nothing by his suit against the other named defendants, and that the defendants Great Southern Oil & Refining Association, O. B. Colquitt, C. U. Connellee, H. A. Wroe, L. S. Brotherton, and Thomas Duncan take nothing by their cross-action against the defendants A. E. Shahan and R. D. Lindley. The Great Southern Oil & Refining Association and the sureties on its appeal bond from the justice court alone filed a motion for a new trial, which was overruled, and they excepted and gave notice of appeal. The appeal does not appear to have been perfected, but on June 9, 1920, they sued out a writ of error and assigned errors in this court for a reversal.

[1] The first assignment of error asserts that—

The court "erred in admitting in evidence, over the objection of the defendant Great Southern Oil & Refining Association, the resolution alleged to have been passed on March 27th, in regard to salaries, the objection urged thereto being that the said resolution was not signed by anybody."

The proposition is that—

"Before a resolution of a company or corporation is admissible in evidence it must be authenticated by the signatures of the president and secretary (or other proper officers) under the seal of the corporation."

In support of the assignment and proposition articles 1160 and 3713, Vernon's Sayles' Statutes are cited. The articles cited relate to corporations, and, since it was admitted at the trial that the Great Southern Oil & Refining Association is a joint-stock company, we are inclined to the opinion they have no application to such companies or associations. But the evidence seems to be uncontradicted that the resolution in question was shown to be the original resolution adopted by the board of directors of the Great Southern Oil & Refining Association at its meeting March 27, 1918. Besides, if the admission of the resolution was error, the error was harmless, inasmuch as all the facts show the resolution was shown by other undisputed evidence which was admitted without objection. Paul Cooper testified:

"I was employed by the directors of the Great Southern Oil and Refining Company in March to act as secretary. I acted as secretary of that concern two months. My salary was agreed upon. There was a resolution adopted at the final meeting of the board of directors with reference to my salary, and this resolution was to the effect that I be instructed to draw a draft on the treasurer for my two months' salary. I drew the draft and took it to Mike Murphy, the treasurer. He was present when the resolution was offered. The draft shown me is the one I drew. I presented it forthwith to the treasurer. The draft shown me is dated at Dallas, Tex., May 27th, and is for $200, payable to Paul P. Cooper, drawn by Paul P. Cooper, secretary of the Great Southern Oil & Refining Association, for two months' salary, drawn upon Mike Murphy, treasurer. I do not remember whether Mike Murphy remained treasurer of the new organization. J. W. Ogburn was president. There was a similar draft drawn with reference to J. W. Ogburn's salary at the time, and a similar resolution offered with reference thereto. This salary was never paid to me by the Great Southern Oil & Refining Association or by any other person. Nothing was being done by the Great Southern Oil & Refining Association during the two months. During the period of two months I performed all the duties I was called upon to perform as secretary of the Great Southern Oil & Refining Association."

J. W. Ogburn testified:

"My name is J. W. Ogburn, and I reside at Pecos, Reeves county, Tex. I was president of the Great Southern Oil & Refining Association for two months. I was the first president. Paul P. Cooper was secretary of the Great Southern Oil & Refining Association. He was secretary for two months, and I was president during that time. Paul P. Cooper was employed by the directors of the company at a salary of $100 per month. I resigned as president on

(231 S.W.)

or about May 27, 1918, and Paul P. Cooper resigned at the same time. There was a meeting of the board of directors of Great Southern Oil & Refining Association at the time that Paul P. Cooper resigned as secretary. At the time he resigned as secretary there was due him $200 as salary. The board of directors were to pay him out of the first receipts from the sale of stock, or in any other way. Paul P. Cooper served as secretary during all the time that I served as president. During the time he served he performed all of the duties required of him as secretary of the association."

The material fact shown by the resolution was the amount of salary to be paid to the secretary of the association. J. W. Ogburn, who was president of the association at the time the resolution was adopted, and at the time that Paul P. Cooper was employed, was permitted to testify, without objection, that the directors of the association employed Paul P. Cooper at a salary of $100 per month, and at the time that Paul P. Cooper resigned as secretary there was due him $200 as salary. No testimony whatever was introduced contradicting the evidence showing the employment of Paul P. Cooper. Without considering for any purpose the resolution objected to, the evidence is amply sufficient to support the verdict and judgment.

[2, 3] The second assignment of error to the effect that the court erred in permitting the witness Paul Cooper to testify that during the time the salary sued for by him was accruing he performed all the duties he was called upon to perform, as secretary of the Great Southern Oil & Refining Association, because such statement was the conclusion of the witness, will also be overruled. The testimony was the statement of fact and properly admitted in evidence. But if its admission was error because the mere conclusion of the witness, no harm was done the defendant thereby for the reason that the same testimony was given by the witness Ogburn without objection. The plaintiff Cooper testified:

"I attended the meetings, had numerous conferences with Mr. Ogburn, and did everything I was called upon to do."

The witness Ogburn, at the instance of the plaintiff, testified without objection:

"Paul Cooper served as secretary during all the time that I served as president. During the time he served he performed all of the duties required of him as secretary of the association."

[4] The question, What disposition was made of the draft alleged to have been drawn in favor of J. W. Ogburn for his salary as president of Great Southern Oil & Refining Association? was asked by said association

of the plaintiff, Paul Cooper, and, upon objections by the defendants Shahan and Lindley that the inquiry related to "outside matters, was not a part of the suit, was not pleaded, and would not be binding unless the conditions with reference to the Ogburn matter were the same," etc., was not allowed. It is not made to appear how the testimony sought to be elicited by the question would throw any light on the matter under investigation or assist the jury in arriving at a correct conclusion upon any branch of the case, and we think no material error, if any, was committed in excluding it. The testimony bore solely upon the issues made by the cross-action, and, if it was relevant to any issue involved in that branch of the case, it is, in our opinion, manifest that it is so lacking in probative force, in the absence of other testimony, that its exclusion furnishes no ground for a reversal.

[5-7] Nor do we think the court erred in holding that the provision in the contract between the Great Southern Oil & Refining Association and A. E. Shahan, in evidence, providing in substance that Shahan would pay the salaries of the officers of Great Southern Oil & Refining Association, related only to salaries thereafter accruing and had no reference to salaries already accrued, but then unpaid. There is no ambiguity in the contract, or uncertainty as to the intention of the parties from the language employed. Words are always to be taken in the common sense in which they are used, and where the language employed is unmistakable and certain resort may not be had to parol evidence to show that the intention of the parties was other than that clearly expressed. The rule that parol evidence is not admissible to vary the terms of a written contract is elementary, and the language used in the contract in question presents no exception to this general rule.

[8, 9] The seventh assignment of error is as follows:

"The court erred in holding that, under the facts offered in evidence by Great Southern Oil & Refining Association through its witness Colquitt, the defendants, Shahan and Lindley could properly urge the statute of frauds as against their alleged oral promises to pay the alleged debt herein sued for by the plaintiff, Cooper, and that they were not estopped from so doing."

We conclude this assignment is well taken. Shahan and Lindley were stockholders and directors of the Great Southern Oil & Refining Association, and the evidence would authorize the finding that, while they were such officers and subsequent to the execution of the written contract mentioned, Shahan and Lindley entered into an oral contract with the association whereby they agreed to pay the salaries of the officers of the association, including the salary of the plaintiff involved in this suit. Besides, there is substantial evidence to the effect that Shahan and Lindley were the moving spirits in the whole organization; that the association was becoming involved in financial difficulties; that Shahan and Lindley were exerting themselves to secure a former governor of this state, as its president and head, upon the theory that, with his prestige and financial ability, a wreck of the organization in which they were financially interested might be avoided; that, upon the assurance of Shahan and Lindley that there were no outstanding liabilities against the association, Ex Governor Colquitt was induced to become a stockholder and president of the association; that very soon thereafter various creditors began to press their claims, and threatened to place the association in the hands of a receiver, and that Mr. Colquitt then told Shahan and Lindley that he would get out and have nothing more to do with the association unless they took care of its debts then due, including the plaintiff's claim; that thereupon Shahan and Lindley made the verbal agreement mentioned to pay plaintiff's claim and other items of indebtedness of the association in consideration of Mr. Colquitt remaining the president and head of the association. The general rule relating to the application of the statute of frauds is that, wherever the main purpose and object of the promisor is, not to answer for another, but to subserve some purpose of his own, his promise is not within the statute, although it may be in form a promise to pay the debt of another, and although the performance of it may incidentally have the effect of extinguishing the liability of another. Lemmon v. Box, 20 Tex. 329. That Shahan and Lindley would profit by the retention of O. B. Colquitt as the president and head of the Great Southern Oil & Refining Association and the payment of its debts to the plaintiff Cooper is manifest. Obviously, therefore, their promise to pay that debt was to subserve a purpose of their own and was not in contravention of the statute of frauds. Evidently their leading object was not to guarantee or secure for the benefit of plaintiff the debt he held against the association, but it was to subserve their own purposes and promote their financial interests or gain. It follows from what we have said that the judgment in favor of the plaintiff Cooper against the Great Southern Oil & Refining Association should be affirmed, and that the judgment in favor of Shahan and Lindley that said association take nothing against them on its cross-action should be reversed, and cause remanded for a new trial on said cross-action, and it is accordingly so ordered.

Affirmed in part, and reversed and remanded in part.

HUBBARD v. HUBBARD. (No. 1216.)

(Court of Civil Appeals of Texas. El Paso. May 19, 1921.)

Divorce 130—Evidence held not to show husband's cruelty.

In view of Vernon's Sayles' Ann. Civ. St. 1914, art. 4633, requiring full and satisfactory evidence, in divorce proceedings, evidence *held* not to support decree granting wife a divorce for cruelty.

Appeal from District Court, Eastland County; E. A. Hill, Judge.

Suit by Pairilee Hubbard against J. M. Hubbard. Judgment for plaintiff, and defendant appeals. Reversed and remanded.

Gilvie Hubbard and Shepherd & Kelly, all of Eastland, for appellant.

Turner & Seaberry, of Eastland, for appellee.

WALTHALL, J. Pairilee Hubbard brought this suit against her husband, J. M. Hubbard, for divorce, for an accounting of amounts of money received by him as rentals from certain real estate, for a partition of the real estate and rentals, and for costs, including attorney's fees.

Appellee alleged her marriage with appellant; that during her married relation appellant was guilty of acts of cruelty, neglect, abuse, and failure of duty, specified in the petition, which rendered their living together insupportable.

The specific acts alleged and upon which evidence was offered are that, while she and her husband were stopping at a hotel in Dallas, in December, 1918, he criticized her personal appearance, told her she was ignorant, called her a bitch, said he could have married another woman more intelligent, better looking, and one he would not be ashamed of; that, when she was sick in bed at Eastland in the summer of 1918, appellant neglected her and failed and refused to care tor her or even respect her in her then condition; that during the time she and appellant lived together appellant abused and slandered her to third persons and repeatedly stated that he was ashamed of his marriage to her; that during their marriage appellant corresponded with another woman, and showered his affections upon her, and neglected appellee and denied her the love that was due from him; that appellant openly accused appellee of having murdered her first husband in order to secure the proceeds of a life insurance policy upon her said husband's life; that during the time of her marriage to appellant he sought by persuasion and threats to force her to turn over to his custody and possession her separate property, consisting of valuable lands, notes, and other property; that on the 15th day of April, 1919,

---

appellant deserted her without cause; and that since that time they have not lived together.

Appellant answered by general demurrer, and special exception, general denial, and specially denied each of the specified acts alleged as grounds for divorce. By cross-action appellant sued for divorce, but does not complain here of the refusal of the court to grant him a divorce.

Both appellee and appellant testified in the case.

The case was tried without a jury, and judgment was rendered granting appellee a decree for divorce, and partitioning the property between appellee and appellant.

The court did not file findings of fact. Appellant insists that the several acts specified as grounds for divorce nor the evidence in support thereof are sufficient to sustain the decree granting the divorce.

We have reviewed the evidence with much care, and in view of the disposition we have concluded to make of the case we have thought it best not to state nor discuss the testimony offered in support of the specific acts charged.

There is such want of allegation and proof of facts which, in our judgment, the decree for divorce should not be sustained.

Article 4633, Vernon's Sayles' Tex. Civil Statutes, prescribes that the decree in divorce proceedings shall be rendered upon full and satisfactory evidence affirming the material facts alleged in the petition. The language used by appellant to his wife, on more than one occasion, was offensive and insulting, and merits the severest condemnation, but, in view of all the undisputed evidence and the circumstances under which the language was used, we have concluded that the decree for divorce was not rendered upon such full and satisfactory evidence as to justify or sustain a decree for divorce. There is no allegation or proof of any act, or threatened act, of physical violence or bodily hurt alleged or proved. The pleadings do not allege nor does the evidence show such acts or conduct on the part of appellant as did produce or was calculated to produce a degree of mental distress which threatened at least to impair the health of appellee. In Bush v. Bush, 103 S. W. 217, it is said that the law is well established by the decisions of this state that, in order to entitle the wife to a divorce in the absence of physical violence, she must show cruel treatment on the part of the husband such as will produce a degree of mental distress which threatens to impair her health. To the same effect is Eastman v. Eastman, 75 Tex. 473, 12 S. W. 1107; McKay v. McKay, 24 Tex. Civ. App. 629, 60 S. W. 318; Bloch v. Bloch, 190 S. W. 528; Bolt v. Bolt, 199 S. W. 309. No threatened impairment of the wife's health is alleged or shown; nor does the evidence justify

the conclusion that the opprobrious epithets used by appellant to appellee, nor his reference to the death of her former husband, produced a degree of mental distress which threatened to impair her health. She continued to live with appellant after his conduct as complained of, and after their separation she went to where appellant was and insisted that he return to his home. But we prefer to base our opinion, reversing and remanding this case, on our conclusion above suggested that the decree granting the divorce is not based upon such full and satisfactory evidence affirming the material allegations in the petition as to justify the divorce granted. Erwin v. Erwin, 40 S. W. 53; Moore v. Moore, 22 Tex. 237; Smith v. Smith, 218 S. W. 602; Lohmuller v. Lohmuller, 135 S. W. 751; Tanton v. Tanton, 209 S. W. 429; Dickinson v. Dickinson, 138 S. W. 205. As said by Judge Fly in Erwin v. Erwin, supra, "From the standpoint of the trial court, this action in granting the decree was entirely consistent and proper," but the statutes relating to divorces are peculiar, and trial and appellate courts must be satisfied with the evidence as being full and satisfactory, affirming the material facts upon which the decree is granted.

It does not seem to us that the conduct of appellant alone as shown by the evidence, and tested by the statute above referred to, was such as to render their living together insupportable.

We need not discuss the other assignments which raise questions of property rights.

The case is reversed and remanded.

SHORT v. WALTERS et al. (No. 6332.)

(Court of Civil Appeals of Texas. Austin. May 4, 1921.)

1. Continuance ⊂=26(11)—Where no commission was issued, although adversary party waived its issuance, there was not due diligence.

Where no commission was issued and placed in the hands of an officer authorized to take depositions, the party asking for a continuance to procure witness' evidence cannot be said to have used due diligence, although his adversary waived the issuance of a commission.

2. Appeal and error ⊂=966(1) — Continuance ⊂=26(1)—Where application for continuance shows failure to use means for procuring testimony, it is addressed to the court's discretion.

When an application for continuance shows that the means provided by law to secure testimony have not been used, the application is addressed to the sound discretion of the trial court, and, unless it clearly appears that such discretion has been abused, the case should not be reversed for overruling the application.

3. Continuance ⇔46(5) — Application addressed to discretion of court should show applicant expected to procure testimony by next court term.

An application for continuance, which is not statutory, and therefore addressed to the court's discretion, should state that the applicant expected to procure the testimony by the next term of court; otherwise denial of continuance is not error.

Appeal from District Court, San Saba County; N. T. Stubbs, Judge.

Action against Joe Short, J. T. Walters, and others, in which Joe Short's application for a continuance was overruled, and he appeals. Judgment affirmed.

N. C. Walker, of San Saba, for appellant. Wilkinson & McGaugh, of Brownwood, for appellees.

KEY, C. J. The only question presented by this appeal is appellant's contention that the trial court erred in overruling his application for a continuance, which reads as follows:

"Now comes the defendant Joe Short in the above styled and numbered cause, and, being duly sworn, states that he cannot safely go to trial at this term of court, on account of the absence of R. A. Weaver, who is a witness on behalf of the said defendant; that the testimony of said witness is material to defendant's defense in this cause, in this, to wit, that defendant's defense in this suit is that the defendant J. T. Walters conveyed the land in controversy to plaintiff, for the purpose of hindering and delaying his creditors; that this defendant expects to prove by said R. A. Weaver, and that said witness will testify, that some time in the early part of 1915 the defendant J. T. Walters placed the lands in controversy in his hands to be sold, at said time stating that, unless he could sell said land, some parties were going to sue him and he wanted to sell this land, or put it in his wife's or his son's name; that said witness was engaged in the real estate business in the city of San Angelo, where the defendant J. T. Walters resided at said time; that said witness R. A. Weaver resided in the city of San Angelo, Tom Green county, Tex.; that defendant has used due diligence to secure the testimony of said witness in this, to wit, that he was served with citation in this case on the 11th day of March, A. D. 1920; that immediately upon being served with said citation, on, to wit the 12th day of March, he wrote Walker & Burleson, attorneys of San Saba, Tex., inclosing said citation and requesting them to represent him in said cause and desiring to know what they would charge him for such services; that, not getting a reply from said attorneys, he instructed his attorney, R. Wilbur Brown, of San Angelo, Tex., to write Walker & Burleson again in regard to handling said case for him; that his said attorney did on the 26th day of March write said attorneys about handling said case; that N. C. Walker answered said letter and requested me to come to San Saba to discuss said case and agree on a fee; that I immediately left for San Saba, which is about 180 miles by rail from San Angelo to San Saba; that I arrived in San Saba on the 31st day of March, and at that time employed N. C. Walker to represent me in this case; not knowing the names of the witnesses that I would need at that time nor exactly what they would testify to, I went back to San Angelo and told my said attorney that I would have Mr. Brown to send Mr. N. C. Walker the names of said witnesses and what they would testify to; that my said attorney, Wilbur Brown, did send Mr. Walker said names of said witnesses with the other papers relating to this case on the 1st day of April, 1920, which was received by my attorney, Mr. Walker, on the 3d day of April; that Mr. Walker on the same day prepared certain interrogatories to said witness R. A. Weaver and other witnesses, and called Mr. Wilkerson up over the telephone, and he said he would waive the issuance of commission and cross same; that on the same day Mr. Walker mailed said interrogatories to Wilkerson & McGaugh, of Brownwood, Tex.; that said attorneys crossed said interrogatories and returned them to Mr. Walker on the 8th day of April, 1920, and on the same day Mr. Walker mailed them to R. Wilbur Brown, of San Angelo, Tex., who at once placed them in the hands of a notary public, who at once took the depositions of all of said witnesses with the exception of said R. A. Walker, who, said notary public certified, was out of the county at that time and could not be found; that the other depositions of said witness, to which was attached said certificate of the absence of, was returned and filed in this court on the 14th day of April, 1920; that a copy of the interrogatories propounded to said witness are attached hereto and marked Exhibit A; that the testimony which witness would have given if he had testified to said interrogatories, or if present, cannot be obtained from any other source, and that a continuance is not sought for delay only, but that justice may be done; that this is defendant's first application for a continuance. Wherefore defendant prays the court to continue this case until the next term of this court. Joe Short.

"Subscribed and sworn to before me this the 15th day of April, A. D. 1920. Jno. H. Moore, Clerk District Court, San Saba County, Tex."

[1, 2] In Tex. & Pac. Ry. Co. v. Hardin, 62 Tex. 367, it was held that, when no commission was issued and placed in the hands of an officer authorized to take depositions, the party asking for a continuance cannot be said to have used due diligence, although his adversary waived the issuance of a commission. It was also held in that case that, when an application shows that the means provided by law to procure testimony have not been used, the application is addressed to the sound discretion of the trial court, and, unless it clearly appears that such discretion has been abused, the case should not be reversed because the application for a continuance had been overruled. In the elaborate opinion in that case, in indicating some

facts which should be stated in such an application for a continuance, the court, among other things, said:

"It is not shown that the evidence of the witnesses would have tended to prove any of the defenses set up in the answer, further than is so shown by the general averment that their testimony is material; nor is it shown that the appellant expected to have their testimony at the next term of the court."

[3] Two of the former cases cited in that opinion hold that an application for a continuance, which is not statutory, and therefore addressed to the discretion of the court, should state that the applicant expected to procure the testimony by the next term of the court. No such statement is made in the application in the instant case; and therefore we hold that the judgment of the trial court should be affirmed, and it is so ordered. Affirmed.

RAWLINGS v. EDIGER. (No. 1755.)

(Court of Civil Appeals of Texas. Amarillo. May 5, 1921. Rehearing Denied June 1, 1921.)

1. Pleading ⬀36(3)—Evidence in support of plea in confession and avoidance admissible despite defendant's admission.

Where the facts pleaded by defendant properly constituted a plea in confession and avoidance, evidence in support thereof was admissible notwithstanding defendant's admission of plaintiff's cause of action under rule 31 for district and county courts (142 S. W. xx).

2. Bills and notes ⬀503—Evidence by defendant to show that third person owned interest in note sued on admissible on issue of no consideration.

In an action on a note, wherein defendant admitted plaintiff's cause of action, and pleaded failure of consideration, it was not error to allow defendant to show that a third person owned an interest in the note, where such fact was pleaded and shown in the presentation of the real defense that defendant had not received the consideration for which the note was given, and that an agreement had been made for rescission of the contract under which it had been given, and for cancellation and return of the note.

Appeal from District Court, Hale County; R. C. Joiner, Judge.

Suit by R. C. Rawlings against Jacob H. Ediger. From judgment for plaintiff, defendant appeals. Affirmed.

H. C. Randolph, of Plainview, for appellant.

C. H. Curl and Williams & Martin, all of Plainview, for appellee.

BOYCE, J. R. C. Rawlings, appellant, brought this suit against Jacob H. Ediger,

appellee, to recover on a promissory note for the sum of $898.50, executed by Ediger and payable to Rawlings. The defendant pleaded failure of consideration and alleged in support of this plea: That the note was given as a part of the consideration for a tract of land contracted to be purchased by the defendant from Geo. W. Littlefield; that the plaintiff made said contract as agent for the said Littlefield; that $708.40 of the note belonged to the said Littlefield; that thereafter the said contract for the sale of said land was rescinded by agreement between all parties interested therein, to wit, the plaintiff, Geo. W. Littlefield, and the defendant, and that as part of such rescission agreement it was agreed that said note should be returned to the defendant; that one Cowart, as partner or agent, acted for the plaintiff in making of said rescission agreement, and that the said Cowart had full authority to act for the plaintiff in such matter; that defendant had never received anything for said note; and that it was, by reason of the facts stated, without consideration. The plaintiff, by supplemental petition, specially denied partnership with Cowart.

The defendant filed admission of plaintiff's cause of action under rule 31 for district and county courts (142 S. W. xx), and offered evidence in support of the allegations of his answer as above stated. The trial judge submitted an issue as to Cowart's agency for plaintiff, and on the answer of the jury thereto entered judgment for the defendant.

All three assignments presented on this appeal are in reference to the effect the admission under rule 31 should have on the introduction of evidence and submission of the case to the jury.

[1] It is first contended that the court should have given a peremptory instruction for the plaintiff, because of such admission. We overrule this assignment. The facts pleaded properly constituted a plea in confession and avoidance (Townes on Pleading, 539–542), and evidence in support thereof was admissible notwithstanding defendant's admission under rule 31 (Fed. Life Insurance Co. v. Wilkes, 218 S. W. 591, and authorities).

[2] Under the other two assignments it is contended that it was error to allow the defendant to show that the said Geo. W. Littlefield owned an interest in said note. If the fact of such ownership had been relied on alone as constituting a defense to the note, and defendant had been contending that plaintiffs could not recover on the note because it was partly owned by said Geo. W. Littlefield, there might be some merit in this contention; but such fact was pleaded and shown merely as a fact, and really an immaterial one, in the presentation of the real defense that defendant had not received the

consideration for which the note was given, and that an agreement had been made for rescission of the contract under the terms of which it had been given and for the cancellation and return of the note. Affirmed.

ELMENDORF v. MULLIKEN. (No. 1230.)

(Court of Civil Appeals of Texas. El Paso. May 19, 1921.)

1. Money paid 🔑8 — Complaint to recover money expended held to show consideration.

A complaint in an action by a stockbroker against another stockbroker alleging that defendant agreed with plaintiff that, if the latter would advertise certain stock in newspapers, defendant would reimburse plaintiff for all sums so expended by him, and plaintiff, relying upon such agreement, so advertised the stock and expended a certain sum, was not subject to the criticism that it failed to show a consideration for the alleged promise of defendant, or that the contract alleged, being unliquidated and uncertain as to its duration, was void for uncertainty.

2. Contracts 🔑9(1)—Uncertainty immaterial after performance.

Uncertainty as to length of time stock was to be advertised under an agreement whereby defendant stipulated to reimburse plaintiff was immaterial in an action for reimbursement by plaintiff, who had expended money in advertising the stock.

3. Trial 🔑260(9)—Refusal of charge not erroneous where matter covered by general charge.

Court did not err in refusing a special requested charge defining the elements of a contract where the general charge correctly covered the subject-matter of the requested charge and in a manner not objected to.

Appeal from El Paso County Court at Law; J. M. Deaver, Judge.

Suit by Grover Mulliken against H. F. Elmendorf. Judgment for plaintiff, and defendant appeals. Affirmed.

Dyer, Croom & Jones, of El Paso, for appellant.

Jones, Jones, Hardie & Grambling, of El Paso, for appellee.

HIGGINS, J. Mulliken sued Elmendorf to recover the sum of $702, alleging, in substance, that plaintiff and defendant were both engaged in the business of selling stocks and bonds; that defendant agreed with plaintiff that, if the latter would advertise the stock of the Homer-Claiborne Oil Company in the El Paso Times and El Paso Herald, the defendant would reimburse plaintiff for all

sums so expended by him; that, relying upon said agreement, plaintiff did so advertise the stock from December 15, 1910, to January 15, 1920, and in so doing expended the sum of $702, which sum defendant became obligated to pay and had refused so to do. The defendant interposed a general demurrer and general denial. Verdict was returned and judgment rendered as prayed for.

[1] Error is first assigned to the action of the court in overruling the demurrer upon two grounds, viz.:

First. That the petition fails to show a consideration for the alleged promise of defendant.

Second. That the contract alleged being unlimited and uncertain as to its duration was void for uncertainty.

Neither of these objections to the petition are well taken. As to the first the petition shows that plaintiff expended the money for which he sues relying upon the defendant's promise to reimburse him. This shows a sufficient consideration for the promise. McKinney v. Rowson & Co., 146 S. W. 643; 13 Cor. Jur. subject, Contracts, art. 150, pp. 315, 316, and 317; Simpkins, Contracts and Sales (3d Ed.) p. 52; Rose v. San Antonio & Mex. Gulf Railroad Co., 31 Tex. 49; Curlin v. Hendricks, 35 Tex. 225.

[2] As to the second the petition shows performance by plaintiff, and this entitled him to recover. The uncertainty as to the length of time the stock was to be advertised becomes immaterial in view of such performance. A contract may be so uncertain that it cannot be specifically enforced in equity, but may nevertheless be the basis for a remedy at law in favor of a party who has wholly or partially performed it. 13 C. J. art. 59, p. 268; Worthington v. Beeman, 91 Fed. 232, 33 C. C. A. 475.

The advertising contract pleaded by plaintiff was terminable at the will of either party thereto, and performance under the same entitled plaintiff to reimbursement for the moneys expended by him in advertising.

[3] The remaining assignment complains of the refusal of a special charge requested by defendant defining the elements of a contract. It is practically the same charge the refusal of which was held to be error in Hubbard City C. O. & G. Co. v. Nichols, 89 S. W. 796. In that case, however, the general charge failed to instruct the jury as to the essential elements of a contract whereas in the instant case the general charge does so. It correctly covers the subject-matter of the requested charge and in a manner not objected to by appellant.

The general charge having sufficiently covered that phase of the case the refusal of the requested charge presents no error. M., K. & T. Ry. Co. v. Criswell, 103 S. W. 695; Whitney v. Tex. Cen. R. R. Co., 50 Tex. Civ.

App. 1, 110 S. W. 70; Gaar Scott Co. v. Burge et al., 49 Tex. Civ. App. 599, 110 S. W. 181.

Affirmed.

AMERICAN NAT. INS. CO. v. DIXON.
(No. 5541.)

(Court of Civil Appeals of Texas. Austin. May 11, 1921.)

Insurance ⟜133(1)—Life insurance policy provision that, if insured die within six months, only one-half of amount will be paid, contravenes statute prohibiting settlement for less than face of policy.

A condition in an insurance policy that, if insured's death occurred within six calendar months from its date, the beneficiary would receive only one-half of the amount mentioned therein, and the full amount if death occurred thereafter, contravened Rev. St. 1911, art. 4742, subd. 3, providing that no life insurance policy shall contain any provision for settlement for less than the amounts insured on the face of the policy, plus dividend and less indebtedness and premiums.

Appeal from McLennan County Court; Geo. N. Denton, Judge.

Suit by Harvey Dixon against the American National Insurance Company. Judgment for plaintiff, and the defendant appeals. Affirmed.

J. D. Williamson, of Waco, and Williams & Neethe, of Galveston, for appellant.

Giles P. Lester and Joe W. Taylor, Jr., both of Waco, for appellee.

KEY, C. J. The statement of the nature and result of this suit contained in appellant's brief is as follows:

"This suit was instituted by Harvey Dixon, alleging that he was the beneficiary in a certain policy issued by the appellant on the life of Patsy C. Dixon, said policy being No. 971132. Appellee contended that under the terms of the policy he was entitled to recover the sum of $410, the amount mentioned in one portion of the policy, less amounts which were paid by the appellant, and the statutory 12 per cent. damages and a reasonable attorney's fee. Appellant contended that appellee was entitled to recover the sum of $205, because the policy provided that one-half only of the above sum of $410 should be payable if death occurred within six calendar months from its date, and

the uncontradicted evidence showed that the insured died within six months after February 9, 1914, the date of the policy.

"The sole question in this case is 'does the provision of the policy that only one-half of above sum payable if death occurs within six calendar months from date and the full amount, if death occurs thereafter,' contravene article 4742, subdivision 3, of the Revised Statutes of the State of Texas."

At the time this case was submitted in this court, the case of First Texas State Ins. Co. v. Smalley, which involved the foregoing question, was pending in the Supreme Court, and, at the suggestion of the appellant in this case, its decision has been delayed to wait the decision of the Supreme Court in the case referred to. That case has recently been decided by the Supreme Court, and the opinion is reported in 228 S. W. 550, and it was there held:

"1. Under Rev. St. 1911, art. 4742, subd. 3, providing that no life insurance policy shall contain any provision for settlement for less than the amounts insured on the face of the policy, plus dividends and less indebtedness and premiums, a policy cannot contain the prohibited provisions, though issued on the industrial plan in small amounts and for weekly or biweekly premiums.

"2. A condition on the face of a life insurance policy immediately following the statement of the amount of the insurance, providing for payment for death from certain diseases having their beginning during the first 12 months of the policy, is void under Rev. St. 1911, art. 4742, subd. 3, prohibiting provisions for settlement for less than the amounts insured on the face of the policy, etc.

"3. The construction of Rev. St. 1911, art. 4742, subd. 3, as applied to a condition on the face of a life insurance policy reducing the amount of insurance in case of death from certain diseases beginning within one year, is not involved in such doubt as to make controlling the ruling of the insurance commissioner approving a form of the policy."

That case is quite similar to the instant case, and the decision there rendered by the Supreme Court is adverse to appellant in this case.

The other questions presented in appellant's brief have received due consideration, and are decided against it.

No error has been shown, and the judgment is affirmed.

Affirmed.

GULF, C. & S. F. RY. CO. et al. v. HAMRICK.
(No. 6557.)

(Court of Civil Appeals of Texas. San Antonio. May 11, 1921. Rehearing Denied June 1, 1921.)

1. **Courts ⊙169(3)—Total of items comprises amount in controversy in county court.**

Under Const. art. 5, § 16 (Rev. St. art. 1764), the county court has no jurisdiction of causes where the matter in controversy exceeds $1,000, exclusive of interest, the matter in controversy not being the amount prayed for or the amount stated generally in the petition, where the items going to make up the total value of damages are specifically stated, and the aggregate sum differs from the amount prayed for or stated generally, the total of the items specifically set out comprising the "matter in controversy" in case of such conflict.

2. **Appeal and error ⊙1178(8)—Court, where jurisdictional amount exceeded only by inadvertence, will remand for amendment.**

Ordinarily, in cases of appeals from the county court, which had no jurisdiction on account of the amount of the matter in controversy, the proper practice is to reverse the judgment and remand, with instructions to the county court to dismiss the cause, but where it was only by amended petition that the jurisdictional amount was exceeded, and defendant appellant, by exception, and in the motion for new trial, raised the jurisdictional question only in the most general terms, while the excess in amount was hidden by a miscalculation due to inadvertence, the Court of Civil Appeals will not order dismissal, but merely remand, that plaintiff may amend if he so desires.

3. **Railroads ⊙5½, New, vol. 6A Key-No. Series—Judgment fixing lien against properties of dismissed defendant owning road under federal control erroneous.**

After dismissal of defendant railway company from the suit which continued against defendant Director General of Railroads, it was error for the trial court to render judgment fixing a lien against the properties of the railroad to secure payment of judgment rendered against the Director General.

Appeal from Johnson County Court; O. O. Chrisman, Judge.

Suit by J. T. Hamrick against the Gulf, Colorado & Santa Fé Railway Company and another. Judgment for plaintiff, and defendants appeal. Reversed, and cause remanded.

Brown & Lockett, of Cleburne, and Terry, Cavin & Mills and O. B. Wigley, all of Galveston, for appellants.

S. C. Padelford, of Fort Worth, for appellee.

SMITH, J. Appellee, as plaintiff below, sued the railway company and the Director General of Railroads for damages resulting from alleged improper handling of a ship-

ment of 93 head of appellee's cattle from Cleburne to the North Fort Worth market. The railway company was dismissed from the suit, and the Director General has appealed from an adverse judgment.

[1] Appellee, in his trial petition, alleged generally that his damages amounted to $967.60, and prayed for recovery in that amount. In addition to, and in explanation of, these general allegations, however, he also set out the specific items comprising his total damages, the first item being a shrinkage in the weight of the cattle amounting to a loss of $297.50, and the other item being the depreciation in the selling value of the cattle resulting in a loss of $1.50 per hundredweight on 49,000 pounds, which, correctly calculated, amounts to $735 (and not $670 as alleged by appellee). As will be seen, the two items, of $297.50 and $735, aggregate a total alleged damage of $1,032.50.

The county court has no jurisdiction of causes where the "matter in controversy" exceeds $1,000, exclusive of interest. Const., art. 5, § 16 (article 1764, R. S.). The matter in controversy is not the amount prayed for, nor the amount stated generally in the petition, where the items going to make up the total value or damages are specifically stated and the aggregate sum thereof differs from the amount prayed for, or stated generally. The total of the items specifically set out comprises the "matter in controversy" in case of such conflict. Ry. v. Berry, 177 S. W. 1187; Wilson v. Ware, 166 S. W. 705; Ry. v. Coal Co., 102 Tex. 478, 119 S. W. 294; Times Co. v. Hill, 36 Tex. Civ. App. 389, 81 S. W. 806; Burke v. Adoue, 3 Tex. Civ. App. 494, 22 S. W. 824, 23 S. W. 91; Tel. Co. v. Hawkins, 85 S. W. 847. Here the total of the items of damage specifically set out was in excess of $1,000, and for the purpose of determining jurisdiction the amount so ascertained will control, notwithstanding the general allegations fixed the amount of damages at a sum within the jurisdictional amount, and the prayer for recovery was only for that sum. The fact that there was an excess of only $32.50 does not matter. In Tel. Co. v. Hawkins, supra, the excess was only 25 cents; in Wilson v. Ware, supra, $1.61. Nor does it matter that appellee in his petition calculated the loss of $1.50 per hundredweight on 49,000 pounds of beef to be $670, since the correct sum of this alleged loss was $735, and the actual total of the specific items of damage alleged by appellee is $1,032.50, of which amount the county court was without jurisdiction. The judgment must be reversed.

[2] Ordinarily, the proper practice, in cases of this character, as prescribed by the Supreme Court in Ry. v. Coal Co., supra, is to reverse the judgment, and remand, with instructions to the court below to dismiss the cause. But in this case, in his original peti-

tion the plaintiff alleged 'damages in the amount of $800, which gave the court jurisdiction. It was by an amended petition that the jurisdictional amount was exceeded. The defendant, by exception, and in the motion for new trial, raised the jurisdictional question, but only in the most general terms, and as the excess in jurisdictional amount was hidden by miscalculation, obviously due to an inadvertence, we are not disposed to order a dismissal, but only to remand, so that the plaintiff below may amend, if he so desires. This course is authorized by the authorities, we believe. Ross v. Anderson. 1 White & W. Civ. Cas. Ct. App. § 1032; Ry. v. Barnett, 27 Tex. Civ. App. 498, 66 S. W. 474; Braggins v. Holekamp, 68 S. W. 57; Burke v. Adoue, 3 Tex. Civ. App. 494, 22 S. W. 824, 23 S. W. 91; Ry. v. Hamilton, 108 S. W. 1002.

The matters complained of by the Director General in the second to seventh assignments of error are not likely to arise in another trial. The statements under the 'eighth to fourteenth assignments of error are insufficient to entitle those assignments to consideration, and the fifteenth, complaining of the insufficiency of the evidence to support the verdict, becomes immaterial.

[3] As stated, the plaintiff dismissed the railway company from the suit. Notwithstanding this fact, however, the court below rendered judgment fixing a lien against the properties of the railway company to secure the payment of the judgment rendered against the Director General of Railroads. This was error, of course. The railway company not being a party to the suit, the court was without authority to render any sort of judgment against it.

The judgment is reversed, and the cause remanded.

**DAVIS et ux. v. CAMPBELL-ROOT LUM-
BER CO. (No. 6374.)**

(Court of Civil Appeals of Texas. Austin.
April 27, 1921. Rehearing Denied
June 1, 1921.)

**1. Appeal and error ⚖⇒1071(6) — Failure to
embrace undisputed facts in findings harmless.**

Failure of trial court to expressly embrace undisputed facts in his findings, if error at all, was harmless.

2. Fraudulent conveyances ⚖⇒58—Intent to defraud not necessary.

If a conveyance of land was voluntary and not upon a consideration deemed valuable in law and the grantors did not have other property within state subject to execution sufficient to pay the debt, the conveyance was void under the statute, whether or not it was the intent of the grantor to defraud.

**3. Fraudulent conveyances ⚖⇒220—Immaterial
that creditor's note was secured by chattel
mortgage in action to set aside conveyance
of land.**

In action upon promissory note for foreclosure of attachment lien upon land claimed to have been fraudulently conveyed, it was immaterial that the note sued upon was secured by chattel mortgages, in the absence of a showing that such mortgages gave any real security for the note or that anything was realized thereon.

4. Husband and wife ⚖⇒254—Property acquired from rents and revenues of wife's separate property constituted community.

Property paid for in 1901 out of the rents and revenues of the separate property of wife in part, and joint earnings of herself and husband, and in part by her children by a prior marriage, constituted community.

**5. Husband and wife ⚖⇒268(2)—Partition did
not affect community property as against
creditor.**

Whatever may have been the effect of a voluntary partition and division of community property among children, wherein husband was given a child's part for his share, and a child later acquired the land, as between the parties themselves, it could not have the effect to change the status of the property from community to separate as to creditors without notice.

6. Fraudulent conveyances ⚖⇒76(1)—$20 consideration held nominal.

A consideration of love and affection and a sum of $20 for land conveyed was merely a nominal consideration which was not valuable in law as against a creditor, where it was grossly inadequate in proportion to the value of the land conveyed.

Appeal from District Court, Coryell County; J. H. Arnold, Judge.

Action by the Campbell-Root Lumber Company against C. F. Davis and wife. Judgment for plaintiff, and defendants appeal. Affirmed.

Mears & Watkins, of Gatesville, for appellants.

Clay McClellan, of Gatesville, for appellee.

Findings of Fact.

BRADY, J. Appellee sued upon a promissory note and for foreclosure of an attachment lien upon certain land, which it was claimed was conveyed by C. F. Davis and his wife, M. A. Davis, the makers of the note, to Jas. C. Davis, in fraud of creditors. It was claimed that the deed to Jas. C. Davis was void as to plaintiff, and that Mrs. M. A. Davis was liable on the note because the debt was incurred for the benefit of her separate property. Judgment was rendered for the full amount of the note and for foreclosure of the attachment lien upon so much of the property as was found not to be homestead, but judgment was rendered in favor of Mrs.

M. A. Davis upon the finding that the property was community. The defenses are sufficiently indicated by the findings of the trial court.

We adopt the findings of fact made by the court below, which are as follows:

"(1) I find that the defendants, C. F. Davis and M. A. Davis, made, executed and delivered to plaintiff their certain promissory note in writing of the description and under the circumstances in all things as set out in plaintiff's original petition; that the note is dated the 25th day of November, 1916, is for the sum of $1,081.40, is due and payable on or before October 1, 1917, to the order of Campbell-Root Lumber Company, with interest thereon from date until paid at the rate of 10 per cent. per annum, and that the makers agree to pay 10 per cent. additional on the note and interest then owing in the hands of an attorney, or collected by suit, and that the note is signed by the defendants, C. F. Davis and M. A. Davis.

"(2) I find that the debt evidenced by the note was incurred during the years of 1908 and 1909 and long prior to the 24th day of April, 1913.

"(3) I find that C. F. Davis and M. A. Davis are husband and wife and have been living together as such for a period of 26 years previous to the filing of this suit.

"(4) I find that the debt evidenced by the note sued on was incurred for lumber and building material bought by the defendants, C. F. and M. A. Davis, from the plaintiff, Campbell-Root Lumber Company, for the purpose of improving that certain real estate described in the pleading, but that the real estate so improved did not constitute the separate property of the defendant M. A. Davis, and that the debt incurred by her was not incurred for necessaries for herself and family, or under such other circumstances as under the laws of this state would render her personally liable for the debt, she being a married woman at the time it was incurred.

"(5) I find that at the time of the marriage of the defendant C. F. Davis, with the defendant, M. A. Davis, she, the said M. A. Davis, then owned in her separate right about 120 acres of the M. Draper survey and 40 acres of the C. S. Thomas survey in Coryell county, Tex., and that said two defendants at once moved upon said land and have continuously since said time and do now use, occupy, and enjoy same as a part of their homestead.

"(6) I find that about the 26th day of November, 1901, by a deed of that date, recorded in volume 75, p. 164, the defendants, C. F. and M. A. Davis, acquired about 450 acres of land in Coryell county, Tex., fully described in paragraph 4, subdivision (a) of plaintiff's original petition; that the grantor in said deed was the Watkins Land Company, and the grantee Mrs. M. A. Davis, but that said deed does not contain any recitals that the conveyance was to the separate use and benefit of Mrs. M. A. Davis; that the conveyance was not in fact so made, but that the land was acquired after the marriage of C. F. and M. A. Davis with the community funds and became their community property.

"(7) I find that the lumber and building material for which the debt herein sued on was incurred was used in the erection of a residence and other improvements of a part of the 450 acres of land hereinabove last mentioned, and that since the erection of said improvements the defendants, C. F. and M. A. Davis, have resided upon said land and have used a part of same, including the residence and improvements just mentioned, in connection with the 160 acres more or less owned by M. A. Davis at the date of her marriage, as the home of the said C. F. Davis and M. A. Davis, and that their homestead was so constituted at the date of the conveyance of their son, Jim Davis, herein next mentioned.

"(8) I find that on the 24th day of April, 1913, by deed of that date not filed for record until January 25, 1918, defendants, C. F. Davis and M. A. Davis, conveyed to their son, Jim Davis, the 450 acres of land above mentioned, less 311 acres thereof theretofore conveyed to J. M. Gray and others by a deed dated January 29, 1913, recorded in volume 58, p. 447, Deed Records of Coryell County, Tex.; that the consideration upon which the conveyance to Jim Davis was made was recited in the deed to have been $20 cash in hand paid and the love and affection of the defendant, C. F. Davis and M. A. Davis, for their son, Jim Davis; that the payment of the $20 in cash was not the consideration inducing the conveyance to the said Jim Davis and was not considered in the agreement therefor, but was paid for the reason only that the attorney preparing the deed suggested the necessity for the payment of a sum of money in order to make the deed valid and binding; that at the time of the conveyance Jim Davis was a minor and had not been by his parents emancipated and given the right to have and use his own earnings; that at the time of the conveyance the land conveyed was of the reasonable market value of $15 per acre; that no consideration deemed valuable in law was paid for the conveyance, but it was a voluntary conveyance and a gift of the land conveyed from C. F. Davis and M. A. Davis to their son, Jim Davis.

"(9) That on April 24, 1913, the date of the conveyance to Jim Davis aforesaid, the defendant C. F. Davis was insolvent and owned no other property in this state subject to execution sufficient to satisfy his debts, and that plaintiff was at such time and had been long prior thereto a creditor of said C. F. Davis as evidenced by the debt herein sued on.

"(10) I find that this suit was filed on the 26th day of June, 1919, and that on this date writ of attachment was duly issued and was levied on all the lands hereinabove mentioned including the 139 acres conveyed to Jim Davis as aforesaid.

"(11) I find that previous to her marriage to the defendant C. F. Davis, M. A. Davis had been married to one Blackwell and had by him eight children, some of whom resided with the defendant M. A. Davis at and after the time of her marriage to C. F. Davis, upon the lands hereinabove mentioned as her separate property and found to be the homestead of the defendants C. F. Davis and M. A. Davis; that it is not disclosed by the evidence how many children resided with her at any particular time, but that some of the children were with the defendants, M. A. Davis and C. F. Davis, at the time of the purchase of the lands from the Watkins Land Company, above mentioned, and contributed by their labor to the growing and cultivating of the crops on the homestead of the said C. F. Davis and M. A. Davis, with the proceeds of which all of the deferred payments to the said Watkins Land Company, set out in the conveyance from them, was made. Nothing of the kind is pleaded, but defendants upon the trial hereof sought to establish that an interest in the land so acquired from the Watkins Land Company was recognized as vesting in the children of M. A. Davis, because they had contributed by their labor on the lands of Mrs. Davis to the payment of the Watkins notes; that after the conveyance from C. F. Davis and M. A. Davis to J. M. Gray and others of the 311 acres of land, above mentioned, the proceeds of said sale was divided among C. E. Davis, M. A. Davis, and said children in some manner expressed by the defendants C. F. Davis and M. A. Davis, as intended to satisfy the claim of the children and the claim of C. F. Davis, and to give M. A. Davis the remainder of the land acquired from the Watkins Land Company, which was afterwards conveyed to Jim Davis as her interest. I find the fact to be that whatever sort of distribution was attempted to be made, it was at most but the consummation of a desire on the part of Mrs. Davis to give her children the money because they had worked for her and Mr. Davis, and in this manner had helped them to pay for the land, and did not change the status of the title to the property.

"(12) I find that plaintiff had no notice actual or constructive as to the condition of the property rights of C. F. Davis, M. A. Davis, Jim Davis, and the children of M. A. Davis by her previous marriage, except that conveyed by the records of this county, and at the time its debt was incurred and at the time of all the conveyances aforesaid, and at the time of the levy of this attachment did not know and was not charged with the knowledge that the lands conveyed to Jim Davis were other than the community property of C. F. Davis and M. A. Davis as on their face and by the record they appeared to be.

"(13) I find that no damage has accrued to the defendants in any of the particulars alleged by them in their cross-actions herein."

The trial court also filed the following conclusions of law:

"1. I conclude that plaintiff is entitled to recover of the defendant C. F. Davis the amount of its debt herein, to wit, $1,496.83, with interest at the rate of 10 per cent. per annum from the 25th day of June, 1919, and all costs of suit.

"2. I conclude that the debt sued on is not such a debt as under the law Mrs. Davis, while a married woman, was permitted to make and that she is not bound thereby.

"3. I conclude that the 450 acres of land aforesaid, including that conveyed to Jim Davis by C. F. Davis and M. A. Davis, was acquired during coverture with community funds, and though standing in the name of M. A. Davis, became and was the community property of C. F. and M. A. Davis until the date of their conveyance of same.

"4. I conclude that the homestead of defendants, C. F. Davis and M. A. Davis, had been

at all times herein mentioned the 160 acres owned by M. A. Davis when she married C. F. Davis, and that on the 24th day of April, 1913, it included, also, the resident and contiguous land to the extent of about 40 acres out of the land and premises conveyed to Jim Davis on that date so that the whole of the lands used for homestead purposes would be 200 acres.

"5. I conclude that the conveyance to Jim Davis was voluntary and was a gift; that at the time plaintiff was a creditor of C. F. Davis; that at the time C. F. Davis was insolvent and owned no other property in this state subject to execution sufficient to satisfy his debts; and that as to plaintiff the conveyance to Jim Davis was therefore void, except as to that part of the land conveyed used by C. F. and M. A. Davis for homestead purposes, being the 40 acres of land more or less last above mentioned.

"6. I conclude that as between all the parties the conveyance to Jim Davis of said 40 acres more or less used for homestead purposes was valid and binding, and he is entitled to recover the title and possession of same.

"7. I conclude that as to the 139 acres of land more or less conveyed to Jim Davis by C. F. Davis and M. A. Davis on the 24th day of April, 1913, less the 40 acres more or less dedicated to homestead purposes, plaintiff is entitled to a foreclosure of its attachment lien as the same existed on the 26th day of June, 1919, for the payment of its debt sued on herein.

"8. I conclude that the defendants should recover nothing on their cross-actions herein."

Opinion.

[1-3] Appellant complains that the trial court did not include in his findings of fact that the note sued on was secured by a chattel mortgage on 50 acres of cotton and cotton seed, and that the note of which it was a renewal was also secured by a mortgage on a grain crop. Granting that these facts were ultimate facts and not mere evidentiary ones, they are undisputed in the record. Under our view of the law, the failure of the trial court to expressly embrace these facts in his findings, if error at all, was harmless. It was not shown that such mortgages gave any real security for the note, or that anything was realized thereon. In these circumstances, it is immaterial that the note was secured by chattel mortgages. In so far as it is suggested that they negative any intent on the part of appellant to defraud appellee, it may be answered that the question does not depend upon the intent. If the conveyance was voluntary and not upon a consideration deemed valuable in law, and the grantors did not have other property within the state subject to execution sufficient to pay the debt, the conveyance was void under the statute. Neither do we see any of the elements of estoppel in the pleadings or the evidence, nor any waiver by appellee of its right. Therefore we overrule the assignment raising these questions.

[4, 5] It is next urged by appellant that the court erred in the eleventh paragraph of the findings of fact, wherein it was found that

the property in controversy was the community property of C. F. and M. A. Davis, because of the partition and division made by them and their children several months before the conveyance to their son, Jas. C. Davis. We have carefully read the testimony upon this issue, and we think the proof was entirely inadequate to show any interest of Mrs. M. A. Davis, as her separate estate, in the property foreclosed upon. The property seems to have been paid for out of the rents and revenues of the separate property of Mrs. Davis, in part, and the joint earnings of herself and husband, and, in part, by her children by a prior marriage. Under the law as it existed at the time this property was acquired and paid for, the rents and revenues from the wife's separate property constituted community. The joint labor and earnings of herself and husband were also such, and the payment by the children of a part of the purchase money did not, under the evidence, create any separate interest in Mrs. Davis. Whatever may have been the effect of the voluntary partition and division among the children, wherein Mr. Davis was given a "child's part" for his share, and Jas. C. Davis later acquired the land in controversy, as between the parties themselves, it could not have the effect to change the status of the property from community to separate as to creditors. Appellee was, at the date of such partition and of the conveyance to Jas. C. Davis, a creditor of C. F. Davis, and had no knowledge or notice of the partition and of the deed to Jas. C. Davis until after it was placed of record several years subsequently. For these reasons, we conclude that the trial court did not err in finding that the property was community.

[6] Although perhaps not properly raised under the assignment, appellant urges the proposition that the conveyance to Jas. C. Davis was upon a consideration deemed valuable in law, and was therefore not a gift or voluntary conveyance within the purview of the statute. This is especially true because the deed was made for love and affection and for the sum of $20, which was actually paid in cash by the grantee. The evidence fully supports the trial court's findings on this issue. It is undisputed that the question of a cash payment, or any payment at all, did not enter into the discussion of the conveyance, until an attorney suggested the payment of $1 to make it binding. Thereupon Jas. C. Davis stated that if it took $1 to make the deed good, $20 would make it better, and it was for this reason the latter amount was recited and was actually paid. In view of the gross inadequacy of this price in proportion to the value of the land conveyed, we think it was but a nominal consideration. The consideration recited and inducing the conveyance were not such as are deemed

valuable in law as to a creditor, and the conveyance was void under the statute.

All assignments have been given careful consideration and are overruled. The judgment is affirmed.

Affirmed.

BAREFIELD v. ALLEN et al. (No. 1170.)

(Court of Civil Appeals of Texas. El Paso. May 5, 1921.)

Appeal and error ⟞773(4)—Case not briefed affirmed in absence of fundamental error.

Where a case has not been briefed, and an examination of the record fails to disclose any error fundamental in its nature, the judgment of the court below will be affirmed.

Appeal from District Court, Eastland County; E. A. Hill, Judge.

Action between T. E. Barefield and W. J. Allen and others. From an adverse judgment, the former appeals. Affirmed.

Slay, Simon & Smith, of Fort Worth, for appellant.

Carrigan, Montgomery, Britain & Morgan, of Wichita Falls, Scott, Brelsford & Smith, of Eastland, and Lee, Lomax & Smith, of Fort Worth, for appellees.

PER CURIAM. This case has not been briefed. An examination of the record fails to disclose any error fundamental in its nature. The judgment is therefore affirmed.

SINTON STATE BANK v. TYLER COMMERCIAL COLLEGE. (No. 2424.)

(Court of Civil Appeals of Texas. Texarkana. May 12, 1921.)

1. Pleading ⟞111 — Plea of privilege prima facie proof of right to transfer.

Under Vernon's Ann. Civ. St. Supp. 1918, art. 1903, defendant's plea of privilege was prima facie proof of its right to have the case transferred to another county for trial.

2. Venue ⟞7—Proof of plaintiff held not to show case within exceptions to venue statute.

In an action by a commercial college against a bank, on which was drawn a check given the college in payment for its scholarship and stationery, where defendant bank filed plea of privilege to be sued in the county where it had its office and transacted business, allegations and proof by plaintiff college that its contract with its student was made in the county of suit, and that by a telegram sent to it in such county in reply to one sent to defendant bank the bank agreed to pay the check, did not show a case within any of the exceptions to Vernon's Sayles' Civ. St. art. 1830, declaring that no person who is an inhabitant of the state shall be sued out of the county in which he has his domicile.

Appeal from Smith County Court; W. R. Castle, Judge.

Suit by the Tyler Commercial College against the Sinton State Bank. From a judgment for plaintiff, defendant appeals. Judgment reversed, and cause remanded, with instructions.

One Gerdes, residing in San Patricio county, purchased of appellee a "scholarship" entitling him to instruction at its college in Tyler, in Smith county, and to certain stationery for use in connection with such instruction. In payment for the scholarship and stationery Gerdes offered appellee his check for $137.50 in its favor on the appellant bank, incorporated under the laws of Texas and having an office and transacting business at Sinton, in said San Patricio county. Before it accepted the check appellee telegraphed appellant at Sinton to ascertain if it would pay same, and in reply, by a telegram sent January 19, 1920, was assured it would; but when the check was afterwards presented to it appellant refused to pay it, assigning as a reason for such refusal that Gerdes had in the meantime instructed it not to pay same. Appellee then sued appellant in a justice court in Smith county. The latter by a proper plea asserted a right it claimed to have the cause transferred to San Patricio county for trial. In an affidavit controverting said plea appellee insisted it had a right to sue in Smith county by force of the twenty-fourth exception to the general rule prescribed in article 1830, Vernon's Statutes, because, it alleged, a part of its cause of action arose in that county, and by force of the seventh and ninth exceptions to said article, because, it alleged, its suit was founded on fraud and trespass committed in said Smith county, in that it was induced by appellant's telegram delivered to it in said county there part with its scholarship and stationery to Gerdes. Appellee's contention was sustained by the justice of the peace, who overruled appellant's plea and rendered judgment against it in appellee's favor for the sum it sued for. Thereupon appellant prosecuted an appeal to the county court of Smith county, where it renewed its insistence that the cause be transferred to San Patricio county for trial. That court, however, also overruled the plea, and, notwithstanding the exception of appellant to its action in that respect, the notice appellant then gave of an appeal from the order overruling its said plea, and its refusal to answer further, tried the cause on its merits and rendered judgment against appellant in appellee's favor for said sum of $137.50. The appeal by appellant is from both the order overruling its plea of privilege and the judgment against it on the merits.

E. P. Price, of Tyler, for appellant.
Brooks & Johnson, of Tyler, for appellee.

WILLSON, C. J. (after stating the facts as above). [1, 2] By force of the statute (article 1903, Vernon's 1918 Supplement) the plea of privilege was prima facie proof of a right in appellant to have the case transferred to San Patricio county for trial. In an effort to discharge the burden which therefore rested upon it to show that it was entitled to maintain its suit in Smith county notwithstanding said plea (Insurance Co. v. Robinson, 202 S. W. 354; Bank v. Sanford, 228 S. W. 650), appellee made the allegations referred to in the statement above, and at the hearing of the plea proved (1) that its contract with Gerdes was made in Smith county, and (2) that by a telegram sent to it at Tyler in reply to one it sent to appellant at Sinton the latter agreed to pay the check. It is plain, we think, that such proof did not show the case to be within any of the exceptions invoked to article 1830, Vernon's Statute, declaring that—

"No person who is an inhabitant of this state shall be sued out of the county in which he has his domicile."

The foundation of appellee's cause of action against appellant was not fraud or trespass on its part, but was its promise to pay the check. As that promise was made in San Patricio county, when appellant delivered the telegram to the telegraph company at Sinton for transmission to appellee at Tyler, it is clear no part of appellee's cause of action against appellant arose in Smith county. For anything appearing in the record to the contrary, the connection appellant had with the transaction between appellee and Gerdes was not other than the sending of that telegram in reply to the one appellee sent it.

The judgment will be reversed, and the cause will be remanded, with instructions to the court below to order the cause transferred to the justice court of precinct No. 1, San Patricio county, for trial, as provided in article 1833, Vernon's Statutes. McKay v. King-Collie Co., 228 S. W. 991.

PRIDDY et al. v. CHILDERS. (No. 1759.)

(Court of Civil Appeals of Texas. Amarillo. March 30, 1921. On Second Motion for Rehearing June 1, 1921.)

On Motion for Rehearing.

1. **Appeal and error ⬩263(3)—Refusal of requested charge not fundamental error reviewable in absence of exception.**

An assignment, "The court committed material error in failing and refusing to give to the jury defendant's special requested peremptory instruction to find for the defendants, "did not present fundamental error, so that it could be considered in the absence of an exception, and on failure to present by bill of exceptions, where it would require the court in its consideration to look to the evidence and statement of facts.

2. **Appeal and error ⬩730(1) — Requested charge held not in fact a charge requiring consideration under general assignment of error.**

A requested charge, "You are instructed that the evidence introduced in this case is insufficient to sustain a verdict for the plaintiff, and you will therefore find for the defendants and so say by your verdict," is not in fact a charge, and, not presenting fundamental error, an assignment that the court erred in refusing to give "defendant's special requested peremptory instruction to find for the defendants" was too general to entitle it to consideration.

3. **Appeal and error ⬩742(5)—Proposition held not to cure defect in too general assignment.**

A proposition following a too general assignment that the court erred in refusing defendant's requested peremptory instruction that, "If the evidence introduced on the trial is insufficient under any theory of the case to sustain a verdict for the plaintiff, the court should on request of the defendants give peremptory instructions to the jury to find for the defendants, and a refusal to give such requested instruction is such error as will require a reversal of the case on appeal," did not specify wherein the evidence was insufficient and did not cure the defect in the assignment.

4. **Judgment ⬩238 — Recovery authorized against one under allegation that two parties to contract made promise.**

When plaintiff alleges that two parties to a contract made him a promise, although under the rule at common law as to joint and several contracts that is a joint promise, yet the allegation necessarily means that each of them promised, and, although he has alleged the promise of the two, he can recover against one upon proof that he promised, although he fails to prove the promise of the other.

5. **Appeal and error ⬩731(1), 742(6) — Assignment of error to verdict should be followed by proposition, and held too general to be considered.**

An assignment of error that "the verdict of the jury is contrary to the evidence and the law in the case" should be followed by appropriate proposition or statement and is too general to be considered.

6. **Appeal and error ⬩731(5), 742(6) — Assignment of error to sufficiency of evidence should be followed by proposition, and held too general to be considered.**

An assignment of error that "the evidence introduced on the trial of this case is wholly insufficient to sustain the verdict of the jury," should be followed by an appropriate proposition or statement and is too general to be considered.

7. **Trial ⬩352(1)—Special issues held not objectionable as invading province of jury.**

In action by broker to recover commissions for furnishing purchaser for oil and gas lease, court did not err in submitting special issues as to whether defendant had revised the price of the lease at the time the plaintiff brought the prospective purchaser to his office, and whether he did not revise the price after plaintiff brought the purchaser there, as against an objection that the said issue was a comment by the court upon the weight of the testimony and invaded the province of the jury in that it unduly emphasized a particular part of defendant's testimony.

On Second Motion for Rehearing.

8. **Trial ⬩139(3) — Peremptory instruction properly denied where evidence sufficient as to one of two defendants.**

Where there were two defendants, and plaintiff's right to recover of them rested upon different grounds and was attempted to be sustained by proof of different facts, the court properly refused to give peremptory instruction in favor of defendants if he thought the evidence was sufficient to sustain the judgment as to one of them.

Appeal from District Court, Wichita County; Edgar Scurry, Judge.

Suit by F. T. Childers against W. M. Priddy and another. Judgment for plaintiff, and defendants appeal. Affirmed.

Martin & Oneal, of Wichita Falls, for appellants.

Harvey Harris, of Wichita Falls (Thelbert Martin, of Austin, on the brief), for appellee.

On Motion for Rehearing.

HALL, J. Appellee Childers, a real estate broker, sued W. M. Priddy and Del S. Brasher, to recover commissions alleged to be due him under a contract made with appellants for the sale of a certain oil and gas lease of a tract of land in Wichita county. Appellee alleged in substance that on or about the 26th day of April, 1919, the defendants listed with him for sale an oil and gas lease on certain premises described in his partition, at $5,000 per acre, cash, agreeing to pay him a commission of 10 per cent.; that on or about that date he procured purchasers who were ready, willing, and able to take the lease at the price and upon the terms given; and that the defendants failed and refused to comply with the contract by assigning the lease. Appellants answered by general demurrer and general denial. Appellee filed his first supplemental petition, alleging that he obtained a confirmation of the price per acre only a few moments before the purchasers were carried to the defendant's place of business; that said confirmation was given by the defendant Brasher at Priddy's place of business; and that Brasher was acting for himself and Priddy. The case was submitted to the jury upon special issues, and the jury found in effect that Brasher (1) had an interest in the lease; (2) that such interest was ³/₁₀₀ of the profits of sale; (3) that Brasher was authorized by Priddy to place the property with plaintiff for sale at $5,000 per acre; (4) that Priddy had not revised the price of the lease at the time the plaintiff brought the prospective purchasers to his office; and (5) that he did not revise the price until after plaintiff brought the purchasers there.

[1, 2] In the original opinion we considered the first assignment of error under the mistaken impression that it presented fundamental error. Upon reconsideration, we have concluded that it does not. The first assignment of error is:

"The court committed material error in failing and refusing to give to the jury defendant's special requested peremptory instruction to find for the defendants."

The instruction is as follows:

"You are instructed that the evidence introduced in this case is insufficient to sustain a verdict for the plaintiff, and you will therefore find for the defendants and so say by your verdict."

The notation made by the court on this request is:

"Presented to counsel for plaintiff and the court before the court read his main charge to the jury, and is by the court refused."

The court's action in refusing this request was not excepted to, nor is it presented here by any bill of exception. The assignment does not present fundamental error, because it requires this court, in its consideration, to look to the evidence and the statement of facts. The Supreme Court held in Houston Oil Co. of Texas v. Kimball, 103 Tex. 94, 122 S. W. 533, that an assignment of error which requires the appellate court to look into the record and consider the evidence does not present fundamental error. In the case of Walker et al. v. Haley (Sup.) 214 S. W. 295, the court held that such an instruction "is not a 'charge' at all, * * * but only the means of giving effect to the sustaining of a demurrer to the evidence, and which, if er-

roneous at all, is so, not because of any defect in the direction, but because of the court's mistaken view as to the effect of the proof." See, also, Shumaker v. Byrd (Sup.) 216 S. W. 862. Since the requested charge is in fact not a charge, and does not present fundamental error, our conclusion is the assignment is too general to entitle it to consideration.

[3] The first proposition following the assignment in appellants' brief is:

"If the evidence introduced on the trial is insufficient under any theory of the case to sustain a verdict for the plaintiff, the court should, upon request of the defendants, give peremptory instructions to the jury to find for the defendants, and a refusal to give such requested instruction is such error as will require a reversal of the case on appeal."

This proposition does not specify wherein the evidence is insufficient and does cure the defect in the assignment.

[4] The second proposition under the first assignment is:

"An averment by plaintiff of joint employment of him as a broker by two defendants to procure a purchaser for an oil and gas lease is not sustained by proof of employment of him by only one defendant, which employment is not participated in by the other defendant, and such variance is fatal where an instructed verdict is requested by defendants."

If this proposition could be considered, the contention therein could not be sustained, because in the case of McDonald v. Cabiness, 100 Tex. 615, 102 S. W. 721, which is a suit in many respects similar to this, Judge Gaines said:

"A plaintiff need not prove all his allegations; it is sufficient if he prove enough of them to make a case. When a plaintiff alleges that two parties to a contract made him a promise, although, under the rule at common law as to joint and several contracts, that is a joint promise, yet the allegation necessarily means that each of them promised. Hence we see no good reason why, although he has alleged the promise of the two, he could not recover against one upon proof that he promised although he may fail to prove the promise of the other."

See, also, Negociacion Agricola y Ganadera de San Enrique, S. A., v. Love, 220 S. W. 224. (9).

The assignment is therefore overruled.

[5] The second assignment is:

"The verdict of the jury is contrary to the evidence and the law in this case."

[6] The third assignment is:

"The evidence introduced on the trial of this case is wholly insufficient to sustain the verdict of the jury."

Neither of these assignments is followed by an appropriate proposition or statement, and they are too general to be considered.

[7] The fourth assignment is:

"Because the court committed material error in charging the jury special issues Nos. 4 and 5, in the court's main charge, wherein the court emphasized the fact of the defendant Priddy having changed his price on the lease described in plaintiff's petition, and the said issue was a comment by the court upon the weight of the testimony and invaded the province of the jury, and for the further reason said issue unduly emphasized that particular part of the defendant's testimony and caused the jury to believe that the court was of the opinion that the defendant Priddy changed the price of said lease after Brooks, Morrison, and Knight came to his office and had notified him of their desire to purchase said lease."

We think these issues were properly submitted and are not subject to the objections set out in the assignment.

No reversible error being pointed out, the original opinion is withdrawn, and the judgment affirmed.

On Second Motion for Rehearing.

[8] We agree with appellants' counsel that there is considerable confusion with reference to the right to appeal and assign error upon the action of the trial court in giving or refusing a peremptory instruction when the request is based upon the sufficiency or insufficiency of the evidence; but since the request made by appellant in this case is not a "charge," as decided by the Supreme Court in Walker et al. v. Haley, 214 S. W. 295, the matter must be properly presented in this court before it is entitled to consideration. The request made by appellant is as follows:

"Gentlemen of the jury, you are instructed that the evidence introduced in this case is insufficient to sustain a verdict for the plaintiff, and you will therefore find for the defendants and so say by your verdict."

There were two defendants in the case, and plaintiff's right to recover of them rested upon different grounds and was attempted to be sustained by proof of different facts. If the court thought the evidence was sufficient to sustain the judgment as to one defendant and not as to the other, it would have been improper to grant the request.

The second motion for rehearing is overruled.

SOLOMON v. SCHWARTZ BROS. & CO.
(No. 6570.)

(Court of Civil Appeals of Texas. San Antonio. May 18, 1921.)

Sales ⟣175—Purchaser could not cancel items of order and then sue for nondelivery.

Buyer under contract could not cancel certain items of his order and then sue for damages for failure to deliver such items.

Appeal from Maverick County Court; W. A. Bonnet, Judge.

Suit by L. Solomon against Schwartz Bros. & Co. Judgment for defendants, and plaintiff appeals. Affirmed.

Sanford & Wright, of Eagle Pass, for appellant.

Ben V. King, of Eagle Pass, for appellees.

FLY, C. J. This is a suit for damages in the sum of $547.50, alleged to have accrued by reason of the breach of a contract to deliver certain goods on or before July 1, 1919, instituted by appellant against appellees. There was really but one issue, and that was as to whether there was a contract made by and between the parties for the delivery of certain goods on or before July 1, 1919, and on that issue the jury found there was no such contract, and judgment was rendered that appellant take nothing by his suit, and that appellees recover of appellant the sum of $363.22 which he admitted he owed them in payment for certain merchandise.

The evidence was conflicting as to what the contract was between the parties, appellant swearing that the goods were to be delivered on or before July 1, and appellees' testimony showing they were to be delivered as they could get them. The jury decided in favor of appellees, as they well might do in view of the contradictory statements made by appellant, and the unsatisfactory evidence he gave. There is no force or merit in the contentions of appellant, and his only assignment is overruled.

There was no unreasonable delay in filling the order, and the authorities as to what constitutes unreasonable delay, cited by appellant, are based on the facts of each case, and cannot be decisive on the facts of this case. The evidence of appellees, which was credited by the jury, shows that there was never any positive understanding that the merchandise was to be delivered on July 1, 1919. Appellant by his acts waived an agreement to deliver by July 1, if such agreement had been made. He contradicted himself flatly at different times in his testimony. When it suited him he canceled an item in the order made by him, and then sued for damages for failure to deliver that very item. He seemed to think that the order was not binding on him as to certain articles he had ordered, and yet he demands strict enforcement of the order so far as appellees are concerned. He admitted that some of the goods were to be delivered July 1, and some July 15. The order had written or printed on it:

"This order is taken subject to delay in delivery and to reduction in quantity, in whole or in part, if the commercial production of the mills or manufacturers is curtailed or interfered with through war, or embargo or by government act or requirements."

The case was purely one of fact, and properly submitted to the jury.

The judgment is affirmed.

———

LANDA et al. v. F. S. AINSA CO., Inc.
(No. 1231.)

(Court of Civil Appeals of Texas. El Paso.
May 12, 1921. Rehearing Denied
June 2, 1921.)

1. Venue ⟸7—Action for breach of written contract properly brought in county in which it was performable.

Seller's action for breach of a written contract by which seller had sold goods to be shipped to specified city was properly brought in the county in which such city was situated under Rev. St. 1911, art. 1830, subd. 5; the contract being performable in such county.

2. Venue ⟸16½—Cause of action properly joined with another regardless of whether venue was properly laid in county in which action on other cause of action was properly brought.

Seller's cause of action for breach of a sale's contract was properly joined with cause of action for breach of a similar contract, in order to avoid a multiplicity of suits, regardless of whether venue as to former contract was properly laid in the county in which the action for breach of latter contract was properly brought.

Appeal from District Court, El Paso County; Ballard Coldwell, Judge.

Action by the F. S. Ainsa Company, Incorporated, against Harry Landa and others. From an order overruling plea of privilege filed by defendants to be sued in the county of their residence, they appeal. Affirmed.

Beall, Kemp & Nagle, of El Paso, for appellants.

Dyer, Croom & Jones, of El Paso, for appellee.

HIGGINS, J. This is an appeal from an order overruling a plea of privilege filed by appellants to be sued in Comal county where they reside. There were several defendants who were partners and engaged in business at New Braunfels in said county, under the firm name of Jos. Landa. The material facts are undisputed and are as follows:

The parties entered into and signed a memorandum of the sale of certain flour, the material portions whereof read:

"Joseph Landa, New Braunfels, Texas sell(s), and F. S. Ainsa Co. buy(s), the following commodities, on the terms and conditions stated herein:
Time of shipment, within sixty days.
Destination, El Paso, Texas.
Routing, seller's option.
Terms of payment, cash. Draft, with bill of lading attached, through———Bank of———.
Prices in this contract are for delivery to carrier at shipping point, with freight allowed to El Paso, Tex., on basis freight rate in effect on date of sale. * * *
"Invoices against this contract are payable in New Braunfels, Tex., with interest at the rate of 8 per cent. per annum after maturity."

The flour was shipped from New Braunfels. The bill of lading consigned the same to order of Jos. Landa, destination El Paso, Tex., notify F. S. Ainsa Co.

To cover the purchase price Landa drew a sight draft on F. S. Ainsa Company and attached the bill of lading thereto. The draft and bill were sent to an El Paso bank and taken up by appellee. The flour was then delivered to appellee, and it was alleged that same was wormy, weevil infested, had a bad odor, and inferior to the sample upon which the sale was made. This suit was to recover damages sustained by the failure to deliver flour conforming to sample.

[1] Under the authorities, the memorandum of sale and the bill of lading when taken up by appellee obligated appellants to deliver the flour in El Paso county. The obligation being in writing and performable in El Paso county, a suit for damages for its breach may be maintained in that county under subdivision 5, art. 1830, R. S. Seley v. Williams, 20 Tex. Civ. App. 405, 50 S. W. 399; People's Ice & Mfg. Co. v. Interstate Cotton Oil Ref. Co., 182 S. W. 1163; Callender, Holder & Co. v. Short, 34 Tex. Civ. App. 364, 78 S. W. 366; Darragh v. O'Connor, 69 S. W. 644; Cecil v. Fox, 208 S. W. 954; Gaddy v. Smith, 116 S. W. 164; Bell County Co. v. Cox, 33 Tex. Civ. App. 292, 76 S. W. 607; Harris v. Salvato, 175 S. W. 802.

The two cases cited by appellants are not in point. In our opinion they are clearly distinguishable.

[2] In the suit appellee also sought to recover damages for the breach of another contract for the sale of flour which contract was made about the same time as the one above discussed. Venue in El Paso county as to the cause of action upon this latter contract is not so clearly shown by the evidence, but in order to avoid a multiplicity of suits it was proper to embrace the suit thereon in this action. Middlebrook v. Bradley Mfg. Co., 86 Tex. 706, 26 S. W. 935.

Affirmed.

———

176

231 SOUTHWESTERN REPORTER

(Tex.

DOOL v. CITY OF WACO et al. (No. 6342.)

(Court of Civil Appeals of Texas. Austin. April 27, 1921.)

Master and servant �286(40)—Negligence in warning of danger of using defective fuses in exploding dynamite held for jury.

In an action against a city for personal injuries received from the delayed explosion of a stick of dynamite in a sewer ditch being constructed by the city, where it appeared that defendant had failed to warn plaintiff against additional danger involved in the use of defective fuses, evidence *held* to require the submission of the question to the jury.

Appeal from District Court, McLennan County; Erwin J. Clark, Judge.

Action by J. O. Dool against the City of Waco and others. Judgment for defendants on a directed verdict, and plaintiff appeals. Reversed and remanded.

Alva Bryan, Geo. W. Barcus, and John Maxwell, all of Waco, for appellant.

Street, Willis & Coston, of Waco, for appellees.

KEY, C. J. This is a damage suit brought by appellant against appellee city of Waco for injuries alleged to have been received by the plaintiff on account of the delayed explosion of a stick of dynamite, in a sewer ditch which was being constructed by the city. After hearing the testimony, the trial court instructed a verdict for the defendant; and the plaintiff has appealed and assigns error against that instruction.

Counsel for appellee make the contention that the undisputed evidence shows that the plaintiff's injuries resulted proximately and solely from his own negligence, and therefore the city of Waco is not liable, although it is subject to the Employers' Liability Act (Vernon's Sayles' Ann. Civ. St. 1914, arts. 5246h-5246zzzz), and therefore cut off from pleading contributory negligence as a defense. In other words, the contention is that, notwithstanding the act referred to, if the defendant was guilty of negligence as charged by the plaintiff, on account of its failure to properly warn him, and on account of the use of a defective fuse, nevertheless, if the testimony given by the plaintiff shows, as contended by appellee's counsel, that the plaintiff was fully aware of all of the risks and danger in which he placed himself, and did so voluntarily, then the proximate cause of the injury was not the defendant's negligence, but the negligence of the plaintiff in pursuing the course he did.

The correctness of the proposition asserted may be conceded, but it does not apply to all the aspects of this case. Among other things, the plaintiff testified as follows:

"Prior to, the time that I went to work using the dynamite out there on that ditch, I had never had any experience in handling dynamite. I reckon that the dynamite was about 6 inches under the ground, and there was about 18 inches of fuse on the outside. They was all about the same distance in the ground, and about the same length. I don't know why that one fuse would not light easily. I lighted three of them, and was trying to light the fourth one. I lit the three of them without any trouble, but when I got to the fourth one, I kept trying to light it three or four times, and it wouldn't catch easily, and these others had burned down 8 or 10 inches, and I got out, thinking that the fourth one wasn't on fire. I didn't know that it was on fire, but when I got back to the ditch it was on fire. In addition to these four fuses that I have been testifying about, there were about four others in that ditch—something like that. I did not know at that time that sometimes fuses would burn slow—that is, that some fuses would burn slow and others fast, and I didn't know that some fuses would light easy and others would light hard. Nobody didn't give me any warning at all with reference to fuses, only Mr. Rody told me that there wasn't no danger in it."

The witness Wm. Tisdale testified that he had had considerable experience in blasting with dynamite, and, among other things, testified as follows:

"If a fuse is defective, sometimes it won't light at all, and then again you can light one, and it will burn a piece and go out. Where a fuse is hard to light, it is caused generally from the powder in the defective fuse."

The testimony of the latter witness tended to show that some fuses were more difficult to light and burned more slowly than others, and the testimony of plaintiff tended to show that he was not aware of that fact, and that the defendant had failed to so inform him, or give him any warning against additional danger involved in the use of such fuses. In other words, if the plaintiff had been given proper warning upon that subject, it may be that he would have waited longer before going back to the ditch, and thereby avoided injury. That question of fact the plaintiff had the right to have submitted to the jury, and therefore we hold that the trial court committed error in directing a verdict for the defendant; and on account of that error the judgment is reversed, and the cause remanded.

Reversed and remanded.

⟐⟐For other cases see same topic and KEY-NUMBER in all Key-Numbered Digests and Indexes

TROTTER v. STATE. (No. 317.)

(Supreme Court of Arkansas. May 9, 1921.
Dissenting Opinion June 13, 1921.)

1. Homicide ⟠⇒309(1)—Court's mistake in use of term "voluntary manslaughter" instead of "involuntary manslaughter" in instruction held error.

In a homicide prosecution in which there was evidence sufficient to warrant a finding that defendant was guilty of involuntary manslaughter, error in defining involuntary manslaughter under Crawford & Moses' Dig. § 2356, as "voluntary manslaughter," without defining involuntary manslaughter in any other instruction, held prejudicial error, since the jurors, not being lawyers, and not understanding the difference between voluntary and involuntary manslaughter, could not have known that court by such instruction had intended to define involuntary manslaughter, and by mistake had used the words "voluntary manslaughter."

2. Criminal law ⟠⇒844(1)—General objection to instruction defining involuntary manslaughter as voluntary manslaughter held sufficient.

A general objection to instruction defining involuntary manslaughter as defined by Crawford & Moses' Dig. § 2356, as "voluntary manslaughter" held sufficient; such error being one of substance, and not of form.

3. Criminal law ⟠⇒814(17)—Refusal of instruction on circumstantial evidence where such evidence is not alone relied on held proper.

In a homicide prosecution in which the state did not depend wholly upon circumstantial evidence, refusal of instruction as to the sufficiency of evidence to justify conviction in a case in which the "state relies upon circumstantial evidence" held proper.

4. Homicide ⟠⇒188(5)—General reputation, but not personal opinion of witness as to deceased's character, admissible.

In a homicide prosecution in which defendant claimed to have acted in self defense, that deceased was a person of violent and dangerous disposition could be proved by testimony as to the general reputation of deceased, but not by the individual opinion of a witness concerning the deceased's character.

5. Homicide ⟠⇒346—Appellate court on appeal from conviction for voluntary manslaughter may affirm conviction of involuntary manslaughter.

Upon appeal from conviction for voluntary manslaughter in which there was evidence which would have warranted a finding that defendant was guilty of involuntary manslaughter, and in which court committed prejudicial error by failure to instruct upon involuntary manslaughter, the appellate court, instead of reversing the judgment and remanding the case for a new trial, will enter a judgment affirming conviction of involuntary manslaughter subject to the Attorney General's election within 10 days to have cause remanded for a new trial for voluntary manslaughter.

McCulloch, C. J., and Smith, J., dissenting.

⟠⇒For other cases see same topic and KEY-NUMBER in all Key-Numbered Digests and Indexes
231 S.W.—12

Appeal from Circuit Court, Drew County; Turner Butler, Judge.

Andrew Trotter was convicted of voluntary manslaughter, and he appeals. Reversed, and judgment affirming conviction of involuntary manslaughter entered subject to the right of the Attorney General to elect within 10 days to have cause remanded for new trial for voluntary manslaughter.

Henry & Harris, of Monticello, for appellant.

J. S. Utley, Atty. Gen., and Elbert Godwin and W. T. Hammock, Asst. Attys. Gen., for the State.

WOOD, J. Appellant was indicted for murder in the first degree in the killing of Fannie Read. He was tried and convicted of voluntary manslaughter. From the judgment sentencing to imprisonment in the state penitentiary for a period of 5 years, he appeals to this court.

The appellant, a negro 18 years of age, and Fannie Read, a negress about 30 years old, on the 8th of August, 1920, were living in illicit cohabitation at Tennessee Spur in Drew county, Ark. On the night of that day, and near the house in which they were living, a gun was discharged, and appellant and Fannie Read was observed running close together for a short distance. They stopped and were scuffling, when a gun was fired again, and Fannie fell. She was shot in the right groin with birdshot or buckshot, and died from the effects of the wound.

It could serve no useful purpose to discuss in detail the testimony. There was evidence to warrant the jury in finding the appellant guilty of voluntary manslaughter. The testimony of appellant was in part as follows:

"I had some puppies there, and there was something the matter with the chickens, and I got up [out of bed] to see what the trouble was. Fannie was out there with the gun and said, 'You son of a bitch, I told you I was going to get you,' and then she shot and ran. I ran after her to take away the gun. While we were tussling over it, it went off and shot her. We were up close together. Both of us had hold of the gun. She grabbed my broken arm. I snatched it, and it went off. I didn't know the gun was loaded, but I saw her unbreech it while going down the road. She got the gun out of her room. It was my gun—a single-barrel shotgun. I didn't shoot her. I could not have shot at her. My arm was in a sling and in splints from my wrist to my shoulder, and I could not get the gun up to my shoulder."

The above testimony, if believed, would have warranted the jury in finding appellant guilty of involuntary manslaughter. The court gave the following instructions on manslaughter:

(8) Manslaughter is the unlawful killing of a human being without malice, express or implied, and without deliberation.

(9) Manslaughter must be voluntary upon a sudden heat of passion, caused by a provocation apparently sufficient to make the passion irresistible. This is voluntary manslaughter.

(10) If the killing be in the commission of an unlawful act, without malice and without the means calculated to produce death, or in the prosecution of a lawful act done without due care and circumspection, it shall be manslaughter. This is voluntary manslaughter.

(11) Under the indictment in this case it is competent, if the proof justifies it, to find the defendant guilty of murder in the first degree, murder in the second degree, voluntary manslaughter, or involuntary manslaughter.

(16) If you have a reasonable doubt as to whether it is murder in the second degree or voluntary manslaughter, you should convict only of manslaughter. If you have a reasonable doubt whether it is voluntary or involuntary manslaughter, you should convict only of involuntary manslaughter.

[1] The appellant objected and excepted to the ruling of the court in giving each of the above instructions. While the court told the jury that they might find appellant guilty of involuntary manslaughter, there is no instruction informing the jury as to the punishment prescribed for such offense.

The testimony showed that the gun from which the fatal shot was fired was a single-barrel shotgun. According to the testimony of the appellant, after Fannie Read fired the gun, he ran after her for the purpose of disarming her, and was trying to snatch the gun away from her when the same was discharged, causing her death. If the jury believed that such was the intention of appellant, this conduct on his part was not unlawful, but the jury were warranted in concluding that the death of Fannie Read was thus caused without due care and circumspection on the part of the appellant.

The court, in its instruction No. 10, told the jury that, if the killing was in the prosecution of a lawful act done without due care and circumspection, it was voluntary manslaughter. Applying the above instruction to the testimony, if the jury believed and accepted the testimony of the appellant, they had no alternative but to find him guilty of voluntary manslaughter. Instead of telling the jury that such conduct in the prosecution of a lawful act done without due care and circumspection was involuntary manslaughter, the court told the jury just the opposite. This was fatal error and highly prejudicial to the appellant, because, if the jury had been told that, if they believed that the killing was done in the prosecution of a lawful act, but without due care and circumspection, they might find the appellant guilty of involuntary manslaughter, the jury under the evidence then would have been authorized to find, and might have found, the appellant guilty of involuntary manslaughter.

[2] The jurors were not lawyers and did not understand the difference between voluntary and involuntary manslaughter. Under their oaths they had to try the case according to the law as declared by the court. The court, in its instructions, made no distinction between voluntary and involuntary manslaughter. The instructions concerning manslaughter were in irreconcilable conflict, and the jury, in attempting to follow them, would be led into inextricable confusion. The mistake of the court in giving conflicting and confusing definitions was not merely one of verbiage or a clerical misprision, which the jurors could themselves observe and correct. The jurors, being laymen, could not correct the mistake of the court. The fact should be noted here that the framers of the Revised Statutes and the Legislature of 1837, which adopted the "Revised Statutes" defining "manslaughter" as set forth in section 1, and "voluntary manslaughter" as set forth in section 2, do not designate the offense prescribed in section 3 as "involuntary manslaughter." Chapter 44, § 3, Revised Statutes. The offense set forth in this section was first designated by our court as "involuntary manslaughter" in Harris v. State, 34 Ark. 469–479. The first digesters who designated it as such were Crawford & Moses, section 2356, C. & M. Digest. When the Legislature itself has not undertaken to define "involuntary manslaughter," and only the Supreme Court and digesters have undertaken to do so, how could a jury of laymen know the difference between voluntary and involuntary manslaughter? They could not know, and even if they did know, they are nevertheless bound to take the law from the trial court. The mistake was one which the court alone could correct. The court was not asked by the state to correct it, and did not correct it. The appellant, by his general objection to that particular instruction, called the court's attention to such defects as rendered the instruction fundamentally wrong. The error was one of substance, and not of form. It was an inherent defect. Therefore a general objection to that particular instruction was sufficient to direct the attention of the court to it. Fones v. Phillips, 39 Ark. 17–40, 43 Am. Rep. 264.

2. Appellant complains of the ruling of the court in refusing to give its prayer for instruction concerning the effect of circumstantial evidence, as follows:

(A) You are further instructed that when the state relies upon circumstantial evidence to justify the conviction of a person charged with crime, then such chain of circumstances, as a matter of law, must not only be inconsistent with defendant's innocence, but must be so convincing of his guilt as to exclude every other reasonable hypothesis, and must establish in the minds of the jury an abiding conviction, to a moral certainty, of the truth of the charge, and unless this is done in this case then it is your duty to acquit the defendant.

[3] There was no error in the ruling of the court. This was not a case in which the state depended wholly upon circumstantial evidence for the conviction of appellant.

[4] 3. J. D. Ratterree testified that he knew the general reputation of Fannie Read while she lived in the town of Monticello for turbulence and violence, or peace and quietude; that such reputation was bad. The witness was asked: "From that reputation did you consider her a dangerous woman?" The court would not permit the witness to answer the question, and the appellant duly excepted to the ruling of the court. This ruling of the court was correct. The individual opinion of a witness concerning the character of the deceased is not competent testimony because that does not tend to prove that the accused had knowledge of the fact that the deceased was a person of turbulent, violent, and dangerous disposition. But, when such is the general reputation of the deceased, it tends to show that the accused had knowledge of such character, and, where it is doubtful as to who was the probable aggressor, such testimony is competent because it tends to throw light upon that issue.

"The reputed character of the deceased on a charge of homicide," says Mr. Greenleaf, "may be evidential as indicating his reasonable apprehension of attack upon an issue of self-defense; for in a quarrel or other encounter the opponent's violent or turbulent character, as known to the accused, may give to his conduct a significance of hostility which would be wanting in the case of a man of ordinary disposition. It is the essence of this principle, however, as all courts concede, that the reputed character of the deceased should have been known to the accused." 1 Greenleaf on Evidence, p. 42, § 14.

See 1 Wharton's Criminal Evidence, p. 246; Underhill on Evidence, §§ 324, 325; Palmore v. State, 29 Ark. 248, 261, 262, and cases there cited; Coulter v. State, 100 Ark. 561-564, 140 S. W. 719.

[5] 4. The jury returned a verdict of guilty against the appellant for voluntary manslaughter, and fixed his punishment at a longer term in the state penitentiary than the shortest period prescribed for that offense. Therefore it is manifest that, if the jury had had an opportunity to return a verdict of guilty against the appellant for involuntary manslaughter and had found him guilty of such offense, they would not have fixed his punishment at a shorter period than one year, which is the longest period prescribed as punishment for that offense. The prejudice to appellant in the granting of Instruction No. 10 will be cured if the punishment of appellant is fixed at one year in the state penitentiary instead of five.

For the error in granting the state's prayer for instruction No. 10, the judgment convicting the appellant of voluntary manslaughter must be reversed, but, as a conviction for this offense includes the conviction also for involuntary manslaughter, and as it is obvious that the jury would have assessed the maximum punishment for that offense, unless the Attorney General elects, within ten days to have the cause remanded for a new trial for voluntary manslaughter, the judgment of the circuit court will be modified, and a judgment will be entered here affirming the conviction of involuntary manslaughter, and certified by the clerk of this court to the keeper of the state penitentiary reducing the sentence of the appellant to imprisonment in the state penitentiary for one year for "involuntary manslaughter." Brown v. State, 34 Ark. 232–239; Noble v. State, 75 Ark. 246–250, 87 S. W. 120; Routt v. State, 61 Ark. 594, 34 S. W. 262; Harris v. State, 119 Ark. 85–94, 177 S. W. 421.

McCULLOCH, C. J., and SMITH, J., dissent. They think the judgment should be affirmed.

McCULLOCH, C. J. (dissenting). Instructions numbers 8, 9, and 10 are in the language of the statute defining manslaughter and the error in number 10 in declaring that the facts related constitute voluntary manslaughter was obviously clerical. It was a mere "slip of the tongue" and the meaning of the court was obvious to any one who took notice of the language used. If appellant's counsel took notice of the error they ought to have called the attention of the court to it by a specific objection. If they did not notice it then it is not conceivable that the jury took sufficient notice of it to be misled by the incorrect statement. In other words, this is an instance, I think, where it is peculiarly essential that a specific objection should have been interposed to the incorrect language in an instruction. The trial judge repeated the precise language of the statute and manifestly intended to write the word involuntary instead of voluntary. Perhaps the error was made by the stenographer who transcribed the instruction. At any rate it is presumable that the trial judge would have corrected the error if his attention had been called to it, for it may be assumed that he did not intend to give two definitions of voluntary manslaughter. The objection to this instruction was formal and general, the same as made to the other 26 instructions of the court covering all of the grades of homicide.

The error is, therefore, harmless and should be disregarded.

SMITH, J., joins in this dissent.

STATE ex rel. ATTORNEY GENERAL v. EAGLE LUMBER CO.   (No. 13.)

(Supreme Court of Arkansas.   May 30, 1921.)

Taxation ⊜⇒380—Stock of foreign corporation not taxable where not of value exceeding value of other property assessed in state.

Under the rule that the taxable value of shares of stock of a corporation is ascertained by deducting the value of its tangible property otherwise assessed from the market value of its shares of stock, the capital stock of a foreign corporation was not taxable where the value of such stock did not exceed the aggregate value of its other property assessed in the state, and the corporation did not own other property elsewhere.

Appeal from Ouachita Chancery Court; James M. Barker, Chancellor.

Action by the State, on the relation of the Attorney General, against the Eagle Lumber Company. From a decree for less relief than demanded, both parties appeal. Reversed, and cause dismissed, on defendant's appeal.

J. S. Utley, Elbert Godwin, and George Vaughan, all of Little Rock, and Wm. T. Hammock, of Heber Spring, for appellant.

Gaughan & Sifford, of Camden, for appellee.

McCULLOCH, C. J. The Attorney General instituted this action on behalf of the state of Arkansas against the defendant, Eagle Lumber Company, a foreign corporation, to recover unpaid taxes alleged to be due on its capital stock since the time it began doing business in this state in the year 1899 up to the time of the commencement of the suit in 1919. The facts are undisputed and are set forth in a written stipulation signed by counsel on both sides.

The defendant is a private corporation, organized under the laws of the state of Iowa, and it began doing business in the state of Arkansas on March 3, 1899, and complied with the laws of the state with respect to foreign corporations doing business in the state. Its authorized and paid-up capital stock was originally $250,000, and subsequently raised to $500,000, "all of which," according to the recitals of the agreed statement of facts, "has always been employed in Arkansas." The written stipulation as to facts reads as follows:

"(2) The tangible assets of the company consist wholly of a sawmill, lumber, logs, and merchandise at Eagle Mills, and of timber lands situated in Ouachita, Dallas and Calhoun counties, all in the state of Arkansas. It owns no property located elsewhere, and for all the years covered by this suit its sole business was the manufacture and sale of timber products at Eagle Mills, Ark.

"(3) * * *

"(4) The company has paid due state and local taxes on all of its tangible property, real

and personal, including certain "moneys and credits" to the proper authorities in Arkansas in accordance with the revenue laws of this state.

"(5) It is agreed as a stipulation of fact that during the period of years covered by the complaint herein the shares of stock representing the capital stock of the company had the same value and no greater than the aggregate property owned by the corporation, all of whose physical assets had an actual situs within the state of Arkansas. It is further stipulated that during said period the property of the company assessed in Arkansas was valued for taxation in the several counties in which it was located at an amount equal to the actual average assessment of other similar property in the state of Arkansas.

"Provided it is further agreed that, if the court holds that the company as a foreign corporation is in any event taxable in Arkansas upon its intangible property or its capital stock, the extent of its liability for such taxes is stipulated to be $1,000 and no more, unless the proper basis for assessment be held to be 50 per cent. of true value as per the Tax Commission order recited in paragraph 6 herein.

"(6) * * *

"(7) It is further agreed that, if all issues of law are finally determined adversely to the defendant, judgment will be entered against the company for $2,000 (or in lieu thereof $1,000), in the event the court upholds as the true taxable criterion the actual average assessed basis rather than the Tax Commission's 50 per cent. basis. * * *"

The court rendered judgment in favor of the state for the recovery of the sum of $1,000, and both parties have appealed.

The Attorney General and his associate counsel argue with much earnestness the question whether the intangible property or capital stock of a foreign corporation doing business in this state is subject to assessment against the corporation for the purposes of taxation. That question is very thoroughly covered by the learned counsel on each side. But it seems to us that under the stipulation of facts in this case it is not proper for us to decide that question, for the reason that the capital stock has no value in excess of the value of the property otherwise taxed in this state, and that the corporation owns no property elsewhere, either tangible or intangible. The substance of the agreement is that all of the capital of the corporation is and has always been employed in the state of Arkansas, that all of its tangible assets are situated in the state of Arkansas, and that it owns no property located elsewhere, that the shares of stock have the same value as the aggregate property owned by the corporation, and that it has paid taxes on all of its tangible property, including moneys and credits.

The rule announced in the decisions of this court is that the taxable value of shares of stock of a corporation is ascertained by deducting the value of its tangible property otherwise assessed from the market value of the shares of stock. State ex rel. v. Bodcaw Lbr. Co., 128 Ark. 505, 194 S. W. 692; State ex rel. v. Ft. Smith Lumber Co., 131 Ark. 40, 198 S. W. 702; Crossett Lumber Co. v. State, 139 Ark. 397, 214 S. W. 43; State ex rel. v. Gloster Lumber Co., 227 S. W. 770. Under the agreement of facts there is no taxable value of the capital stock, as it does not exceed the aggregate value of the other property assessed in this state. Nor is it shown in the agreed statement of facts that they own any other property elsewhere. We do not, therefore, feel at liberty to follow counsel far enough in the argument to decide the question not applicable to the facts set forth in the record.

The court erred in rendering a decree against the defendant for any sum, and the decree is therefore on the appeal of the defendant reversed, and the cause is dismissed.

FISHER v. STATE. (No. 21.)

(Supreme Court of Arkansas. May 30, 1921.)

1. Homicide ⟹122—Illicit relations between deceased and defendant's wife no justification.

In a prosecution for homicide, where it was shown that defendant killed deceased at a railroad station some distance from either of their homes, but there was evidence that deceased had been in the habit of visiting defendant's wife, and urging her to procure a divorce, a requested instruction that defendant was entitled to prove the illicit relations between deceased and defendant's wife, and that the jury might consider such circumstances as exculpating the defendant, or in mitigation of the punishment, was properly refused, since that fact did not justify or excuse the homicide, under Crawford & Moses' Dig. §§ 2338–2383.

2. Witnesses ⟹203—Prosecuting attorney can testify to communications made to him officially.

In a prosecution for homicide, the deputy prosecuting attorney can testify that, prior to the killing, defendant consulted him regarding criminal prosecution against deceased for illicit relations with defendant's wife, and was informed he did not have sufficient evidence, since the attorney was not consulted as an attorney for defendant, and there was no confidential relationship between them.

3. Homicide ⟹163(2)—Good character of deceased admissible only after defendant has attacked character.

In a prosecution for homicide, evidence on behalf of the state that deceased was a man of good character for peace and quietude is not admissible unless defendant has attacked the character of deceased.

4. Homicide ⟹163(2)—Evidence deceased had borrowed a pistol when visiting defendant's wife held not to make evidence of good character admissible.

In a prosecution for homicide, evidence on behalf of defendant, and that, on several occasions, when deceased was going to visit defendant's wife, he had borrowed a pistol to take along with him, is not an attack by defendant on the good character of deceased for peace and quietude, and does not render admissible evidence on behalf of the prosecution as to deceased's character in that respect.

Appeal from Circuit Court, Cross County; R. E. L. Johnson, Judge.

George Fisher was convicted of murder in the second degree, and he appeals. Reversed and remanded.

Killough, Lines & Killough, of Wynne, for appellant.

J. S. Utley, Atty. Gen., and Elbert Godwin and W. T. Hammock, Asst. Attys. Gen., for the State.

HART, J. George Fisher was indicted for the crime of murder in the first degree, and was convicted of the crime of murder in the second degree, his punishment being fixed by the jury at 21 years in the state penitentiary. From the judgment of conviction, the defendant has duly prosecuted an appeal to this court.

It appears from the record that the defendant shot and killed Jess Moore with a pistol, in the town of Wynne, in Cross county, Ark., on the 16th day of July, 1920. According to the witnesses for the state, Jess Moore, with two other men beside him, was sitting down near the depot, in the town of Wynne, when the defendant, George Fisher, approached them, and sat down beside them, being the farthest away from Jess Moore. He spoke to them as he came up, and, after sitting there a few minutes, he arose, and said, "Jess you have done me dirty," and then shot Jess Moore twice with a pistol. Jess Moore rose up and exclaimed, "Oh, George, don't do that." At the time, he was staggering around on the sidewalk. The defendant replied, "You have done enough to me," and shot him twice more. The deceased was unarmed at the time, and made no attempt to shoot, or otherwise injure the defendant.

According to the testimony of the witnesses for the defendant, the defendant lived at the town of Tilton, just north of the town of Fair Oaks, where Jess Moore lived. Both of these towns are situated in Cross county, and not far from Wynne, the county seat. The wife of the defendant ran a boarding house at Tilton, and the deceased was accustomed to go there every other night, ostensibly for the purpose of eating supper, but, in reality, to visit the defendant's wife. It finally came to the knowledge of the defendant that the deceased was visiting his wife. Finally the defendant's wife went to St. Louis, Mo., on a visit to her relatives, and on her return stopped at Wynne, and did not come home. The defendant went over there to induce her to come home, but was unable to do so. He was on his way to the depot to take a local freight train for his home when the shooting occurred. According to the defendant's testimony, the deceased made an effort to shoot him, and he shot him in his necessary self-defense.

A daughter of the defendant testified at the trial that she found a letter from the deceased to her mother, in which he urged her to act in such a way that her husband would leave her, so that he, the deceased, might then get to live with her. The deceased said in his letter that he could not live without her. Some testimony was introduced by the defendant tending to show that he was insane at the time of the killing.

No complaint is made by the defendant that the evidence is not legally sufficient to support the verdict, and it is only necessary to say that a reading of the evidence for the state shows that it was amply sufficient for that purpose.

[1] It is insisted by counsel for the defendant that the court erred in refusing instruction No. 1 asked by the defendant, which is as follows:

"The jury are instructed that defendant had a right to show all the circumstances connected with the killing of the deceased, and to prove the illicit relations, if any, between deceased and wife of defendant, and that they may take all such facts and circumstances into consideration as exculpating the defendant, or in mitigation of the punishment."

The court was right in refusing this instruction. The fact that the deceased may have had illicit relations with the wife of the defendant did not excuse or justify the homicide, under our statutes. Crawford & Moses' Dig. §§ 2338–2383.

[2] It is also insisted that the court erred in admitting the testimony of Giles Dearing. The latter was deputy prosecuting attorney of the county, and the court permitted him to testify before the jury that the defendant came to his house on the evening before the killing, and asked him a number of questions relative to whether the deceased and the defendant's wife had violated the criminal laws. From the information elicited by the questions, the deputy prosecuting attorney told the defendant that there was not sufficient evidence to warrant him in prosecuting the deceased, and advised him that he might get a divorce from his wife. The defendant did not consult Dearing for the purpose of employing him as his attorney. He only consulted him as a public prosecutor. His testimony did not concern any communication made to him as attorney by the defendant as his client, or his advice thereon. Therefore no confidential relation existed between them which would prevent the witness from testifying concerning the matters talked about without the consent of the defendant.

Again, it is contended by counsel for the defendant that the court erred in permitting witnesses to testify for the state that the reputation of the deceased for being a peaceable and law-abiding citizen was good.

[3] In Bloomer v. State, 75 Ark. 297, 87 S. W. 438, the court held that it is well settled in this state that evidence on the part of the prosecution that the deceased was a man of good character for peace and quietude should not be admitted, unless the defendant had undertaken to attack the character of the deceased. See, also, Kelley v. State, 226 S. W. 137.

The Attorney General conceded that the reputation of the deceased for peaceableness is not admissible as original evidence against one charged with murder where self-defense is relied upon. He contends, however, that the evidence of the defendant himself conflicted with the evidence in behalf of the state, and made an issue on the question of who was the aggressor. The defendant, in order to corroborate his own testimony that the deceased was the aggressor, introduced several witnesses, who testified that the deceased asked to borrow a pistol from them, and gave as a reason that he was going to walk from Fair Oaks to Tilton in the nighttime, and did not want to do so without having a pistol. They refused to let him have a pistol.

Another witness testified that the deceased approached him in the same way, and that he let him have a pistol on one occasion to carry with him from Fair Oaks to Tilton, in the nighttime.

Another witness testified that he frequently let the deceased have his pistol to carry with him on his night trips from Fair Oaks to Tilton, and that on each occasion the deceased would return the pistol to his store on the day following. After the witness heard that the deceased was visiting the defendant's wife at Tilton, he refused to let him have his pistol any more.

[4] It is insisted by the Attorney General that this testimony introduced by the defendant was sufficient to bring the case within the rule announced in Carr v. State, 227 S. W. 776. We cannot agree with the Attorney General in his contention. We do not think what the defendant proved concerning the deceased was equivalent to proving his general character as a violent, quarrelsome, and fighting man. It is clear that the proof made in the Carr Case by the defendant as to the character of the deceased was of an entirely different nature from the proof made in the case at bar. In that case, the defendant

offered to prove that the deceased had had numerous fights; paid a fine for each one of them; that he had had several quarrels with other persons; that he had beat up others; that he had killed a negro; and these matters all came along in such consecutive order that the court was of the opinion that they showed the general reputation of the deceased to be that of a violent, turbulent, and fighting man. Here, the deceased did not own any pistol, did not habitually carry one, and only wanted to carry it on the occasions when he went from Fair Oaks to Tilton in the nighttime. On each occasion that he borrowed the pistol, he returned it on the next day. The evidence does not show that he went armed on other occasions. He was unarmed at the time he was killed. It was not shown that he had any previous difficulties with the defendant, or any other person. The mere fact that testimony was introduced tending to show that he visited the defendant's wife, and returned home in the nighttime, and borrowed a pistol frequently on such occasions, does not establish his general reputation as being that of a violent, quarrelsome, and fighting man.

The character of the deceased as being peaceful and quiet is presumed to be good until the contrary appears, and, the testimony of the defendant not being sufficient to show that the general reputation of the deceased in that respect was that of a quarrelsome and fighting man, the state was not entitled to introduce original evidence upon that subject.

It necessarily follows that, if the proof was incompetent, it was prejudicial to the defendant.

For the error in admitting it, the judgment must be reversed, and the cause will be remanded for a new trial.

**ILLINOIS BANKERS' LIFE ASS'N v. DOW-
DY. (No. 26.)**

(Supreme Court of Arkansas. May 30, 1921.)

Insurance ⬯361—Insured's direction to bank authorized to collect premiums to pay premium and charge to insured's account held sufficient payment.

Where insurer authorized bank to collect premiums, and insured with a sufficient deposit to cover the premium directed cashier to pay the premium and to charge amount thereof to his account, before the premium became due, and the cashier agreed to do so, there was a timely payment of premium, though amount thereof was not actually entered against depositor's account until after expiration of the period of grace for payment of premium.

Appeal from Circuit Court, Van Buren County; J. M. Shinn, Judge.

Action by Tom M. Dowdy against the Illinois Bankers' Life Association. Judgment for plaintiff, and defendant appeals. Affirmed.

T. E. Helm, of Little Rock, and Garner Fraser, of Clinton, for appellant.
M. P. Hatchett, of Clinton, for appellee.

SMITH, J. On the trial from which this appeal comes the court gave, over the objection of appellant, an instruction reading as follows:

"No. 2. If you find from a preponderance of the evidence in this case that the said Tom M. Dowdy, as the agent of his wife, the said Julia A. Dowdy, during the latter days of December, 1919, or the early days of January, 1920, directed the cashier and assistant cashier of the Bank of Shirley, or either of them, to pay the premium due or coming due on said policy, and that said Tom M. Dowdy, from the time of such direction to the expiration for the payment of said premium, had sufficient funds on deposit in said bank to his credit to pay said premium, you will find for the plaintiff."

This instruction, in effect, directed a verdict against the appellant insurance company, as there is no dispute about the facts which the jury was there told would warrant a finding for the plaintiff.

The court refused to given instructions asked by appellant which were the converse of the instruction set out above. These instructions declared the law to be that the insured had no right to rely on the promise of the officers of the bank to pay the premium, and that the payment of the premium was not made until the insurance company had received credit therefor on the books of the bank, and that such payment must have been made and credit given within 30 days of the due date of the premium.

Mrs. Dowdy was the insured, and her husband, Tom M. Dowdy, was the beneficiary. It was his custom to pay the premiums, and the payments were ordinarily made by him in the manner in which he had directed the payment in dispute to be made.

The premiums on the policies were ordinarily payable quarterly, although policy holders had the option of paying the premium semiannually or annually in advance, the due dates being January 1st, April 1st, July 1st, and October 1st of each year. The insurance company mailed out in advance to the policy holders notices of the time within which their premiums would be due and the place where they would be payable, and there were a number of policy holders in appellant company residing in Shirley, Van Buren county, Ark.

It was the custom of the company to send to the Bank of Shirley a list of its policy holders residing there with a statement of the premium due by each and signed receipts for premiums to be delivered when payments were made; and for this service the insurance company paid the bank a collection charge of one per cent. The names of the policy holders were written on a printed form, which contained the following direction to the bank:

"Please report as soon as all are paid and in any case not later than the maturity of said collections. Remit to cover all collections and return all unpaid notes and receipts."

Mrs. Dowdy died March 11, 1920, and payment of the policy on her life, which was for $1,000, was refused for the alleged reason that the premium due thereon January 1, 1920, was not paid at that time nor within the 30 days of grace thereafter allowed for payment. The policy in question provided that failure to pay premiums at maturity "shall render the policy absolutely null and void, and the same shall be forfeited without further notice or action of the directors of the association, unless reinstated as herein provided." The bank had no authority to collect premiums after the 30 days of grace had expired.

It was shown that a few days before January 1, 1920, Mr. Dowdy inquired of the cashier of the bank whether the insurance list had been received, and was told that it had not been received. Dowdy thereupon directed the cashier of the bank to pay the premium when the list was received from the company and to charge the amount thereof to his account, and the cashier agreed to do so. Dowdy was a customer of the bank, and carried a deposit there sufficient to have covered the premium. He supposed his request had been complied with and that the premium had been paid in accordance with his request and his usual method of paying premiums.

The cashier of the bank made up his report on February 7th, and mailed it to the company with draft to cover the premiums collected, and the list of such premiums included the January premium on the Dowdy policy. It was the custom of the cashier to make up and forward this report after the expiration of the 30 days of grace. The premium due on the Dowdy policy was $3.17, but the charge ticket made therefor by the cashier of the bank against Mr. Dowdy was not actually entered against his account on the books of the bank until February 12, 1920. The transmittal letter of February 7th miscarried in the mails, and after an exchange of letters and telegrams in regard to it a duplicate list and draft went forward to the company, which was not received by the company, however, until after the date of Mrs. Dowdy's death.

Under the facts thus stated the court did not err in giving the instruction set out above. This case is ruled by the cases of Sovereign Camp, W. O. W., v. Newsom, 142 Ark. 132, 219 S. W. 759, N. Y. Life Ins. Co. v. Allen, 143 Ark. 143, 220 S. W. 808, and Security Life Ins. Co. v. Bates, 144 Ark. 345, 222 S. W. 740.

In the case of New York Life Ins. Co. v. Allen, supra, the authority of an agent to collect and the fact of collection of a premium note were in dispute. The payment of the premium was there claimed to have been made in a manner substantially identical with the method of payment employed here by Dowdy. In that case the court said:

"Allen [the insured] had already told the cashier to pay the note and charge his account with the amount. He had money to his personal credit in the bank more than sufficient to discharge his indebtedness to the insurance company. This direction to the cashier was sufficient, we think, to show a payment to the cashier if he had authority to receive it."

The doctrine thus announced was reaffirmed in the case of Security Life Ins. Co. v. Bates, supra.

No error appearing, the judgment is affirmed.

ARKANSAS ANTHRACITE COAL CO. et al. v. STATE. (No. 18.)

(Supreme Court of Arkansas. May 30, 1921.)

Taxation ⊜117—Local corporations owning property are subject to franchise tax as "doing business," though they merely leased coal lands.

Under Crawford & Moses' Dig. §§ 9799–9801, providing that every corporation organized and doing business under the laws of the state shall make report to the Arkansas Tax Commission, that upon the filing of such report the Tax Commission shall refer the same to the auditor, who shall charge and certify to the treasurer a tax of one-tenth of 1 per cent. on that part of the subscribed or issued capital employed in Arkansas, and in view of section 9820, imposing franchise taxes on corporations having no capital stock employed in the state, etc., domestic corporations which owned and leased coal lands are liable to the tax, even though they were not conducting active operations, but had purchased the property merely for the purpose of doing business in the future, for, as such corporations could not function without the authority of the state and no investment could be made, such investment constituted doing business, though the corporations were largely dormant and inactive.

[Ed. Note.—For other definitions, see Words and Phrases, First and Second Series, Doing Business.]

Appeal from Pulaski Chancery Court; Jno. E. Martineau, Chancellor.

Actions by the State of Arkansas against the Arkansas Anthracite Coal Company and another. From a decree for the State, defendants appeal. Affirmed.

Rose, Hemingway, Cantrell & Loughborough, of Little Rock, for appellants.

J. S. Utley, A. L. Rotenberry, and J. C. Marshall, all of Little Rock, for the State.

McCULLOUGH, C. J. Two consolidated actions are involved in this appeal, each instituted by the state of Arkansas against domestic corporations to recover unpaid franchise taxes under the statute which provides that every corporation "organized and doing business under the laws of this state for profit, shall make a report in writing to the Arkansas Tax Commission," the form and substance of such report being specified, and that upon the filing of such report the Tax Commission shall report the same to the Auditor of State "who shall charge and certify to the Treasurer of State for collection * * * from such corporation a tax of one-tenth of one per cent. upon that part of its subscribed and issued * * * capital stock employed in this state." Crawford & Moses' Digest, §§ 9799-9801.

The articles of incorporation of the Arkansas Anthracite Coal Company define its purposes to be "to buy, own and sell lands, mineral rights, oil, gas and timber rights; conduct mining operations; to run a general mercantile business; to manufacture lumber; to build, own and operate switches and tramroads; to buy, own and sell stocks of railroads and other corporations; to operate stone quarries; to manufacture stone and brick; to lay out cities." This corporation has a paid-up capital of $597,000, which is invested in mining rights and coal lands situated in this state.

The articles of incorporation of the Arkansas Anthracite Mining Company define its purposes to be:

"The mining of coal and other minerals; the operation of railroads, steamboats, barges and tramroads; the buying, owning and selling of lands, merchandise, stocks in other companies; the selling of coal and other minerals, and the establishment of agencies for that purpose."

This corporation has a paid-up capital of $100,000, and invested the same as the other corporations.

The property owned by the two corporations constitutes a single coal field of about 15,000 acres. The coal company has made a lease of a tract of 328 acres of its mineral rights to a certain person, which said lease lapsed without any development work being done. The mining company leased 160 acres to an individual, who assigned the lease to another corporation, which has mined coal and paid royalties to the mining company annually from the year 1918, up to the commencement of these actions. The coal company owns all of the capital stock of the mining company, which it received in consideration of a conveyance of 5,000 acres of its mineral right holdings to the mining company. This conveyance to the mining company was executed to enable the latter to mortgage the property for a loan of $50,000 to use in paying a bonus to a certain railroad company for building a railroad to the coal field. The reason for this was that it did not suit the purposes of the coal company to incur this obligation, and the mining company was organized for the purpose of assuming the obligation under the arrangement just described. Neither of the corporations has transacted any other active business, if it be held that the above-recited transactions constitute "active business." The trial court rendered a decree for the recovery from each of the corporations of the several amounts claimed by the state as franchise taxes.

It is the contention of learned counsel for the corporations that neither have been "doing business" within the meaning of the statute, and that neither is liable for the payment of the franchise tax under the statute. The contention is that the corporations have been and are holding the property in which the capital stock is invested merely for the purpose of doing business in the future, and that this does not fall within the terms of the statute. Counsel argue that the words "doing business" as used in the statute should be interpreted to mean activity in the prosecution of the business specified in the charter. We do not so interpret the statute. The purpose is to exact the payment of a tax on the exercise of the franchise (St. Louis S. W. Ry. Co. v. State, 106 Ark. 321, 152 S. W. 110), and a corporation necessarily exercises its franchise in the investment of its capital in other property, for it derives its authority to make the investment from the franchise granted by the state. It cannot function at all except under the powers granted to it in the franchise. The statute applies to all active corporations—those which are functioning and not those which are dormant. A corporation must be both organized and active in order to be liable for the franchise tax. A corporation may have been duly organized and may remain or become inactive and dormant, but if it functions at all it is, as before stated, alive and active. This view of the meaning of the statute is strengthened by the fact that the tax is laid according to the amount of capital stock "employed" in this state, which shows that the employment of capital stock was construed as constituting the doing of business in the exercise of the franchise.

This view is also very much strengthened by the provision in section 9820, Crawford & Moses' Dig., to the effect that all corporations, both domestic and foreign, "qualifying * * * to do business in this state or organized under the laws of this state," shall pay an annual franchise tax of $10, where such corporation has no capital stock employed in this state, or has less than $13,333 of its capital stock employed. This shows that the lawmakers intended to impose a franchise tax on all live corporations in this state, whether actively engaged in business or not.

In the recent case of State ex rel. v. Gloster Lumber Co., 227 S. W. 770, we decided that a domestic corporation was, under a statute applicable "to 'all corporations doing business in this state,'" liable to general taxes on its stock, all of which was invested in property and business wholly situated and operated in another state, and in disposing of the question we said:

"The theory of counsel for appellee is that a corporation organized under the laws of this state and domiciled here does not come under the requirement of the statute if it has no tangible property here and is not visibly operating some kind of business here in this state. That is not, we think, the correct interpretation of the statute. The words used in the statute are very broad. 'All corporations doing business in this state' is the language used. A corporation organized and domiciled here is necessarily doing business here if it is doing business at all. Its life and existence are here and all of its business activities necessarily emanate here primarily if it functions at all. Its domicile is the fountain head of all its activities."

The same principle controls in the present case for the reasons already stated. Our decision in the recent case of Linton v. Erie Ozark Mining Co., 227 S. W. 411, has no application, for it only reached to the question that a foreign corporation which had not filed its articles of incorporation and obtained permission to do business in the state was not, by merely owning property in the state and leasing it, doing business here within the meaning of the statute, which prohibits corporations from doing business in the state without complying with the laws thereof. The decisions of the Supreme Court of the United States cited by counsel are not applicable, for they relate to a federal statute imposing an excise tax on the net income of corporations doing business in any of the states or territories of the United States. Flint v. Stone-Tracy Co., 220 U. S. 107, 31 Sup. Ct. 342, 55 L. Ed. 389, Ann. Cas. 1912B, 1312; McCoach v. Minehill, etc., R. Co., 228 U. S. 295, 33 Sup. Ct. 419, 57 L. Ed. 842; United States v. Emery, 237 U. S. 28, 35 Sup. Ct. 499, 59 L. Ed. 825. In Flint v. Stone-Tracy Co., supra, which was followed in the later cases, the court said:

"It is therefore apparent, giving all the weight of the statute effect, that the tax is imposed, not upon the franchises of the corporation irrespective of their use in business, nor upon the property of the corporation, but upon the doing of corporate or insurance business and with respect to the carrying on thereof. * * * "

We conclude, therefore, that the decree of the chancery court is correct, and the same is affirmed.

WOODALL v. STATE.   (No. 19.)

(Supreme Court of Arkansas.   May 30, 1921.)

1. Criminal law ⬤⟺465—Exclusion of opinion as to defendant's sanity by witness who had not detailed facts proper.

In a homicide prosecution, defended on the ground of insanity, refusal to permit witness to give her opinion as to whether defendant was insane, without first detailing the facts upon which opinion was based, *held* proper.

2. Homicide ⬤⟺27—Rule as to insanity as constituting defense stated.

In a murder prosecution, the defendant, to establish insanity, must prove by a preponderance of evidence that at the time of killing he was under such a defect of reason from disease of the mind as not to know the nature and quality of the act he was doing, or, if he did know nature thereof, that he did not know that it was wrong, or, if he knew the nature and quality of the act and knew that it was wrong, that he was under such duress of mental disease as to be incapable of choosing between right and wrong as to the act done, and unable, because of the disease, to resist the doing of the wrong act, which was the result solely of his mental disease; it being insufficient that his reason was temporarily dethroned, not by disease, but by anger, jealousy, or other passion, or that he was so morally depraved that his conscience ceased to control or influence his actions.

3. Homicide ⬤⟺270—Whether defendant was insane at time of killing held for jury.

In prosecution for homicide defended on the ground of insanity, where there was testimony that defendant was a victim of paranoia in its persecutory stage, but where there was also testimony that the disease had not progressed to that stage, and also testimony that defendant was not insane at all, the question of whether he was sane or insane at the time of the killing *held* for the jury.

4. Criminal law ⬤⟺49—When delusional insanity constitutes a defense.

The rule that where one labors under a partial delusion only and is in other respects sane, insanity is no defense, but that he must be considered as if the facts with respect to which the delusion exists were real, is applicable only where the testimony proves or tends to prove that the disease is in its first or earliest stage of development, since in such case he, notwithstanding his mental delusion, may still be able to exercise his will and control his actions with reference to delusions, but where the disease has progressed to its second or persecutory stage or subsequent stages, and he is no longer able to control his will and actions, the defense of insanity is available.

5. Criminal law ⚌740—Whether defendant was afflicted with mental disease question for jury, but whether mental disease rendered him irresponsible is an issue of law.

Where the defense is insanity, it is an issue of fact for the jury to determine whether the accused at the time of the act was afflicted with a mental disease, and an issue of law as to whether the mental disease is such as to render him irresponsible.

Appeal from Circuit Court, White County; J. M. Jackson, Judge.

Lee Woodall was convicted of murder in the second degree, and he appeals. Reversed and remanded.

J. N. Rachels, of Searcy, and G. G. McKay, of Bald Knob, for appellant.

J. S. Utley, Atty. Gen., and Elbert Godwin and W. T. Hammock, Asst. Attys. Gen., for the State.

WOOD, J. The appellant was indicted for the crime of murder in the first degree in the killing of L. S. Rudisill. He entered a plea of not guilty, and the only defense offered was insanity. He was convicted of murder in the second degree, and, from a judgment sentencing him to a period of 20 years in the state penitentiary, he appeals.

First. Mrs. R. S. Woodall testified that she was the mother of the appellant. The record shows that during the progress of her examination the following took place:

"Q. Was he [Lee Woodall] at the time of the killing, and had he been for some time prior thereto on the subject of his trouble with L. S. Rudisill, sane or insane?

"Mr. Miller (prosecuting attorney): I object on the ground that the witness has not detailed any of the facts and circumstances sufficient to express an opinion.

"Court: The objection will be sustained to it; I don't think she has detailed sufficient facts and circumstances to testify as to that.

"Mr. Rachels (attorney for defendant): We might as well settle this.

"Court: I am familiar with the decision, and it is not necessary to argue the matter. I have ruled on it, and you can save your exceptions.

"Mr. Rachels: Note my exceptions. He objects to my qualifying the witness.

"Mr. Miller: No; I do not.

"Court: She has not detailed facts sufficient to justify her in expressing an opinion as to his sanity, yet she may be able to do so after awhile."

The record shows that after the above ruling, Mrs. Woodall was examined at length, and testified in detail as to the appellant's conversations with her concerning his trouble with Rudisill and his manner during such conversations, showing what appellant said and did and how his mind was affected. At the conclusion, she was asked:

"Q. I believe you said a while ago that·upon the question of his trouble with Rudisill he was insane? A. He was."

[1] Counsel for appellant contends here that the court erred in not permitting the witness during the early part of her examination to answer the question propounded to her as above set forth. The ruling of the court at that juncture was correct. For at this time the witness had not detailed sufficiently the facts upon which she based her opinion. The record shows that the witness later during her examination fully stated the facts upon which her opinion was based, and was permitted to express the opinion that on the subject of his trouble with Rudisill, appellant was insane. The ruling of the court was in conformity with the rule announced by this court in Bolling v. State, 54 Ark. 588–599, 16 S. W. 658; Smith v. State, 55 Ark. 259–62, 18 S. W. 237; Schuman v. State, 106 Ark. 362, 153 S. W. 611; Dewein v. State, 120 Ark. 302, 311, 179 S. W. 346; Hankins v. State, 133 Ark. 38–63, 201 S. W. 832, L. R. A. 1918D, 784.

Second. The appellant next contends that the court erred in its ruling in giving certain instructions on its own motion and in refusing prayers of appellant for instructions on the issue of insanity. The court, on its own motion, gave 14 instructions on this issue, and it appears that counsel for appellant presented 19 prayers for instructions on the same issue, which the court refused.

In Bell v. State, 120 Ark. at page 553, 180 S. W. 195, this court, having under consideration rulings of the trial court in giving and refusing prayers for instructions on the issue of insanity where the crime charged was murder in the first degree, announced the law as follows:

"Where one is on trial for murder in the first degree, and the state proves the killing under circumstances that would constitute murder in the first degree if the homicide was committed by a sane person, then if the killing is admitted and insanity is interposed as a defense such defense cannot avail, unless it appears from a preponderance of the evidence: First, that at the time of the killing the defendant was under such a defect of reason from disease of the mind as not to know the nature and quality of the act he was doing; or, second, if he did know it, that he did not know that he was doing what was wrong; or, third, if he knew the nature and quality of the act, and knew that it was wrong, that he was under such duress of mental disease as to be incapable of choosing between right and wrong as to the act done, and unable, because of the disease, to resist the doing of the wrong act which was the result solely of his mental disease. * * *

"But it must be remembered that one who is otherwise sane will not be excused from a crime he has committed while his reason is temporarily dethroned, not by disease, but by anger, jealousy, or other passion; nor will he be excused because he has become so morally depraved 'that his conscience ceases to control or influence his actions.' In other words, neither so-called 'emotional' nor 'moral' insanity will justify or excuse a crime."

In commenting upon the numerous prayers for instructions, at page 556 of 120 Ark., at page 196 of 180 S. W., we said:

"It is not surprising that in the multiplicity of prayers for instructions on this issue, many of them conflicting, long, and involved, that the trial court, being under the necessity of ruling promptly and not having the time to investigate, should have failed to give a consistent and harmonious charge in conformity with the law as above announced, which we find to be the case. We cannot comment upon each assignment of error and upon the separate prayers in which error appears without unnecessarily extending this opinion. * * * Instead of the numerous instructions that were given, it would have been far better if the court, after announcing the law as to the burden of proof and declaring the above tests, had instructed the jury that if they believed from the preponderance of the evidence that the appellant was insane they should acquit him, otherwise they should convict him of the crime charged. If counsel had succinctly presented their respective contentions in a few plain prayers embodying the above tests, doubtless the errors that crept into the court's charge would have been avoided."

[2] What we said above in Bell v. State is apposite to this case. In the case at bar the court did not heed the admonition and follow the suggestion of this court in Bell v. State, supra, and as a result we find that the court's charge on the issue of insanity is inconsistent and well calculated to mislead the jury. While some of the instructions given by the court on its own motion correctly declare the law in conformity with the law as announced by this court in Bell v. State, supra, other instructions were entirely out of harmony with the law as there declared, and were contradictory and inconsistent in themselves. The same may be said with reference to the prayers of appellant for instructions. While some of them declared the law in conformity with previous decisions of this court, others did not.

The court told the jury, in several of the written instructions given on its own motion, that, if the appellant at the time of the killing was laboring under a mental delusion, and the killing was the result of such delusion and the appellant was unable to control his act, the jury should acquit him, provided they found the imaginary facts, if real, would justify or excuse the crime. For instance, the court gave instruction No. 10, as follows:

"You are further instructed that, upon a consideration of all the testimony in the whole case, including the testimony tending to show defendant's insanity or mental incapacity for the commission of crime, if you find he was at the time of the act of killing laboring under a mental delusion, and was unable to control his act, then you should acquit the defendant, provided you find that the imaginary facts, if real, would justify or excuse the crime."

In Bolling v. State, supra, we approved the rules announced in McNaughten's Case, and one of them is to the effect that—

"If the defendant labors under a partial delusion only, and is in other respects sane, he must be considered in the same situation as to responsibility as if the facts with respect to which the delusion exists were real."

We also recognized this as announcing a correct legal principle in Smith v. State, 55 Ark. 259–263, 18 S. W. 237. It will be observed that the court in its instructions applied this principle broadly and without qualification or limitation, which makes all the instructions containing this provision in direct conflict with the rule or doctrine as announced in the third test in Bell v. State, supra, and which had been firmly established in previous decisions of this court. Williams v. State, 50 Ark. 511–518, 9 S. W. 5; Green v. State, 64 Ark. 523–534, 43 S. W. 973; Metropolitan Life Ins. Co. v. Shane, 98 Ark. 132, 135 S. W. 836.

Commenting upon the legal tests there laid down in Bell v. State, supra, we said:

"The second and third of these tests are applicable in every case where the evidence tends to prove, as it does here, that the accused. at the time of the alleged criminal act, was afflicted with that disease of the mind termed by medical experts, alienists, and authors on medical jurisprudence as 'paranoia,' which has progressed to the 'stage of persecution.' This disease manifests itself and is characterized by systematized delusions; that is, a delusion based on false premises, pursued by a logical process of reasoning to an insane conclusion. Taylor v. McClintock, supra. The victim of this disease, in its first stage, has apparently a sound mind upon all subjects except those coming within the particular sphere of his delusion, and he may then be able to control his actions with reference to his delusion. Hence the reason for the rule announced in McNaughten's Case, 10 Clark & Finley Rep. 199–211, and recognized by us in Bolling v. State, supra, that where one labors under a partial delusion only, and is not in other respects insane, he must be considered in the same situation as to responsibility as if the facts with respect to which the delusion exists were real. But where the disease has progressed to its second stage, according to Wharton & Stillé, in their excellent work on Medical Jurisprudence, pp. 828–1031b: The patient passes on to the formation or delusion of suspicion and persecution. He believes he is the object of evil designs of others; he is talked about and maligned; he is shunned, his plans are thwarted, he is unjustly dealt with, he is defrauded of his rights. * * * He may fasten his suspicion upon some particular person or persons. He meditates plans of protection, and then of resentment. He has now become the persecuted paranoiac, the most dangerous of all the insane.'

"In this second stage of the disease the mind of the victim of paranoia may have become so completely dominated by the disease as to render him incapable of controlling his actions with reference to the subject-matter of his delusions. The disease may have progressed to the extent that, in the language of Dean on Md. Jur. 497, 'The reason has lost its empire over the passions and the actions by which they are manifested to such a degree that the individual can neither repress the former nor abstain from the latter.' But he adds: 'It does not follow that he may not be in possession of his senses. The maniac may judge correctly of his actions without being in a condition to repress his passions and to abstain from the acts of violence to which they impel him.' Hence the reason for the third test mentioned above, approved by the best of modern authorities."

In the more recent case of Hankins v. State, 133 Ark. 38, at page 47, 48, 201 S. W. 832, 834 (L. R. A. 1918D, 784) we said:

"In approving these rules of McNaughten's Case, the court did not hold that the doctrine of irresistible impulse caused by disease of the mind would not be a good defense in cases where the evidence adduced warranted it. In Bolling v. State, supra, the court was of the opinion that the evidence did not warrant an instruction on irresistible impulse. * * * Now, it seems to us, en passant, that this court, in Bolling v. State, supra, did not have the correct view of the evidence on the issue of irresistible impulse, for the testimony tended to prove that Bolling was afflicted with paranoia, or delusional insanity, which had progressed to the stage of suspicion and persecution, in which state the homicidal tendency or mania is most pronounced."

[3, 4] In the record now before us, there is testimony tending to prove that the appellant was afflicted with a disease of the brain, known as "partial insanity," "monomania," or, in modern psychiatry, as "paranoia," and that this disease had progressed to its second, or persecutory stage. There is also testimony from which the jury might have found that it had not progressed to that stage, and also testimony from which the jury might have found that the appellant was not insane at all. Such being the testimony, it was peculiarly a question of fact for the jury to determine whether or not the appellant was sane or insane according to the tests laid down in Bell v. State, supra. The rule that, "where one labors under a partial delusion only and is in other respects sane, he must be considered as if the facts with respect to which the delusion exists were real," according to the doctrine of Bell v. State, supra, and Hankins v. State, supra, is limited in its application solely to those cases where the testimony proves, or tends to prove, that the disease, paranoia, is in its first or earliest stage of development.

Paranoia is a progressive disease of the brain. Webster defines it as follows:

"A chronic form of insanity characterized by very gradual impairment of the intellect, systematized delusion, and usually by delusions of persecutions or mandatory delusions producing homicidal tendency. In its mild form paranoia may consist in the well-marked crotchetiness exhibited by persons commonly called cranks."

See, also, the New Int. Enc., "Paranoia": 1 Wharton & Stillé's Med. Jur. p. 827, 1031 (a) (b), (c); 2 Clevenger's Med. Jur. of Insanity, p. 860 et seq. 865; Americana, Ency. Brit. In its first and earliest stage the manifestations of delusion indicating a disease of the mind are yet so mild and unpronounced that its victim, notwithstanding his mental delusion, may still be able to exercise his will and control his actions with reference to these delusions. Where such is the case, there is no room for the doctrine of irresistible impulse caused by a disease of the brain. But where the disease has progressed or evoluted to its second or persecutory stage, or subsequent stages, and its form and hallucinations are such as to indicate that its victim, because of the disease, is no longer able to control his will and actions, then the doctrine of irresistible impulse as laid down in the third test, supra, is applicable. See Legal Medicine (Stewart) p. 405, § 158.

[5] Where the defense is insanity, as was said in Hankins v. State, supra:

"It is an issue of fact for the jury to determine whether the accused at the time of the alleged act was afflicted with a mental disease, and an issue of law as to whether the mental disease is such as to render him irresponsible. Therefore the issue of responsibility or irresponsibility in such cases should be submitted to the jury under proper instructions."

And in that case, after approving the legal tests or rules as announced in Bell v. State, supra, we further said:

"These legal rules for determining the issue of guilt or innocence, where the defense is insanity, give the jury a simple and definite guide, announced by those learned in the law, and they cover every possible phase of testimony that may arise in any case."

In cases where the defense is insanity, if counsel in the preparation of their prayers for instructions and trial courts in framing their charges to the jury will but follow the legal test or rules as approved and announced by this court in the recent case of Bell v. State, supra, and Hankins v. State, supra, they cannot go astray. As was said in Kelly v. State, 226 S. W. 137:

"In those cases the whole subject was gone into as thoroughly as could be done by the writer, who voiced the opinions of the court. We deem it unnecessary here to do more than call the attention of court and counsel to those cases which must have been overlooked in the framing of the charge to the jury."

For the error in the rulings of the court in its instructions to the jury, the judgment is reversed, and the cause will be remanded for a new trial.

———

GREGG et al. v. SANDERS et al. (No. 15.)

(Supreme Court of Arkansas. May 30, 1921.)

1. Eminent domain ⟐⟐145(1) — "Just compensation" in benefits received where public use for which land taken enhances value of remainder.

It is the general rule that, where the public use for which a portion of a man's land is taken so enhances the value of the remainder as to make it of greater value than the whole was before the taking, the owner has received "just compensation" in benefits within the meaning of Const. art. 2, § 22.

[Ed. Note.—For other definitions, see Words and Phrases, First and Second Series, Just Compensation.]

2. Eminent domain ⟐⟐145(1)—Rule of damages reduced by benefits not applicable to case of improvement district constructing improvement paid for by special assessment.

The rule that where property is taken, but the public use for which it is taken so enhances the value of the remainder that there is no diminution in the original value, such special benefits constitute just compensation to the owner within the Constitution, has no application to a taking by an improvement district organized to construct an improvement to be paid for out of special assessments levied on contiguous land benefited; the benefits by the improvement cannot be applied in measuring the compensation to be paid the property owner to reduce the amount to be recovered.

Appeal from Pike Chancery Court; James D. Shaver, Chancellor.

Suit between T. J. Gregg and others and H. C. Sanders and others. From judgment for the latter, the former appeal. Affirmed.

Jno. W. & Jos. M. Stayton, of Newport, for appellants.

Geo. A. Hillhouse, of Newport, and Brundidge & Neelly, of Searcy, for appellees.

McCULLOCH, C. J. The Newport levee district was created as an improvement district by the Legislature (Acts 1917, p. 1285), for the purpose of constructing a levee along the bank of White river, through the city of Newport and contiguous territory. The right of eminent domain was conferred for the purpose of acquiring lands to be used in the construction of the levee. The cost of the improvement included, of course, all costs of acquiring rights of way and other expenses to be paid for by assessments on benefits accruing to the real property affected by the improvement. Appellees are the owners of a tract of land containing approximately 17 acres situated just outside of the city of Newport and fronting on White river, and in the construction of the levee the district took and used about five acres of said land of appellees, all of which land so taken fronted on White river. The remainder of the land of appellees is within the bounds of the district, and the benefits thereto from the construction of the levee have, of course, been assessed and will be taxed proportionally for the construction of the improvement. It is not shown in the present record how the district acquired the right of way over the land of appellees, and, as no point is made in this case on that proposition, we assume that the lands were taken without the exercise of the right of eminent domain in the manner prescribed by the statute.

Appellees instituted this action against the district to recover damages laid in the aggregate sum of $3,500, and specified as being the sum of $3,000, the value of five acres taken and used by the district, and the further sum of $500 for damages to the remainder of the land. Appellants (said district and its commissioners), in addition to denials of the allegations of the complaint with respect to the extent of the injury and amount of damages recoverable, pleaded that "the benefits received by said land, local and peculiar to the same, over and above the benefit which said tract receives in common with the other lands in Newport levee district, greatly exceeds the value of the land taken by said district for the right of way of its levee over the lands of the plaintiffs."

The cause was tried before a jury on conflicting testimony in regard to the value of the land taken and the injury or benefit to the remaining land not taken, and the jury returned a verdict in favor of appellees, fixing the damages at the aggregate sum of $1,500, without apportioning the same between the items of damages charged in the complaint.

The court in one of its instructions told the jury, over the objections of appellants, that in ascertaining the amount of damages for taking the land the jury "should not take into consideration any benefits which may accrue by the building of the levee to the remainder of the original tract." An exception was saved to this ruling of the court, and the only question presented on this appeal is whether or not the court erred in holding that appellees' right of recovery for the value of the lands taken and used by the district in the construction of the levee could not be reduced by the benefits accruing to the remainder of the tract.

[1] The only provision in the Constitution of this state in which it is attempted to regulate or restrict the right of eminent domain for public purposes is in section 22, art. 2,

of the Constitution of 1874, which declares that—

"Private property shall not be taken, appropriated or damaged for public use, without just compensation therefor."

The inquiry which, therefore, must always arise in the interpretation of a statute authorizing the taking of property or in any proceeding to recover compensation therefor, is: What is "just compensation" under the given state of facts? Counsel for appellants contend that decisions of this court in Cribbs v. Benedict, 64 Ark. 555, 44 S. W. 707, and City of Paragould v. Milner, 114 Ark. 334, 170 S. W. 78, have established the rule of "just compensation" in cases similar to this to be that—

"Where the public use for which a portion of a man's land is taken so enhances the value of the remainder as to make it of greater value than the whole was before the taking, the owner in such case has received just compensation in benefits."

Such is undoubtedly the rule established by the great weight of authority in cases where property taken for general public use and compensation is to be awarded at the expense of the public. Many cases on that subject are referred to in Cribbs v. Benedict, supra, and there are many other cases to the same effect decided before that time and since.

The rule has been generally applied in instances of the taking of land for use as a public highway or park or such other public use where the compensation is to be awarded out of public funds. The case of City of Paragould v. Milner, supra, is an instance of that character, and we have no doubt as to the correctness of that rule as applied to the facts of such a case. Cribbs v. Benedict, supra, was, however, a case where there was involved an improvement district formed under general statutes for the purpose of constructing a drainage ditch, and we announced the same rule in that case. The question of damages was not, however, involved in that case further than to determine whether or not the statute which failed to provide for the payment of damages was valid, and this rule was merely stated as one of the reasons for holding the statute to be valid without providing for the payment of compensation other than impliedly by the benefits which would accrue from the construction of the improvement. This was stated only as one of the reasons why the statute was valid, and the decision was undoubtedly correct, even though we concluded that this particular reason for so holding was unsound.

[2] We have reached the conclusion that the application of that rule, in a case where an improvement district which is organized for the purpose of constructing an improvement to be paid for out of special assessments levied on contiguous lands benefited by the improvement, cannot be applied in measuring the compensation to be paid to a property owner whose land is taken for the construction of the improvement so as to reduce the amount to be recovered to the extent of the benefits accruing to the other lands in the district which are to be specially taxed for the purpose of paying for the improvement.

It is found, on examination, that all of the cases cited in Cribbs v. Benedict, supra, are those which relate to payment of compensation for property taken for public use where the question of special benefits arising from a purely local improvement to be paid for by special assignments did not arise. In a few cases, like the present one, the authorities are to the contrary. It is readily seen that the application of this rule to the payment of compensation for property taken by an improvement district constitutes a double charge for the benefits accruing to the remainder of an owner's land where a part has been taken for the construction of the improvement. The benefit to the remaining portion of the land is paid for by the owner in special assessments levied to defray the cost of the improvement, and if the owner is compelled to credit the amount of these benefits on the compensation to which he is entitled for that portion of his land which has been taken, the effect is to charge him twice for the benefits. In other words, he will be paying for the benefits in the assessments which are levied against his property, and also the second time when he credits it on the compensation which is due him for his property which has been taken.

Mr. Hamilton, in his work on Taxation by Assessment (volume 1, § 67), states the rule as follows:

"Whatever method of exacting compensation from the property owner for benefits enuring to him is adopted, the property owner cannot be charged twice for the same benefit. * * * So if, under the local statute, certain benefits may be made the basis of a local assessment against the property, such benefits cannot be set off against damages as the property owner can subsequently be compelled to pay therefor in such assessment proceedings."

This rule was announced by the Supreme Judicial Court of Massachusetts in the case of Garvey v. Inhabitants of Revere, 187 Mass. 545, 73 N. E. 664, though that court has steadily adhered to the general rule hereinbefore stated that compensation may be made for property taken for public use in the benefits to accrue to the remainder of the property of the same owner. This doctrine was also announced by Judge Mitchell with much force in the case of State ex rel. v. District Court, 66 Minn. 161, 68 N. W. 860. In that case the court dealt with a statute, one section of which authorized the appraisal of damages for property taken for use in providing a local improvement, and another section which provided for the assessment of such special benefits which was to form the basis of taxes levied to defray the cost of the improvement. The Minnesota court had, in other decisions, announced the general rule as hereinbefore recited with reference to the reduction of damages by compensation in benefits, and reiterated that rule in the case just cited, but held that the rule had no application to an instance where the cost of the improvement for which the land was taken was to be defrayed by the imposition of taxes based upon special benefits. The court said:

"But counsel's contention is that where, as under this statute, the cost of the acquisition of the land is to be defrayed by special assessments upon the property specially benefited thereby, a deduction of special benefits to the remainder of the tract from the value of the part taken is unconstitutional, for the reason that this remainder is subject to assessment, to the extent of these same special benefits, to defray this same cost, which would result either in the owner being taxed twice for the same improvement, or else in depriving him of his property without just compensation. It is very clear that, if the statute will accomplish this result it, or some part of it, is unconstitutional and void.

"We need not stop to inquire what are benefits 'resulting from such taking,' which are to be deducted in the condemnation proceedings—whether they are only those resulting from the mere taking of the land by the city, disassociated from the appropriation and improvement for the purpose for which it is taken, or whether they also include those that will result from such appropriation and improvement, although it is very difficult to conceive what benefits can result to the residue of a tract from the mere act of taking a part of it. But it is very evident from the language of section 8 that the benefits for which assessments are there required include the same benefits which are required to be deducted by section 7. Moreover, the language of section 8 is mandatory and not merely permissive. It not only requires such assessments to be made, but also that they shall be made on all property benefited. Hence, if all the provisions of both sections are carried into effect, the result will be either that the landowner will be deprived of his property without just compensation, or else he will be taxed unequally, by being compelled to pay twice for the same thing."

It is true that in that case the court held that the two sections were in conflict and that the last one, which provided for taxation upon the whole of the benefits without taking into consideration the damages, was void. We have no such question as that in the present case, but the decision of the Minnesota court is persuasive to the extent that it lays down the principle that it would constitute a double charge against the property owner to make him contribute out of benefits received to the cost of improvement by paying assessments, and also by compelling him to credit the benefits which accrue from the improvement on the compensation to which he is entitled for damages on account of other portions of his land being taken.

The theory upon which rests the proceedings for the construction of local improvements by the imposition of special assessments on contiguous property is that the improvement is public in its nature to the extent that the right of eminent domain may be authorized, but it is local to the extent that special benefits accrue to the adjoining property. The improvement is paid for out of special assessments based on such benefits, and when property is taken for use in the construction of the improvement, full compensation must be awarded in order to satisfy the requirements of the Constitution without deduction of the benefits which are to accrue to the owner on the remainder of his property. Damages to the property not taken may, however, be balanced off against the benefits which accrue, for damages must necessarily be taken into account in the estimate of benefits There are authorities to the effect that if the benefits to the remaining property exceed the damages to the property taken, such benefits may be used in the reduction of the damages and the excessive benefits over damages may be the basis of a local assessment. And it has been held that it is proper "to deduct the amount of the special tax levied for a given improvement, from the amount of the benefits received from such improvement, and to treat the amount thus obtained as the net amount of benefits to be deducted from the amount of damages." Hamilton on Taxation by Assessment, § 67; Carroll v. City of Marshall, 99 Mo. App. 464, 73 S. W. 1102; Village of Grant Park v. Trah, 218 Ill. 516, 75 N. E. 1040. There is no question, however, presented in the facts of the present case as to whether the benefits will exceed the amount of taxes assessed against them. It does not appear even that the jury awarded any damages for injury to the remainder of the property not taken, though they may have done so under the testimony and instructions of the court. No point is raised that the benefits exceeded the taxes levied and should be, to that extent, credited on the compensation to be allowed for the damages to the property taken. At any rate, we are convinced that the true rule is that, whether the taxes levied amount to the full amount of the appraised benefits or not, there can be no deduction of any part of the benefits from the compensation to be allowed to a property owner for that portion of his property which is taken and used in the construction of the improvement, for the reason that he pays for his benefits in taxes, the same as other property owners, and it would destroy the rule of equality to require him to contribute to the common use any part of his property without compensation.

There was no error committed, and the judgment should be affirmed. It is so ordered.

HARTON v. DURHAM.   (No. 16.)

(Supreme Court of Arkansas.   May 30, 1921.)

Reformation of Instruments ⬦45(4) — Evidence held to support decree of reformation.

In vendor's suit to reform description in a deed, evidence that the deed was prepared by purchaser and included a description of land not a part of the "B. land" intended to be conveyed *held* to support decree of reformation excluding such land.

Appeal from Faulkner Chancery Court; Jordan Sellers, Chancellor.

Action by B. M. Harton against O. E. Durham, in which defendant cross-complained, seeking reformation of a deed, and the cause being transferred to the chancery court, decree was rendered in defendant's favor reforming the deed, and plaintiff appeals. Affirmed.

J. C. & Wm. J. Clark, of Conway, for appellant.

R. W. Robins, of Conway, for appellee.

McCULLOCH, C. J. Appellant instituted this action against appellee in the circuit court of Faulkner county to recover damages sustained by reason of an alleged breach of the covenants of warranty of title contained in a deed which purported to convey, among other tracts of land, one described as "all that part of the north half of the north half of section twenty-one (21) in township six (6) north, range fourteen (14) west, lying in Conway county, Arkansas." Appellee answered, alleging that the above-described tract of land was included in the deed of conveyance to appellant by mistake, and he asked that the answer be taken as a cross-complaint, that the cause be transferred to the chancery court, and that the deed be reformed so as to exclude said tract from the conveyance. The cause was transferred, and on final hearing the chancery court rendered a decree in appellee's favor reforming the deed.

The facts of the case, as disclosed in the evidence adduced by appellee, are as follows:

Mrs. Mary M. Barnes owned a tract of unimproved timber lands containing a little less than 800 acres, situated partly in Faulkner and partly in Conway counties, Ark., and known as the "Barnes land." The tract included the whole of section 16, township 6 north, range 14 west, which

is intersected by Cadron creek, the boundary line between the two counties mentioned above. The remainder of the land owned by Mrs. Barnes is described in the deed as "all that part of the north half of the north half of section 21, township 6 north, range 14 west, situated in Faulkner county." In other words, Mrs. Barnes owned all that part of the north half of the north half of section 21 east of Cadron creek in Faulkner county, but did not own that part of said north half of the north half of section 21 lying west of Cadron creek in Conway county.

Appellee was a member of a copartnership composed of himself and W. S. Cazort and Guy Farris, engaged in the real estate business in the city of Conway, and Mrs. Barnes listed her lands with them for sale at the net price of $20,000. Appellant knew that the lands were listed with appellee's firm for sale, but opened negotiations direct with Mrs. Barnes and offered her $20,000 for the lands. Mrs. Barnes declined to negotiate with appellant and referred him to appellee's firm, with whom appellant then began negotiations, which resulted in an agreement for the sale of the lands for the sum of $21,500 of which $20,000 was to go to Mrs. Barnes and the remainder to appellee's firm as commission on the sale.

The firm of selling agents did not have a description of the land by sections or subdivisions thereof, and the only description they had was that which mentioned the land as the "Barnes land." They furnished to appellant an abstract of title to the Faulkner county lands, and after examination by appellant's attorney a deed was prepared by the latter and turned over to one of the members of appellee's firm to forward to Mrs. Barnes for execution at her home in New York. The deed thus prepared by appellant's attorney correctly described the "Barnes land," as above set forth, and also purported to convey "all that part of the north half of the north half of section twenty-one (21) in township six (6) north, range fourteen (14) west, lying in Conway county, Ark.," which was not owned by Mrs. Barnes. The members of appellee's firm were, as before stated, unacquainted with the accurate description of the land, and the deed was forwarded to Mrs. Barnes without a verification of the descriptions to ascertain whether or not the lands were correctly described in the deed.

When Mrs. Barnes received the deed she declined to execute and deliver it until the money was paid over to her in New York, and appellant declined to send the money to New York until the deed was executed. In order to bring about the sale, appellee, Durham, agreed to have Mrs. Barnes convey the land to him, and he in turn to make the conveyance to appellant. Appellee was in Hot Springs at the time this controversy arose, and arrangements were made with him by conversation over the telephone by one of the members of the firm. This arrangement was carried out, and Mrs. Barnes erased appellant's name from the deed which had been prepared by his attorney and inserted the name of appellee, Durham, and executed the deed in that form and forwarded the same to one of the banks in Conway for delivery. In the meantime appellee had returned home, and a deed was prepared for him to execute conveying the land to appellant, and the same description was used as in the other deed, including the tract in section 21 lying west of Cadron creek. The two deeds were delivered simultaneously when the payment was made by appellant.

It is shown that appellee was not interested in the sale further than to earn the commission, and that he accepted the deed from Mrs. Barnes and in turn conveyed to appellant merely as the most convenient way of consummating the sale in the emergency which arose by reason of the fact that Mrs. Barnes refused to execute the deed until the money was paid over in New York and appellant refused to pay the money until the deed was ready for delivery at his home in Conway. Appellee shows further that there was no intention on his part or on the part of appellant to negotiate and consummate a sale for any other lands except the tract known as the "Barnes land," which was wild timbered land with which appellant was more familiar than appellee, and that the inclusion of the tract in section 21 west of Cadron creek not owned by Mrs. Barnes and partly in cultivation was the result of a mistake in the preparation of the deed. These facts being sufficiently proved, appellee is entitled to the relief which was granted by the chancery court. The facts are, however, disputed by appellant, but, after careful consideration of the testimony, we are of the opinion that the findings of the chancellor are well supported by the testimony, and that the proof is "clear, unequivocal, and decisive" that the tract of land in question was included in the deed by mistake.

There is a sharp conflict in the testimony on the point whether or not a member of appellee's firm furnished a memorandum containing a description of the land. Suffice it to say that the preponderance of the testimony on this subject is not against the findings of the chancellor. But, aside from that question, it is undisputed that appellant knew that he was buying a tract of wild and unoccupied timber land owned by Mrs. Barnes, and that he was not to get any cultivated lands. The tract in controversy contains 18 acres, of which 11 acres is in a high state of cultivation.

Our conclusion is that the decree of the chancellor was correct, and the same is affirmed.

COSBY v. HURST. (No. 14.)

(Supreme Court of Arkansas. May 30, 1921.)

1. **Attorney and client ⟨key⟩182(3), 192(2) — Lien at common law was on evidence in hands of attorney, and not on debt itself, and complaint must show possession of evidence of indebtedness.**

A common-law lien of an attorney employed to collect an indebtedness was on the evidence of indebtedness in the hands of the attorney and not on the debt itself, and hence in an action in equity by an attorney against his client to have his lien fixed on proceeds of insurance policy, complaint did not state facts which would confer a lien, where it did not allege that the policy or other evidence, if any, was in the possession of the attorney.

2. **Equity ⟨key⟩48—Sole basis of suit to recover money is inadequacy of legal remedy.**

The basis of a suit in equity for the sole purpose of recovery of money is the inadequacy of legal remedy, and hence equity has no jurisdiction of a suit by an attorney against his client and an insurance company to recover compensation for his efforts in bringing about a settlement under a life policy on the ground of insolvency of the client, on the theory of equitable garnishment; there being no allegations setting forth grounds for equitable relief.

3. **Equity ⟨key⟩136—Formal statement of no adequate remedy at law ineffective.**

Nothing is added to a complaint in equity by the formal statement that plaintiff has no adequate remedy at law, being a mere conclusion.

Appeal from Washington Chancery Court; Ben F. McMahan, Chancellor.

Suit by G. A. Hurst against C. A. Cosby and another. Decree for plaintiff, and the named defendant appeals. Reversed and remanded, with directions.

John Mayes, of Fayetteville, for appellant. W. N. Ivie, of Rogers, and H. L. Pearson, of Fayetteville, for appellee.

McCULLOCH, C. J. Appellee is an attorney at law and a member of the Washington county bar, and he instituted this action against appellant in the chancery court of that county to recover the amount of fees alleged to be due for professional services rendered in connection with a claim of appellant against an insurance company. It is alleged in the complaint that appellant made claim in the sum of $1,000 against the Fayetteville Mutual Benefit Association under a policy issued to appellant's wife, now deceased, that appellant employed appellee to collect the claim from said insurance company, and that appellee "prepared the necessary papers and presented the matter to the Fayetteville Mutual Benefit Association in the usual manner," that after such presentation and after investigation made by the said company the latter notified appellee that the claim would be allowed, and would be paid as soon as reached in the regular order of business; that subsequently appellee was notified by the insurance company that payment would be made on June 15, 1919, and that a check was made out by the company payable to appellee as attorney for appellant, but that after the performance of said services by appellee, and before the delivery of the check, appellant employed another attorney to handle the claim for him, and notified the said insurance company not to turn over the check or make any payment to appellee. The complaint contains the further allegation that appellant is insolvent, and the prayer of the complaint is that a lien be declared in appellee's favor for the amount of his fee in the sum of $150 on said claim against the insurance company, which said company was made a defendant in the action. Appellant appeared by attorney, and demurred to the complaint on the ground that it did not state a cause of action within the jurisdiction of the chancery court, and also filed a motion to transfer the cause to the circuit court. The court overruled the demurrer and the motion to transfer, and, the defendant declining to plead further, decree was rendered against him and against the Fayetteville Mutual Benefit Association for the recovery of the sum of $150, which was declared to be a lien on appellant's claim against said insurance company.

[1] It is conceded by counsel for appellee that there is no statutory lien in appellee's favor, for the reason that there was no judgment rendered and no action instituted on appellant's claim against the insurance company. Crawford & Moses Digest, §§ 628, 6304. But it is contended that appellant had a common-law lien, independent of the statute, on the papers in his hands evidencing appellant's claim against the insurance company. The validity of this sort of claim was recognized by this court in the case of Gist v. Hanly, 33 Ark. 233. But the difficulty with appellee's contention is that he has not set forth in his complaint a state of facts which would confer a lien, in that he does not allege that the policy or other evidence, if any, of appellant's claim against the insurance company was turned over to him and still remains in his possession. Such a lien at common law was, as we understand, on the evidence of indebtedness in the hands of the attorney, and not on the debt itself. This being true, appellee has not shown in the complaint that he had in his possession any papers on which he was entitled to a lien.

[2, 3] It is next contended by counsel for appellee in support of the decree that the allegations of insolvency were sufficient to confer jurisdiction on the chancery court, and that the insurance company, as appellant's debtor, having been made a party to the suit, appellee is entitled to an equitable garnishment. The mere allegation of insolvency was not, however, sufficient to show that the remedy at law was inadequate and it does not show a cause of action cognizable in equity. The basis of a suit in equity for the sole purpose of recovery of money is the inadequacy of legal remedies. Davis v. Arkansas Fire Ins. Co., 63 Ark. 412, 39 S. W. 258; Euclid Avenue National Bank v. Judkins, 66 Ark. 486, 51 S. W. 632; Horstmann v. La Fargue, 140 Ark. 558, 215 S. W. 729; Henslee v. Mobley, 280 S. W. 17. There are no allegations which set forth grounds for equitable relief. Newman v. Neel, 227 S. W. 977. Nothing is added to the force of the complaint by the formal statement that appellee had no adequate remedy at law. That was a mere conclusion, and according to the facts alleged there was no reason why a garnishment in an action at law would not have afforded an adequate remedy.

The court erred in refusing to transfer the cause to the circuit court, and for that reason the decree is reversed, and the cause is remanded, with directions to transfer the cause, unless further grounds are stated for equitable relief.

T. A. THOMAS & SONS v. WOLFE. (No. 27.)

(Supreme Court of Arkansas. May 30, 1921.)

Master and servant ⟬=219(5)—Risk of unloading logs held assumed.

Danger attendant upon unloading logs from wagon standing on rough, sloping ground, in passing on the lower side thereof to a point between the front and hind wheels, and releasing the bumper which held the logs in place on the wagon by knocking or pulling out the buck pin, was obvious, and servant doing so assumed the risk or injury, where he was intelligent and experienced in this particular character of work, and was cognizant of a defect in the bumper which caused the buck pin to hang, as well as the sloping condition of the yard where he stopped the wagon for the purpose of unloading.

Appeal from Circuit Court, Clark County; Joe Hardage, Special Judge.

Suit by G. W. Wolfe against T. A. Thomas & Sons. Judgment for plaintiff, and defendants appeal. Reversed, and cause dismissed.

Jno. H. & D. H. Crawford, of Arkadelphia, for appellants.
W. H. Mizell, of Arkadelphia, for appellee.

HUMPHREYS, J. Appellee instituted suit against appellants, a partnership composed of T. A. Thomas and his sons, in the Clark circuit court, to recover damages in the sum of

$8,500, on account of the loss of a leg, occasioned through the alleged negligence of said appellants in providing a defective wagon from which, and a rough, sloping yard upon which, to unload logs.

Appellants filed an answer denying that the injury resulted on account of their negligence, and interposed the further defenses of assumed risk and contributory negligence by appellee. The cause was submitted upon the pleadings, evidence, and instructions of the court which resulted in a verdict and judgment in favor of appellee for $500. From the judgment, an appeal has been duly prosecuted to this court.

At the conclusion of the evidence, appellants requested the court to direct a verdict in their favor, which the court refused to do, over their objection and exception. Appellants now insist that the court committed reversible error in refusing to grant the request.

The facts necessary to a determination of this question are as follows: Appellee was 48 years of age, and experienced in cutting and hauling logs. Appellants were operators of a sawmill. They employed appellee to haul logs to their log yard situated upon their tramway. They maintained a contrivance called a log boom in the yard for the purpose of pulling the logs by a wire cable from the yard and loading them upon the tram cars. The wire cable was short, and this necessitated the unloading of the logs near the tramway. In loading the logs on the cars by this process, trash and dirt were drawn toward the tramway, which made the ground rough and sloping at that point. Nathan Thomas, one of the appellants, told appellee in unloading to drive as close to the track, or tramway, as he could conveniently do, so that the logs, when unloaded, could be picked up easily by the loader. Appellants furnished appellee an 8-wheel wagon, for the purpose of hauling the logs, which contained a defect in the front bumper block that caused the buck pin to stick, so that it had to be knocked loose with an ax in order to release, or throw out, the bumper block. The purpose of removing the bumper blocks was to permit the logs to be rolled off the wagon. The pin could have been removed with the use of a cant hook by one standing at the front end of the wagon, or by going to a point between the front and hind wheels on either the upper or lower side of the wagon, or under the wagon. There was no danger incident to removing the pin by the cant-hook method or by pulling or knocking it out from the upper side or under the wagon, but there was great danger incident to removing it if standing on the lower side of the wagon. It was possible for an active, alert man, without being injured, to remove it while standing on the lower side of the wagon.

The condition of the yard at the point where appellee was directed to unload the logs, as well as the condition of the bumper, was obvious, and known to appellee. In obedience to instructions theretofore given, appellee, on the morning of August 11, 1919, drove the wagon loaded with logs in the open space near the tramway and boom, so that it stood on rough, sloping ground. He passed on the lower side of the wagon, and, when he reached a point between the front and hind wheels, he knocked the pin loose with an ax, which released the front bumper block, and, before he could get out of the way, a log rolled off and crushed his leg, which necessitated amputation. Appellee was alone when the injury occurred. He had knocked out the bumper and unloaded logs in the same way and at the same place before that time without being injured.

According to the undisputed facts detailed above, the danger attendant on unloading logs from a wagon standing on rough, sloping ground, in passing on the lower side thereof to a point between the front and hind wheels and releasing the bumper which held the logs in place on the wagon by knocking or pulling out the buck pin, was obvious. The danger was obvious, and necessarily appreciated by appellee, for he was intelligent and experienced in this particular character of work. He was cognizant of the defect in the bumper which caused the buck pin to hang, as well as the sloping condition of the yard where he stopped the wagon for the purpose of unloading the logs. There were other methods by which he could have released the bumper with safety to himself; for example, by the use of the cant hook, or by going on the upper side or under the wagon and knocking or pulling out the buck pin. The undisputed facts bring the instant case clearly within the doctrine of assumed risks. Precedent for the application of that doctrine to the facts in the instant case will be found in the cases of Williams Cooperage Co. v. Kittrell, 107 Ark. 341, 155 S. W. 119; Wisconsin & Ark. Lbr. Co. v. Price, 125 Ark. 480, 188 S. W. 1171; St. L. S. W. Ry. Co. v. Compton, 135 Ark. 563, 205 S. W. 884; Hunt v. Dell, 226 S. W. 1055.

For the error in refusing to direct a verdict in favor of appellants, the judgment is reversed, and the cause dismissed.

WILSON et al. v. MATTIX et al. (No. 17.)

(Supreme Court of Arkansas. May 30, 1921.)

1. **Drains ⟂16—County court held not to have authority to dissolve drainage district.**

Neither Crawford & Moses' Dig. § 3607 et seq., nor any other sections confer authority on the county court to dissolve drainage districts after they have been organized, and in absence of statute it cannot exercise that authority.

2. **Courts ⟂183—County court held without jurisdiction to restrain unlawful acts under void district organization.**

The county court has no jurisdiction to relieve property owners by injunction against unlawful acts of the commissioners in attempting to proceed under a void drainage district organization.

Appeal from Circuit Court, Craighead County; R. H. Dudley, Judge.

Proceedings by A. B. Wilson and others against J. E. Mattix and others to dissolve a drainage district. Complainants obtained judgment in the county court, and on defendants' appeal to the circuit court the proceedings were dismissed, and complainants appeal. Affirmed.

H. M. Mayes, of Jonesboro, for appellants.

Basil Baker and Horace Sloan, both of Jonesboro, for appellees.

McCULLOCH, C. J. This is a proceeding instituted in the county court of Craighead county to dissolve a drainage district which had been previously organized pursuant to the general statute providing for the organization of such districts by an order of the county court. Crawford & Moses' Digest, § 3607 et seq.

Appellants are the owners of real property in the district, and after the district had been organized and put into operation by the assessment of benefits, issuance of bonds, the letting of a contract for the construction of the improvement and after the work of constructing the improvement had been begun, they filed their petition in the county court praying for an order of the court dissolving the district. They alleged, in substance, that the lands in the district were generally uncultivated and of little value, that the cost of the construction of the improvement, when considered in comparison with the value of the lands, was prohibitive, and that the imposition of the tax on the land would be so burdensome as to constitute confiscation of the property, and that the commissioners had increased the cost from the sum of $60,000, as first estimated, to the sum of $130,000, as finally estimated as the actual cost of the construction. It was further alleged in the petition that the commissioners were proceeding with the construction of the drainage ditch without first obtaining an outlet for the discharge of the water. There was also a general allegation that the improvement, as contracted for, is improvident and will not result in the benefit of the property in the district. There are other allegations not of sufficient importance to mention.

The commissioners of the district appeared by their attorneys as parties for the purpose of resisting the order of dissolution, and on the hearing the county court made an order declaring the district dissolved, and appointed a committee of property owners "to ascertain all claims and charges of any and all persons or firms against said district and to ascertain the financial condition of said district." The order of the court further enjoined the commissioners from proceeding with the construction of the ditch and ordered that the funds on hand to the credit of the district be applied to the payment of current accounts against the district, and the remainder tendered to the purchaser of the bonds, and further that, if the committee should find that bonds had been issued and sold, and the money received by the commissioners, the sum found to be due "shall be by the clerk of this court extended against said lands on the ditch tax book * * * in proportions as assessments have been made and filed by the commissioners of said district, and the same shall be collected by the collector of Craighead county for the year 1921 and paid out in full liquidation of the proper claims against said district." In other words, the court dissolved the district and made a general order winding up its affairs and provided for payment of its indebtedness. The commissioners filed an affidavit and bond for appeal and prosecuted their appeal to the circuit court, and in that court they filed a written motion to dismiss the cause on the ground that the county court had no jurisdiction to adjudicate the dissolution of the district. The circuit court sustained the motion and dismissed the proceedings. The record of that court recites that the cause was heard on the motion of appellees, and the record brought up from the county court. An appeal has been duly prosecuted to this court.

[1] The statute confers no authority upon the county court to dissolve drainage districts. Crawford & Moses' Digest, § 3607 et seq. On the contrary, the statute (section 3609) provides that the order of the county court establishing such a district "shall have all of the force of a judgment," and that, if no appeal from said order be taken within 20 days, "such judgment shall be deemed conclusive and binding upon all the real property within the bounds of the district, and upon the owners thereof." Another section of the statute (3630) provides that the district shall not cease to exist upon the completion of the system, but shall continue for the

purpose of maintaining the ditches and keeping them clear from obstructions, etc. A search of the statute from end to end fails to disclose any provision which, either in express terms or by implication, can be construed to confer authority on the county court to dissolve the district after it has been organized. The county court, in the absence of a statute, cannot exercise that authority. Morrilton Waterworks Imp. Dist. v. Earl, 71 Ark. 4, 69 S. W. 577, 71 S. W. 666; Hall v. Callaway, 94 Ark. 49, 125 S. W. 1015; Taylor v. Wallace, 143 Ark. 67, 219 S. W. 314.

The case last cited is conclusive of the question now under discussion. In that case we held that, inasmuch as the general statute in regard to organization of road improvement districts (Act 338 of the General Assembly of 1915) did not confer authority upon the county court to remove commissioners, the power could not be exercised by that court. In disposing of the question, we said:

"The power conferred upon the county court to appoint three road commissioners at the time of making the order establishing the road district, pursuant to the terms of the act, is a special, and not a general, power. No such power exists in the county court except by enactment of the General Assembly. The general power of supervision by the county court over roads conferred by the Constitution invests said court with no such power or authority. The delegation of power being special, the extent thereof is limited to the express grant."

[2] Nor does the county court possess jurisdiction to exercise the relief to the property owners by injunction against unlawful acts of the commissioners in attempting to proceed under a void organization. If it be conceded that the petition contains allegations which would justify relief in the proper court, it is certain that the county court has no jurisdiction to grant the relief sought in the prayer of the petition.

Judgment affirmed.

POE v. POE. (No. 23.)

(Supreme Court of Arkansas. May 30, 1921.)

1. Divorce ☞29—Remedy of divorce for indignities only for unavoidable evils.

The remedy of divorce, under Crawford & Moses' Dig. § 3500, as to indignities, is for evils which are unavoidable and unendurable, and which cannot be relieved by reasonable exertion by the parties.

2. Divorce ☞29—Cruelty of wife to stepchildren in absence of husband not ground.

Where defendant wife, who was sued for divorce on account of indignities to her husband, consisting of cruel treatment of his children by his first wife, had merely whipped the children in the absence of plaintiff husband, she having treated them kindly at other times, the husband is not entitled to divorce under Crawford & Moses' Dig. § 3500, as to indignities.

3. Divorce ☞286—Allowance of alimony will not be disturbed except for changed conditions.

In the absence of any showing that the court's allowance of alimony to defendant wife until further order was too much, it must be presumed the allowance was fair, and it will not be changed until the conditions of the parties make it necessary for the chancellor to order or modify it.

Appeal from Garland Chancery Court; J. P. Henderson, Chancellor.

Suit by H. E. Poe against Laura Poe. From decree for defendant, plaintiff appeals. Affirmed.

H. E. Poe brought this suit against his wife, Laura Poe, to obtain a divorce on the statutory grounds of cruel and barbarous treatment endangering his life and of such indignities offered to his person as render his condition in life intolerable.

The wife denied the allegations of the complaint and asked for alimony.

It appears from the record that the first wife of the plaintiff was killed in a cyclone, and that some of their children were injured so badly that they were carried to a hospital for treatment. The defendant was a nurse in the hospital and nursed the plaintiff's children while there. This led to the plaintiff's hiring her to become his housekeeper. She went to his home as housekeeper and remained there in that capacity until their marriage, about two years after they first became acquainted.

Edgar Poe, the oldest son of the plaintiff, was a witness for him. According to his testimony, he was 13 years of age, and during most of the time that plaintiff and defendant lived together as husband and wife, the latter treated the children well. Sometimes she would whip them, and sometimes she would make them do without their dinner. Sometimes they had been doing wrong, and sometimes they had not, when she punished them. She struck the witness four or five times with something other than a switch. She hit him once with a shovel and once with a stick of stove wood. One time she hit him in the mouth and knocked six of his teeth loose, and it was about a month before his mouth got well.

The defendant was a Seventh Day Adventist and would not let the children do any work on Saturday, but sometimes attempted to make them work on Sunday. At one time his stepmother bruised his face and eye when she attempted to correct him, and also choked him so that she left her finger prints on his throat when she got through. All the matters testified to happened while the plaintiff was away from home.

Albert Poe, the second son of the plaintiff, testified that most of the time their stepmother treated the children well, but that she whipped them with the first thing she could get her hands on; that she would get mad quickly, and at one time got mad and tied him and his older brother with a rope; that his father was out in the back yard when this was done. He also corroborated the testimony of his brother about their stepmother hitting him in the mouth with a shovel and knocking six of his front teeth loose. The teeth became tight again in about a month.

The plaintiff was a witness for himself. According to his testimony, a great many Seventh Day Adventist preachers called at his home, and he objected to this. His wife was good to her stepchildren the greater part of the time, but when she got mad she used no judgment and would whip them with anything that she got her hands on. She could not control her temper. He was not present at any time when she abused the children, except once when she tied two of them with a rope. He went into the house and cut the rope. His oldest son, Edgar, left home while the plaintiff was absent, because he could not get along with his stepmother. The defendant wrote the plaintiff about this and said that Edgar had run away. She said in her letter that she did not think the matter was serious, but that she had not seen Edgar since he left. Edgar went to his aunt's home when he left. The plaintiff went to see Edgar before he returned home. When he got home, he asked his wife what she meant by treating his children the way she did while he was gone. He told his wife that it looked like she could not get along with his children while he was away. His wife told him that it was all Edgar's fault and that she had not hurt him. The plaintiff then told her that they would have to move from the country into town because his work was in town. The defendant said that she would not go to town with him, and he then took his children to their aunt's and left home. This was in May, 1919, and the plaintiff and the defendant have not lived together since. The plaintiff made no effort to find any particular place to live, but told the defendant that if she wanted to go to town that he would find a place, but it was on the condition that she would treat the children better. He further stated that she had never offered to go back to him.

On cross-examination he admitted that he had been keeping company with other women since he and his wife had separated. He further admitted that he could not afford

to take his wife back the way his children felt about her. He also stated that there was no possible chance for him and his wife to ever live together and get along, and that he was afraid to trust his children with her. His children showed great distress at being carried back to the defendant, and he did not have the heart to do this.

Two other witnesses for the plaintiff testified that they had worked at the plaintiff's house and had seen the defendant whip the children "awful hard." One of them said that the husband would bring home meat to be cooked, and that the defendant refused to cook it because it was against her religion to eat meat. She would only feed them on milk, potatoes, and bread.

The defendant was a witness for herself. She admitted tying the two boys together one time with a rope, but said that she was playing with them. She denied positively that she had whipped the children severely, as testified to by them. She said that she had only whipped them moderately for the purpose of correcting them, and had required them to do but little work on Sunday. She stated that the plaintiff had left their home in the country in May, 1919, and had willfully remained away ever since. She continued to reside at their home after the plaintiff had left for nearly a year and left there because her husband came home during her absence and took the furniture out of the house. She stated that she had always treated her husband kindly and still wanted to make up and live with him. He left her on account of her alleged mistreatment of his children. She denied having mistreated them and asked him not to leave her. Her testimony was corroborated by that of her mother, who had made frequent and lengthy visits at their home while they lived together as husband and wife.

Several other witnesses in the neighborhood testified that they visited the home of the plaintiff and defendant frequently, and that the defendant always treated the plaintiff well and never cruelly whipped or mistreated his children.

The chancellor found the issues in favor of the defendant and dismissed the plaintiff's complaint for want of equity. He allowed the defendant alimony in the sum of $20 per month until further orders of the court.

A decree was entered of record according to the findings of the chancellor, and to reverse the decree the plaintiff has prosecuted this appeal.

James D. Hogue, of Little Rock, for appellant.

A. J. Murphy, of Hot Springs, for appellee.

HART, J. (after stating the facts as above). The grounds for a divorce are statutory merely. Among other causes, our statute provides that the chancery court shall have power to dissolve and set aside a marriage contract where either party shall be guilty of such cruel and barbarous treatment as to endanger the life of the other, or shall offer such indignities to the person of the other as shall render his or her condition intolerable. Crawford & Moses' Digest, § 3500.

[1] In the first place, it may be said that the remedy of divorce, under this clause of our statute, is for evils which are unavoidable and unendurable and which cannot be relieved by reasonable exertion by the parties seeking the aid of the courts. Meffert v. Meffert, 118 Ark. 582, 177 S. W. 1.

[2] In the second place, it may be said that the main grounds relied upon by the plaintiff in support of his bill for divorce is cruel treatment by his wife to his children by his first wife.

In discussing similar statutes it is generally held by text-writers that mistreatment of a stepchild in itself alone will not afford grounds for a divorce. It is only where the cruelty towards the child is habitual or exercised with the intent of causing suffering to the parent that a cause of divorce on this account will arise. Bishop on Marriage, Divorce and Separation, vol. 1, par. 1586; Nelson on Divorce and Separation, vol. 1, par. 301; 9 R. C. L. § 129, p. 347; 19 C. J. p. 50; Barker v. Barker, 25 Okl. 48, 105 Pac. 347, 26 L. R. A. (N. S.) 909; Friend v. Friend, 53 Mich. 543, 19 N. W. 176, 51 Am. Rep. 161; Melvin v. Melvin, 130 Pa. 6, 18 Atl. 920; and Rigsby v. Rigsby, 82 Ark. 278, 101 S. W. 727.

The stepmother might be guilty of great cruelty to her stepchildren, and yet not be guilty in that respect to her husband. This is well illustrated in the present case. According to the testimony of the children and of the father, the stepmother had a very violent temper which she could not control, and when she got mad she would whip them with the first thing she got her hands on. The whippings were all done in the absence of the husband, and according to the testimony of the children themselves, their stepmother whipped them only when she became mad at them. The stepmother denies having whipped them too severely at any time. If the testimony of the children is to be accepted, it does not show that the stepmother whipped them because she was mad at their father and intended by so doing to make him suffer. The children testified that for the most part she treated them kindly. So it may be said that the plaintiff has failed in the respect just set forth to establish any grounds for divorce under the statute. The testimony showed that on account of their difference in religion, the mistreatment of plaintiff's children by his first wife by the defendant, and from other causes, that their marriage was an unhappy one. Our statute, however, has not made these things a ground

of divorce, and the parties must bear the consequences of having made an unwise marriage.

Therefore the chancellor was right in dismissing the plaintiff's complaint for want of equity.

[3] No point is specially made on the fact that the chancellor allowed the defendant alimony in the sum of $20 per month. This allowance was in the usual form, "until the further orders of the court." It does not appear from the record that the allowance was too much. In the absence of any showing to that effect, it must be presumed that the allowance was fair, and it will not be disturbed until the changed conditions of the parties make it necessary for the chancellor to alter or modify it.

It follows that the decree must be affirmed.

THOMAS v. STATE.   (No. 24.)

(Supreme Court of Arkansas.   May 30, 1921.)

1. Perjury ⊕=13—Defendant who induced his wife to make false affidavit cannot be guilty of "perjury," offense being "subornation of perjury."

Where defendant induced his wife to make a false affidavit, and it was charged that he coerced her into making the same, he is not guilty of "perjury," which is defined by Crawford & Moses' Dig. §§ 2588 and 2589, as a willful and corrupt swearing of any material matter in any cause, or the willful and corrupt swearing to any affidavit, but can only be guilty of "subornation of perjury," defined in section 2592, as the procuring of any other person by any means whatsoever to commit any willful and corrupt perjury, etc.

[Ed. Note.—For other definitions, see Words and Phrases, First and Second Series, Perjury; Subornation of Perjury.]

2. Perjury ⊕=13—Where defendant induced his wife to swear to false affidavit, he is not guilty of subornation of perjury unless she knew of the falsity.

Under Crawford & Moses' Dig. § 2592, defendant who induced his wife to make a false affidavit as to the loss of an automobile is not guilty of subornation of perjury unless the wife knew that the statements in the affidavit were false, for the offense consists in procuring any other person to commit any willful and corrupt perjury.

Appeal from Circuit Court, Lincoln County; W. B. Sorrells, Judge.

Lee Thomas was convicted of perjury, and he appeals. Reversed, and cause remanded.

H. K. Toney and L. Dewoody Lyle, both of Pine Bluff, for appellant.

J. S. Utley, Atty. Gen., and Elbert Godwin and W. T. Hammock, Asst. Attys. Gen., for the State.

⊕=For other cases see same topic and KEY-NUMBER in all Key-Numbered Digests and Indexes

SMITH, J. Appellant, Lee Thomas, was tried and convicted under an indictment charging him with the crime of perjury. The indictment alleges that he falsely, willfully, and corruptly made affidavit before a notary public that a certain automobile, owned by his wife, had been stolen, when in truth and in fact it had not been stolen, and that the false affidavit was made for the purpose of collecting certain insurance against the theft of the car.

The testimony in the case shows that Thomas did not make the affidavit, but that it was made by his wife in his presence. Thomas admits the recitals of the affidavit were false, and that he knew they were false; but he says his purpose was to deceive his wife about the car and make her believe it had been stolen. The testimony tended to show that Mrs. Thomas did not know the recitals in the affidavit she made were false.

At the trial the court charged the jury that—

"It is not necessary to sustain a conviction that the defendant be present at every step of the commission of the crime, but if the defendant was present at any time, and while present aided or assisted, encouraged, or being present consented to its commission, then he would be guilty."

The court refused to give an instruction requested by appellant which told the jury that a conviction could not be had unless the affiant, Mrs. Virgie Thomas, appellant's wife, knew that the car had not been stolen at the time she made the affidavit.

It is apparent from the instruction given and the one refused that the cause was submitted upon the theory that, if appellant had induced his wife to make a false affidavit in regard to the theft of the car, and was present when the affidavit was made, he was as guilty of the crime of perjury as he would have been if he had himself made the false affidavit. Appellant was not indicted as having coerced his wife, in his presence, to commit the crime of perjury.

[1] We think a fundamental error was made in the trial of the cause. Under the laws of this state, one who, himself, swears falsely and corruptly, commits the crime of perjury. If he induces another to do so, he commits the crime of subornation of perjury. These are distinct offenses and are separately defined in our statutes.

The definition of "perjury" as contained in sections 2588 and 2589 of C. & M. Digest is as follows:

"Sec. 2588. Perjury is the willful and corrupt swearing, testifying or affirming falsely to any material matter in any cause, matter or proceeding before any court, tribunal, body corporate or other officer having by law authority to administer oaths.

"Sec. 2589. The willful and corrupt swearing, affirming or declaring falsely to any affidavit, deposition or probate authorised by law to be taken before any court, tribunal, body politic or officer shall be deemed perjury."

"Subornation of perjury" is defined in section 2592 as follows:

"Sec. 2592. Subornation of perjury is the procuring of any other person, by any means whatsoever, to commit any willful and corrupt perjury in any cause, matter, proceeding, affidavit, deposition or probate in or concerning which such other person shall be legally sworn, affirmed or declared."

Appellant's offense, under the state's testimony, consisted in inducing his wife to make a false affidavit, and that offense is not perjury, but is subornation of perjury.

The conviction must therefore be reversed, because appellant has been convicted upon a charge for which he was not indicted.

[2] Inasmuch as the cause is to be remanded, and appellant may be reindicted for the offense of subornation of perjury, we take occasion to say that the instruction requested by him set out above should be given when he is placed upon his trial for subornation of perjury.

In 21 R. C. L. p. 276, it is said:

"Subornation of perjury is the crime of procuring another to commit perjury either by inciting, instigating or persuading the guilty party to do so. It is necessary that the perjury be actually committed to complete the crime. The suborner must also be aware that the person suborned intended to commit perjury."

A similar statement of the law is found in Wharton's Criminal Law, vol. 2 (11th Ed.) § 1593; 30 Cyc. 1423; 21 Standard Enc. of Procedure, 828.

Such is the necessary meaning of section 2592 of C. & M. Digest, set out above. It is not sufficient that the suborner procures another person to testify falsely; but the requirement of the statute is for the person procured, "by any means whatsoever, to commit any willful and corrupt perjury," that is, the person swearing, must know the fact sworn to is false.

The judgment of conviction will therefore be reversed, and the cause remanded.

LOUISVILLE WOOLEN MILLS v. KINDGEN.

(Court of Appeals of Kentucky. May 20, 1921.)

1. **Master and servant ⟜358—Involuntary appearance before Compensation Board held not to estop prosecution of common-law action by infant unlawfully employed.**

After an infant, through his statutory guardian, had begun a common-law action for injuries received by him while he was employed in violation of law, and thereby elected to pursue that remedy instead of to claim compensation under the Workmen's Compensation Act, which election he was authorized to make by Ky. St. Supp. 1918, § 4911, the subsequent appearance of the guardian in proceedings before the Compensation Board begun by the master, in which the guardian attacked the jurisdiction of the Board and offered evidence to show that the employment was willful and in known violation of law, does not estop the plaintiff from pursuing his common-law action after the Compensation Board had decided it was without jurisdiction because the employment was in violation of law, especially where the judge before whom the common-law action was pending had decided in a previous case, as yet unreversed, that a decision by the Compensation Board that the employment was in violation of law, was a prerequisite to a suit at common law.

2. **Master and servant ⟜358—Court's acceptance of finding of Compensation Board that infant was unlawfully employed held error.**

Since a finding by the Compensation Board that the employment of an infant was willful and in known violation of law is not a prerequisite to the infant's right to elect to sue at common law under Ky. St. Supp. 1918, § 4911, it was technical error for the court in an action by the infant begun before proceedings were instituted before the Compensation Board to accept as final the Board's finding that the employment was in known violation of law.

3. **Master and servant ⟜358—Infant unlawfully employed held not estopped from prosecution of common-law action by reliance on finding of Compensation Board.**

An infant is not estopped from prosecuting a common-law action for injuries while he was employed in violation of the law by insisting in that action that the master, who had instituted proceedings before the Compensation Board to have compensation awarded to the infant, was concluded by the Board's finding that the employment of the infant was willful and in known violation of law, though the Board had no jurisdiction to make such finding after the infant had previously elected to proceed at common law.

4. **Election of remedies ⟜12—Adoption of erroneous remedy is not election against proper remedy.**

One who prosecutes an action or suit upon a remedy which he erroneously supposed he had, and is defeated therein, is not

concluded by his election from prosecuting his action or suit in the proper forum.

5. **Election of remedies ⟜7(1)—Appearance before tribunal chosen by adversary whose jurisdiction is contested is not election.**

A party does not elect a remedy by his involuntary appearance before a tribunal in a proceeding instituted by his adversary, in which proceeding he contested the jurisdiction of the tribunal.

6. **Appeal and error ⟜1051(2)—Erroneous acceptance of finding by Compensation Board sustained by undisputed evidence is harmless.**

Error by the trial court, in an action at law for injuries to an infant servant, in accepting as final the decision of the Compensation Board that the infant was employed willfully and in known violation of law, is not prejudicial to the master, where that fact was established by undisputed evidence in the action at law, in view of Civ. Code Prac. §§ 134, 338, 756, preventing reversal for error not operating to substantial prejudice of appellant.

7. **Appeal and error ⟜854(2)—Correct judgment not reversed for erroneous reason.**

A judgment, if correct, will not be reversed, though based by the trial court upon an erroneous reason.

8. **Master and servant ⟜95—Infant held unlawfully employed.**

In an action for injuries to an infant servant, evidence on behalf of the master that plaintiff furnished an employment certificate issued by the superintendent of schools as required by Ky. St. § 331a, subsec. 3, which correctly showed his age to be 15, and authorized employment only for filling boxes, but that the employer's superintendent put the infant to work at a carding machine contrary to the express prohibition of subsection 9, shows conclusively that the employment of the infant was willful and in known violation of the law.

9. **Appeal and error ⟜1060(1)—New trial should be granted for prejudicial denial of right to be heard in person and by counsel.**

A litigant has a right to be heard by himself and counsel, and, if this is denied him by the court, a new trial should be granted, provided the error was sufficiently prejudicial to warrant the conclusion that the litigant had not had a fair and impartial trial.

10. **Appeal and error ⟜516—Argument objected to must be made part of bill of exceptions.**

Improper argument of counsel will not be considered on appeal unless made a part of the record by bill of exceptions.

11. **Appeal and error ⟜688(2)—Party must show nature of argument which he claims he was prohibited from making.**

Asserted error in denying to a party the right to make an argument on an issue cannot be considered on appeal unless the proposed argument is brought before the appellate court by bill of exceptions.

⟜For other cases see same topic and KEY-NUMBER in all Key-Numbered Digests and Indexes

12. Appeal and error ⟐⟐688(2)—Record held not to show denial of right to make proper argument.

In an action for injuries to an infant employee, where the court properly directed the jury to render a verdict for plaintiff and submitted to them only the question of damages, asserted error in denying leave to defendant's counsel to argue from the evidence as to mitigation of damages is not established where no avowal was made of the proposed argument, where there were no facts in evidence tending to mitigate the damages, and where defendant's counsel was permitted to argue on the measure of damages which was the only issue submitted to the jury.

13. Master and servant ⟐⟐218(7), 228(1)—Contributory negligence and assumption of risk not defenses to recovery by illegally employed infant.

In an action at law for injuries to an infant while he was willfully employed in known violation of law, contributory negligence and assumption of risk are not available to the master as defenses.

14. Trial ⟐⟐118—Counsel cannot argue to jury against adverse rulings of the court.

Rulings by the court in the course of the trial adverse to the contentions of counsel, even if erroneous, are the law of the case for that trial, and counsel is not permitted to argue to the jury against such rulings.

15. Appeal and error ⟐⟐714(5)—Court can consider undenied statement in brief in connection with silence of record.

Though the briefs of counsel cannot be considered as the record before the Court of Appeals, that court can consider a statement in appellee's brief that appellant's counsel was permitted to argue on the only question submitted to the jury which was undenied by appellant's reply brief in passing upon an asserted error in refusing to permit appellant's counsel to argue a specified issue, where the record was silent as to what, if any, argument was permitted.

16. Damages ⟐⟐132(12)—$10,000 for loss of right arm of 15 year old boy held not excessive.

In an action by a 15 year old boy for the loss of his right arm after attempts had been made to save it for several weeks after the accident, during which he suffered excruciating pain, a verdict for $10,000 damages is not so excessive as to show passion or prejudice on the part of the jury, and will not be set aside.

Appeal from Circuit Court, Jefferson County, Common Pleas Branch, Fourth Division.

Action by Bernard Kindgen, by his statutory guardian, against the Louisville Woolen Mills. Judgment for plaintiff, and defendant appeals. Affirmed.

Baskin & Vaughan, of Louisville, for appellant.

Richard P. Dietzman, Chas. Carroll, Martin T. Moran, and Geo. A. Schuler, all of Louisville, for appellee.

THOMAS, J. This action was brought in the Jefferson circuit court by the appellee and plaintiff below, Bernard Kindgen, an infant, by his statutory guardian, against the appellant and defendant below, Louisville Woolen Mills, seeking to recover damages against the defendant in the sum of $30,000 resulting from injuries sustained by plaintiff while he was employed by defendant, as alleged, in "willful and known violation" of the Child Labor Law (subsection 9 of section 331a, Kentucky Statutes), and upon trial there was a verdict against defendant for the sum of $10,000, which the court declined to set aside upon defendant's motion for a new trial and rendered judgment against it for that amount, to reverse which defendant prosecutes this appeal.

To understand the grounds urged before us for a reversal, it will be necessary to give a brief history of the proceedings had in the case from the time of the filing of the petition to the rendition of the judgment, and also to state some of the undisputed and admitted facts upon which the suit was based. The injury sued for occurred on October 11, 1918, and was caused by plaintiff having his right arm caught in the flywheel of some machinery while he was at work at and around a carding machine and while he was employed to oil and clean that and perhaps other pieces of machinery, and his arm was mashed, lacerated, and torn so that it had to be amputated some weeks afterwards, when it became evident that it could not be saved, and during which time plaintiff suffered intense and excruciating pains. There were also injuries to other parts of his body. At the time of his employment, as well as at the time of the injury, he was but slightly past 15 years of age, of which fact defendant had knowledge through a certificate furnished it by plaintiff at its request, but, notwithstanding it through its foreman in charge continued plaintiff in its employ and assigned him to the work above stated. The petition relies solely upon the prohibited employment of plaintiff as a ground for recovery, making no reference to any act of negligence committed by defendant. The answer contained two paragraphs, the first of which was a denial, and the second relied on contributory negligence, which was denied by a reply, the latter pleading being filed May 19, 1919. On June 7, 1919, an amended answer was filed in which defendant set up the fact that it was operating under our statute commonly known as Workmen's Compensation Act, being chapter 33, p. 354, Session Acts 1916, as amended by chapter 176, p. 690, Session Acts 1918, and being chapter 137, vol. 3, present Kentucky Statutes; that the plaintiff had by writing accepted the provisions of that act, and it alleged that the Workmen's Compensation Board, provided for therein, had exclusive jurisdiction of the matters complained of in the petition, and it relied upon the facts so pleaded by it in abatement of the jurisdiction of the circuit court in which the suit had been brought. A reply to that pleading denied the exclusive jurisdiction of the Workmen's Compensation Board, and it further alleged that plaintiff sustained his injuries while he was "employed in willful and known violation" of the Child Labor Law, hereinbefore referred to, and that he, through his guardian, had elected to sue and recover damages for his injuries as if the Workmen's Compensation Act "had not been passed" (section 30 of that act, now section 4911, Kentucky Statutes); that reply to the amended answer was filed October 4, 1919, and on the 15th of that month an amended reply was filed by plaintiff in which he alleged that in June, 1919, and after the issues herein had been made up by the filing of the original reply, defendant, ignoring the pendency of this suit, applied to the Compensation Board, as provided by section 4932, vol. 3, of the Statutes, for the purpose of procuring a settlement of the claim; that defendant therein (plaintiff here) appeared before the Board and demurred specially to its jurisdiction upon the ground that he, through his guardian, had exercised the election which the Compensation Act gave him in section 4911, supra; and that the Board was thereby ousted of jurisdiction to consider the case in any of its phases, or to legally pass upon any question connected therewith. This objection to its jurisdiction was overruled by the Board, and it proceeded to hear evidence and determine whether plaintiff had been employed in "willful and known violation" of the Child Labor Law, which it found to be true and rendered an opinion to that effect. Its judgment stopped at that point, saying:

"And this award is limited to the ruling upon said issue. Bernard Kindgen, through his statutory guardian, has not elected to claim compensation under section 30 of the act" (now section 4911 of the Statutes).

Plaintiff filed with that amended reply a copy of the opinion and award of the Board of Compensation, and alleged that defendant, by invoking its jurisdiction, was estopped to deny that award, and that the finding of the Board that plaintiff was employed in "willful and known violation" of the Child Labor Law was conclusive upon it. On November 22, 1919, defendant filed a responsive pleading to that amended reply, but styled it "amended answer," in which it alleged that plaintiff appeared before the Board in the proceedings instituted by the defendant as above related, and that, after its plea to the jurisdiction was overruled,

each party introduced evidence as to the age of plaintiff at the time he was employed and at the time he was injured, and as to other facts bearing upon the nature of the employment, and that such appearance was an election on his part to prosecute the action before the Board; and it pleaded such facts in abatement of the common-law action in the circuit court. The record shows no responsive pleading to the one last referred to, and the parties went to trial, with the result above indicated.

At the close of all the evidence defendant moved the court to dismiss the action without prejudice, which was overruled, and it then moved for a peremptory instruction in its favor, which was also overruled, and both of which motions seem to have been made upon the ground that plaintiff, by his involuntary appearance before the Compensation Board and the introduction of testimony before it after its jurisdiction had been challenged, elected to proceed before it, and thereby waived his right to prosecute the common-law action. After the overruling of those motions and after the court had instructed the jury, the record shows this:

"After the instructions had been given and before argument counsel for defendant offered to argue with the testimony as admitted as a basis therefor circumstances in mitigation of damages, to which plaintiff by counsel objected, and the court sustained the objection to which the defendant, by counsel, excepted."

The court gave to the jury only one instruction, the first part of which directed a verdict for plaintiff, and the latter part of which stated the correct rules for the measurement of the amount of recovery, of which no criticism is made on this appeal. The alleged errors of the court in the rulings hereinbefore recited, with the peremptory instruction to find for plaintiff, constitute the errors relied on for a reversal of the judgment.

It is seriously insisted that the court erred in refusing to sustain defendant's motion to dismiss the common-law action without prejudice, and, failing to do that, in overruling its motion for a peremptory instruction upon the grounds, as stated, that plaintiff in appearing before the Compensation Board, though involuntarily and at the behest of defendant, waived his right to further prosecute this action, and thereby ousted the circuit court of any jurisdiction thereof. We cannot agree with counsel in this contention; but, if we should give the effect contended for to plaintiff's action in appearing before the Board under the circumstances, we are then of the opinion, as will hereinafter appear, that the alleged error of the court in overruling the motions referred to did not prejudicially affect the rights of defendant under the facts of this case.

[1] In disposing of this question we cannot

dismiss from our minds the inconsistent position (as it appears to us) assumed by counsel in its discussion. The ground of the contention is that in going before the Board, though involuntarily and for the purpose of responding to the proceedings instituted before it by defendant, plaintiff thereby abandoned his common-law action. The argument is founded upon the provisions of section 4911, supra, of the Statutes, which says:

"If a claim to compensation be made under this section, the making of such claim shall be a waiver and bar to all rights of action on account of said injury or death of said minor as to all persons, and the institution of an action to recover damages on account of such injury or death shall be a waiver and bar of all rights to compensation under this act."

In support of this point it is argued in brief that whichever of the two remedies is first adopted by the guardian of the infant if not killed, or by his representative if he is killed, ipso facto becomes the exclusive one, and it cannot thereafter be abandoned, but must be prosecuted to a finality. It is therefore said that in going before the Board, and in remaining before it until it determined the preliminary question as to the nature of the employment of plaintiff, he was compelled to thereafter prosecute his claim exclusively before that Board. But this conclusion, as we construe counsel's contention, destroys the grounds upon which it is made; for, if the first election constitutes the exclusive remedy, plaintiff in this case ousted the Board of jurisdiction by ignoring the Workmen's Compensation Act and bringing his suit for damages in the circuit court in defiance of the terms of that act. Just here it may be said that in the case of Frye's Guardian v. Gamble Bros. (afterwards appealed to this court and reported in 188 Ky. 283, 221 S. W. 870) the learned judge who tried this case, and before whom *that* one was pending, had construed section 4911 of the Statutes to mean that, before the guardian of an injured infant employee could make his election to ignore the provisions of the Compensation Act and sue at law for the recovery of damages to his ward, the Compensation Board should first determine the preliminary fact that the ward had been "employed in willful and known violation" of law, and at the time of the trial in this case that ruling of his honor had not been reviewed and reversed by this court. So that at the time of the making up of the pleadings in this case, and during the occurrences complained of, it had been judicially determined by the very court before whom this cause was pending that such proceeding for a determination by the Compensation Board was an essential prerequisite to the maintenance of a common-law action, although plaintiff in this case disputed that fact throughout the trial.

[2] It was held by us in the Frye Case that no such determination by the Compensation Board was necessary to enable the guardian or the administrator of the infant to make the election given by section 4911, and, of course, it results that the determination by the Board in this case of the nature of the employment of plaintiff was without any foundation in law, and, technically, the court erred in accepting its finding as to the unlawful nature of plaintiff's employment as final. But there is considerable authority, however, supporting the contention of plaintiff's counsel in their brief in this case, that defendant is bound by that finding, since it voluntarily went before the Board after the institution of this suit for the very purpose of obtaining, among other things, that adjudication. Stevenson v. Miller, 2 Litt. 306, 13 Am. Dec. 271; Asbury v. Powers, 65 S. W. 605, 23 Ky. Law Rep. 1622; Doniphan & Smoot v. Gill, 1 B. Mon. 199; and Bledsoe v. Seaman, 77 Kan. 679, 95 Pac. 576.

[3] But, whether this be so or not, we are thoroughly convinced that plaintiff is not estopped from prosecuting this common-law action in the circuit court by his appearance before the Board under the circumstances stated; nor is he estopped to do so by insisting in his common-law action that defendant is bound by the judgment or award of the tribunal to which it applied, and before which it forced plaintiff, for the purpose of obtaining that specific adjudication.

[4] The supposed authority to the contrary relied on by defendant's counsel, is 15 Cyc. pp. 259 and 260, wherein the text says:

"Any decisive act of a party, with knowledge of his rights and of the facts, determines his election in case of conflicting and inconsistent remedies."

But on the same page it is said that—

"The mere commencement of any proceeding to enforce one remedial right, in a court having jurisdiction to entertain the same, is such a decisive act as constitutes a conclusive election, barring the subsequent prosecution of inconsistent remedial rights."

And, further along, on page 262 of the same volume, it is said that one who prosecutes an action or suit based upon a remedy which he erroneously supposed he had and is defeated therein is not concluded by his election from prosecuting his action or suit in the proper forum. Such an erroneous proceeding does not constitute such a "decisive act of the party" as is required to create a binding election. See Hillerich v. Franklin Insurance Co., 111 Ky. 255, 63 S. W. 592, 23 Ky. Law Rep. 631.

[5] But, for an election, which was superinduced by the "decisive act of the party," to be binding, it should be one of his own voluntary choosing, and not one growing out of his involuntary appearance before a tribunal in a proceeding instituted by his adversary, and which proceeding he contested

by all of the methods known to the practice. At the time of plaintiff's appearance before the Board, as we have seen, the very court before whom his cause was pending had held that the Board had jurisdiction to determine a necessary preliminary fact to the maintenance of his common-law action, and that judgment of the court was in force and unreversed, and it was to save his rights under that ruling that he appeared before the Board in response to a notice procured by defendant. The opinion in the Frye Case from this court settled the question of the jurisdiction of the Board to determine the preliminary question adversely to the way it had been held by the trial court, thus demonstrating that the Board was without jurisdiction of the proceedings instituted before it by the defendant after this suit was filed. If there were no other reasons for denying the binding effect of plaintiff's appearance before that Board, under the conditions appearing, we would hesitate long to give it such effect under the facts and circumstances of the case. We therefore conclude that the court did not err in overruling the motion to dismiss the cause without prejudice, nor in failing to peremptorily instruct the jury to find for defendant.

[6] It is next insisted that, in view of this court's opinion in the Frye Case, the court committed error in accepting as final the finding of the Board in the proceeding instituted before it by defendant to the effect that plaintiff had been "employed in willful and known violation" of law. Besides what has already been said concerning this contention, we may here add that the court was justified in assuming the existence of that fact, and in peremptorily instructing the jury accordingly, under the undisputed and admitted facts in the record as proven by defendant's witnesses; and the practice in this jurisdiction is that a judgment will not be reversed for an error which does not operate to the substantial prejudice of the appellant. Civil Code, §§ 134, 338, and 756. Numerous cases are cited in the notes to the sections referred to in substantiation of the rule.

[7] As an outgrowth of that rule, it has been constantly and uniformly held by this court that a judgment, if correct, will not be reversed, though based by the trial court upon an erroneous reason. Prewitt v. Wilborn, 184 Ky. 638, 212 S. W. 442; Lunsford v. Hatfield Coal Co., 166 Ky. 119, 178 S. W. 1166; Graves County v. First National Bank, 108 Ky. 194, 56 S. W. 16, 21 Ky. Law Rep. 1656; Shewmaker v. Yankey, 66 S. W. 1, 23 Ky. Law Rep. 1759; Dudley v. Goddard, 12 S. W. 302, 382, 11 Ky. Law Rep. 480; and Davison v. Johnson, 113 Ky. 202, 67 S. W. 996, 24 Ky. Law Rep. 27, and other cases therein cited.

[8] At the trial defendant read the testimony of its superintendent and foreman, who, it seems, employed plaintiff, and who also assigned him to his work. That witness testified that some two months or more before the accident he was furnished plaintiff with an employment certificate issued by the superintendent of schools in and for the city of Louisville, as is required by subsection 3 of section 331a, supra, of the Statutes. That certificate is filed with the deposition of the witness, and it shows that plaintiff was born on June 11, 1903, and in it plaintiff was permitted to be employed by the defendant, Louisville Woolen Mills, but prohibits it from employing him at any work except filling boxes." Instead of assigning to him the work mentioned in the certificate, the superintendent admits that he put him to work at a carding machine and imposed upon him the duty of oiling and wiping that machine and perhaps other machines around it, all at a place surrounded with other dangerous machinery, and all of which was directly in contravention of the express provisions and prohibitions of subsection 9 of the last section referred to. This testimony, as we have said, was introduced by defendant itself. It is true the witness says that he instructed plaintiff to not clean the machine or oil or wipe it while in operation, but he admits that he employed plaintiff "to operate or work at a carding machine in the mill," and further says that, "It was the duty of those working at a piece of machinery to keep it oiled and cleaned." Defendant also introduced its general manager, but neither proved nor offered to prove any material fact by him militating in the least against the violations of defendant as shown by the testimony of the superintendent, or which would in any wise relieve defendant of the charge of employing plaintiff "in willful and known violation" of law, as denounced by the statute supra. These were the only witnesses introduced or offered to be introduced by defendant, and if it possessed other testimony contradicting the fact as to the nature of plaintiff's employment, or any other one affecting its liability, there is nothing in the record to indicate it. In addition to the testimony of defendant's superintendent, the plaintiff himself testified to the character of his work, and under this testimony there is no contradiction of the fact that plaintiff was employed and put at work in a manner expressly denounced by the statute, which necessarily makes a case where the employment was in "willful and known violation" thereof. Under these circumstances, and following the rules of practice supra, there can be no escape from the conclusion that the court did not err in peremptorily instructing the jury to find for plaintiff, the amount to be measured by correct rules for the ascertainment of damages and of which no complaint is made.

[9] The next complaint of counsel is that relating to the argument proposed to be made

In "mitigation of damages" as embodied in the above excerpt from the bill of evidence. In disposing of this question it is needless for us to discuss the point, so ably argued by counsel, that a litigant has the right to be heard by himself and counsel, and if this is denied him by the court a new trial should be granted, provided the error was sufficiently prejudicial, in the opinion of the court, to warrant it in concluding that the complaining litigant has not had a fair or impartial trial. This guaranteed rule of practice is so fundamental as to require no citations of authorities by us to sustain it. But the record in this case presents no such question to us.

[10] It is the rule in this jurisdiction, by which this court has uniformly been guided, that improper argument of counsel will not be considered on appeal unless it is made a part of the record by a bill of exceptions, so that it may be determined from the argument itself whether it was proper or improper, and, if improper, whether it was sufficiently prejudicial to authorize a reversal of the judgment. The same rule prevails without exception, so far as we are aware, in all other jurisdictions. Some of the later cases from this court so holding are: Sparks v. Sipple, 140 Ky. 542, 131 S. W. 389; C. & O. R. Co. v. Stapleton, 154 Ky. 351, 157 S. W. 702; United Furniture Co. v. Wills, 158 Ky. 806, 166 S. W. 600; Pine Mountain Manufacturing Co. v. Bishop, 160 Ky. 575, 169 S. W. 1010; St. Paul, etc., Insurance Co. v. Kendle, 163 Ky. 146, 173 S. W. 373; and Chreste v. Louisville Railway Co., 173 Ky. 486, 191 S. W. 265.

[11] The converse of this rule must necessarily follow, since the reason requiring alleged improper argument to be brought before the appellate court in the manner indicated exists with as much force where a proposed proper argument was rejected by the court as where an improper argument was allowed over objections.

[12] There was no sort of avowal made by defendant's counsel in this case as to the nature of the argument that he expected to make or would have made but for the refusal of the court to permit him. Nor did he avow the substance of the proposed argument, or any facts or circumstances in the case looking to "the mitigation of damages," which he desired to discuss; the reason for which was, doubtless, that he could not well do so, since there are no such facts or circumstances appearing in the record.

[13] He had no right to discuss before the jury any contributory negligence of plaintiff, or any assumption of risk by him, since neither of these defenses were available to the defendant in a suit for damages to an infant employed in violation of the Child Labor Law. L., H. & St. L. R, R. Co. v. Lyons, 155 Ky. 396, 159 S. W. 971, 48 L. R. A. (N. S.) 667; Sanitary Laundry Co. v. Adams,

183 Ky. 39, 208 S. W. 6, and cases referred to therein.

[14] Neither could he argue the ruling of the court in holding as a matter of law that defendant was liable to the extent of the damages sustained, nor could he argue any other adverse ruling of the court during the trial, since those errors, if they were such, were for the time being, at least, the law of the case, and counsel under such circumstances is not permitted to take a contrary position before the jury, and cannot in his argument assail such rulings of the court in that trial. Harrison v. Park, 1 J. J. Marsh. 170, and Smith v. Morrison, 3 A. K. Marsh. 83. It is not claimed by counsel that he was deprived of the right to discuss before the jury every issue submitted to it by the instructions of the court, i. e., every fact legitimately bearing on the "measurement" of damages, which is an entirely different thing from "mitigation" of damages.

[15] On the contrary, it is stated in brief for plaintiff that defendant's counsel did argue before the jury facts legitimately bearing on the measurement of damages, and in a reply brief that statement is not denied. True it is that records before this court are not made up in briefs of counsel, but we think we can look to the circumstances related, together with the silence of the record as to defendant's counsel being entirely deprived of any argument, in reaching the conclusion that counsel was permitted to argue to the jury the only issue upon which argument could legally be made, which was the one relating to the measurement of damages. Somewhat fortifying the above position is the opinion in the case of Warner v. Commonwealth, 84 S. W. 742, 27 Ky. Law Rep. 219. In that case complaint was made by the appellant that his counsel was not permitted to read to the jury a certain writing or document pertaining to the Guiteau trial. One of the reasons given in the opinion for disallowing this supposed error was that—

"There was no avowal made as to what his counsel intended to read from the book, and this court cannot say that appellant was prejudiced in any way by the court's refusal to allow the extract to be read to the jury."

If it is essential that a proposed writing offered to be incorporated into the argument of counsel and as a part of it, but which the court refused, should be made a part of the record by an avowal, we see no reason why the same principle would not apply where the proposed argument was entirely verbal. Under the condition of the record we see no reason to sustain this contention.

[16] Lastly it is insisted that the verdict is excessive; but we think not. As stated, plaintiff's right arm was fearfully mangled. In the language of the plaintiff himself, it was "all chewed up." This condition of the arm was also testified to by the physicians

who amputated it. Some weeks passed in an effort to save the arm, but a gangrenous condition set up, and it had to be amputated. The flesh was all torn from it practically from the elbow to the wrist, leaving the bone exposed, and during that time plaintiff suffered great pain. He sustained other injuries to his head, side, and other parts of his body, which likewise produced considerable pain, but eventually healed without permanent impairing results. We held in the case of L. & N. R. R. Co. v. Copley, 177 Ky. 171, 197 S. W. 648, that a verdict for $12,000 for the loss of a leg was not excessive, and for the same injury a verdict for $15,000 was upheld as not excessive in the case of Standard Oil Co. v. Titus, 187 Ky. 580, 219 S. W. 1077. It is probably true that the loss of a right arm to a right-handed person is greater than the loss of a leg, not taking into consideration the element of pain and suffering following the injury. But however that may be, a verdict for $10,000 for the loss of an arm was upheld as not excessive in the case of L. & N. R. R. Co. v. Cason, 116 S. W. 716, and a verdict for a like amount for disfiguring an arm and rendering it practically useless was also upheld in the case of Gnau v. Ackerman, 166 Ky. 258, 179 S. W. 217. Plaintiff was a healthy young man before he sustained his injuries, and, judging from his testimony, he was at least reasonably intelligent. His power to earn money by physical efforts is largely curtailed, if not destroyed, and this, too, at the very beginning of his active life. In view of all the facts and in the light of the cases referred to, we cannot say that the verdict was superinduced by passion or prejudice on the part of the jury, or that it was not sustained by the testimony in the case.

Finding no error prejudicial to the substantial rights of the defendant, the judgment is affirmed.

BARDIN v. COMMONWEALTH.

(Court of Appeals of Kentucky.   May 27, 1921.)

1. Criminal law ⟜1056(1)—Failure to except to oral instruction estopped defendant from objecting on appeal.

In prosecution for removal of tree designating lot boundary under Ky. St. § 1256, defendant's failure to except to the action of the court in orally instructing the jury estopped him from objecting on appeal that instruction was not in writing.

2. Jury ⟜34(3)—Court not empowered to direct verdict against defendant whose plea is not guilty.

Under Const. Bill of Rights, § 7, and under the federal Constitution, guaranteeing to an accused the right to a trial by jury, the court has no right to direct a jury to find defendant

guilty where his plea is not guilty, though the evidence of his guilt may be convincing and wholly uncontradicted.

3. Criminal law ⟜308—Accused entitled to every reasonable doubt in favor of presumption of innocence.

An accused is entitled to every reasonable doubt in favor of the presumption of his innocence.

4. Criminal law ⟜742(1)—Jury sole judge of credibility of witnesses.

The jury is the sole judge of the credibility of the witnesses.

5. Criminal law ⟜741(1)—Weight of evidence for jury.

It is for the court to say what evidence is competent and to decide whether it is admissible, but after its admission it is for the jury to say what weight should be attached to it.

6. Municipal corporations ⟜678 — Trustees could order removal of tree in alley.

Town trustees have a right to order removal of a tree in an alley.

7. Boundaries ⟜56—Whether tree was in an alley and ordered removed by town authorities held for jury.

In a prosecution for removal of a tree alleged to have shown the boundary of a lot, in violation of Ky. St. § 1256, defended on the ground that the tree was in the alley, and that the town authorities had ordered its removal, the question of whether the tree was situated in the alley and had been ordered removed by the town authorities held for the jury.

Appeal from Circuit Court, Green County.

L. P. Bardin was convicted of removing a tree designating the boundary of a lot, and he appeals. Reversed for further proceedings, with directions.

J. H. Woodward, of Greensburg, for appellant.

Chas. I. Dawson, Atty. Gen., and W. P. Hughes, of Frankfort, for the Commonwealth.

QUIN, J. Ky. Stats. § 1256, provides:

"If any person unlawfully, but not with felonious intention, take, carry away, deface, destroy or injure any property, real or personal, or other thing of value not his own, or willfully and knowingly, without a felonious intention, break down, destroy, injure or remove any monument erected to designate the boundaries of this state, or any county, city or town thereof, or the boundaries of any tract or lot of land, or any tree, mark, or post or stone planted for that purpose he shall be fined not less than ten nor more than two thousand dollars."

Appellant was indicted for the offense denounced by the foregoing statute, upon trial was found guilty and fined $100, and to reverse the judgment entered in accordance with said verdict he has prosecuted this appeal.

⟜For other cases see same topic and KEY-NUMBER in all Key-Numbered Digests and Indexes

Appellant urges as error the court's oral instruction to the jury to find him guilty, a point well taken, and because of which a reversal must be ordered.

[1] Section 225 of the Criminal Code requires that instructions in criminal cases shall be given in writing, a provision that has been rigidly enforced, except in misdemeanor cases, where the requirement may be waived. Appellant's failure to except to the action of the court in so instructing the jury estops him from objecting on appeal that the instruction was not in writing. Mobile & Ohio R. R. Co. v. Commonwealth, 122 Ky. 435, 92 S. W. 299, 28 Ky. Law Rep. 1360; Adams Express Co. v. Commonwealth, 163 Ky. 275, 173 S. W. 764; Whitaker v. Commonwealth, 188 Ky. 95, 221 S. W. 215, 10 A. L. R. 145.

[2] Although it is stated on the brief that appellant objected to the action of the court in instructing the jury, the record fails to show that such was a fact. A court is without right to direct a jury to find a defendant guilty where his plea is not guilty.

By section 7 of the Bill of Rights of our Constitution it provided that the ancient mode of trial by jury shall be held sacred, and the right thereof remain inviolate, subject to such modification as may be authorized by the Constitution.

A similar provision found in the federal Constitution guarantees to accused the right to a speedy and public trial by an impartial jury.

[3-5] It is difficult to understand upon what principle it can be maintained that one accused of crime has had a trial by an impartial jury within the meaning of the Constitution where the court has instructed the jury peremptorily to find him guilty. There cannot well be a trial of the cause by a jury unless that body deliberates upon and determines it. Accused is entitled to every reasonable doubt in favor of the presumption of his innocence, and, since the jury is the sole judge of the credibility of the witnesses, it is never proper for the court to direct a verdict of guilty where there is a plea of not guilty, notwithstanding the fact that the evidence of his guilt may be convincing and wholly uncontradicted. Under the constitutional guaranty that a person charged with the commission of a crime is entitled to a trial by jury, the accused person has, in every case where he has pleaded not guilty, the absolute right to have the question of his innocence or guilt submitted to a jury, no matter what the state of the evidence may be. It is for the jury to find the ultimate fact of guilt upon the evidence, under instructions of the court as to the law. It is for the court to say what evidence is competent and to decide whether it is admissible, but after its admission it is for the jury to say what weight should be attached to it. The attempt on the part of the court to re-

turn a verdict for the jury, which in effect is what was done by the trial court in the present instance, is nothing more than trespassing upon the province of the jury, a right not vested in the court under facts such as are presented by this record.

A plea of not guilty on the part of the defendant cannot be understood as other than denying the truth of the indictment, or the denial of the truth of what the witnesses for the commonwealth have sworn to.

In United States v. Taylor (C. C.) 11 Fed. 470, it is said:

"It is not well settled in the federal courts that in civil cases, where the facts are undisputed and the case turns upon the questions of law, the court may direct a verdict in accordance with its opinion of the law; but the authorities which settle this rule have no application to criminal cases. In a civil case the court may set aside the verdict, whether it be for the plaintiff or defendant, upon the ground that it is contrary to the law as given by the court; but in a criminal case, if the verdict is one of acquittal, the court has no power to set it aside. It would be a useless form for a court to submit a civil case involving only questions of law to the consideration of a jury, where the verdict, when found, if not in accordance with the court's view of the law, would be set aside. The same result is accomplished by an instruction given in advance to find a verdict in accordance with the court's opinion of the law. But not so in criminal cases. A verdict of acquittal cannot be set aside, and therefore, if the court can direct a verdict of guilty, it can do indirectly that which it has no power to do directly."

Likewise in People v. Warren, 122 Mich. 504, 81 N. W. 360, 80 Am. St. Rep. 582, the court said:

"When, in addition to that right [the right of a trial judge to direct a jury in relation to the trial of the case], it was held that, in cases where the facts were admitted, the trial court might direct the jury to return a verdict of guilty, the border line separating the functions of the trial judge from the province of the jury was reached. If another step is to be taken, and, in addition to the right to direct the verdict, it is held the judge may, when the jury is unwilling to follow the direction of the court, compel a verdict, then the border line is passed, the judge has entered upon the province of the jury, the constitutional guaranty of a right of trial by jury in criminal cases is overthrown, and the judge has drawn to himself power which has not been exercised by any trial judge since the days of Magna Charta."

This very question was decided by this court in Lucas v. Commonwealth, 118 Ky. 818, 82 S. W. 440, wherein it is said that the provision of the Code declaring that all issues of fact where the punishment exceeds a fine of $16 shall be tried by a jury, and that an issue of facts arises upon a plea of not guilty (Civil Code, §§ 180, 182), was designed to preserve inviolate the right of trial by jury as guaranteed by the Bill of Rights. We take the following excerpt from said opinion:

"In view of these salutary provisions of the Constitution and Criminal Code of Practice, we are unable to conceive of a case in which the trial court would be authorized to instruct the jury to find the accused guilty, except upon his confession of guilt by formal plea to that effect, made in open court, in the presence of the jury selected and sworn to try him. In this case, though a demurrer has been properly sustained to the appellant's plea in bar, his additional plea of not guilty was still before the court and jury, and, as we have already seen, it raised an issue of fact to be tried and determined by the jury; and though the appellant introduced no proof, and that of the commonwealth clearly established his guilt, the jury alone were authorized to declare him guilty, and they should have been allowed to perform their duty under proper instructions, and without coercion from the court. They were the sole judges of the credibility of the witnesses, and of the weight to be given their testimony."

To the same effect see 6 Enc. Pl. & Pr. 689; 16 C. J. 937; Gregory's Criminal Law, § 994, and note to Konda v. United States, 166 Fed. 91, 92 C. C. A. 75, found in 22 L. R. A. (N. S.) 305, and in which the annotator has collated a vast number of authorities.

The present indictment was brought about by the act of appellant in felling a walnut tree that stood at the corner of the lot of the Methodist parsonage in Greensburg, where it borders on a public alley. There were five witnesses on each side. Those who testified for the commonwealth were of the opinion the tree belonged to the parsonage lot. Among the witnesses was a surveyor whose testimony is thus recorded in the bill of exceptions:

"They employed me to come and run the line. We started at the Vaughn corner and run to Water street, and then we surveyed up Water street 957 feet. This lacked 4 feet of getting to the spring house."

This statement, though unintelligible to us, was doubtless understood by those at the trial and who were familiar with the location of the spring house. However, one witness locates the spring at the walnut tree, and another says the survey "left the tree on the parsonage property."

[6] According to appellant's proof the tree was in the alley, and the town authorities had ordered its removal, and one of the town trustees assisted appellant in cutting down the tree. There was a sharp conflict in the evidence, making it peculiarly one triable by a jury. If the tree was in the alley, the trustees had the right to order its removal. This was pointed out in Town of Lagrange v. Overstreet, 141 Ky. 43, 132 S. W. 169, 31 L. R. A. (N. S.) 951, where the court sustained as valid an ordinance providing for the reconstruction of the sidewalk of Overstreet's property, thereby necessitating the removal of a locust tree owned by him that was standing in the sidewalk. Although the real purpose of the ordinance was to secure the removal of the tree, the court held that, unless the action of the board was unreasonable or arbitrary, its action was authorized by the statute. Both Lagrange and Greensburg are cities of the sixth class.

[7] Whether the trustees had ordered the removal of the tree and whether the tree stood in the alley or on the parsonage lot are matters that can and should be shown without much difficulty and in such a manner as to remove any doubt as to the facts.

For the reasons stated, the judgment is reversed for further proceedings consistent herewith.

———

CINCINNATI, N. O. & T. P. R. CO. et al. v. OWSLEY.

(Court of Appeals of Kentucky. May 27, 1921.)

1. **Railroads** ⬳356(3)—**Trespassers becoming licensees by user.**

The mere use of a railroad track by the public does not convert the users from trespassers into licensees, except when and where the use is habitual by such large numbers of people as to put upon the company the duty of anticipating their presence on the track.

2. **Railroads** ⬳355(2)—**Joint right in passway.**

Where track leading from city street to a mill was laid longitudinally in what was an open passway if not a public street, which constituted the only means of reaching the mill, and had been used for such purpose prior to the construction of the track and continuously since the construction thereof, and where such track and the passway were partly upon the property of the mill company and partly upon the property of the railroad company, buggy driver, who drove along track to the mill to make purchase thereat, was neither a trespasser or a licensee, and since the railroad enjoyed the right of way jointly with the public it was required to keep a lookout to avoid injuring persons thereon at least during business hours.

3. **Negligence** ⬳136(9)—**Contributory negligence for jury.**

The question of contributory negligence is usually for the jury, and it is only when the evidence leaves no room for differences of opinion among reasonable men that it becomes a matter of law for the court.

4. **Railroads** ⬳400(12) — **Contributory negligence of buggy driver on mill track held for jury.**

Mill customer, driving buggy along open passway constituting only means of reaching mill on which there was a longitudinally laid mill track used merely as a housing or storage track, struck by a string of freight cars backed from the main track on the mill track into the rear of her buggy while sitting in buggy with curtains down, talking to the miller, *held* not contributorily negligent as a matter of law; the question being for the jury.

5. Railroads ⨌400(14)—Negligence under last clear chance doctrine held for jury

In action for injuries to buggy driver struck on infrequently used mill track by freight train, the applicability of the last clear chance doctrine *held* for the jury.

6. Damages ⨌216(8)—Instruction as to permanent impairment of earning power erroneous, in absence of evidence as to permanency of injuries.

In personal injury action, instruction on measure of damages, allowing a recovery for permanent impairment of earning capacity, in absence of evidence that injuries were permanent, *held* erroneous.

7. Evidence ⨌554—Physician's testimony as to a certain disease inadmissible, in absence of showing that plaintiff had such disease.

In personal injury action, testimony of physician testifying for plaintiff in answer to question as to whether plaintiff had received an injury to her nervous system that: "She has. Whether it will last or not I don't know; sometimes these shocks are very lasting; sometimes there is traumatic hysteria, which is one of the worst diseases a physician is called on to treat" —*held* improper in so far as it referred to traumatic hysteria there being no evidence that plaintiff had such disease.

8. Appeal and error ⨌1050(1) — Erroneous admission of evidence as to disease in personal injury action prejudicial if size of verdict might be attributed thereto.

In a personal injury action, erroneous admission of physician's testimony as to a certain disease which plaintiff was not shown to have suffered from, though ordinarily harmless, would become prejudicial if the size of the verdict might be attributed thereto because not otherwise justified by the evidence.

9. Damages ⨌131(1) — $1,500, for being bumped around in buggy struck by freight cars without visible injuries, held excessive.

In action for injuries to one driving a buggy struck by train, where there was no evidence that the driver was permanently injured, and where she testified that she was bumped around three or four times in the buggy while it was being demolished; that her head and back were hurt, and still bothered her at the time of the trial; that she walked to her home, a distance of about three miles, immediately after the accident, and did not go to the doctor for some five or six days thereafter; that she had visited the doctor but one time, and the doctor testified that she saw no bruises—verdict of $1,500 *held* excessive.

Appeal from Circuit Court, Lincoln County.

Action by Millie Ann Owsley against the Cincinnati, New Orleans & Texas Pacific Railroad Company and others. Judgment for plaintiff and defendants appeal. Reversed with directions.

John Galvin, of Cincinnati, Ohio, K. S. Alcorn, of Stanford, and Emmet Puryear and T. J. Hill, both of Danville, for appellants.

CLARKE, J. McKinney is a town of about 500 inhabitants. Its Main street, running east and west, is intersected at right angles by the appellant railroad company's main and passing tracks and a spur track known in this record as the mill track. The passing track and the mill track join the main track at a switch, a short distance south of Main street. The mill track runs nearly parallel to the other two tracks north of Main street some distance past the McKinney Mill Company's flourmill, which is about 90 feet north of Main street and faces the railroad tracks. There is a platform across the entire front of the mill, which is at its northern end about 8 feet, and at its southern end about 5 feet from the nearest rail of the mill track.

About noon on November 25, 1918, the appellee, driving a horse and buggy, came from her home in the country to the mill for some flour. She came west on Main street across the main and passing tracks, and drove north along the mill track to a point thereon opposite the front door of the mill. The buggy top was up and the curtains were down, and while she was sitting in the buggy, talking to the miller about the flour, the defendant company's local freight crew backed a string of cars from the main track on the mill track and into the rear of plaintiff's buggy. Seeking to recover for injuries alleged to have been thus sustained, she instituted this action, and this is an appeal by the defendants from a verdict and judgment for $1,500 in her favor.

The grounds urged for a reversal are that the court erred (1) in refusing defendant's motion for a peremptory instruction, (2) in the instructions given, (8) in the admission of evidence, and (4) that the verdict is excessive.

1. It is contended that the verdict should have been directed for defendants (a) because plaintiff failed to prove such user of the track as made her a licensee, and (b) because she was guilty of contributory negligence as a matter of law.

[1] (a) The rule is thoroughly established that the mere use of a railroad track by the public does not convert the users from trespassers into licensees, except when and where the use is habitual by such large numbers of people as to put upon the company the duty of anticipating their presence on the track. Adkins' Administrator v. Big Sandy & Cumberland Railroad Company et al., 147 Ky. 30, 143 S. W. 764; Chesapeake & Ohio Railway Co. v. Warnock's Adm'r, 150 Ky. 74, 150 S. W. 29; Corder's Adm'r v. C. N. O. & T. P. R. R. Co. et al., 155 Ky. 536, 159

S. W. 1144; C. & O. R. R. Co. v. Dawson's Adm'r, 159 Ky. 296, 167 S. W. 125; C. & O. R. R. Co. v. Berry's Adm'r, 164 Ky. 280, 175 S. W. 340.

[2] Plaintiff's proof does not show the number of persons using the track at the place of the accident, and it is from this fact, counsel for defendants argue she had not proven herself a licensee under the above rule, and this is probably true; but that rule is not applicable to the facts of this case. Plaintiff was in no sense a licensee upon defendant's track, whose right to the protection of a lookout duty depended upon her conversion from a trespasser. Upon her evidence, which was not contradicted by any witness for defendant, she had as much right in her buggy at the place of the accident as did the defendants with their train. The uncontradicted evidence is · that this mill track is laid longitudinally in an open passway (if not a public street of the town) that leads from Main street to the mill; that same is now and always has been the only means of reaching the mill; that it was so used before the railroad was constructed, and has been habitually and constantly so used since by all members of the public having business at the mill; that the mill track and the passway are partly upon the property of the mill company and partly upon the property of the railroad company.

We held in Southern Ry. in Ky. v. Caplinger's Adm'r, 151 Ky. 749, 152 S. W. 947, 49 L. R. A. (N. S.) 660, that,

"Railway companies that have been privileged to lay tracks and run engines and trains in streets of cities and towns are obliged at all times of the day and night to anticipate the presence of travelers on the street and to take such precautions relating to speed warning and lookout as may be reasonably sufficient to avoid injury to them."

· This is because at such places the railroad company has not the exclusive right of way, but enjoys it jointly with the public. So upon the evidence here the defendant has not the exlusive right of way over the land upon which this mill track is located by only a joint right of use with the mill company and that section of the public having business at the mill. Hence, applying the very same principles as were applied in the Caplinger Case to the slightly different, but entirely analogous, facts of this case, there can be no doubt that defendants in their use of this track owed to that section of the public having business with the mill, of which plaintiff was a member at the time of the accident, a lookout duty during business hours at least, and the court did not err in refusing to direct a verdict upon the theory she was a trespasser.

[3-5] (b) The question of contributory negligence is usually for the jury. It is only when the evidence leaves no room for differences of opinion among reasonable men that it becomes a matter of law for the court. This mill track touched the other tracks only at its northern end, and was used merely as a housing or storage track. The extent of its use by the defendant is not shown, but, being located and used as above indicated, it certainly is not such a track as we may assume was used constantly or frequently by the defendants. In fact a contrary presumption would seem to be more reasonable; and, under all the circumstances proven in this case, we do not think it can be said that plaintiff was guilty of contributory negligence as a matter of law. But even if it might be conceded that she was thus negligent, she was nevertheless entitled to have her case go to the jury under the last clear chance doctrine, since there is much evidence, practically uncontradicted, that her peril could easily have been discovered and her injuries avoided had defendants maintained a lookout on the rear of the backing train, as was their duty. Hence the court did not err in overruling the motion for a directed verdict.

[6] 2. The criticism of the first instruction given by the court is based upon the assumption that plaintiff's right of recovery was dependent upon her status as a licensee on the track as a result of the habitual use of same by large numbers of the public, and has no pertinency under our view of her relationship to the defendants in the use of the track. The criticism of the instruction upon the measure of damages is more serious, in that it allowed a recovery for any permanent impairment of her power to earn money when there was no evidence that her injuries are permanent. This was error of course, and that it was prejudicial is probable, as will appear when we come to consider the complaint that the verdict is excessive.

[7, 8] 3. Dr. Carpenter, testifying for plaintiff, was asked, over the defendants' objection and exception, "Has she received an injury to her nervous system?" and answered:

"She has. Whether it will last or not I don't know sometimes these shocks are very lasting; sometimes there is traumatic hysteria, which is one of the worst diseases a physician is called on to treat."

Defendants asked to have this testimony excluded, which the court refused to do. The form of the question is objectionable, and that part of the answer should have been excluded which refers to traumatic hysteria, since there was no evidence that plaintiff had any such disease. This error seemingly trivial and ordinarily harmless, would become prejudicial like the one just referred to above, if the size of the verdict might be attributed thereto, because not otherwise justified by the evidence.

[9] 4. The evidence is not at all satisfactory that the plaintiff was seriously or substantially injured. There is no evidence whatever that she has been permanently in-

jured. She states that she was bumped around three or four times in the buggy while it was being demolished; that her head and back were hurt, and still bothered her at the time of the trial. She walked to her home, a distance of about three miles, immediately after the accident, and did not go to a doctor for some five or six days thereafter, and but the one time. The doctor testifies that she saw no bruises of any kind, that the pupils of plaintiff's eyes were enlarged, that she was nervous and trembling, and that she would probably be more easily shocked now than she would have been before the accident, but the effect of the doctor's testimony as to the extent of the injury is very much lessened by her practical admission upon cross-examination that the plaintiff was more frightened than hurt by the accident.

We are therefore of the opinion that the size of the verdict must be ascribed to passion and prejudice, unless it may be accounted for by the errors above pointed out, both of which indicated a permanent injury not proven. In either event a reversal must be ordered.

Wherefore the judgment is reversed, with directions to grant defendants a new trial and for proceedings consistent herewith.

———

McKEE v. McKEE.

(Court of Appeals of Kentucky.　May 27, 1921.)

1. Divorce ⬥⇒27(18)—Testimony as to numerous quarrels not sufficient to establish cruel and inhuman treatment.

In wife's divorce action, testimony as to numerous quarrels is insufficient, standing alone, to establish cruel and inhuman treatment.

2. Divorce ⬥⇒130—Evidence held to establish wife's right to an absolute divorce for cruel and inhuman treatment.

In wife's divorce suit, evidence that husband struck and whipped wife, and pulled out her hair, held sufficient to establish her right to an absolute divorce for cruel and inhuman treatment, as against husband's contention that his acts were in self-defense.

3. Divorce ⬥⇒130—Right to inflict corporal punishment on other spouse in self-defense must be clearly established.

The right of one spouse to inflict corporal punishment on the other in absolutely necessary defense of himself or some member of the family must be clearly established to justify such corporal punishment in other spouse's divorce action on ground of cruel and inhuman treatment.

4. Divorce ⬥⇒201—Court had jurisdiction on appeal of question of alimony, where defendant entered appearance pending appeal.

Where defendant in divorce suit, while brought before the Court of Appeals on a warning order, had entered his appearance by filing a written stipulation during the pendency of the appeal, the court had jurisdiction to determine the question of alimony.

5. Divorce ⬥⇒227(2), 240(5), 308—Wife held entitled to $25 allowance, $15 allowance for child, and $25 attorney's fee.

Where the husband at the time of the divorce suit was capable of earning and was earning $200 a month, and owned a farm valued between $1,000 and $1,600, the wife was entitled to an allowance of $25 a month for her maintenance, $15 a month for the maintenance of a child allotted to her, and $25 for attorney's fee.

Appeal from Circuit Court, Boyd County.

Suit by Clara B. McKee against Harlan McKee. From a judgment giving her insufficient relief, plaintiff appeals. Reversed, with directions.

J. F. Stewart, of Ashland, for appellant.

THOMAS, J. The appellant and plaintiff below, Clara B. McKee, sued the appellee and defendant below, Harlan McKee, in the Boyd circuit court, to obtain judgment against him for a divorce, for alimony, and for the custody of their two infant children, Elmer McKee and Garnett McKee, whose ages are seven and two years, respectively. After the taking of testimony by plaintiff only the cause was submitted, and the court rendered judgment, in which it dismissed the petition for alimony and for an absolute divorce, but decreed a divorce a mensa et thoro, and plaintiff was given the custody of the younger child, Garnett McKee, and she was allowed $15 per month for its support, which the defendant was ordered to pay at the 1st of each month beginning July 1, 1919, and defendant was adjudged to pay the cost of the litigation including an allowance of $25 to plaintiff's attorney. The defendant was adjudged the custody of the older child, Elmer McKee. From that judgment plaintiff appeals, insisting that the court erred in not granting to her an absolute divorce, in disallowing her alimony, in giving to defendant the custody of Elmer McKee, and in making an insufficient allowance to her attorney.

The grounds relied on in the petition for the procurement of the divorce are: (1) Six months' cruel and inhuman behavior toward plaintiff, in such a manner as to indicate a settled aversion toward her and to permanently destroy her peace and happiness; and (2) such cruel beating and injury to the person of plaintiff by the defendant as indicates an outrageous temper in him and probable danger to her life or danger

⬥⇒For other cases see same topic and KEY-NUMBER in all Key-Numbered Digests and Indexes

of suffering great bodily injury from her remaining with him. The petition alleged that plaintiff was a healthy, able-bodied young man, and was capable of earning and was earning at the time of the filing of the suit $200 per month, and that he owned a farm in the state of Ohio valued at between $1,000 and $1,600. The answer denied the grounds of divorce, and put in issue the right of plaintiff to the custody of the children; but the averments relating to the financial standing and ability of defendant were undenied.

From the admissions in the pleadings, and from the uncontroverted testimony in the case, it appears that plaintiff at the time of giving her deposition in March, 1919, was 24 years of age, having married in 1911, when she was only 17 years of age. The defendant is a few years her senior. The parties lived together on a farm in Ohio, near the city of Ironton, until about the 1st of December, 1917, when they moved to Ashland, Ky., where defendant procured a position with a railroad company at a salary of $200 per month, and where the parties continued to reside until the separation on December 4, 1918. The farm in Ohio, worth at least $1,250, is still owned by defendant. Both of the parties appear to be reasonably industrious, and to have performed their respective duties in establishing, providing for, and maintaining the material necessities of the home; but defendant was more or less exacting in regard to the personal expenses of his wife, even to the degree of penuriousness, and he was quite demanding of her as to the purposes for which she would expend the few and small amounts of money with which he would intrust her. She does not seem to have been lavish in her desires for dress; but, whether so or not, she was by no means gratified in that respect.

Defendant also appears to have harbored an unfounded jealousy toward plaintiff, and he criticized her because, as he claimed, she would not wear in his presence a cheap hat which he admired, and which she had made by covering a frame costing only 10 cents. He likewise became incensed because his wife attended a neighbor while in childbirth, and he became very much enraged when his wife exhibited to him an anonymous letter stating that he, on some of the numerous nights while away from home late, was in company with some lewd women; and he very much objected to her taking in sewing for some neighbors whereby she could obtain some extra pin money, and which does not appear to have interfered in the least with her attention to her household duties. Defendant, while living upon the farm, spent the greater portion of many nights away from home fox hunting, and he indulged in the same practice of absenting himself from home at night after their removal to Ashland.

In addition, it appears that defendant at times during his married life was addicted to the drinking habit, and to make matters worse plaintiff herself is shown to have possessed what the witnesses called "a high temper."

[1, 2] As stated, the facts down to this point are either admitted or proven by uncontradicted testimony. The only contrariety in the testimony (which, according to our view, is slight) is in that part of it relating to the acts of cruelty on the part of defendant as furnishing the grounds for divorce. He admits in his testimony numerous quarrels with his wife, but which standing alone, would be insufficient to establish the charges against him; but his conduct, according to his own testimony, did not stop with quarreling alone, for on one occasion, which was two days before the separation, he struck plaintiff in the face with his fist and knocked her on the floor, where she remained unconscious for some minutes, and caused her nose to bleed freely and caused her to wear a black eye for more than a month. He applied to her vile names, and on another occasion, prior to the last one, he corporally punished her and pulled from her head a large quantity of hair. It is also shown by her testimony, and not denied by him, that he would brutally treat the children and he beat one of them at one time to such an extent that its back was blistered for days, and plaintiff came in for her share of denunciation for protesting against the child's treatment. The wife testified, and it stands uncontradicted, that on a number of occasions defendant would say to her that he had no affection for her, and that there were a number of women in Ashland that treated him better than she did. She also testified that—

"I went over to Mrs. Clark's to get some goods to make her some dresses, and when he saw them he came and struck me, and said he would kill me. He knocked me, and when I came to he said I had no witness to prove it after he had whipped me."

She testified that, while drinking, defendant would choke her until her breath was nearly gone. Defendant admits striking plaintiff, and also admits pulling out her hair; but he claims that he did so in self-defense.

[3] Our examination of the testimony fails to support his excuse for his conduct. We are not prepared to say that one spouse may never inflict corporal punishment upon the other in the absolutely necessary defense of himself or herself or some member of the family; but the testimony should clearly establish the right to do so, which is by no means true in this case. On the contrary, according to the testimony of plaintiff, each of the difficulties and each of the cruel punishments of her by her husband was without

excuse, and we are by no means convinced from the testimony of defendant himself that he was blameless, since his petty jealousies and his exacting disposition, according to his own theory seem to have been at the bottom of the trouble.

Another circumstance, not to be overlooked, is that on two prior occasions, after receiving physical chastisement, plaintiff sued defendant for the same relief she seeks in this action. On each occasion the suits were dismissed at his solicitation as he admits, and upon his promise, as testified to by plaintiff, that he would reform his future conduct toward her. On one of the occasions, after the dismissal of the suit, he claimed to have been religiously converted; but in a few weeks he resumed his old course and when plaintiff reminded him of his conversion he became offended, because she "ridiculed his religion." We recite these circumstances, as showing that defendant's insinuation of entire blame on the part of plaintiff can scarcely be true; for, if so, he would have hardly pursued the unnatural course of seeking her return to him, and the dismissal of the prior suits on each of those two occasions.

The high temper of plaintiff was an unfortunate fact, but it was one that defendant should have taken into consideration in his treatment of and his dealings with and demeanor toward her, and to have tempered them, even to exhaustion, with all the gentility and kindness due from a husband to a member of his family, especially his wife. At any rate her temper, howsoever bad, would not alone authorize him to resort to the infliction of corporal punishment upon her in order to "put her under his thumb," as testified to by the plaintiff, and not denied by defendant. From the testimony in this record we entertain no doubt that, if defendant had freed himself of the faults and foibles hereinbefore referred to, and had exercised that patience, gentleness, and kindness toward defendant, which is due from a husband to his wife, followed by even a modicum of affection, instead of a renunciation of it, the matrimonial bark would still be sailing on smooth waters, instead of being wrecked by the tempestuous storms which we think the testimony shows were generated by him. Entertaining this view, it results that the court was in error in dismissing plaintiff's petition and in refusing to grant her a divorce.

[4, 5] While defendant was brought before this court on a warning order, he had entered his appearance by filing a written stipulation during the pendency of the appeal, and we therefore have jurisdiction to determine the question of alimony. From the admitted facts as to defendant's earning capacity, and considering the property he owns, it is easily apparent that an allowance of $25 per month for the maintenance of defendant and the $15 per month for maintenance of the child allotted to her, making a total sum of $40 per month, is exceedingly reasonable, and by the same token we conclude that plaintiff's attorney should be allowed an additional sum of $25.

The testimony in the record is not sufficient to show any error in the judgment concerning the custody of the children, and that portion of it will not be disturbed.

Wherefore the judgment is reversed, with directions to enter a judgment as herein indicated, and to retain the case on the docket, so that the questions of alimony and the custody of the children may be readjusted according to future alterations in conditions, if any.

———

GROVE LODGE NO. 274, I. O. O. F., v. FIDELITY PHENIX INS. CO.

(Court of Appeals of Kentucky. May 27, 1921.)

1. Appeal and error ⟺302(5)—Objection that verdict is contrary to law does not raise error in giving and refusing instructions.

To say in a motion for a new trial that a verdict "is contrary to law" is too general, and will not raise the error, if any, in giving and refusing instructions.

2. Insurance ⟺92—Evidence held not to show agency for defendant insurer.

In action for fire loss, evidence *held* not to show that person claimed to have acted for insurer in making parol insurance contract was insurer's agent.

3. Principal and agent ⟺21—Agency may be shown by agent's testimony.

While the declarations of an agent made out of court may not be proven to establish his agency, his testimony in court is competent as to the fact of his agency.

Appeal from Circuit Court, Owen County.

Action by Grove Lodge No. 274, I. O. O. F., against the Fidelity Phenix Insurance Company. From judgment for defendant, plaintiff appeals. Affirmed.

J. G. Vallandingham, of Owenton, for appellant.

J. W. Cammack and Cammack & Baker, all of Owenton, for appellee.

THOMAS, J. Appellant lodge, plaintiff below, sued the appellee and defendant below, insurance company, to recover $600. It was alleged in the petition that plaintiff held a contract with defendant whereby the latter agreed to insure and indemnify plaintiff against damage or loss produced by fire to its lodge building and its paraphernalia and furniture therein, located in the village of

Poplar Grove in Owen county. The lodge room owned by plaintiff was the second story of a frame building, the first story of which was occupied by a Mr. Slaughter as a dealer in general merchandise. It was alleged that the contract was entered into on June 12, 1917, and that on the 20th of that month the property was destroyed by fire, and that defendant denied all liability, and refused to pay any part of the insurance, although it had been notified of the loss. The answer was a denial of all the affirmative allegations made in the petition, and after evidence heard the jury, under the instructions of the court, of which no complaint is made in the motion and grounds for a new trial, returned a verdict in favor of defendant, followed by a judgment, dismissing the petition, of which plaintiff makes complaint on this appeal.

[1] To say in a motion for a new trial that a verdict "is contrary to law" is too general, and will not raise the error, if any, in giving and refusing instructions. American Credit Co. v. National Clothing Co., 122 S. W. 840; Charles Taylor Sons Co. v. Hunt, 163 Ky. 120, 173 S. W. 333; Nicholson v. Patrick, 160 Ky. 674, 170 S. W. 20. But if the motion in this case had been sufficiently specific to raise the question, there could be no reversal because of any error in the instructions, since they submitted to the jury in appropriate language the issues: (a) The supposed authority of J. F. Brock, the alleged agent, through whom the insurance contract was alleged to have been procured; and (b) whether he, as such alleged agent, made the contract with plaintiff in such a way as to bind defendant.

[2] Briefly noticing issue (a), the testimony in the case leaves no doubt in our minds that, as between himself and the defendant company, Brock was not its agent. In fact it is proven by a high officer of the defendant, who appoints all of its agents in the territory of which Kentucky is a part, that Brock was not, nor had he ever been, defendant's agent to solicit or procure insurance. He held no commission or authority from the company, which, according to the testimony, was invariably given to its appointed agents. However, the defendant might be liable to members of the public for the acts of Brock, if it held him out as its agent and dealt with him in such a manner as to induce the belief that he was authorized to represent it in negotiating for and procuring insurance. The only evidence upon this point was the testimony of Brock, who stated without qualification that he was an agent of defendant; but, curiously enough, it is not shown, even by himself, that he ever wrote a policy or that he did anything more than to assist the local agent at Owenton, Ky., in procuring some local risks in his neighborhood, for which the local agent paid him an agreed percentage of the premium. It furthermore

appears that a Mr. Kemper, who was some sort of general agent for the territory, carried Brock with him on one or two occasions to see certain proposed risks in the neighborhood, and to assist him in procuring the insurance thereon, but this occurred in the fall after the summer in which the contract sued on was alleged to have been made. Brock says that he was a member of the lodge, and that either on the 2d or the 9th day of June, 1917, the question of insuring defendant's property came up in meeting, and that he then and there agreed to the contract sued on, and further agreed that plaintiff should have 30 days in which to pay the premium of $15. Notwithstanding his express testimony to that effect, he wrote a letter to the defendant's agent at Owenton on June 12, in which he said:

"Inclosed find papers so you can copy applications for storeroom and for hall. Maybe you can get enough out of what I have down to know what they want. What is the cause of taking so long to get the policies? The first time I am in town, I will come in and see you. Date these policies the 15th, as that is when the others expire."

With the letter he inclosed a form for $250 insurance on the storeroom, or first story of the building, $500 on the second story, and $100 on its contents. The agent, Duvall, testified that he answered that letter on the 15th of June, which was the same day he received it, and stated to Brock, in substance, that he had declined insurance on that building a number of times, and also said:

"I would be very glad to place this business for you if I could, but it is simply impossible, as I haven't a company."

It is true that Brock says he did not receive that letter, but the one he wrote to the agent clearly shows that he did not have authority to issue policies, nor to bind the defendant by contract, and there is ample testimony in the case to show that neither the company nor any of its agents had done any act to induce the belief that Brock was authorized to bind the company by oral contract without the issuance of a policy, or to do anything more than take an application for a policy; it being doubtful if their prior relations with him were such as to inspire the belief that he even had authority to take applications. The extent of the negotiations between defendant's agent at Owenton, with and through whom all insurance contracts had to be effected, and Brock, seems to be that the agent agreed with the latter to pay him for all insurance which he solicited and secured for the agent, and we think such one would not possess the apparent authority to waive all of the proven universal methods of procuring a policy and to bind the company upon a verbal contract of insurance contrary to such methods. At any rate, those issues were submitted to the jury, as stated, and it on sufficient evidence determined them against plaintiff.

[3] It is said, however, that the court erred in permitting Duvall to testify as to the fact of his agency, but there is no merit in this contention. The rule which counsel for plaintiff seeks to invoke is that the declarations of an agent made out of court may not be proven to establish his agency, but the rule does not go to the extent of disqualifying a supposed agent from testifying in court as to the fact of his agency. Peyton v. Old Woolen Mills, 122 Ky. 361, 91 S. W. 719, 28 Ky. Law Rep. 1308; Rice & Hutchins' Co. v. J. W. Croghan & Co., 169 Ky. 450, 184 S. W. 374; California Insurance Co. v. Settle, 162 Ky. 82, 172 S. W. 119; Ethington v. Rigg, 173 Ky. 355, 191 S. W. 98. If, however, we should apply the rule as contended for, it would operate in this case more to the detriment of plaintiff than to defendant, since the strongest evidence of the alleged agency of Brock is his own testimony.

Finding no prejudicial errors in the record, and the verdict being supported by sufficient testimony, the judgment is affirmed.

CURRY et al. v. HINTON (two cases).

(Court of Appeals of Kentucky. May 27, 1921.)

1. Mines and minerals ⟡59 — Evidence held to sustain finding that leases were executed for three, instead of five, years.

In suits to declare oil and gas leases void because, when executed, they were for three years, while, when recorded, they had been forged to provide for a five-year term, evidence held to sustain the court's finding that the leases as originally executed were for a term of only three years.

2. Mines and minerals ⟡74—Where lease for three years was altered, so as to call for five-year term, innocent purchasers could only hold for three.

Where oil and gas leases were executed for a period of only three years, and by forgery changed to five years before record, lessor's rights cannot be defeated on the ground that the lease had fallen into the hands of innocent purchasers.

3. Estoppel ⟡92(2) — Lessor accepting payment of rent held not estopped to claim forgery.

Where oil and gas leases were executed for three years, and forged to include five years before recording them, the fact that lessors accepted payment for the third year after learning of the forgery did not estop them from asserting the forgery and claiming expiration of the lease at the end of the third year.

Appeal from Circuit Court, Allen County.

Suits by J. W. Hinton and by W. S. Hinton against C. M. Curry, trustee, and James P. McClosky, to declare certain oil and gas leases given by the plaintiffs void. Judgments for plaintiffs, and defendants appeal. Affirmed.

J. Franklin Corn and T. W. & R. C. P. Thomas, all of Bowling Green, for appellants.

Oliver & Dixon, of Scottsville, for appellees.

TURNER, C. On February 21, 1916, the appellees, W. S. and J. W. Hinton, father and son, each executed and delivered to Huntsman & Dixon three separate oil and gas leases covering three distinct tracts of land in Allen county; the lease of W. S. Hinton covering a tract of 25 acres, more or less, and the two leases of J. W. Hinton covering two separate tracts, containing, respectively, 30 and 74 acres. The three leases were identical in their terms, except as to the names of the parties, and the W. S. Hinton lease was lodged for record in the Allen county court on the 29th of October, 1917, and the certificate of recordation is dated the 17th day of November, 1917. The two leases executed by J. W. Hinton were likewise lodged for record on the 29th day of October, 1917; but the certificate of recordation as to each of them is dated the 15th day of November, 1917.

Each of the leases on its face was given for the sole and only purpose of mining and operating for minerals, oil and gas, and they each as recorded were to remain in force for a term of five years from date and as long thereafter as oil, gas, or minerals might be produced therefrom. The lessees agreed in each of them to begin a well on the premises within one year from the date thereof, or pay rentals at the rate of 25 cents per acre for each additional year such beginning was delayed until a well was begun. The lessees on the 28th day of November, 1917, transferred and assigned each of these leases to C. M. Curry, trustee, and Curry, trustee, transferred and assigned, on the 24th day of January, 1919, a one-sixth interest in each of them to James P. McClosky. No well was begun on any of the leases during the first year, nor had one been begun when these suits were brought, but the Hintons accepted the rentals for the years beginning in February, 1917, and February, 1918.

At about the time the second rentals were due, in February, 1918, for the third year of the lease, the Hintons learned that the leases as recorded showed that they were for a term of five years, and notwithstanding they then and have ever since claimed that the original leases were executed for only a term of three years, they accepted the rentals for the third year. In 1919, after the expiration of the three years from the date of the leases, each of the Hintons filed an equitable action, alleging, in substance, that at the time of the execution and delivery of each of the three leases to Huntsman & Dixon, or their agent, each of said leases provided on its face that it should be in force for a term of only three years from its date, and that notwithstanding this provision the leases as recorded in the county clerk's office each showed on its face that it was to be in force for a term of five years, and they alleged that either by fraud, mistake, or oversight the "five" was inserted in the original leases in lieu of the "three," and they prayed for a judgment declaring each of the leases void and of no further binding force, and that each of the same be canceled and held for naught.

The defendants answered denying the material allegations of the petitions, and alleging affirmatively that the leases as originally executed were for a term of five years, and in addition there was a plea of innocent purchasership by Curry, trustee, and McClosky. The circuit court held that the leases as originally executed were for a term of only three years, and canceled each of them, or rather, in effect, held that they had expired, and from that judgment Curry, trustee, and McClosky have appealed.

[1] The question of fact involved is not in doubt; only three depositions were taken, and all for the plaintiffs. Both of the plaintiffs stated, in substance, that the leases were to expire at the end of three years, and that the figure "3." distinctly appeared in each of the leases as prepared by the agent of the lessees. Not only so, but Smith, the agent of Huntsman & Dixon, who was a deputy county court clerk, and who took the leases for the lessees, testified clearly and explicitly that he first undertook to get these leases for a term of five years, and that he had been authorized by Huntsman & Dixon to take only five-year leases, and, finding that he was unable to get them for that period, he went to a telephone in the neighborhood and called up Huntsman, and notified him that he could not get these and certain other leases, except for a term of three years, and that Huntsman directed him then to go on and take them for three years, and that in accordance with such directions he did take the leases, and that they were taken for a term of three years. The evidence of all three of the witnesses introduced further showed that the leases at the time of their execution were turned over to Smith as the agent of Huntsman & Dixon, and that they then showed they were for a term of three years only.

This evidence, taken for the plaintiffs, is not controverted by any one, and the deposition of neither Huntsman nor Dixon appears in this case. The conclusion is therefore irresistible that the court's finding of fact, that the leases as originally executed were for a term of only three years, must be approved.

[2] The question of innocent purchase is likewise of little difficulty owing to a recent decision of this court in a similar case. In the case of Lowther Oil & Gas Co. v. McGuire, 189 Ky. 681, 225 S. W. 718, a tract of land had been conveyed by Marcum and wife to John W. Flynn in July, 1910, but the deed had not been put to record. While the title was thus in John W. Flynn, it was levied on and sold by the sheriff under an execution against John W. Flynn. McGuire became the purchaser at the execution sale, and a deed was made to him by the sheriff; but after McGuire's purchase at the sale the name of John W. Flynn was erased from the original Marcum deed, and the name of Charles W. Flynn was inserted therein, and the deed was then recorded, showing Charles W. Flynn to be the vendee. While it was so on the record in the name of Charles W. Flynn, and without notice of the fraud, Lowther and others took an oil and gas lease from Charles W. Flynn, and in an action between McGuire and the lessees of Charles W. Flynn it was expressly held that they were not entitled to the benefits of bona fide or innocent purchasers; the court saying:

"A fraudulent material alteration of a deed is in law a forgery. 19 Cyc. 1374; Devlin on Real Estate, vol. 1, § 461a; Bardin v. Grace, 167 Ala. 453, Ann. Cas. 1912A, 537. It is likewise true that a forged deed is absolutely void and is ineffectual for any purpose. Authorities supra; Devlin on Real Estate, vol. 2, § 726; 18 Corpus Juris, pp. 224 and 242. In such cases purchasers from the vendee in the void instrument obtain no better title than that possessed by their vendor, and are not entitled to the protection afforded to bona fide and innocent purchasers. Authorities supra; 13 Cyc. 591. In the last citation upon this point the text says: 'But where the deed is regarded as absolutely void, it is held that even such a purchaser (innocent or bona fide) can obtain no title. And no title can be obtained even by an innocent party under a deed which is forged.' The text on page 242 of the volume of Corpus Juris referred to says: 'But where the deed is regarded as absolutely void it is held that even such a purchaser can obtain no title.' Section 726 of Devlin on Real Estate, referred to, says, inter alia: 'The provision of the statutes that deeds affecting the title of land shall be void as against subsequent purchasers and creditors without notice, if not recorded, has no application to deeds which are forged.' Other authorities announcing the same doctrine are Pry v. Pry, 109 Ill. 466; Cole v. Long, 44 Ga. 579; De Wolf v. Hayden, 24 Ill. 525, and Crawford v. Hoeft, 58 Mich. 1. It is therefore clear that this defense is not available under the facts of this case."

In the case quoted from there was an alteration of a name and the insertion of another name in lieu thereof; the alteration being apparently made for the purpose of making it appear that John W. Flynn, the defendant in the execution, and whose title McGuire had bought at the sale, never had any title, while in this case the alteration was a change in a figure, showing that a lease was for longer period than it was executed for. In each instance there was a material alteration—in the one case, for the purpose of defeating one's title under an execution sale; and in the other, for the purpose of making it appear that a lease was in force for two years longer than it actually was, possibly with the purpose in view of making it more valuable to prospective purchasers or persons contemplating development.

[3] The claim that appellees are estopped to assert that the leases were for only a term of three years, because they accepted in February, 1918, the rentals for the third year, cannot be sustained. At that time it is admitted that the lease was in force, and that it would remain in force for another year, and although the plaintiffs then had notice that a fraud had been perpetrated or a mistake made, and that the leases as recorded showed that they were for a term of five years, instead of three years, they, in recognition of the fact that the leases still had another year to run, in no wise precluded themselves from asserting the fraud by accepting the rentals for that year. It is likewise undenied that they each wrote to the then holders of the leases about that time, giving notice that they had only one year more to run.

The judgments of the lower court are in accord, not only with the merits, but with the law, and they are each affirmed.

ARNETT v. ELKHORN COAL CORPORATION.

(Court of Appeals of Kentucky. May 31, 1921.)

1. **Pleading** ⬤⇒216(1)—**On demurrer to petition only petition and exhibits filed with it can be considered.**

On a demurrer to the sufficiency of the petition, the court cannot consider anything except the allegations of the petition and the exhibits filed with and made a part of it.

2. **Quieting title** ⬤⇒34(1)—**Petition claiming ownership and possession of land and setting forth matter of adverse claims is sufficient.**

A petition, alleging that plaintiff was the owner of land and in its actual possession and that defendant was wrongfully claiming to be the owner of the oil and gas which were a portion of the land, designating the nature of defendant's claim as nearly as practical without describing its chain of title, but so as to show the claim was hostile to plaintiff's title, is suffi-

cient to state a cause of action under Ky. St. § 11.

3. **Quieting title** ⬤⇒35(2)—**Petition showing defendant claimed under plaintiff's grantor without showing date of plaintiff's deed is insufficient.**

Where a petition to quiet title alleged that plaintiff was the owner of the land in controversy, that he acquired title by conveyance from a named grantor, and that defendant claimed ownership of the oil and gas in the land under a conveyance of such oil and gas from the same grantor, the conveyance to defendant but not that to plaintiff being attached to the petition as an exhibit, the petition is insufficient to state a cause of action if it does not show that plaintiff's deed was prior and therefore superior to defendant's conveyance from the common source of title.

4. **Mines and minerals** ⬤⇒55(2)—**"Exception" of lease in conveyance of oil and gas in land does not show ownership of lease by grantor.**

In a deed conveying the oil and gas in a certain tract of land, a clause, stating there was an oil and gas lease in the land which was excepted from the conveyance, was an "exception," which is a description of some part of the thing granted which the grantor retains and does not convey or something to which another holds title already and which is not intended to be conveyed, and does not, as would a reservation, indicate that the lease referred to belonged to the grantor, who was also grantor of plaintiff in a suit to quiet title.

[Ed. Note.—For other definitions, see Words and Phrases, First and Second Series, Exception.]

Appeal from Circuit Court, Magoffin County.

Suit to quiet title by Elbert Arnett against the Elkhorn Coal Corporation. Judgment for defendant on plaintiff's electing to stand on his petition after demurrer thereto was sustained, and plaintiff appeals. Affirmed.

Augustus Arnett, of Salyersville, for appellant.

E. W. Pendleton, of Prestonsburg, A. W. Young, of Morehead, E. C. O'Rear, of Frankfort, and W. G. Deering, of Louisville, for appellee.

HURT, C. J. The appellant, as the plaintiff below, by his petition in equity against the appellee, as defendant, averred that he was the owner with a legal title thereto, and in the actual possession of a tract of land, which was described, in Magoffin county, and that he purchased the land from one Lewis Hoskins and wife, and came into its possession and ownership through a deed made by Hoskins and wife. He further averred that the defendant was setting up claim to ownership of the oils and gases in the land, and thereby casting a cloud upon his title to his

injury and damage. He filed with his petition a deed from Lewis Hoskins and wife to the Northern Coal & Coke Company, dated September 11, 1903, which he averred was the basis of the defendant's claim of title. He prayed for a judgment, quieting his title to the land, and requiring the defendant to release all of its claims thereto, and for a recovery of damages against the defendant. The foregoing constituted all the averments of the petition, and the deed from Hoskins and wife to the Northern Coal & Coke Company was the only exhibit filed with or made a part of the petition.

The defendant interposed a general demurrer to the petition which was sustained, and the plaintiff electing to stand upon his petition, and declining to amend it, the court adjudged that it be dismissed, and from the judgment the plaintiff has appealed, and the only question before this court is whether the petition stated facts sufficient to constitute a cause of action in behalf of the plaintiff.

[1, 2] At the outset, it is proper to say that upon a demurrer to the sufficiency of the petition, the court is not authorized to look to or to consider anything except the allegations of the petition and the exhibits filed with and made a part of it. In the instant case there were exhibits on file as evidence, and otherwise, which were not any part of the petition and cannot be considered upon the question presented, although it seems that the trial court took into consideration these exhibits. If the plaintiff had been content to have averred that he was the owner of the land and in its actual possession, and that the defendant was wrongfully claiming to be the owner of the oil and gases therein, which were a portion of the land, and to have designated the nature of the defendant's claim as nearly as it was practical to do without describing its chain of title, but so as to show that the claim of ownership by defendant was hostile and adverse to his title, a sufficient cause of action would have been stated under section 11, Ky. Stats. Kincaid v. McGowan, 88 Ky. 91, 4 S. W. 802, 9 Ky. Law Rep. 987, 13 L. R. A. 289; Campbell v. Disney, 93 Ky. 41, 18 S. W. 1027, 13 Ky. Law Rep. 919; Whipple v. Earick, 93 Ky. 121, 19 S. W. 237, 14 Ky. Law Rep. 85; Magowan v. Branham, 95 Ky. 581, 26 S. W. 803, 16 Ky. Law Rep. 233; Williams v. Lowe, 175 Ky. 369, 194 S. W. 342; Brown v. Ward, 105 S. W. 964, 32 Ky. Law Rep. 261; Henderson v. Clark, 163 Ky. 192, 173 S. W. 367; Hall v. Pratt, 142 Ky. 561, 134 S. W. 900; Cumberland Co. v. Kelly, 156 Ky. 397, 160 S. W. 1077; Perry v. Eagle Coal Co., 170 Ky. 824, 186 S. W. 875.

[3] The plaintiff, however, went further and averred how he became the owner of the land, which he did by purchasing it from Lewis Hoskins and wife, and accepting a deed of conveyance from them for the land, which he had caused to be recorded. He thereby averred that his source of title emanated from the deed made to him by Hoskins and wife, but he did not file with his petition the deed nor allege the date thereof. He also undertook to state the source of the defendant's claim of title, and filed with his petition, as a part of it, a deed of conveyance from Lewis Hoskins and wife to the Northern Coal & Coke Company, which he alleged was the basis of defendant's claim to the oil and gases, and this deed shows that Hoskins and wife sold and conveyed the oil and gases in the land to the Northern Coal & Coke Company on the 11th day of September, 1903. While it was not necessary to his cause of action that he should have alleged from whom or the manner in which he acquired title to the lands, nor to have alleged that his vendor had conveyed the oil and gases to another under whom the defendant claimed title, but having undertaken to set out his own and the defendant's claim of title showing that they claimed under a common vendor and that such vendor had conveyed the oil and gases to the predecessor in title of the defendant, it was necessary for him to make averments showing that his title was superior to that of the defendant by alleging that the conveyance to him from Hoskins was prior, and therefore superior, to the conveyance from Hoskins to defendant's vendor, and having failed to do so, the court construing the pleading more strongly against the pleader, according to the well-settled rule, was compelled to conclude that the conveyance from Hoskins to the defendant's vendor was prior to the conveyance from Hoskins to plaintiff, and that Hoskins had thus parted with title to the oil and gases in the land, and had no title thereto when he conveyed the land to plaintiff. The facts necessary to constitute a cause of action for a wrong of the defendant must be alleged and will not be presumed. Reid v. Lyttle, 150 Ky. 304, 150 S. W. 357; Daugherty v. Northern Coal & Coke Co., 174 Ky. 423, 192 S. W. 501; Samuels v. Louisville Ry. Co., 151 Ky. 90, 151 S. W. 37; Johnson v. York Coal & Coke Co., 182 Ky. 303, 206 S. W. 611. The terms of the deed from Hoskins to the Northern Coal & Coke Company shows that it was not a mere license granted to it to take oil and gases from the land, but amounted to a separation of the oils and gases from the remaining portions of the land, and a conveyance in fee simple of the portions of the land consisting of them to the vendee in the deed.

[4] After the granting and habendum clauses in the deed, an exception appears in the following language, viz.:

"It is understood that there is an oil and gas lease on this land, and the same is excepted from this conveyance."

The language of this exception could only mean what it says, and that is, there was then in existence a lease in the ordinarily accepted meaning of the term, upon the land, which authorized some one to operate on the land and to take therefrom oil and gas, and to pay the lessor or the owner holding the rights of the lessor a royalty proportioned to the quantity taken, and that Hoskins was accepting the rights and benefits under this lease for the lessor and lessee in the lease, or for the benefit of their transferees. It will be observed that Hoskins does not indicate by the language of the deed that he held any interest whatever in the lease, as would be inferred, if it was a reservation instead of an exception. An exception in a deed is intended to describe some part of the thing granted, which the grantor retains title to and does not convey, or something to which another holds title already and which is not intended to be conveyed, and the exception may be for the benefit of the grantor himself, or it may be for the benefit of another who already has acquired title to the portion of the thing, which is affected by the exception. The exception may be a description of a portion of the thing granted, which previously to the grant had been conveyed to another, and not necessarily so conveyed by the grantor, but by a prior grantor. Passing over the question which might arise as to the validity of the exception on account of its vagueness and uncertainty, there is nothing in the deed from Hoskins to the Northern Coal & Coke Company from which it could be inferred that he was the owner, at the time of the conveyance, of any beneficial interest in the lease, or that he owned same at the time that he conveyed the land to plaintiff; nor does plaintiff aver that he was the owner of any beneficial interest in the lease at the time of the institution of his action. The exception, in the deed from Hoskins to the Northern Coal & Coke Company, of a lease relating to oil and gas upon the property, being an exception of the rights under the lease of the lessor and lessee, without anything indicating that Hoskins had any interest therein, and there being no way of determining from the deed or the pleading whether the exception was made because Hoskins desired to retain the benefit of a lessor in the lease for himself, or to protect himself against the consequences of his conveyance of the oils and gases, with a warranty of title, to the vendee, because another was then the owner of the benefits, which might accrue to a lessor of the lease, and the petition failing to assert any right or interest in the lease, on the part of the plaintiff, it cannot be assumed that he had any interest therein, or that his vendor ever had any. The plaintiff failing to show that any wrong was done him by the defendant, the court was not in error in having sustained the demurrer.

The judgment is therefore affirmed.

EASTHAM et al. v. EASTHAM et al.

(Court of Appeals of Kentucky. May 24, 1921.)

1. Deeds ⊚=134—Difference between "limitation" and "condition."

The difference between a "limitation" and a "condition" is that in the case of a "limitation" the estate determines as soon as the contingency happens without any act on the part of the person next in expectancy, while in the case of a "condition" the estate continues beyond the happening of the contingency unless the grantor or his heirs, or the devisor or his heirs, take advantage of the breach of condition and make an entry or claim in order to avoid the estate.

[Ed. Note.—For other definitions, see Words and Phrases, First and Second Series, Condition; Limitation.]

2. Deeds ⊚=151—Grantee takes estate freed of void condition.

If the condition expressed in a deed is void, the grantee takes the estate freed of the condition.

3. Deeds ⊚=147—When conditions are void.

A condition is void if it is impossible at the time of its creation, or afterwards becomes so by the act of God or of the grantor, or if it is contrary to law, or to public policy, or is repugnant to the nature of the estate.

4. Deeds ⊚=134—Held to convey an estate upon limitation and not upon condition.

Husband's deed of land to wife during her life, or, should she survive him, while she remained his widow, and at his death, "or should she marry again, then this property goes to * * * children * * * by his first and second wife," conveyed an estate upon a limitation ending on her remarriage and not upon a condition, for the words "should she marry again" did not create a condition by defeating an estate already limited, as the grantee in the first instance took only during her widowhood.

Appeal from Circuit Court, Pulaski County.

Suit by R. L. Eastham and others against Chauncey Eastham and others. From judgment rendered, defendants appeal. Reversed and remanded.

Wm. M. Catron, of Somerset, for appellants.

Ben V. Smith & Son, of Somerset, for appellees.

CLAY, J. In the year 1903, R. L. Eastham, in consideration of the love and affection which he had for his wife and children, conveyed to his wife three acres of ground on Mt. Vernon street in the city of Somerset, and his undivided one-half interest in a business house fronting on the public square in said city. The deed contains the following provision:

"The second party is to have the first described property so long as she lives or remains his widow, should first party die first. At the death of second party, or should she marry again, then this property goes to the children of the first party by his first and second wife."

R. L. Eastham had two children, Rouse and Robert Eastham, Jr., by his first wife, and four children, Chauncy, Bert, Bess, and Louise, by his second wife. Bess Eastham died in infancy and without issue, and her interest passed to her father, R. L. Eastham.

In the month of October, 1919, R. L. Eastham sued Lola Eastham for divorce. She filed an answer and counterclaim denying the allegations of the petition, and asking a divorce from R. L. Eastham. On final hearing she was granted a divorce and given the custody of the children.

While the suit for divorce was pending, R. L. Eastham and his wife, Lola, entered into an agreement settling their property rights. By this agreement R. L. Eastham paid to Lola Eastham the sum of $1,500 cash, and agreed to pay her the sum of $1,000 more in two equal installments, for which he executed his notes. On the other hand, she agreed to convey and did convey to R. L. Eastham all her interest in the property conveyed to her by the deed above referred to.

This suit was brought by R. L. Eastham and Lola Eastham, in her own right and as guardian of the infant defendants, and by Rouse Eastham and Robert Eastham, Jr., against Chauncy Eastham, Bert Eastham, and Louise Eastham, for a construction of the deed of 1903 above referred to, and for a sale of the three acres of land on Mt. Vernon street and a division of the proceeds. The court held that, under the deed in question, Lola Eastham took a life estate with remainder to the children of R. L. Eastham by his first and second wives, that R. L. Eastham was now the owner of said life estate, as well as an undivided one-sixth in remainder owned by Bess Eastham to which he acquired title by descent and by the deed which Lola F. Eastham executed to him. It was further adjudged that the property be sold and the proceeds divided in accordance with the terms of the judgment. The infant defendants appeal.

It is conceded that, if the estate which Lola Eastham acquired under the deed of 1903, and which she reconveyed to R. L. Eastham, terminates in case she marries again, there is no way by which the proceeds of the sale may be properly divided, and no sale is desired.

[1-3] The difference between a "limitation" and a "condition" is that in the case of a "limitation" the estate determines as soon as the contingency happens, without any act on the part of him who is next in expectancy, while in the case of a "condition" the estate continues beyond the happening of the contingency, unless the grantor or his heirs, or the devisor or his heirs, take advantage of the breach of the condition and make an entry or claim in order to avoid the estate. 21 C. J. p. 930. Furthermore, if the condition be void, the grantee takes the estate freed of the condition, and the condition is void if impossible at the time of its creation, or afterward becomes so by the act of God or of the grantor, or if it is contrary to law or to public policy, or repugnant to the nature of the estate. 21 C. J. 930; Plumb v. Tubbs, 41 N. Y. 442; Union Pac. R. Co. v. Cook, 98 Fed. 281, 39 C. C. A. 86; Jones v. Chesapeake, etc., R. Co., 14 W. Va. 514; Mahoning County Com'rs v. Young, 59 Fed. 96, 8 C. C. A. 27; Conrad v. Long, 33 Mich. 78; Outland v. Bowen, 115 Ind. 150, 17 N. E. 281, 7 Am. St. Rep. 420; 2 Blackstone, Com. p. 156.

Counsel for appellees have prepared an able and interesting brief in support of the proposition that Lola Eastham took, under the deed in question, an estate on condition, and that the condition is ✸oid. Particular stress is placed upon the following discussion of the question in section 254, Graves on Real Property:

"Section 254. *Marriage as a Limitation or Condition Subsequent.*—It will conduce to clearness to illustrate the difference between a limitation and a condition by the not uncommon case of a gift to a widow dependent on her not marrying again. Let us suppose first that land is given a widow while she remains unmarried (durante viduitate): Is this a limitation or a condition? And if she marries, does she forfeit the estate, or does it expire by limitation? It is not difficult to see that it is a limitation merely, without the semblance of a condition. How long is the land given the widow? While she remains unmarried, or what is the same thing, until she marries. Nothing is said about her life; it is not limited until her death, but until her marriage. When, therefore, she marries, she has enjoyed all the estate that was given her, and cannot complain that she has lost anything by forfeiture; the land was given her until her marriage, and on that event, the estate ends by limitation. And while the estate might have continued until the widow's death, if she had remained unmarried, yet it is not true that on her marriage a larger estate limited is thereby cut short and defeated. The estate is until her marriage, and when that takes place whether sooner or later, the entire estate given has been enjoyed, and is at an end without entry by the grantor.

"But suppose land is given to a widow for life, with a condition superadded that she shall not marry; and with a proviso that if she does marry, the grantor may enter upon the land immediately, and resume possession. Here the limitation is for life, which is equal to until death. But this is not all. There is superadded or imposed on the limitation a condition, viz., that the widow shall not marry. Suppose, however she does marry, what is the result? Will her estate, in case the grantor enforces the condition and takes the land from her, end by limitation? Clearly not, for the estate limited was for her life, and would not end by limitation until her death; whereas her estate is divested and ends on her marriage—perhaps many years before her death. Hence the estate has died a violent death; the estate limited to the widow was larger than that which she had enjoyed; the entry of the grantor cuts it short before the time limited. The widow forfeits for breach of condition.

"It may be objected that in the two cases just put the practical effect is the same, whether we regard the language as importing a limitation or a condition; that in either case, if the widow does not marry, her estate continues until her death; while if she does marry, her estate is at an end. But there is an important difference. If the land is given to the widow until she married, the effect of her marriage is to terminate her estate ipso facto, and immediately. No entry by the grantor is required in order to terminate her estate. If the widow remains in possession, it is as tenant by sufferance, or by virtue of some new estate given her by the grantor. When, however, the land is given to the widow for life on condition that she does not marry, the effect of her marriage is not to end her estate ipso facto; for a life estate was given her, and that does not expire by limitation or marriage. The grantor must re-enter and take the land, or the widow will remain in possession by virtue of her old estate. In other words, she is liable to forfeit the life estate on her marriage, but if the grantor waives the forfeiture (as he may) the life estate continues to its natural termination."

[4] Let us apply the above test to the language of the deed which is as follows:

"The second party is to have the first described property so long as she lives or remains his widow, should first party die first. At the death of second party, or should she marry again, then this property goes to the children of the first party by his first and second wife."

Clearly, this is not a case where land is deeded to the grantee for life with a condition superadded that she shall not marry, and with a proviso that, if she does marry, the grantor may enter upon the land immediately and resume possession. The grant is for life or during her widowhood. Not only is the duration of the estate measured by the words, "so long as she lives," but by the words, "or remains his widow." Hence the words, "should she marry again," do not have the effect of defeating an estate already limited, for the grantee in the first instance took only during her widowhood. In other words, the case is one where the estate has already filled out the measure of its limitation, and the words, "should she marry again," no more create a condition than do

the words, "at the death of the second party." They merely provide for a limitation over upon the expiration of an estate already limited. This conclusion finds support in Coppage v. Alexander's Heirs, 2 B. Mon. 313, 38 Am. Dec. 153, the only Kentucky case dealing directly with the question. There the language of the will was:

"I give unto my beloved wife, Mary Alexander, the half of my land I now own during her widowhood or life."

In holding that the devise was a limitation expressive of the duration of the estate, and not a condition, the court said:

"But waiving the question just mooted, as to the effect of a condition clearly expressed, restricting the marriage of a widow, as unnecessary now to be determined, we are clearly of opinion, looking at the whole contents of the will, that the devise to his wife during widowhood or life, was intended by the testator, and should be construed, as a limitation expressive of the duration of the estate, and not as a condition subsequent or prior. 1 Roper on Legacies, chap. 13, 558, 526, et seq.; Richards v. Baker, 2 Atk. 321. The testator having made a liberal provision for his wife, in slaves and other property, according to his circumstances, and vested the same in her absolutely, he leaves to her in addition, the one half of his little farm as a home in effect, during her life if she remained a widow, or during her widowhood only, in case she married. The happening of either event was intended to terminate the estate. It was intended as a benefit durante viduitate and no longer. The estate is not vested for life, to be forfeited if she married, but is vested during her widowhood only, in the event of her marriage, and must cease with the termination of her widowhood, as one of the periods to which it was limited, and upon the accrual of which it was made to expire. Vance and Wife v. Campbell's Heirs, 1 Dana, 230."

The only difference between the two cases is that in the case at bar there is a limitation over, and this is always regarded as a strong circumstance in favor of the construction that the estate is upon limitation rather than upon condition. Frye's Case, 1 Vent. 208; 2 Bl. Comm. 155; In re Miller, 159 N. C. 123, 74 S. E. 888. We are therefore constrained to hold that Mrs. Eastham acquired under the deed in question an estate upon limitation and not upon condition. Therefore her estate ends when she marries again, and so does the estate which she conveyed to her husband.

Judgment reversed, and cause remanded for proceedings not inconsistent with this opinion.

TOWN OF NORTONVILLE v. WOODWARD.

(Court of Appeals of Kentucky. May 31, 1921.)

1. **Evidence ⬤48 — Judicial notice taken of regular meetings of board of council of town.**

Court will take judicial notice of regular meetings of board of council of towns, and that a meeting was a regular meeting, although minutes denominated it "first called meeting."

2. **Municipal corporations ⬤183(1) — Filling vacancy of marshal held "appointment," and not "election."**

Where office of town marshal became vacant, and the council filled the vacancy, ascertaining the choice by secret ballot, there was an "appointment," and not an "election," within the meaning of the Constitution and statutes, and the fact that the ballot was secret did not in any way invalidate it.

[Ed. Note.—For other definitions, see Words and Phrases, First and Second Series, Appoint— Appointment; Election.]

3. **Municipal corporations ⬤183(4)—De facto marshal not entitled to salary.**

A de facto town marshal is not entitled to recover any salary, and can retain only that paid him.

4. **Municipal corporations ⬤111(2) — Ordinance must have enacting clause.**

An ordinance is not valid unless it has an enacting clause, under Ky. St. § 3700.

5. **Contracts ⬤125—Against public policy for officer to agree to accept less than fixed salary.**

An agreement by officer to accept less than fixed salary of an office to which he is elected or appointed is void, as against public policy, and a town marshal was not bound by an agreement to accept appointment and to serve for $25 per month when the salary was fixed by ordinance at $50.

6. **Evidence ⬤175—Oral testimony inadmissible to show action of city council.**

Oral testimony of an official as to what action a city council took on a given subject is inadmissible, as a city can only speak through its records.

Appeal from Circuit Court, Hopkins County.

Action by S. L. Woodward against the town of Nortonville. Judgment for plaintiff, and defendant appeals. Affirmed.

J. A. Jonson, of Madisonville, for appellant. Letcher R. Fox and Laffoon & Waddill, all of Madisonville, for appellee.

SAMPSON, J. The appellant town of Nortonville is and was at all the times herein mentioned a town of the sixth class. In January, 1910, there was a vacancy in the office of marshal of the said town, and the new city council, on coming into office, undertook, on January 3d, to fill it by appointing or

electing appellee, S. L. Woodward, to said office. Its first regular meeting on the night of Monday, January 3d, was for the purpose of organization and election of a chairman and other officials of the board, and a marshal. By statute such meetings are fixed on the first Monday in January. The following is a copy of the minutes of that meeting:

"First called meeting of the new board of trustees of Nortonville, Ky., January 3, 1910. Purpose of meeting was to qualify as councilmen for town and to elect chairman, marshal, clerk, and treasurer for same.

"All the board members for 1910 were present and were qualified by Judge J. R. Harrison as councilmen for town. House was now declared ready for applications for marshal. Mr. S. L. Woodward and Mr. T. W. Wiggins made. After hearing applications heard by the clerk, a ballot was made and a vote taken by secret ballot and counted by the chairman and clerk, which showed two votes for S. L. Woodward and two votes for T. W. Wiggins. Chairman J. W. Gatlin cast his vote for S. L. Woodward, which untied the vote and elected S. L. Woodward marshal for the town of Nortonville, Ky.

"Motion duly made and seconded to adjourn to meet January 5, 1910, for further business.

"J. W. Gatlin, Chm.

"C. M. Oates, Clerk."

[1, 2] Although the minutes of the meeting denominate it the "first called meeting," it was, in fact, the regular meeting of the board of council, and of this fact the court takes judicial notice. At such meeting the council had the right to fill a vacancy in the office of marshal. This was an appointment, not an election, within the meaning of our Constitution and statutes, and the mere fact that members of the council, in ascertaining the choice of that body for marshal, took a secret ballot did not in any way invalidate the appointment of Woodward.

That part of our Constitution reading, "In all elections by persons in a representative capacity, the voting shall be viva voce, and made a matter of record," has no application to the facts of this case, because the marshal was not, in the constitutional sense, elected, but only appointed, the statute so designating the act of filling such vacancy.

Another meeting of the council was had on January 5th, but, as Woodward was not ready to execute bond, it was adjourned until the 18th, at which time the council again met, and the marshal's bond was executed and approved by the council. At this meeting the minutes of the regular meeting were read and approved.

Woodward insists that, when he was installed as marshal on the 18th of January, the date of the execution and approval of the bond, he was a de jure, not a de facto officer, and entitled to the regular fixed compensation and emoluments of the office. The city insists that it entered into a verbal agreement and contract with Woodward before his election, by which he was to accept the office of marshal and perform all the duties thereof for a salary of $25 per month and the fees, and a per cent. of the taxes, and to prove this it called several of its ex-officials who participated in the election of Woodward as witnesses, and also introduced a number of reports and claims made out by Woodward against the city in which his salary was fixed at $25 for a part of the time, at $35 for a part of the time, and at $45 for the balance of the time.

[3] This litigation was commenced in 1917 by Woodward, against the city, to recover $1,548, with interest, alleged by him to be the balance due on his salary and fees while marshal, on the basis that the regular fixed salary of marshal was $50 per month during his incumbency. His contention is that the city was financially unable, at the time the service was performed, to pay him his full salary, and that he agreed to accept a less sum on account until the city became able to pay in full. He served as marshal from January, 1910, until September, 1916, and resigned before bringing this suit. The city defends on the theory that Woodward agreed before his election to accept $25 per month as salary, instead of $50, as fixed by ordinance, and that he was paid said sum as it came due until the city council voluntarily raised it to $35 per month, after which time he received that sum until again raised to $45 per month; that he has received in full all salary and fees due him according to the contract, and is estopped by his conduct to claim the full salary fixed by the ordinance. It also insists that the attempted election of Woodward by the city council by secret ballot was invalid, and that he was never more than a de facto marshal, and not, therefore, entitled to recover any salary, but can only retain that heretofore paid him. If he was merely a de facto officer, this contention must be sustained.

Before his election, the city council, by ordinance regularly enacted, fixed the salary of the marshal at $50 per month, and this ordinance had not been repealed, amended, or changed from its passage in 1909 up to the time of this litigation, unless the change was effected by the following minute made March 21, 1911, and found in the records of the city council:

"Regular meeting board of trustees, town of Nortonville, Ky., March 21, 1911.
"Order called by chairman, J. W. Gatlin. Roll call by clerk, J. W. Gatlin, pres., W. E. Laffoon, pres., L. P. Payne, pres., C. M. Stephens, pres., J. N. Oates, absent.

231 S.W.—15

"Regular move and seconded by all voting aye that board allow Marshal Woodward a $10 raise on the month, making his salary $35 per month.
"Regular move and seconded to adjourn to meet call of chairman. J. W. Gatlin, Chm.
"C. M. Oates, Clerk."

No other order or ordinance was made or passed by the council affecting the marshal's salary.

[4] It will be observed that this minute has no enacting clause. It cannot therefore be a valid ordinance. Bates v. City of Monticello, 173 Ky. 244, 190 S. W. 1074, Ky. St. § 3700. Had it been a valid ordinance, it could have only affected the salary of Woodward after his qualification under his subsequent election by the people, and not for the term which he was serving at the time of the passage of the same.

[5] It is a general rule that an agreement by an officer to accept less than the fixed salary of an office to which he is elected or appointed for his compensation is void, as against public policy. Mechem on Public Officers, § 377; 29 Cyc. 1426; Bodenhofer v. Hogan, 142 Iowa, 321, 120 N. W. 659, 134 Am. St. Rep. 422, 19 Ann. Cas. 1073; 22 R. C. L. 538. It would therefore appear that, if it be conceded that Woodward actually agreed, as contended by the city, to serve as marshal for $25 per month when the salary was fixed by ordinance at $50, he was not bound thereby, the agreement being against public policy, and void.

[6] Moreover, there was no competent evidence offered by the city to prove such an agreement. A city can only speak through its records, and there was no record of the city reciting or entering such an agreement. Oral testimony of an official as to what action the city council has taken on a given subject is inadmissible. The records alone are competent evidence of such facts.

It becomes wholly unnecessary for us to determine what the status of the parties would be if the city council had passed a valid ordinance fixing the marshal's salary at a different sum. It cannot be doubted, however, that the lawmaking body of the city could, before election of Woodward, have passed an ordinance fixing his salary at a less sum. It had the means of protecting the city, but failed to exercise them.

It follows from what has been said that Woodward was entitled to recover the full salary of marshal, as provided by the city ordinance at the time of his election, and the trial court did not err in so holding.

Judgment affirmed.

EARLY & DANIEL CO. v. C. S. EVANS & CO.

(Court of Appeals of Kentucky. May 31, 1921.)

Sales ⊂⇒181(13)—Evidence held to show that consignee sold wheat for shipper, and not as its own.

In an action by consignee of wheat against consignor to recover expenses of handling and selling the wheat, which had been bought for export and was rejected, evidence *held* to show that plaintiff in selling the wheat was acting for defendant, and did not sell the wheat as its own.

Appeal from Circuit Court, Jessamine County.

Action by the Early & Daniel Company against C. S. Evans & Co. Judgment for defendants, and plaintiff appeals. Reversed, and remanded for new trial.

John H. Welch, of Nicholasville, and Hunt, Bennett & Utter, of Cincinnati, Ohio, for appellant.

Bronaugh & Bronaugh, of Nicholasville, for appellees.

CLAY, J. On October 24, 1915, the Early & Daniel Company of Cincinnati, Ohio, purchased of C. S. Evans & Co. of Nicholasville, Ky., 8,000 bushels of No. 2 red winter wheat at $1.59 per bushel f. o. b. Nicholasville, Ky., for shipment to Newport News, Va., "subject to Newport News weights and inspection." On May 4th or 5th C. S. Evans & Co. shipped eight carloads of wheat to Newport News. Bills of lading with drafts attached were sent to the Early & Daniel Company, and the drafts paid. Upon the arrival of the cars in Newport News, four were accepted and four were rejected on account of garlic, and the Early & Daniel Company were notified of the rejection by wire dated and received May 14th. On the same day the Early & Daniel Company sent to C. S. Evans & Co. a copy of the telegram and inclosed it in a letter containing the following:

"Will advise further as soon as get more particulars."

On the same day the Early & Daniel Company sent the following telegram to J. H. Graves, manager C. & O. Elevator, Newport News:

"Advise, if you can, what usual manner of handling rejected garlic wheat also send samples of cars [names of cars omitted] deliver grain growers enough our two wheat to take place of these cars and handle the rejected wheat for us."

On May 18th the Early & Daniel Company wrote to C. S. Evans & Co. that they had no definite information from the C. & O.

Elevator as to the manner in which the rejected cars could be handled, and saying:

"However, we are afraid that these cars will not do for export."

On May 19, 1915, the Early & Daniel Company wrote C. S. Evans & Co., advising them that the exporters would not accept the garlic wheat, saying:

"Under the circumstances, we cannot use the wheat at any discount. All we can see for you to do is to make a sale to a Virginia mill. If you want us to assist you in this matter, we will do all we can. Have instructed the elevator at News to send us an elevator receipt and upon receipt of same, will draw on you for amount of drafts paid."

On May 24th the Early & Daniel Company again wrote C. S. Evans & Co. that they had been advised that the wheat could not be mixed for export, and adding:

"Now, gentlemen, under the circumstances, we cannot accept this wheat on contract. Will be compelled to draw back on you with elevator receipts attached just as soon as they arrive. However, if you want us to help you dispose of this wheat, we will gladly do so without any cost to you, or. that is, any charge for our services."

On May 25th C. S. Evans & Co. wrote the Early & Daniel Company, acknowledging the receipt of the letter of May 24th, and adding:

"We also note you say you cannot use this wheat on contract. We do not understand this part of your letter, as any wheat sold, even though it does not grade, should be applied on contract at grade difference, as the writer explained to you when in your office a few days ago."

On May 26th the Early & Daniel Company wrote C. S. Evans & Co. as follows:

"Had the wheat been shipped to Cincinnati or any terminal market, your position of taking in at the market difference would probably be correct. But in this instance, you sold us a specific grade of wheat for export, and have shipped a wheat which cannot be blown or cleaned or mixed in with other stock and be brought up to No. 2 grade. We do not object to your corresponding with Mr. Graves, and have written him to give you all the information or assistance he can. Just as soon as you have had reply from him, will thank you to get in touch with us. Would suggest that you act quickly, as the wheat is there now subject to your order."

On June 2d the Early & Daniel Company wrote to C. S. Evans & Co. that they had not received elevator receipts on the four cars of rejected wheat, and adding:

"If you care to make disposition in the meantime, advise us and we can arrange it. If we can be of any assistance in disposing of this wheat, call on us."

On June 7th C. T. Ashley, a member of the firm of C. S. Evans & Co., went to Newport News to look after the wheat. He called on Mr. Graves, the manager of the C. & O. Elevator, and was referred by him to Mr. Scheer, the chief inspector. Scheer assured him that the wheat would grade as No. 2 wheat, which was satisfactory. Upon Ashley's return from Newport News, the Early & Daniel Company sent the following telegram to C. S. Evans & Co.:

"Newport News elevator wires to-day that loading orders have been received enabling them to mix out the garlic wheat advantage of this should be taken now to save further loss. Therefore we will sell to best advantage to-day. Responsibility for the loss to rest with you or the C. & O. R. R. Company."

However, the telegram, when received by C. S. Evans & Co., read as follows:

"Therefore, we will sell to best advantage to-day's responsibility for the railroad company."

On the same day the Early & Daniel Company wrote C. S. Evans & Co. as follows:

"In reference to our wire to-day. We received a wire from A. H. Graves, Mgr. C. & O. Elevator, Newport News, advising that at this time he could mix your wheat our and get a grade of No. 2.

"We wired you that we would sell wheat in stock at further loss which we did at $1.23 f. o. b. vessel Newport News to-day.

"Now, gentlemen, we cannot account for Graves changing his grade at this late date. We, of course, are going to stand by the original grade. We had advice from Graves at that time that the wheat would not grade at No. 2 for export and could not be cleaned or, blowed and brought up to No. 2 grade by mixing in with other stock we had on hand there at that time.

"We were within our rights in refusing this wheat from you on Graves' advice that the wheat would not do for export, and we cannot accept it at this late date only at the market difference.

"As soon as we get the matter straightened out, that is, the deal finally put through, we will render bill against you for loss, and if you have any claim, it is against the C. & O., as we cannot and do not intend to stand in between on this transaction.

"Trust we have made ourselves clear and undoubtedly our action in selling the wheat at News was satisfactory to you as we did not get reply."

In addition to identifying the various letters and telegrams, E. B. Terrill, who represented the Early & Daniel Company, testified in substance as follows: The purchase of the wheat was made over the telephone and then confirmed by a letter from C. S. Evans & Co. The wheat was purchased for export, and Evans & Co. were informed of this fact. The first communication which he received from Evans & Co. was the letter of May 25th. The wheat was sold on June 15th at the price of $1.23, which was the market price at Newport News at that time. He never received any authority from Evans & Co. to sell the wheat. J. H. Graves, the general agent of the Chesapeake & Ohio Railroad at Newport News, identified the correspondence which passed between him and the Early & Daniel Company. A representative of Evans & Co. called to see him in regard to the four cars of rejected wheat, and was sent by him to H. M. Scheer, the inspector for the Newport News Chamber of Commerce. Scheer testified to the rejection of the wheat and to the fact that sometimes wheat which is rejected on account of garlic is mixed out in shipments where certificates do not require "free from garlic."

For the defendants C. T. Ashley, a member of the firm, testified that he made the sale over the telephone to Mr. Terrill. He did not admit to the Early & Daniel Company that the wheat was not up to contract. Rejected wheat did not apply on contract in any market. The Early & Daniel Company did not notify him that they would handle the wheat for his account. After receiving several letters and telegrams from the Early & Daniel Company, he went to Newport News. He saw Mr. Graves and was referred to his chief clerk. He called him the inspector. He told Mr. Scheer that he came there to handle the wheat himself. Scheer said that he was going to take it and grade it as No. 2 wheat. This was satisfactory to him. On cross-examination he stated that he was in Newport News on the 7th. He did not call up the Early & Daniel Company to let them know what had been done with the wheat. It was their understanding that the wheat was for export, and the cars were all billed for export. He supposed that, where wheat was shipped for export and was not up to proper grade, it would be the shipper's wheat. He did not at any time offer to take back the wheat or repay the Early & Daniel Company. He simply let the wheat alone except for the conversation and correspondence he had with Mr. Terrill. All along the Early & Daniel Company were trying to work it in with some other wheat they had. He did not think that he had letters showing that it was for his account. No matter what the wheat weighed or how it graded, the inspection at Newport News was to control. He did not know what became of the wheat.

The suit was brought to recover $2,034.87, loss on the wheat. $10.60 for shortage in weight, and $30.24 for failure to load the cars to their full capacity. A trial before a jury resulted in a verdict and judgment for defendant. Plaintiff appeals.

It is conceded that the evidence respecting the item of $30.24 for failure to load the cars to their full capacity was sufficient to make a question for the jury, but insisted that the verdict on the item of $2,034.87, loss on the wheat, and $10.60 for shortage in weight, is flagrantly against the evidence.

In addition to believing from the evidence that the contract was made and the wheat paid for, the jury, before finding for the plaintiff, were required by instruction No. 1 to believe from the evidence: (1) That the four carloads of wheat were rejected at Newport News; (2) that plaintiff within a reasonable time thereafter notified the defendant of the rejection and refused to accept the rejected wheat; (3) that the defendant refused and failed to take charge of said wheat after receiving said notice of refusal to accept; (4) that by reason of such failure plaintiff became liable for storage or other charges; (5) that plaintiff notified defendant that it would sell said wheat; and (6) that plaintiff did sell said wheat on the open market for a fair and reasonable price. By instruction No. 2 the jury were told to find for the defendant if they believed from the evidence that, after the wheat was rejected by the inspector at Newport News, the plaintiff took charge of said wheat on its own account and kept and sold the wheat as its own.

Taking up the evidence with reference to the issues submitted in the foregoing instructions, the testimony of H. M. Scheer, the chief inspector at Newport News, and the letters and telegrams from J. H. Graves established beyond any controversy the fact that the wheat in question was rejected. A copy of the telegram notifying the Early & Daniel Company of the rejection of the wheat was mailed on May 14th, the day of its receipt, to Evans & Co., and therefore it cannot be doubted that Evans & Co. were advised of the rejection of the wheat. But the words, "Handle the rejected wheat for us," in the telegram from the Early & Daniel Company to J. H. Graves, are seized upon to show that the Early & Daniel Company did not refuse to accept the wheat. In our opinion these words are of no probative force when considered in the light of all the letters and telegrams which passed between the parties. Not only were Evans & Co. notified of the rejection of the wheat by the inspector at Newport News on May 14th, but on May 18th, which was within a reasonable time, Evans & Co. were notified that the Early & Daniel Company could not use the wheat at any discount and would draw on Evans & Co. for amount of drafts paid. This was a clear and express notice that the Early & Daniel Company could not use the wheat and would hold Evans & Co. responsible for the price. Not only so, but on May 24th Evans & Co. were again notified that the Early & Daniel Company could not accept the wheat on the contract, and that the company would be compelled to draw back on them with elevator receipts attached just as soon as they arrived. Mr. Ashley not

only admitted the receipts of these various letters and telegrams, but also admitted that the rejected wheat would not apply on contract in any market, and that the grading in Newport News was final, even though the weight and grade were erroneous. While the correspondence was going on, Evans & Co. showed no disposition to protect the Early & Daniel Company in the transaction. Although Evans & Co. were notified by various letters and telegrams that the Early & Daniel Company had refused to accept the wheat, Evans & Co. never at any time notified the Early & Daniel Company that they would take charge of the wheat. It is true that Ashley went to Newport News. All that he did was to inquire about the wheat, and, when informed that it would then be graded out as No. 2 wheat, he said that was satisfactory to him. He did not then oppose the arrangement or ask that the wheat be delivered to him. On the contrary, he acquiesced in the arrangement. That being true, all the circumstances show that he failed and refused to take charge of the wheat, and even his own testimony does not tend to establish the contrary. There is no dispute as to the items of storage and other charges for which the Early & Daniel Company became liable, and there can be no doubt that this liability arose from the failure of Evans & Co. to take charge of the wheat. The Early & Daniel Company telegraphed Evans & Co. on June 14th that they would sell the wheat that day to the best advantage. "Responsibility for loss to rest with you or C. & O. R. R. Co." The testimony for Evans & Co. is to the effect that the telegram when received read, "Responsibility for the railroad company." But, however this may be, Evans & Co. do not deny receiving the letter written by the Early & Daniel Company on the same day, advising Evans & Co. that the wheat was sold at $1.23, and that as soon as the matter straightened out they would render a bill against Evans & Co. for the loss, and, if Evans & Co. had any claim, it was against the Chesapeake & Ohio Railroad. It is undisputed that the wheat was sold. Terrill testifies that $1.23 was the market price at Newport News on the day of the sale, and defendant did not attempt to show the contrary.

While an occasional expression in one of the letters or telegrams affords a very unsubstantial basis for an argument to the contrary, the letters and telegrams construed as a whole, and viewed in the light of the conduct of the parties, show unmistakably that the Early & Daniel Company in selling the wheat was acting for Evans & Co. and did not sell the wheat as its own.

In our opinion there is no escape from the conclusion that the verdict of the jury on the issues submitted by instructions Nos. 1 and 2 is flagrantly against the evidence.

The same is true with respect to the item of $10.60 for shortage in weight. The shortage was proved, and there is no evidence to the contrary.

Judgment reversed, and cause remanded for new trial consistent with this opinion.

JOHN R. COPPIN CO. v. RICHARDS.

(Court of Appeals of Kentucky. May 31, 1921.)

1. **Landlord and tenant ⟵169(11)—Responsibility for injury to contractor's workman by elevator held for jury.**

In an action against the proprietor of a building for the death of an electrician engaged by independent contractors installing fixtures, whether a servant of defendant, or servant of a tenant of the building, started the elevator which caused the injury, held for the jury.

2. **Appeal and error ⟵1001(1)—Finding supported by evidence of probative value not disturbed.**

A finding of a jury will not be disturbed, where the proven facts and circumstances were such that a reasonable person would have deduced the conclusion arrived at by the jurors; but if the evidence was not of such probative value as to sustain the deduction, inference, and belief in the mind of a reasonable person, the judgment should be reversed.

3. **Negligence ⟵134(10)—Degree of proof required.**

When the evidence shows that the injury may have resulted from any one of two or more causes, only one of which was due to defendant's negligence, and the inference that the injury resulted from one cause was no stronger than that it resulted from the other or others, a verdict for the plaintiff cannot be sustained.

4. **Negligence ⟵134(2)—May be proven by circumstantial evidence.**

Negligence, like any other fact, may be proven by circumstantial evidence, that is, by proving facts from which a reasonable person could readily infer the ultimate fact of negligence.

5. **Negligence ⟵52—Warning of starting of elevator required.**

An electrician employed by an independent contractor who was working in and about an elevator shaft in defendant's building was entitled to due warning of the starting of the elevator.

6. **Negligence ⟵87—Electrician in elevator shaft held not guilty of contributory negligence.**

An electrician was not guilty of contributory negligence in working in an elevator shaft, where he had been told by the owner of the building that he could work in the shaft and that the elevator would remain on the third floor for a while, having the right to expect a warning from the persons in charge of the elevator before it moved.

7. **Negligence ⟵65—Risk of injury by elevator not assumed by contractor's workman.**

An electrician employed by an independent contractor, installing electrical appliances in and about an elevator shaft in defendant's building, did not assume risks of danger to him occasioned by negligence of defendant's servants, consisting in starting the elevator without giving warning.

Appeal from Circuit Court, Kenton County, Common Law and Equity Division.

Action by W. L. Richards, administrator, against the John R. Coppin Company. Judgment for plaintiff, and defendant appeals. Affirmed

O. M. Rogers and Wm. J. Deupree, both of Covington, and Clore, Schwab & McCaslin, of Cincinnati, Ohio, for appellant.

T. J. Edmonds and R. C. Simmons, both of Covington, for appellee.

SAMPSON, J. The $7,000 judgment which this appeal seeks to reverse was recovered by the administrator of Sidney Harris, in the Kenton circuit court, against the John R. Coppin Company, Incorporated, for the death of Harris in an elevator accident upon the averment and proof by circumstantial evidence that the death was the result of the negligence of the agents and servants of the corporation. Harris was a young man about 24 years of age, in good health and a trained electrical worker. He was engaged by a firm of electricians, independent contractors, to help them install lights and electrical fixtures in the garage part of the John R. Coppin Company's store building in the city of Covington. To do the work Harris and his associates were required to carry the wire from a connection in the ceiling of the first story of the building through the hole made in the floor for the elevator shaft to the basement. The wire had to be incased in conduits so as to make it safe, and attached to the walls of the building and the supports of the elevator in the shaft so as to make it secure. While laying on the floor of the first story with his head and shoulders extending into the elevator shaft, his face downward, engaged in connecting the electric wire or conduit to some part of the shaft equipment or building, the elevator car which was at the third floor above noiselessly descended and caught and killed Harris. The defendant company denied negligence on its part and pleaded contributory negligence on the part of Harris. A trial resulted in a verdict for $7,000, on which the judgment, from which this appeal is prosecuted, was rendered.

The John R. Coppin Company appeals, assigning as grounds for reversal of the judgment the following:

(1) The pleadings do not support the judgment.

(2) The court admitted incompetent evidence of the plaintiff over the objection of the defendant company.

(3) The court should have sustained defendant's motion, made both at the conclusion of plaintiff's evidence and at the conclusion of all the evidence, for a directed verdict in its favor.

(4) The court erroneously instructed the jury as to the law of the case.

Each of these contentions will be considered, but before we do so a statement of the facts somewhat in detail will be given.

The Coppin Company owned a large seven-story building in the city of Covington, in which was located three elevators, two of which were near the front of the building and used for carrying passengers, while the third was in the rear of the building and was used for carrying freight between the basement and the fourth story, its terminus. The accident to and death of Harris happened in the freight elevator shaft. The Coppin Company uses the first, second, and third stories of the building in its retail store business, and employed the seventh floor and the basement for storage purposes. The fourth floor is leased to and occupied by the Kenton Pharmaceutical Company, a patent medicine concern, which has the use of the freight elevator to carry its goods up and down, and had storage in the basement. This last-named company had three persons in its employ at the time of the accident, a pharmacist, an expressman, and a porter named Lee. The expressman was out of the building and had been for some time. The pharmacist never used the elevator, except upon rare occasions when the porter Lee was out, and says he did not use or attempt to use it on the day of the accident, and there is no evidence or even suggestion that he did do so. We will consider Lee's connection with the elevator later.

The Coppin Company employed a number of people both men and women in and about the store, but none of these used the freight elevator on the morning of the accident except Steinborn, the shipping clerk, and four porters named Davenport, Page, Harris, and Brogan, unless some one not accustomed to use it did so, and there is no evidence of this.

The real question of fact in the case being who started the elevator which killed Harris, we see by the process of elimination that only the four porters of the Coppin Company, the pharmaceutical company's porter Lee, and the deceased and the other two electricians need be considered, for they are the only ones shown to have had the opportunity to set the elevator in motion.

It is not seriously argued, nor could it be, that Harris or any of the electricians started the car, for every motive and reason is against such inference, and the direct evidence shows they did not do so. Coming now to the porter Lee who was in the basement at the time Harris met his death, the evidence shows that he had been working around the place for some months, and on the morning of the accident had carried a load of express from the fourth floor of the building down on the freight elevator to the first floor and to the basement, where he left it and began looking about some boxes. While thus engaged, the porters of the Coppin Company took the elevator to the third floor. Lee waited a short time for the elevator to return and then called up to those in charge of it on the third floor and asked for it, but was told that the elevator was in use but he could have it later. He then sat down on a box in the basement to wait for the elevator which he desired to use in taking his truck back to the fourth floor. He was close to the elevator shaft, and the electricians were working in it above connecting the wires and conduits. Harris, the deceased, called to Lee to hand him a wrench which was in the basement. Lee looked for it, but did not at first see the wrench, whereupon Harris told Lee it was on a box, and Lee took it and tried to reach it up to Harris, who was lying on his stomach on the floor above with his head and shoulders projecting into the elevator shaft and looking down at Lee.

Finding the distance too great, Lee procured a keg and stood on it and reached the wrench to Harris. When he stepped down, he glanced up the shaft and saw the elevator noiselessly descending and very near Harris, who was engaged in his work. The eminent peril of Harris so excited Lee that he began to scream, "Stop the elevator!" but, before Harris did or could move, his head and shoulders were caught between the elevator car and the edge of the concrete floor and so mashed that he died shortly thereafter. It is insisted by appellant company that Lee started the car, or at least it argues that the inference to be drawn from the evidence is as great that he started the car, as that any other person, including the Coppin Company's employés, started it. This insistence is based upon the fact that he was accustomed to operating the car and had been waiting for it to carry his truck to the fourth floor, that he was close to the cable by which the elevator was operated, and that his desire for the elevator had prompted him to pull the cable and cause the car to descend. But there is no evidence to support this theory. Lee testified he did not start the car; that he was not in reach of the cable, and did not intend to or try to operate the car. He says the rule was to call "elevator" when one wanted to use the car, and if it was in use the one using it would inform the one wanting it and he would have to wait.

When told that morning that the car was in use, Lee sat down to wait, and did wait. There is no presumption that Lee would have violated the rule about the elevator that morning, especially when there was absolutely no evidence that he had ever done so before. The evidence shows that it only took the elevator a few seconds to travel from the third floor to the first floor. Lee could not have started the elevator unless he did so before Harris asked him to hand up the wrench. When this request was made by Harris, the wrench could not be found by Lee, and he looked around for it, and when he found it he tried to hand it up to Harris, but found he could not reach him, so he obtained a keg and stood upon it so as to pass the wrench to Harris, who was then reaching down through the elevator hole as far as he could. After reaching the wrench to Harris, he stepped down from the keg and glanced up into the shaft and saw the elevator coming down, but not quite to the first floor. Lee was sitting down when Harris asked for the wrench. These facts conclusively prove that Lee did not start the elevator, for if he had done so the car would have reached the first floor where Harris was long before it did. In other words, the time occupied by Lee in finding and handing up the wrench was much greater than that required for the elevator car to run from the third floor to the first floor, and Lee did not have an opportunity to operate the cable during that time. Aside from this, every other circumstance appears to refute the theory that Lee started the car, and this we will advert to later.

The only other persons about the building which the evidence tends to show had an opportunity to start the elevator were the four porters in the employ of the Coppin Company, working on the third and seventh floors. These men, Davenport, Page, Harris, and Brogan, were in charge of and operating the elevator; they had raised it from the basement to the third floor and were loading it with rubbish to be carried to the basement. While they each say, except Brogan, who did not testify, they did not start the elevator and were not on the third floor where it was when it started down, they all admit they had the car in control and could have operated it at any time by pulling the cable. There is much conflict in their testimony. The stuff they had loaded was on the car, but other stuff was yet to be loaded before it went down, according to their contention as gleaned from the evidence. However this may be, the fact is the car started on its downward course while at the third floor in the possession and under the control of the porters of the appellant company,

and it is insisted by appellee administrator that the inference, deduction, and belief may reasonably be drawn and had, from these facts and circumstances proven, that the car was set in motion by one or the other of the four.

[1-3] This brings us to the only serious question of law on this appeal, which is: Did the court err in overruling defendant's motion for a directed verdict and in submitting the case to the jury? Were the proven facts and circumstances such that a reasonable person would have deduced the conclusion that the elevator car was set in motion by the hand of the Coppin Company's agents. If it was the judgment should not be disturbed, but if the evidence was not of such probative value as to sustain the deduction, inference, and belief in the mind of a reasonable person that the car was started on its death dealing course by the hand or agency of the appellant company, then the judgment should be reversed. The motion of the Coppin Company for a peremptory instruction to the jury to find for it was based upon the idea that there was no direct or other evidence of any probative value that the elevator car was set in motion by appellants or its agents or servants, or at most there was such slight circumstantial evidence as is wholly insufficient to support the verdict, and which evidence was equalized by other circumstances which rendered it impossible to determine with any degree of certainty whether the injury and death of Harris was the result of one or the other of two or three causes only one of which would fix liability on the Coppin Company. In other words, appellant insists that the inference to be drawn from the proven facts is equally consistent with its nonliability as with its liability; that there is an equilibrium of evidence, and that in such case it is the duty of the trial court to take the case from the jury because a verdict would be the result of mere speculation on its part. This court has frequently recognized the rule that when the evidence shows that the injury may have resulted from any one of two or more causes only one of which was due to defendant's negligence, and the inference that the injury resulted from one cause was no stronger than that it resulted from the other or others, a verdict for the plaintiff cannot be sustained. L. & N. R. R. Co. v. Guest, 106 S. W. 817, 32 Ky. Law Rep. 670; Cochran's Adm'r v. Krause, 144 Ky. 202, 137 S. W. 1053; McDonald v. Lou. Car Wheel & Supply Co., 149 Ky. 801, 149 S. W. 1142; The Lack Malleable Iron Co. v. Graham, 147 Ky. 161, 143 S. W. 1016.

This doctrine is confidently relied upon by the Coppin Company on this appeal.

[4] It may be stated as a well-recognized principle that negligence, like any other fact, may be proven by circumstantial evidence;

that is, by proving facts from which a reasonable person could readily infer the ultimate fact of negligence. Direct evidence by an eyewitness was not any more necessary in this case to prove the contested fact than in any other case. The question of fact to be determined by the jury was, who started the elevator on the downward trip at the time it struck and killed appellee's decedent, and this fact could as well be established by circumstantial evidence as any other fact, such as the striking of a blow or the firing of a shot which took the life of a human being.

In describing the nature and efficacy of circumstantial evidence, Prof. Greenleaf, in his most excellent work on Evidence, gives the following illustration:

"If a witness testifies that he saw A. inflict a mortal wound on B., of which he instantly died; this is a case of direct evidence; and, giving to the witness the credit to which men are generally entitled, the crime is satisfactorily proved. If a witness testifies that a deceased person was shot with a pistol, and the wadding is found to be a part of a letter addressed to the prisoner, the residue of which is discovered in his pocket; here the facts themselves are directly attested; but the evidence they afford is termed circumstantial, and from these facts, if unexplained by the prisoner, the jury may or may not deduce, or infer, or presume his guilt, according as they are satisfied, or not, of the natural connection between similar facts, and the guilt of the person thus connected with them."

Other writers have held that the difference between circumstantial evidence and that which is denominated direct evidence is merely one of logic and of no practical significance; that all evidence is more or less circumstantial; all statements of witnesses, all conclusions of juries, are the result of inference, the difference being only in degree.

It is conceded by all parties to this litigation that the elevator car would not start without the aid of an outside agency. Some one must pull the cable to set it in motion, but once in motion it would travel in the direction it was going to the terminus of the shaft and there rest until again set in motion by an independent agency. It follows, therefore, that some one, either the servants of the appellant company, those of the pharmaceutical company, or the electricians engaged in work in the shaft, started the elevator.

With these facts conceded, let us look into the situation as it existed at the instant the elevator started from the third floor landing on its downward course immediately before it struck and killed Harris. The servants of the Coppin Company had been using the car at the third floor to load some stuff. The car was in their possession and under their control; some of the stuff to be loaded was on the elevator, but other articles were to be placed upon it, and the Coppin Company's servant or some of them had left the elevator to go for the remainder of the load.

The third floor was exclusively used and occupied by the Coppin Company. There were no persons on that floor except the servants of the company, and they all had easy access to the elevator. The pharmaceutical company occupied the fourth floor, and there was but one man in its service on that floor at the time, and he could not have reached the elevator, but could have reached the cable. He testified he did not start the elevator nor touch the elevator cable before the car started on that morning. All the other persons who had opportunity to start the elevator were on lower floors. The electricians did not have any use for the elevator and did not start it nor do anything to set it in motion. The colored porter, Lee, in the basement, testified he did not start the elevator, and he is partly corroborated by other witnesses; besides, had he started it he could have, and likely would have, stopped it by the same means by which he started it when he realized the peril to which Harris was exposed with his body projecting into the shaft, and would not have begun screaming, "Stop that elevator!" as he did immediately before the car struck Harris. His cries, "Stop the elevator!" were intended no doubt for the one who started it, and, being a part of the res gestæ, plainly supports the theory that he did not start the elevator. So with the car in the possession of and under the control of the servants of the Coppin Company, at the third floor, used exclusively by that company, we think the circumstances are such that a reasonable person might well conclude that some one of the said four servants of the Coppin Company who were working in connection with the car started the elevator. At least, the facts and circumstances tend much stronger to support this inference and deduction than that the elevator was set in motion by some person in the basement or the electricians than whom there were no others.

It cannot be said that the evidence as to negligence or no negligence on the part of the servants of the Coppin Company are equal or at equilibrium. On one side the facts are that the elevator was in the possession and under the control of the servants of the Coppin Company who had the right and power to move it, it was at the third floor, which floor was occupied and used exclusively by the Coppin Company, and all of the servants of the Coppin Company were in position to set the elevator in motion. On the other side, there were no other persons in the building who had possession of the car or who were on the floor of the building from which it started at the time it began to move, and while all persons in the employ of the Coppin Company testifying denied starting the elevator, the circumstances which surround the unfortunate happening are such as to convincingly indicate that neither the porter Lee or any other person in the basement or shaft started the elevator, because they were put in danger by it, and the conduct of Lee after he discovered the elevator moving downward was such as to negative the slight inference that he started it and to raise and support the inference that he did not do so. It is always to be presumed that one will not do anything which will directly imperil his life or that of his associates with whom he is on good terms, and this presumption, in the absence of evidence to the contrary, operated to exonerate Harris, Hanly, and Ensly who were working in and about the elevator shaft. We therefore conclude that the verdict of the jury is supported by sufficient evidence to sustain it.

[5] No one will seriously contend that the appellant company and its agents in charge of the elevator car did not owe Harris and the other men working in and about the elevator shaft the duty of giving reasonable and timely warning of the starting of the elevator under the facts of this case. This is true even though Harris was not in the employ of the Coppin Company but was working for an independent contractor. There was such a relation between the company and Harris as imposed upon the company this duty. The company's assistant superintendent, Macklin, directly in charge of the work of installing the electrical apparatus and of the moving of the goods from the third floor by the porters, knew that the electricians were working in and about the shaft, for he had started them there and had seen them there only a few moments before the accident. He also knew the danger of operating the elevator car while these men were so engaged. He knew that the car was at the third floor and would soon come down, but he did not instruct or warn the operators of the elevator to look out for or signal the electricians on the movement of the car. As the servants of the Coppin Company moved the car up the shaft that morning, one member of the crew told the electricians that they could now work in the shaft as the car would be at the third floor for a while, which plainly evidenced the speaker's knowledge of the danger of operating the car while persons were in or about the shaft, and that he anticipated that the men would likely go to work in the shaft.

All the employés of the Coppin Company knew that the electricians including Harris were at work in and about the shaft, and that the elevator could not move up and down the shaft with safety to them while they were so engaged. With this knowledge it was plainly the duty of the persons in charge of the elevator car to give reasonable and timely notice of the movements of the car, and a failure to do so rendered them and their principal liable in damages for the injury inflicted, regardless of the fact that Harris was in the employ of an independent contractor. National Concrete Con. Co. v. Duvall, 150 Ky. 198, 150 S. W. 46; Otis Elevator Co. v. Wilson, 147 Ky. 676, 145 S. W. 391; Standard Oil Co. v. Titus, 187 Ky. 560, 219 S. W. 1077.

[6] Harris was not guilty of contributory negligence, for he was instructed to work in the elevator shaft by one having authority to regulate the movements of the elevator, and he was expected to be there, and had the right to expect a warning from the persons in charge of the elevator before it moved. As the elevator car descended noiselessly, he could not be expected to hear it, especially when he was engaged in work at which he made more or less noise. His face was down and his attention fixed upon his work, which was exactly beneath where he lay. He had been told that the elevator would remain at the third floor for a while and that he could work in the shaft. If he failed to use reasonable care to get out of the way of the elevator after he knew, or by the exercise of ordinary care could have known, of the descent of the car, and his injury resulted from such failure, his administrator was not entitled to recover. This question was one of fact for the jury and was properly submitted and found against appellant.

[7] But it is said that Harris assumed the ordinary risks of the business and of the known danger of the particular work he was doing, and this is true; but he did not assume the risks of danger to him occasioned by the negligence of the servants of the Coppin Company, nor of the negligence of any one. He had a right, in view of the fact that his presence in the shaft was to be anticipated, to expect those having the elevator in charge to give reasonable and timely notice of its movements, and would not noiselessly slip down upon him and take his life.

Nor is it important, under the facts of this case, that the plaintiff was unable to show by direct evidence which of the servants of the Coppin Company started the elevator, for the Coppin Company owed Harris the duty to instruct each of them in the operation of the elevator while the electricians were in or about the shaft, and it is admitted by Macklin, the assistant superintendent, that he did not so instruct them or any one of them. This was gross negligence which, if it contributed to bring about the injury, as it appears it did, renders appellant company liable.

Judgment affirmed.

LOWERY v. COMMONWEALTH.

(Court of Appeals of Kentucky. May 27, 1921.)

1. **Burglary ⬤⟹28(6)—No variance where indictment charged breaking into store of corporation, and evidence showed owner was partnership.**

Where the evidence showed that the storeroom was that of L., a copartnership, there was no variance from an indictment charging breaking into the storeroom of L., a corporation, the averment as to the corporate character of L. being mere descriptio personæ.

2. **Indictment and information ⬤⟹171—Material variance defined.**

A variance is not material unless it misleads accused in making his defense, or may expose him to the danger of being again put in jeopardy for the same offense.

3. **Criminal law ⬤⟹695(6)—Objection to evidence as a whole unavailing, where part is competent.**

Even if evidence of certain witnesses was incompetent as respects a recital therein of accused's confession, in that it was obtained from him in violation of the Anti-Sweating Law, yet where other portions of the evidence as to arrest of accused when he was trying to dispose of stolen goods was competent, accused's motion to exclude the evidence as a whole was properly overruled.

4. **Criminal law ⬤⟹1130(2)—Blanket objection to overruling objections to evidence insufficient.**

A general statement in accused's brief that every objection by accused was overruled, and that this was error in each instance, without pointing out specific errors, *held* unavailing.

Appeal from Circuit Court, Daviess County.

Robert Lowery was convicted of feloniously breaking into a storehouse with intent to steal, and appeals. Affirmed.

Aud & Higdon, of Owensboro, for appellant.

Chas. I. Dawson, Atty. Gen., and Thos. B. McGregor, Asst. Atty. Gen., for the Commonwealth.

CLARKE, J. The appellant, Robert Lowery, and another were charged jointly by indictment with the crime of feloniously breaking into a storehouse with intent to steal, which is a crime denounced by section 1164, Ky. Statutes.

Appellant upon a separate trial was convicted, and his punishment fixed at confinement in the penitentiary for five years. For reversal of that judgment he urges that the court erred: (1) In overruling his motion for a directed verdict; (2) in refusing to exclude the evidence of all of the commonwealth's witnesses; (3) in failing to properly instruct the jury; and (4) in the admission of incompetent evidence.

[1, 2] 1. The right to a peremptory instruction is claimed because of an alleged fatal variance between the charge in the indictment and the evidence. The indictment in the accusatory part charges the commission of the crime in general language, and in the descriptive part alleges that:

"The said Robert Lowery and Ed Ervin and each of them, acting jointly and together, each aiding, assisting and abetting the other in Daviess county, Ky., on the —— day of ——, 1920, and before the filing of this indictment, with force and arms willfully, unlawfully, and feloniously did break into and enter into a storeroom of Levy's, a corporation, duly created and existing by virtue of the laws of Kentucky," etc.

The evidence shows that the storeroom broken into was Levy's, a copartnership, and not a corporation; that Levy's had been a corporation, but that shortly before the robbery the corporation had been dissolved, and the store had since been operated under the same name, but as a copartnership. This is the variance that counsel for defendant insist is fatal, and entitled him to a directed verdict, but we are unable to agree with this contention. It is clearly shown by the proof that the store of Levy's referred to in the indictment was the store of Levy's broken into. The clause "a corporation duly created and existing by virtue of the laws of Kentucky" is merely descriptio personæ, and might have been omitted without affecting the validity of the indictment. The variance cannot possibly have misled the defendant in making his defense, nor can he again be placed in jeopardy for the same offense. It is therefore not a fatal variance.

This court in Commonwealth v. Brown, 123 Ky. 20, 93 S. W. 605, 29 Ky. Law Rep. 434, approved the rule as stated in 22 Encyclopedia of Pleading and Practice, 551, that—

"Variances are regarded as material in criminal cases only when they mislead the defendant in making his defense, and may expose him to the danger of being again put in jeopardy for the same offense."

To the same effect are Commonwealth v. Jarboe, 89 Ky. 143, 12 S. W. 138, 11 Ky. Law Rep. 344; Sutton v. Commonwealth, 97 Ky. 308, 30 S. W. 661, 17 Ky. Law Rep. 184; Sutton v. Commonwealth, 154 Ky. 799, 159 S. W. 589. The cases of McBride v. Commonwealth, 13 Bush, 337, Carter v. Commonwealth, 76 S. W. 337, 25 Ky. Law Rep. 688, and similar cases relied upon by appellant, are not applicable here. In those cases the defendant was charged with stealing the property of a named person, and the proof was that he had stolen the property of an entirely different person, whose name was not even idem sonans. Manifestly in those cases the variances were fatal because they were such as would have misled the defendant in making his defense, and he would have been in danger of again being put in jeopardy for the same offense. The precise question here involved was before this court in Commonwealth v. Vineyard, 118 Ky. 645, 82 S. W. 289. The indictment in that case charged that the defendant stole certain manila ropes from the Columbia Stave Company, and that same was a duly incorporated company. This court held that by reason of the provisions of section 128 of the Criminal Code the indictment was sufficiently certain without an averment that the Columbia Stave Company was an incorporated company, and that although the indictment averred that it was a corporation, this was an unnecessary allegation, and need not have been proved.

[3] 2. It is insisted that the evidence of each of the commonwealth's three witnesses was incompetent, and should have been excluded because each of them recited a confession of guilt by the defendant, which it is insisted was obtained from him in violation of the provisions of section 1649b, Ky. Statutes, known as the Anti-Sweating Law. We are of the opinion that the confession was not obtained from the defendant in violation of this act; but, even if it were otherwise, we could not, because of the condition of the record, reverse the judgment therefor. Thomas Barneby, an Indianapolis detective and the first witness for the commonwealth, testified that he arrested the defendant while he was trying to sell a trunk full of women's garments to a pawnbroker in Indianapolis; that the defendant at first claimed he bought the goods from an unknown man in Columbus, Tenn., but later confessed that he and Ervin broke into the store of Levy's in Owensboro, Ky., and took them therefrom. The defendant did not object to any of the witness' statements with reference to the confession, but at the close of his evidence objected to the testimony as a whole and moved the court to exclude it from the jury, which motion the court overruled, and the defendant excepted. The evidence of this witness that he arrested the defendant when he was attempting to sell the goods to a pawnbroker in Indianapolis, which goods were later identified by Mr. Levy as being the goods that were stolen from his storeroom in Owensboro when same was broken into as charged in the indictment, was clearly competent, even if the evidence with reference to the confession was not; hence the defendant's motion to exclude all of the evidence of this witness was properly overruled.

As said in Harrod v. Armstrong, 177 Ky. 317, 197 S. W. 816, where numerous like cases are cited:

"The uniform and unvarying rule as announced and adhered to by this court is that for an objection to be available it must be specifically directed to that portion of the testimony which is incompetent, and that to object to evidence as a whole when there is contained in it both competent and incompetent testimony will not be sufficient to authorize this court to reverse the judgment because of the error complained of."

The same rule was even more recently approved and applied in Hall v. Commonwealth, 189 Ky. 72, 224 S. W. 492. For the same reason the court did not err in refusing to exclude the whole of the evidence of the other two witnesses for the commonwealth.

3. The two complaints of the instructions given by the court are that there was no evidence to show that the defendant had anything to do with breaking into the store, and that no reference was made in the instruction to the charge in the indictment that the storehouse broken into was that of Levy's, a corporation. The first complaint is based upon the assumption that defendant's confession of guilt was incompetent, and should have been excluded, which, as we have seen, is not true; but, even if the confession should be excluded, there is ample evidence, though circumstantial, of defendant's guilt to carry the case to the jury and authorize the instructions given. The second complaint has already been disposed of in passing upon defendant's second ground for a reversal.

[4] 4. Counsel do not point out any error of the court in the admission of evidence, but content themselves with this statement:

"It will be noticed that every objection made by defendant in the trial of this case was overruled by the trial judge, and we think that each time he overruled the objection an error was committed."

We have several times expressed our unwillingness to search the record for possible errors of the court, where none is pointed out in brief, and announced the rule that under such circumstances it will be assumed the judgment is correct. Brown v. Daniels, 154 Ky. 267, 157 S. W. 3; Garvey v. Garvey, 156 Ky. 664, 161 S. W. 526; McCorkle et al. v. Chapman, 181 Ky. 607, 205 S. W. 682.

That rule seems equally applicable to possible errors in the admission of evidence upon a jury trial; and we might assume, we think, the trial court did not err in this respect here, where many objections were made and overruled and no such errors are called to our attention by counsel in their brief. We have, however, examined the court's rulings in each instance, and find no error prejudicial to appellant's substantial rights. Wherefore the judgment is affirmed.

**COMMONWEALTH v. LOUISVILLE & N.
R. CO.**

(Court of Appeals of Kentucky. May 25,
1921.)

1. **Indictment and information ⚬125(16)—
Railroads ⚬255(8)—Indictment charging
railroad with failure to provide waiting room
not duplicitous or demurrable.**

Indictment against a railroad, charging it
with failing and neglecting to provide a convenient and suitable waiting room in its depot at a town, *held* not duplicitous or subject
to demurrer, though prolix, redundant, and
pleonastic; it sufficiently charging the offense
denounced by Ky. St. § 772, and not charging
that against which section 784 is directed.

2. **Indictment and information ⚬110(22)—
Charge of offense in language of statute sufficient.**

It is sufficient that the offense be charged
in the indictment in the language of the statute.

3. **Railroads ⚬226—Waiting room, which is
dark, stuffy, too small, or dirty, not "suitable
waiting room."**

A waiting room provided by a railroad at
a station is not suitable or convenient for
waiting passengers, within Ky. St. § 772, requiring the railroad to provide suitable waiting rooms, if it is too small, dark, stuffy, dirty,
or indecent.

4. **Railroads ⚬255(8)—Indictment for failure
to provide suitable waiting room should not
couple word "public" with "passengers."**

Indictment against a railroad for failing to
provide a convenient and suitable waiting room
as required by Ky. St. § 772, should not have
coupled the words "and public" to the word
"passengers" in the allegation that the room
provided was too small to accommodate "passengers and public"; evidence of the sufficiency
of the room to accommodate passengers alone
would warrant acquittal of the railroad, if
the size of the room alone was questioned.

5. **Indictment and information ⚬125(16)—
Charge of two offenses relative to waiting
room readers indictment bad for duplicity.**

The two offenses of failing to provide a
suitable and convenient waiting room, as required by Ky. St. § 772, and failing to heat
and ventilate the waiting room, as required by
section 784, cannot be charged in one indictment without rendering it bad for duplicity.

Appeal from Circuit Court, Ohio County.

The Louisville & Nashville Railroad Company was indicted for neglecting to provide
a suitable waiting room in its depot. Demurrer to indictment sustained, and the
Commonwealth appeals. Judgment reversed,
for trial consistent with the opinion.

See, also, 189 Ky. 309, 224 S. W. 847.

Chas. I. Dawson, Atty. Gen., Thos. B.
McGregor, Asst. Atty. Gen., and C. E. Smith,
of Hartford, for the Commonwealth.

B. D. Warfield, of Louisville, and Thos.
E. Sandidge, of Owensboro, for appellee.

SAMPSON, J. The commonwealth prosecutes this appeal from a judgment of the
Ohio circuit court, holding demurrable an indictment charging the Louisville & Nashville
Railroad Company with failing and neglecting to provide a convenient and suitable waiting room in its depot at Centertown and dismissing the indictment. The indictment, in
so far as necessary to an understanding of
this case, reads as follows:

"Accuse the defendant, Louisville & Nashville Railroad Company, of the offense of failing, neglecting, and refusing to provide convenient and suitable waiting room at its depot in the town of Centertown, committed in
manner and form as follows, to wit:. Said
Louisville & Nashville Railroad Company, a
corporation duly organized, created, and incorporated under the laws of the state of Kentucky, and engaged in the operation of passenger trains in and through Ohio county, after the 1st day of March, 1920, and within 12
months next before the finding of this indictment, did willfully and unlawfully fail, neglect,
and refuse to provide a convenient and suitable
waiting room at its depot in the town of Centertown, an incorporated town of the sixth
class, in said county; that said waiting room
in said depot, its said passenger depot, was
on said date not convenient and suitable for
the accommodation of the passengers of said
company and the public, there being only one
waiting room for white passengers, which said
waiting room so provided, was too small for
the accommodation of said passengers and
the public, and was frequently during said time
not kept open for the use or accommodation of
said passengers, and was and is not sufficiently
lighted, heated, and ventilated, and was not
supplied with suitable or sufficient furniture,
fixtures, and conveniences for the accommodation of said passengers and the public, and
was not kept and maintained in decent order
and repair."

In sustaining the demurrer to the indictment the learned and careful trial judge entered the following order:

"This indictment coming on to be heard on
demurrer of the defendant thereto, and the
court having heard argument of counsel for
commonwealth and defendant on the question
of duplicity, and being sufficiently advised it is
of the opinion that the present indictment
states two offenses, viz. one for not maintaining a convenient and suitable waiting room at
Centertown, which offense arises under section
772 of the Kentucky Statutes, and is punishable by a fine of from $100 to $500; the other
for not keeping the said waiting room at said
town open, heated, and ventilated, which latter
offense arises under section 784 of Kentucky
Statutes, and is punishable by a fine of from
$10 to $20, and of which offense this court has
no jurisdiction, and the commonwealth attorney declining to elect which offense he would
prosecute, it is hereby ordered and adjudged
that said demurrer be sustained, and said
indictment is hereby dismissed, to which plaintiff objects and excepts."

⚬For other cases see same topic and KEY-NUMBER in all Key-Numbered Digests and Indexes

Section 772, Kentucky Statutes, in so far as relevant reads as follows:

"Every company operating a railroad in this state shall provide a convenient and suitable waiting room and water-closet or privies at all depots in cities and towns, and at such stations as the Railroad Commission may require on its lines, and keep and maintain the same in decent order and repair."

The relevant part of section 784 reads as follows:

"All companies shall keep their ticket offices open for the sale of tickets at least thirty minutes immediately preceding the schedule time of departure of all passenger trains from every regular passenger depot from which such trains start or at which they regularly stop, and shall open the waiting room for passengers at the same time as the ticket office, and keep it open and comfortably warmed in cold weather until the train departs."

[1] From a reading of the sections of the statute copied above, and the indictment, it will clearly appear that the indictment is not duplicitous or subject to demurrer, although it is prolix, redundant, and pleonastic. It sufficiently charges the offense denounced by section 772, Kentucky Statutes, but it does not charge the offense against which section 784 is directed, and as but one offense is charged, although there are surplus words somewhat indicating a purpose to include another offense, the indictment is not duplicitous. It is subject to criticism, and that part of it which relates to heating and lighting the waiting room of the depot should have been omitted, for it appertains to the offense denounced by section 784 of Kentucky Statutes only.

Manifestly the indictment under consideration was drawn under section 772, and was intended to charge the defendant company with the offense of failing to provide convenient and suitable waiting room in its depot at Centertown, and not to charge it with failing to "open the waiting room for passengers at the same time as the ticket office and keep it open and comfortably warm in cold weather," as required by section 784.

[2] The offense covered by section 772 is charged in the indictment in the language of the statute, which this court has held sufficient in many cases. L. & N. R. R. Co. v. Commonwealth, 144 Ky. 525, 139 S. W. 756.

[3] But the statute, section 784, is not followed, nor are there words of like import or meaning employed in the indictment, so as to charge the offense therein denounced. If the indictment had not contained the clause, "and was frequently during said time not kept open for the use and accommodation of said passengers," and had omitted the word "heated" appearing in another line, there would have been no indication that the pleader intended to charge the defendant company with the offense covered by section 784, and as the words, taken alone, do not charge the offense denounced by section 784, or any offense, the indictment was not and could not be duplicitous. Nor was the indictment bad for any of the other reasons assigned in brief of appellee company, even though after charging the offense named in section 772 in general terms, it proceeded to charge defendant company with specific acts which rendered the waiting room in the depot inconvenient and unsuitable for the purposes for which it was intended, by setting forth (1) that the waiting room was too small; (2) was not sufficiently lighted or ventilated; (3) was not supplied with suitable furniture and fixtures; and (4) was not maintained in decent order and repair. If the waiting room was too small to be suitable or convenient for the traveling public which used the depot to board defendant's trains, and this fact was proven to the jury, it should have found the defendant company guilty of the offense charged in the indictment. So should the jury have found the defendant guilty on proof that the company had failed to sufficiently light or ventilate the waiting room, for a room not sufficiently lighted or ventilated would not be a suitable or convenient room in which to wait at a depot for a train. And if the company failed to provide a room with suitable fixtures, such as seats, it would be liable on this indictment, or failed to maintain the waiting room in decent order and repair, it would be subject to the penalties denounced by the statute. In other words, a waiting room is not suitable or convenient for waiting passengers which is too small, dark, stuffy, or which is dirty or indecent.

[4, 5] The indictment is subject, however, to the criticism that it is too broad in some of its terms. The railroad is only required to provide a suitable and convenient waiting room for persons waiting to take passage on its trains or to transact business with the company, and is under no obligation to provide a waiting room of any character whatever for the general public. The indictment should not have coupled the words "and public" to the word "passengers," and proof that the waiting room was too small to accommodate "passengers and the public" would not sustain a conviction; but evidence of the sufficiency of it to accommodate the passengers alone would warrant an acquittal of the defendant company, if its size alone was questioned. While we have written in the cases of I. C. R. R. Co. v. Commonwealth, 52 S. W. 818, 21 Ky. Law Rep. 569, I. C. R. R. Co. v. Commonwealth, 90 S. W. 602, 28 Ky. Law Rep. 802, L. & N. R. R. Co. v. Commonwealth, 144 Ky. 625, 139 S. W. 931, I. C. R. R. Co. v. Commonwealth, 179 Ky. 28, 200 S. W. 17, and Commonwealth v. L. & N. R. R. Co., 189 Ky. 309, 224 S. W. 847, that on a trial under an indictment similar to the one under consideration the commonwealth may introduce evidence of the failure of the company to have

its waiting room open and heated in cold weather for at least 30 minutes before the time of departure of trains, we think the better practice would be to exclude all such evidence, for it relates more to the operation than to the providing of a suitable and convenient waiting room, and should be allowed only on the trial of an indictment under section 784, Kentucky Statutes. If it be the purpose of the commonwealth in a given case to charge the defendant company with failure to provide a suitable and convenient waiting room, the indictment should contain nothing about a failure of the company to keep it open and comfortable in cold weather, nor should evidence be received on the subject; but if the commonwealth wants a conviction under section 784 for failure to have the waiting room open, or for a failure to have it comfortably warm in cold weather, it should draw its indictment under this section, and confine its evidence to that which will sustain this charge, and not offer or be allowed to introduce evidence which would sustain a conviction for failure to provide a suitable and convenient waiting room kept in decent order and repair. The two offenses cannot be charged in one indictment, without rendering it bad for duplicity. The Legislature never so intended, else it would not have passed the two statutes, covering different acts or omissions, and prescribing different penalties for their violation.

For reasons indicated the judgment is reversed for a trial consistent with this opinion.

ADAMS et al. v. BATES.

(Court of Appeals of Kentucky. May 31, 1921.)

1. Life estates ⬉28—Petition held to state cause of action for voluntary waste.

A petition alleging that the owner of an undivided share of certain land, the rest of which was owned by plaintiffs, unlawfully and unnecessarily cut and destroyed timber from much of the land, prior to the expiration of a life estate therein formerly owned by him, without the knowledge or consent of plaintiffs, who owned the fee in remainder, *held* to state a cause of action for voluntary waste, as allowed by Ky. St. §§ 2328–2336.

2. Remainders ⬉17(2)—Action for waste committed by grantee of estate for life of grantor need not be delayed until after grantor's death.

Under Ky. St. §§ 2329, 2330, the owners of a remainder in fee after an estate for the life of their grantor, need not delay until after the death of the grantor the bringing of an action for waste committed by the grantee of the life estate.

3. Remainders ⬉17(3)—Statute begins to run against owners of remainder in fee after life estate from time of commission of waste by grantee of such estate.

Where the grantee of an estate for the life of grantor committed waste thereon during grantor's life, the five-year period of limitation fixed by Ky. St. § 2515, began to run against the owners of the remainder in fee from the time of the commission of such waste, they having the right to sue before the expiration of the life estate.

4. Limitation of actions ⬉177(2) — Plaintiff need not allege facts showing action not barred by statute.

The plaintiff, in an action for waste by the grantee of an estate for the life of grantor, need not allege when the cause of action accrued or state facts showing it is not barred, as the statute of limitations, if relied on as a defense, must be pleaded by the party seeking its protection.

5. Limitation of actions ⬉187—Infancy must be pleaded to bar running of statute.

One relying on infancy as a bar to the running of the statute of limitations must plead the fact.

6. Judgment ⬉747(5)—Judgment in suit to quiet title between parties to action for waste held bar to assertion of title by defendant.

In an action against the grantee of a life estate for waste, a judgment in a previous action between the same parties to quiet title *held* a bar to grantee's assertion of title by deed from a third party.

Appeal from Circuit Court, Knott County.

Action by Robert Adams and others against Robert Bates. Judgment for defendant, and plaintiffs appeal. Reversed and remanded, with directions.

Smith & Combs, of Hindman, for appellants.

A. J. May, of Prestonsburg, for appellee.

SETTLE, J. This action was brought by the appellants, Robert Adams and others, named in the petition as plaintiffs, against the appellee, Robert Bates, seeking to recover of the latter damages for the alleged wrongful cutting and appropriation by him of valuable standing timber on and from a tract of land in Knott county, particularly described in the petition. It is alleged in the petition that one John B. Adams, then domiciled in Knott county, died in 1882, intestate, survived by his wife, Lucy Adams, and seven children, the appellants being five of the seven; that John B. Adams owned at the time of his death several tracts of land, including that described in the petition, and that, in a partition subsequently made of these lands, the tract described in the petition was allotted to the widow as dower, in full of her share as widow in the entire landed estate of the decedent; that thereafter the widow, Lucy Adams, by a second marriage, became the wife of Jason Craft, who, while living with her on the dower land, by purchase and through a deed from Margaret Adams, a sister of appellants and daughter of John B. Adams, acquired title to her remainder interest as an heir at law of the latter in the land allotted the widow as dower, which was an undivided seventh thereof, subject to the life estate of Mrs. Craft.

It appears from other averments of the petition that Lucy Craft and Jason Craft, by a joint deed executed in 1890, sold and conveyed to the appellee, Robert Bates, their joint and several interests in the land described in the petition; that of Lucy Craft being her dower, or life estate therein, and that of Jason Craft the undivided seventh in remainder conveyed him by Margaret Adams. The deed from the Crafts to the appellee, Bates, also conveyed him whatever right, actual or potential, either of the grantors might have had in the interest of the other in the land. The deed thus executed was accompanied by the delivery to Bates of the possession of the land thereby conveyed. He thereafter purchased of another child and heir at law of John B. Adams, deceased, his undivided one-seventh interest in remainder in the dower land, and received of the vendor a deed therefor. Appellee remained in exclusive possession of the land in question from the date of its conveyance to him in 1890, certainly, until the death in 1917 of Lucy Craft, which had the effect to terminate the life estate she conveyed him in the land. Whether he is yet in possession thereof the petition fails to disclose. It does allege, however, that he now is the owner in fee simple of an undivided two-sevenths of the land, and that the appellants, as children and heirs at law of John B. Adams, deceased, own, by like title, the remaining five-sevenths; or, more accurately speaking, an undivided interest of one-seventh each.

It also alleges, in substance, that the appellee unlawfully cleared and destroyed timber from much of the land, none of which clearing or destruction of timber was reasonably necessary for the upkeep of the land or its use by the life tenant; and that such unnecessary clearing of the land and destruction of timber by appellee was without appellants' knowledge or consent, and all done prior to the death of Lucy Craft, the former widow of John B. Adams, and, consequently, before the termination of the life estate which she, in conjunction with her second husband, conveyed him in the land. By its final averment the petition lays the damages to the land and to the joint owners rights of property therein, resulting, as alleged, from the appellee's wrongful cutting and destroy-

ing of timber thereon, at $10,000, for five-sevenths of which amount judgment was prayed by the appellants.

The defense interposed by the appellee to the cause of action alleged in the petition was set forth in an answer of five paragraphs, the first of which traversed substantially the averments of the petition, except such as alleged the sale and conveyance to appellee by Lucy Craft and Jason Craft of their respective interests in the land in question, including the remainder interest therein acquired by the latter of Margaret Adams. In the second paragraph it was alleged that the land described in the petition never belonged to John B. Adams, but was a part of a large tract formerly owned by one Robert Hamilton, the father of Lucy Adams, later Lucy Craft, and, in the division of Robert Hamilton's lands among his heirs at law after his death, was allotted, with another parcel, to his son, James Hamilton, who, in 1893, sold and conveyed it to the appellee; and that his claim of title to and possession of the land, notwithstanding his previous purchase of the interest of Lucy Craft and that of her daughter Margaret therein, from and since the execution to him of the Hamilton deed, has been under and by virtue of that deed. In the third paragraph, divers patents were mentioned granting to various persons, assignors, or grantors, as claimed, of Robert Hamilton, lands alleged to have embraced, in whole or in part, the tract described in the petition. This paragraph also alleges that the land in controversy had been held in actual possession by appellee under claim of the title conveyed him by the James Hamilton deed, adversely to appellants and all others, for more than 15 years before the institution of their action, and pleaded the statute of limitations of 15 years as a bar to the latter's claim of title thereto; and also as to their claim to damages for appellee's cutting of timber thereon.

The fourth paragraph of the answer admits the cutting by appellee of 65 poplar trees on and from the land in question, and alleges that it was done in the necessary clearing of a small part of the land actually required for its reasonable cultivation and improvement; and that the material from trees so cut was necessary for use, and was used in inclosing the land. In the fifth paragraph it was alleged that the clearing of land and cutting of timber complained of in the petition was done and committed more than five years before the institution of the action, and that any right of action the appellants may have had for the recovery of damages therefor was and is barred by the statute of limitations of five years, which was formally pleaded.

The appellants filed a general demurrer to the answer and each paragraph thereof and, without waiving their right to insist upon the demurrer, also filed a joint and several reply which, after traversing the affirmative allegations of the answer, substantially averred that all matters pleaded therein in support of appellee's claim of title to the land in question through James Hamilton and others, alleged to be superior to that conveyed him by Lucy and Jason Craft, and also to that asserted by appellants, were put in issue, litigated and determined in an action brought against him by appellants in the Knott circuit court to quiet their title as heirs at law of John B. Adams to a remainder interest of five-sevenths then asserted by them in the land; in which action, as also alleged in the reply, every contention as to title now urged by appellee in the case at bar was decided by the judgment of the Knott circuit court against him and in behalf of appellants; and which judgment, as further alleged, declared the appellants the owners in remainder of five-sevenths of the land in controversy, and awarded them their costs expended in the action; moreover that the appellee prosecuted an appeal from the judgment to the Court of Appeals, and it was by that court affirmed, all of which occurred before the death of Lucy Craft.

The judgment referred to was pleaded in the reply in estoppel of and as a bar to the claim of title to the land attempted to be asserted by appellee in the present action. Following the filing of the reply, the case was submitted on the appellants' demurrer to the appellee's answer, whereupon the circuit court refused to sustain it as to the answer, but held that it should be extended or carried back to the petition and sustained to that pleading; and this was done because of the court's opinion that appellants' right to recover of appellee damages for the cutting of timber by the latter complained of in the petition was confined by the statute of limitations to five years next before the institution of the action, and that, as the petition did not allege that such cutting of the timber by appellee was done within five years next before the institution of the action, it failed to state a cause of action; appellants refused to plead further, and the petition was dismissed. Excepting to all of these rulings and the judgment entered thereon, they have appealed.

[1] While the petition is in some respects awkwardly expressed, and some of its averments of fact barely sufficient to present the full meaning of the pleader, we have reached the conclusion that, considered as a whole, it reasonably well states a cause of action for voluntary waste as allowed by Ky. St. §§ 2328 to 2336, inclusive. Section 2328 provides:

"If any tenant for life or years shall commit waste during his estate or term, of anything belonging to the tenement so held, without special license, in writing, so to do, he shall be

subject to an action for waste, shall lose the thing wasted, and pay treble the amount at which the waste shall be assessed."

Section 2329 permits the bringing of such action by one who has the remainder or reversion in fee simple after an intervening estate for life or years; and also by one who has a remainder or reversion for life or years, each being entitled to recover such damages as it shall appear he has suffered by the waste complained of. Section 2330 gives an heir the right to bring and maintain an action for waste done in the time of his ancestor, as well as in his own time. Section 2332 makes a tenant in common, joint tenant, or parcener who commits waste liable to his cotenants jointly or severally for damages, while section 2334 provides:

"If, in any action for waste, the jury find that the waste was wantonly committed, judgment shall be entered for three times the amount of the damages assessed."

[2, 3] No claim seems to be made in this action for punitive damages. The appellants only seek to recover actual damages for waste committed upon the land by the grantee of the life estate, limited to the injury caused to the remainder interest of each of them; and while the entire value of the timber destroyed is placed at $10,000, they only demand the recovery together of five-sevenths thereof, or a seventh each, recognizing that appellee, as the owner of two-sevenths of the land in remainder at the time the waste was committed, is entitled to credit on the total value of the timber destroyed for two-sevenths thereof. Appellants are not, therefore, suing appellee as a joint tenant for waste committed by him to the land since the termination of the life estate he purchased therein from the widow of John B. Adams. They did not have to delay until after the termination of the life estate by the death of Lucy Craft, formerly widow of John B. Adams, the bringing of the present action against her grantee for waste committed by him to or upon the land before her death. On the contrary, it might have been brought at any time before her death and the consequent termination of the life estate therein she conveyed appellee. Hence we agree with the circuit court that the statute of limitations began to run against appellants' claim for damages when and from the time they might or could have sued therefor; and as the period of limitation fixed by section 2515, Ky. Stats. applies, if the cutting of timber by appellee on the land complained of occurred more than five years before the institution of the action, the statute will bar a recovery.

[4] We do not, however, agree with the circuit court that the failure of the petition to allege that the cutting of timber on the land, causing the waste complained of, occurred within 5 years before the institution

of the action, made it bad on demurrer. It is true the petition does not state when the timber was cut, whether 5 or 20 years before suit. Its averments go no farther, than to say the cutting was done before the termination of the life estate purchased by appellee of Mrs. Craft, and though her death is alleged to have occurred at a date much less than five years next before the institution of the action, no inference can be drawn from that averment as to when the timber was cut, or the statute began to run. Besides, we time and again have held that it is unnecessary for the plaintiff to allege in the petition when the cause of action accrued, or to state such facts as will show it is not barred by the statute of limitations; but that the statute of limitations, if relied on as ground of defense, must be pleaded by the party seeking its protection. Chiles v. Drake, 2 Metc. 146, 74 Am. Dec. 406; Yager v. President, etc., Bank of Ky., 125 Ky. 177, 100 S. W. 848, 30 Ky. Law Rep. 1287; Green County v. Howard, 127 Ky. 379, 105 S. W. 897, 32 Ky. Law Rep. 243. "The reason for the rule," as was said in Green County v. Howard, supra, "is that there may have been something obstructing the running of the statute."

[5] It is claimed in the brief of appellants' counsel that the running of the statute has been obstructed in the case at bar by the infancy of the appellants, or some of them; and that by reason thereof the statute was suspended during the time their disability prevented them from suing. We have failed to find in any of the pleadings an averment or intimation that the appellants, or any of them, were infants when the waste sued for was committed, and if such infancy existed, or is intended to be relied on, it must, like the statute of limitations, be pleaded. It follows from the conclusions we have expressed that the ruling of the circuit court sustaining the demurrer to the petition, was error.

[6] As all claims of title asserted by appellee in his answer to the land involved in this action, except as admitted in the petition, were rejected by the judgment in the previous action between the parties, it is only necessary to refer to the opinion of this court in Bates v. Adams, etc., 182 Ky. 100, 206 S. W. 163, to ascertain the rights both of appellants and appellee in the land. That opinion settles every question of title raised in the case at bar, and fixes it in the parties respectively as we have already stated. Hence, the circuit court should have sustained appellants' demurrer to all of the answer, except the paragraph pleading the statute of limitations of five years, the paragraphs putting in issue the quantity of timber cut by appellee, its value to the land as standing trees at the date of the cutting; whether it was used in fencing the land and such use

was reasonably necessary for that purpose, and whether or not appellants had knowledge of and acquiesced in the cutting of the timber when it was done. Upon the return of the case to the court below, it should require the pleadings to be so reformed as to properly present the issues as above stated.

For the reasons stated, the judgment appealed from is reversed, and cause remanded, with directions to the circuit court to overrule the demurrer to the petition, sustain the demurrer to such of the paragraphs of the answer as have been indicated, and for further proceedings consistent with the opinion.

———

FRANKFORT ELEVATOR COAL CO. v. WILLIAMSON.

(Court of Appeals of Kentucky. May 27, 1921.)

1. **Negligence ⬗136(27)—Contributory negligence of person injured by falling coal pile held for jury.**

In action against a coal company by a customer for injuries received from collapsing coal pile when he was loading coal purchased from the pile, defendant's negligence and plaintiff's contributory negligence in violating instructions in loading from the pile and going near an obviously dangerous condition *held* for jury.

2. **Appeal and error ⬗216(1)—Appellant cannot complain of failure to give instruction not offered.**

Appellant cannot complain of failure to give requested instruction where it was not offered for appellant.

3. **Trial ⬗260(1)—Failure to give instruction covered by others not error.**

Failure to give a requested instruction was not error, where the instructions given embraced the same idea.

4. **Appeal and error ⬗1003—Verdict not disturbed unless clearly against weight of evidence.**

The verdict of a jury will not be disturbed unless clearly and palpably against the weight of evidence.

Appeal from Circuit Court, Franklin County.

Action by James Williamson against the Frankfort Elevator Coal Company. From judgment for plaintiff, defendant appeals. Affirmed.

Leslie W. Morris, E. C. O'Rear, and J. C. Jones, all of Frankfort, for appellant.

B. G. Williams, of Frankfort, J. T. Gooch, of Madisonville, and W. C. Marshall, of Frankfort, for appellee.

TURNER, C. During the severe winter of 1917-18 the appellant operated two coalyards in Frankfort, Ky., one in North Frankfort and the other in South Frankfort.

On the 21st of January, 1918, the appellee went to appellant's North Frankfort yard, and while there by invitation as one of its customers, and while loading his small sled in connection with one of appellant's employés, was severely injured by the collapse or spreading of a large pile of coal in appellant's said yard, and for the injuries so received, as claimed, by reason of the negligence of appellant, and its officers and employés, this action was brought.

The petition alleges, in substance, that the defendant operated the coalyard in question, and that he (plaintiff), together with the public, was invited to go and be there as the customer of the defendant, for the purpose of buying and receiving coal from it, and that on or about the 21st of January, 1918, while he was so upon the premises of the defendant for the purpose of buying and receiving coal, and while upon the ground at or near one of its large banks or piles of coal from which defendant's agents and employés were then and there, and had been immediately previous thereto, taking coal, and while plaintiff, together with an employé of the defendant, was loading and placing coal upon his (plaintiff's) sled, said bank or pile of coal, consisting of heavy blocks and smaller ones, by reason of the negligence and carelessness of the defendant and its officers and agents, fell, and with great force and weight precipitated against and upon the plaintiff said coal, whereby he was violently knocked down by said mass and pile of coal, as a result of which he was seriously, painfully, and permanently injured.

The answer was a traverse of the plaintiff's petition, and in the second paragraph it was pleaded, in substance, that upon the occasion in question the plaintiff had been directed by the agents and servants of the defendant in charge of the coalyard to have the coal loaded upon his sled from certain cars which were loaded with coal and at the time in the yard, but that the plaintiff, in violation of these instructions, and of his own accord, and without authority from the defendant, undertook to load his sled from the pile of coal in the yard, and in so doing he got under the edge of the pile of coal and pulled the blocks of coal from under the same until, with his own hands, the pile was so loosened that it fell, although he had been previously warned in time to have prevented his injury to get out from under the pile of coal, but that he failed to heed the warning, and voluntarily, and without defendant's consent, engaged in loading the coal himself, although the defendant had at the time ample hands to load the same, and that the plaintiff had failed upon the occasion in question to exercise ordinary care for his own safety in getting in and about the pile of coal and taking coal therefrom to load on his sled,

and that his injuries, if any, were due to his own negligence.

The affirmative matter of the answer was traversed on the record.

On a trial the jury returned a verdict for the plaintiff for $1,200, upon which judgment was entered, and, the defendant's motion and grounds for a new trial having been overruled, it has appealed.

A reversal is asked upon three grounds:
(a) Because the court failed to give the peremptory instruction asked for the defendant.

(b) Because the court erred in giving instruction number one at plaintiff's instance.

(c) Because the verdict of the jury was palpably against the evidence and because of the failure of the court to grant a new trial for that reason.

[1] The plaintiff's evidence showed that he went to the coalyard on the day named and took a one-horse sled with him for the purpose of getting $2 worth of coal; that he went to the office and got the sled weighed, and the lady there in charge told him to go out in the yard and get the coal; that he had gotten coal there a number of times before in quantities of from $1 to $2 worth at a time; that after he weighed his sled he went out in the yard and met one of appellant's employés, who asked how much coal he wanted, and, when he told him $2 worth, he said, "All right; right here is a good place to get under; somebody has already knocked down about what you want; good, dry coal, already laying down here;" that there were picks and shovels about there, and he and the employé proceeded to load the sled; that in the big pile of coal there was a hole or tunnel from which people had been taking coal; that the hole was higher than his head and went back under the pile 25 or 30 feet or more, but that the coal which he and the employé loaded on the sled was already knocked down and was dry coal, lying on the ground as if somebody had recently left it there, and that it was all disconnected from the main big pile of coal; that at about the time he thought he had his $2 worth loaded on the sled he saw a large lump down on the ground separate from the big pile, and he thought that lump together with what he had would complete his load, and that he took a fork and was prising or lifting that lump, with his back to the main coal pile, when the whole thing collapsed and spread over him; that the weather had been for some time very cold and was still very cold, and the coal pile was covered with snow and ice and apparently frozen hard.

Some of the material points in appellee's evidence are corroborated. For instance, it is shown by several witnesses that the hole or tunnel was there and had been there for some time, and that they themselves had gotten coal at or out of tunnel, and that it was customary for purchasers of small quantities of coal to go to the coal piles in the yard and load their own sacks or small vehicles, and that such small customers usually sought, as appellee did, to get dry coal, free from snow or ice, which could best be procured at or in the tunnel.

Again, appellee's testimony was corroborated by a disinterested witness upon the material question whether or not he had prized the last large lump of coal from out of the base of the big pile, and thereby by his own act loosened it so as to cause the collapse or spread.

Much of the evidence of the defendant was to the effect that appellee had been directed specifically to load his sled from the cars that were on the tracks in the yard, and that in violation of those instructions he had gone to the large pile of coal. The defendant likewise introduced considerable evidence tending to show that the last large lump of coal which the plaintiff sought to place upon his sled was in the edge of the large pile of coal, and a part of the foundation of the pile, and that, when he loosened it by his own efforts, it caused the whole pile to collapse, and thereby his injury was brought about.

It is first said that the peremptory instruction should have been given, because, as claimed, appellee admitted in his cross-examination that Barrett and Wiley, two of the officers of appellant, had warned him of the danger of going at or near the mouth of the tunnel, and told him it was dangerous.

It is true that the plaintiff stated on cross-examination that Barrett and Wiley said the place was dangerous, and that Barrett was the manager and Wiley the yard boss; but an examination of the plaintiff's whole testimony, and an examination of the evidence of both Barrett and Wiley, who testified for appellant, discloses that the conversation with Barrett and Wiley to which he referred in that evidence was one after the injury. This is apparent from the fact that the plaintiff in another part of his evidence specifically and positively states that he had not been warned before the accident of any danger about getting coal from or near the mouth of the tunnel, and from the further fact that neither Barrett nor Wiley claims to have given him any such warning before the accident, and from the additional fact that it appeared that both Barrett and Wiley visited him more than once after the accident, either at the hospital or at his home.

We are convinced that no fair interpretation of the evidence can make this statement of appellee mean that he was warned by Barrett and Wiley, or either of them, before the accident happened.

But it is said that the facts of this case bring it within the rule that, where a danger is so obvious and imminent that one of ordinary prudence under like circumstances would not have subjected himself to it, there can be no recovery, and that therefore the peremptory should have been given.

We confess that this is the only question in the case which has given us any difficulty; for at first blush it would seem that any ordinarily prudent man would hesitate to go in or near to the mouth of a hole or tunnel in a great pile of loose coal. But when we consider that the hole had been there for some time, that the pile of coal was frozen hard, and that those going there occasionally to get coal did not know whether there were any supports in the tunnel or not, and did not know what, if any, steps had been taken to make it safe, and yet could see from the physical facts that coal had been recently taken out of or down from near the mouth of the tunnel, and when we consider that one of the employés of appellant at work in its yard invited appellee to go to that special place to get his coal, and there worked with him in loading his sled, the employé presumably having better opportunity for knowledge of its danger than appellee, we have reached the conclusion that the conditions and circumstances were not such as to make it an obvious and imminent danger which would preclude this appellee from a recovery.

Not only so, but it is testified in this record by Wiley, the yard boss of appellant, that on the Saturday afternoon before this accident, which happened on Monday, he had caused this large pile of coal to be cut down or trimmed down, and that the way he left it on Saturday afternoon it was not dangerous.

It is comparatively easy after an accident to look back and reason out from the conditions and circumstances with which one was acquainted and say that any reasonable person might have known that it was dangerous; but it is quite another thing, in the ordinary activities of life, for persons in their daily conduct to see and appreciate in advance the danger which subsequently appears to have been so plain.

At any rate, in this case the question of obvious danger was submitted by the court to the jury, and in the light of all the facts there was no such condition as authorized peremptory action by the court on this question. When the evidence is such that reasonable men might differ as to the fair inferences and conclusions which should be drawn from it, it should be submitted to the jury.

In its motion and grounds for a new trial the defendant only complained of error of the court in giving instruction No. 1 asked by the plaintiff, and in its brief it is conceded that the instruction as given is almost identical with the one approved by this court in the case of Ferguson & Palmer Co. v. Ferguson's Adm'r, 114 S. W. 297; but it is complained that the court did not give in this case another instruction which was ordered to be given in that case, to the effect that the defendant was under no obligation to keep its premises safe at places where customers were not invited to be, and that, if the plaintiff at the time he was injured was at a place not provided for the use of customers such as he, they should find for the defendant.

[2, 3] It is sufficient answer to this question to say that no such instruction was offered for appellant, and besides the instructions given embraced the same idea.

The claim that the verdict is palpably against the weight of the evidence cannot be sustained. It is true that upon two of the vital issues in the case the weight of the evidence appears to be against the plaintiff. There are several witnesses who testify that the plaintiff was directed by the young lady in the office to load his sled from the cars and was not directed to go out in the yard, and there were several witnesses who testified that the large block of coal which the plaintiff purposed to load on his sled, and which he was attempting to load when the accident happened, was prized loose by him from the base or foundation of the coal pile at or near the mouth of the tunnel, and that that caused the collapse, and consequently his injury.

[4] It may be admitted that upon these two important questions the weight of the evidence appears to have been against the plaintiff, and it may be admitted that this court would as an original proposition in considering the evidence have made a different finding of fact; but these things furnish us no cause for setting aside the verdict. The jury were the triers of the facts, and we are not authorized to disturb their verdict unless it is clearly and palpably against the weight of the evidence, which it is not in this case. Lou. & Interurban R. R. Co. v. Roemmele, 157 Ky. 84, 162 S. W. 547.

Judgment affirmed.

PEOPLE'S SAV. BANK & TRUST CO. v. KLEMPNER BROS.

(Court of Appeals of Kentucky. April 29. 1921.)

1. **Sales ⟺201(1)—Possession must be delivered before title passes.**

Possession of personal property must be delivered actually or symbolically before title passes.

2. **Sales ⟺218½—Possession of carrier presumptively possession of consignee.**

Presumptively possession of the carrier is possession of the consignee, but such presumption may be rebutted.

3. **Sales ⟺201(4) — Whether possession of carrier possession of consignee buyer question of shipper's intention.**

Whether the possession of a carrier is the possession of the consignee buyer depends on the purpose and intention of the shipper; that is, whether the shipper intended to relinquish the right to dispose of the property in a different way, or whether he intended that the absolute title and possession should pass from him.

4. **Sales ⟺201(4)—Evidence conclusive that debtor consignor did not intend title or possession of goods to vest in creditor consignee.**

Where a debtor agreed with his creditor to ship to the creditor two carloads of merchandise to be applied on the debt, but, when he did so, retained the bills of lading and pledged the same with a draft drawn by him on the creditor consignee to a bank, it was conclusive evidence that he did not intend either the title or the possession of the goods to vest in the creditor consignee until the draft was paid, but intended to keep title in himself for the benefit of the bank and to pledge the merchandise represented by the bills of lading for the payment of the draft, and the creditor consignee, having secured possession of the goods, without surrender of the bills of lading, from the railroad, is liable to the bank for the value of the merchandise in the cars.

Appeal from Circuit Court, Jefferson County, Common Pleas Branch, Third Division.

Action by the People's Savings Bank & Trust Company against Klempner Bros. From judgment on verdict partially for plaintiff and partially for defendants, plaintiff appeals, and defendants cross-appeal. Judgment affirmed on the cross-appeal, and reversed on the original appeal.

Baskin & Vaughan, of Louisville, for appellant.

Hugh B. Fleece, of Louisville, for appellee.

TURNER, C. On and prior to the 5th of September, 1918, Joseph Schetzer was doing business at Memphis, Tenn., in the name of Memphis Iron & Metal Company, and during the same period Klempner Bros., of Louisville, Ky., were engaged in business at that place.

Previous to that time there had been several business transactions between them which resulted as of that date in an indebtedness by Schetzer to Klempner Bros. of something over $1,000, and, as alleged, Klempner Bros. bought from Schetzer two carloads of merchandise to be shipped to them and applied upon such indebtedness.

On the 1st of November Schetzer shipped from Memphis one carload of scrap iron and one carload of Manchester bagging, consigned to Klempner Bros. at Louisville. The bills of lading for these two carloads of merchandise show Klempner Bros. to be the consignees, and are what are known as straight or nonnegotiable bills of lading.

Although Klempner Bros. were designated as consignees in the bills of lading, on the day of shipment Schetzer, still being in possession of the bills of lading, went to appellant bank at Memphis, and there drew his draft on Klempner Bros. at Louisville for $1,400, apparently what he conceived to be the value of the two carloads of merchandise, and attached to the draft the two bills of lading and then sold the draft with the two bills to the appellant bank, which placed the face value thereof, $1,400, to Schetzer's credit in the bank.

The draft with the two bills of lading attached was forwarded in the usual course to Louisville and reached there on the 5th of November, and Klempner Bros. were so notified on that day by the Louisville bank, and were again called up by phone by officers of the bank on November 6th; and on that day one of the members of the firm went to the bank, inspected the draft and bills of lading, and declined to pay same, assigning as a reason that the weights given in the bills were not proper. The draft was protested for nonpayment, and about 10 o'clock of that day one of the carloads of merchandise shipped from Memphis on the 1st of November was placed on a siding or switch in the yard of Klempner Bros.' place of business, and the other car reached there a few days later, and in some way not explained in the record Klempner Bros., without being in possession of the bills of lading, got possession of and appropriated to their own use the contents of the two cars.

Subsequently, on the 22d of November, while Schetzer was in Louisville, the draft remaining unpaid, Klempner Bros. and Schetzer had a full settlement, which showed Klempner Bros. indebted to Schetzer in the sum of $698.04, which they that day paid to him by check.

This is an action by the Memphis bank against Klempner Bros. on the draft, and the defense, in substance, is that on the 5th of September, 1918, while Schetzer was indebted to them, appellees bought from him two carloads of merchandise to be shipped to them at Louisville, and that at the time by agreement between them and Schetzer the two cars of merchandise were to be applied on the indebtedness of Schetzer, and that the two carloads of merchandise so shipped by Schetzer on November 1, 1918, were the two carloads of merchandise so purchased by them, and to be so applied, and were the same two carloads of merchandise represented by the two bills of lading attached to the draft upon which the plaintiff sued; and it is their theory that, as they had previously purchased from Schetzer this identical merchandise to be applied to the payment of their debt, when Schetzer delivered the same to the carrier at Memphis consigned to them at Louisville, they became the owners of the merchandise, and Schetzer no longer had any interest therein, and the bills of lading being nonnegotiable, the plaintiff bank acquired no right or interest in the property represented by the bills of lading.

The lower court directed a verdict for the plaintiff for the value of the carload of Manchester bagging apparently because the evidence showed the two carloads of merchandise contracted for by appellees to be applied on their debt were to be scrap iron, but directed a verdict for the defendants for the value of the one carload of scrap iron, and from the judgment on that verdict the plaintiff has appealed, and the defendants prosecute a cross-appeal.

Going to the heart of the controversy and brushing aside all collateral questions, the case must be determined upon the question whether the title to the merchandise in the two cars passed to Klempner Bros. upon their consignment to them by Schetzer on November 1st; for, if the title passed to them notwithstanding they had never been in possession of the bills of lading, then the assignment of the bills of lading by Schetzer to the bank, and the attaching of them to the draft sold by Schetzer to the bank, gave to the bank no interest or title which Schetzer did not have. But if, on the contrary, the retention by Schetzer of the bills of lading, which represented the merchandise in the two cars, had the effect of retaining in him the title to the merchandise, then his assignment of the two bills of lading to the bank, attached as they were to the draft, operated as a pledge of the merchandise to the bank to secure payment of the draft, although the bills of lading were nonnegotiable.

So that the whole question is: Was the title to the merchandise in the cars in Klempner Bros. at the time Schetzer assigned the bills of lading to the bank, or did their retention by Schetzer retain the title in him?

In discussing this question we shall assume for the sake of argument that the one carload of scrap iron shipped on the 1st of November was part of the merchandise alleged to have been previously purchased by Klempner Bros. from Schetzer to be applied upon Schetzer's indebtedness to them, although that question is in issue, and it is claimed by appellant that there is no evidence to sustain it.

[1] It is the rule that possession of personal property must be delivered either actually or symbolically before the title passes, and here the question is whether the possession of the carrier was the possession of the consignees, although the bills of lading, which are the evidence of title, were never delivered to them, but were retained by the shipper and pledged by him on the same day the shipment was made.

[2] Presumptively the possession of the carrier is the possession of the consignee, but that is only a presumption, and may be rebutted, and it is the claim of appellant here that it is positively and conclusively rebutted by the fact that the shipper, instead of sending the bills of lading to the consignees, not only retained them, but pledged them, and thereby pledged the property which

they represented to the bank to secure the payment of the draft; while, on the other hand, the appellees claim that they, having previously purchased the merchandise under an agreement that it was to be applied to an existing indebtedness of the shipper, not only took upon its consignment to them the title, but the possession of the carrier was their possession.

[3] Ordinarily the possession of a carrier is the possession of the consignee, but whether that is true or not depends upon the purpose and intention of the shipper; that is, whether the shipper intended to relinquish the right to dispose of the property in a different way or whether he intended that the absolute title and possession should pass from him. In this case if Schetzer had intended to comply with his agreement to ship the carload of scrap iron to appellees to be applied on his debt, he would not have retained possession of the bills of lading, but would have promptly mailed them to appellees. The very fact that, instead of mailing to them the bills of lading or delivering the same to some one for them, he on the same day of the shipment, while they were still in his possession, pledged them and the merchandise which they represented to the bank, is convincing that he had no intention of passing the title or possession of the merchandise to appellees until the draft was paid and they thereby got possession of the bills of lading.

In Hutchinson on Carriers, § 194, it is said:

"If, however, the circumstances are such that upon delivery of the goods to the carrier they become the property of the consignee, the carrier holds them as the agent of such consignee, and their destination cannot afterwards be changed without his consent. If, for instance, the consignee is the vendee of the goods, or if he has made advances upon them with the agreement that they shall be shipped to him to be sold in order that he may retain the proceeds for his reimbursement, or if, being a creditor of the consignor, the goods are delivered to the carrier to be shipped to him in satisfaction of his debt according to a previous agreement to that effect, the title to the goods will vest in him upon delivery to the carrier, and if their destination is afterwards altered, except under such circumstances as entitle a vendor to stop them in transitu, the carrier will become responsible to him for them. The legal presumption is that, when goods are sent to a consignee, the title to them vests in him as soon as the shipment is made. It is solely, however, a question of intention or of agreement, and may be shown to be otherwise."

In case of Freeman v. Kraemer, 63 Minn. 242, 65 N. W. 455, Freeman & Co. shipped to Stevenson at Duluth some merchandise in response to a letter from Stevenson offering certain prices for certain kinds of merchandise, and the shipment was consigned to Stevenson. Notwithstanding the merchandise was consigned to Stevenson, Freeman & Co.

drew a draft on him for the price of the merchandise and attached to it the bill of lading, both being sent to a Duluth bank for collection. When the draft reached Duluth Stevenson refused to pay it because the car had not yet arrived, although, in fact, it had arrived, and the railroad company delivered the merchandise to Kraemer, who had bought the goods from Stevenson, the consignee. A peremptory instruction was given to find for the bank against Kraemer, and the court, in affirming that judgment, based its opinion wholly upon the intention of the shipper as ascertained from the facts which are strikingly similar to those in this case, and said:

"We are of the opinion that the order appealed from should be affirmed. It clearly and conclusively appears from the evidence that the sale or contemplated sale from plaintiff to Stevenson was to be a cash transaction. No indicia of ownership was given to Stevenson. On the contrary, the bills of lading were forwarded by plaintiff, with the drafts attached to them, in such a manner as to make the intended delivery of the bills to Stevenson concurrent with the payment of the drafts for the purchase price of the property. From the circumstances, it conclusively appears that plaintiff did not intend to vest the title to the property in Stevenson until the goods were paid for."

In that case, as here, there was a contention by the defendant that as the indicia of ownership was conferred on the consignee the title had vested in him because the goods had been consigned to him, and in response to that contention the court said:

"Appellants contend that plaintiff had conferred indicia of ownership on Stevenson, and that this gave Stevenson power to vest title by estoppel in appellants. In view of the authorities just cited, it is hardly necessary to say that merely shipping the goods addressed to the consignee, while retaining the bills of lading, confers no indicia of ownership on the consignee."

Other authorities holding that the presumption that a consignee is the owner of goods when delivered to the carrier may be rebutted and the real intention of the shipper shown are: Judson v. Minneapolis & St. Louis R. R. Co., 131 Minn. 5, 154 N. W. 506; White & Co. v. Century Savings Bank, 229 Fed. 975, 144 C. C. A. 257; Petitt v. First National Bank of Memphis, 4 Bush, 334; Douglas, Receiver, v. People's Bank, 86 Ky. 176, 5 S. W. 420, 10 Ky. Law Rep. 243, 9 Am. St. Rep. 276; Hawkins v. Alfalfa Products Co., 152 Ky. 152, 153 S. W. 201, 44 L. R. A. (N. S.) 600; Emery's Sons v. Irving National Bank, 25 Ohio St. 360, 18 Am. Rep. 299; Bank of Rochester v. Jones, 4 N. Y. (Comstock) 497, 55 Am. Dec. 290.

[4] It is our conclusion, therefore, that although there had been a previous agreement by Schetzer to ship to Klempner Bros. the two carloads of merchandise to be applied

on his indebtedness to them, his retention of
the bills of lading and his pledge of the same
to the bank on that day, not only furnish
conclusive evidence that he did not intend
either the title or the possession of the goods
to vest in Klempner Bros. until the draft
was paid, but that he intended to keep the
title in himself for the benefit of the bank
and to pledge the merchandise represented
by the bills of lading for the payment of the
draft.

Prior to the shipment Schetzer had both
title to and possession of the merchandise.
He might have sold it and applied the proceeds to his indebtedness to Klempner Bros.,
or he might have kept or otherwise have used
the money. Klempner Bros. had no interest
or equity in the same prior to that time. All
they had was Schetzer's promise to ship
same to them to be applied on his debt, and,
since the goods remained in Schetzer's possession, he might have complied with his
promise to them or he might have disposed
of the goods to others.

It cannot be denied that on the day he
shipped them Schetzer might have mortgaged
the goods to the bank and that Klempner
Bros. could not have successfully asserted
claim to the goods as against the bank; but
what he did, in fact, was only to adopt a
different method of putting them in lien to
the bank.

There should have been a directed verdict
for the plaintiff for the full value of the
merchandise in the two cars.

It therefore results that the judgment is
affirmed on the cross-appeal and reversed on
the original appeal for proceedings consistent
herewith.

COMMONWEALTH POWER RY. & LIGHT CO. v. VAUGHT.

(Court of Appeals of Kentucky. May 24, 1921.)

1. Municipal corporations ⬅️806(3) — One opening doorway in sidewalk is negligent, if he fails to guard the opening.

It is negligence to leave open a cellar door in a much-frequented pavement, without pre-caution being taken to protect the hole; so, where defendant's servants opened a doorway in the sidewalk, and plaintiff, who was carrying a heavy box out of a building, backed into the opening, defendant is liable, unless it had a servant on guard to warn plaintiff of his dan-ger, or plaintiff failed to use ordinary care for his own safety.

2. Municipal corporations ⬅️821(17)—Wheth-er defendant's servants, who opened doorway in pavement, took precautions to warn trav-elers, question for the jury.

Where plaintiff, while carrying a box out of a building, stepped into an open doorway in the sidewalk, the question whether defendant's servants, who had opened the doorway, took precautions to guard against such injury by leaving a servant on watch, held, under the evi-dence, for the jury.

3. Damages ⬅️132(1)—Award of $2,500 dam-ages held not excessive for injury to hand, testicles, etc.

Where an expressman, while backing out of a house with a heavy box, stepped into a door-way in the sidewalk, which had been opened by defendant's servants, and the box fell upon him, injuring his hand, testicles, etc., an award of $2,500 cannot be deemed excessive, where he was 40 years old and earning a salary of $75 per month; it appearing that he suffered much pain and was permanently injured.

4. Appeal and error ⬅️301—Matters not as-signed as ground for new trial cannot be re-viewed.

Where defendant complained of plaintiff's failure to submit to an operation to lessen in-jury, and for that reason the damages were ex-cessive, such matter cannot be reviewed, where not made ground for new trial.

5. Trial ⬅️122—Comment on defendant's fail-ure to call one of physicians appointed to ex-amine plaintiff proper.

Where, at the instance of defendant, two physicians were appointed to examine plaintiff, but defendant called only one of them, it was permissible for plaintiff's counsel to comment on the failure of defendant to call the other.

Appeal from Circuit Court, Boyle County.

Action by James Vaught against the Com-monwealth Power Railway & Light Company. From a judgment for plaintiff, defendant ap-peals. Affirmed.

John W. Rawlings and George E. Stone, both of Danville, for appellant.

Henry Jackson and Jay Harlan, both of Danville, for appellee.

TURNER, C. In January, 1919, the ap-pellee was employed by the Southern Express Company, at Danville, Ky., as a deliveryman, and in that capacity it was his duty to de-liver and to receive from shippers packages handled by the express company. On one day in that month it became his duty to go to and receive from a second-story apartment on Main street in Danville for shipment a large box weighing 300 or 400 pounds. The entrance to the stairway leading to this apartment was in an offset or small court between two buildings, and the pavement there extended into the offset between the two business houses, and this offset or court was a part of the pavement used by the pub-lic. At or near the entrance to the stairway was an iron cellar door, composed of two iron gratings built into the pavement, and which, when closed, were a part of the side-walk. This door was an entrance to the cellar of one of the buildings, and the two gratings, when lifted, one to the east and one to the west, stood approximately upright, but with a slight slant. outward, and when so opened left an aperture of approximately 3x4 feet, and the depth of the cellar was about 4 or 5 feet.

Appellant entered the stairway and left his wagon at the curb. In bringing the large box down the stairway he had no assistance, other than that of one or two small boys, and it is not clear from the evidence what actual assistance they rendered him. At any rate, in bringing the box down the stairway, it was necessary for him to come down backwards, having hold of the front end of the box, which was 3 or 4 feet long, and, either with the assistance of the boys or by dropping the other end from step to step, he managed to thus take the box down.

According to the plaintiff's evidence, the door or gratings were closed when he entered the stairway, but were opened by appellant's agents while he was in the apartment, and without notice to him, and he says that when he backed down the steps with the box, and out onto the street, he straddled one of the iron gratings that were approximately upright and fell into the hole, the large box falling on top of him; that in his contact with the iron grating his testicles were mashed and bruised, and in some way not explained one of the knuckles on his left hand was permanently knocked down. He was confined to his home for about 3 weeks, and was unable to return to his work for 39 days, while he was confined to his home the doctor visited him twice, and after he was able to get out he frequently went to the doctor's office for treatment.

In this action for damages the jury returned a verdict for $2,500 in favor of the plaintiff, and the defendant's motion for a trial having been overruled, it appeals. Four grounds for reversal are insisted upon: (1) Error in the instructions; (2) excessive damages; (3) the failure of appellee to minimize his damages by submitting to an operation; (4) improper argument of counsel.

[1, 2] 1. It was admitted that the defendant's agents and employés opened the door into the cellar, but it was the defense that the grating was open when appellee entered the building, and that an agent or employé was left on guard at the opening to warn persons using the sidewalk. There was some conflict on this issue; one of appellant's employés testifying that he warned appellee against backing into the cellar, while appellee states that he received no such warning, and one or two other witnesses state that the agent so claiming to have warned appellee was at the time of the injury down the street, some little distance away, looking into a window. So that it is apparent that the controlling question of fact in the case was whether appellant had an agent on guard at the door, and whether that agent warned appellee.

In giving its instructions the court carefully followed the rule laid down in the case of De Haven v. Danville Gaslight Co., 150 Ky. 241, 150 S. W. 322, in which case it was held to be negligence as a matter of law to leave open a cellar door in a much-frequented pavement, without precaution being taken to protect the hole; the court holding expressly that to leave such a door open unguarded was negligence as a matter of law. In that case on a trial the jury found a verdict for the defendant, and upon appeal this court reversed that judgment, because the court had submitted to the jury the question whether the defendant's agents had negligently suffered the door to remain open, and laid down the rule that to permit a door in a sidewalk to remain open without being guarded was negligence per se.

In accord with that ruling the lower court in this case instructed the jury, in substance, that they should find for the plaintiff, unless they should believe from the evidence that the defendant's agent was present immediately before and at the time of the accident and warned the plaintiff of his danger, or unless they should believe from the evidence that the plaintiff on that occasion failed to use ordinary care for his own safety, and that his failure contributed · to the injuries to such an extent that they would not have been received, but for such failure, and that, if they believed either of these two things, they should find for the defendant. It will be seen that the latter part of the court's instruction covered the defendant's plea of contributory negligence.

The instruction submitted the only issues upon which the defense was based, for it is not to be questioned that, if the defendant's agents opened this cellar door on the pavement and left it open without a guard, it was guilty of negligence per se, and the questions have been fairly submitted—in fact, we may say submitted with unusual clarity. The instructions offered by the defendant in effect proposed to submit to the jury the issue whether the defendant's agents had negligently left the door open and unguarded, the very thing which the court condemned in the De Haven Case.

[3] 2. Appellee is 40 years of age and at the time of his injury was getting a salary of $75 per month. The appellant's argument is that the damages are excessive, because appellee was only shown to have been away from his work 39 days, and because no permanent injury was shown. It is true that he remained only that length of time away from his employment, but he states in his evidence that since the injury he has not been able to do his customary work and usual lifting without pain, and that he still, at the time of the trial, nearly 9 months after the in-

juries were received, suffered from the same, and that at the time of the injury he "suffered death and was crazy from pain."

So far as the injury to his knuckle is concerned, one of the doctors introduced testified that it will always be in the same condition, and the plaintiff and his physician each testify that he is still suffering from a bad stricture as a result of the accident; the plaintiff stating that, even at the time of the trial, he had great difficulty in urinating, and that it was painful. His physician states that his urethra was injured, and that he had a stricture as a result of the injury, which caused him trouble in urinating, and the plaintiff himself states explicitly that he never had any trouble of that nature before the injury. The physician states, in answer to the question whether the plaintiff was permanently injured:

"I would say so, without a surgical operation for the stricture, requiring after care, and to be sounded occasionally for rest of life to keep scar tissue stretched. The injured hand will remain as it is, knuckle down."

From this evidence it is apparent that the jury was authorized to find, not only that the injury to the knuckle was permanent, but that the stricture resulting from the injury to the testicles and urethra would remain permanent in the absence of an operation, and even if such an operation were had, and the stricture should thereby be removed in a measure, still there would be required for the rest of his life occasional soundings, which apparently would involve not only much inconvenience for the whole life of the man, but would be accompanied by considerable pain. From this evidence the jury was fully authorized in finding that each of the injuries was in a proper sense a permanent injury, and, that being true, the verdict cannot be said to be excessive, and especially in the light of the common knowledge that an injury to the testicles, even though slight, involves the most excruciating pain.

[4] 3. The complaint of appellee's failure to minimize his damages by submitting to an operation, even if otherwise available, cannot be considered. An examination of the grounds for a new trial discloses that this was not one of them.

[5] 4. During the trial, on motion of the defendant, Drs. Montgomery and Jackson were appointed by the court to ascertain the condition of the plaintiff. Appellant then introduced Dr. Montgomery, and, in substance, he stated that his examination disclosed that plaintiff was not suffering from a stricture, but failed to introduce Dr. Jackson. The plaintiff thereafter introduced Dr. Jackson, who had been plaintiff's regular physician, who reiterated, after his examination of the appellee under order of the court, that he was suffering from a stricture.

During the argument by plaintiff's counsel, in referring to this, he said, "Mr. Rawlings did not seem anxious to have the jury know the result of the examination after it was made." And again in the same connection he said: "I do not blame this defendant for not wanting the result of the examination after it was objected to." And it is claimed that these statements constituted an improper argument. Counsel in argument is within his rights in referring in a proper way to things that take place during a trial, and in such argument may make any reasonable deduction or fair inference that may be drawn from such occurrence. The two doctors had been appointed upon the motion of the appellant, and its failure to introduce one of them after having him appointed was a subject to which counsel of the other side might fairly refer, and draw therefrom any reasonable or just inference. The reference, even if error, was trivial.

On the whole case, we see no error prejudicial to the substantial rights of the appellant, and the judgment is affirmed.

KOZY THEATER CO. et al. v. LOVE et al.

(Court of Appeals of Kentucky. Feb. 4, 1921.
Rehearing Denied June 10, 1921.)

1. Landlord and tenant ⟸83(1)—Privilege to "renew" or extend not identical, but construction depends on intention.

While there is a distinction between a privilege to "renew" and one to extend a lease, the term "renew" etymologically contemplating something more than a mere state of passivity, the question whether a covenant is one to renew or extend depends on the intention of the parties as shown by the entire lease and their interpretation thereof before the controversy arose; consequently, where a lease gave the lessees privilege to renew for two successive terms, and the lessees gave notice of their desire to continue the lease, whereupon, without execution of a new lease, the lessor assented and received rents without objection, the lease must be construed as providing for an extension so that the lessees may at the expiration of the second term continue for another.

[Ed. Note.—For other definitions, see Words and Phrases, First and Second Series, Renew.]

2. Landlord and tenant ⟸86(2)—Notice of desire to continue lease given by only two of the several lessees held binding.

Where only two of the several lessees gave notice of desire to continue under an agreement to renew, such notice will be deemed valid and binding, the lessees remaining as the same, the notice having been given for the benefit of all.

⟸For other cases see same topic and KEY-NUMBER in all Key-Numbered Digests and Indexes

3. Landlord and tenant ⬅84—Surrender by one lessee of corporate charter held not to invalidate an extension.

Where during the original term of a lease which provided for an extension one of the several lessees surrendered its corporate charter and thereafter became a copartnership, that fact will not warrant the lessor which consented to one extension in refusing another; for, having waived the matter once, it was waived for all time.

4. Frauds, statute of ⬅58(2)—Verbal consent to extension not objectionable on the ground that it was within the statute of frauds.

Where a lease provided for renewal, the lessor's verbal consent to an extension, the parties treating the covenant as one providing for extension, cannot be questioned on the ground that it was within the statute, because there could be no renewal without the execution of a new lease.

5. Corporations ⬅298(1)—Informal acts of directors of corporation binding where authorized by by-laws or custom.

While it is the general rule that a corporation can act only through its directors at an official meeting regularly held, and that its acts can be proven only by the records of such meeting, there are many exceptions, and the rule may be modified by by-laws or customs, so, where the stockholders and directors of the lessor corporation acquiesced in the action of the secretary in consenting to an extension while the stockholders of the lessee corporation acquiesced in the request of its president for an extension, the action of such officers is binding on both corporations.

6. Landlord and tenant ⬅85½—Though provision be deemed one for renewal, lessor cannot evict lessee who tendered new lease.

Where a lease provided for renewal for two successive terms, and the lessor, after consenting to one renewal or extension, no new lease being executed, assigned the reversion, the assignees cannot by assertion that the provision was one for renewal, and not extension, evict the lessees by refusing to sign a renewal lease which was tendered.

7. Landlord and tenant ⬅85½—Assignees of reversion take lease as construed by the parties.

The assignees of the reversion subject to a lease which contained a provision for renewal take the same subject to the construction of the original parties, and where they had construed it as for an extension the assignees are bound.

8. Partnership ⬅64—That corporate lessee transacted business in name of its president will not warrant refusal of extension of lease.

Where theater property was leased to a number, including the president and stockholders of lessee corporation, the fact that the corporate lessee did business under the name of its president will not warrant the lessor in refusing to grant an extension under Ky. St. § 199b, forbidding any person to carry on or conduct business under an assumed name until a statement has been filed in the county clerk's office giving the name to be used and the names and addresses of the persons so engaged, but excepting Kentucky corporations; for it was not a violation of the law for the corporate lessee to so do business under the name of an individual lessee.

9. Names ⬅10—Contract executed by one doing business under assumed name is voidable only.

A contract executed by party doing business under a name other than his own without complying with Ky. St. § 199b, is not void, but voidable only at the option of the party not in fault, and enforceable against the one at fault.

10. Corporations ⬅50—Lessee corporation's surrender of charter and doing of business under old name held not to warrant refusal to extend as to other tenants.

Where property was leased to a number of tenants, including two corporations, the fact that one of the corporations during the original term surrendered its charter and continued to do business under the old name as a corporation, without complying with Ky. St. § 199b, requiring the filing of such name, will not warrant the lessor in refusing to grant an extension or renewal to the other lessees pursuant to the terms of the lease.

Appeal from Circuit Court, McCracken County.

Forcible detainer proceedings by Quincy B. Love and another against the Kozy Theater Company and others, begun in justice court. From a judgment of restitution entered in the circuit court on a trial without a jury of the traverse of a like judgment upon inquisition of the justice, defendants appeal. Reversed and remanded.

Bradshaw & McDonald, of Paducah, for appellants.

Hendrick & Burns, of Paducah, for appellees.

CLARKE, J. The Palmer Hotel Company, a Kentucky corporation, owns its hotel property in Paducah and the adjacent building known in this record as the Kentucky Theater.

On July 1, 1918, the hotel company by written contract leased the Kentucky Theater "for the period of one year from July 1, 1918, with the privilege to the lessees to renew this lease at the expiration thereof under like terms for a period of one year from July 1, 1919, and a like privilege to renew for one year from July 1, 1920 and a like privilege to renew for one year from July 1, 1921," to the six appellants, Kozy Theater Company, Arcade Theater Company, Lawrence Dallam, Leo F. Keller, Rodney C. Davis, and R. R. Kirkland. It was stipulated that the lessees were to pay to the lessor $1,800 a year rental "payable at the rate of $150 per month during the period of this lease or any renewals thereof," and "at the expiration of this lease * * * no notice to quit shall be necessary, and the lessor shall have the right to enter and take possession."

Appellants took possession, paid the rent for the first year as due, and on June 14, 1919, caused to be written and delivered to Mr. J. C. Utterback, secretary, treasurer, and general manager of the hotel company, the following letter:

"Mr. J. C. Utterback, Secy. Palmer Hotel Co., Paducah, Ky.—My Dear Sir: Please be advised that we wish to exercise our right to continue the lease for the Kentucky Theater for one year from July 1, 1919, as provided in the original lease, bearing date of July 1, 1918, and hereby bind ourselves for the said period to all conditions of the said original lease. Very respectfully, Kozy Theater Co., Inc., by Rodney C. Davis, Pres. Arcade Theater Co., by Leo V. Haag, Manager."

Upon receipt of the above letter Mr. Utterback told Mr. Davis, who was himself one of the lessees and also president and general manager of the Kozy Theater Company, that "it is allright and agreeable to us." Mr. Utterback informed the other officers and directors of the notice and his consent to a continuance of the lease for another year, and they informally approved of his action, but no new lease was executed, nor was any formal action taken with reference thereto by the hotel company.

The lessees through Mr. Davis paid to Mr. Utterback, who accepted same for the hotel company, rent at $150 per month for July and August, 1919; and each month thereafter during the year ending July 1, 1920, paid the same amount to appellant Quincy B. Love, to whom and one Green the hotel company on August 8, 1919, leased both the hotel and Kentucky Theater buildings for a term of 15 years. Love, having acquired Green's rights under their lease in April, 1920, assigned to appellee Rehkopf all of his rights to the Kentucky Theater. Love and Rehkopf then notified appellants that they could not retain the theater after July 1, 1920. Appellants, however, gave Love and Rehkopf written notice before July 1, 1920, that they intended to exercise their option to renew their lease for another year, and tendered to them for execution renewal lease for another year with the same renewal privileges for subsequent years and upon the same terms and conditions as contained in their original lease of July 1, 1918. Love and Rehkopf refused to execute the new lease or accept tendered rentals, and on July 2, 1920, filed this forcible detainer proceeding against appellants.

This appeal is from the judgment of restitution entered in the circuit court upon a trial before the court without a jury of the traverse of a like judgment upon the inquisition before the justice of the peace who issued the warrant.

[1] This court uniformly has recognized a technical distinction between a covenant to renew and a covenant to extend a lease, but has been just as consistent in holding that whether the privilege is to renew or extend depends upon the intention of the parties as shown by the entire lease and their interpretation thereof before the controversy arose, and that the mere fact it is called a privilege to renew is not conclusive. Illustrative cases are Brown v. Samuels, 24 Ky. Law Rep. 1216, 70 S. W. 1047; Ky. Lumber Co. v. Newell & Co., 32 Ky. Law Rep. 396, 105 S. W. 972; Grant v. Collins, 157 Ky. 36, 162 S. W. 539, Ann. Cas. 1915D, 249; Miller v. Albany Lodge, 168 Ky. 755, 182 S. W. 986; Mullins v. Nordlow, 170 Ky. 169, 185 S. W. 825; Gault v. Carpenter, 187 Ky. 25, 218 S. W. 254; Hunt v. McCord, 179 Ky. 1, 200 S. W. 2. See, also, Elliott on Contracts, § 4556.

The true rule to be gathered from these authorities as well as upon principle is that such a covenant in a lease, like any other, will be construed according to its terms if these are certain, but, if there is any doubt of what was meant by what was said in the lease, the actions of the parties before a controversy arose may be examined to ascertain their own interpretation of its meaning, since they better than anybody else knew what they meant by what they said. But in this connection it must be borne in mind, as was well said in Ky. Lumber Co. v. Newell, supra, that:

"The word 'renew' etymologically contemplates something more than passivity in suffering a state to continue as it was; but it is not so much a question of what the term strictly means as what did the parties to the writing mean to express in its use."

And that its meaning when used in a lease in connection with a privilege for an additional term is rarely ever free from doubt, and usually must be explained by some other clause in the lease or by extraneous evidence or both, is attested by the frequency with which the question is litigated and the lack of harmony in the decisions from different courts in attempting to construe its meaning and effect when so used. But, as said in Grant v. Collins, supra, after reviewing numerous authorities:

"The apparent conflict in the cases, as will thus be seen, turns rather on the difference in the facts than on a different conception of the law."

And the facts upon which nearly all of the cases turn will be found on examination to be additional clauses in the leases or the acts of the parties which explain what they meant by "a privilege to renew."

Just what legal import ought to be ascribed to the word "renew" in this connection, in the absence of explanatory facts, is really the question upon which the courts disagree.

Some hold it requires the execution of a new lease, which, however, may be waived; others that there is no distinction between a privilege to renew or extend; while still other courts among which is our own take a middle ground. Our court has gone no farther in an effort to define the term when so used than to hold, as in the Newell Case, that it means "something more than passivity," and as in Miller v. Albany Lodge, supra, that by its use "some positive act on the part of the parties or notice by the tenant is required."

Nor need we now attempt a definition, which manifestly would be difficult, since an additional clause in this lease and the acts of the parties explain what they meant by its use sufficiently for the purpose of this case.

The additional clause which we have heretofore quoted, as in the Grant v. Collins Case upon which appellees so confidently rely, makes it clear a simple holding over and payment of rent beyond the first period was insufficient to satisfy the terms of the lease, but there the analogy between the two cases ends.

In the case at bar the lessees, or rather some of them, gave timely notice of their desire and intention to "renew," or, as they expressed it, to continue the lease, and Mr. Utterback, the general manager of the lessor corporation, not only gave express verbal assent thereto, but thereafter accepted the stipulated rent with the approval of all of the directors and stockholders who knew that same was being paid by the lessees in the exercise of their contract right of renewal.

This certainly was no simple holding over by sufferance under the statute as in the Grant v. Collins Case. It was not so understood by either party, but was very clearly the performance of what each party not only believed, but actually agreed to be a "renewal" or continuance of the original contract, and therefore their interpretation thereof; hence, upon authority of all of the Kentucky cases and most others, we must so construe it, unless, as contended by appellees: (1) The notice was without force or effect because not signed by all the lessees; or (2) the assent by Utterback to a renewal and his actions thereafter are not binding upon the lessor or its assigns because (a) not in writing, and (b) it was not approved at a formal meeting of the board of directors.

[2, 3] 1. There are cases, such as Buchanan v. Whitman, 151 N. Y. 253, 45 N. E. 556, and James v. Pope, 19 N. Y. 324, cited by appellees, and with which we do not disagree, to the effect that a landlord is entitled to hold all of the original lessees to a renewal or extension, and that, some having retired from the business, those remaining cannot enforce the privilege for an additional term. But that rule has no application here, since all of the original lessees continued as such,

and the notice signed by two of them was given for all, and so understood not only by Utterback, but also by appellees Love and Rehkopf. This is shown by the fact that they gave notice to each of the original lessees to quit possession, and made all of them defendants to this action for forcible detainer. Even if the notice for this reason was defective, which we do not hold, that question clearly has been waived by not only the original lessor, but by its assignees as well. by accepting rent from the lessees on the second year knowing it was paid for all and as tenants under an extension of the original lease, and not as tenants by sufferance. But it is argued the Arcade Theater Company by surrendering its charter as a corporation and becoming a copartnership within the first period so changed its character as to call for the application of the rule.

Whatever might have been the rights of the lessor had it upon this account refused to extend the original contract at the end of the first year, it is clear that, having agreed to the extension presumably with knowledge of the facts, it could not thereafter terminate the contract and evict all six lessees because of this change in the character under which one of them was operating. Nor do we think, after once having waived the question, it could later during the continuance of the thus extended contract refuse another extension upon this ground alone, especially where it is not claimed the change in the character of one of the lessees in any wise prejudices the substantial rights of the lessor. Certainly, if the original lessor could not do so, its assignees cannot, since they hold and can have no greater rights under the contract than their assignor had at the time of the assignment.

[4] 2. (a) The contention that the verbal assent of Utterback to the "renewal" construed and called by them a continuance of the contract for an additional term is within the statute of frauds, and therefore without binding effect, is based upon the theory that there could be no renewal except by the execution of a new lease. But obviously there is no merit in this contention, upon the construction given the contract by the parties, and therefore adopted by us as the true one, that a new lease was not required, since the lessees, by giving notice and holding over, hold under the original contract, and not the notice; and the giving of the notice is not an agreement within the statute of frauds. 16 R. C. L. 885.

The recent case of Cincinnati, N. O. & T. P. Ry. Co. v. Depot Lunch Room, 190 Ky. 121, 226 S. W. 887, is not in point, because there was no provision whatever for an additional term in the expired lease, and the verbal promise of a new lease relied upon there in defense of forcible detainer was an entirely independent promise in no wise connected with the original contract and within the statute of frauds. So also with the other cases cited by appellant on this question.

[5] (b) The only authority cited in support of the contention that a corporation can act only through its directors at an official meeting regularly held and that its acts can be proven only by the records of such a meeting is a statement found in Bastin v. Givens, Adm'x, 170 Ky. 201, 185 S. W. 835, of the general rule which with all its force was applicable to the facts of that case. But there are many exceptions to this general or strictly legal rule, as was recognized in Star Mills v. Bailey, 140 Ky. 194, 130 S. W. 1077, 140 Am. St. Rep. 370, which alone is cited in the Givens Case on the question. In Thompson on Corporations, after stating the general rule substantially as it was stated in the Givens Case, many exceptions thereto are set forth in section 1074, which is in part as follows:

"The rule that the board of directors must act as a body or a unit is not iron clad. It has already been seen that a by-law may be created by custom or usage. For similar reasons a board of directors may by acting separately and in an individual capacity establish a custom or usage that will be binding upon them and upon the corporation. Thus where it appeared that from a long practice or a customary usage corporate business was transacted by securing the separate consent of the directors or that the business was customarily transacted at either a casual or an informal meeting of the board it was held as a matter of law to constitute a sufficient approval in the absence of any law or by-law restricting the directors to a different mode. * * * Another exception to this general rule requiring directors to act as a body is shown in a case where the directors themselves owned all of the stock of the corporation and authorized the president to sell all the assets, and it was held that it was immaterial that such authority was not given at a regular meeting of the directors. Acquiescence by the stockholders in the action taken by the directors separately, and where such action was carried out by the corporation, was held sufficient to render the acts valid."

In support of this text in whole or part we cite of the many available authorities: Elk Valley Coal Co. v. Thompson, 150 Ky. 614, 150 S. W. 817; Herring v. Dix River, etc., Co., 23 Ky. Law Rep. 642, 63 S. W. 576; Ford Lumber & Mfg. Co. v. Cobb, 138 Ky. 174, 127 S. W. 763; Paducah Wharfboat Co. v. Mechanics' T. & S. Bank, 164 Ky. 729, 176 S. W. 190; Deposit Bank of Carlisle v. Fleming, 19 Ky. Law Rep. 1947, 44 S. W. 961; German National Bank v. Butchers', etc., Co., 97 Ky. 34, 29 S. W. 882, 16 Ky. Law Rep. 881; German National Bank v. Grinstead & Co., 21 Ky. Law Rep. 674, 52 S. W. 951; Pittsburg, etc., R. Co. v. Woolley, 12 Bush, 451; 10 Cyc. 1102; Fletcher's Cyc. of Corp. vol. 3, pp. 3049 and 3398; Cook v. Jones, 96 Ky. 283, 28 S. W. 960, 16 Ky. Law Rep. 469.

The appellants in the instant case not only offered to prove a customary usage in transacting corporate business that brought this transaction within the first of the three exceptions to the general rule set out above, which was erroneously excluded by the trial court, but they also offered and were permitted to introduce evidence bringing the transaction within the other two named exceptions to that rule.

It is clear, therefore, that the lessor, the Palmer Hotel Company, and its assigns, Love and Rehkopf, are bound by the acts of Mr. Utterback; and for the same reasons upon like evidence the Kozy Theater Company became bound by the acts of Mr. Davis, its president and general manager, in both the execution and extension or "renewal" of the original contract at the expiration of the first period.

[6, 7] This being true, it is apparent Love and Rehkopf could not terminate the contract at the end of the second year upon notice to appellants to surrender possession. It is likewise clear it seems to us that, even if the privilege had been technically one for a renewal requiring the execution of a new lease, appellees could not take advantage of their own refusal to execute same and evict appellants after they had signed and tendered it to them for that purpose. But, however that may be, the appellees took the lease as it already had been construed by the original parties thereto, and appellants before the expiration of the second year did all and more than they were required under that construction to perfect their right to a further extension thereof.

[8] In this view of the case we need only notice one of the several other questions argued in briefs; that is, whether or not the lessees, because of their failure as a whole and of one of their number to comply with section 199b, Kentucky Statutes, are deprived of their right to urge their contract in defense of this action. Section 199b of the Statutes forbids any person or persons to carry on, conduct, or transact any business in this state under an assumed name until a statement has been filed in the county clerk's office of the county where they propose to operate giving the name to be used and names and addresses of the persons so engaged.

But by subsection 4 of this section it is provided that the act shall not apply to Kentucky corporations or "be deemed or construed to prevent the lawful use of a partnership name or designation, provided that such partnership name or designation shall include the true real name of at least one of such persons transacting business." It is shown by the letter head upon which the notice of renewal was written that the lessees have been operating the Kentucky Theater and several others under the name of the

· Kozy Theater Company, which is a Kentucky corporation; and Mr. Davis, one of the lessees and also president of the Kozy Theater Company, and R. R. Kirkland, another lessee, testify that the funds derived by the lessees from operating the Kentucky Theater are kept in bank under the name "R. C. Davis, Manager of the Kozy Theater Co."; that checks against the account are so signed, and no business was done under any other name. There is no other evidence on the question, and therefore none that the lessees have been or are doing any business under any name except that of one of their number, which is not a violation of the act. Commonwealth v. Siler, etc., 176 Ky. 802, 197 S. W. 453. Besides the only business involved here is the execution and extension of the lease which was done in the real names of the parties. The Arcade Theater Company, one of the lessees, is sued as a Kentucky corporation, and only as such is it a party to this action, but it is shown by proof that during the first year of the contract it surrendered its charter, and the same stockholders have continued its business under the same name but as a copartnership.

[9, 10] Even if it be conceded, which we do not so decide, that this fact would have warranted a refusal by the landlord to grant an extension had it been the sole lessee (see Somerset Stave & Lumber Co. v. Brown, 173 Ky. 194, 190 S. W. 680), we are sure that fact alone would not justify a refusal to grant an extension to the other lessees. A contract executed by a party who is amenable to, but has not complied with, section 199b, Ken-

tucky Statutes, is not void, but voidable only at the option of the party not in fault, and enforceable against the party at fault. Warren Oil & Gas Co. v. Gardner, 184 Ky. 411, 212 S. W. 456. Surely, then, the landlord cannot elect to treat the obligation of one of several joint tenants as void, and thereby release him from the contract, and then urge that release, which was optional with him, as a reason for violating his valid covenant with his other tenants, and which all are insisting upon performing. To so construe the statute would impose its severe penalties upon parties not amenable thereto, and that, too, upon an unwarranted application of the rule that the landlord is entitled to have all the lessees comply with the covenant of renewal, since here the landlord can, if he will, enforce the extended contract against all of the same lessees bound when he acquired the property.

Therefore with reference to such facts the statute can only be fairly and reasonably construed to mean that, when a party makes a contract with several as to one of whom it is voidable at the option of the first party, and he elects to avoid it as to that one, the contract must be treated as having been made only by those who had the right to make it in determining their rights and obligations thereunder.

In our opinion the appellants are entitled to hold the premises under their exercise of the option provided in the lease, and appellees did not have the right to evict them.

Wherefore the judgment of restitution is reversed, and the cause remanded for proceedings consistent herewith.

STATE v. HOWARD. (No. 22674.)

(Supreme Court of Missouri, Division No. 2. May 26, 1921.)

1. **Homicide 254—Evidence sustaining conviction of murder in second degree.**

Evidence *held* sufficient to sustain conviction of a woman for murder in the second degree.

2. **Criminal law 829(1)—Requested instructions covered by others given properly refused.**

It is not error to refuse requested instructions covered by other instructions given.

3. **Criminal law 628(6)—Permitting witnesses to testify, although not indorsed on information, held not error.**

In a prosecution for murder in the second degree, it was not error to permit witnesses to testify, although their names had not been indorsed on the information, where they were not known to the state until a few days before the trial and no advantage was sought to be taken of defendant, nor any motion to quash filed, nor continuance asked.

4. **Witnesses 269(1)—Cross-examination of defendant relative to same matters inquired about in chief held not error.**

In a prosecution for murder in the second degree, where defendant's examination in chief covered a broad field, it was not error to cross-examine relative to the same matters inquired about in chief.

Appeal from Criminal Court, Jackson County; Ralph S. Latshaw, Judge.

Mattie Howard was convicted of murder in the second degree, and she appeals. Affirmed.

On September 4, 1919, the prosecuting attorney of Jackson county, Mo., filed, with the clerk of the criminal court of said county, a second amended verified information, charging defendant with murder in the second degree. She was arraigned, entered a plea of not guilty, and the trial of the cause commenced before a jury on October 20, 1919.

State's Evidence.

The state offered substantial evidence tending to prove the following facts:

That Joe Morino, an Italian, was engaged in the jewelry and pawnbroker's business in Kansas City, Mo., and also loaned money; the Touraine is a kitchenette hotel, consisting of a parlor, kitchen, bath, etc., located at 1412 Central avenue, Kansas City, Mo.; that apartment 301 is located on the west side of said hotel; that between 12:15 and 12:30 o'clock, on the night of May 22, 1918, defendant came to the office of said hotel, and asked the clerk for a room. The deceased, Joe Morino, was with her at the time. They were taken by the clerk to apartment 301,

and both expressed themselves as being satisfied with same.

Mr. Geraulty, in charge of the office, who took them up to examine apartment 301, testified that the following occurred:

"When they came downstairs I walked over to the desk and he (Morino) walked over to the door with his back turned towards the street and she (defendant) registered. I handed her the pen and I turned the register around and she registered, 'Mr. and Mrs. B. Stanley, City of Detroit.' She gave me a $20 bill and I gave her the change, $8—$12 for the apartment, and I gave her a receipt for a week, 22d to 29th."

The porter carried her grip up to 301, and in about 15 minutes defendant and deceased came down; he turned the key over to defendant, and witness never saw them any more. The leaf of the hotel register was identified and offered in evidence. The clerk said he could not be mistaken as to defendant being the woman who registered, as above indicated.

On Thursday, May 23, 1918, deceased, Morino, received a telephone call from the woman in apartment No. 301, requesting him to call there, and a settlement would be made for a check which had been returned marked "Insufficient funds." Two or three persons were present at the time of this call, and remembered that deceased asked for the "Mattie Howard check." Morino left his place of business about 8 o'clock that night, and was never seen alive again.

On the night of May 23, 1918, the night clerk in the Touraine hotel saw two women and a man come into the lobby of the hotel, and, after stating that they were going to apartment No. 301, left the lobby and ascended the stairs. The clerk did not think defendant was one of the three. Later, the same night, about 1 o'clock on the morning of May 24th, two women and a man emerged from the alley running along the side of the hotel, and got into a taxicab, which had been previously summoned.

The driver of said taxicab identified defendant as one of the women, and also identified the man with her, from Exhibit No. 10, as introduced by the state. The driver asked them where he was to drive, and the man answered, "Straight ahead;" and told the driver to turn off the light in back part of cab as quickly as he could. The driver further testified that he took the women to the Frederick Hotel, and later took the man to a hotel at Thirty-Third and Paseo, but discovered, on turning around, that the man did not enter above hotel, but was coming down the steps. The driver later identified the man after seeing him at Tenth and Main streets, Kansas City.

There was some evidence tending to show that defendant left Kansas City on the morning of May 24, 1918, and went to Picher,

Okl., where she was seen in the afternoon. From Picher defendant traveled between Joplin and Springfield, Mo., finally going to Trinidad, Colo., and later going to Raton, N. M., where she was arrested with Sam Taylor, the man alleged to have been with defendant the night she got into a taxicab at the Touraine Hotel.

J. W. Lees arrested defendant and Sam Taylor at Raton, N. M. They were both occupying the same house. Defendant was known as Mattie Howard, and at the time she and Sam Taylor were arrested at Raton, N. M., there was found in their room the following burglar tools: A bottle of nitroglycerine, a sawed-off shotgun, jimmies, fuses, peet soap, chisels, keys, cartridges, 45 automatic, blackjack, etc.

Much evidence was introduced by the state showing the conduct of defendant at various times. It was shown, by numerous exhibits introduced for the purposes of comparison of handwriting, that defendant had numerous aliases, and seldom used the same name on two occasions.

Joe Morino, the deceased, was found dead in said apartment No. 301 of the Touraine Hotel, on the morning of May 25, 1918. His head was badly beaten, and a blackjack was found on the floor of the hallway where deceased was lying. The coroner, Dr. Snyder, and James Willis, an embalmer, testified that, in their opinion, deceased had been dead 35 or 40 hours, when found on the morning of May 25, 1918. It appears from the evidence that when discovered, decomposition had so far advanced that when the apartment door was opened the stench filled the entire third floor of the hotel.

Defendant admitted at the trial that she knew where Morino's place of business was, and had been in there three or four times.

W. M. Mohler, of the St. Louis police department, testified that he met defendant in St. Louis, Mo., on March 22, 1919. She wanted to get into communication with her lawyer at Kansas City, and was going under an assumed name. She told witness she "had an apartment in Kansas City, and there was an Italian found dead in it; we being away from the city."

C. V. Floyd, a witness for the state, testified that he saw defendant in a restaurant at Kansas City, Mo., in May, 1918; that she wrote a note which was handed to him in the restaurant. This was about 6:30 p. m., on May 23, 1918. Witness read an account of the death of Joe Morino in the Star. After reading the account, he got out the note, and found it corresponded in detail with the place where Morino was killed. The note read:

"You will greatly please me by calling Home —Main 3085 Bell Grand 1780 Apt. 301."

Witness said he did not call her up as requested.

Defendant's Evidence.

Appellant practically contradicted all of the material testimony offered by the state as to her alleged connection with the murder of deceased. She denied having been at the Touraine Hotel, or that she had anything to do with the murder of Morino. She and some of her witnesses undertook to show by their testimony that defendant was not in Kansas City, Mo., when the homicide occurred.

As it is not the province of this court to pass on the weight of the evidence, we have set out the foregoing testimony taken from a 690-page transcript, in order to determine whether defendant's demurrer to the testimony at the conclusion of the whole case should have been sustained, and in order to pass upon the instructions given and refused. The rulings of the court during the progress of the trial, as well as the instructions given and refused, will be considered, as far as necessary, in the opinion.

The jury returned into court the verdict:

"We, the jury, find the defendant guilty of murder in the second degree, as charged in the information, and assess her punishment at 12 years in the state penitentiary."

Appellant filed motions for a new trial and in arrest of judgment. Both motions were overruled, the defendant was duly sentenced, judgment entered thereon and an appeal duly granted her to this court.

Jesse E. James, of Kansas City, for appellant.

Jesse W. Barrett, Atty. Gen., and Marshall Campbell, Asst. Atty. Gen., for the State.

RAILEY, C. (after stating the facts as above). 1. As no brief has been filed here, in behalf of appellant, we have carefully read the brief of respondent, as well as the 690-page record, to ascertain whether any reversible error was committed against appellant during the progress of the trial. While no special attack was made on the second amended information upon which the case was tried, we have examined same and find it sufficient as to both form and substance. Section 3231, R. S. 1919; State v. Davis, 217 S. W. loc. cit. 90; State v. Johnson, 192 S. W. loc. cit. 442; State v. Fairlamb, 121 Mo. loc. cit. 145, 25 S. W. 895; State v. Reed, 117 Mo. loc. cit. 613, 23 S. W. 886; State v. Dale, 108 Mo. 205, 18 S. W. 976; State v. Lowe, 93 Mo. loc. cit. 572, 574, 5 S. W. 889.

[1] 2. Appellant's demurrer to the evidence, at the conclusion of the case, was properly overruled. There was sufficient substantial evidence offered by the state, as heretofore shown, to warrant the jury in finding as they did in this case.

3. While all the instructions given by the court were formally objected to by defendant, yet we find in the record no specific objection to either. On the other hand, the

court gave remarkably clear and liberal instructions in behalf of appellant, covering every possible phase of the defenses made at the trial, while those given in behalf of the state were in conventional form and properly declared the law. The instructions, taken as a whole, were clear, forceful, and properly declared all the law necessary to enable the jury to intelligently dispose of the issues in the case.

[2] 4. Instruction numbered 13, asked by defendant, and refused by the court, was completely covered by instructions 6 and 8, given in behalf of defendant, which presented the law in much better form.

5. Appellant's instruction numbered 14 was properly refused, because the subject-matter thereof was fully covered by instructions 8 and 9, given in behalf of defendant.

6. Defendant's instruction numbered 15 was fully covered by instruction 8, given in behalf of appellant, and was therefore properly refused.

[3] 7. Objection was made during the progress of the trial to the examination of several witnesses offered by the state, on the ground that their names were not indorsed on the information. In each instance the prosecutor satisfied the court that the names of these witnesses were not known to the state until a few days before the trial, and that no advantage was sought to be taken of defendant. No motion to quash was filed, nor was a continuance asked by defendant to meet the testimony of these witnesses. As this was a case of circumstantial evidence, in which the testimony of the state, as well as that offered by defendant, covered a wide range, in which new witnesses were necessary, and as defendant did not ask for a postponement of the case, the court committed no error in permitting said witnesses to testify. State v. Kehoe, 220 S. W. loc. cit. 963; State v. Stegner, 276 Mo. 428, 207 S. W. 826; State v. Webb, 205 S. W. 187; State v. Ivy, 192 S. W. 733; State v. Jackson, 186 S. W. 990; State v. Robinson, 263 Mo. loc. cit. 324, 172 S. W. 598; State v. Walton, 255 Mo. 233, 164 S. W. 211; State v. Barrington, 198 Mo. 23, 95 S. W. 235.

[4] 8. Some objections were made to the cross-examination of defendant, but, in view of the broad field covered by her examination in chief, we are of the opinion that the cross-examination permitted by the court related to the same matters inquired about in chief, and hence no error was committed in allowing the state to examine her in respect to those subjects. State v. Drew, 213 S. W. loc. cit. 107; State v. Sherman, 264 Mo. loc. cit. 381, 175 S. W. 73; State v. Mitchell, 229 Mo. loc. cit. 698, 129 S. W. 917, 138 Am. St. Rep. 425; State v. Miller, 190 Mo. loc. cit. 463, 464, 89 S. W. 377; State v. Avery, 113 Mo. loc. cit. 498, 499, 21 S. W. 193.

9. Several other matters are presented in the motions for a new trial and in arrest of judgment, but after reading the record carefully, and considering same, we find no errors of which defendant can legally complain. We are of the opinion that defendant had a fair and impartial trial, and was properly convicted on substantial evidence.

The judgment below is accordingly affirmed.

WHITE and MOZLEY, CC., concur.

PER CURIAM. The foregoing opinion of RAILEY, C., is hereby adopted as the opinion of the court. All concur.

STATE ex rel. TUNE et al. v. FALKENHAINER et al., Judges. (No. 22578.)

(Supreme Court of Missouri, in Banc. April 30, 1921. Rehearing Denied May 24, 1921.)

Prohibition ⚫28 — Witnesses ⚫16 — Circuit court had inherent power to issue subpoena duces tecum to secretary of board of complaint of city.

The circuit court of the city of St. Louis had inherent power to issue a subpoena duces tecum requiring the secretary of the board of complaint of the city to produce a letter addressed to the board, despite the latter's claim of privilege, which, in the first instance, was solely for the circuit court, and the question of malice in writing the letter being one of fact which the Supreme Court cannot consider on application for prohibition.

Graves, J., and Walker, C. J., and Woodson, J., dissenting.

Proceeding for writ of prohibition by the State of Missouri, on the relation of Louis T. Tune and others, constituting the Board of Complaint of the City of St. Louis, against Victor H. Falkenhainer and another, Judges. Writ denied.

See, also, 191 S. W. 1078; 273 Mo. 255, 200 S. W. 1062; 199 Mo. App. 404, 203 S. W. 465.

Everett Paul Griffin, of St. Louis (Charles H. Daues, City Counselor, of St. Louis, of counsel), for relators.

Douglas W. Robert and Charles Claflin Allen, both of St. Louis, for respondents.

HIGBEE, J. This is an original proceeding for a writ of prohibition to prohibit the respondents, judges of the circuit court of the city of St. Louis from enforcing a subpoena tecum requiring Marsh to produce a letter addressed to the complaint board on the ground of privilege.

The charter of the city of St. Louis provides that the complaint board shall receive "complaints against any department, board, division, officer, or employé of the city, or against any public utility corporation, and examine the same. It shall recommend to the proper city or state authorities any action deemed advisable." The relators are the members and secretary of this board. The petition alleges that Samuel J. Douglas is an employé of the city of St. Louis in the department of streets and sewers; that Douglas brought an action in the circuit court against Lawrence McDaniel and George S. Thomas for libel, based on a letter written by them November 29, 1916, making certain false charges against him, in this, that he uses vile and obscene language to women and children who pass him; that he curses and swears at children, etc., to his damage in the sum of $50,000; that Douglas brought an action of mandamus against relators in the St. Louis Court of Appeals to obtain a copy of said letter for his use in the preparation and as evidence in the trial of said action, which is still pending in the said circuit court; that the Court of Appeals held that said letter was privileged, and that the court could not compel its production as evidence upon the trial of said cause; that thereafter said Douglas sued out a writ of certiorari in the Supreme Court, alleging that the decision of the Court of Appeals was in conflict with decisions of the Supreme Court, and that the Supreme Court held that said decision was not in conflict with any of its prior decisions and quashed the writ of certiorari; that on March 29, 1920, Hon. Victor H. Falkenhainer, judge of said circuit court, presiding in division 1 of said court, on the application of said Douglas issued a subpœna duces tecum directed to relator Marsh, secretary of said complaint board, to produce said letter at the trial of said cause; that on May 20, 1920, relators filed a motion to quash said subpœna, citing said decision of the Court of Appeals holding said letter to be a privileged communication, but said judge overruled said motion; that said Marsh is ready and willing to appear in said court in response to said subpœna, but is unwilling to produce said letter because the Court of Appeals held it to be a privileged communication; that Hon. Karl Kimmel is now presiding judge in division 1 of said circuit court; that Judge Falkenhainer is now presiding judge in division 13 of said court; and that Judge Kimmel threatens to enforce said subpœna and compel the production of said letter on the trial of said cause, all of which is contrary to the decision of said Court of Appeals.

The respondents' return to the preliminary rule sets out the amended petition filed in the Douglas libel action and the subpœna duces tecum, and avers that in the proceedings in the Court of Appeals (State ex rel. Douglas v. Tune, 199 Mo. App. 404, 203 S. W. 465) and in this court (State ex rel. Douglas v. Reynolds, 276 Mo. 688, 209 S. W. 100)

no showing was made that the libel was predicated upon a letter that was maliciously written, as was averred in the amended petition in the libel suit, and that said court properly overruled the motion to quash said subpœna; that thereafter Judge Falkenhainer was transferred to division 13 of said court, and Judge Kimmel was assigned to division 1 thereof; that the acts done by respondents and each of them respectively were done and intended to be done in discharge of their official duties, and that said subpœna was issued for the reason that the suit was an action for libel on a petition which averred that the letter mentioned in said subpœna was written falsely and maliciously by defendants, and an issue has been joined on a general denial filed by said defendants; that said action has been continued from time to time on account of the pendency of this proceeding. Wherefore they pray, etc.

Relators challenge the sufficiency of the return and move for the issuance of a peremptory writ of prohibition.

The foregoing statement, it is believed, is sufficient for the consideration of the questions arising in this cause. The facts are fully recited in the opinion of Judge Graves in State ex rel. Douglas v. Reynolds, 276 Mo. 688, 209 S. W. 100.

1. Relators charge that the circuit court exceeded its jurisdiction in issuing the subpœna to respondent Marsh to produce in court the letter on which the action was predicated, because it was held to be privileged by the Court of Appeals. The opinion of Judge Graves notes the absence of an averment in the petition for the writ of mandamus of an allegation that the letter was maliciously written.

"In other words, as far as the petition before us for review is concerned, we must presume, under the law, that the letter was sent in good faith and without malice." (276 Mo. 694, 209 S. W. 101.)

On page 695 of 276 Mo., on page 102 of 209 S. W., Judge Graves, speaking for the court in bank, said:

"The petition for mandamus shows the board to which it was addressed was at least a governmental agency provided for the good of the city government. Complaints made to such a body, at the very least, must be held to be qualifiedly privileged, and the qualified privilege cannot be destroyed without a charge of malice. To destroy the patent qualified privilege of this letter, absence of good faith, and presence of malice, should have been charged. No such charge is made and upon this theory alone the Court of Appeals reached a right result in refusing the writ."

There can be no doubt that the letter in question is qualifiedly privileged.

Finley v. Steele, 159 Mo. 299, 60 S. W. 108, 52 L. R. A. 852, was an action for libel based on a letter written by the members of a school board to the county superintendent, making accusations against Miss Finley, the teacher of the school, and asking him to revoke her certificate. Judge Burgess reviewed many cases. At the foot of page 305 of 159 Mo., at page 109 of 60 S. W. (52 L. R. A. 852), the learned judge said:

"It is announced in Marks v. Baker, 28 Minn. 162, that 'the rule is that a communication made in good faith, upon any subject-matter in which the party communicating has an interest or in reference to which he has a duty, public or private, either legal, moral or social, if made to a person having a corresponding interest or duty, is privileged; that in such case the inference of malice * * * is cast upon the person claiming to be defamed.'

" 'Malice in such case is not shown by the mere fact of the falsity of the publication.' Henry v. Moberly, 6 Ind. App. 490; Stewart v. Hall, 83 Ky. 375."

Again, on page 307 of 159 Mo., on page 110 of 60 S. W. (52 L. R. A. 852), it was said:

"They not only had an interest in regard to the way in which the school was being conducted, but in preferring the charges against the plaintiff were simply discharging their duty as members of the school board, and it makes no difference that the exact words of the statute were not used, or that some word not embraced therein was used, the purpose and intent was the same. There was no actual malice proven, and the use of such word or words did not take away the privileged character of the communication. Intent makes the libel in such circumstances.

"The communication was made on a proper occasion, from a proper motive, and was based upon a reasonable cause. It was made in apparent good faith, and under these circumstances the law does not imply malice—and as there was no proof of express malice the plaintiff was not entitled to recover. The judgment is affirmed."

The ruling in Finley v. Steele has been frequently approved. See Peak v. Taubman, 251 Mo. 390, 418, 434, et seq., 158 S. W. 656.

The rule permitting criticism of public officers, is the same as that which governs the criticism of all matters of public interest, such as public institutions, places of entertainment, books, pictures, and other matters, and under it it is permissible to criticize fairly and without malice or view to injure or prejudice in the eyes of the public. McClung v. Star Chronicle Pub. Co., 274 Mo. 194, 202 S. W. 571. But the qualified privilege to criticize public acts of public officials does not exist where defendant was actuated by malice. McClung v. Pulitzer Pub. Co., 279 Mo. 370, 214 S. W. 193. See, also, Diener v. Publishing Co., 230 Mo. 613, 132 S. W. 1143, 33 L. R. A. (N. S.) 216; Id., 232 Mo. 416, 135 S. W. 6; Ex parte Harrison, 212 Mo. 88, loc. cit. 92, 110 S. W. 709, 16 L. R. A. (N. S.) 930, 126 Am. St. Rep. 557, 15 Ann. Cas. 1; Cornelius v. Cornelius, 233

Mo. 1, loc cit. 30, 135 S. W. 65; Tilles v. Publishing Co., 241 Mo. 609 (syl. 6), 145 S. W. 1143; Link v. Hamlin, 270 Mo. 319, loc. cit. 336, 193 S. W. 587; Yancey v. Commonwealth, 135 Ky. 207, 122 S. W. 123, 25 L. R. A. (N. S.) 455, and annotations.

McKee v. Hughes, 133 Tenn. 455, 181 S. W. 930, L. R. A. 1916D, 391, Ann. Cas. 1918A, 459, was an action for libel on a petition to revoke the license of a merchant. In that case it was argued that the petition was not privileged because the council had no authority to revoke the license. The court said:

"Can it be that ordinary laymen, in the exercise of such a right, may be thus caught on such a fine point of law, to their undoing, as is insisted in this case? The juster view is that these men but advance the above mode of action as a suggestion for the consideration of the members of the council, deemed by them competent to judge and act as public officials, and that they are not liable if they acted in good faith or without malice. The right of petition * * * in the Bill of Rights should not be allowed to become a trap for the petitioner to be sprung by any such hairtrigger of technical law."

See 25 Cyc. 385 C.

However, in some jurisdictions communications of the character of this letter are held to be within the protection of the Bill of Rights. Thus an application to the Governor for a pardon, charging that the district judge "changed the venue of the case for the purpose of making the costs excessive," alleged "to be untrue and written and published with actual malice without any foundation whatever," was held to be absolutely privileged. Connellee v. Blanton (Tex. Civ. App.) 163 S. W. 404.

2. The complaint board is a governmental agency created for the express purpose of investigating complaints against any department, board, officer, or employé of the city. It therefore had an interest and a duty to perform in connection with complaints of this character. The complainants were interested, as citizens of St. Louis, in having the matters complained of investigated, and are therefore privileged in making complaints, if made in good faith and without malice. State ex rel. v. Reynolds, 276 Mo. loc. cit. 695, 209 S. W. 100; 25 Cyc. 389.

3. It is urged, however, that the decision of the Court of Appeals is res adjudicata because this court held it was not in conflict with any of its prior decisions. On this point Judge Graves, on page 701 of 276 Mo., on page 104 of 209 S. W., State ex rel. Douglas v. Reynolds, supra, said:

"In the instant case the Court of Appeals did not have before it a libel suit, nor the law of libel. Privilege or qualified privilege in libel law was not before it nor discussed by it. * * * It held that public policy demanded that complaints to this general welfare board should not be made public. * * * Certain it is that there is no conflict between their opinion and Finley v. Steele, supra, or any of the cases following that case. The subject-matters discussed are wholly different."

The relator Douglas prayed for an order to permit him to inspect or make a copy of the letter, basing his claim on the ground that it was a public document, which the court denied. 276 Mo. 698, 209 S. W. 100. It was not claimed that McDaniel and Thomas had any connection with that case. It was res inter alios acta. Henry v. Woods, 77 Mo. 277, loc. cit. 281; Strottman v. Railroad, 228 Mo. 154, loc. cit. 182, 128 S. W. 187, 30 L. R. A. (N. S.) 377; 23 Cyc. 1237.

4. But a fundamental reason why the rule should be discharged is that the circuit court had inherent power to issue the subpœna (40 Cyc. 2167), and the question of privilege or no privilege is, in the first instance, one solely for the trial court. Issue is joined between the litigants on the question of defendants' malice in writing the letter. It must be obvious that it is a question of fact of which this court cannot take cognizance in a proceeding of this character.

While the federal grand jury was investigating the charge of treason against Aaron Burr, he applied to the court for a subpœna duces tecum to the President to produce a certain letter addressed to him by Gen. Wilkinson, together with documents accompanying the said letter, also the military or naval orders given by the President at or near the New Orleans station concerning the said Burr. Chief Justice Marshall heard arguments touching the authority of the court to subpœna the President, or to require him to produce state papers. There was no precedent. It was admitted that such a writ would not run against the king of England, and it was argued by the district attorney that the court had no power to subpœna the chief magistrate or to order the production of state papers to be read in evidence; that the documents called for might contain matter which should not be disclosed.

The Chief Justice could perceive no foundation for the opinion that the issuance of the subpœna would be discourteous to the President. He held that the law does not discriminate between the President and a private citizen, and that the propriety of introducing any paper into a case depends on the character of the paper, not on the character of the person holding it. A subpœna duces tecum, then, may issue to any person to whom an ordinary subpœna may issue, directing him to bring any paper of which the party praying it has a right to avail himself as testimony. The Chief Justice, continuing, said:

"When this subject was suddenly introduced, the court felt some doubt concerning the propriety of directing a subpœna to the chief magistrate and some doubt, also, concerning the propriety of directing any paper in his possession, not public in its nature, to be exhibited in court. The impression that the questions which might arise in consequence of such process were more proper for discussion on the return of the process than on its issuing was then strong on the minds of the judges.

"The court can perceive no legal objection to issuing a subpœna duces tecum to any person whatever, provided the case be such as to justify the process. The court would not lend its aid to motions obviously designed to manifest disrespect to the government, but the court has no right to refuse its aid to motions for papers to which the accused may be entitled and which may be material in his defense.

"These observations are made to show the nature of the discretion which may be exercised. If it be apparent that the papers are irrelative to the case, or that, for state reasons, they cannot be introduced into the defense, the subpœna duces tecum would be useless, but, if this be not apparent, if they may be important in the defense, if they may be safely read at the trial, would it not be a blot on the page which records the judicial proceedings of this country if, in a case of such serious import as this, the accused should be denied the use of them? * * *

"The second objection is that the letter contains matter which ought not to be disclosed. At present it need only be said that the question does not occur at this time. * * * If it does contain any matter which it may be imprudent to disclose, which it is not the wish of the executive to disclose, such matter, if it be not immediately and essentially applicable to the case, will of course be suppressed. * * * Everything of this kind, however, will have its due consideration on the return of the subpœna."

1 Burr's Trial, 182–187.

It is sufficient to add that the subpœna was served and the documents called for were forwarded by Mr. Jefferson to the district attorney. Justice Marshall reserved the right to pass upon their admissibility at the trial. The precedent, thus established, has ever since been followed.

The rule is stated in 40 Cyc. 2169:

"It is the duty of a witness served with a subpœna duces tecum to appear and produce the book or paper mentioned in the writ, if it is in his possession. The fact that a subpœna requires a witness to produce books and papers which he cannot lawfully be required to produce does not affect the legality of the issuance of the subpœna or the obligation of the witness to appear in obedience to it, and, if he has doubts as to whether or not he should produce the document called for, he may submit it to the inspection of the court, which may decide on the question of its production. * * * But it has also been held that a witness is not bound to produce a paper in compliance with a subpœna duces tecum until he has been sworn as a witness to enable him to state on oath his reasons why he should not be compelled to produce it."

In Hull v. Lyon, 27 Mo. 570, it was held, Scott, J., delivering the opinion of the court, that—

"Whether a communication is a privileged one is a question for the court."

In Peak v. Taubman, 251 Mo. 391, 158 S. W. 656, in an opinion by Woodson, P. J., 251 Mo. loc. cit. 434, 158 S. W. 668, the court said:

"It is for the court, and not the jury, to say when words are of a privileged character."

In Hamil v. England, 50 Mo. App. 338, it was held that an attorney who advised about and drew up a fraudulent bill of sale could be compelled to testify as to what was said to him by his client, and that the trial court erred in holding that such communication was privileged. If the advice had been in a letter written by the attorney to his client, would this court have prohibited the enforcement of a subpœna duces tecum for its production in evidence?

In 1 Thompson on Trials, § 730, the learned author says a subpœna duces tecum is defined to be:

"A process by which a court, at the instance of a suitor, commands a person, who has in his possession or control some document or paper that is pertinent to the issues of the pending controversy, to produce it for use at the trial."

In section 175 it is said:

"The papers are required to be stated or specified only with that degree of certainty which is practicable, considering all the circumstances of the case, so that the witness may know what is wanted of him, and may have the papers at the trial so that they can be used, if the court shall then determine them to be competent and relevant evidence.'"

Section 300 reads as follows:

"Whenever, in the practical application of these rules, the question of privilege arose, it was not * * * the right of the witness to judge, except where the matter might incriminate him, whether the matter inquired of was privileged or not. That was the province of the court. If the production of a document was called for, and the witness declined to produce it, upon the ground that the reading of it in evidence would be prejudicial to his interests, or to the interests of the party for whom the witness acted as attorney, the witness was required to submit the document to the inspection of the court, and if the judge, after perusing it, differed from the witness, he would direct it to be read; or if a witness swore that a question put to him could not be answered without a disclosure of secrets communicated to him by his client, it was for the court to determine, from the nature of the inquiry, whether the principle of protection extended to it or not; and if the court decided that it did not, the witness, should he refuse to answer, would be guilty of a contempt, nor would the court even hear counsel upon the plea of the witness' objection."

In State ex inf. v. Standard Oil Co., 218 Mo. 1 (116 S. W. 902), it was said:

"Nor does the Constitution interfere with the power of the court to compel the production of documentary evidence under a subpœna duces tecum." Syl. 11.

"The rule seems to be well settled that, although the determination of a question of fact is thereby involved, it is for the court to determine the admissibility, materiality, relevancy, or competency of evidence, or the competency of witnesses; and it is error for the judge to submit to the jury the competency of evidence, or to instruct them that they may exclude such testimony as they see is improper." 38 Cyc. 1513.

5. It is solemnly asserted by the relators that the trial court exceeded its jurisdiction in issuing the subpœna duces tecum to require Marsh to produce the letter in question held to be privileged by the Court of Appeals, which, as we have seen, was in an action involving other issues and between other parties. It was held by this court, in the opinion by Judge Graves, that the letter is qualifiedly privileged, but, if it be shown to have been written maliciously, its qualified privilege is lost. It was held by Chief Justice Marshall that the writ will issue for the production of state papers, and that the question of privilege is to be determined when they are offered in evidence. It is charged in the amended petition in the circuit court and in the application for the subpœna duces tecum that the letter was false and malicious. It is apparent that its production is essential in the trial of the action. Its admissibility in evidence is a question for the trial court. It would be a manifest usurpation and invasion of the jurisdiction of the trial court were we to assume to rule on the issue presented by the pleadings in this case.

The preliminary rule was improvidently granted and is quashed. The writ is denied.

ELDER and DAVID E. BLAIR, JJ., concur.

JAMES T. BLAIR, J. (concurring). I concur in the principle announced in paragraph 4 of the opinion and concur in the result. The objections (1) that the letter is absolutely privileged and (2) that the question of privilege is res adjudicata may be presented to the trial court for what they are worth. The witness should not be permitted to decide a question of availability of evidence. Prohibition will not lie merely to prevent a trial court from making ruling on evidence, erroneous or otherwise. Neither, it seems to me, are there present any circumstances of the character usually held sufficient to render the remedy by appeal inadequate. Further, the inadequacy of appeal as a remedy is of no great consequence in view of the presence of jurisdiction in the trial court to rule on the question of evidence when it is presented to it.

GRAVES, J. (dissenting.) Samuel J. Douglas has now, and for a long time has had, pending in the circuit court of the city of St. Louis, a libel suit against Lawrence McDaniel and George E. Thompson. This suit has for its basis a letter written by these two gentlemen to the complaint board of the city of St. Louis. From the filing of the libel petition Douglas has made a persistent fight to secure this letter for use in the trial of his libel suit. See his divers efforts in the following cases in the Court of Appeals and in this court: State ex rel. Douglas v. Tune et al. (App.) 191 S. W. 1078; State ex rel. Douglas v. Tune et al., 273 Mo. 255, 200 S. W. 1062; State ex rel. Douglas v. Tune et al., 199 Mo. App. 404, 203 S. W. 465; State ex rel. Douglas v. Reynolds et al., Judges, 276 Mo. 688, 209 S. W. 100.

The situation as to all these cases, except the last named above, is fairly stated in State ex rel. v. Tune et al., 199 Mo. App. loc. cit. 410, 203 S. W. 465. In the instant case we are only concerned with the case in 199 Mo. App., supra, and our own case in 276 Mo., supra.

The present case is in prohibition, wherein the complaint board of St. Louis is seeking to prohibit the circuit court from enforcing a writ of subpoena duces tecum issued by the circuit court (now having for disposition the aforesaid libel suit) requiring this complaint board and its secretary to produce this letter for use in the trial of the cause.

Douglas had made a previous attempt to get this letter or a copy thereof for use in the libel suit. This time it was by mandamus against the complaint board and its secretary. See 199 Mo. App. 404, 203 S. W. 465, supra. In that case the St. Louis Court of Appeals, in closing its opinion (199 Mo. App. loc. cit. 415, 203 S. W. 468), said:

"Our conclusion is that the respondents here were justified in their refusal to permit relator to have an inspection of the letter, assuming such letter was in their control, and in refusing to allow the relator to make a copy of it. That is as far as we go in this case, except to say that neither our court nor the circuit court in which the action for libel is pending, can compel the production of the letter for the purposes sought by relator. Whether the circuit court in which the action for libel is pending can proceed with the case, in the absence of the original letter, and allow parol testimony to be given as to its contents, is a question which is not now before us and which we do not decide."

This opinion was brought before us by certiorari in State ex rel. Douglas v. Reynolds et al., 276 Mo. 688, 209 S. W. 100, and

we decline to quash it. It stands as the law upon the questions therein adjudicated.

The petitioners (relators) for our writ of prohibition plead the final adjudication of Douglas' right to the use of this letter in his libel suit in their petition herein, and say that, notwithstanding such final adjudication of the question, the circuit court is calling for the letter for such use by its subpoena duces tecum, issued upon the application of Douglas, which subpoena the court has refused to quash, notwithstanding the adjudication in the St. Louis Court of Appeals.

The respondents (circuit judges) appear here through the counsel for Douglas, and in their return urge that the present action is between different parties, is different in the form of action, and is different in subject-matter. However, by exhibits and allegations in the petition (not denied in the return) the matter as to whether or not there has been an adjudication of the same question in the former action is in the record before us. This outlines the situation.

I. It is urged by learned counsel for the respondents that the petition for the subpoena duces tecum was granted because of what we said in 276 Mo. 688, 209 S. W. 100, supra. They urge that we ruled that the letter was only qualifiedly privileged and not privileged.

In the case of State ex rel. Douglas v. Reynolds, 276 Mo. 688, 209 S. W. 100, we did not rule that the letter was qualifiedly privileged, and not absolutely privileged. The Court of Appeals had ruled that it was against public policy to permit communications of this character to be made public, and we do not quash their judgment, because we had never ruled upon a similar state of facts, and there was no conflict of opinion. What we did say was that the letter, under the facts, was "at least qualifiedly privileged," and in the absence of a charge of malice the Court of Appeals could have justified its judgment upon that ground. It had not done so, however.

We did not rule that the letter was only qualifiedly privileged. We were not trying to determine the question of qualified privilege or absolute privilege, but we did rule that, even if the letter was qualifiedly privileged the defects in the pleadings were not such as would permit its use, absent in the pleadings the charge of malice. We went further and said that the whole discussion was beside the real issue. So that, if this opinion was the occasion for the issuance of the subpoena duces tecum, there was no justification for the issuance of it.

II. If there had been a prior adjudication of the rights of Douglas to use this letter in the trial of his libel suit, and that adjudication against him, then will prohibition lie? We have ruled that prohibition will lie where an appeal would not be an adequate remedy. To refuse prohibition, it must appear that the party has another remedy, by appeal or otherwise, which is adequate, prompt, and efficient. State ex rel. Knisely v. Jones, 274 Mo. 374, 202 S. W. loc. cit. 1122.

In this case the parties would have to go through the trial of a libel suit, and be subject to all the expenses and inconveniences thereof, when, if the trial court adheres to its expressed views, they would have to appeal to this court, to have the question of res adjudicata determined. In such case the appeal would not be an adequate, efficient, and prompt remedy. Relators have been in court four times at the instance of Douglas upon the right of Douglas to use this letter in the trial of his libel suit. Now he insists that they come for a fifth time by the cumbersome route of appeal. It is time that the question be settled, but an appeal is wholly inadequate as the remedy, in view of the undisputed facts before us. So we hold that, if in fact the plea of former adjudication is good, the writ should go.

III. The question ruled by the St. Louis Court of Appeals was that Douglas could not compel the production of this letter for the use he desired; i. e., for use in the trial of his libel suit. 199 Mo. App. loc. cit. 415, 203 S. W. 465. This was the mandamus case in the St. Louis Court of Appeals. Douglas was the relator in that case, and the complaint board and its secretary were the respondents. Hon. Douglas W. Roberts represented Douglas in that case, as he does the respondents for Douglas in this case. In this case the relators are the complaint board and its secretary, and the nominal respondents two circuit judges of St. Louis, but the real respondent, and the one interested in upholding the circuit judge, is none other than Douglas, through his counsel. Douglas does not have to be an actual party to the suit, if in fact, as here, he is defending the action by his own counsel.

It would be to throw aside all of our experiences to say that Douglas is not the real respondent in the present action. We know by whom all such cases are defended even if the counsel for Douglas were not actually (as here) defending the action. The whole brief for respondents here shows that counsel are here for Douglas. So that we rule that there is identity of parties in the two cases; in other words, whatever our judgment here, it would bind Douglas. Titus v. North K. C. Development Co., 264 Mo. 229, 174 S. W. 432; 15 R. C. L. loc. cit. 1010. In the latter it is said:

"The courts look beyond the nominal parties, and treat all those whose interests are involved in the litigation and who conduct and control the action or defense as real parties, and hold them concluded by any judgment which may be rendered, as, for example, those who employ counsel in the case, assume the active management of the proceeding or defense, or who

pay the costs and do such other things as are generally done by parties; in other words, by participating in the proceedings one is estopped by the judgment as to any questions actually litigated and decided therein. One who instigates another to do a wrongful act, and, when the wrongdoer is sued, takes upon himself and conducts the defense of the case, is estopped from again litigating with the plaintiff in that action the issues there decided. Similarly, where a suit is prosecuted or defended by one person at the instance of another, and for the latter's benefit, the judgment will be binding and conclusive upon the latter. In all such cases the strict rule that a judgment operates as res judicata only in regard to parties and privies expanded to include such persons as parties, or at least as privies."

So, too, there is the same subject-matter; i. e., the use of this letter by Douglas in the trial of his libel suit. And this in the face of the fact that the question of such use has been fully and finally determined against him (in the mandamus suit) by the St. Louis Court of Appeals.

There can be res adjudicata as to certain questions in a case without involving the whole case. Such is the situation here. The right of Douglas to use this letter is a matter finally determined, and, as this matter appears upon the face of the record before us, our writ should go. Under the facts an appeal would be wholly inadequate. For these reasons I dissent.

WALKER, C. J., and WOODSON, J., concur in these views.

HARRINGTON v. HOPKINS et al.
(No. 22336.)

(Supreme Court of Missouri, in Banc.   April 1, 1921.   Motion for Rehearing Denied May 24, 1921.)

Schools and school districts ☞101—Repairing and furnishing not the "erection of buildings," for which annual tax rate may be exceeded.

Const. art. 10, § 11, limiting the annual tax rate, but providing that the limit may be exceeded for the erection of buildings, does not authorize an excess in the rate limit for repairing and furnishing buildings.

Appeal from Circuit Court, Clinton County; Alonzo D. Burnes, Judge.

Suit by William R. Harrington against James O. Hopkins and others to restrain the collection of a tax. Decree for plaintiff, and defendants appeal. Affirmed.

This suit was instituted in the circuit court of Clinton county by the plaintiff against the defendants to restrain the collection of a tax of 90 cents on the $100 valuation of all taxable property situated in the

Lathrop school district of that county. The trial was before the court, which resulted in a decree enjoining the collection of the tax, and in due time the defendants appealed to this court. The facts are as follows:

The respondent, William R. Harrington, is a resident of the school district of Lathrop, in Clinton county, Mo., a qualified voter thereof, and owns a large amount of real estate and personal property within said school district. Said school district is a city or town district, having a board of education, consisting of six directors. The defendant James C. Hopkins is the county clerk, and the defendant John L. Thompson collector, of said county. The defendants Frank L. Porter, Albert C. Fagin, John B. Scott, E. D. Rogers, Bedford Trice, and Thos. G. Klepper constitute the board of education of said school district.

This suit is brought to restrain the levy and collection of a tax of 90 cents on each $100 of the assessed valuation on all property taxable for school purposes in the district. At a meeting of the said board of education held on the 16th day of March, 1920, it was ordered that a proposition to levy a tax of 90 cents on each $100 of the assessed valuation of property in the district, for a repairing and furnishing fund, be submitted to the voters at the annual election in said district to be held April 6, 1920, and that notice thereof be given. The secretary of the board gave notice by publishing the same in the Lathrop Optimist for more than 15 days prior to the election. The proposition was printed on the ballots, with other propositions submitted, and was carried by a vote of more than two-thirds of the qualified voters of said district voting at said election. The original notice given to the newspaper was for a repairing and furnishing fund, but the printer, failing to proof it, published it as a repairing and "finishing" fund. The ballots, however, had it correctly spelled. The claim of the respondent that there was no legal notice given is based solely upon this misspelled word in the notice.

The levy is attacked by the respondent on the ground that it is in violation of sections 11 and 12 of article 10 of the Missouri Constitution, and that it was not levied for the purpose mentioned in the notice and printed on the ballots, but for the purpose of paying teachers. A temporary writ of injunction was issued. The case was tried by agreement, on the 17th of June, 1920, taken under advisement by Judge Burnes, and on the 4th of August the court found for the plaintiff, and made the temporary restraining order final, from which judgment the defendants constituting the board of education of said district appealed.

In pursuance to the foregoing election, the board of directors of said school district made and certified to the clerk of the county court of that county an estimate of the

amount of money necessary to sustain the said school for the year 1920, which was as follows:

"To the County Clerk of Clinton County, Missouri—Dear Sir:

"We, the board of directors of district No. Lathrop, county of Clinton, Missouri, herein submit an estimate of the amount of funds necessary to sustain the public school for the period of —— months, amount of cash on hand, and the approximate rate to be levied on the taxable property in said district for the year beginning July 1, 1920.

"This estimate is based on a district valuation of seven hundred and seventy-nine thousand dollars ($779,000), an enumeration of 365 pupils, a total number of days' attendance of 45,677 days, and the services of 13 teachers.

For School Purposes (Secs. 10846, 10791, 10796, 10825):

For teachers' fund	$12,000
Amount on hand	3,500
Estimate from public funds	200
Amount under state aid law	3,700
Amount to be raised by levy	5,300
Rate necessary for raising this amount, 87 cents.	

For incidental fund (Secs. 10846, 10791, 10796, 10798, 10825):

Amount on hand	$4,000
Amount to be raised by levy	000
Rate necessary for raising this amount, 13 cents.	

For Building Purposes (Secs. 10791, 10797, 10798, 10825):

For fund repairing and furnishing	$7,000
Amount on hand	600
Amount to be raised by levy	7,000
Rate necessary for raising this amount, 90 cents.	

For sinking fund, amount of bonds falling due (Sec. 10782):

Amount on hand	——
Amount to be raised by levy	3,000
Rate necessary for raising this amount, 40 cents.	

For annual interest (Sec. 10783):

Amount on hand	——
Amount to be raised by levy	779
Rate necessary for raising this amount, 40 cents.	

Total amount to be levied on the taxable property of the district	$ ——
Total rate necessary	240 cents

"We estimate that a levy of 240 cents on the $100 valuation will be sufficient to raise above amount.

"Done by order of the board this 6th day of May, 1920.   Jno. B. Scott, President.

"Frank L. Porter, District Clerk."

As previously stated, Harrington, being a property owner of said district, brought this suit to enjoin the levy and collection of said taxes and to remove the cloud upon the title to his real estate. The basis of this suit, as stated by counsel for respondent, is as follows:

"(a) Because the notice of the election was not given as required by law, the same being for a repairing and *finishing* fund, and the ballots cast at said election being for a repairing and *furnishing* fund, a separate and distinct fund from the fund named in the notice.

"(b) Because said 90 cents tax is fraudulent and void, because the levy of said tax was ordered and made for a private and not a public purpose, the real purpose of the levy of said tax being to reimburse the board of directors of said district, 'and others,' for money wrongfully taken by said directors from the sinking fund belonging to said district, and that the real purpose and object of the levy of said tax is to raise sufficient money to pay a note of $7,000 executed by the members of the board of directors of said district to procure money to make restitution to and pay back, and replace in said sinking fund of said district the money so wrongfully taken therefrom as aforesaid.

"(c) Because said 90 cents tax is illegal and unconstitutional, because in excess of the highest rate of taxation authorized by section 11, article 10, of the Constitution of 1875.

"The case was submitted upon the pleadings and evidence, and judgment was rendered for the respondent as prayed in his petition. After the usual steps, appellants appealed to this court. The question for decision is: Is this 90 cents tax valid? If it is, the judgment must be reversed; if not, the judgment must be affirmed. We contend that the tax is not valid, and hence that the judgment must be affirmed."

Daniel H. Frost and W. S. Herndon, both of Plattsburg, for appellants.

John A. Cross, of Lathrop, R. H. Musser, of Plattsburg, and Pross T. Cross, of Lathrop, for respondent.

WOODSON, J. (after stating the facts as above). While there are several propositions presented and discussed by counsel for the respective parties, yet, according to the view we take of the case, it will be necessary to consider but one of them, and that is stated by counsel for respondent in the following language:

"The limitation upon the powers of school directors in section 11, article 10, of the Constitution, are absolute, and cover all taxes of every kind and description, and said 90 cents, being in excess of the constitutional rate, is void."

That section of the Constitution, in so far as this case is concerned, reads as follows:

"* * * For county purposes the annual rate on property, in counties having six million dollars or less, shall not, in the aggregate, exceed fifty cents on the hundred dollars valuation. * * * For school purposes in districts composed of cities which have one hundred thousand inhabitants or more, the annual rate on property shall not exceed sixty cents on the hundred dollars valuation and in other districts forty cents on the hundred dollars valuation: Provided, the aforesaid annual rates for school purposes may be increased, in districts formed of cities and towns, to an amount not to exceed one dollar on the hundred dollars valuation, and in other districts to an amount not to exceed sixty-five cents on the hundred dollars valuation, on the condition that a majority of the voters who are taxpayers, voting at an election held to decide the question, vote for said increase. For the purpose of erecting public buildings in counties, cities or school

districts, the rate of taxation herein limited may be increased when the rate of such increase and the purpose for which it is intended shall have been submitted to a vote of the people, and two-thirds of the qualified voters of such county, city or school district, voting at such election, shall vote therefor. The rate herein allowed to each county shall be ascertained by the amount of taxable property therein, according to the last assessment for state and county purposes. * * *"

The language of the section just quoted is too plain to need construction. It limits the collection of all taxes in a school district such as this to $1 on the $100 valuation for all school purposes; that is, the rate cannot be increased in such a district for all school purposes in a sum in excess "of one dollar on the hundred dollars except for the purpose of erecting public buildings," etc., and there is no pretense that this 90 cents was voted for the purpose of erecting a schoolhouse, or other public buildings, but solely to repair and furnish a building already existing. In no sense can the words "furnishing" and "repairing" be construed to mean the "erection of public buildings," as those words are used in the Constitution.

We find no error in the record, and therefore affirm the judgment of the circuit court.

All concur.

GRAMS v. NOVINGER. (No. 13918.)

(Kansas City Court of Appeals. Missouri. May 23, 1921.)

1. Vendor and purchaser ⟐143 — Purchasers taking possession without receiving abstract held to waive its being furnished within specified time.

Where plaintiff purchaser after first payment, and before receiving abstract, took possession of the land, she waived any right to rescind on account of failure to furnish an abstract of title in the time agreed upon; her action being a choice against rescission for such nonperformance.

2. Trial ⟐155, 383—Defendant's demurrer to evidence admits truth of plaintiff's evidence for purposes of motion only.

The truth of all the evidence on plaintiff's part is admitted by defendant's motion in the nature of a demurrer to plaintiff's evidence at the close thereof for the purpose of the demurrer only, and this applies as well where trial is to the court.

3. Trial ⟐382—Court sitting without jury may give mandatory instruction only when it could do so were the trial by jury.

A court sitting without a jury must pass on witnesses' credibility and the weight of their testimony, and may give mandatory instruction only when that could have been done had the case been tried by jury.

Appeal from Circuit Court, Adair County; J. A. Cooley, Judge.

"Not to be officially published."

Suit by Raymon R. Grams against Isaac A. Novinger. Judgment for defendant, and plaintiff appeals. Affirmed.

J. E. Rieger and W. F. Frank, both of Kirksville, for appellant.
Campbell & Ellison, of Kirksville, for respondent.

ARNOLD, J. This is a suit to rescind a contract for the purchase of 40 acres of land and to recover the amount of first payment on the purchase price thereof.

After making an examination of the tract plaintiff entered into a contract with defendant, on October 2, 1919, for the purchase of 40 acres for the sum of $5,400; $500 in cash was paid at the time, the balance to be secured by deeds of trust on the land purchased and on a lot in the town of Gilman, Iowa. Defendant agreed to execute and deliver a warranty deed to plaintiff on October 15th, and to furnish an abstract showing merchantable title.

The testimony shows that defendant appeared at plaintiff's home in Gilman, Iowa, on October 14, 1919, and stated that he had been to the county seat of the county in which Gilman is located, had made an examination of her title to the Gilman property, and found same to be good, and asked that plaintiff give him a deed of trust to the property; that plaintiff refused to do this because defendant had not brought with him an abstract of the 40 acres in Adair county, Mo. Defendant then told plaintiff to move on the land, and he would close the deal as soon as plaintiff came down. Plaintiff, accordingly, moved to Missouri on October 19th or 20th and onto the land, with her household goods and stock, taking possession thereof on October 21, 1919.

According to plaintiff's testimony defendant directed her to come into Kirksville on October 22d, saying that he would close the deal; that she went as directed, but was unable to find him; that she did not see defendant from October 25th or 27th until November 5th; that no abstract had been furnished her up to that time, and none has been furnished since.

Further, plaintiff testified that one night, soon after their arrival at the place, they were so disturbed by noises about the house that they left in fright, went to the home of a neighbor, and asked that defendant be called by telephone. Defendant came to see plaintiff, and she demanded her abstract of title or her money back, stating the house was "haunted" and unfit for human habitation; that defendant then promised to close the deal on the following day. This was not done, and on October 27th plaintiff and family abandoned the farm, and on December 29th this suit was filed to rescind the contract and to recover $500 first payment and $300 expenses incurred in moving from Gilman, Iowa, to the farm.

The petition alleges the facts practically as set out above. The answer admits the execution of the contract as alleged, and states that defendant was ready to deliver the abstract on October 15, 1919, as provided therein, and that any delay in delivering said abstract was due to the request of plaintiff to await the coming of her attorney from Iowa to examine the same. Further the answer is a general denial of the allegations of the petition.

By agreement the cause was tried to the court without the intervention of a jury. At the close of plaintiff's evidence and on motion of defendant's counsel in the nature of a demurrer to the evidence, the court gave the following declaration of law:

"That under the pleadings and the evidence and the law, the plaintiff cannot recover, and the finding and judgment must be for the defendant."

Judgment was entered accordingly. Motion for new trial was overruled by the court, and plaintiff appeals.

Plaintiff claims she made a prima facie case, proved a contract, its breach by defendant in the delay, and failure to perfect title, her offer to perform her part of the contract, and resultant damages. Plaintiff contends that—

"The furnishing of an abstract showing good title is the first act on the part of either plaintiff or defendant after plaintiff showed her good faith by paying $500" on the contract.

The contract entered into between the parties is not set out in the record, and we are therefore unable to learn and apply its specific terms. We are left to assume from the petition and answer that the covenants of the contract were mutual, and, if so, this contention of plaintiff is not tenable. The inference is that the terms of the contract, in the absence of anything to the contrary, were to be carried out by the parties mutually, as is customary in such cases.

[1] The testimony tends to show that on October 14, 1919, plaintiff agreed to move onto the land, not having received the abstract of title; that she did actually move on the land October 20th or 21st, and took possession thereof without having received the abstract. By this action plaintiff waived any right she may have had to rescind on account of failure to furnish an abstract of title in the time agreed upon. This conclusion is to be drawn from plaintiff's own testimony. By thus taking possession of the property as though this contract were in force, plaintiff chose against a rescission on account of nonperformance of the covenant about the

abstract. Boulware v. Crohn, 122 Mo. App. 571, 99 S. W. 796.

[2] Plaintiff declares that "the truth of all the evidence on plaintiff's part is admitted by motion of defendant," in referring to defendant's motion in the nature of a demurrer at the close of plaintiff's evidence. This may be considered to be correct for the purposes of the demurrer, and discussion or citations relative thereto are unnecessary and would be unprofitable. As claimed by plaintiff, this is true when the cause is tried before a jury, or where the court sits as a jury. The citations of plaintiff are directly in point on this proposition, but are erroneously applied. Plaintiff urges that the time in the delivery of the abstract was of the essence of the contract. Whether this was specially stipulated in the contract or not we have no way of determining, not having the contract before us; but, considering it pro and con, we find ourselves face to face with the waiver of plaintiff in taking possession of the land without the delivery of the abstract.

In Boulware v. Crohn, supra, the court held:

"But a condition precedent may be waived by the party entitled to insist on its performance"—citing O'Fallon v. Kennerly, 45 Mo. 124; Estel v. Railroad, 56 Mo. 282; Melton v. Smith, 65 Mo. 315; Dobbins v. Edmonds, 18 Mo. App. 307.

[3] Plaintiff insists upon the further point that the trial court may not give a mandatory instruction unless the case is tried by a jury, and cites Eaton v. Cates (Sup.) 175 S. W. 950. In that case it is said:

"That it was the province of the court to pass upon the credibility of the witnesses and the weight to be given to their testimony in exactly the same sense that a jury should do in the trial of a cause, and the trial court has no more authority to give a mandatory instruction for the plaintiff, when trying a case without the aid of a jury, than it would have to so instruct a jury when it is trying a case"—citing Crossett v. Ferrill, 209 Mo. 704, 108 S. W. 52; Bartlett v. Boyd (Sup.) 175 S. W. 947.

There is much controversy between the parties as to what the abstract does, or does not, show. The testimony tends to prove that plaintiff was never individually in possession of the same, and her attorney testifies that he did not examine it until after this suit was filed. It is therefore clear that the question as to whether the title is good or not is not before us. The case was tried by both parties on the issue as to whether or not an abstract showing merchantable title was delivered, or tendered, by defendant; and the facts as to what the abstract did or did not show are not before us.

The trial court, under the theory upon which the case was tried, followed the law's well-worn paths in ruling on the evidence. A careful examination of the record fails to show any error in that respect. The demurrer to the evidence was properly sustained.

Judgment is affirmed.

All concur.

━━━━━

KINNEY v. KINNEY.　(No. 14016.)

(Kansas City Court of Appeals. Missouri. May 23, 1921.)

1. **Divorce ⟜235—Alimony largely discretionary.**

Allowance of alimony is addressed to the discretion of the court, to be exercised under established principles and in view of circumstances of each party, such as the ability of husband and condition and means of wife and the parties' conduct.

2. **Divorce ⟜240(5)—Award of $60 per month to wife, with custody of child, where husband has remarried and is earning about $125 per month, held not excessive.**

Where the wife secured the care and custody of a minor child and allowance of $125 per month alimony, which was not paid, and court reduced the alimony to $60 per month, and defendant, who was earning about $125 per month and had again married, appealed, held that, in view of circumstances, the amount of alimony would not be changed.

3. **Divorce ⟜245(2)—Wife's securing allowance for child's support may be considered as ground for reducing her alimony.**

A divorced husband is required to support a minor child, regardless of his duty to pay alimony to his divorced wife; but, if a successful effort is made by the wife to secure separate support for the child, the court may reduce the alimony to be paid the wife, where the husband has again married.

4. **Divorce ⟜282 — Defendant, not objecting below that petition failed to ask alimony, waived the defect.**

Where defendant husband filed motion to modify decree in reference to alimony, and went to trial on that motion and did not raise the question that the petition did not ask for alimony until on appeal, waived the objection.

Appeal from Circuit Court, Jackson County; C. A. Burney, Judge.

"Not to be officially published."

Petition by Louise Kinney against Louis Kinney. Decree for plaintiff, defendant moved to modify the decree fixing alimony at $125 per month, on hearing it was reduced to $60 per month, and defendant appeals. Affirmed.

Stubbs & Stubbs, of Kansas City, for appellant.

Burns & Watts, of Kansas City, for respondent.

━━━━━━━━━━━━━━━━

⟜For other cases see same topic and KEY-NUMBER in all Key-Numbered Digests and Indexes

BLAND, J. On May 4, 1918, plaintiff filed in the circuit court of Jackson county, Mo., a petition for divorce. After alleging five grounds for divorce, and that one male child of the age of one year had been born of the marriage, plaintiff ended the petition with the following prayer:

"Wherefore plaintiff prays the court for a divorce from the bonds of matrimony contracted as aforesaid, for the custody of said minor child, and for such other and further relief under the premises as may be just and proper, and for her costs."

Service was had upon defendant, but he made default. On May 12, 1919, the court entered judgment, granting plaintiff the divorce, giving her the custody of the minor child, and awarding her alimony in the sum of $125 per month. On August 26, 1919, defendant filed a motion to modify the decree, in so far as it fixed the amount of alimony, and upon a hearing of said motion the court reduced the alimony to $60 per month. Defendant has appealed, alleging that the amount last fixed by the trial court is excessive.

The facts show that plaintiff and defendant were married on July 13, 1916, that they lived together as husband and wife until January 1, 1918, and that there was born of the marriage a son, who, at the time of the hearing of defendant's motion, was 2½ years of age. Defendant has never paid any alimony, but plaintiff has been living with her mother, who supports her and her child; plaintiff's father and mother being separated. The mother has some private means, the amount of which is not given in the evidence. Plaintiff's health was good prior to her marriage, but at the time of the trial it was very poor. She had made no attempt to obtain employment, not being able to do hard work. Neither plaintiff nor defendant owned any property.

About two weeks before the hearing of defendant's motion he remarried. At the time of the trial on his motion he was employed by his father, who was in the cigar business, at a salary of $125 per month and expenses while on the road. He and his wife lived with his parents, paying no board. His father had advanced to him quite a sum of money since his marriage to plaintiff, some of which is expected to be returned. The amount expected to be returned is approximately $4,000, which was charged on the father's books against defendant. This indebtedness arose since defendant's marriage to plaintiff, and was for debts created for their living expenses and money advanced toward the maintenance of defendant, plaintiff, and their child while defendant was in the army.

Defendant had been working for his father for five months prior to the trial on the motion, and during that time he had paid about $100 on the indebtedness owing to his father. Defendant at one time had money with which he could have paid his father in part, but paid other debts with it. The father testified that the arrangement he had with his son for the repaying of the indebtedness was "whatever less than his salary he draws, the balance is credited on the indebtedness." It appears that defendant's parents are persons of some means, and the father evidently permits him to pay as he desires. Defendant and his father regarded the $4,000 as an indebtedness which the son would be required to pay, but plaintiff testified that she never understood that defendant was to repay his father. It is quite plain that the indebtedness of defendant to his father is not of the kind that ordinarily exists between debtor and creditor; the advancement of money was not made upon a strictly business basis, and defendant may repay the same at his convenience.

[1-3] The allowance of alimony is addressed largely to the sound discretion of the court, to be exercised with reference to established principles and in view of the circumstances of each party to the cause, such as the ability of the husband and condition and means of the wife and the conduct of the parties. Viertel v. Viertel, 212 Mo. 562, 575, 111 S. W. 579; Blair v. Blair, 131 Mo. App. 571, 110 S. W. 652. From the circumstances of this case it is very difficult for this or any other court to determine the amount of alimony that should be allowed. The trial court no doubt awarded the sum of $60 per month, in view of the fact that plaintiff had the custody of the child and would use this money in part for his support; the support of the child not having been provided for otherwise. Of course, defendant is required to support the child, regardless of his duty to pay alimony to his divorced wife; but, if a successful effort is made on the part of plaintiff to secure separate support for the child, the circuit court may, and no doubt would, reduce the amount of alimony to be paid plaintiff. Under the circumstances of this case we are not disposed to interfere with the alimony awarded by the trial court.

[4] The point is made that the petition does not ask for alimony, and therefore the court had no right to grant the same. The petition states facts which would authorize the court to grant alimony to plaintiff, if prayed. It would seem that alimony in some amount naturally goes with a divorce to the wife. Section 1806, R. S. 1919. However, defendant filed his motion to modify the decree in reference to alimony, and went to trial on that motion, and at no time during the trial or before the case reached this court suggested that the petition did not in express terms pray for alimony. We think that under the circumstances there is no question but that defendant waived the matter of the petition failing to ask for alimony. Mellor v.

Mo. Pac. Ry. Co., 105 Mo. 455, 16 S. W. 849, 10 L. R. A. 36; Garner v. Kansas City Bridge Co., 194 S. W. 82. It is therefore unnecessary for us to decide whether the language in the prayer of the petition, "for such other and further relief under the premises as may be just and proper," was sufficient upon which the court might have properly granted alimony.

The judgment is affirmed.

All concur.

HARTWEG v. KANSAS CITY RYS. CO.
(No. 13901.)

(Kansas City Court of Appeals. Missouri.
April 4, 1921. Rehearing Denied
May 23, 1921.)

1. Appeal and error ⟐⟐766—Appeal dismissed for violation of statute and court rule requiring a clear and concise statement of the case.

Whenever a violation of Rev. St. 1919, § 1511, and Court of Appeals rule No. 16 (169 S. W. xvii), requiring a clear and concise statement of the case, is such as to compel a court to spend time and labor in ascertaining what should have been clearly and concisely presented in such statement, the appeal will be dismissed.

2. Appeal and error ⟐⟐757(1)—Statement of the case held sufficient.

Where the first part of appellant's statement of the case presents a fairly clear and concise statement, the appeal will not be dismissed, though the following pages contained testimony, argumentative matters, and references to issues of law, in violation of Rev. St. 1919, § 1511, and court rule No. 16 (169 S. W. xvii), requiring a clear and concise statement of the case, since the court in such case can obtain a concise statement from the first pages of statement, and disregard the following pages, even though they were made a part of the statement.

3. Carriers ⟐⟐315(1)—Testimony that car started with jerk admissible in action for premature starting.

In an action for negligence in causing a street car to start while a passenger was alighting, in which it was claimed by defendant that the way plaintiff said she fell was contrary to physical laws, testimony that the car started with a jerk was admissible, though the starting of the car with a jerk was not pleaded; such testimony being material as evidential matter.

4. Negligence ⟐⟐119(1)—Proof of all acts alleged unnecessary.

It is not necessary to prove all the acts of negligence alleged.

5. Carriers ⟐⟐303(5)—Employés required to ascertain whether passengers are alighting before starting street car.

Employés, having stopped a street car to allow passengers to alight, were required to ascertain whether any passenger was alighting before starting car without a reasonable time and opportunity having been given passengers in which to alight.

6. Appeal and error ⟐⟐1033(5)—Appellant cannot complain of favorable instruction.

In alighting passenger's action for injuries sustained on premature starting of car, defendant could not complain of an instruction requiring the jury to find that employés knew that passenger was in the act of alighting at the time the car was started, though such fact was not alleged; such instruction being favorable to defendant.

7. Carriers ⟐⟐318(10)—Evidence held to show car started before passenger had reasonable time to alight.

In suit for injury to an alighting passenger, evidence held to show that a street car was started before she had a reasonable time and opportunity to alight.

8. Trial ⟐⟐191(11)—Instruction on measure of damages held not to assume defendant's negligence.

In personal injury action, instruction on measure of damages, "If your verdict is for plaintiff, * * * the jury will take into consideration the nature and extent of her injuries, if any, sustained by the direct result of the negligence, if any, of defendant as set out in other instructions," held not to assume defendant's negligence.

9. Evidence ⟐⟐589—Alighting passenger's testimony as to how she fell on premature starting of car held not contrary to physical laws.

In passenger's action against street railroad for damages sustained on premature starting of car while passenger was in the act of alighting therefrom, where the car was facing the west and the passenger was facing the north while in act of stepping off car, her testimony that she was thrown to the right striking the ground in a sitting posture and falling backwards upon pavement held not contrary to physical laws.

Appeal from Circuit Court, Jackson County; Thomas J. Seehorn, Judge.

"Not to be officially published."

Action by Lottie M. Hartweg against the Kansas City Railways Company. Judgment for plaintiff, and defendant appeals. Affirmed.

Richard J. Higgins, of Kansas City, Kan., and Ben T. Hardin, of St. Louis, for appellant.

Atwood, Wickersham, Hill & Popham, of Kansas City, Mo., for respondent.

TRIMBLE, P. J. [1, 2] Respondent's motion to dismiss appeal will be overruled. It is grounded upon the charge that appellant's statement violates section 1511, R. S. 1919, and our rule 16 (169 S. W. xvii), in that it is not "a clear and concise statement of the case," and includes testimony of witnesses as well as argumentative matters and ref-

⟐⟐For other cases see same topic and KEY-NUMBER in all Key-Numbered Digests and Indexes

erences to issues of law. There is a tendency on the part of some, in preparing a statement of an appellant's case, to trench very closely upon a violation of the spirit and letter of both the rule and statute. This course is not to be commended; and whenever it results in not clearly and concisely presenting the case to the court, so as to compel us to expend time and labor in ascertaining what should be clearly and concisely presented in the statement, the rule and statute thus violated will be enforced by the appropriate penalty of dismissal of the appeal. Appellants gain nothing by a long, involved, and argumentative statement; indeed, they lose much, for a case well stated is more than half argued and ably so, especially if the 'merits thereof are with the side presenting it. But to present arguments before the case is opened to the court, or to rehearse testimony before its bearing and applicability can be perceived, cannot fail to create the impression that reliance is placed more upon argumentative assertions of counsel than upon the inherent facts and justice of the case. In the present instance the first four pages of appellant's statement present a fairly clear and concise statement of the case and what it involves, and therefore the other pages following between that and the "assignment of errors" can be disregarded as no real part of the statement, even though, as printed, it may appear to be a part of it. Inasmuch as the court is not delayed or put to the expenditure of time and labor by this addition or extension to the statement (to obviate which is the purpose of the rule), we overrule the motion to dismiss the appeal.

Plaintiff's action is to recover damages for injuries sustained while attempting to alight from one of defendant's cars, as the alleged result of defendant's negligent management of the car. She recovered judgment in the sum of $1.500, and defendant has appealed.

The record discloses that plaintiff was a passenger on the street car in question proceeding westwardly toward the intersection of Seventh street and Central avenue in Kansas City, Kan., which was her destination, and at which she desired to alight. Plaintiff's evidence is that, as the car approached the regular stopping place at said intersection, she gave the required signal with the electric button requesting the car to stop there. It did so, and at this time plaintiff was standing on the door leading into the rear vestibule in readiness to alight whenever the car came to a stop and her turn came to get off. When the car stopped, the conductor opened the door of the car leading to the street, and several passengers standing in front of plaintiff began to alight, and plaintiff followed closely behind these alighting passengers—some three or four in number—and was immediately behind the

last of these in front of her, a lady by the name of Stratton. The car was crowded, and the passengers in the disembarking line followed as close one to another as they could walk. The car stood motionless as those ahead of plaintiff alighted therefrom, and plaintiff, following closely behind Mrs. Stratton as stated, was on the step in the act of stepping to the ground when the car suddenly started. Plaintiff was facing north as the car started, and she was thrown to the right, striking the ground in a sitting posture, and fell backwards prone upon the pavement. She was carried to a nearby drug store and then removed to her home in an automobile and put to bed. Her injuries were serious and painful.

The petition set forth her status as a passenger approaching her destination and ready to alight as above stated, that the car in obedience to plaintiff's request had come to a standstill at the regular stopping place, and then alleged that while plaintiff "was upon the platform and steps of said car and engaged in leaving the same, while the same was at rest as aforesaid, and before defendant had allowed her reasonable time or opportunity to leave the same, the defendant and its servants in charge thereof negligently and carelessly caused and permitted said car to start in motion and to move forward, thereby causing plaintiff to be thrown from said car violently into and upon the street and hard pavement, grievously and permanently injuring her as hereinafter set out"; that defendant was negligent and careless in that the operatives of the car "negligently caused and permitted said car to start in motion and move forward while she was upon the platform and steps thereof and in the act of alighting therefrom, and in that they negligently failed to hold said car and keep the same standing until plaintiff had reasonable time and opportunity to alight from it in safety; and plaintiff says that as a direct result of said negligent and careless acts and omissions of defendant, and each of them, acting severally and concurrently with each other, she was caused to fall from said car as aforesaid, and as a direct result thereof sustained the following injuries," etc.

[3, 4] It is urged that error was committed in allowing plaintiff to testify that the car "started with a jerk" when no negligence in starting the car with a jerk was pleaded. An examination of the record discloses that defendant's objection to this testimony was sustained, and that afterward no objection was made to plaintiff's testimony as to how she fell. We do not, however, regard the petition as pleading two separate specific acts of negligence, but as merely pleading one act of negligence stated in two ways. Plaintiff's case is not one where she is on the car not intending to get of and is negligently thrown off by either a jerk or same

other negligent act; but it is one where she is in the act of stepping to the ground, and, while in that act, the car is negligently allowed to move, whereby she is caused to fall. The negligence is in causing or permitting the car to start at all while she is in that position. Whether there was a jerk or not was not an element of the negligence alleged, and therefore did not have to, be pleaded, while it was material as evidential matter, especially in view of defendant's contention that the way plaintiff says she fell is contrary to physical laws. The negligence was in the premature start of their car, and it was not necessary to prove two pleaded and concurrent acts of negligence, for, as we have said, two different negligent acts were not pleaded, but only one, stated perhaps in two different ways; and, if two were pleaded, each was fully sufficient to support the cause of action, and it is not necessary to prove all of the acts of negligence alleged. Rogers v. Kansas City Rys. Co., 204 S. W. 595; Hoffman v. Dunham, 202 S. W. 429. Plaintiff's instruction submitting her case required the jury, before it could return a verdict for her, to find that, while plaintiff was on the platform and steps of the standing car and engaged in leaving the same, and before she had reasonable time and opportunity to leave the car, the same was negligently caused and permitted to start and move forward, whereby, as a direct result of such negligence, if any, plaintiff was thrown down and injured. It was therefore within the petition and the evidence.

[5, 6] This instruction did not broaden the issues. The ground of such charge is that the jury were also required to find that those in charge of the car knew of plaintiff's position at the time the car was started, whereas nothing of this kind was alleged in the petition. The operatives of the car concededly stopped it to allow passengers to alight, and it was their duty to know whether plaintiff or any one else was alighting at the time they started it up before a reasonable time and opportunity had been given them to alight, so that it was immaterial whether the operatives knew or did not know plaintiff was in the act of alighting. Hence the instruction required the jury to find too much before returning a verdict in plaintiff's favor, but of this the defendant cannot complain. Teske v. Kansas City Rys. Co., 204 S. W. 577, 579; Morris v. Kansas City Rys. Co., 223 S. W. 784, 795; Paul v. Metropolitan St. Ry. Co., 179 S. W. 787; Raber v. Kansas City Rys. Co., 204 S. W. 739, 740.

[7] There is no merit in the claim that the evidence failed to show that the car was started before plaintiff had reasonable time and opportunity to alight. Neither is there any virtue in the point that in using the phrase "highest reasonably practical care" in said instruction 1 the jury were permitted to apply it to any negligence, whether specified in the petition or not. It could not, under the language of the instruction, apply to anything other than either the duty of the car operatives to know whether plaintiff was getting off the car at the time it was started or to their duty not to start it or permit it to start while she was alighting. As applied to the former, it was unnecessary, and therefore harmless, as we have already stated, and was proper as applied to the latter. At all events, it could not possibly be regarded as leading the jury to believe it applied to any negligence whatever, whether within or without the petition.

[8] Plaintiff's instruction on the measure of damages began by saying:

"If your verdict is for the plaintiff, then in estimating and determining her damages, if any, the jury will take into consideration the nature and extent of her injuries, if any, sustained as a direct result of the negligence, if any, of defendant, as set out in the other instructions herein," etc.

How this assumes the negligence of defendant we are wholly unable to see. The phrase "as set out in the other instructions" does not tell the jury that negligence existed, but merely confined the jury to the claim of negligence relied upon, and referred to the other instructions for an explanation and definition of what was the negligence so claimed and relied upon.

[9] We are also unable to see how plaintiff's fall was so contrary to well-known physical laws as to conclusively disprove her testimony. . The car was facing and started west. The plaintiff was stepping off the car, facing north as she did so. There was no claim that the jerk of the car was so violent as to instantly jerk her feet from under her. Besides, there were other forces reasonably operating to produce the fall she sustained. The point cannot be sustained. Hoffman v. Dunham, 202 S. W. 429; Benjamin v. Metropolitan St. Ry., 245 Mo. 598, 609; Reisinger v. Kansas City Rys. Co., 211 S. W. 909; Jacobs v. Kansas City Rys. Co., 217 S. W. 579.

The judgment is affirmed.

The other Judges concur.

LANGE v. MIDWEST MOTOR SECURITIES CO. (No. 13891.)

(Kansas City Court of Appeals. Missouri. May 23, 1921.)

1. Appeal and error ⊜759—Brief need not contain separate assignments of error.

It is not necessary for a brief to contain separate assignments of error, provided the errors complained of and the points insisted upon are separately and succinctly set forth in the points and authorities, with the proper citations relied upon.

2. Chattel mortgages ⊜162—Seizure of automobile by mortgagee after default not conversion.

After condition broken the chattel mortgagee is regarded as the absolute owner, at least for the purpose of possession and due foreclosure, so that where chattel mortgagee, after default in monthly payments on chattel mortgage on an automobile, took charge of and drove off with the automobile, which had been left parked outside a railroad station by the mortgagor's husband while he saw her off on the train, there was no conversion.

3. Chattel mortgages ⊜162—Acceptance of overdue previous installments not a waiver of future defaults.

That previous installments under a chattel mortgage are accepted after default may constitute a waiver of the right to declare the entire indebtedness due for those defaults, but such fact will not constitute a waiver as to a default thereafter which is not waived.

4. Payment ⊜33—Check not only insufficient, but also conditional, not operative as payment.

Where check sent to chattel mortgagee by chattel mortgagor after default was not only insufficient to meet the amount due, but was coupled with a condition, and was not accepted, it could not be regarded as payment, or as curing the default and restoring the status quo between the mortgagor and mortgagee based on the mortgage.

Appeal from Circuit Court, Jackson County; Daniel E. Bird, Judge.

"Not to be officially published."

Action by Margaret M. Lange against the Midwest Motor Securities Company. Judgment for plaintiff, and defendant appeals. Reversed.

Thomson & Brasher, of Kansas City, for appellant.

J. W. Hawes, of Kansas City, for respondent.

TRIMBLE, P. J. Plaintiff brought suit for $1,500 actual and $5,000 punitive damages for the conversion of an automobile. There was a verdict and judgment in her favor for $1,250 actual and $250 punitive damages, and from this defendant appealed.

It is conceded that at the time of the taking of the automobile the defendant held a chattel mortgage thereon, given by plaintiff in part payment of the purchase price thereof. Said note was for $1,000, payable in monthly installments of $75, due on the first of every month, beginning October 1, 1917, with interest at 8 per cent. on each installment, and to continue every month up to and including August 1, 1918, and on September 1, 1918, a final installment of $175 was to be paid with interest. The interest on each installment and the interest on the unpaid balance of the principal sum were to be paid at the maturity of each installment, and in case of default in the payment of any installment when due then all remaining installments should immediately become due and payable; and there was provision for the payment of a reasonable attorney's fee in case of default. The mortgage provided that the automobile should remain in the possession of the mortgagor until default be made in the payment of the said debt or interest, or some part thereof, but in case of a removal or attempted removal of said automobile from Jackson county, Mo., or any unreasonable depreciation in the value thereof, or in case the mortgagee should deem itself insecure, it could take said property into its possession. There was the usual further provision for a sale under the chattel mortgage, upon the mortgagee's taking possession of the property, either in case of default or as above provided, and there was also a provision in which the mortgagor agreed to exonerate the mortgagee, and hold it harmless from all damages or trespass in entering any premises where the property could be found, and in the taking possession of the same.

Plaintiff made the monthly payments from October, 1917, to April, 1918, both inclusive, but never paid any of them on the first of the month, the payments ranging from the 9th to as late as the 21st of the month on the first day of which they respectively fell due; but it seems that up to and including the one of April 1, they were accepted and credited on said note on the dates they were paid, and there is an admission on the part of defendant in the record that "all the rest of everything was paid up to the 1st day of May" though the defendant repeatedly urged plaintiff to make the payments promptly.

The trouble began with regard to the installment due on May 1, 1918. Plaintiff concedes that she did not pay it on that date, and she made no attempt to make such payment until on May 16, 1918, when she, through her husband, acting as her agent, mailed defendant a check for $77.22, together with a letter telling defendant to "kindly hold check till Saturday," which condition postponed the cashing of the check till May 18th. Plaintiff says she doesn't know why her husband wrote such a condition, as she gave him no authority to do that, but clearly, as the husband was concededly her agent, and the defendant had no means of knowing that the condition was unauthorized, she cannot invoke lack of authority on the part of her agent in the transaction with defendant.

The automobile in question was taken by defendant about 9 o'clock in the evening of May 17, 1918. Plaintiff, in order to leave Kansas City for a trip to Omaha, and then to Minnesota, had her husband to drive her in the automobile from her residence in the city to the union depot, where she took a train and went away on that trip. While her husband was in the depot seeing his wife off on the train, he left the car parked outside, and defendant's representatives took charge of it, and after explaining to a policeman that they were taking it under the chattel mortgage, drove off with it to the police station, where the matter was again explained to the policeman's superiors and, their approval being obtained, the car was placed by defendant in a garage. When the husband, after having seen his wife off, returned to the place where he had parked the car, he found it was gone.

Plaintiff's check for $77.22 was, as stated, mailed to defendant on May 16, 1918, but at that time defendant had already placed the note in the hands of its attorneys. And in the afternoon of that date, said attorneys mailed a letter, having a special delivery stamp on it, to plaintiff, telling her they had the note, an installment of which fell due on May 1, 1918; that the interest to May 17 was $6.86, making a total of $81.86; that the note and mortgage provided that, in the event of default in the payment of any installment when due, and the matter was placed in the hands of an attorney, the latter's fee should also be paid; that since the dictation of the foregoing portion of the letter, their client (the defendant) had handed them the check plaintiff had sent defendant with instructions to hold it until Saturday next; that the check could not be accepted under those conditions; that the attorney's fee would be $10, provided the matter was adjusted by not later than 10 o'clock the next morning by the payment in cash at their office of the amount due to that date, making a total of $91.86; that if they did not have a remittance of that amount by 10 o'clock Friday morning May 17, 1918, they would place a writ in the sheriff's hands, and take the car.

It is not precisely clear what was done with the check plaintiff sent on May 16, 1918. There is some intimation in the record that it was returned to plaintiff, and did not appear again until it was produced at the taking of plaintiff's deposition. There is no question, however, that it was never cashed or sought to be cashed by defendant. And it is conceded that, aside from sending the check on the condition named, no attempt

was ever made to pay the installment due May 1, 1918, nor was there any offer on the part of plaintiff to do so, then or at any time thereafter.

According to defendant's evidence, when no response was had to the letter, defendant's representative went, on May 17, 1918, to the drug store, which plaintiff says she had bought of her husband, and which he was assisting in running as her agent, and tried to see plaintiff. The note and mortgage were signed "M. M. Lange," and the representative did not know she was a woman, but assumed the person was a man. The clerks informed him "Mr. Lange" was not in. He went several times, and, failing to see him, left his telephone number. About 6 o'clock that evening, after the representative had gone home, he received a telephone message from a man who said his name was Lange; and the representative then told his business, and that he had been at the store several times in regard to the note. The man replied that "M. M. Lange" was the wife of his dead brother; that she had taken the car on the Thursday before to Minnesota; that she would not be back before October, and might never return; that he didn't know what she intended to do about the automobile; he admitted that he had been looking after the previous payments on the note for her, but was not involved in the matter, and had nothing to do with this payment; that she had taken the car and left, and he didn't care.

The representative thereupon informed one of the defendant's officers about this, and the two went together in an automobile to the drug store, and from there to plaintiff's home. According to their evidence, the plaintiff (whom they did not know personally) came to the door and informed them that "Mrs. Lange" was not at home, but had gone to Minnesota, and finally refused to give any further information, and shut the door. Not knowing that the person to whom they had been talking was Mrs. Lange herself, they left, going down town. Later the same evening, about 8 o'clock, they returned to plaintiff's home. While they were waiting in front of the house, the automobile in question was driven up and Mrs. Lange got into it and started to the depot. Defendant's representatives followed, and, on the way down there, defendant's evidence is that plaintiff stopped her car and gave them a "good tongue lashing" when they demanded the car. Plaintiff says she asked them why they followed her, and that they told her they represented the defendant, and that, when she asked them if their following her had "anything to do with the car," they said "No," and that they didn't want the car. She, however, says they also got in the driveway at her home, apparently as if to prevent the car being driven out.

Plaintiff denies that she told defendant's

representatives that Mrs. Lange was not at home; and her husband denies that he telephoned that M. M. Lange was his dead brother's wife, or that she had taken the car and gone to Minnesota.

The petition charged that, in addition to taking the car, defendant concealed it from plaintiff; and plaintiff's husband claimed that he did not learn what had become of it for a week or 10 days, but finally admitted that he received a letter from defendant's attorneys about the 21st of May, and plaintiff herself says she got a letter on May 23, saying they had taken it.

[1] Respondent's motion to dismiss appeal because of defects in appellant's brief is wholly without merit. The statement is a fairly impartial and comprehensive statement, easily understood, and gives a reasonably clear view of what the case is about, and what is involved. We fail to see wherein it can be said to violate the rule or the statutes in regard to statements. Under the law as it now stands, the brief does not have to contain separate "assignments of error," provided the errors complained of and the points insisted upon are separately and succinctly set forth in the "points and authorities" with the proper citations relied upon. This was done, and the motion to dismiss must be overruled.

[2] The demurrers to the evidence offered by plaintiff should have been sustained. We fail to see wherein plaintiff made any case to be submitted to the jury. According to the evidence in her own behalf, there was a default in the payment of the installment and interest due on May 1, 1918, and that default was still in force when the car was taken. Nor was there ever any effort on plaintiff's part to pay the installment due May 1, 1918, or the debt thereafter, when the check for $77.22, sent long after the default and with a condition attached, was not accepted.

"After the condition of payment in a chattel mortgage is broken, the mortgagee is entitled to the possession." Edmonston v. Jones, 96 Mo. App. 83, 91, 69 S. W. 741, 743.

"The mortgagee does not need the consent of the mortgagor to take possession after condition broken. He can take possession as he may. He can replevin the property. He may take it wherever he finds it. It is his property." Meyer Bros. Drug Co. v. Self, 77 Mo. App. 284, 293.

After condition broken the mortgagee of personal property is regarded as the absolute owner, at least for the purpose of possession and due foreclosure. Robinson v. Campbell, 8 Mo. 365.

"It is well settled that, after condition broken, the legal title to mortgaged chattels vests in the mortgagee. The right of the mortgagee to seize mortgaged chattels, after condition broken, is a license coupled with an interest, which cannot be revoked by the mortgagor. It is a part of the consideration of the mortgage, and to allow the mortgagor to revoke it would be a fraud upon the rights of the mortgagee, and would very much impair the value of chattel mortgages as securities. The right to seize carries with it, by necessary implication, the right to do whatever is reasonably necessary to make the seizure—including the right to peaceably enter upon the premises of the mortgagor. There is one restriction, however, which the law imposes upon this right. It must be exercised without provoking a breach of the peace." Willis v. Whittle, 82 S. C. 500, 501, 502, 64 S. E. 410.

[3] The fact that previous installments were accepted after they were in default may be a waiver of the right to declare the entire indebtedness due for those defaults, but such fact will not constitute a waiver as to a default thereafter which was not waived. 27 Cyc. 1532, 1533. See, also, Bowens v. Benson, 57 Mo. 26; Baldridge v. Dawson, 39 Mo. App. 527; Connorsville Buggy Co. v. Lowry, 104 Mo. App. 186, 77 S. W. 771. There was no question of waiver raised by the pleadings.

[4] According to plaintiff's admissions as to the amount due and the time for which interest was to be paid thereon—30 days—together with the provisions of the mortgage as to what interest there had to be paid, the amount of the check, $77.22, was not sufficient to meet the amount due. Nor is this all. The check was sent coupled with a condition, and was not accepted. It could not be regarded as payment, or as curing the default and restoring the status quo between the mortgagor and mortgagee based on the mortgage. Johnson-Brinkman Comm. Co. v. Central Bank, 116 Mo. 558, 22 S. W. 813, 38 Am. St. Rep. 615; Hall & Robinson v. Missouri Pac. R. Co., 50 Mo. App. 179, 183.

As we view the case, the judgment must be reversed. Hence it is unnecessary to notice the other alleged errors as to the allowance of punitive damages, or in regard to the instructions.

The judgment is reversed.

All concur.

ORR v. RUSSELL et al. (No. 13909.)

(Kansas City Court of Appeals. Missouri.
May 2, 1921. Rehearing Denied
May 23, 1921.)

1. Pleading ⬤⟹54—Each separate count must be a complete statement of cause of action.

While each separate count in a petition must be a separate complete statement of a cause of action within itself, and must contain all the facts necessary to constitute the cause of action which it asserts, this may be accomplished by appropriate reference to pertinent matters which have been already stated.

2. Appeal and error ⬤⟹170(3)—Pleading ⬤⟹406(5)—Defects in pleading disregarded on appeal, where substantial rights not affected; defective reference from one count to another waived by failure to object.

In an action for commissions for real estate, where the second count by reference adopted all of the allegations of the first count so far as the same were applicable, objection to the sufficiency of the reference was waived by defendant's failure to object to the introduction of any evidence and going to the trial on the issues as presented by the second count, which stated a good cause of action, particularly in view of Rev. St. 1919, § 1276, declaring that the courts shall in every stage disregard any defects in the pleadings which shall not affect substantial rights of the parties, and no reversal shall be had by reason of such defects.

3. Pleading ⬤⟹252(2)—Though plaintiff elected to go to trial on the second count, the first count of the petition did not become an abandoned pleading.

Though plaintiff elected to go to trial on the second count of the petition, and amended his petition by interlineations, the first count was not an abandoned pleading, and an instruction based thereon cannot be complained of.

4. Appeal and error ⬤⟹1033(5) — Defendants cannot complain of instruction placing undue burden on plaintiff.

Where an instruction as a prerequisite to recovery of commissions required plaintiff to establish numerous facts which were stated conjunctively, defendants cannot complain that the instruction as a condition to recovery required as proof of consideration plaintiff's promise to withhold action against the vendor oil company, on the ground that such element was not pleaded, for that merely placed an additional burden on plaintiff.

Appeal from Circuit Court, Jackson County; O. A. Lucas, Judge.

"Not to be officially published."

Action by John M. Orr against William J. Russell and others and C. C. Outhier and others. On trial plaintiff dismissed as to all but the last-named defendants, and from a judgment for plaintiff they appeal. Affirmed.

L. A. Laughlin, of Kansas City, for appellants.

Goodwin Creason and Dwight M. Smith, both of Kansas City, for respondent.

ARNOLD, J. This is an action for commissions growing out of the sale of real estate.

In 1917, William J. Russell and H. R. Payton were the owners in fee of 80 acres of land, composing the west half of the original town site of Oilton, Okl. The land was thought to be good property for the development of oil and gas. The owners sold a few lots, or parts of lots, for building sites, reserving the oil, gas, and mineral rights, which was done pursuant to an agreement or arrangement between the owners.

Russell engaged plaintiff herein to arrange for the sale of lots, or otherwise interest capital in investing in the enterprise. Shortly thereafter Russell and Payton formed the Oilton Oil & Gas Company, an Oklahoma corporation, turning this Oilton property into the company, Payton and Russell owning the larger amount of the stock. Russell had charge of the sale of the stock and engaged plaintiff in the undertaking, and through him Russell and others succeeded in selling $15,000 to $20,000 worth of the stock of the company. Plaintiff then, through Russell, brought the company into negotiations with defendants C. C. Outhier, G. G. Brinton, and George Stock, resulting in the sale to them of the property, then valued at $100,000. It was for the commissions on this sale that the present suit is based; such services being placed at 10 per cent. of the value of the property.

Defendants Outhier, Brinton, and Stock previously had entered into a trust agreement, or common-law corporation, known as the Consolidated Oil Wells Company; they being the trustees of said trust relation. Defendant Outhier, by the terms of the trust agreement, was the president, with power to purchase and sell properties.

When negotiations for the purchase of the Oilton Oil & Gas Company's properties were begun, plaintiff informed defendants that he would look to them for his commission if the property was transferred to them, or he would be compelled to institute proceedings at the outset to insure the payment to him of his commission. As shown by plaintiff's evidence, Outhier then told Orr that if he (Orr) would refrain from taking any action which would complicate or block the deal, defendants would pay him his commission and protect themselves out of the shares of the Consolidated Oil Wells Company stock that were to go to the stockholders of the Oilton Oil & Gas Company in payment of the purchase price of the land in question. March 20, 1919, Orr, for the consideration of 2,500 shares of stock of the Consolidated Oil Wells Company, released the Oilton Oil & Gas Company only, from further liability on his commission; which said shares were not issued. Whereupon Orr repudiated the release of March 20, 1919. The sale and transfer were consummated between the Oilton Oil & Gas Company and defendants.

On June 17, 1919, plaintiff instituted suit for said commission directed against Russell, Payton, Oilton Oil & Gas Company and Outhier, Brinton and Stock. Soon after the institution of said suit Orr entered into another agreement with Payton whereby, in consideration of the issuance to him of 2,500 shares of stock in the Consolidated Oil Wells Company, he released Payton and the Oilton Oil & Gas Company only, from any further liability for commissions. Outhier, Brinton and Stock were not named in this agreement, but the next day, June 18, 1919, they entered into a stipulation with plaintiff whereby plaintiff agreed to a dismissal of the cause as to Payton and the Oilton Oil & Gas Company.

The petition alleged two causes of action with two counts in each, the first count in each cause being based on contract and the second on quantum meruit for the same services. During the trial of the case and on motion plaintiff elected to go to trial on the second count of the first cause of action, and also dismissed as to all defendants excepting O. O. Outhier, G. G. Brinton, and George Stock. The case then went to trial on the one cause of action, to wit, to recover from defendants reasonable compensation for services rendered by plaintiff in accordance with the agreement between plaintiff and defendants, resulting in a verdict for plaintiff in the sum of $1,500. Defendants demurred.

The following is a copy of the petition upon which the case was submitted to the jury (omitting the prayer):

"Plaintiff for his second count against defendants, and each of them, hereby adopts and makes a part hereof, as fully as if the same were herein rewritten and incorporated, each and all of the allegations in the first count of this petition, as amended so far as the same are applicable hereto, and alleges and states that the reasonable value of the services therein rendered were and are $15,000; that he made demand for the same in January, 1919, and subsequent dates thereto, but that no part of said sum has been paid by said defendants, or any of them, and that each and all of them are indebted to this plaintiff for the full amount of $15,000, together with interest thereon at the rate of 6 per cent. per annum from January, 1919."

Plaintiff contends that the appeal should be dismissed "because appellants' brief contains no statement of points, authorities and legal propositions separate and apart from the argument as required by rules 15 and 16 [169 S. W. xiii, xiv] of this court," and because "it does not distinctly and separately allege the errors committed by the inferior court," as required by rule 17 (169 S. W. xiv).

An examination of the brief complained of convinces us that it substantially complies with the rules of this court, and the appeal will not be dismissed on this ground.

[1, 2] Defendants contend that the reference in said second count, adopting "each and all of the allegations in the first count of this petition, as amended, as far as the same are applicable thereto," is not sufficient, and argues that this is not an unequivocal adoption of the allegations of the first count, but leaves it to the pleader to determine what allegations are applicable and what are not. In County of Moniteau ex rel. v. Lewis et al., 123 Mo. App. 673, 100 S. W. 1107, this court held:

"The rule is that each separate count in a petition must be a complete statement of a cause of action within itself, that it must contain all the facts necessary to constitute the cause of action which it asserts. [Weber v. Squier, 51 Mo. App. 601; Bliss on Code Plead. § 121.] But this may be accomplished by appropriate reference therein to pertinent matters which have been already duly and fully stated and which need not be formally set forth at length in each successive count."

That was done in this petition. The petition states a good cause of action;, but if there were any defects therein, defendants waived the same by failing to object to the introduction of any evidence, and going to trial upon the issues presented by the petition, upon the theory offered by plaintiff. If this were not a sufficient answer to the contention of defendants, section 1276, Rev. Stat. 1919, would seem to settle the question finally, as follows: "The court shall, in every stage of the action, disregard any error or defect in the pleadings or proceedings which shall not affect the substantial rights of the adverse party; and no judgment shall be reversed or affected by reason of such error or defect."

[3] Defendants further complain that the court erred in giving instruction D-1 (evidently meaning P-1) for plaintiff, because plaintiff dismissed as to defendant Russell, thereby abandoning his original petition, and under the instruction was permitted to recover on another cause of action altogether. The record shows this state of facts: Plaintiff, by permission of the court, amended his petition by interlineation so as to charge defendants individually, as follows:

"And as a part of the purchase and exchange price of said property and stock agreed with said Russell and Payton in their individual and official capacity as aforesaid and this plaintiff to pay this plaintiff ten per cent. of the purchase and exchange price of said properties."

The trial proceeded upon the pleadings as amended and the first count of the petition was not an abandoned pleading. The instruction complained of fairly presented to the jury the issues thus made, and is not error,

[4] Defendants also claim that the instruction is faulty because it permits a recovery if the jury found "that said trustees agreed with said Orr that if he (Orr) would withhold filing suit or taking action against the Oilton Oil & Gas Company that would prevent said sale being consummated" because there is no such allegation in the petition.

The petition, as amended, alleges that defendants did purchase and take over the property with the knowledge of plaintiff's claim for commission, as set out, and as a part of the purchase price thereof agreed with plaintiff and Russell and Payton to pay this plaintiff 10 per cent. of the purchase and exchange price of said properties. In the instruction complained of, the various elements of plaintiff's cause are stated conjunctively, and the jury were required to find each fact in his favor before it could return a verdict for him. The instruction would have been good without requiring the jury to find that the moving consideration of defendants' agreement to pay the commission to plaintiff was his promise to withhold taking any action against the Oilton Oil & Gas Company that would prevent the sale being consummated. By requiring such finding, the court placed upon plaintiff an additional burden that was not strictly necessary to sustain his cause of action under the allegations of the petition; the defendants are not prejudiced thereby, and the instruction will not therefore work a reversal.

The judgment is affirmed.

All concur.

FIDELITY & CASUALTY CO. OF NEW YORK v. KANSAS CITY RYS. CO. (No. 14027.)

(Kansas City Court of Appeals. Missouri. May 23, 1921.)

1. Master and servant ⟨⟩330(1)—Presumption of liability raised by proof of ownership of automobile negligently driven by employé.

In an action against an automobile owner for negligence of the driver, proof that at the time of the collision the defendant was the owner of the automobile, and that the driver was in its employ, creates the presumption that the driver at such time was acting in the line of his employment, but such presumption may be overcome by evidence of facts showing the contrary.

2. Evidence ⟨⟩10(3)—No judicial notice of city streets.

Courts do not take judicial notice of the streets of a city, of their direction, or relation to each other.

3. Master and servant ⟨⟩332(2)—Automobile owner's responsibility for chauffeur's negligence held for jury.

In an action against an automobile owner for negligence of chauffeur, where there was

evidence that it was the chauffeur's duty after making certain trip to take the automobile back to the garage, that he started out with the purpose of stopping for his dinner on the way to the garage, and that the accident happened while on such trip, but where there was no evidence that the place of the collision was not upon the direct route to the garage, refusal to direct verdict for owner on ground that chauffeur was not acting in the line of employment at time of collision *held* proper.

4. Master and servant ⟨⟩332(2)—Chauffeur's departure from scope of employment for jury.

Where it was chauffeur's duty to take automobile to the garage, a slight deviation from the direct route for the driver's benefit would be a mere incident, and not necessarily out of the line of his duty to his employer, but whether the servant thereby departed from the scope of employment would depend upon the degree of deviation and all the attending circumstances, and would be a question for the jury unless the degree of deviation is so marked and unusual as to authorize court to declare as a matter of law that driver had departed from scope of employment, or so slight as to authorize court to declare that servant was still executing the master's business.

5. Municipal corporations ⟨⟩706(8)—Instruction making operation of automobile at excessive rate of speed in violation of ordinance negligence held not supported by evidence.

In action for negligence of automobile driver, where there was no evidence as to the speed at which the automobile was driven prior to its reaching a point 125 feet distant from the point of collision, instruction that an ordinance made it unlawful to drive an automobile at a greater rate of speed than 20 miles an hour, and that the driving of automobile at a greater rate of speed constituted negligence, *held* erroneous, notwithstanding evidence that automobile was traveling at a rate of speed in excess of 20 miles per hour just prior to the collision, where, under such ordinance, such rate of speed, to constitute presumptive evidence of negligence, must have been continued for a distance of 200 feet.

6. Appeal and error ⟨⟩882(12)—Defendant's requested instruction on burden of proof held not to adopt plaintiff's instruction.

Defendant by requesting instruction that the burden of proof was on plaintiff to prove that defendant was guilty of negligence "as submitted to you in these instructions," and "where defined in these instructions," did not adopt plaintiff's instruction on negligence so as to be precluded from complaining thereof.

Appeal from Circuit Court, Jackson County; Thomas B. Buckner, Judge.

Suit by the Fidelity & Casualty Company of New York against the Kansas City Railways Company. Judgment for plaintiff, and defendant appeals. Reversed and remanded.

Chas. N. Sadler, John E. Connors and E. E. Ball, all of Kansas City, for appellant. Rollin E. Talbert, J. C. Rosenberger, and

W. G. Butts, all of Kansas City, for respondent.

BLAND, J. This is a suit for damages to an automobile. There was a verdict and judgment for plaintiff in the sum of $404.96 and defendant has appealed.

The facts show that on April 13, 1918, an automobile driven by one Steffey who was in the general employment of the defendant as a chauffeur collided with an automobile owned and being driven west by one J. Cohn on the north side of Fifteenth street, a street running east and west in Kansas City, Mo. At the time of the collision Steffey was driving at a high rate of speed on the north and wrong side of said street, in an opposite direction to Cohn.

Steffey on the morning of the day in question, was called to defendant's office at Fifteenth street and Grand avenue, in Kansas City, Mo., and was directed to bring defendant's automobile which was in defendant's garage at Thirty-First and Cherry streets in said city, to that office. Steffey drove the car to defendant's office, where he called for defendant's paymaster and took him to Second street and Grand avenue. After waiting at the latter place for the paymaster to finish paying the men, Steffey took him back to the office at Fifteenth and Grand, where the paymaster was discharged. It was Steffey's duty to take the car back to the garage at Thirty-First and Cherry streets but he started out Fifteenth street for the purpose of stopping for his dinner on his way to the garage. When he reached a point about 50 feet west of Vine street, a street running north and south, and intersecting at right angles Fifteenth street, he was driving on the westbound car track, and came alongside of a truck which was to the south, and going somewhat slower in the same direction. The driver of the truck indicated that he was going to make a left-hand turn into Vine street. Steffey was going too fast to stop, and testified that, in order to keep from striking the truck as it made the turn, he speeded up his car and turned it toward the north, in order to go around the truck. He collided with Cohn's automobile before he was able to return to the middle or south side of the street. The accident happened 25 feet east of Vine street, which was 50 feet wide. Steffey testified that he was going at the rate of 15 to 18 miles per hour, but plaintiff's testimony shows that he was going at the rate of from 20 to 30 miles per hour. Cohn's automobile was materially damaged. After the accident Cohn assigned to plaintiff, who had a policy of insurance upon the car, all his right to any cause of action that he might have against the defendant.

There are a number of specific allegations of negligence in the petition, one of which is founded on ordinance No. 38759 of Kansas City, section 26 of which is pleaded in the petition. Said section provides that every person operating a motor vehicle "shall drive the same in a careful and prudent manner, and at a rate of speed that shall not endanger the property of another or the life or limb of any person or persons, provided that driving in excess" of 20 miles per hour at the place of the collision "for a distance of more than two hundred feet shall be presumptive evidence of driving at a rate of speed which is not careful and prudent."

[1] Defendant's first point is that its demurrer to the evidence should have been sustained, for the reason that there was a total failure of proof that Steffey was acting for the defendant, and within the scope of his employment, at the time of the collision. Plaintiff made out a prima facie case by showing that the automobile, at the time of the collision, was the property of defendant, and that Steffey was in its employ, such facts raising the presumption that Steffey was acting in the line of his employment, which presumption would take flight on the appearance in evidence of facts showing the contrary. Guthrie v. Holmes, 272 Mo. 215, 236, 198 S. W. 854, Ann. Cas. 1918D, 1123; Glassman v. Harry, 182 Mo. App. 304, 170 S. W. 403; Shamp v. Lambert, 142 Mo. App. 567, 121 S. W. 770. The question then presents itself as to whether this presumption in favor of plaintiff has been overcome.

[2-4] The evidence shows that it was the intention of Steffey to stop for his dinner on his way to the garage. Courts do not take judicial notice of the streets of a city, their direction, or their relation to each other. Breckinridge v. Amer. Central Ins. Co., 87 Mo. 62; Vonkey v. City of St. Louis, 219 Mo. 37, 117 S. W. 733. There is nothing in the record to show that the place of the collision was not upon the direct route from defendant's office at Fifteenth street and Grand avenue to its garage at Thirty-First and Cherry streets. Nothing appears to indicate that at the time of the collision there was anything more than an unexecuted intention on Steffey's part to deviate from that route for the purpose of going to his dinner. The intention to deviate being unexecuted, and not yet having become operative, it might be said that at the time of the collision the automobile was being used in the business of defendant. Fitzgerald v. Boston & Northern Ry. Co., 214 Mass. 485, 101 N. E. 1085. But, assuming that there was an executed intention on the part of Steffey to deviate, a slight deviation from the direct route for the benefit of the driver would be a mere incident, and not necessarily out of the line of his duty to his employer. From the evidence now before us there appears nothing otherwise than that the deviation, if any, was merely in-

cidental, and was not such as to take the driver outside of the scope of his employment.

Whether the servant has departed from the scope of his employment would depend upon the degree of deviation, and all the attending circumstances. In some cases the deviation might be so slight as to authorize the court, as a matter of law, to declare that the servant is still executing the master's business. Where the decree of deviation is marked and unusual, such as where the chauffeur takes his employer's car on a frolic of his own, or on a "joy ride," the court, as a matter of law, would declare that he has departed from the scope of his employment, such as was done in the case of Guthrie v. Holmes, supra. The cases falling between these extremes will be regarded as involving a question of fact to be left to the jury. Defendant should be well satisfied in this case, under the facts as they now appear, that the matter of whether Steffey was acting within the scope of his employment was left to the jury. Slothower v. Clark, 191 Mo. App. 105, 179 S. W. 55; Krzikowsky v. Sperring, 107 Ill. App. 493; Ritchie v. Waller, 63 Conn. 155, 28 Atl. 29, 27 L. R. A. 161, 38 Am. St. Rep. 361; 20 Enc. of Law [2d Ed.] p. 166; 26 Cyc. p. 1536; Whatman v. Pearson, 3 Law Rep. Common Pleas Cases, 422.

Complaint is made of plaintiff's instruction No. 2, which told the jury that at the time of the collision an ordinance was in force in Kansas City making it unlawful for any person to drive an automobile at a greater rate of speed than 20 miles per hour upon the streets of the city; that if they found that defendant's car was being driven upon "Fifteenth street in Kansas City at a greater rate of speed than twenty miles per hour, * * * then such acts * * * constituted negligence," and their verdict should be for plaintiff. Defendant contends that the ordinance says that the operation of an automobile in excess of 20 miles per hour at the place of collision is presumptive negligence only if it is operated at such a rate of speed for a distance of two hundred feet or more, and that the ordinance does not provide that the operation of an automobile at a greater rate of speed than 20 miles per hour even for that distance shall conclusively be deemed to be negligent, but only presumptive negligence.

Plaintiff attempts to answer this contention by calling our attention to the fact that there is no excuse offered by the defendant to justify the conduct of Steffey in driving at a greater rate of speed than 20 miles per hour; that defendant contented itself by attempting to show that Steffey was driving at less than that rate of speed; that, there being no evidence of justification, the court was right in telling the jury that if they believed the driver exceeded 20 miles per hour, the limit specified in the ordinance, his conduct was negligent. Plaintiff cites in support of this contention Young v. Dunlap, 195 Mo. App. 119, 190 S. W. 1041, 1044.

[5] However, plaintiff attempts to make no answer to the claim that the ordinance does not make a speed of 20 miles per hour presumptive evidence where it is not shown that such rate of speed was continued for a distance of 200 feet. Plaintiff's evidence shows that defendant's automobile was traveling at a rate of speed in excess of 20 miles per hour just prior to the collision, but there is no evidence on either side as to what speed defendant's automobile was traveling prior to its reaching a point 125 feet distant from the point of collision. Some time after reaching the point first mentioned, defendant's automobile was speeded up. So there was no evidence tending to show even that defendant's automobile during the last 125 feet of its journey was proceeding at the same rate of speed that it was at the time plaintiff's evidence shows that it was going at a greater rate than 20 miles per hour. We think there is no question but that the instruction was erroneous.

However, plaintiff contends that defendant, by its instruction No. 10 adopted plaintiff's instructions, and that the error, if any, was common to both plaintiff and defendant. Defendant's instruction No. 10 reads as follows:

"The court instructs the jury that the burden of proof is on the plaintiff to prove to your satisfaction by the preponderance or greater weight of the credible testimony that the defendant was guilty of negligence as submitted to you in these instructions, and this burden of proof continues and abides with the plaintiff throughout the entire trial; and unless you believe and find from the evidence in the case that the plaintiff has proved by a preponderance of the credible testimony to your satisfaction that the defendant was guilty of negligence, as defined in these instructions, and that such negligence was the direct and proximate cause of the injuries complained of, then your verdict must be for the defendant."

Defendant's instruction No. 11 is as follows:

"By negligence as used in the instructions of the court is meant a failure to use ordinary care. Ordinary care is such care as an ordinarily prudent person would exercise under the same or similar circumstances."

Defendant's instruction No. 4 tells the jury that if they believe that the driver of defendant's automobile was in the exercise of ordinary care, and that Cohn was negligent as defined in other instructions, their verdict should be for the defendant. Defendant's instruction No. 8 tells the jury that if the collision was the result of a mere accident without the fault of negligence of any one, their verdict should be for the defendant, and then defines "accident." ·

[6] It appears that defendant's instruction No. 10 covers merely the burden of proof. It was the intention of the defendant in giving it to tell the jury what that burden consisted of. In directing the attention of the jury to the burden of proof, defendant told them that the burden of proof was on plaintiff to establish by the preponderance of the credible testimony that defendant was guilty of negligence as submitted to them by the instructions, and that they must find that plaintiff had proved by the preponderance of the testimony that defendant was guilty of negligence as defined in the instructions before they could return a verdict for plaintiff.

It does not appear that it was the intention of defendant to adopt plaintiff's instructions, but to have the court define the burden of proof, and to confine the jury, in reference to the burden of proof in relation to the issues of negligence, to the evidence introduced and the instructions of the court. Of course it would have been the duty of the jury to consider only the evidence and instructions of the court, regardless of defendant's instruction No. 10, so that the instruction in that regard added nothing to the case. This is not a case where the defendant, in one of its instructions, referred to some definition in another instruction, and that definition was not contained in any of defendant's instructions, but was contained in plaintiff's instruction and was a wrong definition, such as was assumed in the case of Quinn v. A., T. & S. F. Ry. Co. (Mo. App.) 193 S. W. 933; nor is it a case where defendant's negligence was submitted to the jury in plaintiff's instruction alone, and defendant adopted plaintiff's manner of submission, or referred in terms to an instruction or instructions of plaintiff. It is not apparent that defendant, in asking its instruction No. 10, intended to adopt plaintiff's instruction as its own.

The judgment will be reversed, and the cause remanded.

All concur.

BALDWIN v. KANSAS CITY RYS. CO.
(No. 13877.)

(Kansas City Court of Appeals. Missouri.
May 2, 1921. Rehearing Denied
May 23, 1921.)

1. Negligence ⬤⟹117—Contributory negligence must be pleaded.

Where contributory negligence is not pleaded as a defense, defendant has no right to have that issue submitted.

2. Damages ⬤⟹158(3)—Injury to woman's pelvic organs and consequences thereof sufficiently pleaded.

In husband's action for loss of his wife's society and services, petition alleging injury to her pelvic organs, its effect on her health, etc., held sufficient pleading to render admissible testimony of her fainting spells, irritability, inability for the sexual relations, condition of uterus, melancholy conditions, and inability to walk.

3. Trial ⬤⟹256(13)—More limited instruction, if desired, must be asked for.

Defendant, by failing to ask a more limited instruction on the question of damages, thereby waived any generality in the instruction given.

4. Trial ⬤⟹219—Instruction need not define meaning of "society, assistance, and domestic services," where evidence indicates their meaning.

In a husband's action for loss of his wife's "society, assistance, and domestic services," it was unnecessary that an instruction define these terms, as they were not used in a technical sense, and the evidence advised the jury of their meaning.

5. Damages ⬤⟹99—Husband and wife ⬤⟹209(3)—Husband entitled to damages for loss of wife's society and services, without direct proof of value thereof.

The husband is entitled, as a matter of law, to the society and services of his wife, although the family may be in such circumstances as to eliminate the necessity of the performance of manual labor by the wife; and any negligent act of another that would deprive the husband of this right is an unwarrantable invasion thereof, for which damages are recoverable without direct proof of value, being inferable by the jury from the fact of loss of society.

6. Carriers ⬤⟹287(5)—However long a stop may be, street car must not be started without looking to situation of passengers boarding same.

A street car should not be started merely because a sufficient length of time has elapsed to permit a passenger and those in front of her to board the car safely, for, however long a stop may be, due care requires that a conductor should look to his car before signaling to start.

7. Damages ⬤⟹158(3)—Husband and wife ⬤⟹209(3)—Husband entitled to damages for loss of "consortium"; loss of wife's sexual ability admissible under general pleading of loss of consortium.

The right of consortium is the right, growing out of the marital relation, which the husband and wife have each to enjoy the society and companionship of the other; and a husband, suing for injuries to his wife, is entitled to be paid for his loss of conjugal fellowship, the society and affection expressed in the word "consortium," and under a pleading of such loss evidence of the wife's inability to perform the sexual act is admissible.

[Ed. Note.—For other definitions, see Words and Phrases, First and Second Series, Consortium.]

8. Appeal and error ⚷═232(2)—Objections to evidence, not made below, not considered.

Appellant may not be heard on appeal to object to the admission of evidence on new or other grounds than those stated below.

9. Damages ⚷═158(3) — Testimony of wife's fainting spells held admissible.

In husband's action for injuries to his wife, testimony as to her fainting spells *held* properly admitted as tending to prove allegations of the petition as to her nervous condition.

10. Evidence ⚷═509—Expert physicians could give opinions as to wife's injuries.

In husband's action for injuries to his wife, physicians, who were qualified as experts, could, as such, give their opinions or conclusions as to the nature and effect of conditions found.

11. Damages ⚷═133—$5,000 for injuries rendering plaintiff's wife an invalid held not excessive.

In husband's action for injuries to his wife, a verdict of $5,000 *held* not excessive; the wife having been rendered a permanent invalid by injury to her pelvic organs and too weak to undergo an operation to obtain relief.

Appeal from Circuit Court, Jackson County; Allen C. Southern, Judge.

"Not to be officially published."

Action by Lee K. Baldwin against the Kansas City Railways Company. From a judgment for plaintiff, defendant appeals. Affirmed.

R. J. Higgins, of Kansas City, Kan., and Chas. N. Sadler and E. E. Ball, both of Kansas City, Mo., for appellant.

T. J. Madden and Harry R. Freeman, both of Kansas City, Mo., for respondent.

ARNOLD, J. This is a suit by a husband for loss of society and domestic services of his wife on account of injuries sustained by her due to alleged negligence of defendant. Trial in the circuit court resulted in a verdict and judgment for plaintiff in the sum of $5,000. Defendant appealed.

Plaintiff's evidence shows that on November 30, 1916, Annie Baldwin, the wife of plaintiff, attempted to board one of defendant's south-bound Woodland Avenue street cars on Main street, just north of Thirteenth street, in Kansas City. The car had stopped at the usual place for receiving and discharging passengers, and there were several persons waiting to board the car at that point. Mrs. Baldwin was the third person to attempt to enter the car. It was a pay-as-you-enter car, the rear vestibule being separated into two parts, the rear one for entrance and the other for exit of passengers, the two parts being separated by an iron rod or stanchion at the steps. The conductor stood with his back against the rear wall of the vestibule, facing the front of the car, and by means of

a lever, without leaving his position, could open and close the doors to the places of entrance and exit. The seats in the car were occupied, or practically so, but there was ample room inside for the reception of persons waiting at the stopping place. Mrs. Baldwin followed immediately the two persons who preceded her onto the car, placed her right foot on the step, took hold of the iron rod or stanchion, and, placing her full weight on the step, raised her left foot from the pavement in the act of lifting it on to the step, when the car, without the door being closed or any warning given, was quickly started forward and went on its way. The forward movement of the car caused plaintiff's wife to lose her balance, her body sank down, and her left foot dragged on the pavement.

After the car had run a short distance, the woman clinging to it in this manner, her right foot slipped off the step, her body swung around, so that her face was to the rear, and her hand slipped down the rod, allowing the lower portion of her body to drag along on the pavement, a distance of 40 to 45 feet farther, when her hold with her right hand gave way, and she was precipitated to the pavement upon her back, with her feet to the rear, at a point 80 to 85 feet from where the car first stopped.

The defendant offered some testimony to the effect that the woman boarded the car after it was started, looked around, and, on discovering that her husband was not on the car, attempted to alight, fell, and was injured. There was, however, proof by disinterested bystanders that the matter occurred as hereinabove stated, and we must accept that version which the jury by their verdict found to be the true one. Defendant urges that plaintiff's version of how the accident occurred is so at variance with well-known physical laws and common experience as to justify us in rejecting it. We see nothing incompatible with natural laws or physics in plaintiff's version of the occurrence, and therefore conclude that defendant's position relative thereto is wholly untenable.

The petition charges negligence in the premature starting of the car, and pleads the resulting injuries in detail, including the charge that—

"As a direct result of said injuries and conditions resulting therefrom plaintiff has lost and been injured in the enjoyment of the society, assistance, and services of his wife, including that of the marriage relations, and she has had to have care, nursing, and medical treatment, and will continue to require same in the future."

Defendant's answer is a general denial.

Counsel for defendant complain that the trial court erred in giving instruction No. 1 for plaintiff, and argue that, under said instruction—

"Even though the plaintiff's wife was not attempting to board the car when the signal to start same was given, and attempted to board it afterward, and while it was yet standing still, under that instruction plaintiff would have a right to recover."

The proof is ample that the signal to start was not given until Mrs. Baldwin was in the act of entering the car and the case of Quinn v. Railway, 218 Mo. 545, 118 S. W. 46, cited by defendant is not in point. The instruction required the jury to find that plaintiff's wife was in the act of boarding the car "while it was standing."

[1] Further defendant complains that instruction No. 1 offends because it "failed to require plaintiff to exercise ordinary care for his wife's safety." This contention is not well taken for the reason that contributory negligence is not pleaded as a defense, and defendant had no right, therefore, to have that issue submitted. Meily v. Railroad, 215 Mo. 567, 114 S. W. 1013; Boesel v. Wells-Fargo & Co., 260 Mo. 463, 169 S. W. 110; Lester v. United Rys. Co., 219 S. W. 666. Instruction No. 1 is further criticized "because not based upon the testimony and the pleaded cause." The evidence abundantly sustains the charge in the petition of the premature starting of the car while plaintiff's wife was in the act of boarding same. There was no variance between the proof and the submission. Baldwin v. K. C. Rys. Co., 214 S. W. 274.

[2] Error is also charged in instruction No. 2, asked by plaintiff and given by the court, for the reason that it permits the jury to take into consideration the testimony of fainting spells, irritability, inability for the sexual relations, condition of uterus, melancholy conditions, and inability to walk, claiming that same were not pleaded, and that testimony relating thereto was erroneously admitted. It was specifically alleged in the petition that—

"As a result of said injuries plaintiff's wife was rendered insensible and unconscious, and wholly unable to walk or move, or to use any parts or organs of her body, head, or limbs. Her nervous system and mental faculties were disorganized and deranged; she has suffered from inflammation of and hemorrhages from the bowels, kidneys, and other internal organs; the urinary, genital and all the pelvic organs were displaced, wrenched, and injured, inflamed and diseased, and her back, spine, and sides were bruised, sprained, wrenched, displaced, weakened, and diseased; her general health and physical strength and mental vigor, as well as her entire nervous organization, have been weakened and affected."

[3-5] The evidence as a whole was sufficient to support a finding that the injury caused these conditions. The instruction specifically limited the jury in their findings to the diminution and impairment to the husband of the society, assistance, and domestic services of his wife. Defendant failed to ask a more limited instruction, thereby waiving any generality, if any. Bridges v. Dunham, 183 S. W. 703; Furnish v. Railway Co., 102 Mo. 669, 15 S. W. 315, 22 Am. St. Rep. 800. It was unnecessary to define in the instruction the words "society, assistance, and domestic services," as they were not used in a technical sense. The evidence fully advised the jury of their meaning. The husband is entitled, as a matter of law, to the society and services of his wife, although the family may be in such circumstances as to eliminate the necessity of the performance of manual labor by the wife; and any negligent act of another that would deprive the husband of this right is an unwarrantable invasion thereof. In Furnish v. Railway Co., supra, where it was urged that, as no evidence was offered of the value of the wife's society and services, the instruction should not have been given, the Supreme Court said:

"To this it may be said that the nature of the subject does not admit of direct proof of value and that, when the fact of the loss of society is established by testimony, the assessment of reasonable compensation therefor must necessarily be committed to the sound discretion and judgment of the triers of fact."

This same principle is declared in Reeves v. Lutz, 179 Mo. App. 61, 162 S. W. 280, citing Met. St. Ry. Co. v. Johnson, 91 Ga. 466, 18 S. E. 816, and Bruce v. United Rys. Co., 175 Mo. App. 568, 158 S. W. 102.

[6] What we have said as to instructions given on behalf of plaintiff sufficiently answers most of the objections urged on account of the refusal of instructions offered by defendant. However, it may be said that instruction O was properly refused, because it assumed that defendant had a right to start the car after a sufficient length of time had elapsed to permit plaintiff and those in front of her to board the car in safety. In answer to defendant's contention, we call attention to the case of Nelson v. Railway Co., 113 Mo. App. 702, 88 S. W. 1119, and cases therein cited. In that case it is said:

"However long a stop may be, due care requires the conductor to look to his car before giving the signal to start."

[7-10] Again it is claimed that the court erred in admitting incompetent, immaterial, and irrelevant evidence; i. e. (a) that of consortium, (b) fainting spells, and (c) testimony of physicians as to their conclusions of the nature and effect of conditions found. The right of consortium is the right growing out of the marital relation which the husband and wife have each to enjoy the society and companionship of the other. A husband, suing for injuries to his wife, is entitled to be paid for his loss of conjugal fellowship, the society and affection expressed in the word "consortium." There was evidence introduced relative to the wife's inability to perform the sexual act. This was objected to by de-

fendant solely on the ground that it was not pleaded and called for a conclusion. The court properly overruled the objection as made, and defendant may not now be heard to object on new or other grounds. Testimony as to fainting spells was properly admitted as tending to prove the allegations of the petition as to the nervous condition of plaintiff's wife. The record shows that the physicians were qualified as experts and, as such, could give their opinions. Taylor v. Railway Co., 256 Mo. 191, 165 S. W. 327; Moore v. Met. St. Ry. Co., 189 Mo. App. 555, 176 S. W. 1120; Bragg v. Mt. St. Ry. Co., 192 Mo. 331, 91 S. W. 527; Stobile v. McMahon, 196 Mo. App. 93, 190 S. W. 652.

Defendant claims the trial court erred in permitting counsel for plaintiff, in his closing arguments to the jury, to make improper remarks. We have examined the record as set out in defendant's points and authorities and fail to find anything improper or prejudicial in these remarks. The only utterances bordering on impropriety were those brought out by defendant's remarks on the absence of plaintiff's wife from the trial. We must rule against defendant, therefore, on this contention.

[11] The only remaining question to be determined is the claim that the verdict of $5,000 is excessive. The evidence tends to show that prior to the injury complained of plaintiff's wife was a fairly healthy woman; that she was able to, and did, take care of her household, social, marital, and other duties, and that since the alleged injury she has been an invalid; that she suffers from nervous spells, is weak, thin, and emaciated; her lower limbs shrunken and flabby. The doctors pronounce her permanently injured and too weak to undergo an operation to obtain relief. Plaintiff is deprived of her assistance and services. He carries her about and provides help to look after her. She hobbles about on crutches and has her meals brought to her. At the time of the trial, as shown by the testimony, she had been injured two years and six months and was gradually wasting away. With this state of facts before us, we are unable to say the verdict is excessive.

For the reasons herein stated, the judgment is affirmed.

All concur.

BUEHLER v. WAGGENER PAINT & GLASS CO. (No. 14054.)

(Kansas City Court of Appeals. Missouri. May 23, 1921.)

1. Damages ⬅️216(8)—No error in instruction as to damages for impairment of earning capacity after injured employee reached 21.

Where an employee was injured by an elevator gate being pulled down on his head, it was not error to instruct the jury, if they found his earning capacity would be impaired after he reached the age of 21, to allow him such damages as would be a reasonable compensation therefor, evidence that plaintiff quit several positions on account of his injuries, his earning power being thereby reduced by his inability to continue steadily at work, though he was able to fully perform his duties, and received full compensation therefor while actually at work, being such that the jury might find that he would continue to suffer such inability during the rest of his life.

2. New trial ⬅️163(2)—Sustaining motion on one ground overrules other grounds.

Where a motion for new trial is based on several grounds, the sustaining of motion on one ground necessarily overrules the other grounds.

3. Appeal and error ⬅️1005(4) — Denial of motion for new trial based on evidence not disturbed.

Denial of motion for new trial based on ground that verdict was against weight of evidence was not reviewable, weight of evidence being for trial court.

4. Damages ⬅️132(3)—Verdict for $5,000 for injury causing acute meningitis of brain and resulting inability to work steadily held not excessive.

Where plaintiff, as the result of an elevator gate being brought down upon his head by a fellow employee, suffered from acute meningitis of the brain and was unable to continue steadily at work thereafter, a verdict for $5,000 was not excessive.

5. Trial ⬅️233(3)—Instruction referring jury to petition for date of plaintiff's injury held not error.

In an action for injuries to an employee, an instruction to find for plaintiff if the jury found from the evidence that on or about a certain date plaintiff was injured, etc., was not erroneous, as referring the jury to the petition for the date of the injury instead of telling the jury what the date was, where there was no conflict in the evidence as to the date and the jury could not have been misled.

6. Trial ⬅️192 — No error in instruction assuming undisputed fact that defendant's employee was acting within scope of his employment.

In an action for injuries to a factory employee, an instruction that if the jury found that, while plaintiff was entering upon defendant's elevator, the operator negligently pulled or jerked the gate down upon plaintiff's head, was not erroneous, as assuming that the operator was acting within the scope of his employment, the undisputed evidence showing that either the man who ran the elevator or the last man on it pulled the gate down, and that the operator named was the one who was running the elevator at the time of the injury.

7. Negligence ⬅️139(1) — Instruction defining "ordinary care" held correct.

An instruction that "negligence" means the failure to exercise ordinary care, and "ordinary care" means such care as ordinarily careful and prudent persons usually exercise under the same or similar circumstances shown by the evidence in this case, is not erroneous for failure to insert between the words "circumstances" and "shown" the words "as those," and the criticism that the jury might construe the phrase "shown by the evidence in this case" to mean such care as an ordinarily careful person usually exercises, is hypercritical, and without merit.

Appeal from Circuit Court, Jackson County; Allen C. Southern, Judge.

"Not to be officially published."

Action by Oliver Buehler, by his next friend, Mary Buehler, against Waggener Paint & Glass Company. Verdict and judgment for plaintiff, and from the action of the trial court in sustaining defendant's motion for a new trial, plaintiff appeals. Judgment reversed, and cause remanded, with instructions to reinstate verdict.

McCanles, Kennard & Trusty and E. H. Gamble, all of Kansas City, for appellant.

J. C. Rosenberger and Rollin E. Talbert, both of Kansas City, and Warren L. White, of Springfield, for respondent.

BLAND, J. This is an action for damages for personal injuries. Plaintiff recovered a verdict and judgment in the sum of $5,000, but the trial court sustained defendant's motion for a new trial, on the ground that the court erred in giving instructions, and plaintiff has appealed.

The facts show that on April 4, 1919, plaintiff, a boy 17 years of age, was in the employ of defendant as a helper in the art glass department on the fourth floor of its plant in Kansas City, Mo. About quitting time on that day, plaintiff and three other men entered the elevator at the fourth floor, to descend to the street. The opening into the elevator shaft was guarded by a gate 5 feet wide. This gate was constructed of three pine boards, running crosswise. These boards were about an inch in thickness and 2½ or 3 inches in width, and were held together and braced by other pieces of similar boards. The gate worked up and down, and was supported by a counterweight connected to the gate by a rope which passed over two pulleys. The gate was raised to a height of about 6½ or 7 feet and as plaintiff walked under it the operator of the elevator took hold of the gate, and pulled it down, striking plaintiff on the top of his head. Plaintiff would have been knocked down if he had not grabbed hold of the latticework. He staggered, holding to the latticework, until he reached the first floor. He was dazed, and stumbled against the gate when he was leaving the elevator at the first floor. He lived about four blocks distant, and walked home. He was suffering greatly and felt like "he

wanted to pitch over frontwards." "I was just the same as a drunken man."

When plaintiff reached home he sat down in a chair for a short time, and then went to bed on a couch. This was about 5 or 5:30 that afternoon. He did not eat any supper that night. His mother bathed his head, and gave him some tablets to quiet him. He did not undress that night. His head was hurting him where he had been struck; there was a swelling at that point about the size of a hen's egg. The next morning, which was Saturday, he did not eat very much breakfast, but went back to work and worked until noon, the regular quitting time. He worked, but he was "in misery all the time." The foreman asked him what was the matter, and he replied "I feel kind of dazed like." He did not tell the foreman what had happened the day before. He went home, had his dinner, and went to bed, but got up about 9 o'clock that evening. He was suffering from his head, and could not sleep. This kept him up all night. He stayed in bed the next day (Sunday), and Sunday night his mother gave him some medicine and put cold rags on his head, but he was not relieved. On Sunday or Monday, Dr. Davis was called. The doctor came on two different days. Plaintiff remained home Monday and Tuesday, in bed most of the time, not able to sleep, and suffering from his head, back of his neck, and his eyes. The back of his neck was numb and stiff, and he could not move it. The following Wednesday he went back to work, and worked until Saturday, "sometime toward noon," when he quit on account of his head, from which he was suffering all the time. He told his foreman the reason for his quitting. He remained at home about four weeks, and then went to work for the American Railway Express Company as a freight handler. He worked at this four or five weeks, when he quit "on account of my head." "I got worse." He earned $12 per week while working for the defendant, and went to work for the express company at $80 per month, and was raised to $90 per month shortly after he went there. He suffered from his back, head, eyes, and his hearing. At the time of the trial, which was on January 19, 1920, he was still suffering from his eyes, head, and the back of his neck. His eyes pained him and "he has some kind of a blur before me." The back of his neck was "kind of stiff." Since his injury he goes to bed about 9 o'clock, and lies in bed an hour or an hour and a half before he can get to sleep, then he will sleep until about 12 o'clock, when he will get up on account of his head, and not being able to sleep any longer. Before his injury he was a bright, active boy, and played baseball, basketball, and football, and was interested in sports of this kind, but since his injury he does not engage in any such sports, feeling as though he did not want to do anything. Before his injury he was a good-natured boy, but since he has become morose, nervous, and irritable; his memory is impaired, and he hesitates before attempting to express himself, and has some stoppage in his speech; he is restless, and cries out in his sleep, and has dizzy spells.

While he was working for the American Railway Express Company, he laid off two weeks at one time, and four or five nights at another. He worked on the night shift on account of his head. He could stand night work better than he could day work. He could sleep better during the day than at night. In September plaintiff worked for the Forrester-Nace Box Company, and worked there for a week or two, earning $18 to $20 per week, when he quit and went to Eldorado, Kan., for a vacation and rest, on account of his nervousness and the condition of his health. When he returned he went to work for the Marcus Roofing Company, where he worked four or five weeks, earning $18 per week for two weeks, after which he was paid $21 per week. He quit working for the Marcus Roofing Company voluntarily, and remained from work until the 6th day of December, when he went back to the American Railway Express Company, and worked until the 29th day of December. He had not worked since.

Plaintiff's mother testified that, on the night of the injury, she looked at plaintiff's head, and saw it had a ridge across it; that he remained in bed all night, but was restless, groaning, complaining and could not sleep; that he stayed in bed from noon the next day until Tuesday at 5 o'clock; that he stayed in bed "lounging around." He complained of his head, back, and eyes bothering him; he complained from the following Wednesday until Saturday, when he came home about 11 o'clock and said that he had quit his job because he could not work. She testified that at the time of the trial plaintiff was very nervous, had spells, and she had to give him medicine to quiet him; that he sleeps very little, will dress and come down stairs sometimes in the middle of the night, at which times he would be very nervous. She testified that for 10 years before his injury he did not have headaches; that now he has dizzy spells, and would get up in the morning and hold his head, saying, "I am dizzy."

Plaintiff's father testified as to the difference in plaintiff's nature, disposition, and habits since his injury; that he is very hightempered since the injury, and "gets up and down at night;" that "he gets to hollering, and one thing or another;" that he was not this way before he was injured.

Dr. McLaughlin, on behalf of plaintiff, testified that about eight weeks before the trial he examined plaintiff, and ascertained the nature of his complaint; that he found that plaintiff was suffering from acute meningitis

of the brain; that plaintiff had dimness of vision, pain in the head, nervousness, and a fear of his physician, wanting to know if he had to be operated upon; that his reflexes were paralyzed, indicating a disease of the brain; that plaintiff had unsteadiness of gait, indicating cerebral irritation; that a lesion and concussion of the brain can be caused from a blow on the head; that there is an alteration of the brain structure in concussion, and often there is a rupture of some minor blood vessel of the brain, causing a congestion of the brain; it might be one or many, and involving the whole brain or a portion of it. He testified that plaintiff had high blood pressure and rapid pulse, which was an unusual and abnormal condition for a boy of his age; that high blood pressure and a rapid pulse were often indicative of a nervous condition, due to some injury, or, at least, to some lesion; that an injury to the brain of the kind described would render a boy's disposition morose, and cause him to lose his boyish ambition to play; that, if there is an inflammatory condition present, it causes unnatural depression, anger, and irritability; that such condition of the brain affects the eyes by pressure, and produces partial paralysis of the optic nerve; that it affects the patient's ability to walk steadily; that it causes headaches and aphasia, the latter being loss of memory and inability to articulate; that he found plaintiff suffering from an impaired memory and inability to use the tongue; that the condition in which he found plaintiff's brain was, in his opinion, permanent in character; that the trend of such an injury is toward becoming chronic, or to grow worse. The doctor gave it as his opinion that the condition in which he found plaintiff could have been brought about "while the boy was standing upright, by having a heavy object brought down on his head."

On cross-examination, Dr. McLaughlin testified that plaintiff suffered from acute meningitis at the time he examined him, and that this condition could terminate in chronic meningitis. On redirect examination he testified that the high blood pressure, the test of the reflexes, the examination of plaintiff's face and eyes, and seeing him stagger, were all objective symptoms, as distinguished from subjective; that plaintiff had no indication of a syphilitic condition. He testified that statistics show that sometimes a very slight trauma may produce such an injury as that from which plaintiff suffered. On recross-examination he was asked, if a young man had suffered an injury such as the doctor's examination showed, what would have been the immediate symptoms after receiving the injury. He answered, "shock, possibly not unconsciousness, but in a semi-conscious condition, dizziness, inability to control himself, partial relaxation of the muscles, unsteadiness, rapidity of the heart, sickness at the stomach, etc.;" that there might not form immediately a blood clot, but there would be a rupture of a blood vessel in the head; that a man would be immediately dazed and stunned; that "he would not probably be unconscious, but he would be sick, in a state of shock, and almost in a state of collapse;" that he might be able to speak and answer questions with seeming intelligence, but he would not answer them as he would were he in a normal condition. He testified that meningitis could pass from the acute to the chronic stage in six or eight weeks, and not that it would, as defendant contends he testified.

Dr. Davis, on behalf of defendant, testified that he was called to attend plaintiff after his injury, and found a lump on his head; that there was no external evidence of fracture; that he did not prescribe any medicine except a cathartic, and told the boy's mother to put him to bed and keep him quiet; that he suggested to plaintiff's mother that there was a possibility of a blood clot having formed as the result of plaintiff's injury, that a blow on the head is liable to rupture the small blood vessels, and cause such a clot; that neurasthenia, aphasia, and hysteria are symptoms of a head injury; that there had been instances known to the medical profession where a man received a blow on the head that at the time seemed insignificant, but grew into a serious injury, and had become permanent. The doctor testified that he made no examination of plaintiff; that nothing was told him at the time to suggest a serious injury, and that he did not see plaintiff afterwards; that at the time of his seeing plaintiff he did not think the injury plaintiff had received would produce the results complained of; that, in the absence of any other cause for plaintiff's condition than the blow he received on the head, he would say that the things plaintiff suffered from could have been caused by such a blow. He further testified that the usual symptoms of a blood clot forming after an injury were paralysis and unconsciousness; that usually it would require a blow sufficient to render the patient unconscious at the time he received it to cause an after effect of neurasthenia, aphasia, insomnia, and the things complained of by plaintiff; that it is not usual that an injury such as plaintiff received would result in plaintiff's condition; that sometimes this condition could result from receiving a blow that did not render the patient unconscious, but that such cases were rare.

[1] Defendant complains that the court erred in giving plaintiff's instruction No. 3, which told the jury that if they found plaintiff was injured, and as a result thereof his earning capacity or earning power would be impaired or diminished after he reached the age of 21 years, that they would allow him such sum in damages as they should believe and find would be a reasonable and fair compensation for any such impairment of his earning capacity. It is insisted that there is no evidence of any impairment of plaintiff's earning capacity, either present or future, and certainly no evidence to base the submission of impairment of earning capacity for three years in the future, plaintiff being approximately 18 years of age at the time of the trial. This complaint is based on the contention that plaintiff had lost no earnings, but that when he worked he received greater recompense than he did while working for the defendant; that the evidence fails to show that he quit work at the various times on account of his injury. The evidence expressly shows that plaintiff quit his employment with the defendant and his employment with the American Railway Express Company on account of his injury, and substantially shows that he quit work at Forrester-Nace Box Company on account of it. There is no direct evidence that he quit the other jobs on account of his injury, but there is a plain inference from the evidence that this was the cause of it, it having been apparently assumed at the trial that his injury was the cause of his quitting work at all times, although the direct question was not asked.

While the evidence is conflicting, there is substantial evidence, if believed, and the court and jury believed it, that, as the result of plaintiff's receiving the blow on his head, he suffered a serious and permanent injury, which has interfered materially with his ability to work in the 10 months that transpired from the time of his injury to the time of the trial. He did not suffer earning impairment by being unable to fully perform his duties while at work and to receive full compensation therefor, but his earning power was reduced by his inability to continue steadily at work. The evidence was of such a character that the jury might well say that he would continue to suffer such inability during the rest of his life, although the instruction does not direct the jury to allow anything for permanent injuries. We think there is no question but that there is some evidence tending to show impairment of plaintiff's earning capacity after he reaches the age of 21 years. Garner v. K. C. Bridge Co., 194 S. W. 82, 84, 85; Brohammer v. Lager, 194 S. W. 1072; Kibble v. Q., O. & K. C. R. R. Co. (Sup.) 227 S. W. 42; Nelson v. United Rys. Co., 176 Mo. App. 423, 158 S. W. 446; State ex rel. v. Reynolds, 257 Mo. 19, 165 S. W. 729; The cases of Panos v. Car & Foundry Co., 147 Mo. App. 570, 126 S. W. 815; Haire v. Schaff, 190 S. W. 56; Brown v. Planing Mill Co., 217 S. W. 332; Moses v. Klusmeyer, 194 Mo. App. 684, 186 S. W. 958; Davidson v. Transit Co., 211 Mo. 320, 109 S. W. 583, are not applicable to the facts of this case. If defendant desired to have plaintiff's damages on this score restricted to nominal damages, assuming that this is a case where such an instruction would have been proper, it should have requested an instruction to that effect. State ex rel. v. Reynolds, supra; Sang v. St. Louis, 262 Mo. 454, 463, 171 S. W. 347; Hoover v. Ry. Co. (Sup.) 227 S. W. 77, 79. Instead of this, defendant had given an instruction telling the jury that they should "only award him (plaintiff) such sum as in your opinion is a fair and reasonable compensation for injuries which he sustained."

[2, 3] Defendant contends that the verdict is against the weight of the evidence. The trial court did not sustain the motion for a new trial on this ground. The trial court having sustained the motion for a new trial, and having assigned the reason therefor, it necessarily overruled the motion as to the other grounds alleged in the motion. Callison v. Eads, 211 S. W. 715; Thiele v. Citizens' Ry. Co., 140 Mo. 319, 335, 41 S. W. 800. The matter of the weight of the evidence is exclusively for the trial court, and it having refused to sustain the motion for a new trial for that reason, its action in so doing is not reviewable by this court. Harmon v. Irwin, 219 S. W. 392; Robertson v. Kochtitzky, 217 S. W. 543; Abernathy v. Mo. Pac. Ry. Co., 217 S. W. 568; Terry v. K. C. Rys. Co., 228 S. W. 885.

[4] The trial court likewise ruled against the defendant in relation to its assignment in the motion for a new trial that the verdict is excessive, but defendant again makes the point in this court. Plaintiff's injuries have been fully set forth and discussed, supra, so it is unnecessary for us to again go into the matter. Suffice it to say that we are unable to agree that the verdict is excessive.

[5] It is insisted that plaintiff's instruction No. 1 is erroneous. This instruction reads as follows:

"You are instructed that if you believe and find from the evidence that on or about the 4th day of April, 1919, the plaintiff was in the employ of the defendant, and in the scope of his employment at the time complained of, and that he was entering upon the elevator on the fourth floor, and if you further believe and find from the evidence that while the plaintiff was entering upon the elevator at the fourth floor, if he was doing so, and while plaintiff was exercising ordinary care for his own safety, if you so find the elevator operator, Malcolm Faulkner, negligently, as negligence is elsewhere defined, pulled or jerked the elevator gate down upon the plaintiff's head, and that the plaintiff

was thereby injured, then your verdict will be for the plaintiff."

It is insisted that the instruction refers the jury to the petition for the date of plaintiff's injury, and that it should have told the jury when that date was. There was no conflict in the evidence as to the date on which plaintiff claims he was injured; therefore the date could have been omitted from the instruction entirely. In the circumstances, of course, the jury could not have been misled. Defendant's authorities holding that the instructions should not refer the jury to the pleadings for the issues in the case, are clearly not in point.

[6] It is insisted that the instruction is further erroneous in that it assumed that Faulkner, an employee of the defendant, was acting within the scope of his employment when he pulled the elevator gate down upon plaintiff's head, and that whether Faulkner was acting within the scope of his employment was a disputed fact. We find no dispute in the evidence in regard to this matter. The undisputed evidence shows that this was both a passenger and a freight elevator, and either the man who ran the elevator or the last man on it pulled the gate down. Faulkner was the man who was running the elevator at the time. In addition to this, defendant assumed in its instructions that Faulkner was acting within the scope of his employment.

[7] Complaint is made of plaintiff's instruction No. 2, which reads as follows:

"'Negligence,' or 'negligently,' as used in these instructions, means the failure to exercise ordinary care, and 'ordinary care' means such care as ordinarily careful and prudent persons usually exercise under the same or similar circumstances shown by the evidence in this case."

It is insisted that the words "as those" should have been inserted between the words "circumstances" and "shown," and that the instruction is erroneous, as it might be construed by the jury to mean that the phrase "shown by the evidence in this case" referred to such care as an ordinarily careful person usually exercises. We think the criticism of this instruction is hypercritical, and without merit.

The judgment is reversed, and the cause remanded, with instructions to the trial court to reinstate the verdict.

All concur.

MAYFIELD v. GEORGE O. RICHARDSON MACHINERY CO. (No. 13712.)

(Kansas City Court of Appeals. Missouri. May 2, 1921. Rehearing Denied May 23, 1921.)

1. **Evidence ⟚450(8)—Parol evidence admissible to elucidate indefinite warranty.**

Where a tractor sold was "to be of specification as shown in" a designated circular, in which, among the specifications of the machine, was the specification "number of plows pulled (slow speed) 8–12" and it was warranted "capable of doing as good work as similar articles of other manufacturers," *held* that neither the contract provision that no promises of an agent as to a warranty shall be binding unless ratified by the seller at its home office nor the parol evidence rule rendered inadmissible evidence that the buyer told defendant's agent that he was going to use a certain variety of 18-disc plow, and the agent said it would be all right, since the contract was indefinite as to the kind and size of plow stated, not showing whether 12, 14, or 16 inch plows were meant, or whether they were disc or moldboard plows; and under the evidence it took no more power to pull an 18-disc plow similar to that specified than it did to pull one of nine 14-inch moldboard plows, which was within the number of plows the circular specified the tractor could pull.

2. **Sales ⟚426—Under contract providing for return and rescission on failure of warranty as exclusive remedy, seller, by refusing to accept return, becomes liable for the usual damages for breach of warranty.**

Where contract for sale of a tractor provided that, on failure of warranty, the purchaser's only right would be, after due notice, to have another tractor or a return of the freight money and notes given for the purchase price, and on such failure of warranty, although the purchaser complied with the conditions precedent, and did return the tractor, the seller neither gave the purchaser another in its stead nor returned the money and notes as agreed, the seller's right to confine the purchaser to the contract remedy as exclusive was lost or waived, such exclusive remedy being conditioned upon the seller's compliance therewith; and the buyer was restored to the right to recover the usual damages for breach of warranty.

3. **Sales ⟚426 — An exclusive remedy for breach of warranty must be clearly expressed.**

A provision in a sale contract for a particular and exclusive remedy for breach of warranty will not constitute a limitation of the purchaser's remedies for breach of warranty unless such an intention is clearly expressed by the language and terms of the warranty.

4. **Sales ⟚442(16)—Purchaser on breach of warranty held entitled to recover not only freight money, but also amount he was compelled to pay on notes given for the goods.**

Where warranty of tractor sold was broken in that the tractor was worthless, the purchaser was entitled to recover not only the damages sustained on account of the breach of war-

ranty itself, but also the damages arising from the seller's violation of its agreement to return his money and notes, which would include not only freight money paid by him, but also the amount he was finally compelled to pay to get rid of the notes after litigation thereon.

5. **Sales ⟚442(6,7)—On breach of warranty of tractor, expense in endeavoring to make machine work held recoverable.**

On sale of a tractor warranted to be well made, and to work as well as others of similar character, the purchaser, on breach of the warranty, was entitled to recover the expense he had been put to in endeavoring to make the machine work.

6. **Sales ⟚442(5)—On breach of warranty of tractor, purchaser entitled to recover loss of season's use of land.**

Where a tractor proved worthless, the purchaser was entitled to recover the loss of rental value of one season's use of the land he was to plow, the machine having been sold for plowing purposes and warranted to pull a certain number of plows.

7. **Damages ⟚22 — Damages for breach of contract should compensate for actual loss naturally and proximately resulting.**

The general rule of damages for breach of contract is that the compensation should be equal to the injury, subject to the condition that the damages be confined to those naturally and proximately resulting from the breach, and be not uncertain or speculative, nor outside the contemplation of the parties.

8. **Appeal and error ⟚1170(7) — Admission of evidence held not reversible error in view of verdict which could be corrected by remittitur.**

If evidence of expense incurred in buyer's attempt to make machine work, and the rental value of land, the use of which he lost, were erroneously admitted, the judgment need not be set aside under Rev. St. 1919, § 1513, where verdict was only small amount more than it should have been, and could be corrected by remittitur.

9. **Sales ⟚437(2)—Interest not allowable on buyer's recovery for seller's breach unless asked in pleadings.**

Interest cannot be allowed buyer on recovery for seller's breach of contract and of warranty where not asked in the pleadings.

10. **Appeal and error ⟚1140(2)—Excessive recovery remediable by remittitur.**

Excessive verdict is remediable by requiring a remittitur of an amount in excess of the recoverable items.

Appeal from Circuit Court, Buchanan County; Thos. B. Allen, Judge.

Action by William A. Mayfield against the George O. Richardson Machinery Company. Judgment for plaintiff, and defendant appeals. Affirmed.

Ryan & Zwick, of St. Joseph, and Ellis, Cook & Dietrich, of Kansas City, for appellant.

⟚For other cases see same topic and KEY-NUMBER in all Key-Numbered Digests and Indexes

Culver, Phillip & Voorhees, of St. Joseph, for respondent.

TRIMBLE, P. J. This is an action for damages for various breaches of a written contract governing the purchase and sale of a 30 horse power farm tractor. Plaintiff, at the time of the purchase and the execution of said contract, and the alleged breaches thereof, resided in Oklahoma. Defendant is a Missouri corporation, with its principal office at St. Joseph.

The contract called for the purchase of the tractor, aforesaid, "tractor to be of specification as shown in circular M-2-14," and the clause containing the warranty and other agreements and conditions now in question is as follows:

"The articles specified * * * are warranted * * * to be of good material, well made, and with proper management, capable of doing as good work as similar articles of other manufacturers. If said machinery, or any part thereof, shall fail to fill this warranty, written notice by registered letter shall be given to said corporation, St. Joseph, Missouri, and to the party through whom the machinery was purchased, stating wherein it fails to fill the warranty, and time, opportunity and friendly assistance give to reach the machinery and remedy any defects. If the defective machinery cannot be made to fill the warranty, it shall be returned by the purchaser to the place where received and another furnished on the same terms of warranty, or money and notes to the amount represented, by the defective machinery shall be returned, and no further claim be made on said corporation."

The circular M-2-14 was given to plaintiff at the time contract was made; and among the many specifications of the machine therein contained, was the following: "Number of plows pulled (slow speed) 8-12."

The plaintiff agreed to pay the freight from factory to the point where plaintiff was to receive it, and receive credit therefor on the price, and to execute notes aggregating $2,500 for the purchase price, as follows: One note for $835, due September 1, 1914; one for $835, due September 1, 1915; and one for $830, due September 1, 1916. Said notes were made payable at the Capron State Bank, Capron, Okl., and they provided for interest at 7 per cent. per annum if paid on or before maturity, and 9 per cent. per annum from date if not so paid. There was also a provision for the payment of attorney's fees in case the notes were placed in the hands of an attorney for collection. The notes were executed at Capron, Okl., before the machine was shipped.

The contract and notes were executed and delivered, and the tractor was shipped by defendant to plaintiff at Capron, Okl., on June 4, 1914. Plaintiff took the tractor out to his farm, but the tractor was unsatisfactory, and worthless, not being of good

231 S.W.—19

material or well made, nor would it do the work according to the rating and terms of the contract. Plaintiff promptly notified defendant by registered letter, and defendant made two attempts to remedy the tractor's defects, but without success. Thereupon plaintiff returned the tractor to the place where he had received it, notified the defendant by registered letter, and demanded the return of his notes and the freight he had paid, which it is conceded was $140. The defendant, however, refused to take the tractor back, declined to replace the defective machine with another, and also refused plaintiff his notes and money.

At some time before the maturity of the notes, but whether before or after the rejection of the tractor does not appear, the defendant negotiated the notes to the Union National Bank of Massilon, Ohio. After their maturity, said bank brought suit on them, the first thing plaintiff knowing of said bank having the notes being when he was sued. Believing and being advised that, under the law as it then stood in Oklahoma, the notes were nonnegotiable, and that he had a good defense to them on account of the equities between him and the payee, plaintiff resisted payment under the authority of Randolph v. Hudson, 12 Okl. 516, 74 Pac. 946. The trial court upheld plaintiff's contention as to the nonnegotiability of said notes; and upon appeal, the Supreme Court of Oklahoma, in Union National Bank v. Mayfield, 169 Pac. 626, affirmed the judgment. However, later, the Supreme Court of Oklahoma reversed the judgment, and held that the notes were negotiable. Union National Bank v. Mayfield, 174 Pac. 1034, 2 A. L. R. 135. The Union National Bank being holder for value, and without notice, was not affected by any equities between the maker and payee, so plaintiff herein was compelled to pay said notes, which he did on October 18, 1918, with interest at 9 per cent., making the total payment amount to $3,700. Thereafter, on November 30, 1918, plaintiff brought this suit for the breaches aforesaid. The case was tried on May 13, 1919.

The damages claimed and sought to be recovered by plaintiff was the amount he was compelled to pay on said notes plus the freight he had paid, and also the damages he had sustained by way of expense in trying to operate said tractor, and the loss of the rental value ($2 per acre) of one season's use of the land which the seller knew plaintiff was intending to plow with said tractor and sow in wheat. Over the objections of defendant, the trial court admitted evidence as to these items, and, under instructions, authorized the jury to return a verdict in favor of plaintiff for the amount he was finally compelled to pay on said notes, as well as for the expenses he had incurred in trying to operate the tractor and for the rental value of the land for the season, the use of which he lost by reason of the failure of the tractor to do the work it was warranted to do. The jury returned a verdict in plaintiff's favor for $3,897.75, and defendant has appealed.

No complaint is made as to the sufficiency of the evidence to establish the jury's finding that the tractor was worthless, and not in accordance with the contract and warranty. The record contains ample evidence that the flywheel was smaller than the one designed for it, that the crank shaft was too short, and had been pieced or lengthened out, that the "compression" was bad, that little power could be developed, that the flywheel was "wobbly" on its shaft, and that the tractor would not do the work according to the terms of the contract. In other words, there was ample evidence that the machine was not "well made and, with proper management, capable of doing as good work as similar articles of other manufacturers," and the evidence amply tends to show that the tractor was worthless.

[1] Defendant's first complaint is that certain evidence was improperly admitted. This evidence was that, in plaintiff's locality, when a tractor was used, disc plows were ordinarily used; that it took less power to pull disc plows than it did moldboard plows; that two 8-inch disc plows wouldn't pull any harder than the one 14-inch moldboard plow; that the power required to pull a plow of 18 discs would about equal the power required to pull 9 plows each having a 14-inch moldboard; that when plaintiff was considering buying the tractor he told defendant's agent that he was going to use an Emerson 18-disc plow, and the agent said it would be all right; that in attempting to plow with it plaintiff used an Emerson 18-disc plow, and could not develop enough power to pull it, except at such a shallow depth as was wholly insufficient; that the soil in which the tractor was attempted to be used was the same kind of land in that community which is cultivated and sown in wheat.

The defendant's objection to this line of evidence is that, the warranty being express, there could be no implied warranty of fitness to do the purchaser's particular work, or to pull a particular plow, a particularly large plow of the purchaser's selection of disc type rather than of moldboard, or to plow at a particular depth on purchaser's land. The objection to the evidence as to what plaintiff, prior to the purchase, told defendant's agent what work he proposed to do with the tractor, and the size of the plow he was going to use with it, and the agent's reply thereto, further rests upon the fact that the contract contains a provision that "no promises, whether of agent, employe, or attorney, concerning the articles herein purchased, the working of or warranty thereon * * * shall be binding on said corporation unless made and ratified in writing by an executive officer at its home office;" and also upon the rule that all verbal statements and representations are merged in the written contract, and, if not appearing therein, are excluded thereby. Doubtless the objection would be good as to either one or both of these grounds had the evidence been introduced and relied upon to create or enlarge the warranty contained in the contract, but it was not offered for that purpose.

So far as the use of the tractor for plowing is concerned, the warranty is that the machine will be capable of doing as good work as similar articles of other manufacturers, and, concededly, plowing is such work as is necessarily within the scope of a farm tractor. Indeed, the contract, by specific statement that the tractor shall "be of specification as shown in circular M–2–14" made the circular a part of it, and defendant's answer admits that the defendant sold plaintiff the tractor "of the specification as shown in defendant's circular M–2–14." Now, as hereinbefore stated, this circular said the number of plows that could be pulled at slow speed was from 8 to 12. There was nothing else stated as the size or kind of plows meant, and clearly the contract was indefinite on this subject, not showing whether 12, 14, or 16 inch plows were meant, nor whether they were disc or moldboard plows. The evidence is that, when the tractor in question was demonstrated to plaintiff by defendant's agent, the demonstration was made with an 18-disc Emerson plow; that plaintiff told defendant that this was what he was going to use with the tractor, and purchased an 18-disc Emerson plow of that (the Emerson) company, and the defendant loaded it into the car and sent it along with the tractor when it was shipped to plaintiff. The evidence is further that, when the defendant's agents tried unsuccessfully to make the plow work, no complaint or objection was made that the tractor was overloaded. Under the evidence it took no more power to pull an 18-disc Emerson plow than it did to pull one of nine 14-inch moldboard plows, which was within the number of plows the circular specified the tractor could pull. The demonstration by the agent was with an 18-disc Emerson plow. The contract being indefinite as to the kind and size of plows stated, it was proper to show that both disc and moldboard plows were used in plaintiff's locality, and also to show the acts and conduct of the parties to the contract in order to throw light on the question of how defendant interpreted the contract as to the matter that was definite and obscure therein.

[2] It is next contended that, under the contract, in case of a failure of warranty,

the only right of the plaintiff purchaser was, after due notice of such failure, to have another tractor or a return of the freight money and notes given for the purchase price. In other words, the contention is this was to be the full extent of defendant's liability for the breach of warranty, and the contract made this measure of his damages therefor exclusive. Hence the defendant says the only recovery plaintiff is entitled to have, if any, is the freight money he paid (shown to have been $14, and conceded to be that much), and the value of the notes, i. e., the amount plaintiff would have had to pay had he redeemed them at the earliest opportunity.

There is an almost innumerable array of authorities stating, in general terms, the rule that parties to a contract may stipulate for a special remedy in case of a breach of warranty, and where this is done they are limited and bound by the remedy thus provided, and such stipulation furnishes the basis of the complainant's rights as to the breach of warranty and the measure of damages for the breach; but, in almost every one of the many cases we have examined, the suit was either one wherein the purchase price was all that was demanded or defended against, or where the complaining purchaser had failed to follow out the procedure stipulated as a condition precedent to an enforcement of the warranty. Of course, in such cases, the question of whether the complaining purchaser was entitled to anything other than a release from or a return of the purchase price was in no wise involved. But the present case does not fall within the category of either of the above classes of cases. Here, the plaintiff purchaser did comply with the conditions precedent, and did return the tractor; and the defendant neither gave plaintiff another in its stead nor returned the "money and notes" it agreed to do.

The only case to which we have been cited, or which, in our independent investigations, we have been able to find, which is squarely in point, and upholds defendant's contention, is Helvetia Copper Co. v. Hart-Parr Co., 142 Minn. 74, 79, 171 N. W. 272, 274. The warranty in that case contained a clause similar to the one herein, providing for return of the article purchased, if it was not as warranted, and for a refund of the purchase price, "and no further claim is to be made." Plaintiff in that case offered to return the article, but the company refused to give another or to refund the money. Suit was for general damages, and the trial court submitted the case on the theory that the refusal of the company to give another machine or to refund the money entitled plaintiff to sue for all damages he sustained. The appellate court said:

"This we think was error. We do not understand that a refusal to receive a return of the tractor and to refund the price made, perhaps, in good faith, and under a bona fide claim that refundment was not due, will give rise to the right to sue for damages for breach of warranty, a right which was expressly contracted away."

The court goes on to say they do not "find any decision directly in point," but that—

"The contract provides the remedy for its breach by defendant. Breach by defendant will not give rise to another remedy."

It seems to us that the purchaser's right to sue for general damages for the breach was not unconditionally "contracted away," but that the agreement to make no further claim on the company was conditioned on the agreement of the company to either give another machine or refund the money. In the case of American Foundry, etc., Co. v. Board of Education, 131 Wis. 220, 226, 110 N. W. 403, 406, the court say:

"Upon being so notified of the * * * failure the plaintiff was bound by the contract to do the one thing or the other."

The agreement of the company that it would do this is the basis and the condition, and the only consideration, for the purchaser's giving up his right to general damages. In the Wisconsin case just cited, the suit was by the seller for the balance of the purchase price, but the defendant purchasers counterclaimed for general damages in excess of the amount they had paid. The jury found a verdict not only releasing defendants from paying the balance due on contract, but also gave them a verdict for the amount they had paid, and for other damages they had sustained. The plaintiff appealed, but the verdict was sustained, and the judgment was affirmed. In 24 R. C. L. 250, § 528, it is said:

"The parties to a sale may, by an express provision, limit the right of the buyer, in case of a breach of warranty, to a return of the goods and recovery of the price, and where such is the case the buyer cannot maintain an action for damages *unless* he has tendered a return and the same has been refused by the seller." (Italics ours.)

In the same volume of said work, at page 253, § 531, it is said:

"If the buyer has duly tendered a return, and the seller refuses to accept the same, the buyer may then resort to his action for damages or defend against an action for the price."

[3] No doubt, if the parties to a contract agree upon a particular remedy for a breach of warranty, and expressly and clearly intend to unqualifiedly limit the remedy of the purchaser to the one therein prescribed, the contract will be given this construction, but such contracts do not constitute a limitation

of the purchaser's remedies for a breach of warranty unless such intention is clearly expressed by the language and terms of the warranty. Nave v. Powell, 52 Ind. App. 496, 96 N. E. 395. It is elementary that where the form and wording of the contract is the work of one of the parties, if there is any ambiguity in the meaning or construction of any part of it, such will be resolved against him and in favor of the other party; and it is also elementary that courts will construe the language of a contract, where there is room for construction, according to the intention of the parties, and this intention will be gathered from the language used in a contract as a whole, and from the surrounding facts and circumstances.

Now, the contract in this case clearly, it seems to us, does not unconditionally limit the purchaser's rights to a return of the machine and the receipt of another, or a return of the purchase money. Such limitation follows, and is coupled with, and is necessarily dependent upon, the agreement of the company that it will do either one of the two things above mentioned. To say that the purchaser agreed that, at all events, he would make no other claim on the company, is to read something into the contract that is not there. In Wilson v. Nichols, 139 Ky. 506, 514, 97 S. W. 18, it is held that contracts, such as in the case at bar, do not leave the buyer entirely without remedy if he sustains damages by reason of the failure or refusal·of the seller to comply with his warranty (i. e., giving him a good machine or returning his "money and notes"), since, if the purchaser is compelled to and does return the machine because the seller fails or refuses, in a reasonable time after notice, to comply with his warranty, the purchaser has a cause of action against the seller for damages resulting to him. In Allen v. Tompkins, 136 N. C. 208, 211, 48 S. E. 655, it is said that, if the seller, upon demand for a new machine in accordance with the terms of his contract, refuses to comply therewith, then the provision as to remedy no longer applies, and the purchaser may have recourse to the ordinary remedies for a breach of warranty. In Warder v. Robertson, 75 Iowa, 585, 588, 39 N. W. 905, 906) it is said:

"When the breach occurred, and they [the sellers] neglected to perform their undertaking, he [the purchaser] had the right, independent of the contract, to rescind the sale because of such breach and neglect. It was competent for the parties to make provision as to the course to be pursued in case of a failure of the warranty. * * * But when plaintiffs [the sellers] neglected to perform the undertaking on their part, the performance of which was precedent to defendant's right to avail himself of the remedy provided by the contract, its remedial provisions were *abandoned*, and he could avail himself of such remedies as would have been open to him if that condition had never been embodied in the contract." (Italics ours.)

It is true, in the case the return of the machine may have been permissive, rather than mandatory, but the principle enunciated and here considered would seem to apply equally to a case where the return was mandatory on the purchaser. And it would seem that in a great many of the cases where it is said, in general terms, that a contract, such as the one in the case at bar, gives a purchaser an "exclusive remedy" and limits him to that, the meaning is that he is limited to the course to be pursued, and not that he is limited to a mere rescission of the contract if he has pursued the course prescribed, and the other party has refused to perform on his part. The purchaser has the right of rescission, independent of the contract, and if the provision as to rescission—i. e., return of machine and receipt of another, or get his money back—is violated by the seller, what consideration has been given the purchaser for surrendering his right to pursue his legal remedy for all damages lawfully accruing to him from the breach?

That such is the proper effect to be given to the refusal of the company to comply with the agreement on its part is further supported by the fact that the contract nowhere expressly says the purchaser is, at all events, limited to a rescission of the contract (which, of course, he is, if his only recourse is to merely get his money back), and also by the fact that the contract elsewhere provides that all warranties shall be void if the purchaser does not comply with the terms of the contract on his part. To say that the contract limits the purchaser's damages on account of a broken warranty to merely a return of the purchase price, even if the seller does not comply with his agreement to give a new machine or return the price, while at the same time the contract provides that, if the purchaser violates the terms of the contract on his part, the seller is relieved of its warranty, is to put a construction on the whole contract that we are unwilling to adopt.

The idea expressed by the court in the Helvetia Copper Co. Case, supra, that breach by defendant will not give rise to another remedy, may be proper in that case in view of the sole ground upon which that suit was brought, namely, on a breach of the warranty itself, and not a breach of the agreement to comply with the obligation of the seller to give a new machine or return the purchase price. But such theory cannot be applied to the case at bar, since the petition declares on different breaches of contract, including the breach in relation to the warranty, as well as the breach of the agreement that the company, upon failure of the warranty, and notice thereof, and return of the property, would either give plaintiff a good machine or return the freight money and notes.

[4] We are, therefore, of the opinion that

the plaintiff was entitled to at least recover not only the damages he had sustained on account of the breach of warranty itself, but also the damages arising from defendant's violation of its agreement to return his "money and notes." This would at least include not only the $140 freight money and the value of the notes as of the time he could have first redeemed them without a contest as to their validity, but the amount he was finally compelled to pay in order to get rid of them, when the Supreme Court of Oklahoma at last decided the notes were negotiable. The plaintiff was not required to decide for himself, and at his own risk, the question of law as to the negotiability of the notes. Had he done so, and paid the notes without making his defense, he would doubtless have been met here with that objection.

[5] The contention of defendant that plaintiff is not entitled to recover the expense he was at in endeavoring to make the machine work because the contract of purchase clearly contemplates that the purchaser should use the machine to determine whether it came up to the warranty, proceeds on the assumption that the purchaser's damages are limited, at all events, to a return of the purchase price, and ignores the breach of the company's contract that the machine was well made, and would work as others of similar character, and that, if it did not, they would give him another or return his purchase "money and notes."

[6] The same is true as to the loss of the rental value ($2 per acre) of one season's use of the land he was to plow. This was not under any implied warranty of fitness of the machine, for the contract expressly provided that the machine would pull from 8 to 12 plows and would do that work as well as other tractors of similar kind. The machine was sold for plowing purposes, and was purchased for that work, as shown by the contract itself, and this feature does not therefore rest upon the oral promise of defendant's agent. Nor was such loss not within the reasonable contemplation of the parties, nor could it be excluded as being within the category of lost profits. The rental value of land is something definite and easily capable of being ascertained, not subject to elements of uncertainty, contingency, competition, etc., as are profits in a business.

[7] The general rule of damages for breach of contract is that the compensation should

be equal to the injury, subject to the condition that the damages be confined to those naturally and proximately resulting from the breach, and be not uncertain or speculative, nor outside the contemplation of the parties. Minneapolis Threshing Machine Co. v. Bradford, 227 S. W. 628.

[8-10] Even if the plaintiff were not entitled to recover the expense incurred in the unavailing attempt to make the machine work, nor the loss of the $2 per acre rental value of the land he lost the use of, still this would not necessarily call for a reversal of the case. The $140 freight expense is concededly correct and recoverable. The amount plaintiff was compelled to pay on the notes October 18, 1918, was a little over $3,700, and this, with the freight bill of $140, would aggregate $3,840. The verdict, being for $3,-897.75, is only $57.75 more than the amount plaintiff was actually compelled to pay out in cash on the freight and notes themselves, to say nothing of any other item of damage. If, in addition to the amounts thus actually paid out in cash by plaintiff on these two items alone, he be given interest at 6 per cent. from the time they were paid until the date of the trial, May 19, 1919, the result would be to bring the total far above the verdict, and more than wipe out the aforesaid $57.75. We do not construe the petition as asking for interest, however. Certainly it does not specifically ask for it, and hence interest cannot be relied upon to absorb the aforesaid $57.75. This would not call for a reversal of the judgment and a remand of the cause. Even if it were error to admit the evidence as to the last two items of damage, we cannot "believe that error was committed * * * materially affecting the merits of the action." Section 1513, R. S. 1919; King v. St. Louis, 250 Mo. 501, 514, 157 S. W. 498; Jones v. Prudential Ins. Co., 173 Mo. App. 1, 17, 155 S. W. 1106; Bierderman v Interstate, etc., Co., 172 Mo. App. 1, 12, 154 S. W. 843. If it were erroneous to admit the evidence, and interest be not allowable, still the excess of the verdict could, in that case, be remedied by requiring a remittitur of that amount. Reading v. Chicago, etc., R. Co., 188 Mo. App. 41, 48, 49, 173 S. W. 451. We do not, however, regard the evidence as being inadmissible, and hence will not require a remittitur, but will affirm the judgment as it stands. It is so ordered.

All concur.

RUENZI v. PAYNE, Agent.   (No. 13966.)

(Kansas City Court of Appeals.   Missouri.
May 23, 1921.)

1. **Railroads ⚖═313—Omission of statutory signal prima facie negligence.**

Under Rev. St. 1919, § 9943, the operation of a fast passenger train through and over the streets of an incorporated city without ringing the bell is prima facie negligence.

2. **Railroads ⚖═317—Violation of speed ordinance held negligence.**

The operation of a train across city streets at an excessive rate of speed in violation of city ordinance constitutes negligence.

3. **Railroads ⚖═316(4)—Speed of 50 miles an hour common-law negligence.**

The running of a train through a city and across the streets at a rate of 50 to 60 miles an hour constitutes common-law negligence.

4. **Railroads ⚖═338—Contributory negligence no defense under humanitarian rule.**

Contributory negligence of pedestrian struck at crossing is no defense against railroad's violation of humanitarian rule.

5. **Railroads ⚖═350(25)—Contributory negligence of pedestrian with obstructed view held for jury.**

In an action for the death of a 65 year old pedestrian struck by a west-bound passenger train after she had crossed two tracks without having been able to view the third track to the east because of buildings obstructing the view in that direction before reaching first track, where she was not familiar with schedule of trains, and her attention was attracted to a freight train approaching in the opposite direction on the second track, making it impossible to hear the passenger train, the question whether she was contributorily negligent in not looking to the east after entering on the first track, and before crossing such third track, held for the jury.

6. **Railroads ⚖═327(5)—Failure to look both ways for trains held negligence.**

One who knowingly approaches a railroad crossing must look both ways for approaching trains, and failure to so do is negligence precluding recovery, but such rule is not so unyielding that it must be applied in all its rigor under all circumstances; the measure of caution to be observed depending upon the circumstances.

7. **Railroads ⚖═324(1)—Care required of pedestrian.**

A pedestrian approaching a railroad crossing is required to exercise merely that degree of care which should be expected of an ordinarily careful and prudent person in the same situation, in view of all the circumstances, and is not held to the greatest degree of care.

8. **Railroads ⚖═312(4)—Lookout required.**

Employees operating a train through city toward street crossing track at the rate of from 50 to 60 miles an hour are required to keep a sharp lookout for persons crossing the track.

9. **Railroads ⚖═338—Discovered peril doctrine applied.**

Train operatives who in violation · of law negligently place themselves in a situation where they know they cannnot avoid injuring a traveler after her peril is, or with ordinary care could have been, discovered, are in the same situation as if they had discovered her peril in time and had negligently failed to act.

10. **Railroads ⚖═350(33)—Negligence under humanitarian rule held for jury.**

In an action for the death of a pedestrian struck by train at a crossing, where it was claimed that deceased was contributorily negligent, the applicability of the humanitarian rule held for the jury.

11. **Trial ⚖═252(9)—Instruction on contributory negligence held contrary to the evidence.**

In action under Rev. St. 1919, § 4217, against railroad for death of pedestrian at crossing, the giving of an instruction that, if the train could not have been seen or heard by her while she was approaching the crossing and before she had reached a place of danger, she could not have been held negligent for having failed to see or hear the train before reaching such place of danger, held erroneous; the evidence being the other way.

Appeal from Circuit Court, Boone County; D. H. Harris, Judge.

Action by William Ruenzi, administrator of the estate of Julia Bell, deceased, against John Barton Payne, Agent, substituted for defendant Walker D. Hines, Director General of Railroads. Judgment for plaintiff, and defendant appeals. Reversed and remanded.

McBaine & Clark and Jas. E. Boggs, all of Columbia, for appellant.

Don C. Carter, of Sturgeon, and J. M. Johnson and Donald W. Johnson, both of Kansas City, for respondent.

TRIMBLE, P. J. The administrator-plaintiff herein, under the fourth clause of the death statute (now section 4217, R. S. 1919), brought this suit, praying a recovery of $2,000 because of the death of Julia Bell, who was killed at the Wabash Railroad crossing on Ogden street in the city of Sturgeon, Mo. Verdict and judgment for the above-named amount were obtained, and the defendant has appealed.

Sturgeon is a city of the fourth class, and Ogden street, 80 feet wide, runs north and south and, being the main business street of the town, is a much-traveled thoroughfare. The Wabash Railroad runs east and west through the town and crosses Ogden street at right angles. Mrs. Bell was 65 years old and a widow with no children, but she had several brothers and sisters. She was proceeding as a pedestrian north along the sidewalk on the west side of Ogden street about 5:40 p. m. of August 29, 1919, and, as stated, attempted to cross over the main line of the Wabash Railway, when she was struck and instantly killed by the Wabash west-bound fast passenger train, the road being then in the control of and operated by the Director General.

Many years before this Mrs. Bell had lived in Sturgeon, but she was a visitor and stranger there at the time, having been in town only about a week, and knew nothing of the schedule of trains nor of the running of this fast train through the town without stopping.

In proceeding north along the west side of the street, there are three tracks to be encountered, first, the house track, next, the passing track, and, last, the main track, on the last of which Mrs. Bell was killed. According to plaintiff's evidence, the passing or middle track was 8 feet north of the first or house track, the main track was 8 feet north of the middle track, and it was 32 feet from the south rail of the first track to the north rail of the main line or last track. According to defendant's plat, the middle track was 10 feet 3 inches north of the first track, the main track was 13 feet 5 inches north of the middle track, and the two rails of each track were 5 feet apart, making it 38 feet 8 inches from the south rail of the first track to the north rail of the main line or last track.

The house and passing track, after beginning somewhere west of Ogden street, ran east to and across said street, parallel with the main track, and continued thus eastward beyond Ogden street for a distance of 380 feet to a switch where the said two tracks merged into the main line. The depot was immediately west of Ogden street and on the north side of the main track. From the depot eastward to the above-mentioned switch the ground on which all the tracks lay was practically level, but from the switch continuing on eastward there was considerable down grade to a point about 200 yards from a bridge, which bridge is said to be "hardly a quarter" of a mile east of the switch, and from said point to and past the bridge going east there was a heavy up grade.

South of and alongside the first or house track, and from Ogden street eastward, there was a line of buildings, a coal house, oil tanks and two or three elevator buildings. These obstructed a view of the tracks and of a train approaching from the east, by any one going north along the west side of Ogden street, until the first track was reached. When this point was reached a pedestrian could see down the main track at least to the switch, a distance of 380 feet as heretofore stated. After passing over the first track a pedestrian could see east along the main track for a distance of "a quarter of a mile or further," and when on the second or middle track one could see east along the main track for two miles.

About 80 or 100 feet south of the crossing and 'on the west side of the street is a chicken house, and plaintiff's evidence is that when Mrs. Bell, in her northward journey along the sidewalk, reached the chicken house, a freight train headed east and on the middle track 125 feet west of the crossing began moving, emitting steam, puffing and making a noise which she could hear, but she could not see the freight train on account of the string of cars on the first track extending west from Ogden street. She looked in that direction until she came to the first track where the car jutted out over the sidewalk. Here she made a little detour out into the street around the end of the car and back to the sidewalk again. As she came around the end of the projecting car she was looking at the puffing freight engine as it was moving slowly toward the crossing emitting clouds of steam and making a noise as heretofore stated. It was then 50 or 60 feet west of the crossing. She acted as though she decided, from the slow rate the freight was moving and the distance it was away, that she had plenty of time to cross, and thereupon hastened her speed and continued on north, watching the freight train. Various persons in the vicinity who knew the fast passenger from the east was due and was coming, and who observed that her attention was wholly absorbed by the freight train, and that she had not at any time looked eastward, and was therefore unaware of the approach of the passenger train, began shouting warnings to her. She could not hear what the shouters were saying because of the noise the freight train was making. The evidence in plaintiff's behalf is that the shouts excited her, at least she acted that way; that "she acted like she didn't know whether she could get across for the freight or not"; that, although she had theretofore accelerated her speed, yet when she got in the center of the middle track she broke into a run and continued north, all the time keeping her eyes on the moving freight train. She had reached the north rail of the main track and was just ready to step over it when the fast passenger from the east, 10 minutes late and coming at the rate of 50 or 60 miles an hour, struck her and hurled her body a distance of 80 or 90 feet toward the other or west end of the depot platform, killing her instantly. She at no time looked eastward, and there is no evidence that she ever was conscious of the approach of the train that struck her. There is no question but that the train was going at great speed, as the engineer himself (a witness for defendant) says he was going 50 miles an hour. All of the evidence is that the train approached and crossed Ogden street without slackening speed, and the evidence in plaintiff's behalf, from various disinterested sources, is that no bell was rung nor whistle sounded after the station signal was given "over the hill about a mile from town," except a whistle blown at or shortly before the instant it struck her.

The petition contained five charges of negligence, namely:

(1) Failure to perform the statutory duty of ringing the bell while passing through the town and approaching the crossing.

(2) Running the train through the city at a rate of speed in excess of six miles per hour in violation of a city ordinance prescribing that limit.

(3) Common-law negligence in running the train through the city at a highly dangerous and negligent rate of speed.

(4) Obstructing the sidewalk at the crossing of the house track and failing to have a watchman at the crossing to warn pedestrians of the approach of the train.

(5) A violation of the humanitarian rule in that the operatives of said train had time and opportunity to discover the peril of deceased and that she was oblivious thereto in time, by the exercise of ordinary care, to have warned her of the approach of said train by the sounding of the whistle or the ringing of the bell, and thereby to have avoided the injury, but they negligently failed to discover the peril of deceased and negligently failed to sound the whistle or ring the bell after they had discovered, or in the exercise of reasonable care should have discovered, her peril and the fact that she was oblivious to the same. The answer was a general denial coupled with a plea of contributory negligence.

[1-3] The defendant offered a general demurrer both at the close of plaintiff's evidence and at the close of all the evidence, and now insists that the demurrer should have been sustained. Unquestionably the evidence was more than amply sufficient to support practically all of the charges of negligence on the part of the defendant alleged in the petition. Running a fast passenger train through and over the streets of an incorporated city without ringing the bell was prima facie negligence under the statute (section 9943, R. S. 1919). Day v. Missouri, etc., R. Co., 132 Mo. App. 707, 714, 112 S. W. 1019; Roberts v. Wabash R. Co., 113 Mo. App. 6, 9, 87 S. W. 601. It was also negligent to run the train at such an excessive rate of speed in violation of the ordinance on that subject. Stotler v. Chicago, etc., R. Co., 200 Mo. 107, 98 S. W. 509; Kellny v. Missouri Pac. R. Co., 101 Mo. 67, 13 S. W. 806, 8 L. R. A. 783; Gratiot v. Missouri Pacific R. Co., 116 Mo. 450, 21 S. W. 1094, 16 L. R. A. 189. And, regardless of any ordinance, there was unquestionably common-law negligence in running the train at such a high and dangerous rate of speed through the city and across the streets thereof.

[4] So that, so far as concerns all of the aforesaid charges of negligence except the violation of the humanitarian theory, the question of what disposition should have been made of the demurrer depends upon whether the decedent must be declared to be guilty of contributory negligence as a matter of law. Contributory negligence would constitute no defense against the charged violation of the humanitarian rule. Lloyd v. St. Louis, etc., R. Co., 128 Mo. 595, 29 S. W. 153, 31 S. W. 110. The demurrer was general in its terms, namely, that under the law and the evidence the verdict must be for the defendant. It did not separate the other charges from the one in relation to the violation of the humanitarian rule, and hence it might perhaps be said that the mere action of the court in overruling the demurrer could not be held reversible error, since it was not up to the court to apply a general demurrer to certain of the pleaded charges only, when the defendant did not take the trouble to make the demurrer specific, but offered it generally as to all, including the negligence as to the violation of the humanitarian rule. Torrance v. Pryor, 210 S. W. 430, 432. But, as in the Torrance Case, the question of whether decedent was guilty of contributory negligence as a matter of law is material, since the case was submitted not only on the alleged violation of the humanitarian rule, but also on all of the other charges of negligence alleged in the petition.

[5] According to plaintiff's own evidence, Mrs. Bell, when she passed around the car and over the first track, was 21 feet from the south rail of the main track, and there was no obstruction to prevent her at that point from seeing east down the main track certainly to the switch 380 feet away and for a quarter of a mile or more, had she looked in that direction. There is some claim in plaintiff's briefs that if the train at that time, or before she reached the first track, was beyond the level stretch extending to the switch, it could not have been seen, on account of the slope in the grade that began at the switch and went east to within about 200 yards of the bridge. We find nothing in the record disclosing that, if the train was in the depression caused by the down grade there, it could not have been seen. Besides, Oden, one of the plaintiff's witnesses, says that if, after Mrs. Bell crossed the first track, she had looked to the east, she would have seen the train coming, for it was in sight and he saw it. At this time she was at least 20 feet from the main track, and could have stopped there in a place of safety. She was watching the freight engine 50 or 60 feet away moving slowly toward the crossing, puffing and blowing off steam, and at the shouted warnings she appeared excited and continued hurriedly on her way until, when she got in the center of the middle track, she broke into a run or "dog trot" to and upon the main track in the attempt to get across it. Had she looked east when on the middle track she would have seen the train, for necessarily it was nearer the crossing than when she pass-

ed over the first track. According to plaintiff's evidence the middle track was 8 feet from the main track, and according to defendant's evidence it was 13 feet 5 inches distant. This was a rather narrow space, taking the widest measurement, for an elderly woman to have stopped in and stood while the freight train passed behind her and a fast passenger went in front of her on the main track. But clearly she did not break into a run from the center of the middle track in order to beat the passenger across, because all the evidence is that she was at all times watching the freight train and never once looked east and never did become conscious of the approach of the passenger train. We have no means of knowing whether deceased knew the freight train was on the middle track. Ordinarily it would seem that it would be comparatively easy for her to see that the freight train, only 50 or 60 feet away, was on the middle, and not on the main, track; and yet, in view of the evidence that she was excited by the warning shouts and all the time kept watching the freight train, and, after getting off the middle track, continued at her increased pace to and across the main track, the inference is at least not unwarrantable (and therefore permissible to the jury) that she, in her excitement, became uncertain as to which track the freight train was on, and, in obedience to the warning shouts, endeavored to get surely out of the way as soon as possible by getting clear of both tracks. She was not guilty of contributory negligence in attempting, when she came around the car, to cross in front of the freight train, because it was coming at such a rate of speed and was far enough away to enable her to rightly judge that she could safely attempt to cross in front of it. The warning shouts and the excitement they produced on her evidently created in her mind the idea that there was greater danger from the freight train than she had thought, and hence she endeavored to get out of all possible danger by getting off of and beyond both tracks. She ought not to be held conclusively guilty of contributory negligence because she did not look east at the time she was on the middle track, because her mind was at that moment absorbed in the danger which she thought threatened her from the freight train. To expect her to look east at that time, and under those circumstances, would be demanding of her a high and extraordinary degree of care, and not the ordinary care of an ordinarily prudent and careful person. At least we cannot, as a matter of law, say she should at that time have looked east in order to be in the exercise of ordinary care.

But, regardless of whether she was negligent in not looking east when and after she reached the middle track, the fact remains that when she came around the car on the first track she was at least 8 feet from the middle track and 20 or 21 feet from the main track. At that time she was in a place of safety, and if she had looked east then, she could have seen the approaching passenger train, and would have learned the real source of danger and the peril of proceeding further. Hence the question narrows down to whether Mrs. Bell must be deemed to have been conclusively guilty of contributory negligence because she did not, upon passing around the car on the first track and before reaching the middle track, take the precaution to also look east, notwithstanding the situation and circumstances then confronting her. Here was a woman 65 years of age approaching a crossing where there were three parallel tracks all comparatively close together. She comes to the first track, on which is a line of standing cars, the east one thereof projecting out over the sidewalk, so that she walks out into the street and back again in a detour around the car and over the track. Before she reaches this first track she hears the noise and movement of a train located west of the crossing and on the other side of the line of standing cars. She cannot see the train because of the standing cars, but she knows it is moving east toward the crossing, and knows, too, that it is not on the track on which the standing cars are; hence she knows there is no danger in attempting to pass over the first track. She is a visitor in town and is unaware of the fact (which the others in that vicinity did know) that a fast train, which went through the town at high speed without stopping, was past due and was momentarily expected. Up to the time she reached the first track there is no opportunity to see east of the crossing, for a line of buildings obstructs the view in that direction. Even if the passenger train did whistle a mile from town, it was before she reached the first track, and would not be likely to attract her attention, especially as she heard and was paying attention to the puffing and movement of the freight train. Her attention is somewhat engaged in making the detour from the sidewalk in order to get around the obstruction which the defendant wrongfully placed on the walk. With her mind at least partially on the matter of getting around the car on the first track, but more largely on the freight train, which she could hear, but could not see, approaching the crossing, she goes around the car and over the first track. She is looking west to catch sight of and watch the freight train, and, thinking that she can cross in safety, she proceeds on north still watching the train, when on account of the shouts, which she could not understand, she becomes excited and breaks into a run either in obedience to the shouts or because the shouts have raised a lack of confidence in her judgment as to the danger from the freight train, and when on the main track she is struck by another train of whose approach she was totally unaware. Under these circumstances was she conclusively guilty of contributory negligence because she did not also take the precaution to look east for danger from that source? As said by Gill, J., in McNown v. Wabash R. Co., 55 Mo. App. 585, 590:

"The announcement of the principles of law controlling this character of cases is often easier than their application to a given state of facts."

[6, 7] It has been several times held by the Supreme Court, and it is well settled not only in decisions of that but of the other courts of our state, that when one knowingly approaches a railroad crossing he must look both ways, and, if he does not, it is negligence that will defeat a recovery. Burge v. Wabash R. Co., 244 Mo. 76, 94, 148 S. W. 925; Dyrcz v. Missouri Pac. R. Co., 238 Mo. 33, 47, 141 S. W. 861; Baker v. Kansas City, etc., R. Co., 122 Mo. 533, 544, 26 S. W. 20; Kelly v. Chicago, etc., R. Co., 88 Mo. 534; Weller v. Chicago, etc., R. Co., 120 Mo. 635, 23 S. W. 1061, 25 S. W. 532; Vandeventer v. Chicago, etc., R. Co., 177 S. W. 834; State ex rel. v. Reynolds, 214 S. W. 121. But in all of the cases of which we are aware where the injured person was held guilty of contributory negligence in not looking both ways there were no circumstances which reasonably called for the attention of the injured person in the exercise of care to avoid injury, such as exist in this case. The deceased is not to be held to the exercise of the greatest degree of care, but only that degree of care which should be expected of an ordinarily careful and prudent person in her situation, and in view of all the surrounding circumstances.

"In determining the issue of contributory negligence there is no inflexible formula to apply to all cases. Each must be ruled in view of the peculiar characteristics it exhibits. Acts which in one state of circumstances might be justly pronounced obviously and conclusively negligent may be consistent with ordinary prudence in a changed condition of the surroundings." Kenney v. Hannibal, etc., R. Co., 105 Mo. 270, 284, 285, 15 S. W. 983, 986.

Also, as stated in this and other cases, before we can hold, as a matter of law, that she was guilty of contributory negligence, the evidence must be such as to permit of no other conclusion than that she was negligent, giving plaintiff the benefit of every reasonable inference that may be drawn from the evidence. Whenever the question as to whether a person acted as an ordinarily prudent person would have acted under the same or similar circumstances arises on a state of facts on which reasonable men may fairly arrive at different conclusions, then the question is one for the jury. McNown v. Wabash R. Co., 55 Mo. App. 585. The rule that one

approaching a crossing must look both ways or be guilty of contributory negligence as a matter of law "is not so unyielding that it must be applied in all of its rigor under all circumstances." Baker v. Kansas City, etc., R. Co., 122 Mo. 533, 544, 26 S. W. 20. In Weller v. Chicago, etc., R. Co., 120 Mo. 635, 647, 23 S. W. 1061, 1063, it is said:

"The measure of precaution to be observed by a traveler depends often upon the circumstances and surroundings."

In 20 R. C. L. 112, it is said:

"The acts required to be done with a view to the preservation of safety will depend, necessarily, upon the circumstances of the case; the standard of care being that exercised by ordinarily prudent persons under like circumstances."

On page 115 of the same volume of said work it is said:

"But a person may be so situated as to be disabled without fault on his part to look or listen for perils by which he may be menaced. His attention *may have been distracted to legitimate objects.* It has been said that contributory negligence will not in all cases be imputed as a matter of law to a person who receives an injury from a danger simply from the fact that it might have been seen, because the nature of his duties, *or the surrounding circumstances, may be such as to distract his attention* to other objects. It is only in a plain case that a failure to look or listen can be said to be negligence as a matter of law; the issue in this respect being ordinarily for the jury's determination." (Italics ours.)

In 1 Thompson on Neg. § 189, it is said that—

"Contributory negligence will not in all cases be imputed to a person who received an injury from a danger which might have been seen, and avoided if seen, because the nature of his duties, or the surrounding circumstances, may be such as to distract his attention to other objects."

Now, of course, the very presence of the tracks was a warning of danger, and nothing could legitimately engage the attention of decedent and cause her to omit looking to the east except something that was an apparent danger to her which called for attention. But the freight train moving toward the crossing she was about to pass over was such a legitimate object of her attention, and it was one that would reasonably and naturally occupy her attention and would lead her to understand that it was because of danger from it that the shouted warnings were given. Under these circumstances are we justified in saying that unquestionably a reasonably prudent person under those circumstances would have also looked east? We think we are not. She was not going forward exercising no care. She was exercising care toward what she thought, and from her standpoint what she had reason to think, was the source of danger to her, and from which she exercised care to escape. The noise and puffing of the engine pulling the freight train would naturally keep her from hearing the rumble of the approaching west-bound train even if it, at that time, had been close enough to have given warning by its natural rumble and roar. There is no evidence, however, that she ought to have heard its roar, and, since the train was coming at the rate of from 76 to 88 feet a second, it was a considerable distance down the track east of the crossing before deceased got on the middle track. In other words, there was a combination of circumstances surrounding this elderly lady which could easily and naturally draw her mind wholly toward the apprehended danger on the west and put her into a state of mind which might excuse her for failing to take the added precaution of looking to the east. We cannot say that conclusively an ordinarily prudent and careful person in her situation, acting with ordinary prudence, would have looked east; and hence we feel constrained to hold that the question of her contributory negligence was for the jury.

[8-10] It is urged that there is no room for invoking the humanitarian rule because the deceased suddenly passed from a place of safety to one of danger so closely in front of a fast approaching train that there was no time for anything to have been done to save her. But the evidence does not conclusively show this to be the case. At the time plaintiff came around the car on the first track the train was close to, if indeed it had not reached, the switch. The operatives of the train were running it at from 50 to 60 miles per hour and approaching a place where they knew persons might likely be at any moment. It was their duty to keep a sharp lookout for such and if, in violation of law, they negligently place themselves in a situation where they know they cannot avoid injuring a traveler after her peril is, or with ordinary care could be, discovered, they are in the same situation as if they had discovered her peril in time and had negligently failed to act. Goben v. Quincy, etc., R. Co., 226 S. W. 631, 633. But the case need not rest upon this narrow basis, for there is sufficient evidence in the case to enable the jury to reasonably find that the operatives did have time to avert the tragedy either by sounding the whistle, ringing the bell, or slackening the speed even in a slight degree. When she came around the end of the car she was looking west, and continually looked in that direction as she went on toward the track. She was in the range of the engineer's vision the entire time she was traveling from the first track to the main line. Her obliviousness to danger was apparent to every one in that vicinity observing her from various vantage points, some of them not as good as the engineer had. While the train was thus traveling from the switch to the crossing, the train operatives, though they could not stop, could at least have given a warning, or, if they had slackened speed, she would have had time to take that final step to life and safety which she was not permitted to take. According to the plaintiff nothing of the kind was done, and according to the defendant's evidence the train operatives did not discover her until the train was 25 feet from the crossing.

From what has been said in the foregoing, we are of the opinion that the demurrer to the evidence was properly overruled under the peculiar circumstances of this case.

Complaint is made of several of the instructions, only one of which we shall discuss. This is plaintiff's instruction No. 7. In reality, it is four instructions in one, each paragraph being in fact an instruction separate and complete in itself. The first three paragraphs or instructions embodied in instruction No. 7 are on the subject of decedent's contributory negligence, and the last paragraph thereof is an instruction as to where was the burden of proof as to plaintiff's contributory negligence.

[11] The first paragraph or complete instruction on contributory negligence told the jury that, if they believed from the evidence that the approach of the passenger train "could not have been seen or heard by the deceased while she was approaching said crossing and before she had reached a place of danger, the deceased cannot be held negligent for having failed to see or hear said train before reaching such position of danger." But, as we have heretofore shown, even plaintiff's evidence shows that, after deceased was on or had crossed the first track, she could have seen the passenger train had she looked then, and defendant's evidence is to the same effect. Consequently the instruction embodied in the first paragraph of instruction No. 7 is framed upon a theory that is contrary to all the evidence in the case, and hence is erroneous. It permits the jury to find decedent was not guilty of contributory negligence if she could not have seen or heard the train until after she was in danger when there is not only no evidence to support such a theory, but the evidence is the other way. We have not overlooked plaintiff's very urgent insistence that "the real peril of deceased began when she started on her detour around the obstruction"—i. e., the car on the first track. But, as we have heretofore endeavored to point out, she was not in a place of danger either then or after she had gotten off the first track. She was then in no danger of being struck either by the freight or the passenger train, had she stopped where she was; and unquestionably, if she had looked east at that time, she could have seen the passenger train coming on the main track from which she was still 20 feet distant.

As the case will have to be reversed and remanded for the above-mentioned error, we need not notice the other complaints as to the instructions. It may be well to observe, however, that on another trial it would be advisable to omit any instruction submitting the case on negligence in leaving the car jutting out into the sidewalk, etc., as there may be some question as to whether that negligence can be regarded as a proximate cause of the death sued for. Also there is no reason for leaving out of the petition the "slackening of speed" as one of the ways in which the defendant failed to observe the humanitarian rule, and then inserting it in the instruction submitting that issue, thereby raising the question of whether the issues have been broadened. While it may be true that a charge of a breach of the humanitarian duty of itself notifies the defendant to prepare to meet that issue, and therefore it includes the issue of whether the defendant performed every reasonable effort which might reasonably have been exerted to avoid the injury, still is not that the case only where the failure to observe the humanitarian rule is alleged in such general terms as to include every reasonable act to avoid injury? Is it true where the petition, instead of alleging in general terms that such duty was not performed, specifies the acts which the defendant negligently failed to do as being the things wherein the duty was not observed? We do not pass upon this question, nor upon whether the general language of defendant's instructions 3 and 4 is sufficient to make the claimed broadening of the issues in plaintiff's instruction harmless on the ground of common error.

The judgment is reversed, and the cause is remanded for a new trial.

All concur.

NOAH v. L. B. PRICE MERCANTILE CO.
(No. 14001.)

(Kansas City Court of Appeals. Missouri. May 23, 1921.)

1. Continuance ⊜31 — Defendant held not negligent in failing to procure testimony of court stenographer on surprise by testimony differing from former testimony.

Where plaintiff's witness testified in a deposition and in a former trial that he did not see the defendant's wagon strike plaintiff, and in this trial that he did, and that his unsigned deposition incorrectly represented his testimony, *held*, that defendant, who sought continuance for surprise, was not lacking in diligence for failure to procure the testimony of the party taking down the deposition and the circuit court stenographer, both being temporarily absent so that they could not be procured as witnesses, and cross-examining the

witness as to the deposition did not cure the error in denying continuance.

2. Appeal and error ⊜966(1) — Continuance ⊜7 — Granting continuance is within the sound discretion of the trial court.

Granting a continuance rests in the sound discretion of the trial court, and is not an absolute or arbitrary discretion, but one subject to review; if unsoundly exercised or refusal of continuance to a party surprised by testimony and who exercised due diligence is arbitrary, reversal will be necessary.

3. Continuance ⊜54 — Where plaintiff consented to oral application and waived motion, affidavit, and oath, application containing essential elements held sufficient.

Objection that the overruling of a motion for continuance could not be disturbed because the application was insufficient will be overruled where plaintiff consented that defendant's application might be made orally and in open court and waived motion and affidavit in writing and oath to application, and the application as a whole contained all the essential elements pointing out the surprise in change of testimony of plaintiff witness since former trial and deposition; witness claiming his former testimony was not correctly reported, and designating the name of official stenographer and party taking deposition, and that neither could be procured and showing proper diligence.

4. Continuance ⊜31 — Facts shown by application held to entitle defendant to continuance.

Where defendant asked a continuance on the ground of surprise because plaintiff's witness' testimony was different from that given by him in a deposition and on a former trial, witness stating that his testimony was erroneously reported, and the party taking the deposition and the court stenographer could not be procured, the circumstances entitled defendant to postponement.

5. Depositions ⊜98 — Deposition used by plaintiff in former trial admissible to contradict plaintiff's contentions, although witness is within jurisdiction.

In an action for personal injuries, a deposition taken by plaintiff in a former trial of the case in which the witness' evidence contradicts plaintiff's present contentions was admissible in view of Rev. St. 1919, § 5467, providing that a deposition may be read if witness resides out of state, the only exception being when witness is present at trial, and the witness' presence within the jurisdiction could not prevent its reading, and, where taken previously and used by plaintiff, he could not be surprised thereby.

6. Trial ⊜228(3), 296(3) — Instruction held error as giving probable understanding that plaintiff had right to be where he was when struck and injured, but error not reversible in view of other instructions.

In an action for injuries from being struck by defendant's wagon as it was being driven into a barn where plaintiff was sitting, plaintiff's instruction that, if they found, among other things, that plaintiff was sitting in the barn

(221 S.W.)

between the north side of the driveway and the office, "where he had a right to be," etc., was erroneous, as the jury might understand this to be a statement that plaintiff had a right to be where he was, but the instruction does not constitute reversible error, inasmuch as it elsewhere required jury to find that the defendant negligently drove out of the driveway.

7. Appeal and error ⚓843(2)—Assignment of excessiveness of verdict need not be noticed where reversed on other grounds.

In a personal injury action, the question whether the verdict for damages is excessive need not be decided where a new trial is awarded upon other grounds.

Appeal from Circuit Court, Jackson County: Daniel E. Bird, Judge.

Action by E. W. Noah against the L. B. Price Mercantile Company. Judgment for plaintiff, and defendant appeals. Reversed, and remanded for new trial.

Ball & Ryland, of Kansas City, for appellant.

Samuel E. Swiggett, Rollin E. Talbert, and Rosenberger & Reed, all of Kansas City, for respondent.

TRIMBLE, P. J. Plaintiff, claiming to have been injured through being run over by a wagon negligently driven by defendant's servant while in the prosecution of the master's business, brought suit to recover damages therefor. In his first action he suffered a nonsuit, and thereafter he brought this action, recovering therein a verdict and judgment for $6,000, from which the defendant has appealed.

Defendant is in the business of selling merchandise at retail throughout Kansas City, and perhaps adjacent towns, by means of solicitors who canvass from house to house working under foremen who are in charge of a group of solicitors. Each of these foremen is furnished with a wagon and horse by which the goods to be sold are hauled by the foreman to the locality intended to be canvassed, and there the goods are distributed to the solicitors of that group, who thereupon proceed to canvass that locality, make sales, and account to the foreman therefor.

Defendant kept its horses at a livery barn in Kansas City. It was a two-story structure 70 feet wide north and south, and 50 feet deep east and west, and faced west on an alley 15 feet wide running north and south. The barn office, 12 feet square, was in the northwest corner of the barn, and the north side of the barn entrance, 12 feet wide, was 7 feet south of the south side of the barn office. A driveway 12 feet wide ran from the entrance east apparently the full depth of the barn. This driveway had no partitions marking its boundaries, they being merely

imaginary lines, and the driveway was therefore merely a 12-foot space used in driving vehicles into the barn.

Customarily, a number of chairs stood in the 7-foot space between the driveway and the office, and here those about the barn were accustomed to sit when not engaged in their work.

Plaintiff was one of defendant's solicitors who worked under a foreman named Woods. As he was on a commission, he worked when he chose, and on the day of the alleged injury he was not working, but had come to the barn to tell his foreman that he had been absent on account of his brother's death. It was while seated in one of the chairs in the 7-foot space above referred to, waiting to see his foreman, that plaintiff claims to have received the alleged injury some time about noon of August 5, 1916.

Plaintiff's evidence as to the occurrence of the injury consisted of his testimony and that of a man by the name of McBreen, a saloon keeper; and, according to their evidence, the facts are as follows:

Plaintiff was seated about halfway between the office and the driveway at a point nearly opposite, but perhaps slightly east of, the door in the south side of the office, not far from the southeast corner thereof. He had been sitting there about 15 minutes, with his back to the north and his face to the south, talking to a negro who was sitting in a chair a foot and a half or two feet west of him, when McBreen, in a single buggy with an attractive horse, drove into the barn and east along the driveway until the rear of his buggy was from 12 to 16 feet east of the entrance. McBreen got out of the buggy and began unhitching the horse from the south side thereof. Plaintiff, attracted by the horse, sat with his face to the southeast looking at him. While in this position, Himan, a foreman of defendant, and in charge of one of its wagons, drove rapidly into the barn and driveway but, instead of keeping the horse and wagon confined thereto, they were allowed to veer out of the driveway to the north until they struck and ran over plaintiff, and then the horse and vehicle curved back southeast into the driveway again, striking the buggy standing there, and at this point the horse was caught by Roll, the proprietor of the stable, who was helping McBreen unhitch. As the horse and wagon made this curved course out of the driveway the wagon struck the negro and plaintiff, turning them in their chairs over on the cement floor, the negro falling upon plaintiff, and the left wheel of the wagon passing over plaintiff's leg, injuring his shin, and bruising him in various places about the body.

Plaintiff says he did not see the horse and wagon enter the barn, as his attention was fixed on the McBreen horse. He says the first thing he knew he was knocked over, the negro was thrown on top of him, and he was run over. He says he saw the wheel as it ran over his leg and the horse was going at that time "pretty fast," and that the horse and wagon continued on for 15 or 16 feet past him.

Plaintiff's evidence as to the entrance of the wagon into the barn and what occurred just before and at the moment plaintiff was struck was given by McBreen. He testified that his buggy had been driven along the driveway until its rear end was 14 or 15 feet east of the entrance; that his own horse was about 20 feet east of the entrance and about 5 feet south of the center of the driveway, and his buggy was south of the center of the driveway; that he was standing on the south side of his horse, helping to unhitch it, and was about 18 to 20 feet east of the entrance, when Himan drove in "awfully fast, because I heard a noise, and I just happened to look around, and saw the horse coming in pretty fast." "It looked as though he was coming in at a trot." McBreen also said that as the horse came in the driver was not guiding him aright; the horse's head was turned to the north over toward the office instead of straight east along the driveway; that he heard "some of the boys" holler, and he looked around, and plaintiff and the negro were knocked over by the wagon, the chairs were upset, the two men were on the floor, and they and the chairs were all "mixed up there and scrambled"; that the horse after passing plaintiff, continued east and south until he reached a point near the south side of the driveway close to his buggy, where it stopped, the end of a shaft knocking a piece of the rubber out of the tire on the hind wheel of witness' buggy.

McBreen further testified that he heard the holler and looked around before the accident, and saw what occurred; that, judging from the way the horse entered the barn, Himan must have driven up the alley from the south; that the hollering began before the horse came into the barn, and when he looked around the horse and vehicle were coming into the barn faster than they ought and completely out of their direction; that part of the horse was in the barn and the wagon was still in the alley when he looked around; that he saw the wagon come in the door and saw it strike the negro and plaintiff; that while his horse was between him and them he could easily see over the horse, and when he heard the racket he quit unhitching and looked around; that as he drove into the barn himself he had no difficulty whatever in going along the driveway past the plaintiff and the negro sitting where they were, and that he noticed plaintiff sitting there as he drove in. He denied positively having testified on

the formal trial that he did not see the wagon hit plaintiff or anybody and did not know anything about it until after the alleged occurrence.

There was also evidence on the part of both plaintiff and McBreen that Himan, upon reaching the point in the alley where he turned to come into the barn, had a clear view of, and could easily have seen, plaintiff where he sat for a distance of 35 or 40 feet before reaching him, and that he could easily have stopped the horse in 5 or 6 feet. Plaintiff denied that he was intoxicated at the time, and McBreen says he saw nothing to indicate that he was.

These two witnesses, plaintiff and McBreen, were all that testified for the plaintiff concerning the matters surrounding the infliction of the injury, and, after a medical witness had testified as to the nature and extent of the injuries, plaintiff rested.

Thereupon defendant presented an application for a continuance based on surprise at McBreen's testimony at the present trial and the change therein from what it was at the first trial and in his deposition taken before that. The plaintiff waived the necessity of reducing the application to writing, and also the making of the affidavit thereto, and upon said waiver the application was made orally. Inasmuch as it will be better to here set forth defendant's evidence and contention as to what happened at the barn, in contrast to what plaintiff contends happened, we will not go further into the application at this time except to say that, upon plaintiff's objection that McBreen's testimony at this trial was substantially the same as before, and that defendant had shown no diligence, the court overruled the application for continuance, the defendant excepting.

Upon the commencement of defendant's testimony, the plaintiff for the first time asked to have the witnesses put under the rule, and, over the objections of defendant, this was done.

Thereupon Himan testified that he, in company with Klein on the seat beside him, drove the horse into the barn in a walk; that one cannot see into the interior of the barn till he gets in the doorway; that he saw plaintiff seated in a chair a few feet directly east of the door on the north side of the door line, sitting right close up to the north line of the driveway; that he stopped in the entrance until the rig ahead of him could get out of the way and Klein spoke to plaintiff, and then witness drove on in going east along the driveway and not getting over the north line thereof; that as he started to go into the barn plaintiff, who was sitting right close up to the line, started to get up and pull his chair back; he was sitting right close to the side of the horse as it passed him, and the plaintiff, as he started to pull his chair back, fell over it; whether the chair fell or plaintiff slipped at the time he was not positive. Witness was looking and driving straight ahead, but could not help but see plaintiff fall, as the latter was then at the side of the wagon, witness being on the right-hand side of the seat and Klein on the left next to plaintiff; that he did not know plaintiff was hurt; that he saw him sprawled out on the floor, but he got up immediately; that he is positive the wagon did not run over plaintiff's leg; that there was no jolt, and he did not know plaintiff was struck, and plaintiff made no claim that he was struck, but did at the office show his leg and said it was lucky he was not hurt very much; that the men were sitting further to the south than they usually sat; that he saw plaintiff, in backing his chair from the wagon, as he was sitting pretty close, fall out of his chair, his head to the north, and he was pretty tall; that the negro never moved, never fell out of his chair, but sat still; that the horse went two or three feet and stopped; that the men were sitting too close to the driveway, closer than any one usually sat; that if plaintiff was struck at all it was because, in trying to get further back, he fell out of the chair and stretched his legs out until they came in contact with the wheel, which was his fault, as the wagon would not have hit him; that the horse was 20 years old and quiet and under control; that plaintiff was intoxicated; that it would have been impossible for the horse to have taken any such course as plaintiff says it did, or for the wagon to have struck plaintiff seated where he claims he was, because of the posts.

Roll, the proprietor, testified that the plaintiff was sitting right along the driveway, could not say exactly where, but closer to the line of the driveway than the office; that, when McBreen came in, he, the witness, started to help him to unhitch, and just then Himan came in with his wagon, and, in order to make room for him, witness took hold of McBreen's horse and the buggy shaft and pulled them forward a little to allow Himan room to come in; that when he did this Himan, who had stopped in the entrance, came in, the horse proceeding in a walk; witness had hold of McBreen's horse when he heard a chair turn over, but this was out of witness' sight, owing to the horse; that he did not know whether the wagon struck anything or not, as he was where he could not see; that Himan came to a stop at the door, and then came in a walk, the horse stopping the second time of its own accord, and that he did not catch him; that the horse was headed due east as he came in. His statement that he did not think the horse and wagon got out of the limits of the driveway was stricken out as a conclusion, whereupon he said he could not say whether

they did or not; it would depend on what were considered the limits; that plaintiff was intoxicated. On cross-examination he was asked if he would say plaintiff and the colored boy were about halfway between the north line of the driveway and the office, and answered "Yes"; that he did not see what overturned plaintiff's chair, as he could not see it from where he was; that he did not see plaintiff on the floor at all, as he had gotten up before he got around there; that plaintiff "sort of laughed it off"; that he did not seem to be hurt at all"; but this was stricken out as a conclusion; that the plaintiff's trousers were torn a little above the bottom, and plaintiff went away and came back saying he was "going to get a new pair of trousers for that anyway."

Klein testified that he was on the wagon with Himan, sitting to the left of the latter; that when they drove into the barn entrance they stopped, and plaintiff was sitting very close to the horse and wagon; that witness spoke to him; that he had known plaintiff for a long time, and plaintiff was drinking "pretty heavy," he could hardly stand up; that when the McBreen horse was out of the way they went ahead, and the plaintiff "went to move his rocking-chair, and he fell and went against the left wheel"; that the wagon did not strike his chair nor knock it over, nor was the negro's chair struck, nor did he fall; that Himan's horse took no such course as plaintiff said it did; that it was impossible because of the posts that were there; that plaintiff got up out of his chair, but, being drunk, fell back over it.

Thus it is seen that the issue of whether plaintiff was struck and injured by the wagon through the negligence of defendant's driver or whether he fell and in the fall stuck his leg out in the way of the wagon as it came by and was hurt through his own negligence depends upon evidence that covers a very small and narrow compass, namely, as to what occurred as Himan drove in and at the moment he passed plaintiff. The nub of the case lies in this narrow limit. Wherever plaintiff was seated in the seven-foot space, the alleged injury could have happened as the defendant's witnesses claim, since it is conceded that plaintiff is over six feet tall, and if he was intoxicated as they say he was, and fell and sprawled out on the floor in an effort to get out of his chair, his foot and shin could have struck against the wagon wheel as they claim it did through no fault of defendant's driver; and, as plaintiff did not see the wagon come into the barn, McBreen's testimony as to what occurred before the injury and as to how it happened is a very important and pivotal matter in the case.

In the cross-examination of McBreen he admitted that on October 26, 1916, a little over two months after the alleged injury (the second trial was had nearly four years thereafter), the plaintiff took his deposition, which was before the first trial; that he announced before he was examined that, regardless of the correctness with which it was written up, he would not sign any deposition that he gave. He also said in cross-examination at the present trial that he understood when the deposition was taken that the plaintiff was taking it and had a right to take his deposition as one of the witnesses to the occurrence. He could give no reason at the trial for having thus refused, before the deposition was taken, to sign any that might be taken, but said:

"I just had an idea I would not sign any papers in regard to the case, that is all." "I don't know exactly why. I took a notion I would not sign my name on it."

He further said, in cross-examination, that his testimony in the deposition was taken down in shorthand, and that he never signed the deposition.

This unsigned deposition, which was filed in the first suit, was then presented to him, and he was cross-examined in regard thereto. According to the deposition, McBreen testified as to matters in general pretty much as he did in the present trial, but as to certain vitally important matters his testimony was wholly different and in no way can it be said his testimony is substantially the same, as plaintiff claims.

In the deposition the witness said the first thing that attracted his attention to anything unusual was that he heard some one holler, he thought it was Roll, who was helping unhitch; that witness was facing south (instead of north as he now claims), and had his back turned, and he looked around and saw the horse coming in; that the horse, when he first saw him, was on the north side of the driveway where he, the witness, was, and Mr. Roll had the horse by the head, and the horse had stopped; that he did not see the wagon run over plaintiff or over anything, or strike plaintiff; that he did not see plaintiff or the negro until after the incident was over; that plaintiff had his pants torn, but he did not see his injured leg that day, but did afterwards; that when he. (McBreen) drove into the barn he saw two or three fellows sitting there, but did not notice the plaintiff; that he had no difficulty in driving in. When asked if any one was sitting out in the driveway, he replied, "Well, I drove in all right," and when asked where the sitting men were with reference to the north line of the driveway, he said, "They were on the north side, how far I could not say." He said several times he had his back turned to the men when Himan drove in, and could therefore give no evidence as to how the incident occurred.

But McBreen positively denied having thus testified at the taking of his deposition or at the first trial, and said he had at both times testified as he did at this last trial, and asserted that his testimony given at the taking of the deposition was not taken down or reported correctly by Diffendorfer, the notary and shorthand reporter thereof, with whom, however, he was not acquainted and whose name he did not know.

In the first suit between the parties the plaintiff took and filed therein the deposition of W. S. Buck, who at the time of the alleged injury was the defendant's general manager. At the time of the second trial, however, plaintiff was working in Lincoln, Neb., for Buck, who had gone into the mercantile business for himself. Defendant offered in evidence the deposition thus taken by plaintiff and filed in the former suit. Plaintiff objected to the defendant using the deposition on the ground that Buck was in the city and available. Plaintiff's counsel in making the objection said he was "reliably informed" Buck was in the city, and that he knew he was because counsel had called his office over the telephone. The court ruled that the deposition would not be admissible unless defendant made a showing that Buck was not in the city, and, upon ascertaining that defendant had not had Buck subpœnaed, sustained the objection to the deposition, the defendant excepting.

In the deposition Buck testified that plaintiff came to the defendant's office shortly after noon on the day of the injury; that one of his trousers' legs was torn, a slit about three or four inches long about an inch from the bottom; that plaintiff limped some; that he showed witness "a black and blue place" on his leg about three or four inches above the ankle joint, the skin of which was not broken, but it looked like drops of water were oozing through; that he mentioned no other injuries, and said something about having been run over by somebody down at the barn; that the bruised place had not been dressed yet; and that he made no complaint of any pain or suffering from it, and was able to get about, though he was "pretty drunk," "so drunk he could hardly stand."

Defendant also offered in evidence the petition filed by plaintiff in the former case "for the purpose of showing what was then said about the ground of recovery, and showing the difference between the petition in this suit," and as an admission or statement of what was originally stated by this plaintiff in his pleading and as different and distinct from what he now states in his pleading. The plaintiff objected on the ground that the petition was wholly irrelevant, incompetent, and immaterial to any issue in the case, and the court sustained the objection. Counsel for defendant urged its admissibility because its statements bore on the "credibility of the plaintiff's present story." To this the court replied that plaintiff had a right to file a new petition, and, sustaining the objection, excluded the petition. The defendant then offered the record of the court showing the former nonsuit as some evidence tending to show that McBreen had not testified at that trial as he had in this one, but the court refused to admit it in evidence.

The evidence of plaintiff's medical witness as to his injuries was that plaintiff came to him along in the afternoon; that he had marks and bruises on his hip, back, and left leg between the knee and ankle; that there was not much visible sign of injury outside of the bruise on his leg; that nothing else required treatment and he gave none except to the leg; that as to that the leg was red, swollen, and painful; that the outside layer of skin had been rubbed off, but it was not cut; the blood was exuding through the skin, not running, but coming through the pores; that he continued to treat it for two months, and for a time it got worse; it swelled, and a tumor or pus formed which fluctuated; that when he ceased treating him the place was not cured; there was some inflammation and pain there; that the periosteum or covering of the bone was injured; that the last time he examined him was about a week before the last trial; that the leg looked like anybody's legs now except that one of the muscles was not attached to the ankle; that the result of the long-continued inflammation caused a scar to come in the covering of the bone, through which scar the blood cannot circulate as freely, so that nourishment is impaired, and as the nerves are constricted there it gives rise to tenderness and pain when the leg is pressed at that point; that the leg is weaker than the other and the condition is permanent.

[1] The first point made by appellant is that the court should have granted a continuance on the ground of surprise at the testimony of the witness McBreen. As hereinbefore stated and shown, the vital part of the evidence as to defendant's liability is concentrated in that which has to do with the coming of Himan into the barn and what occurred at the moment he passed plaintiff. The latter admits he did not see Himan come into the barn, and the first thing he knew he was knocked over. The evidence of McBreen that he saw the whole thing is therefore the very heart and vitals of plaintiff's case. It is the only evidence plaintiff has from an apparently disinterested source as to what did occur at the crucial point. Consequently its importance canot be overestimated. But in the vital particulars above noted McBreen's evidence at the second trial (four years after the occurrence) is directly contrary to that which manifestly appears to have been his evidence in his deposition

231 S.W.—20

taken a little over two months after the alleged injury occurred, and to that given by him at the former trial. There is no explanation on his part as to any change. He merely denies that there is any change, and boldly asserts that his testimony was not correctly taken down.' It will not do to say that his testimony is substantially the same, because clearly it is not. The motion for a continuance asserts that he testified at the former trial the same as he did at his deposition. For the purpose of passing on the propriety of the continuance, this must be accepted as true; besides, it is not conceivable that there could have been an enforced nonsuit if he had testified in the former trial as he did at the last. Clearly defendant could not anticipate that McBreen would change his testimony after having twice testified that he did not see the occurrence nor what preceded it. Consequently defendant ought not to be charged with a lack of diligence in not being prepared to meet his bold assertion that he testified the same way before. Nor will it meet the situation to say that McBreen was cross-examined upon the deposition, and that, plaintiff not objecting, the deposition was introduced in evidence by defendant, and therefore it got the benefit thereof. The trouble is McBreen swore that the deposition did not correctly contain his testimony, and, owing to the temporary absence of the shorthand man and notary, Diffendorfer, and of the stenographer of division No. 1 of the circuit court of Jackson county, wherein the first trial was had, defendant was thus caught, unexpectedly and through no fault on its part, without means of obtaining affirmative and competent proof of exactly what McBreen did testify to on those two former occasions, and had no means of impeaching him in the most effective way possible by showing, by the men who took his evidence down, that he testified differently on said occasions. The contention that defendant has shown a lack of diligence because it did not procure a transcript of McBreen's testimony on the former trial, and did not obtain Diffendorfer's deposition as to what McBreen testified to in his deposition, is without merit, since there was no reason to anticipate that McBreen, after having twice testified that he did not see the occurrence, would face about and swear that he did see it. Besides, as to his testimony at the former trial, what good would a transcript of that have done? Defendant had the deposition taken at the instance of plaintiff and by a notary of his selection, but McBreen nullifies it by coolly saying his testimony was not correctly reported. It would seem that under the circumstances defendant could rightfully claim to be surprised. It was thus caught without the means of combating the strange and startling change of front on the part of this witness.

"Surprise in its legal acceptation, it is said, denotes an unforeseen disappointment in some reasonable expectation against which ordinary prudence would not have afforded protection." Peers v. Davis' Adm'rs, 29 Mo. 184, 190; Fretwell v. Laffoon, 77 Mo. 26.

"Where there is a clear case of surprise and the party complaining is wholly free from negligence, so that without the interposition of the court injustice would be done, a continuance should be granted or a new trial awarded." Gidionson v. Union Depot R. Co., 129 Mo. 392, 400, 31 S. W. 800, 802.

And surprise is one of the statutory grounds for granting a new trial. Section 1453, R. S. 1919.

"The general rule is that when a party or his counsel is taken by surprise, in a material point or circumstance which could not have been anticipated, and when want of skill, care, or attention cannot be justly imputed, and injustice has been done, a new trial should be granted." 3 Bouvier, 3210.

In practice, surprise is:

The "situation in which a party is unexpectedly placed, without any fault of his own, which will be injurious to his interest." 37 Cyc. 15.

[2] In Withers v. State, 23 Tex. App. 396, 5 S. W. 121, defendant claimed surprise and asked for a continuance because a witness testified directly contrary to what he had sworn to on a former trial, and it was held that the court erred in refusing the continuance. There is no question but that the granting of a continuance rests within the sound discretion of the trial court, but it is not an absolute or arbitrary discretion; it is one that is subject to review if the discretion has been unsoundly exercised.

"A trial court has no right to arbitrarily refuse a continuance to a party to a suit where there has been due diligence in preparing for trial and when it would work injustice or oppression." Laun v. Ponath, 105 Mo. App. 203, 206, 79 S. W. 729, and cases cited.

[3] It is urged by plaintiff that the action of the court in overruling the continuance cannot be disturbed because the application was not sufficient. It was, however, not overruled on this ground, but because of a lack of diligence. Plaintiff consented that the application might be made orally in open court and waived motion and affidavit in writing and further waived oath to the application. It is not, therefore, the formal written application called for in the statute. But, taking it as a whole, it contains all the essential elements of a good application. It is manifest from the oral motion that the difference in McBreen's testimony was clearly pointed out, and that, owing to the temporary absence of Diffendorfer, who took and transcribed the deposition, and of the official stenographer in division No. 1, defendant could

not meet the change in McBreen's testimony, and that it was impossible to obtain proof to show that fact. The name of the official stenographer was not mentioned, but the man himself was designated, as well as the position he held in an adjoining and co-ordinate branch of the court, and the particular number of the division was given, and the fact that his substitute, acting in his temporary absence, could not read his notes, was fully stated. The necessity of the presence of the witnesses was not dreamed of until McBreen testified as he did, and the importance and imperative need of getting the proof and the temporary impossibility of doing so was all so clearly stated, together with defendant's surprise at the evidence McBreen gave, that it manifestly appeared that the witnesses were "not absent by the connivance or consent of the defendant, and that the application was not made for vexation of delay," even though those particular words were not used by defendant in moving for the continuance.

[4] We think that under the circumstances of this case defendant was surprised and entrapped by the sudden and unaccountable change in the testimony of the witness; that, in view of the situation, defendant was entitled to a postponement of the trial in order that it might have a fair opportunity to impeach the witness by showing that he had changed his testimony in so far as it bore upon the crucial points in plaintiff's case. Hence we entertain the view that a new trial should be granted.

[5] As, in our view, the judgment should be reversed and a new trial granted, it becomes unnecessary to pass upon the question whether there was reversible error in excluding the deposition of Buck and plaintiff's petition in the other case. So far as the latter is concerned, it was admissible for the reason at least as it alleged that "the entrance into said barn was obstructed by other horses and vehicles" when in the present case plaintiff contended that McBreen's horse and buggy was so far inside as to constitute no obstruction and that defendant's driver did not stop his horse at the entrance because there was a horse and buggy in the way. As the case is to be retried we need not say whether this error was cured by plaintiff's belated waiver of objections to the introduction of the petition on a later day and after defendant had closed its case, upon which waiver no action was taken by the court which had theretofore ruled that the petition was not evidence. Buck's deposition, taken by the adverse party and filed in the other case, certainly contained important evidence in defendant's behalf. At the time the deposition was taken, Buck was defendant's general manager, but at the time of the trial he was plaintiff's employer. He was not present in court, and the deposition it-

self showed that he resided in Kansas. Section 5467, R. S. 1919, provides that a deposition may be read if the witness resides out of the state, and this fact may be established by the deposing witness. Michael v. Mathels, 77 Mo. App. 556, 561. The only exception is when the witness is present at the trial.

"The fact that this witness may have been within the jurisdiction of the process of the court at the time of the trial did not prevent the reading of the deposition." Benjamin v. Metropolitan St. Ry., 133 Mo. 274, 287, 34 S. W. 590, 598.

The deposition was taken by plaintiff in the former suit. The other party sought to use it in the second trial, but did not file it in this case nor give notice of intention to use it. A deposition taken and filed in a cause is common property, and either is entitled to use it if otherwise competent. Watson v. Race, 46 Mo. App. 546, 562. In Samuel v. Withers, 16 Mo. 532, there were two depositions of Bristow taken by defendant, one in a former suit, and the other in the trial of the reported action. Witness himself introduced in evidence the deposition taken in the former suit. The court held that "under the circumstances of this case" it was error to admit the deposition, as it was not filed in the second suit nor notice given of intention to use it. In Cabanne v. Walker, 31 Mo. 274, it was held that this rule is dispensed with when the ends of justice require it. And in Parsons v. Parsons, 45 Mo. 265, 267, court, after mentioning the rule, cites Samuel v. Withers, 16 Mo. 532, and then says, "See, however, Cabanne v. Walker, 31 Mo. 214," 31 Mo. 274. In Adams v. Raigner, 69 Mo. 363, 364, the deposition taken in a former case was held admissible, even though not filed in the case tried, and even though notice was not given; the rule not being "considered indispensable" where no surprise would result. Inasmuch as plaintiff took and filed the deposition in the other case, we do not see how he could have been surprised by its use. However, upon a retrial of the case

all question as to its admissibility can be removed by refiling it in this case.

[6] Plaintiff's instruction A ought not to have told the jury that, if they found, among other things, that plaintiff was sitting in the barn between the north side of the driveway and the office "where he had a right to be," since, regardless of the question whether this does not submit a question of law to the jury, it is not altogether certain that a jury might not understand this phrase as being a statement of the court that he had a right to be there. The instruction comes very near evading the issue as to just where plaintiff sat. Plaintiff says he sat halfway between the office and the line of the driveway. Defendant says he sat very close to that line, too close in fact. Now, he could do this and yet not say the instruction constitutes reversible error, inasmuch as it elsewhere required the jury to find that the defendant negligently drove out of the driveway, though, as there were no boundaries for the driveway, they being mere imaginary lines, it might be difficult to say whether it was negligent to get a half inch or so over the line which nevertheless might be considered as out of the driveway. It seems that it would be better to have submitted the question whether plaintiff was sitting in the space above mentioned a sufficient distance away from the driveway to be reasonably safe from passing vehicles in the driveway.

The instruction on the measure of damages should not allow the finding of a greater sum of special damages for medical expense than is warranted by the evidence. The evidence showed $150 while the instruction allowed the jury to find on that item "not exceeding $500."

[7] The question of whether the verdict is excessive need not be noticed in view of a new trial being awarded for the reason and upon the ground herein above stated.

The judgment is reversed, and the cause remanded for a new trial.

All concur.

TEXAS-MEXICAN RY. CO. v. RIO GRANDE
& E. P. RY. CO. (No. 2810.)

(Supreme Court of Texas. May 11, 1921.)

1. **Carriers ⟝12(2)—Commission's order dividing through rate on shipment of terminal carrier's coal over its own and initial carrier's lines held valid.**

Where the Railroad Commission established a joint through rate from one point to another, and where the terminal carrier purchased coal at the point of commencement for shipment between such points without an agreement with initial carrier as to division of the through rate, the commission's order, dividing the through rate for shipment of such coal in proportion to the local rates of the carriers, *held* valid, as against contention that terminal railroad was not entitled to a revenue prorate for hauling its own coal over its own line.

2. **Carriers ⟝12(2) — Terminal carrier not entitled to switching charges on its coal billed for through shipment, but stopped at intermediate point without notice to initial carrier.**

Where Railroad Commission established a joint through rate between two points, and where terminal carrier purchased coal at point of commencement and billed coal for shipment to such other point, it was not entitled to switching charges on cars stopped by it at the intermediate point where initial carrier's line terminated and its own line commenced, without informing initial carrier as to the cars so stopped and the number or identity thereof.

Error to Court of Civil Appeals of Fourth Supreme Judicial District.

Action by the Texas-Mexican Railway Company against the Rio Grande & Eagle Pass Railway Company. Judgment for plaintiff was reversed, and judgment rendered for defendant by the Court of Civil Appeals (173 S. W. 236), and plaintiff brings error. Reversed in part and affirmed in part.

Greer & Hamilton, of Laredo, for plaintiff in error.

A. Winslow, of Laredo, and N. A. Rector, of Austin, for defendant in error.

PIERSON, J. Defendant in error, Rio Grande & Eagle Pass Railway Company, owns and operates a line of railway from Minera to Laredo, where it connects with the Texas-Mexican Railway Company, running eastward through Pescadito to Corpus Christi. Prior to the transactions out of which this suit arose, the Railroad Commission of Texas had established a joint through rate of 80 cents per ton on coal from Minera to Pescadito moving over the lines of plaintiff in error and the Texas-Mexican Railway Company. The local rates on the same commodity for the two roads were, for de-

fendant in error, from Minera to Laredo 65 cents per ton, and for the Texas-Mexican Railway Company from Laredo to Pescadito 55 cents per ton. The Texas-Mexican Railway Company was the purchaser of coal at the mines at Minera on defendant in error's line, and billed and shipped same over defendant in error's line and its own via Laredo to Pescadito. The two roads had no agreement as to the division of the through rate, and the controversy arose between them as to the division thereof. In order to determine the controversy the Texas-Mexican Railway Company submitted the matter of the proper division of said rate to the Railroad Commission of Texas for its decision, and in its application to that body set out eight certain carload shipments of coal, which were shipped on through bills of lading from Minera to Pescadito, and that afterwards said shipments were distributed by it to certain points on its line; and, after setting out in detail the facts relating thereto, it concluded its application to the Commission in the following language:

"The Texas-Mexican Railway Company desires a ruling from your honorable body whether it is entitled to a division of the through rate upon company coal shipped from Minera, Texas, and which coal actually moves to Pescadito, Texas, and we would be pleased to have this ruling cover all shipments of company coal moving from Minera, Texas, to Pescadito, Texas."

After a hearing the Commission entered the following order relating thereto:

"It is now, hereby, ordered by the Railroad Commission of Texas, that the revenue, accruing under the freight rates applicable for the transportation of the shipments in question, the same being carload shipments of soft coal from Minera, Texas, to Pescadito, Texas, shall be divided between the carriers, participating in the haul thereof, in proportion to the local rates of said Companies actually applying to and from the point of interchange, being Laredo, Texas, through which the shipments actually moved; the local rates to be used as factors, being as follows:

"For the Rio Grande & Eagle Pass Ry. Co. sixty-five (65) cents per ton.

"For the Texas-Mexican Ry. Co. fifty-five (55) cents per ton."

About October 29, 1912, the defendant in error began requiring the San Tomas Coal Company, which was acting as agent for plaintiff in error in the shipment of its coal to Pescadito, to prepay the 80 cents through rate charges between the two points, and continued thereafter to so require freight charges to be paid in advance. Plaintiff in error brought this suit against defendant in error in the district court of Webb county, alleging that the total tonnage for the 17 months, beginning October 29, 1912, and ending March 1, 1914, was 18,286.22, on which it paid to defendant in error the gross sum of $14,616.60 at the rate of 80 cents per ton; and that under the division as provided by the Railroad Commission's order it would be entitled to a prorate amounting to 36.7 cents per ton. It sought to recover the 36.7 cents on all coal actually hauled to Pescadito, $2 per car switching charges on those cars stopped at Laredo, and 15 cents per ton on the prepaid freight on the cars stopped at Laredo. Defendant in error contested the validity of the Railroad Commission's order No. 1427, contending that a railroad is not entitled to a revenue prorate for hauling its own coal over its own line. It admitted that it owed plaintiff in error 15 cents per ton on the prepaid shipments stopped at Laredo. It further alleged and charged that said billings to Pescadito were fraudulently made by plaintiff in error for the purpose of getting a prorate that it was not entitled to receive, and in substance that the hauling to Pescadito was a mere subterfuge to avoid defendant in error's local rate of 65 cents per ton on coal from Minera to Laredo; that plaintiff in error was not entitled to switching charges on the cars stopped at Laredo, and that said cars had been stopped at Laredo without giving notice to it of said stoppage or of any rebilling, and plaintiff in error had failed and refused to give any information to defendant in error as to any cars stopped at Laredo. It further alleged that if the Railroad Commission's order is held valid, it applies only to the eight cars of coal specially mentioned in plaintiff in error's application to the Railroad Commission and to all similar shipments from Minera on through shipment to Pescadito made subsequent to the promulgation and notice of said order.

All of the cars, 482 in number, were billed through to Pescadito, but only 271 were actually hauled through to Pescadito, and 211 were stopped at Laredo. The district court held the Railroad Commission's order valid, and gave judgment for plaintiff in error for a full prorate on all shipments hauled to Pescadito; for the 15 cents per ton on prepaid freight on cars stopped at Laredo, and for $2 switching charges on cars stopped at Laredo. The Court of Civil Appeals for the Fourth District reversed the judgment of the district court and rendered judgment for defendant in error, except as to the 15 cents per ton on prepaid freight charges on cars stopped at Laredo, for which it gave judgment for plaintiff in error.

[1] The first question that presents itself is the validity of the Commission's order No. 1427. This court in Cause No. 2811, Railroad Commission of Texas v. Rio Grande & Eagle Pass Railway Co., 230 S. W. 974, opinion delivered May 4, 1921, involving the immediate controversy herein, has held said order valid in all respects and applicable to company coal. Upon the authority of that opinion the judgment of the Court of Civil Appeals is reversed, and that of the district court is affirmed as to the division prorate on the 271 cars hauled through to Pescadito.

Defendant in error admitted that it is liable to plaintiff in error for the 15 cents per ton on the prepaid freight on cars stopped at Laredo, and therefore the judgments of the Court of Civil Appeals and of the district court in that respect are affirmed.

It is earnestly urged by defendant in error that said order No. 1427 of the Commission is retroactive except as to the eight cars of coal shipped prior to the date of the order, and therefore unconstitutional and void as to them.

Defendant in error does not contend that the order is retroactive as to the eight cars, but only as to all those except the eight cars shipped prior to its date. If it is not retroactive as to the eight cars, it is not retroactive as to any.

This order of the Commission is only applying and putting into practical effect its order establishing the through rate. A division thereof where the carriers fail to agree upon same is incident to and an application of the other rate theretofore made by the Commission. In the absence of the Commission's order the court would decree the reasonable division of the through rate, not only as to the eight cars, but also as to all shipments in controversy between the parties. It is clear that the Commission's order dividing the through rate in proportion to the local rates is the reasonable one and the one the court would make, and the result in the instant case would be the same.

Plaintiff in error, Texas-Mexican Railway Company, contends that it is entitled to receive from defendant in error switching charges at Laredo, $2 per car on 209 of the cars that were stopped there, for conveying said cars from the transfer track to its coal bins and shops.

[2] Plaintiff in error billed all its shipments of coal, 482 cars, on through billing from Minera to Pescadito, the shipment extending over a lengthy period of time. Without notifying defendant in error of its purpose to do so, or of its having done so, it stopped its said shipments at Laredo, receiving the said cars on the transfer track. Thereafter it failed and refused to notify or inform defendant in error as to the cars so stopped at Laredo, the number of cars or their identity. It must be held to have received the cars as through shipments and to have voluntarily transferred them to its coal bins and shops, irrespective of its rights as a shipper to stop its shipments in transit by giving notice. We conclude that plaintiff in error is not entitled to recover the switching charges.

The judgment of the Court of Civil Appeals is reversed, except as to the switching charges and the 15 cents per ton on prepaid freight charges on cars stopped at Laredo, and the judgment of the district court is reformed as to the sum of $418 switching charges, which is here rendered in favor of defendant in error. In all other respects the judgment of the district court is affirmed.

The costs of the Court of Civil Appeals are awarded against plaintiff in error, and the costs of this court against defendant in error.

———

REA et al. v. LUSE et al. (No. 244–3326.)*

(Commission of Appeals of Texas, Section A. June 1, 1921.)

1. Fraud ⟷41 — Vendor's complaint held to state cause of action for deceit.

Vendor's complaint, in an action against purchaser, alleging that purchaser misrepresented that maker of notes received in part payment of the purchase price was solvent, that deed of trust had been executed on certain land to secure such notes, and that such land was of certain value, *held* to state a cause of action for deceit.

2. Fraud ⟷59(3)—Measure of damages.

In vendor's action against purchaser for deceit in inducing execution of land contract by misrepresentations that maker of notes received in part payment of purchase price was solvent, that deed of trust had been executed to secure such notes, and that such land was of certain value, vendor's measure of damages was the difference between the value of the land parted with and the value of what he received in the transaction.

3. Liens ⟷7—Purchaser, who accepted notes in part payment on strength of recitals as to security for notes, entitled to equitable lien.

Where notes recited that they were secured by a deed of trust on certain land, and where deed of trust purporting to secure payment of such notes was forged, one who received notes in part payment of the purchase price for other land on the strength of the recitals in notes and deed of trust as to the execution of such deed of trust to secure notes *held* entitled to an equitable deed of trust lien on the land, though no deed of trust was in fact executed.

4. Vendor and purchaser ⟷259 — Vendor held not entitled to vendor's lien on other land to secure payment of third person's notes transferred to vendor in part payment of purchase price.

A vendor who accepted from purchaser in part payment of the purchase price third person's notes, which recited that they were secured by deed of trust on other land, and did not appear to be purchase-money notes, *held* not entitled to a vendor's lien on such other land to secure payment of the notes.

5. Appeal and error ⟷1094(5) — Supreme Court bound by finding of Court of Civil Appeals on conflicting evidence.

The Supreme Court is bound by the finding of the Court of Civil Appeals, reversing judgment of trial court entered on verdict of jury, where evidence was conflicting.

Appeal from Court of Civil Appeals of Seventh Supreme Judicial District.

Action by Mrs. Mary L. Waller Rea and husband against Mrs. P. L. Luse and husband, in which defendants set up a cross-action interpleading A. F. Luse as one of the defendants. Judgment for defendants on the cross-action was reversed, and the cause was remanded by the Court of Civil Appeals (207 S. W. 942), and defendants appeal. Judgment of Court of Civil Appeals affirmed.

Kimbrough, Underwood & Jackson, of Amarillo, for appellants.

W. H. Russell, of Hereford, for appellees.

TAYLOR, P. J. The case presented for review grew out of an exchange of properties between A. F. Luse and Mrs. P. L. Rea on one hand, and Mrs. Mary Waller Rea on the other. Mrs. P. L. Luse, joined pro forma by her husband, sued Mrs. Rea, joined pro forma also by her husband, for breach of warranty of covenants contained in a deed conveying Mrs. Rea's land to Mrs. Luse as a part of the exchange referred to. It is not necessary to state the nature and result of the suit filed by plaintiffs, as the judgment on the direct action was not appealed from.

The case for review arises on the cross-action set up by Mrs. Rea against plaintiffs in the direct action, and A. F. Luse, who was interpleaded as one of the defendants in the cross-action. It is alleged in the cross-petition that Mrs. Rea agreed to sell to A. F. Luse her two sections of land in Deaf Smith county subject to the indebtedness thereon, in consideration that he pay her therefor $14,000 in notes executed by O. H. Bennett, secured by a vendor's lien on 5½ sections of land in Culberson and El Paso counties; that Luse agreed to procure from Bennett a deed of trust on the land covered by the vendor's lien to further secure the payment of the notes; that Mrs. Rea was induced to execute the contract by Luse's statement to her, falsely made, that he had sold to Bennett the lands to be embraced in the deed of trust for a total consideration of $28,000, and that the $14,000 in notes represented one-half of the actual purchase price; that the lands were reasonably worth $28,000, and their market value was at least that amount; that before the final consummation of the contract Luse represented to Mrs. Rea that he had procured the deed of trust from Bennett in accordance with his agreement. It is further alleged that the lands embraced in the purported deed of trust were waste lands, worthless, and without market value; that the purported signature of Bennett was not in fact genuine, and was a forgery. It was alleged that the value of the lands and improvements contracted to be conveyed by Mrs. Rea to Luse was not less than $50,000, and that the incumbrances to which they were subject aggregated about $25,000; that the consideration pretended to be given by Luse for Mrs. Rea's equity of $25,000 was the Bennett notes for $14,000 and $168 in cash; that Bennett was insolvent; and that the security to the notes was worthless.

While the evidence discloses that Mrs. Rea received other property in the trade besides the Bennett notes, no complaint is made that she was deceived in any matters other than those relating to the value of the notes.

The cross-petition sets out that A. F. Luse in his dealings with Mrs. Rea acted for his undisclosed principals, Mrs. P. L. Luse and her husband, and alleges the ratification by them of the terms of the contract and the fraudulent acts of A. F. Luse, and the acceptance by them of the benefits thereof; also that upon the pretended consummation by A. F. Luse of the obligations devolving upon him under the terms of the contract, he cause Mrs. Rea to convey her two sections of land in Deaf Smith county to Mrs. P. L. Luse. These allegations were made the basis for interpleading A. F. Luse as a party defendant. The prayer was for damages in the sum of $25,000. The answer to the cross-action consisted of general and special exceptions, and a general denial.

Mrs. Rea testified that the land conveyed by her to Mrs. Luse was worth $51,200, and that she conveyed it subject to an indebtedness of about $29,000; that she received therefor $14,000 in notes executed by O. H. Bennett, $800 in money, and 160 acres of land in El Paso county. She testified also that A. F. Luse represented that Bennett was solvent and that the land securing the payment of the Bennett notes was worth from $7 to $8 per acre, and that the notes represented one-half of the value of the land; that some time in the spring of 1917, but prior to the consummation of the contract, she had the Bennett notes and trust deed forwarded to her at her bank in Del Norte, Colo.; that she endeavored to sell the notes, but failed; that she then became a little suspicious of the transaction, and returned to Amarillo, Tex.; that she there had a talk with Bennett, in the course of which he promised to pay the notes; that later, in the early part of June (1917) she sent her representative to Hereford for the purpose of finally closing the trade, which he did, delivering at that time the deed from Mrs. Rea

to Mrs. Luse; that she would not have executed the deed had she known Bennett was insolvent; that she then tried to sell the notes in Amarillo, and, failing to do so, made inquiries concerning Bennett, learning that he was notoriously insolvent; that subsequently she had a conversation with Bennett in which he admitted signing the notes, and promised to pay them; but in which he further stated that he did not execute the deed of trust, and that it was a forgery.

Mrs. Rea testified also that she later traded the Bennett notes for two houses and lots in Shamrock, Tex., one in Clarendon, Tex., and 160 acres of land in New Mexico; that she endorsed the notes, the purchaser having required her to do so before he would take them in the trade.

There was no evidence bearing upon the allegations of the cross-action other than Mrs. Rea's, which is summarized above, and certain documentary evidence introduced by her in support of her oral testimony. The deed from A. F. Luse to Bennett is not in evidence.

It was agreed in open court that no vendor's lien was retained therein, or in the Bennett notes, on the land described in the deed of trust. The deed of trust is in evidence, as are also the four Bennett notes aggregating the sum of $14,000, payable to Mrs. Rea, and signed by Bennett. The notes contain the recital that their payment is secured by a deed of trust lien on the land described in the deed of trust, but no reference is made to a vendor's lien. There is an allegation in the cross-petition that the deed of trust dated March 5, 1917, was filed for record March 19 of the same year in the records of Culberson county, Tex. There is no allegation that it was recorded in El Paso county.

The case was submitted on special issues, in response to which the jury found that A. F. Luse, as an inducement to Mrs. Rea to make the contract, represented that O. H. Bennett was financially responsible for the amount of the Bennett notes; that she relied upon the representations made by A. F. Luse; and that they were a material inducement to her to enter into the contract, and were untrue; that Bennett was insolvent, and that the deed of trust, purporting to have been executed by him and delivered to Mrs. Rea, was a forgery. No other issues were submitted by the court, nor was the submission of others requested.

The trial court entered judgment on the cross-action in favor of Mrs. Rea for the face value of the Bennett notes. It is apparent from the judgment recitals that the trial court found as a basis for the judgment that the notes were worthless.

The Court of Civil Appeals was of opinion that the pleadings and evidence present two groups of fact, which, if taken separately, would respectively make the cause an action for deceit on one group, and for breach of contract on the other; that in the event the case be viewed as an action for deceit the measure of damages would be that announced in George v. Hesse, 100 Tex. 44, 93 S. W. 107, 8 L. R. A. (N. S.) 804, 123 Am. St. Rep. 772, 15 Ann. Cas. 456; that if the case should be viewed as one involving a breach of contract by Luse, Mrs. Rea might recover for the breach, and the measure of her recovery would be the difference in the value of notes actually received and their value had they been secured as contracted for; that if the failure of the notes to be secured was the only ground of recovery, a suit for breach of contract and the application of the consequent measure of damages would be proper. The court's conclusion was that the cross-action so combined the facts as to make it in effect an action for deceit. It is stated in the opinion that the value of the 160 acres conveyed to Mrs. Rea in the deal was not proved, and that no evidence of the value of the Bennett notes was offered, except that bearing upon Bennett's insolvency and his failure to execute the deed of trust.

The Court of Civil Appeals was also of opinion that before Mrs. Rea could recover the face value of the notes under the facts stated, it devolved upon her to show that they were worthless, stating in this connection that the record pointedly suggests an equitable lien against the land described in the deed of trust, and also an equitable vendor's lien; and that a court of equity might be authorized to decree an equitable lien against the land. The conclusion of the Court of Civil Appeals, contrary to that of the trial court, was that the evidence was not sufficient to justify a conclusion that the notes were wholly worthless, and that the cause should therefore be reversed and remanded for another trial. 207 S. W. 942.

[1] The gravamen of the complaint is deceit. Plaintiffs in the cross-petition apparently so viewed their cause of action. The matters complained of are the fraudulent acts of A. F. Luse that induced Mrs. Rea to part with her land. Mrs. Rea did not attempt to rescind her contract and tender back the notes and property received therefor. In this important particular the case is unlike Bank of Miami v. Young (Com. of Apps.) 208 S. W. 656, cited by plaintiffs in error. She did not seek to establish an equitable deed of trust lien on the land agreed to be given as security. She proceeded, as was her right, to sell the notes, after having been advised by Bennett that the deed of trust was a forgery, and set up this cross-action for damages. The trial court also apparently viewed the action as one grounded in deceit, as he submitted to the jury only such special issues as would aid in ascertaining whether or not the allegations of fraud were true. The gist of the complaint is that Luse traded Mrs. Rea, among other things, unsecured and worthless notes for her land, fraudulently inducing her to accept them, to her damage, under the belief that they carried the security agreed upon, to wit, a deed of trust executed by Bennett.

[2] The measure of damage in such case is the difference between the value of that parted with by the party defrauded, and that received (George v. Hesse, supra), and is the measure that should have been applied herein by the trial court. Whether this rule was applied by the trial court, or whether the judgment is the same as would have been reached by its application, in view of our conclusion as to the proper disposition to make of the case in the state of the record as we find it, need not be determined.

There is no finding by the jury of the value of any of the property. The evidence was undisputed that Mrs. Rea's equity in the land conveyed by her was worth about $22,000. There is evidence tending to prove that the Bennett notes were worthless. There is also evidence tending to prove that they had some value.

[3, 4] The fact that Mrs. Rea traded the notes for other property is a circumstance tending to prove they had value; nor does the fact that she indorsed them establish conclusively that they were without value. The Court of Civil Appeals is of opinion that the recitals in the trust deeds and notes are such that an inference could be drawn that an equitable deed of trust, and also vendor's lien arose, that might have been enforced by Mrs. Rea in a court of equity. We concur in the holding with respect to the equitable deed of trust lien, but not as to the vendor's lien. It does not appear from the record that the Bennett notes were purchase-money notes. On the other hand, the agreed statement of facts, which is no more, practically, than an agreement as to what the testimony was, contains the ambiguous statement that Luse stated the notes represented one-half of the value of the land. We think, however, the inference that an equitable deed of trust lien might have been enforced by Mrs. Rea is not material in this suit, except as a circumstance tending to show what the value of the notes was while in the hands of Mrs. Rea. The recital in the notes that their payment was secured by trust deed might have tended to enhance their market value, and was probably weighed by the trial court in determining their value. Mrs. Rea disposed of the notes before bringing suit, having elected to sue for damages for fraud, rather than attempt to foreclose a lien, or rescind and sue for breach of contract. In such a suit the recitals in the notes creating a lien as it were by estoppel, could have had no bearing except upon the issue of value.

[5] The Court of Civil Appeals found that the evidence was not sufficient to justify the conclusion that the notes were wholly worth-

less. As there was evidence that the notes had some value, as well as evidence that they were worthless the Supreme Court is bound by the finding. Griffis v. Payne, 92 Tex. 293, 47 S. W. 973.

The judgment of the trial court on the cross-action recites that it is for the face value of the notes, which precludes the idea that the amount of the damage may have been ascertained upon any other theory than that the notes were worthless. There was left therefore no basis for an affirmance of the trial court's judgment, such as might have existed if the judgment had been silent as to the finding upon which it was rendered. Under this state of the record, the Court of Civil Appeals, entertaining as it did the view that the evidence was insufficient to justify a conclusion that the notes were wholly worthless, could not properly make any other disposition of the cause than to reverse and remand it for another trial.

Defendants in error insist in their briefs filed in the Court of Civil Appeals that the judgment should not be permitted to stand, on the ground that the only evidence of forgery offered on the trial was the hearsay evidence of Mrs. Rea that Bennett told her the deed of trust was a forgery. It appears that this testimony was adduced on cross-examination by defendants in error. They urged an objection to its admission, which was sustained. The objection was then withdrawn and the testimony permitted to stand. On the following day the objection was renewed in the form of a motion to strike, which was overruled. The assignments raising the question of whether the judgment in this state of the record should be permitted to stand was not passed upon by the Court of Civil Appeals. As this question and the questions raised by the other assignments of error in the Court of Civil Appeals will doubtless not arise on another trial, it is not necessary that they be determined.

We recommend that the judgment of the Court of Civil Appeals, directing that the cause be reversed and remanded for another trial, be affirmed.

PHILLIPS, C. J. The judgment recommended in the report of the Commission of Appeals is adopted and will be entered as the judgment of the Supreme Court.

HOLMES et al. v. TENNANT. (No. 220–3349.)

(Commission of Appeals of Texas, Section A. June 1, 1921.)

1. Mortgages ⊕=32(5)—Whether deed is mortgage depends on extinguishment of debt.

When a conveyance of land grows out of a pre-existing debt or loan of money, it must clearly appear that such debt is extinguished or it will be held that the conveyance is a mere change in the security.

2. Mortgages ⊕=39 — Whether conveyance a mortgage or conditional sale held question of fact.

In trespass to try title, whether a conveyance of land to mortgagee was a conditional sale or mortgage held a question of fact.

3. Trusts ⊕=13—Rule requiring payment of part of consideration for land not applicable in cases of express trust.

The rule requiring persons claiming that land is held in trust to show that they paid some part of the consideration is not applicable in cases of express trusts.

4. Mortgages ⊕=137—Mortgagor remains owner of land.

A mortgagor of land remains the owner thereof and holds it subject to the rights of the mortgagee.

5. Mortgages ⊕=596, 597—Mortgagee held not entitled to invoke defense of stale demand.

Since mortgagor of land remains the owner thereof and holds it subject to the rights of the mortgagee, the latter, or one holding his interest under a will, is not entitled, in a suit by mortgagor to have a trust declared in the land, to invoke the defense of stale demand.

Error to Court of Civil Appeals of First Supreme Judicial District.

Suit by Mrs. I. R. Holmes and others against Jos. A. Tennant. From a judgment of the Court of Civil Appeals (211 S. W. 798) affirming a judgment for defendant, plaintiffs bring error. Judgments of trial court and Court of Civil Appeals reversed, and cause remanded for another trial.

A. B. Wilson, A. O. Blackwell, and Andrews, Streetman, Logue & Mobley, all of Houston, for plaintiffs in error.

Moody & Boyles and Wm. W. Anderson, all of Houston, for defendant in error.

TAYLOR, P. J. Mrs. I. R. Holmes, widow, A. N. McKay, Flora B. Lee, Margaret St. John Lee, James H. Lee, and Caroline Lee Hoskinson and husband, plaintiffs in error, sued J. A. Tennant, defendant in error, to recover 500 acres of land out of the Richardson Pearsall one-third league in Harris county, Tex. Plaintiffs in error are the assignees and legal representatives of T. W. Lee, I. R. Holmes, and A. M. and J. H. York. Defendant in error is the son of J. H. Tennant, and acquired whatever title he has directly through his father's will.

The first count in the petition states a cause of action in trespass to try title. The second alleges in detail the facts on which claim of title is based. Defendant in error pleaded the three, five, and ten year statutes of limitation, and not guilty.

The court instructed a verdict in favor of

defendant in error, and judgment was rendered accordingly. The Court of Civil Appeals affirmed the judgment. 211 S. W. 798.

The following rather full chronological statement of the facts is necessary to a clear understanding of the first question presented: John L. Carson was the common source of title. In February, 1893, he conveyed to T. W. Lee. On August 3, 1893, a written contract was entered into between J. H. Tennant, La Porte Wharfage & Improvement Company, and La Porte, Houston & Northern Railway Company, by which the Wharfage & Improvement Company agreed to cause to be conveyed to Tennant, together with other property, the land in question, with full power of sale, as collateral security for certain advances in money made by Tennant to the railway company for the purpose of completing the railroad. On September 11, 1893, T. W. Lee, at the request of the Wharfage & Improvement Company, deeded the land to Tennant. On the same date, and as a part of the same transaction, a second contract was made between the Wharfage & Improvement Company, the railway company, and Tennant, reciting, among other things, that Tennant should have power to sell the land in case the indebtedness owing him was not paid, but further that on payment thereof within the time agreed Tennant should reconvey the land to A. M. York, I. R. Holmes, T. W. Lee, and J. H. York, or to such persons as they might direct. On August 2, 1894, the railway company, T. W. Lee, I. R. Holmes, the two Yorks, and J. H. Tennant made another contract in which it is recited that the advances made by Tennant under the prior contracts of August 3d and September 11th amounted at that time to about $20,000. By the terms of the agreement other property was added to the security already held by Tennant on condition that the time of payment be extended to January 1, 1895. It was stipulated that on payment of the indebtedness Tennant should, among other things to be done by him, reconvey to the Wharfage & Improvement Company, or its order, all lands which were conveyed to him as collateral by the original contract. The contracts of August 3d and September 11th were by express provision made a part of the last contract, which was signed as follows:

"The La Porte, H. & N. R. R. Co., by A. M. York, Prest.; A. N. York, T. W. Lee, J. H. York, I. R. Holmes, J. H. Tennant."

On February 4, 1896, there was an execution sale of the land under a judgment against Lee, J. H. York, and others to the judgment creditor, American Tube & Iron Company, which is not a party to this suit. On February 28, 1896, J. H. Tennant sued the Wharfage & Improvement Company, the railway company, and T. W. Lee in the district court of Harris county, seeking foreclosure of a mortgage lien on the land here

in controversy, alleged to have been created by virtue of the contracts of August 3d and September 11th, and the deed made by Lee to Tennant. The petition sets out the terms of the contracts, and alleged the amount due Tennant thereunder on January 1, 1895, was $21,500; that by virtue of various credits made on the indebtedness between that time and April 1, 1895, the balance due on January 1, 1896, including principal and interest, was $5,388.60. Foreclosure of the mortgage lien was prayed for. On October 8, 1897, Tennant amended his petition. He set out, in addition to the transactions alleged in the original petition, the contract of August 2, 1894, making the two Yorks and I. R. Holmes additional parties defendant, and alleging that they were personally liable to pay the debt sued on. Judgment and foreclosure were prayed for against them also. By a third amended original petition filed October 14, 1897, the Galveston, La Porte & Houston Railway Company, and its receivers, were made parties defendant as successors of the La Porte, Houston & Northern Railway Company. On April 20, 1898, J. H. Tennant, father of defendant in error, conveyed to O. C. Drew, trustee, by special warranty deed, the land in controversy. On the same date a contract was executed in duplicate between J. H. Tennant, O. C. Drew, and T. W. Lee, conditioned as follows:

"That the said J. H. Tennant has this day by the agreement and consent, and at the request of T. W. Lee sold and conveyed to said O. C. Drew, trustee, the following described land and premises: [Here follows a description of the land involved in this suit.]

"The said T. W. Lee is desirous of purchasing said land, and the said J. H. Tennant hereby agrees and binds himself to sell the said land to the said T. W. Lee for the sum of $6,608.61, with 8 per cent. interest from this date, and the taxes on said land for the years 1894, 1895, 1896, 1897, 1898.

"It is agreed that, if at any time up to the 1st day of May, 1899, but not thereafter, the said T. W. Lee shall pay the said J. H. Tennant the said sum of $6,608.61 with 8 per cent. per annum interest from this date to the date of conveyance, and shall also pay the taxes for 1894, 1895, 1896, 1897, and 1898, with 8 per cent. interest on said taxes from the date said Tennant may have paid the same, then the said O. C. Drew, trustee, shall convey said property to the said T. W. Lee, or any one to whom the said Lee may direct said conveyance to be made to.

"It is further agreed that in the event the said T. W. Lee does not pay the amount hereinbefore provided for on or before the 1st day of May, 1899, that then, on or after said date, the said trustee shall convey said land to the said J. H. Tennant, his heirs or assigns, in fee simple, and it is expressly understood and agreed that time is of the very essence of this contract, and that this contract of sale of said land shall be of no force or effect·beyond said 1st day of May, 1899, and said Lee's option to buy the same on the terms hereinbefore stated shall absolutely cease and expire on said date; that when such deed is made by said trustee it shall bind the parties hereto, their heirs and legal representatives, to warrant and forever defend against any and all claims whatsoever arising by, through, or under them, or either of them. * * *"

On May 2, 1898, the foreclosure suit brought by Tennant was continued by consent. On October 25, 1898, it was continued generally by agreement, and on December 5, 1898, was again continued generally. On May 13, 1899, the case was dismissed for want of prosecution, and on March 20, 1899, a motion to reinstate was sustained. On May 18, 1899, O. C. Drew as trustee conveyed the land to L. E. Brown, a feme sole, by special warranty deed. On November 14, 1899, the case was again dismissed for want of prosecution. On November 17, 1899, L. E. Brown conveyed the land to J. H. Tennant by deed recorded March 3, 1904. J. H. Tennant, now deceased, bequeathed the land to his son, defendant in error, who leased it in 1906 to W. E. Gay. Defendant in error claims that he has subsequently been continuously in possession of the land through his tenants, paying taxes thereon. The two Yorks in 1910 deeded the land to one of the plaintiffs in error. The other plaintiffs in error are the legal representatives of Lee and Holmes, deceased. There is evidence that the fair market value of the land was largely in excess of the amount specified in the contract of April 20th.

[1] The first question presented is whether the conveyance of April 20, 1898, together with the contract of the same date, set out above, was a conditional sale or mortgage.

It is stated in the brief of defendant in error, filed in the Court of Civil Appeals that on April 20, 1898, Tennant already had a mortgage on the land in suit, concerning the validity of which there was no question, and that a suit was then pending to foreclose it; that there is no evidence of a claim of indebtedness by Tennant against Lee, or any one else, thereafter.

[2] It is not necessary to discuss the evidence further, in view of the fact the contract is set out in full, than to point out that its subsequent to its execution the foreclosure suit was continued by agreement, was dismissed, and later reinstated, all subsequent to the execution and delivery of the conveyance and contract under consideration.

It is stated in Ruffier v. Womack, 30 Tex. 332, that—

"When the transaction grows out of a pre-existing debt or loan of money, it must clearly appear that such debt is extinguished, or it will be held that the new arrangement is a mere change in the security. * * * If by it there was a continuing obligation against the appellees for the debt, the transaction must be declared a mortgage, although it was expressly stated in the deeds that the debt was fully sat-

isfied, and that it was expressly understood and agreed that the contract was intended as a conditional sale, and not a mortgage."

The rule stated has been reiterated frequently by the courts of the state. Soell v. Hadden, 85 Tex. 182, 19 S. W. 1087; De Bruhl v. Maas, 54 Tex. 472; Alstin v. Cundiff, 52 Tex. 462; Gray v. Shelby, 83 Tex. 408, 18 S. W. 809. Our conclusion is that it is a question of fact, under the rule laid down and the evidence stated, whether the conveyance and agreement of April 20, 1898, taken together, constitute a mortgage or conditional sale.

The conclusion reached above is not at variance with the view expressed in the opinion of the Court of Civil Appeals in regard to that question. The court was of opinion further, however, that it was immaterial that the instruments referred to amounted only to a mortgage, for the reason that Lee's title passed out of him prior to his death through the execution sale of February 4, 1896; that neither Holmes nor the Yorks are in any way connected with the title by the evidence.

Whether there is evidence that Holmes and the Yorks had an interest in the land in controversy is the second question presented. The agreement of September 11, 1893, contains the following stipulation:

"On the payment of said amount * * * he (J. H. Tennant) shall reconvey and deed the said 500 acres of land to said A. N. York, I. R. Holmes, T. W. Lee, and J. H. York, or to such persons as they may direct the deed to be made to."

The contract of which the foregoing excerpt was part, as well as the prior contract of August 3d, was by express reference made a part of the contract of August, 1894. The last amended original foreclosure petition filed by Tennant contained allegations to the effect that the defendants, Lee, the two Yorks, and Holmes were partners doing business in the name of the Wharfage & Improvement Company; that on August 3, 1893, Tennant and the defendants as the Wharfage & Improvement Company, entered into a contract in writing, etc.; that on September 11, 1893, the defendants, the Wharfage & Improvement Company, and said parties composing the same, in pursuance of said contract and for the purposes therein mentioned, caused the said T. W. Lee, the then record owner of said 500 acres of land, to execute and deliver to said Tennant a good and sufficient deed therefor; that by reason of the contracts, agreements, and understandings referred to defendants were liable to the plaintiff Tennant for the indebtedness sued on.

A. O. Blackwell testified as follows, omissions therefrom being freely noted:

"I was well acquainted with T. W. Lee, J. L. Holmes, and the two Yorks. I was their attorney. I know the time the 500 acres of land [the land in controversy] were acquired and who paid for it. It was paid for by the La Porte Improvement Company. I recall in a general way the contract * * * dated August 2, 1894. * * * It was the same La Porte Wharfage & Improvement Company spoken of in that contract. I have seen the stockbook of said company. The stockbook was lost with the other records in the storm of 1900. All the records * * * were destroyed. I had charge of the office entirely, the legal department, the engineering, and the bookkeeping, titles, and everything else in connection with it. They used the name La Porte Wharfage & Improvement Company for a year or two after they came down here in connection with one or two matters. I think this tract of land was practically the only one. There may have been one other. * * * After it ceased to do business in its name the two Yorks, Holmes, and Lee looked after and controlled the property. It was a corporation; that is, there were articles of incorporation. * * * The records of the old Wharfage & Improvement Company, and most of the records of the Land Immigration Company were held by Mr. Holmes. All the companies were in a disorganized state at the time of the storm, and Mr. Holmes was undertaking to reorganize under the name of La Porte Improvement Company. * * * Almost all the records of our company, including title papers, were destroyed or so damaged by water that they were illegible. * * * The stock was all in the original stockbook just as it was issued. * * * The stock had not even been torn out, but a record had been made of it and it had been divided into four shares. * * * It was all signed. * * * I do not absolutely recall that contract in 1894 by which the stock was to go back to the improvement company, instead of the individuals. * * * They were at that time negotiating for the sale in 1894 of the La Porte, Houston & Northern Railroad Company (to promoters of a new railroad), * * * and they had hypothecated certain other lands in addition to this 500-acre tract. * * * The agreement was with the promoters that that 500 acres should be absolutely clear and turned over. That was the first agreement that was made, that that 500 acres should be released by the new organization of the railroad company, and turned over to the four members of the company clear. * * * Then it was agreed by the new promoters of the railroad company, who were to take over all the security that they should place $40,000 or $50,000 worth of bonds in between the Yorks and Holmes and Lee, and a possible foreclosure, and that was supposed to be ample. * * * That was the exact situation."

It is not necessary to summarize more of the testimony, or to discuss the refusal of the Court of Civil Appeals to consider—and perhaps for a sufficient reason—testimony more pertinent to the question under consideration than any that has been quoted or stated. It is apparent from that already summarized that an issue of fact was raised as to whether there was an interest in the land in Holmes and the Yorks at the time

of the execution of the contracts and conveyance mentioned above.

While the agreement of August, 1894, provided that on payment of certain indebtedness the land should be reconveyed to "the La Porte Wharfage & Improvement Company, or such persons as they may direct," and while Lee and the two Yorks and Holmes as defendants in the foreclosure suit pleaded defensive averments indicating a repudiation by them of any connection with the mortgage sought to be foreclosed, we cannot conclude that as a matter of law Holmes and the Yorks had no interest in the land, and that Lee did not hold such interests as they may have had in trust for them. Pomeroy's Eq. Jur. (4th Ed.) vol. 3, p. 224; Janes v. Throckmorton, 57 Cal. 368. Nor do we feel warranted in concluding as a matter of law that Tennant held the land in trust. It was, in our opinion, a question of fact, under the evidence stated, whether Lee conveyed the land to Tennant subject to a trust agreement dehors the deed and contract, which operated as a defeasance for the benefit of the assignees and legal representatives of Holmes and the Yorks to the extent of a three-fourths interest in the land. Anding v. Davis, 38 Miss. 574, 77 Am. Dec. 658.

There was evidence, in our opinion, that Lee held the land in trust on acquiring it from Carson. A. O. Blackwell testified, in addition to his testimony quoted above, to the effect that the La Porte Wharfage & Improvement Company paid for the land; that while he could not give all the reasons why Lee was selected to hold the title, it was placed in his name entirely for convenience in handling.

But, whether Lee held the title in trust or not, there is evidence that Lee conveyed to Tennant under a mortgage agreement to reconvey, on the condition stipulated, to Lee and his associates, or to such person as they might direct. This is a circumstance tending to prove that Tennant held not only as a mortgagee, but in trust as well, for his associates named.

[3] If Lee held the title entirely for convenience, it cannot be assumed that the trust, if any, under which Tennant held, was a resulting trust. It was not necessary therefore to show that the Yorks or their associates paid any part of the consideration for the land; the rule requiring such showing not being applicable in cases of express trusts. Oberlender v. Butcher, 67 Neb. 410, 93 N. W. 764; Perry on Trusts (6th Ed.) § 132; Pomeroy on Eq. Jur. (4th Ed.) § 1040.

Defendant in error relies on the defense of stale demand. Whether that defense is applicable under the facts is the third question presented.

[4, 5] If it should be found that the deed and contract of April 20, 1898, constitute a sale, the question of stale demand would not

arise. In the event it should not be so found, then defendant in error holds as devisee the interest of his father as mortgagee. A mortgagor of land remains the owner thereof and holds it subject to the rights of the mortgagee. Duty v. Graham, 12 Tex. 427, 62 Am. Dec. 534; Willis v. Moore, 59 Tex. 628, 46 Am. Rep. 284; Williamson v. Huffman, 19 Tex. Civ. App. 314, 47 S. W. 276 (error refused); Denison, etc., Ry. Co. v. Smith, 19 Tex. Civ. App. 114, 47 S. W. 278 (error refused). The mortgagee, or one holding the interest of the mortgagee under his will, is not entitled, in a suit of this character, to invoke the defense of stale demand. The conclusion reached follows, we think, from the holdings in the following cases: Duren v. Railway Co., 86 Tex. 287, 24 S. W. 258; N. Y. Tex. Land Co. v. Hyland, 8 Tex. Civ. App. 601, 28 S. W. 206 (error refused); Loomis v. Cobb (Civ. App.) 159 S. W. 305 (error refused); Broussard v. Cruse (Civ. App.) 154 S. W. 347 (error refused).

It is not necessary to discuss the assignments relating to the defenses urged under the statutes of limitations further than to say that the evidence does not show conclusively a limitation title in defendant in error.

It is not necessary to pass upon other assignments raising subsidiary questions that may not arise on another trial.

We recommend that the judgments of the trial court and Court of Civil Appeals be reversed, and that the cause be remanded for another trial.

GREENWOOD, J. The judgment recommended in the report of the Commission of Appeals is adopted, and will be entered as the judgment of the Supreme Court.

We approve the holding of the Commission of Appeals on the questions discussed in its opinion.

PHILLIPS, C. J., did not sit in this case.

MORRISS v. HESSE. (No. 217–3342.)

(Commission of Appeals of Texas, Section B. June 1, 1921.)

1. Evidence ⟨=⟩390(1)—Parol evidence is inadmissible to show covenant against incumbrances did not include tenant's occupancy.

In action for breach of covenant against incumbrances, consisting of retention of possession of the premises by a tenant of the vendor for several months after the conveyance, parol evidence was inadmissible to show that the grantees bought the land subject to the occupancy of the tenant, and undertook to arrange for themselves with the tenant to get possession.

2. Covenants ⟨=⟩131—Interest not allowable on damages from breach of covenant from date of accrual of cause of action to the judgment.

In action for breach of covenant against incumbrances, consisting of retention of possession of the premises by a tenant of the vendor for several months after the conveyance, it was improper to allow interest on the amount specially found by the jury to be the value of the diminution of the use and enjoyment of the land by such occupancy from the date of the accrual of the cause of action therefor, there being no jury finding awarding such interest; but interest on such amount was recoverable only from the date of the judgment of the trial court on the finding.

Error to Court of Civil Appeals of Fourth Supreme Judicial District.

Action by Charles W. Green against Nellie Hesse and another, in which, by plea, A. G. Morriss was made a party. Judgment for Nellie Hesse against said Morriss was affirmed by the Court of Civil Appeals (210 S. W. 710), and Morriss brings error. Judgments of the district court and the Court of Civil Appeals reversed, and judgment rendered for defendant in error.

Will A. Morriss and W. H. Lipscomb, both of San Antonio, for plaintiff in error.

Don A. Bliss, of San Antonio, for defendant in error.

KITTRELL, J. This action, in the form in which it is presented to us, is one severed as between the two parties from an action brought by one Charles W. Green against Wm. Hesse and Nellie Hesse, on a vendor's lien note given by A. G. Morriss and W. A. Morriss as part of the purchase money of certain lands in Kerr county.

Wm. Hesse having died, Nellie Hesse and her children made A. G. Morriss a party to the action, and sought to recover damages from him, on the ground that the land, when sold to them, was in possession of a tenant of Morriss, who would not surrender possession of the premises, and who held the same from August, 1909, until the latter part of November, 1909.

The Court of Civil Appeals correctly states that—

"For the purposes of this appeal, the cause of action thus asserted may be said to have been one based upon the covenant against incumbrances in the deed from said A. G. Morriss to Nellie Hesse, implied from the use of the words 'grant and convey' and a general warranty of title, which covenant was alleged to have been breached by such failure to deliver possession."

Defendant in error pleaded in the trial court that she was damaged $1,000 by the loss of an onion crop, and $500 by the appropriation by Morriss of the landlord's share of the rent; and $2,500 by the incumbrance of the lease, but the court submitted to the jury but one issue, which was as follows:

"By what amount, if any, was the value of the use and enjoyment of the land by an owner of the fee-simple title diminished by Burk (the tenant's) occupation or use of the same, or such part of the same as you may believe from the evidence he occupied or used, and during such time as you may believe from the evidence that he occupied or used the same after the deed for the land by A. G. Morriss to Mrs. Hesse?"

The answer of the jury to the question was: "We, the jury, answer, $250." The court entered judgment for $331.25, the $81.25 being the interest at 6 per cent. from and after the death of Wm. Hesse. No complaint is made of the amount of the interest allowed, the contention being that none should be allowed.

The Court of Civil Appeals affirmed the judgment of the trial court, and A. G. Morriss applied for writ of error on two grounds:

(1) That the Court of Civil Appeals erred in overruling the assignment of error directed against the action of the trial court in refusing to permit him to prove by parol that the Hesses bought the land subject to the occupancy of the tenant, and undertook to arrange for themselves with the tenant to get possession.

(2) That the Court of Civil Appeals erred in sustaining the action of the trial court in allowing interest on the sum of $250—the amount of damages found by the jury.

[1] We are of the opinion that the Court of Civil Appeals properly determined the question raised by the first assignment of error. Justice Moursund clearly differentiates the case of Johnson v. Elman, 94 Tex. 168, 59 S. W. 253, 52 L. R. A. 162, 86 Am. St. Rep. 845, cited by plaintiff in error, from a number of other cases in which it is held that parol evidence is inadmissible to enlarge or restrict the warranty in a deed; and we can add nothing to what he has said in his able opinion. Morriss v. Hesse, 210 S. W. 710.

[2] We are of the opinion that the second assignment of error is well taken. The question is clearly ruled by the case of San Antonio & A. P. Ry. Co. v. Addison, 96 Tex. 61, 70 S. W. 200. The holding in that case, in so far as applicable to the case at bar, is to the effect that interest cannot be allowed from the date of accrual of the cause of action to the date of judgment, in the absence of a finding of the jury awarding such interest.

"The issues of the fact having been submitted to a jury, the verdict constituted the sole basis for the judgment."

The recent case of So. Gas., etc., Co. v. Adams et al., 227 S. W. 945, by Section A of the Commission of Appeals, applies this doctrine to cases submitted to a jury upon special issues, and is therefore in all fours with the present case.

We recommend that the judgments of the district court and of the Court of Civil Appeals be reversed, and that judgment be rendered in favor of defendant in error for $250, with 6 per cent. interest per annum thereon from June 22, 1918, the date of the trial court's judgment.

PHILLIPS, C. J. The judgment recommended in the report of the Commission of Appeals is adopted and will be entered as the judgment of the Supreme Court.

MOORE et al. v. AMERICAN LUMBER CO. et al. (No. 187-3231.)

(Commission of Appeals of Texas, Section A. June 1, 1921.)

1. **Appeal and error ⊜⟶1108—Rights under stipulations in deeds made subsequent to application for writ of error cannot be determined.**

Whether a party is entitled to mineral rights in the land in controversy by virtue of stipulations made in the deeds conveying the land subsequent to the filing of the application for writ of error could not be determined by a review of the record.

2. **Appeal and error ⊜⟶781(6)—Case dismissed where issues have become merely academic.**

In an action in trespass to try title, questions brought up on error *held* to have become merely academic, the parties having settled and adjusted their differences, so that the case should be dismissed.

Error to Court of Civil Appeals of Ninth Supreme Judicial District.

Suit by M. G. Moore and W. H. Ratliff against the American Lumber Company and others. Judgment for plaintiffs as against all the defendants except as against the American Lumber Company, for which judgment was entered, and the other defendants and plaintiffs brought error to the Court of Civil Appeals, which reversed and remanded in part, and affirmed in part the judgment (203 S. W. 429), and the plaintiffs bring error. Motion to dismiss at cost of plaintiffs in error granted.

W. H. Ratliff and K. R. Craig, both of Dallas, and Carter, Walker & Cousins, of Hemphill, for plaintiffs in error.

H. B. Short, of Center, Jno. W. Minton, of Hemphill, W. D. Gordon, and F. J. & C. T. Duff, all of Beaumont, and Terry, Cavin & Mills, of Galveston, for defendants in error.

TAYLOR, P. J. This was a suit by M. G. Moore and W. H. Ratliff to try title to a league of land granted to John Moore in 1835. The defendants were American Lumber Company, J. O. Toole, W. F. Goodrich, H. B. Arnold, Harry Youngblood and wife, and R. L. Weathersby and wife.

J. O. Toole disclaimed as to 500 acres in the northeast corner of the league, and also as to 1,107 acres in the south portion, and as to the remainder pleaded not guilty. The American Lumber Company answered by plea of not guilty, and also claimed the entire league under the limitation statutes. It is not necessary to state the answers of the other defendants.

The case was submitted to the jury upon special issues as between all parties except the American Lumber Company, in whose favor the trial court peremptorily instructed a verdict for 1,107 acres of the league. Judgment was entered in favor of Moore and Ratliff as against all the defendants for all the land sued for, except as to the American Lumber Company, in whose favor judgment was entered for 1,107 acres.

The case was appealed to the Court of Civil Appeals by writ of error, J. O. Toole and the other defendants except the American Lumber Company being plaintiffs in error in one writ as against Moore and Ratliff, and Moore and Ratliff being plaintiffs in error in the other writ as against the American Lumber Company. The Court of Civil Appeals reversed and remanded the cause as between plaintiffs in error, Toole and others, and defendants in error, Moore and others, and affirmed the judgment of the trial court as between Moore and Ratliff, plaintiffs in error, and American Lumber Company, defendant in error.

Writ of error was granted by the Supreme Court "only on ground of conflict as to peremptory charge question."

An agreed motion to dismiss was filed on January, 28, signed by counsel for Moore, as plaintiff in error and American Lumber Company, as defendant in error, respectively. Notice thereof was given by the clerk of the Supreme Court to the attorneys of record of all parties to the suit. The only reply raising any question as to the dismissal of the writ was a letter from one of the attorneys of record for J. O. Toole, from which the following is an excerpt:

"It would be unfortunate indeed if private parties could control this case and prevent the 'jurisprudence of this state' from being benefited by having a question of such grave importance in the opinion of the Supreme Court 'finally settled for the benefit of posterity as to whether this John Moore, born in 1830, was the original grantee of this land and did not execute the deed attested by Thos. J. Rusk and others under which defendants in error hold, dated October 3, 1835. * * *

"It is my intention to appear on February 1st, before the honorable Commission of Appeals in the interest of a judicial determination of 'this great question' which must finally be passed upon by the Supreme Court itself later on."

The cause was set for submission by the Commission of Appeals the second time, after being passed on first submission. The material subsequent developments in the case are stated in a letter sent by us (Section A of the Commission) to the attorneys of record of all the parties to the suit, copy of which follows:

"Application for writ of error was made and the writ granted, in the case styled M. G. Moore et al., Plaintiffs in Error, v. American Lumber Co., Defendants in Error, and J. O Toole et al., Plaintiffs in Error, v. M. G. Moore et al., Defendants in Error. The application for the writ is signed by W. H. Ratliff and K. R. Craig, Dallas, Tex., and Carter, Walker & Cousins, Center, Tex., all as attorneys for M. G. Moore et al. On January 28, 1921, an agreed motion to dismiss in the case of M. G. Moore v. American Lumber Co. was filed, signed by the attorneys for M. G. Moore et al., and also by F. J. and C. T. Duff, and Terry, Cavin & Mills, attorneys for American Lumber Company. The motion states that all matters in the cause in which the motion is filed had been adjusted and settled, and that it has been agreed that the cause be dismissed.

"On February 17, an affidavit in support of the motion was filed, copy of which is inclosed herewith.

"It was stated in open court by W. R. Cousins, one of counsel for plaintiffs in error, on the call of this case for submission, that all of the issues in controversy in the cause in which writ of error was granted have been settled by the parties; that the settlement was finally consummated by the American Lumber Company acquiring all of the interests of J. O. Toole here in controversy. Mr. John W. Minton, attorney of record for Toole, who was present at the time, did not controvert the statements made.

"The Supreme Court does not desire to pass upon questions involved if they are only moot questions. Unless the statement that all issues in controversy pending in the causes in which the application was granted have been settled are controverted by March 1st, we will recommend to the Supreme Court that the motion to dismiss be granted."

[1, 2] No affidavit has been filed controverting the statement that all matters in the cause have been adjusted and settled, unless an affidavit made by one of the attorneys of record for J. O. Toole verifying the statements contained in a letter from him (the attorney) addressed to the Commission of Appeals, and a letter from J. O. Toole to his attorney attached thereto, may be regarded as controverting the matters stated.

Mr. Toole in the letter to his attorney dated February 2, 1921, says:

"While I have sold my interest in the Moore land except I retained the mineral right, I want this case to go through the courts and be rendered for the good it will do others. * * * I do not want the case dismissed, but do not know that I have a right to say more."

Independent of whether defendant in error, Toole, is in position to question an agreed motion to dismiss as between Moore and the lumber company, it seems clear that the questions herein have become merely academic. Whether Toole is entitled to mineral rights in the land in controversy by virtue of stipulations made in the deeds conveying the land subsequent to the filing of the application for the writ herein could not be determined by a review of this record; nor would a dismissal of the cause by the Supreme Court affect any rights growing out of such subsequent conveyances. Furthermore, it appears that the Court of Civil Appeals on appeal by Toole reversed and remanded the cause to the trial court as prayed for by him. We recommend that the motion to dismiss at the cost of plaintiff in error be granted.

PHILLIPS, C. J. The judgment recommended in the report of the Commission of Appeals is adopted, and will be entered as the judgment of the Supreme Court.

HOUSTON OIL CO. OF TEXAS v. JORDAN et al. (No. 234-3418.)

(Commission of Appeals of Texas, Section B. June 1, 1921.)

Adverse possession ⬤⇒94—Taxes must be paid before becoming delinquent under five-year statute of limitations.

Compliance with the five-year statute of limitations requires that the payment of taxes for each of the five years be made before they have become delinquent for said year.

Error to Court of Civil Appeals of Ninth Supreme Judicial District.

Actions by the Houston Oil Company of Texas against L. N. Jordan and others, and against John W. Robbins and others, consolidated. From judgment of Court of Civil Appeals (212 S. W. 544), affirming judgments of the district court, the plaintiff brings error. Affirmed in part, and reversed in part and rendered.

H. O. Head, of Sherman, and Kennerly, Williams, Lee & Hill, and Fred L. Williams, all of Houston, for plaintiff in error.

K. W. Denman, of Lufkin, for defendants in error.

POWELL, J. This is an action in trespass to try title, instituted in the district court of San Augustine county, Tex., by the Hous-

ton Oil Company of Texas, for the recovery of 25 acres of land claimed by L. N. Jordan and wife, Laura Jordan, and L. A. Jordan and wife, Mary Jordan. In the same court, at the same time, the same company was suing John W. Robbins et al. for the recovery of 50 acres of land in the same survey. By agreement of all the parties, the causes were consolidated and tried together before the court, without a jury. Judgment was entered in favor of the plaintiff in error for the 50-acre tract, and in favor of L. N. Jordan and wife for the 25 acres. No conclusions of law or findings of fact were filed by the trial court.

Robbins et al. excepted to the judgment as to the 50-acre tract and gave notice of appeal. They filed assignments of error in the trial court, but filed no brief in the Court of Civil Appeals. The latter court, finding no fundamental error apparent on the face of the record, affirmed the judgment of the trial court, awarding the 50 acres to plaintiff in error. See 212 S. W. 544.

The Houston Oil Company of Texas perfected its appeal from the judgment awarding the 25 acres to L. N. Jordan and wife and filed briefs in the higher court. The Court of Civil Appeals, in passing upon that phase of the case, says:

"We therefore conclude at the outset that plaintiff in error showed a superior title to the 25 acres in controversy as against the Jordans, and should have recovered, unless the judgment of the court should be sustained upon the theory that defendants in error showed title by limitation under the five years' statute. After a careful consideration of the record, in connection with the plea of five years' limitation, we have concluded that the evidence was sufficient to warrant the judgment in favor of the defendants in error upon that plea."

And, again, said court held:

"In the case last mentioned, it seems to have been, in effect, held that the five-year statute of limitations does not require, in order to acquire title by adverse possession that taxes be paid before they become delinquent, but only that such taxes be paid concurrently with the possession held by the occupant, and before adverse suit to recover the land. If these decisions announce the correct rule, then, unquestionably, the payment of taxes in this case by the Jordans, and those with whom they are in privity, was a sufficient compliance with the statute, and entitled defendants in error to judgment under their plea of limitation of five years, the other elements being present."

Since the opinion of the Court of Civil Appeals in this case was filed, the Supreme Court of Texas, in an excellent opinion by Justice Greenwood, has passed upon this very question and overruled the views of the Court of Civil Appeals, aforesaid. See Baker v. Fogle, 110 Tex. 301, 217 S. W. 141, 219 S. W. 450.

The case at bar is clearly ruled by the authority just referred to, and in that case the Supreme Court holds that compliance with the five-year statute of limitations requires that the payment of taxes for each of the five years be made before they have become delinquent for said year. The reasons for this rule, so fully stated by the Supreme Court, are sound and convincing.

The undisputed evidence in this case shows that the taxes were not so paid during any five-year period of the possession of the land in question by the Jordans, or those with whom they were in privity. For instance, the taxes for the years 1911, 1912, and 1913 were paid on January 4, 1915.

The only proper judgment in this case, under the evidence, is one in favor of plaintiff in error for the 25-acre tract.

Therefore, we recommend that that portion of the judgments of the district court and the Court of Civil Appeals awarding the 50-acre tract to plaintiff in error be affirmed; that that part of the judgments of the district court and the Court of Civil Appeals awarding the 25 acres to L. N. Jordan and wife be reversed, and a judgment here rendered decreeing that tract, also, to plaintiff in error.

PHILLIPS, C. J. The judgment recommended in the report of the Commission of Appeals is adopted, and will be entered as the judgment of the Supreme Court.

TEMPLE HILL DEVELOPMENT CO. v. LINDHOLM et ux. (No. 231–3410.)

(Commission of Appeals of Texas, Section A. June 1, 1921.)

1. **Appeal and error ⇐722(1)—Appellant may either adopt assignments in motion for new trial or independent assignments.**

An appellant may adopt either the assignments of error set out in his motion for new trial or the assignments filed independently of those in the motion.

2. **Appeal and error ⇐265(1)—On exception to judgment, exceptions need not be taken to findings of court.**

Where trial is before court without jury and judgment is excepted to, exceptions need not be taken to the findings of fact and conclusions of law as a prerequisite to review.

3. **Appeal and error ⇐1008(1), 1114—Findings by court are not conclusive on appeal, where a statement of facts appears in the record.**

Findings of fact by court sitting without jury are not conclusive on appeal, where a

statement of facts appears in the record; and, where the Court of Civil Appeals has not passed on their sufficiency to support the judgment, the cause should be remanded for it to pass thereon.

Error to Court of Civil Appeals of Fourth Supreme Judicial District.

Suit by the Temple Hill Development Company against Eric A. Lindholm and wife. Decree for defendants, and plaintiff appealed to the Court of Civil Appeals, which affirmed the judgment (212 S. W. 984), and the plaintiff brings error. Judgment of the Court of Civil Appeals reversed, and cause remanded to that court to pass upon the sufficiency of facts.

Wm. C. Church and T. F. Mangum, both of San Antonio, for plaintiff in error.

Barrett, Eskridge & Barrett, of San Antonio, and Hood Boone, of Pharr, for defendants in error.

TAYLOR, P. J. Plaintiff in error, Temple Hill Development Company, brought this suit against Eric Lindholm and wife, defendants in error, to recover two lots in an addition to the city of San Antonio and to enjoin defendants in error from residing thereon.

Plaintiff in error claims under a written contract, the terms of which it alleges were violated by defendants in error in failing to comply with certain building restrictions under which the lots were purchased.

Trial was before the court without a jury. Judgment was rendered in favor of defendant in error. Motion for new trial, challenging the correctness of the court's findings, and questioning whether the facts supported the judgment, was overruled. Plaintiff in error excepted to the overruling of the motion, and gave notice of appeal. It also requested the court to file findings of fact and conclusions of law. The request was complied with, and the findings and conclusions were filed, subsequent to the overruling of the motion for new trial. No assignments of error were filed by plaintiff in error separate from those set up in the motion.

The Court of Civil Appeals affirmed the judgment of the trial court (212 S. W. 984), without determining whether the facts support the judgment, or without testing the court's findings by the evidence as disclosed by the statement of facts.

The Court of Civil Appeals, speaking upon this point, says:

"There was no exception taken and properly preserved in the record or any assignment made challenging the accuracy of the court's findings, which appellant requested to be filed, and in the absence of such an assignment we are not at liberty to question the accuracy thereof, and, as the court found all the facts against appellant and in favor of the appellees, they will not be disturbed."

Plaintiff in error complains of the court's failure to consider the assignments as presented, especially with respect to the accuracy of the findings and the sufficiency of the facts to support the judgment.

[1] The assignments presented in plaintiff in error's brief in the Court of Civil Appeals are substantially the same as those set up in its motion for a new trial. It is settled that an appellant may adopt either the assignments of error set out in his motion, or the assignments filed independently of those in the motion. Barkley et al. v. Gibbs et al., 227 S. W. 1099, not yet [officially] reported.

[2] It is also settled that where there is a trial before the court without a jury and the judgment of the court is excepted to, it is not necessary that exceptions be also taken to the court's findings of fact and conclusions of law as a prerequisite to review, under due assignments of error. Hess & Skinner Engineering Co. v. Turney, 109 Tex. 208, 203 S. W. 593; Goodman v. U. S. Peck & Co. (Civ. App.) 192 S. W. 785.

[3] The findings of fact are not conclusive on appeal, where, as in this case, a statement of facts appears in the record. Voight v. Mackie, 71 Tex. 78, 8 S. W. 623; Leiber v. Nicholson (Com. App.) 206 S. W. 512.

We are of the opinion that the judgment of the court of Civil Appeals should be reversed, and that the cause be remanded to that court in order that it may pass upon the sufficiency of the facts to support the judgment; and we so recommend.

PHILLIPS, C. J. The judgment recommended in the report of the Commission of Appeals is adopted, and will be entered as the judgment of the Supreme Court.

We approve the holding of the Commission of Appeals on the question discussed.

FIRST NAT. BANK OF NAVASOTA v. TODD. (No. 222-3356.)

(Commission of Appeals of Texas, Section A. June 1, 1921.)

1. Chattel mortgages ⬩139 — "Subsequent mortgagees in good faith" against whom mortgage, unless filed as required, is void, defined.

Under Rev. St. 1911, art. 5655, declaring that, in absence of change of possession of the property, a chattel mortgage, unless filed in the county where the property is situated or the mortgagor resides, shall be void as against "subsequent mortgagees in good faith," a mortgagee must have advanced a consideration for the mortgage and had no notice of the unrecorded lien, in order to be a mortgagee in good faith.

2. Chattel mortgages ⬩157(2) — Holder of prior unfiled mortgage claiming superiority held to have burden of proof as to good faith of subsequent mortgagee.

Where intervener in chattel mortgage foreclosure asserted, as ground for giving preference to his unfiled prior mortgage, that there was no consideration for plaintiff's mortgage and that plaintiff took it with notice of his lien, and plaintiff did not allege that it had advanced a valuable consideration or was without notice of intervener's mortgage, but was content to rely on intervener's failure to prove his case, intervener had the burden of proving his allegations; the fact that proof of a negative allegation was required not changing the rule with reference to burden of proof.

3. Appeal and error ⬩882(12)—Error in placing burden of proof held not invited.

Error of instruction in placing the burden of proof on plaintiff, over his objection, is not invited, though plaintiff claimed and was allowed the opening and concluding argument, to which under Rev. St. 1911, art. 1953, the party having the burden of proof is entitled.

4. Chattel mortgages ⬩139 — Extension of note sufficient consideration as against prior unfiled mortgage.

If the consideration, or part thereof, for a chattel mortgage, was the extension of the note secured, there is a sufficient consideration to entitle the mortgagee to protection, under Rev. St. 1911, art. 5655, as a subsequent mortgagee in good faith, as against a prior unfiled mortgage.

Error to Court of Civil Appeals of First Supreme Judicial District.

Action by the First National Bank of Navasota against R. A. Barker. Judgment for intervener, J. S. Todd, was affirmed by the Court of Civil Appeals (212 S. W. 219), and plaintiff brings error. Reversed and remanded for new trial.

Lewis & Dean, of Navasota, for plaintiff in error.

I. W. Stephens, of Fort Worth, and T. P. Buffington, of Anderson, for defendant in error.

SPENCER, J. Plaintiff, First National Bank of Navasota, instituted this suit to recover of R. A. Barker upon two notes executed by the latter, one given January 20, 1916, for the sum of $5,416.20 payable to the bank, the other executed December 1, A. D. 1915, payable to A. P. Terrell in the sum of $441.80, which note had been transferred to the bank; and to foreclose a chattel mortgage lien executed by Barker on January 20, 1916, to secure the payment of these notes.

J. S. Todd intervened, claiming as assignee of Evans Snyder Buell Company, asserting a prior and superior lien to the chattels covered by the mortgage; contending that the bank's lien was inferior to the chattel mortgage lien which had been transferred to him, because taken to secure a pre-existing debt without having advanced any new consideration, and with notice by the bank of the superior and equitable right of Evans Snyder Buell Company under the mortgage.

Plaintiff held the note of Barker for the sum of $6,949.30, dated August 20, 1915, and due on November 1, 1915, secured by chattel mortgage executed by Barker upon the same date on 120 steers branded "AB" on the left shoulder—and other live stock not necessary to enumerate—located in Brazos county, Tex., where the mortgage recited that the defendant resided. This mortgage was duly filed in the office of the county clerk on August 20, 1915.

Plaintiff introduced in evidence the mortgage of January 20, 1916, describing 165 steers branded "AB" on the left side, and other cattle, located in Brazos county, Tex. The mortgage recites that it is given in renewal and continuation of the original one, and that 61 head of steers described in the mortgage of August 20, 1915, having been sold, as well as some mules and horses described therein, that the renewal mortgage was taken to include additional live stock to take the place of that sold and traded. This mortgage was filed and registered in the office of the clerk of the county court of Brazos county, Tex., at 2:45 p. m. on January 21, A. D. 1916.

Intervener introduced in evidence the following instruments: (1) Mortgage executed by R. A. Barker, dated January 5, 1916, describing 120 head of steers branded "B" on left thigh. The mortgage recites that the cattle are located in Grimes county, Tex.; that R. A. Barker is a resident of said county; and that the mortgage is given to secure the payment of a note dated January 5, 1916, by R. A. Barker and J. A. Barker in the principal sum of $3,614.31. This mortgage was filed in the office of the clerk of the county court of Grimes county on the 8th day of January, 1916. (2) Mortgage dated January 21, 1916, executed by R. A. Barker, describing 80 head of steers branded "B" on left thigh. The mortgage recites that Barker is a resident of Grimes county, Tex.; that the cattle are located in Brazos county, Tex.; and that it is given to secure the payment of one note for the sum of $2,304.54, executed by R. A. Barker and J. S. Barker, dated January 8, 1916. This mortgage was filed in the office of the county clerk of Grimes county on January 21, 1916. (3) Mortgage executed by R. A. Barker on February 5, 1916, describing 200 head of steers branded "AB" behind the left shoulder. The mortgage recites that R. A. Barker is a resident of Brazos county, Tex.; that the cattle are located in said county; and that it is given in lieu of the two previous mortgages, but with no intention of impairing or in any wise affecting the same. This mortgage was filed in the office of the county clerk of Brazos county, Tex., on February 5, 1916.

Intervener alleged that the Evans Snyder Buell Company had advanced the money and purchased the cattle described in the mortgage for Barker, and that the cattle were at that time unbranded; that Barker agreed to brand them "B" on the left thigh, but in fraud of the mortgagee's rights, he branded them "AB" on the left side behind the shoulder; that Barker had falsely stated in the first two mortgages that he was a resident of Grimes county, Tex., and that the cattle were located there, when in fact he was a resident of Brazos county, Tex., and the cattle located in that county, and that because of these misrepresentations the Evans Snyder Buell Company was deceived and induced to register the mortgages in Grimes county, and that upon discovery of the true facts as to the brand, and of the residence of Barker, and the location of the cattle, the mortgage of February 5, 1916, was taken to protect the mortgagee against fraud prepetrated.

The jury found in answer to special issues submitted to it that the steers described in plaintiff's mortgage of January 20, 1916, were the same steers as those described in the mortgage given Evans Snyder Buell Company, January 5, 1916; that at the time plaintiff took its mortgage it did not know that the cattle described therein were the same cattle as those described in the mortgage of January 5, 1916; that the plaintiff at the time of the taking of the mortgage did not part with anything of value in consideration for the giving of the mortgage by R. A. Barker.

The district court rendered judgment in favor of plaintiff for the amount of the notes and for a foreclosure of its mortgage lien; subject, however, to the lien of intervener and in favor of intervener for the amount of the notes and foreclosure of the mortgage lien, declaring the same superior to the mortgage lien of plaintiff. Upon appeal, the Court of Civil Appeals affirmed the judgment. 212 S. W. 219.

[1] The mortgages of January 5, 1916, and January 8, 1916, respectively, to the Evans Snyder Buell Company not having been filed in the county where the undisputed evidence shows the cattle were located, nor in the county of mortgagor's residence, were absolutely void as against subsequent mortgagees or lien holders in good faith. Article 5655, Revised Civil Statutes 1911.

Under the term "subsequent mortgagees in good faith" mentioned in the article is meant that the party claiming as such advanced a consideration for the taking of the mortgage and that he had no notice of the unrecorded lien. Bowen v. Wagon Works, 91 Tex. 385, 43 S. W. 872.

[2] The court in submitting the case charged the jury as follows:

"In this case, the burden of proof is on the plaintiff to prove its case by a preponderance of the evidence, and by a preponderance of the evidence is meant the evidence of greater weight and probable degree of truth. Now, bearing in mind the foregoing, you are instructed to decide the following special issues:

"Special Issue No. 1. At the time the plaintiff took its mortgage of date January 20, 1916, on the cattle described in said mortgage, you will find whether or not, as a consideration or part consideration for said mortgage, the said plaintiff, at the time of the taking thereof, parted with anything of value in consideration for the giving of said mortgage by the defendant, R. A. Barker."

To which the jury returned a negative answer.

It is a well-established general rule of the law of evidence that the burden of proof of any particular issue is upon the party who asserts and relies upon it, unless expressly assumed by the other party with whom the issue is joined. The intervener in this case asserts that the plaintiff acquired its lien with notice of superior lien and equitable right of Evans Snyder Buell Company, and that no consideration other than the securing of a pre-existing debt was advanced by the bank for the taking of the mortgage.

Having asserted and relied upon these issues to defeat the rights of plaintiff accruing under its duly filed chattel mortgage which, upon its face, imports a consideration, the burden of proof was upon intervener to establish facts supporting such issue or issues. The fact that, to establish the superiority of intervener's lien, required proof of a material negative allegation—that there was no consideration advanced by plaintiff for the taking of the mortgage—did not change the rule with reference to the burden of proof. It will be observed that plaintiff made no allegation charging that it advanced a valuable consideration for the taking of the mortgage, or that it was without notice of the unrecorded mortgage of the intervener, but was content to rely upon intervener's failure to prove his case. In this respect, the remarks of the Supreme Court in Boswell et al. v. Pannall, 107 Tex. 433, 180 S. W. 593, are applicable. In that case the plaintiff's right to recover the land for which he sued depended upon proof of notice to a subsequent purchaser that the conveyance by plaintiff was obtained by fraud, and that the subsequent purchaser had notice thereof. The defendant Boswell especially pleaded want of notice and the payment of a valuable consideration. The court said:

"The court's charge has direct application to this special defense, and as applied thereto is a correct charge; Barrow voluntarily made and relied upon this defense, and assumed the burden to prove it by a preponderance of the evidence. He need not have done so; he could have relied entirely on the failure of the plaintiff, Pannell, to prove his case, standing upon his bare denial of the plaintiff's allegations of fraud and notice of fraud, and confined his defense to evidence rebutting the plaintiff's case. But Barrow did not see proper to go to trial upon pleadings which would not require the court to charge any defense to the jury except the defense that if the plaintiff, Pannell, had failed to establish his case by a preponderance of evidence, to return a verdict for him."

Intervener seems to have recognized that the burden of proof was upon him, with reference to the establishment of the material allegations of his petition, as he called the vice president of the bank as a witness before resting his case, and examined him concerning the transaction.

By analogy, the rule announced by the Supreme Court in McAlpine v. Burnett, 23 Tex. 650, is applicable here and decisive of the question involved. In that case, the plaintiff sought to foreclose a vendor's lien as against subsequent vendees; there being no recitation in the deeds under which they held calculated to give them notice of the lien. Judge Roberts for the court said:

"The question then is, must the last vendees, Hamlett and Perry, assume the burden of proof, and allege and prove, that they are bona fide purchasers for a valuable consideration, paid before notice of the lien; or, must McAlpine & Company, to follow their lien, allege and prove, that they had notice, or had not paid a valuable consideration for the lot. We are of opinion, that the burden rests upon the party claiming the lien. They are seeking to set up and enforce a tacit equity against persons standing on a legal title, complete and fair on its face; and therefore they must assert and establish the facts which constitute their equity."

It is our conclusion, therefore, that the court erred in charging the jury that the burden of proof was upon the plaintiff in this case.

We found in our research that the decision by the Court of Civil Appeals for the Sixth District in Maloney v. Greenwood et al., 186 S. W. 228, is not in accord with the conclusion we have reached.

[3] The contention that plaintiff's counsel invited the error by demanding the opening and concluding argument is untenable. Plaintiff's counsel objected without avail to the court's action in instructing the jury that the burden of proof was upon it. Having placed the burden of proof upon plaintiff, the court was no doubt actuated in allowing it the opening and concluding argument because of statutory provision, as well as the recognized rule of law, that the party on whom the burden of proof rests is entitled to open and conclude the argument. Article 1953, Revised Civil Statute 1911. This action alone, we think, prompted the court's ruling with reference to the order of argument.

[4] Intervener contends that the consideration by plaintiff was a pre-existing debt, and that therefore this does not constitute a new

consideration. If the consideration, or a part of the consideration, for the mortgage of January 20, 1916, was the extension of the note, then there is a sufficient consideration to entitle the plaintiff bank to protection as a subsequent mortgagee in good faith. This, however, is a question of fact for the jury, under appropriate instructions, to determine. Ingenhuett v. Hunt et al., 15 Tex. Civ. App. 248, 39 S. W. 310, writ of error denied, 93 Tex. 710, 42 S. W. xvi.

We recommend, therefore, that the judgments of the district court and court of Civil Appeals be reversed and remanded to the district court for a new trial.

PHILLIPS, C. J. The judgment recommended in the report of the Commission of Appeals is adopted, and will be entered as the judgment of the Supreme Court.

We approve the holding of the Commission of appeals on the question discussed in its opinion.

———

SHAW et al. v. FIRST STATE BANK OF ABILENE. (No. 237–3423.)*

(Commission of Appeals of Texas, Section A. June 1, 1921.)

1. **Vendor and purchaser** ⟨⟩274(1)—**Delivery of vendor's lien note to representative, together with the release, held not negligence on the part of the holder.**

Where plaintiff holding a vendor's lien note against defendant sent a release to the representative of a loan company to take up the note in making a loan on the land to the amount of the difference between the purchase price of a part thereof sold to a third party and the indebtedness to plaintiff, and the representative procured checks both from the third party and from defendant, but misappropriated them, a judgment for defendant cannot be sustained on the ground that plaintiff's negligence in delivering the release was the proximate cause of the injury to defendant, where the representative did not use it to obtain defendant's check, which was given solely because the third party's attorney approved the transaction.

2. **Bills and notes** ⟨⟩452(1)—**Failure of creditor to notify debtor that debt had not been paid not negligence.**

Failure of creditor bank to notify its debtor that a note had not been paid until after the death of one to whom the debtor had intrusted funds for its payment and who had misappropriated them, *held* not actionable negligence available as a defense in an action on the note.

3. **Principal and agent** ⟨⟩70—**Same person may be appointed agent for collection and payment by different parties.**

Where a loan was made to take up a vendor's lien note, and the owner appointed a representative of the loan company to make payment, the holder of the note may appoint same person as its agent to receive payment; the interests not being adverse.

4. **Principal and agent** ⟨⟩92(2)—**Payment of note is complete when funds have reached hands of agent authorized to receive it.**

The payment of a note or other obligation is complete when money intended for its payment or discharge has reached the hands of an agent authorized to receive it.

5. **Principal and agent** ⟨⟩124(3) — **Whether representative of loan company was agent of holder of vendor's lien note authorized to receive payment of the note held for the jury.**

Where a landowner, who desired to take up vendor's lien note to free a portion of the property from the lien, appointed the agent of a loan company to make payment and the holder of the vendor's lien sent the note accompanied by a release to the agent, who misappropriated the funds, the question, in an action by the holder of the note, whether such agent was agent of the holder authorized to receive payment of the note, *held*, under the evidence, for the jury.

Error to Court of Civil Appeals of Third Supreme Judicial District.

Action by the First State Bank of Abilene against C. M. Shaw and wife and A. H. Richardson. Judgment for defendants was by the Court of Civil Appeals affirmed as to defendant Richardson, and reversed and rendered as to defendants Shaw and wife (214 S. W. 442), and the latter defendants bring error. Judgments of the Court of Civil Appeals and the district court reversed and remanded as to plaintiffs in error Shaw for determination of an issue; otherwise affirmed.

Harrison & Cavin, of Eastland, and Wright & Harris, of San Angelo, for plaintiffs in error.

D. M. Oldham, Jr., of Abilene, Blanks, Collins & Jackson, of San Angelo, and W. D. Girand, of Abilene, for defendant in error.

SPENCER, J. Defendant in error, First State Bank of Abilene, Tex., instituted this suit to recover of C. M. Shaw and wife, Laura M. Shaw, plaintiffs in error, upon a vendor's lien note executed by them for the sum of $2,900, and to foreclose the lien upon the lands described in the note.

The facts, necessary to a determination of the question presented, are: That plaintiffs in error owned a 257-acre tract of land, against which two vendor's lien notes were outstanding, the one in suit and another for the sum of $4,100. A. H. Richardson had agreed to purchase, and subsequently did purchase, 63 acres out of this tract. It was desired to release the 63 acres from the lien. C. R. Miller, an attorney of Brownwood, represented Richardson in the transaction. To release the 63 acres, it was necessary to pay both notes. The proceeds to be derived from the 63 acres being insufficient for this purpose, an additional amount was contracted for with a Fort Worth Loan Company. B. E. Hurlbut represented the loan company in making the loan.

Defendant in error, the holder of the note in suit, upon request of Hurlbut, sent it,' accompanied by a release, to the Brownwood National Bank, with instructions to notify Hurlbut that it was there.

Miller inspected the note and release, and, having made certain objections to the latter, it was, at the request of Hurlbut, returned to defendant in error bank for correction. After having made certain corrections, the bank returned it direct to Hurlbut. Hurlbut presented the corrected release to Miller, falsely stating to him that he had paid the note, but that the loan company had demanded the original note before it would close the loan, and that he had sent it to that company.

Relying upon these representations, Miller procured a check for the amount of the purchase price of the 63 acres from his client, Richardson, payable to Shaw and wife, or bearer, and delivered it to Hurlbut. The latter presented this check and another one from the loan company, to Shaw and wife, who indorsed and returned them to Hurlbut. Hurlbut did not inform plaintiffs in error that he held the release, or that he had paid the note, but advised them that he would pay the note. The note was in fact never paid.

Richardson was made a party defendant, but, judgment rendered in his favor, which was affirmed by the court of Civil Appeals, not having been appealed from, further mention of the issue made between him and the bank is unnecessary.

In addition to the general denial, plaintiffs in error specially pleaded: (1) Payment of the note to B. E. Hurlbut, a duly authorized agent of the bank; (2) that the bank having furnished Hurlbut with a release reciting the payment of the note, it thereby clothed him with authority to collect the note, and, Hurlbut having induced them to pay him the amount of the note, the bank is estopped to deny payment; and (3) that the bank negligently failed to notify them until after Hurlbut's death of the nonpayment of the note, and but for which negligence they could and would have induced Hurlbut to replace the money.

The jury found that the bank was negligent in sending the release to Hurlbut; that it was negligent in failing to notify Shaw prior to May 16 of the nonpayment of the note; that if Shaw had been notified prior to Hurlbut's death of the nonpayment of the note, he could and would have induced Hurlbut to replace the amount owing upon the note at the time it should have been paid.

The court found, which findings were incorporated in the judgment, that Shaw, by his acts, made Hurlbut his and his wife's agent for the purpose of paying the note; (2) that Hurlbut made no false representations at the time the checks were delivered by him to the Shaws; (3) that Hurlbut cashed the checks and misappropriated the funds; and (4) that but for the conversion of the funds by Hurlbut, as the result of the bank's negligence, no injury would have resulted to defendants in error.

The trial court rendered judgment in favor of plaintiffs in error, denying recovery of the note and a foreclosure of the lien. The Court of Civil Appeals, however, reversed and rendered the judgment in favor of defendant in error. 214 S. W. 442.

The honorable Court of Civil Appeals held that the act of the bank in delivering the release to Hurlbut was not the direct and proximate cause of any injury to plaintiffs in error; (2) that the failure of the bank to notify Shaw, prior to Hurlbut's death, of the nonpayment of the note was not actionable negligence upon which defendants in error could predicate a defense; and (3) that the finding of the trial court that Hurlbut was the agent of plaintiffs in error to pay the note was inconsistent with the presumptive or implied finding that the checks were delivered to Hurlbut as the agent of the bank.

[1, 2] The holding of the honorable Court of Civil Appeals upon the first two propositions is, in our opinion, undoubtedly correct. Shaw does not claim to have been misled by anything that Hurlbut stated to him. He simply trusted him to cash the check and pay the note. Shaw did not know of the existence of the release until after the death of Hurlbut. He placed no reliance upon its execution or existence. The only effect of intrusting the release to Hurlbut was that it made it possible for him to get possession of the checks, and this possession, coupled with the duty to deliver them to plaintiffs in error, placed him in a position which invited his appointment, by plaintiffs in error, as agent to pay ·the note. Under the facts found, there is, we think, no estoppel in the case.

[3] With reference to the third conclusion —that the finding of the trial court that Hurlbut was the agent of plaintiffs in error to pay the note was inconsistent with the theory that Hurlbut was the agent of the bank to collect the note—we think that the honorable Court of Civil Appeals erred.

The interests of plaintiffs in error in paying the note and that of the bank in receiving payment thereof were not necessarily adverse. No reason is perceived why one, an agent to pay a note, may not also be the agent of the holder to collect it or to receive the payment thereof. The fact that the agency to collect or receive payment of a stipulated demand and the agency to pay the same merge in one person violates no rule or principle of law, and the same person may act as agent for payee and payor in the transaction unless their interests are adverse.

[4, 5] It is a well-established rule that the payment of a note or other obligation is complete when money intended for its payment or discharge has reached the hands of an agent authorized to receive it. Golden v. O'Connell, 76 W. Va. 282, 85 S. E. 533, 2 A. L. R. 460.

If, therefore, Hurlbut was in fact the authorized agent appointed by the bank to collect the note or receive payment thereof, payment to him of money intended to discharge it would operate as a payment of the same, notwithstanding he may have been the agent of plaintiffs in error to pay it. The question of his agency to collect the note or receive payment thereof is, of course, one of fact, to be determined by the court or jury.

We recommend that the judgments of the Court of Civil Appeals and the district court be reversed and remanded as to plaintiffs in error Shaw for a determination of this issue, and that otherwise it be affirmed.

PHILLIPS, C. J. The judgment recommended in the report of the Commission of Appeals is adopted, and will be entered as the judgment of the Supreme Court.

We approve the holding of the Commission of Appeals on the questions discussed in its opinion.

———

MISSOURI, K. & T. RY. CO. OF TEXAS v. MERCHANT et al. (No. 229–3406.)*

(Commission of Appeals of Texas, Section A. June 1, 1921.)

1. **Railroads ⬥═350(8)—Driver of auto struck held not conclusively shown to have seen train in time.**

Evidence in action for collision of train with auto truck *held* not to conclusively show that the driver saw the train in time to stop before going on the crossing, and so was guilty of contributory negligence.

2. **Railroads ⬥═346(5)—Burden of showing contributory negligence on defendant.**

The law presumes that one killed at a railroad crossing was doing whatever was reasonably necessary for his safety, so the company sued for his death must prove he was not, to relieve itself of the consequences of its failure to give the crossing signal.

3. **Railroads ⬥═348(6)—Jury may consider evidence most favorable to plaintiff.**

On the issue of contributory negligence of deceased, the jury had the right to consider the evidence most favorable for plaintiff from the position of deceased just before and at the moment of the collision, rejecting all evidence most favorable to defendant.

4. **Railroads ⬥═350(16)—Failure to look and listen not conclusive of contributory negligence.**

Whether one killed at a railroad crossing was guilty of contributory negligence is an issue of fact under all the circumstances, not foreclosed necessarily by establishing that he did not look or listen.

5. **Trial ⬥═240—Charge on ordinary care of deceased held argumentative.**

Charge that "no one is required to anticipate that another will fail to obey the law, and you are therefore charged that in passing on the issue" whether deceased "exercised ordinary care in approaching the crossing, he had the right to expect that defendant's" trainmen would give the required crossing signals, is argumentative.

6. **Appeal and error ⬥═1064(1)—Argumentative charge on ordinary care of deceased held prejudicial.**

It is misleading in a crossing accident case, in which there are sharply contested issues of negligence and contributory negligence, relative to whether signals were given and as to whether one of ordinary prudence in the position of deceased would have stopped his truck before going on the crossing, to give the argumentative charge that "no one is required to anticipate that another will fail to obey the law, and you are therefore charged that in passing on the issue" whether deceased "exercised ordinary care in approaching the crossing, he had the right to expect that defendant's" trainmen would give the required crossing signals; and its effect would not be necessarily counteracted by the fact that the case was submitted on special issues, or that the jury found that deceased looked and listened for the train.

Error to Court of Civil Appeals of Sixth Supreme Judicial District.

Action by Odelle Merchant and another against the Missouri, Kansas & Texas Railway Company of Texas. Judgment for plaintiffs was affirmed by the Court of Civil Appeals (212 S. W. 970), and defendant brings error. Reversed and remanded for new trial.

Chas. C. Huff, of Dallas, and Dinsmore, McMahan & Dinsmore, of Greenville, for plaintiff in error.

Clark & Sweeton, of Greenville, for defendants in error.

TAYLOR, P. J. Defendants in error, Mrs. Odelle Merchant and her son, Charles Merchant, Jr., brought this suit against C. E. Schaff, receiver of the Missouri, Kansas & Texas Railway Company of Texas, plaintiff in error, for damages growing out of the death of Charles Merchant, Sr., husband of one of defendants in error and father of the other. The case was submitted on special issues, and on the responses given judgment was rendered in favor of defendants in error. The Court of Civil Appeals by majority opinion affirmed the judgment. 212 S. W. 970.

This is an ordinary crossing case in which the collision was between an auto truck driven by Charles Merchant and one of plaintiff in error's passenger trains. The negligence alleged is that plaintiff in error failed to give the statutory crossing signals and failed to keep a lookout. The defenses pleaded are the general issue and contributory negligence. The averments of contributory negligence are so framed as to charge negligence on the part of Merchant either in failing to stop, look, or listen on approaching the crossing, or, in the event he knew of the approach of the train, in racing with it to clear the crossing first.

The jury found in response to the special issues submitted that Merchant, before driving his truck upon the track, looked and listened for the approach of train; that plaintiff in error failed to give the statutory signals in not blowing the whistle or ringing the bell at least 80 rods from the crossing and while approaching it, and that the failure to give the signals was the proximate cause of Merchant's death; that a man of ordinary prudence, under the circumstances surrounding Merchant at the time he approached the crossing, would not have stopped his car for the purpose of ascertaining whether a train was approaching. On motion of plaintiff in error requesting a modification of the findings made, the Court of Civil Appeals adopted as its own the jury findings.

It is not disputed that the pike road upon which Merchant was driving runs for 600 yards through open country, obliquely with and across the railway at the crossing upon which he met his death; that the road is slightly elevated, and the railway track is a little down grade in approaching the crossing; that the rails of the track at the crossing projected above the ground about 3 inches; that Merchant at the time of the accident was driving an automobile truck loaded with six barrels of gasoline; that the regular south-bound passenger train was running about 50 minutes late at a speed of about 40 miles an hour. With the exception of a small clump of bushes a little nearer the crossing than the whistling post, there was nothing on the ground to obstruct Merchant's view of the track as he approached the crossing.

It appears from the evidence that Merchant, as he drew near the crossing, steered his truck so as to hit the rails at right angles. W. E. Milsap, a truck driver who was on the pike when Merchant was struck, testified that the crossing was rough; that on the south side of the road where the wheel ordinarily travels the rails were from three to five inches high above the ground; that in order to go over the rail it was necessary to slow up and pull to the extreme left of the road and hit it square. C. H. Combs, who witnessed the accident from the gallery of his home near the crossing, testified that he could not say how far deceased was from the railway when he made the turn to, hit the rail square, but that he was "right close to the road"; and, further, "that it (the truck) was going very slow then"; that "just before the train got to the crossing he (Merchant) seemed to release his engine and it peartened up." It is undisputed that the whistle was blown before the crossing was reached. Defendants in error's contention was that it was not blown until too late. Upon this point the testimony conflicts. One of the witnesses testified that "right after the train blew" he heard the crash, and that at about the time he heard the one he heard the other commence. T. J. Freeman, who was across the track from the truck as it approached the crossing, testified that "when it began to blow and I looked at the man and saw him coming with his eyes straight ahead steering for the crossing, I got scared and broke and ran and waved my hand and tried to signal the man in the car to stop." The witness was not definite in his statement as to how far the truck was from the crossing when the blast of the whistle began, but his conclusion was, after stating that he was "somewhat rattled" by the examination, that it must have been between 20 feet and nearer.

There was other testimony not necessary to refer to tending to support the judgment predicated on plaintiff in error's negligence in not giving the crossing signals as required by the statute. The principle question for determination is whether the trial court erred in not peremptorily instructing a verdict for plaintiff in error on the ground that Merchant was guilty of contributory negligence.

[1-3] Plaintiff in error's first contention in respect to the alleged contributory negligence is that inasmuch as Merchant saw the train as he approached the crossing, and nevertheless attempted to cross the track in front of it, he was, as a matter of law, guilty of negligence.

The conclusion that Merchant saw the train within time to have stopped his truck before going upon the crossing is based upon the following facts and findings, viewed by plaintiff in error as undisputed: That as Merchant approached his view of the train was wholly unobstructed for a distance of at least 600 yards before the train reached the crossing; that Merchant was driving five or six miles per hour and could have stopped his truck in a distance of 16 feet; that when Merchant was 230 feet away from the track the train was 1,500 feet from the crossing; that Merchant, in approaching the crossing, looked for the train (the jury having so found); that having looked he necessarily saw it.

Chief Justice Willson, in dissenting from the majority opinion, says:

"It thus appearing that Merchant looked for the train, and that there was nothing to prevent him from seeing it, it seems to me the only reasonable inference is that he did see it approaching the crossing before he drove thereon. If he did, I think the inference that he was guilty of negligence in attempting nevertheless to cross the track is not escapable."

We do not concur in the view expressed in the dissent. The vice in it, in our opinion, is in assuming that Merchant necessarily saw the train when he looked. The jury concluded, evidently, that he did not, and the testimony tends to establish the conclusion. It tends to prove also that Merchant knew nothing of the approach of the train prior to the warning blast of the whistle, and there is some evidence that this blast was not sounded until after the truck was nearer than 20 feet to the crossing.

Merchant's line of approach to the crossing formed an angle of about 45 degrees with the line of the track. The train was running at a rate of speed eight or ten times as fast as that at which Merchant was driving. The train was at his right and back of him. The steering wheel of the truck was on the left side. W. H. Norman testified that the truck had a flat body built up at the side with side boards or slats, and had something like a cab over the seat, that the top of the cab was built out of plank and that the sides were solid and without glass; that the back of the cab had curtains; that when a man was sitting in the seat the body of the truck, as built up, was higher than he was. Back of the seat in the truck were six tanks of gasoline about four feet high. C. H. Combs testified that "from any point along that road, if a man cast his eyes to the right, if he looked far enough around, he could see a train at the top of the hill." The truck was loaded, and under the evidence could not have been stopped within a shorter distance than 16 feet, even at the slow speed at which it was moving. It could be stopped within that distance only in the event the brakes were working well. One of the witnesses testified that when he first saw Merchant he was driving at the rate of about 10 miles per hour. Before reaching the crossing he decreased his speed to about one-half that rate. Just before going upon the crossing he "peartened his engine."

The law presumes that Merchant was in the exercise of due care, and was doing whatever was reasonably necessary for his own safety; and it devolved upon plaintiff in error to prove that he was not, in order to relieve itself of the consequences of failing to give the crossing signals as required by law. Lee v. I. & G. N. Ry. Co., 89 Tex. 583, 36 S. W. 63. The testimony was not, in our opinion, such as to leave no room for ordinary minds to differ as to the conclusion to be drawn from it touching the degree of care used by Merchant. The jury had a right to consider the evidence most favorably for the plaintiff from the position of the deceased just before and at the moment of the collision, rejecting all evidence most favorable to plaintiff in error. Kirksey v. So. Traction Co., 110 Tex. 190, 217 S. W. 139. In view of the circumstances pointed out, we think it does not conclusively appear that the deceased saw the train before it was too late, or that he began racing with it while he was farther than 16 feet from the crossing. We concur in the view of the Court of Civil Appeals, as expressed in the majority opinion, that Merchant at the time he entered upon the right of way, situated as he was, would not necessarily have known of the approach of the train even by reasonable observation. The testimony would warrant abundantly the contrary conclusion, but does not establish it as a matter of law.

[4] Plaintiff in error's second proposition is that Merchant was guilty of negligence as a matter of law, in that the uncontradicted evidence shows that he drove towards a railway crossing with which he was familiar, under conditions permitting him to see the approaching train for a distance of more than 600 yards before reaching the crossing, and drove upon it without looking for a train.

The law presumes that Merchant was doing whatever was reasonably necessary for his own safety. Plaintiff in error did not establish as a matter of law that he did not look for the approaching train or take some precaution for his safety.

But regardless of whether this was established, the single act of whether Merchant looked for the approaching train is not necessarily the test of whether he was guilty of contributory negligence. Whether under all of the circumstances he was negligent was an issue of fact, which would not have been foreclosed necessarily against defendant in error by a finding that Merchant did not do the specific acts of either looking or listening. Addendum to Trochta et al. v. M., K. & T. Ry. Co. of Texas, 218 S. W. 1088.

In our opinion plaintiff in error failed to establish as a matter of law that Merchant was negligent.

[5, 6] Plaintiff in error objected to the giving of the following special charge requested by defendants in error:

"You are instructed that no one is required to anticipate that another will fail to obey the law, and you are therefore charged that in passing on the issue of whether or not deceased, Chas. Merchant, exercised ordinary care in approaching the crossing, he had the right to expect that defendant's employees in charge of the train would give the signals required by law in approaching the crossing."

The objections urged were that the charge is upon the weight of the evidence and argumentative. Clearly, in our opinion, it is argumentative, and, taken in connection with the special issues submitted, was calculated to mislead the jury.

Defendants in error relied for recovery on a negative finding by the jury in response to the inquiries concerning the crossing signals. Plaintiff in error endeavored to defeat recovery by having the jury find that a man of ordinary prudence, situated as Merchant was, would have stopped his truck before going upon the crossing; also that Merchant neither looked nor listened for the approach of the train. The issues relating to plaintiff in error's negligence and Merchant's contributory negligence were sharply contested. In connection with these issues, the following instruction was given in the main charge:

"It was the duty of Charles Merchant, deceased, in approaching the defendant's crossing on the public road where his death occurred, to exercise ordinary care, or that degree of care which a person of ordinary prudence would have exercised under the same or similar circumstances, to avoid being struck by a train on the defendant's railroad. A failure to exercise such care on his part would be negligence."

The jury was called upon to answer whether a man of ordinary prudence in Merchant's position would have stopped his truck before going on the crossing. The requested charge complained of, in addition to instructing generally that no one is required to anticipate that one will fail to obey the law, instructed them specifically, in effect, that in passing on the issue of whether Merchant exercised ordinary care in approaching the crossing they should take into consideration that he had a right to expect plaintiff in error's employés to give the crossing signals. The requested charge was calculated to cause the jury to excuse Merchant from using that degree of care for his safety, which, in the absence of such a charge, they might have believed did not constitute ordinary care on his part under the circumstances. It was also calculated to suggest that the court believed Merchant did not hear the signals which he had a "right to expect" to be given, and that they were therefore not given.

The jury found that a man of ordinary prudence would not have stopped his truck under the circumstances surrounding Merchant; also that the failure of plaintiff in error to give the signals was the proximate cause of Merchant's death. The fact that the case was submitted on special issues, or that the jury found Merchant looked and listened for the train, would not necessarily counteract the effect of the charge complained of. Regardless of whether it misstates the law, it was calculated, in our opinion, to mislead the jury, and should not have been given. As stated by Judge Gaines in the case of McDonald v. I. & G. N. Ry. Co., 86 Tex. 1, 22 S. W. 939, 40 Am. St. Rep. 808, in commenting on a somewhat similar charge:

"This may have been proper as an argument to the jury, but it was not proper to be given as an instruction by the court."

We recommend that the judgments of the trial court and Court of Civil Appeals be reversed, and that the cause be remanded for another trial.

PHILLIPS, C. J. The judgment recommended in the report of the Commission of Appeals is adopted, and will be entered as the judgment of the Supreme Court.

We approve the holding of the Commission of Appeals on the questions discussed in its opinion.

MARTIN et al. v. KIESCHNICK et al.[*]
(No. 211–3308.)

(Commission of Appeals of Texas, Section A. June 1, 1921.)

1. Venue ⊜17—Statute as to where suit to enjoin execution shall be brought one of venue, and so waivable.

Rev. St. 1911, art. 1830, subd. 17, providing that no one shall be sued out of the county of his domicile, except when suit is brought to enjoin execution it shall be brought in the county where the judgment was rendered, is one of venue only, and not of jurisdiction; so defendant may waive his privilege.

2. Venue ⊜17—Claim of privilege not waived by following general demurrer in the same answer.

Right of a defendant under Rev. St. 1911, art. 1830, subd. 17, to have action to enjoin execution tried in the county of the judgment, is not waived though the general demurrer filed contemporaneously with the plea in abatement precedes it in the arrangement in the answer, and there is a proviso to article 1902 allowing a defendant in his answer to plead as many several matters, whether of law or fact, as he shall think necessary for his defense, that he shall file them all at the same time "and in due order of pleading."

3. Venue ⊜17—Claim of privilege waived by invoking action on general demurrer and acquiescing in action thereon.

Defendant's claim of privilege to have action determined in another county, asserted by plea in abatement, is waived by his invoking action of the court on the general demurrer, and abiding by its act in sustaining the demurrer and dismissing the action; whereas, if it had merely sustained the plea of privilege, it would under Rev. St. 1911, art. 1833, have transferred the case.

Error to Court of Civil Appeals of Third Supreme Judicial District.

Suit by Richard Kieschnick and wife against Horace Martin and others. Decree dismissing the cause was affirmed by the

Court of Civil Appeals (208 S. W. 948), and plaintiff brings error. Affirmed.

W. A. Morrison, of Cameron, and O. D. Graham, of Thorndale, for plaintiffs in error.

E. A. Wallace, of Cameron, for defendants in error.

SPENCER, J. Defendants in error filed this suit in the district court of Milam county, Tex., on September 22, 1916, seeking to restrain the enforcement of an execution issued out of the justice court, precinct No. 1 of Crockett county, Tex., upon a judgment rendered by that court against the Thorndale Mercantile Company. Plaintiff in error, the Thorndale Mercantile Company, a corporation, and Horace Martin, constable of precinct No. 8, Milam county, Tex., were named as defendants in the original petition. These defendants filed an answer on October 16, 1916, consisting of a general demurrer and general denial. By an amended petition filed March 27, 1917, plaintiff in error W. M. Johnigan, justice of the peace, precinct No. 1, Crockett county, Tex., was made a party defendant.

Plaintiffs in error filed a joint amended answer consisting of a general demurrer, followed by several special exceptions calling in question the jurisdiction of the district court of Milam county to hear and determine the cause because of the venue being laid in virtue of subdivision 17 of article 1830, Revised Civil Statutes of 1911, in Crockett county, Tex. The answer also contained a special exception aimed at the allegations of plaintiff's petition seeking to recover punitive damages, and a demurrer for the benefit of the plaintiff in error Johnigan alone. The court granted a temporary order restraining the enforcement of the execution. The writ was made returnable to the district court of Milam county, Tex. Upon final hearing, the court sustained the general demurrer and all the special exceptions and dismissed the cause.

Appeal was taken by defendants in error to the Court of Civil Appeals and that court being of opinion that plaintiff in error Johnigan had waived his privilege to have the cause tried in Crockett county, Tex., reversed and remanded the cause. 208 S. W. 948.

[1-3] The question for our decision is: Did plaintiff in error W. M. Johnigan waive the plea of privilege accorded by article 1830, subd. 17, which reads:

"Art. 1830. No person who is an inhabitant of this state shall be sued out of the county in which he has his domicile, except in the following cases, to wit: * * * (17) When the suit is brought to enjoin the execution of a judgment or to stay proceedings in any suit, in which case the suit shall be brought in the county in which such judgment was rendered or in which such suit is pending."

The clause quoted is not a jurisdictional statute, but is one of venue only. It determines the venue of actions to be instituted under it, but does not confer jurisdiction over the subject-matter. It is not of that class of exceptions to be found in the statute which are provided for the exclusive benefit of plaintiffs, and which give to them exclusively the choice between different counties in selecting a place in which they will commence their actions. It is not mandatory in the sense that no court, other than the court of the county in which the judgment—the execution of which is sought to be enjoined—was rendered would have jurisdiction, but is controlling if invoked by defendant by the filing in due order of pleading of a proper plea. A defendant may waive his right to invoke it just as he may waive his right to be sued in the county of his domicile. State of Texas v. Snyder et al., 66 Tex. 687, 18 S. W. 106.

Article 1902, Revised Civil Statutes 1911, provides that the defendant in his answer may plead as many several matters, whether of law or fact, as he shall think necessary for his defense and which may be pertinent to the cause, provided that he shall file them all at the same time and in due order of pleading. In Graham v. McCarty & Brown, 69 Tex. 323, 7 S. W. 342, Judge Acker says that—

"'Due order of pleading' requires that a plea in abatement should precede answer to the merits, of either law or fact, is elementary."

In construing the same cause, Judge Roberts for the Supreme Court says:

"The special exceptions of the defendants in the nature of a plea of privilege, being matter alone pleadable in abatement, and being filed after a general demurrer and general denial was properly overruled by the court. They were not filed in 'due order of pleading.' (O. & W. Dig., article 426.) The fact that the matter embraced in the special exceptions was shown in the petition, so that 'the truth of the plea appeared of record,' would dispense with its being pleaded formally under oath, and with the necessity of the adducing other proof in support of it; nevertheless, it was a dilatory plea, (however it might be presented,) which must precede a general demurrer and general denial. Paschal's Digest, articles 1 to 4." Compton v. Stage Co., 25 Tex. Supp. 67.

In each of these cases the records show that the plea in abatement was filed subsequent to the filing of the general demurrer and general denial and not contemporaneously therewith, as in the present case. The language quoted is not authority for holding that where the plea in abatement is filed contemporaneously with the general demurrer and general denial, and the general demurrer precedes the plea in abatement in the arrangement in the answer, that the plea in abatement is thereby waived. That question was not before the court in either case. Where the pleas and defenses are filed contemporaneously, we think the rule announced in Hagood v. Dial, 43 Tex. 625, is controlling. It is there said:

"Whilst the privilege of being sued only in the county of his residence, which our statute, with specified exceptions, gives a defendant, is waived if not asserted before answering to the merits, we think it is not waived where (as in this case it is fair to conclude) the plea asserting it was filed contemporaneously with other defenses. It was held very early by this court that the common-law rules of pleading were inapplicable under our system to this plea. (Richardson and Wife v. Pruitt, 3 Tex. 228.) It is evident that the defendant did not intend by his exceptions and pleas to the merits to waive his privilege which he had already asserted; and, we think, that as to this point the court ruled correctly."

Under the ruling in the Hagood Case, supra, we do not think that plaintiff in error, Johnigan, waived his privilege to have the cause of action against him determined in Crockett county, because the plea in abatement filed contemporaneously with the answer to the merits precedes the general demurrer in its arrangement in the answer; but we do think that he waived his privilege for the reason that he invoked the action of the trial court upon the general demurrer and special exceptions nine and eleven. Special exception No. 9 was aimed at the allegation of plaintiff's petition seeking to recover punitive damages, and special exception No. 11, in the nature of a general demurrer, called in question the right of the plaintiff to maintain the suit against Johnigan because all the alleged actions and omissions of Johnigan relied upon for recovery were performed in his official capacity and in performance of his official duties as justice of the peace. The court sustained, not only the general demurrer, but these special exceptions.

The court in passing upon this general demurrer passed upon the legal sufficiency of the plaintiff's petition, and the cause of action was evidently dismissed in pursuance to the court's ruling in sustaining the general demurrer. Had the court merely sustained the plea in abatement and taken no action upon the general demurrer, it would not have dismissed the cause of action, but would have transferred it to Crockett county, as required by article 1833, Revised Civil Statutes 1911. Hickman v. Swain et al., 106 Tex. 431, 167 S. W. 209. This act of the court, acquiesced in by plaintiff in error Johnigan, was tantamount to a waiver by him of his privilege to have the cause of action determined in Crockett county.

We recommend, therefore, that the judgment of the Court of Civil Appeals reversing and remanding the cause be affirmed.

PHILLIPS, C. J. The judgment recommended in the report of the Commission of Appeals is adopted, and will be entered as the judgment of the Supreme Court.

MILLHOLLON v. STANTON INDEPENDENT SCHOOL DIST. (No. 244—3438.)*

(Commission of Appeals of Texas, Section A. June 1, 1921.)

1. Statutes ⬀195—Expression of one thing excludes another.

The expression of one thing excludes another.

2. Schools and school districts ⬀103(2)—Trustees of school district held not to have right to call election for levy of maintenance tax.

As Loc. & Sp. Laws, 35th Leg. (1917) c. 128, creating the Stanton Independent School District, provides in section 19 that the trustees may themselves levy an annual maintenance tax, the trustees, notwithstanding section 23 declares that in all matters not provided for they shall be vested with the rights, powers, and privileges conferred and imposed by the general laws, have no authority to call an election for levy of a maintenance tax pursuant to the general laws, for the local act supersedes the general laws, and hence is void, violating Const. art. 7, § 3, declaring that the Legislature may authorize an additional ad valorem tax to be levied and collected in all school districts, provided that a majority of the qualified property taxpaying voters voting at an election to be held for that purpose shall vote such tax, and a tax sought to be levied pursuant to the election should be enjoined.

Error to Court of Civil Appeals of Eighth Supreme Judicial District.

Injunction suit by J. E. Millhollon against the Stanton Independent School District. Relief denied, and plaintiff appealed, defendant assigning cross-errors. Judgment affirmed by the Court of Civil Appeals (221 S. W. 1109), and plaintiff brings error. Judgments of trial court and Court of Civil Appeals reversed, and case remanded.

Stephen W. Pratt, of Cisco, Royall G. Smith, of El Paso, and Thos. R. Smith, of Colorado, Tex., for plaintiff in error.

Morrison & Morrison, of Big Springs, for defendant in error.

GALLAGHER, J. The Stanton independent school district was originally incorporated for school purposes only, under the general laws of Texas, and as so created and constituted, lawfully and properly issued and sold certain bonds still outstanding, and by an election duly held the board of trustees were duly authorized to levy and collect an annual tax sufficient to pay the interest on, and create a sinking fund for, the ultimate retirement of such bonds.

The Thirty-Fifth Legislature, by special act appearing as chapter 128, on page 510, of the published local and special laws of the regular session of such Legislature, incorporated the Stanton independent school district, including therein its former territory and also additional territory.

This act creates the district, defines its boundaries, provides for the election of a board of trustees and the perpetuation thereof by subsequent elections, authorizes such board of trustees to organize, appoint necessary officers, levy, assess, and collect taxes, and receive all money apportioned to said district out of the available free school fund, and to exercise general authority in the matter of establishing and conducting public free schools in said district.

On July 25, 1918, by order of the board of trustees of said district, an election was held therein on proper petition to determine whether or not a tax, not to exceed 50 cents on the $100 assessed valuation of property within the district, should be levied for the support of public schools therein. The election resulted in favor of the tax levy, and no complaint of irregularities therein is made.

The board of trustees thereafter for the year 1918 levied a tax of 50 cents on the $100 valuation of all property in the new district, and directed, in accordance with the provisions of said act, that fifteen cents of such tax on the property in the old district be placed in the sinking fund, and that the remaining 35 cents of such tax on the property in the old district, and the entire 50 cents tax on the property in the newly added territory, be applied to maintenance.

J. B. Millhollon, the plaintiff in error, was the owner of certain property taxable for said year which was situated in the new territory added to the district by said act. Such property was regularly assessed, and the tax so levied against the same for said year amounted to $101.22. Millhollon failed to pay this tax.

The assessor and collector of taxes for said district was about to seize and sell certain personal property belonging to said Millhollon to satisfy such unpaid tax, whereupon Millhollon sued out a temporary injunction, restraining said school district, its board of trustees, and its assessor and collector of taxes, from seizing or selling any property belonging to him for the purpose of collecting such tax. On final hearing the trial court entered an order restraining the collection of 15 cents on the $100 of such tax so levied, but permitting the collection of the remaining thirty-five cents of such tax. The Court of Civil Appeals affirmed the judgment of the trial court, 221 S. W. 1109.

Plaintiff in error contends that the special act of the Legislature creating said school district does not, either expressly or by implication, confer on its board of trustees the right or power to order an election to determine whether or not a maintenance tax of 50 cents on the $100, or any lesser sum, shall be levied and collected, but attempts to confer the power to levy and collect such tax without any such election, in violation of the Constitution, and that the tax complained of is, on that account, illegal and uncollectable.

[1, 2] The constitutional provision invoked is a part of article 7, § 3, and is as follows:

"And the Legislature may authorize an additional ad valorem tax to be levied and collected within all school districts, heretofore formed or hereafter formed, for the further maintenance of public free schools, and the erection and equipment of school buildings therein; provided, that a majority of the qualified property taxpaying voters of the district, voting at an election to be held for that purpose, shall vote such tax, not to exceed in any one year fifty cents on the one hundred dollar valuation of the property subject to taxation in such district."

The provisions of the special act of incorporation upon which this contention is based are contained in sections 19 and 23 thereof. Section 19 of that act reads in part as follows:

"The board of trustees of said Stanton independent school district, as heretofore provided for, shall have the power and it shall be their duty, to levy and collect an annual ad valorem tax not to exceed fifty cents on the one hundred dollar valuation of taxable property within said district for the maintenance of the public free schools therein, and a tax sufficient to pay interest on, and create sinking fund to pay at maturity the bonds heretofore issued by what is known as Stanton independent school district organized under general laws of this state and which is a part of the district provided by this act: provided further, that the tax to pay interest on, and create a sinking fund to meet bonds at maturity shall only be levied and collected on the property located within the bounds of the district originally formed; and provided further that said tax in said original district shall not exceed fifty cents on the one hundred dollars valuation of taxable property."

The remainder of the section has no relevancy to the issue under discussion. Section 23 of said special act is as follows:

"As to all matters not provided for in this act, the board of trustees of the independent school district created hereunder shall have and exercise and are hereby vested and charged with all the rights, powers, privileges and duties conferred and imposed by the general laws of this state, now in force or hereafter to be enacted, upon the boards of trustees of independent school districts organized under the general laws of this state."

The Court of Civil Appeals held that section 23 of said special act conferred upon the board of trustees of said school district the rights, powers, privileges, and duties conferred and imposed upon boards of trustees of independent school districts by the general laws of the state, including the right and power to call such election, submit the issue of the tax levy to the voters of the district and on an affirmative vote to levy the tax complained of. We think the court erred in so construing such section. It is true that the general statute provides for such an election as the trustees here called. Were the special act silent in respect to the power, this general statute would control. But the special act is not silent as to the power. In express contradiction of the general statute it provides that the trustees themselves may levy the tax. This is contrary to the Constitution, and renders the special act void. The special act also excludes entirely the application of the general statute to the power exerted since it declares in effect that only as to matters not covered by it shall the general laws control.

The enumeration of one thing in a statute is, according to the well-known maxim, the exclusion of another. This part of the act is in substance an express declaration that the general statute shall not control with respect to the levying of the tax, since that is a matter embraced within the special act, the act declaring in substance that only as to matters not embraced in the special act shall the general laws control.

Since the Legislature has in effect declared that the general laws shall not apply with respect to the power, we do not see how those laws can be looked to as authority for the exercise of the power. The Legislature must be taken at its word. The application by the courts of the general statute cannot be warranted where the Legislature has in effect declared that the general statute should have no application to the given subject.

We recommend that the judgments of the district court and the Court of Civil Appeals be reversed, and the case remanded to the district court for proceedings in accord with this opinion.

PHILLIPS, C. J. The judgment recommended in the report of the Commission of Appeals is adopted and will be entered as the judgment of the Supreme Court.

We approve the holding of the Commission of Appeals on the question discussed in its opinion.

PENDLETON v. HARE.   (No. 232-3413.)*

(Commission of Appeals of Texas, Section A. June 1, 1921.)

1. Evidence ⚫➡80(1)—It is presumed that laws of foreign state are like those of forum.

In an action against the ancillary administrator in Texas for legal services rendered the Oklahoma executor, it will be presumed in the absence of proof as to the laws of Oklahoma in reference to probate of wills and handling estate of decedent that they are similar to the laws of Texas.

2. Executors and administrators ⚫➡111(1) — Reasonable attorney's fees are expenses of administration.

Within Rev. St. 1911, arts. 3623, 3458, reasonable attorney's fees are expenses of administration.

3. Executors and administrators ⚫➡111(3)— In contracting with attorney for services in probate of will, executor acts in representative capacity.

An executor who contracts with an attorney for legal services in connection with the probate of a will, which is the first essential and indispensable step toward carrying out the trusts imposed, is acting, not in his individual but in his representative capacity.

4. Executors and administrators ⚫➡111(3)— Executor may bind estate for reasonable attorney's fees in connection with probate of will.

Under Rev. St. 1911, arts. 3623, 3458, respectively declaring that executors and administrators shall be allowed all reasonable attorney's fees necessarily incurred by them in the course of administration, and that expenses of administration, etc., shall have priority, the executor of a decedent is entitled to procure legal services for the probate of a will, though not personally interested therein, for, if the statute does not authorize such expenditures, it does not forbid the same, and the probate of the will is the first essential step toward carrying out the trusts declared.

5. Executors and administrators ⚫➡521—Attorney's services in will contest in other state may be charged against estate in Texas in hands of ancillary administrator.

Where the executor of an Oklahoma decedent engaged an attorney to probate the will, and the attorney resisted the contest interposed by the decedent's heirs, his claim for legal services may, where the assets in Oklahoma were exhausted, be made a charge against the personal estate in the hands of the ancillary Texas administrator, the executor having abandoned his application to be appointed administrator with the will annexed in the state of Texas, for the ancillary administrator bears the same responsibility as if he were the sole administrator or executor, and privity arises from his obligation to pay the debts of the estate, including the expenses of administration.

Error to Court of Civil Appeals of Sixth Supreme Judicial District.

Suit by W. S. Pendleton against Silas Hare, administrator of Samuel Bailey. A judgment for plaintiff was reversed by the Court of Civil Appeals (214 S. W. 948), judgment being rendered for defendant, and plaintiff brings error. Judgment of the Court of Civil Appeals reversed, and that of trial court affirmed.

W. S. Pendleton, of Shawnee, Okl., J. W. Hassell, of Denison, and Head, Dillard, Smith, Maxey & Head, of Sherman, for plaintiff in error.

F. H. Reilly, of Shawnee, Okl., and J. A. L. Wolfe and J. H. Wood, both of Sherman, for defendant in error.

SPENCER, J. Plaintiff in error, W. A. Pendleton, instituted this suit against Silas Hare, administrator of the estate of Samuel Bailey, to recover the value of attorney's fees for services rendered the estate in Oklahoma.

The facts necessary to a determination of the issues are:

That Samuel Bailey died in Pottawatomie county, the place of his residence, leaving a will in which B. F. Hamilton was named executor and Sherman Spencer the sole beneficiary.

The estate consisted of real and personal property situated in Oklahoma of the value of $6,000 and personal property in Texas consisting of $54,000 on deposit in a Denison Bank and $1,700 in notes executed by a party in Oklahoma and secured by mortgage on Oklahoma real estate.

With knowledge before Bailey's death that he had been appointed executor, Hamilton employed plaintiff in error, a practicing attorney, to assist in the proceedings to probate the will, and in the conduct of the administration and settlement of the estate. After Bailey's death, F. H. Reilly, another attorney, was employed, and the two were thereafter associated in the case; Pendleton being the leading lawyer.

Upon the will being offered for probate, its probate was resisted by Amelia Parker and others. The contest was long and stubborn, but terminated in a judgment probating the will.

On October 1, 1912, while the contest in Oklahoma was pending, W. G. McGinnis filed an application to be appointed and was appointed temporary administrator of the estate in Texas. Hamilton intervened, asking that he be appointed temporary and permanent administrator. Amelia Parker and others intervened to contest the appointment of Hamilton.

After considerable litigation in the district and county courts of Grayson county, it was agreed by all the parties that defendant in error should be appointed permanent administrator of the estate in Texas to take charge of and hold the estate pending the outcome of the Oklahoma contest, and, upon termination of the contest to distribute the estate among the parties entitled to receive it. Defendant in error qualified as administrator, and on February 14, 1917, which was after the termination of the Oklahoma contest, filed his final report as administrator; but its approval was objected to by Amelia Parker and others, plaintiff in error, T. G. Cutlip, and the state of Oklahoma.

During the hearing of the contest on the final reprrt, Sherman Spencer compromised with Amelia Parker and others, and the court then approved the final report, but required the administrator to hold a sufficient amount, pending the result of the litigation of Pendleton, Cutlip, and the state of Oklahoma to pay any judgments that they or any of them might finally recover, and directed that the remainder be paid over to Sherman Spencer.

Plaintiff in error presented his claim to Hamilton, executor, who allowed it for a reasonable fee, without stating the amount. The executor disbursed all of the funds in Oklahoma without paying plaintiff in error's claim.

On February 15, 1917, plaintiff in error presented his claim for $10,000 to defendant in error, Silas Hare, administrator, who refused it on the same day, and this suit was instituted the following day.

Upon a trial before the court without a jury, a judgment was rendered in favor of plaintiff in error for $7,500. Upon appeal the Court of Civil Appeals reversed and rendered the judgment. 214 S. W. 948.

[1] There is no proof in the record as to what the laws of the state of Oklahoma are with reference to the probate of wills and the handling of estates of decedents, and in the absence of which it will be presumed that they are similar to the laws of this state. Western Union Tel. Co. v. Bailey, 108 Tex. 427, 196 S. W. 516.

[2-4] The defendant in error insists that the claim for attorney's fees, which for the most part represents services rendered in establishing the will, is not a charge against the estate, but that, having been contracted for by the executor upon behalf of himself individually and for Sherman Spencer, sole beneficiary under the will, it is the individual obligation of the executor and Sherman Spencer.

There is no statute in this state that requires the executor named in the will to propound the same for probate; but article 3262, Revised Civil Statutes of 1911, permits him to do so; and if, in response to such commission, the executor in good faith makes application to have the same probated, and a contest follows, necessitating the employment of an attorney, and the will is admitted to probate, a reasonable attorney's fee for the services performed is a claim against the estate within the purview of articles 3623 and 3458, Revised Civil Statutes of 1911.

Article 3623 reads:

"Art. 3623. Executors and administrators shall also be allowed all reasonable expenses necessarily incurred by them in the preservation, safe-keeping and management of the estate, and all reasonable attorney's fees that may be necessarily incurred by them in the course of the administration."

Article 3458 declares that—

"The claims against an estate shall be classed and have priority of payment as follows:

* * *

"2. Expenses of administration and the expenses incurred in the preservation, safe-keeping and management of the estate."

In an opinion by Judge Walker of the Commission of Appeals, adopted by the Supreme Court, it is held that reasonable attorney's fees are expenses of administration within the meaning of the clause of the statute quoted. Williams v. Robinson, 56 Tex. 347.

The executor was not personally interested in the probate of the will. In contracting with Pendleton he was acting, not in his individual capacity, but in his representative capacity as executor under it. Portis v. Cole, 11 Tex. 157. The probate of the will was the first essential and indispensable step toward carrying out the trust imposed by it. The statute authorized him to take such step. The employment of an attorney to uphold the will was consistent with his duty as executor to effectuate and complete the purposes of his trust.

If, however, the language employed in the statute is not sufficiently broad to include, as expenses of administration, reasonable attorney's fees incurred in establishing the will, it certainly does not expressly or impliedly prohibit them. In the absence of such statutory inhibition, we may look to the adjudicated cases for enlightenment in determining the rule to be applied, and in so doing find that the decided weight of authority holds, and we think properly so, that where the executor has acted in good faith in employing an attorney in proceedings to probate the will, and the will is established, the estate is chargeable with the expense of reasonable attorney's fees thus necessarily incurred. Re Estate of Frank Hentges, 86 Neb. 75, 124 N. W. 929, 26 L. R. A. (N. S.) 757, and notes; Henderson v. Simmons, 33 Ala. 291, 70 Am. Dec. 590.

Defendant in error relies upon Renn v. Samos, 37 Tex. 240, and Gilroy v. Richards, 26 Tex. Civ. App. 355, 63 S. W. 667, as supporting a contrary view. In the Renn Case the will had been probated, and the heirs of the testator instituted suit against the legatees named in the will for the purpose of setting aside the same, charging fraud upon the part of the defendants in the pretended execution of the will, and in procuring its probate. The plaintiffs in that suit prevailed, but the trial court allowed defendants attorney's fees notwithstanding that they were convicted of fraud by the verdict. The appellate court held that that was a personal action against the defendant, and not against the representatives of the estate of Renn. Having been convicted of fraud, it is not surprising that the appellate court denied recovery. A contrary ruling would encourage fraud.

In the Gilroy Case the Court of Civil Appeals refused to allow a claim against the estate for money paid by the wife as attorney's fees for defending the suit to contest her husband's will. The record in that case reveals that the will did not name an executor, but the wife was appointed temporary administrator. No proceedings other than the probate of the will were ever taken. No duty was imposed under the terms of her appointment as temporary administrator, requiring her to offer the will for probate nor to employ counsel to resist the contest to probate, and her action in resisting the contest to probate the will was not in discharge of any duty imposed by law or by the will, but was her individual act. These facts differentiate that case from the one presented by this record.

[5] In defense of the action, defendant in error further urges that, though the attorney's fee may be a proper charge against the estate in Oklahoma, it can form no basis for a claim against the administrator in Texas, as there is no privity between the executor in Oklahoma and the ancillary administrator in Texas. In support of this contention he relies upon Stacy v. Thrasher, 6 How. 44, 12 L. Ed. 337, and McLean et al. v. Meek, 18 How. 16, 15 L. Ed. 277, which establish the rule that a judgment against an administrator in one state will not support an action against another administrator in a different state, because, in contemplation of law, there is no privity between them. The correctness of the rule announced in those cases is not questioned; but it has no application to the facts of this case. The distinction, as regards privity between administrators appointed by law under different political jurisdictions and privity between testamentary executors, is clearly drawn in Hill v. Tucker, 13 How. 458, 14 L. Ed. 223. It is there said:

"The executor's interest in the testator's estate is what the testator gives him. That of an administrator is only that which the law of his appointment enjoins. * * * But though the executor's trust or appointment may be limited, or though there are several executors in different jurisdictions, and some of them limited executors, they are, as to the creditors of the testators executers in privity, bearing to the creditors the same responsibilities as if there was only one executor. The privity arises from their obligations to pay the testator's debts, wherever his effects may be, just as his obligation was to pay them."

In the same case the court, in discussing the want of privity between administrators deriving their powers from different jurisdictions quotes from Stacey v. Thrasher as follows:

"An administrator under grant of administration in one state stands in none of these relations—of privity—to another administrator in another state. Each is privy to the testator, and would be estopped by a judgment against him, but they have no privity with each other in law or estate. They receive their authority from different sovereignties, and over different property. The authority of each is paramount to the other. Each is administrator to the ordinary from which he receives his commission. Nor does the one come by succession to the other into the trust of the same property, incumbered by the same debts, as in the case of an administrator de bonis non, who may truly be said to have an official privity with his predecessor in the same trust, and therefore liable to the same duties."

The view that the executor and administrator, cum testamento annexo, in different jurisdictions, are, as regards the creditors of the estate, in privity with each other, bearing to the creditors the same responsibilities as if there was only one executor, is clearly stated in a well-reasoned opinion by the Supreme Court of Georgia in Latine v. Clements, Adm'r, 3 Kelly, 426. In that case a judgment creditor of a Virginia executor brought an action upon the Virginia judgment against the Georgia administrator with the will annexed. The court held that they were in privity with the testator and with each other, and that an action would lie against the Georgia administrator with the will annexed.

The fact that the will was never probated in this state does not render the rule announced inapplicable in this case. The Oklahoma executor filed an application to probate the will in Texas, along with his application to be appointed administrator with the will annexed of the estate in Texas, but abandoned the application upon advice of Reily that its probate in Texas was unnecessary, as there was no real estate involved, and because the personal property could be distributed through the probate court of Grayson county upon certified copies of the judgment of the Oklahoma court establishing the will. The will was sufficient to pass all the personal or movable property of the testator wherever situate, and in recognition of this rule of law defendant in error properly distributed the estate in Texas, which consisted exclusively of personalty, under the terms of the will. The Oklahoma executor and the Texas administrator both recognized the authority of the will. In the distribution of the estate, that instrument alone governed each of them. The Texas administrator was appointed because of the want of power of the Oklahoma executor to act in this state. Upon the qualification of the former as administrator, and the undertaking upon his part to distribute the estate through the Texas courts in accordance with the terms of the will, he became the representative of the estate, and therefore in privity with the testator and with the executor.

It is our conclusion that the claim was a valid charge upon the estate in the hands of any administrator, and therefore upon the estate in the hands of the Texas administrator.

We recommend, therefore, that the judgment of the Court of Civil Appeals be reversed, and that of the trial court affirmed.

PHILLIPS, C. J. The judgment recommended in the report of the Commission of Appeals is adopted, and will be entered as the judgment of the Supreme Court.

———

RICHARDSON et al. v. BERMUDA LAND & LIVE STOCK CO. (No. 218-3343.)

(Commission of Appeals of Texas, Section A. June 1, 1921.)

1. Corporations ⬦⟹382—Note held not in violation of prohibition of use of corporation's funds for other than legitimate object of its creation.

Under Vernon's Sayles' Ann. Civ. St. 1914, art. 1164, providing that no corporation shall employ or use its stock, means, assets, or other property for any other purpose than to accomplish the legitimate objects of its creation, the execution of a note by a land and live stock company to pay a railroad contractor a certain sum upon the completion of a railroad line adjacent to the corporation's land was within the power of the corporation.

2. Corporations ⬦⟹464—Note held not within prohibition of creation of indebtedness by corporation.

A note by a land and live stock company to pay a certain sum on the completion of a railroad line adjacent to its land, being so conditioned as to prevent the use of its means or assets, until the facilities contracted for were delivered, was not within the prohibition of Vernon's Sayles' Ann. Civ. St. 1914, art. 1165, of the creation of any indebtedness by a corporation except for money paid, labor done, or property actually received.

Appeal from Court of Civil Appeals of Fourth Supreme Judicial District.

Suit by Mary I. Richardson and another, executors of Asber Richardson, against the Bermuda Land & Live Stock Company. From a judgment of the Court of Civil Appeals affirming a judgment in favor of the defendant (210 S. W. 746), plaintiffs appeal. Reversed and remanded for trial on merits.

Denman, Franklin & McGown and Frank S. Huson, all of San Antonio, for appellants.

Alex C. Bullitt, of San Antonio, for appellee.

TAYLOR, P. J. A contract executed October 5, 1908, by the Bermuda Land & Live Stock Company, defendant in error, of which the following is a copy, forms the basis of the controversy involved in this suit:

"Whereas, we own the following described land, the same being situated in Dimmit county, Texas, known as survey No. ——; and whereas, said land will be greatly enhanced in value by the construction of a standard gauge railroad from a point on the I. & G. N. Railroad now in operation, into Dimmit county, Texas: Therefore, for value received, and as an inducement to Asher Richardson and his associates, and their assigns, to build a standard gauge railroad from a point on the I. & G. N. Railroad near Artesia to Asherton, on Moro creek, in Dimmit county, I, or we, agree and promise to pay to Asher Richardson and his associates at San Antonio, Texas, the sum of two thousand dollars, with eight per cent. (8%) interest per annum from maturity until paid.

"Said sum of two thousand dollars to become due and payable upon the completion of said railroad to Asherton and putting the same in operation, providing same is done on or before June 1, 1909.

"Should this note not be paid at maturity and suit is brought to collect same, then I agree to pay an additional 10% as attorney's fees."

Suit was filed on the contract by Asher Richardson. Subsequent to his death it has been prosecuted by Mary I. Richardson and Littleton V. Richardson, independent executors of his estate, and plaintiffs in error here. The following is a summary of the allegations of the petition material to this discussion: Defendant in error, Bermuda Land & Live Stock Company, is a corporation chartered for the purpose of buying, selling, and raising live stock, and has the power to hold, purchase, sell, mortgage or otherwise convey such real and personal estate as the purposes of the corporation require. In conducting its business it owns and operates a large pasture in Dimmit county, Tex., in which there were no railroad facilities prior to the building of the railroad referred to in the contract. The pasture was 25 or 30 miles from the nearest railroad. Defendant in error executed the contract sued on as an inducement to Richardson to build the road next to its land. This railroad was the first to enter Dimmit county. It extends from Asherton to Artesia, a distance of 30 miles or more, passing next to defendant in error's land, affording it a valuable means of transportation. Defendant in error believed that the railroad would tend to greatly increase its business and the value of its land, and its purpose in executing the contract was to increase its corporate business and the value of its land. Richardson built the railroad and put it in operation within the time agreed upon, and by reason thereof defendant in error was provided with a means of transportation which has greatly increased its business. The increased value of its business, as well as the increase in the value of land resulting from the building of the railroad, is far in excess of the amount of the note

sued on. The sum agreed in said contract to be paid was reasonable as an expenditure for the benefits received, and was an ordinary, usual, and customary expenditure for such a corporation, under the circumstances, to obtain such facilities. The note is past due and unpaid.

The trial court sustained a general demurrer and special exception. The ground of the exception was that the petition shows that the defendant in error is a private corporation organized under the laws of Texas, and does not show that the contract sued on was executed to evidence an indebtedness created for money paid, labor done, or property actually received.

The Court of Civil Appeals affirmed the judgment of the trial court under the view that it was not within the power of defendant in error to execute the contract sued on; that the contract was ultra vires and void, and defendant in error was not estopped from setting up its invalidity. 210 S. W. 746.

[1] The provisions of articles 1164 and 1165 (Ver. Sayl. R. S. 1914) are made the basis of the court's holding that defendant in error was without authority to make the contract. The former provides that no corporation "shall employ or use its stock, means, assets, or other property, directly or indirectly, for any other purpose whatever than to accomplish the legitimate objects of its creation * * * "; the latter, that no corporation "shall create any indebtedness whatever except for money paid, labor done, * * * or property actually received."

The provisions of article 1164 are identical with the provisions of article 665 of the Revised Statutes of 1895, and article 589 of the prior revision. It is clear from the opinions of the Supreme Court construing its provisions as contained in the former statutes that the execution of the contract sued was not in violation of such provisions. Northside Ry. Co. et al. v. Worthington, 88 Tex. 562, 30 S. W. 1055, 53 Am. St. Rep. 778; Bond v. Terrell Mfg. Co., 82 Tex. 309, 18 S. W. 691; Commanche Cotton Oil Co. v. Browne, 99 Tex. 660, 92 S. W. 450; Ft. Worth City Co. v. Smith Bridge Co., 151 U. S. 294, 14 Sup. Ct. 339, 38 L. Ed. 167. It can hardly be questioned that the expenditure of a reasonable amount by defendant in error for the purpose of securing such improved transportation facilities to and from its land as would greatly increase its business was an expenditure to accomplish, and aid directly in accomplishing, the objects for which it was created.

[2] The more serious question in the case is whether the execution of the contract sued upon was in violation of that provision of article 1165 relating to the character of indebtedness that a corporation is prohibited from creating.

Articles 1164 and 1165 were taken by the 1911 codifiers of the statutes from chapter 166 of the General Laws passed in 1907 at the regular session of the Thirtieth Legislature. Laws of Texas, vol. 13, p. 309. That part of section 5 of the act from which the articles referred to were carved, is as follows:

"No corporation, domestic or foreign, doing business in the state, shall employ or use its stock, means, assets or other property, directly or indirectly, for any other purpose whatever than to accomplish the legitimate objects of its creation or that permitted by law, nor shall it issue any stock or create any indebtedness whatever except for money paid, labor done, which is reasonably worth at least the sum at which it was taken by · the corporation; or property actually received reasonably worth at least the sum at which it was taken by the company."

The remaining part of section 5 contains provisions forbidding such corporation to use its assets, property, stock, means, or funds, in the interest of any political party or candidate for office, etc., and provides a penalty for the violation of any of the provisions of the section.

The caption of the act in full is as follows:

"An act on the subject of private corporations, prescribing the terms and conditions on which they may be chartered, and providing the amount of capital stock to be paid in, and when the remainder shall be paid; also prescribing the method by which the capital stock of private corporations may be increased and decreased; also providing for the dissolution of corporations, and the procedure incident thereto; also forbidding any such corporation to use its assets, property, stock, means or funds in the interest or for the success of any political party or candidate for office, or for the defeat or success of any questions submitted to a vote of the people, or for any purpose other than to accomplish the legitimate objects of its creation."

The other sections of the act are not pertinent.

The caption, in so far as it is material here, declares that the purpose of the act was to forbid any such corporation to use its assets, property, means, or funds for any purpose other than to accomplish the legitimate objects of its creation. It suggests no further restriction on the powers of the corporation in this connection than that stated. The first four lines of section 5, brought forward in the 1911 revision as article 1164, makes effective the declared purpose of the act in almost the identical language of the caption.

That part of section 5, quoted above, not incorporated in article 1164, was brought forward in the revision as article 1165. It appears in general to be a legislative enactment of section 6 of article 12 of the Constitution, which declares that—

"No corporation shall issue stock or bonds except for money paid, labor done or property actually received, and all fictitious increase of stock or indebtedness shall be void."

Unless the indebtedness referred to in article 1165 was a general term used by the Legislature to include stock and bonds and such evidences of indebtedness as should constitute the capital of a corporation, it is a distinct limitation upon article 1164. It is questionable whether the Legislature intended by the act of 1907 to place any further limitation upon the use by a corporation of its means or funds than that stated in article 1164, and in the caption of the act. It is not necessary, however, under our view of the effect of the contract declared upon, and in view of the allegations of plaintiffs in error, to construe the act further than to determine whether the contract comes within the terms of that provision relating to the creation by a corporation of "any indebtedness whatever," brought forward as article 1165.

What the Bermuda Land & Live Stock Company did, as appears from the allegations, was to enter into a contract with Richardson and his associates for the purpose of securing transportation facilities to be so used in the conduct of its business as to directly promote the purpose for which it was created. The contract was so conditioned as to render it impossible for the means or assets of the company to be used pursuant to its terms for any purpose until the facilities contracted for were delivered. The company did not, by the execution and delivery of the contract, lend its credit to plaintiffs in error. By the terms of the contract no indebtedness was created against the company until the transportation facilities were available to it for use. The promise to pay did not mature into an indebtedness and become payable except upon the "completion of said railroad to Asherton and putting the same in operation." A purchaser of the contract would have acquired it at his peril. The promise to pay did not become a binding obligation against the company until that which was to be received by it had been actually received. If the contract executed is within the prohibition of article 1165, a corporation is without power to purchase on its credit. There is, in our opinion, nothing in that part of the act of 1907 quoted above, the effect of which was to prohibit defendant in error from entering into the contract declared upon. H. & T. C. Ry. Co. v. Diamond Press Brick Co., 222 S. W. 204.

In the case cited the brick company, a corporation authorized to manufacture and sell brick, entered into a contract with the railway company, agreeing to hold it harmless from all damages it might suffer by reason of its constructing a spur track to the brick company's plant. The railway company built the track as agreed. Judgment was recovered against the railway for personal injuries sustained by him at a crossing over the spur track. The railway company sued the brick company on its contract of indemnity for the amount it was compelled to pay under the judgment. The brick company pleaded that the contract was ultra vires, and the trial court sustained demurrers to the railway's petition. It was stated in the opinion that—

"A corporation is empowered to enter into a contract to enable it to carry on the business and accomplish the purpose of its existence, unless prohibited by law or the provision of its charter. The language of the agreement now under consideration leaves no room to doubt that the contract was made in order to accomplish the purpose for which the corporation was created."

In view of our conclusion that the contract sued on does not represent a form of indebtedness prohibited by article 1165, it is not necessary to determine whether the contract benefits received by defendant in error under the contract were "property actually received."

The trial court and Court of Civil Appeals erred, in our opinion, in holding that the general demurrer and special exceptions should have been sustained.

We recommend that the judgments of both courts be reversed, and that the cause be remanded for trial on its merits.

PHILLIPS, C. J. The judgment recommended in the report of the Commission of Appeals is adopted and will be entered as the judgment of the Supreme Court.

We approve the holding of the Commission of Appeals on the question discussed in its opinion.

PERRY v. SMITH et al. (No. 165-3164.)

(Commission of Appeals of Texas, Section B. June 1, 1921.)

1. Deeds ⟂166—Consent to placing mechanic's lien upon property held not waiver of condition in deed.

Consent by a grantor that grantee place a mechanic's lien upon the land was not a waiver of a condition in the deed that a gin and mill be constructed and operated, the company placing the mechanic's lien upon the land being charged with knowledge of the conditions in the deed, and that its lien was subject to be defeated by a breach of such condition.

2. Deeds ⟂156—Right of re-entry after condition subsequent broken not assignable at common law.

The right of re-entry after condition subsequent broken is not assignable under the English common law.

3. Deeds ⟂156—Right of re-entry after condition subsequent broken assignable.

The question of assignability of the right of re-entry after condition subsequent broken should be governed by the same rule which is applied to the assignability of an interest in land in the adverse possession of another, and the right of re-entry after condition subsequent broken is assignable in view of Rev. St. 1911. art. 7733(4), notwithstanding the act of 1840. which makes the common law of England the rule of decision in the state.

Error to Court of Civil Appeals of Eighth Supreme Judicial District.

Action by L. H. Perry against Sidney Smith and others. From a judgment of the Court of Civil Appeals (198 S. W. 1013) affirming a judgment of the trial court, the plaintiff brings error. Reversed and rendered.

W. W. Moores, of Stephenville, for plaintiff in error.

Pittman & Taylor and J. A. Johnson, all of Stephenville, for defendants in error.

McCLENDON, P. J. On November 12, 1912, S. N. Keith and wife conveyed, for the recited cash consideration of $10, unto Sidney Smith, three acres of land in Erath county, subject to certain conditions, among which were that two acres of the land were to be used by the grantee for gin and mill purposes only, upon which the grantee was to erect a gin and mill building of certain capacity and within a certain time, and providing that, if for any cause the gin and mill be not erected or cease operation on said premises, the land thereby conveyed should revert to the grantors. Smith went into possession, and in January, 1913, made a contract with Higginbotham Company to construct the improvements required under the deed, for which a mechanic's lien was given. In May, 1914, Smith and wife conveyed the land and improvements to Higginbotham Company, in consideration of the debt thus created, which company in turn sold the land to one Holt. The condition for keeping the gin and mill in operation was breached, and after the breach, but before re-entry, on April 1, 1915, Keith and wife conveyed the land to L. H. Perry. This suit was brought by Perry against Smith and his vendees in trespass to try title to recover the land conveyed, upon the ground that the title had reverted to Keith and wife, and that Perry by his deed from the latter had succeeded to their rights. The cause was tried in the district court without a jury, and judgment was rendered for defendants, the court finding that the conditions above named had been broken, but that Keith had waived his right to insist upon the condition on account of having known of the execution of the mechanic's lien to Higginbotham Company and having verbally consented to its being placed upon the land. The Court of Civil Appeals affirmed this judgment, upon the holding that the right of re-entry after condition subsequent broken is not assignable, and therefore no title passed by the conveyance from Keith and wife to Perry. 198 S. W. 1013.

The case presents two questions for determination: First, whether the trial court's holding that the condition in the deed was waived is supported by the evidence; and, second, whether the English common-law doctrine that the right of re-entry after condition subsequent broken is not assignable is in force in this state.

[1] The only testimony tending to show a waiver of the conditions in the deed is to the effect that after the execution of the deed, and before the improvements were put upon the property, Keith knew of and consented to the placing of a mechanic's lien thereon. We are unable to conclude that such fact amounted to a waiver of the condition. There is no intimation that Keith agreed that the condition would not be insisted upon, or that the lien should be other than subordinate to the title acquired by Smith under his conveyance. At the time this lien was created, no breach of the condition had occurred, and the debt secured by the lien was incurred for the purpose of carrying out the terms of the condition. Higginbotham Company and those claiming under it were charged with knowledge of the conditions in the grant to Smith, and its lien upon the real estate was subject to be defeated by a breach of the same condition which would defeat the title acquired by Smith under his deed. The bare fact of knowledge of and consent to a lien upon the property would not, in our opinion, amount to an estoppel or waiver, in so far as conditions not then broken were concerned.

[2] The second question presents no little difficulty. The Court of Civil Appeals has correctly announced the rule under the English common law. Whether that doctrine is in force in this state under the act of 1840, which makes the common law of England the rule of decision in this state, is a question requiring an examination not only into the common-law rule, but into its basis and its applicability to our system of jurisprudence as applied to lands and interest therein. The particular question of the assignability of the right of re-entry after condition subsequent broken has never been presented to the Supreme Court of this state in a case where the question was necessary to a decision, in so far as we have been able to find.

The doctrine of the nonassignability of titles or interests in lands, not in the actual possession of the grantor, has been quite generally by jurists and text-writers ascribed to a dislike for maintenance. As expressed by Coke:

"The reason hereof is for the avoiding of maintenance, suppression of right, and stirring up of suits, and therefore nothing in action, entrie or re-entrie, can be granted over; for so under colour thereof pretended titles might be granted to great men whereby right might be trodden downe and the weake oppressed, which the common law forbiddeth as men to grant before they be in possession." Coke on Littleton, 218b.

Lord Mansfield says:

"Our ancestors got into very odd notions on these subjects, and were induced by particular causes to make estates grow out of wrongful acts. The reason was the prodigious jealousy the law always had of permitting rights to be transferred from one man to another, lest the poorer should be harassed by rights being transferred to more powerful persons."

During the reigns of Edward I and Edward III repeated statutes were passed against maintenance and champerty, "which arose from the embarrassments which attended the administration of justice in those turbulent times, from dangerous influences and oppression of men of power." 4 Kent's Com. p. 514.

By the Statute of 32 Henry VIII, c. 9, entitled "The Bill of Bracery and Buying of Titles," any one selling or buying a title to property of which for the preceding year he or those under whom he claimed, had not either been in possession or received the rents, was subjected to the penalty of forfeiting the value of the lands, one half to the crown and the other half to the informer; an exception being made were one in possession purchased an outstanding adverse title or claim. Introductory to this statute is a recital of conditions which brought forth its enactment, as follows:

"The King, our sovereign lord, calling to his most blessed remembrance that there is nothing within this realm that conserveth his loving subjects in more quietness, rest, peace, and good concord than the due and just ministration of his laws, and the true and indifferent trials of such titles and issues, as been to be tried according to the laws of this realm, which his most royal majesty perceiveth to be greatly hindered and letted by maintenance, embracery, champerty, subordination of witnesses, sinister labour, buying of titles, and pretensed rights of persons not being in possession, whereupon great perjury hath ensued, and much inquietness, oppression, vexation, troubles, wrongs and disinheritance hath followed among his most loving subjects, to the great displeasure of Almighty God, the discontentation of his majesty, and to the great hindrance and let of justice within this his realm, for the avoiding of all which misdemeanors, and buying of titles and pretensed rights, and to the intent that justice may be more fully and indifferently ministered, and the truth in causes of contention plainly tried between his subjects of this realm; be it enacted, etc."

Lord Coleridge, in referring to the period of English history in which these statutes were passed, says:

"It may be that the danger of the oppression of poor men by rich men, through the means of legal proceedings, was great and pressing; so that the judges of those days, wisely according to the facts of those days, took strict views on the subject of maintenance." Badlaugh v. Newdegate, 1 Q. B. D. 7.

But, independently of these statutes, it is no doubt correct that at common law titles and interests in lands were not assignable, unless the grantor was in possession. This doctrine is usually ascribed to practices of the feudal system, under which livery of seizin "delivery of corporeal possession of the land or tenement * * * was held absolutely necessary to complete the donation." 2 Blackstone's Com. 311. Modern scholars, however, have rejected this explanation, assigning as the true basis of the doctrine the fact that our Anglo-Saxon forbears had no mental conception of title as separate from the subject of title, and consequently mere rights as distinguished from things were not the subject of contract. This view is ably maintained by Prof. Maitland in an article entitled "The Mystery of Seisen." 2 L. Q. Rev. 495.

Whatever view may be taken of the origin of or reasons for the general doctrine of non-assignability of titles to or interests in lands not in possession of the grantor, it is quite clear that none of those reasons existed in the Republic of Texas at the time the common law was adopted as the rule of decision in civil matters. Neither the English statutes nor the English common law upon the subject of maintenance have ever been held to be of force in Texas. Bentinck v. Franklin, 38 Tex. 458. In that case it was said that there is no law prohibiting champerty in force in this state. Whenever the doctrine under discussion has been invoked, the Supreme Court has declined to enforce it, notable examples of which are to be found in upholding the assignability of choses in action generally (Nimmo v. Davis, 7 Tex. 26); the right of expectant heirs (Hale v. Hollon, 90 Tex. 427, 39 S. W. 287, 36 L. R. A. 75, 59 Am. St. Rep. 819; Barre v. Daggett, 105 Tex. 573, 153 S. W. 120); transferability of land held adversely in the possession of another (Carder v. McDermett, 12 Tex. 546; Campbell v. Everts, 47 Tex. 102).

Our Supreme Court has repeatedly pointed out that the evils sought to be obviated by the English rule would be more likely to flourish under conditions here by an adoption of that rule. Chief Justice Hemphill quoted with apparent approval from Stoever v. Whitman's Lessee, 6 Bin. 421, where it is said that—

"From the equality of the condition of persons in this country, there was no danger of maintenance from the influence of powerful individuals, and the abundance and the cheapness of land rendered it necessary to admit of its transfer with almost as much facility as personal property. For these reasons, when deeds and devises of land have been considered in our courts, it has never been made a question whether the grantor or devisor was in or out of possession, and to make it now would disturb what has been looked upon as settled." McMullen v. Guest, 6 Tex. 275.

In Stewart v. Railway, 62 Tex. 246, we read:

"While it is the policy of the courts to discourage groundless and vexatious litigation, the Constitution declares that: 'All courts shall be open, and every person for an injury done him in his lands, goods, persons or reputation shall have remedy by due course of law.' The policy that dictated the English statutes had for its object the protection of the poor against the wealthy and influential, when their rights formed the subject of litigation before the courts. Here the conditions of society in a great measure are very different. To enable the poor in many cases to secure an adjudication upon disputed rights, it is necessary that the right of the attorney to contract for a contingent interest in the subject-matter of the litigation, by way of compensation for professional service, should be recognized."

From the earliest times it has been the policy of our law to permit the free transfer of all classes of property and rights in property, except in those cases where such rights were from their very nature purely personal to the grantor, or where assignability was in contravention of some rule of public policy or statute law.

In Graham v. Henry, 17 Tex. 164, it is said:

"In general, whatever is susceptible of exclusive, individual appropriation may be the subject of bargain and sale; so that property considered as an exclusive right to things, implies not only a right to use, but a right to dispose of them. Whatever exclusive right a man has in anything, he has a right to dispose of absolutely, as he pleases, provided he makes no disposition of it prohibited by law. It matters not what advances he has made towards acquiring the ultimate dominion, or absolute and complete proprietorship; the moment he has acquired an exclusive interest, though it be but a contingent and executory interest, he may dispose of it at pleasure, subject only to the condition that it is not forbidden by law."

In Johnson v. Newman, 43 Tex. 628, the court had for decision the assignability of the right of citizens of Texas under the Constitution of the republic to acquire land grants. The court say:

"Though at the date of this contract Mitchell had neither a title to the land in controversy nor the certificate under which it has been acquired, still there was, undoubtedly, guaranteed to him by the Constitution the right to this amount of land on his complying with the requirements to be prescribed by law. This right, though neither real nor personal property in esse, was nevertheless an inchoate right to get that quantity of land out of some part of the public domain at the time, and in the manner to be afterwards provided and determined by the government. It was a right or interest of such character as to be the subject of a contract. Emmons v. Oldham, 12 Tex. 26; Graham v. Henry, 17 Tex. 167; Babb v. Carroll, 21 Tex. 679; Andrews v. Smithwick, 24 Tex. 488."

In discussing the effect of the act of 1840, which made the common law of England the rule of decision in this state in civil matters, Chief Justice Brown, in Grigsby v. Reib, 105 Tex. 600, 153 S. W. 1125, L. R. A. 1915E, 1, Ann. Cas. 1915C, 1011, says:

"We conclude that 'the common law of England' adopted by the Congress of the republic was that which was declared by the courts of the different states of the United States. This conclusion is supported by the fact that the lawyer members of that Congress who framed and enacted that statute had been reared and educated in the United States, and would naturally have in mind the common law with which they were familiar."

If we examine the decision of other states, we find that the authorities are not in accord in holding that the right of re-entry after condition subsequent broken is not assignable. The following is from 4 Kent's Commentaries, p. 513:

"The ancient policy which prohibited the sale of pretended titles, and held the conveyance to a third person of lands held adversely at the time to be an act of maintenance, was founded upon a state of society which does not exist in this country."

A very recent edition (1920) of a standard text on real property has this to say:

"In any jurisdiction where one disseised is without the interposition of a statute accorded the right to transfer land in the adverse possession of another, it would seem that the grantor should have the right to transfer the right of re-entry after a breach of the condition has occurred, since after breach his right of entry is absolute, as is that of one disseised." Tiffany on Real Property (2d Ed.) vol. 1, § 86.

The decisions in Pennsylvania and New Jersey support this view. McKissick v. Pickle, 16 Pa. 140; Bouvier v. Railway, 67 N. J. Law, 281, 51 Atl. 781, 60 L. R. A. 750.

The latter case is well considered, and the history of the doctrine of nonassignability is ably reviewed. The rules of the common law were in force in that state in similar manner as under our statute of 1840. The conclusion reached is summarized in the following quotation:

"I think that in any case, wherever the English law against maintenance is not in force, a right of entry for condition broken should be held transferable after breach of the condition."

[3] From the foregoing discussion it is evident that the question of assignability of the right of re-entry after condition subsequent broken should be governed by the same rule which is applied to the assignability of an interest in land in the adverse possession of another. In the latter class of cases, our Supreme Court, as above stated, has spoken in no uncertain terms. In the leading case of Carder v. McDermett, above, the court say:

"The fact that persons out of possession may sell titles which have no foundation in law, and which may be purchased for no other purpose than vexation and the profits of litigation, is no sufficient reason why all lawful owners, ousted of possession, shall be deprived of control over their property. This would be punishing the community in order that some pests might not escape. If the ancient rules of the common law with respect to the nonassignability of mere rights or choses in action and also with respect to the modes of conveyance of real property were still recognized, then there might be some reason for the rule. For at common law no interest could be conveyed, except where the grantor was in actual or constructive possession of the thing granted. And this was on the general ground that such conveyance would multiply suits, and be transferring lawsuits to strangers. Hence a debt or other chose in action could not be assigned (2 Story, 1039), nor could a right of entry or action in real property. This notion against the assignment of choses in action has long since been exploded, but in relation to assignments of rights of entry has more firmly maintained its ground. And under the earlier mode of conveyance by feoffment there was some reason for holding that a right of entry could not be assigned by one out of possession. For, as the livery of seizin was a component part of the transfer by feoffment, it was necessary, in general, that the feoffer should have actual possession at the time of the livery made, although it seems that under some special circumstances, when livery could not be made upon the land, it might be made within view, and was thus effectual to transfer the right of entry, and was so far an exception to the general rule that a right of entry could not be transferred by one out of possession.

"But, under the modern and ordinary forms of transfers, no actual possession is necessary to give validity to conveyances. The seizin by deed draws to it the constructive possession. And if there were any good reason for relaxing the ancient law with respect to the necessity of actual possession to the validity of a transfer, making constructive possession sufficient, there seems no good reason why the mere usurpation of a possession should invalidate a conveyance, when actual possession was not necessary to make it good.

"There are some refined distinctions between the effect of a disseizin and dispossession, and in a very elaborate disquisition appended to the cases of Doe v. Oliver and the Duchess of Kingston, in Smith's Leading Cases, it is maintained that, according to the present state of the law in England, where a title has been reduced by actual disseizin to a mere right of entry, it can be neither devised nor granted, yet, when there is only adverse possession, it may be devised, and, if there be no maintenance, it may also be conveyed.

"But it is not necessary to trace the effect of these distinctions, as they will not control the decision. For we are of opinion that whether the owner be disseized or dispossessed, or by whatever name his being put out of possession may be denominated, yet that he has such right as will enable him to make a valid conveyance, effectual in law to support an action to try the title. This doctrine exists in some of the states."

In concluding this discussion, it may not be out of place to advert to the fact that the statute which created the action of trespass to try title was adopted at the same session of the Congress that adopted the common law in civil matters. In that enactment all fictitious actions at common law were abolished, and a simple method of procedure was applied to all actions for the recovery of real property. In so far as possession was concerned, that act only required that the plaintiff allege "that he was in possession of the premises or entitled to such possession." R. S. art. 7733(4).

In view of the grounds upon which the English common-law doctrine is predicated, the lack of unanimity in other American states in adopting that doctrine, and the fact that our own Supreme Court has declined to apply the doctrine in cases brought clearly within its purview and application, we are constrained to conclude that the right of re-entry after condition subsequent broken should be held assignable in this state.

We conclude that the judgments of the district court and Court of Civil Appeals should be reversed, and judgment rendered in favor of plaintiff in error for the land sued for.

PHILLIPS, C. J. The judgment recommended in the report of the Commission of Appeals is adopted, and will be entered as the judgment of the Supreme Court.

___

WISDOM v. CHICAGO, R. I. & G. RY. CO.
(No. 247–3445.)

(Commission of Appeals of Texas, Section A. June 1, 1921.)

1. Appeal and error ⬄1094(5) — Supreme Court bound by Court of Civil Appeals' holding as to insufficiency of evidence to sustain verdict.

Determination by Court of Civil Appeals as to insufficiency of evidence to sustain the verdict is binding on the Supreme Court on writ of error to review the judgment of the Court of Civil Appeals.

2. Appeal and error ⬄987(1)—Duty of court of Civil Appeals to set aside judgment for insufficiency of evidence to sustain verdict.

It is the duty of the Court of Civil Appeals to set aside a verdict, and the judgment rendered thereon, where in its opinion the evidence is insufficient to sustain the verdict.

3. Appeal and error ⬄1175(5)—Court of Civil Appeals not authorized to render judgment in reversal for insufficiency of evidence.

The Court of Civil Appeals, on reversing judgment for insufficiency of conflicting evidence to sustain the verdict, has no right to render judgment, but must remand the case to the lower court for new trial.

4. Carriers ⬄303(1)—Degree of care railroad owes alighting passenger stated.

A railroad owed an alighting passenger that high degree of care which a very prudent and cautious person would have exercised under the circumstances to enable her to alight in safety.

5. Carriers ⬄303(8)—Railroad required to furnish safe steps, or aid passenger in alighting.

It was railroad's duty to furnish such steps as would enable a woman passenger to alight in safety, and, if the steps were defective or unsafe, to render such assistance to her as would make the use of steps as safe as if they had been the safest then known.

6. Carriers ⬄303(8) — Required to assist alighting passenger where need of assistance is apparent.

When safe and proper facilities for alighting are furnished, carriers are not required to assist passengers in ordinary cases to alight from trains, but if the circumstances of the particular case make it reasonably apparent that such assistance is needed, it is the carrier's duty to render such assistance.

7. Carriers ⬄320(25) — Whether alighting passenger should have been assisted is a question for the jury.

Whether an alighting passenger was in need of assistance, and whether such need was reasonably apparent to employés, and whether failure to render such assistance constituted negligence, are questions for the jury to be determined under the facts in each case.

Error to Court of Civil Appeals of Second Supreme Judicial District.

Suit by Geneva Wisdom against the Chicago, Rock Island & Gulf Railway Company. Judgment for plaintiff was reversed, and judgment was rendered for defendant by the Court of Civil Appeals (216 S. W. 241), and plaintiff brings error. Judgment of Court of Civil Appeals reversed, and case remanded to the district court for new trial.

R. E. Carswell, of Decatur, and Carden, Starling, Corden, Hemphill & Wallace, of Dallas, for plaintiff in error.

Lassiter & Harrison, of Fort Worth, and McMurray & Gettys, of Decatur, for defendant in error.

GALLAGHER, J. Plaintiff in error, Miss Geneva Wisdom, brought this suit against defendant in error, Chicago, Rock Island & Gulf Railway Company, to recover damages for injuries alleged to have been sustained by her in alighting from one of said company's trains at Paradise, Tex., which injuries are alleged to have resulted from the negligence of said company.

Miss Wisdom was a passenger on one of the company's trains. On the arrival of the train at Paradise she emerged from the coach with a grip in her hands, which, on starting to descend from the platform of the coach to the platform of the station, she took in both hands and held in front of her. This grip contained four or five books, a number of dresses, and two pairs of shoes. Estimates of its size and weight varied, but there was testimony that it was about two feet long, and heavy.

There were three steps, and as she stepped from the platform of the coach onto the first step her foot, in some manner, slipped and she fell backward and slid, feet foremost, down the steps onto the station platform below. She was wearing at the time, shoes, or pumps, of a fashionable make, with heels about three inches high. The heel from one of these shoes was wrenched off during her fall.

She did not ask for assistance in attempting to alight from the car. The auditor was standing at her left as she started to descend the steps. The conductor and brakeman were standing on the station platform, one on either side of the steps, for the purpose of assisting passengers to alight. The auditor testified that it was the duty of the brakeman to assist passengers in getting off the train, and the brakeman testified that he did assist passengers who preceded Miss Wisdom. None of the employees of the company rendered any assistance, though the auditor and brakeman testified that they attempted to do so after she slipped and began to fall.

The testimony concerning the condition of the steps was conflicting. There was testimony that the steps were covered with rubber mats, and that the rubber on the top step was entirely gone in places, and the step worn slick. There was also testimony that the rubber mat, though not worn through, was worn smooth and slick in places, and the photograph submitted supports this description of the same. There was other testimony to the effect that there was nothing wrong with the steps. There was a handrail on either side of the steps, extending from just above the top step to the bottom step. One witness testified that when Miss Wisdom stepped on the first step her foot slipped forward and the heel of one shoe caught on the edge of the step and was pulled off. Practically all the witnesses agree in saying that she slipped on the first step; that her feet went out from under her, and she fell backward and bumped, feet foremost, down the steps to the platform of the station.

There was testimony to the effect that she received painful and permanent injuries as the result of such fall.

There was a trial by jury. The court's charge authorized a recovery if the employees in charge of the train failed to take hold of her arm, and thus assist her in alighting from the train, and if such failure was negligence and the proximate cause of her injuries, or if the step, or steps, were worn slick or slippery, and in consequence of such condition she slipped, or stumbled and fell, and if permitting such steps to be in such condition was negligence and the proximate cause of her injuries.

There was a verdict for the plaintiff, and judgment was entered in accordance therewith. The railway company appealed, and a majority of the Court of Civil Appeals held that the evidence was insufficient to support the verdict, and reversed the judgment of the trial court, but, instead of remanding the case for another trial, rendered judgment for the railway company. 216 S. W. 241. This writ of error was granted by the Supreme Court to review the judgment so rendered.

[1, 2] We do not understand the Court of Civil Appeals to hold that there is no evidence of negligence on the part of the railway company in this case. Such holding would have been erroneous as a matter of law, because, while the evidence is conflicting, there is some evidence in the record to the effect that the top step, or the rubber mat thereon, was old and worn slick, and that plaintiff in error slipped on this step. From this evidence, if believed, the jury might have reasonably inferred that the condition of this mat or step was the cause of the fall suffered by her, and that in furnishing a step in that condition defendant in error did not exercise that high degree of care for her safety which it was required to exercise in furnishing her facilities to alight from its train. A majority of the Court of Civil Appeals, as we understand the opinion rendered in this case, merely held that the evidence was, in their opinion, insufficient to sustain the verdict. This holding involves a question of fact within the exclusive jurisdiction of the Court of Civil Appeals, and this court is bound by such holding. A majority of that court being of such opinion, it was not only within its power, but it was its duty, to set the judgment and verdict rendered thereon,

aside. Choate v. S. A. & A. P. Ry. Co., 91 Tex. 406, 410, 44 S. W. 69.

[3] While the Court of Civil Appeals had the power to reverse the judgment of the trial court, and could have remanded the case for another trial, it does not follow, there being a conflict in the evidence, that it could properly render judgment for defendant in error, as it did do. The law applicable to this feature of this case is clearly expressed by the Supreme Court in the case of Choate v. Railway Co., supra, and we quote from the opinion in that case as follows:

" 'Whether there be any evidence or not is a question for the judge; whether it is sufficient evidence is a question for the jury.' 1 Greenleaf, Ev. § 491. So that it is elementary that whether there be any evidence or not to support an issue is a question of law, and not of fact; and it follows that the decision of the Court of Civil Appeals upon such a question is subject to review by this court.

"Nor do we concur in the opinion that the Court of Civil Appeals have the right to conclusively determine the facts of any case. Our Bill of Rights contains the emphatic declaration that 'the right of trial by jury shall remain inviolate.' Const. art. 1, § 15. It is the province of the jury to determine questions of fact; but it is in the power of the trial judge to set aside the finding and to award a new trial. The Court of Civil Appeals has the same power upon appeal. But clearly the trial court cannot set aside the verdict of the jury and substitute its finding instead of the finding of a jury, and render judgment accordingly. To say that the Court of Civil Appeals may do so when there is any conflict in the evidence is to concede to that court a power over the facts greater than that possessed by the judge who heard the evidence, who had the witnesses before him, and had the opportunity of judging of their credibility by their appearance and manner of testifying."

We, therefore, hold that the Court of Civil Appeals erred in rendering judgment for defendant in error, instead of remanding the case to the district court for another trial.

[4] Defendant in error owed to plaintiff in error that high degree of care which a very prudent and cautious person would have exercised under the circumstances to enable her to alight from its train in safety. St. L., A. & T. Ry. Co. v. Finley, 79 Tex. 85, 88, 15 S. W. 266.

[5] It was the duty of defendant in error to exercise such care in furnishing steps on which plaintiff in error could safely descend from its train. There was, as before stated, evidence tending to show that the steps furnished were defective, and more or less unsafe, and if such was the case, then it was its duty to render such assistance to her in alighting from its train as would make the use of such steps as safe as if they had been the safest then known. Mo. Pac. Ry. Co. v. Wortham, 73 Tex. 25, 28, 10 S. W. 741, 3 L. R. A. 368; T. & P. Ry. Co. v. Miller, 79 Tex. 78, 84, 15 S. W. 264, 11 L. R. A. 395, 23 Am. St. Rep. 308.

[6, 7] The courts of this state have never construed the law to require carriers, when safe and proper facilities for alighting are furnished, to assist passengers, in ordinary cases, to alight from their trains. If, however, the circumstances of a particular case make it reasonably apparent that such assistance is needed, it becomes the duty of the carrier to furnish the same. It is for the jury to determine, under all the facts in evidence in each such case, whether assistance was needed, whether such need was reasonably apparent, and whether a failure to render the same constituted negligence. T. & P. Ry. Co. v. Miller, 79 Tex. 78, 83, 84, 15 S. W. 264, 11 L. R. A. 395, 23 Am. St. Rep. 308; I. & G. N. Ry. Co. v. Williams, 183 S. W. 1185–1187 (writ refused); M., K. & T. Ry. Co. v. Buchanan, 31 Tex. Civ. App. 209, 72 S. W. 96, 97 (writ refused); St. L. S. W. Ry. Co. v. Kennedy, 96 S. W. 653, 656 (writ refused).

If this issue is raised by the evidence on another trial, the suggestions here made and authorities cited furnish the rule by which it should be determined.

We recommend that the judgment rendered by the Court of Civil Appeals be reversed, and the case remanded to the district court for another trial.

PHILLIPS, C. J. The judgment recommended in the report of the Commission of Appeals is adopted, and will be entered as the judgment of the Supreme Court.

We approve the holding of the Commission of Appeals on the questions discussed in its opinion.

HUDMON v. FOSTER et al. (No. 215–3329.)

(Commission of Appeals of Texas, Section A. June 1, 1921.)

1. Action ⊝48(1) — Rule against multifariousness not applied where the causes of action grow out of the same transaction.

The rule against multifariousness, the improper joining in one suit of distinct and independent matters, is to be construed with, and so as not to restrict, the policy of avoiding a multiplicity of suits; so that the matters relied on for recovery in the petition growing out of the same transactions, exceptions to the petition on the ground of multifariousness, should not be sustained, and plaintiff put to necessity of separate actions.

2. Appeal and error ⊝1040(3) — Erroneous sustaining of exceptions on ground of multifariousness not harmless.

The erroneous sustaining of exceptions to a petition on the ground of misjoinder of causes of action, and requiring plaintiff to proceed on one only of them, is not harmless because he fails to recover on the cause tried, on the ground of insufficiency of the evidence.

Error to Court of Civil Appeals of Third Supreme Judicial District.

Action by W. Earle Hudmon against W. M. Foster and another. Judgment for defendants was affirmed by the Court of Civil Appeals (210 S. W. 262), and plaintiff brings error. Reversed in part and remanded.

H. O. Lindsey, of Waco, for plaintiff in error.

Allan D. Sanford, of Waco, for defendants in error.

SPENCER, J. Plaintiff in error, W. Earle Hudmon, filed this suit on September 10, 1913, against Eugene Early, W. M. Foster, and H. H. Shear. On May 12, 1916, an amended original petition was filed in which H. H. Shear was excluded as a defendant.

The amended petition alleged in substance that plaintiff, being financially embarrassed and very much in need of money, applied to defendants for a loan to meet his pressing needs; that as a result of the application, he entered into a contract with defendants, the terms of which are: That defendants did not have the entire amount desired, but that they would endeavor to find some person who would advance a balance to make up a loan of $17,500; that as compensation for finding such person and securing the money, plaintiff should transfer and assign to them capital stock amounting to $5,000 of a corporation to be thereafter formed, with its domicile at Hamilton, Tex., for the purpose of manufacturing cotton seed products; that the loan should be evidenced by notes of Hudmon payable to the order of Early & Foster to be held by them for the benefit of the parties making the loan; that contemporaneously with the execution of the notes, and for the purpose of securing the notes, Hudmon should hypothecate and deposit with them certificates of stock in the corporation to the amount of $30,000, and should execute and deliver to defendants a contract providing and creating a lien upon the stock; that, on a failure to pay the notes or either of them when due, defendants should have authority to foreclose the lien upon giving ten days' written notice to Hudmon.

Plaintiff further alleged that the provisions in the contract requiring him to deliver the certificates of stock was merely a device by defendants to conceal the real intent of the transaction; that the transferring of the stock was interest on the loan; and that this amount, when added to the 10 per cent. interest specified in the notes, rendered the total rate of interest paid highly and grossly usurious; and that, if the $5,000 capital stock be considered payment for services, it was greatly and extravagantly disproportionate thereto, and for that reason extortionately usurious.

Plaintiff further alleged that defendants controlled shares of stock in the corporation amounting to $30,000, and that he owned the balance of $30,000 upon which defendants held the hypothecation contract; that, the mill proving unprofitable, it became necessary to sell, and they did sell, the same for $57,500, thereby sustaining a loss of $2,500; that the defendants refused to bear any part of the loss, but by threats to foreclose under the hypothecation contract compelled plaintiff to bear the whole loss, to his damage in the sum of $1,250.

He also charged that by threats to foreclose said lien, they refused to pay the proper authorities any part of the certain taxes—state, county, and municipal—due on the mill property for which they were equally liable, but, by force of such threats, compelled plaintiff to pay all the taxes amounting to $600, for which they and their interest in the property were equally bound.

Defendants answered by general demurrer, by special exception directed at the petition on account of the alleged misjoinder of causes of action, and by general denial. The court sustained the special exception as to the misjoinder of causes of action and ordered a dismissal of the petition unless the plaintiff amended his petition.

Plaintiff elected to proceed upon the actions for usury, as indicated by his second amended petition filed May 19, 1917.

Upon a trial of this issue, before the court, without a jury, judgment was rendered in favor of defendants. Upon appeal and original hearing the Court of Civil Appeals upheld the action of the trial court in sustaining the exception, as to the misjoinder of causes of action, and reversed and remanded the judgment on the usury question on account of the insufficiency of the evidence. Upon motion for rehearing, the trial court judgment was in all things affirmed. 210 S. W. 262.

The honorable Court of Civil Appeals was of opinion that the question of multifariousness was a matter largely within the discretion of the trial court, and that as no injury to plaintiff had been shown because of the sustaining of the exceptions, the judgment should not be disturbed.

[1] Misjoinder of causes of action, or multifariousness, has been thus defined:

"Multifariousness in equity pleading is the improperly joining in one bill distinct and independent matters and thereby confounding them; as for example the uniting in one bill of several matters perfectly distinct and unconnected against one defendant, or the demand of several matters of a distinct and independent nature against several defendants in the same bill." Whart. Law Dic.; National Bank v. Texas Investment Co., 74 Tex. 433, 12 S. W. 101.

The Supreme Court declared at a very early date that—

"A leading principle in our law and system of procedure is to avoid a multiplicity of suits, and to settle in one action the respective claims of parties when they are of such a nature as to admit of adjustment in that mode." Thomas v. Hill, Admr., 3 Tex. 270; Fitzhugh v. Orton, 12 Tex. 4.

The rule against multifariousness should not be construed to restrict the policy of our law which enjoins the avoidance of a multiplicity of suits, but should be construed with reference to it; so that, without conflict, each may perform its office within its respective sphere. In filing suits, parties plaintiff are as much entitled to invoke the one as they are compelled to obey the other. The discretion, with reference to joinder of causes of action, reposed in the trial court, must be exercised consistent with the rule which enjoins the multiplicity of suits, and if the matters relied upon for recovery in the petition grow out of the same cause or transaction and subject-matter of dispute, the petition is not subject to exceptions as multifarious. Walcott v. Hendrick, 6 Tex. 415; Railway Co. v. Graves, 50 Tex. 181.

In our opinion, the court was not warranted in sustaining the exceptions on the ground that the petition was multifarious. The matters relied upon for recovery grew out of the same transaction, and therefore plaintiff should not be put to the necessity of bringing four separate suits instead of one. Wills Point Bank v. Bates, Reed & Cooley, 76 Tex. 329, 13 S. W. 309.

[2] Defendants insist that, as the Court of Civil Appeals found that no injury had resulted to plaintiff, the cause should not be reversed. We recognize the rule that a misjoinder of causes of action will not require a reversal of a judgment if the erroneous action of the court in allowing such misjoinder resulted in no injury to the defendant (Thompson v. Griffin, 69 Tex. 139, 6 S. W. 410; Railway Co. v. Watkins, 88 Tex. 20, 29 S. W. 232), but this rule has no application where, as in this case, exceptions to the petition were sustained upon the ground of misjoinder of causes of action when in fact there was no misjoinder.

The Court of Civil Appeals having affirmed the judgment of the trial court upon the questions of usury, based upon the sufficiency of the evidence, the judgments in that respect should be affirmed; but for the error committed in sustaining the exceptions on account of the misjoinder of causes of action, we recommend that the judgments of the Court of Civil Appeals and of the district court be reversed, and the causes remanded to the district court for trial of the excluded causes.

PHILLIPS, C. J. The judgment recommended in the report of the Commission of Appeals is adopted, and will be entered as the judgment of the Supreme Court.

HARLAN et al. v. ACME SANITARY FLOORING CO. et al. (No. 185–3228.)

(Commission of Appeals of Texas, Section B. June 1, 1921.)

1. Appeal and error ⬾722(1)—Appellant not restricted to assignments in motion for new trial.

Appellant is not restricted to the assignments in the motion for a new trial, but may file assignments of error independently of those specified in such motion.

2. Trial ⬾181—Statute requiring objection to charge before submission to jury not applicable to peremptory instruction.

Acts 33d Leg. (1913) c. 59, requiring an objection to the charge to be made before given to the jury, is not applicable to a peremptory instruction.

Error to Court of Civil Appeals of Eighth Supreme Judicial District.

Action by Lee Harlan and others against the Acme Sanitary Flooring Company and others. Judgment for defendants, affirmed by the Court of Civil Appeals (203 S. W. 412), and the plaintiffs bring error. Judgment of Court of Civil Appeals reversed, and case remanded, with instructions.

Edwards & Edwards and A. S. Thurmond, all of El Paso, for plaintiffs in error.

Thornton Hardie, C. W. Croom, and Jones, Jones & Hardie, all of El Paso, for defendants in error.

KITTRELL, J. This action was brought by plaintiffs in error against defendants in error, based on allegations that plaintiffs were induced by fraudulent representations made by defendants to buy 60 shares of the stock of the Acme Sanitary Flooring Company. The representations were alleged to have been that the company was fully incorporated, with a paid-up capital stock of $25,000, but more money was needed for working capital, and, if the plaintiffs would take $6,000 worth of stock, the company would have $12,-000 working capital. The plaintiffs were to receive treasury stock, which they thought they were receiving and did receive; whereas they did not, and for that reason, and others, alleged they were deceived, defrauded, and suffered damages. In view of the disposition made of the case, no further statement of the pleadings is necessary.

At the close of the testimony for plaintiff,

the trial court of its own motion, and without argument being heard, directed the jury to return a verdict for defendants. Plaintiffs filed a motion for a new trial, containing four grounds of alleged error, which, while different in phraseology, were substantially the same in legal effect, in that every one directed attention to the error which counsel conceived the trial court had committed in directing on its own motion, and without argument, a verdict for defendants. Plaintiffs in error also filed assignments of error, two in number, in the office of the clerk, and these were used in the brief as the basis for the propositions on which they rested their appeal. Both the motion for a new trial and the assignments of error filed with the clerk were duly indexed as a part of the record.

The Court of Civil Appeals refused to consider the assignments and affirmed the judgment. It based its action on two grounds:

First. That the statute requires that the assignments in the motion for a new trial shall constitute the assignments of error, and that neither of the assignments presented in the brief were true copies of any paragraph of the motion for a new trial.

Second. That the plaintiff in error failed to object to the peremptory instruction in favor of defendant before it was given to the jury.

[1] The holding of the Court of Civil Appeals on the first ground is contrary to, and in conflict with, the holding of the Supreme Court in the case of Hess & Skinner v. Turney, 109 Tex. 208, 203 S. W. 593. The holding in that case has recently been reaffirmed in a case not yet officially reported. Barkley et al. v. Gibbs et al., 227 S. W. 1099. In the memorandum of approval by the Supreme Court of Judge Sadler's opinion in that case, Chief Justice Phillips uses the following language:

"We have expressly ruled in Hess & Skinner v. Turnay, 109 Tex. 208, 203 S. W. 593, that under article 1612 as amended by the act of 1913, an appellant is entitled to have considered assignments of error filed independently of those specified in his motion for a new trial. He may adopt the assignments in his motion for new trial or not, as he chooses."

The question may therefore be treated as no longer an open one, and it follows that the holding of the Court of Civil Appeals on the first ground stated in its opinion was erroneous.

[2] The holding of that court on the second ground is also erroneous, because of its being contrary to and in conflict with the holding of the Supreme Court in Walker v. Haley, 214 S. W. 295, Decker v. Kirlicks, 216 S. W. 385, and Shumaker v. Byrd, 216 S. W. 862. The holding in those cases is that the requirement of chapter 59, Acts of the 33d Legislature, that objection to the charge must be made before it is given to the jury, has no application to a peremptory instruction. Justice to the Court of Civil Appeals of the Eighth District requires that it be said that its opinion in the instant case was delivered before the cases last cited were decided.

We recommend that the judgment of the Court of Civil Appeals be reversed, and that the case be remanded to that court, with instructions to consider the assignments.

PHILLIPS, C. J. The judgment recommended in the report of the Commission of Appeals is adopted, and will be entered as the judgment of the Supreme Court.

We approve the holding of the Commission of Appeals on the question discussed in its opinion.

BAKER v. SHAFTER. (No. 213–3312.)

(Commission of Appeals of Texas, Section A. June 1, 1921.)

1. **Appeal and error ⟺930(3)—In absence of objection, it will be presumed that special issues conform to pleadings and evidence.**

In an action against a railway company for personal injuries sustained in a crossing accident, in the absence of any objection to the special issues submitted or request for special charges correctly submitting the issues, those submitted will be presumed to conform with the pleadings and evidence, and treating the issues submitted as embracing the only theory relied upon by plaintiff, it follows that, the jury having found plaintiff guilty of negligence, such negligence bars recovery unless the pleadings or evidence raise the issue of discovered peril, so that, under Rev. St. 1911, art. 1985, all facts necessary to support the judgment can be deemed found.

2. **Negligence ⟺83—Doctrine of "discovered peril" stated.**

The doctrine of discovered peril involves the exposed condition brought about by the plaintiff's negligence; the actual discovery by defendant's agents of plaintiff's perilous situation in time to avert, by use of all means at their command, commensurate with their own safety, injury to him, and the failure thereafter to use such means.

[Ed. Note.—For other definitions, see Words and Phrases, Second Series, Discovered Peril.]

3. **Negligence ⟺119(6) — Discovered peril must be pleaded.**

To invoke the doctrine of discovered peril, it must be pleaded.

4. **Railroads ⟺345(1) — Issue of discovered peril held not raised by pleading.**

In action against railroad for injuries in a crossing accident, pleadings which failed to assert the actual discovery by defendant's agents of plaintiff's perilous situation in time to have averted the accident by the use of means at their command commensurate with their own safety are lacking in one of the essential elements of discovered peril.

5. Judgment ⚖=251(1), 256(2)—Judgment must conform to issues pleaded; courts may not ignore findings and pass judgment.

Judgments must conform to issues raised by pleadings and upon which case was tried, and courts cannot ignore jury's findings and render judgment upon theory of discovered peril in an action for personal injuries in railroad crossing accident where such matter was not pleaded.

Error to Court of Civil Appeals of Fourth Supreme Judicial District.

Action by Victor Shafter against the International & Great Northern Railway Company and James A. Baker, its receiver. Action dismissed as to the Railway Company. Judgment for plaintiff, and the receiver appealed to Court of Civil Appeals, which affirmed the judgment (208 S. W. 961), and the receiver brings error. Reversed and remanded.

Jno. M. King, of Houston, and Marshall Eskridge, F. C. Davis, and Arthur V. Wright, all of San Antonio, for plaintiff in error.

J. D. Childs, of San Antonio, and Martin Faust, of New Braunfels, for defendant in error.

SPENCER, J. Victor Shafter instituted this suit to recover of the International & Great Northern Railway Company and its receiver, James A. Baker, for personal injuries alleged to have been sustained by reason of the negligence of the defendants. The answer was a general denial, and a plea of contributory negligence. The suit was dismissed as to the railway company.

Upon the issue of liability, the court submitted but two issues to the jury, both of which were answered in the affirmative. They are:

"No. 1. Was the defendant, James A. Baker, receiver of the International & Great Northern Railway Company, his agents and employés, guilty of negligence in operating its engine at the time and place, under the circumstances, in running its engine over the plaintiff and inflicting the injuries which you may find from the evidence were so inflicted on the plaintiff?

"No. 2. Was the plaintiff guilty of negligence in attempting to cross the railroad tracks of the defendant at the time and place and under the circumstances which you may find from the evidence he so undertook to cross said tracks when he was struck by the engine of the defendant?"

The court rendered judgment for plaintiff in the sum of $3,000, and, upon appeal, the Court of Civil Appeals affirmed the judgment. 208 S. W. 961.

It will be observed that, in each of the special issues submitted, the element of proximate cause was omitted. It also appears that neither of the parties requested a finding upon this issue, and that the only objection to the special issues submitted was that by plaintiff in error to special issue No. 1—the objection being that there was no evidence warranting its submission.

[1] Plaintiff's pleading properly raised the issue of defendant's negligence as the proximate cause of the injury, and defendant's pleading specifically charged that plaintiff's contributory negligence was the proximate cause thereof. In the absence of any objection to the special issues submitted, the failure of the parties to request special charges correctly submitting the issue, it will be presumed that the issues were in conformity to the issues joined by the pleadings and the evidence, and the answers thereto will be interpreted in the light of the issues tendered and relied upon for recovery. If, therefore, we treat the issues submitted as embracing the only theory relied upon by plaintiff for recovery, it would follow that, as the jury found that plaintiff was guilty of negligence, such negligence bars a recovery. However, plaintiff contends that, as the pleadings and the evidence raise the issue of discovered peril, all facts necessary to support the judgment of the trial court will, under article 1985, Revised Civil Statutes, be deemed as found, thus rendering the finding of the jury that plaintiff was guilty of negligence immaterial.

The honorable Court of Civil Appeals held that, while there was no specific plea of discovered peril, it is involved in the general issue of proximate cause, and raised in a general way by the allegations that the operative in charge of the engine failed to stop it, and that, as there was evidence upon which a finding sustaining such an issue could be predicated, therefore, in support of the trial court's judgment, plaintiff's negligence should be treated as the remote, and not the proximate, cause of the injury.

[2, 3] The doctrine of discovered peril involves three elements, viz: (1) The exposed condition brought about by the negligence of the plaintiff; (2) the actual discovery by defendant's agents of his perilous situation in time to have averted—by the use of all the means at their command, commensurate with their own safety—injury to him; and (3) the failure thereafter to use such means. To invoke the doctrine of discovered peril, it must be pleaded. Stewart v. Portland, etc., Ry. Co., 58 Or. 377, 114 Pac. 936.

[4] The allegations of the pleadings relied upon as raising the issue are:

Plaintiff alleged:

"Plaintiff further avers that at said time and place it was the duty of defendants:

"(a) To operate their switch engines, at all hours while in motion, at said crossing in charge of and under the control of careful and competent firemen, engineers, and other operatives, switchmen, or watchmen, by keeping a close and careful watchout ahead for pedestrians and others who might be on or in places of danger near the tracks, so as to be able to see them and prevent their injury by said heavy and dangerous instrumentalities thus propelled along such public streets, and to so adjust the speed of such switch engines as to have them under perfect control, and be able to stop them in short order when necessary to preserve human life or limb that might be lawfully on the said tracks, which the defendants, their servants, and employees negligently failed to do on this occasion, and which they could or should have done, and they then and there failed to keep such proper lookout, and if they had done so they could have stopped said engine and prevented said injury to plaintiff, which they failed to do, and thus their negligence became and was the proximate cause of plaintiff's said injuries. * * *

"(c) It was also the duty of defendants to maintain safe, proper, and up-to-date appliances and machinery with which the operatives were to operate and control their switch engines while in the streets of said city at the time and place in question, in order to stop said engines in short and proper order in case of persons suddenly getting on their tracks in front of such moving engines, and the defendants either negligently failed to equip and furnish their switch in question on this occasion with such safe appliances or equipments, or the operatives of said switch engine negligently failed to use the same, and thereby said failure of duty on the part of defendants became and was a proximate, contributing cause to plaintiff's said injuries."

Defendant pleaded:

"That plaintiff had frequently, prior to the accident, passed over said tracks at this point, and well knew that there might be expected engines and cars to be passing over said tracks and across Lakeview avenue at any time. But, notwithstanding this knowledge, plaintiff walked diagonally across said tracks, and without stopping, looking, or listening negligently stepped immediately in front of a moving engine, and, before his peril was discovered by the operatives thereof, suffered the accident complained of; wherefore he cannot recover."

It will thus be seen that there is no allegation charging the second essential element of discovered peril; that is, that the operatives in charge of the train discovered plaintiff's perilous situation in time to have averted injury to him. Neither was the issue submitted nor requested to be submitted to the jury for a finding.

[1] It is apparent, we think, that plaintiff did not rely upon discovered peril for a recovery. In this condition of the record, it is improper to inject such an issue into the case. The judgment must conform to the issues raised by the pleading, and upon which the case was tried. Courts are not at liberty to ignore the findings of the jury in response to issues tried and submitted, and to render judgment based upon a theory not relied upon for recovery.

The case, in our opinion, will, of necessity, have to be reversed, and, as the Court of Civil Appeals found that there was evidence raising the issue of discovered peril, the ends of justice will be best subserved by remanding the cause for another trial. Camden Fire Ins. Co. v. Yarbrough, 215 S. W. 842, and authorities there cited.

Therefore, we recommend that the cause be reversed, and remanded for a new trial.

PHILLIPS, C. J. The judgment recommended in the report of the Commission of Appeals is adopted and will be entered as the judgment of the Supreme Court.

DUNN v. JACKSON. (No. 228–3404.)

(Commission of Appeals of Texas, Section A. June 1, 1921.)

1. **Habeas corpus ⚷99(1)—Parent is natural guardian of his children, as respecting right to habeas corpus.**

The parent is the guardian by nature of his children, and his right to their custody is paramount, but this right may be forfeited by misconduct or lost through misfortune.

2. **Habeas corpus ⚷99(3)—Interests of child prevail in proceedings for custody.**

A parent may surrender the custody of his child to a third person, and on habeas corpus proceedings by the parent to regain the custody the paramount interest of the child becomes the dominant issue.

3. **Habeas corpus ⚷85(1)—Third person may defeat habeas corpus by father to regain custody of child by showing it is not to the benefit of the child.**

Where a parent who surrendered custody of his child to a third person brought habeas corpus to regain the custody, the third person has the burden of establishing facts necessary to overcome the legal presumption in favor of the parent's custody, but it is sufficient if the third person show that the best interests of the child demand that it remain in his or her custody, and it is improper to grant the parent the custody of the child, regardless of all else, unless his unfitness be shown.

4. **Habeas corpus ⚷99(6)—Wishes of child of sufficient age to judge for itself should be considered in habeas corpus proceedings.**

In determining the custody of a child, its wishes, where sufficiently mature to judge for itself, should be consulted, and weighed with the other testimony, but the child's choice is not necessarily a controlling factor.

5. **Habeas corpus ⚷99(1)—Father, though suitable, is not entitled to custody of child at all events.**

Where the father of a baby on his wife's death gave her into the custody of her maternal grandmother, who cared for the infant until she was 14, the mere fact that the father, who had married again and had other children, was a proper person to have the custody of the infant, does not entitle him to its custody, regardless of the wishes of the infant, who had became estranged from her father, stepmother, and half-sisters, and the maternal grandparent should be allowed to retain custody where for the best interests of the child.

Error to Court of Civil Appeals of Sixth Supreme Judicial District.

Habeas corpus proceedings by J. T. Jackson to recover from Mrs. L. A. Dunn the custody of his minor child. Judgment for plaintiff was affirmed by the Court of Civil Appeals (212 S. W. 959), and defendant brings error. Judgments of Court of Civil Appeals and of district court reversed, and cause remanded for new trial.

R. R. Taylor, of Jefferson, for plaintiff in error.

Schluter & Singleton, of Jefferson, for defendant in error.

SPENCER, J. This habeas corpus proceeding was instituted by J. T. Jackson to regain the custody of his minor child, Annie Jackson, from the custody of the child's maternal grandmother. The father was awarded custody of the child, and from this order respondent appealed to the Court of Civil Appeals, which court affirmed the judgment of the trial court. 212 S. W. 959.

The findings of fact and conclusions of law by the trial court are as follows:

"(1) I find that Annie R. Jackson was born in February, 1905, in Marion county, Tex., and while she was an infant only two weeks old her mother died, and her grandmother, Mrs. L. A. Dunn, was present at the death of Mrs. J. T. Jackson, her daughter, and that the applicant herein, J. T. Jackson, consented for Mrs. L. A. Dunn to take his infant daughter and care for her, and consented at that time not to retake the custody of the child from its grandmother.

"(2) Mrs. Dunn took the care and custody of Annie Jackson, and cared for her tenderly and well from that time to this date.

"(3) J. T. Jackson remarried after his first wife's death, and to this marriage were born two children, both girls. The older is past ten years of age, the younger is eight years of age.

"(4) A great deal of the time since J. T. Jackson's second marriage he has lived in Marion county, but for the last several years he has lived in Louisiana.

"(5) I find that Mrs. L. A. Dunn is of good moral character and an indulgent grandmother, but for the past three years has been practically an invalid, but is now somewhat improved; that she and her husband have separated and are not now living together, but she is living with a single son about 25 years of age, and she and this single son and another son who is working in the oil fields of Louisiana, and a daughter who is married are very fond and almost passionately attached to Annie Jackson, and that she likewise is very fond of them and does not want to leave them. The grandmother does not oppose Annie going with her father if she wishes to go.

"(6) I find that J. T. Jackson is a man of honorable deportment and integrity, is kind and good to his family, but of a temperament that is not enthusiastically demonstrative in his affections; that he loves his daughter and is able and is always a proper person to have the care and custody of his own children; that he is now earning $140 per month and is working in Marion county, but has only recently moved to Marion county from Louisiana, and his second wife and two daughters have not yet returned to Marion county, but will do so at once; that he is diligent, industrious, and able to educate and care for and educate his daughter and desires her care and custody.

"(7) I find that the stepmother of Annie Jackson long desired that she be brought to her father's home and raised with her half-sisters, and the only reason that it has not been heretofore done is that Annie's father regretted very much to deprive the grandparents of the child for whom they had formed such strong attachment.

"(8) I find that in recent years there has become an estrangement from some cause of the child against her father, stepmother, and half-sisters, and that she now bears no more affection for them than if they were rank strangers about whom she knew nothing, and I am unable to determine what the cause is.

"(9) I find that J. T. Jackson has not contributed a great deal to the support and maintenance of his daughter Annie, and that her support and maintenance has been furnished by her grandparents and two uncles and an aunt. I find that several years ago, when Annie was small, her stepmother purchased goods and made up some clothing or wearing apparel for Annie and sent them to her, and that Annie's aunt and grandmother returned the clothing with no explanation whatever, but that they now say they were returned because they were too small and cheap and poorly made; and I am led to believe there is a very decided dislike on the part of the grandmother, uncles, and aunt of Annie towards Annie's stepmother, without any apparent cause that I am able to find.

"Conclusions of Law.

"(1) I conclude that the parents are the natural guardians of their minor children and entitled to their custody as against the world, except in instances where the parents are of such character that the association of the child with the parent would be injurious to either the physical, moral or educational welfare of the child, and the burden is on those seeking to establish such unfitness by clear and satisfactory proof.

"(2) I conclude that the agreement of J. T. Jackson with the grandmother of Annie to never retake the custody of Annie from her grandmother cannot in any way alter, change, or affect the right of J. T. Jackson to the custody of his daughter, nor his parental and legal obligations to care for, educate and maintain her.

"(3) I conclude that the welfare of Annie, according to the law, should be the sole criterion in determining her custody, and unless it is satisfactorily shown to me that the parent is an improper person to have the custody of his child, I conclude that the welfare of the child will be better served by being in the custody of the parent than in the custody of any one else; therefore, on the foregoing findings of fact, I awarded the custody of Annie Jackson to her father."

The findings of fact reveal that the minor is offered two homes equal in so far as material comforts are concerned; one by the father and the other by the maternal grandmother. This condition, unfortunate in the sense that the designation of one of the two robs the other of the girl's affections and constant association which both cherish, is due to the fact that the father, because of the mother's death, placed her, when but two weeks of age, in the care and custody of the grandmother, consenting not to retake the child from her custody.

[1, 2] The parent is the guardian by nature of his children and his right to their custody is paramount, but this right may be forfeited by misconduct or lost through misfortune; but where he has surrendered this custody to a third person, who performs the duties incumbent upon him as the natural guardian, a new condition is created which inures to the benefit of the child. The law does not prohibit such a transfer by the parent, but, on the contrary, allows the child to reap the benefit therefrom, and upon a habeas corpus proceeding by the parent to regain custody of the child the paramount interest of the child becomes the dominant issue. Legate v. Legate, 87 Tex. 248, 28 S. W. 281.

In the case of the State v. Deaton, 93 Tex. 243, 54 S. W. 901, Judge Brown, speaking for the Supreme Court upon this question, quotes with approval from Weir v. Morley, 99 Mo. 484, 12 S. W. 798, 6 L. R. A. 672, as follows:

"What is for the best interest of the infant is the question upon which all cases turn at last, whatever may be said in the opinion about contracts; and the answer returned is that the custody of the child is by law with the father, unless it appears by satisfactory evidence that the best interest of the child demands that he should be deprived of that custody, and upon him who so avers devolves the burden of proof; the presumptions are against it."

[3] Under this just rule, the burden of proof rested with the respondent to establish facts necessary to overcome the legal presumption in favor of the parent's custody. It does not require, however, that respondent prove the parent disqualified by misconduct or misfortune; but the burden resting upon respondent is met by establishing that the best interests of the child demand that she remain in the custody of respondent.

The trial court, as shown by its conclusion of law, proceeded upon the theory that the

231 S.W.—23

parent is entitled to the custody of the child unless respondent establish by clear and satisfactory evidence that the parent is an improper person to educate and rear her. This places a greater burden upon respondent than the law demanded. No such burden rested primarily with respondent. Of course, if respondent had established that the parent was an improper person and respondent a proper person, able and willing to care for the child, she would have been entitled to retain custody of her. The parent's fitness, however, was not an insurmountable obstacle to the retention of the custody by respondent, because the parent's right must yield when the best interests of the minor demand it.

[4, 5] The error of the court is made manifest in the third conclusion of law. The court recognizes that the welfare of the child is the sole criterion in determining her custody, but because it was not shown that the parent was an improper person, indulged the presumption, in disregard of the evidence as to the best interests of the child, that her best interest would be best served by being in the custody of the parent. The effect of this holding was to utterly ignore, as immaterial to a decision of the cause, the expressed wishes of the child, who was nearly 14 years of age at the time she testified, to remain with her grandmother, the strong attachment she had formed for her grandmother in response to the affection bestowed upon and care taken of her by the grandmother and the severing of ties formed during the most impressionable period of her life, by taking her from the only home she had ever known and placing her in a home whose inmates she had no more affection for than if they were rank strangers.

These things were matters of vital importance in determining the important question of fact as to whose custody would be most beneficial to the child's interest; and the evident failure to consider them, coupled with the court's requirement that respondent prove the relator an improper person to educate and rear the child, necessitate, we think, a reversal of the cause.

The wishes of a child whose custody is in controversy may, if it be of a sufficiently mature age to judge for itself, be consulted and weighed with other testimony in determining the issue; but its choice is not necessarily a controlling factor. Ellis v. Jesup et al., 74 Ky. (11 Bush) 403; Neville v. Reed, 134 Ala. 317, 32 South. 659, 92 Am. St. Rep. 35; Workman v. Watts, 74 S. C. 546, 54 S. E. 775; State v. Richardson, 40 N. H. 272; Hurd on Habeas Corpus (2d Ed.) 531.

We recommend therefore that the judgments of the Court of Civil Appeals and of the district court be reversed, and the cause remanded for a new trial.

PHILLIPS, C. J. The judgment recommended in the report of the Commission of

Appeals is adopted, and will be entered as the judgment of the Supreme Court.

We approve the holding of the Commission of Appeals on the question discussed in its opinion.

SAN ANTONIO & A. P. RY. CO. v. BEHNE et ux. (No. 163–3159.)

(Commission of Appeals of Texas, Section B. June 1, 1921.)

1. **Negligence ⊜⇒56(3)—Law of proximate cause applicable to violations of statutory and common-law duty.**

It is not the rule that violation of a statutory duty imposes liability for any injury traceable to the wrongful act, regardless of whether it might have been foreseen or anticipated; but the rule is that where the act or omission is wrongful or negligent, whether as a result of failure to observe a statutory or common-law duty, liability, in either case, is limited to proximately caused injuries, and the rules for determining proximate cause are the same in either case.

2. **Negligence ⊜⇒59—Foreseeableness of injury as "natural and probable result" element of proximate cause.**

Foreseeableness or anticipation of injury is a necessary element of proximate cause; and while actual anticipation is not the test, nor is it material whether the particular injury might have been foreseen, it is requisite that the injury be of such a general character as might reasonably have been anticipated and that the injured party should be so situated with relation to the wrongful act that injury to him or to one similarly situated might reasonably have been foreseen; the phrase "natural and probable result" meaning what should reasonably be anticipated in the light of common experience applied to the surrounding circumstances.

3. **Railroads ⊜⇒113(10)—Insufficient drainage held not proximate cause of drowning in flood.**

Failure of a railroad to have sufficient opening for flood water in bridging a creek as required in Rev. St. art. 6495, whereby in a not unprecedented flood its bridge was washed away, *held* not the proximate cause of the death of one who was drowned when thrown from a tree downstream in which he had taken refuge from the flood, when the tree was struck by the bridge washed against it by the flood waters.

Error to Court of Civil Appeals of Third Supreme Judicial District.

Action by Albert Behne and wife against the San Antonio & Aransas Pass Railway Company. Judgment for plaintiffs was affirmed by the Court of Civil Appeals (198 S. W. 680), and defendant brings error. Judgments of the district court and Court of Civil Appeals reversed and rendered.

Henderson, Kidd & Henderson, of Cameron (Boyle, Ezell, Houston & Grover, of San Antonio, of counsel), for plaintiff in error. U. S. Hearrell and R. B. Pool, both of Cameron, for defendants in error.

McCLENDON, P. J. This action was brought by Albert Behne and wife as plaintiffs, against the San Antonio & Aransas Pass Railway Company, as defendant, to recover for the death of their son Ed Behne, who was drowned by being thrown from a tree in which he had taken refuge from the flood waters of Elm creek; the tree having been struck and felled by a bridge of defendant company, which had been washed by the flood waters against the tree.

The cause was tried before a jury upon special issues, and upon the answers by the jury of all issues favorably to plaintiffs, judgment was rendered for the latter. This judgment was affirmed by the Court of Civil Appeals. 198 S. W. 680.

Liability is predicated upon the failure of the railway company in constructing its roadbed and tracks to provide the necessary drainage in accordance with the natural lay of the land, as required by statute (R. S. art. 6495).

The controlling question is whether the failure of the railroad company in this particular was the proximate cause of the death of plaintiff's son. The Court of Civil Appeals, in an elaborate opinion, has given a very full and accurate statement of the pleadings and evidence. In the conclusion we have reached, which is that the complained of wrongful acts of defendant were not, in contemplation of the law, the proximate cause of the drowning of the plaintiffs' son; the following statement of the facts, which are in the main undisputed, will suffice to a clear understanding of that issue:

Elm creek at the point of intersection with defendant's railway flows in an easterly direction—the railway at that place running approximately north and south. The valley of Elm creek is about 4,000 feet in width. Across this valley the railway beginning at the south was constructed upon a solid earth dump some 6 or 7 feet high, extending from the high-water mark on the south to a distance of about 2,132 feet. On the north side of the valley was a similar dump or embankment, extending about 846 feet. Between these dumps was the bridge proper across the channel of the creek, 154 feet in length, and trestle work connecting with the bridge, and to the north of it, extending some 832 feet to south end of the north dump, leaving an open space, represented by the length of the bridge and trestle work, of approximately 982 feet, or about one-fourth of the width of the valley. The bridge proper was a few feet higher than the dump. Just below and to the east of the railway was an open tract of sparsely wooded land, containing some six or seven acres through which the creek meandered, and through this tract extended a public road, the regular thoroughfare from Cameron to Ben Arnold. The railway had been constructed for quite a number of years, during which time there had been a number of floods as high as that in question, the waters of which had run over the dumps on either side of the bridge, and on several occasions these dumps had been washed away; but the bridge and track had always remained intact.

On the occasion in question, Ed Behne, with two of his brothers and an uncle, had driven from their home some miles distant to the open tract of land below the railway, unhitched their team in the creek bottom, and were fishing. They expected to camp there that night. About 7 o'clock in the evening a heavy rain came up and the creek began to rise rapidly. In a few minutes they began preparation to leave by hitching up their team, but before they could get out of the creek bottom, the water had risen so rapidly that they were compelled to take refuge in the trees. They had been in the trees some 30 minutes when the railroad bridge and a part of the track was washed away and struck the trees in which they had taken refuge. Two of the Behne boys and their uncle were drowned. The third Behne boy, Manuel, succeeded in reaching another tree, from which he was rescued the following day. The evidence, though conflicting, was sufficient, we think, to warrant the jury finding that the flood was not unprecedented, either in height or in the rapidity with which the water rose. It was clear, however, from the evidence that in the rapidity with which the water rose and the force with which it struck the railway embankment, trestle, and bridge, it was, at all events, quite unusual. There was a great deal of testimony upon this point, but it is not necessary to notice it in detail. The evidence showed that the open tract upon which the Behne boys and their uncle were fishing was frequently used by campers and camping parties, and was often resorted to during the fishing season by fishermen, and that the public road running through it was frequently used. It was also in evidence that Elm creek was subject to sudden rises and that during seasons of flood neither human beings nor animals made use of the flooded area of the open tract of land, or of the roadway.

[1] The holding of the Court of Civil Appeals is to the effect that the statute, noncompliance with which is the basis of the suit, was enacted for the protection of persons, as well as property, and that its violation constituted a wrongful act as a matter of law and imposed liability for any injury which could be traced to such unlawful act, regardless of whether the injury were one of a kind or nature which might have been foreseen or anticipated. As we construe the opinion of the Court of Civil Appeals, a distinction is drawn between an act which is wrongful or negligent per se, as in violation of statute, and one which results from a failure to exercise ordinary care, in so far as the doctrine of anticipation of injury, as applied to proximate cause, is concerned.

The conclusion thus reached is not in accord with the holdings of our Supreme Court. We do not find that any distinction is drawn as regards the rule that liability for a wrongful act is limited to such injuries as are proximately caused by such wrongful act, whether the act be wrongful per se, as for the failure to comply with a statutory duty, or wrongful at common law, as being a failure to exercise ordinary care. The difference between the two classes of wrongful acts rests solely in the method of determining whether they be wrongful. When it is shown that a statute has been violated, wrongfulness or negligence follows per se, as a matter of law; whereas, if the dereliction complained of depends for its wrongful character upon the principles of the common law, it is usually a question of fact whether there has been a failure to exercise ordinary care.

When it has been once determined that the act or omission complained of is wrongful or negligent, whether as a result of failure to observe a statutory or common-law duty, liability, in either case, is limited to proximately caused injuries. And the rules for determining proximate cause are the same in either case. Railway v. Barry, 98 Tex. 250, 83 S. W. 5; Burnett v. Fort Worth Co., 102 Tex. 31, 112 S. W. 1040, 19 L. R. A. (N. S.) 504; Railway v. Wilkes (Tex. Civ. App.) 159 S. W. 126; Railway v. Dobbins (Tex. Civ. App.) 40 S. W. 861; Waterman Lumber Co. v. Beatty, 110 Tex. 227, 218 S. W. 363.

Quoting from the Burnett Case, above:

"It is almost universally held that the violation of a statutory duty is negligence per se. But, as we understand it, this is the difference between negligence at common law, usually a question of fact, and the violation of a statutory duty—'only this and nothing more.' When a plaintiff sues for the neglect of the provisions of a statute, or of the ordinance of a city, and proves such violation and that he has been injured as the approximate cause thereof, he has established the first postulate of his case, that is the negligence of the defendant."

The exact point is decided in the Waterman Lbr. Co. Case, above, in the following language by Associate Justice Greenwood:

"There is no doubt that it is essential to the maintenance of an action for damages for a personal injury, founded on the violation of a statute, to establish not only a violation of the statute but that the violation was the proximate cause of the injury. Though the violation of the statute would be negligence per se, the action would fail without a showing of proper causal connection between the negligence and the injury. Shearman & Redfield, Law of Negligence (Street's Ed.) § 27; Railway v. Bigham, 90 Tex. 225, 38 S. W. 162; Railway v. Campbell, 241 U. S. 510, 60 L. Ed. 1125; Stirling v. Bettis Mfg. Co., 159 S. W. 916; Elk Cotton Mills v. Grant, 140 Ga. 727, 48 L. R. A. (N. S.) 656, 79 S. E. 836. It follows that there was the same necessity for a proper application of the thoroughly settled law of proximate cause in this case as in the ordinary negligence case involving no violation of a statute."

[2] The doctrine that foreseeableness or anticipation of injury is a necessary element to proximate cause is now so well established in this state that it is hardly necessary to do more than state the rule. The leading cases which announce this doctrine are Seale v. Ry., 65 Tex. 274, 57 Am. Rep. 602; and Ry. v. Bigham, 90 Tex. 223, 38 S. W. 162. In the Seale Case the rule is stated in this language:

"When a defendant has violated a duty imposed upon him by the common law, he should be held liable to every person injured, whose injury is the natural and probable result of the misconduct; and that the liability extends to such injuries as might reasonably have been anticipated, under ordinary circumstances, as the natural and probable result of the wrongful act."

This rule is clear and definite, and should, we think, produce little, if any, confusion, provided the language used be given its reasonable interpretation. Some controversy has arisen in other jurisdictions and among text-writers upon the question whether anticipation of injury should be limited in application to determining the question of negligence vel non; one view being that in determining whether the act complained of is negligent—that is actionably so—anticipation of probable consequences is controlling; but that whenever it is determined that the wrongdoer should reasonably have anticipated that the act might be injurious to some one, negligence is established and liability extends to every injury which naturally flows therefrom, regardless of whether reasonable foresight might anticipate it. It may well be that difference between these two views is more apparent than real, and that the conflict arises more from a confusion of terms or the infirmities of language than from a substantial divergence of views. It is clear to our mind that in the definition of "proximate cause" above quoted, the two portions of the definition are used synonymously as expressing the same thought. To say that an injury is the "natural and probable consequence" of a given act is but saying in other words that it is such an injury as might "reasonably have been anticipated, under ordinary circumstances, as the natural and probable result of that act." One sui juris is legally charged with the duty of antici-

pating all consequences of his conduct which under ordinary circumstances flow therefrom as the natural and probable result. To meet the requirements of this rule, actual anticipation is not the test; nor is it material whether the particular injury might have been foreseen. But it is requisite that the injury be of such a general character as might reasonably have been anticipated; and that the injured party should be so situated with relation to the wrongful act that injury to him or to one similarly situated might reasonably have been foreseen.

The basis for this rule is in the Bigham Case given to be that one ought not to be held responsible for those consequences of his acts which, in the light of common experience, and having a due regard for the rights of others, he could not be expected reasonably to have anticipated. "It would seem that there is neither a legal nor a moral obligation to guard against that which cannot be foreseen, and under such circumstances the duty of foresight should not be arbitrarily imputed."

The chief difficulty arises, not in determining what the rule is, but in applying it to each particular case when it arises—a difficulty frequently adverted to by the courts.

"The difficulty is to apply them [the rules under discussion] to a given state of facts, and we recognize fully that their application to one state of facts can rarely be a precedent for any other case, because it is hardly possible for two cases to be identical. Whether a certain result could be anticipated from a given act or omission is usually a question of fact, and becomes a question of law only when but one reasonable conclusion can be drawn from the facts." Ry. v. McDonald, 208 S. W. 912.

It would, for the reason last announced, not be profitable to review the many cases in which the doctrine of anticipation of injury has been applied in this state. From them, however, it will be seen that our Supreme Court has uniformly applied what might be termed a practical, common sense test, the test of common experience. The expression "natural and probable result" has been used and interpreted to mean what should reasonably be anticipated in the light of common experience applied to the surrounding circumstances. "Since every event is the result of a natural law, we apprehend the meaning is that the injury should be such as may probably happen as a consequence of the negligence, under the ordinary operation of natural laws." Bigham Case. above.

In the Seale Case, liability was denied for injuries to a person who was burned in trying to extinguish a fire caused by negligence of the defendant. It was said:

"That one exercising due care, and incurring no risks, in extinguishing a fire, should have the flames communicated to her clothes, and thereby lose her life, is something so improbable that the anticipation of it should not be charged to any one under such circumstances. Such a thing might happen, but it would be only from some casualty which could not possibly be foreseen; and, in such cases, as we have seen, the original negligence cannot be regarded as the proximate cause of the injury."

In the Bigham Case, the negligence of a railway company in having a defective fastening upon a gate to its stock pens was held not to be the proximate cause of injuries to the owner of cattle in the pen who was injured by being run over by the cattle in their frightened escape through the gate, while he was in the act of securing the gate with a rope. Liability for injury to the cattle thus escaping was, however, held to exist.

In the recently decided case of Ry. v. Bennett, 110 Tex. 270, 219 S. W. 198, the following clear and concise application of the rule is given by Chief Justice Phillips:

"Under the authority of Seale v. Railway Co., 65 Tex. 274, 57 Am. Rep. 602, and Railway Co. v. Bigham, 90 Tex. 223, 38 S. W. 162, the negligence of the defendant's employés in the origin of the fire cannot be justly regarded as the proximate cause of the injury to Bennett. The test of this question is, ought the defendant and its agents to have reasonably foreseen that as the consequence of the negligence which caused the explosion in the tank car, the injury to Bennett, or like injury to some other employé in his situation, would probably result? In the language of Judge Gaines' opinion in the Bigham Case, nothing short of prophetic ken could have anticipated the happening of the combination of events which resulted in Bennett's becoming overheated. No one standing at the stage of the entire happening which had to do with the gas explosion in the tank car could have regarded it as other than a bare possibility, at best, that at a later period of a fire thus produced in an open inclosure, an employé of the company, in attempting to extinguish it, would get so close to the fire or stay in such a situation so long as to be injured by the heat of the fire."

[3] We think a proper application of the principles above announced leads to the conclusion that the failure of defendant company to provide proper drainage as required by the statute was not the proximate cause of the death of plaintiff's son. Conceding that the flood was not so unprecedented, either in height or suddenness, as to be without the purview of the statute, and that defendant should reasonably have anticipated its happening, and that it might result in washing away the bridge; nevertheless, the chain of circumstances which brought about plaintiff's position of peril was so unusual and improbable as to be wholly without the sphere of events which defendant ought reasonably to be held to have anticipated. That the events of this chain were possibilities is, of course, conceded. This is demonstrated by the fact that they did happen, and as a result of the operation of natural laws. But the extreme improbability of the resultant death of plaintiff's son rests in the fact that it could only happen at a time of heavy flood, unusual in its suddenness and under such circumstances that no one could be presumed to be, except by the barest stretch of the imagination, in the path of the destroying agency—the washed away bridge. The causal connection between the negligence which put in motion that agency, and the injury, is not controlled by the fact that the agency acted directly upon the injured party. That causal connection was broken in contemplation of law by the intervention of disconnected and independent agencies, brought into being by a chain of circumstances so improbable as to render them in law unforeseeable. The breaking away of the bridge was indeed a cause, and an immediate cause, of the injury. Without it, the injury would in all probability not have happened. But the relation between the wrongful act complained of and the ultimately resultant injury is so remote as to require resort, not to probabilities, but to fantastic speculation in bare possibilities, if not indeed to "prophetic ken"; which the law does not require.

We conclude that the judgments of the district court and Court of Civil Appeals should be reversed, and judgment rendered in favor of defendant company.

PHILLIPS, C. J. The judgment recommended in the report of the Commission of Appeals is adopted, and will be entered as the judgment of the Supreme Court.

———

WAGGONER et al. v. KNIGHT.
(No. 239–3427.)

(Commission of Appeals of Texas, Section A. June 1, 1921.)

1. Judgment ⊸333—Answer to motion for correction of judgment entry could raise issue as to fraud in rendition of judgment.

Where all the parties to an action in which a judgment was rendered were served with notice of motion to correct the judgment entry, it was permissible for the answer to the motion to raise the issue of fraud in the rendition of the judgment and to ask that it be annulled.

2. Judgment ⊸741—In proceedings on motion to correct judgment entry, where answer to motion alleged invalidity, order held res judicata as to validity of judgment, though issue was not expressly decided.

Where all the parties to the action in which a judgment was rendered were before the court on a motion to correct the judgment entry, and where the answer to the motion had raised the issue of fraud in the rendition of the judgment and had asked to have it annulled, the judgment on the motion correcting the judgment entry with no express disposition of issue as to the alleged fraud *held* res judicata as to validity of judgment in subsequent action making attack thereon.

3. **Judgment** ⊂⊃**333**—**Answer to motion for correction of judgment entry held to raise issue as to fraud in its rendition.**

Answer to motion to correct judgment entry, alleging that judgment was procured by fraud, raised the issue of fraud, though movant did not deny allegations of fraud, since the motion to correct the minute entry of the judgment was in effect an assertion that the judgment was free from fraud, making denial of allegations as to fraud unnecessary.

Error to Court of Civil Appeals of Seventh Supreme Judicial District.

Suit by Olga V. Knight, as guardian of the estate of Mrs. C. E. Rogers, a lunatic, against W. T. Waggoner and another. Judgment for defendants was reversed, and the cause remanded by the Court of Civil Appeals (214 S. W. 690), and defendants bring error. Judgment of Court of Civil Appeals reversed, and judgment of trial court affirmed.

Miller & Miller, of Fort Worth, for plaintiffs in error.

M. M. Hankins and W. T. Perkins, both of Quanah, for defendant in error.

TAYLOR, P. J.   In the early part of the year 1906, Mrs. C. E. Rogers, divorced wife of J. J. Rogers, sold to Joe Terry the land here in controversy. Terry conveyed to W. T. Waggoner, who had furnished the money for the original purchase. L. H. Mathis, attorney for Mrs. Rogers, negotiated the sale to Terry, and out of the proceeds thereof was paid by her a commission of $150. All of the purchase money was paid to Mrs. Rogers except the balance due the state, and the amount of delinquent taxes.

In the fall of 1906, Mrs. Rogers not having given possession, and rumors having gained currency to the effect that she was insane, suit was instituted by Waggoner in trespass to try title to recover the land. The cause was numbered 3067 on the docket of the court. On January 29, 1907, the case came on for trial. No appearance was made for Mrs. Rogers. Counsel for Waggoner suggested to the court that he had been advised there was some question as to her sanity. The court thereupon appointed L. H. Mathis to represent her.

Mathis answered as guardian ad litem, setting up in substance that while Mrs. Rogers was abnormal in some respects, she was, at the time of the sale of the land, sane; that she had received its full value in the trade, and it was to her interest that the trade should stand. Waggoner replied setting up the terms of the trade, and further that the money received by Mrs. Rogers, except the

amount of the commission paid Mathis and a small amount expended by her for necessaries, was still on deposit in the National Bank of Wichita Falls to her credit. The prayer was for recovery of the land, or, in the alternative, for the recovery of the money paid Mrs. Rogers, and for protecting liens.

The court found that the trade was made by Terry in good faith, was just and fair, and free from fraud; that Mrs. Rogers was sane at the time she sold the land; and that she received full and fair value therefor. Judgment was rendered on the findings that Waggoner recover the land. Soon thereafter Mrs. Rogers gave possession. Thus the matter stood until 1909.

In the early part of that year, J. J. Rogers and Mrs. Olga V. Knight, his daughter—also the daughter of Mrs. Rogers—filed a lunacy charge against her. Upon hearing she was adjudged a lunatic, and, following the judgment, was confined in the State Asylum. Mrs. Knight was appointed guardian of the estate, and as such received from her mother the balance of the proceeds of the sale of the land.

In February, 1911, Mrs. Knight as guardian filed this suit in the ordinary form of trespass to try title to recover the land. The cause was numbered 4030 on the docket. By amended petition upon which the case was tried, an attack was made upon the judgment in Waggoner v. Rogers in cause No. 3067. The allegations made the basis of the attack are to the effect that Mrs. Rogers was insane at the time of the sale of the land, and has been insane continuously since; that Waggoner and Terry planned together to get the land from Mrs. Rogers for less than its true value, and to that end, knowing that she was insane, procured the making of the conveyance from her to Terry; that Waggoner, by filing suit numbered 3607 and prosecuting it to judgment, endeavored to cover up the fraud practiced to get the land; that L. H. Mathis, the guardian ad litem for Mrs. Rogers, was disqualified as such by reason of his interest in the suit. Waggoner, in reply, pleaded, among other defenses, that of res adjudicata.

The following facts constitute the basis of the plea: After the filing of the suit by Mrs. Knight as guardian, Waggoner ascertained that a clerical error had been made in entering the judgment on the minutes in Waggoner v. Rogers, cause No. 3607, in that the land, instead of being described correctly as section No. 2, was described incorrectly as section 92. He thereupon filed a motion in cause No. 3607 asking a correction of the minute entry to the end that the minutes would properly describe the land and truly reflect the judgment actually rendered. Notices were issued and served upon Mrs. Rogers, Mathis, and Mrs. Knight as guardian of

Mrs. Rogers. Mrs. Knight appeared by counsel, one of whom, M. M. Hankins, was appointed by the court to represent Mrs. Rogers as guardian ad litem. On July 18 and 19 answers to the motion were filed by the guardian and guardian ad litem, respectively, in which they pleaded limitation in bar of correcting the entry, and a general denial. They pleaded also specially the same facts in resisting the motion to correct the judgment entry as were pleaded by Mrs. Knight in this cause (No. 4043) as a basis for setting the judgment aside. The prayer following the response to the motion was, as it is in this case, that the deed and judgment be canceled and set aside. Judgment was rendered in the proceeding in which the motion was made, making the correction as prayed for. No express mention was made in the judgment of the issue of fraud raised by the special answers of the guardian and guardian ad litem. The Court of Civil Appeals reversed the judgment, but on appeal to the Supreme Court it was affirmed. 108 Tex. 328, 193 S. W. 136.

The facts set out in the foregoing statement relating to the motion to correct constitute the basis of the plea of res adjudicata set up in this cause.

Upon the trial the court instructed the jury peremptorily to find for Waggoner. The Court of Civil Appeals by a majority opinion reversed the cause and ordered it remanded for another trial. 214 S. W. 690.

It is urged in the application for the writ that the judgment of the Court of Civil Appeals should be reversed and that of the trial court affirmed, on two grounds: First, that no testimony was offered tending to raise the issue of fraud in the rendition of the judgment in cause No. 3607; second, that plaintiff in error's plea of res adjudicata was good. If either contention is correct the trial court judgment should be affirmed.

Judge Hall in the minority opinion states as follows the fundamental question to be decided:

"Under the Texas practice, when a motion is made by plaintiff in a judgment to correct the judgment entry, and all parties have been duly served with notice of the motion, is it permissible for the defendant in the judgment to raise the issue of fraud in its rendition and ask that it be annulled?"

If such proceeding was permissible in connection with the consideration of the motion to correct, and the judgment rendered in the proceeding disposed of the issue of fraud raised by the special answers, plaintiff in error's plea of res adjudicata was good.

It is the view of the majority of the Court of Civil Appeals that the court's judgment upon the motion had no other effect than to merely correct the clerical error pointed out and make the judgment in cause No. 3607 speak the truth. In support of this view

Coleman v. Zapp. 105 Tex. 491, 151 S. W. 1040, is cited, and the following excerpt is quoted therefrom:

"A proceeding of such character, whose only purpose is to have the judgment entry speak truly the judgment as rendered, neither asserts nor seeks the enforcement of any new right; it presents no issue between the parties except in respect to the accuracy of the record and otherwise involves the adjudication of nothing between them. It is powerless to reopen the controversy as closed and sealed by the judgment and makes no such attempt. The inquiry under it is not what judgment might or ought to have been rendered, but only what judgment was rendered; and such is the sole issue to be determined. If an amended or corrected entry be ordered, the status of the parties and their relative rights, as decreed and fixed by the judgment, remains untouched and unaltered, in no sense adjudicated anew, but only judicially evidenced as originally determined."

The foregoing excerpt, as will be seen by an examination of the opinion of which it is a part, follows immediately a quotation to the effect that frequent decisions of the Supreme Court have settled the right to have a judgment amended after the expiration of the term at which it was obtained, when through mistake or clerical error the record fails to speak truly the judgment actually rendered. The language of the excerpt is carefully qualified, however, so as to apply to proceedings "whose only purpose is to have the judgment entry speak truly." It is apparent that it does not apply to such a proceeding after its scope has been enlarged with a view to determining other issues. It is not the effect of the excerpt, nor is it held in the opinion from which it was taken, that issues other than that of correcting the entry may not be set up and determined in a proceeding of that character, where the parties at interest are all before the court. As pointed out by Judge Hall, the court expressly approves, in the opinion in the Zapp Case, the joinder in one proceeding of the scire facias and attachment proceedings considered in connection with the motion. It has been recognized that such practice is permissible where the several causes arise out of the same transaction. Hammond v. Atlee, 15 Tex. Civ. App. 267, 39 S. W. 600; Smart v. Panther, 42 Tex. Civ. App. 262, 95 S. W. 679; Clevenger v. Mayfield (Civ. App.) 86 S. W. 1062. A contrary holding in this case would be inconsistent with the settled policy of the Texas practice to avoid a multiplicity of suits.

[1, 2] It was the duty of the court to hear in the proceeding on the motion the issues raised by the pleadings. All of the parties at interest were before the court. A guardian ad litem was appointed to represent Mrs. Rogers, and through his answer on her behalf the issue of fraud was raised. The pleading

raising the issue was not withdrawn, nor was any objection urged to its consideration.

It is urged that regardless of whether the issue of fraud was raised, the judgment did not dispose of it; and in this connection attention is directed to the fact that the judgment on the motion is silent as to the issue of fraud; also, that no evidence was offered upon any issue other than that of limitation. The Supreme Court held in Hermann v. Allen, 103 Tex. 382, 182 S. W. 115, that a judgment is logically to be taken as disposing of all the issues pending for decision under the pleadings, unless the court excludes some of them from the effect of the adjudication.

In that case the suit was by Allen to recover damages for the wrongful suing out and service upon him of a writ of injunction in a former suit. The former suit was by Hermann and another against Allen and another, restraining Allen from removing his house situated on Hermann's land. In the suit filed by Hermann, Allen pleaded in reconvention his right to the house, and that he should recover damages suffered by reason of the service on him of the writ wrongfully sued out by Hermann. In that suit the pleadings put in issue (1) the right of Allen to move the house, and (2) the right of Allen to recover damages by reason of Hermann's interference with that right. The judgment determined the first issue in Allen's favor, but made no mention of the second. In the suit by Allen seeking to recover damages for the service upon him of the injunction writ, Hermann pleaded res adjudicata based on the judgment in the suit by Hermann and another.

Judge Williams, in holding the res adjudicata plea good, states that while Allen was not bound to plead in reconvention his damages in the former suit, and was not bound in the event he did so plead to prosecute his plea to final judgment, nevertheless he could not go to trial and submit his cause for decision upon pleadings raising such an issue, and afterwards be heard to say it was not involved in the final judgment, merely' because he introduced no evidence to sustain it and no mention was made of it.

In the later case of Trammell v. Rosen, 106 Tex. 132, 156 S. W. 1161, plaintiff sued to recover on certain purchase-money notes and to foreclose the lien. Defendant set up his homestead rights in one of the lots covered by the lien and sought to recover damages for the taking of the homestead by sequestration. The judgment was for recovery on the notes and for foreclosure of the lien, but did not expressly dispose of either the homestead or damage issue. It was held that both issues were disposed of by the plaintiff's judgment for debt and foreclosure.

The majority opinion holds that the Supreme Court cases discussed are not pertinent in determining the question presented, for

the reason that final judgment had already been rendered in cause No. 3607 at the time the motion to correct was presented, and that the only jurisdiction then remaining in the court as to that cause was its jurisdiction to correct the judgment as entered. The reason assigned is without force, if it was permissible for defendants in error through their allegations of fraud to invoke the jurisdiction of the court as upon an independent action. The majority recognize in the following language that it was permissible for defendants in error to raise the issue of fraud in the proceeding in the motion:

"We do not mean to say that, if the appellees had answered the issues tendered in appellant's answer to the motion, and the court had actually heard and decided the issues thus made and rendered judgment thereon, we would not consider the matter as being finally disposed of. In such case, under our liberal system of practice, the proceeding and judgment thereon might properly be regarded as a proceeding in an independent action, though it was filed in and took the number and style of the original suit."

If issue was joined on the plea of fraud, the effect of the conclusion reached by the majority, in view of its holding quoted above, is that the plea of res adjudicata should not have been sustained on the fraud plea because issue was not joined, rather than because of a lack of jurisdiction in the court.

[3] The issue of fraud in procuring judgment was raised by defendants in error by the allegations of their special answer. It was not necessary, as pointed out in the minority opinion, that plaintiff in error deny the allegations in order to join the issue. Inasmuch as the motion to correct the minute entry of the judgment was in effect an assertion that the judgment was free from fraud, no denial was necessary. Issue was therefore joined on the charge of fraud. The purpose thereafter of the proceeding on the motion was no longer merely to correct the judgment entry, but was to determine the issues raised as upon an independent action.

The pleadings put in issue (1) plaintiff in error's right to correct the judgment, and (2) the validity of the judgment. Neither issue was excluded from the scope of the court's action. The judgment determined the first in plaintiff in error's favor, but made no express disposition of the second. It follows, we think, from the holdings of the Supreme Court in the Trammell and Hermann Cases, that both issues were disposed of by the judgment. Plaintiff in error's plea of res adjudicata is therefore good.

This conclusion was reached in the minority opinion of the Court of Civil Appeals. In concurring therein no attempt has been made to add to Judge Hall's clear and logical discussion of the questions presented. What has been said is but little more than a free summary of the salient points of the majority and minority opinions of the Court of Civil Appeals, made with a view to presenting as a connected whole, the statement of the case, and the majority and minority holdings discussed, together with our concurrence in the latter.

We recommend that the judgment of the Court of Civil Appeals be reversed and that of the trial court affirmed.

PHILLIPS, C. J. The judgment recommended in the report of the Commission of Appeals is adopted, and will be entered as the judgment of the Supreme Court.

HAYNES v. WESTERN UNION TELE-GRAPH CO. (No. 227-3401.)

(Commission of Appeals of Texas, Section A. June 1, 1921.)

1. Pledges ⟨⇒⟩56(1)—Collateral to be sold at public auction after advertisement and notice to pledgor in absence of agreement to contrary.

The pledgee's right to sell collateral held by him to secure his debt, and the manner in which such right shall be exercised, are proper matters of contract, though, in the absence of an agreement, the law confers upon the pledgee the right to sell at public auction after due advertisement and after reasonable notice to the pledgor of the time and place of sale.

2. Evidence ⟨⇒⟩69—Pledgee presumed to follow law as to manner of sale in absence of evidence.

In the absence of evidence as to the terms of the contract of pledge or the procedure by which the pledgee's lien was foreclosed, it will be presumed that the pledgee in selling collateral followed and did not violate the law as to the manner of sale.

3. Appeal and error ⟨⇒⟩1094(1)—Court of Civil Appeals has exclusive jurisdiction over questions of fact.

The Supreme Court on writ of error to review judgment of Court of Civil Appeals will not consider questions of fact, the Court of Civil Appeals having exclusive jurisdiction.

Error to Court of Civil Appeals of First Supreme Judicial District.

Suit by R. B. Haynes against the Western Union Telegraph Company. Judgment for plaintiff was reversed and judgment rendered for defendant by the Court of Civil Appeals (212 S. W. 260), and plaintiff brings error. Reversed and cause remanded, with instructions.

C. G. Krueger, of Bellville, and Walters, Storey, Blanchard & Battaile, of Houston, for plaintiff in error.

Hume & Hume, of Houston, for defendant in error.

GALLAGHER, J. R. B. Haynes, plaintiff in error, was indebted to the City National Bank of San Antonio in the sum of $3,000 evidenced by note and secured by the deposit as collateral of certain shares of the capital stock of the Sealey Mattress Company, of the alleged value of $6,000.

Some time in October, 1908, the San Antonio Bank agreed with Haynes and the Sealey National Bank of Sealy to hold the note until November 1, 1908.

C. T. Sanders, cashier of the Sealy Bank, subsequently, for a valuable consideration, agreed with Haynes that he would procure or furnish the money to take up the loan, and notified the San Antonio Bank of this arrangement and requested the San Antonio Bank to notify him before offering said collateral for sale.

The San Antonio Bank, on November 3, 1908, delivered to the Western Union Telegraph Company, defendant in error, for transmission and delivery, the following message:

"San Antonio, Texas, Nov. 3, 1908.
"To C. T. Sanders, Cashier Sealey National Bank, Sealy, Texas:
"Unless Haynes loan is retired previously, will sell collateral ten o'clock Wednesday, November 4th.
　　　　"[Signed]　City National Bank."

The telegraph company transmitted the message, but did not deliver it to Sanders until 11:20 a. m. on November 4th.

The San Antonio Bank sold the collateral and applied the proceeds to liquidate the debt which amounted at that time to $3,074.

Sanders testified that had said telegram been delivered to him in time he would have wired the money to the San Antonio Bank.

Haynes testified that he was in Kansas City at the time and relied solely on his agreement with Sanders.

The record does not disclose the terms of the contract of pledge under which the stock was deposited, nor the details of the foreclosure sale. Neither Sanders nor Haynes made any effort to set the sale aside, or to redeem the collateral from the purchaser.

The telegraph company pleaded general demurrer and general denial. The trial was before the court. The company offered no witnesses and introduced no evidence except what was claimed to be the original telegram which it undertook to transmit and deliver to Sanders.

Judgment was rendered in favor of Haynes for $2,926, and the company appealed.

The Court of Civil Appeals reversed and rendered the judgment in favor of the company on the theory that it devolved on plaintiff in error, before he could recover the value of his collateral in excess of the debt secured, to show affirmatively that the San Antonio Bank made a valid sale of the collateral at public auction after the due advertisement and reasonable notice to him of the time and place of sale, and that no such showing was made. 212 S. W. 260.

[1] The right of a pledgee to sell collateral held by him to secure his debt, and the manner in which such right shall be exercised, are proper matters of contract. Jones on Collateral Securities, p. 862, § 730, from which we quote as follows:

"It is, of course, competent for the parties to agree by express terms that upon the pledgor's default, or upon his failure to keep the security good, the pledgee may sell at public or private sale at his option without giving notice of his intention or the time or place of sale, or upon giving a specified notice of such time and place."

In the absence of an agreement, the law confers upon the pledgee the right to sell at public auction after due advertisement and after reasonable notice to the pledgor of the time and place of sale. Luckett v. Townsend, 3 Tex. 119, 49 Am. Dec. 723.

[2] The evidence in this case fails to disclose the terms of the contract of pledge, or the procedure by which the pledgee's lien was foreclosed. The presumption is that the bank in this matter followed the law and not that it violated it.

In the case of Williams v. Talbot, 27 Tex. 159, 168, 169, the defendant's title depended upon the validity of a contract of sale, or bond for title executed by the original grantee of the land. The law prohibited such original grantee from selling the land prior to receiving final title. The grant of final title and the contract of sale under which defendants claimed, both bore the same date, and there was no evidence whether the contract of sale was executed before or after the grant of final title. The court in that case on this point said:

"The final title for the league of land in dispute, and the contract between the grantee, Purdy, and Robertson, both bear date on the 30th of December, 1834; and in the absence of all testimony on the subject, it must be presumed that the contract was not executed until after the consummation of the grant. It is always to be inferred, in the absence of testimony to the contrary, that parties have acted within the scope of their legitimate authority. It will never be presumed that they have violated the law when the reverse is equally consistent with the facts disclosed to the court."

The rule thus declared by the Supreme Court is applicable to this case. There being no presumption that the bank, in effecting a foreclosure of its lien by sale of the collateral, acted contrary to law or exceeded the scope of its legitimate authority, and there being no evidence to that effect, there is nothing to show that the sale was not fully binding on plaintiff in error. It follows, therefore, that the Court of Civil Appeals erred in reversing and rendering the case.

[3] Defendant in error was appellant in the Court of Civil Appeals, and in its brief in said court assigned various alleged errors not considered by that court because of its holding above discussed. Some of these assignments involve questions of fact, over which the Court of Civil Appeals has exclusive jurisdiction.

We therefore recommend that the judgment of the Court of Civil Appeals be reversed and the cause remanded to that court for further consideration, and with instructions, in event it overrules all of appellant's other assignments of error, to affirm the judgment of the trial court.

PHILLIPS, C. J. The judgment recommended in the report of the Commission of Appeals is adopted and will be entered as the judgment of the Supreme Court.

We approve the holding of the Commission of Appeals on the question discussed in its opinion.

LAIDACKER v. PALMER et al.
(No. 219–3347.)

(Commission of Appeals of Texas, Section A. June 1, 1921.)

Judgment 💠⊃525—Recital as to rights of co-defendants as claimed in their answer held not adjudication between them.

A judgment awarding a 50-acre tract to defendants E. and J., as against O., another defendant, who had filed a cross-bill against them, and reciting that "as to said defendants" E. and J., J. was the owner of the west half and E. of the east half of the tract, "as will appear from their answer to said cross-bill," *held* not to vest any title in J. as against E., being a mere recital, as respects their rights against other, as to the partial contents of their joint answer to the cross-bill of O., and the only issue joined by their answer and the only matter concluded by the judgment being the right of O. to recover against E. and J.

Error to Court of Civil Appeals of Ninth Supreme Judicial District.

Trespass to try title by N. E. Laidacker against V. K. Palmer and another. Judgment for defendants was affirmed by the Court of Civil Appeals (210 S. W. 739), and plaintiff brings error. Affirmed.

W. D. Gordon, Crook, Lord, Lawhon & Ney, and Thos. J. Baten, all of Beaumont, for plaintiff in error.

Marshall & Harrison, of Liberty, for defendants in error.

SPENCER, J. Plaintiff sued defendants in trespass to try title to the 25-acre tract of land described in the petition. Defendant answered by general demurrer, general denial, plea of not guilty, and plea of 5 and 10 year statute of limitations. It was agreed that Emil Bourdreaux was the common source of title. In support of his chain of title, plaintiff offered in evidence a judgment of the district court of Liberty county, Tex., rendered the 27th day of February, 1903, in the case of W. L. Hill et al. v. Charles G. Bruce et al., being numbered 3409 on the dockets of that court. The portion of the judgment relied upon as vesting title in Jacob C. Baldwin reads:

"It is further ordered, adjudged, and decreed by the court that the defendant Charles G. Bruce take nothing by reason of his cross-bill against the defendant Emil Bourdreaux and Jacob C. Baldwin, and that said Emil Bourdreaux and Jacob C. Baldwin do have and recover of and from the said defendant Charles G. Bruce the following described tract of land, to wit: 50 acres of land, it being a part of the east one-half of said Jesse Devore league of land, and being the same tract marked on the map as Bourdreaux 25 acres and Baldwin 25 acres, and more particularly described by metes and bounds as follows: [Here follows a description of said 50-acre tract.]

"That as to said defendants Jacob C. Baldwin and Emil Bourdreaux, that the said Baldwin is the owner of the west one-half of said 50-acre tract and the said Bourdreaux is the owner of the east one-half thereof, as will appear from their answer to said cross-bill now on file in this cause."

The plaintiff also offered in evidence the following deeds: Deed from Jacob C. Baldwin to David Hannah, dated February 15, 1906; deed from David Hannah to J. G. Stoval and J. W. Pelt, dated March 3, 1906; deed from J. G. Stoval and wife and J. W. Pelt and wife to Charles G. Bruce, dated January 3, 1916.

Defendants offered the following deeds in evidence in support of their chain of title: Deed from Emil Bourdreaux to Jacob C. Baldwin, dated February 27, 1903; deed from Emil Bourdreaux and wife, Mary J. Bourdreaux to J. J. Reavis, dated November 16, 1912; deed from J. J. Reavis and wife, Euna Reavis to defendant, dated November 16, 1912.

The trial court permitted, without objection, testimony by Mary J. Bourdreaux to the effect that, at the time of the deed by Emil Bourdreaux to Jacob C. Baldwin, in which she did not join, she was using and occupying the land in question, as her homestead, and that she continued to claim, use, and occupy it until the date of sale to J. J. Reavis. Upon the conclusion of the evidence, the court, at the request of defendants, gave the following peremptory instructions:

"Gentlemen of the jury, the evidence shows that, at the date of the deed from E. Bourdreaux to J. C. Baldwin, to wit, February 27, 1903, the land described therein as being the same land in controversy was the homestead of E. Bourdreaux. You will therefore return a verdict for defendants."

Upon appeal, the Court of Civil Appeals affirmed the judgment. 210 S. W. 739.

The only issue in the case is, Does the judgment in cause No. 3409 vest title in this land to J. C. Baldwin? Plaintiff recognizes this as the only issue by stating in his brief, filed in the Court of Civil Appeals, that, under the evidence offered, if Jacob C. Baldwin acquired title to the 25-acre tract which was set apart to him by the court against Emil Bourdreaux, the plaintiff is entitled to recover in this suit; if he did not, the plaintiff is not entitled to recover.

The title to the entire tract of 50 acres, of which the 25 acres in controversy is a part, was in Emil Bourdreaux at the date of the judgment of February 27, 1903. In that judgment the court awarded the 50 acres of land to Emil Bourdreaux and Jacob C. Baldwin, as against Charles G. Bruce, the defendant in that suit. But we do not think that the judgment undertakes to divest the title out of Bordreaux and into Baldwin. The portion of the judgment relied upon as having that effect is nothing more than a mere recital as to the partial contents of their answer to the cross-bill of Bruce. The only issue joined by their answer, and the only matter concluded by the judgment, was the right of Bruce to recover as against Bourdreaux and Baldwin, but this was not an adjudication of any rights between Bourdreaux and Baldwin. As said in Finley v. Cathcart, 149 Ind. 478, 48 N. E. 586, 589 (63 Am. St. Rep. 292):

"It is affirmed in Jones v. Vert, 121 Ind. 140, that party, to successfully invoke the doctrine of former adjudication, must be one who, in the former action, tendered to the party against whom he invokes it an issue to which the latter could have demurred or pleaded; and, where two or more defendants make an issue with the plaintiff, a judgment determining that issue in favor of the defendant does not settle the question between codefendants."

The record does not reveal that there was any issue between Bourdreaux and Baldwin. If, by appropriate pleadings, one had assailed the title of the other, and thereby put in issue the question of title as between them, a different question would be presented. But, instead of this, it appears that they filed a joint answer to the cross-bill of Bruce, indicating that they were not adversaries in that suit. Therefore the recital of the judgment as to what their answer contained as to the ownership of the land cannot be held an adjudication of the title as between them. Railway v. Railway, 88 Tex. 509, 18 S. W. 956.

In view of the conclusion reached, we recommend that the judgment of the Court of Civil Appeals and of the trial court be affirmed.

PHILLIPS, C. J. The judgment recommended in the report of the Commission of Appeals is adopted, and will be entered as the judgment of the Supreme Court.

CITIZENS' NAT. BANK OF STAMFORD v. STEVENSON. (No. 224–3392.)

(Commission of Appeals of Texas, Section B. June 1, 1921.)

1. Banks and banking ⚖=233 — Federal statutes control on any point with reference to national banks, including organization and issuance of stock.

A national bank, being incorporated by the federal government, and subject to its laws in its organization and issuance of stock, is subject to the federal statutes, which are supreme and controlling; if the federal and state provisions on any point with reference to national banks conflict, the state rules must yield.

2. Banks and banking ⚖=242 — Facts held to constitute a payment of money for stock.

Where the president of plaintiff national bank, to assist defendant in the purchase of the bank's stock, arranged with another bank to make defendant a loan, to be evidenced by his note, indorsed by the president of plaintiff bank personally, and further secured by the bank stock to be issued to defendant, and the note was prepared and signed by defendant and indorsed by the president of plaintiff bank and accepted by the other bank, which passed the amount of the note to the credit of plaintiff bank subject to its check, and sent in a slip showing the same, and the stock was issued to defendant, who indorsed it in blank and forwarded it to the other bank to be deposited as collateral security for his note, the facts constituted a payment for the stock in money to plaintiff bank as completely and conclusively as would have an actual transfer of cash, and plaintiff bank can recover on the last of notes given it by defendant when it took up his note from the other bank.

3. Banks and banking ⚖=260(2) — One national bank may lend, taking a note secured by stock of another such bank.

It is not illegal for one national bank to loan money and take a note therefor secured by the stock of another national bank.

4. Evidence ⚖=20(2) — That banks daily make loans secured by stock of other banks is matter of common knowledge.

It is a matter of common knowledge that state and national banks are almost daily making loans secured by the capital stock of other banks.

Error to Court of Civil Appeals of Eighth Supreme Judicial District.

Suit by the Citizens' National Bank of Stamford against J. H. Stevenson. From judgment for defendant, plaintiff appealed to the Court of Civil Appeals, which affirmed (211 S. W. 644), and plaintiff brings error. Judgments of the trial court and Court of Civil Appeals reversed, and cause remanded to the trial court, with instructions to render judgment for plaintiff, on recommendation of the Commission of Appeals.

Andrews & Combes, of Stamford, for plaintiff in error.

Stinson, Chambers & Brooks, of Abilene, for defendant in error.

POWELL, J. In its petition for writ of error, the plaintiff in error states the nature and result of the suit with commendable clearness and brevity as follows:

"This suit was originally brought by plaintiff in error against defendant in error in the district court of Jones county, on the 8th day of August, 1917, for the principal, interest, and attorney fees of a certain promissory note, of date the 1st day of December, 1916, executed by the defendant and payable to the order of the plaintiff for the principal sum of $958.65, due June 30, 1917, bearing interest from maturity until paid at the rate of 10 per cent. per annum, and providing for 10 per cent. attorney fees, on which there was then due, exclusive of interest, the sum of $1.054.51, in which suit the plaintiff, in due form of law, filed its affidavit and bond in attachment, which was duly approved, and the attachment was duly issued in conformity with law on August 8, 1917, and was duly levied on August 9, 1917, on the north one-half of section 21 of the Deaf and Dumb Asylum lands situated in Jones county, Tex., patent No. 311, volume 3, save and except the east 200 acres of said one-half section which had been designated by the defendant as a homestead, a copy of which writ of attachment, with the officer's return thereon, was filed with the county clerk of Jones county for record, and was recorded in the attachment records of said county whereby the plaintiff acquired an attachment lien against said property to secure the amount due on the note sued on. By its first amended original petition plaintiff prayed for judgment for principal, interest, and attorney fees due on said note, and for costs of suit and for the foreclosure of its attachment lien against said property. The defendant below answered that the obligation sued on was given by the defendant to the plaintiff for the purchase of stock in said bank, and was an illegal contract, and contravened the Constitution and statutes of the state of Texas, and therefore void, and prayed that plaintiff take nothing by said suit. and that he go hence without day and recover his costs. The cause was tried before the court without the intervention of a jury, and resulted in a judgment that plaintiff take nothing by its suit, and that the note sued on be canceled and defendant recover his costs. In

⚖=For other cases see same topic and KEY-NUMBER in all Key-Numbered Digests and Indexes

due time plaintiff filed its motion for new trial, which was overruled, and the cause was brought to the Court of Civil Appeals at Forth Worth, and transferred by the Supreme Court to the Court of Civil Appeals at El Paso, where it was affirmed."

The majority opinion of the Court of Civil Appeals referred to will be found in 211 S. W. 644. Associate Justice Higgins filed a vigorous dissent in a very able and exhaustive opinion. 211 S. W. 646.

As we view it, the controlling question in this appeal is whether or not, when the stock was first issued by the bank, it had been paid for in money. If so, then the note was not void, and Stevenson was liable upon it, as well as the various renewals thereof given from time to time. As bearing upon the above issue, the findings of fact of the trial court, adopted by the Court of Civil Appeals, are:

"The dealings between the parties leading up to and culminating in the execution of the note sued on are substantially as follows: The Citizens' National Bank of Stamford, Tex., incorporated with a capital stock of $30,000, determined to increase its capital stock to $100,000, and thereupon solicited the defendant, by its cashier, to purchase of this issue. The defendant replied that he had no money with which to make a purchase. The defendant testifies that the cashier then replied that he would make him able to buy; that thereafter he executed his demand note for $600, payable to the plaintiff. This latter statement is denied by the cashier, he testifying that defendant executed a 30-day note, payable to the Western National Bank of Fort Worth, Tex. The trial court made the following finding of fact with reference to above and the after dealings of the parties:

" 'That defendant was informed that the money would be procured by him signing his note to the Western National Bank of Fort Worth, which he, on June 25, 1909, accordingly did. This note was for $600, representing the purchase price of five shares of stock of the value of $120 each; that the said note of the defendant was a demand note, and was placed by the plaintiff, or J. S. Morrow, acting for the plaintiff, with the said Fort Worth bank, and indorsed by the said J. S. Morrow, and the testimony authorizes the conclusion of fact that the money for the face value of the same was placed to the credit of plaintiff on the books of the Western National Bank; that several days thereafter the plaintiff notified the Comptroller of Currency that the necessary amount of capital stock had been subscribed and paid to the plaintiff, and thereupon the Comptroller of Currency issued his certificate to the effect, authorizing the said increase of capital stock as applied for by the plaintiff.

" 'That about the time of the execution of the said note by the defendant to the Western National Bank of Fort Worth, Tex., five shares of the stock of plaintiff, of the par value of $100 per share, was issued, but not delivered, to the defendant, but placed by the plaintiff with the Western National Bank of Fort Worth, as collateral security for the note of the defendant. That thereafter and in about 30 days, the defendant executed his note to the plaintiff to cover the amount of his note to the Western National Bank of Fort Worth, whereupon the note executed by the defendant to said Western National Bank was redeemed or paid and satisfied, and at the time of the execution of the note by defendant to plaintiff, in lieu of the Fort Worth bank note, the plaintiff then delivered said five shares of stock of plaintiff to the defendant. That defendant in this case from time to time renewed his note so given to the plaintiff, culminating in the final note sued on in this case for the sum of $958.65, the interest being added in as the note was renewed from time to time.' "

The record is strikingly free from controverted issues of fact. The facts are all undisputed, except with reference to the note executed by Stevenson to the Western National Bank of Fort Worth. In the first place, Stevenson testified very positively that he never did sign a note to said bank, but only and always to the plaintiff in error. The trial court found against this contention. Again, there was some dispute in the evidence as to whether or not the Fort Worth Bank note was payable on demand, or in 30 or 60 days. The lower court found that it was a demand note, but not presented for payment until 30 days after its execution. The case was very fully developed.

The federal statutes governing the increase of capital stock and the issuance thereof by national banks provide:

"Any association formed under this title may, by its articles of association, provide for an increase of its capital from time to time, as may be deemed expedient, subject to the limitations of this title. But the maximum of such increase to be provided in the articles of association shall be determined by the Comptroller of the Currency; and no increase of capital shall be valid until the whole amount of such increase is paid in, and notice thereof has been transmitted to the Comptroller of the Currency, and his certificate obtained specifying the amount of such increase of capital stock, with his approval thereof, and that it has been duly paid in as part of the capital of such association." U. S. Comp. St. § 9679.

Article 1146 of Vernon's Sayles' Revised Civil Statutes of Texas, carrying out provisions of the Constitution of Texas, is as follows:

"No corporation, domestic or foreign, doing business in the state, shall issue any stock whatever, except for money paid, labor done, which is reasonably worth at least the sum at which it was taken by the corporation, or property actually received, reasonably worth at least the sum at which it was taken by the company. Any corporation which violates the provisions of this article shall, on proof thereof in any court of competent jurisdiction, forfeit its charter, permit or license, as the case may be, and all rights and franchises which it holds under, from or by virtue of the laws of this state."

[1] The defendant in error invoked the Texas law in an effort to avoid his note. The plaintiff in error is a national bank, incorporated by the federal government as one of its agencies, and subject to its laws. In its organization and issuance of stock it is subject to the federal statutes, which are supreme and controlling. It is well settled that, if the federal and state provisions upon any point with reference to national banks conflict, the state rules must yield. See Davis v. Elmira Savings Bank, 161 U. S. 275, 16 Sup. Ct. 502, 40 L. Ed. 700; Easton v. State of Iowa, 188 U. S. 219, 23 Sup. Ct. 288, 47 L. Ed. 452; F. & M. National Bank v. Dearing, 91 U. S. 29, 23 L. Ed. 196. The latter case is cited with approval by the Supreme Court of Texas in the case of Boerner v. Traders' National Bank, 90 Tex. 443, 39 S. W. 285.

In the case at bar, if the stock was paid for at all, it was paid in money. That being true, we are not called upon to consider possible conflicts between state and federal law. A payment in cash would comply with either law.

[2] Do the facts in this case constitute a payment of money for the stock? On this point the majority of the Court of Civil Appeals held:

"There is no pretense in this case that there was any money paid into the plaintiff's bank by the Fort Worth bank. It is only claimed that a credit was given upon the books of the Fort Worth bank, and then the amount placed to the credit of the capital stock upon the books of plaintiff. Credit of this nature is not equivalent to cash within the meaning of the Constitution and statutes."

No authority is cited by that court to sustain said ruling. We find none. We do not think it sound or correct. It is contrary to our daily experiences in the commercial world, and especially transactions between banks. A large majority of transfers of money between banks are made on paper. Deposits are made, subject to check by those in whose favor they are made. The money is paid out on such checks, and frequently transferred from one bank to another in such manner. In fact, we are sure that, as a rule, the actual cash is not transferred from one bank to another in payment of a credit or collection due it in one case out of ten.

In this case, J. S. Morrow, president of the Stamford Bank, assisted Stevenson in the purchase of five shares of stock in his bank. In order to enable him to buy the same, he arranged with the bank at Fort Worth to make Stevenson a loan, which was to be evidenced by the latter's note, indorsed by Morrow personally, and further secured by the bank stock to be issued to Stevenson. The note was prepared accordingly. It was signed by Stevenson and indorsed by Morrow. It was accepted by the Fort Worth bank, and the latter placed the amount of the note to the credit of the Stamford bank, subject to its check, and sent in a slip showing the same. The Comptroller of the Currency of the United States was advised that the money had been paid in, and the increase of the capital stock was authorized by him. Then the stock was issued to Stevenson. He indorsed it in blank. It was then forwarded to the Fort Worth bank, to be deposited with it as collateral security for the Stevenson note. As we view it, these facts constitute a payment of the money to the Stamford bank, just as completely and conclusively as would an actual transfer of the cash to the vaults of the latter. We are sustained in this view by several of the authorities, to a few of which we refer.

Morse on Banks and Banking, § 451, says:

"A credit given for the amount of a check by the bank upon which it is drawn is equivalent to and will be treated as a payment of a check. It is the same as if the money had been paid over the counter on the check and then immediately paid back again to the account."

The above text is quoted with approval by the Supreme Court of Nebraska in the case of Bartley v. State, 53 Neb. 810, 73 N. W. 744, as follows:

"It was conceded on the argument by counsel for the accused that if the latter had drawn from the depository bank the actual cash and then redeemed the warrant therewith, proof thereof would be sufficient to sustain the charge of embezzlement of money. As we view it, the legal effect of the transaction, as it actually occurred, is not materially different. The defendant, as state treasurer, drew his check upon the Omaha National Bank for $201,884.05, payable to the order of the president thereof, and delivered the same to the payee, which, in connection with the acceptance of the check by the bank, the entry of the transaction upon the books thereof, and the surrender of the warrant to the defendant, constituted a segregation or separation of the amount of dollars expressed in the check from the general mass of money in the bank as the portion belonging to the state, and passed the title to the latter. In contemplation of the parties, and in the eye of the law, the segregation was as full and complete as though Mr. Millard, the president of the bank, upon the delivery of the check to him had stepped into the vault, counted out $201,884.05, placed it upon the counter, charged the state with that amount on the bank books, credited the Chemical National Bank with a like sum, delivered the warrant to the defendant, and then returned the money to the vault from whence it came; or as if the check had been made payable to the defendant's own order, by himself presented to the paying teller at the bank for payment, who selected from the mass of money in the bank the sum represented by the check, placed the same in a pile on the counter, and then, by direction of the defendant, applied the same in payment of the warrant. To constitute embezzlement it was not necessary that the defendant himself should have acquired the physical or manual possession of the money. He, by his check, authorized and directed the bank to pay the money called for therein to 'J. H. Millard, Pt.' The bank was thereby empowered to select and transfer the money to the payee, which, in contemplation of law, it did, although there was no actual handling of a dollar in the entire transaction. In the language of Morse, Banks and Banking, § 451, 'A credit given for the amount of a check by the bank upon which it is drawn is equivalent to, and will be treated as, a payment of the check. It is the same as if the money had been paid over the counter on the check, and then immediately paid back again to the account or for the use for which the credit is given.' See Oddie v. National City Bank of New York, 45 N. Y. 735."

Again, the same text is cited with approval by the Supreme Court of Oregon, in case of State v. Ross, 55 Or. 450, 104 Pac. 596, 106 Pac. 1022, 42 L. R. A. (N. S.) 601, 613. That court, continuing, says:

"3. When the Trust Company placed to the credit of 'Steel, Treasurer, Education,' the amount of a check, it thereby acknowledged that it had received the amount of the check in money, and is at least prima facie sufficient to establish the receipt of the money by the Trust Company."

Judge Williams, of our own Supreme Court, in case of Anderson v. Walker, County Judge, 93 Tex. 119, 53 S. W. 821, expresses the same view as follows:

"It is an undisputed fact that a credit to the county was entered upon the bank books, and this, prima facie, represented so much money on deposit belonging to the county." See Newmark on Bank Deposits, § 181.

In our view, therefore, this stock was actually paid for in money. The issuance thereof was lawful, and the first note executed by Stevenson was valid and binding, as were the several renewals thereof, including the note in suit, executed from time to time. Having held this stock was paid for, it is not necessary to pass upon the question so ably discussed by Judge Higgins in his dissent, and in which he holds that the certificate of the Comptroller of the Currency that the money had been paid in was conclusive, and not subject to collateral attack.

[3, 4] It is suggested that the note to the Western National Bank was void, because it is illegal for one national bank to loan money and take a note therefor, secured by the stock of another national bank. We know of no such law of either state or nation. We have been cited to no such law. It is within the common knowledge of us all that state and national banks are almost daily making loans secured by capital stock of other banks. It has been distinctly held that one national bank can make a loan secured by the stock of another national bank. The United States

Supreme Court, in the case of National Bank v. Case, 99 U. S. 628, 25 L. Ed. 448, speaks as follows:

"There is nothing in the argument on behalf of the appellant that the bank was not authorized to make a loan with the stock of another bank pledged as collateral security. That is an ordinary mode of loaning, and there is nothing in the letter or spirit of the National Banking Act that prohibits it. But if there were, the lender could not set up its own violation of law to escape the responsibility resulting from its illegal action."

The transaction between Morrow and Stevenson, in our view, was entirely legitimate. If Morrow was good enough to help Stevenson to get this stock with his bank, even to the extent of indorsing his note personally, that fact should not afford Stevenson any cause for complaint. If Morrow was careless of his bank's interest in later making to Stevenson a loan without security, to pay his debt to the Fort Worth bank, the only room for complaint was on the part of the other stockholders of the bank. Stevenson should not be heard now to try to avoid a valid obligation, even though the bank stock purchased did not prove profitable. Investments are frequently made which turn out likewise.

No fraud on the part of plaintiff in error or its officers was alleged in the pleadings filed by Stevenson. None was shown. There is no evidence showing any promise, or agreement, on the part of the Stamford bank or its officers, to take care of Stevenson's note to the Fort Worth bank at its maturity. The whole case, as heretofore stated, seems to us to present a state of facts which doubtless happens time and time again, each day in Texas, and which we deem lawful.

As we view the case, the only proper judgment in the lower court would have been one in favor of plaintiff in error for the full amount sued for, with foreclosure of its attachment lien. We would recommend the rendition of such a judgment here except for the fact that we think, as a practical proposition, the trial court and its clerk can more conveniently assess the damages and work out other details. In fact, the record here does not disclose an entirely accurate or detailed description of the 200-acre homestead tract to be excluded from the attachment lien foreclosure. Therefore, we recommend that the judgments of the district court and the Court of Civil Appeals be reversed, and the cause remanded to the former, with instructions to render judgment in favor of plaintiff in error for the full amount due upon the note sued upon, as per its terms, including principal, interest, and attorney's fees, for costs of court and a foreclosure of its attachment lien, all as prayed for in its first amended original petition.

PHILLIPS, C. J. The judgment recommended in the report of the Commission of Appeals is adopted, and will be entered as the judgment of the Supreme Court.

We approve the holding of the Commission of Appeals on the question discussed in its opinion.

MASSILLON ENGINE & THRESHER CO. v. BARROW et al. (No. 210–3305.)

(Commission of Appeals of Texas, Section A. June 1, 1921.)

1. Homestead ⬅=89—Both widow and remainderman cannot have homestead in same land.

A son, living with his widowed mother upon land which she claimed as her homestead, was precluded from asserting a homestead interest in the same land which she claimed as a homestead, for one claiming merely an interest in remainder is without any right to possession necessary to found a claim of homestead.

2. Homestead ⬅=84—Tenants in common held to have impressed tract with homestead character.

Where surviving widow and children, upon death of the husband and father, became tenants in common of a tract of community land of the mother and deceased, and one son lived upon the tract, and had inclosed and was using not more than 20 acres of it, and another son was living upon contiguous land which he had purchased and built a house on, and his inclosure extended onto the tract and within its compass, and upon such tract were the barn, some fruit trees, and a plot of ground not exceeding 10 acres which he was farming, the sons subjected the land to homestead purposes.

3. Homestead ⬅=84—Tenants in common may impress land with homestead.

Tenants in common may impress the tract owned in common with the character of a homestead, provided such use does not prejudice the rights of other cotenants.

4. Homestead ⬅=37—Homestead interest of tenants in common not confined to land actually inclosed by them.

The homestead interest of tenants in common is not confined to the land actually inclosed by them, but is coextensive with their undivided interest in the entire tract, and, so long as it is unpartitioned, it is not within their power to designate their homestead by metes and bounds.

5. Homestead ⬅=37—Inclosure of part of tract by tenants in common does not limit their homestead to inclosed part where remainder is wild land.

The law does not absolutely protect the entire tract of land, up to the amount of 200 acres, upon which the homestead may be located, regardless of the use to which a part of it may be devoted, but merely limits or restricts the homestead to that acreage, and the owner may, by a use inconsistent with the homestead purpose, abandon a part of that which

the law would otherwise protect; but, where the uninclosed land of a tract held by tenants in common was wild, uncultivated land not used for any purpose, such use was not inconsistent with homestead purposes, so that, as to tenants in common who had inclosed part of the tract, and were living thereon as their homestead, their homestead right extended to their undivided interest in the whole tract, for, in such case, until there is an inconsistent use, the law implies an intent to use, and therefore a constructive use, of the entire tract for homestead purposes.

Error to Court of Civil Appeals of Ninth Supreme Judicial District.

Suit by Clarence Barrow and others against the Massillon Engine & Thresher Company. Judgment for plaintiffs was affirmed by the Court of Civil Appeals (203 S. W. 933), and defendant brings error. Modified and affirmed.

H. E. Marshall, of Houston, and A. W. Marshall, of Anahuac, for plaintiff in error. Stevens & Stevens, of Houston, for defendants in error.

SPENCER, J. Clarence Barrow and wife. Rosa, Lee Barrow and wife, Josephine, and J. M. Barrow and wife, Jane, instituted this suit in the district court of Chambers county, Tex., naming the Massillon Engine & Thresher Company, a corporation, and F. R. Lafour, sheriff of Chambers county, Tex., as defendants, seeking to restrain the sale of the lands described in the petition—the corporation having procured the issuance of an order of sale upon a judgment which the corporation had secured in the district court of Chambers county, Tex., against Clarence. Lee and J. M. Barrow, and this order of sale having been placed in the hands of the sheriff. Lee and J. M. Barrow having died during the pendency of the suit, the proper heirs were made parties thereto.

The basis of the judgment against the three Barrows was this: On October 7, A. D. 1903, in order to better secure the corporation in the payment of an indebtedness which the Barrow brothers owed it, the three brothers, joined by their wives, executed and delivered a mortgage upon their undivided interest in the two tracts of land which are the subject of this controversy—one consisting of 540 acres; the other of 160 acres. Upon the indebtedness becoming due, and upon default in the payment thereof, that suit was instituted, but the wives were not made parties thereto. Judgment for the amount of the indebtedness, with foreclosure of the mortgage lien, was rendered; the judgment directing an order of sale upon the lands upon which such lien was foreclosed.

The present suit for injunction is predicated upon the alleged ground that the land in question constituted, at the time of the execution of the mortgage, the homestead of the plaintiffs, and that the mortgage was not executed for the purpose of paying or securing the payment of any lien for purchase money, taxes, or improvement upon such homestead.

The court issued a temporary restraining order, and, upon final hearing, perpetually enjoined the foreclosure, by order of sale, of the judgment lien against the land claimed as homesteads by the plaintiffs, and in this final order decreed that, in so far as the judgment in the foreclosure suit purported to fix a lien against the land described in the judgment, it be canceled and held for naught. Upon appeal, the Court of Civil Appeals affirmed the judgment. 208 S. W. 933.

J. S. Barrow died in 1892, leaving surviving him seven children—Clarence, Lee, and J. M. being of this number—and his wife, Eliza Jane Barrow, the mother of these children. It is admitted that the 540-acre tract, known as the Banda tract, was the separate property of J. S. Barrow, and the 160-acre tract, known as the Barrow tract, the community property of the marriage.

[1] Clarence and Lee Barrow and the heirs of J. M. Barrow, deceased, each claimed a homestead right to an undivided interest of 200 acres of the entire tract of land, although each was entitled to but an undivided interest of approximately 67 acres. The land was divided subsequent to the giving of the mortgage. Clarence Barrow lived in the house with his mother upon the 540-acre tract of land. His claim to a homestead interest is based upon his own evidence, as follows:

"I married at home, but do not remember how long I had been married at the time I signed this mortgage. I was living on the old place. We took an undivided interest in the land, and it had never been divided. I never had built a home or house on any part of the 700 acres before this mortgage was given, but I lived on the homestead. My mother was living in the old Barrow homestead, and had been living there since the death of my father. I was living there with my mother. She remained there and occupied it up until the time of her death. She used that as her homestead. I did not rent land from my mother, just worked with her. I think the Banley (Banda) is all prairie, and the Barrow is all prairie except a little bit in the woods. Nobody occupied that, outside of the little field John had, and what Lee had, and what my mother had, there in the old home place, all that land was out. We had about 40 acres under fence, and the rest of it was wild range land, and there was no attempt to utilize it. Outside of what we were farming and our pasture, the rest of it was outside."

He also testified that, before and after the execution of the mortgage, he and his brothers got their firewood and posts from the 16

acres of timbered land on the bayou. This tract was on the Banda survey, and was subsequently set aside in partition to Clarence Barrow. It is quite clear from the undisputed evidence that the alleged claim of Clarence Barrow to a homestead right is coextensive with and confined to the identical land used by his mother as her independent homestead. No act of his indicated an intention to devote any of the land, outside of that held and used by the mother, to homestead purposes. No contention is made that she abandoned her homestead, or waived her right thereto; but, on the other hand, it is admitted that she continued to exercise the right of homestead possessions given her under the Constitution until her death. This right was, we think, exclusive, and precluded Clarence Barrow and the other heirs absolutely from asserting a homestead interest in the same land which she claimed as a homestead, while her right of possession continued and was exercised. This identical question was before the Supreme Court of Kentucky in the case of Merrifield v. Merrifield, 82 Ky. 526. That court said:

"But both she [the widow] and D. B. Merrifield [the son] cannot have a homestead in the land. It was decided in the case of Maguire, Helm & Co. v. Burr, 4 Ky. Law Rep. 659, that joint owners of a tract of land, upon which they both live in separate buildings with their families, are each entitled to a homestead, although the land has not been divided. But this court has never gone so far as to determine that both the widow and remainderman can, at the same time, have a homestead in the same land, nor do we think the statute can be so applied and extended. The theory of the homestead exemption is that the debtor requires a prescribed amount in value of land to be set apart for the support of himself and dependent family, but to accomplish such a beneficent object he must have the right to occupy and use it; * * * but a party having merely an interest in remainder is without any right to the possession, and, in the meaning of the law, not in possession."

Defendant in error relies upon the decision of the majority in Ward v. Walker (Tex. Civ. App.) 159 S. W. 320, in which writ of error was denied, as decisive of the question that the child of a survivor owning an undivided interest in land devoted to homestead purposes by the survivor may, by living with the latter, acquire a homestead interest in the same land designated and used by the survivor as a homestead. In our opinion the decision of the majority upon that question was erroneous.

In that case the plaintiffs were seeking to enforce the specific performance of a contract concerning land. C. K. Walker and wife, defendants against whom specific performance was sought, interposed the defense that the land was their homestead, and that, as the wife did not join in the contract, the contract was void as to them. They occupied and claimed the same land as a homestead as did the father. The trial court refused to decree specific performance against them or the other tenants in common, named as defendants in the action. From this judgment the plaintiff appealed. The Court of Civil Appeals affirmed the judgment as to C. K. Walker and wife, upon the ground that the land was their homestead, but reversed and remanded, with instructions to the trial court to enter judgment against W. C. Walker, C. W. Walker, and L. M. Walker, decreeing specific performance by them as to their undivided interest in the land described in the contract. The latter applied for writ of error, but C. K. Walker and wife, being satisfied with the judgment, did not join in the application for the writ, and neither did the plaintiffs apply for a writ of error to correct the judgment of the Court of Civil Appeals as to C. K. Walker and wife.

We have examined the application for writ of error in that case, and find that there is no assignment in the application directly or indirectly calling in question the correctness of the majority's opinion upon the homestead question. Therefore, the refusal of the application for the writ cannot be considered an approval of the majority's holding upon that question.

[2] The 160-acre Barrow tract was the community property of Eliza Jane Barrow and J. S. Barrow, and, upon the death of J. S. Barrow, the children and the mother became tenants in common. At the date of the giving of the mortgage, Lee Barrow lived upon this tract, and had inclosed and was using not more than 20 acres of it. J. M. Barrow purchased from one Wallis less than an acre of land—out of a tract of land not the subject of this litigation, but contiguous to the land in controversy—upon which he had erected a house, and was living at the date of the transaction. The evidence reveals that the inclosure extended onto the Barrow tract, and that, within its compass, but upon the Barrow tract, were the barn, some fruit trees, and a plot of ground not exceeding 10 acres, which he was farming.

[3, 4] Under these facts, it cannot be doubted, we think, that it was the intention of Lee and J. M. Barrow to subject, and that they did subject, the land so used to homestead purposes. It is well settled that, as tenants in common, they had a right to impress the land with the homestead character, provided such use did not prejudice the rights of the other cotenants. Clements v.

Lacy, 51 Tex. 150. Their homestead interest was not confined to the land actually inclosed, but was coextensive with their undivided interest in the entire tract; and, so long as it was unpartitioned, it was not within their power to designate their homestead by metes and bounds. Jenkins v. Volz, 54 Tex. 636; Brown et al. v. McLennan et al., 60 Tex. 48.

[5] The homestead rights of Lee and J. M. Barrow to the extent of their undivided interest in the entire tract is not to be defeated, and their homestead right confined to the amount of land actually inclosed and used by them, merely because the entire tract was not used. The law does not absolutely protect the entire tract of land up to the amount of 200 acres, upon which the homestead may be located, regardless of the use to which a part of it may be devoted. It merely limits or restricts the homestead to that acreage, and the owner may, by a use inconsistent with the homestead purpose, abandon a part of that which the law would otherwise protect.

The uninclosed land of the Barrow tract was not put to a use inconsistent with homestead purposes. In fact, it was wild, uncultivated land, not used for any purpose. In a case of this character, until there is such inconsistent use, the law implies an intent to use, and therefore a constructive use of, the entire tract for homestead purposes, and prohibits the creation of liens thereon except for the purposes stated in the Constitution. McDougall et al. v. McGinniss et al., 21 Fla. 362; Morrissey v. Donohue, 32 Kan. 649, 5 Pac. 27.

It is our conclusion that the mortgage lien attempted to be created upon the undivided interest of Lee and J. M. Barrow in the Barrow tract is invalid; but that otherwise it is a valid and enforceable lien.

We recommend, therefore, that the judgment of the district court be modified, so as to permit the carrying out of the order of sale, under the terms of the judgment in the original suit, of the undivided interest of Clarence Barrow in the Barrow survey, and of Clarence Barrow and the other defendants in error of their undivided interest in the 540-acre tract of land; and, as so modified, that the judgment be affirmed.

PHILLIPS, C. J. The judgment recommended in the report of the Commission of Appeals is adopted, and will be entered as the judgment of the Supreme Court.

ROBERTS et al. v. ARMSTRONG.
(No. 225-3393.)

(Commission of Appeals of Texas, Section A.
June 1, 1921.)

1. Appeal and error ⟨⟩1213—Judgment on former appeal not conclusive where pleadings and facts differ.

Where the pleadings and facts on second trial were not identical with those on the first, the opinion and judgment of the Court of Civil Appeals on the former appeal did not so finally and fully adjudicate both the law and the facts as to justify the trial court on the second trial in striking out the answer of defendants, containing both general denial and other defensive pleas, and in rendering judgment for plaintiff without proof of any facts except the value of the rents sued for.

2. Vendor and purchaser ⟨⟩18(½)—Optionee did not acquire title by option contract.

By an option contract the optionee did not acquire any title to the land involved, but at most secured only the right to acquire an interest in the land by complying, at his election, with the stipulations on his part.

3. Vendor and purchaser ⟨⟩196—Owner entitled to rents and crops until title defeated by exercise of option.

The holder of an option contract covering land can occupy no better position than the holder of a mortgage duly recorded prior to the owner's contract of tenancy and prior to planting of the crop; in case of a mortgage the owner of the land remains such until his title is defeated at foreclosure sale, and in the case of an option he remains the owner until the holder of the option tenders full compliance with its terms and becomes entitled to receive a conveyance in accordance therewith, the owner in either case being entitled to the rents and crops until his title is actually defeated.

4. Crops ⟨⟩5—Crops pass under deed unless severed, but are personal property.

Though annual crops, the fruits of industry, so long as they are attached to the land, pass with the deed thereto unless actually or constructively severed, yet they are for general purposes classed as personal property.

5. Mortgages ⟨⟩372(4)—Owner cannot sever crops or rents by reservation on foreclosure sale.

When there is a foreclosure under power of sale in a deed of trust, the owner is not an actor in the transaction, and cannot sever the crops or rents by reserving them at the time of sale.

6. Evidence ⟨⟩13—Maturity of crops matter of common knowledge.

It is a matter of common knowledge that the cultivation of crops of corn and cotton in Wharton county at the time of tender by plaintiff optionee and demand by him was practically complete, and that such crops were either partly matured or rapidly approaching maturity.

7. Vendor and purchaser ⟨⟩196—Option contract gave optionor right to reserve crops and rents.

Option contract covering the sale of land, properly construed, *held* to have given the owner and optionor the right to reserve his growing crops and the rents arising out of them when the optionee elected to exercise his option.

Error to Court of Civil Appeals of First Supreme Judicial District.

Suit by R. A. Armstrong against G. C. Gifford, wherein B. C. Roberts and others, executors of defendant, were made parties defendant in his stead on his death. From judgment for plaintiff, defendants appealed to the Court of Civil Appeals, which affirmed (212 S. W. 227), and defendants bring error. Judgments of the trial court and Court of Civil Appeals reversed, and case remanded for further proceedings on recommendation of the Commission of Appeals.

Hall & Barclay and Kelley & Hawes, all of Wharton, and Williams & Neethe, of Galveston, for plaintiffs in error.

Gaines & Corbett, of Bay City, for defendant in error.

GALLAGHER, J. R. A. Armstrong, defendant in error, instituted this suit in the district court of Wharton county against G. C. Gifford, and alleged that said Gifford by a contract in writing dated February 21, 1913, in consideration of $1,000, gave him an option on 531 acres of land in said county at $60 per acre, and that said option was to be exercised, if at all, on or before August 1, 1913.

It was further alleged that said contract provided that the consideration for the purchase of said land under said option should be paid one-half cash and the remainder in one, two, three, and four years, and that said Armstrong was given the right to sell said land on or before August 1, 1913, on the same terms, and that said Gifford would make a deed to the purchaser, and that in such event said Armstrong should receive as his compensation the excess of the purchase price over $60 per acre.

It was further alleged that crops of corn, cotton, and other things were grown on the said land during the crop year of 1913, and that the reasonable rental or rental value of such crops when matured was $2,835.89, and that said Gifford received that amount as rentals on said land for said year.

It was further alleged that on July 31, 1913, Armstrong sold said land to G. A. Harrison, and that said Harrison then and there tendered compliance with the terms of said option and demanded a deed to said land, and that Gifford refused to accept said tender or make said deed.

⟨⟩For other cases see same topic and KEY-NUMBER in all Key-Numbered Digests and Indexes

It was further alleged that by such tender and demand Harrison became entitled to the land together with the rentals on said land for the year 1913, that such rentals were in excess of the purchase price of said land under the terms of said option contract, and that it was agreed between Armstrong and Harrison that such rentals should pass to Armstrong as his compensation in the premises.

It was further alleged that after such tender and refusal Gifford conveyed said lands to Harrison, and that it was also agreed by and between Gifford, Armstrong, and Harrison that Armstrong should have a right to sue for and recover such rents in his own name, provided he, or Harrison, or both were entitled on account of such tender and demand under the terms of such option contract to a deed which would have passed such rents or crops.

G. C. Gifford died before a trial was had, and his executors, B. C. Roberts and Mrs. Annie Gifford, plaintiffs in error herein, were made parties defendant in his stead.

Said executors answered by general and special exception, general denial, and by special pleas, alleging, among other things, that said option contract was entered into when only a small portion of said land, if any, had been planted, and before any of such crops were in existence, that nothing was said in the negotiations resulting in said contract about purchasing such crops or the rents therefrom, and that it was never contemplated by the parties that said option contract should cover either the crops or rentals on said land for said year.

They further alleged that said Gifford, without any idea that Armstrong intended under such option contract to claim the crops or rents for said year, proceeded to advance money to the tenants, and that Armstrong allowed him to make such advancements until a few days before the expiration of such option contract.

They especially denied that Harrison offered to comply with the terms of the option contract, and alleged the fact to be that Harrison was unwilling to purchase the land unless Gifford would agree that the rents should go with the land, which he had theretofore declined to do, on the ground that the option contract did not require him to do so.

They further denied that the tender and demand on July 31, 1913, as alleged by Armstrong was made in good faith, and alleged that Harrison never offered to execute the notes required by such option contract, and that Harrison never intended to execute and deliver to Gifford notes for the deferred payments bearing interest from the date of the deed so demanded, but that the tender of the cash consideration was made under an agreement between Armstrong and Harrison that they would divide any recovery which might be had by reason of the refusal of such tender and demand for a deed.

A trial was had before a jury, and under a peremptory instruction of the court a verdict was returned for the defendants, and judgment entered in accordance therewith.

Armstrong appealed, and on hearing of such appeal the judgment of the trial court was reversed, and the cause remanded. 196 S. W. 723.

The executors then filed an amended answer consisting of a general denial, repetition and elaboration of their former pleadings, and certain additional allegations raising issues not made in such former pleadings.

Armstrong excepted to such amended answer and to the several paragraphs thereof on the ground that the opinion and judgment of the Court of Civil Appeals in said cause was res adjudicata of all matters so set up by said amended answer of said executors, and said demurrers were sustained by the court, and the court ordered that no evidence be admitted upon the trial of said cause except as to the value of the crops and rents in controversy.

The judgment of the trial court further recited that the matters in controversy were submitted to the court, and that the court heard evidence only as to the value of the crops received by Gifford after deducting therefrom the amounts received by the tenants and the amounts advanced in raising and gathering the crops, and that it was agreed that rents so collected by Gifford for said year amounted to $2,635.89.

Judgment was rendered in favor of Armstrong against said executors for said sum, with interest from January 1, 1914, and costs of suit.

Said executors appealed, and on hearing of such appeal said judgment was affirmed. 212 S. W. 227.

Said executors applied for and obtained a writ of error, and the case is before us for hearing on said writ.

The Court of Civil Appeals on the first appeal in this case construed the contract sued on adversely to the contention of plaintiffs in error, and held that their testimony failed to establish a defense thereto, and ended the opinion with the statement that the court was not in possession of sufficient facts upon which to render judgment, and that the judgment of the trial court would therefore be reversed, and the cause remanded.

The judgment of the court was as follows:

"This cause came on to be heard on the transcript of the record, and the same being inspected, because it is the opinion of this court that there was error in the judgment, it is therefore considered, adjudged, and ordered that the judgment of the court below be reversed, and the cause remanded for further proceedings in accordance with the opinion of this court."

[1] Plaintiffs in error in their first assignment submit that the Court of Civil Appeals erred in holding that the opinion and judgment on the former appeal so finally and fully adjudicated both the law and the facts as to justify the trial court upon the second trial in striking out their answer containing both general denial and other defensive pleas and rendering judgment for defendant in error without proof of any facts except the value of the rents.

The statement of facts on this appeal shows that the court on the trial here appealed from announced that in his judgment all matters and things in controversy in this cause were fully settled by the opinion of the Court of Civil Appeals, that the judgment and mandate of said court were then presented and considered, a copy of the same being attached to such statement of facts and being made a part thereof, and that no further evidence was introduced or permitted than to show the value of the rents in controversy, and that it was agreed by the parties in open court that the value of such rents was $2,635.89, and that upon such admission and the said judgment and decision of said Court of Civil Appeals the court entered judgment for such rents with interest and costs.

In Magnolia Park Co. v. Tinsley, 96 Tex. 374, 73 S. W. 5, it appeared that the Court of Civil Appeals, on a former appeal of the case, had held that defendants had title to a part of the land in question, and that plaintiffs were entitled to recover a part, but, after reversing a judgment in favor of the defendants, remanded the cause for the sole reason that the jury had not found the number of acres the plaintiffs were entitled to receive. 59 S. W. 629. Of this judgment the Supreme Court said:

"Upon the former appeal the Court of Civil Appeals for the Third Supreme Judicial District did not render judgment declaring the rights of the parties, but said: 'The record is not in such condition as will authorize this court to render judgment.' That court decided a question of law which is involved in this appeal, but the decision does not bind the Court of Civil Appeals or this court on this appeal. Kempner v. Huddleston, 90 Tex. 184."

In the case of Kempner v. Huddleston, 90 Tex. 184, 37 S. W. 1066, so cited, the Supreme Court, in answer to a certified question from the Court of Civil Appeals inquiring whether the decision of that court on the first appeal of the case was conclusive of the question then decided, but again presented in the appeal then pending, replied:

"We answer that the former decision of the court in this case constitutes no bar to the further consideration of the same question upon a second appeal. Burns v. Ledbetter, 56 Tex. 282; Railway v. Faber, 77 Tex. 153; Bomar v. Parker, 68 Tex. 435.

"In Railway v. Faber, cited above, the court said: 'Upon a second or other subsequent appeal this court adheres to its former rulings unless clearly erroneous.'

"The question as to whether the court will reconsider, upon a second appeal, what it has formerly decided in the same case, must always be addressed to the discretion of the court and determined according to the particular circumstances of that case."

The court, in Frankland v. Cassaday, 62 Tex. 418, 419, 420, considered a case on its third appeal in which the record showed that the pleadings had undergone no change, and that the issues of law and fact were identical with such issues on the former appeal, the statement of facts on the former appeal having been used instead of depositions or witnesses. In the opinion in that case the court lays down the rule as follows:

"Recurring to the rule stare decisis relied on by the defendant in error, the general rule is thus stated by Wells in his treatise on Res Adjudicata and Stare Decisis, § 613: 'It is a well-settled principle that the question of law decided on appeal to a court of ultimate resort must govern the case in the same court, and the trial court, through all subsequent stages of the proceedings, and will seldom be reconsidered or reversed, even if they appear to be erroneous.

"The application of this rule, however, contemplates that the facts on the second appeal shall be substantially the same, or rather, perhaps, that they shall not be such as to affect materially the legal questions involved under the first appeal."

We sustain this assignment and hold that the trial court misconstrued the effect of the decision and judgment of the Court of Civil Appeals on the first appeal in this cause, and erred in refusing to put defendant in error on proof of his case (except as to the amount or value of the rent in question), and in striking out the answer of plaintiffs in error and refusing to hear any competent testimony which they might have seen fit to offer. It follows that the Court of Civil Appeals also erred in affirming the judgment of the trial court. Magnolia Park Co. v. Tinsley, supra; Kempner v. Huddleston, supra; Frankland v. Cassaday, supra; Ogden v. Bosse, 23 S. W. 730; Miller v. Burgess, 154 S. W. 590; Mitchell v. Western Union Telegraph Co. 28 Tex. Civ. App. 445, 56 S. W. 442 (writ refused).

Plaintiffs in error by proper assignments submit for construction the option contract declared on, and contend that the same did not authorize defendant in error nor the purchaser produced by him to demand the rents and growing crops in addition to the land.

The contract declared on simply gave an option to purchase the land. None of its terms purported to deal either with crops or rents arising out of the same.

The land was cultivated by tenants and planted in corn, cotton, and other crops. The rents reserved were in part money rent, in part the ordinary "third and fourth" of the crops, and in part the share of said Gifford in crops raised by tenants "on the halves" as shown by statement attached to the pleadings of plaintiffs in error, and which the statement of facts recites is the basis of the calculation and agreement as to the amount of such rents.

[2] The defendant in error did not, by the option contract, acquire any title to the lands. At most, he secured only the right to acquire an interest in the lands by complying, at his election, with the stipulations on his part. Oil & Pipe Line Co. v. Teel, 95 Tex. 586, 592, 68 S. W. 979. Gifford was the owner of the land at the time the crops were planted. He could not know that the defendant in error would ever avail himself of the right to purchase under the terms of the option contract. If he let the land lie idle, and defendant in error did not elect to take the land, he would lose a year's rental. If he rented the land as he did do, he necessarily expended time, attention, and skill in selecting and contracting with his tenants. Some of his tenants cultivated a part of said lands for a share of the crops, Gifford furnishing the land, seed, and supplies, and the tenant furnishing the labor, under an agreement that the proceeds of the crop should be equally divided. It seems from the statement of facts and the exhibit to the pleadings on which the same purports to be based that Gifford's entire one-half interest in these crops was classed as rents. According to the contention of defendant in error, Gifford was compelled to let the land remain uncultivated and risk losing the entire rental value of the land for the year, or to have it put in cultivation and risk losing his time, skill, and labor expended in the premises, as well as the seed furnished and the use of his teams, tools, and other supplies.

[3] We have found no cases directly in point with reference to the rights of the holder of an option contract, but we are of the opinion that such holder can occupy no better position than the holder of a mortgage duly recorded prior to the contract of tenancy and prior to the planting of the crop. In case of a mortgage the owner of the land remains such until his title is defeated at foreclosure sale, and in the case of an option he remains the owner until the holder of the option tenders full compliance with its terms and becomes entitled to receive a conveyance in accordance therewith. In either case the owner is entitled to the rents and crops until his title is actually defeated.

[4] While annual crops, the fruits of industry, so long as they are attached to the land, are held to pass with a deed thereto unless actually or constructively severed, yet they are for general purposes classed as personal property. Willis v. Moore, 59 Tex. 628, 637, 638, 46 Am. Rep. 284; Temple Trust Co. v. Pirtle, 198 S. W. 627, 628; Kreisle v.

Wilson, 148 S. W. 1132, 1134; Colonial Land & Loan Co. v. Joplin, 196 S. W. 626, 629 (writ refused by committee of judges); Colonial Land & Loan Co. v. Joplin, 184 S. W. 537, 539.

The Supreme Court in Willis v. Moore, supra, 59 Tex. 638, 46 Am. Rep. 284, says:

"A mortgagor is entitled to sever in law or fact the crops which stand upon his land at any time prior to the destruction of his title by sale under the mortgage; this results from his ownership and consequent right to the use and profits of the land, and the mortgage is taken with knowledge of that fact."

The court in the same case, in speaking of the manner in which such severance may be made (59 Tex. 639, 46 Am. Rep. 284), says:

"The Court of Appeals of Maryland, in Purner v. Piercy, 40 Md. 223, in speaking of what constitutes severance, say: 'There is nothing in the vegetable or fruit which is an interest in or concerning land, when severed from the soil, * * * whether grain, vegetables, or any kind of crop (fructus industriales), the product of periodical planting and culture; they are alike mere chattels, and the severance may be in fact, as where they are cut, and removed from the ground, or in law, as when they are growing, the owner in fee of the land, by a valid conveyance, sells them to another person, or when he sells the land, reserving them by an express provision.' To the same effect is the case of Titus v. Whitney, 1 Harrison, 85."

[5] Of course, when there is a foreclosure under power of sale in a deed of trust, the owner is not an actor in the transaction, and cannot as a part thereof sever the crops or rents by reserving them at the time of sale. The case of Colonial Land & Loan Co. v. Joplin, 196 S. W. 626, 628, involved a judicial foreclosure and sale. The trial court, following the analogy of growing crops held that certain nursery stock growing on the mortgaged premises was personal property, and that the lien of the deed of trust did not attach thereto, and severed such nursery stock by express provision in the decree and ordered the land and nursery stock sold separately and refused to order the proceeds of the sale of the nursery stock applied on the mortgage debt, a large part of which remained unpaid after applying the full proceeds of the sale of the land.

The Court of Civil Appeals affirmed the judgment, and in its opinion said:

"Whatever may be the rule in other jurisdictions, with us neither annual crops, whether growing or standing in the field ready for harvesting, nor anything else actually annexed to the land, and not intended by the parties to its being put there to become a permanent accession to the freehold, constitute a part of the realty, but are regarded as personal property; and as such the title thereto remains in the maker of a mortgage upon the land, which does not by specific provision include them, and he may sever them in law or in fact at any time prior to the destruction of his title by sale under his mortgage. No sale under the mortgage, and therefore no extinguishment of the mortgagor Nursery Company's title, having occurred at the time the court, through the receiver, in September, 1914, took charge of and henceforth stood in its place as to its property, no good reason occurs to us as to why the court could not cause the severance in this instance, and thereby do the same thing the mortgagor might have done.

"The first of the above-stated rules of law was declared by our Supreme Court in Willis v. Moore, 59 Tex. 628, 46 Am. Rep. 284, and the other in Hutchins v. Masterson, 46 Tex. 551, 26 Am. Rep. 286, supra, and both pronouncements are still the law in Texas, having been reaffirmed by that and other of our courts a number of times.

"If, therefore, under the evidence and conditions shown here, it was not intended by the parties, in giving and accepting the trust deeds, that the nursery stock should become a permanent accession to the soil, or if it is to be considered as in the nature of a crop produced by annual labor, and consequently subject to the same rule of law, it was personalty, and not affected by the trust deed liens.

"That under both suppositions its character was fixed as personalty, we think, is quite free from doubt."

An application for writ of error was refused by the committee of judges.

Defendant in error did not claim that there was anything in the circumstances attending the making of the contract tending to show that the parties intended that the purchaser of the land under such option should be entitled to the growing crops or the rents arising out of the same. He stood on the letter of his contract.

According to the allegations of the plaintiffs in error the deceased, G. C. Gifford, at all times denied that it was the intention of the parties that crops or rents should pass to the purchaser on the exercise of the option, and also denied that a proper construction of the option contract so required, and at all times asserted his right to reserve his crops and rents in the consummation of a sale under such option.

[6] It is a matter of common knowledge that the cultivation of crops of corn and cotton in that part of the state at the time of the tender and demand alleged was practically complete, and such crops either partly matured, or rapidly approaching maturity.

[7] We therefore sustain these assignments, and hold that a proper construction of the option contract gave the deceased, G. C. Gifford, the right to reserve his growing crops and the rents arising out of the same.

The other questions raised in the application are rendered immaterial by our holding on the question just discussed.

The condition of the record is such that we do not feel justified in recommending that the case be reversed and rendered, and we therefore recommend that the judgment of the trial court and the Court of Civil Appeals be reversed and remanded for further proceedings in accordance with this opinion.

PHILLIPS, C. J. The judgment recommended in the report of the Commission of Appeals is adopted, and will be entered as the judgment of the Supreme Court.

We approve the holding of the Commission of Appeals on the question discussed in its opinion.

SIMPSON v. GREEN. (No. 223–3369.)

(Commission of Appeals of Texas, Section A. June 1, 1921.)

1. Frauds, statute of ⊜125(1)—Statute does not declare parol sale of land void, but merely provides means of resistance.

The statute does not declare a parol contract for the sale of land to be illegal and void, but merely provides a means of successful resistance in case the statute is not complied with.

2. Frauds, statute of ⊜106(4)—Consideration need not be expressed in writing.

It is not necessary that the consideration of a contract for sale of lands should be expressed in the writing.

3. Frauds, statute of ⊜103(1)—Deed deposited in escrow held not insufficient as memorandum.

A deed deposited in escrow is not insufficient as a memorandum because in the form of an executed contract.

4. Frauds, statute of ⊜106(4)—Recital of consideration of deed in escrow held sufficient to meet requirements of statute.

In trespass to try title where the statute of frauds was interposed as a defense and it appeared that the vendor had executed an ordinary warranty deed and deposited it in escrow to be delivered on acceptance of title and payment of purchase money, the recital of the deed as a money consideration in a specified amount held sufficient to meet the requirements of the statute, though an auto was taken in part payment prior to its execution, and the balance in cash deposited where the deed was executed and deposited.

5. Frauds, statute of ⊜127—Decree enforces prior oral contract reduced to writing and not memorandum.

When a sufficient memorandum of a prior oral contract has been made and signed and suit for enforcement is brought, it is the oral contract that is enforced, and not the memorandum by which such contract is proved.

6. Escrows ⊜1—Valid contract of sale necessary to make deposit of deed a genuine "escrow."

A valid contract of sale is necessary to render the deposit of a deed in pursuance of the same a genuine "escrow" (citing Words and Phrases, Escrow).

⊜For other cases see same topic and KEY-NUMBER in all Key-Numbered Digests and Indexes.

7. **Escrows** ⟶8(2)—Deposit of deed sufficient to meet statute of frauds held an irrevocable escrow.

Where there is a prior verbal contract of sale, and the recitals in the deed placed in escrow, in themselves or in connection with other writings submitted therewith, meet the requirements of the statute of frauds, the deed so deposited is a genuine escrow, and therefor irrevocable, and the prior verbal contract is thereby rendered enforceable.

8. **Specific performance** ⟶16—All circumstances must be taken into consideration in determining whether remedy inequitable.

All circumstances in evidence must be taken into consideration in determining whether specific performance in a given case would be inequitable.

9. **Specific performance** ⟶121(3)—Evidence insufficient to show that enforcement for contract of sale would be inequitable.

In a suit for trespass to try title and for specific performance of a contract for the sale of land at the price of $4,500, the land being alleged to be worth $6,000 and defendant's rental interest in the crops worth $1,500, and there being an incumbrance for unpaid purchase money, evidence *held* insufficient to show that a decree for specific performance would be inequitable.

Error to Court of Civil Appeals of Second Supreme Judicial District.

Suit by William Simpson against Jesse Green. Judgment for defendant was affirmed by the Court of Civil Appeals (212 S. W. 263), and plaintiff brings error. Reversed and remanded as recommended by the Commission of Appeals.

McMurray & Gettys, of Decatur, for plaintiff in error.

R. E. Carswell, of Decatur, and Sullivan, Hill & Minor, of Denton, for defendant in error.

GALLAGHER, J. Wm. Simpson, plaintiff in error, sued Jesse Green, defendant in error, in trespass to try title to recover 175 acres of land. He alleged Green sold him the land sued for, for $4,500, of which sum $50 in cash, together with an automobile accepted at a valuation of $300, were paid at the time; the balance to be paid in cash when Green furnished Simpson an abstract showing good title in Green to the land.

Simpson further alleged that Green, in pursuance of said agreement, executed a deed purporting to convey said land to him for a cash consideration of $4,500 and placed the same in escrow in the hands of one Frank Turner to be held until Simpson should approve the title and pay the remainder of the purchase money. He further alleged that he thereafter waived the furnishing of the abstract, accepted the title to said land, and offered to pay the balance of the purchase price, but that Turner refused to de-

liver the deed on the ground that Green was unwilling for him to do so. Simpson prayed for judgment for title to the land and for possession of the deed held by Turner.

Green, besides pleading general denial pleaded that the contract of the sale of said land by him was oral and unenforceable, because in violation of the statute of frauds.

He also pleaded that he was young and inexperienced and ignorant of the real value of the property in question, and that Simpson was a shrewd business man, and trader of long experience and familiar with the value of such property, and thereby had decided advantage in the negotiations.

He further alleged that the land was worth $6,000, and that his rental interest in the crops thereon was worth $1,500.

He further alleged before he executed the deed to the land he offered to rescind the trade and return the $50 received by him, but that Simpson refused, and that after the deed was executed and delivered to Turner he again sought to rescind the trade, and offered to return both the $50 and the automobile received by him, and that such offer was again refused by Simpson.

He further alleged that when the deed was executed and delivered to Turner, Simpson represented to him that he could not withdraw from his prior verbal contract, but was legally bound to consummate the same, and that Simpson knew that such representations were false and fraudulent, and that he, said Green, was ignorant of the law and believed the same, and that thereby Simpson acquired his land for a consideration wholly inadequate and unconscionable.

Frank Turner was also made a party defendant and answered by disclaiming any interest in the litigation, asserted that he held the deed as stakeholder willing to deliver it to the party entitled thereto, and tendered the deed in court and asked to be discharged with his costs.

The trial was before the court, and the trial judge found that a verbal contract of sale was made substantially as alleged, and that $50 cash was paid on the purchase price at the time; that Green became dissatisfied and offered to return the $50 and rescind the trade, but Simpson insisted that the trade was binding and enforceable and that he was going to have the land; that Green was ignorant of the law and believed the representations so made, and because of such belief executed a general warranty deed conveying the land to Simpson for a recited consideration of $4,500 in hand paid, and that said deed was placed in the hands of Frank Turner until Green furnished abstract of title and Simpson paid the balance of the purchase money; that at the same time Simpson delivered the automobile to Green and deposited with Turner, or in his bank, $2,000 to be paid to Green on delivery of the deed and agreed to pay the balance of the purchase money when abstract was furnished and deed delivered to him; that shortly thereafter Green again sought to be released from the trade and tendered to Simpson $50 in cash and offered to return the automobile and, upon Simpson's refusal to accept the same, deposited $50 in Turner's bank to Simpson's credit and left the automobile at his house; that shortly thereafter Simpson waived the furnishing of an abstract, tendered Turner the balance of the purchase money, and demanded delivery of the deed, which demand was refused.

The trial court rendered judgment for the defendant in error, and the Court of Civil Appeals affirmed the judgment. 212 S. W. 263. A writ of error was granted by the Supreme Court.

The Court of Civil Appeals held that the parol contract of sale and no other was the one sought to be enforced, and that the deed did not constitute such memorandum thereof as to make it enforceable under the statute of frauds.

This holding is the basis of plaintiff in error's first assignment.

The statute of frauds of this state, so far as applicable, is as follows:

"No action shall be brought in any of the courts in any of the following cases, unless the promise or agreement upon which such action shall be brought, or some memorandum thereof, shall be in writing and signed by the party to be charged therewith. * * * (4) Upon any contract for the sale of real estate. * * *" Rev. St. 1911, art. 3965.

[1] The contract under consideration is not declared by the statute of frauds to be illegal and void. The statute merely provides a means of successful resistance in case it is not complied with. It is not compliance with the statute which constitutes the contract. The statute presupposes its legality, the enforcement of which is only suspended by the statute until its provisions are satisfied. Robb v. San Antonio St. Ry. Co., 82 Tex. 392, 395, 396, 18 S. W. 707; Bringhurst v. Texas Co., 39 Tex. Civ. App. 500, 87 S. W. 893, 896 (writ refused); Edwards v. Old Settlers' Association, 166 S. W. 423, 427 (writ refused); Crutchfield v. Donathon, 49 Tex. 691, 696, 30 Am. Rep. 112.

[2] The rule is settled in this state that it is not necessary that the consideration of the contract of sale of lands should be expressed in the writing. Thomas v. Hammond, 47 Tex. 42, 55; Fulton v. Robinson, 55 Tex. 401, 404, 405; Ellett v. Britton, 10 Tex. 208, 210; Adkins v. Watson, 12 Tex. 199, 201.

The sufficiency of the memorandum of a prior verbal contract was discussed in Morrison v. Dailey, 6 S. W. 426, 427, in which case the Supreme Court announced the rule in this state to be as follows:

"Upon the question presented by the proposition in the demurrer, that the terms of the contract are not sufficiently shown in the memorandum, the decisions are in conflict. The weight of authority seems to be in favor of the rule that all the material terms of the contract should appear in the writing. Riley v. Farnsworth, 116 Mass. 225; Grace v. Denison, 114 Mass. 16; Drake v. Seaman, 97 N. Y. 230; Gault v. Stormont, 51 Mich. 636, 17 N. W. 214; Minturn v. Baylis, 33 Cal. 129; Soles v. Hickman, 20 Pa. St. 180. But the contrary rule is not without authority to support it. Ellis v. Bray, 79 Mo. 227; O'Neil v. Crain, 67 Mo. 251; Holman v. Bank, 12 Ala. 369; Johnson v. Ronald's Adm'r, 4 Munf. 77; 1 Reed, St. Frauds, par. 419. The courts which held the affirmative of the question seem to base their conclusion upon the ground that, by the use of the word 'agreement' or the word 'contract,' the statute meant all stipulations agreed to by the parties. On the other hand, it is considered by some of the authorities that the object of the statute so far as lands are concerned, was to abrogate parol titles, and that this was sufficiently accomplished by a memorandum of the promise to convey the land, to be signed by the vendor, without requiring the other terms of the agreement to be stated. We need not decide which is the better reason, for we regard is as now settled, in this state, that all the terms of the contract need not appear in the memorandum. In Fulton v. Robinson, 55 Tex. 401, a receipt which named the vendee, and recited that it was 'part of the purchase money of my own headright, lying on Rush Creek, in the Cross timbers,' and which was signed by the vendor, was sufficient under the statute of frauds. The memorandum before us is quite similar to that, but is more explicit. It states the price, and that it was to be paid partly in cash and partly on a credit, and shows the rate of interest. If that memorandum was sufficient, this must be. The decision in the case cited lays down a rule of property; and, though we may consider it against the weight of authority, and the better reason, we are not at liberty to depart from it. It is not without both reason and authority to support it."

The deed executed by defendant in error and placed in the hands of Turner to be delivered to plaintiff in error upon payment of the purchase money was an ordinary general warranty deed from Green to Simpson reciting a consideration of $4,500 in hand paid, and conveying the land in question by appropriate description.

[3, 4] Defendant in error contends that this deed was insufficient as a memorandum under the statute because it was in the form of an executed contract, and recited a consideration of $4,500 in hand paid, when in fact an auto was taken as part payment, and all the consideration had not then been paid. The auto was taken at or prior to the execution of the deed at an agreed cash value, and $2,000 in cash was deposited with Turner, or in his bank, at the time the deed was

executed and deposited, and the deed was to be delivered on payment of the remainder of the purchase money. We therefore hold that these objections are untenable, and that the recitals in the deed were in themselves sufficient to meet the requirements of our statute of frauds. McCown v. Wheeler, 20 Tex. 372; Johnson v. Elmen, 94 Tex. 168, 173, 59 S. W. 253, 52 L. R. A. 162, 86 Am. St. Rep. 845; House v. Holland et al., 42 Tex. Civ. App. 502, 94 S. W. 153.

In McCown v. Wheeler, supra, a deed had been delivered which was in proper form, except that the name of the grantee was blank. In discussing the value and effect of this deed, the court said:

"Whether the deed, upon the filling of the blank with the name of the grantee, would have been valid as a deed or not, it was of value to the plaintiff. For if so filled up and afterwards acknowledged by the grantor, it would have been good. And in a suit for specific performance by the plaintiff against his grantor, it would be admissible evidence of the contract of sale, though not operative as a deed."

The remaining question to be considered is whether the delivery of the deed to Turner under the facts and circumstances in evidence was a sufficient delivery in law available in avoidance of the statute of frauds.

The contract of deposit was the joint act of the parties. Defendant in error executed and deposited the deed to be delivered when plaintiff in error accepted the title and paid the balance of the purchase money. Plaintiff in error at the same time deposited a check for $2,000, which check was cashed, the proceeds of which were held in Turner's bank to be paid to defendant in error when his title was accepted. It is true this contract of deposit rested in parol, but that it may so rest is conceded by defendant in error. The fact that it was participated in by both parties met the requirement of mutuality and took it out of the class of cases where the deposit and instructions accompanying the same are the ex parte acts of the depositor. Cooper v. Marek, 166 S. W. 58, 60; 21 C. J. p. 870, § 12; Davis v. Clark, 58 Kan. 100, 48 Pac. 563.

The Court of Civil Appeals, in Cooper v. Marek, supra, says:

"A delivery made by the depositor alone will not be sufficient to constitute a valid escrow."

The case of Davis v. Clark, supra, involved an agreement for a loan of money on a note and mortgage on real estate. The note and mortgage in pursuance of an agreement between the parties were delivered to a third party to hold in escrow until the borrowed money was actually paid or delivered for the use and benefit of the wife of the mortgagor, she having joined in both note and mortgage. The note and mortgage were duly executed and deposited according to agreement, but before the payment of the money to the wife the mortgagor, upon whose separate property the mortgage was given, died. After his death the money was paid and the note and mortgage delivered to the mortgagee. It was contended that the death of the mortgagor revoked the authority of the holder, and that his subsequent delivery of the note and mortgage was without authority and void. The court held the contrary, and in the course of the opinion said:

" 'An escrow is an obligatory writing (usually, but not necessarily, in the form of a deed) delivered by the party executing it to a third person, to be held by him until the performance of a specified condition by the obligee, or the happening of a certain contingency, and then to be delivered by the depository to the obligee, when it becomes of full force and effect.' 6 Am. & Eng. Ency. Law, 857. This definition, which seems to be collected out of all the authorities, applies fully to the instruments in question in this case. They were delivered by the Harshes to W. M. Clark, in pursuance of an agreement with Mr. Book, to be held by Mr. Clark until the performance of a specified condition by Mr. Book, and then to be delivered to him. Contrary to the view of the plaintiffs in error, the depository of an escrow is regarded as an agent of both obligor and obligee, and he can neither return the deed or other instrument to the former without the latter's consent, nor deliver it to the latter without the consent of the former, save upon fulfillment of the agreed conditions. Roberts v. Mullenix, 10 Kan. 22; Grove v. Jennings, 46 Kan. 366, 28 Pac. 738; Lessee of Shirley v. Ayres, 14 Ohio, 307; Cannon v. Handley, 72 Cal. 133, 13 Pac. 315. * * * According to these decisions, the depository of an escrow is not the agent of the depositor, merely, and the agreement of deposit cannot be rescinded by him alone, and the escrow withdrawn at his will.''

Defendant in error contends that notwithstanding there was a valid mutual contract of deposit in pursuance of a prior verbal contract of sale, and the deed in question so deposited, it was not an escrow and remained revocable at the option of plaintiff in error in the absence of proof of an enforceable contract of sale, independent of the recitals in the deed, and independent of the mutual agreement for the holding and ultimate delivery of the same.

[5] When a sufficient memorandum of a prior oral contract has been made and signed and suit for enforcement is brought, it is the oral contract that is enforced, and not the memorandum by which such contract is proved.

[6] The authorities hold that a valid contract of sale is necessary to render the deposit of a deed in pursuance of the same a genuine escrow. 21 C. J. p. 866, § 2; 10 R. C. L. p. 622, § 3; 3 Words and Phrases, First Series, p. 2464; Fitch v. Bunch, 30 Cal. 208, 212; Miller v. Sears, 91 Cal. 282, 27 Pac. 589, 25 Am. St. Rep. 176; Stanton v. Miller,

58 N. Y. 192, 202; Holland v. McCarty, 178 Cal. 597, 160 Pac. 1069; Thomas v. Birch, 178 Cal. 483, 173 Pac. 1102; Anderson v. Messenger, 158 Fed. 252, 85 C. C. A. 468; Clark v. Campbell, 23 Utah, 569, 66 Pac. 496, 54 L. R. A. 508, 90 Am. St. Rep. 716; Kopp v. Reiter, 146 Ill. 437, 34 N. E. 942, 22 L. R. A. 273, 37 Am. St. Rep. 156.

[7] Where there is a prior verbal contract of sale and the recitals in the deed placed in escrow in themselves, or in connection with other writings submitted therewith, meet the requirements of the statute of frauds of the jurisdiction in which the suit arises, we think the better reasoning sustains the proposition that the deed so deposited is a genuine escrow, and therefore irrevocable, and that the prior verbal contract so evidenced is thereby rendered enforceable. 2 Elliott on Contracts, p. 570; 10 R. C. L. p. 629, par. 11; Griel v. Lomax, 89 Ala. 420, 6 South. 741; Johnston v. Jones, 85 Ala. 286, 4 South. 748; Campbell v. Thomas, 42 Wis. 437, 24 Am. Rep. 427; Moore, Kappel & Co. v. Ward, 71 W. Va. 398, 76 S. E. 307, 43 L. R. A. (N. S.) 390, Ann. Cas. 1914C, 263; Thayer v. Luce et al., 22 Ohio St. 62; Minn. & Oregon Land & T. Co. v. Hewitt Investment Co. (D. C.) 201 Fed. 752, 759; Bronx Inv. Co. v. National Bank of Commerce, 47 Wash. 566, 92 Pac. 380; McGee v. Blankenship, 95 N. C. 563; Blacknall v. Parish, 59 N. C. 70, 78 Am. Dec. 239.

Mr. Elliott, in his work on Contracts (volume 2, p. 570), speaking of the necessity for delivery of the memorandum relied on to avoid the statutes, says:

"However, when a deed is placed in escrow beyond the control of the grantor it is sufficient as a memorandum."

The rule with reference to the sufficiency of a delivery in escrow as satisfying the statute of frauds is thus stated in 10 R. C. L. p. 629, par. 11:

"If, after an oral contract for the sale and purchase of land, the vendor makes, executes and delivers in escrow a deed for the land, reciting the consideration, and containing the terms and conditions of the sale, it has been held that this will amount to a compliance with the statute of frauds, and the contract if so alleged and proven will be enforced."

The statute of Wisconsin declares every contract for the sale of lands void unless such contract or a memorandum thereof expressing the consideration is in writing and subscribed by the person by whom the sale is made. Wis. Stat. § 2304.

The Supreme Court of that state, in discussing the sufficiency of the recitals in a deed to meet the requirements of the statute and render its deposit in pursuance of a prior verbal contract to convey a genuine escrow in Campbell v. Thomas, 42 Wis. 437, 24 Am. Rep. 429, says:

"The only writing subscribed by Thomas, which relates to any such contract, is the deed he deposited with Judge Hand. That instrument expresses a consideration, and if it contained the whole contract, we should have no difficulty in holding that it answers the requirements of the statute."

The court in the same opinion discusses the case of Thayer v. Luce & Fuller, 22 Ohio St. 62, and concludes the discussion with the following reference thereto:

"We so far adopt it here as to hold that, if a person who has made a parol agreement to sell land sign an instrument in the form of a conveyance of such land, to the vendee, and deposit it in escrow, if such instrument contains the terms of the parol agreement, including the consideration, it is a sufficient compliance with the requirements of the statute of frauds."

The Court of Civil Appeals which decided this case has since adopted the view expressed by the Supreme Court when it granted this writ and applied the same in the case of Townsend v. Day, 224 S. W. 283, 286.

The Court of Civil Appeals for the Eighth District has also adopted the same view and has applied the same in the case of Pearson v. Kirkpatrick, 225 S. W. 407, 409.

Defendant in error cites, among other cases, Main v. Pratt, 276 Ill. 218, 114 N. E. 576; McLain v. Healy, 98 Wash. 489, 168 Pac. 1, L. R. A. 1918A, 1161; Seifert v. Lanz, 29 N. D. 139, 150 N. W. 568; Foulkes v. Sengstacken, 83 Or. 118, 158 Pac. 952, 163 Pac. 811, to sustain his contention that an enforceable contract must be shown independent of the recitals in the deed.

In the case of Seifert v. Lanz there was a valid written contract signed by the husband, and it was held that the wife, by joining her husband in the execution of the deed in pursuance thereof, and joining her husband in depositing the same in escrow with said contract, adopted such contract and rendered the deed so executed and deposited a binding conveyance of the homestead as to her. The recitals in the deed in the other cases were held wholly insufficient in themselves to meet the requirements of the statute of frauds, and therefore the effect of the delivery in escrow of a deed which does contain such recitals was not before the court in any of such cases.

We have failed to find any case holding the escrow revocable or the sale unenforceable where a deed containing recitals sufficient to meet the requirements of the statute of frauds was deposited under a mutual agreement between the vendor and vendee in pursuance of a prior complete verbal contract of sale.

We therefore hold that the recitals contained in the deed deposited by defendant in error with Turner, being sufficient to meet the requirements of our statute of frauds, rendered the prior contract of sale enforceable and such deposit a genuine and irrevocable escrow.

Turner, with whom the deed was deposited, was trustee for both parties, and he was required by law to deliver the deed to plaintiff in error when he tendered compliance with the terms of the contract of deposit. 10 R. C. L. p. 633, § 15.

The trial court found that specific enforcement of the contract would be inequitable, and defendant in error contends that there is evidence in the record supporting such finding, and that therefore the judgment should be affirmed regardless of the holding of this court on the sufficiency of the recitals in the deed to avoid the statute of frauds.

The defendant in error, Green, was at the time of the transaction a young man 23 years of age. He inherited one-fourth of the tract of land in controversy, and in November, 1916, bought the remaining three-fourths from his brothers and sisters for $3,000. He owed $1,900 on the place at the time of the transaction in August, 1917, and was afraid he would have to enter military service, and he wished to settle his business before he went to the war. He had lived at home with his mother all his life, and his experience in trading was limited; but there is no intimation that he did not possess the capacity of the average man of his age and opportunity. The place was rented to tenants on the third and fourth at the time of his transaction.

Green spoke to Simpson about buying this land before he purchased the interest of the other heirs and told him if he would pay $4,000 he could have the whole place, but Simpson refused.

About August, 1917, Simpson approached Green and asked him if he still wanted to sell, but Green said he was not caring much about selling. Simpson asked him to go with him and see the place and arranged for some one to take Green's place at work, and they went together to look at the land.

Simpson offered to trade some horses and mules on the place. Green refused to consider the proposition, but told him he would take $4,300 and the automobile. Simpson laughed at him and said it was more than the place was worth.

They met again next day and traded colars, and after some dickering they agreed on $4,200 and the automobile, and Simpson gave him $50 on the trade. Green agreed to pay the taxes and pay off the incumbrance and furnish an abstract.

Two days later Green, having decided that he did not wish to carry out the trade, offered Simpson his money back and offered to pay him for his trouble in going to look at the place, but Simpson refused and said he had bought the place and was going to have it. The same day a relative of Green's offered Simpson the $50 back and $50 more on top of it to let Green keep the place, but

he refused and insisted that he was going to have the place.

They finally called parties to witness that Green was to execute the deed and furnish an abstract, and Simpson was to put $2,000 in the bank, and Turner was to hold the deed and the money until the remainder of the purchase money was paid. This was done, and Green received the automobile that day.

About two weeks later, Green concluded not to carry out the trade and took the automobile back to Simpson and offered to pay back the $50 and to pay him for his trouble in going to look at the place. This offer was refused, Simpson repeating that he had bought the place and intended to have it, and Green left the automobile and deposited the $50 in the bank to Simpson's credit. The place, with the accruing rents, was sold to Simpson for $4,500; the automobile being taken at $300.

The testimony of witnesses with reference to the value of the land ranged from $25 to $40 per acre. The rents actually collected amounted to $969.14.

The rule with reference to enforcement of contracts for the sale of real estate by decree for specific performance is laid down in 25 R. C. L. p. 271, § 72, as follows:

"Specific performance is granted to a greater extent in cases of contracts respecting real property than in cases respecting personal property. While in the latter case the jurisdiction to grant it is limited to special circumstances, in the case of real estate specific performance is decreed almost as a matter of course when the contract has been properly established and is unobjectionable in any of its features which address themselves to the chancellor's discretion. Under such circumstances the vendee is entitled to have the contract specifically enforced irrespective of his right to recover damages for its breach."

The effect of inadequacy of consideration in determining whether specific performance will be decreed is stated in section 10, p. 208, of the same authority, as follows:

"It is, however, the generally accepted rule, both in England and this country at the present time, that mere inadequacy of price does not in itself constitute a sufficient reason for a court of equity to withhold specific performance of the contract."

The rule with reference to inadequacy of price is thus stated in 36 Cyc. p. 609:

"In the language of a leading case, 'unless the inadequacy of price is such as shocks the conscience, and amounts in itself to conclusive and decisive evidence of fraud in the transaction, it is not itself a sufficient ground for refusing a specific performance;' or, to state the rule more in accordance with modern conceptions of fraud, inadequacy of consideration or of the subject-matter, standing alone as a defense, must be so gross as to lead to an inference, satisfactory to the court, of fraud or mistake in the making of the contract"—citing authorities.

The rule with reference to the effect of hardship in the contract sought to be specifically enforced is thus stated in section 22, p. 224, 25 R. C. L.:

"Although courts of equity may decline to enforce those contracts which are inequitable or unfair, it is not their province to undo a bargain merely because it is hard. The courts are not concerned with the question of the wisdom of bargains of persons competent to deal with their own affairs, and hardship will not ordinarily prevent specific performance of a contract which was fairly and justly made, when it results from miscalculation or from contingencies which might have been foreseen, and for which the complainant is not at fault"—citing authorities.

The Supreme Court of Missouri, in the case of Evans v. Evans, 196 Mo. 1, 93 S. W. 969, 975, held that the purchase of property worth $5,000, for $2,600 was not so inequitable as to prevent specific performance, notwithstanding the purchase was by an uncle and it was claimed that he knowingly misrepresented the value of the lands to his nephews to secure the trade.

[8, 9] All circumstances in evidence must be taken into consideration in determining whether specific performance in a given case would be inequitable. The situation of defendant in error in this case with reference to liability to military service at the time of the contract, his desire to have his business in shape in case he should be compelled to go to war, the incumbrance on the land for unpaid purchase money, the price he had shortly theretofore paid for the three-fourths interest in this very land, the uncertainty as to the amount likely to be realized from the yearly rents at the time of the trade, the difference of opinion among the witnesses as to the value of the land, the absence, according to his own testimony, of any undue solicitation inducing him to enter into the trade, or any element of fraud or oppression in connection therewith, in our opinion clearly refutes any contention that the enforcement of specific performance would be inequitable, and such contention of defendant in error is therefore overruled.

We recommend that the judgment of the district court and the Court of Civil Appeals be reversed and the cause remanded for further proceedings in accord with this opinion.

PHILLIPS, C. J. The judgment recommended in the report of the Commission of Appeals is adopted, and will be entered as the judgment of the Supreme Court.

We approve the holding of the Commission on the question discussed in its opinion.

CLARK v. TEXAS CO-OP. INV. CO.
(No. 221-3353.)

(Commission of Appeals of Texas, Section A. June 1, 1921.)

1. **Sales ⬤⇒390—Defrauded buyer may stand by contract and recover damages, or he may rescind.**

One who has been induced by fraud to enter into a contract has his choice of remedies, either to stand by the bargain and recover damages for fraud, or he may rescind and return the thing bought and receive back what he paid.

2. **Limitation of actions ⬤⇒28(1)—Action for fraudulently inducing plaintiff to subscribe for stock construed as one for rescission not governed by the two-year statute.**

Where plaintiff alleged he was fraudulently induced to subscribe for stock, and his allegations further showed a purpose to recover what he paid, that the certificates had not been issued, and that he had received nothing and consequently could make no offer of restoration, and that the notes he executed were worthless, in that they had been canceled by defendant, he appeared to have repudiated the contract and to seek restoration of the status quo, so that his action was, in effect, for rescission, and the two-year statute was not applicable.

3. **Appeal and error ⬤⇒1114—Where Court of Civil Appeals had not passed on questions over which the Supreme Court has no jurisdiction, the case must be remanded.**

Where the Court of Civil Appeals considered but one assignment, and certain others are necessarily determined by its conclusion thereon, but several assignments present questions of adjective law, over which the Supreme Court has no jurisdiction, these and other assignments should be passed upon by the Court of Civil Appeals, to which the cause should be remanded.

Error to Court of Civil Appeals of Second Supreme Judicial District.

Suit by James Clark and others against the Texas Co-operative Investment Company. Judgment for plaintiffs, and the defendant appealed to the Court of Civil Appeals, which reversed and rendered judgment for defendant (212 S. W. 245), and plaintiff named brings error. Judgment of Court of Civil Appeals reversed, and cause remanded to that court for consideration of assignments not disposed of and for the further orders.

See, also, 216 S. W. 220.

Padelford, Turner & Doyle, of Cleburne, and D. W. Odell, of Fort Worth, for plaintiff in error.

Capps, Cantey, Hanger & Short, of Fort Worth, and Ramsey & Odell, of Cleburne, for defendant in error.

TAYLOR, P. J. James Clark, plaintiff in error, sued the Texas Co-operative Investment Company, defendant in error, and the Texas Organization Company, to recover $1,500 and interest thereon. The court gave a peremptory instruction in favor of the organization company, and submitted the cause to the jury as between the remaining parties. Judgment on the cause submitted was for plaintiff in error. · The Court of Civil Appeals, by action of the majority, reversed the judgment of the trial court and rendered judgment in favor of defendant in error. 212 S. W. 246.

The original petition alleges that the organization company, in June, 1911, was engaged in selling capital stock of defendant in error preparatory to securing its charter; that defendant in error contracted with plaintiff in error to sell him shares of its stock to the amount of $4,000, he paying to defendant in error at that time $1,000 in cash, at the same time executing and giving his notes for the aggregate sum of $3,000 for the remainder of the purchase price; that as a part of the contract defendant in error agreed that shares of stock of the face value of $5,000 in the Commonwealth Bonding & Casualty Insurance Company, then owned and held by plaintiff in error, would be accepted as collateral security for plaintiff in error's note, and that the stock would be immediately issued and delivered to him; that in May, 1912, he tendered to defendant in error his certificates of shares in the bonding and casualty company and demanded that the $3,000 in shares of stock in defendant in error be delivered to him; that the demand was refused; that he thereupon demanded the return of the $1,000 in cash theretofore paid by him; that both demands were refused by defendant in error.

It is further alleged that on July 10, 1911, plaintiff in error contracted to purchase additional shares in the amount of $2,000, in consideration whereof he paid defendant in error the further sum of $500, and gave additional notes in the sum of $1,500; that the same agreement was made as before with reference to the acceptance of the bonding and casualty company stock as collateral; that thereafter on May 27, 1912, the contract was rescinded and the note canceled, but no part of the $500 so paid was returned to plaintiff in error.

It was also alleged that no certificates of stock were issued or delivered to plaintiff in error; that defendant in error refused to carry out its agreement to accept the stock of the bonding and casualty company as collateral on the $3,000 note; that it repudiated the agreement and claimed to have canceled plaintiff in error's notes, but still retained the $1,500 paid it, and, though often requested to repay the same, refused so to do.

The petition contains other allegations to the effect that defendant in error, by false and fraudulent representations, induced plaintiff in error to enter into the contract to purchase the stock. The prayer was for $1,500 with interest thereon from the date of payment, for costs of suit, and general relief.

The allegations of the original petition are greatly amplified in the sixth amended original petition, upon which trial was had. It is alleged therein also that plaintiff in error offered to transfer the $5,000 of capital stock in the bonding and casualty company to the investment company in accordance with the terms of the agreement, but that defendant in error refused to receive it, and thereafter canceled the $6,000 of stock in the investment company for which plaintiff in error had subscribed, and refused to issue and deliver to him any part thereof; that defendant in error claimed to have canceled defendant in error's notes, and refused to carry out the contract and agreement, or any part thereof, and kept and refused to pay to plaintiff in error the sum of $1,500 in cash, which he had theretofore paid; that defendant in error, though often requested so to do, refused to repay to the plaintiff in error the said sums of $1,000 and $500 in cash, which it obtained from him in the manner stated.

The allegations of fraud set out in the original petition were amplified in the amendment in proportion to the amplification of the other allegations. The prayer was again for $1,500, interest, costs of suit, and general relief. Legal and equitable relief was also prayed for.

It was the conclusion of the majority of the Court of Civil Appeals that the trial court should have instructed a verdict in favor of defendant in error, on the ground that the cause of action was barred by the two-year statute of limitation. The correctness of the conclusion is to be determined by whether the suit is one for damages growing immediately out of the alleged fraud, or for rescission based on fraud. Cooper v. Lee, 75 Tex. 114, 12 S. W. 483; Gordon et al. v. Rhodes & Daniel, 102 Tex. 300, 116 S. W. 40; opinion of Court of Civil Appeals herein, 212 S. W. 245.

[1] It is well settled that one who has been induced by fraud to enter into a contract may rescind it, unless, of course, his right to rescission has been lost. Blythe v. Speake, 23 Tex. 429; 13 Corpus Juris, § 652. The rule governing rescission in such cases is quoted by Judge Roberts in·the last paragraph of the case cited, in the following language:

"A party defrauded in a contract has his choice of remedies. He may stand to the bargain and recover damages for fraud, or he may rescind the contract, and return the thing bought, and receive back what he paid."

[2] Plaintiff in error alleged that he was fraudulently induced to enter into the subscription contract. The purpose of this suit,

as appears from the allegations, is to recover what he had paid under its terms. The certificates of stock which he contracted to purchase were not issued. He had received nothing from defendant in error, and consequently could make no offer of restoration. The notes he had executed were worthless, in that they had been canceled by defendant in error. The allegations disclose that it was the purpose of plaintiff in error, after making the discovery that he had been deceived in the manner stated, to restore the status quo. He repudiates on the ground of fraud any obligation under the agreement, and prays for recovery of what he was induced to part with through the misrepresentations alleged. In other words, his action as pleaded is, in effect, one for rescission.

It was the view of Judge Buck, who wrote the opinion of the Court of Civil Appeals, stating his own and the majority views, that the suit is one for rescission, and that the two-year statute of limitation is not applicable. His reasons, as well as the authority cited in the opinion, support his conclusion (1 Black on Rescission, p. 8), and we concur therein.

[3] Only one of numerous assignments of error was considered by the Court of Civil Appeals. If the conclusion concurred in is correct, the questions presented by some of the other assignments are necessarily determined thereby. Several of the assignments remaining present questions of adjective law, over which the Supreme Court has no jurisdiction. Decker v. Kirlicks, 110 Tex. 90, 216 S. W. 385; Hartt v. Yturia Cattle Co. et al., 228 S. W. 551, not yet [officially] reported. These and other assignments should be passed upon by the Court of Civil Appeals. Kirksey v. Southern Traction Co., 110 Tex. 190, 217 S. W. 139.

We accordingly recommend that the judgment of the Court of Civil Appeals be reversed, and that the cause be remanded to that court for consideration of the assignments not disposed of and for the further orders.

PHILLIPS, C. J. The judgment recommended in the report of the Commission of Appeals is adopted, and will be entered as the judgment of the Supreme Court. We approve the holding of the Commission of Appeals.

GRAVES v. HAYNES. (No. 230-3408.)*

(Commission of Appeals of Texas, Section A. June 1, 1921.)

1. Trial ⟺261 — Requested instruction not technically correct held to require correct instruction.

In an action brought against defendant as seller for losses resulting from cattle being diseased, defended on the ground that defendant acted merely as plaintiff's agent, a requested instruction presenting such defense, while not technically correct in every particular, *held* so nearly so as to require the court to give a proper charge on such defense.

2. Fraud ⟺13(3)—Belief of party misrepresenting fact unimportant.

The fact that seller of cattle may have believed them safe, sound, and free from tick fever, was unimportant, if in fact the buyer believed seller's representations to that effect to be true and relied upon them in purchasing the cattle.

3. Fraud ⟺22(1)—Duty to investigate truth of representation as to diseased cattle.

A buyer of cattle was under no duty to investigate the truth or falsity of seller's representations that the cattle were safe, sound, and free from tick fever.

4. Fraud ⟺20 — Reliance on representations as to diseased cattle.

If buyer of cattle represented to be free from tick fever believed the representations and relied on them and would not otherwise have purchased the cattle, he is entitled to recover damages, although he relied in part on what he saw when he inspected the cattle; but, if he relied in fact on what he saw, he cannot recover.

Error to Court of Civil Appeals of Second Supreme Judicial District.

Action by Allen Haynes against Herbert Graves. Judgment for plaintiff, and the defendant appealed to the Court of Civil Appeals, which affirmed the judgment (214 S. W. 665), and the defendant brings error. Judgment of district court and that of Court of Civil Appeals reversed, and cause remanded to the district court for another trial.

Bryan, Stone & Wade, and Moses & Rowe, all of Fort Worth, for plaintiff in error.

Jno. L. Ward, of Tulsa, Okl., J. H. Evetts, of Temple, and Capps, Cantey, Hanger & Short and David B. Trammell, all of Fort Worth, for defendant in error.

GALLAGHER, J. Allen Haynes, defendant in error, sued Herbert Graves, plaintiff in error, and alleged that he had theretofore purchased from Graves, in Fort Worth, 295 head of cattle to be shipped to Bell county, Tex., for feeding, breeding, raising, and selling purposes, and that such purposes were well known to Graves. He further alleged that Graves falsely and fraudulently represented that said cattle were safe, sound, and free from disease, and that such representations were not true, and that said cattle were then and there diseased with cattle fever, or some other contagious or infectious disease, which rendered them unsound, unfit for the uses intended, and without value. He further alleged that he was ignorant of the condition of the cattle, and from the inspection afforded and made by him he could not detect that said cattle, or any of them, were diseased, and that he relied on said representations and warranties, and believed them to be true and acted thereon by buying and paying for said cattle. He further alleged that 101 head of said cattle died within a very short time after they were delivered to him, and were of no value, and that the remainder of said cattle were either affected, or soon became affected, with said disease and were thereby greatly depreciated in value.

It was further alleged that the term "safe" meant that the cattle came from below the quarantine line and would not contract the fever on being shipped to Bell county.

Graves pleaded general denial, and specially denied that he was the owner of the cattle in question, and alleged that Haynes instructed him to go upon the market at Fort Worth and purchase for him about 300 head of cattle, and that he did so, paying for such cattle and holding them until Haynes came and received them and repaid the money expended by him in the purchase of the same, together with a commission of $6 per car, and the expense incurred in carrying out such commission.

He further alleged that in purchasing and paying for said cattle and paying the expenses incident to holding them until delivery he was acting as agent and commission man for Haynes, and that such was the customary way in which such business was transacted. He further alleged that he, in good faith, used his best skill and judgment in buying said cattle, and that they were in fact from south of the quarantine line and were known as "safe cattle."

There was a trial before a jury, and testimony was introduced tending to sustain the several allegations of the respective parties.

Haynes testified that Graves represented the cattle to be safe, sound, and free from fever, and Graves corroborated him, and further testified that the cattle did come from what is known as safe territory—that is, territory south of the quarantine line—and that they were sound and free from fever at the time they were delivered to Haynes.

There was testimony to the effect that the cattle in question developed cattle fever within a few days after Haynes received them, and that the injury suffered by him in the death of a part, and in the depreciation in value of the remainder, of these cattle, resulted from that disease.

There was expert evidence that cattle fever was contracted solely from the bite of a certain kind of tick, and that cattle north of the quarantine line are free from ticks, and cattle south of the line had, or were supposed to have, such ticks on them; that there was no absolute immunity to tick or cattle fever, but there was a condition known as resistance existing when cattle had spent all their lives in ticky territory; such cattle might develop cattle fever and die of it; that Bell county was at that time south of the line and in ticky territory, and cattle to be shipped there should have been from below the quarantine line, or from ticky territory; that a change of cattle from one part of the ticky territory to another involved a chance of great loss, because of the difference in resistance to the infection of different localities; and that cattle moved from one pasture to another frequently developed such fever and died therefrom.

There was testimony to the effect that both Haynes and Graves were experienced cattlemen.

There was testimony to the effect that Haynes, in company with Graves, went among the cattle and inspected them and noticed that some of the cattle had ticks on them and some did not.

The court, on the issue of agency, charged the jury as follows:

"You are further charged that if you find and believe from the evidence that the said Herbert Graves, in purchasing said cattle, acted as agent only for the plaintiff, Allen Haynes, and as such agent used his best skill and judgment in buying 'safe' and sound cattle that were not afflicted with fever, then and in such event you will find for defendant, unless you should find in favor of plaintiff under some other portion of this charge.

"But, in this connection, you are further instructed that even if you find and believe that said Graves in purchasing said cattle acted as agent of plaintiff only, still if you should further find that in purchasing same he failed to use his best skill and judgment to secure cattle which were 'safe' (as the word is used in the evidence) and sound and not afflicted with cattle fever, or if you find and believe that he fraudulently misrepresented to plaintiff the condition of said cattle, or fraudulently represented that they were 'safe' cattle when they were not (if they were not), and thereby induced the plaintiff to take same, and that at such time some or all of said cattle were afflicted with cattle fever and that some of them died therefrom, then and in such event you will find for plaintiff the market value of such cattle as you may believe so died from fever; and if you further find and believe that others of said cattle had cattle fever or were caused to contract said disease by reason of others of such cattle being so afflicted therewith at the time they were received by plaintiff, and that their market value was thereby depreciated, then and in such event you will find and return a verdict in favor of plaintiff for the difference in the market value of such cattle at the time of such purchase in the condition in which they would have been but for such fever or disease and their value in the condition in which they were in after having such disease."

Plaintiff in error in appropriate terms excepted to the first paragraph of this charge,

cause it limited his right to a verdict in
is favor, if acting as agent, to the contin-
ency that the jury should not find for the
plaintiff under some other portion of the
charge, and because it did not charge affirma-
ively that he should have a verdict in his
avor if the jury found he acted as the agent
·f and in pursuance of a commission from the
·laintiff.

He excepted to the second paragraph there-
)f, because there was no evidence of his fail-
·re to use his best skill and judgment, and no
evidence that he made any fraudulent or willful misrepresentations in the matters referred to in said charge.

The jury returned a verdict for damages
in favor of defendant in error who was plaintiff in the trial court, and judgment was entered in his favor thereon. The Court of
Civil Appeals affirmed the judgment (214 S.
W. 665), and the case is before us for hearing on writ of error granted by the Supreme
Court.

[1] Plaintiff in error assigns as prejudicial
error requiring reversal, the action of the
court in refusing to give to the jury the following special charge requested by him, to
wit:

"If you believe from evidence that in acquiring
the cattle, defendant did so, not for himself, but
upon an order and commission, if any, previously given by the plaintiff, and if you further
believe from the evidence that in executing
such commission, if any, defendant used ordinary care, that is, such care as a person of ordinary prudence would use under the same or
similar circumstances, to purchase for plaintiff
cattle which were sound and free from disease, then and in such event you will find and
return a verdict for defendant, even though you
should believe from evidence that some or all
of the cattle so purchased were affected with
tick fever, at the time they were shipped to
Bell county."

The only affirmative defense relied on by
plaintiff in error was that he acted in the
transaction in question as agent for defendant in error, upon an order or commission
previously given to him.

If such were the facts and he accepted such
agency and undertook to execute such commission, and in doing so exercised reasonable
skill and ordinary care to purchase for defendant in error cattle which were safe,
sound, and free from fever, he discharged
the full measure of his duty, and was not
liable to him even though some, or all, of
such cattle were affected with fever at the
time they were shipped to Bell county.
Mechem on Agency (2d Ed.) §§ 1275, 2410.

The charge of the court did not present this
defense as fully and forcibly as plaintiff in
error was entitled to have it presented. He
was entitled, upon proper request, to have it
presented affirmatively and without being in
any way limited by other portions of the
court's charge. In the case of Wichita Falls

231 S.W.—25

Traction Co. v. Adams, 107 Tex. 612, 614, 615,
183 S. W. 155, 156, the Supreme Court, in an
opinion by Chief Justice Phillips, says:

"In a jury trial where the case is submitted
under a general charge of the court, a party is
entitled to an affirmative presentation of an
issue raised by the pleading and evidence upon
which he relies for the establishment of his
cause of action or his defense. For a proper
application of the law of the case to the different phases of the evidence as a guide for the
jury's action, he is not remitted to inferences
which may be drawn from the charge. Whether
plaintiff or defendant, it is his right, upon proper request, to have the issue affirmatively submitted by the court through an appropriate
instruction grouping the facts which, if determined in his favor, will, under the law, entitle him to the verdict. This, it may be said, is
the distinct office of the special charge under
our practice. El Paso & Southwestern Railroad
Company v. Foth, 101 Texas, 133, 100 S. W.
171, 105 S. W. 322; St. Louis Southwestern
Railway Company v. Hall, 98 Tex. 480, 85 S.
W. 786; Missouri, Kansas & Texas Railway
Company v. McGlamory, 89 Texas, 638, 35 S.
W. 1058; Texas Trunk Railway Co. v. Ayres,
83 Tex. 268, 18 S. W. 648."

The requested charge, while not technically correct in every particular, was so nearly
so as to require that a proper charge be giv-
en. Freybe v. Tiernan, 76 Tex. 286, 291, 13
S. W. 370; Willis v. Smith, 72 Tex. 565, 572,
10 S. W. 683.

[2] Plaintiff in error complains of the action of the trial court in refusing his special
requested charge as follows:

"If you believe from the evidence that in acquiring the cattle, defendant did so for himself
and not for the plaintiff upon an order, if any,
previously given, and if you should further find
from the evidence that at the time the cattle
were delivered to plaintiff some or all of them
were not sound and free from disease, but if you
should find from the evidence that the defendant in good faith believed that said cattle were
sound and free from disease, and that before
accepting same plaintiff went among and inspected the cattle for himself, then and in such
event you will find and return a verdict for defendant."

The fact that the plaintiff in error may
have believed that the cattle were safe, sound,
and free from fever, was unimportant if, in
fact, defendant in error believed the representations to that effect to be 'true and relied
upon them in purchasing the cattle. Buchanan v. Burnett et ux., 102 Tex. 492, 495, 119
S. W. 1141, 132 Am. St. Rep. 900.

[3, 4] Defendant in error was under no
duty to investigate the truth or falsity of
such representations. The Supreme Court,
in Labbe v. Corbett, 69 Tex. 503, 509, 6 S.
W. 808, 811, lays down the rule in the following quotation from another authority:

"When once it is established that there has
been any fraudulent misrepresentations, * * *
by which a person has been induced to enter

into a contract, it is no answer to his claim to be relieved from it to tell him that he might have known the truth by further inquiry. He has a right to retort upon his objector: 'You, at least, who have stated what is untrue, * * * for the purpose of drawing me into a contract, cannot accuse me of want of caution, because I relied implicitly upon your fairness and honesty.'"

If defendant in error believed such representations and relied on them and would not have purchased the cattle if they had not been made, he would not be denied his action, even though he did not rely solely on such representations, but relied in part on what he saw when he inspected the cattle. Buchanan v. Burnett et ux., 102 Tex. 492, 495, 119 S. W. 1141, 132 Am. St. Rep. 900.

However, if he did not rely either in whole or in part on such representations, but relied in fact on what he saw when he inspected the cattle, he could not recover because of the making of such representations. Cresap v. Manor, 63 Tex. 485, 488; Garrett v. Burleson, 25 Tex. Supp. 41, 44.

The court did not err in refusing such requested charge. If this issue is made by the evidence on another trial, the court upon proper request should give a charge in accord with the authorities above cited.

The other assignments urged in the application for writ of error are based on matters which may not arise on another trial, and are therefore not here passed upon.

We recommend that the judgment of the district court and the Court of Civil Appeals be reversed, and the cause remanded to the district court for another trial.

PHILLIPS, C. J. The judgment recommended in the report of the Commission of Appeals is adopted and will be entered as the judgment of the Supreme Court.

We approve the holding of the Commission of Appeals on the question discussed in its opinion.

RICE-STIX DRY GOODS CO. v. FIRST NAT. BANK OF McGREGOR.
(No. 236–3421.)

(Commission of Appeals of Texas, Section A. June 1, 1921.)

Homestead ⬅️128 — Purchaser held estopped to deny validity of mortgage lien on ground that property constituted homestead.

That a purchaser of property subject to a lien takes with knowledge of vendor's recognition of the validity of the lien estops him to deny its validity, notwithstanding any unrevealed intention on the part of the purchaser subsequently to contest its validity on the ground that the property constituted a homestead.

Error to Court of Civil Appeals of Supreme Judicial District.

Suit by the Rice-Stix Dry Goods Com against John F. Gullidge and others. Ju ment for plaintiff was reversed on the peal of defendant First National Bank McGregor (213 S. W. 344), and plain brings error. Reversed, and judgment trial court affirmed, as recommended by Commission of Appeals.

J. D. Williamson, of Waco, for plaintiff error.

D. A. Kelley, of Waco, for defendant in error.

SPENCER, J. Plaintiff, Rice-Stix Dry Goods Company, a corporation, instituted this suit to recover of John F. Gullidge and J. M. Fox, doing business as partners under the firm name and style of Gullidge Mercantile Company, a balance of $1,500 due upon three of a series of five promissory notes, dated April 8, 1914, executed and delivered by them to plaintiff in error and to foreclose the lien created by the execution of a deed of trust by J. F. Gullidge and wife, Lena Gullidge, dated April 8, 1914, upon block 1 of J. F. Gullidge addition to the town of McGregor in McLennan county, Tex., to secure plaintiff in the payment of these notes. Subsequent to the execution of the deed of trust and the recording of it in McLennan county, Tex., Gullidge conveyed the property in question to the First National Bank of McGregor, Tex., and the bank was made a party defendant in the suit and a foreclosure asked against it.

Gullidge answered, admitting the execution of the notes and deed of trust, and that the balance of $1,500 was unpaid and the deed of trust a valid and existing lien. He also alleged that at the time the property was deeded to the bank he was indebted to it personally and as indorser and surety for the Gullidge Company in the aggregate sum of several thousand dollars, and that, in consideration of the conveyance of the property to it, the bank, with knowledge of the deed of trust, agreed to accept the property, which he alleged was reasonably worth $2,500, subject to the deed of trust lien, and to credit him with $500 on his indebtedness to it. In his prayer, he asked that the bank be adjudged primarily liable for the debt, that plaintiff's lien be foreclosed, and that he be adjudged secondarily liable for the indebtedness.

The bank entered a general denial to plaintiff's and defendant Gullidge's petitions, and as against plaintiff specially pleaded that the deed of trust lien was void, invalid, and of no effect under the homestead exemption clause of the Constitution, for the reason that at the time of and long prior to the

---

⬅️ For other cases see same topic and KEY-NUMBER in all Key-Numbered Digests and Indexes

xecution of the deed of trust the property upon which the lien was attempted to be created was the homestead of Gullidge and wife, used and occupied as such by them, and that the recorded deed of trust and the claim of plaintiff under it created a cloud upon its title to the property. It prayed for judgment decreeing the deed of trust null and void, that the cloud cast because of its existence be removed, and that defendant bank be quieted in its title.

Plaintiff replied that Gullidge and wife never claimed the property as their homestead, that any homestead right they might have claimed was abandoned, that the bank, as a part of the consideration, took the property subject to the lien which Gullidge represented was a valid and existing lien and obligated and bound itself to discharge the debt and lien, and that it was estopped to deny the validity thereof. Gullidge adopted these allegations as his reply to the bank's answer. The cause was dismissed as to the defendant Fox.

Upon a trial before the court, without the aid of a jury, the court rendered judgment for plaintiff against Gullidge for the amount of notes, and against Gullidge and the bank, foreclosing the lien upon the property. Upon appeal, the Court of Civil Appeals held that the homestead in disconnected tracts of land depends on the actual use made of it, and that this use is controlling as against the negative declarations of the owner; that the evidence in this case showed that the property was the homestead of Gullidge and wife, and used as such by them at the time of the execution of the deed of trust; that a purchaser of land constituting part of a homestead may, as against one holding a deed of trust executed prior to the sale, assert that the land constituted a homestead, and the deed of trust lien therefore invalid; and that such purchaser is not estopped to deny the invalidity, unless as a part of the consideration he agrees to pay the debt or discharge the lien. As to the latter holding it concluded that the evidence was in an unsatisfactory state, and therefore reversed and remanded the cause. 213 S. W. 344.

In the view we take of the case, it is unnecessary to pass upon but one question, and that is: Is the grantee estopped, under certain undisputed facts of the case, to plead the invalidity of the lien? It is significant that neither Gullidge nor his wife claimed a homestead interest in the property. Both recognized the justness of the debt, which the lien was given to secure. At no time has either of them repudiated the obligation or urged the invalidity of the lien to secure it. The defense comes from without, and over their active and vigorous protest. Mrs. Gullidge is emphatic in her testimony to the effect that it was her understanding, at the time she executed the deed to the bank, that the bank was to satisfy the indebtedness and the lien given to secure it; otherwise, she would not have signed it.

Mr. Gullidge testified positively that he discussed the indebtedness of $1,500 with the bank's representative, who had actual and constructive notice of the lien, and informed him that it was protected by a valid lien and would have to be paid at a certain time. The bank's version of the transaction, as revealed by the testimony of its representative, Cavitt, does not in terms or by implication contradict the issue made by Gullidge. Cavitt testified:

"I did not tell Mr. Gullidge that the bank would be willing to credit him with $500 on that place upon a conveyance of that property to the bank, and the bank would step in his shoes as to the Rice-Stix Dry Goods Company debt. I do not know the language that was used, but the understanding with Mr. Gullidge and I was that we should take the title that he had for that $500, and it was subject to the record. I do not remember just what was said, but I understood there was supposed to be an incumbrance on the property."

The testimony of all the witnesses, including the bank's representative, is to the effect that the property was worth considerably more than $500. In fact, it seems not to be disputed that the land was reasonably worth $2,000. Cavitt's explanation of why the bank gave only $500 for the property, when it was worth considerably more, was that he knew that plaintiff thought it held a lien against the property, and that a contest as to its validity would result in involving considerable expense to the bank. He did not, however, inform Gullidge that the bank intended to contest the validity of the lien. The contention of Gullidge that as part of the consideration for the conveyance the bank assumed the payment of his indebtedness to plaintiff was determined adversely by the trial court, but the facts enumerated show conclusively, as a matter of law, that the bank accepted the property subject to the lien, and with the knowledge that Gullidge recognized it as valid and existing. Therefore the taking of the property subject to the lien and with knowledge of Gullidge's recognition of its validity, operates as an estoppel upon the part of the bank to deny its validity.

The force of these undisputed facts is not weakened by an unrevealed intention that may have lurked in the mind of the bank's representative to subsequently contest the validity of the lien. Knowing at the time of the acceptance of the deed that Gullidge recognized the validity of the lien, and that he considered it as security for the debt, it was its duty, if it intended to treat the lien as invalid, to inform Gullidge of such intention. It ought not, by secret reservation and in defiance of its agreement to take subject to the record, to be permitted to deprive Gullidge of the value which the lien represented to him as security for the debt.

The same rule applied here was applied by the Supreme Court of Minnesota in Alt v. Banholzer, 86 Minn. 57, 29 N. W. 674. In that case, the grantee purchased the mortgaged property with notice of, and took the deed subject to, the mortgage, and then sought to cancel the mortgage because of its invalidity, in that the property conveyed was the homestead, and that the wife did not join in the execution thereof. The court said:

"The point is made by the defendant that the plaintiff [grantee], therefore, acquired only the equity of redemption in the land by such conveyance, and that she has no rights to claim any greater interest therein. If such is the character of the deed, and it does not seem to be questioned by the plaintiff, we think the point well taken. It was entirely competent for the parties to so limit the effect of the conveyance, and to recognize and provide for the payment of the debt, for which the grantor was personally liable, so that, if required to pay the same, he might, in equity, have recourse against the land for his indemnity. The effect of such a conveyance is to make the land a primary fund for the payment of the debt, and to place the mortgagor in the situation of surety therefor only. Johnson v. Zink, 51 N. Y. 836, and cases cited. So the grantee of land, subject to a usurious mortgage which is absolutely void, cannot question its validity. 'He must pay it if he has agreed to; and, if not, he must allow the lands conveyed subject to it to be applied to its payment' "—citing authorities.

The uncontroverted facts showing that the bank took the property subject to the record, which revealed the lien and with knowledge that Gullidge recognized the lien as security to protect his indebtedness, it is, as a matter of law, under such facts, estopped to deny the validity of the lien and the mortgagee is therefore entitled to a judgment of foreclosure.

We recommend, therefore, that the judgment of the Court of Civil Appeals be reversed, and that of the trial court affirmed.

PHILLIPS, C. J. The judgment recommended in the report of the Commission of Appeals is adopted, and will be entered as the judgment of the Supreme Court.

LEMON v. STATE.   (No. 6286.)

(Court of Criminal Appeals of Texas. May 25, 1921.)

1. Larceny ⊛⟿55—Circumstances held not sufficient to overcome presumption of innocence.

In a prosecution for theft, circumstances held not of sufficient cogency to overcome presumption of innocence.

2. Larceny ⊛⟿64(1)—Receiving stolen goods ⊛⟿8(3)—Evidence of possession held not to justify inference of guilt.

Proof that stolen tools were on premises belonging to and under control of the father of one accused of theft and receiving stolen goods, in an outhouse with other tools, would not justify an inference of guilt on the part of the accused, in the absence of any assertion of ownership by the accused.

Appeal from Swisher County Court; J. E. Swepston, Judge.

Bill Lemon, charged with theft and receiving stolen property, was convicted of a misdemeanor, and appeals. Reversed and remanded.

Culton & Taylor, of Tulia, for appellant.
R. H. Hamilton, Asst. Atty. Gen., for the State.

MORROW, P. J. Charged with theft and receiving stolen property, appellant was convicted of misdemeanor; punishment fixed at confinement in jail for 25 days.

Appellant and his brother, John Lemon, were charged, by separate indictments, with the theft of certain tools. The articles had been left by the owner in his field about his tractor. He caused a search of the residence of John Lemon, and there found some of the articles in his possession. He also caused the search of the premises of the father of appellant, and in one of the outhouses, among other tools, he found some articles, to the identity of which with those lost the owner testified. There was evidence that the appellant and his brother John were near the tractor at a time when they might have taken the property.

John Lemon, who had been convicted and satisfied the judgment introduced by the state, testified that he took the property, including some gasoline; that the appellant was present, but took no part in the offense, but protested against his brother doing so. He also declared, on cross-examination, that he had made this same statement upon his trial. The county attorney, who conducted the trial of John Lemon, testified on behalf of the state that John Lemon, on his own trial, did not say that the appellant had no connection with it, but had testified that appellant raised the seat and took the cap off the gasoline tank, in order that John Lemon might pour the stolen gasoline in the car. The circumstances under which this contradicting testimony was given are not made sufficiently clear for us to determine whether any rules of procedure were transgressed therein or not.

[1] The court instructed the jury that the office of the testimony of the county attorney was limited to the impeachment of the statements of the witness John Lemon. The state's case rests upon circumstantial evi-

dence alone. The circumstances consist in the presence of the appellant at the time the offense was committed, the fact that John Lemon put the articles which he stole in the car in which he and his brother were riding, and the fact that some articles identified as stolen were on the premises of the father of appellant. It did not appear that appellant knew any of the articles were in the car. We do not regard these circumstances, either singly or collectively, of sufficient cogency to overcome the presumption of innocence. They are consistent with the defensive theory developed by the state's own witness, John Lemon, that the appellant, while present, took no part in the commission of the offense, but protested against it. The impeaching testimony introduced by the state to discredit John Lemon could not have the effect of affirmative testimony showing appellant's guilt. Giving it its full scope, it could have but discredited the witness relied upon by the state, namely John Lemon.

[2] The evidence of possession does not justify the inference of guilt. None of the property was found in the possession of the appellant. The extent to which the state's testimony on the subject goes is that it was on the premises belonging to and under the control of the father of the appellant; that it was in an outhouse with other tools. There is an absence of any assertion of ownership by the appellant. The inadequacy of this testimony is illustrated by numerous decisions. Casas v. State, 12 Tex. App. 59; Branch's Ann. Tex. Penal Code, § 2463; Russell v. State, 86 Tex. Cr. R. 609, 218 S. W. 1050; Field v. State, 24 Tex. App. 428, 6 S. W. 200; Underhill on Crim. Evidence, § 300, p. 527.

From what has been said, it follows that, in our opinion, the judgment should be reversed, and the cause remanded.

GARNER v. STATE. (No. 6199.)

(Court of Criminal Appeals of Texas. April 20, 1921. Appellant's Rehearing Denied June 8, 1921.)

1. **Homicide** ⟲309(6)—**Charge on provoking difficulty held appropriate.**

In a prosecution for murder, resulting in conviction of manslaughter, only the mitigating and justifying acts being in controversy, not the killing, the words and conduct of defendant immediately preceding the assault made by deceased which resulted in his death *held* to render appropriate a charge upon the law of provoking the difficulty.

2. **Homicide** ⟲309(1)—**Converse of state's charge on provoking difficulty should have been submitted.**

In a prosecution for murder, resulting in conviction of manslaughter, where the court charged submitting the issue of provoking the difficulty from the standpoint of the state, in connection therewith the converse of the charge on defendant's request should have been fully submitted.

3. **Criminal law** ⟲854(6)—**Permitting juror to go home for an hour because of sickness in his family erroneous.**

Under Code Cr. Proc. 1911, arts. 699, 745, in a prosecution for murder, resulting in conviction of manslaughter, where, after ten jurors were selected, impaneled, and sworn, one of them was permitted by the court, without consent of defendant or his counsel, and without being accompanied by an officer, to go to his home, about a mile distant, where a member of his family was sick, and there remain away from the courthouse, separated from the other members of the jury, for about an hour, such action was error, necessitating reversal as in violation of the mandatory provisions of the statute.

Appeal from District Court, Motley County; J. H. Milam, Judge.

Tom Garner was convicted of manslaughter, and he appeals. Reversed.

A. J. Fires, of Childress, G. E. Hamilton, of Matador, and Williams & Martin, of Plainview, for appellant.

R. H. Hamilton, Asst. Atty. Gen., for the State.

MORROW, P. J. The appellant was charged with murder and convicted of manslaughter. His punishment was fixed at confinement in the penitentiary for five years.

[1, 2] We deem it unnecessary to recite the facts further than to say that the killing of the deceased by the appellant was not a controverted issue. It was the mitigating and justifying facts that were in controversy. Upon well-settled principles we think the words and conduct of the appellant immediately preceding the assault made by the deceased which resulted in his death were such as to render appropriate the charge upon the law of provoking the difficulty. The paragraph of the charge submitting that issue from the standpoint of the state is, so far as we discern, without fault. In connection therewith, however, the converse, upon request, should have been more fully submitted.

The appellant, in a special charge, sought to have the court say to the jury:

"You are instructed that you must not only believe that defendant used the language and was guilty of the conduct relied on by the state to show provocation of deceased, but you must further believe that such language and conduct, if any, was reasonably calculated to and did actually provoke a difficulty in which the deceased was killed."

There is other language in the special charge which may have justified its refusal in the form prepared. On another trial, however, if a proper special charge upon the subject is requested, it should be given.

[3] A special venire was present, and, after ten jurors were selected, impaneled, and sworn, one of them was permitted by the court, without the consent of either the appellant or his counsel, and without being accompanied by an officer, to go to his home about one mile distant, where a member of his family was sick, and there remain away from the courthouse, out of the presence of the court and separated from the other members of the jury, for about an hour. The trial judge discovered that he had misapprehended his rights in excusing the juror and requested a waiver of the separation by the defendant and his counsel. This they refused to make. The court thereupon heard evidence. The juror testified that, though he had had conversations, he had talked to no one about the case. Covering the subject, article 745 of the Code of Criminal Procedure says:

"After the jury has been sworn and impaneled to try any case of felony, they shall not be permitted to separate until they have returned a verdict, unless by permission of the court, with the consent of the attorney representing the state and the defendant, and in charge of an officer."

In article 699, it is said:

" * * * When jurors have been sworn in a case, those who have been so sworn shall be kept together and not permitted to separate until a verdict has been rendered, or the jury finally discharged, unless by permission of the court, with the consent of the state and the defendant, and in charge of an officer."

A similar state of facts was before the court in McCampbell v. State, 37 Tex. Cr. R. 607, 40 S. W. 496, save that in that case the separation was with the consent of the accused on trial. Holding that a reversal must result, the court said:

"We hold in this case that the statute provides the modus operandi for an agreement to a separation, and prescribes the method to be pursued in such separation; that is, what shall be done. The provision requiring the juror to be attended by an officer is as imperative as that provision which prohibits the separation of the jury without consent. There can be a consent, but this consent can only be to the separation. There can be no consent to a separation without the juror being attended by an officer. He could as well waive the right of trial by a jury as waive those statutory provisions which secure its purity and efficiency. The accused is not alone interested in this matter. The state has an interest in the life and liberty of the citizen. The state has an interest in the purity of the trial by jury. It is not to the interest of the state to take the life of her citizens, unless it is taken in pursuance of law; hence the Legislature had the right to make the provision contained in article 725. A separation of the jury may result in great injustice to the state,

as well as to the accused, not only in the particular case, but as establishing a bad precedent. If we were to permit this practice, there would be a contest in nearly every case as to whether or not the party made the agreement (as the record shows in this case); and, in addition to that, questions would arise as to whether the juror had been tampered with, for, whether he consented or not, if the juror had been improperly dealt with by any one else, either by word, act, or gesture, it would be a ground for a reversal, and a juror in every such case would be ready to absolve himself. Hence we believe it to be the better policy, independent of the mandates of the statutes, to hold that a juror in a felony case cannot be permitted to separate unaccompanied by an officer. The judgment is reversed, and the cause remanded."

This court has held to this view on numerous occasions. See Gant v. State, 55 Tex. Cr. R. 284, 116 S. W. 801; McDougal v. State, 81 Tex. Cr. R. 179, 194 S. W. 944, L. R. A. 1917E, 930.

Referring to the statutory provisions and the construction thereof in the decisions mentioned, and others, the state, through the Assistant Attorney General, says:

"The state is of opinion that the court committed error in forcing defendant to proceed to trial, after the jury had separated, as shown in said bill, which is such error as to compel the reversal of this case."

In this view we are constrained to concur. The statute naming the conditions under which the jury may be separated is mandatory. It gives effect to sound public policy; it is designed to preserve purity of a jury trial. Its nonobservance has been uniformly held to lay upon this court the imperative duty to order a reversal. In doing so in the instant case we are but obeying the mandate of the lawmaking power, so plain that it requires no interpretation, and based upon reasons so clear that they have not been the subject of controversy. Hitherto when it has been made plain by the record that the statute has been disregarded and the trial court, upon due presentation of the matter, has refused to grant a new trial, this court has amended the error by ordering a reversal of the judgment, and such is the course we must now pursue.

On Motion for Rehearing.

HAWKINS, J. Appellant has filed a motion for rehearing urging that we were in error in our original opinion in holding that the issue of provoking the difficulty was raised by the evidence, and requesting a review of that matter and modification of the opinion.

We have carefully examined the entire statement of facts again, and after having done so are still of the belief that the evidence raises the issue.

The evidence may not be the same upon

another trial. If so, and this issue should be submitted, of course the converse should be submitted in order that appellant's rights would be fully protected.

Motion for rehearing is overruled.

WORLEY v. STATE. (No. 6290.)

(Court of Criminal Appeals of Texas. May 25, 1921.)

1. **Assault and battery ⟜54—Homicide ⟜8—Automobile law held not to change law of homicide, but to add to law of aggravated assault.**

The purpose of Vernon's Ann. Pen. Code Supp. 1918, art. 1022a, being the Automobile Law of 1917, *held* not to be to change the law of homicide, but to add a new clause to the law of aggravated assault.

2. **Homicide ⟜134—Indictment for negligent homicide by use of automobile must charge all essential elements of offense.**

In charging negligent homicide, through the driving of an automobile, the particular act relied upon should be set up, and it should appear from the indictment that all the elements of the offense charged exist, among which is that declared in Pen. Code 1911, art. 1116, relating to apparent danger, and also that declared in article 1119, relating to apparent intention to kill.

2. **Homicide ⟜134—Indictment for negligent homicide by use of automobile held insufficient.**

In a prosecution for negligent homicide by use of an automobile, an indictment omitting the element of apparent danger required by Pen. Code 1911, art. 1116, and being deficient in describing the act relied on, *held* insufficient.

Appeal from Young County Court; W. H. Reeves, Judge.

J. A. Worley was convicted of negligent homicide, and he appeals. Reversed, and cause dismissed.

Marshall & King, of Graham, and Kay, Akin & Kenley, of Wichita Falls, for appellant.

R. H. Hamilton, Asst. Atty. Gen., for the State.

MORROW, P. J. Appellant was convicted for the offense of negligent homicide.

We quote the indictment, omitting the formal part:

"One J. D. Worley did then and there unlawfully operate a motor vehicle, to wit, an automobile upon a public highway of the state of Texas, to wit, a public street of the city of Graham, Young county, Tex., and did then and there while so operating said motor vehicle, willfully, and with gross negligence, collide with and injure another person, to wit, Baxter Harley, the said Baxter Harley being then and

there a pedestrian upon such highway, which said injuries did then and there result in the death of the said Baxter Harley, against the peace and dignity of the state," etc.

In Automobile Law of 1917, § 35 (article 1022a of Vernon's Ann. Penal Code Supp. 1918), we find the following:

"If any driver or operator of a motor vehicle or motorcycle upon the public highways of this state shall willfully or with gross negligence, collide with, or cause injury to any other person upon such highway, he shall be held guilty of aggravated assault, and shall be punished accordingly, unless such injuries result in death, in which event said party so offending shall be dealt with under the general law of homicide."

[1] It was not the purpose or effect of this statute to change the law of homicide, but the object was to add a new clause to the law of aggravated assault. The various elements of the law of homicide are contained in the Code:

Negligent homicide is "such as happens in the performance of a lawful act," and such as "occurs in the performance of an unlawful act." Penal Code, art. 1113.

One who, "in the performance of a lawful act, shall, by negligence and carelessness, cause the death of another, * * * is guilty of negligent homicide of the first degree." Penal Code, art. 1114.

"To constitute this offense, there must be an apparent danger of causing the death of the person killed, or some other." Penal Code, art. 1116.

"To bring the offense within the definition of homicide by negligence, either of the first or second degree, there must be no apparent intention to kill." Penal Code, art. 1119.

[2] Doubtless one, by the use of an automobile, might commit homicide of any degree, depending upon the facts in each particular case. In charging negligent homicide the particular act relied upon by the state should be set out, and it should appear from the indictment that all the elements of the offense charged exist. Among these is that declared in article 1116 that—

"To constitute this offense, there must be an apparent danger of causing the death of the person killed, or some other"; and "to bring the offense within the definition of homicide by negligence, either of the first or second degree, there must be no apparent intention to kill." Article 1119.

From these we understand that it is necessary that the state allege and prove that the danger was apparent to the accused (Talbot v. State, 58 Tex. Cr. R. 324, 125 S. W. 906), and that he, either in the commission of the unlawful act such as is described in the statute or through negligence, caused the injury. Forms coinciding with these views have been long in use. See Willson's

Crim. Forms, edition of 1806, forms 385 and 386.

[3] The indictment before us omits entirely the statutory element of apparent danger and is deficient in describing the act relied upon. Prima facie it is not unlawful to operate a motor vehicle upon a public highway. If in this instance an unlawful operation was intended, the facts making the operation unlawful should have been alleged. If it should be intended to charge that the act of operating the automobile was lawful, but performed in a negligent manner, corresponding averments should be embraced in the indictment.

For the reasons stated, the judgment of the trial court is reversed, and the cause dismissed.

FRANKLIN v. STATE. (No. 6294.)

(Court of Criminal Appeals of Texas. May 25, 1921.)

Criminal law ⊂⊃1090(1)—In absence of statement of facts, bills of exceptions, or fundamental error apparent, judgment affirmed.

A judgment of conviction must be affirmed where there is no statement of facts or bills of exceptions and the proceedings appear to be regular, and no fundamental error is apparent on the face of the record.

Appeal from District Court, Jones County; W. R. Chapman, Judge.

Jessie Franklin was convicted of theft, and appeals. Affirmed.

R. H. Hamilton, Asst. Atty. Gen., for the State.

HAWKINS, J. Conviction was for the theft of property of the value of more than $50. Punishment was fixed at confinement for four years in the penitentiary.

The record is before this court, without any statement of facts or bills of exceptions. The proceedings appear to be regular, and no fundamental error is apparent on the face of the record.

The judgment is affirmed.

CRISP v. STATE. (No. 6234.)

(Court of Criminal Appeals of Texas. May 11, 1921. Rehearing Denied June 8, 1921.)

1. Criminal law ⊂⊃1091(1)—Bills of exception not complying with rule may not be considered.

Bills of exception which do not comply with the rule may not be considered by the Court of Criminal Appeals.

2. Criminal law ⊂⊃1091(4)—Bill of exceptions to admission of evidence held not to comply with rule, and incomplete.

In a prosecution for theft of seed cotton, bill of exceptions to the admission of evidence, reciting that defendant objected to the answer of a witness to the question when he had his cotton weighed how much did he have, unless hearsay, stating that the objection was overruled by the court, and not undertaking to show what the answer of the witness was, or whether he ever answered the question at all, did not comply with the rule, and it was also incomplete in that it did not state the connection in which the question was asked, nor the relevancy of it to the issue involved in the case.

On Motion for Rehearing.

3. Criminal law ⊂⊃1090(8)—Judgment cannot be overturned for admission of hearsay testimony in absence of bill of exceptions to it.

There being legal evidence adduced on trial sufficient to sustain the conviction appealed from, the Court of Criminal Appeals would not be authorized to overturn the judgment, even though it found hearsay testimony in the record, in the absence of a bill of exceptions complaining of the court's ruling in admitting it.

4. Criminal law ⊂⊃1091(1)—Compliance with statute relative to bills of exception necessary.

Substantial compliance with Rev. St. 1911, art. 2059, relative to bills of exception, is necessary to enable the Court of Criminal Appeals to perform its reviewing function; the appellate court must in some authentic way be advised of the nature of the ruling, the character of the objection, the subject-matter to which it related, and the probable influence upon the result.

5. Larceny ⊂⊃65—Evidence held sufficient to sustain conviction of theft of seed cotton.

Evidence *held* sufficient to sustain conviction of theft of more than $50 worth of seed cotton.

Appeal from District Court, Cooke County; C. R. Pearman, Judge.

G. W. Crisp was convicted of the theft of more than $50 worth of seed cotton, and he appeals. Affirmed.

See, also, 220 S. W. 1104.

E. W. Neagle, of Sherman, for appellant. R. H. Hamilton, Asst. Atty. Gen., for the State.

HAWKINS, J. Appellant was convicted for the theft of more than $50 worth of seed cotton, and his punishment assessed at two years confinement in the penitentiary.

It is not necessary to set out the facts in this case, but they show beyond question the appellant to be guilty of the charge against him; indeed, his own confession offered in evidence admits the guilt.

[1, 2] Ten bills of exceptions appear in the

record, and we regret to state that no single one of them complies with the rule, and is in a condition where it may be considered by this court. Most of them object to the admission of testimony, and wholly fail to state what the answer of the witness was. As an illustration, we refer to bill No. 4. The witness, B. F. Rawlings, was asked, "When you had the cotton weighed at Tioga how much did you have?" The bill recites that appellant objected to the answer unless he weighed the cotton himself as it would be hearsay, and states that the objection was overruled by the court, and nowhere undertakes to show in the bill what the answer of the witness was, or whether he ever answered the question at all. The bill is also incomplete in that it does not state the connection in which the question was asked, nor the relevancy of it to the issue involved in the case. This is a fair sample of all the bills, and does not comply with any of the rules heretofore laid down by this court. In Branch's Criminal Laws of Texas, § 47, will be found a general statement that—

"A bill is defective if it fails to set out the evidence admitted, and show that the evidence was in fact not only offered but admitted in evidence before the jury."

See many cases collated under the foregoing general head.

No error appearing from the face of the record, the judgment of the trial court is affirmed.

On Motion for Rehearing.

MORROW, P. J. Conceding that the rulings of the trial court on the introduction of evidence were not properly brought forward by bill of exceptions, appellant insists that some of it so grossly offended against the rule excluding hearsay that cognizance of it should be taken in the absence of bill of exceptions.

[3, 4] There being legal evidence adduced upon the trial sufficient to sustain the conviction, we would not be authorized to overturn the judgment even though we found in the record hearsay testimony in the absence of a bill of exceptions complaining of the court's ruling in admitting it. In support of his view, appellant invokes the clause of the Constitution, which declares that one accused of crime shall be confronted with the witnesses against him. The Constitution confers upon the Court of Criminal Appeals appellate jurisdiction of all criminal cases "with such exceptions and under such regulations as may be prescribed by law." One of the regulations made by the Legislature pursuant to this constitutional provision is that which declares that—

"The defendant, by himself or counsel, may tender his bill of exceptions to any decision, opinion, order or charge of the court or other proceedings in the case." Code of Crim. Procedure, art. 744.

In preparing a bill of exceptions, no form shall be required, but the objection to the ruling or action of the court shall be stated with such circumstances, or so much of the evidence as may be necessary to explain it, and no more, and the whole as briefly as possible. Revised Statutes, art. 2059. A substantial compliance with this apparently simple provision of the statute seems obviously necessary to enable the appellate court to perform its function. The appellate court, called upon to review the action of the trial court, must, in some authentic way, be advised of the nature of the ruling, the character of the objection, the subject-matter to which it relates, and the probable influence upon the result. Bills of exceptions are designed to effect this purpose.

[5] The evidence upon which appellant's conviction rests is not hearsay. The owner of the cotton testified that he weighed and placed in his wagon a certain number of pounds. He was not certain of the accuracy of his scale. A part of the cotton was stolen, and he weighed the remainder at the gin, and found a discrepancy of 577 pounds. We do not gather from his testimony that he learned the gin weight from a ticket, but that he weighed it, and that the ginner placed the weight on the ticket which the witness had lost. The confession of appellant and his confederate and their testimony disclose that they took from the wagon of the owner six sacks of cotton and sold them to the ginner, who testified to their purchase, and he said that the cotton purchased from the appellant and his coprincipal amounted to 696 pounds.

The only controversy developed was whether the cotton which was stolen from the injured party named in the indictment was over the value of $50. The ginner paid $74 for that which he bought. It is claimed by appellant and his confederate that there were nine sacks, three of them having been stolen from another place. The value of the cotton was more than 10 cents per pound. Assuming that the appellant stole but six sacks from the wagon of the injured party, and that those elsewhere were of equal weight, the fact that that, covered by this prosecution, was not worth more than $50 is not conclusive. Aside from this view the circumstances were such as to raise an issue of fact as to whether the amount of cotton which the appellant had stolen from the owner named in the indictment exceeded in value the sum of $50. The solution of this issue against the appellant, in view of the record, we are not warranted in overturning.

The motion is overruled.

DODARO v. STATE. (No. 6282.)

(Court of Criminal Appeals of Texas. May 25, 1921.)

1. Indictment and information ⇐137(1)—Information not subject to quashal because misdesignating court.

Information for unlawfully carrying a pistol presented in the "county court at law of Wichita county" was not subject to quashal on the ground the court was designated by act of the Legislature as the "court of Wichita county at law."

2. Weapons ⇐17(6)—Court did not err in refusing to instruct where issue not raised.

In a prosecution for unlawfully carrying a pistol, the trial court did not err in refusing to instruct that defendant could not be guilty if he carried the pistol from his home to his place of business, etc., when it was not carried habitually between such places, where the issue was not raised as presented in the requested charge.

3. Criminal law ⇐829(14)—Instruction in prosecution for carrying pistol covered proper portion of requested charge.

In a prosecution for unlawfully carrying a pistol, where the court directed the jury not to consider the testimony of the state's witnesses as to what they thought with reference to the intentions of defendant on occasions when he placed the pistol against the side or breast of a witness, this sufficiently covered the proper portion of defendant's requested charge that the jury should not regard testimony of state's witnesses that defendant placed the pistol against the side or breast of one of them, and what he said in that connection, or regard the testimony of the witnesses as to what they thought of his intentions.

4. Weapons ⇐17(3) — Evidence defendant placed pistol against side of witness, and what he said, admissible.

In a prosecution for unlawfully carrying a pistol, evidence that defendant placed the pistol against the side or breast of one of the state's witnesses, and what he said in such connection, was admissible.

Appeal from Wichita County Court; Guy Rogers, Judge.

Pete Dodaro was convicted of unlawfully carrying a pistol, and he appeals. Affirmed.

Mathis & Caldwell, of Wichita Falls, for appellant.

R. H. Hamilton, Asst. Atty. Gen., for the State.

HAWKINS, J. Conviction was for unlawfully carrying a pistol. Punishment was assessed at a fine of $100.

[1] The record shows the information in the case to have been presented in the county court at law of Wichita county. Appellant filed a motion to quash because there is no such court as designated in Wichita county, but that the court was designated by the act of the Legislature as the court of Wichita county at law. The question raised has been decided against appellant in the case of Pelz v. State, 230 S. W. 154, decided April 13, 1921, and not yet [officially] reported.

[2] Appellant requested the court to instruct the jury that appellant would not be guilty if he carried the pistol from his home to his place of business, or from his place of business to his home, when same was not carried habitually between said places. The charge in question would have been a pertinent one under a correct state of facts, but an examination of the statement of facts in this case leads us to the conclusion that the issue was not raised as presented in the requested charge, and therefore the court was not in error in refusing to give the same.

[3, 4] Another charge requested by the appellant was to the effect that the jury be instructed not to regard the testimony of the state's witnesses that defendant placed a pistol against the side or breast of one of the witnesses, and what he said in that connection, and also to exclude from their consideration the testimony of the witnesses as to what they thought the intentions of appellant were at that time. We find in the court's main charge an instruction directing the jury not to consider the testimony of the state's witnesses as to what they thought with reference to the intentions of defendant on the occasion in question. This sufficiently covered that portion of the requested charge which it was proper for the court to give, and it was not error to decline to give that portion which seeks to have the jury disregard the actions of the defendant with the pistol, and what he said at the time.

It is not necessary to state the evidence in the case at length, but it was sufficient to sustain the conviction, and, finding no errors in the record, the judgment is affirmed.

⇐For other cases see same topic and KEY-NUMBER in all Key-Numbered Digests and Indexes

WITT v. STATE. (No. 6204.)

(Court of Criminal Appeals of Texas. May 25, 1921.)

Weapons ⬤=17(5)—Whether defendant was a traveler at time of carrying a pistol held for the jury.

In prosecution for unlawfully carrying a pistol, defended on the ground that defendant was a traveler at the time of his arrest, and as such entitled to carry a pistol, the question of whether defendant's journey had ceased, or had been deflected from, at the time of his arrest, *held* for the jury.

Appeal from District Court, Marion County; J. A. Ward, Judge.

A. W. Witt was convicted of unlawfully carrying a pistol, and he appeals. Reversed and remanded.

P. G. Henderson and J. H. Benefield, both of Jefferson, for appellant.

R. H. Hamilton, Asst. Atty. Gen., for the State.

MORROW, P. J. Conviction is for unlawfully carrying a pistol. The appellant was found with a pistol on his person in the city of Jefferson. He had traveled thereto in an automobile from a town in another county, some 60 miles distant, for the purpose of assembling and transporting some men to his place of residence to work on a road which was under construction. He was employed by a man by the name of Wilson, who referred him to another in Jefferson by the name of Avinger, whom Wilson had also employed. He reached Jefferson about 7 or 8 o'clock in the evening. Wilson had sent Avinger a telegram advising him to be ready to accompany the appellant with certain others to work on the road. Appellant said that after reaching Jefferson he went into a restaurant for something to eat; that he therein made inquiry for Avinger; that from there he went to a restaurant, in care of which the telegram to Avinger was directed, and there made inquiry for Avinger. Failing to find him, he walked on the street to make inquiry for him. The time thus consumed, according to his testimony, was about 15 minutes, when he was arrested.

The state's theory and testimony is that appellant had been in town for a longer time than that, and that he was under the influence of intoxicating liquor. The court, in its charge in connection with the law with reference to travelers, used the following language:

"* * * When a traveler reaches his point of destination, he cannot go about over town with his pistol on his person, either for business or pleasure, but must take it to a place of deposit, and there leave it until he is ready to resume his journey; and where a traveler, upon reaching a town, takes his pistol on his person and travels around over town for business or pleasure, he then becomes a violator of the law, as though he were not a traveler."

"If you believe from the evidence that the defendant was a traveler, then you will find him not guilty, unless you further find from the evidence, beyond a reasonable doubt, that after the defendant reached the town of Jefferson that he went about the town with his pistol on his person, in which event you will find him guilty."

"A traveler is a person who is making a journey to a distant point from his place of residence, or place of starting; but upon reaching his destination he then ceases to be a traveler, while staying at his journey's end, until he is ready to resume his journey or return."

Appellant's theory is that this charge was erroneous and upon the weight of the evidence, in that the jury should have been made to know that the appellant would have a right to stop his car in Jefferson, go to a restaurant for his supper, and to carry his pistol while he was on his journey, and that if, when found in possession of his pistol, his journey had not ended, a conviction should not result.

We are of the opinion that the charge was overrestrictive of appellant's right to have the jury determine, under all the facts before it, whether his journey had ceased or been deflected from, in the sense that it would deprive him of the benefit of the law exempting a traveler from the prohibition of the statute. Irvin v. State, 51 Tex. Cr. R. 53, 100 S. W. 779; Mays v. State, 51 Tex. Cr. R. 32, 101 S. W. 233; Price v. State, 34 Tex. Cr. R. 102, 29 S. W. 473; Brent v. State, 57 Tex. Cr. R. 411, 123 S. W. 593; Quinn v. State, 50 Tex. Cr. R. 209, 96 S. W. 33; Waterhouse v. State, 62 Tex. Cr. R. 551, 138 S. W. 386; Waterhouse v. State, 57 Tex. Cr. R. 590, 124 S. W. 633; Goodwin v. State, 55 Tex. Cr. R. 179, 115 S. W. 1184, 131 Am. St. Rep. 811; Fields v. State, 45 Tex. Cr. R. 563, 78 S. W. 932; Morris v. State, 73 Tex. Cr. R. 67, 163 S. W. 709; Waterhouse v. State, 62 Tex. Cr. R. 551, 138 S. W. 386; Ward v. State, 67 Tex. Cr. R. 604, 136 S. W. 49. Without quoting from them, the principle announced in the authorities cited is that a traveler, by the cessation of the journey on some legitimate business incidental thereto, is not, as a matter of law, a deflection or departure therefrom. Branch's Ann. Penal Code, p. 569.

For the reason stated, the judgment of the trial court is reversed, and the cause remanded.

⬤=For other cases see same topic and KEY-NUMBER in all Key-Numbered Digests and Indexes

RAY v. STATE.   (No. 6293.)

(Court of Criminal Appeals of Texas.
May 25, 1921.)

Criminal law ⟝109(3)—Appeal dismissed in
absence of compliance with law.

Where a transcript is not certified to by the
clerk and the bills of exceptions are not approved by the judge, and the statement of facts
is neither signed by the attorneys nor the judge,
an appeal must be dismissed without passing
upon the merits, under Code Cr. Proc. 1911,
art. 929; Rev. St. 1911, art. 2114.

Appeal from District Court, Wichita
County; H. F. Weldon, Judge.

Floyd Ray was convicted of rape, and appeals. Appeal dismissed.

R. H. Hamilton, Asst. Atty. Gen., for the
State.

HAWKINS, J. Appellant was convicted
for the offense of rape, and his punishment
assessed at death.

The record reaches this court in a most peculiar condition. The transcript is not certified to by the clerk; the only two bills of
exceptions shown in the record are not approved by the judge, and the statement of
facts is neither signed by the attorneys nor
the judge.

While it is unsatisfactory to the court to
dispose of a case of this magnitude without
an opportunity of passing upon the merits of
the case, yet there is nothing to be done in
this case except order a dismissal of the appeal for a failure to comply with the law;
and it is so ordered. Article 929, C. C. P.,
1911; article 2114, R. S. 1911.

Ex parte CATES.   (No. 6334.)

(Court of Criminal Appeals of Texas.   May 18,
1921.   Rehearing Granted June
9, 1921.)

1. Habeas corpus ⟝113(9)—Court without
jurisdiction where no notice of appeal in
transcript.

Where the transcript in a habeas corpus
proceeding showed the application for the
writ, the answer of the officers and the order
denying bail, but no notice of appeal, the
court had no jurisdiction.

On Motion for Rehearing.

2. Habeas corpus ⟝107—Where jury fixed
punishment of applicant at less than capital,
court erred in denying bail.

Where the verdict of the jury upon the
former trial fixed the applicant's punishment
at less than capital and testimony tending to
show a conspiracy between the applicant and

deceased's wife to kill deceased was erroneously admitted, the court cannot say that the
jury upon another trial would be likely to inflict
the death penalty, and the applicant should be
admitted to bail.

Appeal from District Court, Crosby County; W. R. Spencer, Judge.

Application for writ of habeas corpus by
Sam Cates against the State. From an order remanding relator to the custody of the
Sheriff without bail, relator appeals. Reversed, and relator
admitted to bail.

See, also, 227 S. W. 953.

Lloyd A. Wicks, of Ralls, and W. H. Bledsoe, of Lubbock, for appellant.
R. H. Hamilton, Asst. Atty. Gen., for the
State.

HAWKINS, J. The relator filed an application for a writ of habeas corpus before
Hon. Judge W. R. Spencer, judge of the Seventy-Second judicial district of Texas on
March 10, 1921. On April 28, upon a hearing under such application, relator was remanded to the custody of the sheriff without
bond.

[1] The record is before us in such a condition that we are unable to consider it. The
transcript shows only the application for
the writ, the answer of the officers, and the
order denying bail. It nowhere shows notice
of appeal, and there is nothing in the record
advising this court in any way that the order of the district judge remanding applicant without bail was unsatisfactory to him.
This is not an original writ of habeas corpus
presented to this court, and if it can be entertained it must be upon appeal from a
hearing before the district judge, and in the
absence of notice of appeal this court has
no jurisdiction.

The appeal is therefore ordered dismissed.
Ex parte C. P. Shearman et al., 230 S. W.
691, decided May 11, 1921.

On Motion for Rehearing.

This is an appeal from an order of the district judge remanding relator to the sheriff
without bail. At a previous day of the term
the appeal was dismissed because the record
disclosed no notice of appeal from the order
of the district judge.

Upon motion for rehearing we find attached a certificate of the district judge to the effect that notice of appeal was given. Therefore the motion for rehearing is granted, and
the matter will now be determined upon its
merits.

[2] The facts in the case will not be set
out in detail. The main case has been before this court heretofore, and the opinion
will be found reported in 227 S. W. 953. After the mandate in that case was issued, the
present habeas corpus proceedings were be-

gun. Sufficient facts are detailed in the opinion referred to for the purposes of this application for bail; and having in mind the verdict of the jury upon the former trial of the case, which fixed the punishment at less than capital, and the fact that certain testimony admitted upon that trial was held to have been erroneously admitted, and all of the other facts in the case being taken into consideration, we have reached the conclusion that it is a case where we would not be authorized in saying that the jury, upon another trial in the discharge of their duty, would be likely to inflict a death penalty.

Therefore the judgment of the trial court will be reversed, and the relator admitted to bail in the sum of $15,000.

FLEISCHMAN v. STATE. (No. 6230.)

(Court of Criminal Appeals of Texas. May 4, 1921. State's Rehearing Denied June 8, 1921.)

Larceny ⬥⇒7—Defendant not guilty if he took timber from barn of which he had control; "owner."

If defendant, at the time of the commission of his claimed offense of stealing timber, taken from a barn leased to him, had the care, control, and management of the barn from which the timbers were charged to have been taken, conviction could not result; defendant, the lessee of the barn, in possession, being the owner within the meaning of Pen. Code 1911, art. 1329, defining theft.

[Ed. Note.—For other definitions, see Words and Phrases, First and Second Series, Owner.]

Appeal from Smith County Court; D. R. Pendleton, Judge.

M. Fleischman was convicted of larceny, and he appeals. Judgment reversed, and cause remanded.

Bulloch, Ramey & Storey, of Tyler, for appellant.

R. H. Hamilton, Asst. Atty. Gen., for the State.

MORROW, P. J. The appellant leased from Greenberg a 40-acre tract of land with improvements. The lease was in writing, and by its terms the appellant acquired the right to use and occupy the premises during the year 1920.

The state's theory and testimony is to the effect that the appellant disconnected from the barn on the premises "five joists timbers of the value of 50 cents each, and three boxing planks of the value of 50 cents each," and that he appropriated them to his own use.

The appellant's theory and testimony is

that he purchased from Greenberg an old barn, which was also on the premises, and that the lumber, which is the subject of the controversy, is a part of the old barn. It was conceded by the prosecuting witness that the old barn had been sold to the appellant. Appellant was living upon the premises; and there were no reservations in favor of the prosecuting witness contained in the lease. It was stipulated that appellant, at his own expense, should keep in good repair the buildings and barns upon the premises. The ownership was laid in Greenberg.

The appellant requested, and the court refused, an instruction to the effect that if the appellant, at the time of the commission of the alleged offense, had the care, control, and management of the barn from which the timbers were charged to have been taken, a conviction could not result. The state concedes that a reversal should result from the refusal of this instruction. The instruction embodies a correct legal proposition, and should have been given, had it been called for by the fact. Frazier v. State, 18 Tex. App. 434. In the case before us, the property was under the care, control, and management of the appellant. This was not disputed. He had leased it for a year; he was in possession of it, entitled to the use of it, was paying rent for it, and had obligated himself to keep the buildings in repair. He was the owner within the meaning of the statute. Article 1335, prescribing the circumstances under which one may be convicted of theft by taking his own property, does not embrace the prosecution like the present one. As related to criminal prosecution, the facts appear to be novel. If a prosecution can be predicated upon them, it would seem to come under article 1348 of the Code, defining theft by bailee. See Branch's Ann. Tex. Penal Code, § 2522; Lee v. State, 81 Tex. Cr. R. 129, 193 S. W. 313.

The premises were leased or hired to the appellant. From the standpoint of the state, the pieces of timbers described in the indictment were a part of the barn, that is, a part of the realty, and were detached by the appellant, thereby becoming personal property. Conceding this, the property was still under the care, control, and management of the appellant. His possession was exclusive. If he made use of his possession to convert the property, as contended by the state, his offense, if any, would seem to come under the statute, which provides that:

"Any person having possession of personal property of another by virtue of a contract of hiring or borrowing, or other bailment, who shall, without the consent of the owner, fraudulently convert such property to his own use with intent to deprive the owner of the value of the same, shall be guilty of theft." Article 1348, Penal Code.

We, in the case of Lee v. State, supra, cited authorities and discussed in some detail the term "bailee." As the term is applied to personal and not to real property, we are not certain that, under the facts in the present case, a criminal offense was committed, conceding the testimony of the state to be true. The owner had protected himself against any depredations by taking the written obligation of the appellant to make repairs, and this obligation was a protection against losses by reason of detaching the planks from the barn. Appellant was under contract to replace them.

We are clear, however, in the opinion that the appellant is not guilty of the offense charged in the indictment, which is ordinary theft, that is, he is not guilty under article 1329 of the Code, in which theft is thus defined:

"'Theft' is the fraudulent taking of corporeal personal property belonging to another from his possession, or from the possession of some other person holding the same for him, without his consent, with intent to deprive the owner of the value of the same, and to appropriate it to the use or benefit of the person taking."

From what we have said, it follows that the judgment should be reversed, and the cause remanded; and it is so ordered.

On Motion for Rehearing.

HAWKINS, J. A motion for rehearing has been filed on behalf of the state by the honorable Brady P. Gentry, county attorney of Smith county. In connection with the motion he presents an able and ingenious argument, urging that we were in error in holding that appellant was not guilty of theft under article 1329, P. C. He insists that appellant lawfully obtained care, control, and management of the barn, but that he did not obtain lawfully the actual care, control, and management of the severed parts; that the legal care, control, management, and possession of the property ceased by his wrongful act, and that after the severance, by reason of the wrongful act in accomplishing it, the legal care, control, and management reverted to Greenberg.

We cannot agree with the contention urged, for it seems to us to confuse the ideas of legal ownership and possession. The ownership of the property never passed out of Greenberg. Under the lease contract with appellant the possession of the property passed to him, but the legal title to the property, that is, the real ownership, remained in Greenberg. The title to the severed parts of the barn was in him as completely after the severance as before. But the gist of the contention in the motion is that, when appellant by an act unauthorized by his lease contract, severed the timber from the barn, this act in itself revived the possession of Greenberg. We cannot accede to this proposition. That a party may sever from the

realty and thereby reduce it to personalty and become guilty of theft is not an open question in this state. Ex parte Willke, 34 Tex. 155; Harberger v. State, 4 Tex. App. 26, 30 Am. Rep. 157; Alvis v. State, 42 Tex. Cr. R. 424, 60 S. W. 551; Meerschat v. State, 57 S. W. 955; Farris v. State, 69 S. W. 140.

The novelty of the case is presented in the question of alleging and proving possession as required under our theft statute. Whether possession was rightful or even lawful does not always control. It has been held that where property is stolen from one who had himself acquired it by theft, ownership and possession may 'be alleged in the first thief. Looney v. State, 80 Tex. Cr. R. 317, 189 S. W. 954. The question here, to our minds, is not the question of legal ownership, but the question of possession. When Greenberg put appellant in possession of the barn and other property on the leased premises he parted with that character of possession which would permit an allegation of possession in him on a charge of theft of any of the property. If a third party had severed the timbers from the barn, and been prosecuted for theft, it would have been necessary to allege possession in the appellant. There is no question in our minds about the correctness of this proposition. The appellant, being in possession of the barn under his lease contract, was by virtue of the same lease contract in possession of the severed parts of the barn, although his act in committing the severance may have been unauthorized; and so we have a case in which it would be necessary to charge him with theft from his own possession, and, as we said in the original opinion, it is not that character of case coming within the rule as to theft of one's own property.

The motion for rehearing calls our attention to the fact that we were in error in our original opinion, wherein we stated:

"The owner had protected himself against any depredations by taking the written obligation of the appellant to make repairs."

An examination of the lease contract as it appears in the record shows that we were in error in such statement, and that portion of our original opinion will be corrected. However, this inadvertent, erroneous statement does not change the legal announcements in the opinion.

We are very clear in our minds that the former opinion makes the proper disposition of this case in holding that the prosecution could not proceed against appellant under a charge of theft in the ordinary form. In the motion for rehearing the county attorney requests that in the event we should adhere to our former holding, we announce positively and pointedly whether the offense would be theft by conversion or no offense at all. Having made, as we believe, the proper disposition of the case, any announcement along the

Ine suggested would be dicta, and it has always been the policy of this court, to avoid that wherever possible in reviewing a case. Upon investigation of the motion for rehearing the writer has become very much interested in the question presented. While the amount involved in this prosecution is small, yet a positive announcement of the law controlling would be one far-reaching in its character. We regret that no authorities have been cited for our help, and we do not feel, under the circumstances, that we should make a more decisive announcement as to our impressions as to the character of the offense, if any, than is contained in our original opinion. The close of our term is approaching, and many cases are pending where parties are confined in jails of the state. The press of business in an endeavor to dispose of those cases before adjournment has precluded us from making as thorough an investigation as we would desire to make into the legal proposition involved.

The motion for rehearing will be overruled.

BYRD v. STATE. (No. 6191.)

(Court of Criminal Appeals of Texas. May 25, 1921.)

1. **Criminal law ⟝596(2) — Showing of diligence held sufficient to justify continuance for absence of witnesses.**

In a prosecution for unlawfully selling intoxicating liquor, where a continuance because of the absence of defendant's wife, was asked, a showing that the wife had been duly subpoenaed, but was not able to appear because of illness, as certified to by a doctor, *held* sufficient as to diligence.

2. **Criminal law ⟝598(2) — Showing of diligence held insufficient to justify continuance for absence of witnesses.**

In a prosecution for unlawfully selling intoxicating liquor, where a continuance was asked for the absence of a witness, diligence did not sufficiently appear upon a mere showing that a subpoena had been asked but had not been served.

3. **Criminal law ⟝595(4)—Evidence of absent witnesses held so material as to make refusal of continuance error.**

In a prosecution for unlawfully selling intoxicating liquor, evidence of absent witnesses *held* material, so that it was error to refuse a continuance on the ground of the absence of such witnesses.

4. **Criminal law ⟝596(1)—Rule as to cumulative testimony not strictly applied to first applications for continuance.**

The rule as to cumulative testimony is not to be applied strictly to first applications for continuance.

5. **Criminal law ⟝419, 420(1)—Evidence held inadmissible, as hearsay.**

In a prosecution for unlawfully selling intoxicating liquors, evidence of a witness that he was present when the person to whom the liquor was alleged to have been sold pointed out defendant as the man who sold him the liquor *held* objectionable, as hearsay.

6. **Criminal law ⟝1056(1)—Failure to charge as to accomplices held not reversible error.**

In a prosecution for unlawfully selling intoxicating liquor, where no exception was taken to the action of the trial court in failing to charge as to accomplices, and no special charge was asked presenting such issue, such failure was not reversible error.

Appeal from District Court, Red River County; Ben H. Denton, Judge.

John Byrd was convicted of selling intoxicating liquor, in violation of the Dean Law, and he appeals. Reversed.

Prentice Wilson, of Clarksville, and B. B. Sturgeon, of Paris, for appellant.

R. H. Hamilton, Asst. Atty. Gen., for the State.

LATTIMORE, J. Appellant was convicted in the district court of Red River county of selling intoxicating liquor, in violation of what is known as the Dean Law (Acts Second Called Session, Thirty-Sixth Legislature, p. 228).

[1, 2] Appellant applied for a continuance because of the absence of his wife and Mrs. Black. Appellant's wife had been duly subpoenaed but was not able to appear at the trial because of illness, as certified to by a doctor. We are of opinion that sufficient diligence was shown as to this witness. A subpoena had been asked for Mrs. Black, who lived in Titus county, and it did not appear that said process had ever been issued or served upon her, except by the statement of appellant to that effect in his application for a continuance, and this is not sufficient. The facts must be shown. Branch's Ann. P. C. § 315.

The alleged purchaser of the intoxicating liquor was Royce Wilson, who testified that he and one Hargrove drove with appellant in a car 15 miles out from Clarksville to the home of appellant on the morning of Thursday, September 16, 1920, and there procured certain whisky, a part of which was given by appellant to Wilson in payment for his services and the use of his car in making said trip. This witness testified that they left Clarksville about 7 or 8 o'clock in the morning, and returned before noon, and that witness was arrested for his connection with said liquor before noon also. Wilson was corroborated in his story by Hargrove. Appellant denied having gone to his home on the occasion in question, with said men, and denied knowing Wilson at all. He further stated that on the morning of Thursday, September 16, 1920, he left his home, came 15 miles to Clarksville in a buggy, and there got with two men, Smiley and White, and with them went back in a car to his home to look at some cattle, reaching his place about 10 o'clock and remaining around the premises until about 2 o'clock, about which time he left and went back to Clarksville in the car with said two named men, and that he was not with Wilson or Hargrove at all during said day, or at any other time. By his wife and Mrs. Black, who is appellant's daughter, he expected to prove that he spent the night of September 15, 1920, at his said home, and on the morning of Thursday, September 16th, he went in a buggy at about 7 o'clock to Clarksville, and some 3 hours later returned home in a car with Smiley and White, and remained about the place until in the neighborhood of 2 o'clock; that no other car came to said house on said day, and that Royce Wilson was not there and did not come there in a car at all.

[3, 4] There can be no question but that this testimony was material, and in our opinion the continuance should have been granted. The evidence does not come under the head of cumulative testimony, nor is the rule as to cumulative testimony to be applied strictly to first applications for continuance. Buck Smiley, one of the witnesses as to the matters of defense above set out, admitted on cross-examination that he was under indictment himself for selling liquor, which fact made stronger appellant's need for the testimony of the two women. Diligence as to the matter of Mrs. Byrd's testimony was shown, as above stated; and while it does not appear as to Mrs. Black, still it is shown from the record that she was sick at the time of trial, and that diligence would not have availed to procure her testimony.

[5] In view of the reversal of this case made necessary by the refusal of said continuance, we further observe that the evidence of the witness McKinney, to the effect that he was present when Royce Wilson pointed out appellant as the man who sold him liquor, would be objectionable as hearsay.

[6] No exception was taken to the action of the trial court in failing to charge that Wilson was an accomplice, and no special charge was asked presenting this issue; hence the action of the trial court in failing to charge on such testimony would not be reversible error (Branch's Ann. P. C. § 716), but if excepted to, or such charge be requested and refused, error would appear.

For the error in refusing the continuance, a reversal is made necessary, and same is ordered.

PHILLIPS v. STATE.　(No. 6089.)

(Court of Criminal Appeals of Texas. Ap 6, 1921. Rehearing Granted May 4, 19⁵ State's Rehearing Denied June 8, 1921.)

1. Criminal law ☞970(7), 1032(4)—Information for theft falling to use word "fraudulently" subject to motion in arrest or objection on appeal.

Complaint and information charging misdemeanor theft without alleging that the property charged to have been stolen was "fraudulently" taken was defective in substance, and such defect may be raised by motion in arrest of judgment or in the Court of Criminal Appeals for the first time.

On the State's Motion for Rehearing.

2. Larceny ☞29—Information for theft held not to have used words equivalent to "fraudulently."

Information for misdemeanor theft alleging that defendant "did unlawfully take, steal, and carry away," etc., did not use language supplying the omission of the word "fraudulently."

Appeal from Williamson County Court; F. D. Love, Judge.

Tom Phillips was convicted of misdemeanor theft, and he appeals. Judgment reversed, and prosecution ordered dismissed.

See, also, 219 S. W. 454.

Melasky & Moody, of Taylor, for appellant. Alvin M. Owsley, Asst. Atty. Gen., for the State.

LATTIMORE, J. This conviction was for misdemeanor theft, and appellant's punishment was fixed at ten days in jail and a fine of $50.

The widow Struhall owned chickens, and on a certain night six of them disappeared from her hen house, among the number a white rooster with certain yellow feathers on his back, a dominecker hen, a white hen, and a black and two brown hens. Fresh shoe tracks were found next morning in the chicken yard along with a lot of fresh feathers. Three chicken heads and some blood and feathers were found in a nearby vacant lot. For some reason the officers were notified the morning after the loss of the chickens went to the restaurant conducted by appellant about 9 or 10 o'clock that morning and there found on his kitchen table six dressed chickens. Suspicion as to identity of the chickens as being Mrs. Struhall's, and of appellant as being their taker, led to questions as to where and how appellant got said chickens so found in his possession. He said he bought them from two little boys. Pressed for their names, he said he did not know, but later said they were named Willie and Frankie, but he did not know their surnames. He described the chickens before they were dressed as being two brown, one dominecker and some black hens, beside a white rooster with a yellow saddle. He also said he had not paid the boys, but they would be back that afternoon about 6 o'clock for their money. The officers hid across the street that afternoon, but no boys came to appellant's place. About 8 o'clock they again went to see what he had to say, and he then claimed that, though the boys had not come, a man named George had been there and demanded pay for the fowls, but that he had not paid him. The next morning the insistent officers again interviewed appellant, and he said George Kellog had been to see him again the night before and wanted him to pay for the chickens, and that Kellog lived on the Cabiness farm. The officers went out to the Cabiness place, but failed to find Kellog, and they seem to have then proceeded against appellant. The city marshal testified that he knew no boys in Granger, a town of about 1,000 people, named Willie or Frankie, and also when they got to appellant's place the chickens had already been picked and cleaned.

This is the second appeal. See 86 Tex. Cr. R. 624, 219 S. W. 454. The case was reversed at a former time because of the erroneous admission of a statement of appellant. On the instant trial certain exceptions were reserved to the court's charge, in substance that a verdict of not guilty should have been instructed; that the identity of the chickens had not been established; that appellant's explanation of his possession was reasonable, and its falsity not shown; that the material allegations of the information had not been proven. None of these appear to us to be in the nature of exceptions to the court's charge, nor are they sufficient to bring same before us for review.

Appellant asked a peremptory instruction in his favor, and also another special charge. the latter, however, appearing to be covered by the main charge of the trial court. The evidence as to the identity of the chickens is circumstantial, but we are not prepared to say that same is so wanting in weight and sufficiency as to make the verdict of the jury without support or to call for a peremptory charge in favor of appellant. The correspondence in the time of loss by Mrs. Struhall and the acquisition by appellant; the same number of chickens; the same general description by color and sex; one rooster and five hens; the expedition with which the fowls were picked and cleaned, all six of them being so treated in the early morning of one day; the Willie-Frankie story; the failure to find George Kellog; the entire failure of the evidence to account in any satisfactory manner for appellant's possession of the six chickens so closely identified and connected—all seem to us to point with sufficient clearness to appellant's connection with the taking of said chickens as to have justified the jury in their conclusion.

Having found no error in the record, the judgment of the trial court will be affirmed.

On Motion for Rehearing.

[1] By some means we overlooked appellant's motion in arrest of judgment, which is now called to our attention on this rehearing. It appears therefrom that appellant urged, in arrest of judgment, the insufficiency of the complaint and information against him herein, in that same failed to allege that the property charged to have been stolen was "fraudulently" taken. An examination of said complaint and information makes it evident that the complaint is well founded. This is a matter of substance, and not mere form, and may be raised by motion in arrest of judgment, or in this court for the first time. Baldwin v. State, 76 Tex. Cr. R. 499, 175 S. W. 701; Branch's Ann. P. C. § 2425; Vernon's P. C. p. 832.

Because of the failure of said pleadings to contain this necessary allegation, the motion for rehearing must be granted, the judgment reversed, and the prosecution ordered dismissed.

On State's Motion for Rehearing.

HAWKINS, J. At a former day of the term this case was affirmed, then later reversed and ordered dismissed because our attention, on appellant's motion for rehearing, was called to an alleged defect in the information. The state has now filed a motion for rehearing by and through Hon. H. N. Graves, who was county attorney of Williamson county when the prosecution in this case was had. The information alleges that appellant "did unlawfully take, steal, and carry away," etc., omitting, as will be seen, the word "fraudulently." It is now insisted that the allegations in the information are equivalent to the use of the latter word.

[2] It has been so long held by this court that the use of the word "fraudulently" is indispensable in charging theft under our statute it would be unwise to make a departure even if the state's contention were even more meritorious than ingenious. But we cannot agree with the proposition that the words used supply the word "fraudulently." Prim v. State, 32 Tex. 158; Conner v. State, 6 Tex. App. 455; Young v. State, 12 Tex. App. 614; Muldrew v. State, 12 Tex. App. 617; Sloan v. State, 18 Tex. App. 225; Ortis v. State, 18 Tex. App. 282; Ware v. State, 19 Tex. App. 13; Chance v. State, 27 Tex. App. 441, 11 S. W. 457; Doxey v. State (Sup.) 12 S. W. 412; Watt v. State, 61 Tex. Cr. R. 662, 136 S. W. 56; Baldwin v. State, 76 Tex. Cr. R. 499, 175 S. W. 701.

The motion for rehearing is overruled.

SOUTHERN SURETY CO. v. NALLE & CO. et al. (No. 6223.)

(Court of Civil Appeals of Texas. Austin. May 16, 1921.)

1. Constitutional law ⊜276—Statutory provision that change in plan of construction shall not affect liability on contractor's bond held unconstitutional.

Rev. St. art. 5623a, as added by Laws 1915, c. 143, § 2 (Vernon's Ann. Civ. St. Supp. 1918, art. 5623a), in so far as it provides that no change or alteration in the plans, building construction, or method of payment shall affect the liability under a contractor's bond, is unconstitutional.

2. Principal and surety ⊜100(4)—Test stated as to whether modifications affect liability under contractor's bond reserving right to modify.

In determining whether changes in the plans or construction affect the liability under a contractor's bond which referred to and made a part of its plans and specifications reserving to the owners the right to alter or modify the plans and specifications, the test is whether the changes "alter or modify the plans and specifications" of the building contracted to be erected, or do they amount to a contract for a different building?

3. Principal and surety ⊜100(4) — Change from three-story to four-story building may release surety under contractor's bond reserving right to "alter or modify plans and specifications."

In an action on a contractor's bond reserving the right to "alter or modify the plans and specifications," where it appeared that the original contract provided for a three-story hotel, but the plans were subsequently changed so as to provide for a four-story building, held, that such change constituted such a departure from the plans and specifications as to call for a different building, and therefore released the surety in the absence of ratification.

4. Principal and surety ⊜128(1)—Change in plans ratified by surety will not release him.

Where the surety under a contractor's bond consents to, or ratifies, a change in plans, its receipt of additional pay by reason of such change is proof of such ratification or of having consented to the change in advance.

5. Principal and surety ⊜161—Evidence sustaining finding that surety had received additional compensation on account of alterations in plans.

In an action on a contractor's bond, wherein it appeared that the plans, originally providing for a three-story hotel building, were modified so as to provide for a four-story building, evidence held to sustain a finding that the surety had received additional pay on account of such alterations which amounted to a ratification thereof.

6. Evidence ⊜242(2)—Statement of agent of limited authority not part of res gestæ is hearsay.

The statement of an agent of limited authority not a part of the res gestæ is hearsay and, if objected to, should not be admitted.

7. Trial ⊜105(2) — Hearsay testimony not objected to is evidence.

Hearsay testimony, if not objected to, is evidence to be considered by the court or jury for what they may deem it to be worth.

8. Trial ⊜105(2) — Failure to object to evidence of inferior grade a waiver of best evidence.

A party may waive production of the best evidence by failing to object to that of an inferior grade.

9. Evidence ⊜244(8) — Testimony by surety company's agent held competent as admission as against objection that it was hearsay.

In an action on a contractor's bond, where the defense of alterations in the plans was interposed, evidence by the architect that the general agent of defendant surety company told them defendant had received additional pay because of the alterations in the plans held admissible, since defendant was a corporation and could only speak through its agents.

Brady, J., dissenting.

Appeal from District Court, Travis County; Geo. Calhoun, Judge.

Action by Nalle & Co. and others against the Southern Surety Company. Judgment for plaintiffs, and defendant appeals. Affirmed.

Barrett, Eskridge & Barrett, of San Antonio, and Hart & Patterson, of Austin, for appellant.

Brooks, Hart & Woodward, W. A. Barlow, Samuel B. Dickens, and Fiset & Shelley, all of Austin, Mantor & Briggs, Critz, Lawhon & McNair, and S. I. Reinhardt, all of Taylor, Holloway & Holloway, of Dallas, and W. D. Caldwell, of Fort Worth, for appellees.

On Motion for Rehearing

JENKINS, J. As the Supreme Court, since our original opinion herein was written, has held that Rev. St. art. 5623a, as added by Laws 1915, c. 143, § 2 (Vernon's Ann. Civ. St. Supp. 1918, art. 5623a), is unconstitutional, we withdraw that opinion, and substitute the opinion herein for same, and also for our opinion on rehearing, which will be incorporated herein.

Findings of Fact.

On March 23, 1917, Howard Bland, T. W. Marse, and A. J. Zilker, hereinafter called the "owners," entered into a contract with John W. Hood, John W. Hood, Jr., F. J. Strassel, and F. Greenwell, composing the Capital City Building Company, hereinafter referred to as the contractors, for the erection of a three-story fireproof hotel building, on certain lots in the town of Taylor, Williamson county, in accordance with plans and specifications drawn by Henry T. Phelps, architect, for the sum of $47,825. The contractors were to provide and pay for all material and work done, and complete the building in 125 days. Payments to the amount of 85 per cent. of the work done and material placed on the ground were to be made on the 1st and 15th days of each month, as the work progressed.

Of even date with the contractor, the contractors executed to the owners a bond, in the sum of $23,912.50, with the Southern Surety Company, hereinafter referred to as the "surety company," as surety, conditioned for the faithful performance of the contract, and specially that those who furnish material for or performed labor thereon should be paid for same, and might bring suit thereon as though specially mentioned therein. F. M. Coleman, of San Antonio, was the general agent of the surety company. The contractors entered at once upon the performance of their contract.

On May 10, 1917, the owners formed a corporation, under the name of the Blazilmar Hotel Company, hereinafter called the "hotel company," and subscribed for all of the stock of said hotel company, and thereafter remained the sole owners of such stock.

On the 10th day of May, 1917, the owners conveyed the lots upon which the hotel was to be built, and the contract for building the same, to the hotel company. On August 3, 1917, the hotel company entered into a contract with the contractors wherein it was agreed that they should build a fourth story to the hotel, and receive for the walls thereof $8,211.55, with the option of the hotel company to have the same finished in accordance with the specifications for the third story; for which, if so finished, the contractors were to be paid the further sum of $8,740.45. This contract declared that it was a part of the original contract, and the work was to be done as therein provided, and the time for the completion of the building was extended 45 days.

The surety company had no knowledge of the execution of the contract for the fourth story at the time of its execution. It did, however, learn that a fourth story was being added, and received additional pay, by reason of the increased cost of the fourth story.

On or about the ———— day of ————, 1917, the contractors assigned to the surety company all funds and estimates due or to become due for work done or material furnished, or to be furnished or done in the performance of their contract; and on April 20, 1917, the contractors and the surety company notified the owners of such assignment, and that thereafter all money due on said contract

should be paid to the surety company, which was done, including work and material for the fourth story.

The contractors abandoned work on the hotel, and the same was finished by the hotel company at a loss of $1,343.69.

The following parties intervened in this cause, and there was due them by the contractors, at the time of the trial hereof, the amounts set opposite their respective names, to wit: The Blazilmar Hotel Company, $1,343.69; Nalle & Co., $5,107.25; James A. Thompson, $2,954.62; F. B. Seward, $239.13; Fairchild Lumber Company, $454.31; Prewitt Hardware Company, $345.60; Elgin Standard Brick Company, $518; J. Desco & Son, $1,499.85; Torbett & Germond Company, $410.06; C. M. Gossett, $464.33; K. J. Peterson, $48.10; Federal Glass & Paint Company, $323.15; Mosher Manufacturing Company, $350; Southern Architectural Cement Stone Company, $165; Austin Builders Supply Company, $160.95. For which sums the court rendered judgment against the contractors, in favor of said respective parties. Judgment was also rendered in favor of said parties for said respective amounts against the surety company.

The case was tried before the court without a jury. The court filed findings of fact and conclusions of law.

Opinion.

[1] On authority of Williams v. Baldwin, 228 S. W. 557, not yet officially published, we sustain appellant's assignments to the effect that the following portion of the Act of March 31, 1915, art. 5623a, is unconstitutional, to wit:

"No change or alteration in the plans, building, construction or method of payment shall in any way avoid or affect the liability on said bond, and the sureties on said bond shall be limited to such defenses only as the principal on said bond could make." R. S. art. 5623a.

The plans and specifications, which are referred to in the contract and made a part thereof, contain the following clause:

"The owners reserve the right, by conferring with the superintending architect, to alter or modify the plans and this specification in any particular, and the architect shall be at liberty to make any deviation in the construction, detail or execution without in either case invalidating or rendering void the contract, and in case any such alteration shall increase or diminish the cost of doing the work, the amount to be allowed to the contractor or owner shall be such as may be equitable and just, and be determined by the architect."

[2] It has long been customary to insert similar provisions in builder's contracts. This, in part at least, has been occasioned by the rule of strictissimi juris, adopted by courts in reference to sureties, whereby the surety was released if "any" change was

made in the contract, though the same may have been immaterial and in nowise to his detriment. By a provision in the contract similar to that above set out, the surety agrees in advance that "some" changes may be made in the contract. What changes? Not necessarily immaterial ones. They might be very material without avoiding the contract, as for instance in the cost of construction. Stocking v. Fouts (Wash.) 169 Pac. 595, in which the increase in the cost was 20 per cent., though, as said in Doyle v. Faust, 187 Mich. 108, 153 N. W. 725, "there is a * * * limit beyond which, if alterations are made, the surety will be released." The question in all such cases is: What alterations were in contemplation of the parties, as evidenced by the language used in the contract, read in the light of what changes are frequently found to be desirable during the construction of buildings?

We think the test is: Do the changes "alter or modify the plans and specifications" of the building contracted to be erected, or do they amount to a contract for a different building? As has been said: Do the changes destroy the identity of the building?

It was held in the following cases, in which the contracts provide for changes substantially as in the instant case, that the changes did not amount to a new contract, nor release the surety: Dorsey v. McGee, 30 Neb. 657, 46 N. W. 1018 (the change was an addition of a stairway, a change in the character of the hardware, and the location of the cistern); Stocking v. Fouts, supra (the change was in the interior finish); Milavetz v. Oberg, 138 Minn. 215, 164 N. W. 912 (the contract required the changes to be ordered in writing; they were ordered orally); Doyle v. Faust, supra (the change was in the partition walls, windows, and chimney). In Stocking v. Fouts, supra, the court said:

"There was no change in the outward appearance and design of the building, its size, main walls, foundations or floors."

In Doyle v. Faust, supra, it is said: "There was no change in the character or exterior dimensions of the building."

In the following cases it was held that the changes released the surety: House v. Surety Co., 21 Tex. Civ. App. 590, 54 S. W. 303 (the change was from a three to a four story building); Miller v. Ice Co., 66 Ark. 287, 50 S. W. 508 (the change was from a one-story to a two-story building); Rhodes v. Clute, 17 Utah, 137, 53 Pac. 900 (the change was from a frame to a brick building, nearly doubling the cost); Sweatt v. Bonne, 60 Wash. 18, 110 Pac. 617 (a two-story building and a cellar were added); Contracting Co. v. Hudson River Co., 192 N. Y. 209, 84 N. E. 965 (the change was from a masonry to an earth dam with a masonry core).

In House v. Surety Co., supra, the court said:

"The identity of the building was destroyed."

In Rhodes v. Clute, supra, the court said: They (the changes) were so variant, "both in price and construction, as to amount to an abandonment of the contract, and the creation of a new one."

[3] Many other cases in point might be cited, but these are sufficient to show the correctness of the test hereinbefore stated. Applying this test to the instant case, we do not think that a four-story building is a three-story building, with alterations and modifications in its plans and specifications, but that it is such a departure from the plans and specifications as to constitute it a different building.

We are confirmed in this view by the fact that under the provision for changes, as herein set out, the owner could make the same without the consent of the contractor. Does this mean that the owner could compel the contractor to erect one or more additional stories, without the contractor having any voice as to the price to be paid for same? We think not. And if not, there was a limitation contemplated as to what changes could be made. This limitation we think was changes in the building described in the plans and specifications, and not a change to different building.

[4] However, if the appellant consented to or ratified such change, it is not released. If it received additional pay by reason of such change, this is proof, either that it consented to such change in advance, or ratified the same.

[5] The court found specifically that appellant received pay, by reason of the increased cost incurred in the erection of the fourth story. This finding is binding on us, unless it is unsupported by the testimony. In support of this finding, the following facts appear of record:

F. M. Coleman was the general manager in Texas for appellant, and as such signed the bond herein sued on. He lived in the same city (San Antonio) with Hood, the contractor in charge of the work. He testified that their relations were close and confidential. He was informed by Hood of the contemplated change in the contract before the same was made. He knew of it after it was made, and never at any time objected thereto. Under the assignment of the contract to appellant, Coleman had the right to receive and disburse the payments made by the owners after the change in the contract, if he had agreed to such change; otherwise he had no such right. He did receive and disburse such payments, on the estimates of the architect, which showed upon their face that they were for a four-story building.

The architect, Phelps, testified positively that Coleman told him that appellant received additional pay by reason of the addition of the fourth story. This, according to Phelps, was not a casual remark which might not have been understood or correctly remembered by the witness, but was stated in a conversation when the building was in course of construction, and when Coleman was discussing the change from a three to a four story building, and the custom of bonding companies in such cases. Coleman was equally positive in his denial of having made such statement, and denied, as did also Hood, that such additional payment had been made. This raised an issue of fact to be decided by the court. The court decided it in favor of appellee.

Appellant contends that the statement of Coleman, that he received pay by reason of the addition of the fourth story, cannot be considered as legal evidence, for the reason that it was hearsay.

[6-8] It is true that the statement of an agent of limited authority, not a part of the res gestæ, is hearsay, and if objected to should not be admitted. It is also true that hearsay testimony, if not objected to, is evidence to be considered by the court or jury for what they may deem the same to be worth. In this, as in all other cases, the jury, or the court sitting as a jury, are the exclusive judges of the weight to be given to the evidence. Hearsay and secondary evidence are excluded, when seasonably objected to, not because they do not tend to prove the fact to which they relate, but because they presuppose the existence of better evidence. A party may, however, waive the production of the best evidence, by failing to object to that of an inferior grade. Schlemmer v. Ry. Co., 205 U. S. 9, 27 Sup. Ct. 407, 51 L. Ed. 683; Damon v. Carrol, 163 Mass. 404, 40 N. E. 185; Yeager v. Wright, 112 Ind. 230, 13 N. E. 709, 710; State v. Cranney, 30 Wash. 594, 71 Pac. 50–53; Riehl v. Evansville Foundry Ass'n, 104 Ind. 70, 3 N. E. 635; Stern v. Freeman, 4 Metc. (Ky.) 315; Langworthy v. Coleman, 18 Nev. 440, 5 Pac. 67. The same is true as to the testimony of a witness disqualified by reason of interest. Heely v. Barnes, 4 Denio (N. Y.) 73, 74; Donelson v. Taylor, 8 Pick. (Mass.) 391.

In the instant case, no objection was made to the testimony of the witness Phelps. In Henry v. Phillips, 105 Tex. 466, 151 S. W. 533, acts and declarations of Mr. Patillo, deceased, were proven without objection, which tended to show that in executing and delivering a deed to the land in controversy he did not intend thereby to convey title to the grantees. The court said:

"For this purpose it was not admissible, being hearsay evidence and in disparagement of the grantor's deed duly executed."

The fact that such testimony was hearsay added nothing to the fact stated by the court that "such incompetent testimony can never form the basis of a finding of facts." The

same result would have followed had Patillo been present and testified, without objection, that he did not intend to convey title to the grantees. Public policy will not permit a grantor to say that he had a secret mental reservation contrary to the express terms of his deed, and should he so testify, without objection, such testimony would be no basis for a verdict or judgment. This case is not authority against the proposition that hearsay is competent evidence, if not objected to, as is held by the authorities above cited.

[9] We are also of the opinion that the testimony of Phelps would have been admissible even had it been objected to, for the reason that appellant is a corporation, and can speak only through its agents. Coleman was its general agent in Texas. The statement about which Phelps testified was made while the business of which he had control for appellant, namely, the erection of the building, was being transacted. We think, under the circumstances, he was the alter ego of appellant, and that his admission was its admission.

For the reason that appellant consented to or ratified the change from a three-story to a four-story building, by receiving pay for the increased risk, the judgment of the trial court is affirmed.

Motion overruled.

KEY, C. J. I concur in the conclusions announced by Mr. Justice JENKINS in the foregoing opinion, but as I did not concur in the former holding of this court that article 5623a of the Revised Statutes is constitutional, and wrote a dissenting opinion upon that subject, that opinion is not withdrawn.

KEY, C. J. When this case was originally decided by this court, the writer had it noted that he dissented from so much of the majority opinion as held that the provision of the statute, copied in the majority opinion and regulating the liability of sureties upon a contractor's bond, is constitutional. He concurs with Mr. Justice JENKINS in holding that the motion for a rehearing should be granted, and the judgment of the court below affirmed, for the reasons stated in his opinion this day filed. This renders it unnecessary to pass upon the constitutionality of the statute referred to in the original opinion; but, inasmuch as Mr. Justice JENKINS in his opinion on motion for rehearing reiterates the holding that the statute is constitutional, I deem it proper to briefly state some of my reasons for dissenting from that view.

It is well settled by the authorities that in a controversy between citizens of the same state, if a statute is unconstitutional, it cannot, without the consent of the parties, be read into the contract, nor given any effect whatever in determining the rights of the parties; and therefore, if this statute is violative of our federal or state Constitution, then it is not to be read into nor treated as a part of the contract which the surety company entered into when it became surety for the contractors. '

With this preliminary statement, I will proceed to briefly state my views concerning the constitutionality of that statute.

It is conceded in the majority opinion that if, by enacting the statute under consideration, the Legislature meant that a surety would be bound on his bond, though the owner and the contractor should so change the contract as to destroy the identity of the building and make it essentially a different one from that contemplated by the contract, for the performance of which the surety bound himself, the act would be unconstitutional as an undue restriction on the freedom of contract. In that pronouncement I fully concur, and as we do not differ upon that subject no authorities will be cited in support of that proposition.

The majority opinion holds that such is not a proper construction of the statute, but that it was intended to apply to only such changes as are frequently found desirable during the construction of a building, and which do not change its essential character, nor make the contract as changed a radically different contract from the one on which the bondsmen became surety.

The language of the statute is as broad and comprehensive in reference to the liability of sureties as it was possible to make it. It not only declares that no change or alteration in the plans, building, construction, or method of payment shall in any way avoid or affect the liability on the bond, but it adds, "and the sureties on said bond shall be limited to such defenses only as the principals on said bond could make." In other words, if the Legislature had the power so to do, they have rendered it impossible for any one signing such bond to limit his liability to that of surety, and have, in effect, declared that he shall be a principal. The language "no change or alteration in the plans" certainly includes the addition of another story to the building, which is the change that was made in this case; and it seems to me that it is almost equivalent to judicial legislation for the courts to say that such broad and comprehensive language in the statute should be given a restricted meaning, and held not to apply to the change that was made in this case.

In holding that the particular provision of the statute regulating the liability of sureties is unconstitutional, I do not intend to declare the entire act void. That portion of the statute can be eliminated, and a valid law remain, regulating the rights of owners, contractors, materialmen, and laborers.

BRADY, J. (dissenting). The instances have been rare in which I have felt compelled to disagree with my Associates, but in this case I consider it my imperative duty to do so. Ordinarily, I should be content to merely register my formal dissent, but the decision impresses me as being so destructive of the fundamental law of agency, and such an undue regard for the findings of a trial court, as to justify me in writing at length my views.

In the original opinion, while differing upon the question of the constitutionality of the statute, this court unanimously held that there had been such a change in the contract to which appellant bound itself as surety as released it from liability. It was further held that the facts in the case did not raise any issue of estoppel in pais, and it was expressly found by this court that the finding of the trial court, to the effect that the surety received pay on the second contract, was not supported by the evidence. The case is now made to turn upon exactly opposite conclusions as to the facts in relation to the payment of a premium upon the second contract. The basis for this change in opinion is substantially the mere uncorroborated statement of an architect that he heard the general agent for appellant make the admission, about four months after the contract was consummated, that the company had been paid a premium on the supplemental contract.

My dissent is founded on practically two grounds: First, that the evidence, upon which the finding of the trial court and of this court now is based, was incompetent and insufficient to support the finding and judgment predicated thereon; secondly, that, if the evidence be regarded as competent and having any probative value whatever, the finding is so against the overwhelming weight of the evidence that it should not be permitted to stand.

The Supreme Court has set at rest all question as to the unconstitutionality of this statute, and that matter need not be further considered, although I should have liked to suggest the interpretations which, in my opinion, saved the statute from unconstitutionality. This discussion will be limited to the admissibility and competency of the evidence indicated, and its manifest insufficiency to support the finding and judgment.

Out of the multiplicity of cases on the subject, and whatever apparent conflicts there may be in the decisions, the rule is to be clearly deduced that a principal is never to be deprived of his property or rights by declarations and admissions of an agent, not made in the performance of his duties, and amounting to no more than a mere narrative of a past event. Perhaps I could not better begin the treatment of this question than by quo-ing from Greenleaf on Evidence, vol. 1, p. 133, § 200 (16th Ed.), as follows:

"With respect to all verbal admissions, it may be observed that they ought to be received with great caution. The evidence, consisting as it does in the mere repetition of oral statements, is subject to much imperfection and mistakes; the party himself either being misinformed, or not having clearly expressed his own meaning, or the witness having misunderstood him. It frequently happens, also, that the witness, by unintentionally altering a few of the expressions really used, gives an effect to the statement completely at variance with what the party actually did say."

I will now cite and quote from illustrative cases, noting by the use of italics the portions of opinions which I wish to emphasize.

The case of Parr v. Illinois Life Ins. Co., a decision by the Missouri Court of Appeals, 178 Mo. App. 155, 165 S. W. 1152, is directly in point upon the inadmissibility and incompetency of such testimony, where the declarations and admissions of the agent are made subsequent to the transaction and not as a part of the very work or business he is transacting under the authority of his principal. The distinction between such admissions by an agent in relation to a past event and those made contemporaneously with the transaction is pointed out in that case.

In Stone v. Railroad News Co., 153 Ky. 240, 244, 154 S. W. 1092-1094, liability was sought to be fixed upon the corporation by proof of statements or admissions of the general manager after the accident In the course of the opinion it was stated:

"The rule is that the declarations of an officer or agent not forming any part of his official act or act within the scope of the agency, are not admissible against the corporation to prove an antecedent fact, nor, as a general rule, is the admission of the officer or agent of a fact tending to show liability of the corporation receivable against the corporation when made subsequent to the transaction in question, and not properly a part thereof. Elliott on Evidence, vol. 1, page 878, section 255; East Tennessee Telephone Co. v. Simm's Adm'r, 99 Ky. 404 [36 S. W. 171]. Even if any portion of Schuls's evidence was competent for the purpose of impeaching Blackman, *it was not competent as substantive evidence, and cannot, therefore, be considered in determining whether or not a peremptory instruction should have gone.* Rejecting the alleged statements of Blackman, which were clearly incompetent as substantive evidence, there is not the slightest evidence tending to show that the News Company knew, or by the exercise of ordinary care could have known, of the dangerous condition of the bottles or of their liability to explode."

Further instructive cases, which time will not permit me to discuss, are the following: East Tenn. Tel. Co. v. Simms' Adm'r, 99 Ky. 404, 36 S. W. 171; Pac. Mutual Life Ins. Co. v. Walker, 67 Ark. 147, 53 S. W. 675; Davis v. Whitesides, 1 Dana (Ky.) 177, 25 Am.

Dec. 138; Wash v. Cary (Ky.) 33 S. W. 728. In the latter case the court quoted from Storey on Agency, as follows:

"The representation, declaration, and admission of the agent does not bind the principal, if it is not made at the very time of the contract, but upon another occasion. * * * *To hold a declaration or admission of an agent which was not part of the res gestæ to be equivalent to those of the principal would render the situation of every principal perilous indeed. Although such declaration or admission might be false, yet the principal would be bound by them.*"

As further authority along this line may be cited Merrow v. Goodrich, 92 Me. 393, 42 Atl. 797, 69 Am. St. Rep. 512; Noel Construction Co. v. Armored Concrete Construction Co., 120 Md. 237, 87 Atl. 1049, Ann. Cas. 1915A, 1082; Hyatt v. Leonard Storage Co., 196 Mich. 337, 162 N. W. 951; Memphis & V. R. Co. v. Cocke, 64 Miss. 713, 2 South. 495; Moore v. Chicago R. Co., 59 Miss. 243; Mowing Machine Co. v. Pearson, 64 Hun, 638, 19 N. Y. Supp. 485; Johnson v. Ins. Co., 172 N. C. 142, 90 S. E. 124; Stone v. N. W. Sleigh Co., 70 Wis. 585, 36 N. W. 248; Emerson v. Burnett, 11 Colo. App. 86, 52 Pac. 752. In the last-cited case, the declarations of a general manager were sought to be shown to bind the principal, and it was said:

"There is no rule better settled than that the declarations of an agent, to be binding upon his principal, must be made concerning the business which he is authorized to transact, and while he is engaged in its transaction. * * * *The situation is not altered by the fact that Dorr had the general management of the ranch. As a general agent he probably had authority to conduct a variety of transactions; but each one would be distinct from the other, and his declarations concerning a particular transaction could not be a part of the res gestæ, unless made while he was engaged in that identical transaction. The principle of the rule applies to all cases of agency, whether general or special.*"

Fairlie v. Hastings, 10 Ves. Jr. 123, 32 Reprint, 791, contains an excellent exposition of the rule limiting the acts and declarations of agents to matters strictly within their authority, and the dangers of admitting mere narratives of past events, concluding with this statement:

"A party is bound by his own admission; and is not permitted to contradict it. But it is impossible to say, a man is precluded from questioning or contradicting anything any person has asserted as to him, as to his conduct or his agreement, merely because that person has been an agent of his. *If any fact, material to the interest of either party, rests in the knowledge of the agent, it is to be proved by his testimony, not by his mere assertion.*"

In Merchants' Natl. Bank v. Clark, 139 N. Y. 314, 34 N. E. 910, 36 Am. St. Rep. 710, it was said:

"While evidence to show what took place at the time when the notes were offered and received for discount, in order to prove knowledge of the bank of the fact, might be proper, subsequent admissions and declarations by individual directors, or other officers, would be of no effect to bind the bank. What they may have said, not being under oath, cannot be evidence against the bank; and upon that principle, as because the statements were not made in strict relation to any agency for the bank, such evidence is inadmissible."

It was further said that an agent "has no authority to bind his principal by any statements as to bygone transactions." Still other illustrative cases are the following: Terry ·v. Birmingham Natl. Bnk., 93 Ala. 599, 9 South. 299, 30 Am. St. Rep. 87; Western Union Tel. Co. v. Way, 83 Ala. 542, 554, 4 South. 844; Clark v. Goldie, 177 Mich. 653, 144 N. W. 504, 506; Andalman v. Chicago & N. W. Ry. Co., 153 Ill. App. 169, 173; Young v. Grand Lodge of A. O. U. W., 149 Ill. App. 603, 605; Jenks v. Burr, 56 Ill. 450, 452; Pennsylvania Co. v. Kenwood Bridge Co., 170 Ill. 645, 649, 49 N. E. 215; Cleveland, C., C. & St. L. Ry. Co. v. Jenkins, 75 Ill. App. 17, 25; Taplin v. Marcy, 81 Vt. 428, 71 Atl. 72, 76; Raven Red Ash Coal Co. v. Herron, 114 Va. 103, 75 S. E. 752; Rèusch v. Roanoke Cold Storage Co., 91 Va. 534, 22 S. E. 358; Atlas Assur. Co. v. Kettles, 144 Ga. 306, 87 S. E. 1; Aiken v. Tel. Co., 5 S. C. (5 Rich.) 358, 369; Hoffman v. Metropolitan Express Co., 111 App. Div. 407, 97 N. Y. Supp. 838, 841; Flour City Natl. Bnk. v. Grover, 88 Hun, 4, 34 N. Y. Supp. 496, 498; Scovill v. Glasner, 79 Mo. 449, 455; McDermott v. Hannibal & St. J. R. Co., 73 Mo. 516, 519, 39 Am. Rep. 526; Dunnington & Co. v. Louisville & N. Ry. Co., 153 Ky. 388, 155 S. W. 750, 753; Hazelton v. Union Bank of Columbus, 32 Wis. 34, 48; Hynds v. Hays, 25 Ind. 31, 34; Memphis & C. R. Co. v. Maples, 63 Ala. 601, 609; Wicktorwitz v. Farmers' Ins. Co., 31 Or. 509, 51 Pac. 75, 77; First Natl. Bnk. of Portland v. Linn County Natl. Bnk., 30 Or. 296, 47 Pac. 614; Morgan v. Royal Ben. Society, 167 N. C. 262, 83 S. E. 479, 481; Vicksburg & Meridan R. R. v. O'Brien, 119 U. S. 99, 105, 7 Sup. Ct. 118, 30 L. Ed. 290.

In Waggoner v. Snody, 98 Tex. 512, 85 S. W. 1134, our Supreme Court recognizes the rule laid down in most of the cases cited, and it was there said:

"To render the declarations of an agent admissible against the principal, such declarations must have been made concerning an act within the scope of the authority of the agent, *and at the time that the act was being performed by the agent.* If the declarations be made before or after the act was done, it is not a part of the res gestæ, therefore not admissible."

Other Texas cases in effect recognizing the same principle are: North Am. Accident Ins. Co. v. Frazer, 112 S. W. 812; Carson v. St. Joseph Stockyards Co., 167 Mo. App. 443, 151 S. W. 752; Tex. Central R. Co. v. Dumas,

149 S. W. 543; Bullock v. Houston E. & W. T. Ry. Co., 55 S. W. 184, 185; Tex. & P. Ry. Co. v. Johnson, 90 Tex. 304, 38 S. W. 520; Galveston, H. & S. A. Ry. Co. v. Jackson, 53 S. W. 81; Paris & G. N. R. Co. v. Lackey, 171 S. W. 540.

As to the effect of incompetent testimony, as probative and substantive evidence of a fact, our Supreme Court has recently clearly laid down the rule in Henry v. Phillips, 105 Tex. 459, 151 S. W. 533:

"The testimony of the witness to the effect that after the date of the deed's execution by Patillo he listed the property for sale, and inquired often as to whether it could be sold, and of another that Patillo refused to sell him a portion of the land, but offered to sell the entire tract, was not competent testimony to prove any issue in the case. The only relevant purpose for which this testimony could have been offered was for the purpose of showing that Patillo did not execute the deed in question for the purpose of conveying the land therein described. For this purpose it was not admissible, being hearsay evidence and in disparagement of the grantor's deed duly executed. * * * While the admission of this testimony was not objected to by counsel for defendants, that fact would be important only in the event its admission was afterwards complained of as violative of a right reserved to defendants. *Such incompetent testimony can never form the basis of a finding of facts in an appellate court, notwithstanding its presence in the record without objection.* When the appellate court comes to apply the law to testimony constituting the facts of the case, *it can only base its conclusion upon such testimony as is under the law competent. That which is not competent testimony should be given no probative force.* The admission of such testimony is no talisman to give effect to that which is irrelevant and incompetent to sustain or deny a material issue in a case."

It is admitted that the statements made by Mr. Coleman to Mr. Phelps, the architect, were made at least four months after the second contract .was made and the premium paid, if at all. It is further undisputed that the circumstances of these statements were that they were made while these gentlemen and a third party were going to Medina Dam, in Bexar county, on a fishing trip. Mr. Phelps was even unable to definitely fix the month in which it occurred. The parties were in an automobile, and the conversation detailed by the witness was during the trip in the car to Medina Dam. Mr. Phelps could not even fix the place where the alleged admission occurred as to the payment of a premium for the supplemental contract, stating that it .was either on some street in San Antonio or on the road to the fishing place. While Mr. Phelps testified that the conversation related to the custom of surety companies, in charging an extra premium for additional work, and that he was clear in his recollection that Mr. Coleman made the statement that a premium was in fact paid, he fixes the time as several months after the second contract was made, and states that the declaration was volunteered by Mr. Coleman. It is not claimed that there was any argument as to whether or not the premium had been paid, or that the question was in controversy, nor even that any one was claiming that a premium had been paid, but simply was a statement volunteered by Mr. Coleman, in the course of a general conversation on the customs of surety companies. Thus manifestly it is not urged that the alleged declaration of Mr. Coleman was made as the result of deliberate thought upon the question, nor even that his attention had been directed to the fact that it was being 'claimed that the company was bound on the second contract, and that a premium had been paid therefor to the surety company. In these circumstances, I earnestly insist that, not only was the admission inadmissible, upon which absolute liability is now sought to be fixed on the principal, being made long after the event claimed, but that it was not, in any just and proper sense, made while executing any matter intrusted to him by the principal, nor in the course of his duty to his employer.

To my mind, in holding that this testimony, contradicted as it was, in effect, by that of every other witness who testified on the subject, was admissible and competent, the majority have set a dangerous precedent. If this is the law, it is extremely precarious for any person or corporation to undertake to transact business through agents, general or special. As the holding is sought to be justified upon the ground that the principal here is a corporation, and that its general agent must be regarded as the alter ego of the company, it is apparent that the decision is most interesting to all who seek to do business in corporate form. As I see it, there is no real difference, as to this question, between declarations and admissions made by the agent of a corporation and of an individual. After all, the question comes back to whether the admission was made in the scope of the agent's authority, while doing the work or about the business of his principal, and under such circumstances as made it binding upon the employer. Of course, I concede that a general agent ordinarily possesses greater powers than a special or local agent, but I can never assent to the view that declarations such as are here relied upon, made in such circumstances, can absolutely bind the principal, even though a corporation, in the absence of proof that he had authority to make the admissions. In this particular case, adverse parties were careful to show the authority of the agent, made by the vice president and secretary-treasurer of the company, under general authority of a resolution by the board. It is worthy of note, however, that they did not seek to show any authority to make such an admission, nor any custom of its agents to make such.

Believing that the testimony was inadmissible and incompetent, I am of the opinion that it cannot be looked to in support of the finding and judgment of the trial court. Our Supreme Court has so declared in Henry v. Phillips, supra, and that decision has been followed by the Courts of Civil Appeals in cases cited above. The ground of differentiation suggested in the last opinion of the court is to my mind wholly inadequate and unjustified. Mr. Justice JENKINS, in seeking to distinguish Henry v. Phillips from the instant case, has stated that public policy will not permit a grantor to say that he had a secret mental reservation contrary to the express terms of his deed; hence such a statement, even if testified to by the grantor himself, could not form the basis of a verdict or judgment. It may be replied that neither will public policy permit an agent to bind his principal by such a declaration, unless made with authority and in the line of his duty. The objection goes beyond the mere claim of hearsay; it goes to the probative value of the declaration, even if admitted to have been made. The principle recognized in the decisions is that such evidence is incompetent to prove the ultimate fact, being but a mere narrative of a past and consummated transaction, the declaration not shown to have been made with authority, as well as being the purest hearsay. It is wholly lacking in probative value, especially in that the very party who is claimed to have made the declarations was a witness in the case, and denied not only the statements imputed, but positively testified on the ultimate question of fact that no premium was ever paid. Not only has this question been decided by our own courts, but there is strong authority from other jurisdictions to the same effect. In Mima, Queen & Child v. Hepburn, 7 Cranch, 290, 3 L. Ed. 348, it was said that—

"Hearsay evidence is incompetent to establish any specific fact, which fact is in its nature susceptible of being proved by witnesses who speak from their own knowledge."

To the same effect is Hopt v. Utah, 110 U. S. 574, 4 Sup. Ct. 202, 28 L. Ed. 262; In re J. S. Appel Suit & Cloak Co. (D. C.) 198 Fed. 322; Claflin v. Ballance, 91 Ga. 411, 18 S. E. 309; Eastlick v. Southern Ry. Co., 116 Ga. 48, 42 S. E. 499; Suttles v. Sewell, 117 Ga. 214, 43 S. E. 486; State Bank v. Wooddy, 10 Ark. 638.

In the last three cases it was expressly held that the admission of hearsay evidence without objection does not render it legal and admissible testimony, and that it is of no probative value. As was quaintly said in Re Case, 214 N. Y. 199, 108 N. E. 408, "Insufficient evidence is, in the eye of the law, no evidence."

I also call attention to the following line of cases, holding that awards of Industrial

Accident Boards cannot be sustained where based upon incompetent and hearsay evidence, admitted without objection, although such boards are permitted to hear such evidence, and no objection is permitted by the statute: McCauley v. Imperial Woolen Co., 261 Pa. 312, 104 Atl. 617; Valentine v. Weaver, 191 Ky. 37, 228 S. W. 1036; Reck v. Whittlesberger, 181 Mich. 463, 148 N. W. 247, Ann. Cas. 1916C, 771; Carroll v. Knickerbocker Ice Co., 218 N. Y. 435, 113 N. E. 507, Ann. Cas. 1918B, 540.

While convinced that, upon the principles and authorities heretofore stated, the finding in question must fall, I am further fixed in the view that, upon the assumption that the evidence was admissible and competent, the finding is so in the face of the overwhelming weight of the evidence that it cannot stand. The testimony of Mr. Phelps, the architect, that Mr. Coleman had volunteered the admission that a premium had been paid, is disputed by every other witness who undertook to testify on this point. If the premium was paid, by whom was it paid? Not by Mr. Hood, the contractor, for he testified that he never paid it. The owners also testified, and they disclaimed ever having paid it, or having any knowledge of its being paid. Mr. Coleman not only denied that he ever made such a statement, but swears that no premium was collected. He had the sheets from his ledger, and the file of this transaction present at the trial, and accounted for every dollar of the account relating to this contract. It was sought to be shown that the payment for a premium on the second contract was included in certain items of amounts paid to the surety company for insurance, but Mr. Coleman unmistakably showed that the checks or drafts for these amounts did not include a premium for the bond, but embraced only the cost of "liability insurance," which included a different class of undertakings. He gave in detail the numbers of the policies, and excluded any possibility that the premium for the second contract was ever paid. Furthermore, Mr. Coleman testified that he would not have executed a second bond, nor have received a premium therefor, on his own responsibility, but would have referred the matter to the general officers of the company. His reason for this statement, which is corroborated, in effect, by Mr. Hood, the contractor, was that the possible financial troubles of Mr. Hood, arising out of some litigation in Missouri, might have made the second contract an undesirable risk.

If it be conceded that Coleman was an interested witness, there is nothing whatever in this record to indicate that Mr. Hood, the contractor, was other than disinterested, as to this question. If the premium was ever paid, he was certainly the proper person to pay it, since all the funds for the building were paid to him. He positively denied ever paying it. Besides, he states a circumstance strongly corroborating this testimony. He testified that when the question of a second or new bond was being discussed, he insisted that if one was to be given he must have an additional allowance of $250. Of this amount $149 and some odd cents was for the commission to the surety company, based on 1 per cent. of the additional cost, and the $100 for expenses to St. Louis. The reason for this additional amount was that he did not hope to have Mr. Coleman make the new bond, and that it would require a special trip to St. Louis to discuss the matter with the office there. As far as the record discloses, I have not found that this testimony is disputed, nor that any such allowance was ever made or paid to Mr. Hood, for the purpose of paying the premium, or his expenses. As stated above, his testimony is also corroborative of Mr. Coleman's contention that he would not have accepted a premium for the supplemental contract without special authority from the company.

The owners made no such claim; and there is nothing whatever in this record, outside the statement of Mr. Phelps as to the admission of Coleman, which tends to show any payment. This is not all. In one of the opinions now withdrawn, it was stated that Mr. Phelps, the architect, was a disinterested witness. Let us see if he was. The owners who testified stated that they had discussed the necessity for a new bond with Mr. Phelps, who had prepared the supplemental contract, and he had a place therein inserted for the approval of the contract by the surety company. They testified that either Mr. Phelps had convinced them that there was no necessity for a new bond, or that they had looked to him to attend to this phase of the matter, and secure a new bond, if necessary. This is the positive testimony of Mr. Zilker, one of the owners. In view of Mr. Phelps' standing as an architect, and of his dereliction of duty, upon the assumption that he had neglected this important feature of his employment, can it be justly said that he was a disinterested witness?

This statement of the evidence should be sufficient to show that the conclusion of the trial court, approved by this court, was directly opposed to the overwhelming weight of the evidence. It rests wholly on Mr. Phelps' narrative of what he heard Mr. Coleman say, and without any pretense on the part of Mr. Phelps that he had any knowledge of the premium having been paid. In my judgment, this testimony amounts in any event to no more than a mere scintilla of evidence, especially under the circumstances of the alleged admission.

The testimony shows, without dispute, that the admission, volunteered by Mr. Coleman, was made in an automobile, probably while traveling over mountain roads on a fishing trip to Medina Dam. While the parties talked, the little Ford rattled right along, and it is inconceivable that their thoughts were not to some extent upon their adventure. To any one who knows the alluring piscatorial possibilities of Medina Lake, that paradise of Texas fishermen, it seems strange to give so much force and effect to a declaration of this character, even if it were made. I am especially surprised that the Chief Justice of this court, so long and so well known over this state as an ardent, though sometime unsuccessful, disciple of Izaak Walton, should be willing to attribute the serious result he has to the mere casual remark of even a general agent, volunteered under such circumstances.

Levity aside, I earnestly insist that such declaration was casual in every proper sense. It was not made in the line of the duty of the agent, nor in the course of his employment, in relation to a pending subject. It was in reference to an already consummated contract to guarantee the performance of the contractor's obligation to do a work, which entailed an additional cost of practically twenty per cent., and, as this court has held, changed the identity of the original contract. It was made, if at all, not in the course of a discussion as to whether or not the premium was paid, but was merely volunteered; Mr. Coleman not having been apprised that any one was claiming a payment of the premium.

It is not enough to show that the general subject of the conversation was the building in course of erection, to bring the admission within the line of the agent's authority and duty. The specific subject-matter was the acceptance of a consideration for an undertaking of the company, and that was not under discussion. All such considerations as a discussion of the progress being made by Mr. Hood on the building, and whether it was satisfactory, and what were the general customs of surety companies, are all beside the question. The crux of the whole matter is: Was Coleman in this respect about the business of his employer, and following the line of his duty with regard to the very matter of the payment of a premium? If the case is to turn upon whether Coleman was the alter ego of the corporation, then that relation must be tested, not by proof as to his power to make the original contract, nor even his authority to have accepted a premium and to have bound the company on a second contract, but his authority to bind the company by a mere admission long subsequent to the time when such undertaking was assumed, and under the remarkable circumstances disclosed by the record.

I dispute some of the facts cited in the opinion to support the finding in question, as well as the effect given them. It is stated

that the relations of Mr. Coleman and Mr. Hood, the contractor, were close and confidential. I find from the record that Mr. Coleman testified, apparently without dispute, that he only knew Hood a very short time before the first contract was executed, and that he knew of him previously only by hearsay. As to the suggestion that Mr. Coleman knew of the contemplated change before and after it was made, and made no objection, this was utterly insufficient to fix any liability on the company. The agent was under no duty, indeed, had no right, to object to a new contract between the owners and the contractor. As to the circumstance that the company had received an assignment of the funds payable to the contractor under the first contract, and that Coleman had received and disbursed payments on estimates of the architect after the change, this, too, is insufficient to show, in the face of the positive testimony in this record, that the company had undertaken to become surety on the second contract. The statement of facts shows good and sufficient reasons for the making of such assignment, due to actual or probable financial difficulty of Mr. Hood, the contractor, and possible interference with and hindrance of his work from outside parties. The account was a joint control account, requiring the signatures of both Mr. Hood and Mr. Coleman before the building fund could be disbursed, and this for the reason just stated.

The fact that the estimates disclosed on their face that they included lumber and material for the fourth story is of very little, if any, weight, when it is remembered that at the time the new contract was made the building, as originally planned, was only about two-thirds completed, and the new estimates included both work under the old and the new contract. It is obvious that for the protection of the surety company's interest, Mr. Coleman might well have continued to jointly control the disposition of the funds received for the building, even though they included work under the new contract, without binding his principal to an undertaking to which it never assented, and for which it received no consideration.

It should not be necessary for me to say that I have reached the conclusion stated with regret. I am not at all unmindful of the rule requiring an appellate court to sustain the findings of a trial court upon questions of fact, where there is evidence to support them. It is not only a well-settled rule, but a very convenient one in the disposition of troublesome cases. I fear it is too often resorted to. I think I may be permitted to say that no judge has shown greater deference than myself for the conclusions of trial courts on fact questions, but surely there is a limit. There must be boundaries beyond which an appellate court may not go without practically abdicating the function of revising judgments not supported by competent evidence. It is hoped that this language is not too strong, because my respect for the opinion of my Associates is only equalled by my regard for their feelings. To sum it all up, I cannot in good conscience approve the conclusion reached. If the decision must stand, it will have to be over my earnest protest, based upon a conclusion reached only after the most mature deliberation and thought of which I am capable.

I cannot conclude this opinion without acknowledging my great obligation to able counsel for appellant, whose industry and research have made available such a wealth of authority, upon the questions discussed, and whose clear and forcible arguments have greatly assisted me.

PICKRELL et al. v. IMPERIAL PETROLEUM CO. et al. (No. 1779.)

(Court of Civil Appeals of Texas. Amarillo. April 20, 1921. Rehearing Denied June 1, 1921.)

1. Evidence ⬅️571(7)—Jury are not bound by opinion based on disputed facts.

In an action for deceit in the sale of an oil lease, the jury are not bound as to the value of the lease by the opinion of the only witness who testified to such value, where the facts on which the opinion was based were disputed.

2. Evidence ⬅️571(7)—Jury are not bound by opinion of interested witness.

In an action for deceit the jury are not bound to accept the opinion of an interested witness as to the actual value of the property sold, though no other witness expressed an opinion as to such value.

3. Trial ⬅️365(1)—Verdict must be construed in light of circumstances.

A special verdict rendered by the jury must, like many other instruments, be construed in the light of the surrounding circumstances.

4. Judgment ⬅️256(2) — Trial ⬅️365(1) — Special answer held to find value of entire lease not merely of interest in controversy; judgment erroneous as not conforming to special findings.

In an action for deceit in the sale of an undivided seven-sixteenths interest in an oil and gas lease, an answer by the jury to a special issue as to the reasonable market value of the lease and the wells at the time the contract was made by its language refers to the value of the lease as an entirety, and is not limited to the interest in controversy by the fact that the pleadings and evidence related only to such interest so that it was error to render judgment for plaintiff on the basis that the value stated was the value only of the interest in controversy.

5. Mines and minerals ⬅️74 — Purchaser of lease ratifying contract by suing for deceit is liable for interest on purchase-money notes.

Where a purchaser, who was induced by fraud to buy an oil lease in part payment for which he executed notes bearing interest at a stipulated rate, thereafter elected to ratify the contract by suing for damages for the deceit, he is liable for the interest on the purchase-money notes as well as the principal, against which he is entitled to set off the damages occasioned by the deceit.

6. Mines and minerals ⬅️74—Vendor held entitled to attorney's fee on purchase-money notes notwithstanding fraud in sale of lease.

Where a purchaser of an oil lease executed notes for a portion of the purchase price which stipulated for an attorney's fee, the vendor is entitled in an action against him for deceit in which the purchaser did not recognize the obligation of the notes to claim the attorney's fee provided for by the notes, though the purchaser recovers damages for deceit, which are to be offset against his liability for the balance of the purchase money.

7. Assignments ⬅️120—Buyer of notes pending suit thereon can prosecute suit in name of seller.

The buyer of purchase-money notes pending suit between the vendor and the purchaser can prosecute the suit in the name of the vendor without becoming a party thereto.

On Motion for Rehearing.

8. Appeal and error ⬅️1177(8)—Judgment not rendered on verdict on ambiguous issue.

Where the language of an issue submitted to the jury indicated that the jury found the value of an oil lease as an entirety, and not the value of the interest in controversy, but the trial court, which knew the arguments made upon such issue, construed it as a finding of the value of the interest in controversy, the Court of Appeals will not render a judgment on the issue as a finding of the entire value, which would preclude appellee from showing that the jury intended the contrary, but will remand the case for a new trial.

Appeal from District Court, Wichita County; Edgar Scurry, Judge.

Suit by Frank T. Pickrell and another against the Imperial Petroleum Company and others to recover damages for deceit in the sale of an oil lease. Judgment for the plaintiffs for a part only of the amount claimed, and they appeal. Reversed and remanded.

Kay, Akin & Kenley, of Wichita Falls, and McKenzie & Loose, of El Paso, for appellants.

Weeks, Morrow & Francis, of Wichita Falls, for appellees.

BOYCE, J. Appellants, Pickrell and Krupp, brought this suit against appellee Imperial Petroleum Company to recover damages for deceit in the sale by the Petroleum

Company to the plaintiffs of an undivided seven-sixteenths interest in and to a certain oil and gas lease on five acres of land in Wichita county, Tex. There were two oil-producing wells on the land at the time of the contract for sale, and the basis of the suit was alleged false representations made as to the condition and producing capacity of these wells. The jury found that certain false representations as to the condition of the wells had been made by defendants and relied upon by the plaintiffs. The language of the submission of issue No. 6 furnishes the ground of one of the principal contentions on this appeal. The issue and its answer are as follows:

"Special issue No. 6: What was the reasonable market value of the lease and the wells at the time and in the condition you find such wells to have been in at the time the contract was made? Answer: $120,000."

The appellants had agreed to pay $160,-000 for the seven-sixteenths interest in the lease, and the judgment entered by the court allowed the plaintiffs the sum of $40,-000 damages for deceit. Such other of the proceedings and facts in the record of the trial court as is necessary to an understanding of the opinion will be stated in connection with the decision of the particular points raised.

Appellants first contend that the finding of the jury as to the value of the lease is not supported by the evidence; that the trial court was bound to accept what appellants contend is the undisputed evidence, to the effect that the value of the seven-sixteenths interest in the lease sold to the plaintiffs was the sum of $21,875. This evidence consisted of the opinion of the plaintiff Pickrell, and since the exact language used in the giving of this testimony may be material in the decision of another question, discussed later, we will quote it. The witness says:

"I was familiar with the market value of oil leases as to the flush production and settled production on November 18, 1919. From my knowledge of the condition of that well up there, up to the time of the bringing of this suit, wells No. 1 and No. 2 in that lease out there, I would know the market value of that lease in the condition in which it was in on November 18, 1919. The reasonable value, market value, of that lease at that time would be not more than $45,000 or $50,000. That was the full value of the lease. The seven-sixteenths interest would be about $20,000 or $21,-000. It would be seven-sixteenths of the $45,-000 or $50,000, whichever you use was the market value. * * * From my knowledge now I do say that the interest we bought in this property was worth on the market at the time we bought it not to exceed $20,000 or $21,000."

[1, 2] There was testimony to the effect that the wells had been represented as being in good condition, with the flush oil still in them and capable of producing from 2,000 to 2,500 barrels of oil per day, and that they were shut down at the time of the making of the contract on account of lack of facilities to handle the oil. The plaintiffs' evidence tended to show: That well No. 1 was at the time of the execution of the contract "making salt water," and this increased until soon thereafter it was producing only salt water; that the casing in well No. 2 had been raised by gas pressure, and when the gas pressure was released it failed to go back to its seat by about 10 inches, and this was its condition at the time of the contract; that when the well was opened, soon after the sale, it also produced salt water. The defendant's testimony, on the other hand, tended to show that the wells were, at the time of the sale, each capable of producing from 600 to 1,100 barrels of oil per day and had produced no salt water; that the production of salt water in the wells was the result of accidents in swabbing out and putting liners in the wells after the plaintiffs took charge of them. The jury were not bound to accept Pickrell's opinion as to the value of the lease. This opinion was based on the theory that the wells were in the condition detailed by plaintiffs' witnesses, and, as we have seen, this was a matter of dispute. But, even if there were no dispute as to the facts, the opinion of an interested witness need not be accepted absolutely. Buchanan v. Bowles, 218 S. W. 652, and authorities; City of Ft. Worth v. Burgess, 191 S. W. 864.

[3, 4] It is next contended that the court erred in construing the finding of the jury in answer to the sixth special issue, quoted above, to mean that $120,000 was the value of the seven-sixteenths interest in the lease rather than the value of the entire lease, and in entering judgment on such construction of the verdict. A verdict of a jury, we take it, is, like the language of any other instrument, to be construed in the light of the surrounding circumstances (Gibson v. Dickson, 178 S. W. 48; Rushing v. Lanier, 51 Tex. Civ. App. 278, 111 S. W. 1090; G., C. & S. F. Ry. Co. v. Baker, 218 S. W. 12; Adamson Lumber Co. v. King Lumber Co., 227 S. W. 702; Crenwelge v. Ponder [Com. App.] 228 S. W. 145), and we may look to the record to determine what these circumstances were. The contract sued on provides for the sale, transfer, and assignment of "an undivided seven-sixteenths interest in and to a certain oil and gas lease" on the said five acres of land which were particularly described, "said lease being a part of a certain parcel or tract of land, * * * with field notes set out in a certain oil and gas lease duly recorded," etc. The contract further provided:

That "the proceeds from 75 per cent. of seven-sixteenths of the oil runs from the above-described leasehold estate" should be paid to the First National Bank of Wichita Falls, to be applied on the purchase price agreed to be paid for said seven-sixteenths interest; that "it is further understood and agreed that there are now two oil wells upon said above-described leasehold estate"; that the purchasers "shall take charge of said lease from and after the date hereof, * * * and that such oil as is now in storage on said lease at this time shall belong to" the Imperial Company; that the vendors "now have a certain contract and agreement with the Sinclair-Gulf Pipe Line Company, relative to the running of oil from said leasehold estate, and it is understood and agreed that the first party will transfer and assign said contract to second parties along with the leasehold estate"; that "second parties take said lease subject to a certain assignment made on the 14th day of May, 1919, by D. C. Brunson, M. G. Hickman, and A. P. Lever, trustees of the Burk-Brunson Calloway Oil Company, a joint-stock association, covering the above-described leasehold estate," and that said parties agree to carry out the obligations imposed by virtue of said assignment and comply with all the conditions "set forth in the original lease upon said property"; that "a copy of this contract, along with a valid and bona fide assignment of said oil and gas lease," shall be placed in escrow with agreement for delivery, as particularly set out.

The plaintiffs' petition begins with a statement that the defendants had entered into an executory contract with plaintiffs for the sale of "an undivided seven-sixteenths interest in and to an oil and gas lease" upon said five acres of land. The contract is then described, and the petition thereafter, in many places, refers to the transaction generally as a sale of an oil and gas lease. In the allegations of the fraudulent representations made by the defendants it is alleged, among other things:

That one of the defendants fraudulently represented "that the two alleged wells upon said oil and gas lease were good oil wells; * * * that the production of oil from seven-sixteenths of the oil and gas lease owned by defendants would pay more than all of the deferred payments; * * * that the seven-sixteenths interest of said oil and gas lease, as owned by the defendants, was actually worth more than $200,000; * * * that the plaintiffs' income would be very large from the production of said seven-sixteenths from said well; that, if they purchased said seven-sixteenths interest in said oil and gas lease, the production therefrom would net the plaintiffs, at the very lowest, $1,500 per day; * * * that defendants represented to the plaintiffs that a test of said two alleged wells on said oil and gas lease could not be made; * * * that defendants represented that said oil and gas lease and the two wells thereon to be the best in the northwest field."

There are also some references in the defendants' answer to the "seven-sixteenths interest" sold by the defendants to the plaintiff. The case was submitted on special issues, and the court prefaced the submission of the issues as to false representations by this general language:

"Did the defendant L. J. Bryan make the following representations to plaintiffs when they were negotiating for the contract?"

Issue No. 1 inquires whether it was represented "that the two alleged wells upon said oil and gas lease were good oil wells," etc. Issue No. 5 required a finding as to whether it was represented by the defendants that "said two alleged wells, 1 and 2, upon said oil and gas lease, were in good condition for immediate operation, and that they had a contract with the Sinclair Gulf Pipe Line Company whereby, commencing on December 1, 1919, to take all the oil from the said oil and gas lease," etc. We have already quoted special issue No. 6, which furnishes the ground of the controversy presented by this assignment. We have also already quoted the only direct evidence that was given as to the value of the lease, or the seven-sixteenths interest therein. The only other evidence suggested by either party that might have any bearing on this matter is the testimony of the witnesses Pickrell and Bryan, as follows: The witness Pickrell testified:

"This interest that we bought from the Imperial Petroleum Company was a working interest. There was an overriding royalty or seven-sixteenths owned by somebody else. That was owned by Burk-Bronson & Calloway. * * * As to whether I knew that we were taking over the interest of the one who was charged with the drilling of the wells, we were taking over the interest of the one who was operating the wells."

The witness Bryan testified:

"The lease is one of those regular seven-eighths working interest and one-eighth royalty interest, and they acquired seven-sixteenths in it in consideration that they operate it and drill it."

It will thus be seen that throughout the proceedings a distinction was maintained, though not with entire consistency between the oil and gas lease as an entirety and the seven-sixteenths undivided interest which was the subject of the contract. The language of the submission of issue No. 6 would, taken literally, refer to the lease as an entirety, and we do not think that the record is sufficient to warrant a holding that it should be otherwise construed. It is true that the evidence last above referred to makes it appear that the value of the seven-sixteenths interest, which was the subject of the sale, could not properly be mathematically determined from a finding of the value of the entire lease, but the witness Pickrell had figured it in that way in the presence of the jury. The fact of the impropriety of the action of the court in submitting an issue which could not properly form the basis of a judgment is not, under the circumstances, convincing that a construction opposed to the natural and literal meaning of the language should be adopted or that it was adopted by the jury. We conclude that there was error in the entry of the judgment based on this construction of the finding, and the case should be reversed for this reason. We do not think, however, that we should render judgment for the plaintiffs. The trial court evidently thought that the jury understood the finding to be as to the value of the seven-sixteenths interest. The language used under all the circumstances was likely to lead to confusion and misunderstanding. There is such uncertainty as to the meaning of the verdict that we do not feel warranted in rendering a judgment on it. Railway Co. v. Hathaway, 75 Tex. 557, 12 S. W. 999; Moore v. Moore, 67 Tex. 293, 3 S. W. 284.

As already stated, the consideration agreed to be paid for said seven-sixteenths interest in the lease was $160,000. Of this amount $30,000 was paid in cash, and the balance evidenced by nine notes, one payable on the 10th day of each successive month, beginning with the 10th day of January, 1920. The eight notes first maturing being for $15,000 each, and the last note for $10,000. The contract provided that the proceeds from 75 per cent. of seven-sixteenths of the oil runs from the lease should be paid to the First National Bank of Wichita Falls, to be credited upon said notes, until they were fully paid. The plaintiffs paid the first note, but failed to pay the other notes as they matured. The defendants, in their answer, set up these facts, and alleged that the notes had been placed in the hands of attorneys for collection, and prayed for judgment for principal, interest and attorney's fees due on said notes, according to the provisions thereof, and also for a foreclosure of lien on the seven-sixteenths interest in the oil and gas lease. The district judge applied the $40,000 damages, which he concluded under his construction of the verdict the plaintiffs were entitled to recover on their action for deceit, in satisfaction of the notes pro tanto as of the date of their execution and gave the defendants judgment for the balance due on the notes after such application with interest on such balance at the rate stipulated in the notes, but refused to allow the recovery of any attorney's fees on this amount. The judge also found that certain amounts, being 75 per cent. of the oil runs from said interest in said property, had been deposited in the First National Bank of Wichita Falls, and decreed that these amounts be paid to the defendants and credited on the judgment, and foreclosed a lien on the said interest in the oil lease and all oil produced by said interest on said lease from the date of the judgment. The fifth and sixth assignments complain that there were no pleadings that

would authorize the judgment in reference to the moneys in the bank, the proceeds of oil runs from the property, nor as to any oil that might be produced by the property pending the sale. There is no pleading of such matters, and there may be some doubt as to whether this part of the judgment was warranted. We need not decide the question as in view of such doubt the pleadings will doubtless be amended, and the question not likely to occur on another trial.

[5] Under the seventh assignment it is contended by appellant that the effect of the finding of the jury that the contract was induced by defendant's fraud, for which plaintiffs were entitled to recover damages, was to make the defendant's claim for recovery of any unpaid purchase price for said property an unliquidated and uncertain demand; that the defendants in such case were not entitled to recover on the contract, but only such amount as the jury found to be the value of the property at the date of the contract, less the payments that had been made; and that therefore defendants were not entitled to recover interest as provided in the notes, but only legal interest on the amount that might be found to be due from the date of the entry of the judgment. A similar question, though presenting the opposite contention, is raised by the appellees' cross-assignment, which complains of the refusal of the court to allow them the 10 per cent. attorney's fees on the balance that was found to be due on the notes. The fraudulent representations did not render the contract void, it was merely voidable; and the plaintiffs, by their action for damages for deceit, elected to affirm the contract. In such case the defendants were entitled to enforce plaintiffs' obligations under the contract, and the plaintiffs had a cause of action for damages for false representations, though by proper pleading there might be an offset in the same suit of the amounts found to be due on the respective claims of the parties. Allyn v. Willis, 65 Tex. 71; 12 R. C. L., 410; Pomeroy's Equity Jurisprudence (4th Ed.), § 915; Clark on Contracts, § 234; Scalf v. Tompkins 61 Tex. 481; Du Bois v. Rooney, 82 Tex. 173, 17 S. W. 528. In case of such offset the application thereof in this case should be made as of the date of the contract and the notes; and the defendants, if there were any balance unpaid on the notes, would be entitled to recover interest thereon from their date at the stipulated rate. Brown v. Montgomery, 19 Tex. Civ. App. 548, 47 S. W. 808; Tompkins v. Galveston St. Railway Co., 4 Tex. Civ. App. 1, 23 S. W. 25; King v. Bressie, 32 S. W. 729.

[6] Under the case as pleaded, we think also that the defendants would be entitled to recover attorney's fees on the balance that was found to be due after allowance of the offset. This would seem to result from the

application of the principles stated; and the authorities last above cited sustain this conclusion. We do not think there is any conflict in this holding with the case of Laning v. Iron City National Bank, 89 Tex. 601, 35 S. W. 1048, relied upon by the appellant. In that case the holder of certain notes brought a premature suit thereon and wrongfully levied an attachment on the debtor's property. The debtor reconvened in the suit and recovered damages in excess of the amount of the notes. The trial court allowed the plaintiff attorney's fees on the full amount that would be due on the notes without the offset and it was decided by the Supreme Court that—

"There was, in fact, at the time the notes fell due, nothing justly and rightfully due from the defendant to the plaintiff; for, although the unliquidated damages would not operate as an extinguishment of the notes, the claim could by law be so applied by the court."

In two of the cases we have cited there was a balance due after application of the offset and attorney's fees were allowed on this balance. If the plaintiffs, in bringing this suit, had recognized the binding obligation of the notes and offered to pay any balance that might be found to be due on them, if any, after ascertainment of the amount of their damages, a different case might be presented. In such case there might have been no necessity for the defendants to seek any affirmative relief on the notes; their task would have been a defense of the suit for damages. But the plaintiffs were insisting until just before the beginning of the introduction of the evidence upon a rescission of the contract. They had pleaded in the alternative for damages and filed their election to stand on their action for damages just before entering upon the trial. But even then they were denying liability on the notes and insist in this court, as we have stated, that they are not bound by the obligations of the contract. Under such circumstances we think the defendants would be entitled to the indemnity provided by the contract to cover the costs incurred in the enforcement of its obligations.

[7] If the Bryan Oil Corporation be a different person from the Imperial Petroleum Company, and if it did own the notes at the time of the trial, it would not be a necessary party to the suit. Having acquired the rights of the Imperial Company pending the litigation, it could prosecute the litigation in the name of said company. Evans v. Reeves, 6 Tex. Civ. App. 254, 26 S. W. 220.

For the reasons stated, the judgment will be reversed, and the cause remanded.

On Motion for Rehearing.

[8] We cannot assent to the appellants' insistence that it is our duty to render judgment here on the verdict of the jury rather than to remand the cause. While, as we have held, the literal meaning of the issue submitted was not confined to the requirement of a finding as to the value of the seven-sixteenths interest in the lease, and the court was not warranted in placing such construction on the verdict and rendering the judgment accordingly, yet the record and manner of the submission of the issue is such that it is not clear that the jury understood just what was submitted to them. The issue submitted, "What was the reasonable market value of the lease and the wells, etc.?" conceding that there was no intention to limit the finding to the seven-sixteenths interest, is ambiguous. The value of the oil lease would not be the same as the value of the wells, taking the language literally. The value of the lease would be diminished by the one-eighth royalty charge due the lessor, while the value of the wells would include both the lessor's and lessee's interest. The evidence, as we have suggested, tends to show that the interest sold to plaintiffs, being an "operating" interest, might not be of the same value as an "overriding" seven-sixteenths interest owned by the Burk-Brunson & Calloway Company. It was the duty of the court to submit only issues made by the pleading and on the answer to which judgment might be rendered. The jury, composed of reasonable men, probably knew that the court was submitting issues of fact made by the pleading, and that their answers would be the basis of the judgment. They were likely to have been confused as to the meaning of this issue, and may have concluded that the court was submitting the issue made by the pleading, and which he should have submitted; that is, the value of the interest in the lease sold to the plaintiffs. The trial court knew how he understood the question and was in position to know what meaning was given to it in the argument of the case before the jury, and we must assume was impressed with the belief that the jury attached the same meaning to the issue as did the trial court. If we should render the judgment here, we would deprive the appellees of the opportunity of showing the facts as to the argument of the case, etc., as might lead to the conclusion that it would be unjust to render judgment on a construction of the issue which was not adopted in the argument of the case to the jury. There are a number of authorities which sustain us in principle in the conclusion that we ought not, under such circumstances, render judgment here. Howeth v. Anderson, 25 Tex. 557, 573, 78 Am. Dec. 538; H. & T. C. Ry. Co. v. State, 24 Tex. Civ. App. 117, 56 S. W. 231, concluding sentence of opinion; Gose v. Coryell, 59 Tex. Civ. App. 504, 126 S. W. 1168. In Howeth v. Anderson, the Supreme Court said:

"The view we have taken of the case would lead to the rendition of judgment for the dendants upon the verdict, but, as that might eprive the plaintiff of having the case revised pon the evidence, as he might have done had he judgment been adverse to him in the court elow, and he might suffer an injustice by the ase taking a direction which he was not bound o anticipate, the judgment will be reversed ind the cause remanded for further proceedings."

So in this case, if the trial court had finally adopted the construction of the verdict insisted upon by appellants, appellees would have had an opportunity of presenting in a motion for new trial, all the facts which would make it inequitable for the court to render a judgment upon such construction and a rendition of the judgment here would deprive them of this opportunity. In the case of Moore v. Moore, 67 Tex. 293, 3 S. W. 285, where there was a controversy as to the construction of the verdict, it was said:

"It may be that the court correctly interpreted the language of the jury, or it may be that they agreed only that defendant was entitled to one half the land, and failed to agree upon the issues involving the question of title to the other half. As to the true construction of such a verdict, neither the lower court nor this court is permitted to speculate. The verdict must find all the issues made by the pleadings in language which does not admit of mistake. It should be the end, and not the continuation, of the controversy."

We adhere to our former judgment, and the motion for rehearing will be overruled.

———

PAYNE v. WHITE HOUSE LUMBER CO.
(No. 1750.)

(Court of Civil Appeals of Texas. Amarillo. May 11, 1921. Rehearing Denied June 1, 1921.)

1. **Railroads ☞5½, New, vol. 6A Key-No. Series—Substitution of federal agent under Transportation Act.**

The substitution of federal agent appointed under Transportation Act 1920 as defendant in a suit against the Director General and a railroad company, though made without the notice ordinarily required by the state practice, is sufficient where such notice is waived by an appearance by the attorneys who signed the pleadings for the Director General and represented the agent at the trial, making objection and taking bills of exceptions.

2. **Evidence ☞44—Judicial notice that Director General of Railroads was succeeded by Agent of President.**

Where suit was brought against a railroad company and the Director General of Railroads, who was thereafter, before trial of the case, dismissed and succeeded by the Agent of the President under Transportation Act 1920, the

court will take judicial notice of the fact that the latter was agent for the company prior to the trial and that the former Director General was no longer entitled to represent the government at that time.

3. **Commerce ☞89—District Court has jurisdiction of suit to recover demurrage and excess freight charges made in violation of Interstate Commerce Commission rule.**

The district court has jurisdiction of a suit to recover excessive freight charges and demurrage paid under protest, though the initial jurisdiction is with the Interstate Commerce Commission to fix and establish rules and rates; the suit being to recover charges demanded and paid in violation of the Interstate Commerce Commission's rule fixing demurrage charges and freight rates, and not to assail the rule as unreasonable.

4. **Evidence ☞489—Testimony as to what constituted market value admissible where witness testified he knew the market value.**

In an action against a railroad for damages for shortage between weights at points of shipment and destination of certain cars of coal delivered to consignee, testimony of a witness, that the market value of the coal was the price at the mines plus carriage and tax and giving the amount at each place on each shipment, was admissible where he first testified that he knew the market value.

5. **Action ☞48(3)—Causes of action for excessive freight and demurrage charges and damages for shortage of coal properly joined.**

Causes of action against a railroad for excessive freight charges, demurrage charges wrongfully exacted, and damages for shortage of coal delivered, were properly joined, since all grew out of contracts of shipment and were not ex delicto, but ex contractu, and between the same parties.

6. **Witnesses ☞255(7)—Testimony from records made by witness was admissible, though records themselves were exhibits and witness had no independent recollection of facts.**

In an action against a railroad company for damages for shortage of coal delivered to plaintiff, testimony of the manager of plaintiff's business at the place of delivery, as to the weight of two cars of coal upon their arrival, was admissible, though witness testified from his records which were attached to his deposition as an exhibit showing the weight of the two cars, where his duties were to keep correct records of such transactions, the cars were unloaded under his direction, and he weighed the coal and made the entries at the time of unloading and identified the weight sheets from which he testified as original records from his office, although he had no independent recollection of the weights.

7. **Witnesses ☞255(7)—Testimony from original sheets made by witness admissible, though book in which same kept not offered in evidence.**

Where a witness, in an action to recover from a railroad company for shortage of coal delivered to plaintiff, testified as to the weight of certain cars delivered, from certain weight sheets made by him at the time, the fact that the book in which the sheets were kept was not offered in evidence did not render them inadmissible; only the entry in the book relevant to the issue being admissible.

8. Witnesses ⚯255(7) — Testimony as to weight of cars of coal weighed and entered in books by witness at time of unloading admissible, where witness' superior testified as to correctness of entries.

In an action to recover from a railroad company for shortage of coal delivered to plaintiff, testimony of a witness as to the weight of part of two cars delivered was admissible, where the weights were entered by him in the books at the time of unloading, which was part of his duty, and plaintiff's general manager testified as to the correctness of the entries made.

9. Evidence ⚯376(1)—Testimony of witnesses as to weight of cars of coal admissible along with original scale tickets showing weights of cars and coal in pounds.

In an action against a railroad company to recover for shortage of coal delivered to plaintiff, testimony of witnesses who weighed out the cars of coal at the initial points of shipment, that in the line of their duties they kept a record of the weights of the cars when empty and loaded and that each attached the original scale tickets, which corresponded with the entries on their books, was admissible, as were the scale tickets themselves, upon which the weights, gross, tare and net, were stamped when the weighing was done; the figures on the tickets being construed to mean pounds and not tons.

10. Carriers ⚯100(1) — Though cars were bunched owing to washouts, carrier, though without fault, not entitled to demurrage for free time allowed shipper in such case.

Though cars were bunched through no fault of the carrier but owing to washouts over which it had no control, it could not collect demurrage for the free time which the rules grant the shipper under such conditions, making it impossible to get cars for loading and unloading, and which demurrage the rules also stipulate shall be refunded.

11. Appeal and error ⚯926(1)—Where court admitted evidence on issue after sustaining exception, and petition not amended, it is presumed court changed mind.

Where, in an action to recover demurrage charges paid under protest, the court admitted an expense bill to show the amount of demurrage and rendered judgment therefor after having sustained exceptions thereto, and that portion of the petition suing for demurrage was not stricken out, it will be presumed on appeal that the court changed his mind.

12. Carriers ⚯135—Where no objection to bills showing weight of car of coal delivered to consignee, no error in allowing amount stated therein.

In an action to recover for shortage of coal delivered to consignee where there was no ob-

jection to the introduction of a freight bill and expense bill showing the weight of a car of coal, the court was justified in allowing the amount therein stated.

13. Carriers ⚯134—Evidence held to support judgment for shortage in coal delivered, though there was probable chance of loss or error in ascertaining weight thereof.

Evidence *held* sufficient to support the amount of a judgment for shortage in coal delivered to consignee due to its having been shipped in open cars to save money in loading and unloading, though there was probable chance of loss or error in ascertaining the weight thereof.

Appeal from District Court, Hemphill County; W. R. Ewing, Judge.

Action by the White House Lumber Company against Walker D. Hines, Director General of Railroads, and the Panhandle & Santa Fé Railway Company, wherein John Barton Payne was substituted as defendant. Judgment for plaintiff, and defendant John Barton Payne appeals. Affirmed.

Terry, Cavin & Mills, of Galveston, and Hoover, Hoover & Willis, of Canadian, for appellant.

Sanders & Jennings, of Canadian, for appellee.

HUFF, C. J. The appellee lumber company, a corporation, originally filed its petition in the district court, December 2, 1919, against Walker D. Hines, Director General of the United States Railroad Administration, and Panhandle & Santa Fé Railway Company. It sued for damages for alleged shortage between weights at point of shipment and weights at destination of a number of cars of coal shipped from points in Colorado to its offices at White Deer, Pampa, Miami, and Canadian, Tex.; the total shortage alleged to be 21 tons, made up of several thousand pounds shortage on each of the cars named, and alleged to have been the market value of $10 per ton, or a total of $210. All of said shipments occurred during the year 1918. Also it is alleged and claimed the right to a refund of various demurrage charges paid under protest during the year 1918 on a number of different shipments of coal and lumber at destination, Canadian, Tex., alleging that the cars of said shipment were delayed in transit and delivered in such numbers as to exceed the consignee's daily rate of shipment, and also that they exceeded appellee's facilities for unloading within the free time, but for which the demurrage would not have occurred. The total amount of damage claimed was $643.25, with legal interest on same from date of collection.

It is also sought to recover for an overcharge for freight on a car of lumber from Calcasieu, La., to White Deer, Tex., in the sum of $185.22 and legal interest from date of payment of the overcharge. The latter shipment was made during December, 1917, and arrived during January, 1918. Walker D. Hines filed a plea ih abatement, based, first, upon the ground that as to the claim for demurrage and overcharge of freight such matters were fixed by rules of the Interstate Commerce Commission of the United States, and that such Commission has jurisdiction to determine the correctness thereof, and that the district court of Hemphill county did not have jurisdiction of the suit to recover the same, in the absence of a showing in plaintiff's petition that any application had been made to the Interstate Commerce Commission for relief, and further that the matter complained of in the suit occurred while the Panhandle & Santa Fé Railway Company was under the control of the United States Railway Administration, and that at the time of filing the plea, August 18, 1920, such administration was represented by John Barton Payne, Walker D. Hines having been dismissed, and that John Barton Payne should be made a party to the suit, for which reason he asked that the case be continued.

Such plea of abatement having been overruled and exceptions noted, defendant Hines then filed his original answer, in which he excepted to the plaintiff's petition on various grounds and pleaded that the Panhandle & Santa Fé Railway Company was not responsible; that the Interstate Commerce Commission had jurisdiction over the claim for freight and demurrage and that the claim should have been first presented to such Commission; that the cars being in a group arose from the act of God in the nature of an unprecedented washout of the track which caused the cars to accumulate at points without any negligence on the part of defendant; that the coal was shipped in open cars, such as would naturally permit some of it to escape therefrom; that such shipments were for the convenience of the public to save money in loading and unloading, and that the Regional Director had made a ruling that the administration would not pay for loss and damage when so shipped except in certain instances arising from fire, theft, etc. He also pleaded misjoinder of causes of action in that the freight, demurrage, and shortage of coal would require three entirely different adjudications; also, that the shortage would be due to natural causes, such as shrinkage en route. The plaintiff below, appellee here, by supplemental petition, pleaded that since the institution of this suit the President of the United States has appointed John Barton Payne as representative of all railroads under government control, to succeed Walker D. Hines, the appointment being in virtue of an act of Congress, which provided specifically that at the time of such appointment, and

by reason thereof, no pending suit should abate against any carrier originally under government control, and that it then made substitution of Payne in the place of Hines, in accordance with the provision of the act, and prays for judgment in accordance with the original petition. The court substituted Payne by an order entered of record at the same term at which such supplemental petition was filed. No citation or notice to Payne was issued, and defendant Hines excepted to the action of the court. The case was tried before the court without a jury, and the court rendered judgment against John Barton Payne as Federal Agent, for $974.59, with interest thereon from September 1, 1920. John Barton Payne filed a motion for new trial and an appeal bond and brings this case before this court for review.

[1, 2] The first, second, and third assignments of error relate to the action of the court in rendering judgment against John Barton Payne as Agent of the Railroad Administration, for the reason that he had no notice and could not be substituted as a matter of law without being cited, or having notice served upon him, and that the court erred in overruling defendant's motion that the cause be continued for the purpose of citing appellant. The record shows in this case that John Barton Payne, Agent, was substituted for Hines by the supplemental petition and order of court before entering upon the trial of the case. Hines and the railroad appear to have been dismissed by the action of the appellee in filing its supplemental petition. The same attorneys that represented Hines and the railway company represented Payne in his motion for new trial and on his appeal in this case. The case seems to have been fully developed in the trial court on the facts, and counsel representing Payne at that time or at this time show that they represented defendant in the trial court, making objections and taking bills of exception to the action of the court in its various rulings, however, signing it as attorney for Hines and the railway company, except in the motion for new trial. There is a bill of exception in the record taken by the attorneys for Hines, reciting the various facts above set out with reference to the substitution of Payne for Hines, without citation or notice, and stating that the attorneys did not appear for Payne but for Hines. However, the trial court qualifies the bill by stating that if counsel for appellant stated that they were not appearing for Payne in the trial, he did not hear it, and the judgment recites that—

"Both plaintiff and defendant appeared by attorneys, announced ready for trial, and a jury being waived, all matters of fact as well as of law were submitted to the court. The court having heard the pleading read, the evidence offered, the argument of counsel, and being advised as to the law, here renders judgment and decrees in said cause."

To reverse this case upon the assignments made would be upon a bald technicality. This court, in the case of Hines v. Collins, 227 S. W. 332, rather expressed the opinion that in the substitution of the Agent of the Government, under the Transportation Act of 1920 (41 Stat. 456), service upon him might be required. However, the case was not reversed upon that ground, but upon others; but we were then of the opinion that possibly under our practice such notice or service would be required. There seems to be a diversity of opinion among the courts, as to the meaning of that act, or, in other words, the method by which the agent should be made a party. We call especial attention to the case of Gundlach v. Railway Co. (Wis.) 179 N. W. 985, and the case of Kersten v. Hines (Mo.) 223 S. W. 586. These cases seem to hold that it would be sufficient simply to substitute Payne for Hines in the judgment without notice. However this may be, we regard the question as one of the practice for determination by the forum where the litigation is pending, and that the transition from Hines to Payne as party does not abate the suit and does not affect the rights of the complainant, but preserves his rights, and therefore any method by which Payne may be made a party, satisfying the practice in the court where the suit is pending, we presume would be sufficient to continue the litigation to final judgment in the name of Payne. In this state, while notice or citation is ordinarily required to bring in a new party, yet such notice or citation may be waived by making an appearance, and we think under the facts of this case that the court was justified in holding that the attorneys, whose names were signed to the pleadings for Hines, were in fact the attorneys representing John Barton Payne, Agent, under the Transportation Act. We take judicial notice of the fact that he was the agent for the company, some time prior to the trial of this case in the lower court, and that Hines was no longer a Director General or entitled to represent the government at that time. If Hines was dismissed from the case by the appellee in a supplemental petition, and by order of the court, it was rather a strange and anomalous procedure for him to still remain in the trial court and make a complete defense to the cause of action alleged as a party to the suit, when he was no longer a party, and that John Barton Payne should then take advantage of his bills of exceptions and his objections to the testimony and to the action of the court in rendering judgment and present the very same objections to this court for review and at the same time contend that he had not made an appearance in the trial court. To hold that the trial court was not justified in treating appellant as having appeared in the court below, would be to do so in the face of almost a conclusive presumption that he had then made his appearance, and to set aside the findings of the court in the judgment that the defendant did appear by counsel and answer would be in the face of the record. We believe the assignments should be overruled. Smith v. Smith, 123 S. W. 198; Railway Co. v. McCarty, 29 Tex. Civ. App. 616, 69 S. W. 229; York v. State, 73 Tex. 651, 11 S. W. 869; 4 C. J. pp. 1362, 1364, 1365, 1340, 1341; Morris v. Anderson, 152 S. W. 679 (6).

[3] The fourth and sixth assignments deny the jurisdiction of the district court to determine the claim with reference to demurrage and freight charges and assert that the jurisdiction is with the Interstate Commerce Commission. It is asserted that the petition on such claim involved a construction of the rules of the Interstate Commerce Commission and for that reason the district court had no jurisdiction. This is not a suit attacking the rule of the Interstate Commerce Commission fixing demurrage charges or the freight rate as being unreasonable, but is a suit to recover charges demanded and paid in violation of the rule. The petition might have been more specific, but it is apparent the rule or rate fixed by the Commission is not assailed, but it was the act of demanding and receiving demurrage and freight not authorized to be collected under the rules filed with the Interstate Commerce Commission. The initial jurisdiction, of course, is with the Commission to fix and establish rules and rates for terminal charges, or other transportation charges. The petition does not present an administrative question upon which the road's liability depends and does not involve a question of the reasonableness of a practice in interstate commerce, of which the Interstate Commerce Commission has the jurisdiction. We think in an action of this character the only question between the shipper and carrier is what was the legal right of the carrier under its rules and regulations to collect demurrage, and not what they should have been. U. S. Compiled Statutes, § 8572; Railway Co. v. Lewellen, 192 Fed. 540, 113 C. C. A. 414; Railway Co. v. Sonman Shaft Coal Co., 242 U. S. 120, 37 Sup. Ct. 46, 61 L. Ed. 188; U. S. v. Pennsylvania Ry. Co., 242 U. S. 208, 37 Sup. Ct. 95, 61 L. Ed. 251; Railway Co. v. Solum, 247 U. S. 477, 38 Sup. Ct. 550, 62 L. Ed. 1221; Gimbel v. Barrett (D. C.) 215 Fed. 1004; Railway Co. v. Rogers, 75 W. Va. 556, 84 S. E. 248.

[4] The fifth assignment is based on the admission of the testimony of R. H. Stone as to the market value of coal. The witness in effect stated the mine prices of the coal, plus the carriage and tax, was its market value at the various places of destination. The appellant contends that this was not evidence

of its market value. The witness was asked if he knew the market value, and answered, "Sure." He then stated it was the price at the mines, plus carriage and tax, giving the amount at each place on each shipment. We think there was no reversible error in admitting this evidence. Railway Co. v. Hapgood, 201 S. W. 1040; Fowler v. Davenport, 21 Tex. 635, 636.

[5] The seventh assignment urges error in refusing to sustain an exception to the petition, on the ground of misjoinder of causes of action. All three causes grew out of contracts of shipment, and are not ex delicto but ex contractu, and between the same parties. Elder v. Railway Co., 105 Tex. 628, 154 S. W. 975; Railway Co. v. Dowe, 70 Tex. 5, 7 S. W. 368; Harless v. Haile, 174 S. W. 1023(2).

We think no reversible error is shown by assignments 8 and 9. We do not believe it to be necessary to discuss these assignments, which present exceptions to the petition.

[6] The tenth assignment urges error in admitting the testimony of J. H. Ford. The witness testified to the weight of two cars of coal upon their arrival at Miami, and the difference is shown by the invoice and the weights of each car.

Assignment 11 asserts error in admitting an exhibit to Ford's deposition, purporting to show the weight of the two cars of coal. To the oral statement appellant objected that the witness was wholly dependent upon his records and that the records were attached to his deposition and were the best evidence to the exhibit to the deposition because the witness did not remember the weights; that he kept a book and sheets which were merely detached from the original books and only a part of the record, and there was no testimony that he was in the habit of keeping correct records. This witness was the manager of the business at Miami, and his duties were to keep correct records of all business transactions, such as weighing coal, keeping books, etc., and the cars were unloaded under his direction, and he weighed the coal as it was unloaded and made the entries at that time. He said he could only give the correct weight from the sheets and pages; that he examined the weight sheets attached to the interrogatories, which were original records from his office at the time he was in charge of the same. "I find those figures are correct." He had in his hands the original sheet of the weights, names of the drivers, where unloaded, etc. The sheets were in his handwriting and were made by him at the times stated in the sheet. The records, he stated, were then in his hand and "absolutely correct for the reason that I entered it at the time the weights were made and I know them to be correct." These sheets the evidence shows were on what is known as detachable sheets, which are kept in book form. The evidence shows witness, at the time his deposition was taken, was residing in Arizona. We think, although the witness stated he had no independent recollection of the weights, that upon examination of a memorandum made by him at the time the coal was weighed, that he could use the same for the purpose of refreshing his memory, and when he states they were absolutely correct he could give the weights, as shown, and there was no error in admitting that testimony. Railway Co. v. Starts, 42 Tex. Civ. App. 85, 94 S. W. 207; Railway Co. v. Blanton, 63 Tex. 109; Enc. of Evidence, vol. 14, p. 725c; 17 Cyc. p. 387, et seq. We think this testimony admissible, as he testified not only from a memorandum made by himself at the time, but also the original entry on the sheets identified by the witness.

[7] The fact that the book in which the sheets were kept was not offered in evidence did not render the sheets inadmissible. Certainly the appellant does not contend the entire book should be offered. It was only the entry in the book relevant to the issue which is admissible. This court has expressed its views on this character of evidence in the case of Schaff v. Holmes, 215 S. W. 864; Railway Co. v. Arnett, 219 S. W. 232 (1 and 2). In this case the sheets offered were the first permanent original entries and not copied which could have been offered if the books or sheets had been out of the jurisdiction of the court or possession of the party offering them. Railway Co. v. Dilworth, 95 Tex. 327, 67 S. W. 88; Enc. of Evidence, vol. 2, p. 347.

[8] The twelfth, thirteenth, and fourteenth assignments present the same objection to the testimony of the witness W. M. Craven to cars of coal weighed by him for appellee at Pampa, Tex. His testimony was as to the weight of six cars, four of which he weighed and entered himself, and part of two cars, the other part of which were weighed by Robert Coleman. As to that weighed and entered by himself the testimony was admissible for the reasons given by us in considering the tenth and eleventh assignments. As to that weighed by Coleman, the testimony shows the coal weights by Coleman were entered in the books at the time of unloading, which was part of Coleman's duty. Mr. Stone, the general manager for appellee, testified as to the correctness of the entries made and that the books were correctly kept, and we think sufficiently verified the book entries as being kept correctly to admit the entries by Coleman. Part of appellant's objection goes to the weight of the testimony, which we think, after an examination by us, did not go to its admissibility. There was no error in admitting the testimony of Mr. Cravens, and the sheets attached to his deposition.

The fifteenth, sixteenth, seventeenth, eighteenth, and nineteenth assignments are to the action of the court in admitting the testimony of the witnesses Voyles, Froelich, and Moss and sheets of original entry showing the weights of cars weighed by them and entered on such sheets in the course of their respective duties at the time and place of weighing the same. These assignments are overruled for the reasons given in our consideration of the tenth and eleventh assignments.

The twentieth assignment presents no reversible error and will be overruled without further discussion.

The twenty-second, twenty-third, and twenty-sixth assignments present no reversible error, and nothing will be gained by discussing them or giving reasons for overruling them.

[9] The twenty-first, twenty-fourth, twenty-fifth, and twenty-seventh assignments present as error the action of the court in admitting the testimony of John Lane, Howard J. Murray, and Richard Evans, who, the evidence showed, weighed out the cars of coal at the various initial points of shipment of the various cars in which a shortage is asserted. These witnesses show that in the line of their respective duties they kept books of record and weighed out the cars when empty and loaded and kept a record of the two different weights. They each attached the original scale tickets and compared the original scale tickets and entries on their books and testified they correspond. The original scale tickets are attached to their depositions. It seems to be the contention of appellant that these tickets do not show the amount of coal in each car. As illustrating:

One of the tickets shows: 129,000 gross
　　　　　　　　　　　　　　　　44,300 tare
　　　　　　　　　　　　　　　　————
　　　　　　　　　　　　　　　　847 net.

It is urged it cannot be determined whether 847 referred to tons or pounds. The court considered the remainder to be 84,700 pounds, and not tons. The difference between the gross sum, less the tare, is 84,700 pounds. Appellant seems to make the contention that the tickets ought to specify whether it was pounds or tons. If it was tons the judgment of the court has certainly given the appellant the benefit in holding it was pounds. The witnesses show this was the correct weight of the cars, gross and tare. It would, it seems to us, be imputing to the trial court a finding that there was 847 tons on the car, or that the car weighed 44,300 tons and when loaded weighed 129,000 tons, not warranted by the evidence or justified by reason. "Gross" and "tare" have well known meanings in commercial transactions and within the common meaning of the terms as understood by the average man. See Webster's definition of the terms. It is manifest the weigher only set out the thousands and hundreds, not giving the units or tens. If he had not done so, it is only a matter of subtraction and easily made. It is shown by the witness that the weights, gross and tare, were automatically stamped on the tickets when the weighing was done. The original deposition with the scale tickets attached are sent up for our inspection. The figures so stamped are dim, but can be discerned we think, and will support the trial court's judgment. At any rate, we apprehend the trial court's eyes are as good as ours. The weight of each car, giving its number, is given in the freight bills and in the expense bills, which were not objected to and introduced in evidence, and they correspond with the weights on the tickets. The tickets, together with the testimony of the witnesses, were admissible. Appellant's objections we really think only go to the weight of the evidence, and in this particular we are not able to say the trial court misinterpreted it.

[10-11] The twenty-eighth and twenty-ninth assignments are to the effect the court erred in admitting the expense bill to show the amount of demurrage and in rendering judgment for demurrage after having sustained exceptions thereto, and that thereafter there was no amendment filed. The plaintiff did not sue for overcharge on demurrage, but sued for the demurrage paid under protest, on the ground that it was not liable to pay demurrage charges. The appellant alleged that the cars were bunched, but that it was through no fault of the railroad, but owing to washouts, over which it had no control. It seems exceptions to the petition, Nos. 4 and 5, were sustained by the trial court and no amendment was filed by appellee. These exceptions appear to be to the items for freight and demurrage on the ground that they do not allege the freight of the shipment and the rate per hundred pounds, and that the allegations concerning overcharges of freight and demurrage, because the established tariff rates and rules are not set out and do not show the true rate to be charged by law. As to the demurrage there was no recovery sought or had for overcharge, but on the ground that there was collected demurrage when none was due or should have been collected. The demurrage rate is allowed for unloading after 2 days or 48 hours, free time, at the rate of $2 per day for the first five days; $5 for the sixth and each succeeding day. The rules provide when as a result of the act or neglect of the carrier cars are bunched at the original point, in transit, or at destination, and delivered by the carrier line in accumulated numbers in excess of daily shipment, the consignee shall be allowed such free time as he would have been entitled to had the cars been delivered in accordance with the daily rate of ship-

ment. No demurrage shall be collected under these rules for detention through named causes, and demurrage charges assessed or collected under such conditions shall promptly be canceled or refunded, when because of high water or snowdrift it is impossible to get cars for loading or unloading, during the prescribed free time. This provision is part of the causes named. It will be observed that appellant pleaded on account of high water and washouts the cars were bunched at destination. This being true, it was not entitled to collect demurrage for the free time which the rules granted the shipper under such conditions. This was the demurrage collected which the rules stipulated should be refunded and, as we understand the petition, was the demurrage sought to be recovered in this case. The trial court, if he understood the exception when made, evidently reconsidered his action as is manifest, by admitting the evidence as to the demurrage charges demanded and collected, and in rendering judgment for that sum. It seems the record entry was not corrected in that particular in the trial court. That portion of the petition suing for demurrage was not stricken out but is here before this court. Under such circumstances we think we are justified in holding that the trial court changed his mind with reference to the ruling on the exceptions. Texas Land & Loan Co. v. Winter, 93 Tex. 560, 57 S. W. 39; Matheson v. C. B. Live Stock Co., 198 S. W. 641, paragraph 5, and authorities cited.

[12] Assignments 31 and 32 assert there was no evidence of the weight of two certain cars at the point of shipment. The weight of one of the cars was proven by Lane. It would seem appellant has his number wrong in his assignment, and therefore his assignment and propositions are not well taken. The other car, the weight is shown by the freight bill and expense bill, and these instruments show the weight of the car of coal. In the absence of an objection to this testimony, for such purpose the trial court probably was justified in allowing the amount therein stated.

[13] The thirty-third assignment assails the judgment for damages for loss of coal. The appellant seems to think, because there may have been or was a probable chance of loss or error in ascertaining the weight of the coal lost, that the court ought not to have rendered judgment for $187.50. We believe the evidence sufficient to support the judgment of the court.

The judgment will therefore be affirmed.

On Motion for Rehearing.

It is insisted by the appellants strenuously that we erred in holding that the trial court, from the record, was justified in holding that appellant as agent for the government appeared in the trial court. We see no reason for changing our ruling on that point. After the present act of Congress took effect, Hines was appointed as agent of the government and as such represented it in this action, and upon his removal Payne was appointed. The government was represented under the last act through its then agent, Hines, and by order of the trial court Payne was substituted as his successor. We think the record sufficient to show the attorneys who represented Hines were the attorneys for the government and they continued to represent it through Payne. See Payne v. Stockton (Ark.) 229 S. W. 44.

The appellant questions our conclusion as to the effect of Stone's evidence on market value, under the fifth assignment of error. The question was asked him:

"Did that character of coal have a market value at the various places of destination, as shown there at the time it was delivered? Did it have a market value there? A. Sure. It has the market value of the mine cost plus freight. Q. Do you know what the market value was? A. Yes. I know this way that coal is something—"

The court then asked some questions. As we construe his answer to the court, the market value of the coal was the mine price and that his company was charged whatever price was in effect at the time of shipment. The witness in effect stated the coal had a market price, which was the price paid plus the freight, and when asked if he knew said, "Yes," and then proceeded to show how he knew. The answers were sufficient to permit him to give the market price. How he knew was only material as to the weight of his evidence. Because the market price happened to be the same as cost and carriage did not negative the fact that that was not the market price. This witness was an extensive dealer in the commodity at the various points of delivery, and evidently was fully acquainted with the market values. Certainly cost and carriage did not injure the appellant; there was no profit charged; that is, its value was not fixed at the selling price to the consumer. We think the court was justified in admitting the testimony of the witness as to the value of the coal lost.

The motion for rehearing will be overruled.

KURZ et al. v. SOLIZ.   (No. 6575.)

(Court of Civil Appeals of Texas.   San Antonio.   May 26, 1921.)

1. Evidence ☞575—Testimony at former trial inadmissible unless witness absent or dead.

Admission of a portion of transcript of evidence at a former trial of the cause setting out the testimony of a witness was error, where it was not shown the witness was absent from the state or was dead.

2. Appeal and error ☞1051(2)—Admission of evidence harmless where uncontradicted evidence established same fact.

Testimony of witness at a former trial placing the value of appellee's land at $60 an acre, even if error because of absence of showing that the witness was absent from the state or dead, was not injurious to appellant, where the uncontradicted evidence of another witness fixed the value at $30 an acre, and the jury found the value to be $20 an acre.

3. Champerty and maintenance ☞5(8)—Violation of law by attorney does not prevent suitor's recovery.

Under Pen. Code 1911, art. 421, as to barratry, a suitor is not barred from recovery because his attorney had violated the law in obtaining the employment.

4. Vendor and purchaser ☞240—Innocent purchase must be pleaded.

Innocent purchase, for proof thereof to be available, must be pleaded.

Appeal from District Court, Atascosa County; Covey C. Thomas, Judge.

Action by Marcelina Soliz against A. A. Kurz and others.   From judgment for plaintiff, defendants appeal.   Affirmed.

Clamp, Searcy & Clamp, of San Antonio, and Frank H. Burmeister, of Jourdanton, for appellants.

Walter E. Jones, J. R. Garnand, and R. R. Smith, all of Jourdanton, for appellee.

FLY, C. J.   This is a suit instituted by appellee against A. A. Kurz and his wife, Lizzie Kurz, G. W. Kurz and H. J. Ulbrich, for the purpose of annulling and setting aside a certain deed of conveyance to 100.1 acres of land in Atascosa county, being survey No. 79½ on the waters of Palo Alto creek, northwest of Pleasanton, which deed it was alleged was secured from appellee through the fraudulent representations of A. A. Kurz and G. W. Kurz, as to $300 being due as taxes on the land, for which it would be sold.   It was also alleged that a portion of the land had been sold by the Kurz to H. J. Ulbrich, who was an innocent purchaser.   The prayer was that appellee have judgment against A. A. Kurz, Lizzie Kurz, and G. W.

Kurz "for the value of the land, and the interest, less $700 paid to plaintiff and $37.86 taxes paid by defendants Kurz in land so sold to said Ulbrich; that the deed which she executed by reason of the fraudulent acts of defendants A. A. Kurz and G. W. Kurz be canceled in so far as the land not sold to said H. J. Ulbrich is concerned; that the title to all the land except the 51.64 acres of land sold to said H. J. Ulbrich be divested out of the defendants A. A. Kurz, G. W. Kurz, and Lizzie Kurz and vested in plaintiff, and that the said entire tract of land be partitioned among and between plaintiff and defendant H. J. Ulbrich; that a writ of partition issue; that she be placed in possession of that portion of said land that may be set aside to her in the partition thereof; for all costs of suit; and for such other and further relief, general and special, in law and in equity, to which she may be entitled."   The cause was submitted to a jury on four special issues, to which they answered that execution of the deed was procured from appellee by representations upon the part of A. A. Kurz that there were due on the land of appellee delinquent taxes in the sum of $300, for which the land was about to be sold, and that the land at the time the deed was executed had a reasonable market value of $20 an acre.   Upon that verdict judgment was rendered that appellee recover the 100.1 acres of land from appellants, except the 51.64 acres of land sold to H. J. Ulbrich, that appellee recover of A. A. Kurz and G. W. Kurz $1,037.80, the value of the 51.64 acres, less $737.86, the amount paid out by Kurz on the land, and that they be divested of all right, title, and interest in the land, and that H. J. Ulbrich be dismissed from the cause with his costs.

That the evidence was sufficient to show that the deed to the land was procured through the fraudulent representations of A. A. Kurz as to delinquent taxes and the imminence of a sale of the land for the taxes is not questioned by the three assignments, and we conclude that the findings of the jury are amply supported by the facts.

[1, 2] The first assignment of error complains of the introduction in evidence "of that portion of the transcript of the evidence taken at a former trial of said cause, wherein is set out the testimony of H. E. Dixon, a witness for the plaintiff."   The testimony should not have been admitted in the absence of proof that the witness was absent from the state or was dead.   Under the ruling in Boyd v. Railway Co., 101 Tex. 411, 108 S. W. 813, we feel inclined to hold that the evidence was sufficient to show that the witness was absent from the state, and that his testimony, which was as to the market value of the land, was admissible, but, if

the evidence was not admissible, appellants could not have been injured by it, for it was proved by the uncontradicted evidence of L. Morgan Williams that at the time appellee executed the deed to appellants, during the spring of 1919, the land had a reasonable market value of $30 an acre. The witness Dixon placed its value at $60 an acre. Williams was the county clerk of Atascosa county, and the jury seems to have been guided more by his testimony in finding the land was worth $20 an acre. Appellants do not assail the evidence of Williams, and failed to contradict it in any manner. .

[3] The answer of appellants presents no affirmative defense to appellee's claim, except that appellee understood the consideration for her land, and that she received full value for the land, and yet through the second assignment of error it is sought to present in this court the defense that the undisputed evidence shows that the suit "is a manufactured lawsuit." The assignment is:

"Because the undisputed evidence discloses that this suit was not instituted by the plaintiff, Marcelina Soliz, but was caused to be brought by one Roger Watson, acting in conjunction with one Erenie Rodriguez, and is a manufactured lawsuit."

That language it is said will be treated as a proposition, although what is proposed does not appear from it. It is not attempted to be indicated what should be done, "because the undisputed evidence discloses" the matters and things set forth therein, and nowhere in the brief does it appear what should happen, "because the undisputed evidence discloses" the things alleged. Suppose Roger Watson did cause appellee to institute the suit, and acted in conjunction "with one Erenie Rodriguez"; how should that fact cause a reversal of the judgment herein? And how does the fact that the two individuals acted in conjunction in causing the suit to be brought make it "a manufactured lawsuit"? Evidently the jury and trial judge differed with the opinion of appellants that it was "a manufactured suit" after a full investigation of all the testimony offered by the parties. It might be surmised that appellants were endeavoring to invoke the penalty of a violation of the law of barratry as defined in article 421 of the Penal Code of Texas, because that article is cited. That article could not affect the right of appellee to recover, and appellants made no claim that the suit was not brought in good faith, unless the assignment herein copied can be manipulated into such claim. The evidence does not sustain any such claim. However criminal Watson may have been, appellee and her grandson, Erenie Rodriguez, were not shown to have violated any law in connection with the suit. The case

of Ford v. Munroe, 144 S. W. 349, does not support any claim that appellee had "manufactured" a case. That was a case in which an attorney had contracted with one not an attorney to give the latter a part of a fee to be obtained from a third person who was induced by the layman to employ the attorney. It does not hold that the third person could not recover because his attorney had violated the law in obtaining the employment.

[4] The evidence showed that A. A. Kurz was the agent of G. W. Kurz in purchasing the land from appellee, but, if he was not such agent, appellants, not having alleged or proved that G. W. Kurz was an innocent purchaser for value without notice, have nothing upon which to base a claim in this court that he was an innocent purchaser. Even though the proof should show that G. W. Kurz was an innocent purchaser, it would profit him nothing, because he did not plead that he was an innocent purchaser. Freeman v. McAninch, 87 Tex. 132, 27 S. W. 97, 47 Am. St. Rep. 79; Railway v. Harris, 95 Tex. 346, 67 S. W. 315.

The judgment is affirmed.

HUBB-DIGGS CO. v. MITCHELL.
(No. 6367.)

(Court of Civil Appeals of Texas. Austin. May 4, 1921. Rehearing Denied June 1, 1921.)

1. **Monopolies** ⬤⟹17(1)—Contract held to fix price in violation of anti-trust laws.

A contract between wholesale and retail dealers, providing that retailer shall sell tractor at price fixed by manufacturer for sale to retail trade, and requiring wholesaler to reimburse retailer for any decrease in the retail price of tractors, *held* an agreement to fix and maintain price for the sale of a commodity, in violation of Rev. St. 1911, art. 7796, subds. 2, 4, 5.

2. **Pleading** ⬤⟹214(1)—Facts alleged in petition admitted by general demurrer.

Facts stated in petition are admitted by general demurrer.

3. **Judgment** ⬤⟹145(4) — Answer to petition alleging illegal contract held to present a meritorious defense on motion to set aside default.

In retail dealer's action against wholesale dealer to recover reduction in price of tractors, in which it was alleged that retailer had agreed to sell tractors at market price, and that wholesaler had agreed to reimburse retailer on reduction thereof, answer, denying that wholesaler had agreed with retailer as to fixing the price and as to reimbursement of retailer by wholesaler on decline in prices, and alleging that the market value of the tractors was at all times the market price at time of sale to retailer, and that there was no loss or damage to retailer because his reduction of price was voluntary, *held* to present a meritorious defense, on motion to set aside default judgment and for a new trial, as against contention that the agreement alleged in petition was illegal, and that court should not aid party to illegal agreements who has suffered default to go against him.

4. Appeal and error ⟐957(1)—Judgment ⟐ 139—Discretion in setting aside of judgments cannot be arbitrarily exercised.

The discretion enjoined by the court in the matter of setting aside default judgments is not an arbitrary discretion, and is subject to such review, where manifest injustice has been done.

5. Judgment ⟐143(3) — Default entered against corporation set aside, where neither officers nor attorneys of corporation had actual knowledge of service of citation until after judgments.

Where return day stated in citation issued and served upon defendant corporation was incorrect, and where another citation giving the correct return date was served upon the corporation, but where neither the officers of the corporation nor its attorneys to whom such citation had been referred had actual knowledge of the service of the second citation until after default judgment was taken, the default will be set aside; there being an equitable excuse for the failure to appear and answer.

Appeal from Coleman County Court; L. G. Matthews, Judge.

Suit by W. I. Mitchell against Hubb-Diggs Company. Default judgment was rendered for plaintiff, and from an order overruling defendant's motion for a new trial, defendant appeals. Reversed and remanded.

McLean, Scott & McLean, of Fort Worth, and Snodgrass, Dibrell & Snodgrass, of Coleman, for appellant.

Critz & Woodward, of Coleman, for appellee.

BRADY, J. Appellee sued appellant, a corporation, in the county court of Coleman county, for damages for breach of contract, in the sum of $969.50. The petition was filed April 7, 1920, and on the same day a citation was issued and duly served upon appellant, commanding it to appear "on the first Monday in July, 1920, the same being the 5th day of July, 1920." The return day stated in this citation was incorrect, and should have been the first Monday in June, being the 7th day of June. Having discovered the mistake, appellee's attorneys procured the issuance of another citation, giving the correct return date, which was served by leaving a

copy of the citation, together with a certified copy of the petition, at the principal office of the company. The service of the second citation was in time for the June term, and, appellant having made default, appellee, on appearance day, June 8, 1920, took judgment by default for the full amount claimed, with interest and costs of suit.

It appears that the first citation was turned over by the president of the company to its attorneys at Fort Worth, for attention, and that neither they nor the officers of the company had any actual knowledge of the service of the second citation until after judgment was taken.

In response to the first citation, appellant's counsel forwarded a plea of privilege to the clerk, on June 25, 1920, which was filed June 26, 1920, at the same time advising appellee's attorneys that they were filing the plea. The reply of said attorneys informed counsel for appellant that judgment by default had been previously rendered. After some correspondence between the attorneys in which appellee refused to agree to set aside the judgment, appellant, on August 26, 1920, filed motion for new trial, and on September 4th appellee filed contest of the motion. The court heard the matter upon the verified motion of appellant and upon the sworn contest of appellee, together with the evidence introduced at the hearing. The motion was overruled, from which this appeal was taken.

Appellant contends that the court erred in rendering judgment by default for appellee, and in refusing to set the same aside, because the contract alleged was subject to general demurrer as being in violation of the anti-trust laws of the state. A careful consideration of the contract alleged, as the basis for recovery, convinces us that it was violative of several provisions of our statutes against trusts and monopolies.

Article 7796, Revised Statutes 1911, among other things, defines a trust to be a combination of capital, skill or acts between two or more persons, firms, corporations, or associations of persons, or either two or more of them, for any of the following purposes:

"2. To fix, maintain, increase or reduce the price of merchandise * * * or commodities. * * *

"4. To fix or maintain any standard or figure whereby the price of any article or commodity of merchandise, * * * shall be in any manner affected, controlled or established.

"5. To make * * * any contract * * * by which they shall agree in any manner to keep the price of an article or commodity * * * at a fixed or graded figure, or by which they shall in any manner affect or maintain the price of any commodity or article."

These and related provisions of the anti-trust laws have been frequently before our courts. Among the cases dealing with this

question may be cited the following: Wood
v. Tex. Ice & Cold S. Co., 171 S. W. 497; Star
Mill & Elevator Co. v. F. W. G. C., 146 S. W.
604; Segal v. McCall, 108 Tex. 55, 184 S. W.
188; Woods v. American Brew Ass'n., 183
S. W. 127; Am. Brewing Ass'n v. Woods,
215 S. W. 448; Fuqua et al. v. Pabst Brewing
Co., 90 Tex. 298, 38 S. W. 29, 750, 35 L. R. A.
241; Coal Co. v. Lawson, 89 Tex. 394, 32 S.
W. 871, 34 S. W. 919; Brewing Co. v. Temple-
man, 90 Tex. 277, 38 S. W. 27; Tex. Brewing
Co. v. Anderson, 40 S. W. 737; Tex. Brewing
Co. v. Durrum, 46 S. W. 880; Mansur &
Tabbetts Imp. Co. v. Price, 22 Tex. Civ. App.
616, 55 S. W. 764; Pasteur Vaccine Co. v.
Burkey, 22 Tex. Civ. App. 232, 54 S. W. 804;
White Dental Mfg. Co. v. Hertzberg, 51 S. W.
855; Coal Co. v. Lawson, 89 Tex. 394, 32
S. W. 871, 34 S. W. 919; Houck v. Associa-
tion, 88 Tex. 184, 30 S. W. 869; Simmons &
Co. v. Terry, 79 S. W. 1103; State v. Racine
Sattley Co., 63 Tex. Civ. App. 663, 134 S.
W. 401; Jersey Creme Co. v. McDaniel
Bottling Co., 152 S. W. 1187; J. R. Watkins
Medical Co. v. Johnson et al., 162 S. W. 394;
Rawleigh Medical Co. v. Mayberry, 193 S.
W. 199; Armstrong v. Rawleigh Medical Co.,
178 S. W. 582; Pictorial Review v. Pate Bros.,
185 S. W. 309; Rawleigh Med. Co. v. Fitzpatrick, 184 S. W. 549; Rawleigh Med. Co.
v. Gunn, 186 S. W. 385; Newby v. W. T.
Rawleigh Co., 194 S. W. 1173; Whisenant et
al v. Shores-Mueller, 194 S. W. 1175; Pennsylvania Rubber Co. v. McClain, 200 S. W.
586; Dodd v. W. T. Rawleigh Co., 203 S. W.
131; State v. Willys-Overland Co., 211 S. W.
609. These authorities are referred to, not
as being in point upon the facts involved, but
as illustrating the uniformity with which the
principles and policies embodied in our statutes against trusts and unlawful conspiracies
have been recognized and enforced.

[1] In the absence of any authority, we
should not hesitate to hold the contract made
the basis of this suit to be illegal and void,
as in contravention of the statutory provisions heretofore stated. It was, in substance,
alleged that on or about June 7, 1919, appellant sold and delivered to appellee seven
Fordson tractors, the appellant being a wholesale dealer in these articles, and the appellee
a retail dealer. It was alleged that the
market value of the tractors at the residence
of appellee was at all times $930 each, and it
was expressly averred that—

"The said defendant then and there, and at
the time of said sale, agreed with plaintiff that
the same should be sold at said sum of $930."

The plain effect of this averment is that
the parties had agreed to fix and maintain the
price for the sale of a commodity or article of
commerce. It is then alleged that about
June 17th appellant wired appellee that the
manufacturers of the tractors, Henry Ford
& Son, had reduced the price, and wired and

instructed appellee to likewise reduce the
price on the tractors so as to thereafter sell
the same for $791.50 to the retail trade. It
is next alleged that appellant had, by various
contracts and writings, agreed and contracted with appellee to indemnify and save him
harmless from any decline or reduction in
price, and had agreed and contracted with
him to repay and reimburse him—

"for any decrease in the retail price of said
tractors put into effect by plaintiff at the instance or request of defendant; and that by
virtue of and in accordance with said contracts
and agreements with plaintiff he reduced the
retail price of said tractors from $930 each to
$791.50 each."

It cannot be even plausibly argued that
this is not an averment that appellee, in pursuance to contracts and agreements theretofore made, reduced, fixed, and maintained
the retail price of the tractors.

The next paragraph of the petition contains
an allegation to the same effect, and expressly recites that—

The contract for indemnity and reimbursement was dependent "upon the condition of the
plaintiff putting said reduction to effect, and
that said reduction was put into effect at the
instance and request of said defendant, and for
the benefit of defendant, and in accordance with
said contract, agreement and guaranty upon his
part to this plaintiff."

These allegations plainly show contracts
and agreements violative of most, if not all,
of the provisions of the anti-trust statutes
stated above.

In holding the contract, as pleaded, void,
we do not mean to be understood as deciding
that a mere contract of a wholesale dealer
to reimburse a retailer for any decline in
price of merchandise or commodities sold
him would be void when not made in connection with and in pursuance of illegal
agreements fixing, maintaining, or reducing
prices. If the appellee had pleaded such a
contract, disassociated from the contracts
and agreements referred to, a different question would be presented.

[2] While we have held that the contracts
pleaded were violative of the laws against
trusts, if this were the only defense urged
by appellant to the judgment by default, it
may be that we should not grant the relief
of setting the same aside, on the principle
that equity will not aid either party to an
illegal contract. If the facts stated in the
petition were true, as is admitted by general
demurrer, the parties would be in pari delicto; and it would appear that a court should
not aid a party to illegal agreements who
has suffered default to go against him.
However, that is not the only nor indeed the
main defense set up in the answer and in
the motion for new trial.

In addition to a plea of privilege, appellant entered a sworn denial of the averments of the petition. Furthermore, it expressly denied that it ever agreed with appellee to reduce or fix the price of the tractors, and alleged that it did not agree to reimburse appellee for any decline in prices, nor make any guaranties in reference thereto. It was also pleaded, which seems to find support in the averments of the petition itself, that the market value of the tractors was at all times $930, and that there was no loss or damage to appellee, because his reduction of price was voluntary, and he could not therefore impose liability upon appellant. It was also alleged that the appellee did not introduce any evidence as a basis for the default judgment, and that, his claim not being liquidated nor proven by an instrument in writing, it was necessary that evidence should be introduced before a valid judgment by default could be taken.

[3] We are of the opinion that these pleadings show a meritorious defense; and if equitable reasons have been shown why answer was not filed before judgment, or was filed within such time as that appellant was entitled to present its defense, the motion should have been granted.

We do not agree with the contention of appellant that it was not legally served with citation to the June term of court. The officer's return and the evidence upon this point show legal service according to a mode provided by statute, and the attempt to impeach the return and service was unsuccessful.

Nor do we find it necessary to pass upon the interesting question as to whether this was an unliquidated demand upon which evidence was necessary to ascertain the damages before a valid judgment by default could be rendered.

In view of articles 1938 and 1939, Revised Statutes of 1911, and the rule early announced in this state that a judgment by default admits all of plaintiff's cause of action except the damages claimed, there is great force in the suggestion of appellant's counsel that the final judgment by default without the introduction of evidence was erroneous. Holland v. Cook, 10 Tex. 244; Herring v. Herring, 189 S. W. 1105; Dancy v. Rosenberg, 174 S. W. 831. However, as we have stated, we prefer not to decide this question.

[4] As we have indicated, the judgment was upon a contract repugnant to the policy of the state against trusts and unlawful conspiracies, to which the defendant pleaded a meritorious defense, but the chief difficulty we have had in reaching a satisfactory conclusion is upon the question whether appellant has shown equitable grounds for setting aside the judgment. From the sworn answer and motion and the other evidence considered at the hearing, it fairly appears that, while there was legal service of the second citation, the officers of the corporation had no actual knowledge of it until after the judgment was taken. It is further shown that appellant and its counsel were misled into suffering judgment by default to be taken by the erroneous return date stated in the first citation. We find an utter want of bad faith indicated, and while these considerations do not afford a legal excuse, they have a strong appeal in equity. It is insisted, however, that a question of this sort is primarily for the discretion of the trial court. Nevertheless, the discretion is not an arbitrary one, and is subject to review where manifest injustice has been done. The question which has given us the greatest concern is the delay in filing the motion, but it was shown that it was filed at the same term of court, and but for the absence of the trial judge during the last week of the term the motion might have been heard, and the plea of privilege, and even the trial on the merits have been had at the same term.

[5] The correspondence of the attorneys and the other evidence showing the absence of the president of the company, who had peculiar knowledge upon the subject-matter of the litigation and the handling of this matter for appellant, indicates that there was substantial excuse for the delay. Upon the whole, we think the showing made presented an equitable excuse for both the failure to appear and answer before default judgment was rendered, and to sooner present the defenses. Dancy v. Rosenberg, 174 S. W. 831, and authorities there cited.

We are of the opinion that no substantial injustice will be done appellee by ordering the judgment set aside, and the opportunity given to appellant to present its plea of privilege and its answer to the merits; and that the trial court should have granted the motion. The case will be reversed, and the cause remanded.

Reversed and remanded.

CITY OF DALLAS v. MAXWELL
(231 S.W.)

CITY OF DALLAS v. MAXWELL et ux.
(No. 1800.)

(Court of Civil Appeals of Texas. Amarillo.
April 27, 1921. Rehearing Denied
June 1, 1921.)

**1. Municipal corporations ⚖796—City under
duty to erect barriers at necessary points on
streets.**

It is the duty of a city to erect railings or
barriers along its streets at places where they
are necessary to make the same safe for drivers in the use of ordinary care.

**2. Municipal corporations ⚖819(4)—Evidence
held sufficient to sustain finding city's negligence was proximate cause of jitney bus passenger's injury.**

In an action against a city for injuries to
a jitney bus passenger, when the bus went off
the street into a ravine, after hitting a telegraph pole, evidence *held* sufficient to sustain
the jury's finding that the city's negligence in
failing to erect a barrier at the point was the
proximate cause of the accident and the injuries complained of.

**3. Municipal corporations ⚖800(5)—City not
relieved from liability to jitney bus passenger
injured through its negligence and that of
driver.**

The fact that the driver of a jitney bus was
negligent in the operation of his vehicle, which
negligence concurred with that of the city in
not erecting a barrier at the particular point
in causing the car to leave the street and plunge
into a ravine, does not relieve the city of liability for injuries to a passenger, the driver's
negligence, concurring with the negligence of
the city, having been the proximate cause of
the accident.

**4. Appeal and error ⚖1050(1)—Error in ad-
mission of evidence rendered harmless by reception of other like evidence.**

Error in the admission of evidence was rendered harmless by the reception of evidence
from other witnesses without objection tending
to prove the same fact.

**5. Municipal corporations ⚖796—Whether ra-
vine into which jitney bus plunged private or
municipal property immaterial.**

If it was the duty of a city to erect and
maintain a barrier on a street at a point where
a jitney bus left the street and plunged into a
ravine, it is immaterial to the city's liability
under the facts whether the ravine was private
or municipal property.

**6. Damages ⚖158(3)—Testimony of jitney
bus passenger and physician as to injuries
admissible.**

In an action against a city for injuries to a
jitney bus passenger, when the car left the
street and plunged into a ravine, testimony of
the injured passenger, a woman, that the bones
of her nose were broken, the roof of her mouth
pushed up to the top of her nose, etc., *held* admissible, as was also the testimony of a medical
witness to the same effect, plaintiff having
sought to recover for mental anguish and suf-

fering, the result of the disfiguring injuries
which she described.

**7. Municipal corporations ⚖819(7)—Evidence
held to sustain finding jitney bus passenger
did not appreciate dangers of use of street.**

In an action against a city by a jitney bus
passenger, injured when the car left the street
and plunged into a ravine, evidence *held* sufficient to sustain the jury's finding that plaintiff
did not know or fully appreciate and understand
the dangers incident to the use or attempted
use of the street at the particular point by vehicular traffic.

**8. Trial ⚖132—Opening statement of plain-
tiff's counsel informing jury as to effect
of finding not reversible error where withdrawn.**

In an action against a city by a jitney bus
passenger injured when the car left the street
and plunged into a ravine, where, during the
opening argument, plaintiff's counsel stated that
the attorneys for defendant wanted the jury
to say "Yes," and find plaintiff assumed the risk
of riding in the jitney, and that he said they
should answer the question "No," and not
charge her with such risk, but, on objection,
plaintiff's counsel withdrew the statement, there
was no reversible error.

**9. Trial ⚖114—Counsel in argument may
state how much plaintiff should recover.**

It is not improper for counsel in argument
to state to the jury how much they think the
plaintiff should recover.

**10. Damages ⚖132(1)—$10,000 for severe
physical injuries and disfigurement of married
woman not excessive.**

A judgment for $10,575 recovered from a
city by a jitney bus passenger, a married woman, injured when the car left the street at an
unguarded point, and plunged into a ravine, subjecting her to severe physical injuries and disfigurement, *held* not excessive.

Appeal from District Court, Dallas County; W. F. Whitehurst, Judge.

Suit by B. G. Maxwell and wife against
the City of Dallas. From judgment for
plaintiffs, defendant appeals. Affirmed.

Jas. J. Collins, W. S. Bramlett, Allen
Charlton, and Carl B. Callaway, all of Dallas, for appellant.

W. D. Cardwell, of Burkburnett, and Mc-
Cutcheon & Church, of Dallas, for appellees.

HALL, J. Mrs. Laura Maxwell, joined
by her husband, sued the appellant to recover $25,000 damages as the result of personal
injuries charged to have been sustained by
her by reason of the negligence of said city.
It is alleged, in substance, that on or about
December 9, 1916, she was a passenger in a
motor bus, commonly known as a jitney,
which was being operated along Carlisle
street, in said city, and that, at the time of
the accident which occasioned the injuries
complained of, the bus was being driven at

a rate of speed not to exceed 15 miles an hour; that, several years prior to the above-named date, the city had built and constructed at the intersection of Carlisle and Vine streets a concrete or stone culvert, and had constructed, built, and maintained sidewalks and curbing along Carlisle street, at the intersection of Vine street, and that the construction of said culvert was on account of a deep ravine where Vine street ended; that defendant so constructed the culvert and fill in Vine street as to raise the intersection of said streets to the level of Carlisle street on each side of the ravine; that said city owned, maintained, and controlled the ravine where Vine street ended. It appears that Carlisle street runs approximately east and west at the place of the accident; that Vine street extended from the south ends at Carlisle street; and that, on the north side of Carlisle street, at the point where Vine street intersects it and ends, the ravine is approximately 50 feet deep.

Plaintiffs further allege that at all times since the construction of said fill, culvert, sidewalks, and curbs at and near the place, and for more than 24 hours prior to December 9, 1916, defendant had notice of the open and dangerous condition of the street, curb, sidewalks, fill, culvert, and ravine; that for a long time prior thereto said city had negligently and carelessly left said streets, curbs, sidewalks, culvert, fill, and ravine open and exposed, and had negligently and carelessly constructed and maintained the same in an open and exposed condition, to such an extent that said streets, sidewalks, culvert, fill, and ravine were openly and notoriously dangerous to persons and vehicles using said streets; that by the exercise of ordinary care the city could have made said place safe; that the mayor and city engineer knew of its dangerous condition, or by the exercise of ordinary care and diligence could have known, and by the use of ordinary care and diligence could and would have provided suitable curbs, guards, or rails to prevent accidents and injuries to persons and vehicles using said streets; that by failing to use such care the said city was negligent, and that its negligence was the proximate cause of the injuries sustained by the plaintiff, Mrs. Maxwell; that the city had permitted a large pole to be erected in said street near said gulch, which said pole was exposed, and not protected by any curbing; that on the west side of said Carlisle street, where Vine street ended, said ravine was from 40 to 50 feet deep, and extended almost to the width of Vine street; that the curb along the west side of said Carlisle street did not extend to a point even with the east line of Vine street, if extended, but only to within 8 or 10 feet of said east line; that there was no curb on the west side of Carlisle street opposite to where said Vine street ended, and no side-

walk there save and except a string of three boards or planks, which were practically o: a level with said streets; that from the wes side of said board walk, and from 2 to 4 fee to the west of said walk, there was a prec. pice going down into said ravine which et tended along the west side of Carlisle stree. nearly the width of Vine street, and tha: said precipice was wholly unguarded, and without barriers, railing, or curb of any kit. to prevent persons and vehicles from falli.; into said ravine; that at the intersection of said Vine and Carlisle streets, as aforesaid, the said city ordinarily maintains a stree light, and at the hour of the accident, to wit about 6:30 p. m. of said day, said street light was not burning, in consequence of whit the streets were dark, and by reason thereof the driver of the motor bus could not an: did not see said pole into which his motor bus ran, and on account of the failure of said city to have said lights burning, and on account of the negligence of said city t: failing to construct and maintain a curb at that point, and its failure to construct and maintain a barrier to prevent said automo-bile from running into said ravine, its neg-ligence was the proximate cause of the in-juries; that when said motor bus came with-in a few feet of the east line of Vine street. and on the right-hand side of Carlisle street, the driver of said motor bus lost control of the vehicle, and the front part of the right-hand side of the bus struck the pole, which stood about 4 inches within the curb line of said street, swerved to the right, and, when it cleared said pole, it went over said board walk, down into the ravine, and turned over. thereby injuring the plaintiff, Mrs. Maxwell. She alleges her injuries to be as follows:

"That at the time of said accident Mrs. Max-well was a strong, healthy, married woman, 30 years of age; that by reason of the accident she suffered the following injuries: Both the upper and lower jawbones were broken; her nose was mashed, bruised, and broken; some of her teeth were knocked out, and some broken off; the bone of her nose running to the base of the brain was broken and fractured, and on ac-count of the breaking of said bones in her jaws and nose, and the breaking off and knocking out of her teeth, her face has been permanently dis-figured, from which she has suffered great and excruciating physical pain and mental anguish; and said injuries are of a permanent nature. and she has, and will continue through her nat-ural life, to suffer great physical pain and men-tal anguish, mortification, and humiliation; that her limbs were mashed and bruised and lacer-ated; her hips and spine were mashed, bruised. and made sore, from which she has suffered great physical pain and mental anguish; that she suffered internal injuries of the womb. ovaries, stomach, bowels, intestines, and female organs, which said injuries are permanent, and from which the said Mrs. Maxwell will suffer through her natural life, all to her damage in the sum of $20,000."

By trial amendment, plaintiffs pleaded actual notice to the mayor and city engineer the city of Dallas of the defects in the streets causing the accident, alleging that said actual notice was given more than 24 hours prior to the accident. The city answered with a general demurrer, certain special exceptions, a general denial, a plea of assumed risk, contributory negligence, and interposed the two-year statute of limitations as to the claim for certain expenses. The cause was submitted to a jury on special issues, in reply to which the jury found: (1) That the failure of the city in not having a sufficient and adequate guard or barrier along the north line of Carlisle street, at the place and time of the accident, was negligence; (2) that said negligence was the proximate cause of the accident and injuries complained of; (3) that the driver of the bus in which Mrs. Maxwell was riding was negligent in the operation of the vehicle; (4) that at and just prior to the accident the steering gear on the bus was so defective that the driver could not control and guide it; (5) that his negligence was not the proximate cause of the accident complained of; (6) that the negligence of the city, concurring with the negligence of the driver of the bus, was the proximate cause of the accident. In connection with the sixth special issue, the court charged the jury as follows:

"In passing upon the foregoing special issues, you are instructed that, by the term 'concurrent proximate cause,' as used in the above special issue, is meant such act as is wanting in ordinary care, which activity aided in producing the injury, and such act as might reasonably have been contemplated as involving the result under the circumstances."

The jury further found: (7) That, at the time she entered the jitney, Mrs. Maxwell did not know, fully appreciate, and understand the dangers incident to the use or attempted use by vehicular traffic of Carlisle street at its intersection with Vine street. Special issues 8, 9, and 10 relate to the amount of damages sustained. The trial resulted in a verdict for plaintiffs in the sum of $11,200, and interest from January 20, 1920, at 6 per cent. Plaintiff filed a remittitur of $625, and judgment was rendered against the city in the sum of $10,575.

The first error is assigned to the action of the court in refusing to direct a verdict for the city. Under this assignment appellant presents its first proposition, as follows:

"The alleged actionable negligence upon which appellees rest their cause of action are that: (1) There was no curb on the west side of Carlisle street, where Vine street ended; and (2) the ravine or precipice next to the west line of Carlisle street at the end of Vine street was unguarded. Viewed in the most favorable light for appellees, the evidence shows that appellant is not legally liable to appellees for the injury sustained by Mrs. Maxwell, due to the descension of the jitney into the ravine, notwithstanding the want of a curb and unguarded condition of the ravine and its proximity to the west or northwest line of Carlisle street, because: (a) Appellant owed appellees no duty to erect a barrier to prevent the jitney descending into the ravine; or, (b) to erect a barrier of such character as would have prevented the jitney, under the circumstances shown, from descending into the ravine; and (c) the alleged omission or omissions was or were not the proximate cause of the jitney descending into the ravine; hence, the peremptory instruction should have been given."

In reply to this proposition, which we suggest is multifarious, the appellees submit the following counter proposition:

"It was the duty of the city of Dallas to use ordinary care to build and maintain its streets in a reasonably safe condition for the usual travel, and the failure of the city to erect guard rails or barriers to protect the traveling public from falling down a deep precipice or gulch, immediately adjacent to said street and sidewalk, is a question for the jury to pass upon as to whether the failure to erect said barriers or guard rails in each case is negligence, and whether said negligence is one of the proximate causes of the accident resulting from a motor bus being driven at a slow and lawful rate of speed, going over said precipice and seriously injuring plaintiff's wife."

Appellee also submits a second counter proposition, as follows:

"Where a municipal corporation opens up a street, such as the filling in of a gulch and the tearing down of a bridge over said gulch, and invites public travel, it must be made reasonably safe for such use, and if there is a dangerous place, such as a declivity, precipice, or ravine, so close to the street, or the traveled part thereof, whether on city property or private property, as to render it unsafe for travel, in the abuse of a barrier, constitutes a defect in the street, and the municipality is liable if the jury finds said failure to erect a barrier under the circumstances was negligence, and such negligence was the proximate cause of the accident."

Several plats were introduced in evidence —one showing, as before stated, that Carlisle street runs east and west at the point of the accident. Another was introduced by appellant, made by its engineer, which does not indicate the points of the compass, but from which we infer that Vine and Carlisle streets, as shown on that map, do not intersect each other at right angles, and for the purposes of this opinion we will treat them as running in the directions first above stated. That part of article XIV, § 11, of the city charter applicable to the case is:

"The city of Dallas shall never be liable on account of any damage or injury to person or property, arising from or occasioned by any defect in any public street, highway or ground of any public work of the city, unless the specific defect causing the damage or injury shall have been actually known to the mayor or city engineer by personal inspection, for a period of at least twenty-four hours prior to the occurrence of the injury, or damage, unless the attention of the mayor or city engineer shall have been called thereto by notice thereof in writing at least twenty-four hours prior to the occurrence of the injury or damage, and proper diligence has not been used to rectify the defect after actually known or called to the attention of the mayor or city engineer, as aforesaid."

J. H. Lane, the driver of the bus, testified that he was 30 years old, married, and had been living in Dallas 5 years prior to the accident; that the route traveled by him was the regular one prescribed by the city for jitneys to operate over. He testified:

"I will say that I taken mine out on Carlisle, but there were some of them that went down the railroad, and on across the railroad to Cedar Springs, and some of us went out Carlisle to keep from crossing the railroad and pulling that hard hill. I had been engaged in driving a jitney at that time about 8 or 9 months, and was licensed by the city. I went from Austin to Akard on Elm street, and from Akard to Cedar Springs and from Cedar Springs to Carlisle; from Carlisle to Bowen, and out Oak Lawn, and returned the same route. I was permitted by the city, and those who had charge of the inspection of operation of jitneys and of their routes, to go over Carlisle street. Prior to the 9th of December I had been operating my jitney over Carlisle street about a month; had been transferred over there from Oak Cliff. I got the transfer from the city to this line which I have described. My car was inspected once a week by the jitney inspector. I recall the accident at Carlisle and Vine streets on December 9. It was about 6:30 o'clock in the evening. I was traveling in a southwestern direction; was coming to town on Carlisle. At the time there was a little boy in the front seat with me. The steering wheel or steering gear was on the left side, and I was seated on the left side of the front seat, and the boy on the right side. It was a five-passenger Ford. Besides the boy, as I found out later, I had Mrs. Holford and Mrs. Maxwell in the car. They got in the car at Sneed street. With reference to Vine street, Sneed is east one block; north and east of Carlisle and Vine. My automobile had a top on it at that time and I had side curtains. The top was up and the curtains were half up; that is, the curtains were up to the back seat where the ladies sat. I was not running very fast; don't think it could have possibly been over 8 or 10 miles an hour. I am familiar with the speed of such vehicles.

"When I stopped, and the ladies got in, one of the ladies, I don't know which, said, 'Let's fasten up these curtains; it is cold.' I didn't think it had been cold enough to put up the curtains. So I reached back with my left hand. My right hand, when I reached back with my left hand, was on the steering wheel, and I was sitting just like I am now, and reached back that way; was sitting with my face straight ahead, looking straight ahead on the street; don't think I ever turned in the seat. I just reached back and gave the curtains a jerk, and the lady said, 'I will fasten this,' and I says, 'All

right.' Well, I seen that my car had cut to the right some; I don't know how it was, but it seemed like it wanted to go to the right all the time, and I tried to cut it to the left, and could not, and about that time I seen the pole, and it hit the pole in some way, I don't know just how, and then it sorter seemed like it was going the other way. It seemed like it sorter turned a little, and all at once it just turned where that ditch was, and I grabbed the emergency and tried to stop the car, but could not, and we went off then. It seemed like it was all done in a second. I remember the car hitting the pole, and up to that time we were pretty near off. The pole was located right near the curb. It was right at the edge of the ditch or the street gutter, just a little to the right of that. It is right across the street from Carlisle, where Vine street ends. The curb along there, up to that pole, or near the pole, is built up tolerably close to the pole, but there is a piece where there is no curb. I don't remember how many feet it is from the end of the curb to the pole. Could not say whether it was 10, 15, or 20 feet, but I know there is no curb where the pole is, where the car went off. The arc light at the intersection of Vine and Carlisle streets was not on at the time the accident happened. Along Carlisle street, on the right-hand side coming to the city, the way I was coming, there was no curbing. Before you get to Vine street there is a curb. As to the sidewalk, there was two planks, as well as I remember, just two inch planks down there. I don't remember how wide they were, but not very wide. They were not on a very high incline. They were right on the ground.

"I stated a while ago that my machine kept trying to turn to the right. I later found the cause of that. I think my wheels had become toed, and caused the axle to tip forward, and the radius knuckle, the left knuckle on the radius rod, I think, broke. I used every effort in my power to steer my machine back into the street; tried to turn it to the left. I didn't know at that time why I could not do so. I knew something was wrong with the steering gear, but did not know what it was; it would not work. After the car struck the pole and went over the sidewalk, it went right off into that ditch. We measured from the top of the sidewalk down into that ravine where we fell, or where the car landed, and it was 48 feet. As my car went over the embankment, it turned bottom upwards. On that portion of it, if Vine street would be projected across to the north side of Carlisle, where there is a pencil mark there, there is no sidewalk. There is nothing but a board walk. There is not an elevation there to that sidewalk. After the accident I crawled out from down there under the car, and pulled the little boy out, and then ran around to the ladies, and hollered for help. Near the telephone post along where the curb line would come, it is about 3 or 4 feet in some places to where the bluff starts down. I could not say how near it is from the telephone post, because I don't remember exactly, but my recollection is I judge it to be 3 or 4 feet. There is a telephone pole in the board walk, two 12-inch boards there, then from this board it is about 6 or 8 inches in some places to where the precipice starts down. On this little diagram there used to be a bridge across here—banisters—old-fashioned bridge, and they taken the bridge out and filled in there down to this gulch, and they never extended Vine street on across there. Underneath that bridge was this gulch; that gulch is what they filled in and made Vine street run into there. It has been a good long while since the bridge was there; I guess about 8 or 10 years since they filled that in. I lived about middle ways that block from where the accident took place. Would be, I guess, about 200 feet across from the house to the gulch. As my car went over that embankment, it turned bottom upwards. It killed one lady, and injured the other. There were no guard rails or barriers, or anything to prevent the car from going into the ravine. It was dark about that time. I think I had my headlights on, but Ford lights are very dim—mine were."

Several photographs were introduced, showing the conditions surrounding the place of the accident. These views were taken from different points, and served to verify and illustrate the testimony of the several witnesses. B. G. Maxwell testified that the telephone pole on the north side of Carlisle street was just about on the curb line, and where the curb would be if it had been extended along the edge of the precipice made by the fill. He further testified that there was no gutter on that side of the fill. He admitted that the place of danger was open and visible, and its condition could be seen at all times, and stated that Carlisle street was at that time macadamized and graveled, and in that particular was in good condition for traveling. Mrs. Maxwell testified, in substance, that at the time she and her sister-in-law, Mrs. Holford, entered the jitney to go to town, the wind was chilly, and only the back curtains of the jitney had been put up; that the curtain on her side of the vehicle was loose; that she said something about it, and the driver started to reach back to fasten it, and she told him to let it alone, that she would fasten it. She testified that he never did turn around, but reached his hand back for that purpose, and that was when she first entered the jitney. She says, just preceding the accident—

"it seemed like the car kinder jumped on the street a little bit, and the next thing I knew we were going into the ditch. From the boards the embankment slopes down gradually for a few feet, and then goes straight down;" that the last thing she remembered was that she was fixing the curtain.

John Van Wort, the third passenger, who occupied the front seat with the driver, testified in part:

"After the ladies got into the car, one of them complained about the wind blowing in through the curtains, and the curtain on the left-hand side car was flapping. I was seated on the right of the driver on the front seat. After this lady made that remark, the driver turned to fasten the curtain, using his left hand. The car was moving at about 10 or 15 miles an hour. Just about the time he turned around to fasten the curtain, and I think about the time

231 S. W.—28

he fastened it, we hit the telephone pole. The right-hand side of the car hit the pole and glanced off, and it threw the car around. When the car hit the telephone pole it threw the back end of the car to the left, and the car went right down the gutter. The driver put his left hand about like this, to fasten the curtain; then one of the ladies said: 'I will fix it,' and he brought his hand around and put it back to the front, and the lady started to fasten that curtain. I was turned around looking at the lady at the time. After the driver turned round the lady started to fix the curtain; then the car hit the post. That was my testimony on the former trial."

W. J. Powell, assistant city engineer, testified:

"There is a culvert under Carlisle street, and approximately on the south side of Vine street, which terminates in a retaining wall, a concrete retaining wall near the southwest line of Carlisle street, and the top of this wall is 9½ feet from the floor line of the culvert. My recollection is that the top of the wall is approximately flush with the surface of the street to the bottom of the culvert, and it would be approximately 19½ or 20 feet. From the top of that stone wall to the surface of the street is filled in with earth. All of that concrete wall is on Vine street, and is owned by the city."

J. G. Clardy, among other things, testified:

"That he lived near the scene of the accident, and went there immediately after the accident, and found Mrs. Holford dead and Mrs. Maxwell still breathing; that there was no light burning, and they could hardly see to get out; that the ravine or precipice is about 57 feet deep; that there is a two board plank walk along the west side of Carlisle street, but no sidewalk or curb; that the surface of the street was level, and the water ran over it; when it rained, the water from the street ran over the plank walk and down into the ravine; that it washed the dirt away all the time, and made the precipice come nearer the sidewalk; that at the time of the accident there were no boards there—no board sidewalk—just a little path across there."

S. B. Massie testified that during 1916, and a few years prior thereto, he was the city bridge man and foreman of district No. 2; that is, general foreman of the street bridge improvement work; that there is a cement sidewalk on both sides of what is supposed to be Vine street, through there down down that gulch; that for the convenience of pedestrians, school children, and so on, he built a wooden walk on across there by laying three 2x8 boards; that Ben Sira was the superintendent of this department at that time; that, when the street was first graded, there was a bridge where Carlisle first crosses Vine street; that prior to the accident he reported to Ben Sira about the precipice and gulch, and suggested that there should be a barricade, or a fence, or something at the top of the deep gulch, as it was almost straight down, as a good many children passed up and down that way, and that Sira would not let him do it; that a Mr. Alexander got up a petition to that end, and took it to the city hall prior to the accident, petitioning to have the ditch protected in some way.

C. L. Holford testified that on Monday morning, after his wife was killed Saturday night, the employees of the city came with a grader, and opened up a gutter across there but that this was after the accident. J. E. Lee, former commissioner of the city of Dallas, testified in part that he had, during 1911–1913 served as such commissioner, supervisor of streets, highways and bridges; that during that time he went out to the ravine; that the retaining wall was probably half way up to the street level, and probably 30 feet beyond the street line; that the storm sewer extended all the way under the retaining wall, and possibly 25 or 30 feet beyond it; that there were no barriers or guards above the surface of the street.

[1-3] In 13 R. C. L. p. 421, § 346, we find the rule stated as follows:

"It is well settled that it is the duty of a municipal or quasi municipal corporation to erect railings or barriers along the highway at places where they are necessary to make the same safe and convenient for travelers in the use of ordinary care, and that it is liable for injuries to travelers resulting from a breach of its duty in this regard. This is true though the danger arises from structures or excavations outside of the highway, and on the land of adjoining owners, when they are in the general direction of travel upon the highway. Whether or not a railing or barrier is necessary in a given case depends largely upon the circumstances of the particular locality in reference to which the question arises. Among the facts material to be considered are the character and amount of travel, the character of the road itself, its width and general construction, the direction of the road at the place, the length of the portion claimed to require a railing, whether the danger is concealed or obvious to the extent of the injury likely to occur therefrom."

The abstract question has been presented to the courts of this state in several cases, some of which are cited below, and the duty of the city to maintain barriers in the interest of travelers is generally declared, and the failure of the city to use reasonable diligence in the performance of this duty is invariably held to present a question of negligence for the determination of the jury. In some of the cases cited, the courts have reviewed the authorities at great length, and it would result in a needless extension of this opinion to quote from them. This case, as originally tried, was consolidated with the case of C. M. Holford against the city of Dallas, in which Holford sought to recover because of the death of his wife, who was in the jitney at the time of the accident. Rain-

ey, Chief Justice, reversed and remanded the branch of the case now before us, and reversed and rendered the case in favor of the city upon the issue of Holford's right to recover. The rule quoted above, citing some of the cases hereinafter mentioned, is announced in this language:

"It is the duty of a city to see that its streets be made and maintained in a reasonably safe condition for use by the public, but as the statutes furnish no certain way a street is to be fixed, the court erred in charging that the failure to do certain things to make it safe for travel would be negligence. Where there is no statutory law stating what acts constitute negligence, the court should not assume that such acts are negligence. Whether such an act constituted negligence was a question of fact, which should be determined by the jury. * * *"

The evidence shows that Carlisle street, where the accident happened, was kept in good repair, except as to the gulch side of the street; and, as to that, there was no railing or barrier there to prevent travelers from leaving the street. Whether or not such absence of railing or barrier was negligence on appellant's part should have been submitted to the jury to determine, and not assumed by the court. The evidence quoted above is sufficient to sustain the finding of the jury that the city's negligence in failing to erect a barrier was the proximate cause of the accident and the injuries complained of; and the further finding that the driver of the bus was negligent in the operation of his vehicle does not relieve the city of liability, since the jury also found that his negligence, concurring with the negligence of the city, was such proximate cause. City of San Antonio v. Wildenstein, 49 Tex. Civ. App. 514, 109 S. W. 231; Gonzales v. City of Galveston, 84 Tex. 3, 19 S. W. 284, 31 Am. St. Rep. 17; Still v. City of Houston, 27 Tex. Civ. App. 447, 66 S. W. 76; City of Dallas v. McCullough, 95 S. W. 1121; City of San Antonio v. Porter, 24 Tex. Civ. App. 444, 59 S. W. 922; City of Ft. Worth v. Patterson, 196 S. W. 251; Eads v. City of Marshall, 29 S. W. 171.

The evidence, without reciting it here, shows that the appellant had all necessary notice of the defect and danger that its charter required of the injured party. The evidence shows that, while at the moment of the accident the steering gear of the jitney was defective, the driver had no previous knowledge of the defect; on the contrary, it is shown that his car had been duly inspected by the city authorities, as required by the city. By several assignments, appellant attacks the charge of the court upon various grounds. We have spent much time in a careful consideration of the criticisms made by appellant, and we have concluded that it fairly and fully presents the case as made by the pleadings and evidence. The substance of the issues asked and refused was presented, though in somewhat different language, in the charge given by the court. It would needlessly prolong the opinion to discuss each of these assignments in detail.

The tenth and eleventh assignments are based upon the admission of certain testimony elicited from Mrs. Maxwell and her husband as to the extent of her female troubles. This was all objected to, upon the ground that no such injuries were included in the notice served upon the city. It is not necessary for us to decide as to the admissibility of this evidence, since it was withdrawn from the jury, and they were instructed to disregard evidence of all injuries not set up in the notice.

[4] The error, if any, in the admission of the evidence complained of under the twelfth assignment is made harmless by the reception of evidence tending to prove the same fact from other witnesses without objection.

[5] Even though it did not appear that the city had formally accepted the dedication of Vine street, as represented on the plots introduced over appellant's objection, no injury is shown by the thirteenth assignment. A pencil plot was introduced, and this, with the evidence of various witnesses, fully explained the situation at the place of the accident. If it was the duty of the city to erect and maintain a barrier at the point of the accident, it is immaterial under the facts whether the ravine was private or municipal property.

Mrs. Maxwell's injuries were described in the notice served upon the city, in part, as follows:

"Both her upper and lower jawbones were broken; her nose was broken; teeth knocked out and broken off, and her face and head were bruised and mashed and lacerated; that said injuries are of a permanent nature, and will disfigure her face for life, and from said injuries she suffered great and excruciating pain, and on account of same will continue to suffer throughout her natural life, and that, by reason of said injuries, she will be disfigured for life, and on account thereof will suffer great mental anguish."

[6] By the fifteenth assignment it is urged that the court erred in permitting Mrs. Maxwell to testify that the bones of her nose were broken, the roof of her mouth was pushed up to the top of her nose, and the base of her nose was broken; that it was "just bursted open just like my chin; my nose was pushed back." We think this testimony was clearly admissible, as was also the testimony of Dr. Milliken to the same effect. During the argument, counsel for appellees said to the jury:

"Not only has she suffered these injuries, gentlemen, but she must go through life and to her final resting place suffering the mortification and humiliation of having people stare at her because of the injuries to her face and her deformed condition there. In my opinion—and

this is just my opinion—if she got the whole amount she sued for, she would not be compensated for such humiliation."

We think this is proper argument. She sought to recover for mental anguish and suffering—the result of the injuries which she described, and which so disfigured her personal appearance. The mutilation of her face was described in the pleadings, and the facts were proven, by the unchallenged evidence of at least one witness. The shade of difference between the terms "mental suffering," "humiliation," and "mortification" is so dim that lexicographers have not been able to distinguish the one from the other. A physical deformity which is patent to observers may produce these things. As was said by Brady, Justice, in Texas Power & Light Co. v. Martin, 226 S. W. 451:

"The first question raised in the brief relates to the overruling of a special exception of appellant, and to the argument of counsel for appellee as to mental anguish claimed to have been suffered by appellee because of his scarred and disfigured hand. The specific claim is that such sufferings are too remote to be the subject of compensation, and to constitute recoverable damages. This contention was considered by this court in the recent case of Texas Electric Railway v. Whitmore (decided April 14, 1920) 222 S. W. 644."

In the Whitmore Case, the question of mental suffering, or, in other words, humiliation and mortification, as the result of being scarred and disfigured, is discussed at length, and the affirmative of the proposition sustained. The holding in that case is fully sustained by many decisions in this state.

[7] By the nineteenth assignment it is contended that the answer of the jury to the seventh issue submitted to them, and in which they found that Mrs. Maxwell did not know, fully appreciate, and understand the dangers, if any there were, incident to the use or the attempted use of Carlisle street at that point by vehicular traffic, is not supported by the evidence. We cannot assent to this proposition. It is true that she had seen the place of the accident more than once, and with reasonable intelligence should have known that a vehicle leaving the line of the street would meet disaster with its occupants, but she is not bound to foresee and guard against defective vehicles, nor was it an exhibition of foolhardiness for her to take passage in a jitney which defendant's officers had not only licensed to pass the very spot where she was injured, but whose duty it was, by inspection, to provide against any defects in the vehicle. We think this presents the question of contributory negligence, rather than assumed risk.

[8, 9] During his opening argument, counsel for plaintiff said:

"They (the attorneys for the defendant) want you to say 'Yes,' and find that woman (pointing to Mrs. Maxwell) assumed the risk of riding in that jitney, so that she will be deprived of her damages. I say you should answer the question 'No,' and not charge her with that risk."

The court's qualification of the bill shows that, upon objections by defendant's counsel, he further said:

"All right, gentlemen; if the defendant objects to that argument, I withdraw it, and ask you not to consider it, as I will present the issue in another way."

The courts are not in entire agreement upon the question presented by this, the twentieth assignment; some holding that it is highly improper for the jury to be informed by counsel in argument of the legal effect of their finding, but there is a consensus of opinion by the courts in this state that where the information conveyed is such that a jury, composed of reasonably intelligent men, would know the effect of any particular finding, it does not constitute reversible error, especially where the statement is withdrawn, either by counsel or by proper instruction of the court. G. H. & H. Ry. Co. v. Fleming, 203 S. W. 105; Rice v. Garrett, 194 S. W. 673, and authorities cited. Nor is it improper for counsel, in their argument, to state to the jury how much they think the plaintiff should recover. T. & B. V. Ry. Co. v. Dodd, 167 S. W. 238.

[10] The remaining assignments relate to the amount of the verdict. Appellee remitted certain items which were improper. In view of all the evidence, we are not prepared to say that the judgment is excessive. It is therefore affirmed.

DENTON v. KANSAS CITY LIFE INS. CO.
(No. 6317.)

(Court of Civil Appeals of Texas. Austin. May 11, 1921.)

1. Insurance ⚖136(2)—Manual delivery of policy unnecessary, where issued and mailed to agent for delivery.

Manual delivery of an insurance policy is not necessary, where there has been an acceptance of the application and the policy has been issued and mailed to the assured or to an agent of the company for unconditional delivery to the assured.

2. Insurance ⚖136(4) — Delivery of policy during applicant's good health is condition precedent to liability.

Stipulations in a life insurance policy that same is to be null and void unless delivered to the insured or his beneficiary during his lifetime and while in good health are valid and binding and conditions precedent to the liability of the insurer.

3. Insurance ⚖136(4)—Policy delivery not unconditional where agent directed to ascertain applicant's health before delivery.

Where policy, conditioned on delivery during applicant's good health, was mailed to the company's agent to be delivered only after he had ascertained whether applicant had had any attack of grippe, Spanish influenza, or pneumonia since being examined, and applicant, on the day before the mailing of the policy to the agent, was taken with influenza, developing into pneumonia, of which he died before receipt of the policy by the agent, who then refused to deliver it, there was no issuance and transmission of the policy through the mails for unconditional delivery.

4. Insurance ⚖136(4) — Where application provided that the policy should be void unless delivered to assured while in good health there was not an unconditional acceptance of the risk.

Where an application for life insurance itself provided that the policy should be void unless delivered to applicant while in good health, there was no unconditional acceptance of the risk, so that the company was not liable to the applicant's beneficiary upon refusal of its local agent to deliver the policy to her after applicant's death, from a disease contracted after the application was signed.

5. Insurance ⚖136(4)—Implied delivery by placing in mails held not binding, where insurer had no knowledge of subsequent illness of insured.

Under a policy conditioned on delivery during applicant's good health, the company is not liable, though there was an implied delivery by placing the policy in the mails addressed to the company's agent for delivery to the insured, where neither the company nor its agents knew of the illness of the insured subsequent to the acceptance of the application.

6. Insurance ⚖136(4)—Applicant taken with influenza not in "good health" within policy condition of delivery during applicant's good health.

An applicant for a life insurance policy, who contracted influenza on the day before the policy was placed in the mails, and, before the policy was received, died from pneumonia resulting from influenza, was affected with a serious and dangerous disease, which directly contributed to the immediate cause of his death, and therefore, at the time the policy was placed in the mails, was not in "good health" within a policy condition of delivery during applicant's "good health," for the quoted phrase, although not implying that the applicant is free from slight ailments, means that he is not suffering from any serious or fatal illness or disease.

[Ed. Note.—For other definitions, see Words and Phrases, First and Second Series, Good Health.]

7. Appeal and error ⚖854(1)—Court must affirm judgment of lower court if any ground to support it.

It is the duty of the court to affirm the judgment of the lower court if there be any ground to support it.

⚖For other cases see same topic and KEY-NUMBER in all Key-Numbered Digests and Indexes

8. Insurance ⚖=651(2)—Letter from company, instructing local agent to ascertain whether insured in good health before delivering policy, held competent.

In action on a policy conditioned on delivery during applicant's good health, a letter from the general agent of the company to its local agent, directing him to ascertain whether the applicant was in good health, and, if not, to report the fact to the company before delivering the policy, was competent upon the issue of the delivery of the policy and the intention of the company in that respect, in view of plaintiff's contention that delivery of the policy to the local agent was delivery to the insured.

Appeal from District Court, Runnels County; J. O. Woodward, Judge.

Action by Lucy Denton, for herself and as survivor in community of the estate of George V. Denton, against the Kansas City Life Insurance Company. Judgment for defendant, and plaintiff appeals. Affirmed.

A. K. Doss, of Ballinger, for appellant.
Dallas Scarborough, of Abilene, for appellee.

Findings of Fact.

BRADY, J.   Mrs. Lucy Denton, for herself and as survivor in community of the estate of George V. Denton, brought this suit against appellee to recover upon a life insurance policy, alleged to have been issued on the life of her deceased husband. The defenses of the insurance company resolved themselves into the claim that the company was never bound, because there was no delivery of the policy to Mr. Denton, nor to his beneficiary during his lifetime and while in good health. The defenses were based upon certain provisions in the application and policy. It was provided in the application:

"That it is expressly agreed to and understood on my part that this contract is to be null and void and of no binding force whatever, unless my application is received and accepted by the home office of the company, and approved by the medical director, and the policy of insurance is delivered to me or to my beneficiary during my lifetime, and while in good health."

The policy contained a similar provision, as follows:

"That this policy shall not take effect unless the first premium hereon has been paid and this policy delivered to the applicant within thirty days from the date hereof, or unless the applicant is in good health at the time of its delivery."

The court rendered judgment in favor of the insurance company, from which the plaintiff appealed.

The agreed statement of facts was as follows:

"First. On December 4, 1918, George V. Denton, a resident citizen of Runnels county, Tex., made application to the defendant company for a policy of life insurance in the sum of $1,500, payable to his estate; said application as signed by the said George V. Denton being attached and marked 'Exhibit A' and made a part of this agreement.

"Second. That on the date of said application, the said Denton made, executed, and delivered to W. E. Branch, local agent at Ballinger, Tex., for the defendant, a note covering the amount of the first year's premium on said policy, the amount of same being $45.10; that W. E. Branch and A. J. Thorp at said time were both local agents for the defendant, at Ballinger, Tex., and acted concurringly in taking said application and accepting said note in payment of said first year's premium.

"Third. That on said 4th day of December, 1918, said George V. Denton submitted himself for physical examination before Dr. J. G. Douglas, practicing physician residing in Ballinger, Tex., the said Douglas being then and there the duly appointed local medical examiner for the defendant company; and the said Denton was on said date examined by the said Dr. Douglas; that the report of said physician on the physical condition of the said George V. Denton at the time of said examination is hereto attached and marked 'Exhibit B' and made a part of this agreement.

"Fourth. Said application and report of said medical examination were thereupon forwarded to the home office of the defendant company at Kansas City, Mo., and said report of said medical examination thereafter approved by the chief medical examiner for the defendant, and in due course and routine of business a policy of insurance of the kind and character applied for was signed by the defendant in due form on the 2d day of January, 1919, dated said day and date, which said policy was, on the 8d day of January, 1919, duly registered under the laws of Missouri; that immediately thereafter said policy of insurance was transmitted by mail to Texas office and general agent for Texas of the defendant, at Dallas, Tex., to be by him forwarded to the local agents at Ballinger, Tex., that on the 7th day of January, 1919, said policy was forwarded by mail from said Dallas office to the said W. E. Branch at Ballinger, Tex.; that the said Branch was then residing temporarily in Eastland, Tex., and said policy was forwarded from Ballinger to Eastland, with his mail; and thereafter said W. E. Branch, having received said policy at Eastland, Tex., returned same to said A. J. Thorp at Ballinger, for delivery to the insured; that said policy of insurance was received in Ballinger by said A. J. Thorp after the death of the insured; that demand was made on said A. J. Thorp by attorneys for said Lucy Denton, plaintiff, for delivery of said policy, and same was refused, the defendant and its agents retaining possession of said policy, and that same is still in its possession, said policy being hereto attached and marked 'Exhibit C.' That prior to the institution of this suit, payment of the amount represented by said policy was demanded of defendant, and payment refused by defendant; said policy being a part of this agreement.

"Fifth. That on the 2d day of January, 1919, the said George V. Denton was taken sick with influenza; that some five days later said disease developed pneumonia, and that the said George V. Denton died from pneumonia on the 10th day of January, 1919; that the said George V. Denton was in good health from December 4, 1918, to January 2, 1919.

"Sixth. That on the 22d day of March, 1919, the defendant returned to said Mrs. Lucy Denton said note so given and executed by said George V. Denton; that upon the maturity of said note the said Mrs. Lucy Denton, through her attorney, made a tender to the defendant of the amount of the principal and accrued interest on said note, which was then and there refused by the defendant; that the plaintiff has duly qualified as survivor in community of the estate of George V. Denton, deceased, and as such is entitled to bring this suit; that the policy number of the policy of insurance on which this suit is based is No. 172062."

It was also agreed that the local agent at Ballinger, who took the application of George V. Denton, accepted on the same date the promissory note of Mr. Denton, in full settlement of the first premium, and that it was understood between the agent and Mr. Denton that the policy when issued should be returned to the agent at a bank in Ballinger, to be delivered to the insured. The policy did not reach the bank until after the death of Mr. Denton, either the 16th or 17th of January, 1919. The policy contained the usual provision that no agent had the power to modify the contract, to waive any forfeiture, to bind the company by making any promise or representation, or to deliver any policy contrary to the provisions heretofore quoted. It was stipulated that these powers could be exercised only by the executive officers of the company.

The physician who examined Mr. Denton testified that he was the local medical examiner of appellee, and that, at the time he made the examination of Mr. Denton, he was the family physician of the applicant. He further testified that Mr. Denton was taken ill with influenza on January 2d, and continued to suffer with this disease until January 8th, when pneumonia developed, from which he died on January 10th. He also stated that Mr. Denton's fatal illness dated from January 8th, and had not pneumonia developed he probably would have survived; further, that Mr. Denton was in good health from the date of his examination up to the 2d day of January, when he took the influenza, a disease commonly known as "flu."

Appellee offered in evidence the following letter:

"Dallas, Texas, January 7, 1919.

"Mr. W. E. Branch, Ranger, Texas—Dear Mr. Branch: The Kansas City Life Insurance Company instructs our agency, before delivering the inclosed policy No. 172062 to the insured, that we personally question the insured and ascertain whether the insured is now in good health, and whether he or she has had an attack of la grippe, Spanish influenza or pneumonia, since being examined for this policy. If you find the insured now to be in good health and has not had any of the above ailments, since being examined, then have he or she to sign the memorandum attached to this policy, and which is made a part thereof. We are further instructed to have this executed by the insured and witnessed by the agent in each case before delivering the policy.

"If the insured has had an attack of any of the above-mentioned ailments, or is now not in good health, then you will please report this fact to our office by first mail and wait further instructions from the company before offering to deliver the policy. Please forward this memorandum to our office after same has been signed by the insured and witnessed by you, along with your report of delivery of contract. We are requested to make this report the day of delivery. Please bear this in mind.

"Yours very truly,
"W. B. Bolding, Mgr. Policy Dept."

Opinion.

[1] In several forms, appellant presents the proposition that the contract of insurance was fully consummated and a delivery of the policy effected, within the meaning of the application and the policy, when it was issued and placed in the mails for delivery in due course to the insured. It is not claimed that there was manual delivery to the insured, but that a constructive or implied delivery resulted. Among the cases cited to sustain this proposition are Fidelity Mutual Life Ass'n v. Harris, 94 Tex. 25, 57 S. W. 635, 86 Am. St. Rep. 813; Unterharnscheidt v. Mo. State Life Ins. Co., 160 Iowa, 223, 138 N. W. 459, 45 L. R. A. (N. S.) 743. These cases do recognize the rule that manual delivery is not necessary where there has been an acceptance of the application, and the policy has been issued and mailed to the assured, or to an agent for unconditional delivery; and numerous cases are cited in support of the proposition that legal delivery is very frequently accomplished without an actual transfer of manual possession. It will be noted, however, that in each of these, as well as in other cases cited, it is stated that to accomplish such a result the transmission of the policy must be for unconditional delivery. In the Harris Case, it was said by Mr. Justice Williams:

"It does not appear that the agent to whom this policy was sent was to ascertain the condition of Harris' health, or that he had any discretion to hold it in any event; and this distinguishes the case from that of Society v. Pettus, 140 U. S. 226, 11 Sup. Ct. 822, 35 L. Ed. 497, in which the premium was to be collected by the local agent before the policy took effect."

In the Unterharnscheidt Case, which is strikingly similar to the present case in most of its features, it also appeared that the policy was transmitted to the agent of the company for unconditional delivery, in so far as any of the applicable provisions of the application. were concerned. We shall have occasion to briefly discuss these cases hereafter, in an effort to distinguish them from the instant case.

[2] We have examined numerous authorities bearing upon the question under discussion, and find an apparent conflict which we shall not attempt to reconcile. An instructive note on this subject will be found in 17 L. R. A. (N. S.) 1144, and also in 43 L. R. A. (N. S.) 725.

In the first case note, 17 L. R. A., referring to stipulations of this character, it is stated by the editors:

"It may be said generally that such stipulations are valid and binding, and that there can be no recovery if the policy is delivered to assured while he is in ill health, provided that neither the insurer nor any authorized agent had knowledge thereof; and this is true, by the weight of authority, even if the illness arose before the time of the application and medical examination. This is likewise true if the policy is delivered after death, but in ignorance thereof, or even with knowledge on the part of an agent without authority. Still more is it true if never delivered because of the illness or death of applicant."

In Ruling Case Law, vol. 14, p. 898, it is said:

"The application may provide that the contract shall not be complete until delivery of the policy, in which case delivery is essential, unless delivery is waived, as it may be."

It is generally held that such stipulations are in the nature of conditions precedent to the liability of the insurer. Cyc. vol. 25, p. 719; R. C. L. vol. 14, p. 900; Yount v. Ins. Co. (Mo. App.) 179 S. W. 749; Amr. Home Life Ins. Co. v. Melton, 144 S. W. 362; Neff v. Metropolitan L. Ins. Co., 39 Ind. App. 250, 73 N. E. 1041; Clark v. Mutual Life Ins. Co., 129 Ga. 571, 59 S. E. 283; Schwartz v. Germania Life Ins. Co., 18 Minn. 448 (Gil. 404); Oliver v. Mutual Life Ins. Co., 97 Va. 134, 33 S. E. 536; Metropolitan Life Ins. Co. v. Howle, 62 Ohio St. 204, 56 N. E. 908; also same case on subsequent appeal, 68 Ohio St. 614, 68 N. E. 4. Numerous other authorities might be cited to the same effect, and we understand this rule to be virtually approved by our Supreme Court in Ins. Ass'n v. Harris, supra, in the discussion of the case of Schwartz v. Germania Ins. Co., supra.

[3] Keeping in mind the principles above stated, let us consider whether in this case there was any constructive or implied delivery of the policy. It is an undisputed fact that when the policy was issued, registered and transmitted by mail to the general agents of the company at Dallas, Texas, to be in due course forwarded to the local agent for delivery, it was upon express and positive instructions to personally interview the applicant and to require satisfactory evidence that the insured was in good health before a de-

livery of the policy should be made. The instruction to the agents was specifically to ascertain whether the applicant had any attack of la grippe, Spanish influenza, or pneumonia since being examined for the policy. Further, if it developed that such was the fact, the agents were required to report that fact to the home office by first mail, and to await further instructions from the company before offering to deliver the policy. It thus appears that there was not any issuance and transmission of the policy through the mails for unconditional delivery to the applicant. It clearly was not the intention of the company to effect a delivery until satisfied of the good health of the applicant since the date of his examination, and a manual delivery was clearly contemplated, but upon the condition indicated. There is not the slightest evidence that there was any waiver of this condition by the company; nor is there any element of estoppel in the case. It follows, we think, that since the action of the company, in withholding manual delivery until satisfied that applicant was in good health and subject to none of the diseases mentioned, was based upon an express and valid stipulation in the contract; it was a condition-precedent to the liability of the company. The minds of the parties never met, and there was no consummated contract.

[4] It is suggested by appellant's counsel that in this case there had been an application, payment of first year's premium, and unconditional acceptance of the risk with no reservations, and that therefore the insurer could not bind the insured by attempting to impose conditions upon the delivery of the policy not contemplated in the contract, without his consent. The vice in this argument is that it assumes that there was an unconditional acceptance of the application, and an attempt to impose conditions outside its provisions. The facts are to the contrary. The basis for the action of the company in refusing to consummate the delivery until satisfied as to the applicant's health, was a provision in the application itself. This was a part of the contract. It was an agreement the parties could lawfully make, and should be enforced. To hold otherwise would be for the court to make a contract for the parties. Until the proposal was accepted, without reservation, there was no completion of the contract, and no final consummation of delivery. Yount v. Prudential Life Ins. Co. (Mo. App.) 179 S. W. 749, and authorities there cited.

[5] There is another ground upon which we think it should be held that the trial court properly rendered judgment for appellee. If it should be conceded that a constructive or implied delivery was made by the placing of the policy in the mails, nevertheless it was subject, in the absence of waiver or estoppel, to the condition that the insured should then be in good health. This stipula-

tion was contained in the very proposal for insurance, and was binding upon the applicant and his beneficiary. There is no pretense that the company or its authorized agents knew of the illness of Mr. Denton, which began January 2d, and which, in the course of a few days, developed into pneumonia, which caused his death. Several of the authorities cited above recognize the rule that under such conditions even a manual delivery of the policy would not preclude the company from proving the fact, and thus avoiding liability under the very terms of the application and policy. This rule is expressly recognized by our Supreme Court in the case of Ins. Ass'n v. Harris, supra, and is applicable to the facts of this case. It was there held that:

"If the applicant had then been dead or not in good health, the policy would never have been binding; but, as he was alive, it became effectual at once, if he was also in good health, unless other provisions postponed this conclusion."

[6] It is true that "good health," as used in such connection, does not imply that the applicant is free from slight ailments. It means that he is not suffering from any serious or fatal illness or disease, which is usually a question for the court or jury. Under the agreed facts, it appears that the family physician of applicant was unwilling to testify that he was in good health after January 2d, the day before the policy was placed in the mails. It appears that applicant died directly from pneumonia, but that disease was immediately caused by influenza. It is true that the physician also stated that, in his opinion, the fatal illness dated from January 8th, and that if pneumonia had not developed, applicant would probably have survived. We think, however, the testimony on this point was sufficient to justify a finding by the trial court that applicant was affected with a serious and dangerous disease, which directly contributed to the immediate cause of his death, and therefore he was not in good health at the time even when the policy was placed in the mails for transmission to the agents of the company.

[7] It is our duty to affirm the judgment of the lower court, if there be any ground to support it. In our opinion, the judgment is referable to either or both the grounds of support indicated, and we have concluded that it should be affirmed.

We will now briefly consider the two cases mainly relied upon by appellant, Fidelity Mutual Life Ass'n v. Harris, supra, and Unterharnscheidt v. Life Ins. Co., supra.

We have already pointed out that in the Harris Case our Supreme Court qualified the doctrine that where the application and policy provide that it shall not take effect until delivery, a manual delivery is not necessary, but a constructive delivery may result, by

recognizing that the transmission to an agent or to the insured must be unconditional before a delivery could be implied. This condition is clearly recognized by the court in discussing the case of Schwartz v. Ins. Co. supra, which was not challenged, but indeed tacitly approved. Furthermore, the questions really decided in the Harris Case were merely whether the law of Texas or of Pennsylvania should control in determining the validity and construction of the contract; and whether, under the undisputed evidence, there was any liability on the part of the insurance company. The holding was that the law of Pennsylvania should control, and that under the facts the company should not be held liable, although there had been in that case an actual delivery to the assured.

As to the Unterharnscheidt Case, it is concededly more difficult of differentiation. The facts are very like those in the instant case. and the insurance company was held liable, notwithstanding there was no actual delivery. A close analysis of this case, however, discloses that, when the policy was mailed and at the date it should have reached the agent by due course of mail. settlement had been made for the first premium. as found by the jury. The court also found that the undisputed evidence showed that the disease from which the insured died did not develop until several days after the policy should have reached the agent. The court found there was nothing to rebut the presumption that the state of health of the applicant, existing at the date of his application, continued at the time the policy was executed and sent to the agent. The holding of the court may be summarized in this paragraph, at page 234 of 160 Iowa, at page 463 of 138 N. W., at page 748 of 45 L. R. A. (N. S.):

"In other words, the applicant had complied with all the requirements of the contract on his part, and was entitled to receive the policy. He was not responsible for the voluntary absence of the agent, and his rights cannot be abridged or lost by the failure of the agent to perform his duty in the premises."

It thus appears that not only had the first premium been paid, but that the applicant was in a state of good health when the policy was transmitted for delivery. In the instant case, while settlement had been made with the company by the giving of a note, there was evidence tending to show that the applicant was not in good health, when the policy was transmitted with instructions not to deliver if the applicant was not in good health.

If we have not successfully distinguished the Unterharnscheidt Case, nevertheless, we think the great weight of authority, as well as reason, supports our conclusion that the policy in this case never became effective and binding on the company.

[8] There only remains to be considered the question of the alleged error in admitting the letter from the general agents of the company to the local agent. The objections urged were that the letter was ex parte, unknown to and not binding on the plaintiff or her husband, self-serving, and tended to change, novate, and modify the written contract of insurance. We do not think that the letter was subject to any of these objections. It was competent upon the issue of the delivery of the policy, and especially the intention of the company in that respect. It was the contention of the appellant that delivery of the policy to the local agent was delivery to the insured, and it was permissible for the company to show what were the instructions to its agents before it finally accepted the proposal and effected a delivery. As against the objections urged, we hold that the letter was admissible and competent testimony.

Finding no reversible error, the judgment will be affirmed.

Affirmed.

JENKINS, J., being disqualified, did not participate in this decision.

BUSBEE et al. v. BUSBEE et al. (No. 6361.)

(Court of Civil Appeals of Texas. Austin. May 13, 1921.)

1. Appeal and error ⟐⟐753(2)—Judgment affirmed in absence of assignments of error and fundamental error.

Where appellants' brief contains no assignment of error, judgment must be affirmed unless the record discloses fundamental error.

2. Appeal and error ⟐⟐722(1)—Copies of findings of fact designated as assignments of error held not such.

Brief of appellant held not to contain assignments of error, though it referred to copies of certain of the trial court's findings of fact and designated them assignments of error, such alleged assignments not charging that the trial court committed any error, and not being followed up by any proposition in the brief, as required by the rules, although it contained what were called propositions, which were mere recitals of certain testimony contained in the statement of facts, not asserting any proposition of law.

3. Appeal and error ⟐⟐745—Assignments of error may be considered though not filed below.

Where findings of fact and conclusions of law were filed after the final judgment was rendered, under rule 101 (142 S. W. xxiv) appellants had the right to complain thereof by assignments of error presented in their brief,

though not contained in the transcript, and not filed in the court below.

Appeal from District Court, Brown County; J. O. Woodward, Judge.

Action by Lorena Busbee and others against T. B. Busbee and others. Judgment for plaintiffs, and defendants appeal. Affirmed.

A. L. Brantley, of Eastland, and J. L. Alford, of Rising Star, for appellants.

McCartney, Foster & McGee, of Brownwood, for appellees.

KEY, C. J. [1, 2] Appellants' brief contains no assignments of error, and therefore the judgment must be affirmed, unless the record discloses fundamental error. The brief referred to copies certain of the trial court's findings of fact, and designates them assignments of error, the following being a sample:

"First Assignment of Error.

"(T. R. page 40, tenth finding of fact.) I find that T. B. Busbee used $500 belonging to his wife, Mrs. A. L. Busbee, in the purchase of the land involved in this suit, situated in Rising Star, Tex., and that the interest on this money since it was used amounts to the sum of $350, or a total of $850, and that the plaintiffs are entitled to charge against the interest of T. B. Busbee in said community estate two-thirds of said sum or the sum of $566.65 instead of that much interest in said Rising Star land."

It will be noted that the alleged assignments do not charge that the trial court committed any error; nor does the brief follow them up with any proposition, as required by the rules. It is true that it contains what is called propositions, but these are mere recitals of certain testimony contained in the statement of facts, and do not assert any proposition of law.

[3] We do not sustain appellees' contention that the alleged assignments should not be considered because they were not filed in the court below and copied from the transcript, because, as the findings of fact and conclusions of law were filed after the final judgment was rendered, under rule 101 (142 S. W. xxiv) appellants had the right to complain of such findings and conclusions by assignments of error presented in their brief, though not contained in the transcript. Moody v. Bonham, 178 S. W. 1020; Craver v. Greer, 107 Tex. 356, 179 S. W. 862. However, that rule does not dispense with assignments of error, and, as appellants' brief in this case contains no assignments of error, it must be disregarded.

We have discovered no fundamental error, and therefore the judgment is affirmed.

Affirmed.

QUINN v. QUINN.   (No. 670.)

(Court of Civil Appeals of Texas. Beaumont.
May 20, 1921.   Rehearing Denied
June 8, 1921.)

1. Brokers ⟨⟩66—Fact that assistance was
   required in selling land no bar to compensation under agreement to divide commissions.

Where broker agreed to pay one assisting
him half the commission if he should first call
attention of buyer to land listed, the fact that
a sale of a particular farm would not have been
made to the purchaser furnished but for the efforts of the broker in selling vendor's lien notes
and a tract of land for such purchaser would
not prevent a recovery by the assistant of the
agreed compensation.

2. Brokers ⟨⟩66—One who first pointed out a
   farm for sale after listed entitled to agreed
   part of commission, though before listed broker called purchaser's attention thereto.

Where before a farm was listed with a
broker for sale, and when the purchaser was
in no way interested therein, the broker called
it to his attention, but not with a view to making a sale, and agreed to pay one assisting him a
portion of commissions received on sales of
land, and the farm was first pointed out to the
purchaser by such assistant after it was listed, the assistant was entitled to recover the
agreed compensation.

3. Brokers ⟨⟩66—Ordinary rules governing
   rights of real estate agents held not to apply
   to commissions as between brokers.

Where broker agreed to pay to one assisting him one-half of commissions earned from
sales of land brought about through the efforts
of the assistant, the ordinary rules governing
the rights of real estate agents to commissions
for sale of lands had no application; the rights
of the parties being governed by the contract as
made between them.

Appeal from District Court, Jefferson
County; W. H. Davidson, Judge.

Suit by Paul Quinn against B. E. Quinn.
Judgment for plaintiff, and defendant appeals. Affirmed.

Collins, Morris & Barnes, of Beaumont,
for appellant.

Smith, King & Hart, of Beaumont, for appellee.

HIGHTOWER, C. J. The appellee, Paul
Quinn, as plaintiff below, filed this suit in
the district court of Jefferson county against
appellant, B. E. Quinn, to recover $2,049.76,
with interest on that amount at the rate of
6 per cent. per annum from January 14,
1920, and upon trial before the court without
a jury, appellee recovered judgment for the
full amount sued for, and from that judgment B. E. Quinn appealed to this court.

Appellee claimed that the amount sued
for by him was due him by appellant for

services rendered to appellant as a real estate agent and dealer under a parol contract
between them. In the year 1919, and for
several years prior thereto, appellant was
engaged in the real estate business in the
city of Beaumont, and had a well-established business of that character, which consisted
of buying and selling lands and listing lands
of others for sale on commission. Appellee alleged, substantially, that about May 1, 1919,
he entered into a parol contract with appellant to assist him in his real estate business,
and that under such contract appellant had
become liable to him for services rendered for
the amount for which he sued, and which appellant had refused to pay him. Appellee
alleged the nature and terms of the contract
to be as follows:

"That heretofore, to wit, on or about the 1st
day of May, 1919, the defendant employed the
plaintiff, Paul Quinn, to assist him with his said
real estate business in Jefferson county, Tex.,
and on or about said date entered into a binding
and legal agreement and contract with this
plaintiff, to assist him with his real estate business, which said contract and agreement was
oral and, in substance, as follows, to wit: Defendant agreed to furnish an office and to pay
all expenses incident to the conducting of said
real estate business, and to furnish an automobile and defray the expenses of said automobile in its operation and repair, etc.; that
the plaintiff should not be required to pay any
rent or expenses whatever in connection with
the operation of said real estate business, or
any expense in connection with the maintenance or operation of said automobile.

"That under said agreement it was the duty
of plaintiff to seek for purchasers of real estate, and to work to the end that property listed with the defendant's real estate business
should be sold; and by the terms of said agreement it was agreed by and between plaintiff and
defendant that where property was listed with
the defendant for sale, and the plaintiff should
be the first to get in touch or call the attention of a purchaser to any property listed with
the defendant for sale and belonging to others
than himself and one R. E. Smith, and a sale
should be consummated with such person to
whom plaintiff had presented such property first,
then plaintiff was to receive as compensation
on such sale one-half of the gross commission
received as the result of such sale."

This is a sufficient statement of appellee's
pleading to show what he claimed the parol
contract between him and appellant to be.
Appellant's answer consisted of a general
demurrer, general denial, and a special averment as to the terms of the contract that was
made between him and appellee. Appellant's
version of the contract, as contained in his
answer, was as follows:

"Defendant did employ plaintiff to assist him
in his real estate business, and by the terms of
such agreement plaintiff was to distribute literature, put up signs on property listed for

sale, and list new property and new clients, and, on the condition that plaintiff would distribute literature, post signs, and list new business, defendant agreed to give plaintiff one-half of the commission on the sales of property that he (plaintiff) should make and carry through to conclusion without the assistance of defendant; that plaintiff did not carry out the terms of his said employment and did not distribute literature as he agreed to do, and he did not post signs as he agreed to do, and he did not try to list new business as he agreed to do, and, instead of being diligent in his work and complying with the contract, plaintiff would lie around the office, and on several occasions he was found asleep in the office during business hours when clients would come to the office on business, and, though plaintiff breached his contract, yet defendant advanced him certain sums of money hereinafter more specifically alleged, and gave him credit for certain commissions which he had not earned and was not entitled to."

The real controversy between the parties was whether the appellee was entitled to one-half of the commission which was received by appellant for the sale of a certain farm in Jefferson county known as the Richardson-Walker farm, which commission amounted to $5,444.81. It was the contention of appellee that after this farm had been listed for sale with appellant as a real estate dealer, he (appellee) about the 1st of December, 1919, made known to Albert and Herman Dommert the fact that said farm was listed with appellant for sale by its owners, and that he pointed out to said Dommerts on a map in appellant's office the location of this farm, and informed said Dommerts of facts which he considered made the farm a very valuable one, and that at the time he so mentioned this farm to the Dommerts, and after his statement as to its being a very desirable farm, etc., the Dommerts seemed quite interested in the proposition, and that afterwards a sale of the farm to the Dommerts resulted. He further alleged that he was the first to call attention of the Dommerts to the fact that the Richardson-Walker farm was listed with appellant for sale, and that he was the first to present and point out this property to the Dommerts, and that he worked diligently with the view to consummating a sale of said farm to said Dommerts, and that largely through his efforts the purchase of the farm by the Dommerts was brought about.

Appellant, in his answer, specially denied that appellee was the first to call attention of the Dommerts to the fact that the Richardson-Walker farm was listed with him for sale, but, on the contrary, alleged that he (appellant) first informed the Dommerts that said farm was listed with him for sale, and that it was through his own efforts and diligence that the Dommerts became the purchasers of said farm. Appellant further alleged, substantially, that under the parol contract between him and appellee the latter was entitled to no part of the commission received for the sale of said farm, for the reason that according to the terms of the parol contract appellee was only to share in commissions received on new business that had come in to appellant's office after the making of such parol contract—in other words, new business—and that he was only entitled, under the terms of the contract, to share in commissions paid by new clients, and that the Dommerts were not new clients, but that, on the contrary, they were old clients of appellant, before the making of the contract between him and appellee. He further alleged, substantially, that the Dommerts did not agree to purchase said farm, and would not have purchased said farm but for the fact that he (appellant) bound himself to sell for the Dommerts $15,000 worth of certain vendor's lien notes for their full face value, principal and interest, and also but for the fact that appellant agreed and bound himself to sell for the Dommerts or buy from them a tract of land owned by them in Jefferson county of some 539 acres at a net profit of $10 per acre, and he alleged that he did sell said vendor's lien notes and said land for the Dommerts, as he agreed and bound himself to do, and thereby enabled said Dommerts to purchase said farm, which otherwise they were not willing, ready, or able to do, and that therefore appellee was not entitled to any part of the commission received for the sale of said farm.

Upon the trial below the appellee testified that on the 1st of December, 1919, the said Albert and Herman Dommert, who were brothers and who were residents of the state of Louisiana, came to Beaumont, and early in the morning on that day came into appellant's real estate office, and that he (appellee) was alone in the office when they came in, appellant not having come to the office at that time, but came in some hour or so later. He testified, substantially, that while the Dommert brothers were in the office, and before appellant came to the office on the morning in question, he called attention of the Dommerts to the fact that the Quinn Realty Company, which was the business name under which appellant conducted his real estate business, had listed with it for sale the Richardson-Walker farm, and that he pointed out this farm on a map then in the office, and told the Dommerts how the farm was located, etc., about the advantage of good roads, etc., and that at that time the Dommerts seemed interested in what he stated to them about this farm, and that up to that time the Dommerts had not been at all interested in the farm, and never knew that the same was for sale, and especially that they never knew that the same was listed with the Quinn

Realty Company for sale. On that trip to Beaumont the Dommerts did not remain more than a day or two, but returned to their home in Louisiana, and about the 14th of December following they again came to Beaumont, and the sale and purchase of this farm was again discussed with them, both by appellee and by appellant, and they became interested in this farm. The testimony shows that appellant and appellee, on this second trip to Beaumont, accompanied the Dommerts to this farm, which was some five miles west of Beaumont, and it was carefully looked over by the Dommerts, in company with appellant, and after the return to the city of Beaumont negotiations were commenced which resulted in a consummation of a sale of this farm to the Dommerts for the total consideration of $110,000, $40,000 of which was paid in cash. The testimony shows that appellant sold for the Dommerts $15,000 worth of vendor's lien notes for their full face value, and that appellant and another purchased from the Dommerts the tract of 539 acres of land hereinbefore mentioned, at a profit to the Dommerts of $10 per acre. It was testified by the Dommerts that their purchase of the farm in question depended upon their being able to sell said vendor's lien notes and said tract of land at a profit of $10 per acre to them, and that they could not have purchased the farm had they not been able to sell the notes and farm as they did, and in that connection both the Dommerts testified that the sale of these notes and the tract of land before mentioned was consummated entirely by the appellant. Appellee, testified, however, on the trial that on the trip back from the farm to Beaumont on the day that the Dommerts had inspected the farm, they stated, unconditionally, that they were going to buy the farm for the consideration agreed upon, and that they did not claim that they would be unable to do so unless they could sell said vendor's lien notes and said tract of land, and in that connection appellee further testified that appellant voluntarily stated to the Dommerts that he would sell for them said vendor's lien notes and said tract of land at the profit to them of $10 per acre.

[1] It will be seen from the foregoing statement of the pleadings of the parties that they disagreed entirely as to the terms of the parol contract between them. If the parol contract was substantially as alleged by appellee, as we have shown above, and if he first called attention of the Dommerts to the fact that the Richardson-Walker farm was listed with the Quinn Realty Company for sale, and if his efforts in connection with the transaction contributed to the sale to the Dommerts, then he was entitled to share in the commission received on such sale, even though it was not by his efforts alone that the sale was finally consummated. It is true

that it was the contention of appellant that before appellee would be entitled, under the terms of their agreement, to share in any commission received for the sale of land listed with the Quinn Realty Company, he (appellee) must have been the first to make known to the purchaser the fact that such land was so listed, and to present the proposition to the purchaser, and by his own efforts and alone carry out and consummate the deal, unaided in any way by appellant himself; but, as we have already shown, appellee testified that all he was required to do, under the terms of the oral agreement, in order to share in a commission received, was to be the first to call attention of the purchaser to the fact that the land was listed with the company for sale, and to present the proposition to the purchaser first, and to use his best efforts to consummate and assist in the consummation of a sale. The trial court filed no findings of fact or conclusions of law, but, as we view the evidence in the case, as disclosed by the record, it was sufficient to warrant a finding by the trial court that the oral contract between the parties was substantially as claimed by appellee, and the evidence was also sufficient, if given credence by the trial court, to warrant a finding by him that appellee was the first to call attention of the Dommerts to the fact that the Richardson-Walker farm was listed with the Quinn Realty Company for sale, and to present said property to them, and that his efforts to sell said property to the Dommerts contributed largely to the consummation of the sale and purchase of said farm, and that therefore he was entitled, under the terms of the oral contract, to share in the commission that was received by appellant for the sale of said farm, to the extent of one-half thereof, which amount was allowed him by the trial court's judgment. The fact, if it was a fact, that the sale of this farm would not have been made to the Dommert brothers but for the efforts of appellant in selling said vendor's lien notes and said tract of land for them, would not, under the terms of the parol contract as claimed by appellee, prevent a recovery by him. Under the terms of the contract as he claimed it, his right to share in the commission was not conditioned upon his being the sole cause of the sale of property listed with the Quinn Realty Company, but, as he claimed the contract to be, he was only required to use diligent efforts to make sales of property listed with said company and to be the first to point out to a purchaser such property, and then, if negotiations so commenced resulted in a sale by the efforts of both appellant and appellee, and not alone on account of the efforts on the part of appellee, he would be entitled to share in the commission. The only real controversy in the case is as to the terms of the parol contract, and that was a question of fact for the determination of the court, and, as we have said, the evidence of appellee, if given credence, was sufficient to warrant a finding that the terms of the contract were such as claimed by him.

[2] It is strenuously contended by appellant, among other things, that even if the parol contract between himself and appellee was as claimed by the latter, still, under the evidence adduced upon the trial, appellee was not entitled to recover, for the reason that appellant himself was shown to have been the first to point out to the Dommerts the Richardson-Walker farm, which he did one day while he and they were driving out to a farm owned by the Dommerts near Beaumont, some time in the fall of 1919. The road on which the parties were driving ran close to said farm, and while passing thereby appellant did call attention of the Dommerts to said farm, but the undisputed evidence shows that at that time the farm had not been listed with appellant for sale by its owners, and further shows that the Dommerts were in no way interested in the purchase of the farm at that time, and it was not called to their attention with any view on the part of appellant of making any sale of same to them. We hold that the mere calling attention of the Dommerts to the farm, as they were passing along, under these facts, did not constitute a pointing out of the farm to the Dommerts for sale, and that it could not be said, upon such facts, that appellant, and not the appellee, was the first to present this property to the Dommerts for sale.

[3] The ordinary rules governing the rights of real estate agents to commissions for sale of lands have no application to this case, but, on the contrary, the rights of the parties must be governed by the contract as made between them.

What we have said, in effect, disposes of all assignments of error, and it would serve no useful purpose to discuss them separately.

The judgment of the trial court will be affirmed.

**WILMARTH et al. v. REAGAN et al.
(No. 2411.)**

(Court of Civil Appeals of Texas. Texarkana.
May 18, 1921. Rehearing Denied
May 26, 1921.)

1. **Levees ⇐⇒8 — Levee improvement district lawfully created in so far as commissioners' court concerned.**

Where sufficient notice of hearing of the commissioners' court of a county at which a levee improvement district was created was given in compliance with the requirement of Laws 1918 (4th Called Sess.) c. 44, the district was lawfully created in so far as concerns the power of the commissioners' court to create it.

2. **Levees ⇐⇒7—Court of Civil Appeals must treat as concluded questions of boundaries of district, etc.**

In view of Laws 1918 (4th Called Sess.) c. 44, § 6, the Court of Civil Appeals must treat as concluded by order of the commissioners' court of a county creating and organizing a levee improvement district questions of the correctness of the description of the boundaries of the district, and of the inclusion of land which should not have been included.

3. **Levees ⇐⇒5—Quo warranto ⇐⇒8—Existence of district could be questioned only by state.**

Under Laws 1918 (4th Called Sess.) c. 44, § 7, a levee improvement district was a governmental agency, and a body politic and corporate, and its existence and right to act as such could be questioned only in quo warranto proceedings prosecuted by or on behalf of the state.

4. **Levees ⇐⇒11—Plaintiffs held not entitled to maintain suit in so far as it was to annul report of commissioners of appraisement.**

Despite Const. art. 5, § 8, under Laws 1918 (4th Called Sess.) c. 44, §§ 21–23, plaintiffs, attacking an order of the commissioners' court of a county creating a levee improvement district, held not entitled on the allegations of their petition to maintain their suit, in so far as it was to annul the report of the commissioners of appraisement assessing damages and benefits.

5. **Levees ⇐⇒34—Bond election not invalid because held by manager alone.**

In view of Vernon's Sayles' Ann. Civ. St. 1914, arts. 3063, 3077, the mere fact that a levee improvement district's election on the question of issuing bonds was held by the manager alone is no reason for holding it invalid.

6. **Appeal and error ⇐⇒1042(1) — Error in striking petition harmless where it does not appear it was amendable.**

If it was error to strike out the petition instead of treating it as bad on demurrer, such error should be regarded as harmless where it does not appear from anything in the record that plaintiffs offered to amend, or that they could have amended the petition to state a cause of action.

Appeal from District Court, Kaufman County; Joel R. Bond, Judge.

Suit by I. L. Wilmarth and others against J. C. Reagan and others. From judgment for defendants, plaintiffs appeal. Affirmed.

This was a suit by appellants I. L. Wilmarth, Frank R. Lewis, W. A. Tucker, A. L. Trail, and T. J. Gilkey against the Kaufman county levee improvement district No. 9, and against J. C. Reagan, J. J. Roddy, and John Garner as the supervisors, and J. J. Davis, C. C. Ritter, and B. B. Hatley as the commissioners of appraisement of said district. Exceptions having been sustained to the plaintiffs' second amended petition, they asked and obtained leave to file a third amended petition. On motion of appellees, the latter petition, when filed, was stricken out, and judgment was rendered that appellants take nothing by their suit.

The second amended petition is too long to set out here. It appeared from the allegations therein that the purposes of the suit were as follows:

I. To annul the order of the commissioners' court of Kaufman county purporting to have been made in conformity to authority conferred by the Act April 2, 1918 (General Laws, Fourth Called Session, pp. 97 to 117), creating said Kaufman county levee improvement district No. 9; or, in the alternative, to rearrange the boundaries thereof so as to exclude therefrom lands belonging to appellants which, they alleged, had been wrongfully included therein. The grounds relied on for this relief were alleged to be: (1) That "sufficient notice" of the hearing resulting in the passing of said order was not given property owners interested. (2) That the boundaries of the district were not sufficiently described and fixed, in that the field notes thereof were incorrect. (3) That lands belonging to plaintiffs which should not have been were included in the district.

II. To annul the report made by the commissioners of appraisement of the district assessing damages and benefits to lands therein, and to annul an order alleged to have been made by the supervisors of said district approving said report; or, on the alternative, to compel said commissioners of appraisement to reassess said damages and benefits. The ground relied on for this relief was alleged to be that the assessments were discriminatory against appellants in favor of J. C. Reagan, one of the supervisors, and others.

III. To "prohibit" the sale of bonds voted to pay for the proposed improvements in said district, and to "prohibit" the levy of a tax on property in said district to pay such bonds. The ground relied on for this relief was alleged to be that, whereas a manager and two clerks were appointed to hold the bond election, it was held by the manager alone.

John H. Sharp, of Ennis, E. E. Hurt, of Dallas, and Adair Dyer, of Ennis, for appellants.

James A. Cooley, of Kaufman, for appellees.

WILLSON, C. J. (after stating the facts as above). [1] While appellants charged in their second amended petition that "sufficient notice" was not given of the hearing at which the improvement district in question was created, it appeared from the records made a part of said petition by reference thereto, and before the court as exhibits to other pleadings in the case, that the requirement of the Act April 2, 1918 (General Laws, Fourth Called Session, pp. 97 to 117), with reference to notice of such hearing was complied with.

Therefore there was no merit in appellants' contention that the district was not lawfully created, so far as it was based on allegations in said petition questioning the power of the commissioners' court of Kaufman county to create it. The power existed by force of the statute, was invoked by the filing of the petition for the creation of the district, and was exercised after due notice had been given persons concerned.

[2] It may be that the power the court possessed was not properly exercised, in that, as charged in said petition, the boundaries of the district were not correctly described, and in that land belonging to appellants was included which should not have been included in the district. But those were questions the trial court should (as it did) have treated, and which this court must treat as concluded by the order of the commissioners' court creating and organizing the district, in the absence, as was the case, of allegations showing that the action of said commissioners' court was the result of fraud practiced; for, by the express terms of the act (section 6), the commissioners' court had "exclusive jurisdiction [quoting] to determine all issues in respect to the creation, or not, of such district, and of all subsequent proceedings in respect to said district if the same should be created." It has been held that the "exclusive jurisdiction" conferred in such cases forbids a review by another tribunal of questions as to the sufficiency of a description in a petition for the creation of such a district, and as to whether a district as created conforms to such description or not. Parker v. Drainage District, 148 S. W. 351; and see 19 C. J. 641, 664, 680, 681.

[3] If, however, it should be said that the effect of the provision referred to in section 6 of the statute was not to forbid such review by other courts, the review could not be had at the instance of appellants, but must have been at the instance of the state, or on its behalf. By the terms of the act referred to (section 7) the district, colorably, at least, was "a governmental agency and a body politic and corporate," and its existence and and right to act as such could be questioned only in quo warranto proceedings prosecuted by or on behalf of the state. Parker v. Drainage District, 148 S. W. 351; Cochran v. Kennon, 161 S. W. 67; Holt v. State, 176 S. W. 743; Minear v. McVea, 185 S. W. 1048; Crabb v. School District, 146 S. W. 528.

[4] Nor do we think the trial court erred when he concluded that it did not appear from the allegations in said petition that appellants were entitled to maintain their suit so far as it was to annul the report of the commissioners of appraisement assessing damages and benefits to lands in the district, and in so far as it was to annul a decree alleged to have been made by the supervisors (but which, in

fact, was made by the commissioners of appraisement, as appeared from other parts of the record) approving said report. By the terms of the act (sections 21–23) it was the duty of the commissioners of appraisement, after viewing the lands in the district, to assess the "amounts of benefits and damages" to accrue to such lands as a result of the improvements determined upon; to make a report of their findings in those respects; and, at a time and place fixed, after notice to persons concerned, hear and determine objections to the report. It was also the duty of said commissioners of appraisement, after modifying their report so as to make it conform to changes determined upon at such hearing, to make a decree confirming the report as modified. The findings, as so confirmed, it was declared in the act, "shall [quoting] be final and conclusive." If the court below, in the fact of that declaration, had power in any event to annul the report and order of the commissioners of appraisement, it must have been by force of section 8 of article 5 of the Constitution, which confers on district courts "general original jurisdiction over all causes of action whatever for which a remedy or jurisdiction is not provided by law or this Constitution." We do not think a right in the trial court to grant relief in the respects specified can be predicated on the language quoted; for jurisdiction in such cases was provided by law when power to assess benefits and damages to lands in such a district was conferred upon commissioners of appraisement provided for in the act, and a remedy for assessments wrongfully made was provided when owners of lands in the district were given a right to be heard on objections made by them to the assessments.

[5] It is plain, we think, that the suit was not maintainable so far as it was to "prohibit" the sale of bonds voted, and to "prohibit" the levy of a tax to provide a fund to pay the bonds, on the ground that the election at which the bonds were voted was held by the manager appointed to hold it in the absence of clerks appointed to assist in holding it. Conceding that the validity of the election could be questioned otherwise then in a proceeding to contest it (Robertson v. Haynes, 100 S. W. 735; and see Smith v. Reaves, 208 S. W. 545), it is clear the mere fact that it was held by the manager alone would not be a reason for holding it to be invalid (Vernon's Statutes, arts. 3077, 3063; Savage v. Umphries, 118 S. W. 893; 20 C. J. 179).

[6] As, for the reasons stated, we think a case entitling appellants to relief was not made by the allegations in the second amended petition, we hold the trial court did not err when he sustained the exceptions interposed by appellees to same. The case made

by the allegations in the third amended petition was not materially different from that made by said second amended petition, and therefore that petition was also subject to the objection that it did not state a cause of action entitling appellants to relief. If it was error to strike it out, instead of treating it as bad on demurrer, the error should be regarded as a harmless one; for, as before stated, the case made by said third amended petition was not different from that made by the second amended petition, and it does not appear from anything in the record that appellants offered to so amend, or that they could have so amended the petition as to state a cause of action.

The judgment is affirmed.

═══

PEACOCK v. AUG. A. BUSCH & CO.
(No. 699.)

(Court of Civil Appeals of Texas. Beaumont. May 20, 1921.)

1. Evidence ⊜271(18)—Instrument signed by plaintiff held properly admitted when offered by plaintiff.

In an action to recover balance due on note for $2,500, plaintiff was properly permitted to introduce in evidence an instrument signed by plaintiff, and not defendant, whereby plaintiff agreed to reconvey land when an older note was reduced to $2,500, as against an objection that it was in the nature of a self-serving declaration, plaintiff having the right to demand possession of such instrument after reconveying the property to defendant in whose hands the instrument had been originally placed.

2. Evidence ⊜353(9)—Instrument signed only by party offering it held admissible.

An instrument whereby plaintiffs agreed to reconvey land when an old note should be reduced to $2,500 need not be signed by defendant to be binding and effective on plaintiff, and was not inadmissible in an action on a new note for $2,500 when offered by plaintiff, in whose possession it then was, on the ground that witness, testifying that defendant had knowledge of the existence of the instrument and assented to its terms, was mistaken in a statement that defendant had signed, such mistake only going to his credibility.

Appeal from District Court, Falls County; Prentice Oltorf, Judge.

Action by August A. Busch & Co. against Frank Peacock. Judgment for plaintiffs, and defendant appeals. Affirmed.

E. W. Bounds, of Fort Worth, for appellant.

F. M. Fitzpatrick, of Waco, and Frank Oltorf, of Marlin, for appellees.

WALKER, J. On the trial of this case, the appellees, plaintiffs below, offered in evidence the following instrument: .

"Whereas, Frank Peacock and wife Alice Peacock has conveyed to Aug. A. Busch & Co., Adolphus Busch and Edw. A. Faust, doing business under the firm name of Aug. A. Busch & Co., by deed dated October 5th, 1914, part of lots No. 10 and No. 20, block No. 4 according to the official town map of Marlin, Falls county, Texas, said property being described in said deed. Now it is agreed by Aug. A. Busch, Adolphus Busch & Company, acting through H. H. Hartman, Manager Dallas Branch of Aug. A. Busch & Company that said Aug. A. Busch, Adolphus Busch and Edw. A. Faust, doing business under the firm name of Aug. A. Busch & Company, will reconvey said property to Frank Peacock and Alice Peacock within a reasonable time after the amount due Aug. A. Busch & Co., by said Frank Peacock is reduced by payment to twenty five hundred dollars.

"Signed this the 5th day of October, 1914.
        "Aug. A. Busch & Co.,
        "By H. H. Hartman, Mgr."

The only assignment in the record complains of the admission of this instrument, on the ground (copying from bill of exception) that said instrument "came from the possession of the plaintiff, was not signed by the defendant, and was in the nature of a self-serving declaration." The instrument did come from the possession of the plaintiff, and was not signed by the defendant.

Appellee instituted this suit against appellant to recover the balance due on a note for $2,500, dated the 8th day of March, 1916. It was their contention that this note represented the balance due on an old account, which, on the 5th day of October, 1914, amounted to $8,469.52. The record shows that this account was closed by a note on that date, and, to secure the payment of the note, appellant deeded to appellees certain valuable real estate. Appellees reconveyed all this property to appellant on the 24th day of February, 1916.

[1] H. H. Hartman, a witness for appellees, testified that he was the district manager for appellees during the time covered by the deeds above mentioned, and handled this transaction with appellant; that he accepted the deed from appellant on condition that he would have it reconveyed to him when the old note was reduced to $2,500; that appellant did reduce the old note to $2,500, and, under the contract the property was reconveyed to him; that at the time of the execution and delivery by Peacock of the deed he, as manager of appellees, executed the contract, of which appellant complains, and that appellant saw this contract, and signed it at that time. It was the contention of appellant, and he so testified, that he paid the old note in full at the time appellees

redeeded him the property, and that the note sued on was executed by him to cover any possible sum that he might become due in the future; that, after the execution of the note, he bought large bills of goods from appellees, aggregating about $20,000, but paid cash for all goods so bought, and never afterwards became indebted to appellee in any sum; that he never paid appellees any sum on the note sued on, and the credits entered on the note were fictitious.

We do not think this testimony was subject to the criticisms urged. At the time this instrument was offered in evidence, it was properly in the hands of appellees. If their theory of the case is correct, when they executed their obligation to redeeding the property to appellant, they had the right to demand that he surrender to them this written obligation. Appellant no longer had any rights under it, and had no rights to its possession.

[2] Nor was it objectionable as being self-serving. While appellant denied any knowledge of the existence of the instrument until it was shown him on the trial, appellees testified that it was exhibited to him, and he assented to its terms. As it was not necessary for him to sign the contract to make it binding and effective against appellees, it was not made inadmissible on the ground that the witness was mistaken in his statement that appellant had signed it. This mistake in Hartman's testimony only went to his credibility, and, by entering judgment in favor of his principals, evidently the jury believed he was testifying truthfully.

The judgment of the trial court is affirmed.

WIEDNER v. WIEDNER. (No. 696.)

(Court of Civil Appeals of Texas. Beaumont. May 20, 1921.)

1. Divorce ⬤⟲55—Cruelty must not approach mutuality.

Divorces sought for on ground of cruelty will not be granted where the cruelty approaches mutuality and both have indulged therein.

2. Divorce ⬤⟲127(2)—Court not required to accept uncontradicted testimony of party in divorce action.

In an action by husband for divorce on the ground of cruelty, failure of defendant to deny charges made by the plaintiff raised no presumption in favor of the truthfulness of plaintiff's testimony, and, plaintiff being only witness to that fact, court was not required to accept his testimony as true, under Rev. St. 1911, art. 4633.

Appeal from District Court, Milam County; John Watson, Judge.

Suit by W. Wiedner against Louisa Wiedner. Judgment for defendant, and plaintiff appeals. Affirmed.

E. A. Wallace, of Cameron, for appellant. John A. Jones and U. S. Hearrell, both of Cameron, for appellee.

WALKER, J. [1] Appellant filed this suit against his wife, praying for divorce and for partition of certain property which he alleged was community. On a trial to the court without a jury, the divorce was denied, and no order was made affecting the property. This case, on its facts, comes clearly within the rule announced in Haygood v. Haygood, 25 Tex. 576; Beck v. Beck, 63 Tex. 34; Jones v. Jones, 60 Tex. 451; Hale v. Hale, 47 Tex. 336, 26 Am. Rep. 294; Bohan v. Bohan, 56 S. W. 959, denying divorces where the parties are guilty of recrimination. As said by Chief Justice Willie, in Beck v. Beck, supra:

"The cruelty must not approach to mutuality, nor be exercised sometimes by the one and sometimes by the other, though differing somewhat in degree."

[2] By her testimony and that of her witnesses, appellee fully controverted the charges that she had attempted to poison appellant and that she had been guilty of improper conduct with other men. If he is correct in his construction of the record that appellee did not deny that she had struck him, he is the only witness to that fact, and the court was not required to accept his testimony as true. The failure of the defendant to deny charges made by the plaintiff in divorce proceedings raises no presumption in favor of the truthfulness of plaintiff's testimony. R. C. S. 1911, art. 4633. On the facts of this record, we think the decree was properly denied. This disposition of the divorce question leaves nothing before us regarding the property issue.

The judgment of the trial court is in all things affirmed.

WESTERN UNION TELEGRAPH CO. v. BRETT. (No. 686.)

(Court of Civil Appeals of Texas. Beaumont. May 10, 1921. Rehearing Denied May 25, 1921.)

Appeal and error ⊂⊃742(1)—Reference necessary in brief to transcript in connection with statements made under assignments.

Assignments of error, submitted as propositions, cannot be considered on appeal, where there is not a reference in appellant's brief to the transcript or statement of facts, in connection with statements made under such assignments, as required by rule 31 (142 S. W. xiii).

Appeal from Harris County Court, at Law; Roy F. Campbell, Judge.

Suit by F. M. Brett against the Western Union Telegraph Company. Judgment for plaintiff, and the defendant appeals. Affirmed.

Hume & Hume, of Houston, and Francis R. Stark, of New York City, for appellant. S. B. Ehrenwerth, of Houston, for appellee.

HIGHTOWER, C. J. The appellee filed this suit in one of the justice courts of Harris county against the Western Union Telegraph Company, appellant, to recover damages in the sum of $200, alleged to have been sustained in consequence of the negligent failure on the part of appellant to promptly transmit and deliver a message which appellee had sent to one of his sons in the city of Houston, informing him of the serious illness of another of appellee's sons, a brother of the son at Houston. In the justice court appellee recovered judgment for the full amount claimed, and the telegraph company appealed to the county court at law of Harris county, where judgment was rendered against it for $180, and this appeal was prosecuted from the latter judgment.

There are several assignments of error found in appellant's brief, and each is submitted as a proposition of law within itself. Objection is made by appellee to the consideration of any of the assignments, for several reasons; one of the reasons being because there is not a reference in appellant's brief to the transcript or statement of facts in connection with any statement made under these assignments, as is required by rule 31 for briefing causes in this court (142 S. W. xiii). We find, upon inspection of appellant's brief, that the objections interposed by appellee to the consideration of these assignments are well taken, and should be sustained by this court. Rule 31 provides:

"To each of said propositions there shall be subjoined a brief statement, in substance, of such proceedings, or part thereof, contained in the record as will be necessary and sufficient to explain and support the proposition with reference to the pages of the record."

See Caffrey v. Bartlett Western R. Co., 198 S. W. 810; Hirsch v. Patton, 49 Tex. Civ. App. 499, 108 S. W. 1018; Beaumont Traction Co. v. Edge, 46 Tex. Civ. App. 448, 102 S. W. 746; Railway Co. v. Scott, 156 S. W. 294; Railway Co. v. Pemberton, 106 Tex. 463, 161 S. W. 2, 168 S. W. 126; Bain v. Coats, 228 S. W. 571.

Fundamental error is not claimed, and we have discovered none. The judgment will therefore be affirmed.

⊂⊃For other cases see same topic and KEY-NUMBER in all Key-Numbered Digests and Indexes

FISHER et ux. v. GULF PRODUCTION CO.
(No. 685.)

(Court of Civil Appeals of Texas. Beaumont.
May 18, 1921. Rehearing Denied
June 1, 1921.)

I. Homestead ⚖══122—Wife's right to homestead ceases on acquiring a new one, and husband's deed estops him.

A husband, acting in good faith, may select the homestead of the family, and when he has acquired a new home, and his wife has removed with him to the newly acquired homestead, a prior deed made by him without her concurrence to the former homestead becomes as to the husband operative as an estoppel against his right to recover the property, and the wife's right, being that of homestead only, ceases when a new homestead has been acquired and she removes thereto.

2. Homestead ⚖══123—Acceptance of money held ratification of transaction barring action for misrepresentations.

Where a husband and wife contracted to sell their homestead and the wife subsequently refused to join, notwithstanding that with the proceeds of the sale they had acquired a new homestead, and had removed thereto, their act in accepting the purchase money for the land with full knowledge of the material facts *held* a ratification, precluding them from recovering for false representations inducing the execution of the earnest money receipt by the wife.

3. Cancellation of instruments ⚖══37(4)—Pleading readiness to repay, if required, held not a tender.

In a suit to cancel a deed on the ground that it was procured through misrepresentations, a statement in plaintiffs' petition that, if they were required to pay money received as a condition precedent to recovery they were ready to do so, *held* not a tender.

Appeal from District Court, Chambers County; D. F. Singleton, Judge.

Action by E. H. Fisher and wife against the Gulf Production Company. Judgment for defendant, and plaintiffs appeal. Affirmed.

E. B. Pickett, Jr., and C. H. Cain, both of Liberty, for appellants.

J. Llewellyn, of Liberty, and D. Edw. Greer, of Houston, for appellee.

O'QUINN, J. Appellants, E. H. Fisher and Martha Fisher, husband and wife, brought this suit against appellee, Gulf Production Company, to set aside and cancel a deed of date October 31, 1918, to a tract of 69.72 acres of land, on the grounds of fraud, deception, and misrepresentation in the procurement of the deed.

The record does not disclose when this suit was filed, but on March 15, 1920, appellants filed their amended original petition herein, alleging fraud, deception, and misrepresenta-

tion in the procurement of said deed, and that same was made to and operated upon Mrs. Martha Fisher, to the effect that she, having signed the earnest money receipt for the $50, was bound in law to sign the deed, and that she could be required to do so, and that she believed and relied upon said misrepresentations so made to her, and unwillingly signed said deed, and further alleging fraud, in that the deed contained a recitation that it conveyed all the land owned by appellants in Chambers county, and further that the stipulation in the assignments of Keeble to Mrs. Martha Fisher of his interest in the royalty in the oil produced on said land recited that it was not to become operative until appellee had received the sum of $35,000 in royalty out of and from oil produced by said land, which she did not understand was to have been in said assignment.

Appellee answered by general and special exceptions, general denial, and specially that, by reason of the uncertainty in the description and lines of the tract of land conveyed, the clause in said deed which recited all lands owned by appellants in Chambers county merely intended to include the one tract bought, and no more, and that it followed the descriptive clause in the contract of sale given in the earnest money receipt, and that the acknowledgment of Martha Fisher was regular on its face, and, believing it stated the truth, appellee paid appellants the full consideration called for in said deed, without notice or knowledge of any vice or irregularity in either the execution or acknowledgment of said deed, and that appellants, without any manner of protest or notice to appellee, accepted and ever since have retained the full sum of money paid by appellee as consideration for said land, and had purchased a new and permanent home therewith, where they were living long before and at the time of the trial, and that by the acceptance and retention of said money and the purchase and occupation of said new home appellants had fully ratified said deed and its acknowledgment, and were estopped to rescind said deed or to sue for said land. At the conclusion of the evidence, the court, on motion of appellee, instructed the jury to return a verdict in its favor, which was done, and judgment thereon entered for appellee, from which appellants have appealed.

Appellants present five assignments of error, all leveled at the action of the court in instructing a verdict for appellee, contending the same was error, and especially by reason that the evidence raised and supported (1) a question of fact as to whether Mrs. Martha Fisher's execution of the deed conveying her homestead to appellee was induced by fraud and misrepresentation; and (2) also as to whether certain conditions regarding the $1/_{192}$ royalty assigned to Mrs. Fisher were secretly and fraudulently inserted in said as-

⚖══For other cases see same topic and KEY-NUMBER in all Key-Numbered Digests and Indexes

signment. As we view the record and construe the law, there is but one question necessary to be discussed, and that is the effect of appellant's having acquired and removed to another home, after deeding the land in controversy to appellee.

The undisputed evidence shows that the land in question was the separate property of appellant E. H. Fisher, husband of appellant Mrs. Martha Fisher; that same was the homestead of appellants on October 26, 1918, and had been for many years; that in August, 1918, a well which was being drilled near their said homestead by Walter Keeble and others acting with him was brought in, producing a considerable quantity of oil, and has since continued to produce oil in paying quantities; that on October 26, 1918, appellants executed and delivered to said Walter Keeble an earnest money receipt for $50, in which they contracted to sell and to convey to said Walter Keeble the land in question for $31,860, the said sale and conveyance to be concluded within 15 days from the date of said receipt, the said receipt reciting that said land was all the land appellants owned in Chambers county; that the said land was at the time under lease to the United Petroleum Company, which said lease provided for the payment of a one-eighth royalty to the owners of the land; that Keeble and those with whom he was associated had agreed with appellee to convey the land to appellee, or to have same conveyed to it, subject to the lease contract with the United Petroleum Company, for $35,000, retaining a $1/32$ royalty; that on October 31, 1918, in pursuance of said contract with Keeble, appellants executed and delivered to appellee, who was taking the same from Keeble, a general warranty deed in usual form, with joint and privy acknowledgments, to the land in question, for the said consideration of $31,860 cash, which was paid to appellants by appellee by draft on the South Texas Commercial National Bank of Houston, Tex., which said draft was accepted by appellants, duly indorsed by both, and cashed the next day; that shortly thereafter appellant E. H. Fisher purchased some 700 acres of land in Harris county, Tex., paying for same out of the money received from appellee for the land in question, and with his wife, Martha Fisher, removed to said land in Harris county, and have since that time occupied same as their home; that, at the time said deed to appellee was executed, appellant Mrs. Martha Fisher stated that she did not want to sign said deed, that she had backed out and was not going to sign same, and that they (she and her husband) were not getting enough for said land; that after considerable discussion, she contending that she was not going to sign the deed, and Keeble and others urging that, having signed the earnest money receipt, she was in law bound to sign said deed, she finally signed same, but testified on the trial that she did not willingly do so, and that she did not state to the officer taking her acknowledgment that she did not wish to retract it; that at the time appellants executed the said deed Keeble assigned his interest in the $1/32$ royalty agreed to be paid to him and his associates to Mrs. Martha Fisher as an inducement for her to sign said deed, the same amounting to $1/192$ royalty interest in the oil produced from said land, to become operative when appellee had received the sum of $35,000 as a royalty from said land.

The gist of appellants' propositions under their assignments of error is that a deed to the homestead, which has been procured by fraud and deception of the grantee practiced upon the grantors, and particularly upon the wife, is not a valid conveyance, the rule, both of law and in equity, being that fraud renders all contracts void ab initio, and the rule of law also being that the delivery of a deed which is not voluntary, but is brought about by misrepresentations of fraudulent deception, does not pass title, and especially asserting that the deed which Mrs. Fisher made to her homestead was void as to her rights, if same was procured by fraud of the grantee, or if her acknowledgment was not taken as required by statute, and appellee (grantee) had notice of such failure to comply with the statute in the taking of her acknowledgment, and further that, if said deed was procured by fraud, an estoppel could not be invoked against Mrs. Fisher.

To this contention appellee replies that a deed to the homestead, signed by the husband, even though not signed by the wife, becomes operative after the property is abandoned as a homestead, and the property could not be recovered by the husband because he is estopped by the deed, and could not be recovered by the wife because her homestead rights ceased when her husband acquired, and she removed with him to, another homestead, and that, as the land in question was the separate property of appellant E. H. Fisher, and he having legally bound himself to convey same to Keeble or his heirs or assigns by the contract evidenced by the earnest money receipt, and as he had procured a new home, and with his wife was living thereon, that said contract to convey was enforceable at the time of the filing of this suit, and the trial of same, had it not already been consummated, for the reason that the land involved was no longer the homestead of appellants.

There is no evidence to show, nor do appellants contend, that any fraud was perpetrated or attempted as to appellant E. H. Fisher, either in the making of the contract to sell or in the execution of the deed. No fraud is charged as to the execution by Mrs. Fisher of the contract of sale, but said charges of fraud are confined entirely to the procurement of her signature to and acknowledgment of the deed in question. No fraud is charged as to the conduct of E. H. Fisher toward his wife, Martha Fisher, relative to the execution of either the contract to sell or the deed in question. There is no intimation, either in the pleadings or the proof that he in any manner attempted any fraud upon her rights; but, to the contrary, the record shows he acted perfectly open, frank, and honorable with his wife throughout.

[1] We believe that the contention of appellant is well taken. It is the well-settled law of this state that the husband, acting in good faith, may select the homestead of the family, and that when he has acquired a new home, and his wife has removed with him to the newly acquired homestead, a prior deed made by him without her concurrence, to the former homestead, becomes operative as to the husband as an estoppel against his right to recover the property, and the wife's right, being that of homestead only, ceases when a new homestead has been acquired and she removes thereto. Marler v. Handy, 88 Tex. 421, 31 S. W. 636; Slavin v. Wheeler, 61 Tex. 654; Parker v. Schrimsher, 172 S. W. 175; Irion v. Mills, 41 Tex. 310; Hudgins v. Thompson, 211 S. W. 586; Smith v. Uzzell, 56 Tex. 315; Wynne v. Hudson, 66 Tex. 9, 17 S. W. 110; Randleman v. Cargile, 163 S. W. 352.

[2, 3] Again, appellants having accepted the purchase money for the land (their homestead) with full knowledge of all the material facts concerning the execution of the contract of sale (earnest money receipt) and the final deed of conveyance, and having retained same and purchased a new home therewith, to which they have removed and on which they have since lived, and having never at any time made any actual tender of said money back to appellee, or to any one (the statement in their petition that, should the court hold that they were required to repay said money as a condition precedent to recovering the land, then they are ready to do so, is not even an offer to do equity or refund the money, but only a statement by way of pleading, and is not a tender), is in our opinion a ratification of said sale and deed, and precludes appellants from recovering herein. As apropos to this case, we quote Judge Reese in Burke-Mobray v. Ellis, 44 Tex. Civ. App. 24, 97 S. W. 322, a case in some features very similar to the instant case. He says:

"The undisputed evidence shows that appellant accepted the purchase price of the land from Roberts with full knowledge of all the material facts concerning the sale, protesting only that she had rather Roberts had not sold the land. It is true that appellant testified that she took the money with the sole intention of paying it back to Ellis if he would take it, and that she at once put it in the bank; but she kept it, and never at any time made any actual tender of it to Ellis. It remained in her possession and subject at all times to whatever disposition she chose to make of it, from the time it was paid to her in the early part of May, 1901, until paid into the registry of the court on April 27, 1905. She gave no notice to Ellis of her intention for nearly a month after receiving the money. The mere offer to do equity by the payment of money to Ellis as contained in her petition was not, in the circumstances, sufficient. If the bare acceptance of the money from Roberts did not constitute such a ratification of the delivery of the deed as to bind appellant, her subsequent conduct with regard to it would do so. If it be true, as testified by her, that she accepted the money for the sole purpose of repaying it to Ellis, it was incumbent upon her at once to disavow the sale to Ellis, and tender back the money, and to follow up such tender by depositing the money in the registry of the court, when the suit was filed. She was seeking affirmative relief of a court of equity in the cancellation of the deed, and it was incumbent upon her promptly to tender the money to Ellis, and upon his refusal to take it to place it beyond her own control, and subject to the control of the court, for Ellis, upon a determination of the suit in her favor. Weaver v. Nugent, 72 Texas, 277, 10 S. W. 458, 13 Am. St. Rep. 792; Werner v. Tuch (N. Y.) 27 N. E. 845, 24 Am. St. Rep. 443. As it is, appellant, knowing that the value of her land was wildly fluctuating on account of the excitement from the prospect of obtaining oil at Sour Lake, kept herself in a position, at all times, from the receipt of the money until the actual payment into the registry of the court four years afterwards, either to press her suit for the land, or abandon it and keep the money. If, by any chance, the land had so depreciated in value during these four years as that it would have made it to her advantage to keep the money, which might have happened, appellant could have abandoned her suit and kept the money, and appellees could not have helped themselves. She kept herself in a position to take advantage either of a fall in the value of the land by keeping the money and abandoning her claim to the land, or a rise in such value by prosecuting her claim. This was entirely inconsistent with what was required of her to entitle her to relief from a court of equity by a cancellation of the deed and a recovery of the land. Under the undisputed evidence upon this point, appellants were not entitled to recover, and the court did not err in so instructing the jury."

Usually, abandonment and estoppel are questions of fact for the jury to find, and the court is not authorized to take same from the jury and instruct a verdict; but, as in this case, when the acquisition of the new home is not disputed, but admitted, and where the fact of retention of the purchase money and acquisition of a new home therewith is not questioned, but is also admitted, then the facts are found, and the court is authorized to apply the law to the facts and direct the verdict.

This case does not come within the rule where the husband has acted in fraud of the rights of the wife with regard to the sale of the homestead, nor that other rule where mortgages or other liens have been attempted to be given on the property while same is actually the homestead.

Finding no reversible error in the record, the judgment is affirmed.

DALLAS COUNTY v. BARR. (No. 1793.)

(Court of Civil Appeals of Texas. Amarillo. April 27, 1921. Rehearing Denied June 1, 1921.)

1. **Eminent domain ⟨key⟩280—Right of abutting owner to damages from elevating highway not affected by prior deed from his grantor for highway.**

Right of the grantee of land as abutting on a highway to damages thereto from the elevating of the roadway is not affected by the fact that prior to his deed the land for the highway had been conveyed in fee for highway purposes by the same grantor.

2. **Eminent domain ⟨key⟩101(1) — Damages to abutting property from elevating highway recoverable.**

Under the Constitution as amended in 1876 (Const. art. 1, § 17) to provide that a person's property shall not be taken or "damaged" for public use without adequate compensation, unless by his consent, damages to the land abutting on a highway from elevation of the roadway by a viaduct and approach thereto are recoverable.

3. **Eminent domain ⟨key⟩285—County liable for damage from its elevating highway.**

A county is liable for the damage to property abutting on a highway from its elevation of the roadway.

4. **Eminent domain ⟨key⟩141(3) — Measure of damages difference in value before and after injury.**

The measure of damages to abutting property by the elevation of a highway is the difference in the value of the land before and after the change.

5. **Eminent domain ⟨key⟩300—Finding of damages held supported by evidence.**

Evidence consisting of varying opinions as to value of land before and after elevation of highway *held* to support the jury's finding as to amount of damages therefrom to abutting property.

6. **Eminent domain ⟨key⟩148—Interest from injury allowable as part of damages.**

Interest from time of injury to abutting property from elevation of highway is allowable as part of the damages, though at time of action they are unliquidated.

Appeal from District Court, Dallas County; E. B. Muse, Judge.

⟨key⟩For other cases see same topic and KEY-NUMBER in all Key-Numbered Digests and Indexes

---

Action by J. H. Barr against Dallas County. Judgment for plaintiff, and defendant appeals. Affirmed.

Muse & Muse, of Dallas, for appellant.

Thompson, Knight, Baker & Harris, Allen Charlton, and George Wright, all of Dallas, for appellee.

HUFF, C. J. The appellee, Barr, sued Dallas county and others for damages. The other defendants were dismissed and the cause proceeded to judgment against Dallas county. The damages alleged were to abutting property to a roadway by erecting a viaduct therein and constructing an approach to a bridge across Trinity river. It was alleged that the structure erected in the public road extended across the entire front of appellee's property, 261½ feet, and that its elevation ranged from 12 feet at the west corner to an elevation of 18 feet at the east corner, above appellee's property. The structure blocked and covered the entire roadway and prevented traffic in front of appellee's property. That the structure was composed of concrete, steel, and dirt, and impairs, injures, and destroys the easement of ingress and egress, light, view, and air, belonging to said property, by reason of it abutting on the said road and by reason of it having enjoyed the same for over 30 years. That tne construction of the viaduct damaged appellee's property in the sum of $20,000, and that the structure was erected for public purposes without consideration and without his consent. The appellant answered that as a county it was not liable for such damages; that it was the owner of a 100-foot road-way strip of land, and that appellee and itself each deraigned title from a common source, Mrs. Sarah H. Cockrell; that in 1872 she conveyed by a duly recorded deed the 100-foot strip of land to a toll bridge company, for the purposes recited in the deed for constructing a toll bridge over the Trinity river, and therefrom a causeway, raised road or pike on said 100-foot strip of land, for public travel across the bottom lands; that the county had acquired the title to said bridge and strip of land from said company and for more than 80 years had been in possession thereof, with an elevated road thereon, and making valuable improvements upon said road; that the appellee, with actual and constructive notice of the foregoing, acquired his land in 1901; that he holds under a junior title in point of time of conveyance and recordation and that his said land was burdened with the servitude imposed by the senior conveyance and the user aforesaid of the public highway. The facts justify the conclusion that the title to the 100-foot strip of land upon which the road or causeway was erected is in Dallas county and has been used as a highway for 80 years or more and before the appellee purchased his block of land. Mrs. Cockrell executed her deed to the toll company, upon the condition that it would locate and build a bridge across the river and a causeway over the strip of land which was completed in 1872, and after the bridge was completed the 100-foot strip was used by the public as a highway. After Dallas county took over the bridge in 1882, and the highway known as the Dallas and Ft. Worth Pike, it has worked the road or pike and improved it for public use as a highway. The tract of land owned by appellee is out of a block of land designated in a plat made and entered in a judgment in a partition suit between the heirs and Mrs. Cockrell, which is designated on the map as block 4. This plat and the field notes of his deed shows that the land of appellee only goes to the north line of the 100-foot strip upon which the roadway was established. That is, the evidence shows that appellee did not own the fee to any part of the 100-foot strip, but that the same was owned by the county, but controlled by it for road purposes. The facts establish that if the title was not in the county to the fee, it had an easement by prescription for the highway for the use and benefit of the public, and that appellee's land abutted thereon, and that he acquired his right to his land and went into possession long after the county's rights attached and bought his land with knowledge of the highway and with reference thereto. His tract of land is about three acres, and he had filled it up so as to make it 3 or 4 feet higher than the roadway on the highway some time in 1908. His work in filling had been gradual, but he had raised the grade of his lot something over 14 feet, and he had access to his land and egress from it to the highway and ingress and egress to and from the highway to his land; that he had two or three places where a passageway or roadways were prepared to enter his land from the roadway. The highway owned and worked by the county is a continuation of Commerce street in the city of Dallas, on the east side of the river. This highway crossed the bridge and connected with Commerce street. On the east side of the river there were a number of railroad tracks over which trains were being operated. The bridge was old and considered unsafe and inadequate for the growing traffic. It would seem the city, county, and the terminal road companies made some arrangement to put in a new bridge high enough to be above high water and of sufficient height to place a viaduct over the river and railroads. The work was completed some time in 1916, and on the west side of the river and in front of Barr's land the county elevated the road and erected an approach and a viaduct therein the entire length of appellee's property, the viaduct being 226 feet in front, so that it rendered his land inaccessible from that part on which the viaduct is placed and the remainder of his front, 135 feet, the roadway was raised about 4 or 5 feet on an average above appellee's land. The viaduct is something near 19 feet above the land at the east corner thereof; that is, including the railing on the concrete structure of 226 feet, and an average height of 12½ feet, above his land, and an average of 4 or 5 feet on the 135 feet raised by dirt, in making the approach to the viaduct and bridge. The land is wholly inaccessible from the viaduct. It is admitted that the work was done by the county and others, without the consent of appellee, and without compensation unless his deed from Mrs. Cockrell to him amounted to such consent. That he has not been paid for any damages, and that he made his claim for damages to the county in proper form, which was refused. The case was submitted to a jury on two issues: The value of the land before the erection of the viaduct and its value after such erection. The jury found its value before was $10,000, and after the erection $2,000, and the judgment was rendered for the difference, $8,000, against appellant county, from which this appeal is prosecuted.

[1, 2] Appellant, by assignments, asserts the judgment is erroneous because there is no cause of action against the county shown, setting out various grounds in which it is asserted the facts fail to show a cause of action. We will endeavor to consider the grounds relied upon for reversal without specifically setting out the assignments themselves or discussing them as made by the brief. The defense of appellant and all his propositions are bottomed upon the assumption that the appellee's cause of action is for taking his land without his consent and without compensation. In this the appellant places its defense upon a false premise. This suit is for damages to abutting property. The mere fact that the title to the 100-foot strip of land was in the county for highway purposes does not justify the county so to use this strip for public use as to damage abutting property within the meaning of the Constitution. The title to the fee in the 100 feet is not a material fact in this case, as we conceive the issues. Under the old Constitution, prior to the amendment in 1876 (article 1, § 17), as we understand the authorities, an actual invasion of another's land and the taking thereof was required to authorize a recovery; but such is not now the only ground of recovery. Conceding that the deed by Mrs. Cockrell to the toll company, and by that company to the county, conveyed the 100-foot strip for highway purposes, and that such servitude was impressed upon this strip of land when appellee bought from the party to whom the land was set over in the judgment referred to in the statement of facts, the plat in the judgment shows appellee's property was abutting upon the highway. These facts at least tend to show that ap-

pellee and his vendors bought and sold this land with reference to this plat. In such case, the appellee acquired as appurtenant to his land all such rights, privileges, easements, and servitude as were represented by the map to belong to the land or to be in the owners thereof, and the sale and conveyance of the land, in accordance with the map, implies a grant or covenant for the owner of the land that the road shall never be appropriated by the owner of the road, inconsistent with that represented by the deeds to appellee, or the map, especially so where the change would tend to lessen the value of the land sold. Lamar County v. Clements, 49 Tex. 347; Oswald v. Grenet, 22 Tex. 94. We do not think the effect of Mrs. Cockrell's deed placing the title of the strip of land in the county for highway purposes estops appellee from asserting damages from the use of that land so as to injure the appellee's abutting property. The deed concluded any recovery for any damages to the land sustained by reason of the location of the highway which had occurred prior to the time appellee purchased it. The question really presented, as we understand the question, is whether in changing the grade or elevating the roadway above the appellee's land, or in erecting a viaduct in front of the land, he can recover damages. Under our Constitution no person's property can be damaged for public use without his consent and without adequate compensation. There was no compensation paid in this case, and the consent of appellee was not secured to effect the change. Whatever may have been the rule under the former Constitutions of this state, allowing compensation for the taking of land and in changing the grade of roads or streets, we believe the rule now to be, under our present Constitution, that—

"All damages resulting to abutting property by reason of lowering or raising the street in front of it is within the constitutional provisions in question and compensation must be made therefor. It is immaterial whether the whole surface of the street in front of it is raised or lowered, or only a part of it, as where a causeway is built in the middle or an embankment on one side or a sidewalk is only raised or lowered." 1 Lewis, Eminent Domain, § 348, and chapter "2, In Constitution."

In this case the testimony shows a viaduct was erected in the road, constructed of concrete and steel for 226 feet, and as part of the approach to the bridge 135 additional frontage was raised. The viaduct was 18 feet above at one point and more than 12 at another. This would come, it seems to us, under the general recognized right of recovery for damages.

"The construction of viaducts, bridges, and tunnels and approaches thereto, for the purpose of carrying streets over or under railroad tracks, streams or other obstructions, though often a great public utility, is frequently attended with great damage to property abutting on such improvements. All such damages are within the Constitution and may be recovered." Id., § 349.

The appellant cites the cases of Northern Transp. Co. v. Chicago, 99 U. S. 635, 25 L. Ed. 336, and Smith v. Corporation of Washington, 20 How. 135, 15 L. Ed. 858, and many other decisions as asserting the proposition:

"That persons appointed or authorized by law to make or improve a highway are not answerable for consequential damages, if they act within their jurisdiction and with care and skill, is a doctrine almost universally accepted alike in England and in this country."

The same high tribunal, rendering the opinion in the two cases above, later held that the amendment of the Constitution of Illinois, authorizing a recovery for damages sustained for public use, modified the former rule. The latter case arose over the construction of a viaduct near the complainant's property, for which damages were claimed. The Supreme Court distinguished the case then in hand from those above cited and approved the rule announced by the Supreme Court of Illinois, and quoted from the case of Railway Company v. Ayres, 106 Ill. 518:

"Under this constitutional provision a recovery may be had in all cases where private property has sustained a substantial damage by the making and using an improvement that is public in its character—that it does not require that the damage shall be caused by a trespass or an actual physical invasion of the owner's real estate, but if the construction and the operation of the railroad or other improvements is the cause of the damage, though consequential, the party damaged may recover."

The Supreme Court of the United States said, in the interpretation of the later Constitution of Illinois, that they concurred in the opinion expressed by the Supreme Court of that state, and that the use of the word "damaged" was not meaningless and could have been used with no other intention than that given by the state court. Chicago v. Taylor, 125 U. S. 161, 8 Sup. Ct. 820, 31 L. Ed. 638. Our own state Supreme Court has followed the Illinois rule in the interpretation of our Constitution, in a suit for damages to private property occasioned by grading and paving Elm and Preston streets in the city of Dallas, and in the exercise of lawful authority conferred upon the city by its charter. In speaking of the change in our Constitution, our court said:

"In other states, in whose laws a like change has been made, the right to recover damages where there has been no direct or physical invasion of the property is now recognized. Chicago v. Taylor, supra. The same doctrine was announced by this court in the case of Railway Co. v. Hall, 78 Tex. 169, 14 S. W. 259." Cooper v. City of Dallas, 83 Tex. 239, 18 S. W. 565, 29 Am. St. Rep. 645.

The change in our Constitution has been recognized by our Supreme Court and by our Courts of Civil Appeals, as giving a cause of action to owners of property for damages sustained by works for public use, in a number of cases, some of which are the following: Powell v. Railway Co., 104 Tex. 219, 135 S. W. 1153, 46 L. R. A. (N. S.) 615; Lumber Co. v. Railway Co., 104 Tex. 8, 133 S. W. 247, 36 L. R. A. (N. S.) 662, Ann. Cas. 1913E, 870; Southwestern Tel. & Tel. Co. v. Smithdeal, 104 Tex. 258, 136 S. W. 1049; Id., 103 Tex. 128, 124 S. W. 627; Railway Co. v. Eddins, 60 Tex. 656; Railway Co. v. Fuller, 63 Tex. 467; Railway Co. v. Edrington, 100 Tex. 496, 101 S. W. 441, 9 L. R. A. (N. S.) 988; Railway Co. v. Hardin, 168 S. W. 1017; Texarkana v. Lawson, 168 S. W. 867; City of Marshall v. Allen, 115 S. W. 849; Shows v. City of Dallas, 172 S. W. 1137; Moore v. City of Dallas, 200 S. W. 870.

[3] It is insisted by appellant that the county cannot be held liable for damages where it is performing duties pertaining to public roads and bridges imposed upon it by law. It appears, in some portion of appellant's brief and argument, that it is contended, and it would have us infer, that the constitutional provision only applies to railway companies and others engaged in public work or service for the use of the public. The Constitution itself makes no such distinction as to who are liable for damages to the property of a citizen which is occasioned by work for the use of the public. It would seem the purpose of the safeguard in that document is to protect the individual against the sovereign power of the state, and that it gives him compensation where the public damages his property for its use. The majority in this country is the sovereign power, but the Constitution protects the minority in the enjoyment of their property. The individual cannot be made to suffer alone and sacrifice his property to the public use, but those for whose use it is appropriated or damaged must bear the burden. "Eminent domain" is simply the right or power of a sovereign state to appropriate private property for the purpose of promoting the general welfare. The sovereign power is in the state; but, for road and bridge purposes, it has delegated that power to the counties of the state, who may sue and be sued. So it may, and does, grant to public service corporations the right of eminent domain; but in granting such powers it is coupled with the declaration that counties or corporations shall not take, damage, or destroy the private property of the citizens in order to accomplish the contemplated purpose. The state, nor any of its agencies, in promoting the general welfare, can damage the property of the citizen without compensation, whether it be through county, city, railroad, or any public service corporation. Railway Co. v. Fuller, supra. It was several times held under the old Constitution of this state that counties could not take property for public use without compensation. Travis County v. Trogdon, 88 Tex. 302, 31 S. W. 358; Bounds v. Kirven, 63 Tex. 159; Norwood v. Gonzales, 79 Tex. 218, 14 S. W. 1057; Hamilton v. Garrnett, 62 Tex. 602; Watkins v. Walker, 18 Tex. 592, 70 Am. Dec. 298; see also, Heverbekken v. Hale, 109 Tex. at page 113, 204 S. W. 1162. We see no reason why under the present Constitution, the county may damage such property for public use without being liable therefor, as it was liable before for the taking.

[4] The assignments which assert error in refusing to submit the cost or expense in making the necessary way of ingress or egress to appellee's land from the present viaduct or causeway, we think, present no error. It is now generally recognized that the measure of damages is the difference in the value of the land before the erection of the structure and after its erection.

[5, 6] Appellant also urges that the evidence fails to establish the value of appellee's land before the structure in the road and after, as found by the jury. There is no witness who gave his opinion that the value was as fixed by the jury. The witnesses, in giving their opinion, range widely. Some fixed it at a value of $30,000 before; some at $150 per front foot; some at $125 per front foot, before the erection, and that after the erection it depreciated from 25 to 50 per cent.; others that its value was enhanced by the structure several thousand dollars. It seems from the record that by agreement of the parties to this suit before the trial court, the jurors were permitted to view the premises as they then existed. In fixing the value we think much must be left to the judgment of the jury in considering the opinion of the witnesses as to the value of property. The evidence, we think, will support the findings of the jury in this case. Houston Belt, etc., v. Vogel, 179 S. W. 268; Buchanan v. Bowles, 218 S. W. 652, and authorities there cited. Interest may be allowed as damages. It is proper, we think, in this case, to calculate it from the date of the injury, and not from the date of the judgment. The fact that the amount claimed at the time of filing the suit was unliquidated does not affect the right to recover interest as part of the damages in this kind of action. Watkins v. Junker, 90 Tex. 584, 40 S. W. 11; Railway Co. v. Schofield, 72 Tex. 496, 10 S. W. 575.

We find no reversible error assigned, and the judgment of the trial court will be affirmed.

ATER et ux. v. MOORE. (No. 6378.)

(Court of Civil Appeals of Texas. Austin. April 27, 1921. Rehearing Denied June 1, 1921.)

. **Wills** ⬤==384 — Sustaining of an exception to part of answer held harmless if error.

In a contest of a will, any error in sustaining an exception to paragraph, containing averments that property was valued at $20,000 and contestants only received $5 each, was harmless, where the terms of a will were undisputed and the value of the estate was proven without controversy in the amount alleged.

2. **Wills** ⬤==153—Advice given by third party not fraud on part of beneficiary.

It was not fraud on the part of beneficiary under a will that a third person gave advice to testator without any inducement or solicitation on the part of the beneficiary, who had no participation whatever therein.

3. **Pleading** ⬤==8(16) — Allegations of undue influence held mere conclusions.

Averments in will contest that execution was procured by undue influence exerted by testator's wife, who possessed great influence over the testator, and that by her insistence and by her pleading she procured him to execute the will and to cut off contestants, were but conclusions of the pleaders and did not state facts.

4. **Wills** ⬤==155(3) — Not undue influence for wife to plead with testator.

It does not constitute undue influence for a wife to plead with her husband to make a will in a certain manner, nor even to insist thereon, provided her solicitations and importunities do not overthrow the will and destroy the free agency of the testator.

5. **Wills** ⬤==277—Facts to be pleaded in will contest.

Good pleading requires that, in stating the grounds of a will contest, facts should be averred and not conclusions, and when grounds of contest embrace fraud, duress, or undue influence, a subsequent will, revocation, or the like, such matters, not being ultimate facts but conclusions of law to be drawn from facts, must be pleaded, not in the language of the statute, but the facts relied on must be stated.

6. **Wills** ⬤==167—Not revoked by mere expression of desire on part of testator.

Mere expression of a desire by testator to change his will cannot have the effect of revoking it or of changing any of its provisions, in view of Rev. Civ. St. art. 7859, providing manner in which wills may be revoked.

7. **Wills** ⬤==177—Not changed by expression of desire and unintentional deception.

Where testator inherited money after executing his will, which he did not desire to have pass by the will, and went to his partner for advice, and the latter unintentionally deceived him by telling him that such property would not pass under the will, the will was not revoked or changed in any manner and should be probated as written.

Appeal from District Court, Lampasas County; F. M. Spann, Judge.

Contest of will of A. H. Moore, deceased, by Mr. Guy Ater and wife against Mrs. Carrie Moore. From an adverse judgment, contestants appeal. Affirmed.

W. H. Browning, of Lampasas, and G. T. Shires, of Waco, for appellants.

W. B. Abney, of Lampasas, for appellee.

BRADY, J. The appeal is from an order probating a will. The questions presented for our decision relate to the rulings of the trial court in sustaining exceptions to parts of the answer of the contestants, who are the appellants. It was alleged by contestants that by the terms of the will the entire estate of the deceased was given to Mrs. Carrie Moore, the surviving wife, and to A. H. Moore, Jr., child of the testator, A. H. Moore, by his second wife. It was further alleged that the property was of the value of $20,000, and that the will cut off the contestants with only the nominal sum of $5 each; they being children of A. H. Moore, deceased, by a former wife. The exception to the paragraph containing these averments was to the effect that they were wholly insufficient to prevent the probate of the will, because the testator had the legal right to devise his estate as he saw fit. It is urged by appellants that it was error to sustain the exception, as the plea was introductory merely, and was entitled to be considered in connection with another part of the answer alleging undue influence.

[1] It is perhaps sufficient answer to this contention to say that the plea of undue influence was itself inadequate to present any issue. It may be added that the error, if any there was in sustaining this exception, was harmless because the terms of the will were undisputed, and the value of the estate was proven without controversy in the amount alleged by appellants.

The next question to be considered is the sustaining of an exception to the fourth paragraph of contestants' plea alleging undue influence by the wife of the testator. The ground of the exception was that no facts were set forth from which any undue influence could be inferred. It is claimed for appellants that this part of the answer was entitled to be considered in connection with the previous allegations, and also with a subsequent part in which the issue of fraud was sought to be raised.

[2] An examination of the latter part of the answer discloses that the alleged fraud consisted merely in advice given the testator by a third party, and it is not claimed that this was through any inducement or solicitation of the wife, nor that she had any participation whatever in the same. Therefore the fourth paragraph had no bearing

upon the plea of fraud, and was not entitled to be considered in that connection.

[3, 4] As to the sufficiency of the plea of undue influence, it was alleged that the execution of the will was procured by undue influence exerted by the wife, who possessed great influence over the testator, and that by her insistence and by her pleading she procured him to execute such will, and to cut off contestants with only the sum of $5 each.

As we understand the law, these averments were but conclusions, and do not state facts. It does not constitute undue influence for a wife to plead with her husband to make a will in a certain manner, nor even to insist thereon, provided her solicitations and importunities do not overthrow the will and destroy the free agency of the testator. No such facts are alleged, and we think the pleading of undue influence wholly insufficient.

[5] In 40 Cyc. 1269, it is said:

"Good pleading requires that in stating the grounds of the contest facts should be averred, and not conclusions. * * * When the grounds of contest embrace fraud, duress, or undue influence, a subsequent will, revocation, or the like, such matters, not being ultimate facts but conclusions of law to be drawn from facts, must be pleaded, not in the language of the statute, but the facts relied on must be stated."

This is a fair statement of the rule obtaining in this jurisdiction. That mere pleading with a testator and insistence that he make his will in a particular way is not itself sufficient to invalidate the will, and does not constitute undue influence, see the following authorities: Berry v. Brown, 148 S. W. 1117; Smith v. Smith, 153 S. W. 918; 40 Cyc. 1144 et seq., c. 1, 3, and 7.

[6, 7] The remaining question to be decided is whether the court erred in sustaining an exception to the plea of contestants to the effect that a short time before his death A. H. Moore expressed a desire to make a change in his will, because he had inherited certain property from his father and mother, alleged to be of the value of $5,000 or more, which he desired should not pass by the will. It was also alleged in this connection that Mr. D. T. Briggs, partner of testator, who had written and prepared the will, and in whom Mr. Moore had unlimited confidence, advised Mr. Moore, in response to his questions, that the will would not convey the property which he had inherited from his father and mother since the making of the will, or that he did not think it would. It was further averred that if the testator had been correctly advised upon the legal effect of his will as to the property in question; he would have changed his will; and that he was deceived and misled by the statement of the opinion given him by Mr. Briggs,

although it was not charged that Briggs intentionally deceived the testator. By reason of these facts, it was averred that, however honest the advice and opinion of Mr. Briggs might have been, it had the effect of unduly influencing the testator and of preventing him from making any change in his will, and constituted a legal fraud. The exception addressed to this pleading was in substance that the expression of the desire of the testator to change his will, and the conversations with Mr. Briggs, all occurred long subsequent to the execution of the will, and were wholly insufficient to revoke the will in any particular, as the methods of revocation of wills are provided by statute, which were not alleged to have been done.

We have carefully considered the facts pleaded upon this issue, and have reached the conclusion that the trial court ruled correctly. Article 7859, Revised Civil Statutes, provides, in effect, that no revocation of any will, nor any clause thereof nor devise therein, can be made except by a subsequent will, codicil, or declaration in writing, executed by the testator; or by the testator's destroying, canceling, or obliterating the will, or causing it to be done in his presence.

In Morgan v. Davenport, 60 Tex. 230, our Supreme Court held that a legal revocation can only be accomplished by one or more of the modes prescribed by statute. To the same effect, also, is Locust v. Randle, 46 Tex. Civ. App. 544, 102 S. W. 946. Therefore we are of the opinion that the mere expression of a desire by Mr. Moore to change his will could not have the effect of revoking it, or of changing any of its provisions. Neither do we think the facts alleged, with relation to the advice given by Mr. Briggs could have the effect of revoking the will, or of changing the legal effect of any part thereof, in so far as it may be claimed that this operated as a revocation of the will.

Independently of the question of revocation, we are also of the opinion that the facts were insufficient to prevent the probate of the will, which the record shows was executed with all the formalities and under the solemnities required by law, and it further appearing that it had never been revoked. At most, these facts show a mistake on the part of the testator as to the legal effect of his will, and this under the advice of a third party, who was a layman and whose opinion the testator had sought. It is not alleged that either of the beneficiaries under the will had brought about this mistake, or had been in any wise instrumental in so doing; and it is not even alleged that the advice was given by his partner wrongfully, or with any intention to deceive. Furthermore, the averments upon this point do not specifically exclude the notion that Mr. Moore might have sought the advice of his partner with a view of changing his will, if it did not have the effect of conveying the property he had subsequently inherited, so as to insure that the original devisees would receive this property also; although there is a general allegation that if he had known the true effect of his will he would have changed it. Again, except for the mere general statement just mentioned, Mr. Moore might have received correct advice as to the legal effect of his will from some other source after having consulted Mr. Briggs, or he may have decided to act upon his own judgment. It is true, as we have stated, that this pleading itself contained the statement that the testator had implicit confidence in Mr. Briggs, and relied implicitly upon his judgment; and further that the testator died in ignorance of the fact that the property inherited by him after the execution of the will would pass by the will, but believed at the time of his death that at least a part of such property would go to the contestants. However, in any event, we are of the opinion that these facts do not constitute either undue influence or legal fraud, nor do they fall within any recognized ground of invalidating a will, and are wholly insufficient to deny the admission of the will to probate, as was sought to be done by contestants.

We overrule all assignments, and, no reversible error having been shown, the judgment is affirmed.

Affirmed.

FOLEY BROS. DRY GOODS CO. v. McCLAIN et al. (No. 677.)

(Court of Civil Appeals of Texas. Beaumont. May 20, 1921. Rehearing Denied June 1, 1921.)

1. Libel and slander ⬧⇒89(1)—Petition held to state cause of action, though not alleging special damages.

Petition of store employé against the company operating the store alleging a slander by having charged her with theft held to state a cause of action, the utterance or statement complained of being slander per se, so that the petition did not need to allege special damages.

2. Libel and slander ⬧⇒41—No recovery in case of qualified privilege unless malice present.

There can be no recovery for a slanderous utterance made under circumstances entitling it to a qualified privilege unless defendant's agent, in making the statement, was actuated by actual or express malice, or other evil motive.

3. Libel and slander ⬧⇒45(2)—Statement of store manager relative to theft by employé held qualifiedly privileged.

Utterance or statement, charging female employé of large store with thievery, made

by the store's manager in his office in the presence of other executives and employés when he was investigating a claim of theft held qualifiedly privileged and not to be made a basis for damages, actual or exemplary, unless the employé charged with the theft could show the statement was actuated by actual or express malice or want of good faith.

4. Libel and slander ⬧⇒101(4) — Plaintiff has burden in case of qualified privilege to show statement was actuated by malice.

Where a slanderous utterance is shown to have been conditionally privileged, plaintiff must take the burden of showing that it was actuated by actual or express malice or want of good faith.

5. Libel and slander ⬧⇒112(2)—Evidence insufficient to justify finding of malice in making charge of theft.

In an action by a female store employé against the company for slander by its manager in charging her with theft, evidence held insufficient to warrant the jury's finding that the manager's utterance, made under conditions entitling it to a qualified privilege, was actuated by actual or express malice.

Appeal from District Court, Harris County; W. E. Monteith, Judge.

Action by Hazel McClain and another against the Foley Brothers Dry Goods Company. From judgment for plaintiffs, defendant appeals. Judgment reversed, and cause remanded.

Garrison, Pollard, Morris & Berry, and Maurice Epstein, all of Houston, for appellant.

Wm. Masterson and Samuel Schwartz, both of Houston, for appellees.

HIGHTOWER, C. J. This was an action for slander brought by the appellee, as plaintiff below, against the defendant, and resulted in a verdict and judgment in favor of the plaintiff for $3,000, from which this appeal was prosecuted. We find in appellant's brief what seems to be a sufficiently full and clear statement of the nature and result of the suit, and which is in no respect questioned by the appellees, and the same is adopted by this court, as follows:

"This suit was instituted by Hazel McClain, a minor, through her father, Thomas McClain, as next friend, to recover both actual and exemplary damages alleged to have been sustained by her by reason of certain alleged slanderous statements made by the appellant. She alleged in her petition substantially as follows:

"That on or about the 14th day of November, 1918, she was employed by the defendant (appellant), Foley Brothers Dry Goods Company, as a wrapper of goods and merchandise in the neckwear department, on the first floor of the store; that on or about said date, and while so employed, a co-worker of the plaintiff on said floor, to wit, a saleslady by the name of Bessie York, brought a package of goods to the plaintiff unwrapped, with the request that the plaintiff wrap the same, as it was her duty to do; that Bessie York presented therewith a duplicate slip, which showed the value of the goods to be $4.50, stating at the time to the plaintiff that same had been paid for by her, and requested of plaintiff that no charge check be entered therefor; that she believed and relied upon the statements made by said Bessie York, and acting upon the truth thereof, having no reason to doubt the same, if, in fact, said statements were false, which is not admitted, but expressly denied, and so believing, she wrapped the said package of goods as she was requested to do, attaching thereto, as is customary in such cases, a duplicate slip, delivering the same to the cashboy to be carried to the delivery department; that shortly thereafter the package was returned to her unwrapped, with the request that she furnish duplicate check; that she advised the party so requesting that the duplicate check was attached to said package when delivered to the cash boy, and that she was unable to attach said duplicate slip; that shortly thereafter she was approached by one Muenster, an employé of the defendant as floorwalker, who had charge of the floor, who demanded of plaintiff the duplicate check or slip for said goods, and that he was advised by the plaintiff that the same was delivered to the cash boy; that notwithstanding her statement or explanation, she was then required by said Muenster to go with him to one Fred Kennedy, who was the superintendent of defendant's store, and who, in such capacity as superintendent, had authority to hire and discharge employés, including the plaintiff, who also interrogated the plaintiff regarding said package, and the duplicate slip, and who was likewise advised by plaintiff that same had been wrapped, and said slip attached under the circumstances as heretofore stated; that thereupon the said Kennedy stated to the plaintiff in a loud voice, and in the presence and hearing of various other parties, that the goods had been stolen, and that plaintiff was implicated in the thievery, as much to blame therefor as the said Bessie York, meaning and intending to say thereby that both the plaintiff and Bessie York were guilty of the theft of said goods.

"The plaintiff further averred that she was then required by said Kennedy, as superintendent, to go to one George Cohen, who was the manager of said defendant's store, and who has some interest therein, as a member thereof, who likewise interrogated the plaintiff regarding the wrapping of said package and the duplicate slip attached thereto, and that said Cohen then and there told plaintiff and said to her in a loud voice, and in the presence and hearing of one Muenster and Kennedy, and various other persons whose names are to the plaintiff unknown, that she, plaintiff, was as much implicated in the thievery of said goods as was the said Bessie York, thereby charging and meaning and intending to charge and say that both the plaintiff and the said Bessie York were guilty of theft of goods; that she immediately thereafter was discharged.

"Plaintiff averred that she had nothing whatever to do with said articles of merchandise except as above alleged, and after having made said explanation, the said agents, servants, and employés of the defendant company falsely intending to injure the plaintiff, and to bring her into public disgrace, scandal, shame, and humiliation, and to injure her in her good name, fame, credit, and reputation, did falsely, wickedly, maliciously speak and publish said charges, statements and accusations to and of and concerning this plaintiff, to her great damage, viz., $10,000 actual damages, and punitive damages $5,000.

"The defendant answered by general and special demurrers, general denial, and specially alleged that, if said statement was made, the same was a privileged communication, and was not made in the hearing or presence of any one save and except the employés of the defendant company whose duty it was to investigate and truthfully ascertain the true facts surrounding the wrapping of said package, and that said statements, if made, were made in the discharge of their duty that they owed to the defendant company, its officers and representatives.

"The case was submitted to the jury upon special issues, which special issues and the answers thereto are as follows:

" 'Special Issue No. I: Did or did not parties other than Mr. George Cohen, Mr. Fred Muenster, and Mr. John Kennedy hear the statement set out in plaintiff's petition by and between them and Miss Hazel McClain in Mr. George Cohen's private office?'

"To which the jury answered: 'They did.'

" 'Special Issue No. II: Give the name or names of the parties who overheard the statement set out in plaintiff's petition.'

"To which the jury answered: 'Parties unknown to us.'

" 'Special Issue No. III: Did or did not the parties who heard said statement understand what was said at the time same was uttered?'

"To which the jury answered: 'They did.'

"Special Issue No. IV: Did or did not the parties who heard said statement understand to whom it was said at the time same was uttered?'

"To which the jury answered: 'They did.'

"Special Issue No. V: Was or was not such statement actuated by malice toward the said Hazel McClain as the term "malice" will be hereinafter defined?'

"To which the jury answered: 'It was.'

" 'Special Issue No. VI: What amount of actual damages, if any, do you find the plaintiff, Hazel McClain, entitled to recover herein by reason of said statement so made to her?'

"To which the jury answered: '$1,500.'

" 'Special Issue No. VII: What amount of exemplary damages, if any, do you find the plaintiff, Hazel McClain, is entitled to recover herein by reason of said statement so made to and about her?'

"To which the jury answered: '$1,500.' "

By supplemental petition filed, plaintiff joined issue with defendant on its plea of privilege, both in law and on the facts. After the verdict of the jury had been returned, the defendant moved to set the same aside, which motion was overruled, and judgment was entered upon the verdict in favor of the plaintiff for $1,500 actual and $1,500 exemplary damages. Afterwards, defendant filed its motion for new trial, which was also overruled.

By the first assignment of error, complaint

is made that the trial court erred in overruling appellant's general demurrer. It is contended that this action of the court was error, because the petition did not state a cause of action against appellant, in that it failed to allege any slanderous or defamatory statement concerning plaintiff involving the commission of a crime. Also, it is contended that the petition failed to allege in haec verba any language used by appellant concerning the plaintiff that could be made the basis for slander, or that imputed to plaintiff the commission of any crime, or which charged plaintiff with an offense upon which an action could be predicated. Also, it is contended that the petition failed to allege special damages, and that, since the language attributable to appellant, the use of which plaintiff complained of, was not actionable per se, the petition showed no cause of action, in the absence of an allegation of special damages.

[1] After careful consideration of this assignment, we have reached the conclusion that it cannot be sustained. The natural and reasonable inference or conclusion that would be drawn by the ordinary mind from the statement and language alleged to have been made and used to and concerning appellee by defendant would be that appellee was implicated criminally in the theft of goods, or, in other words, that she was guilty of a criminal offense. Therefore the utterance or statement complained of, as shown in the petition, was slanderous per se, and, this being so, it was not necessary, in order to show a cause of action, that the petition should allege special damages. Belo v. Fuller, 84 Tex. 450, 19 S. W. 616, 31 Am. St. Rep. 75; Publishing Co. v. Jones, 83 Tex. 302, 18 S. W. 652; Baten v. Houston Oil Co., 217 S. W. 394. In the last-mentioned case, the authorities are fully reviewed by Associate Justice Walker, who wrote the opinion in the case. The first assignment will be overruled.

By the second and third assignments, complaint is made of the action of the trial court in overruling certain special exceptions interposed by appellant to the plaintiff's petition. We have given them consideration, but think they are untenable, and, without further discussion, overrule them.

The fourth and fifth assignments complain of the refusal of the trial court to peremptorily instruct a verdict in favor of appellant. The theory of appellant upon which the peremptory instruction was requested was, and the contention here is, that the uncontradicted evidence in the case showed conclusively, that the statement or utterance or charge sought to be made the basis of this suit was, in contemplation of law, a privileged communication; and further, that there was no evidence whatever showing or tending to show that defendant's manager, Cohen, in making such statement, charge, or utterance, was actuated by actual

or express malice, or by any evil motive, and that therefore the verdict should have been instructed in favor of appellant.

The sixth and seventh assignments, in effect, complain of the refusal of the trial court to grant appellant a new trial, on the ground that the communication, utterance, or charge complained of was shown by the undisputed evidence to be privileged, and that the evidence was insufficient to warrant the finding of the jury that appellant was actuated by actual or express malice in making such utterance, statement, or charge to and concerning the appellee.

It is the contention of counsel for appellee that the statement or charge of which appellee complains was not privileged, either absolutely or conditionally, and that, since the statement or utterance complained of was slanderous per se, it was not necessary, in order to a recovery by her of actual damages, that actual or express malice on the part of appellant be shown. Appellee further contends that if the occasion on which the utterance or statement complained of was made was such as constituted the same a conditionally privileged communication, that then it was incumbent upon appellant to establish its specially pleaded defense of privilege, by proving all the elements which go to constitute that defense. And in this connection, it is contended by, counsel for appellee that the burden of proof was upon appellant to show, not only that the slander complained of was uttered in the presence and hearing of persons mutually interested in the matter under investigation, and concerning which they had corresponding duties, but that the burden was upon appellant to also prove that the utterance was justified by the occasion; and also that the burden rested upon appellant to prove that the utterance was made in good faith, and in the honest belief of its truth, and also that the burden was upon appellant to prove that there existed just and probable grounds for entertaining such belief. And counsel for appellees contend that this burden was not discharged by appellant, since there was no proof offered by it to show that the statement or utterance to appellee by its manager, Cohen, was justified in any way, and since there was no proof by appellant that the statement or utterance to appellee was made in good faith, and in the honest belief of its truth, and since it was not proved by appellant that there existed any just or probable grounds for holding such belief, if it was held, the defense of privileged communication was not established.

[2] If the occasion on which the slanderous utterance or statement complained of was made to appellee was such as to clothe the same with the qualified privilege contended for by appellant (it is not contended here that the same was absolutely privileged), then, before appellee was entitled to recover

any damages because thereof, it was incumbent upon her to prove that appellant's said manager, Cohen, in making such statements or utterance to appellee, was actuated by actual or express malice, or by other evil motive, and, if there was an absence of such proof, she was not entitled to recover even actual damages. We understand it to be the law of this state that, where the slanderous utterance complained of is shown to be conditionally or qualifiedly privileged, the law itself raises the presumption of good faith and want of malice. It follows, therefore, that before the plaintiff, in a suit of this character, can recover either actual or exemplary damages, where the qualifiedly privileged character of the utterance has been shown, it would be incumbent upon the plaintiff to meet and defeat that defense, by proving by facts and circumstances reasonably sufficient on that point that the utterance was actuated, by actual or express malice, or the lack of good faith. Railway Co. v. Richmond, 73 Tex. 568, 11 S. W. 555, 4 L. R. A. 280, 15 Am. St. Rep. 794; Cranfill v. Hayden, 97 Tex. 544, 80 S. W. 609; Warehouse Co. v. Holloway, 34 Colo. 432, 83 Pac. 131, 3 L. R. A. (N. S.) 696, 114 Am. St. Rep. 171, 7 Ann. Cas. 840; Simmons v. Dickson, 110 Tex. 230, 213 S. W. 612, 218 S. W. 365; McClung v. Pulitzer Publishing Co., 279 Mo. 370, 214 S. W. 193; Odgers on Libel and Slander (5th Ed.) 225.

In Warehouse Co. v. Holloway, supra, we find this language was used by the Supreme Court of Colorado:

"It seems to us that, when the case is shown to have been privileged, the burden of showing that the defendant has lost his privilege is cast upon the plaintiff. The presumption which attaches to a writing, written on a privileged occasion is that it was written in good faith and upon probable cause. As said by Justice O'Brien in Hemmens v. Nelson, 138 N. Y. 524 [20 L. R. A. 440, 34 N. E. 342]: 'The question is not whether the charge is true or false, nor whether the defendant had sufficient cause to believe that the plaintiff sent the letter, or acted hastily, or in a mistake; but the question is, the occasion being privileged, whether there is evidence for the jury that he knew or believed it to be false. The plaintiff [defendant] may have arrived at conclusions without sufficient evidence, but the privilege protects him from liability on that ground until the plaintiff has overcome the presumption of good faith by proof of a malicious purpose to defame her character, under cover of the privilege.'

" 'This kind of malice,' says Justice O'Brien in the case cited, 'which overcomes and destroys the privilege, is, of course, quite distinct from that which the law, in the first instance, imputes with respect to every defamatory charge, irrespective of motive. It has been defined to be an "indirect and wicked motive which induces the defendant to defame the plaintiff." Odgers, Libel and Slander, 267.' "

In Railway Co. v. Richmond, supra, it was said by the Supreme Court of this state:

"We understand the law to be that a communication made in good faith in reference to a matter in which the person communicating has an interest, or in which the public has an interest, is privileged if made to another for the purpose of protecting that interest, and that a communication made in the discharge of a duty and looking to the prevention of wrong towards another or to the public is so privileged, when made in good faith. In such cases, although the statements made may have been untrue, malice cannot be implied from the fact of publication, and to sustain an action in which the existence of evil motive must be proved."

In Cranfill v. Hayden, supra, our Supreme Court used this language:

"If a defamatory publication is absolutely privileged, the occasion justifies the language, and no action arises. If the defamatory words are not justified, malice is implied, for the reason that every act intentionally done to the damage of another, without legal justification, or excuse, is in the eye of the law malicious. But a defamatory publication which is conditionally privileged occupies a middle ground; that is to say, the publication is privileged provided it was actuated by a sense of duty growing out of the occasion, and provided it was not malicious. When the court finds that the publication is conditionally privileged, the effect of the holding is to cast upon the plaintiff the burden of proving that malice prompted the act—not merely malice which arises by implication of law, but malice in fact, otherwise denominated actual malice. In other words, if the publication be conditionally privileged, malice is not implied from the mere fact of the publication."

In Simmons v. Dickson, supra, in an opinion of the Commission of Appeals of this state, Section B, approved on this point by the Supreme Court, is was said:

"It is conceded that the publication was conditionally privileged, and that, to be actionable, it must have been published with actual or express malice; the burden of proof being cast upon the plaintiff to establish actual malice. Plaintiff contends, however, and the Court of Civil Appeals held that the jury might infer such malice from the vehemence of the language used and the disproportion between the epithets applied to the plaintiff and the charges made against him. We are unable to concur in this conclusion. It is but the assertion in different language of the proposition that malice can be inferred or presumed from the fact of publication. When a publication is conditionally privileged, the law raises the presumption of good faith and want of malice; and to hold, in such case, that malice may be inferred from the character of the language used alone, would, in our opinion, destroy the force of the privilege. This view, we think, is in accord with the great weight of authority in this country, and with previous holdings of our Supreme Court."

As supporting the holding of the court in that case, Judge McClendon cited Warehouse Co. v. Holloway, supra, Railway Co. v. Richmond, supra, and Cranfill v. Hayden, supra. We think it is clear, from the authorities above cited, that in an action of slander, if it be shown that the slanderous utterance was conditionally privileged, then, before the plaintiff would be entitled to recover, proof must be reasonably sufficient to show that the slanderous utterance was actuated by actual or express malice towards the plaintiff, or by some other evil motive or bad faith.

The next question that follows for determination in this case is whether the slanderous utterance complained of by the appellee on the part of appellant's manager, Cohen, was conditionally or qualifiedly privileged. The undisputed evidence in this case, as reflected by the record before us, bearing upon the question as to whether the occasion which gave rise to the utterance complained of was such as to clothe the same with the privilege claimed for it by appellant, establishes the following facts:

The appellee, a young lady about 16 years of age, was employed by appellant in its dry goods establishment in the city of Houston. Her duties were to wrap and check articles of merchandise sold by appellant in its establishment, either to general customers or to employés themselves in the establishment. There were many employés in the establishment, some of whom waited on purchasers of goods and made sales to them, and others, like the appellee, who wrapped up and checked the articles sold, after the sale had been made. Many of these employés were young ladies called salesladies, one of whom was a young lady named Bessie York. Under the rules and regulations of appellant's establishment, which were promulgated for the conduct of its large business as a mercantile concern, it was required that, when one of the salesladies had made a sale of goods to a purchaser, the articles sold would be sent or carried by the saleslady to one of the wrapping clerks, like the appellee, and at the same time the saleslady making the sale would make out two checks, or lists, one called the original, and the other the duplicate check, or list, each check, or list, showing the items purchased, and also the price thereof, and this would be so whether the articles were to be paid for in cash by the purchaser, or whether the same were to be charged to the purchaser on the books of appellant. These checks, or lists, both original and duplicate, would be delivered to the wrapping clerk, together with the articles of merchandise sold, and it was the duty, if the purchase was made by a stranger to the establishment, or rather any person other than an employé, to check over these lists accompanying the articles sold, and ascertain whether the articles actually delivered to the wrapping clerk corresponded with the articles mentioned in the list, both in kind and price, and also it was the duty of the wrap-

ping clerk to ascertain from the list whether the transaction was a cash transaction or whether the purchase was to be charged. This would be disclosed by notation made by the saleslady on the lists, both original and duplicate. If it was a cash transaction, cash would be paid to the saleslady by the purchaser, and this would also accompany the articles sent to the wrapping clerk, and it was then her duty to wrap up the articles sold for the purchaser, and to wrap within the package the duplicate list, as we have described it, and to then send to the cashier the cash paid therefor, accompanied by the original list or check. If the transaction was not a cash one, that is to say, if the purchase was a credit transaction, both lists, as we have explained, would accompany the articles purchased to the wrapping clerk, and that the purchaser was to be charged on appellant's books therefor, and the duplicate would be wrapped up with the articles purchased, and the package handed by the wrapper to the purchaser, but the original slip, showing the transaction, would be sent by the wrapping clerk to the cashier, just the same as if the sale had been made for cash. If one of the employés, like Miss Bessie York, should desire to purchase any article of merchandise from appellant, the same procedure would be followed with reference to making the original and duplicate lists showing the articles purchased and the price to be paid therefor, and whether the same was paid for in cash by such employé or was to be charged on appellant's books, and the duplicate check, as in the case of a regular purchaser, would be wrapped up with the articles purchased, and the package would be sent to a department in appellant's establishment known as the delivery department, but could not be delivered, under appellant's rules and regulations, at that time to the employé making the purchase, and there would be a red tag on such package sent to the delivery department; but the wrapping clerk handling such purchase was required, under appellant's rules and regulations, to send the original list or check showing such articles and the price thereof, and whether it was a cash transaction or charge account, to appellant's cashier. These rules and regulations were clearly understood by the appellee.

Shortly before noon on the 14th day of November, 1918, Miss Bessie York, who, as we have shown, was one of the young lady salesladies in appellant's establishment, carried several articles of merchandise, of the aggregate value of $4.50, to appellee to be wrapped up for her, stating to appellee that she was making the purchase for herself, and that it was a cash transaction, and that she was paying the cash therefor. Appellee took the articles and wrapped them up, and she testified that these articles were accompanied by what purported to be a duplicate list showing the items purchased and the price charged therefor, and that she inclosed this duplicate list, along with the articles which she wrapped up in the package, and sent the same by one of the little cash boys in the store to the delivery department, which package, under appellant's rules, would have been delivered to Bessie York that evening after the store had closed, or that evening at the closing hour for business. No original check or list was turned over to appellee by Bessie York at the time these articles were brought to her by Bessie York, and she saw no original list or check that had been made by Bessie York, if one was made. Notwithstanding, however, the fact that no original list or check accompanied this purchase, she wrapped up the articles and sent them to the delivery department without having the original list or check to send to appellant's cashier, as appellant's rules required, and in doing this, appellee violated and disobeyed appellant's rules, and was aware of such violation and disobedience at the time of handling this package for Bessie York. Appellee testified, however, that she believed what Bessie York had stated to her about purchasing the articles for herself, and believed that it was a cash transaction by Bessie York, and, as claimed by her, she had no "room or reason" to doubt what Bessie York stated to her. She testified that if Bessie York stole these articles of merchandise, or intended to steal them, she was not aware of such intention, and had no reason to believe or suspect any bad faith or wrong purpose on the part of Bessie York at the time she handled the transaction for her. Shortly after (the time is not definitely stated) this package was sent by appellee to the delivery department, one of the cash boys in the store came to appellee with the package opened, holding the same in his hand, and inquired of appellee for the duplicate list that was supposed to accompany or be in the package at the time it was sent to the delivery department. Appellee replied that she put the duplicate list in the package when she sent it to the delivery department, and that she did not know what had become of such list. Shortly after that, on the same evening, a Mr. Muenster, who occupied the position of floorwalker in appellant's store on the same floor where appellee worked, came to appellee and inquired of her about the duplicate list that was supposed to accompany this package, and appellee explained to him, as she did to the cash boy, that she had put the list in the package, and that she knew nothing more about it. Mr. Muenster went away, but shortly returned to appellee, and told her that Mr. Cohen, appellant's president and general manager, wanted to see her in his private office, and thereupon appellee started, in company with Mr. Muenster, to Mr. Cohen's private office, which was situated on the mezzanine floor above, and when she reached

that office, the Bessie York package was lying on Mr. Cohen's office desk, and in the presence of Mr. Muenster and Mr. Kennedy, who was appellant's general superintendent, Mr. Cohen asked appellee, substantially, what she knew about the package, and why the same did not contain the duplicate list that should have been in the package at the time it was sent by her to the delivery department. Appellee stated to Mr. Cohen, then and there that Bessie York had brought the articles of merchandise to her to be wrapped up, and stated to her that she was purchasing them for herself, and that she was paying cash for them, and that Bessie York gave her a duplicate list of the articles showing the items and price, etc., and that she placed the duplicate list in the package when she sent it to the delivery department, and that she did not know what had become of the duplicate list, and did not know what Miss York's purpose was in handling the transaction as she did, and that she did not suspect that Bessie York intended to steal the articles or that she had any criminal intention with reference to them. She stated that she had wrapped the package for Bessie York, and sent it to the delivery department, because Bessie York had asked her to do so, and admitted that she knew that the original list or check should have accompanied the articles when brought to her for wrapping, under the rules and regulations of appellant's establishment, which list would have been sent to the cashier. Whereupon, in the presence of appellant's superintendent, Kennedy, and Mr. Muenster, the floorwalker, Mr. Cohen, appellant's president and general manager, said and stated to appellee: "Well, it behooves you to tell us what you know about this package, because it doesn't look straight," and appellee replied: "Mr. Cohen, I told you all I know about the package." Thereupon Mr. Cohen said to appellee, "Well, it looks like to me that you are as much implicated in this thievery as Bessie York is." Thereupon Mr. Kennedy, superintendent, stated, "Yes, George, I quite agree with you in the fact that she is as much implicated in it as Bessie York." Appellee testified that both Mr. Cohen and Mr. Kennedy spoke in a loud tone of voice in using the language to her just quoted, and that Mr. Cohen seemed to be angry. Mr. Cohen then told appellee to return to her station on the first floor and to not say anything to any one about what had occurred, and thereupon appellee went back to her station and resumed her duties on the first floor.

On the following morning, appellee returned to appellant's store at the usual hour, and appellant's superintendent, Kennedy, told her that she was discharged from further employment by appellant, and she was paid what was then due her, and her connection with appellant's establishment ceased. At the time she was informed by

the superintendent of her discharge, she had
gone up as was usual on the second floor
where the young salesladies put away their
coats, etc., on coming to work, and after she
was informed that she was discharged, she
went back down on the first floor, and had
there stopped and was talking to one of the
young salesladies on that floor, and had
been there about 10 minutes, so she testified,
when appellant's floorwalker, Muenster, approached her, and stated to her, substantially, in the presence of the young lady to
whom she was talking, and others, that she
was no longer an employé in appellant's
store, and requested her to leave the store
and, upon her failing to do so, promptly,
Muenster took her by the arm, as she says,
for the purpose of ejecting her from the
store, and that she was compelled to strike
him in order to extricate herself, after which
appellee left appellant's establishment.

[3] It was shown by the evidence of appellee herself, as well as others, that appellant's floorwalker, Muenster, was authorized,
and that it was his duty, under his employment with appellant, to see that customers
were properly waited on in appellant's store,
and to see that all employés on the floor discharged their duties and observed and obeyed
the rules and regulations of appellant in the
conduct of its business, and further, that it
was his duty to investigate and correct any
breach or violation of such rules and regulations by the employés on that floor. It was
also shown, without dispute, that appellant's
superintendent, Kennedy, was authorized,
and that it was his duty, to employ and discharge the employés in appellant's establishment, including the appellee, and to generally superintend the business of the store. It
was also shown without dispute that George
Cohen was the president and general manager
of the Foley Brothers Dry Goods Company,
and had supreme direction and control of all
other employés in appellant's establishment.
In short, it was shown by the undisputed
testimony that appellant's floorwalker,
Muenster, its superintendent, Kennedy, and
its president and general manager, Cohen,
were all authorized, and it was their duty,
to enforce the rules and regulations of appellant governing the conduct of its mercantile business, and to investigate any irregularities by employés under them, and to prevent any and all disobedience and violations
of such rules and regulations by such employés. This duty each of these men owed
to the Foley Brothers Dry Goods Company,
and the proof shows, without dispute, we
think, that each of these men was in the discharge of his duty at the time the slanderous
utterance or statement complained of by appellee was made. The proof shows, without dispute, that there were many employés
in appellant's establishment, some of the testimony indicating that the aggregate number

of employés would exceed, perhaps, 250. It
is manifest that it was necessary for the
conduct of such a large establishment that
rules and regulations should be promulgated
and enforced; and we hold, as a matter of
law, upon the facts of this record, that appellant's manager, Cohen, in making the utterance or statement complained of, and
sought to be made the basis of this suit, did
so in the discharge of his duty to appellant,
and that, therefore, such utterance to appellee was qualifiedly privileged, and the trial
court should have so held as a matter of
law. It was clearly announced in the case
of Railway Co. v. Richmond, supra, and also
in Cranfill v. Hayden, supra, that any utterance or communication made by one to
another in the discharge of a duty owed by
the one making the utterance is qualifiedly
privileged, and cannot be made the basis of
an action for damages, either actual or exemplary, unless it be shown by the party
complaining of the utterance or communication that the same was actuated by actual
or express malice or want of good faith.
The holding in those cases was expressly approved and adhered to in Simmons v. Dickson, 110 Tex. 230, 213 S. W. 612, 218 S. W.
365. See, also, Railway Co. v. Floore, 42 S.
W. 607, in which writ of error was denied
by the Supreme Court of this state. In that
case the court used this language:

"All such matters commonly "charged to be
libelous, clearly showing that it was a business
matter in which the railway company was interested, and such communication appearing to
have been sent only to persons concerned in
the matter, the court should have charged the
jury that the communication was privileged,
and that a recovery could not be had without
proof that the privilege was exercised in malice. * * *"

And in the Richmond Case, supra, it was
said by our Supreme Court:

"We understand the law to be that a communication made in good faith in reference to
a matter in which the person communicating
has an interest, or in which the public has an
interest, is privileged if made to another for
the purpose of protecting that interest, and
that a communication made in the discharge of
a duty and looking to the prevention of wrong
towards another or the public is so privileged
when made in good faith. In such cases, although the statements made may have been
untrue, malice cannot be implied from the fact
of publication, and to sustain an action in
which the existence of evil motive must be
proved."

As sustaining its view on the point, the
court quoted from Harrison v. Burk, 5 El. &
Bl. 848, as follows:

"A communication made bona fide upon any
subject-matter in which the party communicating has an interest, or in reference to which
he has a duty, is privileged if made to a person having a corresponding interest or duty,

although it contained criminatory matter which without this privilege, would be slanderous and actionable. * * * 'Duty,' in the preferred canon, cannot be confined to legal duties which may be enforced by indictment, action, or mandamus, but must include moral and social duties of imperfect obligation."

"When words imputing misconduct to another are spoken by one having a duty to perform, and the words are spoken in good faith and in the belief that it comes within the discharge of that duty, or where they are spoken in good faith to those who have an interest in the communication and a right to know and act upon the facts stated, no presumption of malice arises from the speaking of the words, and therefore no action can be maintained in such cases without proof of express malice. If the occasion is used merely as a means of enabling the party to utter the slander to indulge his malice, and not in good faith to perform a duty or make a communication useful and beneficial to others, the occasion will furnish no excuse."

We repeat that the occasion on which the utterance complained of by appellee was made to her was, upon the undisputed facts of this case, such as to give the utterance a qualifiedly privileged character, because the utterance complained of was by one who had a duty to perform to another, and therefore, under the authorities, the utterance was qualifiedly privileged.

[4] But the able counsel for appellee in this case contend that, if this court should conclude that the utterance complained of was qualifiedly privileged, nevertheless, such utterance being slanderous per se, the burden of proof rested upon appellant to show want of malice, and that the utterance was made in good faith, and in the belief of its truth. We have already shown, by the authorities above cited, that this contention cannot be sustained, but, on the contrary, such authorities clearly hold that, where the utterance is shown to have been conditionally privileged, the plaintiff must then take the burden of showing that the same was actuated by actual or express malice or want of good faith.

[5] This brings us to the question as to whether there was sufficient evidence in this case to warrant the jury's finding that the utterance complained of was actuated by actual or express malice, or want of good faith. Appellee contends that the evidence was sufficient to warrant such finding by the jury. We cannot, without making this opinion too long, go into the evidence in detail, but we shall state, substantially, all facts and circumstances which we think could reasonably have any bearing upon the point. The evidence is undisputed that this young lady, the appellee, at the time of the occurrence complained of, had been in appellant's employ about a month, in the discharge of the same duties as she was performing at the time of the occurrence. She testified that she knew appellant's floorwalker, Muenster, and the superintendent, Kennedy, and its president and manager, George Cohen, and that she saw these gentlemen on an average of once or twice a day during her employment; that up to the time of the occurrence complained of she had never observed anything in the conduct of either of these gentlemen towards her to indicate any unkind or disrespectful feeling for her; that up to the time of the occurrence, no disobedience or irregularity on her part had been called to her attention or complained of by either of the gentlemen mentioned, and the substance of her testimony, in short, is that she knew of no reason why either of these gentlemen should entertain any unkind or unfriendly feeling for her. She further testified that Miss Bessie York, on the very evening that the conduct which appellant was investigating occurred, was discharged, and that such discharge was because appellant's manager believed that Bessie York was guilty of the theft of the articles of merchandise concerning which the investigation was instituted, or that she intended to steal the same, and there was not a fact or circumstance, as we view this record, offered by the appellee showing or tending to show that appellant or any of its employés in authority entertained any unkind feeling for Bessie York, or that her discharge was because of anything other than the belief on the part of appellant's manager of her guilt relative to the said articles of merchandise. It is true that appellee testified that the words uttered and spoken to her by appellant's manager, Cohen, and of which she complains, were uttered in a loud and angry tone, and, if this be true, it is also true, perhaps, that it was not absolutely necessary that the utterance should have been made in such tone, nor that the language used should have been so strong. It was clearly held, however, in Simmons v. Dickson, supra, substantially, that, when the utterance complained of is conditionally privileged, the law raises the presumption of good faith and want of malice, and that it cannot be held in such a case that malice may be inferred from the character of the language used alone, because such an inference would have the effect to destroy the defense of privilege. The court used this language:

"Plaintiff contends, however, and the Court of Civil Appeals held, that the jury might infer such malice from the vehemence of the language used and the disproportion between the epithets applied to plaintiff and the charges made against him. We are unable to concur in this conclusion. It is but the assertion, in different language, of the proposition that malice can be inferred or presumed from the fact of publication. When a publication is conditionally privileged, the law raises the presumption of good faith and want of malice; and to hold, in such a case, that malice can be inferred from the character of the language used alone, would, in our opinion, destroy the force of the privilege."

So it is contended here by counsel for appellee, among other things, that the mere disobedience of rules by the appellee, or the irregularity of which she was guilty in handling the package of articles delivered to her by Bessie York, would not require such strong language or epithet as was applied to her by appellant's manager for such disobedience, and that therefore that fact may be considered by a jury as strongly indicating actual malice and want of good faith on the part of appellant's manager. If we concede the contention, we would, in effect, hold contrary to the law as just quoted. It is further contended by counsel for appellee, in effect, that the jury might have reasonably inferred malice on the part of appellant's manager and those engaged with him in the investigation, because, at the time of the utterance complained of, appellee had explained and declared to all three of the gentlemen engaged in the investigation that she knew nothing about the motive that prompted Bessie York in bringing the articles to her as she did, and that she had no "room or reason" to suspect Bessie York of any wrong intention, and that, since there was no evidence that appellant made any further investigation to see what actuated Bessie York in thus handling the articles, the jury was authorized to infer malice or bad faith; but in this connection we repeat that appellee herself expressly testified that Bessie York was discharged by appellant because its manager believed that she was guilty of the theft of the articles, or that she intended to steal them. Appellee also contends that the action of appellant's floorwalker, Muenster, on the next morning, when appellee was discharged, in speaking to her as he did, and attempting to remove her from the store, was a cogent fact and circumstance showing malice and bad faith on the part of appellant towards her, but it must be remembered that, at the time of this conduct on the part of Muenster, the utterance complained of had already occurred, and we feel sure that we would not be justified in concluding that the conduct of Muenster in this regard should be construed as proof of actual malice attributable to appellant in making the utterance complained of by its manager, Cohen.

It is true, as contended by counsel for appellee, that the record, as made by appellee's testimony, shows without contradiction by any witness that she was not guilty of any criminal intention or purpose in handling the Bessie York package as she did, and that therefore the charge that she was guilty of theft of the package, or as much so as Bessie York, was false, but it has been too often held by the appellate courts of this state that, where a finding of actual malice is necessary to sustain a recovery for a slanderous utterance which is conditionally privileged, malice cannot be found from the falsity of such statement alone. Laughlin v. Schnitzer, 106 S. W. 908, and authorities there cited. In the case cited it was said:

"It was necessary in order for plaintiff to recover, that the jury should find that the words were spoken with some degree of express malice, but this fact they could not find from their falsity alone. Bradstreet v. Gill, 72 Texas, 121, 9 S. W. 753, 2 L. R. A. 405, 13 Am. St. Rep. 768."

Taking the record before us in its entirety, we have reached the conclusion, giving consideration to every fact and circumstance that could reasonably be said to show malice or lack of good faith on the part of appellant's employés, whose conduct is complained of by appellee, that such evidence as a whole was insufficient to warrant the finding of the jury that appellant was actuated by actual malice in making the utterance to appellee of which she complains, and we are therefore constrained to hold that the finding of the jury that there was such actual malice has no reasonable support in the evidence, and that the sixth and seventh assignments, which, in effect, make complaint of that finding, must be sustained.

We will not say, however, that, upon the record as a whole, there is no fact or circumstance that might have a tendency to prove malice, but only hold that the evidence, as developed and shown by the present record, was not sufficient to warrant a finding by the jury that there was such actual malice. It may be that we would be justified in holding that the evidence on that point is so weak as to require the judgment to be reversed and rendered. But it appears to us that the case was tried for appellee upon the theory that the burden was upon appellant to disprove malice on its part, and it may be that other evidence can be produced by the appellee upon another trial sufficient to show that the slanderous utterance made the basis of this action was actuated by malice, and, if so, appellee would be entitled to recover in some amount. We therefore overrule the fourth and fifth assignments, which complain, in effect, of the refusal of the trial court to peremptorily instruct a verdict in appellant's favor.

What we have said above, in effect, disposes of all other assignments in appellant's brief, and it is unnecessary to notice them further.

Being of the opinion that the slanderous matter complained of was qualifiedly privileged, and that therefore the burden of proof was upon appellee on the issue of malice and want of good faith, and that the finding of the jury that there was actual malice is not reasonably supported by the evidence in the record before us, it follows that the judgment should be reversed, and the cause remanded, and it will be so ordered.

TECUMSEH OIL & COTTON CO. v. GRESHAM. (No. 1811.)

(Court of Civil Appeals of Texas. Amarillo. May 4, 1921. Rehearing Denied June 1, 1921.)

1. Novation ⚎7—Seller could not substitute other party in its place.

A company which contracted to deliver cottonseed oil could not substitute some other party in its place and require the buyer to deal direct with such party in receipt of instructions for the delivery of the oil or settlement therefor.

2. Customs and usages ⚎19(3)—Evidence insufficient to show custom that seller might require buyer to deal with other party direct.

Evidence held insufficient to show that under the usages and customs of the trade defendant seller had the right to satisfy its contract by requiring the buyer to deal direct with another party for the oil.

3. Sales ⚎173 — Receiver of buyer company held to have furnished cars for shipment, though cars belonged to other.

Receiver of a company, the buyer of cottonseed oil, had authority to use for the acceptance of the oil from the seller company certain cars belonging to another company, so, though he offered no other cars, he did not fail to furnish cars for the shipment.

4. Receivers ⚎90—Need not carry out executory contract, but estate is liable for breach.

Though a receiver may not be forced to carry out executory contract, the estate is not, by his rejection of the contract, released from liability for its breach.

5. Sales ⚎418(12)—Buyer which resold entitled to recover for seller's failure to deliver.

Where the buyer of oil, if deliveries had been made as contracted, could, through its receiver, have performed its resale contract, the original seller of the oil, not having delivered, could not successfully claim that the original buyer was not damaged by the failure to deliver, on the ground that, as the resale price was less than the purchase price, no profit would have been realized from the resale, since the original buyer's damages for failure to make deliveries included not merely loss of profits from the resale, but also liability incurred for breach of the resale contract.

6. Sales ⚎181(11) — Evidence insufficient to show buyer refused to pay for car of oil on demand.

In suit by the trustee of a company which purchased cottonseed oil against the seller for failure to deliver, evidence held insufficient to support defendant seller's claim that the buyer company, prior to its bankruptcy, failed and refused to pay for a tank car of oil on demand, which operated as a repudiation of the contract.

Appeal from District Court, Grayson County; Silas Hare, Judge.

Suit by O. S. Gresham, trustee, against the Tecumseh Oil & Cotton Company. From judgment for plaintiff, defendant appeals. Affirmed.

See, also, 211 S. W. 458.

J. F. Holt and Wolfe & Freeman, all of Sherman, for appellant.

Wood, Jones & Hassell, of Sherman, for appellee.

BOYCE, J. In August, 1915, the Tecumseh Cotton Oil Company, hereinafter referred to as the Tecumseh Company, agreed to sell to the Sherman Cotton Oil & Provision Company, hereinafter referred to as the Sherman Company, three tank cars of cottonseed oil, to be delivered in November, 1915, at "35 cents per gallon, loose, f. o. b. Oklahoma common points, in tank cars of 160 barrels capacity each, to be furnished by buyers," cars to be shipped and routed at "buyer's option" and paid for on "sight draft against bill of lading for invoice amount." The contract was made subject to the rules of the Interstate Cotton Seed Crushers' Association. Two of these rules involved in the discussion of the controversy between the said parties are as follows:

"Section 8. Rule 28. In case of contracts for oil for specified shipments it shall be the duty of the seller to notify buyer at least ten days previous to the expiration of the period in which the tank cars might be forwarded, in time to reach seller, in time to admit of shipment of the oil within the contract period. In case seller does not give such instructions within the period specified, it shall be the duty of the buyer to ask by wire for such instructions, confirming by letter and then failing to receive them may upon wire notice, given forty-eight hours in advance, through any recognized cotton oil broker in good standing, buy the oil contracted for, holding the seller for any loss and expense incurred in such repurchase and accounting to him for any profits earned in it over the contract price."

"Section 1. Rule 25. Failure on the part of the buyer to forward cars in the proper time and give due notice thereof shall entitle the seller, at his option, to cancel the contract."

About November 1st the Sherman Company wrote the Tecumseh Company that it ex.) TECUMSEH OIL & COTTON CO. v. GRESHAM 469

(881 S.W.)

ad resold these three cars of oil to Peet Bros. Manufacturing Company, of Kansas City, and asked for delivery as early in the month as possible. The Tecumseh Company acknowledged receipt of this letter and notified the Sherman Company to have two cars at Oklahoma City during the first half of November for loading by the Southwestern Cotton Oil Company, from whom the Tecumseh Company had purchased two tanks of oil, and to have the other car at Tecumseh on November 9th for loading by the Tecumseh Company. It may be inferred, though the evidence is not very full as to this point, that under the contract of resale from the Sherman Company to Peet Bros. Manufacturing Company was to furnish the cars for loading said oil, and that the cars that were furnished were furnished by Peet Bros. Manufacturing Company on this contract. The Sherman Company instructed the Tecumseh Company to load said cars on arrival and ship to Peet Bros. Manufacturing Company "in accordance with their instructions, making draft on us at Sherman, in accordance with the terms of our contract." One car was duly delivered under the contract; another was loaded and shipped from Oklahoma City. The Southwestern Company, which loaded this car, drew draft on the Tecumseh Company with bill of lading attached. The Tecumseh Company paid this draft and in turn drew draft on the Sherman Company with bill of lading attached. The evidence is not sufficient to show that this draft was ever presented to the Sherman Company for payment. The draft was drawn on November 18th, and on November 19th the bank in which it had been deposited delivered the unpaid draft and the bill of lading back to the Tecumseh Company. It is not shown what became of this car of oil except that it was never delivered to the Sherman Company. On November 19th the Sherman Company was adjudged a bankrupt, and the appellee, O. S. Gresham, was appointed receiver, and later trustee in bankruptcy, and immediately upon appointment was authorized to carry out the contract with the Tecumseh Company, and could and would have paid for said oil if it had been delivered. On November 20th communications by phone and letter were had between the representatives of the Tecumseh Company and the receiver for the Sherman Company, the result of which is summed up in the two following letters:

The Tecumseh Company wrote the Sherman Company as follows:

"Referring to the two tanks crude oil sold you for November shipment, f. o. b. Oklahoma points, kindly furnish tanks on instructions from the Interstate Cotton Oil Refining Company to take care of this sale, in accordance with contract, and make settlement direct with them at our contract price."

To this letter the receiver replied in part as follows:

"This is not satisfactory to me. I find the contract between the Tecumseh Oil & Cotton Company and the Sherman Cotton Oil Provision Company is for three tank cars prime, crude oil; that papers have passed on one tank car, leaving undelivered two tank cars; that one of these two tank cars has been loaded by the Southwestern Cotton Oil Company, Oklahoma City, Okl., to whom the Sherman Cotton Oil Provision Company were instructed to forward tanks; that the bill of lading and invoice were presented to the Sherman Cotton Oil Provision Company on the evening of the 18th instant for payment; and that the party presenting the invoice was requested to present them the next morning for payment, to which he agreed. The terms of this contract were sight draft, bill of lading attached, and I demand that papers be passed through the bank in accordance with the contract on this tank car immediately. I further understand that the last tank car has been forwarded to the Southwestern Cotton Oil Company, Oklahoma City, Okl., in accordance with your instructions, and I demand that papers on this tank car likewise be handed to me promptly on receipt. The contract referred to is between the Tecumseh Oil & Cotton Company and the Sherman Cotton Oil Provision Company, and I cannot agree to look to any one but the Tecumseh Oil & Cotton Company to fulfill their contract, and unless any demands are complied with and I am immediately advised of your intention to so comply, I will be compelled to protect the equity of the Sherman Cotton Oil Provision Company in this transaction by proceeding in accordance with the rules governing this transaction."

Nothing further appears to have been done by either party in reference to the matter until on December 1st the Tecumseh Company notified the receiver that it had canceled the contract "account your noncompliance with the contract."

This suit was brought by the said O. S. Gresham, trustee, to recover as damages the difference between the contract price of the two undelivered tanks of oil and the market value of same at the time when the oil should have been delivered. Under appropriate pleading by the respective parties, evidence of the foregoing facts, and such other facts as we may state in our discussion of the case, was introduced, and on the close of the evidence the court instructed the jury to render a verdict for the plaintiff for the sum of $3,853.18, this being shown to be the difference betwen the contract price and market value of the oil, and there being no issue as to such matter the controversy being as to liability.

Two assignments are presented: One that the court erred in refusing to give appellants requested peremptory instruction, and the other complaining of error in the giving of the peremptory instruction for the plaintiff. The same questions, to a large extent, are presented under both assignments, and we may dispose of them by a general discussion.

[1, 2] One proposition made under the assignments is that the request made by the appellant company to furnish tank cars on instructions from the Interstate Cotton Oil Company was a sufficient offer by the Tecumseh Company to perform the contract, and that it was discharged on refusal of the trustee to accept the oil thus tendered. In this connection it was shown that the Tecumseh Company had purchased two tanks of oil from the Interstate Company for delivery at Guthrie, Okl., a common point, and that such oil "could have been delivered on this contract." If the rights of the parties are to be determined by the terms of the contract, without reference to any usage or custom, it is clear that the letter of November 20th is not a legal offer on the part of the Tecumseh Company of compliance with the contract. There was nothing in the contract that would authorize the Tecumseh Company to substitute some other party in its place and require the buyer to deal direct with such party in receipt of instructions for delivery of the oil or settlement therefor. There were no contractual relations between the Sherman Company and the Interstate Company, and the Tecumseh Company was not authorized by the terms of the contract itself to require the Sherman Company to assume such relations and deal "direct" with the Interstate Company as was demanded by the Tecumseh Company in this offer. But the appellant contends that "under the usages and customs of the trade" it had the right to satisfy its contract in this way. If we concede that a showing of such a custom would be permissible under the terms of the contract, the evidence is not sufficient to establish that such usage and custom existed. The evidence is sufficient to show that in such contracts the seller may deliver oil made by other mills and require the buyer to send his cars to be loaded by such other mills, but the same witnesses who testified as to such custom further testified that under the usage the purchaser could not be required in such case to deal "direct" with the third person, as was proposed by appellant. But, even if the appellant could, in the first instance, have demanded that the Sherman Company furnish cars and take delivery from the Interstate Cotton Oil Company and settle with it, as was proposed, it could not do so in this case if the trustee had the right (a matter we will presently consider) to demand that delivery be made in the tank cars already furnished. Those cars were furnished on notice given by the Tecumseh Company under the rule we have quoted, and the Sherman Company could not, under such circumstances, refuse delivery at such time and place and demand that cars be furnished at some other place.

[3] Another proposition presented under these assignments is that these two tank cars belonged to Peet Bros. Manufacturing Company; that the receiver had no authority to use them for acceptance of the oil; that he offered no other cars, and thus failed to furnish cars for the shipment, and the appellant had the right to cancel the contract for this reason. It appears from the evidence that the trustee rejected the contract with Peet Bros., but the evidence does not disclose when this rejection was made. It does appear that the receiver was, immediately after his appointment, authorized to carry out the contract of purchase with the Tecumseh Company, and to this end to pay the draft against the car that had already been shipped, and it may be inferred that the rejection of the contract with the Peet Bros. Manufacturing Company was made later. While the tank cars may have been furnished by Peet Bros. Manufacturing Company, this was done under a contract between the Sherman Company and the said manufacturing company, and the fact remains that the Sherman Company had caused the cars to be furnished under its own contract with the Tecumseh Company. One of these cars was already in use, being loaded and presumably on its way to Kansas City, and the other furnished and ready for filling. The loaded car was under the control of the possessor of the bill of lading issued by the railway company, and the receiver was, under the contract, entitled to this control on payment of draft for the purchase price due the Tecumseh Company. As to this car it would seem clear enough that the appellant company could not deny the right of the trustee to the use of the car and at the same time appropriate it to his own use, by retaining the bill of lading and making its own disposition of the car of oil. The right to the use of both cars was dependent upon the terms of the contract between the Sherman Company and Peet Bros. Manufacturing Company. Just what this contract was does not appear, except that the Sherman Company was selling the oil to Peet Bros. Manufacturing Company, and that said manufacturing company was to pay therefor the sum of 34½ cents per gallon. The manufacturing company does not appear to have been objecting to the oil being loaded into these cars; the settlement of the right as to the use of the cars was a matter for adjustment between the Sherman Company and the manufacturing company. The appellant did not refuse to deliver the loaded car, or load the other one, on the ground that the cars belonged to Peet Bros., and that the trustee had no right to use them. If any such objection had been raised at that time, it might possibly, if it had been shown to be

a valid one, have been met in some way, but the appellant did not at that time claim that the Sherman Company had failed to furnish cars at the time and place it had been notified to do so, but insisted that the said company accept delivery of said oil at some other time and place. It is our opinion that the appellant has not successfully maintained this proposition.

[4, 5] The proposition just discussed is followed by another, to the effect that, since Peet Bros. Manufacturing Company had furnished the cars under the contract with the Sherman Company, it had the right to insist on delivery of the oil to it upon acquisition by the receiver, and that, if this had been done, the receiver would have sustained a loss on the transaction, so that he suffered no damages from the appellant's refusal to deliver the oil. This contention is based on the fact that Peet Bros. Manufacturing Company was to pay the Sherman Company 34½ cents per gallon for the oil, while the Sherman Company was to pay the Tecumseh Company 35 cents per gallon therefor. A trustee has the right to accept or reject the executory contracts of the bankrupt, but it may be true that the trustee's use of the cars would be such an acceptance of the contract with Peet Bros. Manufacturing Company as would preclude a subsequent rejection. So that one premise of the proposition, to wit, that the receiver or trustee would have been bound to have delivered the oil to Peet Bros. Manufacturing Company after accepting it loaded in cars belonging to said company, is supported by some reason. But, if we concede that this premise is established, yet the conclusion contended for by appellant does not follow. It is true that the trustee would not, in such event, have made a profit on the whole transaction, and would have even sustained a slight loss. On the other hand, the failure to deliver the oil and the final rejection of the manufacturing company's contract subjected the bankrupt's estate to the liability of a claim for. damages on the part of Peet Bros. Manufacturing Company for a breach of its contract, the measure of which would be the difference between its contract price and the market value of the oil, and perhaps, in addition, compensation for the expense, etc., incurred in furnishing the cars for receipt of the oil; for, while a trustee may not be forced to carry out an executory contract, the estate is not by its rejection released from liability for its breach. Central Trust Co. v. Chicago Auditorium Association, 240 U. S. 581, 36 Sup. Ct. 412, 60 L. Ed. 811, L. R. A. 1917B, 580; Planters' Oil Co. v. Gresham, 202 S. W. 154, § 17; Collier on Bankruptcy (12th Ed.) pp. 968, 969. So the fulfilling of the contract with Peet Bros. Manufacturing Company would have saved the bankrupt estate from this liability, and in this way there was a consequent damage from the failure of the appellant to deliver the oil. Gresham v. Tecumseh Oil & Cotton Co., 211 S. W. 458. It is true that such case was decided on the theory that it was shown that the oil would not have gone to the buyer, but the reasoning in that case, in connection with our conclusion as to liability of the bankrupt estate in case the oil was not delivered to the buyer, supports our decision of this proposition.

It is also urged that the evidence shows that the loaded car was actually shipped and delivered to Peet Bros. Manufacturing Company under the contract, and the judgment in effect makes the appellant responsible for the delivery of four cars instead of three. The evidence does not support this conclusion. As we have seen, it does not appear what became of this car of oil; but it does appear that the appellant had possession and control of it through the possession of the bill of lading, and presumably disposed of it to its own advantage. It refused to deliver the bill of lading to the trustee, and did not at the time claim that the car had been delivered to Peet Bros. or to the trustee in satisfaction of the contract, but recognized that it still owed two cars of oil on this contract.

[6] Another contention made by appellant is that the Sherman Company "prior to bankruptcy failed and refused to pay for said tank car of oil on demand therefor, and this operated as a repudiation of said contract, especially as to said one tank car." We think the evidence is also insufficient to support this claim. The plaintiff offered testimony to the effect that on the afternoon of November 18th a clerk from the office of the Tecumseh Company presented to a clerk in the office of the Sherman Company an invoice of a car of oil with bill of lading attached; that the manager of the Sherman Company was at such time out of the office temporarily, the Tecumseh Company clerk had no authority to make such payment, and the employee of the Tecumseh Company promised to return the next morning to receive payment. The testimony offered by the Tecumseh Company tends to contradict the statement that any one from its office presented such invoice to the Sherman Company for payment, and is to the effect that a draft on the Sherman Company with bill of lading attached was deposited in the Merchants' & Planters' Bank at Sherman on November 18th, and was returned by the bank to the Tecumseh Company on the next day unpaid. The draft was introduced in evidence, and there is no notation of refusal of payment on it, and there is no evidence that the bank presented it to the Sherman Company for payment, and on November 20th the Tecumseh Company was not claiming that the contract had been canceled by any failure or re-

fusal on the part of the Sherman Company to make payment for this oil.

We find no reversible error presented by any of the propositions made under the two assignments, and the judgment will be affirmed.

BARMORE v. DARRAGH et al. (No. 6574.)

(Court of Civil Appeals of Texas. San Antonio. March 30, 1921. Rehearing Denied June 1, 1921.)

1. Wills ⊂470—All provisions looked to in ascertaining testator's intention.

All the provisions of a will should be looked to in ascertaining the testator's intention.

2. Wills ⊂601(1)—Statute does not prohibit subsequent provision from limiting absolute estate previously given.

The rule that an absolute disposition may be limited by a subsequent clause in a will, where the intention is clearly expressed, is not affected by Rev. St. 1911, art. 1106, raising a presumption of fee-simple devise, "if a less estate be not limited by express words."

3. Wills ⊂545(3)—Devise over on devisee's death effective only on devisee's predeceasing testator.

A provision in a will that an estate shall take a certain course in case of the death of a named person operates only in case the person's death occurs before testator's death; but such rule is inapplicable where, after an absolute devise, the contingency named whereby the estate devised should go to devisee's sister was not his death merely, but his death "before his sister * * * without heirs of his body."

4. Wills ⊂608(1)—Rule in Shelley's Case held inapplicable.

The rule in Shelley's Case is directed against a devise over to the "heirs" of the first taker, and hence is inapplicable to an absolute devise followed by a provision that if the devisee should die before his sister and without heirs of his body the estate shall go, not to his heirs, but to his sister.

5. Wills ⊂545(3)—Devise held to give life estate; "in case"; "without heirs of his body."

Where an absolute devise was followed by a provision that "in case" devisee died before his sister without "heirs of his body" his share should go to his sister, the devisee, on surviving the testator, did not take title absolutely but on his death without issue the devise over to his sister, if living, would take effect; "in case" meaning "in the event," and "without heirs of his body" meaning "without issue."

[Ed. Note.—For other definitions, see Words and Phrases, In Case.]

6. Wills ⊂457—To effectuate intention, words may be given other than technical import.

In harmonizing conflicts to effectuate the ascertained intention of the testator, words and

phrases may be given meanings other than their technical import.

7. Wills ⊂447—Construction consistent with lawful intention adopted.

Where words or phrases are susceptible of two constructions, one consistent with an intention to do that which the testator may lawfully do, and the other consistent with an intention to do that which he may not lawfully do, the one construction will be adopted and the other rejected.

8. Wills ⊂439—Intention not to be conjectured.

Courts must not indulge in and give effect to mere conjecture as to the intention of a testator, since to do so would be assuming the power to make rather than to construe the will.

9. Wills ⊂495, 506(4)—Clause held to give remainder to children of devisee of life estate; "heirs of his body"; "issue of his own body"; "inherit"; "take."

Where an absolute devise was followed by a paragraph, the first clause of which directed that the estate devised should go to devisee's sister if she survived him dying without "heirs of his body," and the second clause of which provided "but if he dies leaving issue of his own body then his said heirs shall inherit" his estate, such second clause was an alternative of the first clause, and would be given effect as giving the property, in case devisee was survived by issue of his body, to those of such issue who were living at his death; "heirs of his body" and "issue of his own body" being construed to mean simply "children," and "inherit" to mean "take," although technically "inherit" is a word of limitation, and "take" is a word of purchase.

[Ed. Note.—For other definitions, see Words and Phrases, First Series, Issue of the Body; First and Second Series, Heirs of the Body; Inherit; Take.]

10. Wills ⊂538—Devise over on death of another is presumed to refer to death before testator's death.

A clause in a will devising over to another an estate given to testatrix's daughter in fee by a previous clause, "in case of the death of" the daughter and her named child, impliedly conditioned the devise over upon the death of the daughter and her child before testatrix's death, so that where the daughter and her child survived testatrix the devise over lapsed.

11. Wills ⊂601(1)—Clause following absolute devise held to give devisee life estate with remainder to surviving children.

Where an absolute devise was followed by a provision that in case the devisee at her death shall leave children, "which includes B. [her child by a former marriage], her children shall inherit her estate, share and share alike," the devisee was limited to a life estate with remainder over to those of her children who might survive her; the clause "which includes B." being treated as surplusage and ineffective, and the provision that the property should pass "share and share alike" being conclusive of testatrix's intention that it pass by purchase, not by limitation.

12. Wills ⚓467—Direction for education of grandchild held precatory.

A clause in a will, following devises of life estates in the property to testatrix's son and daughter, in which testatrix enjoined them to "take care of B. [the son of the daughter by a former marriage] and properly educate him, to be paid for out of the estate which I give to my said two children * * * until the said B. shall have received his education," was precatory merely; it being left to the will of the son and daughter whether its provisions should be regarded.

13. Wills ⚓849 — Clause restricting giving away of estate received under will held void.

A clause in a will directing that the rights that a beneficiary receives under the will shall revert to others, if he gives any of the estate he inherits under the will to any of certain named kin, is void.

Appeal from District Court, Bexar County; W. S. Anderson, Judge.

Suit by John Greenleaf Darragh and others against John Darragh Barmore. From judgment for plaintiffs, defendant appeals. Reversed and rendered.

See, also, 227 S. W. 522.

J. Ed. Wilkins, of San Antonio, for appellant.

Cobbs, Blankenbecker & Wiggin, of San Antonio, for appellees.

SMITH, J. Annie Pendleton Shepherd Darragh, a widow, died testate on December 15, 1918, leaving an estate consisting of very valuable property, which was sought to be disposed of in a will which was probated on January 8, 1919. To obtain a construction of that will, this suit was instituted by John Greenleaf Darragh and Mabel Darragh Jenkins, son and daughter, respectively, and the only children, of the said Annie Pendleton Shepherd Darragh, against John Darragh Barmore, minor son of Mabel Darragh Jenkins by a former marriage. John L. Jenkins, present husband of Mabel Darragh Jenkins, joined his wife as a party plaintiff in the suit. The will in question, omitting formal parts, reads as follows:

"First: I give and bequeath to my beloved children, John Greenleaf Darragh and Mabel Darragh Jenkins, all of my estate, real, personal and mixed, choses in action, bonds and securities and moneys of whatever kind or character, wheresoever situated, share and share alike, except as hereinafter specially provided in reference to certain personal property.

"Second: I give to my daughter, Mabel Darragh Jenkins, all of my household and kitchen furniture, linens and furnishings, beds, bedding, crockery ware, glass ware, silver ware, cooking utensils and everything pertaining to kitchen and household use, also all of my personal effects, clothing, etc., all jewelry, ornaments, etc., except one certain topaz ring that was my husband's which I give to my son, John Greenleaf Darragh, together with a certain diamond stick pin with colored stone, which I likewise give to him.

"Third: I give to my said two children jointly all the dining room furniture, to be divided equally between them, the manner of division shall be agreed upon by them; and I also further give to my son, John, the right to select any one or two pieces of china and one or two pieces of silver ware.

"Fourth: In case John Greenleaf Darragh dies before his sister, Mabel Darragh Jenkins, without heirs of his body, all of his portion of the estate shall go to my said daughter, Mabel Darragh Jenkins; but if he dies leaving issue of his own body, then his said heirs shall inherit his portion of said estate.

"Fifth: In case of the death of my daughter, Mabel Darragh Jenkins, and in case of the death of John Darragh Barmore, her child, then the said John Darragh Barmore, if living, or his heirs, as hereinabove stated, shall take her estate; but in case that the said Mabel Darragh Jenkins at her death should leave children, which includes John Darragh Barmore, her children shall inherit her estate, share and share alike.

"Sixth: I give and bequeath to John Darragh Barmore, child of Mabel Darragh Jenkins, his grandfather's watch, and to John Greenleaf Darragh, my son, his father's gold watch chain.

"Seventh: It is the wish and is so enjoined upon John Greenleaf Darragh and Mabel Darragh Jenkins, that they shall take care of John Darragh Barmore and properly educate him, to be paid for out of the estate which I give to my said two children, John Greenleaf Darragh and Mabel Darragh Jenkins, until the said John Darragh Barmore shall have received his education. It is understood that whatever rights John Darragh Barmore receives under the provisions of this will shall lapse and revert to my said children or their heirs, in case he gives any part whatsoever of the estate he inherits hereunder to any of his Barmore kin, including his father and grandfather.

"Eighth: I hereby appoint John Greenleaf Darragh and Mabel Darragh Jenkins my executors of this my last will and testament and direct that my estate be administered without the intervention of any proceedings of any court, and that no action be taken in any court in the administration of my estate other than by probating this will and filing such inventory as the law requires.

"I further direct after probating said will the said estate shall be closed and no further proceedings shall be had therein; and I further direct that no bond or other security shall be required of my said executors and that they administer the same without bond."

Upon a hearing before the court without a jury, the lower court found, among other essential facts not material here, that John Greenleaf Darragh and Mabel Darragh Jenkins were the only children of testatrix;

that John Greenleaf Darragh is unmarried and without issue, and that John Darragh Barmore, appellant herein, is the only child of .Mabel Darragh Jenkins, and was born to her of a former marriage. The court further found that it was the intention of testatrix to leave her real property to appellees John Greenleaf Darragh and Mabel Darragh Jenkins, share and share alike. Upon these findings of fact the court concluded, as a matter of law, that the will should be construed to vest in appellees, share and share alike, the fee-simple title to all the real property of testatrix at her death, and that any declarations or expressions used in the will that might be construed to limit the purpose to create a fee-simple title in appellees were null and void, as repugnant to the fee-simple title, and that it appeared from the entire will and from the testimony relative thereto that it was the intention of the testatrix to vest the absolute title in appellees. Upon these conclusions the court rendered judgment for appellees, vesting absolute title in them, and from this judgment John Darragh Barmore, through his guardian ad litem, brings this appeal.

Although it may be inferred from the trial court's conclusions that parol evidence was introduced upon the trial, no statement of facts appears with the record, from which we assume that the only evidence actually introduced was the will itself. However, we can conceive of no parol testimony that should be given the effect of modifying or destroying the intention of the testatrix as expressed in the instrument, and if the finding of the court is in conflict with the intent as expressed in the will, such finding will be disregarded here.

Appellant's contention as to the meaning of the will is set forth in the first and only proposition contained in his brief, which is as follows:

"Paragraph 1, taken in connection and with the limitations placed thereon by paragraphs 4, 5, and 7 of the will convey to John Darragh a qualified defeasible fee subject to be defeated upon his death without issue and convey to Mabel Darragh Jenkins only a life estate."

Appellees contend that under the terms of the will the fee simple to the whole of the estate, together with full power to convey, passed to John Greenleaf Darragh and Mabel Darragh Jenkins, share and share alike, immediately upon the death of the testatrix.

Appellant in his brief asserts only the one proposition quoted, cites only two authorities, and only meagerly discusses his proposition. Appellees, however, have gone very thoroughly into the whole case and the authorities bearing thereon, and we find it convenient to consider and discuss the question involved along the lines and in the order they are so fully presented by appellees.

The will must be so construed as to effect the purposes of the testatrix, if this can be done without contravening any established rule or statute. Let us see where that course will lead us in this case:

If we consider paragraph 1 of the will alone, title to the whole property must vest absolutely in Mabel Darragh Jenkins and John Greenleaf Darragh, share and share alike. But this would have occurred, exactly, had there been no will at all, since the statutes provide for just such disposition in the absence of a will. Accordingly, the making of the will would have been a perfectly futile thing, unless the testatrix had some further purpose to effect. Was this further purpose the disposition of certain personal property belonging to testatrix? If that was all, then such purpose was fully effectuated in paragraphs 2, 3, and 6, which serve no other purpose and have reference to no other part of the estate. And paragraph 8 provides in the usual way for the appointment of executors, and serves no other purpose.

Paragraphs 1, 2, 3, 6, and 8, then, within themselves, constitute a will that is complete and sufficient for the purpose of disposing of all the real, personal, and mixed property belonging to the estate, and for the administration thereof. If there had been no will the statutes would have made exactly the same disposition of the estate, except as to the peculiar division of the household goods and heirlooms. And if there had been no will, the probate court, under the statute, would have appointed as administrators of the estate either or both of the very executors named in the will, although it would not, of course, have relieved them of the trouble of making bond. Accordingly, if we give effect only to paragraphs 1, 2, 3, 6, and 8 of the will, the only purposes thereof were to divide in a particular way the household goods and heirlooms, and relieve the children of testatrix of the necessity of making bond as executors of the large estate involved. When we read the entire instrument, it seems to us to be obvious that the will was not solemnly made for such trivial purposes alone.

But, if such were the only purposes of the will, or even if there was the added purpose to direct the doing of things already provided for and required by the law, then either and all of such purposes were very fully and clearly effectuated in paragraphs 1, 2, 3, 6, and 8, and nothing further could have been written to strengthen or elucidate them.

These conclusions bring us to a consideration of the remaining provisions of the instrument, embraced in paragraphs 4, 5, and 7. If the only purpose in the mind of the testatrix, in making her will, was to devise to her two children the fee in the entire estate, as contended by appellees, then why did she add these further provisions? Any good-faith effort to ascertain the intention of testatrix must embrace a consideration of the whole instrument and every provision and clause therein, and it will not do simply to ignore the provisions in the three paragraphs mentioned. They must be read and considered in connection with all the other provisions, and they must be given effect, unless, indeed, to do so will contravene the law. If they are in real or apparent conflict with other provisions of the will, they must be harmonized therewith, if that can be done, since the law imposes upon the courts the solemn duty of putting into effect the expressed objects in the mind of the testatrix.

And, first, we will look at the fourth paragraph of the will, which provides:

"In case John Greenleaf Darragh dies before his sister, Mabel Darragh Jenkins, without heirs of his body, all of his portion of the estate shall go to my said daughter, Mabel Darragh Jenkins; but if he dies leaving issue of his own body, then his said heirs shall inherit his portion of said estate."

It must be borne in mind that in the first paragraph of the will testatrix had definitely and clearly devised to her son a full half interest in the estate, without any exception, reservation, or limitation, except as to certain personal property, the disposition of which in subsequent paragraphs is clear and is not to be questioned. But now, in the fourth paragraph, the provisions of the instrument return to the subject of disposition of the estate, and very clearly show an intention on the part of the testatrix to resume or continue control of the property not specifically disposed of in the second, third, and sixth paragraphs, in which the absolute devise in the first paragraph is confirmed as to certain personal property, and direct in detail the course of its disposition. And having arrived at this close-up view of the intention of testatrix, it becomes obvious, it seems to us, that she did not intend that her son should have the power of alienating his portion of such estate, but the same should remain intact and pass on to his sister upon his death without living issue of his body.

The fifth paragraph of the will provides:

"In case of the death of my daughter, Mabel Darragh Jenkins, and in case of the death of John Darragh Barmore, her child, then the said John Greenleaf Darragh, if living, or his heirs, as hereinabove stated, shall take her estate; but in case that the said Mabel Darragh Jenkins at her death should leave children, which includes John Darragh Barmore, her children shall inherit her estate, share and share alike."

Here again the testatrix evidences an intention, as in the case of the devise to her son, to preserve intact the portion of the estate devised to her daughter, so that upon the latter's death the same should pass to her children. The language of the provisions of this paragraph differs very materially, if strictly construed, from the language of the corresponding provision with reference to the portion of the estate sought to be devised to John Greenleaf Darragh, and yet it is apparent that it was the intention of testatrix to pass the estate on through each of her children upon the same terms and conditions, and with the same limitations and restrictions, and that intention should be respected if the law will so permit.

The seventh paragraph of the will provides:

"It is the wish and is so enjoined upon John Greenleaf Darragh and Mabel Darragh Jenkins, that they shall take care of John Darragh Barmore and properly educate him, to be paid for out of the estate which I give to my said two children, John Greenleaf Darragh and Mabel Darragh Jenkins, until the said John Darragh Barmore shall have received his education. It is understood that whatever rights John Darragh Barmore receives under the provisions of this Will shall lapse and revert to my said children or their heirs, in case he gives any part whatsoever of the estate he inherits hereunder to any of his Barmore kin, including his father and grandfather."

The first clause of this paragraph is, of course, plain enough and amounts, in effect, simply to a request of the children of testatrix to see to the education of the grandchild, John Darragh Barmore, to be paid for out of the estate in question. Appellees contend that this clause has a tendency to confirm the absolute devise in the first paragraph in that testatrix here refers to "the estate which I give to my two said children, John Greenleaf Darragh and Mabel Darragh Jenkins." But if that is the effect of this reference, it is more than overcome by the further references in the second clause of the same paragraph to "the rights John Darragh Barmore receives under the provisions of this will," and to "the estate he inherits hereunder." In so far as it has a bearing upon the question of the intention of testatrix, it may be said that the seventh paragraph, taken as a whole, indicates that while she desired her two children to have the use and benefit of the estate, testatrix did not want it to get beyond the reach of this grandchild. The direct purpose of the seventh paragraph, however, was, of course, to request that John Darragh Barmore be educated, and to prevent any part of the estate from passing through him to his Barmore connections.

To sum up the purposes which we think were in the mind of testatrix when she made her will, we find that she desired her children, John Greenleaf Darragh and Mabel Darragh Jenkins, to use and enjoy, upon equal terms, the whole of the estate so long as they each lived, but that this estate should remain intact, and, except the personal property in which the fee is specifically confirmed in the second, third, and sixth paragraphs, should pass to the children of said devisees; and, further, that if either John Greenleaf Darragh or Mabel Darragh Jenkins should die without children, then his or her portion of such estate should pass to the other.

Appellees urge that the devise of the certain personal property mentioned in paragraphs 2, 3, and 6 of the will must take the same course as the devise of all the balance of the estate; that the first paragraph is an absolute devise of the whole estate; and that if we should hold (as appellees significantly surmise we will do) that the devise of the estate other than the articles mentioned in those paragraphs is limited by paragraphs 4 and 5, then we must hold also that the limitations apply with equal force to the kitchen utensils, etc., specifically distributed in paragraphs 2, 3, and 6. But this position is in our opinion insupportable, notwithstanding its apparent logic. We think the testatrix sought in paragraphs 2, 3, and 6 to except the articles therein mentioned from the operation of the provisions of paragraphs 4 and 5. This is made obvious, we think, by the very nature of those articles, by the significant fact that testatrix singled them out, and, reiterating the gift in fee, specifically distributed them in a peculiarly appropriate way among the devisees, and by the further fact of the omission of any provision for a subsequent devise over as to these articles. The provisions of paragraphs 2, 3, and 6 are, as to the articles mentioned, confirmatory of the absolute devise in paragraph 1, while the provisions of paragraphs 4 and 5 are in positive derogation thereof.

Having ascertained as best we could the intention of the maker of the will, it becomes the duty of the court to give effect to this intention, if that can be done with due respect and regard to public policy, to the common law, and to the statute law of the state. Appellees urge that the language of paragraphs 4 and 5 is confused and of doubtful import, and the purposes thereof obscure, and cannot serve to limit the devise so clearly expressed in the first paragraph. While it is true that the language of this paragraph is peculiar, to say the least of it, we think that the intention of the testatrix as therein expressed is unmistakable and enforceable.

So, keeping in mind the first paragraph of the will, in which the testatrix devises her estate in equal shares to her two children, and paragraphs 2, 3, and 6, in which the fee in certain personal property is confirmed by specific distribution, we pass on to a construction, in their order, of the fourth and fifth paragraphs, the provisions of which give rise to this litigation. The fourth paragraph will be quoted again:

"In case John Greenleaf Darragh dies before his sister, Mabel Darragh Jenkins, without heirs of his body, all of his portion of the estate shall go to my said daughter, Mabel Darragh Jenkins; but if he dies leaving issue of his own body, then his said heirs shall inherit his portion of said estate."

Appellant, John Darragh Barmore, contends that this provision, taken in connection with and as a limitation upon the first paragraph, conveys to John Greenleaf Darragh a qualified defeasible fee in the estate, subject to be defeated upon his death without issue. Appellees urge, on the contrary, that, whether so intended by testatrix or not, the provisions of this paragraph cannot operate as a limitation upon the fee passing directly to John Greenleaf Darragh under the first paragraph. Appellees base this contention upon several contentions, which will be now considered.

[1] First, it is urged that the first paragraph of the will "creates an absolute estate in fee simple," and that "a subsequent paragraph which attempts a limitation over to another upon the absolute estate already devised is repugnant to and inconsistent with the absolute property in the first devisees and is void." It is true that the first paragraph, when taken alone, and ignoring all the other provisions of the will, creates an estate in fee simple in the named beneficiaries. But we are not permitted to look alone to the first or any particular paragraph of the instrument, or to ignore any provision or provisions, or all the provisions but the first or any particular one. We must look to all the provisions when we set about in good faith to ascertain the intention and give effect thereto. This rule, now thoroughly settled by the decisions, is well stated by Mr. Justice Stayton, in McMurry v. Stanley, 69 Tex. 227, 6 S. W. 412, and quoted with approval by Chief Justice Gaines in Dulin v. Moore, 96 Tex. 135, 70 S. W. 742:

"In construing the will all of its provisions should be looked to for the purpose of ascertaining what the real intention of the testatrix was; and, if this can be ascertained from the language of the instrument, then any particular paragraph of the will, which, considered alone, would indicate a contrary intent, must yield to the intention manifested by the whole instrument."

[2] In support of their proposition now under discussion, appellees cite a number of authorities, including article 1106, R. S., as follows:

"Every estate in lands which shall hereafter be granted, conveyed or devised to one although other words heretofore necessary at common law to transfer an estate in fee simple be not added, shall be deemed a fee simple, if a less estate be not limited by express words or do not appear to have been granted, conveyed or devised by construction or operation of law."

We do not, by any means, undertake to question the value or justice of this provision of the statute. But we do not regard it as material here, because it appears to us that the limitations in the fourth paragraph of the will are in fact by "express words," the meaning and purpose of which are unmistakable. The rule embraced in article 1106 is after all but the rule of the decisions, and while it is followed in some of the authorities cited by appellees, none of them goes further than the statute in question. Let us quote further from McMurry v. Stanley, supra:

"There are cases that hold that an absolute power of disposition, given to the first taker for his own benefit, renders a subsequent limitation void for repugnancy, and the decisions were made by courts for whose opinions we have the highest respect. We, however, doubt the propriety of applying such an arbitrary rule in the construction of testamentary papers, for it would often defeat the intention of a testator, as clearly expressed as may be the intention to confer on the first taker a particular estate, with power to dispose of a part or the whole of the property. At most it is but a rule, technical in its nature, based upon the presumed intention of a testator, which ought never to be given a controlling effect when, by the clear language of a will, it appears that the testator did not intend that the first taker should have an absolute estate in fee for his own use and benefit. Any other ruling may make the intention of a testator to depend on a presumption of fact, when the testator, by his own language, has made his intention clear and thus left no occasion for indulging in presumptions.

"It is always dangerous to adopt arbitrary rules for the construction of testamentary papers. It is no doubt true that, when an estate is given in one part of a will, in clear and decisive terms, such estate cannot be taken away or cut down by any subsequent words that are not as clear and decisive as the words of the clause giving the estate. As said by the Court of Appeals of New York: 'The rule that a limitation over to one cannot be based upon a primary devise of an absolute estate to another is founded entirely upon the supposed intention of the testator. When provisions are irreconcilably conflicting, one must give way to the other, and that must be adopted which seems to accord most clearly with the testator's primary object in executing the instrument; but when, by limiting the character of the first estate, the second may also be preserved, it is clearly the duty of the court to do so, unless such a construction is subversive of the general scheme of the will, or forbidden by some inflexible rule of law.' Wager et al. v. Wager, 96 N. Y. 174."

[3] Appellees' next proposition is best stated by quoting it:

"Where, as in this case, the absolute title to the real property is devised to appellees in fee simple by the first paragraph of the will, the devise over in case of their death which is provided for in the fourth and fifth paragraphs is, upon well-settled principles of law, construed to mean the death of the appellees occurring during the lifetime of testatrix. Since, however, appellees survived the testatrix, the limitations and contingencies provided for in the fourth and fifth paragraphs of the will are read out of the will, and the will is to be construed as if said paragraphs were not contained therein."

It is true that where it is provided in a will that an estate shall take a certain course "in case of the death of" a named person, the courts now construe such words to mean "in case such person dies before the testator dies." St. Paul's Sanitarium v. Freeman, 102 Tex. 376, 117 S. W. 425, 132 Am. St. Rep. 886; Johnston v. Reyes, 183 S. W. 7. This holding is now the established rule, and the contention of appellees is undoubtedly correct, in the abstract. But the provision in the fourth paragraph of the Darragh will does not furnish a concrete example for the application of this rule, because here the contingency named is not merely "in case John Greenleaf Darragh dies," but is "in case John Greenleaf Darragh dies before his sister, Mabel Darragh Jenkins, without heirs of his body." The contingency contemplated, then, is not merely the death of John Greenleaf Darragh, which is not a contingency at all, but a certainty, but comprises two events, to wit: (a) The death of Darragh prior to the death of his sister, and (b) his death without heirs of his body, neither of which events is certain, and neither of which has yet occurred. St. Paul's Sanitarium v. Freeman, supra.

[4] In connection with the phase of the case now under discussion, appellees have much to say of the rule in Shelley's Case, which they ingeniously invoke to support their contention that under the terms of the will the estate was conveyed in fee simple to appellees. While it is true that this venerable rule has not always met with a cordial reception into the jurisprudence of Texas (Tendick v. Evetts, 38 Tex. 275), and that in even a comparatively recent case the Supreme Court of the state recommended to the Legislature that it be repealed (Lacey v. Floyd, 99 Tex. 112, 87 S. W. 665), it has nevertheless finally found a secure place in that jurisprudence; and while its application may in some cases work hardships, sometimes real but more often merely apparent, it is just as firmly a part of our system as if it had been crystallized into a statute. It has been said somewhere that, as a matter of fact, the rule was created for the purpose of obstructing, rather than effectuating, intention; but that may be said of almost any rule of law, as this is. It is not a rule of construction, or of intention. It is essentially a wise rule, for, while it has been buffeted about by the Legislatures and courts of many lands, and railed at and berated through all that period it has nevertheless survived for more than half a thousand years. But this rule does not apply to the fourth paragraph of the Darragh will, as appellees urge upon us. We think that

under that paragraph of the will the course of the devise is affirmatively deflected from a conflict with the rule in Shelley's Case. That rule is directed against a devise over to the heirs of the first taker. And if in the first clause of the fourth paragraph it had been provided that in event of the death of Darragh, the ancestor, before the death of his sister his heirs should take the estate, the rule in question would apply. But that is not the case here. On the contrary, the provision is that if Darragh should die before his sister and without heirs of his body the estate shall go, not to his heirs, but to a named beneficiary, to wit, his sister, and the rule in Shelley's Case is thus avoided.

[5] In their original brief appellees treat as one the two clauses of the fourth paragraph of the will, but in their more extended supplemental brief or argument they treat the two clauses separately, as we think must be done. Let us analyze these clauses for a moment: The first provides that if John Greenleaf Darragh dies without heirs of his body, his sister, Mabel Darragh Jenkins (if living) shall take his part of the estate. That clause completely provides for the contingency described, and must be tested by its own terms in determining its validity, notwithstanding the requirement that the second clause, as well as all the other parts of the instrument, must be looked to in aid of construction and in determining intention. The first clause, then, provides, simply and unmistakably, that if John Greenleaf Darragh dies before Mabel Darragh Jenkins, and "without heirs of his body," then Mabel Darragh Jenkins shall take the estate given him in the first paragraph of the will. The provision is complete, and, in our opinion, valid, and must be given effect in accordance with the clear intention of the testatrix. The second clause provides that if John Greenleaf Darragh "dies leaving issue of his own body, then his said heirs shall inherit his portion of the estate." This provision is intended, obviously, as an alternative course for the estate to take if it should be deflected from the course fixed in the first clause because of the failure of the basic contingency therein provided for—the death of Darragh before that of his sister. The second clause, when considered alone, raises innumerable questions, both of intention and construction, but when considered in connection with the first clause becomes more simple. What is meant, in the first clause, by "heirs of his body"? And in the second by "issue of his own body"? And by "inherit"? And by "his said heirs"? Surely, by "heirs of his body" testatrix did not mean to describe that class of persons who by inheritance take in succession from generation to generation, which is the technical meaning of the phrase when considered alone and without reference to the context of the instrument in which it is used.

It has been said that these words may have a double import—one, an import of designation, by which it is intended to elect those heirs in being at the time of the death of the first taker; and the other an import of inheritance, meaning descendants through all future time so long as there are any. Moreover, the term may be construed to mean, simply, children, if it is apparent from the context of the instrument in which it is used that such was the intention of the testator. Simonton Case, 93 Tex. 50, 53 S. W. 339, 77 Am. St. Rep. 824. The same may be said of the term "issue of his own body," as used in the second clause of the fourth paragraph. Undoubtedly, the testatrix had in contemplation the same heirs when she used these expressions. The second clause, as stated, is an alternative of the first clause; in the first it directs a course in the absence of certain heirs, and in the second directs another course in the presence of certain heirs. Of course, the same heirs were in contemplation in both instances. And in the second clause it is provided that if Darragh dies leaving "issue of his own body" then his said heirs "shall inherit," etc. To what "heirs" does testatrix refer? The word "heirs" is used in the first clause, but not in the second. Unquestionably, she had reference, however, to the "heirs" mentioned in the first clause and to the "issue" mentioned in the second clause; throughout the paragraph she had in mind the same heirs, whoever they were. And there is the word "inherit" in the second clause of the fourth paragraph. Is it not probable that she means that in the event provided for in this clause the heirs testatrix had in mind should "take" rather than "inherit" the estate referred to? And yet the respective meanings of the two words are different and in legal effect in irreconcilable conflict. "Inherit" is a word of limitation; "take" is a word of purchase. A testator can direct who shall "take" an estate; but he cannot say who shall "inherit" it. If the testatrix here used the word "inherit" advisedly, then she undertook to do that which in law she could not do; if she inadvertently used it in the place of the word "take," then she was doing that which the law permitted her to do.

[6-8] The courts may, as we have said, look at the context of a will when in search of the intention of the testator in case of ambiguity or uncertainty, and upon ascertaining such intention may harmonize and reconcile inconsistencies and apparent conflicts, and in accomplishing these objects may give to words or phrases meanings other than their technical import. When the intention is clearly ascertainable, the courts will go far in rearranging and modifying words and phrases in order to effectuate that intention, and where such words or phrases are susceptible of two constructions, one consistent

with an intention to do that which the testator may lawfully do, and the other consistent with an intention to do that which he may not lawfully do, the one construction will be adopted, and the other rejected. Hancock v. Butler, 21 Tex. 804. On the other hand, however, the courts must not indulge in and give effect to mere conjecture as to the intention of a testator; that would be assuming the power to make, rather than construe, the will. Philleo v. Holliday, 24 Tex. 38. Now, with these general principles in view, we will endeavor to state our conclusions as to the meaning and effect of the fourth paragraph of the will in question, which for convenience we will restate:

"In case John Greenleaf Darragh dies before his sister, Mabel Darragh Jenkins, without heirs of his body, all of his portion of the estate shall go to my said daughter, Mabel Darragh Jenkins; but if he dies leaving issue of his own body, then his said heirs shall inherit his portion of said estate."

The primary intention of the testatrix was, obviously and of course, to keep the estate in her children and grandchildren. Her first step to that end, as expressed in the first clause, was to provide that if John Greenleaf Darragh should die before his sister, Mabel Darragh Jenkins, and without heirs of his body, all of his portion of the estate should go to his said sister. We think, as to this clause, the case comes squarely under the decision in St. Paul's Sanitarium v. Freeman, supra, and that, surviving the testatrix, John Greenleaf Darragh did not take title absolutely, but that on the condition of his death without heirs of his body the devise over to Mabel Darragh Jenkins, if living, will take effect. In the Freeman Case, one Julian Reverchon was the testator, and after his death Freeman, the first taker, who had never married, brought suit, as Darragh has here done, to have the will construed and to determine the question of whether he was entitled to a fee-simple title in the devised property, or whether the estate he held in the property was subject to be defeated by his death without issue. In the second paragraph of his will Reverchon devised all his property in fee to Freeman, but in a subsequent paragraph it was provided that—

"In the event the said Robert M. Freeman shall die without issue, then * * * all of my said property willed as aforesaid (shall) be given to" the sanitarium.

The clause of the Darragh will now under consideration provides that "in case"—which means "in the event"—"John Greenleaf Darragh dies before his sister, without heirs of his body"—which as here used means the same as "without issue"—"all of his portion of the estate shall go to my said daughter, Mabel Darragh Jenkins." It is obvious that the purpose, effect, and meaning of the two provisions are identical. In each instance it is provided, simply, that in event of the death of the first taker without issue the estate shall go to the second taker. The question now under discussion was the only question before the court in the Freeman Case, except one of construction of an incidental phrase, which is also in point here. The opinion in that case, written by Chief Justice Gaines, is thoroughly applicable to and decisive of the question here, and it was there held that should Freeman die at any time without issue the limitation over to the sanitarium shall take effect, and the judgment of the trial court that Freeman was entitled to the property in fee simple was reversed and rendered. In deference to that decision we hold, then, that the effect of the provisions of the first paragraph and the first clause of the fourth paragraph, when construed together, as they must be is not to pass the fee simple to John Greenleaf Darragh upon the death of testatrix, but that upon the condition of his death without issue the limitation over to Mabel Darragh Jenkins will take effect. In so holding, we are not unmindful of the earnest reasoning of counsel, and the great care and ability with which they have presented their contention that Mrs. Darragh intended and the effect of the law requires that her son should, upon her death, be vested with the fee simple to the estate devised. Such an intention could not have been better expressed than by designedly omitting this clause from the will; but, the clause being present, and designedly· so, it cannot be ignored, but must be considered, and if its purpose can be lawfully effected that must be done.

[8] This brings us to the second clause of the fourth paragraph of the will. Primarily, it is the alternative of the first clause, which provides for disposition of the estate if Darragh die without leaving heirs of his body, and stipulates that if Darragh dies "leaving issue of his own body, then his said heirs shall inherit his portion of said estate." If this clause is considered alone, without testing its purposes by reference to any other provisions of the will, it would probably come within the rule in Shelley's Case, and therefore be without effect. We have endeavored to show that it was the apparent purpose of testatrix that the estate should go to her two children for their use and enjoyment, and upon the death of either without children, or living issue of the body, as the case may be, the corpus of the estate should pass to the survivor, but in case of children in one case, and of living issue of the body in the other, such children or issue should take the estate of their respective ancestors. And the question is, Can this purpose be given effect under the peculiar language of this clause? If given their general signification, the words "issue of his own body" are words

of limitation, and not of purchase, and in this case would offend the rule in Shelley's Case. On the other hand, if the testatrix intended the words to designate the bodily issue of John Greenleaf Darragh who may be in being at the time of his decease, then the provision does not so offend. In the one case the intention is to do that which cannot lawfully be done; in the other the intention is to do that which can lawfully be done. Are the words as here used susceptible of the last construction, that is, may these words reasonably be construed to designate, and give the property to, persons in being at the time of the death of John Greenleaf Darragh; such persons being the issue of the latter's own body? We think so. Without reference to the general purposes of the testatrix as disclosed by the whole will, which we think favors such construction, the very language of the clause embracing these words, "if he dies leaving issue of his own body," imports such meaning, and raises the presumption that she did not mean to make the devise over to a class of persons who take in succession from generation. to generation. These observations bring us inevitably to the conclusion that by the second clause of the fourth paragraph of her will Mrs. Darragh intended, and thought she was giving expression to such intention, that if her son be survived by issue of his own body, such issue then in being should take the estate, and such being the intention, and the language being subject to that import, it will be given that effect. Our construction, then, of the fourth paragraph of the will, both clauses thereof included, in connection with the first paragraph, is this: That by its terms John Greenleaf Darragh is given a life estate in one-half of the property of testatrix other than that specifically devised in fee in paragraphs 2, 3, and 6. If he is survived by his sister, Mabel Darragh Jenkins, but not by issue of his own body, his sister will take such estate; but if he is survived by issue of his own body, then those of such issue who are living at the time of his death will take the estate.

[10] We come now to the fifth paragraph of the will, relating to the estate given to Mabel Darragh Jenkins. It is segregated into two clauses; the second being the alternative of the first, which is as follows:

"In case of the death of my daughter, Mabel Darragh Jenkins, and in case of the death of John Darragh Barmore, her child, then the said John Greenleaf Darragh, if living, or his heirs, as hereinabove stated, shall take her estate. * * *"

We have shown that where a devise is made over to one "in case of the death" of another, and no other contingency is interposed, the death contemplated is one occurring before the death of the testator, and applying that rule to the clause quoted, the provision "in event of the death of" Mabel Darragh Jenkins and John Darragh Barmore means in event of their deaths before the death of testatrix. The law construction writes the phrase to read this way:

"In case of the death of my daughter, Mabel Darragh Jenkins, before the death of testatrix, and in case of the death of John Darragh Barmore before the death of testatrix, then the said John Greenleaf Darragh, if living, or his heirs, as hereinabove stated, shall take her estate."

It is probable that testatrix intended there to provide that if both Mrs. Jenkins and her child died before Darragh died, then Darragh or the heirs of his own body would take. But it is not so expressed, and it would be repugnant to a settled rule of construction to write that contingency into the provision. So the contingency provided for by implication—the death of both Mrs. Jenkins and her son before the death of testatrix—did not occur, and is now impossible of occurrence, and accordingly the devise lapses.

[11] The second clause of the fifth paragraph, as an alternative of the first clause, provides that "in case that the said Mabel Darragh Jenkins at her death shall leave children, which includes John Darragh Barmore, her children shall inherit her estate, share and share alike." The clause would be simple, but for the phrase "which includes John Darragh Barmore" and the use of the word "inherit." The purpose of affirmatively designating the son as one of the children of his mother is to us inexplicable. But as the reference seems harmless, and without any influence upon the intention or construction of the clause, it should be treated as surplusage and of no effect for any purpose. For reasons which we have already set up in discussing the use of the word "inherit" in the fourth paragraph, it must be held that that word was likewise inadvertently used in the fifth. It is obvious that the devise over is to the children who may survive the first taker, and that a word of purchase, rather than of limitation, was intended. This purpose, it seems to us, is emphasized by the use of the qualifying words "share and share alike." It is quite unlikely that testatrix would attempt to exercise a control over the estate that the law does not permit by directing its course of inheritance after the death of the first taker, but it is inconceivable that she would undertake to say in what proportions it should thus descend. We think the provision that the property pass share and share alike to the children is conclusive of the intention that it pass by purchase, and not by limitation. So we hold that the second clause of the fifth paragraph of the will limits Mabel Darragh Jenkins to a life estate, with remainder over to those of her children who may survive her.

[12, 13] We will discuss again for a mo-

ment the seventh paragraph of the will. The first clause is precatory merely, and it is left to the will of John Greenleaf Darragh and Mabel Darragh Jenkins whether its provisions shall be regarded. The second clause directs that the rights that John Darragh Barmore receives under the provisions of the will shall revert to others if he gives any of the estate he inherits under the will to any of his Barmore kin. This provision is, of course, for obvious reasons, void. This brings us to the end of the will so far as construction is concerned.

The judgment of the trial court is reversed and here rendered as follows:

(1) That John Greenleaf Darragh and Mabel Darragh Jenkins take a life estate, share and share alike, in the property owned by testatrix at the time of her death, other than the personal property specifically devised in fee and distributed by the provisions of paragraphs 2, 3, and 6.

(2) That if John Greenleaf Darragh dies before the death of Mabel Darragh Jenkins, without heirs of his body then living, the said Mabel Darragh Jenkins shall take his share of the estate, other then mentioned in paragraphs 2, 3, and 6, but if he is survived by issue of his own body, such issue living at the time of his death shall take said estate.

(3) That upon the death of Mabel Darragh Jenkins her children shall take that property in which in said will she is given a life estate. Reversed and rendered.

COBBS, J., entered his disqualification, and did not participate in this decision.

FORT WORTH ELEVATORS CO. v. KEEL & SON et al. (No. 7892.)

(Court of Civil Appeals of Texas. Galveston. April 1, 1921. Rehearing Denied April 28, 1921.)

1. **Sales 200(2)—Where wheat shipped consigned to shipper's order, title passes on the payment of draft attached to bill of lading and delivery of the bill of lading, though weighing at destination necessary.**

Where wheat is purchased and shipped by rail consigned to shipper's order, and drafts for the price are sent through banks, with bills of lading attached, and such drafts are paid by the purchaser, and bills of lading delivered to him, title passes to the purchaser, notwithstanding that the wheat must be measured or weighed at destination to definitely determine the exact sum to be paid for the entire mass.

2. **Carriers 88—Carrier relieved of liability for shipment on delivery to purchaser's agent.**

Where a seller of wheat shipped it by rail to his order, with a draft and bill of lading attached, and the carrier delivered it to a wharf

company, which was the agent of the purchaser authorized to receive it, the carrier thereafter owed no legal duty relative to the protection of the wheat.

3. **Carriers 134—Wharves 20(7)—Evidence held to show proximate cause of loss of wheat due to act of God.**

In an action by a purchaser of two carloads of wheat brought against the seller, the carrier, and a wharf company, where it appeared that during a flood the wharf company hauled the cars into the yards of a railroad company, where they were destroyed by fire caused by the flood waters reaching an adjacent car of unslacked lime, the undisputed evidence held to show that the proximate cause of loss of the wheat was due to a storm properly classified as an act of God.

4. **Wharves 20(1)—Removal of wheat by wharf company to place where destroyed held remote and not proximate cause of loss.**

In an action by a purchaser of wheat against the seller, the carrier, and a wharf company for loss of the wheat by fire due to flood waters produced by a storm reaching a car of unslacked lime, where it appeared that the wharf company, after the wheat had been delivered to it, was forced to haul the cars to another point and to leave them in the yards of a third party where the loss occurred, the removal by the wharf company, if negligence, was the remote, and not the proximate, cause of the loss.

5. **Wharves 20(7) — Evidence sustaining finding that loss from storm could not have been prevented by defendant.**

In an action by a purchaser of two carloads of wheat against the seller, the carrier, and a wharf company to which it had been delivered, where it appeared that because of a storm flood waters gathered to a height forcing the wharf company to move the cars to a place where they were destroyed by fire, caused by water reaching unslacked lime, evidence held to support a finding that the damage by high water from the storm could not be prevented by the wharf company at a reasonable expense and without injury to others.

6. **Wharves 20(1)—Wharf company held not obligated to raise tracks above level of flood waters of previous storms to prevent injury to wheat delivered to it.**

In an action by a purchaser of wheat against the seller, the carrier, and a wharf company to which it had been delivered, for its loss by fire occurring through flood waters reaching a car of unslacked lime at a point to which the wharf company had been forced to move the cars in an effort to protect them, held that the wharf company could not be charged with anticipation of the severity of the storm, and was not obligated to go to great expense to raise its track beyond the level of flood waters of previous storms.

7. **Wharves 20(1)—Removal of wheat by wharf company to escape floods held not actionable negligence.**

In an action by a purchaser of wheat against a wharf company to which it had been delivered for its loss by fire caused by flood waters reaching an adjacent car of unslacked lime in the yards of a third party, to which the wharf company had moved it to escape the floods, such removal *held* not under the evidence actionable negligence, it being made in good faith in the stress of grave and impending danger, and with the view of saving the property from injury.

Appeal from [District Court, Galveston County; Robt. G. Street, Judge.

Action by the Fort Worth Elevators Company against Keel & Son and others. Judgment for defendants, and plaintiff appeals. Affirmed.

Maco & Minor Stewart, of Galveston, Albert J. De Lange, of Houston, and Jules Damiani and W. N. Zinn, both of Galveston, for appellant.

James B. & Charles J. Stubbs, of Galveston, and Davis & Davis, of Gainesville, for appellee Keel & Son.

Lee, Lomax, Wren & Smith, of Fort Worth, for appellee Gulf, C. & S. F. Ry. Co.

Terry, Cavin & Mills, of Galveston, and Thompson, Knight, Baker & Harris, and Geo. S. Wright, all of Dallas, for appellee Wharf Co.

LANE, J. This suit was brought by appellant, Fort Worth Elevators Company, on the 19th day of December, 1916, against J. Z. Keel and W. L. Keel, parties composing the firm of Keel & Son, the Gulf, Colorado & Santa Fé Railroad Company, hereinafter referred to as the Santa Fé Company, and the Galveston Wharf Company, hereinafter called the Wharf Company, to recover the sum of $2,364.53, the value of two cars of wheat. The plaintiff in its original petition, in effect, alleged:

That on the 6th day of August, 1915, it and the defendants Keel & Son entered into a contract whereby the latter agreed to sell and deliver to the former at Galveston, Tex., for export, two cars of No. 2 bulk wheat, containing 1,000 bushels each, for which the purchaser agreed to' pay the seller $1.20½ per bushel, or a gross sum of $2,410, less $45.47 unpaid freight charges from Gainesville, Tex., to Galveston, Tex.; that it was the understanding and agreement of the contracting parties that the weight and grades of the wheat as ascertained at Galveston should govern in the final settlement between said parties, and that the contract of sale and purchase should not be complete until all of the wheat had arrived at Galveston for export, and had been inspected, weighed, and accepted by the purchaser; that thereafter in due time Keel & Son, the sellers, did deliver the two cars of wheat to the Santa Fé Railroad Company, to be by said company transported to Galveston and to be there delivered to the purchaser, Fort Worth Elevators Company, and that the Santa Fé Company executed and delivered to Keel & Son a

bill of lading for each of said cars of wheat, showing that each contained 1,000 bushels, that said bills of lading contained a stipulation that the wheat should be delivered to shippers' order, notify the Fort Worth Elevators Company; that such bills 'of lading with drafts attached thereto for the purchase price of the wheat were sent to the Fort Wort Elevators Company by Keel & Son on the 7th day of August, 1915, and that they were received by the Fort Worth Elevators Company at Fort Worth, Tex., on the 7th day of August, 1915, and that said drafts were paid in full, less the sum of $45.47, part of the freight charges, the net sum so paid being $2,364.53, that being the sum which the purchaser had contracted to pay Keel & Son for the wheat; that the sum so paid was the reasonable market value of the wheat at Galveston at the time of the conversion thereof by the defendants.

"That said payments aforesaid were made to the shipper because the plaintiff relied absolutely and implicitly upon the correctness of said drafts and bills of lading and upon the agreement of the defendant shipper and the obligation of the defendant railway company to deliver to the plaintiff at Galveston, Tex., the quality and quantity of wheat contracted for, and that such payments were made in accordance with the custom prevailing in the grain trade of the state of Texas and the custom commonly used by and between the plaintiff and the shipper; that the said bills of lading and each of them were properly indorsed by the shipper, and that the plaintiff, upon the payment of the drafts attached to such bills of lading, became the owner and holder thereof, and that it is now, and has been at all times since the payment of the aforesaid drafts, the owner and holder of said bills of lading, and of each of them, and the defendant railway company became thereby bound to deliver the grain as described in said bill of lading to the plaintiff at Galveston, Tex., for export."

That it was well known to all the defendants that said wheat was intended for export to points without the United States by water from Galveston; that the defendant Wharf Company, as well as the Santa Fé Company, was a common carrier and public transportation company, maintaining lines of railroad and transportation facilities connected with the line of railway of the Santa Fé Company, terminating at the water's edge at the port of Galveston, and connected with an elevator owned, maintained, and operated by said Wharf Company.

"That the railway had no facilities at Galveston for the delivery of grain and in contracting to so deliver said grain for export said railway bound and obligated itself to arrange for some connecting line at Galveston to be by it selected for the exchange of said grain from the line of said railway to an elevator necessary to handle said grain; or from cars to shipside for export, and plaintiffs allege upon information and belief and assert it to be a fact that the railway company by some arrangement, the terms of which are unknown to the plaintiff, *delivered the said grain to the Wharf Company for delivery to plaintiff at ship's side or in the elevator of said Wharf Company, and that the said Wharf Company accepted and received such grain for such delivery to the plaintiff.* (Italics ours.)

"That plaintiff has no knowledge of the facts, if any, as to what disposition was made of said grain after delivery was made by the said shipper to defendant railway, other than the conflicting claims made by defendant railway and defendant wharf company to plaintiff as to the whereabouts of such grain, the truth concerning such shipment of said grain being wholly within the knowledge of the defendant railway and the Wharf Company, both of said defendants knowing all the facts concerning the same, and none of said facts being known to plaintiff. Defendant railway advised plaintiff that said grain was delivered to said Wharf Company, which latter company contends that said grain was not delivered to it by said railway company, but that it was retained by the said railway, and plaintiff had made demand upon said shipper, railway, and said Wharf Company for delivery of said grain in accordance with the terms of said contract and bill of lading, but said defendants have failed and refused, and still fail and refuse, to deliver same to plaintiffs, but have converted said grain to their own use or to the use of one or the other of them, the facts of such conversion being wholly within the knowledge of defendants and not at this time known to the plaintiff.

"That the said railway has converted said grain to its own use, and, pleading in the alternative, plaintiff says that if said railway has not converted same, then in that event said railway did deliver same to the Wharf Company, which latter company converted same to its own use; that defendant shipper by reason of the obligation to deliver said grain to plaintiff at Galveston, Tex., under its contract with the plaintiff, is jointly and severally bound with said railway company and said Wharf Company, and with each of them, to deliver said grain at Galveston, Tex., to plaintiff, but that each and all of the defendants have failed and refused to deliver such grain to the plaintiff, although demand has ofttimes been made therefor, on each and every one of them; that by reason of the failure and refusal of the defendants and each of them to deliver said grain to the plaintiff, the plaintiff has thereby been damaged in the sum of $2,364.53, together with interest thereon from the 7th day of August, 1915, until paid, at the rate of 6 per cent. per annum and all costs herein incurred."

Prayer was for judgment against all the defendants for the sum of $2,364.53, and interest thereon from August 7, 1915.

Keel & Son answered plaintiff's complaint by general denial and by special pleading that—

"On August 6, 1915, by contract with the plaintiff over the telephone, they sold to the plaintiff for shipment during that week 3,000 bushels of bulk wheat, basis No. 2, for the price of $1.20½ per bushel cash, payable upon the loading of said wheat for shipment to Galveston, Tex., which wheat was to be delivered to plaintiff at Galveston and in the final settlement Galveston official weights and grades were to govern; that in compliance with said contract, defendants, on August 7, 1915, at Gainesville, Tex., delivered to the defendant railway company 3,000 bushels of No. 2 wheat, which was loaded in three cars of said railway company, each car containing 1,000 bushels, and for the usual customary freight charges, said railway company agreed and undertook to transport said three cars of wheat from Gainesville to Galveston, and there deliver them to the order of defendants."

They then alleged the drawing of the drafts as alleged by plaintiff, and the payment thereof by plaintiff. They further alleged that by the payment of the drafts attached to the bill of lading plaintiff became the owner of and entitled to possession of the wheat; that the bills of lading specified that the plaintiff was to be notified at Galveston of the arrival of the wheat at that point; that one of the cars of wheat sold by them to the plaintiff, under the contract by which the two cars in controversy were also sold, arrived at Galveston on the 9th day of August, 1915, and was inspected and received by the plaintiff on the said day. The other two cars, being the ones mentioned in the petition, arrived at Galveston on August 13, 1915, and were inspected and accepted by the plaintiff, but were afterwards, on August 16, 1915, destroyed by fire while in the yards of either said railway or other railroad company or Wharf Company; said two burned cars contained each 1,000 bushels of No. 2 wheat, fully complying with said contract, and the plaintiff was promptly and instantly notified by said railway company of the arrival of said wheat.

They allege that said two cars of wheat were the property of plaintiff upon its arrival at Galveston and had been its property since loaded at Gainesville for shipment, and that it was so treated by plaintiff, and that plaintiff is now suing as the owner thereof.

"That while Galveston official weights and grades were to control in the final settlement, the property passed to the plaintiff regardless of such weights or grades, which merely determined whether the plaintiff would be owing defendants anything additional or whether the plaintiff would have any claim against these defendants for shortage in weight or grade."

Keel & Son also filed their cross-bill against the other defendants, and alleged that the wheat was destroyed by fire at Galveston while in possession of the Santa Fé Company, but in view of the disposition we shall make of this appeal, in so far as it affects them, we deem it unnecessary to further refer to the pleading setting up their cross-action.

The defendant Gulf, Colorado & Santa Fé Railroad Company answered: First, by general denial; second, that if it be found that it did receive the wheat under the contract of shipment as alleged by the plaintiff, then it says that it did transport and deliver the same at Galveston under said contract, and did comply with all its obligations under said contract, in that it did transport said wheat with reasonable dispatch to Galveston, and there after due notice deliver the same to the plaintiff, but that if it should be held that said wheat was in its possession as a common carrier at the time of its loss, and that it had not been legally delivered to the plaintiff, and that this defendant had not complied with all its obligations with reference to said wheat, and that its possession and control of said shipment had not terminated, then it says that said shipment was damaged and destroyed by the unprecedented storm and flood of August 16, 1915, which occurred at Galveston; that such storm and flood were of such unprecedented violence and character that it, or its action and consequence, could not have been anticipated, or its consequences averted by the performance of any duty defendant owed to plaintiff, and that the loss of said wheat and its value was due to such unprecedented storm and flood without any fault or negligence of defendant, and that such storm and flood was and were an act of God, for the consequences of which the defendant cannot be held liable; third, that if it be found that it undertook to transport said wheat as alleged by plaintiff, and that under such undertaking it failed to make delivery to the plaintiff as alleged, then it says that the bill of lading upon which said shipment was made provided that no carrier or party in possession of said shipment should be liable for any loss of same, or damage thereto, caused by the act of God. This defendant alleged further as follows:

"That the shipments in question were interstate or foreign shipments, controlled by the laws of the United States, Statutes of Congress, and the decisions of the United States courts, and this defendant says that not only at common law is it not liable for the damages alleged, but it is not liable by virtue of said provision in the bill of lading referred to above, and under the laws and decisions of the United States courts. That the question of this defendant's liability in this case is in all things governed by the United States laws and decisions."

The defendant Wharf Company answered: First, by general denial; second by specially denying that the wheat in controversy was ever delivered to it; third, that if said wheat was ever delivered to it, it received the same, not as a common carrier, but as a warehouseman only, without any knowledge or information as to the ultimate destination thereof, and that it received and held said wheat as such warehouseman in accordance with the orders of the owner, thereafter to be given, etc. It then alleges the damage and destruction of the wheat by the unprecedent-

ed storm and flood of August 16, 1915, as the act of God, as did the defendant Santa Fé Company.

By supplemental petition, filed on the 19th day of May, 1919, the plaintiff denied generally the allegations of the defendants, Santa Fé and Wharf Companies, and says that it was not advised as to the facts concerning the loss or destruction of the wheat in controversy, that such facts are wholly within the knowledge of said defendants, and that if said wheat was destroyed as alleged by defendants it was by reason of their fault and negligence.

By supplemental answer both the defendants Santa Fé Company and the Wharf Company denied the allegations of the plaintiff's supplemental petition, and, further replying to same, say: That the pleadings of plaintiff show that the negligence charged occurred more than two years prior to the setting up of any cause of action based upon the negligence charged, and therefore such cause of action so based was barred by the two-year statute of limitation at the time said supplemental petition was filed.

After the trial of the case had begun the plaintiff filed its trial amendment reading as follows:

"(1) The allegations herein are not set up as a cause of action on which recovery is sought, but in reply to and in avoidance of the attempt by defendants to escape liability by showing the loss through the act of God.

"(2) The wheat in controversy was delivered to defendant Gulf, Colorado & Santa Fé Railway Company, which issued its bill of lading therefor, and plaintiff seeks recovery thereunder, said Gulf, Colorado & Santa Fé Railway Company being the initial carrier, and at all times liable—defendant Galveston Wharf Company if it received said wheat and had same in its possession, as is sought to be shown by the Gulf, Colorado & Santa Fé Railway Company, did receive and hold same as a common carrier.

"(3) Defendants, Gulf, Colorado & Santa Fé Railway Company and Galveston Wharf Company, on this trial have introduced evidence by which they seek to show the wheat in controversy was destroyed in a fire occurring in a railroad yard other than that of either of said defendants. If they do so show, then plaintiff says such loss was not by act of God without the negligence of defendants, but, on the contrary, said defendants and each of them were guilty of negligence in their method of handling and in their placing of said wheat, such handling and placing being exclusively in the knowledge of defendants, who themselves and through their servants and agents so handled and placed said wheat, and plaintiff is not informed on the subject.

"(4) Among the acts of negligence of defendants and each of them concurring with any act of God that may be attempted to be proven plaintiff asserts the following:

"(a) Defendants and each of them failed to place said wheat above the reach of flood waters as to the height of which they had full knowledge in advance.

"(b) Defendants and each of them maintained their tracks and yards at such low level above mean low tide as that same was not a safe place over which to transfer and on which to handle and place said wheat.

"(c) Defendants and each of them removed said grain from the B yard near the elevator of defendant Galveston Wharf Company, and placed same on low ground where defendants and each of them knew, or by the use of reasonable diligence could and should have known, the wheat would be destroyed.

"(d) Defendants and each of them placed said wheat at some point unknown to plaintiff, but known to defendants where said wheat came in contact or in such close proximity to inflammable materials as to result in the loss and destruction thereof.

"(e) Defendants and each of them failed to place said wheat above the danger of flood waters, though informed of the danger in sufficient time to have done so.

"(f) Defendant Gulf, Colorado & Santa Fé Railway Company together with others so constructed a causeway across Galveston Bay as to raise the height of the waters on Galveston Island, thereby making it necessary for said company to have raised its own yards and tracks.

"(g) Defendants and neither of them notified consignee of plaintiff of the arrival of the wheat within a reasonable time.

"(h) Defendants themselves placed or permitted to be placed combustibles, after notice of the approach of the storm, in such way as to bring about the loss."

After addressing special exceptions to each paragraph of said trial amendment, the defendants Santa Fé Company and Wharf Company filed answers, denying each and every allegation in said trial amendment contained, and pleaded the two-year statute of limitation in bar of any recovery based upon the acts of negligence for the first time set up in said trial amendment.

In an effort to condense, as much as possible, the allegations of 13 separate pleadings filed by the several parties, covering 52 pages of the record, we have made the foregoing statement, believing that it contains the substance of all material allegations in the pleadings, and is sufficient for the presentation of the issues presented by this appeal.

There were demurrers and many special exceptions filed by the several defendants addressed to the pleas of the plaintiff to which we have not referred in the statement made, for the reason that all such demurrers and exceptions were overruled by the court, and no attack is made upon such ruling on this appeal.

J. Z. Keel, of the firm of Keel & Son, was called as a witness by plaintiff, Fort Worth Elevators Company, and testified that on the evening of the 5th day of August, 1915, he had a talk over the phone with Jules Smith, representative of the Fort Worth Elevators Company, he being at Gainesville, Tex., and Mr. Smith at Fort Worth, Tex.; that by that talk he sold Mr. Smith for his company 3,000 bushels of wheat at $1.20½ per bushel, delivered · at Galveston, Tex.; that he confirmed such sale by letter, the material parts of which are as follows:·

"Gainesville, Texas, Aug. 6, 1915.
"Fort Worth Elev. Co., Fort Worth, Texas—
Dear Sirs: As per phone talk, your Mr. Jules Smith and our Mr. J. Z. Keel, beg to confirm sale to you of 3,000 bus bulk wheat, hard, soft or mixed wheat, @ $1.20½ bu. del. Galveston for shipment this week, usual Galveston official weights and grades to govern settlement. * * *
"Truly yours,   Keel & Son, by H. B. K."

That on the same day on which the above letter was written Keel & Son delivered to the Gulf, Colorado & Santa Fé Railroad Company the two cars of wheat now in controversy for shipment to Galveston, Tex., for which said Santa Fé issued its two bills of lading, by which it contracted to transport said two cars from Gainesville. Tex., to Galveston, Tex., and there deliver same to the order of Keel & Son; that on the same day Keel & Son indorsed said bills of lading in blank and attached thereto two drafts reading as follows:

"Gainesville, Texas, Aug. 6, 1915. 191.
"On demand pay to the order of the Lindsay National Bank, Gainesville, Texas, $1,180.00, eleven hundred eighty-one and 00/100 dollars in current funds.
"Keel & Son, by J. M. Kemplin. 175.
"To Fort Worth Elev. Co. Fort Worth, Texas."

· "Gainesville, Texas, Aug. 7, 1915. 191.
"On demand pay to the order of the Lindsay National Bank, Gainesville, Texas, $1,183.53, eleven hundred eighty-three and 53/100 dollars in current funds.
"Keel & Son, by H. B. Keel. 177.
"To Fort Worth Elevators Co. Fort Worth, Texas."

That these bills of lading and drafts were on the 7th day of August, 1915, presented to the Fort Worth Elevators Company by the Fort Worth National Bank, and that the drafts were on said date fully paid by the Fort Worth Elevator Company, and upon such payments the bills of lading and drafts were delivered to said Elevator Company; that on the 6th day of August, 1915, Keel & Son received from the Fort Worth Elevators Company the following letter:

"Aug. 6, 1915.
"Messrs. Keel & Son, Gainesville, Texas—
Gentlemen: We confirm purchase from you last night of three cars basis #2 wheat $1.20½ delivered Galveston, which business we are glad to have done with you.
"Yours very truly,
"The Fort Worth Elevators Co."

And that Keel & Son also received from said Elevator Company the following instrument (the date of receipt not shown):

"Fort Worth, Texas, 8/6/15.

"Keel & Son, Gainesville, Texas. This confirms purchase from. you to-day, by (phone) per J. G. S, to Mr. Keel 3 cars —— bushels #2 wheat (basis) at 120½ per bu. basis delivered Galv. export for shipment this week To be billed O/N the Ft. Worth Elvs. Co. and routed Galveston, Tex. Galveston weights and grades shall govern in final settlement on this contract and a 3¢ bu. margin shall be left to guarantee same. Inspection, trackage (if any) and exchange charges to be paid by shipper.

"To insure payment of drafts, always immediately advise shipment, rendering separate invoice on each car, giving car number and initial, number of pounds, bushels, bags or bales, point of origin and destination.

"It is understood, when designation grades and weights are to determine final settlement, that the grades and weight of commodities herein contracted for shall be determined either at point of inspection or final unloading point, at option of the Fort Worth Elevators Co.

"We reserve the right without further notice, to extend the time of shipment, or cancel the contract or buy for shippers account, if for any reason any portion of the herein contracted goods are not shipped within contract time.

"It is further agreed that this contract is not complete until all shipments made to apply herein have arrived at destination and have been inspected, weighed and accepted.

"We will not pay exchange on drafts drawn against us at sight or on demand, nor will we honor drafts when exchange is added in invoice or amount of draft.

"Send all papers to us at Fort Worth, and drafts to Farmers' & Mechanics' Nat. Bank.

"It is also agreed and understood that this confirmation is a part of the contract, and its receipt, without objection or notification to us at once of error herein, shall be understood by us as an acknowledgment and acceptance of the contract as set forth above.

> "The Fort Worth Elevators Co.
> "Per R. M. Kelso."

Testifying further, the witness said:

"The trade was made over the telephone on the evening of the 5th, and they sent us what they call their confirmation. We did not make any reply to that, but I sent them a confirmation. We did not receive this confirmation from them before we shipped out this carload of wheat; we shipped the carload of wheat on the 6th, before we received this contract. I don't know whether we received it before we shipped the next two cars; I don't know when this was received; I didn't see it."

Testifying further he said that he paid no attention to the terms of the instrument above set out, purporting to state terms of the sale contract; that he paid no attention to the terms of this paper, because the only contract his firm had with the said Elevator Company was oral. The foregoing testimony was in no way disputed.

The undisputed evidence shows that the Fort Worth Elevators Company made arrangements with the Wharf Company to handle its grain coming into Galveston for the year 1914 and for 1915; that the grain was to be handled through the Wharf Company's elevators, and that under such arrangement the Wharf Company had handled such business during the years 1914 and 1915; that the Santa Fé Company had been informed of the aforesaid arrangement between the Elevator Company and the Wharf Company, and that it did, on the 10th of July, 1915, receive a letter from the manager of the Wharf Company again informing it that the Wharf Company would handle, through its elevators "A" and "B," grain for the Fort Worth Elevators Company; that it was understood by the arrangement made that whenever cars containing grain came into Galveston under order notify Fort Worth Elevators Company the railroad companies, including the Santa Fé, would give notice to the Wharf Company on behalf of the Fort Worth Elevators Company of the arrival of such cars, and then deliver them to the Wharf Company; that the two cars were brought into Galveston by the Santa Fé Company on the 12th day of August, 1915, and that on the 13th day of the same month they were, in accordance with the general agreement between the Santa Fé Company and the Wharf Company, placed on the elevator "B" track, of the Wharf Company at or about Twenty-Ninth street, and in about 300 feet of its elevator "B"; that the Santa Fé Company notified the Wharf Company by letter on the same day that the two cars in controversy had arrived, and that the same had been ordered to the elevators of the Wharf Company as per its request; that at the time these cars were delivered to the Wharf Company the storm that struck Galveston on the 16th day of August, 1915, had been reported in the Gulf, and the United States Weather Bureau had issued storm warnings at Galveston; that the "B" yard of the Wharf Company at Twenty-Ninth street is at an elevation of about 6½ feet above mean low tide, and that the floor of a car placed in said yard would be about 10½ feet above mean low tide; that the storm waters in the storm of August 16, 1915, at Galveston, reached a total height of about 12 to 13 feet in the "B" yard at Twenty-Ninth street.

It was shown that on the morning of the 15th of August, 1915, at 8 a. m., the wind had a velocity of 7 miles an hour from the north; at noon it had increased to 13 miles northeast, and at 8 p. m. it was 20 miles an hour northeast. At midnight on the 15th it was still 20 miles, but had backed to the north. On the 16th at 1:45 a. m. it changed to the northeast, and was blowing 30 miles at 2:20 a. m.; 35 miles at 6 a. m.; 40 miles at 9:30 a. m.; 45 at 11:20 a. m.; 50 miles at 12:35 p. m.; 55 miles at 1:17 p. m.; 60 miles at 3:05 p. m.; 65 miles at 3:50 p. m.; 70 miles at 6:42 p. m., and it continued to blow 70 miles or over until 4 a. m. of the 17th. At 9:57 p. m.

he maximum of wind on the 16th occurred, 5 miles from the northeast, with an extreme velocity of 110 miles. The maximum during the storm occurred at 2.37 a. m. on the 17th; 83 miles east, with an extreme velocity of 120 miles at 2:30 a. m.

It was shown that about 10 a. m. of the 16th the superintendent of the Wharf Company tried to get in touch with the railroad officials so as to get permission to pass over their main lines with a view to hauling cars of wheat, then on its tracks, across the causeway over the bay to the mainland, but that he failed to get in communication with said officials, and that at about 1 a. m. he directed the employés of the Wharf Company in charge of the switch engines of his company to hitch onto said cars of wheat and start with them to the mainland; that said employés did hitch onto 59 cars of said wheat, including the 2 cars in controversy, and started to haul them to the main land, but when they got to Fifty-First street the railroad track was so obstructed by the storm waters that it was impossible for them to proceed further; and then, learning that the mainland could not be reached, they undertook to return with their train of cars to the "B" yards of the Wharf Company, from whence the cars had been taken, but again the fury of the storm and the flood waters caused thereby frustrated their plans, and they were forced to back the cars of wheat, including those in controversy, into the yards of the Trinity & Brazos Valley, known as the Valley yards.

It was shown that there was a car of unslacked lime in the Valley yards close to where the two cars in controversy were placed, and that the rising waters, driven by the wind of the hurricane, entered the car of lime and produced a fire, which spread to the two cars of wheat and destroyed them and their contents.

It was shown that none of the agents, officers, or employé of the Wharf Company knew of the existence of said car of lime, or had any reason to suspect that it was in the yard. In other words, we think the evidence shows that after the Wharf Company was advised of the probable intensity or force of the hurricane it made every reasonable effort to take plaintiff's wheat to the mainland, and that in being frustrated in so doing it had it placed in the safest place which could be reached.

It was also shown that the point in the Valley yards where this wheat was placed was about the same elevation above low mean tide as was the point from which it was taken in the "B" yards, and that such damages as would have resulted from high water alone would have been practically the same in each of said yards.

It was shown that on the 8th day of September, 1900, a violent hurricane struck Galveston Island, and that it resulted in the drowning of 8,000 to 10,000 people, the destruction of thousands of houses, and of various kinds of property of the value of hundreds of thousands of dollars. It was shown that hurricanes of considerable violence had struck the Gulf coast of Texas in the years 1875, 1886, 1900, and 1909, and that none of them except the one of 1900 did any great damage to life or property in the city of Galveston. It was shown that the hurricane of 1900 was the most severe and disastrous storm that had ever struck the Texas coast up to the hurricane of 1915. It was shown, however, that the hurricane of 1915 lasted much longer than that of 1900, and that as a result thereof the flood waters on the bay front, along the wharves, and in the vicinity of all railway yards on the island, were from 2 to 3 feet higher than they were in 1900. It was shown that after the 1900 storm and before the storm of 1909 the people of Galveston with the aid of the state of Texas, constructed a sea wall about 17 feet in height, along the Gulf coast, beginning at the extreme northeastern part of the island and extending southwestwardly around the city of Galveston for 5 miles or more, which it was thought would protect the city against material damage from storms of the intensity of that of 1900, should such storms again occur. Evidencing the faith the people of Galveston had in the sea wall as a protection against future storms, Lewis Fisher, mayor of Galveston, and other prominent citizens of Galveston, signed, published and caused to be sent broadcast the following circular:

"Galveston Tribune, July 23, 1909.
"Editorial, Volume 1, Page 12.
"The Sea Wall Does Its Work.

"Galveston's famous sea wall has had its first severe test and has done the thing it was built to do. It has turned back the assaults of the storm-driven sea upon the low sand island from a second grave disaster.

"The greetings sent out to the world by the leading citizens of Galveston will not only allay present fear for those now on the island, but will strengthen the confidence felt by the world in the ability of the engineers to make the Island City permanently safe from the sea.

"The greeting follows:

"The city of Galveston sends greetings to her sister cities, the people of the United States, and of the world, in that in this hour it has just passed through a most formidable storm, manifesting in its course some of the most violent incidents of cyclonic disturbances, and its great sea wall has completely vindicated its efficiency and protected the city against dangers from the sea, leaving such insignificant damages as are incident to all storms. The city's great business interest and its people have safely passed through a most severe hurricane, the sea wall proved a complete success, the city's great wharves and shipping interests suffered no damage, and not a life was lost on the island."

The faith of the people in the sea wall as an absolute protection, as expressed in the foregoing circular, however, was shattered by the unprecedented storm of 1915, which caused the flood waters to reach a height of 2 to 3 feet above those of the storm of 1900 in the railway yards.

There was evidence amply sufficient to sustain a finding that neither the Santa Fé Company nor the Wharf Company could have raised their railroad tracks to such heights as would have prevented damage to the plaintiff's wheat from the flood waters of the hurricane of 1915 at a reasonable cost and expense, and without injury to property of others.

The cause being tried before a jury the court instructed a verdict for the defendants Keel & Son, and submitted the following special issues:

"(1) Would the hurricane of 1915 have been reasonably anticipated by a person of ordinary prudence in the position of the defendants? Answer Yes or No.

"(2) Could damage by high water from the hurricane of 1915 have been provided against by the defendants at a reasonable expense and without injury to others? Answer Yes or No."

To the first question the jury answered "Yes" and to the second "No," and they also found in favor of Keel & Son as instructed by the court.

Upon the verdict of the jury and the evidence the court rendered judgment in favor of the defendants. From such judgment the Fort Worth Elevators Company has appealed.

[1] By the first assignment of error appellant insists that the court erred in instructing a verdict for Keel & Son. Its contention is that Keel & Son had contracted to deliver the wheat to it in Galveston; that said wheat had not been delivered to the Fort Worth Elevators Company at the time of its destruction, and hence title thereto had not passed to said company. There is no merit in this contention. The facts hereinbefore stated clearly show that the wheat had been delivered to appellant's agent at Galveston, and that the ownership thereof had passed from Keel & Son to appellant.

Where goods are purchased and are shipped by rail, consigned to shipper's order, and drafts for the price are sent through banks with bill of lading attached, and such drafts are paid by the purchaser and bills of lading delivered to purchaser, title to such goods passes to the purchaser. Where the entire shipment is sold and paid for, as in this case, but must be measured or weighed at destination, with a view of definitely determining the exact sum to be paid for the entire mass, the title passes to the purchaser, notwithstanding the necessity of such measurement or weighing. Robinson & Martin v. Houston & Tex. Cent. R. Co., 105 Tex. 185,

146 S. W. 537; Boaz & Co. v. Schneider & Davis, 69 Tex. 128, 6 S. W. 402. This proposition is, we think, too well settled to require citation of other authorities.

By assignments 2 to 7, inclusive, it is insisted: First, that the answer of the jury to special issue No. 2 is unsupported by the evidence, and is contrary to all of the evidence, in that the evidence is undisputed and conclusive that the Santa Fé Company and the Wharf Company could have raised a sufficient number of their respective tracks to accommodate all loaded cars in their possession to such height as would have placed cars standing thereon above the storm waters of the storm of 1915, without injury to the rights or property of others; second, that the submission of special issue No. 2 was error, in that the jury should have been asked whether a person of ordinary prudence in the position of the defendants would have raised the tracks above high water, and whether such raise could have been accomplished without material injury to others; third, that the court erred in not rendering judgment for the plaintiff on the answer of the jury to special issue No. 1, because defendants were carriers and are liable to plaintiff for having failed to comply with their contract to deliver the cars of wheat to plaintiff at Galveston, and because defendants as carriers are liable as insurers; and, fourth, that the court erred in excluding the testimony of A. P. Hall to the effect that subsequent to the storm of 1915 the Santa Fé Company had raised a portion of its railroad tracks in the city of Galveston, at a cost of approximately $40,000 to $50,000 to such height that the bottom of cars standing thereon would be above the heights reached by the storm waters of the storm of 1915, and that there was no reason why the remaining portion could not be so raised, for the reason that such testimony was admissible on the question of the practicability and reasonableness of cost of such improvements.

[2] In so far as these assignments, or any of them, relate to the cause of action alleged against the Gulf, Colorado & Santa Fé Railway Company they are overruled. We have reached the conclusion, as before stated, that the uncontroverted and undisputed evidence showed that the Santa Fé Company received the two cars of wheat at Gainesville, Tex., for transportation to Galveston, Tex., to be there delivered to the plaintiff; that it did so transport said wheat, and that it did deliver same to the Wharf Company at Galveston, for the plaintiff, in accordance with the general contract and agreement then existing between the plaintiff and the Wharf Company, and between the Wharf Company, as the authorized agent of plaintiff, and the Santa Fé Company. The undertaking of the Santa Fé Company relative to these cars of wheat as a carrier had been promptly and fully performed. The

wheat had been delivered by the Santa Fé Company to the Wharf Company, which had been directed by the Elevator Company to receive the same at Galveston, several days before the storm reached Galveston and before it was destroyed. It is therefore clearly apparent that the questions of whether the Santa Fé Company should have anticipated the approach of the storm of 1915, or as to whether it could have raised its railroad tracks so as to place cars standing thereon above the reach of the storm waters of the storm of 1915, with reasonable expense and without injury to others, or as to whether it could have reasonably foreseen that the wheat standing in the "B" yards would have been damaged from the rising waters, were not material or pertinent inquiries in view of the facts found by us. The Santa Fé Company owed the plaintiff no legal duty relative to the wheat in controversy after it had delivered the same to the Wharf Company, the agent of the plaintiff authorized to receive the same at. Galveston.

Having disposed of the assignment relating to the liability of Keel & Son, and having also considered and disposed of assignments 2 to 7, inclusive, in so far as they relate to the liability of the Santa Fé Company, we now come to consider said assignments as they relate to the Galveston Wharf Company.

[3, 4] The jury found that the storm of 1915 would have been reasonably anticipated by a person of ordinary prudence in the position of the defendants. We think this finding, in the light of all the facts and circumstances, must be construed as a finding only that the defendants should have anticipated that a storm of more or less violence would probably strike Galveston as it did in 1915, and not as a finding that they should have anticipated a storm of the violence and duration of that of 1915, a storm of much longer duration than that of 1900, which up to that time was by far the most violent storm that had ever visited Galveston, nor as a finding that they should have further anticipated, notwithstanding the seawall, that the storm of 1915 would cause flood waters to rise to the unprecedented heights of 12 to 13 feet above mean low tide in the railway yards and along the wharf front as it did, the same being a height of about 2 or 3 feet greater than reached by the flood waters of the disastrous storm of 1900. Notwithstanding, however, the finding of the jury to special issue No. 1, we have reached the conclusion from the undisputed evidence that the proximate cause of the loss of the wheat in controversy was the storm of 1915, and that said storm is properly classed as an act of God, and that the defendant Wharf Company is not liable therefor. While it must be conceded that had plaintiff's wheat been left on "B" track it would not have been wholly lost, and that its removal from said yard to the Valley yards and its being placed and left close to a car of unslacked lime concurred with the storm in producing the loss, and while but for said removal the total loss would not have been suffered, still such removal, even if it could be said to be negligence on the part of the Wharf Company, was the remote and not the proximate cause of such loss. We think the law as declared in Barnet v. Railway Co., 222 N. Y. 195, 118 N. E. 625, Bergman v. Railway Co., 64 S. W. 999, G., C. & S. F. Ry. Co. v. Darby, 28 Tex. Civ. App. 229, 67 S. W. 129, Hunt v. Railway Co., 74 S. W. 69, G., C. & S. F. Ry. Co. v. Texas Flour Mills, 143 S. W. 1179, G., H. & S. A. Ry. Co. v. Crier, 45 Tex. Civ. App. 434, 100 S. W. 1177, Wells Fargo & Co. Express v. Porter, 203 S. W. 987, and Fentiman v. Railway Co., 44 Tex. Civ. App. 455, 98 S. W. 939, is applicable to the facts of the present case, and acquits the Wharf Company from any liability for the loss of plaintiff's wheat.

[5] However, a further discussion of the scope and import of the inquiry of the court as propounded by special issue No. 1 and as to what the jury intended to find by their answer thereto becomes immaterial in view of the finding of the jury in answer to special issue No. 2. To this issue the jury answered in effect that the damage by high water from the storm of 1915 could not have been provided against by the defendant at a reasonable expense and without injury to others. This answer was amply supported by evidence. After much testimony as to the extent of the raising of almost the entire southern part of the city of Galveston lying along the Gulf coast to a height of from 6 to 8 feet since the storm of 1900, thus preventing storm waters from flowing south or east, had been heard, Mr A. D. Dickey, a civil engineer of long experience, testified as follows:

"It would be impracticable from an engineering standpoint to raise the level of the railroad tracks and yards that we have been discussing so that the storm level of 1915 would not enter box cars, unless some arrangements could be made to raise the grade of almost the entire city south of these railroad yards. It could not be accomplished satisfactorily by any system of drainage in my judgment."

Again:

"If you raise these yards out there, and the storm water in time of storms was sufficiently high to come over the embankments, it would wash out great gullies and would damage property immediately adjacent to railroad yards. The water would then be up as high as grade of your tracks on yards and would extend back over the city to same level. It would raise water all over the city. In case of storm the more embankments you would put out there the higher water you would have in the city, and the longer it would take water to recede, and the longer it would stay in city. In addition to that, it would be very difficult to take care of drainage from the south towards the north and towards the bay. It would be a very difficult engineering problem.

"As to raising the tracks out yonder, the whole side of the town was raised and the drainage all thrown towards the bay. So the raising of the tracks out there did not interfere with the drainage, because it was all taken care of at the same time. It would have been a very difficult proposition if you had undertaken to raise these railroad tracks round there and carry it in on the embankment. It would have been an entirely different proposition."

Independent, however, of the finding of the jury that the tracks of the defendants could not have been raised so as to have placed cars standing thereon above the heights reached by the storm water of 1915, there is, we think, a controlling reason why the judgment rendered in favor of the Wharf Company should be affirmed. The undisputed evidence shows that the loss of plaintiff's wheat was caused by the storm of 1915, an act of God, and not by reason of any negligent act of the Wharf Company. In the case of G., C. & S. F. Ry. Co. v. Flour Mills Co., supra, it is said:

"The occurrences which have been held in some of the cases to be acts of God are spoken of as unprecedented, but it is manifest that an occurrence need not be unprecedented in the literal sense of that word in order to be regarded as an act of God. Any definition of the term which includes the idea that it must be an occurrence the like of which has never happened before would so restrict the application of the rule as to practically abrogate it. Under such a definition, a tidal wave, an earthquake, a volcanic eruption, or a storm, it matters not how violent or destructive such disturbance might be, would not be an act of God, unless it was more violent than any of like kind that had preceded it. It goes without saying that this is not the rule. All that is required in this regard to make an occurrence of this kind an act of God is to show that it was so unusual that it could not have been reasonably expected or provided against."

And in Fentiman v. Railway Co., 44 Tex. Civ. App 455, 98 S. W. 939, it is said:

"The flood which destroyed plaintiff's goods was an act of God; to say that it was not His act because as great a flood occurred at the same place in 1844 would be to hold that God is incapable of causing two floods of the same character in the same place."

It is shown that the citizens of Galveston during the period between the great storm of 1900 and the one of 1915 were so confident that their properties situated in the business portion of said city were free from flood waters that they made no changes in the levels of their buildings in which were stored large stores of food, clothing, and other properties of the value of millions of dollars; that these business men were of experience, not men of only ordinary skill and judgment, but of large business capacity and prudence; that they lived, invested their money, and kept their properties in the business portion of Galveston, where the waters reached a height of about 6 or 7 feet in the storm of 1915, with a feeling of safety, inspired no doubt with the thought that it was not probable that there would be a recurrence of a storm of the severity of the one of 1900, and that, should such possibly recur, the great sea wall would protect them, their families, and their properties. How, then, can it be held that a failure of the Wharf Company to build its tracks above the heights reached by the storm of 1915 was negligence, as that term is understood in law? What act did the defendant do to endanger or neglect to do for the protection of property in its possession that a person of ordinary prudence situated as it was would or would not have done?

Under the decisions quoted from above and those cited, the courts have held that the storm of 1900, the smaller storm of 1909, and the greatest storm of history on the Gulf coast in August, 1915, were acts of God and of such nature that man was not legally charged with the duty of anticipating their occurrence, and not answerable in damages proximately caused by such storms or hurricanes.

[6] Under these decisions we feel constrained to hold that this defendant was not charged with the duty of anticipating the severity of the storm of 1915, and was not obligated to go to the great expense of undertaking to raise its tracks on the "B" yard or on any other part of its property beyond the level of the flood waters of the storms of 1900 and 1915. A holding of the court that this defendant was charged with such duty would do violence to the decisions of the courts of this state.

[7] Appellant insists by its ninth assignment that the court erred in not instructing a verdict for it, in that the undisputed evidence shows that the Wharf Company removed the wheat in controversy from its "B" yard and placed same in the Valley yards, over which it had no control; that it was there destroyed by fire by reason of being placed near a car containing unslacked lime, which was set on fire by the storm waters coming in contact with the unslacked lime, and that if said wheat had not been so removed from "B" track it would not have been destroyed. This contention cannot be sustained. The undisputed evidence shows that as soon as it became apparent to the officials of the Wharf Company that the wheat might be damaged by the storm they did everything within their power to protect the same; that they attempted to move the wheat to the mainland, and, upon being frustrated in this attempt by the storm, they then tried to get it back to the "B" yards, and were again frustrated, and as a last resort they placed the cars containing the

wheat in the Valley yard, where there happened to be located a car of unslacked lime, which was later ignited, and from which the fire spread to and burned the two cars of wheat in controversy. We find as a matter of law that the removal shown by the evidence was not an act of actionable negligence. Such removal was made in good faith, in the stress of a grave and impending danger, and with the view of saving said property from injury.

As we have heretofore shown, even if it should be said that it was negligence upon the part of the Galveston Wharf Company to move the cars of grain from the "B" yards to the Valley yards, under the circumstances there could be no liability against the Wharf Company by reason of such movement, because under the law the Wharf Company could not be charged with the damage to said grain by the storm waters and the lime fire, as the proximate result of such movement of the cars. If these cars of grain had been permitted to stand upon the tracks of the "B" yards, the damage to the grain by water would have been practically the same as the damage by water in the Valley yards. The additional damage by fire caused by the lime was not the probable and natural result of the placing of the cars in the Valley yards. The defendant could not have reasonably anticipated that the damage by fire would result when the cars were placed in those yards.

We have considered all of the assignments, and in view of our conclusion that the loss of appellant's wheat was due to the act of God, as hereinbefore expressed, we think it useless to prolong this opinion by a further discussion of other matters complained of by assignments 2 to 7, inclusive, or by the remaining assignments.

The judgment is affirmed.

Affirmed.

BROWNFIELD v. BRABSON et al.
(No. 1814.)

(Court of Civil Appeals of Texas. Amarillo.
May 18, 1921.)

1. Lost instruments ⬅=8(1)—Possession not indispensable prerequisite to presumption of existence of deed.

Possession is not an indispensable prerequisite to the presumption of the existence of a deed, but it is essential that the claim of title be made in some tangible form calculated to bring notice to those who are adversely affected thereby, so as to create a presumption of acquiescence in such claim by the adverse parties.

2. Lost instruments ⬅=8(3)—Execution of quitclaim deed for consideration does not show acquiescence of heirs in presumed deed.

Where plaintiffs claimed title to land under presumed existence of a deed, the giving of a quitclaim deed by heirs of alleged grantor would not tend to show any acquiescence on their part in any claim by plaintiffs if supported by a full-paid consideration.

3. Evidence ⬅=87—Presumption of conveyance one of fact and not of law.

The presumption in favor of the existence of a conveyance of land is one of fact and not of law.

4. Trespass to try title ⬅=35(1)—Plaintiff confined to proof of title specially pleaded.

Except as to title by limitation where plaintiff in trespass to try title elects to plead his title specially, he is confined to the proof of the title so pleaded.

5. Trespass to try title ⬅=35(1)—Title by limitations not permissible under general allegations.

A showing of title by limitations is not permissible under the general allegations of a petition of trespass to try title, but must be specially pleaded.

6. Trespass to try title ⬅=35(1)—Presumption of execution of deed asserted under general allegation.

The presumption of the execution of a deed may be asserted under the general allegations of a trespass to try title petition.

7. Adverse possession ⬅=71(1)—Conveyance of interest held to support plea of five years' limitation as a deed and not quitclaim.

A conveyance by grantors of all their right, title, and interest in certain described lands, followed by the habendum clause of a general warranty deed, is a deed to the land, and not a mere quitclaim of the grantor's interest, and will support a plea of five years' limitation.

8. Adverse possession ⬅=80(2)—Deed must contain sufficient description to support plea of five years' limitation.

A deed to support a plea of five years' limitation must contain such a sufficient description that it will appear from its terms or reference to other instruments of record in the chain of title that it conveys the very land in controversy, so that its registration will put the adverse party on notice that the land is thus being claimed, as an owner of land is not bound to run down references to facts outside the chain of title to ascertain the meaning of the deed.

9. Adverse possession ⬅=82—Five-year statute begins to run from registration of deed.

The five-year statute of limitations begins to run from the time of registration of the deed on which the plea is based.

10. Adverse possession ⬅=93—Payment of taxes for five years held sufficient.

Where deed was registered September 7, 1904, payment of taxes for the years 1904 to 1908, inclusive, was sufficient to sustain a plea of five-year limitations, it not being necessary to pay taxes for the year 1909.

⬅=For other cases see same topic and KEY-NUMBER in all Key-Numbered Digests and Indexes

11. **Adverse possession ⇐90—Title may be acquired to undivided interest in land.**

Title may be acquired to an undivided interest in land under the five-year statute of limitations by payment of taxes.

12. **Adverse possession ⇐115(1)—Whether party claiming under five-year statute paid taxes properly held for jury.**

In trespass to try title, where a party claimed land under five-year statute, whether defendant had paid the taxes for five consecutive years as required by the statute *held* for the jury.

13. **Adverse possession ⇐90—Taxes must be paid under proper description.**

It was not sufficient, under the five-year statute of limitations, that taxes were paid, where payment was made on a wrong description, so that no credit of taxes was made on the assessment of taxes against the tract of land in question, since such payment would not afford owner of legal title any notice that some one else was paying taxes on his land.

14. **Adverse possession ⇐94—Payment of taxes after delinquency insufficient.**

Payment of taxes after delinquency is insufficient under the five-year statute of limitations.

Appeal from District Court, Terry County; W. P. Leslie, Special Judge.

Suit by Mollie J. Brabson and others against M. V. Brownfield. Judgment for plaintiffs, and the defendant appeals. Reversed and remanded.

Roscoe Wilson and Percy Spencer, both of Lubbock, for appellant.

G. E. Lockhart, of Tahoka, for appellees.

BOYCE, J. Mollie J. Brabson and others brought this suit against M. V. Brownfield to recover the E. ½ of survey 39, block A-1, certificate 1445, E. L. & R. R. R. R. Co., in Terry county, Tex. The petition was in the regular form of trespass to try title, and in addition thereto contained what plaintiffs style a "special plea," which set out the chain of title from T. C. Reade, the patentee, down to J. M. Brabson; the plaintiffs being the surviving wife and heirs of the said Brabson. It was alleged that the deed from the patentee, Reade, to Geo. T. Keith, under whom the plaintiffs claim, had been lost or destroyed; but that the plaintiffs and those under whom they claim, had claimed and asserted ownership of said land for more than 35 years, paying taxes thereon, and that such claim was made with the acquiescence of the said Reade and his heirs, so that there should be a presumption of a conveyance from the said Reade to the said Keith. The defendant answered by plea of not guilty and plea of five years' limitation; also by cross-action he sought a recovery of the land under title acquired by the five-years limitation. The appeal is from a judgment for the plaintiffs entered on a verdict return in their favor under peremptory instructions from the trial judge.

The survey, containing 640 acres of land, was patented to T. C. Reade on February 7, 1881. Geo. T. Keith conveyed the E. ½ of the survey, the land in controversy, to E. S. Rogers, on November 3, 1883. E. S. Rogers paid the taxes on 320 acres of land out of the section for the year of 1891. The taxes for the years 1882 to 1896 on 320 acres of land out of the section were paid by J. S. Daugherty after delinquency. Rogers conveyed the land to J. M. Brabson by deed dated November 17, 1896. Brabson paid taxes on the land for the years 1897 to 1911, inclusive, except for the years 1904, 1907, and 1909. The taxes for some of the years were paid before delinquency and occasionally after the taxes for one or more years had become delinquent. The plaintiffs introduced in evidence a quitclaim deed from one of the heirs of T. C. Reade, who had acquired the interest of the other heirs, whereby the grantor quitclaimed to the plaintiffs her interest in said land. This deed was executed April 20, 1915. All of the deeds referred to were properly recorded. J. M. Brabson died in 1912, and the plaintiff Mollie J. Brabson is his surviving wife and the other plaintiffs are his heirs. This suit was filed on the 18th day of October, 1916.

The defendant's plea of five years' limitation was based on a deed executed by N. M. Viser, dated November 3, 1903, and recorded in September, 1904. This deed was in the terms of a general warranty deed and the said Viser thereby conveyed to the defendant "all that certain tract or parcel of land lying and being situated in Terry county, Texas, the same being my ¾ interest in section 39, block A-1, certificate No. 1445, E. L. & R. R. R. R. Co. survey." It appears that another person, with whom Viser had no privity of title, owned the northwest quarter of the section at this time. One W. M. Viser had acquired title to the southwest quarter of the section in the year 1887, but no privity of title is shown between the said W. M. Viser and N. M. Viser. The said Brownfield paid, or attempted to pay, taxes on 480 acres of land out of the section, from 1905 to 1915. During some of these years, however, the taxes were paid on a wrong description, and some of them were paid after delinquency. We will make a fuller statement of such matters when we come to discuss the question of the sufficiency of the evidence to sustain the plea of limitations.

The disposition of the appeal under the assignments presented requires a decision of the following questions: (1) Whether the evidence is sufficient to warrant a conclusive presumption of the existence of a deed of conveyance from the patentee, Reade, to Geo. T. Keith. (2) If not, could the plaintiffs, having specially pleaded their title, rely on a conveyance from the heirs of T. C. Reade, which was not pleaded? (3) Is the conveyance from Viser to Brownfield such a deed as will support the plea of five years' limitation? (4) Does the evidence show such payment of taxes as will sustain the plea? We will dispose of these questions in the order stated.

[1-3] (1) There was never any possession taken under claim of deed from Reade to Keith. The only tangible claim of title made by plaintiffs and those under whom they hold was in the registration of the deeds from Keith down to Brabson and payment of taxes by those holding under such deeds. These payments were not made regularly, and, so far as the evidence discloses, were not conclusively shown to have been paid for any five consecutive years; so that, even if possession had been taken under these deeds, the evidence would not conclusively sustain a plea of five years' limitation. Possession is not an indispensable prerequisite to the presumption of the existence of a deed, but it is essential that the claim of title be made in some tangible form calculated to bring notice to those who are adversely affected thereby, so as to create a presumption of acquiescence in such claim by the adverse parties. The circumstances of and consideration for the execution of the quitclaim deed by the heirs of Reade are not shown. So that such fact has little probative force in establishing an acquiescence on the part of such heirs in the claim of Brabson. So far as the evidence shows, the heirs of Brabson may have paid a full consideration for the rights acquired under the quitclaim, and, if such were the fact, the execution of the quitclaim deed would not tend to show any acquiescence at all on the part of the heirs of Reade. The principles of law applicable to the matter of presumptions in favor of the existence of a conveyance have been well settled by the decisions of this state, and have been recently discussed by us at some length, and we refer to a few of these authorities in lieu of a further discussion of the question here. Taylor v. Watkins, 26 Tex. 688; Baldwin v. Goldfrank, 88 Tex. 249, 31 S. W. 1066; Herndon v. Vick, 89 Tex. 469, 35 S. W. 143; Hutchison v. Massie, 226 S. W. 695. The presumption is one of fact and not of law, and the evidence in this case does not warrant such a conclusive presumption of the existence of such a deed as to justify a peremptory instruction in favor thereof. We need not decide whether under the evidence the plaintiffs were entitled to have the issue submitted to the jury.

[4-6] (2) "It is well settled that, except as to title by limitation, where the plaintiff elects to plead his title specially he is confined to the proof of the title so pleaded."

Molino v. Benavides, 94 Tex. 413, 60 S. W. 875; Rule v. Richards, 159 S. W. 389(8). The exception in favor of the plea of limitations is allowed because a showing of title by limitations is not permissible under the general allegations of a petition of trespass to try title, but must be specially pleaded. So that a special pleading thereof in the petition is not to be regarded as a more particular statement of what might have been shown under the general allegations, as would be true in the ordinary case of the special pleading of the title. Erp v. Tillman, 103 Tex. 574, 131 S. W. 1060, and authorities cited. We take it that the presumption of the execution of a deed by Reade could have been asserted under the general allegations of a trespass to try title petition. Buie v. Penn, 172 S. W. 549, on motion for rehearing. So that the case does not present an exception to the general rule.

[7, 8] (3) As to the third question for decision, the appellee contends that the deed from Viser to Brownfield did not purport to convey the land itself, but only the grantor's interest therein, and will not support a plea of five years' limitation. We have not thought it necessary to determine whether or not the first part of the proposition is well taken (see Roseborough v. Cook, 108 Tex. 364, 194 S. W. 131; Barksdale v. Benskin, 194 S. W. 402, writ of error granted), as we think it must be held that the conveyance is of a three-fourths interest in the land itself, and not merely the grantor's chance of title to such interest. In the case of Garrett v. Christopher, 74 Tex. 453, 12 S. W. 67, 15 Am. St. Rep. 850, a conveyance by the grantors of "all our right, title, and interest in" certain described lands, followed by the habendum clause of a general warranty deed, was held to be a deed to the land, and not a mere quitclaim of the grantor's interest. In Kempner v. Beaumont Lumber Co., 20 Tex. Civ. App. 307, 49 S. W. 412, the conveyance was in the form of a general warranty deed, conveying "all my right, title, and claim and interest, being an undivided one-half interest," and it was held that the instrument was a deed and not a quitclaim. In White v. Frank, 91 Tex. 66, 40 S. W. 964, it was said of similar language in a deed that—

"The words first used—'all my interest'— taken in connection with what follows, are evidently intended to define the quantity of her [the grantor's] interest, and not to limit the conveyance to such interest as she might hold in an undivided half of the lands. The grantor practically asserts that she holds an undivided one-half interest in the lands, and that she conveys that interest. It does not purport merely to release her interest in the land, whatever that interest may be."

We think this statement is properly applicable to the language of the deed under consideration. But the troublesome question in considering the sufficiency of the deed to support the statute of limitations is whether the deed, on its face, is to be construed as conveying an undivided interest, or whether by the use of the words "my three-fourths interest" it invites the introduction of parol evidence as to the surrounding circumstances to ascertain whether an undivided three-fourths interest in the entire tract is intended to be conveyed or some particular three-fourths of the section. It is the law that a deed, to support this plea of limitation, must contain sufficient description as that it will appear from its terms, or reference to other instruments of record in the chain of title, that it conveys the very land in controversy so that its registration will put the adverse party on notice that the land is thus being claimed. Kilpatrick v. Sisneros, 23 Tex. 137; Acklin v. Paschal, 48 Tex. 176; Randolph v. Lewis, 163 S. W. 649 (opinion on motion for rehearing and authorities). The owner of the land is not bound to run down references to facts outside the chain of title to ascertain the meaning of the deed. Brokel v. McKechnie, 69 Tex. 32, 6 S. W. 623; Young v. Traban, 43 Tex. Civ. App. 611, 97 S. W. 147. So, if the terms of this deed would convey either an undivided interest or a specific three-fourths of the land if it had been divided, and it were shown that the grantor claimed title to such divided interest, then we doubt whether it would be sufficient to sustain the plea; for, if it did not purport to convey an undivided interest in the entire section, the owners of the east half had no means of record of knowing what part of the land was intended to be conveyed by the deed. We have concluded that we should construe the instrument as a conveyance of an undivided three-fourths interest, as the language used in its natural significance is more appropriate to express that meaning, and would be really inappropriate if the intention was to convey a specific divided portion of the section. We conclude, therefore, that the deed is sufficient to sustain a plea of limitations to an undivided three-fourths of the one-half section of land in controversy.

[9-14] (4) The defendant's deed was registered on September 7, 1904, and limitations would begin to run from such time (Harvey v. Cummings, 68 Tex. 599, 5 S. W. 513), and would be complete on September 7, 1909, if all taxes were paid by defendant as they became due during such time and the possession was sufficient. It would not have been necessary that he pay the taxes for the year 1909. Club Land & Cattle Co. v. Wall, 99 Tex. 591, 91 S. W. 778, 122 Am. St. Rep. 666. The defendant paid taxes, intending to pay them on his interest in the land, on 480 acres of land for the years 1904, 1905, 1906, 1907, and 1908. Payment of taxes on the land in such way would have been sufficient to sustain the plea of limitations to an undivided three-fourths interest, therein. Dowdell v. McCardell, 193 S. W. 182; Yarbrough v. Whitman, 50 Tex. Civ. App. 391, 110 S. W. 471. The taxes for the years 1906 and 1908, however, were paid on the wrong abstract number, and J. M. Brabson appears to have paid the taxes for 1906 on the E. ½ of the section, under proper description, several months before the defendant paid taxes for such year, and the said Brabson paid taxes for the year 1908 on the same day that defendant paid the taxes. We have had some doubt as to whether, after Brabson had paid the taxes on the land on a correct description, the defendant could thereafter pay taxes on the same land, and thus bring himself within the provisions of the statute. But the Supreme Court has held that although there may have been a double payment of the taxes, yet such payment by the person claiming under limitations is sufficient. Thomson v. Weisman, 98 Tex. 170, 82 S. W. 503. It does not appear whether the defendant rendered the land for taxes for the years 1906 and 1908, nor does it appear that the payments of taxes made by the defendant for either of those years were credited to the assessment of taxes against the land which followed the correct abstract number on the tax rolls. It does appear from the tax rolls that the taxes for 1908 on the entire section, described as abstract No. 798, certificate No. 1445, survey No. 39, E. L. & R. R. R. R. Co. grantee, 640 acres (which was the correct description of the land) were assessed to "unknown owners," and that J. M. Brabson paid taxes for that year on the E. ½ of the survey as thus assessed, and the inference is that the payment made by plaintiff on another abstract number, though correctly describing survey number, was credited on the tax rolls to another survey under the abstract number on which payment was made. The evidence would not, we think, have warranted a peremptory instruction in appellant's favor on this issue. Conn v. Houston Oil Co., 218 S. W. 139; Dutton v. Thompson, 85 Tex. 115, 19 S. W. 1026; Henning v. Wren, 32 Tex. Civ. App. 538, 75 S. W. 910. If payment was made on a wrong description, so that no credit of taxes was made on the assessment of taxes against this tract of land, such payment would not have afforded J. M. Brabson any notice that some one else was paying taxes on his land. The appellant concedes that, while he intended to pay the taxes for the years 1909 and 1910, his payments were made under a mistaken description, and were credited to the assessment against other lands. This mistake was discovered in 1912, after the unpaid taxes for 1909 and 1910 had become delinquent, at which time the appellant, according to his oral testimony, paid such taxes. Payment of such taxes after de-

linquency is insufficient. Baker v. Fogle, 110 .Tex. 301, 217 S. W. 141, 219 S. W. 450. The defendant, in January of the years 1912, 1913, 1914, and 1915, paid taxes on the land for the respective preceding years; but these payments did not complete the title by limitations even if the plaintiffs were held to their claim acquired by the quitclaim deed executed in 1915. If plaintiffs sustain their claim under J. M. Brabson, limitations would be suspended for a period of one year following his death; but the title, based on a quitclaim deed from the heirs of T. O. Reade, would not be subject to this suspension. No question is raised as to the sufficiency of the possession by the defendant, Brownfield, to sustain the plea of limitations, and we have not considered such matter.

We are of the opinion, therefore, that the plaintiffs were not entitled to the peremptory instruction given in their favor; neither was the defendant entitled to a peremptory instruction on his plea of limitations, either as a defense or as supporting his cross-action. Even if the evidence was insufficient to make an issue in plaintiff's favor as to the existence of a deed from the patentee Reade to Geo. T. Keith, the justice of the case requires that we remand the cause rather than reverse and render judgment here.

The judgment of the trial court will accordingly be reversed and the cause remanded.

———

BALLEW & HUSTON et al. v. BLAKENY. (No. 2394.)

(Court of Civil Appeals of Texas. Texarkana. March 23, 1921. On Rehearing, April 21, 1921.)

I. Stipulations ⬤=14(12) — Costs improperly charged in judgment against bank under stipulation.

Where it was agreed at the trial that "the First National Bank is a mere stakeholder, and that the bank has the $600, which is claimed by the plaintiff, and the defendants B. & H. put up $300, and the plaintiff put up $300. The bank does not claim the money. No judgment shall be rendered against the bank, except for $600, which is a mere depository"— the court erred in entering judgment against the bank for $600, and "for court costs"; the bank never having made any claim to the money and being willing to pay it to the rightful owners, both before and after the suit was filed.

2. Brokers ⬤=106—In action against agent to recover earnest money deposited, principal was necessary and proper party defendant, and there was no error in rendering judgment against both.

In action against real estate agent to recover a deposit in a bank as earnest money on a sale of land, part by plaintiff and part by the agent, the owner of the land, as principal, was a necessary and proper party to the suit, and there was no error in rendering judgment against the owner, as well as the agent and the bank, where he entered a general denial to the petition in claim of the earnest money for default in the contract, and did not file a disclaimer of any legal interest in the money, and did not testify that he never authorized his agent to make the contract of sale; but the judgment should provide that a payment to the plaintiff by the bank of the amount of the deposit should be in full satisfaction of the entire judgment.

Appeal from Henderson County Court; Joe A. McDonald, Judge.

Suit by R. J. Blakeny against Ballew & Huston and others. Judgment for plaintiff, and defendants appeal. Modified and affirmed.

The appellee brought the suit to recover $600 deposited as earnest money with the First National Bank as stakeholder. The defendants each made answer. The case was submitted to the jury on special issues, and on the answers of the jury the court entered judgment for the $600 in favor of the plaintiff. The plaintiff and Ballew & Huston, as agents of A. B. Moore, agreed in writing and signed on October 14, 1919, the following:

"The parties of the first part, Ballew & Huston, acting as agents of A. B. Moore, agree to sell to R. J. Blakeny, party of the second part, 58 acres of land. [Here follows description by field notes.] Each party agrees to put up a forfeit of $300 in First National Bank of Malakoff, Texas."

A. B. Moore, the owner of the land, appointed Ballew & Huston his agents to dispose of it. The price of the land was to be $70 per acre cash. Plaintiff and Ballew & Huston, as agents, each put up the $300 cash required of them. Plaintiff pleaded and testified that he was ready and willing to perform his part of the contract, but that the other parties to the contract failed and refused to convey the land described in the contract to him. Ballew & Huston pleaded and claimed in the evidence that the above written agreement made by them as agents did not contain all the agreement between the parties, but that by mutual mistake the following part of the agreement was left out of the said writing:

"There shall first be taken off the north end of the Moore tract 75 acres for Mrs. L. R. Clark, and then 58 acres for Mr. Miller, and after these tracts are surveyed and cut off R. J. Blakeny is to have a 58-acre tract, and the same is to lie immediately south of the Cook tract of 73 acres."

The defendants testified that they offered to plaintiff a deed describing the 53-acre tract south of the 73 acres, and that he refused to accept it. It was agreed in the trial by the parties that:

"The First National Bank is a mere stakeholder, and that the bank has the $600, which is claimed by the plaintiff, and the defendants Ballew & Huston put up $300 and the plaintiff put up $300. The bank does not claim the money. No judgment shall be rendered against the bank, except for $600, which is a mere depository."

The jury answered the issues submitted (1) that there was no agreement such as pleaded by the defendants, and (2) that any such agreement was not left out of the original agreement by mutual mistake.

Miller & Miller, of Athens, for appellants. Justice & Justice, of Athens, for appellee.

LEVY, J. (after stating the facts as above). [1] The first assignment of error predicates error in entering judgment "for court costs" in favor of the plaintiff against the First National Bank. This was error, both in view of the pleadings and evidence and the agreement of the parties. The bank has never made claim to the money, and was willing to pay it to the rightful owners, both before and after suit was filed. The assignment of error is sustained, and the judgment is modified in that respect.

[2] The second assignment predicates error in rendering judgment against A. B. Moore. Ballew & Huston were acting, in making the contract of sale and in the deposit of the earnest money, as agents for A. B. Moore, and the effect and extent of the judgment is merely to adjudicate against A. B. Moore, in favor of the plaintiff, any interest A. B. Moore may have in the earnest money so deposited for him and in his behalf. A. B. Moore entered a general denial to the plaintiff's petition in claim of the earnest money for default in the contract, and did not file a disclaimer of any legal interest in the money, and did not testify that he never authorized his agents to make the contract of sale. The contract of sale was for him and in his behalf as owner of the land, and as principal in the agreement he was a necessary and proper party to the suit. The assignment is overruled.

The third assignment assails the sufficiency of the evidence to show such nonperformance of the contract of sale as to entitle the plaintiff to recover the money sued for. We conclude that this assignment should be overruled.

There is no reversible error in the fourth assignment of error, and it is overruled.

The judgment is modified and affirmed.

On Rehearing.

PER CURIAM. The motion for rehearing is granted only in so far as it seeks to modify the judgment of the county court. The judgment authorizes a recovery and execution against each of the defendants severally and jointly for the $600 sued for. The judgment should be corrected, so as to provide that the payment to the plaintiff by the bank of the $600 should be in full satisfaction of the entire judgment.

HAMNER et al. v. BOREING.

(Court of Appeals of Kentucky. June 7, 1921.)

1. Appeal and error ⇔1189(3)—Reversal of judgment in creditor's suit held to bar relief to general creditor not party to appeal.

A suit by B. to set aside fraudulent conveyances by a debtor and subject the property to the payment of his debt was consolidated with suit by other creditors to have the conveyances adjudged preferential and for the benefit of all creditors. Judgment was rendered dismissing B.'s petition but adjudging that he was a judgment creditor of the debtor, and also adjudging that the transactions between the debtor and his wife operated as an assignment for the benefit of all creditors and that the proceeds should be applied on the judgments against the debtor. Held, that under the judgment B. was only a general creditor and was not a necessary party to an appeal by a party claiming under the conveyances, and a reversal of the judgment on such appeal prevented him from obtaining payment of his judgment from the property conveyed, though he was not made a party to the appeal.

2. Appeal and error ⇔327(10)—Assignments for benefit of creditors ⇔295(5)—All creditors not necessary parties to suit or appeal.

In an action to have a preferential conveyance by a debtor adjudged to operate as an assignment for the benefit of all creditors, all of the creditors are not necessary parties under Ky. St. § 1912, relating to parties in suits concerning conveyances in fraud of creditors, nor are they all necessary parties to an appeal in such case.

Appeal from Circuit Court, Laurel County.

Consolidated actions by John R. Boreing and others against W. B. Catching and others. From a judgment in favor of Boreing, C. D. Hamner, receiver of the First National Bank of London, appeals. Reversed, with directions.

Hazelwood & Johnson, of London, for appellant.

H. C. Faulkner, of Hazard, and H. C. Clay, of London, for appellee.

TURNER, C. In August, 1914, the appellee, John R. Boreing, filed an equitable action in the Laurel circuit court against W. B. Catching and others, wherein he alleged he had a judgment for something over $3,000 against Catching upon which an execution had been issued and returned "no property found."

He asked for a general order of attachment against the property of W. B. Catching, and attacked certain conveyances made by Catching to his wife and others, as well as certain conveyances made by the wife to others, as being without consideration and as having been made to defraud the creditors of W. B. Catching. He sought specifically to subject to the payment of his debt

the property so alleged to have been fraudulently conveyed.

About that time other creditors of Catching instituted their several actions in the Laurel circuit court, some of them seeking the same remedy that Boreing had sought, while others attacked certain transactions between Catching and his wife, and between his wife and others, merely as being preferential, and asked that the property so conveyed be adjudged to be for the benefit of all the creditors of W. B. Catching.

These suits were all consolidated, and after full preparation a judgment was entered dealing in detail with the several transactions involved, and among other things it was adjudged that Boreing was not entitled to any of the relief sought in his petition, and the same was dismissed, and a judgment for costs given against him in favor of the defendants therein; it being recited, however, in the judgment that he was the owner of and entitled to collect from Catching the judgment upon which his suit was based.

In another subdivision of the judgment then entered, it was adjudged that certain transactions between Catching and his wife operated as an assignment of the property and effects of W. B. Catching for the benefit of all his creditors, and that the proceeds of the same should be applied, after the payment of costs, to "the foregoing judgments against W. B. Catching and such other valid claims against him as hereafter be filed herein properly proven and allowed by the court; no further proof of the judgment herein rendered against W. B. Catching being required."

From that judgment the receiver of the First National Bank of London, to which institution Catching was largely indebted, and who as receiver claimed the property for the bank embraced in the conveyances which had been declared preferential, appealed, but did not make Boreing a party to this appeal.

Pending the appeal, Boreing presented in this court certain supplementary parts of the record, which had not been copied by the receiver, and asked to be permitted to prosecute an appeal from the judgment upon his own account upon the record as thus made up, which this court declined to permit him to do.

Upon a final hearing this court reversed the judgment of the Laurel circuit court and held the deeds so adjudged by the lower court to be preferential embraced only such property as the receiver of the bank was entitled to, and that such property was part of the bank's assets, and directed a judgment entered dismissing all pleadings and petitions seeking to cancel and set aside the conveyances mentioned.

The whole history of the litigation up to that time will be found in the case of Best, Receiver, v. Melcon, 183 Ky. 785, 210 S. W. 662.

Upon the return of the case to the Laurel circuit court, a judgment was entered setting aside so much of the former judgment as adjudged the conveyances in question preferential, and adjudged the property therein conveyed to be sold and the proceeds collected by the receiver.

After the proceeds of the sale had been brought into court, the appellee Boreing entered a motion that his proportionate part of the proceeds of that land, amounting to $993.35, be paid to him, and this motion the circuit court sustained and directed its officers to pay that amount to Boreing, and from that action of the court this appeal is prosecuted by the present receiver of the London bank.

This action was taken by Boreing upon the theory that the original judgment of the Laurel circuit court, adjudging that the several conveyances involved were preferential, was to the extent of his claim against W. B. Catching proportionately for his benefit, and that as he was not a party to the appeal wherein the judgment was reversed, it was still in force and effect in so far as his rights were involved.

[1] The fundamental error in this position is in the assumption that any judgment was ever entered in the Laurel circuit court for his benefit as an individual. The effect of the judgment, so far as he was concerned, was that he was a general creditor of W. B. Catching, but that he was not entitled to have certain property described by him subjected to the payment of that judgment, and therefore his petition was dismissed and a judgment for costs entered against him.

He sought one kind of relief solely for his own benefit, which was denied him, while the plaintiffs in some of the other suits sought a different kind of relief, not only for their own benefit, but for the benefit of all the creditors of Catching, and that relief was by the circuit court granted to them, and Boreing, being a general creditor of Catching, was only incidentally the beneficiary of their action, and as an individual was granted no relief whatsoever against anybody, but, on the contrary, was dismissed out of court with a judgment for costs against him.

It is perfectly clear that from the time that Boreing's petition was dismissed with costs and all relief denied him, he occupied the position only of any other general creditor of W. B. Catching, and occupying that position, he was not a necessary party to any appeal by the receiver of the bank to reverse that judgment any more than any other general creditor of Catching would have been, and therefore, when the mandate of this court was filed in the lower court and, in accordance therewith, the judgment of that court set aside, Boreing had no more claim upon the proceeds of that property than any other general creditor of Catching. When his petition was dismissed, he was just as effectually out of court as if he had never filed it, and occupied no position different from that of any other general creditor who had filed a claim in the action.

[2] In an action to have a preference adjudged and that it operate as an assignment for the benefit of all creditors, all the creditors are not necessary parties any more than all are necessary parties in the settlement of a decedent's estate. Ky. Stats. § 1912. Certainly then they are not all necessary parties to an appeal in such case.

The judgment is reversed, with directions to set aside the order appealed from.

SCOTT et al. v. THACKER COAL MINING CO. et al.

(Court of Appeals of Kentucky. March 22, 1921. Rehearing Denied June 21, 1921.)

Boundaries ⊜3(3)—Natural object held to control over courses and distances.

The calls for courses and distances in a patent *held*, on the evidence, to be controlled by a call for a natural object, under the rule that, where there is a conflict between courses and distances and natural objects, the latter will control.

Appeal from Circuit Court, Pike County.

Action by Martha Scott, revived in the name of her heirs, Emery Scott and others, against the Thacker Coal Mining Company, in which defendant by counterclaim interpleaded the heirs of Richard Daniels, deceased. Judgment in favor of the Daniels heirs, and the Scott heirs appeal. Reversed, with directions.

See, also, 160 Ky. 365, 169 S. W. 830.

Willis Staton, of Pikeville, for appellants. P. B. Stratton, J. J. Moore, J. F. Butler, and J. S. Cline, all of Pikeville, for appellees.

TURNER, C. In June, 1900, Martha Scott leased certain lands on the Tug fork of Big Sandy river in Pike county to the Thacker Coal Mining Company for coal mining purposes. Prior thereto, in December, 1897, Richard Daniels and his wife leased to the same company for the same purposes adjoining tracts of land.

The coal company opened up the mining operations on these tracts of land, and, having failed for a time to pay to Martha Scott the royalty to which she thought she was entitled on certain lands claimed to have been embraced in her boundary, she originally brought this suit, asking judgment for the amount of such royalties.

The coal company answered, admitting its

operations under the lease from Mrs. Scott, and alleging that it was also operating under certain leases from Daniels on adjoining lands, and alleging that both Scott and Daniels were claiming that a certain tract of land upon which the company was operating was embraced in their several leases, and each claiming the royalties therefrom, and made its answer a counterclaim against the heirs of Daniels, and asked that the controversy between them be settled, and that it be directed by the court to whom it should pay the royalties.

The Daniels people came in and asserted their title to the disputed boundary, and the circuit court, upon a trial, in effect adjudged that neither of the parties had shown title in themselves, and therefore declined to adjudge the royalties to either.

They each appealed to this court from the judgment, and it was reversed, with directions to the lower court to establish the line and dispose of the royalties between the parties. Scott v. Daniels, 160 Ky. 365, 169 S. W. 830.

Upon the return of the case there was additional preparation, and upon a hearing the court adjudged the disputed boundary to the Daniels heirs, and from that judgment the Scott heirs have appealed.

Martha Scott is a daughter of Ephraim Hatfield and claims under a deed from him, and Ephraim Hatfield claimed under two patents, one issued in 1850 to Ferrell Evans, and the other to Ephraim Hatfield in 1867; the Daniels people claim under certain other patents, but only claim to the Evans or Hatfield line; and so the vital thing in the controversy is a proper determination of where the Evans or Hatfield line is located, the lines of the Evans and Hatfield patents being the same so far as they affect the land in controversy.

Hatfield was the owner in 1867 of the Evans patent of 350 acres, and a patent was then issued to Hatfield for 793 acres, embracing the Evans 350-acre patent, together with certain other previously patented lands, and still other lands claimed to have been vacant.

It is agreed between the parties that the calls in the two patents in question—the Evans and Hatfield patents—only affect this controversy after they leave the bank of the river at the mouth of Bear Tree Hollow. The evidence shows that the survey made for appellants at that point begins right at the bank of the river at or near the mouth of that small branch, while that made for the appellees, or at their suggestion, began some 75 to 90 feet away from the bank of the river, and that made only a slight divergence between them up to the point where the real disputed call comes in, which will be hereafter noticed. But, inasmuch as appellants' survey began immediately at the bank of the river, and the previous call in

the two patents calls for "two sycamores on the bank of said river," we have concluded that the beginning point at the mouth of that branch was more accurate in appellants' survey. From that point on the calls in the Evans patent are as follows:

"Thence S. 21° W. 20 poles to a lynn and beech in Bear Tree Hollow; thence leaving the calls of said former survey [referring to a 150-acre previous survey made for Evans] S. 18° E. 52 poles to a white oak, hickory and sarvis on top of a ridge; S. 20° W. 134 po. to two chestnut oaks, on top of the ridge between Sugar Camp branch and Pound Mill branch; S. 83° W. 22 poles to a black oak and two hickories on the top of said ridge; S. 19° W. 53 poles to three white oaks; S. 4° W. 140 poles to a white oak, sourwood and gum in the gap at the head of the branch that empties into said river at said Evans' house."

The calls from that point in the Hatfield patent are as follows:

"Thence S. 21° W. 20 poles to a lynn and beech in the Bear Tree Hollow; S. 18° E. 52 poles to a white oak, hickory and sarvis on top of the ridge; S. 20° W. 134 poles to two chestnut oaks on top of the ridge between the Sugar Camp and Pounding Mill branch; S. 83° W. 22 poles to a black and two hickories on top of sd. ridge; S. 19° W. 53 poles to two white oaks; S. 4° W. 140 poles to a white oak, sourwood and gum in the gap at the head of the branch that empties into the river just above sd. Hatfield's house."

Appellants claim that the call S. 20° W. 134 poles should be extended so as to reach the natural object called for at B, while appellees claim it should stop at A, and thence run with the ridge to C, and thence on the east and west ridge.

All the evidence in the record shows that the house referred to in these calls was occupied by Evans when his survey was made and patented in 1849 and 1850, and that the same house was occupied by Hatfield when his survey and patent were made and issued in 1866 and 1867.

The survey upon which Evans' patent was issued calls for two chestnut oaks on top of the ridge between Sugar Camp branch and the Pond Mill branch. So that we have in one survey a stream called the Pond Mill branch, and in the patent issued on that survey we have a stream called the Pound Mill branch, and in a subsequent one embracing the same land, and with the same calls, we have a stream called the Pounding Mill branch.

For a long time during the preparation of this case, before the first appeal, these were all treated as referring to the same stream, to wit, Pounding Mill branch, as shown on the map herewith filed, which, as will be observed, flows into the Tug river, its general direction being south, on the opposite side of the ridge from the Sugar Camp or Ferrell Evans branch, the latter branch flowing north into the same river on the other side of a considerable bend in the river. But after the case had been submitted for hearing in the circuit court before the first appeal the appellees had the order of submission set aside upon a showing in affidavits that they had learned that at one time in the past what is shown on the map as Fish Trap branch had been called Pond Mill branch, and that therefore the call in the two patents "S. 20° W. 134 poles to two chestnut oaks on top of the ridge between Sugar Camp and Pound, or Pounding Mill branch" really meant the ridge running north and south between the waters of said Fish Trap branch and Sugar Camp branch, and did not refer to the ridge running east and west between the headwaters of the Sugar Camp branch and the Pounding Mill branch. Accordingly the order of submission was set aside, and one of the appellees in a second deposition given by her states that she was born about 1850 in this immediate locality, and that in her childhood she had heard older persons refer to the Fish Trap branch as Pond Mill branch, and that there yet remains evidence of an old dam on the Fish Trap branch showing that in days gone by there had been a milldam there.

This evidence was taken by the appellees in an effort to explain away the call in the two patents for the ridge between the waters of Sugar Camp and Pound or Pounding Mill branch, because in the absence of a satisfactory explanation of that call it is recognized that the courses and distances in the patent must give way before the natural objects called for in them. In other words, even though the call for 134 poles gives out at a point which does not reach the ridge called for, in order to reach such natural object it will be extended so as reach it, thereby following the well-recognized rule of law that courses and distances must give way to well known natural objects.

But this evidence that in her childhood the Fish Trap branch had been called at times the Pond Mill branch is not substantiated by the other reliable evidence in the record. On the contrary, in the many deeds and patents and surveys which are introduced in evidence in this record, many of them older than the witness claims to be, that stream is referred to only as the Fish Trap branch, and not in one single instance, so far as our search of the record discloses, has it been referred to as the Pond Mill branch.

Our conclusion therefore is, from the whole evidence and from an examination of all these surveys and patents, that the ridge called for between the waters of Sugar Camp branch and Pound or Pounding Mill branch is the ridge running east and west, or approximately east and west, and which the call in question when extended reaches at or about the point of that ridge where it turns north, which is shown to be the dividing ridge between the headwaters of those two streams.

That this conclusion is proper must be apparent when we consider that, if it be conceded that Fish Trap branch was once sometimes called Pond Mill branch, the point on the ridge running north and south at which appellees claim the 134-pole call gives out is not in fact on the ridge between Fish Trap branch and Sugar Camp branch, but is on a ridge between the Fish Trap branch and the headwaters of the Tinnie branch, which runs into the river east of the mouth of Sugar Camp branch; there being a spur or ridge shooting off from the north and south ridge which divides the waters of the Sugar Camp branch from the waters of Tinnie branch and another small branch, and makes it impossible for the waters of Sugar Camp branch to reach the point where they claim that call gives out and should stop.

On the other hand, the map on file and all the evidence shows that, if the call of 134 poles is correct and must stop at the point where it gives out, it does not reach the ridge between Sugar Camp branch and Pounding Mill branch by nearly 200 poles at the nearest point, and it is therefore argued by appellants that the 134-pole call is manifestly a mistake, and that it was intended originally to be a 314-pole call, the figures "1" and "3" being by mistake transposed, which would in fact and does reach the ridge at the nearest point between the waters of Sugar Camp branch and Pounding Mill branch.

The evidence that the Fish Trap branch was ever known or called Pond Mill branch being unsatisfactory, and the fact being apparent that, if it had been, the 134-pole call would not end at a point on a ridge between the waters of Fish Trap or Pond Mill branch and the waters of Sugar Camp branch, the conclusion seems irresistible that there must have been some mistake in the distance of the original call, and that the call for the natural object—that is, the ridge between the waters of Pounding Mill branch and Sugar Camp branch—must prevail.

It has long been the rule in this state that, in the location of lines from descriptions in title papers, if there is a conflict between courses and distances and natural objects called for, the latter will control, and the courses and distances will be changed or modified so as to conform to the natural objects called for.

Natural objects have a fixed place; they are there for all time, while courses and disances as shown by title papers are merely records made by men and which may or may not be accurate. And not only so; it is a matter of practical knowledge that surveyors ordinarily make up their reports long after they have actually run the lines, if in fact they do actually run them. And the rule is therefore based upon the sound assumption that, if there is a mistake, it is in the courses and distances, and not in the fixed location of natural objects. Kentweva Coal & Lumber Co. v. Helton, 170 Ky. 211, 185 S. W. 838; Rush v. Cornett, 169 Ky. 714, 185 S. W. 88; Gilbert v. Parrott, 168 Ky. 599, 182 S. W. 859.

Our conclusion that the call in question should be extended to the natural object called for is further strongly fortified by a right at the head of the main fork of the branch called the Sugar Camp branch which flows into the river right at or near Hatfield's house, being the same house formerly occupied by Evans, and called for in both patents.

It is conceded by the parties on both sides that the surveyor will not close if the lines are run as contended by either party, and we confess that after long, diligent, and earnest labor we have been unable to reach any conclusion in any way satisfactory to ourselves except to apply the rule that we have applied as to the natural objects involved.

We have prepared and file herewith a small map to be published with this opinion, giving some idea of the nature of this controversy.

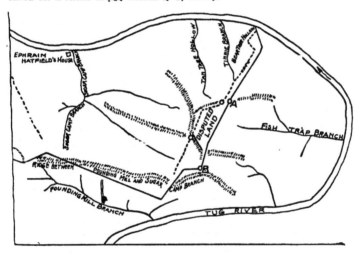

subsequent call in the patent for another natural object, to wit:

"S. 4° W. 140 poles to a white oak, sourwood, and gum in the gap at the head of the branch that empties into the river just above said Hatfield's house."

Although the course fixed in this call is clearly wrong, the map on file as well as all the evidence shows that there is such a gap

It results from what we have said that when the Hatfield or Evans line is located with reference to these natural objects, it embraces the disputed land in plaintiffs' conveyance, and it and the royalties should have been adjudged to them.

The judgment is reversed, with directions to enter a judgment, as herein indicated.

CLARKE, J., not sitting.

COMMONWEALTH v. MILBURN.

(Court of Appeals of Kentucky. May 31, 1921.)

1. **Criminal law ⟨⟩814(20) — Instruction to convict of petit larceny properly refused, where evidence showed market value of stolen property more than $20.**

In a prosecution for receiving stolen property, it was not error to refuse an instruction, authorizing the jury to punish defendant as in case of petit larceny; there being no conflict of evidence as to the value of the whisky stolen being in excess of $20.

2. **Criminal law ⟨⟩736(1)—Whether certain persons were accomplices of defendant held for the jury on conflicting evidence.**

In an action for receiving stolen property, where the evidence was conflicting as to whether certain alleged accomplices possessed such guilty knowledge of the property having been stolen as made them in law accomplices of defendant, it was proper for the court to submit the question to the jury.

3. **Criminal law ⟨⟩1134(4)—Court cannot reverse order granting new trial in felony case.**

The court, on an appeal by the commonwealth, can review any ruling of the trial court and declare its opinion of the law thereon, but it cannot, in a case of felony, reverse an order granting a new trial.

Appeal from Circuit Court, Daviess County.

John Milburn was found guilty of receiving stolen property. From an order granting a new trial, the commonwealth appeals. Conclusion that grant of new trial was unauthorized certified to trial court as the law of the case.

Chas. I. Dawson, Atty. Gen., Thos. B. McGregor, Asst. Atty. Gen., and C. E. Smith, of Hartford, for the Commonwealth.

Aud & Higdon, of Owensboro, for appellee.

SETTLE, J. The appellee, John Milburn, jointly with Dorris Hawkins, Berry Tichenor, and Herman Lyons, was indicted in the Daviess circuit court for the crime of unlawfully, willfully, and feloniously receiving stolen property from Robert Bryan, knowing at the time that it had been stolen. The property, as charged in the indictment, consisted of a number of cases of whisky, of greater value than $20, belonging to Hugh Herr, and had been stolen from him. The appellee was accorded a separate trial, which resulted in a verdict from the jury finding him guilty of the crime charged and fixing his punishment at confinement in the penitentiary for a period of one year. Within proper time he filed a motion and grounds for a new trial, which motion was sustained, and a new trial granted him by the circuit court. To this ruling the commonwealth by its attorney excepted, and from the order granting the new trial has appealed.

It appears that the appellee was granted a new trial: First, because of the opinion of the trial court that he was prejudiced in his substantial rights by its failure to give an instruction under which the jury might have determined whether he was guilty, as in a case of petit larceny, and have inflicted upon him the same punishment provided for that offense, if they found that the stolen property he was charged to have received was not of as great value as $20; second, that the court also erred to appellee's further prejudice in failing to instruct the jury, as a matter of law, that certain witnesses, whose testimony was given in behalf of the commonwealth, were accomplices of appellee, instead of instructing them, as was done, that they should determine from the evidence whether they were such.

[1] Regarding the first of these supposed errors, it is sufficient to say that an instruction authorizing the jury to find appellee guilty as in a case of petit larceny, and to inflict upon him the punishment applicable to that offense, would not have been proper, as there was no evidence on which to base such instruction. The only evidence as to the value of the whisky was that it was of superior brands, known as "Old Stone" and "Hill & Hill"; that its market value was $100 per case of 12 quarts, and that two or more cases of the stolen whisky were twice in appellee's possession, at least one of which he retained by leaving it at the house of a friend. There was a contrariety of evidence as to whether he had any knowledge that the whisky had been stolen, but no conflict of evidence as to its value. We repeatedly have held that such an instruction as that in question is improper, in the absence of evidence to support it. Klette v. Commonwealth, 165 Ky. 430, 177 S. W. 258; Stephens v. Commonwealth, 164 Ky. 265, 175 S. W. 353.

[2] The second supposed error referred to is as unsubstantial as the first. The evidence was quite conflicting as to whether the alleged accomplices who testified on appellee's trial were in fact such. Notwithstanding the fact that some of the alleged accomplices were jointly indicted with appellant, the evidence was conflicting as to whether they or any of them possessed such guilty knowledge of the whisky's having been stolen as made them in law accomplices of appellee. Personally, one might well believe from the circumstances that they were, but whether they were was a matter to be determined from the evidence; hence it was proper for the court to submit the question to the jury for decision, as was done. This action of the trial court has received our approval in the following cases: Anderson v. Commonwealth,

181 Ky. 311, 204 S. W. 71; Richardson v. Commonwealth, 166 Ky. 570, 179 S. W. 458; Elmendorf v. Commonwealth, 171 Ky. 410, 188 S. W. 483; Levering v. Commonwealth, 132 Ky. 666, 117 S. W. 253, 136 Am. St. Rep. 192, 19 Ann. Cas. 140; Smith v. Commonwealth, 148 Ky. 69, 146 S. W. 4.

[3] We cannot, however, agree with counsel for the commonwealth that the order of the circuit court, granting appellee a new trial, should be reversed, and a judgment of conviction entered against him in that court upon the verdict of the jury. The order granting a new trial in a criminal prosecution is not a final judgment, and cannot be reversed, by this court on appeal. It has authority, on appeal by the commonwealth, to review any ruling of the trial court complained of as error, and to declare its opinion of the law thereon, but it cannot, in a case of felony, reverse a judgment of acquittal or an order granting a new trial. Commonwealth v. Hourigan, 89 Ky. 305, 12 S. W. 550, 11 Ky. Law Rep. 509; Commonwealth v. Brogan, 163 Ky. 748, 174 S. W. 473; Commonwealth v. Brand, 166 Ky. 753, 179 S. W. 844.

It is our conclusion that the action of the court below in granting appellee a new trial was unauthorized on any of the grounds urged therefor, and this conclusion is hereby certified to that court as the law of the case.

RIDDLE v. JONES.

(Court of Appeals of Kentucky.   June 8, 1921.)

1. **Easements ⟐⟐36(3) — Conveyance held to show signature to grant of easement was genuine.**

In an action to restrain the use of a passway across plaintiff's farm, evidence *held* to show that the signature of plaintiff's grantor to an instrument conveying the passway to defendant's predecessor in title was genuine and not forged.

2. **Easements ⟐⟐53—Witnesses ⟐⟐140(19)—Conveyance held quitclaim deed so that grantor had no interest which disqualified him as witness.**

A warranty deed to a farm, conveying all the right vested in the grantor to use the passway now existing over plaintiff's land, was only a quitclaim deed so far as that passway was concerned, and therefore the grantor had no interest in the maintenance of the passway which would make him incompetent to testify to the signature of plaintiff's deceased grantor to the instrument creating the passway.

3. **Easements ⟐⟐36(3)—Evidence held not to show undue influence in obtaining conveyance of easement.**

Evidence which only showed that the owners of adjoining farms were close friends and consulted each other in business transactions does

not show undue influence by one in obtaining from the other an easement for a passway across the farm.

4. **Easements ⟐⟐24—Exchange of roads establishes sufficient consideration for grant of each easement.**

An instrument trading a road to defendant across the farm owned by plaintiff to a highway in exchange for a road across defendant's farm to another farm owned by plaintiff's grantor, who executed the instrument, shows sufficient consideration for the grant of each easement.

5. **Easements ⟐⟐12(3)—Indefiniteness of road description is cured by passway established on ground.**

Even if the description of a proposed easement for a passway from defendant's farm to a highway would be too uncertain to be enforced while the conveyance remained executory, it is sufficient after it has been executed by the establishment of the passway upon the ground.

6. **Easements ⟐⟐3(2)—Presumed to be appurtenant and not in gross.**

Easements creating private passways are never presumed to be personal or in gross when they can be construed to be appurtenant to the land, since the law favors such construction as will create a covenant running with the land.

7. **Easements ⟐⟐3(2)—Passway held to be appurtenant and not in gross.**

An instrument granting an easement for a passway across plaintiff's farm, which stated that it was to be for the use of the two farms and no other, shows that it was appurtenant and not in gross.

8. **Acknowledgment ⟐⟐5—Acknowledgment unnecessary to make instrument binding on parties and privies with notice.**

The acknowledgment of an instrument conveying real estate is primarily to entitle the instrument to be recorded, and the absence of such acknowledgment does not render the instrument void as between the parties and their privies in estate without notice.

9. **Descent and distribution ⟐⟐129—Easements ⟐⟐22—Heir or gratuitous grantee is bound by unacknowledged conveyance, though having no notice.**

An heir or gratuitous grantee is bound by the unacknowledged written instrument conveying an easement over the premises, though he has neither actual nor constructive notice of its execution, and he takes his estate incumbered with the easement.

Appeal from Circuit Court, Owen County.

Action by Susie G. Riddle against Robert C. Jones to enjoin trespass on plaintiff's land by passing across it in going from defendant's farm to the turnpike. From a judgment dismissing the petition, plaintiff appeals. Affirmed.

W. A. Lee, of Owenton, for appellant.
J. G. Vallandingham, of Owenton, for appellee.

THÓMAS, J. The appellant and plaintiff below, Susie G. Riddle, owns an estate for her life in a farm located in Owen county containing about 200 acres, the south line of which is the New Liberty and Garnett turnpike. Her interest was conveyed to her by deed of gift from her father, Thomas Gayle, which he executed on December 12, 1908; but the grantee was not to have possession until the death of her father, the grantor, which occurred on April 23, 1917. Adjoining the 200 acres on the north is a tract of land containing 183 acres, known in this record as the Brock farm, but which was conveyed to J. C. Jones, the father of appellee and defendant below Robert C. Jones, by deed dated March 1, 1907, and which was executed pursuant to a contract theretofore entered into on January 1, 1907. Adjoining the Brock farm on the north is one containing about 100 acres, known in this record as the Cull farm, and it was also owned by Thomas Gayle, the father of plaintiff, from a time prior to 1907 till he conveyed it by deed of gift to another daughter before his death. J. C. Jones died on August 31, 1914, leaving surviving him the defendant, Robert C. Jones, and other heirs who inherited the Brock farm, but which is now owned entirely by the defendant; he having purchased the interest of the other joint tenants.

On April 15, 1918, plaintiff filed this action against defendant seeking to enjoin him and his tenants from trespassing on her land by passing over and across it in going from defendant's farm to the New Liberty and Garnett turnpike, and she obtained a temporary restraining order issued by the clerk of the Owen circuit court enjoining defendant from the commission of any of the acts complained of, but which was afterwards dissolved by the circuit judge upon a hearing pursuant to notice. Defendant answered traversing in the main the allegations of the petition and affirmatively alleging that he owned a right of easement to travel from his farm across that of plaintiff to the turnpike, which easement was created by a writing which Thomas Gayle, plaintiff's father, and J. C. Jones, the defendant's father, jointly executed for the mutual benefit of their respective farms on January 7, 1907, and which (omitting dates and signatures) reads:

"This agreement made and entered into Between Thomas Gayle & J. C. Jones, we to (two) have this day traded roades, I Thomas Gayle have this day traded J. C. Jones a roade through my farme for one through the Brock farme to get to the Cull farme, said roade is to bee for the use of these too farmes & no other. Said pass way is gated, each party to keepe up his gates."

At that time there was a road leaving the turnpike and traversing plaintiff's 200-acre tract to the Brock farm and passing through it to the Cull farm. It left the pike at the corner of the yard to the residence of Thomas Gayle and passed through some lots, and upon it there were a number of gates, as there were also gates at some points in it where it traversed the Brock farm. That passway had been used by the owners and occupants of the Cull and the Brock farms, and perhaps others in the neighborhood north of plaintiff's land, in practically the same location as it was when this suit was filed, for more than 50 years, but which use plaintiff claims was all the while permissive only; but whether so or not it is immaterial in this case, since defendant relies on the writing hereinbefore inserted.

Plaintiff, by reply, sought to avoid the effect of that writing by (1) a plea of non est factum; (2) undue influence exercised upon Thomas Gayle by J. C. Jones whereby the former was induced to sign it, if he did so; (3) a plea of no consideration; (4) that if mistaken in all of the above the paper was too indefinite to be enforced; and (5) that it by its terms did not create an appurtenant easement, but only one in gross which terminated with the death of J. C. Jones. Proper responsive pleadings made the issues, and upon submission, after extensive proof taken, the larger part of which is wholly incompetent and irrelevant, the court dismissed the petition, and to reverse that judgment plaintiff prosecutes this appeal.

[1] There is scarcely any substantial testimony in the record supporting the plea of non est factum, relied on in avoidance (1). Even the plaintiff herself in giving her testimony under oath would not say that the signature of "Thomas Gayle" to the writing relied on by defendant was not made by her father. When asked the direct question by her attorney, she answered:

"The 'Gayle' looks natural, but the 'Thomas' does not. I can't say positively whether it is or not."

Her brother, English Gayle, who was perhaps her most active witness, said that, "I think that my father did not sign the signature." He gave as his reasons for so thinking that he had compared the signature with others made by his father, and he concluded there was a discrepancy between them, and that his father had frequently told him that he had not given or sold a road through his farm (which was incompetent), and because of these two reasons witness thought his father did not sign the writing. A sister of plaintiff is the only witness who says positively that her father did not sign it, but she gave no satisfactory reason for her opinion. Opposing this testimony is that of Fred Jones, a brother of defendant, who testified that he saw Thomas Gayle sign his name to the writing in contest. A number of witnesses who were familiar with the handwriting of plaintiff's father testified that from their familiarity with it they believed the signature in question was genuine. Bank cashiers with whom Thomas Gayle did business also testified that according to their best opinion the questioned signature was made by him. Fortifying all of the above positive oral testimony, the original deed, which Thomas Gayle executed to plaintiff, was filed in the case and has been brought to this court for our inspection, as has also the paper expressly granting the easement in question, and the two signatures are so similar in their construction and contour as to leave no doubt in the mind of even a layman as to such subjects that the two signatures were made by the same person. There are also some original checks signed by Thomas Gayle brought here with the record, and to them, in signing his given name, he would write it "Tom" or "Thom," but the surname "Gayle" signed thereto is identical with the same name on the writing in question, and it is shown beyond dispute that Mr. Gayle, when executing any writing relating to real estate or any interest therein, would always write his given name in full, while he would abbreviate it in his signatures to other writings. We therefore not only have the finding of the chancellor upon this issue of fact, but we find the testimony in the record overwhelmingly supporting his conclusion thereon.

[2] But it is said that the witness Fred Jones was an incompetent one under the provisions of section 606 of the Civil Code of Practice, since he was liable on his warranty in his deed conveying his interest in the Brock farm, and he was therefore a party in interest, though not one in name, and was forbidden, under the provisions of the section of the Code referred to, from testifying to the execution of the grant by Thomas Gayle. This would perhaps be true if the facts assumed by plaintiff's counsel were true, but which the record shows to be otherwise. The deed executed by Fred Jones was only a quitclaim deed so far as the passway in question was concerned. It says on that subject:

"This deed conveys to grantee all the right vested in grantor (Fred Jones) to use the passway now existing and used through the lands of R. C. Jones and Thomas Gayle's land."

That language contains no warranty concerning the passway, and Fred Jones having no interest, direct or remote, in the subject-matter of the litigation, he was a competent witness to prove the facts to which he testified.

[3] In support of avoidance (2), the only testimony offered or introduced was that of a number of witnesses showing that Thomas Gayle and J. C. Jones were fast friends and almost inseparable in their associations.

Each had great confidence in the other, and they consulted each other about their business transactions and affairs. This character of testimony is so wholly insufficient to establish the fact for which it was introduced that we deem it unnecessary to further consider this ground.

[4] Avoidance (3) is equally as unsupported as is the one last considered. The writing on its face shows a sufficient consideration for its execution. Thomas Gayle was as much interested in having a passway over the Brock farm to his Cull farm, lying as we have seen to the north of defendant's farm, as J. C. Jones was interested in having a passway from his farm over Gayle's farm to the turnpike. The parties by the very language they employed "traded roades," Gayle giving one to Jones through his farm in consideration of the latter giving one through his farm to the former. There could scarcely be expressed a more substantial consideration.

[5] In disposing of avoidance (4), we might assume for argument's sake (but which we are unwilling to indorse as a correct proposition under the facts in this case) that if the writing in dispute was purely executory, it would not be enforceable because of uncertainty and indefiniteness of its terms. But, long before this suit was brought, and almost immediately after the execution of the disputed writing, the parties to it located the passway across each of their farms where it has been maintained and used constantly since that time and without objection till a short while before the filing of this suit. If the contract at the time it was executed was not enforceable because of uncertainty, that defect was removed by the act of the parties which cured the uncertainty of its terms by the actual location of the passway upon the ground (Bowling v. Rouse, 90 S. W. 1073, 28 Ky. Law Rep. 1037), and after such location and mutual user, it does not lie in the mouth of either party, or any privy of his, with notice (though for a valuable consideration) to repudiate the agreement because of its alleged indefinite and uncertain terms (O. & O. Ry. Co. v. Richardson, 98 S. W. 1042, 30 Ky. Law Rep. 426).

[6] Avoidance (5) is also easily disposed of. Easements consisting of private passways are never presumed to be personal (or in gross) when they can be construed to be appurtenant to the land. The law favors such construction of the grant as will create a covenant running with the land. As said in the case of Hammonds v. Eads, 146 Ky. 162, 142 S. W. 379:

"This [a passway in gross] is never to be presumed when it can be fairly construed to be appurtenant to some other estate; that an easement is appurtenant and not in gross when it appears that it was granted for the benefit of the grantee's land."

See, also, Johns v. Davis, 76 S. W. 187 (not elsewhere reported).

[7] It appears from the face of the writing here involved that the easement therein granted was "for the benefit of the grantee's land," for it says that "said roade is to bee for the use of these too farmes & no other." There is no doubt about the passway in question being an appurtenant one and running with the title to the lands for the benefit of which it was created, and not one in gross.

[8] But it is insisted that though the writing may not be inoperative, for any of the reasons discussed above, it was not legally executed because it purports to convey an interest in land and it was not acknowledged according to law. It has been frequently held by this court that the statutory requirement as to the acknowledgment of deeds was primarily for the purpose of enabling the grantee to place them on record so as to give constructive notice to the world; for unless their execution be proven according to the statutory requirements, they cannot be recorded. But the omission of such requirements does not prevent the writing from conveying an enforceable interest as between the parties and their privies in estate with notice. 19 Corpus Juris, 907.

[9] But an heir or a gratuitous grantee who obtained their interest without the payment of a valuable consideration is bound by the unacknowledged written instrument, although he has neither actual nor constructive notice of its execution, and takes his estate incumbered with the burdens which the unacknowledged and unrecorded instrument creates. Having paid no valuable consideration, such privies in estate have no intervening equities to be protected, because of the absence of notice, and their rights are subordinate to prior equities though they be secret ones. This is in conformity with the rule that an heir or a gratuitous grantee takes no greater interest than was possessed by his ancestor or grantor. Field's Heirs v. Napier, 26 Ky. Law Rep. 240, 80 S. W. 1110. The plaintiff, Mrs. Riddle, obtained her land from her father under a deed of gift from him, while defendant inherited a part of his farm and purchased his other interest in it after actual knowledge of the existence of the writing in question. Both plaintiff and defendant, therefore, are bound by its terms, and they are each obligated to permit the other to use the passway for the purpose for which it was created, and neither of them can close or obstruct it to the detriment of the other.

Other points are discussed, most of which are based upon wholly irrelevant issues and which are supported by equally irrelevant and incompetent testimony, and none of which do we deem it necessary to consider.

Wherefore the judgment is affirmed.

BARRIGER v. BRYAN et al.

(Court of Appeals of Kentucky. June 8, 1921.)

Principal and agent ☞103(11)—Agent to sell land authorized to sell for cash, and principal not bound by other sale, in absence of ratification.

The owner of land who authorizes his agent to sell authorizes a sale for cash only, and where there is no acceptance by the owner of cash given in part payment, nor any other act on his part from which ratification may be inferred, he is not bound by any act of his agent by the terms of which the latter undertook to sell the property on terms different from those of cash as authorized.

Appeal from Circuit Court, Simpson County.

Suit by J. M. Bryan and others against D. S. Barriger. From judgment for plaintiffs, defendant appeals. Reversed for further proceedings.

Rodman Grubbs, Grubbs & Grubbs, and William Marshall Bullitt, all of Louisville, and G. T. Finn and L. B. Finn, both of Franklin, for appellant.

John B. Rhodes and Sims, Rodes & Sims, all of Bowling Green, and Geo. W. Roark and G. C. Harris, both of Franklin, for appellees.

QUIN, J. Appellant owned a farm of 227 acres near the city of Franklin. Being a nonresident of the state, he secured the services of a boyhood friend, an attorney, to look after this farm. For a number of years said representative had entire charge of the place, including the renting thereof, the care of the property, the erection of outbuildings, attention to repairs, painting, etc.; in fact, he did everything the owner could have done had he been present. As an attorney he represented appellant in certain litigation pertaining to the property and in the purchase of a portion of the farm; he also negotiated a loan with a local bank to take care of the purchase price.

From 1914 to 1917 many letters were written by appellant to his agent, in which he impressed upon the latter that the writer's purpose was to get the property in condition for sale. The agent made repeated efforts to dispose of the property, and on July 30, 1917, submitted an offer of $60 per acre, which included the crops. This offer was declined by appellant in a letter written to his agent on the 13th of the following month. Under the impression he was vested with full authority to contract for the sale of the property at $60 per acre, the agent, on August 11, 1917, entered into a written contract with appellees by the terms of which he undertook to sell the property to appellees for the sum of $60

---

per acre, payable one-third in cash, the balance in equal payments due in one and two years, possession to be given January 1, 1918. Said agent, on behalf of appellant, further agreed, at the owner's expense, to have the farm divided as appellees might desire. As soon as appellant received notice of the execution of the contract of sale, he immediately telegraphed his agent, declining to approve the sale and stating that his price for the farm was $100 per acre, and he would not accept $60. Thereupon the purchasers instituted this suit, seeking the specific performance of the contract, and upon trial the prayer of their petition was granted and the commissioner was ordered to execute a deed conveying the land to appellees. This appeal followed.

Appellees contend that Harris, the agent, was authorized to sell the property for $60 per acre, and to enter into a binding contract at that price, and only in the event he received an offer for a less amount was he required to submit it to his principal for approval. It is the contention of appellant that he never authorized Harris to sell the land, but merely requested him to find a purchaser and to submit to him for approval any offer he might receive.

Appellant's letters prior to December, 1916, are susceptible of the construction for which appellees contend, viz. an authorization to Harris to sell the property for $60 per acre; but appellant testifies that on the date last above mentioned, while on a visit to Franklin, he had a talk with Harris in which he expressly told him (Harris) that the price for the farm from that date would be $100 per acre, though he might consider offers for a less amount. The substance of this conversation as given by appellant finds corroboration in the testimony of two other witnesses.

Harris admits having had this conference with appellant, but, as he understood it, appellant merely suggested that they ask $100 per acre for the land; he did not understand appellant to withdraw his former price of $60. No letters subsequent to December, 1916, throw any light upon the subject. One cannot read the letters and the testimony of the witnesses without the mind being left in doubt as to what was the real understanding between the parties in regard to the disposition of the property. Color is given to the theory of appellant in the fact that in the letter of July 30, 1917, Harris submitted for approval an offer of $60 per acre. If, as appellees contend, Harris had authority to close a deal at that price, he would not have had any reason to submit it to his principal for approval. But we do not find it necessary to decide this question, in view of a further

point raised by counsel, which is decisive of this appeal.

Granting that appellant had the authority to sell, it is insisted Harris exceeded his authority in the making of said contract. A mere contract to sell implies a sale for cash. The right of an agent to sell on credit land placed in his charge depends largely upon his contract of employment. It is a general rule stated by the text-writers and supported by many authorities that, in the absence of special authority, the agent must sell for cash only; he cannot sell on credit, nor even for part cash and part in time payments. Unless there is proof of an established usage of trade or business to the effect that such an authority vests in the agent the power to sell on credit (and no such custom is shown here), an authority or direction to sell real estate does not carry with it the right to sell on credit. Where there is no acceptance by the principal of the cash given in part payment, nor of any other act on his part from which a ratification might be inferred, he is not bound by any act of his agent by the terms of which the latter undertakes to sell property upon terms different from those authorized, such, for example, as Harris undertook to do in the contract sued on. See C. J. 617; 21 R. C. L. 886; Mechem on Agency, § 814; Paige on Contracts, § 1747; Burks v. Hubbard, 69 Ala. 879; School Dist. v. Ætna Ins. Co., 62 Me. 330; Stengel v. Sergeant, etc., 74 N. J. Eq. 20, 68 Atl. 1106; Lumpkin v. Wilson, etc., 5 Heisk. (Tenn.) 555; Horst, etc., v. Lightfoot, etc., 103 Tex. 643, 132 S. W. 761. At most Harris had nothing other than a mere authority to sell.

The record does not show any authority vested in him to sell upon terms other than cash, from which it follows that in the execution of the contract relied upon he exceeded his authority to such an extent that it is not binding on his principal. Nor was he authorized to agree to bear the expense of subdividing the farm. This subdivision was made necessary by a sale to three persons (appellees), each of whom intended to pay a given part of the purchase price and to receive land in proportion to the amount of their individual investment.

These conclusions in no wise reflect upon the integrity and honesty of Mr. Harris, who seems to have been actuated by none other than the best of motives; the only difference being that, from our reading of the record, we are of the opinion he was not authorized to bind appellant by the contract whose specific performance was sought in this suit.

For the reasons given, the judgment will be reversed for further proceedings consistent herewith.

SHOCKEY v. SHOCKEY.

(Court of Appeals of Kentucky. June 7, 1921.)

1. **Divorce ⚖93(1)—Petition held to sufficiently allege abandonment, but not cruelty.**

In a wife's suit for divorce, a petition, alleging that at a specified date the husband without fault on the wife's part willfully abandoned her and since then had not contributed anything to her support, and that while they lived together he frequently beat and abused her, rendering her life burdensome and condition intolerable, sufficiently alleged abandonment to constitute a cause of divorce, but did not state a cause of divorce for cruelty.

2. **Divorce ⚖36—Separation not "abandonment" and does not authorize divorce until after five years.**

"Abandonment" as a cause of divorce is something more than separation, and, where it is not shown which one left or abandoned the other, separation does not entitle the wife to a divorce until she has been separated from the husband for five years without any cohabitation.

[Ed. Note.—For other definitions, see Words and Phrases, First and Second Series, Abandon—Abandonment.]

3. **Witnesses ⚖60(2)—Abandonment is matter of proof, and wife is not competent witness.**

Abandonment as a cause for divorce is a matter of proof, and the wife is not a competent witness to establish it.

4. **Divorce ⚖108—Evidence of cruelty without allegation thereof does not authorize decree.**

In a wife's suit for divorce, evidence tending to prove cruelty will not support a judgment on that ground, where the allegations of the petition as to cruelty were insufficient.

Appeal from Circuit Court, Fayette County.

Suit by Alice Shockey against Jones Arche Shockey. From a judgment dismissing the petition, plaintiff appeals. Affirmed.

R. S. Crawford, of Lexington, for appellant.
Hogan L. Yancey, of Lexington, for appellee.

SAMPSON, J. Appellant, Alice Shockey, sued her husband, James Arche Shockey, in the Fayette circuit court in July, 1919, for divorce, averring that—

They were married "January 3, 1916, and lived together as man and wife from the time of their marriage until December, 1917, at which time the defendant without fault on the part of plaintiff willfully abandoned her, and since said date has not contributed anything to her support. The plaintiff says that during the time they lived together he procured divers sums of money from her and wasted same in drunkenness and dissipation and frequently beat and abused her, rendering her life burdensome and condition intolerable."

The petition also alleges that plaintiff is, and has been for more than five years, a resident of Fayette county, Ky., and that the cause of divorce arose and existed in Fayette county, Ky., within five years next before the commencement of this action. The defendant was summoned but made no defense. The county attorney of Fayette county filed a report in which he said:

"I must object to the granting of the relief sought by the plaintiff on the ground that the allegation of cruelty is insufficient and that the proof which was taken only on that ground is insufficient."

The case was then remanded to rules, and the plaintiff given leave to retake her depositions, but she did not do so.

The cause being submitted for judgment, the court dismissed the plaintiff's petition at her cost, and she appeals.

The brief for appellant, the only one in the record, consists of one typewritten page without citation of authority.

[1] The petition sufficiently avers abandonment on the part of appellee, to constitute a cause of divorce to appellant, but it does not state a cause of divorce for cruelty, although it does allege that defendant "frequently cruelly beat and abused her, rendering her life burdensome and condition intolerable."

[2, 3] A divorce may be granted only for one of the causes set forth in the statute. Living apart without cohabitation for five consecutive years next before the application for divorce is a ground to either party, and the party not in fault may have a divorce if he or she be abandoned by his or her spouse for one year. The proof in this case shows merely that plaintiff and defendant separated. It does not show which one left or abandoned the other. Abandonment constituting a cause of divorce is something more than separation. A wife who merely separates from her husband is not entitled to a divorce until five years have elapsed without any cohabitation between them. Abandonment is a matter of proof, and the wife is not a competent witness to establish it.

Ignoring her deposition on this subject, there is absolutely no evidence as to how, why, and where the parties separated, and no proof whatever that defendant abandoned plaintiff more than one year before the institution of this action.

[4] There is some evidence tending to prove that defendant was cruel to plaintiff; but as the allegations of the petition as to cruelty are wholly insufficient to support a judgment on this ground, it cannot be considered, for proof without allegation is nothing.

Judgment affirmed.

⚖For other cases see same topic and KEY-NUMBER in all Key-Numbered Digests and Indexes

FOXWELL v. JUSTICE.

(Court of Appeals of Kentucky.   June 8, 1921.)

1. Covenants ⟐39—Deed with warranty cannot be defeated by extrinsic facts as to prior sale of mineral or knowledge of grantee.

A deed purporting to convey a fee-simple title with warranty cannot be construed to embrace a reservation of mineral merely because the grantor had previously conveyed such mineral or because his prior deed for the mineral was of record, or even because his grantee with warranty had actual knowledge of the prior sale of the mineral; such facts being insufficient to defeat the grantee's cause of action on the covenant of warranty.

2. Mines and minerals ⟐55(4)—One in possession of surface under separated title holds mineral as trustee for owner.

Under Ky. St. § 2366a, one in possession of the surface under a separated title holds possession of the mineral as trustee for the legal owner of the same.

3. Covenants ⟐102(1)—Eviction not condition to right of action for breach of warranty in favor of one who could not acquire possession.

There is an exception to the general rule that eviction is a condition precedent to the right to sue on a warranty in favor of one who did not and could not acquire possession under his deed.

4. Pleading ⟐229—Amended pleadings must be in furtherance of justice and not substantially change claim or defense.

The only limitation on the right to file amended pleadings in the trial court, under Civ. Code Prac. § 134, is that they must be in furtherance of justice, and not substantially change the claim or defense.

5. Pleading ⟐237(8), 238(3)—Offered amendment should be supported by affidavit, and court may refuse to file same if it appears to change issues.

When an amendment is offered during the trial, unless filed merely to conform the pleadings with the proof, the party offering it should show by affidavit why it was not sooner tendered, and the court may refuse to file it when it appears it changes the issues in a substantial way.

6. Appeal and error ⟐959(1)—Discretion of court in refusing amendments not disturbed unless abused.

The action of the trial court in admitting or rejecting amendments to pleadings will not be disturbed on appeal, unless there has been a manifest abuse of discretion.

7. Pleading ⟐236(7)—Refusal to file amended answer changing issues, etc., not abuse of discretion.

In an action to recover for breach of a warranty in a deed the value of minerals previously conveyed by defendant grantor to another, where defendant grantor's amended answer was tendered at the submission, after all of the proof had been heard, and it changed the substantial issues, etc., it cannot be said the trial court abused its sound discretion in refusing to file it when tendered.

Appeal from Circuit Court, Webster County.

Action by Henderson Foxwell against J. A. Justice. From judgment for defendant, plaintiff appeals. Affirmed.

Bourland & Blackwell, of Dixon, and Cox & Grayot, of Madisonville, for appellant.
Bennett & Withers, of Dixon, and N. B. Hunt and J. C. Worsham, both of Henderson, for appellee.

CLARKE, J.   In 1914 Henderson Foxwell, an aged colored man of good character and business ability, but illiterate, sold and conveyed to a neighbor, J. A. Justice, a white man, the absolute fee-simple title to 148 acres of land, with covenant of general warranty and without reservation of any kind.   He had, however, in 1903, or 11 years theretofore, sold and conveyed all of the mineral in the same land to the St. Bernard Mining Company by a deed which was promptly recorded.

In 1917, Justice instituted this action at law to recover of Foxwell for breach of the warranty in his deed the value of the minerals, alleging, in addition to the foregoing facts, that defendant at the time through his son, who negotiated the sale, represented to him that he had not sold the minerals. Defendant answered, denying the alleged representations about the minerals, and by counterclaim averred that plaintiff knew of the prior conveyance of the minerals; that he executed the deed under the mistaken belief that it conveyed only the surface, and that "he in ignorance thought and supposed that said deed reserved said coal and mineral rights, and stated truly the agreement and contract between the parties." He prayed for a reformation of the deed, and upon his motion the cause was transferred to equity. Demurrers to the petition and counterclaim for reformation as amended were overruled, and the affirmative allegations of the latter were traversed by reply.

The parties announced ready for trial at a subsequent term, and by agreement the proof was heard in open court and the law and facts submitted to the court. After all of the proof was in, defendant tendered an amended answer and counterclaim, in which he offered to refund the purchase money, $6,800, with interest, and asked a cancellation of the deed. Plaintiff objected to the filing of this pleading, and it was made part of the record, but not filed. The court rendered judgment against defendant for $1,480, and he has appealed.

For reversal, defendant insists the court erred (1) in overruling the demurrer to the petition and awarding damages, (2) in denying a reformation of the deed, and (3) in refusing to file his amended answer and counterclaim asking a cancellation, and in refusing him that relief.

Counsel for defendant concede the deed to plaintiff was sufficient in form and terms to have conveyed the minerals if at the time defendant had owned them, and that it did not have that effect simply because same had been theretofore conveyed to another. They contend, however, that minerals underlying land are excluded from a conveyance which describes the land by metes and bounds (1) by an exception or reservation in the deed, and (2) without any such exception or reservation where, as here, the minerals previously have been "severed in ownership and the right thereto vested in some other person." Counsel thus state their position:

"The appellant believes that it is the law of this state that the conveyance made to the St. Bernard Mining Company of such coal and mineral rights on the 25th day of August, 1903, made and constituted a separate and distinct estate of such coal and mining rights, and that subsequent conveyance of the surface would not include the coal, unless apt, inclusive words should be used in such conveyance showing a clear intention upon the part of the grantor to convey and warrant the title to such estate.

"The deed of record in D. B. 39, at page 350, being sufficient in form was notice to the world, appellee included, that a distinct, individual, and separate estate had been created, and that it no longer would pass by mere description of the surface, but would be excluded from any subsequent conveyance of the surface as clearly and certainly as if expressly reserved by the language of the deeds."

They contend most earnestly such a rule was announced in Kincaid v. McGowan, 88 Ky. 91, 4 S. W. 802, 9 Ky. Law Rep. 987, 13 L. R. A. 289, and has been approved in Kennedy v. Hicks, 180 Ky. 562, 203 S. W. 318, Big Sandy Co. v. Ramey, 162 Ky. 236, 172 S. W. 508, Webb v. Webb, etc., 178 Ky. 152, 198 S. W. 736, and Gabbard v. Sheffield, 179 Ky. 442, 200 S. W. 940.

Upon examination, however, it will be found that counsel are mistaken in their interpretation of the McGowan Case and the other named cases cited it only in support of the now thoroughly established doctrine that separate fee-simple estates in land may exist in the surface and in the minerals thereunder; that one person may own the one and another the other, and that each such estate is subject to the laws of descent, devise, and conveyance.

[1] The state of facts which existed in the McGowan Case and induced the holding there that apt words were required to convey a separated estate in the minerals, upon which counsel for defendant especially rely, does not exist here. There the grantor conveyed a 2,200-acre boundary, but excepted from conveyance several small tracts within that boundary, the surfaces only of which had theretofore been conveyed to others; and the question for decision was whether the minerals under the small excluded tracts passed to the grantee or remained in the grantor. The court held, as was eminently proper, that since the small tracts had been excepted out of the large boundary, and thereby necessarily excluded from the conveyance, the grantor's separated title to the minerals therein did not pass because of the absence of apt words expressing such an intention by the parties. The court was construing the deed and merely stated in effect that apt words would have been required to overcome the natural inference from such exclusions. Manifestly neither that case nor any of those cited sustains the contention here made, that the apt words of this deed which counsel concede import a fee-simple title and a warranty thereof, must be construed to mean something less, because of extrinsic facts. Under such a contention a warranty becomes meaningless and a champertous deed an impossibility; obviously such a contention cannot be supported by reason or authority.

It is equally clear that the fact the prior deed to the St. Bernard Mining Company for the minerals was of record, or even that plaintiff had actual knowledge of the sale of the minerals, is insufficient to defeat a cause of action upon a covenant of warranty.

The rule is thus stated in 15 C. J. 1230:

"The fact that either or both parties knew at the time of conveyance that the grantor had no title in a part or a whole of the land does not effect the right of recovery for a breach of covenant."

This statement of the rule was quoted with approval in Helton, etc., v. Asher, 135 Ky. 758, 123 S. W. 285, and has been applied in numerous other cases, including Jones v. Jones, 87 Ky. 82, 7 S. W. 886, 9 Ky. Law Rep. 942; Cornelius v. Kinnard, 157 Ky. 50, 162 S. W. 524; Downs v. Nally, 161 Ky. 432, 170 S. W. 1193.

The only authority cited by the defendant to the contrary is Sanders v. Rowe, 48 S. W. 1083, 20 Ky. Law Rep. 1082, which seemingly sustains his contention so far as actual knowledge is concerned. But that case, when cited upon the same question in Helton v. Asher, supra, was distinguished upon the ground that the relief there granted, a rescission, was rested upon fraud or mistake, and when cited in Ison v. Sanders, 163 Ky. 605, 174 S. W. 505, upon the question of fraud or mistake was held not to be controlling. Hence as it has been construed it is au-

FOXWELL v. JUSTICE
(281 S.W.)

thority, if at all, only to the effect that actual knowledge by the grantee of the defective title of the grantor is competent but not controlling evidence, upon the question of fraud or mistake in an action on the warranty, which proposition is supported by reason as well as authority. 15 C. J. 1230; New York, etc., Coal Co. v. Graham, 226 Pa. 348, 75 Atl. 657.

[2, 3] The petition does not allege an eviction, usually a condition precedent to a right to sue on a warranty, but this was not necessary here, since it is thoroughly established in this jurisdiction that the one in possession of the surface under a separated title thereto holds possession of the minerals as trustee for the legal owner of same (Ky. Stats. 2366a; Farnsworth v. Barret, 146 Ky. 556, 142 S. W. 1049); and an exception to the general rule that an action on the warranty does not accrue until there has been an eviction is recognized in favor of one who did not and could not acquire possession under his deed (15 C. J. 1304; Butt v. Riffe, 78 Ky. 352; Laevison v. Baird, 91 Ky. 204, 15 S. W. 252, 12 Ky. Law Rep. 786; Smith v. Jones, 97 Ky. 670, 31 S. W. 475. And see Fitzhugh v. Croghan, 2 J. J. Marsh. 429, 19 Am. Dec. 139.

Hence the court did not err in overruling the demurrer to the petition, and as the defendant does not contend, as he could not, that the evidence of damage was not sufficient to support the judgment of $1,480 therefor, the judgment must be affirmed unless defendant by way of counterclaim was entitled to a reformation or a cancellation of the deed.

2. Fraud is not charged against plaintiff, and if defendant's counterclaim sufficiently alleges a mutual mistake, which we do not think it does, such mistake is not established by the evidence. The only evidence, if any, of a mistake upon the part of plaintiff is such as is inferrable from his constructive knowledge of the prior conveyance of the minerals to the St. Bernard Company, and this if not entirely negligible upon such an inquiry as this is certainly not of that clear and convincing character which is always required for the reformation of a written contract which does not appear upon its face to be either ambiguous or incomplete. McMee v. Henry, 163 Ky. 729, 174 S. W. 746; Ison v. Sanders, supra; Pickrell & Craig Co. v. Castleman Blakemore Co., 174 Ky. 1, 191 S. W. 680.

3. Even if we might concede that the evidence is sufficient for a cancellation of the deed upon the theory that the minds of the parties did not meet, upon both sides of which proposition there is much evidence, we could not for that reason reverse the judgment herein because that affirmative defense was not seasonably presented.

A broad discretion is lodged in the trial court by section 134 of the Civil Code of Practice in the matter of filing amended pleadings "in the furtherance of justice" and to insure an orderly procedure.

[4] The only limitation, however, upon the right to file same is that they must be in the furtherance of justice, and do not substantially change the claim or the defense. Ford v. Providence Coal Co., 124 Ky. 517, 99 S. W. 609, 30 Ky. Law Rep. 698; City of Louisville v. Lausberg, 161 Ky. 361, 170 S. W. 962.

[5] But when an amendment is offered during the trial, unless filed merely to conform the pleadings with the proof, the party offering it should show by affidavit why it was not sooner tendered (Cincinnati Railroad Co. v. Crabtree, 100 S. W. 318, 30 Ky. Law Rep. 1000; Christen v. Christen, 184 Ky. 822, 213 S W. 189); and the court may refuse to file same when it appears that it changes in a substantial way the issues. See cases cited under section 134 of the Code, note 41.

[6] The action of the lower court in admitting or rejecting amendments will not be disturbed on appeal, unless there has been a manifest abuse of discretion. Lanman, etc., v. Louisville Dry Goods Co., 138 Ky. 798, 129 S. W. 111; Robards v. Robards, 110 S. W. 422, 33 Ky. Law Rep. 565.

[7] The amendment in the instant case was tendered at the submission, and after all of the proof had been heard. It changed the issues in a substantial way. Neither it nor the proof suggested any equitable terms upon which a cancellation could have been ordered. The case had been pending for more than a year, and there was no showing why the amendment was not sooner tendered or requested for a continuance. Under such circumstances it cannot be said the court abused a sound discretion in refusing to file the amendment when tendered, and certainly such an abuse is not manifest or clear.

For the reasons indicated, the judgment is affirmed.

JONES v. BLACK et al.

(Court of Appeals of Kentucky. June 7, 1921.)

Deeds ⟹134—Conveyance to grantee so long as she remains the wife or unmarried widow of grantor limits the estate and is not a condition for defeating it.

In a husband's deed conveying land to his wife, the words "so long as she shall remain the wife or the unmarried widow of the party of the first part" do not have the effect of cutting short or defeating a larger estate before the time fixed for its determination, but measure in the first instance the duration of the entire estate conveyed, and are words of limitation, and not of condition, and the limitation is valid.

Appeal from Circuit Court, Knox County.

Suit by J. R. Jones, guardian for Stanley Black and others, against W. C. Black and others. Judgment dismissing the petition, and the guardian appeals. Affirmed.

Hiram H. Owens, of Barbourville, for appellant.

P. D. Black, of Barbourville, for appellees.

CLAY, J. On January 7, 1909, William Carson Black conveyed to his wife, Etta Shaffer Black, a house and lot located in Barbourville, by deed containing the following habendum:

"To have and to hold unto the party of the second part, Etta Shaffer Black, so long as she shall remain the wife or the unmarried widow of the party of the first part, W. C. Black, with covenant of general warranty."

Etta Shaffer Black, who died September 25, 1917, was survived by her husband, W. C. Black, and four infant children, Stanley Black, Russell Black, John A. Black, and Mary Black. In the month of August, 1919, J. R. Jones was appointed and qualified as guardian of the children.

This suit was brought by Jones, as guardian of the infants, against the infants and W. C. Black, their father, and the grantor in the above-mentioned deed, for the purpose of selling the property and reinvesting the proceeds. The petition alleged, in subtance, that Etta Shaffer Black acquired a fee-simple title by the deed referred to, and that upon her death the property descended to her children subject to the curtesy of her husband, W. C. Black. In addition to filing a demurrer to the petition, W. C. Black filed an answer and cross-petition pleading that Etta Shaffer Black's interest in the property terminated with her death, and thereupon the property reverted to him. The demurrer to the answer and cross-petition was overruled, but the demurrer to the petition was sustained, and the petition dismissed. Plaintiff appeals.

It will be observed that the property was conveyed to the wife "so long as she shall remain the wife or the unmarried widow of the party of the first part." These words do not have the effect of cutting short or defeating a larger estate before the time fixed for its determination, but measure in the first instance the duration of the entire estate conveyed. That being true, they are words of limitation, and not of condition, and the limitation is valid. Coppage v. Alexander's Heirs, 2 B. Mon. 313, 38 Am. Dec. 153; Vance v. Campbell, 1 Dana, 229; Chenault v. Scott, 66 S. W. 759, 23 Ky. Law Rep. 1974. And, since the estate was to continue only so long as the grantee remained the wife or widow of the grantor, it necessarily follows that her estate terminated with her death, and the title to the property did not pass to her children. Having no title to the property, they could not maintain an action for its sale and a reinvestment of the proceeds. Hence the petition was properly dismissed.

Judgment affirmed.

CLAY et al. v. THOMAS et al.

(Court of Appeals of Kentucky. March 4, 1921. Rehearing Denied June 17, 1921.)

1. Appeal and error ⟹162(1)—Acceptance of voluntary satisfaction of judgment does not bar appeal, when judgment not for full amount sought.

Under Civ. Code Prac. § 757, providing that the enforcement of a judgment for only part of the demand sued for shall not prevent an appeal as to the part not recovered, the acceptance of a voluntary satisfaction of a judgment will not bar an appeal when the judgment is not for the full amount sought, but a contrary rule prevails where there is a valid settlement of a cause of action.

2. Trusts ⟹317—Trustees not entitled to allowance for making sale in addition to that allowed by terms of will.

Where two heirs, acting as trustees, purchased part of the property from the other heirs, and resold the same at a large profit, whereupon the court ordered distribution among the heirs of the amount received from the resale, less expenses incurred in effecting the same, they were not entitled to an allowance for making the sale in addition to the amount allowed them under the will, in view of a clause that the allowance therein provided for should be in lieu of all other compensation.

3. Trusts ⟹283(2)—Trustees accounting for profits on resale of property purchased from beneficiaries entitled to discount on purchase-money notes, on distribution of proceeds.

Where two heirs, being trustees, purchased trust property from the other heirs, and their esale was decreed to be trust property, for the enefit of all the heirs, they were entitled to the amount of a discount deducted from the urchase-money notes.

.. Trusts ⟏283(2)—Trustees on distribution of proceeds of resale of trust property purchased from beneficiaries may deduct reasonable amount expended for services of employee in caring for land until it was disposed of.

On accounting for the proceeds of the resale of trust property by two heirs, acting as trustees which they had purchased from beneficiaries, they were entitled to deduct the amounts paid for special services rendered and salary and expenses paid to an employee in caring for the land until it was disposed of; the allowance being reasonable.

5. Trusts ⟏283(2)—Trustees, on distribution of proceeds of resale of trust property purchased from beneficiaries may retain interest on expenses incurred before sale.

The trustees of an estate on distribution of the proceeds of a resale of the trust property among themselves and other heirs were entitled to deduct from the latter's share the amount of interest on items of expense incurred before the sale; the sale having inured to the benefit of all the heirs.

6. Trusts ⟏283(2)—Trustees on distribution of proceeds of resale of trust property cannot deduct for depreciation of property not included in sale.

Where two heirs, as trustees of an estate, purchased property thereof from all the heirs, and resold the same with the exception of a certain mill site, whereupon the court ordered the deeds to them canceled and the proceeds of the resale distributed among all the heirs, less expenses incurred in making the sale, the trustees were not entitled to deduct the amount of depreciation in the mill property, they having paid for it only the amount of the other heirs' respective interests, and the amounts due the other heirs having already been charged with a greater sum already paid them by the trustees.

7. Trusts ⟏283(2)—Trustees, on distribution among heirs of proceeds of resale of part of trust property, may recover losses by operation of mill, which was not resold.

On accounting for the proceeds of the resale of part of trust property, the trustees were entitled to reimbursement for loss sustained by them on account of the operation of a mill prior to its sale by them, and for such a period thereafter as was necessary to the disposition of logs and other supplies theretofore provided for; they having operated the plant under the belief they were the owners of it by purchase from the other heirs.

8. Trusts ⟏283(2)—Trustees, on distribution of proceeds of resale of trust property purchased from beneficiaries, not entitled to credit for taxes paid on proceeds belonging to other heirs.

On distribution among the heirs of an estate of the proceeds of a resale of trust property, two of them, as trustees, were not entitled to credit for the taxes paid on the proceeds belonging to the other heirs; they not having shown what taxes they paid thereon.

9. Appeal and error ⟏1011(1)—Determination of trial court as to amount of trustee's land sold with trust property not disturbed where evidence conflicting.

Where two heirs of an estate, being trustees, sold some land of their own along with land belonging to the estate, the determination of the lower court as to the amount thereof will not be disturbed, where the evidence was conflicting as to the respective amounts.

10. Trusts ⟏283(2)—Trustees, on distribution of proceeds of resale of trust property, not entitled to credit for enhanced value of property by reason of general warranty deed executed by them.

Where the trustees of an estate purchased property thereof and resold part thereof at a considerable profit, whereupon the deeds to them were canceled, and the court ordered a distribution of the proceeds of the resale among all the heirs, less expenses incurred in making the sale, the trustees were not entitled to credit for the enhanced value of the property, by reason of a general warranty deed executed by them, though they received only covenants of special warranty.

11. Trusts ⟏283(2)—Heirs, by accepting benefits of sale of trust property by trustees, estopped to assert liability of each trustee for entire amount of judgment, contrary to provisions of deed.

Where two heirs of an estate, being trustees, purchased property of the estate from all the heirs and resold part thereof, whereupon the deeds to them were canceled and a distribution of the proceeds of the resale among all the heirs ordered, the other heirs, having elected to stand by the deed from the trustees to the purchaser at the second sale, were estopped to assert that the estate of each of the trustees was chargeable with the entire amount of the judgment, contrary to the terms of payment as fixed in the deed.

Appeal from Circuit Court, Clark County.

Suit by James T. Clay and others against Irma T. Thomas and others. From a judgment entered after an accounting directed by the Court of Appeals (178 Ky. 199, 198 S. W. 762, 1 A. L. R. 738), plaintiffs appeal, and defendants cross-appeal. Affirmed and reversed in part on both original and cross-appeals, with directions.

T. E. Moore, of Hazard, Ben Williams, of Frankfort, and Harmon Stitt, of Lexington, for appellants.

B. R. Jouett and Pendleton & Bush, all of Winchester, John R. Allen, of Lexington, and E. S. Jouett, of Louisville, for appellees.

QUIN, J. James M. Thomas owned considerable property in Rockcastle and Jackson counties. He died testate in 1905, leaving surviving him two sons, W. R. and R. L. Thomas, and two daughters Mrs. T. E. Moore and Mrs. Mary Thomas Ireland. Three of these children have since died, leaving descendants.

The two sons and a son-in-law, Thomas E. Moore, Jr., were appointed executors and trustees of the will. An ex parte proceeding was filed by the trustees, and others interested, seeking authority to sell decedent's property to the two sons. A judgment granting the relief sought was entered, and the property was sold to the two sons, who agreed to pay for the interest of each sister $47,500, or at a valuation of $190,000, for the entire property. Within three years after their purchase the two sons disposed of the property for over $400,000.

This suit was filed by Mrs. Ireland and the children whose interests had been sold, to secure their proportion of the profits realized by the purchasers, on the ground that the trustees had no authority to sell to themselves individually the trust property. This court, in an opinion reported in 178 Ky. 199, 198 S. W. 762, 1 A. L. R. 738, sustained the petitioners, and held that the sale of the property would be treated as a sale by the trustees to inure to the benefit of all. The lower court was directed to ascertain the exact sum actually collected from the sale, and the amount, if any, still due. A deduction was ordered for such expenses, if any, as were incurred in effecting the sale, or in perfecting titles, also for the amount of taxes paid by the purchasers after they acquired the property. These sums to be credited on the purchase price with interest, the balance to be prorated among those entitled thereto, the Moore children and Mrs. Ireland to be charged with $47,500, which had been previously paid them. Upon the return of the case supplemental pleadings were filed, proof taken, an accounting had, and judgment entered.

Complaining the lower court failed to follow the mandate of this court in many important matters, and for other alleged errors, Mrs. Ireland, her two children, and the Moore children have taken this second appeal. T. E. Moore, Jr., is the only surviving trustee.

A motion by appellees to dismiss the appeal was passed to a hearing on the merits. This motion was based on a previous settlement of the judgment. After entry of the judgment below executions were issued, and these were withheld pending a conference between counsel. On the day appointed the judgment was paid, and the executions indorsed satisfied. Undoubtedly it was considered by some that this settlement or payment would be taken as a finality, and no appeal would be taken, nor is any reflection cast on counsel because they so understood it. On the other side it is said that counsel then representing appellants were not authorized to make any settlement prejudicial to the rights of their clients, one of whom was an infant. It is apparent those attending the conference at which the money was paid held different views as to the effect of their negotiations.

[1] Civil Code, § 757, provides in part that: "* * * When a party recovers judgment for only part of the demand or property he sues for, the enforcement of such judgment shall not prevent him from prosecuting an appeal therefrom as to so much of the demand or property sued for that he did not recover."

Construing this section of the Code, we held in Hendrickson v. New Hughes Jellico Coal Co., 172 Ky. 568, 189 S. W. 704, that an indorsement of satisfaction of the judgment, interest, and cost on the margin of the order book did not preclude an appeal by plaintiff. See, also, Cravens v. Merritt, Jr., 178 Ky. 727, 199 S. W. 785.

The acceptance of a voluntary satisfaction of a judgment will not bar an appeal when the judgment is not for the full amount sought. A contrary rule prevails where there is a valid settlement of the cause of action. Under the state of the present record the satisfaction of the executions did not bar appellant's right to appeal.

[2] Appellants claim the judgment is erroneous in several respects. These we will take up in the order of their presentment, and then discuss the items involved on the cross-appeal.

1. An allowance of $16,000 to the trustees for making the sale: After making certain devises and bequests testator in clause 11 of his will provided that the residue of his property, with the exception of the property in Jackson and Rockcastle counties, was given to his trustees to hold in trust for the benefit of his four children according to certain directions therein contained; among other things, that they should operate the lumber plant at Ford, Ky., until the logs and standing timber on the Kentucky river could be manufactured and sold, but for a period not longer than three years after his death, and the trustees were given general power to manage and control said business. With the exception of the property in Rockcastle and Jackson counties the will provided that the trustees should take testator's other property not specifically disposed of, with the general directions to reduce same to cash as soon as this could be done to advantage. Among other things, the trustees were to pay the taxes upon all the property, including the Jackson and Rockcastle lands, until the Ford property was sold, and then distribution is ordered of the proceeds.

In clause 12 the Jackson and Rockcastle properties were given equally to his four children, to be held, managed, and disposed of by the three trustees named in paragraph 11, being the two sons and son-in-law heretofore mentioned. The same not to be sold until the expiration of at least three years after his death, with the right on the part of the trustees to postpone the sale until as much as 10 years after his death.

Clause 16 reads as follows:

"For their services as trustees each of said trustees named in paragraph eleven, and their successors, shall receive an annual allowance of six hundred dollars.

"And inasmuch as it will be necessary for my son, Robert L. Thomas to give his entire personal attention to the business, because of his actual familiarity therewith, I desire in consideration of his doing this, that he shall receive as compensation therefor the additional sum of $1,200.00 per annum. It is understood that the allowance herein provided for shall be in lieu of all other compensation to said trustees in their capacity of both trustee and executors and cease with the three-year period."

The executors and trustees received the compensation for the three years provided by the last-mentioned clause.

Appellees claim the trustees were compelled to expend much time and energy in disposing of this property, clearing titles, keeping off squatters, etc., and for their services for consummating and completing the deal and disbursing the money they were entitled to a sum in addition to that mentioned in clause 16. The property consisted of approximately 20,000 acres, covering an area of some 31 square miles, and was situated about 12 miles from a railroad. The lower court ordered an allowance to the executors of $16,000, but on cross-appeal they are asking that it be fixed at $25,000. It is their contention that testator particularly arranged for additional compensation for these services. It is argued that testator specifically excluded from the operation of the trust in clause 11, the Jackson and Rockcastle properties, and provided the term the Ford plant should be operated, and in fact they were named as special trustees for a different purpose in clause 12; that the two paragraphs create separate and distinct trusts; this is on the theory that no allowance or compensation was fixed for the trustees named in paragraph 12. It is admitted that the trustees referred to in the two clauses are the same. Furthermore it is said the trustees were to render no service and do nothing with the Rockcastle and Jackson county property until three years after the testator's death, except, of course, the payment of taxes, and as it was impossible to fix, with any degree of accuracy, proper compensation for services to be rendered under paragraph 12, none was in fact fixed, and hence the insistence that an allowance should be made of not less than $25,000 for the services so rendered. A vast amount of work was done by the trustees, including the care of and attention to the property, keeping it clear of squatters, looking after pending litigation affecting the property, as well as the clearing of titles and the work incident to the final sale.

T. E. Moore, Jr., one of the trustees, found the purchaser. He is counsel for the appellants, and not only is not asking any allowance for the services so rendered by him, but is resisting any allowance to the trustees other than that fixed in clause 16. But for the provision of clause 16 it could not be satisfactorily contended that the trustees were not entitled to adequate compensation for the arduous duties they were compelled to perform in the care, management, and control of this vast area of land. But we find it impossible to escape the positive instructions of testator found in this clause. In the language of the will:

"It is understood the allowance herein provided for shall be in lieu of all other compensation to said trustees in their capacity of both trustee and executor, and to cease with the three-year period."

We must assume testator meant exactly what he said in his carefully prepared will. It was his manifest intention that, aside from the compensation fixed for the services rendered for the three-year period as provided in clause 11, the trustees and executors were not to receive other compensation for any services rendered by them. They were not compelled to accept the trust, and their acceptance of it must have been in accordance with the provisions of the will. In the appointment of his two sons and his son-in-law as executors and trustees testator doubtless had in mind that they represented the recipients and beneficiaries of practically three-fourths of his large estate, and it was not his desire or wish that Mrs. Ireland's remaining one-fourth should be charged with any fees or commissions for any services rendered by them. He evidently reasoned they would be glad to render these services free of charge or cost to their sister; his aim being to make them equal in the distribution of the proceeds of this, the largest item of his estate. The ultimate result of allowing additional fees or commissions to the trustees would be that Mrs. Ireland alone would be the one to pay, charged as she would be with her one-fourth. We are satisfied testator had no such intention; indeed he very positively expressed himself to the contrary. To make a charge against the estate each would be chargeable with his or her one-fourth, and to the extent that any allowance on this account should be made it would in reality affect only Mrs. Ireland. To disallow this item enhances the estate to that extent, and since Mr. Moore has waived his claim to any commission it follows that Mrs. Ireland is relieved of a charge of one-fourth or $4,000, and the net sum payable to the estate of the two sons is decreased only a little more than $1,000. We think the lower court erred in making any allowance to the executors and trustees on this account.

[3] 2. $8,190, discount deducted from the purchase money. Objection is raised to this item allowed by the lower court: It is ar-

gued the purchase-money notes which were discounted were as good as government bonds, and there was no reason for discounting same. In discounting these notes the executors did nothing more than would have been done by them or any other good business men in the conduct of their own affairs. Many considerations might justify the holders of notes in discounting them. As no good reason is pointed out why this allowance should not stand, it will not be disturbed.

[4] 3. $5,000, allowance to J. W. Fowler: Fowler was an employee of the Ford Lumber & Manufacturing Company, on a nominal salary. While so employed he made purchases of land for W. R. and R. L. Thomas, individually, and likewise performed various services for the estate of decedent. He seems to have been familiar with the entire property; he knew all the corners; he went over the land with the purchasers, and spent several days with the attorneys in going over the titles after the sale of the property had been agreed to, as likewise going on the property with surveyors, representing the purchasers. That he rendered very valuable services is conceded. He went over the land to see if any depredations had been committed; he either surveyed or assisted in surveying the lands when purchased, and seems to have had general supervision over the property. The objection to this allowance is not so much to the amount, as it is to the apportionment of same; it being contended the major portion of his services were rendered for the Thomases or the Ford plant, and not for the estate, but the evidence satisfies us that Fowler did render a considerable amount of valuable services for the estate, and the allowance of $5,000 is not excessive, and should be sustained.

4. Allowance of $4,500 to Fowler for salary and expenses: Item 3 was an allowance for special services rendered by Fowler in caring for the land until it was disposed of. Item 4 represents a nominal salary he received and his general expenses. As in the preceding item we think this allowance was within reasonable limits. The salary was for a period of over three years, the amount of which is not objected to, and for the reasons given as to item 3 we do not think the court erred in allowing this sum.

[5] 5. Allowance of $4,000, interest on items of expenses incurred before the second sale: While there was no specific exception to this item, we find no ground to disallow it. Since the court has held that the sale inured to and for the benefit of all the children, the court very properly allowed interest on the items paid by the Thomases until the final disposition of the property.

[6] 6. $15,100, depreciation in the Livingston mill property: This mill site, with approximately 150 acres, was located in Rockcastle county, and some distance from the Jackson county lands. This property was included in the original purchase by the Thomases, and was authorized by the judgment in the ex parte proceedings. The Jackson county lands consisted of about 20,000 acres, valued at $170,000, and the Livingston mill site at $20,000, a total of $190,000, these being the valuations according to the evidence in the ex parte proceedings, and upon which Mrs. Ireland and the heirs of Mrs. Moore were paid their one-fourth. The Livingston mill property was not included in the sale of the Jackson county lands; hence no part of the proceeds of that sale was distributed among the heirs. The $15,100 allowed by the court was arrived at by deducting from the original purchase of $20,000 the sum of $2,000, received from the sale of a house on the property and $2,900, insurance. The lower court was evidently of the opinion that, as the Thomases had paid $20,000 for the mill site, they were entitled to have that amount returned to them, less the amount realized from the sale of the house and the sum collected on the insurance, but in so holding it seems the court erred. At most the Thomases only paid $10,000 for the mill property, being the one-fourth interest of their two sisters, as they paid nothing to themselves. The lower court's judgment directed that the amounts due Mrs. Ireland and the estate of Mrs. Moore should be charged with the sum of $47,500, which had been paid by the two brothers under the first sale. This being true, the estate of the two Thomases would receive credit for the full amount paid by them; hence they would not be out anything on the deal. Why allow the Thomases $20,000, when they had only paid $10,000, or why $10,000, if they receive credit for the sum so paid? The mill property belongs to the estate and in the event of sale the proceeds should be equally distributed according to the terms of the will. It follows the Thomases are not entitled to any credit on this account.

[7] From the sale of the house and the insurance all but $1,000, retained by R. L. Thomas, was put back into the business. Accordingly his estate should be charged with this amount. On the counterclaim appellees are asking an additional allowance of $20,900, on account of the operation of the Livingston mill. This is composed of two items: First, the sum of $17,000, which it is claimed the Thomases lost in the operation of the mill; second, the remainder is the net amount received from the sale of the house and insurance, with the exception of the $1,000 retained by R. L. Thomas. Appellees contend it was the desire of testator that this property should be operated in connection with the Jackson county lands after his death the same as it had been during his lifetime, and that its operation in fact added to the salable and marketable value of said property; that for this reason and no other was the property operated, and as the court set

aside the deed to all the property, including the Livingston mill, appellants cannot reap the benefits or proceeds of the sale of the Jackson county property, and not submit to a charge for the loss growing out of the operation of the Livingston mill; if the deed was void for one purpose it was void for all, and appellants must accept the losses as well as the profits. There is much merit in this contention, but the state of the record is such that it is impossible to tell how much of the alleged loss was sustained in the operation of the Livingston mill until it was sold to Ritter, etc., upon a return of the case the court will make inquiry into this matter, permitting the parties to introduce such proof on this matter as may be desired. If the mill property was operated subsequent to the sale to Ritter, etc., which seems to have been the case, the estate is not chargeable with any losses after said date, except those incurred in the prudent operation of the mill incident to the disposition of the logs and other supplies theretofore provided for. The Thomases or their estates are entitled to reimbursement or credit for such loss as may have been sustained on account of the operation of the Livingston mill up to the sale to Ritter, etc., and the subsequent period above referred to, because they were in good faith operating the plant under the belief they were the owners of it, as well as the landed estate. If they were holding the other property as trustees for the estate, a like result would follow in regard to this property. This disposes of the items involved on the original appeal.

We will now consider those on the cross-appeal.

[6] (a) Appellees are asking that credit be entered for $15,000, as the amount of taxes payable since 1912 on the one-half of the proceeds of sale belonging to appellants. This amount is based on the idea that the state and county rate for the years involved was $1 on each $100 of taxable value and $1.50 as the average rate for city taxes in the state. It is said that Lexington, where appellees lived, is known to be much higher than the average city in its tax rate. We are impressed with the novelty of this claim, especially that part forming the basis upon which it is sought to fix the amount of the liability. If appellees paid taxes on the amount stated, this is and was a fact capable of exact proof, and none is offered. Loss of the tax receipts would not offer an excuse for failure of proof. It is said appellees used this money as their own in connection with other money, but they do not show what, if any, taxes they paid thereon. This claim cannot be allowed.

(b) Claim for $15,000 additional on account of interest on items of expense before the second sale seems to have been waived.

[7] (c) Included in the total acreage conveyed to Ritter and associates was a con-

siderable area owned individually by the Thomas brothers. Appellants contend this is 2,553.24 acres; appellees insist it is 3,200 acres. The difference is caused by contradictory statements in the depositions of T. E. Moore, Jr. The court fixed this item at 2,637.61 acres. The total purchase price of $473,170.15 for something over 23,000 acres is figured on the basis of $20.66¾ per acre. The lower court allowed on this account $54,-507.24. In giving his second deposition Mr. Moore says he had not seen the original deed for about five years, at the time he first testified; that he had since found he made some errors in stating the acreage sold. In the second deposition he fixes it at 2,553.24 acres. The deed from the Thomases to Ritter, etc., did not specify which of the tracts conveyed were owned by the Thomas brothers, but from the derivation of title and examination of the deed books the witness said he ascertained the total acreage owned by them. Eleven of the 12 tracts mentioned include 2,428.09 acres. The acreage of one, the Lear tract, is not given. The witness on cross-examination conceded an omission of 147 acres from one tract. This admission, the unstated acreage in the Lear tract, and the further fact that in some instances the conveyance was for so many acres more or less, leads to the conclusion the lower court fixed the exact acreage as near as could be under the evidence.

[10] (d) $50,000, enhancement in the value of the property by reason of the general warranty deed executed by the Thomases. The last and largest items made the basis of the counterclaim is that of $50,000, claimed as the enhanced value of the property due to the general warranty deed executed by the Thomas brothers. The Thomases, when they purchased the property, received only covenants of special warranty. The lower court adjudged that appellants were responsible and liable to account to appellees for their proper proportion of any loss that might be sustained growing out of the general warranty clause in the deed to Ritter, etc.

It is testified the purchasers would not have taken the property in the absence of a general warranty deed, and there is much proof in the record that this character of deed added considerable to the salable value of the land. Appellees do not base their claim upon the mere right to be indemnified, but insist they should receive credit for the amount to which the value of the property was enhanced by reason of the general warranty covenant. This position is not without merit. When appellees sold this land after their purchase from appellants, in order to effectuate a sale they were compelled to execute a deed of general warranty. This deed was made by them individually under the belief that the sale to them under the order of court was valid. Therefore, upon the resale of the property, appellants incurred no responsibility for the marketability or warranty of title, nor did they join in the deed.

It is conceded that had appellants not asked for a ratification of the sale, and a distribution of the proceeds, they might with propriety, question the reasonableness and legality of this claim. Only a part of the consideration of the sale of the land was paid in cash; deferred payments extended over a period of seven years. The grantee was given power under the deed to deduct for any loss of the land conveyed. Of $40,000 retained in nonnegotiable notes, but $10,000 was held as a security for any loss under the warranty. The activity shown by the purchasers in their use of the property, the cutting of timber, building of railroads and switches, would have a tendency to stir up any hostile or probable claims during these eight years of their occupancy, but the record does not show the pendency of any such claims or suits.

Unquestionably the general warranty deed added to the value of the property, an enhancement that inured to the benefit and profit of appellees to the extent of one-half. The Thomas brothers could not have been compelled to incur an individual liability on account of this warranty. They voluntarily assumed it under the mistaken belief the property belonged to them. This court held the deed voidable, and that the sale to Ritter, etc., would be treated as having been made by the Thomases as trustees. They made no effort to be relieved of their individual liability under the warranty, nor can they, under the circumstances, maintain their counterclaim for the added value of the land brought about by the warranty.

However, the burden of the responsibility growing out of the warranty should be borne alike by all. We doubt if the method adopted by the lower court is a sufficient protection to appellees. This can only be done through the execution of bond in an amount not exceeding one-half of the purchase price, with interest, by which appellees will be afforded proper protection and indemnity for their warranty. Upon the return of the case and in the settlement thereof the lower court will see that such a bond, within reasonable limits as to time and amount, is executed.

[11] From the gross proceeds of the sale of the property the court made certain deductions, and found that the shares of Mrs. Ireland and the Moore children amounted to $159,608.41. Adding certain items of interest and crediting them with amounts previously paid the net amount due Mrs. Ireland's trustee is fixed at $29,974.11, and a like sum due the Moore children.

In the distribution of the proceeds, the share due the estate of W. R. Thomas was paid, one-third each to his widow, Carrie Hanson Thomas, his daughter, Ethel T. Rounsavall, and his son, Hanson Thomas. The share due Robert L. Thomas was retained by him. The judgment accordingly directed that the amount due Mrs. Ireland's trustee and the Moore children be paid one-half by the executors of R. L. Thomas and one-sixth each by Mrs. Carrie H. Thomas, Mrs. Ethel T. Rounsavall, and Hanson Thomas. In so doing it is said the court erred, the contention being that appellees are co-obligors, and the estate of each of the Thomas brothers is chargeable with and liable for the entire amount of the judgment. The importance of this point is pressed with great earnestness because of the fact that Hanson Thomas is shown to be insolvent. No objection is made to an order of contribution as between appellees for their proportion of the judgment, but as to those entitled to recover it is said they should not be limited to certain appellees for stated amounts; that, on the contrary, the estates of the Thomas brothers are liable for the entire amount of the judgment. Generally speaking, the rule contended for is correct.

But whether a trust obligation and its resultant liability is several or joint depends largely upon the facts. In the present suit the sale to Ritter, etc., was approved, and a settlement was asked upon the basis of the proceeds of that sale. Before the execution of the deed to Ritter, etc., W. R. Thomas died intestate; hence under the law of descent his widow and children took his interest in the land. In 1912 R. L. Thomas and the widow and heirs of W. R. Thomas conveyed the land to Ritter, etc., and it was provided in the deed that payments should be made one-half to R. L. Thomas and one-sixth each to Mrs. W. R. Thomas and her two children, and the purchase money was paid accordingly. While the deed to the Thomas brothers was set aside, appellants elected to stand by the deed from the Thomases to Ritter, etc. Appellants were not compelled to accept the conditions of sale as fixed by that deed, but, having elected so to do, they must abide by its terms. Those terms were agreeable to the grantors. In accepting the sale price appellants must acquiesce in the method of payment adopted by the parties.

It is evident appellants were satisfied the property brought a good price; at least they were unwilling to risk a resale. With full knowledge of the terms of the sale they adopted them as their own; therefore they cannot complain because the court prorated the judgment in exact accord with the terms of the deed. This disposes of all the items questioned on the original and cross-appeal.

For the reasons herein given the judgment appealed from be affirmed and reversed in part on both the original and cross-appeals as herein indicated. As to the item of loss incurred in the operation of the Livingston mill, up to the time of the sale to Ritter, etc., the case will be reversed for the purpose of allowing the parties to take such further proof as they may desire, with instructions to the court to enter judgment for such an amount as appellees may show themselves entitled on this account.

TURNER v. COMMONWEALTH.

(Court of Appeals of Kentucky. June 7, 1921.)

1. **Larceny ⊜68(1)—Evidence held to make question for jury.**

On a trial for chicken stealing, evidence *held* sufficient, as against motion for peremptory charge to take the case to the jury.

2. **Criminal law ⊜1213—Habitual criminal act does not inflict cruel punishment contrary to Constitution.**

Ky. St. § 1130, providing for increased punishment upon a second conviction and for life imprisonment upon a third conviction for felony, does not violate Const. § 17, prohibiting excessive fines or cruel punishment.

3. **Criminal law ⊜589(2)—Denial of continuance because defendant physically and mentally unable to prepare defense not abuse of discretion.**

The refusal of a continuance, asked for on the ground that defendant was old and broken down in health and physically and mentally in no condition to confer with his counsel or prepare his defense, was not an abuse of discretion, where the evidence as to physical and mental condition preponderated against the motion and the issues were few and simple, the defense was ably conducted, and there was no contention that defendant could have procured any other evidence.

4. **Criminal law ⊜625—Refusal to postpone trial for investigation of defendant's sanity held not error.**

Under Cr. Code Prac. § 156, authorizing the court to postpone proceedings in a criminal case until a jury be impaneled to inquire into defendant's soundness of mind, if the court be of the opinion that defendant is insane, the refusal to postpone the trial for the purpose of having defendant examined by physicians was not error, where there was no affirmative showing that he was insane, and the court took the testimony of the county physician and jailer which removed any doubt as to his sanity.

5. **Jury ⊜72(3)—Denial of motion that sheriff in summoning extra jurors be instructed to make no distinction between men and women not error.**

A motion to instruct the sheriff that in summoning extra jurors no distinction be made between men and women was properly overruled, as the statute prescribes the method of summoning jurors, and, unless the sheriff asks advice, the court has no authority to direct how his duty shall be performed.

6. **Criminal law ⊜1171(6)—Remark of counsel on motion prior to trial not prejudicial when no juror shown to have been present.**

A remark of the commonwealth's attorney on a motion for an inquest of lunacy before trial, that every time defendant had been tried he pretended to be crazy or sick, but that the testimony in such cases showed he was neither sick nor crazy, was not prejudicial to defendant's substantial rights, where it was not shown that any of the jurors who tried the case were present when the remark was made.

7. **Criminal law ⊜394—Arresting officer may search person of prisoner and use evidence thus obtained.**

Notwithstanding Const. § 10, prohibiting unreasonable searches and seizures, an arresting officer has the right without a warrant to search the person of a prisoner lawfully arrested and take from his person and hold for the disposition of the court any property connected with the offense and which may be used as evidence against him, and hence, where a person was arrested for chicken stealing while carrying a sack containing chickens, the officer had a right to open the sack and use the evidence thus obtained against defendant.

8. **Arrest ⊜63(4)—Officers held to have sufficient ground for believing felony committed to justify arrest without warrant.**

Where a person known to have been previously convicted as a chicken thief was seen by officers going towards a city with a sack filled with chickens and given a ride asked to be let out at the edge of the town, falsely pretending that he lived there, and told the officers that he had bought the chickens, they had reasonable grounds to believe that he had committed a felony authorizing them to arrest him without a warrant under Cr. Code Prac. § 36.

Appeal from Circuit Court, Fayette County.

Robert Turner was convicted of chicken stealing, and he appeals. Affirmed.

W. P. Kimball, R. E. Lee Murphy, and Taylor N. House, all of Lexington, for appellant. Chas. I. Dawson, Atty. Gen., and W. T. Fowler, Asst. Atty. Gen., for the Commonwealth.

CLAY, J. Robert Turner was convicted of the offense of chicken stealing, and his punishment fixed at confinement in the penitentiary for a period of two years. He appeals and assigns numerous grounds for a reversal of the judgment.

[1] Briefly stated, the facts are these: Ernest McMeekin is a farmer and lives on Harrodsburg pike in Fayette county. He was the owner of several chickens. About 4 o'clock on the afternoon of December 21, 1920, Turner was on the Harrodsburg pike not far from McMeekin's home, and was walking toward Lexington with a sack on his back. At the same time, Ernest Thompson, the night chief of police of the city of Lexington, and one or two others, were in the city automobile en route to Lexington. They saw Turner and recognized him. After running past him, they stopped, and one of the men in the car asked Turner if he wanted to ride to the city. Turner said that he

did and got into the machine. They asked him what he had, and he said he had a sack of chickens. When they reached the city limits, Turner said that he lived there and asked them to stop. Thompson said:

"Oh, no, Bob, what do you want to get out here for? You live over on the other side of town. Where did you get those chickens?"

Turner replied that he had bought them. Thompson said, "Oh, no, you didn't," and brought Turner on down to the police station. In the sack were several hens and a Plymouth Rock rooster. They put an advertisement in the paper in regard to the chickens. On seeing the advertisement, McMeekin discovered that several of his chickens were gone and then went to the police station. He was able to identify the rooster because it was a pet rooster and belonged to his brother's little girl, and the other chickens resembled those which he had lost. While he identified the chickens as his, he was doubtful if he could have identified them if the rooster had not been with them. 'It further appeared that twice before Turner had been convicted and sentenced to the penitentiary for the same offense.

On the other hand, Turner testified that he was out in the country setting steel traps and met a colored fellow by the name of George Cole, who lived in the South Elkhorn neighborhood, and who sold him the chickens and sack for $7.50, or $1.25 apiece. He further claims that a white man was present and witnessed the transaction. Neither Cole nor the white man appeared as a witness, and no effort was made to procure their testimony.

Here, then, we have a case where McMeekin lost certain chickens. Though he was candid enough to admit that he might not have been able to identify the other chickens had it not been for the presence of the rooster, he was certain that the rooster was his, and equally certain that the other chickens were his, in view of the presence of the rooster and of the fact that they corresponded to the chickens which he had lost. On the day on which the chickens disappeared, Turner was in the neighborhood and was seen going from the direction of the McMeekin farm toward Lexington carrying the chickens in a sack. After entering the automobile and reaching the city limits, he pretended that he lived there and wanted to get out, though, as a matter of fact, he lived on the other side of town, some distance away. On being asked what he had in his bag, he said they were chickens and that he had bought them from a man by the name of Cole. Thus, on the one hand there was evidence that he was in the neighborhood where the chickens were stolen and was in possession of the chickens. On the other hand, there was his unconfirmed statement that he had bought the chickens. In our opinion the evidence of his guilt was not only sufficient to take the case to the jury, but to sustain the verdict. It follows that the court did not err in overruling the motion for a peremptory made at the conclusion of the evidence for the commonwealth and afterwards renewed at the conclusion of all the evidence.

[2] Another error relied on was the refusal of the court to sustain the demurrer to the indictment. The indictment set forth two former convictions for the same offense. The demurrer challenged the validity of the Habitual Criminal Act, which provides in substance that every person convicted a second time of felony, the punishment of which is confinement in the penitentiary, shall be confined in the penitentiary not less than double the time of the first conviction; and if convicted a third time of felony, he shall be confined in the penitentiary during his life. Section 1130, Kentucky Statutes. The point is made that the act violates section 17 of the Constitution, which provides that excessive bail shall not be required, nor excessive fines imposed, nor cruel punishment inflicted. In reply to this contention, it is sufficient to say that the statute has been attacked on several occasions, not only on the ground that it violates section 17 of the Constitution, but on numerous other grounds, and its validity always has been sustained. Boggs v. Commonwealth, 9 Ky. Law Rep. 342, 5 S. W. 307; Herndon v. Com., 105 Ky. 199, 48 S. W. 989, 20 Ky. Law Rep. 1114, 88 Am. St. Rep. 303; Hall v. Com., 106 Ky. 898, 51 S. W. 814, 21 Ky. Law Rep. 520; Chenowith v. Comth., 11 Ky. Law Rep. 562, 12 S. W. 585; White v. Com., 20 Ky. Law Rep. 1942, 50 S. W. 678; Hyser v. Comth., 116 Ky. 418, 76 S. W. 174, 25 Ky. Law Rep. 608; Taylor v. Com., 3 Ky. Law Rep. 783.

[3] Another ground urged for reversal was the refusal of the court to grant the defendant a continuance. In his affidavit filed in support of the motion, the defendant stated that he was old and broken down in health, and that he was not in a condition, physically or mentally, to confer with his counsel or prepare his defense. No other evidence was offered in support of the motion. The commonwealth introduced the county physician and jailer, whose evidence tended to show that the defendant was physically able to stand the ordeal of a trial, and that his condition had not been such as to prevent him from preparing the case. Furthermore, the record shows that the indictment was returned on December 29, 1920. Defendant was arraigned on January 5, 1921, and entered the plea of "not guilty." The case was assigned for trial on February 3, 1921, but the trial did not take place until February 14, 1921. It is not contended that there was any other evidence which the defendant could have procured. The issues in the case were few and simple. His defense was ably conducted.

In view of these circumstances, and of the further fact that the evideence as to his physical and mental ability to prepare for and stand the trial greatly preponderates over the evidence to the contrary, it is clear that the court did not abuse a sound discretion in refusing a continuance.

[4] Another contention is that the court erred in overruling the motion to have two physicians appointed by the court to determine the question of defendant's sanity before going into trial. The Code authorizes the court to postpone the proceedings in a criminal case until a jury be impaneled to inquire whether defendant is of unsound mind, but only in the event that the court be of the opinion that there are reasonable grounds to believe that the defendant is insane. Criminal Code of Prac. § 156. Notwithstanding the lack of an affirmative showing by the defendant that he was then insane, the court took the precaution to inquire of the county physician and the jailer with reference to the defendant's actions while in jail, and their testimony was calculated to remove any doubt as to defendant's sanity. That being true, the court did not have reasonable grounds to believe that the defendant was insane, and there was no error in refusing to postpone the trial for the purpose of having the defendant examined by two physicians.

[5] When the jurors were being called and examined, and when the regular panel was exhausted, the defendant moved the court to instruct the sheriff that in summoning extra jurors no distinction be made between men and women. The motion was properly overruled because the statute prescribes the method of summoning jurors, and unless the sheriff asks the advice of the court, the court is without authority to direct the sheriff how his duty shall be performed.

[6] Another insistence is that the court erred in overruling the defendant's motion to discharge the jury panel, because the commonwealth's attorney, in arguing the motion to have an inquest of lunacy before defendant was put on trial, made the following remark in open court:

"Every time he (meaning defendant) has been tried in this court, he pretended to be crazy or sick when the time comes for his trial; but the testimony in the cases showed he was neither sick nor crazy."

We need go no further than to say that the bill of exceptions fails to show that any of the jurors who tried the case were present in court when the remark was made. That being true, it cannot be said that the remark was prejudicial to the substantial rights of the accused.

[7, 8] Still another contention is that the principal evidence in this case was obtained by unreasonable search and seizure, contrary to section 10 of the Constitution, and to the rule laid down in the case of Youman v. Comth. 189 Ky. 152, 224 S. W. 860. An examination of that case will show that it distinctly recognizes, as a long-established exception to the rule against search and seizure, that an arresting officer has the right without a warrant to search the person of a prisoner lawfully arrested, and take from his person and hold for the disposition of the court any property connected with the offense for which he is arrested and which may be used as evidence against him. 2 R. C. L. § 25, p. 467. Here, the defendant had been out in the country and was going toward the city with a sack filled with chickens. The officers who took him in the automobile knew him and knew of his prior convictions as a chicken thief. When they reached the edge of town, the defendant, pretending that he lived there, asked to be let out of the machine. As a matter of fact, he did not live there, but lived on the other side of town, and it was much nearer to his home to go as far as the officers intended to go. When asked what he had in the sack, he stated that they were chickens, and said to the officer that he had bought them. Our Code authorizes an arrest without a warrant where the officer has reasonable grounds to believe that the person arrested has committed a felony. Section 36, Criminal Code; Wright v. Comth., 85 Ky. 123, 2 S. W. 904, 8 Ky. Law Rep. 718; Morton v. Sanders, 178 Ky. 836, 200 S. W. 24. In view of the conduct of the defendant and all the circumstances surrounding the transaction, it seems to us that the arresting officer had reasonable grounds to believe that the defendant had committed a felony. Therefore he had the right to arrest the defendant and the further right, after the defendant was under arrest, to open the sack and use the evidence thus obtained against the defendant.

A reversal is asked on the ground of improper argument by the commonwealth's attorney. It appears that the court promptly sustained an objection to the remarks complained of, and admonished the jury not to consider them. In view of this action by the court, we are not prepared to say that the remarks of the commonwealth's attorney were such as to prejudice the substantial rights of the defendant.

Other questions are raised, but we deem it unnecessary to discuss them. It is sufficient to say that the defendant had a fair trial, and we perceive no reason for disturbing the verdict.

Judgment affirmed.

BEALE v. STROUD et al.

(Court of Appeals of Kentucky. June 3, 1921.)

1. **Infants ⚖️41—Purchaser at sale of land has no remedy for loss of land where there is no express warranty and no representations.**

The purchaser of land belonging to an infant at a sale for reinvestment of the proceeds in a suit brought by the infant's guardian has no remedy against the infant for his loss of the land because of an outstanding paramount title where there was no express warranty of the title and no representation, fraudulent or otherwise, inducing the purchase.

2. **Judicial sales ⚖️52—No implied warranty of title and doctrine of caveat emptor applies.**

There is no warranty of the title of lands sold under a judgment of the court by the owner or any party to the action, and the doctrine of caveat emptor applies with full vigor where the purchaser does not act upon representations of the owner inducing the purchase.

3. **Judicial sales ⚖️52—Purchaser will be relieved before confirmation but not afterwards if he will acquire no title.**

If before confirmation of a judicial sale the purchaser discovers that he will acquire no title by reason of the purchase or other equitable consideration making it unjust and unfair to require him to pay the purchase money, and such facts are made known to the court, he will be relieved from paying for the land, but after confirmation he will not be relieved from complying with his bid on the ground that he has acquired or will acquire no title unless he has relied on representations of the parties causing him to make the purchase.

4. **Partition ⚖️116(1)—Implied warranty of title does not run to alienees.**

The implied warranty of title between joint owners or coparceners on a partition of land does not protect any one except the former coparceners and their heirs and does not embrace an alienee of a coparcener who purchases after the partition is made.

5. **Partition ⚖️116(1)—Purchaser of coparcener's share at judicial sale not entitled to benefits of implied warranty of title.**

Where one of the coparceners among whom land was partitioned was an infant and her guardian brought suit to sell the share allotted to her for reinvestment of the proceeds, the purchaser at such sale was in no more favorable position than any other alienee as respected the right to rely on the warranty of title implied from the partition.

6. **Infants ⚖️98—Conveyance of land with warranty presumed unauthorized when petition does not allege authority.**

In an action on an infant's alleged warranty of title, where the petition alleges that on a sale of the land for reinvestment of the proceeds the commissioner conveyed the land with warranty of title, but does not allege that the court directed the commissioner to convey the land with such warranty, it must be presumed that the insertion of the warranty in the deed

was an unauthorized act on the part of the commissioner.

7. **Infants ⚖️42—Warranty of title in commissioner's deed not binding on infant.**

Under Civ. Code Prac. § 494, subsection 2, providing relative to the sale of lands of infants for reinvestment that the court shall cause the title of the property to be conveyed without warranty, a warranty inserted by the commissioner in his deed was not binding on the infant, especially where the court did not direct the insertion of such warranty.

8. **Infants ⚖️29—Retention of land in which proceeds of sale invested only estops infant to attack validity of sale.**

Where land of an infant was sold for reinvestment of the proceeds, and the purchaser lost the land by reason of an outstanding paramount title, the retention by the infant after arriving at her majority of the land in which the purchase money was invested only estopped her from denying the validity of the sale of whatever title she had.

9. **Partition ⚖️116(1)—Parties not presumed to have assumed obligations not implied by law.**

While coparceners when making a voluntary partition may doubtless warrant the title to each, where the partition is compulsory, they cannot be presumed to have assumed any obligations other than those implied by law from the nature of the proceedings where the warranty inserted in the deed was no different in its terms from that which the law would imply.

10. **Partition ⚖️116(1)—Parties do not acquire new title.**

The parties to a suit for the partition of land do not acquire any new or additional title to the land, but only the segregation of their interests.

11. **Partition ⚖️96—Court or commissioner cannot give warranty unless authorized by parties.**

Under Civ. Code Prac. § 499, subsection 7, providing relative to partition suits that, if the report is confirmed, a commissioner to be appointed for the purpose shall by deed convey to each party the land allotted to him, any warranty other than that implied by law is unauthorized where the parties did not seek or desire a conveyance with terms other than as provided by law.

Appeal from Circuit Court, Calloway County.

Action by A. B. Beale against Eva Stroud and others. From a judgment dismissing the action, plaintiff appeals. Affirmed.

Rainey T. Wells, of Murray, for appellant.
A. D. Thompson, of Murray, and J. O. Speight, of Mayfield, for appellees.

HURT, C. J. T. J. Tucker owned a tract of land which he sold and conveyed to one Holland. Thereafter Tucker executed a mortgage upon the land to one Hale to secure a debt which he owed to the latter. Hale instituted an action against Tucker to enforce the mortgage lien, which resulted in a judgment to that effect, and a sale of the land under the judgment to satisfy the debt. Hale became the purchaser of the land at the decretal sale, the sale was confirmed, and the land conveyed to Hale by a commissioner of the court. Hale died, and his heirs, several in number, instituted an action for a partition of the lands which they had inherited from him. The court decreed a partition and an allotment to each of his or her portion in severalty. The tract which Hale had purchased at the decretal sale, in his action against Tucker, was allotted to the appellee Eva Stroud (nèe Hale), who was then an infant. The report of the commissioner to make the partition and allotment was confirmed, and a deed executed to each of the partitioners for the lands allotted to him or her, respectively, by a commissioner of the court. Thereafter the guardian of the infant Eva Stroud instituted an action to secure a sale of the lands allotted to her in the partition and the reinvestment of their proceeds in other lands. A judgment was rendered to that effect, and the land which Hale, the ancestor, had purchased at the sale under the judgment in his favor against Tucker, and which in the partition had been allotted to Eva Stroud, was adjudged to be sold and was purchased at the sale by the appellant, Beale. The report of sale was duly confirmed, the purchase price paid, and the land conveyed to Beale by a commissioner. Holland, in an action for that purpose recovered the land from Beale and ousted him from its possession, the court having adjudged that Holland was the owner of a paramount title, and for such reason adjudged him the owner and entitled to the land.

Beale, by this action, sought to recover of Eva Stroud, and other children of Hale, in the way of damages for the loss of the land, the sum of money which he had paid for it, as its purchaser under the judgment in favor of the guardian for a sale and reinvestment of the proceeds. A general demurrer was sustained to his petition as amended, and the action was dismissed, and from the judgment he has appealed.

[1-3] Beale, having lost the land which he had purchased and paid for, to all appearances in good faith believing that he was acquiring by his purchase a good title thereto, naturally has the sympathy of a court of equity. He avers in the petition that Eva Stroud is now the owner and in possession of the land in which the money paid by him for the land which he had lost was invested, and it is insisted that this fact creates an equity in his favor. However, there is no averment in the petition to the effect that Eva Stroud made any express warranty of the title to the land, or by any representation, fraudulent or otherwise, induced the purchase of it by Beale, and in the absence of such facts he has no remedy against her. She was an infant, and by reason of such fact the court was invested with jurisdiction to sell the land, and did so by a judgment to that effect. Perhaps one of the oldest principles applicable to a judicial sale, and which has been uniformly adhered to in this jurisdiction, is that there is no warranty of the title of lands sold under a judgment of court by the owner or any party to the action, and the doctrine of caveat emptor applies with full vigor to such a sale. The purchaser must beware of what he purchases at such a sale. The court adjudges to be sold and conveyed to the purchaser such title as the parties have to the land, and nothing more. If, before confirmation, the purchaser discovers that he will acquire no title by reason of the purchase, or other equitable consideration, making it unjust and unfair to require him to pay the purchase money and he makes such facts known to the court, he will be relieved from the necessity of paying for the land, but after the confirmation of the sale he will not be relieved from complying with his bid upon the grounds that he had acquired, or will acquire no title by his purchase unless he can show that he has relied on representations made by the parties which has caused him or induced him to make the purchase. The court having made the sale, there is no warranty of title to be relied upon, and the purchaser at such a sale, where he does not act upon representations of the owner which induce the purchase, takes his chances on the title which he may acquire, and, having obtained all that he purchased, cannot justly complain of the parties or the court. Williams v. Glenn's Adm'r, 87 Ky. 87, 7 S. W. 610, 9 Ky. Law Rep. 941, 12 Am. St. Rep. 461; Farmers' Bank v. Peter, 13 Bush, 594; Henning v. Sweeney, 4 Ky. Law Rep. 986; Taylor v. Bank of Woodford, 4 Ky. Law Rep. 437; Fearons v. Gallagher's Heirs, 7 Ky. Law Rep. 298; Cooper v. Hill, 6 Ky. Law Rep. 742; Humphrey's Ex'r v. Wade, 84 Ky. 391, 1 S. W. 648, 8 Ky. Law Rep. 384; Elkin v. Gill, 9 Ky. Law Rep. 971; Fox v. McGoodwin's Adm'r, 56 S. W. 515, 21 Ky. Law Rep. 1776; Kentucky Union Co. v. Commonwealth, 128 Ky. 610, 108 S. W. 931, 110 S. W. 398, 33 Ky. Law Rep. 9, 49, 587; Dotson v. Merritt, 141 Ky. 155, 132 S. W. 181.

[4] The appellant relies for a right to recover against the brothers and sisters of Eva Stroud, who, before the partition of the lands of Hale, were joint owners with her of all the lands inherited by them, including the land in controversy, and had by reason of the partition between them of the jointly owned lands warranted the title of the lands

set apart to Eva Stroud. Appellant claims that, although he, as a purchaser of the latter land at a judicial sale cannot rely upon any warranty of the title to it as against the parties to the action in which the sale was had, his purchase embraced any warranty of the title made prior thereto which runs with the land, and for such reason he can require them to make good his loss upon the warranty made by them to their coparcener, Eva Stroud. The doctrine that a judicial sale of land embraces and passes to the purchaser the benefits of a previous warranty of a title to it, which was of such a character as would run with the land, was upheld by this court in Thomas v. Bland, 91 Ky. 1, 14 S. W. 955, 12 Ky. Law Rep. 640, 11 L. R. A. 240, and appellant's contention in the instant case would be sound if the warranty to title which arises by implication for the benefit of each coparcener where a partition of land jointly held is made ran with the land allotted to each coparcener and extended to an alienee of the coparcener's after the partition was made. The warranty of title which the law raised by implication by each of the joint owners of the lands for the benefit of each of the owners, when a partition to the land in severalty is made, does not extend to nor protect any one, except the former coparceners and their heirs, and does not embrace an alienee of a coparcener, who purchases after a partition is made, and such warranty does not run with the land. Such implied warranty exists against an alienee from one of the parceners after partition made, but does not exist in his favor as against any of the parceners, and he must look alone to his immediate vendee. Jones v. Bigstaff, 95 Ky. 395, 25 S. W. 889, 15 Ky. Law Rep. 821; Sawyers v. Cator, 8 Humph. (Tenn.) 280, 47 Am. Dec. 608; Weiser v. Weiser, 5 Watts (Pa.) 279, 30 Am. Dec. 313; Compton v. Mathews, 3 La. 128, 22 Am. Dec. 167; Weston v. Roper Lumber Co., 162 N. C. 165, 77 S. E. 430, Ann. Cas. 1915A, 931.

The above-described warranty did not formerly exist as between joint tenants and tenants in common, but only as between coparceners, and the reason assigned for limiting its operation to coparceners was that they could be compelled to make partition, but joint tenants and tenants in common could not be required to make partition, and, a partition being a matter of agreement in all cases between themselves, they were required to look to and abide by such agreements as to warranty of title that they might agree upon. The same reason would seem to limit the existence of an implied warranty to instances of compulsory partition between coparceners, and thus would not apply when the partition was voluntary. The rules which denied the right of compulsory partition between joint tenants and tenants in common having been abrogated

by statutes, and the reason for their existence forgotten, the rules relating to the implied warranty between coparceners came by analogy to be applied to tenants in common by inheritance where the facts are as in the instant case. Morris v. Harris, 9 Gill. (Md.) 19; Huntley v. Cline, 93 N. C. 458; Patterson v. Lanning, 10 Watts (Pa.) 135, 36 Am. Dec. 154. In some jurisdictions it is held that a warranty is not implied except in instances of compulsory partition, but in this state it has been broadly held, ignoring all distinctions between holdings by joint tenants, tenants in common, and coparceners, where there is a unity of title and possession, that an implied warranty attaches to every partition of land, and exists though no warranty is expressed in the deeds. Venable v. Beauchamp, 3 Dana (Ky.) 321, 28 Am. Dec. 74. This implied warranty is, however, a special one with regard to the damages for its breach as well as the persons who may take advantage of it, and extends no further and may be relied upon by no other persons, except as heretofore stated.

[5] The partition between Hale's heirs was compulsory, and there is no doubt but under all the authorities an implied warranty existed, but it could only be invoked by the coparceners themselves or their heirs, and would not extend to benefit an alienee of any one of them after partition made, and Beale, as a purchaser of the share of the lands allotted to Eva Stroud at a judicial sale, could not occupy a more favorable position as regards the implied warranty between the coparceners arising from the partition than he would occupy if he had purchased the share allotted to her directly from her. In the latter instance he could not invoke the implied warranty, and, being a purchaser at a judicial sale, which was confirmed without objection upon his part, there was no warranty upon her part upon which he can rely for recoupment.

The foregoing conclusions would be very clear but for the fact that they are somewhat beclouded by allegations in the petition as amended to the effect that the commissioner of the court who executed the deed of conveyance to Beale, in pursuance of his purchase of the land, under the judgment in the action maintained for a sale of the lands which were allotted to Eva Stroud, incorporated in the deed a clause of general warranty, and provided in the deed that the infant Eva Stroud would warrant and defend the title to the land. It is also averred that previous thereto, in the action to partition and after the report of the partition by the commissioners had been made, and a commissioner had been appointed to sign, execute, and deliver to each of the tenants in common a deed for the lands allotted to each of them in severalty, the appellees, the cotenants of Eva Stroud, by the commissioner, executed to her a deed for the lands allotted to her, and by its terms did "warrant and contract to defend the title to the premises therein conveyed." The partition recites that copies of the deeds are filed with the petition, but they are not in the record, and the foregoing are the essential averments in regard to them. The question is presented as to the effect that such stipulations in the deeds executed by the commissioner has upon the rights of the parties, and upon the principles governing their rights, as heretofore stated.

[6-8] In reference to the action by the guardian of Eva Stroud to procure a judgment to sell her lands, as an infant, for reinvestment, and in which Beale became the purchaser, it is not averred that the court directed the commissioner to convey the lands to him with a warranty of title, but the allegation is that the commissioner so conveyed it after the purchase and confirmation of the sale, and hence it must be concluded that the insertion of a clause attempting to bind the infant to warrant the title to Beale was an unauthorized act on the part of the commissioner. If the court had undertaken to have such express warranty included in the deed, its act would have been without authority, expressly contrary to the statutes, and void. Subsection 2 of section 494, Civ. Code Prac., concerning judicial sales, provides as follows:

"The court shall cause the title of the property to be conveyed by a commissioner to the purchaser, without warranty."

In jurisdictions where the courts are empowered to cause the lands of an infant to be sold under judgments rendered for that purpose by the guardians of an infant, or trustees appointed for that purpose, it has been held that a warranty incorporated in the deed of the guardian or trustee is not binding upon the infant. Young v. Lorain, 11 Ill. 641, 52 Am. Dec. 463; Brackenridge v. Dawson, 7 Ind. 388. Liability upon a warranty must exist, if at all, from the contract of the party sought to be bound, or from operation of law. In the present instance it cannot be pretended that the infant contracted, and there is no law which creates the obligation for her, nor is there any authority which authorized the commissioner to contract for her, and the appellant must be presumed to have known such facts. The retention of the land in which the money was invested after arriving at her majority would only estop her from denying the validity of the sale of whatever title she had to the land which was sold, and she does not attempt to assail the validity of the sale,

[9-11] Doubtless coparceners having a unity of title and possession, when making a voluntary partition, may make such contract with reference to warranting the title to the portion allotted to each as they may choose to do, but, where the partition is compulsory, they cannot be presumed to have assumed any obligations other than is implied by law, from the nature of the proceedings. It is not averred that the court in proceeding to partition the lands between the children of Hale undertook or directed its commissioner to include a warranty of title in the deed to Eva Stroud, and that the commissioner was without such authority there can be no question. The court could not in such a proceeding impose an obligation which the law does not impose or authorize. The parties did not acquire any new or additional title to the lands, but the only thing accomplished was the segregation of the interests of each. The authority of the court and its commissioner in such a proceeding with reference to the deeds to be made is governed by subsection 7, § 499, Civ. Code Prac., which is as follows:

"If the report be confirmed, a commissioner to be appointed for the purpose shall, by deed, convey to each party the land allotted to him."

The law annexes the only warranty which exists arising from such conveyances. Any other warranty being unauthorized, unless made by the parties, would leave nothing but the implied warranty imposed by law. There is no averment that any of the parties to the proceeding sought or desired the conveyances with terms other than are provided by law in such cases, and the allegation in regard thereto is that the parties by the commissioner "did in said deed warrant and contract to defend the title." Dismissing any contentions as to the authority of the commissioner or court, in the premises, as well as the extent of obligations assumed by the parties to the proceeding for the acts of the commissioner, it seems that the terms of the deed imposed upon the coparceners only the same obligation which was implied if none had been expressed in the deed, but which only extended to the parceners, and not to an alienee of one of them; for, after all, it could and was nothing more than a partition deed, and, the warranty therein expressed not being different from the terms which would be used for the expression of the warranty annexed by law to a partition, it could not be presumed that in such a deed it was intended to embrace more, and hence would not run with the land.

The judgment is therefore affirmed.

LEWIS, Clerk of Court, v. JAMES, Inspector, et al.

NASH, Clerk of Court, v. STATE TAX COMMISSION et al.

(Court of Appeals of Kentucky.   June 14, 1921.)

1. Officers ⬤⟿100(2) — Prohibition against change of salaries applies only to salaried officers.

Const. § 235, prohibiting a change in the salary of a public officer during his term, relates only to salaried officers, and therefore does not apply to a county court clerk, whose compensation is wholly by specific fees and commissions.

2. Officers ⬤⟿100(1)—Requirement of services without compensation does not violate provision against change of compensation unless existing laws authorize compensation.

A statute enacted during the term of office of a county court clerk, imposing upon such clerk the duty of collecting motor vehicle licenses without providing any compensation for such collections, does not violate Const. § 161, forbidding a change in compensation of any officer during his term of office, unless by legislation existing at the time of the clerk's election he was entitled to compensation for such services.

3. Officers ⬤⟿99—Legislature can add to duties without providing additional compensation.

The Legislature can add to the duties of an office after the incumbent has been elected and require the incumbent to perform those duties, though no compensation is provided for the performance thereof, since the duties of an office for which no compensation is provided are considered ex officio duties, which the incumbent must perform by reason of his holding the office.

4. Officers ⬤⟿94—Neither state nor county is liable to officers in absence of legal obligation.

Neither state nor county ever becomes indebted to any of its officers by implication, and such officers, in order to hold a state or county responsible for a claim, must show a legal obligation on the part of the county or state to pay it, especially in view of Ky. St. § 1749, forbidding compensation for any ex officio services rendered or to be rendered by an officer.

5. Licenses ⬤⟿14(1)—Motor Vehicle Act of 1920 was intended to embrace all statutory law on subject.

Acts 1920, c. 90, providing for the regulation and licensing of vehicles, was clearly intended to embrace all the statutory law pertaining to the regulation of the use of motor vehicles and the licensing and operation thereof.

6. Statutes ⬤⟿225 — Previous motor vehicle acts can be considered in ascertaining intention in subsequent act.

The previous legislation for the operation of motor vehicles, especially Acts 1914, c. 69 (Ky. St. c. 88b), may be considered in ascertaining the intention of the General Assembly in enacting Acts 1920, c. 90.

7. Clerks of courts ⬤⟿26—Motor Vehicle Act of 1920 impliedly prohibits commission for collecting licenses.

The Motor Vehicle Act of 1920, sections 3, 5, 17, 18, of which prescribe the duties of clerks of the county courts in relation to the collection of license fees from motor vehicles, and provides specific fees as compensation for many of the services required, but not for the collection of the fees, and do require that all the fees shall be paid over to the State Tax Commissioner, impliedly prohibits the clerks from retaining the 5 per cent. commission allowed them for collecting other license fees.

8. Clerks of courts ⬤⟿26—Authority in Motor Vehicle Act to deduct fees "under this act" does not authorize deduction of commission allowed by other statute.

The provision of Motor Vehicle Act 1920, § 18, subsec. j, requiring the clerk to make an accounting for all moneys received by him under the act after the deduction of his fees "under this act," does not authorize the deduction of the 5 per cent. commission allowed the clerk by another statute for the collection of other license fees.

9. Clerks of courts ⬤⟿26—General statute allowing commissions on licenses collected not read into Motor Vehicle Act.

The provision of Ky. St. § 4195, allowing the clerk of the county court 5 per cent. commission on licenses collected by him under the terms of that statute, cannot be read into the Motor Vehicle Act 1920, which requires the clerk to collect the license fees for motor vehicles in a method different from that required for other licenses.

10. Clerks of courts ⬤⟿26—Statute giving fees for specific acts in addition to commissions does not indicate intention to allow commission on motor vehicle licenses.

The fact that Ky. St. § 1720, allowed the clerk of the county court specific fees for specific acts in connection with the issuance of licenses, on which he was allowed a 5 per cent. commission for collection by section 4195, does not show that the Legislature intended the 5 per cent. commission also to apply to the fees for motor vehicles' licenses collected by him under the Motor Vehicle Act of 1920, which also prescribed specific fees for specific acts, but did not allow a commission.

11. Clerks of courts ⬤⟿26—Statute authorizing commission on moneys other than licenses does not authorize commission on motor vehicle licenses.

Ky. St. § 4242, allowing the clerk of the county court 5 per cent. commission on public moneys collected by him, which manifestly applies to moneys other than license taxes for which a specific commission of the same amount was allowed by section 4195, does not give him a commission on motor vehicle license taxes collected by him.

Separate suits by S. H. Lewis, Clerk of the Fayette County Court, against Henry E. James, Inspector, and others and by J. B. Nash, Clerk of the Franklin County Court, against the State Tax Commission and others for injunction. The cases were heard together. On motion before a judge of the Court of Appeals to dissolve the temporary injunction granted by the circuit court. Motion granted, and temporary injunction dissolved.

Geo. C. Webb, of Lexington, Logan & Myatt, of Louisville, and Morris & Jones, of Frankfort, for plaintiffs.

Chas. I. Dawson, Atty. Gen., for defendants.

HURT, C. J. The General Assembly at its regular 1920 session enacted a statute which is chapter 90 of the acts of that body. It is entitled:

"An act relating to vehicles; regulating their use and operation upon the public highways of this commonwealth; providing for the registration and licensing of motor vehicles, fixing the amount of the license and manner of payment thereof; providing for the registration and licensing of operators of motor vehicles and the amount of such license; providing a method of registration of motor vehicles; preventing illegal traffic in motor vehicles; providing penalty for the violation of this act, and repealing any and all conflicting laws."

By the provisions of the act, a license tax was imposed upon the owners of motor vehicles, for the privilege of operating same, or permitting the operation of same, upon any public highway, as defined in subsection (f) of section 1 of the act, as well as a license tax upon the privilege of operating a motor vehicle as a chauffeur, upon a public highway, as defined in the act. For the regulation and control of the operations of motor vehicles the owners and chauffeurs were required to register with the Tax Commission through the medium of the clerks of the county court, upon whom the act imposed a great many duties with regard to such registration, furnishing application blanks therefor, receiving applications, issuing receipts provided for in the act, collection of license taxes, distributing plates and badges, keeping records, and probably other duties. In the act, the duties of the clerks are stated as follows in section 17 thereof:

"Sec. 17. *Duties of the Clerk.* (a) It shall be the duty of the clerk in each county to see that the provisions of this act in his county are enforced, and in doing so he shall: (b) Take all applications as provided in this act. (c) Issue the receipts provided for in this act on blanks furnished by the commission. (d) Collect the fees due the state as provided for in this act. (e) Distribute the registration plates and badges furnished by the commission and keep a complete record in his office for the benefit of the public of all such registrations in his county, and to notify the owner or chauffeur of the receipt by him of the duplicate badges or plates. (f) Remit and report each Monday to the commission all moneys collected

under him during the previous week, together with the duplicates of receipts issued by him during the same period, all checks to be made payable to the State Treasurer. (g) Account to the commission for all registration plates, badges and receipt forms consigned to him, at such time or times as the commission may direct; give the commission timely notice of a probable deficiency of plates or other supplies."

As compensation to the clerk for the services required of him by the provisions of the act, it is provided that he may collect from the licensees the following fees for the following specific services:

(1) For filing an application for registration, receiving license fee, and giving to the applicant a receipt containing the registration number and the information included in the application, and two plates bearing the number, the sum of 30 cents.

(2) For delivering to one who has lost a registration receipt, upon application filed, the sum of 40 cents.

(3) For receiving from a licensee a statement as to his loss of a registration plate or plates, receiving 50 cents for each plate or plates desired to be duplicated and giving receipt therefor, the sum of 40 cents.

(4) Notifying, by mail, the licensee of the receipt of the duplicate plate or plates, taking up the receipt above mentioned and delivering to the licensee the duplicate plate or plates, the sum of 40 cents.

(5) When a vehicle is sold, receiving the indorsed receipt of the original owner and the bill of sale, and retaining same, receiving the transfer fee of one dollar, and issuing a receipt bearing the same date and information as is required in the original receipt, except the change in name and address, the sum of 40 cents.

(6) For receiving registration plates, and indorsed receipts from a licensee, who has "junked" a vehicle, and forwarding these, with a copy of bill of sale, to the State Tax Commission, the sum of 40 cents.

(7) For receiving application for a chauffeur's license, receiving license fee, delivering a receipt containing the name and address, registration number and description of the applicant, and a numbered metal badge to the applicant, the sum of 40 cents.

(8) For duplicating receipt and badge of a chauffeur, who has lost the original, the sum of 40 cents.

Section 18 of the act, among other provisions, contains the following:

"Sec. 18. *Duties of the Commission.* (a) It shall be the duty of the commission to carry out the provisions of this act, and in so doing shall: * * *

(i) *Disposition of Funds.* Receive all moneys forwarded by the clerk in each county and turn over same to the auditor for the benefit of the state road funds; and out of this fund shall be paid the expenses of said commission incident to the enforcement of this act, said payment being made in the manner provided by law for payment of salaries and expenses.

"(j) *Settlements.* Shall at the end of each fiscal year make a settlement of the accounts showing the receipts and expenditures, and file same with the Auditor of Public Accounts for the state. And they shall further require an accounting from the clerk in each county for all moneys received by him under the provisions of this act, after the deduction of his fees under this act, and for all receipts, forms, plates and badges consigned to him."

Section 22 of the act provides as follows:

"Any and all laws and parts of laws in conflict herewith are hereby repealed."

Each of the plaintiffs, who is a clerk of a county court, one for the county of Fayette, and the other for the county of Franklin, instituted an action against the State Tax Commission, and the individual members thereof, and the former included as defendants to his action the Inspector and Examiner and the Treasurer, but each of the actions involves the same question for decision, and were heard together in the trial court. A demurrer was sustained to the petition of the clerk of the Fayette county court, so far as it concerned the Inspector and Examiner and the Treasurer. The plaintiffs claim that they are entitled to retain 5 per centum of the moneys collected by them and paid over to the treasurer of the state, through the Tax Commission, from the license taxes imposed upon the owners of motor vehicles and chauffeurs, as compensation for their services in receiving and remitting such taxes. Averring that the defendants were demanding that they pay over to the state the entire sum of such taxes, and threatening to inflict penalties upon them for failing to do so, the plaintiffs ask an injunction against the defendants, to restrain them from taking such action. The circuit court being of the opinion that section 4195, Ky. Stats., applied to the collection and remission of the taxes in controversy, and that the plaintiffs were entitled to retain the 5 per centum of the sum of all license taxes collected and paid over by them under chapter 90 Session Act 1920, a temporary injunction restraining the members of the Tax Commission from requiring the plaintiffs to account for or to pay over the 5 per centum, and the question is now before me, as a judge of the Court of Appeals upon the motion of the Tax Commission and Attorney General, to dissolve the injunction.

The following facts are conceded: (1) Chapter 90, Session Acts 1920, was enacted after the plaintiffs had been elected and inducted into their respective offices, and (2) the duties imposed upon them by that act were duties which they had not theretofore been required to perform, either with or without compensation. Both plaintiffs and defendants invoke sections 161 and 235 of the Constitution, the former of which provides that—

"The compensation of any city, county, town or municipal officer shall not be changed after his election or appointment, or during his term of office"

—and that latter prohibits a change in the salary of a public officer during the term for which he is elected. The plaintiffs contend that 5 per centum of all public moneys which a county clerk is required to collect and pay into the treasury was a fixed fee for such service pertaining to the office when they were elected and inducted into office, and that it is beyond the power of the General Assembly to require them to perform any such service and to deny such compensation, and that the statute should not on that account be so construed; while the defendants contend that to permit the plaintiffs to retain the 5 per centum in controversy would be to authorize a change in their compensation during their terms of office, and hence violative of the cited provisions of the Constitution.

[1] The compensation of the office of county court clerk arising wholly from specific fees and commissions, it is apparent that section 235 of the Constitution is not involved, because that has relation only to salaried offices.

[2] It is also apparent that the invoking of the section 161 of the Constitution is without need upon the part of either the plaintiffs or defendants, unless the Legislature has by existing legislation attempted to authorize the plaintiffs to retain as compensation 5 per centum of the license taxes, which they are required to collect and pay over, by chapter 90, supra, or to take away from them some fixed source of compensation of their offices, and if such legislation does not exist it is unnecessary to decide whether section 161, supra, would or would not effect it. In the light of the conclusion which has been arrived at, it is altogether unnecessary to discuss the effect of 161 or 235, supra, upon the rights of officers, with the distinction to be drawn between offices to which a fixed salary is attached and those of which the compensation is specific fees and commissions.

[3] It is very well settled that it is within the power of the Legislature to add to the duties of an office after an incumbent has been elected, and during his term of office, and he will be required to perform those duties although no compensation is provided at all for the performance of the additional duties. It has been consistently held that to add to the duties of a salaried office during the term of an incumbent does not entitle the incumbent to any additional compensation on account of. added duties, and, as applied to an office, the compensation for the duties of which are specific fees for certain specific duties of the office, that the incumbent will not be entitled to compensation for any other

duties than those for the performance of which compensation is provided. The other duties of such an office are considered ex officio duties, which the incumbent must perform by reason of his holding the office. 29 Cyc. 1424; Mitchell v. Henry County, 124 Ky. 883, 100 S. W. 220, 30 Ky. Law Rep. 1051; Brown v. Laurel County Fiscal Court, 175 Ky. 747, 194 S. W. 907; James v. Duffy, 140 Ky. 607, 134 S. W. 459, 140 Am. St. Rep. 404; Spalding v. Thornbury, 128 Ky. 533, 108 S. W. 291, 108 S. W. 906, 31 Ky. Law Rep. 738; Jefferson County v. Waters, 114 Ky. 48, 70 S. W. 40, 24 Ky. Law Rep. 816; Locke v. City of Central, 4 Colo. 65, 34 Am. Rep. 66; and many other cases of the same and similar holdings.

[4] Hence, although chapter 90, supra, required the plaintiffs, as a duty of their respective offices, to collect the license taxes therein provided for, and to pay over same to the state, their right to have and retain a commission of 5 per centum, or any other sum, would depend entirely upon whether authority for such action can be found in the statutes of the state now existing, for it has been heretofore held that neither a state nor county ever becomes indebted to any of their agents by implication, and that such agent, in order to hold a state or county responsible for a claim, must show a legal obligation on the part of state or county to pay it. Wortham v. Grayson County Court, 13 Bush, 53. This principle is emphasized by section 1749, Ky. Stats., which provides that—

"No fee bill shall be made out, or compensation allowed hereafter, for any ex officio services rendered or to be rendered by an officer."

[5] To determine the merits of plaintiff's contention the result depending upon a construction of the present statutes applicable to such subjects will make necessary the ascertainment as to whether or not the Legislature, in enacting chapter 90, intended that the clerks should have the right to a commission of 5 per centum on the license taxes as claimed by them. This is arrived at from all the provisions of chapter 90, supra, and from a consideration of any other existing statutes which are in pari materia with it. The provisions of chapter 90, supra, which have been cited, and the other provisions of that chapter, indicate very clearly that the Legislature intended that it should embrace all of the statutory law intended to be enacted, pertaining to the subject of regulating the use of motor vehicles, the licenses for operating same, and the collection and disbursement of the license taxes arising from that source. It is intended to be a very comprehensive act, and the provision in it by which it is declared that all laws and parts of laws in conflict with its provisions were repealed indicates clearly that it was meant to embrace all statutory provisions pertaining to the subjects legislated about. It is also clear that the Legislature intended to adopt a different system for the collection and disposition of the funds arising from the license taxes imposed by chapter 90 than is applied to other license taxes imposed by other laws. The entire funds arising from licenses imposed by chapter 90, supra, are to be devoted to the improvement and building of the public roads in the state, while the great bulk of other license taxes imposed come into the general expenditure fund of the state.

[6] The previous legislation in regard to licenses for the operation of motor vehicles may be looked to to ascertain the intention of the General Assembly in enacting chapter 90, and especially the act of 1914 (chapter 69), which is chapter 88b, Ky. Stats., and which is repealed by the repealing clause of chapter 90, and the other acts preceding it. It will thus be seen that the previous legislation required the collection and paying over to the treasury of the license taxes upon motor vehicles, without any commission allowed to any official, whose duty it was to make the collections, from which it appears, that the policy of the state has been, from the first legislation upon that subject, to require the collection of these taxes without any cost to the state treasury in the way of a percentage to the collector, and such policy must at least be persuasive of the purpose of the Legislature, when it enacted chapter 90, supra, and wherein is not incorporated any provision for a percentage to the clerks.

[7] Looking now broadly to the requirements of chapter 90, which for the first time imposed the duty of collecting the license taxes upon the operation of motor vehicles upon the county clerks, it is found that section 3 of that act provides that the clerk shall receive and file the application for a license, and shall receive the license tax and give to the owner a receipt containing the registration number, and the information included in the application, and two plates bearing the number, and for this service the statute provides as follows:

"For services performed, the owner shall pay the county clerk the sum of thirty cents for registration."

When a licensee has lost the registration plates and applies for duplicates, subsection (c) of section 3, supra, requires him to pay and the clerk to receive the sum of 50 cents for each plate, and to issue to the licensee a receipt therefor, "and for which service the owner shall pay the clerk the sum of forty cents." The same subsection provides that upon receipt of the duplicate plate or plates, the clerk shall notify the licensee, by mail, and the licensee shall return to the clerk the receipt given him for the payment of the price of the duplicate plates, and upon the delivery of the plates, the statute provides, "And for this service the owner shall pay

231 S.W.—34

the clerk the sum of forty cents." When a purchaser of a vehicle from a licensed owner desires a transfer, he is required to present an indorsed receipt, pay the transfer fee of $1 to the clerk, and for which the clerk gives him a receipt, subsection (d) par. 4, of section 3 of the act thus provides that "for his services hereunder, the purchaser shall pay the clerk a fee of forty cents." When the clerk collects the tax from an applicant for a chauffeur's license, issues him a receipt, and gives him a numbered metal badge, subsection (a) of section 5 of the act thus provides, "And for his services, the registrant shall pay to the clerk a fee of forty cents." Subsection (d), par. 4, of section 3 of the act provides that, when a purchaser "junks" or otherwise renders the automobile unfit for future use, he will be relieved of the duty of transferring registration by the delivery of registration plates, indorsed receipt, and a second copy of the bill of sale to the clerk, who will return the plates, receipt, and copy of the bill of sale to the Commission, "and for these services the purchaser shall pay the clerk the sum of forty cents." Subsection (f) of section 17 of the act, supra, requires the clerk to report and remit to the Commission on each Monday all moneys collected by him during the previous week, and subsection (d) of the same section indicates the moneys to be collected and remitted as "the fees due the state as provided for in this act." Subsection (j) of section 18 of the act provides that at the end of each fiscal year the Tax Commission shall "further require an accounting from the clerk in each county for all moneys received by him under the provisions of this act, after the deduction of his fees under this act," etc. The legislative intention to require the clerk to pay over the entire sum of the license taxes collected by him under the act, and to compensate him for his services only to the extent provided for in the act, could not very well be expressed more strongly than is done by the foregoing language.

[8] It is suggested that the language of the statute, "deducting his fees under this act," means the 5 per centum claimed by the plaintiffs; but this contention is necessarily not well grounded, since the fees to be deducted are those provided for by the act, and nowhere in the act is a commission of 5 per centum to the clerk provided for. The language manifestly has reference to the fees above enumerated to be paid to the clerk by the licensees, because they are the only fees provided for under the act, and the language was used to make the meaning clear, as the fees are collected by virtue of the act, and, the writer having broadly provided that "all moneys collected under the act" were to be accounted for, the language above stated was then added, to except, for the officer, the fees allowed to him under the

act. By the terms of the act the Legislature provided at least, for the compensation it intended for the clerk to have for collecting the license taxes, along with the other services it required of him, for some of which no compensation was provided at all, and although the compensation may be considered scant and insufficient and as imposing an onerous duty upon the clerk beyond the value of his compensation, with that question the courts can have nothing to do, as that was a question wholly within the legislative discretion. The failure of the Legislature to provide any compensation for the clerk for the responsibility of holding and remitting the funds collected from the license taxes does not authorize the clerk to have a claim against the state on that account, as heretofore stated, unless there is some statute which authorizes such compensation. It is clear enough that chapter 90, supra, does not contain any provision permitting the clerk to retain any per centum of the taxes collected, but requires him to pay over to the treasury, not a part, "but all the moneys collected under him during the previous week," and the Tax Commission is required to cause the clerk to account, not for a part of the sum of the taxes collected, but "for all the moneys received by him under the provisions of this act, after the deduction of his fees," etc. If the Legislature did not intend to preclude by the above language the right of the clerk to retain a percentage of the taxes collected, there could be no reason for the use of the word "all" when referring to the moneys to be paid over to the treasury, in defining the duties of the clerk, and its reiteration, when the duties of the Tax Commission are defined.

The plaintiffs, however, contend that sections 4195, 4242, Ky. Stats., control their rights in the premises and entitle them to retain the 5 per centum of the license taxes in controversy. Section 4195 is as follows:

"When such license is granted, the county clerk shall fill up the original stub. The original he shall deliver to the person to whom it is granted, and shall, within two days thereafter, forward the duplicate to the Auditor of Public Accounts, who shall charge * * * the tax to him, and the clerk shall, once each month, pay the license tax collected into the state treasury; and said clerk, as compensation for his services, shall be allowed 5 per cent. commission on all license tax collected and accounted for by him."

Section 4242, Ky. Stats., provides as follows:

"Each circuit and county clerk shall make out an account of all taxes and other public money received by him up to the first day of each circuit court; and said report shall show in detail of whom said moneys were received, for what and when received, and shall be verified by him and entered of record; and he shall pay over the public money remaining in his hands to the trustee of the jury fund, until otherwise provided by law, so much thereof as the court may by order direct as being necessary for the payment of the jurors; and the original account certified with the order of the court, shall be transmitted with the balance of the funds to the auditor. The clerk shall be allowed 5 per cent. commission on ,said sums reported and paid by him. * * * "

[8] As a reason for the contention that sections 4195 and 4242, Ky. Stats., apply and entitle the plaintiffs to the percentage of the taxes claimed, it is insisted that neither of the sections have been repealed, nor in any manner modified, and should be read into the provisions of chapter 90, supra. That they have not been repealed nor modified by chapter 90, nor any other statute, seems to be true, as neither of them bear any relation or were ever intended in any way to have effect upon the collection of license taxes, for the operation of motor vehicles. The statutes, supra, are sections of an act of March 15, 1906, and that statute imposed a great many license taxes, many of which were to be granted by the clerk of the county court, who was made the collector of certain of the license taxes, therein designated. The statute of March 15, 1906, which is now chapter 108, Ky. Stats., also provided that all licenses should be granted by the clerk of the county court, when not otherwise provided by law. There were imposed other license taxes, where the licenses were to be granted by other officers, and the collection of the taxes imposed upon others. Section 4195, supra, authorized the payment to the clerk of a commission of 5 per centum upon the sum of the license taxes, collected by him, and paid to the Treasurer, under chapter 108, Ky. Stats., and upon the license taxes designated for his collection, by the provisions of that chapter. The taxes collected from those licenses the clerk was required to report to the auditor within two days, and once in each month to pay the taxes into the treasury. The section, supra, could have had no relation to a tax upon motor vehicles, as at the time of its enactment no such licenses were required. The things for the doing of which the clerk was authorized to license and to collect the taxes and to receive a commission for collecting were all specifically designated in the statute of which section 4195 is a part. Such section is in full force and effect touching the purposes for which it was enacted. While a license tax created since the enactment of that statute, with no provisions as to its collection, or other specific arrangement different from the licenses provided for in chapter 108, supra, which are designated as collectible by the clerk, would fall under the provisions of section 4195, supra, a license tax thereafter created, although to be collected by the clerk, is neces-

sarily subject to the conditions provided for by the statute creating it, if any different conditions are imposed, such as to apply to the motor license taxes, provided for by chapter 90, supra. When license taxes were imposed upon the operation of motor vehicles upon the highways, the taxes were made payable to the Secretary of State, and afterwards to the Commissioner of Motor Vehicles, as a subordinate of the Secretary of State, and no commissions were allowed or paid for the collecting of the taxes. When by chapter 90, supra, the duty of collecting the license taxes for the operation of motor vehicles were imposed upon the county clerks, it was upon different terms and under different regulations from those governing the collection of other license taxes, which they are now and had been theretofore authorized to collect, and one of the conditions was that they should pay the entire tax collected by them into the treasury upon each Monday, and another was that by the terms of the statute imposing the duty no commission for the collection was provided for, but in terms was denied. If section 4195, supra, should be attempted to be added to chapter 90, no requirement of it would be consistent with the requirements of chapter 90 with reference to the duties of the clerk.

[10] It is suggested that, in addition to a commission of 5 per centum upon the license taxes, which the clerk was authorized to collect, under chapter 108, Ky. Stats., he was also entitled to collect a specific fee for issuing a license (section 1720, Ky. Stats.), and for such reason the fees allowed him for specific duties performed by him, under chapter 90, supra, was not in payment for his services in collecting and remitting the taxes. The difference in the two statutes is that chapter 108, Ky. Stats., expressly allows the commission, and section 1720, supra, expressly provides the fee, for granting a license, while chapter 90, supra, expressly provides the fees for certain specific services, among which is collecting the taxes, and, by the strongest implication amounting to an express denial, denies any commission or percentage for holding and remitting the money, and imposes such duty and others upon the clerk as ex officio duties without compensation. Section 4195, supra, was in force when chapter 90 was enacted, and, having been in force for many years, theretofore, the Legislature is presumed to have known of its requirements and limitations, and to have considered same when enacting chapter 90, but it cannot be held that it contemplated or intended that the collection of taxes provided for in that chapter should be subject to the conditions of section 4195, since the latter statute expressly provided for the payment of the taxes once each month by the clerk to the auditor, and the retention of 5 per centum as a commission, while the

moneys collected by the clerk under chapter 90 the Legislature provided should be remitted to the treasury through the Tax Commission once each week, and, instead of expressly providing for the retention of a percentage, expressly required the remission of the entire sum collected. Hence if by any construction section 4195 could be added to chapter 90 as a part of it, all of its provisions would be inconsistent with the provisions of chapter 90, and would fall under the effect of the repealing clause in the latter statute.

[11] Section 4242, supra, manifestly applies to public moneys which it was the clerk's duty to collect, under chapter 108, Ky. Stats., and other statutes, other than license taxes, since section 4195 applied to license taxes specially. Under the law, the clerk had the duty of collecting special taxes, such as taxes upon deeds, mortgages, powers of attorney, and in some instances certain taxes upon property, and such like, and section 4242 was a direction as to all such public moneys, and other than license taxes. If such section was attempted to be added to and read with the provisions of chapter 90 all the provisions of it would be contradictory of the provisions of chapter 90, unless the single sentence, which provides that the clerk shall be allowed a commission upon the sums collected and paid over by him could be held consistent with it, and to insist that the one sentence, which manifestly refers to public moneys, then authorized to be collected, by statutes then in force, and to moneys other than license taxes, should be lifted out of the section, discarding the other provisions of it and its context, and held to apply to the taxes collected under chapter 90, is not supported by any sound reason. Hence it is concluded that neither section 4195 nor 4242 has any application to the provisions of chapter 90, supra.

It is therefore concluded, that the clerks of the county court cannot retain 5 per centum of the license taxes collected by them under the provisions of chapter 90, supra, and the temporary injunction granted by the circuit court is dissolved.

Judges THOMAS, SETTLE, CLARKE, and CLAY considered the motion with me, and concur in the conclusion reached.

STANGE et al. v. PRICE.

(Court of Appeals of Kentucky. June 3, 1921.)

1. **Corporations** ⟐⟐514(1)—Plea denying existence of nul tiel corporation.

In the language of common-law pleading, a plea denying the existence of a corporation is called a plea of nul tiel corporation.

2. **Corporations** ⟐⟐514(1)—Pleading ⟐⟐111—Pleading of nul tiel corporation is in abatement, and, if sustained, additional parties may be ordered.

The objection raised by plea of nul tiel corporation will be considered in abatement rather than in bar, and when it appears the objection is well taken it furnishes ground for order requiring additional parties to be made.

3. **Pleading** ⟐⟐111—After plea of nul tiel corporation sustained, defendant entitled to dismissal in absence of tendered amendment.

Where a plea of nul tiel corporation is filed and sustained, defendant is entitled to dismissal of the action without prejudice in the absence of a tendered amendment making new parties and correcting the mistake or misnomer in the petition.

4. **Pleading** ⟐⟐106(1)—Plea in abatement does not deny right of action, and must give better writ.

A plea in abatement offers an objection to form rather than substance, and does not deny the right of action itself, and as a general rule such a plea must give plaintiff a better writ.

5. **Parties** ⟐⟐94(2)—Mere mistake or misnomer in plaintiff's name pleadable in abatement only.

A mere mistake or misnomer in plaintiff's name, which does not affect his or its capacity to sue in the right name, is pleadable in abatement only, and when the establishment of the truth of the matters alleged will not bar a future action of the same property, but will merely abate the present action, it cannot be said the matter answered is a plea in bar.

6. **Parties** ⟐⟐95(5)—Amended petition setting up that plaintiff which sued a corporation was in fact a partnership permissible.

Where defendant, sued by a claimed corporation, filed a plea in abatement shortly after the discovery by him of the fact that plaintiff was not a corporation, and on the same day an amended petition was tendered in which it was stated that the allegation that plaintiff was a corporation was a mistake, and as a matter of law it was a partnership composed of two named parties doing business under a corporate name, the court in furtherance of justice should have permitted filing of such pleading, and erred in sustaining objection to its filing and dismissing the action.

Appeal from Circuit Court, Boyle County.

Action by Herman Stange and another, partners doing business under the name of the Western Tin & Japan Manufacturing Company, against Thomas J. Price. From a judgment for defendant, plaintiffs appeal. Reversed for further proceedings not inconsistent with the opinion.

Chas. C. Fox, of Danville, for appellants. Puryear & Clay, of Danville, for appellee.

QUIN, J. This action was instituted by the Western Tin & Japan Manufacturing Company, as a corporation, seeking to recov-

er a balance due on account for merchandise
sold defendant (appellee). The answer was
made a counterclaim, in which, after denying the material parts of the petition defendant claimed certain credits to which he was
entitled in the way of freight charges, etc.
A reply made up the issues. Thereafter defendant filed a plea in abatement shortly
after the discovery by him of the fact that
plaintiff was not a corporation. On the
same day an amended petition was tendered
in which it was stated that the allegation
that plaintiff was a corporation was a mistake, and as a matter of fact it was a partnership composed of Herman Stange and
Victor L. Stange, and as such partners they
were trading and doing business under the
firm name of Western Tin & Japan Manufacturing Company, and in said name sold
and delivered the merchandise set out in the
petition. An objection to the filing of this
amended petition was sustained, and the action was dismissed; hence this appeal.

[1] In the language of common-law pleading, a plea denying the existence of a corporation is called a plea of nul tiel corporation.
Whether such a plea should be construed
in bar of the action or in abatement thereof
the authorities are not agreed. 14a C. J.
828.

[2] The rule in this state is that such an
objection will be considered in abatement
rather than in bar, and when it appears that
the objection is well taken, as is instanced
in the present case, it furnishes ground for
an order of court requiring additional parties to be made. Woodson, etc., v. Bank of
Gallipolis, 4 B. Mon. 203; Jones, etc., v.
Bank of Tennessee, 8 B. Mon. 122, 46 Am.
Dec. 540; Wood, etc., v. Friendship Lodge,
106 Ky. 424, 50 S. W. 836, 20 Ky. Law Rep.
2002; Higdon v. Wayne County Security Co.,
154 Ky. 337, 157 S. W. 708. See, also, Baltimore & Potomac R. R. Co. v. Fifth Baptist
Church, 137 U. S. 568, 11 Sup. Ct. 185, 34
L. Ed. 784.

[3] Where such a plea is filed and sustained, the defendant is entitled to a dismissal of the action without prejudice in
the absence of a tendered amendment making new parties and correcting the mistake
or misnomer in the petition.

[4] A plea in abatement offers an objection to form rather than substance, and
does not deny the right of action itself, and
as a general rule such a plea must give the
plaintiff a better writ. Andrew Stephens
on Pleading, § 71.

[5] The mere mistake or misnomer in
plaintiff's name, which does not affect his
or its capacity to sue in the right name, is
pleadable in abatement only, and when the
establishment of the truth of the matters
alleged will not bar a future action of the
same property, but will merely abate the
present action, it cannot be said the mat-

ter answered is a plea in bar. Oregon Central Railroad Co. v. Wait, 3 Or. 91.

In Newman on Pleading & Practice, §
219b, it is said:

"If there be a mistake in the name of either
the plaintiff or defendant, it will not be as fatal
to the action now as it formerly was. If the
plaintiff sued by a wrong name, it was formerly
a matter defeating the action, if relied on by
appropriate plea; but now the defect can be
reached only by motion to correct the mistake
and state the name of the party correctly. It
is true that, when an action is brought and the
proof shows no liability to the plaintiff who has
sued, there can be no recovery by him against
the defendant; and if the person to whom the
liability exists is shown to be another and different person, there can be no amendment allowed which changes the real parties to the
action. But where it appears that the liability
is to the person who really brings the suit, and
that there is merely a mistake in the true name,
or a misnomer as it is called, the court will usually allow an amendment correcting the mistake upon such terms as may be just."

This text finds support in Baumeister, etc.,
v. Markham, 101 Ky. 122, 39 S. W. 844, 41
S. W. 816, 72 Am. St. Rep. 397, which was
a suit instituted by Pauline Markham
against Baumeister and others to recover
damages for injuries which plaintiff claimed
she sustained when she stepped into a hole
in a sidewalk in the city of Louisville. The
point was made that plaintiff was in fact
the wife of Randolph Murray, and therefore
Markham was not her name. In speaking
on the subject under consideration the court
says:

"It is a rule of practice recognized by this
court that, if the defendant to an action, though
sued in the wrong name, was in proper person
before the court and litigated with the plaintiff
about the subject of controversy, a judgment
against him on the merits of the case is as valid
and effectual as if he had disclosed, and the action had been rendered in his true name.
"There is no reason why the same rule may
not as well apply to the case of a plaintiff suing in an assumed name, if the defendant has
not been thereby prejudiced. Therefore, if appellee be the identical person who received the
injury complained of, as is so, the judgment in
her favor should not be held invalid for the
only reason she chose to sue in a name adopted for the stage, and by which she is generally
known, for appellants have not been thereby
misled, nor can she maintain another action for
the same cause against them or either of them."

The right of a person or persons to conduct business in this state under an assumed name is recognized by Ky. Stats. § 199b,
provided such person complies with the statute by the filing in the office of the county
clerk of a certificate setting forth the information required by said section.

The Messrs. Stange were privileged to
conduct business under the name of the
Western Tin & Japan Manufacturing Com-

pany, and it was under this designation that they transacted business with the defendants, nor were they known to the defendants by any other name. The business belonged to them and they were the real persons at interest. The fact that it was conducted under a trade-name rendered the business none the less an individual enterprise, and rendered them no less responsible for its obligations. Since it was competent for them to assume such name as they desired any contract made by them under said name would be binding upon them. If a suit instituted in their name had been prosecuted to judgment, without objection, they would afterwards be estopped from denying the binding 'effect of the judgment, should the result be unfavorable to them. As said in 14 Enc. Pl. & Pr. 278:

"There is nothing so sacred in a name that right and justice should be sacrificed to its sanctity."

After all it is not so much the name as the identity of the person who causes the name to be employed. In a suit instituted by the Messrs. Stange in their trade-name the proceedings, so far as they are concerned, would not be wanting in respect to real parties plaintiff, and after judgment they would be estopped to raise the point that the suit was not brought in the name of a natural person, a partnership, or a corporation.

Since the partners are capable of suing, an action brought in their true name or in the trade-name of their adoption will be binding upon them whenever it appears the suit was instituted at their instance. This is not a case of fictitious parties; the parties are real; though acting under an assumed name, they are nevertheless real persons. See Clark Bros. v. Wyche, 126 Ga. 24, 54 S. E. 909. To the same effect is Charles v. Valdosta Foundry & Machine Co., 4 Ga. App. 733, 62 S. E. 493, in which latter case appears this statement:

" * * * The person who thus sues in a trade or business name cannot, in his real name, be afterwards heard to dispute any judgment rendered in the case in which he was a party plaintiff under the assumed or trade name."

Of course, these authorities recognize the fact that defendant is entitled to be sued by a real party in interest, and, if he decides to contest the point that he is not so sued, he can do so by a plea in abatement setting up the names of the real parties plaintiff, as was done by the defendant. But the effect of such plea, as we have seen, is not in bar of the action, but merely an abatement of it until such time as proper amendments are seasonably offered curing the defect complained of. This is not a case where plaintiff is a nonentity, as il-

lustrated in Steamboat Burns, 9 Wall. 237, 19 L. Ed. 620; and Steamboat Penbinaw v. Wilson, 11 Iowa, 479, where it was held a steamboat could not be made a party to an action. Likewise it has been held that the estate of a decedent has no legal personality such as can have a status in court. Estate of John Columbus v. Monti, 6 Minn. 568 (Gil. 403). Nor can a suit be instituted in the name of one's property. Western & Atlantic Ry. Co. v. Dalton Marble Works, etc., 122 Ga. 774, 50 S. E. 978.

Civ. Code Prac. § 134, provides in part that:

"The court may, at any time, in furtherance of justice, and on such terms as may be proper, cause or permit a pleading or proceedings to be amended, by adding or striking out the name of a party; or, by correcting a mistake in the name of a party or a mistake in any other respect; or by inserting other allegations material to the case. * * * And, if a proceeding taken by a party fail to conform in any respect to the provisions of this Code, the court may permit an amendment of such proceeding, so as to make it conformable thereto. And, if the allegations of a pleading be so indefinite or uncertain that the precise nature of the claim or defense is not apparent, the court may require the pleading to be made definite and certain by amendment. The court must, in every stage of an action, disregard any error or defect in the proceedings, which does not affect the substantial rights of the adverse party; and no judgment shall be reversed or affected by reason of such error or defect."

For instance, in Woodram, by, etc., v. Cincinnati & Kentucky Southern Ry. Co., 38 S. W. 703, 18 Ky. Law Rep. 945, it was held that, while a suit cannot be maintained in the name of a next friend for the benefit of an infant, plaintiff should have been permitted to file an amended petition curing the defect, after a demurrer had been sustained to the pleading.

In Pike, Morgan & Co. v. Wathen, 78 S. W. 187, 25 Ky. Law Rep. 1264, where appellant had been sued in the lower court as a corporation, it was held on a petition for rehearing that, in the absence of proof of defendant's corporate existence, which was denied in the answer, the burden was on plaintiff to prove defendant was a corporation, and upon failure to make the requisite proof plaintiff was not entitled to recover, but the action was reversed, with instructions to permit the parties to amend their pleadings, if desired. And in Teets v. Snider Heading Mfg. Co., 120 Ky. 653, 87 S. W. 808, 27 Ky. Law Rep. 1061, where defendant, sued as a corporation, filed a plea in abatement stating that it was a partnership doing business under the designation by which it had been sued, the action of the lower court in dismissing the action was held error, and plaintiffs were accorded the right to file an amended petition withdrawing the averment that defendant ,was a corporation and making the firm members defendants.

A good statement of the rule applicable to the facts of this case is found in Porter, etc., v. Cresson et al., 10 Serg. & R. (Pa.) 257, from which we take the following excerpt:

"The distinction as to proper parties between plaintiffs and defendants, the former being pleas in bar, the latter in abatement, has no principle for its foundation, and time and good sense will finally prevail, and require equally in both cases that defendant should take advantage of it by plea in abatement. It is more convenient to all parties that advantage should be taken of it in limine, by plea in abatement, and that parties should, after issue joined, proceed on the merits, than that a defendant should on the trial be allowed to defeat a plaintiff on a mere matter of form. The subject is very fully considered by Sergt. Williams, in his very comprehensive note to Cabbell v. Vaughan, 1 Saund. 291. From the time of the Year Books to this time misnomer might be pleaded in abatement, when the plaintiff misnames himself (22 Edw. III, c. 34) and we ought not to be more strict than in the days of the Year Books; and in Brooke, Misnomer, 73, it is said that in an action by a corporation or a natural body misnomer of the one or the other goes only to the writ. But, if there was no such company as Cresson, Wistar & Co., then there could be no person in rerum natura to maintain the action; that would be in bar, for there could be no one to maintain the action by any name. Here there was a company, such a one as is described in the bill, to whom the defendants bound themselves by the name of trade. This cannot be stronger than a plaintiff misnaming himself, and according to the ancient and modern doctrine it is a plea in abatement, where there is a mistake in the name or description of any existing party having a right to sue, and, if this can be pleaded in abatement, it ought not to be received in bar."

[8] Plaintiff on the same day in which the mistake in its name was made to appear having tendered an amended pleading alleging the facts as hereinabove stated, the court in furtherance of justice should have permitted the filing of this pleading, and because of the failure so to do the judgment must be and is reversed for further proceedings not inconsistent herewith.

CLONINGER v. COMMONWEALTH.

(Court of Appeals of Kentucky. June 7, 1921.)

1. **Criminal law ⬅1160—New trial will not be granted unless verdict is palpably and flagrantly against the weight of the evidence.**

In view of amendment of March 23, 1910, to Cr. Code Prac. § 281, authorizing the Court of Appeals to review the decisions of the trial court upon motions for new trial, a decision upon the ground that the evidence was insuffi-

cient to support the verdict is reviewable, but a new trial will not be ordered where the trial was fair, unless the verdict is palpably and flagrantly against the weight of the evidence.

2. **Homicide ⬅11—Guilt of murder requires malice aforethought or predetermination to kill without lawful reason existing at the time.**

Before one can be guilty of murder he must be actuated by malice aforethought in doing the acts resulting in death, which means a predetermination to kill without lawful reason, which must exist previous to the killing, but it is immaterial at what previous time the intention was formed if it then existed.

3. **Homicide ⬅231—Malice may be shown by threats or by circumstances.**

Malice aforethought may be shown by proof of threats or inferred from defendant's actions and the circumstances of the crime or manner of its commission.

4. **Homicide ⬅11—Circumstances establishing malice stated.**

If the jury believed that accused armed himself and sought deceased for the purpose of killing or seriously injuring him with or without bringing on an altercation and shot him to death, malice aforethought was established.

5. **Homicide ⬅332(2)—Verdict of guilty held not result of passion or prejudice, and not palpably or flagrantly against the evidence.**

The jury is the judge of witnesses' credibility and of the facts in a criminal case, and its verdict of guilty of murder cannot be disturbed where not so contrary to the evidence as to appear to be the result of passion or prejudice and not palpably or flagrantly against the evidence.

Appeal from Circuit Court, Harlan County.

Thomas Cloninger was convicted of murder, and he appeals. Affirmed.

Hall, Jones & Lee of Harlan, for the appellant.

Chas. I. Dawson, Atty. Gen., and Thos. B. McGregor, Asst. Atty. Gen., for the Commonwealth.

HURT, C. J. The appellant, Thomas Cloninger, at Baxter, a railroad station near Harlan, shot John Callahan to death. He made use of a pistol, and discharged five shots, and the result was the instant death of his victim. Each of the shots took effect, and one penetrated Callahan from his back. Cloninger, having been charged with the crime of willful murder, by indictment, upon a trial was found to be guilty by the verdict of the jury, and his punishment fixed at imprisonment during life. He was denied a new trial, and a judgment rendered in accordance with the verdict, and from the judgment he has appealed.

While in his motion for a new trial the appellant assigned various alleged errors of the trial court as grounds for granting him a new trial, upon this appeal he has abandoned all but the alleged error in refusing to set aside the verdict of the jury upon the ground that the verdict is against the evidence, and is not supported by a sufficiency of evidence.

[1] Formerly the well-established rule was to refuse a new trial upon the ground that the verdict was against the evidence, if there was any evidence which conduced to prove the guilt of the crime charged, but since the amendment of March 23, 1910, to section 281 of the Criminal Code, which authorizes this court to review the decisions of the trial court upon motions for a new trial, a decision upon the ground that the evidence was insufficient to support the verdict is reviewable by this court. But it has also consistently been held that a new trial will not be ordered by this court where the trial was fair, unless the verdict is palpably and flagrantly against the weight of the evidence. Wilson v. Com., 140 Ky. 1, 130 S. W. 794; Blanton v. Com., 147 Ky. 812, 146 S. W. 10; Lucas v. Com., 147 Ky. 744, 145 S. W. 751; Crews v. Com., 155 Ky. 122, 159 S. W. 638; Edmonds v. Com., 149 Ky. 242, 147 S. W. 881; May v. Com., 164 Ky. 112, 175 S. W. 17; Chaney v. Com., 149 Ky. 472, 149 S. W. 923; Black v. Com., 154 Ky. 144, 156 S. W. 1043. In the latter case it was said:

"There is seldom a criminal case tried in which there is not sharp conflict in the evidence introduced for the commonwealth and the accused, and we have adopted the sound rule of not interfering in criminal cases, or indeed civil cases, with the finding of the jury upon disputed questions of fact unless it affirmatively, and, we might say, at first blush, appears that their verdict is so contrary to the evidence as to make it appear that it was the result of passion or prejudice."

There are many sound reasons for the above rule, among which are that the jury sees and hears the witnesses and probably is acquainted with their characters, habits, and degrees of intelligence, and know the objects mentioned, and thus is enabled to more correctly estimate the weight to be given circumstances, and the inferences to be drawn from them, and there are other reasons not necessary to be here enumerated.

[2-4] The appellant, by his brief, does not seem to contest the fact that the evidence was such as from which the jury might have properly found him to be guilty of voluntary manslaughter, but it is seriously insisted that there was no evidence, or at least not a sufficiency of it, to justify the jury in finding him to be guilty of murder. A detailed statement of the testimony of the various witnesses will not be attempted, nor is such necessary to indicate the basis of the opinion arrived at, but it is necessary to state the es-

sential facts to indicate the basis of the theories of the commonwealth and the appellant, respectively. The victim of the homicide was engaged in assembling a wagon near the depot at Baxter, and had been so engaged since the early morning of the day upon which he was slain at about half after 11 o'clock. Several persons other than the accused and the deceased were about the grounds, but no one seems to have been giving his attention to Callahan until attracted by the report of the first pistol shot discharged by the appellant. The accused resided with his son, Harmon Cloninger, about one-half mile from the depot. Harmon Cloninger and deceased were enemies, and exercised their dislike by causing each other to be arrested and tried for alleged offenses three or four times during the previous twelve months. Just two days before the homicide Callahan had caused Harmon Cloninger to be arrested upon a charge of violating the laws prohibiting the sale of liquor, and at the trial before the magistrate the accused was present and exhibited some feeling upon the subject. Two or three months previous to the homicide the accused had remarked that if Callahan should "cross his path" he would kill him. On the evening before his death Callahan stated to an acquaintance that the Cloningers, father and son, owed him a debt, that he had given them a sufficient time in which to pay it, and that he was intending to take steps to compel payment, and, if he could not secure the payment of the debt by law, he would have recourse to some other means. These statements by Cloninger and his victim about each other were, however, not communicated to either. On the day of the homicide Harmon Cloninger was about the depot for an hour or more while Callahan was engaged in assembling the wagon, and had come there, he claimed, to purchase cartridges or cartridge shells, and did purchase them from a merchant in Baxter. He returned to his home, where the accused was, near 11 o'clock, and after having dinner returned to the depot, the accused accompanying him. Before leaving his home for the depot, the accused put his revolver in his pocket, which he did, as he claimed, with the intention of making a sale of it at Baxter. He claimed that his purpose in going to Baxter was to pay a small debt which he owed to a merchant there, and to secure some tobacco, but he did not pay the debt, although he saw the individual to whom he owed it, and who testified that he was unable to remember whether or not the accused was indebted to him, nor did he obtain the tobacco desired. Harmon Cloninger claimed that he returned to the depot for the purpose of seeking the company of certain persons to go with him upon a hunt for rabbits. Within 5 to 15 minutes, as estimated by the different persons who deposed to seeing the Cloningers coming to or arriving at the depot, the accused had gone to a place where Callahan was at work assembling the wagon, and several persons were attracted by the report of a revolver and, looking in that direction, saw Callahan holding his hand in front of his face, and accused shooting him. After he fell, the accused discharged one more shot into him, but he claims that was done accidentally. The accused then immediately returned to his home, claiming on the way, and after his arrival there, that Callahan had broken his arm, by striking him with a monkey-wrench, but refused to permit his arm to be examined. There were no weapons of any kind found upon or about the body of Callahan, except a pocketknife, which was closed, in one of his pockets. A glove was upon one of his hands, and its mate was lying near his other hand. A monkey-wrench was lying upon the hounds of the wagon several feet from where the body lay. A short time after the accused arrived at his home, according to several witnesses, he was under the influence of intoxicating liquors, but he claims to have gotten in that condition after Callahan was killed. Upon the trial the appellant testified that after arriving at the depot from his home he visited a toilet which was situated near where Callahan was at work, and when he came out of the toilet he engaged Callahan in a friendly conversation, but the latter without provocation abused him, threw a monkey-wrench, or something of similar character, at him, and which struck upon the arm and knocked him to the ground, and then advanced upon him, continuing to strike at him with his hand, or at least there is no testimony to the effect that Callahan had any object in his hand. When the accused arose from the ground, according to his statement, he commenced to shoot, and continued until Callahan fell. Harmon Cloninger corroborates the accused fully in the above statement, except as to the conversation which the accused claimed to have had with his victim before the fighting commenced, and other witnesses, two of whom are brother-in-laws of Harmon Cloninger, corroborated the accused in part by testifying that Callahan, after their notice was attracted by the shooting, was striking at accused with one hand, and apparently trying to seize him with the other, while accused was engaged in shooting, and one of the witnesses deposed that the accused was knocked or thrown back upon the ground, so that his hand rested upon it, before he discharged the first shot. This witness also testified that Callahan was holding his hand in front of his face. From this evidence it does not appear whether Callahan was assaulting the accused or whether he was attempting to save himself by seizing the pistol, or knocking it out of the hand of the accused. The arm of the accused was not broken, and had no visible mark at any time which indicated that he had received a blow upon it sufficiently forcible to knock him to the ground, or in fact any kind of blow.

Of course, before one can be guilty of murder, he must be actuated by malice aforethought in doing the acts which result in the death of another. This means that a predetermination to kill, and that without lawful reason, must exist previous to the act of killing, but it is immaterial at what time previously the predetermination was formed, if it existed at the time of the killing. The existence of malice aforethought may be shown by proof of threats, or may be inferred from actions of the accused, from the circumstances of the crime, and the manner of its commission. The jury, in arriving at its verdict, necessarily determined that the accused did not commit the homicide in his necessary or apparently necessary self-defense, and the degree of his crime was in that instance dependent upon whether he committed the crime in a sudden affray, or in a heat of passion, superinduced by sufficient provocation, wthout previous malice, or whether he was actuated by malicious motives. In determining this question, the jury was entitled to take into consideration the facts and circumstances which it believed from the evidence to be established. If it believed from the evidence that the accused, with the purpose of killing or doing serious bodily harm to the deceased, armed himself, sought out the deceased, and either with or without bringing on an altercation with him shot him to death, there could be no question of the existence of malice aforethought upon his part and it cannot be said that the facts and circumstances proven and the inferences to be drawn from such facts and circumstances were not sufficient to support a finding that the accused had predetermined to commit the homicide.

[5] The jury is the judge of the credibility of the witnesses and what the facts of a criminal case are, and its verdict will not be disturbed unless it is so contrary to the evidence as to appear to be the result of passion and prejudice, and a consideration of the facts and circumstances heretofore detailed indicates clearly that there is no reason to set aside the verdict upon the ground that it is palpably or flagrantly against the evidence. The trial was fair and uncommonly free from error.

The judgment is therefore affirmed.

DENNIS v. FIRST STATE BANK OF ELKHORN CITY.

(Court of Appeals of Kentucky. June 7, 1921.)

Banks and banking ⟨key⟩54(3)—Cashier liable for negligence in making loans, though authorized.

A bank cashier who permitted a depositor, whom he knew or could have known by exercising ordinary diligence, was insolvent and a nonresident of the state, with no property therein subject to execution, to overdraw his account, and accepted from him and discounted a note in the amount of the overdraft, indorsed by sureties whom he knew to be insolvent, was liable to the bank for his negligence, whether or not he had authority to make such loans.

Appeal from Circuit Court, Pike County.

Action by the First State Bank of Elkhorn City against Percy V. Dennis. Judgment for plaintiff, and defendant appeals. Affirmed.

Picklesimer & Steele, of Pikeville, for appellant.

J. E. Childers, of Pikeville, for appellee.

TURNER, C. This is an action by the plaintiff bank against the defendant Dennis, its former cashier.

The original petition alleged that the defendant, while he was such cashier, permitted one Johnson to overdraw his account in said bank in the sum of $300, and also accepted a note in the sum of $300 from said Johnson, and that neither the note nor the overdraft had been paid by the said Johnson, or by any one for him, and that neither of them was collectible. It was alleged that at the time of these transactions it was against the rules of the bank, and against the contract of employment of defendant as such cashier, to permit overdrafts, and that it was agreed that, should he as such cashier permit overdrafts, he was to be personally liable to the bank for the full amount of the same. And it was further alleged that, under the contract of employment of defendant as cashier, and under the law and custom in force at the time, the defendant had no right or authority to loan money on a note unless the loan was approved by its board of directors. And it was, in substance, alleged that the defendant, in violation of his contract of employment, and of the law and custom in force at the time, permitted Johnson by the overdraft and by discounting his $300 note, to become indebted to the bank in the sum of $600, neither of which sums has ever been collected or can be collected.

It was further alleged that during the defendant's incumbency as cashier he negligently failed to cause to be protested a note for $300 executed by one Bowling, and indorsed by certain other parties, and that because of such negligent failure to protest payment could not be enforced against the indorsers, and the note was not collectible as against Bowling.

An answer seems to have been filed to the original petition, but was lost, and there is an agreement of record traversing its allegations.

Subsequently, however, an amended petition was filed, wherein it was alleged that the man Johnson, whom the defendant permitted to overdraw his account, was at the time both insolvent and a nonresident of this state, and had no property in this state subject to execution, and that these facts were either known to the defendant or could have been known to him by the exercise of ordinary diligence. It was further alleged that the overdrafts and notes, executed by Johnson and discounted by the bank, are not now collectible by the bank, and never were at any time collectible by the bank, and that the principal and sureties in the note were at all times insolvent, and that this fact was known to the defendant, or could have been found out by him by the exercise of diligence. It was further alleged in the amendment that during the period defendant was cashier of the bank there was in force a resolution adopted by the bank, the existence of which was known to the defendant, whereby the cashier was to be held responsible for all loans and discounts not authorized or directed by the board of directors, and that neither of the loans to Johnson was so authorized or directed by the board of directors, or any of them.

The allegations of this amendment, so far as the record discloses, were undenied.

The action was originally brought in equity and was prepared and tried out as an equitable action without objection. After the taking of all the evidence, the cause was submitted, and the court entered a judgment against the defendant for $700, being the amount of the $300 Johnson note discounted by the cashier, the $300 note accepted by the cashier to cover the overdraft, and the $100 Bowling note which the defendant failed to have protested.

It is apparent that under the state of the pleadings there could have been no other judgment as to the two Johnson transactions, for the allegations of the amendment, which are undenied, are that the defendant, knowing Johnson to be insolvent, and knowing him to be a nonresident, and knowing that he had no property in this state subject to execution, and knowing that the sureties or indorsers on his said note were each insolvent, was negligent in contracting such an obligation for the bank; and under those undenied allegations it is immaterial whether he had authority to make such loans or not. For, if he had such authority, it was unmistakable negligence to contract such debts for the bank.

As to the failure to have the Bowling $100 note protested, it is sufficient to say that the defendant in his evidence practically admits his negligence in that respect and avows his willingness to be held responsible for that amount.

Notwithstanding the state of the pleadings, the case was tried out on its merits, and it may not be improper to say that we have fully examined the evidence and approve of judgment of the chancellor.

The judgment is affirmed.

IRVINE DEVELOPMENT CO. v. CLARK.

(Court of Appeals of Kentucky. June 3, 1921.)

1. **Evidence ⬅=474½—Neither agency nor extent can be established by opinion evidence.**

Neither an agency nor the extent thereof can be established by opinion evidence.

2. **Contracts ⬅=28(3)—Evidence insufficient to show that plaintiff had contract with defendant development company to drill oil well.**

In an action against a development company for labor performed in drilling an oil well on the property of a third party, an oil company, evidence *held* insufficient to show against defendant development company either an express or an implied contract to pay plaintiff for drilling the well, showing rather that plaintiff's contract was with the oil company.

Appeal from Circuit Court, Clark County.

Action by H. W. Clark against the Irvine Development Company. From judgment for plaintiff, defendant appeals. Reversed and remanded.

J. T. Metcalf, of Winchester, J. C. Jones, of Frankfort, J. Barton Rettew, of Philadelphia, Pa., and Morris & Jones, of Frankfort, for appellant.

C. F. Spencer and C. S. Moffett, both of Winchester, for appellee.

CLARKE, J. This is an appeal by the defendant from a judgment for $2,329.50 rendered against it in favor of the plaintiff, now appellee, for labor performed by him in drilling an oil well upon the property of another than the defendant, namely, the New York-Irvine Oil Company, called hereinafter the "oil company."

Considerable portions of the briefs are devoted to a discussion of whether or not the petition is a declaration upon an express or an implied contract, but it will not be necessary for us to consider that question, because of our conclusion that there is no evidence to sustain either and that the court erred in overruling defendant's motion for a directed verdict made at the conclusion of plaintiff's

evidence and renewed after all of the evidence had been heard.

Plaintiff had a written contract with defendant to drill an oil well on the A. S. Pasley lease owned by defendant at $1.50 per linear foot, which contract contained the provision that the defendant was to pay plaintiff "$50 per day in case of any delay in drilling on said lease if said party of the first part (plaintiff) is on the lease and ready to drill and the delay is the cause of the second party (defendant)."

Mr. H. C. Jordon was the resident manager of both the defendant and the oil company, both of which were nonresident corporations. Shortly after plaintiff began to drill the well upon the Pasley lease, operations were estopped by an injunction, and Jordon directed plaintiff to move his rig onto the Hiram Reed lease, which was some five or six miles distant from the Pasley lease and was owned by the oil company. Plaintiff drilled two wells upon the Reed lease and at the direction of Jordon presented his bill therefor to and was paid by the oil company. After the completion of these two wells upon the Reed tract, Jordon directed plaintiff to move his rig to the Wince Friend lease, also owned by the oil company, and to drill a well upon that lease, and it is to recover for the work done by plaintiff upon the Friend lease that he has instituted this action. It is at once apparent that plaintiff was not entitled to recover of the defendant development company for the work he performed upon the lease of the oil company, an entirely different corporation, either under an extension of his written contract with the former or upon a quantum meruit, unless Jordon, who was the agent for both corporations in directing plaintiff to perform the work, was acting as the agent of defendant. There is no evidence whatever that in so doing he was acting as defendant's agent, except the bare statement of the plaintiff in answer to a leading question of his own counsel, and that this is not true and was so understood by the plaintiff before he drilled the well on the Friend lease is shown beyond doubt by his own testimony. He admits that when he had completed the two wells upon the Reed lease, and before he moved to the Friend lease, he was directed by Jordon to present his bill for drilling the two wells upon the Reed lease to the oil company; that he did so; and that the company paid same by check. He further admits that he knew Jordon was the agent of both companies and that the oil company and not defendant owned the Friend lease; that he asked Jordon to which company he should present his bill for drilling the well upon the Friend lease, and was directed to present it to the oil company, which he did; and that he never presented any bill for same to the defendant or suggested in any way to Jordon or the defendant that he was looking to it for payment prior to the institution of this action.

[1] The rule is thoroughly established that neither an agency nor the extent thereof can be established by opinion evidence. It is thus stated in 2 C. J. 948:

"A witness on the issue of agency must state only the facts and circumstances concerning the various transactions, leaving the court or jury to determine whether or not an agency was created, and hence may not give his opinion or state his conclusions as to the existence of the agency or the nature and extent of the agent's authority."

[2] There is therefore absolutely no evidence that Jordon had any authority to bind defendant for work he might order for the oil company, plaintiff does not even so state; and his statement that in so doing Jordon was acting for defendant is proven by his own admissions on the facts to be but an unwarranted conclusion and without probative value.

Hence plaintiff by his evidence did not prove against defendant either an express or an implied contract to pay him for drilling the well upon the Friend lease owned by the oil company. Nor was his case made out by the evidence for the defendant.

Jordon testified that he employed the defendant to perform the work here involved for the oil company and not the defendant development company, and that he so informed the plaintiff at the time. That this is true is conclusively established by letters introduced by the defendant which plaintiff wrote to Mr. Jordon and to the oil company.

Just after plaintiff moved his rig to the Friend lease and started drilling the well on same, he wrote a letter to Mr. Jordon in which he said, among other things:

"What company will I charge the account to? I believe you told me one time but I have forgotten and I have no contract to refer to."

A few days later he made out a bill to the New York-Irvine Oil Company and mailed it to Mr. Jordon as its agent for the expense of moving his drilling outfit from the Reed to the Friend lease. About a month later he wrote Mr. Jordon a letter which begins:

"Will drop you a few lines to see if you have heard from the New York-Irvine Oil Company. I have not heard from the Move Bill and I think it is time. I paid out my money a long time ago for them."

This letter ends with, "Please give me a reply in regard to the New York-Irvine Co. without delay." When he completed drilling the well, he sent his bill therefor and for plugging same to the "New York-Irvine Company." A few weeks still later, he wrote Mr. Jordon another letter, in which he said:

"I begin to want to see some money. I have written to-day to the New York Company. If they don't make me reply I will have to give it to attorney."

The letter to the New York Company above referred to was sent by registered mail, and is as follows:

"Furnace, Ky. 5/11/1918.
"New York-Irvine Oil Co., New York, N. Y.
—My Dear Sirs:　A long time ago I sent your man Jordon at Winchester, Ky., the move bill to the Wince Friend farm $1,067.50 later sent him the bill for drilling the well (4/8) $1,242.00 I have called his attention to the fact these bills has not been paid he replies he had written also wired you and it appeared you give it no attention Please give this your attention and send me check by return mail for the bills $2,329.50 as I will be compelled to put it in attorney's hands for collection.
"Yours truly,　H. W. Clark."

Great stress is laid by counsel for plaintiff upon the fact that he refused to sign a written contract with the New York-Irvine Oil Company for drilling the wells upon the Reed lease which Mr. Jordon delivered to him in duplicate while he was drilling those wells. It is insisted that his refusal to sign this contract was notice to the defendant through its agent Jordon that he was unwilling to perform work for the oil company; but, even if this were true, that fact would not be sufficient to charge defendant for work that plaintiff was performing upon the property of another and not under contract with or by direction of defendant or Jordon as its agent.

Equally unfounded is the contention that the work done by plaintiff on the Friend lease as directed by Jordon was done for defendant under an authorized extension of the written contract with reference to the Pasley lease. The sum of the argument in support of this contention is that the provision, in that contract quoted above, for the payment by defendant of $50 per day during any delay for which plaintiff was not responsible, authorized Jordon to employ plaintiff's time for defendant during the delay occasioned by the injunction and that he was so acting when he directed plaintiff to drill the wells on the Reed and Friend leases, or at least that plaintiff was justified in so assuming. Obviously, however, such a provision and any contingency that might arise thereunder could not possibly be construed into an authority for Jordon to employ plaintiff to perform work for another than the defendant. But even if such an extension of the contract might be presumed as to the work done on the Reed tract upon the assumption that plaintiff reasonably believed he was there for defendant and by its consent, which is not true of course, it could not possibly apply to work done on the Friend lease, because plaintiff knew before he left the Reed lease that he was working for the oil company and not defendant.

Wherefore the judgment is reversed, and the cause remanded for another trial consistent herewith.

PEOPLE'S BANK OF SPRINGFIELD v. TRUE.

(Supreme Court of Tennessee.　June 18, 1921.)

1. **Banks and banking ⚖116(2)—Cashier not presumed to have communicated knowledge to bank when interest antagonistic.**

Where defendant gave a note to L., who was acting on behalf of his father, and the father, in subsequently selling the note to the bank of which L. was cashier, negotiated both with L. and the president of the bank, there was no presumption that L. communicated to the bank his knowledge of the facts out of which the note arose, as in assisting in the sale of the note for the benefit of his father he was acting in a capacity where his interest was antagonistic to that of the bank.

2. **Bills and notes ⚖343—Grantee giving note by way of restitution liable to purchaser having knowledge of fraudulent transaction.**

If property was conveyed to defendant to prevent the grantor's creditors from reaching it, defendant could not escape liability on a note executed by him to the grantor by way of turning back to the grantor part of the proceeds of the lands, though a purchaser of the note knew of the fraudulent transaction, as the note was not in furtherance of the fraud but in disaffirmance thereof.

Appeal from Chancery Court, Robertson County; J. W. Stout, Chancellor.

Suit by the People's Bank of Springfield against H. C. True. From a decree for plaintiff, defendant appeals. Affirmed.

Hamilton Parks, of Nashville, and R. L. Peck, of Springfield, for Bank.

A. L. Dorsey, of Springfield, for True.

GREEN, J. This suit was brought by the People's Bank of Springfield, hereafter called complainant, against H. C. True, hereafter called defendant, to recover the balance due on a note of $7,000. An answer was filed denying liability, and by way of crossbill defendant sought to compel a cancellation of the note.

The note was executed payable to his own order by defendant, indorsed in blank by him, and delivered to R. F. Long for the benefit of his father, E. B. Long, and negotiated by the latter to complainant. Two payments were made on the note, one of $500 and one of $1,000.

On the hearing the chancellor found that complainant was an innocent purchaser of the note for value before maturity and decreed in its favor. From this decree defendant has appealed to this court.

A mass of proof was taken in the case, which, however, we do not find it necessary to review. Whatever may be the merits of the case between defendant and the Longs, we must agree with the chancellor that the complainant is an innocent holder of the note.

Undoubtedly the complainant took the note for value. It gave in consideration thereof another note for $3,000 signed by J. A. Long & Co. and another note for $2,000 signed by R. E. Glover & Co., in addition to $1,500 cash. This made a total consideration of $6,500. The first payment of $500 was made on the note before the bank bought it. It is not denied that the bank obtained the note before its maturity, and the only debatable question is whether the bank took the note under such circumstances as to charge it with notice of defenses alleged to exist in favor of defendant as against the Longs.

There are two theories as to the origin of this note—the facts incident to its execution. One theory is advanced by the complainant, and the other by the defendant. It will not be necessary to determine which of these theories is correct, since upon either theory the bank is still entitled to recover.

The defendant says that he, along with other gentlemen in Robertson county, became involved in a land speculation in Texas. He says that as a result of this venture his associates, among whom was E. B. Long, became indebted to him in the sum of about $11,000; that to satisfy this indebtedness E. B. Long conveyed to defendant certain lands which he (Long) owned in Robertson county, Tenn.; that later E. B. Long's associates refused to contribute to him anything on account of the joint indebtedness to defendant which Long had settled as aforesaid. Defendant says that when it became apparent to Long that the others would not reimburse him, Long began to make demands on defendant to give back his lands or the proceeds thereof. Defendant says that Long was quite persistent in these demands and kept after him all the time; that finally, while he did not conceive that he owed Long anything, he turned over to R. F. Long the $7,000 note here in suit with the understanding that said note was not to be collected. Defendant says that his agreement with R. F. Long was that the father, E. B. Long, should have the profits of the sale of the Robertson county lands conveyed as aforesaid by E. B. Long to defendant, together with some other personal property. Defendant insists that the note was only delivered to R. F. Long as a sort of protection to E. B. Long, in case defendant should die or anything should happen to him, and defendant reiterates that it was fully understood by both the Longs that the $7,000 note was not to be collected.

R. F. Long was at that time the cashier of the complainant bank. Defendant contends that since R. F. Long was fully advised as to the conditions under which the note was executed and knew that it was not to be collected, the complainant bank became affected with the knowledge which R. F. Long had, and that it is not an innocent holder of the note.

It is fair to say that R. F. Long utterly denies that he had any such understanding as is claimed with defendant, but he claims that he took, the note understanding that it was to be paid promptly. In fact, R. F. Long says that the note originated in an entirely different way, as will hereafter appear.

It is manifest, if we accept defendant's theory of the facts, that R. F. Long was acting in these negotiations with defendant as the agent of the father, E. B. Long.

It appears otherwise in the proof that when the $7,000 note was negotiated to the complainant, E. B. Long conducted such negotiation with both R. F. Long, the cashier, and H. T. Stratton, the president, of complainant. It is not insisted that Stratton had any knowledge of the agreement said to have existed to the effect that the note should not be collected.

[1] So far as the knowledge of R. F. Long is concerned, there is no presumption that he communicated such knowledge to his principal, the complainant, for in assisting about the sale of the note to complainant for the benefit of his father, R. F. Long was acting in a capacity where his interest was antagonistic to that of complainant. Provident, etc., Assurance Society v. Edmonds, 95 Tenn. 53, 31 S. W. 168; Wood v. Green, 131 Tenn. 583, 175 S. W. 1139; Smith v. Bank, 132 Tenn. 147, 177 S. W. 72.

Had R. F. Long been the sole representative of the complainant in this transaction as well as of his father, then the complainant would have been charged with the knowledge of R. F. Long under Smith v. Bank, supra. The testimony, however, shows that Stratton was looking out for the complainant's interest in the purchase of the note and represented complainant, partly, at least. Stratton knew nothing of the agreement that the note was not to be paid, and for the reasons stated, under the authority cited, the knowledge of R. F. Long cannot be imputed to the complainant.

The complainant's theory with reference to the origin of the note sued on is that E. B. Long became very much involved as a result of the land speculations in Texas referred to above. Complainant insists that nothing was due to defendant whatever as a result of these operations and denies that E. B. Long conveyed his lands to defendant for any such a purpose. It claims that the whole purpose of this conveyance was to cover up E. B. Long's property and to prevent it from being reached in satisfaction of the numerous debts which he had incurred in Texas and at home. Complainant contends that the $7,000 note was given by way of turning back to E. B. Long part of the proceeds of his lands which had been fraudulently conveyed to defendant and sold by the latter.

[2] The defendant insists that if this be the truth of the matter, there can be no recovery upon the note by the complainant. This upon the idea that the note grew out of a fraudulent transaction and that a court of equity will not lend its aid under such circumstances.

We think that such argument rests on a misconception of the present situation. The note, according to complainant's theory, was not given in furtherance of a fraudulent transaction, but was given by way of restitution of the proceeds of the property fraudulently conveyed. Even, therefore, if the complainant had knowledge of the original fraudulent conveyance as it appears from the bill it did have, it still may recover on the note.

"While a fraudulent grantee is under no legal obligation to reconvey, it is said he is under a moral obligation to do so, and all subsequent acts done by him in execution of this duty should be favorably considered in equity. If in fulfillment of his moral obligation he makes a reconveyance, such act will be binding on him, and if the rights of no innocent third person have intervened, the fraudulent grantor will become revested both in law and equity with the title previously conveyed to his grantee; and the grantee will be estopped from thereafter setting up any claim to the property." 20 Cyc. 619.

This rule is recognized in at least two cases in Tennessee.

In Stanton v. Shaw, 62 Tenn. (3 Baxt.) 12, a purchaser of real estate to defeat his creditors procured the title to be taken in the name of the third person. This third person subsequently reconveyed to the true owner. It was held that the creditors of the third party, not having attempted to subject the property to their debts while it was in the name of said third party, could not reach it after the reconveyance to the real owner, although the reconveyance was, of course, voluntary.

In Insurance Co. v. Waller, 116 Tenn. 1, 95 S. W. 811, 115 Am. St. Rep. 763, 7 Ann. Cas. 1078, property was fraudulently conveyed to a wife as trustee to put it beyond the reach of her husband's creditors. Later she reconveyed to the husband. The conveyance was upheld, and the husband held to be vested with the entire legal and equitable title to the property, so as to enable him to recover upon insurance policies covering the property and issued in his name.

The lands conveyed to defendant had been sold by him, and if this conveyance was in truth fraudulent, it was his duty to restore the proceeds of the sale. A note given for such purpose cannot be considered as in furtherance of any fraud, but is rather in disaffirmance and should be approved.

For the reasons stated, we think there was no error in the decree of the chancellor, and it must be affirmed.

HAYNES v. STATE.

(Supreme Court of Tennessee. June 20, 1921.)

Criminal law ☞749—Jury must fix sentence of one under 18 years of age.

The jury must fix the sentence of one under 18 years of age convicted of crime, the Indeterminate Sentence Law having no application to persons under the age of 18 years convicted of crime punishable by imprisonment in the penitentiary, under Shannon's Code, §§ 4433a5, 7202a1, 7213, and a verdict which does not do so is void.

Error to Criminal Court, Davidson County; Frank M. Garard, Judge.

John Haynes was convicted of murder in the second degree, and brings error. Reversed and remanded for new trial.

R. O. Boyce and M. P. Estes, both of Nashville, for plaintiff in error.

Wm. H. Swiggart, Jr., of Nashville, for the State.

HALL, J. The plaintiff in error, John Haynes, was convicted of the crime of murder in the second degree by a jury in the criminal court of Davidson county. At the time of his conviction he was under 18 years of age.

The trial judge instructed the jury as follows:

"If you find the defendant not guilty of murder in the first degree, or if you have a reasonable doubt as to his guilt of that offense, you will acquit him of that offense and your next inquiry will be whether or not he is guilty of murder in the second degree; if you convict him of this offense, that is all you need to say in your verdict; and it then becomes the duty of the court to sentence the defendant to serve an indeterminate sentence, or period of time, in the penitentiary of the state from 10 to 20 years."

By section 7202a1 of Shannon's Annotated Code (section 1, c. 8, Acts 1913), it is provided as follows:

"Whenever any person over eighteen years of age is convicted of any felony or other crime committed after the passage of this law [after February 21, 1913] and punishable by imprisonment in the penitentiary, the court imposing such sentence shall not fix a definite term of imprisonment, but shall sentence such person to the penitentiary for an indefinite period, not to exceed the maximum term nor to be less than the minimum term provided by law for the crime for which the person was convicted and sentenced, making allowance for good time as now provided by law."

The law, as it stood before the passage of chapter 8 of the Acts of 1913, was as follows:

"It is the duty of the jury to ascertain in their verdict, the time, within the limits prescribed by law, during which an offender is to be imprisoned in the penitentiary." Shannon's Annotated Code, § 7213 (Acts 1829, c. 23, § 76).

By section 4433a5 of Shannon's Annotated Code (Acts 1907, c. 599, § 4; Acts 1917, c. 97, § 4), it is provided as follows:

"All boys under the age of eighteen years who have been convicted of an offense punishable by confinement in the penitentiary shall be sentenced to and confined in said training and agricultural school under the provisions of this chapter. All boys convicted of an offense punishable by imprisonment in the penitentiary shall be transported to and from the said reformatory at the expense of the state and taught some trade or pursuit and employed and kept at some useful and elevating occupation."

It will be noted that the statute first above cited applies to all persons over 18 years of age who may be convicted of any felony or crime committed after its passage, and punishable by imprisonment in the penitentiary, and is known as the "Indeterminate Sentence Law." It has no application to persons under the age of 18 years who may be convicted of any felony or other crime punishable by imprisonment in the penitentiary.

Plaintiff in error, being under 18 years of age, and excluded from the operation of the act of 1913, was subject to have an assessment of punishment only under the law as it stood before that statute was passed, and independent of it, in the reform school, under chapter 599, Acts of 1907, which act expressly applied to him, for a term of imprisonment to be fixed by the jury. Shannon's Annotated Code, § 7202.

The jury not having fixed or assessed the punishment of the plaintiff in error as provided by statute in such cases, we think the verdict was void. Martin v. State, 130 Tenn. 509, 172 S. W. 311; Gass v. State, 130 Tenn. 581, 172 S. W. 305; State v. Ragsdale, 10 Lea, 671; Mayfield v. State, 101 Tenn. 673, 49 S. W. 742; Fitts v. State, 102 Tenn. 141, 50 S. W. 756.

The verdict of the jury being void, the judgment based on it cannot stand. It is therefore reversed, and the case is remanded for a new trial.

STATE ex rel. ATTORNEY GENERAL v. COLORED TENNESSEE INDUSTRIAL SCHOOL et al.

(Supreme Court of Tennessee. April 30, 1921.)

1. Appeal and error ⚖=>894(2), 907(3)—Evidence presumed to sustain finding, when not before the court at law, but not in equity.

In a case coming from a court of law, where there is no bill of exceptions, the Supreme Court will presume that there was sufficient evidence to sustain the finding below; but on appeal in a chancery case the hearing is de novo, on the transcript of the record filed, and in the absence of any evidence, before the court to support the decree below, it cannot be sustained.

2. Appeal and error ⚖=>596—Appellees' counsel should direct insertion of portion of record material to his clients.

Under Acts 1905, c. 85, where counsel for appellees is given notice of the portion of the record which appellant desires sent up, it is his duty to direct the insertion of such portion of the record as may be material to his clients.

3. Corporations ⚖=>613(1) — Intervener held not entitled to question authority to bring suit to dissolve.

Where the Attorney General filed a bill to dissolve a corporation, and after final decree a judgment creditor filed a petition setting up his judgments, and sought payment, but for some time after his intervention raised no question as to the Attorney General's authority to bring the suit, he was precluded from questioning such authority.

Appeal from Chancery Court, Davidson County; John T. Lillyett, Chancellor.

Suit by the State, on the relation of the Attorney General, against the Colored Tennessee Industrial School, in which Bedford Taylor intervened. Decree for complainant, and intervener appeals. Reversed and remanded for rehearing.

W. C. Cherry, of Nashville, Sp. Counsel, for the State.

R. S. West, Sadler & Goodman and J. C. Napier, all of Nashville, opposed.

GREEN, J. The bill in this case was filed by the state, on the relation of the Attorney General, to dissolve the Colored Tennessee Industrial School, purporting to be a corporation, and to recover from it certain property in its possession, alleged to have been obtained from the state upon false representations. A receiver was appointed for the defendant corporation upon the filing of the bill.

The corporation and certain individual defendants answered.

According to decrees rendered in the cause, proof appears to have been heard by the Chancellor. A final decree was passed dissolving the corporation, and ratifying the action of the receiver, who had taken possession of its property and turned it over to the state, or rather to various institutions of the state.

Prior to the appointment of said receiver one Bedford Taylor brought two suits against this corporation, one before a magistrate and one in the circuit court. After the receiver was appointed, Taylor applied for permission to prosecute said suits against the receiver; but such permission does not appear to have been granted him by the chancellor. Nevertheless said suits were prosecuted to judgment in the circuit court of Davidson county; no defense being made to either of them.

After obtaining these judgments against the corporation, Bedford Taylor filed a petition in the chancery court, setting up such judgments, and by decree of the chancellor they seem to have been allowed as a claim against the corporation.

Aside from the assets of the corporation taken over by the receiver and turned over to the state, there was a balance of $2,000 in the hands of the treasurer of the state, remaining out of an appropriation of $10,000 made by the Legislature for the benefit of this institution.

It appears from the record before us that litigation was had over the validity of this $10,000 appropriation, and that said appropriation was held valid by this court; but that the court directed it to be expended under the supervision of three commissioners appointed by this court.

Taylor insisted in his petition that he was entitled to have a pro rata payment of his indebtedness out of the assets of the corporation which the receiver took over and later passed on to the state. Taylor also claimed that he was entitled to reach this $2,000 remaining unexpended in the hands of the state treasurer.

The chancellor held that the state was entitled to recover the assets of the corporation which the receiver found as representing the fund obtained from the state upon false pretenses, and he also held that the balance of the fund with the state treasurer was only to be expended at the discretion of the commissioners, and was not liable to any debts of the corporation.

The decrees in the case recite, as said before, that these conclusions of the chancellor were reached upon the record before him and upon proof, including the former decree of this court appointing the commissioners to expend the state appropriation and defining their powers.

Taylor has appealed to this court, acting under the provisions of chapter 85 of the Acts of 1905. He gave notice as to what portion of the record below he desired to have sent up and this notice was duly served upon adverse parties. They paid no attention to it, and the transcript before us contains only those portions of the record designated by Taylor. In this transcript there is no proof, not even the former decree of this court upholding the state appropriation and appointing the commissioners.

[1] In a case coming from a court of law, where there is no bill of exceptions, this court will presume there was sufficient evidence to sustain the finding of the court below. In a chancery case, however, upon appeal, the hearing in this court is de novo upon the transcript of the record filed. In the absence of any evidence before us to support the decree below, it cannot be sustained. Shelby County v. Bickford, 102 Tenn. 402, 52 S. W. 772; Hearst v. Proffit, 115 Tenn. 560, 91 S. W. 207; Leiberman, Loveman & O'Brien v. Bowden, 121 Tenn. 496, 119 S. W. 64.

Chapter 35 of the Acts of 1903 has been commended by this court in Leiberman, Loveman & O'Brien v. Bowden, supra, and the practice thereunder indicated as follows:

"The act of 1903 was designed to save costs to litigants and to abridge voluminous records. It establishes a practice which is to be commended and encouraged. Under this act counsel for appellant is authorized, after giving notice to adversary counsel, to designate only such portion of the record as he conceives is material to the proper presentation of the case to the appellate court. If the opposing counsel conceives the portion of the record designated insufficient, he is authorized, to direct the insertion of the remainder of the record, or such additional portion thereof as may be material to his client. If he fails to designate such additional portion of the record after receiving notice from opposing counsel, he is in no attitude to complain of the transcript thus made up in accordance with the statute. It is not necessary that his consent shall be given to a limited or abridged transcript in order to give this court jurisdiction in the case." Leiberman, Loveman & O'Brien v. Bowden, supra.

So far as we can now see, the court below would not have been justified in turning over the assets of the defendant corporation to the state to the exclusion of creditors except upon the trust fund theory. While there may have been abundant proof below to sustain this theory, it is not contained in this record. And while the chancellor may have been entirely justified, construing the decree of this court appointing these commissioners and defining their duties with respect to the state appropriation, in holding that said fund was not available to creditors of this corporation, this former decree is not before us.

[2] As stated in Leiberman, Loveman & O'Brien v. Bowden, supra, when an appeal is taken under chapter 35 of the Acts of 1903, it is the duty of counsel for appellee after notice to direct the insertion of such portion of the record as may be material to his clients.

[3] Taylor insists that the suit herein was improperly brought and that the Attorney General was without authority in the matter. It is urged that such a suit must have been brought by the District Attorney General. The Attorney General relies on special authority from the Legislature. This question was not raised below until some time after Taylor had intervened in the suit and sought to obtain the benefits thereof. We think his course in coming into the case in this way precluded him from questioning the propriety of the suit.

It follows, for the reasons above stated, that the decree below must be reversed. In accordance with the practice adopted in Hearst v. Proffit, supra, this case is remanded to the chancery court for a rehearing, with leave to both parties to introduce such testimony as they desire.

The commissioners, Thompson, Cherry, and Vertrees, will pay the costs of this appeal, and the cost below will remain as taxed by the chancellor.

We think Taylor is not entitled to raise other questions made by him.

PENNINGTON v. FARMERS' & MERCHANTS' BANK.

(Supreme Court of Tennessee. May 28, 1921.)

1. **Banks and banking ⊕=153 — Bank held to become bailee of bond and not only box in which kept.**

Where purchaser of Victory Bond from bank understood the bond was to be placed in her father's tin box in the vault, but relied upon the promise of the bank president to take care of the bond for her and his assurance that it would be safely kept, the bank clearly became a bailee of the bond itself, and not a bailee of the father's box, and the bank was liable, if at all, for its loss by robbery, under Thomp. Shan. Code, § 2099, and not under sections 2100, 2102.

2. **Bailment ⊕=12—Care to be exercised by bailee.**

Bailee under a bailment for the sole benefit of the bailor is bound to use a degree of diligence and attention adequate to the performance of his undertaking, and care and diligence which would be sufficient as to goods of small value or of slight temptation might be wholly unfit for goods of great value and very liable to loss and injury.

3. **Banks and banking ⊕=154(9) — Whether proper care was exercised as to bond deposited held for jury.**

In an action against a bank to recover the value of a Victory Bond left with the bank for safe-keeping and stolen by burglars, whether bank exercised proper care held for the jury.

4. Banks and banking ⇐154(7)—Usage and custom as affecting care exacted of bailee.

Usage and custom in a particular business reflect on the care exacted of a bailee, but in an action against a bank to recover value of bond stolen from vault by burglars it was not competent to permit defendant to prove what one or two other banks may or may not have done toward safeguarding their valuables, the business policy of burglary insurance companies, nor advertisements of bank, where plaintiff relied wholly on personal assurances from the bank president.

Appeal from Circuit Court, Maury County; W. B. Turner, Judge.

Action by Minnie Pennington against the Farmers' & Merchants' Bank. Judgment for defendant, and plaintiff appealed to the Court of Civil Appeals, which transferred the case. Reversed and remanded.

Sam Holding, of Columbia, and L. H. Hammond, of Mt. Pleasant, for appellant.

Percy S. Chandler, of Mt. Pleasant, and Hughes, Hatcher & Hughes, of Columbia, for appellee.

GREEN, J. Plaintiff brought this suit to recover from defendant the value of a $1,000 Victory Bond which belonged to her and had been lodged in the bank's vault for safe-keeping. The bank was robbed, its vault being blown open by burglars, and plaintiff's bond, along with other valuable papers, taken.

The circuit judge directed a verdict in favor of the defendant, and the plaintiff appealed in error to the Court of Civil Appeals. That court transferred the case to this court, conceiving that the constitutionality of an act of the Legislature was involved.

The form of charter provided by our statutes for banks and trust companies, under which statutes defendant is incorporated, contains, among other things, the following:

"It shall have the right to construct a vault on its real estate, or to rent any vault already constructed or to be constructed, which, in the judgment of the directors, will provide reasonable means of safety against loss by theft, fire, or other cause, in which vault may be fixed or placed safes, boxes, or receptacles for the keeping of jewelry, diamonds, gold, bank notes, bonds, notes, and other valuables, which boxes, safes, or receptacles may be rented by the corporation to other persons or corporations, on such terms as may be agreed by the parties."

"In no event shall the corporation be liable for any loss of said jewelry, diamonds, gold, bank notes, bonds, notes, or other valuables thus lost by theft, robbery, fire, or other cause, the said corporation not being the insurer of the safety of said property, nor in any manner liable therefor. The corporation is not required to take any note or property thus deposited, as the person who rents a safe, box, or receptacle, is, for the term of his lease, the owner thereof."

Sections 2101, 2102, Thompson's Shannon's Code.

The circuit judge was of opinion that these sections were applicable to this case, and that under the provisions of section 2102 defendant could not be held liable for the loss of said bond, kept as hereafter described.

We cannot agree with the learned trial judge in this conclusion.

We think such sections cover a case where a particular box or space in its vaults is rented or leased by the bank. This is made clear by the provision that the person renting the box or receptacle is, for the term of his lease, the owner thereof. A rental contract is clearly contemplated. The customer selects his space, fills it as he pleases, and takes his chances under the statute.

We have no such a case before us. Plaintiff's father had a tin box which the bank had presented to him. He kept his valuable papers in this box. The bank undertook to care for the box without charge. Mr. Pennington had rented no space or receptacle in the bank's vault, and the bank was free to keep his box where it thought proper. The plaintiff's bond was placed in this box belonging to her father so intrusted to the bank.

We think this bailment was undertaken by the bank under the authority of another provision of its charter, namely, the following:

"It shall have power to take and receive on deposit, specially as bailee, any jewelry, plate, money, specie, securities, valuable papers, or other valuables of any kind, and, upon a consideration to be agreed upon by the parties, to guarantee the safe preservation and redelivery of the same; also the power to guarantee the payment of bonds and mortgages owned by other persons, or to guarantee titles to real estate for a consideration to be agreed on by the parties." Section 2099, Thompson's Shannon's Code.

Sections 2100, 2101, of Thompson's Shannon's Code, relied on by defendant, are attacked as unconstitutional; it being asserted that such legislation is arbitrary and unreasonable and discriminatory in favor of banks. We do not think this legislation is applicable to the case before us, and therefore have no occasion to pass on the constitutionality of the enactment.

Nevertheless, as the constitutional question was fairly raised on the record, we retain jurisdiction of the case and will dispose of the other questions.

Plaintiff's proof tends to show that she was the daughter of a substantial farmer, who kept an account with defendant bank. She herself had a savings account at this bank. Some months before the robbery her father determined to give her $1,000. He so informed the president of the bank, and the latter drew a check to plaintiff's order, which the father signed and took to her.

The father testifies that the president of the bank asked him to have his daughter to do business with that institution. The father said that he could not interfere, and told the bank president that he must speak to plaintiff about the matter himself. It appears from the father's testimony that he and the bank president had previously had some conversation about the rate of interest the bank was paying on savings deposits, which was only 3 per cent., and the father insisted that he should have 4 per cent. for his savings. The bank president would not yield, and the matter was arranged by the father buying Liberty Bonds from the bank with his savings.

Plaintiff testifies that before she received the $1,000 check from her father the bank president called her up and told her he understood she was to receive this present and asked her if she would not buy a bond from him. She says that after some negotiation over the telephone she agreed to buy the bond and the bank president said he would take care of it for her. She states that when her father gave her the check she indorsed it and sent it back to the bank by her father, and that he paid $995 to the bank for a Victory Bond and brought her back $5.

The father testified further that at the suggestion of the president of the bank the daughter's bond was put in his (the father's) box by the bank official himself, and the box carried back by the latter into the vault.

[1] It appears from the testimony of plaintiff that, although she understood the bond was to be placed in her father's box, she relied on the promise of the bank president to take care of her bond for her and his assurance that it would be safely kept. She was not familiar with the interior of the bank's premises.

Upon these facts we think the bank clearly became a bailee of the bond itself and not a mere bailee of the father's box. According to plaintiff's proof the president of the bank undertook to take care of the bond, and he himself selected the father's box as a receptacle for the bond.

The case, therefore, is entirely different from Sawyer v. Old Lowell National Bank, 230 Mass. 342, 119 N. E. 825, 1 A. L. R. 269, and that line of cases, holding that the acceptance of a box, chest, package, or envelope, does not charge the depository as a bailee of the contents of such receptacle. As appears from the note to the case just mentioned (1 A. L. R. 272), there is a conflict of authority as to the liability of a bank under such circumstances. We do not get to this question in considering the propriety of the directed verdict below.

It is insisted for the plaintiff that the deposit of this bond with defendant bank, in view of the particular facts of this case, was a bailment for mutual benefit of the parties. The argument is quite forceful. Plaintiff's testimony, indeed, indicates that the promise of the bank's president to take care of the bond was part of the consideration for her purchase of this security from the bank.

[2] We may concede, however, that the bailment was for the sole benefit of the plaintiff. Nevertheless, a mandatory is bound to use a degree of diligence and attention adequate to the performance of his undertaking. The degree of care required is essentially dependent upon the circumstances of each case. It is materially affected by the nature and value of the goods and their liability to loss or injury. That care and diligence which would be sufficient as to goods of small value or of slight temptation might be wholly unfit for goods of great value and very liable to loss and injury. Jenkins v. Motlow, 33 Tenn. (1 Sneed) 248, 60 Am. Dec. 154;. Kirtland v. Montgomery, 31 Tenn. (1 Swan) 452; Colyar v. Taylor, 41 Tenn. (1 Cold.) 373; Mariner v. Smith, 52 Tenn. (5 Heisk.) 203; Cicalla v. Rossi, 57 Tenn. (10 Heisk.) 67.

Ridenour v. Woodward, 132 Tenn. 620, 179 S. W. 148, 4 A. L. R. 1192, was a case of an alleged conversion by the bailee. The court held that not every parting of possession by the bailee of the thing intrusted to his care was a misappropriation, and suggested that the old cases went too far in this respect. It was repeated, however, that the care required of an accommodation bailee was "to be measured * * * with reference to the nature of the thing placed in his possession."

Plaintiff's bond was a coupon bond negotiable by delivery. She states that the president of the bank told her there was no necessity for registering the bond; that it would be safe at the bank. Plaintiff's proof tends to show that the bank was robbed at night; that there was no night policeman in the town of Mt. Pleasant, where the bank was located, and the bank had no burglar alarm nor night watchman, nor did it burn lights in its building at night. Mr. Pennington's tin box was placed in the vault along with other like boxes belonging to customers. The vault was an old one, built of brick, without steel lining. It had an iron or steel door. In the vault there were a nest of safety deposit boxes and two safes. Neither the safety deposit boxes nor the safes were disturbed by the burglars. Only the tin boxes were rifled. One of the safes was burglar proof. In this safe the bank kept its money and its own bonds and bonds belonging to relatives of some of its officers. There was not room in this safe to put tin boxes, but plenty of room to place plaintiff's bond and the bonds belonging to the bank's other patrons.

[3] We think the evidence detailed and other proof appearing in the record entitled

the plaintiff to have her case go to the jury. It should have been left to the jury to say, under all the circumstances, in view of the nature of plaintiff's property, whether the bank had exercised adequate care for the protection of said property.

We find no error in the rulings of the trial judge on evidence that are of consequence.

[4] Usage and custom in a particular business reflect on the care exacted of a bailee. Kelton v. Taylor, 79 Tenn. (11 Lea) 264, 47 Am. Rep. 284; Railway Co. v. Manchester Mills, 88 Tenn. 653, 14 S. W. 314. We do not think it competent to prove, however, what one or two other banks may or may not have done toward safeguarding their valuables. Likewise we think the proof offered as to the business policy of the burglary insurance companies was incompetent. They are influenced by many reasons in determining what risks they will undertake. So, also, the advertisements of defendant bank were irrelevant, as plaintiff relied wholly on personal assurances from the bank president when she placed her bond there.

Reverse and remand for a new trial.

BRICKEY v. STATE. (No. 3.)

(Supreme Court of Arkansas. May 23, 1921.
Rehearing Denied June 20, 1921.)

1. Criminal law ⚖596(3), 606—Overruling of motion for continuance, not verified and based only on impeaching evidence, discretionary.

Under Crawford & Moses' Dig. §§ 1270, 3130, the court did not abuse its discretion in overruling motion for continuance, which was in due form, but was not verified, either by defendant appellant or his attorney for him, while another witness testified on behalf of defendant to substantially the same facts set up in the motion, tending to impeach the testimony of the state's witness.

2. Criminal law ⚖641(1)—Right to be heard by counsel not denied defendant, to whom continuance refused for absence of counsel.

Where defendant's regularly employed counsel did not appear on account of engagement elsewhere, and instead of granting defendant continuance the court appointed counsel to represent him, the right to be heard by counsel guaranteed to persons accused of crime by Bill of Rights, § 10, was not denied.

3. Criminal law ⚖593—Denial of continuance for absence of employed counsel except for sickness or unavoidable casualty discretionary.

It is never an abuse of discretion for the court to refuse to grant a continuance on account of the absence of employed counsel, unless caused by sickness or other unavoidable casualty; absence from the court where causes are pending in which he is employed as counsel, on account of causes pending in other courts in which he is also employed as counsel, not being an unavoidable casualty.

4. Criminal law ⚖1144(17)—Presumption sentence pronounced in due time according to statute.

In the absence of any showing to the contrary, it will be presumed that sentence was pronounced in due time according to Crawford & Moses' Dig. § 3229.

5. Criminal law ⚖977(3)—Defendant, who did not object, waived time specified for pronouncing sentence.

Where defendant did not make any objection at the time to the pronouncement of sentence, though he was given an opportunity to do so, he must be held to have waived the matter of the time for pronouncing sentence specified by Crawford & Moses' Dig. § 3229.

Appeal from Circuit Court, Van Buren County; J. M. Shinn, Judge.

Willie Brickey was convicted of selling intoxicating liquor, and he appeals. Affirmed.

J. Allen Eades, of Morrillton, for appellant.

J. S. Utley, Atty. Gen., and Elbert Godwin and W. T. Hammock, Asst. Attys. Gen., for the State.

WOOD, J. On the 9th of March, 1921, the same being an adjourned day of the regular February term of the Van Buren circuit court, the appellant was convicted of the crime of selling intoxicating liquors, and by judgment of the court sentenced to imprisonment in the state penitentiary for one year. From that judgment he prosecutes this appeal.

[1] Appellant urges as his only ground for reversal of the judgment that the court erred in overruling his motion for a continuance. He assigns three reasons why the court erred:

First. Because of the absence of H. G. Wolverton, a material witness, who was summoned before the court convened, and who was sick and unable to attend. The motion for continuance was in due form, but was not verified, either by the appellant or his attorney for him, and, furthermore, another witness testified on behalf of appellant to substantially the same facts set up in the motion tending to impeach the testimony of the state's witness. The court did not abuse its discretion under these circumstances in overruling the motion. Sections 1270 and 3130 of Crawford & Moses' Digest; Morris v. State, 103 Ark. 352, 147 S. W. 74; James v. State, 125 Ark. 269, 188 S. W. 806; Burris v. Wise & Hind, 2 Ark. 33, 40; State Life Ins. Co. v. Ford, 101 Ark. 513, 142 S. W. 863.

[2] Second. The appellant set up that the cause should be continued on account of the absence of J. A. Eades, who was unable to attend court because the adjourned term was at a day when the circuit court was in regular session at Morrilton, requiring the attorney's presence at the latter court. The affidavit of Eades in support of this ground of the motion shows that he had been employed by the appellant to defend him, and his fee had been paid; that he appeared in attendance at the regular term of the Van Buren circuit court, but that court was adjourned until the 7th of March on account of the absence of the regular judge; that he could not appear at the adjourned day because on that day the regular term of the circuit court was in session at Morrilton, and he could not be present at both courts, and was compelled, on account of his business in the latter court and the duty he owed his clients there, to attend that court. Of those facts he duly notified the presiding judge of the latter court, and also the prosecuting attorney, and requested a continuance of the cause to the regular fall term of the Van Buren circuit court. The regularly employed attorney being absent, the court appointed Garner Fraser, an attorney in attendance at the adjourned term of the Van Buren circuit court, to represent the appellant, who prepared and filed his motion for continuance, and conducted his defense.

[3] The court did not err in refusing appel-

lant's motion to continue because of the absence of employed counsel. The right to be heard by counsel guaranteed to persons accused of crime by the Bill of Rights, article 2, § 10, Constitution of 1874, was not denied the appellant in this case. On the contrary, when his regularly employed counsel did not appear, the court appointed counsel to represent him. Counsel who are employed to represent clients having cases pending in courts must so arrange their business as to be able to appear to represent their clients when those cases are called for trial. The business of the courts cannot be controlled, interrupted, or made to conform to the business interests of attorneys. The fact that an attorney may have cases for clients pending in different courts whose terms convene at the same time, and which condition may render it impossible for the attorney to be in attendance at one of the courts, is no imperative reason for the continuance of the causes in which he is employed in the court which he does not attend. These are matters addressed to the sound discretion of the presiding judge of the court, who must conduct the public business intrusted to him in a manner most conducive to the interests of the public whom he serves. It is never an abuse of discretion for the court to refuse to grant a continuance in a cause on account of the absence of employed counsel, unless such counsel is absent by reason of sickness or some other unavoidable casualty. The absence of an attorney from a court where causes are pending in which he is employed as counsel, because of causes pending in other courts in which he is also employed as counsel, is not an unavoidable casualty.

[4, 5] Third. The appellant contends that the court erred in sentencing the appellant on the day after the verdict of guilty was returned against him. The appellant relies upon section 3229 of Crawford & Moses' Digest, which provides in part as follows:

"Upon the verdict of conviction in cases of felony, the court shall not pronounce judgment until two days after the verdict is rendered unless the court is about to adjourn for the term and then in not less than six hours after the verdict, except by the defendant's consent."

The record shows that the jury returned a verdict on the 9th of March, and the record entry of March 10th is as follows:

"The defendant was this day brought into open court, and, being informed of the nature of the indictment, plea, and verdict, was asked if he had any legal cause to show why sentence should not be pronounced against him, and, none being shown, it is adjudged." etc.

The record does not show when the Van Buren circuit court adjourned. In the absence of any showing to the contrary, it will be presumed that the sentence was pronounced according to law. Moreover, the appellant did not make any objection at the time to the pronouncement of the sentence, and he was given an opportunity to do so. He therefore must be held to have waived the time specified in the statute.

We find no errors in the record, and the judgment is therefore affirmed.

TAYLOR v. WALKER. (No. 35.)

(Supreme Court of Arkansas. June 6, 1921.)

1. Fixtures ⊜14—Machinery parts added under agreement for removal on expiration of lease did not become part of realty.

Machinery parts installed by tenant in a gin plant and which lessor had agreed that lessee might remove upon expiration of lease did not become a part of the real estate.

2. Appeal and error ⊜901—Refusal of instructions not error in absence of showing that they were not covered by other instructions given.

Refusal of requested instructions will not be held error in the absence of a showing that, in so far as they correctly declared the law, they were not covered by other given instructions.

3. Replevin ⊜96—Rendition of verdict in solido not ground for reversal.

Where action in replevin was tried upon the theory that the various articles replevied constituted a single unit of value, and where the testimony on both sides related to the value of the property as a whole, the rendition of the verdict in solido, instead of fixing the value of each specific article, as required by Crawford & Moses' Dig. § 8653, is not ground for reversal; the statute having been waived.

4. Replevin ⊜96—Statute providing for fixing value of each article not jurisdictional.

Crawford & Moses' Dig. § 8653, providing for the fixing of the value of each specific article replevied, held not jurisdictional, but may be waived and will be held to be waived where the property replevied is treated as parts of a single unit.

Appeal from Circuit Court, St. Francis County; J. M. Jackson, Judge.

Suit by George P. Walker against Rena Taylor. Judgment for plaintiff, and defendant appeals. Affirmed.

R. J. Williams and Walter Gorman, both of Forrest City, for appellant.

Mann & Mann, of Forrest City, for appellee.

SMITH, J. This is a suit in replevin for various parts of a System gin plant. The litigation arose in the following manner: Appellant, Mrs. Taylor, owned a plantation, which she leased to the Beck Company, a corporation, for a term of five years. This lease was dated August 4, 1906, and covered the five-year period beginning January 1, 1907. On May 7, 1908, a second lease was executed for a five-year period beginning at the expiration of the first lease. Each lease included "the steam gin and sawmill, together with all buildings of every kind" being on the land. These leases were transferred by the Beck Company to George P. Walker on January 8, 1909.

Before the termination of the last lease a disagreement arose between Mrs. Taylor and Walker, chiefly over delay in payment of rent, and she served notice on him to vacate. He vacated the premises, but left the ginhouse locked and refused to surrender the key. Thereupon Mrs. Taylor put another lock on the ginhouse. She refused, on demand, to surrender certain pumps, belts, pulleys, gins, presses, and other fixtures, whereupon Walker brought replevin therefor. This suit was commenced September 21, 1915.

It was shown on behalf of Walker that the old ginhouse was in a dilapidated and dangerous condition, and the gin was moved across the road into a new building. According to Walker, it was not only agreed that he should retain ownership and control of any new machinery installed by him, but it was also agreed that he should have the right to remove the building at the expiration of his lease if he desired to do so. In erecting the new plant Walker used the old engine and certain shafting and a fan belonging to the old plant. All other parts were new.

At the trial testimony was offered as to the value of these new parts as a unit comprising a ginning plant and the usable value thereof. The jury returned into court the following verdict:

"We, the jury, find for the plaintiff for the possession of the property, and fix the value at $650, and find a fair rental value of said property to be $800 for the five years said property was held by the defendant."

After the verdict had been read, but before the jury had been discharged, counsel for Mrs. Taylor objected to its form, for the reason that it did not specify the separate value of the various parts of the gin which had been replevied.

[1] It is insisted that a verdict should have been directed in Mrs. Taylor's favor, upon the ground that the property replevied had become a part of the real estate, and was not therefore the subject of replevin. Without a full recitation of the testimony on this issue, it suffices to say that, according to the testimony which tends to support the verdict, Walker was unable to operate the gin on account of its age and condition, whereupon it was agreed that he might install such new parts as were neces-

sary, with the privilege of removing them upon the expiration of his tenancy. Under this agreement the new parts of the ginning plant did not become a part of the real estate, but remained the lessee's personal property, and were therefore subject to a suit in replevin. Buffalo Zinc & Copper Co. v. Hale, 136 Ark. 10, 206 S. W. 661; Cameron v. Robbins, 141 Ark. 607, 218 S. W, 173; Vanhoozer v. Gattis, 139 Ark. 390, 214 S. W. 44; Heim v. Brook, 133 Ark. 593, 202 S. W. 36; Bache v. Central O. & C. Co., 127 Ark. 397, 192 S. W. 225, Ann. Cas. 1918E, 198.

[2] At the trial from which this appeal comes instructions numbered from 1 to 11 were asked in Mrs. Taylor's behalf, but none were given, and counsel complained of this refusal. It is not shown, however, that these instructions, in so far as they correctly declared the law were not covered by other instructions which were given.

Complaint is also made that the court erred in giving instructions, but no error is pointed out in the instructions given. Reed v. State, 102 Ark. 391, 147 S. W. 76, Ann. Cas. 1914B, 811; Bass v. Starnes, 108 Ark. 357, 158 S. W. 136.

It is finally insisted that the jury was permitted to return a verdict in solido. This point appears, however, not to have been raised until the jury had returned its verdict, although the jury had not then been discharged.

[3, 4] It appears that the cause was tried upon the theory that the various articles replevied constituted a single unit of value, and the testimony on both sides related to the value of the property as a whole. The request that the articles be separately valued could not have been complied with by the jury even if the request had been made when the jury first retired to consider of its verdict, because, as has been said, each side had treated the property in dispute as a single unit of value.

The statute does provide (section 8653, C. & M. Digest) for fixing the value of each specific article replevied; but this requirement is not jurisdictional. It may be waived (Hobbs v. Clark, 53 Ark. 411, 14 S. W. 652, 9 L. R. A. 526; Neal v. Cole, 223 S. W. 18), and will be held to be waived in a case where, as in this, the property replevied is treated as parts of a single unit.

It is also objected that the verdict returned included the usable value, not only of the property replevied, but of other property used in connection with it owned by Mrs. Taylor. It is not made to appear, however, that such is the case. It is true that property owned by her was used in connection with other property owned by Walker, and that it took all of the property to make a complete gin plant. But there was no question in the case about what property was owned by her, or what parts of the plant had been installed by Walker, and no objection appears to have been made that the testimony in regard to usable value was not confined to the parts installed by Walker.

No error appearing, the judgment is affirmed.

ROAD IMPROVEMENT DIST. NO. 9 OF SEVIER COUNTY v. BENNETT et al. (No. 37.)

(Supreme Court of Arkansas. June 6, 1921.)

Highways ⇐=142—Statute held not to authorize circuit court to set aside whole assessment of benefits.

Acts Sp. Sess. 1920, No. 407, creating road improvement district No. 9 of Sevier county, did not by section 9 thereof confer on the circuit court on appeal from the county court power to set aside the whole assessment of benefits to pay for constructing a road, but only provided a method for attacking, on appeal to the circuit court, assessments of benefits against particular tracts of land for good cause shown by the property owner or owners of the particular tract or tracts; section 7 providing a method for attacking the whole assessment of benefits in the chancery court.

Appeal from Circuit Court, Sevier County; Jas. S. Steel, Judge.

Proceedings for the creation of Road Improvement District No. 9 of Sevier county, contested by J. W. Bennett and others. From judgment creating the district, objectors appealed to the circuit court, which set aside judgment levying an assessment of benefits to pay for construction of a road, and the district appeals. Judgment reversed, and cause remanded for further proceeding.

Lake & Lake, of De Queen, for appellant. E. K. Edwards, of Lockesburg, and B. E. Isbell, of De Queen, for appellees.

HUMPHREYS, J. This is an appeal from the judgment of the Sevier circuit court, setting aside a judgment of the county court levying an assessment of benefits to pay for constructing a road in road improvement district No. 9 of Sevier county. Appellees, four landowners in said district, prosecuted the appeal from the judgment of the county court under section 9 of Act No. 407 of the Special Session of 1920 of the General Assembly of the State of Arkansas, creating the district. The issue tried and determined in the circuit court on appeal related to the assessment as a whole, and the issue as to the validity or invalidity of the individual assessments made upon the lands of appellees was not developed or determined. Section 9 of said special act, under which the appeal was taken, did not confer

upon the circuit court power on appeal to set aside the whole assessment. It only provided a method for attacking, on appeal to the circuit court, assessments of benefits against particular tracts of land for good cause shown by the property owner, or owners, of the particular tract, or tracts. This construction must be given section 9 of the act aforesaid, because section 7 of the same special act provides a method for attacking the whole assessment of benefits in the chancery court of said county. If both sections provide a method for attacking the assessment of benefits as a whole, there is wanting in the act any remedy or redress for unjust or inequitable assessments of benefits against individual tracts of land, since section 7 of said act provides in unmistakable terms for a remedy or redress against an unjust or inequitable assessment as a whole by suit in the chancery court. The conclusion is irresistible that the remedy or redress provided in section 9 has relation to redress for unjust or inequitable assessments of benefits against particular tracts of land, for it is quite unlikely that the Legislature would give two remedies for correcting unjust or inequitable assessments as a whole and no remedy for correcting individual assessments. The circuit court was therefore without jurisdiction to set aside the entire assessment of benefits in the district and should have limited the inquiry to the validity of the assessments against the particular tracts of land owned by the appellees herein.

Appellees insist, however, that this cause should be dismissed, and have filed a motion for that purpose, because, during the pendency of the appeal here, the General Assembly of this state passed an act repealing the special or local act by which the district in question was created. The repealing act bears number 291 and was approved March 21, 1921. Section 1 of the repealing act is as follows:

"That Act No. 407 of the General Assembly, approved February 20, 1920, entitled 'An act to create road improvement district number nine of Sevier county,' be and the same is hereby repealed."

Section 2 of the repealing act provides, among other things, for a continuation of the district and the commissioners thereof for the purpose of paying the indebtedness thereof. Said section, in part, is as follows:

"On the expiration of said six months (referring to the time in which claims against the district may be presented to the commissioners) it shall be the duty of the commissioners to levy upon the real property of the district a tax sufficient to pay the indebtedness thereof. If the assessment of benefits of the district has been made and confirmed, said tax shall be based upon such assessment of benefits. If the assessment of benefits has not been made and confirmed, it shall be by the assessed value of the property for State and county taxation as it appears upon the county assessment."

The insistence of appellant is that the repealing statute, approved March 21, 1921, is void, because it impaired the obligation of contracts and, in that respect, infringes upon both the Constitution of the state and of the United States. So far as the issue involved on this appeal is concerned, it is unnecessary to determine whether the repealing act is valid or void. The issue here is whether the circuit court had jurisdiction on appeal to set the judgment of the county court, levying the assessments of benefits against the property in the district, aside, in whole. It follows from our conclusion that it did not; that the levy of assessment of benefits as a whole must stand, whether the repealing act be valid or void. If the repealing act is void, the judgment levying the assessment of benefits will stand as a whole under the original act creating the district, because not attacked by suit in the chancery court under section 7 of the original act. If the repealing act is valid, the act itself provides for a continuation of the district for the purpose of paying the indebtedness thereof and authorizes the commissioners to base the assessment of benefits upon the confirmed assessment of benefits levied under the judgment of the county court. It not being necessary to pass upon the validity of the repealing act, we withhold any opinion as to what might be deemed valid claims against the district within the meaning of claims, as used in section 2 of the repealing act.

The motion of appellees to dismiss the appeal is therefore overruled, and, for the error indicated, the judgment of the circuit court is reversed, and the cause remanded for further proceedings.

FEDERAL TRUCK & MOTORS CO. v. TOMPKINS. (No. 36.)

(Supreme Court of Arkansas. June 6, 1921.)

Evidence ⬤⟿441(9)—Warranty cannot be ingrafted by parol upon complete unambiguous sales contract.

Where complete sales contract is unambiguous and contains no warranty, a warranty cannot be proven by parol testimony.

Appeal from Circuit Court, Franklin County; James Cochran, Judge.

Suit by the Federal Truck & Motors Company against Sam Tompkins. Judgment for defendant, and plaintiff appeals. Reversed and remanded.

Willard Pendergrass, of Altus, and Evans & Evans, of Booneville, for appellant.
J. P. Clayton, of Ozark, for appellee.

SMITH, J. On September 7, 1919, appellee made a contract to purchase a secondhand truck from the appellant company. By the terms of the contract $500 of the purchase price was to be paid in cash. Appellee gave his check for $100 and agreed to pay the balance of $400 when the truck was delivered to him at his place of business in Ozark. He also agreed, on delivery of the truck, to execute 10 notes, each for $75, payable one every 30 days. Under the agreement, appellant company was to send the truck from Ft. Smith, where the sale was made, to Ozark, but was unable to make delivery, and so notified appellee. Thereafter, on September 20th, appellee, accompanied by one Dodgins, went to Ft. Smith. Dodgins examined the truck, passed judgment upon it and approved it, and was employed by appellant company to drive the truck to Ozark. Thereupon the parties entered into the following contract:

"Original.
"Retail Car Contract.
"Ft. Smith, Ark., 9/20/19.
"Federal Truck & Motors Co. (Distributor)—Gentlemen: Please enter order for one model 1½ ton truck, secondhand, to be delivered on or about 9/20/19 (barring delays in transportation or other causes beyond our control), according to the following plan and specifications:

Price as per contract..........................$1,250.00

Catalogue Specifications.
Freight from factory............................ • • •
War tax.. • • •
  Total $1,250.00
Total price of extra equipment:
Deposit .... $ 500.00
Credit 500.00
In notes of $75 each 30 days................   750.00

"It is understood and made a part of this agreement that title or ownership of car as above described does not pass to purchaser until final cash payment is made.
  "(Salesman) George W. Malecot.
"Dated: Accepted 9/20/1919, at Federal Truck & Motors Co.
"By: S. L. Tompkins (Purchaser)."

Appellee proceeded to use the truck in his business, and, after three of the notes had been paid and two others had matured, proposed to pay the balance if allowed proper discount. This proposition was not accepted, and appellee thereafter refused to make other payments, and this suit was begun in the court of a justice of the peace to enforce payment of the notes.

The case reached the circuit court on appeal, and at the trial there appellee interposed the defense of a breach of warranty. He testified that before completing the payments he discovered that the truck was worn out, and instead of being only eight months old and in good condition as warranted, it had been in use for three years and was about worn out. Over appellant's objection the cause was submitted to the jury on this issue, and there was a verdict and judgment in appellee's favor, from which is this appeal.

Appellee defends the judgment of the court below on the theory that he was deceived and induced, by false representations in regard to the age and condition of the truck, to make the contract. But the case was not tried or submitted on that issue. In the instructions submitting the case to the jury the court said:

"The defendant admits the execution of the notes, the sale of the motor truck, but says that the truck was warranted or guaranteed to him to be in good condition and not to have been run to exceed eight months and to be as good as new. He says that it was not as good as new and it was not in good condition and it was run more than eight months and that the warranty has proven to be false. * * *"

Having thus stated the issue, the court told the jury to find for appellee if the testimony supported his contention.

The court was in error in submitting the question of warranty. The contract set out above is apparently a complete contract of sale. There appears to be no ambiguity about it requiring explanation, and no warranty is incorporated therein. In Lower v. Hickman, 80 Ark. 508, 97 S. W. 681, this court said:

"1. A warranty is so clearly a part of a sale that where the sale is evidenced by a written instrument it is incompetent to engraft upon it a warranty proved by parol. The character of the written instrument is not important, so long as it purports to be a complete transaction of itself, and not a mere incomplete memorandum or receipt for money or part of a transaction where there are other parts of it other than warranties. It may be a complete contract signed by both parties and comprehensive and exhaustive in detail, and contain many mutual agreements, terms and stipulations, or it may be a simple bill of sale, or sale note evidencing the sale. The principle is the same in any of these transactions, and oral evidence of a warranty is almost universally excluded when a complete written instrument evidences the sale. It is not important that the instrument be signed by both parties, for acceptance of the other may be equally binding, and the principle here invoked is as often applied to unilateral as to bilateral instruments. For the statement of the principles involved and the many applications thereof, see"—citing cases.

What was there said is equally applicable here. See, also, Johnson, Berger & Co. v. W. J. Hughes & Co., 83 Ark. 105, 108 S. W. 184; Arden Lumber Co. v. Henderson Iron Works, 83 Ark. 240, 103 S. W. 185; Barry-Wehmiller Machinery Co. v. Thompson, 83 Ark. 288, 104 S. W. 137; Bradley Gin Co. v. Means Machinery Co., 94 Ark. 130, 126 S.

W. 81; Morris v. S. W. Supply Co., 136 Ark. 507, 206 S. W. 894; Sweet Springs Milling Co. v. Gentry, Buchanan & Co., 142 Ark. 234, 218 S. W. 380, 219 S. W. 1013.

For the error of submitting the question of breach of warranty, the judgment is reversed, and the cause will be remanded for a new trial.

———

SANDERSON et al. v. MARCONI. (No. 29.)

(Supreme Court of Arkansas. June 6, 1921.)

1. Trial ⟷177—Where each party requested peremptory instruction, the court may decide the issue.

Where each party requested a peremptory instruction, that was tantamount to an agreement that the court might decide the issues, and it was not error to give a peremptory instruction for one of the parties; the evidence being sufficient to sustain the verdict.

2. Indemnity ⟷16—Evidence held to sustain judgment in favor of indemnitor against bondsmen who compromised liability.

Where plaintiff asserted that he delivered to defendants $700 in cash and securities to indemnify them against loss as sureties on the appearance bond for plaintiff's son, that the son fled the country, and that defendants compromised the judgment against them for $350, evidence held sufficient to sustain the judgment in plaintiff's favor notwithstanding defendants' contention that the return of none of the money was contemplated.

3. Appeal and error ⟷260(2)—Exclusion of evidence not excepted to cannot be reviewed.

Where no exception was reserved to the exclusion of evidence, the matter cannot be reviewed.

Appeal from Circuit Court, Miller County; Geo. R. Haynie, Judge.

Action by Louis Marconi against M. E. Sanderson and others. From a judgment for plaintiff, defendants appeal. Affirmed.

T. E. Webber, Jr., and M. E. Sanderson, both of Texarkana, for appellants.

Jno. N. Cook, of Texarkana, for appellee.

McCULLOCH, C. J. The plaintiff, Louis Marconi, instituted this action against the defendants alleging that he delivered to them the sum of $700, consisting of $600 in cash and a bond of the United States of the denomination and value of $100, to indemnify them against loss as sureties on the appearance bond of plaintiff's son, and that the defendants accepted said sum and executed said bond on condition that the funds would be returned to him in the event plaintiff's son complied with the terms of the bond, and that the defendants should use such part of the funds so paid over as would be required to discharge their liability in event of forfeiture on the bond. Plaintiff alleged that there had been a forfeiture of the bond and a judgment in favor of the state which had been compromised by defendants on the payment of the sum of $350, and the prayer of the complaint was for the recovery of the balance of the money so paid over. Defendants answered, admitting the receipt from plaintiff of said funds and government bond, but denied that plaintiff delivered the money to defendants "with any promise or assurance whatever from said defendants that any part of this money would be returned in case a forfeiture was taken upon said bond." The answer contained a further statement:

"That the plaintiff well understood, and it was so explained to him, * * * that if he executed said bond that his son * * * would flee the country and would not be in attendance when his case was called in said court, and that, if plaintiff put up the money for said bond, the whole of the same * * * would be entirely lost to him. The plaintiff further understood * * * that none of the money would be returned to him in case the son failed to appear under the requirements on said bond."

There was a trial before a jury which resulted in a verdict in favor of the plaintiff for the sum of $350. This verdict was rendered on the peremptory direction of the court.

The facts of the case, as related in the pleadings and set forth in the testimony, are that plaintiff's son was arrested and held in custody on a charge of felony, and in order to induce one of the defendants, Frank Carrara, to sign a bail bond, the plaintiff delivered to one of the banks in Texarkana, where Carrara resided, the sum of $600 in money and a government bond of the denomination of $100, and drew a check in Carrara's favor for the amount of the money. Carrara signed the bond, and the accused, after being liberated on the bond, fled the country. A forfeiture was taken on the bond, and judgment was rendered against the sureties in the sum of $500, which appellants compromised for the sum of $350 and paid it. The contention of plaintiff is that he paid over the money under a promise that it was to be returned to him if there was no forfeiture under the bond, and that any part of it not used in paying a judgment on the bond such part was to be returned to him. The defendants contend that there was no express promise to return the money, but, on the contrary, that the money was received from plaintiff with the understanding that none of it was to be returned to him in any event, whether there was a forfeiture on the bond or not. One of the defendants offered to testify concerning an agreement that the money was paid with the understanding that the accused was to flee the country, but the court excluded that testimony on the ground that such agreement was not pleaded in the answer. There was no exception saved to the ruling of the court in that regard.

[1, 2] The state of the proof is such that the jury might have found that the agreement between the parties was that the money was to be paid over to defendant Carrara as compensation to him for making the bond, and that no part of it was to be returned in any event, or the jury might have found from the testimony that the money was paid over to Carrara merely to indemnify him against any loss which he might sustain by reason of becoming surety on the bond. Each party asked for a peremptory instruction, and the court granted the plaintiff's request and refused the request of the defendants. This was tantamount to an agreement that the court might decide the issue, and it was not error to give a peremptory instruction under those circumstances, if the evidence was legally sufficient to sustain the verdict, no other instructions being asked for or given. St. Louis S. W. Ry. Co. v. Mulkey, 100 Ark. 71, 139 S. W. 643, Ann. Cas. 1913C, 1339. There was, as before stated, sufficient evidence to warrant the jury in finding that, while there was no express promise to return the money, there was in fact an agreement that the money was paid to Carrara as indemnity against loss, and under those circumstances there was an implied promise to return any of the money not used in discharging liability under the bond.

[3] It is argued here that there was evidence offered sufficient to show that the contract was unlawful in that it was expressly agreed that the money was paid over in consideration of the fact that the defendants would make the bond and the boy was to flee the country. There was no exception saved to the ruling of the court excluding this testimony; therefore we are not called on to decide anything in that regard. Even if the language of the answer be regarded as sufficient to present this issue, the findings of the court on the request for a peremptory instruction are sustained by sufficient evidence on such issue.

The judgment is therefore affirmed.

HAWKINS v. RANDOLPH.   (No. 34.)

(Supreme Court of Arkansas.   June 6, 1921.)

1. Contracts ⊂⇒92—Whether a party had mental capacity determined by facts of particular case.

The question of whether a party to a contract had mental capacity must be determined under the facts of the particular case.

2. Mortgages ⊂⇒319(3)—Evidence showing release by 80 year old mortgagee invalid for want of mental capacity.

In action to set aside on the ground of mental incapacity a release, by 80 year old plaintiff mortgagee, of mortgage for $10,000 in consideration of defendant mortgagor's agreement to pay plaintiff $480 per year during the remainder of his life, evidence held to show plaintiff's incapacity.

3. Contracts ⊂⇒96—Between persons in fiduciary relationship closely scrutinized.

Transactions between persons connected by fiduciary relations will be closely scrutinized, not only in technical cases of fiduciary relationship, but in all cases where the relation between the parties gives one the controlling influence over the other.

4. Contracts ⊂⇒94(8)—Will not be set aside for mere inadequacy of consideration.

Where the parties are capable of contracting, the court will not set aside their contracts for mere inadequacy of price, but where the inadequacy is accompanied with other facts showing concealment on the part of the one who obtains a benefit, on account of old age, ignorance, incapacity, etc., on the part of the one granting the benefit, equity will readily grant relief.

5. Pensions ⊂⇒2—"Pension" defined.

A pension is the regular allowance paid to an individual by the government in consideration of past services or in recognition of merit, and to the payment of which the whole resources of the government are pledged.

[Ed. Note.—For other definitions, see Words and Phrases, First and Second Series, Pension.]

Appeal from Franklin Chancery Court; J. V. Bourland, Chancellor.

Suit by Robert H. Randolph against S. B. Hawkins. Decree for plaintiff, and defendant appeals. Affirmed.

Robert H. Randolph brought this suit in equity against S. B. Hawkins to annul and set aside a contract whereby the plaintiff released in favor of the defendant a mortgage on a tract of land to secure an indebtedness of $10,000.

On the 7th day of July, 1919, R. H. Randolph executed to S. B. Hawkins a deed to 183 acres of land in Franklin county, Ark., for the consideration of $12,500. Of this amount $500 was in cash, and the balance in five promissory notes. The first note was for $2,000, and the remaining four notes were for $2,500 each. The first note fell due on January 1, 1920, and one each year thereafter. Hawkins gave Randolph a mortgage on the land purchased to secure the payment of these notes. The defendant paid the first note when it fell due, and subsequently the parties entered into a contract as follows:

"This agreement, made and entered into this 9th day of March, 1920, between S. B. Hawkins, party of the first part and R. H. Randolph, party of the second part, witnesseth, that in consideration of the release of a certain mortgage dated September 10, 1919, and the return to the said S. B. Hawkins of the notes secured by said mortgage, it is hereby understood, contracted and agreed that the said party of the first part, his heirs and assigns, executors and administrators, shall pay unto said R. H. Randolph or his assigns, during the period of his natural life the full sum of four hundred and eighty dollars (480.00) each and every year during such life, payable quarterly on the first days of April, July, October and January, beginning on the 1st day of April, 1920, with the amount of $120.00 and paying said amount as aforesaid at the beginning of each quarter thereafter so long as said R. H. Randolph shall live. It being the idea of this contract and the intention of the parties to afford said party of the second part an annuity of $480.00 for the term of his natural life, payable quarterly in advance, and that at the time of his death such payments shall cease and no further obligations shall thereafter rest upon the said S. B. Hawkins by virtue of this contract or the securities surrendered in consideration of this contract.

"In witness whereof, the parties have hereunto set their hands this 9th day of March, 1920."

Pursuant to the terms of the contract, Randolph on the same day executed a release deed to Hawkins to the property described in the mortgage. The object of this suit is to cancel the contract and the release deed executed by Randolph to Hawkins.

R. H. Randolph was a witness for himself. According to his testimony he resided on his land in Franklin county, Ark., but transacted his business at Mulberry, in Crawford county, Ark. For many years he had transacted his business with a bank at that place of which S. B. Hawkins was the cashier. Randolph was an uneducated man, could not read or write, except to sign his name. Hawkins had acted as his confidential adviser for about 30 years. Randolph was a widower without children, and was about 80 years of age when he conveyed his land to Hawkins and took a mortgage back to secure the payment of the purchase money. The contract which is the basis of this lawsuit was written by the attorney of Hawkins in a back room of his bank. The lawyer commenced to read the contract to Randolph, and Hawkins took it from him, saying that the contract was all right, and that it was not necessary to read it over to Randolph.

Randolph was just getting over a case of influenza, and did not recollect signing the release deed. Hawkins gave Randolph a certificate on the bank for $120 on April 1, 1920. Subsequently he mailed Randolph a quarterly payment for a similar amount. Randolph then began to realize what had been done, and sent the money back to Hawkins.

On cross-examination Randolph admitted that he had attended to his own affairs all of his life and felt that he was competent to do so when at himself. He stated that he was sick when the contract in question was executed. He admitted that he boarded with Jack Underwood in March, 1920, but denied telling him that he wanted to sell his land for the reason that the road and other taxes were eating it up. He denied telling Underwood that he would like to turn his mortgage over to some one and draw $40 a month on it like he (Underwood) was doing with the government. Randolph further stated that as soon as Mr. Chew explained the meaning of the contract to him he immediately authorized him to bring this suit.

The defendant, S. B. Hawkins, was a witness for himself. He admitted having known Randolph for 30 years, and that he had bought the land from him at the time and on the terms described above. In March, 1920, Randolph came to Hawkins, and wanted him to pay him a pension. Randolph called it a pension. He reminded Hawkins that he had sold the land to Stewart, and that the mortgage would be in the way. Randolph wanted to release the mortgage so that Hawkins could go on with his trade. Hawkins wrote for his attorney to come down, and on the next day the attorney came to town, and the contract in question was executed. Hawkins asked Randolph how much he wanted, and Randolph said that he would have to have $440 per year. Hawkins replied: "That is all right. If that will keep you comfortable, it is all right with me." The attorney prepared the papers, and they were signed in duplicate the next day. After he had acknowledged the release deed Randolph said: "You ought to have this recorded." Hawkins replied that he would mail it right away. Randolph then said: "No; that is a valuable paper, it might miscarry or get lost in the mail. You ought to send it by some one." Hawkins said: "All right, I will send it by my son and have it recorded," and did so. Randolph came to Hawkins a few days later, and said he ought to have $480 a year. Hawkins said: "All right, Uncle Bob, if you need $480, we will make it $480." Hawkins then took both copies, and changed them to read $480 per year. On the 1st day of April, 1920, Hawkins placed $120 to Randolph's credit, and Randolph seemed satisfied. On July 1, 1920, Hawkins mailed him a check

for $120, and Randolph returned it. When they first talked about the contract in question, Randolph told Hawkins that the taxes were eating him up, and the people were wanting him to invest his money.

C. R. Starbird, the attorney for Hawkins, said that when he first got to the bank, Randolph was there waiting for him. Hawkins introduced them, and sent them into the back room to fix up the business. From the way Randolph commenced talking, Starbird thought that he wanted to make a will. Randolph replied that he did not want to make a will, but that Hawkins was to give him a pension. He told Starbird that he wanted one just like Uncle Jack Underwood was drawing. Starbird then asked him what amount the pension was to be, and Randolph said that they had not yet agreed on the amount. Hawkins was called into the room, and Starbird told him that they would have to agree on the amount. Hawkins said, "Uncle Bob, tell us how much you want." Randolph said that he thought about $440 a year. Hawkins said, "That is all right," and left the room. Starbird then took a memorandum of the contract and prepared it at his office, and then mailed it to Hawkins.

According to the testimony of Jack Underwood, Randolph was boarding at his house and told him that a new road was being built past his place, and that he had sold his land to get rid of the taxes which were eating it up. He stated further that he had a mortgage for $10,000 on his land, and that the taxes would eat that up; that he wished some one would take that, and give him a pension like he (Underwood) was drawing. Underwood then suggested that he should talk with Hawkins about it, and Randolph said that he would go right up and see Hawkins about it. A few days later Randolph told Underwood about the execution of the contract in question.

Mrs. Jack Underwood testified that she heard Randolph tell her husband that the taxes were eating him up, and that he wished he could arrange to have some one pay him a pension just like her husband drew from the government, and that he would turn over his $10,000 mortgage for it. Subsequently she heard Randolph tell her husband that he had drawn his pension.

Mrs. Bettie Conatser testified that Randolph told her that he had released the mortgage which Hawkins had given him, and that Hawkins had agreed to pay him $40 a month as long as he lived.

A physician who treated Randolph for influenza in March, 1920, testified that he could not see that Randolph's mind was affected by the disease.

An employee of the bank of which Hawkins was the cashier took Randolph's acknowledgment to the release deed, and corroborated Hawkins as to what took place when the contract and deed were executed.

The chancellor found in favor of the plaintiff, and it was decreed that the contract of March 9, 1920, should be canceled, and that the release deed should also be canceled.

It was further decreed that the mortgage on the land and the four notes given by Hawkins to Randolph in payment of the land should be in full force and effect. The defendant Hawkins has duly prosecuted an appeal to this court.

Evans & Evans, of Booneville, J. P. Clayton, of Ozark, and Starbird & Starbird, of Alma, for appellant.

Sam R. Chew, of Van Buren, for appellee.

HART, J. (after stating the facts as above). [1] We think the decision of the chancellor was correct. In the case of Kelly's Heirs v. McGuire, 15 Ark. 555, the court recognized that the law does not seem to have attempted to draw any discriminating line by which to determine how great must be the imbecility of mind to render a contract void, or how much intellect must remain to uphold it. The reason that no exact general rule as to incapacity to contract can be laid down is because each case will be found influenced by its own peculiar circumstances. In discussing the subject the court said:

"While the solemn contracts between men, should never be disturbed on slight grounds, yet it may, perhaps, be assumed, as a safe general rule, that, whenever a person, through age, decrepitude, affliction, or disease, becomes imbecile, and incapable of managing his affairs, an unreasonable or improvident disposition of his property, will be set aside in a court of chancery. In Re James Barker, 2 John. Ch. Rep. 232. * * *

"If a contract is freely and understandingly executed, by a party, with a full knowledge of his rights, and of the consequences of the act, it must stand. This court disclaims all jurisdiction to interfere on account of the improvidence or folly of an act done by a person of sound, though impaired, mind. But, on the other hand, contracts have been set aside and canceled, when want of consideration, or the improvident nature of the transaction has raised the presumption that fraud and misrepresentations were employed. Shelford on Lunacy, 267. When a gift is disproportionate to the means of the giver, and the giver is a person of weak mind, of easy temper, yielding disposition, liable to be imposed on, the court will look upon such gift with a jealous eye, and strictly examine the conduct and behavior of the person in whose favor it is made, and if it can discover that any acts or stratagems, or any undue means have been used, to procure such gift; if it see the least speck of imposition, or that the donor is in such a situation with respect to the donee as may naturally give him an undue influence over him; in a word, if there be the least scintilla of fraud, a court of equity will interpose"—citing cases.

[2] The court has continued to recognize this as the general rule since that time. Campbell v. Lux, 225 S. W. 653, and Nelson v. Murray, 224 S. W. 486. In the application of the doctrine to the facts of the present case it may be said that the evidence shows that Randolph freely and willingly entered into the contract in question and executed the deed of release to the mortgage; but his action, measured as it must be by the testimony of the witnesses as to the circumstances surrounding the transaction, does not show that intelligent participation characteristic of one who understands what he is doing and comprehends the nature of his act.

[3] The evidence shows that Randolph and Hawkins had lived on terms of the closest friendship for 30 years, and that Randolph always advised with Hawkins in regard to his affairs. He had full confidence in his judgment and integrity. He was an uneducated man, and usually followed the advice of Hawkins in all his business transactions. Courts regard with a jealous eye transactions between persons connected by fiduciary relations. The principle is not confined to technical cases of fiduciary relationship. It is applicable to all cases where the relation between the parties gives one the controlling influence over the other.

[4] It is true that where the parties are capable of contracting, courts will not set aside their contracts for mere inadequacy of price, but where the inadequacy is accompanied with other facts showing concealment on the part of the one who obtains a benefit on account of old age, ignorance, incapacity, etc., on the part of the one granting the benefit, courts of equity will readily grant relief.

The direct testimony of the witnesses, standing alone, shows that Randolph had always been capable of attending to his own affairs, and that he still had intellect enough to make a disposition of his property, but his situation and the surrounding circumstances are proper to be taken into consideration in determining whether a court of equity should interpose. Randolph was over 80 years of age and was an ignorant person, unable to read or write. Hawkins had been his confidential adviser for 30 years. Randolph had already sold him his farm, and had taken a mortgage back to secure most of the purchase price. His fears about the taxes eating up his lands were groundless; for after the sale he had nothing to do with paying the taxes on the land. Hawkins owed Randolph $10,000, which was secured by a mortgage on the farm. Randolph exchanged this secured indebtedness, which bore interest at the rate of 6 per cent. per annum for an agreement on the part of Hawkins to pay him an amount annually which would be less than the interest. The only benefit that he could possibly derive was to receive this payment

uarterly instead of annually. While his
mortgage was taxable, there is nothing to
how that exorbitant taxes were about to be
assessed against it.

[5] The whole substance of the transaction
was to give up a secured debt of $10,000,
bearing interest at 6 per cent. per annum,
for an unsecured debt of $480 annually for
the rest of his life. If Randolph had lived
20 years longer, which is altogether improbable, these small payments would not
have consumed the principal, much less the
interest. The interest would have amounted
to $600 per annum as against $480 under the
new contract. It is evident that Randolph
thought that he was getting a pension, and
that Hawkins knew that he thought so. This
fact is shown, not only by the testimony of
Hawkins himself, but by the testimony of
the witnesses introduced by him. Now a
pension is a regular allowance paid to an
individual by the government in consideration
of past services, or in recognition of merit.
The whole resources of the government are
pledged to the payment of pensions. Here,
as we have already seen, Randolph already
had the obligation of Hawkins to pay him
$10,000, with 6 per cent. interest per annum,
and in addition this obligation on the part of
Hawkins was secured by a mortgage on the
land. Randolph exchanged this for the unsecured promise of Hawkins to pay $480 per
annum as long as he lived.

The record shows that the amount promised was no more than sufficient to support
Randolph in his old age if he continued in
reasonable health. If he became sick and
his expenses thereby materially increased, it
will be readily seen that he had deprived
himself of the means of being supported and
cared for in that condition, while if he had
retained his property he would have had
ample means for that purpose. It is just
such conditions and situations as this that
equity scrutinizes closely and always inter-
poses to grant relief.

It follows that the decree will be affirmed.

———

SPIVEY et al. v. SPIVEY. (No. 30.)

(Supreme Court of Arkansas. June 6, 1921.)

Appeal and error ⟺300—Judgment affirmed
where appellant failed to file motion for new
trial with prayer for appeal within 30 days
after decision.

Under Crawford & Moses' Dig. § 1314, providing that, if verdict or decision is rendered
within three days of adjournment of term, a
motion for a new trial with an alternative
prayer for appeal in case motion for new trial
be overruled may be presented to the court
for its action and be acted on within 30 days
of verdict or decision, and on overruling mo-

tion court may indorse on motion grant of appeal and fix time for filing bill of exceptions, an
appellant attempting to appeal by proceeding
under this statute does not comply with statute
where motion was filed on day of adjournment,
but not presented to court within 30 days, no
alternative prayer for appeal was asked, and
no time fixed by the court overruling the motion
for filing bill of exceptions, and judgment must
be affirmed.

Appeal from Circuit Court, Desha County;
W. B. Sorrells, Judge.

Suit by Bush Spivey and others against
Madora Spivey in the probate court. From
judgment for defendant in the circuit court
on appeal, plaintiffs appeal. Affirmed.

John T. Cheairs, Jr., of Tillar, for appellants.

Danaher & Danaher, of Pine Bluff, and De
Witt Poe, of Arkansas City, for appellee.

McCULLOCH, C. J. Appellants are the
next of kin and heirs at law of Louis Spivey,
who died testate, and by his will disposed of
all his property except a certain sum of money. The testator by his will gave certain land
and personal property to his widow, and the
balance of his estate, except the sum of money
not disposed of, was devised to certain of
his relatives, and to his wife's grandchildren,
these last being the descendants of children
born to the widow of the testator by a former
marriage.

The executor named in the will administered on the estate, and this proceeding was begun in the probate court to require the executor to pay appellants the sum of money
not disposed of by the will. The case was
heard in the probate court, and an appeal
was duly prosecuted to the circuit court,
where a trial of the issue was had. The decision there turned upon the question of the
duty of the testator's widow to elect whether
she would take under the will or not. The
court rendered judgment in favor of the widow on August 25, 1920, and on the following
day adjourned for the term. A motion for a
new trial was filed on August 26th, the day
of adjournment, but the motion was not
presented to the court until the 28th day of
September, when the same was heard by the
judge in vacation and overruled. In overruling the motion for new trial the court did
not indorse on the back of the motion therefor an order granting an appeal and specifying a time within which a bill of exceptions
might be filed.

In prosecuting this appeal appellant has
proceeded under section 1314, C. & M. Digest,
which reads as follows:

"Sec. 1314. The application for a new trial
must be made at the term the verdict or decision is rendered, and except for the cause
mentioned in subdivision seven of section 1311,
shall be within three days after the verdict or

decision was rendered, unless unavoidably prevented: Provided, that where the verdict or decision is rendered within three days of the expiration or adjournment of the term, a motion for a new trial, with an alternative prayer for appeal to the Supreme Court in case said motion be overruled, may be presented, upon reasonable notice to the opposing party or his attorney of record, to the judge or chancellor, or his successor in office, of the district in which said verdict or decision is rendered, wherever he may be found, at any time within thirty days from the date of the verdict or decision, and such judge or chancellor shall pass upon said motion and indorse his ruling thereon, upon the back of the motion, either granting the motion or overruling same; and if said motion be overruled he shall also indorse upon said motion, his order granting an appeal to the Supreme Court, and his further order specifying a reasonable time allowed in said cause for filing a bill of exceptions. Upon filing such motion and the judge's order thereon, with the clerk of the court where the cause is pending it shall become a part of the records and files of the cause, and shall have the same legal force and effect as if same had been filed in term time, as now provided by law."

It is insisted that this statute has not been substantially complied with, and that there is therefore no bill of exceptions bringing into the record for review the testimony in the case.

This contention appears to be well taken. The statute requires that the motion for a new trial be presented to the court for its action and be acted upon by the court within 30 days of the date of the verdict or decision. This was not done within the time limited by law; nor did the court fix the time within which a bill of exceptions might be filed. The statute not having been substantially complied with, appellants are in the same attitude they would be in if they had permitted the term to lapse without having filed a motion for a new trial or of having had the same passed upon by the court during the term at which it was filed, and the judgment must therefore be affirmed. Feild v. Waters, 229 S. W. 735, and cases there cited.

———

BRIN BROS. v. LYON BROS. (No. 39.)

(Supreme Court of Arkansas. June 6, 1921.)

1. Sales ⬡==168(2)—Seller estopped from contending that buyer was bound to inspect within reasonable time after receiving shipment.

Where the buyer on receipt of goods wrote to seller that they had been prematurely shipped, and would not be opened until the buyer's customers got in their cotton, and the seller did not answer for over a month, he cannot, where the buyer, on later opening the goods, rejected them as unequal to the sample, contend that the buyer should have inspected within a reasonable time after delivery.

2. Account stated ⬡==6(1)—Letter by buyer, setting forth premature shipment and that goods would not be immediately inspected, held not acquiescence and account stated.

Where on receipt of a shipment the buyer stated that it was prematurely shipped, and would not be opened or inspected for some time, etc., such letter was not an acquiescence by the buyer in the seller's statement of the account to entitle the seller to recover on an account stated, though the goods did not equal sample.

3. Appeal and error ⬡==172(1)—An issue of account stated, not presented in trial court, cannot be presented on appeal.

The issue of account stated, not presented in the trial court, cannot be presented for the first time on appeal.

Appeal from Circuit Court, Faulkner County; Geo. W. Clark, Judge.

Action by Brin Bros. against Lyon Bros. From a judgment for defendants, plaintiffs appeal. Affirmed.

Holland & Edmondson, of Conway, for appellants.

R. W. Robins, of Conway, for appellees.

HUMPHREYS, J. Appellants, a firm of importers residing in Dallas, Tex., instituted suit against appellees, a firm of merchants residing in Republican, Ark., in the Faulkner circuit court, to recover $408.47, representing the price of laces and other notions ordered by appellees from appellants on the 5th day of August, 1920, and shipped, by parcels post, on the 22d day of said month. Appellees interposed the defense that the merchandise delivered was not equal in quality to the samples exhibited when the order was made, and the return thereof within a reasonable time after discovering the defects. The cause was submitted upon the pleadings, evidence, and instructions of the court, which resulted in a verdict and judgment against appellants, from which an appeal has been duly prosecuted to this court.

The evidence adduced on behalf of appellants tended to show: That merchandise, corresponding to the samples exhibited to appellees by appellants' salesman when the order was made, on the 5th day of August, 1920, was shipped by appellants to appellees on the 22d day of said month. That subsequently a statement of the account, covering the shipment, was mailed by appellants to appellees. That, on September 10, 1920, in response to the statement of account, appellees wrote appellants the following letter:

"We are in receipt of your statement asking us for payment. We call your attention to the fact that when we bought these goods from your salesman we told him that we didn't need the goods for a while, that we wanted them for our fall business, but you shipped the goods at once.

"This is to advise you that we have the merchandise here in our house, haven't never looked at it, as we didn't want to open it up until our customers got out some cotton so that they would have some money to pay for what they got. We are going to ask that you give us some time until our customers get some cotton out."

That on the 23d day of October, 1920, appellees again wrote appellants, as follows:

"Answering your registered letter dated 19th, will say that we have to-day opened up your merchandise we bought from you, and this is to advise you that they didn't open up to our satisfaction, as some of the goods seemed to be much cheaper merchandise than we bought. "Owing to cotton conditions this fall we never opened up your goods until a few days ago, and it seems to us also you prefer putting us out of business. This is to advise you that we are to-day returning to you every dollar's worth of your goods you shipped us, and as to the future we don't want to buy anything from you. Goods shipped by express."

That the price of the goods decreased considerably between the 5th of August and the 29th day of October, 1920.

The evidence adduced on behalf of appellees tended to show that, when the order for the merchandise was given, on the 5th day of August, it was understood that shipment should not be made until later in the season; that, when the goods arrived, appellees received, but did not open and inspect, them, and, shortly after receiving them, wrote the letter of September 10, 1920, to appellants, heretofore set out in full; that, after writing the letter aforesaid, the goods were retained unopened in the store of appellees until two or three days before appellees wrote the letter of date October 23, 1920, to appellants; that, two or three days before writing the last letter, appellees opened the goods and shipped them back to appellants by express, on the 29th day of said month.

The cause was submitted to the jury upon the theory that appellants could not recover if the goods were inferior to the samples exhibited when the order was made, provided the appellees rejected them within a reasonable time after they should have been delivered under the contract. The instructions given by the court, presenting these questions of fact for determination by the jury, were not objected to by appellants. For that reason, the substance, as well as the form, of the instructions must be regarded as correctly presenting the issues of fact for determination by the jury, involved in

231 S.W.—36

the theory upon which the cause was submitted.

[1] Appellants, however, presented instructions which the court refused to give, over their objections and exceptions, embodying the idea that the duty rested upon appellees of inspecting and rejecting the goods within a reasonable time after receiving same, if they did not conform to the samples exhibited when the order was made. We think this theory untenable, in view of the fact that there was evidence tending to show that the goods were prematurely shipped, when regarded in connection with the contents of the letter written by appellees to appellants of date September 10, 1920. In that letter, the attention of appellants was called to the fact that, according to the contract, the goods had been prematurely shipped; that they were in the house unopened, and that appellees did not want to open them until their customers got out some cotton so that they would have money with which to buy them. A direct request was also made in the letter that time be granted them until their customers got their cotton out. So far as the record shows, no answer was made by appellants until the 19th day of October. Appellants, therefore, silently acquiesced in the goods remaining in appellees' store unopened until that date. Appellants' own conduct clearly estopped them from asking instructions to the effect that appellees were bound to inspect and reject them, if inferior to sample, within a reasonable time after receiving the shipment. We think the cause was submitted to the jury upon the correct theory.

[2, 3] Appellants insist that they should have been permitted to recover as upon an account stated; that on August 22d, they presented an account for the goods to appellees, which was not disputed, but, in effect, acknowledged as being correct by appellees in letter of date September 10, 1920. We do not so interpret the letter. The letter informed appellants that the goods had been ordered by agreement for fall trade, and had been prematurely shipped; that they had not been opened, and would not be until later. The letter at most was an admission of liability upon condition that the goods should conform to the samples when inspected. The facts surrounding the transaction do not render the account presented on August 22d an account stated. Again, the issue of an account stated was not presented or insisted upon in any form in the trial court, and cannot be insisted upon for the first time on appeal.

No error appearing, the judgment is affirmed.

VAUGHAN v. ODELL & KLEINER.
(No 33.)

(Supreme Court of Arkansas.   June 6, 1921.)

1. Brokers ⬤⇒88(4) — In suit for procuring purchaser to whom owners refused to sell, direction of verdict for defendants held error.

In an action for commission for procuring a purchaser of timber, which the owners refused to sell to the purchaser procured, held, that it was error to direct a verdict for defendants.

2. Brokers ⬤⇒86(1)—Finding for broker in suit for procuring purchaser to whom owners refused to sell warranted.

Evidence in action for commission for procuring a purchaser of timber to whom the owners refused to sell held to warrant a finding for the broker.

3. Brokers ⬤⇒63(1)—Owners preventing sale cannot set up their refusal to deed as ground of defense to claim for commission.

Where owners of timber by their own misconduct prevent fulfillment of the contract of sale on their part, they cannot set up their refusal to carry out the contract by executing a timber deed as a ground of defense to the broker's claim for his commission.

4. Estoppel ⬤⇒59—One preventing the doing of a thing cannot benefit by the nonperformance.

He who prevents a thing from being done shall not avail himself to his own benefit of the nonperformance which he has occasioned.

Appeal from Circuit Court, Arkansas County; W. B. Sorrells, Judge.

Suit by T. L. Vaughan against Odell & Kleiner.   Judgment for defendants, and plaintiff appeals.   Reversed and remanded.

James E. Hogue, of Little Rock, and J. E. Ray, of Stuttgart, for appellant.

John L. Ingram, of Stuttgart, for appellees.

HART, J.   T. L. Vaughan brought this suit against Odell & Kleiner in the circuit court to recover a broker's commission for effecting a sale of certain timber belonging to the defendants.

In the circuit court a verdict was directed for the defendants, and from the judgment rendered upon the verdict the plaintiff has duly prosecuted an appeal to this court.

T. L. Vaughan was a witness for himself. According to his testimony he made a contract for Odell & Kleiner to sell the timber on a thousand acres of land which they owned in Arkansas county, Ark.   They gave him a price of $6 per acre for the timber, and Vaughan was to get all over that price for his commission.   Odell & Kleiner did not think that he could get over $7 an acre for the timber.   Vaughan sold the thousand acres of timber of Odell & Kleiner to Carver & Russell of West Plains, Mo., for $8 an acre,

and a written contract for the purchase of the timber was duly signed by Carver & Russell, and they deposited $1,000 in a bank at West Plains to guarantee the performance of their contract to purchase the timber.   Vaughan then went to Stuttgart and reported to Odell & Kleiner what he had done.   They told him that there was another 40 acres of timber which was not included in the contract.

The contract was subsequently modified to include this 40 acres, and some changes were made in the time of making some of the payments of the purchase money.   The total purchase price under the modified contract was $8,320, of which $4,000 was to be paid in cash when the deed was signed, and of the remainder, $2,000 was to be paid in ninety days and $2,320 in four months.   It was also agreed that the deposit of $1,000 formerly made in the bank at West Plains should be applied on the first payment.   Subsequently Vaughan made a contract to sell the timber for Carver & Russell to R. R. McIntosh for $11,520.   Under this contract McIntosh was to pay the $7,320 due from Carver & Russell to Odell & Kleiner.   When Odell & Kleiner found out that Carver & Russell had made a contract to sell the timber for more than they had paid for it, they refused to execute a deed to the timber to Carver & Russell under their other contract.   When the contract was originally entered into between Carver & Russell and Odell & Kleiner by Vaughan, the latter made an investigation of the solvency of Carver & Russell and found that they were financially able to carry out the contract on their part.

On cross-examination Vaughan admitted that he had brought suit against Carver & Russell to recover his commission and that his complaint in that case states that Carver & Russell "have no property in this state from which the money due herein could be made, except that which comes from the interest which they have from the property herein described, and are wholly insolvent." Vaughan explained that what he meant by that was that Carver & Russell had no property in this state, except the timber which they had contracted to purchase from Odell & Kleiner and which the latter had refused to convey to them.

R. R. McIntosh was a witness for the plaintiff and testified that he made a contract with Vaughan to purchase the timber in question for $11,520, of this amount he was to pay Odell & Kleiner $7,320 in cash; that he was anxious to buy the timber and was able to pay for it at the time he entered into a written contract for the purchase of it as above stated.

E. C. Carver was also a witness for the plaintiff.   According to his testimony Odell & Kleiner gave him an extension of time within which to pay for the timber, and before the extension of time had expired, Vaughan made a contract with R. R. McIntosh for them to sell him the timber for $11,520. The contract provided that he was to pay for them to Odell & Kleiner $7,320 of this amount. They were prevented from carrying out this contract because Odell & Kleiner refused to convey the timber to them. Subsequently McIntosh purchased the timber from another party for $16,500 and sold it for $19,000.

Some evidence was adduced by the defendants tending to show that Carver & Russell had failed to perform the contract on their part and that they were unable to carry out their contract for the purchase of the timber without borrowing money with which to pay the purchase price. Other evidence tended to show that the contract of purchase had been abandoned before they made a contract through the plaintiff to sell the timber to R. R. McIntosh.

[1, 2] In this state of the record, the court erred in directing a verdict for the defendants. The evidence for the plaintiff warranted the jury in finding for him. According to the evidence adduced in his behalf, he was the agent of the defendants to sell the timber for them and was to receive as his commission all that he might sell the timber for above $6 per acre. In other words, under the original contract, he sold to Carver & Russell 1,000 acres of timber at $8 per acre, and under the modified contract he sold them 1,040 acres at $8 per acre, amounting in the aggregate to $8,320. He was to have all over $6 per acre that he could get for the timber as his commission. The original contract for the sale of the timber to Carver & Russell was in writing. Odell & Kleiner made some objections to it because it did not include an additional 40 acres of timber which was in the tract they intended to sell. The contract was modified so as to include this tract, and the modified contract was also in writing. This was a valid and binding contract, and, according to the evidence of the plaintiff, the purchasers were able to complete the contract and were anxious to do so. They were able to pay the purchase money upon the execution and delivery to them of a timber deed, and the defendants refused to execute such a deed.

[3] It is true that under the contract between the plaintiff and the defendants, the sale was to be completed and the plaintiff was to receive as his commission any excess over $6 an acre which the defendants might receive for the purchase price of the timber. However, according to the evidence for the plaintiff, the defendants by their own misconduct in refusing to execute a timber deed to Carver & Russell prevented the fulfillment of the contract on their part, and the defendants cannot set up their own refusal to carry out the contract by executing a timber deed as a ground of defense to the plaintiff's claim for his commission.

[4] It is a well-settled and sound principle of law that he who prevents a thing from being done shall not avail himself to his own benefit of the nonperformance which he has occasioned. We think this rule was recognized by the Supreme Court of Massachusetts in Munroe v. Taylor, 191 Mass. 483, 78 N. E. 106. In that case the broker was to receive all over a certain stipulated price as his commission. He sold the land at a price largely in advance of the stipulated amount and entered into a binding contract for the sale of the property. In that case it did not appear that at any time the defendant had refused to make a proper deed of conveyance. It was the plaintiff's contention that having found a customer who became bound to buy, his commission had been earned. The court held that he was entitled to a commission only in the event of procuring the consummation of the sale, and not on procuring the execution of a contract of sale which was never performed. He failed to make out his case by not introducing evidence tending to show that the defendant had wrongfully refused to carry out the contract upon his part. This is clearly shown by the concluding part of the opinion. It reads as follows:

"What the plaintiff really undertook was not only to find a purchaser at a fixed price, but to effect a sale, which meant a payment of that price, and this having been done he would have earned the excess, but until the consideration became payable, or the defendant refused to convey, he could not demand any remuneration, or maintain an action for breach of the contract."

The rule was also recognized by this court in Lewis v. Briggs, 81 Ark. 96, 98 S. W. 683. In that case the owner of the land was to receive $8,000 net, and the balance of the purchase price was to be paid to the broker as a commission for the sale of the land. The court held that under the terms of the contract the broker did not make out a case for recovery against the owner by showing that he secured a contract with solvent parties to purchase the land. In discussing the question the court said:

"He must under this contract show either that defendants have received some part of the balance of the purchase money to which they were entitled, or that the parties who agreed to purchase were ready, willing and able to perform their part of the contract, and that they were prevented from doing so by the default or failure of the defendants to perform their part of the contract."

In concluding the opinion the court said that under the contract so long as the purchase price was unpaid, and so long as the defendants were not to blame for its nonpayment, they were not liable. This was a clear recognition of the rule as we have stated it. Upon the principle stated in these cases, the broker might have a claim for his services if the sale had failed through the fault of the defendant.

As above stated, in the case at bar, it is fairly inferable from the plaintiff's testimony that Carver & Russell were solvent and were able to carry out the contract on their part, and that they were anxious to do so, but were prevented by the failure of the defendants to execute the timber deed.

It follows that for the error in directing a verdict for the defendants, the judgment must be reversed, and the cause will be remanded for a new trial.

STATE v. CARROLL et al. (No. 22682.)

(Supreme Court of Missouri, Division No. 2.
May 26, 1921.)

1. Bail ⟝82—Proceedings by scire facias to forfeit bail held, in form and effect, a civil case.

In a proceeding by the state by scire facias to forfeit a bail bond given in a prosecution for forgery, where the judgment fixed no punishment and required no appearance of the surety, but was, in form, a money judgment, for which execution might issue, not against the person, but against the property of the surety, the case is, in effect and form, a civil case, and on appeal may be dismissed for failure to comply with the requirements as to assignments of error, brief, or appearance.

2. Appeal and error ⟝434, 719(1), 773(2)—Appeal from judgment forfeiting recognizance in criminal prosecution dismissed where no errors assigned.

Rev. St. 1919, § 4106, requiring the Supreme Court to consider errors whether assigned or not, applies only to appeals authorized by sections 4066-4113, and not to an appeal from a judgment forfeiting a recognizance in a prosecution for forgery, in view of section 4086, so that, where appellant has failed to assign error, file brief, or appear, the appeal will be dismissed.

Appeal from St. Louis Circuit Court; Vital W. Garesche, Judge.

Proceeding by the State against E. J. Carroll, principal, and Henry Streutker, surety, by scire facias, upon a forfeiture of a recognizance. Judgment for plaintiff, and defendant surety appeals. Appeal dismissed.

T. J. Rowe, Jr., of St. Louis, for appellant.
Jesse W. Barrett, Atty. Gen., and J. Henry Caruthers, Sp. Asst. Atty. Gen., for the State.

WHITE, C. This is a proceeding by scire facias upon the alleged forfeiture of a recognizance wherein Emmett J. Carroll, charged with the crime of forgery, was principal, and Henry Streutker, appellant, was his surety.

The transcript of the record which was sent here shows that the cause against Carroll was pending in the circuit court of St. Louis, June 20, 1919, was assigned to division No. 10 of that court, and on October 14, 1919, was continued to the next term of court. The record recites that on October 17, 1919, the defendant failed to appear; a forfeiture was declared, and scire facias ordered. The scire facias was issued on the 10th day of November, 1919. December 2, 1919, the defendant's surety, Henry Streutker, appeared and filed his answer. January 23, 1920, the proceeding was continued until the next term of the court. The record then shows that on March 12, 1919 (evidently a clerical error for March 20, 1919), Henry Streutker not having sufficient reason shown why the state of Missouri should not recover its debt and costs according to the terms of the bond, it was ordered that judgment be entered against him for the sum of $1,500. The record recites that Streutker filed his motion for new trial March 16, 1920; it was overruled March 22d; March 29th, Streutker filed his affidavit for appeal, and the appeal was allowed to this court. There being no bill of exceptions, the motion for new trial does not appear in the record. The answer of defendant Streutker is not copied in the transcript of the record.

I. The appellant has filed in this court no assignment of errors, no brief, and made no appearance. If this case is to be treated as an appeal from a judgment on an indictment or information, it would be the duty of this court to consider all that appears in the record, and to determine whether any error has been committed, in obedience to section 4106, R. S. 1919, regardless of that failure of the appellant. Otherwise it should be treated as a civil case, and the appeal should be dismissed for failure.

The reason why this court has assumed jurisdiction of proceedings by scire facias to forfeit bail bonds and recognizances where the amount is less than $7,500 is stated in the case of State v. Hoeffner, 137 Mo. 612, loc. cit. 614, 615, 38 S. W. 1109, where the court said:

"If the charge shows a felony then the proceedings in that case would be a continuation of the prosecution for felony, and this court would have jurisdiction to make effective that charge, on the familiar principle of law that, where jurisdiction of the main question attaches, every incident necessary to make that jurisdiction effectual follows as a matter of law."

In the case of State v. Epstein, 186 Mo. 89, 84 S. W. 1120, Judge Gantt expressed it in this way (186 Mo. loc. cit. 98, 84 S. W. loc. cit. 1122):

"As an appeal upon the main charge of felony must be heard in this court, so also must the auxiliary proceeding thereon be heard in this court on appeal."

The above-cited cases were approved in the late case of State v. Wilson, 265 Mo. loc. cit. 10, 175 S. W. 603. It will be noticed that the reasons given by this court for retaining jurisdiction of such cases is because it is auxiliary to a felony of which it had jurisdiction, not because the case in itself confers jurisdiction. The court which has jurisdiction of the felony case must retain authority to enforce any judgment which is rendered in that felony case.

[1] The judgment fixes no punishment and requires no appearance of the judgment de-

fendant. In form it is a money judgment, for which execution may issue, not against the person of the defendant, but against his property. In effect and form it is a civil case.

[2] II. But whatever view may be taken of the nature of the proceedings, there can be no room to say that section 4106, R. S. 1919, requiring this court to consider errors whether assigned or not applies, because that section applies only to appeals authorized by article 15, c. 25, Revised Statutes of 1919. Section 4086 of that article provides that—

"In all cases of final judgment rendered on any indictment or information, an appeal to the Supreme Court of Appeals shall be allowed the defendant."

This is not a judgment rendered upon any indictment or information, and the defendant in an indictment or information has not appealed. The surety on a recognizance has appealed from a judgment against him in this collateral proceeding. He must comply with the rules of this court in order to secure a review of the proceeding. Having failed to do so, the appeal should be dismissed.

It is so ordered.

RAILEY and MOZLEY, CC., concur.

PER CURIAM. The foregoing opinion by WHITE, C., is adopted as the opinion of the court.

All concur.

———

STATE v. HIGHTOWER. (No. 22602.)

(Supreme Court of Missouri, Division No. 2. May 26, 1921.)

1. **Rape** ⚫⟹52(4)—**Evidence held to establish the age of prosecutrix at less than 15 years.**

In a prosecution for rape, evidence *held* clearly sufficient to establish the age of prosecutrix at less than 15 years.

2. **Rape** ⚫⟹57(1)—**Evidence held to make out a case for the jury.**

In a prosecution for rape, evidence *held* sufficient to make out a case for the jury, so that overruling defendant's demurrer to the evidence was not error.

3. **Criminal law** ⚫⟹855(4)—**Court did not abuse its discretion in refusing to discharge jury for misconduct of prosecutrix.**

Where the jury found the defendant guilty of rape under the revolting and brutal circumstances testified to by prosecutrix, the jury's assessment of minimum punishment is so surprising in its moderation that it cannot be held that the trial judge abused his discretion in refusing to discharge the jury because of an alleged threat of the prosecutrix, outside of the courtroom and in the presence of some of the jurors, that she would get a gun and shoot the defendant.

Appeal from Circuit Court, Jackson County; E. E. Porterfield, Judge.

James Hightower was convicted of rape, and he appeals. Affirmed.

Horace Kimbrell, of Kansas City, for appellant.

Jesse W. Barrett, Atty. Gen., and Robert J. Smith, Asst. Atty. Gen. (R. W. Otto, of Union, of counsel), for the State.

DAVID E. BLAIR, Judge. Defendant was convicted of rape, and was sentenced on the verdict to imprisonment in the penitentiary for five years, and has appealed.

The prosecuting witness, Nettie Neal, was 13 years old and defendant 26. Both are negroes. Nettie had been adopted by and lived with Addie Searles, whom she called her aunt. After attending a dance in Kansas City, on the night of September 7, 1919, Nettie and defendant boarded an Independence car at Tenth street and Troost avenue and occupied the same seat. There is a conflict in the evidence as to whether defendant induced her to get on this car. Her story is that he offered to take her home and she did not know what car she boarded; that he had nothing to say to her until she sat down in the same seat with him. They met at Tenth and Troost, and Nettie testified she did not know who defendant was. At or near the public square in Independence both left the car. From this point their stories differ widely. Nettie testified that defendant took her to a box car in the Missouri Pacific yards, and pushed her up into the car and ravished her under threats of killing her. This occurred between 1 and 2 o'clock in the morning. She testified that defendant wore a black and white striped shirt and a vest, but no coat.

Defendant testified that when the car stopped at Independence he was the first one off and saw nothing more of the girl; that about a block from the car he met two other negroes, a man and a woman, who were friends; the woman was his cousin; that all three then proceeded directly to the home of defendant and found his wife in bed, and that it was then 1:30 a. m. Defendant denied having ravished the girl. He admitted wearing a black and white striped shirt, but denied wearing a vest.

Another negro testified to seeing defendant and the girl leave the car together and walk south toward the railroad yards, and still another negro testified to seeing defendant and the girl at another point further from the square and going toward the railroad yards.

⚫⟹For other cases see same topic and KEY-NUMBER in all Key-Numbered Digests and Indexes

Lester Olden and Annie Jenkins testified to meeting defendant alone about a block from the square and going with him to defendant's home, and fix the time of arrival as 1:30 a. m. Defendant's wife testified to the fact and time of their arrival, and that about 2 a. m. she sent defendant to the lunch stand of another negro, Albert Chinn, for some fish, and that he returned about 4 a. m. Chinn corroborated her on this point, and said defendant remained at his place about two hours playing cards. These witnesses accounted for defendant's presence at the time the prosecuting witness fixes for the assault at the box car.

Shortly before 2 a. m. a police officer found the girl in a dazed and almost unconscious condition, partly in and partly outside the box car, and carried her into the station, and then she was taken to the office of a white doctor, who treated her. She was shortly afterward treated by a negro doctor, who testified to the abundant evidences of her ravishment.

Defendant was arrested two or three days later, and before being accused of the crime asked the chief of police, Nealy A. Harris, "Are you arresting me for the crime on this little girl Saturday night?" Defendant did not deny this statement when testifying. He was taken to the hospital, where the girl positively identified him as her assailant. The police visited defendant's home soon after his arrest, and found a black and white striped shirt and a pair of trousers with blood stains on them. Defendant accounted for the stains by saying that he had been injured by a drill falling on him two or three months previous, which caused a boil in his groin, and that the blood and pus from this caused the stains on his shirt. The underwear worn by him that night had been washed by his wife. She said that garment had not been blood-stained.

This statement covers the facts sufficiently for an understanding of the case.

[1] The assignments of error made by appellant in his brief are that there is no competent or substantial proof that the prosecutrix was under the age of 15 years at the time of the alleged assault; that the court should have sustained defendant's demurrer to the evidence at the conclusion of all the evidence; and that the court should have discharged the jury because of the misconduct of the prosecutrix in the presence of jurors, which misconduct tended to inflame the jurors against defendant.

On the question of her age, testatrix testified as follows:

"Q. How old are you? A. Thirteen.
"Q. When were you thirteen? A. I don't know.
"Q. Was it September? A. Yes, sir."

Mrs. Searles testified on this point as follows:

"Q. She lives with you then? A. Yes, sir.
"Q. And has how long? A. Ever since she was something over a year old.
"Q. And she is past 13 now, is she? A. She was 13 last September, but I don't know the exact date."

The evidence was clearly sufficient to establish the age of prosecutrix at less than 15 years. The defense offered no evidence to the contrary. The girl was before the jury. The contention is trivial.

[2] Likewise the contention that the demurrer to the evidence should have been given must be overruled. The facts already stated are sufficient to make out a case to submit to the jury. The case can be made very much stronger by setting out the testimony in detail. We have read the testimony and find it sufficient to support the verdict.

[3] A brief recital from the bill of exceptions is necessary to an understanding of the remaining assignment of error. At the opening of court on the morning of the second day of the trial the following record was made by counsel for defendant:

"The jury having been taken from the room, the following proceedings were had out of the presence and hearing of the jury, as follows, to wit:

"Horace S. Kimbrell, having been duly sworn, testified as follows:

"Mr. Kimbrell: My name is Horace S. Kimbrell; I am the attorney representing James Hightower. This morning before court convened, and while the judge of this court was opening the door to the courtroom, the prosecuting witness, Nettie Neal, in the presence of the judge of this court and several of the jurors trying this cause, stated that she would get a pistol and shoot the defendant. That one of the jurors stated to the prosecuting witness that she ought not to kill him; that if she should kill him she would be in danger of being hanged herself.

"The Court: She was talking to me, and what she said was, 'I will kill him.' That is what she said. She didn't say who she was going to kill. She didn't mention the defendant or call his name, or mention him at all. That is all I know.

"Mr. Kimbrell: The defendant asks the court to discharge this jury from any further consideration of this case for the reason that just before court convened this morning, in the corridor of the courthouse, the prosecuting witness, Nettie Neal, in the presence of the judge of this court and several of the jurors trying this cause, stated that she would get a pistol and kill the defendant. A dismissal of the jury is asked for the reason that the statement made by the prosecuting witness outside of the courtroom and while court was not in session, inflamed the minds of the jurors against this defendant, so that he cannot have a fair and impartial trial of this cause.

"The Court: Motion overruled.

"To which ruling and action of the court the defendant then and there at the time duly excepted and still excepts."

It will be seen there is conflict between Judge Porterfield and Attorney Kimbrell as to what was said at the courtroom door. Mr. Kimbrell testified that the prosecutrix said she would get a pistol and shoot the defendant, and that one of the jurors said she ought not to kill him, as she would be in danger of being hanged herself. Even accepting Mr. Kimbrell's testimony, we do not believe the occurrence calls for a retrial of the case. In the first place, the discharge of a jury is largely within the discretion of the trial judge. State v. Bersch, 276 Mo. 397, loc. cit. 420, 207 S. W. 809; State v. Gray, 172 Mo. 430, 72 S. W. 698; Kennedy v. Holladay, 105 Mo. 24, 16 S. W. 688. Here the trial judge himself witnessed the entire incident and saw testatrix and the jurors, and could determine for himself the effect of the incident and whether the threats of the prosecutrix were mere idle talk and so understood by the jurors, or were a deliberate attempt to influence the jurors. The prosecutrix is referred to in the record all the way through as "this little girl," and it is very apparent from her testimony that she was very ignorant. She was in the first grade at school at age 13, indicating either partial feeble-mindedness or woeful neglect. The jury had previously heard her testify, and probably gauged her intelligence and her responsibility. The judge doubtless saw and considered all these things. He overruled the motion to discharge the jury, and the trial proceeded to verdict. When his attention was again called to the incident in the motion for new trial, he doubtless would have granted a new trial if there had been the slightest room for belief that the incident inflamed the minds of the jury against defendant. The verdict of the jury finding defendant guilty under the revolting and brutal circumstances testified to by the prosecutrix and assessing the minimum punishment is surprising in its moderation. By no possible view can we arrive at the conclusion that the jury was inflamed against defendant, or that the incident had the slightest effect on the minds of the jurors.

The information is in approved form. The instructions are clear and entirely proper and sufficient under the testimony. The verdict is unassailable.

Therefore, finding no error in the record, the judgment is affirmed.

All concur.

STATE v. BLOOMER. (No. 22646.)

(Supreme Court of Missouri, Division No. 2. May 26, 1921.)

1. **Indictment and information** ⚖=110(11)—**Information for grand larceny in language of statute held sufficient.**

An information for grand larceny, which followed the language of the statute (Rev. S. 1919, § 3312) defining grand larceny, was sufficient.

2. **Larceny** ⚖=57—**Evidence held to warrant finding that defendant attempted to convert hogs with knowledge of prosecutor's ownership.**

On a trial for stealing hogs, evidence held to warrant the jury in finding that defendant attempted to convert the hogs to his own use and make away with them after he knew they belonged to the prosecuting witness, even if he thought in the first place that they belonged to one whose hogs he was caring for, under an arrangement that he was to have one-half the increase.

3. **Larceny** ⚖=75(2)—**Instruction not erroneous because not in terms requiring finding that taking was felonious and without owner's consent.**

On a trial for larceny, an instruction, requiring the jury to find that defendant stealthily took, and carried away hogs, the property of the prosecuting witness, without any honest claim of ownership, and well knowing that he had no interest or claim of interest, and with intent to convert them to his own use and permanently deprive the owner of the use thereof and his property therein, was not erroneous because not in terms requiring the jury to find that the taking was felonious and without the owner's consent, as under the facts hypothesized the taking would be felonious and without the owner's consent.

4. **Criminal law** ⚖=1169(1)—**Larceny** ⚖=63—**Question asked defendant on cross-examination as to acts of third person not erroneous or harmful.**

On a trial for stealing hogs running on an open pasture, a question asked defendant on cross-examination as to whether he heard a witness testify that he drove down as many as 13 or 14 with two sows was not erroneous or harmful to defendant, where his answer indicated that such witness was assisting him in driving up his hogs, as it simply explained how he rounded up the hogs.

Appeal from Circuit Court, Barry County; Charles L. Henson, Judge.

Levi Bloomer was convicted of grand larceny, and he appeals. Affirmed.

T. D. Steele, of Monett, for appellant. Jesse W. Barrett, Atty. Gen., and Albert Miller, Asst. Atty. Gen., for the State.

WHITE, C. The appeal is from a conviction of grand larceny. The defendant was charged with having stolen 13 hogs of the

---

ue of $185, the property of one W. C. oper.

Cooper lived on a farm in Barry county, out two miles distant from the farm on which the defendant Bloomer lived. The country between the two places was hilly and open pasture. In the spring of 1919 Cooper had a number of hogs, about 33 shotes and 6 sows. In March, 1919, those shotes were about 8 months old, and were allowed to run at large in the open country. Cooper, in a search for his hogs one day found one of his sows crippled. Extending his search on the 22d day of March, he found 13 of his hogs in the pasture of the defendant. A day or two later he returned with a companion, and found 7 of those hogs, 5 of which had been crated by Bloomer in preparing to haul them away. Bloomer said he sold them to Bill Wiley. When Cooper turned his shotes out to range they were not earmarked. When he found them in Bloomer's pasture they had fresh earmarks. Bloomer refused to give up the hogs; Cooper brought a replevin suit, and recovered some of them. His hogs were identified by himself and two or three other witnesses.

It was claimed by Bloomer he and one Mr. Potter, from whom he rented the farm on which he lived, had an arrangement by which he was to take care of Potter's hogs for one-half of the increase. He had rounded up these shotes in the belief that they belonged to Potter and had marked them.

The evidence for the state tended to show that the shotes weighed about 75 pounds each, and were worth about 14 cents a pound, which would make the 13 hogs aggregate in value about the amount alleged in the information. A number of witnesses testified, who knew Cooper's hogs, saw those in dispute, and described the circumstances under which they ran at large. Cooper demanded the hogs of Bloomer, who thereafter attempted to keep them, and did dispose of some of them so that Cooper recovered only a portion of them in his replevin suit.

The appellant has filed no brief, and in order to consider the errors which are assigned for reversal one must have recourse to the motion for new trial and motion in arrest. These assign a defective information, error in instructions in overruling the defendant's demurrer to the evidence, failure to instruct on all the law of the case, admission of immaterial evidence, and improper cross-examination of defendant.

[1] I. The motion in arrest says the information does not charge an offense against the law of the state of Missouri. The information follows the statute (section 3312, R. S. 1919), defining grand larceny. State v. Swearengin, 234 Mo. loc. cit. 552, 137 S. W. 880. It is suggested that in charging the offense the information omits the word "steal," and some argument is presented on that theory. The copy of the information as set out in the record, however, contains the allegation that the defendant "unlawfully and feloniously did then and there, steal, and carry away," etc., following the language of the statute. The information is sufficient.

[2] II. The demurrer to the evidence was properly overruled. Cooper identified his hogs and reinforced his identification with proof that they were his, and showed the circumstances under which they came into the defendant's possession. The defendant refused to give them up, and there was sufficient evidence from which the jury might find that he attempted to convert them to his own use and make away with them after he knew they belonged to Cooper, even if he had thought they were Potter's in the first place.

[3] III. Instruction No. 1 is objected to. It requires the jury to find and believe beyond a reasonable doubt that at the place and time designated in the instruction:

"The defendant did then and there steal, take, and carry away 13, or any less number of, hogs, about eight months old, weighing about 75 pounds each, of the property of W. C. Cooper, of any value, without any honest claim of ownership in them, and well knowing he had no interest or claim of interest in them, and with the intent to convert the same to his own use and to permanently deprive the owner of the use thereof and of his property in them," etc.

It was not necessary for the instruction further to require, in terms, that the taking was without the owner's consent. To find that he did steal and carry them away with intent to convert to his own use and permanently deprive the owner of the same would be a sufficient finding that it was without the owner's consent. State v. Richmond, 228 Mo. loc. cit. 364, 128 S. W. 744. Likewise, it was not necessary to use the word "feloniously" in the instruction because the jury was required to find the facts, as set out in the part of the instruction copied above, which would constitute felonious taking. State v. Massey, 274 Mo. loc. cit. 589, 204 S. W. 541; State v. Rader, 262 Mo. 136, 171 S. W. 46.

[4] IV. A careful reading of the record does not show any error in the admission or exclusion of evidence. The defendant was sworn on his own behalf, and testified as to the contract he had with Potter, how Potter's hogs ran on the open range, and how he looked up the increase and drove up the hogs in question. He also introduced a witness named Benton Bowen, whose testimony indicates that he assisted the defendant in rounding up the hogs. The defendant on cross-examination then was asked this question:

"Q. You heard Bowen testify that he drove down there as many as 13 or 14 with two sows; drove them over there?"

This was objected to, the objection was overruled, the defendant excepted, and the defendant answered:

"That Benton Bowen was telling about? We never got any sow right at the present time with these unmarked shotes that Will Cooper has claimed for."

This indicates from his own testimony that Bowen assisted him in driving up his hogs. The matter he testified about was how and in what manner he had got possession of the hogs which he was charged with stealing. The connection of Benton Bowen with the matter simply further explained how he rounded them up. There was no impropriety in the question, and defendant was not harmed by it. State v. Ivy, 192 S. W. loc. cit. 736.

V. There is no reason for the complaint that the court did not instruct on all the law of the case. The jury were properly instructed as to what it was necessary to find in order to convict upon circumstantial evidence, presumption of innocence, reasonable doubt, and every principle involved in the case. No instruction was asked for by appellant except one in the nature of a demurrer to the evidence; no element necessary for the jury's consideration and omitted has been pointed out in the motion for new trial.

Finding no error in the record, the judgment is affirmed.

RAILEY and MOZLEY, CC., concur.

PER CURIAM. The foregoing opinion by WHITE, C., is adopted as the opinion of the court.

All concur.

STATE ex rel. MISSOURI MOTOR BUS CO. v. DAVIS, Judge, et al. (No. 22561.)

(Supreme Court of Missouri, in Banc. May 24, 1921.)

1. Receivers ⇍131—Court may order sale of property in hands of receiver before final judgment, where necessary to preserve interests of parties.

Where certain motorbusses in the hands of a receiver were stored at considerable expense, their operation had resulted in considerable losses, and they were rapidly depreciating in value, the court appointing the receiver had the power, even before final decree, to order the property sold, though the receiver was not appointed to effect a sale.

2. Prohibition ⇍5(3)—Application for held a collateral attack on order for sale of property by receiver.

Where the owner of certain motorbusses in the hands of a receiver appeared at the hearing

of the latter's motion for an order of sale, but did not move to modify the order and did not appeal therefrom, his application for a writ of prohibition to prevent the sale before final judgment was a collateral attack and could not be sustained.

Application for writ of prohibition by the State of Missouri, at the relation of the Missouri Motor Bus Company, a corporation, against Charles B. Davis, Judge of Division No. 14 of the Circuit Court of the City of St. Louis, and H. S. Albrecht, temporary receiver of the Missouri Motor Bus Company, to prevent a sale by the receiver, before a final decree, of certain property of relator as ordered by the court. Preliminary rule discharged.

E. H. Wayman, of St. Louis, for relator.
Marshall & Henderson, of St. Louis, for respondents.

JAMES T. BLAIR, Judge. Relator seeks a writ of prohibition to prevent the sale by a receiver, before final decree on the merits, of certain motorbusses. In the suit in which the receiver was appointed the Commonwealth Finance Corporation sought to impress a trust or an equitable lien on the property of relator, including the vehicles here involved, and sought also the cancellation of certain chattel mortgages upon that property and the appointment of a receiver to take the property in charge. A receiver was appointed and took charge of the property. Some months thereafter a motion was filed asking that an order be made for the sale of the motorbusses belonging to relator and then in the hands of the receiver. A hearing was had and evidence was heard and a sale was ordered. Thereupon relator applied to this court for a writ of prohibition.

The record filed by relator shows that upon the hearing of the motion for the order of sale evidence was introduced which strongly tended to show that the vehicles were stored at an expense of $150 per month; that their operation had been attempted and had resulted in considerable losses; that they were rapidly depreciating in value both because of declining prices and because of deterioration of the vehicles themselves while kept idle and in storage; that the expense of insurance and of watchmen to guard the vehicles was large. Relator participated in this hearing.

[1, 2] "A court of equity appointing a receiver to take possession of property, pending a litigation concerning the rights of the parties thereto, is vested with the power of selling the property in the receiver's hands whenever such a course becomes necessary to preserve the interests of all parties. Thus in an action to determine the rights of conflicting claimants to a steamboat which was placed in the hands of a receiver pendente lite, and was operated under his direction for two

years, the court, upon being satisfied that it was highly inconvenient and unfit to continue in possession and operate the boat for a longer period, ordered it sold, although the bill on which the receiver was allowed was not framed for the purpose of effecting a sale. And a sale may be decreed in such case, although the rights of the parties to the property have not yet been ascertained and established." High on Receivers (4th Ed.) § 192. The case cited in support of this rule is Crane et al. v. Ford et al., Hopkins' Ch. (N. Y.) loc. cit. 116. The same rule, in substance, is laid down in Beach on Receivers (Alderson's Ed.) p. 553; Alderson on Receivers, § 598; Gluck & Becker on Receivers, § 35. "The general rule is that the court should not order a sale of the receivership property prior to the final decree, but there are exceptions to the rule, especially where the property is of a nature liable to deterioration or loss or likely to cause great expense for its upkeep." Tardy's Smith on Receivers (2d Ed.) p. 1784. This court recognized the same doctrine in State ex rel. v. Woodson, 161 Mo. loc. cit. 458, 61 S. W. 252, and applied it in State ex rel. v. Shelton, 238 Mo. 281, loc. cit. 295, 142 S. W. 417. In that case, as in this, the applicant for our writ of prohibition appeared at the hearing of the motion for the order of sale, but did not move to modify and did not appeal therefrom, and it was held that the effort to prohibit the enforcement of the order of sale was a collateral attack and could not be sustained. As in that case, so in this, the court had jurisdiction to order a sale, in proper circumstances, prior to final judgment. It heard evidence which proved or tended to prove facts which justified the order, and that "order, though irregular and improvident, cannot be assailed in a collateral action, and such action will not lie to set aside the order of sale and proceedings thereunder." High on Receivers (4th Ed.) § 196, quoted and approved in State ex rel. v. Shelton, supra.

The preliminary rule is discharged.

All concur.

THOMAS et al. v. GOODRUM et al.
(No. 20600.)

(Supreme Court of Missouri, in Banc. May 24, 1921.)

1. Bills and notes ⬚497(5)—Burden on holder to prove that he or person under whom he claims acquired title as holder in "due course."

At common law and under Negotiable Instrument Act 1905, every holder is deemed prima facie to be a holder in due course, but when it is shown that the title of any person who has negotiated the instrument was defective, the burden is on the holder to prove that he or some person under whom he claims acquired the title as holder in due course; "in due course" implying in the holder his own good faith in the acquisition of the instrument as well as his want of notice of any infirmity which would by reason of such notice affect the instrument in his hands.

2. Bills and notes ⬚358—Holder of notes as collateral for pre-existing debt not innocent purchaser.

Where a mortgage and investment company, interested with others in the purchase of cut-over lands, advanced money to such others for the purpose of acquiring the lands, and later took from them, as collateral security for such advancements, notes of purchasers of the lands, the company stood in the same position in relation to the notes as the one of its associates in the land deal in whose name the sale to such purchasers was made for the benefit of all.

3. Jury ⬚28(17)—Pleading ⬚411—Where defendant in suit in equity to cancel notes set up counterclaim at law, plaintiff could not claim trial by jury; objection to counterclaim in suit to cancel notes waived by failure to demur.

In a suit to cancel certain promissory notes, where defendant filed a counterclaim at law to recover on one of the notes, the error, if any, was waived by plaintiffs' failure to demur and by their express waiver of a trial by jury, so that the court could examine the entire controversy as in purely equitable cases.

4. Vendor and purchaser ⬚37(4)—Representations inducing purchase of land held statements of fact not expressions of opinion.

In an action to cancel certain promissory notes on the ground of misrepresentations as to the location and productivity of certain land for which the notes were given, representations that the land would and did produce from one-half to a bale of cotton per acre and similar statements as to the productivity of land of the same character in the same locality held not expressions of opinion, but statements of fact depending on local experience of local conditions of soil and climate made by one who knew to one known by him to be ignorant and to have had no opportunity to ascertain for himself.

5. Vendor and purchaser ⬚37(4)—Excessive purchase price may be element of fraud.

Freedom of the parties to fix their own price does not preclude the courts from considering excessiveness of price as evidence of fraud; and, if the price is so glaringly excessive that an honest man would hesitate to receive it unless convinced that the purchaser was not laboring under a mistake as to the real conditions, then knowledge of the seller and excusable ignorance of the purchaser may be sufficient to sustain the charge of fraud.

6. Vendor and purchaser ⬚45—Representations as to value held not fraudulent as matter of law.

Where purchasers went to look at cut-over land and were at liberty to take a plat of the land and go over it and to interview farmers in the neighborhood, but failed to do so, representations of vendors that the land was worth $25 an acre, for which price it was sold to the purchasers, *held* not, as a matter of law, ground for relieving the purchasers of their contract obligations.

Woodson, J., dissenting.

Appeal from Circuit Court, Barton County; B. G. Thurman, Judge.

Suit by Legran Thomas and another against D. C. Goodrum and others. Judgment for defendants, and plaintiffs appeal. Affirmed.

G. W. Barnett, of Sedalia, for appellants. Martin & Martin and E. L. Moore, all of Lamar, for respondents.

BROWN, C. This suit was instituted in the Barton circuit court February 8, 1917. The petition states, in substance, that defendants are owners and holders of four negotiable promissory notes executed by plaintiffs to one W. L. Perkins January 19, 1914, each being for the sum of $3,967.72 with interest at 6 per cent., being given for a part of the purchase price of about 1,026 acres of land in Little River county, Ark., at $25 per acre, and upon which plaintiffs had paid $11,000 at the time of the transaction; that the notes were procured from plaintiffs by fraud and misrepresentations as to the situation and character of the land; that the defendants trust company and investment company were owned and controlled by the defendant Goodrum who had some interest in the land which the plaintiffs could not state; that he was present in Arkansas and assisted in the perpetration of the fraud, and received the notes whether for himself or for said corporations or either of them with full knowledge of the facts and circumstances constituting it. These were substantially as follows: Plaintiffs were residents of Sedalia engaged in farming, and, in addition thereto, were dealers in implements and hardware in Hughesville. Two real estate agents named Hale and Hootman came to them at Hughesville with plats and pictures and literature regarding these lands in Little River county, Ark., and represented that Perkins and one Trice owned a large quantity of these lands, that it was wonderfully productive, would take care of a great amount of stock by reason of the Bermuda grass growing in that region, and so glowingly represented the quality and variety of products that could be raised upon it that plaintiffs became greatly interested and were induced to visit it. They arrived in Ashdown, Little River county, Ark., where the lands were situated, on January 3, 1914, and were there received by Trice, a confederate of Perkins and Goodrum, and interested in the sale of the lands. He took them to breakfast, and afterward to the office of Perkins and himself, where he procured teams, and with one

Gladdis, who was employed by Trice and Perkins to assist them in effecting the sale, he drove out to look at lands in the vicinity of Ashdown. During the trip they showed plaintiffs choice lands in that vicinity which they falsely stated were no better than the lands Perkins was offering them, and including one tract which Trice falsely represented he had sold for $25 per acre. They also said that the timber lands they were selling were, when the undergrowth was cleared out, producing from one-half bale of cotton to one bale per acre, and when cleared would produce from one to one and one-half bales, which would sell for $65 to $80 per bale. They also represented 736 acres to be in one compact body, which was untrue. There were also two tracts, one of 130 acres about 2½ miles east of the main body, and another one mile west, both of which Perkins represented to be better than the other lands, which was also false, it being the less valuable. That as a matter of fact the lands were worth less than $10 per acre, and the lands of that quality, including those in controversy, would not when cleared produce more than one bale to 3 acres. It also charges that all of these statements were not only false, but known to Perkins and Trice at the time to be false, and were made for the purpose of deceiving plaintiffs and inducing them to buy the lands at $25 per acre. It further states, in substance, that they were strangers in the locality, and that for the purpose of preventing them from ascertaining the truth the defendants and Perkins kept them from coming in contact with disinterested persons from whom they might or could ascertain the truth.

The defendant C. D. Goodrum filed a separate answer in which he disclaims any interest in the subject-matter of the suit and asks to be dismissed with his costs. The defendants Goodrum Trust Company and the Goodrum Mortgage & Investment Company filed a joint answer in which: First, they admit the execution of the notes and mortgage mentioned in the petition and deny generally all its other allegations; second, they plead laches by which they say the plaintiffs have forfeited their right to the equitable relief asked in the petition, as follows: (1) By taking possession of the lands and remaining in possession for more than two years before bringing the suit with a full knowledge of all the facts and circumstances of the transactions without making any complaint or offer to rescind or surrender the same; (2) by paying on December 30, 1914, $572 upon the purchase price of said land without complaint; and (3) by paying on March 1, 1915, the further sum of $1,000 upon said purchase price. The third count declared upon the note first maturing, stating it to be due and unpaid and asking judgment thereon. The issues were tried as if a reply had been filed, although none appears in the record. A jury was waived by the parties, and the cause went to trial before the court upon the issues presented by the pleadings, and after hearing the evidence the court found the said issues for the defendants, dismissing the defendant O. D. Goodrum with his costs, dismissing the plaintiffs' petition as to the other defendants, and also finding the issues for said last-mentioned defendants upon their counterclaim and rendering judgment thereon for the sum of $4,715, with interest from the date thereof at the rate of 6 per cent. per annum with costs.

The facts are that at the time of these transactions in the beginning of 1914 the plaintiffs resided in Pettis county, Mo., and were engaged in the implement and hardware business in Hughesville and also in farming. The three defendants resided in Lamar. O. D. Goodrum seems from the testimony to have been the progenitor of the other defendants, which natural enough, took his name. The Goodrum Mortgage & Investment Company was the elder of these, and Mr. Goodrum was its president. His testimony shows that its existence had gradually faded away until he could not state whether it was a corporation or not, or whether he was president or not, but only that it owned some interest in these notes, and the Goodrum Trust Company had been regularly incorporated for the purpose of succeeding it. Mr. Goodrum, although his testimony was not characterized by naïveté, acknowledged that he was its president, that it had an interest in the notes in question which it held as collateral security, and that the expiring mortgage and investment company, or its unnamed members, as the case might be, had a further interest in it. These collateral interests had been acquired by the advancement of money to the Southern Realty Company, a corporation doing business in Ashdown, Little River county, Ark., of which Perkins was president and manager and with which Trice, a former real estate dealer at Lamar, had his office. Trice and Goodrum had become acquainted in a business way at Lamar, and when Trice left and went to Ashdown and became associated with the realty company, the latter corporation continued its relation with the Goodrum Company to the extent of securing advancements from the latter upon their land transactions in Little River county, Ark.

Hootman and Hale were real estate agents in Sedalia and also agents of the Southern Realty Company for the sale of certain "cutover" pine lands in Little River county, Ark., of which there was a considerable quantity. This description implies lands which had once served their purpose as timber lands, the large pine having been removed, and the remaining pine being interspersed with scrub oak usually found in such localities.

Hootman and Hale approached plaintiffs in Sedalia with maps, pictures, and literature glowing with favorable representations of these lands, and plaintiffs became interested and went down to see for themselves. The lands were adjacent to the Kansas City Southern Railroad and near Ashdown, a city of 2,000 or 3,000 people. They were nicely entertained at the home of Trice, taken to Texarkana, which was only about 23 miles distant, and also to Red Bluff, another nice town about 10 miles east, and then taken over the lands around Ashdown, including some of the lands in question. It is during this trip to Ashdown that the misrepresentations charged in the petition are alleged principally to have been made. These consisted of statements that all the lands except 130 acres west of Ashdown were in a compact body, which was not the case, as they were scattered to some extent; also that Perkins, Gladdis, and Trice represented to them that similar lands in that vicinity were selling for $25 per acre. This the defendants allege was true. The plaintiffs also testified that Perkins, Gladdis, and Trice stated to them that lands of the character of those purchased by them would upon the clearing of the underbrush raise from one-half bale to a bale of cotton without further clearing. This statement, if made, was untrue, as none of the evidence for either party sustained it. The witnesses on both sides testified either that land in this condition was unfit for cotton raising and would not produce a crop or that they had never tried it.

The plaintiffs also testified that they were informed by Perkins and Trice that the same land would produce from one bale to one and a half bales per acre when in cultivation. The evidence on both sides was to the effect that a bale to from 3 to 5 acres was all that could be expected. In this 1,000-acre tract less than 100 acres had been cleared. This was mostly, if not entirely, in the detached 130 acres known as the Mose Hill tract. The most of this clearing had been abandoned.

As to the value of the land there was a great diversity in the evidence. The plaintiffs' witnesses, of which there were quite a number, estimated its value per acre at from $3 to $10, while the defendants' witnesses estimated it at from $10 to $30. These wide differences are explainable mostly by the standpoint from which the witness spoke. Most of them were farmers who had been unsuccessful, while others spoke from a purely speculative standpoint. This evidence, so far as we consider it necessary, will be mentioned as we proceed with the opinion.

In arranging for the initial payment of $11,000 plaintiffs had given their note to Perkins for 500-odd dollars, which was paid by Thomas to Mr. Goodrum with interest on September 30, 1914, without complaint as to the bargain. On January 16, 1915, he wrote Perkins as follows:

"Mr Perkins Dear sir i thought i would write you a few lines to let you know that i cannot pay the interest on them notes i had the colery in my hogs i lost almost all of them i can not get the money from the Bank and the only way i can pay the interest is to sell the land Let me sell my interest in that land to you send me a bid on it i have about 6000 in that land i will take the property in Hughesville as part of the pay i am hardly able to be round yet this is woring me to think i can not get around and see after my business you send me a bid and i will try to sell to you now is the time to make money for you for you can sell this land for a good prise in a short time you and Mr. Goodrum fix this up with your selves if you dont buy the land as i cant do anything with it. Let me know by return maile what you will do this is all for this time and wish you prosperes year good By"

On the 25th of the same month he wrote Goodrum as follows:

"Dear sir i received your statement about the interest on them nots i can not pay the interest now the coten crop down there was light and no prise it did not make mutch and i had the colery in my hogs and lost all of them so i cant pay i wrote to Mr. Perkins about it .they have the land to sell again let me sell my part of the land to you i have about 6000 dolars in that land and i will take the Hughesville property and 2000 dolars for it this is the only way i can pay the interest Grimes is down there you will half to write him down there you see Mr. Perkins and try to fix it with him this is all i can do so Good By."

On the 28th of the same month he again wrote Goodrum as follows:

"Dear sir i received your statement and you say you must have settlement i can not pay the interest now as i toled you the trade that i spoke of is the one thousand dolar morge you hold against the Grimes property in favor of S. W. Mcclure in Hughesville Mr. Perkins said he turned them over to you i will take the one thousand dolar note and two thousand dolars in money for my one half interest in the land 1026 acres in have paid 6000 in have no other way of paying the interest let me hear from you in regard to this i have bin sick for three months and i want to fix this up as soone as i can. i would of came over to see you before now but i am not able to come i guess you can understand what i mean by the one thousand dolar note Mr. Perkins got this note from S. W. McClure in his trade at Hughesville i hope you will understand me"

On February 7, 1915, he again wrote Goodrum as follows:

"Mr. Goodrum Dear sir i received your statement in regard to the interest i can not send the money But have Two propositions to make you if you will receive a note for the interest and give me one year to pay it at 7 per cent interest fill out a note for one half of the interest and send it to me and i will sine it and send it back to you and you send one to Grimes for the other half of the interest the other proposition is if you will give me the mortgage that you holde in favor of S. W. McClure i will turne over all of my interest in the Arkansas land this mortgage is on the Grimes property in Hughesville if neater these propositions suts you you will have to sell the land let me know by return maile what you intende to do about it"

On February 12, 1915, he wrote Goodrum as follows:

"Mr. Goodrum Dear sir i received your statement you acuse me of something that is not true i toled you that if could not pay the interest now you said i had laide down it i did not i sent you three or four ofers to fix it with you and it seames as none of them suits you you said you would have to sell the land if thes ofer dose not suite you you will have to sell"

On September 7, 1915, he again wrote Goodrum on this subject as follows:

"Mr. C. D. Goodrum Dear sir i have Bin wanting to come and see you in regarde to the Thomas & Grimes nots you Holde and i thought i would write you and finde out when it would sute you the Best. you let me know By return maile when it will sute you Best for me to come yours Truly"

[1] 1. A careful consideration of the evidence, and especially of the testimony of Mr. C. D. Goodrum, impresses us with the conviction that, so far as the rights of the two defendant corporations are concerned, they stand in the shoes of Perkins, and are entitled only to such rights as the latter would have were he in court making his defense as payee and holder of the notes. One will not be permitted to take the wrongdoer under his protection and shield him from the consequences of his fraud. If he claims its fruits he must be entitled to a place among the injured.

For many years this honest doctrine was expressed in the rule that, where the title to negotiable paper was vitiated in the hands of the first holder by fraud perpetrated by him in its inception, the burden rested upon each subsequent holder to show his title in due course; that is to say, that he acquired it in good faith before maturity for value, or, if not, that some other holder in due course had intervened between himself and the fraudulent payee. This doctrine was firmly established in Missouri in Hamilton v. Marks, 63 Mo. 167, in which the authorities, both English and American, were carefully reviewed, and has been constantly followed by this court. Keim v. Vette, 167 Mo. 389, 67 S. W. 223; Campbell v. Hoff, 129 Mo. 317, 31 S. W. 603; Johnson v. McMurry, 72 Mo. 278; Henry v. Sneed, 99 Mo. 407, 12 S. W. 663, 17 Am. St. Rep. 580.

The same doctrine was carefully preserved by the Negotiable Instrument Act of 1905 in the following language:

"Every holder is deemed prima facie to be a holder in due course; but when it is shown that the title of any person who has negotiated the instrument was defective, the burden is on the holder to prove that he or some person under whom he claims acquired the title as holder in due course." Section 10029, R. S. 1909.

No words could be selected to express more plainly the rule that, if the title of the payee is defective by reason of his own fraud, the burden would rest upon his indorsee to prove that he himself was a holder in due course; that is to say, that he acquired it in good faith without notice of the infirmity of the indorser's title. The words "in due course" in every section of the act in which they are used imply in the holder his own good faith in the acquisition of the instrument as well as his want of notice of any infirmity which would by reason of such notice affect the instrument in his hands.

[2] Goodrum's testimony shows that the two corporation defendants were creatures of his own. They both bore his name. While the first was, as is indicated by its name, a mortgage investment company, the trust company was, as he says, organized to take over its business. He does not even know who was interested in it, but he managed it during its life, and when his fellow townsmen Trice went to Ashdown to associate himself with Perkins, of the Southern Realty & Trust Company, Mr. Goodrum went down, looked over the ground, made some investments for himself, and furnished the realty company money to acquire this very land. When the land was sold the realty company put up the Perkins security as collateral to cover these advancements. This title as collateral for these advances is the only title proved by his testimony, and when the trust company was organized to succeed to the business of its predecessor it took over these notes. Being asked, Mr. Goodrum declined to state any amount advanced on them. He was the mouth of his corporation. When it spoke it spoke through him, and when he refused to speak it was the corporation that remained silent.

When he, having all the facts relating to the title in his possession, testified as to such facts, the evidence superseded the presumption arising from his possession of the notes with the blank indorsement of the payee disappeared, and we must look to the testimony for information as to the true title, and, doing so, we find the only title to be that they were delivered to the mortgage and investment company, and are now held as collateral security for money advanced to the Southern Realty Company through Trice and Perkins in the acquisition of the land before the sale to plaintiffs. This being true, the defendants stand in the same position as would Perkins, in whose name the sale was made for the benefit of all as their respective interests were then fixed.

[3] 2. Another preliminary question presents itself. The cause of action stated in the petition was equitable in its nature, and the cancellation of the four notes given by the plaintiffs to Perkins was the remedy sought, which the court could grant only in the exercise of its equitable jurisdiction. That the three parties named as defendants, all of whom were within the jurisdiction of the court, were proper parties to the suit under the allegations of the petition, is admitted. The counterclaim set up in the answer is purely an action at law by two of the defendants alone, and therefore triable by jury as to them. If this was unauthorized by sections 1806 and 1807 of the Revised Statutes of 1909, the count was subject to demurrer under the provisions of sections 1808 and 1809, and the effect of a failure to demur would be the same as in case of the petition. Without determining the interesting questions which arise upon the propriety of this counterclaim under our Code, we hold that the error, if any, was waived by the plaintiffs in the course of pleading, and that their express waiver of a trial of the issues by jury was an election to join issue in a trial by the court without a jury upon all the questions presented by the pleadings.

Without inquiring to what extent the equitable issues presented by the petition and the issues at law presented by the counterclaim were identical, we must recognize that the equitable remedy sought covered the entire field of the controversy, and it is our duty to examine it as in cases of purely equitable cognizance.

[4] 3. This case grows out of a real estate transaction incident to the building up of a new community upon an old foundation. The pine lands of Little River county, Ark., had been "cut over." The products had gone to the mills for manufacture, and the people who accomplished that work had sought other fields in which to continue their chosen activities. The land agents had come to develop its latent possibilities as an agricultural community. These cut-over lands seem from the evidence to have been of different qualities, or, more correctly speaking, perhaps, different degrees of the same quality. There were some tracts of bottom land upon which the fertility of the higher lands had been deposited and which were therefore more productive. There were "flats" upon which the water stood a considerable portion of the year, and when it escaped or evaporated they became dry and baked; and there were "knolls" which were fairly productive. The principal crop upon which the tillers of these lands depended was cotton, and the tillable land outside the bottoms would when cleared and cultivated produce that product in quantities of one bale, weighing 500 pounds, to from 3 to 5 acres. Very naturally these real estate people sought a market for these lands in the more thickly set-

tied portions of the country where lands were more valuable and productive, and real estate agents sought those regions as a field for purchasers. Among others Mr. C. Y. Trice, a real estate agent of Lamar, Mo., went to Ashdown to look over the conditions, and became associated with Mr. W. L. Perkins in the organization of a corporation for the purpose of handling this land under the name of the Southern Realty & Trust Company. He went back to Lamar and talked with Mr. C. D. Goodrun, who was the head of a Real Estate Mortgage Investment Company in that city. Mr. Goodrum made several visits to Ashdown, and in his corporate capacity consented in proper cases to furnish money to the Southern Realty & Trust Company for the purpose of dealing in these lands. Among the activities of the Southern Realty Company was an agency in Sedalia handled by Hootman and Hale, who were furnished with literature descriptive of the Arkansas lands and so worked upon the feelings of some Pettis county people, including the plaintiffs, that they assembled a party including plaintiffs to go to Ashdown and see for themselves. Mr. Goodrum got on the Kansas City Southern train somewhere in Barton county and traveled along with them. The result was that plaintiffs were shown these lands and agreed to purchase about 1,000 acres if they could turn in a stock of goods, with the house in which it was situated, at Hughesville, Pettis county, as a part of the purchase price, which was fixed at $25 per acre. It was during this trip and their stay of a few days in Ashdown and vicinity that plaintiffs say they were grossly deceived as to the character and value of these lands. They say.that they were assured by Trice and Perkins as well as by Mr. Gladdis, whom they employed to talk for them, that the land would and did produce when the undergrowth was removed and the land planted in cotton the same year without other clearing, from a half bale to a bale of cotton per acre. That this statement, if made, was grossly false is not denied. Also the further statement is attributed to Perkins and his associates that land of the character of that in question, when cleared, produced, a bale to a bale and a half of cotton per acre, which is also an exaggeration of its productiveness. The witnesses on both sides practically agreed that the land would not produce cotton before clearing it of timber and putting it in a state of cultivation, and that when properly cultivated it would take from 2 to 4 or 5 acres to produce a bale of cotton. These false representations are positively denied by the living witnesses Perkins and Gladdis to whom they are attributed by plaintiffs, while Trice, another party charged with them, or some of them, is dead.

It is said by respondents that these representations as to the productive quality of the land are simply expressions of opinion, and do not, therefore, constitute false representations of fact. We cannot agree with this. These were not expressions of opinion which any person could form from the inspection of the soil, but of fact depending upon local experience of local conditions of soil and climate in the production of the staple crop of that particular locality. If a stranger desired to know whether cotton was produced under these conditions, he could only learn by asking some one who knew. If he desired to know the average quantity produced per acre, he would be driven to the same expedient. Of his own knowledge he would have no foundation upon which to form an opinion. It was in no sense an expression of judgment, but a fact stated by a person who knew to a person known by him to be ignorant and to have had no opportunity to see and ascertain. The very foundation upon which one of the parties was seeking and the other giving information was the known ignorance of the seeker and knowledge of the giver. The respondents cite us to Wilson v. Jackson, 167 Mo. 135, 66 S. W. 972, and Brown v. Mining Co., 194 Mo. loc. cit. 700, 92 S. W. 699, to sustain their contention that this information was simply an expression of opinion. In the first case cited the court says that it was not represented that the land had produced, but that it could produce, the articles mentioned in abundance, and that the words were not spoken for the purpose of information, but as a matter of opinion or judgment. We are unable to see that the facts of the Mining Company Case have any bearing upon this, but the court makes clear the difference in this respect between "opinion" and "information" as we have already stated it. We think the statements charged are statements of fact with reference to a matter about which the plaintiffs are not presumed to have any knowledge other than such as they could obtain through answers to their inquiries, and that they were so vital to the value of the land for the agricultural use for which it was especially recommended as to constitute an important element in the trade. There is, however, an element of uncertainty in all such estimates that admits a considerable margin of variation. That the production would vary with weather conditions, with the manner in which the crop was cultivated, as well as local conditions of soil and drainage, is evident, and to this margin must be added some concession to the commercial instinct before we reach the line beyond which the only admissible inference is falsehood. This is the line which separates error which the law excuses from falsehood which, when told for gain, it denounces as fraud.

In this case both Trice and Perkins are charged with having made these false statements to plaintiffs. Trice, being dead, cannot deny the charge against him. Perkins denies having made these false statements, and it is necessary to consider the weight which we must give the testimony of plaintiffs in that respect.

Eight months after the sale, and while Grimes was living upon and presumably cultivating the land or preparing it for cultivation, the plaintiffs paid a note given by them in connection with the transaction without suggesting to Perkins, the payee, that they had been deceived. They were unable to pay their interest as it became due, and in the correspondence in which they sought terms that would enable them to do so we find no indication of a charge of bad faith, although it covered a year and a half succeeding the transaction. It indicates simply that the obligation they had assumed was beyond their ability to perform, and that they desired to get out of it on any terms which would release them from it. There is nothing in the record to indicate that the charge of fraud was made against Mr. Perkins, Mr. Trice, Mr. Goodrum, or any other party interested in the sale until the first note became due in January, 1916, when Mr. Barnett was employed to look into the matter with a view of protecting the plaintiffs and incidentally to determine whether any valid defense existed. Taking all these matters into consideration, we cannot say that the charge of misrepresentation as to the productive quality of the land is sustained by the evidence with that definiteness and certainty required in equity to overturn and cancel a contract in writing voluntarily made in compliance with all the formalities prescribed by law.

[5] 4. It is said that the consideration for which these notes were given—that is to say, the 1,026 acres of "cut-over" pine land in Southwestern Arkansas—was so glaringly inadequate as to afford, of itself, evidence of fraud. That the land was represented by Perkins and his associates interested in the transaction to be worth $25 per acre is shown not only by his admission in testimony, but also appears upon the face of the transaction itself. There seems to be nothing in the law which denounces as fraudulent a sale of property for a good round price, provided the sale is fairly made without deception as to facts relating to its value. In other words, a person has the right to say that his land is worth so much and to refuse to take less. He may ordinarily prescribe the conditions upon which he will part with his title, and the law will not compel him to take less nor forbid a purchaser to bid the price. He must, however, deal fairly and openly and without the practice of that deception which the law characterizes as fraud.

This freedom of action does not preclude the courts from taking purchase price into consideration as evidence of fraud in the sale. It is generally an element of the fraud, and if the price is so glaringly excessive that an

honest man would hesitate to receive it unless convinced that the purchaser was not laboring under a mistake as to the real conditions, then knowledge of the seller and excusable ignorance of the purchaser may be sufficient to sustain the charge of fraud.

[6] In this case the land had once been valuable for its pine timber. When this had been removed, the stumps and pine roots that permeated the clay of the soil and the trees too small to be worked into lumber for the markets remained, and it had been left by the lumbermen as being no longer valuable to them. Some of it, as we are told in the evidence, had been forfeited for taxes. The sale of these lands to farmers became interesting to enterprising real estate dealers who gathered upon the ground. Mr. Trice was one of these, Mr. Goodrum followed him with money to invest in the enterprise, and a company was organized in Ashdown for that purpose by Mr. Perkins, who acquired considerable tracts of this land which he definitely describes as 5,000 or 25,000 acres. We notice these things because the record shows two classes of people in Little River county from among whom this testimony has been produced. The occupants of the farms seem mostly to be poor and to have conservative opinions of its value. The speculative class say little of the price they paid, but have liberal ideas of the price it should and does sometimes bring when they sell it. The parties to this case represent both kinds. In fact, they are both represented in the person of these plaintiffs, who purchased at $25 per acre and are now trying to let go at about $14 per acre. Under these circumstances the evidence covers a wide range of value—from $3 to $30 per acre. It is hard to say that this testimony is not founded upon an expression of real opinion, formed from the standpoints of these various witnesses. We cannot, under this evidence, characterize as willfully false the statement of Perkins in selling this land that it was worth, and that other lands of a similar character in that locality were worth, the price received by him in this sale. The parties sustained no relation of confidence toward each other. They were absolute strangers. The plaintiffs might have relied upon the statements of Hale and Hootman, Sedalia agents of Perkins, but they did not. They went there to look for themselves, and were at liberty to take a plat of the land and go to it, and to interview farmers struggling with the same proposition. Perkins had the right to assume that plaintiffs, as men of ordinary intelligence, knew that he would represent the value of the land in the interest of the sale. Under these circumstances they had no right to consider the statements of value as anything but statements of the seller to be pitted against their own judgment in the negotiation. In Anderson v. McPike, 86 Mo. loc. cit. 300, we said:

"It is equally clear that 'a mere false assertion of value, where no warranty is intended, is no ground of relief to a purchaser, because the assertion is a matter of opinion which does not imply knowledge, and in which men may differ; mere expression of judgment or opinion does not amount to warranty. Every person reposes at his peril in the opinion of others, when he has equal opportunity to form and exercise his own judgment."

This doctrine has been frequently repeated in this court. Cornwall v. Real Estate Co., 150 Mo. 377, 51 S. W. 736; Coal Co. v. Halderman, 254 Mo. loc. cit. 640, 163 S. W. 828; Wingfield v. Railroad, 257 Mo. loc. cit. 365, 166 S. W. 1037.

The plaintiffs had a fair trial in a forum of their own choice, and we see nothing in the record to justify us in interfering with the result.

The judgment of the Barton county circuit court is therefore affirmed.

RAGLAND and SMALL, CC., concur.

PER CURIAM. The foregoing opinion by BROWN, C., is adopted as the opinion of the court.

All the Judges concur, except WOODSON, J., who dissents.

STATE v. LIKENS. (No. 22622.)

(Supreme Court of Missouri, Division No. 2. May 26, 1921.)

1. Criminal law ⟨⇒⟩1170½(5)—Witnesses ⟨⇒⟩277(4)—Cross-examination of defendant charged with murder not erroneous and in no event harmless.

In a prosecution for murder, defendant having testified in chief in regard to a conversation he had with his father at the house of deceased the day before the killing, cross-examination as to whether he had not stated to his father at the time that he was looking for the God damn son of a bitch that turned his cattle out, to which defendant replied that he did not use the language, and as to whether he told them that he was mad enough to kill there at that time, to which he answered in the negative, was not erroneous, and was in no event harmless.

2. Witnesses ⟨⇒⟩277(2)—Cross-examination of defendant showing for what length of time he had carried pistol, proper.

In a prosecution for murder, cross-examination of defendant if he had his gun with him when he went for his mail on the day of and just preceding the killing was proper, as going to show what length of time on the day he had carried the pistol which he had testified he used when he killed deceased.

3. Criminal law ⟨⇒⟩778(11)—Instruction on flight, though not submitting defendant's explanation, not reversible error.

In a prosecution for murder, instruction on flight, though not submitting to the jury for their consideration as an explanation of defendant's flight the possibility of mob violence, barely suggested by his testimony, *held* not reversible error.

4. Homicide ⟨⇒⟩309(5)—Instruction on manslaughter in fourth degree properly refused.

In a prosecution for murder, defendant being guilty of murder in the first or second degree, or justified in the killing on the ground of self-defense, requested instruction on manslaughter in the fourth degree was properly refused.

5. Homicide ⟨⇒⟩254—Conviction of murder in the second degree sustained.

Evidence *held* sufficient to sustain conviction of murder in the second degree.

6. Homicide ⟨⇒⟩312—Verdict of guilty of murder in the second degree sufficient.

Verdict, "We, the jury, find defendant [naming him] guilty of murder in the second degree, and do assess his punishment at imprisonment in the penitentiary for 15 years," was sufficient.

Appeal from Circuit Court, Lawrence County; Charles L. Henson, Judge.

J. C. Likens was convicted of murder in the second degree, and he appeals. Affirmed.

I. V. McPherson, of Aurora, and W. B. Skinner, of Mt. Vernon, for appellant.
Jesse W. Barrett, Atty. Gen., and Albert Miller, Asst. Atty. Gen., for the State.

DAVID E. BLAIR, Judge. Defendant was convicted in the Lawrence county circuit court of murder in the second degree, and sentenced on the verdict to imprisonment for 15 years in the state penitentiary, and has appealed.

The information charged murder in the first degree, but the state elected to try for second degree murder. Defendant killed one Fred Snyder on the 2d day of July, 1918, in Lawrence county. The wife of deceased was a sister of the defendant. Her father, Wheat Likens, lived with deceased and his wife at the time of the killing. The defendant had been living upon a nearby farm, containing about 200 acres owned by Wheat Likens. Because of arrears in rent he had shortly before been dispossessed by legal proceedings. The deceased had thereafter put in a crop of oats on a part of that farm.

Shortly before the killing the defendant had returned to the Likens place. Some of his cattle had gone into the oatfield of the deceased, and the controversy over this and over the previous dispossession of defendant was largely the cause of the hard feelings between deceased and the defendant which led to the killing. Shortly before the killing the defendant discovered that his cattle had been driven out of the oatfield of the deceased, and he claimed that they had been

⟨⇒⟩For other cases see same topic and KEY-NUMBER in all Key-Numbered Digests and Indexes abused and beaten. He became very angry, and talked with neighbors and others on the public highway, and made threats to kill the man responsible for beating his cattle. The day before the killing, and immediately after making these threats, he went to deceased's house, and asked for the deceased, who happened to be away at the time.

On the morning of the killing the deceased and his son Carl were plowing corn near the oatfield, when deceased discovered that a number of shocks of oats had been thrown down, and went to that part of the field and set up the shocks again. Early in the afternoon he left his team with Carl and started across toward the oatfield again, and after he had been gone a few moments Carl heard several shots. Climbing on top of his cultivator he raised himself to a sufficient height to be able to see over higher ground between, and saw defendant standing in the oatfield near a large sycamore tree, and saw smoke, apparently from the revolver shots. The defendant moved around aimlessly for a moment or two, and walked toward the road and turned back again, and, as Carl started in that direction, the defendant walked across the field and disappeared in the timber. The son found his father dead, lying face downward on the ground. It was discovered that there were three pistol bullet wounds in the back and one on the front of the body.

The defendant disappeared from the neighborhood immediately, and no one saw him after Carl Snyder watched him enter the timber, until in February, 1919, when he was arrested at his brother's home in Dade county, some 30 miles from the scene of the killing. The sheriff of Lawrence county and the sheriff of Greene county scoured the country, looking for the defendant, immediately after the killing, and until a late hour that night, but found no trace of him. On receipt of word that the defendant had been seen at his brother's home in Dade county, the officers watched that place one evening, and failed to locate the defendant. They returned early the next morning and concealed themselves in some brush and sprouts near the house, and finally the defendant appeared, followed by a dog, and started in their general direction, when they were discovered by the dog. The defendant approached their place of concealment, apparently to investigate the cause of the dog's excitement, and the officers commanded the defendant to throw up his hands. The defendant jumped, and immediately turned and started to run. One of the officers shot the defendant with a shotgun, and brought him to his knees. The officers captured him, and upon search found a revolver in his pocket.

At the trial the defendant testified that on the afternoon of the killing he had been down to get his mail at the mail box on the public road, and as he returned past the oatfield he saw the deceased setting up the oat shocks. His testimony in chief as to what transpired there was as follows:

"Q. Go ahead. Tell what took place over there. A. I walked on down the road, going towards home, and when I got down to pretty near even with him he was looking up that way and spoke, and I spoke to him. He says, 'Come out this way, Charley.' I walked out to pretty close to where he was, and he said, 'Somebody is tearing my oats down;' and I said, 'Somebody has been beating my cattle up,' and he said, 'I am not going to stand up with this any more; I will fix this with you;' and started towards me, and put his hand back in his hip pocket, and I pulled my gun and started shooting. He wheeled, and looked like he had started to get his gun ready. It seemed as if he was trying to do something, and I shot three more shots at him and he fell.

"Q. Why did you draw your gun and shoot him? A. Because I thought he was going to shoot me.

"Q. You did it to prevent that? To save yourself? A. Yes, sir."

Search of the scene immediately after the killing showed that deceased had no weapon whatever. All the articles that were found on his person were a watch, a small piece of tobacco, and an ordinary unopened pocketknife in the hip pocket of his overalls. No weapon or missile of any kind was found anywhere near where the deceased was lying.

The defendant explained his leaving the vicinity by stating that he started to go to one of the neighbors, and then happened to think if he remained in the neighborhood he might be the object of mob violence, and so left. He claimed to have been at his brother's in Dade county from that time until his arrest. He left his cattle without any provision for their care and attention. He did not deny having attempted to flee at the time the officers sought to arrest him, and made no explanation of his conduct at the time. He offered testimony tending to show that he sustained a good reputation as a quiet, peaceable, and lawabiding citizen.

Defendant's counsel has filed no abstract of the testimony, and has favored us with no assignment of errors, brief, or argument. The points suggested for our consideration as alleged error by the motion for a new trial and the motion in arrest of judgment, are as follows: .

(1) The admission of illegal and incompetent testimony offered by the state, and the exclusion of legal, competent, and material evidence offered by the defendant.

(2) Improper cross-examination of defendant on matters not testified to by him in chief.

(3) The giving by the court of illegal and improper instructions, and the refusal of the

court to instruct on all the law of the case, particularly upon manslaughter in the fourth degree.

(4) The insufficiency of the evidence to support the judgment.

(5) The information fails to charge any crime under the laws and Constitution of this state, and is too vague, indefinite, and uncertain to inform the defendant of the accusation against him.

(6) That the verdict is not sufficient in form or substance to support the judgment.

We have carefully studied the transcript of the evidence, and have failed to find any testimony offered by the state and admitted over the objection of the defendant, or any evidence offered by the defendant and excluded by the court, where we regard the court's action as prejudicial to the substantial rights of the defendant. Numerous exceptions were saved by the defendant during the course of the trial to adverse rulings of the court, but we fail to find reversible error in such rulings in the light of the entire record. Our attention has not been specially directed to any particular testimony which was introduced by the state or excluded when offered by the defendant. No good purpose can be served by detailing the circumstances attending the various rulings appearing in the record.

[1] Error is claimed in permitting improper cross-examination. We note that defendant testified in chief in regard to a conversation he had with his father at the deceased's house the day before the killing. In cross-examination on this matter he was required to answer if he had not stated to his father at that time that he was looking for the God damn son of a bitch that turned his cattle out, to which defendant replied: "I didn't use that language." And again: "Q. You didn't tell them that you were mad enough to kill there at that time? A. No, sir." This is said to have been improper. He had testified in chief to a conversation with his father at that time and place, and the state was entitled to bring out all the conversation, and "need not categorically follow what was said in his chief examination." State v. Foley, 247 Mo. loc. cit. 638, 639, 153 S. W. 1010. In any event he denied the threats, and his case was not prejudiced by his answer or the fact that the questions were asked.

[2] Again, defendant was asked on cross-examination if he had his gun with him when he went for his mail on the day of and just preceding the killing. To this question defendant's counsel objected. It was entirely proper to show for what length of time on that day he had carried the pistol, which he had testified that he used when he killed the deceased. The testimony shows that defendant left his house and went for his mail and immediately returned, and on such return had his trouble with the deceased. Even without this testimony the inference could be drawn that he took the pistol when he left his house, because the testimony disclosed no opportunity for him to procure it elsewhere.

The instructions given by the court fully covered the issues raised by the testimony given by the witnesses, and included instructions on murder in the second degree, self-defense, the presumption of intended death from the use of a deadly weapon upon a vital part of the deceased if used without just cause or excuse, the effect of statements made by defendant, good character of defendant, the fact that the information is a mere formal charge, the presumption of innocence attending the defendant throughout the trial, reasonable doubt, and credibility of witnesses. These are all substantially in the form repeatedly approved by this court.

[3] The instruction on flight is as follows:

"If the jury find and believe from the evidence that the defendant, immediately after the commission of the homicide alleged in the information, fled from the country and absented himself from his usual place of abode, and concealed himself for the purpose of avoiding arrest and trial of said offense, you may take that into consideration as a circumstance in passing upon his guilt or innocence."

While it is true that this instruction fails to submit to the jury for their consideration as an explanation for defendant's flight the possibility of mob violence, barely suggested by defendant's testimony, yet under the evidence we do not believe the instruction as given is reversible error. An instruction in substantially the same form was condemned in State v. Harris, 232 Mo. loc. cit. 320, 134 S. W. 535, and the judgment in that case was reversed solely because the instruction on flight was not broad enough to include defendant's explanation of his leaving the state. However, the facts in the two cases are entirely different. In the Harris Case the defendant denied the killing, and there was a conflict in the evidence as to his identity. He was a negro, and he was charged with shooting an innocent bystander, looking on at a street brawl. Witnesses testified that they knew said defendant, and saw him at the time, and that he did not fire the shot. Defendant introduced evidence to the effect that he fled because he feared mob violence, which the evidence tended to show had actually been incited against him because of the killing.

In the case of State v. Schmulbach, 243 Mo. loc. cit. 538, 147 S. W. loc. cit. 968, an instruction, telling the jury that flight "raises the presumption of guilt," without also submitting to the consideration of the jury threatened mob violence as a reason for defendant's flight, was held to be erroneous. "There was evidence that the shooting immediately created great excitement, that armed men scoured the country for defendant, that threats of mob violence were made, and that sentiment was much aroused against him." Schmulbach had shot down a police officer of Joplin while he was taking defendant's wife to the city jail.

There was no evidence of threatened mob violence in the case at bar. All the testimony on this point appears in defendant's cross-examination, and is as follows:

"Q. Now, after the shooting what did you do? A. Well, I turned back out to the road.

"Q. What did you go back to the road for? A. I thought I would go to Cameron's and tell them what happened.

"Q. Then you changed your mind? A. I went out to the road, and I happened to think that the folks were liable to come in there and mob me.

"Q. What folks had told you they were liable to come in there and mob you? A. My brother told me for one.

"Q. Did they know you were going to kill him, to be mobbed for? A. No, sir.

"Q. Somebody had told you prior to that time that they were liable to come in there and mob you? You happened to think of that, and you turned and went back? A. I turned back and went this old road.

"Q. And disappeared in the woods? A. Yes, sir. To the place where I came from."

At the time he left the vicinity no one had talked to the defendant since the killing. The remark made by his brother could not possibly have referred to the state of mind of the public caused by and existing after the killing. It may be that his brother had said this to him in an endeavor to dissuade him from carrying out threats made against the deceased. Defendant's conduct at the time of his arrest several months after the killing indicated a persisting purpose of trying to escape arrest and trial.

If there had been substantial testimony tending to show that defendant fled to escape mob violence rather than to avoid arrest and trial for the offense charged against him, the instruction should be held bad. But there was no error in giving the instruction in this form under the evidence before us. Defendant certainly could not have been prejudiced by the omission under the facts in this case, since it would require a very great stretch of imagination for the jury to find that he fled to escape mob violence, and his resort to such explanation has every appearance of an afterthought.

[4] The record shows that defendant's counsel requested an instruction on manslaughter in the fourth degree. There is no evidence in the record on which to base such an instruction. Defendant was guilty of murder in the first or second degree, or was justified on the ground of self-defense. There was no quarrel at the scene of the killing, and no physical encounter, other than the shooting. There was nothing to indicate the act was done in the heat of passion. Defendant is the only living witness to what transpired at that time, and all his testimony tended to show that he acted in self-defense to prevent an apparent assault by the deceased. The court did not err in refusing to give this sort of an instruction.

[5] There is ample testimony to support the verdict. There had been serious trouble between defendant and deceased over the possession and use of the farm, and over defendant's cattle. There was substantial evidence of threats by defendant that indicated deceased as the object. Even if defendant had not admitted the killing, there was abundant evidence that he fired the fatal shots, and his immediate flight and subsequent resistance to arrest point eloquently to the fact of his guilt. All these facts fully justify the verdict returned by the jury.

The information follows substantially the form used in indictments and informations repeatedly held by this court to be good. It is not necessary to set it out in this opinion or to cite authorities in its support.

[6] The point that the verdict is not sufficient in form or substance to support the judgment is entirely without merit. The verdict was as follows:

"We, the jury, find the defendant, J. C. Likens, guilty of murder in the second degree, and do assess his punishment at imprisonment in the penitentiary for 15 years."

It carries its own proof of its entire sufficiency.

Finding no reversible error in this record, the judgment of the trial court is affirmed.

All concur.

JENKINS v. JENKINS. (No. 21652.)

(Supreme Court of Missouri, Division No. 2. May 26, 1921.)

Courts ⟐231(40)—Appeal from judgment for profits and rents of which widow had been deprived held not within jurisdiction of Supreme Court.

Where widow died prior to rendition of judgment in her suit to have dower assigned and homestead set off, and to compel an accounting for rents and profits arising from the use of the land, and the suit was revived in the name of her administrator, an appeal from the judgment for the administrator for the amount of the rents and profits of which she had been deprived was not within the jurisdiction of the Supreme Court; the title to the land not being affected by the judgment, and the jurisdiction being therefore in the Court of Appeals.

Appeal from Circuit Court, Macon County; Vernon L. Drain, Judge.

Suit by Jane Jenkins, for whom Joseph Jenkins, as administrator of the estate of Jane Jenkins, deceased, was substituted, against Thomas Jenkins. Judgment for plaintiff, and defendant appeals. Cause transferred to Court of Appeals.

Ben Franklin, of Macon, for appellant. Nat. M. Shelton, of Macon, for respondent.

WHITE, C. This suit was brought in the circuit court of Macon county by Jane Jenkins, the widow, against Thomas Jenkins, son of Thomas L. Jenkins, deceased, for the purpose of having dower assigned and homestead set off in 80 acres of land left by Thomas L. Jenkins at his death, and to compel an accounting for the rents and profits arising from the use of said land from May, 1910. Thomas L. Jenkins died in May, 1910; this suit was filed in June, 1918.

The plaintiff, Jane Jenkins, died before judgment was rendered in the case, and the suit was revived in the name of Joseph Jenkins, administrator of her estate. The court heard the evidence before the death of Jane Jenkins, and rendered judgment after her death, assessing the value of the rents and profits of which she had been deprived at $500, and rendered judgment in favor of the administrator for that amount; and the widow's right to dower and homestead having determined at her death.

This court is without jurisdiction. The title to real estate, though incidentally involved, is not affected by the judgment. Kennedy v. Duncan, 224 Mo. 661, 123 S. W. 856; Stough v. Steelville Elec. L. & P. Co., 217 S. W. loc. cit. 519, and cases cited. The Duncan Case is directly in point.

The cause is transferred to the Kansas City Court of Appeals.

RAILEY and MOZLEY, CC., concur.

PER CURIAM. The foregoing opinion by WHITE, C., is adopted as the opinion of the court.

All the Judges concur,   .

STATE ex rel. DOLMAN v. DICKEY et al. (two cases). (Nos. 22343, 22344.)

(Supreme Court of Missouri, Division No. 2. May 26, 1921.)

1. **Appeal and error ⚖=238(3), 281(1)—In the absence of motion for new trial and arrest of judgment, nothing but record proper can be considered.**

In the absence of motion for a new trial and arrest of judgment, nothing but the record proper can be considered by the appellate court.

2. **Appeal and error ⚖=1201(1)—Petition deemed amended in case of remand for trial on particular issue.**

Where the Supreme Court first reversed outright a judgment for relator commanding the issuance of tax bills for public work, but on rehearing remanded the case for determination of whether the contract was severable and recovery could be had for part of the work, the petition on retrial must be considered as amended and to deal solely with that issue.

3. **Appeal and error ⚖=1096(1)—Propriety of former judgment not reviewable.**

Where a judgment of mandamus commanding the issuance of tax bills for a public improvement was reversed and the cause remanded solely on the issue whether portions of the contract were severable and recovery could be had on them, relator, who merely introduced the previous record and did not relitigate the issue as to whether he was entitled to a general recovery, cannot, where judgment went in his favor on the second trial, by filing an affidavit for appeal, reopen in the appellate court the question of his right to a general recovery, for in such case the appeal is on the record proper, and, as the petition will be construed as amended to present only the issue of whether items were severable, etc., the previous issue was wholly unpresented, and, if relator desired to obtain reconsideration of the former judgment, he should have directly presented that issue in the lower court.

4. **Appeal and error ⚖=1097(1)—Party to appealing from judgment in his own behalf cannot obtain review of former adverse ruling of appellate court in same cause.**

Where former judgment for relator was reversed and the cause remanded solely to determine whether he could partially recover, he cannot, by appealing from the judgment in his behalf for partial recovery, reopen the original litigation.

5. **Contracts ⚖=171(1)—Rule as to severability of items stated; "severable contract."**

If part of a contract to be performed by one party consists of several distinct and separate items and the price to be paid by the other is apportioned to each item to be performed or is left to be implied by law, such contract is in general "severable," and the same rule holds where the price to be paid is clearly and distinctly apportioned to different parts of what is to be performed, though the latter in its nature is single and entire.

[Ed. Note.—For other definitions, see Words and Phrases, First and Second Series, Severable Contract.]

Appeal from Circuit Court, Buchanan County; Thomas B. Allen, Judge.

Petition by the State, on the relation of John E. Dolman, against C. E. Dickey and others for writ of mandamus. From a judgment for relator, respondents appeal, and relator also appealed. Affirmed.

On November 9, 1916, relator filed, in the circuit court of Buchanan county, Mo., a petition for mandamus to compel respondents to issue and deliver to him certain tax bills, to pay for the construction of pavement on a street in St. Joseph, Mo., a city of the first class. The relator is the assignee of the Standard Construction Company, the contractor in the performance of the work. Respondents made their return, and the circuit court aforesaid, after hearing the evidence, found the issues in favor of relator and granted a peremptory writ. Said defendants, in due time, appealed the cause to this court. Upon a hearing of the case, we reversed it outright, as shown in the opinion of Commissioner White, reported in 280 Mo. 536, 219 S. W. at page 363 and following. Relator filed in this court a motion for rehearing. In support of said motion, this court was requested to hold that the contract mentioned in petition was severable, and that the work on the sidewalk and curbing mentioned therein was substantially complied with, etc. Thereupon, at the instance of relator (280 Mo. 536, 219 S. W. 368), the opinion of Commissioner White was modified and the cause remanded, in order that the trial court might ascertain whether the construction of the curbing and sidewalk was in accordance with said contract, and could be separated from the paving, in determining the price to be paid for same, etc. The motion for rehearing, after said modification, was thereupon overruled. Upon the filing of the opinion and mandate of this court in the circuit court aforesaid, the latter proceeded to dispose of the case upon the petition and return aforesaid under the directions of this court for the purposes aforesaid.

It appears from defendants' bill of exceptions herein that relator, in the retrial of the case, offered in evidence the bill of exceptions and record in the case made up at the former trial. Other evidence was offered by relator in support of his contention.

On March 29, 1920, the circuit court entered the following judgment after said retrial:

"Now on this day comes the plaintiff by John E. Dolman, its attorney, and also come the defendants, by Charles W. Meyer, their attorney, and the mandate and opinion of the Supreme Court in said cause, remanding the same to this court for further proceedings with reference to the sidewalk, curb and driveways, having been filed and the said cause in accordance with said opinion, now coming on to be heard and the record upon the former trial of this cause, the bill of exceptions and the original contract having been introduced in evidence and the court having heard the arguments of counsel and being fully advised in the premises, finds that the sidewalks, curbing and driveways can be separated from the paving of the roadway and that the prices therefor are different from the price charged for said driveway, to wit: For all curbing taken up and reset per linear foot, fifteen cents. For new (artificial concrete stone) curbing furnished and set per linear foot, forty-four cents. For (artificial concrete stone) sidewalk per square foot, fourteen cents and for concrete driveways per square foot, twenty cents.

"And the court further finds that all of said sidewalks, curbing and driveways were constructed in accordance with the contract, and that plaintiff is entitled to have tax bills issued therefor according to the terms of said contract, but that under said decision of the Supreme Court, plaintiff is not entitled to have tax bills issued in payment for the paving of the roadway provided for in said contract.

"It is therefore ordered, considered and adjudged that a peremptory writ of mandamus issue against said defendants and against the board of public works of the city of St. Joseph as now constituted and the city engineer of said city, commanding them to issue and deliver tax bills to said John E. Dolman, relator herein, for all sidewalks, curbing and driveways constructed under said contract, in accordance with the prices contained therein and that the city engineer certify, authenticate and sign the same to the end that the same may be established as a lien against the several pieces and parcels of land liable for such improvement.

"That plaintiff have and recover interests on said tax bills at the rate of 8 per cent. per annum from the date of his demand therefor, to wit, January 27, 1915, and that said relator have and recover of said defendants his costs in this behalf expended and hereof let execution issue."

On April 2, 1920, defendants filed a motion for a new trial, which was overruled on April 14, 1920. Defendants, in due time and in a proper manner, appealed to this court.

Relator filed no motion for a new trial, nor did he file any motion in arrest of judgment. He filed an affidavit for appeal on April 24, 1920, and took leave to file a bill of exceptions during the May term, 1920, of said court.

Relator's affidavit for appeal, which was sustained, reads as follows:

"Comes now the relator, John E. Dolman, in the above-entitled cause, and moves the court for an appeal to the Supreme Court of the State of Missouri. John E. Dolman, being first duly sworn, on his oath states that he is the relator in the above-entitled cause and that this appeal is not made for vexation or delay, but because he believes himself aggrieved and injured by the judgment of the court in this cause. J. E. Dolman.

"Subscribed and sworn to before me this 16th day of April, 1920," etc.

The respective appeals will be disposed of separately in the opinion.

A. F. Lindsay, City Counselor, and C. W. Meyer, Asst. City Counselor, both of St. Joseph, for appellants.

John E. Dolman, of St. Joseph, for respondent.

RAILEY, C. (after stating the facts as above). [1-4] I. Relator insists that on the record aforesaid, he is entitled to have this court reconsider the law of the case as declared in the opinion of Judge White. It is true that the Supreme Court, in a few cases, when properly presented, has reconsidered its former ruling on the second appeal, but such practice is an exception to the general rule, and is not to be encouraged. According to our conception of the law, relator is in no position to ask at our hands a reconsideration of the former ruling, denying the writ of mandamus, for he is here without any record upon which that matter can be considered.

We remanded the original case, at the instance and request of relator, in order to give him a chance to recover tax bills for the curbing and sidewalk, if the trial court should find that the contract was severable, etc. The jurisdiction of the circuit court, upon a retrial of the case, was limited solely to the above issue. In granting relator's request for a retrial of the above matter, it was upon the theory that the petition and writ were to be considered as amended, so as to deal alone with the above issue. Both court and counsel proceeded in the second trial upon this theory, as shown by the proceedings and judgment rendered. The record proper, then, in the second trial, consisted of the petition and writ as amended, the return of defendants, and the judgment heretofore set out. As shown by the record, relator offered testimony upon the retrial of the case, and, after judgment was rendered in his favor, upon the issues thus presented, he filed no motion for a new trial or in arrest of judgment, but simply filed the affidavit for appeal heretofore mentioned, and has sought to bring the case here without the evidence, or without any matters of exception, which may have occurred during the progress of the trial. It has long since become elementary law in this state that in the absence of a motion for a new trial, and in arrest of judgment, nothing but the record proper can be considered by the appellate court. State v. Griffin, 98 Mo. loc. cit. 674, 675, 12 S. W. 358; State v. Wray, 124 Mo. loc. cit. 542, 543, 27 S. W. 1100; State v. Handley, 144 Mo. loc. cit. 118, 119, 45 S. W. 1088; State v. Revely, 145 Mo. 660, 47 S. W. 787; Harding v. Bedoll, 202 Mo. 625, 100 S. W. 638; Stark v. Zehnder, 204 Mo. loc. cit. 449, 102 S. W. 992; Gilchrist v. Bryant, 213 Mo. 442, 111 S. W. 1128; Groves v. Terry, 219 Mo. 595, 117 S. W. 1167; State ex rel. v. Adkins, 221 Mo. loc. cit. 120, 119 S. W. 1091; Hays v. Foos, 223 Mo. 421, 122 S. W. 1038; Betzler & Clark v. James, 227 Mo. 375, 126 S. W. 1007; St. Louis v. Henning, 235 Mo. 44, 138 S. W. 5; Blanchard v. Dorman, 236 Mo. 416, 417, 139 S. W. 395; Realty Co. v. Brewing Co., 247 Mo. 29, 152 S. W. 31; Haggerty v. Ruth, 259 Mo. 168 S. W. 537; McKee v. Donner, 261 Mo. 378, 379, 168 S. W. 1198; Case v. Carland, 264 Mo. 463, 175 S. W. 200; State ex inf. v.

Morgan, 268 Mo. loc. cit. 271, 187 S. W. 54; Tracy v. Tracy et al., 201 S. W. 902; Pennewell et al. v. Pennewell et al., 204 S. W. 183; Hoskins v. Nichols et al., 213 S. W. 888; State v. Baugh, 217 S. W. loc. cit. 280.

Numerous other authorities in this state, to the same effect, can be found reported. The petition and writ, considered as amended, the return of defendants, considered as amended to correspond with same, and the judgment entered on the second appeal, constitute the record proper in this case, but not in the former proceedings. State ex rel. Combs v. Staten et al., 268 Mo. loc. cit. 295, 296, 187 S. W. 43, 44. As heretofore shown, there is nothing for review before us on relator's appeal but the record proper, and, having received all he asked for in this proceeding, he has no legal ground for complaint under the present appeal.

2. Relator's appeal is likewise without merit, for the obvious reason that he has appealed from a judgment in his own behalf, without complaining of any error in the trial. No judgment was rendered against him in the trial court, and he got all he claimed in the retrial of the case.

3. The authorities cited by relator for reopening the original controversy, as he has attempted to do by simply filing an affidavit for appeal in the second trial, do not sustain his contention. It will be found, upon examination of the records in those cases where the original opinion was reconsidered upon a second appeal, that on the retrial the evidence was introduced as in the first trial, instructions asked, motions for new trial filed, etc. If the trial court refused to follow our ruling, there would be no necessity for a reconsideration of the case on appeal; but if it followed our ruling, then the complaining party might again appeal, and we would then determine whether the original judgment should stand. In this orderly way of procedure, the trial court would not be ignored in the proceeding, and the whole record would be before us on the second appeal for our consideration.

In support of this conclusion, we call attention to the leading case in this state of Hamilton v. Marks et al., 63 Mo. 170 and following, cited and relied upon by relator. The case was formerly tried, and will be found reported in 52 Mo. at page 78 and following, 14 Am. Rep. 391. On a retrial of the case, evidence was heard, instructions asked, and the case was again tried as formerly. This court then had before it, in the usual manner, the record and proceedings of the second trial, showing that the matters complained of were again before this court for its consideration.

We are not aware of any rule of legal procedure in this state, by which relator can have the original judgment and proceedings herein reconsidered, as he has attempted to do in this case, on appeal from a judgment in his own favor, and that, too, by ignoring the trial court, and failing to produce for our consideration the evidence and other proceedings had before the trial court.

Defendants' Appeal.

[5] 4. Judge White's opinion (280 Mo. 536, 219 S. W. 363, and following) contains a very full statement of the facts, as they were presented in the original trial, and hence it is not necessary to incumber this record with a reproduction of same. The evidence adduced by relator at the second trial was amply sufficient to sustain the judgment rendered in the present case, if the contract can be construed as authorizing the severance made by the trial court in its judgment. We have examined the authorities cited by defendants in support of their contention that the contract in controversy is not severable, yet we do not think the weight of authority is with the defendants in respect to this matter. In our opinion, the principle of law which should apply in a case of this character is very clearly and forcefully stated in Amsler v. Bruner et al., 173 Ill. App. 337, 338, as follows:

"If the part of a contract to be performed by one party consists of several distinct and separate items, and the price to be paid by the other is apportioned to each item to be performed or is left to be implied by law, such a contract is in general severable, and the same rule holds where the price to be paid is clearly and distinctly apportioned to different parts of what is to be performed, though the latter in its nature is single and entire."

The principle of law above announced is supported by the following authorities: Keeler v. Clifford, 165 Ill. 544, 46 N. E. 248; Siegel v. Eaton & Prince Co., 165 Ill. 550, 46 N. E. 449; Barlow Mfg. Co. v. Stone, 200 Mass. 158, 160, 161, 86 N. E. 306; Dibol & Plank v. W. & E. H. Minott, 9 Iowa, 403; Pierson et al. v. Crooks et al., 115 N. Y. loc. cit. 554, 555, 22 N. E. 349, 12 Am. St. Rep. 831; Wooten v. Walters, 110 N. C. loc. cit. 255, 14 S. E. 734, 736; Williams v. Robb, 104 Mich. 242, 246, 247, 62 N. W. 352; 2 Parsons on Contracts (9th Ed.), § 4, pp. 672-674; Hammon on Contracts, § 463, p. 907; 13 Corpus Juris, § 528, par. 4, p. 563; 7 A. & Eng. Ency. of Law (2d Ed.) par. 4, p. 95; 3 Elliott on Contracts, § 2046, pp. 229-231, and cases cited. The rulings of our appellate courts upon kindred questions, while not directly in point are in line with the law as declared in above authorities. Neil v. Ridge, 220 Mo. 233-257, 119 S. W. 619; Porter v. Paving & Construction Co., 214 Mo. loc. cit. 18 and fol., 112 S. W. 235; Haag v. Ward, 186 Mo. 325, 348;[1] Reinert Bros. Const. Co. v. Whitmer (App.) 206

S. W. 888; City of Maryville v. Cox, 181 Mo. App. loc. cit. 263, 264, 167 S. W. 1166; Joplin ex rel. v. Freeman, 125 Mo. App. 717, 722, 103 S. W. 130; City of Marionville, to Use, v. Henson, 65 Mo. App. 397.

It does not appear from the record before us that defendants are liable to sustain any loss or damage should the judgment below be enforced. In our opinion, the ends of justice will best be subserved by overruling defendants' contention.

5. In view of the conclusions heretofore reached, the judgment of the trial court, as to relator and defendants, is hereby affirmed.

WHITE and MOZLEY, CC., concur.

PER CURIAM. The foregoing opinion of RAILEY, C., is hereby adopted as the opinion of the court.

All concur.

STATE v. EDELEN.   (No. 22580.)

(Supreme Court of Missouri, Division No. 2. May 26, 1921.)

1. Criminal law ☞1134(3)—Defects in information may be remedied on new trial after reversal for other reasons.

An objection that an information was not sworn to by the prosecuting attorney or any other person, and the prosecutrix's affidavit was not sworn to and filed with the information, need not be formally decided, where the cause must, for other reasons, be reversed and remanded, for such matters may be voided upon new trial.

2. Criminal law ☞1134(3)—No decision on qualification of jurors where new trial granted.

Upon appeal from a criminal prosecution, whether court erred in overruling defendant's challenge to the qualification of certain jurors need not be decided, where the cause is reversed and the matter not likely to arise upon new trial.

3. Criminal law ☞1171(1)—State's dramatic attempt to browbeat defendant witness by presenting questions on matters not covered by main examination held to require reversal.

In a prosecution for forcible rape, where prosecutrix's clothing was in evidence, cross-examining appellant as to condition of such clothing and as to his knowledge of how she acquired certain marks, bruises, and injuries, which matters were not referred to in the main examination of defendant as a witness, and which questions were presented in a dramatic manner, constituted error prejudicial to defendant's rights and affected extent of his punishment assessed by the jury, and indicates an intention to browbeat and discredit defendant before the jury, requiring reversal of conviction.

4. Criminal law ⚖️696(5)—Error to refuse to strike out evidence, though question was not objected to.

In a prosecution for forcible rape, it was error to refuse to strike that part of a physician's testimony where he was asked his opinion of what made certain discolorations on prosecutrix's garments, and replied that he thought she had been mistreated, for, while the question might properly have been objected to on the ground that witness' answer would invade the province of the jury, yet the defendant was not bound to anticipate that the witness would, in legal effect, give it as his opinion that defendant had raped the prosecutrix.

5. Criminal law ⚖️811(2) — Instruction that jury should consider physical strength of prosecutrix and defendant held reversible error as a palpable comment on a portion of state's evidence.

In a prosecution for forcible rape, instructing the jury to consider the physical strength, ability, and power of prosecuting witness and defendant and the condition of prosecutrix's clothing *held* erroneous as a palpable comment on a portion of the state's evidence, particularly since the court failed to advise the jury to consider evidence of the conduct of prosecutrix, who testified to a different state of facts on the trial from what her evidence disclosed at preliminary trial, so that the instruction was not only unfair and in violation of Rev. St. 1919, § 4083, but in contravention of law, and requires reversal.

Appeal from Circuit Court, Clark County; N. M. Pettingill, Judge.

Glen Edelen was convicted of rape, and his motions for new trial and in arrest of judgment were overruled and sentence passed, and he appeals. Reversed and remanded for new trial.

On November 25, 1919, the prosecuting attorney of Clark county, Mo., filed with the clerk of the circuit court, in vacation, an information, which, omitting caption, reads as follows:

"Now comes James H. Talbott, prosecuting attorney within and for the county of Clark and state of Missouri, basing his information upon the affidavit of one Golda Hoffeditz, herein filed, gives the court to understand and be informed that one Glen Edelen, on or about the 24th day of August, 1919, at and in the county of Clark and state of Missouri, in and upon one Golda Hoffeditz, unlawfully, violently, and feloniously, did make an assault, and her, the said Golda Hoffeditz, then and there unlawfully, forcibly, and against her will, feloniously did ravish and carnally know. Contrary to the form of the statutes in such cases made and provided and against the peace and dignity of the state. [Signed] James H. Talbott. Prosecuting Attorney within and for the County of Clark and State of Missouri."

The affidavit mentioned in the information, without caption, reads as follows:

"Golda Hoffeditz, being duly sworn on her oath, states that one Glen Edelen, on or about the 24th day of August, 1919, at and in the county of Clark and state of Missouri, in and upon one Golda Hoffeditz, unlawfully, violently, and feloniously, did make an assault, and her, the said Golda Hoffeditz, then and there unlawfully, forcibly, and against her will, feloniously did ravish and carnally know. Contrary to the form of the statutes in such cases made and provided, against the peace and dignity of the state.

"[Signed] Golda Hoffeditz.

"Subscribed and sworn to before me this 17th day of November, 1919.

"[Signed] James M. Wadmore,
"Clerk of the Circuit Court of
Clark County, Missouri."

On December 1, 1919, defendant filed a motion to quash said information, which was overruled by the court. On December 8, 1919, defendant was arraigned, and entered a plea of not guilty. On December 8, 1919, appellant was placed on trial before a jury.

The state's evidence, in a general way, tended to show the following facts:

Prosecutrix, Golda Hoffeditz, 19 years of age, lived with her parents on a farm. Appellant, 22 years of age, lived with his mother on a farm about 2½ miles distant from the said prosecutrix. Both lived in the vicinity of the town of Revere, Clark county, Mo. On the night of August 23, 1919, appellant, in a Ford touring car, took prosecutrix to Farmington, where they attended a picture show. They left Farmington on their trip homeward about 11 o'clock p. m., returning the same route they had gone until they reached the town of Anson, at which place appellant grabbed the wheel and turned into another and different route, which was hilly and not much traveled and on which route there were few or no houses, and which led through, along, and over private ways and a road that was narrow with brush on either side. Here, according to the testimony of prosecutrix, appellant stopped the car, and while in the front part of said car forcibly ravished prosecutrix. He then took prosecutrix to her home, arriving there about 2:30 a. m., August 24th. Here appellant left prosecutrix at the gate, continuing on to his home. When they got to the gate at prosecutrix's home, appellant asked her if he could come back and prosecutrix answered, "Try it if you want to get run off the place." Appellant said if he could not come back he wanted his ring; whereupon prosecutrix returned his ring, received from appellant her ring, and went upstairs and called her mother. She informed her mother of appellant's treatment of her and exhibited her torn and blood-stained clothing and wounds she sustained. When prosecutrix came down stairs to breakfast that morning she made complaint to her father. She did not eat any breakfast. The testimony showed that she had a scratch on her chest, mark across her back and stomach; her arms were red from her wrists to her elbows. There was a mark on her wrist and her knees were discolored. Her private parts bore bruises. Dr. McConnell, the family physician, was called the afternoon of August 24th, and made an examination of prosecutrix. He, in company with Dr. Bridges, made an examination of her later in the day. Dr. McConnell testified that he found a discoloration on her back; that she complained of tenderness of the chest and knees; that he had theretofore treated her for the flu, which left her in a nervous condition; that he saw no discoloration about her private parts that would indicate that anything had happened; that there was some laceration of the female organs and a slight bloody secretion. Dr. Bridges testified that prosecutrix had some marks on her body; that a mark on her knee had begun to discolor; that there was a scratch on her shoulder; that her foot was bruised; that her private parts were tender with the serum mucus coming from the vagina.

Defendant's Evidence.

The testimony on the part of appellant was to the effect that on several occasions shortly preceding the night of August 23, 1919, he had taken prosecutrix to Farmington, sometimes alone with her, at other times in company with his brother and sister of his deceased wife; that on these occasions appellant and prosecutrix would ride with their arms about each other and would stop and "visit" on the way; that on these occasions he would have his arms around prosecutrix, feeling her body; that she would sit in his lap and permit him to hug and kiss her. Appellant admits that on the night of August 23d, in returning home from Farmington, he left the main road at Anson, because it had been freshly worked and made travel thereon difficult. He testified that he and prosecutrix stopped on the way and that he had sexual intercourse with her while he was upon his knees in the front part of the car, but that he did not force her. The testimony further shows that at this time prosecutrix weighed about 93 pounds and appellant about 160 pounds.

Such other parts of the testimony, the instructions, rulings of the court, etc., as may be deemed necessary or important, will be considered in the opinion.

On December 4, 1919, the jury found defendant guilty and assessed his punishment at imprisonment in the penitentiary for 25 years. Defendant, in due time, filed his motions for a new trial and in arrest of judgment. Both motions were overruled, and on the following day the court rendered judgment and passed sentence upon appellant in conformity to the terms of the verdict.

Thereupon defendant duly appealed the cause to this court.

Perry S. Rader, of Jefferson City, and T. L. Montgomery and J. A. Whiteside, both of Kahoka, for appellant.

Jesse W. Barrett, Atty. Gen., and Albert Miller, Asst. Atty. Gen., for the State.

RAILEY, C. (after stating the facts as above). [1] On December 1, 1919, appellant filed his motion to quash the information heretofore set out, upon four grounds, two of which read as follows:

"(1) Because the information is not verified by the prosecuting attorney, or any one else.

"(2) Because the information is not based upon the official oath of the prosecuting attorney. * * *"

The information was not sworn to by either the prosecuting attorney or any other person. It purports, on its face, to be based on the affidavit of Golda Hoffeditz, which contains substantially the same facts as are set out in the information. The affidavit of the prosecutrix, supra, was sworn to and filed with the information. The sufficiency of the latter is properly challenged by the motion to quash. It is strenuously insisted by appellant that the trial court committed reversible error in overruling his motion to quash said information. We will postpone a consideration of this subject until we determine whether it is necessary to reverse and remand the cause for a new trial upon some other ground. If it should become necessary to reverse and remand the case, the subject-matter of above complaint can be obviated by the filing of an amended information covering the foregoing objection.

[2] 2. Appellant assigns as error the action of the court in overruling his challenge as to the qualification of certain jurors to sit in the trial of the case. This proposition, like the preceding one, would not probably arise upon a retrial of the cause, and hence will be postponed until other questions, hereafter mentioned, are determined.

[3] 3. Appellant earnestly contends that with the sanction of the trial court his constitutional and statutory rights were ruthlessly stricken down by counsel employed to assist the state, who compelled him, under the ruling of the court and against his protest, to testify before the jury as to prejudicial matters not brought out or referred to in his examination in chief. We were much impressed with the seriousness and importance of this charge at the oral argument in this court, and will endeavor to set out the substance of the testimony, with the rulings of the court in respect to this matter, while considering same.

While the prosecutrix was upon the stand, the clothes and underclothes which she claims to have worn were produced before the jury, each item identified, some of which were torn, and some had spots on them.

The cross-examination of defendant was conducted by Mr. Hartzell. The first three pages of same, taken literally from the transcript on file, read as follows:

"Q. Do you know how the prosecuting witness got that black and blue mark six inches long and half an inch wide on her back. (Defendant's counsel objects, because this is the defendant and there was no evidence about it in his examination in chief.)

"By the Court: The objection is overruled. (To the overruling of which objection defendant's counsel did then and there at the time duly except and saves herein his exception.)

"Q. Do you know how that black and blue mark on the back of the prosecuting witness, about six inches long and from a half to an inch wide, got there? A. No, sir.

"Q. You don't know how she got that? A. I do not.

"Q. Do you know anything about a scratch on her breast? A. No, sir.

"Q. You don't know how she got that? A. No, sir.

"Q. Do you know about the mark on her foot? A. No, sir.

"Q. Do you know how she got that? A. No, sir.

"Q. Do you know anything about' the mark on her knee? A. No, sir.

"Q. Do you know how she got that? A. No, sir.

"Q. Did you ever see those clothes before? A. Yes, sir.

"Q. Where did you see them last? A. On Goldie Hoffedits. (Defendant's counsel objects, because this is the defendant and was not examined about it.)

"By the Court: The objection is overruled. (To the overruling of which objection defendant's counsel did then and there at the time duly except and saves herein his exception.)

"Q. Look at the garment I now show you as spoken of as the dress of the prosecuting witness; did she have that on that night? A. She did.

"Q. Do you know anything about that hole in the dress? A. No, sir.

"Q. Look at the garment called the skirt; did you see that that night? (Defendant's counsel objects, because this is the defendant and for same reasons.)

"By the Court: The objection is overruled. (To the overruling of which objection defendant's counsel did then and there at the time duly except and saves herein his exception.)

"A. Yes, sir.

"Q. Look at the garment spoken of as the skirt; did you see that that night? (Defendant's counsel objects because this is the defendant, and for same reasons.)

"By the Court: The objection is overruled. (To the overruling of which objection defendant's counsel did then and there at the time duly except and saves herein his exception.)

"A. No, sir.

"Q. Did you know of that condition that night? A. No, sir.

"Q. Did you see it that night. A. No, sir.

"Q. Look at the garment known as the drawers in the record; have you seen that before?

(Defendant's counsel objects, because this is the defendant and for same reasons.)

"By the Court: The objection is overruled. (To the overruling of which objection defendant's counsel did then and there at the time duly except and saves herein his exception.)

"A. No, sir.

"Q. Feel of them and see if you ever felt them that night? (Defendant's counsel objects, because this is the defendant and for same reasons.)

"By the Court: The objection is overruled. (To the overruling of which objection defendant's counsel did then and there at the time duly except and saves herein his exception.)

"A. Yes, sir; I probably did."

Practically all of that part of the cross-examination above quoted, including the clothes exhibited in connection with same, related to matters which had not been brought out or referred to in chief. In addition thereto, the truth of the matters referred to in said questions was assumed, although defendant was standing upon the general issue, and with some evidence contradicting some of the assumed facts. By way of illustration, the first question above quoted reads:

"Q. Do you know how the prosecuting witness got that black and blue mark six inches long and half an inch wide on her back?"

This question improperly related to matters not referred to in chief, and it assumed that the alleged marks upon the body of prosecutrix existed, in the face of the general issue pleaded by defendant.

The evidence in regard to the matters above referred to had been placed before the jury in detail. It is evident from the dramatic way in which the above questions were propounded and the answers obtained, with the sanction of the court, that they were very prejudicial to the rights of defendant, and had much to do with the extent of the punishment in this case. We feel constrained to observe, after reading the above examination, that the questions propounded were intended to browbeat and discredit defendant before the jury, and evidently had the desired effect. The foregoing cross-examination of defendant, in respect to matters not brought out or referred to in his direct examination, was not only prejudicial, but in direct conflict with our organic and statutory law. Section 23 of article 2 of our Constitution; section 4030, R. S. 1919; State v. Drew, 213 S. W. 106, 107; State v. Bowman, 272 Mo. loc. cit. 501, 199 S. W. 161; State v. Goodwin, 271 Mo. loc. cit. 81 and fol., 195 S. W. 725; State v. Swearengin, 269 Mo. loc. cit. 185, 190 S. W. 268; State v. Pfeifer, 267 Mo. loc. cit. 30, 183 S. W. 337; State v. Kyle, 177 Mo. 659, 76 S. W. 1014. The above cross-examination of defendant was not only improper, but the dramatic manner in which the prosecutrix's clothes were paraded before the jury as a part of this improper cross-examination was well calculated to intensify a feeling of prejudice against appellant.

[4] 4. Appellant complains of the ruling of the trial court in refusing to strike out a part of the testimony of Dr. Bridges. The latter testified in chief, at the instance of the state, that he noticed discoloration on some of prosecutrix's clothing. The following then occurred:

"Q. Under your opinion, what made those discolorations on those garments? A. *I thought she had been mistreated.*" (Italics ours.)

The court thereupon overruled defendant's motion to strike out the above answer as simply a conclusion of the witness. While the question, as asked, might properly have been objected to on the ground that the answer of the witness would be an invasion of the province of the jury, yet the defendant was not bound to anticipate that the witness, in answering the question, would, in legal effect, give it as his opinion that defendant had raped the prosecutrix. Under the circumstances, the trial court should have sustained defendant's motion to strike out said answer.

[5] 5. Appellant complains of the action of the court in giving to the jury at the instance of the state instruction numbered 6, which reads as follows:

"*The court instructs the jury that in determining whether or not the defendant forcibly ravished the prosecuting witness you may take into consideration the physical strength, ability, and power of the prosecuting witness and the defendant at the time of the alleged offense, the physical condition of the prosecuting witness, and the condition of her clothing immediately after time it is charged the act complained of was committed,* together with all the testimony and other facts and circumstances in the case." (Italics ours.)

The foregoing instruction is a palpable comment on a portion of the evidence given in behalf of the state. Why should the court emphasize the fact that the jury ought to consider the physical strength of defendant and the prosecutrix, as well as the latter's clothing, etc., leaving in the background the substantial evidence tending to show that the prosecutrix, at the preliminary trial, testified to a different state of facts from what her evidence disclosed at the trial? Why was it necessary for the court to call especial attention to the matters aforesaid, and yet fail to advise the jury to consider the conduct of prosecutrix while with defendant on prior occasions? Instruction 8, given in behalf of defendant, properly advised the jury to consider all the facts in evidence. This was sufficient, without emphasizing the above facts, as indicated in said instruction. The giving of same was not only unfair to defendant and a violation of our statute (section 4088, R. S. 1919), but in contravention of

the law, as declared in numerous decisions of this court, some of which are as follows: State v. Adkins, 225 S. W. loc. cit. 982, 983; State v. Fish, 195 S. W. loc. cit. 998; State v. Malloch, 269 Mo. loc. cit. 239, 190 S. W. 266; State v. Rogers, 253 Mo. loc. cit. 412, 161 S. W. 770; State v. Shaffer, 253 Mo. loc. cit. 337, 161 S. W. 805; State v. Mitchell, 229 Mo. loc. cit. 697, 129 S. W. 917, 138 Am. St. Rep. 425; State v. Rutherford, 152 Mo. loc. cit. 133, 53 S. W. 417; State v. Reed, 137 Mo. loc. cit. 139, 38 S. W. 574; State v. McCanon, 51 Mo. 160.

In State v. Adkins, 225 S. W. loc. cit. 982, 983, we reversed and remanded the cause on account of the giving of an instruction very similar to the one above mentioned.

6. Other matters have been briefed by appellant's counsel, including the validity of the information, etc., but as these questions are not likely to arise on a retrial of the case, we have not deemed it necessary to pass upon same.

On account of the errors heretofore pointed out, the cause is reversed and remanded for a new trial.

WHITE and MOZLEY, CC., concur.

PER CURIAM. The foregoing opinion of RAILEY, C., is hereby adopted as the opinion of the court.

All concur; DAVID E. BLAIR, J., in separate opinion and WALKER, J., in separate opinion, in which DAVID E. BLAIR, J., concurs.

DAVID E. BLAIR, J. (concurring). I am unable to agree with the conclusion reached in paragraph 3 of the majority opinion. In the statement of facts it appears that defendant had testified that he and the prosecutrix stopped on the way home and that he had sexual intercourse with her, but did not force her. With this admission from defendant it was proper to ask defendant for an explanation of the condition of the body of prosecutrix and of the clothing which she testified she wore on the night of the alleged assault. The questions may be objectionable on the ground that they assumed the truth of the matters referred to therein, but no such objections were made thereto by defendant. The objections made were that the various questions were improper cross-examination of the defendant.

Even though the defendant had not been asked in direct examination to explain the condition of prosecutrix and her clothes, if the bruises were received by her and her clothes were torn at the time of the alleged assault, such facts tended strongly to contradict defendant's testimony that prosecutrix willingly yielded to him. As was said in State v. Foley, 247 Mo. loc. cit. 638, 153 S. W. 1019:

"Can he be asked by his counsel 'to tell what happened there,' actually tell part of it, and then take refuge in the statutory privilege? We think not. The state need not categorically follow what was said in his chief examination."

I agree with the conclusions reached in paragraphs 4 and 5 of the majority opinion, and therefore concur in the result reached by the learned Commissioner.

WALKER, J. I concur in the majority opinion with the modification that it should hold that the motion to quash the information was properly overruled. Although neither the affidavit of the prosecuting attorney nor the prosecuting witness was indorsed on the information, the latter alleges that it was based upon the affidavit of the prosecuting witness, which was filed with the clerk and is to the same effect as the information. This procedure constitutes a sufficient compliance with the requirements of sections 3849 and 3850, R. S. 1919, and has met with the approval of this court in State v. Schnettler, 181 Mo. 173, 175, 185, 79 S. W. 1123.

DAVID E. BLAIR, J., concurs herein.

STATE v. NELSON. (No. 22620.)

(Supreme Court of Missouri, Division No. 2. May 26, 1921.)

1. Homicide ⊜⟹309(2)—Evidence held to justify charge of manslaughter.

Evidence from which it could have been found that deceased was killed by a second shot fired after he had retreated some distance justifies a charge on manslaughter, although defendant claimed he fired only one shot and the evidence of the circumstances surrounding the firing of that shot showed that it was either justified or unprovoked, but such instruction, since Acts 1919, p. 256, abolishing all degrees of manslaughter, should be given generally under Rev. St. 1919, § 3236.

2. Homicide ⊜⟹297—Every fact which would justify must be submitted.

In prosecution for homicide, any fact which the evidence tends to show would justify the killing must be submitted to the jury in order to sustain his conviction, even though requests of defendant for submission of such facts were not in proper form.

3. Homicide ⊜⟹300(12)—Failure to charge on self-defense against attack by companions of deceased held error.

Where the evidence showed that deceased and his two companions were acting togther, and that the assault upon defendant, which he claimed as justification for the shooting, was made by one of the companions, it was error to give an instruction on self-defense, which related only to defense against deceased, and did not include the right of defendant to defend himself against an attack by any one of the three companions.

Appeal from Criminal Court, Jackson County; E. E. Porterfield, Judge.

Aaron Nelson was convicted of manslaughter in the fourth degree, and he appeals. Reversed and remanded.

Dickinson & Hillman, of Kansas City, for appellant.

Jesse W. Barrett, Atty. Gen., and Marshall Campbell, Sp. Asst. Atty. Gen., for the State.

WHITE, C. On December 2, 1919, the defendant, a colored man, was put upon his trial charged in the information with murder in the second degree, in that he killed one Walter L. Bell, a white man. The jury, December 3d, found him guilty of manslaughter in the fourth degree, and assessed his punishment at two years in the state penitentiary. He appealed from that judgment.

The defendant was a small lame negro; he kept a low-grade rooming house for Negroes and Mexicans at 305 West Fifth street, in Kansas City, Mo. On the night of June 1, 1919, Walter L. Bell and two companions, Frank Weeks and Alva Bebee, were rounding up the drinking places in Kansas City. They had been drinking at various places, chiefly a species of wine called "Dago Red." This liquor, designated by counsel for defendant as a "moral anæsthetic," possessed a quality which animated the drinker with an immediate and urgent desire for more. About 12:30 that night the three men went up the stairs to the entrance of Nelson's place, and were admitted because Nelson knew Bebee. It appears that Nelson had an arrangement by which he could observe who was coming and admit only his friends. They asked Nelson for wine; he offered them beer. Having partaken of Dago Red, they did not want beer. They were in Nelson's parlor for a few minutes, and what happened there for a time was of little significance, according to the hazy recollection of Bebee and Weeks. They asked Nelson to play some pieces on his Victrola; he played two pieces, and they paid him 10 cents for it. While they were there, according to Weeks, some one reached in from another room, and pulled Bell in there, and Weeks reached in and pulled him back.

After the pieces were played on the Victrola two colored persons came in; Weeks was uncertain whether it was a man and woman or two men. The three then started to leave, impelled to a rather expeditious exit by a gun in Nelson's hand, and pointed toward them. No explanation is given by either Weeks or Bebee as to the cause of Nelson's menacing them with his weapon. He followed them to the head of the stairs as they were starting down with the gun pointing towards them. Bebee had in his hand a quart bottle from which they had emptied the Dago Red before they went up to Nelson's place. With this bottle he struck Nelson over the head, cutting him and shattering the bottle. Nelson then fired down the stairway. The Dutch courage instilled by the potent Dago Red was inadequate to brace them against firearms, and the three fled precipitately down the stairs. They ran, according to Bebee, but "running" according to Weeks was not sufficiently descriptive of the expeditious flight; he said they "fell down the steps." They got to the street and ran west on Fifth street, when another shot was fired and Bell, who was behind, fell to the sidewalk; he was dead when one of the witnesses got to him.

Several witnesses heard the second shot and some testified it came from a window up stairs, and one swore it was fired from the sidewalk at the foot of the stairs. The bullet struck Bell nearly in the center of the back of the neck, at the root of the hair; it passed between the vertebræ and out through the mouth, breaking two upper teeth. There was an abrasion on the forehead, contusions in front of the right ear, and cuts on top of the head. There was a fracture of the skull. The opinion of the physician who made the post mortem was that the bullet passed through the vertebræ and caused almost instant death; that after being wounded the deceased could not have run any distance, but would have collapsed at once. The physician further said the fracture of the skull might have been caused by his fall forward on the sidewalk after he was shot.

Nelson testified that he was in his parlor when the bell rang; he went to the door, and the three men came in and began at once to hit him with the bottle; he always carried a gun at that time of night. He was somewhat stunned by the blows, and fired only once. His pistol was found by the officers hidden behind the piano, and two empty, freshly fired shells were found in it. He admitted that after he had fired he went back in a room and told some girl who was in there that the law would be there soon.

Defendant introduced evidence of several witnesses, who swore that he had a good reputation as a peaceable and law-abiding citizen.

[1] I. Appellant assigns error to the action of the trial court in giving the jury an instruction authorizing a conviction for manslaughter. The argument is that there was an attack with a deadly weapon which justified his firing in self-defense. If his testimony, and the more favorable interpretation of the state's testimony, should be applied, it is argued, it was self-defense or nothing. Any fact which the jury might believe would mitigate the homicide would justify an acquittal. The argument proceeds upon the theory that Bell was hit by the first shot which Nelson sent down the stairs.

The state's evidence tends to show that the fatal shot was fired while the three men were flying down the street after Nelson had run a distance of from 60 to 90 feet from the foot of the stairway, and that it was the second shot which killed him. At that time there was no room whatever for self-defense. The act of 1919 abolished all degrees of manslaughter. Acts of 1919, p. 256; State v. Bird, 228 S. W. 751, loc. cit. 753. On another trial with the same evidence an instruction on manslaughter generally should be given under section 3236, R. S. 1919.

II. Appellant assigns error to the giving of Instruction No. 9, as follows:

"The court instructs the jury that if you find and believe from the evidence that the defendant shot and killed the deceased, and at the time he shot him defendant apprehended, and had reasonable cause to apprehend, that the deceased was about to kill defendant, or to do him some great bodily injury, then he had the right to shoot in his own defense. It is not necessary that the danger should have been actual and about to fall on him, but it is necessary for him to have apprehended it, and that there should have been at the time he shot the deceased reasonable cause for such apprehension. It is for you to say from the evidence in the case whether the defendant did apprehend, and had reasonable cause to apprehend, that such impending harm was about to fall on him at the time he shot. If you find and believe from the evidence that he did not have reasonable cause to apprehend that such danger was impending at the time he shot, then he is not justifiable, his apprehending himself in danger is not sufficient; he must have had reasonable cause to apprehend it, and of that you are to determine from all the facts and circumstances in the case."

It will be noticed that this instruction authorizes an acquittal on the ground of self-defense only if the "defendant apprehended, and had reasonable cause to apprehend, that deceased was about to kill defendant or do him some great bodily injury."

[2] The defendant asked several instructions covering self-defense in which the jury were directed to acquit if the defendant had good reason to believe, and did believe, he was in such danger from any or all of the defendants. These were all refused. Whether these instructions were in proper form we need not consider.

It is said by this court in the case of State v. McBroom, 238 Mo. loc. cit. 499, 141 S. W. 1121:

"In a criminal case every issuable fact necessary to establish the state's case must be submitted to the jury."

Any fact which the evidence tends to show would justify a homicide must be submitted to the jury for determination in order to authorize a conviction. State v. Harris, 232 Mo. loc. cit. 328, 134 S. W. 535; State v. Starr, 244 Mo. loc. cit. 180, 148 S. W. 862; State v. Schmulbach, 243 Mo. loc. cit. 538, 147 S. W. 966. For instance, where a defendant charged with a crime has fled, and there is evidence to show some other cause of the flight than an attempt to escape justice, it is error to give the ordinary instruction on the presumption of the right to flight without considering the qualification of such facts.

[3] In this case the three companions were together, and were acting together, and the assault upon the defendant was made by Bebee and not Bell. From the evidence it is possible to infer that the first shot was the fatal one. The instruction should have incorporated a direction that if the jury found the three persons, or any one of them, assaulted the defendant, and he believed, and had reasonable cause to believe, they or either of them was about to kill him or do him great bodily injury, he had a right to shoot in self-defense. This precise question was passed upon by this court in the case of State v. Adler, 146 Mo. 18, loc. cit. 23, 24, 25, 47 S. W. 794. Under that authority the Attorney General confesses error.

Other errors are assigned to the action of the court in the conduct of the trial which we deem it unnecessary to review, because the same incidents probably would not occur in another trial.

The judgment is reversed, and the cause remanded.

RAILEY and MOZLEY, CC., concur.

PER CURIAM. The foregoing opinion by WHITE, C., is adopted as the opinion of the court.

All the Judges concur.

STATE v. McBRIDE. (No. 22656.)

(Supreme Court of Missouri, Division No. 2. May 26, 1921.)

1. Indictment and information ☞30 — Indictment for larceny not insufficient as to return by grand jury, etc.

An indictment for larceny of an automobile, having the proper recitals and charging the offense in the language of the statute defining grand larceny (Rev. St. 1919, § 3312), being signed in due form by the prosecuting attorney, as required by section 3888, and indorsed a true bill by the foreman of the grand jury, in accordance with section 3882, is not insufficient for lack of showing it was returned by a lawfully constituted grand jury and that it was not signed by the foreman.

2. Indictment and information ☞193 — Irregularity in indictment for larceny cured by statute of jeofails.

If there was any irregularity in an indictment for larceny of an automobile or failure to state that the grand jury had been regularly impaneled for the county, it was cured by the statute of jeofails (Rev. St. 1919, § 3908).

3. Witnesses ☞350 — Defendant subject to cross-examination to prove prior convictions.

Despite Rev. St. 1919, § 4036, limiting cross-examination of defendant to matters referred to in his examination in chief, etc., under section 5439, a defendant who takes the stand in his own behalf is subject to cross-examination to prove prior convictions of criminal offenses to affect his credibility, and it is proper to show what crime he has been convicted of as well as the mere fact of conviction.

4. Criminal law ☞723(3) — Argument of prosecuting attorney referring to prevalence of particular crime, etc., not error.

In a prosecution for larceny of an automobile, it was not error for the prosecuting attorney, in argument to the jury, to refer to the prevalence of the particular crime, and to urge the jury to do their duty with that in view, and to argue that it would be a reflection on them to fail to convict and assess the maximum punishment under the evidence before them.

5. Criminal law ☞713 — Arguments of prosecuting attorney referred to and based on evidence legitimate.

The prosecuting attorney's statements to the jury in argument, whether he characterizes defendant, the quality of his crime, or urges the jury to do their duty, are always legitimate when referred to and based upon the evidence before the jury.

6. Criminal law ☞875(3) — Verdict under indictment finding defendant guilty as charged in information not error.

In a prosecution under an indictment, verdict finding defendant guilty as charged in the information was not error.

7. Larceny ☞77(2) — Instruction in relation to recent possession of stolen property sustained by evidence.

In a prosecution for larceny of an automobile, instruction in relation to the recent possession of stolen property held sustained by evidence.

Appeal from Criminal Court, Jackson County; E. E. Porterfield, Judge.

John McBride was convicted of grand larceny, and he appeals. Judgment affirmed.

Bellemere & Langsdale, of Kansas City, for appellant.

Jesse W. Barrett, Atty. Gen., and Robert J. Smith, Asst. Atty. Gen., for the State.

WHITE, C. The appellant was convicted in the criminal court of Jackson county of grand larceny. He was charged with having stolen, August 4, 1919, a Ford automobile of the value of $500, the property of W. C. Eldridge.

The evidence for the state showed that Monday, August 4, 1919, Eldridge owned a Ford automobile, for which he had paid $585 a month before. On that date he parked his car at Electric Park, in Kansas City, about 8:30 p. m. He returned an hour later and found his car gone. He next saw the car on August 9th, at Lawrence, Kan., where he identified it and took it away. He identified it as his car by a number of articles he had left under the back seat, besides the regular kit of tools that came with the car. He also identified it by appliances he had attached to it; a switch on the dash, a coil lock, wiring for the tail light, a cut-out, and other things. When he recovered the car the city license plate was absent; the motor number on the car had been changed.

The undersheriff at Lawrence, Kan., arrested the defendant with the car. The defendant gave his address as Kansas City, and his name as William Hunter; the jailer booked him by that name. He said he had worked for the Metropolitan Street Railway. He exhibited a bill of sale dated the 6th day of August, 1919, whereby one C. V. Emery sold and assigned the automobile to William Hunter. He said he left Kansas City after the bill of sale was made. The defendant claimed to own the property, but made no attempt to retain it or recover possession after it was taken from him by the sheriff. He attempted an alibi. Some relatives of his wife testified that he was visiting his wife's sister at a farm near Lawrence, Kan., on Sunday and Monday, August 3 and 4, 1919, and remained there until 10:30 at night, Monday, August 4th, which would cover the time at which the automobile disappeared.

Defendant also introduced witnesses to prove they saw him purchase the automobile in Kansas City, August 6th. He denied that he gave his name as William Hunter, but testified that he knew a man by that name; that William Hunter was a motorman on the Roanoke line; that the bill of sale from Emery to Hunter, which was offered in evidence, was in Hunter's possession when the defendant bought from Hunter the automobile in question. Neither Hunter nor Emery was produced at the trial. Defendant explained that on Friday before the Monday on which the car is said to have been stolen he met a man in Kansas City with a Ford car for sale. The man told him he was going to St. Joseph and would return and let him have it for $500 when he came back, if in the meantime he did not sell it. He said he would be back Tuesday, August 5th. Tuesday morning the defendant arrived in Kansas City and Hunter showed up with the car; he paid Hunter $500 for it and the trade was concluded the next day, the 6th, by the

231 S.W.—38

delivery of the car and the bill of sale. The defendant explained that he had the money in his pocket to pay for it, some of which he obtained from his wife and the rest he had carried.

The jury returned a verdict of guilty and assessed the defendant's punishment at three years' imprisonment in the penitentiary. From that judgment he appealed. He has filed no brief, and we have recourse to the motion for new trial to find if any errors have been committed and preserved for review.

[1] I. It is claimed that the indictment is insufficient, in that it is not shown it was returned by a lawfully constituted grand jury, and that it was not signed by the foreman. The indictment has the proper recitals, and charges the offense in the language of the statute defining grand larceny (section 3312, R. S. 1919). It is signed in due form by the prosecuting attorney (section 3885, R. S. 1919), and indorsed "a true bill" by the foreman of the grand jury, in accordance with section 3882, R. S. 1919. State v. Campbell, 210 Mo. loc. cit. 215, 109 S. W. 706, 14 Ann. Cas. 403.

[2] We cannot discover in the indictment any irregularity or failure to state that the grand jury had been regularly impaneled for Jackson county. If there was such irregularity, it was entirely cured by the statute of jeofails (section 3908, R. S. 1919).

[3] II. The defendant while on the witness stand testified that he had served a term in the Missouri state penitentiary at Jefferson City. On cross-examination the state's attorney asked him what he was in the state penitentiary for. This was objected to; objection overruled and exception saved. The witness stated he was in for grand larceny. The state's attorney then asked him what he was in Sing Sing prison in the state of New York for. Defendant denied that he ever was in Sing Sing. To this question the defendant's attorney objected, and, after the arguments of some length which followed, the court overruled the objection and the state's attorney changed the form of his question and asked the defendant if he had served a term of three years in the state prison at Sing Sing, N. Y., for robbery. Defendant answered in the negative. To all this there was objection and exception.

Section 5439, R. S. 1919, provides that any person who has been convicted of a criminal offense is a competent witness, but the conviction may be proved to affect his credibility, either by the record or by his own cross-examination. This section repeatedly has been held to apply to a defendant who takes the stand in his own behalf, notwithstanding the provision of section 4036, which limits the cross-examination of defendant to matters referred to in his examination in chief, but provides that a defendant in such case "may be contradicted and impeached as any other witness in the case." State v. Howe, 228 S. W. loc. cit. 479; State v. Spivey, 191 Mo. loc. cit. 111, 90 S. W. 81; State v. Sovern, 225 Mo. loc. cit. 591, 125 S. W. 769; State v. Corrigan, 262 Mo. 209, 171 S. W. 51; State v. Johnson, 192 S. W. loc. cit. 442.

If the defendant may be impeached as any other witness, it is not only proper to show that he had been convicted but to show of what crime he had been convicted. If the prosecutor knew or had information that the defendant had served a term in the penitentiary of New York, it was entirely proper for him to ask the witness about it, although he may not have had a record of such conviction in a form to be admissible in contradiction of the witness. He took his chance on that. We cannot infer, because he failed to produce the record after the defendant denied his conviction, that the question was not asked in good faith. The question of the prosecutor, when he asked the witness what he had served in Sing Sing for, was improper as assuming that the defendant had been in the penitentiary. The objection, however, was not to the form of the question but to the substance, and we cannot say the defendant was harmed by the question, since it only tended to elicit the same answer that the succeeding question brought. He had the advantage of his denial, and in the argument had the advantage of the failure of the state to attempt to contradict him in regard to it. There was no reversible error in the cross-examination.

[4, 5] III. In his closing argument the prosecuting attorney, Mr. Lee, used this language:

"I said any automobile thief that comes into this courtroom could get on the witness stand; * * * if you should come down here with testimony such as has been given in this case and lay it before a jury of 12 men and they brought in a verdict of not guilty, wouldn't you be ashamed of that jury?"

The prosecutor then urged the jury to fix the maximum punishment, and used this language:

"I say nothing will stop the stealing of automobiles in this community until jurors will go out in the jury room and be bold enough, when the testimony warrants it, to write a verdict assessing the maximum punishment, and you are demonstrating you are good citizens and believe in the enforcement of the law when you do that."

It is not error for the prosecutor, in his argument to the jury, to refer to the prevalence of crime and urge the jury to do their duty with that in view, and argue that it would be a reflection upon them to fail to convict under the evidence before them. State v. Sherman, 264 Mo. loc. cit. 385, 175 S. W. 73; State v. Banks, 258 Mo. loc. cit. 493, 167 S. W. 505; State v. Rogers, 253 Mo. 399, loc. cit. 415, 161 S. W. 770; State v. Hyland, 144 Mo. loc. cit. 313, 46 S. W. 195; State v. Elvins, 101 Mo. loc. cit. 246, 13 S. W. 937; State v. Zumbunson, 86 Mo. loc. cit. 113.

From the cases cited it appears that that sort of argument is not error, whether the prevalence of crime appears from the evidence or is a matter of common knowledge in a community. We are unable to find any authority which says that a prosecutor may not urge the jury to fix the maximum punishment where he believes the evidence would warrant it. The prosecuting attorney's statements to the jury in his argument, whether he characterizes the defendant, the quality of his crime, or urges the jury to do their duty in the case, are always legitimate when referred to and based upon the evidence before the jury, as was the argument in this case.

[6] IV. The prosecution was on an indictment. The verdict of the jury as set out in the bill of exceptions finds the defendant guilty of grand larceny as charged in the "information." This is assigned as error in the motion for new trial. This same form of verdict returned upon a like indictment has been held without error by this court because in no way prejudicial. State v. Taylor, 261 Mo. loc. cit. 223, 224, 168 S. W. 1191.

[7] V. No feature of the instruction is lacking so far as the counsel for defendant has pointed out in his motion for new trial. The jury was fully instructed as to the presumption of innocence, reasonable doubt, and the defendant's attempted alibi. The usual instruction in relation to the recent possession of stolen property was fully sustained by the evidence as set out above. The instruction gave the defendant the benefit of any explanation he might produce of his possession, which was admitted.

Finding no error in the record, the judgment is affirmed.

RAILEY, and MOZLEY, CC., concur.

PER CURIAM. The foregoing opinion by WHITE, C., is adopted as the opinion of the court.

All the Judges concur.

STATE v. PEARSON. (No. 22585.)

Supreme Court of Missouri, Division No. 2.
May 26, 1921.)

. **Criminal law ⟲273—Plea of guilty confesses only truth of fact stated in information,
not guilt of violation of statute against offense charged.**

By his plea of guilty defendant charged with
illegal voting confessed only the truth of the
facts stated in the information; the plea did
not involve a plea of guilty of violation of the
statute against illegal voting unless the information correctly charged commission of such
crime, and defendant can take advantage of
any defect in the information by appeal or on
writ of error.

2. **Elections ⟲328(2)—Information failed to
charge illegal voting in violation of statute.**

Information that defendant falsely applied
for and received a ballot and cast it at the
election without having a lawful right to vote in
the township, in that he was not then and there
a resident and qualified voter in such election
precinct of such township in such county, and
was not then and there a citizen of the county
for a period of a year before the day of the
election, which he knew, did not charge a violation of R. S. 1919, § 3209, in that defendant
voted at an election when he was not a qualified
voter, in view of Const. art. 8, § 2, defining
the residence necessary for a qualified voter,
and Rev. St. 1919, § 4748, requiring that a
voter shall reside in the state one year and
in the county at least 60 days preceding election, etc.

Error to Circuit Court, Pemiscot County;
Sterling H. McCarty, Judge.

Isaac Pearson was convicted of illegal voting, and he brings error. Judgment reversed, and defendant discharged.

C. G. Shepard, of Caruthersville, for plaintiff in error.

Jesse W. Barrett, Atty. Gen., and Albert
Miller, Asst. Atty. Gen., for the State.

WHITE, C. On information filed November 14, 1920, in the circuit court of Pemiscot county, defendant was charged with illegal voting on the 2d day of November, 1920.
On the 17th of November, at the same term
of court, the defendant appeared in person
in court, waived arraignment, pleaded guilty to the information as charged, and his
punishment was fixed at two years' imprisonment in the penitentiary. Afterwards a writ
of error was sued out in this court by the
defendant.

[1] I. By his plea of guilty the defendant
confessed only the truth of the facts stated
in the information. It did not involve a plea
of guilty of violation of the statute against
illegal voting unless the information correctly charged the commission of that crime.
He could take advantage of any defect in the
information by appeal or by writ of error.
State v. Kelley, 206 Mo. loc. cit. 693, 105 S. W.

606, 12 Ann. Cas. 681; State v. Reppley, 278
Mo. loc. cit. 339, 213 S. W. 477.

[2] II. The information charged that on the
—— day of November, 1920, while an election was being held in Virginia township,
Pemiscot county, state of Missouri (setting
out the different offices, national, state, and
county, for which the election was being
held), the defendant appeared at polling precinct No. 1 of Virginia township, of Pemiscot
county, falsely applied for and received a
ballot, and cast said ballot at said election.
Then the information states the offense thus:

"Without having a lawful right to vote therein, in this, to wit, that he, the said Isaac Pearson, was not then and there a resident and
qualified voter in said election precinct of said
township in said county, and was not then and
there a citizen of Pemiscot county, Mo., for a
period of one year before the date of said
election, all of which the said Isaac Pearson
then and there well knew."

Apparently the information attempts to
charge an offense in violation of section 3209,
R. S. 1919, in that he knowingly voted at an
election when he was not a qualified voter.
Section 2, art. 8, of the Missouri Constitution,
defines the residence necessary for a qualified
voter. First, he shall have resided in the
state for one year, and in the county, city, or
town where he offers to vote at least 60 days,
immediately preceding the election. Section
4748, R. S. 1919, requires that a voter shall
reside in the state one year, and in the county 60 days, immediately preceding the election, "and shall vote only in the township
in which he resides, or, if in a town or city,
then in the election district therein in which
he resides." It will be noticed that the information does not charge that Pearson was
not a resident of the state one year' next
before the election, but that he was not a
resident of Pemiscot county. A voter is not
required to be a resident of the county for
more than 60 days. It further says that he
was not a resident at the time "in said election precinct in said Virginia township."
The statute does not require that he shall
live in the precinct in which he voted, but
only that he shall vote in the township in
which he resides. The information fails to
charge that defendant was an illegal voter
either in not having resided in the state for
the requisite time, or in the county for the
requisite time, or in failing to reside in the
township in which he sought to vote. The
information therefore charges no offense.

The judgment is reversed, and the defendant discharged.

RAILEY and MOZLEY, CC., concur.

PER CURIAM. The foregoing opinion by
WHITE, C., is adopted as the opinion of the
court.

All concur.

⟲For other cases see same topic and KEY-NUMBER in all Key-Numbered Digests and Indexes

STATE v. HENDERSON. (No. 22684.)

(Supreme Court of Missouri, Division No. 2.
May 26, 1921.)

Receiving stolen goods ⬅3—Knowledge of information leading reasonably prudent man to believe property to be stolen not sufficient guilty knowledge.

The knowledge by person receiving stolen property of such facts as would put a reasonably prudent man exercising ordinary caution on his guard, or such as would cause such a man exercising such caution, under the circumstances, to believe that the property had been stolen, will not supply the knowledge that property was stolen necessary to a conviction for receiving stolen property.

Appeal from St. Louis Circuit Court; Wilson A. Taylor, Judge.

Devereaux Henderson was convicted of receiving stolen property knowing it to have been stolen, and he appeals. Reversed and remanded.

Edward J. McCullen and Edward W. Foristel, both of St. Louis, for appellant.

Jesse W. Barrett, Atty. Gen., and Albert Miller, Asst. Atty. Gen. (R. W. Otto, of Union, of counsel), for the State.

WHITE, C. The appeal is from a judgment, upon conviction, in the circuit court of the city of St. Louis, of receiving stolen property knowing it to be stolen.

One Adolph Kroner, of Kansas City, on July 28, 1917, was the owner of a Buick automobile which on that day was stolen from where it stood in front of the Union Depot. Subsequently the car, identified by the motor number, was in possession of the defendant in St. Louis, and sold by him to one H. A. Woerman. Defendant claimed he bought the car in St. Louis from a man named King. A large volume of evidence appears, offered by the state, to show the defendant's guilty knowledge which evidence it is unnecessary to review.

The only point urged here for reversal is the giving by the court of the following instruction:

"By the term 'knowing' that the property was stolen is not meant absolute personal and certain knowledge on the part of the defendant that the property mentioned in the indictment had been stolen, but such knowledge and information in his possession at the time he received the same, if you believe he did receive it, as would put a reasonably prudent man, exercising ordinary caution, on his guard, and would cause such a man, exercising such caution, and under circumstances which you believe defendant received the property, to believe and be satisfied that the property had been stolen. The mere naked fact of the possession of said property by the defendant raises no presumption that the defendant knew that said property had been stolen by another."

An instruction of which the above is an exact copy was condemned by this court as reversible error in a similar case. State v. Ebbeller, 222 S. W. loc. cit. 397. The ruling in that case has been approved and followed in several later cases.

The judgment is reversed, and the cause remanded.

RAILEY and MOZLEY, CC., concur.

PER CURIAM. The foregoing opinion by WHITE, C., is adopted as the opinion of the court.

All concur.

STATE v. WILSON. (No. 22665.)

(Supreme Court of Missouri, Division No. 2.
May 26, 1921.)

1. Homicide ⬅127—Information for murder held sufficient.

An information for murder in the conventional form and properly verified held to fully state the facts and not subject to attack.

2. Criminal law ⬅1038(3)—Defendant not requesting instructions cannot complain of those given which properly declared the law.

Where the instructions given properly declared the law of the case, and no additional declarations of law were requested, defendant had no valid ground of complaint in regard to the instructions.

3. Criminal law ⬅1159(2)—Not province of Supreme Court to pass upon weight of evidence.

It is not the province of the Supreme Court to pass upon the weight of the evidence, but only to ascertain whether the party charged with crime has been fairly and properly tried, and, if convicted, whether there is substantial evidence tending to sustain the conviction.

4. Homicide ⬅254—Evidence sufficient to support conviction for killing in hold-up.

Evidence held sufficient to support defendant's conviction for murder in the second degree in killing a Chinese laundryman in a hold-up in the laundry.

Appeal from Circuit Court, Jackson County; E. E. Porterfield, Judge.

Lewis Wilson was convicted of murder in the second degree, and he appeals. Affirmed.

The information was as follows:

"Now comes Hunt C. Moore, prosecuting attorney for the state of Missouri, in and for the body of the county of Jackson, and upon his oath informs the court that Lewis Wilson, whose Christian name in full is unknown to said prosecuting attorney, late of the county aforesaid, on the 16th day of April, 1919, at the county of Jackson, state of Missouri, in and upon one Charlie Wing, then and there being feloniously, wilfully, premeditatedly, on purpose and of his malice aforethought did make an assault, and a certain revolving pistol, which was then and there loaded with gunpowder and leaden bullets, and by him the said Lewis Wilson in his hands then and there had and held, he, the said Lewis Wilson, did then and there feloniously, wilfully, premeditatedly, on purpose and of his malice aforethought, discharge and shoot off at, upon, and against him the said Charlie Wing, and he, the said Lewis Wilson, with the leaden bullets aforesaid out of the pistol aforesaid then and there, by force of the gunpowder aforesaid, by the said Lewis Wilson shot off and discharged as aforesaid, then and there, feloniously, wilfully, premeditatedly, on purpose, and of his malice aforethought, did strike, penetrate, and wound the said Charlie Wing in and upon the body of him, the said Charlie Wing, thus and thereby then and there feloniously, wilfully, premeditatedly, on purpose, and of his malice aforethought, giving to him, the said Charlie Wing, with the leaden bullets aforesaid, so as aforesaid discharged and shot off out of the pistol aforesaid, by the said Lewis Wilson, one mortal wound, of which said mortal wound the said Charlie Wing on the said 16th day of April, in the year aforesaid, the said Charlie Wing at the county of Jackson and state of Missouri, died; and so the prosecuting attorney aforesaid, upon his oath aforesaid, in the manner and by the means aforesaid, feloniously, wilfully, premeditatedly, on purpose, and of his malice aforethought, did kill and murder, against the peace and dignity of the state."

On May 26, 1919, the prosecuting attorney of Jackson County, Mo., filed, in the criminal court of said county, a verified information, in which defendant was charged with feloniously killing one Charlie Wing, on the 16th day of April, 1919, in the county and state aforesaid, with a revolving pistol loaded with gunpowder and leaden bullets.

On May 31, 1919, defendant was arraigned and entered a plea of not guilty.

On defendant's application a change of venue was awarded and the cause transferred to division 2 of the criminal court of said county.

On September 15, 1919, the trial of defendant was commenced before a jury.

State's Evidence.

The evidence on the part of the state shows substantially the following facts: That Charlie Wing, a Chinaman, whose name in the Chinese language was Chen Young Shung, was, at the time of his death, about 78 years of age, and was the owner of a laundry at 20 East Missouri avenue, in Kansas City, Mo.; that his brother, Harry Wing, whose Chinese name is Chin Me Shung, was working with him at the laundry on the 16th day of April, 1919, the day of the killing; that deceased was working in a rear room in the laundry, and his brother was working in the front room; that about 9:30 to 10 o'clock at night two negroes came into the front room, and one of them grabbed hold of Harry Wing from behind, and the latter screamed; that deceased came out of the back room, and appellant, who had grabbed Harry Wing, shot and killed Charlie Wing; that after the shot was fired deceased kept going towards appellant, traveling 13 or 14 feet; that appellant hit him four or five times before going away; that Harry Wing recognized the appellant in the room that night; that he had been there before to borrow some money; that Harry Wing recognized defendant as the man who shot and killed Charlie Wing; that he recognized him by his size, by a scar on his face, and by the color of his clothing; that defendant came back to the laundry a few days after the killing; that Harry Wing then saw him, again recognized him, and went to find some one who could speak English, in order to have him arrested.

A Chinese association of Kansas City, Mo., offered a reward of $500 for the conviction of the man who did the killing.

The testimony of Harry Wing was given to the court and jury through an interpreter named Willie Toi.

Defendant's Evidence.

Appellant testified, in substance, that he had lived in Kansas City ever since 1898; that he was a common laborer, enlisted in the army in 1911, and was discharged in 1914; that he was taken into the army under the Selective Draft Act (U. S. Comp. St. 1918, U. S. Comp. St. Ann. Supp. 1919, §§ 2044a–2044k); that he had never been convicted of any offense; that he never, on the night of April 16, 1919, or at any other time, entered the laundry of a couple of Chinamen on Missouri avenue, and held them up or attempted to hold them up; that he had nothing to do with the hold-up of that place, or the shooting of the Chinaman, and knew nothing about it; that he knew the women who worked at the laundry, Bertha Davis, Mollie King, and a girl named Gussie; that on the evening of the hold-up, April 16, 1919, he was at 1219 Baltimore avenue, helping a fellow in a cigar store and pool hall whose name was Turner Brown; that he commenced work that day about 5:30 to 6 o'clock, and worked until 12 or 12:30 at night; that he, Turner Brown, and Lackey then walked to Walnut street; that he (defendant) caught a car and went east; that Brown caught a Vine street car; that he (defendant) lived at 923 Michigan street, and had lived there about two months; that he worked at the pool hall when he did not have a steady job; that when arrested he was working at the Albany Hotel, Ninth and Charlotte, and had been working there about two weeks; that he heard about the killing of the Chinaman the next day; that after he heard of the killing

he was eu ʝ ʋ big ye   n cross-exami
s; that after this he went down to   defendant was li
y and paid the girl the dollar he   Gussie May H
  that she told him Charlie got   that she was wo
he told her he saw it in the paper;   day of killing; t
d been down at the laundry about   told her the nex
)efore the killing; that he had been two big yellow
sands of times before the killing,   up, and shot his
ə worked at Armour's, knew the   big negro, but is
walked by there; that he knew   Henry Jerden,
vis, Mollie King, and Gussie; that   half of defendant
ed money from the girls, but not   he knew nothin
~hinaman; that he went down to   that the purporte
·y the next evening after the kill-   is not true; that
aw the brother of deceased there   the alleged stater
e; that he and the brother spoke;   Mr. Wasson, said
·itness) had a heavy scar on his   jury. It states,
it had been there some time;   Jerden is 24 yea
s there two years before the trial;   1919, shortly.aft
  Payne owned the barber shop,   to his house, and
endant was working and Turner   spotted out," and
s manager.   go out with Alfr
amination defendant testified that   that Jerden unde
tes he could go out and get 100   somebody, and s∢
rsons who have scars on one or   that he met thes
of their necks.   they went to the
  rown testified, in substance, that 20 East Missoui
6, 1919, he was manager of the   that Clark staye
ınd cigar stand at 1219 Baltimore   went inside with
hat he knew defendant, and the   pulled out his gui
ked for him when he was not em-   to "throw up the
where; that he usually commenced   ran into a back
t 5:30 to 6 o'clock, and worked   ducked behind a
12 o'clock at night; that he took   as the latter rai
his home, with defendant, after   he (Jerden) ran
up on the night of the killing.   Carr any more u
examination witness testified that   he came to Jerd

"We, the jury, find the defendant guilty of murder in the second degree, as charged in the information, and assess his punishment at ten years in the state penitentiary."

Defendant, in due time, filed motions for a new trial and in arrest of judgment. Both motions were overruled.

While matters stood in this shape it was agreed between counsel for the state and for the defendant, with the consent of the trial court, that the records and proceedings in the case of State v. Jerden, charged with killing Charlie Wing on April 16, 1919, should be incorporated as part of the bill of exceptions in the Wilson Case. The record in the Jerden Case shows that he was convicted for the murder of Charlie Wing aforesaid, and that no appeal was taken by him. Defendant Wilson, in due time, after sentence was pronounced and judgment entered upon the verdict aforesaid, appealed to this court.

Kimbrell & Wofford, of Kansas City, Mo., for appellant.

Jesse W. Barrett, Atty. Gen., and Robert J. Smith, Asst. Atty. Gen., for the State.

RAILEY, C. (after stating the facts as above). [1] 1. The information in this case is in the conventional form, properly verified by the oath of the prosecuting attorney, states the facts very fully, and is not subject to attack. State v. Taylor, 190 S. W. 330; State v. Conley, 255 Mo. loc. cit. 194, 195, 164 S. W. 193; State v. Clay, 201 Mo. loc. cit. 681, 100 S. W. 439; State v. Privitt, 175 Mo. 224, 75 S. W. 457; State v. Rice, 149 Mo. loc. cit. 466, 51 S. W. 78.

[2] 2. The court gave eight instructions to the jury, numbered from 1 to 8, inclusive. While all of them were formally objected to by counsel for appellant, yet no specific objection was made to either in the trial court, nor does any specific objection appear in the record before us. We have carefully read and considered each of said instructions. They presented fully and fairly to the jury the law necessary to guide the latter in passing upon the merits of the case. We are of the opinion that the instructions given properly declared the law of the case, and, as no additional declarations of law were requested, appellant has no valid ground of complaint in respect to the instructions.

3. Upon a careful reading of the entire record we find no adverse rulings of which defendant can legally complain. On the contrary, both the trial court and prosecuting attorney treated him with the utmost fairness during the trial, excluded no part of his material testimony, and no remarks were made by either the court or prosecuting attorney which, in any manner, created a prejudice against appellant. We therefore find no error in the record, relating to the trial, of which defendant can legally complain.

4. After the motion for a new trial and in arrest of judgment had been overruled, counsel for defendant, with the consent of the trial court and prosecuting attorney, was permitted to incorporate as a part of the bill of exceptions herein the record and proceedings in the case of State v. Jerden, tried in the same court, in which the defendant therein was convicted of the murder of Charlie Wing on April 16, 1919, and no appeal taken from the judgment of conviction. We know of no precedent for this mode of procedure and are not fully advised as to its purpose. From a purely humanitarian viewpoint, however, regardless of either law or precedent on the subject, we have, with great care, read all the records and proceedings in both cases.

[3] As we have often said it is not the province of this court to pass upon the weight of the evidence. We are only concerned to the extent of ascertaining whether the party charged with crime has been fairly and properly tried, and, if convicted, whether there is substantial evidence tending to sustain the conviction.

[4] In this case Harry Wing, one of the parties "held up" positively identified defendant Wilson as the negro who shot and killed his brother, Charlie Wing, at the laundry on April 16, 1919. He knew defendant before the shooting, as the latter admitted he had been to the laundry a great many times and had met Harry Wing. In addition to the foregoing, Harry Wing identified defendant as the man who killed his brother by the scar on his face, by his size, and color. The defendant admitted he had such a scar, and the evidence shows he was a large man. Harry Wing also testified as a witness in the case against Jerden, and gave substantially the same evidence as he did in this case. We have no hesitation in holding that defendant was convicted upon substantial evidence. He has received an exceedingly fair trial, free from prejudice, and we find no legal grounds for disturbing the verdict. The judgment below is accordingly affirmed.

WHITE and MOZLEY, CC., concur.

PER CURIAM. The foregoing opinion of RAILEY, C., is hereby adopted as the opinion of the court. All concur.

In re BOWARD'S ESTATE.

LIBBY v. BOWARD.

(No. 22097.)

(Supreme Court of Missouri, Division No. 2.
May 26, 1921.)

1. Homestead ⟨⟩135—Rights of parties must
be determined by law in force at time of
homestead owner's death.

The rights of all the parties interested in
a decedent's homestead, his administrator, his
son, and his creditor, must be determined by
the law in force on the date of decedent's
death.

2. Homestead ⟨⟩134—Title to homestead vested in heirs of decedent free from payment
of debts contracted after it was acquired.

Under Rev. St. 1899, § 3620, when a decedent died on August 8, 1900, title to his homestead real estate at the time became vested in
his heir or heirs, subject to the homestead
right of the widow and minor children, free
from the payment of debts contracted after the
homestead was acquired.

Appeal from Circuit Court, Linn County;
Fred Lamb, Judge.

In the matter of the estate of C. F. Boward, deceased, wherein O. F. Libby, as administrator, petitioned for order of sale of
certain homestead property to pay a claim,
H. W. Boward contesting. From an order
of sale, contestant appealed to the circuit
court, which sustained the order, and contestant appeals. Reversed without remand.

Both counsel for appellant and respondent
have filed clear and intelligent statements in
this court, and there appears to be no disagreement between them as to the facts. We
accordingly adopt respondent's statement,
which reads as follows:

"Charles F. Boward died intestate in Linn
county, Mo., on August 8, 1900, leaving surviving him Sophrona E. Boward, his widow,
and one minor son, H. W. Boward, the appellant herein, and seized and possessed of a
house and lot in the city of Brookfield, in said
Linn county, which premises then as well as
now were of about the value of $1,000. The
title to said premises was acquired, and the
deed thereto recorded some time prior to the
death of said Boward. From the time said
premises were acquired and up to the time of
the death of said Boward, he, with his wife
and minor son, occupied the same as a homestead, and after his death the same passed to
and was occupied as a homestead by the widow
and minor son until the son attained his legal
majority, and thereafter by the widow until her
death, which occurred in August, 1918. After
the homestead was acquired and the deed thereto recorded, the said Charles F. Boward became indebted to one Con Yagel, which indebtedness was still outstanding and unpaid at the
time of the death of said Boward in the year
1900.

"After the death of said Boward, the respondent herein, O. F. Libby, was by the probate court of Linn county, Mo., appointed administrator of the estate of the deceased, duly
qualified, and since which time has been, and
is now, so acting. The administrator upon assuming the duties of his office ascertained that
the deceased left no personal estate except his
household goods and furniture, which were
claimed by the widow and were turned over to
her as her absolute property. It was also ascertained by the administrator that the said
Boward owned no real estate at the time of his
death except the house and lot which was then
his homestead.

"The debt due from the deceased to the said
Con Yagel, was duly presented to and allowed
by the probate court as a demand against the
estate of said deceased and assigned to the
fifth class of demands. There were no other
debts or demands allowed against said estate.
The administrator believed that under the
homestead law then in force (Session Laws of
1895, p. 185; section 3620, R. S. Mo. 1899)
the sale of said property to pay said allowed
demand would have to be postponed until the
minor reaching his majority and the death of
the widow.

"The widow died at Linn county, Mo., in August, 1918, and the son, who is the appellant
herein, having become 21 years of age some
years prior to the death of his mother, the
homestead interest in said premises was thereby terminated, and soon thereafter the administrator filed his petition in the probate court
for an order of sale of said real estate for the
purpose of paying the demand of Yagel. The
petition for the sale was duly sustained, and
the sale ordered by the probate court. From
this order the said H. W. Boward appealed to
the circuit court of Linn county, Mo., and upon a hearing of the matter in that court the
order of sale made by the probate court was
in all things sustained, and the appellant brings
the case to this court by appeal. It is conceded
by the appellant that the proceedings in the
probate court for the sale were in all respects
regular and are not called in question."

Letters of administration were granted to
Mr. Libby by the probate court of Linn county, Mo., on September 13, 1905.

The demand of Con Yagel was allowed in
the probate court on December 13, 1905, for
$428.55.

A petition for the sale of the property in
controversy was filed in the probate court of
Linn county, Mo., at the November adjourned
term, 1918. The order of sale was made by
the probate court on February 24, 1919.

Appellant alleges in his statement that no
question arises as to the regularity of the
proceedings, and all the facts are admitted
in the record, so that there is presented on
this appeal but two questions: First. Was
the claim so stale as to preclude the order
of sale? Second. Did the property which was
the homestead of Charles F. Boward in his
lifetime upon the death of his widow become

subject to the payment of his debts or immediately pass to his son, Henry F. Boward?

Judgment was entered in behalf of respondent on June 25, 1919. Defendant in due time filed motions for a new trial and in arrest of judgment. Both motions were overruled, and the cause duly appealed by him to this court.

Bailey & Hart, of Brookfield, for appellant.

C. C. Bigger and O. F. Libby, both of Laclede, for respondent.

RAILEY, C. (after stating the facts as above). I. It is conceded that Charles F. Boward, the owner of the land in controversy, died on August 8, 1900; that at the time the Con Yagel debt in question was contracted, as well as prior thereto, said Charles F. Boward, with his wife and this defendant, who was then a minor, held and occupied the land aforesaid, worth about $1,000, as their homestead; that the Yagel debt was not secured by a lien of any kind on said land.

[1] It is contended by both parties to this litigation that the rights of all the parties in interest must be determined by the law which was in force on August 8, 1900, when Charles F. Boward died. This contention is sound and supported by our former rulings, some of which are as follows: Brown v. Brown's Adm'r, 68 Mo. loc. cit. 390; Register v. Hensley, 70 Mo. loc. cit. 194; Davidson v. Davis, 86 Mo. 440; Burgess v. Bowles, 99 Mo. 543, 12 S. W. 341, 13 S. W. 99; Quinn v. Kinyon, 100 Mo. loc. cit. 553, 13 S. W. 873; Linville et al. v. Hartley, 130 Mo. 252, 32 S. W. 652; Keene v. Wyatt, 160 Mo. loc. cit. 9, 60 S. W. 1037, 63 S. W. 116; Brewington v. Brewington, 211 Mo. 48, 109 S. W. 723; Bushnell v. Loomis, 234 Mo. loc. cit. 384, 385, 137 S. W. 257, 36 L. R. A. (N. S.) 1029; Balance v. Gordon, 247 Mo. loc. cit. 131, 152 S. W. 358; Wright v. Hetherlin, 277 Mo. loc. cit. 112, 209 S. W. 871; Regan v. Ensley, 222 S. W. loc. cit. 774.

In Balance v. Gordon, 247 Mo. loc. cit. 131, 152 S. W. 361, Judge Lamm, in clear and explicit language, declared the law of this state in respect to above matter as follows:

"Under the doctrine of the Bushnell-Loomis Case, we hold that the rights of creditors, as well as those of the widow and minor children, must be measured by the law in existence at the death of the householder."

Pursuing this subject further, we will endeavor to point out in the succeeding proposition the law as it existed in this state on August 8, 1900, when Charles F. Boward died.

2. In 1895 the General Assembly passed an act (Session Acts 1895, p. 186), a part of which was carried into the revision of 1899 as section 3620, and which reads as follows:

"If any such housekeeper or head of a family shall die, leaving a widow or any minor children, his homestead to the value aforesaid shall pass to and vest in such widow or children, or if there be both, to such widow and children, and shall continue for their benefit without being subject to the payment of the debts of the deceased, unless legally charged thereon in his lifetime, until the youngest child shall attain its legal majority, and until the death of such widow; that is to say, the children shall have the joint right of occupation with the widow until they shall arrive respectively at their majority, and the widow shall have the right to occupy such homestead during her life or widowhood, and upon her death or remarriage it shall pass to the heirs of the husband; and the probate court having jurisdiction of the estate of the deceased housekeeper, or head of a family, shall, when necessary, appoint three commissioners to set out such homestead to the persons or persons entitled thereto."

The section above quoted was in full force and effect on the 8th day of August, 1900, when Charles F. Boward departed this life. The rights of the parties to this litigation must, therefore, be determined under the act of 1895, supra. In construing the latter act, it is well to take an inventory of the homestead as it existed immediately prior to the law of 1895.

In 1875 the Legislature passed a law (Session Acts 1875, pp. 60, 61) which authorized the probate court to sell the homestead property, for the payment of debts contracted after the acquisition of same, subject to the homestead rights of the widow and minor children. On the death of the widow, and at the majority of the youngest child, the purchaser under the probate sale would take the fee-simple title to said property. The foregoing construction of the act of 1875 is sustained by the following authorities: Wilson v. Wilson, 255 Mo. loc. cit. 535, 164 S. W. 561; Balance v. Gordon, 247 Mo. loc. cit. 128, 152 S. W. 358; Robbins v. Boulware, 190 Mo. 33, 88 S. W. 674, 109 Am. St. Rep. 746; Keene et al. v. Wyatt et al., 160 Mo. 1, 60 S. W. 1037, 63 S. W. 116; Anthony v. Rice, 110 Mo. 223, 19 S. W. 423; Poland v. Vesper, 67 Mo. 727.

[2] As the homestead property is exempt from execution and attachment for debts acquired subsequently to the acquisition of the homestead, it is manifest that the Legislature, in the enactment of section 3620, R. S. 1899, intended to cut off the right to sell the homestead property for the payment of debts subsequently contracted, even if the youngest child has reached his majority and the widow is dead. In other words, we have held in legal effect that, when Charles Boward died on August 8, 1900, the title to the homestead real estate at that time became vested in his heir or heirs, subject to the homestead rights of the widow and minor children, free from the payment of debts con-

This conclusion is clearly sustained by the following authorities: Broyles v. Cox, 153 Mo. 242, 54 S. W. 488, 77 Am. St. Rep. 714; In re Powell's Estate, 157 Mo. loc. cit. 156, 57 S. W. 717; Keene et al. v. Wyatt et al., 160 Mo. 1, 60 S. W. 1037, 63 S. W. 116; Balance v. Gordon, 247 Mo. loc. cit. 127, and fol., 152 S. W. 358; Armor v. Lewis, 252 Mo. loc. cit. 574, 578, and fol., 161 S. W. 251; Ehlers v. Potter, 219 S. W. loc. cit. 916.

Upon a careful review and consideration of this subject, we are well satisfied with the conclusion reached in the foregoing cases, and hold that, under the act of 1895, as it stood on the 8th day of August, 1900, the probate court of Linn county, Mo., had no legal right to order a sale of the property in controversy for the payment of the Yagel demand.

The position of this court in respect to above matter is strongly supported by the subsequent legislative construction placed upon section 3620, R. S. 1899, by the General Assembly, in 1907, when it passed an amendatory act (Laws 1907, p. 301), which authorized the probate court, under the circumstances of this case, to order the sale of the homestead property subject to the rights of the widow, provided the heirs of the husband were persons other than his children, etc. It is manifest that the Legislature, recognizing the law as declared by this court, which precluded a sale of the homestead property absolutely under the act of 1895, concluded to modify the same, by allowing said property to be subjected to the pay-

Cruts first. The latter entered a plea of not guilty, and his trial was commenced before a jury on November 8, 1920.

It appears from the evidence that defendants are brothers, and that D. W. Bailey, mentioned in the information, is their uncle. The latter, on April 14, 1920, owned 160 acres of unimproved land, lying north of the farm of Rainey Cruts, and east of land owned by D. W. Cruts. D. W. Bailey, and three of his sons, who were then living with him, on the afternoon of April 14, 1920, went to the west side of said 160 acres, and burned the grass and leaves east of the east side of D. W. Cruts' land. They had finished that part of the work, had gone to the south side of said 160 acres, north of the land belonging to Rainey Cruts, and were burning east on the Bailey land, when Rainey Cruts saw the smoke and telephoned his brother Dan. The latter was in the field at work, and his wife and Mrs. Cook communicated to him the telephone message from Rainey. Shortly afterwards Rainey put his pistol in his pocket, and went out into the field where Dan was at work. After some conversation, Dan went to his own home, put a pistol in his pocket, and returned to where Rainey and the women were. The two men then walked on over to where Bailey and his sons were burning the trash, and the two women claimed to have followed along, 40 to 50 steps in the rear, but did not come clear up to where Bailey and his boys were located. Rainey says he had a fork, which he left at a point some distance from where Bailey and sons were at work. As the main controversy relates to what occurred when the two Cruts boys came up to where Bailey and his three boys were, we have deemed it best to set out the substance of the testimony, as given by the eyewitnesses.

Dan W. Bailey testified that no part of the fire reached the fence of either of the Crutses; that at one place the fire got up within a foot or two of Rainey's fence, but they put that fire out and started to continue burning where they had left off, to put out the above fire. Just about this time, the defendants appeared on the land of Rainey, on the opposite side of the fence from Bailey's. Dan Bailey then describes what occurred, in substance, as follows: That Rainey Cruts said, "We come over here to see about this fire." That he seemed to be awfully mad. That he said to Rainey: "You needn't mind about that, Rainey. We will take care of the fire. We don't aim for the fire to get out." That Rainey said: "That is all right; just so it don't get into the fence." That just then Dan Cruts commenced accusing John Bailey, his son, of attempting to hit him with the fork. That Dan Cruts then said: "Don't hit me with that fork. Don't hit me with that fork." That these remarks were addressed to John Bailey. That Dan Cruts

then grabbed a rock, threw it at John, and it hit the top rail of the fence; and just at that time both defendants commenced shooting. They got the guns from out of their pockets. That just as soon as Dan Cruts threw the rock, he put his hand in his pocket, and then just as Rainey threw his gun on witness, Dan Cruts threw his gun on John Bailey. That John Bailey was doing nothing when Dan Cruts said, "Don't hit me with that fork." That John was just standing there with the fork on his shoulder. That Dan Cruts shot John Bailey in the right arm. Witness, who had been formerly judge of the county court, testified as follows:

"Mr. Hutchinson: Now, go ahead, Judge, and tell what happened. When the shooting commenced what did you do, if anything? A. I didn't do a thing. The first—when they first throwed their guns down on me I didn't think they would shoot, and the first shot Rainey Cruts shot he shot me in the abdomen; the second shot he shot me in the leg; and Dan Cruts, the third shot that he shot hit John's arm, and the fork just fell off his shoulder, back of his shoulder, and his arm just fell down by his side, and he just turned around and around. Dan Cruts turned then on to me and shot two shots at me, and Rainey Cruts shot two shots at my head. The first two shots—the first shot was in my abdomen, and the next shot in my leg, and the next two shots he held the gun or aimed right on my head—he aimed to hold his gun on my head.

"Q. Did the last two shots Rainey Cruts fired—did they hit you? A. There was two shots hit my hat, and I felt one strike one of my ears.

"Q. What did you say, if anything, during that time? A. I didn't say a word. * * *

"Q. How long was it from the time they were throwing the rock and the shots were fired? How long a time elapsed? A. Just immediately. Just as quick as he throwed the rock they both went to shooting at the same time—right then.

"Q. How fast were the shots fired? A. Just as fast as they could make their pistols revolve.

"Q. From where you were standing at the time they came up, did you advance towards them after they stopped? A. No, sir.

"Q. Did you draw the fork on them you had in your hand? A. No, sir.

"Q. Did you attempt to stick the fork in Rainey Cruts? A. No, sir.

"Q. Did you walk up to the fence and put your foot on the fence? A. No, sir.

"Q. Did you see your son advance toward Dan Cruts? A. No, sir; he never advanced a bit.

"Q. He never advanced a bit? A. No, sir.

"Q. Did he take the pitchfork off his shoulder? A. No, sir; he had the pitchfork on his shoulder when the third shot was fired.

"Q. And then what became of it? A. It just fell backwards over his back, and his arm fell down by his side, and he just turned around and around."

Witness testified that the fence was rotted down, and was about 3 or 3½ feet high; that he never at any time got on the same side of the fence with Rainey and Dan Cruts; that he was about 16 feet from Rainey when the shots were fired, and that he was never any closer to him; that one of the shots struck him above the right knee.

There was some other testimony of witnesses, as to threats and swearing of both defendants after the shooting was over. The testimony of John Bailey, Oscar Bailey, and Rolla Bailey, who were with their father at the time the above transactions occurred, is practically the same as that of D. W. Bailey. The doctors testified, in substance, that one of the pistol balls struck Dan W. Bailey in the abdomen and lodged against his hip bone.

Defendant's Evidence.

Mrs. Dan W. Cruts and Mrs. Cook both testified, in substance, that they were 45 or 50 steps away when the shooting commenced; that they saw Dan W. Bailey and John Bailey, with their pitchforks, advancing towards defendants like they were going to jab them; that John Bailey was after Dan Cruts, and old man Bailey was after Rainey Cruts; that Rainey fired the first shot, and they then turned back home and saw nothing more of the shooting.

Rainey Cruts, the defendant, testified, in substance, that after he and his brother spoke to Dan Bailey, and they exchanged some words about the fire, Dan Bailey then said, "What are you fellows looking for?" and was mad; that defendant then said to him, "I don't care for you burning it, just so you don't get in the fence"; that about that time Dan Bailey took a chew of tobacco, and "kinda" nodded his head, and the boys reached on their shoulders for their forks; that John started at Dan and said, "G—— d—— you!" and Dan Cruts said, "Now, stand back, John," two or three times, and finally reached over to pick up a rock, and John "kinda" stopped; that he (witness) reached over and tapped his brother on the arm and told him not to do that, and his brother Dan dropped the rock; that about the time witness says he got straightened up and turned his head, his uncle Dan Bailey was right at his face almost with a fork; that he would take a little stroke at witness and then gouge; that he hit defendant, jabbed him on the arm, and produced a knot there as large as an egg. Defendant further testified as follows:

"So he just got right across on me. Well, I didn't want to kill him, and the first shot I intended to shoot him in the leg, and he just kept coming, and I just went to shooting wherever I could shoot, and the last shot, the last time he gouged the fork clear past my head, and when he did I just jammed the gun right down on his head. I don't suppose the gun was over that far from his head. When I done that he went back to the back of the fence row just as fast as he come across and throwed his fork down, and that settled it."

Dan W. Cruts corroborates his brother Rainey as to what occurred at time and place of shooting.

Several witnesses testified that defendant had the reputation of being a peaceable, quiet, and law-abiding citizen. Some of the witnesses testified that the general reputation of Dan W. Bailey for truth and veracity was not good, and that he had the reputation of being a quarrelsome, turbulent man. Witnesses were likewise introduced as to the good character of. Dan Bailey for truth and veracity, and they testified that he had the reputation of being a peaceable, quiet man.

After the instructions were read to the jury, the latter returned into court the following verdict:

"We, the jury, find the defendant, Rainey Cruts, guilty, as charged in the information, and assess his punishment at imprisonment in the penitentiary for the term of two years."

Defendant, in due time, filed motions for a new trial and in arrest of judgment. Both motions were overruled, and the cause duly appealed by him to this court.

Lorts & Breuer and Holmes & Holmes, all of Rolla, for appellant.

Jesse W. Barrett, Atty. Gen., and Robert J. Smith, Asst. Atty. Gen., for the State.

RAILEY, C. (after stating the facts as above). [1] 1. Under proposition 1 of appellant's "Points and Authorities," it is asserted that—

"In a prosecution under section 3262, R. S. 1919, defendant may be convicted of an assault without malice, and the jury should be so instructed if the evidence warrants it."

Section 3262, supra, reads as follows:

"Every person who shall, on purpose and of malice aforethought, shoot at or stab another, or assault or beat another with a deadly weapon, or by any other means or force likely to produce death or great bodily harm, with intent to kill, maim, ravish or rob such person, or in the attempt to commit any burglary or other felony, or in resisting the execution of legal process, shall be punished by imprisonment in the penitentiary not less than two years."

It is appellant's contention that he was entitled to an instruction, under the evidence, by virtue of section 3693, R. S. 1919, leaving it to the jury to determine whether the assault was committed with malice aforethought, or with intent to kill, or do some great bodily harm, without malice aforethought. Said section 3693, R. S. 1919, reads as follows:

"Upon an indictment for an assault with intent to commit a felony, or for a felonious assault, the defendant may be convicted of a less offense; and in all other cases, whether prosecuted by indictment, information or before a justice of the peace, the jury or court trying the case may find the defendant not guilty of the offense as charged, and find him guilty of any offense, the commission of which is necessarily included in that charged against him."

Several authorities are cited by defendant in support of above contention. We are not disposed to criticize the cases cited, when applied to the facts referred to therein. In construing the two sections of our statute above quoted, we should keep in mind the particular facts of each case coming before us. It may be conceded, for the purposes of the case, that instances may arise under said sections in which it would be proper to submit to the jury the question as to whether defendant might be convicted for a lower offense than that called for in section 3262, supra; but in each case the facts must be sufficient to warrant the court in submitting said issue to the jury.

If the evidence in behalf of the state be taken as true, defendant Rainey Cruts armed himself with a loaded pistol and went to the scene of trouble, where Dan W. Bailey and his three sons were at work on their own premises, engaged in the legitimate business of burning trash thereon. When defendant and his brother approached the division fence, the state's evidence shows that all of the Baileys were standing from 10 to 15 feet from the fence, with their respective forks on their shoulders; that they remained in that condition, and made no effort to advance on defendant and his brother, or to harm either of them; that defendant thereupon pulled his pistol, and without any provocation shot Dan Bailey once in the right leg above the knee, once in the abdomen, and fired two more shots, which went through his hat. On the other hand, defendant testified that he put his hand on his brother, told him not to throw the rock at John, and, as he turned his head, Dan W. Bailey was almost at his face with the pitchfork, with which he commenced hitting and gouging defendant, without any justification or excuse therefor. He testified that on the first shot he intended to shoot his uncle Dan in the leg, as he did not want to kill him, but his uncle "kept coming, and I just went to shooting wherever I could shoot, and the last shot, the last time he gouged the fork clear past my head, and when he did I just jammed the gun right down on his head." On the state's theory, was defendant guilty of a murderous assault on his uncle, without provocation, with a loaded pistol, or did he shoot Dan Bailey in self-defense? Both theories were submitted to the jury under appropriate instructions, and a verdict returned to the effect that defendant intentionally shot his uncle without provocation.

The physical facts in this case speak louder than words. It is undisputed that defendant shot Dan Bailey in his right leg above the knee; that he shot him in the abdomen, tried to shoot him in the head, and only missed the latter by a small margin, as two holes were shot through his uncle's hat. The plea of self-defense having been eliminated by the verdict of the jury, it left the case with defendant having shot his uncle, as disclosed by the physical facts, without either justification or excuse. Taking the physical facts, in connection with the remaining testimony in the case, we are of the opinion that the trial court committed no error in refusing to instruct as to a lower grade of assault. State v. Feeler, 226 S. W. loc. cit. 17, 18; State v. Ray, 225 S. W. loc. cit. 973; State v. Foster, 281 Mo. 618, 220 S. W. loc. cit. 960, 961; State v. Jones, 217 S. W. 22, 23; State v. Burns, 278 Mo. loc. cit. 449, 213 S. W. loc. cit. 117; State v. Wansong, 271 Mo. loc. cit. 56, 57, 58, 195 S. W. 999; State v. Webb, 266 Mo. 672, 182 S. W. 975; State v. Webb, 205 S. W. 190; State v. Curtner, 262 Mo. loc. cit. 218, 170 S. W. 1141; State v. Maguire, 113 Mo. loc. cit. 675, 21 S. W. 212; State v. Doyle, 107 Mo. loc. cit. 43, 44, 17 S. W. 751.

[2] 2. Appellant's second contention is that—

"Under the law a man not only has the right to shoot another in the necessary defense of himself, but has the same right in defense of his brother, and the jury should be so instructed where the evidence warrants it."

See section 3233, R. S. 1919; State v. Turner, 246 Mo. 598, 152 S. W. 313, Ann. Cas. 1914B, 451.

We have no disposition to controvert the above proposition, where the facts in the case justify the defendant in affording his brother protection. The above principle of law, however, has no application to the facts in this case. Defendants were granted a severance, and the case of State v. Rainey Cruts is the only one pending here for our consideration. It is not claimed, by either the state or defendant, that the latter shot any one but Dan W. Bailey. Appellant is on trial here for shooting his uncle, and not for shooting some other person, while the latter was assaulting his brother. It is not claimed that Dan W. Bailey was assaulting defendant's brother when he was shot by appellant. On the contrary, the latter testified, as heretofore shown, that he shot Dan Bailey, because he claimed the latter was hitting and jabbing him with a pitchfork.

The above contention is without merit and overruled.

[3] 3. Defendant's third contention reads as follows:

"It was error for the court to admit, as a part of the res gestæ, evidence as to the act of Dan Cruts (brother of defendant) in shooting at John Bailey (son of prosecuting witness), and to refuse, by proper instruction, to withdraw such evidence from the consideration of the jury in determining defendant's guilt."

The court admitted as res gestæ everything that occurred from the time defendant and his brother came into the presence of Dan W. Bailey and his three sons, until the shooting was over, and the two Cruts boys left. The conversation, acts, and proceedings between said parties, under the circumstances aforesaid, were so interwoven as to present a single, continuous, and inseparable transaction. The facts present a typical case, involving the doctrine of res gestæ. State v. Pfeifer, 267 Mo. loc. cit. 28, 29, 183 S. W. 337; State v. Katz, 266 Mo. loc. cit. 502, 503, 181 S. W. 425; State v. Anderson, 252 Mo. loc. cit. 98, 99, 158 S. W. 817; State v. Vaughan et al., 200 Mo. 1, 98 S. W. 2; State v. Cavin, 199 Mo. 154, 97 S. W. 573; State v. Woodward, 191 Mo. loc. cit. 633, 90 S. W. 90; 10 Ruling Case Law, § 157, p. 974.

The Missouri cases supra conclusively sustain the trial court in holding that the entire transaction which took place at the time of the shooting was a part of the res gestæ to be considered by the jury in passing upon the case.

[4, 5] 4. Defendant's instruction A was properly refused because it was a comment on a portion of the testimony. State v. Adkins, 225 S. W. 981; Jones v. Ry. Co., 228 S. W. loc. cit. 784, and cases cited. It was likewise properly refused because instruction 4, given by the court, correctly declared the law and covered the question complained of by appellant. State v. Hitsabeck, 132 Mo. loc. cit. 358, 34 S. W. 38.

5. We have examined all the matters complained of by appellant, and find no error in the record of which he can legally complain. The case was carefully tried by court and counsel, and the verdict is fully sustained by substantial evidence.

The judgment below is accordingly affirmed.

WHITE and MOZLEY, CC., concur.

PER CURIAM. The foregoing opinion of BAILEY, C., is hereby adopted as the opinion of the court.

All concur.

STATE v. RITTER. (No. 22597.)

(Supreme Court of Missouri, Division No. 2. May 26, 1921. Rehearing Denied June 8, 1921.)

1. Arson ⬤➡22—Indictment and information ⬤➡110(7)—An indictment not defective because not stating owner of the building containing goods burned.

An indictment under Rev. St. 1919, § 3288, declaring that every person who shall set fire to or burn any goods or merchandise which is insured with intent to defraud the insurers shall be guilty of arson, need not state the name of the owner of the building in which the goods were located, and is sufficient if it follows the statute, for ownership of the building is immaterial.

2. Witnesses ⬤➡278—Exclusion of answers by witness to question, whether she expected in making statement not to be prosecuted, held not error.

In a prosecution for arson, where one of defendant's colleagues was asked whether she did not, in making a statement to designated person, entertain the hope that she would not be prosecuted and the statement was not definitely identified, the exclusion of answers that the witness did not entertain any such hope was not error, even though there should be great latitude in cross-examining a witness connected with the crime who testifies on behalf of the state.

3. Criminal law ⬤➡371(7)—Testimony as to statements made by defendant as to his connection with other incendiary fires admissible.

In a prosecution for arson where it was contended that defendant induced the witness to consent to the burning of her household goods, etc., testimony by the witness as to statements made by defendant concerning his connection with other incendiary fires is admissible to show intent, for such statements were in the nature of admissions, and it is immaterial whether they occurred before or after the fire in question.

4. Criminal law ⬤➡369(11)—Evidence of statement by defendant as to his previous connection with incendiary fires admissible.

In a prosecution for arson where the witness testified that defendant induced her to consent to the burning of her household goods, etc., testimony by the witness as to defendant's statement concerning his connection with previous incendiary fires was admissible to prove that the fire in question was of incendiary origin and to prove the corpus delicti or connect defendant therewith.

5. Witnesses ⬤➡370(1)—Evidence of bias of witness against codefendant inadmissible where severance was granted.

While it is always competent as affecting the credibility of a witness to show his bias against the accused, evidence that the witness was biased against accused's codefendant is inadmissible where severance was granted.

6. Witnesses ⬤➡360—State entitled to rebut showing that witness kept house of ill fame.

Where defendant in cross-examination of witnesses of the state attempted to show that principal witness had kept a house of ill fame, it was permissible for the state to show that the house of such witness did not bear that reputation, regardless of the propriety of the inquiries of defendant's counsel.

7. Witnesses ⬤➡270(3) — Facts improperly brought out on cross-examination may be rebutted.

If counsel chooses to examine a witness as to facts not admissible in evidence, the other party has a right to examine him as to the evidence so given.

(221 S.W.)

8. Witnesses ⬅360—Evidence of good character, inadmissible.

Where there was no direct attack, the mere fact that the state on cross-examination propounded questions to defendant's witness reflecting upon his standing does not warrant the admission of independent evidence as to the good character of the witness for truth and veracity.

9. Criminal law ⬅1172(1)—Number and prolixity of instructions do not warrant reversal.

Where the instructions were correct, the mere fact that they were numerous and prolix in verbiage does not warrant reversal.

Appeal from St. Louis Circuit Court; John W. Calhoun, Judge.

Joseph Ritter was convicted under Rev. St. 1919, § 3288, of arson in the third degree, and he appeals. Affirmed.

Carl M. Dubinsky and Abbott, Fauntleroy, Cullen & Edwards, all of St. Louis, for appellant.

Jesse W. Barrett, Atty. Gen., and Albert Miller, Asst. Atty. Gen., for the State.

WALKER, J. The appellant was convicted, in the circuit court of the city of St. Louis, of arson in the third degree, under section 3288, R. S. 1919, and his punishment assessed at fifteen years' imprisonment in the penitentiary, which was reduced by the trial court to five years. From this judgment he appeals.

The offense for which the appellant was convicted was the burning of certain household goods in the possession of one Bertha Trader, located in an apartment occupied by her on Delmar avenue, in the city of St. Louis, with the intent to injure and defraud the insurers of said property. Bertha Trader testified for the state. Her testimony was to the effect that she (the appellant) and one Fendelman entered into a conspiracy to burn the goods in the apartment in which she resided for the purpose of securing the insurance on same; that the appellant brought the greater part of the goods and placed them in the building for the purpose; that he introduced Fendelman to her as the man who would start the fire and stated that his name was Jones. The appellant testifying in his own behalf denied any connection with the matter, except as an insurance adjuster. The property was insured in the sum of $800 in one company and $1,000 in another. Upon an adjustment of the loss the two insurance companies paid the sum of $800; of this amount Bertha Trader received $250, and the balance was retained by the appellant. The latter was at the time a member of the firm of Bersch, McMahan & Ritter, whose ostensible business was that of a fire insurance adjuster, engaged in business under the name of the Independent Adjustment Company, and as such it represented Bertha Trader in the settlement of her claims against the insurance companies. The burning of the goods as testified by Bertha Trader was effected by the starting of a fire in a wardrobe in one of the rooms of the apartment. Fendelman, who, under the conspiracy, was to start the fire, was seen in the immediate vicinity of the building at the time.

There is much testimony as to the particulars of the fire, the adjustment of the claim by Ritter for Mrs. Trader, and his retention of the money when the losses were paid, not necessary to be set forth in detail.

Fendelman was indicted jointly with the appellant. A severance was granted resulting in the conviction as heretofore stated.

[1] I. Appellant contends that the indictment is insufficient, in that it does not allege the name of the owner of the building in which the goods burned were located. This allegation was not necessary. The section under which the indictment is framed is several. The offense denounced therein with which the appellant was charged was the burning of goods with the intent to defraud the insurers.

This offense is charged in the language of the statute, and hence there is no merit in the contention, for the reason that the crime having been defined by the statute which embodied all the constituent elements of the offense, the indictment following same is sufficient. This measure of the sufficiency of a statutory charge was last approved by this court in State v. Bersch, 276 Mo. loc. cit. 411, 207 S. W. loc. cit. 813. Stated more concretely as applicable to the law and facts at bar, the offense consisted, as stated, in the burning of the goods to defraud the insurers. State v. Greer, 243 Mo. 599, 147 S. W. 968. Ann. Cas. 1918C, 1163. The location of such goods other than that they were in the city of St. Louis, where the charge was preferred, which fact is alleged in the indictment, was immaterial.

[2] II. It is contended that error was committed in the striking out of the answer of the witness Bertha Trader to an inquiry made of her by the counsel for the appellant on cross-examination, as follows:

"In making the statement to Mr. McDaniel, did you not, by reason of making said statement, entertain the hope and expectation that you would not be prosecuted?"

To this she answered, "No, sir," which answer on the motion of counsel for the state was stricken out. What this statement was concerning which the inquiry was made does not appear. Although this inquiry was repeated, followed by a like ruling as at first, it was confined in each instance to the witness' hopes and expectations, dependent upon her having made the statement alleged to have been made to McDaniel and not to her testimony at the trial to which no reference was made. If the inquiry had been directed to ascertaining her hopes and expectations, dependent upon her testimony, the exclusion of her answer, if in the affirmative, would have been error, and if found upon a consideration of all the other facts to have been prejudicial, it would have been sufficient to have worked a reversal. Numerous rulings are to be found, declaratory of the latitude permissible in the cross-examination of witnesses shown to have been connected with the crime for which the accused was being tried. Proofs of promises, inducements, and the hopes and beliefs of the witness may be adduced to affect his credibility; but a vague inquiry as to an alleged statement of the witness, of which not even the purport is shown, cannot be made to serve that purpose.

The facts at bar, therefore, clearly distinguish this case from rulings here and elsewhere, recognizing the right of cross-examination to ascertain if a witness' testimony is animated by any other purpose than a statement of the facts. State v. Shelton, 223 Mo. loc. cit. 134, 122 S. W. 732, and cases; Stevens v. People, 215 Ill. 593, 74 N. E. 786; People v. Langtree, 64 Cal. loc. cit. 259, 30 Pac. 813; People v. Moore, 181 N. Y. 524, 73 N. E. 1129; State v. Kent, 4 N. D. loc. cit. 598, 62 N. W. 631, 27 L. R. A. 686; Lee v. State, 21 Ohio St. 151.

[3] III. Error is assigned in the admission in evidence of statements made by appellant to Bertha Trader as to his connection with other incendiary fires. These statements were in the nature of voluntary admissions of the commission by the appellant, of other crimes of a like nature to that charged. They were admissible as tending to show intent, and it is immaterial whether they occurred before or after the commission of the crime for which he was being tried. State v. Bersch, 276 Mo. loc. cit. 415, 207 S. W. 809, and cases.

[4] Furthermore, the admission of this testimony was authorized as tending to show that the fire in question was of incendiary origin, and also to prove the corpus delicti, or connect the appellant with same. State v. Cox, 264 Mo. loc. cit. 413, 175 S. W. 50, and cases.

[5] IV. It was attempted to be shown that one of the state's witnesses was biased or hostile to Fendelman, and hence that the exclusion of his testimony as to such bias was error. It is always competent, as affecting the credibility of a witness, to ascertain the state of his mind against the accused. State v. Horton, 247 Mo. loc. cit. 665, 153 S. W. 1051; State v. Miller, 71 Mo. 590. This rule, however, has never been extended to the admission of proof of witness' bias against others. State v. Montgomery, 28 Mo. 594.

Fendelman, although he had been jointly indicted with the appellant, had been granted a severance and was not a party to the action. It was therefore immaterial what the witness' feelings may have been toward him.

[6, 7] V. It is further contended that error was committed in admitting testimony as to the prior conduct of Mrs. Trader to rebut the attack upon her character made by the appellant. Appellant's counsel had attempted in the cross-examination of certain witnesses for the state to show that Mrs. Trader had kept a house of ill repute or one bearing that reputation in the neighborhood. The evident purpose of this examination was to show that she was a woman of unchaste character and thereby affect her credibility. In rebuttal the state was permitted to show that her house did not bear that reputation. The testimony, therefore, did not, as contended by appellant, constitute proof of specific acts to sustain the witness' character. Where an inquiry is made, as at bar, the state may be permitted to rebut the testimony thus offered by proof of the actual facts. Although the trial court may therefore have erred in permitting counsel for the appellant to make the inquiry in the manner in which it was made (People v. Christy, 65 Hun, loc. cit. 353, 20 N. Y. Supp. 278; White v. Comm., 96 Ky. loc. cit. 184, 28 S. W. 340; Griffin v. State, 14 Ohio St. loc. cit. 63), this did not preclude the state from disproving same; ruled otherwise, the appellant would be enabled to profit by his own error.

The propriety of the trial court's ruling in this behalf may be tersely stated in the language of a well-recognized treatise on evidence (1 Greenl. Ev. § 468), cited with approval in Olive v. State, 11 Neb. loc. cit. 28, 7 N. W. 452, as follows:

"If the counsel chooses to cross-examine the witness as to facts not admissible in evidence, the other party has a right to examine him as to the evidence so given." 22 C. J. pp. 483, 484, § 582, and cases.

[8] VI. Error is assigned in the refusal of the trial court to admit testimony to show the good character of Fendelman, who testified for the defense. His character had not been directly questioned, but, on cross-examination, inquiries were made of him reflecting upon his standing; and later the appellant offered to show that Fendelman was a man of good reputation for truth and veracity. The rule as to the admission of testimony of this character in both civil and criminal cases has been very exhaustively considered by Graves, J., en banc, in Orris v. Railroad, 279 Mo. 1, 214 S. W. 124, in which it is held:

"Neither proof of mere contradictory statements nor a rigid cross-examination of the party will authorize the introduction of evidence, as to his general reputation for truth and veracity; such things go to the credit to be given testimony of witness, rather than to his reputation for truth and veracity."

The opinions of the Courts of Appeals, holding to the contrary, which are cited by appellant in his brief, are expressly overruled. The ruling in the Orris Case, so far as it applies to criminal cases, is but an affirmance of the doctrine announced in the early case of State v. Thomas, 78 Mo. 327, which was subsequently given express approval in State v. Fogg, 206 Mo. loc. cit. 716, 105 S. W. 623, in which the court said:

"It is urged by counsel for appellant that the court committed error in the exclusion of the testimony offered to prove the defendant's reputation in the neighborhood in which he resided for truth and veracity. This testimony was properly excluded for the reason that the defendant's reputation for truth and veracity had not been assailed, and the mere fact that there was a conflict between his testimony and that of the prosecuting witness is not in contemplation of law such an attack upon his reputation for truth and veracity as would warrant the court in admitting the testimony as to such reputation, for the purpose of bolstering up the testimony of the defendant, when such reputation had been in no way assailed. As applicable to this proposition we know of no rule of law which makes any distinction between the defendant as a witness and any other witness in the case; therefore, we take it that the rule as announced in State v. Thomas, 78 Mo. 327, is decisive of this question."

We therefore overrule this contention.

[9] VII. We have carefully reviewed the instructions, not only those given, but those refused; while the former are numerous and somewhat prolix in verbiage, they correctly present the applicable law under the evidence and are not subject to such criticism as to warrant a reversal.

The instructions refused, where not covered by those given, are subject to such objections as to prevent our interfering with the ruling of the trial court in regard thereto; they are either not authorized by the facts, or are a comment on same, or incorrectly declare the law. We do not deem it necessary, therefore, to review them separately.

The testimony as to the appellant's guilt is ample to sustain the verdict. He was fairly tried and the judgment is therefore affirmed.

All concur.

STATE v. RONGEY. (No. 22678.)

(Supreme Court of Missouri, Division No. 2. May 26, 1921.)

1. Homicide ⬅292(4)—An instruction as to striking with a pair of heavy shoes held reversible error where not justified by evidence.

In a prosecution for assault with intent to kill, it was error to instruct the jury that they should convict the defendant if they found that he committed the assault with a large and heavy pair of shoes, which defendant then wore, and should find that such shoes were deadly weapons, where there was no evidence that he wore such shoes, or that appellant stamped and kicked his victim on head and face as stated in the instruction.

2. Homicide ⬅292(4)—Assumption in instruction without supporting evidence that defendant was wearing heavy shoes was error.

In a prosecution for assault with intent to kill, an instruction directly assuming without evidence to support it that defendant was wearing heavy shoes when he made the assault was error, the question whether the heavy shoes were deadly weapons being also submitted.

3. Homicide ⬅292(4)—Instruction assuming without evidence that defendant assaulted another with a weapon is erroneous.

In a prosecution for assault with intent to kill, an instruction assuming, without sustaining evidence, that defendant assaulted another with a weapon, and providing that, if said weapon or as used was not a deadly one, then the defendant might be convicted of assault to kill without malice, and punished as provided by Rev. St. 1919, § 3263, is erroneous.

4. Homicide ⬅292(4)—Instruction as to deadly weapon held erroneous in the absence of evidence.

In a prosecution for assault with intent to kill, an instruction that if defendant intentionally used upon prosecuting witness a deadly weapon, or a weapon, as used, likely to produce death, he is guilty, *held* erroneous, because there was no evidence that defendant had a weapon, and no evidence that he had on the heavy shoes, which another instruction mentioned as a weapon, or tending to show that any such boots or shoes were deadly weapons, for such an instruction required evidence of use of a weapon such as would be construed in law to be deadly.

5. Homicide ⬅90—Instruction authorizing a conviction for assault with intent to kill where defendant simply used fists is error.

An instruction authorizing jury to convict defendant under Rev. St. 1919, § 3263, of committing an assault with intent to kill, although he simply used fists and bruised the head and face of prosecuting witness thereby, and had no instrument of any kind in his hands, is error.

6. Criminal law ⬅1134(3)—Where a conviction is reversed, other questions not likely to arise on retrial need not be considered.

Where a criminal case must be reversed, it is unnecessary to consider other questions not likely to recur upon retrial.

Appeal from Circuit Court, St. Francois County; Peter H. Huck, Judge.

Braz Rongey was convicted of assault with intent to kill. His motion for new trial was overruled, sentence pronounced, and he appeals. Reversed, and remanded for new trial.

On May 1, 1920, the prosecuting attorney of St. Francois county, Mo., filed in the cir-

⬅For other cases see same topic and KEY-NUMBER in all Key-Numbered Digests and Indexes

cuit court of said county a verified information, which, without caption and signature, reads as follows:

"Comes now W. E. Coffer, prosecuting attorney within and for the county of St. Francois, and state of Missouri, on behalf of the state of Missouri, upon his oath of office and upon his knowledge, information, and belief, does inform the court and does state and charge that one Braz Rongey, late of the county of St. Francois and state of Missouri, on the 6th day of April, 1920, did, at and in the county of St. Francois and state of Missouri, with force and arms, in and upon the body of C. J. Adami, there being, feloniously, willfully, on purpose, and of his malice aforethought, make an assault; and that the said Braz Rongey, then and there, him, the said C. J. Adami, on purpose and of his malice aforethought, willfully and feloniously and with great force and brute violence with his hands and clenched fists, and with some blunt instrument which he then and there held in his hands, the nature and character and description of which said blunt instrument is to the prosecuting attorney unknown, but which blunt instrument was then and there a dangerous and deadly weapon, did strike, beat, and wound the said C. J. Adami, and with a large and heavy pair of shoes, which said shoes the said Braz Rongey then and there had and wore upon his feet, and which said large and heavy shoes were then and there, as used, dangerous and deadly weapons, did then and there strike, kick, stamp the said C. J. Adami in and upon a vital part of the body, to wit, the mouth, temples, chest, sides, and body of his, the said C. J. Adami, with such brute force and violence, and in such a cruel and unusual manner, as to likely produce death or great bodily harm, with intent then and there him, the said C. J. Adami, on purpose and of his malice aforethought, willfully and feloniously to kill and murder; contrary to the form of the statutes in such cases made and provided, and against the peace and dignity of the state."

On May 21, 1920, defendant waived arraignment, entered a plea of not guilty, and commenced the trial of his cause before a jury on the same day.

State's Evidence.

The evidence on behalf of the state was, in substance, as follows: On April 6, 1920, at a school election in Bonne Terre, St. Francois county, Mo., at about 5:30 or 6 o'clock in the afternoon, C. J. Adami was returning from the voting place and passed appellant. The latter stepped up behind Adami and, with a sharp blow, struck him behind the ear. Adami fell on his face and stomach on the concrete walk, and was unconscious. Appellant followed him down, struck him several licks with his fist, then took him by the shoulder, turned him over, and hit him several licks again on the other side of his face. Adami made no resistance, and appellant told him to get up, that he wanted to knock him down again. While Adami was down on the ground, appellant gave him a short, sharp kick in the side, between the hip and shoulder. Appellant had on boots or shoes when he kicked Adami. The latter's face was badly bruised, his mouth was bloody, and his eyes were black and bloodshot; his face was dark and bruised; his body and head were sore from the effects of the licks; his wrist was swollen and painful. Appellant said he had whipped Adami because the latter fired him, and caused him to lose his job. In the difficulty, Adami's metal pencil and fountain pen were badly bent by the licks of appellant.

Defendant's Evidence.

Appellant produced several witnesses who testified that he hit Adami with his fist, but did not kick him, nor did he hit him with a blunt instrument.

H. B. Rongey (defendant) testified, in substance, that he waited until Adami got far enough from the polling place, walked up to him, and said, "Now, I got you," and when he turned around defendant knocked him down. Some man ran out and started to pick Adami up, but defendant said: "Leave him alone, let him stay there," and he left him there. Adami then got up, staggered around, and fell back over the sidewalk, with his head in the gutter. Two or three men came up, and defendant asked them if he (Adami) had any friends there, and said, "If he has, and they want any, I'll give them some, or take some, makes no difference to me." Defendant then said, "Now take him up, and let Mr. Crane look at him." Defendant claimed that Adami fired him, and would not pay him $52.50 that the company owed him. Defendant testified that—"I never kicked him, and I never hit him with nothing but my bare fist; I whipped him with my fists." Appellant said he never aimed to kill him, but just to give him a good whipping.

On cross-examination, appellant admitted he had been arrested once in Missouri and once in Illinois; was fined for fighting in Illinois. He said he would have pleaded guilty to an assault if they had let him, but was not guilty of an assault with intent to kill.

After the giving of instructions, the jury returned into court the following verdict:

"We, the jury, find the defendant, Braz Rongey, guilty of assault with intent to kill, with malice aforethought, as he stands charged in the information, and assess his punishment at imprisonment in the penitentiary for a term of three years.

"C. B. McClintock, Foreman."

The instructions and rulings of the court will be considered, as far as necessary, in the opinion.

Defendant in due time filed his motion for a new trial, which was overruled. The court sentenced defendant, and entered judgment accordingly. Appellant in due time filed an affidavit for appeal, which was allowed him to this court.

Marsalek & Stahlhuth, of St. Louis, for appellant.

Jesse W. Barrett, Atty. Gen., and Robert Smith and R. W. Otto, Asst. Attys. Gen., or the State.

RAILEY, C. (after stating the facts as above). [1] 1. Appellant assigns as error the action of the trial court in giving to the jury instruction numbered 1. A portion of said instruction complained of, reads as follows:

"First. If, upon consideration of all the evidence in the case in the light of the court's instructions, you find and believe from the evidence that, at the county of St. Francois and state of Missouri, on the 6th day of April, 1920, the defendant made an assault upon the prosecuting witness, C. J. Adami, with his hands and clenched fists, *or with a large and heavy pair of shoes, which said shoes the defendant then and there had and wore upon his feet,* and shall find that said *large and heavy* shoes were *deadly* weapons, that is to say, weapons likely, *as used,* to produce death or great bodily harm, did then and there strike, *kick, stamp, and wound* the prosecuting witness in and upon the *head, face,* and body of him, the said C. J. Adami, in such manner and with such force as under the circumstances was likely to produce death or *great bodily harm,* and that he did so willfully, and on purpose, and with malice aforethought, with the intent to kill the said C. J. Adami, *or to do him some great bodily harm,* you will find the defendant guilty of an assault *with intent to kill* with malice aforethought, as charged in the information, and assess his punishment at imprisonment in the penitentiary for a term of not less than two years, unless you shall find that the defendant acted in self-defense, as set forth in other instructions." (Italics ours.)

2. There was no evidence adduced at the trial which tended to show that defendant was wearing large and heavy shoes when the assault was made, nor is there any evidence in the record tending to show that appellant stamped and kicked Adami upon the head and face at all, much less with the alleged large and heavy shoes. The instruction is clearly erroneous, because it submitted issues to the jury without any evidence in the case upon which to base the same. State v. Bailey, 57 Mo. 131; State v. Chambers, 87 Mo. 406; State v. Herrell, 97 Mo. 105, 10 S. W. 387, 10 Am. St. Rep. 289; State v. Allen, 116 Mo. loc. cit. 555, 22 S. W. 792; State v. Edwards, 203 Mo. loc. cit. 539, 102 S. W. 520; Stetzler v. Met. St. Ry. Co., 210 Mo. loc. cit. 714, 715, 109 S. W. 666; State v. Stenzel, 220 S. W. loc. cit. 884; State v. St. John, 94 Mo. App. 229, 68 S. W. 374.

Judge Fox, in State v. Edwards, 208 Mo. loc. cit. 539, 102 S. W. 520, very clearly declares the law of this state in respect to above matter, as follows:

"In the discussion of the complaint lodged by the appellant against this instruction we must not overlook the fundamental rules as applicable to the giving of instructions either in civil or in criminal cases; that is, that it is essential in both criminal and civil cases that, in order to authorize an instruction upon any particular subject involved in the cause, there should be at least some substantial evidence upon which to predicate the instruction, and it is error in either a civil or criminal cause to give an instruction without any evidence to support it."

The jury, having been turned loose under this instruction, were authorized to conjecture that defendant was wearing, at the time of the assault, heavy shoes, without any substantial evidence tending to show said fact. The instruction was erroneous as given, and the court committed reversible error in giving the same as above indicated.

[2] 3. The concluding paragraph of the first clause of said instruction 1 reads as follows:

"Whether the *large and heavy shoes* were deadly weapons, and whether such weapons, as used, if you shall find that they were used, were used in such manner and with such intent by the defendant on the occasion under consideration, are matters to be determined by you under all the facts and circumstances in evidence in the case." (Italics ours.)

Here, again, was a direct assumption on the part of the court, without evidence to support it, that defendant was wearing heavy shoes when he assaulted Adami. In the preceding proposition we held the instruction was erroneous, because it submitted to the jury the issue as to whether defendant was wearing heavy shoes, without any evidence on the subject, but, as shown in the above quotation, the court assumed that the shoes worn by defendant at the time of assault were heavy shoes, and then proceeded to submit to the jury the question as to whether heavy shoes were deadly weapons. Tested by the authorities cited in the preceding proposition, the above-quoted portion of said instruction 1 is clearly erroneous.

[3] 4. The second paragraph of said instruction 1 reads as follows:

"If you find from the evidence that such assault was made by the defendant with intent to kill or do great bodily harm, but that it was made without malice aforethought, or that the *weapon* used was not a *deadly one,* or one likely, *as used,* to produce death or great bodily harm, you will find the defendant guilty of an assault with intent to kill without malice, and assess his punishment at imprisonment in the penitentiary for a term of not less than two nor more than five years," etc. (Italics ours.)

The above quotation *assumes* without one particle of evidence to sustain the assumption that defendant assaulted Adami with a *weapon,* and then provides that, if said *weapon,* or *as used,* was not a *deadly* one, then defendant might be punished as provided in section 3263, R. S. 1919. The authorities cited under proposition 2 of this opinion apply with equal force to the second section of said instruction 1 above quoted. We find, upon a careful reading of the record, *that no evidence whatever was produced* tending to show that a deadly *weapon*, or any other kind of *weapon*, was used by defendant in assaulting Adami. Hence, the second paragraph of said instruction is erroneous, as given.

[4] 5. The first section of said instruction 1 contains the following:

"You are further instructed that if one person intentionally uses upon another a deadly weapon, that is, a weapon which, *as used*, is likely to produce death, at a vital part of the body, and in such manner or with such force as is likely to result in death, he is presumed by such use and such force to have intended to kill, and, if he so uses such weapon or such force without just cause or provocation, he is presumed to have acted with malice aforethought."

The above portion of said instruction is erroneous for two reasons: First, because it deals with a "*weapon*," and there is no evidence in the case showing that defendant had a *weapon*, when assaulting the prosecuting witness; second, because there is no evidence in the record showing that any *weapon* was used, or that defendant had on *heavy shoes* when the assault was made, *nor is there any evidence tending to show that the boots or shoes worn by defendant were deadly weapons.* In other words, before such an instruction should be given as that above quoted, it would have to appear *from the evidence* that a *deadly weapon* was used, *or* that such weapon was used *as would be construed in law to be a deadly weapon.* State v. Harris, 209 Mo. 423, 108 S. W. 28; State v. Stubblefield, 239 Mo. 526, 144 S. W. 404; State v. Fair, 177 S. W. 355.

Without undertaking to quote from above authorities, it may be stated that they expressly condemn such an instruction as that above quoted, under such circumstances as are disclosed in this record.

[5] 6. Instruction numbered 2 given by the court reads as follows:

"The court further instructs the jury that it is not incumbent upon the state to prove that the assault made upon the prosecuting witness by the defendant was made with a deadly weapon in order to convict him of assault with intent to kill, with malice aforethought, but all that is required is that you find and believe from the evidence beyond a reasonable doubt that on or about the 6th day of April, 1920, the defendant, without good cause, did assault * * * the prosecuting witness in and upon the head, face, or body with * * * clenched fists, * * * with such force and in such manner as was likely under the circumstances to produce * * * great bodily harm, and that defendant made said assault willfully, on purpose, and with malice aforethought.

"In connection you are further instructed that the law presumes a person intends the natural and probable consequences of his acts, and if you believe from the evidence in the case that defendant assaulted the prosecuting witness, C. J. Adami, in a manner likely to produce * * * greatly bodily harm, the law presumes that he intended to kill him, or do him some great bodily harm."

This instruction is vigorously assaulted by defendant upon several grounds, most of which have been previously considered. The criticisms of instruction 1 apply with equal force to the above instruction. The last paragraph of instruction 2, above quoted, is especially condemned as unsound, under the circumstances of this case, in State v. Stubblefield, 239 Mo. loc. cit. 530, 144 S. W. 404, and following. In other words, instruction 2, as framed, authorized the jury to convict defendant under section 3263, R. S. 1919, for a felony if he simply used his fists and bruised the head and face of the prosecuting witness thereby, although he had no instrument of any kind in his hand.

In the case of State v. Webb, 266 Mo. 672, 182 S. W. 975, and following, a majority of the court en banc had ever gone in this state in holding that an assault with a large ring on the finger would warrant a conviction for a felonious assault. The dissenting opinion, concurred in by two of the other judges en banc, at page 688 and following, pointed out the class of cases which had come before the court in which a felonious assault was involved and a presumption indulged.

Instruction 2 given in this case does not properly declare the law, whether tested by the Stubblefield Case or that of State v. Webb, supra, as it authorized the conviction of defendant for a felonious assault although the injuries were inflicted solely with defendant's naked fists, and without any instrument used in connection with same.

7. It is undisputed that defendant made an inexcusable assault upon the prosecuting witness, for which he ought to be punished. In fact, defendant concedes that he was guilty of an assault for which he should be punished, but insists, and correctly so, *that on the facts presented in this record* he was not properly convicted of a *felony*, under the provisions of either section 3262 or 3263 of the Revised Statutes of 1919. We may say in passing that, in our opinion, defendant's own conduct during the trial of the case, as shown by the record, was largely responsible for the verdict in this case.

[6] In view of what has already been said, it is unnecessary to consider any other questions in the case, as they may not likely appear upon a retrial of same.

On account of the errors heretofore pointed out, the cause is reversed, and remanded for a new trial.

WHITE and MOZLEY, CC., concur.

PER CURIAM. The foregoing opinion of RAILEY, C., is hereby adopted as the opinion of the court.

All concur.

STATE v. CALDWELL. (No. 22621.)

(Supreme Court of Missouri, Division No. 2.
May 26, 1921.)

1. Homicide ⟺112(5)—Doctrine of self-defense not available, where defendant brought on difficulty.

One who brings on a difficulty for the purpose of killing his adversary or wreaking his vengeance upon him is not protected by the doctrine of self-defense.

2. Homicide ⟺300(3)—Instruction on provoking difficulty held not misleading.

In a prosecution for assault with intent to kill, instruction that one who brings on a difficulty for the purpose of killing his adversary cannot avail himself to the right of self-defense *held* not misleading, in view of other instructions on self-defense.

3. Homicide ⟺119—One who is struck by another's fist not entitled to resort to use of deadly weapon in self-defense.

One who is struck by the fist of another is entitled in self-defense to use only such force as is necessary to repel the assault, but not to resort to the use of a deadly weapon.

4. Homicide ⟺244(1)—Doctrine that one assaulted may act upon appearances held inapplicable under the evidence.

In a prosecution for assault with intent to kill, the rule that one assaulted may act upon appearances *held* inapplicable under the evidence.

5. Homicide ⟺145 — One who uses deadly weapon on another's body presumed to know that result is likely death.

One who uses a deadly weapon upon some vital part of another's body must be presumed to know that the effect is likely to be death.

6. Homicide ⟺145—Intent inferred from assault with deadly weapon.

Intent will be inferred from the making of an assault with a deadly weapon.

7. Criminal law ⟺823(5)—Failure to define words "just cause or excuse" held not to render instruction objectionable in view of definition of "malice."

In a prosecution for assault with intent to kill, instruction that defendant was guilty if the assault was done without "just cause or excuse" without defining the quoted words *held* not erroneous, in view of other instructions defining "malice"; since quoted words are included in word "malice" in so far as it means the intentional doing of a wrongful act without just cause or excuse.

[Ed. Note.—For other definitions, see Words and Phrases, First and Second Series, Just Cause; Malice.]

8. Criminal law ⟺822(1)—Instructions construed together.

In passing on the sufficiency of an instruction, the court will construe all the instructions together.

9. Criminal law ⟺823(5) — Instruction held not objectionable for failure to charge on self-defense in view of other instructions.

In a prosecution for assault with intent to kill, instruction that defendant was guilty if the shooting of prosecuting witness was done without a just cause or excuse without charging therein on defendant's right of self-defense, *held* not error, in view of other instructions on self-defense.

10. Homicide ⟺244(1)—Evidence held insufficient to show self-defense.

In a prosecution for an assault with intent to kill, in which defendant claimed to have acted in self-defense, evidence *held* to sustain conviction.

11. Criminal law ⟺1159(2)—Verdict, supported by substantial evidence, not disturbed.

The Supreme Court will not disturb a verdict, where there is sufficient substantial evidence to sustain it.

Appeal from Circuit Court, Andrew County; Alonzo D. Burns, Judge.

C. F. Caldwell was convicted of an assault with intent to kill, and he appeals. Affirmed.

P. C. Breit and L. W. Booher, both of Savannah, for appellant.

Jesse W. Barrett, Atty. Gen., and J. Henry Caruthers, Sp. Asst. Atty. Gen., for the State.

WALKER, J. Appellant was charged by information in the circuit court of Andrew county with an assault with intent to kill. Upon a trial he was convicted and his punishment assessed at one year's imprisonment in a county jail and a fine of $500. From this judgment he appeals.

David Waldon was the janitor of the First National Bank Building in Savannah. The appellant, a dentist, had his office on the second floor of that building. The parties on January 1st and 2d had some disagreeable words, and during the second quarrel, appellant said he would "blow a hole through Waldon." The next morning they met on a street corner in Savannah, and when within 8 or 10 feet of each other the appellant said, "Now, damn you," drew a pistol, and shot Waldon twice. Before the shooting Waldon either assaulted the appellant with his fists, or was attempting to disarm the latter, but failed in so doing. The wounds received by Waldon were dangerous, but did not prove fatal, and after the extraction of the bullets and a week's stay in a hospital he recovered. Testimony of witnesses who saw the parties when the last shot was fired is to the effect that Waldon had his hands up, and was making no effort to assault the appellant. One of the witnesses heard the appellant, a few minutes after the shooting say: "I told the black s—— of a b—— I would kill him." Appellant, testifying in his own behalf, said that, while en route from his home to his office on the morning of the assault, he met Waldon at a street corner; that the latter rushed upon him and struck him repeatedly with his fists upon the head and face; that the appellant said to Waldon, "stay back" or "stand back"; that after the first blows appellant succeeded in getting off his overcoat and wraps, it being a very cold morning, and drew his revolver, and fired in order to stop the attack on him. After the first shot Waldon continued to strike him and when he fired the second shot Waldon stepped back, and appellant proceeded on his way to his office.

There was testimony to the effect that on the day, or following the day of the assault, there were bruises on appellant's cheek and forehead. The officer who arrested appellant, however, a few minutes after the shooting, and other witnesses, contradicted this testimony. The appellant was about 47 years of age, and weighed 145 or 150 pounds, was reasonably active, and in good health. Waldon, to employ the language of the state's witnesses, was "an old decrepit negro, about 63 years of age."

I. Appellant assigns error in the giving, by the trial court, of the following instruction:

"The jury is instructed that a person who brings on a difficulty for the purpose of killing his adversary or wreaking his vengeance on him cannot avail himself with the right of self-defense in order to shield himself from the consequences of wounding or injuring his adversary, however imminent the danger in which he may have found himself during the progress of the affray, and if in this case the jury believe that from the evidence that the defendant prepared himself with a pistol previous to the difficulty with the witness David Waldon, on the 8d day of January, 1919, and sought, brought on, or entered voluntarily into the encounter with Waldon, in order to wreak his malice on him, then there is no self-defense in the case."

[1, 2] This instruction correctly declares the law in regard to the limitation of the doctrine of self-defense. Other instructions were given, both at the request of the state and the appellant, which clearly presented the applicable law under the evidence, and hence the instruction complained of cannot be interpreted to appellant's prejudice. For example, instruction numbered 5, given at the request of the state, was as follows:

"The defendant admits the shooting and wounding, but claims that he acted in self-defense. Upon this question the court instructs you that if you find from the evidence that when defendant shot and wounded said Waldon he had reasonable cause to believe, and did believe, that said Waldon was about to take his life or do him some great personal injury; and, further, that he had reasonable cause to believe, and did believe, that it was necessary for him to shoot and wound said Waldon in order to protect himself from such danger, then he ought to be acquitted on the ground of self-defense.

Whether defendant had reasonable grounds to believe that such danger existed, and whether he shot and wounded said Waldon in the honest belief that it was necessary for the protection of his life or person, are questions which you must determine from all the evidence in the case. If you believe from the evidence that the defendant shot and wounded the said Waldon unnecessarily, and when he did not have reasonable cause to believe that the said Waldon was then about to kill him or do him great bodily harm or personal injury, then and there is no self-defense in the case, and you cannot acquit the defendant on that ground."

And also instruction numbered 4, given at the request of the appellant, which is as follows:

"The court instructs the jury that if you find and believe from the evidence that Dr. C. F. Caldwell was at the time of the difficulty on his way from his home to his place of business, on a public thoroughfare, and that David Waldon first assaulted defendant, then defendant was under no obligation to retreat, but had a right to stand his ground and to use force in resisting such assaults as was necessary to protect himself from great personal injury or bodily harm. And if defendant at the time he shot David Waldon had reasonable cause to apprehend, and did apprehend, that David Waldon was about to do defendant some great personal injury or bodily harm, and that the danger was imminent and about to fall, and that defendant shot to avert such apprehended danger, then such shooting was justifiable and you should acquit the defendant on the ground of self-defense; and in this connection you are instructed that it is not necessary in order to acquit on the ground of self-defense, that the danger should in fact be real or actually impending; all that is necessary is that defendant had reasonable cause to believe and did believe that the danger was real and about to fall upon him; and if the defendant acted in a moment of apparently impending danger from an assault by David Waldon, it was not necessary for him to nicely gauge or measure the proper quantity of force necessary to repel the assault, but that he had a right to use any means for his own protection that was reasonably necessary under the circumstances. And the question for you to determine is not what you think it was necessary for the defendant to have done or not done at the time he shot David Waldon, but the question is what the defendant might have reasonably believed, and had good reason to believe, was necessary for him to do under all the circumstances."

[3, 4] If it be conceded, as certain witnesses for the appellant testified, that Waldon struck, or attempted to strike, appellant with his fist, the extent to which the doctrine of self-defense would be applicable would be to authorize the appellant to interpose only sufficient force to repel the assault, but not to resort to the use of a deadly weapon. There is nothing in the nature of the attack of Waldon upon the appellant, if it was made, or in any of the attendant circumstances upon which the appellant would be authorized to base a rea-

sonable apprehension of immediate danger, or that Waldon was about to do him great personal injury. The rule, therefore, that one assaulted may act upon appearances finds no support in the evidence in this case to explain, much less palliate, the appellant's conduct in arming himself with a pistol and in shooting Waldon, to repel a nonfelonious assault. As to who brought on the difficulty was submitted to the jury for its determination. The reasonable inference, in view of all the facts, especially those in regard to the preceding quarrels of the parties and the appellant's arming himself with and the subsequent use of a deadly weapon, is that he provoked the difficulty.

An instruction in like form to that complained of was approved by this court in State v. McGuire, 69 Mo. loc. cit. 200, and in numerous later cases.

The criticized instruction, therefore, which is definitive in its nature, when read in connection with the other instructions, was not error.

II. The following instruction given at the instance of the state is also assigned as error.

"The court instructs the jury that he who uses upon any other at some vital part any deadly weapon must in the absence of qualifying facts be presumed to know that the effect is likely to be death, and, knowing this, must be presumed to do it wickedly or from a bad heart. If, therefore, the jury believe from the evidence in this case that the defendant willfully, feloniously, on purpose, and of his malice aforethought made an assault on one David Waldon, as charged in the information, by shooting and wounding said David Waldon with a pistol in some vital part with a manifest design to use such weapon upon him, and without a sufficient reason, cause, or extenuation, then it must be presumed that the defendant intended to kill said Waldon."

[5] This instruction correctly states the law, defining the presumption arising from the use of a deadly weapon, and in like words has been approved by this court. State v. Weeden, 133 Mo. 76, 34 S. W. 473; State v. Grant, 144 Mo. 66, 45 S. W. 1102.

[6] This instruction sufficiently declares the intent with which the assault was committed, and it is in conformity with established precedents. State v. Harrod, 102 Mo. 590, 15 S. W. 373; State v. Frazier, 137 Mo. 332, 38 S. W. 913; State v. Hudspeth, 159 Mo. 195, 60 S. W. 136; State v. Painter, 67 Mo. 84. In addition, it may be said generally that, the act with which appellant is charged being wrong in itself, the intent may be inferred from its unlawful commission. State v. Lentz, 184 Mo. 237, 83 S. W. 970.

III. Another instruction complained of is as follows:

"If you believe from the evidence beyond a reasonable doubt that the defendant at the county of Andrew, in the state of Missouri, on or about the 3d day of January, 1919, did shoot and wound David Waldon, with the felonious intent to kill said Waldon, but without malice aforethought, and that said shooting and wounding was done without just cause or excuse, you will find the defendant guilty, and assess his punishment at imprisonment in the penitentiary not less than 2 years nor more than 5 years, or imprisonment in the county jail not less than six months, or by fine of not less than $100 and imprisonment in the county jail not less than three months, or by fine of not less than $100."

[7, 8] The objections urged to this instruction are that it does not define the words "just cause or excuse," and that it fails to include defendant's right of self-defense. It is exceedingly elementary that instructions must all be construed together, whatever right of self-defense the appellant was entitled to was defined in other instructions, and there was neither reason nor necessity for its incorporation in this instruction. A like criticism may be made of appellant's second objection, in regard to the definition of the words "without just cause or excuse." In the light of the other instructions no doubt could arise in the minds of the jurors as to what would have constituted just cause or excuse for the defendant's act.

In a legal sense as relating to an offense of this character the words "without just cause or excuse" are included within the meaning of the word "malice," in so far as that term means the intentional doing of a wrongful act without just cause or excuse; or, as we said in the early case of State v. Hays, 23 Mo. loc. cit. 325, malice is a term of law directly importing wickedness and excluding a just cause or excuse. This, it is true, was said in a case of homicide, but so far as it defines a state of mind, it is equally applicable to the case at bar. Malice, therefore, having been correctly defined in other instructions, the words "without just cause or excuse," if technically considered, are included within that definition; if considered in their ordinary sense they required no explanation other than that afforded by their own evident meaning. An examination of the cases cited by appellant in support of this assignment of error fails to disclose their relevancy in the matter under consideration. Hence it is unnecessary to review these rulings. There is therefore no merit in this contention.

[9] IV. We have heretofore adverted to the fact that the appellant's right of self-defense was not ignored, but clearly defined in accordance with the facts. The instruction, numbered 1, given at the request of the state, therefore, in which it is claimed by appellant that this defense should have been defined, not having purported, nor did any other single instruction purport, to cover the entire case, and the defense having been once defined, and the instructions as a whole embracing all of the issues and the law ap-

plicable thereto, this contention is not entitled to serious consideration.

[10, 11] V. The contention that "the evidence of the prosecuting witness was false, perjured," etc., has no substantial foundation. On the contrary it was supported by other testimony, and, viewed in the light of all the circumstances, it appeals to the unbiased mind as being true. The testimony in the Prendible Case, cited by appellant (165 Mo. 329, 65 S. W. 559) discloses a state of facts authorizing the conclusion that the witnesses for the state were guilty of perjury. No semblance of similarity to such facts is found in the case at bar. The rule announced in the Prendible Case has, therefore, no application here. The jury heard the testimony. It is sufficiently substantial to establish the appellant's guilt and to authorize the verdict; we will not disturb it.

The judgment of the trial court is therefore affirmed.

All concur.

LAVELLE v. METROPOLITAN LIFE INS. CO. (No. 21692.)

(Supreme Court of Missouri, Division No. 2. May 26, 1921.)

1. Courts 231(23)—Constitutional question must be raised at earliest practical opportunity, in order to give Supreme Court jurisdiction.

A litigant must raise his constitutional question at the earliest practical opportunity, and keep the same alive throughout the case, if he desires this court to consider it on appeal, and in an action on an insurance policy, where the defendant insurer did not raise the question by a demurrer or objection to introduction of evidence, but contested right of recovery on the merits, the question may not be presented to this court for hearing in order to give it jurisdiction, less than the jurisdictional amount being involved.

2. Courts 231(23)—Supreme Court has no jurisdiction, where constitutional question injected into case by exception to ruling excluding depositions.

Where a constitutional question was sought to be injected into an action on an insurance policy to give appellate jurisdiction, when the court excluded depositions, by objection that the court's construction of the statute of Illinois rendered such statute unconstitutional as a violation of Const. U. S. art. 14, § 1, and Const. Ill. art. 2, § 2, the Supreme Court will refuse to entertain jurisdiction; the case having been tried on its merits.

3. Courts 487(1)—Where no constitutional question is presented and less than jurisdictional amount is involved, Supreme Court must transfer case to Court of Appeals.

On appeal to Supreme Court, where no valid constitutional question is presented, and the amount involved is less than jurisdictional amount of $7,500, this court is without jurisdiction, and must transfer the cause to the Court of Appeals.

Appeal from St. Louis Circuit Court; J. Hugo Grimm, Judge.

Action by Lizzie Lavelle against the Metropolitan Life Insurance Company. Judgment for plaintiff, and defendant appeals. Cause transferred to St. Louis Court of Appeals.

This action was commenced by plaintiff on August 19, 1918, before a justice of the peace, in the city of St. Louis, Mo., on a policy of insurance, dated June 30, 1909, and delivered at Chicago, Ill., by the defendant, a life insurance corporation organized under the laws of New York, but engaged in the insurance business under the laws of both Missouri and Illinois, in which John Lavelle, plaintiff's husband, was the insured. The policy was for $500, and in favor of this plaintiff, as the beneficiary therein. Among other things, it contains the following:

"*Incontestability.*—This policy constitutes the entire contract between the parties and shall be incontestable, except for nonpayment of premiums, after two years from its date."

Plaintiff is a resident of Chicago, Ill., and, with her said husband, was living there when the application for insurance was executed. The policy was delivered to said John Lavelle in the city of Chicago aforesaid. The insured died in Chicago on March 18, 1910. Plaintiff obtained judgment on said policy before said justice of the peace, and after the cause was appealed by defendant to the circuit court aforesaid she filed in the latter an amended petition, in which she pleaded the legal effect of said policy and alleged a compliance with its terms and provisions and a refusal of defendant to pay the amount due on said policy after due notice had been given and demand of payment had been made. The amended petition alleged that, under the common law and statutory law of Illinois, the defendant was estopped from contesting the validity of said policy, because no action was taken by it to contest the same within two years from the date thereof. Plaintiff likewise pleaded, and offered in evidence, in bar of defendant's right to contest said policy, the following decisions of the Illinois Supreme Court, to wit: Monahan v. Metropolitan Life Insurance Co., 283 Ill. 136, 119 N. E. 68, L. R. A. 1918D, 1196; Weil v. Federal Life Ins. Co., 264 Ill. 425, 106 N. E. 246, Ann. Cas. 1915D, 974; Flanigan v. Federal Life, 231 Ill. 399, 83 N. E. 178; Royal Circle v. Achterrath, 204 Ill. 549, 68 N. E. 492, 63 L. R. A. 452, 98 Am. St. Rep. 224.

When plaintiff offered in evidence each of the Illinois Supreme Court decisions, heretofore mentioned, no objection was interposed to the admission of either, upon the ground that said decisions, or either of them, violated any provision of the Constitution of the United States or of the state of Illinois. No objection was made that either of said decisions violated, or was in conflict with, the provision of any Constitution.

The premiums were paid on the policy according to the requirements of the latter, and no part of same was ever repaid to plaintiff or her husband, although said premiums, amounting to $27.56, were paid into court on March 20, 1919, as a tender, etc. The defendant filed no answer or other pleading in either the justice's court or the circuit court.

Appellant defended the action on the theory that John Lavelle, at the time he made his application for insurance, had a cancer which finally resulted in his death less than two years from the date of said policy; that defendant had no knowledge of insured's diseased condition prior to his death, and delivered to him the policy aforesaid under the belief that he was in sound health. It appears from the evidence that the policy sued on was delivered to John Lavelle on June 30, 1909, that he died on March 18, 1910, that on April 1, 1910, defendant denied liability on demand by beneficiary, and this action was commenced on August 19, 1918. Appellant offered at the trial substantial evidence tending to show that deceased, for some time prior to his death, was possessed of a cancer, and ultimately died from the effects of same. The court excluded this testimony for reasons hereafter mentioned, and exceptions were duly saved as to said ruling.

Under a peremptory instruction from the trial court, the jury, on March 27, 1919, returned a verdict for plaintiff, including principal and interest, in the sum of $769.75, for which amount judgment was duly rendered, etc. Defendant in due time filed its motion for a new trial, which was overruled, and the cause duly appealed to this court. Such other facts as may be deemed important will be considered in the opinion.

Fordyce, Holliday & White, of St. Louis, for appellant.

James J. O'Donohoe, of St. Louis, for respondent.

RAILEY, C. (after stating the facts as above). [1] 1. As the amount involved in this litigation is less than $7,500, it becomes necessary at the outset, to determine whether this court has jurisdiction over the cause. It is the well-established law of this state that a litigant must raise his constitutional question, if he desires this court to consider same on appeal, at the earliest practical opportunity during the progress of the trial below, and to keep the same alive through-

out the case. Huckshold v. United Rys. Co. of St. Louis, 226 S. W. 852, 853; State v. Kramer, 222 S. W. loc. cit. 824; State v. Missouri Dental Board, 221 S. W. loc. cit. 73; Bealmer v. H. Fire Ins. Co., 220 S. W. loc. cit. 957, 958; McManus v. Burrows, 217 S. W. loc. cit. 514; Republic Rubber Co. v. Adams, 213 S. W. loc. cit. 81, 82; Meredith v. Claycomb, 212 S. W. loc. cit. 863; State v. Howe Scales Co. of Ill., 277 Mo. 213, 210 S. W. loc. cit. 9, 10; Strother v. Railroad, 274 Mo. loc. cit. 276 and following, 203 S. W. 207; Littlefield v. Littlefield, 272 Mo. loc. cit. 166, 197 S. W. 1057; Carson v. Railway Co., 184 S. W. 1039; Garey v. Jackson, 184 S. W. 979; Hardwicke v. Wurmser, 264 Mo. 138, 174 S. W. 808; Stegall v. Pigment & Chem. Co., 263 Mo. 719, 173 S. W. 674; Dubowsky v. Binggeli, 258 Mo. 197, 167 S. W. 999; Miller v. Connor, 250 Mo. 677, 157 S. W. 81; George v. Railroad, 249 Mo. loc. cit. 199, 155 S. W. 453; Pickel v. Pickel, 243 Mo. loc. cit. 666, 147 S. W. 1059; Milling Co. v. Blake, 242 Mo. 23, 145 S. W. 438; Ross v. Grand Pants Co., 241 Mo. loc. cit. 299, 145 S. W. 410; Canning & Packing Co. v. Evans, 238 Mo. 599, 142 S. W. 319; Hartzler v. Met. St. Ry. Co., 218 Mo. 562, 117 S. W. 1124; State v. Gamma, 215 Mo. 100, 114 S. W. 619; Lohmeyer v. Cordage Co., 214 Mo. 685, 113 S. W. 1108; Sublette v. Railroad, 198 Mo. 190, 95 S. W. 430.

In Lohmeyer v. Cordage Co., 214 Mo. loc. cit. 689, 690, 113 S. W. 1108, 1110, Judge Lamm very clearly and forcefully stated the law, in respect to the matter under consideration, as follows:

"But it must be taken as settled law that in so grave a matter as a constitutional question it should be lodged in the case at the earliest moment that good pleading and orderly procedure will admit under the circumstances of the given case; otherwise it will be waived."

In George v. Railroad, 249 Mo. loc. cit. 199, 155 S. W. loc. cit. 454, Judge Graves discusses this question from a common-sense viewpoint, as follows:

"If a law is plainly relied upon by the plaintiff, as here, and defendant desires to challenge that law upon constitutional grounds, it should be done at the earliest practical moment, and in addition a finger should be placed upon the provisions of the Constitution violated. This has been so long and well ruled that the mere mention of the ruling should suffice."

The amended petition, on which the case was tried, as heretofore shown, pleads the laws of Illinois, and asserts therein that the policy in controversy became incontestable after two years from its date. Appellant could have filed an answer to the amended petition, and raised therein the constitutional questions now relied on to confer jurisdiction on this court. It could have demurred to said petition, and presented said questions in its demurrer. It could have objected to the introduction of any evidence under the petition, for the alleged reason that the Illinois laws relied on were in conflict with certain provisions of the Illinois Constitution, as well as those of the United States. Instead of raising its alleged constitutional questions at the earliest practical opportunity, as above indicated, appellant contested plaintiff's right of recovery on the merits throughout the trial, until her case in chief was closed, without even intimating that it desired to present a constitutional question for the consideration of the court. The plaintiff was sworn as a witness, testified at length in chief, and upon cross-examination offered in evidence the policy and the laws of Illinois, as well as other facts heretofore set out. No constitutional question was either raised or discussed up to this point. At the conclusion of plaintiff's case in chief, the record recites the following:

"Mr. Robb: Our position is that, as the insured died before the two-year period expired, there really is no contestable period to apply at all in the case."

The defendant thereupon interposed a demurrer to the evidence, as follows:

"The court instructs the jury that, under the pleadings and evidence for the plaintiff, your verdict must be in favor of the defendant."

The above demurrer was overruled, and defendant thereupon offered its evidence, hereafter referred to in the succeeding proposition. If the appellant, acting through its counsel, were desirous of having this court consider its alleged constitutional questions, they should have been presented to the trial court by timely action, and as indicated by our former rulings. Having failed to comply with the plain requirements of this court in respect to foregoing matter, we hold that there is no constitutional question legally presented for our consideration.

[2] 2. Aside from the conclusion heretofore reached, does the record disclose any real constitutional question in the case, even if the alleged one had been presented at the proper time and in a proper manner? Defendant contended at the trial that the insured was possessed of a cancer when the policy was executed, and that he died from the effects of same, less than two years after the date of the policy. Appellant offered in evidence the depositions of several witnesses tending to establish the above fact. The court excluded said depositions, on the ground that the policy was incontestable after two years from its date. Defendant likewise offered in evidence the Illinois statute and the case of Des Moines Life Insurance Co. v. Seifert, 210 Ill. 157, 71 N. E. 349, as well as other evidence, which was excluded, tending to show that the insured died from the effects of a cancer, and that defendant, by reason thereof, had the right to contest the policy sued on in this cause. The constitutional question was attempted to be injected into the case as follows:

"Mr. Robb: Save our exception to the court's ruling, on the ground the policy is governed by the statute of Illinois, which requires an incontestable provision to the effect that the policy shall be incontestable two years from date, *and that under the construction placed thereon by the court the defense is out off two years from the date of the policy, even though the insured dies in the two-year period, and renders the statute unconstitutional, and in violation of section 1 of article 14 of the Amendments to the United States Constitution, and section 2 of article 2 of the Constitution of the state of Illinois.*" (Italics ours.)

It will be observed that defendant does not claim the Illinois statute is unconstitutional, but that the construction placed thereon by the trial court renders it invalid, etc. If appellant's contention should be sustained in respect to foregoing matter, it would open wide the floodgates and allow practically every case to be brought here, where an erroneous ruling is complained of during the progress of the trial. Whenever an objection was made to the introduction of testimony, and it was overruled, the losing party could insist that the ruling of the court deprived him of certain constitutional rights, etc. The same is true with regard to the giving or refusing of instructions, or in respect to any other adverse ruling of the court.

In discussing the law with respect to a justice of the peace in the state of Iowa, we held, in Howland v. Railway Co., 134 Mo. loc. cit. 479, 36 S. W. loc. cit. 30, that:

"His jurisdiction to decide contrary to law was just as great as to decide in conformity with law. His power to decide right necessarily included the power to decide wrong. Error does not diminish jurisdiction. There is a broad and turnpike-like distinction between the existence of jurisdiction and its mere exercise."

The above quotation was cited with approval in Garey v. Jackson, 184 S. W. loc. cit. 982, where a constitutional question, like the one at bar, was sought to be injected into the case. We have uniformly refused to entertain jurisdiction in respect to a constitutional question, presented under the circumstances of this case, as shown by the following authorities: Huckshold v. U. Rys. Co. of St. Louis, 226 S. W. 852, 853; Bealmer v. Hartford Fire Ins. Co., 220 S. W. loc. cit. 957; McManus v. Burrows, 217 S. W. loc. cit. 514; Strother v. Railroad, 274 Mo. loc. cit. 276, 203 S. W. 207, and following; Garey v. Jackson, 184 S. W. 979; Stegall v. American Pigment & Chem. Co., 263 Mo. loc. cit. 723, 173 S. W. 674; Canning & Packing Co. v. Evans, 238 Mo. loc. cit. 604, 605, 142 S. W. 319; Sublette v. Railroad, 198 Mo. 190, 95 S. W. 430. We have no disposition to shirk our responsibility in passing upon real constitutional questions, when fairly and timely presented, but we cannot consistently assume jurisdiction on such facts as are presented in this record, where simply an alleged erroneous ruling of the trial court is complained of in admitting or rejecting testimony.

[3] 3. Having reached the conclusion that no valid constitutional question is presented, we are without jurisdiction to proceed further by reason of the amount involved. We accordingly transfer the cause to the St. Louis Court of Appeals for its determination.

WHITE, C., concurs.

PER CURIAM. The foregoing opinion of RAILEY, C., is hereby adopted as the opinion of the court.
All concur.

STATE v. LEE.　(No. 22670.)

(Supreme Court of Missouri, Division No. 2. May 26, 1921.)

1. **Rape ⬤⟳20—Indictment held sufficient.**

Indictment charging that defendant did feloniously and violently make an assault upon one E., and did forcibly and against her will feloniously ravish and carnally know her, the said E., *held* sufficient to charge rape under Rev. St. 1919, § 3247.

2. **Criminal law ⬤⟳1038(3), 1056(1)—Instructions sufficient, in absence of a showing that defendant requested others, and in absence of exception as to failure to give others.**

Where it did not appear from the record that defendant offered any instructions aside from those given, nor that any request was made for an instruction upon any other branch of the case outside of the questions properly covered by the instructions given, and where no exception was saved as to failure to instruct, appellant's contention that the court failed to instruct the jury upon all phases of the offense *held* without merit.

3. **Criminal law ⬤⟳713—Prosecuting attorney's statement that defendant was charged with raping a white woman not objectionable, though indictment did not charge prosecutrix was white.**

In prosecution for rape, where the prosecutrix, a white woman, was present in court and testified, prosecuting attorney's statement, when jury was being impaneled, that defendant was charged "with raping a white woman" *held* not objectionable, though indictment did not charge that prosecutrix was a white woman.

4. **Criminal law ⬤⟳1044—Defendant could not complain of testimony of witnesses whose names were not indorsed on indictment, in absence of motion to quash indictment or motion for continuance.**

Defendant could not complain of the testimony of witnesses, even if their names had not been indorsed on the indictment, unless he moved to quash the indictment, or asked for a continuance to meet such testimony.

5. **Criminal law ⬤⟳628(7)—Admission of testimony of witnesses whose names were not indorsed on indictment held not error.**

Admission of testimony of witnesses whose names were not indorsed on indictment, where prosecutor explained to the court that he had just learned of their importance, *held* not error.

6. **Criminal law ⬤⟳406(3) — Written admissions, not obtained by promises or threats, admissible.**

In a prosecution for rape, the court did not err in admitting defendant's written statement containing admissions, where the evidence was clear and convincing that no promises or threats were made as an inducement for him to sign the statement.

7. **Criminal law ⬤⟳406(1) — Testimony of police chief, as to defendant's admissions in his presence, admissible.**

In prosecution for rape, testimony of chief of police, as to admissions made in his presence by defendant as to his guilt and connection with the crime, *held* admissible.

Appeal from Criminal Court, Jackson County; Ralph S. Latshaw, Judge.

Walker Lee was convicted of rape, and he appeals. Affirmed.

Appellant was charged by indictment, with the crime of rape. It is alleged, that on June 28, 1920, at the county of Jackson and state of Missouri, said defendant did feloniously and violently make an assault upon one Elizabeth Dahmm, and did forcibly and against her will feloniously ravish and carnally know her, the said Elizabeth Dahmm.

State's Evidence.

There was substantial evidence as to defendant's guilt, offered on the part of the state, which tends to show the following facts: Mrs. Elizabeth Dahmm lived, with her husband, about two miles east of Independence in Jackson county, Mo., about one-half block from the track of the Chicago & Alton Railroad. They owned about two acres of ground, which was used as a garden and orchard. Her husband was absent from home on the date hereafter mentioned, and Mrs. Dahmm, on said date, was at her home alone. The railway track is elevated above the ground on which Mrs. Dahmm lived. On the 28th day of June, 1920, an extra gang of laborers were at work on the Chicago & Alton Railroad, between Independence, Mo., and the residence of Mrs. Dahmm. The defendant had been a member of this railroad gang, and on the morning of the 28th of June, 1920, quit work, but loafed around with the rest of said gang until about 1:30 o'clock in the afternoon of said day. Several of the railroad employees testified that after 1:30

o'clock above mentioned, they saw the defendant running down the railroad track beyond the home of Mrs. Dahmm and near her place; that he then had on a pair of blue overalls, and when they saw him about 4 o'clock he had changed his pants and had on yellow overalls.

Mrs. Dahmm testified, in substance, that she was standing at the front door of her house, when defendant approached and wanted some matches; that she went to get him some matches, and on her return, while she was looking in some other direction, he struck her a violent blow on the side of the head, which rendered her unconscious; that when she came to, she was lying on the bed in another room, with the defendant on top of her, having sexual connection with her, and that he then struck her with a club, which he had in his hand, and rendered her ·unconscious; that after finally coming to, she managed to go a short distance to the home of Mrs. Tutter, who afterwards called for a doctor, and had the chief of police at Independence notified as to the assault.

Dr. M. P. Woods, a physician at Independence, Mo., of 20 years' standing, testified, that he was called to treat Elizabeth Dahmm on or about the 28th of June, 1920, in Mrs. Tutter's yard at about 4:30 p. m.; that he found her suffering from a shock, and she was in a contused condition; that he could not arouse her; that he found a number of wounds about her face and neck, a large contusion over the left eye, a cut across the right eye and to the skull; that there was a wound on the back and upper part of her head, on the right side, 2½ to 2¾ inches in length; that she had, on the right side of her face, bruises, as if you could see the imprint of the object with which she must have been struck; that it was not a tear, but seemed to be a strike or knock; that her eyes were swollen, and one was shut; that her face was discolored, and she was bleeding from these various wounds and from her nose; that she had some marks on her neck, around her throat, and around the side of her neck; that there were marks of violence on her neck, finger prints, and some scratches through the skin; that her condition was caused by violence.

A. Tannehill, a member of the police force, with Chief of Police Harris, went out to the scene of the trouble, and Tannehill found, at the home of Mrs. Dahmm, in the bedroom, a puddle of blood on the bed, and some other blood on the floor, which had dried; that he found a stick 30 feet from the house, lying in the weeds. This stick was preserved, and introduced at the trial. The evidence on behalf of the state disclosed that the stick was shown to defendant after his arrest, and he admitted to the chief of police and others that it was the stick with which he assaulted Elizabeth Dahmm.

After the assault, the defendant was at the station about 4 o'clock p. m., preparing to leave for Glasgow, Mo. None of the railroad men at that time knew of the assault, and no one in the town knew of it, except Chief of Police Harris. Just before defendant took the train for Glasgow, he had a talk with Chief Harris, and volunteered the statement that—

"The man who committed that crime ought to be tarred and feathered out in the middle of the street, and I think I can give you some evidence."

He then said to Chief Harris that two fellows had caught the train going east, and if he would wire to Glasgow he might catch them. At this time, Mrs. Dahmm was in the sanitarium at Independence, having been taken there by Chief Harris.

The defendant took the train for Glasgow, and after a more minute description of the assailant had been obtained from Mrs. Dahmm, a telegram was sent, calling for the arrest of defendant. He ran nearly six miles, fleeing from the officer, before he was arrested. After being brought back to Jackson county, when approaching Independence, he asked Chief Harris to take him on to Kansas City, as he did not want to stop at Independence. The chief complied with his request, and placed him in the jail at Kansas City until the following morning. When the chief came for defendant to take him to Independence, he protested against going, and said he wanted to plead guilty. Without any threats or promises from anybody, he then told the Chief of Police and the Assistant Prosecuting Attorney that he was guilty of the crime charged against him, and wanted to plead guilty. At his request, a written statement as to what occurred was prepared and signed by him, in regard to the assault, but he changed front and denied therein that he had committed the rape. Said statement was offered in evidence, and is in words and figures following, to wit:

"July 2, 1920.

"Statement of Walker Lee, made July 2, 1920, to Chief Harris and Will S. Guinotte, Assistant Prosecuting Attorney, at the office of the Prosecuting Attorney at Kansas City:

"My name is Walker Lee. I am 36 years old, and a single man. I have lived at Roanoke, Mo., all my life. My mother, Mary Jane Lee, is living there now. I came to Independence, Mo., on June 19, 1920, and was employed by the Chicago & Alton Railway as a section hand. I worked on track near Alton avenue, which was about two blocks from Mrs. Dahmm's house. At night I slept in the boarding car with the other hands.

"I quit the job on the railroad the morning of the 28th of June, 1920. Lloyd Snoddy and Pat Casey, two colored boys who lived at Glasgow, quit at the same time. We were going to Glasgow that night to get our pay. I shot 'craps' that morning, and ate dinner about 12 o'clock at the boarding car. I loafed around after dinner. About 2 o'clock I walked east on the

cks about two blocks, where I passed a use that sits about 50 feet from the tracks. walked on up the track a little ways, and then me back and went down to this house to get drink. A woman came to the door and I ked her for some matches, and she said 'to me on in,' and she gave them to me. There as a piece of stovewood by the door, and I cked it up and held at my side. The woman iked me where I lived and what I was doing, nd I told her that I had been working on the ailroad and was going home to Glasgow. Her ead was turned away from me, and I hit her ver the head with the club. I do not remember how many times I hit her. I then ran ut of the house and went back to the boarding ar. I was passed down to Glasgow on the 5:27 train, and then to Mexico where I caught he Wabash to Moberly, where I went to see my sister, Minnie Lee, who works at the Woodland Hospital. I came back to Slater Tuesday night and Tuesday morning, Wednesday morning, the officers at Slater tried to arrest me. I got away, and went to Gallatin, where I was arrested by two officers from Glasgow, and taken back and confined in the jail at Glasgow, Mo. I was returned to Independence by Chief Harris Thursday. This statement is made of my own free will and accord, no threats or promises having been made by any one, but because it is the truth.   [Signed] Walker Lee.
"Witnesses:
    "Will S. Guinotte."

The evidence shows, that after defendant was arrested and brought to Jackson county, Mrs. Dahmm identified him as the man who assaulted and raped her.

Defendant's Evidence.

The only testimony offered in behalf of appellant was that given by himself, in which he testified that he was 37 years of age; that on the 28th of June, 1920, after quitting his job, he came back to the bunk car and went to the railroad pond to take a swim; that he found other boys in the pond, and did not go in, but watched the others for about one hour; that he then came back, talked to the foreman, and, with the other railroad employees, received a pass to go to Slater; that the police officer who brought him to Kansas City tried to get him to make a statement, by saying there was a mob waiting for him; that Chief Harris told him of the crime the day it was committed; that he did not admit to the officers that he had ever seen the club before; that he did not go to the house of Elizabeth Dahmm on the 28th of June, 1920; that he did not ask her for matches; that he did not have the conversation with her on said date; that there was no blood on his hat and overalls; and that he did not commit this crime.

Other testimony in the case tends to corroborate the statement to the effect that defendant was the man who made the assault on Mrs. Dahmm, as heretofore stated.

The court gave five instructions covering

the case, which were not objected to by defendant, and the jury thereafter returned into court the following verdict:

"We, the jury, find the defendant, Walker Lee, guilty of rape as charged in the indictment and assess his punishment at death."

Defendant in due time filed motions for a new trial and in arrest of judgment. Both motions were overruled, he was thereafter sentenced and judgment entered, in accordance with the statute, and an appeal was duly granted him to this court.

Knox & Gibbs, of Kansas City, for appellant.

Jesse W. Barrett, Atty. Gen., Robert J. Smith, and Robert W. Otto, Asst. Atty. Gen., for the State.

RAILEY, C. 1. Defendant is not represented here by counsel, although he has been convicted of one of the most atrocious crimes known to our law, that of rape. We, therefore, feel the responsibility devolving upon us of making a thorough examination of the law and facts to ascertain whether defendant has had a fair and impartial trial, and to determine whether he has been convicted upon substantial evidence.

[1] While no assault has been made upon the indictment, we have examined the same and find it to be in proper form. Section 3247, R. S. 1919; State v. Warren, 232 Mo. 185, 199, 134 S. W. 522, Ann. Cas. 1912B, 1043; State v. Burries, 126 Mo. 565-566-567, 29 S. W. 842.

2. The court gave five instructions to the jury, which were not objected to by appellant, as to either form or substance. They clearly, properly and fairly declared the law by which the jurors were to be governed in arriving at their verdict. As no complaint was made, or objection urged, against the instructions given, we have not deemed it necessary to set them out.

[2] 3. It does not appear from the record that defendant offered any instructions, aside from those given, nor does it appear that any request was made of the court to instruct upon any other branch of the case, outside of the questions properly covered by the instructions given. The complaint, therefore, in defendant's motion for a new trial, that the court failed to instruct the jury upon all phases of the offense, is without merit, and especially so as no exception was saved as to the alleged nondirection of the court in respect to said matter. State v. Cook, 207 S. W. loc. cit. 833; State v. Wansong, 271 Mo. loc. cit. 59, 195 S. W. 1002; State v. Pfeifer, 267 Mo. 23, 183 S. W. 337; State v. Smith, 190 S. W. loc. cit. 1060; State v. Gifford, 186 S. W. loc. cit. 1060; State v. Taylor, 267 Mo. 41, 183 S. W. 299; State v. Snyder, 263 Mo. loc. cit. 668, 173 S. W. 1078; State v. Sykes, 248 Mo. 708, 154 S. W. 1130; State v. Chis-

sell, 245 Mo. loc. cit. 554, 555, 150 S. W. 1066; State v. Dockery, 243 Mo. 592, 147 S. W. 976.

[3] 4. Defendant, when the jury was being impaneled, objected to the statement of Mr. Curtin, assistant prosecutor, to the effect that he was charged "with raping a white woman by the name of Elizabeth Dahmm," etc. The court sustained the objection on the theory that the indictment did not say Mrs. Dahmm was a white woman, but told the prosecutor he could say to the jury that the evidence would show Mrs. Dahmm was a white woman. To our mind the objection made was without merit, as Mrs. Dahmm was present and testified in the case. The jury could see from her appearance she was a white woman. The court, however, sustained defendant's objection to said statement of the prosecutor, and no exception was saved as to the ruling of the court in respect to this matter.

[4] 5. Appellant's counsel objected to the testimony of several witnesses offered by the state, on the ground that the names of said witnesses were not indorsed on the copy of the indictment furnished defendant. The indictment on file in the case, as shown by the record here, had the names of said witnesses endorsed thereon. The alleged copy of the indictment, which defendant had, was not produced in evidence. No motion to quash the indictment was filed by defendant, nor was a continuance of the case asked. Even if the original indictment did not have the names of witnesses indorsed thereon, defendant was in no condition to complain of the testimony of said witnesses, unless he moved to quash the indictment, or asked for a continuance to meet the testimony thus offered. State v. Kehoe, 220 S. W. loc. cit. 963; State v. Ferguson, 278 Mo. 119, 212 S. W. loc. cit. 343; State v. Stegner, 276 Mo. 428, 207 S. W. 826; State v. Webb, 205 S. W. 187; State v. Ivy, 192 S. W. 733; State v. Jackson, 186 S. W. 990; State v. Robinson, 263 Mo. loc. cit. 324, 172 S. W. 598; State v. Walton, 255 Mo. 233, 164 S. W. 211; State v. Rasco, 239 Mo. loc. cit. 553, 554, 144 S. W. 449; State v. Jeffries, 210 Mo. 302, 109 S. W. 314, 14 Ann. Cas. 524; State v. Barrington, 198 Mo. 23, 95 S. W. 235; State v. Myers, 198 Mo. 225, 94 S. W. 242.

[5] (a) Defendant's complaint that a few of the witnesses, whose names were not on the original indictment, were not competent to testify by reason of that fact, is not tenable, as the prosecutor explained to the court he had just learned of their importance, etc. Under the foregoing authorities, the court committed no error in permitting said witnesses to testify.

[6, 7] 6. Appellant in his motion for a new trial contends that the court committed error, to his prejudice, in permitting the state to read to the jury the written statement of defendant, heretofore set out. The evidence is clear and convincing that no promises or threats were made to defendant as an inducement for him to sign said statement. On the contrary, we are satisfied from the record before us beyond a reasonable doubt that defendant voluntarily and of his own free will and accord made the statement aforesaid, as well as the oral admissions, relating to his guilt, etc. The court, therefore, committed no error in permitting said statement to be read in evidence; and likewise committed no error in permitting Chief Harris and Judge Pendleton to testify as to the admissions made in their presence by defendant, as to his guilt and connection with the crime charged against him. State v. Thomas, 250 Mo. loc. cit. 211, 157 S. W. 330; State v. Brooks, 220 Mo. loc. cit. 83, 84, 119 S. W. 353; State v. Armstrong, 203 Mo. loc. cit. 558, 559, 102 S. W. 503; State v. Spaugh, 200 Mo. loc. cit. 596, 597, 98 S. W. 55; State v. Barrington, 198 Mo. loc. cit. 109, 110, 94 S. W. 235; State v. Jones, 171 Mo. loc. cit. 406, 71 S. W. 680, 94 Am. St. Rep. 786; State v. Meyers, 99 Mo. loc. cit. 119, 12 S. W. 516; State v. Patterson, 73 Mo. 695.

7. After reading and considering the record herein with painstaking care, we have not been able to find any error of which defendant can legally complain. The case was carefully and well tried by the court and counsel upon each side. There is nothing in the record to indicate that defendant had other than a fair and impartial trial, before an unprejudiced jury. It is to the credit of the state that a case of this character has been tried within its limits, and punishment administered to a person found guilty of the detestable crime of rape, under the orderly administration of legal procedure, rather than by a resort to mob law.

The judgment of the trial court is affirmed, and the cause remanded to the criminal court aforesaid, to be proceeded with in accordance with its judgment.

WHITE and MOZLEY, CC., concur.

PER CURIAM. The foregoing opinion of RAILEY, C., is hereby adopted as the opinion of the court.

All concur.

BORACK v. MOSLER SAFE CO. et al.
(No. 21673.)

(Supreme Court of Missouri, Division No. 2.
April 7, 1921. Rehearing Denied
May 26, 1921.)

1. **Appeal and error ☞1005(4) — Order, granting new trial on ground that verdict is against weight of evidence, reversed.**

Supreme Court will not interfere with action of trial court in granting new trial on the ground that the verdict of the jury was against the weight of the evidence, if there is any substantial evidence which would support a different verdict, but, if the evidence is such that a different verdict could not be allowed to stand, an order granting a new trial will be reversed, even though such order was bottomed by the trial court on the ground that the verdict was against the weight of the evidence.

2. **Municipal corporations ☞705(4, 11)—Negligence per se to violate ordinance relating to manner of turning at intersections; violation of traffic ordinance, to be actionable, must be proximate cause of injury.**

A violation of an ordinance, requiring vehicles in turning to the left into another street to turn to the right of and beyond the center of the intersecting street before turning, is negligence per se, and the violator is liable in damages for all injuries proximately caused thereby, but violator cannot be required to respond in damages if the injury was caused by an occurrence over which the violator had no control, and which he could not have reasonably foreseen as the result of such violation.

3. **Municipal corporations ☞705(11)—Cutting corner in violation of city ordinance held not proximate cause of death.**

Violation by a teamster of a city ordinance, requiring vehicles in turning to the left into another street to turn to the right of and beyond the center of the intersecting street before turning, was not the proximate cause of the death of plaintiff's decedent, occasioned by one wheel of the wagon getting in the rail of a street car track, causing a violent jerk, and one of the horses to slip and fall against the tongue of the wagon in such manner as to cause the end of the tongue to strike the deceased, who was on a temporary sidewalk selling newspapers, and decedent's widow was not entitled to recover.

Appeal from St. Louis Circuit Court; Robert W. Hall, Judge.

Action by Rosa Borack against the Mosler Safe Company and others. From an order granting a new trial after a verdict for defendants, defendant Ernest J. Weis appeals. Reversed and remanded, with instructions to reinstate the verdict and re-enter judgment for defendant Weis.

W. H. Douglass, of St. Louis, for appellant.

Edw. W. Foristel, of St. Louis (James T. Roberts, of St. Louis, of counsel), for respondent.

DAVID E. BLAIR, J. The action is for damages in the sum of $10,000 for death of the husband of respondent, plaintiff below, due to alleged negligence of the defendants. Trial by jury resulted in a verdict for the defendants Mosler Safe Company and Ernest J. Weis. The trial court sustained a demurrer to the evidence as to defendant George F. Kiesel. The trial court sustained plaintiff's motion for a new trial on two grounds:

First, "because the verdict was against the weight of the evidence"; and, second, "because the court erred in refusing to give the jury an instruction declaring the law to be that a police officer has no right by an act of his own to violate a valid subsisting city ordinance."

Defendant Weis appealed from the order setting aside the verdict and granting a new trial.

Plaintiff is the widow of Abraham Borack, a blind news vendor, who was killed on or about September 14, 1916, as a result of a blow from the tongue of a dray wagon owned and operated by defendant Weis. Said defendant was engaged in hauling material for a building being erected at the northeast corner of Broadway and Washington avenue in the city of St. Louis. In the course of this work a fence had been built around the structure between it and the curb, and a narrow sidewalk had been constructed alongside the fence for use by the public. Defendant's driver had hauled several loads of material, and in unloading the same had caused serious obstruction to traffic, because the stopping of his team and wagon at the proper place for unloading prevented passengers on the street cars from boarding and leaving the same. In the position he had theretofore assumed the team and wagon were on the north side of Washington avenue with the team to the west. Having noticed the obstruction referred to, the traffic officer on duty on that corner directed said driver on his next trip to come in another way, that is, to come south on Broadway and turn toward the east on the north side of Washington. By coming around in this manner the team and wagon would be stopped far enough to the east of the unloading point to avoid interference with passengers getting on and off the street cars and the movement of such cars on Washington.

In obedience to these instructions and on his next trip the driver drove his team south on Broadway, and stopped just north of the north line of Washington until he received a signal from the traffic officer. He testified that he remained there 15 or 20 minutes waiting for the congestion at that corner to be relieved. Upon receiving a signal from the officer he drove his team and wagon east on Washington, turning in a wide swing to the left of the intersection of the two streets, in order to bring his said wagon and team to a position with the left wheels close to the temporary sidewalk on the north side of Washington with the rear of the wagon at the proper place for unloading. In making this turn one wheel of the wagon caught in the rail of the street car track, and caused a violent jerk, and one of the horses slipped and fell against the tongue of the wagon in such manner as to cause the end of the tongue to strike the deceased, who was on or near the temporary sidewalk, selling his newspapers. The injury resulted in his death. At that place the pavement was composed of wooden blocks. These were more or less slippery at all times, and particularly so at the time of the accident, because it had been raining. At that point the pavement sloped more because of the location there of a drainage sewer. It appears from the evidence that horses are liable to slip and fall on wooden block pavement at any time, and especially when the pavement is wet, and there is no way to prevent the same. All the foregoing facts were shown by plaintiff's witnesses.

An ordinance of the city of St. Louis was introduced by plaintiff, which provided that—

"A vehicle in turning to the left into another street, shall turn to the right of and beyond the center of the intersecting street before turning."

The violation of this ordinance and the careless and negligent driving and management of the team by the driver constitute the main charge of negligence in the petition. The petition also alleged that defendant negligently overloaded the wagon in violation of another city ordinance introduced in evidence, so that it was impossible for the horses to pull the same with safety, and that this caused the fall of the horses and the resulting injury to the deceased.

The answer was a general denial and plea of negligence on the part of deceased. The reply was a general denial of the new matter alleged in the answer.

Defendant Weis interposed a demurrer to plaintiff's evidence, and also a demurrer to all the evidence introduced in the case, both of which were overruled by the court and exceptions saved.

I. The evidence of plaintiff did not disclose any overloading of the wagon, but rather that it was not loaded quite as heavily as usual. The court did not submit the question of the overloading of the wagon to the jury, and clearly such charge of negligence was not sustained by any evidence, and need not be further considered.

[1] II. If the record discloses any substantial evidence of negligence on the part of defendant's driver in the handling of the team which contributed to the injury of the deceased, this court will not interfere with the action of the trial court in granting a new trial on the ground that the verdict of the jury is against the weight of the evidence. But if the evidence is such that a verdict for plaintiff would not be allowed to stand, the order granting a new trial will be reversed, even though such order was bottomed by the trial court on the ground that the verdict is against the weight of the evidence. This has been so frequently and consistently ruled that citation of authorities is unnecessary.

[2] III. This brings us then to a consideration of the plaintiff's evidence. The ordinance of the city of St. Louis required vehicles, in turning to the left into another street, to turn to the right of and beyond the center of the intersecting street before turning. It is the general rule in this state that the violation of such an ordinance is negligence per se, and the violator is liable in damages for all injuries proximately caused thereby. Brannock v. Elmore, 114 Mo. 55, 21 S. W. 451; Schlereth v. Mo. Pac. Ry. Co., 96 Mo. 509, 10 S. W. 66.

Assuming for the purpose of the case, but without so deciding, that the defendant's driver under the circumstances here shown was guilty of negligence per se in driving to the left of the intersection of the streets, as claimed by plaintiff, yet defendant would not be liable for the death of plaintiff's decedent, unless such negligence was the proximate cause of his death. Even though defendant's driver was negligent in driving to the left in violation of the ordinance, defendant cannot be required to respond in damages if the injury to deceased was caused by an occurrence over which the driver had no control, and which he could not reasonably have foreseen as the result of such negligence. This is the rule laid down in Daneschocky v. Sieble, 195 Mo. App. 470, 193 S. W. 966, cited by respondent, and it is undoubtedly the general rule.

[3] Taken by itself, the sudden jerk of the wagon and slipping of a horse and fall of the horse against the wagon tongue, causing it to strike and injure deceased, could be nothing more than an accident. Plaintiff's evidence shows the driver was experienced in his work; that he did not make a sharp turn, but, on the contrary, made a wide turn. No jerking of the team or any act of the driver tending to cause the horse to fall is shown. The plaintiff's evidence further shows that there is no way to prevent horses from falling on wooden block pavement, either wet or dry.

It is clear that the turning to the left of the intersection of the streets had no tendency to increase the likelihood of a horse slipping and falling. Such accidents are as frequent in one place in the street as another. If the turn had been made to the right of the intersection, and in making such turn the same thing had occurred, we would not hesitate to characterize it as a mere accident. The turn to the left was probably no sharper than if it had been made to the right of the intersection, for in turning into the north side of Washington the driver would start to turn sooner. That would be all the difference. The driver could not have been expected to anticipate the fall of the horse as a result of such turn. The occurrence was a mere accident not reasonably to have been foreseen as a result of his alleged negligence.

A good illustration of results that might, and reasonably would, occur from a violation of an ordinance of this sort would be where a vehicle coming west bound along the north side of Washington avenue would collide with the team headed eastward on the wrong side of the street. If a collision of that sort had occurred, with or without negligence on the part of the driver of such other vehicle and knocked down defendant's horse and caused the injury to deceased, the result could be said to have been one the driver of defendant's team could reasonably have anticipated and naturally resulted from his violation of the ordinance. The accident here did not come within the class of accidents that reasonably resulted from the violation of the ordinance.

It therefore appears from the evidence of plaintiff and as a matter of law that the negligence of defendant's driver was not the proximate cause of the injury to plaintiff's decedent, and the trial court should have sustained defendant's demurrer at the close of plaintiff's case, and as defendant's evidence did not in any wise tend to strengthen plaintiff's case, the court again erred in refusing to give a peremptory instruction for defendant at the close of all the evidence. Since there was no evidence of negligence of defendant that was the proximate cause of the death of plaintiff's husband, there was no reason for the trial court to set aside the verdict of the jury as being against the weight of the evidence.

This being our view of the evidence, there is no necessity of discussing the proposition of law involved in the refusal of plaintiff's instruction. The verdict of the jury was for the right party.

It therefore follows that the order granting a new trial should be reversed, and the cause remanded, with instructions to the trial court to reinstate the verdict of the jury and re-enter judgment thereon in favor of defendant Weis.

All concur.

STATE v. BAIRD. (No. 22676.)

(Supreme Court of Missouri, Division No. 2. May 26, 1921.)

1. Criminal law ⟐⟐814(17)—When instruction on circumstantial evidence is necessary.

In a homicide prosecution, the court must instruct the jury in regard to circumstantial evidence, where the defendant's guilt is established wholly by circumstantial evidence, and where the fact of the homicide by the defendant depends upon circumstances, but not where the only resort to circumstantial evidence is to show the manner in which the homicide took place.

2. Criminal law ⟐⟐814(17) — Failure to instruct on circumstantial evidence held not error.

In a homicide prosecution, where defendant admitted having killed deceased, and there was nothing for the jury to determine from circumstantial evidence, except whether the defendant or the deceased was the aggressor, and whether there was justification for the act, or facts which would mitigate the crime, failure to instruct on circumstantial evidence *held* not error.

3. Witnesses ⟐⟐337(2)—Defendant may be impeached by evidence as to his veracity and morality, but not as to his character as a quarrelsome citizen.

Where defendant, charged with murder, took the stand in his own behalf, the state could impeach him, under Rev. St. 1919, § 4036, and show his bad reputation for truth, veracity, and morality; but it had no right to show his character as a quarrelsome, turbulent citizen, since such evidence did not tend to impeach him as a witness, but was an attack upon his character as a defendant.

4. Criminal law ⟐⟐776(1)—Evidence held to warrant instruction on good character.

In a prosecution for murder, evidence *held* to warrant an instruction on good character.

5. Criminal law ⟐⟐1137(5)—The state, having produced evidence as to defendant's character, could not complain that his character was not in issue.

In a homicide prosecution, the state, having treated defendant's character as in issue, and having produced evidence tending to show bad character, could not complain that the issue was not before the jury, because the defendant had not himself put his character in issue.

6. Criminal law ⟐⟐776(1)—Meaning of words "whenever necessary," within statute requiring instruction on good character.

The words "whenever necessary," within Rev. St. 1919, § 4025, requiring court to instruct on defendant's good character "whenever necessary," is not limited to cases where the defendant himself has offered evidence of his good character, but includes any case where his character is put in issue, and there is sufficient evidence to warrant a finding that his character is good.

7. Estoppel ⟐⟐68(1)—Parties bound to positions assumed.

Parties to a litigation are bound to positions they assume therein.

8. Estoppel ⟐⟐62(2)—State bound by a position assumed.

The state is bound by a position assumed by it in a criminal proceeding.

Appeal from Circuit Court, Pemiscot County.

Everett Baird was convicted of murder in the second degree, and he appeals. Reversed and remanded.

Mayes & Gossom, of Caruthersville, for appellant.

Jesse W. Barrett, Asst. Atty. Gen., and J. Henry Caruthers, Sp. Asst. Atty. Gen., for the State.

WHITE, C. The appellant, March 23, 1920, in the circuit court of Pemiscot county, was convicted of murder in the second degree, and his punishment fixed at imprisonment in the penitentiary for a term of 15 years. He was charged with having killed one Will Jenkins on the 10th day of August, 1919.

Jenkins and Baird were farmers, and lived near each other; their two houses being about 100 yards apart. It seems that Jenkins was making a crop on the shares for Baird. The two men had had some difficulty; the evidence showed that each had made violent threats against the other. The house of the two men fronted east, and it appears that a division fence, somewhere near midway between the two houses, separated their respective inclosures; Baird's house being on the south. To the rear, and a little to the north of Baird's house, was his barn. North of the barn, across the fence, was Jenkins' cornfield. There was no witness to the homicide, except the defendant himself. Jenkins' body, a few moments after he was shot, was found a few feet from the division fence, inside his cornfield, among the cornstalks. The state attempted to show the shot which killed Jenkins was fired from a window in the loft of Baird's crib, which window was about 18 or 20 feet south of where Jenkins' body lay. He was killed with a shotgun, and according to the testimony the wounds ranged downward, indicating that he was shot from an elevation. Baird admitted he killed Jenkins with a shotgun, and explained to several persons who testified for the state how it occurred. It is claimed by the state that those explanations were inconsistent.

According to the evidence offered by the defendant, on the morning before the tragedy, about 8:30 in the morning, Baird went away from home to a little town called Netherlands. While he was gone, his wife and Jenkins' wife had a quarrel about vegetables in the garden. It seems that the gardens of the two were inclosed together. A short time afterwards Jenkins appeared at the milk house in Baird's yard where Mrs. Baird was, and abused her violently, threatening to kill the defendant. He had a shotgun at the time and went off through the field; Mrs. Baird thought, hunting for her husband. Mrs. Baird then brought out her husband's shotgun, and when he returned from town she told him of the altercation. Soon afterwards Jenkins appeared with his gun, apparently "stalking" the defendant, peeping around his barn, as if to discover where he was. After watching for a time, the defendant stepped out in the open, and after a few remarks and gestures, from which appellant claimed he thought Jenkins was about to shoot him, he fired the fatal shot. Eleven shot took effect in Jenkins' head, killing him instantly. Evidence was offered by defendant to prove that Jenkins was a violent, turbulent, quarrelsome character. Evidence also was offered by the state as to the defendant's character, which will be noted later in the opinion.

The evidence indicates that Jenkins fell where he lay, about 18 or 20 feet north of the window in the loft of the defendant's barn, and about 5 feet north of the division fence. The stalks of corn near the body showed the marks of a shot. With the view we take of the case, it is unnecessary to set out the evidence at greater length.

[1] I. The appellant assigns error to the failure of the court fully to instruct the jury on all the questions of law involved in the case. He claimed the court should have instructed in regard to circumstantial evidence. The court must instruct the jury in regard to it, where the guilt of the defendant is established wholly by circumstantial evidence. Where the fact of the homicide by the defendant depends upon circumstances, such an instruction is necessary, but not where the only resort to circumstantial evidence is for the purpose of showing the manner in which the homicide took place. State v. Gartrell, 171 Mo. loc. cit. 519, 17 S. W. 1045; State v. Crone, 209 Mo. 316, loc. cit. 331, 108 S. W. 555; State v. Bobbitt, 215 Mo. loc. cit. 43, 114 S. W. 511; State v. Massey, 274 Mo. 578, 204 S. W. loc. cit. 543.

[2] In this case the defendant admitted that he killed Jenkins; nothing was left for the jury to determine from circumstance, except as to who was the aggressor, and whether there was justification for the act or facts which would mitigate the crime. Such instruction in this case was not necessary.

[3] II. Error is further claimed in the failure of the court to instruct on the good character of the defendant. The statute (section 4025, R. S. 1919) requires the trial court, whether requested or not, to instruct the jury upon all questions of law arising in a criminal case, which instructions must include, "whenever necessary, the subjects of good character and reasonable doubt."

The defendant did not put his character in issue—offered no evidence as to good character. He took the stand in his own behalf, and the state had the right to impeach him "as any other witness." See section 4036,

R. S. 1919. The state, in rebuttal, recalled three witnesses, B. F. Allen, William Foley, and C. L. Lefler. Allen testified as follows, without objection:

"Q. How long have you known Everett Baird? A. Known Everett Baird as far as I remember. I got acquainted with Everett Baird about 1906 or 1907, as well as I remember.

"Q. Ask if you are acquainted with his general reputation for truth and veracity in the neighborhood in which he has lived? A. Never heard that discussed.

"Q. Ask whether or not you are acquainted with his general reputation as to being a dangerous, quarrelsome, and turbulent character? A. Yes, sir; I am acquainted with it.

"Q. Is that good or bad? A. It is not bad for quarreling— (Interrupted:)

"Q. Dangerous? A. —and dangerous.

"Q. The full question? A. Not dangerous for quarreling and fighting, unless you impose on him.

"By the Court: You say it is not bad for that?

"Witness: No, sir; it is not bad."

Foley testified that he did not know the defendant's general reputation in the neighborhood in which he lived for being a dangerous, quarrelsome, turbulent character.

Lefler testified without objection, as follows:

"Q. Mr. Lefler, I will ask whether or not you are acquainted with the general reputation of the defendant in this case for being a dangerous, quarrelsome, and turbulent character? A. Yes, sir.

"Q. Is that good or bad? A. Well, it is not so bad.

"Q. Is it good or bad? A. Well, lately he has been a pretty good man; used to be, when he got whisky in him, of course, he didn't care much.

"Q. Since whisky gone out, he's done pretty well? A. Different man before whisky went out.

"By the Court: How long back, do you say? "Witness: I guess for a year or two."

The state had a right to show that defendant had a bad reputation for truth and veracity, and that his general reputation for morality was bad; but it had no right, for the purpose of impeaching him as a witness, to show that he was of bad character as a quarrelsome, turbulent citizen. State v. Beckner, 194 Mo. 281, loc. cit. 294–296, 91 S. W. 892, 3 L. R. A. (N. S.) 585; State v. Shuster, 263 Mo. loc. cit. 602, 173 S. W. 1049; State v. Edmundson, 218 S. W. loc. cit. 865. Such evidence did not tend to impeach the defendant in his character as a witness, but was an assault upon his character as a defendant. State v. Beckner, supra, 194 Mo. loc. cit. 294, 91 S. W. 892, 3 L. R. A. (N. S.) 585. It was an attempt to show he possessed the very qualities which would affect his tendency to commit the crime of which he was charged.

[4] It is claimed by the state that this evidence is not sufficient to warrant an instruc-

tion upon good character, because it is not substantial evidence of good character. This court has held that "whenever necessary," as used in the section of the statute quoted, means "whenever there is any substantial evidence of general reputation of such character offered in evidence." State v. Cook, 207 S. W. loc. cit. 833; State v. Byrd, 213 S. W. 37. The case of State v. Anslinger, 171 Mo. loc. cit. 608, 609, 71 S. W. 1041, is cited by the state in support of the propriety of the court's refusal to give such instruction. In that case a witness was charged with illegal and fraudulent voting. The character witness testified that the defendant was a hard-working and industrious man, and the court held (171 Mo. loc. cit. 609, 71 S. W. 1041) that there was not the slightest evidence upon the trait of character involved in the charge which rendered it necessary for the information of the jury to instruct upon the subject of good character; that a man might be a hardworking man, and still be dishonest; it would not affect the trait of character which would lead him to vote illegally.

In this case the questions were addressed to the very trait of character involved in the commission of the crime charged, whether the defendant was turbulent and dangerous. Allen testified that he was acquainted with Baird's reputation; that it was not bad for quarreling and fighting. Lefler testified that he once had a bad reputation when he could get liquor, but that of late his reputation for being quarrelsome was not bad. This evidence was brought out by the state; it was not objected to by the defendant, and was proper for the jury's consideration; that is, the state made an assault upon the defendant's character as a defendant, and the evidence tended to show the reverse of what was intended. We are unable to say that there was no substantial evidence that the defendant had a good character in that respect.

[5, 6] Further, having deliberately attacked the character of the defendant, treating the matter as being in issue, having made the attack with the expectation of proving a bad character, and having produced evidence tending to show the contrary, the state is not in position to say that the issue was not before the jury. "Whenever necessary," as used in the statute, is not limited to cases where the defendant himself has offered evidence of his good character, but it must include any case where his character is put in issue and there is sufficient evidence to warrant a finding by the jury that his character is good.

[7, 8] The position of the state in this respect is like that of a party to a suit who offers evidence as if an issue had been tendered by the pleading in the case, when in fact the pleading tendered no such issue.

He cannot, therefore, claim there was error in submitting such issue to the jury; the court would err if it failed to submit the issue to the jury. Chouquette v. Southern Elec. Ry. Co., 152 Mo. loc. cit. 263, 264, 53 S. W. 897; Fisher & Co. Real Estate Co. v. Realty Co., 159 Mo. loc. cit. 567, 62 S. W. 443. Parties to litigation necessarily are held bound to positions they assume therein. Green v. City of St. Louis, 106 Mo. 454, loc. cit. 458, 17 S. W. 496. We see no reason why this rule should not be applied to the state in a criminal proceeding. We therefore are of the opinion that the court erred in refusing to instruct the jury on the question of defendant's character.

Other errors are assigned, which we deem it unnecessary to consider, because like circumstances probably will not occur in another trial.

The judgment is reversed, and the cause remanded.

RAILEY and MOZLEY, CC., concur.

PER CURIAM. The foregoing opinion by WHITE, C., is adopted as the opinion of the court.

All concur.

PETER HAUPTMANN TOBACCO CO. v. UNVERFERTH. (No. 21425.)

(Supreme Court of Missouri, Division No. 2. May 26, 1921.)

1. **Justices of the peace ⬢⟲161(3) — Appeal from default judgment in justice court an appearance.**

By an appeal to circuit court from a default judgment of justice court defendant entered his appearance in the case, and he was in court for all purposes of his case in the circuit court, and it made no difference whether he went to trial on a plea in abatement or on the merits, or made default after his motion to discharge a garnishment and for dismissal of the case had been overruled; such motions being utterly futile for the purpose of attacking the jurisdiction of the justice court over his person or property brought before that court by garnishment or under a writ of attachment.

2. **Justices of the peace ⬢⟲44(3)—Jurisdiction in tort action determined by demand.**

In an action in conversion, based on tort, and not on a written instrument, jurisdiction of justice court is determined by the demand in the pleadings, and it is immaterial that plaintiff's loss may have been in excess of $500.

3. **Trover and conversion ⬢⟲66—Embezzlement held question for jury.**

Evidence in action based on claim of abstraction of money by defendant from plaintiff's safe *held* to make a case for the jury.

Appeal from St. Louis Circuit Court; Glendy B. Arnold, Judge.

Action by the Peter Hauptmann Tobacco Company against Henry Unverferth. There was a judgment for plaintiff, which was affirmed in the Court of Appeals (200 Mo. App. 482, 207 S. W. 283), and the case certified to the Supreme Court. Affirmed.

Anderson, Gilbert & Hayden, of St. Louis, for appellant.

D. J. O'Keefe, of St. Louis, for respondent.

DAVID E. BLAIR, Judge. Appeal from the circuit court of the city of St. Louis to the St. Louis Court of Appeals. The judgment of the circuit court was there affirmed, and the case was certified here as being contrary to a previous decision of the Springfield Court of Appeals in the case of Lively v. Munal-Jones Lumber Co., 194 S. W. 741.

The opinion of the St. Louis Court of Appeals was by Reynolds, P. J., and was reported in 200 Mo. App. 482, 207 S. W. 283. We content ourselves with making reference to the case as there reported for a full statement of the facts and the opinion of the court. In brief, plaintiff (respondent here) instituted suit by attachment before Robert Walker, a justice of the peace of the city of St. Louis, against defendant for $500 for money of the plaintiff alleged to have been taken by the defendant from a safe belonging to plaintiff. Defendant was in the habit of receiving money from plaintiff's drivers and placing it for safe-keeping in sealed envelopes in said safe which was in the office at the stables of the plaintiff, where defendant worked as head stableman. Defendant lived with his family over the stable and had access to the office and safe at all times. He reported the loss of the money, and it was thereafter charged that he took the money and checks amounting to something over $600.

The demand in the suit filed was for $500, the limit of the money jurisdiction of the justice court. The checks amounted to about $100. A garnishment was issued on said attachment and served upon two banks, one of which was the Broadway Savings Trust Company, which answered that it had in its possession the sum of $918.72 as the property of the defendant.

The writ of attachment was issued on a form in which the name of Charles S. Luce, another justice of the peace in the same district, was used instead of the name of Robert Walker, the justice of the peace who issued the writ. Return to this writ was made by the constable showing service on June 4, 1914, by delivering a true copy to defendant and by summoning the Broadway Savings Trust Company and the Northwestern Bank as garnishees. The garnishment against the Northwestern Bank was subsequently dismissed.

When the error in naming Justice Luce was discovered, an amended writ was issued on June 18, 1914, correcting said error. This writ was dated and made returnable on the same dates as the original writ, to which writ constable made the return that he served it on defendant June 4, 1914, and summoned the Broadway Savings Trust Company as garnishee. Thereafter, and on September 1, 1914, the justice issued a new writ of attachment and summons returnable September 18, 1914, to which the constable made a non est return as to defendant and that he served the attachment by attaching money of the defendant in the hands of the Broadway Savings Trust Company. On October 1, 1914, the justice issued his alias writ to a special constable, commanding him to summon defendant to appear October 15, 1914, to which writ such special constable made return under oath that he served the summons by leaving a true copy thereof at the usual place of abode of the challenger with a member of his family over 15 years of age. On October 15, 1914, the justice rendered judgment against defendant by default in the sum of $500. It does not appear whether judgment was rendered against the garnishee. After the rendition of such default judgment in the justice court, defendant appealed the case to the circuit court.

In the circuit court the defendant filed his motion to discharge the garnishment, setting out that he appeared therein solely for the purpose of the motion. This motion detailed the proceedings before the justice of the peace, which we have only briefly outlined above, and averred that the proceedings in the justice court were null and void, and that the justice was without jurisdiction and prayed for a release of the garnishment and that the judgment in the justice of peace court be set aside and that the action be dismissed. This motion was overruled by the circuit court. Thereupon defendant filed his plea in abatement, stating that he appeared specially and only for the purpose of his plea in abatement and under protest, etc. The plea in abatement was tried first and resulted adversely to defendant. The trial of the case on the merits resulted likewise, and judgment was entered against the defendant for $500. Motion for a new trial and in arrest of judgment in the attachment proceedings and on the merits were overruled, and the defendant has appealed.

The main contention of defendant is that the justice of the peace acquired no jurisdiction of his person or his property, because there was no valid process; that the original writ of summons and attachment was void because returnable before another justice than the justice issuing same; that such void process could not be amended; that the writ of October 1, 1914, conferred no jurisdiction on the justice; that the statute does not authorize the appointment of a special constable to serve process in attachment suits, and that therefore service thereunder on the defendant was a nullity; that where the justice court acquired no jurisdiction the circuit court acquired none on appeal, and such appeal does not cure defective service or want of service.

The Court of Appeals sustained the action of the trial court and held that by going to trial on the merits the defendant lost the benefit of his plea to the jurisdiction of the justice over his person and refused to determine the validity of the attachment, because that question was deemed not material for the reason that defendant had given bond covering the personal judgment rendered against him.

The opinion of that court recites its rulings in the case of Powell v. Railway Co. (App.) 178 S. W. 212, wherein it had previously held that defendant in that case waived his right to challenge the jurisdiction of the justice court by taking an appeal to the circuit court, and further recited that said Powell Case had been certified to the Supreme Court, where it was still pending at that time.

[1] In the case of Cudahy Packing Co. v. Chicago & Northwestern Railway Co. (No. 21471) 230 S. W. 82, handed down in April, 1921, Division 1 of this court in an able and exhaustive opinion by James T. Blair, J., reviewed all the cases in this state on the vexed question of the effect of the taking of an appeal from the justice court to the circuit court, and, with the concurrence of all the judges of that division, held that the taking of such an appeal by the defendant "constitutes such an appearance as to waive defects in or absence of summons or service." By his appeal from the justice court the defendant entered his appearance in the case in that court, and he was in court for all purposes of his case in the circuit court. It made no difference whether he went to trial on a plea in abatement or on the merits or made default after his motion to discharge the garnishment and for dismissal of the case had been overruled. After he had entered his appearance by taking such appeal these motions were utterly futile for the purpose of attacking the jurisdiction of the justice court over his person or his property brought before that court by garnishment under the writ of attachment.

Another question raised by defendant and one not discussed in the opinion of the Court of Appeals is that the amount involved exceeded the jurisdiction of the justice court. The amount of cash missing exceeded $500, and no voluntary credit was given on the claim. To support this contention defendant cites the case of Trapp v.

Mersman, 183 Mo. App. 512, 167 S. W. 612. The action there was based on a note on ,which an amount in excess of the jurisdiction of the justice was due, and it was held that the written instrument, and not the memorandum of plaintiff as to the amount claimed, determined the jurisdiction of the justice court; that such memorandum did not amount to a voluntary credit on the note, so as to' bring it within the jurisdiction of the justice.

[2] In the case before us the action is based on tort and not on a written instrument. The jurisdiction of the justice court is determined by the demand. It is immaterial that plaintiff's loss may have been ·in excess of $500. Plaintiff is permitted to waive recovery for a part of its loss, if it wishes. The defendant is in no position to object to such reduction. Burden v. Hornsby, 50 Mo. 238.

[3] Defendant contends there was no evidence to support the judgment of the trial court, either on the merits or upon the attachment. It is unnecessary to set out the evidence at length, because it is fully reviewed in the opinion of the Court of Appeals. It tends to establish that defendant received the money exceeding $500 and put it in a safe under his control, and that he was the only one present having keys to the inner door of the safe. The regular watchman was on duty from 5 o'clock the evening before until after 5 o'clock the next morning and did not leave premises during the night. There was a vicious watchdog loose in the stables at night that would not permit strangers to enter. This watchman saw defendant come down to the office at about 5 o'clock on the morning the money was missing. This was an hour earlier than he usually came down stairs. The watchman saw no one except defendant about the place. A police officer saw defendant at 6:40 or 6:45 in the morning trying to open the safe, and afterwards saw him running south away from the stables and asked him what was the matter, and defendant stated that the money was gone. Defendant gave several reasons for opening the safe. Search of his rooms was made, but none of the money was found. The Court of Appeals held that there was sufficient evidence to make a case for the plaintiff to submit to the trier of the facts. We agree with that court that there was sufficient evidence to make out a case for plaintiff. The same evidence which entitled the plaintiff to have the case submitted on the merits was sufficient on the plea in abatement on the ground that the damages for which the action was brought arose from the commission of a felony. The findings of the trial court conclude the matter.

Finding no error in the record, the judgment of the trial court is affirmed.

All concur.

BURTON v. HOLMAN et al.   (No. 22083.)

(Supreme Court of Missouri, Division No. 2. May 26, 1921.)

1. Wills ⬖400—Instructions held not ground for reversal as against contention that jury might have been misled into considering mental capacity an issue.

In a contest of a will on the ground of undue influence, in which the mental capacity of testatrix was not questioned either in the pleadings or during the trial, the granting of an instruction that if the testimony of the attesting witnesses was true the instrument was the will of testatrix unless jury should further find that it was the result of undue influence, and refusal to instruct that mental capacity was not an issue, held not ground for reversal, since jury could not have been misled as to whether mental capacity of testatrix was an issue.

2. Trial ⬖418 — Defendants, by presenting own evidence, waived overruling of demurrer to plaintiff's evidence.

Defendants, by presenting their own testimony, instead of standing upon their demurrer to plaintiff's evidence in chief, waived their right to object to the overruling of such demurrer, as it then became the duty of the jury to pass upon the evidence as a whole.

3. Trial ⬖139(1) — Demurrer to plaintiff's evidence properly overruled if there is any substantial evidence to support cause of action.

If there is any substantial evidence tending to support plaintiff's cause of action, the court did not err in overruling demurrer to plaintiff's evidence.

4. Wills ⬖163(2)—Undue influence presumed on showing of confidential relationship between testatrix and beneficiary.

Where a fiduciary or confidential relationship is shown to have existed between testatrix and beneficiary of will, undue influence will be presumed, and beneficiary has the burden of showing that he did not exercise such undue influence.

5. Trial ⬖156(3)—Plaintiff given benefit of legitimate inference on defendant's demurrer to the evidence.

On defendant's demurrer to the evidence at the conclusion of the whole case, it is the court's duty to give plaintiff the benefit of every inference which a fair-minded jury of ordinary intelligence might legitimately draw from the evidence.

6. Wills ⬖324(3) — Whether will making testatrix's physician and confidential adviser a beneficiary was procured by undue influence held for jury.

In daughter's contest of mother's will on ground of undue influence, claimed to have been exerted by the mother's physician and trusted confidential adviser, made a beneficiary, the question of undue influence held for the jury.

7. Trial ⌐186—Instruction held properly refused as a comment on a part of evidence.

In daughter's contest of mother's will on ground of undue influence claimed to have been exerted by mother's physician and confidential adviser named as a beneficiary in the will, instruction that the mother had the right to dispose of the property as she saw fit, "and, although the jury may believe from the evidence that she made an unjust and improper disposition of her property by will and cut off some of her relatives with but little who had as strong or stronger claim on her generosity as others who received more of her will, such facts are no evidence of undue influence taken alone," *held* properly refused, being an unwarranted comment on a part of the testimony, and being in conflict with plaintiff's instruction properly declaring the law, and directing the jury, in passing upon undue influence, to consider all the facts and circumstances shown by the evidence.

Appeal from Circuit Court, Randolph County; A. W. Walker, Judge.

Suit by Mary H. Burton against H. Frank Holman, administrator of the estate of Martha Harlow, deceased, and others. Judgment for plaintiff, and defendants appeal. Affirmed.

This suit was commenced by plaintiff, in the circuit court of Randolph county, Mo., on August 9, 1918, in vacation, to contest the will of her mother, Martha Harlow, a resident of said county, who died about April 26, 1918. The will was duly probated in said county, and is set out in the abstract of record. The executor named in the will and the heirs of testatrix having refused to administer upon said estate, the probate court of Randolph county, on May 8, 1918, appointed defendant, H. Frank Holman, public administrator of said county, to take charge of the estate, and he is now the acting administrator of said estate. The other defendants are designated as beneficiaries in said will.

The controversy, as presented in the petition, is clearly stated in respondent's brief, as follows:

"The entire gist of the action is alleged to be undue influence exercised by the principal defendant, Dr. T. H. Dinwiddie, who was the practicing physician and trusted confidential adviser of the deceased, Martha Harlow."

Appellants state the issues involved as follows:

"The petition, while being very verbose, bases its right to set the will aside on undue influence only."

The answer of the real defendants, Dinwiddie and the trustees of the Baptist Church of Higbee, is a general denial of undue influence.

The testatrix, Martha Harlow, was the widow of John F. Harlow, who died about 1898, while living at Higbee, in said county. Plaintiff is the only child of testatrix and John F. Harlow. The will in controversy is dated April 4, 1903. By the third and seventh paragraphs of the will plaintiff was given $500 and the household and kitchen furniture left by her mother. The eighth paragraph of said will reads as follows:

"I will, devise and bequeath to T. H. Dinwiddie, lots nine (9) and ten (10) in block one (1), in Owen's division of Higbee, in Randolph county, Missouri, to have and to hold in fee simple forever, and I also will and bequeath to said T. H. Dinwiddie the sum of one thousand dollars."

The evidence tends to show that testatrix was about 76 or 78 years old when the will was made on April 4, 1903. Respondent contends that the estate left by testatrix was of the value of $6,500 or $7,000. Appellants contend that it was worth about $7,300. The latter amount is named as the value by Wisdom Burton, one of plaintiff's witnesses.

The will, after providing for the payment of testatrix's debts, and the other bequests mentioned, left the remainder of her estate to James E. Rucker and John H. Botts, as trustees of the Baptist Church of Higbee, Mo. As appellants are insisting that the cause should be reversed, with instructions to sustain the will, in order to avoid repetition, we will consider the evidence on the merits, the instructions, and the rulings of the court in the opinion.

The jury returned a verdict rejecting the will; judgment was entered in due form on the verdict; appellants, in due time, filed motions for a new trial and in arrest of judgment. Both motions were overruled, and they duly appealed the cause to this court.

J. H. Whitecotton, M. J. Lilly, W. B. Stone, and Edmund Burke, all of Moberly, for appellants.

Willard P. Cave, of Moberly, for respondent.

RAILEY, C. (after stating the facts as above). 1. There was no controversy at the trial over the pleadings or evidence thereunder as to the sufficiency of testatrix's mental capacity to make the will in controversy. Counsel for plaintiff, in his opening statement to the jury, after calling attention to the testimony which would show Dr. Dinwiddie was the family physician of testatrix, and was her confidential business adviser, said:

"If we show you these, then we say we do not think there will be any lingering doubt in your mind *that this will was procured by the undue influence of the defendant Dinwiddie.*" (Italics ours.)

Counsel for appellants, after stating to the jury their theory of the case, said:

"Now, I think the testimony will disclose these *facts, that the will was made of her own free will without influence or suggestion from a living soul.* If these facts turn out as I believe they will turn out, I don't believe you will have any trouble on earth in sustaining this will." (Italics ours.)

In appellants' original brief, it is said:

"The petition, while being very verbose, bases its right to set the will aside *on undue influence only.*" (Italics ours.)

In appellants' reply brief, it is said:

"It is admitted by the respondent that this action is based upon the exercise of *undue influence* by Dr. Dinwiddie over the mind of Martha Harlow, deceased, and therefore respondent claims that said will was procured by the *undue influence* of Dr. Dinwiddie." (Italics ours.)

In respondent's brief, it is said:

"The entire gist of the action is alleged to be *undue influence* exercised by the principal defendant, Dr. T. H. Dinwiddie, who was the practicing physician and trusted confidential business adviser of the deceased, Martha Harlow."

The plaintiff did not ask a verdict at the hands of the jury, upon the idea that testatrix did not have sufficient mental capacity to make the will. Nor does it appear from the record, that plaintiff's counsel argued or even suggested any such question before the jury. Appellants made formal proof as to the execution of the will by Jones and Wayne, who testified, without contradiction by any one, that testatrix was of sound mind and executed the will in their presence, etc. There was absolutely no controversy over the mentality of Mrs. Harlow, at any stage of the proceedings.

[1] The court, therefore, gave to the jury, at the instance of plaintiff, instructions A and D, which, in legal effect, told the jury if the testimony of Jones and Wayne was found by them to be true then they should find that the instrument produced was the will of testatrix, unless they should further find that it was the result of undue influence, etc. In said instructions A and D the jury were not directed to find for plaintiff under any circumstances. We are at a loss to understand how appellants could have been injured on account of the giving of said instructions.

In the case of Byrne v. Byrne, 250 Mo. loc. cit. 642, 157 S. W. 609, relied on by appellants, the facts were different. The meaning of the petition was doubtful, and the testimony produced at the trial was an issue in the case. On page 642 of 250 Mo. (157 S. W. 611) Judge Graves said:

"The *prima facie* case showed mental capacity, and even the evidence for the plaintiff is not sufficient to show mental incapacity. Under the pleadings and under the evidence there is no question *that this issue, if it was an issue,*

should have been taken out of the case by the instruction aforesaid. We do not think it was a *live* issue, either by proof or pleading, *but the petition is so peculiarly worded that the jury may have been misled, although no instruction was asked by plaintiff upon mental incapacity.* * * * Standing alone, under the facts of this case, it might not be such error as would necessarily work a reversal, but its refusal evidently contributed its mite to the result, *in an exceedingly close case.*" (Italics ours.)

The instruction mentioned by Judge Graves as having been refused is similar in form and substance to appellants' instruction 1 refused in this case.

On the facts heretofore set out, testatrix's mental capacity to make the will was not questioned in the pleadings or in the trial of the case. It would be a reflection upon the intelligence of the jury to hold that they might have been misled as to the mental capacity of testatrix to make the will in controversy. We accordingly hold that no reversible error was committed on account of the giving of said instructions A and D, nor in refusing appellant's instruction 1, although no harm would have resulted from the giving of same, and informing the jury thereby that mental incapacity was not an issue in the case.

[2] 2. Appellants, under proposition II of their "Points and Authorities," contend that the trial court committed error in overruling defendants' demurrer to plaintiff's evidence in chief. The law of this state is thoroughly settled adversely to appellants' contention. Instead of standing upon their demurrer to plaintiff's evidence in chief, appellants put before the jury their own testimony, and thereby waived their right to object to the overruling of said demurrer, as it then became the duty of the jury to pass upon the evidence as a whole. Bowen v. Ry. Co., 95 Mo. loc. cit. 275, 276, 8 S. W. 230; Guenther v. Ry. Co., 95 Mo. loc. cit. 289, 8 S. W. 371; McPherson v. Ry. Co., 97 Mo. loc. cit. 255, 10 S. W. 846; Hilz v. Ry. Co., 101 Mo. loc. cit. 42, 13 S. W. 946; Riggs v. Railroad, 216 Mo. loc. cit. 310, 115 S. W. 969; Riley v. O'Kelly, 250 Mo. loc. cit. 660, 157 S. W. 566; Lareau v. Lareau, 208 S. W. loc. cit. 243; State v. Jackson, 223 S. W. loc. cit. 728, and cases cited; State v. Mann, 217 S. W. loc. cit. 69, and cases cited.

Under the foregoing authorities, appellants' contention supra is without merit.

[3] 3. It is further insisted by defendants that their demurrer to the evidence, interposed at the conclusion of the whole case, should be sustained. If there was substantial evidence offered at the trial tending to support respondent's contention that the will in controversy was the result of undue influence upon the part of Dr. Dinwiddie over the mind of testatrix at the time of its execution, the trial court cannot be convicted of error in overruling said demurrer.

Appellants, at page 10 of their reply brief, very frankly state the law of this case, as follows:

"We admit that it is the law of this state that 'when a confidential relation is shown to exist between the testator and the recipient of his bounty, an exerted influence will be presumed to have induced the bequest, and the onus is cast upon the beneficiary to make explanation of the transaction and establish its reasonableness."

[4] The law, in respect to this subject, is very clearly and concisely stated by this court in Sittig v. Kersting, 223 S. W. loc. cit. 749, as follows:

"Under such circumstances (e. g., the showing of the existence of a fiduciary or confidential relation), the law presumes the bequest was the result of undue influence, and the burden is thus thrown upon the recipient of the bounty to show that it was not."

To same effect are the following cases: Kleinlein v. Krauss, 209 S. W. loc. cit. 936; Grundmann v. Wilde, 255 Mo. loc. cit. 116, 164 S. W. 200; Byrne v. Byrne, 250 Mo. loc. cit. 646, 157 S. W. 609; Cornet v. Cornet, 248 Mo. 184, 154 S. W. 121; Mowry and Kettering v. Norman, 204 Mo. loc. cit. 189, 103 S. W. 15, and cases cited; Roberts v. Bartlett, 190 Mo. loc. cit. 699 and fol., 89 S. W. 858; Dausman v. Rankin, 189 Mo. 688, 88 S. W. 696, 107 Am. St. Rep. 391.

[5] In considering the demurrer to the evidence, therefore, at the conclusion of the whole case, it becomes our duty to give respondent the benefit of every inference which a fair-minded jury of ordinary intelligence might legitimately draw from the evidence. It is equally as well settled that, where respondent has produced substantial evidence as to the merits of her case, it is not the province of this court to pass upon the weight of the evidence, nor have we any legal right to do so. Keeping in mind the foregoing principles of law, which should guide us in the consideration of this case, we will pass to a review of the testimony relating to the subject of undue influence.

The evidence of plaintiff tends to show that defendant Dr. Dinwiddie, a man said to be worth $20,000 to $25,000, who was neither related to plaintiff nor her mother, about the year 1899, became the administrator of the estate of John F. Harlow, deceased, who was the husband of testatrix, and shortly thereafter became the family physician of Mrs. Harlow, and continued as such up to the time of her death, in 1918; that during all of said period he was the confidential business adviser of Mrs. Harlow; that the latter was about 76 or 77 years of age when the will in controversy was executed on April 4, 1903; that, during the month of February, 1903, commencing with the 12th and ending with the 27th of said month, Dr. Dinwiddie made 12 visits to testatrix, and presented an account against her estate for said services, together with a bill for other services, amounting in the aggregate to $260.

Wisdom Burton testified that, shortly after the death of John F. Harlow, Dr. Dinwiddie became the physician of testatrix, "and from that time until she died he attended to her business and was her business confident to the most minute detail."

Dr. Nichols testified that Dr. Dinwiddie had been acting as the family physician of Mrs. Harlow, and continued as such physician, and looked after her business affairs.

R. I. Hines testified that, on one occasion, Dr. Dinwiddie, in speaking of testatrix, remarked that "the old lady couldn't pay for a load of wood without he said so."

Walter Shiftlett testified as follows:

"Q. What, if anything, in the way of presents and matters of that kind did he make to the old lady back in 1901, 1902, 1903, 1904, and 1905? A. Well, I have been there Christmas times and maybe around her birthday and she nearly would always have something that she said Doctor Dinwiddie gave to her—several times it was a small bottle of whisky and little dishes and glasses or something of that kind. I know a number of times she showed me little dishes that she said Doctor Dinwiddie gave to her."

Mrs. Dolly Shiftlett testified that, shortly after Mr. Harlow's death, Dr. Dinwiddie became the family physician of testatrix, and continued as such up to the time of her death; that he looked after the business of Mrs. Harlow wholly. This witness was a grandchild of testatrix, and testified that the latter was always on pleasant and congenial terms with plaintiff and the mother of witness.

Mr. Willard P. Cave testified in favor of plaintiff, as follows:

"To the best of my recollection, knowledge, and belief, the instrument was written at the request of the defendant, Dr. T. H. Dinwiddie, in my office, and taken away by him. I gave a receipt for the charge made for preparing the will, and it was delivered, with the will, to Dr. Dinwiddie, who took it away from my office."

He said he never saw testatrix, and did not know her.

Dr. Dinwiddie testified that he had treated Mrs. Harlow off and on from the date of her husband's death, up to the time of her death; that he was her regular physician; that he collected interest for her on notes that she had out; that he looked after property she had a mortgage on, to see if it was worth the money, "and attended to her business for her in a general way." He admitted that he borrowed $3,000 from testatrix, and owed a part of same at her death; that he was to pay her 5 per cent. interest on the loan, and that he never got less than 6 per cent. on his loans; that the credits on said $3,000 note were in his handwriting. Dr. Dinwiddie denied that he took the draft of the will to Mr. Cave and denied in toto the facts which Cave testified about. He also testified that he had nothing to do with the will, or the making of same, and that he never knew of its contents until after the death of Mrs. Harlow, although he had heard it intimated that she had made a will before she died.

T. H. Walton testified, in behalf of defendants, that Mrs. Harlow told him in 1911 she would not sell the home where she was living; that she wanted it to go to Dr. T. H. Dinwiddie at her death, "for her appreciation of what he had done for her."

E. E. Newman was cashier of the Higbee Savings Bank. He said Dr. Dinwiddie was a director in said bank, and that Mrs. Harlow's will was kept in the vault of said bank with other wills.

The evidence of plaintiff tends to show that the value of the estate left by Mrs. Harlow at her death was about $7,000, and that about $3,500 in value of her property was willed to Dr. Dinwiddie, while but $500 and the household and kitchen furniture was given to plaintiff, her only child, by the provisions of the will.

[6] The foregoing is a fair outline of the testimony relating to the subject of undue influence. In view of the law on this subject, as stated at the commencement of this proposition, we hold, without the slightest hesitation, that the trial court was clearly right in overruling appellants' demurrer to the evidence at the conclusion of the whole case.

[7] 4. The trial court is charged with error in refusing defendants' instruction numbered 3, which reads as follows:

"The court instructs the jury that Martha Harlow in making her will had the right to dispose of her property as she wished and to give all or so much of the same thereof to any one of her relatives, or even to other persons not her relatives, as she saw fit or deemed proper; and, although the jury may believe from the evidence that she made an unjust and improper disposition of her property by will, and cut off some of her relatives with but little who had as strong or stronger claim on her generosity as others who received more of her will, *such facts are no evidence of undue influence taken alone*, and raise no presumption of the invalidity of the will, provided the jury find that while making the will she had a sound and disposing mind and memory." (Italics ours.)

This instruction is palpably erroneous, and was properly refused, because it was an unwarranted comment on a part of the testimony in the cause. Andrew v. Linebaugh, 260 Mo. loc. cit. 663; Rice v. J. C. B. & T. Co., 216 S. W. loc. cit. 751; State v. Adkins, 225 S. W. loc. cit. 982, 983. It was in conflict with plaintiff's instruction E, which properly

declared the law, and directed the jury, in passing upon undue influence, to consider all the facts and circumstances shown by the evidence.

5. We have carefully examined and fully considered all the questions presented by the record and in the briefs of counsel. We are of the opinion that no error was committed by the trial court of which appellants can legally complain. The judgment below was for the right party, and is accordingly affirmed.

WHITE and MOZLEY, CC., concur.

PER CURIAM. The foregoing opinion of BAILEY, C., is hereby adopted as the opinion of the court. All concur.

VAN HORN v. VAN HORN. (No. 17302.)

(St. Louis Court of Appeals. Missouri. May 3, 1921. Rehearing Denied June 7, 1921.)

Divorce ⚌132—Evidence held insufficient to establish plaintiff's right to divorce on the ground of indignities.

In an action by a husband against his wife for divorce on ground of indignities, evidence *held* insufficient to establish the husband's right to divorce

Appeal from Circuit Court, St. Louis County; John W. McElhinney, Judge.

"Not to be officially published."

Action for divorce by Charles G. Van Horn against Leota L. Van Horn. From a decree for defendant dismissing the bill, plaintiff appeals. Affirmed.

Marion C. Early and Ivon Lodge, both of St. Louis, for appellant.

Rassieur, Kammerer & Rassieur, of St. Louis, for respondent.

BRUERE, C. This is a suit for divorce brought by the husband. He seeks divorce on the ground of indignities stated in the petition as follows:

"That for more than two years prior to said separation defendant constantly nagged and abused plaintiff, applying to him vile epithets, frequently threatened to strike and injure plaintiff, and upon several occasions assaulted plaintiff by striking him and because of her ungovernable temper frequently flew into such rages of temper that she would seize upon and throw at plaintiff anything she could get in her hands, and frequently threatened bodily injury to plaintiff, and, further, defendant became so insanely jealous of plaintiff that he was unable to conduct in a proper way his business as a restaurant keeper because of her interferences and frequent displays of bad temper and jealousy in and around their home and his place of business, and plaintiff states that such conduct upon the part of defendant continued until he was unable to endure it any longer."

The answer admits the marriage, also the separation, and denies the other allegations of the petition. It further sets up that the plaintiff was not an injured and innocent party; that he was infatuated with a certain woman named therein with whom, since said separation, he spent most of his time; that the separation was caused by plaintiff, at his own instance, because he tired of defendant and for no other reason; that plaintiff compelled defendant to enter into a contract of separation; that defendant had frequently assured plaintiff of her love and devotion and had requested plaintiff to resume cohabitation with her, but that plaintiff had refused absolutely to entertain her request and had refused her said advances; and that plaintiff was not entitled to the relief sought by him. The allegations of the answer were denied by a reply.

The lower court found the issues for the defendant and dismissed the bill. The plaintiff has appealed.

The learned trial court, in support of said decree, filed an opinion and memorandum of his findings of facts. Said memorandum follows:

"A special feature of this case is the agreement of the parties on the 10th day of August, 1916, to live separate and apart, which contained the clause that each party to this contract should be free to go and come without the hindrance or interference from the other, and each party agrees not in any way to interfere with or disturb the other. The practical interpretation of this by the parties, and one which appears reasonable under all the circumstances, was to allow liberties to each other in their relations and attentions to other persons, which, without such understanding and agreement, might be intolerable indignities between husband and wife. Of course, it could not be construed as intended to permit or condone gross offenses, such as infidelity, which are not here charged or shown.

"Accordingly, the special attentions of the plaintiff to a lady friend, shown by the evidence, were not intolerable indignities to the defendant, since she had consented thereto, at least until she signified her objections thereto or withdrew her consent. This she did not do. So the case must be determined on the charges of indignities on the part of the defendant up to the time of the separation. The evidence shows that in the last two years the parties lived together there was some disputes, difficulties, loud language, and, perhaps, on two or three occasions, use of offensive language, and, perhaps, a slight push or something of the kind, with intervals of peace and quiet.

"The business in which both were engaged and their domestic surroundings were conducive to irritation and disturbance. It is not shown that the quarreling and exhibition of high temper were wholly, or for the most part, on the side of the defendant.

"Under all the circumstances, the acts and conduct of the defendant did not amount to indignities of such a nature or so frequently repeated as to be intolerable to the plaintiff. He may have become tired of his wife and wanted to put her away, even as early as April, 1915, when he sent her to California; but this was not due to misconduct on her part.

"The provision for separate maintenance in the contract was moderate. It was rightfully due to defendant as a wife, and especially for her services and assistance to her husband in his home and in building up his business. She ought not to be deprived of it without proof of good cause for divorce."

Appellant urges that the finding and decree of the lower court should have been in his favor.

The lower court denied plaintiff a divorce on the ground that the evidence disclosed that the indignities, on the part of the defendant, complained of, were isolated acts of misconduct and not of such frequent occurrence as to render plaintiff's condition intolerable.

We have carefully read all the evidence in this case and have reached the same conclusion arrived at by the learned trial judge who tried this case.

The marriage between the parties hereto took place on the 8th day of April, 1907. The parties continued to live together until September, 1916.

The plaintiff testified that during the time he lived with his wife they were constantly disagreeing and quarreling. His testimony consisted largely of statements of mere general conclusions. No facts were stated. We are left entirely in the dark as to the cause of their quarrels; thus such testimony has no probative force.

These disagreements and quarrels may have been due to a lack of conciliatory temper in both parties; if so, they constituted no ground for divorce. Webb v. Webb, 44 Mo. App. 229; Holschbach v. Holschbach, 134 Mo. App. 247, 114 S. W. 1085.

Aside from his statements of mere general conclusions, concerning the demeanor of the wife, the acts and conduct of the wife, testified to and complained of, are few and far apart.

The only substantial evidence, relating to the grounds of divorce relied on, is the evidence concerning the use of offensive epithets on the part of the wife.

Plaintiff lived with his wife almost eight years. Plaintiff's testimony discloses that defendant called him offensive names on two occasions only. The first occurrence was while they were living over the Jefferson Avenue restaurant in 1914. The other occurrence, testified to by him, happened when they were living on Kings highway in 1915. Witnesses for plaintiff testified that they heard the wife use offensive epithets on two occasions; the occurrences mentioned by them were the same as testified to by the plaintiff.

The defendant denied calling her husband offensive names. She testified that her husband compelled her to sign the contract of separation; that she did not desire to be separated from him; that she was in love with her husband and desired to go back to him.

. Several witnesses, intimately acquainted with both husband and wife, who daily associated with them for a long period of time, while employees in the restaurant business conducted by the husband, with the aid of the wife, testified that the defendant was a woman of good character; that they had never heard defendant use any bad language and had never witnessed any difficulty between husband and wife.

We do not think that the evidence shows that the conduct of the wife was such as to render plaintiff's condition intolerable, or that her behavior toward the plaintiff was of such a nature as to tend to the subversion of the marriage relation.

"The statute undoubtedly contemplates a course of conduct of one spouse toward the other, whereby the latter's condition is rendered intolerable through repeated acts constituting indignities." Dowling v. Dowling, 183 Mo. App. cit. 462, 167 S. W. 1079.

Such conduct on the part of the defendant is not shown in this case. See, also, Holschbach v. Holschbach, 184 Mo. App. 249, 114 S. W. 1035; Scholl v. Scholl, 194 Mo. App. 559, 185 S. W. 762; Webb v. Webb, 44 Mo. App. 229; Hooper v. Hooper, 19 Mo. 357; Mahn v. Mahn, 70 Mo. App. loc. cit. 342; Kempf v. Kempf, 34 Mo. 211; Van Horn v. Van Horn, 82 Mo. App. loc. cit. 82.

Moreover, we think the evidence in this case presents a case where we should defer to the finding of the trial court. The lower trial court had the advantage of having the witnesses before him and the opportunity of observing their demeanor on the witness stand, and thus in a better position to judge of their credibility than is this court.

Appellate courts, in divorce cases, will defer to the finding of the trial judge and will not reverse his findings unless it appears incorrect.

We are not in entire accord with the conclusion reached by the lower court that, in view of the agreement of the parties on the 16th day of August, 1916, the special attentions of the plaintiff to a lady friend, shown by the evidence, were not to be considered.

The evidence discloses that apart from plaintiff's constant association with said lady friend, plaintiff called her endearing names and was seen to kiss her on several occasions. We do not think the parties contemplated by said agreement that such conduct could be indulged in without objection.

Before a party is entitled to a decree of divorce, it must appear from the evidence that the complainant is not only the injured, but also the innocent, party. On a careful reading of the record in the case we are impressed that the plaintiff is not altogether the innocent party.

In view of the result reached here, it becomes unnecessary to pass upon respondent's contention that this appeal should be dismissed because of the alleged violation by appellant of Rule 18, Rules of Practice (169 S. W. xvii) of this court.

The decree of the circuit court of St. Louis county dismissing plaintiff's bill is proper. The Commissioner recommends that the judgment be affirmed.

PER CURIAM. Thee opinion of BRUERE, C., is adopted as the opinion of the court.

The judgment of the circuit court of St. Louis county is accordingly affirmed.

ALLEN, P. J., concurs.
BECKER, J., concurs in the result.
DAUES, J., not sitting.

INSURANCE AGENCY CO. v. BLOSSOM et al. (No. 16211.)

(St. Louis Court of Appeals. Missouri. Feb. 8, 1921. Rehearing Denied June 7, 1921.)

1. Corporations ⟢111—Officer and director had right to sell shares held.

The vice president and treasurer of a company, also a director and a stockholder, had the same right of disposition over the shares he held in the corporation as he had over any other personal property owned by him, and he was under no legal obligation to refrain from selling them, even though a sale of them was harmful to the corporation and the corporation at the time was insolvent.

2. Corporations ⟢174—Purchaser of stock acquired merely right in management and interest in property after payment of debts.

The purchaser of corporate stock acquired no title to the assets of the company, but simply acquired a right in the management of the corporation and an interest in its property remaining after payment of its debts.

3. Corporations ⟢65—Though property of corporation a trust fund for payment of debts, shares of stock fully paid for are not such a fund.

The property of every corporation is regarded as a trust fund for the payment of its debts, but shares of capital stock fully paid for and held by a stockholder are not such a trust fund, nor is the owner a trustee.

4. Appeal and error ⟨⟩172(1)—Contention not pleaded cannot be raised.

A contention not pleaded in complaint cannot be raised on appeal.

5. Corporations ⟨⟩333 — Judgment creditor could hold officer of company who received assets in reorganization.

If the vice president and treasurer, who was also a director and stockholder of a company, received any of its assets on reorganization, the transfer inured to the benefit of the company's judgment creditor, and he could hold the officer and director liable.

6. Corporations ⟨⟩603—Sale of stock did not cause dissolution.

The mere sale of stock of a company to an individual is not cause for dissolution of the company.

Appeal from St. Louis Circuit Court; Vital W. Garesche, Judge.

"Not to be officially published."

Suit by the Insurance Agency Company, a corporation, against Dwight B. Blossom, individually and as one of the trustees under dissolution of the Webb Motor Fire Apparatus Company, a corporation, and another. From judgment for defendants, plaintiff appeals. Affirmed.

Greensfelder & Levi, of St. Louis, for appellant.

Jesse McDonald and Arnold Just, both of St. Louis, for respondents.

BRUERE, C. This is a suit in equity. The pith of the lengthy petition in the case is: That the plaintiff obtained a judgment on the 20th day of October, 1914, in the circuit court of the city of St. Louis against the Webb Motor Fire Apparatus Company, on a debt due June 1, 1912. That execution was issued thereon, at the April term, 1915, in said court, and returned unsatisfied, and that the judgment remained unpaid. That the defendant, Dwight B. Blossom, was a director and officer of said company, and as such assented to the organization of a corporation, known as the "Webb Company." That pursuant to an agreement entered into, between the stockholders and officers of the Webb Motor Fire Apparatus Company and the stockholders and officers of the Webb Company, all the assets of the Webb Motor Fire Apparatus Company were transferred to the Webb Company and removed from the state of Missouri to the state of Pennsylvania. That the stockholders and officers of the Webb Motor Fire Apparatus Company misappropriated all the assets of the Webb Motor Fire Apparatus Company to their own use instead of applying the same to the payment of its debts. That the defendant, Dwight B. Blossom, received, for his participation in the above transaction, $4,150 par value of preferred stock and $4,150 par value of the common stock of the Webb Company. That at that time Dwight B. Blossom was the owner of 82,300 shares of the capital stock of the Webb Motor Fire Apparatus Company, the par value of which was $82,300, for which he had only paid $41,150; leaving a liability against him on account of said unpaid stock of $41,150. That the defendant, Dwight B. Blossom, was guilty of violations of the corporation laws of the state of Delaware, in that, as director of the Webb Motor Fire Apparatus Company, he had ordered dividends to be paid, in amounts greater than plaintiff's claim, out of property of the said corporation other than its surplus and net profits. The petition concludes by declaring that, because of the matters therein stated, the said Dwight B. Blossom became a trustee for the benefit of the plaintiff and became liable to plaintiff to the amount of its judgment against the Webb Motor Fire Apparatus Company; it prays judgment for said amount. The answer is a general denial.

The circuit court found the issues in favor of the defendants and entered up a judgment for the defendants. Plaintiff appeals from said judgment.

The facts in the case are not controverted. The case is such that it demands a detailed statement of facts. The facts are: The plaintiff is a judgment creditor of the Webb Motor Fire Apparatus Company. The debt on which the judgment was obtained accrued during the month of May, 1912. The Webb Motor Fire Apparatus Company was a Delaware corporation doing business in the city of St. Louis, Mo. The defendant, Dwight B. Blossom, was the vice president and treasurer of that company until July 1, 1912. He was the owner of 82,300 shares of stock of said company of the par value of $82,300, for which he paid par, in cash. On April 17, 1912, he was also a creditor of said company to the extent of $89,282.53. The company became financially involved, and on April 17, 1912, a contract was entered into, between G. E. Blakeslee, on behalf of himself and his associates, and certain stockholders of the Webb Motor Fire Apparatus Company, including Dwight B. Blossom, the defendant, whereby the said Blakeslee agreed to cause to be issued trustees' certificates, representing preferred and common stock in a proposed new corporation, in exchange for stock held by said stockholders of the Webb Motor Fire Apparatus Company. Said contract further provided that the stockholders of the old company were to receive the same number of shares in the new company as they held in the old; the shares were to be divided 50 per cent. preferred and 50 per cent. common stock of said new corporation. The total number of shares to be thus exchanged totaled 206,900. Of these Dwight B. Blossom was to receive 41,150 preferred and 41,150 shares of common stock. The old company was capitalized for $300,000; the new company was to have a capital stock of $1,500,000. The contract further provided that 12 notes of the proposed corporation for $3,273.55 each, payable in 1, 2, 3, 4, 5, 6, 7, 8, 9, 10, 11, and 12 months, respectively, should be executed and delivered to Dwight B. Blossom in part payment of the amount of $89,282.53, then due said Blossom from the said Webb Motor Fire Apparatus Company, and that for the remaining $50,000, of said indebtedness the said Blossom was to receive $50,000 of the preferred stock and $25,000 of the common stock of said new corporation. The contract further provided that G. E. Blakeslee should furnish, within 30 days of the date thereof, a sum not less than $50,000 to be used in paying claims against the Webb Motor Fire Apparatus Company. It was further provided that there should be sold, on or before the 1st day of July, 1912, at par, $120,000 of the preferred stock of said new corporation, which said $120,000 would carry with it a stock bonus of $60,000 of the common stock. The contract was to be consummated on or before the 1st day of July, 1912. Pursuant to the provisions of said contract, the Webb Company was organized under the laws of the state of Delaware, and the stock was exchanged, and the notes were delivered to Mr. Blossom. About $8,000 was paid by the Webb Company to Mr. Blossom on the notes. There were no dividends paid on the stock of the Webb Company. Said company became insolvent and went into the hands of a receiver in August, 1913. The stock of the concern became worthless. It appears from the evidence that the Webb Motor Fire Apparatus Company continued in active business in the city of St. Louis after the consummation of the aforementioned contract and until September, 1912. Some time in the month of September, 1912, the assets of the Webb Motor Fire Apparatus Company were transferred from St. Louis, Mo., to the Webb Company located in Allentown, Pa. The record does not disclose the kind of assets transferred nor the disposition that was made of them by the Webb Company. At the trial the plaintiff abandoned the charge, made in his petition, that Dwight B. Blossom was liable on account of unpaid stock; the evidence being that he paid par for said stock.

Counsel for appellant ask a reversal of the judgment rendered herein, based on ten assignments of errors. Consistent with an understanding of the points raised, we can condense them to five and state them as follows:

[1-3] 1. Complaint is made that the court erred in failing to find, as a matter of law, that the contract entered into between Dwight B. Blossom and the parties-named in the contract was in fraud of the creditors of the Webb Motor Fire Apparatus Company.

We hold that there is no evidence in this case upon which to base such a finding.

Dwight B. Blossom had the same jus disponendi over the shares he held in said corporation as he had over any other personal property owned by him.

He was under no legal obligation to refrain from selling them, even if a sale of them was harmful to the corporation, and the corporation at the time of sale was insolvent. The fact that Mr. Blossom was a director in the corporation at the time he disposed of his stock did not restrict in any way his right to sell his stock therein. The right to sell is not given to him as a director but as a stockholder. The purchaser of Mr. Blossom's stock acquired no title to the assets of the Webb Motor Fire Apparatus Company, but simply acquired a right in the management of the corporation and an interest in its property remaining after the payment of its debts. It is elementary law that the property of every corporation is regarded as a trust fund for the payment of its debts, but the shares of capital stock, full paid and held by a stockholder, are not such a trust fund, nor is the owner a trustee. The sale of the stock of said corporation did in no way reduce its corporate assets nor impair plaintiff's right to follow said assets and have them sold under execution in order to satisfy its said judgment. The rights of the creditors of the Webb Motor Fire Apparatus Company being in no way impaired because of the contract, we are unable to see how the contract could be held to be in fraud of creditors.

[4] 2. Appellant complains that the court erred in not holding Mr. Blossom liable for plaintiff's claim against the corporation because the evidence showed that the corporation paid the debt he held against it, at a time when he was a director thereof and when plaintiff's claim was unpaid and the corporation was insolvent. There is no evidence in the record that the money paid him in part payment of his debt against the Webb Motor Fire Apparatus Company came out of the assets of said corporation. The evidence shows that the money Mr. Blossom received came from the Webb Company.

But suffice it to say that this contention cannot be raised because not pleaded.

[5] 3. Appellant complains that the court erred in not holding Mr. Blossom liable to plaintiff because the evidence established the fact that the defendant received $25,000 from the Webb Motor Fire Apparatus Company. If Blossom received any of the assets of the Webb Motor Fire Apparatus Company, as charged by appellant, the transfer inured for the benefit of plaintiff and he could hold Blossom liable; but such is not this case. The $25,000 represented no part of the assets of the Webb Motor Fire Apparatus Company; it was Webb Company stock, paid Mr. Blossom as part of the purchase price due him

on account of the sale of his Webb Motor Fire Company stock. Appellant, however, contends that because Blossom paid nothing for this stock of the Webb Company, it being bonus stock, he should be held liable as a trustee. There is no such issue pleaded in this case; nor has appellant a judgment against the Webb Company.

4. Appellant complains that the court erred in not holding Blossom liable because the evidence showed that Blossom participated in transferring all the assets of the Webb Motor Fire Apparatus Company, while it was insolvent, from the state of Missouri to the Webb Company in the state of Pennsylvania.

The record discloses that Blossom resigned as director of the Webb Motor Fire Apparatus Company on July 1, 1912; after said date he was not a stockholder in said company, therefore he could not have had a voice in directing its affairs. The company continued in active business in the city of St. Louis until September, 1912; the assets of the said corporation were not removed until some time during the month of September, 1912.

[6] (5) Appellant complains that the court erred in holding that Blossom was not liable because the evidence showed that he, as director of the Webb Motor Fire Apparatus Company, failed to comply with the corporation laws of the state of Delaware by not adopting the method therein prescribed for effecting a dissolution of said corporation.

What we have heretofore said regarding assignment of error marked 4 above applies with equal force to this contention. However, we may add that the sale of the stock of the Webb Motor Fire Apparatus Company to G. E. Blakeslee did not create a dissolution of that corporation.

We are of the opinion that on the facts presented in the record the finding and judgment of the circuit court of the city of St. Louis is correct. The Commissioner recommends that the judgment be affirmed.

PER CURIAM. The opinion of BRUERE, C., is adopted as the opinion of the court.

The judgment of the circuit court of the city of St. Louis is accordingly affirmed.

REYNOLDS, P. J., and ALLEN and BECKER, JJ., concur.

GERTH v. CHRISTY.   (No. 16354.)

(St. Louis Court of Appeals. Missouri. May 3, 1921.)

1. Brokers ⚖=88(2)—Whether defendant employed plaintiff to effect an exchange held for the jury.

In an action for commission, the question whether defendant employed plaintiff broker to effect an exchange of lands so as to entitle plaintiff to commission held, under evidence, for the jury.

2. Appeal and error ⚖=961—New trial ⚖=99 —The granting of new trial for newly discovered evidence rests largely in discretion of trial court.

The granting of a new trial on the ground of newly discovered evidence, which is an exceptional procedure, rests largely in the discretion of the trial court, and any doubt as to whether the discretion has been soundly exercised is to be resolved in favor of the ruling.

3. Appeal and error ⚖=961—Appellate court will interfere with denial of new trial on the ground of newly discovered evidence only in clear case.

It is only in a case entirely free from doubt that the appellate court will interfere with the action of the trial court in denying a new trial requested on the ground of newly discovered evidence.

4. New trial ⚖=102(9)—Denial of new trial on ground of newly discovered evidence not an abuse of discretion, though witness was not friendly with movant.

The denial of a new trial on the ground of newly discovered evidence that a witness who testified at the former trial would testify that plaintiff, a real estate broker, proposed that the witness should charge defendant a commission, and that plaintiff should charge the other party to the exchange, was not an abuse of discretion, though defendant's counsel made affidavit that he and the witness were not on speaking terms, and that the witness would not confer with him prior to trial, where it appeared that the witness answered all questions willingly and fully and stated his connection with the real estate transaction, so there was sufficient opportunity for defendant to have brought out the alleged newly discovered evidence.

Appeal from Circuit Court, Clark County; N. M. Pettingill, Judge.

"Not to be officially published."

Action by Ed A. Gerth against J. A. Christy. From a judgment for plaintiff for part of the relief sought, defendant appeals. Affirmed.

J. A. Whiteside, of Kahoka, for appellant. C. T. Llewellyn, of Kahoka, for respondent.

BECKER, J. Plaintiff brought suit in two counts, seeking to recover $454.50 as a commission for services rendered defendant as a real estate agent in an exchange of defendant's farm for another farm.

Upon trial the jury returned a verdict in favor of the defendant on the first count, and in favor of plaintiff, in the sum of $100 on the second count. From the judgment resulting the defendant in due course appeals.

It appears that the defendant was the owner of a farm which he desired to trade for a farm in the school district in which his children were attending school. According to plaintiff's testimony, defendant asked him "to find him a trade" for his farm. This is, however, denied by the defendant. It is conceded that the defendant's farm was in point of fact traded for the farm of one Henry Hoffeditz, in the desired school district, and that plaintiff was present and took part in the negotiations pending over the exchange of the farms. Plaintiff claims that in the negotiations he represented the defendant, while defendant in turn claims that he thought plaintiff in the negotiations was representing Hoffeditz.

[1] Appellant assigns as error the action of the learned trial court in refusing his instruction in the nature of a demurrer offered at the close of the entire case. This point is not well taken.

Plaintiff testified that the defendant requested plaintiff to "find him a trade" for his farm, and it is conceded that the plaintiff, through his efforts, interested Henry Hoffeditz, who was the owner of a farm, in the matter of a trade, and after various negotiations the defendant did in point of fact trade his farm for that of Hoffeditz. While it is true the defendant denied that he had requested plaintiff to find a trade for his farm, and that throughout the negotiations he was of the belief that he, the plaintiff, represented Hoffeditz, the evidence, though conflicting, clearly makes the case one for the jury.

[2-4] In the defendant's motion for new trial one of the grounds set up therein was that of newly discovered evidence, and it is here urged that the court should have sustained the motion for a new trial on that ground.

The alleged newly discovered evidence is to the effect that one Crandall would testify that in the summer of 1916, about the time that the contract for the exchange of the farms of the defendant and Hoffeditz was executed, the plaintiff proposed to said Crandall that he (Crandall) should charge the defendant a commission on the said exchange of farms, and that he (Gerth) would charge the said Hoffeditz a commission on the deal. The motion for new trial recites that the information that Crandall would testify to these facts did not become known to the plaintiff or his attorney until after the trial of the case had been concluded. The affidavit of said Crandall was filed in support of the said motion, as was also the affidavit of the defendant's attorney to the effect that the said Crandall, though he had been a witness for the defendant in the trial of the case, had not been on speaking terms with said defendant's attorney for several years prior to the time of the trial of said case and had refused prior to the date of the trial to confer with him as to what he would testify to, but that the said Crandall told him he would tell what he knew when he got on the

witness stand; that the only information that he had as attorney or otherwise with reference to what said Crandall would testify to he had received from his client, Christy, the defendant in the case; that he had examined the said Crandall when he was on the stand as a witness as to all matters which had been so reported to him; and that it was only four days after the trial that he learned that Crandall would testify to the facts set forth in the motion for new trial.

With reference to the granting of motions for new trial on the ground of newly discovered evidence, Judge Sherwood, speaking for our Supreme Court, in the case of Cook v. St. Louis & Keokuk R. R. Co., 56 Mo. 380, said:

"Coming as they must from those who have been made to bite the dust in the forum, and are writhing under the tortures of a recent and unaccepted defeat, it is to be observed that they are regarded with a jealous eye, and construed with remarkable strictness by the courts, who invariably hold that they should be tolerated, not encouraged, viewed with aversion rather than favor, granted as an exception, and refused as a rule. * * * The granting of new trials because of evidence subsequently discovered rests for the most part with the trial court; and any doubt as to whether the discretion vested in this regard in that tribunal has been soundly exercised is to be resolved in favor of its ruling. It is only in a case entirely free from any element of uncertainty as to the impropriety of such ruling that appellate courts feel themselves called upon to interfere. People v. Superior Court of New York [5 Wend. 114, and cases cited]. * * *"

The record discloses that Edward Crandall, as a witness for defendant, among other things, testified that he occasionally did a real estate business and had gladly given him his aid to bring about an exchange of farms between Christy and Hoffeditz without any intention of charging for his services, in that he was anxious to have Christy living within their school district; that while he had taken Christy to look over the Hoffeditz farm he had not been instrumental in closing the deal; that he remembered a conversation between plaintiff and defendant in which plaintiff (Gerth) said he was going over to Illinois to see a man who owed him some money, and that inasmuch as Hoffeditz was living within a short distance of this man, he (Gerth) would run down and see him while he was there; that he did not remember whether Christy requested Gerth to talk to Hoffeditz when he made that trip or not. In answer to the question, "Do you know whether or not Christy employed Gerth to make the exchange of farms with Hoffeditz?" he answered:

"No; I don't know. Q. Was Gerth interested in making an exchange? A. Yes, sir; I think he took quite a good deal of interest in it."

Crandall further testified that Christy came to see him and find out if he owed him anything for his services in the matter and told him he did not, and when asked as to whether anything was said about Gerth by Christy at that time he said:

"No; I don't think so; not to my memory. Q. At any other time? A. Yes; there was, at Mr. Gerth's request; I mentioned to Christy that he was expecting a commission or some pay out of it; he is expecting pay for his work. Q. What was the conversation between Christy and you? A. It was very little; just a few words. Christy said he didn't employ him and didn't owe him anything."

In view of the record we are of the opinion that it sufficiently appears that ample opportunity was afforded defendant during the examination to have brought out fully any and all information that the witness Crandall had upon the subject in question. Judging from Crandall's testimony, he was a fair and impartial witness and answered all questions put to him willingly and fully. And this was evidently the view the learned trial court took of the matter as evidenced by the fact that defendant's motion for new trial was overruled. In the light of all the facts in the case, we are unwilling to rule that the trial court abused its discretionary power in an arbitrary or wrongful manner.

Holding, as we do, that there was substantial testimony sufficient to take the case to the jury, and that there were no errors committed by the trial court which affected the merits of the case, the judgment should be, and the same is hereby, affirmed.

ALLEN, P. J., concurs.
DAUES, J., not sitting.

In re SCHILL'S ESTATE.

NEWELL v. SCHILL.

(No. 16338.)

(St. Louis Court of Appeals. Missouri.
May 8, 1921.)

Judgment ⊜=342(2)—Judgment making allowance to widower as separate property could not be set aside after term.

Order of the probate court, made at the June term, 1915, making an allowance to a widower from his deceased wife's estate as his absolute property, not changed or appealed from during the term specified by the statute regarding appeals from the probate court, Rev. St. 1909, § 290, was a final judgment, and at the subsequent December term the probate court could not by sustaining exceptions to the settlement filed by such widower as executor of his wife's deceased administrator set aside the allowance made to him at the previous term.

Appeal from St. Louis Circuit Court; Wilson A. Taylor, Judge.

"Not to be officially published."

In the matter of the estate of Magdalena Schill, deceased, wherein Julius Schill, as executor of the will of Martin Schill, deceased, administrator of the estate of Magdalena Schill, filed settlement in the probate court, to which James P. Newell, public administrator, excepted. From judgment for the public administrator, the executor appeals. Judgment reversed, and cause remanded, with directions to enter judgment overruling exceptions filed to the settlement.

Koenig & Koenig, of St. Louis, for appellant.

Jones, Hocker, Sullivan & Angert, of St. Louis, for respondent.

BIGGS, C. Martin Schill was the widower of Magdalena Schill, deceased, and administrator of her estate. Upon the death of Martin Schill, Julius Schill, as executor of the last will of said Martin Schill, filed a settlement in the probate court showing the nature and kind of assets that said Martin Schill had in his hands as administrator of the estate of Magdalena Schill. James P. Newell, public administrator, who had taken charge of the estate of said Magdalena Schill, filed exceptions to this settlement, and thereby arose the controversy.

The only question in controversy between the parties involves the right of Martin Schill to take $400 out of the assets of the estate of his deceased wife under the provision of section 120, R. S. of Mo. 1909, then in force, which amount was duly allowed to him by order of the probate court, and to retain same as his absolute property, in view of the fact that said Martin Schill during his lifetime and by order of the probate court received the sum of $1,000 as a partial distribution out of the assets of the estate of his deceased wife; said sum being allowed to him by reason of his right to have a child's share in said estate as provided by the statutes.

The probate court and the circuit court upon appeal sustained the exceptions and ordered Julius Schill, executor of Martin Schill, to restate the settlement of the account of the deceased administrator up to the time of his death, omitting therefrom the item of $400 for which he took credit.

After the customary preliminaries, Julius Schill as such executor has duly perfected an appeal to this court.

It appeared that Martin Schill in his lifetime, and while in charge of the estate of his wife, filed his formal application in the probate court for an allowance of $400 as his absolute property under section 120 of the Statutes of 1909. On June 28, 1915, and during the June term of that court, an order was made sustaining the application, and the widower was duly allowed $400 as his absolute property. No appeal was prosecuted from this order making the allowance within the statutory period. Thereupon the said Martin Schill appropriated to his own use the said sum of $400 out of the estate, and after his death, as stated, his executor filed the settlement of Martin Schill as such administrator of his deceased wife, showing that said sum had been retained by said Martin Schill. This settlement was filed in the probate court at the December term, 1915, and on January 10, 1916. Thereafter exceptions were filed to the settlement, and for the first time the question was raised as to the right of said Martin Schill to take the $400 as his absolute property made to him under the order of the probate court without deducting same from his share in the estate of his deceased wife.

As stated, the order of the probate court made at the June term, 1915, making the allowance to said Martin Schill as his absolute property, was never thereafter changed or appealed from during the time specified by the statute regarding appeals from the probate court (section 290, R. S. 1909). Thereafter at the subsequent December term the probate court by sustaining exceptions to the settlement filed by Julius Schill, executor, thereby in effect set aside the allowance referred to. This appellant contends was beyond the jurisdiction of the court, as the order of allowance was a final judgment after the lapse of the term.

In Re Estate of Fritch, 179 Mo. App. 434, 164 S. W. 659, this court held that the action of the probate court in allowing a widow a sum of money in lieu of a year's provisions as authorized by section 115, R. S. 1909, was a final judgment and could not thereafter at a subsequent term be modified by the probate court. As was held in that case, it is clear that the allowances to the widow or widower of $400 as absolute property come within the same category as allowances in lieu of provisions provided for in sections 114 and 115.

Respondent has not favored us with any brief attempting to justify the action of the probate court and the circuit court. It appears under the Fritch Case that this allowance became a final judgment after the lapse of the term, and hence the probate court was without power thereafter to set the order aside. It results that the judgment of the circuit court should be reversed, and the cause remanded, with directions to enter a judgment overruling the exceptions filed to the settlement of Julius Schill as such executor, and that same should be certified to the probate court of the city of St. Louis.

PER CURIAM. The foregoing opinion of BIGGS, C., is adopted as the opinion of the court.

The judgment of the circuit court is accordingly reversed, and the cause remanded, with directions as recommended by the Commissioner.

ALLEN, P. J., and BECKER, J., concur. DAUES, J., not sitting.

CARROLL et al. v. MURPHY et al.
(No. 17214.)

(St. Louis Court of Appeals. Missouri. May 3, 1921.)

1. **Wills ⬅=>52(1)—Burden on proponents as to issue of sanity.**

Under Rev. St. 1919, § 521, the burden is on proponents of a will to show testator was of sound mind at the time the will was made.

2. **Wills ⬅=>327—Courts may peremptorily instruct on lack of capacity if evidence permits.**

In will contests, courts may give a peremptory instruction when there is no substantial evidence to sustain the issue of mental capacity to make a will.

3. **Wills ⬅=>324(2)—Issue of insanity for jury on substantial evidence.**

If there was any substantial evidence tending to show that testatrix was sane when she made her will, the issue of her sanity should have been submitted to the jury.

4. **Wills ⬅=>324(2)—Evidence held to make prima facie case of testatrix's mental capacity.**

In suit by testatrix's brothers to set aside her will for mental unsoundness, evidence held sufficient to make out a prima facie case that testatrix had mental capacity to make a will, tending to show that testatrix knew what property she had, the names of the persons naturally within the range of her bounty, etc., so that the question of her capacity to make a will was for the jury.

Appeal from St. Louis Circuit Court; Victor H. Falkenhainer, Judge.

"Not to be officially published."

Suit by John Carroll and others against Mary Murphy and others. Verdict for plaintiffs, and from an order granting defendants new trial, plaintiffs appeal. Affirmed.

Robt. M. Zeppenfeld, of St. Louis, for appellants.

Frank H. Fisse and Henry H. Oberschelp, both of St. Louis, for respondents.

BRUERE, C. This is a suit to set aside the will of Mary Carroll. The validity of the testament is assailed on two grounds: First, because the testatrix was not possessed of a sound mind at the time the will was made. Second, because the will was procured through the undue influence of the defendants, Mary Murphy and Mrs. B. Wilson.

⬅=>For other cases see same topic and KEY-NUMBER in all Key-Numbered Digests and Indexes

The plaintiffs are brothers of the testatrix. The defendant Ellen Sullivan is the sister, the defendants Ellen and Nora Sullivan are nieces, and the defendant John Carroll is a nephew, of the testatrix. Said defendants, together with the defendants Mary Murphy, Mrs. B. Wilson and Francis Gilfillan, are also legatees under said will.

The will is in words and figures as follows:

I, Mary Carroll, single and unmarried, of city of St. Louis, Missouri, make and declare, this my last will.

I direct the payment of all my just debts and funeral expenses and expenses of last illness.

I bequeath two hundred dollars ($200.00) to Father Gilfillan, of the New Cathedral Parish, St. Louis, Mo., on Lindell boulevard for masses.

I bequeath five hundred dollars ($500.00) each to my cousin, Mrs. Mary Murphy, my sister, Ellen Sullivan; my nephew, John Carroll.

I bequeath two hundred dollars ($200.00) to Mrs. B. Wilson, 5075 Delmar avenue.

I bequeath one dollar ($1.00) to each of my brothers, John, Maurice, and Tom Carroll.

All the remainder of my estate I give, bequeath and devise absolutely, share and share alike, to Ellen and Nora Sullivan, the two daughters of my sister, Ellen Sullivan, county Kerry, Ireland.

I nominate and appoint my friend, Miss Kate Martin, executrix of this my last will and request she be not required to give any bond as such.

In witness whereof, I have hereunto set my hand and seal this 26th of February, 1918.

　　　　　　　　her
　　　　Mary X Carroll. [Seal.]
　　　　　　　mark
Henry H. Oberschelp, Witness.

Signed, sealed, declared and published as her last will and testament by said testatrix Mary Carroll, in our presence and we, in her presence and at her request subscribe our names as witnesses.　　Forest H. Staley, M. D.
　　　　　　　　Henry H. Oberschelp.
　　　　　　　　Dorothy E. Wright.

At the trial, in support of the will, the defendants introduced the attesting witnesses, Dr. Forest H. Staley and Dorothy E. Wright. They testified to the execution of the will, its attestation in the manner and form provided by the statute, and the sanity of the testatrix. The defendants also introduced the will and rested.

Thereupon the court, over objections of the defendants, gave to the jury a peremptory instruction for the plaintiffs, requiring the jury to find that the paper writing in question was not the last will and testament of Mary Carroll. The jury returned a verdict in accordance with said instruction.

Defendants in due time filed their motion for a new trial which was sustained by the court. From the order granting a new trial plaintiffs appealed.

The only point presented is whether or not the lower court erred in holding, by its order granting a new trial, that the question of testamentary capacity of the testatrix should have been submitted to the jury.

Appellants' sole contention is that the proponents did not make out a prima facie case because they failed to show that the testatrix was of sound mind at the time the will was executed.

[1] Under the provisions of section 521, Revised Statutes of Missouri 1919, the burden is on the proponents of the will to show that the testator was of sound mind at the time the will was made. Bensberg v. Washington University, 251 Mo. 641, 158 S. W. 330; Turner v. Butler, 253 Mo. loc. cit. 215, 161 S. W. 745; Balak v. Susanka, 182 Mo. App. 458, 168 S. W. 650.

[2] In will contests courts may give a peremptory instruction when there is no substantial evidence to sustain the issue of mental capacity to make the will. Teckenbrock v. McLaughlin, 209 Mo. 539, 108 S. W. 46; Bensberg v. Washington University, supra; McFadin v. Catron, 138 Mo. 197, 38 S. W. 932, 39 S. W. 771.

[3] If there was substantial evidence introduced in this case, showing that the testatrix was sane at the time she executed the will, then this issue should have been submitted to the jury. On this question, proponents introduced the two subscribing witnesses, Dr. Forest Henry Staley and Dorothy E. Wright.

In substance Dr. Forest Henry Staley testified he was a physician at Barnes Hospital on February 28, 1918. On the morning of said day, at about 9 o'clock, Mary Carroll, the testatrix, was brought to said hospital in a very burned and very severe condition. He examined her, and found that she could not live, because of the extensive burns. "It was found that she was a Catholic, and a priest was summoned to look after her religious side and about— she remained in about the same condition, and when she came in she was perfectly conscious, and responded to questions readily. Her mind was clear and alert." Between 12 and 1 o'clock he went to see her again, and asked her if she did not want to make a will, and she told him that she did, and he called the head nurse, and she took the dictation of the will. The will was drawn up. He got all the facts from the testatrix. Mary Carroll signed the will in presence of the subcribing witnesses. While witness was drawing up the will he wanted a lawyer to check up his work, and a call was put in for Mr. Oberschelp. Before Mr. Oberschelp came the will was completed, it was read to Mary Carroll, and after she read it she signed it. Soon after Mr. Oberschelp came the will was shown to him, and he noticed that no provision had been made therein for an executor, and he suggested that another will be drawn up, and an executor be named therein. The question was put to the testatrix whom she wanted as executrix, and she named Mary Murphy. She was told that Mary Murphy could not act, because she was a married woman, and she then named Kate Martin. Mr. Oberschelp then wrote the second will, which is the will in question. The provisions in the second will are the same as in the first will. After this second will was written, it was read to Mary Carroll, and then handed to her, and she read it, and said that it was her last will and testament, following which she signed it in the presence of the subscribing witnesses. The witnesses to the will signed it at testatrix's request. Mary Carroll was over 21 years of age. On cross-examination witness testified that Mary Carroll told witness when she was making the will what property and money she had. He wrote the words in the first will, "I, Mary Carroll, being of clear mind and with full conscience," and meant by that statement that Mary Carroll "was conscious and her mind was clear—certainly, from the way she responded to questions and the way she engaged in conversation." Miss Bridge took the dictation, and everything he dictated he got from Mary Carroll. He asked Mrs. Carroll how she wanted to dispose of her property and her money, and she told him and started out by saying, "I give five hundred dollars to my cousin, Mary Murphy," etc., just in the way the will is written. "She told me how many brothers she had, and named them, and that one was a policeman, who lived in the city." She mentioned a Mrs. Wilson, her cousin. He wrote down the persons she mentioned, and the amounts she desired to give each, exactly as she gave them to him. Mr. Oberschelp, the attorney, came not later than 15 minutes after he drew up the first will. It took just a few minutes to write and execute the second will. It was executed in 15 or 20 minutes after the attorney came. Mary Carroll realized she was going to die; she asked for the priest. There was a slight difference in the condition of Mary Carroll between the period from 9 o'clock to 1:30 and the period from 1:30 to the time she died. She began to have difficulty in breathing about 3 o'clock. She died of shock. The symptoms of the severe shock did not come on until just preceding her death. Mary Carroll was able to articulate up to the time she died. She died about 4 o'clock. He saw her about 10 minutes before she died, and she was still able to talk; she asked for a drink of water. Mary Carroll was apparently not in much pain. She was asked if she was in much pain, and she answered she was not. The second will was executed about 2 o'clock.

On redirect examination witness testified he never knew Mary Carroll before the day he saw her at the Barnes Hospital. Witness asked Mary Carroll how much she desired to bequeath her brothers, and she replied, "I don't care to give them anything." Witness told her she would have to give them something in order for the will to be legal, and she said she would leave a dollar to each of them. Every bit of information

witness got for the preparation of the will he got solely from Mary Carroll. Mary Carroll of her own free will volunteered every bit of information that appears in the will. She told witness she had money in the bank and some Liberty Bonds besides. Mary Carroll told the subscribing witnesses to the will to sign the will as witnesses, and after the will was read to her it was handed to her, and she read it and made her mark and said that it was her last will and testament.

In substance Dorothy E. Wright, a student nurse at Barnes Hospital, testified that she saw Mary Carroll about 2 o'clock on the day the will was executed. She saw "Mr. Oberschelp recopying the will, and when he got through he read it carefully to Mary Carroll, and asked her if she agreed to all the details, and if it was the way she wanted it, and she indicated in the affirmative that she was perfectly satisfied with it, and then he asked her if she wished Doctor Staley and myself to witness it, and she indicated again in the affirmative." Mary Carroll signed the will in witnesses' presence, and she attested it. Testatrix was asked by Mr. Oberschelp if she wished to leave anything more to her brothers, and she answered in the negative. Witness was not sure whether Mary Carroll said yes or no, or whether she merely nodded, in response to Mr. Oberschelp's question.

On cross-examination witness testified when she got there all the business of making the will was over and testatrix was merely answering questions with a word or a nod, she was able to say, "yes or no." Witness saw Mary Carroll sign two wills. "Testatrix had to be questioned as to all the provisions that were made, and in a measure she was aroused to respond."

The requisite test of mental capacity, sufficient to make a valid will, as laid down by our Supreme Court, is:

"The rule in this state is that one, who is capable of comprehending all his property and all persons who reasonably come within the range of his bounty, and who has sufficient intelligence to understand his ordinary business, and to know what disposition he is making of his property, has sufficient capacity to make a will." Holton v. Cochran, 208 Mo. loc. cit. 410, 106 S. W. 1064; Couch v. Gentry, 113 Mo. loc. cit. 255, 20 S. W. 890; Riggin v. Westminster College, 160 Mo. loc. cit. 579, 61 S. W. 803; Mowry v. Norman, 223 Mo. loc. cit. 474, 122 S. W. 724; Winn v. Grier, 217 Mo. loc. cit. 445, 117 S. W. 48; Sehr v. Lindemann, 153 Mo. loc. cit. 288, 54 S. W. 537; Martin v. Bowdern, 158 Mo. 379, 59 S. W. 227; Byrne v. Fulkerson, 254 Mo. loc. cit. 120, 162 S. W. 171.

[4] Measured by the above test, we think the evidence was sufficient to make out a prima facie case that the testatrix had sufficient mental capacity to make a will.

Dr. Staley stated the facts and acts of the testatrix, connected with the making of the will; these tended to show that the testatrix knew what property she had, the names of the persons who naturally came within the range of her bounty, and the disposition she was making of her property. He testified that the testatrix told him that her property consisted of money in bank and Liberty Bonds. No effort was made to prove that the information given him was not true. The testatrix further gave Dr. Staley the name of her relatives. The persons mentioned by her are the persons stated in the petition as the heirs of the testatrix.

Dr. Staley testified that the testatrix of her own free will volunteered every bit of information that appears in the will; that he wrote down the persons she mentioned and the amounts she desired to bequeath to each, exactly as she gave them to him; that, in telling him what she desired to give each legatee, she used the words, "I give five hundred dollars to my cousin, Mary Murphy," etc., just in the way the will is written.

After the will was read to the testatrix she read it, and said it was her last will and testament. Dr. Staley testified that her mind was clear and alert when she came to the hospital, and that there was but a slight change in her condition until just a few minutes before she died. This evidence tended to show that testatrix knew the business she was engaged in and the disposition she was making of her property.

We think the evidence, introduced at the trial, was sufficient to make out a prima facie case, and that the question as to the testatrix's mental capacity to make a will was for the jury to decide.

The action of the lower court sustaining the motion for a new trial was proper and should be affirmed, and the Commissioner so recommends.

PER CURIAM. The opinion of BRUERE, C., is adopted as the opinion of the court.

The judgment of the circuit court of the city of St. Louis is accordingly affirmed.

ALLEN, P. J., and BECKER, J., concur. DAUES, J., not sitting.

VOGELSANG et al. v. BOARD OF EDUCATION OF CITY OF CAPE GIRARDEAU. (No. 16350.)

(St. Louis Court of Appeals. Missouri. June 7, 1921.)

1. Appeal and error ⚖=882(12)—No complaint of error in instruction adopted by complainant.

Appellant will not be heard to complain about an error in an instruction, where he adopted the same error in his own instructions.

2. Schools and school districts ⚖=84—Clause in construction contract relating to insurance held not to include derrick.

A section of a contract to construct a school building, requiring the school board to take out insurance to cover "all work incorporated in the building and all material for the firm in or about the premises," did not include a derrick owned by the contractors and furnished and used by them.

Appeal from Cape Girardeau Court of Common pleas; John A. Snider, Judge.

"Not to be officially published."

Action by August Vogelsang and Henry Vogelsang, composing the firm of Vogelsang Bros. Construction Company, against the Board of Education of the City of Cape Girardeau. Judgment for plaintiffs, and defendant appeals. Reversed in part, and remanded, with directions.

L. L. Bowman and Spradling & Burroughs, all of Cape Girardeau, for appellant.

Edw. D. and David B. Hays, of Cape Girardeau, for respondents.

BECKER, J. This action was instituted in two counts. In the first count plaintiffs seek to recover the sum of $300 as a balance due on a contract made to build an addition to the Lincoln School in Cape Girardeau, Mo., while by the second count plaintiffs seek to recover $120.74 for damages sustained by them as the result of defendants' failure to maintain insurance according to the terms of the building contract, on the work which the plaintiffs were doing on another and different building from the one named in the first count. The case was tried to the court and a jury, and resulted in a verdict for plaintiffs on each count. From the resulting judgment, defendants appeal.

As to the first count, it appears that in the contract entered into between plaintiffs and defendants, whereby plaintiffs agreed to build an addition to the Lincoln School for a sum approximating $10,000, it was provided, among other things, that plaintiffs should furnish—

"and set up in the basement one S–36–7 Ideal cast iron sectional boiler, or equal, having the capacity of 8,150 square feet, provided with fire draft and clean-out door complete, and a full set of complete shaking and dumping grates."

The boiler which plaintiffs installed in the building was a Capital boiler which had been used about four years. The building, according to the contract, was to be built according to certain drawings and specifications furnished by the architect and made a part of the contract, and all of the work under the contract was required to be done—

"under the direction of said architect and his decision as to the true construction and meaning of the drawing and specifications shall be final."

When plaintiffs had finished the building, the architect, after making an inspection, issued to the plaintiffs his final inspection certificate for the final payment; but when the time for payment arrived some member of the board of education raised the question as to whether or not the Capital boiler installed in the school by plaintiffs under the contract was a compliance with the terms of the said contract, which called for an "S-36-7 Ideal cast iron sectional boiler, or equal," notwithstanding the approval by the architect and the agreement in the contract that the architect's decision should be final.

To settle the controversy it was agreed between plaintiffs and defendants, and for the purpose of determining whether or not plaintiffs had complied with their contract, that a competent licensed inspector should examine the boiler placed in the school—

"within 30 days and report the condition and value of the boiler to the board of education, and if his report shows the condition of the boiler to be good and its value equal to a new Ideal boiler, such as specified by the architect to be placed in the above-named building, the obligation of the Vogelsang Bros. Construction Company will have ceased; or if the board of education fails to have this examination and report made within 30 days, the obligation of said contractors shall cease. Should this report show the boiler to be inferior or of less value than the boiler specified by the architect, then the said Vogelsang Bros. Construction Company agrees to purchase and install one Ideal boiler manufactured by the American Radiator Company, of the size and kind specified by the architect. To protect the school board in this obligation and agreement, the said Vogelsang Bros. Construction Company agrees to allow the board of education to hold back a sum of $300, which amount will be paid the said Vogelsang Bros. Construction Company upon the final settlement of the above matter."

In conformity with the said agreement a licensed inspector made a special inspection of the boiler, and made a written report thereof, which set out several defects which in his opinion needed to be remedied; but nowhere in said report is there anything said as to whether the Capital boiler installed therein is as good as and equal in value to a new Ideal boiler, nor from said report can that question be determined. It is conceded that the said inspection was the only one made under the agreement between the plaintiffs and defendants for an inspection of the boiler.

The plaintiffs made the changes suggested in the inspector's report, with the exception of putting in a fusible plug, which it is contended was not essential, and also that the type of Ideal boiler specified in the contract did not have a fusible plug on it. Plaintiffs, after the report of the inspector and the mak-ing of the changes therein outlined, made demand for the $300 withheld under said written agreement, but defendants refused payment.

At the trial plaintiffs adduced substantial testimony tending to prove that the Capital boiler installed in the building had a much greater heating capacity than the size S-36-7 Ideal boiler, and that there would be an economy in the use of the larger or oversize boiler in the matter of the coal consumed for the purpose of heating the building, and there was also testimony tending to show that the boiler installed was "equal" to the boiler specified in the contract to which it was required to measure up.

[1] Appellants complain that instruction numbered 3 given for plaintiffs below contains error, in that it told the jury that the school building was to be equipped with "one S-36-7 Ideal cast iron sectional boiler, or equal, having a capacity of 3,150 square feet," when in point of fact the contract required such boiler to be a new S-36-7 Ideal boiler." From an examination of the instructions given at the request of appellants, defendants below, it appears that their instruction numbered 3 contains the identical error. It needs no citation of authority that under these circumstances appellants will not be heard to complain, since they adopted the same error in their own instructions. But see Smart v. Kansas City, 208 Mo. 162, 105 S. W. 709, 14 L. R. A. (N. S.) 565, 123 Am. St. Rep. 415, 13 Ann. Cas. 932; Lange v. Mo. Pac. Ry. Co., 208 Mo. 458, 106 S. W. 660.

The instructions given fully and fairly presented the case to the jury, and it is readily apparent from a reading of the record in this case that the judgment for plaintiffs on the first count is for the right party, and, finding no error therein prejudicial to appellants' rights, we rule that the judgment thereon should be affirmed.

As to the second count: Plaintiffs were erecting a school building for defendants under a written contract, one of the stipulations of which was as follows:

"The owner shall, during the progress of the work, maintain full insurance on said work, in his own name and in the name of the contractor, against loss or damage by fire, lightning, or cyclone. The cost of said insurance shall be prorated between the owner and contractor, the contractor paying the full amount for the actual time consumed in the completion of his contract. The policies shall cover all work incorporated in the building, and all materials for the same in or about the premises, and shall be made payable to the parties hereto, as their interest may appear."

During the course of the construction of the building a derrick belonging to plaintiffs, which they had upon the grounds and were using in and about the work of the construction of the said building, was wrecked by a cyclone, to plaintiffs' damage in the sum of $120.74. It appears that defendants had failed to take out insurance as required under the terms of the contract, which fact, however, was unknown to plaintiffs, who relied upon the said provision of the contract, and had not taken out any insurance to protect themselves. There is no question but that the derrick was wrecked by the cyclone, and that the damage sustained by plaintiffs is the amount alleged in their petition.

[2] A reading of the section of the contract above set forth, which requires defendants to take out insurance to cover "all work incorporated in the building and all material for the same in or about the premises," clearly cannot be construed to include a derrick owned by the contractors, and furnished and used by them in and about the construction of the building. It therefore follows that, even though the defendants below had complied with the contract with reference to taking out insurance, such insurance would not have availed plaintiffs with reference to the damage they suffered by the wrecking of their derrick by a cyclone.

The second count in plaintiffs' petition, therefore, fails to set out facts sufficient to constitute a cause of action. This matter was specifically called to the attention of the learned trial court in defendants' motion in arrest of judgment, but was overruled. It follows that the judgment against defendants on the second count of plaintiffs' petition should be, and the same is, reversed.

The result following from the foregoing views is that the judgment is reversed, and the cause remanded with directions to the trial court to enter judgment for plaintiffs for $361.50, with interest at the rate of 6 per cent. per annum from the date of the judgment in the court below.

ALLEN, P. J., concurs.
DAUES, J., not sitting.

STATE ex rel. YOUNGMAN v. CALHOUN, Circuit Judge. (No. 17409.)

(St. Louis Court of Appeals. Missouri. May 3, 1921. Rehearing Denied June 7, 1921.)

1. Evidence ⬤⟞456—Parol evidence inadmissible to show the meaning of a word which is not ambiguous.

In a contract for the sale of physicians' practice, a provision that the sellers will not "establish" themselves as practicing physicians and surgeons within five miles of a specified place is not ambiguous with respect to the quoted word, and parol evidence is not admissible to show the intention of the parties as to its meaning.

2. Prohibition ⬤⟞10(2)—Want of jurisdiction held to appear as a matter of law on the face of a judgment awarding an injunction so that prohibition would lie.

The word "establish" as used in a contract for the sale of a physicians' practice, and providing that the sellers would not establish themselves as practicing physicians and surgeons within five miles from a specified place, was unambiguous, and did not call for extrinsic evidence to show the intention of the parties as to its meaning, and hence a judgment, awarding an injunction and involving a construction of such word contrary to its plain meaning, showed an excess of jurisdiction as a matter of law as distinguished from a matter of fact, and, there being no adequate remedy by appeal, error, or otherwise, prohibition would lie to prevent the enforcement of such injunction.

3. Contracts ⬤⟞202(2)—Contract in restraint of trade strictly construed.

A contract by which physicians sold their practice and agreed to refrain from establishing themselves as practicing physicians and surgeons within five miles from a specified place is one clearly in restraint of trade and personal liberty, and should not be construed to extend beyond its fair import.

4. Good will ⬤⟞6(4)—Contract for sale of a physicians' practice construed in respect to restriction on sellers as to continuing practice.

A contract by which physicians sold their practice and agreed not to "establish" themselves as physicians and surgeons within a radius of five miles of specified premises, held not violated by the sellers, where they established an office outside of the five-mile limit, though they occasionally made calls on patients within such limits, and received calls at their office from patients living within the prescribed limits.

"Not to be officially published."

Original proceedings by the State, on the relation of Jacob A. Youngman, against Hon. John W. Calhoun, Judge of the Circuit Court of the City of St. Louis, for a writ of prohibition. Temporary writ made permanent.

Brownrigg, Mason & Altman, of St. Louis, for relator.
Frank A. Habig, of St. Louis, for respondent.

BECKER, J. This is an original proceeding by the relator to prohibit respondent, as a circuit judge, from undertaking to enforce against the petitioner certain portions of a judgment or decree of injunction entered in the circuit court of the city of St. Louis, in a case in which Louis P. Habig is plaintiff and Jacob A. Youngman, the relator herein, is defendant.

In response to a preliminary rule in prohibition respondent made a return, which, by consent of counsel, is to be taken as a demurrer to the application filed by the relator and to our said preliminary writ, and we have the case under submission as on motion for judgment on the pleadings.

The facts are substantially as follows: Louis A. Habig and Jacob A. Youngman are both physicians. Dr. Habig, up until the spring of 1919 was practicing medicine in the state of Illinois, while Dr. Youngman practiced in the city of St. Louis, and was the owner of the property known as 5817 Gravois avenue, which he used both for his residence and for his office. Dr. Youngman sold his said home to Dr. Habig, who moved into the house and took up the practice of medicine. The property was sold and conveyed to Dr. Habig by Dr. Youngman and his wife with the following agreement included in and as a part of the contract of sale, namely:

"The owners agree not to establish themselves as a practicing physician and surgeon within a radius of five miles of the above premises after December 1, 1919, for a period of five years."

Shortly after the said sale Dr. Youngman made a visit to Florida, and upon his return opened an office at the corner of Grand and Lafayette avenues, in the city of St. Louis, for the practice of medicine, and began making calls within the said prohibited district. Thereupon suit was filed by Dr. Habig to enjoin Dr. Youngman from opening or maintaining the said office and to enjoin him from practicing medicine or surgery in any manner with any former patients, or any other persons living within the prohibited district. After the suit was filed, but prior to the hearing of the application to show cause, Dr. Youngman, admitting that his new location was within the prohibited district, closed his office at Grand and Lafayette avenues, and made a tender of all fees he earned at such office, as well as the costs of the suit. Upon final hearing the temporary injunction which had theretofore been issued was made permanent. Among other things, the injunction prohibits Dr. Youngman from making calls within the district, or treating patients or residents of the district who might call at his office, which is now established at Sappington, Mo., concededly outside of the district. Thereupon relator filed this application for a writ of prohibition on the ground that the decree of the said respondent as judge of the circuit court of the city of St. Louis is in excess of his jurisdiction and the jurisdiction of the said court in said cause to the extent that said decree enjoins the said petitioner from engaging in the practice of medicine or surgery in any manner with any of his former patients or any other patients or persons, and from engaging in the practice of medicine or surgery in any manner with any of his former patients or any other pa-

tients or persons within a radius of five miles or less from the said premises, when in fact the petitioner did not bind or obligate himself, under the said contract of sale, further than to refrain from establishing or maintaining an office for the practice of medicine or surgery within the said district, and prays that said respondent be prohibited from in any way undertaking to enforce against petitioner the said judgment or decree, unless it be to the extent of preventing the said petitioner from opening or establishing an office for the practice of medicine and surgery within the said district, during the period of five years from the 1st day of December, 1919.

The decree of injunction issued by learned respondent judge against the relator herein is thus assailed on the ground that said injunction is in part at least in excess of the jurisdiction of the said court. It is no longer open to controversy but that—

"if the facts of a given case show either want of jurisdiction or excess thereof, together with an absence of an adequate remedy at law or in equity, a case is made warranting the issuance of the writ. It should be observed that, although want of jurisdiction and excess of jurisdiction are commonly referred to and considered as separate grounds for the issuance of the writ, there is in principle little distinction between them, as each means an attempt by a court or person to take judicial action without judicial power or authority for such action." State ex rel. Term. Ry. Co. v. Tracy, 237 Mo. 109, loc. cit. 118, 140 S. W. 888, 890 (37 L. R. A. [N. S.] 448).

Plaintiff's petition below charges specifically that the defendant is violating the terms of a written contract, which contract is set out therein in hæc verba. That portion of the contract of sale which Dr. Youngman is alleged to be violating is as follows:

"The owners (meaning Dr. Youngman and his wife) agree not to establish themselves as a practicing physician and surgeon within a radius of five miles of the above premises after December 1, 1919, for a period of five years."

[1, 2] At the outset it is necessary for us to determine whether the phrase, "to establish themselves as a practicing physician and surgeon," is ambiguous. We note that learned counsel for respondent specifically deny that this phrase is ambiguous, and to this viewpoint we readily agree, and since we are of the opinion that these words as used in the contract have an ordinary meaning, plain and unambiguous when read in connection with the other portions of the contract, it follows that extrinsic evidence as to their meaning is not necessary, nor would such evidence be admissible on the trial of the case on its merits. Thus, then, the controversy resolves itself upon the application before us into a question of jurisdiction as a matter of law as distinguished from matter

of fact, and therefore, since it is readily apparent that the ordinary remedies by appeal, error, etc., would not furnish adequate relief to relator, we have before us a question properly invoking the discretion of this court whether or not upon the record before us relator is entitled to a writ of prohibition.

[3] The contract in question is clearly one in restraint of trade and personal liberty, and as such should not be construed to extend beyond its fair import. Haldeman v. Simonton, 55 Iowa, 145, 7 N. W. 493; Bowers v. Whittle, 63 N. H. 147, 56 Am. Rep. 499; Barron v. Collenbaugh, 114 Iowa, 71, 86 N. W. 53.

[4] Under the contract in question Dr. Youngman bound himself not to establish himself as a practicing physician or surgeon within a certain district for a definite period of time. It is conceded that in opening an office at Grand and Lafayette avenues, in the city of St. Louis, Dr. Youngman violated this agreement, and prior to the trial of the case below he gave up his office at said location, and tendered into court the fees which had come to him as a practicing physician while located at said place, and at the same time tendered the costs of the suit up to the date of such tender. At the time of the hearing of the case Dr. Youngman had established an office at Sappington, Mo., a place admittedly more than five miles distant from Dr. Youngman's former residence and location on Gravois avenue, which he had sold to Dr. Habig.

What did the parties to this contract mean by the language in the bill of sale to the effect that Dr. Youngman would not establish himself as a practicing physician and surgeon, etc.? After mature reflection we can come to no other view than that the parties to the contract intended thereby that Dr. Youngman should not maintain an office for the practice of medicine or surgery within the prescribed district, and nothing more. In other words, it was intended by this portion of the contract to restrain Dr. Youngman from opening up an office as a practicing physician or surgeon at any point within five miles of the home which, under the agreement of sale, was sold by Dr. Youngman to Dr. Habig. We cannot read the language of this agreement as intending to mean that Dr. Youngman was not at any time within five years to call upon or prescribe for any person living within a radius of five miles of his former home. It would seem as though Dr. Habig was satisfied with the protection afforded, namely, that Dr. Youngman, for the specific period of time, would not open up and establish an office for the practice of medicine within five miles of his former residence and office.

In the light of this view it is clear that the decree entered below by the learned circuit judge, in so far as it restrains and enjoins Dr. Youngman, in his practice of medicine and surgery, from making calls within said prescribed district, or treating patients living within said district, or from treating former patients or residents of such district who might call at his office, even though it is established outside the said district, goes beyond the terms of said contract, and is therefore to that extent in excess of the jurisdiction of the said learned trial judge, respondent here.

Our temporary writ of prohibition heretofore issued herein prohibits the respondent herein from in any way undertaking to enforce against the petitioner its said judgment or decree except in so far as it enjoins him from opening or establishing an office for the practice of medicine or surgery within a radius of five miles of 5617 Gravois avenue, St. Louis, Mo., for a period of five years from December 1, 1919, until the further order of this court. For the reasons indicated above the temporary writ should be made permanent. Accordingly it is so ordered.

ALLEN, P. J., concurs.

McNEILL et al. v. WABASH RY. CO.
(No. 16249.)

(St. Louis Court of Appeals. Missouri. May 3, 1921. Rehearing Denied June 7, 1921.)

1. Action ⬩27(3) — Consignee may sue on common-law liability.

Where a carrier undertook to transport breeding ewes to an independent stockyard in St. Louis, but they were delivered to yards in Illinois, and sold for immediate slaughter, the consignee may recover on the carrier's common-law liability, regardless of the written contract, and may show that wrong destination was inserted therein by mistake.

2. Evidence ⬩433(6) — Consignee may show that written contract did not express destination.

Consignee of live stock may show that the written contract did not express the correct destination, and that after the receiving agent attempted to correct it it was again changed by another agent of the carrier.

3. Carriers ⬩212—Delivery of sheep to same consignee at wrong yards held not to exonerate carrier.

Where a carrier had knowledge that the shipper was the owner of breeding ewes consigned to an agent at the independent stockyards at St. Louis, the fact that the carrier wrongfully delivered them to the same agent at other yards, where they were sold for immediate slaughter, will not exonerate the carrier, which was advised if sent to the yards where delivered they would be sold for slaughter, for the consignee is to be regarded as an agent of the owner to receive only at the proper destination.

4. Carriers ☞230(1)—Waiver of right of action for misdelivery by acceptance of proceeds from sale of breeding ewes held for jury.

Where an owner of breeding ewes, which had been delivered by carrier to the wrong yards, where they were slaughtered, accepted the proceeds of their sale, did not waive as a matter of law his right of action against the carrier which made the misdelivery, but the question should be submitted to the jury.

5. Estoppel ☞119—Where reasonable minds can differ, question of waiver is for jury.

Question of waiver is one of intention depending on the circumstances of the case, and if reasonable minds can draw different conclusions it is for the jury.

6. Carriers ☞229(5)—An award of $2,125 for misdelivery of 218 breeding ewes which, as a result, were sold for slaughter, held not excessive.

In an action against a railroad company for damages for the conversion of a shipment of 218 breeding ewes, which as a result was sold for slaughter, the award of $2,125 *held*, under the evidence, not excessive.

Appeal from Circuit Court, Audrain County; E. S. Gantt, Judge.

Action by J. P. McNeill, Mark L. McNeill, and A. H. McNeill, a partnership doing business under the name of J. P. McNeill & Co., against the Wabash Railway Company. From a judgment for plaintiffs, defendant appeals. Affirmed.

N. S. Brown, of St. Louis, and A. C. Whitson, of Mexico, Mo., for appellant.

Abbott, Fauntleroy, Cullen & Edwards, of St. Louis, for respondents.

BRUERE, C. This is an action against the defendant, a common carrier, for alleged damages resulting to the plaintiffs by reason of the wrongful delivery by the defendant of certain live stock belonging to the plaintiffs. Plaintiffs recovered, and defendant prosecutes the appeal.

The cause of action stated in the petition is as follows:

"That on the 16th day of January, 1918, the plaintiffs delivered, and the defendant received, 218 head of sheep, being breeding ewes, which defendant agreed for in consideration of certain freight charges paid, well and safely to carry from Mexico, Mo., to St. Louis, Mo., and at the latter place to deliver the same to the plaintiffs, or their agents or assigns; but the defendant, in violation of its said agreement, and in total disregard of its duty as common carrier as aforesaid, so carelessly and negligently conducted itself in the premises that said property was not delivered to the plaintiffs, its agents, or assigns, in St. Louis, Mo., and that said defendant failed and neglected to deliver said property at its destination to the plaintiffs, or to any one for them, but on the contrary the said defendant wrongfully diverted said stock to National Stockyards, in the state of Illinois, and delivered them to a live stock commission firm, who were engaged in the business of receiving and selling such sheep for immediate slaughter, and that by reason of the delivery by the defendant of said sheep to said parties in the state of Illinois, and by reason of its failure to deliver them to the point of destination, to wit, St. Louis, Mo., said breeding ewes and all of them were sold for immediate slaughter, and were slaughtered, and that plaintiffs received on account of the sale and slaughter of said sheep the sum of $1,799.81; that the total value of said sheep, as breeding ewes, was $4,360, and that, by reason of the wrongful acts of the defendant above set forth, plaintiffs were damaged in the sum of $2,560.90."

The answer contains a general denial, and, in addition, pleads:

(1) That the sheep referred to in plaintiffs' petition were received and transported by the defendant under and subject to the terms of a written contract, whereby it was agreed between the plaintiffs and defendant that defendant should transport the sheep from Mexico, Mo., to the National Stockyards, at Illinois, and there deliver the same to the Woodson-Fennewald Commission Company, the consignee named in the contract; that defendant fully complied with the provisions of said contract and transported said sheep from Mexico, Mo., to the National Stockyards, Ill., and made delivery thereof to said Woodson-Fennewald Commission Company.

(2) That the plaintiffs appointed the said Woodson-Fennewald Commission Company its agents to receive and take delivery of said sheep at its destination and that the said commission company received the sheep, as the agent of the plaintiffs, and sold the same at the National Stockyards, Ill., for and on behalf of the plaintiffs, that the plaintiffs received the proceeds of said sale, and by so doing waived any right they had or may have had to have said sheep delivered at St. Louis, Mo., and that plaintiffs therefore were estopped from asserting their claim for damages set up in the petition.

In their reply, plaintiffs denied, under oath, that they executed the contract set up in the answer, and averred therein that they made a contract with the defendant to transport said sheep to the Independent Stockyards, St. Louis, Mo., and gave defendant directions in writing to that effect; that by mistake the agents of the defendant, in writing said contract, inserted the destination as National Stockyards, Illinois, but that said mistake was discovered before the sheep were shipped; and, being advised of its mistake, the defendant corrected and agreed to correct said contract by making the destination Independent Stockyards. The reply further admitted that the sheep were delivered wrongfully to the National Stockyards by defendant, and that thereafter, and by reason of said conversion, the sheep were sold by mistake, and plaintiffs received what they brought at said sale, to wit, $1,799.81, and which amount was $2,560.90 less than their real value.

The facts in this case are briefly as follows:

About the middle of January, 1918, the plaintiffs purchased from the firm of Mason & Carter 218 breeding ewes. The ewes had been bred and were to bring lambs the following April. The plaintiffs gave directions to Mason & Carter to ship the sheep from Mexico, Mo., to plaintiffs' home at Salem, Mo. Mr. Carter, a member of the firm of Mason & Carter, saw Mr. Richards, defendant's freight agent at Mexico, Mo., about shipping the sheep to Salem, Mo. Mr. Richards informed Mr. Carter that the sheep would have to be shipped to St. Louis, Mo., and then rebilled from St. Louis to Salem, Mo. Mr. Carter then communicated with Mr. E. L. Woodson, a member of the firm of Woodson-Fennewald Live Stock Commission Company, and told him he was billing two loads of sheep to plaintiffs at Salem, Mo., and that Mr. Richards would not bill them through to Salem, and requested Mr. Woodson to see a Mr. Clem, live stock agent for the defendant, and see if he could not get them shipped through to Salem without unloading them.

Mr. Woodson saw Mr. Clem, and was told by him to bill the sheep to the Independent Stockyards, St. Louis, Mo., and then rebill them over the Frisco to Salem. Mr. Woodson informed Mr. Carter what Mr. Clem had said, and Mr. Carter told him the sheep would be billed to the Woodson-Fennewald Commission Company at the Independent Stockyards at St. Louis, and then rebilled to Salem, Mo. Arrangements were made for Mr. Andrew McNeely, manager of the Woodson-Fennewald Commission Company, at the Independent Stockyards, St. Louis, Mo., to take charge of the sheep at the Independent Stockyards, and rebill them to Salem, Mo., to plaintiffs.

Mr. Carter then told Mr. Richards, defendant's freight agent, to bill the sheep to the Woodson-Fennewald Commission Company at the Independent Stockyards at St. Louis, Mo. Mr. Richards then prepared a live stock contract, to which was attached an offer of shipment, and which the plaintiffs were to sign. Mr. Carter noticed that the offer of shipment read "from Mexico, Mo., to St. Louis U. D.," and he told Mr. Richards he wanted the sheep to go to the Independent Stockyards, and asked him if the letters U.

D. meant that they would be shipped to the Independent Stockyards. Mr. Richards replied that they did, and that they billed them on the U. D. track to go to the Independent Stockyards, St. Louis, Mo.

Mr. Carter further noticed that on the back of the contract were written the words "From Mexico, Mo., To Natl. Stockyards, Ill.," and he called Mr. Richards' attention to the mistake, and told him to bill the sheep to the Independent Stockyards; that if they went to the National Stockyards, to the Woodson-Fennewald Commission Company, the sheep would be sold for slaughter. He told Mr. Richards to correct the mistake. Mr. Richards promised to do so, and did change the contract on the back thereof, by scratching out the words "Natl. Stockyards, Ill.," and writing in lieu thereof the words "St. Louis U. D.," but failed to make the correction in the body of the contract.

The contract names the Woodson-Fennewald Commission Company consignee. Their name appears only on the back of the contract. Mr. Carter suggested that Mr. Richards write a new contract, but Mr. Richards assured him that the train crew would not see the contract, but would get the waybill. Mr. Carter thereupon executed the contract and offer of shipment on behalf of the plaintiffs.

The destination of the sheep, according to the waybill accompanying the shipment, was St. Louis U. D. The sheep were received for shipment by the defendant on the 16th day of January, 1918, and duly arrived at defendant's station at Bremen avenue, St. Louis, Mo. The Independent Stockyards are located at said Bremen avenue. The destination named in the original waybill, accompanying the shipment, was changed by defendant's agent at Bremen Avenue Station by writing on said waybill in blue pencil the words "National Stockyards." As to why this change was made, the evidence does not disclose.

The Woodson-Fennewald Commission Company were located at the National Stockyards, East St. Louis, Ill., but maintained a branch house at the Independent Stockyards, Bremen avenue, St. Louis, Mo., which was conducted for them by the McNeely & Son Commission Company. The sheep in question were not delivered to the Independent Stockyards, St. Louis, Mo., but were delivered by the defendant to the National Stockyards Company, at East St. Louis, Ill.; they were unloaded into their pens, and, a few hours after they received them, the said Yards Company delivered them to the Woodson-Fennewald Commission Company at said last-named place.

The season for the sale of breeding ewes had closed at the National Stockyards at the time the sheep were delivered to the Woodson-Fennewald Commission Company, and at said time the great majority of the sheep consigned to said commission company at the National Stockyards, Ill., were sold for immediate slaughter. Mr. Little, who had charge of the sheep department of the Woodson-Fennewald Commission Company, not knowing that the sheep were not to be put on the market for sale, sold the sheep within a few hours after they were delivered to him by the Stockyards Company, and the sheep were immediately thereafter slaughtered. The plaintiffs had no knowledge that the defendant had delivered the sheep to the National Stockyards Company until after they were killed.

The net proceeds of the sale of the sheep amounted to $1,799.81, which amount the Woodson-Fennewald Commission Company paid plaintiffs. The defendant offered no evidence other than the shippers' contract, heretofore mentioned, which was admitted in evidence.

The jury returned a verdict in favor of the plaintiffs for $2,125. At the close of plaintiffs' case, and again at the close of all the evidence, the defendant asked a peremptory instruction, in the nature of a demurrer to the evidence, which the court refused to give. Counsel for defendant insist that said instruction should have been given.

[1, 2] (1) They argue that the plaintiffs are precluded from recovering in this action because of the written contract. They contend that the destination of the sheep, according to the written contract, was the National Stockyards, and that delivery of the sheep was made at said destination.

This suit is not founded on a breach of the written contract, but on the alleged breach of the common-law duty of defendant to deliver the sheep to the consignee according to plaintiffs' direction. Plaintiffs were not compelled to sue on the written contract, but could sue defendant on its common-law liability as a common carrier. Defendant pleaded and introduced the written contract as a defense. Plaintiffs had a right to set up and prove that the written contract, by reason of the mistake made therein, did not effectuate the intention of the parties, and therefore was not binding on them. Barlow v. Elliott, 56 Mo. App. 377; Leitensdorfer v. Delphy, 15 Mo. 160, 55 Am. Dec. 137; Lupe v. Atlantic & Pacific R. R. Co., 3 Mo. App. 77; Deierling v. Railroad, 163 Mo. App. loc. cit. 296, 146 S. W. 814; Creamery Co. v. Railroad, 128 Mo. App. 422, 107 S. W. 462; Short v. Thomas, 178 Mo. App. 417, 163 S. W. 252; Wernick v. Railroad, 131 Mo. App. 37, 109 S. W. 1027.

The evidence disclosed beyond question that the parties at no time intended to ship the sheep to the National Stockyards, Ill., but intended that the shipment should be made to the Independent Stockyards, St. Louis, Mo. The words "Natl. Yards, Ill.," written in the body of the contract, were inadvertently writ-

ten therein by defendant's agent. The mistake was discovered before the shipment was made, and defendant endeavored to correct it by eliminating the said words, and writing in lieu thereof, on the back of said contract, the words "St. Louis U. D."

Moreover, defendant's agent, the one who wrote the contract, made out the waybill for the shipment. In the waybill the sheep were billed to St. Louis U. D.; St. Louis U. D. meaning Independent Stockyards, according to the interpretation of said agent. This waybill accompanied the shipment, and was the order that controlled the train crew in handling the shipment. Defendant, therefore, was not misled because of the written contract in making delivery of the sheep at the National Stockyards, Ill.

It is evident from the testimony that the reason the sheep were carried to the National Stockyards, Ill., and there delivered, was on account of the unauthorized act of defendant's agent at Bremen avenue, St. Louis, Mo., who changed the destination of the shipment and rebilled the sheep to the National Stockyards, Ill. This act was the cause of defendant's wrongful delivery and conversion of the sheep. The issue raised by the pleadings regarding the execution of the written contract was for the jury to decide.

[3] (2) Counsel for defendant further contends that the defendant had the right to assume that the consignee, the Woodson-Fennewald Commission Company, were the owners of the sheep, and therefore the delivery to said consignee discharged the defendant from liability, although the place of delivery was not the place appointed by the plaintiffs. To this contention we cannot agree. It will be seen from the statement of the facts in this case that the defendant had notice that the sheep belonged to the plaintiffs, and that the consignee was merely their agent to receive the sheep at the Independent Stockyards, St. Louis, Mo., and reship them to Salem, Mo. Defendant, therefore, had no right to indulge in the presumption contended for.

The law governing the question under discussion is tersely stated by the Supreme Court of the United States in the case of Southern Express Co. v. Dickson, 94 U. S. 550, 24 L. Ed. 285. Said case is decisive of this question. The court there says:

"Where it is known that the goods are the property of the shipper, and have been shipped by him for delivery to the consignee as his agent at a distant place, can the carrier deliver the goods to such consignee or to their order at another place? * * * We think the rule is that, where the consignor is known to the carrier to be the owner, the carrier must be understood to contract with him only, for his interest, upon such terms as he dictates in regard to the delivery, and that the consignees are to be regarded simply as agents selected by him to receive the goods at the place indicated."

See, also, Smith Co. v. Railroad, 145 Mo. App. 394, loc. cit. 406, 407, 122 S. W. 342; Hutchinson on Carriers, vol. 1, § 177, vol. 2, § 736; Wichita Poultry Co. v. Southern Pac. Ry. Co., 197 Mo. App. 578, 198 S. W. 82; Cooper v. Bank of British North America (C. C.) 30 Fed. 171; Bank of British North America v. Cooper, 137 U. S. 473, 11 Sup. Ct. 160, 34 L. Ed. 759; Bartlett v. Steamboat Philadelphia, 32 Mo. 256.

It was the duty of the defendant to deliver the sheep according to the plaintiffs' direction, and to make delivery at the place appointed by the plaintiffs, to wit, at the Independent Stockyards, St. Louis, Mo., and a delivery at the National Stockyards, Ill., although to the same consignee, did not relieve defendant from its responsibility.

[4, 5] (3) The defendant further contends that the plaintiffs waived the conversion by receiving the proceeds of the sale of the sheep. In dealing with this question it must be borne in mind that the plaintiffs had no knowledge of the wrongful delivery of the sheep until after the sheep were slaughtered. Defendant was guilty of a conversion in delivering the sheep at the National Stockyards. The slaughter of the sheep was due to said conversion. The wrongful act of the carrier, the cause of the loss to the plaintiffs, had been committed when plaintiffs accepted the proceeds of the sale of the sheep.

Let us suppose that the plaintiffs had accepted the sheep from the defendant after they were slaughtered. Could it be contended that plaintiffs' act in accepting the sheep constituted a waiver of the conversion, as a matter of law? We think not.

Waiver is a question of intention. What constitutes waiver depends upon facts of each particular case. If reasonable minds might draw different conclusions from the facts, the question of waiver is one for the jury, and not for the court.

The plaintiffs contend that they did not take the proceeds of the sale of the sheep in satisfaction of the wrong done them by the defendant; that the loss sustained by them for the miscarrying of the sheep to a wrong and bad market, and having them sold for slaughter, was not intended to be waived, and was not affected by plaintiffs' acceptance of the proceeds of sale.

There was ample evidence to sustain plaintiffs' contention. It was a question of fact to be determined by the jury. The court was not authorized to declare, as a matter of law, that plaintiffs had waived the conversion. Arrington v. Wilmington & Weldon R. R. Co., 51 N. C. 68, 72 Am. Dec. 559; Lesinsky v. Great Western Dispatch, 10 Mo. App. 134, loc. cit. 141; Atkisson v. Steamboat Castle Garden, 28 Mo. 124; People's

State Savings Bank v. Railroad, 192 Mo. App. 614, 178 S. W. 292; Fairbanks, Morse & Co. v. Baskett, 98 Mo. App. loc. cit. 67, 71 S. W. 1113; Lake Shore, etc. Railroad Co. v. W. H. McIntyre Co., 60 Ind. App. 191, 108 N. E. 978; Lester v. Delaware, L. & W. R. R. Co., 92 Hun, 342, 36 N. Y. Supp. 907; 10 Corpus Juris, § 330; McSwegan et al. v. Pennsylvania R. R. Co., 7 App. Div. 301, 40 N. Y. Supp. 51.

[6] (4) Respondents further contend that the verdict is excessive. The evidence discloses that a few days prior to the conversion of the sheep plaintiffs paid $3,833.50 for them. There was evidence showing that immediately after they were shipped the price of breeding ewes was from $2 to $2.50 a head higher. Other evidence tended to show that the sheep were worth $20 per head. The verdict of the jury is supported by the evidence.

It would needlessly lengthen this opinion to consider appellant's other assignments of errors. It is sufficient to say that we find no error which would warrant a reversal of the judgment herein.

The judgment of the circuit court of Audrain county should be affirmed, and the Commissioner so recommends.

PER CURIAM. The opinion of BRUERE, C., is adopted as the opinion of the court. The judgment of the circuit court of Audrain county is accordingly affirmed.

ALLEN, P. J., and BECKER, J., concur. DAUES, J., not sitting.

———

ELMS et al. v. MUTUAL BENEFIT LIFE INS. CO. (No. 15596.)

(St. Louis Court of Appeals. Missouri. May 3, 1921. Rehearing Denied June 7, 1921.)

1. Appeal and error ⟷927(3)—Cause considered most favorably to appellant on appeal from nonsuit.

On appeal from a judgment for defendant after denying plaintiffs' motion to set aside a nonsuit, the cause must be considered in the light most favorable to plaintiffs.

2. Insurance ⟷146(3) — Plain forfeiture clause will be enforced.

While the law does not favor forfeiture, especially in the case of insurance contracts, the courts cannot do otherwise than to enforce a contract plainly providing for forfeiture when no statutory law intervenes to prohibit it.

3. Insurance ⟷349(1)—Policy held to provide for forfeiture for nonpayment of premium.

A life insurance policy written before the enactment of the nonforfeiture statutes (Rev.

St. 1919, §§ 6151–6153), expressly providing that in case of nonpayment of premium the insurer should not be liable for payment of any part of the sum insured for, but that the policy should cease and determine, clearly provides for forfeiture which must be enforced.

4. Insurance ⚽═349(4)—Provision for deduction for indebtedness held not to apply where policy was forfeited.

The provision of the insuring clause that the company would pay the amount of policy after deducting all indebtedness to the company applied to a payment while policy was in force, and was not inconsistent with a subsequent clause forfeiting the policy for nonpayment of premiums.

5. Insurance ⚽═368(1)—Clause giving right to paid-up insurance not inconsistent with forfeiture clause.

There is no inconsistency between a clause in life insurance policy providing for its forfeiture for nonpayment of a premium when due and a clause that, if two years' premiums have been paid, the insured, on default of payment of a subsequent premium, may receive a paid-up policy for an equitable sum upon the demand and surrender of policy within three months from lapse.

6. Insurance ⚽═360(3)—Reserve under policy held forfeited for nonpayment of premiums.

Even if the reserve under a life insurance policy which lapsed from nonpayment of premiums be construed to be the company's profits, the insured is not entitled thereto when the policy expressly provided for forfeiture of all profits thereunder.

7. Insurance ⚽═390—Voluntary application of reserve of paid-up insurance does not waive forfeiture.

Where a life insurance policy expressly providing for forfeiture for nonpayment of premiums had lapsed, the insurance company did not waive its right to forfeit by voluntarily applying, when the insured failed to surrender his policy and demand the cash surrender value within the time limited, the reserve earned under the policy to the purchase of paid-up insurance which had expired before the death of insured.

8. Insurance ⚽═360(3)—In absence of statute forfeited reserve is property of company.

Before the enactment of nonforfeiture statutes (Rev. St. 1919, §§ 6151–6153), the reserves earned on the policy which provided for forfeiture of the insurance and all profits in the event of nonpayment of premiums were the property of the company, so that the beneficiaries under the policy could not recover such reserves from the company on the theory it converted the property of insured to its own use by applying the reserves to a paid-up policy of insurance.

Appeal from St. Louis Circuit Court; Glendy B. Arnold, Judge.

Action by Edward C. Elms and others against the Mutual Benefit Life Insurance Company. From a judgment for defendant after denying plaintiffs' motion to take a nonsuit, plaintiffs appeal. Affirmed.

Igoe & Carroll and Anderson, Gilbert & Hayden, all of St. Louis, for appellants.

Jones, Hocker, Sullivan & Angert, of St. Louis, for respondent.

BIGGS, C. This is an action upon a policy of life insurance. The policy in the sum of $1,000 was issued upon the life of Rossington Elms and was dated March 31, 1871. The premiums were paid until March 3, 1906. The one due that day was not paid nor was any subsequent premium paid. The insured died October, 1912.

The petition is in two counts, the first being a straight suit on the policy, and the second on the theory of a conversion of the reserve standing to the credit of the policy at the time it lapsed, which is alleged to have been the sum of $765.49.

The answer to the first count, after denying the performance of the terms and conditions of the policy on the part of the plaintiffs, set up that the insured failed to pay the premium of $44.46 due on March 3, 1906, and as a result the policy·lapsed, and under its terms the company became exempted from the payment of any sum. It is further averred that under the policy it was provided that after two or more premiums had been paid the company upon the lapse of the policy for the nonpayment of any subsequent premium would issue a paid-up policy insuring an equitable sum, payable at death, provided application was made for such paid-up insurance and the policy surrendered to the company within three months after its lapse. It is then averred that no application was made nor was the policy surrendered for paid-up insurance within three months after its lapse for the nonpayment of the·premium due March 3, 1906.

Defendant's answer to the second count denied that on March 3, 1906, or at any time there was a reserve or cash value standing to the credit of the policy of $765.49 as alleged by plaintiffs, and denied that either the insured or plaintiffs were entitled to any reserve or cash value under said policy upon its lapse for the nonpayment of the premium.

The cause was tried by the court sitting as a jury, and upon request of the defendant at the close of the case the court declared the law to be that plaintiffs were not entitled to recover under either count of the petition. Following the usual preliminaries, plaintiffs have appealed.

No question of pleading arises in the case, and the facts are undisputed. The foregoing statement and substantive portions of the pleadings may be considered as facts established in the case; the parties, however, differing only as to the legal effect of the olicy stipulations and subsequent action f the company after the lapse of the policy ollowing the default in the payment of preliums. It was conceded that the defendant vas duly notified and denied liability for iny sum, and that all premiums were paid rom 1871 to the premium due March 3, 1905, out that no further premiums were paid by the assured or by any one. It was further admitted no demand was made within three months after the lapse or at any time for the paid-up insurance provided in the policy. The provisions of the policy material to the issues are as follows:

"And the said company does hereby promise and agree to and with the said assured well and truly to pay or cause to be paid the said sum insured, at their office in the city of Newark, to the said Catherine Elms or assigns, within ninety days after due notice and proof of the death of said Rossington Elms. And in case the said assured should die before the decease of the said Rossington Elms, then the amount of this insurance shall be payable to their children or to their guardian if under age, within ninety days after due notice and proof of interest and of the death of said Rossington Elms, deducting therefrom all indebtedness of the party to the company, together with the balance, if any, of the year's premium."

The forfeiture provision is as follows:

"In case the said premium shall not be paid on or before the several days hereinbefore mentioned for the payment thereof, at the office of the company in the city of Newark, or to agents when they produce receipts signed by the president or treasurer, then, and in every such case, the said company shall not be liable to the payment of the sum insured, or any part thereof, and this policy shall cease and determine; but after two or more full years premiums have been paid hereon the company will issue a paid-up policy insuring an equitable sum, payable at death, provided application be made for same, and the policy with the profits thereon be duly surrendered within three months after its lapse."

"And it is further agreed by the within assured that in every case where this policy shall cease or become or be null and void all previous payments made thereon and all profits shall be forfeited to the said company; and that if it be assigned, written notice shall be given to the company and their assent thereto obtained."

It was further shown that in the year 1879 and in 1895 the company adopted new forfeiture systems which were applied to all future policies of the company and were also made applicable to all prior policies which had been issued. By these systems the insured in the event of a lapse was given in lieu of the paid-up insurance provided in the policy the right or option of withdrawing the reserve on the policy either in cash or having the reserve applied to the purchase of extended insurance, upon condition, however, of a demand being made therefor and a surrender of the policy to the company within three months after lapse. It was provided in the system that in the event of a failure to make demand or surrender the policy within three months for paid-up insurance provided in the policy or for the cash surrender value or for extended insurance the reserve should be applied to the purchase of extended insurance.

It was further undisputed as was shown by certain letters written to plaintiffs' counsel and by other evidence that in June, 1906, after the policy in the instant suit had lapsed on March 3, 1906, in view of the fact that the policy was not surrendered or any demand made for the cash or for a paid-up policy, the company applied the reserve on the policy to the purchase of extended insurance, which resulted in the policy being continued in force for the full amount of $1,000 for a period of four years and twenty-four days or until March 27, 1910, more than two years prior to the death of the assured.

The Missouri nonforfeiture statutes (sections 6151, 6152, 6153, R. S. 1919) were not enacted until 1879, which was after the date of the policy in suit, and hence there is no contention that they are applicable. The policy in suit being unaffected by that law, we need only consider its terms in determining whether the beneficiaries had any rights thereunder at the time of the death of the insured October, 1912, in view of the concession that the policy lapsed on March 3, 1906, for failure to pay premiums.

[1] Plaintiffs' learned counsel have not formally assigned errors in the action of the trial court. The suit was tried before the court without a jury, and after the cause was taken under advisement the court sustained the defendant's demurrers to the evidence and granted to the plaintiffs the right to take a nonsuit. Failing in their motion to have the nonsuit set aside, plaintiffs have appealed and are entitled to have the cause viewed in the light most favorable to them. Such matter, however, is of little consequence, as there are no disputed questions of fact in the case.

We are able to glean from the points and arguments of counsel that it is contended by plaintiffs that no forfeiture was provided in the policy; that, granting such provision, the same was waived by the defendant by reason of it formally subjecting the policy to its nonforfeiture system adopted in 1879 whereby it granted to the assured the right to extended insurance under certain conditions and stipulations; that the provision in the policy providing for deducting any indebtedness thereon and also unpaid premium is inconsistent with and negatives the idea of forfeiture, and also the provision requiring a surrender of the policy and profits is claimed to be inconsistent with the claim of forfeiture, the result being that two constructions are possible under the policy, and the one favoring the assured should be adopted.

[2] While the law does not favor forfeitures, especially in the case of insurance contracts, where the parties plainly by their contract provide for them, and no statutory law intervenes to prohibit them, the courts cannot do otherwise than enforce the contract as written by the parties themselves. Ashbrook v. Ins. Co., 94 Mo. 72, 6 S. W. 462; Smoot v. Ins. Co., 138 Mo. App. 438, 120 S. W. 719; Mitchell v. Ins. Co., 179 Mo. App. 1, 161 S. W. 362.

[3] The policy here provided upon failure to pay the premium that "then and in every such case the said company shall not be liable for the payment of the sum insured or any part thereof, but the policy shall cease and determine." This was followed by a provision giving to assured after the payment of two or more premiums the right to have a paid-up policy for an equitable sum payable at death, provided application be made for same and the policy with the profits thereon be duly surrendered within three months after its lapse.

This provision plainly and clearly provides for a forfeiture, and in view of the fact that the nonforfeiture law of Missouri cannot be applied to the policy we are powerless to do anything but to enforce the contract as written.

[4] It is argued by plaintiffs that the forfeiture clause is inconsistent with the provision of the prior insuring clause which says that upon assured's death the company would pay the amount of the policy, after "deducting therefrom all indebtedness of the party to the company together with the balance, if any, of the year's premium." Of course, if the policy was forfeited, there could be nothing to deduct. The provision referred to giving the company the right to deduct any indebtedness due the company manifestly applied to a payment made by the company while the policy was in force, and not where the policy has been forfeited under its terms prior to the insured's death. Ruane v. Ins. Co., 194 Mo. App. 214, 186 S. W. 1188.

The case of Kline v. National Ben. Ass'n, 111 Ind. 462, 11 N. E. 620, 60 Am. Rep. 703, relied on by plaintiffs, is wholly unlike this case. There the policy acknowledged the receipt of six assessments and then provided for a forfeiture for failure to pay assessments. The company contended the policy was forfeited because one of the assessments that it acknowledged was paid was not in fact paid, and it was held that as against the beneficiary the company was estopped by the recital in the policy acknowledging the receipt of the six assessments from asserting that one of them was not paid. Furthermore the court in construing the contract as a whole found that it did not entitle the company to declare a forfeiture. The court said (111 Ind. loc. cit. 466, 11 N. E. 623, 60 Am. Rep. 703):

"The only clause which professes to give a right to declare a forfeiture is the brief clause contained in the orders given by the assured, and this cannot be allowed to prevail against the statements in the application, the acknowledgment in the policy, the provision that it shall be incontestable except for fraud, and the recitals of the binding receipt."

[5] Nor is there any inconsistency between the forfeiture clause and the provision following which gives to the assured on default the right to a paid-up policy for an equitable sum upon demand and surrender of the policy within three months from lapse.

[6] The right to paid-up insurance was conditioned upon the owner making application therefor "and the policy with the profits thereon be duly surrendered to the company within three months after its lapse." It is contended by plaintiffs that defendant has construed this policy and stated that these "profits" amounted to the sum of $765.49. Defendant does not admit that the profits on the policy amounted to $765.49 at date of lapse, but that the "reserve," an entirely different thing, amounted to that sum, which reserve was voluntarily and without obligation on its part applied to the purchase of extended insurance under its nonforfeiture systems adopted in 1879 and 1895.

However, granting that the profits amounted to that sum, the policy plainly and unequivocally forfeits all profits to the company upon failure to pay premiums.

[7] But say plaintiffs granting a right of forfeiture same was waived by reason of the company after the death of Rossington Elms admitting in letters to plaintiffs' counsel that it had applied the reserve that had accumulated on the policy at date of lapse to the purchase of extended insurance. The letters do not admit any liability under the original policy, but state same became valueless under its provision for nonpayment of premium. It is then stated that after lapse and upon failure of the assured to request a paid-up policy under the provisions of the original policy the company had applied the reserve to the purchase of extended insurance in view of the fact that the insured had not surrendered the policy for paid-up insurance or for cash surrender value.

The sole benefit accruing to assured under the policy terms upon lapse was to have paid-up insurance for an equitable sum upon complying with the conditions. The other benefits, namely, cash surrender value and the right to extended insurance, were accorded the policy voluntarily by the company when there was no obligation to do so by the terms of the original contract. Such action should not be construed as a waiver of the rights of the company to enforce the plain provisions of the written contract. The company, although not obligated, gave to the assured upon his default the benefit of extended insurance for a term of about four years, as the accumulated reserve carried the policy that length of time. Had the assured died within that time, his beneficiaries would have received the full face of the policy.

[8] The second count proceeds on the theory that at the time of the default the reserve belonged to the assured, and that the company was guilty of conversion in applying it to the purchase of extended insurance. Under the terms of the policy the assured had only a conditional right to paid-up insurance upon lapse. If the policy had unconditionally given to the assured upon default a right to a cash surrender value, there would be merit in plaintiffs' contention that a conversion existed.

In view of the fact that there was no statute in effect at the time governing the disposition of the reserve, and where, as here, the policy did not accord to the assured the benefits of the reserve upon lapse either for cash surrender value or for paid-up or extended insurance, the reserve belonged to the company, and not the assured. Payne v. Ins. Co., 195 Mo. App. 512, 191 S. W. 695; State ex rel. v. Vandiver, 213 Mo. 187, 214, 111 S. W. 911; Wilhelm v. Prudential Ins. Co., 227 S. W. 897, not yet officially reported.

One of the purposes in enacting the non-forfeiture statutes was to give to the assured benefits arising from the reserve in the form of extended insurance, thereby clearly indicating that absent the statute the reserve belonged to the company.

It follows that the court properly declared the law as applied to the facts, and that the judgment should be affirmed.

PER CURIAM. The foregoing opinion of BIGGS, C., is adopted as the opinion of the court.

The judgment of the circuit court is accordingly affirmed.

ALLEN, P. J., and BECKER, J., concur. DAUES, J., not sitting.

HEATH v. BECK. (No. 15015.)

(St. Louis Court of Appeals. Missouri. May 3, 1921. Rehearing Denied June 7, 1921.)

1. Appeal and error ⬅494 — When certified copy of decree on one count not filed, it is not reviewable.

Where counts in equity for reformation of a contract and at law for damages were tried separately, and defendant brought the case to the Court of Appeals by the short method of appeal, but filed only a certified copy of the judgment for damages, and not a certified copy

of the decree on the equity count as required by Rev. St. 1919, § 1479, the judgment for damages is the only judgment before the court for review, especially where the order granting the appeal shows that it was the only judgment appealed from.

2. Vendor and purchaser ⬅343(1) — Purchaser entitled to recover for breach of vendor's oral agreement to plat land so as to give outlet.

Where a vendor in selling part of a tract of land orally agreed to plat the rest of the tract in such manner as to afford the purchaser an outlet to a roadway connecting with the public road, a reformation of the contract to include such provision was not necessary in order to permit a recovery of damages.

3. Appeal and error ⬅846(3) — Judgment affirmed if sustainable on any theory when no declarations of law asked or given.

In an action tried by the court without a jury, where no declarations of law were asked by either party or given by the court, the judgment will be affirmed if it may be sustained upon any theory supported by the evidence.

4. Evidence ⬅427 — Oral agreement by vendor to open street does not vary written contract and deed.

An oral agreement by the vendor contemporaneous with the written contract of sale to open a street through the land to give the purchaser an outlet did not conflict with, or vary the terms of, the written contract or deed, and oral evidence thereof was not inadmissible as varying or contradicting the terms of the writing.

5. Appeal and error ⬅173(6) — Frauds, statute of ⬅144 — Defense held waived.

The defense that the contract sued on was within the statute of frauds (Rev. St. 1919, § 2169) was waived and could not be raised for the first time in the Court of Appeals, where the statute was not pleaded, no objection based on the statute was made to evidence of the verbal contract, no instruction on that theory was offered, and the statute was not referred to in the motion for a new trial.

6. Frauds, statute of ⬅125(1) — Does not render contract void but is rule of evidence.

Rev. St. 1919, § 2169, does not render a contract void, but goes merely to the remedy, and as such is a rule of evidence.

Appeal from Circuit Court, St. Louis County; G. A. Wurdeman, Judge.

"Not to be officially published."

Action by Richard Heath against George Beck. Judgment for plaintiff, and defendant appealed to the Court of Appeals, which transferred the cause to the Supreme Court (204 S. W. 43), but the cause was subsequently retransferred to the Court of Appeals (225 S. W. 993). Affirmed.

Hans Wulff and John Porter, both of St. Louis, for appellant.

George H. Brooks, of Webster Groves, and Joseph C. McAtee, of Clayton, for respondent.

BIGGS, C. This cause, having been transferred to the Supreme Court (204 S. W. 43), was retransferred here, as that court concluded after an examination of the record that title to real estate was not involved (225 S. W. 993). In the Supreme Court opinion referred to, the substance of the pleadings and issues in the cause are stated thus:

"The petition is in two counts. The first alleges that respondent bought from appellant a parcel of land in St. Louis county for a money consideration of $350, and bought it upon the representation that appellant would plat the rest of the same tract in such manner as to afford respondent an outlet from his parcel to a roadway running over appellant's property and connecting with a public road; that upon this representation appellant finally prevailed upon respondent to purchase the parcel mentioned at the price stated, payable in installments; that a written agreement was drawn which embodied the contract to purchase, except that it did not contain the agreement concerning the roadway appellant had promised to secure to respondent; that appellant repeated his assurances and thereby induced respondent to sign the agreement as presented; that in November, 1909, respondent made final payment, and appellant executed and delivered to him a warranty deed to the land; that upon the receipt of each installment and the final payment appellant repeated his assurances and representations, and respondent relied thereupon in making the payments and in accepting the deed, which did not contain an agreement for the roadway; that appellant caused the tract he retained to be surveyed and a plat to be made which showed a roadway as orally agreed, but did not file the plat, and afterward sold the property without reserving a roadway and without notifying the purchaser of the existence of the oral agreement therefor. It is then alleged that respondent's property is valueless without the roadway; that appellant's failure to reserve an outlet for respondent's benefit was in fraud of respondent's right, and respondent is without an adequate remedy at law; that the representations were made to deceive respondent and defraud him and accomplished that purpose; that a reformation of the written agreement to cause it to include the provision concerning the outlet is necessary in order to prevent appellant from succeeding in working a fraud upon respondent. The prayer is for such a reformation of both the agreement and the deed.

The second count incorporates or purports to incorporate the facts set up in the first count, and then states that, 'relying upon the promise of defendant to furnish him an outlet and roadway to said premises as therein described, plaintiff purchased from defendant a strip of land,' which the petition then describes, 'and paid him therefor the sum of $350. Plaintiff states that, contrary to the said agreement and the terms thereof, defendant has failed and refused and still fails and refuses to furnish him with said outlet; that he as sold the property over which it was to be established to one Wolff, without notifying the said Wolff of the said agreement; that the said property is value-

less; and that by reason of the premises plaintiff has been damaged in the sum of $350,' for which judgment is prayed. On the first count the trial court reformed the agreement and the deed as prayed. On the count for damages the court rendered judgment for respondent for $300."

The so-called equity count and the second count which sounds at law for damages were tried separately. After a hearing on the first or equity count there was a decree for respondent reforming the agreement and deed, after which appellant filed a motion for a new trial. Later on the cause was heard on the second count for damages, and the court, as stated, rendered judgment for respondent on that count.

[1, 2] Thereafter a motion for new trial being overruled, the appellant brings the cause here by the short method of appeal, but failed to file in this court a certified copy of the decree rendered on the equity count as required by section 1479 of the R. S. of 1919, but did file a certified copy of the judgment for damages rendered on the second count. The court's decree, however, is copied in appellant's abstract of the record. Under such circumstances, the only judgment properly before us for review is the judgment for damages on the second count of the petition. The certified copy of the order granting the appeal filed here discloses that the appellant appealed only from the judgment of the court on the second count for damages. Under such circumstances, we decline to review the action of the Court on the first count. As stated by the Supreme Court, the first count seems designed to reform respondent's evidence for use in the trial upon the second count and in view of the sale to the innocent purchaser Wolff who is not a party to the cause, the reformation of the contract and deed could in no way affect the title to the property. Furthermore, such reformation is unnecessary in order to permit a recovery on the other count.

[3] The second count for damages was tried before the court without a jury. No declarations of law were asked by either party or given by the court. Under such circumstances, it is well established that the duty of this court is to affirm the judgment, if it may be sustained upon any theory supported by the evidence.

Appellant's objections to the judgment on the second count are twofold: First, that the court erred in allowing testimony as to the alleged contemporaneous oral promise on the part of appellant to establish the right of way and consequently in allowing a recovery upon an oral contract contemporaneous with the written agreement; and, second, that the oral contract referred to provided for an easement in other land than that covered by the deed and written contract, and consently **said** contract not being in writing **void** under the statute of frauds.

6] As to the first proposition. The oral .tract referred to does not in any way cont **with** or vary the terms of the written **itract**. In speaking of the rule of law .ich **presumes** that the written contract **ibodies** the entire agreement between the rties **and** therefore that extrinsic evidence **inadmissible** to vary or contradict the rms **thereof**, this court in the case of Bows **v. Bell**, 193 Mo. App. 210, loc. cit. 218, 2 **S. W.** 1068, 1070, says:

"**Among** these numerous exceptions is one, rmly **established**, to the effect that even where written contract exists between the parties)uching the same general subject-matter, exrinsic evidence may nevertheless be admissible 1 proof of a prior or contemporaneous collatral parol agreement between them, separate nd distinct from that contained in the writing tself, and not inherently in conflict with the atter"—citing cases.

The verbal agreement sued on, and which respondent's evidence tended to substantiate,)y which appellant promised to open a street :hrough his land, was entirely consistent with the terms of the contract and deed, and the oral evidence did not vary or contradict or impair any of the obligations contained in the said contract and deed or in any way tend to defeat their operation.

As to the statute of frauds: Defendant asserts that the verbal contract sued on cannot form the basis for a judgment, for the reason that it provides for an easement in land, and is therefore void under the statute of frauds, not being in writing. It may be admitted that the contract referred to concerns an interest in land and therefore comes within the statute of frauds (section 2169, R. S. 1919).

[5, 6] Defendant's answer was a general denial. He nowhere pleads the statute, nor did he object when evidence of the verbal contract sued on was introduced on the ground that the agreement .came within the statute of frauds. Neither did the defendant offer any instructions on that theory. The statute was nowise referred to in the motion for new trial and seems to be raised for the first time in this court. While the statute of frauds may have been available to the defendant as a conclusive defense, still it was not so unless the statute was properly invoked, for it is well established that the statute of frauds is an affirmative defense and may be waived, and is so waived unless it is pointedly brought to the attention of the trial court either by pleading by objection to the evidence on that ground or by request for instructions. The statute does not render a contract void, but goes merely to the remedy and as such is a rule of evidence. We think the defense was clearly waived under the rules established by the following authorities: Schmidt v. Rozier, 121 Mo. App. 306, 98 S. W. 791; Railroad v. Clark, 121 Mo. 169, loc. cit. 186, 25 S. W. 192–906, 26 L. R. A. 751; Moormeister v. Hannibal, 180 Mo. App. 717, loc. cit. 725, 163 S. W. 926; Ewart v. Young, 119 Mo. App. 483, loc. cit. 485, 96 S. W. 420; Gifford Co. v. Willman (Kansas City Court of Appeals) 187 Mo. App. 29, 173 S. W. 53.

No error appearing in the record, the judgment should be affirmed.

PER CURIAM. The foregoing opinion of BIGGS, C., is adopted as the opinion of the court.

The judgment of the circuit court is, accordingly, affirmed.

ALLEN, P. J., and BECKER, J., concur. DAUES, J., not sitting.

HUNTER v. AMERICAN BRAKE CO.
(No. 16364.)

(St. Louis Court of Appeals. Missouri. May 3, 1921. Rehearing Denied June 7, 1921.)

1. **Negligence** ⟳134(10) — **Evidence that an injury resulted from one of two causes insufficient.**

In a personal injury action there can be no recovery, if the evidence goes no farther than to show that plaintiff's injury resulted from one of two causes, for one of which and not the other defendant could be held liable, but it devolves on plaintiff to adduce substantial evidence showing that the cause for which defendant is liable produced the result.

2. **Trial** ⟳156(3)—**In passing on a demurrer the evidence should be viewed most favorably to plaintiff.**

In passing on defendant's demurrer to the evidence, it should be viewed in the light most favorably for the plaintiff.

3. **Negligence** ⟳43—**Care required as to invitee using wall as passway.**

Where railroad employés necessarily used as a passway a wall in defendant's plant in switching cars, defendant is liable for injuries suffered by a switchman, if there was coal on the wall of such a character as to render the place not reasonably safe, where defendant knew of the presence of the coal, or in the exercise of ordinary care could have known thereof, in time by the exercise of ordinary care to have removed it, and it is unnecessary for the injured switchman to show more than that coal was on the wall.

4. **Negligence** ⟳136(22) — **As to switchman stumbling on coal left on passway in building held question for jury.**

In an action by a switchman, who, while using a narrow wall in defendant's plant as a passway in connection with his duties of placing cars in the plant, stumbled on small pieces of coal left on the wall, which were not more than an inch square, *held* that, under the circumstances, the question whether the leaving of such pieces of coal on the wall was negligence was for the jury.

5. Appeal and error ⚖=1066 — Instruction allowing jury to assume fact unsupported by evidence reversible error.

In an action by a switchman, who claimed that, while using a low wall in defendant's plant as a passway, he fell as a result of stepping on small pieces of coal, an instruction which allowed the jury to assume that coal was dropped on the wall by the defendant's cranes, used in unloading coal cars, was prejudicial error, where there was no evidence that coal was at any time so dropped; the evidence being sharply conflicting as to whether there was any coal on the wall, and defendant, if not responsible for presence of the coal, being liable only if it remained there for a sufficient length of time to enable defendant to discover and remove it.

6. Negligence ⚖=139(2)—Instruction held erroneous, as imposing absolute liability for invitee's injury.

Where a railroad switchman, who fell while using a wall in defendant's plant as a passway in connection with his duty of placing a car in the building, claimed that the fall was the result of stumbling on pieces of coal, a general instruction for plaintiff, reciting that, if defendant failed to keep the wall free from lumps of coal, and as a direct result plaintiff was caused to fall, verdict should be for plaintiff, was erroneous and misleading, because placing an absolute duty on defendant, when it was bound only to exercise reasonable care.

7. Negligence ⚖=138(1) — Instruction objectionable in not requiring finding of negligence.

Where a railroad switchman, who, while in the course of his duty in placing cars in defendant's plant, stumbled while using a wall as a passway, claimed that the fall was the result of stepping on the coal left on the wall, an instruction purporting to cover plaintiff's entire case that if the jury should find that defendant in the exercise of ordinary care could have known that lumps of coal were on the wall, and that in walking on the wall plaintiff's foot was liable to strike a lump, causing him to fall, and if defendant failed to keep the wall free and clear of such lumps, and plaintiff was thereby caused to fall, defendant was liable, was objectionable, as not in terms requiring the jury to find that defendant's conduct constituted negligence.

Appeal from St. Louis Circuit Court; J. Hugo Grimm, Judge.

"Not to be officially published."

Action by Clarence Hunter against the American Brake Company. From a judgment for plaintiff, defendant appeals. Reversed and remanded.

Anderson, Gilbert & Hayden, of St. Louis, for appellant.

Edw. W. Foristel, of St. Louis (James T. Roberts, of St. Louis, of counsel), for respondent.

ALLEN, P. J. This is an action for personal injuries sustained by the plaintiff while upon the premises of the defendant corporation, as an invitee, alleged to have been occasioned by defendant's negligence. The trial below, before the court and a jury, resulted in a verdict in favor of plaintiff in the sum of $10,000. The trial court, however, required plaintiff to remit from the verdict the sum of $3,000 as a condition to the overruling of defendant's motion for a new trial. From a judgment in the sum of $7,000, entered accordingly, the defendant prosecutes this appeal.

At the time of plaintiff's injury, to wit, February 24, 1918, he was in the employ of the Terminal Railroad Association, in the city of St. Louis, as a switchman; his duties being to assist, in such capacity, in switching cars in and out of industrial plants. When injured, he was a member of a switching crew engaged in placing a loaded car in a building or large shed on the premises of the defendant company located at the southeast corner of Broadway and Tyler street in said city; Broadway extending north and south, and Tyler street extending east and west. At the time in question a switching tract entered defendant's premises from Tyler street, curved to the southwest, and entered the building mentioned through a large opening in what is termed the east wall thereof. It appears, in fact, that the building extended approximately from the northeast to the southwest, and that this track entered the northeast end thereof, and extended through the building, about 130 or 140 feet, to what is termed the west wall. The track was parallel with and a short distance from the southeast wall of the building, or the south wall, as it is termed; and immediately north of the track, and parallel therewith, was a concrete wall, referred to as a retaining wall, which began at a point a short distance outside of the building near the opening mentioned, where it was 1 foot in height, and, extending into the building, sloped upward until it attained a height of about 3 feet 8 inches above the grade of the track, or about 4 feet 9 inches above the level of the floor or ground on the north side of the wall. It appears that the wall reached the said height of 3 feet 8 inches at a point about 41 feet inside of the building, and that from that point on to the west or southwest end of the building, a distance of approximately 100 feet, the wall continued at that height, the top thereof being level and about 20 inches in width, except at places where pieces had been broken therefrom. When a coal car was upon this track in the building, the side thereof was but a short distance from this wall. Plaintiff testified that there was "just room enough for a car to go in there." And other

---

⚖=For other cases see same topic and KEY-NUMBER in all Key-Numbered Digests and Indexes

testimony of plaintiff indicates that the distance between the side of a coal car, when on this track, and the retaining wall, would be about 10 inches. A witness for the defendant said:

"I suppose there would be 2 feet, or probably a foot and a half, between the side of the car and the retaining wall."

At the time of plaintiff's injury this train crew was backing a train or "string" of cars into this building for the purpose of placing therein a loaded car that was at the end of this train. It appears that in the performance of his duties as switchman it was necessary for plaintiff to walk along the top of this retaining wall in entering defendant's building in advance of the train of cars, in order to give signals as to the placing of the car to be left on this track. It was conceded below, by defendant's counsel, that plaintiff "had to use this wall, and was using it in the performance of his duties," and it is frankly conceded here that plaintiff "was upon the premises in pursuance of a purpose which existed for the mutual advantage of appellant and his employer, and that he was therefore an invitee, to whom appellant owed the duty of exercising ordinary care to furnish a reasonably safe place." It appears that defendant knew of this use of the wall, and that an employé of defendant was charged with the duty of keeping the wall free from obstructions.

The petition alleges that, while plaintiff was thus walking along the top of this retaining wall, in the performance of his said duties, his right foot struck a piece of coal on the top of the wall, causing him to stumble and fall between the wall and the side of a coal car upon said track, whereby he was injured as set out in the petition. The petition contains three assignments of negligence, viz.: (1) In failing to keep the top of the wall free and clear of obstructions and obstacles; (2) in failing to provide sufficient light in the building; and (3) in failing to warn plaintiff of the danger. The case, however, went to the jury alone, on the first assignment, supra. The answer is a general denial. The ruling of the trial court in refusing to peremptorily direct a verdict for defendant is assigned as error; and this assignment makes it necessary for us to state the evidence in some detail.

Plaintiff was injured on Sunday shortly after noon. He testified that he walked along this retaining wall ahead of the cars that were being moved in, "in order to protect the rear end of the train." According to all of the testimony there was one car standing on this track at the west end thereof. This was a "coal car," and according to plaintiff's testimony it was, at the time, partly loaded with coal, though according to the testimony for defendant the car was loaded with steel billets. Plaintiff's

testimony is that he walked on this wall from the entrance to the building to the end of the track—i. e., to the west end of the car that was standing at the end of the track—and then turned about and started to walk toward the east, walking beside this coal car. He said:

"I probably took about 8 or 10 steps, and my right foot rolled on a piece of coal, letting me down in between the wall and the car that was already in there. All my weight came on my left foot, and my left knee went under me like that. I seen those cars coming, and I whistled and hollered, 'Oh, George!' [calling to George Wood, foreman of the switching crew]. I threw myself over on this wall, got up between the wall and threw myself on the wall, and that is all I remember until Woods came and got me by this leg. When he got a hold of this leg, and put it out from under me, I came to. It knocked me out."

The testimony shows that it was defendant's custom to unload coal from cars standing upon this track into bins north of the retaining wall, by means of an "overhead conveyor" or traveling crane, which operated a device referred to in plaintiff's testimony as a "clam shell." Plaintiff testified that this clam shell traveled back and forth over this wall in unloading coal; that it would lift a ton of coal at a time. He said:

"It comes down, and has jaws on it, and pulls it up, and it runs on a crane, which carries it across this wall over to the bin."

This was the first time that plaintiff had been in the building that day, and it appears that no other cars had been moved upon this track on that day.

On cross-examination, plaintiff testified that, after walking to the west end of the car which was standing in this building, and after having turned to retrace his steps, he walked to a point "about 75 feet inside of the shed"—i. e., 75 feet from the entrance at the northeast side of the building; that neither in walking into the building, on top of this wall, nor in thus retracing his steps, did he perceive any coal upon the wall until after his injury. Further testifying in this connection, he said:

"I never did see the entire chunk of coal. I seen some coal my foot turned on and left the crumbles there."

When asked if he had any idea as to how large the piece of coal was before his foot struck it, he said that he had not.

On cross-examination, plaintiff further testified that he did not know "how far the rear car in the string of cars was from the car that was standing there" when he fell. He said, however:

"The string of cars I was assisting in putting in was moving at the time I fell. • • • I don't know whether they had come together or not."

When asked if he had seen coal fall from cars frequently when they were being switched into the building, he said that coal sometimes fell from the cars.

On redirect examination plaintiff was asked how far the moving cars were from him when he fell, and he said:

"Just as I fell, I seen the cars coming along the end of the shed. I do not know where they were brought to a stop. I was laying between this coal car and the walk."

One Maus, the "head man" of the switching crew, testified that he did not see plaintiff fall, but that when the cars came to a stop he went forward and found plaintiff sitting on the wall. He said that he "found in a space of probably 10 or 15 feet several lumps of coal scattered about this wall in small pieces." On cross-examination he said that plaintiff was "apparently in the middle of this 15-foot space * * * in which there were lumps of coal scattered about"; that the "coal was in small pieces, the largest probably a little bit larger than an inch square." He further testified that when he reached plaintiff the latter was lying near the east end of the car that was in the building; that plaintiff was about 10 feet from that end of the car.

One Wood, the foreman of the switching crew, testified upon receiving a signal the moving cars were stopped when the end car was about 6 feet from the car that was in the building; that he went forward and found plaintiff lying on top of the wall, apparently unconscious, "somewhere near the end of the car that was in there, pretty well back in the shed." On cross-examination, referring to plaintiff's position on the wall, he said:

"He was alongside the car that was there."

Being questioned further as to this, he said:

"I think that he was in by that car that was already in there. I do not know whether he was right at the end of it."

When asked if he did not know that the car that was in the building was a car partly loaded with steel, he answered:

"I know they loaded steel cars to the end of the wall."

On being recalled for further cross-examination, plaintiff testified as follows:

"When I went along this wall the first time, toward the inside end, I passed right along the side of the car that was standing in there. I went clear down to the rear end of it. I presume about two-thirds of its contents had been unloaded. I am certain that the remainder that was there was coal, and not steel billets. As I passed alongside the car, I was within two or three feet of it. I had no difficulty in seeing there was coal in the car."

The testimony for defendant tends to show that no coal was on the wall at the time of plaintiff's injury. One Bienecke, employed by defendant as a foreman, testified that he worked upon these premises on the night prior to plaintiff's injury and until about 11 o'clock of that day; that between 8 and 9 o'clock on this Sunday morning he walked along the entire length of the retaining wall and saw no coal lying on it at any place. His testimony is that there was a car of steel at the west end of this track, which was received the previous day, and that no coal had been received on that track since February 18, six days prior to plaintiff's injury. He said that there were two overhead cranes used by defendant for unloading coal from cars upon this track, but that neither of them had been operated on that Sunday morning, and that no coal had been unloaded there for a period of six days prior to plaintiff's injury. According to his testimony the cranes carried large buckets into which the coal was shoveled.

One Farrar, an employé of defendant, testified that he heard plaintiff call when hurt, and went to the place where plaintiff was lying; that he noticed that there was no coal on the wall at the time.

In behalf of appellant it is argued that plaintiff failed to establish that the piece of coal, if any, upon which he stumbled and fell, was on the wall prior to the time of plaintiff's injury for such a length of time as to charge defendant with notice of its presence. In other words, it is said that, if there was any coal on the top of this wall at the place where plaintiff fell, it was not shown that defendant had any actual knowledge thereof, nor was it shown that the coal in fact was upon the wall for any length of time prior to the injury, so as afford any ground for a finding that defendant, by the exercise of ordinary care, could have known of its presence there. And in this connection it is urged that there is no evidence that any coal ever dropped from these traveling cranes, while there is evidence that coal sometimes fell from the sides of coal cars as they were being moved in, and that consequently it is quite as reasonable to suppose that the piece of coal, if any, which caused plaintiff's injury, fell from the coal car that was being moved into the building.

[1-3] It is true, as appellant urges, that there can be no recovery if the evidence goes no farther than to show that the plaintiff's injury resulted from one of two causes, for one of which, and not the other, the defendant may be held liable. It devolves upon the plaintiff to adduce substantial evidence tending to show that the cause for which defendant is liable produced the result. And if the evidence leaves this matter purely to conjecture and speculation, then plaintiff's case must fail. See Coin v. Lounge Co., 222 Mo. 488, 121 S. W. 1, 25 L. R. A. (N. S.) 1179, 17

Ann. Cas. 888. But the evidence in this case, as set out above, leaves no room for the argument that this piece of coal, which, it is said, caused plaintiff to fall, came from the coal car which was being moved into the building. The evidence is abundant that this moving coal car, at the end of the train, was stopped before it reached the point where plaintiff fell. The testimony for plaintiff is that when he fell he was at the side of the stationary car, and perhaps 10 feet west of the east end of that car. While there is some testimony of plaintiff to the effect that the place where he fell was about 75 feet from the east entrance to the building, which might place him east of the east end of this stationary car, this was obviously a mere estimate of the distance mentioned, and is not be utilized to defeat a recovery, since in passing upon the demurrer the evidence must be viewed in the light most favorable to plaintiff. As shown above, plaintiff testified positively that he had taken but 8 or 10 steps from the west end of this stationary car; the car being 40 feet in length. He said that he fell "down in between the wall and the car that was already in there," and later he said, in substance, that when he fell he looked up and saw the moving cars entering the building. Furthermore, the testimony of Wood, supra, is that when he reached plaintiff the latter was at the side of the car that had been standing on the track, and that the incoming cars stopped 6 feet from this stationary car.

It is quite clear, therefore, that this moving coal car did not reach the point where plaintiff's injury occurred, and that, if there was coal upon the top of the wall at that point, it could not have fallen from that car, and if the coal fell upon the wall from the side of the stationary coal car, beside which plaintiff fell—if that car was in fact loaded with coal—the inference is that this occurred, if at all, on some day prior to that of plaintiff's injury, for all of the evidence is that no coal was unloaded there on that day, and defendant's evidence is that no coal had been unloaded there for a period of six days prior to the time of plaintiff's injury.

It is true that there is no testimony that any coal, at any time, dropped from the clam shell or bucket operated by the overhead crane; but it was not necessary for plaintiff to show how the coal came upon the wall. If in fact there was coal upon the wall of such character as to render the place not a reasonably safe place for plaintiff to pass over in the performance of his duties, then defendant may be held liable for injury thereby resulting to plaintiff, while in the exercise of ordinary care for his own safety, provided defendant knew of the presence of such coal or by the exercise of ordinary care could have known thereof, in time, by the exercise of ordinary care, to have removed the same.

[4] While plaintiff's evidence tends to show that there was coal upon this wall, it appears that the coal consisted of small pieces or particles, none being more than about one inch in thickness. And hence the question arises whether, in any event, defendant could be found negligent in permitting such small lumps or pieces of coal to remain upon this wall; i. e., whether the defendant, in the exercise of ordinary care, ought to have anticipated that the presence of such small pieces of coal thereupon would be likely to cause injury to one required to pass over such wall. The presence of pieces of coal of the size indicated by this evidence, upon an ordinary walk or passageway, might, perhaps, constitute no evidence of a negligent breach of duty on the part of the proprietor of the premises owing to an invitee thereupon, though this we do not decide. In the case before us these small obstructions were upon a wall 20 inches in width, which was in close proximity to a railroad track, the top of the wall being 3 feet 8 inches above this track and a greater distance above the floor or ground on the west side of the wall. There is some conflict in the testimony as to the amount of light in this building, and at about the place where plaintiff fell. We have not considered it necessary to set out this testimony. As said, the assignment of negligence as to insufficient light was abandoned by plaintiff; and it is not contended by defendant that plaintiff was guilty of contributory negligence in not seeing the pieces of coal upon which he is said to have stepped. But, in view of the danger to be apprehended from even small obstacles left upon the wall, we are of the opinion that, under all of the conditions present, while the court could not so declare as a matter of law, the jury could with propriety find that the presence of such small pieces of coal on the wall—if there for such time as to enable defendant, by the exercise of ordinary care, to discover and remove the same—constituted negligence on the part of defendant as for a failure to exercise ordinary care to keep such place reasonably safe for plaintiff's use as an invitee thereupon; and this appears to be tacitly conceded by appellant's argument.

For the reasons indicated, we think that the demurrer to the evidence was properly overruled.

[5] Complaint is made of plaintiff's instruction No. 1, purporting to cover the whole case and directing a verdict. This instruction is as follows:

"The court instructs the jury that if you believe and find from the evidence that on the 24th day of February, 1918, the defendant, in the yard of its plant, mentioned in the evidence, owned and maintained the shed, track, and concrete wall mentioned in the evidence; and that in placing railroad cars upon said track under said shed it was necessary for plaintiff and other switchmen attached to the switching crew placing such railroad cars upon said track under said shed to walk upon the top of said concrete wall, and that on said day the plaintiff was employed by the St. Louis Merchants' Bridge Terminal Railway Company as a switchman, and that he was engaged in placing railroad cars upon said track under said shed for the use of the defendant, and that in order to do so he walked along the top of said wall; and that defendant prior thereto unloaded or caused to be unloaded coal from cars on said track by means of an overhead conveyor, and dropped lumps of coal upon the top of said wall, and that the defendant knew, or by the exercise of ordinary care could have known, that it was necessary for plaintiff to walk along the top of said wall for the purpose of placing said railroad cars upon said track under said shed in defendant's said plant, and that defendant knew, or by the exercise of ordinary care could have known, that lumps of coal were on the top of said wall and that in walking along the top of said wall plaintiff's foot was likely to strike a lump of said coal, and that it was likely to cause him to fall and be injured thereby; and if you find that the defendant failed to keep said wall free and clear of such lumps of coal, and that as a direct result thereof plaintiff's right foot did strike a lump of coal lying upon the top of said wall and that he was caused to fall thereby and that as a direct result thereof plaintiff was injured, as mentioned in the evidence, and that at said time plaintiff was exercising ordinary care for his own safety, then your verdict must be for the plaintiff."

It will be noticed that this instruction permits the jury to find that prior to the time of plaintiff's injury the defendant unloaded coal from cars on this track by means of the overhead conveyor, "and dropped lumps of coal upon the top of said wall." As we have said, there is no evidence whatsoever that any lumps of coal were dropped from this conveyor at any time. It was consequently error to permit the jury to so find, without any evidence upon which to predicate such finding; and under the circumstances we are of the opinion that this error cannot be regarded as other than prejudicial. In authorizing the jury to find that coal was dropped from the conveyor upon this wall, the court, in effect, declared that there was evidence from which they might conclude that such was the fact. There was a direct and sharp conflict in the testimony as to whether any coal was upon the wall at the time. If it was there, and remained there for a time sufficient to enable defendant, by the exercise of ordinary care, to discover and remove it, it mattered not how it came there. But, in view of this sharply contested issue of fact in the case, we think that it was prejudicial error to authorize the jury to assume that coal was in fact allowed to fall upon the track from the conveyor, when there is no testimony whatsoever that, in operating such conveyor, any coal was ever known to fall therefrom. See Small v. Polar Wave Ice & Fuel Co., 179 Mo. App. 456, loc. cit. 465, 162 S. W. 709, and cases cited; Scott v. Smelting Co., 187 Mo. App. 344, 173 S. W. 23; Cowan v. Hydraulic Press Brick Co., 222 S. W. 924.

[6] The instruction is faulty in another respect. The language following the last semicolon therein tells the jury that if they find "that the defendant failed to keep said wall free and clear from such lumps of coal," and that as a result thereof plaintiff's foot struck a lump of coal, etc., then to find for plaintiff. The effect of the language used in this portion of the instruction is to convey to the jury the idea that defendant was under an absolute liability to keep the wall free from such lumps of coal at its peril; whereas defendant's duty was to exercise ordinary care to that end. While the various portions of the instruction, hypothesizing separate matters to be found, are in the conjunctive, nevertheless the phraseology of this latter part of the instruction is such as to appear to predicate liability upon defendant's failure, alone, to keep the wall free and clear of lumps of coal. Note the language following this semicolon, viz.:

"And if you find that the defendant failed to keep said wall free and clear of such lumps of coal, and that as a direct result thereof plaintiff's right foot did strike a lump of coal lying upon the top of said wall and that he was caused to fall thereby and that as a direct result thereof plaintiff was injured, * * * then your verdict must be for the plaintiff."

We think that this part of the instruction was of such character as to have the effect of misleading the jury, under the circumstances, and hence prejudicial, especially in view of the fact that plaintiff's case is by no means a strong one—though we hold it to be one for the jury—and the evidence is highly conflicting as to the facts which we regard as necessary to establish negligence on the part of defendant.

[7] This instruction is further complained of on the ground that it does not require the jury to find that defendant's conduct in permitting these pieces or particles of coal to remain upon the wall—even though defendant could have discovered the same by the exercise of ordinary care—amounted to negligence. It is true that the instruction does not in terms require the jury to find that to permit such pieces of coal to remain upon the wall, if defendant could have discovered them by ordinary care, constituted negligence. (In this connection see State ex rel. Long v. Ellison, 272 Mo. 571, 199 S. W. 984; Greenstein v. Foundry Co. [Sup.] 178 S. W. 1179; Burrows v. Likes, 180 Mo. App. 447, loc. cit. 452, 453, 166 S. W. 643.) However, among the findings required, is one that appears to be tantamount thereto, viz. that defendant knew, or by the exercise of ordinary care could have known, "that lumps of coal were

on the top of said wall, and that in walking along the top of said wall plaintiff's foot was likely to strike a lump of said coal, and that it was likely to cause him to fall and be injured thereby." And consequently the instruction should perhaps not be condemned as fatally bad on this ground.

Upon a retrial, if one be had, a large portion of this instruction should be entirely recast. Other questions raised need not be discussed.

The judgment must be reversed, and the cause remanded. It is so ordered.

BECKER, J., concurs.

NORTH v. NATIONAL LIFE & ACCIDENT INS. CO. OF NASHVILLE, TENN. (No. 16469.)

(St. Louis Court of Appeals. Missouri. March 8, 1921.)

1. Insurance ⬧525—Where insured could not lie in bed because of bad heart, he was "confined to bed" within policy.

The provision of an industrial insurance policy for payment of sick benefits when insured is necessarily confined to bed does not mean that insured should be confined to her bed all of the time, but should be bedridden in a substantial sense, and insurer cannot escape paying sick benefits because insured could not lie in bed owing to a bad heart.

[Ed. Note.—For other definitions, see Words and Phrases, Second Series, Confined to bed.]

2. Insurance ⬧360(3)—Policy not forfeited for nonpayment of premiums when insured was entitled to sick benefits sufficient to pay premiums.

Courts do not favor forfeitures and will not enforce them against equity and good conscience, so that an insurance policy will not be declared forfeited for nonpayment of premiums where insurer held, when the premium became due, more than enough money due the insured as sick benefits to pay the same.

3. Insurance ⬧360(3) — Specific order from insured to apply sick benefits in payment of premiums not necessary.

Insurer need not have a specific order from the insured to apply sick benefits due to the payment of premiums, since such application is for insured's benefit, and his consent will be presumed, and equity requires the insurer to make such application.

4. Insurance ⬧585(1) — Deceased's husband held entitled to sue on industrial insurance policy for sick benefits, though not administrator.

Where an industrial insurance policy provided that its production by the company with the receipt for the sum insured, signed by the beneficiary, was conclusive evidence that such sum had been paid and that all claims under the

policy had been fully satisfied, the insurer cannot arbitrarily select a person of the designated class to whom payment is to be made, and action on the policy for sick benefits accrued at insured's death could be brought by deceased's husband in possession of the policy, although not appointed administrator of insured.

5. Appeal and error ⬧1068(4) — Instruction omitting requirement that damages for delay in payment of loss insured against must be limited to 10 per cent. cured by verdict.

In an action on an industrial insurance policy, an assignment of error that the court in its instruction relating to damages for vexatious delay did not limit the recovery to an amount "not to exceed 10 per cent. on the amount of the loss" is not well taken, where, although the record shows damages in excess of the 10 per cent., yet less than 10 per cent. was included in the verdict returned.

Appeal from St. Louis Circuit Court; George H. Shields, Judge.

Action by John North against the National Life & Accident Insurance Company of Nashville, Tenn. Verdict and judgment for plaintiff, and the defendant appeals. Affirmed.

George P. Burleigh, of St. Louis, for appellant.

Crittenden Clark, of St. Louis, for respondent.

BRUERE, C. This is an action of assumpsit, on an insurance policy of the kind known as industrial insurance. It was commenced before a justice of the peace, and appealed to the circuit court of the city of St. Louis. A verdict and judgment in said circuit court in favor of the plaintiff, from which judgment defendant appeals.

The defendant issued a policy of insurance to one Ella North the deceased wife of plaintiff. The policy bears date the 19th day of May, 1913. The provisions of the policy pertinent to the issues raised in this case are as follows:

(1) "In further consideration of the payment in advance of the premium stated in schedule below, on or before every Monday hereafter during the life of the insured, the National Life & Accident Insurance Company doth hereby agree, subject to the conditions herein, to pay to the beneficiary the amount of death benefit provided herein within 24 hours after due proof of death has been furnished the company, and in case of sickness or accident to pay to the insured the weekly benefits named in schedule below according to the terms hereof." The schedule above referred to contains: Weekly premium 20 cents; name of insured Ella North; maximum weekly allowance for sickness or accident $4.00; amount payable beneficiary in event of death $43. John North.

(2) "Weekly benefits for sickness will only be paid for each period of seven consecutive days that the insured is, by reason of illness, necessarily confined to bed and there visited profes-

sionally by a duly licensed and practicing physician."

(3) "The insured, however, shall not be entitled to sick or accident benefits when premium payments are in arrears for two weeks or more."

(4) "Should the insured die when the premium payments on this policy are four weeks or more in arrears this company shall not be liable for any sum under this policy."

(5) "The production by the company of this policy and of a receipt for the sum insured, signed by the beneficiary, or an executor or administrator, or legal representative of the insured, shall be conclusive evidence that such sum has been paid and that all claims under this policy have been fully satisfied."

On December 5, 1915, the assured, Ella North, took sick. A physician saw her on the 8th of December, 1915, and found her suffering from heart trouble. She was unable to be confined to her bed at times; her ailment being such that she could not get her breath while in a reclining position. During her sickness, and up to the time of her death, she was under the care of physicians. It further appears that during that time she was unable to perform her household duties, was unable to wait on herself, and that her sister, a nurse, and her neighbors administered to her wants. On the 9th day of December, 1915, Ella North filed a claim for a sick benefit with the defendant, accompanied with a certificate executed by a licensed and practicing physician, showing the nature of her sickness as provided by the terms of the policy. One or two like claims and certificates were likewise filed at the beginning of each week thereafter. The insured died February 23, 1916. It is admitted by the defendant company that all premiums due under the terms of the policy were paid up to December 20, 1915; no premiums were paid after said date.

The plaintiff sues for the sick benefits under the policy, and the amount of the death benefit provided therein, together with a reasonable amount for vexatious refusal to pay, and for attorney fees and interest. The sick benefits amount to $40, computed at $4 a week for 10 weeks, and the death benefit amounts to $43. The case was tried before a jury, and the jury assessed plaintiff's damages at the sum of $196.26, as follows, to wit:

Amount due under policy	$ 83 00
Interest	10 26
Damages	20 00
Attorney fees	100 00
	$196 26

At the close of the whole case the defendant requested the trial court to give an instruction in the nature of a demurrer to the evidence, which the court refused to give. This action of the court is assigned as error on the ground that the defendant had declared a forfeiture of the policy for nonpayment of premiums.

Under the facts in this case the decisive question for determination is whether or not it was the duty of the defendant to apply so much of the moneys in its hands, due the insured under the terms of the policy on account of sick benefits, to the payment and satisfaction of the unpaid premiums as was necessary in order to prevent a forfeiture of the policy.

So far as we are aware this precise question has not been passed upon by the appellate courts of this state.

While some courts hold to a contrary view, the greater weight of authority is that it is the duty of insurance companies to apply such moneys to the payment of premiums when due, so as to prevent a forfeiture of the policy.

[1] The amount of the premiums due defendant at the time of the death of the insured, February 23, 1916, amounted to $2. The jury found that on February 23, 1916, there was due the insured under the terms of the policy, on account of sick benefits, the sum of $40, $4 of which was due December 16, 1915. The insured was not in default on December 16, 1915; all premiums had been paid up to December 20, 1915. The company itself was in default in its payment of the sick benefits due insured. There was no excuse for defendant to refuse payment of the claims for sick benefits filed with it by the insured. Its ground for refusal to pay, as declared by its claim inspector to the insured, was that the insured was not confined to bed. Under the facts in this case, it would be rank nonsense to hold that because the insured could not lie in bed, owing to the bad condition of her heart, she was not entitled to sick benefits. That provision of the contract heretofore set out does not mean that the insured should be confined to bed all the time, but means that the insured must be "bedridden in a substantial sense." Hays v. General Assembly American Benevolent Ass'n, 127 Mo. App. 195, 104 S. W. 1141; Bradshaw v. American Benevolent Ass'n, 112 Mo. App. loc. cit. 437, 87 S. W. 46; Ramsey v. General Accident, Fire & Life Ins. Co., 160 Mo. App. 236, 142 S. W. 763.

[2] It is not conscionable to hold the insured in default for his premiums and at the same time absolve the insurer from payment of the sick benefits. The courts do not favor forfeitures and will not enforce them when to do so would be against equity and good conscience. It would be strange equity and bad morals to hold that the defendant had the right to declare the policy forfeited because of nonpayment of premiums when it had in its hands at the time said premiums became due more than enough money belonging to the insured to pay the premiums.

[3] Appellant contends that the defendant could not, without specific orders from the insured, apply part of the moneys in its hands, due the insured, to pay the premiums

due. No reason is given to support this contention. It is not necessary that specific orders from the insured be received before applying said moneys to the satisfaction of the premiums. Such application being for the benefit of the insured, his consent thereto will be presumed.

Furthermore, the defendant had the undoubted right to deduct the amount applied to pay premiums from the sum due insured for sick benefits under the law of set-offs.

The plainest principles of equity and a just regard for the rights of the insured required the defendant to apply the moneys in its hands due the insured to the satisfaction of the premiums when due, so as to keep the policy alive.

We hold that the defendant had no right to declare the policy forfeited and that the policy was in force at the time of the death of the insured. Russum v. St. Louis Mutual Life Ins. Co., 1 Mo. App. 228; North American Accident Ins. Co. v. Bowen (Tex. Civ. App.) 102 S. W. loc. cit. 167 (not officially reported); American National Ins. Co. v. Mooney, 111 Ark. 514, 164 S. W. 276; Albrecht v. People's Life & Annuity Ass'n, 129 Mich. 444, 89 N. W. 44; Union Cent. Life Ins. Co. v. Caldwell, 68 Ark. 505, 58 S. W. 355; Brady v. Coachman's Benevolent Ass'n (City Ct.) 14 N. Y. Supp. 272; Smith v. St. Louis Mutual Life Ins. Co., 2 Tenn. Ch. 727; Girard Life Ins. Co. v. Mutual Life Ins. Co., 97 Pa. 15; Franklin Life Ins. Co. v. Wallace, Adm'r, 93 Ind. 7; Rogers v. Union Benevolent Society, 111 Ky. 598, 64 S. W. 444, 55 L. R. A. 605; Supreme Lodge O. M. P. v. Meister, 204 Ill. 527, 68 N. E. 454; Supreme Lodge of Patriarchs of America v. Welsch, 60 Kan. 858, Appendix, 57 Pac. 115;[1] Fraternal Aid Ass'n v. Powers, 67 Kan. 420, 73 Pac. 65; Youndhoe v. Grain Shippers' Mutual Fire Ins. Ass'n, 126 Iowa, 374, 102 N. W. 137.

[4] The appellant next contends that under the terms of the policy the plaintiff was not entitled to any sick benefits due to the insured for the reason that the sick benefits passed to the administrator of the deceased, who alone could sue for same.

There is no provision in the policy stating specifically to whom sick benefits, due and unpaid at the time of the death of the insured, are to be paid. The policy, however, does provide, as heretofore noted, that the production by the company of the policy and of a receipt for the sum insured signed by the beneficiary was conclusive evidence that such sum had been paid and that all claims under the policy had been fully satisfied. Under this clause the insurer cannot arbitrarily select a person of the designated class to whom payment is to be made.

In this case the plaintiff was in lawful possession of the policy and a payment to him, under the express provisions of the above clause in the policy, would completely protect the defendant from all further claims under the policy. Renfro v. Metropolitan Life Ins. Co.. 148 Mo. App. 258, 129 S. W. 444; Wilkinson v. Metropolitan Life Ins. Co., 63 Mo. App. 404; Clarkston v. Metropolitan Life Ins. Co., 190 Mo. App. 624, 176 S. W. 437; Wilkinson v. Metropolitan Life Ins. Co., 64 Mo. App. 172; Jones v. Prudential Ins. Co., 173 Mo. App. 1, 155 S. W. 1106; Metropolitan Life Ins. Co. v. Brown, 186 S. W. 1155 (not officially reported).

We therefore hold that the plaintiff is entitled to the indemnity due under the health clause of the policy.

[5] Appellant's last assignment of error is that the court in its instruction, relating to damages for vexatious delay, did not limit the recovery to an amount "not to exceed 10 per cent. on the amount of the loss."

The appellant further contends that while the jury found the amount due under the policy to be $83, the amount assessed as damages for vexatious delay was $30—an amount far exceeding the statutory limitation of 10 per cent.

This last contention as to the amount assessed by the jury for vexatious delay is not supported by the record. An inspection of the items making up the verdict, hereinbefore set out, will disclose that while the item on vexatious delay reads, "Damages $30.00," only $3 is included in the total amount of the verdict returned. Wherefore, the giving of the instruction complained of was harmless error.

Appellant's objections to the other instructions given or refused by the court are necessarily ruled against it in view of what we have herein said in passing on the other assignments of error.

The judgment herein is for the right party, and should be affirmed. The commissioner recommends that the judgment of the lower court be affirmed.

PER CURIAM. The opinion of BRUERE, C., is adopted as the opinion of the court.

The judgment of the circuit court of the city of St. Louis is accordingly affirmed.

REYNOLDS, P. J., and ALLEN and BECKER, JJ., concur.

---

[1] Reported in full in the Pacific Reporter; reported as a memorandum decision without opinion in Kansas Reports.

FORRESTER v. WALSH FIRE CLAY PRODUCTS CO. (No. 16231.)

(St. Louis Court of Appeals. Missouri. May 3, 1921. Rehearing Denied June 7, 1921.)

1. **Master and servant ⟺289(15)—Contributory negligence in stepping on loose board held for jury.**

Where plaintiff, a carpenter, constructed a runway for wheelbarrow men which was some two inches lower than the door through the foundation wall, but the same was accepted, and at a time considerably later in order to avoid it a wheelbarrow man stepped on a loose board which had been placed to lessen the jar and was thrown to the ground and injured, the question of his contributory negligence under the circumstances held for the jury.

2. **Master and servant ⟺101, 102(8)—Ordinary care to furnish reasonably safe place held limit of duty.**

A master is bound only to use ordinary care to furnish his servant a reasonably safe place of work, and an instruction that it is his duty to furnish a reasonably safe place of work is defective.

3. **Trial ⟺252(11)—Instruction held broader than evidence in allowing recovery if loose board was placed on runway by foreman or agent.**

Where plaintiff stepped on a loose board on a runway in a building in the course of construction and when it tilted was thrown to the ground and injured, an instruction allowing recovery if defendant, its agent or foreman, placed the loose board on the runway was erroneous, where the evidence as to whether the foreman placed the board there was sharply conflicting; for, unless defendant or its authorized agent placed the board on the runway, it was necessary to recovery that defendant either had knowledge of the presence of the board or should have known that fact as a result of ordinary care, while the instruction permitted recovery even if a fellow servant placed the board on the runway regardless of any ordinary care.

4. **Trial ⟺251(1)—Instruction must not be broader than the pleadings.**

Instruction must not be broader than the pleadings.

5. **Trial ⟺251(8)—Instruction should be limited to the defect complained of.**

Where the defect complained of was a runway inside of a building, an instruction that it was the duty of defendant to use ordinary care in keeping the entry of the building safe was defective.

6. **Damages ⟺216(2)—Instruction should not allow recovery for injuries complained of.**

The instruction should not allow recovery for injuries complained of, but only those established by evidence.

7. **Appeal and error ⟺1064(1)—Instruction held reversible error.**

In personal injury action by servant who stepped on loose board on a runway and was injured, where the evidence whether the board was placed there by foreman or an irresponsible agent was sharply in conflict, an instruction that it was the duty of the master to furnish a reasonably safe place of work, and that if the master, its foreman or agent, placed the board, it would be liable, is reversible error; the duty of the master being too broadly stated, and the instruction also making the master liable though an irresponsible agent had placed the board on the runway and it had not had sufficient time to discover its presence, etc.

Appeal from Circuit Court, Audrain County; E. S. Gantt, Judge.

"Not to be officially published."

Action by Daniel G. Forrester against the Walsh Fire Clay Products Company. From a judgment for plaintiff, defendant appeals. Reversed and remanded for new trial.

R. D. Rodgers, of Mexico, and J. O. Barrow, of Vandalia, for appellant.

Robert A. May, of Louisiana, Mo., and J. W. Buffington, of Mexico, Mo., for respondent.

BIGGS, C. This is a negligence case growing out of the relation of master and servant, wherein defendant appeals from a judgment against it for $2,000, contending in the main that the evidence convicted plaintiff of contributory negligence as a matter of law and hence its demurrer to the evidence should have been sustained, and that the court below committed error in instructing the jury on behalf of plaintiff.

The charge of negligence is a violation of defendant's duty to use ordinary care to furnish plaintiff a reasonably safe place to work, and it is not contended that the evidence was insufficient to warrant the submission of the cause to the jury on that charge. As stated, defendant asserts that the evidence shows plaintiff's contributory negligence beyond an inference to the contrary.

The plaintiff was employed to do rough carpenter work. For some time prior to July 3, 1917, defendant had been engaged in erecting, among other buildings, a brick structure known as a machinery room at its plant in Audrain county. This building was 36 feet wide and 125 feet long, and while the outer walls were being constructed of brick and before the laying of the joists and other inside work was begun, it was necessary to have on the inside of the building scaffolds and runways to enable the bricklayers to construct the walls. The runways were used for the purpose of conveying materials, such as brick and mortar, about the building for use by the brickmasons.

⟺For other cases see same topic and KEY-NUMBER in all Key-Numbered Digests and Indexes

On July 3, 1917, at the time plaintiff received his injuries, the north wall of this building had been constructed some six feet above the top of what was known as the foundation wall, which foundation wall extended some seven feet above the level of the ground. A doorway seven feet wide was left in the north wall, the bottom of the door being the top of the foundation wall. Outside of the doorway and opposite thereof was a platform on a level with the top of the foundation wall. In order to get the material into the building, a runway built of boards was constructed from the ground to this platform. The laborers with wheelbarrows would wheel the material from the ground up the runway to the platform and then over the platform and through the seven-foot doorway in the north wall and then on to another runway on the inside of the building, and thence to the scaffolds or platforms where the bricklayers were at work. That part of the runway immediately adjacent to the said doorway and on the inside of the building is the source of contention between the parties, the plaintiff contending that it was negligently maintained by permitting a loose board to be and remain thereon.

Plaintiff, as stated, was a carpenter and had constructed this part of the runway about a week previous to the accident. By reason of the supports or horses which supported the runway being too short, the runway where same joined the doorsill was not high enough to make the same even or flush therewith, and resulted in there being a drop of from two to four inches from the doorsill to the runway. There is evidence tending to prove that this fact was called to the attention of defendant's foreman at the time by the plaintiff, and he accepted the runway as being sufficient, and stated those running the wheelbarrows could use it in that condition.

After the plaintiff had finished constructing this runway, he was required to work in other parts of the plant and was not again on the runway until July 3d, the date of the accident. At that time he was ordered by the defendant to go into the machinery room and construct a scaffold along the south wall thereof for the use of the brickmasons. After gathering up his tools, plaintiff started towards his place of work following the course of the wheelbarrow men by going up the runway onto the platform and over the platform to the doorway in the north wall. His view of the runway on the inside of the building was obstructed by the brick wall until he arrived at the doorway. After passing through the doorway and proceeding about two or three steps over the runway on the inside of the building, plaintiff observed a man with a wheelbarrow coming towards him on the runway. The runway being only 2 feet wide, there was not room for the two to pass, and plaintiff thereupon stepped back with an idea

of getting onto the doorsill of the doorway and thereby allowing the wheelbarrow man to pass. As he did so and in making his steps backward, he stepped on the end of a loose board which had been placed just inside and next to the doorsill and across the runway. This loose board was about 3½ feet or 4 feet long, 12 inches wide, 2 inches thick, and had been placed against the doorsill on the inside to lessen the jar of the wheelbarrows as they passed from the doorsill to the runway. Plaintiff testified that the wheelbarrow could not pass him and he glanced back to see for a way to go back and get out of the way; that in glancing backward he noticed this board and intended to step onto the board and then onto the foundation wall at the doorway, where there was plenty of room. When plaintiff stepped on the board, it being loose, it tilted, and he fell to the ground some 7 or 8 feet, receiving injuries.

Plaintiff testified:

"Q. When you say you stepped on the board intending to step on the foundation, how many steps was necessary for you to take backwards? A. About a couple of steps. I just made one step backwards and noticed this board. I just made one step back with this foot. Q. Which foot? A. Right foot, and aimed to step on back with my left foot onto this board, and when I stepped back it gave way, and that is as far as I got."

The board was laying right inside the foundation wall across this two-foot runway. One end of the board was lying flush with one side of the runway, and the other projected over the east side of the runway, and on this projecting part plaintiff stepped, and naturally the board tilted, as it was not nailed or fastened in any way to the runway.

Plaintiff's witness Taylor testified that on the morning of the day plaintiff was injured this board was caused to be placed on the runway by two of defendant's foremen in order to lessen the jar of the wheelbarrows as they passed from the doorsill to the runway. Both of these foremen, however, testified that they knew nothing about the board being there until after the plaintiff was injured.

Plaintiff had no occasion to pass over this runway after he had constructed it, until at the time of his injury. The only opportunity he had to observe the condition of the board laying across the runway was on the one occasion as he passed over it, at which time he was carrying his tools in his arms, which consisted of nail bar, nails, saw, hammer, and square. Plaintiff noticed the board as he passed through the doorway and stepped over it, but did not observe whether or not it was nailed to the runway. Plaintiff testified that he thought it was nailed sufficient to hold him when he stepped on the projecting end, and that he did not know it was laid loose, and had no chance to give that a thought, as he was backing back to get out of the way of the wheelbarrow man.

On cross-examination plaintiff testified:

"Q. There was no occasion for you stepping out on this board when there was a two-foot runway for you, wide enough for you to walk on? A. Yes, sir. Q. And if you had been watching where you were going you could have stayed on that two-foot runway and walked back to the foundation wall in the doorway perfectly easy? A. If I had taken my time and delayed the wheelbarrow man and inspected this run in every way, shape, or form when I went in there, I might have stayed on the run and turned around and walked back; but just at the spur of the moment I saw this man coming, and my intention was to step back and let him pass, and in so doing I made a step back with my left foot on this loose board with the intention of stepping onto this foundation, but I never got on the foundation."

[1] It will be observed that plaintiff had no other opportunity to observe the condition of this board and to know that it was loose except by passing over it on this one occasion. He did not know whether the board was nailed or not. There can be no question but what the board could have been rendered secure by having it nailed to the runway. Of course, if plaintiff knew that the board was loose or had ample opportunity to observe its condition, it might well be said that his act in stepping on the board was negligence as a matter of law. Where, as here, the plaintiff had no such knowledge or had no opportunity to observe its condition except on this one occasion, we hold that it cannot be said that his act in stepping on the projecting end of the board was contributory negligence on his part as a matter of law. We think under all the facts and circumstances, the question was one for the jury, and that the court did not err in refusing the defendant's peremptory instruction. The facts in this case are strikingly like those in Doyle v. M., K. & T. Trust Co., 140 Mo. 1, 41 S. W. 255, where the Supreme Court held that the question of plaintiff's contributory negligence was a jury question.

Unless he knew or had reason to suspect the contrary, plaintiff had the right to assume that defendant had performed its duty and that the runway was reasonably safe for travel. In determining the question plaintiff is entitled to the full force of all the evidence, and we do not think it could be well said that plaintiff's act, under the circumstances, in stepping on the projecting board, was so clearly a negligent one that reasonable minds could form no other conclusion but that he was negligent. In other words, it ought not be said as an irresistible conclusion that plaintiff was guilty of contributory negligence. Hutchinson v. Safety Gate Co., 247 Mo. 71, loc. cit. 113, 152 S. W. 52; Koerner

v. St. Louis Car Co., 209 Mo. 141, loc. cit. 157, 158, 107 S. W. 481, 17 L. R. A. (N. S.) 292; Curtis v. McNair, 173 Mo. 270, 73 S. W. 167.

[2, 3] Complaint is made of the instructions given on behalf of plaintiff. Instruction No. 5, which covers the whole case and authorizes a verdict for plaintiff, is as follows:

"The court instructs the jury that it is the duty of the master to furnish a servant a reasonably safe place in which to work, and that this duty on the part of the master is a continuing one, and although you may believe from the evidence that when plaintiff entered defendant's employment, the place in which he was required to work was a reasonably safe place, yet if you find from the testimony in this case that said place was thereafter by the carelessness and negligence of defendant, its agent or foreman, rendered dangerous and unsafe by the placing of the loose board on the runway detailed in evidence, and that by reason of such carelessness or negligence the plaintiff was injured without fault or carelessness on his part, then it will be your duty to render a verdict for the plaintiff."

This instruction is faulty, in that it places the duty on the master to furnish a reasonably safe place in which to work, when it is well established that the duty of the master in that regard is to use only ordinary care to that end. A more serious objection, however, arises by reason of the fact that the instruction authorizes a verdict for plaintiff in the event the defendant, its agent or foreman, placed the loose board on the runway.

As heretofore stated, plaintiff's witness Taylor testified that two of defendant's foremen caused the board to be placed on the runway on the morning of the day on which plaintiff was injured. Plaintiff's instruction No. 1 authorized a verdict for the plaintiff upon a finding of such facts among others. This instruction No. 5 goes further and permits a recovery for plaintiff in the event the jury found that the loose board was placed on the runway by any agent of the defendant. The witness Taylor was contradicted by both foremen, who testified that they knew nothing about a board being on the runway until after the plaintiff was injured. The jury may have concluded that Taylor was mistaken in his testimony and that the two foremen had no knowledge of the board being on the runway, but they may have concluded that some other agent or workman employed by the defendant placed the board on the runway. Defendant had a number of workmen and agents about the plant, and the jury may have thought that some of these agents placed the board on the runway. Of course, if defendant's foreman had placed the board thereon, this was actual knowledge of the fact on the part of the defendant; but in the event the jury should conclude, as it had a right to do under this instruction, that some one other than the foreman placed the board thereon, as long as such person was an agent of defendant, they were given authority to find defendant liable.

If one other than the defendant or its authorized agent had placed the board, it would have been necessary for the plaintiff to have proved, either knowledge on the part of the defendant of such fact, or that it should have known such fact by the exercise of ordinary care on its part.

[4] There is no evidence in the case of defendant's knowledge of the loose board being on the runway, except through Taylor's testimony, and the evidence does not disclose, except through such testimony, what length of time the board had been on the runway. If during the progress of the work a loose board was placed on the runway by a fellow servant of plaintiff or by some one not authorized, before defendant would be liable it would be necessary for it to either know of such fact, or that it should have known of it by the exercise of ordinary care. The instruction is broader than the evidence, in that it permits a recovery for plaintiff in the event any agent of the defendant placed the board on the runway and without further requiring that the defendant either knew of such fact, or should have known of such fact by the exercise of reasonable diligence. Instructions must not be broader than either the pleadings or evidence. Degonia v. Railway, 224 Mo. 564, 123 S. W. 807; State ex rel. v. Ellison, 270 Mo. loc. cit. 654, 195 S. W. 722.

[5] Error also lurks in other instructions given on behalf of plaintiff. Whether such error is material or prejudicial, we need not here say. For instance, instruction No. 3 for the plaintiff told the jury that it was the duty of the defendant to make and keep the entry into the building reasonably safe for travel. As stated, the duty of the defendant was to use ordinary care to that end. Besides this, there was no complaint against the entry into the building, but only as to the condition of the runway on the inside of the building. While the form of this instruction was held not to be reversible error in Garard v. Coal & Coke Co., 207 Mo. loc. cit. 258, 105 S. W. 767, the instruction should upon a retrial be reformed so as to place upon the defendant the duty of using ordinary care to make and keep the runway reasonably safe for travel.

[6] Also plaintiff's instruction No. 1 authorized a verdict for plaintiff on the finding of certain facts causing the injury complained of. The plaintiff should be allowed damages, not for the injuries complained of, but only for those injuries established by the greater weight of the evidence. The injuries complained of in the petition were greater than those established by the evidence.

[7] Where the question of defendant's liability is a close one, it is all-important that the jury be properly instructed on the law as applied to the facts. The errors in the instructions are not such as could be termed nonprejudicial.

It follows that the judgment should be reversed, and the cause remanded for a new trial.

PER CURIAM. The foregoing opinion of BIGGS, C., is adopted as the opinion of the court.

The judgment of the circuit court is accordingly reversed, and the cause remanded for a new trial.

ALLEN, P. J., and BECKER, J., concur. DAUES, J., not sitting.

In re DWYER'S ESTATE.

DWYER et al. v. DWYER et al.

(Nos. 16375, 16376.)

(St. Louis Court of Appeals. Missouri. May 3, 1921.)

1. Descent and distribution ⚖=47(1)—Pretermitted heir held to take by descent and not by purchase.

A child of decedent, inadvertently omitted from the enumeration of children in the will, who was admitted as an equal participant by agreement of all the heirs, took by descent, and not by purchase.

2. Executors and administrators ⚖=495(1)—Executors held not entitled to commissions on property not included within the power of sale in the will.

Under Rev. St. 1919, § 220, providing that executors shall be allowed a commission of 5 per cent. on personal property and on money arising from the sales of real estate, executors were not entitled to commissions on the interest of a pretermitted heir, or on the value of real estate in which the widow was given a life estate, and as to which the executors were not given a power of sale, though under an agreement by the heirs the pretermitted child was allowed to take an equal interest in the real estate, and the widow conveyed the home place by quitclaim deed to the heirs for the purpose of permitting a distribution of the same among the children.

3. Conversion ⚖=16(5)—Executors and administrators ⚖=495(1)—Discretionary power of sale not exercised does not work a conversion and executors not entitled to commissions on value of land as personalty.

A will providing that testator's real estate should be sold by his executors, and the proceeds of the same after payment of debts and legacies to be equally divided between testator's children, and that the executors should use discretion as to when the real estate should be sold, and if such real estate was not sold within five years after testator's death it was to be divided in kind among the children, *held* not to work a conversion of the real estate into personalty, where before the expiration of five years after death of testator the children by an agreement and conveyances among themselves divided the real estate in kind, and such devise did not confer title on the executors, but was a devise directly to the children subject to a discretionary power of sale, and hence the executors were not entitled to commissions on the value of such real estate on the ground that the same was personal property, under Rev. St. 1919, § 220.

Appeal from St. Louis Circuit Court; John W. McElhinney, Judge.

"Not to be officially published."

In the matter of the estate of Timothy Dwyer, deceased. Application of Arthur Dwyer and William Dwyer, executors of de-
cedent, for an allowance by the circuit court, on appeal from the probate court, of commissions, to which application Pearl Dwyer and others filed exceptions. From a judgment allowing the claim in part the exceptors appeal, and the executors present a cross-appeal. Reversed and remanded.

Henry Higginbotham, E. McD. Stevens, and Robert W. McElhinney, all of Clayton, for appellants.

Emerson E. Schnepp, of St. Louis, for respondents.

BECKER, J. This is an appeal, first, by the executors of the will of Timothy Dwyer; and, second, a cross-appeal by the legatees and devisees of said will, as exceptors, from an allowance, by the circuit court of St. Louis county, to the said executors, of commissions from said estate, said cause having gone to the circuit court on appeal by said executors from the probate court, from an order sustaining in part the exceptors' exceptions to their annual and final settlements.

Clauses 2 and 5 of the will, which are pertinent to the issues in this case, read as follows:

"(2) I give and devise unto my wife Elizabeth Dwyer my home place in the northeast corner of the Denny and Clayton roads, now occupied by us, containing forty acres, more or less; to have and to hold for and during her natural life; with the remainder upon her death to my children hereinafter named, or their descendants, in equal parts, the children of any deceased child taking the interest of their parent in said estate."

"(5) All my other personal property first to be sold and the proceeds thereof collected by my executors, and all the rest and remainder of my real estate to be sold by my executors hereinafter named and the proceeds of both personal and real estate, after deducting the debts and legacies above mentioned, to be equally divided between my said children above named, or their descendants if any of them should be dead.

"My executors are directed to use discretion as to the time when said real estate shall be sold, and in no case sacrifice same, and if not sold within five years after my death, it may be divided in kind among my children or their descendants if a majority of my children then living so desire; if any of my children shall be then dead their descendants shall take their parent's share."

The testator died in February, 1914, leaving surviving him a widow and eight children. Seven of the children were specifically named in the will, but the eighth child, John, had inadvertently been omitted. Two of the testator's sons were named as executors of the will. They duly qualified as such and administered upon the estate, but up to February, 1916, the executors had failed to exercise the power to sell the real estate under the will. Some time after the probate of the will the pretermitted heir, John Dwyer, executed and delivered a quitclaim deed to the executors for all of his right, title, and interest in and to the estate, in consideration of which he was to receive a proportionate share of the estate the same as each of the other children of the testator.

The widow, on her part, decided that she wanted to move off the home place, the 40-acre tract left her for her life, and to move to the town of Clayton, and upon the children of the testator executing a lease to her for life on a house in Clayton owned by them, at the rental of one cent per year, and the said children agreeing to pay her the sum of $40 per month as long as she should live, the widow made a quitclaim deed to the executors to all of her right, title, and interest in and to the 40-acre tract devised to her in the will. The executors thereupon took possession of all of the real estate including the home place, managed the same, collected the rents, made repairs, and paid the taxes for a period of two years or more with the full knowledge and consent of all of the children.

In the early part of 1916, the children being desirous of having the estate finally closed, held various conferences, and finally agreed to divide the property in kind among themselves. By mutual consent of all the heirs, the valuation of each parcel of the real estate was agreed upon, and according to the total of these valuations, $8,500 was the approximate sum that each child's share amounted to, and so the various parcels were grouped into eight shares each share approximating as near as possible said value of $8,500. Any share having a value greater or less than $8,500, the excess or deficiency thereof was to be deducted from or added to the distributive share of the heir (who accepted such share of the real estate) on final settlement of the estate. In this manner all of the shares of real estate would be equalized.

The deeds to the several parcels of land were executed by all of the heirs and the executors as well. Two of these eight divisions or shares went to the executors themselves. Prior to the execution and delivery of the said deeds the executors prepared and had each of the heirs sign a written agreement. These agreements were uniform, excepting as to the description of the property and the price thereof, and read as follows:

"In consideration of a distribution of $8,500 to be made to each of the eight children, we, the undersigned, agree to purchase from the executors of the estate of Timothy T. Dwyer, the following described property. * * *"

Then follows the description of the property and the price to be paid therefor by such heir as was to receive the deed for such

231 S.W.—43

property. It will be noted that there was included in this distribution of the real estate the one-eighth interest therein which John Dwyer, the pretermitted heir, had quitclaimed to the executors, and also the home place, consisting of 40 acres, which had been quitclaimed to the executors by the widow.

Upon final settlement of the estate the executors took credit for a payment to themselves of $3,573 as a 5 per cent. commission on the sale of all of the said real estate which had been divided among the heirs on the basis of the total agreed valuation thereof of $70,260.37. In due course exceptions were filed to the final settlement of the executors, by the heirs, with the exception of the son John.

There was a trial in the probate court, and a trial de novo in the circuit court on appeal. The judgment of the circuit court, so far as it is material on appeal here, in effect sustained the exceptions to commissions charged by the executors upon the one-eighth share that belonged to the pretermitted heir John Dwyer, and upon the home place, consisting of 40-acres, which under the will was given to the widow for life, which said two items aggregated the sum of $32,750, $28,500 of which as having been agreed upon by all of the heirs and executors as the value of the home place of 40 acres, and the sum of $4,250 as the value agreed upon for John Dwyer's share in the said real estate. The value of these two parcels of real estate, which had been included in the real estate divided among the heirs, was deducted from the total valuation of the said real estate, which, in effect, reduced the allowed commissions by the sum of $1,635.18.

From the judgment of the circuit court the executors and the heirs, with the exception of John, filed cross-appeals. We have before us, therefore the sole question as to whether or not, under the facts set out above, the executors are entitled to a commission of any part of the $70,260.32, the agreed value of the real estate, which was divided among the heirs in the manner above set forth. Section 229, R. S. of Mo. 1909 (section 220, R. S. of Mo. 1919), with reference to compensation, allows executors—

"as full compensation for their services and trouble a commission of 5 per cent. on personal property and on money arising from the sale of real estate."

[1, 2] It is readily apparent that the one-eighth interest that the pretermitted heir, John Dwyer, had in the real estate in question, came to him by descent and not by purchase. That this is so is due to the fact that John was not named in the will, and therefore his share could in no event be construed as being included in the power of sale given the executors by the terms of the will, and

therefore could in no event be subject to a charge as for commission on the part of the executors. And the same is true with reference to the home place, which under the provisions of the will went to the widow for life, with remainder over to the children the testator named in the will. Consequently, when no provision was made in the will for the sale by the executors of the home place the executors as such would not be entitled to any commission thereon against the estate, and this is so even though the widow quitclaimed her life estate to the executors.

[3] The other parcels of real estate, under paragraph 4 of the will, were directed to be sold by the executors therein, and the proceeds, after deducting the debts and legacies, were to be equally divided between the children of the testator named in the will. The executors in said will were further specifically directed—

"to use discretion as to the time when said real estate shall be sold and in no case sacrifice same, and if not sold within five years after the death of the testator, it may be divided in kind among my children or their descendants, if a majority of my children then living so desire."

Having in mind that it is the testator's intention which is the determining factor as to whether equitable conversion takes place or not, we must take the will from the four corners, and in the light thereof determine the testator's intention. Should we conclude that under the provisions of this will there was an equitable conversion of these particular parcels of real estate, then, even though we were to hold that the acts of the heirs in dividing the same parcels among themselves was a reconversion, it is clear, in light of Gilbreath v. Cosgrove, 193 Mo. App. 419, 185 S. W. 1181, the executors would be clearly entitled to their commission; but if we conclude that under the terms of the will there was no equitable conversion, then no commissions are due the executors as such under our statute. O'Bannon's Estate, 142 Mo. App. 268, 126 S. W. 215.

It has frequently been ruled that if the act of converting is left to the option, discretion, or choice of the executors or others charged with making it, no equitable conversion takes place, because no duty to make the change rests on them. In other words, to bring about equitable conversion, the character of land or money must be definitely and imperatively fixed to the property by will or other instrument. Did the testator here then intend that the said parcels of real estate snould be converted into personalty and be distributed as personalty, whether an actual sale of the said real estate took place or not? We think not, for the testator gave a power of sale to the executors named in his will,

but only at the discretion of his executor and upon condition that a sale could be made without sacrificing the property, and conditioned also that if the real estate was not sold within a period of five years then the property could be divided in kind among said children if a majority then living so desire.

As we construe this clause of the will it was not the intention of the testator to thereby definitely require that said parcels of land be sold, but rather intended thereby to create a power of sale in his executors, discretionary and conditional. In other words, there is here lacking an imperative and absolute direction to convert, irrespective of all contingencies, and independent of all discretion. We have therefore, come to the conclusion that the doctrine of equitable conversion could not become effective under this power until at least an actual sale had been made by the executors thereunder. Compton v. McMahan, 19 Mo. App. 498. We are clearly of the opinion that under the terms of the will in question the testator did not devise said parcels of land to his executors, but to his children, subject to the discretionary and conditional power of sale conferred on his executors, and the proceeds thereof, in the event of the exercise of the power of sale, after deducting the debts and legacies, to be equally divided among his said children. Eneberg v. Carter, 98 Mo. 647, 12 S. W. 522, 14 Am. St. Rep. 664; Williams v. Lobban, 206 Mo. 399, 104 S. W. 58.

Under the record in this case we are unwilling to rule that the executors exercised the power of sale given them in the will. We are inclined to the view and so hold that the heirs merely made a voluntary partition of the land in question after the debts of the estate and special legacies were paid. That in doing so they were clearly within their rights needs no citation of authority. We rule that the parcels of land were real property at the time of its division, and that there was no sale of it to the heirs as was intended by the testator by the power of sale granted in the will. Consequently, if there was no sale the executors were not entitled to treat these parcels of land so portioned among the heirs as personal property, and to collect a commission of 5 per cent on their valuation. In re O'Bannon's Estate supra.

The learned trial court having in its judgment overruled the exceptions to the final settlement of the executors as to the allowance of their commissions as to these said parcels of land which were partitioned by the heirs among themselves, excepting John Dwyer's share and the home place, in which a life estate was given the widow under the terms of the will, it follows, from what we have said above, that the same was error, and that the judgment herein should be and the same hereby ordered reversed, and the cause remanded, with directions to proceed to enter a judgment in the circuit court in conformity with the views herein expressed.

ALLEN, P. J., concurs. DAUES, J., not sitting.

———

ENSIGN v. CRANDALL. (No. 16372.)

(St. Louis Court of Appeals. Missouri.
May 3, 1921.)

1. Bills and notes ⟁497(5)—Where instrument was obtained through fraud, plaintiff has burden of showing he was a "holder in due course."

Under Rev. St. 1919, § 841, declaring that the title of any person who negotiates a negotiable instrument is defective when he obtained the instrument through fraud, and section 845, declaring that, when it is shown that the title of any person who negotiated the instrument was defective, the burden is on the holder to prove that he, or some person under whom he claims, acquired title as a holder in due course, the holder of a note procured through fraud and misrepresentation of the payee has, regardless of the fact that the defense was set up by the answer, the burden of showing that he was a "holder in due course," defined by section 838 as one who took the instrument regular and complete on its face before maturity, and without notice of any infirmity, and in good faith, for value.

[Ed. Note.—For other definitions, see Words and Phrases, First and Second Series, Holder in Due Course.]

2. Bills and notes ⟁537(6)—Plaintiff making prima facie showing that he was a holder in due course is entitled to directed verdict unless the showing is controverted.

Rev. St. 1919, § 845, declaring that, when the title of any person who negotiated a negotiable instrument is shown to be defective, the holder has the burden of showing that he, or some one under whom he claims, obtained the instrument before maturity as a holder in due course, does not affect the burden of proof in the strict sense, but places on plaintiff the burden of producing evidence, so, where plaintiff introduced evidence showing prima facie that he acquired a note procured through fraud as a holder in due course, he is, where defendant introduced no controverting evidence, entitled to the direction of a verdict.

3. Bills and notes ⟁537(6)—Evidence held insufficient to carry to the jury the issue as to whether plaintiff was a bona fide holder.

In an action on a note shown to have been procured though the payee's fraud, where plaintiff introduced evidence establishing prima facie that he was a bona fide holder, testimony that plaintiff had previously collected notes for the payee, as well as testimony that the checks given in payment could not have passed

through banks according to the stamps thereon, held insufficient to carry to the jury the question whether plaintiff had notice of the infirmity of the notes, and it was improper for the trial court to refuse to direct a verdict in his favor.

Appeal from Circuit Court, Clark County;
N. M. Pettingill, Judge.

Action by Charles B. Ensign, doing business as C. B. Ensign & Co., against Edgar Crandall. From a judgment for defendant, plaintiff appeals. Reversed, and cause remanded.

W. L. Berkheimer and John M. Dawson, both of Kahoka, for appellant.
Chas. Hiller and T. L. Montgomery, both of Kahoka, for respondent.

ALLEN, P. J. This is an action upon two promissory notes, each for the sum of $375, executed by the defendant on April 4, 1913, payable to the order of the Night Commander Lighting Company, a corporation, two years after the date thereof, with interest from maturity at the rate of 6 per cent. per annum. Plaintiff sues as the holder in due course of said notes. The trial below before the court and a jury, resulted in a verdict and judgment for the defendant, and the plaintiff has brought the case here by appeal.

The petition is in two counts, one upon each of the notes. In each count, after alleging the execution and delivery of the note therein mentioned to the said payee named therein, it is alleged that the payee indorsed and delivered the same to the Jackson Brokerage Company; that the latter, for valuable consideration paid to it by plaintiff, indorsed the note in blank and delivered it to plaintiff, who thereby became the owner and holder thereof prior to the commencement of the suit; that plaintiff is an innocent purchaser thereof, "without notice whatever of any infirmity in the title thereto or his immediate indorser." Each count concludes with the usual prayer.

The answer admits the execution of the notes in suit and their delivery to the Night Commander Lighting Company, but denies each and every other allegation in the petition. Further answering, the defendant alleges that at and prior to the execution of these notes one Rickey was an agent of the Night Commander Lighting Company, and local manager of its business conducted at Quincy, Ill.; that prior to the execution of these notes the defendant became a surety upon a bond executed by Rickey to said company, conditioned on the faithful performance by Rickey of his duties as such agent and manager; and that, at the time of the execution and delivery of the notes sued upon, one Jones, president and manager of said company, falsely and fraudulently represented to defendant that Rickey was short in his accounts with the company, and owed the company a large sum of money; all of which was false and untrue, and known so to be by said Jones. And it is averred that the defendant, relying upon said false and fraudulent statements, and in order to discharge his supposed obligation as surety on the bond, did, on said April 4, 1913, execute three promissory notes to the said Night Commander Lighting Company, each for the sum of $375, due respectively in one, two, and three years from said date, and delivered the same to said company. And it is alleged that Rickey was not then, nor has he ever been, short in his accounts with said Night Commander Lighting Company, but has faithfully performed all of his duties as the agent and manager of said company, and that defendant was in no wise liable on said bond. And it is further averred that the Night Commander Lighting Company and the Jackson Brokerage Company are one and the same, and owned by the same individuals; and that plaintiff, when the notes in suit were assigned to him, knew all of said facts, and participated in the fraudulent purpose of said indorser, and is not in good faith the owner of the notes in suit, in due course, for value before maturity, and that the same are void.

Other allegations touching the alleged fraud are made which need not be noticed. And the answer alleges that of the three notes so executed and delivered by defendant, one thereof, viz., that due one year after said date, was, at its maturity, presented by the Jackson Brokerage Company to a bank in Wyaconda, Mo., where the notes are made payable, for payment, purporting to have been indorsed by the Night Commander Lighting Company and by the Jackson Brokerage Company; that said brokerage company was organized for the purpose of taking and holding notes payable to the Night Commander Lighting Company, so that said brokerage company might pose as an innocent purchaser thereof for value in due course of business. And it is averred that when said note, payable one year after date, became due, it was protested for nonpayment, and has never been paid—

"because of the facts in this answer set forth, all of which was known to this plaintiff when the notes sued on were assigned to plaintiff for collection, and are held by him with the knowledge of the fraudulent acts of the indorsers of said notes sued on, and he is not in good faith the owner and holder for value in due course, and should not recover."

The reply puts in issue the new matter of the answer.

At the trial the notes were introduced in evidence, bearing indorsements purporting to be those of the Night Commander Lighting Company and the Jackson Brokerage Company, each indorsement being made "per G. W. Mayes." Plaintiff, by deposition, testified that he purchased the notes in suit on November 9, 1914, from the Jackson Brokerage Company, the latter being represented by G. W. Mayes, who brought the notes to plaintiff's office; that the notes bore the indorsement of the Night Commander Lighting Company, known to him to be the genuine and authorized indorsement of the company, and were indorsed by the Jackson Brokerage Company, through Mayes, "one of the proprietors and chief owner of the Jackson Brokerage Company, a partnership," in his presence, in his office in Chicago.

Plaintiff's further testimony is that, in the transaction in question, he purchased the two notes in suit, together with six other notes, aggregating a total face value of $2,835, for which eight notes he paid $1,940. And he introduced in evidence two canceled checks, both dated November 9, 1914, drawn by him on the Continental Commercial Bank of Chicago, one for the sum of $1,000, and the other for the sum of $940, the former being payable to the Night Commander Lighting Company and the latter to the order of the Jackson Brokerage Company. Plaintiff testified that these checks were thus made payable, one to the Night Commander Lighting Company and the other to the Jackson Brokerage Company, at the request of Mayes, from whom he purchased the notes. Each of the checks is stamped paid, and, in addition to the indorsement of the payee, bears the indorsement of the Jackson City Bank, of Jackson, Mich., to the order of the Corn Exchange National Bank, of Chicago, and bears the "clearing house stamp," purporting to show that it was "paid through the Chicago Clearing House" on November 10, 1914, at 10 a. m. And plaintiff testified that both checks were paid by the Continental Commercial Bank, upon which they were drawn, and charged to his account.

When asked if he knew of any infirmities or other defenses in favor of the maker of these notes when he purchased them, he said that he did not; that, on the contrary, he was informed that they had been given in settlement of an account between the maker and the Night Commander Lighting Company; and that he purchased the notes before maturity in the usual course of business. He further testified that on said November 9, 1914, he wrote to defendant a letter, a copy of which appears in the deposition, and which purports to be a letter notifying the defendant of plaintiff's acquisition of the notes in suit, and requesting defendant to mail to plaintiff a check or draft for each note when the same should become due.

With this deposition, and exhibits attached thereto, in evidence, plaintiff rested.

As a witness in his own behalf, defendant testified that he was a resident of Wyaconda, where he was engaged in the implement business; that he knew J. E. Jones, who was president of the Night Commander Company, and that, in the course of his business, he bought goods from that company through its "branch house" in Quincy, Ill., which was in charge of one Rickey, mentioned in the answer as manager thereof. And defendant's evidence shows that he became surety on a bond for Rickey, as alleged in the answer, and that, at the time of the execution of the notes in suit, Jones, as president of the Night Commander Lighting Company, falsely represented to him that Rickey was short in his accounts with said company, and thus obtained the two notes sued upon, together with another note for $375 due one year after said date, in settlement of the alleged shortage, and purporting to be in discharge of defendant's obligation as surety on said bond. It is unnecessary to set out the evidence relating to this matter in detail. It is sufficient to say that testimony both of defendant and of Rickey, the latter testifying as defendant's witness, tends to show that the notes in suit were in fact procured by fraud on the part of the Night Commander Lighting Company, through its president, Jones. And this testimony stands uncontradicted in the record.

Defendant's own testimony shows nothing tending to show any knowledge by plaintiff of the fraud said to be practiced upon defendant in procuring these notes. Rickey testified that the Night Commander Lighting Company had its principal place of business in Jackson, Mich., 209 miles from Chicago; that Jones was president and general manager of that company, and president and general manager also of the Jackson Brokerage Company, and that Mayes was secretary and treasurer of both companies. He stated that the Jackson Brokerage Company was organized "to take over the notes that were taken by the Night Commander Lighting Company"; but, on plaintiff's motion, this was stricken out. He was then asked what the Jackson Brokerage Company did, and he answered: "They took the paper from the Night Commander Lighting Company for collection." The court allowed this answer to stand. The witness testified that he knew plaintiff, C. B. Ensign. When asked what connection plaintiff had "with the position of this company," he answered: "I know he collected papers for the Night Commander Lighting Company." Again, the witness was asked concerning the business relations between plaintiff and the two companies mentioned on or about November 9, 1914, and he answered: "Charles B. Ensign collected papers and notes for the Jackson Brokerage Company, and for the Night Commander

Lighting Company." And there is testimony as to the presentation and dishonor of the note first falling due, as alleged in the answer.

In behalf of defendant, one Martin, a local bank clerk, testified, in substance, that in his opinion the checks above mentioned, if executed in Chicago on November 9, 1914, could not have passed through the Jackson bank, 209 miles from Chicago, then through the Corn Exchange Bank of Chicago, as indicated by the indorsements thereon, and have reached the clearing house in Chicago at 10 o'clock on the following day. On cross-examination, however, he testified that he had never been in Jackson, Mich., or in Chicago, knew nothing about "how they handled papers there," except by hearsay, and had no knowledge of the time schedule of the trains operating between the two places.

One Lang, a local bank cashier, likewise testified that, in his opinion, these checks could not have pursued the course mentioned and have reached the Chicago Clearing House by 10 o'clock on November 10, 1914. But, on cross-examination, he stated that, if the check was cashed in Jackson on November 9, it could have reached the Chicago Clearing House by 10 a. m. on the following day.

In rebuttal, one Wilkerson, an agent for the Chicago, Burlington & Quincy Railroad, testified that about 10 trains per day were operated each way between Chicago and Jackson, Mich., the fast trains, which usually carry mail, making the trip in about 4 hours.

For plaintiff, the court gave 12 instructions. Eight instructions offered by plaintiff were refused, including a peremptory instruction to find for plaintiff on both counts. Six instructions offered by defendant were given.

[1] Appellant makes 20 assignments of error. One of these assignments is that the court erred in refusing to peremptorily direct a verdict for the plaintiff. As shown above, the defense of fraud between the original parties set up by defendant in his answer was shown by uncontradicted evidence adduced by the defendant. In his answer, defendant alleged that plaintiff had full knowledge of this fraud when he purchased the notes. And plaintiff's reply puts in issue the averments of the answer, except the admissions therein made. And in this situation the question as to where the burden of proof rests is one of vital consequence in the case. Judged alone by the state of the pleadings, it would appear that the burden of proving that plaintiff had knowledge of the infirmity in the note, or took the note in bad faith, would rest upon the defendant. But section 845, Rev. St. 1919 (section 10029, Rev. St. 1909), provides as follows:

"Burden of Proof on Holder When Defective Title is Shown.—Every holder is deemed prima facie to be a holder in due course; but when it is shown that the title of any person who has negotiated the instrument was defective, the burden is on the holder to prove that he or some person under whom he claims acquired the title as holder in due course. But the last-mentioned rule does not apply in favor of a party who became bound on the instrument prior to the acquisition of such defective title."

In this connection, it should be noted that section 841, Rev. St. 1919 (section 10025, Rev. St. 1909), provides as follows:

"Title, When Defective.—The title of a person who negotiates an instrument is defective within the meaning of this chapter when he obtained the instrument, or any signature thereto, by fraud, duress or force and fear, or other unlawful means, or for an illegal consideration, or when he negotiates it in breach of faith, or under such circumstances as amount to a fraud."

It is clear that, under section 841, supra, the title of the Night Commander Lighting Company to the notes in suit was shown to be defective, within the meaning thereof, by proof that defendant's signature to the notes was obtained by fraud. Consequently, by the terms of section 845, supra, the burden was placed on the plaintiff "to prove that he or some person under whom he claims acquired the title as holder in due course." A holder in due course is defined by section 838, Rev. St. 1919 (section 10022, Rev. St. 1909), as follows:

"Holder in Due Course.—A holder in due course is a holder who has taken the instrument under the following conditions: (1) That it is complete and regular upon its face; (2) that he became the holder of it before it was overdue, and without notice that it had been previously dishonored, if such was the fact; (3) that he took it in good faith and for value; (4) that at the time it was negotiated to him he had no notice of any infirmity in the instrument or defect in the title of the person negotiating it."

It cannot be doubted that plaintiff, in his case in chief, adduced substantial evidence tending to show that he was a holder in due course; for plaintiff's testimony tends to show that he purchased the notes (each regular upon its face) before maturity, in good faith, and for value, and that, at the time they were negotiated to him, he had no notice of any infirmity in the title of the person negotiating them. Plaintiff (appellant here) contends that the defendant adduced no evidence below of any probative force or value tending to controvert the evidence for plaintiff which tends to show that he was a holder in due course; and that, with the case in this posture, it became the duty of the trial court to peremptorily direct a verdict for the plaintiff.

[2] Whether, in a case of this character, a verdict may be directed for a plaintiff, who thus has cast upon him the burden to prove that he is a holder in due course, where he adduces evidence tending to show that he acquired the instrument as a holder in due course, and the defendant adduced nothing having a tendency to contradict or overthrow this, is a question as to which there has been a lack of harmony in the cases in which the question has arisen in this state. In the recent case of German American Bank v. Smith, 202 Mo. App. 133, 208 S. W. 878, this court held that, under such circumstances, the court should direct a verdict for the plaintiff. In Hill v. Dillon, 176 Mo. App. 192, 161 S. W. 881, the Springfield Court of Appeals reached a contrary conclusion, applying the rule stated in Gannon v. Laclede Gas Light Co., 145 Mo. 502, 46 S. W. 968, 47 S. W. 907, 43 L. R. A. 505, which is there said to have been established from the time of our earliest reported cases, and which has since been followed in a long line of decisions, viz.:

"That when either party to a controversy submits testimony (other than written instruments that call for the court's construction of their meaning and import) to sustain his or her burden of proof, the other party, though offering nothing to contradict it is entitled to have the jury pass upon the whole case, and determine the credibility of the witnesses and the weight to be given to their testimony."

But in Downs v. Horton, 209 S. W. 595, the Springfield Court of Appeals, disapproving Hill v. Dillon, and other cases of like tenor, held that, although the note, upon which plaintiff was suing as an indorsee, was admittedly procured by the fraud of the payee's agent, plaintiff, by oral testimony, unimpeached and uncontradicted, could discharge the burden of proof placed upon him by section 845 of the Negotiable Instruments Law, supra, so as to entitle him to a directed verdict. The case was certified to the Supreme Court, where, in an opinion by Commissioner Ragland (230 S. W. 103, not as yet [officially] reported), the decision of the Springfield Court of Appeals was sustained. The subject is elaborately discussed in those opinions, and the earlier cases considered. It is held that section 845, supra, is merely declaratory of the common-law rule of decision which prevailed in this state prior to the adoption of the Negotiable Instruments Law. But it is held by the Supreme Court in the Downs Case, in effect, that what we may term the doctrine of the Gannon Case, supra, in respect to the right to direct a verdict for one having the burden of proof, does not here apply, for the reason that the burden placed upon the holder by section 845, supra, is, it is said, not the "burden of proof in its strict sense," but is the burden of producing evidence at some stage of a trial to make or meet a prima facie case—sometimes called the "burden of the evidence"—which may shift during the progress of the case. In this view, when plaintiff made a prima facie showing that he acquired the title to these notes as a holder in due course, he discharged the burden resting upon him, and it then devolved upon defendant to adduce evidence tending to overcome the prima facie case thus made; and, if defendant failed in this, plaintiff was entitled to a directed verdict.

[3] It is earnestly and ably contended by respondent's learned counsel that there is substantial evidence in this record tending to controvert the prima facie showing made by plaintiff that he was a holder in due course, so as to make it a question for the jury to say whether plaintiff took the notes without knowledge of the defect of infirmity in the payee's title thereto, and in good faith, as was held by the Springfield Court of Appeals to be the case in Depres, Bridges & Noel v. Galloway, 224 S. W. 998. We have given very careful consideration to this argument of respondent's counsel, but we are forced to the conclusion that there is here no evidence of any probative force or value tending to overthrow the prima facie showing made by plaintiff in respect to this matter. In this connection it may be noted that section 842, Rev. St. 1919 (section 10026, Rev. St. 1909), provides that—

"To constitute notice of an infirmity in the instrument or defect in the title of the person negotiating the same, the person to whom it is negotiated must have had actual knowledge of the infirmity or defect, or knowledge of such facts that his action in taking the instrument amounted to bad faith."

It is true that Rickey testified, in substance, over objections of plaintiff's counsel, that plaintiff had "collected papers and notes" for the Jackson Brokerage Company and the Night Commander Company; but the fact that plaintiff had at some time collected notes for these companies would not warrant any inference of knowledge on his part of the defect or infirmity in the title to these notes; nor could it be inferred therefrom that plaintiff took the notes under circumstances amounting to bad faith. Neither can it be said that the fact that the plaintiff, who was shown to have had previous business dealings with these companies, was familiar with the indorsements upon the paper, knowing such indorsements to be genuine and authorized, sufficed to raise any inference that plaintiff had knowledge of such infirmity or defect in the title to the paper, or that he took the same in bad faith.

And, obviously, the testimony which was introduced, over plaintiff's objections, for the purpose of showing that the checks in evidence, dated November 9, 1914, could not have been deposited in a bank in Jackson, Mich., and have reached the Chicago Clearing House by 10 o'clock on the following morning, if admissible at all, under the circumstances, availed defendant nothing. The uncontradicted evidence for plaintiff is that he paid value for the notes, and that these two canceled checks which were introduced in evidence were, in fact, paid by the bank upon which he drew them, and charged to his account.

It follows, therefore, that though, under the evidence in this record, defendant was defrauded by the payee's representative, Jones, plaintiff, suing as a holder in due course, was entitled, as a matter of law, to recover on the notes, and the trial court erred in refusing to peremptorily direct a verdict for plaintiff. In this view it is unnecessary to discuss the numerous other assignments of error made.

The judgment is consequently reversed, and the cause remanded.

BECKER, J., concurs.

WILLIAMS v. JOHN T. HESSER COAL CO.
(No. 16556.)

(St. Louis Court of Appeals. Missouri. May 3, 1921. Rehearing Denied June 21, 1921.)

1. Master and servant ⟫8(2)—Employment for another year presumed from continuance in service.

Where the contract between a coal company and a sales agent was for the employment of the agent at $1,800 per year, payable monthly, for at least two years, with a certain bonus, the hiring was on a yearly basis, and where at the end of the second year and the end of the third year the agent continued in the company's service without a new agreement, a presumption of fact arose that the employment was to continue through another year.

2. Master and servant ⟫43—Cause of discharge question of fact.

In an action by a coal company's sales agent for breach of his contract of employment, whether plaintiff's discharge was for disability or failure on his part to perform his duties *held* a question of fact.

3. Appeal and error ⟫1010(1)—Finding of fact not interfered with when supported by substantial evidence.

The finding of fact made by the lower court sitting as a jury will not be interfered with by the Court of Appeals, where there is substantial evidence in the record to support it.

4. Master and servant ⟫40(3) — Evidence held to show wrongful discharge.

In an action by a coal company's sales agent for breach of his contract of employment, evidence *held* sufficient to sustain finding that plaintiff's discharge was not because of disability or failure on his part to perform his duties.

5. Damages ⟫140—Verdict for sales agent in action for wrongful discharge held not excessive.

In an action by a coal company's sales agent for breach of contract of employment, whereby plaintiff received $150 per month, plaintiff having been out of work for four months, and then having secured employment at $115 per month, and having been discharged when the contract had six months to run, judgment in plaintiff's favor for $670, being $150 a month for four months, plus $35 a month for two months, was not excessive.

Appeal from St. Louis Circuit Court; William T. Jones, Judge.

Action by R. H. Williams against the John T. Hesser Coal Company, a corporation. From judgment for plaintiff, defendant appeals. Affirmed.

John W. Mueller, of St. Louis, for appellant.

Henry H. Oberschelp, of St. Louis, for respondent.

BIGGS, C. This is an action for damages for the alleged breach of a contract of employment.

The charge in the petition is that—

"By an agreement and contract duly entered into between defendant, a corporation, acting through its duly authorized officer and representative at Cincinnati, Ohio, and plaintiff, located at Richmond, Va., defendant employed plaintiff as general sales agent at the rate of $1,800, per annum, payable monthly, for a period of at least two years from February 1, 1912; that in accordance with said agreement plaintiff entered upon the performance of his duties thereunder, and was and remained in defendant's employ during three full years from said February 1, 1912, and during the first six months of the fourth year, until July, 1915, when, contrary to and in violation of said contract, which had become and was effective at least until the end of said fourth year, viz. until February 1, 1916, defendant, without any good or justifiable cause or excuse, wrongfully dismissed from its employ and discharged plaintiff, who was at all times ready and willing to carry out said contract and perform his duties thereunder, and defendant thus breached said contract, and damaged plaintiff in the sum of $1,500, for which, and interest and costs, plaintiff prays judgment against defendant."

After the defendant had filed a general denial the cause was tried before the court without the aid of a jury, and judgment was rendered for plaintiff for the sum of $753.75, from which the defendant in the proper manner has perfected an appeal to this court.

Defendant's contentions in the main are that the petition fails to state a cause of action; that the defendant's demurrer at the close of the evidence should have been given; that the court erred in finding that the contract in suit was such as to be capable of renewal in the absence of a new agreement at the termination of the term originally agreed upon; that error inhered in the ruling of the court, to the effect that the contract of employment constituted a yearly contract and was renewable automatically without a writing or memorandum required by the statute of frauds, and that the court erred in not ruling that the contract of employment was one at will and determinable at any time by the defendant.

After several conferences between the plaintiff and the president of defendant company, the parties entered into a written agreement evidenced by letters between them. On February 5, 1912, plaintiff wrote to the defendant company, stating that he had no desire for a formal contract, and gave his understanding of their agreement as follows:

"That I am employed at the rate of $1,800 per annum, payable monthly, for a period of at least two years from February 1, 1912, and a bonus of $1.00 per car on all commercial coal in excess of 160 cars per month."

On February 7, 1912, the defendant company through its president replied to the plaintiff's letter as follows:

"Answering your letter of the 5th, I will say the terms you mention are perfectly satisfactory and in accordance with my understanding of our agreement. Your letter of the 5th inst. and this reply constitute all the agreement necessary. The only additional qualification I will include in the agreement is that it may terminate at the option of the company in case of disability, failure or any other reason on your part to perform the duties of the office. I have always inserted this in all such agreements, feeling that it is only justice to the company to have this understood. I trust you will have no objection to it.

"Your official title should be general sales agent, which you are in fact."

Thereupon the plaintiff took up the duties of his office, and served the defendant as its sales agent at Richmond, Va., for the entire period of the two years mentioned in the letter of February 5th. At the expiration of the two years plaintiff continued as such sales agent without any new written agreement either verbal or written, for 1½ years thereafter, or until August 1, 1915, at which time the defendant terminated the employment, giving as a reason therefor that the office was being operated at a loss, and had been for the six months prior thereto. After his discharge the plaintiff was out of employment for four months, and then secured a position at $115 per month. The damage claimed by the plaintiff is his salary from August until the following February 1st, which would be the end of the fourth year from the date of the contract, at the rate of $150 a month, less what he had been able to earn within that time.

In accordance with the contention of plaintiff the court below construed the contract between the parties as evidenced by the letters as a yearly employment of plaintiff which was automatically renewed by the plaintiff continuing in the service from year to year without any new agreement, and, being a yearly employment, the statute of frauds had no application.

Defendant's complaints against the judgment may be answered by a solution of the question as to whether the contract embodied in the letters constituted an employment by the year, to be terminated only at the end of each year, or is one at will that could be terminated by either party at any time after the expiration of the two-year period.

[1] The question is one of the intention of the parties to be gathered from the contract between them. In this case it may reasonably be inferred, not only from the circumstances and conditions surrounding the parties, but from the language used in the contract that a yearly employment was intended.

At the time the contract was made the plaintiff gave up permanent employment, and removed to Richmond, and took charge of the defendant's business, under a contract which employed him "at the rate of $1,800 per annum, payable monthly, for a period of at least two years from February 1, 1912." The fact that the contract was to run for a minimum of two years indicates an intention to provide a yearly employment. The agreement between the parties is something more than a mere hiring at so much per year in that it contains a provision which indicates an intention that the hiring shall be on a yearly basis. Arnold v. Railway Steel Spring Co., 181 Mo. App. 612, 110 S. W. 617; Id., 147 Mo. App. 451, 126 S. W. 795; Bell v. Warehouse Co., 205 Mo. 475, loc. cit. 489, 103 S. W. 1014; Morris v. Briggs Photo Supply Co., 192 Mo. App. (Kansas City Court of Appeals) 145, loc. cit. 150, 179 S. W. 783; Bradner v. Rockdale Powder Co., 115 Mo. App. 102, 91 S. W. 997; Warden v. Hinds, 163 Fed. 201, 90 C. C. A. 449, 25 L. R. A. (N. S.) 529, note; Resener v. Watts, Ritter & Co., 73 W. Va. 342, 80 S. E. 839, 51 L. R. A. (N. S.) 629.

It being conceded that at the end of the second year and also at the end of the third year plaintiff continued in the defendant's service without a new agreement, the presumption arose that the employment was to continue through another year. Such a presumption is one of fact, and does not alter, but continues, the terms of the original contract, and does not convert an express into an implied contract, but simply raises an inference of fact that the parties agreed to extend the operation of the old contract for another year. Morris v. Briggs Photo Supply Co., supra; Bell v. Warehouse Co., supra; 1 Labatt on Master and Servant, 230. See note to the case of Stewart Dry Goods Co. v. Hutchison, 177 Ky. 757, 198 S. W. 17, L. R. A. 1918C, 706. We think the court properly construed the contract as providing for a yearly employment.

[2-4] Defendant claims that, irrespective of whether the defendant had a right to discharge plaintiff at will, it had the right to terminate the employment at its option, as provided in its letter to the plaintiff of February 7th, "in case of disability, failure or any other reason on your part to perform the duties of the office." As to whether the discharge of plaintiff was because of disability or failure on his part to perform his duties was a question of fact in the case which the lower court, sitting as a jury, solved in favor of plaintiff, and which finding will not be interfered with by us in the event there is substantial evidence in the record to support it. We find ample evidence to support such finding, as the letters between the parties indicate that defendant had no complaint to make of the manner in which plaintiff performed his services, but concluded to discon-

tinue the Richmond office in order to reduce expenses. While it is true that defendant's evidence tended to show that plaintiff had not sold as much coal as was contemplated by the parties, and that the office at Richmond was conducted at a loss, still, as stated, there was evidence tending to show that the defendant did not blame this condition on the plaintiff.

[5] Nor can the verdict be said to be excessive, as contended by the defendant. Under the contract plaintiff received $150 per month. He was out of work for four months, and then secured employment at the rate of $115 per month, which was $35 per month less than his salary under the contract. Plaintiff having been discharged on August 1, 1915, the contract at that time had six months to run, or until February 1, 1916. During this period plaintiff was idle four months, and the remaining two months he was employed at $115 per month. This justified a judgment in plaintiff's favor as given by the court for $670, being $150 per month for four months plus the $35 per month for two months. The judgment of the court for $670, with interest from September 14, 1916, at 6 per cent., amounting to $83.75, making a total judgment of $753.75, was warranted by the law and the evidence, and should be affirmed.

PER CURIAM. The foregoing opinion of BIGGS, C., is adopted as the opinion of the court.

The judgment of the circuit court is accordingly affirmed.

ALLEN, P. J., and BECKER, J., concur. DAUES, J., not sitting.

KENEDY PASTURE CO. et al. v. STATE et al. (No. 3043.)

(Supreme Court of Texas. May 18, 1921.)

1. **Courts** 🠔247(10)—**Court of appeals' judgment as to boundary respected, where whole case does not depend upon boundary controversies.**

Although the Supreme Court might determine boundary disputes where necessary on other matters properly appealed in an action of trespass to try title, yet where the whole case does not depend upon the determination of the boundary controversies, the finality of the judgment of the Court of Civil Appeals as to them should be respected.

2. **Appeal and error** 🠔1094(2)—**Findings of trial court and Court of Civil Appeals upon questions of fact are conclusive on Supreme Court.**

Upon error to review an action in trespass to try title, where the trial court's judgment on boundary disputes involved questions essentially of fact supported by evidence, the findings of the trial court and the Court of Civil Appeals are conclusive on the Supreme Court.

3. **Public lands** 🠔198—**Treaty of Guadalupe Hidalgo does not protect Mexican land grants not in existence when the treaty was signed.**

The provisions of the treaty of Guadalupe Hidalgo, protecting Mexican land grants, cannot be construed to protect a grant made to one by a Mexican state in April, 1848, which was after the signing of such treaty.

4. **Public lands** 🠔199—**A nation may not grant title to land to which it has no title.**

A nation cannot grant land to private individuals in territory to which it has no title, and a de facto possession could not supply that title.

5. **Public lands** 🠔199—**Power of Mexican government to grant land in territory ceded to this country ended with signing of treaty.**

Treaties take effect from the date signed, and where disputed territory is ceded as by the treaty of Guadalupe Hidalgo, the power of the ceding government to grant land within it ends with the signing of the treaty.

6. **Public lands** 🠔223(1)—**Party having paid for land and had it surveyed prior to 1836 acquired inchoate and equitable title protected by treaty.**

Where land between the Nueces and the Rio Grande rivers was surveyed for grantee who paid the Mexican authorities for it prior to 1836, when it was finally claimed by the Texas Republic, such grantee acquired an inchoate or equitable title having its origin prior to December 19, 1836, which would be protected by the treaty of Guadalupe Hidalgo.

7. **Public lands** 🠔210—**Copies of original letters, shown to be genuine and found in Mexican archives, held admissible to show equitable title.**

Copies of letters found in the archives of a Mexican town held admissible in evidence, after admission of evidence as to genuineness of the originals, as compared copies to show equitable title in the grantee from a Mexican state prior to the ceding of the territory by Mexico, in an action in trespass to try title.

8. **Public lands** 🠔209—**Abandonment of grant must be shown by unequivocal act evidencing intention, and mere failure to assert right is insufficient.**

In an action in trespass to try title, plaintiff's contention that, if a grantee from a Mexican state acquired an inchoate right to the land, he thereafter abandoned it, is not well taken, where there was no unequivocal act on his part evidencing such intention, since his mere failure to assert such right could not operate as a forfeiture of it, besides such was a question of fact, concluded by the trial court's judgment.

9. **Public lands** 🠔210—**Parties buying from state held innocent purchasers as against record of invalid Mexican grant.**

In a proceeding by the state and purchasers from it, in trespass to try title, opposed by claimants under a Mexican grant, where such grant was void, its record, with the field notes accompanying it, in the county, or the filing of a copy of it and the field notes in the Land Office, afforded no character of notice to such purchasers, and a resurvey, based upon the void grant, was wholly without authority and the filing of the field notes thereof could not operate as notice, so that, even if diligently pursued, such knowledge could only lead to ascertainment of the void grant, and the purchasers from the state are innocent.

10. **Public lands** 🠔210—**Parties purchasing from the state not required to search Mexican records of ancient towns.**

Parties purchasing land from the state were not under the duty of searching through the records of ancient towns of foreign country for evidence of an adverse right, which was only discovered long after their rights accrued by extraordinary effort, in the archives of a Mexican town, for there can be no presumption of notice, where inquiry, pursued with ordinary diligence, would have been futile.

11. **Public lands** 🠔209—**Parties, allowing rights to slumber 70 years in buried records in foreign country with no possession, held not entitled to establish claim against innocent purchasers.**

Where parties, claiming land against the state and holders of title from state, permitted the meager and fragmentary evidence of their right to slumber more than 70 years in the buried records of a foreign jurisdiction, with no possession on their part, with the land vacant and the state's claim openly asserted by appropriation at an early day, its resurrection now will not be suffered to defeat the title of innocent settlers, who purchased from the state in good faith.

12. **Public lands** 🠔223(1)—**Claimants under Mexican grant cannot complain of judgment for innocent purchasers whom they did not reimburse.**

Where purchasers of land from the state had not paid the full money consideration when they first learned of defendant's claim under predecessor's inchoate right to title from a Mexican state, but had completed their settlement, improved the land, and paid the principal part of the consideration, and defendant claimant made no offer to reimburse them for consideration paid or improvements, or in any way to perform what equity would require, they are in no position to complain of a judgment protecting the rights of such purchasers.

13. Public lands ⊂⇒203 — Appropriation void on its face does not give character of "titled land" or "land equitably owned" within constitutional provision.

An appropriation under a Mexican grant void upon its face cannot in its very nature give land the character of "titled land" or "land equitably owned" within the contemplation of Const. art. 14, § 2.

Error to Court of Civil Appeals of Third Supreme Judicial District.

Trespass to try title by the State of Texas and others against the Kenedy Pasture Company and others. Judgment for plaintiffs, and the defendants appealed to the Court of Civil Appeals, which affirmed the judgment and denied rehearing in part and granted it in part (196 S. W. 287), and the defendants bring error. Judgment of the trial court and of the Court of Civil Appeals affirmed.

G. R. Scott, Boone & Pope, of Corpus Christi, James B. Wells, of Brownsville, Ike D. White and E. Cartledge, both of Austin, and Herbert Davenport, of Brownsville, for plaintiffs in error.

B. F. Looney, Atty. Gen., G. B. Smedley, Asst. Atty. Gen., Ball & Seeligson and C. W. Trueheart, all of San Antonio, John L. Terrell, of Dallas, and Lyndsay D. Hawkins, of Breckenridge, for defendants in error.

PHILLIPS, C. J. This suit involves about 30,000 acres of land in Willacy County—formerly a part of Cameron County. There are a great many parties to it and a number of complicated issues.

In the main, it is a controversy between the State and those holding under the State, on the one side, and John G. Kenedy, a large number of Mexicans, some interveners and the Kenedy Pasture Company, a corporation, on the other, concerning the title and the location of what the latter parties claim is the Santa Rosa de Abajo Grant, a grant made by the Mexican Government, and to which all of these parties except the Kenedy Pasture Company assert title.

The Abajo Grant, if located as these parties contend it should be, comprises part of forty-nine sections of land, now claimed by the State and those holding under the State, besides an additional strip of land and an insert lying immediately to the west of those sections.

The Kenedy Pasture Company claims certain of these forty-nine sections and parts of sections as included within the real boundaries of the original Mexican grants, the E Paistle and the Las Barrosas, both owned b it and lying immediately to the east an south of the sections. To such sections an parts of sections it also asserts a limitatio title.

The suit also embraces a controversy between those of the parties called the Fan Heirs and those claiming the Abajo Grant over the strip and the inset lying immediately west of the forty-nine sections. This strip and inset are claimed by the latter as within the true lines of the Abajo Grant. The Fant Heirs claim the same land as a part of the Arriba Grant, a survey owned by them and lying to the west of the Abajo and the forty-nine sections.

The effect of the contention of Kenedy and the other parties adverse to the State an the claimants under the State, is to locate the western boundary lines respectively of the Abajo, the El Paistle and the Las Barrosas Grants more than a mile further west than as maintained by the latter, and the northern line of the Las Barrosas slightly further north.

We subjoin two sketches which show with approximate correctness the situation of these grants and the land in controversy. The first shows the grants if located as contended for by the State and the parties in common with it. The broken lines indicated on the second show their location according to the contention of the parties adverse to the State and the claimants under it.

The El Paistle and Las Barrosas Grants were confirmed by the Legislature in 1852. There is no question as to their validity. They were surveyed and patented for Mifflin Kenedy in 1873. This was prior to the locations made on the Abajo Grant under the authority of the State. They were conveyed in 1892 by Mifflin Kenedy to the Kenedy Pasture Company.

In 1904 the State, in a suit against D. R. Fant and D. Sullivan, recovered, as excess land of the Arriba Grant, what is delineated on the sketches as the "Crocker Land"—the tier of eleven sections lying to the west of the other thirty-eight sections here involved.

The State's suit, here, for the benefit of itself and those holding title under it, was for the land comprising these forty-nine sections. In its petition the land was substantially described as being bounded on the north by Olmos Creek; on the east by the west boundary lines of the El Paistle and Las Barrosas Grants as patented; on the south by the Las Barrosas as patented; and on the west by the east boundary line of the Arriba as established by the judgment in the suit of the State against D. R. Fant and D. Sullivan.

The thirty-eight numbered sections, other than the Crocker Land, shown on the sketch-

⊂⇒For other cases see same topic and KEY-NUMBER in all Key-Numbered Digests and Indexes

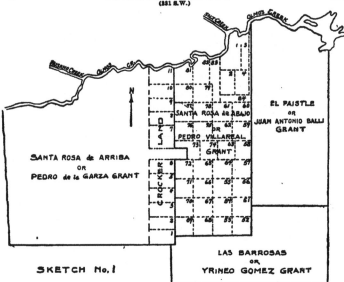

SKETCH No. 1

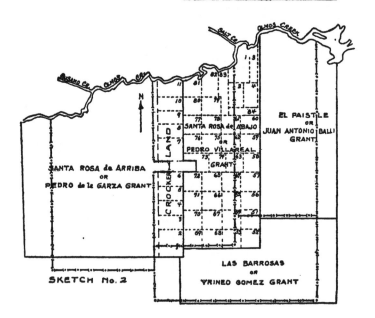

SKETCH No. 2

es; viz., Sections Nos. 81, 82, 83, 1, 3, 80, 79, 2, 4, 84, 77, 78, 61, 60, 76, 75, 62, 59, 73, 74, 63, 58, 72, 65, 64, 57, 71, 66, 55, 56, 70, 67, 54, 51, 69, 68, 53, and 52, were surveyed in the years 1879 and 1881 under railroad certificates owned by F. J. Parker, the nineteen odd numbered sections being surveyed for Parker, and the nineteen even numbered sections for the School Fund. The nineteen odd numbered sections were patented to Parker in 1888.

The Fant Heirs hold title to these nineteen odd numbered sections under the patents issued Parker: viz., Sections Nos. 81, 83, 1, 3, 79, 77, 61, 75, 59, 73, 68, 65, 57, 71, 55, 67, 51, 69, and 53.

Of the nineteen even numbered sections surveyed for the School Fund, nine: viz., Sections Nos. 66, 64, 72, 54, 70, 62, 76, 78, and 74, were sold to settlers in 1898, 1904 and 1908 on condition of settlement, the payment of one-fortieth of the purchase price and the execution by the purchasers of their obligations for the balance.

The remaining ten of the even numbered sections are held by the State for the School Fund, unsold.

The eleven sections delineated on the sketches as the "Crocker Land," lying to the west of the thirty-eight sections, were likewise sold by the State to the Crockers, in 1908 and 1909, on condition of settlement, payment of one-fortieth of the purchase money and execution by the purchasers of their obligations for the balance.

These purchasers from the State all completed their occupancy as required by law. Since their purchase they have continuously held possession of these several sections, as have the Fant Heirs of the nineteen sections held under the Parker title from the State, interrupted only by the extension of a fence by the Kenedy Pasture Company along what it claims are the true western lines of the El Paistle and the Las Barrosas. This fence was extended not in right of the Abajo Grant, but in right only of the Kenedy Pasture Company's claim as to the true location of the El Paistle and Las Barrosas. The right of these parties holding under the State remained unquestioned by the adverse claimants to the Abajo until the filing of a suit in Cameron County in 1904, which was consolidated with this suit.

Under the contention of the State and those in common with it as to the location of the Abajo Grant, the thirty-eight sections surveyed under the railroad certificates, alone, are upon the Abajo, and the Crocker eleven sections lie without it and to the west.

According to the contention of Kenedy and the other parties adverse to the state and its claimants as to the location of the El Paistle and Las Barrosas Grants, those two grants, as shown by the second sketch, conflict with the sections along the east of the

thirty-eighth sections, with Crocker Section No. 1 and a part of Crocker Section No. 2 and the southern portions of Sections 68 and 69 and a part of the southern portion of Section 53; and if the Abajo be located as contended by them, it includes all of the remaining land of the forty-nine sections and, in addition, the strip and the inset to the west of them.

The trial court and Court of Civil Appeals sustained the contention of the State and its claimants as to the location of all three of these grants.

The facts concerning the Mexican title to the Abajo Grant asserted by Kenedy, the Mexican defendants and the interveners, and notice of it by the claimants under the State, are substantially these:

In 1832, Antonio Canales, a Survey General of the Mexican State of Tamaulipas, surveyed the land claimed to be comprised by the Abajo Grant and which then lay within the State of Tamaulipas, for Pedro Villareal, who was in possession of the land at that time. Following the survey and prior to 1835, Villareal paid to the proper Mexican authorities the purchase money for the land —$165.00, the amount at which it was appraised. His expediente was forwarded to the Governor of the State of Tamaulipas, and his right to receive final title or a grant was recognized by the authorities of the State.

Years later, on April 12, 1848, after the establishment of Texas independence and after the signing of the Treaty of Guadalupe Hidalgo, a purported grant to the land was issued to Villareal by the Governor of the State of Tamaulipas.

Villareal was in possession of the land in person or by representatives until 1850 or 1860. Since that time there has never been any possession by him or any one claiming under him. He nor any one claiming under him has ever paid any taxes on the land. It was rendered for taxes for his heirs but twice, in 1880 and 1881, by W. A. Crafts as attorney. In 1882 it was assessed against "Unknown Owners."

The grant issued to Villareal by the Mexican Governor of Tamaulipas and the field notes claimed to have been made by Canales, were filed by W. A. Crafts as attorney for the heirs of Villareal in the office of the County Clerk of Cameron County on August 8, 1879, and recorded as one instrument.

The field notes were filed by Crafts with the County Surveyor of Cameron County and a re-survey of the land requested, August 18, 1879.

In November, 1879, the County Surveyor made the re-survey as requested by Crafts. The field notes of the re-survey were filed in the Surveyor's office, December 15, 1879, and in the General Land Office, December 31, 1879 reciting that they were of a re-survey of a grant "made for the heirs and assigns of Pedro Villareal to whom the land was originally granted by the State of Tamaulipas and surveyed by Canales, original map and field notes bearing date of December 21, 1832, and recorded in Clerk's office of Cameron County."

On February 3, 1887, a certified copy of the Cameron County record of the grant to Villareal and the field notes, was filed as one instrument in the General Land Office.

In the deed from the estate of F. J. Parker to R. and J. Driscoll and D. R. Fant, conveying the nineteen sections claimed by the Fant Heirs and through which they deraign title, and also in the deed from the Driscolls to D. R. Fant, the ancestor of the Fant Heirs, it was recited that those sections were located over a Spanish grant to Pedro Villareal which had become forfeited to the State of Texas.

At the time F. J. Parker located his surveys on the Abajo Grant he had notice that Judge James B. Wells, of Brownsville, had seen what purported to be a grant to the Abajo issued to Pedro Villareal on April 12, 1848, by the Governor of the State of Tamaulipas, and that it appeared on its face to be an original grant.

When the parties claiming under the State acquired title to their portions of the Abajo, there were on file in the General Land Office a number of official maps on which was indicated a survey of the Abajo Grant, there appearing within the lines of the survey on these maps the words, "Santa Rosa de Abajo, Pedro Villareal." As found by the trial court, the purchasers from the State of the nine even numbered sections of the thirty-eight, and of the Crocker sections, had notice of these maps, which we infer to mean actual notice.

Aside from the grant issued by the Mexican Governor of Tamaulipas to Villareal on April 12, 1848, the title of Villareal to the Abajo rested entirely upon the evidence afforded by copies of certain letters from Mexican officials dated in the years 1832, 1833 and 1834. These letters, after a prolonged search instituted by Jno. G. Kenedy for evidence of the Villareal title, were found by Frank C. Pierce, an attorney for Kenedy, in the archives of the Municipality of Reynosa, Mexico, in 1904 or 1905. It does not appear that any of the claimants under the State had any notice of these letters, or of the matters to which they purport to relate, until after this controversy over the land began.

In 1878, or prior thereto, F. J. Parker built a fence along or near the supposed east line of the Arriba Survey, which the trial court found to be approximately the west line of the Abajo. This fence extended from south of the south line of the Abajo north to a point south of Los Olmos Creek, thence running west, south of the creek, enclosing the Arriba Grant and other lands.

In 1883 the Kenedy Pasture Company, the owner of the El Paistle Grant, built a fence along the west line of that grant as claimed by it, being located approximately upon what the Kenedy Pasture Company and the other parties here adverse to the State and its claimants assert to be the dividing line between the Abajo and the El Paistle Grants, and extending from Los Olmos Creek on the north to the Las Barrosas Grant, as patented, on the south.

In the year 1885, or prior thereto, Mrs. King, who owned certain land north of Los Olmos Creek, erected a fence from a half mile to a mile north of the creek, running east and west parallel thereto and connecting the Kenedy Pasture Company fence on the east.

In the year 1885 D. R. Fant erected a fence extending east and west a short distance north of the south boundary line of the Abajo and connecting the fence erected on the west line of the Abajo with the Kenedy Pasture Company fence on the east.

In 1886 the Kenedy Pasture Company erected a fence along the north line of the Las Barrosas Grant, as patented, extending from the Kenedy Pasture Company fence on the east of the Abajo along the south line of the Abajo and connecting with the Parker fence erected along the west line of the Abajo. When this fence was erected by the Kenedy Pasture Company, D. R. Fant removed the fence which had been erected by him in 1885 along the south line of the Abajo.

In 1885 D. R. Fant extended the old Parker fence on the west line of the Abajo north across Los Olmos Creek, so as to connect with the east and west fence of Mrs. King above mentioned. This connection completed the enclosure of that part of the Abajo included within the boundaries of the Parker fence on the west and the Kenedy Pasture Company's fence running through the eastern portion of the survey of the Abajo as fixed by the trial court, there being included however in the enclosure certain other lands north of Los Olmos Creek.

About the year 1885 D. R. Fant ran a division fence from a point on the west line of the Abajo, and at about the southern portion of the off-set in the west line, connecting the Parker fence on the west with the Kenedy Pasture Company's fence on the east and dividing the Abajo into two enclosures, each containing about 5,000 acres of land. About the same time Fant also erected some fences for the purpose of enclosing certain small pastures near the ranch headquarters, some of such enclosures being east and some being west of Parker's old fence. The fences erected by the Kenedy Pasture Company were kept up by it; and the Parker fence and other fences erected by D. R. Fant, and

Mrs. King's fence running north of Los Olmos Creek, were kept up by Fant continuously from the time of their erection and were sufficient to turn stock.

When the Kenedy Pasture Company built its fence in 1833 along what it claims to be the west line of the El Paistle Grant, there was brought within the enclosure the eastern portion of the Abajo as the Abajo was located by the trial court, being that portion shown east of the broken line on sketch No. 2 extending north and south through the Abajo. This part of the Abajo as fixed by the trial court has since been in the continuous and exclusive possession of the Kenedy Pasture Company. The whole enclosure however of which it was thus a part comprised more than 5,000 acres of land, and there was no segregation of that part of the Abajo thus enclosed from the other land within the enclosure.

About the year 1885 D. R. Fant dug three wells on different ones of the nineteen odd numbered sections on the Abajo Grant claimed by the Fant Heirs, for the purpose of supplying water for cattle; and continuously from 1883 the Fant Heirs and their predecessors in title have grazed cattle on those sections and excluded other stock therefrom, except in isolated instances.

Since 1878, or earlier, and for a continuous period of more than ten years, F. J. Parker, the Driscolls and D. R. Fant, whose title is held by the Fant Heirs, had open, adverse possession of the strip of land and-inset lying to the west of the Crocker lands, using and enjoying such strip and inset enclosed by a substantial fence, and such strip and inset being claimed as a part of the Arriba Grant owned by them.

The case was tried without a jury, and the trial court found, among other things, that the purported grant of the Abajo Survey, issued by the Governor of the Mexican State of Tamaulipas to Pedro Villareal, of date April 12, 1848, was void.

It further found that while this grant was void and vested no title in Villareal, yet prior to December 19, 1836, Villareal acquired in accordance with the laws of Mexico in force at that time, the right to a grant of the Abajo Survey, and hence an equitable title to the Abajo Grant, good as against the State of Texas and as against purchasers from the State with actual or constructive notice of such equitable title. This holding that Villareal acquired an equitable title to the Abajo Grant was based upon the evidence afforded by copies of the letters of Mexican officials found in the archives of the Municipality of Reynosa, Mexico, which have been referred to in a previous part of this statement.

The court found that the Fant Heirs, holding the nineteen odd numbered sections on the Abajo under patents from the State,

and the purchasers from the State of the nine of the remaining nineteen even numbered sections on the Abajo, were innocent purchasers for value of those sections without either actual or constructive notice of the Villareal equitable title to the Abajo Grant, and hence that their respective titles to those sections were superior to that equitable title.

It found that the Kenedy Pasture Company had failed to establish title by limitation to that part of the Abajo Grant within its fences.

It found that the Fant Heirs had title under the Ten Years Statute of Limitation to the strip and inset lying to the west of the Crocker land.

It found that the Fant Heirs had title under the Three and Five Years Statutes of Limitation to all of the odd numbered nineteen sections on the Abajo lying west of the fence built by the Kenedy Pasture Company through the eastern portion of the Abajo extending from Los Olmos Creek and south to the north line of the Las Barrosas Grant.

As has already been stated, the court fixed the location of the Abajo, the El Paistle and the Las Barrosas Grants as contended for by the State and those claiming under the State.

Judgment was accordingly rendered as follows:

In favor of the Fant Heirs for the nineteen odd numbered sections on the Abajo Grant and for the strip and inset lying to the west of the Abajo Grant and the Crocker land.

In favor of the Crockers for the eleven sections lying to the west of the Abajo Grant. In favor of purchasers from the State, Tindall and wife, Mrs. Jeffers and Sam M. Boyd for nine of the nineteen even numbered sections on the Abajo Grant surveyed for the State and purchased by them: to-wit, Sections Nos. 66, 64, 72, 54, 70, 62, 76, 78 and 74.

In favor of John G. Kenedy, the Mexican defendants and the interveners for the remaining ten of the nineteen even numbered sections on the Abajo surveyed for the State; to-wit, Sections Nos. 80, 82, 4, 60, 2, 84, 52, 56, 58 and 68.

It was further adjudged that the Kenedy Pasture Company take nothing and that the State of Texas take nothing except its rights securing the unpaid purchase money due it on the sections adjudged to the purchasers from it.

The judgment was affirmed by the Court of Civil Appeals.

The important questions in the case are the validity of the grant made by the Governor of the Mexican State of Tamaulipas, April 12, 1848, to Pedro Villareal; whether, independently of the grant, Villareal acquired an equitable right or title to the land comprised in the so-called Abajo

Grant, as found by the District Court and Court of Civil Appeals; and if Villareal did acquire such a right or title, whether the purchasers from the State, Tindall and others, and the Fant Heirs, holding under patents from the State, have title to their respective sections superior to the Villareal right or title, as innocent purchasers for value without notice.

[1] The disputes as to the boundaries of the Abajo, the El Paistle and the Las Barrosas Grants and the limitation questions involved in those disputes, we do not feel called upon to determine. They are boundary controversies, pure and simple. It is evident that as to them there would have been no case except for the disputes over the location of the lines of those grants. Cox v. Finks, 91 Tex. 318, 43 S. W. 1. The limitation title asserted by the Kenedy Pasture Company to the eastern tier of sections and parts of sections and parts of some of the southern sections as delineated upon the sketches, as embraced within the El Paistle and Las Barrosas Grants, grows out of the disputes as to the boundaries of those grants, and is but a part of the controversy over their boundaries. The limitation title asserted by the Fant Heirs to the strip and inset west of the Crocker lands is equally but a part of a boundary dispute. The right of the whole case does not depend upon a determination of the boundary controversies, and we therefore have jurisdiction of it. But no other part of the case is concerned in the boundary disputes. Their adjudication affects, and can affect, no other issue. They are in the case as independent boundary controversies, of which, ordinarily, the jurisdiction of the Court of Civil Appeals would be final. All other issues in the case lie entirely without them, and the settlement of those issues in no wise involves their adjudication. With this true, we do not feel that a review of the boundary controversies is imposed upon this court.

Since the presence of other distinct issues, in no way involving the questions of boundary, gives the case an independent character other than that of a "boundary case," the boundary disputes do not, as we have said, affect our jurisdiction of the case. And if for the settlement of these other issues it were necessary to determine the boundary disputes, we would determine them. That would be essential to our jurisdiction over the other issues. Such was the condition in West Lumber Co. v. Goodrich (Tex. Com. App.) 223 S. W. 183. That case was an action for conversion involving the question of the boundaries of the land—analogous to Steward v. Coleman County, 95 Tex. 445, 67 S. W. 1016, as well as purely a dispute over the land depending entirely upon the ascertainment of its true boundaries. Since the case in respect to the action for con-

version necessarily involved the boundary question, we felt warranted in approving the opinion of the Commission of Appeals in its determination of that question. In such a case the determination of the boundary controversy as involved in one phase of the case would necessarily determine it as to all phases. The settlement of the purely boundary dispute would result from its determination in the adjudication of the other part of the case, and as necessary to a consistent holding and judgment. But there is no such situation here as was presented in West Lumber Co. v. Goodrich. The boundary disputes here are independent and separable controversies. The other parts of the case do not involve them. The determination of the other issues does not depend upon their settlement. We therefore are of opinion that the finality of the judgment of the Court of Civil Appeals as to them should be respected.

[2] Aside from this, the questions of boundary and limitation here were essentially questions of fact. It cannot be reasonably contended that there is no evidence supporting the trial court's judgment in their regard; and we would therefore not be authorized in reversing that part of the judgment. Findings of fact by the trial court and the Court of Civil Appeals, with evidence to support them, are conclusive upon this court.

[3] The land in controversy lies in what was at one time the Mexican State of Tamaulipas, between the Nueces and Rio Grande rivers. This is the foundation of the claim, very earnestly pressed by Kenedy and others holding under Villareal, that the Governor of Tamaulipas had authority to issue Villareal a grant on April 12, 1848, and that the grant of that date in Villareal's favor is accordingly valid and protected by the Treaty of Guadalupe Hidalgo. This is a far-reaching contention, so we will examine it. It involves the sovereignty of Texas over this territory, and is a direct challenge of that sovereignty at the time this grant was issued.

One of the things demanded by General Houston of Santa Anna following the victory of San Jacinto was that he require his subordinate commanders the immediate withdrawal beyond the Rio Grande of all Mexican troops in Texas; and this was done. This was the first assertion by the new-born Republic of dominion clear to the utmost Mexican border. On December 19, 1836, the Congress of the Republic declared that the sovereignty of Texas extended to the Rio Grande, defining the southern and western boundary of Texas as beginning at the mouth of that river, and running thence up its principal stream to its source. In the annexation of Texas to the United States as a State, the Rio Grande was accepted as the boundary between Texas and Mexico.

It is fair to say that upon no other terms would Texas have consented to the annexation.

The acceptance of that boundary line was the basis of President Polk's policy in the opening of the war with Mexico. Its dispute by Mexico led to the war. Early in 1846, following the annexation of Texas in the previous December, President Polk ordered General Taylor to advance to the Rio Grande, which he did. The Mexican commander at Matamoras demanded General Taylor's withdrawal to the Nueces. He refused. On April 23rd the Mexicans crossed the river and ambushed a body of the American troops. Two weeks later they attacked General Taylor in the Battle of Palo Alto,—May 8, 1846, in which they were repulsed. On the next day Taylor drove them back across the river in a disastrous rout. And on the 18th of May General Taylor crossed the Rio Grande and occupied Matamoras.

The attack upon the American troops of April 23rd was the occasion of President Polk's message to Congress, declaring that Mexico had passed "the boundaries of the United States" and had shed American blood "upon American soil," and that in consequence a state of war existed.

The territory between the Nueces and the Rio Grande remained largely under the actual possession and jurisdiction of Mexico until 1846. But after the establishment of Texas independence through the defeat of Santa Anna's army, his recognition of Texas sovereignty, and particularly the resolution of the Congress of the Republic of December 19, 1836, that jurisdiction was never a rightful one. It was but a de facto possession.

Such as it was it came to a complete end when early in 1846 United States troops in behalf of Texas and for the enforcement of her rights with respect to this very area, occupied the territory and ousted the Mexicans from it. This has never been doubted. Not only was Mexican authority at an end in the territory early in 1846, but in September, 1847, United States troops had captured the Mexican capital and the entire country was subject to their arms.

With no right at all to this territory after 1836, it would be strange to admit the sovereignty of Mexico over it in 1848, when two years before the sovereignty of Texas had been perfected by reducing the territory to possession. It is equally anomalous to contend that in 1848 Mexican de facto possession of it continued, when in 1847 the entire country, with its capital, was in the hands of American troops and the defeat of Mexico an accomplished fact.

While Mexico's ouster from the territory was in progress, the Legislature of Texas, on April 29, 1846, enacted a joint resolution, declaring:

"That the exclusive right to the jurisdiction over the soil included in the limits of the late Republic of Texas was acquired by the valor of the people thereof, and was by them vested in the Government of the said Republic, that such exclusive right is now vested in and belongs to the State, excepting such jurisdiction as is vested in the United States, by the Constitution of the United States, and by the joint resolution of annexation, subject to such regulations and control as the Government thereof may deem expedient to adopt."

This was a reaffirmation of the sovereignty of Texas over all territory within the borders of the Republic as defined by the resolution of December 19, 1836, and proclaimed both its rightful and actual jurisdiction over this territory.

The Treaty of Guadalupe Hidalgo was signed February 2, 1848. It recognized the Rio Grande River as the boundary between Texas and Mexico, which was a recognition of the right of Texas to the entire area between the Nueces and the Rio Grande. It stipulated that the civil rights of Mexicans within the territory ceded by Mexico, as they existed under the laws of Mexico when the treaty was signed, should be protected.

The proposition asserted by the claimants under the Mexican title is therefore, that though the jurisdiction of Mexico over this territory was never rightful after 1836; though such jurisdiction as it exercised was terminated early in 1846 by its complete ouster from the territory by American troops,—not only so, but with the entire country of Mexico reduced by September 1847; and though this grant was issued in April, 1848, more than two months after the signing of the treaty of peace and Mexico's recognition in the treaty of the right of Texas to the territory, still, that a Mexican official, in April, 1848, had authority to exercise the sovereign power of granting away land within it; and that his acts in derogation and repudiation of the sovereignty of Texas, must, in the courts of Texas, be accepted as valid. The proposition largely sets aside the freedom from Mexican rule accomplished by the establishment of Texas independence. It ignores the constant proclamation of both the Republic's and the State's sovereignty over this territory after December 19, 1836, and the consummation of their rightful claim by effective possession. It asserts the authority of Mexico to grant land in Texas to which it had no right and of which it had no actual control. It attempts to extend the protection of the Treaty of Guadalupe Hidalgo to rights not in existence when the treaty was signed, but attempted to be created afterward. It is refuted by the decisions of this court and plain principles of international law.

[4] It is a novel proposition to say that a sovereignty having no right to given terri-

tory, long after its dispossession, its defeat in a war growing out of dispute over the territory, and its express recognition of the superior right by the provisions of a solemn treaty, may lawfully exercise the sovereign authority of disposing of it by grant. If this be the law a mere de facto jurisdiction over territory once obtained by an unlawful sovereignty, is of a greater force, though terminated, than the lawful sovereignty's de jure and de facto possession and control combined. It is met by the simple proposition that a nation cannot grant away territory to which it has no title.

Considerations of policy and justice of course require of a de facto government the preservation of order and the adjustment of private rights and claims between individuals. For this reason the acts of the de facto government in actual possession of disputed territory in the ordinary administration of its laws, in so far as they affect private rights, are valid. Its acts affecting public rights, however, are void, since they are necessarily in derogation of the rightful, the de jure, sovereignty. The granting of the public domain is of course an act affecting public rights. It has never been otherwise considered. Titles to land in ceded or even conquered territory acquired from a former sovereignty when it had the right to grant them are of course valid, even as against the succeeding sovereignty. But it is plain that this rule cannot apply to a grant of land in territory to which the sovereignty issuing the grant had at the time no right, even though it was in possession. If the sovereignty had no right to the territory, its possession was not rightful. An unlawful, even though an actual possession of land, cannot confer the power of disposing of the title. This is as true of nations as it is of individuals. In cases of disputed territory, when the true boundary is ascertained or adjusted by agreement, grants made by the unlawful sovereignty in the territory to which as thus ascertained it had no right, whether it had possession at the time of the grants or not, unless confirmed by express agreement, fail and are of no effect against the sovereignty to which the territory of right belonged. They fail simply because of want of title in the grantor. A de facto possession cannot supply the title. These principles are well established and are a part of the accepted law of nations. Coffee v. Groover, 123 U. S. 1, 8 Sup. Ct. 1, 31 L. Ed. 51.

Not only is a grant of land void where a part of territory to which the sovereignty making it had at the time no lawful right, even though it was in possession, but certainly after the signing of a treaty which recognizes the superior right of the opposing sovereignty, its power of granting away the territory is at an end. If its possession is not rightful, clearly its jurisdiction can obtain only for strictly municipal purposes. Until actual delivery of the territory it subsists for those purposes alone—to preserve the public order, the settlement of disputes between individuals and the like. But after the signing of the treaty its powers of sovereignty except strictly for those purposes, cease. It distinctly has no power to grant land or franchises. Such a power is one of the highest attributes of sovereignty, and its exercise would necessarily operate as a denial of the rights of the succeeding sovereignty. Davis v. Police Jury, etc., 9 How. 280, 13 L. Ed. 188; Trevino v. Fernandez, 13 Tex. 664.

This court has never recognized the right of Mexico after early in 1846 to grant land in this territory. It has denied such right in every instance where it has considered the question of such authority. It has, in fact, never recognized the validity of any Mexican title to land in this territory originating after December 19, 1836, the date the Congress of the Republic proclaimed that the sovereignty of Texas extended to the Rio Grande. The only Mexican titles to land in the territory which it has recognized as within the protection of the Treaty of Guadalupe Hidalgo, except such as the Legislature has confirmed, have been either those granted prior to December 19, 1836, or those which prior to that date were good in equity and hence in good conscience entitled to the sanction of Texas courts. This is plainly declared in Haynes v. State, 100 Tex. 426, 100 S. W. 912, where concerning lands in this same territory claimed under Mexican title it was said:

"The land was surveyed for the State in 1884, and there is, of course, no question of the State's right to it unless the plaintiff in error has shown a right to the land which originated at a date prior to the 19th day of December, 1836, and which right is protected by the treaty of Guadalupe Hidalgo between the United States and Mexico."

This is because the sovereignty of Mexico over this territory after December 19, 1836, was never rightful, and Mexico accordingly had no power after that date to create titles to land within it.

To the same effect is State v. Gallardo, 106 Tex. 274, 166 S. W. 369, where in relation to a Mexican title to land within the same territory and its protection by the Treaty of Guadalupe Hidalgo, it was said:

"The rights of the defendants should be determined, therefore, by the character of the title under which they claim as it existed on December 19, 1836."

In State v. Bustamente, 47 Tex. 320, there was before the court a grant by the Mexican Governor of Tamaulipas to land in this same territory, dated January 2, 1848—three months before the date of the grant in the present case—the land having been surveyed in 1835. The authority of the Mexican Governor to make such a grant was denied in the opinion of Chief Justice Roberts in these words: .

"The proof was therefore not sufficient, unless the Governor of Tamaulipas had, on the 2d day of January, 1848, the right to grant this land east of the Rio Grande, under the treaty of Guadalupe Hidalgo, concluded one month thereafter, to wit, on the 2d day of February, 1848.

"We are of opinion that he had not such right. Texas claimed the territory, in defining its boundaries, on the 19th of December, 1836. In 1846, the claim was perfected by possession and the actual exercise of exclusive jurisdiction, and from that time it was lost by the State of Tamaulipas, in Mexico, for all purposes whatever, whether of judicial action or the exercise of powers relating to eminent domain. And it never afterwards recovered such lost powers. The action of the Governor, in making concession, was without authority, and neither advanced nor prejudiced the imperfect title previous to the 19th day of December, 1836. Halleck's Int. Law, page 798, section 22; Trevino v. Fernandez, 13 Tex. 664; Davis v. Police Jury of Concordia, 9 How."

It is said by counsel for the claimants under the Mexican title here that this part of Chief Justice Robert's opinion was dicta, since the court was considering a title under the Act of 1870 which related only to Mexican titles originating prior to December 19, 1836, whereas this title was shown by the date of the grant to have originated January 2, 1848. The holding cannot be disposed of in this way. It was not dicta. It is overlooked that there was a survey of the land made under Mexican authority in 1835, shown to have been presented with the claim as in part the basis of the right. The title was therefore one plainly within the Act of 1870, as the court recognized in simply holding the evidence insufficient and remanding the case for further trial. The same title was before the court again in the Haynes Case, 100 Tex. 426, 100 S. W. 912, where it is shown that the title plainly originated prior to December 19. 1836. and where because of that fact and its being good in equity on that date, it was upheld against the suit of the State.

In State v. Cuellar, 47 Tex. 295, there was before the court another Mexican grant made in 1848—November 21st—of land within what was the State of Tamaulipas. Concerning the power of the Mexican Governor to make a grant of the land, "in 1848," this was said by Judge Roberts:

"In reference to the first proposition, there can be no pretense that the instrument signed by Alejo Gutierez, in 1848, is, or possibly can be, a conveyance, in the nature of a grant, to a tract of land in the State of Texas, by virtue

of any power vested in him as an officer of a foreign country (Tamaulipas), at the time he signed the paper."

In the Haynes Case, 100 Tex. 426, 100 S W. 912, the Mexican grant, the same as before the court in the Bustamente Case, ⁊ dated January 2, 1848, and was to land ⁊ already stated, also in the former Merⁱꜜ State of Tamaulipas. The title was sustained, not because of the grant, but because the title was, on December 19, 1836, good ⁊ equity. The title as based upon the gr⁊ was entirely discarded by the court. It ⁊ plain from the decision that the title wo⁊ have been rejected by the court had it po⁊ sessed no other foundation than the gra⁊

In the Sais Case, 47 Tex. 307, it was ⁊ tinctly affirmed that Mexico entirely lo⁊ all control of this territory early in 18⁊ since which time Texas has constantly ex⁊ ercised jurisdiction over it. The holding ⁊ the Gallardo Case, 106 Tex. 274, 166 S. ⁊ 369, is to the same effect.

If this territory was under the de jure ⁊ de facto jurisdiction of Texas early in 18⁊ and that jurisdiction has since continued as is the legal and historical ·fact, it is id⁊ to say that in 1848 it was still subject ⁊ Mexican sovereignty and that the Mexi⁊ government had then the authority to d⁊ pose of land within it.

The grant considered in Clark v. Hills, ⁊ Tex. 141, 2 S. W. 356, cited by the claimar⁊ under the Mexican title, had been express⁊ confirmed by the Legislature. There is ⁊ intimation in that opinion, as there is no⁊ in any opinion of this court, that the Mexi⁊ government had authority to grant lands ⁊ Texas north or east of the Rio Grande aft⁊ the signing of the Treaty of Guadalupe Hi⁊ algo, or for that matter, after it lost its d⁊ jure jurisdiction in 1836.

In the opinion rendered in Texas-Mexi⁊ Railway Co. v. Locke, 74 Tex. 370, 12 S. ⁊ 80, Chief Justice Stayton spoke of there bei⁊ no evidence that the lands in controvers⁊ originally titled to the Mexican predecessor⁊ of the defendants, did not belong to them "⁊ July 4, 1848," the date the Treaty of Guada⁊ lupe Hidalgo was proclaimed, and if the⁊ did, that they were protected "in so far a⁊ valid titles against the State of Coahui⁊ and Texas on March 2, 1836." The isolate⁊ use of that date in such connection does no⁊ affect the question here, much less contro⁊ it. The grants upon which the Mexica⁊ titles rested in that case were issued in 183⁊ when the territory where the land lay wa⁊ within the rightful jurisdiction of Mexic⁊ The opinion makes no pretense of holdin⁊ that Mexico had the right to grant away lan⁊ in ·Texas up to July 4, 1848, or any tim⁊ after it lost its rightful sovereignty ov⁊ Texas.

[5] With respect to the rights of eithe⁊ government under a treaty, the treaty tak⁊ effect from the date it is signed. Haver ⁊.

Yaker, 9 Wallace, 32. Only as between individuals is its effect postponed to the date of proclamation, and this only upon the ground of notice.

As early as 13 Texas (Trevino v. Fernandez, 13 Tex. 664) this court fully recognized the doctrine already referred to, that where disputed territory is ceded by a treaty, the power of the ceding government to grant land within it ends with the signing of the treaty. It would be idle to conclude a treaty relating to disputed territory, if between its signature and proclamation the ceding government has the full right to grant the territory all away.

The Mexican grant here was in our opinion clearly void under the repeated decisions of this court, and, aside from express authority, upon plain and just principles of law. Not at this late day is it to be held that the authority of Mexico to dispose of the public domain of Texas existed after its sovereignty was ended by the valor of the Texas patriots and it was completely dispossessed from the soil.

[6] While the grant issued by the Mexican Governor to Villareal was void and conveyed no character of title, we are of opinion—contrary to the contention of the State—that the District Court and Court of Civil Appeals were right in their conclusion that there was evidence showing that the Abajo Grant was surveyed for Villareal and that he paid the Mexican authorities for it prior to 1836, and that by such authorities his right to the land was recognized, affording him an inchoate or equitable title having its origin prior to December 19, 1836. True, the proof was meager and fragmentary, as such proof would naturally be, adduced at this remote period, particularly in view of the destruction by French troops in 1864 of Victoria, the capital of Tamaulipas, with its archives. But we do not think it can be fairly said that there was no evidence to the effect stated.

[7] This proof rested largely in the official letters found in 1904 by Pierce, Kenedy's attorney, in the archives of the Mexican town of Reynosa. Complaint is made of the admission of the copies of the letters, but there was evidence of the genuineness of the originals, and the copies were admissible in our opinion as compared copies. The letters do not distinctly recite that the Abajo had been surveyed for Villareal or that he paid for that particular survey. But they do fairly show that a survey within that jurisdiction was made for Villareal, that he had paid for the land so surveyed, all prior to 1836, and that also prior to that year his expediente, or instructive dispatch, had been forwarded the Governor for the issuance of final title. The Governor, as shown by the letters, received the expediente and directed that Villareal, with other persons named,

appear at his office for the receipt of title. The forwarding of Villareal's expediente to the Governor would reasonably afford the presumption that he had paid for the land to which it related. Haynes v. State, 100 Tex. 426, 100 S. W. 912. Independently of the official letters, it was found by the Court of Civil Appeals that the Abajo was surveyed for Villareal in 1832 by Canales, Surveyor General of Tamaulipas. It was proved conclusively that Villareal was in possession of the Abajo until 1850 or 1860. These facts in connection with the letters show, at least circumstantially, that the land referred to in the letters as surveyed for Villareal, paid for by him and to which his right was recognized by the Mexican authorities, was the Abajo Survey. At all events, while the proof is not clear, we think that under it this holding is more in consonance with right and fairness than would be a contrary one.

[8] With respect to the State's contention that if Villareal acquired an inchoate right to the land he thereafter abandoned it, there was not shown any unequivocal act on his part evidencing such an intention. A mere failure to assert his right could not operate as a forfeiture of it. Besides, this was a question of fact, concluded by the judgment of the trial court; and as we have held upon the other fact questions, we will not review it.

[9-11] The holding of the trial court that the Fant Heirs and the purchasers from the State were purchasers for value of their respective sections without notice of the inchoate right of Villareal, should in our opinion be also sustained. There is hardly room for controversy upon this question. The grant issued Villareal being void, its record with the field notes accompanying it in Cameron County, or the filing of a copy of it and the field notes in the Land Office afforded, of course, no character of notice. The resurvey by Cocke of the Abajo at the instance of Crafts was based upon the void grant. It was hence wholly without authority, and the filing of the field notes could not, therefore, operate as notice. Whatever actual knowledge F. J. Parker, the predecessor in title of the Fant Heirs, had of Villareal's right, even if diligently pursued, would have led only to the ascertainment of the void grant. But any notice to him would not affect purchasers under him if they were innocent. Holmes v. Buckner, 67 Tex. 107, 2 S. W. 542. His deed to the Driscolls and Fant and the deed of the Driscolls to Fant, the ancestor of the Fant Heirs, which referred to the Villareal Grant, expressly contradicted the existence of any right in Villareal, by the recital that the land had been forfeited to the State. The only actual notice of anything in relation to Villareal's right had by those claiming under the State was of the maps in the Land Office, upon which was

indicated a survey of the Abajo for Villareal. But there is nothing whatever to show that those maps had any relation to Villareal's equitable right, or that they were referable to any title in Villareal's save that which the void grant purported to evidence. Inquiry produced by everything in the case having any character of actual notice would have led inevitably, we think, only to the void grant, shown to be void upon its face. Crafts, the attorney for Villareal, who was instrumental in filing the grant for record, in obtaining a re-survey of the Abajo and in thus affording evidence of Villareal's right, was not shown to have had any knowledge of the equitable right in Villareal, or of any right except that founded on the void grant. Inquiry of him would have given no knowledge in any way concerning Villareal's equitable right. Nobody, it appears, had any knowledge of the letters, without which there was no evidence of any right at all in Villareal, until 1904, when Pierce after prolonged search discovered them in the town of a foreign country. It is not to be held that those holding under the State were under the duty of searching through the records of ancient towns of a foreign country for evidence of an adverse right, which was only discovered, long after their rights accrued, by extraordinary effort. There can be no presumption of notice where inquiry pursued with ordinary diligence would have been futile. Slayton y. Singleton, 72 Tex. 209, 9 S. W. 876. Those now claiming the land against the State and the holders of its title permitted the meager and fragmentary evidence of their right to slumber for more than seventy years in the buried records of a foreign jurisdiction. With no possession on their part, with the land vacant, and the State's claim openly asserted by appropriation at an early day, its resurrection now should not be suffered to defeat the title of innocent settlers who bought from the State in good faith.

[12] There is no question as to full value having been paid for the Fant title. The purchasers from the State had not paid the full money consideration at the time when from this controversy they first learned of Villareal's inchoate right. But they had all long before completed their settlement upon the land. This was the chief part of the consideration to the State in its sale of the land to them. They had therefore paid the principal part of the consideration. They had also improved the land. The claimants of the Villareal right made no offer to requite them for the consideration paid, or for their improvements, or in any way perform what equity would in any event require at their hands. With this true, they are in no position to complain of the judgment protecting the rights of these purchasers in their sections by an award of such sections to them,

or of the protection of the right of the State to the balance of the purchase money due on them.

[13] When the land was surveyed for the State and under the Parker certificates there was no evidence in the Land Office or elsewhere within the State of any appropriation of it in the right of Villareal save that which was referable alone to the Mexican grant, which was void upon its face. An appropriation void upon its face cannot, in its very nature, give land the character of "titled land" or "land equitably owned" within the contemplation of section 2, article 14 of the Constitution.

The right of the entire case was in our opinion attained by the trial court. Its judgment and the judgment of the Court of Civil Appeals are affirmed.

WHITNEY HARDWARE CO. v. McMAHAN et al. (No. 2987.)

(Supreme Court of Texas. May 25, 1921.)

1. Husband and wife ⏘102—Married woman liable for tort in connection with removal of roof on her building.

A married woman owning a rented building would be liable for a tortious wrong in negligently and carelessly removing the roof and not replacing it until after the tenant's property was damaged by rain; such liability being independent of her capacity to contract for repairs, and independent of her liability for an act or omission of agents.

2. Husband and wife ⏘102—Wife liable for tort, though connected with contract.

For a tortious wrong a married woman must respond in damages, though the wrong be committed in an attempt to perform a contract, whether binding or not on the married woman.

3. Husband and wife ⏘102—Wife, as well as husband, liable for wife's torts.

The statutes dealing with the rights of husband and wife leave the wife, as well as the husband, liable for the torts of the wife.

4. Husband and wife ⏘152, 213—Feme covert liable for breach of contract and negligence in management and control of her separate estate.

The power granted to a married woman by Acts 1913, c. 32 (Vernon's Sayles' Ann. Civ. St. 1914, arts. 4621. 4622, 4624) to manage and control her separate estate and the rents to be derived therefrom carried with it the incidental and collateral power to contract with her tenant to repair her store building and to employ others to make such repairs, and she would be liable for the breach of her contract and the proximate results of negligence on the part of those employed by her in leaving the roof off during a rain and destroying tenant's property, without protection from her coverture.

Certified Questions from Court of Civil Appeals of Fifth Supreme Judicial District.

Suit by the Whitney Hardware Company against E. K. McMahan and others in the district court, which was appealed to the Court of Civil Appeals, which has certified the question whether the complaint states good cause of action against Mrs. Effie McMahan, a married woman. 231 S. W. 1117. Answered that plaintiff's petition was not subject to general demurrer.

J. J. Averitte and Wear & Frazier, all of Hillsboro, for appellant.
R. M. Vaughan, of Hillsboro, and Fred V. Lowrey, of Dallas, for appellees.

GREENWOOD, J. The Whitney Hardware Company, appellant, sued Mrs. Effie McMahan, her husband, E. K. McMahan, and her brother-in-law, Waul McMahan, appellees, to recover damages in the sum of $2,500.

The petition alleged that appellant was a corporation engaged in business as a retail merchant, owning a stock of hardware in a brick building belonging to appellee Mrs. Effie McMahan as her separate property and rented by her to appellant; that the building got out of repair to such an extent as to be untenantable; that thereupon Mrs. McMahan, acting individually and by agent, on or about August 1, 1915, contracted with appellant to put the building in a good tenantable state; that instead of properly repairing the building in compliance with her contract, the appellees, each acting as an individual and as agent for the others, duly authorized, negligently removed, without the knowledge of appellant, a part of the roof of the building and failed to restore same until after a heavy rain; and that as the proximate result of the removal of the roof and of the failure to restore it, appellant's stock was damaged in the sum for which a recovery was sought.

The Court of Civil Appeals certifies to us the question: Does plaintiff's petition state a good cause of action against Mrs. Effie McMahan, a married woman, or was it subject to a general demurrer?

[1, 2] Under the averment that Mrs. McMahan in person carelessly removed and failed to restore a part of the roof of the building, proximately causing damage from rain to appellant's stock of hardware, she would be liable for a tort, independent of her capacity to contract for repairs, and independent of her liability for an act or omission of agents. For a tortious wrong a married woman must respond in damages, though the wrong be committed in an attempt to perform a contract, whether binding or not on the married woman. 26 R. C. L. 758; Stock v. Boston, 149 Mass. 414, 21 N. E. 871, 14 Am. St. Rep. 430.

[3] Our statutes dealing with the rights of husband and wife have been uniformly construed as leaving the wife, as well as the husband, liable for the torts of the wife. McQueen v. Fulgham, 27 Tex. 464; Crawford v. Doggett, 82 Tex. 140, 17 S. W. 929, 27 Am. St. Rep. 859.

[4] At common law the wife had no capacity to enter into a contract. The statutes creating and safeguarding her separate estate gave her no general power to contract. Kavanaugh v. Brown, 1 Tex. 484. The act of March 13, 1848 (Acts 2d Leg. c. 79) empowered her to contract debts for necessaries furnished herself and children and for expenses to benefit her separate property. Prior to 1913 there was no other statutory grant of power to the wife to bind herself personally by contract. The act of 1913 (Laws 1913, c. 32 [Vernon's Sayles' Ann. Civ. St. 1914, arts. 4621, 4622, 4624]) eliminated the express grant of capacity to incur obligations for expenses for the benefit of her separate property. The act contained words which seem to have continued the wife's statutory obligation for necessaries furnished herself and children.

The history of the 1913 act repels the conclusion that it authorized the wife to contract as if free from disability, except when expressly forbidden. Both houses passed the act when it did confer such authority. Because of the Governor's objections to the policy of giving the wife so wide a contractual capacity, the bill was recalled from his office; and the manifest purpose of the radical change in the terms of the act was to diminish the power to contract which the wife would have had under the bill on its prior passage. Red River National Bank v. Ferguson, 109 Tex. 293, 206 S. W. 923.

As enacted, instead of conferring on the wife the capacity to make all contracts not specially inhibited, the act enlarged her rights and powers; first, by giving to her "the sole management, control, and disposition of her separate property, both real and personal," subject to provisos as to the incumbrance, conveyance, or transfer of certain property; second, by placing the personal earnings of the wife, the rents from the wife's real estate, the interest on bonds and notes belonging to her and dividends on stocks owned by her under the control, management, and disposition of the wife alone, subject to restrictions on incumbrances and transfers; and, third, by providing that the specific items of community property confided generally to the wife's control and management, as well as her separate property, should not be subject to the payment of debts contracted by the husband. The act also declared bank deposits to be presumptively the separate property of the party in whose name they stood in the dealings of banks in honoring checks and orders on such deposits. The act relieved all community property, except the personal earnings of the wife and the income, rents, and revenues from her separate property, along with the husband's separate property, from being subjected to the payment of debts contracted by the wife, except those contracted for necessaries furnished her or her children, and, in the same connection, forbade the wife from being joint maker of a note or surety on any obligation without the joinder of her husband.

As clearly stated by Mr. Bishop:

"Every statute carries with it so much of collateral right and remedy as will make its provisions effectual; or, as Lord Coke expresses it, 'when the law granteth any thing to any one that also is granted without which the thing cannot be.'" 2 Bishop on Law of Married Women, § 21.

As incidents to the wife's power of exclusive management and control of her separate property and of the specified portions of the community, she became vested with all such contractual power relative to same, as is requisite to make her power effectual.

The right to control and manage a store building or an improved farm, and to receive the rents, would be or would soon become valueless if the holder of the right were denied the power to make a binding rental contract and the power to make engagements for repairs or betterments.

The Supreme Court of Illinois decided that an action would lie against a married woman for work done in the improvement and cultivation of her farm, under a statute authorizing her to take the title to real estate free from her husband's control and interference, during coverture, and to possess and enjoy it as if she were unmarried. In the course of an instructive discussion, the court said:

"For, how can she possess and enjoy a separate estate which is made subject to her sole control, the same as though she were unmarried, unless she can put it to the same uses that an unmarried woman might? An unmarried woman has the same legal capacity, the same right of control over her own property, if of full age, as a man may have. * * * In Mitchell v. Carpenter, 50 Ill. 470, the court said: 'It may be said that a married woman cannot adequately enjoy her separate property unless she can make contracts in regard to it. This is true, and hence her power to make contracts so far as may be necessary for the use and enjoyment of her property must be regard-

ed as resulting by implication from the ... If she owns houses, she must be permit... contract for their repair or rental. If she ... a farm, she must be permitted to bargain ... its cultivation and to dispose of its produc... Cookson v. Toole, 59 Ill. 520, 521.

The Supreme Court of Maine held that ... statutory right of a married woman to "... age" real estate included the power to ... mit to arbitration a question of damage the... to. In so holding, the court said:

"To manage property is (vide Webster Dict.) to conduct the concerns of it; and ... power to manage it must of necessity inclu... the power to make valid contracts respecti... it, by means of which she could acquire rig... against those dealing with her in relation ... it." Duren v. Getchell, 55 Me. 248.

In Frecking v. Rolland, the New Io... Court of Appeals said:

"The statute of March 2, 1860, 'concern... the rights and liabilities of married wom... provides that a married woman may carry ... any trade or business or perform any la... or services on her sole and separate accou... and that the earnings therefrom shall be ... sole and separate property. The power of ... married woman to make contracts relating ... her separate business is incident to the po... to conduct it. It cannot be supposed that the Legislature, while conferring the power up... a married woman to enter into trade or bu... ness on her own account, intended that ... common-law disability to bind herself by c... tract should continue as to contracts made ... carrying on the business in which she ... permitted to engage. The power to engage ... business would be a barren and useless ... disconnected with the right to conduct it ... the way and by the means usually employed." 53 N. Y. 425.

The power granted by the statute to Mr... McMahan to manage and control the sto... building, belonging to her separate esta... and the rents to be derived therefro... carried with it the incidental and coll... eral power to make a contract with he... tenant to repair the store building and ... employ others to make needed repairs. She would be liable for the breach of her contra... and for the proximate results of negligen... on the part of those employed by her, witho... protection from her coverture.

We answer to the question certified tha... plaintiff's petition was not subject to a ge... eral demurrer in behalf of Mrs. McMaha...

MILLS et al. v. MILLS. (No. 3271; Motion No. 5091.)*

(Supreme Court of Texas. June 1, 1921.)

1. Appeal and error ⟷1082(2) — Supreme Court is without jurisdiction of assignments of error not passed upon by Court of Civil Appeals.

Where the Court of Civil Appeals in its disposition of the case did not consider assignments of error presented by appellants relating to certain testimony, the Supreme Court is without jurisdiction of such assignments.

2. Appeal and error ⟷1114—Judgment remanding to district court modified to one remanding to Court of Civil Appeals which failed to pass on certain assignments.

Where the Supreme Court has reversed judgment of Court of Civil Appeals and remanded the cause of the district court, and it is learned that the Court of Civil Appeals did not pass on certain assignments regarding testimony, the judgment remanding to the district court will be changed to a remand to the Court of Civil Appeals.

Error to Court of Civil Appeals of Fifth Supreme Judicial District.

On rehearing. Plaintiffs' and defendant's motions for rehearing overruled. Former judgment (228 S. W. 919) reversing judgment of Court of Civil Appeals (206 S. W. 100) permitted to stand, but the remand to the district court is changed to a remand to the Court of Civil Appeals for consideration of assignments of error on testimony questions.

Shurtleff & Cummings, of Breckenridge, and Chas. L. Black, of Austin, for plaintiffs in error.

Wear & Frazier and J. E. Clarke, all of Hillsboro, for defendant in error.

PHILLIPS, C. J. In approving the report of the Commission of Appeals in this case, and in accord with its recommendation, we originally reversed the judgment of the Court of Civil Appeals and remanded the case to the District Court for further trial.

[1] It has come to our attention that the Court of Civil Appeals in its disposition of the case did not consider certain assignments of error presented by the appellant there relating to the admissibility of certain testimony, but reversed the judgment of the District Court upon another and independent ground.

The Supreme Court is without jurisdiction of the assignments of error relating to this testimony, and the Court of Civil Appeals should not be denied the opportunity of determining them.

[2] Both motions for rehearing, filed respectively by the plaintiffs in error and the defendant in error, will be overruled. Our judgment reversing the judgment of the

Court of Civil Appeals will stand, but instead of the cause being remanded to the District Court, as was done originally, it will be remanded to the Court of Civil Appeals for its consideration of the assignments of error on the testimony questions.

GARZA et al. v. CITY OF SAN ANTONIO (No. 230–3409.)

(Commission of Appeals of Texas, Section B June 1, 1921.)

1. Taxation ⟷620—Delinquent taxes on tract assessed to husband cannot be enforced against part of the tract assessed in name of wife for part of period.

The taxes for ten years on five acres of land assessed as belonging to defendant's husband cannot be collected by foreclosing a tax lien for all of the taxes on two of the five acres assessed as the property of defendant for only six years.

2. Taxation ⟷643—To foreclose lien for delinquent taxes must allege and prove nonpayment.

In suits for taxes and foreclosure of liens therefor, it is essential to allege and prove nonpayment and consequent delinquency.

3. Taxation ⟷644—Assessment roll not proof of nonpayment of taxes.

In a suit to collect delinquent taxes, a mere copy of the assessment roll does not prove nonpayment.

4. Taxation ⟷644—Delinquent tax rolls are prima facie evidence of nonpayment of taxes.

The delinquent tax rolls required by Statutes, art. 7685 et seq., are prima facie evidence of nonpayment of taxes.

5. Appeal and error ⟷931(1)—No presumption evidence sufficient to support judgment by court without jury, where agreed statement of facts contains all the evidence.

In a suit for the collection of delinquent taxes tried by the court without a jury, there is no presumption that there was evidence sufficient to support the judgment, where there is an agreed statement of facts containing all the evidence; presumptions being indulged only in the absence of proof and not against proof.

6. Taxation ⟷647—Description of land ordered to be sold for taxes held insufficient.

In a suit to foreclose a lien for delinquent taxes, where the petition, in connection with the assessment roll, described the property as containing five acres, a judgment describing the land as consisting of two acres was not sufficient to identify the property with reasonable certainty; the portion ordered to be sold being left almost wholly to inference and conjecture.

7. Taxation ⟷615—In suit to recover delinquent taxes all legal requirements must be strictly complied with.

Where a state or municipality seeks to recover a judgment against a citizen for taxes, by virtue of which his property may be seized and sold, all legal requirements must be strictly complied with, and the rule applies with the same force to the description of the property in a judgment as to proof of nonpayment.

Appeal from Court of Civil Appeals of Fourth Supreme Judicial District.

Suit by the City of San Antonio against Carolina C. Garza and husband. From a judgment of the Court of Civil Appeals affirming a judgment for plaintiff (214 S. W. 488), defendants appeal. Reversed and remanded.

J. D. Childs, of San Antonio, for appellants.

J. H. Cunningham and R. J. McMillan, both of San Antonio, for appellee.

KITTRELL, J. This suit was brought to recover back taxes for many years on property described as follows:

"One tract of land described as old city lot No. A-6, new city block No. A-6, situated on Trueheart street, situated within the corporate limits of the city of San Antonio, in Bexar county, state of Texas."

It is alleged that said defendant Carolina C. Garza is now, and was for the fiscal years mentioned, the owner of the hereinafter described property, and the description is given as above set forth.

The description on unrendered roll for 1899 is as follows: 1 tract city block A-6 32x140, five acres Trueheart Street, Land 5000, Imp. 3000, total value $8000. That for 1900 (unrendered) is 1 tract city block A-6 E. S. Trueheart Street, five acres, and the same description and same value as that of 1900 is used as the basis of assessment on down to and including 1908, or nine years.

For all the years from 1899 to 1908, both inclusive, ten years, the property is assessed as belonging to Leonardo Garza. In the assessment blank or roll for 1908 are these words: "For 1909 trans. to Carolina Garza."

In 1909 the property was rendered by Leonardo Garza for Carolina Garza by the following description: 1 tract city block A-6 E. S. Trueheart Street. Feet front 2 acres, former value land $5000, Imp. $3000. Present value land $2000, Imp. $3000. Total value $5000. On the assessment blank or roll are these words: "In 1908 Tract C. B. A-6 Ass'd to Leonardo Garza, Sr., 12/22."

The assessment for 1910 (unrendered) is in the name of Carolina C. Garza by the following description: 1 tract city block A-6 E. S. Trueheart 2 acres land $3000, Imp. $3050. Total value $6050.

The property was unrendered for 1911. The description was the same. Total value $6000. Carolina C. Garza named as owner.

The assessment in 1912 as to owner, description, and value was the same as for 1911.

For 1913 Carolina C. Garza is named as owner, and the rendition was by Leonardo Garza as 1 tract city block A-6 E. S. Trueheart. Feet front 2 acres, Land $3000. Imp. $3000. Total value $6000.

For 1914 Carolina C. Garza is named as owner, and the property is described as follows:

Lot No. 1, tract A-2 City block A-6 E. S. Ave. D. Feet front 2 acres. Former value land $3000. Imp. $200.

Present value land $7170 Imp. I. D.
                                   8180 $2040 5
  Total value   10220

The taxes alleged to be due and alleged not to have been paid were for the several years stated as follows: For 1899, $136.00; 1900, $136.00; 1901, $133.60; 1903, $116.40; 1902, $133.60; 1903, $140.00; 1904, $145.70; 1905, $135.60; 1906, $135.40; 1907, $128.40.

It will have been seen from the statement above made that up to and including 1908 the property described on the assessment blank or roll was assessed as belonging to Leonardo Garza, and the quantity was given as five acres. For and including 1909 down to and including 1914 the property was assessed as belonging to Carolina C. Garza, and the quantity was named as two acres. The taxes alleged to be due and unpaid for the respective years after 1908 are in the amounts as follows: For 1909, $71.35; 1910, $87.40; 1911, $92.88; 1912, $98.88; 1913, $92.80; 1914, $148.76.

Judgment was rendered against Carolina C. Garza, joined pro forma by her husband, Leonardo Garza, for the taxes on—

"that certain tract of land fronting on Trueheart street, within the corporate limits of the city of San Antonio, Bexar county, Tex., and situated in city block A-6, consisting of two acres of land."

The amount of taxes named in the judgment is, for each year from 1899 to 1914, both inclusive, exactly the amounts alleged in the petition.

It was further adjudged that the plaintiffs recover of Carolina C. Garza, joined pro forma by her husband, Leonardo Garza, Sr., penalties at the rate of 10 per centum per annum, and interest at the rate of 6 per centum per annum, etc., for the fiscal years 1899 to and inclusive of the fiscal year 1914, in the total amount of $3,195.59.

[1] As has been shown, from 1899 till and including 1908 the property was assessed for taxes as five acres belonging to Leonardo Garza, while from 1909 to and including 1914 it was assessed and taxed as two acres belonging to Carolina C. Garza, plaintiff in error; yet judgment for the entire taxes, penalties, and interest was rendered against plaintiff in error, and her two acres ordered to be sold for the payment of the taxes on the entire five acres, including those which accrued for ten years, before, so far as the

record reveals, she had any interest in any part of the property.

Such rendition of judgment is not, in direct terms, made the basis of complaint in the application; but attention is called to it, to the end that the error may not be again made.

Assuming, for the purpose of argument, that the description·is sufficient, and that proof of nonpayment of the taxes had been made, it is clear to our minds that the taxes for ten years on five acres of land belonging to Leonardo Garza cannot be collected by foreclosing a tax lien for all of the taxes on two acres, which, so far as the record reveals, had been assessed as the property of Carolina Garza for only six years.

[2, 3] The first assignment of error in the application is, in substance, that in suits for taxes and foreclosure of liens therefor it is essential to recovery to not only allege but prove the nonpayment and consequent delinquency. The proposition is sound, and the assignment is well taken.

There is not a word of testimony in the statement of facts to the effect that the taxes had not been paid, nor is there any evidence, direct or inferential, that the taxes on the other part of the five acres had been paid.

The statement of facts consists of two parts: First, certified copies of assessments for the several years, as above set forth. Second, certified copies of the various ordinances which were from year to year enacted by the city council, under and by virtue of which the property was assessed for taxation.

Manifestly a mere copy of the assessment roll does not prove nonpayment. The real defendant, Carolina Garza, and the nominal defendant, Leonardo Garza, both filed denial of the allegations of the petition, and thereby the plaintiffs were put to the necessity of proving nonpayment.

In Clegg v. State, 42 Tex. 611, Justice Moore said:

"The bare fact of the assessment of· the tax" does not "authorize suit for its collection. This cannot be done until the taxpayer is in default by his failure to pay."

It is fundamental and elementary that, having alleged nonpayment as an essential prerequisite to recovery, the plaintiffs were bound to prove the allegation.

In Henderson v. White, 69 Tex. 104, 5 S. W. 374, Chief Justice Willie said:

"It should be made clear that the taxes had not been paid," and the fact should not "be left to inference or conjecture."

[4] It has been held in this state that when the delinquent tax rolls required by statute (Rev. St. 1911, art. 7685 et seq.) to be made out are offered in evidence, they are prima facie evidence of nonpayment (Rouse v. State, 54 S. W. 32; Watkins v. State, 61 S. W. 532);

but no such delinquent rolls are offered in evidence. Indeed, there is absolutely no evidence except the copies of the assessments and of the ordinances.

[5] Defendants in error in their brief present the contention that it will be presumed there was evidence sufficient to support the judgment when the case is tried before the court without a jury. The proposition is sound when there is no statement of facts, but where there is a statement of facts which (as in the present case) it is agreed contains all the evidence heard, we cannot presume that to be a fact which the record before us shows is not a fact. As is said in Withers v. Patterson, 27 Tex. 496, 86 Am. Dec. 643:

"Presumptions are indulged in the absence of proof and not against proof."

[6] The second assignment of error is to the effect that the description of the property on the assessment rolls in the petition and in the judgment is insufficient to identify the property. The proposition presents a question by no means free from difficulty. The property is described in the petition as:

"One tract of land described as old city block No. A–6, new city block A–6, situated on Trueheart street. situated within the corporate limits of the city of San Antonio, Bexar county, state of Texas."

That description is definite, and the mean ing it conveys is that old city block A–6 and new city block A–6 are the same, and that the whole block was meant; and when read in connection with the assessment it meant the block contained five acres.

The description in the judgment is:

"That certain tract of land fronting on Trueheart street, within the corporate limits of the city of San Antonio, Bexar county, Tex., and situated in city block A–6, consisting of two acres of land."

The inquiry inevitably suggested is, "What two acres?" and the record furnishes no answer.

Repeatedly the property is described in the assessment as "city block A–6, east side Trueheart street, five acres," but there is nothing in the statement of facts or in the judgment to show what two acres of the five were foreclosed on and ordered to be sold. There are no means of identification pointed out or furnished by the evidence before us.

In the case of Henderson v. White, 69 Tex. 104, 5 S. W. 374, the land was assessed as 160 acres belonging to unknown owners. One Heath paid half the taxes due. The deed under which appellant claimed purported to convey to his grantor all the 160 acres except what Heath had paid the taxes on.

The Supreme Court says:

"It is impossible to tell what particular portion of the land was sold for the half of the taxes that were unpaid. * * * We do not know, except from conjecture or inference, that Heath paid taxes upon a portion of the land owned by himself. * * * Such doubts should not exist in the case of a tax sale. If land is sold for the taxes due upon it, there should be no doubt that the land sold and the land assessed are identically the same; and, further, it should be made clear that the taxes had not been paid, and neither of these facts should be left to inference or conjecture."

As has been said, the description in the petition, taken in connection with the assessment up to and including 1908, indicates that city lot No. A–6 contained five acres, while the decree refers to two acres in city block A—6, but what two acres is left wholly to "inference and conjecture."

In the opinion of the Court of Civil Appeals the cases of Slaughter v. City of Dallas, 101 Tex. 315, 107 S. W. 48, and City of San Antonio v. Terrill, 202 S. W. 361, are cited. We have carefully examined both cases; also the case of Hermann v. Likens, 90 Tex. 448, 39 S. W. 282, cited in the Slaughter Case. Both of the cases involved suits for taxes, and the defense was based on invalidity of the assessments for want of sufficient description. The description in both cases was, under the facts, held to be sufficient, and we see no reason to question the correctness of the holding; but in the instant case we are not called upon to pass upon the question of the validity or invalidity of assessments.

The question presented in the record before us is whether the judgment of foreclosure identifies the land foreclosed on as the land described in the petition.

It is necessary, of course, to examine the assessments as they appear in the statement of facts, and when we do so we find that for ten years the property was assessed as five acres, the property of Leonardo Garza, and at the end of that time and for six years later is assessed against plaintiff in error as two acres, but no deed or any parol testimony is offered to show what two acres is meant, and the two acres are not described by lines, or shape or boundaries of contiguous lots or blocks, or in any other way that would enable any purchaser to segregate them from the rest of the five acres. The law applicable to the question is stated in 37 Cyc. p. 1313, as follows:

"The tax judgment * * * in particular must contain such a description of land affected as will suffice to identify it with reasonable certainty, and the description must correspond with that in the petition at least so far as to show that the same tract or parcel of land was intended."

It is obvious that the judgment in the record before us does not meet such requirement, nor are there in this case, as there was in each of the cases referred to above, any, so to speak, assisting facts or data to so guide and direct any person as to enable him to locate the lines and boundaries of the two acres which were part of the five which were assessed as the property of Leonardo Garza.

[7] We are of the opinion that the description in the judgment is wholly insufficient, in that what land is foreclosed on and ordered to be sold is left almost wholly to "inference and conjecture." It is established law that where the state or any municipality resorts to the courts to recover a judgment against a citizen for taxes, by virtue of which the property of the citizen may be seized and sold, all legal requirements must be strictly complied with. Henderson v. White, supra.

As has been held by the Court of Errors and Appeals of New Jersey:

"Statutes derogatory to the rights of property, or that take away the estate of a citizen, are to be construed strictly." Taxpayers' Protective Ass'n v. Kirkpatrick, 40 N. J. Eq. 56, 41 N. J. Eq. 347, 7 Atl. 631.

The rule of law so laid down applies with the same force to the matter of a description in a judgment as it does to the matter of proof of nonpayment of the taxes sued for.

We recommend that the judgments of the district court and Court of Civil Appeals be reversed, and the case be remanded to the district court to be tried in accordance with this opinion.

PHILLIPS, C. J. The judgment recommended in the report of the Commission of Appeals is adopted, and will be entered as the judgment of the Supreme Court.

We approve the holding of the Commission of Appeals on the questions discussed in its opinion.

CAWTHORN v. CITY OF HOUSTON.
(No. 233-3416.)

(Commission of Appeals of Texas, Section B.
June 1, 1921.)

1. Municipal corporations ⬦⇒742(4)—Requirement of 90 days' notice of injury to mayor and council must be alleged if applicable, unless waived, or the city estopped.

Under Houston City Charter, art. 9, § 11, requiring a party injured in person or property to give the mayor and council written notice thereof within 90 days, notice is a condition precedent to right of action, so that plaintiffs, suing the city, must affirmatively allege the prescribed notice, if applicable to the facts pleaded, unless the city has waived the charter provisions or become estopped by its officers' actions from asserting it.

2. Municipal corporations ⬦⇒741(1)—Charter requiring injured party to give 90 days' notice to mayor and council before beginning suit upheld.

The provision of Houston City Charter, art. 9, § 11, requiring persons injured by the city to give the mayor and council notice within 90 days thereafter, will be upheld, and must be strictly complied with, and is only a prerequisite to the assertion in court of a claim of liability by the injured party.

3. Municipal corporations ⬦⇒741(1)—Charter provision requiring notice within 90 days after injury applies to one injured while hauling sand for city.

In a personal injury action against the city, where the negligence complained of resulted in the caving in of a sand bank upon the plaintiff while he was hauling sand for the city, Houston City Charter, art. 9, § 11, requiring giving of notice to mayor and council within 90 days after injury, is applicable.

4. Municipal corporations ⬦⇒741(1)—Requirement of notice of injury applies to city employees.

The provision of Houston City Charter, art. 9, § 11, before suing the city within 90 days after personal injury, that party shall have the mayor and city council notified of the injury, is in derogation of common law, and should be construed with reasonable strictness, and applies to city employees as well as others.

5. Municipal corporations ⬦⇒733(1)—In hauling sand and adjusting damages for injuries to one therein engaged, the city acts in its proprietary capacity.

In hauling sand with its teams and distributing it generally, the city of Houston was undoubtedly acting in its proprietary capacity, and in adjusting claims for damages arising therefrom it continues to act in that capacity, and the courts recognized the distinction between proprietary and governmental capacity.

6. Municipal corporations ⬦⇒741(3)—Mayor and council may waive strict compliance with provision requiring notice of personal injury before bringing suit.

The mayor and commissioners of the city of Houston are not prohibited from waiving

the requirement of Charter, art. 9, § 11, that a party injured through the city's negligence must notify the mayor and city council within 90 days thereof as a prerequisite to bringing suit, and they should be permitted to do so, a waiver being the voluntary relinquishment of a known right.

7. Municipal corporations ⬦⇒742(6)—Whether city commissioner waived strict compliance with charter provision for notice of personal injury held a jury question.

In an action against the City of Houston for personal injuries, whether the acts of a commissioner, acting for the mayor and council, constituted a waiver of strict compliance with Houston Charter, art. 9, § 11, requiring notice to mayor and council of personal injury within 90 days as a prerequisite to a suit, is a question which plaintiff was entitled to have submitted to the jury.

8. Municipal corporations ⬦⇒741(3)—A commissioner as agent for commissioners and mayor may waive strict compliance with charter provision.

A city commissioner, being authorized by the mayor and commissioners to approach a claimant for personal injuries and offer him a compromise and invite him to their office to discuss it, may be deemed authorized to waive strict compliance with Houston City Charter, art. 9, § 11, requiring notice.

9. Municipal corporations ⬦⇒741(3)—City held estopped by conduct of its officers from requiring strict compliance with charter provision.

Whether or not the mayor and council intended to waive strict compliance with Houston City Charter, art. 9, § 11, requiring notice within 90 days after injury, where the mayor and commissioners, through their agent, one of the commissioners, so conducted themselves so as to lull claimant into a sense of security and cause him to think they were waiving such charter provision, the city is estopped to assert noncompliance therewith.

Error to Court of Civil Appeals of Ninth Supreme Judicial District.

Action by J. H. Cawthorn against the City of Houston. From a judgment sustaining a general demurrer to plaintiff's petition, the plaintiff appealed to the Court of Civil Appeals, which affirmed the judgment (212 S. W. 796), and the plaintiff brings error. Judgments of the district court and Court of Civil Appeals reversed, and cause remanded to the former for trial in conformity with opinion.

Rowe & Kay, of Houston, for plaintiff in error.

W. J. Howard, of Houston, for defendant in error.

POWELL, J. This is an action in damages, instituted in the district court of Harris county, Tex., by J. H. Cawthorn against the city of Houston, in which the plaintiff sought judgment in the sum of $30,000 for alleged personal injuries sustained by him on or about June

13, 1916, as the result of defendant's negligence. The original petition is copied in full in the opinion of the Court of Civil Appeals, and no useful purpose would be subserved by recital of details here, especially as they have no important bearing upon the controlling questions on this appeal. Suffice it to say that Cawthorn was an employee of the city, driving a wagon which was engaged in hauling sand from a sand bank belonging to said city, and distributing such sand to various parts of the municipality as needed; that, while loading his wagon one day, the sand bank caved in on him, resulting in his serious injury. The petition was in the usual form of an action for damages for personal injuries resulting from negligence.

The defendant in error interposed the following demurrers to plaintiff's original petition, to wit:

"I. Now come the defendants, and with leave of court file this their first amended original answer, and as in their original answer demur to plaintiff's petition that the same shows no cause of action against them, and of this they pray judgment.

"II. For further demurrer those defendants would show that by the provisions of section 11, article IX, of the City Charter of the City of Houston, it is provided that as a condition precedent to liability notice of claim for damages shall be given the city as therein provided, and plaintiff's petition wholly fails to show any such notice was given."

Section 11 of article 9 of the charter of said city just referred to, and which is all important in this opinion, reads as follows:

"Sec. 11. Before the city of Houston shall be liable for damages for personal injuries of any kind, or for injuries to or destruction of property of any kind, the person injured, or the owner of the property injured or destroyed, or some one in his behalf, shall give the mayor and city council notice in writing of such injury or destruction, duly verified, within ninety days after the same has been sustained, stating in such written notice when, where, and how the injury or destruction occurred, and the apparent extent thereof, the amount of damages sustained, the amount for which claimant will settle, the actual residence of the claimant by street and number at the date the claim is presented, and the actual residence of such claimant for six months immediately preceding the occurrence of such injuries or destruction, and the names and addresses of the witnesses upon whom he relies to establish his claim, and a failure to so notify the mayor and city council within the time and manner specified herein shall exonerate, excuse, and exempt the city from any liability whatsoever. * * *"

The city, also, in its answer, specially pleaded the provisions of said section of the city charter, and alleged failure on the part of Cawthorn to comply therewith, and denied any liability to him in consequence of such failure.

By way of replication to said demurrers and plea of defendants in error Cawthorn pleaded as follows:

"I. That the provisions of the city charter of the city of Houston pleaded by the defendant in paragraph 11 of its said answer have no application to an injury such as sustained by the plaintiff, wherein the acts of the defendant were the direct and proximate cause of said injury as set forth by plaintiff in his original petition.

"II. That the provisions of the City Charter of the City of Houston pleaded by the defendant in paragraphs I, II and III of said answer were waived as a condition precedent or a prerequisite to the defendant's liability in this cause, because the defendant, acting by its authorized agents and one of its commissioners, Matt Drenan, shortly after the plaintiff had sustained the injuries complained of in his original petition, and within ninety days after said injuries were inflicted, knowing and being fully advised as to the cause, nature, and extent of the plaintiff's injuries, visited the plaintiff for the purpose of offering, and did offer, to the plaintiff a written instrument for the plaintiff to sign, which paper related to the injuries of plaintiff and compensation in money to plaintiff by reason thereof, with authority from the mayor and commissioners so to do, and also said commissioners invited plaintiff to appear before the commissioners while in session with a view of adjusting and settling for a consideration said injuries, and which the plaintiff attempted to do, but was unable to get said commissioners together at the time agreed upon although the said mayor and commissioners, at various and sundry times, agreed to take up the plaintiff's claim, and see what could be done for him, all of which was within 90 days from the infliction of said injuries, and then and thereby the defendant waived said notice, and became estopped from the operation thereof in its favor.

"III. Plaintiff, further pleading herein, says that defendants are estopped from now here pleading the said charter provision requiring the plaintiff to give the said ninety days' notice of his claim for injuries, as alleged by him:

"1st. By reason of the facts alleged in his petition.

"2d. By reason of the foregoing facts herein alleged.

"3d. This plaintiff here and now alleges that said defendant's officers, knowing of plaintiff's injury as alleged, and knowing his ignorance of said charter provision, through its officers, Matt Drenan, one of its commissioners, and other officers and agents of the defendant city of Houston, fraudulently put the plaintiff off from time to time, leading him to believe that they would compensate him for the injury sustained by him, until said ninety days had expired from the date of said injury, and by reason of which said facts the said defendant city of Houston, and its officers, defendants herein, are now here estopped from pleading said charter provision or now claiming any benefit or right thereunder."

Upon consideration of the pleadings above outlined, the city's general demurrer was sustained. Cawthorn failed to amend, and the court dismissed his suit. Plaintiff in error prosecuted his appeal to the Court of Civil Appeals, which court affirmed the judgment of the trial court. See 212 S. W. 796.

Cawthorn, in due course, filed application in the Supreme Court for writ of error, which was granted.

[1] The charter of the city of Houston is a special one, granted by the Legislature of Texas, and its provisions have the same effect as other statutes of the state, and the public, as well as the courts, must take notice of them. The section in question is a condition precedent to the right of action, and it is incumbent on the plaintiff to affirmatively allege the giving of the prescribed notice. See Dillon on Municipal Corporations (5th Ed.), § 1618; City of Dallas v. Shows, 212 S. W. 633.

It was necessary, therefore, to plead compliance with this provision, if the latter applied to a state of facts as pleaded here, unless said provision of the charter was waived by the city, or the latter was estopped from asserting it by reason of the action of its officers. Did it so apply?

[2] It is conceded by all parties hereto that charter provisions like the one now under discussion, and which obtain in practically all the larger cities, have been uniformly upheld. Not only so, but the higher courts have, almost without exception, required strict compliance therewith. Numerous authorities from all the states could be cited, but we content ourselves with referring to a few in Texas, as follows: Parsons v. City of Ft. Worth, 26 Tex. Civ. App. 273, 63 S. W. 889; Luke v. City of El Paso (Civ. App.) 60 S. W. 363; English v. City of Ft. Worth (Civ. App.) 152 S. W. 179; City of Ft. Worth v. Shero, 16 Tex. Civ. App. 487, 41 S. W. 704 (writ of error denied by the Supreme Court); City of Dallas v. Shows, 212 S. W. 633.

McQuillin on Municipal Corporations, § 2715, says in this connection:

"Such requirements are enacted in furtherance of the public policy, and their object and purpose is to protect the municipality from the expense of needless litigation, and give it the opportunity for investigation, and allow it to adjust differences and settle claims without suit."

This eminent authority might have added, as some others do, that such provisions also enable the cities to get their proof in hand before the witnesses scatter, and while the facts are fresh in their minds. In other words, such notice aids the governing boards of cities to know the facts and to pay claims without suit, where just, or to conserve the evidence for litigation where that becomes necessary. After all, such notice does not affect the question of liability of the city for its acts. It is only a prerequisite to even the assertion in court of a claim of liability by the injured party.

[3] But while conceding that, as a general rule, this provision of the charter is applicable and should be enforced, Cawthorn contends that it does not apply in his case for two reasons: (1) That the negligence complained of was the act of the city itself, and notice was unnecessary; (2) that the city was acting in its proprietary, as distinguished from its governmental, capacity, and is liable to Cawthorn as an employee, just as a private employer would be.

Let us consider said contentions in their order. Counsel for Cawthorn seriously urged that, under the decision of the Supreme Court of Texas in case of City of Houston v. Isaacks, 68 Tex. 116, 3 S. W. 693, the provision of the charter now under discussion does not apply to a case where the injury is the result of an act of the city itself. The case of Houston v. Isaacks, supra, announced a correct principle of law, and has been often followed by the higher courts of Texas. However, the first case in which the Court of Civil Appeals of this state so construed said authority as to uphold the contention now being urged by Cawthorn was the case of Shows v. City of Dallas (Civ. App.) 172 S. W. 1137. A writ of error was granted by the Supreme Court in this case. The opinion therein was later written by Presiding Judge Sonfield, of Section A of the Commission of Appeals. See City of Dallas v. Shows, 212 S. W. 633. In that opinion the court says:

"The provision in defendant's charter requiring notice of the injury as a condition precedent to a suit for such injury is valid. It is wholly immaterial that the injury was the result of the act of the city itself. City of Houston v. Isaacks, 68 Tex. 116, 3 S. W. 693, does not hold otherwise. In that case the court had under consideration a charter provision to the effect that the city should not be liable to any person for damages caused from the defective condition of streets, ways, crossings, etc., unless same remained in such condition ten days after special notice in writing given to the mayor or street commissioner. The court held such notice unnecessary when the defect was caused by the action of the city itself. The question therein involved was notice of the defect, not of an injury the result of such defect."

The Commission of Appeals in the case just quoted further held that, even though the injury was the act of the city itself, injuries to the person cannot be recovered unless a provision of a city charter similar to the one at bar has been complied with.

This recommendation of the Commission of Appeals was adopted by the Supreme Court, and said holding approved by the latter. Consequently this contention of Cawthorn's must be overruled.

[4] The next inquiry is whether or not injuries to employees, as distinguished from the public generally, are within the requirement of the charter provision in question. We have carefully reviewed all the authori-

ties cited, and made considerable independent investigation. We find no authority sustaining Cawthorn's contention in this connection. In attempting to construe provisions like the one now being considered, we are in complete accord with Section A of the Commission of Appeals in the case of City of Dallas v. Shows, supra, when that court says:

"The requirement of notice of injury as a condition precedent to an action, while valid and in accord with sound public policy, is in derogation of common right, and should therefore be construed with reasonable strictness, and not extended by implication beyond its own terms, or held to apply to such damages as are not within its clear intent. 28 Cyc. 1450."

The language of the provision is all inclusive, and broad enough to cover personal injuries to any one. Reading all the provisions of said section, separately and in connection with each other, we think the article covers and includes injuries to employees as well as others. Not only so, but there would seem to be as much reason for requiring this notice of employees as of others. It is true the employee works for the city, and some of the authorities of the city would be more likely to have independent knowledge of his injuries than of accidents to outsiders. But in most cases the mayor and commissioners, who alone have power to settle claims for damages, do not know the employees personally. Furthermore, this article of the city charter requires much more information than the mere happening of the accident and the time and place thereof. We think employees are within the provision of the charter, and this contention of Cawthorn's should also be overruled.

Counsel for Cawthorn seems to confuse the article of the charter in question with another article of said charter, which requires notice of defects in sidewalks, and which does actually affect the liability of the city upon a trial of a case in court on its merits. The article in question has nothing to do with the determination of the liability of the city upon the trial of a case on its merits. For that reason, if a city should be liable to its employees just as a private employer is, that would have nothing to do with the section of the charter now under discussion.

[5] We think the Court of Civil Appeals in this case correctly held this provision of the charter applicable to the case at bar, and that the general demurrer was properly sustained by the trial court, unless the city had waived strict compliance therewith, or had so acted as to be estopped from demanding it of Cawthorn as a condition precedent to his right to bring this suit.

Upon these latter points the Court of Civil Appeals held: (1) It had serious doubts whether or not any of the officers of the city of Houston had authority to waive this provision in its charter; (2) if it had such authority, the waiver must be by the mayor and commissioners, and not by one commissioner alone; (3) that the action of Commissioner Drennan was not a waiver of the provision of the charter, but only an invitation to Cawthorn to present his claim to the council as by law provided.

The Court of Civil Appeals cites no authority to sustain any of said rulings nor does the city of Houston do so. The important inquiry, then, in that connection, is whether or not the doctrine of waiver and estoppel can be applied to municipalities and their governing boards in a state of facts like those at bar. The courts of last resort in several states have answered this inquiry in the affirmative, within certain bounds. We call attention to a few of such authorities. The Supreme Court of Illinois in the case of City of Chicago v. Sexton, 115 Ill. 230, 2 N. E. 263, says:

"We hold simply that a municipal corporation may be estopped by the action of its proper officers, when the corporation is acting in its private, as contradistinguished from its governmental, capacity, and has lawful power to do the act."

Again, the Supreme Court of Nebraska, in the case of Trust Co. v. City of Omaha, 63 Neb. 280, 88 N. W. 523, 93 Am. St. Rep. 442, says:

"The correct rule, therefore, is, and should be, that the doctrine can be appealed to effectively, as against a municipal corporation, only when it is acting in its private as contradistinguished from its public or governmental capacity. There may be, and probably are, exceptions to the rule stated, as when a municipality has gained a clear and decided advantage by the act relied on to operate as an estoppel, and equity will prevent it from retaining the advantage, and at the same time deny its binding force."

The Supreme Court of Texas is in accord with the Nebraska decision just quoted, as will be seen from its opinion in the case of Krause et al. v. City of El Paso, 101 Tex. 216, 106 S. W. 121, 14 L. R. A. (N. S.) 582, 130 Am. St. Rep. 831. In that case certain individuals owned a brick house located on a triangular lot in the business portion of the city of El Paso, and the building encroached on the street. However, it had been erected after the owners had complied with the ordinance covering erections of buildings and laying out of street lines. The owners had also built sidewalks along the said building lines, as demanded by the city authorities. After many years, the city ordered the removal of said building, as it was in the street. The district court and the Court of Civil Appeals sustained the city's contention. Justice Brown, writing the opinion in this case said:

"To justify a reversal of the judgments of the Court of Civil Appeals and district court it must appear that the city was estopped to claim the ground as a part of the public highway, or that the facts show that the city had abandoned the use of that part of the street. The defendants in error submit the proposition that a municipal corporation cannot convey the public streets of a city to private individuals for private use. Therefore the title to the streets cannot pass from the corporation to the citizen by estoppel."

Again, he said:

"Ordinarily a municipal corporation is not subject to estoppel by reason of the negligent or unauthorized acts of its officers, but it is generally recognized that there are exceptions to that rule."

Still further he said:

"Why should a municipal corporation, which has led a citizen into error and caused him to expend large sums of money in the erection of permanent improvements upon a portion of the highway, after 20 years' occupancy, be permitted to destroy the improvements without compensation, simply to assert a legal right? A sense of justice common to all civilized people revolts at such a rule of legalized wrong."

The Supreme Court, in the case just quoted, reversed the judgment of the lower court, and perpetually enjoined the city of El Paso from removing said house from its then location. It applied the doctrine of estoppel in said case.

It will be seen from the above opinion that in Texas the doctrine of estoppel not only applies generally where the city is acting in its proprietary capacity, but also by reason of the negligence or unauthorized acts of its officers, where the equities of the situation demand it.

In the light of the above authorities, let us now consider their application to the case at bar. In hauling sand with its own teams and distributing it generally over the city, the latter was undoubtedly acting in its proprietary capacity, and in adjusting claims for damages arising therefrom it continues to act in that capacity. The courts of Texas recognize the distinction aforesaid between the capacities in which a city acts. The Supreme Court in the case of Ostrom v. City of San Antonio, 94 Tex. 523, 62 S. W. 909, speaks as follows:

"A municipal corporation proper—a city, for example—acts in a twofold capacity, certain functions are conferred upon it in the interest of the public at large and certain others for the peculiar advantage of its own inhabitants. For the unlawful acts of its officers in performing functions of the former class, the corporation is held, as a rule, not to be responsible; but for their torts in discharging duties of purely corporate character, the corporation is liable."

In the case just quoted the Supreme Court held that the cleaning of the city streets and

disposal of garbage is not the performance of a duty primarily resting on the state, but is the exercise of a corporate power, as distinguished from a governmental function, for the abuse of which the city is liable.

[6] The mayor and commissioners of the city of Houston are vested with broad general powers. They have the right to do everything in the management of the city's affairs which is not prohibited by its charter. They alone have authority to adjust and settle claims for damages against the city. The provision in question is one of procedure only, and is but an aid to the mayor and commissioners in passing upon the liability of the city in any given case. Whether or not they could waive this provision after the 90 days had expired we do not say. We doubt it. But they are not prohibited from waiving it during the 90 days' period. The charter does not prohibit a waiver at any time. If the mayor and commissioners are willing to investigate a given case themselves, and attempt to compromise the same during the 90 days period, we see no reason why they should not be permitted to do so. The provision is solely for their convenience. We think they can waive strict compliance with this provision. A waiver, in law, is the voluntary relinquishment of a known right, and if, under the facts, a jury can say that the mayor and commissioners intended to waive strict compliance with this provision, such compliance would not be necessary as a condition precedent to the maintenance of this suit for damages. The question of waiver is ordinarily one for a jury, where intention of the parties is not clear. For a case in point, and a charge approved, see Railway Co. v. Hendricks, 49 Tex. Civ. App. 314, 108 S. W. 747, in which a writ of error was denied by the Supreme Court.

[7] We differ with the Court of Civil Appeals as to a reasonable interpretation of the acts of Drennan, as they apply to this question of waiver. We think the reasonable conclusion from it all is that a strict compliance with the charter provision was waived, if plaintiff's allegations were true, and only a partial compliance therewith in a reasonable time was the desire of the city. But, at any rate, Cawthorn was entitled to have the jury pass upon the facts and interpret the intention of the city officials therefrom.

[8] The Court of Civil Appeals say that it certainly cannot be held that one commissioner can waive this provision. That is not the point. Cawthorn alleges that Commissioner Drennan was authorized by the mayor and his colleagues to approach the claimant and offer him a compromise and invite him to their office to discuss it. The mayor and other commissioners could authorize Drennan to act for them. If he was their agent, they were all bound. It follows from what has been said that we think the Court

of Civil Appeals erred in its various holdings relative to the question of waiver.

[9] Again, the doctrine of estoppel applies to this case, in our opinion. No matter whether the mayor and commissioners intended to waive strict compliance with the charter provisions or not, we think the evidence raises the issue of estoppel. If, from the allegations of Cawthorn, the mayor and commissioners, through their agent, Drennan, so conducted themselves as to lull the claimant into a sense of security, causing him to think they were waiving said charter provision, and if an ordinarily prudent person, under the same or similar circumstances, would have so concluded, then the city is estopped to demand strict compliance with the charter provisions. If the allegations of Cawthorn are true, there is much reason to conclude that, as a matter of law, the city is estopped. But we rather think this question of estoppel, and all issues of fact in connection therewith, should be submitted to the jury under appropriate instructions for their determination.

This charter provision is hard enough, at best, on those who are injured by the city. It is in derogation of common right. City officers' must not act in such a way as to lead people into a trap, and cause them to delay strict compliance with the charter provision until the 90 days have expired.

We think the jury should be given a chance, upon a trial of the case, to pass upon the questions of waiver and estoppel as above outlined. If said issues are decided in favor of Cawthorn, then he can maintain his suit, without either pleading or proving strict compliance with said charter provision. As we view it, the general demurrer was erroneously sustained for the reasons hereinbefore set out.

Therefore we recommend that the judgments of the district court and the Court of Civil ·Appeals be reversed, and the cause remanded to the former for a trial in conformity with our views.

PHILLIPS, C. J. The judgment recommended in the report of the Commission of Appeals is adopted, and will be entered as the judgment of the Supreme Court.

We approve the holding of the Commission of Appeals on the questions discussed in its opinion.

─────────

HAUPT et al. v. MICHAELIS. *
(No. 232-3414.)

(Commission of Appeals of Texas, Section B. June 1, 1921.)

1. Wills ⊜=439—Intention of testator must control.

The intention of testator, if not inconsistent with some established rule of law or with public policy, must control in the construction of a will; and it is the duty of the defendants to ascertain such intention, and to give force and effect to the scheme that the testator had in his mind for the disposition of his estate.

2. Wills ⊜=488—Parol evidence inadmissible where will is free from doubt.

Where the instrument is free from doubt, and the intention of the testator is expressed with sufficient intelligence and clearness to make the will incapable of more than one construction, there is no need of parol evidence, and such evidence will not be admitted to show that the will did not express the intention of the testator.

3. Wills ⊜=488—Evidence of surrounding circumstances not admissible to contradict expressed intention.

Evidence of surrounding circumstances is inadmissible to show that testator's intention was different from that signified by him in the use of the words in the will.

4. Wills ⊜=488—Extrinsic evidence admissible where intent of testator ambiguous.

Where a will is ambiguous to the· extent that the intention of the testator cannot be ascertained from the language of the will itself, extrinsic evidence is admissible.

5. Wills ⊜=470—Intent of testator must be arrived at by considering entire will.

All parts of a will must be construed together, and the intention of the testator must be arrived at by considering the whole, and not from detached, segregated, and isolated words, sentences, or clauses.

6. Wills ⊜=460—Words or sentences may be transposed to show testator's intent.

In construing a will, words, clauses, or sentences, or even whole paragraphs, may be transposed to any extent with a view to show the intent of the testator.

7. Wills ⊜=441—Law at time of execution may be considered in determining intent.

The law at the time of the execution of a will may be considered in ascertaining testator's intent.

8. Evidence ⊜=65—Testator presumed to have known that in absence of will his children would inherit equally.

It is a matter of common knowledge that, in the absence of a will, all testator's children will inherit equally, and testator will be presumed to have known the law in that respect.

9. Wills ⊜=535—Holographic will construed to exclude one of testator's children.

Testator having six children, including a married daughter, who had a husband and two children, in his lifetime divided his lands into five parts, and made deeds, respectively, to the children other than the daughter, and in his will recited the fact of such division, and provided ·that L., the daughter's husband, and his two children should receive no part of his lands. The will further recited that the daughter was entirely incompetent, and ·had to be taken care of all her life. The daughter had lived in the home of testator for five years preceding testator's death. Her husband never visited her during that time, and she suffered from intense and continuous melancholia. *Held*, that it was the evident intent of testator to exclude the daughter from any interest in the land.

Error to Court of Civil Appeals of Fourth Supreme Judicial District.

Suit by G. B. Haupt and others against M. G. Michaelis. Judgment for plaintiffs was, on defendant's appeal, reversed in part and affirmed in part (212 S. W. 274), and plaintiffs bring error. Reversed on recommendation of the Commission of Appeals, and judgment of trial court affirmed.

Will G. Barber and T. J. Saunders, both of San Marcos, for plaintiffs in error.
W. W. Searcy, of Brenham, and R. E. McKie, of San Marcos, for defendant in error.

KITTRELL, J. This action as originally filed in the district court was in the form of trespass to try title, but the concrete question, as the case is presented to us, is, What is the proper construction of the holographic will of W. W. Haupt?

To the end that our opinion may be complete within itself, and that there may be no necessity to refer back to the original case out of which this appeal grew, we will set forth in condensed form the facts:

The will which we are called upon to construe bears no date, but was executed some time in 1905 or 1906, the exact time not being important to be known.

The maker of it died in 1907, but the son, who by common consent took charge of all his (the testator's) papers, seeing the will was not dated or witnessed, thought it had no validity as a will and it was not offered for probate until about seven years after the testator's death.

Its probate was contested, but the judgment admitting it to probate was sustained by the Court of Civil Appeals (212 S. W. 274), and writ of error was refused by the Supreme Court.

A guardian was appointed for one of the daughters of W. W. Haupt, Mrs. Alice Landers, who had become insane, and by order of the court her interest in the land, which is the subject of litigation in this proceeding, was sold to defendant in error. The daughter inherited one-sixth of the community interest of her mother, one-twelfth of the whole, and the purchaser (defendant in error) claimed that she took one-sixth of her father's one-half under his will. Therefore he, by his purchase under the sale by the guardian, got title to one-sixth of the whole. The remaining five heirs contended that their sister Mrs. Landers took no interest in the land under the will of her father.

Plaintiffs in the court below (plaintiffs in error here) obtained judgment in the district court, decreeing that Mrs. Landers took nothing under the will, and that they were adjudged entitled to recover one-twelfth of the land, which judgment was reversed by the Court of Civil Appeals, and defendant in error was adjudged to be entitled to one-sixth of the land instead of one-twelfth.

If, as plaintiffs in error contend, Mrs. Landers was excluded as a devisee by the will of her father then the judgment of the Court of Civil Appeals must be reversed. On the other hand, if she was included as a devisee by the terms of the will, its judgment must be affirmed.

The will of W. W. Haupt, as it appears in the statement of facts, is in terms as follows:

"As I am past my threescore years and ten, it becomes my duty to provide for the future.

"My land is all surrounded by fence which my son Lewis (and every one in the neighborhood knows it boundaries).

"I have already laid off my field in 50 acre lots and all the children have drawn shares and measured off and selected their lots and are satisfied with their selection. These are on the M. M. McCarver League. The balance of my land lies on the west end of the McCarver tract. Some, or in all on the McCarver tract 400 acres.

"That is held as pasture land and each heir should have an undivided interest in said pasture—as 150 acre on the West end of the McCarver league. As I expect the most of my children to build houses on West end of McCarver League, I desire that each one should occupy all the land necessary to accommodate the necessity of the land around the house.

"Their is one exception to this rule. I don't want A. P. Landers to ever have any interest whatever in any part of this land. Nor his two children, Willie & Johnnie. His wife, my daughter Alice, has lived with me five years and she is entirely incompetent to do anything & has to be taken care of all her life.

"My wife, Sarah Ann, as long as she lives must be provided from the products of this place, as far as it is able to do so, with all the necessaries & comforts of this life. I have a few dollars in the Wood National Bank, the Ed. Green First National Bank, both of San Marcos, and the Groos Bank of Kyle, all of which is at her disposal and mine. Now to sum up, there is not a child of mine, who would not spend the last dime for their mother's comfort. As for A. P. Landers I ask no favors from him and done want any. As for his two sons Willie & Johnnie, my children can give them money if they choose, but they must be deny any of my land.

                    "[Signed] W. W. Haupt."

There are certain facts material to be understood in order to properly interpret the above will, which facts we will state in as condensed form as is consistent with clearness. The testator had six children, two sons and four daughters, all of whom were grown and married.

One of the daughters, Mrs. Alice Landers, had a husband and two grown sons. Their family home was in Hopkins county, but for five years before the will was made she had been an inmate of the home of her parents in Hays county. She was the victim of intense melancholia, and lived as a recluse in her room. Though she had been raised in the neighborhood, she declined to see any of her former friends, and had no intercourse even with the members of her father's family. Her meals were carried to her room, and when addressed she replied only in monosyllables. She did not perform any of the duties of the household or assist in their performance. Her husband did not visit her during the entire five years, nor did either he or his and her sons contribute in any measure whatever to her support, but she was maintained entirely by her father.

While she was living in that way at her father's house the other five children divided the field which was on the McCarver tract, and consisted of about 250 acres into five equal parts, and it was testified by four of the plaintiffs, children of W. W. Haupt, that the division was made by their father's direction, and that the reason he gave for dividing it into five parts instead of six was that if any of it was given to Mrs. Landers she would get no benefit from it, and it would be the same as giving it to her husband and sons, and he did not want them to have any of it; that she had been in his house for five years, and was unable to attend to any business, and would have to be taken care of the rest of her life.

It is shown by record evidence that the testator ratified and confirmed the division by making a deed, in which his wife joined, to each child for the land he or she had drawn in the division, making five such deeds, none of which was made to Mrs. Landers.

With the title to the 250 acres standing in that condition the will was made. After her father's death Mrs. Landers was, pursuant to medical advice, placed in a sanitarium in San Antonio where persons afflicted with nervous and mental ailments were treated. How long she remained there is not revealed by the record, but about December 27, 1907, her son took her out of the sanitarium and carried her to Sulphur Springs, Hopkins county. It appears that when she was next seen by any of her father's family she was in the asylum for the insane at Terrell, Tex.

The widow of W. W. Haupt died in 1912, intestate, and Mrs. Landers inherited one-sixth of her community interest in the land on the Dunn league, and, in order to prove the title he claimed to one-sixth of the entire 2,830 acres, defendant offered in evidence orders of the county court of Hopkins county, which showed that on July 8, 1912, A. P. Landers was, pursuant to his own application, appointed guardian of his wife's person and estate, and that in a supplemental inventory filed March 5, 1914, he inventoried one-sixth of the 2,830 acres in the Dunn tract as property belonging to his wife's estate, and that the interest was appraised at $6,050.

He showed also that on March 12, 1914, he was empowered to sell the one-sixth interest, and that he made the sale the same day; that the sale was confirmed March 19, 1914, and that for a recited cash consideration of $6,050 he on March 24, 1914, made a deed in his capacity as guardian to M. G. Michaelis to the said one-sixth interest.

We have had the benefit of briefs and arguments of marked ability, but counsel on both sides admit that they have been unable to find any case exactly like the instant case; or, as it is expressed by counsel for plaintiffs in error:

"We have found no case just like this, and of the many cases examined no one can be said to really be a precedent on the facts for the decision of any other."

A large part of the briefs is devoted to discussion of the question when and to what extent is parol evidence admissible for the purpose of construing the meaning of a will, and a very large number of authorities are cited from the reports, not only of this state, but from the courts of other states and of England, and from text-books which are everywhere recognized as reliable authority; but there are certain basic fundamental rules of construction and rules prescribing when, and to what extent, parol evidence is admissible in such cases, which are followed and applied in all jurisdictions, and it is unnecessary to go beyond the limits of our own reports in order to find cases in which those rules have been recognized and applied.

[1] That the intention of the testator, if not inconsistent with some established rule of law, or with public policy, must control, and it is the duty of the courts to ascertain such intention and to give force and effect to the scheme that the testator had in his mind for the disposition of his estate, is a cardinal and fundamental rule of interpretation, and is so familiar that no citation of authority is necessary.

The rule was so laid down in Texas at least as early as the case of Philleo v. Holliday, 24 Tex. 42, and perhaps earlier.

[2] Where the instrument is free from doubt, and the intention of the testator is expressed with sufficient intelligence and clearness to make the will incapable of more than one construction, there is no need of parol evidence, and such evidence will not be admitted to show that the will does not express the intention of the testator. A. & E. Encyc. of Law, vol. 30, p. 675; Cyc. vol. 40, p. 1428.

[3] Where the will is plain and unambiguous, no evidence of surrounding circumstances is admissible, and direct evidence of inten-

tion, as by the testator's declaration, is never admitted for the purpose of showing that his intention was different from that signified by him in the use of the words of the will. Ency. of Ev. vol. 14, pp. 504, 505, 506; Lenz v. Sens, 27 Tex. Civ. App. 442, 66 S. W. 111.

The rules of law above set forth have been established almost from time immemorial, and are recognized and applied by all courts in cases where the will under consideration was plain and unambiguous; that is, where it was capable of but one construction.

[4] When the will is not of that character, but is ambiguous to the extent that the intention of the testator cannot be ascertained from the language of the will itself, another rule of law equally as well established is applicable, and is necessary to be invoked. As an accurate statement of the consensus of judicial opinion, it is phrased in Cyc. vol. 40, p. 1431, as follows:

"Where the language of the will is uncertain and doubtful, or contains a latent ambiguity, extrinsic evidence may be admitted for the purpose of explaining the will, the situation of the testator, and the facts and circumstances surrounding him at the time of the execution of a will, such as evidence as to the facts that the will was written by the testator himself, and that he was not a professional man, or as to the condition of his family, and the amount and character of his property, or as to his feelings toward, and his relations to, the persons affected by the will, or as to the condition of the beneficiaries. Such evidence, however, is not admissible where the language of the will is plain and unambiguous."

In the statement of the rule of law just quoted the term "latent ambiguity" is used, and it may be helpful to say at this point that it is made evident by examination of the latest text-books, and the decisions of our own courts, that the distinction between "latent" and "patent" ambiguities is now practically ignored and disregarded; and the courts, without regard to the distinction, endeavor to arrive by the most direct way at what the testator meant when he wrote the will. Gardner on Wills, 388–389; Page on Wills, 988; Schouler on Wills, 581; Jarmon on Wills, vol. 1 (6th Ed.) 400–402; Meyers v. Maverick, 28 S. W. 716.

Among the numerous authorities cited in Cyc. in support of the rule of evidence above quoted is the case of Hunt v. White, 24 Tex. 643. That case was decided as early as 1860, and has been consistently followed to this time. In the course of his opinion Chief Justice Wheeler quoted from Phillips on Evidence, and cites Greenleaf to the effect that to allow parol evidence where the will is plain and unambiguous would be "inconsistent with the rule * * * which has been universally established for the construction of wills, namely, that the testator's intention is to be collected from the words used in the will, and words which he has not used cannot be added."

However, it is held in the same case that "it is competent to admit parol evidence * * * to explain a will * * * by showing the situation of the testator in his relation to persons and things around him; or, as it is often expressed, by proof of the surrounding circumstances, in order that his will may be read in the light of the circumstances in which he was placed at the time of making it."

It is also said that while the intent "must be ascertained from the meaning of the words in the instrument and from those words alone," yet, as the testator "may be supposed to have used language with reference to the situation in which he was placed to the state of his family, his property, and other circumstances relating to himself individually and to his affairs, the law admits extrinsic evidence of those facts and circumstances, to enable the court to discover the meaning attached by the testator to the words used in the will, and to apply them to the facts of the particular case."

The substantial meaning of the authority last cited, and of all others that we have examined, and the idea sought to be conveyed, is tersely and felicitously phrased by the Supreme Court of Kentucky in the following language:

"In other words, as it has often been expressed, it is incompetent by this character of proof to show what the testator intended to say, but did not, but it may be shown what was intended by what he did say." Eichhorn v. Morat, 175 Ky. 80, 193 S. W. 1013.

[5] It is of course elementary that all parts of the instrument must be construed together, and the intention of the testator be arrived at by considering the whole, and not from detached, segregated, and isolated words, sentences, or clauses.

[6] In this connection it is logically in order to set forth yet another rule of construction which has long been applied by the courts of Texas and all other jurisdictions, and which is peculiarly applicable to the instant case.

"There is no more clearly established rule of construction, as applicable to wills, than that words, or clauses of sentences, or even whole paragraphs, may be transposed to any extent, with a view to show the intention of the testator. Pond v. Bergh, 10 Paige, 140. Words and limitations may be transposed, supplied, or rejected. But it must appear, either from the words of the will, or extrinsic proof, admissible in aid of the words, that the transposition does really bring out the true intent of the testator, and thus render what was before obscure, clear. * * * There is no doubt that a particular construction of words, although somewhat variant from their more natural and obvious import, may be strengthened by reference to extraneous circumstances." 1

Redf. on Wills (4th Ed.) pp. 481–2, quoted in Hawes v. Foote, 64 Tex. 27.

Extraneous facts are always admissible in aid of the construction of wills to the extent of explaining doubts, or removing uncertainties, when with that aid the intent is clear, Currie v. Murphy, 35 Miss. 473.

We have been prompted to deal at length with the question of the admissibility of parol evidence, rather by reason of deference to the earnest contention of the respective counsel, than because we believe a determination of the question was essential to a proper decision.

We are of the opinion that the will is capable of being correctly interpreted without reference to any of the testimony admitted over objection of defendant in court below (defendant in error here) by applying to the will and the undisputed facts the recognized rules of construction above set forth.

It is proper to say in this connection that it is revealed by the statement of facts that, in reply to the objection made to the introduction of the parol testimony as to declarations of the testator, counsel for plaintiffs in the court below stated that he would not insist upon any statement of W. W. Haupt as to what he was going to, or did, put in his will, but contended that any declaration of the testator as to why he wanted any person to take and another not to take, an interest in the land was competent as a circumstance bearing on the construction of the will. The testimony appears to have been admitted, limited to the purpose indicated.

As we have said above, we believe the will can be properly construed without reference to any evidence except that which is undisputed.

The testator refers first in specific terms to his "field" which was in the McCarver tract, and following the order of his will we will deal first with that property. We can pretermit, for the purpose of argument, all the testimony as to the declaration of the testator as to his reasons for so dividing the 250 acres as to exclude Mrs. Landers from any interest therein, since it has already been shown that he made deeds dividing the 250 acres among five of his children, and that Mrs. Landers was not one of the five.

The contention has been pressed that a construction of the will which would exclude Mrs. Landers from any interest in the land would operate gross injustice, but, as has been seen, not only did the testator in the solemn form of a deed to each of five children so divide the 250 acres as to exclude Mrs. Landers, but his wife, the mother of Mrs. Landers, joined in the execution of each and all of those deeds.

Certainly it cannot be contended that the mother would have harbored any intention to do her daughter injustice. As to the 250 acres, those deeds clearly manifest the purpose and intent of the testator concerning Mrs. Landers.

Referring to the division so made he says: "I have already laid off my field in 50-acre lots, and all the children have drawn shares," etc.

It is obvious that that statement is not literally true, because Mrs. Landers was not included in the division, though it was made with solemn formality. To conform that statement to the truth, and express the manifest meaning and purpose of the testator, we must supply between the words "all the children" and the words "have drawn" the words "to whom I intend to give any of my land."

There is abundant authority in law for so supplying words, where they serve to make clear the meaning and intention of the testator. Hawes v. Foote, 64 Tex. 27, and authorities therein cited.

Proceeding to the third paragraph of the will, we find as part of a sentence a clause which reads as follows: "*And each heir should have an undivided interest in said pasture*" (italics ours). As we construe the brief and argument of counsel for defendant in error, he bases his contention in the main on that clause.

Arguing on the basis of the words italicized, he strenuously insists that there is no doubt or ambiguity in the will. If there were no language following these words explanatory of the meaning of the testator, or if these words could properly, and in accordance with recognized and controlling rules of construction, be separated and segregated from what precedes and what follows, the contention would unquestionably be correct.

There are, however, phrases explanatory of the testator's meaning, and we are not at liberty to disregard accepted canons of construction.

It is manifest that the testator meant to make an exception which would apply to one of his children, and we are of the opinion that the words, "their is one exception to this rule," should be transposed so as to immediately follow the clause, "*And each heir should have an undivided interest in said pasture.*"

This is true, because, the purpose to make an exception being obvious, the reason for the exception was meant to follow the declaration that there should be one, and the reason is that he did not want either the husband of his daughter or her sons ever to have any interest whatever in any part of his land.

The statement that he expected "most" (which implies, but not all) of his children to build on the west end of the McCarver Field tract clearly establishes no "rule," since he evidently contemplated that there might, and probably would, be one or more exceptions to, so to speak, his expectation.

When we consider the obvious purpose to prevent the son-in-law and grandsons from ever by any possibility benefiting by his will, the transposition made above is justified, if not imperatively demanded. This view is strengthened, if indeed not conclusively proved correct, by the further language in paragraph 6:

"My daughter Alice [Mrs. Landers], has lived with me for five years and is entirely incompetent to do anything & has to be taken care of all her life."

The statement is abundantly justified by the evidence, showing her husband had neither visited his wife nor contributed in any measure to her support in five years.

It appears to us that the plan and purpose of the testator to limit the division of his land to five children is further shown by the statement that if his children chose they could give the grandsons money, but they must be denied any part of his land.

If all the children, including Mrs. Landers, were to get only an equal share of the land, there could have been no reason for the apprehension that any of them out of his or her one-sixth would give a part to the sons of a sister who was to receive as much as each of the others.

There is no room for doubt that W. W. Haupt's controlling and dominant purpose was to so devise his land that his son-in-law and grandsons could never by any possibility have any interest in it; yet if his daughter had become a beneficiary under the will, and had died the day after her father died, a life estate of one-third would have vested instantly in the husband, and title in fee simple to all her share in her sons.

If she survived, as she did, the husband, as the law then was, would have had the management and control of all the property and been entitled to half the rents and revenues.

If she was meant to be included in the terms of the devise, then the will meant nothing, since its effect would have been in no wise different from the operation of the statute of descent and distribution.

[7] It has been held in high authority that the law of the state at the time of the execution of a will may be considered in ascertaining the intention of the testator. Peet v. Peet, 229 Ill. 341, 82 N. E. 376, 13 L. R. A. (N. S.) 780, 11 Ann. Cas. 492.

[8] The presumption is entitled to be indulged that the testator knew that if he made no will all his children would inherit equally, as that is a matter of common knowledge; and, if the instrument be given the interpretation contended for by defendant in error, to all intents and purposes it amounted to no will, and the manifest plan of the testator becomes no plan, and the purpose which was obviously uppermost in his mind to exclude his son-in-law and grandsons from any possible interest would be thwarted and defeated.

Neither the husband nor the grown sons of Mrs. Landers had contributed to her support in five years, and it is evident that the testator realized that her support would have to be furnished by his wife and children, as the remaining 125 acres of the McCarver tract produced no revenue, and the revenue from the Dunn tract was very small.

Defendant in error lays much stress upon the arrangement made between Mrs. Haupt and her children as to the remaining 125 acres of the McCarver tract, of the benefit of which Mrs. Landers was the recipient to the extent of about an amount equal to that which each of the other five children had received out of the same tract.

We do not attach great importance to that transaction, first, because it is clearly shown that the money was used to meet the expense of keeping Mrs. Landers in a sanitarium: and, second, because we are unable to see how it is in any way helpful in interpreting the will made a year or more before by W. W. Haupt.

We do not deem it necessary to consider the assignments of error relating to giving and refusing charges, as under the facts in evidence they do not raise questions of substantive law.

If the court believed the meaning of the will to be doubtful and was unable to determine whether or not Mrs. Landers was excluded from an interest in the land, there is abundant authority in support of its action in submitting the question to the jury as a mixed question of law and fact.

[9] We are of the opinion that, regardless of the parol testimony, the court could and should have construed the will as expressing the intention of the testator to exclude Mrs. Landers from any interest in the land in question; therefore whether there were or were not errors committed in the trial becomes an immaterial question.

We are of the opinion that the judgment of the district court was correct, and that it was erroneously reversed.

We therefore recommend that the judgment of the Court of Civil Appeals be reversed, and that of the district court be affirmed.

PHILLIPS, C. J. The judgment recommended in the report of the Commission of Appeals is adopted, and will be entered as the judgment of the Supreme Court.

GILLIAM v. MAHON et al. (No. 241–3433.)

(Commission of Appeals of Texas, Section B. June 8, 1921.)

1. Wills ☛439—Cardinal rule of construction is to ascertain intention.

The cardinal rule in the construction of every will is to arrive at the intention of the testator, which must be given effect unless contrary to public policy or forbidden by some inflexible rule of law.

2. Wills ☛601(1)—Provision giving fee to wife held not cut down by subsequent ambiguous provision.

A will providing that "I give and bequeath to my wife all my real and personal property, * * * also my granddaughter to have equal share with all my heirs when the property is divided," gave the property to the wife in fee, as the clear gift in fee could not be cut down by the subsequent ambiguous clause.

Error to Court of Civil Appeals of Fifth Supreme Judicial District.

Suit by R. A. Gilliam, guardian and executor, against Mittie Gibson Mahon and others to construe a will. A judgment of the district court was reversed by the Court of Civil Appeals (215 S. W. 124), and plaintiff brings error. Reversed, and judgment of the District Court affirmed.

Cockrell, Gray, McBride & O'Donnell, of Dallas, for plaintiff in error.

J. J. Eckford and Lee Richardson, both of Dallas, for defendants in error.

KITTRELL, J. The action out of which the appeal in this case arose was brought for the purpose of construing the will of S. A. Mahon, who died at Dallas, on November 16, 1912. He left surviving him a widow, Alice A. Mahon, who, subsequent to his death, became hopelessly insane and so remains.

S. A. Mahon had been married prior to his marriage with Alice A. Mahon, and by his first marriage had one son, whose death preceded that of his father by several years. The defendant in error, Mittie Mahon, is a daughter of that son, and consequently a granddaughter of the testator, S. A. Mahon.

At the death of said testator his heirs were Sidney A. Mahon, a son, Nettie Pauline Mahon, a daughter, and Margaret Mahon Brickel, a daughter, who were all children of the testator and his wife Alice Mahon; and the fourth and last heir was, and is, the said Mittie Mahon, a daughter of the son by the first marriage of the testator, as above stated.

The daughter, Margaret Mahon, prior to 1912 married Joseph H. Brickel, and survived her father, but died in the year 1918, leaving a will in terms as set forth below, which will was duly probated in Dallas county. The construction of that will is in no wise in-volved in this proceeding, except to show proper parties. It reads as follows:

"Nov. 30, 1917, Monravia, Calif.

"This my will dated Nov. 30, 1917. I want Mr. R. A. Gilliam, with the assistance of my sister, Nettie, to administrate my affairs.

"First, Lucile Brickel to have my one-half of home place owned with her.

"All my other property I want my mother, Mrs. Alice Mahon, to have, and if the income is not enough with her own to give her every comfort I want such property as can be sold even at a sacrifice to be used for that purpose.

"At my mother's death I want my sister Nettie to have one-half of the property, and the other half to be equally divided between my niece, Mittie Mahon, and my sister-in-law, Mrs. Mittie Gibson Mahon and Mrs. Lyda Thompson Mahon.

"Mrs. J. H. Brickel.

"Mrs. Margaret Mahon Brickel."

The will left by S. A. Mahon at the bottom, and just above the signature, bears date September 12, 1912, and reads as follows:

"State of Texas, County of Dallas:

"Dallas, Texas, Sept. 23, 1912.

"Know all men by these presents that I, S. A. Mahon, of the state of Texas, county of Dallas, have this day executed my will and testament, being of good mind, willed to my wife, Alice A. Mahon, of the above state and county in the event of my death I give and bequeath to my wife Alice A. Mahon, all my real and personal property and all my interest in the New York Life Insurance Co. All debts to be paid, also my granddaughter Mittie Mahon to have equal share with all my heirs when the property is divided.

"Witness my hand this Sept. 12, 1912.

"[Signed]   S. A. Mahon."

The case was tried in the district court without a jury, and the trial judge phrased his conclusion of law as follows:

"The court is of the opinion, and so decrees, that the will of the said S. A. Mahon vested in the said Alice A. Mahon, his surviving wife, all the estate, real, personal and mixed, owned by the said S. A. Mahon at his death, and so construes the will, and has entered decree herein accordingly."

The Court of Civil Appeals construed the will as vesting only a life estate in Mrs. Alice A. Mahon, and reversed the judgment of the district court, and rendered judgment for appellants in that court (defendants in error here). Defendants in error filed no brief or written argument in this court, resting their case on their brief in the Court of Civil Appeals and oral argument in this court.

Plaintiff in error makes the same contention here as he made in the Court of Civil Appeals, and presents in his application for writ of error two assignments, which, taken together, mean the same thing, viz.: That the will vested a fee-simple estate in Alice A.

Mahon as the district court held; and that the Court of Civil Appeals erred in holding to the contrary. Under these two assignments he states four propositions, which, in view of the facts and the terms of the will, can be fully and fairly condensed as follows:

"Where by its terms a will purports to vest a fee-simple title absolute in the first taker, coupled with an unlimited power of control and disposition, a subsequent direction in the will limiting any undisposed residue over to others is void, and the first taker's fee-simple title is unaffected thereby, since, where the first clause clearly vests a fee-simple title in the wife, such title will not be disturbed or cut down by a subsequent clause which is uncertain and ambiguous in its meaning."

The counter contention of defendants in error can be stated fairly in the following form:

"That effect should be given to the entire instrument according to the intention of the testator, and when in the first clause of the will he gives all his property to his wife, and in the second clause says his granddaughter is 'to have' an equal share when the property is divided, the will should be construed as vesting an estate in the wife only for life, or until the same shall be divided, and after her death, or when the property is divided to vest the title in the heirs, including the granddaughter. Since no power of disposition is given by the terms of the will the wife is vested only with an estate for life or until the property is divided, as the expression of the intention or desire on the part of the testator that his granddaughter should have a certain interest has the same force and effect as if the estate had been devised in express terms."

In support of the contentions thus phrased defendants in error cited in the Court of Civil Appeals the following Texas cases: Faulk v. Dashiell, 62 Tex. 652, 50 Am. Rep. 542; McMurry v. Stanley, 69 Tex. 227, 6 S. W. 412; Lake v. Copeland, 82 Tex. 464, 17 S. W. 786; Cleveland v. Cleveland, 89 Tex. 445, 35 S. W. 145; Cottrell v. Moreman, 136 S. W. 124; Dulin v. Moore, 96 Tex. 135, 70 S. W. 742; Wiess v. Goodhue, 98 Tex. 280, 83 S. W. 178; Haring v. Shelton, 103 Tex. 10, 122 S. W. 13.

[1] Most, if not all, of these cases are familiar to the profession, and we shall not undertake to analyze them all or point out their application to the question under discussion. All of them support the rule which prevails in all jurisdictions, that the cardinal rule in the construction of every will is to arrive at the intention of the testator, which intention must be given effect unless it be contrary to public policy or be "forbidden by some inflexible rule of law." There is no difference of opinion between opposing counsel as to the rule—indeed, could not be, as it is not only elementary and fundamental, but inherently logical and just. They differ only upon the question of its application to the facts revealed by the record.

[2] The rule applicable to the instant case is a rule of construction, the purpose of which is to arrive at, or gain, the testator's intention, and which is applied for no other purpose. As is said in Wager v. Wager, 96 N. Y. 174, which case is quoted from by Judge Stayton in McMurry v. Stanley, 69 Tex. 227, 6 S. W. 412:

"The rule that a limitation over to one cannot be based upon a primary devise of an absolute estate to another is founded entirely upon the supposed intention of the testator."

The rule referred to can be correctly and more fully phrased as follows:

"Where the first clause of a will in clear, unambiguous language gives and bequeaths to one devisee all the property real and personal of which the testator dies possessed, such estate so given cannot be disturbed, cut down, or diminished by a subsequent clause, which is uncertain and ambiguous in its meaning."

That rule of law has been long established and applied. Careful examination of the cases of McMurry v. Stanley, 69 Tex. 227, 6 S. W. 412, and Dulin v. Moore, 96 Tex. 135, 70 S. W. 742, which are strongly relied upon by defendants in error, reveals that the clause of the will in each case which was held to limit the devisee was clear, direct, and unambiguous, and left no doubt as to the intention and desire of the testator, which was, under the terms of the instrument, capable of being practically carried out.

Such is the nature and effect of the first clause of the will of S. A. Mahon, which, in clear and unambiguous terms, vested an estate in fee in his wife in all his property. The clause referring to the granddaughter is secondary only. Were it as clear as the first it would be our duty to reconcile the two, but in view of its ambiguous character the primary clause cannot be affected by it. If the second clause were given effect the result would be to incorporate all of the heirs of the testator as beneficiaries, though there is no direct intimation on the part of the testator that they were to share, and though they are wholly unmentioned or referred to as beneficiaries under the will. This being true, the rule applicable to the situation forbids such a construction, and demands that the will be construed as vesting an estate in fee to all the property in the wife, provision for whom appears to have been the primary and controlling purpose of the testator, and as to whom only did he express his intention in clear and effectual legal terms.

The following cases support the conclusion reached: Howard v. Carusi, 109 U. S. 725, 27 L. Ed. 1089;[1] Ide v. Ide, 5 Mass. 500; Thornhill v. Hall, 2 Cl. & F. 22; article 1106, Rev. Stat. Tex.; Feegles v. Slaughter, 182 S. W. 10.

It follows from what has been said that the construction put upon the will by the district court was correct, and that the Court

[1] 3 Sup. Ct. 575.

of Civil Appeals erred in holding to the contrary. We therefore recommend that the judgment of the latter court be reversed, and that of the district court be affirmed.

PHILLIPS, C. J. The judgment recommended in the report of the Commission of Appeals is adopted, and will be entered as the judgment of the Supreme Court.

STEED et ux. v. GULF, C. & S. F. RY. CO.
(No. 216–3339.)

(Commission of Appeals of Texas, Section B. June 1, 1921.)

1. Negligence ⟺59—One liable only for injury reasonably anticipated.

A person is liable for such injuries only as might reasonably have been anticipated as the natural result of his acts.

2. Carriers ⟺305(1)—Conductor's temporary blocking of aisle not proximate cause of woman passenger's falling while waiting for him to let her pass.

The act of a conductor of a passenger train in temporarily obstructing the aisle as he stood therein, bending over to speak to some one, as a woman passenger approached walking to the rear, held not the proximate cause of her falling before she reached him as she halted to wait for him to let her pass.

3. Carriers ⟺283(2)—Conductor not negligent in temporarily blocking aisle.

The conductor of a passenger train was not negligent in temporarily obstructing the aisle by standing therein, bending over to speak to some one, as a woman passenger approached, walking to the rear, and lost her balance before she reached him as she halted to wait for him to let her pass.

4. Evidence ⟺571(9)—Conductor's opinion on hypothetical case held incompetent.

In action for injuries to woman passenger by falling in aisle while waiting for conductor to let her pass, testimony of the conductor that a woman walking to the rear of a car in motion might become overbalanced while attempting to stop to wait until one obstructing the aisle should let her pass was without probative value, being a mere opinion on a hypothetical case, and, in any event, had reference to a permanent blocking of the aisle, and not to a temporary blocking of the aisle, which was the character of the blocking disclosed by the evidence in the case at bar.

Error to Court of Civil Appeals of Sixth Supreme Judicial District.

Action by S. A. Steed and wife against the Gulf, Colorado & Santa Fé Railway Company. Judgment for plaintiffs was reversed and rendered by the Court of Civil Appeals (209 S. W. 772), and plaintiffs bring error. Judgment of the Court of Civil Appeals affirmed.

B. Q. Evans, of Greenville, and W. ⸳ Shields, of Eastland, for plaintiffs in err.⸳ Dinsmore, McMahan & Dinsmore, of Greenville, for defendant in error.

POWELL, J. S. A. Steed and his wife Mrs. Lena Steed, sued the Gulf, Colorado & Santa Fé Railway Company, in the district court of Hunt county, Tex., for $15,000. wherein they allege as the damages accruing to them by reason of personal injuries sustained ⸳ Mrs. Steed while a passenger on one of the company's trains on the afternoon of April 25, 1916, between Garland and Celeste, Texas. Upon the theory, as alleged, that the conductor, in obstructing the aisle as he did, was guilty of negligence which proximately caused Mrs. Steed to fall as she did, the plaintiffs recovered judgment against the defendant for $4,000. The judgment was based upon a general verdict of the jury. From said judgment, the railway company perfected its appeal to the Court of Civil Appeals, where the judgment of the district court was reversed and rendered in favor of defendant in error. See 209 S. W. 772.

While Mrs. Steed's testimony on practically all material points is at variance with all the other evidence, including the testimony given by disinterested witnesses, the Court of Civil Appeals, in deference to the verdict of the jury, found the following facts:

"On the afternoon of April 25, 1916, appellee Mrs. Steed, then a passenger on one of appellant's trains, while walking from the front end to the rear end of the car she was in, fell to the floor thereof, and thereby was injured. Her account of the accident was, substantially, as follows: The conductor was at about the middle of the car, standing in the aisle, bent over, talking to some one, as she approached him. When she got near to him he straightened up, looked at her, and then again bent over toward the person he was talking to, thereby obstructing the aisle, she said, so that she could not pass on. She endeavored to stop, intending to wait in the aisle until the conductor 'got ready to let her pass,' but, instead, because the train was moving rapidly in a direction opposite to the one in which she was moving, lost her balance and fell to the floor. At the time she fell she was so close to the conductor, she said, that she 'could have touched him.' If he had not stooped over as he did, she further said, she could have gone 'around him and scrouged by him.'"

Based upon the findings of fact just set out, the Court of Civil Appeals held:

"Keeping in mind the rule that required appellant's conductor to use the care a very cautious, prudent, and competent person would have used for Mrs. Steed's safety when he saw her walking toward him in the aisle of the car (Ry. Co. v. Halloren, 53 Tex. 46, 37 Am. Rep. 744; St. John v. Ry. Co., 80 S. W. 235), we nevertheless are of the opinion the trial court erred when he refused appellant's request iat he instruct the jury to return a verdict in s favor; for we do not think the facts proven 'arranted a finding that said conductor acted s such a person would not have acted. We iink a very cautious, prudent, and competent erson reasonably would not have expected or oreseen that injury to Mrs. Steed would reult from his obstructing the aisle as the conluctor did, and therefore we think that the inury she suffered should have been regarded as lue to an accident for which appellant was not 'esponsible. Ry. Co. v. Brown, 75 S. W. 807."

There was only one allegation of negli4 gence in this case, and that was the act of the conductor in blocking the aisle. No allegation of negligence was based either on the rough handling of the train, if it gave her a shove, or the presence of foreign articles in the aisle, if she was caused to fall. As a matter of fact, the accident occurred in an ordinary chair car, apparently equipped in the ordinary manner, and constructed in the usual way. There is no proof that the train was handled roughly, or that any foreign obstacle in the aisle caused her to fall. Again, there is neither allegation nor proof that the conductor, in leaning forward, struck the plaintiff, or touched her at all and caused her to fall. As a matter of fact, she never touched the conductor. She says, herself, she could have touched him. But she did not do so. In her pleadings, she avers that she was within about two seats of the conductor when the accident occurred. She never did testify just how far, in distance, she was from him. She is very indefinite in that regard. However, many witnesses do testify rather accurately on that point, and the reasonable conclusion from all the testimony is that she was from three to six feet distant from the conductor when she fell.

[1] It is the well-settled law of this state that a person is only liable for such injuries as might reasonably have been anticipated as the natural result of his acts. The rule has been clearly stated by our Supreme Court in several leading cases, as follows:

In case of Seale v. Railway Co., 65 Tex. 274, 57 Am. Rep. 602, that court says:

"When a defendant has violated a duty imposed upon him by the common law, he should be held liable to every person injured, whose injury is the natural and probable consequence of the misconduct; and that the liability extends to such injuries as might reasonably have been anticipated, under ordinary circumstances, as the natural and probable result of the wrongful act."

We quote further from the same case, as follows:

"That one exercising due care, and incurring no risks, in extinguishing a fire, should have the flames communicated to her clothes, and thereby lose her life, is something so improbable that the anticipation of it should not be charged to any one under such circumstances. Such a thing might happen, but it would be only

from some casualty which could not possibly be foreseen; and, in such cases, as we have seen, the original negligence cannot be regarded as the proximate cause of the injury."

Justice Gaines speaks as follows in case of Railway Co. v. Bigham, 90 Tex. 223, 38 S. W. 162:

"Ought the agents of the company to have foreseen that, as a result of the imperfect fastening of the gate, the injury, or any injuries similar in character, would probably result? In our opinion, nothing short of prophetic ken could have anticipated the happening of the combination of events which resulted in the injury to the person of the plaintiff. The act of the defendant in permitting the fastening to its gate to become insecure was in itself lawful; and since it was clearly out of the range of reasonable probability that an injury to the person of any one should result, it should be held as a matter of law that the negligence of the company gave no right of action for such injuries."

Coming on down to later decisions, we also refer to a very able opinion by our present Chief Justice Phillips, in the case of Railway Co. v. Bennett, 110 Tex. 262, 219 S. W. 198, as follows:

"Under the authority of Seale v. Railway Co., 65 Tex. 274, 57 Am. Rep. 602, and Railway Co. v. Bigham, 90 Tex. 223, 38 S. W. 162, the negligence of the defendant's employés in the origin of the fire cannot be justly regarded as the proximate cause of the injury to Bennett. The test of this question is, ought the defendant and its agents to have reasonably foreseen that as the consequence of the negligence which caused the explosion in the tank car, the injury to Bennett, or like injury to some other employé in his situation, would probably result? In the language of Judge Gaines' opinion in the Bigham case, nothing short of prophetic ken could have anticipated the happening of the combination of events which resulted in Bennett's becoming overheated. No one standing at the stage of the entire happening which had to do with the gas explosion in the tank car could have regarded it as other than a bare possibility, at best, that at a later period of a fire thus produced in an open enclosure, an employé of the company, in attempting to extinguish it, would get so close to the fire or stay in such a situation so long as to be injured by the heat of the fire."

[2] Applying the above rules of law to the facts in this case, we are clearly of the opinion that the railway company is not liable to Mrs. Steed for the injuries she sustained. In the first place, it must be remembered that the aisles in the passenger coaches are for the common use of all. The train crew and the passengers are alike entitled to their use. They all have the same right to pass up and down these aisles, but each must use them with reasonable regard for the rights of others. No one has the right to permanently obstruct such passageways. The conductor not only had the right to be in this aisle,

but it was his duty to be there in the discharge of his obligations not only to the company, but to the passengers as well.

[3] Under the testimony of Mrs. Steed herself, he was looking after his passengers when leaning over to speak to them at the time of her accident. We believe, with the Court of Civil Appeals, that this conductor was doing nothing more than a very cautious, prudent, and competent employé would have done under the same circumstances, and that, laying aside the question of proximate cause, there was no negligence of any kind in his conduct. He says he would have stepped aside at the proper time and allowed Mrs. Steed to pass; that he would have done this when she reached him. There is no proof to the contrary, for Mrs. Steed fell before reaching him, and gave him no opportunity to step aside and permit her to pass.

[4] But, even if the conductor had actually blocked the aisle temporarily, he could not have anticipated the injuries here alleged. It is true, attorneys for plaintiffs, on cross-examination, gained certain admissions from him in answer to hypothetical questions, which amounted to declarations that, under certain circumstances, he might have anticipated the fall of Mrs. Steed. For instance, the following evidence:

"I was right slap in the aisle, but not quite all of the aisle was taken up by me. That distance across that aisle was 27 or 28 inches. As to whether or not, if I was standing there in that aisle like I said I was, she didn't have an inch to get by me on, I would have stepped out of the way and let her by. Yes, sir; that is proper, and it is my duty to do that. If a lady is coming down the aisle, it is my duty to step out and let the lady go by, and it is safer for our passengers for me to do that. No, sir; it is not my purpose to block the aisle when people are walking on it, and that would be dangerous, if I did. If a person should be coming right on to where I am standing, if a lady should be walking in the opposite direction from the way the train is going and meeting me, I would not block the aisle. I would be liable to unbalance the woman. Yes, sir; I would be liable to cause the woman to lose her balance and she might fall. I have been a conductor a long time and have done that."

Because of the testimony just quoted, which Chief Justice Willson said was admitted without objection, the latter, on motion for rehearing, expressed a desire to reverse his original opinion in this case. But a majority of that court adhered to its original opinion, stating that the evidence just quoted was without probative value on the issue of negligence vel non of the conductor, because a mere opinion of the witness on a hypothetical case, and for that reason incompetent as evidence. In support of this view, the case of Henry v. Phillips, 105 Tex. 459, 151 S. W. 533, is cited. In that case our Supreme Court, in a splendid opinion by Justice Dibrell, held:

"While the admission of this testimony was not objected to by counsel for defendants, that fact would be important only in the event its admission was afterwards complained of as violative of a right reserved to defendants. Such incompetent testimony can never form the basis of a finding of facts in an appellate court, notwithstanding its presence in the record without objection. When the appellate court comes to apply the law to testimony constituting the facts of the case, it can only base its conclusion upon such testimony as is under the law competent. That which is not competent testimony should be given no probative force. The admission of such testimony is no talisman to give effect to that which is irrelevant and incompetent to sustain or deny a material issue in a case."

We are of the view that the majority of the Court of Civil Appeals were correct in their holding with reference to this opinion testimony of the conductor. But, be that as it may, a reasonable construction of his evidence would not lead to the conclusion that even he anticipated the alleged injury to Mrs. Steed. What he evidently intended to say was that a "permanent" blocking of the aisle might lead to serious injuries to passengers. He also testified that he was careful of the welfare of his passengers; that he was not in the habit of blocking the aisle; that he always stepped aside at the proper time and let people pass; that he would have done so in the case at bar. He knew he frequently blocked the aisle temporarily, and he did not have such obstruction in mind in talking about serious injuries to passengers.

Operatives of railway companies can be charged only with the anticipation of such injuries as would reasonably result, in the light of common experience, applied to surrounding circumstances. Tested by this rule, what do we find in this case? Happily, the case is within our common experience. Hundreds and thousands of us travel each day on passenger trains. We watch people go up and down the aisles in passenger coaches almost every day. We know how they act ordinarily. We know how these aisles are used. The train crew, in ordinary practice, as a passenger reaches them, usually step aside. They do not do so when passengers are from 3 to 50 feet distant from them. Such a stepping aside would involve needless delay in the discharge of their duties. Furthermore, passengers are occasionally delayed a minute or so in passing a conductor in the aisle. Such delay, in the absence of special notice to the conductor, is the only natural result to be anticipated from a temporary blocking of the aisle. We believe it is the only result that would follow in the case of an average person. The company in this case

(231 S.W.)

had no notice that Mrs. Steed was afflicted in any way. It was only required to exercise the same care for her safety as it would for that of other ordinary passengers. The experience of those traveling on trains in passing conductors in the aisles, year after year, and in the common knowledge of all, is such as to render it wholly unreasonable to require a conductor to anticipate that a woman approaching him, seeing him, and knowing the aisle was temporarily, at least partly, obstructed, would be caused to fall and sustain serious injuries. The record is silent as to the cause of Mrs. Steed's fall. She says she slipped, or became excited, or stumbled. At any rate, the fall was the result of an intervening cause, which could not have been reasonably anticipated to flow naturally from the temporary presence of the conductor in the aisle. In the natural order of things, a person of average health would have acted thus in this situation: She would have gone ahead until she actually reached the conductor and then given him a chance to step aside; if he had not done that promptly, she would have asked him to do so. If he then failed to step aside in a reasonable time, the company would have been liable for such damage as would reasonably have been anticipated. Even then, there would be some doubt whether the fall and serious injury of the passenger should be anticipated as the natural result of the delay. Mrs. Steed just collapsed and neither gave the conductor an opportunity to step aside, nor requested him to do so.

We dislike to override the verdicts of juries, but we think all reasonable minds will agree with us that the railroad company should not be held liable in this case. If it should be so held, passengers could stand up in the aisles of coaches every day when the conductor is performing his usual duties, and temporarily obstructing the aisles, and faint away, and sue for and recover heavy damages. Such a rule would work the greatest possible injustice to railway companies. The floodgates would be opened to much litigation if any such rule should be established by our courts.

We have found no case exactly in point on the facts. We doubt if such a case as this has ever before found its way into the appellate courts. The case most nearly in point, that we have discovered, is that of De La Pena v. Railway Co., 82 Tex. Civ. App. 241, 74 S. W. 58. In that case, the railway company had blocked a crossing with cars, and the plaintiff desiring to cross the track, took a path running along the right of way for the purpose of going around the cars, stepped into a hole, or open drain, and was injured. In passing on the question as to the proximate cause of the injury in that case, the court said:

"The obstruction of the crossing was not that which, in a natural and continuous sequence, unbroken by any new independent cause, produced the accident which resulted in plaintiff's injury, and hence was its proximate cause."

We think the trial court should have instructed the jury, as requested by the railway company, to return a verdict for the defendant, and that the Court of Civil Appeals correctly reversed the judgment for plaintiffs and rendered one for the defendant in error. Therefore we recommend that the judgment of the Court of Civil Appeals be affirmed.

PHILLIPS, C. J. The judgment recommended in the report of the Commission of Appeals is adopted, and will be entered as the judgment of the Supreme Court.

POE v. CONTINENTAL OIL & COTTON CO. et al. (No. 227–3403.)

(Commission of Appeals of Texas, Section B. June 1, 1921.)

1. Master and servant ⬥358 — Common-law remedy in lieu of compensation available to employee without statutory notice.

Where an employer fails to give an employee notice that his industry is being operated under the Workmen's Compensation Act, as required by Vernon's Sayles' Ann. Civ. St. 1914, arts. 5246x, 5246xx, the employee may sue for damages for personal injuries based upon common-law liability, in the absence of waiver of notice.

2. Election of remedies ⬥1—Valid available remedies essential.

The doctrine of election does not apply unless the party has two valid and available remedies when he makes his election.

3. Master and servant ⬥358—Common-law remedy not waived by making compensation claim after limitation.

Where an injured employee, more than six months after his injury, attempted to obtain an adjudication before the Industrial Accident Board, under the Workmen's Compensation Act (Vernon's Sayles' Ann. Civ. St. 1914, arts. 5246h–5246zzzz), he did not waive his right to sue at common law for want of the statutory notice, the doctrine of election of remedies being inapplicable, plaintiff, by reason of his failure to apply within the time prescribed by the act, having no valid or enforceable remedy before the Accident Board.

4. Master and servant ⬥358—Application for compensation not waiver of want of notice to employee.

An attempt of an injured employee to obtain an adjudication before the Industrial Accident Board under the Workmen's Compensation Act (Vernon's Sayles' Ann. Civ. St. 1914, arts. 5246h–5246zzzz), after the lapse of the time al-

---

⬥For other cases see same topic and KEY-NUMBER in all Key-Numbered Digests and Indexes

lowed within which to make application for compensation, is not a waiver of the employer's failure to give notice to the employee of his industry being operated under the act, want of notice being material only in event of an effort to enforce rights in the courts, and the employee not having intended to abandon his common-law remedy, but merely to get an equitable and prompt adjustment by way of compromise before the board.

5. Master and servant ⬤⟾397—Compensation Board not a court.

The Industrial Accident Board created by Workmen's Compensation Act (Vernon's Sayles' Ann. Civ. St. 1914, arts. 5246h–5246zzzz), is not a court, but an administrative board, where interested parties may reach amicable adjustments quickly, by way of compromise.

6. Estoppel ⬤⟾88(1) — Effort to compromise not estoppel to assertion of rights in court.

A mere effort to reach a compromise is not an estoppel to the assertion of one's rights in court.

7. Statutes ⬤⟾239 — Laws depriving citizens of rights strictly construed.

Laws depriving citizens of rights possessed by them should be strictly construed.

8. Master and servant ⬤⟾358—Reservation before compensation board held to prevent implied waiver of common-law remedy.

Where an injured employee agreed upon dates for a hearing before the Industrial Accident Board of his claim for compensation under the Workmen's Compensation Act (Vernon's Sayles' Ann. Civ. St. 1914, arts. 5246h–5246zzzz), but reserved in writing a stipulation that the agreement was made without prejudice to any rights, claims, and defenses of any party, his attempt to obtain an adjudication before the Board, which allowed a plea of limitation, was insufficient to imply a waiver of his rights to sue at common law for want of notice.

Error to Court of Civil Appeals of Eighth Supreme Judicial District.

Action by C. C. Poe against Continental Oil & Cotton Company and others. From a judgment of the Court of Civil Appeals (211 S. W. 488), affirming a judgment for defendants, plaintiff brings error. Reversed and remanded.

J. W. Moffett and Sayles & Sayles, all of Abilene, for plaintiff in error.

Frank S. Anderson, of Galveston, for defendants in error.

POWELL, J. On June 20, 1917, C. C. Poe filed this action for damages in the sum of $15,000 in the district court of Taylor county, Tex., against John Guitar, who was doing business under the firm or trade name of Continental Oil & Cotton Company, alleging he had sustained personal injuries on October 8, 1915, while in the employ of the latter, and because of the negligence of Guitar. The petition further alleged that the injuries were sustained by Poe while operating a certain device, known as a "go-devil," for removing and conveying cotton seed.

On September 12, 1917, plaintiff in error filed his first amended original petition, naming the Georgia Casualty Company, also, as a party defendant. This latter pleading was occasioned by the original answer of the defendant. In his amended petition Poe sued as before for his damages against Guitar, basing his allegation upon the common-law liability of the latter for his injuries. In the alternative, the petition prayed for a recovery against the said Casualty Company, under the terms of the Workmen's Compensation Act (Vernon's Sayles' Ann. Civ. St. 1914, arts. 5246h–5246zzzz).

By way of replication to Poe's amended petition, the defendants filed amended pleas in abatement on February 13, 1918, the contents of which have been accurately stated by the Court of Civil Appeals, as follows:

"That on and prior to October 8, 1915, defendant Guitar was a subscriber to and a member of the Georgia Casualty Company, a corporation authorized to transact business in the state of Texas and under the provisions of the Employers' Liability Act, c. 179, Acts of Thirty-Third Legislature [Vernon's Sayles' Ann. Civ. St. 1914, arts. 5246h–5246zzzz], was authorized to insure the payment of compensation to injured employees, and that Guitar had paid a year's premium in advance, and received a receipt therefor, and the casualty company had issued to Guitar a policy of insurance, a copy of which policy was attached and made a part of the pleas; that on October 8, 1915, Poe was employed by defendant Guitar, and while acting in the course of his employment claims to have received the injuries described in his petition; that on and prior to October 8, 1915, Guitar had in all respects complied with the provisions of the Employers' Liability Act and had given notice in writing and print to all persons under contract of hire with him, including Poe, that he had provided for payment of compensation for injuries to his employees with the Georgia Casualty Company, as provided by sections 19 and 20, pt. 3, of the act (Vernon's Sayles' Ann. Civ. St. 1914, arts. 5246x, 5246xx), and that Poe had actual notice that Guitar had so provided for such payment of compensation, and thereafter continued in the employment of Guitar; that after sustaining his alleged injury the plaintiff elected to file, and filed, with the Industrial Accident Board claim against the casualty company for compensation under the terms and provisions of the Employers' Liability Act, and that thereafter Poe and the casualty company submitted the matters in dispute in respect to said claim to the Industrial Accident Board, and on January 17, 1917, said Board determined the claim upon its merits, and adjudged that the casualty company was released and discharged from the payment of compensation for the injuries alleged in plaintiff's petition, and that the judgment and order of the Board was res adjudicata and a bar to any further claim to recover compensation for the injuries declared upon by plaintiff. The order of the Industrial Accident Board was made a part of the plea, and reads as follows:

"January 17, 1917.

"'O. C. Poe, Employee, v. Continental Oil and Cotton Company, Employer; Georgia Casualty Company, Insurer.

"'On this, the 17th day of January, A. D. 1917, after due notice to all parties at interest, came on to be considered by the Industrial Accident Board the claim of compensation filed with said Board by C. O. Poe against the Georgia Casualty Company, as the insurer for the Continental Oil & Cotton Company, subscriber; and,

"'It appearing to the Board that the questions involved herein have not heretofore been settled by agreement of the parties interested herein; and

"'It further appearing to the Board that the said C. C. Poe is not entitled to recover by reason of failure to make claim in the manner and within the time provided in the act;

"'It is therefore ordered, adjudged, and decreed by the Industrial Accident Board that the said Georgia Casualty Company be and the same is hereby fully released and discharged from the payment of any and all compensation by reason of the alleged injuries in the above case.'

"It was further alleged that Poe had thereby made an election of remedies, and was bound by his election and the Board's order."

The trial court heard the amended pleas in abatement on the day of their filing, sustained the same, and abated the suit. It decreed further that the defendants, and each of them, go hence without day and recover all their costs.

Before passing upon said pleas in abatement, evidence was introduced in the trial court showing the proceedings before the Industrial Accident Board in this connection. Those facts, as found by the Court of Civil Appeals, briefly stated, were: that on August 9, 1916, some 10 months after the accident, attorneys for Poe made their first attempt to obtain an adjudication before the Accident Board; that many letters were passed between said Board and the attorneys for the interested parties; that the hearing was postponed from time to time by agreement; that a decree was finally entered by the Board on January 17, 1917; that said decree released defendants from any liability, because Poe had not filed his claim within 6 months after the accident occurred; that there was no trial before said Board on the facts with reference to the merits of the case.

From the judgment of the trial court, Poe appealed to the Court of Civil Appeals, which court affirmed the judgment of the lower court. See 211 S. W. 488. Poe, in due course, filed an application in the Supreme Court for writ of error, which was granted.

[1] In disposing of the case, the Court of Civil Appeals found that Guitar had not given Poe the notice that his industry was being operated under the Workmen's Compensation Act, as required by articles 5246x and 5246xx, Vernon's Sayles' Revised Civil Statutes of Texas; that said notice was essential if Poe was to be denied the right to sue for and recover damages for personal injuries, based upon common-law liability; that the want of such notice can be waived by the injured employee at his option. We think the Court of Civil Appeals is correct in all its rulings set out above.

It will be seen, then, that Poe had a valuable right after the accident. He had the right to commence his suit under the common law at any time within two years after the accident. He certainly did not expressly waive that right. If he relinquished it at all, it was by implication to be deduced from acts and circumstances.

[2, 3] The principal contention of defendants in error was that the doctrine of election of remedies applied; that Poe had one remedy at common law and another under the Workmen's Compensation Act; that he was put upon his election; that he did elect to claim under the latter, and made an effort to obtain his rights before the Accident Board; that, by reason of the exercise of said election, he waived and forfeited his common-law rights, and could not thereafter be heard to assert them.

The Court of Civil Appeals correctly disposed of that contention by overruling it. There is some conflict in the authorities as to the application of this doctrine, where one enforceable remedy is selected and suit commenced and withdrawn before final judgment. But the higher courts are a unit in support of the proposition that the doctrine does not apply unless the claimant actually has two valid and available remedies at the time he makes his election. This rule was clearly announced by Justice Key in the case of Bandy v. Cates, 44 Tex. Civ. App. 38, 97 S. W. 711, as follows:

"As to the question of estoppel by election, which is the other defense relied upon, we do not feel called upon to decide whether there is such inconsistency between the two remedies—a judicial sale and a sale by trustee—as to render the doctrine of election applicable. In order to sustain a defense founded upon that doctrine, it must be made to appear that the plaintiff actually had two valid, available, and inconsistent remedies, and that he undertook to pursue one. His supposition that he had a particular remedy and his effort to enforce it is immaterial, and does not constitute an election, unless the remedy in fact existed. Morris v. Rexford, 18 N. Y. 552; Kinney v. Kiernan, 49 N. Y. 164; McNutt v. Hilkins, 80 Hun, 235, 29 N. Y. Supp. 1047; In re Van Norman, 41 Minn. 494, 43 N. W. 834; Gould v. Blodgett, 61 N. H. 115.

"As the debt was barred by the statute of limitation at the time Cates undertook to foreclose his lien in the former suit, he was not entitled to the relief sought, and therefore his action in that case did not constitute such election as would cut him off from his right to have the trustee foreclose his lien, which was his only valid remedy. No error has been shown, and the judgment is affirmed."

The writ of error was denied by the Supreme Court of Texas in the case of Bandy v. Cates, supra, and it has been followed with approval in numerous cases, for instance, the case of Brodkey v. Lesser (Civ. App.) 157 S. W. 457.

Applying the above authorities to the instant case, we find that, at the time Poe's attorneys wrote their first letter to the Accident Board, he had no valid or enforceable remedy there. It had been barred by the statute of limitation for almost 4 months. Therefore Poe cannot be said to have elected a remedy he could not, under the law, enforce. This is exactly in line with the facts in the case of Bandy v. Cates, supra.

We think what we have said should dispose of the controlling point in this case; for it is equally as illogical to hold that a man would waive a valid remedy for a nonenforceable one as it would be to say that he elected an unenforceable remedy and waived a valid right. To so charge a man is to reflect upon his sanity. Such a waiver, if made at all, was at a time when it would have been without any consideration.

[4-6] After correctly disposing of the doctrine of election of remedies, the Court of Civil Appeals says:

"But if we are correct in our holding that the written or printed notice could be waived by appellant, and that he did waive it by claiming the benefit of the act, presenting his claim to the Board, and invoking its action, then it follows that the parties occupy the same attitude as if notice in the first instance had been given in the manner prescribed by law, and the further conclusion would necessarily ensue that the present suit cannot be maintained perforce of the third section, part 1, of the act. Article 5246i, Vernon's Sayles' R. S."

In this conclusion, as we view it, the court is in error. If Poe had intended to abandon his common-law remedy, then his act in attempting to obtain an adjudication would be a waiver of said want of notice. The Court of Civil Appeals seems to think that such attempt alone is to be construed as such a waiver. We do not think so. The want of notice would be material only in event of an effort to enforce rights in the courts. It is more reasonable to assume that Poe was willing to hold his common-law suit in abeyance until he could ascertain the possibility of getting an equitable adjustment before the Accident Board. He probably thought such a settlement could be had promptly. If the Accident Board can be said to be useful in any respect, it is largely as an administrative board where interested parties can reach amicable adjustments quickly. It is a field for compromise. The Supreme Court of Tex-

as, in case of Middleton v. Texas Power & Light Co., 108 Tex. 96, 185 S. W. 556, held that the board is not a court. That decision was followed by the Commission of Appeals in case of Insurance Association v. Roach, 222 S. W. 159, which latter decision overruled a number of cases cited by counsel for defendants in error, but which are immaterial in this case.

It is more reasonable to assume, then, that the Accident Board was approached by Poe only as a medium through which a compromise might be obtained. A mere effort to reach a compromise has never been held to be an estoppel to the assertion of one's rights in court. See Insurance Co. v. Calvert, 101 Tex. 128, 105 S. W. 320.

[7] We are heartily in accord with the Court of Civil Appeals at San Antonio in its statement that "laws depriving citizens of rights possessed by them should be strictly construed." See Kampmann v. Cross (Civ. App.) 194 S. W. 437. This Workmen's Compensation Act was under discussion there.

[8] Not only was there no express waiver by Poe of his common-law rights, but in two instances, when agreeing upon dates for the hearing before the Board, he reserved in writing the following: "This agreement is made without prejudice to any rights, claims, and defense of any party." In the face of this express reservation, we fail to see how any one could think Poe was waiving his common-law rights. That should have been sufficient to overcome any implied waiver, no matter how strong the facts. It seems to us it would certainly do so in this case, where the only action from which such a waiver could be implied was an attempt on Poe's part to obtain an adjudication before the Accident Board. Such evidence of waiver is insufficient. If it is to be implied at all where the doctrine of election of remedies does not apply, then it must be upon additional and more convincing circumstances than the one present in this case.

The utter injustice that would result from the decision of the lower courts in this case cries out to us in ringing tones. Here was an employee who had been injured. He had one valid common-law remedy which was a valuable right. The defendants in error want the courts to say that he waived that most valuable right and submitted himself to the Accident Board; where, after they had succeeded in getting him that far along, he is met, not with a fair, square trial upon the merits of the case, but is confronted with a technical plea of limitation. He really gets no trial upon the merits. In other words, defendants in error would deprive this man of a chance to see whether any one should compensate him for his injuries. The courts should be slow in laying down any such rule. Whenever it is possible, injured parties must be accorded their chance to be compensated. If, under the facts, one theory in connection with an alleged waiver is as plausible as the other, then the courts should find in favor of the theory which preserves to a man his valuable rights. Employees who exercise due care in the discharge of their duties have already been deprived of many of their former rights in court by the enactment of this Workmen's Compensation Statute. The courts will not be too ready to take away any more by judicial construction. We think Poe still had his right to prosecute his common-law suit against Guitar, if the want of notice is still apparent upon another trial.

Therefore, we recommend that the judgments of the district court and Court of Civil Appeals be reversed, and the cause remanded to the former for another trial not inconsistent herewith.

PHILLIPS, C. J. The judgment recommended in the report of the Commission of Appeals is adopted and will be entered as the judgment of the Supreme Court.

We approve the holding of the Commission on the question discussed in its opinion.

WAGGONER et al. v. ZUNDELOWITZ.
(No. 226–3400.)

(Commission of Appeals of Texas, Section B. June 1, 1921.)

1. Mines and minerals ⬳74—In suit to rescind transfer of interest in lease instruction for defendants held not error, if misrepresentations were all as to facts.

In a suit to rescind an assignment of interest in an oil lease, based on defendants' false representations to obtain an option on plaintiff's interest in the lease transferred to them, an instruction to find for defendants if plaintiff discovered their falsity before he signed, and, knowing thereof, executed the transfer, was not erroneous, if none of the misrepresentations involved an opinion, but were all statements of actual facts.

2. Mines and minerals ⬳74—A false statement, claimed to obtain a transfer of interest in lease, held a statement of fact.

A false statement that an oil well being drilled was to be a dry hole, claimed to have been made to obtain an option on an interest in a nearby lease, was not an expression of an opinion, but a statement of fact based on apparent knowledge.

3. Appeal and error ⬳215(1)—Instruction as to false representation held correct on appeal, in absence of objection thereto.

Where, in an action based on alleged false representation, most of which appeared to be not merely matters of opinion, an instruction, proper as applying to misrepresentations as to facts, must be held correct on appeal, in absence of objection that it did not distinguish between kinds of misrepresentations and apply the law accordingly.

4. Appeal and error ⬳1033(5)—Instruction that plaintiff, suing to rescind, must have discovered falsity of all representations before waiver established, held harmless.

In an action to rescind and cancel the sale of an oil lease on the ground of misrepresentations by the buyer as to the nonproductivity of a well on adjacent property, an instruction that plaintiff must have discovered the falsity of all the representations, and not merely the material ones, before he could be held to have waived the fraud by signing the transfer, was not prejudicial to plaintiff.

5. Mines and minerals ⬳74—Waiver of fraud affecting rescission of transfer of interest in lease not dependent on knowledge that transferee knew representations were false.

Waiver of fraud by execution of transfer of interest in oil lease with knowledge thereof does not depend on knowledge that the transferee knew he was falsifying when he made representations amounting to statement of opinion to procure an option on such interest, whether such option was binding or not.

6. Mines and minerals ⬳74—Falsity of an opinion representation to obtain option on interest in lease held not material as affecting right to rescind.

Falsity of an opinion representation that a nearby well looked like a dry hole, made to obtain an option on an interest in an oil lease, was not material as affecting right to rescind the transfer of such interest, where nothing was done to prevent a fair test of the well, and the assignor did nothing to inform himself in relation thereto.

7. Appeal and error ⬳1067—Failure to instruct that party suing to rescind must have had knowledge before he could waive fraud held not prejudicial.

Where plaintiff, after discovering the falsity of defendant's representation that an oil well on land near his lease was a dry hole, signed a transfer of his lease to defendant, he was not prejudiced by the failure of the court to charge that he must have known that defendant knowingly falsified before he could be adjudged to have waived the fraud; the discovery of the falsity leading inevitably to the conclusion that defendant knew it was false when made.

8. Mines and minerals ⬳74—Fraud in obtaining option on interest in lease waived by transfer after notice of misrepresentations as to nearby well.

If waiver of fraud in obtaining an option on an interest in an oil lease depended on knowledge of the false representations about a nearby well, the fraud was waived by a transfer without further inquiry, after being advised by others that the well was a good producer; it having come in the same or the previous day, and being the talk of the town.

9. Mines and minerals ⬳74—Charge as to waiver of fraud by signing transfer properly refused for failing to submit sufficiency of knowledge of fraud.

In an action to rescind a transfer of an interest in an oil lease on the ground of fraud in obtaining an option, a special charge that plaintiff did not waive the fraud by signing the transfer after discovering the falsity of representations, unless he knew of defendant's bad faith, was properly refused for failing to submit the question as to whether or not the knowledge he had was sufficient to put him on inquiry.

10. **Mines and minerals ⊂⇒74—In suit to rescind transfer of interest in lease, charge as to waiver of fraud held erroneous as to necessity of knowledge of bad faith.**

In an action to rescind a transfer of an interest in an oil lease on the ground of fraud, a charge that, unless the plaintiff, before he executed the transfer, knew all the facts with reference thereto, the representations were false, and that the defendant at the time knew the facts and failed to communicate the same, was erroneous, as not confining the necessity of the plaintiff's knowledge of bad faith to the one opinion representation that a well being drilled on nearby land was to be a dry hole.

11. **Mines and minerals ⊂⇒74—Fraud in obtaining option on interest in lease may be waived by executing final assignment if assignor only knows material facts.**

Fraud in obtaining an option on an interest in an oil lease may be waived by execution of the final assignment, if assignor only has knowledge of the material facts, and need not know all the facts with reference to the transaction.

12. **Trial ⊂⇒194(11)—Charge on fraudulent representations held erroneous as weight of the evidence.**

In an action to cancel an oil lease on the ground of fraudulent representations, a requested charge, stating as a matter of law that a certain fact was material and a certain other fact, taken alone, was not material, *held* erroneous as on the weight of the evidence.

13. **Trial ⊂⇒261—Special charge properly refused, unless correct in all its parts.**

A special charge should be refused unless correct in all its parts; the trial court being under no obligation to separate the correct from the incorrect portions.

14. **Appeal and error ⊂⇒1002—Verdict on conflicting evidence not disturbed.**

Where the evidence was conflicting, verdict rendered by the jury will not be disturbed on appeal.

Error to Court of Civil Appeals of Seventh Supreme Judicial District.

Suit by A. Zundelowitz against Ed Waggoner and another. From a judgment of the Court of Civil Appeals, reversing a judgment for defendants (211 S. W. 598), defendants bring error. Reversed, and judgment of district court affirmed.

Bullington, Boone, Humphrey & Hoffman, of Wichita Falls, for plaintiffs in error.

Carrigan, Britain & Montgomery, of Wichita Falls, for defendant in error.

POWELL, J. This suit was filed in the district court of Wichita county, Tex., by A. Zundelowitz against Ed Waggoner and W. W. Silk, praying for a rescission and cancellation of a certain transfer and assignment of an oil and gas lease, executed by defendant in error on May 14, 1917, and further praying, in the alternative, for his damages in the sum of $18,000. All of the parties had been jointly interested in an oil lease covering 348½ acres of land, the interest of Zundelowitz being an undivided one-fourth. On the date last mentioned, the latter conveyed his interest therein to Waggoner for a cash consideration of $37.50 per acre. Waggoner then conveyed to Silk an undivided one-half of this interest he had purchased from Zundelowitz.

The petition alleged that an oil well was being drilled on the Burnett ranch about one mile from said lease; that about May 12, 1917, Waggoner and Silk became informed that the well above mentioned was being brought in, and was showing up for a good well; that they then conspired together to defraud Zundelowitz out of his interest in the lease on said 348½ acres; that in pursuance of said conspiracy they made certain false representations to him with reference to said well and lease, and concealed certain other information with reference thereto, thereby obtaining an option from the latter on May 13, 1917, covering his one-fourth interest in said lease; that the assignment was executed, as aforesaid, the next day; that at that time he was still in ignorance of the true facts about the oil well development near the lease.

Waggoner and Silk answered by general and special exceptions and general denial; they specially denied that they defrauded Zundelowitz, or concealed any information from him which it was their duty to impart; they further pleaded that Zundelowitz had the same opportunity to know of the development on the Burnett ranch and the bringing in of the Gulf Production well thereon, as they did, and that he was fully advised even before the option was signed; that in any event, before the final assignment was executed to Waggoner on May 14, Zundelowitz did have knowledge of all the material facts about the development on the Burnett ranch, and, even if he had been defrauded in the beginning, his act in executing the final assignment and completing the executory contract and option amounted to a waiver and condonement of the alleged fraud, and a ratification and confirmation of the option contract which he alleged Waggoner had secured by misrepresentation and concealment. The answer further alleged that the actions and conduct of Zundelowitz in the premises estopped him from seeking to cancel his transfer of his undivided interest in said lease, or to seek damages by reason thereof.

The case was tried before a jury, which, in response to a general charge of the court, returned a general verdict for Waggoner and Silk. Complying with the jury's verdict, the judgment of the court was that Zundelowitz take nothing by his suit, and that Waggoner and Silk go hence and recover their costs.

In due course, Zundelowitz appealed from the judgment of the trial court to the Court of Civil Appeals at Fort Worth, whence the case was transferred to the Court of Civil Appeals at Amarillo. The latter court entered judgment reversing the judgment of the trial court and remanding the case for another trial. See 211 S. W. 598. Waggoner and Silk, in due time, filed a motion for rehearing in the Court of Civil Appeals, which was overruled. In due course thereafter they sued out a writ of error to the Supreme Court, which was granted.

The controlling questions on this appeal involve paragraph 6 of the general charge of the court, and special charge No. 2, requested by Zundelowitz in connection therewith, and refused by the court. Said paragraph No. 6 is as follows:

"If you find and believe from the evidence that Ed Waggoner did make the representations as alleged by A. Zundelowitz, and that said representations were false, and that said Ed Waggoner knew them to be false, and that A. Zundelowitz did rely upon the same, and was induced thereby to sell said lease to the said Waggoner, nevertheless, if you further find and believe from the evidence that A. Zundelowitz discovered the falsity of said representations, if they were false, before he signed the transfer of said lease to the said Waggoner, and, having said knowledge and knowing the falsity of said representations, if they were false, signed and delivered the transfer of said lease to the said Waggoner, you will find for the defendants."

Said special charge No. 2 is as follows:

"In connection with paragraph 6 of the court's charge, you are charged that, before you can find for the defendants under said paragraph, you must believe that A. Zundelowitz, before he executed and delivered the transfer of the lease, knew all the facts with reference to the transaction; that is, he must have known that the representations were false, and he must have known that Ed Waggoner at the time said representations were made knew the facts with reference to said well, or had information with reference to same, and failed to communicate the facts within his knowledge, and it would not be sufficient simply for you to find that A. Zundelowitz had information before he made said transfer that the well had been brought in."

The Court of Civil Appeals, apparently ignoring the fact that both the pleadings and evidence account for many fraudulent representations as being involved in the issue of waiver, or ratification of the alleged fraud, limits its discussion of the correctness of the above charge to only one phase of the testimony, to wit: Zundelowitz testified:

"I wanted to set this trade aside because he [Waggoner] said it was to be a dry hole, and on the basis of that he was going to sell it. It made a big difference to me whether it was going to be a dry hole. If I had known the well was a producing well, I would not have sold it for $37.50."

In line with the above limitation of the evidence, said court announces the following general principles of law:

"1. Ordinarily, misrepresentation of a material fact will be sufficient to support an action for fraud, whether the person making it knew that it was false or not. One making a statement of fact as a basis of negotiations is bound to know whether it is true, and bad faith is not in such cases a necessary element of an action for fraud. In this case, however, the statement in reference to the well was made in the form of the expression of an opinion, and it is generally true that a statement of an opinion will not form the basis of an action for fraud. There are exceptions to this rule, however. Where an opinion is expressed for the purpose of deceiving as to a matter which has within the knowledge of the person expressing it ceased to be a matter of opinion, and is thereby made the means of a misrepresentation or concealment of a fact, it may form the predicate for actionable fraud. Houston v. Darnell Lumber Co., 146 S. W. 1063; Olston v. Oregon Water Power & R. Co., 52 Or. 343, 96 Pac. 1095, 97 Pac. 538, 20 L. R. A. (N. S.) 926; 20 Cyc. 18; 12 R. C. L. p. 248; Mudsill Mining Co. v. Watrous, 61 Fed. 163, 9 C. C. A. 415.

"2. Fraud which renders a contract voidable may be waived or condoned, and the contract ratified by the party defrauded, but acts relied upon as ratification must be done after the person defrauded 'has obtained full knowledge of all the material facts involved in the transaction, has become fully aware of its imperfection and of his own rights to impeach it, or ought and might, with reasonable diligence, have become so aware.' 2 Pomeroy (3d Ed.) par. 964; North American Accident Insurance Co. v. Miller, 193 S. W. 758; Ingram v. Abbott, 14 Tex. Civ. App. 583, 38 S. W. 626; Black on Rescission and Cancellation, par. 591.

"3. If bad faith on the part of Waggoner in making the representation as to the well was material in determining whether fraud had been committed, it necessarily follows that knowledge on the part of Zundelowitz as to such bad faith was also a material fact in determining whether he had waived the fraud by executing the transfer. The charge of the court does not therefore correctly present the issue of ratification as made by the evidence. This was called to the court's attention, both by objections to the charge and by the request for instructions referred to. We think the charge requested should have been given."

Said court assigns no other reason for reversing and remanding the judgment of the trial court.

According to the view of the Court of Civil Appeals, before Zundelowitz can be held to have waived the alleged fraud, three things were necessary: (1) False representations must have been made; (2) Waggoner must have known that they were false when he made them; (3) Zundelowitz must have known, not only their falsity, but also that Waggoner knew they were all false when made.

[1] If none of the alleged misrepresentations involved an opinion, but all were statements of actual facts, then we are sure no one will contend for a moment that paragraph 6 of the court's general charge is erroneous, so far as Zundelowitz is concerned. Numerous authorities can be cited in support of this proposition, but we content ourselves by referring to a very excellent opinion by Justice Lurton of the United States Circuit Court of Appeals in the case of Simon v. Goodyear Metallic Rubber Shoe Co., 105 Fed. 573, 44 C. C. A. 612, 52 L. R. A. 745. In that case, the very contention Zundelowitz here makes was before the court. It is also true that the facts in that case are similar to those in the case at bar, in that in each case there was a preliminary contract, binding on its face. That court, speaking through the distinguished jurist above named, said:

"But it is said that plaintiff did not have full knowledge of the deceit, in that he did not know before full performance that Rodenbach or his principal knew the falsity of his representations, and that this fact was not discovered until it came out in the evidence in this case. But plaintiff did discover as early as May, 1895, that the factories which had been operated before April 18, 1895, by the Rubber Reclaiming Company were in full operation, each for itself, and that each was in the market, actively competing for old rubber waste. The actionable misrepresentation, upon plaintiff's theory of the case, was that these factories were out of business, and therefore would not be competitors in the market for the material he undertook to collect and sell to plaintiff. It was not of the essence of his case that Rodenbach knew his representations to be false. If he made the representation, which it is claimed he did make, with the purpose of procuring the contract in question, and with the intent that the plaintiff should act upon it, without knowledge as to whether it was true or not, it would be a false representation within the rule. Cooper v. Schlesinger, 111 U. S. 148, 155, 4 Sup. Ct. 360, 28 L. Ed. 382; Iron Co. v. Bamford, 150 U. S. 665, 14 Sup. Ct. 219, 37 L. Ed. 1215. Fraud is not waived unless there be conduct inconsistent with a purpose to disaffirm the contract after full knowledge of the facts which constitute the fraud, and raise an election whether the defrauded party will go on with the contract, or disaffirm what has been done. Mining Co. v. Watrous, 9 C. C. A. 415, 61 Fed. 163; Alger v. Keith (decided by this court November 7, 1900) 105 Fed. 105; Moxon v. Payne, 8 Ch. App. 881. But full knowledge of a fraud does not mean that the party defrauded shall have knowledge of all of the evidence tending to prove the fraud. If he have knowledge of the material facts which go to make up the case of deceit as practiced upon him, it is sufficient to make him elect whether he will go on with the contract, or stop short and sue for the loss he has already suffered. Bach v. Tuch, 26 N. E. 1019, 126 N. Y. 53.

"When the plaintiff learned, as he did in May, 1895, that the several factories which had been operated by the Rubber Reclaiming Company had not gone out of business of reclaiming old rubber, but were actively prosecuting that business, and in the market, each for itself, competing for waste rubber, he knew the material facts which went to make his case for deceit. By thereafter deliberately proceeding with the execution of the contract, he waived the deceit and affirmed the contract. Upon this ground the direction to the jury to find for the defendant was correct, and the judgment is accorungly affirmed."

[2, 3] The only misrepresentation which could possibly be construed as being merely an opinion is the one centered upon by the Court of Civil Appeals. On cross-examination, Zundelowitz testified that Waggoner said, in speaking of the new well, "that it was to be a dry hole, and on the basis of that, he was going to sell it." This was not an expression of an opinion. It was a statement of fact, based upon apparent knowledge. It was not a statement that it looked like a dry hole, or might be one. He is alleged to have said, "it was to be one." We doubt if any of the misrepresentations involved only an opinion. If it be said that Zundelowitz contradicted himself on the exact language used by Waggoner, then the jury should have been asked to pass upon which part of his testimony was true, and, therefore, whether a statement of fact or only an opinion. No such instruction was requested by Zundelowitz. In any event, as most of the alleged misrepresentations were, undoubtedly, not matters merely of opinion, paragraph 6 of the court's charge was correct, in the absence of an objection by counsel for Zundelowitz that it did not distinguish between the kinds of misrepresentations and apply the law accordingly. No such objection is found in the record. The objections were that the charge was erroneous because it did not require that Zundelowitz know that Waggoner knew all the representations were false when made. Therefore paragraph 6 must stand, as we view it.

[4] Paragraph No. 6 of the general charge of the court requires that Zundelowitz must have discovered the falsity of all the representations of Waggoner, and not merely his material representations, before the former could be held to have waived said fraud. That charge was prejudicial to Waggoner, but Zundelowitz cannot be heard to complain.

[5] But, admit, for the sake of argument,

that Waggoner told Zundelowitz the well was likely to be a dry hole, and that said statement was an opinion, and not one of fact, we still believe paragraph 6 of the court's general charge correct, and that it was not necessary for said charge to include an instruction that Zundelowitz's waiver of this fraud depended upon his knowledge that Waggoner knew he was falsifying when he made his representations.

There is an authority of excellent standing which has passed upon the very contention made in this connection by counsel for defendant in error. The Supreme Court of California, in a very recent case, has expressly overruled the same in a very similar fact case. See Thomas v. Birch, 178 Cal. 483, 173 Pac. 1102. In that case, the majority stockholders of an oil company decided to discourage the minority stockholders, depreciate the value of the stock of the corporation, and buy them out for a nominal consideration. The company had four small producing wells. A fifth was being drilled, and when nearing completion it made a very favorable showing for a large producer. It finally came in that way, but was purposely choked off by the conspirators. In April, 1911, the injured parties sold their stock, having given an option on it about 60 days before. The plaintiffs admitted that they knew about the value of this well No. 5 before they finally sold their stock, but said they did not know that the conspirators had practiced their fraud upon them until two years later. The trial court sustained a general demurrer to the petition, and the Supreme Court of California affirmed that action. The court held that the evidence showed that plaintiff, before finally selling the stock, knew that well No. 5 had been opened for production, and all about the value thereof, and the effect of its development upon the value of the stock, and that nothing else was material. We quote from the court's opinion in the California case as follows:

"A binding contract arose for the first time when Birch, on April 18, 1911, made payment and took the stock. But the plaintiff's own pleading alleges that on April 10, 1911, eight days before payment of the purchase price, he learned that well No. 5 had been opened for production, and the further allegations, fairly construed, amount to an admission that he then learned all about the well and its value and the effect of its development upon the value of the shares. At that time it was still within his power to revoke the option and retain his stock. Instead of so doing, he allowed the defendant to go on and consummate the purchase, took the agreed price, and then, after a lapse of some three years, charges fraud in a transaction which he voluntarily carried into effect, after full knowledge of the facts. This he cannot do."

In the case just about quoted, the conspirator expressed an opinion, just as in the case at bar. He said that well No. 5 would not be a good producer. It is exactly like the present case on the facts. The only difference in the cases is that the California court held that the conspirators had no option on the stock binding upon its face. We have considerable doubt about the binding effect of the option in the instant case, but we waive that, and admit for present purposes, that it is binding. We do not think its binding effect is material, and we believe that the California court would have rendered the same decision, had the option in that case been binding. In discussing this very proposition, that court said:

"Strong authority may be cited for the view that, even if there had been a contract of purchase and sale, binding upon both parties, the seller could not, where he discovered the fraud while the contract remained wholly executory, deliver the property and receive the purchase price, and still maintain an action for damages for the fraud. McDonough v. Williams, 77 Ark. 261, 92 S. W. 783, 8 L. R. A. (N. S.) 452, 7 Ann. Cas. 276; Thompson v. Libby, 36 Minn. 287, 31 N. W. 52; Baird v. Mayor of N. Y., 96 N. Y. 567, 576. In Thompson v. Libby, supra, the court said: 'To allow a person who has discovered the fraud while the contract is still wholly executory to go on and execute it and then sue for the fraud looks very much like permitting him to speculate upon the fraud of the other party. It is virtually to allow a man to recover for self-inflicted injuries.' It is not necessary, for the purposes of the present case, to go so far."

In connection with the practice of permitting a person, after knowledge that he has been the victim of false representations, to go ahead with an executory contract, and then try to "rue back," we are in accord with the United States Circuit Court of Appeals in the case of Kingman v. Stoddard, 85 Fed. 740, 29 C. C. A. 413. The court there says:

"For example, if one by the imposition of fraudulent practices has been induced to purchase goods, and after their receipt discovers the fraud, he may rescind, or may affirm and have his action for the deceit. But if, before delivery of the goods, he has discovered the fraud, he may not then accept the goods, and still have an action for deceit. He had sustained no injury prior to the discovery of the fraud. He was under no legal obligation to execute a contract imposed upon him through fraud. Fraud without damage, fallen or inevitable, is not actionable. The loss arises from his acceptance of the goods. This being done with knowledge of the fraud, he has voluntarily brought upon himself the injury. 'Volenti non fit injuria.' With respect to an executory contract voidable by reason of fraud, the defrauded party, with knowledge of the deceit practiced upon him, may not play fast and loose. He cannot approbate and reprobate. He must deal with the contract and with the wrongdoer at arm's length. He may not, with knowledge of the fraud, speculate upon the advantages or disadvantages of the contract, receiving its benefits, and at the same time repudiate its obligations. Grymes v. Sanders, 93 U. S. 55, 62; McLean v. Clapp, 141 U. S. 429, 12 Sup. Ct. 29. Fraud is not actionable when the defrauded party, before performance and after knowledge of the fraud, voluntarily ratifies and exacts performance of the contract by the other party thereto."

Paragraph 6 of the court's charge was onerous enough on the plaintiffs in error, in our judgment, whether the representations were matters of fact or opinions. For the same reason, special charge No. 2, requested by Zundelowitz, would have been erroneous.

[6] Further, if it be held that this particular representation about the dry hole was an expression of an opinion only, then we doubt if it was material in any event, for it probably could not be the basis of an action for fraud. The Court of Civil Appeals announces some rules in this connection, and in support thereof cites, among other cases, that of Mudsill Mining Co. v. Watrous et al., 61 Fed. 163, 9 C. C. A. 415. Justice Lurton, in that case, lays down the following rules in this same connection, with which we are in hearty accord. He says:

"It is perhaps too well settled to admit of controversy that a misrepresentation, in order to constitute fraud, must be an affirmative statement of some material fact, and not a mere expression of opinion. Gordon v. Butler, 105 U. S. 553; Development Co. v. Silva, 125 U. S. 247, 8 Sup. Ct. 881. This distinction between the misrepresentation of a fact and the expression of an opinion is peculiarly applicable in the sale of a property so speculative and uncertain as a silver mine. In Jennings v. Broughton, 17 Beav. 234, which was a case brought to set aside the sale of shares in a mining venture on account of fraud in the sale. Knight Bruce, L. J., said: 'First, in the statements or representations concerning the mine, was there any untrue assertion material in its nature; that is to say, which, taken as true, added substantially to the value or promise of the mine, and was not evidently conjectural merely?'

"The representations made verbally, and which it is alleged were false, related alone to the average richness of the exposed body of ore. Though in form the affirmation of a fact, yet, when applied to the subject-matter of the negotiation, it was in its very nature conjectural, and amounted to an expression of opinion. But this rule that a mere expression of an opinion will not constitute fraud must not be pushed beyond the reason for the rule. If a false statement is to be given immunity because it is mere 'puffing' or 'trade talk,' and only the expression of an opinion, it is because the party to whom the opinion is addressed has no right to rely upon the mere expression of an opinion, and is assumed to have the ability and opportunity of forming his own opinion and coming to an independent judgment. In speaking of the difference between the legal effect of a representation as to a fact and the expression of an opinion, Mr. Pomeroy says: 'The reason is very simple: While the person ad-

dressed has a right to rely on any assertion of a fact, he has no right to rely upon the mere expression of an opinion held by the party addressing him, in whatever language such expression be made. He is assumed to be equally able to form his own opinion, and to come to a correct judgment in respect to the matter, as the party with whom he is dealing, and cannot justly claim, therefore, to have been misled by the opinion, however erroneous it may have been.' Pomeroy, Eq. Jur. par. 878.

"If, therefore, the party making false statements as to a matter conjectural in its character, and therefore relating to a matter of opinion, actively intervenes to prevent investigation and the discovery of the truth, and such intervention be effective in the concealment of the facts and in the deception of the buyer, a clear case of operative fraud is made out. In every such case immunity will not be extended to false expressions of opinion, upon the ground of 'puffing' or 'trade talk,' if it appear that the vendor has, by his conduct, prevented investigation, and induced reliance upon the statements of the seller. In such a case the subsequent conduct of the seller in actively preventing the buyer from the formation of an independent opinion so connects itself with the original misrepresentation as to become part and parcel of the false statement, and amounts in law to the false affirmation of a fact. A false representation may, and most often does, consist in language alone, expressed or written; but it may also consist in conduct alone, or external acts. Whenever the purpose is to induce belief in the existence of a fact which does not exist, every word and act intended to produce conviction and induce action becomes a misrepresentation if, through their instrumentality, the party upon whom they are practiced is induced to act. 2 Pom. Eq. Jur. § 877. The gravamen of the alleged fraud lies in the allegation that when the complainants undertook to examine this property, and form an independent judgment as to its value, through the active and willful intervention of defendants, their samples were rendered untrustworthy by the secret admixture of silver in a form in which it did not exist in this mine; that the purpose was to give to these samples, otherwise representative of the average value of the ore in sight, a false and fictitious value, which would confirm the untrue statements expressed theretofore as to the silver contents of the mine. Now, it must be evident that, if this was done, a most abominable fraud was practiced, and that no court would suffer a contract resting upon such a foundation to stand."

It will be seen that the liability in the case just quoted was based, not alone upon the fraudulent representations expressing an opinion, but also upon the active and operative fraud thereafter practiced by defendants in "salting" the mine and preventing a fair test. In the case at bar, it became the duty of Zundelowitz to investigate this opinion expressed by Waggoner. If he did not do so, he could not predicate a case of fraud thereon. If he had made such an investigation, Waggoner would still not have been liable, because of said opinion representation, unless he had gone further and done something to prevent Zundelowitz from making a fair test of said well. As the latter made no effort to inform himself about the well, and as Waggoner did nothing to prevent his doing so, we are of the view that said representation was immaterial, and could have been eliminated entirely. Paragraph 6 of the court's charge was not required to take it into account.

[7] If the jury found, under paragraph 6 of the court's charge, that Zundelowitz discovered the falsity of Waggoner's representation that the well looked like a dry hole, then that inevitably led to the conclusion, as we see it, that Zundelowitz knew that Waggoner knew it was false when made. On the same day the representation was made the well came in. It was not a dry hole. Waggoner was an experienced oil man and scout. He kept up with the news in matters of that kind. The whole town was excited. Zundelowitz, knowing the representation was false, must have known that Waggoner was not innocent in that connection. For this reason, Zundelowitz was not prejudiced, in any event, by failure of the court to charge that he must have known that Waggoner knowingly falsified before he could be adjudged guilty of waiver.

It seems to be the theory of counsel for Zundelowitz that the latter was bound by the option contract; that he could not take any steps to rescind the same until he knew of some fraud on the part of Waggoner authorizing the rescission; that such rescission could be based only upon the theory that Waggoner knowingly told an untruth when he said the well looked like a dry hole; that the jury should have been instructed that his act in executing the final contract could not be a waiver of his right of rescission, unless he knew beforehand of Waggoner's bad faith.

[8] Without abandoning any of our views already expressed, let us concede for the purpose of the discussion that the waiver by Zundelowitz did depend upon his knowledge of the fraud of Waggoner in making said representation about the dry hole. The jury returned its verdict upon one or both of the following theories: (1) That no false representations were made; (2) that if they were made Zundelowitz discovered the falsity thereof before signing the final transfer, and waived the said fraud. If the verdict was upon the former theory, then the charge on waiver prejudiced no one. If it was upon the latter theory, we must assume that the jury found that Zundelowitz knew there was a fine well out there near this lease before he executed the final contract, and that Waggoner had told him an untruth the afternoon before, in saying that it was to be a dry hole. Paragraph 6 of the court's charge required the jury to find that much. It did not require much stretch of the imagination for

Zundelowitz to go a step further and conclude that Waggoner knew the false statement was false when he made it. Viewing the matter as ordinarily prudent persons would, we think the information Zundelowitz did have was enough to require him, as a matter of law, to delay the final execution of his assignment until he could inquire into those matters, and see if he had a right to rescind his option contract. He says Waggoner told him Sunday afternoon that the well looked like a dry hole. Early the next morning, he was advised by others that it was a good producing well. It had come in on Sunday, and possibly Saturday before. It was the talk of the town. Under these circumstances, it became his duty to make further inquiry before closing the deal. He did not do so, but went ahead and signed the transfer. When he did that, he ratified and waived the fraud, and special charge No. 2, requested by his counsel, was immaterial. The general charge was sufficient.

[9] At any rate, if he was not required, as a matter of law, to pursue his inquiry, after getting all that information, the special charge in this connection should have been so framed as to submit to the jury the question as to whether or not the knowledge he already had was sufficient to put him upon inquiry before executing the final transfer. Only in the event they answered that in the negative should the jury in any case have been told that the waiver depended upon knowledge by Zundelowitz of the bad faith of Waggoner. The special charge did not so provide and it was, in any event, properly refused.

[10] Said special charge is, of course, in error in not confining the necessity of Zundelowitz's knowledge of Waggoner's bad faith to the one representation involving only an opinion.

[11] Not only was special charge No. 2 erroneous in the respects above mentioned, and therefore properly refused by the trial court, but it was further contended that it was erroneous in this: Said special charge required that Zundelowitz know "all the facts with reference to the transaction," before he could be held guilty of waiver in executing the final assignment. The Texas courts have never announced any such law. From the very beginning, the only knowledge required is of the material facts. See Mitchell v. Zimmerman, 4 Tex. 75, 51 Am. Dec. 717; Lemmon v. Hanley, 28 Tex. 219; Jackson v. Stockbridge, 29 Tex. 394, 94 Am. Dec. 290; Carson v. Kelley, 57 Tex. 379; Miller v. Jannett, 63 Tex. 82; Putman v. Bromwell, 73 Tex. 465, 11 S. W. 491; Barrett v. Featherstone, 89 Tex. 567, 35 S. W. 11, 36 S. W. 245; Downes v. Self, 28 Tex. Civ. App. 356, 67 S. W. 897; Furneaux v. Webb, 33 Tex. Civ. App. 560, 77 S. W. 828; Katzenstein v. Reid & Co., 41 Tex. Civ. App. 106, 91 S. W. 360.

In fact the Court of Civil Appeals seem

to take no issue with the authorities on this point. In approving the special charge in this connection, that court says:

"We do not think that this omission vitiates the charge, as this qualification would be implied; besides, the explanation which follows this general statement in the charge leaves no room for mistake as to the meaning thereof."

We think the other matters discussed in this opinion control the case, and that it is not necessary to pass upon the correctness of the views of the Court of Civil Appeals just above quoted, and we do not do so.

[12] Furthermore, we are of the view that said special charge is clearly upon the weight of the evidence, and should not have been given. This charge states, as a matter of law, that a certain fact is material, and a certain other fact, taken alone, is not material. The most that Zundelowitz could contend for would be to have the jury pass upon the materiality of certain facts and representations. Ordinarily, this is the province of the jury in cases of this kind. This charge, in two respects, deprives the jury of that privilege. We refer to the case of Evans v. Goggan, 5 Tex. Civ. App. 129, 23 S. W. 854. In that case, the court says:

"It was not proper for the court to instruct the jury that a given fact—the one stated in the charge—would constitute ratification. The jury had the right to look at all the facts showing the true effect of the use of the piano. It may be that the fact stated would be deemed by the jury as sufficient, or that it, considered with other facts, was not sufficient. We are constrained to say that the charge was not the law of the case."

[13] It is elementary that a special charge should be refused unless correct in all its parts. The trial court is under no obligation to separate the correct from the incorrect portions. For the many reasons stated, the trial court, in our judgment, properly refused said special charge.

[14] This was peculiarly a fact case. There was sharp conflict in the testimony. Zundelowitz had his chance before the jury, and we think the charge of the court was more than fair to him. As a matter of fact, he never did testify to anything which would indicate that he was influenced in the final execution of the assignment by his knowledge, or lack of knowledge, of Waggoner's bad faith in making the representations. Zundelowitz assigned several inconsistent reasons as the cause of his desire to rescind the Waggoner assignment. After a careful analysis of the testimony we are inclined to the view that, if his testimony was true, he gave the real reason when he said he executed the option, relying upon Waggoner's promise to share the profits with him on a resale. He testified that Waggoner promised to give him all over the $37.50 per acre that

his one-fourth interest should sell for. If that had been true, then the $37.50 per acre was only a matter of form, and Zundelowitz did not care how good a well had come in on the Burnett ranch. In fact, the better the well, the more his profits would be. He stated that some one told him, after the final transfer had been signed, that Waggoner would not be fair and carry out that agreement about the profits; that he believed said latter statement, and began to take action accordingly. Believing that, as he says he did, and hearing that the lease had sold for $300 per acre, we assume that he was unwilling to see others make that much out of his former holdings. If we are correct in this view, then none of the other representations induced the contract, and therefore were not in the case. But we gladly concede to the jury the privilege and duty of passing upon these facts in evidence and settling the conflicts therein. They performed their duty under a charge of the court, against which Zundelowitz had no cause to complain. They have spoken, and we think the judgment of the trial court, reflecting their verdict, should be affirmed.

Therefore we recommend that the judgment of the Court of Civil Appeals be reversed, and that of the district court affirmed.

PHILLIPS, C. J. The judgment recommended in the report of the Commission of Appeals is adopted and will be entered as the judgment of the Supreme Court.

———————

MORRISON et al. v. NEELY et al.
(No. 229—2407.)

(Commission of Appeals of Texas, Section B. June 8, 1921.)

1. **Appeal and error ⟜724(1)—Statute as to sufficiency of assignment of error liberally construed.**

   Vernon's Sayles' Ann. Civ. St. 1914, art. 1612, making an assignment of error directing court's attention to errors complained of sufficient, is to be liberally construed.

2. **Appeal and error ⟜750(4)—Assignments of error held to attack sufficiency of evidence to sustain findings of fact.**

   Under Vernon's Sayles' Ann. Civ. St. 1914, art. 1612, assignments of error sufficient to direct the court's attention to the fact that appellant claimed that the evidence was not sufficient to support the judgment *held* to present question as to sufficiency of evidence to support the findings of fact of the trial court, though the assignments do not directly and specifically attack the findings of fact.

3. **Appeal and error ⟜1094(1)—Sufficiency of evidence to support judgment exclusively a question for the Court of Civil Appeals.**

   The Supreme Court has no jurisdiction to pass upon the sufficiency of the proof to support the judgment; such question being within the exclusive province of the Court of Civil Appeals.

Error to Court of Civil Appeals of Second Supreme Judicial District.

Action by Byron B. Byrne against Earl Morrison and others, in which W. H. Neely and wife and another filed a cross-action against defendant Morrison and one Hastings. Judgment for plaintiff on the main action. Judgment for Neely and wife on the cross-action, affirmed by Court of Civil Appeals (214 S. W. 586), and Morrison and another bring error. Remanded to Court of Civil Appeals, with instructions.

L. W. Sandusky, of Colorado, Tex., for plaintiffs in error.

R. G. Smith, of El Paso, M. Carter, of Colorado, Tex., and J. E. Starley, of Pecos, for defendants in error.

KITTRELL, J. The action out of and from which the appeal in this case arose was based on a certain bond for title executed by plaintiffs in error to one Bryon B. Byrne to three certain sections of land in Culberson county by plaintiffs in error, on which bond one W. H. Neely and his wife and one Wood were sureties. Byrne recovered the judgment he sought, and secured relief he was satisfied with, in the form of a decree for specific performance, and none of the defendants has appealed from that judgment.

The case as presented in the Court of Civil Appeals was an appeal by Morrison and Hastings from a judgment of $2,412.20 upon a cross-action against them by W. H. Neely for money had and received, and not accounted for.

To all intents and purposes the question of title to none of the land is in fact involved; for, while there are a number of instruments in addition to the bond for title, in the form of contracts, deeds of trust, and deeds offered in evidence, it is clear that by the unappealed-from judgment in favor of Byrne title to three sections passed into him, and by a deed of which neither the regularity, validity, nor effect is called in question the title to the rest of the land passed into Byrne's mother, who paid a valuable consideration for it.

The result as to the land left no question to be appealed, except, as has been said, that of whether or not the trial court rightly adjudged that plaintiffs in error were debtors to Neely for balance of money had and received.

While this is true, there are certain facts necessary to a clear understanding of the case, or which will at least be helpful to that end. The case was tried before the court without a jury, and was evidently tried with ability and most painstaking care, and the findings of fact, which cover in small typewriting 20 pages of the record, are abundantly sustained by the evidence, and all findings of values and debts and credits are set down in itemized detail with mathematical accuracy.

In the main the testimony as to sales (so far as not revealed by record evidence) and of receipts and payments by plaintiffs in error was given by Morrison.

The material facts stated in as condensed form as is practicable are:

(1) That about May 1, 1914, W. H. Neely owned eleven sections of school land bought in the usual statutory way from the state, none of which had been paid for in full, and on all of which he was more or less delinquent in interest payments.

(2) He had complied with the law as to occupancy of eight sections, but as to the other three he had not.

(3) Besides his indebtedness to the state Neely owed quite a number of other debts which were pressing him, and he proposed to Morrison and Hastings in effect that they should take charge of all his lands, taking title in his own name, and sell, trade, or in any wise that they might see fit handle the same, borrowing money, if necessary, and when the lands had been sold and his debts had been paid, including a compensation to them of $1,000, pay him whatever remained.

(4) Eight of the sections were under mortgage, and the note was held by the Roscoe State Bank, and Morrison and Hastings agreed to buy in these eight sections at the sale under the deed of trust, which was given April 20, 1912. Morrison bought these sections for $1,006 on September 1, 1914, at trustees sale.

(5) Neely and wife also made a contract with Morrison and Hastings to live out the rest of the necessary three years on the other three sections, and when he had done so to make deed to Morrison and Hastings.

(6) It was admitted that Neely lived out the necessary time and secured certificate to that effect, which was duly recorded.

(7) On September 4, 1915, after said contract last mentioned was made, Morrison and Hastings executed the bond for title which was the basis of the action in this case, as before stated.

(8) Morrison and Hastings on October 20, 1914, borrowed $3,000 and gave a deed of trust on all the eleven sections as security for the debt, borrowing the money in their own names.

(9) After certain brokerage fees and expenses were deducted, they received net $2,688.33, out of which was repaid to them or to Morrison the $1,006 paid out at the foreclosure sale, and an additional sum allowed by the court on Morrison's testimony sufficient to make the total $1,075.21, for which, among a large number of other items, Morrison and Hastings were allowed credit.

On August 14, 1915, Morrison and Hastings, and Morrison as agent for Neely, made a deal with Byron B. Byrne whereby they exchanged him all the eleven sections for property known as the "brick garage," which included an automobile accessory and repair shop, a tin shop, a large amount of material on hand, and two new and two secondhand automobiles, all of a reasonable value of more than $4,000. Byrne was to take the land with the incumbrance of $3,000 on it which had been borrowed by Morrison and Hastings, and assumed the state debt.

Neely agreed to the trade, but the property was never turned over to him; Morrison and Hastings' explanation being that Byrne could not close the deal and make transfer free from incumbrance.

In order to get possession the contract and bond were put in escrow with a bank which had a claim in such form against Byrne or the property, or both, that Byrne could not make delivery, and Morrison and Hastings, without the knowledge of Neely, went security for Byrne at the bank for $2,000, and the "garage" was turned over to Morrison and Hastings on September 22, 1915, and they kept it in possession and operated it at a loss until February 28, 1916.

They took no inventory of stock, kept no invoice or books of account, but disposed of most, if not all, of the stock, including all the automobiles, and on February 26, 1916, proposed to Byrne that, if he would pay or arrange to have paid at the bank the $2,000 note, they would turn back to him the property.

The arrangement was carried out, and the court found that the value of the property turned back was $750. Byrne's mother paid the note, and Morrison and Hastings conveyed her eight of the sections of land, she assuming the $3,000 note they had given for the borrowed money.

In October, 1913, after the deed of trust under which the Roscoe State Bank sold the eight sections of land was given, Neely deeded three sections to one Spruill for lands in Mitchell county, but before the foreclosure on Neely's land by the bank a vendor's lien was foreclosed on Spruill's land, and the subsequent foreclosure on Neely's land made it impossible for the trade to be carried out. Spruill was not made a party to the action in any way, nor was it sought by Morrison and Hastings to have him made a party.

About the first of the year 1915 Neely, to use the language of the trial court, "entered into some kind of land trade" with one Witten to convey him some of the sections of land on which the Roscoe State Bank had a lien, and Neely through his son took possession and held the Witten land (which was in Ward county) during the year 1915, but the trade fell through on account of failure of Witten's title to the Ward county land.

Witten was not a party to the case in the trial court, nor was it sought by Morrison and Hastings to have him made a party, nor when the testimony was produced relative to the Spruill and Witten deals did any party to the suit ask to have trial stayed to make parties.

It has been very difficult to cull out from such a complexity of trades and deals and deeds the facts necessary to be understood, but the above is a summary in as condensed form as is consistent with clearness.

The Court of Civil Appeals, in affirming the judgment of the trial court, held that—

"The assignments do not directly and specifically attack the findings of fact filed by the trial judge, and it is well settled that the question of the sufficiency of the proof to sustain the findings of fact cannot be raised merely by an attack upon the judgment for the lack of such proof." 214 S. W. 586.

The writ was granted on the ground that the assignments were sufficient to challenge the correctness of the judgment. We are of the opinion that they were sufficient to direct the attention of the court to the errors complained of, which meets the requirement of the statute, since that constitutes all the functions of an assignment of error.

[1] When article 1612, R. S. 1911, relating to the filing of assignments of error, was amended by the act of 1913 (V. S. R. S. art. 1612), after prescribing what is necessary to be done by an appellant, the provision was added, "but an assignment shall be sufficient which directs the attention of the court to the error complained of," which clearly indicates that the statute should be liberally construed, and it has been uniformly so construed. The principle upon which this court has acted in passing upon the question is clearly stated in Land Co. v. McClelland, 86 Tex. 179, 23 S. W. 576, 1100, 22 L. R. A. 105:

"They [the rules and statutes] should be given a reasonable and practical construction, and not one calculated to embarrass suitors in the appellate tribunals by unnecessary restrictions, * * * so as to cut off the approach of such parties as seek relief in good faith from the consequences of supposed errors committed to their prejudice in the trial courts."

See Orange Lumber Co. v. Ellis, 153 S. W. 1181; Hess & Skinner v. Turney, 109 Tex. 208, 203 S. W. 593; Barkley v. Gibbs, 227 S. W. 1099.

[2, 3] While it is true, as is said by the Court of Civil Appeals, the assignments in the instant case "do not specifically attack the findings of fact of the trial court," yet they are sufficient to "direct the attention of the court" to the fact that appellant complained that the evidence was not sufficient to support the judgment; a question the determination of which is the exclusive province of the Court of Civil Appeals, as the Supreme Court has no jurisdiction to pass upon the sufficiency of the proof to support

any given judgment. Since the assignments were sufficient to direct the attention of the court to an error complained of, which it only had the right to pass upon, it should have considered them.

We recommend that the case be remanded to the Court of Civil Appeals, with instructions to consider the assignments.

PHILLIPS, C. J. The judgment recommended in the report of the Commission of Appeals is adopted, and will be entered as the judgment of the Supreme Court.

We approve the holding of the Commission of Appeals on the question discussed in its opinion.

EVANS et ux. v. HOUSTON OIL CO. OF TEXAS et al. (No. 224–3391.)

(Commission of Appeals of Texas, Section A. June 8, 1921.)

1. **Adverse possession ⚖=60(2)—Possession with owner's permission not adverse possession.**

Occupancy of land by one who entered thereon by permission of the owner did not give occupant title by adverse possession, since the possession in such case was that of the owner.

2. **Adverse possession ⚖=47—Owner's entry on land to cut timber broke continuity of adverse claimant's possession except as to land inclosed by claimant.**

Owner's entry upon land to cut timber therefrom interrupted the running of the statute of limitations in favor of adverse claimant as to all of such land except that portion inclosed by claimant, since owner's entry on land carried with it constructive possession of all the land not in claimant's actual possession.

3. **Adverse possession ⚖=50—Purchase of other land three-quarters of a mile distant from land occupied did not preclude purchaser from obtaining title to land occupied by adverse possession.**

Adverse claimant in possession of land claimed did not by purchase from owner thereof of another tract of land three-quarters of a mile distant from land so occupied and claimed acknowledge owner's title to the land so occupied so as to preclude him from obtaining title thereto by adverse possession, but such purchase was merely a circumstance for the jury to consider in connection with other facts and circumstances in evidence in determining whether the adverse claimant's possession was adverse during a continuous period of 10 years at any one time.

4. **Adverse possession ⚖=115(1)—Whether plaintiff's possession of land was adverse held for jury.**

Whether plaintiff, claiming to have acquired title by adverse possession, had actual, continuous, adverse possession for a period of 10 years, held for the jury.

Error to Court of Civil Appeals of Ninth Supreme Judicial District.

Suit by Jubal Evans and wife against the Houston Oil Company of Texas and others. Judgment for defendants affirmed by the Court of Civil Appeals (211 S. W. 605), and plaintiffs bring error. Judgments of district court and Court of Civil Appeals reversed, and cause remanded, with directions.

Coleman & Lowe, of Woodville, for plaintiffs in error.

Kennerly, Williams, Lee & Hill, of Houston, H. O. Head, of Sherman, and P. O. Settle, of Houston, for defendants in error.

GALLAGHER, J. Jubal Evans and wife, plaintiffs in error, sued the Houston Oil Company of Texas and others, defendants in error, for an undivided 160 acres of the W. S. Brown survey in Tyler county to be surveyed so as to include their improvements, claiming that they had acquired title thereto under the 10-year statute of limitation.

It was agreed that the defendants in error owned the land sued for unless plaintiffs in error had acquired title thereto under the 10-year statute. A trial was had before a jury. The court instructed a verdict in favor of defendants in error and judgment was so rendered.

The Court of Civil Appeals, by divided court, affirmed such judgment. 211 S. W. 605.

The survey in question contains 960 acres and is oblong in shape, being nearly two miles long from east to west.

Jubal Evans was the principal witness, and his testimony on direct examination is in substance as follows:

He moved on that survey in June, 1887, and lived on it with his family 16 or 17 years, leaving it in 1903 or 1904. He lived on the east end or east corner of the survey. He did not own any land on the survey at the time he moved onto it, but he afterwards purchased 160 acres where he lived, which tract was totally in the pine woods.

He had other improvements on said survey besides his home. He had a field of 12 or 15 acres down on the creek about three-fourths of a mile from his home place. He claimed 160 acres around that field and down to the creek to be surveyed so as to include the field. He hired 3 acres of this land cleared in the summer of 1887. He cleared and put into cultivation 5 acres the first year, and he put the entire field in cultivation the second year. He cultivated the land embraced in that field every year from 1887 to 1903, and he claimed 160 acres of that land each and every year while he stayed there and has claimed it ever since he left.

Evans was then taken on cross-examination and testified in substance:

A. F. Hester was on said survey logging

and running timber down the creek to the Reliance Lumber Company. Hester moved up there in 1887 and built a camp house on said survey and told him to take charge of it, and he did so and boarded Hester's men. Evans did not intend to stay there at first, but he kept on living there with his family. After about one year Hester pulled up and left and went to logging three or four miles away. He wanted Evans to go with him, but Evans declined, and said he would just stay where he was and cultivate his field and go to and fro to his work with Hester. When Hester built this little house and had Evans move into it he was running the camp for the Reliance Lumber Company and was its woods foreman, working the timber on this survey and running it down to them. He was really a contractor, cutting the timber and running it down and selling it for so much a thousand for the Reliance Lumber Company, which Company then owned the land.

The Reliance Lumber Company, by deed dated September 9, 1893, conveyed to Evans by metes and bounds 160 acres of land out of the northeast part of the survey, reserving the timber thereon. The purchase came about in this way: Hester, one day, in casual conversation with Evans, suggested that maybe he could buy the land he lived on at that time, and said he would see the Reliance Lumber Company. Evans expressed the hope that he could get a place to live on and put his house on.

Hester was agent for the Reliance Lumber Company and attended to their business. Hester procured the deed and delivered it to Evans and carried him for the purchase money, which was paid by Evans in work for Hester. Evans pointed out to Hester the exact land he wanted, so it would cover his house and little field near the house, and the tract purchased was so surveyed. The tract purchased was out in the open pine woods and a more desirable place to live. Evans talked the matter over with his wife, and she favored getting the land to live on, saying she did not want to go down in the creek bottom to live, but that he could still cultivate his field down there.

The Reliance Lumber Company conveyed the land to the Village Mills Company, and said company, on the 9th day of April, 1901, released the timber rights reserved by the Reliance Lumber Company when it conveyed the land to Evans.

The Village Mills Company entered this survey and cut the timber off of the same in 1900 and 1901, but they did not cut any timber off the 160 acres surrounding Evans' field, which he was claiming at the time.

While the Village Mills Company was cutting the timber off this survey, Evans sold them some cordwood. He had deadened the timber in the spring, and he cut it in the fall and sold it to them for $1.15 per cord, which was about the value of the work in getting it out, but it was on the land, and Evans wanted to dispose of it. Evans did not know whether the Village Mills people knew at the time that this wood was cut off the 160 acres he was claiming. It was agreed by the parties that this survey was patented land.

Evans, on re-examination, testified in substance:

Hester was a relative, and, when he testified on cross-examination that Hester was putting out timber for the Reliance Lumber Company, he meant that that company bought the timber. Hester put it out to the man who would give him the most money for it. He said he sold it to the Reliance Lumber Company. He was a timber contractor and picked out floating timber wherever he could find it, put it in the creek, and carried it by water to Beaumont to market.

Hester was not concerned, so far as he knew, with this survey or any other survey in that country, further than getting such floating logs off of it as he could buy. He cut timber off of several surveys around there. It was a fact that in that day and time a fellow floating timber down the creek cut it most anywhere he wanted it. They paid mighty little attention to lines or to the owners.

Evans requested Hester to buy the land he did buy, and Hester was his agent and acted in that capacity in the purchase. Evans told Hester at the time that he claimed the 160 acres down on the creek, being the land here sued for.

Before Evans left the place in 1904 he took a part of the rails inclosing his field in the bottom and carried them to his home place and used them there, but he did not take all the rails away from the field. The reason for the taking of the rails was that Evans was crippled in the hand, and his boys were not old enough to work, and he could not get any one to split any rails for him.

Evans sold his 160-acre home place to Ben Best by deed dated July 24, 1905. He paid taxes on this tract, but never paid any taxes on the land involved in this suit.

A majority of the Court of Civil Appeals held that the undisputed testimony showed that plaintiffs in error entered and resided upon the land at the special instance and request of the owner, and that their entry thereon in 1887, and their subsequent occupancy thereof was permissive, and not adverse, and this holding is the basis of the first assignment submitted by plaintiffs in error.

The entry of Evans upon the land was, under the evidence, at Hester's instance and request, to serve the purpose of the owner and at a place already selected and partially prepared for his coming. He remained in possession of a tract of land embracing the original improvements, living thereon with his family continuously until he purchased the same for a home in September, 1893. He never set up any claim to this tract so purchased, and never by word or act repudiated the title of the owner thereto.

The Supreme Court, in Word v. Drouthett, 44 Tex. 365, 369–370, discussing adverse possession under the 10-year statute of limitation, says:

"The possession must be exclusive, or, as it is generally expressed, it must be 'actual, continued, visible, notorious, distinct, and hostile.' 2 Smith's Lead. Cases, 561 et seq. It must neither be abandoned, yielded up, or held in subordination to, recognition of, or dependent upon the will or right of another. He who would claim by reason of his adverse possession must, as has been said, 'keep his flag flying.' 19 Penn. St. 265. His entry upon the land must be with intent to claim it as his own or hold it for himself; or his intention to do so, if conceived after going into possession for some other purpose, must be manifested by some open or visible act or declaration showing such purpose, in order to set the statute in motion in his favor."

[1] Clearly possession of the home place by plaintiffs in error from their entry upon the land until their purchase of the same was not adverse. Word v. Drouthett, supra; Carter v. La Grange, 60 Tex. 636–638; Udell v. Peak, 70 Tex. 547, 551, 7 S. W. 786.

Possession of the home tract by plaintiffs in error being by permission of the owner, such possession constituted in law actual possession of the same by the owner, and such possession carried therewith constructive possession of all the land claimed by Evans in this suit, except such, if any, as was in his actual adverse possession at that time.

[2] The Village Mills Company, the owner of said survey in 1900 and 1901, entered upon the same during said years and cut the timber thereon. This entry by the owner carried with it constructive possession of all the land claimed by Evans in this suit except such as was in his actual possession at that time. South Texas Development Co. v. Manning (Tex. Civ. App.) 177 S. W. 998, 1000 (writ refused).

Plaintiffs in error make no claim of possession by them of any part of the land sued for, except from the summer of 1887 to and including the year 1903. Upon the facts stated, it is clear that plaintiffs in error did not have adverse possession for 10 continuous years of any of the land sued for, unless their possession of the field of 12 or 15 acres was of that character.

This field was in the bottom, three-quarters of a mile away from the home place. It was in no way incidental to, nor related to, the purposes for which Hester induced Evans to move on to the land, and was in no way connected with the logging business Hester was carrying on. It seems Evans took possession of the same without asking or securing permission of Hester or any one else. Part of it was cleared and put into cultivation in 1887 and the remainder the next year, and it was cultivated every year from then until and including the year 1903, and Evans claimed 160 acres of land, including such field, every year during such time, and still claimed the same at the time of trial.

The defendants in error contend that Evans by entering into an agreement with Hester as the agent of the Reliance Lumber Company, the owner of the land, for the purchase of the home tract of 160 acres, and by subsequently accepting a deed thereto in 1893, recognized and acknowledged the title of the owner and thereby defeated any claim of adverse holding of any part of the land sued for at or prior to that time. This contention is based on the theory that a claim by Evans of an undivided interest of 160 acres in the Brown survey under and by virtue of the 10-year statute was a claim of an interest running through the entire survey, and that the purchase of any part of such survey from the owner was in effect a purchase of a part of the land so claimed by Evans.

A similar question was before the Court of Civil Appeals for the First District in the case of Louisiana & Texas Lumber Co. v. Kennedy, 142 S. W. 989, 990. In that case Kennedy sued the lumber company for an undivided 160 acres of land out of a tract of 276 acres, claiming title thereto under the 10-year statute and asking that the particular land to which he claimed to be entitled be set off and designated by the court. He also claimed that the lumber company had cut timber off the land and asked judgment against it for 160/276 of the value of all the timber so cut. He recovered judgment on this claim in the district court, but the Court of Civil Appeals reversed that part of the judgment and rendered judgment for the lumber company, holding that, while the 160 acres to which Kennedy was entitled was undivided in the sense that its boundaries were not defined, it was located by his possession and improvements and embraced the same, and such land contiguous thereto as the court might designate, and set apart to him in final partition, and that when so designated such land would be considered his from the time his title was perfected, and that, if any timber was cut therefrom after title vested in him by virtue of said statute, he could have his appropriate action.

This field, claimed and cultivated by Evans, is described as three-quarters of a mile from the home place. Certainly no part thereof is embraced in such place, nor does it reasonably appear, were plaintiffs in error entitled to recover the entire undivided interest of 160 acres sued for, that a reasonable selection and designation of the same by the court, or by commissioners of partition under its direction, so as to include such field, would necessarily, or even probably, include any part of the 160 acres so purchased.

[3] We therefore hold that such purchase did not prevent an adverse holding of the field in actual possession of Evans, but that such purchase was merely a circumstance which the jury were entitled to consider in connection with all the other facts and circumstances in evidence in determining whether Evans' possession of such field was adverse during a continuous period of 10 years at any one time.

[4] If, prior to his abandonment of this field in 1903 or 1904 Evans had at any time actual, continuous adverse possession of the same for a period of 10 years, he will be entitled to recover the same in this action, and whether his possession thereof was of such character is a question of fact for the determination of the jury in view of all the evidence which may be before them tending to illustrate and explain it. Word v. Drouthett, 44 Tex. 365, 370.

We recommend that the judgments of the district court and the Court of Civil Appeals be reversed, and the cause remanded to the district court for proceedings in accordance with this opinion.

PHILLIPS, C. J. The judgment recommended in the report of the Commission of Appeals is adopted, and will be entered as the judgment of the Supreme Court.

We approve the holding of the Commission of Appeals on the question discussed in its opinion.

ROBERSON et al. v. HUGHES et al.
(No. 238-3426.)

(Commission of Appeals of Texas, Section B. June 1, 1921.)

1. Appeal and error ⇐672, 719(1)—Jurisdiction of Court of Civil Appeals limited to errors assigned and error of law apparent on face of record.

The jurisdiction of the Court of Civil Appeals is limited to the review of error assigned in the manner prescribed by law and error of law apparent on the face of the record.

2. Appeal and error ⇐672—Holding of court based upon finding of fact not error of law apparent on face of record.

In an action to recover two tracts of land, brought by the children and heirs at law of the first wife of plaintiffs' father against his children and heirs of deceased children by two subsequent marriages, where plaintiffs made no claim to one of the tracts, other than that it was the separate property of their mother by virtue of its having been purchased with her separate estate, the holding of the trial court that the tract was the property of the

children of the second and third marriages, under a finding of fact that it was paid for with funds of those communities, was not error of law apparent on the face of the record, such as the appellate court would have jurisdiction of without its having been assigned.

3. Appeal and error ⇐172(1)—Claim as to time of acquisition of property asserted to be community cannot be made for first time on appeal.

In an action by the children of the first wife of deceased to recover two tracts of land from his children by his second and third wives, the finding of the trial court that title vested in the latter will not be disturbed, where the claim that the land was purchased during the first marriage and plaintiffs inherited their mother's interest therein was raised for the first time on appeal, as the community property of husband and wife is subject to the payment of the debts contracted by either of them during the marriage, and evidence might have been presented by defendants requiring a vesting of plaintiff's interest in a manner not inconsistent with the judgment of the trial court.

4. Appeal and error ⇐994(3)—Evidence to discredit testimony not considered on appeal, where any evidence of sufficient probative force to support court's finding.

In an action by the children of deceased's first wife against his children by his second and third wives to recover certain land, evidence tending to discredit the testimony of defendants' witness as to the identity and payment of certain notes executed by deceased and witnessed by himself during deceased's second marriage will not be considered on appeal, if there was any evidence of sufficient probative force to support the trial court's finding that the land was paid for with funds of the second and third communities.

5. Evidence ⇐383(7)—Evidence held sufficient to support finding tract of land purchased on credit, despite recital in deed of cash consideration.

In an action to recover a tract of land by the children of deceased by his first wife against his children by his second and third wives, testimony of defendants' witness as to the identity and payment of certain notes executed by deceased during his second marriage held sufficient to support the court's finding that the tract was bought entirely on credit and paid for with funds of the second and third communities, despite recitals in the deed that a cash consideration of $300 was paid at the time of its execution during the first marriage.

6. Evidence ⇐236(2)—Notes executed by deceased husband after death of first wife admissible as admission of community debt.

In an action to recover certain land, brought by the children of deceased by his first wife against his children by his second and third wives, certain notes executed by deceased after the death of the first wife were properly admitted, being competent as an admission by the husband of a community debt in a proceeding seeking to charge community property with that debt.

Appeal from Court of Civil Appeals of Sixth Supreme Judicial District.

Action by Mrs. Annie Hughes and others against Mrs. Mattie Roberson and others. Judgment for defendants. From a judgment of the Court of Civil Appeals (214 S. W. 946), overruling all assignments of error brought by plaintiffs, but reversing the judgment for defendants on a ground not assigned, defendants appeal. Reversed, and judgment of district court affirmed.

Nat W. Brooks and Fitzgerald & Ramey, all of Tyler, for appellants.

Johnston & Hughes, of Waco, and Wm. H. Hanson, of Tyler, for appellees.

McCLENDON, P. J. The controlling question in the application is whether the Court of Civil Appeals had the power to reverse the judgment of the trial court for error not assigned. The following statement of the case will sufficiently make clear that issue:

The action, which was to recover two tracts of land, referred to as tracts 1 and 2, was brought by Mrs. Annie Hughes and Mrs. Mollie Pye, the only children and heirs at law of Mrs. Emma L. Moore, who was the first wife of plaintiffs' father, J. W. Moore, against the children and heirs of deceased children of J. W. Moore by two subsequent marriages. Plaintiffs sought by their suit to have the land adjudged the separate property of their mother, upon the allegations that tract No. 1 was paid for entirely with her separate property, and that tract No. 2 was purchased with the proceeds of the sale of a small portion of tract No. 1, as originally acquired by their father. They prayed that the entire title to both tracts be decreed to them as heirs of their mother. Three of the defendants, holding the interest of one child by each of the second and third marriages, filed separate answers, in which, besides a general denial, they alleged that tract No. 1 was purchased with community funds of all three communities. The remaining defendants, besides a general denial, pleaded specially that tract No. 1 was wholly paid for with funds of the last community.

The facts, which were undisputed, except as to the manner in which the land in controversy was paid for, were:

J. W. Moore was married three times: First, in 1856 to Emma L. Vann, who died in 1867; second, in 1867 to Augusta Vann, who died in 1875; and third, in 1877 to Elizabeth Stovall, who died in 1918. J. W. Moore died in 1910. Excepting those who died in infancy, there were eight children born of these marriages—two (plaintiffs) of the first, and three each of the second and third. Tract No. 1, originally containing 132 acres, was conveyed by J. J. Flinn to J. W. Moore by deed dated September 14, 1867, acknowledged in 1895, and reciting a consideration

of $300 paid. On January 11, 1873, J. W. Moore and wife, Augusta, conveyed 12.8 acres of tract No. 1 for the recited consideration of $120 paid. Tract No. 2 was conveyed to J. W. Moore on March 24, 1874, for the recited consideration of $30 paid.

The only testimony tending to establish plaintiffs' allegation that tract No. 1 was purchased with property of their mother was given by plaintiffs themselves and was stricken out on motion of defendants. Alleged error, predicated upon that action of the trial court has been eliminated, since no complaint is made in the Supreme Court of the action of the Court of Civil Appeals in overruling assignments of error relating to that ruling. The trial court found as a fact that tract No. 1 was paid for equally with community funds of the second and third marriages, and upon that finding concluded, as a matter of law, that the title to that tract was vested equally in those communities. Judgment was rendered accordingly; one-sixteenth interest in each tract being awarded to each of the plaintiffs as heirs of their father, and the remaining interest in each tract being decreed in defendants. The evidence upon which this finding of fact was based will be given below.

Plaintiffs alone appealed from that judgment, urging 24 assignments of error, 22 of which complained of the exclusion or admission of evidence, and the other 2 complained of the findings of fact that no part of the consideration for tract No. 1 was paid with funds of the first community, and that that tract was paid for with funds of the second and third communities. Those two assignments are based upon the recitals in the deed to tract No. 1 that the consideration was $300 paid.

The Court of Civil Appeals overruled all assignments of error, but reversed the judgment and remanded the cause for further trial upon the holding that, under the finding of fact that tract No. 1 was acquired during the first marriage, title thereto vested, as a matter of law, in the first community, subject to the right in the other communities to be reimbursed for the funds used to discharge the purchase-money obligation. 214 S. W. 946. Writ of error was granted, because the error upon which the trial court's judgment was reversed was not assigned.

[1] From the foregoing statement it will be seen that none of the assignments question the correctness of the trial court's conclusion of law that the title to tract No. 1 vested in the second and third communities because it was paid for with funds of those communities. The Court of Civil Appeals is a court of review, and its jurisdiction to review rulings of the trial court is limited by statute. For the purposes of this case, that jurisdiction authorizes review of only two

classes of error: First, error assigned in the manner prescribed by law; and, second, error of law apparent upon the face of the record, which latter has been defined as "such error as is fundamental in character, or one determining a question upon which the very right of the case depends, or such an error as being readily seen lies at the base and foundation of the proceeding and necessarily affects the judgment" (Wilson v. Johnson, 94 Tex. 276, 60 S. W. 242; Houston Oil Co. v. Kimball, 103 Tex. 103, 122 S. W. 533, 124 S. W. 85), and, again, as "such manifest error as when removed destroys the foundation of the judgment" (Oar v. Davis, 105 Tex. 484, 151 S. W. 794).

[2] The question presented resolves itself, therefore, into the further inquiry whether the error of the trial court in holding that tract No. 1 was the property of the second and third communities, under the finding of fact that it was paid for with funds of those communities, constituted fundamental error, or error of law apparent upon the face of the record. We think, under the holding of Oar v. Davis, above, that question must necessarily be determined in the negative. That suit was brought against the wife and her second husband, by her children by her first husband, to cancel a deed which the children had made to their stepfather, conveying lands which were the separate property of their father. The children sued for the entire title to the land as sole heirs of their father, upon the allegation that the land was by mistake included in a deed by which they conveyed other lands to their stepfather. The mother was made a party defendant, upon the allegation that she asserted homestead rights in the property. The trial court found that the land was the separate property of plaintiffs' father, and was included by mistake in the deed to the stepfather, and that the mother had abandoned her homestead rights in the property. Upon these findings of fact the trial court concluded as a matter of law that the children (plaintiffs) acquired by inheritance from their father the entire title to the property, and rendered judgment in their favor accordingly. The mother urged upon motion for rehearing in the Court of Civil Appeals, for the first time, that under the finding of the trial court that the property was the separate estate of her first husband she as a matter of law, under our statutes of descent and distribution, inherited a life estate in an undivided one-third interest therein, and that the trial court erred in not awarding her such interest.

It was contended that this error was fundamental, and should be considered by the appellate court, even though not assigned. The opinion of the Supreme Court is well considered, and reviews the previous adjudications of that court upon the much-discussed question of what constitutes fundamental error. The conclusion that the error thus raised was not fundamental is stated in the following quotation:

"If the error complained of is one of law, it neither lies at the base and foundation of plaintiffs' cause of action, nor is it such an error of law as is apparent upon the face of the record. To determine whether it be an error of law at all depends upon the issue of title made by the pleadings and the evidence adduced to sustain or deny the respective rights of the parties. In the absence of any claim on the part of Mrs. Oar in her pleadings, or in the presentation of her claim to any part of the land in controversy, other than that claimed through the deed to her husband and the right of the homestead, which claims were litigated, the court might well presume that, if she was entitled to a one-third life interest in the land, she had waived such claim. Whether this view be sound or not, there is no phase of the law under which we can treat the supposed error of law as one of a fundamental character. As suggested by Judge Talbot, if a claim had been made by Mrs. Oar to the land by virtue of inheritance, plaintiffs might have shown by reason of some conveyance or other arrangement she had parted with such interest. We therefore think the Court of Civil Appeals was right under the circumstances in refusing to consider the assignment of error."

[3] The analogy in principle between that case and the case before us is so complete as to require little discussion. Plaintiffs made no claim in their pleadings to tract No. 1, other than that it was the separate property of their mother, by virtue of having been purchased with her separate estate. So far as the record shows, the only controverted issues of fact were those which bore upon the time and manner of payment of the consideration. Conceding that the legal title to tract No. 1 vested in the first community, still—

"Nothing is clearer in our law, as declared both by statute and by repeated decisions of this court, than that the community property of the husband and wife is subject to the payment of the debts contracted by either of them during the marriage, * * * and that the heirs of the wife, on her death, are entitled, not to one-half of the community property as it may then exist, but to one-half of what may remain, after the discharge of the debts to which such property is liable. Articles 4627, 3592, Rev. Stats.; Jones v. Jones, 15 Tex. 147; Carter v. Conner, 60 Tex. 60." Stone v. Jackson, 109 Tex. 387, 210 S. W. 953.

The powers of the community survivor to deal with community property are very broad. Among those powers is that of discharging community debts, and appropriating community property in reimbursement. It will readily be seen, therefore, that had the issue been made that the title vested in the first community, and that plaintiffs inherited their mother's interest therein, evidence might have been presented which would have required a vesting of that interest in a manner not inconsistent with the judgment of the trial court. The question presented is, we think, clearly ruled by the decision in Oar v. Davis.

[4, 5] Defendants in error, plaintiffs below, present in the form of counter propositions two cross-assignments of error, complaining of the action of the Court of Civil Appeals in the following particulars:

First, it is urged that the trial court erred in permitting in evidence two notes purporting to have been given by J. W. Moore in 1872 and 1874 in payment of tract No. 1; and, second, that the evidence was not sufficient as a matter of law to overcome the presumption that consideration for that tract was paid when the deed was executed, in view of the recital in the deed of a consideration of "$300 paid." These cross-assignments call for a statement of the evidence upon which was based the trial court's finding that tract No. 1 was paid for with funds of the second and third communities. They are so nearly related that we will consider them together.

One of the defendants testified that, after the death of J. W. Moore, she and her mother, the third wife, found among J. W. Moore's papers the original deed to tract No. 1, and with it the two notes mentioned above. The 1872 note reads as follows:

"By the 24th day of December next I promise to pay to J. J. Flynn, or bearer, the sum of two hundred ninety-six and 15/100 dollars, in gold, with ten per cent. interest from date until paid, for land sold and deeded to me by him on the Lafata league, Smith county, Texas, on the 14th day of September, 1867, it being for value received.

"1872.

"Witness: A. G. Tommie. [No signature; the note being torn where signature should appear.]"

A. G. Tommie, the subscribing witness to the 1872 note, testified in substance that he was well acquainted with J. W. Moore, having known him in Troupe county, Ga., before Moore moved to Texas in 1866; that he knew Flynn well, and worked for him 4 years; that upon the occasion of the execution of the 1872 note, which witness identified as having been executed by Moore and witnessed by himself, Flynn had sent him to Moore to make a trade for a wagon and yoke of oxen as a credit on a note that Moore had originally given for tract No. 1. The trade was made, and the agreed amount, which figured a little more than the interest on the original note, was credited thereon, and the 1872 note executed by Moore for

231 S.W.—47

the balance. His testimony is based upon personal knowledge gained at the time the 1872 note was made; he having seen the original note given for tract No. 1, which, when the 1872 note was made, was almost "out of date." He further testified to a custom in those times of receipting a paid note by tearing off the signature of the maker. The 1874 note was dated January 1 of that year, payable to order of J. J. Flynn, for $324.97, and recited the same consideration as the 1872 note. The signature to this note was also torn off. It bore indorsements of payment as follows: $7.25 in 1879, and "one hundred [torn] four and 52/100" in 1874.

[6] We need not notice the evidence which, it is urged, tends to discredit the testimony of the witness Tommie, since it is within our province only to determine whether there be any evidence of sufficient probative force to support the trial court's findings. That the foregoing testimony was sufficient to support that court's finding that tract No. 1 was bought entirely on credit, and was paid for in 1872 and subsequent years, seems to us too clear to admit of serious doubt or call for discussion. The only question regarding the testimony which we think deserves mention is the admissibility of the declaration in the 1872 and 1874 notes that they were given to pay for the land. These notes were executed by the husband after the death of the first wife, and the question arises as to the competency of the husband's admission or acknowledgment of a community debt in a proceeding seeking to charge community property with that debt. Under the broad principles laid down in Stone v. Jackson, above, and the authorities therein reviewed, we think these notes were properly admitted in evidence. The precise question was decided in Word v. Colley, 143 S. W. 257, in which a deed to community realty was upheld, which was made under deed of trust by the surviving husband to pay a community debt, the only evidence of which was the written declaration of the husband made after the death of his wife. Writ of error was refused in that case. In the present case the written declarations of the surviving husband are corroborated by the testimony of the witness Tommie to the effect that he saw the original purchase-money note at the time of the first renewal in 1872.

We conclude that the judgment of the Court of Civil Appeals should be reversed, and that of the District Court affirmed.

PHILLIPS, C. J. The judgment recommended in the report of the Commission of Appeals is adopted, and will be entered as the judgment of the Supreme Court.

FARMERS' & MERCHANTS' STATE BANK OF BALLINGER v. CAMERON et al.

(No. 190—3239.)

(Commission of Appeals of Texas, Section B. June 8, 1921.)

1. Appeal and error ⇐1094(2)—Finding of usury approved by Court of Appeals not reviewed.

Whether usury entered into notes being a matter demonstrable by calculation, and none being presented in the record to show that it did not, and the trial court's finding that it did having been approved by the Court of Civil Appeals, it is not within the province of the Commission of Appeals to consider the matter.

2. Usury ⇐137—Held paid and received by purchase under deed of trust, allowing recovery of penalty.

Usury is paid and received, allowing recovery of double penalty under Vernon's Sayles' Ann. Civ. St. 1914, art. 4982, where holder of usurious note secured by deed of trust, at trustee's sale thereunder bought, for more than was due, excluding usury, and the full amount of the bid was credited on the note, and a deed was made by the trustee to the purchaser; the title to the property thereby passing to him.

3. Mortgages ⇐282(4) — Proceeding against mortgaged property before action against its purchaser necessary.

Before a purchaser of land, who had assumed, as part of the consideration, a deed of trust thereon, can be proceeded against personally on the secured notes, the land which is the primary fund for payment thereof must be exhausted by sale under the deed of trust.

Error to Court of Civil Appeals of Eighth Supreme Judicial District.

Action by S. M. Cameron and others against the Farmers' & Merchants' State Bank of Ballinger. Judgment for plaintiffs was affirmed by the Court of Civil Appeals (208 S. W. 1167), and defendant brings error. Affirmed.

Jno. I. Guion and M. C. Smith, both of Ballinger, for plaintiff in error.

R. B. Truly, of Eastland, and Snodgrass, Dibrell & Snodgrass, of Coleman, for defendants in error.

Statement of the Case.

KITTRELL, J. The facts out of which this case arose, stated as concretely as is consistent with clearness, are as follows:

On April 20, 1910, the Camerons executed their note to the bank for $4,600 payable at three months. There had been a previous note for $3,000 given, or at least credits to that amount in favor of the Camerons had been entered on the books of the bank, somewhere between two and three weeks before April 20, 1910, in contemplation of the use

of the money in buying a lot of mares out on the Rio Grande border.

They bought to the extent of $4,600, or $1,600 in excess of the deposit, and their drafts to the extent of $4,600 were paid by the bank. The entire indebtedness was on April 20th put into one note for $4,600, and the jury found that $138 interest was paid by the Camerons on the day the note was given, but it was extended for the full amount, and was again extended when it fell due.

Other notes were given from time to time, and certain payments were made, and other money borrowed or other advances made to or for the Camerons by the bank over a period of time of about four years; the total number of notes in the way of extensions of the original note and additional amounts for new advances being 14.

The series of loans and payments and extensions finally culminated in one note for $10,530, dated March 31, 1914, bearing 10 per cent. interest, and due January 1, 1915, with interest from maturity until paid.

The Camerons, coincident with the execution of said note, executed a deed of trust on five several tracts of land situated in Runnels county. The deed of trust was in the usual form.

Default having been made in payment of the note, the trustee in due and regular form sold the land at public sale on April 6, 1915, for the purpose of paying the notes, less the credits.

It appears that there were a number of bidders, but the highest bidder was the bank, and the land was adjudged and knocked off to it for the amount of its bid, which was $8,750, the full amount of which was credited on the note, and a deed made by the trustee to the bank, of which institution he was cashier.

The Camerons on September 25, 1915, filed suit against the bank to recover upon an alleged claim of usury, alleging as a summary of all their specific allegations as follows:

"That the actual indebtedness due from plaintiffs to defendants at the time of the sale of said land was only the aggregate sums hereinbefore mentioned, to wit, $10,900; less actual payments and credits hereinbefore set out in the aggregate sum of $5,893.24; making actual indebtedness due from plaintiffs to defendant the sum of only at the time of the sale $5,007.35."

They plead that, the property having been sold for $8,750, and the acceptance of said bid, and the crediting of the $8,750 on the indebtedness, the said defendant collected $3,742.65 usurious interest, and prayed judgment for double that amount, and prayed in the alternative for the difference between $8,750 and $5,007.35, which is $3,742.65.

The case was submitted on 42 special issues prepared by the court and other special issues submitted at request of counsel.

The judgment recites that defendants had "received and collected from the plaintiffs • • • $3,577.15 usurious interest, and judgment was rendered for double that amount, or for $7,154.30.

Defendant by way of cross-action alleged, in substance, that certain parties, Terry by name, had executed to the British & American Mortgage Company, Limited, their note for $3,000 secured by deed of trust on two of the tracts of land for which plaintiffs had given the bank a deed of trust, being the first two tracts described in plaintiffs' petition, aggregating 341½ acres; that, while the note and security were valid and subsisting, the Terrys conveyed the two tracts to the plaintiffs, who assumed the payment of the $3,000 note executed by the Terrys; that later, July 1, 1912, the Camerons agreed with the mortgage company upon an extension of payment of the note for five years from November 1, 1912, at 8 per cent., payment to be made in certain installments not necessary to enumerate. Later the time of payment of certain of the installments was extended.

Defendant alleged that it owned the $3,000 note by assignment in writing from the mortgage company, and that certain specified installments of interest had not been paid, wherefore they had declared the whole debt due.

The proof showed that the mortgage company on September 7, 1916, for value received, assigned the trust deed and the $3,000 note to the defendant bank without recourse. When the transfer was taken, the note for $240 first mentioned in the extension agreement had been paid. The bank paid it before the transfer. It had paid the first three principal notes, and the interest note had been taken up. This had been done without request of the Camerons.

The bank prayed for personal judgment on the note against the Camerons, alleging they were notoriously insolvent, and prayed that, if any judgment be recovered against it, it be offset by the judgment on the $3,000 note.

In response to a special issue the jury answered that the bank bid solely for the equity of the Camerons in the land. The court adjudged that the bank take nothing by its cross-action.

Opinion.

The case may properly be determined upon the assumption that the transactions out of which the litigation arose were tainted with usury. As we construe the record, and the assignments of error, there is in the application for writ of error no serious attack made upon the findings of the jury by the motion for a new trial, or upon the con-clusions of the Court of Civil Appeals as to the question of usury.

[1] Whether usury entered into the notes was a matter demonstrable by calculation, and none is presented in the record to show that it did not, and, the trial court's finding that it did having been approved by the Court of Civil Appeals, it is not within our province to consider the question.

[2] The plaintiff in error contends, as we interpret the application for writ of error, that even if it be conceded that usury had been paid, nevertheless the sale under deed of trust was "involuntary" payment, and that by reason of that fact the defendant bank did not in fact "collect" or "receive" usurious interest so as to bring its action within the purview of article 4982, V. S. C. S. This is the first of the only two questions presented by the application.

In a technical sense the sale may have been, indeed was, involuntary as to plaintiffs, but it was certainly not "involuntary" as concerns the defendant bank. Pursuant to the provisions of the deed of trust, it sold the property and bid $8,750, and the property was knocked off to it (the bank), and the whole amount of the bid was credited on the debt, and the bank received a deed to the property.

What does, and what does not, constitute "payment" of usurious interest is a question which has been frequently before the courts, and is one by no means free from difficulty. We have not been able to find any case entirely like the instant case. Before the writer became a member of the court the case of Gunter v. Merchant, 213 S. W. 604, was decided by this section of the Commission in a very clear and instructive opinion by Judge Sadler, which was approved by the Supreme Court. The facts of that case and this were wholly different, but the question of what constituted payment was discussed at length. It is the law that to reserve out of a loan interest in advance at a rate beyond the legal limit does not constitute payment of usury.

Where the plaintiff, appellee, borrowed $200 and gave his note for $235 and afterwards made five payments of $17.50, aggregating $87.50, plaintiff was held entitled to recover only the $87.50 or double that amount; the $35 not having been in contemplation of law actually paid. Rosetti v. Lozano, 96 Tex. 57, 70 S. W. 204.

Where usurious interest was included in a note given in renewal of a note bearing usurious interest, it was held recovery could not be had under the penalty statute until the usurious interest was actually paid, and including the interest in a renewal note was not actual payment (First Nat. Bank v. Lasater, 196 U. S. 115, 25 Sup. Ct. 206, 49 L. Ed. 408; National Bank, etc., v. Ragland, 181 U. S. 45, 21 Sup. Ct. 536, s. c. 45 L. Ed. 738), and giving additional note for usurious interest is not payment (Brown v. Bank, 169 U. S. 416, 18 Sup. Ct. 390, 42 L. Ed. 801).

The usurious interest must actually have been paid, and where all payments were credited on the principal and the usurious note has not been fully paid, the penalty cannot be recovered. Allen v. Bank, 175 S. W. 485.

Obviously none of the cases above cited are in "all fours" with the instant case, but are helpful in enabling us to arrive at what we conceive to be a correct conclusion.

The property was sold by due and regular course of procedure in accordance with the provisions of the deed of trust, and, if it be conceded that only $5,007.35 of the $8,750 was really due on the note outside of the alleged amount of usury, certainly the sale was good as to the amount concededly due. It was so adjudged in Hemphill v. Watson, 60 Tex. 679.

In the absence of authorities directly in point we are left to deal with the question in the light of general principles. Concededly the title to the property passed to the defendant by the sale, regardless of whether the part of the bid made up of usurious interest be taken into consideration or not. Hemphill v. Watson, supra. The entire bid was credited on the note, and the record reveals no attempt by cross-action or otherwise on the part of defendant to recover the deficiency on the $10,530 note. If the note secured by the deed of trust had been for only $8,750, and the bid had been credited on the note, the debt would have been fully discharged, in other words, have been "paid" by plaintiffs, and the payment would to the extent of all the bid above $5,007.35 have been in the form of usurious interest, and would have been recited in the trustee's deed as part of the consideration received from defendant for the property. If, as defendant contends, that much of the bid was the same as no payment at all, yet the defendant treated it as payment, and the trustee received it as such, and to the extent of $3,742.-65 it was part of the bid. We can see no distinction in legal effect between that situation and proceeding, and what actually took place.

It is settled law that no cause of action to recover back usurious interest accrues until such interest has been paid. Cyc. vol. 39, p. 1034. It is likewise the law that it is not necessary that the payment be made in money, but it is sufficient if it be made in property. As a general rule the right to recover usury cannot be exercised so long as any part of the debt which is justly due, principal and interest, remains unpaid. Authorities supra.

In some jurisdictions the general rule of law prevails that money paid voluntarily as usurious interest cannot be recovered. The ground of such holding is that the parties are held to be in pari delicto. In such states the rule has been applied in cases wherein the payment of the usurious interest is obtained by exercise of power of sale. The sale being made under power conferred by the borrower himself, it is treated as if he had made it. R. C. L. vol. 27, p. 271. It seems to us that the rule just stated is applicable in this state where recovery is allowed where usurious interest is paid voluntarily. The property was sold under a power conferred by the Camerons; and the title passed out of them by the sale, in consideration of at least the valid portion of the debt, and, as we have said, there is no evidence revealed by the record of any attempt to collect the difference between the bid of $8,750 and the $10,530 note and interest, aggregating $10,900, which fact evidences that the bank treated the debt as paid. This being true, if the authorities cited are applicable, as we think they are, the question presented whether the sale and the crediting of the bid on the debt and receiving a deed to the property by the bank was equivalent to a payment by the Camerons and the receipt by the bank of usurious interest must be answered in the affirmative.

The defendant took title to the property upon a bid for it of $8,750 and thereby to that extent the debt of plaintiff was paid, and we are unable to escape the conclusion that plaintiffs actually "paid" and the defendant actually "received" usurious interest. We cannot conceive by what process of reasoning the bid and the crediting of it on the debt thereby pro tanta discharging the debt can be held to be sufficient consideration to pass title to the land, and at the same time not operate as "payment" of usurious interest included in the note.

[3] The second and remaining question presented for determination is no less difficult than the first. Two of the tracts of land described in plaintiff's pleadings and included in the deed of trust given by the Camerons to the bank had previously been conveyed by the Terrys to the Camerons, the latter assuming, as part of the consideration for the conveyance, a deed of trust upon the land which had previously been given by the Terrys to a mortgage company to secure a note for $3,000. Later the bank acquired by purchase the notes given by the Terrys to the mortgage company, together with the deed of trust lien securing it. In the present suit the bank by way of cross-action and counterclaim sought a personal judgment against the Camerons upon their assumption of this note, but did not ask for a foreclosure of the deed of trust lien, nor did they pray to have the land securing the $3,000 note subjected to the payment of the note as a primary fund. The trial court rendered judgment against the bank upon this cross-action and counterclaim, and the Court of Civil Appeals affirmed that judgment.

This ruling, we think, was correct under the authority of Harris v. Masterson, 91 Tex.

171, 41 S. W. 482. We do not deem it necessary to enter upon an elaborate analysis of that case, or to set forth the certified questions and answers thereto. It is sufficient to say that that case holds that, where a vendee who is personally liable upon vendor's lien notes conveys the land to a third party, and the latter assumes the payment of the notes, the land becomes a primary fund for the payment of those notes, and the holder of the notes can be required by the original vendee to exhaust the vendor's lien upon the land before personal judgment can be rendered against the vendee upon his personal obligation upon the vendor's lien notes, and personal judgment thereon can be rendered only in case of and to the extent that the land fails to satisfy the notes.

In the present case, when the Terrys sold the land to the Camerons, and the latter assumed the deed of trust obligation which the Terrys had given to the mortgage company, the land thus conveyed became the primary fund for the payment of those notes, and before personal judgment could be recovered against the Terrys that primary fund would have to be exhausted. When the land was later sold by the bank in satisfaction of the latter's second lien, the sale was, by stipulation in the conveyance, made subject to the deed of trust given by the Terrys to the mortgage company; and before personal judgment could be rendered against the Camerons, upon their assumption of the Terry $3,000 note, the bank would have to exhaust the primary fund, that is, the land conveyed by the Terrys to the Camerons, before the Camerons could be required to respond personally upon their assumption of the $3,000 note. As the bank did not ask for this relief, but only prayed for personal judgment against the Camerons upon their assumption of the $3,000 note, the trial court, we think, correctly denied the relief prayed for, and the Court of Civil Appeals correctly affirmed that judgment.

We therefore recommend that the judgments of the district court and Court of Civil Appeals be affirmed.

PHILLIPS, C. J. The judgment recommended in the report of the Commission of Appeals is adopted, and will be entered as the judgment of the Supreme Court.

PULLMAN CO. v. GULF, C. & S. F. RY. CO.
(No. 215–3330.)

(Commission of Appeals of Texas, Section B.
June 8, 1921.)

1. **Trial ⬅141—Charge, submitting undisputed question, properly refused.**

A requested charge, submitting an undisputed question, is properly refused.

2. **Trial ⬅261—No error to refuse a charge in part incorrect.**

It is not error to refuse a requested charge in part incorrect; the court not being required to separate the proper from the improper, and give a modified charge.

3. **Appeal and error ⬅1082(2)—Holding of intermediate court not questioned by petition for error is not reviewable.**

The holding of the Court of Civil Appeals that the giving of a charge was error, not having been called in question in the application for writ of error to that court, is not before the Commission of Appeals for review.

4. **Appeal and error ⬅1068(3)—No reversal for erroneous instruction, where judgment was the only one proper under the evidence.**

Judgment will not be reversed for erroneous instruction where under the evidence no other judgment than that rendered could properly be rendered.

Error to Court of Civil Appeals of Second Supreme Judicial District.

Action by John B. Scripture against the Gulf, Colorado & Sante Fé Railway Company and the Pullman Company, with cross-action by the Railway Company against the Pullman Company. The Court of Civil Appeals affirmed judgment for plaintiff against the Railway Company, but reversed the judgment for the Pullman Company as between it and the Railway Company (210 S. W. 269), and the Pullman Company brings error. Judgment of Court of Civil Appeals reversed, and judgment of district court affirmed.

Etheridge, McCormick & Bromberg, of Dallas, for plaintiff in error.

Lee, Lomax & Smith, of Fort Worth, and Terry, Cavin & Mills, of Galveston, for defendant in error.

KITTRELL, J. While the controversy in this case as it is presented to us is between the two companies, the names of which appear in the title of the case, it was not an original action as between them. In the action out of which the case arose one Scripture was the original plaintiff, and the parties to this action were both defendants. Scripture was a passenger in a Pullman Company car attached to a train of the railroad company, and in stepping from the train to a box in alighting was injured. He made both corporations defendants, but before the trial actually began dismissed his action as to the Pullman Company. The railroad company had, however, made the Pullman Company a defendant by cross-action, praying that, in event of any recovery by plaintiff against it, it have judgment over against the Pullman Company for a like amount. There was a contract between the two corporations, the interpretation of which was to a large extent a controlling feature of the litigation; at least in the Court of Civil Appeals. In the district court of Denton county, in which county the injury occurred, plaintiff recovered a substantial verdict against the railway company, but a verdict was returned against the railway company on its cross-action against the Pullman Company. The Court of Civil Appeals of the Second District affirmed the judgment as to the railway company, but reversed it as between the two corporations (Gulf, C. & S. F. R. Co. v. Scripture, 210 S. W. 269). Both corporations applied for a rehearing, which was denied both. Writ of error was refused the railway company as between it and the plaintiff Scripture. The Pullman Company obtained writ of error on the ground that the Court of Civil Appeals erred in holding that the trial court erred in refusing the special charge asked by the railway company; its contention being that it was undisputed that the vestibule of the Pullman Coach was brilliantly lighted, all the witnesses so testifying, and the railway company so admitting in definite positive terms in its brief in the Court of Civil Appeals.

The ground of action set up by the plaintiff are correctly stated by the Court of Civil Appeals, as follows:

"Plaintiff charged negligence on the part of both defendants in failing to give him a reasonable opportunity to alight safely from said car; in failing to have sufficient light on the platform of said car; in failing to stop the train at Krum a sufficient length of time to enable plaintiff to safely disembark; in failing to have sufficient light on the ground or platform upon which plaintiff landed; in failing to assist plaintiff to alight; in failing to place the box upon which plaintiff was to step securely fixed on the ground; in failing to have the ground where the box was placed reasonably level and smooth, so that the box placed thereon would not overturn, etc."

The answer of the railway company to the allegations of the plaintiff consisted only of a general denial, and allegation of contributory negligence on the part of plaintiff, on three grounds, not necessary to set forth.

This statement is necessary in view of the contention of the parties before us as to the requested charge as to the light in the vestibule, and of the admission made by the railway company with reference thereto.

The allegations of the cross-action by the railway company were as correctly stated by the Court of Civil Appeals as follows:

"The defendant railway company pleaded that there was a contract existing between it and the Pullman Company by virtue of which the Pullman Company was to provide its own employees and servants for the collection of fares charged for the sleeper, and for the services of receiving and discharging passengers from said cars, and that by the terms of said contract the Pullman Company had agreed to indemnify and save harmless the railway company against all liability and claims for injuries to persons arising from the acts or omissions, whether negligent or wrongful or otherwise, of the employees of the Pullman Company in the line of their employment. It further alleged that, if it were true that plaintiff sustained the injuries alleged by him as the result of the failure to afford him a reasonable opportunity to safely alight from said sleeping car and train at Krum, or because of insufficient light on the platform or at the place he attempted to get off the car, or because a sufficient time was not allowed him to alight from the car, etc., said acts of negligence, if any, were the acts of the Pullman Company's employees."

The only assignments of error of the railway company which the Court of Civil Appeals discussed, and on which it based its holdings, were the fifteenth and sixteenth.

The first of these assignments was directed against the thirteenth paragraph of the charge of the court, which reads as follows:

"Now, if you believe from the evidence that the plaintiff was injured, and you further believe that his injuries were proximately caused by the negligent failure, if any, of the Pullman employees to assist him in disembarking from said train or in improperly placing the footstool for him to step upon, if you believe that it was improperly placed, or if you believe that his injuries were proximately caused by failure, if any, of the Pullman porter to notify the employees of the railroad of the presence of the plaintiff at said place wishing to disembark from said train, and you find this failure of said porter, if he did so fail, to be negligence, that is, a failure to use a high degree of care, and you find that these acts of negligence, if any, were the proximate cause of his injuries, if any, and that he would not have been injured but for said acts, then the railroad company would be entitled to a judgment over against the Pullman Company for whatever sum, if any, you find in favor of the plaintiff against the railway company."

The railway company made the giving of this charge the sixteenth ground of its amended motion for a new trial, it being given in that part of the court's general charge, which he stated applied to the controversy between the two corporations, and made its giving, as has been said, its fifteenth assignment of error in its brief.

It also specifically objected in writing and saved bill of exceptions to the giving of said paragraph 13, on the ground that the charge required it to show that the act of the Pullman employees which contributed to the injury was a negligent act, whereas, by the terms of the contract between it and the Pullman Company, it was entitled to indemnity whether the act of the porter was negligent or not.

The sixteenth assignment of error of the railway company was based upon the refusal of the trial court to give the following special charge No. 8, requested by it, which, nitting certain preliminary and explanatory recitals, not necessary to be set forth, was as follows:

"Now, therefore, if you believe that plaintiff was injured, but that such injury was due to and proximately caused by the failure, if any, of the Pullman Company's porter to properly and safely place the foot box, or the failure, if any, of the Pullman Company to furnish sufficient light in the vestibule of its sleeping car 'rom which plaintiff was alighting, or failure, f any, of the said Pullman Company's employees in charge of such car to stop or request the stopping of defendant's train until plaintiff could alight therefrom; and if you further believe that the omissions, if any, of said Pullman Company employees in the respects here stated were in line of their employment— you will find in favor of said Gulf, Colorado & Santa Fé Railway Company against said Pullman Company for the amount of the verdict, if any, you may return in plaintiff's favor and against said railway company.

"You are further instructed in this connection that under said contract, even though you may believe that the omissions, if any, of the said Pullman Company's employees in the respect above stated were not negligent or wrongful, still, if you further believe that the injury, if any, sustained by plaintiff arose from such acts or omissions, you will nevertheless find in favor of said railway company and against said Pullman Company for the amount of the verdict, if any, rendered in plaintiff's favor against said railway company."

The refusal of the trial court to give said special charge No. 3 was duly excepted to, and bill of exceptions duly taken, and such refusal was made the forty-sixth ground of the motion for a new trial filed by the railway company.

That portion of the contract between the two companies which was offered in evidence by the railway company, in so far as it is pertinent to the question to be determined, is as follows:

"The Pullman Company agrees to indemnify and save harmless the Railway Company against all liabilities and claims for loss or damage to, or destruction of property, and for injuries to persons or deaths, as follows: * * *

"Subdivision (d). All claims and liabilities arising from the acts or omissions whether negligent or wrongful, or otherwise, of employees of the Pullman Company in line of their employment."

In its original opinion the Court of Civil Appeals, while setting forth the fact that the record disclosed that the railway company objected to the thirteenth paragraph of the charge, which was made the basis of the fifteenth assignment of error, yet it stated no affirmative holding or conclusion upon the question, but proceeded to deal with the sixteenth assignment of error, directed against the refusal of the trial court to give special charge No. 3, and stated the conclusion that said charge should have been given; therefore the assignment was sustained, and the judgment as between the Pullman Company and the railway company was reversed on the ground that the trial court erred in refusing special charge No. 3, but, finding, as it stated, that "the negligence of the appellant [the railway company] in starting the train at the time it did without first learning whether the Pullman passenger had alighted was established without controversy," therefore it affirmed the recovery against the railway company. In its opinion on motion for rehearing the Court of Civil Appeals deals with both assignments of error, and states with reference to paragraph 13 of the charge:

"If the railway company was entitled to the presentation of the defense of the terms of that provision in contract between it and the Pullman Company, such defense did not in any sense depend on the question of negligence of the Pullman Company's employees in causing, or contributing to cause, the injury to plaintiff, but was entirely independent of the question of negligence. If the railroad company had the right to enforce the contract of indemnity according to its terms—and no question is here raised as to such right—we are of the opinion that it was positive error to limit such right to indemnity to a showing of negligence on the part of the Pullman Company."

The Court of Civil Appeals held that the charge was reversible error. This being true, we are confined to a discussion of two questions: (1) Whether the trial court properly refused to give special charge No. 3, requested by the railway company, which refusal was made the basis of its sixteenth assignment of error; and, (2) whether under the undisputed facts any other judgments could have been properly rendered as between the two corporations, except the one rendered in favor of plaintiff in error. In the application for writ of error the assignment is to all intents and purposes made that, regardless of whether paragraph 13 was or was not correct, the judgment rendered by the trial court as between the two corporations was the only judgment which could properly have been rendered.

[1, 2] As to the first of the two above-stated assignments, we are of the opinion that the trial court properly refused special charge No. 3, requested by the railway company, and that the Court of Civil Appeals erred in holding such action error on the part of the trial court. This is true for the following reasons:

(1) There was absolutely no dispute that the vestibule of the Pullman Car was brilliantly lighted. The appellant railway in its brief in the Court of Civil Appeals asserted in most emphatic and unqualified terms that there was no possible ground for the contention that the accident could be attributed in any degree to want of sufficient light in the vestibule. Its own conductor said he saw

the light from the Pullman vestibule flashing so brightly on the ground that he could see the Pullman porter 230 feet away.

The following authorities support the statement that to have given a charge on an undisputed question would have been reversible error: Hardy v. De Leon, 5 Tex. 230 (citing Boardman v. Reed, 6 Pet. [U. S.] 328, 8 L. Ed. 415); Wintz v. Morrison, 17 Tex. 372, 67 Am. Dec. 658; I. & G. N. Ry. Co. v. Stewart, 57 Tex. 166; Railway Co. v. Gilmore, 62 Tex. 391; Denham v. Trinity Lumber Co., 73 Tex. 84, 11 S. W. 151; Railway v. Harvin, 59 S. W. 629; Western Union Tel. Co. v. Burgess, 60 S. W. 1024.

(2) Because had it been that a part of the requested charge was correct and a part incorrect, it would not have been obligatory on the trial judge to have separated the proper from the improper parts; nor to modify the charge. Hardy v. De Leon, supra; Wells v. Barnett, 7 Tex. 584; Rosenthal v. Middlebrook, 63 Tex. 339; Gulf, etc., v. Shieder, 88 Tex. .167, 30 S. W. 902, 28 L. R. A. 538; Ft. Worth v. Daniels, 29 S. W. 695; Cyc. vol. 38, p. 1708 et seq.

It is manifest, when considered in the light of the foregoing authorities, and the requested charge was properly refused. The charge having been properly refused, the Court of Civil Appeals erred in reversing the judgment on the ground of such refusal.

[3, 4] However, that court held it to have been reversible error to have given paragraph 13 of the charge, which holding is not called in question by the application for writ of error; therefore is not before us for review; hence, if the contention of plaintiff in error that the only judgment was rendered as between it and the railway company which could properly have been rendered be not sound, then as a practical question it is not material whether the refusal of special charge No. 3 was error or not.

We are brought then logically to inquire whether as between the two corporations any judgment could properly have been rendered except the one that was rendered. The question will probably be more felicitously stated by saying that we are called upon to determine whether there was any evidence upon which a verdict holding the Pullman Company liable could be based on another trial. In order that we might correctly determine that question we have repeatedly carefully read, not only the statement of facts, but the record, and even after we had prepared an opinion we again examined carefully the application for the writ, in which is set forth fully and fairly all the evidence bearing upon the question, where the responsibility for the injury rested. That evidence was given both by the employees of the railway company and the plaintiff; in the larger part, by the former.

We were at first inclined to give a degree of importance to the testimony of the plaintiff as to the placing of the step box and the action or nonaction of the Pullman porter which we are satisfied upon further examination it is not entitled to. It is at best but a matter of opinion and so far as it was not negative in form was but the expression of "an idea," and did not possess the probative force that was sufficient to carry the case to the jury on the question whether the Pullman porter was negligently, or otherwise, responsible in any degree for the accident. This being true, there is no evidence to sustain a verdict against the Pullman Company. On the other hand, the inexcusable negligence of the employees of the railway is conclusively established by their own evidence, as the Court of Civil Appeals found, with unquestionable correctness.

We have reached the conclusion that there is no evidence sufficient to show that the Pullman porter did anything he ought not to have done, or left anything undone that he ought to have done, or that he was in any measure responsible for the injury to the passenger. It is made clear by the evidence that coincident with the passenger putting his foot on the step box the train was negligently put in motion with a jerk, and the passenger was thrown under the train, and that but for the presence of mind and promptness of the porter would likely have been killed.

It is obvious from the opinion of the Court of Civil Appeals that had that court reached the conclusion that the refusal of special charge No. 3 was correct, it would have affirmed the judgment of the trial court as between the two companies. That charge was properly refused by the trial court for the reasons we have already given, hence no ground was left for reversal of the judgment as between the two companies.

The contention of plaintiff in error that the only judgment has been rendered as between the two corporations that could properly have been rendered must be sustained.

We therefore recommend that the judgment of the Court of Civil Appeals be reversed, and the judgment of the district court be affirmed.

PHILLIPS, C. J. The judgment recommended in the report of the Commission of Appeals is adopted, and will be entered as the judgment of the Supreme Court.

TEXAS & N. O. R. CO. v. GERICKE.
(No. 233-3415.)

(Commission of Appeals of Texas, Section A.
June 8, 1921.)

**1. Master and servant ⚙=204(1)—Assumption
of risk defense under federal act.**

In action for an injury to an employee engaged in painting a bridge used in interstate commerce, the common-law doctrine of assumed risk, if supported by the facts, is a complete defense.

2. Master and servant ⚙=226(1) — Risk of master's negligence not assumed.

An employee does not assume negligence of his employer as a risk ordinarily incident to his service.

3. Master and servant ⚙=217(19)—Risk of unsafe place assumed by servant having knowledge of danger.

An employee placed by his employer in a position where he could not guard himself against danger by any reasonable amount of care on his part can assume that his employer had made such provision for his safety as was reasonably necessary to protect him from injury, and was not required to use even ordinary care to see whether this had been done, and he can therefore be held to have assumed the risk of the master's failure to take such precaution only when he knew it had not been taken or when in the ordinary discharge of his duty he must have acquired such knowledge.

4. Master and servant ⚙=217(16)—Risk of failure to give warning of vehicles not assumed by bridge painter on scaffold known to be too low.

Though a railroad bridge painter, who was working on a scaffolding on the under side of a bridge over a highway, and could not see approaching vehicles, knew that the scaffolding was too low to permit high-topped wagons to pass under it, so that he assumed the risk of injury from that defect, such knowledge does not show assumption of risk by him of his employer's failure to have watch kept to give warning of the approach of vehicles if such watch was reasonably necessary for the employee's protection.

5. Master and servant ⚙=288(5)—Assumption of risk question for jury.

If the evidence shows with such certainty that reasonable minds cannot differ as to its effect that the employee knew or must necessarily have known in the ordinary discharge of his duties that his master was not taking precaution for his safety, the charge denying recovery on the ground of assumption of risk would be proper.

6. Master and servant ⚙=280—Evidence held to show bridge painter on scaffold did not assume risk.

In an action for an injury to a railroad bridge painter when the scaffolding on which he was working and which was hung under a bridge over a highway was struck by a wagon, evidence held to sustain the jury's finding that he did not know of the master's failure to have

watch kept for approaching vehicles which would strike the scaffold, though it showed that shortly before the accident another wagon had struck the scaffold, but stopped before any injury was done when some one called a warning.

7. Appeal and error ⚙=994(2)—Credibility of plaintiff as witness for the jury.

The credibility of plaintiff as a witness and the weight to be given his testimony in view of his interest is for the jury.

Error to Court of Civil Appeals of Ninth Supreme Judicial District.

Action by Louis Gericke against the Texas & New Orleans Railroad Company. Judgment for plaintiff was affirmed by the Court of Civil Appeals (214 S. W. 668), and defendant brings error. Affirmed.

Baker, Botts, Parker & Garwood and McMeans, Garrison & Pollard, all of Houston, for plaintiff in error.

Presley K. Ewing, of Houston (L. E. Blankenbecker, of San Antonio, of counsel), for defendant in error.

GALLAGHER, J. Louis Gericke, defendant in error, brought this suit against the Texas & New Orleans Railroad Company, plaintiff in error, and two other corporations, to recover damages for personal injuries sustained by him while in the service of the railroad company and at work on a bridge belonging to said company which extended over and across Third street in the city of Houston.

The street at this point was about 30 feet wide, with cement walls on either side. The bridge was supported by iron girders, the ends of which rested on the respective cement walls. These girders had a perpendicular thickness of between 24 and 36 inches, and the cross-ties were laid directly upon them. The distance from the bottom of the girders to the surface of the street below was estimated by the witness to be between 15 and 20 feet.

Gericke belonged to a painting crew and was engaged at the time he was injured in cleaning the rust and dirt off the girders, preparatory to painting them. He was working on a scaffold swung by block and tackle from the cross-ties above. This scaffold had been erected only a short time before, under the personal supervision of one Stoner, the company's vice principal, and foreman of the gang in which Gericke was working. Stoner testified that it was placed as high up toward the bridge as the men could work while standing on it, and higher than convenient to work upon, and that he thought it would clear everything. He had twice before painted the same bridge in the same way.

Gericke had worked for the company about a week, but he was during that time engaged in painting a bridge over the bayou, and there was no danger from passing traffic beneath it. When he was at work his view was obstructed by the girders, and he could not see vehicles approaching on the street from either direction. It was therefore impossible for him to discover their approach and protect himself from injury therefrom. After he began work, and before the accident, a high-topped wagon came along the street. It got right against the scaffold and somebody "hollered" and the wagon stopped. Then Gericke and the men working with him raised the platform to let the wagon pass. They then lowered it to the place where Stoner had directed it to be placed, and it was at that place when the accident in question occurred.

Stoner always looked out for danger and for accidents, and saw that the work was left in proper shape when they quit in the evening. Stoner did not work on the platform, but was on the ground and all around the work. When he had left the work before, he had always left one Languish, the "straw boss," in his place.

Gericke testified that while he was so working he did not believe there was any danger because the boss (Stoner) was there; that he expected Stoner to look out for his safety while he was upon this scaffold over the street; that he did not know that Stoner was liable to go away while he was on the scaffold at work, nor that he had gone away at the time he was hurt.

Languish was on the work all the time. He did not work on the scaffold. He was on the ground or elsewhere about the work.

Gericke testified that he thought if Stoner should go away Languish would take his place and look out for his safety. There is no evidence that Stoner, when he left the work just a few minutes before Gericke was injured, advised Languish that he was leaving, or requested him to look after the work, or the safety of the men on the scaffolds. Stoner testified that he did not place a watchman under that bridge to give warning to approaching vehicles, or to warn the men on the scaffold; that he thought the scaffolds were high enough to clear the traffic, though he knew that high wagons like the one in question did use the street, and that such wagons had passed under the bridge when he had painted it before, but had always cleared the scaffolds.

About two or three hours after Gericke began work on this platform another high-topped wagon approached without warning, and struck the platform on which he was working, causing him to fall therefrom to the street below, from which fall he suffered permanent injuries.

The railroad company was engaged in interstate commerce, and the bridge in question was so used by it at the time.

Gericke sought recovery on the ground that the company, through its said vice principal, knew, or should have known, in the exercise of ordinary care, that the scaffold provided for him to work upon was liable to come in contact with passing vehicles, and thereby subject him to danger of injury, and that it was the duty of the company to keep a lookout for passing vehicles, or to maintain a watchman to do so, he being unable, in the discharge of his duties, to look out for himself, and that he expected this to be done, and thought it was done.

The railroad company answered by general denial and pleas of contributory negligence and assumed risk, alleging the use by it of the bridge in question in its business as a carrier of interstate commerce.

Gericke dismissed his suit against one of plaintiff in error's codefendants, and the jury acquitted the other of negligence, and the issues on this appeal are those arising between Gericke and the company.

The case was submitted to the jury on special issues and a verdict returned, which, as between Gericke and the company, finds as follows:

"(1) That a person of ordinary prudence, on the occasion in question, in the relation the defendant railroad company then occupied to the plaintiff, as a means of maintaining the working place reasonably safe, would have taken or seen to the taking, under all the attendant circumstances, of some reasonable precaution by lookout for vehicles, or by warning to plaintiff, to prevent a passing wagon from striking the scaffold in a manner to endanger plaintiff's safety; (2) that the defendant railroad company, on the occasion in question, failed to take or see to the taking of any such precaution; (3) that such failure on its part was negligence towards plaintiff, that is, a failure to exercise such care towards him as an ordinarily prudent person would have exercised under the same or similar circumstances; (4) that such negligence was a proximate cause of alleged injury to plaintiff; * * * (8) that the plaintiff, on the occasion in question, was not guilty of negligence as defined by the court, in not raising the scaffold high enough to clear vehicles, such as the alleged wagon, or in lowering the scaffold enough to come in contact with such vehicles; (9) that the plaintiff did not know, nor was it obvious, nor must it necessarily have been known to him, in the ordinary discharge of his own duties, that the defendant railroad company was taking, or would take, no precautions for his safety by lookout for vehicles, such as the wagon in question, or by warning the plaintiff, as submitted to the jury in special issues 1 and 2; (10) that $10,000 was fair and adequate compensation for the alleged injuries sustained by plaintiff on the occasion in question."

Judgment was entered in accordance with such findings.

The Court of Civil Appeals held that the findings of the jury were sustained by the evidence, and affirmed the judgment. 214 S. W. 668.

Plaintiff in error makes no complaint of the findings of the jury to the effect that it was negligent in providing for the safety of defendant in error, that such negligence was the proximate cause of his injury, and that he was not guilty of negligence contributing thereto.

Plaintiff in error's first assignment complains of the refusal of its requested peremptory instruction, which is as follows:

"In this case you are instructed that the undisputed evidence shows that the plaintiff, at the time he was injured, was engaged in interstate commerce, and the undisputed facts show that he, while so engaged, assumed the risk, and that his injury was the result of one of the risks ordinarily incident to the business in which he was engaged, and it is further shown by the undisputed evidence that the plaintiff has failed to show by a preponderance of the evidence any negligence upon the part of the defendant, Texas & New Orleans Railroad Company, which was the proximate cause of plaintiff's injury. You are therefore instructed to return a verdict for the defendant, Texas & New Orleans Railroad Company."

[1] Plaintiff in error being engaged as a carrier of interstate commerce, and using the bridge in question in discharging its duties as such, the common-law doctrine of assumed risk, if supported by the facts, became available as a complete defense to this suit. Seaboard Air Line Ry. Co. v. Horton, 233 U. S. 492, 34 Sup. Ct. 635, 58 L. Ed. 1062, 1069, L. R. A. 1915C, 1, Ann. Cas. 1915B, 475; Chicago, R. I. & G. Ry. Co. v. De Bord, 109 Tex. 20, 24, 192 S. W. 767, 768.

[2] An employee does not assume negligence of his employer as a risk ordinarily incident to his service.

Mr. Justice Yantis, speaking for the Supreme Court in Chicago, R. I. & G. Ry. Co. v. De Bord, 109 Tex. 20, 23, 24, 192 S. W. 767, 768, says:

"The rule is too well settled to require the citation of authorities that under the common-law doctrine of assumed risk the plaintiff in a negligence suit does not assume any risks or dangers arising from the negligence of the defendant of which he has no knowledge; but it is equally well settled that at common law plaintiff does assume the risks and dangers caused by the negligence of which he did have prior knowledge."

[3] Defendant in error, having been placed by plaintiff in error, acting by its vice principal, at work in a place exposed to dangers from which he could not by reason of his necessary position in the discharge of the duties of his employment, guard himself by any reasonable amount of care on his part, had the right to assume that plaintiff in error had made such provision for his safety as was reasonably necessary to protect him from injury while so engaged, and was not required to use even ordinary care to see whether this had been done or not. Only when he actually knew that such provision for his safety had not been made, or when in the ordinary discharge of his duty he must necessarily have acquired such knowledge, can he be held to have assumed the risk of injury from such failure. M., K. & T. Ry. Co. v. Hannig, 91 Tex. 347, 351, 43 S. W. 508; T. & N. O. Ry. Co. v. Bingle, 91 Tex. 287, 288, 42 S. W. 971; Barnhart v. K. C., M. & O. Ry. Co. of Tex., 107 Tex. 638, 646, 184 S. W. 176; I. & G. N. Ry. Co. v. Hinzie, 82 Tex. 623, 630, 18 S. W. 681; Chicago & N. W. Ry. Co. v. Bower, 241 U. S. 470, 36 Sup. Ct. 624, 60 L. Ed. 1107, 1110.

The Supreme Court, in the case of Railway v. Hannig, supra, says:

"We understand the law to be that when the servant enters the employment of the master, he has the right to rely upon the assumption that the machinery, tools, and appliances with which he is called upon to work are reasonably safe, *and that the business is conducted in a reasonably safe manner.* He is not required to use ordinary care to see whether this has been done or not. He does not assume the risks arising from the failure of the master to do his duty, unless he knows of the failure and the attendant risks or in the ordinary discharge of his own duty must necessarily have acquired the knowledge. Bonnet v. Railway Company, 89 Tex. 72; Railway v. Bingle, ante p. 287." (Italics ours.)

The Supreme Court, in the case of Barnhart v. Railway Company, says:

"The plaintiff had the right to rely upon the master to furnish him a safe place to work, and he need make no inspection to ascertain whether the master has discharged this duty."

The Supreme Court, in the case of Railway v. Hinzie, says:

"It is true also that he [plaintiff] knew that cars would probably at any moment be switched onto the side track on which he was at work; but this would not necessarily, or even probably, import that he knew that appellant would neglect to give him adequate warning of their approach, and that it was hence unsafe for him to perform the work in obedience to his orders. The mere fact that he knew that cars would be probably switched in upon the side track would not preclude a recovery by him, unless he also knew that it was unsafe to continue his labors; and this was a question for the jury. Wood's Mast. & Serv. § 775."

[4] Notwithstanding defendant in error may have known that the platform on which he was working was hung too low to allow a wagon of the kind in question to pass under it without coming in contact with it, and might be held to have assumed the risk of injury incident to that defect alone, if a proper watch was kept, still, if he was ignorant of the fact that no watch was kept, and

the failure to keep such watch caused or contributed to his injury, then he could not be held' to have assumed the risk resulting from such failure; such risk being one superadded to the risk assumed by the negligence of the company. Poindexter v. Receivers, Kirby Lumber Co., 101 Tex. 322, 325, 107 S. W. 42; T. & N. O. Ry. Co. v. Kelly, 98 Tex. 123, 135–137, 80 S. W. 79; Mo. Pac. Ry. Co. v. Somers, 78 Tex. 439, 442, 443, 14 S. W. 779; Chicago & N. W. Ry. Co. v. Bower, 241 U. S. 470, 36 Sup. Ct. 624, 60 L. Ed. 1107, 1110.

In the case of Poindexter v. Receivers, supra, plaintiff was injured by a rivet from a leather belt striking his eye by reason of the breaking of such belt. He alleged negligence in using an old and defective belt and in using a defective pulley. There was evidence from which the jury might have found that, if the belt was defective, plaintiff knew of the defect, but the evidence, on the other hand, tended to show that he was justifiably ignorant of any defect in the pulley. Discussing the doctrine of assumed risk, as arising out of these circumstances, the Supreme Court says:

"But, if the belt was a safe one, and the danger of its breaking and throwing off such objects, when used upon proper pulleys, was one of the ordinary risks of the service which plaintiff assumed, this would not include an assumption of the risk caused by defendant's negligence in having a defective pulley, if it caused the belt to break. Or, if it were shown that the belt was defective, and that plaintiff knew of its condition and assumed the risk incident to such defect alone, still he would not be precluded from recovering, if the defective condition of the pulley caused or contributed to his injury. Missouri Pac. Ry. Co. v. Somers, 78 Tex. 442, 443; Texas & N. O. Ry. Co. v. Kelly, 98 Tex. 137. The risk resulting from the defective pulley would be one superadded by the defendant's negligence to that assumed, and for an injury caused or contributed to by it the defendants would be liable."

The recovery by defendant in error in this case is predicated on a finding by the jury that plaintiff in error was negligent in failing to take some reasonable precaution by lookout for vehicles, or by warning to him to prevent passing wagons from striking the scaffold on which he was working in a manner to endanger his safety, and that such failure to take such reasonable precaution was the proximate cause of his injury.

Whether the injuries received by defendant in error resulted from a risk assumed by him under this state of the record depends on whether he knew of the failure of the company to take such precaution; if he did know such fact, he assumed the risk of injury therefrom, but, if he did not know such fact, he did not assume such risk.

The jury found that defendant in error did not know, that it was not obvious to him, and that it was not necessarily known to him, in the ordinary discharge of his own duties, that plaintiff in error would take no precaution for his safety by a lookout for vehicles, such as the wagon in question, or by warning to him. The Court of Civil Appeals held the evidence sufficient to support such finding. The real issue raised by this assignment, therefore, is whether there is any evidence to sustain such finding.

[5] If the evidence shows, with such certainty that reasonable minds cannot differ, as to its effect, that the defendant in error knew, or must necessarily have known in the ordinary discharge of his duties, that plaintiff in error was not taking, or would not take, precaution for his safety by keeping a lookout for passing vehicles, or by warning to him, then the charge under consideration should have been given; otherwise it was properly refused.

[6] We have reviewed the entire evidence in this case. The application for the writ of error adopts for its statement of facts the facts as recited by the Court of Civil Appeals in its opinion in this case. The Court of Civil Appeals held in accordance with the verdict of the jury that the defendant in error did not know such precautions for his safety were not being taken, but, doubtless through oversight alone, failed to recite all the testimony.

Plaintiff in error seems to rely for its proof of such knowledge on the fact that a high-topped wagon had passed under the bridge a short time before the accident, and that defendant in error assisted in raising the platform to let the wagon pass and in then lowering the platform to the place it occupied before.

Defendant in error testified on this identical point as follows:

"During the time we were putting it up one wagon struck it while I was working awhile on there. It just got right against it, and somebody hollered, and the wagon stopped. It was too low then, and I saw it when the wagon struck it. Nobody was hurt at that time; it never hit it hard to hurt anybody. I was standing on one of the planks then. When they hollered, the wagon stopped, and we raised this board and let them go through and then we put it back. The scaffold had not been raised or lowered while I was working on it. It remained at the same place where I put it under the direction of my foreman. I do not know how [high] the scaffolding was above the street. * * * I think it was a good while after the first wagon hit it before this wagon hit it. I continued to work on the scaffold. No other wagon hit it. Mr. Stoner was standing under the bridge when we finished putting up the scaffold. I do not know what became of him. * * * I think I worked about two hours before I was hurt, about a couple of hours. When the first wagon struck the girder I had my head alongside of the girder. I did not stop and get down. I did not see the wagon. Somebody just hollered, you know, and he wagon was right against it there. I did not go on working. We raised the board. We stopped working and got under the girder. I could see the wagon and the street then. I do not know where Mr. Stoner was then. I do not know whether he was there or not. The fellow that was working with me said, 'Raise it and let him get over.' * * * I say that one wagon came along there, and that somebody hollered, and that Bonwell and I raised the plank and let the wagon go under. The hollering came from on the ground there under the bridge. I do not know who it was that hollered. I thought Mr. Stoner was down there watching under there, keeping a lookout for wagons that would pass under. The connection I thought Mr. Stoner had with this hollering at the time this first wagon passed under there when we raised the plank was to stop it so it would not knock me off. * * *

"I did not know, at the time I got hurt, or at any time before I got hurt that there was nobody down on the ground keeping a lookout. I expected Mr. Stoner, the boss, to look out for my safety while I was engaged in that work. I did not know at the time I was injured, or beforehand, that the defendant company never used a watchman, or never had any body to keep a watchout. I had only worked for the company seven days, and over on the other side of the bridge. I testified that there was no occasion for any watchout."

[7] The credibility of defendant in error as a witness and the weight to be given to his testimony as one of the parties in interest was for the jury. The jury found that he did not know that no precaution was taken for his safety, and we cannot say that there is no evidence to support such finding. Neither can we say that the evidence shows with such certainty that reasonable minds cannot differ as to its effect that he did know that plaintiff in error was taking, or would take, no precaution for his safety by lookout for vehicles, such as the wagon in question, or by warning to him.

This case is very similar to the case of Grace & Hyde Co. v. Kennedy, decided by the United States Circuit Court of Appeals for the Second Circuit, and reported in 99 Fed. 679, 40 C. C. A. 69. In that case the defendant was constructing a shed over the width of the sidewalk on one side of an avenue in the city of New York. In consequence of the extent of the public use of the street in the daytime, the work was done at night. Two derricks were employed in placing the material used in constructing the shed in proper position. These derricks were secured by guy lines extending across the avenue. About 5 o'clock in the morning a mail van came along this avenue and struck one of the guy lines, causing it to sway and knock the plaintiff from his position to the ground, from which fall he suffered injury.

The case was presented to the jury by the plaintiff upon the theory that, inasmuch as the work was necessarily done at night upon a street which was frequently occupied by passing vehicles of various kinds, and as the necessary guy ropes which extended into the street must be fastened where they were in danger of collision with a passing vehicle, if unobserved in the darkness by the driver of the vehicle, it was the duty of the defendant to take such precaution against injury to his employees as to render the place of their work reasonably safe. The defendant, among other defenses, relied on assumed risk. There was a verdict for plaintiff, which on appeal was affirmed. The issue of assumed risk was disposed of by the court in its opinion as follows:

"The subject which is contained in the defendant's assignment of error that the plaintiff assumed the risk of his position and of the conditions as they existed was fully considered in Railway Co. v. Archibald, 170 U. S. 665, 18 Sup. Ct. 777, 42 L. Ed. 1188, and it is sufficient to say that the plaintiff did not assume the risk of the employer's neglect to furnish a reasonably safe system of protection against the danger from injury by passing vehicles, and that there is no adequate evidence that he continued to remain at work with the knowledge of the insufficiency of the protection which was actually furnished. The judgment is affirmed, with costs."

We therefore hold that the peremptory charge requested by plaintiff in error was properly refused.

The other assignments in the application for writ of error in this case are controlled by the provisions of law above set out, and the authorities cited in support of the same. We have carefully considered all of such assignments, and in our opinion they present no reversible error.

We therefore recommend that the judgment of the Court of Civil Appeals in this case be affirmed.

PHILLIPS, C. J. The judgment recommended in the report of the Commission of Appeals is adopted, and will be entered as the judgment of the Supreme Court.

HUMPHREY et al. v. NATIONAL FIRE INS. CO. OF HARTFORD, CONN.
(No. 221-3355.)

(Commission of Appeals of Texas, Section B. June 1, 1921.)

1. Insurance ⟹308, 548 — Anti-technicality statute not applicable to breaches which could in no event contribute to loss, such as breach of provision for examination after loss.

Vernon's Sayles' Ann. Civ. St. 1914, art. 4874a, providing that no breach by insured of warranty or condition of fire insurance policy shall avoid it unless contributing to the loss, does not apply to any provision the breach of which could in no event contribute to loss, and hence does not apply to breach of condition that insured shall submit to examination after fire occurs, as such breach could not contribute to the fire.

2. Insurance ⟹548 — Policy requirement of examination of insured after loss held a material condition.

A fire insurance policy provision requiring insured to submit to examination after loss is a material one, and if breached the insurer would be deprived of a valuable right for which it had contracted.

3. Abatement and revival ⟹40 — Insurance ⟹615—Pleading ⟹111—Refusal to submit to examination after loss does not avoid policy, but only suspends right of recovery until examination, and hence is pleadable in abatement, not in bar; sustaining plea in abatement effective only as dismissal of premature action.

Failure or refusal to submit to examination after loss does not bar recovery, but merely suspends the right of recovery until the condition of examination is complied with; and such failure or refusal is therefore to be pleaded in abatement, and not in bar, and, if the plea be sustained, its only effect is dismissal of suit as prematurely brought.

4. Abatement and revival ⟹40, 85—Plea of failure to submit to examination, being in abatement, waived if not made at proper time.

Under Vernon's Sayles' Ann. Civ. St. 1914, arts. 1902, 1909, 1910, 1947, and rules 7 and 24 for District Courts (142 S. W. xvii, xix), as to order of pleas in abatement, where, in action on fire insurance policy, failure of insured to submit to examination was not pleaded except as one of several special defenses, in insurer's answer, it was not filed in due order, as a plea in abatement, and not being called up at the first term of court, and no special ruling being asked thereon before a trial on the merits, the plea was waived.

5. Insurance ⟹548 — Requirement that insured submit to examination must be reasonably enforced.

A provision in a fire policy requiring insured to submit to examination after loss may be availed of by insurer only if it fixes a reasonable time and place for such examination, whether such qualification is expressed in the policy or not.

6. Insurance ⟹640(2) — Insurer can defend on ground of insured's failure to submit to examination only if pleading and proving that the time and place of examination were reasonable.

To avail itself of the failure of insured to submit to examination after loss under a fire policy, insurer must not only plead the policy clause providing for examination, but must plead and prove that it fixed a reasonable time and place for such examination.

7. Insurance ⟹665(3) — Evidence held to support jury finding that time and place fixed for examination were unreasonable.

In action on a fire insurance policy, evidence *held* to support a finding of the jury that the time and place fixed by insurer for insured's examination after loss were unreasonable.

8. Insurance ⟹548—Insured has right to have attorney present at examination after loss.

Under a fire insurance policy requiring insured to submit to examination after loss, it is insured's right to have his or her attorney present at the examination.

9. Insurance ⟹548—Insured, failing to submit to examination after loss on reasonable notice, may do so later.

Insured, refusing to comply, even on reasonable notice, with a fire policy requirement of examination after loss, could later recede from that position and offer to submit to such examination.

Error to Court of Civil Appeals of First Supreme Judicial District.

Action by Julia C. Humphrey and husband against the National Fire Insurance Company of Hartford, Conn. Judgment for plaintiffs was reversed and rendered by the Court of Civil Appeals (211 S. W. 811), and plaintiffs bring error. Judgment of Court of Civil Appeals reversed, and that of district court affirmed.

Marsene Johnson, Elmo Johnson, Roy Johnson, and Marsene Johnson, Jr., all of Galveston, and Black & Smedley, of Austin, for plaintiffs in error.

Mart H. Royston, of Galveston, for defendant in error.

POWELL, J. Julia C. Humphrey, joined pro forma by her husband, sued the National Fire Insurance Company of Hartford, Conn., in the district court of Galveston county, Tex., for the recovery of $1,500 due under a policy issued by the latter to her on July 10, 1915, covering her separate personal property located in her rented home in the city of Galveston. The insured property was almost totally destroyed by fire in the early morning hours of January 1, 1916. The petition was in the usual form of a suit for recovery of damages on a fire insurance policy.

The defendant in error, among other defenses, alleged a violation of the following provisions of the policy, to wit:

"The insured, as often as required, shall exhibit to any person designated by this company all that remains of any property herein described, and submit to examination under oath by any person named by this company, and subscribe the same, and, as often as required, shall produce for examination all books of account, bills, invoices and other vouchers or certified copies thereof, if originals be lost, at such reasonable place as may be designated by this company or its representative and shall permit extracts and copies to be made thereof."

And again:

"No suit or action on this policy for the recovery of any claim shall be sustainable in any court of law or equity, until after full compliance by the insured with all the foregoing requirements, nor unless commenced within two years next after the fire."

The case was submitted to the jury upon special issues, to which answers were returned as follows:

"(1) What was the total value of the property covered by the policy in the house at the time of the fire? Answer: $3,281.00.

"(2) What was the amount of loss and damage by fire of the property covered by the policy? Answer: $2,500.00.

"(3) Was any other request ever made of Mrs. Julia C. Humphrey to submit herself for examination by the agents of the company, than such as is testified to by witness Bucklew? Answer: No.

"(4) Was the time designated in the notice given by the witness Bucklew to Mrs. Humphrey for her to submit herself for examination by the agents of the company a reasonable time? Answer: Unreasonable.

"(5) Did Mrs. Humphrey knowingly refuse to submit herself to examination by agents of the company? Answer: Yes."

Upon the jury's findings, the court rendered judgment for plaintiff in error in the sum of $1,250, that being one-half of the $2,500 assessed by the jury as her loss and damage. She had two policies, each for the sum of $1,500, and defendant in error was in no event liable for more than half of said total loss.

Defendant in error appealed from said judgment to the Court of Civil Appeals at Galveston, which court reversed and rendered the judgment of the trial court because the jury had found that Julia Humphrey, the insured, had knowingly refused to submit herself to examination by agents of defendant in error on January 3, 1916. See 211 S. W. 811. The same Court of Civil Appeals had reversed and remanded a similar judgment in this case on a former appeal. See 199 S. W. 865.

Plaintiffs in error, following the last judgment of the Court of Civil Appeals, revers-ing and rendering their judgment, sued out a writ of error in due course to the Supreme Court, which was granted.

The controlling questions on this appeal are involved in the construction of the provision of the policy with reference to examination of the insured, and already set out in hæc verba herein.

[1] Plaintiffs in error contend that said provision of the policy is within the purview of article 4874a (Acts of 1913) of Vernon's Sayles' Ann. Civil Statutes of the State of Texas, and is therefore precluded as a defense. Said article of the statutes reads as follows:

"That no breach or violation by the insured of any of the warranties, conditions or provisions of any fire insurance policy, contract of insurance, or application therefor, upon personal property, shall render void the policy or contract, or constitute a defense to a suit for loss thereon, unless such breach or violation contributed to bring about the destruction of the property."

We cannot agree to this contention. Several months after the writ was granted in this case, said statute was construed by section A of the Commission of Appeals, with the approval of the Supreme Court, and it was held:

"It seems conclusive that no promissory warranties, conditions, or provisions of a fire policy, the breach of which could in no event contribute to bring about the loss of the property insured, are within the purview of the act invoked." McPherson v. Fire Ins. Co., 222 S. W. 211.

The doctrine announced in the case of McPherson v. Ins. Co., supra, was followed by section A of the Commission of Appeals in the case of Ins. Co. v. Levy, 222 S. W. 216, and by section B of the Commission of Appeals in case of Insurance Co. v. Waco Co., 222 S. W. 217.

So, whatever may have been the conflicting views in this connection heretofore, the rule is now well settled. The provision authorizing an examination of the insured after the fire occurs could, in no event, contribute to the fire. Therefore it is not within said statute.

[2] We are also of the view that the Court of Civil Appeals in this case has correctly held that the provision in question is a material one in such contracts, and that if the same were breached, the insurer would be deprived of a valuable right for which it had contracted. R. C. L. vol. 14, p. 513; notes to 52 L. R. A. 425, 426; Gross v. Ins. Co. (C. C.) 22 Fed. 74; Fleisch v. Ins. Co., 58 Mo. App. 596.

Before proceeding to a discussion of whether or not there was any breach of said provision by the insured, we think it best to consider the same and ascertain the nature thereof, and the penalty for its breach. The insured agrees, at reasonable times and places, as often as required, to submit to examination by agent of insurer, and to submit all relevant books of account, bills, invoices, vouchers, etc. It is clear that the chief purpose of this privilege to the insurer is the ascertainment and adjustment of the loss which has already occurred. The insurance company, in its policy, evidences in many ways its desire to avoid the necessity of litigation in the settlement of its losses. It reserves the right to have the benefit of the examination provided for before suit can be sustained.

[3] What is the penalty for breach of said provision? In reading the policy in question, it will be found that in many instances forfeiture is the penalty for breach of warranties and conditions. In other cases, it is provided that in certain events the company will not be liable. But, for a violation of the provision for an examination of the insured, it is only provided that—

"No suit or action on this policy for the recovery of any claim shall be sustainable in any court of law or equity until after full compliance by the insured with all the foregoing requirements, nor unless commenced within two years next after the fire."

It is evident that the only penalty for breach of said provision is to delay the time when suit may be sustainable. If the insured refuses to submit to the examination, when reasonably requested so to do, he only delays the time when he can recover on his policy. He only postpones the date when he can enforce payment. If he offers to submit himself to the examination, after a refusal, any time within two years after the fire, he can then go into court. We are of the view that this provision is in no sense one in bar of recovery, but one in abatement, and that the defense should be so pleaded. If such a plea should be sustained by the court, its only effect would be a dismissal of the case because prematurely brought. That this provision is a plea in abatement, rather than one in bar, is not only clear to us from the wording of the same, but it has been so construed by many appellate courts, to a few of which we shall refer.

Justice Pelham of the Court of Appeals of Alabama, in case of Fire Ins. Co. v. Toilet Goods Co., 10 Ala. App. 395, 64 South. 635, speaks in this connection as follows:

"It was held in Weide v. Germania Ins. Co., Fed. Cas. No. 17,358, 1 Dill. 441, that the failure or refusal of the insured to submit to an examination on oath under the usual stipulations of a policy containing such a requirement does not work a forfeiture of the policy, but only causes the loss not to be payable until the condition is complied with, and that such refusal should be pleaded in abatement and separately from defenses in bar of recovery in all events at any time. The effect of the refusal of the assured to answer questions on oath under the terms of the policy is not to forfeit or avoid the policy and bar recovery on it, but to suspend the right of payment or recovery until the answers are given in compliance with the condition. Objection that the action is prematurely brought, that the assured refused to submit to an examination, should be raised by plea in abatement. 19 Cyc. 926 (3). We think that, for the reasons given, the trial court is not to be put in error for sustaining demurrers to the pleas numbered 2, 4, 5, and 6."

Justice Atkinson, of the Supreme Court of Georgia, in the case of Rosser v. Ins. Co., 101 Ga. 716, 29 S. E. 286, uses the following significant language:

"The defendant, in its plea, alleged that the suit had been brought before the expiration of the time limited in the policy within which, after receiving proofs of loss, it was not bound to pay. This plea, if sustained, would have had the effect only to defeat this particular action. The cause of action itself would still have survived, and the plaintiff could, after the expiration of the time limited in the policy in which the insurer was not bound to pay, bring his action anew. It was a plea in abatement. It alleged a ground for abating the suit in the present case, but was not a good defense to the action upon its merits."

Justice Mitchell of the Supreme Court of Pennsylvania, in the case of Plate-Glass Co. v. Ins. Co., 189 Pa. 255, 42 Atl. 138, 69 Am. St. Rep. 810, announces the following relevant rule:

"The policy provides that, in case of disagreement as to the amount of loss, it shall be ascertained by appraisers, and, further, that no action shall be brought on the policy until after compliance with all its requirements, among which is that relating to appraisers. Such appraisement, or the effort to have it, would be at the most a condition precedent to an action by the insured, and the failure to have it a ground for a plea in abatement by the company."

It is clear to us, as stated by the authorities just cited, that provisions like the one in question present only matters in abatement, and that if such provisions are pleaded and sustained, the only result would be a dismissal of the suit as having been prematurely brought.

The Supreme Court of Washington goes even further, and holds, in construing exactly the same provisions, as follows:

"When we look to the words of the policy, which it is well settled must be strictly construed against the insurance company, we do not find that it provides that no action shall be 'commenced,' but that no action shall be 'sustainable.' At the time plaintiffs sought to sustain their action by proofs, the examination had been signed and was in the hands of the defendant. All that the policy required had been performed." Barbour v. Ins. Co., 101 Wash. 46, 171 Pac. 1030.

The Washington case indicates that compliance with this provision of the policy might be had after the suit has been instituted and without the necessity of a dismissal of the case, even though such a plea in abatement be sustained. We cite this case only to show the trend of authority in some quarters. We do not desire to be understood as going this far, although we are heartily in accord with the Texas authorities which uniformly hold that forfeitures are not favored.

[4] If the said provision is one in abatement, then it should be pleaded in due order and action asked thereon in compliance with the statutes and court rules in such cases provided. They are:

Article 1910 of Vernon's Sayles' Revised Civil Statutes of Texas, reads as follows:

"Pleas to the jurisdiction, pleas in abatement, and other dilatory pleas and demurrers, not involving the merits of the case, shall be determined during the term at which they are filed, if the business of the court will permit."

Article 1947 of the same Statutes reads as follows:

"When a case is called for trial, the issues of law arising on the pleadings, and all pleas in abatement, and other dilatory pleas remaining undisposed of, shall be determined; and it shall be no cause for the postponement of a trial of the issues of law that a party is not prepared to try the issues of fact."

Rule 24 for the District Courts (142 S. W. xix) provides as follows:

"All dilatory pleas, and all motions and exceptions relating to a suit pending, which do not go to the merits of the case, shall be tried at the first term to which the attention of the court shall be called to the same, unless passed by agreement of parties with the consent of the court; and all such pleas and motion shall be first called and disposed of before the main issue on the merits is tried."

Due order of pleading is essential, and pleas in abatement must precede pleas to the merits or in bar. Articles 1902 and 1909 of Vernon's Sayles' Revised Civil Statutes, and Rule No. 7 for the District Courts (142 S. W. xvii).

Was there any effort to comply with said statutes or court rule? The facts in this connection are:

The original petition in this case was filed January 28, 1916. The record does not disclose the date of filing or the contents of the insurer's original answer. The record does disclose the fact that the first amended answer of insurer was filed November 18, 1916. Said answer is not in the record. But on the said 18th day of November, the insured filed

her first supplemental petition, and it is in the record. Said petition, answering said first amended answer, shows that said answer set up two special exceptions, neither of which referred to the provision of the policy in question here. Said provision did constitute the sixth special answer in bar.

The opinion of the Court of Civil Appeals on the first appeal was handed down on December 21, 1917 (199 S. W. 865).

The insured filed her first amended original petition on March 22, 1918, and the second amended answer of defendant in error, in reply thereto, was filed next day. Said answer, in consecutive order, was as follows: A general demurrer; three special exceptions, none of which related to the provision now under discussion; a general denial and several special defenses. The third among the latter alleged a violation of the provision in issue herein.

It is quite clear that, as a plea in abatement, the same was not filed in due order, was not called up at the first term of court, and no special ruling was asked thereon before a trial on the merits. Under all these circumstances, we think this plea was waived, and that the judgment of the district court should have been affirmed.

If we are correct in viewing this plea as one in abatement, then we are sustained in our view last expressed by the opinion of the Supreme Court of Texas in the case of Blum v. Strong, 71 Tex. 321, 6 S. W. 167. On motion for rehearing, Justice Gaines wrote vigorously, concluding as follows:

"We therefore conclude that the appellants, by proceeding to trial upon the merits of the case, without specially invoking the action of the court upon the plea in abatement, must be held to have waived it; and that it matters not so far as the disposition of this appeal is concerned, whether it should be considered a sufficient plea or not."

We believe this is one plea in abatement in which the rule requiring action at the first term of court after suit is filed should be rigidly enforced. If this plea in abatement had been passed upon at the first term of court in 1916 and sustained, the insured could have dismissed her case, and then submitted to the examination, thereby preserving her rights. But, by not urging the plea and permitting it to pass along from term to term, two years might elapse, and then the insured lose her right of action entirely. If the plea be sustained after the lapse of two years following the fire, and the cause then dismissed, a new suit would then be barred. It is evident that this plea in abatement should be handled by the court in strict compliance with the statutes and court rules covering pleas in abatement. Otherwise, gross injustice would result.

[5] But, whether a plea in abatement or not, we think this provision of the policy

cannot affect the right of the insured to recover unless she violated an attempt on the part of the insurance company to reasonably enforce it. In construing this provision, we are in hearty accord with the opinion of the Court of Appeals of New York State, in the case of Porter v. Ins. Co., 164 N. Y. 504, 58 N. E. 641, 52 L. R. A. 424. In that case, in construing this same provision, the court concludes as follows:

"Finally, it should be noted that the condition alleged to have been violated in this case applied only after the capital fact of a loss. The object of the provision was to prescribe the manner in which an accrued loss was to be adjusted and ascertained. The liability of the defendant having become fixed by the happening of the event, upon which the contract was to mature, conditions which prescribe methods and formalities for ascertaining the extent of it or for adjusting it, are not to be subjected to any narrow or technical construction, but construed liberally in favor of the insured."

We think that, under the express terms of this provision, before the insured is under any duty to submit to such an examination, the insurance company must fix a reasonable time and place therefor. But, if the provision does not expressly so require, then it should be so construed. In passing upon a provision of a similar nature, the Supreme Court of Minnesota concurs in our view. See Johnson v. Ins. Co., 129 Minn. 18, 151 N. W. 413, L. R. A. 1916F, 1149, Ann. Cas. 1916A, 154. In fact, the Court of Civil Appeals, in its opinion in this case, does not seem to take issue with us.

[6] The jury did find that the insured knowingly refused to submit herself to the examination on January 3, 1916. But they expressly found, also, that the time set was unreasonable. In order to avoid the effect of that finding the Court of Civil Appeals held that the issue was not authorized by the pleadings or supported by the testimony, and reversed and rendered the judgment of the district court. Our answer to said views of the Court of Civil Appeals is:

In the first place, we think before the insurance company can impose any obligation upon the insured in this connection, it must plead its defense and prove it. It did plead the provision of the policy. As we view it, it could not discharge its burden of proof in establishing said defense, until it had shown the jury that the time and place fixed were reasonable. In other words, the burden of pleading and proof in this particular matter was with the insurance company.

[7] Was the jury justified, under the facts in evidence, in finding that the time fixed for the examination was unreasonable? We think they were amply justified in so finding. What are the facts in this connection, construed in the strongest light for the insur-

ance company? The demand served upon insured was as follows:

"Jan. 3, 1916.

"Mrs. Julia C. Humphrey, née Peebles, Galveston, Texas—Dear Madam: You are hereby demanded to appear at Charles Neynaber a Notary Public Office 221–22nd Street, Galveston Texas at 2:30 p. m. of this date and there submit to examination under oath relative to a fire and the alleged damage caused by said fire to the property insured under policy No. 56086 of the National Fire Insurance Co. of Hartford, Conn.

"The said fire is reported to have occurred on Jan. 1, 1916, in the house located at 2901 Avenue G.

"This demand is made in accordance with the above named and numbered policy and I would particularly call your attention to lines 81 to 85 inclusive.

"[Signed] National Union Fire Ins. Co., "By Sam Bucklew."

Lines 81 to 85 of the policy referred to are set out in the provision of the policy under discussion and includes the duty of bringing to the examination all books of account, bills, invoices, and other vouchers, etc.

It is somewhat difficult to determine from the record just when this notice was actually delivered to insured. Neynaber, the insurer's notary, said it was delivered on Monday or Tuesday just after the fire, and the insured agreed to come for the examination the next day after notice was delivered. Bucklew, the adjuster of the company, testified he gave her this notice on Sunday afternoon about 4 o'clock, and that the insured refused to appear at the time he had fixed, but told him she would meet him at the office of her attorney on Monday morning. It is not essential to settle these conflicts in the testimony. The law of Texas imposed no duty upon the insured to take any steps until Monday morning in her preparation to comply with this demand. The law justly recognizes the right of our people to rest on Sunday. The adjuster himself knew this, for he says he dated the notice on Monday, the day following, so he would be sure it was in legal form.

So, let us see the situation as it confronted the insured on Monday morning, January 3. She was required to appear for the examination at 2:30 p. m. that day. As a woman who had just lost her home and nearly all her clothes, she probably had other urgent duties that shortly after the fire. Aside from those facts, however, the notice itself required that she bring books of account, invoices and vouchers covering the lost property. The jury might well have found it impossible for her to have done this in half a day. The property consisted of furniture and household goods in general. It takes time to get up invoices of the numerous articles involved in property of this character.

[8] Again, the proof shows she wanted to

consult her attorney. She had a right to do this. In our view, it was her privilege to have him present at the examination. The provision does not specify a private examination. We are in full sympathy with the view announced by the Court of Appeals, in Missouri in the case of Thomas v. Insurance Co., 47 Mo. App. 169. The court there says:

"When insurance companies proceed to take these examinations, it is tantamount to a declaration of intention to contest the claim, and it would seem the part of prudence that the assured have his attorney at hand when anything so important is being done. To deny so reasonable a request bears the appearance of an attempt to take an undue advantage of the plaintiff in a secret examination, or an effort to manufacture a mere technical defense for this case. It cannot be allowed to succeed."

That she did not have time to gather the data required by the insurance company and arrange with her own counsel before 2:30 p. m. that day seems to us almost an inevitable conclusion. Certainly, the jury was fully justified in finding the time fixed unreasonable. That being true, the insured, as before stated, owed no duty to respond to the demand, and this provision cannot avail the company anything in this instance. We think the Court of Civil Appeals erred in ignoring this finding of the jury and rendering judgment against the insured.

[9] But, even if the time fixed for the examination had been reasonable, she could have refused to comply, and later tendered herself to the company. That would have been a compliance with the provisions of the policy, in our judgment. We are sustained in this view by the Circuit Court of Appeals of the United States in the case of Insurance Co. v. Rose, 228 Fed. 290, 142 C. C. A. 582. Justice Woolley affirmed the judgment of the lower court for the insured, and spoke as follows in this connection:

"The court correctly charged that the insured was required to submit himself and his papers to examination as a condition precedent to a right of action on the policy. It appears that in November, 1912, the insured submitted himself and his papers to examination, but in December, 1912, he withdrew himself and his papers from examination. As held by the learned trial judge, the declination to submit to further examination arrested the performance of the condition precedent required of the insured, and if nothing further had been done, no right of action would have accrued to him. But in February following, the insured, contemplating suit, receded from this position and openly offered to submit himself and his papers to examination."

The undisputed facts in this case show that, while the insured failed to appear at the time set on the afternoon of January 3,

she did tender herself to Neynaber on Wednesday, January 5, just two days later. He sent her to Miss Dau, saying she was the one to examine her. The insured submitted to an examination by the representative of the state fire marshal of Texas at that time. We say that these facts are undisputed. They are testified to by the insured, by one of her attorneys, and by Miss Dau. Neynaber said he would not deny it. So, it appears that very quickly after the time fixed by the company, she did go to the very office it had designated and tendered herself to the very notary and stenographer it had employed for this work. If these agents of the company did not then conduct the examination the company desired, they should, at least, have notified their principal of her offer to submit to the examination. If they had done that, it would then have become the duty of the company to make an effort to fix another date for the examination. If its agents failed in the performance of their duty, the insurance company cannot complain.

The jury found that the insurance company never attempted to fix another date for an examination. Consequently, there is no merit, as we view it, in the defense pleaded.

The insured contends that her appearance and testimony upon the first trial was a compliance with this provision, and that the suit could be sustained by the time of the second trial. We do not think it necessary to pass upon this point. We will say, in passing, that we find no evidence in the record showing any effort on the part of the insured to conceal any information. On the very morning of the fire, she had the company's agent meet her at the scene of the fire and talked with him freely. She and her attorney both discussed the matter fully with the adjuster. Her attorney visited the scene of the fire with the latter on January 3. Two days later she offered herself for examination to the agents the company had designated. She did submit to an examination conducted by an agent of the state fire marshal of Texas. It seems that she testified on the first trial of this cause in the district court. Consequently, long before the final trial, the company should have had all the information it desired. Certainly, it could have had it by the exercise of reasonable diligence. We find it difficult to escape the conclusion that the insurance company was more desirous of preserving its defense than of ascertaining the information it alleged it desired. It occurs to us that the judgment of the Court of Civil Appeals would work a very grave injustice.

For the many reasons discussed, we think the Court of Civil Appeals erred in reversing and rendering the judgment of the trial court. As we view it, the latter court entered the only proper judgment.

Therefore, we recommend that the judgment of the Court of Civil Appeals be reversed, and that of the district court affirmed.

PHILLIPS, C. J. The judgment recommended in the report of the Commission of Appeals is adopted, and will be entered as the judgment of the Supreme Court.

TEXAS EMPLOYERS' INS. ASS'N v. BOUDREAUX et al. (No. 234–3417.)

(Commission of Appeals of Texas, Section A. June 1, 1921.)

1. Master and servant ⬤⟷386(5)—Statutes of descent looked to in apportioning compensation among dependents.

The statutes of descent and distribution (Rev. St. 1911, arts. 2469, 2462) must be looked to for a rule by which to apportion compensation among dependents for the death of a servant under the Workmen's Compensation Act, pt. 1, § 8a, as added by Laws 1917, c. 103 (Vernon's Ann. Civ. St. Supp. 1918, art. 5246–15).

2. Constitutional law ⬤⟷70(3)—Courts not concerned with wisdom of legislative enactment.

The courts are not concerned with the wisdom of the plan adopted by the Legislature in apportioning compensation under the Workmen's Compensation Act, as amended by Laws 1917, c. 103 (Vernon's Ann. Civ. St. Supp. 1918, arts. 5246–1–5246–91), to the dependents of a deceased servant.

3. Master and servant ⬤⟷388—Compensation for death payable directly to dependents.

Compensation awarded under the Workmen's Compensation Act, as amended by Laws 1917, c. 103 (Vernon's Ann. Civ. St. Supp. 1918, arts. 5246–1–5246–91), for death of a servant is neither the community nor separate property of the deceased, and does not pass to the estate of the deceased to be administered upon, but is payable directly to those to whom it is awarded.

4. Master and servant ⬤⟷386(1)—Compensation for death arises out of contractual relation and is in lieu of damages.

Compensation for death of employé under the Workmen's Compensation Act, as amended by Laws 1917, c. 103 (Vernon's Ann. Civ. St. Supp. 1918, arts. 5246–1–5246–91), arises out of the contractual relation between the employer and the deceased employé, and is in substitution for damages ordinarily recovered by statute because of the death of the employé due to the negligence of the employer.

5. Master and servant ⬤⟷386(5)—Compensation for death distributed as community property.

Where husband and father is killed in an accident, compensation under the Workmen's Compensation Act, as amended by Laws 1917, c. 103 (Vernon's Ann. Civ. St. Supp. 1918, arts. 5246–1–5246–91), partakes more nearly

of community than of separate property, and should be distributed according to the statute of descent and distribution applicable in distributing community property, one-half going to the wife and one-half to the children, under Rev. St. 1911, art. 2469.

6. Master and servant ⬤⟷418(6)—Court's findings on question of lump sum compensation reviewable.

District court's findings upon question of whether judgment in a compensation proceeding should be rendered in a lump sum are findings of fact and subject to be reviewed on appeal to the Court of Civil Appeals the same as other fact issues are subject to review, under Workmen's Compensation Act, as amended by Laws 1917, c. 103, pt. 1, §§ 15, 18, and part 2, § 5 (Vernon's Ann. Civ. St. Supp. 1918, arts. 5246–33, 5246–37, 5246–44).

Error to Court of Civil Appeals of Ninth Supreme Judicial District.

Proceedings under the Workmen's Compensation Act by Mrs. Regina Boudreaux to obtain compensation for the death of her husband, opposed by the Gulf Production Company, subscriber, and the Texas Employers' Insurance Association. From a judgment of the Court of Civil Appeals (213 S. W. 674) affirming an award of compensation, the Insurance Association brings error. Judgment of Court of Civil Appeals reversed, and cause remanded to that court for a review of findings and the conclusion of trial court with respect to whether case was one calling for a lump sum award and for further orders.

Harry P. Lawther, of Dallas, for plaintiff in error.

Crook, Lord, Lawhon & Ney, of Beaumont, and Gremillion & Smith, of Crowley, La., for defendants in error.

TAYLOR, P. J. The Gulf Production Company was a subscriber to the Employers' Liability Act, as amended in 1917 (Acts 1917, c. 103 [Vernon's Ann. Civ. St. Supp. 1918, §§ 5246–1–5246–91]), and carried a policy of insurance with the Texas Employers' Insurance Association. Israel Boudreaux was in the employ of the production company and was covered by the policy. Boudreaux sustained injuries while so employed which resulted in his death. The deceased left surviving him a wife and three children, two of whom were minors. The other was a married daughter, neither a minor nor dependent upon the father for support.

The Industrial Accident Board found that the wife and two minor children were entitled to receive as compensation under the act the weekly sum of $11.15; that the attorneys representing the beneficiaries were entitled to receive for their services 15 per cent. of the first $1,000 to be paid the beneficiaries by the insurance association and 10 per cent. of the remainder. The Board further found that the amounts to be paid both the beneficiaries and the attorneys should be paid in weekly instalments as they accrued. An award was made by the Board in accordance with the findings.

The insurance association, plaintiff in error, brought this suit to set aside the award of the Board. Trial was before the court without a jury, and resulted, in part, in the court's setting aside the award. Judgment was rendered, however, against the association; but the award, instead of being made payable in weekly benefits, was made payable in a lump sum, on the ground that the case was a special one in which manifest hardship and injustice would result unless the compensation was required to be so paid.

The judgment was for $3,446.75, one-third to be paid the attorneys representing the beneficiaries, and two-thirds to be paid the beneficiaries. Under the terms of the decree one half of the amount awarded the beneficiaries was payable to the widow of the deceased, and the other half, to the two minor children in equal parts.

There were two assignments of error in the Court of Civil Appeals; First, that the trial court erred in adjudging the case a special one where hardship would, result from paying the compensation in weekly instalments rather than in a lump sum; second, that the court erred in distributing the amount awarded the wife and minor children in the proportion of one-half to the wife and one-fourth each to the two children, rather than equally among the three.

The Court of Civil Appeals overruled the assignments, under the view that the compensation awarded defendants in error was distributed as required by the terms of the act; and under the further view that the findings and conclusions of the trial judge as to whether compensation should be paid in a lump sum were final and conclusive, and not subject to be reviewed on appeal. 213 S. W. 674.

The assignments of error contained in the application for the writ are that the Court of Civil Appeals erred in overruling the assignments set out, substantially, above.

Plaintiff in error points out, in connection with its contentions made under the assignment relating to the distribution of compensation, that title to the compensation does not come to the beneficiaries by inheritance from the deceased, but vests in them originally; that the act names the beneficiaries and provides that they alone shall receive compensation; that no provision is made in the act for the payment of a greater proportion of compensation to one beneficiary than to the other; that the act makes no reference to either separate or community property or to different degrees of relationship to the deceased, or to the whole blood or half blood, or to bastards, such as is made in the statutes of descent and distribution; that it includes among the beneficiaries named stepmothers, who are not named in those statutes; and insists that by reason of the matters pointed out the compensation awarded the beneficiaries should be distributed among them equally.

The effect of the contention made is to place an unwarranted limitation upon the office of the statutes of descent and distribution in the administration of the act. It is true that the provision of the act naming the classes of beneficiaries both modifies and limits the operation of the statutes, but to such extent only as arises from the fact that not all of those designated as heirs in the statutes are designated as beneficiaries under the act, and from the further fact that one class, stepmothers, is designated by the act that is not named in the statutes.

In the original draft of section 8a, besides the surviving husband and wife, only dependent parents, dependent children, and dependent brothers and sisters of the deceased employé were designated as beneficiaries. By amendment adopted while the section was under consideration, two other classes of beneficiaries were added, dependent grandparents and dependent stepmothers. House Journal, 35th Legislature, p. 1082.

[1, 2] It is not necessary to decide what the proper rule of distribution would be in a case in which a stepmother is claimant as a beneficiary. Suffice it to say in this case that the amendment, merely adding, as it does, a class of beneficiaries not known to the inheritance statutes, did not have the effect of changing the original plan of the act with respect to the distribution of compensation. Whether the beneficiaries designated stand in different degrees of relationship to the deceased employé, or whether some be of whole and some of the half blood, or whether the beneficiaries are identical with the heirs of the deceased employé, the statutes of descent and distribution must be looked to for a rule by which to apportion the compensation. The courts are not concerned with the wisdom of the plan. No other is provided by the act, and no modification of the full operation of the statutes as rules of apportionment is warranted by the provisions of the act, other than the modification incident to the designation of classes of beneficiaries not identical with the classes of heirs designated in the statutes.

The beneficiaries to whom the compensation was awarded in this case are the surviving widow and two minor children of the deceased. As the wife and children (in the event they were the only survivors of the father) would take as heirs and distributees under the statutes, so do they partake as beneficiaries of the compensation awarded. The extent of the modification of the inheritance rule in this case is that the married daughter, an heir of the deceased under the statutes, does not partake of the compensation, not being designated a beneficiary by the act.

[3] The statutes of descent and distribution furnished one rule for distributing the community estate of a deceased husband to his surviving wife and children, and another for distributing among them his separate estate. Articles 2469 and 2462, R. S. 1911. The compensation awarded in this case is neither the community nor separate property of the deceased. It does "not pass to the estate of the deceased to be administered upon," but is payable directly to those to whom it is awarded.

Some difficulty arises, therefore, in determining which statute is applicable as a rule of distribution in this case. If the statute relating to the distribution of community property is to be applied, the apportionment should be one-half to the surviving wife and one-fourth each to the two minor children; if the statute relating to the distribution of the separate property is to be applied, the apportionment should be made equally, one-third to the wife and one-third each to the two children.

[4, 5] The compensation provided by the act arises out of the contractual relation between the employer and the deceased employé. When awarded for death of the employé, it is in substitution for damages ordinarily recovered by statute because of the death of the employé due to the negligence of the employer. Middleton v. Texas Power & Light Co., 108 Tex. 96, 185 S. W. 556. It is measured by the current wages of the deceased, and is to all practical purposes to supply to his beneficiaries the means of support which were afforded by his wages prior to his death. Its payment is provided for "from week to week as it accrues," except in special cases. The right of the deceased to have compensation paid his beneficiaries in case of his death was acquired by him during coverture. His wages flowing from his contract of employment under which he was working at the time of his death were community property. The compensation measured by his community wages and having its source, as it were, in the same contract of employment, partake more nearly of the nature of community than of separate property; and it should be distributed, in our opinion, according to the statute of descent and distribution applicable in distributing community property. Under this statute the apportionment provided is one-half to the wife and one-half to the children. Article 2469, R. S. 1911. Only two of the children being beneficiaries, the proportion should be, as between the wife and children, one-half to the former and one-fourth each to the latter.

The conclusion that this apportionment of the compensation should be made was reached by the Industrial Accident Board, the trial court, and the Court of Civil Appeals, and we concur therein.

[6] The Court of Civil Appeals did not review the evidence touching the question of whether judgment should have been rendered in a lump sum, being of opinion that the trial court's findings upon this question were final, and not subject to be reviewed on appeal. This holding is the basis of the complaint made in the remaining assignment of error.

Were the findings of the trial court with respect to whether the case was one calling for a lump sum settlement subject to review by the Court of Civil Appeals?

Section 18, part 1, of the act, provides that the compensation shall be paid from week to week as it accrues, unless the liability of the association is redeemed as provided elsewhere in the act.

Section 15, part 1, of the act, is as follows:

"In cases where death or total permanent incapacity results from an injury, the liability of the association may be redeemed by payment of a lump sum by agreement of the parties thereto, subject to the approval of the Industrial Accident Board hereinafter created. This section shall be construed as excluding any other character of lump sum settlement save and except as herein specified; provided, however, that in special cases where in the judgment of the Board manifest hardship and injustice would otherwise result, the Board may compel the association in the cases provided for in this section to redeem their liability by payment of a lump sum as may be determined by the Board."

The act provides further (article 5246–44, Vernon's Sayles' Statutes, 1918 Supp.) that—

"If the final order of the Board is against the association then the association and not the employer shall bring suit to set aside said final ruling and decision of the Board, if it so desires, and the court shall in either event determine the issues in such cause instead of the Board upon trial de novo and the burden of proof shall be upon the party claiming compensation. In case of recovery the same shall not exceed the maximum compensation allowed under the provisions of this act."

Under the provisions of the foregoing article the trial court had authority to determine the issues in the case, including the issue as to whether or not the compensation should be paid in a lump sum. This issue is necessarily one of fact. Facts only could make it appear whether the case is a special one.

Evidence was introduced upon this issue by defendants in error. It is not necessary to to set it out. The trial court heard the case de novo, and made its findings upon all the issues, including the issue with respect to a lump sum award. We see no reason why these findings are not subject to the same haracter of review on appeal to which findings upon other fact issues are subject. The Court of Civil Appeals, in our opinion, has power to review, and should review, the findings upon the issue of a lump sum settlement. Choate v. S. A. & A. P. Ry. Co., 91 Tex. 406, 44 S. W. 69.

We recommend that the judgment of the Court of Civil Appeals be reversed, and that the cause be remanded to that court for a review of the findings and conclusion of the trial court with respect to whether the case was one calling for a lump sum award, and for further orders.

PHILLIPS, C. J. The judgment recommended in the report of the Commission of Appeals is adopted and will be entered as the judgment of the Supreme Court.

We approve the holding of the Commission of Appeals on the questions discussed in its opinion.

——————

ROBERTS v. STATE. (No. 6218.)

(Court of Criminal Appeals of Texas. May 4, 1921. Rehearing Denied June 1, 1921.)

1. Criminal law ⟷598(9)—Issuance of subpœna for witness in another case is not sufficient diligence to require continuance.

The issuance of subpœna for the absent witness in another case against the same defendant, which did not secure the attendance of the witness, is not sufficient diligence to entitle accused to a continuance of the case on trial.

2. Criminal law ⟷598(8)—Failure to issue compulsory process to compel attendance of witness defeats right to continuance.

The failure of accused to avail himself of the compulsory process to which he is entitled to compel the attendance of a witness in his behalf defeats his right to a continuance because of the absence of such witness.

3. Criminal law ⟷608—On hearing application for continuance, court need not accept telegram stating presence of witness could not be obtained.

In ruling on an application for continuance because of the absence of a witness, the court is not bound to accept a telegram from a physician that the witness could not appear because of the sickness of his child.

4. Criminal law ⟷597(1)—Testimony of absent witness held not shown to be of controlling importance.

In a prosecution for assault with intent to murder, testimony by an absent witness that defendant was subject to attacks of temporary insanity, though relevant, would not be of controlling importance to justify continuance, where the witness could not testify to defendant's mental condition at the time of the assault, and other witnesses had testified to his periods of insanity.

5. Homicide ⟷151(2)—Presumption and burden of proof as to mental derangement stated.

In a prosecution for assault with intent to murder, when it was not claimed that defendant was permanently or continuously insane, the existence of defendant's mental derangement at the time he shot his wife was not a presumption following the proof that, upon other occasions, he had become temporarily deranged; and it being conceded that his mental derangement was an exception, it was defendant's burden to prove that it prevailed at the time the offense was committed.

6. Homicide ⟷179—Testimony as to defendant's demeanor when arrested competent on issue of insanity.

In a prosecution for assault to murder, where the defense was insanity, it was not error to permit the sheriff to testify as to the demeanor of defendant when he was arrested.

7. Criminal law ⟷465—Sheriff can give opinion of defendant's sanity, based on observation of defendant while in custody.

In a prosecution for assault to murder, where the defense was insanity, it was not error to permit the sheriff to give his opinion that accused was sane, based on his observations of accused while in custody.

On Motion for Rehearing.

8. Criminal law ⟷539(2) — Voluntary testimony by defendant in own behalf can be used against him on subsequent trial, or in different case.

Where a defendant voluntarily takes the stand in his own behalf, his testimony is subject to the same rules as apply to other witnesses, and such testimony can be used against him at a subsequent trial of the same case, or on the trial of a different case arising from the same transaction, even though he was not warned before he gave the testimony.

Appeal from District Court, Walker County; J. A. Platt, Judge.

P. H. Roberts was convicted of assault with intent to murder, and he appeals. Affirmed.

A. T. McKinney, Jr., and M. E. Gates, both of Huntsville, for appellant.

R. H. Hamilton, Asst. Atty. Gen., for the State.

MORROW, P. J. Conviction is for assault with intent to murder; punishment fixed at confinement in the penitentiary for a period of eight years.

The injured party was the wife of the appellant. The tragedy is described by the state's witness, Miss Ethel Sprott, appellant's stepdaughter. There had been a separation; at least the appellant had been away from his home for some days. Upon his return, he asked his wife if he could come back home. Not receiving a favorable reply, he drew his pistol. The witness jumped in the lap of her

⟷For other cases see same topic and KEY-NUMBER in all Key-Numbered Digests and Indexes mother, was ordered by the appellant to get out, and, failing to do so, he shot her; and upon her falling, her mother ran, and was also shot. The appellant then shot himself. Other witnesses, including appellant's wife, gave a description of the shooting ,which coincided with that of the young woman whom we have mentioned.

Upon his arrest, there ,were found upon the person of appellant several letters which had been written by him. One was to his brother, one to his wife's brother, one to his stepdaughter, and one to the minister. In these letters he expressed affection for his wife, resentment at her treatment of him, and an intention to kill her and commit suicide. He also complained of mistreatment by his stepdaughter, and in his letter to his brother he gave minute information touching the amount of money that he owed, and the name of each of his creditors.

Appellant was engaged as a guard of convicts in the penitentiary, and had been so engaged for a long time. He introduced testimony of a nonexpert witness to the effect that, at the time of the occurrence, or about that time, his mind was unsound. The state's testimony combated this theory, and this was the controverted question before the jury.

An application for a continuance was made because of absence of a witness by whom he expected to prove acquaintance with the appellant and knowledge of his general conduct, disposition, and behavior for 18 years; that when worried or provoked, his mind became unbalanced; and details of incidents in the conduct of appellant which the witness would relate as a predicate for his opinion were embraced in the application. The application disclosed that no subpœna had been issued to the witness, though he lived in a nearby town; that, in the companion case for shooting Miss Ethel Sprott, the witness had been subpœnaed; that a telegram from the doctor had been received stating that "the son of the witness had typhoid fever, and that it was impossible for him to come."

[1, 2] Diligence to procure the attendance of an absent witness is not established by showing that, in another case against the accused pending in the same court, a subpœna for the witness had been issued. The law gives one accused of crime the right to compulsory process to secure the attendance of his witnesses, and imposes upon him the duty to cause the issuance of such process where he has knowledge of the witness and his whereabouts within the state. If, with such knowledge, he fails or refuses to avail himself of the privilege of issuing process and seeking to have it served, he is not in a position to demand that the court postpone his case because of the absence of the witness. The precedents upon this subject are definite. Isham v. State, 49 S. W. 594; Vanderberg v. State, 66 Tex. Cr. R. 583, 148 S. W. 315; Cyc. of Law & Procedure, vol. 9, p. 197.

The reasons for this ruling embraced in the previous decisions of this court are deemed sufficient, and a restatement of them is unnecessary.

[3, 4] Even if the deligence was not wanting, the abuse of the trial judge's discretion in overruling the application is not apparent. He was not bound to accept the telegram from the doctor as conclusive evidence that the attendance of the witness could not be secured during the trial. The facts developed in the trial of the case, while they reveal the relevancy of the testimony of the absent witness, disclose that it was not of controlling importance. It was not the contention of the appellant that he was permanently insane, or that he was suffering from a malady continuous in its operation. It ,went to the extent only of asserting that he was subject to recurrent or fitful attacks of mental derangement, consequent upon excitement or agitation brought about by disturbing emotions. The absent witness, according to the application, would have testified to this general condition of the appellant's mind, but could not have testified that at the time the offense was committed his reason was dethroned. His testimony circumstantially pointed to this conclusion, and in this respect was cumulative of much other testimony which was before the jury.

[5] The crucial point in the case was the condition of appellant's mind at the time he shot his wife, and the existence of mental derangement at that time ,was not a presumption following the proof that, upon other occasions, he had become temporarily deranged. It being conceded that mental derangement was an exception, it was appellant's burden to prove that it prevailed at the time the offense was committed. Leache v. State, 22 Tex. App. 279, 3 S. W. 539, 58 Am. Rep. 638; Webb v. State, 5 Tex. App. 596; Wooten v. State, 51 Tex. Cr. R. 428, 102 S. W. 416; Hunt v. State, 33 Tex. Cr. R. 252, 26 S. W. 206.

It seems that the appellant had testified on a former occasion that he had no knowledge of what took place at the time the alleged offense was committed. The bill does not make it plain whether this occurred upon this trial or of another case. Assuming, however, that it was in a trial of another case, there was no error in admitting it. The rule prevailing in this state, as we understand, is that where one, upon the trial of his case, voluntarily becomes a witness, and testifies to facts which are relevant and material, they may be used against him in a retrial, or on the trial of another case involving the same transaction. Jones v. State, 64 Tex. Cr. R. 510, 143 S. W. 622; Smith v. State, 75 S. W. 298; Preston v. State, 41 Tex. Cr. R. 300, 53 S. W. 127, 881; Williams v. State, 225 S. W. 178. We are, by appellant, referred to Somers v. State, 54 Tex. Cr. R. 475, 113 S. W. 533, 130 Am. St. Rep. 901, but it deals with a different question and is not in point in this case.

[6, 7] There was no error in permitting the sheriff to describe the demeanor of the appellant at the time of his arrest. This testimony was admissible as bearing upon the issue of insanity. Lane v. State, 59 Tex. Cr. R. 595, 129 S. W. 353; Hurst v. State, 40 Tex. Cr. R. 378, 46 S. W. 635, 50 S. W. 719; Mikeska v. State, 79 Tex. Cr. R. 109, 182 S. W. 1127. Nor did the court err in permitting the sheriff to give his opinion, based upon the conversation with the appellant and his conduct while in his custody, touching his insanity. Turner v. State, 61 Tex. Cr. R. 97, 133 S. W. 1052; Cannon v. State, 41 Tex. Cr. R. 467, 56 S. W. 351; Lane v. State, 59 Tex. Cr. R. 603, 129 S. W. 353; Burt v. State, 38 Tex. Cr. R. 397, 40 S. W. 1000, 43 S. W. 344, 39 L. R. A. 305, 330; Plummer v. State, 86 Tex. Cr. R. 495, 218 S. W. 499.

The record reveals no error which would authorize a reversal of the judgment. It is therefore affirmed.

On Motion for Rehearing.

HAWKINS, J. [8] In our original opinion we held that, where a defendant voluntarily becomes a witness in his own behalf, his testimony, where relevant and material, may be used against him in a retrial of the same case, or the trial of another case, where his statements on the former trial are pertinent. Appellant urges that we were in error in so far as our announcement goes to the extent of permitting the former testimony of an accused to be reproduced against him in an entirely new case. Upon principle and reason we do not think we fell into error in so holding.

In Johnson v. State, 39 Tex. Cr. R. 625, 48 S. W. 70, the defendant was charged with theft, in the county court, and with burglary, in the district court. He entered a plea of guilty to theft, and upon his trial for burglary his plea of guilty was introduced against him, over his objection that he had not been warned of the consequences at the time he entered this plea of guilty to the theft charge. It was held legitimate evidence on the trial of the burglary charge, upon the theory that the plea of guilty in the misdemeanor case was freely and voluntarily made. In Collins v. State, 39 Tex. Cr. R. 441, 46 S. W. 933, while defendant was being tried the second time he was cross-examined with reference to a certain statement made by him while on the witness stand on the first trial of the case. An objection was urged to the testimony, because appellant was not warned or cautioned under the statute relative to confessions before his evidence was given on the former trial. Judge Henderson, in discussing the question, used the following language.

"It is contended here that, although he voluntarily took the stand, such testimony could not be used adversely to him, unless he had been warned before making the same, although he was a witness in his own behalf. If this contention is right, then the statements so made could not be used by the jury that tried the first case, because he had not been warned. If the failure to warn could be used to prevent his testimony at a former trial from being used at a subsequent trial, then the same reason would preclude its use at the first trial."

Later on in the opinion, discussing the same matter, he said:

"A defendant having taken the stand in his own behalf, it is presumed that he does so after having advised with his counsel, and after full knowledge that he can become a witness on his own behalf; and that when he does so he is to be treated while on the stand as any other witness, and his testimony so given can be used against him at any subsequent trial. If this were not so, he would testify under a ban, and not with that freedom which the law seems to apprehend."

Wharton's Criminal Evidence (10th Ed.) p. 1371, § 664, discussing the question now under consideration, says:

"In the earlier cases, confessions under oath were generally excluded. The reason for this was that the 'examination of the prisoner should be without oath, and of the others, upon oath,' so that where the accused was examined on oath the confession was rejected, because of the illegal manner in which it was taken, and not merely because of the oath. But, when the disqualifications of the accused were removed, and he was allowed to become a witness in his own behalf at his own election, the rule ceased when the reason ceased. Hence, the mere administration of an oath to the accused will not render the confession involuntary; nor the fact that the confession was made under oath, as a witness, or otherwise, in prior judicial proceedings, if no compulsion nor undue influence was used."

If an accused, not under arrest, makes a statement of a criminative character, it may be used against him in any prosecution wherein it may become pertinent. An accused can become a witness only by his own voluntary act; and when he thus voluntarily takes the witness stand, and under the sanction of an oath speaks, it is as any other witness; and if his statements while testifying become pertinent to an issue arising in the subsequent trial of the same case, or of another case, we can see no valid reason why the state may not prove the statement against him. If A. were on trial in the county court for a misdemeanor, and should testify that he was 19 years of age, and subsequently was on trial for a felony in the district court, and, in an effort to secure the benefit of the "juvenile law," should swear he was only 16 years of age, it would seem illogical and contrary to principle to deny the state the right to prove his former statement on that issue. If B. should have testified on the misdemeanor trial that A. was 19, and then change his testimony on the trial of the felony, and swear A. was only 16, certainly it would not be questioned but that the state could attack B. by showing his former testimony. In principle, we can see no distinction. When A. voluntarily takes the witness stand in his own behalf, the safeguard under the law of "confessions" is waived by him; in the eyes of the law he becomes as any other witness; if, while testifying, he makes inculpatory admissions, they may be proven against him in any case where pertinent.

The holding here is not in conflict with Mathis v. State, 84 Tex. Cr. R. 514, 209 S. W. 150. In that case a witness, while testifying in a civil suit, declined to answer a question because it would criminate him. He was compelled by the court to answer. On a subsequent trial of the witness on a criminal charge, the state proved against him his unwilling and forced statement. This court properly held it was error.

For the reasons stated, we adhere to our original opinion, and the motion for rehearing is overruled.

ROBERTS v. STATE. (No. 6217.)

(Court of Criminal Appeals of Texas. May 25, 1921.)

Criminal law ⟝594(1)—Court held not within its discretion in overruling application for continuance for absence of witness.

In a prosecution for assault to murder, where the defense was insanity, *held* not within discretion of trial judge to overrule an application for continuance on account of absence of a witness on the question of insanity where there was sufficient diligence and absent witness' testimony was probably true, was material, and likely to change the result.

Appeal from District Court, Walker County; J. A. Platt, Judge.

P. H. Roberts was convicted of assault to murder, and he appeals. Reversed and remanded.

A. T. McKinney, Jr., and M. E. Gates, both of Huntsville, for appellant.

R. H. Hamilton, Asst. Atty. Gen., for the State.

MORROW, P. J. Conviction is for assault to murder Miss Ethel Sprott. It is a companion case to No. 6218, 231 S. W. 759, against the same appellant, wherein he was convicted for an assault with intent to murder his wife. The transaction detailed in that case discloses the facts in this one.

The defense was insanity. The first application for a continuance on account of the absence of the witness Parrott was presented and overruled. That the diligence appears sufficient was not controverted. The evidence of the absent witness bore upon the issue of insanity, which issue was strongly supported by facts and circumstances as well as the opinion of nonexpert witnesses.

In the companion case we declined to reverse on account of the absence of the same testimony, but in that case the record excluded any legal diligence to secure his attendance. In the case before us that the diligence required had been exercised was not contested. The testimony was manifestly material to the only defensive issue presented. We find no basis for a conclusion that the testimony of the absent witness was not probably true; that is to say, there is no sufficient reason for assuming that he would not have recited the facts set up in the application and given his opinion based thereon that the appellant was at times insane to a degree rendering him incapable of comprehending the distinction between right and wrong. The other evidence in the case rather discredits the idea that the witness would not have given the testimony. We think it cannot be said, as a matter of law, that it would have had no effect upon the verdict. Upon the record, we are of the opinion that it was not within the discretion of the learned trial judge to overrule the application, and that in the light of the facts developed a new trial should have been awarded. Roberts v. State, 67 Tex. Cr. R. 580, 150 S. W. 627; Barlow v. State, 61 Tex. Cr. R. 64, 133 S. W. 1050; Webb v. State, 5 Tex. App. 596.

Upon the other points presented the record is in every essential sense like that in the companion case, and for the reason therein stated are, in our opinion, without merit.

Upon the ground indicated, the judgment is reversed, and the cause remanded.

⟝For other cases see same topic and KEY-NUMBER in all Key-Numbered Digests and Indexes

McGOWEN v. STATE. (No. 6232.)

(Court of Criminal Appeals of Texas. June 1, 1921.)

1. **Jury** ⬅110(3)—Accused may waive challenge of juror not householder or freeholder.

All of the grounds of challenge for cause stated in the statute, including that of failure of a juror to be a householder or a freeholder, may be waived by the accused.

2. **Jury** ⬅109—Court may not of own motion set aside juror.

Where accused waives his grounds of challenge for cause and accepts a juror, the trial court may not of his own motion stand said juror aside and proceed without him.

3. **Criminal law** ⬅1166½(6)—Reversible error for court to stand aside accepted juror.

In a homicide case, it was prejudicial error for the court of his own motion to stand aside a juror, where accused waived his ground of challenge.

Appeal from Criminal District Court, Bowie County; P. A. Turner, Judge.

Columbus McGowen was convicted of manslaughter, and appeals. Reversed and remanded.

Keeney & Dalby, of Texarkana, for appellant.

R. H. Hamilton, Asst. Atty. Gen., for the State.

LATTIMORE, J. Appellant was charged in the criminal district court of Bowie county with the offense of murder, and upon his trial was found guilty of manslaughter, and his punishment fixed at confinement in the penitentiary for a period of two years.

[1–3] The case must be reversed for error which is admitted and confessed by the Assistant Attorney General. It appears from bill of exceptions No. 1 that the fifth juror who was examined upon his voir dire was asked no question by either party as to whether or not he was a householder or freeholder in this state. He was duly accepted as a juror and was sworn to try the case, and took his place in the jury box. Later he informed the court that he was not a householder or a freeholder. Thereupon the trial court asked appellant's counsel what he desired to do in the premises, and upon appellant's counsel declining to make any statement or further object to the presence and service of said juror, the trial court of his own motion stood said juror aside and proceeded with the formation of the jury to try the case; appellant excepting to the standing aside of said juror. It seems well settled both by statute and decisions in this state that all of the grounds of challenge for cause stated in our statute, save three, among which

three is not found that of failure to be a householder or a freeholder, may be waived by the accused. It has been held that, where the accused waives his ground of challenge for cause and accepts a juror, the trial court may not of his own motion stand said juror aside and proceed without him. Lowe v. State, 226 S. W. 674; Crow v. State, 230 S. W. 148, recently decided. For the error of the trial court in standing aside said juror of his own motion after he had been accepted and sworn, the case must be reversed. It would have been proper for the court, after discovering the facts making said juror subject to challenge for cause, to have offered to appellant an opportunity to exercise said challenge with knowledge of the facts, and, upon his failure or refusal to challenge said juror for cause, to have permitted him to continue as such juror throughout the trial of the case. The above requiring reversal, the other errors complained of will not noticed.

For the error mentioned, the judgment of the trial court will be reversed, and the cause remanded.

PATTERSON v. STATE. (No. 6169.)

(Court of Criminal Appeals of Texas. May 25, 1921.)

1. **Criminal law** ⬅1101—Where there is but one statement for two cases tried simultaneously, court will consider record not containing statement as being before it without same.

Where two persons are indicted separately for complicity in the same crime and are tried simultaneously and identical transcripts in each case with but one statement of facts filed, the appellate court will treat the record not containing the statement of facts as being before it without such statement, as the record in the appellate court must be complete in each case.

2. **Criminal law** ⬅655(1)—Remarks of judge to jury not reversible error, in view of instructions, and where rights of accused not prejudiced.

Remarks of the judge to the jury before the trial of one accused of robbery that they should pay close attention to the testimony, and thereby avoid controversy among themselves and reach a verdict more speedily and satisfactorily, were not reversible error, where the court on objection instructed the jury not to consider his statement as evidence, or as tending to show guilt or innocence, and the remarks were not calculated to prejudice the rights of the accused.

3. **Criminal law** ⬅406(1)—Oral statement of accused, leading to finding of pistol with which offense committed, admissible.

Under Code Cr. Proc. 1911, art. 810, excluding oral statements made by the accused while under arrest unless they conduce to establish his guilt, such as finding the instrument with which the offense was committed, a statement so made by one accused of robbery, which led to the finding of the pistol claimed to have been used, was admissible.

4. Criminal law ⚘1170(2)—Error in exclusion of evidence of no weight where same testimony given by state's witness.

In a prosecution for robbery, error in the exclusion of evidence as to certain exculpatory statements made by defendant at the time of his arrest was of no weight where such evidence was fully placed before the jury by the arresting officer.

5. Criminal law ⚘426—No error in rejection of testimony of one indicted for participation in same offense as to exculpatory statements by him similar to those of defendant.

In a prosecution for robbery with firearms, where defendant did not testify, there was no error in the rejection of the testimony of another indicted for participation in the same offense, as to exculpatory statements made by him to the arresting officer at the time of his arrest, as he could not testify on defendant's behalf, and the arresting officer testified as to similar statements by defendant.

6. Criminal law ⚘1170½(6)—Question as to whether accused had been charged with robbery at former time not reversible error where court refused to permit answer and instructed jury not to consider question.

In a prosecution for robbery with firearms, a judgment of conviction will not be set aside because defendant's accomplice was asked if it was not true that he and defendant had both been arrested and charged with robbery with firearms at a former time, where the court refused to permit an answer and instructed the jury not to consider such question.

Appeal from Criminal District Court, Tarrant County; George E. Hosey, Judge.

E. C. Patterson was convicted of robbery with firearms, and he appeals. Affirmed.

R. H. Hamilton, Asst. Atty. Gen., for the State.

LATTIMORE, J. Appellant was convicted in the criminal district court of Tarrant county of the offense of robbery with firearms, and his punishment fixed at confinement in the penitentiary for seven years. This is a companion case to that of the State of Texas v. J. M. Williams, 231 S. W. 110, recently decided by this court, and reversed for error in refusing to allow the appellant in that case to give testimony as to certain statements claimed by him to have been made to the arresting officer, which were rejected by the trial court, but by us deemed to have been material in his behalf. It appears that said Williams and this appellant were indicted separately for complicity in the same criminal transaction, and by some character of agreement between the state and said defendants they were tried simultaneously, and identical transcripts in each

case are here on file, with but one statement of facts, to which, apparently under the same agreement of the attorneys in the trial court, we are referred in both cases.

[1] Inasmuch as the matter appears without precedent, we have considered said single statement of facts in both these cases, but must decline so to do hereafter. The spirit of the law, if not its letter, requires the filing and preservation as part of the record of each case upon appeal of a complete transcript and statement of facts pertaining to said case; and, if it be permissible to consolidate and try simultaneously cases wherein there be separate indictments, yet in case of appeal the record in the appellate court must be complete in each case, or this court will be compelled to consider and treat such records as do not contain statement of facts as being before us without such statement of facts. Gumpert v. State, (No. 6163) 229 S. W. 330.

[2, 3] Reference is here made to what we said in our opinion in the Williams Case, supra, as to the remarks of the court below in impaneling the jury, also with regard to what was said by the accused in connection with the pistol found by the officers, and we approve what was so said as applicable to the instant case.

[4] Bill of exceptions No. 6 in the instant case is identical with the same bill as discussed in the opinion in the Williams Case, supra, but in following out the statements made by the trial court in his qualification to said bill, and examining that part of the statement of facts referred to by said trial judge, we find that the matters complained of as being desired in evidence and rejected, as described in said bill of exceptions, are of no weight in the instant case, for the reason that said evidence was fully placed before the jury by the officer who arrested appellant and said Williams; said officer testifying that the statements apparently rejected by the court were later in the testimony of said officer fully narrated as having been made by this appellant.

[5] The error for which said Williams Case was reversed, viz. that Williams was not allowed to testify to certain statements made by him to the arresting officer after he was in custody, is of no avail to this appellant. Under our practice Williams could not have been introduced as a witness on behalf of appellant, they being indicted for participation in the same criminal transaction and offense; and appellant has therefore no ground for complaint on this appeal, based on the rejection by the trial court of all or any part of Williams' testimony, as relating to the guilt or innocence of this appellant. As stated by us above, however, it appears from the statement of facts referred to in the qualification of bill of exceptions No. 6 that the arresting officer testified

fully to the statements made by this appellant after his arrest, which are substantially those offered by Williams while on the witness stand, the rejection of which was held by us to be error on his appeal. This appellant did not take the stand or offer to testify as a witness.

[6] By bill of exceptions No. 14 complaint is made that while Williams was on the stand testifying he was asked by the state's attorney if it was not true that he and appellant had both been arrested and charged with robbery with firearms at a former time. Upon objection to this question the trial court promptly refused to require or permit any answer, and both verbally and in writing instructing the jury not to consider or allude to said question so asked, as same was improper. We do not think the asking of such question presents reversible error. This court could not lay down the rule that for the mere asking of a question as to whether or not one accused of crime had not theretofore been arrested or convicted, even though the accused had not taken the witness stand, a judgment of conviction should be set aside solely because such question was asked; it appearing that it was not answered, and that the court did all in its power to prevent any injurious effects.

We do not deem it necessary to set out the evidence, as the facts are identical with those appearing in our opinion in the Williams Case, supra, and are ample to support the verdict and judgment.

Finding no reversible error in the record, the judgment will be affirmed.

GILES v. STATE. (No. 6135.)

(Court of Criminal Appeals of Texas. June 1, 1921.)

1. Criminal law ⚡597(1)—On first application for continuance state cannot contest truth of testimony of absent witness.

In a prosecution for murder, on defendant's application for a continuance to secure the testimony of absent witnesses, the state could not contest the truth of the absent testimony, but only defendant's diligence to secure the same; the application being her first.

2. Criminal law ⚡594(1)—Continuance erroneously denied where impossible to secure attendance of absent witnesses.

In a prosecution for murder, defendant's application for a continuance to secure the testimony of absent witnesses should have been granted; the witnesses being at some unknown point in another part of the state, so that it was impossible to secure their attendance without a postponement, and the evidence showing that efforts to secure their attendance were made in good faith and diligently pursued.

3. Criminal law ⚡613(3)—Absence of complete diligence in securing absent testimony does not necessarily justify denial of new trial.

Testimony to support a defensive theory, otherwise resting upon defendant's testimony alone, being such as the law regards with favor, the absence of complete diligence to secure such testimony of absent witnesses does not necessarily justify the overruling of a motion for a new trial.

4. Homicide ⚡234(1)—Evidence held to show presence of accused accounted for in manner consistent with innocence.

In a prosecution for murder, evidence *held* to show that defendant's presence was accounted for in a manner consistent with her innocence.

Appeal from District Court, Wharton County; M. S. Munson, Judge.

Lottie Giles was convicted of murder, and she appeals. Reversed.

Mathis, Teague & Mathis and Wander & Williamson, all of Houston, for appellant.

O. M. Cureton, Atty. Gen., and C. L. Stone, Asst. Atty. Gen., for the State.

MORROW, P. J. Appellant was convicted for the murder of H. C. McCormick; punishment fixed at confinement in the penitentiary for a period of 25 years. The uncontroverted evidence may be thus summarized:

Washington Giles, husband of appellant, was charged by the justice court with a misdemeanor, growing out of the mistreatment of a dog. Giles was out upon his farm some two miles from the county seat. His family consisted, besides his wife, of his mother, Polly Giles, two adopted children, a boy and girl, aged 9 and 10 years respectively, and a brother, Osborne Giles. Pitman, a constable, went in an automobile to the home of appellant, taking with him a warrant, and on his way overtook McCormick, also an officer, who joined him. On arriving on the premises, Washington and Osborne Giles were plowing in the field, and continued to plow until they reached the end of the turn row, when they left their plows in the field and came with their stock to the home.

The transaction took place in the evening before sundown. Pitman advised Washington Giles of the charge against him and the necessity for his arrest. Giles protested, asserting that he was not guilty of the offense and declined to submit to arrest. During the controversy Giles fled. Pitman drew his pistol and pursued him. Giles took refuge in the house. Pitman requested the appellant, who at the time was present, to tell her husband to come out and talk to him. She complied with this request. Giles came to the door, when the officer seized his arm, and a struggle ensued, at the termination of which Giles said that he would go on condition that his wife accompany him. Pursuant to this, Giles stepped out upon the gallery and the appellant went in the house to make some preparation for the trip. During her absence Giles again asserted his unwillingness to submit to the arrest. He was then seized by the officer, who struck him on the head with a pistol. During the struggle, in which McCormick also participated, the appellant came out of the house.

It is an uncontroverted fact that during the conflict Osborne Giles came out of the house with a rifle in his hand, and presented it in a threatening manner; that Washington Giles became possessed of Pitman's pistol; that he fired, and killed the deceased, McCormick, one shot taking effect. Pitman fled, and Giles fired at him. Subsequently, Washington and Osborne Giles fled, taking with them the pistol and the gun. They were pursued, and three or four days later were killed, appellant, in the meantime, having been arrested and placed in jail.

Concerning her conduct during the encounter, appellant's testimony and that of Pitman are in sharp conflict. That of Pitman goes to show that, before the phase of the difficulty in which the fatality occurred, she had taken part in opposition to the officer; that when Washington Giles was fleeing, and Pitman was pursuing him with a pistol in his hand, she seized Pitman, and endeavored to hold him; that, while Pitman was endeavoring to pull Giles out of the house, she interposed in his aid; that during the fatal struggle she aided Giles in forcing the pistol out of the hand of Pitman. Thereafter she said: "Now, you got them;" that this was immediately preceding the shot which killed the deceased.

Appellant testified that just before the officers arrived she had been fishing on the creek nearby, and was just returning when she, on approaching the house, heard her husband whistling a religious tune, and at the time saw the two Giles plowing; that she also saw an automobile nearby, and the two gentlemen—McCormick and Pitman—whom she did not know at the time; that soon after she saw her husband running, followed by Pitman with a pistol in his hand. She was not aware of the occasion for the trouble, and became very much excited, and asked Pitman not to kill her husband; that Pitman then told her that he had come to arrest him, and he said that she should try to obtain her husband's consent; that she did ask him to accompany Pitman, and during the conversation her husband came to the door. His arm was seized by Pitman, and, believing that it was about to be broken, she asked Pitman not to break it; that at the same time she urged her husband not to further resist, upon which Giles indicated his willingness to go if the appellant would accompany him. To this she assented, but stated that she would have to make some preparation relative to her wearing apparel, as she had been fishing; that Pitman consented to wait until she could do so, and that, while she was changing her clothes, her attention was attracted by a controversy on the outside, and upon rushing to the door she observed Osborne and Washington Giles, Pitman, and McCormick "tussling," as she expressed it. She exclaimed, "What is the matter?" and Osborne told her that her husband had been snatched off the gallery and hit on the head with a gun. She heard her husband say, "Go and get my gun, and kill him," upon which Osborne Giles extricated himself, and she saw blood running down her husband's head, and asked the officers not to kill him. At that time, Osborne, whom she described as a boy, appeared with a gun, and she said, "Oh, son, don't kill him." Upon the presentation of the gun the officers released Washington Giles and ran, leaving him in possession of the pistol, whereupon he said, "I have got to die for this anyway, and I might as well take some one with me." She insisted that she took no further part than that described by her, that she used no words of encouragement, that she made no effort to aid her husband or his brother, and that her entire words and conduct were directed toward peace and prevention of injury.

She made application for a continuance, to secure the testimony of the two children who were members of the family. In the application it was asserted that they were present during the transaction, and in a position to hear and see all that was said and done, and by them her version of the affair, as given in her testimony, would be supported, and that given by Pitman controverted.

At the time of the trial, the only eyewitnesses were the appellant and Pitman. The admitted principals, Washington and Osborne Giles, had been killed, Polly Giles, the mother-in-law of appellant, had become deranged, and the two children were absent. These children had become members of the family of appellant and her husband some years preceding the tragedy.

Appellant was indicted on the 18th of November, and arrested on the 24th of that month, and on the same day caused a subpoena to be issued for the absent witnesses, directed and sent to Jackson county, where, according to her information, the witnesses were at the time. This subpoena was returned by the sheriff on the 26th day of November, accompanied by a letter stating that the witnesses could be found in the city of Victoria in Victoria county; and on the 29th of November a subpoena was obtained and sent to the sheriff of Victoria county, reaching him on the 1st of December, and returned on the 12th of that month, which was Sunday, the trial being set for the 13th. From this return, it appeared that the witnesses had gone from Victoria county to North Texas, for the purpose of picking cotton. These witnesses were negroes, and it was alleged that it was customary at this season of the year to visit the various counties for the purpose of picking cotton.

The application was the first one, and the diligence was contested. In the contest it was asserted that, at the time the subpœna was issued to Jackson county, appellant was aware that the witnesses could not be found there; that the same was true with reference to the issuance of subpœna to Victoria county; that, as a matter of fact, the location of the witnesses was known to the appellant, but the subpœnas were purposely not issued to their proper addresses. In the contest, it was also contended that the children were not present at the time of the homicide.

No evidence appears to have been heard in support of the allegation that the subpœnas were not issued in good faith, or that appellant had purposely caused their issuance to a county in which they would not be found, knowing their true whereabouts, save the affidavit of Mr. Pitman, a state's witness, stating that the witnesses were with Eliza Smith in Kingsville, Kleberg county, and that they had accompanied Eliza Smith from Jackson county to Victoria county, and from Victoria county to Kingsville. This affidavit, so far as it purports to state facts, supports, rather than controverts, the position assumed in the application touching the whereabouts of the children, and the same is true of the information received from the sheriff of Jackson county. He stated in returning the subpœna that, from the best information obtainable by him, "they were in Victoria, just west of the depot on the north side of the G. H. & S. A. R. R. on the Beeville branch." The return of the sheriff of Victoria county indicates that the witnesses had been there, it stating that "they were in North Texas, picking cotton, exact location not known."

In Pitman's affidavit, attached to the contest, he states, in substance, that he did not see either of the children at the time of the tragedy. Two other witnesses made affidavits that they went to the house about 30 minutes after the tragedy, and, upon arrival, saw the body of the deceased lying in the yard, and at the same time saw Polly Giles and the two children coming from the back way in the direction of the creek. The application was overruled without further evidence. On the trial, however, Pitman and the affiants gave, in substance, the same testimony as above mentioned touching the witnesses at the time of the homicide, but no further testimony concerning their whereabouts at the time the subpœnas were issued at the time of the trial.

Considering the negro character, the fact that in the nighttime the old negress Polly Giles and the two children were not found alone at the immediate spot where the dead man lay does not conclusively produce the inference that they were not on the premises at the time he was killed.

Upon the trial, appellant testified that she had written and caused to be written letters of inquiry, and had received personal information relative to the whereabouts of the children; and that subpœnas were issued in accord with the information thus obtained; that at the time of the trial she had no specific knowledge of their whereabouts other than that contained in the information adduced in response to the subpœnas. She also testified that the children were present at the time of the homicide; that one of them came to the house with her; and that, while she did not see them during the excitement immediately antecedent to the struggle, she saw them immediately afterwards. It is also shown that, at the time of the trial on the information received, the witnesses were in Kingsville. A subpœna for them was sent to the sheriff there, and was returned later not executed.

Testimony was developed upon the trial that the witness Pitman was very bitter against appellant; that he was jailer, and, while she was in jail, abused her. The sheriff testified, among other things, that he found her sleeping upon an iron cot, with nothing but a newspaper upon it; and that, in consequence of that, and other conditions, he took her out of jail to his home.

[1, 2] The application being the first, the real issue which the state was authorized to make in its contest was not the truth of the absent testimony, but the diligence to secure the testimony. Sneed v. State, 100 S. W. 922; Steel v. State, 55 Tex. Cr. R. 556, 117 S. W. 850; Branch's Ann. Penal Code, § 321. To be diligent it is not required nor expected that the impossible should be accomplished. Mapes v. State, 14 Tex. App. 134; Donahoe v. State, 28 Tex. App. 13, 11 S. W. 677, and other cases in Branch's Ann. Penal Code, § 318. After receiving information that the witnesses were in North Texas at some unknown point, it was obviously impossible to secure their attendance without a postponement of the trial.

In the case before us, we are impressed with the view that the compliance of the law demanded of the appellant nothing more than was done to secure the attendance of the absent witnesses. If, as intimated in connection with the contest, the relatives of the absent witnesses were seeking to avoid the service of process upon them, the appellant's difficulty in securing them may have been increased, but the justice of postponement of the trial for a reasonable time to enable her to overcome the difficulty is emphasized, rather than diminished, in the absence of evidence connecting her with the effort to avoid their attendance.

[3] It may be possible that those in charge of the absent children may have been frightened at the prospect of bringing them to the county by memory of the fact (which is disclosed by the record) that, in consequence of the tragedy, both the husband and brother-in-law of the appellant, who were connected with the homicide, had been killed, and her two nephews, who were not shown to have been connected with it, were hanged. Whatever may have been the reason for the failure of service of process, we find nothing that would warrant the conclusion that appellant's efforts to secure their attendance were not made in good faith and diligently pursued. Even if the matter of diligence were questionable, the absent testimony, being to support the defensive theory of the appellant, which otherwise rested upon her testimony alone, was such as the law regards with favor. Koller v. State, 36 Tex. Cr. R. 499, 38 S. W. 44; Beard v. State, 55 Tex. Cr. R. 158, 115 S. W. 592, 131 Am. St. Rep. 806; Branch's Ann. Pen. Code, § 329, and cases cited. It being of such character, it does not always happen that the absence of complete diligence would justify the trial court in overruling the motion for new trial. Mitchell v. State, 36 Tex. Cr. R. 278, 33 S. W. 367, 36 S. W. 456; Duffy v. State, 67 S. W. 420; Day v. State, 62 Tex. Cr. R. 452, 138 S. W. 130; Branch's Ann. Penal Code, § 319.

[4] Appellant's conviction rests upon the theory that she was a principal actor in the homicide. Assuming that the conflict arose and proceeded as the state's witnesses described it, her presence was accounted for in a manner consistent with her innocence. The state's testimony suggests that the intention to kill the deceased was not formed in the mind of Washington Giles until after, under appellant's persuasion, he had agreed to submit to the arrest, and the appellant had agreed to accompany him. From the state's standpoint, it appears that the appellant was not present when Washington Giles indicated that he had changed his mind about submitting to arrest, she being at that time in the house, making preparation for the trip.

From Pitman's testimony the following quotation is taken:

"There was nothing done by either of them until after I jerked Washington Giles off the gallery and hit him in the head with the pistol, and then the boy (meaning Osborne Giles) came out of the house with a rifle. After I jerked Washington Giles off the gallery and hit him with the pistol, then she [appellant] came out of the house."

Taking into account the manner of making the arrest, and recalling that appellant was the wife of Washington Giles, and that, on coming out of the house, she beheld him wounded and bleeding in the struggle with his assailant, some participation in the conflict by her is accounted for as not necessarily unlawful. Guffee v. State, 8 Tex. App. 187. The state's evidence, revealing that she may not have known the cause of the renewal of the conflict, there being no direct testimony that she heard or was aware of the fact that Washington Giles had recanted his intention to submit to arrest, suggests that she may have joined in the effort to disarm Pitman with no purpose other than a lawful one—that of protecting her husband from further injury. Her testimony, if believed by the jury, would have made it plain that her purpose was lawful. The testimony of the absent witnesses, according to the application, would have supplemented that of appellant upon this phase of the case.

Considering the character of the diligence used, and the materiality of the absent testimony, as developed upon the trial, we believe that, in refusing a new trial, the learned trial judge fell into error.

For this reason a reversal of the judgment is ordered.

DIBBLES v. STATE. (No. 6268.)

(Court of Criminal Appeals of Texas. June 1, 1921.)

Criminal law ⬅854(3)—Conviction reversed where jurors separated.

A judgment of conviction of a felony cannot stand where the court below with the consent of the accused permitted the jury to separate and go to their respective homes and spend the night, none of them being accompanied by an officer, under Vernon's Ann. Code Cr. Proc. 1016, art. 745.

Appeal from District Court, Hardin County; D. F. Singleton, Judge.

Collie Dibbles was convicted of burglary, and appeals. Reversed and remanded.

Owen M. Lord, of Sour Lake, for appellant.

R. H. Hamilton, Asst. Atty. Gen., for the State.

LATTIMORE, J. This appellant was convicted in the district court of Hardin county of the offense of burglary, and his punishment fixed at confinement in the penitentiary for three years.

It appears from bill of exceptions No. 1 that, after the testimony in the case had been introduced, the court below, with the consent of the appellant, permitted the jury to separate and go to their respective homes and there spend the night, none of them being accompanied by an officer. To this action of the court appellant took his bill of exceptions, which is approved by the trial court without any explanation whatever. This is in violation of the express inhibitions of article 745, Vernon's C. C. P., which forbids the separation of the jury in a felony case in any event except the jurors so separated be in charge of an officer. This court held in Porter v. State, 1 Tex. App. 394, that such separation was not allowable even by the consent of the accused and permission of the judge presiding, unless said jurors were in charge of an officer. So far as we know, there has been no deviation from this holding down to the present. See Sterling v. State, 15 Tex. App. 249; Kelly v. State, 28 Tex. App. 120, 12 S. W. 505. No sort of explanation of the fact of such separation anywhere appears, nor was there even any effort on the part of the state to show no injury. Early v. State, 1 Tex. App. 248, 28 Am. Rep. 409; Burris v. State, 37 Tex. Cr. R. 587, 40 S. W. 284.

For the error mentioned the judgment of conviction will be reversed, and the cause remanded for another trial.

THIELEPAPE v. STATE. (No. 6212.)

(Court of Criminal Appeals of Texas. May 4, 1921. Rehearing Denied June 8, 1921.)

1. **Criminal law ⬅=1097(1)—Single statement of facts accompanying three separate records, etc., objectionable.**

Where defendant was charged with liquor offenses in three indictments, and such three cases, by agreement of counsel for the state and defendant, were tried at the same time before the same jury, three separate charges submitting the law applicable to the cases being given, and three verdicts being returned, while on defendant's appeal there are in the three separate records only one statement of facts, such procedure is objectionable as hampering the Court of Civil Appeals.

2. **Intoxicating liquors ⬅=137—Defendant who used equipment already on premises guilty of having it in possession.**

If defendant moved on premises where there was paraphernalia for the manufacture of intoxicating liquor, and took possession of such paraphernalia and proceeded to use it, he was guilty of having in possession equipment to manufacture intoxicating liquor not for medicinal, etc., purposes, though the equipment was already in existence on the premises when he took charge of them.

3. **Criminal law ⬅=597(3)—Denial of continuance for absence of witnesses whose testimony would establish no defense not erroneous.**

In a prosecution for having in possession equipment for manufacturing intoxicating liquor not for medicinal, etc., purposes, denial of continuance to procure the testimony of witnesses to the fact that the equipment was on the premises when defendant took possession of them held not erroneous, as such evidence could furnish no defense.

4. **Criminal law ⬅=394—Illicit liquor equipment admissible, though discovered by officers without search warrant.**

In a prosecution for having in possession equipment for the manufacture of intoxicating liquor not for medicinal, etc., purposes, such equipment was in evidence, though the officers were not armed with a search warrant at the time they discovered and took possession of it.

5. **Intoxicating liquors ⬅=233(2)—Testimony that defendant had whisky in possession like that in jugs in his barn admissible.**

In a prosecution for having in possession equipment for the manufacture of intoxicating liquor not for medicinal, etc., purposes, testimony that when defendant was arrested, on returning home from a purported visit to his mother-in-law, a small quantity of whisky was found in his possession, or in the car he was driving, of a similar character to the whisky found in jugs at his barn, was admissible.

6. **Criminal law ⬅=663, 858(3)—Equipment taken from defendant properly allowed to remain in courtroom; jury would have had right to take equipment with them during deliberations.**

In a prosecution for having in possession equipment for the manufacture of intoxicating liquor not for medicinal, etc., purposes, equipment found on defendant's premises being admissible, the court properly allowed it to remain in the courtroom until the case was concluded; after it had been properly offered in evidence, the jury, had they desired, would have had the right to take the equipment to the jury room for further examination during deliberations.

7. **Criminal law ⬅=404(3)—Jugs found in defendant's possession admissible to show preparation of container for liquor when made.**

In a prosecution for manufacturing intoxicating liquor, six five-gallon jugs found with other liquor equipment on defendant's premises would be admissible in evidence as tending to show preparation of a container for the liquor when made.

8. **Criminal law ⬅=404(3)—Jugs found in defendant's possession admissible on charge of having equipment in possession.**

In a prosecution for having in possession equipment for the manufacture of intoxicating liquor, not for medicinal, etc., purposes, five-gallon jugs found on defendant's premises with other liquor equipment was discovered by the officers were admissible in evidence as tending to show defendant had been operating the equipment.

9. **Criminal law ⬅=451(1)—Opinion that smoke on defendant's barn looked like fresh smoke admissible as shorthand rendering of facts.**

In a prosecution for having in possession equipment for the manufacture of intoxicating liquor not for medicinal, etc., purposes, testimony of a witness as to the smoked condition of the back of defendant's barn, that it looked like fresh smoke, was admissible as a shorthand rendering of the facts.

On Motion for Rehearing.

10. Intoxicating liquors ⚷236(19)—Evidence held sufficient to sustain conviction of having illicit equipment in possession.

In a prosecution for having in possession equipment for the manufacture of intoxicating liquor not for medicinal, etc., purposes, evidence *held* sufficient to sustain conviction, though the top of a certain kettle enumerated as one of the articles of the equipment and necessary before the equipment could be used to make liquor was not found or accounted for.

11. Criminal law ⚷449(1)—Question of identity of liquor in bottle and in jugs did not involve expert testimony.

In a prosecution for having in possession equipment for the manufacture of intoxicating liquor not for medicinal, etc., purposes, testimony that liquor in a bottle found in defendant's car was of the same kind as that in jugs in his barn did not involve any question of expert testimony.

Appeal from District Court, Parker County; F. O. McKinsey, Judge.

Robert Thielepape was convicted of having in possession equipment for the manufacture of intoxicating liquor not for medicinal or other lawful purposes, and he appeals. Judgment affirmed.

Baskin, Dodge & Bishop and Sam S. Beene, all of Fort Worth, for appellant.

R. H. Hamilton, Asst. Atty. Gen., for the State.

HAWKINS, J. [1] It appears from the records before us that appellant was charged in three indictments with, (a) being in possession of equipment for the purpose of manufacturing intoxicating liquor; (b) with the manufacture of the same; (c) with being in possession of intoxicating liquor in violation of the law. These three cases, by agreement of counsel representing the state and the defendant, were tried at the same time before the same jury; three separate charges submitted the law applicable to the cases, and three verdicts were returned. This is an unusual method of disposing of felony cases in the trial court. We find in the three separate records only one statement of facts. This is objectionable, and hampers this court seriously in the discharge of its duties; it is a practice which attorneys may fall into that the court cannot countenance. We will consider the statement of facts in this instance, but wish to give proper warning that a statement of facts hereafter must accompany the record in each case regardless of the agreement of defendant and counsel for the state.

The conviction in the case now under consideration was under an indictment charging that appellant had in his possession equipment for the manufacture of intoxicating liquor, not for medicinal, sacramental, mechanical, or scientific purposes. The equipment is described in the indictment to be one kettle, one worm, and trough, one funnel, ten barrels, and one furnace. Appellant was convicted and his punishment assessed at confinement in the penitentiary for one year.

The issues presented by appellant in his motion to quash the indictment have all been decided adversely to his contention in Ex parte Gilmore, 228 S. W. 199.

Error is assigned because the court overruled the first application for continuance based on the absence of witnesses Ed Jackson, R. A. Moore, and Earl W. Silby. The qualification to the bill shows that on October 14, 1920, this case was set down for trial for October 26th; subpœnas were not requested for these witnesses until October 20th; no excuse for the delay in having process issued appears from the bill. We are inclined to think there was a lack of diligence in securing process. However, if these witnesses had been present and had sworn to all that is claimed they would, and the jury had believed it all to be true, it is not likely any different verdict would have been reached.

The statement of facts discloses that the appellant some time between the 1st and 15th of April, moved upon a small farm known as the Marti place, and resided there until the 23d of June, when an investigation by the officers resulted in these prosecutions being filed against appellant. Marti, who had formerly lived on this place, moved away in the fall, and between the time he left and appellant's occupation of the premises two young men had been living on the place. The evidence shows that neither they nor appellant had ever been seen doing any farm work while they were living upon the premises. There were two barns on the place, a small and large one. The mother of appellant's wife lived in Fort Worth, and it was the practice of appellant and his wife to make frequent trips from their home to the city of Fort Worth ostensibly to visit the mother. These trips were made in a five-passenger Ford car, and once or twice each week. Early in the morning of the 23d of June the sheriff and other officers visited the appellant's place, he being absent at the time on one of his trips to Fort Worth. In the large barn, under some hay, they discovered three five-gallon jugs, two of them being full of corn whisky, and the other partially filled. There was also discovered at the same time concealed under the hay, a kettle with a ca-

⚷For other cases see same topic and KEY-NUMBER in all Key-Numbered Digests and Indexes acity of about thirty gallons. One of the officers, in walking over the hay, stepped in the kettle, and it was discovered in this manner. In the small barn there was a partition. n one side of it there was a furnace and a worm in a trough, the trough being about 15 feet long made out of 1 by 12 inch lumber, through which there ran two copper tubes or worms. They also found three or four empty five-gallon jugs under the kitchen floor. The furnace described was a large one, being some 6 feet long, and would accommodate the kettle found in the large barn. The furnace was so arranged that a pipe ran from it out at the east or back end of the barn, so the smoke from the furnace would go out near the ground on the east or back side. In the other portion of this small barn were found nine or ten barrels full of mash. In two or three of these barrels the mash had ceased working, had settled down, and was clear, but in the others it was still fermenting. Three sacks of meal were found at the same place the barrels were discovered. The evidence discloses that from six to twelve days are required for this mash to go through fermentation and settle sufficiently to be used in the further process of making whisky. One witness testified that his premises joined the Marti place, and that on one occasion he went down there on some business, and in looking for the parties passed the back end of the small barn, and noticed the same to be all smoked up, and observed the pipe coming out near the ground. He testified that the smoke looked to be tolerably fresh. This witness also testified that during the time appellant lived there, he had, on more than one occasion, while in the field plowing, detected an odor coming from the direction of the barn in question, which smelled like bread cooking, and made him hungry. A lady testified that upon one occasion while appellant was living there she had gone to the place for the purpose of getting blackberries; for some reason they did not get out of their car; appellant's wife came out on the gallery, and witness noticed some one come around the small barn and go in the inside, and noticed smoke coming from behind the barn. After the discovery had been made by the officers as hereinabove detailed, appellant was arrested about noon, as he and his wife and brother returned home from Fort Worth. In the car were found three five-gallon jugs, empty, but with the smell of whisky strong about them. Appellant also had with him at this time three sacks of meal and three packages of sugar, being about $2 worth of sugar to the package. Substantially the foregoing is the testimony offered upon the trial, and it will not be undertaken to state it more in detail, unless it should be necessary to do so in discussing some of the bills of exceptions presented.

[2, 3] Appellant claims that if the witness Silby were present, he would testify that he was with appellant at the time the latter moved upon the place and knew there was hay in the large barn at that time and that there were several barrels in the small barn; that he had also seen one Joe Marti, on several occasions during appellant's absence, go to his barn and take therefrom a suitcase and carry it to his buggy. By the witnesses Tackson and Moore appellant said he could prove that they had aided him in moving to the place and also knew the contents of the barn at the time he moved and saw several barrels filled with slop in the barn. The purpose of this testimony evidently was that it tended to show the equipment for the manufacture of intoxicating liquor was upon the premises at the time appellant took possession thereof. As stated heretofore by us, we cannot see that the testimony of these witnesses could have in any way affected the result of the trial. If a party should move in and take possession of a furnished house, the furniture would no less be in his possession and under his care and control after he had moved in than if it had been acquired subsequently. If appellant moved upon the premises in question, all of the paraphernalia for the manufacture of intoxicating liquor being upon the premises at the time, yet, if appellant took possession thereof and proceeded to use the equipment, as the evidence in this case indicates that he did, it could furnish no defense to him because the equipment was already in existence on the premises when he took charge of them. We therefore find no error on the part of the court in overruling appellant's application for continuance. Branch's Crim. Laws, § 239, and many cases cited; Clowers v. State, 228 S. W. 226.

[4] In his bills of exceptions Nos. 3 and 4 appellant complains of the action of the court, first in not sustaining his motion to have the equipment in question returned to him, and, second, to the introduction of such equipment in evidence, because the officers were not armed with a search warrant at the time they discovered and took possession of the property. We will not discuss this question at length, but regard the case of Rippey v. State, 86 Tex. Cr. R. 539, 219 S. W. 463, as decisive of the matters raised by appellant in these bills, and following that case, we conclude there was no error in the action of the court with reference to this equipment.

[5] Witnesses testified that when defendant was arrested upon returning home a small quantity of whisky was found in his possession, or in the car he was driving, of a similar character to the whisky found in the jugs at the large barn. That is to say, that both were "white corn whisky." Appellant excepted to the court permitting the witnesses to so testify. There was no error in this.

The testimony may have been of little weight, but it was not inadmissible.

[6] By other bills appellant assigns error in permitting the equipment found upon the premises to be brought into the court and exhibited to the jury and permitting it to remain in the courtroom during the arguments, and until the jury retired. The state had a right to produce before the jury the equipment discovered upon the premises of appellant and not depend upon a description thereof by a witness who had seen it. The various articles constituting the equipment being proper evidence in the case, it is proper for the court to let them remain in the courtroom until the case was concluded; and after they had been properly offered in evidence, the jury, if they had desired, would have had the right to take them to the jury room for their further examination during deliberation upon the case.

[7, 8] Appellant complains because the court permitted to be exhibited before the jury six five-gallon jugs, which had been found at the time the other equipment was discovered, because it was no part of the equipment described in the indictment. As stated in the beginning of this opinion, appellant was tried upon three charges at once. Upon the charge of manufacturing intoxicating liquor there is no question but the introduction of these jugs in evidence would have been permissible, as tending to show preparation of a container for the liquor when made. No charge was asked limiting this evidence to any particular case, or any particular charge. We do not believe the court would have been authorized in giving such a charge had it been requested. If the state had been able to show by an eyewitness that appellant had been operating the equipment in question in the manufacture of intoxicating liquor, it certainly would have had a right to do so; on the charge for having equipment in his possession, it likewise had a right to offer any legitimate evidence as a circumstance tending to prove the same thing.

[9] Appellant also reserved a bill of exceptions because the state was permitted, over his objection, to prove by one witness the smoked condition of the back side of the small barn, and who, in connection with his testimony, said it "looked like fresh smoke," on the ground that the same was a conclusion of the witness, and not a statement of fact. It would be almost impossible for a witness to so describe the appearance of a smoked wall as to enable a jury to draw a conclusion as to whether it was fresh smoke or otherwise, and we believe this explanation from the witness that it "looked like fresh smoke" comes within the rule of a shorthand rendering of the facts, and was permissible under the circumstances. Branch's Anno. P. C. p. 73, § 132.

We find no errors in the record, and the judgment is affirmed.

On Motion for Rehearing.

LATTIMORE, J. [10] This case is before us upon appellant's motion for rehearing. He urges that we were in error in holding the evidence sufficient because of the fact that the top to a certain kettle which is enumerated as one of the articles of the equipment for making intoxicating liquor, which was found in appellant's possession by the officers, was not found or accounted for. It was stated by a gentleman who examined the equipment in the presence of the jury that the top of the kettle would be necessary in order to make liquor with said equipment. Various parts of said equipment were apparently not in actual use on the day that the officers searched the premises and found same. There was such quantity of affirmative evidence satisfactorily establishing the fact that the manufacture of liquor was being rather extensively carried on on the premises in appellant's possession, that we would not feel inclined to hold said evidence insufficient because the officers did not find and take into their possession the top of the kettle which could easily have been overlooked by them, they not being experts and not knowing the importance that the top of said kettle might play in making the contraband article.

The questions raised in said motion relative to the conflict between the Dean Law (Acts 36th Leg. [2d Called Sess.] c. 78) and the Volstead Act (41 Stat. 305) will not be here discussed because they have been fully settled against appellant in other decisions of this court.

We did not dispose in the original opinion of appellant's application for continuance on account of the absence of witnesses Tackson, Moore, and Silby, on the ground of insufficient diligence to procure their presence, but upon the proposition that the testimony alleged to be expected from said witnesses did not appear to us to be such as could have materially affected the result of the trial.

[11] That the liquor found in a bottle in the car of appellant was of the same kind as that in the jugs in his barn was material matter such as could be testified to by persons having opportunity to make the comparison. We do not understand that ability to testify to such fact called for any question of expert testimony, and believing that we correctly disposed of the case upon the original hearing, appellant's motion for rehearing is overruled.

THIELEPAPE v. STATE. (No. 6214.)

(Court of Criminal Appeals of Texas. May 4, 1921. Rehearing Denied June 8, 1921.)

Intoxicating liquors ⬤=236(19)—Evidence held to sustain conviction of illicit manufacture.

Evidence *held* sufficient to sustain conviction for the manufacture of intoxicating liquor not for medicinal, etc., purposes.

Appeal from District Court, Parker County; F. O. McKinsey, Judge.

Robert Thielepape was convicted of manufacturing intoxicating liquor, and he appeals. Affirmed.

Baskin, Dodge & Bishop and Sam S. Beene, all of Fort Worth, for appellant.
R. H. Hamilton, Asst. Atty. Gen., for the State.

HAWKINS, J. In this case appellant was convicted for the manufacture of intoxicating liquor, and his punishment assessed at confinement in the penitentiary for one year.

The legal questions presented are identical with those passed upon by the court in a case against this same appellant in cause No. 6212 (231 S. W. 769), in which he was charged with the possession of equipment for the manufacture of intoxicating liquor. A discussion of the same questions in this case would only be a repetition, and we refer to the case decided this same day for a statement of the facts, and our views upon the legal questions presented.

As we gather from the record, the contention of appellant was that the whisky found upon his premises at the time the officers made the investigation was not manufactured by him, but by parties who had previously occupied the premises. The court instructed the jury upon this issue and pertinently told them:

"Although you may believe from the evidence that the whisky testified about by witness was found on the premises on which he (appellant) lived, yet you cannot convict the defendant unless you believe from the evidence beyond a reasonable doubt that the same was manufactured by him."

The court also gave a proper charge upon circumstantial evidence.

The jury were fully warranted in reaching the conclusion that appellant himself had been engaged in the manufacture of intoxicating liquor. The evidence shows that the mash in the majority of the barrels found on appellant's premises was, at the time of the discovery, still in a state of fermentation. The evidence is further to the effect that it takes from six to twelve days for this fermentation to cease, and at the time the officers made the raid in question, the appellant had been upon the premises for more than two months. Sacks of meal were discovered in connection with the barrels containing the mash, and appellant had in his possession, in his car, at the time of his arrest, three more sacks of meal, and a quantity of sugar. An honest jury could hardly have reached any other conclusion than was reached by the jury in this case.

The judgment is affirmed.

On Motion for Rehearing.

LATTIMORE, J. This case was affirmed at a former time and comes before us upon appellant's motion for rehearing. No sufficient reasons appearing in said motion for believing our former opinion incorrect, and concluding that the case was properly disposed of, the motion for rehearing will be overruled.

━━━━

THIELEPAPE v. STATE. (No. 6213.)

(Court of Criminal Appeals of Texas. May 11, 1921. Rehearing Denied June 8, 1921.)

Intoxicating liquors ⬤=236(6½)—Evidence held to sustain conviction of having liquor in possession.

Evidence *held* to sustain conviction of having in possession intoxicating liquors not for medicinal, etc., purposes.

Appeal from District Court, Parker County; F. O. McKinsey, Judge.

Robert Thielepape was convicted of having in possession intoxicating liquors not for medicinal, etc., purposes, and he appeals. Affirmed.

Baskin, Dodge & Bishop and Sam S. Beene, all of Fort Worth, for appellant.
R. H. Hamilton, Asst. Atty. Gen., for the State.

HAWKINS, J. Appellant was convicted for having in his possession intoxicating liquors not for medicinal, mechanical, scientific, or sacramental purposes, and his punishment assessed at one year in the penitentiary.

This is a companion case to Nos. 6212 and 6214 (231 S. W. 769, 773) against the same appellant, decided last opinion this day, May 4th. The same legal questions are presented in this case as were disposed of in the others, and therefore we pretermit a discussion of them again. The evidence is also set out practically in full in one of those cases, and it will not be necessary to repeat it here further than it has reference to the particular charge we are now considering. The evidence fully authorized the jury in reaching the conclusion that appellant not only had intoxicating liquor in his possession, but that he was holding it in his possession for the purpose of unlawfully selling it. At the time his premises was raided two five-gallon jugs of corn whisky were found under some hay in his barn, and another five-gallon jug partially filled was found in the same place. Equipment for making intoxicating liquor was found upon his premises, and there was evidence to the effect that he had been using it. Some nine or ten barrels of mash in various stages of fermentation, and corn meal, were found in his barn. Appellant was in the habit of making one or two trips a week to Fort Worth in his car, and at the time of his arrest, upon approaching home, three empty five-gallon jugs were found in his car, together with three sacks of corn meal and a quantity of sugar. The jugs seem to have borne about them the unmistakable odor of whisky, and the jury was fully warranted in reaching the conclusion that the whisky found in appellant's possession was held by him for the unlawful purpose of sale and barter.

Having disposed of the legal questions involved in the other cases, and believing the evidence in this case sustains the verdict, the judgment of the trial court is affirmed.

On Motion for Rehearing.

LATTIMORE, J. This case was affirmed at a former time and comes before us upon appellant's motion for rehearing. No sufficient reasons appearing in said motion for believing our former opinion incorrect, and concluding that the case was properly disposed of, the motion for rehearing will be overruled.

McCLURE v. STATE. (No. 6275.)

(Court of Criminal Appeals of Texas. June 1, 1921.)

1. Criminal law ⊕═507(7)—Prosecutrix in an incest case held to be an accomplice.

Where incestuous relations extending over a period of many years existed between defendant and prosecutrix, his stepdaughter, 19 years of age, she was an accomplice within the rule as to accomplice testimony.

2. Criminal law ⊕═511(5)—Testimony of prosecutrix, as accomplice, held not sufficiently corroborated.

Testimony of neighbors to having seen defendant and prosecutrix together in places which would have afforded opportunity for the commission of the crime was not sufficient corroboration to establish incest by accomplice testimony of prosecutrix, where defendant produced a large number of witnesses who testified that he bore a good reputation for virtue and chastity.

Appeal from District Court, Wise County; F. O. McKinsey, Judge.

R. C. McClure was convicted of incest, and he appeals. Reversed and remanded.

McMurray & Gettys, of Decatur, for appellant.

R. H. Hamilton, Asst. Atty. Gen., for the State.

LATTIMORE, J. Appellant was convicted of incest in the district court of Wise county, and his punishment fixed at five years in the penitentiary.

[1] The indictment was for incest alleged to have been committed with appellant's stepdaughter, a young lady 19 years of age. She testified to an act of intercourse with appellant, and as to the fact that he had given her various presents, and to a conversation had with her mother, appellant's wife, in which she told her mother of continued incestuous relations with appellant extending over a period of many years, and that he was the father of two children to which she had given birth. She was an accomplice under all our authorities. Branch's Ann. P. C. pp. 588, 589.

[2] Appellant asked an instructed verdict at the close of the testimony, basing such request on the lack of corroboration of the young woman. A test of the sufficiency of such corroboration might be made by applying the familiar rule of considering the weight of the testimony in the record, aside from that of the accomplice witness, and ascertaining if same would tend to show the accused guilty of the act charged. A Mr. Foreman testified that about the date fixed by the prosecutrix he was working in a field adjacent to that in which she and her two half-sisters were hoeing; that appellant was harrowing in another nearby field. On more than one occasion on that day this witness said he saw prosecutrix leave her work and go toward the house as if for water, and saw her enter an orchard, and at the same time he would see appellant leave his team and go also into said orchard, and that after being out of sight for 15 or 20 minutes the girl would go out of the orchard and appellant would also go out of the same place and back to his team. He said this all occurred in the daytime and in plain sight of himself and of the two daughters of appellant; they being about 12 and 14 years of age respectively. Mr. and Mrs. Porter and Mr. Phillips testified they were neighbors of the McClures, and had often seen appellant and the prosecutrix on the public road together, going to and from the town of Decatur, and had seen them going to church together; that sometimes appellant was accompanied by his wife, the mother of prosecutrix, and sometimes she was not along.

This is all of the corroborating testimony. There does not appear anything in it which, in and of itself, would tend to connect appellant with any criminal knowledge of the young lady. Our Assistant Attorney General, in his brief for the state, admits it to be insufficient for corroboration, and we are of opinion that he is correct. Appellant placed on the stand in his own behalf a large number of his neighbors, who testified that he bore a good reputation as to his conduct toward women and for virtue and chastity. It was not even proven by others that the young lady had given birth to any children, nor was she examined by any physician or other persons who testified as to any physical evidence of penetration, and in fact there was no evidence in the record aside from her own, to show that she had ever had intercourse with any man. A letter written by prosecutrix to appellant stating that what he had done was known, and unless he deeded all he had to her mother and left the country his case would be put in the hands of the authorities, was in evidence.

Because of the insufficiency of the corroborating evidence, the judgment of the trial court must be reversed and the cause remanded; and it is so ordered.

HUNT v. STATE. (No. 6165.)

(Court of Criminal Appeals of Texas. June 1, 1921.)

1. Criminal law ⚷511(1)—Evidence corroborative of accomplice held sufficient.

In prosecution for automobile theft, evidence in corroboration of an accomplice *held* sufficient.

2. Larceny ⚷41—State required to prove that automobile found in defendant's possession was that claimed to have been stolen.

In prosecution for theft of automobile, the state was required to prove that the car which had been proved to have been in defendant's possession was the one claimed to have been stolen.

3. Larceny ⚷62(2)—Want of consent not inferred from other circumstances, where owner, though a witness, did not testify with reference thereto.

Where the owner of alleged stolen property is present and testified before the jury, and fails to give direct and positive testimony as to want of consent to the taking of the property, such want of consent will not be inferred from other circumstances in evidence.

Appeal from District Court, McLennan County; Richard I. Munroe, Judge.

F. S. Hunt was convicted of automobile theft, and he appeals. Reversed and remanded.

McCutcheon & Church and Geo. Clifton Edwards, all of Dallas, for appellant.

R. H. Hamilton, Asst. Atty. Gen., for the State.

HAWKINS, J. Conviction was for theft of an automobile. Punishment was assessed at 10 years in the penitentiary.

Sims, an accomplice, testified that he and appellant stole a new Ford car in Waco on a certain Saturday night from a certain place described by him; that they carried this car out in the country, changed the motor number on it, and put a highway license number on it which had prior to that time been taken out in Bell county preparatory for use on a stolen car; that it was taken out in the name of J. H. Hines; appellant took the car north, and afterwards reported to witness that he had sold it in Dallas; witness was unable to recall the highway license number they put on the car, or the motor number; after this car was taken they discovered in it a bathing suit, which they threw away.

The owner of the car, Roy Poole, testified that his car had been stolen from the point where Sims claimed he and Hunt got it. Poole had left a bathing suit in his car, which he never saw again. This car was taken on June 12th. On June 17th Powell bought a car from Hunt in Dallas, bearing at that time motor number 3886427, and license number 490006. Hunt transferred to Powell a state license purporting to have been issued to J. H. Hines by the Bell county tax collector, bearing numbers corresponding to the ones on the car. This license was introduced by the state. Powell sold the car to Maxwell, and Poole got it back from Maxwell. When Poole lost his car a tassell which had been pulled off a dress was in it, and when the car was recovered this same tassell was found under one 'of the seats, and it was partly in this way the car was identified.

This is a companion case to two other cases against Hunt which were decided in March of this year, 229 S. W. 869, 230 S. W. 406, but not yet [officially] reported, and many questions raised in this case were decided, in them, and will not be discussed at length again.

[1] A special charge was requested, directing the jury to return a verdict of not guilty, because there was not sufficient evidence to corroborate the accomplice. There was no error in refusing to give this charge. We believe the car was sufficiently identified as the Poole car, and appellant was found in the possession of it recently after the theft, and we think the corroboration sufficient.

[2] The court was also asked to charge the jury to acquit appellant, unless they believed from the evidence beyond a reasonable doubt that the car sold to Powell belonged to Poole. This charge should have been given. See Hunt Cases, supra, and authorities cited.

The charge requested with reference to the effect of the introduction of the license receipt in evidence was erroneous; but a charge as indicated in the other opinions should have been given.

Appellant's contention that the theft of an automobile is a misdemeanor, regardless of the value of the car, was fully discussed in one of the opinions heretofore rendered in a case against the same appellant, and therefore will not be discussed again here.

We have expressed our views upon all questions, save one, raised by the record in this case, in the other cases referred to. The records are very similar, and some of the same errors appear in this record as were disclosed in the others.

In appellant's motion for new trial he urges that he is entitled to the same:

"Because the state did not prove as required by law, positively, and in terms, the want of consent requisite to conviction; the owner of the car alleged to have been stolen being present and testifying, twice, in the case, for the state."

[3] An examination of the statement of facts discloses that the ground for the motion for new trial is well taken. While Roy Poole, the owner of the alleged stolen car, testified to all the circumstances from which the jury might infer that it was taken without his consent, it appears that at no time during his examination was he asked in regard to his want of consent. If the state relied upon the fact that the circumstances might justify the conclusion that he did not consent, it was not sufficient. Where the owner of the alleged stolen property is present and testifies before the jury, and fails to give direct and positive testimony as to his want of consent to the taking of the property, such want of consent will not be inferred from other circumstances in evidence. This question will be found fully discussed in Caddell v. State, 49 Tex. Cr. R. 133, 90 S. W. 1014, 122 Am. St. Rep. 806, in which a great many cases are reviewed and cited.

For the errors herein pointed out, and others discussed in the former opinions referred to, the judgment is reversed, and the cause remanded.

BEAN v. STATE. (No. 6247.)

(Court of Criminal Appeals of Texas. June 1, 1921.)

Homicide ⟺325—Failure to charge on law of homicide in defense of one's person after threats held not reversible error.

In prosecution for murder of sister's husband after the husband had assaulted and seriously injured his wife and had threatened to kill her entire family, and after the wife had taken refuge with defendant, in which defendant claimed to have shot from his house in defense of himself, sister, and others of the family while deceased was advancing toward the house, the court's failure to instruct on the law of homicide in defense of one's person in a case wherein the accused relies upon threats accompanied by a demonstration, where no special charge was asked correcting the omission, and where the fatal shot and the infliction of the injuries from which death appeared to result took place after deceased had fled from the premises pursued by defendant, held not reversible error.

Appeal from District Court, Polk County; L. Manry, Judge.

Isaac Bean was convicted of murder, and he appeals. Affirmed.

R. H. Hamilton, Asst. Atty. Gen., for the State.

LATTIMORE, J. Appellant was convicted in the district court of Polk county of murder, and his punishment fixed at confinement in the penitentiary for five years.

Appellant killed his brother-in-law. The facts showed that the sister of appellant, wife of deceased, had received at the latter's hands continued cruel treatment beginning soon after her marriage and culminating shortly before this homicide in a brutal assault upon her by deceased in which two of her ribs were broken and she was otherwise seriously injured. It appears that after said assault she escaped from her home, hid in the woods, and later made her way to her father's house, where her brother, appellant herein, lived. The bad reputation of deceased as being that of a violent and dangerous man seemed fully proven, and it was in testimony that he had repeatedly threatened the extermination of the whole Bean family, stating to one witness that he was going to Livingston and get a Winchester and wipe out the whole family, and to another that he was going into the army, but that before he left he was going to kill out the whole Bean family, and these threats had been communicated to appellant before the homicide. On the night in question deceased came to the home in which the Bean family lived, called out from the gate, and demanded to see his wife. She came to the door, and he then commanded her to accompany him home. She turned back into the house, and he advanced toward the building and was shot by this appellant from a window. Appellant is a negro boy 18 or 19 years old, and the proof further shows that, after shooting at deceased from said window, he pursued the latter a distance of several hundred yards from the house, finally overtaking him, and that he then shot him again, clubbed his gun, and beat deceased over the head until he was dead or practically so. No other motive appears for the killing than that appellant was desirous of protecting his sister and his father's family, and that he was afraid of deceased. The record appears before us without a bill of exceptions either to the taking or rejection of evidence, or to the charge of the trial court. The trial court did not submit the law of homicide in defense of one's person in a case wherein the accused relies upon threats accompanied by a demonstration, but, inasmuch as no special charge was asked correcting this omission, and in view of the further fact that the fatal shot, or the infliction of the injuries from which death appeared to result, took place after deceased had fled from the premises, we would not feel at liberty to hold the failure to give said charge as any serious error. The jury had the facts before them and saw fit to give to appellant the lowest punishment for the offense charged.

Finding no error in the record, the judgment will be affirmed.

THERIOT v. STATE. (No. 6240.)

(Court of Criminal Appeals of Texas. June 1, 1921.)

1. Homicide ⟹309(4)—Evidence of previous difficulties and of fear and excitement on the part of accused held to require submission of the issue of manslaughter.

Evidence of previous difficulties and of fear and excitement of defendant accompanying assaults and threats by deceased, though not sufficient to constitute adequate cause, *held*, on the evidence, to require the submission of the issue of manslaughter.

2. Witnesses ⟹383—Cannot be impeached as to an immaterial matter.

Where defendant's witness on cross-examination denied that he had made a statement that defendant would get the deceased and wouldn't miss him, the state could not impeach such witness on such denial, as the statement referred to was a mere opinion of the witness and immaterial.

3. Criminal law ⟹720(9)—Argument of prosecuting attorney based on immaterial testimony held improper.

Reference by the prosecuting attorney in argument to immaterial testimony brought out on cross-examination of one of defendant's witnesses, consisting of the witness' opinion that defendant would kill deceased, was improper and called for admonition from the court.

4. Criminal law ⟹633(2) — The statute requiring the reading of the indictment held mandatory.

Code Cr. Proc. 1911, art. 717, requiring the indictment to be read to the jury on the trial of a criminal case, is mandatory and not directory merely.

Appeal from District Court, Jefferson County; E. A. McDowell, Judge.

Albert Theriot was convicted of murder, and he appeals. Reversed and remanded.

David E. O'Fiel and C. W. Howth, both of Beaumont, for appellant.

R. H. Hamilton, Asst. Atty. Gen., for the State.

MORROW, P. J. Appellant shot and killed Joseph Luquette for which he is under conviction for murder; punishment fixed at confinement in the penitentiary for five years.

There is evidence of previous difficulty, threats on the part of the deceased, and a demonstration immediately preceding the homicide sufficient to raise the issue of self-defense and of intent to execute the threat.

Appropriate instructions were given upon the subject of murder and self-defense, including the law pertaining to communicated threats.

[1] Complaint is made of the failure to instruct the jury on the law of manslaughter. Some six or seven months preceding the homicide, Darby, a half-brother of the appellant, and the deceased, engaged in a difficulty over an alleged written communication addressed by the deceased to the wife of Darby. There was evidence that some three days before the death of the deceased, while Darby and appellant were together, deceased renewed the difficulty, accompanied by a simple assault upon the appellant and threats to take the life of both. Darby fired at deceased.

It seems that the appellant and the deceased were employees of a refining company, and that on the day of the homicide appellant went to the plant of the company to receive his wages. The deceased, according to the evidence of several witnesses, seeing the appellant, approached him, caught him by the shoulders and turned him around, and in an angry manner declared that he would then settle the argument. One witness said:

> "This young man, the defendant, appeared to be very much excited and afraid. He impressed me as being afraid of the dead man. I think the other man was larger and stronger than this boy, and he looked to be well built and a matured man. He appeared to be angry, and appellant impressed me as wanting to avoid trouble."

Appellant was about 18 years of age, while the deceased was about 21 years old.

The appellant said that as he was walking to the street car with a number of others, the deceased approached him, grabbed him by the shoulder and turned him around, and said:

> "Well, here's where we settle that argument. You and your brother shot at me and missed me. I would just as well be dead as not."

The deceased, according to the appellant, looked angry, and appellant believed that he was about to be shot; that the deceased walked back and forth several times continuing his conversation; that immediately before the shot was fired, deceased walked away, and upon his return, made a quick move indicating that he was going to shoot and kill appellant; that appellant then shot him.

It was appellant's contention that bearing upon the issue of manslaughter was the evidence of previous difficulty, communicated threats, and hostile demonstrations (Williams v. State, 61 Tex. Cr. R. 356, 136 S. W. 771), evidence of sudden meeting, fear, and excitement upon the part of the accused (Anderson v. State, 60 Tex. Cr. R. 314, 131 S. W. 1124; Howard v. State, 23 Tex. App. 265, 5 S. W. 231). There was also evidence of an assault and battery committed by the deceased immediately before the homicide, and threatening words and conduct. Doubtless, singly, neither the assault nor any one of the matters mentioned might be adequate cause, but taken collectively, and viewed in the light of the previous relation between the appellant and deceased, we think the court was not warranted in refusing appellant's request to submit to the jury the issue of manslaughter. Wadlington v. State, 19 Tex. App. 274; Masters v. State, 71 Tex. Cr. R. 608, 160 S. W. 693; Reed v. State, 9 Tex. App. 318; Rutherford v. State, 15 Tex. App. 247; Nelson v. State, 48 Tex. Cr. R. 274, 87 S. W. 143; Pickens v. State, 86 Tex. Cr. R. 657, 218 S. W. 758.

[2, 3] The witness Verette, for the appellant, was asked by the state's counsel, upon cross-examination, if he had not said to one Bohlin that Frank Darby "had shot at a fellow and had missed him, but that Darby's brother would get him and wouldn't miss him." The witness having denied making this statement, Bohlin was called and testified that Verette had made the statement. So far as the inquiry made of Verette bore upon the issues involved, it sought to obtain his opinion that the appellant would shoot the deceased and would not miss him. The opinion of Verette to this effect was not material or legitimate testimony. The impeachment of him was not authorized. Drake v. State, 29 Tex. App. 270, 15 S. W. 725, and other cases collated in Branch's Ann. Penal Code, § 175. The testimony thus adduced was used against the appellant in argument, the prosecution seeking to draw therefrom the inference that Verette had made the statement, which he denied, and which was attributed to him by the witness Bohlin, and that in making it he was acting upon information obtained from the appellant. We find no evidence to support this inference and are of the opinion that the use made of the testimony was improper. Even from the state's standpoint, the evidence had no place in the record other than to discredit Verette, and could not have been available as a substantive fact against the appellant. The court, on appellant's request, should have admonished the jury to disregard the argument. Ex-

ception was made to the ruling of the court in the admission of the testimony, and the use made of it, and is properly brought forward for review.

[4] To one of appellant's bill of exceptions, the court appends the following qualification:

"When this case was called for trial and after announcement of ready by state and defendant, the defendant was by the county attorney duly arraigned, duly entered the plea of not guilty. But after the impaneling of the jury the indictment was not read to the jury. But the defendant having shown no injury suffered by him by reason of the failure to read said indictment, and the court believing the statute on this subject to be directory, the motion for a new trial was overruled."

Code Cr. Proc. 1911, art. 717, declares, concerning the method of trial, that—

"A jury having been impaneled in any criminal action, the cause shall proceed to trial in the following order: (1) The indictment or information shall be read to the jury by the district or county attorney. (2) The special pleas, if any, shall be read by the defendant's counsel, and if the plea of not guilty is also relied upon, it shall also be stated."

The character of subdivision 1 of this statute, whether mandatory or directory, has been the subject of judicial interpretation. In Wilkins v. State, 15 Tex. App. 420, the provision was held mandatory. The court said:

"We are of the opinion that a failure to read to the jury, on the trial of a felony case, the indictment, must be regarded as an omission from which we must apprehend that injury may have resulted to the defendant. * * * We think the reading of the indictment to the trial jury, in a felony case, is mandatory and essential, and that, were we to hold to the contrary, it would be establishing a loose and dangerous practice, and one which would be in direct contravention to the plainly expressed will of the Legislature."

Commenting upon this and other cases to the same effect, Judge Ramsey, in writing the opinion of this court in Essary v. State, 53 Tex. Cr. R. 606, 111 S. W. 927, said:

"The indictment is the basis for the prosecution. Among other things, its office is to inform the appellant of the charge laid against him and one of the purposes of the requirement that it shall be read to the jury at the beginning of the prosecution is to inform them in precise terms of the particular charge laid against the defendant on trial. His plea thereto makes the issue. While it may be thought that this ground of objection is in its nature quite technical, it is, nevertheless, the right of every defendant to have the charge read against him and to have his plea entered therein. Such is the express provision of our statute and this right has been recognised time out of mind by all the decisions of this court. It is of such a substantial nature that in all the decisions of this court it has been treated and regarded as mandatory. That it can be waived is well established but such a waiver cannot be inferred but in a case where the statute has been disregarded the burden rests upon the state to show such conduct and acts upon the part of the defendant as may, in fairness, be treated and regarded as a waiver. In a case involving life and death, it is always unsafe to depart from that order of procedure established by law in this state. This, it clearly appears, was done in this case. No reason is given why it was so done except as we may infer that the failure to follow the statute was the result of mistake or inadvertence. When discovered the error was not cured by the reintroduction of the testimony or any offer so to do, and under the rule obtaining in this state for all these years, the failure to observe this mandatory provision regulating the control of trials, must be held, as we do now hold to be, in itself, violative of his rights and hurtful to his interest."

The state, through its Assistant Attorney General, concedes that the learned trial judge was in error in refusing a new trial upon the ground that it was affirmatively shown that the indictment was not read to the jury which tried and rendered against him the verdict of guilty. We are constrained, in view of the record before us and the precedents cited, to concur in this view. For this and the other errors to which we have adverted, the judgment of the trial court is reversed and the cause remanded.

SHIELDS v. STATE. (No. 6195.)

(Court of Criminal Appeals of Texas. June 1, 1921.)

1. Homicide ⚖=261—Dead bodies not exhumed for examination unless justice demands.

Exhuming and examination of bodies in homicide cases ought not to be allowed in any case, unless it is imperatively demanded under the circumstances and is necessary for the due administration of justice.

2. Homicide ⚖=261—Exhumation of body held not imperatively demanded.

In a homicide case where defendant's theory of the killing of her husband was that he was standing up and the state's theory was that he was lying in bed, held, that court did not err in denying a motion that the body of deceased be exhumed so as to ascertain for the purpose of the jury's knowledge the course of a wound.

3. Criminal law ⚖=1186(1)—Cause not reversed unless wrong may be righted on another trial.

Before the Court of Criminal Appeals will order a reversal of a cause and entail the delay and expense of another trial, it must believe that wrong has been done which can be righted on another trial.

4. Homicide ⚖=340(4)—Errors in charge as to murder immaterial, where conviction was for manslaughter.

Errors in charge as to matters relating to the law of murder and the law of manslaughter are immaterial on appeal, where defendant was convicted of manslaughter and her punishment fixed at the minimum allowed by statute.

5. Homicide ⚖=300(2) — Charge relative to threats held not subject to criticism.

Defendant in homicide case could not criticize a charge relative to threats, where the jury was pointedly told that if deceased had made threats against defendant and it appeared to her from her standpoint at the time that by acts, or words coupled with acts, he manifested an intention to execute such threats, she would be justified in killing him and should be acquitted.

6. Criminal law ⚖=673(2) — Special charge held to cure error.

There was no error in failing to limit purpose for which evidence that defendant had been indicted for a felony was admitted, where a special charge on the matter was requested and given.

7. Criminal law ⚖=1090(12, 13)—Matters not supported by bill of exceptions not considered.

Complaints of matters of argument and of misconduct of the jury, which are not supported in the record by bills of exception setting forth such matters, cannot be considered on appeal.

Appeal from District Court, Potter County; Henry S. Bishop, Judge.

Sallie Shields was convicted of manslaughter, and appeals. Affirmed.

A. M. Mood, of Amarillo, for appellant.
R. H. Hamilton, Asst. Atty. Gen., for the State.

LATTIMORE, J. Appellant was convicted in the district court of Potter county of manslaughter, and her punishment fixed at two years' confinement in the penitentiary.

All the parties to the tragedy were negroes. Appellant was indicted for the murder of her husband. A special venire of 75 jurors was ordered upon motion of appellant. When the case was called for trial, she moved to quash the venire and the return thereon because not drawn, executed, and returned as required by law. This complaint narrowed down to the proposition that the return of the officer as to certain absent veniremen was insufficient. The court overruled the motion, directing that the sheriff amend the return, which order was obeyed; the amendment appearing to be filed on the following day. No objection was made to proceeding before such amendment was made, and no complaint appears to be made of the amended return in so far as same showed the diligence used by the sheriff in attempting to serve said absent veniremen; but complaint is made of the language used

⚖=For other cases see same topic and KEY-NUMBER in all Key-Numbered Digests and Indexes

by said officer in making said amended return, which we deem without support, and a discussion of which would be of no value.

At the close of appellant's testimony in chief she presented to the court the following motion:

"Comes now defendant, by her attorney, A. M. Mood, at the close of her testimony in chief, save the defendant herself, and shows to the court that the defendant has used every effort and diligence on her part, and has examined carefully all persons that she is advised knows anything relative to the wounds that were on the deceased, and the recollection of the undertaker being of a more or less uncertain nature, the defendant now here moves that the court order a proper officer or commissioner or appointee of the court to exhume the body of Will Shields and ascertain for the purpose of this jury's knowledge the course of the one wound that went clear through this negro's body in particular, and as well as to advise the jury as to the location of the entrance definitely of the other wounds, and for cause and reason for such motion this defendant would show to the court that she believes that on account of the theory of the state and the defendant in this case that the exact location particularly of the exit and entrance of the one wound is highly material to her theory of defense in this case."

This motion was overruled, and such action is urged as error. As sustaining her contention that said motion should have been granted, appellant cites the case of Gray v. State, 55 Tex. Cr. R. 90, 114 S. W. 635, 22 L. R. A. (N. S.) 513. In that case there was a sharp conflict as to whether deceased was shot in the front or the back, and the accused claimed that each of the bullets fired by him at deceased were still in his body and that an autopsy would reveal the presence of all of same.

[1, 2] Discussing the circumstances under which the repose of the dead should be disturbed in order to make an examination such as is here desired, the learned judge, writing the opinion for this court in the Gray Case, said:

"It ought not to be allowed in any case unless it was imperatively demanded under the circumstances, and was necessary for the due administration of justice."

We are in accord with this holding, but not with its application to the instant case. The bill taken to the refusal of said motion in the case before us, states that the theory of the state was that the deceased was lying in bed when shot; that of appellant was that both were on their feet and deceased was coming at her when she shot him. Conceding these to be the respective theories of the state and the defense, the question arises: What could be revealed by the autopsy requested, for or against either side? Appellant's theory as to the bullet wounds would appear to be set out in a statement made by the undertaker, who was a defense witness, to the attorney for the appellant, which is as follows:

"When you attempt to refresh my memory by asking me if it is not true that I conveyed it to you that there was one wound a little above his right nipple that went clear through his body, practically straight, one down here about the pit of his stomach that did not go through him, and one wound in his arm: Those locations in my mind at this time are apparently correct as to entry of the bullets, but as to what bullets came out I could not say relative to those, if any."

This testimony of the undertaker was corroborated by his assistant, who said he saw an exit bullet hole in deceased's back, high up; and also by the sheriff, who testified that deceased had a bullet hole near the pit of his stomach, one in his arm, and one in his breast which, according to witness' best recollection, went straight through the body. No other witnesses testified as to the wounds, bullet holes, or anything of that kind; nor did the state by direct testimony or cross-examination of any witness with reference to bullet holes, or the exit or entrance of bullets, in any way appear to thus controvert the testimony just mentioned. The sheriff was the only state witness, and his testimony on this point was in line with the theory of appellant as stated.

We confess ourselves at a loss to see the need for additional testimony on behalf of appellant, on a matter about which all the evidence as to bullet holes was corroborative of appellant's theory. What could she expect from the autopsy? Human experience demonstrates that one lying in bed reclines on one side or the other, or partially so, as much or more than on the back or stomach. A bullet fired from a pistol in the hands of one facing such bed would appear to be as apt to go straight through the body of one lying on his side in such bed, as it would if the parties were standing facing each other. The state made no contention that deceased was shot in the back, nor that he was lying on his back in bed when shot, nor that the wounds were other than as shown above.

Again, examining appellant's own testimony, she said deceased was coming toward her when she shot him, but made no mention of the position of his body, whether straight or stooped, directly facing her, or at an angle; nor does she say how she held the pistol, whether about at a height that would make a bullet striking the breast go straight through, or otherwise.

[3] Conceding that such autopsy would show that deceased was struck in the breast by a bullet that went straight through his body, and by another bullet at or near the pit of his stomach, and by one in the arm, what conflict of evidence would be settled or effected by testimony of these facts? What

stronger proof would this be of the fact that deceased was advancing upon appellant, than that he was lying on one side in the bed when shot? Before this court would order a reversal of a cause, and entail the delay and expense of another trial, we must believe wrong has been done which can be righted on another trial. Reverting to the opinion of Judge Ramsey in the Gray Case, supra, and applying it, we think this motion was properly refused because not imperatively demanded under the circumstances, and not necessary for the due administration of justice.

[4] Appellant excepted to the court's charge for many reasons, but most of said exceptions were to matters relating to the law of murder and to alleged errors in submitting the law of manslaughter, all of which questions pass out of our consideration inasmuch as appellant was convicted of manslaughter and her punishment fixed at the minimum allowed by statute.

[5] We do not think paragraph 5 of the court's charge open to the criticism that it failed to apply the law relative to threats, to the facts. Same pointedly told the jury that if deceased had made threats against appellant, and it appeared to her from her standpoint at the time that by acts, or words coupled with acts, he manifested an intention to execute such threats, she would be justified in killing him and should be acquitted.

[6] An exception was taken to the failure of the trial court to limit the purpose for which evidence of the fact that appellant had been indicted for a felony was admitted; but, inasmuch as a special charge to this effect was requested and given, no error is shown.

[7] In her brief appellant makes complaint of some matters of argument and of misconduct of the jury which are not supported in the record by any bills of exception setting forth such matters, and therefore such questions are not properly before us for consideration.

Finding no error in the record, the judgment of the trial court will be affirmed.

Ex parte GRADINGTON et al. (No. 6339.)

(Court of Criminal Appeals of Texas. June 1, 1921.)

1. Extradition ⊜34 — Requisition paper must be accompanied by certified copy of affidavit or indictment.

Under Act Cong. Feb. 12, 1793,[1] on the subject of extradition, it is absolutely necessary and is an essential prerequisite that a requisition paper be accompanied by a certified copy of the affidavit or indictment.

2. Habeas corpus ⊜85(2) — Burden held on relator to show that warrant of extradition was not based on proper affidavit.

Where extradition warrant issued by Governor contained the recital, "And whereas, said demand is accompanied by a copy of said affidavit, duly certified as authentic, by the Governor of said state," a presumption arose in favor of the legality of the extradition warrant, and the burden was on the alleged fugitive to show in a habeas corpus proceeding that no proper affidavit accompanied the requisition papers and that the Governor was not in possession of the proper papers authorizing the issuance of the warrant.

Appeal from District Court, Bexar County; S. G. Tayloe, Judge.

Proceeding in habeas corpus by Laura Gradington and another to obtain release from custody. From a judgment remanding them to the custody of the sheriff, they appeal. Affirmed.

Linden & Martin, of San Antonio, for appellants.

R. H. Hamilton, Asst. Atty. Gen., for the State.

HAWKINS, J. On March 30, 1921, relators filed an application for writ of habeas corpus before Hon. S. G. Tayloe, judge of the Forty-Fifth district court of Bexar county, Tex. The applications were in proper form and will not be set out in full. The applications were granted, and in response John W. Tobin, sheriff of Bexar county, responded that he was holding the relators by virtue of an extradition warrant issued by the Governor of Texas, directing delivery of the parties to Robert B. Stubbs, agent of the state of Louisiana, to convey the relators back to that state for trial.

Prior to the issuance of the extradition warrant, an affidavit had been filed before a justice of the peace of Bexar county to the effect that the relators were fugitives from justice from the state of Louisiana, and they were held temporarily upon this affidavit.

The record seems to show that the hearing upon the application was begun on April 8, but was continued or postponed until a later date. At the time of the first hearing it is made to appear from the record that the requisition issued by the Governor of Louisiana recited that the relators were charged by "information" in the state of Louisiana, and that a certified copy of the information accompanied the requisition. The warrant of extradition issued by the Governor of the State of Texas upon that requisition followed the recital in the requisition, and recited that a copy of the information accompanies the requisition.

We may infer that between the original hearing, which was begun on April 8, and the final hearing, the Texas authorities holding the relators ascertained that a requisition could not be honored by the Governor of this state unless it was accompanied by a certified copy of an "indictment" or "affidavit" charging an offense against relators in the demanding state; and that the authorities sought from the Governor of Louisiana a new requisition on the Governor of Texas, accompanied by a certified copy of an affidavit, upon which new requisition the Governor of Texas issued a new extradition warrant, and the sheriff of Bexar county, by an amended answer, set up the fact that he was holding the relators under the last extradition warrant which had been placed in his hands. Upon the final hearing of the matter on April 30, the relators were remanded to the custody of John W. Tobin, sheriff of Bexar county, from which judgment they appealed to this court.

There appears in the statement of facts upon the final hearing the following requisition from the Governor of Louisiana.

"Exhibit G.

"State of Louisiana.

"Executive Department.

"The Governor of the State of Louisiana to the Governor of State of Texas:

"Whereas, Ora Jackson, alias Ora Jefferson, and Laura Grandington (colored) stand charged in the parish of Orleans in this state, with the crime of larceny from the person, by affidavit, and it has been represented to me that they have fled from justice and have taken refuge in the state of Texas.

"And, whereas, agreeably to the Constitution of the United States, and an act of Congress passed February 12, 1793, I have made application to his Excellency the Governor of the State of Texas for the surrender of the said parties fugitive from justice, and have also, in pursuance of the powers vested in me by law, appointed Robert B. Stubbs, agent on the part of the state of Louisiana, for the purpose of receiving the said parties from the constituted authorities of the said state of Texas whenever they shall have been surrendered in accordance with such application, and bringing them into this state to be dealt with according to law.

"These are therefore to request and require all persons to permit the said Robert B. Stubbs, agent, as aforesaid, to execute the trust imposed on him and to render all lawful and necessary assistance in the premises.

"This state will not be responsible for any expense attending the execution of the requisition for the arrest and delivery of fugitives from justice.

"In testimony whereof, I have hereunto set my hand and caused to be affixed the Great Seal of the State of Louisiana.

"Witness John M. Parker, Governor of our said state, at the city of Baton Rouge, this the 11th day of April in the year of our Lord nineteen hundred and twenty-one and of the Independence of the United States of America the one hundred and forty-fifth, and of the state of Louisiana one hundred and ninth. By the Governor. Jno. M. Parker. R. H. Flower, Asst. Secretary of State. [Seal.]"

And following that the extradition warrant issued by the Governor of the State of Texas, as follows:

"Exhibit F.

"In the Name and by the Authority of the State of Texas.

"Executive Department.

"To All and Singular the Sheriffs, Constables, and Other Civil Officers of Said State:

"Whereas, it has been made known to me by the Governor of the State of Louisiana that Ora Jackson, alias Ora Jefferson, and Laura Grandington (colored) stand charged by affidavit before the proper authorities, with the crime of larceny from the person committed in said state and that the said defendants have taken refuge in the state of Texas; and whereas, the said Governor, in pursuance of the Constitution and laws of the United States, had demanded of me that I cause the said fugitives to be arrested and delivered to Robert B. Stubbs, who is, as is satisfactorily shown, duly authorized to receive them into custody and convey them back to said state; and whereas, said demand is accompanied by copy of said affidavit duly certified as authentic by the Governor of said state:

"Now, therefore, I, Pat M. Neff, Governor of Texas, by virtue of the authority vested in me by the Constitution and laws of this state, and the United States, do issue this my warrant, commanding all sheriffs, constables, and other civil officers of this state, to arrest and aid and assist in arresting said fugitives and to deliver them when arrested to the said agent in order that they may be taken back to said state to be dealt with for said crime.

"In testimony whereof, I have hereunto signed my name and have caused the Seal of State to be hereon impressed at Austin, Tex., this 14th day of April, A. D. 1921. By the Governor. Pat M. Neff, Governor. S. T. Staple, Secretary of State. [Seal.]"

The affidavit which is required to accompany the requisition was not introduced in evidence, and the contention of relators before this court is that, because the record fails to show that the requisition was accompanied by a certified copy of the affidavit, relators should be discharged.

[1] Under the act of Congress (1 Stat. 302) on the subject of extradition, it is absolutely necessary and is an essential prerequisite that the requisition paper be accompanied by a certified copy of the affidavit or indictment. That has long been the settled law, both by the decisions of this state and the United States. See Ex parte Lewis, 75 Tex. Cr. R. 320, 170 S. W. 1098; Roberts v. Reilly, 116 U. S. 80, 6 Sup. Ct. 291, 29 L. Ed. 544.

[2] While it is necessary that an authenticated copy of an affidavit or indictment accompany the requisition, it does not follow by any means that relator should be dis-

charged because the record in this case fails to show such certified affidavit. In the very case to which we are cited by relators (Roberts v. Reilly, supra), Justice Matthews, delivering the opinion for the Supreme Court of the United States, uses the following language:

"It must appear therefore, to the Governor of the State to whom such a demand is presented, before he can lawfully comply with it: First, that the person demanded is substantially charged with a crime against the laws of the state from whose justice he is alleged to have fled, by an indictment or an affidavit, certified as authentic by the Governor of the State making the demand; and second, that the person demanded is a fugitive from the justice of the state the executive authority of which makes the demand.

"The first of these prerequisites is a question of law and is always open upon the face of the papers to judicial inquiry, on an application for a discharge under a writ of habeas corpus. The second is a question of fact, which the Governor of the State upon whom the demand is made must decide, upon such evidence as he may deem satisfactory. How far his decision may be reviewed judicially in proceedings in habeas corpus, or whether it is not conclusive, are questions not settled by harmonious judicial decisions, nor by any authoritative judgment of this court. It is conceded that the determination of the fact by the executive of the state in issuing his warrant of arrest, upon a demand made on that ground, whether the writ contains a recital of an express finding to that effect or not, must be regarded as sufficient to justify the removal until the presumption in its favor is overthrown by contrary proof. Ex parte Reggel, 114 U. S. 642 (ante, 250). Further than that it is not necessary to go in the present case."

In the instant case, an examination of the extradition warrant issued by the Governor of the State of Texas will disclose the following recital:

"And whereas, said demand is accompanied by a copy of said affidavit, duly certified as authentic, by the Governor of said state."

What effect should be given by this court to the recital in the extradition warrant? Shall it be presumed that the recital of the Governor of the State of Texas that he had before him, accompanying the requisition, a certified copy of the affidavit charging relators with an offense in Louisiana speaks the truth? Or does such recital mean nothing? We are not without authority in our state to answer such question. In Ex parte Stanley, 25 Tex. App. at page 377, 8 S. W. at page 647 (8 Am. St. Rep. 440), this court, speaking through Judge Willson, said:

"In the case we are considering, the warrant recites, but does not set forth in full, the affidavit upon which it is issued. We have found no decision or authority which requires that the warrant should set forth the evidence in full, except the intimation referred to in Thornton's case. The correct rule is, we think, laid down in Donohue's Case, 84 New York, 438, in a syllabus as follows: 'Where the papers upon which a warrant of extradition is issued are withheld by the executive, the warrant itself can only be looked to for the evidence that the essential conditions of its issuance have been complied with, and it is sufficient if it recites what the law requires.'"

Later on, we read the following in the same case:

"We are of the opinion that the warrant is in substantial compliance with the statute. No form for such a warrant is prescribed by law, and when it shows upon its face, with reasonable certainty, as does the warrant in question, that the essential prerequisites to its issuance have been complied with, it must be held prima facie valid."

In Ex parte White, 39 Tex. Cr. R. 497, 46 S. W. 639, Judge Hurt, speaking for the court, after setting out the facts, used the following language:

"The case should have been permitted to rest here, because the presumption obtained that the Governor of this state issued his warrant upon proper authority; that the requisition and the papers accompanying the same were in proper form, etc.—in fact, that a case was presented to him requiring the warrant, arrest, and extradition of relator."

The presumption arising in favor of the legality of the extradition warrant issued by the Governor of the fugitive state is not a conclusive one, and a relator always has the right to go behind such presumption and prove, if he can, that the Governor was not in possession of the proper papers authorizing the issuance of the warrant, but in this case this was not done. The relator stands upon the proposition that in the absence of an affidavit this court should presume that no affidavit was in the hands of the Governor of the State, when the authorities just cited are directly to the contrary. The burden is upon the relator to show that the recitals in the extradition warrant were not true.

The judgment of the trial court remanding the relators to the custody of the sheriff of Bexar county, to be by him delivered to the agent of the state of Louisiana, is in all things affirmed.

DAVIS v. STATE. (No. 6220.)

(Court of Criminal Appeals of Texas. April 27, 1921. Rehearing Granted June 1, 1921.)

1. Criminal law ☞368(1)—Statements as to ownership of grain by those hauling it held res gestæ.

In a prosecution for the theft of grain by one of those engaged in hauling it to the elevator, the warehousemen can testify that others hauling the grain to the warehouse stated it belonged to prosecuting witness, who had telephoned the warehousemen the grain was coming, since such statements were part of the res gestæ of the connection of those parties with the wheat which they were then hauling.

2. Larceny ☞43—Evidence of amount paid and price per bushel is admissible to show quantity of wheat.

In a prosecution for larceny of wheat, the owner of the wheat can show quantity which he sent to an elevator, where he did not remember the number of bushels, by stating the amount of money he received for the wheat and the price per bushel, since the jury could determine the quantity of wheat from such evidence by a mathematical computation.

On Motion for Rehearing.

3. Larceny ☞55—Evidence held not to sustain conviction for theft of wheat.

Evidence that defendant was one of several drivers hauling wheat for prosecuting witness, and that he disposed of a load of wheat for his own account under suspicious circumstances, but which did not show clearly that the owner's wheat was short or that any shortage could have been caused only by theft, held insufficient to sustain a conviction for theft of the wheat.

4. Criminal law ☞318—Inference unfavorable to accused cannot be drawn from absence of testimony available to the state.

No inference unfavorable to accused can be drawn on the failure to produce evidence, where the evidence was available to the state, and it would have been to the state's interest to produce it if it had been favorable to the state.

Appeal from District Court, Randall County; Henry S. Bishop, Judge.

Roy Davis was convicted of theft and sentenced to two years' confinement in the penitentiary, and he appeals. Reversed and remanded on rehearing.

Kinder, Russell & Griffin, of Plainview, for appellant.

R. H. Hamilton, Asst. Atty. Gen., for the State.

HAWKINS, J. Appellant was tried for the theft of 68 bushels of wheat, alleged to have been the property of Embry Finley, convicted, and his punishment assessed at confinement in the penitentiary for two years, from which judgment he appeals.

No exceptions were urged to the charge of the court, and no special charge requested, except one which was a peremptory instruction directing the jury to return a verdict of not guilty because of the insufficiency of the evidence. This peremptory request was refused by the court, and will be discussed later with reference to the sufficiency of the evidence.

[1] Only two bills of exceptions appear in the record. It appears that the owner, Mr. Finley, did not haul the wheat in question himself, but had the appellant, his brother, and two other parties haul it in and deliver it at the elevators. The witness J. B. Gurley was the manager of one of the elevators, and Mr. Finley had told him that he was going to send wheat in, and while Gurley was testifying he was asked by the state if he bought any wheat from Finley, and, if so, how much; whereupon counsel for defendant asked permission to question the witness on this point, and it developed that the witness Gurley would answer that he only knew it was Finley's wheat from what the haulers said, and objected to this testimony on the ground that it would be hearsay. We do not believe the court committed error in permitting the witness to state that the parties who delivered the wheat to the elevator told him it was Finley's wheat. Finley had told him he was going to send the wheat in, and the statements of the haulers at the time they delivered the wheat were res gestæ statements of their connection with the wheat, and, we think, properly admissible.

[2] While the witness Finley was testifying he was asked by the district attorney how much wheat he had sold to the Townsend elevator. He was unable to state the number of bushels, but gave the aggregate amount of money he received from the Townsend elevator and the amount per bushel he received. This was objected to by counsel for appellant on the ground that it was not the proper way to prove the number of bushels of wheat he had sold to the Townsend elevator. We find no error in the action of the court in permitting this character of testimony. The witness may not have remembered the number of bushels delivered to the Townsend elevator, but, if he knew the amount per bushel he received, and the total amount paid him for wheat delivered to that elevator it was pertinent proof which would enable the jury to determine the number of bushels by mathematical calculation; hence we find no error, as presented by appellant in his bill of exceptions No. 2.

The witness Finley testified that he had threshed 1,776 bushels of wheat, and that most of this wheat, something in the neighborhood of 1,600 bushels, had been stored in a granary situated about 200 yards from where appellant lived; the remainder of the wheat being kept at his (Finley's) house. He did

not know the exact number of bushels of
wheat placed in the granary, but estimated
it to be somewhere in the neighborhood of
1,600 bushels. He secured the services of the
appellant and his brother and two other
parties by the name of Morris and Gassaway
to haul and deliver the wheat from the granary in question to the two elevators at
Happy, Tex. Upon checking up on his wheat
he discovered a shortage, and an investigation resulted in developing the fact that on
one day appellant was seen hauling wheat
from the granary to one of the elevators at
Happy, and on the next day was seen in the
town of Canyon, 16 or 18 miles distant, with
a load of wheat. The appellant's conduct
with reference to the sale of the wheat in
Canyon is not consistent with that of an
honest man in relation either to his own
property, or that in his possession rightfully.
He sold this wheat in Canyon under an assumed name, taking a check payable to C. E.
Clark. Afterwards he drew a check payable
to himself, purporting to be signed by C. E.
Clark, for the purpose of transferring the
money to his own account. We cannot agree
with appellant's contention that the evidence
is insufficient to support the verdict of guilty.
His access to the wheat in the granary belonging to Finley is unquestioned, and his
disappearance from home for a day and night
at this particular time is unexplained. The
shortage in the wheat as checked up by
the owner, and the conduct of appellant in
handling the wheat in the town of Canyon
was sufficient, we think, to authorize the jury
to find that the appellant had stolen the wheat
from the owner Finley. This question was
submitted to the jury fairly for their consideration, and they determined that issue
in favor of the state, and against appellant
a proper charge on circumstantial evidence
was submitted. We do not feel authorized
to disturb the verdict and substitute our
judgment for that of the jury upon an issue
of fact.

The judgment of the trial court will be
affirmed.

On Motion for Rehearing.

MORROW, P. J. [3] Upon re-examination
of the evidence, we have reached the conclusion that it is not sufficient to support
the conviction.

Perhaps the most tangible fact against
the appellant is the fact that while he had
access to the wheat of Finley he sold upon
his own account 68 bushels at Canyon and
acted in relation thereto in a manner justly
bringing him under the suspicion of wrong-
doing.

The evidence is wholly circumstantial. To
be sufficient, it must reveal, beyond a reasonable doubt, that Finley's wheat was fraudulently taken, and that the appellant was
the guilty agent. The taking is not satisfactorily disclosed. Finley obtained from the

231 S.W.—50

thresher a quantity of wheat, which, according to the thresher's weights exhibited to
Finley amounted to 1,776 bushels. A part
was left at his home, and a part put in the
granary. No weights or measurements were
made as to either amount, but Finley, according to his estimate or guess, puts the
amount in the granary at 1,600 bushels. He
sold 1,169 bushels to Neff, 439½ bushels to
Townsend, and 32% bushels to Gassaway.
Whether that sold to Gassaway was from the
granary or the home of Finley is not disclosed. The evidence shows that there was
probably a shrinkage in weight during the
time the wheat remained in the granary,
but the amount of the shrinkage is not given.

Four persons, including the appellant, were
employed by Finley to haul his wheat from
the granary to the elevator. He saw none
of it loaded or weighed. Neither of these
persons were used as witnesses.

The persons at the elevator testified that
certain wheat was received from each of
the persons, but the amount delivered by the
appellant and the others who hauled the
wheat respectively was not shown.

Finley's testimony is to the effect that his
means of knowing that there was a shortage
was by the variation between the thresher
weights and the elevator weights as reported
to him.

[4] There is nothing in the record describing the character of the wheat which appellant sold such as to identify it as a part of
that belonging to Finley. No reason is given
for the failure to use the witnesses and persons who had access to Finley's granary, nor
is it shown that the granary was not acces-
sible to others. It is not competent to use
against appellant the inference that may be
drawn from the absence of testimony available to the state, and which, if favorable, it
would be to the interest of the state to introduce. Wilkie v. State, 83 Tex. Cr. R. 490, 208
S. W. 1091; Taylor v. State, 221 S. W. 614;
Parish v. State, 85 Tex. Cr. R. 75, 209 S. W.
681.

If it be assumed that Finley had correctly
guessed the number of bushels placed in his
granary, it cannot be inferred that the appellant got the wheat he sold at Canyon from the
granary for the reason that the amount admittedly sold by Finley exceeds the amount
that he put in his granary. Even if the shortage were established, there would arise from
the testimony and absence of testimony several hypotheses consistent with the innocence of
the appellant; for example, a discrepancy
might have resulted from the loss of weight
or from the difference in the operation of the
scales used at the various places and from
the uncertainty as to how much wheat was
taken by others having access thereto. The
identity of the wheat found in the possession
of the appellant with the stolen property
cannot be assumed.

"There must be legal and competent evidence pertinently identifying the defendant with the transaction constituting the offense charged against him." Branch's Ann. Penal Code, § 1877.

No inference sufficient to support the conviction can be drawn from the fact that appellant was in possession of wheat at Canyon and was guilty of suspicious conduct relating thereto, in the absence of other evidence excluding the theory arising from the fact that Finley lost no wheat, or, assuming that he did, it was the act of others whose opportunity to take it was equal to that of appellant, which theory the state, having means to combat, has failed to disapprove.

The motion for rehearing is granted, the affirmance set aside, and the judgment of the trial court is now reversed, and the cause remanded.

FLORES v. STATE. (No. 6209.)

(Court of Criminal Appeals of Texas. May 4, 1921. Rehearing Denied June 15, 1921.)

1. **Criminal law ⚫=>632—For transfer to juvenile docket, defendant has burden of showing age.**

Under the Juvenile Law (Vernon's Ann. Code Cr. Proc. 1916, art. 1195 et seq.), accused, seeking to have the case transferred to the juvenile docket, has the burden of establishing to the satisfaction of the trial judge that he is under 17 years of age.

2. **Criminal law ⚫=>939(1)—No sufficient reason shown why so called newly discovered evidence should not have been ascertained by counsel.**

Relative to new trial for so-called newly discovered evidence consisting of a statement by defendant as to his age, made to the assistant county attorney before his age became an issue, conceding defendant's ignorance of its importance, *held* no sufficient reason was shown why it should not have been ascertained by counsel, being in a statement of facts in another case used and handled on the trial by counsel for both parties.

3. **Homicide ⚫=>354—Finding relative to death penalty that defendant was not under 17 supported by evidence.**

Jury's finding that defendant was not under 17 at time of commission of crime, within Vernon's Ann. Pen. Code 1916, art. 35, prohibiting death penalty on one under that age at that time, and as to which defendant has the burden of proof, *held* supported by the evidence.

4. **Criminal law ⚫=>729—Inaccurate statement in argument of crime of which defendant had been convicted harmless.**

Though the evidence, as bearing on defendant's credibility, showed merely that he had been convicted of robbery, inaccurate statement of county attorney in argument that it showed he was convicted of robbery with firearms, hav-

ing been promptly corrected, was not prejudicial.

5. **Criminal law ⚫=>363—Evidence of finding of weapon at place of crime admissible as part of res gestae.**

Evidence of the finding at the place of the homicide and immediately thereafter of a weapon is admissible as part of the res gestae.

6. **Criminal law ⚫=>422(1)—When preparation of, or weapons found on, conspirators may be shown stated.**

When parties are charged with acting together in the commission of a crime, evidence of preparation of, or weapons found on, any of them, whether before, during, or so soon after the offense as to shed any fair light on the act or intent of such alleged participants is admissible against any of them.

7. **Criminal law ⚫=>698(3)—Evidence equivalent to that admitted without objection not rejected.**

When evidence is admitted without objection, the same or equivalent evidence from other witnesses will not be rejected.

8. **Homicide ⚫=>281—Evidence held sufficient for submission of issue of participation.**

Evidence on prosecution for murder *held* to authorize submission of the issue of defendant's participation as a principal.

9. **Criminal law ⚫=>1172(6)—No reversal for a charge unless harm might have resulted.**

Even though a charge be not called for by the facts, there will be no reversal for giving it unless it appear that in some way harm might have resulted therefrom.

Appeal from District Court, Falls County; Prentice Oltorf, Judge.

Jose Flores was convicted of murder, and appeals. Affirmed.

J. A. Jones and Robt. F. Higgins, both of Marlin, for appellant.

C. M. Cureton, Atty. Gen., and C. L. Stone, Asst. Atty. Gen., for the State.

LATTIMORE, J. Appellant was convicted in the district court of Falls county of the murder of Oscar Sharp, and his punishment fixed at death.

Appellant was a Mexican, apparently without means of employing counsel, and the trial court is to be congratulated that in his selection of some one to represent the accused he placed the case into the hands of men who have apparently taken every possible step to preserve and present the rights of appellant.

[1] An affidavit was made in form as suggested by our statute that appellant was a juvenile under the age of 17 years at the time of the trial. This was presented to the court below, who heard evidence and rendered judgment against appellant on this issue, and this is complained of here. In the Juvenile Law (article 1195 et seq., Ver-

non's C. C. P.) It appears that the burden of proving that he is under 17 years of age is placed on the accused, and that such facts must be established to the satisfaction of the trial judge. The evidence bearing on this issue in the instant case was conflicting. Appellant, his mother and sister, gave testimony in his behalf, while a number of witnesses who had been more or less familiar with him for a number of years testified to facts and statements from which the conclusion could be reached that he was over 17 years of age at the time of said trial. His sister said that she was 21, and other witnesses testified that she had given her age at 24 years. She was married and had three children, one of whom was 5 years of age. This sister testified that, while she did not know appellant's age, she had two sisters born between herself and appellant. Appellant's mother in her testimony denied the fact that she had any children born between appellant and the sister mentioned, and stated that the only children she had ever borne were Frankie, age 24, Juana, age 21, and appellant, age 16. Many contradictory statements of each of the defense witnesses bearing on the question of appellant's age were proven. The motive of said three witnesses for giving testimony favorable to appellant was strong. We are not able to see from a careful examination of all the testimony that the conclusion reached by the trial judge in this regard was erroneous.

[2] Newly discovered evidence was a ground of appellant's motion for a new trial, which was controverted in this regard by the county attorney, and evidence was heard on the proposition that the matters referred to as newly discovered evidence were known to appellant and his attorneys, or by the exercise of reasonable diligence could have been so known. Said newly discovered evidence consisted of a statement by appellant to the assistant county attorney, of his age, same having been made before that question became an issue in this case. Said statement would hardly have been admissible as original evidence in behalf of appellant, and would probably be held self-serving, and his right to prove same at all seems to be based on the ground that such statement was corroborative of appellant's statement of his age made while on the witness stand, regarding which he was contradicted by testimony for the state. We might conclude this matter by saying appellant must have known that he had made such statement to the assistant county attorney, and therefore cannot claim it to be newly discovered, but, conceding to his ignorance, and to the fact that he was a foreigner and youthful, that its importance was not known to him, and the further fact that he had not made known to his counsel that he had made such statement, still we think it amply

shown on the hearing before the court of the issue made by the replication of the county attorney that said statement of the appellant to the assistant county attorney appeared in a statement of facts in another case of appellant, which statement of facts was present in court during the instant trial, and, according to the evidence heard, was handled and used by both counsel for the state and the appellant. Appellant was questioned as to what he had said about his age on said former trial on the occasion of the instant trial, and apparently reference was had to his testimony on said former occasion as contained in said statement of facts which was present and used by counsel for the state and defense. No sufficient reason is shown why the matters contained in said statement of facts could not have been ascertained by appellant's counsel if they had cared to examine same with reference thereto.

[3] Appellant and his mother testified on the instant trial that he was 16 years of age, and, inasmuch as our statute (article 35, Vernon's P. C.) forbids the infliction of the death penalty upon one not 17 years of age at the time of the commission of the crime, the age of appellant at said time became an issue. In his charge the trial court told the jury unless the evidence led them to believe that appellant was 17 years of age at the time of the commission of the offense, if any, they could not inflict the death penalty; also that the burden of proof rested on appellant to show that at said time he had not arrived at said age. Complaint is made of said charge, and also the failure of the evidence to show that appellant was 17 years old at the time of said homicide. It seems to have been the uniform holding of this court that the burden of proof on this issue is on the accused. Ake v. State, 6 Tex. App. 399, 32 Am. Rep. 586; Ellis v. State, 30 Tex. App. 601, 18 S. W. 139; Wilcox v. State, 33 Tex. Cr. R. 392, 26 S. W. 989; Williams v. State, 77 Tex. Cr. R. 237, 177 S. W. 965. The trial court was correct in his charge in placing the burden of proof upon the defendant to establish his nonage.

We have to some extent discussed the question of appellant's age as involved in his effort to have the case transferred to the juvenile docket. We have given this record careful study on this point, and especially so in view of the infliction of the extreme penalty of the law at the hands of the jury. Appellant swore that he was 16 years of age, and would be 17 on December 3, 1920, the homicide having taken place in the summer of that year. He said he was born in 1903. On cross-examination he stated that he left home in Matamoras, Mexico, in 1915, but could not remember whether it was summer or winter at the time; also that he was 12 years old when he left home. He denied having stated on his former trial for another offense that he was going on 14 years of age when he left home. He admitted having lived in Falls county near the home of witness McDouell, but did not remember whether it was 1910, 1911, or 1912, but said he was 8 years old at that time. He denied having stated on said former trial that he was 17 years old; also denied that he had told the witness McDouell that he was 18 or 19 years old, and that he had been in the army. Appellant's sister testified as above stated with regard to her mother's children between herself and appellant, stating that she did not know her own birthday, nor the year she was born, nor the years either of the other children of her mother were born, and that she knew how old she was because she had been to see her mother 2 or 3 years prior to the trial, but that her mother did not then tell her she was 21, and that she did not remember how old her mother had told her that she was on the occasion of said visit. She denied telling the sheriff that her age was 24. It appears from the record that appellant's mother was not present at the beginning of the trial, but was located in Grayson county and brought as a witness during said trial. She testified as above indicated with regard to the fact that she had had but three children, Frankie, Juana and appellant, and admitted that she had talked with Flores, an interpreter, the night before, and that she had not stated appellant's age correctly, giving as her reason that she did not feel good. On cross-examination she stated that appellant's birthday was December 3d, and denied having told Flores, the interpreter, that it was August 27th, and also denied having told said Flores that she did not know what year appellant was born. She testified that he was born in 1903, but that this was the first time she had ever so stated. She admitted, when asked the night before as to the year of his birth, and if it was not 1901, that she had said she did not know, but this she also explained by saying she was feeling sick. She also admitted having told parties the night before she had not seen appellant since he was 3 years old. She stated she did not know what year her son Frankie was born, nor the year of Juana's birth, nor her own.

Bearing on appellant's age, state witness Flores testified that appellant's mother told him that appellant would be 17 in August, 1920; also that she had told him there was one or two years' difference between the ages of appellant and her daughter Juana; also that she said she did not know if appellant was born in 1901, 1902, or 1903; and that she kept account of his age by the months; that she told him that Juana would be 21 on December 3d. Sheriff Moore testified that he went after appellant's mother to bring her as a witness, and that she told him appellant was 18 years old, and that his

birthday was August 27th; also that appellant's sister Juana had told him she was 24 years old, and that appellant was 18 years of age. Mr. Jennings, county attorney, introduced as a witness for some reason by appellant, testified that Juana told him she was 21 years old, and that appellant was 19. Wesley McDouell testified that he had a store at Satin, Falls county, and knew appellant there in 1913, at which time appellant lived about 100 yards from said store; that he noticed appellant's ability to handle a large boy in scuffling with him, and asked him how old he was; and that appellant said he was 11 or 12 years old. This witness also stated that in the spring of 1920 appellant came to his store, and in a conversation said that he had been in the army, and that he had told the army people he was 28 years old in order to get into the army. McDouell said that he then questioned appellant's statement and told him he was not over 18 or 19, and that appellant said he was correct in his surmise. Gus Guderian testified that appellant worked for him in the fall of 1916 and in the spring of 1917, and that when he first employed him he wanted to pay him less than a man's wages, but appellant told him at the time he was 15 years old; that appellant appeared about as large in 1917, when he left witness' employ, as he was at the time of the trial; that he paid appellant from his employment in 1916 a man's wages. Mr. Donohoo, court reporter, testified that he took down in shorthand appellant's testimony upon a former trial for another offense; that in response to a question as to how old he was when he ran away from home in 1915 appellant said he was going on 14 years of age; also that at said trial appellant's counsel asked him how old he was at the time of the trial, and he said he was 17, and, when asked when he had been 17," appellant replied "In December." We have thus given the testimony at some length bearing on the age of appellant at the time of the commission of this offense. The question was fully submitted to the jury, and by them considered in the light of all the testimony and decided adversely to appellant's contention. In view of the facts as detailed above, we do not feel justified in holding their decision of this question of fact to be unsupported or manifestly against the weight of the testimony.

[4] It was in testimony that appellant had been convicted of robbery prior to this trial. In his argument to the jury on the instant trial the assistant county attorney referred to the fact of said conviction, and stated that appellant had been convicted of robbery with firearms. Objection being made that the testimony did not show said robbery to have been with firearms, the trial court verbally instructed the jury not to consider said statement. No further reference to the matter appears to have been made. No written in-

 action was asked by appellant on the sub-
t. Complaint is now made of this argu-
nt. We do not think the mere misquota-
1 of the evidence, apparently by inadver-
ce, would necessarily call for reversal, and
s is especially true when no charge on the
)ject in writing is presented and refused.
e point involved in the testimony that ap-
lant had been convicted of any felony was
 effect upon his credibility as a witness,
i, it not being controverted that he had
n convicted of robbery, we think a refer-
ce to same as having been committed
th firearms, which reference was promptly
rrected, would not be of serious conse-
ence to appellant.

[5-7] It appears from the record that the
ooting resulting in the death of Sharp was
ard by the sheriff, who hurried to the jail
d went upstairs where he found deceased
 the throes of death. On the trial Mr.
oore, the sheriff, was permitted to testify
iat he found behind the radiator in the jail
1 object variously described, but which
ems to be composed of a short piece of iron
aving some wire wound around it, all being
icased in some rags, one end of which form-
i a loop such as could go around the wrist
nd which was a sort of slug shot or blud-
eon about 15 inches in length altogether.
'his object was introduced in evidence. To
he testimony of Sheriff Moore of the finding
f this object and its introduction before the
ury objection was made by appellant upon
he ground that said weapon was not shown
o have had any connection with the homi-
lde, and that appellant was not shown to
iave had any knowledge of same, and there-
ore could not be bound by the existence or
inding of such object. The record shows
that appellant, Jordan Israel, and others
were prisoners in the Falls county jail, that
appellant was a trusty, and that deceased
was the jailer. On the occasion in question
when deceased came up and entered what is
known as the run-around to feed the prisoners, according to the case as made by the
state, appellant seized him, and Jordan Israel
and a Mexican named Sanchez, with both of
whom appellant had been seen in consultation that morning, also at once took part in
the attack upon deceased. Witnesses said
that Jordan Israel, just before deceased came
up, had something that looked like rags in
one of his pockets, which he transferred to
another pocket, and one witness said he saw
Jordan Israel trying to put something which
looked like rags into the mouth of deceased.
As Sheriff Moore came up the steps Israel was
seen to take from under his bunk and throw
over behind the radiator the object which
was found by Mr. Moore and became the subject of this objection. The trial court, in his
qualification of appellant's bill of exceptions,
states that the object in question was made
of a piece of short iron with wire around it

and a hook about three inches in length, all
wrapped in rags, and that same was flexible
and could easily have been doubled up and
put in the pocket, and that when same was
so doubled up its appearance was such that
it might be taken for a rag. We think the
evidence of Sheriff Moore admissible for various reasons. It was part of the res gestæ
of the transaction. We are also of opinion,
that, when parties are charged with acting
together in the commission of a crime, evidences of preparation of, or weapons found
on, any one of them, whether before, during,
or so soon after the commission of the offense
as to shed any fair light on the act or intent of such alleged participants, would be
admissible against each or all of them. In
addition to the above and applicable to the
instant case as made by the record, we observe that substantially the same description
of said object appears in the testimony of
the witness McCowan, which was admitted
without objection from appellant. This is
the witness who testified that as the sheriff
came up the stairs he saw Jordan Israel
throw behind the radiator a piece of iron
wrapped in rags. It is a well-established
rule that, when evidence is admitted without
objection, the same evidence, or that equivalent from some other witness, will not be rejected.

[8, 9] Appellant's third objection to the
charge of the court as presented in his exceptions taken thereto before the jury retired
is as follows:

"Defendant objects and excepts to the ninth
paragraph of the court's charge, wherein he
authorizes a conviction of defendant for murder in the event the jury may find that he aided in the killing, though the same was brought
about by the act of some one else; there being no evidence in this case upon which to submit the charge of principals, and no evidence
to authorize the charge therein given."

The objection is very general and would
bring in review the entire evidence in the
case. Examining paragraph 9 of the charge
of the court, which is quite lengthy, we conclude that in same the court was submitting
the defensive theory that deceased was killed
by Lee Andrew Massey (as claimed by appellant), and that in this connection the court
instructed the jury that, if they believed the
killing was done by Massey, they should
acquit, unless appellant was connected with
such killing as a principal, and if they had
a reasonable doubt as to the fact that appellant killed deceased, or aided as a principal in such killing, the jury should acquit.
We are unable to see any substantial objection to said charge. A half dozen prisoners
in said jail testified to appellant's active
participation in the killing. He himself, uncorroborated by testimony direct or circumstantial, swore that the killing was done by
Lee Massey, another prisoner. It was prop-

er for the court to submit in charge the defensive theory based on a killing by Massey. This was done. The overwhelming proof showing appellant's guilty participation in the homicide, we can see no possible harm in submitting his right to an acquittal if Massey or any one else actually killed deceased, unless it was shown that appellant was also an actor in the commission of said 'crime. The jury are the judges of the facts, of the credibility of the witnesses; they may accept as true the testimony of one state or defense witness and reject others, and, had the jury accepted the theory that Massey fired the shot, this would not have necessarily compelled them to reject the fact of appellant's guilty participation, and, unless it appear that in some way harm might have resulted from giving a charge complained of, we are required by statute not to reverse, even though the charge be not, strictly speaking, called for by the facts.

The severity of the penalty imposed upon this appellant has led us to carefully consider each contention made by his able counsel, but we are unable to so far agree with any of same as to conclude that a reversal of this cause is necessary or demanded by the record. The crime was most heinous. Made a trusty by the man whom he slew, appellant took his life for no apparent reason except a desire to escape imprisonment as a penalty inflicted by a jury for an act for which deceased was in no way responsible. Apparently appellant was the leader in the murderous plan and its execution, resulting in the unprovoked death of an officer of the law in the discharge of his duty.

We find no reversible error in the record, and the judgment will be affirmed.

On Motion for Rehearing.

HAWKINS, J. Among other things, appellant complains in his motion for rehearing that we were in error in our original opinion wherein the statement was made that appellant had been convicted of robbery prior to the trial in the instant case, and to some extent basing upon that our holding that the argument of the district attorney in his closing address to the jury, in which he referred to the prior conviction, was not reversible error. On account of the severe penalty in this case, we have again examined the bill of exceptions presenting this matter. We find this expression in the latter part of the bill (whether it is a qualification placed there by the judge, or whether the entire bill is a bill prepared by the judge we are unable to say from the context):

"To the extent that the assistant county attorney included 'firearms' in his argument there was no support in the evidence, and the court immediately sustained the objection of defendant and instructed the jury not to consider same. Experienced counsel for defendant pursued the incident no further than the verbal objection, not requesting any written instruction."

The expression in the bill of exceptions that "to the extent that the assistant county attorney used the word 'firearms' in his argument there was no support in the evidence," would justify us in reaching the conclusion that there was support in the evidence as to the conviction for robbery, and the seemingly inadvertent statement in argument that it was with "firearms" does not seem to us sufficient to work a reversal of the case in view of the entire record.

All other matters called to our attention upon the motion for rehearing were considered and exhaustively discussed in the original opinion. We have again examined the assignments of error relative to those same matters, and believe that they were properly disposed of, and to discuss them again would serve no useful purpose, and would be largely a repetition.

The serious nature of the penalty has caused us to give careful consideration to all matters presented, not only in the motion for rehearing, but upon the original consideration of the case, and we have reached the conclusion that the motion for rehearing should be overruled.

BOAZ v. STATE. (No. 5508.)

(Court of Criminal Appeals of Texas. Nov. 10, 1920. Rehearing Denied June 15, 1921.)

1. Criminal law ⟺598(5)—Defendant held not entitled to continuance because of lack of diligence in securing witness.

Where about 14 days elapsed between the filing of indictment for murder and issuance of defendant's subpoena, which was returned not executed in about three days, and the case was set for trial about 10 days thereafter, during which time no further effort was made to secure the witness' attendance, and the affidavit of the witness attached to the motion for new trial indicates that he was at San Antonio, in the army, so that a casual inquiry at camp headquarters would have disclosed his whereabouts, held that affidavit indicates that by exercise of diligence the defendant could have secured the witness' attendance, and hence was not entitled to a continuance.

2. Criminal law ⟺598(5), 939(2)—Defendant not entitled to continuance or new trial for absent witness where not diligent in discovering witness' whereabouts.

Where defendant, prosecuted for murder, had a subpoena issued for a witness, a resident of the county, and the return of subpoena disclosed that witness had left a year before, and was in the army, so that the return indicates that knowledge of his departure, if not possessed by defendant appellant, could have been

⟺For other cases see same topic and KEY-NUMBER in all Key-Numbered Digests and Indexes

acquired by the use of diligence, and witness' deposition taken, and if the subpœna had been issued soon after indictment, such information would have come to defendant in time to secure the witness, defendant was not entitled to continuance because of lack of diligence.

3. Criminal law ☞941(2) — Refusal of new trial for cumulative evidence held not abuse of discretion.

In a prosecution for murder, the trial judge did not abuse his discretion in failing to grant a new trial for absence of witness who could give evidence of deceased's having admitted his correspondence with defendant's wife and defendant's jealousy, where it was disclosed by evidence without controversy that such clandestine correspondence was conducted between the deceased and the defendant's wife, such being merely cumulative evidence upon an uncontroverted issue, and testimony of another witness of an uncommunicated threat by deceased against defendant, where there was also evidence of a communicated threat.

4. Witnesses ☞53(4) — Where defendant proved by his wife that she occupied room with deceased at hotel, it was proper for state to develop from her that no criminal conduct took place.

In a prosecution for murder, where defendant appellant introduced his wife as a witness, and proved by her that she had met deceased and occupied a hotel room with him for several hours with doors locked, it was proper for state, on cross-examination of the wife, to develop that at this meeting no criminal conduct took place, in view of Vernon's Ann. Code Cr. Proc. 1916, art. 811, providing that when the detailed act, declaration, or conversation is given in evidence any other act or declaration necessary to make it fully understood may also be given in evidence.

5. Criminal law ☞829(5) — Instruction that defendant could arm himself in anticipation of attack by deceased not required where jury instructed on self-defense against apparent danger.

Where, in prosecution for murder, the jury were instructed upon self-defense against apparent, as well as real, danger, and upon defendant's right to act upon a demonstration by deceased manifesting an intent to carry out a threat, it was not incumbent upon court to instruct that defendant had right to defend himself in anticipation of an attack by deceased, particularly where it was instructed that defendant had right to seek deceased, and in doing so to arm himself.

6. Criminal law ☞829(5) — Failure to repeat instruction that defendant could use any means at his command to protect himself, and was not bound to retreat, was not error.

In prosecution for murder, where the jury was instructed that the defendant had a right to use any means at his command to protect himself from deceased, who had threatened his life, and that he was not bound to retreat, it was not error to fail to repeat the instruction at the request of the defendant, in reference to instruction on the law of communicated threats.

7. Criminal law ☞829(18) — Refusal to charge upon matters covered by another charge not error.

Where a general instruction that the burden was upon the state to show defendant guilty beyond a reasonable doubt was embraced in the general charge, and the jury were instructed fully on the law of threats, requested instructions which were no more than substantial repetitions of the main charge on such matters were properly refused.

8. Homicide ☞300(7) — Failure to instruct that defendant could continue to shoot as long as danger from deceased continued, as viewed from defendant's standpoint, held not error.

In prosecution for murder, failure to instruct at defendant's request that he had right to continue to shoot as long as the danger continued, as viewed from his standpoint, was not error, where such charge was rendered unnecessary by the circumstances, including an instruction that, if the first shot inflicted mortal wounds, and in firing it appellant was acting in self-defense, they would not consider as a circumstance against him that he fired additional shots, where the evidence showed that each of the wounds was fatal, there being no evidence to require the requested instruction.

On Motion for Rehearing.

9. Criminal law ☞1038(1) — Objection to instruction not made at time of trial will not be considered.

Assignment of error in an instruction will not be considered where no exception was presented to the court specifically pointing out the omission claimed by the assignment, in view of Vernon's Ann. Code Cr. Proc. 1916, art. 743, providing that objections to special charges shall be made at time of trial.

10. Criminal law ☞829(5) — Refusal to charge jury to view facts as they appeared to defendant at time of killing was not error where jury was instructed on self-defense from apparent danger.

In prosecution for homicide, it was not error to refuse a requested instruction that jury should place themselves as nearly as they could in the place of defendant at time of homicide, and view all facts as they appeared to him, from his viewpoint, and not as they appear to jury now, where the court had instructed on the right to defend from apparent danger.

Appeal from Criminal District Court, Dallas County; C. A. Pippen, Judge.

E. H. Boaz was convicted of manslaughter, and he appeals. Affirmed.

Baskin, Dodge, Eastus & Ammerman, of Fort Worth, Puckitt, Mount & Newberry and Reid Williams, all of Dallas, and Black & Smedley, of Austin, for appellant.

J. Willis Pierson, Dist. Atty., M. T. Lively, Cavin Muse, Robert B. Allen, and Robert B. Allen, Jr., all of Dallas, and Alvin M. Owsley, Asst. Atty. Gen., for the State.

☞For other cases see same topic and KEY-NUMBER in all Key-Numbered Digests and Indexes

MORROW, J. Appellant shot and killed McDowell. Indicted for murder, he was convicted of manslaughter, and his punishment fixed at confinement in the penitentiary for a period of five years.

The appellant was about 34 years of age, had been married about nine years; his wife was about 31 years of age, and there was one child. Before the marriage deceased had been a suitor of appellant's wife, and after the marriage there had been conducted between the deceased and Mrs. Boaz a clandestine correspondence, and interviews had taken place, of which the appellant was ignorant at the time. A few days before the homicide, Mrs. Boaz, with her child, left her home in Memphis, Tex., and disappeared. The appellant went to Dallas in search of her, and made inquiry of the deceased over the phone touching her whereabouts, and was denied information. Appellant went to Navarro county in search of his wife, and there, in conversation with a friend of hers, learned of clandestine correspondence that had taken place some time before. He had in the meantime intercepted some of the letters from the deceased, and had concluded from them that the relations between the deceased and his wife were suspicious, if not criminal, and in one of the letters there was embodied, according to the evidence, a threat against the appellant. Returning to Dallas, the appellant went into a barber shop in which the deceased worked, though appellant had not seen him for a number of years, and, according to his theory, did not know him. The deceased, taking a satchel or grip, and putting some articles in it, left the barber shop, and the appellant, hearing the name of the deceased called, followed him, and, according to his theory, overtook him while the deceased was in the act of putting his grip into an automobile; and, upon appellant's accosting deceased and seeking information, the deceased assumed a hostile attitude, and attempted to open the grip, as appellant believed, to secure a pistol, whereupon the appellant shot. There was testimony introduced to the effect that a pistol was seen in the grip in the car of the deceased after the homicide. This, however, was controverted.

It was shown by Mrs. Boaz, who was introduced as a witness on behalf of her husband, that a clandestine correspondence had been conducted between her and the deceased, and that on one or more occasions she had met the deceased in a hotel in Dallas, and had been alone with him in a room with the door locked for a considerable time; that on the occasion of her disappearance she had come to Dallas, and had seen the deceased, and had a meeting with him of the kind described above in the hotel. She also testified upon behalf of appellant that there was a threat against the appellant in one of the deceased's letters, which had come to the knowledge of the appellant, and that, because of the knowledge acquired touching the correspondence, appellant was furious.

The state's theory and testimony indicated that the appellant went into the barber shop where the deceased worked, wearing a handkerchief over his face as a means of disguise, and that, when the deceased left the shop, the appellant followed him; that, before leaving, McDowell stated he was going out to shave a man, and would be back soon. There were three wounds on the deceased, each of them entering the back. A state witness said that, while talking to a man on the street, his companion said, "Look," and he saw McDowell running, and the appellant following him. They were about 40 or 50 feet apart; that he saw the first shot fired, which was fired when they were about 50 or 60 feet distant from each other. The deceased was running, had nothing in his hands that could be seen. They continued to run until the third shot was fired, when McDowell fell; that between the first and the third shots McDowell ran something like 90 feet. Another witness said he saw McDowell put something in the car, and turn as though to crank the car; that he looked up, and appeared surprised and startled, and then turned and ran fast, and the witness saw the appellant with a pistol in his hand. The parties went out of the sight of the witness before the first shot was fired.

[1] The refusal to grant a continuance is made the subject of complaint. The absent witnesses named in the application were Albert Wesley and Joe Davis. It is charged in the application, which was the first, that Joe Davis was a resident of Memphis, Tex., but temporarily stationed at Camp Travis, in San Antonio, and was a member of 353d Motor Truck Company. The indictment was filed on March 11, and the day fixed for the trial was April 8. A subpœna was issued for Joe Davis at the address mentioned in the application March 26, and returned not executed on the 29th of March, 1919. We have discovered in the record no reasons stated for the failure of the appellant to apply for the subpœna for the witness at an earlier date. Fourteen or fifteen days elapsed between the filing of the indictment and the issuance of the subpœna. In the meantime, the case was set for trial the 8th of April. The subpœna was returned not executed some 9 or 10 days before the date of trial, and the record shows no effort of the appellant after the subpœna was returned to secure the attendance of the witness. The affidavit of the witness attached to the motion for a new trial indicates that, during all of the time from March 6 until after April 8, he was at San Antonio with Motor Transport Corps No. 353. In his affidavit it is stated:

"That he was in said camp continuously from the 6th day of March, 1919, and a casual inquiry at his camp headquarters would have disclosed his whereabouts between said date of March 6 and April 8, 1919."

This affidavit indicates that by the exercise of diligence the appellant could have secured the attendance of the witness. The fact that the subpœna was returned on the 29th day of March, 8 days after it was issued, with the statement by the officer that the witness had not been found, would not, we think, excuse further effort on the part of appellant to procure his attendance. The case of Todd v. State, 57 Tex. Cr. R. 26, 121 S. W. 506, is in point. The indictment was filed January 23. The subpœna was returned the 27th day of January, and the trial began the 2d of February. The accused having failed to apply for other process, his diligence was held incomplete. Other cases in point are Holmes v. State, 38 Tex. Cr. R. 370, 42 S. W. 996; Cromwell v. State, 59 Tex. Cr. R. 525, 129 S. W. 622; Jones v. State, 65 Tex. Cr. R. 69, 144 S. W. 252; Giles v. State, 66 Tex. Cr. R. 638, 148 S. W. 317; Dean v. State, 29 S. W. 477; Stephens v. State, 69 Tex. Cr. R. 437, 154 S. W. 996.

[2] The subpœna relied on for Albert Wesley was issued the 5th day of April, and in the return it is disclosed that he had left for Virginia a year before, and was in the army. Wesley was a resident of Dallas county, and the return on the subpœna indicates that knowledge of his departure from the state, if not possessed by the appellant, could have been acquired by him by the use of diligence, and the deposition of Wesley taken if desired. And apparently, if the subpœna for him had been issued soon after the indictment was filed, the information would have come to appellant by means of a return on the subpœna within time to have taken his deposition.

[3] The witness Davis, if present, would have testified that about a year before the homicide he was in the barber shop in the Oriental Hotel, and the barber shaving him stated that he was the suitor of Mrs. Boaz before her marriage, and that before she was married she was a good woman, and that Dr. Boaz was no man at all, and had caused her to do as she had, and further stated that Dr. Boaz knew of correspondence with his wife, was jealous of the barber, and was watching him; that the barber further stated that he was expecting trouble with Dr. Boaz, and would be prepared to protect himself against him. By the witness Wesley the appellant expected to show that he carried letters written by appellant's wife to deceased, and by the deceased to her. In passing upon the motion for a new trial, the court had before it the evidence in the case, which disclosed without controversy, as we understand the record, that a clandestine correspondence was conducted between the deceased and appellant's wife. The testimony

of Wesley, therefore, was but cumulative upon an uncontroverted issue. The testimony of Davis was in part upon a similar issue, though it also tended to show an uncommunicated threat made by the deceased against the appellant. This evidence would have been admissible as bearing upon the question of self-defense, but, inasmuch as it was shown by the evidence, and not disputed, that the deceased had made a threat against the appellant which was communicated to him, we would not feel warranted in holding that the evidence was so important as to show an abuse of discretion by the trial judge in failing to grant a new trial for the absence of the witnesses, the diligence to secure his attendance, falling short of the legal requirements.

[4] The appellant having introduced his wife as a witness, and proved by her that she had had clandestine correspondence with the deceased, and had met him at the Oriental Hotel in Dallas and occupied a room with him for several hours with the doors locked, the cross-examination of his wife, developing that at this meeting no criminal conduct took place, was, we think, germane to the direct inquiry and legitimate cross-examination. The appellant having on his direct examination disclosed the meeting between his wife and the deceased, it was proper for the state to interrogate her as to all that took place between them. Their conduct while in the room was a legitimate subject of inquiry. It was a part of the same transaction, and was within the statute which says:

"When a detailed act, declaration, conversation or writing is given in evidence, any other act, declaration or writing which is necessary to make it fully understood or to explain the same may also be given in evidence." Vernon's Ann. C. C. P. art. 811.

Appellant having called his wife as a witness to prove a part of the transaction, she became competent to prove it all.

[5] The court instructed the jury upon self-defense, embodying the right to defend against apparent as well as against real danger, and also charged upon appellant's right to act upon a demonstration manifesting the intent upon the part of the deceased to carry out a threat. The charge in no way qualified or abridged the right of perfect self-defense. In this state of the record, it was not incumbent upon the court to instruct the jury that appellant had a right to arm himself in anticipation of an attack from the deceased. The complaint of his failure to do so, however, is not tenable, for the further reason that the court gave a charge prepared by the appellant to the effect that the appellant had the right to seek the deceased, and in doing so to arm himself, and that his so doing would not be considered as a circumstance against him, and would in no wise impair

his perfect right of self-defense. Williford v. State, 38 Tex. Cr. R. 393, 42 S. W. 972; Alfred Smith v. State, 81 Tex. Cr. R. 368, 195 S. W. 595.

[6, 7] The court, in the thirteenth paragraph of his charge, having instructed the jury that the appellant had the right to use any means at his command to protect himself, and that he was in no event bound to retreat, was not in error in failing to repeat the instruction at the request of the appellant. And the same is true with reference to the law of communicated threats. Nor does it occur to us that in charging on the law of threats the court failed to instruct the jury to grant the appellant the benefit of reasonable doubt. The instruction given was to the effect that, if they believed that the appellant had been informed that a threat had been made, and that at the time he shot the deceased the latter did, or was doing, some act, or spoke some word, which from appellant's standpoint appeared to him to indicate or manifest an intent on the part of the deceased to carry such threat into execution, the killing would be justifiable; and in the succeeding paragraph the jury was instructed that, if they believed beyond a reasonable doubt at the time the appellant shot him the deceased did or was doing no act, or spoke no word, which from appellant's standpoint reasonably appeared to him to indicate or manifest an intention on deceased's part to carry the threat into execution, then the appellant could not justify upon the ground of threats.

A general instruction to the effect that the burden of proof was upon the state to prove the guilt beyond a reasonable doubt, and that in case of a reasonable doubt they would acquit, was embraced in the charge. We find no exception to the charge upon the ground that the law of reasonable doubt was not sufficiently charged on. The criticism in the brief of counsel is based upon the refusal by the court to give certain instructions requested by the appellant. These instructions, so far as they relate to the subject of the law of threats, were nothing more than substantial repetitions of the paragraphs of the main charge upon that subject. They were no more definite upon the subject of reasonable doubt than was the main charge, and no special charge, specifically directed to the amendment of the supposed omission in the court's charge to fully instruct on the law of reasonable doubt, appears to have been requested. The rule of law applicable to the matter in hand, we think, is given in Powell's Case, 28 Tex. App. 398, 13 S. W. 601, from which we quote:

"With respect to the charge on threats and self-defense, the objection is urged that it requires the jury to believe that the facts existed which constituted self-defense before they could acquit defendant, whereas the law is that if they entertained a reasonable doubt of the existence of such facts they should acquit him. In this case the court charged the rule of reasonable doubt generally, making it applicable to the whole case, and under repeated decisions of this court this was sufficient. McCullough v. State, 23 Tex. App. 620; Ashlock v. State, 16 Tex. App. 13; Barr v. State, 10 Tex. App. 507."

Instances in which this rule has been approved are numerous. See Rose's Notes on Texas Reports, vol. 5, p. 775; Simpson v. State, 81 Tex. Cr. R. 389, 196 S. W. 835; Head v. State, 82 Tex. Cr. R. 214, 198 S. W. 581, and cases collated; Clay v. State, 75 Tex. Cr. R. 387, 170 S. W. 744; Vernon's Tex. Crim. Stats. vol. 2, p. 684.

[8] Complaint is made of the failure to instruct the jury at the request of appellant that he had a right to continue to shoot as long as the danger continued, as viewed from his standpoint. The necessity of such a charge in a given case depends upon the facts and the manner in which the issues are submitted to the jury. Clark v. State, 56 Tex. Cr. R. 295, 120 S. W. 179; Smith v. State, 57 Tex. Cr. R. 455, 123 S. W 698; Woodward v. State, 54 Tex. Cr. R. 89, 111 S. W. 941. There are cases in which such a charge is required to protect the accused under the law of manslaughter. These are cases, however, in which the conviction is for murder. Lagrone v. State, 84 Tex. Cr. R. 609, 209 S. W. 411. There being no charge submitting the theory that the appellant fired the subsequent shots after the danger had ceased, the inquiry is, Does the evidence suggest that in firing the subsequent shots he was under a reasonable apprehension, as viewed from his standpoint, that the danger continued? Lynch v. State, 24 Tex. Cr. App. 350, 6 S. W. 190, 5 Am. St. Rep. 888; Faubian v. State, 83 Tex. Cr. R. 234, 203 S. W. 898; Thompson v. State, 85 Tex. Cr. R. 144, 210 S. W. 801, and cases cited. The court instructed the jury in a special charge that, if the first shot inflicted a mortal wound, and that in firing it the appellant was acting in self-defense, they would not consider as a circumstance against him that he had fired additional shots, or inflicted upon the deceased additional wounds, which were not fired or inflicted in self-defense. The evidence tended to show that each of the wounds was fatal. Looking to the evidence, it appears from appellant's testimony that he followed the deceased out of the barber shop for the purpose of conversing with him. He had seen the deceased put something in a satchel, and carry it with him out of the barber shop. Appellant saw deceased at his automobile, and the appellant said:

"He said he didn't care to have any conversation with me, had had all he wanted out of me, and began to dig in the grip which he had in the automobile, and I reached for my gun. At that time he started back, and I shot him. I thought he was going after a gun in the grip, is the reason I shot. I could not tell what it was, but I saw him put something in the grip, and he was taking it out, trying to open it, and when he saw me pull my gun he started away. He was looking at me when I pulled my gun. I don't know how many times I shot. I don't know whether he turned and ran. I don't know anything at all about that. I don't know whether he stayed there or not. I know I shot. I saw him going into the case. He said angry words. I don't know whether I was shooting him to death as he was running from me. I don't know that I shot him three times in the back; cannot recall anything after I shot him."

The state's theory and testimony is that when the deceased saw the appellant he fled, and that when the first shot was fired they were 40 or 50 feet apart, and that the deceased continued running, the appellant pursuing him, the distance between increasing; that all the shots took effect in the back; that the deceased at the time he fled was without arms. Neither in the testimony of the state nor the appellant do we find any evidence which impresses us as raising an issue calling for a charge upon appellant's right to continue to shoot. Viewing the state's testimony, there was no issue of self-defense—the deceased was fleeing, he was unarmed, he had abandoned the difficulty. In its strongest light, the appellant's testimony raises the issue of self-defense upon previous threats and apparent danger at the time he fired the first shot. He disclaims any knowledge of what subsequently occurred, and, so far as we are able to discern, there is an absence of evidence which requires a charge instructing the jury that the appellant had the right to continue to shoot while, viewed from his standpoint, the danger existed. There was never any danger, real or apparent; from the state's testimony, the deceased was fleeing from the start. The appellant discloses what operated upon his mind at the time he first fired, but furnishes by his evidence no basis for an affirmative charge that the subsequent shots were fired in the belief that the danger had not ceased.

After a careful examination and consideration of each of the matters presented for review in the record, we are constrained to conclude that no error is disclosed which would justify or authorize a reversal of the judgment.

It is therefore affirmed.

On Motion for Rehearing.

HAWKINS, J. [9] Appellant insists in his motion for rehearing that the trial court erred in the fourteenth and seventeenth paragraphs of his charge in shifting the burden of proof on the defensive issues, and that these matters were sufficiently pointed out by the special charges Nos. 5 and 11, which were refused, and that our opinion heretofore rendered is erroneous.

No objection is made now to the fourteenth and seventeenth paragraphs, except that they should have concluded with a statement, "or if you have a reasonable doubt thereof." Without going into a discussion of the many cases cited by appellant in his brief, we desire to revert to the acts of the Legislature in 1913, art. 743, Vernon's C. C. P. No exception was presented to the court's charge specifically pointing out an omission in the particular now complained of, and while the special charges requested contained a proper clause with reference to the "reasonable doubt" as applied to the defensive issues, yet there was nothing in the special charges, or in any objection to the main charge, to pertinently call the court's attention to the matter now urged as error. The last clause in article 743 reads:

"And all objections to the charge and on account of refusal or modification of special charges shall be made at the time of the trial."

If what is now urged as such a serious objection was at the time of the trial overlooked by the able attorneys representing appellant, is it likely any great harm befell appellant by reason thereof? The jurors knew very well what the main issues in the case were, and it is not to be presumed by this court that they indulged in the refinement of analysis in the consideration of the case as do attorneys in discussion of legal propositions. For the court to hold that the requesting of a special instruction, which the trial court could legitimately consider as a substantial repetition of his main charge, can take the place of an objection which should pertinently point out the matter complained of, would virtually work a repeal of the statute. We do not desire to be understood as holding that, where the special charge goes to some substantial matter, it would not in some cases be erroneous to refuse it, even though no objection was presented because of its omission from the main charge; yet, where the complaint only goes to the omission of a few words, we feel that, in justice to the trial courts, and to make effective the law referred to, objectionable omission should be pointed out by exception then made. The case of Walker v. State, 229 S. W. 527, presents very much the same situation, and sustains what we have written.

In the brief and argument upon rehearing we are referred to Johnson v. State, 29 Tex. Cr. App. 150, 15 S. W. 647, and the line of authorities following that case, as laying down a more correct rule than the one announced in Powell's Case, 28 Tex. App. 398, 13 S. W. 599, and others referred to in our original opinion. Perhaps we did not make our meaning clear. Just preceding the reference to the Powell Case this language was used: "We find no exception to the charge upon the ground that the law of reasonable doubt was not sufficiently charged on," and then follows a statement in which we were inaccurate, to the effect that the special charges requested were no more definite upon the subject of "reasonable doubt" than was the main charge. What we were undertaking to say was that, in the absence of an exception pointedly calling the court's attention to an omission as to "reasonable doubt" applied to each defensive issue, the Powell Case announces a correct rule.

[10] Appellant requested the following special instruction:

"You are instructed that, in passing upon the issues in this case, it is your duty to place yourselves as nearly as you can in the place of defendant at the time of the homicide, and to view all the attendant facts and circumstances as they reasonably appeared to him from his standpoint, at the time, and not as they may appear to you now."

We do not think it was necessary to submit this charge. The court had already told the jury that—

"It was not necessary that there should be actual danger, as a person has the right to defend his life and person from apparent danger as fully and to the same extent as he would had the danger been real, provided he acted upon a reasonable apprehension of danger as it appeared to him from his standpoint at the time."

We have carefully examined the other grounds urged in support of the motion for rehearing. They were all considered and discussed in the original opinion, and, we believe, correctly disposed of.

While we might have reached a somewhat different verdict had we occupied the place of jurors, yet, passing upon the case in the light of the record, the judgment must be sustained, and the motion for rehearing is overruled.

CANTER v. CANTER. (No. 655.)

(Court of Civil Appeals of Texas. Beaumont. May 26, 1921.)

Appeal and error ⟲282, 744—In case tried to court, motion for new trial not necessary, but assignments of error must be filed before appeal.

On appeal from a judgment in a case tried before the court without a jury, assignments of error in appellant's brief cannot be considered, where none were filed in lower court, though it is not necessary to file a motion for new trial.

Appeal from District Court, Liberty County; D. F. Singleton, Judge.

Suit by Rhola Smith Canter against Day Canter for divorce. Judgment for plaintiff, and defendant appeals. Affirmed.

O. H. Cain and E. B. Pickett, Jr., both of Liberty, for appellant.
O. R. Wilson and J. Llewellyn, both of Liberty, for appellee.

O'QUINN, J. This is a suit by Rhola Smith Canter against Day Canter for divorce, partition of the community property, and the custody of their five minor children. The case was tried before the court without a jury, and judgment rendered awarding the divorce, dividing the community property, and giving to plaintiff the custody of the children, as prayed for.

Appellant presents three assignments of error: (1) That the court erred in not sustaining his general demurrer to appellee's petition; (2) that the evidence was not sufficient to sustain the judgment; (3) in refusing to hear further evidence on the part of appellant. Appellee objects to this court's considering appellant's assignments of error, because same (1) were not filed in the court below; and (2) because no motion for new trial having been filed, article 1612, Vernon's Sayles' Civ. St., and Rules 101 and 101a for District and County Courts (159 S. W. xi), relating to assignments of error, are mandatory. The record fails to show that any motion for a new trial was filed, or that any assignments of error were filed in the court below before the taking of the transcript from the clerk's office, or at any time. Where a case is tried before the court without a jury, it is not necessary to file a motion for new trial in order to appeal, but in that case it is necessary to file assignments of error. There having been no assignments of error filed, as required by article 1612, Vernon's Sayles' Civ. St., we cannot consider the assignments in appellant's brief. Article 1612, Vernon's Sayles' Civil Statutes; Witherspoon v. Crawford, 153 S. W. 633; Smith v. Smith, 107 S. W. 888; Rules 101 and 101a (159 S. W. xi); Dallam County v. S. H. Supply Co., 176 S. W. 798.

Finding no fundamental error in the record, the judgment is affirmed.

KANAMAN v. GAHAGAN. (No. 7452.)

(Court of Civil Appeals of Texas. Dallas.
May 28, 1921.)

Appeal and error ⚖⇒1195(1)—After affirmance
by Supreme Court, opinion of Court of Civil
Appeals stands as law of case.

Where the Court of Civil Appeals certified
a question to the Supreme Court, which answered it in the affirmative, affirming the opinion of the Court of Civil Appeals, such opinion
of the Court of Civil Appeals, originally handed down, reversing and rendering the judgment,
stands as the law of the case.

Appeal from District Court, Dallas County; Jas. P. Haven, Judge.

On motion for rehearing. Motion overruled, and former opinion affirmed.

For former opinion, see 185 S. W. 619.
See, also, 230 S. W. 141.

Adams & Stennis, of Dallas, for appellant.
M. L. Morris and John W. Pope, both of
Dallas, for appellee.

HAMILTON, J. This cause was appealed
from the Sixty-Eighth district court of Dallas county. On February 5, 1916, this court
delivered its opinion reversing the judgment
of the trial court, and rendering judgment
for appellant, because of fundamental error.
The opinion of this court so deciding the case
is reported in 185 S. W. 619. That opinion
clearly states all the facts and exhaustively
considers the questions presented. For a
full understanding of the issues thoroughly
considered, and the conclusions correctly adduced, we refer to the report of the opinion.

The suit was upon notes executed and delivered by appellant, under appellee's direction, as consideration for certain shares of
stock in a prospective corporation in process
of organization, which was later incorporated and the stock issued. In the course of
events preceding suit, the notes were transferred by the promoters of the corporation
to appellant, their employé; the consideration for the transfer being that he might do
with the notes for them whatever his judgment dictated. Maturity arrived, appellant
failed to pay, and the suit was filed. This
court adduced from the facts that the transactions involved resulted in the issuance of
stock of a corporation in violation of article
12, § 6, of the state Constitution, which provides that—

"No corporation shall issue stock or bonds,
except for money paid, labor done, or property
actually received."

The case having been decided as above indicated, the appellee filed an insistent motion for a rehearing, and the court, in considering this motion, arrived at the conclusion that the holding upon the decisive feature of the case was in apparent conflict with
certain other decisions of our appellate
courts, whereupon the case was presented
to the Supreme Court by this court upon the
following certified question:

"Do the facts and transactions recited in
our statement of the case constitute, within the
meaning of the Constitution and statute, an
issue of corporate stock?"

The Supreme Court has answered this
question in the affirmative, affirming the
opinion of this court above cited. See opinion of Supreme Court in W. I. Kanaman v.
H. I. Gahagan, 230 S. W. 141. The opinion
of this court originally handed down, reversing and rendering the judgment, and published in 185 S. W. 619, therefore stands as the
law of the case, and reference is made to
that decision without further discussion.

The motion for rehearing is overruled.

———

JEMISON et al. v. ESTES. (No. 1229.)

(Court of Civil Appeals of Texas. El Paso.
May 19, 1921.)

1. Trial ⚖⇒255(1)—Charge that jurors were
exclusive judges of facts must be requested.

Failure to charge jurors that they were
the exclusive judges of the facts proved, the
credibility of the witnesses and the weight to
be given to their testimony, held not reversible
error, in absence of request for such instruction, since in absence of such request it will
be presumed that the charge as given was satisfactory.

2. Appeal and error ⚖⇒544(1)—Court cannot
consider propriety of giving charge, in absence of statement of facts.

In the absence of a statement of facts, the
Court of Civil Appeals cannot pass on the
propriety of giving a charge as to jurors being exclusive judges of the facts proved, the
credibility of the witnesses, and the weight to
be given to their testimony.

3. Appeal and error ⚖⇒544(1)—Court will not
pass on whether issues were fully submitted,
in absence of statement of facts.

In absence of a statement of facts, the
Court of Civil Appeals cannot say that the issues made by the pleading and the evidence
were not fully submitted.

4. Trial ⚖⇒352(4)—Issue must be supported
by evidence to be submitted.

To justify the submission of an issue of
fact tendered by the pleading, it must be supported by the evidence.

5. Appeal and error ⚖⇒1062(1)—Error in submission of whether brokers were procuring
cause immaterial, in view of finding that
broker had no contract with owner.

In broker's action for commission, where
the jury found that defendant did not list the
land with broker for sale at the time and

on the terms alleged, and did not agree to pay brokerage commission, and that if there had been such a listing the brokers had in effect abandoned the contract, any error in submission of whether brokers were the procuring cause of the sale of the land would be immaterial.

6. Appeal and error ⟨key⟩218(2)—Failure to submit issue not available on appeal, in absence of request.

Failure to submit issue is not available on appeal, in absence of request therefor.

Error from District Court, Midland County; W. P. Leslie, Judge.

Suit by J. M. Jemison and another against H. P. Estes. Judgment for defendant, and plaintiffs bring error. Affirmed.

Garrard, Baker & Russell, of Midland, for plaintiffs in error.

E. M. Whitaker, of El Paso, and J. M. Caldwell, of Midland, for defendant in error.

WALTHALL, J. J. M. Jemison and W. J. Moran sued H. P. Estes for $1,316, alleging, in substance, that Estes listed for sale certain real estate described at a price then agreed upon, and contracted with Jemison to pay him a commission of 5 per cent. upon his procuring a purchaser at a price of $8 per acre, on a patented basis; that Jemison assigned to Moran a one-half interest in the contract; that Estes knew of such assignment to Moran and acquiesced therein, in that he accepted the efforts of each of plaintiffs to sell the lands and made no objection thereto, and at all times during the negotiations for the sale of the lands Estes accepted efforts of each of plaintiffs, and is now estopped from setting up as a defense that the contract with Jemison could not be assigned. Plaintiffs alleged that they procured a purchaser for said lands in the person of Roy Parks, who was ready, willing, and able to buy said land, and who in fact did buy the lands at the price stated, alleged that they were the procuring cause of the sale by defendant to Parks, in that they brought the parties together, and for a long period of time carried on negotiations between Estes and Parks, carried Parks upon the property, pricing same to him, and did and performed things usually done in such instances, and alleged that Estes ratified the transfer of interest to Moran.

Estes answered by general demurrer, special exception, misjoinder of parties, general denial, specially denied that at the time of the sale of the property to Parks, plaintiffs, or either of them, were the agents for the sale of the lands, or had authority to offer same for sale; denied that either or both of plaintiffs were the procuring cause of the sale of the land; alleged that if plaintiffs, or either of them, ever offered said land

for sale to Parks, said offer or attempt to sell occurred long prior to the sale by defendant, and that plaintiffs were unable to make said sale, and that, if any negotiations for the sale by plaintiffs had taken place, such negotiations had ceased, and that long thereafter Parks and defendant began new and independent negotiations which resulted in the sale of said lands to Parks, and that such sale was not through the efforts of plaintiffs. Defendant denied knowledge of any assignment of any interest in the contract by Jemison to Moran, and denied that he had ratified same.

The case was tried with a jury and submitted on special issues. On issues submitted by the court the jury found:

1. Estes did not contract and list with Jemison, on or about May 1, 1918, the lands described in the plaintiffs' petition, at the price and upon the terms therein alleged.

2. (a) Jemison thereafter transferred to Moran a one-half interest in said contract, in consideration of the efforts of Moran to assist in procuring a purchaser for said lands. (b) Estes did not know of and agree to such agreement and transfer between Jemison and Moran.

3. Neither Jemison and Moran, nor either of them, were the procuring cause of the sale of said lands to Parks.

4. Jemison and Moran discontinued efforts to sell the lands to Parks after the final closing of the Estes sale.

5. Jemison and Moran did not renew such efforts prior to the time Parks told Estes he would take the property at $8 per acre in case he could raise the money.

At the request of plaintiffs the court gave to the jury the following special charge:

"A procuring cause, as used in the sense of a real estate broker procuring for a client a purchaser, means the original discovery of the purchaser by the broker, together with the starting of the negotiations by him, together with the final closing by or on behalf of his client with the purchaser, through the efforts of the broker; and such is true, although the negotiations are left to the owner and seller, after the purchaser was procured."

On the findings of the jury judgment was rendered for Estes. Plaintiffs below bring this case to this court by writ of error.

No statement of facts are found in the record. Plaintiffs in error claim that it is fundamental error—that is, error in law apparent on the face of the record—for the court to fail to instruct the jury that they were the exclusive judges of the facts proved, the credibility of the witnesses, and the weight to be given to their testimony.

[1, 2] In our opinion the matter complained of does not present fundamental error. It certainly could not be deemed affirmative error in the court's charge, in submitting to

the jury the law of the case, for the court not to tell the jury that they are the exclusive judges of the facts proved, the credibility of the witnesses, and the weight to be given to their testimony. Such charges inform the jury only as to their province, power, and duty, and may be properly given. If, however, the plaintiffs in error desired such charge to be given, they should have so requested, and, not having done so, it will be presumed that they were satisfied with the charge as given. In the absence of a statement of facts this court cannot pass upon the propriety of giving such a charge. The record does not present prejudicial error in the matter complained of. None of the cases referred to by plaintiffs in error are in point, and we need not review them.

The second specification of error complained of is that the court should have defined to the jury what was meant by the term "procuring cause." The record presented shows that the court gave a special charge requested by plaintiffs defining that term. As showing fundamental error, plaintiffs in error present the following proposition:

"The plaintiffs' petition seeking a recovery for a sale of defendant's lands under brokerage contract, and the defendant joining issue with him by allegation of abandonment of the part of plaintiffs, and the subsequent sale by the defendant without the assistance of the plaintiffs, it was fundamental error in advising the jury that the plaintiffs would be entitled to recover, if they were the procuring cause of the sale, even though the buyer and seller consummated their own trade, and the plaintiffs were not present at the time of the closing thereof."

[3-5] We are not quite sure that we get the real meaning intended to be conveyed by the proposition. Plaintiffs in error do not indicate in the proposition, nor in the statement thereunder, nor in the argument, the issue submitted of which they complain. The court submitted to the jury the issue as to whether plaintiffs in error or either of them were the procuring cause of the sale of the land, and in connection therewith submitted to the jury the requested special charge defining the term "procuring cause." While issues 4 and 5 are not quite clear in their meaning, the court in said two issues undertook to submit to the jury the facts pleaded in the seventh paragraph of the answer, to the effect that plaintiffs had been unable to consummate a sale to Parks, and had ceased their efforts to do so, and that thereafter Estes and Parks began new and independent negotiations resulting in a sale by Estes to Parks of the land. We might agree with plaintiffs in error that the real, determining issue in the case, as made in the petition, was not submitted to the jury, but not having a statement of the facts, we cannot say that the issues as made by the pleading and the evidence were not fully submitted. The pleading tenders the issue of fact, but to justify its submission it must be supported by the evidence.

The jury found under the first issue, practically, that Estes did not contract and list the land with Jemison for sale at the time and on the terms alleged, and did not agree to pay a commission on a sale, and under subsequent issues they found that if there was such contract and listing, plaintiffs in error had, in effect, abandoned such contract. If these issues were supported by the evidence it would be immaterial whether plaintiffs in error had found a purchaser ready, able, and willing to buy, and that he did buy, the land, and that they were the procuring cause of the sale. Dunn v. Price, 87 Tex. 318, 28 S. W. 681; Newell v. Lafarelle, 225 S. W. 853.

[6] We might add here that, if the court did not submit such issue as the pleading and the evidence disclosed by the record would demand, to have a review of such failure, plaintiffs in error must have requested the submission of such issue, and the court's refusal to submit could be made the basis of a review of such error.

Judge HIGGINS concurs in the result.

Finding no reversible error, the case is affirmed.

W. T. RAWLEIGH CO. v. SMITH et al.
(No. 1215.)

(Court of Civil Appeals of Texas. El Paso. April 28, 1921. Rehearing Denied June 16, 1921.)

1. Appeal and error ⟨⇒⟩989—On question of sufficiency of evidence, only evidence supporting verdict considered.

In determining whether there is sufficient evidence to sustain a verdict, an appellate court must reject all evidence favorable to the losing party and consider only that sustaining the verdict.

2. Monopolies ⟨⇒⟩21—Province of court stated.

In determining whether a contract for sales of goods for resale by the buyer violates the anti-trust statute (Vernon's Sayles' Ann. Civ. St. 1914, arts. 7796–7818), it is the province of the court to construe the original contract and also to construe facts found by the jury as to communications subsequent to the contract in connection with the original contract.

3. Evidence ⟨⇒⟩437—Monopolies ⟨⇒⟩17(1)—Communications subsequent to contract held admissible and to render contract violative of statute.

Though a contract for sales of goods to one purchasing for resale provided that it constituted the sole agreement, and that booklets, bulletins, and literature sent to the buyer should be considered as educational and advisory, and not as altering the contract, evidence of subsequent communications *held* admissible to show that the seller restricted the buyer's territory, fixed the resale prices, and required the buyer to give his entire time to the business, and these facts, when established, render the contract violative of the Anti-Trust Law.

Appeal from District Court, Jones County; W. R. Chapman, Judge.

Action by the W. T. Rawleigh Company against J. F. Smith and others. From a judgment for defendants, plaintiff appeals. Affirmed.

Walter S. Pope, of Anson, for appellant Jno. B. Thomas, of Anson, and E. T. Brooks, of Abilene, for appellees.

HARPER, C. J. Suit was instituted in the district court of Jones county, Tex., by the W. T. Rawleigh Company against W. J. Hendrix, principal debtor, and J. F. Smith, G. L. Goza, and W. A. Howard, as sureties or guarantors, for a balance of $1,543.53, besides interest upon open, verified account for goods, wares, and merchandise sold and delivered to W. J. Hendrix on or about June 10, 1916, and various dates thereafter fully shown on itemized and verified account attached to plaintiff's original petition.

Appellant alleged that appellee W. J. Hendrix on or about December 7, 1917, executed and entered into a written contract with appellant wherein he agreed to pay any balance due plaintiff for goods previously and subsequently purchased at wholesale price f. o. b. Freeport, Ill.; that appended to said contract and as a part of same is a guaranty contract executed on or about the same date by defendants J. F. Smith, G. L. Goza, and W. A. Howard, a copy of all of which was appended to plaintiff's petition in which they bound and obligated themselves to pay said account.

Appellees answered by general and special exception, general denial, denying that said goods, wares, and merchandise were sold under the contract sued on, but alleged that they were sold on a subsequent contract, or else a subsequent enlargement on said original contract; that appellants restricted appellee Hendrix to certain prescribed territory in which to sell said goods, to a certain price for which to sell said goods, and to the sole business of selling said goods, all of which was in violation of the Anti-Trust Laws of Texas (Vernon's Sayles' Ann. Civ. St. 1914, arts. 7796–7818), and in restraint of trade, and hence void. To which answer appellant answered with general and special exceptions and general denial and specially alleged that all communication between appellant and appellee Hendrix after the execution of said contract was merely educational and advisory and did not amount to a new contract or modify or change the contract sued on.

The case was submitted to the jury on the following special issues:

"Question No. 1: Did plaintiff and defendant W. J. Hendrix contract or agree that the territory in which the said W. J. Hendrix was to sell the goods of plaintiff was to be restricted?

"Question No. 2: Did plaintiff and defendant W. J. Hendrix contract or agree that defendant W. J. Hendrix was to sell the goods shipped him by plaintiff at a price fixed or to be fixed by plaintiff?

"Question No. 3: Did plaintiff and defendant W. J. Hendrix contract or agree that defendant W. J. Hendrix was to be restricted alone to the business of selling goods purchased by defendant W. J. Hendrix from the plaintiff?"

All of which were answered in the affirmative, and on which verdict the court rendered judgment that appellant take nothing and appellees recover of appellant their costs.

Motion for new trial was filed, presented, and overruled, and the case is now properly and regularly before this court on appeal.

Assignments 1 and 9 insist that the court should have instructed a verdict for the appellant, and that the judgment entered is contrary to the law and the evidence, and 2, 3, and 4 urge that there is no evidence to support the findings of the jury to the three special issues submitted.

[1] The following are some of the facts relied upon by appellee to support the verdict. We confine ourselves to these matters because the rule is that, in passing upon whether there is sufficient evidence to sustain a verdict, an appellate court must reject all evidence favorable to the losing party, and consider only that sustaining the verdict, and if the jury might have reached such a verdict on the evidence, the court on appeal cannot set it aside. Cartwright v. Canode, 106 Tex. 502, 171 S. W. 696.

The exact question presented is that the evidence in the record has no probative value as a defense to the cause of action asserted by the plaintiff. The appellant objected to its admission by the court, and has assigned errors because it was not competent evidence to vary the provisions of a written contract.

The account sued on is an open verified account showing items for the years 1916, 1917, and 1918. The contract recites:

"Renewal Contract.

"(1) This contract made at the city of Freeport, state of Illinois, a corporation, between the Rawleigh Company, seller, and Hendrix, * * * of Texas, buyer.

"(2) That for and in consideration of the promises hereinafter contained to be kept and performed by the parties hereto, the seller * * * agrees to sell in such reasonable quantities as the buyer may. from time to time desire to purchase goods, wares, and merchandise manufactured or sold by it. But seller shall have the right to limit sales and shipments to the buyer or refuse to make any further sales and shipments should said buyer fail to make payments as agreed.

"(3) All goods sold to be delivered f. o. b. Freeport."

(4) Provides for the price.

(5), (6), and (7) provide for payments and the manner thereof.

(8) Sale of wagon to buyer.

(9) Seller agrees to repurchase all unsold goods.

(10) Provides means of terminating contract. To terminate in all events December 31, 1918.

(11) Agreement to extend by making new contract.

"(12) It is further understood and agreed that any and all booklets, bulletins, folders, leaflets, letters, and all literature of all nature which the seller may mail or send out to the buyer shall in no wise alter, modify, change, or effect this agreement, and shall only be considered as educational and advisory.

"(13) And it is further understood and agreed by and between the parties hereto that this contract includes and does and shall constitute the sole, only, and entire agreement between the parties hereto, and further that this contract cannot and shall not be changed or modified in any particular whatsoever by any employee or representative of the seller in any capacity, unless any such change or modification shall first be specifically reduced in writing and signed by both of the parties hereto, and then any such change or modification shall only be effective after the corporate seal of the seller shall have been duly affixed thereto."

The record discloses that this is a renewal contract of a similar one for the years preceding back to 1916.

Appended to this contract was an agreement executed by appellants Smith, Goza, and Howard by which, "in consideration of the extension of further time to the above-named buyer in which to pay his account for goods previously bought, and in consideration of extending further credit, they jointly and severally guaranteed * * * all moneys due and that may become due said seller under the terms of the above contract."

The defendant Hendrix testified:

"After the contract was executed I received the following:

" 'The W. T. Rawleigh Company, by C. P. Kiplinger, correspondent:

" 'We inclose vouchers describing the territory you selected: Part of Jones county, Texas, west of a line running north and south Stamford, Ruson, and Truby and north of the wagon road running west of Truby to the county line. Please sign and return the original and keep the duplicate for future reference.

" 'We are inclosing this with the understanding that you will select your headquarters in locality. * * *'

"Inclosed with this was the following instrument:

" 'Territory Selection Folder No. 5856. The W. T. Rawleigh Company, Freeport, Ill.

231 S.W.—51

" 'Gentlemen: I have your notice of acceptance of my contract. My selection of territory is described below. Please reserve all the territory for me except the incorporated municipalities therein and make a record of my selection upon receipt of this. I will complete my arrangements and expect to order first shipment of products shortly and will begin selling them promptly after their arrival.'

"I received those instruments after I had signed the contract. I sold a few of their goods out of that territory. I sold a few in the corner of Fisher and Stonewall counties. I wrote the company about it some of the customers in that corner of the counties were wanting me to come over on their territory. There was nobody selling those things on their side. [This letter was not produced.] The substance of this letter was that if I worked my territory as I should and as often as I should and as close as I should that I wouldn't have any use to cross out of it, be no need for me crossing out of it. I replied to that letter and explained it more fully. They replied that they thought I was a little peeved, and in it objected to me having any other territory. I never went out of the territory that they had given me any more after that except to stay all night when I was near the line. Did not sell anything outside of the territory except to leave something to pay for my night lodging. As to whether I followed any other trade or profession during that time I tried to farm a little in 1918. I got letters from them stating that they expected me to put in every day of my time in that business, at least five days in every week, in that business and no other.

"I got letters from them relative to selling their goods only. A letter dated April 15, 1918, contained the following: 'Don't be discouraged, just keep out on the road five and a half and six days each week and you are going to come out all right yet.' "

There are many letters and pamphlets and circulars copied in the statement of facts which have very little, if any, probative value, not copied here because the above will suffice for a predicate for the purposes of this opinion.

The first proposition is that—

"It is the province of the court, not the jury, to construe a written contract and where a contract specifically directs the exact method of its changes and modifications and provides that all letters, leaflets, and writing sent from plaintiff to defendant shall be merely educational and advisory it becomes the duty of the court to examine the evidence offered by the defendant, and if said evidence does not show that the contract has been so changed as its terms provide it was the duty of the court to instruct the jury to return a verdict for the plaintiff."

It will be noted that the appellee opposes a recovery in this case on the grounds that the transaction was in contravention of the Texas anti-trust statutes because under the contract, supplemented by letters and instructions the plaintiff sent Hendrix, who was governed thereby, the latter was required to confine his sales of the plaintiff's products to a designated territory to sell them at a designated retail price, and to devote all his time to this project, to the exclusion of other employment.

[2] It is true that it is the province of the court to construe the original contract, and also, after the jury had found the facts, to construe these after facts in connection with the original in arriving at the legal conclusion as to whether or not the anti-trust statute had been violated thereby.

[3] This court has upon two occasions passed upon these identical questions and has held to the contrary of appellant's contentions. Newby v. Rawleigh Co., 194 S. W. 1173; Whisenant v. Shores Mueller Co., 194 S. W. 1175. These cases were so nearly on all fours of the facts of this one and were so carefully considered that we think a reference thereto for our views fully expressed is sufficient.

We desire also to cite with approval the case of Caddell v. Watkins Med. Co., 227 S. W. 227, where additional logical and potent reasons are assigned for holding transactions of this kind obnoxious to provisions of our anti-trust statutes.

Finding no error, the cause is affirmed.

————

HOME LIFE & ACCIDENT CO. v. JORDAN.
(No. 8529.)

(Court of Civil Appeals of Texas. Dallas. May 7, 1921. Rehearing Denied June 11, 1921.)

1. Master and servant ⬥➡896—Compensation claim held within district court's jurisdiction.

In an injured employé's suit to set aside a decision of the Industrial Accident Board and to recover compensation under the Workmen's Compensation Law (Vernon's Ann. Civ. St. Supp. 1918, arts. 5246—1 to 5246—91), petition *held* to show jurisdiction in the district court, in that it stated a cause of action for compensation for total incapacity under section 10 (article 5246—18), or for partial incapacity, or total and partial incapacity combined, under sections 11, 11a (articles 5246—19, 5246—20), and not a cause of action for compensation for loss of index finger, or for ankylosis of such finger under section 12 (article 5246—21), which would have confined recovery to less than $500.

2. Pleading ⬥➡214(1)—Allegations of fact taken as true on demurrer.

Allegations of fact in petition must be treated as true on demurrer.

3. Master and servant ⬥➡401—Compensation claimant's petition for doctor's bills held insufficient.

In an injured employé's action under the Workmen's Compensation Law (Vernon's Ann. Civ. St. Supp. 1918, arts. 5246—1 to 5246—91), a petition which does not allege that there was

a failure to furnish reasonable medical aid when needed, or within a reasonable time after notice of the injury, nor that the doctor's charges therefor are reasonable, does not state a cause of action for the recovery of such charges.

4. Appeal and error ⬥➡1040(10)—Overruling of exception to allegations held harmless in view of judgment.

Overruling of exception to allegation as to doctor's bills incurred *held* harmless in view of plaintiff's failure to recover therefor.

5. Trial ⬥➡125(4)—Remarks of counsel in argument to jury held to inflame jurors' minds against defendant.

In injured employé's action for compensation against the employer's insurer, employé's counsel's remarks during argument that the plaintiff was an old man without money and without friends, who had suffered a terrible accident, whose health was broken, and whose nervous system was impaired, and that the jury was his only place of refuge, and that the defendant was a rich and powerful insurance company, an artificial person without a soul, that he had represented insurance companies and knew all their tricks, that they hated to pay a poor man what was justly due him, and that he had never heard of an insurance company that was willing to pay an honest claim, that defendant insurance company was no exception to the rule, that plaintiff had not been represented before the Industrial Accident Board, and that the Workmen's Compensation Law (Vernon's Ann. Civ. St. Supp. 1918, arts. 5246—1 to 5246—91) was one of the greatest outrages ever forced on the people of the state, *held* ground for reversal; such remarks tending to inflame the minds of the jurors against the defendant.

6. Appeal and error ⬥➡207—Improper remarks of counsel available on appeal notwithstanding failure to object.

Under Court Rules 39 and 41 (142 S. W. xiii, xiv), improper remarks of counsel in argument to jury are available on appeal, notwithstanding failure of party prejudiced thereby to object; it being the duty of the court on its own motion to confine counsel to legitimate argument.

————

Appeal from District Court, Dallas County; E. B. Muse, Judge.

Suit by Charles Jordan against the Home Life & Accident Company. Judgment for plaintiff, and defendant appeals. Reversed and remanded.

Burgess, Burgess, Chrestman & Brundidge, of Dallas, for appellant.

John White, of Dallas, for appellee.

TALBOT, J. The appellee brought this suit against the appellant to recover the compensation due him under what is known as the Texas Employers' Liability Act or Workmen's Compensation Law of this state (Vernon's Ann. Civ. St. Supp. 1918, arts. 5246—1 to 5246—91), on account of personal injuries alleged to have been sustained as the result of an accident to him while in the employment of the Republic Box Company at Dallas, Tex. Plaintiff alleged, in substance, that the accident and injury complained of occurred on the 29th day of January, 1919, in the course of his employment with the company; that said company at that time held a policy of insurance issued by the appellant covering the Republic Box Company's employés under said act; that the injury consisted in cutting off and severing the index finger on his left hand at the distal phalange, splitting said finger, and injuring the tendons, ligaments, and nerves of his left hand and finger and left arm, and that the injuries produced traumatic rheumatism; that the finger became stiff, and that the injuries totally disabled him for work for a period of 104 weeks, from the 6th day of February, 1919; that his weekly wage was $14.42, and he was entitled to compensation of 60 per cent. thereof, or $8.65 per week for 104 weeks, from the 6th day of February, 1919, making a total of $899.60; that by reason of the policy of insurance issued by defendant, it agreed to compensate plaintiff for his said injuries under the terms of said act; that plaintiff complied with all of the terms of the said Workmen's Compensation Law to be by him complied with; that he submitted his claim to the said Industrial Accident Board, which, on May 6, 1919, heard the same, and on said date rendered its judgment as follows: That on January 29, 1919, the Republic Box Company was a subscriber to said act and carried a policy of insurance with defendant; (2) that on said date plaintiff was an employé of said box company and as such was covered by said policy of insurance; (3) that on said date, in the course of his employment, plaintiff sustained injuries in the manner and to the extent set out in the report of accident, claim for compensation, and evidence in the cause; (4) that the average weekly wage of plaintiff, at the time and prior to the injury, was $14.42, and he was therefore entitled to compensation at the rate of $8.65 per week; (5) that as a result of said injury the plaintiff lost the use of the distal phalange of his index finger of his left hand and thereby became entitled to recover compensation from defendant for the period of 15 weeks, beginning February 6, 1919, and continuing thereafter until the full period of 15 weeks have expired; (6) that John White, as his attorney before the Board, was entitled to pay for his legal services in a sum equal to 15 per cent. of the first $1,000, and 10 per cent. of any sum paid in excess of $1,000; that the Board therefore ordered defendant to pay to plaintiff the sum of $8.65 per week for the period of 15 weeks, from and after February 6, 1919, less any and all sums theretofore paid on the claim, if any, and less the attorney's fees allowed; and further ordered defendant to pay John White, attorney, the amounts aforesaid, as attorney's fees.

Plaintiff further alleged that on May 8, 1919, he gave to all the parties interested notice that he was not willing and did not consent to abide by said final ruling and decision of said Board, and afterwards in due time filed this suit in the district court of Dallas county, Tex., having jurisdiction of the case, for the purpose of setting aside said final ruling and decision of the Board and particularly that part finding that the average weekly wage of plaintiff prior to sustaining such injury was $14.42, and to the finding awarding John White for his services equal to 15 per cent. of the sum paid on the total amount and the final awarding, and decreeing the plaintiff weekly compensation in the sum of $8.65 per week, because said finding and award are contrary to the evidence used in this case. Plaintiff further alleged that weekly payments to him would work a hardship because he was entitled to be paid $8.65 per week for 104 weeks, or $899.60, part of which was due and part to accrue, and because plaintiff owed debts of $500 incurred since his injury, also doctor's bills incurred by reason of the injury; that because defendant had not paid the weekly installment, plaintiff had elected to mature the entire claim of $899.60, and had instituted suit thereon; that he had agreed to pay his attorney, John White, 33⅓ per cent. of the recovery. Wherefore, he prayed that the final order and opinion of the Industrial Accident Board, to the extent complained of by plaintiff, be in all things set aside, and that plaintiff be awarded compensation at the rate of $8.65 per week, commencing February 6, 1919, with full payments now of the matured payments or a sum total of $899.60, and that his said attorney be decreed 33⅓ per cent. thereof, etc.

Defendant answered by plea in abatement that plaintiff's petition showed the only injury sustained by him · was the loss of the third or distal phalange of his index finger on his left hand, and under section 12, pt. 1, of the Workmen's Compensation Law (article 5246—21), he was entitled to recover 60 per cent. of his weekly wages, not less than $5 nor more than $15 per week, for a period of 15 weeks, and that the district court did not have jurisdiction of said sum. Defendant also filed a general demurrer, special exceptions, and a general denial. The plea in abatement and demurrers were all overruled, to which ruling defendant excepted. Defendant specially pleaded that if plaintiff was entitled to recover, it was compensation only for the loss of the distal phalange of the index finger on his left hand, and for that he was not entitled to recover a greater sum than found by the Industrial Accident Board, as shown in plaintiff's petition, amounting to the sum of $129.55, less $34.60 previously paid to plaintiff by defendant. It specially denied any indebtedness to plaintiff in the sum of $500 or other items claimed by him, and prayed that plaintiff be adjudged to accept the sum of $8.65 per week for 15 weeks, as found by the Industrial Accident Board.

At the trial plaintiff and defendant agreed that the following facts were true: That on January 29, 1919, plaintiff was in the employ of Republic Box Company at a wage of $2.50 per day; that notice was given to the employer within 30 days and notice of the injury and claim for compensation was filed with the Industrial Accident Board within 6 months after injury; that all parties were before the Board on the 6th day of May, 1919, on which date it rendered its decision, and that notice was given within 20 days that plaintiff refused to be bound and was not willing to accept or abide by the final ruling and decision of the Board, and that within 20 days thereafter notice was given by plaintiff to the Republic Box Company, the Board, and defendant, and suit was filed in the Forty-Fourth district court, Dallas, Tex., in the county where the injury occurred; that defendant had a policy under the terms of the Texas Employers' Liability Act, insuring the employés of the Republic Box Company at the time of and prior to the accident, and that defendant tendered payment under the terms of the award of May 6, 1919, by the Board, and offered to pay said amount; that defendant has paid the plaintiff $34.60 on his claim; that plaintiff's average weekly wage, calculated under the Compensation Law of the State of Texas, at and prior to the accident, was $14.42 per week, and that 60 per cent. thereof, the compensation, would amount to $8.65 per week, in the event injury is shown under the law by the evidence.

The case was submitted to a jury upon special issues, and upon their answer to the issues and other facts found by the court, the court gave plaintiff judgment against defendant for compensation at the rate of $8.65 per week for 75 weeks, beginning February 6, 1919, less a credit of $34.60 paid to plaintiff by defendant, aggregating $648.75; that payments accrued prior to the trial and unpaid should be paid in a lump sum with 6 per cent. interest per annum on weekly payments from date of their maturity; and that weekly payments not matured should bear interest at the same rate from their maturity. The judgment awarded John White, plaintiff's attorney, one-third of the total amount of the recovery, and directed defendant to pay him such one-third.

The defendant's motion for a new trial having been overruled, it appealed.

The first assignment of error complains of the trial court's action in overruling the defendant's plea in abatement, which was in the nature of a plea to the jurisdiction of the court; the second complains of the court's action in overruling the defendant's general demurrer to the plaintiff's petition; and the complaint of the third is that the court erred in overruling the defendant's special exception to the plaintiff's petition. These assignments present in different form substantially the same question, namely, that the district court did not have jurisdiction because, under the allegations of the petition and the law applicable thereto, the plaintiff could in no event recover as much as $500.

The propositions advanced, so far as is necessary to state, are: (1) That the district court has not jurisdiction in a suit for damages or debt where the amount in controversy is less than $500, exclusive of interest; (2) under the allegations in plaintiff's petition, and section 12, pt. 1, of the Workmen's Compensation Law of the State of Texas, upon which this suit is based, if ankylosis (total stiffness) of the index finger on plaintiff's left hand can be inferred, the limit of his recovery would be for a period of 45 weeks, at the rate of $8.65 per week, or a total of $389.25, which sum is not within the jurisdiction of the district court.

The plaintiff sought to recover not only for the visible wound inflicted upon the index finger of his left hand, but also for the injuries resulting therefrom to the tendons, ligaments, and nerves of his left hand and said finger and for traumatic rheumatism, stiffness of the finger and pain produced thereby, all of which it is alleged totally disabled the plaintiff for work for a period of 104 weeks. The Workmen's Compensation Law of this state awards to the injured employé, in lieu of all other compensation except for medical aid, hospital services, and medicines as provided for the loss of an index finger, or for ankylosis (total stiffness) of such finger, 60 per cent. of the average weekly wages during 45 weeks, and declares that the loss of the third or distal phalange of any finger shall be considered to be equal to the loss of one-third of such finger. The defendant's interpretation of the statute in question seems to be that since it fixes definite payments for definite periods for specific injuries, in lieu of all other compensation, the plaintiff can recover only the compensation given him by the statute for that specific injury, and that allegations to the effect that he sustained injuries to the tendons, ligaments and nerves of his finger, hand, and arm, and the traumatic rheumatism resulted therefrom, so incapacitating him that he was unable to work for a period of 104 weeks, and other allegations of suffering and inconvenience as a result of the specific injury, cannot be allowed to and do not increase either the amount of plaintiff's compensation or the number of weeks for which such compensation is to be paid him; and it is argued by the defendant's counsel that if the allegations in the plaintiff's petition that his finger became stiff can be taken to mean that ankylosis of the joints existed as a result of the injury, even then his compensation under the law would be $8.65 per week for 45 weeks only, and the total of that sum, to wit, $389.25, would not be within the jurisdiction of the district court. The argument is not without force, but we are not prepared to agree with the conclusion expressed. Section 10 of the statute (article 5246—18) is as follows:

"While the incapacity for work resulting from injury is total, the association shall pay the injured employé a weekly compensation equal to sixty per cent. of his average weekly wages, but not more than $15.00 nor less than $5.00, and in no case shall the period covered by such compensation be greater than four hundred and one (401) weeks from the date of the injury."

[1, 2] The plaintiff alleges that the accident complained of resulted in permanent personal injuries to him; that the index finger of his left hand was cut off or split at the distal phalange, and as a direct result thereof the tendons, ligaments, and nerves of the finger and hand and arm were injured, traumatic rheumatism, stiffness of said finger and hand produced, which wholly incapacitated and disabled him for work for a period of 104 weeks. The section of the statute just quoted provides that the injured employé shall be paid the compensation therein specified regardless of the nature of his injury, so long as his incapacity for work resulting from the injury is total, not exceeding a period of 401 weeks. The alleged period of the plaintiff's total incapacity for work as a result of his injuries is 104 weeks, a far less number of weeks than the number for which compensation is allowed by section 10 of the statute, but together with the allegations of the plaintiff's petition presenting a claim for damages in amount clearly within the jurisdiction of the district court. The allegations of the petition presented questions of fact, and for the purposes of the defendant's demurrers the court had to treat them as true. Thus treated, they showed a right of recovery for a sum in excess of $500.

Again, section 11 (article 5246—19) is as follows:

"While the incapacity for work resulting from the injury is partial, the association shall pay the injured employé a weekly compensation equal to sixty per cent. of the difference between his average weekly wages before the injury and his average weekly wage earning capacity during the existence of such partial incapacity, but in no case more than $15.00 per week; and the period covered by such compensation to be in no case greater than three hundred weeks; provided that in no case shall the period of compensation for total and partial incapacity exceed four hundred and one (401) weeks from the date of the injury."

Section 11a (article 5246—20) provides that in cases of the injuries therein enumerated, the incapacity shall conclusively be held to be total and permanent, and that the enumeration shall not be taken as exclusive, but that in all other cases the burden of proof shall be on the claimant to prove that his injuries have resulted in permanent, total incapacity. The pleadings of the plaintiff, it occurs to us, present a case in which he would be entitled to compensation for a period of total incapacity or partial incapacity or total and partial incapacity combined, making it essential to determine the number of weeks of such total, partial, or combined incapacity, as shown by the evidence, not to exceed 401 weeks for total incapacity or 300 weeks for partial incapacity, or 401 for the two combined from the date of the injury, and, as said by defendant's counsel, pain resulting from the effort to work, and other disabling consequences, would be elements to be considered, and the number of weeks of total, partial, or combined incapacity could properly be submitted to the jury for its determination. In either case the amount recoverable would be within the jurisdiction of the district court.

[3, 4] The petition alleged that—

"Plaintiff has unpaid accounts, debts, which aggregate the sum of $500, due and incurred since the date of his injury by reason of plaintiff being incapacitated to work and earn money, also doctor's bills incurred by reason of treatment of his injured finger, hand, and arm, and asked judgment therefor."

These allegations were specially excepted to and the exception overruled. We think this action of the court was error. It was not alleged in this connection that the association failed to furnish reasonable aid, hospital services, and medicines, when needed, or within a reasonable time after notice to the association of the injury, nor that the charges were fair and reasonable. In the absence of such allegations, the plaintiff under the Workmen's Compensation Law showed no cause of action for the recovery of such charges or debts. The defendant, however, suffered no injury by the action of the court in this matter, for the reason that no recovery was had by the plaintiff for said alleged claim.

[5] The defendant's fourteenth assignment of error asserts that the court erred in permitting counsel for the plaintiff, in his closing argument to the jury, to indulge in improper, inflammatory, and prejudicial remarks to the jury. This assignment is well taken and will be sustained. The bill of exception shows that counsel said, in substance:

"That the jury would remember the facts; that they could see the relative position of the parties; that on one hand was his client, an old man without money and without friends; that he had suffered this terrible accident from which he had undergone hours of excruciating pain; that his health was broken and his nervous system impaired by reason thereof; that he had not been able to engage in any kind of employment since the accident, and that the jury was his only place of refuge, and he was seeking from them the rights which had been heretofore denied; that on the other hand the defendant was a rich and powerful insurance company, an artificial person without a soul; that he had represented insurance companies and knew all their tricks; that he knew they hated to pay a poor man what was justly due him; that he had never heard of any insurance company that was willing to pay an honest claim, and that the defendant insurance company was no exception to the rule; that his heart went out to the poor man who was forced to fight a war against an insurance company; that the insurance companies had their agents everywhere, and that when the case of this plaintiff was called before the Industrial Accident Board, the defendant insurance company was represented by its agents and attorneys, and that with the testimony of hired doctors and the appeals of eloquent attorneys, the defendant insurance company induced the Industrial Accident Board to reduce plaintiff's claim to a mere pittance; that in all of these proceedings the voice of the plaintiff was not heard; that this Compensation Law is one of the greatest outrages ever forced on the people of Texas; that he did not have any money to go himself, neither did he have money to send doctors and lawyers to plead his cause; and that his only hope for justice lay in the verdict which he expected the jury to render."

[6] The court in approving the bill indorsed thereon the following:

"This bill is qualified with this statement, that no objection was made to these remarks by counsel for plaintiff save and only in this bill."

It appears that counsel made the objectionable remarks with the knowledge of the court, without rebuke or effort to restrain him. The rules promulgated for the government of the district court declare that counsel shall be required to confine the argument strictly to the evidence and to the arguments of opposing counsel (Rule 39, [142 S. W. xiii]), and the court will not be required to wait for objections to be made where the rules as to arguments are violated (Rule 41 [142 S. W. xiv]). By these rules the "duty devolves affirmatively, first, upon counsel to confine his argument strictly to the evidence and to the

argument of opposing counsel; second, upon the court, on its own motion, to confine counsel to this line of argument." If both the counsel who is making the argument and the court shall fail in the discharge of their duty, the rules give to opposing counsel the privilege, but do not make it his duty, to then present his point of objection. This discretion given to counsel, as to whether he will make the objection at the time, was doubtless based upon the well-known embarrassment, and often prejudice, which generally attend the interruption of argument of counsel by another. Willis & Bro. v. McNeill, 57 Tex. 465. Counsel should never endeavor to obtain a verdict by argument based upon anything other than the facts in the case and the conclusions legitimately deducible from the law applicable to them, and any other practice should be promptly repressed. "Every litigant, whether he is morally good or bad, or rich or poor, is entitled, in a court of justice, to have his rights passed upon and his evidence weighed by an unprejudiced tribunal." The evidence as to the extent or seriousness of the plaintiff's injuries and as to the number of weeks necessary to effectuate a complete recovery from the effects thereof was sharply conflicting. The record does not disclose the remarks of counsel were provoked by opposing counsel; nor is there in the evidence before us anything which warranted their inflammatory character. Jurors are disposed to regard as proper any argument which the court permits the attorneys to make, and the remarks objected to and permitted in this case were well calculated to influence the jury in resolving important issues of fact against the defendant. They could only have the effect of inflaming the minds of the jurors against the defendant, and so far exceeded the bounds of legitimate argument that they alone justify a reversal of the judgment obtained. Western Indemnity Co. v. MacKechnie, 214 S. W. 456; S. A. Pace Groc. Co. v. Guynes, 214 S. W. 794; Metropolitan St. Ry. Co. v. Roberts, 142 S. W. 44; Railway Co. v. Scott, 26 S. W. 999.

There are several other assignments of error, but they have been disposed of against the appellant by what we have already said or present no reversible error, and hence they need not be discussed. Of course, if the incapacity extends beyond one week, compensation shall begin to accrue on the eighth day after the injury.

The judgment is reversed, and the cause remanded.

FIRST NAT. BANK OF JACKSONVILLE v. CHILDS. (No. 6344.)

(Court of Civil Appeals of Texas. Austin. April 13, 1921. Rehearing Denied June 8, 1921.) .

1. Pleading ⟨key⟩111—Controverting plea of privilege need not set out facts required by statute where they are alleged in the petition.

A plea controverting a plea of privilege to be sued in another county was not insufficient because not specifically alleging facts relied on to confer venue, as required by statute, where it pleaded that the suit was founded upon an offense and trespass committed by defendants in the county as set out in the petition to which reference was made, since the averments of the petition were thereby made a part of the controverting plea and the petition stated facts satisfying the statute.

2. Dismissal and nonsuit ⟨key⟩5—Plaintiff may dismiss as to defendant whose plea for change is about to be allowed.

Our statutes provide that plaintiff may take a nonsuit at any time before the decision is announced, and also may discontinue as to any one or more defendants where no cross-action or affirmative relief is sought, and when the discontinuance would not operate to the prejudice of other defendants, so that, where the court had indicated that he would allow the plea of special privilege of one defendant, but not of another, plaintiff could, before the decision, dismiss as to the one whose plea was to be allowed.

3. Pleading ⟨key⟩111 — Not proper to express opinion on matters going to the merits in hearing upon change of venue.

Upon hearing of a plea of special privilege, it is not proper to express any opinion upon matters which are for determination upon the trial of the case upon its merits.

4. Pleading ⟨key⟩111—On plea of privilege, it is sufficient for plaintiff to plead a cause of action, and prove that it arose in whole or in part in county where suit was brought.

Upon pleas of privilege, it devolves upon plaintiff only to plead a cause of action arising in whole or in part in the county of suit, or an offense or trespass committed therein, and that the acts relied on, or a part of them, occurred there, and it is not necessary to prove all the elements finally fixing liability upon the defendant, but it is sufficient for plaintiff to plead a cause of action, and prove that it arose in whole or in part in such county, or that the alleged trespass was committed there.

5. Venue ⟨key⟩8 — Injury alleged held a "trespass" within statute.

Petition for recovery for offense or "trespass" consisting of threats of criminal prosecution and abuse, or other overt acts, held to constitute an action in trespass within the exception to the venue statute, since the petition alleged no mere negligence, but wanton and deliberate acts resulting in the impairment of plaintiff's health, and in physical injuries, force

not being a necessary element in a trespass case.

[Ed. Note.—For other definitions, see Words and Phrases, First and Second Series, Trespass.]

6. Corporations ⟨key⟩503(3)—Defendant corporation not entitled to change where acts complained of were performed in county of suit.

The exception in matters of special privilege authorizing a suit against a corporation, to be instituted where the cause of action, or a part thereof, arose, did not require granting a change of venue where, under the evidence on the plea, the acts chiefly resulting in the injuries alleged by the plaintiff were performed, if at all, in the county where suit was brought.

On Rehearing.

7. Pleading ⟨key⟩111—Prima facie right to change of venue under plea of privilege overcome by evidence.

In an action against a bank and its attorney, evidence tending to show that the attorney acted with the bank's authority in doing alleged wrongful acts constituting trespass, and tending to show ratification or acquiescence, held sufficient to overcome the prima facie right to change arising from the sworn plea of privilege, for such facts need not be proven with the certainty and completeness required to entitle plaintiff to judgment on the merits.

Appeal from District Court, McLennan County; H. M. Richey, Judge.

Suit by W. T. Childs against the First National Bank of Jacksonville, Tex., and Lee G. Carter. A plea of privilege to be sued in another county was overruled as to the defendant Bank, and sustained as to the defendant Carter, as to whom the cause was dismissed, and the Bank appeals. Affirmed.

Lee G. Carter, of Jacksonville, and Sleeper, Boynton & Kendall, of Waco, for appellant. Johnston & Hughes, of Waco, for appellee.

BRADY, J. This suit was instituted by appellee against the appellant bank and Lee G. Carter, in the district court of McLennan county. Both defendants filed pleas of privilege, and asked that the cause be transferred to Cherokee county, the domicile of the corporation, and the residence of the individual defendant. Controverting pleas were filed by the plaintiff, and, upon a hearing, the court sustained the plea of privilege of Carter and overruled the plea of the bank. However, upon the announcement by the judge that it was his intention to sustain the plea of privilege of Carter, the plaintiff moved the court, orally, to dismiss his suit as to said defendant, and the court later sustained his written motion to that effect. The bank has appealed from the order entered on this hearing.

[1] The first question that will be discussed is the claim that the controverting

⟨key⟩For other cases see same topic and KEY-NUMBER in all Key-Numbered Digests and Indexes

plea was insufficient, because it did not specifically allege the facts relied on to confer venue upon the courts of McLennan county, as required by the statute. In the verified controverting plea, the plaintiff pleaded that the suit was founded upon an offense and trespass committed by the defendants, consisting of threats of criminal prosecution, and the abuse and other overt acts more fully set out in the petition, to which reference was made. A similar allegation was made under the claim that the defendant bank was a private corporation, and that the cause of action, or a part thereof, arose in McLennan county. The effect of this was to make the averments of the petition part of the controverting plea, and, we think, was a substantial compliance with the statute. Indeed, there is much to commend the practice where the facts are so fully pleaded in the petition. We have no doubt that, if the plaintiff had attached a copy of the petition to his controverting plea as an exhibit, and had sworn that the facts therein alleged were true, it would have met the purposes of the statute. We see no difference where the facts alleged in the petition are expressly made a part of the controverting plea. Morgan v. Johnson, 15 Tex. 569; Gray v. Steedman Bros., 63 Tex. 95; Huffman v. Hardeman (Sup.) 1 S. W. 575.

[2] The next point to be discussed is the contention that the trial court should not have permitted plaintiff to dismiss as to the defendant Carter, it being claimed that the court was without jurisdiction so to do. Our statutes provide that a plaintiff may take a nonsuit at any time before the decision of the court is announced; and also that a plaintiff may discontinue his suit against any one or more defendants, where no cross-action or affirmative relief is sought by said defendants and when the discontinuance would not operate to the prejudice of the other defendants. It is true that our venue statute, as amended, provides that when a plea of privilege is sustained the cause shall not be dismissed, but shall be transferred to the proper court. It is not believed, however, that it was the intention of the Legislature to prevent the full operation of the statutes as to nonsuit and discontinuance. Under the former practice, when a plea of privilege was sustained the case was dismissed. The history of the amendment convinces us that its purpose was to prevent a dismissal by the court, and not a voluntary dismissal by the plaintiff, when he does not choose to follow up his suit against a defendant whose plea of privilege has been sustained. There could be no valid reason assigned for denying plaintiff the right to discontinue his suit when the venue has been sustained. Ordinarily a defendant could not complain at such action. In this case it is clear that no injury was done either defendant. Nor do we see that

the court was lacking in jurisdiction to enter the order of dismissal. District courts are courts of general jurisdiction, and the court had the power, if it desired to do so, to set aside the order sustaining the plea of privilege of the one defendant and to permit a nonsuit or discontinuance as to him. This was substantially what was done, if not in form.

We are not required in this case, however, to rest the decision on this point upon the view above expressed. The record shows that, when the court announced his intention to sustain the plea of privilege of Carter, but before he had entered any order to that effect, or announced his final decision thereon, the plaintiff asked leave to dismiss his suit as to that defendant. The court announced that plaintiff would be granted time to file a written motion, and both parties would be given time to present authorities. The written motion was thereafter filed, and the following day the court sustained the motion to dismiss. We think it is immaterial that the entry of the order sustaining the plea of privilege of Carter preceded the entry of the order allowing the dismissal. Plaintiff had previously, in open court, and before the decision of the court was actually announced, sought a discontinuance as to such defendant. His right to discontinue the suit could not be prejudiced or affected by a subsequent decision or order sustaining the plea of privilege. Weil v. Abeel, 206 S. W. 735, and authorities there cited; Luter v. Ihnken, 143 S. W. 675; Bates v. Hill, 144 S. W. 288; Rutledge v. Evans, 219 S. W. 218. In the last-cited case, the court held that, where actions were severable, the court may sustain the plea of privilege as to one of the defendants, and transfer the cause as to him, but hold it for trial as to the other defendant.

[3] Appellant has raised several interesting questions as to the failure of the proof to show that Mr. Carter, as attorney for the bank, had authority to do the alleged wrongful acts in behalf of the bank; and also the inadequacy of the evidence to show that the bank had ratified or acquiesced in his actions. It is not thought proper to express any opinion upon these matters, as they are questions for determination upon the trial of the case on its merits.

[4] Upon the hearing of the pleas of privilege, it devolved upon the plaintiff only to plead a cause of action arising in whole or in part in McLennan county, or an offense or trespass committed in that county, and to prove that the acts relied upon, or a part of them, occurred there. In such a proceeding it is not necessary to prove all the elements finally fixing liability upon the defendants. It was sufficient for the plaintiff to plead a cause of action, and to prove that it arose in whole or in part in the county where the suit was brought, or that the

alleged trespass was committed there. At most, it was only necessary to show a probable recovery. We think the showing was sufficient to justify the conclusion and judgment of the trial court.

[5] It is claimed by appellant that no offense or trespass was alleged by plaintiff within the meaning of the venue statute; and also that no cause of action in whole or in part arising in McLennan county was alleged. As to the first of these contentions, we are strongly inclined to the view that this is a case of trespass under the doctrine announced by the Supreme Court in Hill v. Kimball, 76 Tex. 210, 13 S. W. 59, 7 L. R. A. 618. It is true that the court, in the later case of Ricker v. Shoemaker, 81 Tex. 22, 16 S. W. 645, qualified the former case in respect to certain expressions therein. Nevertheless, Mr. Justice Gaines, speaking for the court in the Ricker Case, stated that:

"The words 'when the crime, offense, or trespass was committed' indicate that the word trespass was intended to embrace only actions for such injuries as result from wrongful acts willfully or negligently committed, and not those which result from a mere omission to do a duty."

The holding was that a mere negligent omission would not constitute a trespass. Here the petition alleges no mere negligence, but acts claimed to have been committed wantonly and deliberately, resulting in the impairment of plaintiff's health and in physical injuries. It is not believed that the authorities in this state justify appellant's contention that force is a necessary element in a trespass case. We prefer, however, not to rest the decision alone upon this exception to the general venue statute.

[6] Plaintiff also invoked the exception which authorises a suit against a private corporation to be instituted where the cause of action, or a part thereof, arose. Under the evidence, the acts chiefly resulting in the injuries alleged by plaintiff were performed, if at all, in McLennan county. Therefore, under the pleadings and the evidence, the trial court, for this reason also, was warranted in holding that the venue was properly laid in McLennan county.

We have carefully considered all the assignments in the brief, and conclude that no reversible error has been shown. The judgment will be affirmed.

Affirmed.

On Rehearing.

Counsel for appellant has filed an able argument on motion for rehearing, and it is thought proper, if not necessary, to briefly discuss some of the points of attack upon our original opinion.

It is insisted we were in error in holding that, under the present statutes, a plaintiff is not deprived of his right to take a voluntary nonsuit, or to discontinue his suit against one or more defendants, when a plea of privilege has been sustained. Several authorities have been cited in support of this proposition, but we do not find that they sustain it. We referred to the case of Rutledge v. Evans, 210 S. W. 218, a decision by the Court of Civil Appeals for the Fourth District, in which it was held that, where actions are severable, the court may sustain a plea of privilege as to one of the defendants and transfer the cause as to him, but hold it for trial as to the others. It appears that the Supreme Court has granted a writ of error in that case, and has indicated its opinion that this practice is not permissible, but that the entire cause should be transferred as to all the parties. This would appear to be in line with previous holdings of the Supreme Court, especially Hickman v. Swain, 106 Tex. 431, 167 S. W. 209, but in no case which we have examined does it appear that there was a dismissal by the plaintiff as to one or more of the parties.

We are not convinced that our original opinion upon this question is incorrect, and we are still strongly inclined to the view that our venue statute, as amended, does not prevent a plaintiff from taking a voluntary nonsuit or discontinuance, notwithstanding a plea of privilege may have been sustained. A contrary view would seem to be an unreasonable construction of the statute. If a plaintiff should desire to discontinue his suit and entirely abandon the litigation, upon the sustaining of a plea of privilege, we do not see how a defendant could complain of the exercise of such right, where he has no cross-action, and does not seek affirmative relief. It would seem to be folly to require a transfer of the cause to another court, with the increased costs necessarily resulting, in order to permit the plaintiff to take his nonsuit in another jurisdiction. We are unwilling to impute such an intention to the Legislature, in the absence of language more clearly indicating a purpose to restrict the legal right of the plaintiff, conferred by other statutes, to enter a voluntary dismissal. That our interpretation is the correct one is strongly intimated in the case of Garrison v. Stokes, 151 S. W. 898. There it was indicated that the plaintiff, upon the sustaining of the plea of privilege of one defendant, might have dismissed as to such defendant.

As pointed out in our opinion, however, the correctness of the trial court's ruling does not alone depend on the right of a plaintiff to take a nonsuit after a plea of privilege has been sustained. As we view the record, the plaintiff in this case made his motion orally, and in open court, before the court had made any judicial pronouncement upon the plea of privilege of either defendant, and he was granted leave to file his motion in writing. It is true that on the same day, and before the written motion to dismiss was filed, the court made a docket entry sustaining the plea of privilege of the defendant Carter, and noted the plaintiff's exception thereto. On the following day, however, the written motion to dismiss was filed, and was sustained. We still adhere to the view that, the plaintiff having sought a discontinuance as to Mr. Carter before the decision of the court was announced as to the latter's plea of privilege, his right to a nonsuit and discontinuance as to such defendant was not prejudiced or affected by the subsequent decision and order sustaining the plea of privilege. Furthermore, the bill of exceptions fairly discloses that the trial court refused to approve the order prepared by the defendants for transfer of the cause, and entered an order instructing the clerk not to make entry of the same on the minutes; and, taking the bill as a whole, it substantially appears that the court set aside the order sustaining the plea of privilege before granting the motion to dismiss. It does not appear that there was a formal setting aside of the order sustaining the plea of privilege, but this was what was substantially done, and we do not think that the court was without jurisdiction so to do. An appeal from such order had not been perfected, and, indeed, has never been taken.

For all the reasons indicated, we reiterate the conclusion that there was no error in permitting the plaintiff to take a nonsuit as to the defendant Carter, and in retaining venue over the cause as to the remaining defendant, the bank.

Our opinion is also vigorously challenged because of the claim that it was not proven that Mr. Carter had authority to act for the bank in doing the acts claimed to constitute a cause of action for damages. It is especially urged that we have virtually overruled our decision in the case of First National Bank v. Gates, 213 S. W. 720, which has been cited and approved by other Courts of Civil Appeals. A consideration of the facts and holdings in the cases referred to has convinced us that there is no conflict between these decisions and our holding in this case. In the Gates Case, there were several grounds urged for maintaining the venue in Coleman county as against the Brownwood National Bank. We expressly held, and adhere now to the view, that it was not enough to plead facts sustaining the venue in the county where the suit was brought, but that such facts must be proved. However, our holding there was that the facts proven did not show that the Brownwood National Bank was connected with the alleged fraud, nor the alleged conversion, nor the other matters which it was claimed conferred venue on the courts of Coleman county. Furthermore, there were findings by the jury as to these matters which were adverse to the plaintiff, and which we held were supported by the evidence. In the other cases cited by appellant here, there was

no proof whatever of the authority of the alleged agent to execute the contracts sued on, and this was an indispensable element in fixing the venue.

[7] In the instant case, while we do not think it proper to express an opinion as to the sufficiency of the proof to finally fix liability upon the bank, there was some proof tending to show that Mr. Carter, as attorney for the bank, acted with authority in doing the alleged wrongful acts in behalf of the bank and tending to show ratification or acquiescence in his actions by the bank. The evidence on this point, while circumstantial, was, in our opinion, sufficient to raise the issue, and, for the purposes of venue, was sufficient to overcome the prima facie right to a change of venue arising from the filing of the sworn plea of privilege. We cannot accede to the proposition that, upon the trial of such issues, it was necessary to prove the facts with such certainty and completeness as would entitle the plaintiff to a judgment on the merits. We reiterate the view that "in such a proceeding it is not necessary to prove all the elements finally fixing liability upon the defendant."

We have found nothing in the cases cited, originally, or on rehearing, which militates against this holding. We have given careful consideration to all of the matters urged in the motion, and have concluded that it should be overruled.

Motion overruled.

HULL v. GUARANTY STATE BANK OF CARTHAGE. (No. 643.)

(Court of Civil Appeals of Texas. Beaumont. May 31, 1921. Rehearing Denied June 15, 1921.)

1. **Banks and banking ⊂⇒228 — Evidence held to make issue of fact as to whether president was acting for bank.**

In an action by a bank to recover an overdraft, evidence *held* to make an issue of fact as to whether the president of the bank in purchasing defendant's cotton and promising to put the proceeds in the bank to his credit was acting as president of the bank or individually.

2. **Appeal and error ⊂⇒1011(1) — Trial judge's finding on issue of fact not disturbed.**

Where the trial court was compelled to determine an issue of fact upon diametrically opposed evidence and pass upon the veracity of the witnesses, it is the duty of the Court of Civil Appeals to uphold his finding.

3. **Appeal and error ⊂⇒747(2) — Inconsistency of conclusions not considered when only one party has assigned error.**

Whether the court's conclusions of law which were partly favorable to defendant and partly unfavorable were inconsistent as a whole need not be determined, where there is no cross-assignment of error by plaintiff.

4. Banks and banking ⊃106—Bank not liable for president's failure to deposit money as agreed individually.

Where the president of a bank acted as an individual and not as an official of the bank in purchasing defendant's cotton and promising to deposit the proceeds in the bank to his credit, the bank was not responsible to the defendant for his failure to deposit the proceeds to defendant's credit, though he deposited them to his own credit; it not appearing that any of the other officers knew anything about the nature of the transaction until long afterwards.

Appeal from District Court, Panola County; Chas. L. Brachfield, Judge.

Suit by the Guaranty State Bank of Carthage against E. A. Hull. From a judgment for plaintiff, defendant appeals. Affirmed.

Garrison, Pollard, Morris & Berry, of Houston, and H. N. Nelson, of Carthage, for appellant.

P. P. Long, R. W. Priest, and Woolworth & Duran, all of Carthage, and Edwin Lacy, of Longview, for appellee.

HIGHTOWER, C. J. The appellee, the Guaranty State Bank of Carthage, Panola County, Tex., a banking corporation organized under the laws of this state, filed this suit against appellant, Hull, in the district court of Panola county, claiming that appellant, a customer of the bank, had overdrawn his account in the bank to the extent of $3,042.50, and that on account of such overdraft appellant was indebted to appellee in said sum, and judgment was prayed against appellant for that amount.

Appellant, after interposing a general demurrer and general denial, alleged specially that on and prior to the 18th day of March, 1912, one R. E. Trabue was the acting president of said bank, and that as such president had control and authority over, and the general management of, its business affairs, with authority to make loans, accept and receive deposits, and collect indebtedness due said bank; that for several years prior to said 18th day of March appellant had various and sundry transactions with Trabue in his capacity as president of the bank, wherein appellant had sold and delivered to Trabue, in his capacity as president of the bank, much cotton, which transactions covered a period of several years; that Trabue, as president, would simply pass the amount of the proceeds of such cotton to the credit of appellant, and would then instruct appellant to draw against said amount; that prior to said 18th day of March, said Trabue, as president of said bank, had neglected to pass the proceeds of such cotton to appellant's credit, and that

appellant, on several occasions, called Trabue's attention to such failure, and that Trabue, in his capacity of president of the bank, would promise appellant that he would have the matter attended to; that he (Trabue) had simply overlooked the matter of having the proceeds passed to appellant's account and credit, but that nevertheless he had instructed the employés in the bank to pay any check or checks that appellant might draw against the bank; that appellant did not live in the town of Carthage, but lived about five miles away, and that he had implicit confidence in Trabue, and trusted him to see that proper credits were duly entered as he had promised and agreed to do; that his bank or pass book had not been checked up or balanced for some time, and that when he carried his bank or pass book to the bank and asked the cashier or other officers of the bank to check the same up and place the proper credits there, they usually made excuses that Trabue was not in, but that they would see him and have the proper credits entered, but that Trabue, as president, had instructed them to honor all checks drawn on said bank, and that the same would be promptly paid; that on or about the 18th day of March, 1912, appellant's pass book showed that he was due the bank the sum of $5,165, when in truth he was not due said bank such amount, said Trabue as president of said bank having failed to deposit to appellant's credit money paid to him as president of the bank.

Appellant further alleged that on or about said 18th day of March, 1912, Trabue, as president of said bank, came to appellant's residence late one evening, and told appellant that the bank examiner was checking up the bank, and that he was complaining about the bank books showing overdrafts of appellant; that Trabue brought along with him a slip of paper showing that appellant was due said bank an overdraft of $5,165, which amount corresponded with appellant's pass book and last check; that appellant told Trabue at the time, as president of the bank, that he did not owe the bank such a large amount, and that Trabue told appellant that it was necessary for him to collect said amount, and that if appellant would pay same that he (Trabue) would have his account corrected and all debits properly entered; that appellant then told Trabue that he did not have the money to pay off said amount, but that he had in the town of Carthage 128 bales of cotton; that he would turn the cotton over to Trabue, in his capacity as president of the bank, so that he could liquidate said indebtedness, as shown by the books of the bank, and that appellant could within a few days go to town and have his account checked up and all proper credits allowed; that appellant turned over to Trabue on that day, as president of said bank, said 128 bales of cotton; that they agreed upon a stipulated price for said cotton, which amounted to $6,993.81; that from said amount they deducted $5,165, the amount which Trabue claimed that the bank books showed appellant to be overdrawn, and that Trabue, as president of the bank, executed to appellant his note for $14,125, being the balance that said Trabue claimed was due appellant for cotton purchased by Trabue in his capacity of president of the bank, from him, for which appellant had not been given credit at said bank; that $1,835 of this amount was the balance due from said cotton, after deducting $5,165 to cover said claimed overdraft. Appellant further alleged that Trabue, in his capacity as president of the bank, did not deposit or place to appellant's credit in the bank said sum of $5,165, but turned the same over to the bank by giving the bank a draft on another party, with bill of lading covering the 128 bales of cotton attached to the draft; that such draft was paid, and that the bank received the proceeds of said 128 bales of cotton, but did not credit, and afterwards refused to credit, appellant with said sum of $5,165, as Trabue, in his capacity as president, agreed to do; that in turning over the cotton to Trabue, as president, the same was so done to liquidate and pay off any overdraft which the bank held against appellant, with the understanding that any errors or any credits not theretofore received by appellant would be corrected; that in fact the books of the bank at that time showed that appellant had overdrawn his account $2,065.59, and that afterwards appellant drew checks, subsequent to said 18th day of March, in the aggregate amount of $682.01 which, added to the total amount due, as shown by the books of the bank, would make appellant due the bank the sum of $2,722.57; that against this amount appellant should have been credited with the sum of $5,165 paid to Trabue in his capacity as president, as before stated, which would leave a balance due appellant of $2,412.73; and appellant prayed for judgment over against said bank for the difference between $5,165 alleged to have been paid to Trabue as president of the bank, and for which he alleged the bank received the benefit, and the proceeds thereof, and the sum of $2,722.57, the amount appellant was actually due the bank.

In reply, by way of supplemental petition, appellee alleged that the authority of Trabue for the collection of debts, if any he had, was confined to the acceptance of money, and that if appellant ever turned over to Trabue, as president of the bank, any cotton, the same was not a payment to the bank on appellant's overdrafts, and that the same never came into its possession, with the knowledge that the same was turned over to Trabue in payment of any debt or overdraft of appellants. And

further, appellee answered, substantially, that in purchasing the 128 bales of cotton from appellant, Trabue was not acting for the bank in making such purchase, but that such sale and purchase of such cotton was made between Trabue and appellant as individuals, and that such being so, the bank was not liable or responsible to appellant on account of Trabue's failure to place the proceeds of such cotton to appellant's credit in the bank, and that if Trabue, in so purchasing the cotton, did promise appellant to make such deposit of the proceeds, he did so as the agent of appellant, and not as the agent of the bank, and that the bank was not liable or responsible for such breach of the trust and confidence on Trabue's part.

The case was tried before the court without a jury, and resulted in a judgment allowing appellant a credit of $2,165.81 on the overdraft or claim sued on by appellee, but rendered judgment in favor of appellee for $682.68. This last-named sum was made up by checks that had been drawn by appellant on the bank subsequent to the 18th day of March, 1912. To this judgment appellant excepted, and gave notice of appeal to this court, which has been duly perfected.

The trial judge prepared and filed findings of fact and conclusions of law, as follows:

"Findings of Fact.

"(1) I find that R. E. Trabue, on March 18, 1912, was president of the Guaranty State Bank of Carthage, Tex., and had the right to collect debts due the bank, but had no right to collect anything from solvent persons except money, and that at the time defendant Hull was solvent.

"(2) I find that R. E. Trabue bought cotton from E. A. Hull on the 18th day of March, 1912, in his individual capacity, and that he collected the overdraft of said E. A. Hull, at said Guaranty State Bank, on that date, and that the amount of said overdraft on that date, as shown by the books, was $2,165.81, and that the said R. E. Trabue did not pay said amount to the Guaranty State Bank, as he promised to do.

"(3) I find that there was an agreement between the bank and E. A. Hull to pay 10 per cent. on all overdrafts, and that since the 19th day of March, 1912, the said E. A. Hull drew checks against said bank, which were paid, amounting to the sum of $682.68, and that the interest on the overdrafts up to the filing of this suit is $5.

"Conclusions of Law.

"I conclude, as a matter of law, that R. E. Trabue, as president of the Guaranty State Bank, having collected the amount of the overdraft, due said bank, to the 18th day of March, 1912, the same cannot now be collected by the said bank, although the said R. E. Trabue did not pay the same to said bank.

"I further conclude that the defendant, E. A. Hull, is indebted to said bank in the sum of $682.68, which amount is admitted by the pleadings of said Hull, the same being the amount of checks drawn against said bank, and by it paid, since the 19th day of March, 1912, and that the plaintiff bank is entitled to judgment for said amount of $682.68, plus the sum of $5 interest on said overdraft, after the 19th day of March, 1912, and up to the filing of this suit, together with 10 per cent. per annum on said amount of overdraft since the date of the filing of this suit, February 3, 1913, and judgment will accordingly be entered."

It will be noted from the above that the trial judge, in his second finding of fact, found that Trabue, in purchasing the 128 bales of cotton from appellant on the 18th day of March, 1912, did not act for the bank in making such purchase, but that he bought said cotton from appellant for himself, individually. In other words, the court found as a fact that the cotton transaction between appellant and Trabue, in which the 128 bales of cotton was turned over by appellant to Trabue, was between those parties as individuals, each representing himself, and it is evident from the court's conclusions of law and judgment that the bank could not be held responsible to appellant because of Trabue's breach of promise to put the proceeds of such cotton to the extent of $5,165 to appellant's credit in the bank. We think this view of the trial court as to the law was correct.

Appellant's brief contains three assignments of error, but the third assignment embraces everything that is in the first and second, and our disposition of the third assignment will dispose of them all. That assignment is as follows:

"The undisputed facts, as well as the great weight and preponderance of the evidence, show that on or about March 18, 1912, R. E. Trabue, as president of the Guaranty State Bank of Carthage, Tex., represented to E. A. Hull that he was overdrawn at the bank in the sum of $5,165.87, and that the bank examiner was demanding of the bank that said overdraft be paid; and the pass book of E. A. Hull showing that the amount stated by R. E. Trabue as due was in good faith paid to the said R. E. Trabue as president of said bank, said $5,165.87 would be by the said R. E. Trabue as president passed to the credit of E. A. Hull to liquidate said indebtedness, and the said R. E. Trabue, as president of said bank, failed to place said $5,165.87 to the credit of E. A. Hull, but placed said amount to his own credit, so as to cover an overdraft that he owned the bank, the bank would be liable to E. A. Hull for said amount, and the bank, having received the proceeds of said sum of $5,165.87, would be estopped from claiming that R. E. Trabue had no right as president to collect said money, and that he having failed to place said amount to the credit of E. A. Hull, the bank would not be liable; and the court erred in so holding, under the facts above stated, which are shown by the great weight and preponderance of the evidence, as well as the findings of fact by the court, that E. A. Hull was only entitled to a credit for the actual amount that was due the bank,

and not for the amount represented to be due the bank by R. E. Trabue, and as shown by E. A. Hull's pass book that he actually paid the bank."

This assignment is submitted as a proposition. There is a second proposition under the assignment, which is as follows:

"R. E. Trabue, as president of the Guaranty State Bank of Carthage, having received from the defendant, E. A. Hull, 128 bales of cotton, the proceeds of which were to be used in the liquidation of the statement of an alleged overdraft of $5,165.87 claimed to be due said bank by E. A. Hull, and the proceeds of said cotton having been turned over to said bank, the bank would be estopped from denying liability for the value of said cotton, or the proceeds of the cotton, used by said bank, upon the ground that the amount received for the cotton was applied to the payment of the president R. E. Trabue's indebtedness, or that R. E. Trabue had no authority to take cotton for E. A. Hull's indebtedness, and in so doing he was not acting within his authority or the apparent scope of his authority."

[1, 2] It will be noted, from the quoted assignment and propositions thereunder, that appellant assumes that the uncontradicted testimony showed that in making the purchase of 128 bales of cotton from appellant, Trabue acted in his capacity as president of the bank, and that such a transaction was one made in the interest of the bank by Trabue as its president. If the state of the evidence, as we find it in the record, were such as to authorize us to hold that it was shown without dispute that in making the purchase of this cotton from appellant Trabue acted in his capacity as president of the bank, and that such transaction was one between appellant and the bank, acting through its said president, we would be inclined to hold that the bank would be responsible and liable to appellant for Trabue's failure to deposit the amount of the proceeds of the cotton to appellant's credit in the bank, as Trabue agreed to do. It is not true, however, as claimed by appellant, that the uncontradicted testimony shows that in making the purchase of this cotton Trabue acted for the bank or in his capacity as president of the bank. It is true that Mr. Hull, the appellant, testified that Trabue, throughout the transaction, acted in his capacity as president of the bank, and that appellant turned him over the cotton in his capacity as president of the bank, and would not have turned it over to him as he did as an individual. Trabue testified positively, however, that in making the purchase of this cotton from appellant he represented himself only, and that it was an individual transaction on his part; that he purchased the cotton on his own account, but admitted that he did tell appellant that out of the proceeds of the cotton, when he sold it, he would deposit enough money in the

bank to discharge the amount of appellant's overdrafts in the bank, whatever that amount was found to be, and he admitted, in the same connection, that he failed to make such deposit for appellant's benefit, and that in so failing he breached his promise and contract with appellant, and abused his confidence. We would not be authorized, in view of this contradiction in the evidence between appellant and Trabue, to hold that the trial court's finding, to the effect that the cotton transaction was between Trabue and appellant as individuals, has not sufficient support in the evidence to warrant such finding. On the contrary, it is made clear that this was an issue of fact for the court to determine upon diametrically opposed evidence, and the trial court, sitting without a jury, was compelled to determine that issue of fact and to pass upon the veracity of the witnesses, and having determined the matter in favor of the appellee, it is our duty to uphold it, which we do.

[3, 4] Whether or not the court's conclusion of law, as a whole, is consistent, it is not for us to determine, because there is no cross-assignment on the part of appellee. Our conclusion on the legal proposition involved is that although Trabue failed to keep his promise with appellant by depositing in the bank the amount of money, being the proceeds of the cotton for appellant's benefit or credit, as he agreed to do, and was therefore clearly guilty of a breach of trust, still the bank cannot be held responsible to appellant for such breach of trust, although, as claimed in the assignment, the proceeds of the cotton was deposited in the bank to Trabue's own credit. It was shown by evidence sufficient for the purpose that none of the officers of the bank, other than Trabue, knew anything about the nature of the cotton transaction between appellant and Trabue, and knew nothing, until long after the transaction, of any claimed promise on Trabue's part to deposit the proceeds of the cotton to appellant's credit in the bank. The cotton transaction between appellant and Trabue being a transaction in which Trabue acted as an individual and not as an official of the bank, the bank is not legally responsible for misconduct on Trabue's part, although it resulted in loss to appellant. It was so held, substantially, by the Texarkana Court of Civil Appeals on a former appeal of this case. See 165 S. W. 104.

In dealing with the question as to the liability of a bank for misconduct on the part of one of its officers, in a transaction resulting in loss to another, Ruling Case Law, vol. 3, § 86, p. 457, has this to say:

"In order that the bank may be held liable, it is, of course, necessary that the transaction be with the bank and not with the officer as an individual."

See, also, First National Bank of Allentown v. Williams, 100 Pa. 123, 45 Am. Rep. 365.

No useful purpose would be served by any further discussion, since it is clear that the trial court's second finding of fact has sufficient support in the evidence, and since the law must follow and be conclusive upon that finding of fact, the trial court's judgment is affirmed.

———

HARTFORD LIFE INS. CO. v. PATTERSON. (No. 8521.)

(Court of Civil Appeals of Texas. Dallas. April 2, 1921. Rehearing Denied June 11, 1921.)

1. **Insurance** ⪧84(4) — **Insurer's agreement with agent as to renewal held not to supplant prior agreement.**

Insurance company's agreement with agent providing for continuous renewal commissions upon policies thereafter written, without any limitation with reference to agent's voluntarily ending his service or any other limitation, *held* not to supplant previous agreement providing for continuance to renewals so long as agent did not voluntarily sever his connections with company; there being no such inconsistency between the two agreements as to preclude agent's recovery on renewals upon policies written prior to the execution of the subsequent agreement.

2. **Election of remedies** ⪧7(1)—**Institution of proceeding not a conclusive election.**

The mere institution of a proceeding is not such a conclusive election as will prevent the plaintiff from abandoning it and pursuing an inconsistent remedy.

3. **Pleading** ⪧248(4) — **Plaintiff could amend petition by asserting remedy on contract inconsistent with that first pleaded, that contract had been repudiated.**

Where insurance company being sued by agent for renewal commissions sought to show that cause of action alleged in original petition was a suit for damages for the accepted termination of the contract repudiated by the company, and then set up in bar the plea of limitation, plaintiff could amend the petition so as to plead a cause of action upon theory that contract was a continuing one and had not terminated, notwithstanding amendment asserted an inconsistent remedy.

4. **Election of remedies** ⪧12—**One does not have two remedies to elect between where there is valid defense to one of them.**

A party does not have two remedies between which he must elect, where there is a valid defense to one of them, as where the remedy first sought is defeated by laches or statute of limitations.

5. **Evidence** ⪧271(19) — **Letters written by plaintiff not admissible in his behalf.**

In insurance agent's action against insurance company for renewal commissions in which the company denied the existence of the contract entitling agent thereto, letters written by the agent abounding in argumentative statements *held* inadmissible, without qualification.

6. Appeal and error ⬯1170(7) — Erroneous admission of evidence harmless in view of other evidence.

In an agent's action against an insurance company for renewal commissions the company denied existence of the alleged contract entitling agent thereto, the erroneous admission, on agent's behalf, of letters written by him tending to prove existence of contract, *held* harmless, where the evidence was conclusive in favor of agent to such an extent that the Court of Civil Appeals could not have permitted a finding contrary to that made by the jury to stand, since in such case the court could not say that the error caused the rendition of an improper judgment, under Courts of Civil Appeals Rules No. 62a (149 S. W. x).

Error from District Court, Dallas County; E. B. Muse, Judge.

Action by W. H. Patterson against the Hartford Life Insurance Company. Judgment for plaintiff, and defendant brings error. Affirmed.

Locke & Locke, of Dallas, for plaintiff in error.

Cockrill, Gray, McBride & O'Donnell, of Dallas, for defendant in error.

HAMILTON, J. On April 4, 1893, plaintiff in error, a life insurance company, contracted with defendant in error engaging him as its general agent in Texas. By subsequent amendments and substitutions this contract was changed as to commissions and renewals to be paid to Patterson and a partner who had become associated with him after the date of the first contract. The partner was eliminated before this controversy arose, and the agreements may be and will be stated as existent only between Hartford Life Insurance Company and Patterson. By a new agreement made between the parties on June 1, 1896, Patterson's initial commissions were increased and the period through which he should receive renewal commissions on all policies written through his agencies was fixed to cover the first 10 years of each policy. Other provisions of the contract not contained in previous agreements are not material and accordingly need not be mentioned. The agreement of June 1, 1896, contained the following provision relating to the payment of renewals to Patterson:

"Two dollars per annum out of each succeeding annual payment for nine years on each such policy, provided said payments are made to said company (the date of termination of this contract by limitation fixed in line 79 in no wise discontinuing this compensation, in respect of business done before said date), it being un-

derstood and agreed that in case said party of the second part leaves the service of said company, then all interests in this contract and in compensation for business furnished thereunder shall absolutely cease and determine."

On December 30, 1897, the contract dated June 1, 1896, was expressly amended by still another agreement in the following respect material to this controversy. For the above-copied section relating to payment of renewals was substituted this section:

"The renewal commissions alleged by said contract upon payments made after the first year of each policy upon business hereafter written shall continue to be paid to said parties of the second part during the continuance of the respective policies, subject to all other conditions of said contract."

It seems that about the time of expiration of the above-mentioned 1896 contract by express limitation contained in it, a question arose as to Patterson's right to continuous renewals on business obtained previous to December 30, 1897. This was in 1906. About this time Patterson asserted his right to continuous renewals upon business written prior to December 30, 1897. Patterson based his right to such continuous renewals upon a contract evidenced by a letter from the secretary of the company, written either late in 1906 or early in 1907, amending the renewal provision of the contract of June 1, 1896, so as to provide for continuous renewals unless and until Patterson voluntarily quit the service of the company. The company did not expressly deny nor admit this claim. This letter Patterson claimed was written either in the latter part of 1896 or the first part of 1897. The evidence shows that the letter was written and misplaced or lost, before Patterson made his claim based upon it in 1906. No definite disposition of Patterson's asserted right was made and the incident passed. Patterson continued to collect the renewals upon all business produced prior to December 30, 1897, until the last of 1913 or the first of 1914, when he became connected with the Missouri State Life Insurance Company as a result of some character of consolidation or agreement whereby the Missouri State Life Insurance Company took over all of a certain kind of plaintiff in error's business. The plaintiff in error, in consonance with the terms of a mutual understanding to that effect, after this change collected the premiums on all business previously produced through defendant in error's office. Thereafter remittances of renewals accruing on all policies postdating December 30, 1897, were made to defendant in error by plaintiff in error, but none were made to him on policies antedating December 30, 1897. Prior to 1914 Patterson had collected the premiums on all the policies written in his territory and had remitted to the company the premiums after deducting renewals upon all of them, those for policies written before as well as after December 30, 1897. The company had acquiesced in this with knowledge that Patterson was basing his right to retain renewals for business produced prior to December 30, 1897, upon the lost letter. This letter, as we have stated, contained the provision that Patterson was to have continuous renewals upon all premiums paid for policies from the beginning of his agency in 1898, unless he "voluntarily quit the service of the company."

The letter was written by the secretary of the company, and its contents were divulged to other officers of the company; but no copy of it was carried in the regular files of the company. According to Patterson's testimony, this was to keep the contract secret, because it was more favorable to Patterson than other agency contracts were to other agents. It does not appear that the existence of the letter was known to the officers of the company who participated in the agreement of December 30, 1897. Instead, that contract, it seems, was made with officers of the company who knew nothing of the letter or the agreement evidenced by it. The secretary of the company who wrote the letter was dead when Patterson in 1906 made his claim to continuous renewals by virtue of it.

The contention in the case is as to the right of Patterson to collect continuous renewals upon policies written prior to December 30, 1897. His contention is that the letter gave him the right to such renewals. The plaintiff in error, on the contrary, very vigorously argues that the amendment of December 30, 1897, supersedes all previous agreements as to renewals, and provides for no continuous renewals except upon business thereafter written, as stated in section two of that amendment.

The case was tried below before the court and a jury. The only question submitted to the jury was whether or not the company's secretary wrote the letter in the year of 1896 or in the first part of 1897, as claimed by Patterson. This question was determined by the jury's finding that such letter was written, and judgment was rendered for defendant in error.

Opinion.

[1] Plaintiff in error presents most thoroughly the position that the amendment of December 30, 1897, having specifically provided for continuous renewals only on business thereafter written, all previous understandings inconsistent with it were displaced by it, and that the letter relied upon by Patterson, containing an inconsistent stipulation for renewals, was entirely eliminated and canceled by the act of entering the agreement of December 30, 1897. In the view that the letter affords no basis of recovery because it was supplanted by the last amendment we do not concur. The soundness of the conclusions to which the able and cogent argument of counsel leads from the premises laid down we do not undertake to question. But we do not think the hypothesis from which they proceed is sufficiently related to the facts of this case to allow the propositions for which they contend to control. We cannot agree that the provision of the 1897 agreement to the effect that Patterson should receive continuous renewals on business thereafter written necessarily precludes, in view of all the evidence and circumstances of the case, his collection, by virtue of the letter, of continuous renewals upon business theretofore written.

The agreement established by the letter provided for continuous renewals so long as Patterson did not voluntarily sever his relations with the company. The 1897 agreement provided for continuous renewals upon policies thereafter written without any such limitation with reference to his voluntarily ending his services or any other limitation. We think this difference is insufficient to establish such inconsistency between the two agreements as to render the existence of that evidenced by the letter incompatible with the other and preclude its sustaining defendant in error's right to renewals upon policies written previous to December 30, 1897. This is especially so in view of the construction given the two instruments together by the company as well as by defendant in error, as is to be implied from their continuous acquiescence in the collection of the renewals for many years upon the theory that the contract expressed by the letter authorized it and that nothing else did. The provisions of the letter qualified defendant in error's right to continuous renewals by requiring that he should not voluntarily quit the service of the company. His right to renewals on policies written prior to December 30, 1897, was limited by this provision. The agreement dated December 30, 1897, removed this limitation as to policies written subsequent to that date and provided unconditionally that Patterson should receive continuous renewals upon policies thereafter written. This agreement expressly stated that it should apply to renewals only upon future business. It gave Patterson an added advantage as to such business, but left him bound as to previously written policies by the condition that he could receive his renewals from them only under the provisional stipulation that he should not voluntarily leave the service of the company. The plaintiff in error, for a long period after defendant in error's right to renewals on policies antedating the last contract would have lapsed, if that contract had been intended to cut him off from renewals on such policies, continued to collect them. These collections were made with the knowledge of plaintiff in error that they were claimed as authorized by a letter contract made before the 1897 contract and under no other claim. The two agreements not being necessarily inconsistent and incompatible and the parties by their acts and dealings with each other in relation to the subject-matter having applied them both and given them a harmonious construction so as to allow renewals on policies written prior to December 30, 1897, under the one and renewals on policies written after that date under the other, we do not think the provision in the last amendment for continuous renewals "upon business hereafter written" ought necessarily to be held to imply the exclusion of continuous renewals on all other business. Hence the doctrine contained in the maxim, "Expressio unius est exclusio alterius," contended for by plaintiff in error, does not apply under the facts and situation presented by the case.

Plaintiff in error contends, in the second place, that defendant in error had two inconsistent remedial rights to choose between when he instituted suit, which were these: First, that when the company repudiated the contract (if its existence be conceded), Patterson then at once became possessed of the right to accept such repudiation as a termination of the contract and bring an action for damages because of such wrongful termination of the contract. Second, the company having repudiated the contract, Patterson could decline to accept such repudiation as a termination of the contract and could treat it as continuing and bring suit to enforce it at or after its maturity. These two coexisting and inconsistent rights presenting themselves to defendant in error, it is asserted by plaintiff in error, he was compelled to make an election as to under which he would pursue his remedy; that he did make such election by filing his original petition wherein he chose to treat the contract as ended and upon that theory sued for damages, declaring upon a cause of action which arose the moment of the breach; that this cause of action was barred by limitation; and that plaintiff in error specially pleaded limitation. It is asserted that defendant in error perceived the error of his election of remedies when the plea of limitation confronted him, and that he thereupon filed an amended petition seeking to abandon his first choice of remedies and to substitute for it the inconsistent one secondly above named, which course is prohibited by the doctrine of election of remedies.

[2-4] We have examined with care both the original petition and the amended petition. The doctrine of election of remedies appears not to have been extensively treated by Texas

231 S.W.—52

courts, and no decisive rule seems to exist by which all cases in which the question arises can be tested with reference to it. Whether or not inconsistent remedies exist requiring an election, it seems, must be determined on the facts of each case. However, we do not think the inconsistency contended for by plaintiff in error clearly appears between the two pleadings. We do not construe the original petition as in effect containing a positive acceptance of repudiation of the contract and being a suit for damages upon the theory that defendant in error has elected to treat the contract as ended, and unless a conclusive election appeared from the pleadings plaintiff in error could not invoke the rule against defendant in error. Besides, since there is conflict of authority in the application of this doctrine, conceding the original petition and the amended petition to assert inconsistent rights, we choose to follow those authorities which seem to hold that the mere institution of a proceeding is not such a conclusive election as will prevent the plaintiff from abandoning it and pursuing an inconsistent remedy. Lewis v. Powell, 205 S. W. 737; Johnson v. Bank, 198 S. W. 990. It has been held that a suit for damages confirming a contract is a bar to a suit for rescission; but that a suit for rescission may be abandoned and the remedy for damages for breach pursued. Wright v. Chandler, 178 S. W. 1176. "An original complaint will not constitute an irrevocable election precluding plaintiff from filing an amendment asserting an inconsistent remedy." 20 C. J. 35. The fact that plaintiff in error sought to show the cause of action alleged in the original petition was a suit for damages for the accepted termination of the contract repudiated by it and then set up in bar the plea of limitation would authorize an amendment embodying the assertion of an inconsistent remedial right, and the pursuit of a remedy thereunder. Tullos v. Mayfield, 198 S. W. 1073; 20 C. J. 24. "A party does not have two remedies between which he must elect where there is a valid defense to one of them, as where the remedy first sought is defeated by laches, or the statute of limitations, although there are decisions inconsistent with this rule." 20 C. J., supra These authorities would overcome plaintiff in error's contention, even if it were established or conceded that the amended petition constituted the pursuit of a remedy entirely inconsistent with that sought in the original petition. But, as above stated, we hold that the asserted inconsistency does not in reality exist. The amended petition only more definitely, clearly, and specifically sets out the cause of action pleaded in the first instance. Williams v. Emberson, 22 Tex. Civ. App. 522, 55 S. W. 595.

[5, 6] Numerous letters were introduced in evidence by the defendant in error over the specific objections of plaintiff in error, and after they were introduced the court refused to qualify the effect of certain ones of them by instructing the jury that they were admitted only as proof that the company had notice of Patterson's claim. These letters were not admissible as evidence without qualification. They were letters written by Patterson and in his behalf and abounded in argumentative statements. But we are not prepared to admit that the error was harmful, although the evidence was inadmissible, and immaterial. They related to the letter contract Patterson rested his rights in this suit upon and to other matters and transactions, wholly irrelevant, which preceded that contract. The evidence in behalf of plaintiff in error upon the issue of whether or not the letter contract claimed by Patterson was made was so weak, inconclusive, and negative in character that it can scarcely be denominated as more than proof of a suspicion of a fraudulent claim, or as tending to make an issue of fact as to whether the letter was written in accordance with Patterson's contention. Patterson was supported in his positive testimony with reference to the letter by at least two disinterested and unimpeached witnesses. Plaintiff in error during a period of 17 years after the date on which it contends its liability for renewals was fixed so as to exclude those granted by the letter continued regularly to pay them or allow Patterson to retain them, which was in effect the same, under no claim of right except that given by the letter. All the foregoing is met by evidence on the part of the company's officials, who had succeeded those with whom Patterson dealt, only to the effect that their files and records contained no copy of any contract or letter embracing the stipulations Patterson and his witnesses swore were in the letter, and with statements made by them that they did not believe, and had no reason to believe, that any such contract ever existed. The material evidence taken altogether is practically conclusive of the affirmative of the only issue presented to the jury. We do not think we could permit a finding contrary to that made by the jury to stand. Holding this view of the proof upon the only fact determined by the jury, we believe that the rules by which we are to be guided in such situations clearly require us to overrule the assignments presenting this error. We cannot say the error probably caused the rendition of an improper judgment, or that the result could have been different if such error had not been committed. 62a Rules Texas Courts of Civil Appeals (149 S. W. x); Howell v. West, 227 S. W. 253.

The judgment is affirmed.

UNITED STATES FIDELITY & GUARANTY CO. OF BALTIMORE, MD., v. LOWRY. (No. 6341.)

(Court of Civil Appeals of Texas. Austin. May 18, 1921. Rehearing Denied June 15, 1921.)

1. Master and servant ⬅═367—Traveling salesman held "employé" within Compensation Act, and not an "independent contractor."

A traveling salesman, performing the usual and customary services for his employer, who could rightfully discontinue work or be discharged at any time, and was actually controlled by his employer in the performance of his work, held entitled an employé within the Workmen's Compensation Act, pt. 4, § 1 (Vernon's Ann. Civ. St. Supp. 1918, art. 5246—82), and not an independent contractor although he was not upon the pay roll of the employer, and was not paid wages, receiving his compensation by way of commission.

[Ed. Note.—For other definitions, see Words and Phrases, First and Second Series, Employé; Independent Contractor.]

2. Master and servant ⬅═418(5)—Admission of compensation award in evidence held not reversible error.

In a suit to set aside an award under the Workmen's Compensation Act (Vernon's Ann. Civ. St. Supp. 1918, arts. 5246—1 to 5246—91) it was not reversible error to admit in evidence a certified copy of the award made by the Industrial Accident Board, where it did not appear that the court considered the award in rendering a judgment for any improper purpose, and it was apparent that upon all the facts, which were practically undisputed, the court could properly have rendered no other judgment.

Appeal from District Court, Brown County; J. O. Woodward, Judge.

Action by the United States Fidelity & Guaranty Company of Baltimore, Md. against Mrs. J. S. Lowry, to set aside an award of the Industrial Accident Board in a proceeding under the Workmen's Compensation Law. Judgment for defendant, and plaintiff appeals. Affirmed.

See, also, 219 S. W. 222.

Hunt & Teagle, of Houston, and Seay, Seay, Malone & Lipscomb, of Dallas, for appellant.

Wilkinson & McGaugh, of Brownwood, for appellee.

Findings of Fact.

BRADY, J. Appellant sued to set aside an award of the Industrial Accident Board, made under the provisions of chapter 103, General Laws 35th Leg. (Vernon's Ann. Civ. St. Supp. 1918, arts. 5246—1 to 5246—91), commonly known as the Workmen's Compensation Law. Appellant had insured the Tom Padgitt Company, of Waco, Tex., against loss by virtue of injury to its employés under such act.

d the award was in favor of Mrs. Lowry, the beneficiary and widow of J. S. Low.

The contest was based on the grounds it Lowry was not an employé, but an indendent contractor, or, at least, not such an aployé as comes within the purview of the t. Upon a trial without a jury, judgment as rendered for Mrs. Lowry, giving her mpensation in the sum of $4,500, payable weekly installments.

We desire to give appellant the benefit of full statement of the facts in the case, and erefore copy the following statement from s brief, which is not challenged by appel- e, and is believed to be substantially corect:

"It is agreed by the parties to this suit that, t the time of the death of J. Scott Lowry, the om Padgitt Company had more than three mployés, and on said date carried a policy of nsurance with the United States Fidelity & uaranty Company of Baltimore, Md., of the ind required and permitted by the Employers' Liability Act of the state of Texas, and that aid Tom Padgitt Company was a subscribing ompany, and had complied with all of the requisites of such act, and at the time of the death of said J. Scott Lowry said policy of insurance, issued by said United States Fidelity & Guaranty Company, in compliance with the provisions of said Compensation Act, was in full force and effect; that the United States Fidelity & Guaranty Company has a permit to do business in the state of Texas, and has complied with all the requirements demanded of such companies, and is authorized and permitted to issue the kind of policy above described, which was issued to said Tom Padgitt Company.

"It is further agreed that due notice and claim of beneficiary was made in the time required by law by Mrs. J. S. Lowry, to the Industrial Accident Board of the state of Texas, at Austin, on account of the death of J. S. Lowry, and that all requirements of law in that regard were complied with.

"That at the time of the death of said J. Scott Lowry his average weekly earnings were, and had been for 1 year previous thereto, an aggregate of $1,089.93 per year, and an average weekly wage of $20.95.

"That said J. Scott Lowry was killed in Coke county, Tex., on February 11, 1918, by the overturning of his automobile.

"That on August 17, 1918, said Industrial Accident Board met and awarded on said claim, and within the time required by law; that said United States Fidelity & Guaranty Company gave Mrs. J. S. Lowry and the Industrial Accident Board of the state of Texas all required legal notices incident to appeal from said award, and did within the time required by law appeal from and file suit in the district court of Brown county, Texas; said notice to said Mrs. Lowry and said Industrial Accident Board contained all necessary legal prerequisites of such notice that it was not willing, and did not consent, to abide by the ruling of said board, which was served within the time required by law.

"That J. Scott Lowry left no minor children, no dependent parents nor grandparents, nor stepmother, and no dependent parents or de-pendent brothers and sisters, and that only his widow, the defendant, Mrs. J. S. Lowry, was dependent on him for a livelihood, and that he contributed support to no one except to the defendant, Mrs. J. S. Lowry.

"The award of the Industrial Accident Board was also introduced in evidence over the objection of appellant, as hereinafter appears.

"F. E. Goodman testified as follows:

"'My name is F. E. Goodman. My age is 49, and my residence is in Waco, Tex. I am a farmer, and also vice president of the Tom Padgitt Company of Waco, Tex., wholesale saddlery people. I have been connected with the Tom Padgitt Company for about 30 years.

"'I knew J. S. Lowry in his lifetime, and he was connected with the Tom Padgitt Company. Mr. Lowry was employed by the Tom Padgitt Company as a traveling salesman in West Texas on a commission basis, and had been so employed for several years prior to his death, his duties being such as are ordinarily incident to such work, and he traveled both on the train and in an automobile, principally in the latter.

"'Mr. Lowry resided and made his headquarters at Brownwood, and traveled as far north as the Panhandle, and as far south as Rock Springs, in Edwards county, and, as to how far west he would go, that was optional with him. In covering the territory in question he did not travel under the directions of the Tom Padgitt Company, as the company did not instruct him when and where to go, and Lowry used his own automobile, and paid all of his expenses incident to his traveling, and used his own discretion and judgment as to how and when he should travel, and also as to where he should travel in the territory in question.

"'Between the 1st and 5th of each month, the company settled with Mr. Lowry according to the gross sales made by him and accepted by said company, during the previous month, on a basis of 7½ per cent. average commission.

"'There was nothing in the contract with Mr. Lowry which precluded or prevented him from representing any other company or companies, or carrying any other line that he might decide to handle.

"'Mr. Lowry fixed his own time, and when and where he should travel in the territory in question.

"'There was nothing to prevent Mr. Lowry from carrying passengers in his automobile for a consideration and receiving such consideration. He did not work on a salary, but worked on a commission as fully stated above. I originally made the contract with Mr. Lowry on behalf of the Tom Padgitt Company, and the original contract was in writing, as I recollect it, but afterwards from year to year the contract was either renewed verbally or by correspondence, and for the last few years of his employment there was no formal written contract. The original contract and the subsequent renewals of same had been in existence during the period Mr. Lowry traveled for Tom Padgitt Company, that is, for several years before his death. He first traveled in a horse and buggy; he then bought an automobile. He sold this automobile and bought another, and was then given some railroad territory, in which he covered a few towns on the train, but the most of his territory was covered by automobile, and the machine was his exclusive property. The Tom Padgitt Company did not own any interest in the machine, nor in any way connected with it. Mr. Lowry's agreement with the Padgitt Company was to work this territory as in his judgment he thought best; the matter was entirely in his hands to go and come, day or night, in any way that he saw beneficial; and for such orders as he secured from the trade in that territory that were O. K.'d and approved for shipment by the company and were shipped he received for his services a 7½ per cent. average commission for such orders as were shipped by them, the payment of this commission being paid Lowry by check on Waco between the 1st and 5th of each month following the date of sale, as the records of the Padgitt Company showed that they had shipped of the sales made by Lowry. Mr. Lowry was under his own management as to traveling in the territory. He was allowed to carry such other lines as he wanted to carry. He was allowed the privilege of discontinuing his services at any time, and the Padgitt Company was allowed the same privilege, to discharge him at any time his services were not satisfactory, or that they wanted to put any one else in that territory. The only obligation on the Padgitt Company's part was that their line of goods was not to be sold by any other salesman in that territory as long as Mr. Lowry represented them in the same territory. He was further allowed to carry anybody with him in his car, as it was his car. The upkeep and all expenses incident to his traveling in the territory were to be paid out of the commissions so far as the Padgitt Company was concerned, as they were not interested in any debt of any character nor had any liability on the part of Mr. Lowry so far as the Padgitt Company was concerned.

" 'Mr. Lowry covered some territory that he selected, and some of the territory covered by him was designated by the company; that is, as already stated, his territory extended on the north to the Panhandle, and on the south to Rock Springs, and Brownwood on the east, but his territory was unlimited on the west until he reached El Paso.

" 'Prices and terms were to be made by the Padgitt Company at all times; Lowry had nothing to do with making the prices except according to price lists and other directions furnished by the Padgitt Company, and the company forwarded him price lists whenever there were changes in the market.

" 'The Padgitt Company passed on the responsibility and solvency of the parties to whom Lowry made sales, and his sales were made and orders taken subject to approval by the company when the orders went into the house.'

"Mrs. J. S. Lowry testified:

" 'I am Mrs. J. S. Lowry, and the widow of J. Scott Lowry. J. Scott Lowry lost his life about the 11th of February, 1918. He was working at the time he was killed for Tom Padgitt Company of Waco.

" 'Mr. Lowry was traveling for Tom Padgitt when he was killed, selling Tom Padgitt's line of goods, harness and leather, and everything of the kind in their line. He had been engaged in that business for 18 or 19 years. I know the territory that he covered, because I used to go with him. He went to the Panhandle which was as far as he could go, and

west as far as he could go, and to Rock Springs, and all the towns in between there. Tom Padgitt gave him the territory in which he traveled; he had that territory, and no one else had it. I was familiar with his contract with Tom Padgitt, because I traveled with him, and every once in a while Tom Padgitt would have him come into the house, and I used to go with him.

" 'I handled the correspondence; I would copy the letters he got from Tom Padgitt, and send them on to him, because sometimes he wouldn't get them; he would go through the towns, and other people would get his mail, so I would copy them and send him the copy. They were all the time changing the prices. Some other Lowry would come and get his mail, and he would get no mail. I would keep the letter at home, and send him the original.

" 'There were no other men traveling for the Tom Padgitt Company in his territory. There would be a racket if there was; he couldn't go in anybody's else territory. He got his prices from the Tom Padgitt Company. When we were getting ready for war the prices would come in every week. Whenever the goods went up he would go by what they said; he got instructions as to prices from Tom Padgitt Company.

" 'Sometimes he collected bills from customers for the company; sometimes he would also attend to other business for Tom Padgitt, seeing after some land that Tom Padgitt had down at London, which is out from Brady, in Schleicher county. He often attended to business like that, because he was acquainted with the territory and Padgitt wasn't. Tom Padgitt would want him to go and see if the land was all right; it was land that he had taken in on debts.

" 'I know of Mr. Lowry making collections for Tom Padgitt Company, but these collections would not always be for goods that he had sold; that would be when he would send him off to collect certain bills, when they would get behi'd.

" 'Tom Padgitt used to have Mr. Lowry come in to Waco, and when he did Tom Padgitt would pay his fare there and back; that was for the purpose of going over the stock and taking the price lists and looking the stock over; I used to go with him down there.

" 'Sometimes the crops were bad here, and he would go somewhere else to do business; the crops were bad here, and there wasn't any sale for anything, and they told him to go to Oklahoma, and gave him a territory up there, and that was where he was going when he got killed; he was going up there then, and he turned around and came back when I sent him that letter.

" 'That is the letter Tom Padgitt wrote him which you show me. He may have gone up to Oklahoma to sell some goods, but I don't just, remember about it. He may have done that a little. while; they were sending him up in that territory. I believe he did go up there once for a little while. I think they sent him up there one time. When he was killed he was coming from going up there. Tom Padgitt sent him there, and gave him a territory in Oklahoma. At the time he was on his way home.

" 'I have the letter Tom Padgitt wrote him to go to Oklahoma; that is the letter which you show me. The letter reads: "Tom Padgitt Company. Wholesale Saddlery, Carriages and Buggies. Waco, Texas, January 3, 1918. Friend Lowry: As per your late request, we inclose check for $100. Hope it will reach you in due time. No news. Trade is quiet, although busy on government work. Some of your Oklahoma orders we have to decline on very poor standing. I wish you a better year for 1918. Your friend, Tom Padgitt." I haven't the letter Tom Padgett wrote him to go to Oklahoma; that is the last letter I sent on to him. Mr. Lowry had the other letters, and I haven't that.

" 'Mr. Lowry often wrote Tom Padgitt for instructions as to what to do; they gave him instructions and he did everything they told him to do. I haven't the letters; he destroyed those letters. He got letters nearly every day, and they were destroyed. Sometimes the letters would say for him to go to a certain place, and if he didn't have good trade there to go to some other place. He was supposed to go over the territory every 60 days. Some places he had better trade than others, and wherever he had the best trade he went; wherever he got the best trade for his interest and their interest he went there. If the party to whom he sold goods hadn't made his payments they wouldn't ship the goods, but he wouldn't know that until the 1st of the month; he wouldn't know how many of them had been approved at that time. It was not the situation that when they had inquiries from some retailer in the territory they would send that inquiry to Mr. Lowry, and that he would call on them; he would go there under Padgitt's instructions. They did give Mr. Lowry the benefit of the inquiries, though, if there were such. They never told him just when to go, because he was supposed to make the territory every 60 days. Part of their instructions to him was to send him the price lists so he would know what to charge the customers.' "

Opinion.

The principal issue in this case is whether J. S. Lowry, under the facts stated, was an employé within the purview of the compensation law, or an independent contractor. In support of the contention that he was an independent contractor, appellant cites the following authorities: Western Indemnity Co. v. Prater, 213 S. W. 855; Moore & Savage v. Kopplin, 135 S. W. 1033; Stephenville, N. & S. T. Ry. Co. v. Couch, 56 Tex. Civ. App. 336, 121 S. W. 189; Edmundson v. Coca-Cola Co., 150 S. W. 273; In re Raynes, 66 Ind. App. 321, 118 N. E. 387; Bouvier's Law Dictionary, vol. 2, p. 1532; Words and Phrases, vol. 4, p. 3542; Honnold's Compensation Law, vol. 1, p. 208. None of these authorities appears to sustain appellant's theory. Indeed, the principles recognized in some of them would seem to be adverse. For instance, in Moore & Savage v. Kopplin, 135 S. W. 1033, it was said:

"We will remark, however, only such an employé as is free to do the work he is employed to do in his own way without directions, orders, let, or hindrance from his employer, being responsible to him only for the result, is regarded as such a contractor."

There is also nothing favorable to appellant in the quotation from Bouvier, which is as follows:

"An independent contractor is one who exercising an independent employment contracts to do a piece of work according to his own methods, and without being subject to the control of his employers, except as to the result of his work."

We also regard the rule announced in Honnold's Compensation Law, as applied to the facts of this case, to be against appellant's contention. This author states the rule as follows:

"The Compensation Law does not apply where the injured person is an independent contractor and the relation of the employer and employé does not exist. It is not possible to lay down a hard and fast rule or state definite facts by which the status of men working and contracting together can be definitely defined in all cases, as employés or independent contractors. Each case must depend on its own facts. Ordinarily no one feature of the relation is determinative, but all must be considered together. A contractor is ordinarily one who carries on an independent employment and is responsible for the results of his work, one whose contract relates to a given piece of work for a given price. These characteristics, however, though very suggestive, are not necessarily controlling. Generally speaking, an independent contractor is one who exercises an independent employment and contracts to do a piece of work according to his own methods without being subject to the control of his employers, save as to the results of his work."

None of the adjudicated cases cited by appellant is at all in point on the facts. The case claimed to be most nearly in point (In re Raynes, 66 Ind. App. 321, 118 N. E. 387) is an opinion by the Appellate Court of Indiana upon certified questions. In the language quoted by appellant, the court only undertook to give a concept in a general way of what classes of persons were within the protection of the Workmen's Compensation Act of that state. Furthermore, the court expressly stated that, under the facts certified, there appeared to be nothing inconsistent with the conclusion that the applicant was an employé within the meaning of the act.

We have been cited to no case which holds that a traveling salesman has been held to be an independent contractor, and we have found none. On the contrary, in 15 Cyc. at page 1033, a traveling salesman, whether employed on a salary or selling on commission, is defined to be an employé. See, also, Foley v. Home Rubber Co., 89 N. J. Law, 474, 99 Atl. 624; Industrial Commission v. Ætna Life Ins. Co., 64 Colo. 480, 174 Pac. 589, 3 A. L. R. 1336.

As sustaining the view that Mr. Lowry was an employé, and not an independent contractor, appellee's counsel cite the following authorities: 16 Am. & Eng. Enc. of Law (2d Ed.) p. 187; Waters v. Pioneer Fuel Co., 52 Minn. 474, 55 N. W. 52, 38 Am. St. Rep. 564; City of Tiffin v. McCormack, 34 Ohio St. 638, 32 Am. Rep. 408; Jensen v. Barbour, 15 Mont. 582, 39 Pac. 906; Cockran v. Rice, 26 S. D. 393, 128 N. W. 583, Ann. Cas. 1913B, 570; Muncie Foundry & Machine Co. v. Thompson (Ind. App.) 123 N. E. 196, 197; Wallace v. Southern Cotton Oil Co., 91 Tex. 18–22, 40 S. W. 399; Jernigan v. Houston Ice & Brewing Co., 33 Tex. Civ. App. 501, 77 S. W. 260, 261; Corrigan, Lee & Halpin v. Heubler, 167 S. W. 159–162; 16 Am. & Eng. Enc. of Law (2d Ed.) pp. 191, 192, subd. 9; 14 R. C. L. pp. 78, 79, subd. 16; Bodwell v. Webster, 98 Neb. 664, 154 N. W. 229, Ann. Cas. 1918C, 624, and note 632–634; Tuttle v. Embury-Martin Lumber Co., 192 Mich. 385, 158 N. W. 875, Ann. Cas. 1918C, 664; Sempier v. Goemann, 165 Wis. 103, 161 N. W. 354, Ann. Cas. 1918C, 670.

The act itself defines an employé as follows:

"Every person in the service of another under any contract of hire, expressed or implied, oral or written, except masters of or seamen on vessels engaged in interstate or foreign commerce, and except one whose employment is not in the usual course of trade, business, profession or occupation of his employer." Part 4, § 1, c. 103, Acts 1917, p. 291.

We are very strongly of the view that, independently of the standards or criterions usually employed to determine this question, the language of the act fairly comprehends the service and employment such as the undisputed facts show Mr. Lowry was engaged in when killed. It would seem that he was in the service of another, under a contract of hire, and that his employment was in the usual course of the business or occupation of his employer.

In 26 Cyc. pages 1546 to 1547, it is said that an independent contractor is one who, carrying on an independent business, contracts to do a piece of work according to his own methods, and without being subject to the control of his employer as to the means by which the result is to be accomplished, but only as to the result of the work. To the same effect is Jaggard on Torts, sec. 73, p. 228; and in Sherman & Redfield on Negligence (6th Ed.) p. 396, it is said:

"In actual affairs an independent contractor generally pursues the business of contracting, enters into a contract with his employer to do a specified piece of work for a specified price. * * * The one indispensable element to his character is that he must have contracted to do a specified work, and have the right to control the mode and manner of doing it."

The general rule is thus stated in 16 Am. & Eng. Ency. of Law (2d. Ed.) p. 187:

"Generally speaking, an independent contractor is one who, in rendering services, exercises an independent employment or occupation, and represents his employer only as to the results of his work, and not as to the means whereby it is to be accomplished. The word 'results,' however, is used in this connection in the sense of a production or product of some sort, and not of a service."

In Cockran v. Rice, supra, the Supreme Court of South Dakota emphasized the importance of the feature that the contract must be one to perform a certain definite and specified result, and contemplates a definite beginning, continuance, and ending. It was also stated by that court:

"A test of the relationship between the employer and employé is the right of the employer under the contract to control the manner and continuance of the particular service and the final result. No single fact is more conclusive as to the effect of the contract of employment, perhaps, than the unrestricted right of the employer to end the particular service whenever he chooses, without regard to the final result of the work itself."

And in nearly all of the cases cited by appellee stress is laid upon the test of service for another person as distinguished from the performance of a specific and independent work.

[1] In view of the facts that, properly speaking, Mr. Lowry was performing the usual and customary service for his employer as a traveling salesman, and that he was not doing any specified piece of work, nor undertaking the production of any given result, nor for any specified time, and that he might rightfully discontinue work, or be discharged at any time, and that there is evidence that he was actually controlled by his employer in the performance of his work, at least as to the main features of his employment, such as the soliciting of orders, the prices at which he should sell, and the terms of sale, the allotment of specified territory, and the approval and consummation of his sales by his employers, these considerations are decidedly characteristic of the services of an employé, rather than the contract or undertaking of an independent contractor.

We attach no importance to the point emphasized that Mr. Lowry was not upon the pay roll of the Tom Padgitt Company, and that it was shown that he was not paid wages. In lieu of wages, he received his compensation by way of commissions, and that he was not on the pay roll is thus readily accounted for. Neither do we regard as of controlling importance the fact that Mr. Lowry was performing his duties many miles from the place of business of his employer, and beyond the physical control of such employer. He was where the duties of his employment reasonably required him to be, or at least where he might reasonably have been upon the business of his employer.

In the Foley Case, supra, a traveling salesman lost his wife in the sinking of the Lusitania, while en route to visit his employer's London office. His mission being connected with his employment, it was held that his presence on the ship was not such a consideration as would defeat recovery. It was held that the risk was inherent in the employment itself.

Further discussion of the question is not deemed necessary. We have concluded that upon authority and reason Mr. Lowry must be held to have been an employé within the meaning and purview of our Workmen's Compensation Act.

[2] This disposes of the principal question on the appeal, but it is contended that we should reverse and remand the case because of the alleged error in the admission of the certified copy of the award made by the Industrial Accident Board. This evidence was objected to, and the bill of exception shows that—

"Said award was introduced in evidence and considered by the court in rendering judgment herein."

We agree with appellee's counsel that, even if it was unnecessary to introduce the award of the board for any purpose, it is difficult to see how it could have been prejudicial to appellant, in view of the fact that appellant had attached a certified copy of such award to its petition. It is insisted, however, that since the bill of exception shows that the court considered such award in rendering judgment, it must have influenced him in deciding the merits of the case. We do not think this necessarily follows. It does not affirmatively appear that the award was offered in evidence or considered by the court on the issue of employé or independent contractor, which was the only real question in the case. In view of the novel procedure afforded by the statute, in an appeal to the courts to set aside an award, and the substitution of the judgment of a court to settle the controversy, it may well be that out of an abundance of caution counsel offered and the court admitted in evidence the certified copy of the award for jurisdictional purposes. It does not follow that because the trial judge considered the award in rendering judgment that he considered it for any improper purpose. Young v. Robinson, 185 S. W. 715, and authorities there cited.

In any event, we do not think the introduction of the award in evidence constituted reversible error, for the reason that upon all the facts, which were practically undisputed, the court could properly have rendered no other judgment. Under the evidence, we think the court might properly have instructed a verdict for Mrs. Lowry had there been a jury trial, and therefore the admission of the award in evidence was immaterial, and, if error at all, was harmless.

We do not question the soundness of the decision, upon this point, in Texas Employers' Ins. Ass'n v. Downing, 218 S. W. 112. It not only appears that there was a sharply controverted issue as to whether the plaintiff was totally and permanently disabled, upon which issue the jury might have considered the award, but the Insurance Association, in effect, requested that the testimony should be limited to proof of the fact that a final ruling and decision by the board had been made. It appears that, notwithstanding this request, the court overruled the objection, and practically permitted the award to go to the jury for all purposes. It was under such circumstances that the court held this ruling to be reversible error. The difference, we think, is manifest.

Being of the opinion that no reversible error has been shown, the judgment is affirmed.

Affirmed.

TEXAS ELECTRIC RY. v. JONES.
(No. 8538.)

(Court of Civil Appeals of Texas. Dallas. May 28, 1921. Rehearing Denied June 18, 1921.)

1. Damages ⚖══160 — Allegation that plaintiff was "obliged" to pay held to sustain admission of evidence of reasonableness of doctor's charges; "compelled."

An averment in a petition of a servant for injuries that plaintiff was "obliged" to pay and become liable for medicines and medical treatment in the sum of $200 was sufficient, in absence of special exception, as an averment of the reasonableness of the expenditure; the word "obliged" being synonymous with the word "compelled," which implies reasonableness.

[Ed. Note.—For other definitions, see Words and Phrases, Oblige; First and Second Series, Compel—Compelled.]

2. Trial ⚖══296(2) — Instruction on assumed risk held not to ignore negligence and contributory negligence, in view of other instructions.

In a servant's action for injuries, an instruction which in effect charged the jury that, if plaintiff's injury was not the result of a risk ordinarily incident to his employment, he was entitled to recover, was not objectionable as ignoring the issues of negligence and contributory negligence, where other instructions preceding and following it fully and properly presented the issues claimed to be omitted; the situation not presenting a case of conflicting instructions.

3. Damages ⟜216(8)—Evidence held to support a charge on loss of time and diminished earning capacity.

Where plaintiff pleaded and testified as to his wages at the time of injury, and to the length of time he was unable to work, and physicians testified as to the extent of his injuries, and their permanent effect, the allegations and evidence supported a charge as to reasonable value of time lost and diminished earning power.

Appeal from District Court, Hill County; Horton B. Porter, Judge.

Action by P. J. Jones against the Texas Electric Railway. Judgment for plaintiff, and defendant appeals. Affirmed.

Templeton, Beall, Williams & Callaway, of Dallas, and Wear & Wear, of Hillsboro, for appellant.

Morrow & Stollenwerck, of Hillsboro, for appellee.

HAMILTON, J. This is an action for damages alleged to have accrued by reason of personal injuries inflicted as a proximate result of the negligence of a section foreman acting as an employé of appellant.

Appellee alleged that in May, 1917, he was in appellant's service as a section hand, and in substance he alleged the following: While appellee and other employés of appellant were going from their place of work on appellant's road to another point thereon, and traveling on a motorcar used by appellant to transport them from place to place, the foreman, under whose orders appellant worked, ordered him and other employés to push the motorcar along the track for the purpose of starting the engine used to propel it; that while appellee was thus engaged in moving the car and walking by its side, the engine was started, and the section foreman ordered appellee to jump on the car while it was in motion; that as he attempted to get on the car in compliance with the order, the section foreman, who was operating it, negligently caused it to lurch forward and backward, and at the same time accelerated the speed; that the car was not equipped with handholds, and that the jerks caused appellee to lose his balance and fall in front of it; that, notwithstanding appellee's perilous position thus negligently caused by the section foreman, no effort was made to stop the car, and as a proximate result of the described negligence it ran over appellee's ankle and leg, dislocating and breaking the ankle, fracturing the bone in the leg, and otherwise injuring appellee. Appellant answered by general denial, and also pleaded contributory negligence and assumed risk. The trial before a jury resulted in a verdict and judgment for appellee, and appellant has appealed.

The appeal embodies assignments of error complaining of the admission of evidence

to prove that doctor's bills incurred by appellee were reasonable and proper, and assailing the charge of the court relating to the feature of assumed risk, and also the charge relating to damages for loss of time from labor and for diminished capacity to work.

[1] The trial court admitted evidence to prove that the bill for the physician's services was reasonable and proper. Appellant objected to the evidence on the ground that the petition did not allege that the doctor's bill was a reasonable charge. With reference to doctor's bills and medicine the petition contained this language:

"And [plaintiff] has thereby been obliged to pay and become liable to pay for medicines and medical treatment from doctors in the sum of $200.00."

Appellant did not specially except to the petition on the ground that it contained no allegation of the reasonableness of the bills. It has been held that where the plaintiff alleged he had been compelled to incur expenses for medicine and the services of a physician, the allegation, by intendment, meant that the charges were reasonable, and, in the absence of a special exception to the pleading, was sufficient evidence of the amounts paid or incurred. Railway Co. v. Duck, 69 S. W. 1028; Railway Co. v. Lee, 21 Tex. Civ. App. 174, 51 S. W. 351, 57 S. W. 573; Railway Co. v. Stuart, 48 S. W. 803. "Obliged" in the sense of its use in the appellee's petition is synonymous with "compelled" in the sense of its use in other cases above cited. We therefore think the allegations were adequate to sustain admission of the evidence, particularly since there was no special exception to the pleading suggesting its insufficiency on this feature.

[2] The charge of the court upon assumed risk was as follows:

"You are charged that when the plaintiff, P. J. Jones, entered the employ of the defendant company, if he did, he assumed all the risks ordinarily incident to such employment, if any, and if you believe that his injury, if any, was the direct and proximate result of a risk ordinarily incident to his employment, if any, you will find for the defendant, though, if you should believe from a preponderance of the evidence that his injury was not the direct and proximate result of a risk ordinarily incident to his employment, if any, you will find for the plaintiff."

Appellant takes the position that we ought to reverse the judgment because by this charge the court directed the jury to allow the whole case to turn upon the question of whether or not the injury was the result of a risk assumed by appellee, and ignored the other issues made by the pleadings and the evidence, which were those of negligence vel non and contributory negligence.

The charge as a whole comprehensively presented all features of the case to the jury.

It defined negligence, proximate cause, ordinary care, and contributory negligence in the order stated, and these definitions were followed by the paragraph relating to assumed risk, of which complaint is made. Immediately succeeding this paragraph were two others, which respectively instructed the jury as to the application of negligence and contributory negligence, which had already been defined. These sections of the charge were as follows:

"You are charged that if you believe from the evidence in the case that if in the discharge of his duties as a section hand the plaintiff undertook in the usual way, and without negligence on his part attempted to get upon the motorcar in the control and under the supervision of the section foreman Gibson, and while plaintiff was so doing said foreman negligently operated and controlled said car, caused said car to give a sudden jerk forward, and caused plaintiff to be thrown down or forward in front of said car and to be run over or against, and injured as alleged by plaintiff, then you will find in favor of plaintiff, unless you further find from the evidence that plaintiff was guilty of contributory negligence as defined in the court's charge.

"If you find and believe from a preponderance of the evidence in this case that the plaintiff was guilty of contributory negligence, as that term has been hereinbefore defined, and that as a direct and proximate result of such contributory negligence, if any, he sustained the injuries, if any, complained of, then you will return a verdict for the defendant."

We think the charge as a whole fairly applied the law, and instructed the jury with sufficient clearness, balance, and accuracy as to the rules of law applicable to all the issues of the case. The charge must be considered as a whole, and all of its parts should be taken together in undertaking to determine whether or not the complaining party was prejudiced by it.

"Where an instruction, taken as a whole, fairly and properly expresses the law applicable to the case, no just ground for complaint exists, even though an isolated or detached clause or expression is in itself inaccurate or incomplete." Hartsfield v. Pace, 189 Ky. 98, 224 S. W. 647; Pierce v. Schram, 53 S. W. 716; T. & N. O. Ry. Co. v. Pearson, 224 S. W. 709; Railway Co. v. Walters, 80 S. W. 669.

The question here presented is not to be confused with that sometimes arising from the error of the court in giving conflicting charges upon the same particular issue. In such instances of contradictory charges upon one feature the jury is left to apply either charge, and, even if one be correct, the courts are compelled to review the action, because in such cases it cannot be said that the jury applied the correct charge, rather than the conflicting erroneous one. But no such question of conflict of charges is present in this case, and therefore those decisions relating to it are not in point and have no application.

[3] The objection to the charge assigned with reference to damages for loss of time and for diminished capacity to labor is based upon the proposition that there was no evidence either as to what was the reasonable value of time lost or as to the extent of diminished capacity to labor in the future; and the further proposition is advanced that the charge was in this respect unwarranted and improper, because the petition contained no allegation of the reasonable value of time lost.

Both the petition and appellee's evidence were to the effect that at the time he was injured he was a strong, healthy man, about 50 years old, capable of earning a certain daily wage by manual labor, and that he was then earning it; that after the injuries were received he was incapacitated from doing any work at all until five or six months had passed, and that during this period he lost $1.40 each day, because that was the amount he was receiving when he was injured and thereby completely incapacitated from doing any work during this period. He testified that his ankle still pained him and was stiff, and that his leg hurt constantly, and he gave testimony in detail clearly showing a condition calculated to lessen his capacity to work. His testimony that he was regularly earning a given wage when he was injured, considered in connection with his testimony showing how long after the accident he could perform no work at all, was to be taken by the jury as proof of the reasonable value of lost time. The reasonable value of lost time in the particular instance could be determined by no standard of greater accuracy than that supplied by an ascertainment of what appellee was earning immediately preceding the injuries, in view of the uncontradicted proof that he was an unskilled laborer, dependent entirely upon manual work. The physicians who treated him gave evidence as to the extent of the injuries and suffering totally incapacitating him for a period, and they also testified that the injuries were permanent, and that the injured members would never be sound again. The allegations and the evidence, to say the least, were sufficient to supply a basis of damages for loss of time and for diminished capacity to labor in the future, and hence it was proper for the court to charge the jury that in estimating the amount of damages, if any, they might consider, among other elements of damage, the reasonable value of time lost on account of the injuries, and also appellee's diminished capacity, if any, to labor and earn money in the future.

We are unable to say that any error is presented to justify reversing the judgment, and it is affirmed.

SCRIPTURE v. SCRIPTURE. (No. 8551.)

(Court of Civil Appeals of Texas. Dallas.
May 28, 1921.)

1. **Homestead** ⟨⟨=⟩150(1)—**Divorced wife as
guardian of their minor child could apply to
have deceased husband's homestead set apart
for use of child.**

While a divorced wife could not assert any
claim to the homestead of her deceased husband, yet she, as the duly constituted guardian
of their minor daughter, could apply to the
county court to have the homestead which he
occupied at the date of his death set apart for
the occupation and use of such minor.

2. **Homestead** ⟨⟨=⟩142(1)—**Decedent's homestead may be set over to minor daughter living with decedent's divorced wife.**

Vernon's Sayles' Ann. Civ. St. 1914, art.
3413, provides that exempt property must be
set apart for the use of widow, minor children,
and unmarried daughters remaining with the
family of the deceased, and the qualification
"remaining with the family" does not apply to
minor children, so that a minor daughter under
custody of decedent's divorced wife may have
the use and occupation of the homestead set
over to her.

3. **Homestead** ⟨⟨=⟩142(1)—**Father legally bound
for child's support after divorce giving custody to wife so that such minor may have
homestead set apart.**

The fact that decedent was single when he
died did not affect the right of a minor daughter living with decedent's divorced wife to have
the homestead set aside for such minor's use,
for, notwithstanding the marriage status had
been dissolved by the divorce decree, and the
custody of the child awarded to the mother,
and that they did not live with the father, yet
he was legally bound for the child's support.

Appeal from District Court, Dallas County; W. F. Whitehurst, Judge.

Application by Mrs. M. E. Scripture, as
guardian of the person and estate of Ruth
Scripture, against R. C. Scripture, as administrator of the estate of R. M. Scripture, deceased, for allowance for the support of said
minor, and to set aside deceased's homestead
to such minor's use. From a judgment in
favor of such minor, an appeal was taken
to the district court, which confirmed the
judgment of the probate court, and, his motion for new trial being overruled, the administrator appeals. Affirmed.

Muse & Muse, of Dallas, for appellant.
Baskett & De Lee, of Dallas, for appellee.

TALBOT, J. The nature and result of this
suit is well stated in the brief of the appellant, is acceptable to the appellee, and is as
follows:

Administration was duly taken out upon
the estate of R. M. Scripture, deceased, upon
application therefor filed August 10, 1918.

R. C. Scripture was appointed and duly qualified as such administrator. On January 24,
1919, Mrs. M. E. Scripture, guardian of the
person and estate of Ruth Scripture, the
minor daughter of R. M. Scripture, deceased,
filed application in the probate court for an
allowance for the support of said minor, and
to set aside the homestead of R. M. Scripture,
deceased, to said minor. The administrator,
on February 28, 1919, filed answer to such application, alleging, among other things, that
on February 15, 1913, Mary E. Scripture was
decreed a divorce from R. M. Scripture, and
that the custody of said minor child, Ruth
Scripture, was awarded to her; that said
Mary E. Scripture, guardian aforesaid, and
R. M. Scripture, were by such decree of divorce constituted single persons; that long
prior to such decree of divorce neither she
nor said child had lived upon the farm constituting the alleged estate of the deceased,
and that, continuously since the decree of divorce, neither have lived upon the land claimed to belong to said estate; that said minor
child, under said decree, was not a constituent member of the family of R. M. Scripture, was not such in fact, and did not reside
with him upon said land; that said minor,
Ruth Scripture, was not a constituent member of the household or family of R. M.
Scripture continuously for long prior to his
death, and under her legal status was not
entitled to the rights claimed; that on August 8, 1919, the probate court entered its
order making an allowance of $500 to the
guardian of said minor as and for support,
and setting aside 83.5 acres of land described
in the judgment to said guardian for the use
and benefit of said minor, Ruth Scripture,
during her minority, or so long as her guardian may be permitted to so occupy and use
the land under the order of the proper court
having jurisdiction thereof; and the administrator was directed to deliver said homestead to the said guardian in accordance
with the judgment, to which judgment the
administrator in open court duly excepted,
gave notice of appeal to the district court of
Dallas county, and duly perfected said appeal. On August 31, 1920, upon the hearing
of the cause in the district court, the judgment of the probate court was in all respects
confirmed, except that the order was confined
to two tracts of land, 25.5 acres and 28 acres,
the other tract having been disposed of under
a vendor's lien note. The case was tried upon an agreed statement of facts between the
parties, and, upon motion of the administrator, the court filed his findings of facts
and conclusions of law, adopting the agreed
statement of facts as his findings of fact.
Motion for new trial was overruled, and appeal perfected to this court.

The material facts, as agreed to by the
parties and adopted by the trial court as his

⟨⟨=⟩For other cases see same topic and KEY-NUMBER in all Key-Numbered Digests and Indexes

conclusions of fact, are substantially as follows: R. M. Scripture died July 9, 1918, his first wife having died prior thereto. In 1900 or 1901, subsequent to the death of his first wife, R. M. Scripture married his second wife, M. E. Scripture. One child, Ruth Scripture, was the fruit of the second marriage. She was born October 20, 1902. R. M. Scripture and his second wife, M. E. Scripture, were divorced by decree of the district court of Dallas county, Tex., on the 15th day of February, 1913, and by said decree the custody of Ruth Scripture was awarded to her mother, since which time to the present Ruth has resided with her mother as a member of the family. After her father and mother were divorced, Ruth, a girl about 18 years of age at the time of the trial of this case, never resided or lived with her father. At the time of his death R. M. Scripture resided upon the land described in the petition as his homestead, and by the agreement of the parties said land, for the purposes of this appeal, is to be regarded and treated as the separate estate of R. M. Scripture, deceased. The minor, Ruth Scripture, had, at the time the judgment herein was rendered, no property save and except such interest as she may have as heir to the estate of her father, R. M. Scripture. She is living with and has been supported by her mother since said decree of divorce, except that, during the lifetime of her father, he from time to time gave or sent her money. Mrs. M. E. Scripture had no property, and has been earning a livelihood by her own labor, receiving therefor about $20 per week. The education of the minor, Ruth, has been borne altogether by her mother, and she is "now qualified to enter college."

[1] The contention of the appellant is that a decree of divorce constitutes the husband and wife single persons, and that, in the administration of her father's estate, the guardian of the minor child of the deceased father is not entitled, where the father and mother of said minor child were divorced and the custody of the minor child decreed in said divorce to the mother, and with whom said minor child resided since such judgment as a member of the family of the mother to the date of the death of the father, and where such minor child had never resided or lived with the father from the date of the decree of divorce to the death of the father, to have the homestead of the father, his separate property, set aside for the use and benefit of said minor. On the other hand, the appellee contends that the guardian of a minor child of a deceased father is entitled to have the homestead of the deceased father set apart to the minor child, notwithstanding the father and mother of said minor child were divorced, and the care, custody, and control of said child had been awarded the mother in the divorce proceedings, and said minor child had thereafter lived with her mother, and was

not living with the father at the time of his death, and had not lived with her father on said homestead since said divorce, and that it is not essential to such right that either the parent was married at the time of death or that the minor should have resided with such parent at the time of the latter's death. We think the contention of the appellee is substantially correct, and that the judgment should be affirmed. Mrs. M. E. Scripture, having been divorced from her husband, could not assert, and did not assert, any claim for herself to the homestead of her late husband, R. M. Scripture. Duke v. Reed, 64 Tex. 713. But she was the duly constituted guardian of the minor, Ruth Scripture, the daughter of herself and her said husband, and in this capacity made the application to the county court to have the homestead, which he was occupying at the date of his death, set apart for the use and occupation of their said minor child.

[2] It is made perfectly clear by our Constitution and the adjudicated cases of this state upon the subject that it is not necessary that the minor child reside with the father at the time of his death to entitle it to a right in his homestead. By article 3413, Vernon's Sayles' Civil Statutes, the exempt property must be set apart for the use and benefit of three distinct classes of persons, namely, (1) the widow, (2) minor children, and (3) unmarried daughters remaining with the family of the deceased. The qualification, "remaining with the family of the deceased," applies only to the third class, and has no application to the second class, the minor children. That the minor child may have been awarded by the court in a divorce proceeding to the custody of the mother makes no difference. The Constitution seems "imperative in its command that the homestead shall not be taken from the minor children, so long as their guardian may be permitted, under the order of the proper court having jurisdiction, to use and occupy the same." Even the fact that the minor children are residing with their mother, who has a homestead in her own right, does not destroy their right in the deceased father's homestead.

[3] Again, as argued in effect by the appellee, the fact that the deceased father was a single man does not affect the question. The rights of the minor children do not depend upon such status, but upon their relation to him as children, notwithstanding the marriage of the father and mother has been dissolved by a decree of court, and the custody of the children has been awarded to the mother, and they do not live with the father, yet the father is legally bound for their support and they are entitled to his protection. Creditors have no right to have satisfaction out of the homestead of an insolvent estate which descends as other property subject to the use of the survivor or minor children under order of the court.

The conclusions we have reached are so thoroughly supported by the following cases that further discussion would, it seems, serve no useful purpose. Zapp v. Strohmeyer, 75 Tex. 638, 13 S. W. 9; Hall v. Fields, 81 Tex. 553, 17 S. W. 82; Speer & Goodnight v. Sykes, 102 Tex. 451, 119 S. W. 86, 132 Am. St. Rep. 896; Shook v. Shook, 145 S. W. 682; Hoefling v. Hoefling, 106 Tex. 350, 167 S. W. 210. In the last-cited case, it is held that our laws concerning exemption of homesteads relate to both solvent and to insolvent estates.

The judgment is affirmed.

STATE NAT. BANK OF TEXARKANA v. POTTER. (No. 2437.)

(Court of Civil Appeals of Texas. Texarkana. July 1, 1921. Rehearing Denied July 2, 1921.)

1. Sales ⬦191—Payee, who accepted notes by selling them, bound to ship machinery.

Where defendant maker of notes delivered them to the agent of the payee, on condition the payee would accept them and ship by a given time certain machinery purchased by the maker, the payee accepted the notes by the act of selling them, and was legally bound thereby to ship the machinery.

2. Bills and notes ⬦370—Want or failure of consideration not defense against holder in due course.

The want or failure of consideration of notes is not available as a defense against a bank, which took them without notice in such respect before acquisition; the notes at the time not being due.

3. Bills and notes ⬦56—Notes not void because maker did not affix revenue stamps.

Where the lack of federal revenue stamps on certain notes was rectified before they were put into the course of trade, and before plaintiff bank, a holder in due course, acquired them, such notes are not void merely because the maker himself did not affix the proper stamps.

4. Bills and notes ⬦342—Lack of cancellation of revenue stamps on transfer to holder in due course not a circumstance of suspicion.

The mere fact that federal revenue stamps on certain notes were not marked "Canceled" at the time of the transfer of the notes to plaintiff holder in due course was not such a circumstance of suspicion in and of itself as to put plaintiff purchaser of the notes on inquiry.

Appeal from Smith County Court; D. R. Pendleton, Judge.

Suit by the State National Bank of Texarkana against U. A. Potter. From a judgment for defendant, plaintiff appeals. Judgment reversed, and rendered for plaintiff.

Will D. Pace, of Troup, and Bulloch, Ramey & Storey, of Tyler, for appellant. Brooks & Johnson, of Tyler, for appellee.

LEVY, J. The suit is by the appellant on promissory notes made by appellee and payable to the order of the Williams Mill Manufacturing Company. Appellant alleged that it acquired the notes and became a bona fide owner and holder of same in due course of trade, for a valuable consideration, before maturity of any one of them. The appellee pleaded that the notes were never delivered to the Williams Mill Manufacturing Company as binding obligations at the time, but were conditionally delivered; failure of consideration; and the invalidity of the notes for lack of revenue stamps in conformity with law. After hearing the evidence, the court gave a peremptory instruction to the jury to return a verdict in favor of defendant, and error is predicated on this ruling.

[1, 2] The evidence conclusively shows that the appellant acquired the notes before maturity in due course of trade, without notice of any equities between the maker and the payee. It does appear that appellee delivered the notes to the agent of the payee upon a condition that the payee would accept them and ship the machinery by a given time. The payee did accept the notes, by the very act of selling them, and was legally bound thereby to ship the machinery. The payee having accepted the notes, the maker was legally entitled to make claim to that amount in the bankruptcy proceedings. The want or failure of consideration of the notes is not available as a defense against appellant; there being no evidence that it had any notice in that respect before acquisition, the notes not being at that time due. The trial court seems to have decided as a matter of law, influencing the peremptory instruction, that—

"The notes were invalid and nonnegotiable at the time they were acquired by plaintiff," because they "were not stamped with the revenue stamps by the defendant, nor by his authority, as required by the act of Congress requiring revenue stamps to be affixed and canceled by the maker."

The only evidence introduced at the trial with reference to the stamping of the notes was the testimony of appellee, as follows:

"The notes were not stamped with revenue stamps at the time I signed and turned them over to the agent of the Williams Mill Manufacturing Company, and were not canceled at that time, as they had not been sent in and approved by the company, and were to be sent back to the bank at Troup. They never were sent back to me to stamp, and I never did put revenue stamps on them, nor authorize any one else to do so. The stamps that are now on the notes were not put there by me, or with my knowledge or consent, and the initials and cancellation written on them is not my handwriting. The initials written on the stamps are 'V. A. P.'"

[3, 4] It appears that these stamps were on the notes at the time the appellant acquired them, but the letters "V. A. P." were apparently written on the stamps at a date later than that of acquisition. Clearly the lack of the stamps was rectified before the notes were put into the course of trade and before appellant acquired them, and the notes are not void merely because the maker himself did not affix the stamps. Failure on the part of any maker to affix stamps is a personal punishment to him. The law does not make the notes void because the owner has not affixed the stamps, if the stamps are finally on the notes by the time they are disposed of in the due course of trade. And the mere fact that the stamps on the notes were not marked or canceled at the time of the transfer would not be such a circumstance of suspicion, in and of itself alone, as to put the purchaser upon inquiry.

The judgment is reversed, and, as it appears conclusively that the plaintiff was a bona fide purchaser for value without notice, judgment is here rendered in favor of plaintiff for the debt sued for, interest, and with costs of the trial court and of this appeal.

**COBB et al. v. J. W. ALLEN & BRO.
(No. 2434.)**

(Court of Civil Appeals of Texas. Texarkana.
July 1, 1921. Rehearing Denied July 2,
1921.)

1. **Mechanics' liens** ⟐⟐315—**Contractor's bond held not available to materialmen.**

Where building contract did not provide for the payment of materialmen, and where the contractor's bond was not on its face made for the benefit of the materialman, a materialman could not recover on such bond, notwithstanding Vernon's Ann. Civ. St. Supp. 1918, art. 5623a, providing that the contractor's bond shall be conditioned for the payment of materialmen, and authorizing the materialmen to sue on such bond, since such statute means merely that if the owner shall contract with the contractor to have the contractor pay materialman, and shall give a bond for the performance of the terms of such contract, the materialman has the right to sue on the bond, regardless of whether the terms of the bond so specified.

2. **Constitutional law** ⟐⟐276—**Mechanics' liens** ⟐⟐313—**Statute relating to contractor's bond held void as interference with the right to contract.**

Vernon's Ann. Civ. St. Supp. 1918, art. 5623a, providing that a contractor's bond shall be conditioned for the true and faithful performance of the contract and the payment of all subcontractors, laborers, mechanics, and materialmen, and that such subcontractors and materialmen shall have the right to sue on the bond, regardless of whether their claims are secured by any lien, *held* void, as an unwarranted interference with the right to contract.

⟐⟐For other cases see same topic and KEY-NUMBER in all Key-Numbered Digests and Indexes

Appeal from District Court, Red River County; Ben H. Denton, Judge.

Suit by J. W. Allen & Bro. against Geo. T. Cobb, C. M. Godwin, B. J. Johnson, and H. B. Johnson on a contractor's bond. Judgment for plaintiffs, and the sureties on the bond appeal. Reversed as to Geo. T. Cobb, surety, and affirmed as to other defendants.

T. T. Thompson, of Clarksville, for appellants.

Austin S. Dodd, of Clarksville, for appellees.

LEVY, J. Godwin & Johnson, contractors, entered into a written contract with Mrs. J. C. Barton to erect a residence for her in accordance with certain plans and specifications, furnishing all material and labor for same. The contract price was $11,750, to be paid in partial payments as the progress of the work required, the owner to reserve until final completion and acceptance of the building 20 per cent. of the contract price. The contractors executed the following bond with sureties:

"The State of Texas, County of Red River.

"Know all men by these presents: That we, C. M. Godwin and Beacher Johnson of the city of Denton, Texas, and the city of McKinney, Texas, respectively, do hereby and herein acknowledge ourselves as principals together with the other signers hereto as sureties held and firmly bound unto Mrs. J. C. Barton of the city of Clarksville, Texas, in the sum of $2,000.00, two thousand dollars, for the payment of which well and truly to be made we bind ourselves severally and collectively, our heirs, executors and administrators, firmly by these presents.

"The condition of the above obligation is such that as the above bounden Godwin & Johnson have this day entered into contract with the said Mrs. J. C. Barton for the erection of certain residence building in accordance with plans and specifications mentioned in said contract, now if the said Godwin & Johnson shall faithfully carry out this contract to the full and complete satisfaction of the said Mrs. Barton, then this obligation shall become null and void, otherwise to remain in full force and effect.

"Witness our hands and seals this —— day of April, A. D. 1919.

"[Signed] Godwin & Johnson, Principals.
[Seal.]

"[Signed] H. B. Johnson,

"[Signed] Geo. T. Cobb, Sureties. [Seal.]"

The appellee, a mercantile firm, furnished certain material to the contractors, which was used by them in erecting the residence. The contractors failed to pay for the material, and the appellee (the seller) brought this suit for the amount of the debt against them and the sureties on their bond. The court rendered judgment against all the defendants; and the sureties on the bond appeal, claiming that they are not liable because the bond is not a statutory, but a common-law, bond.

[1] The contract does not provide for the payment of materialmen, and the bond on its face is not made for the benefit of materialmen. The payment of materialmen is not a part of the contractual obligation of the parties. It is evident, then, that the contract and the bond are in the form we find them, because the parties merely elected to so contract, and not for the reason that they undertook to .follow the statute or stipulate in respect to it. In order to hold, then, that the bond is made for the benefit of materialmen, and that they could recover on it, Vernon's Ann. Civ. St. Supp. 1918, article 5623a, would have to be read into the contract, if it can legally be injected into it. It is not thought that the act intends to make a contractual obligation for the parties that they did not contract themselves. The act, properly construed, means only that if the owner shall contract with the contractor to have the latter pay all materialmen and to give a bond for the performance of the terms of the contract, then such contract obligation to pay all materialmen inures also to the benefit of materialmen, and they have the right to sue on the bond regardless of whether or not the terms or wording of the bond so specify. And it would be a sufficient answer to appellee's claim that there is not any such voluntary agreement of the parties. That such is the fact sufficiently appears from the language of the contract.

[2] But another distinct ground exists in the case for denying a recovery against the sureties on the bond. This article of the statute has been held unconstitutional as an unwarranted interference with the right to contract. Hess v. Denman Lbr. Co., 218 S. W. 162, writ of error denied by Supreme Court (see Williams v. Baldwin [Com. App.] 228 S. W. at page 557). If this article of the statutes which it is claimed governs the contract and the rights of the parties in the bond, whether actually incorporated into the writing or not, as invalid, then such law cannot be made a part of such contracts. It is only a valid statute regulating contracts which is, by its own force, read into and made a part of such contracts. It is otherwise as to invalid statutes. Provisions cannot legally be forcibly inserted into contracts in obedience to an unconstitutional statute demanding their insertion. In Railway Co. v. State, 100 Tex. 420, 100 S. W. 766, the Supreme Court said:

"If the statute involved in this litigation is invalid, then the fact that the proceedings in the court are regular will not constitute it due process of law, by which the penalties denounced against the railroad company would be enforced."

This ruling of the Supreme Court is in effect that if a statute is unconstitutional in any respect any attempt to enforce it would be an infringement of the "due process" provision.

The judgment as to the surety George T. Cobb is reversed, and judgment is here rendered in his favor, with all costs of appeal and all costs incurred by him in the trial court, and against appellees. The defendants C. M. Godwin, B. J. Johnson, and H. B. Johnson not appealing, the judgment against them will remain undisturbed.

WILSON v. WILSON. (No. 6345.)

(Court of Civil Appeals of Texas. Austin. April 20, 1921. Rehearing Denied June 8, 1921.)

1. Divorce ⊜⚬223—Awarding of attorney's fee discretionary with trial court.

In a proper case the trial court has authority to render judgment in favor of the wife for attorney's fee, but the right thereto is a matter largely within the discretion of the trial court.

2. Divorce ⊜⚬223—Refusal to award wife attorney's fee held not abuse of discretion.

Where wife was given the only property owned by the husband and wife for the purpose of providing necessaries for herself and minor children placed in her custody, and the payment of expenses and costs incurred by her in connection with divorce suit, and where the husband was in bad health and it was uncertain as to when he would regain his health sufficient to earn his livelihood, refusal to award wife an attorney's fee *held* not an abuse of discretion.

Appeal from District Court, McLennan County; H. M. Richey, Judge.

Suit by W. J. Wilson against Virgie Bell Wilson, in which defendant filed a cross-action. From judgment for defendant on her cross-action giving her insufficient relief, she appeals. Affirmed.

R. L. Henderson, of Waco, for appellant.

Witt, Terrell & Witt, of Waco, for appellee.

JENKINS, J. This was a suit by appellee against appellant for divorce. Appellant filed a cross-action, asking for divorce, custody of minor children, and partition of community property. Judgment was rendered in favor of appellant on her cross-action, awarding to her the custody of the children and the use of all community property, but denying her an attorney's fee. This appeal is from the judgment of the court denying such attorney's fee.

The case was tried before the court without a jury, and the trial court filed the following findings of fact and conclusions of law:

⊜⚬For other cases see same topic and KEY-NUMBER in all Key-Numbered Digests and Indexes

"(1) I find that upon the date of the trial of this case that plaintiff was confined in a sanitarium and did not testify, and that upon the testimony of the defendant given at the trial she was entitled to a divorce upon her cross-action, and as to this there was no contest by the plaintiff, that the employment of an attorney by defendant to represent her was necessary, and that the defendant personally agreed to pay her attorney a reasonable fee, and that a reasonable fee would be $200, and that she employed as her attorney R. L. Henderson, who acted in good faith.

"(2) I find that the plaintiff and defendant are the father and mother of five children, and that it is to the best interest of the three minor children, all being girls, to wit, Mabel Wilson, Itho Wilson and Myra Wilson, that they be awarded to the care and custody of the defendant, Virgie Bell Wilson.

"(3) I find that the only property owned by the plaintiff and defendant consists of the following community property: A house and lot situated at No. 1037 Taylor street, of the approximate value of $2,500, constituting the homestead of plaintiff and defendant; a house and lot situated at 301 Matthew street, Hillsboro, Hill county, Tex., of the approximate value of $1,000; household and kitchen furniture of the approximate value of $500.

"(4) I find that the plaintiff, W. J. Wilson, is about 55 years of age, about 20 years older than the defendant, Virgie Bell Wilson; that he has been for some time in bad health, and for the past several weeks confined in a sanitarium for the benefit of his health, and was upon the date of the trial of this case confined in said sanitarium, that on account of his poor health he has been unable to earn a livelihood for several weeks, and that it is uncertain as to when he will regain his health sufficient to earn a livelihood.

"(5) I find that the defendant, Virgie Bell Wilson, is a woman of approximately 35 years of age, and in good health and in every way competent to earn a livelihood, and, with the aid of the use of the community property set apart to her, able to pay a reasonable fee to the attorney employed by her to represent her in this suit.

"Conclusions of Law.

"(1) I conclude that the defendant is entitled to a divorce on her cross-action.

"(2) I conclude that it is to the best interests of the minor children that they be awarded to the care and custody of the defendant.

"(3) I conclude that it is proper and equitable that the entire community property of the plaintiff and defendant should be and by judgment it is set apart for the use of the defendant in providing for the necessaries for herself and minor children and the payment of expenses and costs incurred by her in connection with this suit, and that it would be inequitable to charge the plaintiff with the attorney's fees incurred by the defendant."

We approve these findings of fact, and adopt them as our own.

Opinion.

[1, 2] In a proper case the trial court has authority to render judgment in favor of the wife for an attorney's fee when sued for a divorce. However, the right to such attorney's fee is a matter largely within the discretion of the trial court. There is no statute requiring judgment for such attorney's fee. We do not think that the trial court abused its discretion in its judgment in this case. We approve the trial court's conclusions of law.

Finding no error of record, the judgment of the trial court is affirmed.

Affirmed.

LOBIT et al. v. DOLEN et al. (No. 681.)

(Court of Civil Appeals of Texas. Beaumont. May 25, 1921. Rehearing Denied June 15, 1921.)

1. Landlord and tenant ⟺66(2) — Landlord held not charged with notice of change of possession from tenants at will to their former agent.

Where persons in possession of land as tenants at will discontinued their ranch business, and soon afterwards gave one formerly in actual possession as their agent the wires and posts in a fence constructed by them, and he thereafter rebuilt the fence, using such posts and wires, the landlord held not charged with constructive notice that there had been any change in the possession where the tenants never surrendered the possession.

2. Landlord and tenant ⟺66(3)—Agent of tenants at will held charged with notice of landlord's rights.

One in actual possession of land for four years as the agent of persons who were merely tenants at will was charged with constructive knowledge of the facts and conditions of their entry, though he did not know to whom the land belonged, as respected his right to hold adversely to the landlord.

3. Landlord and tenant ⟺66(3)—Agent of tenants at will held to stand in employer's shoes, and not entitled to claim adversely until landlords had notice.

Where tenants at will of land used in their stock business discontinued their business, but did not surrender possession, but afterwards gave the posts and wire in their fence to their former agent, who had been in actual possession, and he rebuilt the fence, inclosing part of the land with other land of his own, he stood in his former employers' shoes, and occupied the relation of tenant at will to the landlord, and his possession could not be adverse to the landlord until the landlord had actual or constructive knowledge of his adverse claim.

Appeal from District Court, Harris County; W. E. Monteith, Judge.

Action by J. Lobit and others against I. S. Dolen and others. Judgment for defendants, and plaintiffs appeal. Reversed and rendered.

Maco & Minor Stewart and R. W. Houk, all of Houston, for appellants.

Campbell, Myer & Freeman and Sewall Myer, all of Houston, for appellees.

WALKER, J. As applicable to this appeal, we adopt the statement made by Judge Graves on a former appeal of this case (Dolen v. Lobit, 207 S. W. 143), which is as follows:

"Appellees sued appellants in the court below in trespass to try title to recover 597.85 acres of land in the J. W. Moody survey, in Harris county, Tex. Among other pleas, the latter set up their claim to the land under the statute of 10 years' limitation.

"At the close of the evidence, upon motion of appellees, the court peremptorily instructed a verdict in their favor, upon which judgment was duly entered, and appellants present this appeal.

"A number of assignments of error are urged, differing in form and manner of statement, but all directed against the court's action in giving the peremptory instruction. The main contention is that the question of whether or not appellants' possession and occupancy of the land was as tenants of appellees, or of those who held under the appellees was one of fact for the jury to determine under all of the evidence, and should not have been taken from them by the court. This contention, we think, is easily correct, without giving to the evidence what seems to us to be its full force. As we read the statement of facts, it was well-nigh, if not indeed conclusively, established that no such tenancy existed, and that the independent adverse possession of the land by the Dolens began early in 1898 and continued uninterruptedly down until the time of the trial; but this court is not asked to render judgment in favor of appellants, their sole complaint being that the court below erred in taking the case from the jury. Accordingly, we merely sustain so much of the various assignments as presents that error, and reverse and remand the cause for another trial.

"The issue of tenancy referred to arose out of the following transactions between and among the various persons interested:

"In 1889 or 1890, J. O. Hutcheson and I. B. Baker began the conduct of a partnership cattle business near Cypress, in Harris county, keeping their cattle and horses in pastures known, respectively, as the H. R. pasture, the big pasture, the Kelley hill pasture, and the pony pasture; the last named being used exclusively for cow ponies. From 1891 or 1892 to about June, 1895, appellant I. S. Dolen worked for the firm of Hutcheson & Baker as their ranch foreman, looking after and caring for their stock in these different pastures; they furnished him while engaged in their services the Rock Roberts house to live in. In 1890, the 597.85 acres in controversy, together with other lands, was inclosed by Hutcheson & Baker in what was thus known as the pony pasture, under consent to them that it might

be so inclosed from M. Levy and J. Lobit, predecessors of appellees in title thereto; no rent being paid them for the privilege.

"Hutcheson & Baker sold all their partnership cattle in 1894, delivered them in the spring of 1895, and immediately dissolved their partnership; both members going out of the cattle business. A few cow ponies may have been left over; but, after thus selling their stock, the firm had but a single transaction, which was to fatten some beeves, closing that out in March, 1896. The firm did not use the pony pasture, in which was included the land in controversy, after the delivery of their stock in the spring of 1895, and soon thereafter a prairie fire almost completely destroyed its east string of fence, and seriously damaged the west string. I. S. Dolen ceased working for the firm of Hutcheson & Baker in June, 1895, and Baker died in June, 1896, just before his death giving Dolen his interest in the wire and posts as this fire had left in the east string of the pony pasture fence. J. O. Hutcheson, the other member of the firm, subsequently gave Dolen his interest also in the remnants of wire and posts left in this fence after the fire. Neither Hutcheson nor Baker knew what use Dolen intended to make of these remnants of posts and wire, neither gave him consent to take or use any part of the Moody land, neither knew that he had any intention of fencing or using any of it, and according to the testimony of Dolen, it lay out on the commons, unfenced, and used by the public generally for over two years subsequent to the fire following their discontinuance of its use; but early in 1898 I. S. Dolen having in the meantime bought 87½ acres in the Roberts survey to the south, and 175 acres in the Gary and Barrow surveys to the east and south of the pony pasture as constructed and maintained by Hutcheson & Baker, built a substantial three-strand barbed wire fence so as to inclose within it the 597.85 acres in controversy and the 87½ and 175 acre tracts thus purchased by him. While in doing this he used such posts and wire of the old Hutcheson & Baker fence around their pony pasture as were fit for the purpose, and substantially followed its lines along the north and part of the east sides, he extended its south and east strings in order to include the three additional tracts he had purchased, and drew in its west string to the line between the Merritt and the Moody surveys, thus comprising within what was thereafter generally known in that community as 'Dolen's pasture,' in all 860.85 acres, as against 597.85 acres of the Moody only as used by Hutcheson & Baker.

"Dolen testified, and in all essential features he was corroborated by other witnesses, that from and after the fixing up of this new fence by himself, though never having known who owned it, he intended to and did claim the Moody 597.85 acres openly and notoriously against the world; that he continuously kept, used, and occupied it for the operation of his dairy business until the date of this trial, at all times maintaining his fences and gates up and closed, and keeping his stock within and other people's stock out of it, having actually lived on the adjoining Gary 160 acres since 1900; that Hutcheson & Baker not only had nothing whatever to do with his so taking possession of and occupying the Moody land, by any agreement with him, or otherwise, but neither of them knew of it."

On the trial from which this appeal is prosecuted, Dolen's limitation claim was submitted to the jury, and, on their answer, judgment was entered in his favor for the land in controversy. In addition to the statement as made by Judge Graves, we give the following additional fact from this record.

On the 20th of May, 1901, Captain Hutcheson wrote Mr. Levy the following letter:

"Houston, Texas, 5—20—1901.

"Mr. M. M. Levy, Galveston, Texas—Dear Sir: Yours, requesting me to remove fence from your land on which it was constructed by Mr. I. B. Baker, received and contents noted. We are ready to comply with your request within a reasonable time, but as the writer did not have anything to do with the erection of this fence, and does not know exactly how it lies on your land, will you be kind enough to give me a rough plat of the same, so that I shall know exactly how to conform to your wishes? You will recollect that Mr. Baker, who is now dead, was the managing member of the firm, Hutcheson & Baker, in the cattle business, is the reason that I make this request.

"Very truly yours,

"Dic. J. C. H. [Signed] J. C. Hutcheson."

Captain Hutcheson knew nothing of the circumstances under which the land in controversy was fenced, and in writing this letter had in mind other lands of Lobit and Levy held under fence by the Hutcheson & Baker partnership. The land in controversy was held under contract made by Mr. Baker with Lobit and Levy, for the Hutcheson & Baker partnership. Mr. Levy replied to this letter as follows:

"Galveston, Texas, May 21, 1901.

"Mr. J. C. Hutcheson, Houston, Texas—Dear Sir: Yours of the 20th inst. duly received. Until we will have made sale, we will not ask you to remove the fence. When we do ask you, we will get the field notes and give same to you. You will understand that we have no desire to molest you, nor cause you any unnecessary expense, but of course if we make sale, it will be necessary to remove the fence, unless the party buying will be willing to allow you to keep it there. [Signed] M. M. Levy."

We are unable to distinguish this case on its facts from West Lumber Co. v. Sanders, 225 S. W. 828, an opinion by this court on which the Supreme Court denied writ of error.

[1] Hutcheson & Baker were tenants at will of Lobit and Levy. As such tenants, they never surrendered the possession thus given to their landlords, though they dissolved their partnership, and did not repair the fences after they were partly destroyed by fire. There was never a time, subsequent to their original entry, in which they could

231 S.W.—53

have been called trespassers had they entered on this land. Lobit and Levy did not know that the partnership had abandoned the possession. In fact, they thought that Hutcheson & Baker, as such tenants at will, were holding possession in their name during all these years. Nor are the circumstances in this record sufficient to give them constructive notice of that fact. During the years that Hutcheson & Baker held the land, Dolen was their agent, actually in the possession and control of the land. Had Lobit and Levy gone upon the land during the years 1891 to 1895, they would have found Dolen living near their land, and in actual possession as agent of their tenants. Had they gone there during the years 1895 to 1898, they would have found him living in the same house, and their land still under the fence placed there by their tenants, though in bad repair. Had they gone there during the years 1898 to 1912, when this suit was filed, they would again have found him in possession, holding and pasturing stock on their land, branded as the cattle of their former tenant, Hutcheson. In our judgment, there is not a circumstance in this record, in the absence of actual notice, to give Lobit and Levy notice of the adverse claim of Dolen, even had they gone upon this land in person. In view of the fact that Hutcheson & Baker had the right of entry, and that Lobit and Levy recognized them as their tenants, every circumstance of Dolen's holding could have been understood by them as being in subordination to their title.

[2, 3] What was Dolen's relation to Lobit and Levy? As he was in actual possession of their land for four years as the agent of Hutcheson & Baker, he was vested with constructive knowledge of all the facts and conditions of their entry. The fact that he did not know to whom the land belonged does not aid his limitation claim. Having been in possession for four years, under those who did know, he is vested with knowledge of that fact. As it affected Lobit and Levy, his holding during the years 1891 to 1895 was the same character as the holding of Hutcheson & Baker. He "stood in their shoes." This relation—in law, that of tenancy—having once existed, he could not make his personal entry of 1898 hostile, without visiting upon Lobit and Levy actual or constructive knowledge of his adverse claim. On the facts of this record, that notice was not shown. It seems to us clear that Dolen's claim does not bring him within the well-recognized rule:

"So long as the relation of landlord and tenant exists, the tenant cannot acquire an adverse title as against his landlord. It is equally well settled that one who enters as a tenant is not, merely because of that fact, precluded from subsequently holding adversely to his landlord. To do so, however, it is necessary to renounce the idea of holding as tenant, and to set up and assert an exclusive right in himself. It is also essential that the landlord should have actual notice of the tenant's claim, or that the tenant's acts of ownership should be of such an open, notorious, and hostile character that the landlord must have known it." 1 R. C. L. 747.

In our judgment, there was privity between the holding of Hutcheson & Baker and Dolen, not only on the facts just discussed, but also by reason of the fact that he entered upon the land for the purpose of repairing the fence erected and used by them under their tenancy contract. While it is true that they did not recognize that the placing of this fence on the land made it a part of the realty, and, in giving it to Dolen, did not intend to give him a part of or interest in the realty, yet, under their tenancy, they had the right of entry, and this right they gave to Dolen when they gave him the fence. Under this right, thus given him, Dolen's entry was lawful. Whatever may have been his secret purpose in taking possession of the land, the law made him privy to this tenancy contract, and fixed his status as that of tenant at will. West Lbr. Co. v. Sanders, supra, and authorities therein cited. It follows then that his claim could not become hostile to the owners until he brought himself within the rule above quoted from 1 R. C. L. 747.

As he did not do this, the court erred in not instructing a verdict for appellants.

In making this holding, we recognize that we are in direct conflict with the holding of the Court of Civil Appeals for the First Supreme Judicial District on the former appeal of this case, but, believing that this case is on "all fours" with our disposition of West Lumber Co. v. Sanders, we are left no alternative but to reverse the judgment of the trial court, and here render judgment for appellant. It is accordingly so ordered.

ERWIN et al. v. ERWIN. (No. 6577.)

(Court of Civil Appeals of Texas. San Antonio. May 26, 1921. Rehearing Denied June 18, 1921.)

1. Divorce ⟜93(3)—Petition alleging cruelty, etc., held sufficient.

In a wife's suit for divorce, a petition alleging habitual indifference, neglect, and failure to support, continual and habitual abuse, nagging and cursing, refusal to support and contribute to the support of the wife and their minor children, or to buy them clothes, and acts humiliating to the wife and rendering their living together as husband and wife insupportable, held sufficient in connection with a trial amendment stating times and details of the matters alleged.

2. Divorce ⟜106—Evidence that husband cursed wife and another in her presence held admissible under petition.

In a wife's suit for divorce, evidence that the husband cursed the wife on different occasions and cursed a third person in her presence held admissible under the petition, especially where the case was tried by the court, who was capable of separating the material testimony from the immaterial.

3. Divorce ⟜124—Court must be satisfied that divorce should be granted.

Whether a divorce case be tried with or without a jury, the trial court must be satisfied from all the testimony that a divorce should be granted as a matter of law, and in case of appeal the Court of Civil Appeals must be likewise satisfied.

4. Appeal and error ⟜742(2)—Jurisdictional question considered though not germane to assignment.

A jurisdictional question must be considered, though assigned as part of an assignment not germane to it.

5. Divorce ⟜27(3)—Physical violence not indispensable to show cruelty.

Under Rev. St. art. 4631, authorizing a divorce for excesses, cruel treatment, or outrages by either party, if such ill treatment is of such a nature as to render their living together insupportable, physical violence need not always be shown, and excesses, cruel treatment, or outrages of such a nature as will produce a degree of mental distress, threatening to impair the health of the injured party, is sufficient.

6. Divorce ⟜27(18)—Husband's mistreatment of wife held to entitle her to divorce.

Where a husband was unsanitary in his person, cursed the wife not only in privacy, but in the presence of others, neglected her and refused to furnish her and their children proper clothing, but allowed the wife to work to help support herself and the children while earning good wages himself, neglected her in her sickness, etc., and such acts were not occasional, but persistent, the wife was entitled to a divorce.

Appeal from District Court, Bexar County; W. S. Anderson, Judge.

Suit by Edna Erwin against W. S. Erwin and others. From a decree for plaintiff, defendants appeal. Affirmed.

Chambers, Watson & Johnson, of San Antonio, for appellants.

O. M. Fitzhugh and L. Allen, both of San Antonio, for appellee.

COBBS, J. This suit was brought by appellee for divorce against appellant and settlement and partition of the community estate between them. Briefly stated, it is alleged they were married in Inglefield, Ind., on or about the 13th day of October, A. D. 1907, and lived together as husband and wife until about a year before the institution of the present suit, when, because of the cruelties, excesses, and outrages of appellant, she ceased to live with him as his wife or in the same house with him. The statutory grounds for jurisdiction were sufficiently alleged and proven.

It is alleged that soon after the marriage appellant began a course of cruel, excessive, and inhuman conduct towards her, which continued until plaintiff was forced to leave him, and which rendered their future living together as husband and wife insupportable. Those grounds, generalized, are that, though earning good money, appellant wholly failed and refused to provide the ordinary necessities of life for her and their two minor children, so that she has been compelled by her own labor to supply such necessities, or obtain same as the gift of friends and relatives; that during their whole married life the appellant only furnished her two dresses; that she had to keep roomers and do such other work as she could to obtain means of support for herself and the two minor children. During all this time appellant was amply able to provide of his means such necessities for her and their children, but he willfully failed and refused to do so, to her shame, humiliation, and suffering.

Appellee further alleged he was habitually unclean and even filthy in his personal care of himself, going as much as three months at one time without bathing his body, without excuse, humiliating to her, and which made their living together as husband and wife insupportable.

Appellee further alleged appellant during all their married life together was given to violent outbursts of temper and would go into a rage of anger without excuse, justification, or provocation, and would indulge in the use of the most violent language, cursing, and swearing in the presence of and to appellee, and threatened to do her personal violence at times, which humiliated her and caused her great distress of both body and mind; that such line of conduct has been such as to give her great pain of mind and body, and has caused her to fear unless she separate from appellant and have an order restraining him from coming about or interfering with her, her health will be seriously broken and wrecked, which already has rendered their living together as husband and wife insupportable.

There are two children born to them, Lucille, 12 years old, and Geraldine, approaching 8 years old, who have been supported and cared for by appellee, and neglected and disregarded by appellant, and appellee prays for their custody and control.

In reply to the special exceptions appellee filed a trial amendment more definitely and specifically pleading and setting out the facts, times, etc., and more specifically alleging as to the times abusive language was used and circumstances concerning his rages, cursing, and swearing at and to her.

The appellant filed answer, containing general and specific objections to the petition. It will be observed there is no specific allegation of personal violence.

After hearing all the evidence the court granted the decree of divorce to appellee as prayed for.

[1] We overrule appellant's first, second, third, fourth, and fifth assignments of error, all challenging the sufficiency of the petition to state a cause of action because uncertain in its allegations of what constituted the acts of cruel treatment.

We think the petition and trial amendment sufficiently state a cause of action for divorce. They together state time, place, and material circumstances and acts of cruel treatment sufficiently. It is not necessary to point them out in detail here; the general grounds sufficiently appear as we set them out in the statement of this case and are proven in detail. It is based upon habitual indifference, neglect, and failure to support; continual and habitual abuse upon the part of appellant to appellee, persisted in continuously during the entire period of their married life; nagging, cursing, and abusing her and at her in the presence of others; refusing to support and to contribute to the support of herself and their minor children; refusal to buy her or them clothing; remaining uncleanly and refusing and neglecting to bathe his body, humiliating to her and insupportable.

[2, 3] The sixth, seventh, and eighth assignments of error complain of the action of the court in allowing Edna Erwin, appellee, to testify:

"I ask him to give me a check, and he said, 'Check! check! check! God damn you, that is all you talk about is check!'"

Again:

"My husband came home and asked me where I was going and I told him to the Majestic and he began to curse me. He said, 'God damn you, that is all you do is run around.'"

And again:

"Mr. Henry, the grocer, a little below us, came to the house for his grocery bill, and he came in and cursed Mr. Henry in my presence, and said, 'God damn you, you are afraid you won't get it.'"

These assignments are based on the objection taken at the time that there is no allegation, to support such testimony, irrelevant, immaterial, and prejudicial to the defendant. We think the pleading sufficiently broad enough to admit this testimony. Besides, the case was tried before the court without a jury, who was quite capable to separate the material testimony from the immaterial. Whether a case be tried with or without a jury, the judgment of the trial court, as to whether or not a divorce should be granted as a matter of law, must be satisfied from all the testimony, and so it must be with this court. Golding v. Golding, 108 S. W. 498.

[4] The ninth assignment of error is that the abusive language set out would not justify the dissolution of the marriage; that no evidence was shown that it produced injury to her mind or health, such as to render their living together as husband and wife insupportable. There is also raised in this same assignment the jurisdictional question that the appellee has not resided in the county of Bexar for a period of six months next preceding the filing of this suit. However illogically assigned as a part of an assignment not germane to it, we consider a jurisdictional question wherever it appears. Nevertheless as to this part of the assignment, the testimony is to the contrary, and it is overruled.

[5] Now as to the other questions: A divorce will be granted to either party where either "is guilty of excesses, cruel treatment or outrages toward the other, if such ill treatment is of such a nature as to render their living together insupportable." Article 4631, R. S. The statute is very broad. It will be observed that the statute, in referring to excesses, cruel treatment, or outrages, says "if such ill treatment is of such a nature," etc. In defining the words: "Ill conduct" in a divorce statute, it is held in Doe v. Roe, 23 Hun (N. Y.) 19–26, "does not mean ill conduct which was the cause of the ill treatment of complainant by defendant, alleged as a ground of divorce, but means any ill conduct." Huilker v. Huilker, 64 Tex. 2.

The appellant has well presented his theory in his excellent brief. To our mind his error consists of the fact that he seems to think there must always be shown some physical violence or such cruel treatment as is tantamount to it. He greatly relies on the opinion of this court in Rowden v. Rowden, 212 S. W. 302. We think the rule is well settled that the ill treatment spoken of in the statute means that such excesses, cruel treatment, or outrage must be of such a nature as will produce a degree of mental distress which threatens to impair the health of the injured party.

[6] Of course, we cannot place one standard of law or rule of conduct for one person that does not apply generally. But under the broad terms of the divorce statute that allows the court to ignore the finding of a jury and enter such judgment as convinces the judicial mind it must mean something more than the strict technical rules and standards applied in each case to every person. The same abuse, cursing and recursing, among a class utterly lacking in refinement, would perhaps pass unnoticed, as no possible hurt might be done to either, while such kept up between refined people would be inexcusable, unbearable, and intolerable, and would indeed be "ill treatment" in the highest degree of excesses and cruelty. Hence the reason of the rule that requires the courts to be satisfied, in each case where the divorce is sought, whether or not it should be granted. We do not think the authorities cited by appellant are to the contrary. Take this case for instance; the trial court had the parties before him and heard the testimony of many other witnesses besides the husband and wife. He saw what we cannot observe except from the record, but what we do see is that there is no language or expression from the appellee lacking in refinement, while the testimony shows the man unsanitary in his person, often not bathing his body, cursing her and at her, not only in privacy, but in the presence of others, neglecting her and refusing to give her and her children proper clothing, the father of two nice little girls, allowing his wife to work to help support herself and children, while earning good wages himself, allowing other people to help clothe his wife, neglecting her in her sickness, and many other elements of ill treatment not necessary to set out here, but sufficient to support the court's findings. If such course of conduct would not ultimately, and did not, "render their living together insupportable," it would be hard to conceive a cause that would have that effect. Bahn v. Bahn, 62 Tex. 521, 50 Am. Rep. 539; Eastman v. Eastman, 75 Tex. 475, 12 S. W. 1107.

Appellant's contention that the failure on the part of the wife to bring this suit earlier is to be held against her is not in our opinion justified by the facts. She is rather to be commended for her hesitancy, which was due to her reluctance to go before a court and expose her domestic life, and she waited, hoping for an improvement, until her girls began to arrive at an age to take notice.

From the earliest decision of our courts, it has never been necessary, under the broad terms of the statute granting divorces because of the ill treatment that amounted to cruel treatment, that there should be personal violence or bodily hurt. Sheffield v. Sheffield, 3 Tex. 87; Wright v. Wright, 6 Tex. 16; Eastman v. Eastman, 75 Tex. 473, 12 S. W. 1107; Dawson v. Dawson, 63 Tex. Civ. App. 168, 132 S. W. 381; Jones v. Jones, 60 Tex. 451; Taylor v. Taylor, 18 Tex. 578.

On the subject of divorces this court has been very pronounced against them, except it be made very clear that one should be granted. Lohmuller v. Lohmuller, 135 S. W. 753; Rowden v. Rowden, 212 S. W. 302; Bingham v. Bingham, 149 S. W. 214. We do not intend to limit or qualify those cases. They are authority here. While the pleadings nor evidence set out any physical violence, yet the pleading and evidence show such a line of general, persistent ill treatment, neglect, and disregard for his wife and children as to render their living together as insupportable. It is not a mere occasional instance of "abusive language used only once, or even at intervals," but is that with many other things and acts done, such as said by the late Justice Neill in Dawson v. Dawson, supra:

"It is now generally held, even in jurisdictions where the common law obtains, unaided by statutes such as ours, regarding causes for divorce, that 'any unjust conduct on the part of either the husband or wife, which so grievously wounds the feelings of the other, or so utterly destroys the peace of mind of the other as to seriously impair the health, or such as to utterly destroy the legitimate purpose and object of matrimony constitutes extreme cruelty,' constituting a cause for the dissolution of matrimony."

Many cases of cruel treatment have been based upon charges of the husband reflecting upon the wife's chastity.

No good woman should be compelled to live with a man who so assassinates her character, but that is not the only character of ill treatment that amounts to cruelty to her. The trial court heard all the testimony in this case and granted the divorce.

We find no reversible error assigned, and overrule the assignments.

The judgment of the trial court is affirmed.

POPE v. WITHERSPOON et al. (No. 6488.)

(Court of Civil Appeals of Texas. San Antonio. June 18, 1921.)

1. Trespass to try title ⟐11—Plaintiff need prove title only from common source.

Under Rev. St. art. 7749, making it sufficient to show by deeds a chain of title emanating from a common source, the burden is on plaintiff to deraign his title from the sovereignty of the soil unless there is a common source of title shown.

2. Deeds ⟐38(1)—Description is certain which can be made certain.

Descriptions of land are certain which can be made certain.

3. Trespass to try title ⟐41(2)—Descriptions in deeds held sufficient to show parties deraigned title from common source.

In trespass to try title, deeds introduced by plaintiff to show the title of defendant which contained descriptions varying from those in plaintiff's chain of title held to show that the land referred to was the same land, and to establish a common source of title.

4. Trespass to try title ⟐35(2)—Equitable right cannot be relied on under plea of not guilty.

Though the plea of not guilty in trespass to try title authorizes any defense which defeats recovery, since the suit is possessory, it does not authorize an unforeclosed equity in defend-

ant to defeat the recovery of the land by the true owner having the paramount legal title under the common source, but such equity must be set up by adequate pleading.

5. Subrogation ⟐14(2) — Subsequent incumbrancer held not entitled to subrogation against purchaser of one of several tracts.

Where a number of tracts of land had been sold subject to a vendor's lien, and two of them were resold to a subsequent purchaser who discharged the portion of the lien note chargeable against his tracts, a subsequent incumbrancer for money loaned to the first purchaser has no right of subrogation against the subsequent purchaser, especially where it was not shown the money loaned was applied to the payment of the original vendor's lien note, though the subsequent incumbrance recited the existence of that indebtedness.

6. Vendor and purchaser ⟐257 — Lienholder does not acquire title without foreclosure.

The holder of a lien upon tracts of land acquires no title thereto without foreclosure by proceedings in which all persons who had acquired interests in the land were made parties.

Error from District Court, Nueces County; W. B. Hopkins, Judge.

Trespass to try title by W. C. Witherspoon against W. E. Pope and others. Judgment for plaintiff, and the named defendant brings error. Affirmed on rehearing.

G. R. Scott and Boone & Pope, all of Corpus Christi, for plaintiff in error.

E. B. Ward, of Corpus Christi, and Taliaferro, Cunningham & Moursund, of San Antonio, for defendant in error Witherspoon.

COBBS, J. This is an action in the usual form of trespass to try title to lands. It was tried without a jury. Upon request of defendant, the court made special findings. There is also in the case a statement of facts. The court rendered judgment in favor of defendant in error for the land, and the first question raised here is that the trial court erred in finding that Mrs. H. M. King was the common source of title. As the court's findings are much in the nature of conclusions, we cannot clearly understand it without going to the statement of facts filed. Spearman v. Mims, 207 S. W. 574.

[1] In trespass to try title, the burden is on the plaintiff to deraign his title from and under the sovereignty of the soil, unless there is a common source of title shown. The necessity in this case of showing title from the sovereign is attempted to be obviated by introducing an intervening common source, in the person of Mrs. H. M. King, to which all these claimants are alleged to go in lieu of the sovereign. See article 7749 of the Revised Civil Statutes, providing that it shall not be necessary to deraign title beyond a common source, but suf-

ficient to show by deeds a chain of title emanating from and under such source. Branch v. Deussen, 108 S. W. 164.

[2] Defendant in error introduced muniments of title for the sole purpose of showing the common source, which it is contended did not describe the land in controversy. In regard to descriptions of lands, it is well settled that is certain which can be made certain. Bitner v. Land Co., 67 Tex. 342, 3 S. W. 301.

[3] The court found that the common source of title was Mrs. H. M. King, who conveyed 20 acres out of section No. 50, lot No. 20, of the Flour Bluff and Encinal Farm and Garden tracts in Nueces county.

The petition describes section No. 50 and 20 acres out of section 50, lot No. 20, out of Flour Bluff and Encinal Farm and Garden tracts, and introduces the title, to wit: King to Timmins describes section 50, Encinal and Flour Bluff Farm and Garden tracts; Timmins to Witherspoon describes section 50, lot No. 19, of Flour Bluff and Encinal Farm and Garden tracts. And second one, from and to same parties, describes section 50, lot No. 20, of the Flour Bluff and Encinal Farm and Garden tract.

The main defense of petitioner was urged under the plea of "not guilty." The case was tried by the court without a jury, and judgment was rendered for defendant in error for the land.

To prove the common source of title, the defendant in error introduced a number of consecutive transfers to plaintiff in error, each of the deeds describing the land as being lands out of "Flour Bluff and Encinal Farm and Garden tracts." In the deed of King to Timmins are described various lots, but no section 50, lot 19, and no section 50, lot No. 20, and it is not described as "Flour Bluff and Encinal Farm," etc., but "Encinal and Flour Bluff Farm," etc. Then follow deeds from Timmins of the land as described in Mrs. King's deed. The lots conveyed are Nos. 19 and 20 out of section 50.

Looking to the instruments introduced, and reading the recitals, references, and descriptions therein, the only conclusion that can properly be reached is that the reference is to the same land and identifies it, and that the common source is established. Bateman v. Jackson, 45 S. W. 224; Echols v. Jacob Mercantile Co., 38 Tex. Civ. App. 65, 84 S. W. 1082; Edwards v. Smith, 71 Tex. 159, 9 S. W. 77; Minor v. Lumpkin et al., 29 S. W. 801; Malone v. Long, 128 Md. 377, 97 Atl. 643. It is immaterial that the descriptions of the deed and petition do not exactly correspond, if it is apparent that the same land is meant. Gray v. Kauffman, 82 Tex. 68, 17 S. W. 513.

This assignment is overruled.

The record further shows that Mrs. King retained in her deed to R. L. Timmins the vendor's lien and superior title to secure a part of the purchase money payable in two notes. She transferred the second of these notes to John Tod, together with the superior title to the land. This note was released by Tod to Timmins. Timmins conveyed lot No. 19 out of section 50 to C. G. Witherspoon, on the 17th day of April, 1907; also lot No. 20 out of section 50, April 26, 1907, to C. G. Witherspoon. Then Timmins, subsequent to Witherspoon's purchase, executed a deed of trust to C. W. Ogden, trustee for Mrs. King, to secure two notes for $11,126.91, each describing them as the purchase-money notes for the land given by Timmins to Mrs. King, filed for record January 17, 1907. Tod, who purchased note No. 1 through his agent, Drought, released to Timmins note No. 1 on June 11, 1909, and on July 7, 1909, a release to same note due Mrs. King was executed by Ogden, trustee. October 13, 1908, Timmins executed a deed of trust to J. D. Crenshaw, as trustee for Mrs. Bodet, to secure note for $3,000, reciting it was borrowed—

"for the purpose of paying balance of the purchase money which the above-mentioned vendor's lien was retained to secure, and it is agreed that Mrs. Sophia Bodet be subrogated to all rights and privileges of said vendor's lien."

It was properly filed November 14, 1908. Mrs. Bodet transferred this note and lien to Mrs. Lyle Malone for a valuable consideration, and it was filed for record February 4, 1910. On March 1, 1910, the property described in deed of trust was sold to satisfy note purchased by Mrs. Malone. On October 1, 1910, she sold same through her attorney to Thomas W. Dunlap, which deed was duly filed for record, and she also made to him, on February 17, 1911, her quitclaim deed, also duly filed for record.

On October 5, 1910, Timmins quitclaimed and released to Thomas W. Dunlap all the rights in the described property, and a number of other lots, being same land conveyed by Mrs. King to him. Dunlap sold to Brooks and Brooks sold to Stanfield, retaining vendor's lien. Dunlap sold half interest in the notes to Jess W. Taylor. Dunlap and Taylor brought foreclosure suit, which property, being sold at sheriff's sale, was purchased by Taylor, who sold to S. C. Ingram, and Ingram sold to W. E. Pope.

[4] The chief defense was subrogation, presented under a plea of "not guilty." There were no special equitable defenses specially pleaded. Under the plea of "not guilty" any defense that defeats the recovery may be shown. That is because such a suit is possessory, and any bar that can be properly raised to defeat an entry may be interposed. But we know of no rule of pleading that will authorize a mere unforeclosed equity,

ᴏt properly pleaded, to be used under a plea of "not guilty" to defeat the recovery of the land by the true owner having the superior, paramount legal title under the common source, without an adequate pleading setting up and proving the supposed equities. Under a plea of "not guilty," the introduction generally of mere equities to establish claims of subrogation will not be entertained. See Wilkin ᵥ. Owens & Bros., 102 Tex. 199, 114 S. W. 104, 115 S. W. 1174, 117 S. W. 425, 132 Am. St. Rep. 867, in which the court says:

"It is held distinctly in the case of Fuller v. O'Neil, 69 Tex. 349, that in order to assert an equity of subrogation in property that had been illegally sold the facts must be pleaded. We think this is a correct ruling, and was approved by this court in the case of Crow v. Fidler, 3 Tex. Civ. App. 582, and in Matthews v. Moses, 21 Tex. Civ. App. 496, in which applications were made to this court for writs of error and refused. See, also, Black v. Garner, 63 S. W. 918."

And further on in the same case, discussing Williams v. Wilson, 76 Tex. 69, 13 S. W. 69, the court says:

"Since in an action of trespass to try title a defendant without a plea may show any fact that will defeat the plaintiff's right to recover, since in making out their case they showed the lease and the purchase money that was paid for it, they were held not entitled to recover without tendering the consideration shown to have been paid their ancestor for the land. We think that case clearly distinguishable from this, in which the attempt is to subrogate the parties claiming under the purchase to a lien upon the lands for the purchase money, on the ground that it had been used in paying the debts of the estate and the heirs had derived the benefit thereof."

[5] If the facts showed such a case as, in the administration of justice, should be reversed and remanded to permit petitioner to amend his pleadings, we would do that. But, as we understand the facts, no good would be accomplished by so doing, and therefore it will not be done.

To restate some of the facts: Mrs. H. M. King sold to R. L. Timmins a large number of lots (including the two in controversy), retaining the vendor's liens on all the land conveyed to him to secure two purchase-money notes. The second maturing note, maturing two years after date, she transferred to John Tod. That note being paid, the lien on that note was released by her to Timmins. Timmins, by two several deeds, one dated April 17, 1907, conveyed the two lots, Nos. 19 and 20, sued for to C. G. Witherspoon, who, in turn, having paid the purchase price of said lands to Timmins, secured release therefrom.

In no way does Witherspoon, defendant in error, assume the payment of any sum of money due to Mrs. King. In fact, as the

matter stood, he was in a position, if it had been necessary, to require Mrs. King to foreclose her lien on all the lots, and require that those unsold at the time be sold first, to protect his purchase. We have looked in vain to ascertain from any instrument, recital, or oral testimony, for that matter, where Mrs. King was ever paid by Timmins the amount due her on the other note, except by inferences and presumption. It is admitted by petitioner in error that she executed no release for it. The only evidence by which there is any claim that petitioner paid off any part of that lien, and is subrogated to her lien, or any other equity is claimed by petitioner to be in the recitals of a deed of trust from Timmins to Crenshaw, trustee, of November 13, 1906, which was after Timmins had parted with his title to Witherspoon, made for the benefit of Mrs. Sophia Bodet, in which it is recited, among other things, after describing the land, to further identify the same as the property "conveyed by Mrs. H. M. King to R. L. Timmins * * * and upon which a ,vendor's lien was retained in said deed," etc. The trust deed them continues and says:

"That whereas, R. L. Timmins and Willie R. Timmins, the said parties of the first part, are justly indebted to Mrs. Sophie Bodet, party of the third part herein, as evidenced by one certain promissory note executed by the said parties of the first part, and payable to the order of the said party of the third part, as follows, to wit:

"$3,000   San Antonio, Texas, Nov. 13, 1906.

"One year after date we, or either of us, promise to pay to the order of Mrs. Sophie Bodet, in San Antonio, Texas, the sum of three thousand dollars, with interest from date at the rate of eight per centum per annum, interest payable semiannually. In case this note is placed in the hands of an attorney for collection after maturity, or the same is collected through the probate court, we agree to pay the further sum of ten per centum of the amount due for attorney's fees. The money is borrowed for the purpose of paying off the balance of the purchase money which the above-mentioned vendor's lien was retained to secure and it is agreed that Mrs. Sophie Bodet shall be subrogated to all the rights and privilege of said vendor's lien."

The notes of Timmins to Mrs. King are each for the sum of $11,126.91, dated November 10, 1906, whereas the note in Timmins' deed of trust to Crenshaw trustee, to secure Mrs. Bodet, is dated November 13, 1906, and is for the sum of $3,000. In the former notes they bear interest at 6 per cent. per annum, and in the latter note it bears 8 per cent. interest per annum. There is nothing in that deed of trust except the reference to the deed in describing it by the words, "upon which a vendor's lien was retained in the deed," that pretends subrogation, other than in this subsequently executed trust deed in the language set out. That cannot bind defendant in error by any possible extension of the doctrine of subrogation of petitioner to the rights of Mrs. King, by presumption that the $3,000 was paid Mrs. King on the note. For aught this record shows, Mrs. King may still hold that note, and it would be just as much a lien against those other numerous lots sold to Timmins as against these two, and enforceable against all, unless barred by the statute of limitations.

There is no pretense of any foreclosure of Mrs. King's lien, whether as vendor or under any deed of trust or other procedure, but the claim is made under rights, secured under other foreclosures of subsequent liens to which neither Mrs. King nor defendant were parties or privy in estate, and he cannot be bound thereby. A mere debtor cannot subrogate the stranger who lends money to a lien held by a creditor, regardless of whether the creditor joins or whether the subsequent purchasers join. Mrs. King could not have foreclosed this deed of trust given to secure Mrs. Bodet in that $3,000 note, any more than Mrs. Bodet or her assignee could have foreclosed the deed of trust given to secure Mrs. King, under the language of the deed of trust attempting a subrogation to a note not shown to have any connection with the note held by Mrs. King. The notes are different. The deeds of trust are different, and the transaction different. If paid Mrs. King, there was no legal or equitable subrogation made by any party who had any right to do so. Suppose petitioner was in possession of lands upon which Mrs. King had a lien against Timmins; this would not give him the right to hold possession against defendant, the true owner, for he had no superior title by which to assert such a right. See Baker v. Compton, 52 Tex. 252. Under this authority the vendor may recover the land reciting ownership of unpaid purchase-money notes, but the mere assignee of such notes cannot do so. Subrogation can do no more than to create just such rights as were assigned, and it is clear that Mrs. Bodet herself, under the rights secured to her by the Timmins note, described in the deed of trust, could not defend against defendant in error in trespass to try title under a plea of "not guilty."

[6] It cannot for a moment be held that a person holding a mere lien acquires title without foreclosure. Russel v. Kirkbride, 62 Tex. 457. To do so would have required the making of Witherspoon and all the parties holding the numerous unsold lots, set out in the deed from Mrs. King to Timmins, parties. Williamson v. Conner, 92 Tex. 581, 50 S. W. 697.

Timmins, after he had parted with his title to defendant in error, had no power or authority thereafter to incumber it with any lien against his vendee. Gillum v. Collier, 53 Tex. 593.

While Timmins, as against himself, could substitute a new note and lien to Mrs. King, and impress it as a part of the consideration of the purchase, he did not have the power to extend it to the land he had sold, without the consent of his vendee, based upon some valuable consideration to compel him to bear such imposed burden. However, we do not think he attempted to do so.

We have not discussed the legal effect of other transfers and sales bearing on petitioner's claim of subrogation, because, from what we have said, he was in no position to assert such a claim. But we have determined also that the alleged lien or right of subrogation has not extended to or passed to him by the muniments of title shown.

From the view we take of this case, there is neither pleading nor proof that establishes any right in petitioner of subrogation, and no good purpose would be accomplished by reversing the judgment and remanding for another trial. We, therefore set aside our previous judgment in reversing and rendering, and recall our original opinion, file this in lieu thereof, and grant defendant in error a rehearing. Upon reconsideration of the whole case we find no merit in any error assigned, and we affirm the judgment of the trial court.

SMITH et al. v. WOMACK et al. (No. 6264.)

(Court of Civil Appeals of Texas. Austin. April 6, 1921. Rehearing Denied June 8, 1921.)

1. **Mines and minerals ☞73—Oil and gas lease conveys interest in the land.**

An oil and gas lease giving the lessee power to take and remove oil and like minerals conveys an interest in the land.

2. **Executors and administrators ☞150—Executors not authorized to grant oil and gas lease.**

Where a will gave power to executors and executrixes to do and perform anything in and about the management and control and disposition of the estate, and to carry the provisions of the will into execution, but there were no express terms authorizing sale of mineral rights, the executors, etc., have no authority to grant an oil and gas lease.

3. **Mines and minerals ☞74—Where title to be conveyed would be doubtful, specific performance of contract to purchase oil and gas lease will not be granted.**

Where the title tendered by executors contracting to grant an oil and gas lease on the lands of the testatrix was at best so doubtful that it was not a merchantable title, the purchaser is entitled to refuse and performance will not be enforced.

☞For other cases see same topic and KEY-NUMBER in all Key-Numbered Digests and Indexes

Appeal from District Court, Williamson County; Ireland Graves, Judge.

Action by George W. Smith and others against Frank R. Womack and others. From a judgment for defendants, plaintiffs appeal. Affirmed.

W. H. Nunn and F. D. Love, both of Georgetown, for appellants.

Critz, Lawhon & McNair, of Taylor, for appellees.

KEY, C. J. The following statement is copied from the brief of appellants:

"The appellants, all of the devisees under the will, Mary Shelby Smith, deceased, sued the appellees, Frank R. Womack, and the First National Bank of Taylor, Tex., in the district court of Williamson county, Tex., for the sum of $1,500, and for cause of action allege: That George W. Smith, acting for himself and the other plaintiffs, and the defendant Frank R. Womack, entered into a certain contract in writing, under the terms of which Frank R. Womack deposited in the said First National Bank of Taylor, Tex., the sum of $1,500, with instructions to the said bank that the said money should be turned over and delivered to the said George W. Smith in the event that the said George W. Smith procured to be acknowledged by himself, Fannie Smith, William Wayne Smith, Blanch Smith and Murry Smith, a certain oil lease, in the capacity shown by the said oil lease, and caused same to be delivered to the said Frank R. Womack within 10 days from said date. The said oil lease, having heretofore been prepared, the form, terms and conditions agreed upon.

"That the plaintiffs complied with all of the terms and conditions of the said contract, and caused the said oil lease to be duly acknowledged and delivered within said ten days; but that the defendants then and there refused to turn over and deliver the said $1,500 to the plaintiffs.

"The defendant bank answered, alleging that it held the $1,500 in escrow, and that it stood ready and willing to pay the same to the party entitled thereto, and prayed for judgment of the court directing to whom it should pay same.

"The defendant Frank R. Womack answered that at the time the making of the said contract the plaintiff George W. Smith represented that he, together with the other proposed makers of the lease contract, as the executors of the will of Mary Shelby Smith, deceased, had the power to make the said lease contract; and that the defendant Womack relied upon the said representations so made; that the said George W. Smith and the other executors of the said will did not in fact have the power to make the said oil lease contract under the terms of the said will; and that the said defendant did not learn of the said want of power till after the making of the first named contract; that a copy of the said will is attached to the said answer.

"The following agreement was made in open court, on the trial of the said cause, to wit: 'It is agreed by both parties that the contracts were in fact drawn as alleged, and that copies of them were left in the possession of the law firm of Critz, Lawhon & McNair; that within 10 days from the execution of the mutual contract, the plaintiff George W. Smith turned over to the said law firm of Critz, Lawhon & McNair, which was acting for the defendant Frank R. Womack, a certified copy of the will and of the probate of the will of his deceased wife; that within 10 days of the execution of the mutual contract the plaintiff George W. Smith tendered to the defendant Frank R. Womack the oil lease contract, and that it was executed in the manner required by both the mutual contract and the oil lease contract. It is further agreed by the parties that no objection at this time, or any other time, was urged to the title of the plaintiffs in the property, except the objection of the want of power or authority in the plaintiffs to make the lease contract.' It appeared from the proof that the property covered by the oil lease was the separate property of Mary Shelby Smith, deceased, and is covered by her will.

"The case was tried before the court without a jury, and judgment was rendered for the defendants, from which the plaintiff in due time appealed to this court.

"The only issue made upon the trial of the case was whether the executors under the will of Mary Shelby Smith, deceased, had the power to make the oil lease; it being contended by appellees that the will itself denied such power."

Appellees concede the correctness of that statement, with the following additions thereto; Appellee Frank R. Womack denied that the will of Mary Shelby Smith, through which the plaintiffs derived title, conferred upon the executors or trustees the power to sell the land, or execute the contract referred to in the plaintiffs' petition. That defendant also averred in his answer that he was induced to enter into the contract referred to by the representations of the plaintiff George W. Smith that he and the other parties plaintiff had the power and authority to grant, convey, and deliver to said defendant the contract in question, and to convey the mineral, oil, and gas rights in and under the land described in said lease contract, and that such power and authority was derived from and given by the will of Mary Shelby Smith; which representation defendant Womack alleged was not true but, on the contrary, the will denied to the plaintiffs any such power to convey. Womack also pleaded, in substance, that it was the duty of the plaintiffs to furnish a good marketable title, and that the title furnished was defective, doubtful, and hazardous, and therefore the court was justified in not rendering judgment for the plaintiffs.

There was a nonjury trial, which resulted in a verdict and judgment for the defendants; and the plaintiffs have appealed.

In the court below and in this court, the defendant bank was and is in the attitude of a stakeholder, and is willing to abide the judgment of the court, and pay the money to whichever party it may be adjudged to belong, but asks that it be relieved of all costs.

The trial court filed the following findings of fact, which are conceded to be correct:

"(1) I find that on June 19, 1919, the plaintiff Geo. W. Smith, as first party, and defendant Frank R. Womack, as second party, executed the instrument referred to in the pleadings as the mutual contract, a copy of which is attached to the plaintiffs' first amended original petition and marked 'Exhibit B.'

"(2) I find that on the same date, namely, June 19, 1919, Geo. W. Smith and Frank R. Womack signed the oil lease contract, a copy of which is attached to said amended petition, marked 'Exhibit A.' That at the same time as stated in the so-called 'mutual contract,' defendant Womack deposited with defendant bank the sum of $1,500, to be held by the bank in accordance with the terms of said 'mutual contract.'

"That the oil lease contract (Exhibit A), bearing Womack's signature, was retained by Messrs. Crits, Lawhon & McNair, defendant Womack's attorneys, with the understanding that Geo. W. Smith was to procure the signatures thereto of the plaintiffs, Murry Smith, William Wayne Smith, Blanch Smith, and Fannie Smith, which was afterwards done.

"(3) It was also understood and agreed by Geo. W. Smith and Womack, at the time Womack signed said instruments, that Geo. W. Smith was to furnish to Womack's attorneys, within the 10 days' period referred to in the mutual contract, certified copies of the probate proceedings, showing the probate of the last will of Mary Shelby Smith, the deceased wife of Geo. W. Smith, who was the owner, in her separate right, of the property referred to in the oil lease contract.

"(4) At the time of the execution of the 'mutual contract,' Geo. W. Smith represented to Womack that under the terms of his wife's will, he and the others who subsequently signed the oil lease contract had authority to execute the same; and it was understood at that time that unless thereby Womack could acquire valid title to that which the oil lease contract purported to convey, Womack was not to be required to go forward with the contract.

"(5) Within the 10 days referred to, Smith furnished certified copy of the probate proceedings and Womack's attorneys (also within said period), after examining said papers, informed Geo. W. Smith that in their opinion those who were signatories to the oil lease contract as grantors had no authority under the will to execute such instrument, and that Womack would therefore refuse to go forward with the contract.

"(6) Item third of Mary Shelby Smith's will reads as follows: 'I hereby nominate, constitute and appoint my husband, George W. Smith, and my sister-in-law, Fannie Smith, my sons, William Wayne Smith, Murry Smith, and George Earl Smith, and my daughters, Blanch Smith and May Dee Smith, the independent executors and executrices and trustees to carry out this my will, and no bond or other security is to be required of them or either of them, and I hereby confer upon them full power and authority to carry into execution all the terms, conditions and provisions in this will contained.'

"(7) Item eleventh reads in part as follows: 'It is my will that the executors, executrices and trustees heretofore named who have arrived at the age of twenty-one years at my death may qualify as such by taking and subscribing the oath required by law of executors; and each of my children under the age of twenty-one years at my death may upon arriving at that age likewise qualify by taking such oath.'

"(8) Item twelfth provides, substantially in the language of the statute authorizing the administration of an estate by an independent executor, that the courts shall have no jurisdiction other than to admit the will to probate and permit the returning of an inventory, etc.; and said item reads further as follows: 'And I hereby confer full and ample authority and power upon such of my executors and executrices as may qualify to do and perform any and everything in and about the management, control and disposition of my estate and to carry the provisions of this will into execution.'

"(9) Item fourth is as follows: 'I hereby will, bequeath and devise to my said executors and executrices and trustees all my property and estate, real, personal and mixed, of which I may die seized and possessed, or to which I may be entitled by inheritance, bequest and devise, or otherwise, to hold, manage, and control the same as hereinafter provided.'

"(10) Item fifth reads in part as follows: 'It is my will and I so direct that my said executors and executrices and trustees shall keep, hold and control the corpus of my estate, to lease and rent the same in the best possible manner to secure the largest income or revenue compatible to the interest of my estate, and the income or earning of my estate, including any life insurance of which I am the beneficiary, shall be divided into eight equal parts.' The will further provides that two of the eight shares of the annual income shall be paid over to Geo. W. Smith, and one share to each of the other persons named as executors, executrices and trustees. It further provides that upon each child's reaching the age of 30 years one-eighth of the corpus of the estate shall be delivered to such child, subject, however, to an attempted restraint upon alienation until such beneficiary shall have reached the age of 40 years. Other provisions of item fifth direct more specifically the manner in which the shares of the revenues given to the children shall be applied and handled during their minority, etc.

"(11) Item seventh provides that the one-eighth of the corpus of the estate bequeathed to Fannie Smith (sister-in-law to testatrix) may, at her option, be set apart to her at any time after the death of testatrix, to be used and held by her for her life with full power to sell and convey the same or any part thereof, and at her death any undisposed part thereof to revert to the estate and be divided equally among the children of testatrix or their descendants.

"(12) Substantially the same character of provision is contained in item eighth with respect to the two-eighths share of the corpus of the estate, the income from which is given to Geo. W. Smith for his life, except that he is not given power to dispose of the corpus of such two-eighths interest.

"(13) At the time of the execution of the oil lease contract, Geo. W. Smith, the father, Fannie Smith, the sister-in-law, and Murry Smith, William Wayne Smith and Blanch Smith, three of the children, had qualified as independent executors of the will, and each of them executed the contract in such capacity as well as individually. The other two children, George Earle Smith and May Dee Smith, being minors, had not qualified as executors, and did not join in the execution of the contract.

"(14) The testatrix, Mary Shelby Smith, died prior to January 14, 1918, and her will was filed for probate on that date.

"(15) It was not shown or contended that the oil lease contract was executed for the purpose of raising money to pay debts of the estate of Mary Shelby Smith."

The written instrument denominated a "lease contract," which was tendered by the plaintiffs as a compliance upon their part with the contract sued on among other things, contains the following provisions:

"Know all men by these presents: That we, George W. Smith, Fannie Smith, William Wayne Smith, Blanche Smith and Murrey E. Smith, for ourselves individually, and as independent executors of the estate of Mary Shelby Smith, deceased, late of Jefferson county, Texas, have and do hereby lease unto F. R. Womack, of the county of Williamson and State of Texas, his heirs and assigns, the tract of land herein described for the purpose of exploiting the same for the extraction of minerals therefrom; and we do hereby also grant and convey unto the said F. R. Womack all of the oil, gas and other minerals in and under said land, as also the exclusive right of drilling and operating thereon for oil or gas, together with a right of way for and a right to lay pipe lines to convey water, steam, oil and gas, and a right to have and use sufficient water, oil and gas from the premises to drill and operate any wells that he may bore or drill thereon; and for such other privileges as are reasonably requisite for the conduct of said operations; and a right to remove at any time from said premises any and all property which may have been placed thereon by the said F. R. Womack, his heirs or assigns."

Mrs. Smith added a codicil to her will, which reads as follows:

"Whereas, I, Mary Shelby Smith, of the county of Jefferson and state of Texas, have heretofore made my last will and testament bearing date the 6th day of May, A. D. 1916: Now, I do by this instrument, which I hereby declare to be a codicil to my will, further direct my executors, executrices and trustees to exercise all efforts to pay such debts as my estate should owe at the time of my decease, out of the rents and revenues of my estate, so as to keep my estate, or as much as thereof is possible, intact for the trust estate heretofore created in the original will; and to that end my said executors, executrices and trustees shall use the gross income in the payment of said debts as well as in the payment of the taxes and other necessary expenses of the estate, including the premium on my insurance policy."

Opinion.

As conclusions of law, the trial court held:

(1) That the instrument designated as the "oil lease contract," wherein the grantors purported to "grant and convey unto the said F. R. Womack all of the oil, gas, and other minerals in and under said land," was an attempted conveyance of a part of the land.

(2) That as it was not shown that any debts existed against the estate, it was not made to appear that the executors had power and authority to convey any part of the real estate.

(3) That even if the will could be construed as conferring such power to convey, yet such authority was of so doubtful a character that, in the absence of a prior judicial construction to that effect, the defendant was justified in rejecting the title on account of such uncertainty.

[1] The first conclusion of the trial court, to the effect that the instrument referred to purported to convey an interest in and part of the land itself, is now well settled in this state. See Texas Company v. Daugherty, 107 Tex. 226, 176 S. W. 717, L. R. A. 1917F, 989, decided by our Supreme Court, and other authorities referred to by Chief Justice Phillips in the able opinion prepared by him in that case.

[2, 3] It is quite clear that the will does not, in express terms, confer upon the executors the power to sell, unless it be that such power is conferred by that provision which reads:

"And I hereby confer full and ample authority and power upon such of my executors and executrices as may be qualified to do and perform any and everything in and about the management, control, and disposition of my estate, and to carry the provisions of this will into execution."

Of course, the words "management and control" cannot be construed as conferring power of sale, while in certain circumstances the word "disposition" may be given that meaning. However, when all the terms of the will are taken into consideration, and especially those which direct that the corpus of the estate shall be preserved intact, we do not believe the word "disposition" in this will was intended to confer the power of sale. But if mistaken in that respect, we agree with the trial judge in his last conclusion of law, to the effect that the construction of the will is so doubtful as that the title which was tendered by the plaintiffs was not a merchantable title, and for that reason the defendant had the right to refuse to accept it; and that the trial judge did not err in rendering judgment against the plaintiffs. Roos v. Thigpen, 140 S. W. 1180; Clegg v. Brannan, 190 S. W. 812.

No reversible error has been shown, and the judgment is affirmed.

Affirmed.

BAKER v. HODGES. (No. 698.)

(Court of Civil Appeals of Texas. Beaumont.
May 25, 1921.)

1. Railroads ⬳307(4)—Flagman only required at unusually dangerous crossings.

A railway company's duty to keep a flagman at a public highway crossing only arises where the crossing can be said to be attended with extra hazard or unusual danger, which depends upon the extent of the use of the crossing and the surrounding circumstances.

2. Railroads ⬳350(5)—Negligence in maintaining flagman question of fact.

If a highway crossing over a railroad is used extensively and frequently by the public, and trains are operated over it at frequent intervals, and there are obstructions materially obstructing the view of approaching trains, it is a question for the jury, or for the court sitting without a jury, whether the failure to have a flagman at the crossing constitutes a failure to use such care as an ordinarily prudent person would use under the same or similar circumstances.

3. Railroads ⬳308—Violation of ordinance requiring flagman negligence.

Where a valid city ordinance requires a flagman at a railroad crossing, it is negligence as a matter of law on the part of the railroad company to fail to comply with such ordinance, and if such failure is the proximate cause of an injury to one using the crossing, the railroad company is liable.

4. Railroads ⬳350(5)—Negligence of conductor failing to station flagman at crossing held question of fact.

Where the conductor of a freight train, standing on a passing track for the purpose of allowing a passenger train to pass, knew that the passenger train was soon to arrive, and that the view of persons using the crossing would be greatly obstructed by the presence of the freight train, and that a switch engine near by, puffing and making a noise, possibly prevented persons from hearing the approach of the train, and that the freight train left only a narrow passage over the track, and that the crossing was extensively used, it was a question of fact for the trial court sitting as a jury whether he acted as an ordinarily prudent person in failing to place some member of the crew at the crossing as a flagman until the passenger train had passed.

5. Railroads ⬳337(1)—Failure to have flagman at obstructed crossing held proximate cause of injury.

The failure of the conductor of a freight train waiting on a passing track at a highway crossing for a passenger train to pass to station a member of the crew at the crossing as a flagman was the proximate cause of an injury to one struck by the train, though other persons attempted to warn him of the approach of the train, and he failed to heed the warning, where it appeared that he did not hear their warnings or see their signals.

6. Railroads ⬳316(4)—Speed ordinance immaterial where speed was negligent.

Whether an ordinance limiting the speed of trains to 10 miles an hour applied to the receiver of a railway was immaterial, where the trial judge found as a fact that the receiver was negligent in operating the train at the rate of speed at which it was operated over a crossing, and such finding was supported by the evidence.

7. Railroads ⬳350(11)—Negligent speed held question of fact.

Whether the operation of a train at a speed of 25 miles an hour over the principal crossing in a city or town of 1,200 to 1,400 inhabitants, which was near the depot and station and was obstructed by a long freight train, cut in the middle of the street and leaving a passage of only 16 feet for the use of the public, was negligence, was a question of fact for the trial court sitting without a jury.

8. Appeal and error ⬳742(1)—Statement under assignment as to contributory negligence should be full and fair.

Under rule 31 for Courts of Civil Appeals, an assignment of error, complaining of a finding that plaintiff was not guilty of contributory negligence, should be supported by a full and fair statement of all the evidence in the record bearing upon the question of contributory negligence.

9. Damages ⬳130(2)—Verdict of $3,500 for injuries to shoulder and other injuries not excessive.

Where a farmer, 42 years old, also owning and operating a cotton gin, and in robust health, was confined in the hospital for 12 days and to his house for about 6 weeks as the result of an injury, and 2 years after the accident his shoulder was still so badly injured that he could not raise his arm above his head or chop with an axe or use a hoe, and he had suffered a great deal of physical pain, and his physical capacity for work was reduced fully two-thirds, an award of $3,500 as damages was not excessive.

10. Damages ⬳62(2)—Only ordinary care required in treatment of injuries.

An injured person is only required to use ordinary care and prudence in the treatment of his injuries.

Appeal from District Court, Robertson County; John Watson, Judge.

Action by A. J. Hodges against James A. Baker, receiver of the International & Great Northern Railway Company. From a judgment for plaintiff, defendant appeals. Affirmed.

H. A. Bush and J. L. Goodman, both of Franklin, and Henderson & Ranson, of Bryan, for appellant.

J. C. Scott, of Corpus Christi, K. W. Gilmore, of Houston, and Perry & Woods, of Franklin, for appellee.

HIGHTOWER, C. J. This suit was filed by the appellee, Hodges, as plaintiff below, against the appellant, James A. Baker, in his capacity as receiver of the International & Great Northern Railway Company, for the recovery of damages because of personal injuries alleged to have been sustained by appellee, and also for damages to his automobile. The accident occurred in the town of Franklin, Robertson county, about sundown on the 28th day of November, 1917, while the appellee was driving his automobile along one of the principal streets of that town, and where the same is crossed by the railway track.

It was alleged by appellee that his view of the track upon which the approaching train was traveling was obstructed by a freight train, which had been placed upon a side track near and parallel to the main track, and that the freight train was then cut so as to leave the crossing open for passage, etc. Plaintiff then alleged that there was no flagman at this crossing, and that the train, at the time of the accident, was running at a dangerous and excessive rate of speed, and that those in 'charge of the train gave no warning of its approach to the crossing. The specific grounds of negligence alleged were (1) that appellant failed to have stationed at said crossing where said freight train had been cut a flagman or some other employé, who could and should have warned appellee and other persons about to cross said railway track of the aproach of said passenger train; (2) that appellee was guilty of negligence in placing said freight train and box cars on said side track in such position that they obstructed the view of the crossing and the main line thereabout, so that appellee and any person approaching said crossing from the south of the track could not see the approach of the passenger train which collided with appellee's automobile, until they had passed said freight train and box cars so placed on said side track; (3) that the servants and employés of appellant, in charge of the passenger train, failed to give warning of the approach thereof, by sounding any warning and by failing to ring the bell of the locomotive on the engine, as it approached said crossing in the corporate limits of the town of Franklin, in violation of a duty which appellant owed to appellee and others who might be about to cross said track, and that such failure was in direct violation of an ordinance of the town of Franklin, and also in violation of the statute of this state, which required that the bell on said locomotive should be rung at a distance of at least 80 rods from said crossing, and should be kept ringing until said crossing had been passed; (4) that the servants and employés of appellant, in charge of said passenger train, were at the time of said collision operating and running the same at a rate of approximately 25 miles per hour, which rate of speed at said time and place and in proximity to said street crossing was reckless and dangerous,

and was, besides, in direct violation of an ordinance of said town, which limited the rate of speed of trains to 10 miles per hour.

Appellant answered by general demurrer and special exceptions unnecessary to mention, and then specially alleged that appellee's injuries were the result solely and proximately of his own contributory negligence, in the following respects: (1) Because he failed to note the approach of the train, the warning of which was given by the flash of the headlight, by the bell and whistle, and that if he had been using any care for his own safety he could have heard same; (2) because he was violating the law of the state in approaching a railroad crossing at a rate of speed exceeding 6 miles per hour, and that he was doing same in a reckless and in an intoxicated, or semi-intoxicated, condition; (3) that as he approached said crossing, he was warned by different parties that the train was coming, and he heard same, or could have heard same if he had been paying any attention to his own safety, and that on account of such contributory negligence on his part, which was the proximate cause of his injuries, if any, appellee sustained such injuries, if any, and appellant, therefore, is not liable for same.

The case was tried before the trial court without a jury, and judgment was rendered in favor of appellee for $3,900, to which judgment appellant duly excepted, and has perfected an appeal to this court.

At the request of appellant, the trial judge prepared and filed findings of fact and conclusions of law, which are quite full, and they will serve as a sufficient statement of the facts upon which the judgment appealed from was based, and we copy them in full, as follows:

"(1) I find that Jas. A. Baker is receiver of the International & Great Northern Railway Company, and that he was such receiver on the 28th day of November, A. D. 1917, the date on which plaintiff received the injuries for which judgment is rendered herein; and that, as such receiver, the said Jas. A. Baker did, at the said time, and does now, operate a line of railway through Robertson county, Tex., and through the incorporated city of Franklin, in said county and state, where said injuries were inflicted upon plaintiff.

"(2) I find that, on the 28th day of November, 1917, defendant, for the use and convenience of the public, kept and maintained a public road and street crossing over and across his said line of railway, which was the principal crossing in the said city of Franklin, and located just east of and adjacent to the passenger and freight depot in said city; said street at said crossing being about 80 feet in width.

"(3) I find that the said city or town of Franklin was, on said date, the county seat of Robertson county, that its population was approximately 1,200 to 1,400 inhabitants; that the principal business portion of said town was located on the north side of defendant's railroad, and about ¼ of the population of said town resided on the south side of said railroad; that a large trade territory tributary to said town was also located south of said railroad, and that said crossing was the one mostly used by people residing in and near said town on the south side of said railroad in going to and returning from the business portion of said town, and that said crossing was the principal crossing used by the public generally while passing between the north and south sides of said town.

"(4) I find that, at the point where said railroad crossed said street, at said time, defendant had and maintained a passing track, which was located about 10 feet south of the main line of said railroad, and also had a side track, commonly called the house track, which was located about 39 feet south of said passing track, and that Carter & Maris' lumber office was located about 60 feet south of said house track and on the east side of said street.

"(5) I find that, on said date, plaintiff, in company with two of his neighbors, W. O. Streater and W. A. Sparks, who were riding in his automobile with him, while driving across said railroad at said crossing was struck by a west-bound passenger train, which was then and there within the scope of their employment, and that, by reason of said collision, and as a direct and proximate result thereof, plaintiff was seriously and permanently injured, and his automobile was also badly broken, injured, and demolished as the proximate result of said collision.

"(6) I find that, a few minutes before said collision, the servants and employés of defendant in charge of a local freight train, while acting within the scope of their employment, placed a long string of box cars on said passing track, leaving an opening or cut through same at said crossing only about 16 feet wide, and that the section of said box cars extending eastward from said crossing covered practically all of the said passing track lying east of said street, and said section of cars also extended westward to about the center of said street, the west end of said east string of cars being so placed that the same extended into and across a part of the beaten roadway near the center of said street, thereby obstructing the view and passageway along that part of said street; that said string of box cars were in said position at the time of said collision, and they effectually obstructed the view of persons approaching said crossing from the south, and would and did prevent such persons from seeing the approach of a west-bound train on the main line track while approaching said crossing. I find that the act of defendant's said servants and employés, in placing said string of box cars so that the same extended into and incumbered said street and roadway, was negligence on their part, and that said negligence was a proximate cause of plaintiff's said injuries and damage.

"(7) I find that the servants and employés of defendant, in charge of said freight train, while acting within the scope of their employment, switched said freight train and box cars on said passing track for the purpose of letting said passenger train pass by; that it was then only a few minutes until said passenger train was due to arrive, and the conductor of defendant in charge of said freight train then knew that said passenger train was soon due to arrive; that said conductor knew that said crossing was the principal crossing in said town, and that the same was frequently used by the public; that, at the time of the arrival of said passenger train the locomotive of said freight train was working and moving about only a short distance down to the west from said crossing, being engaged in spotting some cars on one of the side tracks, and the same was then and there puffing and emitting steam, and the bell thereon was ringing, all of which made considerable noises at and about said crossing, all of which was known to said conductor; that, notwithstanding the said conditions then existing at and about said crossing, said conductor, while acting within the scope of his employment, failed and neglected to place a member of his train crew at said crossing, and failed and neglected to have any other person at said crossing, to warn persons about to cross there of the approach of said passenger train. I find that such failure and omission of duty on the part of said conductor, under the peculiar conditions and circumstances then existing at said crossing, was negligence on his part, and that said negligence was a proximate cause of plaintiff's said injuries and damage.

"(8) I find that, on said date, and at the time of said collision, there was in full force and effect a penal ordinance of the said incorporated city of Franklin, providing that it shall be unlawful for any operator, engineer, brakeman, conductor, or other person to run, or cause to be run, in or through the corporate limits of said city of Franklin, any engine, car, or train at a greater rate of speed than 10 miles per hour, and prescribing a penalty for the violation thereof; I find, that said passenger train, at the time and place of said collision, which was within said corporate limits, was being run by the engineer who was a servant and employé of defendant, acting within the scope of his employment, and that said engineer was then and there causing said passenger train to be run through the corporate limits of said city of Franklin at a speed which was greatly in excess of 10 miles per hour, and that the running of said train at said time and place at a greater rate of speed than 10 miles per hour was a proximate cause of the injuries and damages sustained by plaintiff in said collision.

"(9) I find that defendant's said passenger train, at the time it collided with plaintiff's automobile, was being run and propelled by the engineer and servant of defendant in charge thereof, and who was then and there acting within the scope of his employment, at a high, reckless, and dangerous rate of speed, to wit, about 25 miles per hour, and that said engineer, in so causing said train to run at such rate of speed at said crossing and in close proximity to said depot and station, was guilty of negligence, and that said negligence was a proximate cause of plaintiff's said injuries and damage.

"(10) I find that plaintiff was not intoxicated at the time of said collision, and that neither of his companions were intoxicated; that plaintiff did not fail to exercise ordinary care for his own safety while approaching said crossing, nor did the said W. C. Streater or W. A. Sparks fail to exercise such care; that plaintiff did not cause his automobile to be run at a greater rate of speed than 6 miles per hour

.t any point within 30 feet of said main line
rack and crossing; that plaintiff did not fail
o exercise ordinary care to keep his said au-
omobile under control while approaching said
:rossing; that plaintiff and his said compan-
ons, before going upon said crossing and while
approaching the same, each and all looked and
listened and did everything that a person of
ordinary prudence would do under the same or
similar circumstances to discover the approach
of trains at and about said crossing, but neither the plaintiff nor either of his said companions discovered or heard the said passenger
train until they had passed through the cut or
opening in said freight train and around the
west end of the east string of box cars on said
passing track, and it was then too late, by the
use of any means at plaintiff's command, or
that of either of his said companions, to avoid
said collision and his said injuries and damage
occasioned thereby. I find that neither the
plaintiff nor either of his companions were
guilty of negligence in any particular while approaching said crossing, and that plaintiff was
not guilty of contributory negligence.

(The eleventh finding is immaterial to any
contention before this court.)

"(12) I find that, at the time of said collision, plaintiff was a strong healthy man, 42
years of age, and had a life expectancy of 26.72
years; that, as a direct and proximate result
of the negligence of the servants and employés
of defendant, while acting within the scope of
their respective employments, plaintiff was
seriously and permanently injured; that he sustained several cuts and bruises upon his person; that his left clavicle was broken near the
middle, and also at the distal end of same, and
he has been caused to suffer great pain by
reason of his said injuries; that the use of
his left arm and shoulder have been greatly
reduced thereby. I find that, by reason of, and
as a direct and proximate result of, the said
injuries to plaintiff's person, he has been actually damaged in the sum of $3,500 which said
sum, if paid now, would reasonably compensate
him for his said personal injuries.

"(13) I find that plaintiff did not refuse to
follow the advice of his physicians, that he submitted to every reasonable and necessary treatment of his said injuries, and that he was not
guilty of negligence in any particular with respect thereto.

"(14) I find that the automobile which was
being driven by plaintiff at the time of said
collision was at said time the property of plaintiff; that said automobile was, as a direct and
proximate result of the negligence of the servants and employés of defendant, while acting
within the scope of their respective employments, greatly broken and injured, and that
the difference in the market value of said automobile at Franklin, Tex., immediately before
said collision and immediately thereafter, is the
sum of $400 which said sum would reasonably
compensate plaintiff for the injury done to
said automobile in said collision.

"Conclusions of Law.

"(1) I conclude, as a matter of law, that the
act of defendant's engineer and servant in
charge of the passenger train, which collided
with plaintiff's automobile, in causing said train
to be run at a greater rate of speed than 10

miles per hour through the corporate limits
of the city of Franklin, and at the time and
place of said collision, was negligence per se
on the part of said engineer and servant of
defendant, same being in violation of a penal
ordinance of said incorporated city of Franklin.

"(2) I conclude that the defendant is liable
to plaintiff for each and all of the respective
acts of negligence on the part of his said servants and employés, while acting within the
scope of their respective employments.

"(3) I conclude that the said defendant, Jas.
A. Baker, receiver of the International & Great
Northern Railway Company, is justly and legally liable to the plaintiff, A. J. Hodges, in
the sum of $3,900 for actual damages sustained
by plaintiff, as above found, and that plaintiff
should have judgment against defendant for the
said sum, together with all costs of this suit."

By the first assignment of error, appellant
complains of the sixth finding of fact by the
trial court, which was that appellant was
guilty of negligence in having the string of
box cars or freight cars upon the side track
or passing track, as we have shown above,
and that such negligence was a proximate
cause of appellee's injuries. The proposition
under this assignment is that the presence of
the box cars or freight train upon appellant's
track could not constitute an independent
ground of negligence, as found by the trial
court. In support of this proposition, appellant cites the following cases: M., K. & T.
Ry. Co. v. Rogers, 91 Tex. 52, 40 S. W. 956;
I. & G. N. Ry. Co. v. Knight, 91 Tex. 660, 45
S. W. 556; Dillingham v. Parker, 80 Tex. 572,
16 S. W. 335; G., H. & S. A. Ry. Co. v. Harris, 22 Tex. Civ. App. 16, 53 S. W. 599; T.
& P. Ry. Co. v. Eddleman, 175 S. W. 777.
Opposing this proposition, appellee cites H. &
T. C. Ry. Co. v. Stewart (Sup.) 17 S. W. 33;
G., H. & S. A. Ry. Co. v. Michalke, 90 Tex.
276, 38 S. W. 31. In our opinion, the holding
in the Stewart and Michalke Cases are in
direct conflict with the holdings in the Knight,
Harris and Eddleman Cases, and it would
seem that the conflict is irreconcilable. It is
unnecessary, however, for us to attempt to
reconcile such conflict, because we are of
opinion that the trial court's judgment in
this case should be affirmed, even if we
should sustain the first assignment of error.

At this point, it might be well to say that
we sustain every finding made by the trial
court, as quoted above, after eliminating
from our consideration the sixth finding,
made the basis of the first assignment.

The second assignment complains of the
trial court's seventh finding of fact, which
was that appellant's conductor was guilty
of negligence in failing to place some one of
his train crew at the crossing in question to
flag said crossing or to warn persons about
to cross of the approach of appellant's passenger train; the contention being that neither the pleadings nor proof warranted such
finding. The first proposition under said

assignment is, in substance, that in the absence of pleading and proof showing unusual circumstances surrounding the crossing rendering it unusuallly hazardous, negligence cannot be predicated upon the failure of the railway company to keep a flagman at such a crossing. The next proposition under the assignment is that the evidence showed, without dispute, that the appellee was warned of the approach of the passenger train to the crossing, before he attempted to go over the crossing, and that his disobedience of such warning was the proximate cause of his injuries, or at least failure on the part of appellant to have a flagman at the crossing was not the proximate cause of the collision.

[1-3] With reference to the first proposition, it might be conceded that it is well-settled law in this state that a railway company is not bound to keep a flagman or watchman at all public crossings over its track. On the contrary, it has been held in several cases, by our Supreme Court, that the duty to keep a flagman at such a crossing only arises where the crossing can be said to be attended with extra hazard or unusual danger. This will depend upon the extent of the use of the crossing and the circumstances surrounding it. If the crossing be one that is used extensively and frequently by the public, and trains are operated over the crossing at frequent intervals, and there be objects or obstructions of any character at and near such crossing that materially obstruct the view thereof and of approaching trains to the same, then it should be left to the determination of a jury, or court trying the case without a jury, to say whether in failing to have a flagman at the crossing the railway company used such care as an ordinarily prudent person would have used under the same or similar circumstances. This we understand to be the rule announced, substantially, in Railway Co. v. Magee, 92 Tex. 616, 50 S. W. 1013; Railway Co. v. Moore, 107 S. W. 658; Railway Co. v. Walker, 171 S. W. 264; Railway Co. v. Tisdale, 199 S. W. 350. And, of course, in a city where a valid city ordinance requiring a flagman at a railroad crossing is in effect, it would be negligence, as a matter of law, on the part of a railway company to fail to comply with such ordinance, and if that failure should be the proximate cause of an injury to one using the crossing, liability would be established.

[4] The appellee in this case, however, did not contend that it was the duty of appellant to keep a permanent or regular watchman or flagman at the crossing in question at all times, but his contention was and is that under the peculiar facts and circumstances at the time of the collision it was the duty of appellant, through the conductor of its freight train, to place one of the crew of that freight train at the crossing to warn persons about to use it of the approach of the passenger

train, which collided with the automobile in this case. As the findings of the trial court indicate, and which we approve, this freight train had arrived in the town of Franklin just a few moments before the fast passenger train was due to arrive, and the conductor of the freight train put the same on the passing track, for the purpose of getting it out of the way of the passenger train, which he knew was soon to arrive, and he also knew that the view of persons using that crossing from the south side of the main line would be greatly obstructed, or rather that the view of appellant's main line for a long distance east of the crossing would be largely obstructed by the presence of these box cars and freight train on the passing track, and he also knew that the switch engine near there was puffing and making a noise, which would, perhaps, have the effect of preventing persons about to use the crossing from hearing the approach of the passenger train, and he also knew that he had only left a passage of about 16 feet in width over the track at that point. He also must be held to have knowledge, approximately at least, of the use that was made of that crossing by the public, and it was shown by the evidence as a fact that that use was quite extensive. In view of such facts, and we have not stated them all, bearing upon the point, we have no hesitancy in concluding that it was a question of fact for the trial court to determine whether appellant's conductor acted as an ordinarily prudent person would have acted in failing to place some one of his crew at the crossing as a flagman until appellant's passenger train had gone over that crossing. And the trial court having found that such failure on the part of appellant's conductor was negligence, and that such negligence became a proximate cause of the collision which resulted in appellee's injuries, the judgment must be affirmed, unless appellee was guilty of contributory negligence.

[5] With reference to the second proposition under this assignment, which is that the failure to have a flagman at the crossing could not have been the proximate cause of the collision, because, as claimed by appellant, appellee was warned by other persons of the approach of the train, and failed to heed the warning, and that his failure itself was a proximate cause and convicted him of contributory negligence, it is sufficient to say that the undisputed proof is, by both of the persons who claimed to have hallooed and waved at appellee, as he started over the crossing, that appellee did not appear to hear them or to see the signals attempted to be conveyed to him. Therefore this proposition cannot be sustained. That the trial court was warranted in finding that appellant's conductor was guilty of negligence in failing to place a flagman at this crossing on the occasion in question, see the companion

case of Baker v. Streater, 221 S. W. 1043;
8 Am. & Eng. Enc. of Law, 391, 392; G., H.
& S. A. Ry. Co. v. Linney, 163 S. W. 1035; I.
& G. N. Ry. Co. v. Jones, 60 S. W. 978; M.,
K. & T. Ry. Co. v. Hurdle, 142 S. W. 992;
Railway Co. v. Zumwalt, 226 S. W. 1080.

[6, 7] With reference to the third assignment of error, under which it is contended that the ordinance of the town of Franklin, limiting the speed of trains within the corporate limits to 10 miles per hour, had no application to appellant in his capacity as receiver of the railroad, and that, therefore, the speed of the train, if it was over 10 miles an hour, could not be negligence per se, as held by the trial court, we say that we doubt the correctness of such contention, but it is entirely unnecessary to decide that point, for the reason that the trial judge also found as a fact that appellant was guilty of negligence in operating the train at the rate of speed at which it was operated at the time over the crossing, under all the conditions and circumstances then attending, and we think this finding has support in the evidence. The trial judge found as a fact that the train was being operated at a speed of 25 miles per hour over this crossing, which was in close proximity to the depot and station of appellant, and over a crossing used more than any other in the town of Franklin, and which was obstructed, as we have shown, by the long freight train, which had been placed right near the main track, and which had been cut practically in the middle of the street, and a passage left of only 16 feet for the use of the public. Under these circumstances, we think it might well be left to a trial court or jury to determine whether a railway company would be guilty of negligence in operating a train over such a crossing at the speed of 25 miles per hour. We sustain this finding of negligence on the part of the trial court, and also his finding that the speed of the train was a proximate cause of of the collision and appellee's injuries.

[8] The fourth and fifth assignments complain of the finding of the trial court, to the effect that the appellee was not guilty of contributory negligence. We overrule the assignments, and in this connection we cannot refrain from calling attention to the fact that the statement of the evidence subjoined to these assignments and propositions thereunder is not such a full and fair statement of the evidence in this record bearing upon those assignments as the rules contemplate should have been made in appellant's brief. Rule 31 (142 S. W. xiii) for the Courts of Civil Appeals requires, substantially, that counsel for appellant should make a full and fair statement of all the evidence in the record that bore upon this question of contributory negligence; that such statement should be made upon the professional honor of counsel, and while we would not be understood as intimating that counsel for appellant in this

231 S.W.—54

case have purposely omitted evidence found in the record materially bearing upon these contentions, yet after careful inspection of the statement of facts in this connection, we find that counsel for appellant have, in fact, omitted to embrace in this statement in the brief everything that bears materially upon these assignments, and we have been compelled to go largely into the statement of facts to determine these matters. Counsel for appellee have interposed an objection to our consideration of these assignments at all, because of the failure of appellant's counsel to make that full and complete statement of the evidence in support thereof as they should have made. We have given them consideration, however, but it is manifest that they cannot be sustained, and they are overruled.

The sixth assignment complains of the finding of the trial court to the effect that appellee's automobile was traveling at a speed less than 6 miles an hour at the time it approached within 30 feet of the crossing in question. We overrule this contention. Such finding by the trial court has sufficient support in the evidence as we find it in the record.

The seventh assignment complains that the judgment for $3,500 for personal injuries sustained is excessive, it being contended by appellant that the evidence showed that there was no permanent injury to appellee, and that he had not suffered any great pain therefrom, and that he was never disabled for more than 10 or 15 days on account thereof; and, further, it is contended that if there had ever been any pain or injury, same had been caused by appellee's own negligence in failing to follow the advice of his physician; that the use of his left arm and shoulder had not been impaired, and that his earning capacity has not been reduced; and that he had not been damaged in the sum of $3,500.

[9] When we look at the statement which follows this assignment in appellant's brief, we must again complain of its incompleteness. This statement falls far short, in our opinion, of a full, complete, and fair statement and enumeration of all the evidence, or rather the substance of same, bearing upon this contention. Nevertheless, we have considered this assignment, and have gone to the statement of facts for the purpose of acquainting ourselves with all the facts bearing upon this contention. After having done so, we have no hesitancy in saying that the assignment cannot be sustained, and must be overruled. There is proof in this record—positive proof—in substance that at the time of his injuries appellee was a man 42 years of age, in robust health. He was a farmer by occupation, and in connection with that business owned and operated a cotton gin. After he was injured, he was taken immediately to appellant's hospital at Palestine, and was there confined under treatment of

appellant's doctors for 12 days, and he was then removed to his home, and for a period of approximately 6 weeks he was unable to get about, but was confined to his house, and would have to be assisted and helped in order to get around the place. It was shown that his shoulder was so badly injured that he has been unable to raise his left arm above a level with his head, and that he cannot chop with an axe, for the reason that he can only now use one hand for that purpose, and, further, it is shown that he cannot use a hoe in his farming, for the reason that after a very short time in the attempt his shoulder gives him such pain and trouble that he has to desist. This was his condition approximately two years after the injuries had been sustained. It is also shown that he suffered a great deal of physical pain in consequence of the injuries sustained, and he testified, positively, that by the injuries sustained his physical capacity for work had been reduced fully two-thirds. Unquestionably, the testimony shows, at least there is abundant testimony to warrant the finding by the trial court, that the appellee is permanently and seriously injured, and we have no hesitancy in concluding that the court's finding that $3,500 is no more than reasonable compensation for such injuries has abundant support in the evidence.

[10] With reference to the contention that the evidence shows that whatever permanent injuries, if any, appellee has received, was in consequence of his disobedience of his physician's instructions, etc., we have to say that this cannot be claimed to be shown by the undisputed evidence. On the contrary, the evidence is abundantly sufficient to warrant a finding that the appellee used ordinary care and prudence in the treatment of his injuries, and that was the degree of care required of him. T. & P. Ry. Co. v. McKenzie, 30 Tex. Civ. App. 293, 70 S. W. 238; I. & G. N. Ry. Co. v. Duncan, 55 Tex. Civ. App. 440, 121 S. W. 368; West Lbr. Co. v. Keen, 221 S. W. 625.

What we have said already disposes of the eighth, ninth, and tenth assignments, and they, too, are overruled.

The judgment of the trial court will be affirmed.

STONEWALL v. McGOWN. (No. 6576.)

(Court of Civil Appeals of Texas. San Antonio. May 18, 1921. Rehearing Denied June 8, 1921.)

1. **Escrows** ⬚1—Defined and held to have no application to money placed with another to be applied as directed by owner.

An escrow is a written instrument importing a legal obligation which is deposited by grantor, promisor, obligor, or his agent with a stranger or third party to be kept by the depositary until the performance of a condition or happening of a certain event, and then to be delivered over to the grantee, promisee, or obligee, and has no application to money placed in the hands of another to be applied as directed by the owner.

[Ed. Note.—For other definitions, see Words and Phrases, First and Second Series, Escrow.]

2. **Damages** ⬚65 — Action construed as one for misappropriation of funds in which plaintiff was estopped to claim more than damage actually suffered.

In an action by the owner of money placed in the hands of the defendant receiver with instructions as to its application, held, that the action was for a misappropriation of funds, and that the plaintiff could not recover for the reason that the money had been paid as directed by him in releasing liens upon his land, so that he was estopped by equity and good conscience from recovering more than the damages actually suffered, namely, the unexpended balance left after discharging the liens.

Appeal from Bexar County Court; John H. Clark, Judge.

Suit by Gust Stonewall against Floyd McGown, receiver of the Cross S. Farming Company. Judgment for defendant, and plaintiff appeals. Affirmed.

Keller, Russell & Woodhull, of San Antonio, for appellant.

F. C. Davis, of San Antonio, for appellee.

FLY, C. J. This is a suit for $620.62, left by appellant, through his agent, M. L. Harkey, with appellee, for certain purposes, and which it is alleged had been misappropriated by appellee. The suit is based on the following instrument in writing:

"San Antonio, Tex., Jan. 3, 1917.

"Received of M. L. Harkey six hundred twenty and 62/100 dollars, to be applied on liens against farms 57, 58, 59, 60 in section 165 of the Cross S. ranch in Dimmit county, Texas. It is agreed and understood that this money is to be held in escrow until releases are obtained from the Pratt & Hays lien, Cross S. Farming Co. V. L. lien, and the Bankers' Trust Co. V. L. lien, and a guaranty policy on these farms from Stewart Title Guaranty Co., if same can be obtained at $10.00; otherwise Mr. Harkey will pay difference.

"[Signed] Floyd McGown,
"Receiver Cross S. Farming Company."

The cause was tried by the county judge, and judgment rendered in favor of appellant for $10 and all costs.

[1] An escrow is a written instrument which by its terms imports a legal obligation, and which is deposited by the grantor, promisor, or obligor, or his agent, with a stranger or third party, to be kept by the depository until the performance of a condition or the happening of a certain event, and then to

e delivered over to the grantee, promisee, or obligee. 10 R. C. L. § 2, p. 621. Being derived from a French word meaning a bond or writing, and so always used in English, it could have no application to money placed in the hands of another to be applied as directed by the owner.

[2] The facts merely tend to show a misappropriation of funds deposited for a certain purpose. The instructions were in effect, as evidenced by the receipt, that appellee should use the money in paying off certain indebtedness and in paying for a guaranty of title from a certain company. It may be that appellant may have intended that the money should be used in obtaining the releases and getting a guaranty of title, and if each and all could not be obtained then to be returned to the depositor, but it is not apparent how the guaranty of title could have been procured without first paying off the liens. Even though such was the intention of appellant, he is in no position to recover the money, for the reason that the liens on his land have been paid off, and the testimony shows that he has a good marketable title to the land. It would be unconscionable to permit him to have his debts paid, his title to the land perfected, and then recover all the money that was paid out by appellee on the land. Equity and good conscience would estop him from a recovery of more than the damages suffered by him, and under the facts of the case such damages could not have been more than the $10 in appellee's hands after discharging the liens.

Appellant does not claim that all the liens were not paid off, nor that his title to the land is defective, nor does he offer to do equity in regard to the matter. He wants to keep his land, and recover the purchase money paid out by him to obtain title to the land. This will not be permitted.

The judgment is affirmed.

YOUNG et al. v. BLAIN. (No. 666.)

(Court of Civil Appeals of Texas. Beaumont. June 1, 1921. Rehearing Denied June 15, 1921.)

1. Mortgages ⬅️32(1)—Deed absolute on its face may be shown to be a mortgage.

A deed absolute on its face may be shown by the intention of the parties to be security for a debt and in legal contemplation a mortgage.

2. Mortgages ⬅️36—Party asserting that deed absolute on its face is a mortgage has burden of proof.

The party asserting that a deed absolute on its face was in fact a mortgage has the burden of so showing by preponderance of the evidence.

3. Mortgages ⬅️32(2)—For deed absolute on its face to be held a mortgage, it must have been so intended by the parties.

For a deed absolute on its face to be a mortgage, it must have been so understood and intended by both of the parties at the time of its execution.

4. Trial ⬅️143—In case of disputed facts issue should be submitted to jury.

In case of disputed facts, the issue should be submitted to the jury.

5. Mortgages ⬅️39—Evidence insufficient to carry to jury whether deed absolute on its face was a mortgage.

Where defendant admitted the execution of a deed, not pleading non est factum or that it was secured by fraud, but asserting that it was in fact a mortgage, evidence held insufficient to carry that issue to the jury; defendant testifying that she never signed the deed.

6. Witnesses ⬅️345(2)—Witness cannot be impeached by inquiry as to particular crimes.

A witness cannot be impeached by allowing the opposite party to inquire whether he had not been charged with various criminal offenses, for that is not a proper mode of an impeachment even on cross-examination.

Appeal from District Court, Jefferson County; E. A. McDowell, Judge.

Trespass to try title by W. R. Blain against Annie E. Young and others. From a judgment for plaintiff, defendants appeal. Affirmed.

Jno. M. Conley, of Beaumont, for appellants.

W. R. Blain, of Beaumont, for appellee.

O'QUINN, J. This is a suit in trespass to try title to a lot of land in the city of Beaumont, brought by appellee against appellants. Appellants answered by general demurrer, general denial, plea of not guilty, and specially that the lot was, at the time of the execution of the deed in question, part of the homestead of appellant Mrs. Annie E. Young (then Mrs. Annie Sawyer), and that the deed challenged was, in fact, a mortgage.

At the conclusion of the testimony, the court instructed the jury to return a verdict for the plaintiff, upon which judgment was rendered. Appellants filed motion for new trial, which being overruled, they have brought the case here for review.

[1, 2] Appellants' first assignment of error is as follows:

"The court erred to the prejudice of appellants in giving a peremptory instruction to the jury to find for the appellee, and in overruling and denying appellants' exception to the peremptory instruction given by the court to the jury to find a verdict for appellee, for the reason that there was ample and sufficient evidence produced in the trial of said cause raising the issue as to whether or not the deed executed by the appellant Annie E. Young and her husband, Walter Sawyer, and appellee, W. R. Blain, to C. W. Howth, said deed bearing date September 17, 1913, recorded in volume 137, p. 582, of the Deed Records of Jefferson county, Tex., was, in fact, a mortgage."

—which said assignment is submitted as a proposition. The evidence shows that appellant Annie E. Young was, prior to 1911, Annie E. Pipe, wife of E. W. Pipe; that after being divorced from E. W. Pipe, she married Walter Sawyer, and was his wife on September 17, 1913, when the deed in question was executed; that after the death of Walter Sawyer, she married John Blease; that after having been divorced from Blease, she married Walter Young, one of the appellants herein.

Appellee offered in evidence: (1) A deed from J. D. Bendette, Jr., to Mrs. E. W. Pipe to the land in question, dated July 20, 1907; (2) decree of court divorcing Annie E. Pipe from E. W. Pipe; (3) decree of court partitioning the community property of Annie E. Pipe and E. W. Pipe, giving to Annie E. Pipe the land in controversy; (4) deed from Annie E. Pipe to W. R. Blain (appellee), dated August 16, 1912, conveying, among other things, the lot in question; (5) deed from Annie Sawyer and her husband, Walter Sawyer, and W. R. Blain, to C. W. Howth, dated September 17, 1913, conveying the lot in controversy; and (6) deed from C. W. Howth to W. R. Blain, dated December 18, 1914, conveying said lot to appellee.

It also appears from the evidence that in the partition suit between Mrs. Annie Pipe and her divorced husband, E. W. Pipe, she agreed to pay him $300, and the judgment was so entered, and she did not have the money, and that in order to get same she executed a deed to W. R. Blain (appellee), of date August 16, 1912, conveying to him the three lots decreed to her in said partition suit, one of which was the lot here in question, the deed reciting a consideration of $750, $400 cash and one vendor's lien note for $350, payable one year after date. It is not questioned but that this conveyance was simulated, being merely for the purpose of negotiating the note to enable Mrs. Pipe to get the money with which to pay the $300 awarded to E. W. Pipe in said partition suit, and that when the note for the $350 was paid off by Mrs. Pipe, Blain reconveyed all of said property back to her except the lot involved here. It is also shown by the evidence that before said note was discharged by Mrs. Pipe, and before Blain reconveyed said property back to Mrs. Pipe, her then husband, Walter Sawyer, was indicted for felony theft, and that in negotiating relative to said charge with W. R. Blain, appellee, the apparent title to said lot then being in said Blain, she, Mrs. Sawyer, her husband, the said Walter Sawyer, defendant in

said felony theft case, and said W. R. Bla: executed a deed to C. W. Howth, to said ?: in question, dated September 17, 1913. Th is the deed that appellants, in their answ: specially assert was a mortgage, and w⸱ = appellee contends was executed as an abs⸱ lute conveyance of the lot for the purpo⸱ of paying the $200 fee charged to defend sai Walter Sawyer in said felony case.

Appellant Annie E. Young, with referen⸱: to the deed referred to in appellants' answ⸱: as a mortgage, testified as follows:

"Q. Now, Mrs. Pipe, there is in evidenc⸱ : deed introduced by plaintiff, a deed from y⸱ and Walter Sawyer and W. R. Blain to C. ⸱ Howth, that deed being dated September 1⸱ 1917, and reading as follows: 'That An⸱: Sawyer, joined by her husband, Walter Saw⸱⸱: and W. R. Blain, of the county of Jeffers⸱ state of Texas, for and in consideration of th⸱ sum of $200 to us in hand paid by C. W. How⸱ the receipt of which is hereby acknowledg⸱⸱ have granted, sold and conveyed, and by th⸱⸱ presents to grant, sell and convey to the s⸱⸱ C. W. Howth of the county of Jefferson, sta⸱ of Texas, all that certain lot, tract or par⸱⸱ of land,' etc. Now I will ask you if you ⸱⸱⸱ received that $200 which is recited as hav⸱⸱ been paid by Mr. Howth? A. Mr. How⸱ will tell you that he never paid me a thi⸱; Mr. Howth didn't pay me a nickel in God⸱ world, and I will take a dying oath that I nev⸱ received a dime from him. I can't expla⸱ to the court how come to execute that dee⸱ because I never executed nothing but this ⸱⸱⸱ for Sawyer. That is all that I ever signed ⸱ that one paper. I signed a bond for Sawyer because he got into some trouble. He was m⸱ husband at that time. Mr. Sawyer told me ⸱ go and get Mr. Blain, when he was arrest⸱⸱ He was arrested as he was going to get ⸱⸱ the car at the post office, and he said, 'Go ⸱⸱ Mr. Blain,' and I went up to Mr. Blain's of⸱⸱ and told him that he was arrested, and he sa⸱⸱ 'Do you want me to defend him?' and I sa⸱⸱ 'How much will you charge?' and he said '2⸱ to plead his case,' and I had $10 in my pock⸱⸱ and I went up to John Ryan in the money ord⸱⸱ department and I got another $10, and I pa⸱⸱ him his fee, and I said, 'Ain't you going to gi⸱⸱ me a receipt?' and he said, 'You know I am al⸱ right.' I certainly paid him cash, and he knows it too. He knows it, too, that I gav⸱ him $20, and Mr. Howth will be a witness f⸱⸱ that, too. I gave him the $20 and he was ⸱ jail about two days. That was on the 8th day of August, 1913, that he was arrested, and ⸱ was between that and the 12th day I paid hi⸱ the money, and he got him out of jail. H⸱ said to me, 'Are you going to let him stay i⸱ jail?' and I said, 'I don't know nothing abou⸱ it,' and he said, 'Why don't you get a bond' and he said, 'I will go his bond if you wi⸱ deed me a lot,' and I said, 'I don't want to dee⸱ any lot over to you,' and he said, 'You wi⸱ get it back again,' and he got me to sign th⸱ bond. Of course, I couldn't read it mysel⸱ and I just took what they read to me. ⸱ wasn't able to read it myself. If the deed th⸱⸱ they have introduced dated the 17th of Sep⸱ tember, 1913, from W. Sawyer et al. to C. W⸱ Howth, is claimed by Mr. Blain to be a dee⸱

that we executed to secure them on Mr. Saw-yer's bond, I will state that I know nothing of that. They told me that it was a bond that I was signing, and that is all that I know."

On cross-examination she further testified:

"At the time myself and Mr. Blain made that deed to Mr. Howth, there was some improvements on the lot. * * * On September 3, 1914, Mr. Blain deeded this land back to me, but at the time he gave me that deed, I did not understand at that time that he wasn't going to deed it all back to me; that is, this 46 feet on the east end of that property. I didn't owe Mr. Blain a nickel, and I didn't receive a nickel from him, and this is nothing but a pure piece of robbery. Yes, sir, I told my attorney that he refused to deed it back to me. He told me that he wouldn't deed it all, that he was going to keep that lot. I didn't know that I was signing a deed to my property. I thought I was signing a bond. Of course, I didn't owe him anything, and I thought when I signed that paper that I would get it back if I signed it. This paper that you hand me has my signature on it. Yes, sir; that is my signature. And it appears to have been dated on the 17th of September, 1913. At the time I signed it with the intention of getting it back again. At the time this deed was made to Mr. Howth, I will say that I had nothing to do with it, and Mr. Howth will tell you the same thing. I will also state that when we made this deed to Mr. Howth, I did not tell Mr. Blain that I would pay him $200 to represent Walter Sawyer. In fact, I never promised him anything, not a five-cent piece. He said, 'I charge $20 to plead his case,' and I paid him the $20 cash before he took the case. That $20 I paid Mr. Blain was to represent Mr. Sawyer in the courts, not the justice court alone. He charged me $20, and I paid him for it. I suppose Mr. Blain went to the justice court and represented Mr. Sawyer in the examining trial. I don't know for sure whether the grand jury of Jefferson county indicted him after that or not for theft, but he told me (Blain) that I had to get some one to go his bond, and I said I didn't know who to get, and he said. 'You sign a lot over to me, and I will go his bond,' and he said, 'I will give it back to you.' I don't know whether Mr. Blain went before Justice Showers and represented my husband, Walter Sawyer, on his examining trial or not. I was present in court at that time, but I don't know whether it was Justice Showers or not. Yes, sir; it was before one of the justices of peace that the trial was had. I paid Mr. Blain $20 to represent Mr. Sawyer. I don't know what Mr. Blain would charge to represent a man for theft, but I do know he said he would represent Mr. Sawyer for $20, and I paid him, and that was enough, too. It is not a fact that after Sawyer was indicted on a felony theft charge that I made that deed to Mr. Howth, and promised to pay Mr. Blain $200 to represent him. Mr. Blain told me he would plead his case for $20, and I paid him. There was no trial that I know of. There was no evidence against him. He came out of that case. I don't know how much money Walter Sawyer was charged with having taken. I never heard the amount named. I think he was charged with taking $75 and a watch, but I don't know any-thing more about it. I don't know anything more about it than you do."

Appellee W. R. Blain testified:

"There has been certain deeds introduced in evidence concerning this property, one from the defendant to me, and one from me to the defendant, and one from myself and defendant and Walter Sawyer to C. W. Howth. I will now tell about how I first become connected with this matter, beginning at the first transaction that I had with reference to this land. On March 13, 1911, Mr. Howth filed suit for Mrs. Pipe. It was at that time against E. W. Pipe, and in the original petition she applied for a divorce, * * * I think possible he tried the case, I am not positive, but there was no dispute as to the community property in that suit. The only thing involved was the divorce. Subsequently, the suit was filed by me for a division of the community property. * * * There was a settlement made by which Mr. Pipe was to receive a 27½ foot on the north end of the tract and Mrs. Pipe to receive the house in which they lived and the balance of the property. There was a tract 237 feet and the other was 46 feet by 237, and another little piece that she acquired through the Beaumont Improvement Company. There was an agreed judgment between the parties, and a judgment entered in the case. She agreed to pay $300 to E. W. Pipe when the judgment was entered. * * * In the meantime she married Walter Sawyer, and he was arrested, I think the 10th of September, and put in jail on the 10th of September. I made his bond for appearance before the justice of peace for examining trial, and charged her $20 to represent him in the examining trial, and she paid me $10, and I think she borrowed the other $10 from somebody. I told her that I would accept $20 in the examining trial before Judge Showers, and I did it the next morning. He was bound over to the grand jury, and I made that bond. Mr. John Brooks and myself were sureties on this bond. That bond was made on the 11th day of September. The grand jury returned an indictment against him on the 13th day of September, 1913, and on the 17th she came to the office. He was arrested on the 17th of September, and she came to the office some time between 11 and 12 o'clock and told me that he had been arrested, and we had to make another bond for him, that he was in jail, and I told her that I wouldn't make the bond for him unless I was paid a fee in the case for representing him. I told her that if she wanted to employ Mr. Howth and myself to represent him in the felony case, that we would if the fee was paid. She didn't pay any money, and suggested that I take this title to the land in my name and that would be security. I told her that it would not be security, that it was her homestead, but that she could make a deed to Mr. Howth for the 46 feet, and in that way there would not be any question as to the passing of the title out of me. So she and I and Walter Sawyer executed the deed to Mr. Howth. That deed was executed for a $200 fee to represent Walter Sawyer in the felony case pending against him in the district court. It was not for the purpose of securing money on a bond for Walter Sawyer, none in the world. I had signed his bond twice before without any security. That deed was given as a fee for representing him. * * * After this deed was made by myself, Walter Sawyer, and Annie Sawyer to Mr. Howth, Mr. Howth made a deed to me. Mr. Howth and I dissolved partnership. in September, 1914, and at that time we owned this piece of land, and another piece in the A. B. Williams survey about half a mile north of this and an interest in a tract of land in the Bullock survey that we had taken in as fees and he deeded the three tracts to me. That was my part of the fees. That is I got the land in a settlement of our partnership business. That deed was made to me as a settlement of the affairs of our office."

On cross-examination he further testified: "When Mrs. Pipe first came to see me about this Sawyer matter, I don't think there was any complaint filed at that time. I think the complaint was filed afterwards. They had just arrested him, and she came on to the office to see me. When he was first arrested, he was not charged with a misdemeanor, but was charged with a felony for stealing 90-odd dollars and a watch. I don't know whether the bond says that he was charged with a misdemeanor in the justice court or not. In fact, I don't know what the bond says, but I know what I represented him for, and I know what he was charged-with. * * * After he was indicted, he was arrested again on the 17th. This examining trial was had on the 11th. * * * I understood that he had been indicted, and was put in jail when she came to the office. * * * I did not appear before the court on the 16th and have his bond fixed for him. At that time I was not employed in the case. I represented the man in the justice trial for $20, which was paid, and knowing that if he was indicted I felt that he would come back to get me to represent him again, but I didn't consider that I was employed in the case at that time. I was out of the case and paid for it, when the examining trial was over. After he was indicted, she came to the office. and my agreement was to defend him for $200. * * * I have already stated several times the case was dismissed on the motion of the county attorney, and that the case did not go to trial. I convinced the county attorney that he couldn't convict him, and the case was dismissed on his own motion. I had several long conversations with Scurlock about the case. I came to court every time it came up for trial. I don't know how many times it come up for trial, but I know Mr. Sawyer, and myself were in attendance three times. I have a distinct recollection that it was set for trial more than the one time marked on the docket, and I was present every time. The case was filed in the Fifty-Eighth judicial district court of this county, and my agreement was that I would defend him, and my agreement was to get him out if I could for $200. It didn't matter whether I tried the case or not. I considered when the case was dismissed that I had fulfilled my agreement with her. That agreement contemplated that I would try his case, and I would have tried it if it had not been dismissed, but it did not contemplate that if he had been tried and convicted that I would appeal his case for him in the Court of Criminal Appeals. We did not have any understanding about that. My agreement went to the extent that I would defend him in the district court for $200, and he never had a trial in the district court. The surest and best way to get rid of a criminal case is to get it dismissed if you can."

The witness Jean A. Hartnett testified for plaintiff as follows:

"You have exhibited to me a paper which purports to bear my signature, and I have examined the same, and have identified same as my signature. Will also say that I took the acknowledgment as a notary public of this county to that instrument. I was present at the time Mrs. Young, at that time Mrs. Sawyer, and Mr. Blain had a conversation with reference to representing Mr. Sawyer, her husband. I was in the office with Mr. Blain and heard part of the conversation. The part that I heard was this: When Mrs. Sawyer came into the office this day, she had a bond. Her husband was in jail, and had been indicted—I believe he had been indicted, I am not sure. Anyway, she had a bond, and wanted Mr. Blain to represent him and get a bond up, and Mr. Blain refused to represent him unless she paid him a cash fee. She said that she did not have the money, and the question of land was brought up, some land she owned out there. I don't know exactly where it was at the time. When I came back to Mr. Blain's office, Mr. Blain had wrote up a deed, and I took her acknowledgment, wherein she transferred a lot to Mr. Blain for Mr. Blain to represent Sawyer, in that case for theft, I believe."

On cross-examination he further testified:

"As I have already stated in my examination, I have a recollection about this woman having gone over to Mr. Blain's office, and talking over this whole transaction with him, but can't say that there is a distinct recollection. I remember the case and the occasion, and I remember what was said in that conversation; that is, part of what was said. She come in there and wanted Mr. Blain to represent Walter Sawyer, who was then charged with theft, and make bond, and get him out of jail. That was her purpose in coming up there, yes, sir; she said that was her purpose in coming up there, to get Mr. Blain to represent Walter Sawyer and make a bond for him. I also have a recollection about her saying that she wanted Mr. Blain to get him out of jail, as he was in jail at that time. Mr. Blain said that he wouldn't represent him unless she paid him a cash fee."

[3] That a deed, absolute on its face, may be shown by intention of the parties to be a security for debt or any financial risk, and therefore, in legal contemplation, a mortgage, is well settled. The deed in the instant case being absolute on its face—a regular warranty deed—and appellants having pleaded that it was a mortgage, the burden was upon them to show by a preponderance of the evidence that same was intended by the parties to be a mortgage. Brewster v. Davis, 56 Tex. 478; Lowry v. Carter, 46 Tex. Civ. App. 488, 102 S. W. 930; Goodbar v. Bloom, 43 Tex. Civ. App. 434, 96 S. W. 657.

For the deed to have been a mortgage, it must have been so understood and intended by both parties at the time of its execution. Webb v. Burney, 70 Tex. 324, 7 S. W. 841.

[4, 5] Where there is any dispute as to the facts, then the court should submit the matter to the jury; but as we view the record, and under the law, the evidence submitted by appellants did not raise the issue of the deed being a mortgage. Appellants, in their pleading, admit the execution of the deed, but contend that same was intended as a mortgage. But Mrs. Young (Sawyer) nowhere in her testimony says that said deed was intended as a mortgage. In effect, she denies the excution of the deed, saying:

"I can't explain to the court how (I) come to execute that deed, because I never executed nothing but this bond for Sawyer, and that is all that I ever signed, is that one paper."

She further testified:

"If the deed that they have introduced, dated the 17th of September, 1913 (the deed in question), from W. Sawyer et al. to C. W. Howth, is claimed by Mr. Blain to be a deed that we executed to secure them on Mr. Sawyer's bond. I will state that I know nothing of that. They told me that it was a bond that I was signing, and that is all that I know."

It thus appears that appellants' allegations in their answer that the deed was a mortgage is not supported by the proof, and being the only question to be determined, under the pleadings, there was no error in the court's instructing the verdict.

In their answer, appellants do not plead non est factum, but plainly admit the execution of the deed, nor in the admission of its execution do they plead fraud in securing same. Therefore the testimony of appellant Annie E. Young that she "never executed nothing but the bond for Sawyer," and that "they told me it was a bond that I was signing, and that is all that I know," does not support the pleading that the deed was executed but was intended to be and was a mortgage. The assignment is overruled.

[6] Appellants' second, third, fourth, and fifth assignments of error complain that the court erred in not permitting them to ask the witness Jean A. Hartnett if he had not been charged with various criminal offenses, including murder, selling "dope," illegally making intoxicating liquor, and "bootlegging," contending that same was admissible to affect his credibility as a witness. The court did not err in sustaining objections to said questions. Judge Brown, in the case of M., K. & T. Ry. Co. v. Creason, 101 Tex. 336, 107 S. W. 527, says:

"At an early date in the history of this court, it was settled that 'in the impeachment of a witness the inquiry should be confined to his general reputation for truth, and that it should not extend to his general moral character.' Boone v. Weathered, 23 Texas, 675; Ayres v. Duprey, 27 Texas, 594; Kennedy v. Upshaw, 66 Texas, 452. In the case last cited Judge Stayton quoted the rule as above stated from Boone v. Weathered, and said: 'This is in accordance with the great weight of authority.' Boone v. Weathered has been followed by this court in all subsequent decisions, and has in no sense been modified in its application to impeachment of witnesses. However, it is claimed that the rule is not applicable to impeachment of a witness by cross-examination of him, and we are cited to a number of authorities to sustain that proposition, among which is Carroll v. State, 24 S. W. 100, in which the Court of Criminal Appeals depart from the rule established by the Supreme Court both for civil and criminal cases at the time that it had jurisdiction of criminal matters. In G., C. & S. F. Ry. Co. v. Johnson, 83 Texas, 633, this court distinctly applied the same rule to cross-examination of a witness for the purpose of impeachment that was laid down in the case of Boone v. Weathered. In the Johnson Case, a witness being on the stand, the party against whom he had testified, over the objection of the party who had called him, was permitted by the trial court, upon cross-examination, for the purpose of impeaching the witness, to ask him if he was not a deserter from the United States Army. Of which ruling this court said: 'The testimony was wholly irrelevant to any issue in the case. The object of it was to break down the witness' character before the jury and to discredit the testimony. A witness cannot be impeached in such way.' Thus we see that the rule applied by this court has been uniform that, for the purposes of impeachment either upon cross-examination of the witness attacked or by the introduction of other evidence, it must be confined to testimony relevant to the issue of the credibility of the witness. * * * We see no reason for departing from the well-established rule of this court upon the subject. We therefore answer that it was not competent on cross-examination to impeach the witness, Apple, by proving by him that he had been indicted for a felony or other crime."

These assignments are overruled.

No reversible error appearing in the record, the judgment is affirmed.

TAYLOR et al. v. MASTERSON et al.
(No. 6591.)

(Court of Civil Appeals of Texas. San Antonio. June 1, 1921.)

1. Appeal and error ⟜66—No appeal except from final judgment.

No appeal can be prosecuted from any other than a final judgment.

2. Appeal and error ⟜80(1) — No order or decree not precluding further litigation is a "final judgment."

For purpose of appeal, a judgment is only "final" when the whole matter in controversy is disposed of as to all the parties, and no order or decree which does not preclude further litigation is final.

[Ed. Note.—For other definitions, see Words and Phrases, First and Second Series, Final Decree or Judgment.]

3. Appeal and error ⟜80(1) — Judgment for plaintiff disposes of defendant's plea in reconvention or cross-action and is appealable.

Under Rev. St. art. 1997, declaring that there can be but one final judgment in any cause except where otherwise specially provided by law, there cannot be final judgments on both plaintiff's original claim and defendant's plea in reconvention, a plea in reconvention or a cross-action being so much a part of the entire suit that, when judgment is rendered for plaintiff on his claim without mentioning defendant's plea, the judgment will be *held* to have disposed of such plea so as to be appealable.

4. Appeal and error ⟜78(3) — Order sustaining demurrer to pleas held not a final appealable judgment.

An order sustaining a demurrer and special exceptions to defendants' pleas in reconvention, followed by a decree reciting that defendants declined to amend and gave notice of appeal, and stating that "on motion of the defendants this cause is continued until next term of the court," was not a final judgment, but merely an interlocutory order or decree which the appellate court has no jurisdiction to review.

Appeal from District Court, Dimmit County; W. D. Love, Special Judge.

Trespass to try title by H. Masterson and others against J. S. Taylor and others. From an order sustaining a general demurrer and special exceptions to defendants' pleas in reconvention, defendants appeal. Appeal dismissed.

F. Vandervoort, of Carrizo Springs, for appellants.

N. A. Rector, of Austin, for appellees.

FLY, C. J. H. Masterson, and Ellen B. Ross, joined by her husband, J. O. Ross, instituted this action of trespass to try title to 640 acres of land, known as the John Cummings survey against the appellants, J. S.

Taylor, Ella G. Taylor, F. Vandervoort, the Nueces Valley Irrigation Company, Mrs. M. A. Hass, and her husband, Charles Hass. The Taylors opened up the pleadings in behalf of the appellants, by filing a plea consisting of about 16 pages of typewritten matter, which is denominated "Original Plea in Reconvention," and it is followed by pleas in reconvention of each and all of the other defendants, herein named as appellants, as well as by interveners, C. L. Bass, Jay C. Adams, Thomas M. Mills, Ellen Taylor Deutz, and Helen F. Reedy. The death of H. Masterson was suggested, and his heirs were made parties plaintiff. The court sustained a general demurrer and special exceptions to the pleas of appellants, and from that order this appeal has been attempted. After reciting that defendants declined to amend and gave notice of appeal, the decree states: "On motion of the defendants this cause is continued until next term of the court."

[1] With only a few exceptions specially provided for by statute, the rule is fixed and inexorable that no appeal can be prosecuted from any other than a final judgment. The reason for such a rule is the beneficent one of protecting courts and litigants from vexatious, frivolous, and interminable appeals from the numerous orders of a nisi prius court in the trial of causes. The wisdom of the rule has commended it to English and American courts for so long a time "that the memory of man runneth not to the contrary." Without the rule, and a strict enforcement of it, inextricable confusion, a vast amount of useless and unnecessary labor, a vast expenditure of money, indefensible consumption of time, and criminal delay in the preservation of rights or redress of wrongs, would inevitably result.

[2] There can be only one final judgment or decree in a case, and a judgment is only final when the whole matter in controversy is disposed of as to all the parties, and no order or decree which does not preclude further litigation is final. It is the last, the conclusive judgment, which settles all of the issues, as to all of the parties. Nothing more must remain to be done, if the judgment is a final one. As said by Mr. Freeman and cited with approval by the Supreme Court:

"A decree can never be final until the party in whose favor it is can obtain some benefit therefrom without again setting the cause down for further hearing before the court. * * *" Linn v. Arambould, 55 Tex. 611; Railway v. Smith County, 58 Tex. 74; Garza v. Baker, 58 Tex. 483; Trammell v. Rosen, 106 Tex. 132, 157 S. W. 1161; Fort Worth Imp. Dist. v. City of Fort Worth, 106 Tex. 148, 158 S. W. 164, 48 L. R. A. (N. S.) 994; Kinney v. Telephone Co., 222 S. W. 227.

[3] The statute, article 1997, Rev. Stats., is positive in declaring that there can be

but one final judgment rendered in any cause except where it is otherwise specially provided by law, and it cannot be contended that the law has provided that where there is a plea in reconvention two final judgments will be permissible, one on the original claim and the other on the plea of the defendant. On the other hand, pleas in reconvention or cross-actions are considered to be so much a part of the entire suit that when a judgment is rendered for the plaintiff on his claim, without mentioning the plea in reconvention or cross-action, the judgment will be held to have disposed of such plea or cross-action. In the case of Trammell v. Rosen herein cited, the Supreme Court shows a conflict between different Courts of Civil Appeals on this subject, but holds that this court and the Court of Civil Appeals of the Fifth District were correct in holding as herein indicated. The Supreme Court said:

"These decisions of the Courts of Civil Appeals for the Fourth and Fifth Districts, respectively, proceed upon the theory that the general judgment in favor of plaintiff against the defendants adjudicates all matters pleaded in the cross-action as effectually, for all practical purposes, as though the judgment embodied an express finding thereon in a specific sum in favor of defendants, and then deducted that sum from the gross amount found for plaintiff. We think that reasoning is sound, although the form of such judgment is not commendable."

The answers in this case, if they set up any defense at all, would amount to no more than pleas of not guilty and a prayer to be quieted in their title, and it would be a judicial anomaly if there could be a final judgment on their plea and then one on the petition.

[4] The appeal will be dismissed because of a want of jurisdiction to review what was merely an interlocutory order or decree of the court.

DALLAS COUNTY STATE BANK v. CRISMON et al. (No. 8557.)

(Court of Civil Appeals of Texas. Dallas. June 4, 1921.)

Chattel mortgages ⇐138(1)—Superior to mechanic's lien for repairs.

A properly recorded chattel mortgage on an automobile is a lien superior to the lien of a mechanic for repairs made subsequent to the mortgage, though the mortgage obligated the mortgagor to keep the automobile in repair, where it also provided that he should not incumber or permit any incumbrance or lien of any character against it.

Error from Dallas County Court; T. A. Work, Judge.

Suit by the Dallas County State Bank against B. E. Crismon and others. Judgment granting plaintiff insufficient relief, and it brings error. Reversed and rendered.

Holland & Bartlett, of Dallas, for plaintiff in error.

J. R. Golden, of Dallas, for defendants in error.

TALBOT, J. This suit was brought by Dallas County State Bank against B. E. Crismon, Used Ford Corporation, and E. U. Conrad to recover balance due on a note secured by chattel mortgage executed by said Crismon payable to Used Ford Corporation and transferred for value and before maturity to said corporation to said bank, and to foreclose a chattel mortgage on an automobile truck. Conrad was made a party defendant by the bank, he having possession of the truck claiming a mechanic's lien thereon. Defendant Crismon filed no answer. There was no issue as to the amount due the bank or as to the validity of the chattel mortgage held by it. The chattel mortgage was on record, and the defendant in error was therefore affected with notice.

The defendant in error, E. U. Conrad, answered, alleging that during March and April, 1920, he was engaged in the automobile garage business, furnishing material and labor to repair cars for hire, and that while so engaged, the defendant B. E. Crismon brought to him the automobile upon which plaintiff is seeking to foreclose a lien, and requested him to make such repairs on said automobile as were necessary to put said car in good condition so that the same could be operated and used for the purposes for which it was intended that it should be used. That defendant in error repaired said car, furnishing such material and such labor and performing such services as were necessary in connection therewith, and that the reasonable value of the labor, services, and material so furnished, and which were necessary to the continued operation of the car, was in the sum of $217.16, which said amount the said B. E. Crismon, as owner of said car, agreed to pay to defendant in error for such labor, material, and services rendered by him. Defendant in error further pleaded that the mortgage contract obligated the defendant B. E. Crismon to keep the automobile truck in good repair; that the repairs made by the defendant in error were necessary for the preservation and betterment of the automobile and the continued operation thereof; that the value of said car in its broken down condition at the time it was delivered to defendant in error to be repaired by him was approximately $275 or $300; and that the value of the same after it had been repaired by defendant in error was approximately

$650 to $700, and the court found that the repairs made by the said Conrad increased the value of said automobile truck to the extent of the repairs made by him.

The chattel mortgage, among other things, provided that mortgagor "will not incumber or permit any incumbrance or lien of any character whatsoever against the same."

The case was tried before the court without a jury. The court rendered judgment for the bank for $495.60 with foreclosure of its chattel mortgage lien, and for the defendant Conrad for $142.85 with foreclosure of his mechanic's lien, and decreed that same was a superior lien, to the prior recorded chattel mortgage lien held by the bank. From this judgment the bank sued out a writ of error.

There was no controverted issue as to the amount due the bank or as to the validity of the chattel mortgage lien held by it. The only disputed question in the case was and is with reference to the priority of liens shown. In other words, the question involved in the controversy in the county court was and is in this court, whether or not the existing chattel mortgage lien of the bank is superior to the after-acquired and established mechanic's lien of the defendant in error, E. U. Conrad. The counsel for the defendant in error has filed in this court a very interesting, persuasive, and able brief in support of his contention that the established mechanic's lien is the superior lien, but it appears, we think, that the Supreme Court and the Courts of Civil Appeals of this state, which have passed upon the question with possibly one exception, have held to the contrary. American Type Foundry v. Nichols (Sup.) 214 S. W. 301; Ferrel-Michael Abstract & Title Co. v. McCormac et al. (Com. App.) 215 S. W. 559; Jesse French Piano & Organ Co. v. Elliott, 166 S. W. 29; Holt v. Schwarz, 225 S. W. 856. The matter seems to have been very carefully considered and exhaustively discussed in the cases cited, and anything we might say in disposing of this appeal in addition to what is said would be superfluous and useless. In the first case cited the Supreme Court held that a lien of a printer on a printing press and gasoline engine is subordinate to the lien of a chattel mortgage filed for record before the printer began his employment, notwithstanding such statute provides for "a first lien." In that case the court said that the effect of its decision was to subject to the employé's lien the property created by or necessarily connected with the performance of his labor, as that property stood at the time of his employment, but that the court declined, in the absence of clear language regarding it, as have most of the courts of last resort in the United States, to extend the employé's lien so as to attach to and diminish or destroy the interest or right of an innocent lienholder which had vested prior to the employment, and of which the employé

was chargeable with notice. In support of the conclusion reached the Supreme Court quoted from the opinion of the Supreme Court of Michigan in the case of Denison v. Shuler, 47 Mich. 598, 11 N. W. 402, 41 Am. Rep. 734, the following:

"The mortgage was on file and defendants were therefore affected with notice. On general principles it would seem that the lien so carefully reserved by the vendor, the person furnishing the entire original machine, ought to have priority over the subsequent repairers. The engine itself included all the labor and all the material necessary for its production, and when the plaintiff sold it he virtually furnished to his vendees that labor and those materials, and preserved an express lien. The repairers did less. Their expenditure was comparatively small, and they acted in making it under circumstances which charged them with notice of the plaintiff's prior lien. Why should their claim be preferred?"

Following this quotation our Supreme Court said that the final conclusion of the Michigan Supreme Court was the same as that announced by it, and was embodied in the following sentence:

"Had it been intended that the kind of lien in question should operate retrospectively and override prior securities executed to secure purchase money, it is not to be supposed that the Legislature would have left the purpose in any doubt."

In Holt v. Schwarz, supra, the facts were practically the same as in the instant case, and the Court of Civil Appeals for the Fourth District said:

"When the car was delivered to appellants for repair, the chattel mortgage had been duly executed, filed, and registered, was subsisting and unpaid, and appellants had full notice thereof when they performed the work. There is no provision of the statutory law of this state that postpones or subordinates the prior valid chattel mortgage liens to liens of repair shops or mechanics made upon automobiles when such prior chattel liens are in force. If no such lien can be postponed by such repairs, it is unimportant whether the mechanic or repair shop retains possession or not, or whether they increase the value by way of betterments. The mortgagee's rights must be considered. He might not be willing for extensive repairs to be made, so that his securities may be impaired. One dealing with mortgaged property does so at his peril."

These decisions settle the question against the defendant in error, and requires that the judgment of the county court be reversed, and that judgment be here rendered for the plaintiff in error.

The fact that the mortgage contract obligated the mortgagor, Crismon, to keep the automobile in good repair does not materially alter the case. It was also provided in the chattel mortgage that the mortgagor "will not incumber or permit any incumbrance or lien of any character whatsoever against the same." In view of this latter provision it may well be said that it was in the contemplation of the parties that the mortgagor should keep the automobile in repair at his own expense without incumbering it for the cost of such repairs, and hence the interdiction of such incumbrance.

All the material facts were developed in the trial below, and no good would be accomplished by remanding the case for another trial.

The judgment of the trial court will therefore be reversed, and judgment here rendered, establishing the Dallas County State Bank's mortgage lien as a superior lien to the after-acquired mechanic's lien of the defendant E. U. Conrad, and adjudging costs against him. The judgment of the county court below will not otherwise be disturbed.

———

BOARD OF PERMANENT ROAD COM'RS OF HUNT COUNTY et al. v. JOHNSON et al. (No. 8646.)

(Court of Civil Appeals of Texas. Dallas. May 7, 1921. Rehearing Denied June 4, 1921.)

1. **Highways ⚖=103—Change of route for construction of county road not an abuse of "discretion," warranting judicial interference therewith.**

Where the board of permanent road commissioners of a county created under Sp. Laws 33d Leg. (1913) c. 60, in selection of route between two terminals, carefully considered the entire situation, and where there was no evidence of bad faith or perversity, or of moral delinquency, actuating the board or any of its members in receding from the tentative selection of one route and ultimately adopting another route, and where the selection of such other route caused the contribution by the state of $106,000, which the state threatened to withdraw if the road was constructed along the route first selected, the change of routes was not an abuse of discretion, warranting interference, though first route would serve more people and the cost of maintenance would be less, but at most was a mistake of judgment, with which the court will not interfere; "discretion" being defined as the power or right to act officially according to what appears just and proper under the circumstances.

[Ed. Note.—For other definitions, see Words and Phrases, First and Second Series, Discretion.]

2. **Injunction ⚖=74—Courts cannot invade discretion to correct mistakes of judgment.**

Courts cannot invade the discretion of public functionaries to correct mere mistakes of judgment.

Appeal from District Court, Hunt County; Geo. B. Hall, Judge.

Action by J. O. Johnson and others against the Board of Permanent Road Commissioners of Hunt County and others. Judgment for plaintiffs, and defendants appeal. Judgment reversed, and injunction dissolved.

Clark & Sweeton, of Greenville, for appellants.

B. F. Crosby and M. B. Harrell, both of Greenville, for appellees.

HAMILTON, J. This is an appeal from a judgment perpetually enjoining appellants from constructing a certain described paved road in Hunt county.

The board of permanent road commissioners of Hunt county was created under and exists by virtue of a special road law for Hunt county enacted by the Thirty-Third Legislature. It consists of the commissioners' court, the county auditor, and eight citizens, two selected from each of the four commissioners' precincts. Special Laws 33d Leg. p. 190, vol. 16, Laws of Texas. This board, under the provisions of the Hunt county road law, is given unlimited discretion in selecting, laying out, and constructing paved roads.

Appellees alleged substantially that the members of the board, in deliberate and exhaustive exercise of the discretion reposed in them by the provisions of the law, selected and decided to construct a road, designated as the "Jacobia route," which route, in the light of existing facts and conditions and as a matter of justice to the great majority of the citizens to be affected, sound and practical judgment dictated ought to be constructed. But, it was alleged, after the "Jacobia route" had been selected by the board, the state highway department refused to extend state and federal aid for the construction of the road, to augment the county's funds derived from bonds voted by the county, and that this circumstance induced the board to surrender its discretion to the state highway commission, and to yield to the arbitrary demands of the highway commission, which was done in adopting for construction the road the building of which was enjoined.

Appellants answered by general demurrer and general denial. The appeal is presented upon one assignment of error, which is as follows:

"The judgment entered herein is without evidence to support it, is contrary to the law, and is an unwarranted interference with the discretionary powers, duties, and responsibilities of the permanent road board of Hunt county. There is no evidence to show that the road board failed to exercise its own discretion. On the contrary, the undisputed evidence is that it has freely exercised its discretion, that it has chosen the more direct and cheaper route, and that, in doing so, it will save the people of

Hunt county $146,000, besides working in harmony with the state highway department."

We sustain the view asserted by appellants. The record does not reveal in the board's action, purposes and conduct which constitute abuse of discretion in matters of this kind. There is no evidence whatever of bad faith or perversity, or of moral delinquency, actuating the board or any of its members, in finally receding from the tentative selection of the "Jacobia route," and ultimately adopting the "middle route," the construction of which appellees seek to enjoin.

[1, 2] The evidence reflects a long and insistent discussion between the board and the highway commission, throughout which the former strive to persuade the latter to acquiesce in supplying federal and state aid to the construction of the "Jacobia route," and throughout which the highway department insists that it would not accede to the proposal, but would withdraw a contribution of road funds amounting, according to the evidence, to $106,000. The evidence shows that the construction of the route finally adopted will cost $40,000 less than the "Jacobia route"; the former route being a shorter and more direct connection between Greenville and Commerce, the two respective terminals. It also shows that the "Jacobia route" would directly serve a great many more people than the "middle route" finally adopted, and that the cost of maintaining the "Jacobia route" would be less. The evidence also shows the aggregate taxable value of property in the vicinity of the "Jacobia route" to be much greater than that in the vicinity of the other. But, on the other hand, the evidence establishes that the members of the board carefully and patiently considered the entire situation, and weighed the advantages of the "Jacobia route" against the loss to the county's road system the withdrawal of the $106,000 federal and state aid would entail, by virtue of building the "Jacobia route," and that their honest judgment suggested the soundness of building the adopted road and saving the $106,000, rather than building the Jacobia road and losing it. Not even the semblance of corruption or disregard of duty is discoverable in the record. At most, it can be said to disclose only a mistake of judgment; and it is well settled that courts cannot invade the discretion of such public functionaries to correct mere mistakes of judgment.

Before a court is authorized to restrain by injunction the acts of such boards, it must be established that the conduct complained of is tainted with some element of turpitude or its equivalent. When the board was created by the votes of the citizens of Hunt county, as it was, under the provisions of the special law, the people thereby assumed whatever peril there was to be involved in the board's honest, although erroneous, judgment, and they cannot call upon the courts to nullify that judgment, notwithstanding it may not be in accord with the better judgment of others, and notwithstanding that the facts and conditions may persuade the court that effectuating such judgment will operate to impair the highest public interests. The conduct complained of was but the legitimate result and expression of authoritative opinion, and courts may not review such opinions and substitute therefor their own, derived from the same facts upon which the board acted.

Neither may the court say that, because the board has once tentatively expressed its judgment as to the soundest selection of a route, it cannot subsequently abandon that judgment and select another route, in consideration of whatever advantage will accrue from such circumstance as the extension of the $106,000 aid, which otherwise it was thought would have been lost. The exercise of discretion in this matter meant more than merely determining which particular road would directly serve the greater number of citizens in a certain portion of the county, or which road would extend through a locality contributing most to the taxes paid for the bonds. It meant a consideration and weighing of whatever entered as a factor to contribute to or detract from the general welfare of the county from the standpoint of a permanent road system for the entire county. The scope of the board's duties comprehended, in connection with this very matter of choice of routes, a conservation of the road interests of the whole county, and we think it manifest that a proper exercise of discretion permitted, if it did not require, consideration of the $106,000 of proffered aid as an element of legitimate concern in adopting a route for construction of the road.

"'Discretion,' as applied to public functionaries, means the power or right to act officially, according to what appears just and proper under the circumstances. * * * Courts will not interfere with the exercise of such discretion * * * unless it has been abused. * * * In order to constitute an abuse of such discretion, it must appear that it was exercised on grounds, or for reasons, clearly untenable, or to an extent clearly unreasonable." Board of Commissioners of Rio Grande County v. Lewis, 28 Colo. 378, 65 Pac. 51.

In considering the question of abuse of discretion by county commissioners in determining to build a certain road the Amarillo Court of Appeals, speaking through Justice Boyce, in the case of Grayson County v. Harrell, used the following language:

"There is no allegation that the decision of the commissioners' court to improve the Luella road was the result of any corrupt, fraudulent, malicious, or improper motive on the part of the commissioners, or that their decision was not made in good faith. The facts alleged, if true, only show a bad mistake in judgment. In cases of this kind, the discretionary power conferred upon the commissioners' court can only be interfered with by injunction where the proposed action is fraudulent." Grayson County v. Harrell, 202 S. W. 163.

Also see Tippett v. Gates, 223 S. W. 702; Waterbury v. City of Laredo, 60 Tex. 523; Tyree v. Road District, 199 S. W. 644.

There being no evidence in the record showing or tending to show that the adoption of the road was the result of perversity, caprice, or moral delinquency of any nature, but, on the contrary, the evidence clearly showing that the members of the board pursued the dictates of conscience and judgment in the actions complained about, it follows that no abuse of discretion appears, and accordingly the decree is unsupported by the evidence.

The judgment is therefore reversed, and the injunction granted is dissolved.

INDEMNITY CO. OF AMERICA v. MAHAFFEY. (No. 6560.)

(Court of Civil Appeals of Texas. San Antonio. May 11, 1921. Rehearing Denied June 8, 1921.)

1. Appeal and error ⊂⇒434 — Execution of agreement by defendant in error operated as appearance in Court of Civil Appeals.

Execution by defendant in error of an agreement on file among the papers that plaintiff in error could file the transcript and record in the Court of Civil Appeals and file its briefs at any time before a specified date, and that defendant in error might file his briefs at any time prior to two weeks before submission of the cause, operated as an appearance in the Court of Civil Appeals by defendant in error.

2. Insurance ⊂⇒637 — Automobile purchaser's petition seeking to recover on fire and theft policy on car demurrable in not showing assignment of policy to him.

Petition whereby the purchaser of an automobile sought to recover from an indemnity company which had issued a fire and theft insurance policy on the car eight months prior to the sale, the car having been stolen four days after the sale to plaintiff, *held* subject to general demurrer so far as the indemnity company was concerned, plaintiff purchaser of the car not having been a party to the policy, but a stranger, and it never having been transferred or assigned to him, so far as the petition showed.

Error from Tarrant County Court; W. P. Walker, Judge.

Action by H. L. Mahaffey against the Indemnity Company of America and another. Judgment by default against the Indemnity Company after plaintiff had dismissed as to other party, and defendant Indemnity Company brings error. Reversed and remanded.

Bradley, Burns, Christian & Bradley, of Fort Worth, for plaintiff in error.

C. F. Clark, of Fort Worth, for defendant in error.

SMITH, J. [1] We find among the papers an amicus curiæ "suggestion of certain material fatal errors which are apparent upon the record in" this cause, coupled with a motion to dismiss the writ of error because of such errors. The objections pointed out go to the sufficiency of the citation in error and the officer's return thereon. Two of the objections are untenable, while the others are waived by defendant in error, who signed an agreement, on file among the papers here, that plaintiff in error could file the transcript and record in this court, and file its briefs herein at any time before September 3, 1920, and further agreeing that defendant in error might file his briefs any time prior to two weeks before the submission of the cause. The execution of this agreement operated as an appearance in this court by defendant in error; and the motion to dismiss is accordingly overruled. Stephenson v. Chappell, 12 Tex. Civ. App. 296, 33 S. W. 880, 36 S. W. 482.

[2] Mahaffey, plaintiff below, and defendant in error here, alleged that on February 21, 1919, the indemnity company issued a fire and theft policy in the amount of $300 covering a certain Ford automobile; that thereafter, on October 11, 1919, he purchased the car from the then owner; that four days later, on October 15, 1919, the car was stolen and has not been recovered; that when he purchased the car the indemnity policy was in the possession of the Guaranty State Bank of Fort Worth, and that he instructed the bank to have the policy transferred to him, which the bank agreed to do "and led the plaintiff to believe that the * * * bank would have and cause said policy to be transferred to * * * plaintiff, and that plaintiff did believe that the * * * bank would and did have the said policy transferred to said plaintiff"; that if the bank failed to have the policy so transferred, and thereby relieved the indemnity company of liability on the policy, "then and in that event the plaintiff has been damaged by the negligence of the" bank in the sum of $300.

The bank appeared and answered, but the indemnity company made no appearance, whereupon Mahaffey dismissed the bank from the action, and took a default judgment against the indemnity company for the amount of the policy, and the company brings that judgment here by writ of error.

The petition of the plaintiff below discloses: That at the time the indemnity policy was issued the car did not belong to Mahaffey, but was the property of a third party; that the policy was not issued to Mahaffey, but to a third party; that after the policy

---

⊂⇒For other cases see same topic and KEY-NUMBER in all Key-Numbered Digests and Indexes

had been in force about eight months Mahaffey bought the car, which was stolen from him four days later; that at the time Mahaffey purchased the car the indemnity policy was in the possession of the Fort Worth bank, and that Mahaffey instructed the bank to have the policy transferred to him; but that plaintiff cannot allege that the policy was ever so transferred to him.

The petition, in our opinion, was subject to a general demurrer so far as the indemnity company was concerned, and accordingly will not support a judgment by default against that company. If the indemnity company was liable to Mahaffey, it could have been so only by reason of the insurance contract or policy. That contract was made originally with a third party, a stranger to this litigation. It was not made with Mahaffey. He was not a party, but was a stranger to it. It was never transferred or assigned to him, so far as the petition shows, and no contract or privity of contract between the company and himself was alleged, and accordingly no case was made by his petition.

The judgment is reversed, and the cause remanded.

ST. PAUL FIRE & MARINE INS. CO. v. CHARLTON. (No. 8537.)

(Court of Civil Appeals of Texas. Dallas. May 14, 1921.)

1. Indemnity ⚓11—There is no right of action on an indemnity contract until the indemnitee has suffered loss.

In the case of an agreement to pay or a covenant to do a certain act, a recovery may be had as soon as there is a breach of the contract, where as in the case of a covenant of indemnity, strictly, that is of indemnity against loss, no right of action accrues until the indemnitee has suffered a loss against which the covenant runs.

2. Insurance ⚓514—On loss of bonds in mail, insured bank had right of action against insurer under indemnity policy, transferable to plaintiff.

Where a bank was under contract to deliver certain bonds to plaintiff, for which he had paid, and the defendant insurance company contracted to indemnify the bank from loss in transmitting them through registered mail, and they were lost, held, that the bank had sustained a loss entitling it to indemnity from the insurance company, and which the bank could lawfully assign to plaintiff together with the policy.

Appeal from Dallas County Court; T. A. Work, Judge.

Suit by S. A. Charlton against the St. Paul Fire & Marine Insurance Company. Judgment for the plaintiff, and the defendant appeals. Affirmed.

Harris & Graham, of Dallas, for appellant. H. C. Jarrel and S. A. Charlton, both of Dallas, for appellee.

TALBOT, J. The appellee brought this suit against the appellant to recover $200 on an insurance policy issued on August 14, 1917, by the appellant to the State National Bank of San Antonio, Tex., which had been assigned to the appellee. The appellee alleged the issuance of the policy and set out its terms and provisions. He alleged that said bank, on the 20th day of February, 1918, was the owner of two Liberty bonds of the par and market value of $100 each; that he had entered into a contract with the bank for the purchase of said bonds, agreeing to pay therefor the sum of $200; that the bank agreed to deliver the bonds to appellee at Ft. Sill, Okl., title to pass on delivery; that on the day mentioned the bank deposited said bonds as registered mail in the United States post office at San Antonio, Tex., addressed to appellee at Ft. Sill, Okl., and that in order to protect itself and the appellee against loss in transit insured said bonds in appellant's company by the contract of insurance mentioned. The policy insured the bank in case of loss of the bonds, to be paid to the assured in the sum of $200, within "15 days after proof of loss and proof of interest," and provided that—

In case of "loss or misfortune it shall be lawful and necessary to and for the insured to sue, labor, and travel for, in, and about the defense, safeguard, and recovery of the property without prejudice to this insurance, and upon payment of any loss under this policy the assured or assigns, in consideration thereof, agree to convey to the said St. Paul Fire & Marine Insurance Company the unincumbered title in the property lost as absolute owners thereof, and to take all necessary measures in behalf, and at the risk and expense of the said St. Paul Fire & Marine Insurance Company, for the recovery, reissue, or replacement of said property when possible."

Appellant pleaded a general demurrer, special exceptions, and a general denial. The trial court overruled all exceptions to the plaintiff's petition, and upon a trial had before the court without a jury judgment was rendered in favor of appellee for the sum of $226.60, with interest thereon at the rate of 6 per cent. from and after the date of the judgment. Appellant's motion for a new trial was overruled, and it perfected an appeal to this court.

It is contended that the bonds aforesaid, registered and insured under the policy set out above in accordance with the terms and conditions thereof, were lost in the mail; that neither said bonds nor the package containing them ever reached the plaintiff herein and were never delivered to the plaintiff; that the said bank, in due time and in accordance with the said policy, presented proof of loss and proof of interest, and in all things, before the delivery of said package to the post office, the said bank fully complied with all the terms, conditions, and provisions of the said policy; that said bank assigned in writing to S. A. Charlton the title to the Liberty bonds, in order that the plaintiff would be in a position to comply with the terms of the policy upon payment by the insurance company, and so that the plaintiff could convey to the defendant the absolute title to such bonds, upon the defendant paying the loss sustained to plaintiff; that on or about the 6th day of November, 1919, said bank, in writing and for a full consideration, assigned and conveyed to the plaintiff in this cause the cause of action of said bank against the defendant arising as hereinbefore alleged, and said bank assigned to plaintiff the policy of insurance in question, and the claim which it (the bank) may have under and by virtue of said policy, and authorized the said S. A. Charlton to bring, maintain, and prosecute any and all suits necessary to the enforcement of said policy of insurance in his own name; that thereby the plaintiff became the legal owner of the cause of action herein alleged against the defendant, and the defendant became liable and bound to pay to the plaintiff the sum that it had promised and agreed to pay to said bank by reason of the loss of said bonds, to wit, the market value of said bonds, together with 6 per cent. interest thereon.

[1] There is, in general, a well-settled distinction between an agreement to indemnify and an agreement to pay or a covenant to do a certain act. In the latter case a recovery may be had as soon as there is a breach of the contract, whereas, in the case of a covenant of indemnity, strictly, that is, of an indemnity against loss, no right of action accrues until the indemnitee has suffered a loss against which the covenant runs. 14 Ruling Case Law, § 2, p. 44. At common law the rule is that to authorize a recovery on a mere bond of indemnity actual damage must be shown. 14 R. C. L. § 13, p. 55. Appellant invokes an application of the rule of law announced upon the facts alleged in the instant case and asserts that under it the judgment of the court below should be reversed and judgment here rendered in its favor, and, in addition to the authority which we have mentioned, cites the cases of Owen v. Jackson-Hinton Gin Co., 217 S. W. 762, decided by this court, and McBride v. Ætna Life Ins. Co., 191 S. W. 5, decided by the Supreme Court of Arkansas. In those cases the plaintiffs sought to recover upon insurance policies taken out by the employer, not for the benefit of their employés, but merely to indemnify themselves against actual loss from personal injury to the employé, and it was correctly held that the insurer incurred no liability until the employer had paid the loss,

drawing the distinction between an insurance policy which constitutes a contract of indemnity and what is ordinarily termed "liability insurance."

[2] But we are not prepared to hold that the appellee failed to show by his pleadings a cause of action and right of recovery against the appellant. On the contrary, we have reached the conclusion that the facts alleged show a cause of action and right of recovery in the appellee against the appellant and that the appellant's demurrer was properly overruled. The appellee alleged the purchase of the bonds from the bank at San Antonio, Tex., and facts showing the liability of the bank to him under the contract of purchase; the assignment of the policy of insurance and the bank's claim against the appellant on account of the loss of the bonds; and facts sufficient to show that appellee had been subrogated to the rights of the bank under the policy. The allegations were also sufficient to show that inasmuch as the appellee's contract of purchase called for a delivery of the bonds at Ft. Sill, Okl., the title to the same had not, at the time of their loss, passed to the appellee, and that therefore the loss of the bonds constituted a loss to the bank which the policy indemnified it against and the bank's cause of action, and the policy, according to the allegations of the petition, having been assigned to the appellee, he could sue and recover on the policy. The facts alleged, as is pointed out in the trial judge's conclusions, further show that before the shipment and loss of the bonds the bank had received therefor from the appellee $200, the purchase money, and was legally bound to deliver to the appellee two bonds of the par value of $200; that it had owned two such bonds with which to make such delivery; that after the bonds were lost in the mails the bank occupied the same position as before relative to the $200 received from appellee and to the obligation it had assumed to deliver the bonds to appellee, but it had suffered a loss, as it no longer had the bonds with which to make the delivery and with which to discharge its said obligation; that the practical result is that the bank by the loss of the bonds has lost $200, the value of the bonds, since, while it received $200 in payment for the bonds which it had obligated itself to deliver to the appellee, and had lost the bonds which it endeavored to deliver through the mail and which the appellant had insured to indemnify it against such loss, it was still under obligation to the appellee to deliver bonds as it contracted to do. Clearly in this situation the bank had a cause of action against the appellant on the insurance policy issued by it, which together with the policy could lawfully be transferred and assigned to the appellee. At all events, we think the allegations of the appellee's petition were not obnoxious to a general demurrer, and appellant's first and second as-

signments of error asserting that they were will be overruled.

The third assignment of error has, in effect, been disposed of adversely to the appellant by what we have already said, or, if not, it presents no reversible error.

The judgment is affirmed.

BLAYLOCK et al. v. SLOCOMB.   (No. 697.)

(Court of Civil Appeals of Texas. Beaumont. June 1, 1921. Rehearing Denied June 15, 1921.)

1. **Appeal and error** ⟷396—**Exception in notice of appeal not necessary for appeal from temporary injunction.**

As under Vernon's Sayles' Ann. Civ. St. 1914, art 4644, a temporary injunction order may be made in chambers, out of term and without notice or hearing, a notice of appeal is not necessary to give a right of appeal from such order; the general law (article 2084) requiring exceptions to the ruling of the trial court and notice of appeal therefrom having no application.

2. **Appeal and error** ⟷396—**Exception and notice of appeal necessary to perfect appeal from final judgment perpetuating injunction.**

To appeal from a final judgment perpetuating an injunction made in open court upon a hearing in term time in a trial upon the merits of the case, exception and notice of appeal required by the general law (Vernon's Sayles' Ann. Civ. St. 1914, art. 2084) is necessary, and where no exception was taken and notice given the appeal must be dismissed.

Appeal from District Court, Milam County; John Watson, Judge.

Action by S. J. Slocomb against L. L. Blaylock and others. From a judgment for plaintiff, defendants appeal. Appeal dismissed.

S. M. Burns, Jr., of Cameron, and Byers & Cavanagh, of Houston, for appellants.

Chambers & Wallace, of Cameron, for appellee.

O'QUINN, J.   Appellee began this suit in the district court of Milam county, Tex., by his petition filed December 19, 1919, alleging that on said date he was the owner of a certain house and lot in the town of Cameron, Tex., and that same was his business homestead, which he had never abandoned, and that appellants had on the 10th day of December, 1919, levied an execution thereon, and by virtue thereof was advertising the same for sale, and praying for a temporary writ of injunction to restrain said sale, and that ap-

pellants Wilkins & Lange be enjoined from further levying any writ of execution on said property, and that the lien of appellants Wilkins & Lange created by the abstract of judgment theretofore recorded in said Milam county be removed as a cloud upon appellee's title to said property, and that on final hearing the said writ be made perpetual. The temporary writ was issued as prayed for, and hearing thereon set for the next regular term of the district court of said Milam county in January, 1920. The cause came up regularly for trial on March 2, 1920, before the court without a jury, and the court, after hearing the evidence, rendered judgment in favor of appellee that the property in question was appellee's business homestead, and perpetuating the writ of injunction, and granting full relief as prayed for by appellee, from which judgment this appeal is prosecuted.

At the threshold of the case, we are met with the objection of appellee that this court is without jurisdiction to determine this appeal for the reason that appellants did not except to the judgment in the court below, and that no notice of appeal was given from said judgment.

[1, 2] We have carefully inspected the whole record, and find that it fails to show that any exception to said judgment was made or any notice of appeal was given. It is well settled, under article 4644, Vernon's Sayles' Civil Statutes, that since a temporary injunction order may be made in chambers, out of term, without notice or hearing, a notice of appeal is not necessary to give a right to appeal from such order. Young v. Dudney, 140 S. W. 806; Farwell v. Babcock, 27 Tex. Civ. App. 162, 65 S. W. 512. Hence the general law (article 2084, Vernon's Sayles' Civil Statutes) requiring exceptions to the rulings of trial courts, and notice of appeal therefrom, as a condition precedent to the right of appeal, has no application in such cases, but we can find no authority for dispensing with said requirements in an effort to appeal from a final judgment perpetuating an injunction made in open court, upon a hearing in term time in a trial upon the merits of the case in its regular order. We think such exception and notice are necessary to invest this court with jurisdiction to hear this appeal, and for want of same the cause is dismissed from the docket of this court. Western Union Tel. Co. v. O'Keefe, 87 Tex. 423, 28 S. W. 945; Goldman v. Broyles, 141 S. W. 283; Beaumont v. Newsome, 143 S. W. 941; McMillen v. Lumber Co., 149 S. W 734; Harbinson v. Cottle County, 147 S. W. 719.

Appeal dismissed.

ROBERTSON v. STATE. (No. 1.)

(Supreme Court of Arkansas. May 23, 1921.
Rehearing Denied June 27, 1921.)

1. Intoxicating liquors ⬦236(19) — Evidence held sufficient to show defendant manufactured liquor.

In a prosecution for manufacturing whisky, evidence *held* sufficient to sustain a conviction, notwithstanding the fact that the still exploded and he contended no liquor had been distilled, the fact that raw material was poured out on the ground and that whisky was found on the premises warranting the inference of manufacture.

2. Criminal law ⬦1172(6) — Erroneous instruction allowing conviction for manufacture of intoxicating liquor under indictment charging manufacture of spirits harmless.

In a prosecution for manufacturing spirituous liquor denominated as whisky, an instruction that if defendant manufactured alcoholic, ardent, vinous, malt, or fermented·liquors which could be used or drunk as an intoxicating beverage, was harmless, and not prejudicial even though the proof should have been confined to the kind of liquor named, the sole question being whether defendant, whose still exploded, distilled liquor or not.

3. Intoxicating liquors ⬦233(2) — Testimony concerning finding of whisky near defendant's home admissible.

In a prosecution for manufacturing intoxicating liquors, it was proper to permit an officer to testify concerning the finding of whisky near defendant's home, since this had some tendency to prove that liquor was manufactured by defendant on the premises.

Appeal from Circuit Court, Lonoke County; George W. Clark, Judge.

Bill Robertson was convicted of having manufactured alcoholic spirits, commonly known as whisky, and he appeals. Affirmed.

Williams & Holloway and Guy E. Williams, all of Lonoke, for appellant.

J. S. Utley, Atty. Gen., and Elbert Godwin and W. T. Hammock, Asst. Attys. Gen., for the State.

McCULLOCH, C. J. Appellant was convicted under an indictment charging him with having manufactured "one pint of alcoholic, ardent, vinous, and intoxicating spirits, commonly called 'whisky.'" It is undisputed that appellant erected a crude distillery in an outhouse at the home of one Ezell Trice, in Lonoke county, where he lived, and that he attempted to manufacture whisky. Appellant admitted as much in his testimony, but .he denied that he completed the distillation of the whisky from the raw material which he was using. He used a metal coal oil tank or barrel and a wooden keg, into one of which he put the sour mash, and the two containers

were connected with a cane pipe used as a "worm." Appellant testified that he put into the keg a half bushel of chops, two gallons of molasses, and five buckets of water. A hole in the ground was used as a furnace, and the metal barrel was set over it. A fire was built in the furnace, and after the contents of the barrel became heated, an explosion occurred. Appellant's effort to manufacture whisky was thus discovered, and his arrest followed in a few hours, as soon as the services of an officer could be procured.

Appellant freely admitted to the officer, and admitted on the witness stand, that he was attempting to make whisky for his own use, but he claimed that he did not succeed in the effort, which was frustrated by the explosion.

[1] After appellant was arrested and taken to jail, the officer went back to the house of Ezell Trice, and the latter carried him out a short distance from the house and discovered buried in the ground two jugs and a bottle of white "moonshine" whisky. Trice testified that he did not put the whisky there, and did not know it was there until it was discovered on the search made by him and the officers. One of the officers who made the arrest testified concerning the condition of the crude distillery that he found, and also stated that some of the material used in making the liquor had been poured out on the ground.

It is earnestly contended that the evidence is insufficient to establish the fact that appellant manufactured any whisky—that the proof merely shows that he was engaged in an effort to make whisky, but that he did not complete it. We think, however, that the evidence is sufficient to warrant the jury in finding that the operation of the distillery resulted in the manufacture of whisky. The fact that used raw material was poured out on the ground, and also the fact that whisky was found on the premises, is sufficient to warrant the inference that whisky was manufactured there by appellant. The two jugs and the bottle of whisky were found on the premises only a few hundred yards from the house of Trice, who testified that neither he nor his wife put the whisky there, and there is no evidence that any one else besides appellant frequented the premises.

[2] It is next contended that the court erred in giving an instruction to the effect that the defendant could be convicted if the proof showed that he had manufactured "alcoholic, ardent, vinous, malt, or fermented liquors which could be used and drunk as intoxicating beverage," when the indictment specifically charged the manufacture of whisky. Conceding, under the rule announced by this court in Carleton v. State, 129 Ark. 361, 196 S. W. 124, that the particular language of the indictment was descriptive of the offense, and

that the proof must be confined to the kind of liquor specifically named, we are of the opinion that the instruction given by the court was not prejudicial, as the sole issue in this case was whether or not appellant succeeded in manufacturing whisky, which he was undertaking to do at the distillery when the explosion occurred. Appellant admitted that he was attempting to manufacture liquor, and, as before stated, the sole question was whether or not he succeeded in the effort. It is not conceivable that the jury were misled by this instruction, and reached the conclusion that appellant manufactured anything else but whisky. We think the instruction was harmless.

[3] Again, it is insisted that the court erred in permitting one of the officers to testify concerning the finding of whisky near Trice's home. We think that this had some tendency to prove that liquor was manufactured by appellant on the premises, and that the ruling of the court in admitting the testimony was correct.

Judgment affirmed.

TEXARKANA & FT. SMITH RY. CO. v. ADCOCK. (No. 32.)

(Supreme Court of Arkansas. June 6, 1921. Rehearing Denied June 27, 1921.)

1. **Husband and wife ⚖️209(2)—Under Texas statute wife may maintain in her own name action for personal injuries, damages therefor not being community property.**

Since Vernon's Ann. Civ. St. Supp. Tex. 1918, art. 4621a, declaring that all property received as compensation for personal injuries sustained by the wife shall be her separate property, etc., a married woman may for injuries sustained in Texas maintain a separate action, for the recovery cannot be treated as community property for which the husband alone can sue.

2. **Venue ⚖️4—Action for personal injuries is transitory.**

An action for personal injuries against a carrier is one ex delicto, personal, and transitory, and may be maintained in a state other than in which it arose.

3. **Continuance ⚖️24—Will not be granted merely to obtain cumulative testimony.**

In an action against a carrier for personal injuries suffered while passenger was alighting, a continuance will not be granted to obtain the testimony of a brakeman stationed at the door, who was suffering from what was claimed temporary paralysis of the throat, rendering him unable to speak, where other witnesses testified to substantially the same facts as to what the brakeman would testify.

4. **Appeal and error ⚖️231(9)—Errors in verbiage of instruction not reviewed, unless specifically pointed out.**

Inaccuracies in the verbiage of an instruction will not be reviewed, where they were not pointed out by specific objections.

5. **Trial ⚖️260(1)—Refusal of requests covered is not error.**

The refusal of requests covered by the charges given is not error.

6. **Trial ⚖️278—Specific objection to instruction necessary.**

The giving of an instruction not in good form is not error, where specific objection was not made.

7. **Trial ⚖️235(1) — Words emphasizing the fact that the jury is the sole judge of weight of evidence improper.**

Where the court had instructed that the jury are the sole judges of the weight of the evidence and the credibility of the witnesses, it was improper to add by way of accentuation the words "illimitable, final, and unfettered."

8. **Evidence ⚖️598(1)—Mere number of witnesses does not establish weight of evidence.**

In determining the preponderance of the evidence, it is proper for the jury to take into consideration the number of witnesses testifying; but the preponderance is not necessarily in favor of the one who produces the greater number of witnesses to a proposition, that depending entirely on the weight or degree of credit which the jury may give to the testimony of the respective witnesses, taking into consideration their interest, relationship to the parties, manner of testifying, etc.

9. **Carriers ⚖️303(4) — Carrier must allow passenger reasonable opportunity to alight.**

It is the duty of a carrier to allow passengers a reasonable opportunity to alight, and a train must stop at a station long enough for that purpose, and it is the duty of a carrier also to take into consideration any special condition peculiar to any passenger and to the surroundings of the station, and to give a reasonable time under the circumstances.

Appeal from Circuit Court, Miller County; Geo. R. Haynie, Judge.

Action by Mary Adcock against the Texarkana & Ft. Smith Railway Company. From a judgment for plaintiff, defendant appeals. Affirmed.

James B. McDonough, of Ft. Smith, and King & Mahaffey, of Texarkana, Tex., for appellant.

J. M. Carter, of Texarkana, Ark., for appellee.

WOOD, J. This action was brought by the appellee against the appellant. The appellee alleged that she was a passenger on appellant's train from Texarkana, Ark., to Bloomburg, Tex.; that when the appellant stopped its train at Bloomburg, for the purpose of allowing the appellee and other passengers to alight, there were standing on its platform other persons who desired to take passage on that train, and before the appellee, in the exercise of ordinary care, had time to debark, other persons were allowed to board the train in such numbers that appellee thereby was prevented from getting off until the incoming passengers had sufficiently cleared the passageway; that immediately after the passageway was cleared appellee was going down the steps to debark, and the train was put in motion, and the appellee was thrown off her balance. Appellee alleged that the step leading from the coach to the platform was high and dangerous; that the appellant failed to furnish any stool or step on which to alight, and failed to furnish any one to assist her in alighting from the coach; that these acts of negligence caused appellee to fall from the coach upon the hard surface of the platform, and produced serious personal injuries, which she set forth in detail, to her damage in the sum of $3,000, for which she prayed judgment.

The appellant answered, denying specifically the allegations of negligence, and set up as an affirmative defense contributory negligence on the part of the appellee. Appellee testified that she and her husband were passengers on appellant's train, as alleged in her complaint, and that when the train stopped at Bloomburg, Tex., they got up to get off, and when they got to the door people were crowding in so that appellee and her husband could not get out. They started out as quickly as they could. Her husband was ahead of her. She had no baggage, except a little hand satchel. Just as soon as they could get out, her husband stepped off, and she started to get off, and the train gave a jerk and threw her backwards. She first realized that the train was moving when she made her step. Nobody was there to help her off. There was no stool to step on. She then described her injuries, which it is unnecessary to set forth. Other witnesses corroborated the testimony of the appellee.

There was testimony on behalf of the appellant tending to contradict the testimony introduced on behalf of the appellee. It was shown that a white man by the name of Marshall was brakeman on the train on that occasion; that he was at his place on the platform where the passengers get on and off, and had a step stool. Marshall was not present to testify at the trial, and the appellant moved to continue the cause on that account. Appellant alleged that Marshall was present at a former term of the court, when the cause by mutual agreement was continued, and that he could not be present at this term because he was afflicted with paralysis, which at this time rendered him, and for some time to come would render him, unable to talk; that his testimony was material, because the appellant expected to prove by him facts which it set forth, directly contradicting the testimony of the appellee as to the acts of negligence to which she had testified. Appellant alleged that it thought that, if the cause was continued, there would be a reasonable chance of either procuring the attendance of the witness or his deposition.

The motion for continuance was filed December 8, 1920, and accompanying the motion was a certificate of a physician, made on December 2, 1920, to the effect that Marshall was afflicted with throat trouble in the nature of paralysis, rendering him unable to talk, and that he would not be able to attend court. The rulings of the court in the giving and refusing prayers for instructions will be considered as we proceed. The trial resulted in a verdict and judgment in favor of the appellee. The appellant by this appeal seeks to reverse the judgment.

[1, 2] 1. Appellant contends that the appellee cannot maintain this suit, since the injury occurred in Texas, and under the laws of that state damages for personal injuries to the wife are community property, for which the husband alone can sue. The Legislature of Texas in 1915 enacted the following statute:

"All property or moneys received as compensation for personal injuries sustained by the wife shall be her separate property, except such actual and necessary expenses as may have accumulated against the husband for hospital fees, medical bills, and all other expenses incident to the collection of said compensation." Article 4621a of 1918 Supplement to Vernon's Texas Civil and Criminal Statutes.

Since the passage of the above act, compensation for personal injuries sustained by the wife is no longer community property, and such compensation is now the separate property of the wife. In the absence of a decision of the highest court of Texas, holding that under the above statute the husband alone can maintain a suit to recover compensation for personal injuries to his wife, we are constrained to hold that the wife under the above statute should be permitted to maintain a suit in her own name and right. Such would undoubtedly be the proper construction if the injury had occurred in this state under a similar statute, when construed in connection with section 5577 of Crawford & Moses' Digest. That statute expressly confers upon married women the right to sue and to be sued, and to enjoy all rights and to be subject to all the laws as though she were a feme sole.

Learned counsel for appellant cite us to cases of the Courts of Civil Appeals of Texas holding that the husband alone can sue for community property, and that damage for personal injuries to the wife are community property. Ainsa v. Moses (Tex. Civ. App.) 100 S. W. 791; Cone v. Belcher, 57 Tex. Civ. App. 493, 124 S. W. 149; Allemania Fire Ins. Co. v. Angier (Tex. Civ. App.) 214 S. W. 450. But counsel have not directed our attention to any decision of the Court of Civil Appeals of Texas or of the Supreme Court since the passage of the above act holding that compensation for personal injuries to the wife is community property, and that the husband alone can sue for the same. Our own research has not discovered a holding of the courts of Texas to that effect. Therefore we must construe the statute as we believe it should be construed, in harmony with our own laws upon the subject. The action is one ex delicto, personal, transitory, and therefore may be brought in this State. St. L., I. M. & S. R. Co. v. Brown, 67 Ark. 295, 54 S. W. 865; K. C. So. Ry. Co. v. Ingram, 80 Ark. 269, 97 S. W. 55; St. L., I. M. & S. R. Co. v. Hesterly, 98 Ark. 240, 135 S. W. 874; St. L. & S. F. Rd. Co. v. Coy, 113 Ark. 265, 168 S. W. 1106; Hines v. Rice, 142 Ark. 159, 218 S. W. 851.

[3] 2. Appellant next contends that the court erred in overruling its motion for a continuance. On the allegations of negligence set forth in the complaint, the testimony of the absent witness, Marshall, as alleged in the motion for continuance, would have been very material, because he was the brakeman who was stationed at the door where passengers got on and off the train, and his testimony as set out in the motion directly contradicted the testimony of the appellee and her witnesses, tending to sustain the allegations of negligence set up by the appellee. But, upon careful consideration of the testimony of several other witnesses on behalf of the appellant, we find that their testimony tended to establish the same facts as would have been testified to by the witness Marshall, if present. Marshall's testimony, therefore, would have been only cumulative, and the rule has been thoroughly established by this court that the trial court cannot be reversed for overruling a motion for continuance, where the testimony of the absent witness is but cumulative. See Carpenter v. State, 62 Ark. 286, 36 S. W. 900; St. L., I. M. & S. R. Co. v. Fisher, 80 Ark. 376, 97 S. W. 279; A. L. Clark Lumber Co. v. Northcutt, 95 Ark. 291, 129 S. W. 88; James v. State, 125 Ark. 269, 188 S. W. 806; and other cases collated in 1 Crawford's Digest, p. 1023, "Continuance," 12(6).

[4-7] 3. The appellant next contends that the court erred in giving and refusing certain prayers for instructions. We have examined the several prayers in the light of the criticisms by the learned counsel for the appellant, and we find that there are some inaccuracies; but they are mere errors of verbiage, and do not relate to matters of substance. The attention of the trial court should have been drawn to them by specific objection, which was not done. Some of the prayers of the appellant which the court refused were correct, but these were covered by other instructions which the court gave. Instruction No. 5, set forth in marginal note,[1] was not in good form, and, if specific objection had been made to it, the court should not have given it. The jury are the sole judges of the weight of the evidence and the credibility of witnesses. After thus instructing the jury, it was surplusage, and wholly unnecessary and improper, to add by way of accentuation the words "illimitable, final, and unfettered:"

[8] In determining where the preponderance of the evidence lies on the facts at issue, it is proper for the jury to take into consideration the number of witnesses testifying pro and con; but the preponderance is not necessarily in favor of the one who produces the greater number of witnesses to a proposition. That depends entirely upon the weight or degree of credit which the jury may give to the testimony of the respective witnesses, after taking into consideration all the elements or tests by which the credibility of witnesses is determined, such as interest, relationship to the parties, bias, means of information, manner of witness in testifying, etc. See St. L., I. M. & S. R. Co. v. Evans, 99 Ark. 69, 76, 137 S. W. 568; Newhouse Mill & Lbr. Co. v. Keller, 103 Ark. 538-547, 146 S. W. 855; Martin v. Vaught, 128 Ark. 293, 194 S. W. 10. But, while the instruction cannot be approved as a precedent, it is not erroneous in substance, and, in the absence of specific objection, it was not prejudicial error calling for a reversal of the judgment.

[9] The charge as a whole was in conformity with the law applicable to the facts of this record as announced by this court in many decisions, some of them quite recent. In St. Louis Southwestern R. Co. v. Aydelott, 128 Ark. 479, 194 S. W. 873, we said:

"It is the duty of carriers to allow their passengers a reasonable opportunity of getting on and off their trains, and they must stop at stations long enough for that purpose. A reasonable time is such time as a person of ordinary care and prudence should be allowed to take. It is the duty of the carrier, in determining what is a reasonable time, to take into consideration any special condition peculiar to any passenger and to the surroundings at the station, and to give a reasonable time under the existing circumstances, as they are known or

---

[1] No. 5. It is not the number of witnesses who testify in a case that creates the greatest weight of evidence. One witness may be opposed by many witnesses, and still the jury would be justified in accepting this one witness' testimony, as against a number of other witnesses, as to how the thing happened, provided you believe his testimony more nearly comports with the truth; and as to whether their testimony or his more nearly comports with the truth you are the sole, illimitable, final, and unfettered judges.

should be known by its servants, for a passenger to get on or off its trains."

See, also, Payne, Dir. Gen., v. Thurston, 230 S. W. 561.

The issues of negligence and contributory negligence were submitted under instructions free from prejudicial error. There was evidence to sustain the verdict.

The judgment is therefore affirmed.

BATTLE v. DRAPER. (No. 22.)

(Supreme Court of Arkansas. May 30, 1921.
Rehearing Denied June 27, 1921.)

1. Contracts ⬥176(1)—Court construes written contract and declares terms and meaning where it is not ambiguous.

It is the duty of the court to construe a written contract and declare its terms and meaning to the jury where the contract contains no words of latent ambiguity.

2. Contracts ⬥10(1)—Contract of purchaser from mortgagor to bid in land on foreclosure sale did not lack mutuality.

Contract between plaintiff, the purchaser of two tracts of land, and defendant, to whom she sold one of such tracts, whereby defendant, the mortgage executed by plaintiff on the tracts having been foreclosed, agreed to bid in the property, etc., held not to have lacked mutuality.

3. Vendor and purchaser ⬥70—Contract by purchaser to bid in land on foreclosure sale held construable to mean he must bid amount due mortgagee.

Contract between plaintiff, the purchaser of two tracts of land, and defendant, to whom she sold one of such tracts, whereby defendant, the mortgage executed by plaintiff on the tracts having been foreclosed, agreed to bid in the property, etc., held construable to mean that defendant must bid at least the amount due the mortgagee under the foreclosure decree.

4. Frauds, statute of ⬥118(5)—Authority of seller's agent to contract with purchaser that latter should bid in land on foreclosure not required to be in writing.

Authority on the part of the agent of a seller of land to sign the contract with the purchaser that the purchaser should bid in the property on foreclosure sale of mortgage given by the seller, etc., was not required to be in writing.

5. Principal and agent ⬥103(9)—Owner of land authorizing agent to sell, bound by terms of contract made by him.

Where the owner of land gave her agent power to make a contract of sale, she was bound by its terms as soon as he made it regardless of the fact whether he had shown it to her, or stated the terms of it to her before he signed it for her as her agent.

6. Appeal and error ⬥301—Defendant cannot raise for first time on appeal question of excessive verdict.

Defendant, having failed to include in his motion for new trial the ground that verdict was excessive, cannot for the first time raise the question on appeal.

Appeal from Circuit Court, Hempstead County; Geo. R. Haynie, Judge.

Suit by Mattie B. Draper against O. M. Battle. From a judgment for plaintiff, defendant appeals. Affirmed.

Mattie B. Draper brought suit against O. M. Battle to recover damages for the alleged breach of a contract. The defendant denied liability under the contract.

Mattie B. Draper purchased from J. J. Battle two tracts of land in Hempstead county, Ark., known respectively as the Custer place and the Smith place. On the 10th day of October, 1912, she executed a mortgage on said tracts of land in the sum of $19,000 to J. J. Battle to secure a balance of the purchase money. On the 9th day of December, 1912, she sold and conveyed to the defendant, O. M. Battle, a brother of J. J. Battle, the Smith place for $16,000, and retained a lien upon the land for the unpaid purchase money. Most of the purchase money was unpaid, and the sale was made subject to the mortgage she had given to J. J. Battle. Having failed to pay J. J. Battle according to the terms and conditions of the mortgage, he brought suit against her and O. M. Battle in the chancery court to foreclose her mortgage and to cancel her deed to O. M. Battle in so far as it affected his rights under the mortgage. On the 5th day of March, 1915, a decree of foreclosure in favor of J. J. Battle was entered of record in the chancery court. The court rendered judgment in favor of J. J. Battle for the sum of $21,621.45 for his mortgage debt, interest and taxes paid by him. This sum was adjudged to bear interest from date at the rate of 8 per cent. per annum until paid. It was decreed that the deed of Mrs. Draper to O. M. Battle for the Smith place should be canceled in so far as the rights of J. J. Battle under his mortgage are affected. A decree of foreclosure upon default of the payment of the mortgage indebtedness was entered of record in the usual form. The sale was advertised to take place on the 30th day of June, 1915. In order to protect their rights in the premises on that day and before the sale was had, Mrs. Mattie B. Draper and O. M. Battle entered into a contract in writing as follows:

"Whereas, J. J. Battle has a judgment for $21,876.06, principal and interest, against the Custer land belonging to Mattie B. Draper and against the Smith place belonging to O. M. Battle: Now we agree that O. M. Battle is to bid in all this land at the sale to-day, or have it done, and that in payment of the judgment there shall be charged against the Smith land the sum of $15,000 and against the Custer land the sum of balance of the judgment and costs of the case, now estimated at $100. O. M. Battle is to take care of the $15,000, and Mattie B. Draper is to take care of the balance of the judgment; that is, she is to proceed to make a loan on the Custer land and take up her part of the judgment, and O. M. Battle will deed or have deeded to her or her assigns the Custer land. If she fails to do this within 12 months, then this agreement is void, and said O. M. Battle shall own the Custer land absolutely; this agreement being an option by O. M. Battle, given in consideration of a large concession of the indebtedness due her, Mattie Draper, on the Smith place by O. M. Battle. All received for these lands at the sale advertised for to-day over the amount of the judgment coming to these parties, they or either of them may bid said land up, and if a reasonable bid is offered by an outside party, the owner may let his or her land sell, but such sale shall not change the basis of this settlement, and the owner of the land so sold shall have the overplus so bid."

J. J. Battle was the only bidder at the foreclosure sale, and he bid in both the Smith and Custer tracts for his debt, interest, and costs. O. M. Battle did not attempt to bid at the sale. Before 12 months expired Mrs. Draper, through her father, who was her agent in the premises, made a demand of O. M. Battle for a deed to the Custer place in accordance with the terms of the contract of June 30, 1915, and offered to pay him the sum of $7,000 therefor. O. M. Battle waived an actual tender of the money and refused to make the deed. He claimed that the title to the land was then in J. J. Battle, and that there was no liability on his part under the terms of the contract between him and Mrs. Draper of the date of June 30, 1915.

The witnesses in the case variously estimated the value of the Custer tract at from $15 to $35 an acre. J. J. Battle said that there were between 500 and 600 acres in the tract, and that the land was not worth more than $15 per acre. The father of Mrs. Draper said that there were between 600 and 700 acres in the tract, and that the whole tract was worth $20,000. Other witnesses estimated the land to be worth from $20 to $35 per acre.

J. J. Thomas, the father of Mrs. Draper, acted as her agent throughout the entire transaction and signed the contract with O. M. Battle of the date of June 30, 1915, as follows: "Mattie B. Draper, by John J. Thomas, Her Agent."

Other facts will be stated or referred to in the opinion.

The jury returned a verdict in favor of the plaintiff, Mattie B. Draper, against the defendant, O. M. Battle, in the sum of $7,500.

From the judgment rendered, the defendant has duly prosecuted an appeal to this court.

Gulley & Ashton, of Little Rock, for appellant.

L. F. Monroe, of Washington, Ark., and Jno. N. Cook, of Texarkana, for appellee.

HART, J. (after stating the facts as above). It is first insisted by counsel for the defendant that the court erred in giving instruction No. 1 as follows:

"If you find from a preponderance of the evidence that the plaintiff, Mattie B. Draper, through herself or her agent, and within one year from June 30, 1915, offered to pay the plaintiff (defendant) the sum of $7,000 as the balance due on the Custer place, and that the defendant refused said offer, or waived a tender of said sum, and failed to execute a deed to plaintiff to said land, your verdict will be for the plaintiff."

The correctness of this instruction depends upon whether or not the contract between O. M. Battle and Mrs. Mattie B. Draper of the date of June 30, 1915, is ambiguous.

[1] It will be observed that the court construed the contract and declared it valid in giving this instruction. It is well settled in this state that it is the duty of the court to construe a written contract and declare its terms and meaning to the jury where the contract contains no words of latent ambiguity. Paepcke-Leicht Lbr. Co. v. Talley, 106 Ark. 400, 153 S. W. 833, and Wilkes v. Stacy, 113 Ark. 556, 169 S. W. 796.

[2] It is first insisted by counsel for the defendant that the construction is erroneous because the contract lacked mutuality. We cannot agree with counsel in this contention. In Johnson v. Wilkerson, 96 Ark. 320, 131 S. W. 690, the court held that the entire contract must be looked to as a whole in determining the consideration for its various obligations and the question of mutuality of the obligations. The court held further that one condition is sufficient to support several undertakings and promises.

In Kilgore Lumber Co. v. Thomas, 98 Ark. 219, 135 S. W. 858, the court held that mutual obligations imposed by a contract form a sufficient consideration for entering into it. See, also, Fisher v. Skinner, 112 Ark. 190, 164 S. W. 735.

Tested by the principles announced in those cases, it cannot be said that the contract was void for want of mutuality. By the terms of the contract O. M. Battle bound himself to bid in all the land at the foreclosure sale, and that he would take care of $15,000 of the mortgage indebtedness, and that Mrs. Draper should take care of the balance of it, which amounted to about $7,000.

It will be remembered that Mrs. Draper had conveyed the Smith place to O. M. Battle in December, 1912, for the consideration of $16,800, most of which was on deferred payments. The sale was subject to the mortgage of J. J. Battle. The contract further provided that, unless Mrs. Draper paid her part within 12 months, the agreement should be void, and that O. M. Battle should own the Custer land absolutely. The contract then recites that this option is given in consideration of a large concession of the indebtedness due Mrs. Draper on the Smith place by O. M. Battle. Thus it will be seen that, if O. M. Battle had carried out the contract on his part and had bid in the land for the amount of the mortgage indebtedness, interest, and costs, he would have had an absolute title to the Custer place, provided Mrs. Draper did not exercise her option to repurchase under the contract, and Battle would have been released from the payment of the purchase money which he agreed to pay Mrs. Draper on the Smith place in excess of $15,000. He had agreed to pay $16,800. Thus it will be seen that the difference was a substantial sum and was a good consideration for the contract. The agreement on the part of Mrs. Draper to release a part of his indebtedness to her for the purchase price of the place was a sufficient consideration for his agreement to bid in the lands at the foreclosure sale. There was a benefit derived on each side from the contract, and that fills the demand of the law as to consideration. Any benefit conferred on O. M. Battle to which he was not lawfully entitled or any detriment suffered or agreed to be suffered by Mrs. Draper is a good consideration and will support the contract.

[3] It is also urged that the last part of the contract which deals with the question of what the parties should do in case of a reasonable bid being offered and accepted by an outside party is ambiguous. We need not consider this, however, for there was no bid by any outside party exceeding the mortgage indebtedness, as contemplated by the parties. The whole tenor of the agreement shows that O. M. Battle was to bid the amount of the judgment and costs, and the clause of the contract relative to outside parties bidding refers to them bidding more than the mortgage indebtedness and costs. This is shown by the language used, because it provides that such a sale should not change the basis of the settlement, and that the owner of the land so sold should have the overplus so bid. We think the court was right in construing the contract to mean that O. M. Battle must bid at least the amount due J. J. Battle under the foreclosure decree.

The undisputed evidence shows that O. M. Battle did not bid in the land as he had agreed to do, and there was no error in giving the instruction.

[4] It is true the contract was signed by the agent of the plaintiff, and that there was no writing authorizing him to do so, but that does not make any difference. The evidence shows that the agent had authority to sign the contract for his principal, and such authority was not required to be in writing. Davis v. Spann, 92 Ark. 213, 122 S. W. 495.

[5] It is also true, as contended by counsel for appellant, that Capt. Thomas did not show the contract to Mrs. Draper until after it was executed; but that does not make any difference. Mrs. Draper stated that he was her agent in making the contract, and this constituted him as her general agent. She stated specifically that she gave him power to act as her agent in the matter. Therefore, being her general agent to make the contract, she was bound by its terms as soon as her father made it, regardless of the fact of whether he had shown it to her, or stated the terms of it to her before he signed it for her as her agent.

Again it is urged that the judgment should be reversed because the complaint alleges that, if the contract had not been entered into, the plaintiff could and would have raised the necessary funds and would have saved her land from sale under the foreclosure decree. This allegation was immaterial and had no part in the case. It was not treated as material to the issues raised by the pleadings, and no evidence was introduced relative to it. The reason is apparent. The parties had entered into a contract with regard to the matter, and the terms of this contract, if valid and binding, fixed their rights and the measure of damages for breach of it. We have held the contract to be a valid and binding one, and the undisputed evidence shows a breach of it by O. M. Battle. This suit was brought by Mrs. Draper against him within the period of the statute of limitations, and she had a right to maintain it.

[6] The court correctly instructed the jury on the measure of damages. It is claimed that the verdict is excessive. That the verdict was excessive is not made one of the grounds for a new trial, and the defendant, having failed to include it in his motion for a new trial, cannot for the first time raise the question on appeal. Moreover, the evidence for the plaintiff was sufficient to warrant the jury in returning the verdict in the amount found by it.

It follows that the judgment must be affirmed.

HOWELL, Collector, v. LAMBERSON et al.
(No. 45.)

(Supreme Court of Arkansas. June 13, 1921.)

1. Taxation ⟨⟩515—Taxpayer may pay one tax while refusing to pay other taxes on his land.

A taxpayer may pay the amount of any one tax listed against his land while refusing to pay other taxes listed against it.

2. Statutes ⟨⟩181(1)—Primary object in construction to ascertain intention of Legislature from language used.

The primary object in the construction of statutes is to ascertain the intention of the Legislature from the language used.

3. Taxation ⟨⟩561—Collector not liable for failure to collect tax or omission to advise taxpayer, where he made proper effort; "fail" and "omit to advise" implying neglect or omission.

Under Crawford & Moses' Dig. § 3618, providing a penalty if any collector of taxes shall "fail" to collect the drainage tax along with the other taxes, unless enjoined, and Road Acts 1919, vol. 1, p. 529, § 21, providing a penalty if he shall "omit to advise" any taxpayer of the amount of his local road improvement assessment when he pays his general taxes, a collector does not subject himself to the penalty where he demands such taxes and endeavors to collect them at the time he collects the general taxes; the words "fail" and "omit to advise," as used in the acts, importing to become deficient or lacking, to leave unperformed, to omit, to neglect, being applicable only in case of neglect or omission of the collector to perform such duty.

[Ed. Note.—For other definitions, see Words and Phrases, First and Second Series, Fail.]

4. Taxation ⟨⟩561—Collector cannot refuse to accept payment of general taxes because taxpayer refused to pay drainage tax also.

Under Crawford & Moses' Dig. § 3618, imposing a penalty on tax collectors for failure to collect a drainage tax along with the other taxes, and Road Acts 1919, n. 529, § 21, imposing a penalty for omitting to advise any taxpayer of the amount of his local improvement assessment, the collector could not refuse to accept payment of general taxes because the landowner refused to pay his improvement taxes; the statute being directed against the collector and not the landowner, whose rights cannot be taken away without direct and express language to that effect.

Smith and Humphreys, JJ., dissenting.

Appeal from Circuit Court, Craighead County; R. H. Dudley, Judge.

Application of G. W. Lamberson and another for a writ of mandamus against Homer Howell, as Collector of the Revenue of Craighead County, Ark., to compel him to accept payment of certain county and school taxes. From a judgment for plaintiffs, defendant appeals. Affirmed.

On May 17, 1920, G. W. Lamberson and A. D. Lamberson filed a petition in the circuit court against Homer Howell as collector of the revenue of Craighead county, Ark., for a writ of mandamus to compel Howell, as such collector, to accept their payment of said county and school taxes upon certain lands situated in the county and owned by them which the collector had refused to accept.

As a defense to the action, the collector alleged that the petitioners owned lands in drainage districts Nos. 15 and 16 of Craighead county, Ark., and in the Tri-County highway improvement district, and that certain assessments were due and unpaid on said lands in said improvement district.

The collector further alleged that he had refused to accept the tender of the general taxes for the reason that the petitioners had refused to pay at the same time these local assessments due as aforesaid.

The case was tried in the circuit court on an agreed statement of facts substantially as stated above. It was adjudged by the circuit court that the collector be commanded to receive from G. W. Lamberson and A. D. Lamberson the state and county taxes tendered by them upon their lands as described in the complaint, and that he as such collector issue them a tax receipt therefor without payment or tender by them of the local assessments alleged to be due in drainage districts Nos. 15 and 16 in the Tri-County highway improvement district. No injunction had been issued prohibiting the collector from collecting the improvement district taxes. The case is here on appeal.

Lamb & Frierson, of Jonesboro, for appellant.

H. M. Mayes, of Jonesboro, for appellees.

Sloan & Sloan, of Jonesboro, amicus curiæ.

HART, J. (after stating the facts as above). The record shows that the drainage districts were organized under the general drainage act. Section 3618 of Crawford & Moses' Digest, relative to the collection of drainage taxes in such districts, reads as follows:

"The amount of the taxes herein provided for shall be annually extended upon the tax books of the county, and collected by the collector of the county along with the other taxes, and for his services in making such collection the collector shall receive a commission of one per cent.; and the same shall by the collector be paid over to the county treasurer at the same time that he pays over the county funds. If any collector shall fail to collect the drainage tax along with the other taxes, he shall be subject to a penalty of one hundred dollars for each instance in which he shall collect from an individual the other taxes and omit the drainage tax, unless the drainage tax has been enjoined by a court of competent jurisdiction, to be recovered in a suit brought by the commissioners to the use of the district; and the county clerk shall be subjected to a like penalty for each case in which he shall fail to enter the drainage tax on the tax books."

The Tri-County highway road improvement district was created under special act No. 186 of the Acts of 1919 (Road Acts of 1919, vol. 1, p. 510). Section 21 of that act reads as follows:

"The county collector of each of the respective counties in which lands in said road improvement district are situated shall collect the several installments of the assessments of benefits during each year at the time he collects the general taxes, and if he shall omit to advise any taxpayer of the amount of his installment of the assessment of benefits during that year, at the time such taxpayer is paying his general taxes, he shall be subject to a penalty of one hundred dollars for each instance, which may be collected by the commissioners by civil action or by deducting said penalty from any fee due the collector from said district."

It is the contention of the collector that the effect of these statutory provisions is to prohibit him from accepting a tender of the state and county taxes on the lands in question unless the owners would pay the drainage and road taxes due and unpaid upon said lands at the same time.

The agreed statement of facts in this case shows that the plaintiffs tendered to the collector the amount of state, county, and school taxes levied on their lands, but refused to pay the drainage and road improvement taxes on the ground that they had not been legally assessed and levied and that they were going to contest the same. The collector refused the tender on the ground that under the statute he was not allowed to collect the general taxes without also collecting the improvement district taxes. The object of this lawsuit is to compel him to receive the general taxes without the payment of the improvement district taxes.

[1] In the absence of a statute to the contrary, a taxpayer always has the right to pay the amount of any one tax listed against his land while refusing to pay other taxes listed separately against it. Cooley on Taxation (3d Ed.) vol. 2, pp. 808 and 809; 37 Cyc. p. 1164.

Among the cases cited in Cyc. is Colt v. Claw, Collector, 28 Ark. 516. In that case the court said that whether the owner of real estate shall pay all taxes or pay one kind and not another, or let his lands go to sale for all or part, are questions for him and not for the collector to determine. The question of whether this right of the landowner has been taken away by the drainage and road improvement district statutes set out above is the issue raised by this appeal.

[2-4] The primary object in the construction of statutes is to ascertain the intention of the Legislature from the language used,

where that can be done. Tested by this rule, we do not think that either of the statutes referred to makes it obligatory upon the landowner to pay the local assessments imposed upon his land by the drainage improvement districts, or by the road improvement district, when he makes payment of his general taxes, state, county, and school. The language of the statute shows that it is directed against the collector and not against the landowner. The word "fail," as used in the drainage statute above copied, imports to become deficient or lacking, to leave unperformed, to omit, to neglect. Century Dictionary and Bouvier's Law Dictionary. The statute in question provides that if any collector shall fail to collect the drainage tax along with the other taxes, he shall be subject to a penalty of $100 for each instance in which he shall collect from an individual the other taxes and omit the drainage tax unless the drainage tax has been enjoined. We think the word "fail" implies in this statute an imposed duty upon the collector to collect the drainage tax at the same time he collects the general taxes and is applicable only in case of neglect or omission of the collector to perform such duty. The word "fail," as used in the statute, covers both the intentional and unintentional nonperformance on the part of the collector. Where the collector has demanded the tax and endeavors to collect it from the landowner at the time he collects from him the general taxes and the landowner should tender his general taxes and contest the payment of the drainage tax and refuse to pay it, it could not be said that the collector failed to act or to perform his duty in the premises so as to subject himself to the penalty prescribed by the act. In such case he would be guilty of no delinquency, and failure to perform his duty could not be ascribed to him for the reason that he had done all that he was authorized to do in the premises. Under the terms of the statute the collector could not refuse to accept a voluntary payment of the general taxes because the landowner wished to contest the payment of his improvement taxes and on that account refused to pay the same. The language of the statute is in no sense directed against the landowner, and his right to pay his general taxes without paying the improvement taxes cannot be taken away by any supposed intendment on the part of the Legislature. Such a right is a valuable one to the landowner and could in no event be taken away without direct and express language to that effect on the part of the Legislature.

The road improvement district statute uses the words "omit to advise." The reasoning we applied above to the use of the word "fail," in the drainage district statute applies with equal force here.

An argument is also made that a statute

imposing a duty upon the landowner to pay his drainage and road improvement taxes as a prerequisite to his right to pay his general taxes would be unconstitutional. The views we have expressed render it unnecessary to pass upon this question.

It follows that the judgment must be affirmed.

SMITH and HUMPHREYS, JJ., dissenting.

LEWIS et al. v. HARPER. (No. 20.)

(Supreme Court of Arkansas. May 30, 1921. Rehearing Denied June 27, 1921.)

1. Landlord and tenant ⬥61—Tenant cannot dispute title of landlord.

A tenant cannot dispute the title of his landlord while he remains in possession under him, nor acquire possession from the landlord by lease and then dispute his title without surrendering possession.

2. Landlord and tenant ⬥65—Tenant cannot dispute title of purchaser from landlord.

A tenant cannot dispute the title of a purchaser from the landlord.

3. Landlord and tenant ⬥111—Relations ceases upon disavowal of landlord's title.

Where tenant went into possession of land and cleared it, and thus became entitled to two years' free rent, and thereupon disavowed landlord's title, the relation of landlord and tenant then ceased as between them, and the tenant became a trespasser, and landlord could sue at once to recover possession, though the leasehold term had not expired.

Appeal from Circuit Court, Sebastian County; John Brizzolara, Judge.

Action by R. A. Harper against Sherman Lewis and others. Judgment for plaintiff, and defendants appeal. Affirmed.

J. E. London, of Van Buren, and J. B. McDonough, of Ft. Smith, for appellants.

Pryor & Miles, of Ft. Smith, for appellee.

WOOD, J. The appellee brought this action against the appellants. He alleged that he was the owner of certain lands in Sebastian county, Ark., and that he was entitled to the possession of same; that the appellants entered into possession of the lands under an agreement with the appellee and Robert Dunning, who at that time owned an undivided one-half interest. By the terms of the contract the appellants were to clear the lands of standing timber, and as compensation for their services in so doing they were to have the possession of the lands free of rent for two years; that in the year 1919 the appellants disclaimed the title of appellee and Dunning; that they made false and mislead-ing statements to William B. Owen, State Land Commissioner, to the effect that the land was an island and that the title was in the state; they applied to the Commissioner for a deed; that the appellee and Dunning were compelled to go to considerable expense to resist the claims of the appellants; that the Commissioner decided that the lands did not belong to the state. Notwithstanding this decision, the appellants still contend that the lands belong to the state. Appellee further alleged that appellants had committed waste and had refused to allow other tenants of the appellee to cross the lands. Appellee prayed for judgment for possession and damages in the sum of $250 and for rents.

Appellants answered denying all material allegations of the complaint, and they averred that the land in controversy held by them is an island, that it is subject to sale under the act of the General Assembly of 1917; that they applied to purchase the same on May 20, 1919, and that the State Land Commissioner arbitrarily refused their application, and that a mandamus is now pending against him to compel him to make appellants a deed. They alleged that appellee had no title or color of title to the lands.

The testimony on behalf of the appellee tended to sustain the allegations of his complaint. Lewis (one of the appellants) was called as a witness for the appellee, and he testified substantially as follows: That he and his brother went into possession of the lands in February, 1919; that Bob Dunning showed them the land and said he had some land to lease and that he would give them two crops to clear the land or one crop and give him the timber; that they did not agree as to which they would take, but they told him they would cut the timber off for $2 and give him the timber or either they would sell the timber and not cultivate it the next year. They took charge of the lands under that agreement and cleared up some of it. After they went into possession they learned that the land was state land. They then made application to the Commissioner of State Lands to purchase the same, and as soon as they made this application they did not consider themselves any longer tenants of Dunning, under whom the appellee claimed by warranty deed; that after the Commissioner denied their application to purchase the land they brought a mandamus to compel him to do so. The appellants cultivated about 20 acres of the land in controversy in the year 1919, lands which they had cleared, and this year 1920 they had in cultivation between 20 and 25 acres. There were 131 acres on the island which was in their possession. They were to pay no rent for the years 1919 and 1920; that they only sold about 10 cords of wood from the land, and the balance was

---

till there cut up in such lengths as were required for making excelsior. There was no fence around the land when Dunning showed same to appellants. The river was on one side, and a fence on the other between the island and the rest of the farm.

There was further testimony to the effect that at the first of the year 1920 the appellee notified appellants to get out, and they refused to obey the notice, giving as a reason that they considered themselves no longer his tenants, but were holding possession. The appellants offered to prove that the land in controversy was an island, which the court would not permit them to do, and also offered to introduce deeds to show that the title was not in the appellee, which testimony the court refused to allow. At the conclusion of the testimony the court instructed the jury to return a verdict in favor of the appellee, which was done. A judgment was then rendered in favor of the appellee, from which is this appeal.

[1] It appears from the undisputed facts in the record that the appellants went into possession of the lands in controversy under the appellee's grantors. The appellants do not deny, but, on the contrary, admit, that they took possession of the lands in controversy under appellee's grantors, but they set up in defense of the action that appellee's grantors had no title, and hence they say that the appellee acquired none. The appellants have thus placed themselves in the attitude of denying the title of their landlord while holding on and claiming the right to the possession, which they only could have obtained through him. This they cannot do, according to the authorities generally and as held by numerous decisions of this court.

"A tenant cannot dispute the title of his landlord while he remains in possession under him, nor acquire possession from the landlord by lease and then dispute his title without surrendering possession." Burton v. Gorman, 125 Ark. 141, 188 S. W. 561.

"The possession of a tenant is that of his landlord," and "so long as the relation of landlord and tenant exists, the tenant cannot acquire an adverse title as against his landlord." Gee v. Hatley, 114 Ark. 376, 170 S. W. 72.

See, also, Bryan v. Winburn, 43 Ark. 28; Simmons v. Robertson, 27 Ark. 50; Hughes v. Watt, 28 Ark. 153; Pickett v. Ferguson, 45 Ark. 177, 55 Am. Rep. 545; Dickinson v. Arkansas City, etc., 77 Ark. 570, 92 S. W. 21, 113 Am. St. Rep. 170; and other cases cited in appellee's brief.

No question of the right to homestead government lands is involved in this controversy.

[2] The appellants contend that the relation of landlord and tenant did not exist between the appellants and the appellee because the appellee was the purchaser from the appellants' landlord, and they did not take and hold possession under the appellee.

"A tenant cannot dispute the title of an assignee or purchaser of the landlord any more than he could dispute the title of the landlord or lessor himself." Adams v. Primmer, 102 Ark. 380, 144 S. W. 522.

[3] The appellants also contend that they had cleared up the land under the contract which entitled them to the land free of rent for two years, but the law is that upon the disavowal of the landlord's title the relation of landlord and tenant ceases and as between them the tenant becomes a trespasser, and the landlord may sue at once to recover possession, though the leasehold term has not expired. 16 R. C. L. § 631; Merryman v. Bourne, 9 Wall. 592, 19 L. Ed. 683; Walden v. Bodley, 14 Pet. 156, 10 L. Ed. 398. There was no error in the ruling of the court in refusing to allow appellants to offer testimony to show that the lands in controversy belonged to the state.

The judgment of the court was in all things correct, and it is affirmed.

G. H. HAMMOND CO. v. JOSEPH MERCANTILE CO. (No. 6.)

(Supreme Court of Arkansas. May 23, 1921. Rehearing Denied June 27, 1921.)

Brokers ⬅106—Evidence held to warrant instruction that, if plaintiff packing company permitted its broker to sell meat as his own, defendant purchaser was not liable.

In an action by a packing company to recover as for conversion by a mercantile company which purchased certain bacon from the packing company's broker for the sale of its products, evidence *held* sufficient to warrant the court in presenting the case to the jury, on the theory embraced in its instruction that if plaintiff packing company, by its course of conduct and dealings with its broker, and through him with the public, permitted the broker to sell its goods as his own, and defendant company so purchased the bacon in question believing it to be the property of the broker, it was not liable.

Appeal from Circuit Court, Greene County; R. H. Dudley, Judge.

Action by G. H. Hammond Company against the Joseph Mercantile Company. From judgment for defendant, plaintiff appeals. Affirmed.

See, also, 222 S. W. 27.

D. G. Beauchamp, of Paragould, for appellant.

Huddleston, Fuhr & Futrell, of Paragould, for appellee.

WOOD, J. The appellant, a corporation of the state of Michigan and doing business in Arkansas, entered into a contract with one Ray Perkins, of Paragould, Ark., the material parts of which are as follows:

The appellant appointed Perkins its broker for the sale of certain of its products in Paragould, Ark. The appellant was to pay Perkins a commission for his services. Perkins was to keep an account of goods consigned to him by the appellant in books furnished by the latter, which were subject to recall and inspection by the appellant at all times. Perkins was to make weekly reports of the stock on hand and delivery of goods on blanks furnished by appellant. Perkins was to sell the goods on behalf of appellant and on terms prescribed by the appellant. Perkins was to bill no goods from consigned stock to himself under any circumstances. Perkins was to bill all goods on blanks furnished by the appellant, and to forward a duplicate thereof to appellant on the day the goods were delivered. He was to keep the receipts for goods delivered on file subject to the order of the appellant. He was not to handle on consignment any packing house products except appellant's with appellant's consent. Perkins was to account to appellant for all weights shipped. He was to keep all goods in a suitable building, and not mingle them with other merchandise, and to sell and handle the same without expense to the appellant except his commission.

This action was brought by the appellant against the appellee to recover the sum of $308.10. The appellant alleged that the appellee had taken possession of 1,165 pounds of bacon extras, which belonged to the appellant, and that appellee had converted the same to its own use without authority of appellant. This is the second appeal in this case. The complaint remained the same on both trials. On the first trial the answer to the complaint set up that Perkins was in the employ of the appellant as a factor and in possession of its products, with full power and authority to sell, deliver, and collect for appellant's products, either in his own name or in the name of appellant; that appellee purchased the meat in controversy from Perkins as his individual property; that he represented to the appellee that it was his property, being the accumulation of what was known as "overs," and was billed out to the appellee as the individual property of Perkins and paid for by the appellee as such; that the appellee, in purchasing the meat from Perkins, followed the custom and course of trade which had prevailed at Paragould for many years, and was well known to the appellant; that the appellee believed that the meat was the individual property of Perkins, and had no knowledge to the contrary.

The issue as thus raised on the first trial was sent to the jury, and in one of its instructions the court declared as follows:

"If the plaintiff authorized and knowingly permitted its factor, Perkins, to sell overs or any other of its goods, or his own goods, on his individual account as individual owner to customers, * * * and the defendant at the time believed Perkins to be the true owner, or authorized to sell in his own name, then you will find for the defendant."

In passing on this instruction this court explained the difference between factor and broker as follows:

"A factor may buy and sell in his own name, and he has the goods in his possession, while a broker, as such, cannot ordinarily buy or sell in his own name and has no possession of the goods sold."

In passing on the facts as developed at the former trial, we said:

"Perkins was not a factor or commission merchant and had no right to sell the products of the plaintiff in his own name. Therefore the court erred in assuming to the jury that Perkins was a factor, and in telling the jury to find for the defendant if it should further find that the plaintiff authorized or knowingly permitted its factor, Perkins, to sell overs or any of its goods, or his own goods, on his individual account."

For the error in giving the above instruction the court reversed the judgment and remanded the cause for a new trial.

On the second trial the appellee filed an amended answer, in which it alleged that Perkins was an independent dealer in meat products in Paragould, Ark., and was conducting his individual business in connection with that of the plaintiff; that he combined his own and the plaintiff's business in this way to such an extent that his customers could not tell whether they were dealing with him individually or as the agent of the plaintiff; that the plaintiff knew, or should by the exercise of reasonable prudence and care have known, that Perkins was conducting his own individual business in conjunction with the plaintiff's business; that the defendant, acting in good faith and ignorant of plaintiff's alleged interest in said meat, purchased the same according to the custom of trade, and paid Perkins for the same, honestly and in good faith believing Perkins to be the true owner thereof, and that plaintiff company is therefore estopped from now claiming payment from the defendant.

On the issue thus joined at the last trial, the president of the appellee testified substantially as follows: He had been in business at Paragould, Ark., for about 15 years. The day appellee purchased the meat, Perkins came in and said he had some meat that he would sell to the appellee a quarter of a cent under the market price. Witness purchased it of him and paid for it. He had traded with Perkins and his father for 15 years, and had bought meat from them quite a number of times as their individual property. No question ever came up before and nothing had happened to arouse his suspicion that the meat was not Perkins'. Witness knew that Perkins was the broker of the appellant to sell its meat products, and that he had no right to sell appellant's goods as his own individual goods, but he did not sell the meat in controversy as the goods of appellant. Witness did not know anything about the contract between Perkins and the appellant. Witness knew that nobody had a right to sell goods belonging to some one else without authority. Witness did not know that this meat was the property of appellant. Perkins might have bought it from some one else so far as he knew. He supposed that the goods were shipped by the appellant to Perkins. Appellant had done nothing at any time or said anything that would lead witness to believe that the goods were purchased. He trusted Perkins' word that the goods were his. The products that the appellee bought from Perkins were paid for sometimes in cash and sometimes by check. The checks were made payable sometimes to Perkins and sometimes to the appellant. Witness never heard any kick on this. Witness bought the goods from Perkins and not from the Hammond Company. When he bought goods from Perkins that were billed by the Hammond Company he paid the Hammond Company for them. The only time he gave Perkins checks in his own name was when he owned the stuff himself. Witness did not know whether the appellant had any knowledge or information of the individual transactions he had with Perkins or not.

The secretary of the appellee testified that he had been in charge of the office and book affairs of the appellee for about 20 years. During this time appellee had been doing business with Ray Perkins and his father. Witness knew nothing about the contract between appellant and Perkins—made no inquiry about it. Witness knew that the appellee bought the meat in question from Ray Perkins individually and paid for it. Witness had nothing to put him on inquiry that the meat did not belong to Perkins. He would not have bought it if he had known it was Hammond's. Witness knew that Perkins had no right to sell Hammond Company meat as his own and in his own name. The accounts that the appellee paid Perkins in his own name were for goods that Perkins claimed were his own and sold as his own. Witness did not remember how many companies Perkins might have represented. No question ever came up about the purchase of meat. He did not know whether under the contract Perkins had the right to sell the meat in his own name—never saw the contract. Perkins said he was selling his own meat.

Other witnesses testified substantially to the effect that they had bought packing house products from the Perkinses for several years. One witness stated that he had bought meat from Perkins in the name of the Hammond Company. Sometimes Perkins would bill it out to witness in his individual name in average amounts from $75 to $700. Witness had transactions directly with the Hammond Packing Company. They would often send him a statement for comparison. Perkins always protected witness against all advances. Witness would make remittances to Perkins. All checks for individual purchases would be made direct to him.

Another witness stated that he had bought quite a large quantity from Perkins—had had transactions for the Bertig Bros. with Perkins in which Perkins sold Bertig. Bros. meat as his individual property. It did not occur often, and no question was raised about it.

Another witness testified that for 13 years he had bought stuff from Perkins. He would mail checks to both Perkins and the appellant. No question was ever raised. Towards the latter part of his business witness thought Perkins was selling meat on a commission, but never gave it any thought. Witness had bought meat from Perkins as his own product, and would usually pay Perkins individually when he purchased it from him that way, and there was never any complaint on the part of the appellant. Witness did not know whether they ever knew about it or not.

Another witness stated that for 15 years he had bought meat from the Perkinses. He did not know whether he traded with them as individuals or as the agents of the Hammond Company. He would buy stuff from them, and they would send around and collect for it, and he would make the checks payable to Perkins. Witness "thought Ray Perkins was the whole cheese—didn't know any difference."

Ray Perkins testified for the appellee to the effect that he dealt in meats and lards on his own account; that he sold in his own name to a large extent to appellee and other merchants who handled the goods sold by him. These merchants were his customers in buying his individual goods and also the Hammond goods. He would sell them Hammond goods as Hammond's agent and sometimes as his individual goods and collect for them individually. Customers paid sometimes in checks to the Hammond Company and sometimes to witness individually. Witness would get the money and account to the Hammond Company for their part of it and keep his part. There was never any objection by the appellant to this method of conducting the business. Question never arose. Goods billed out to purchasers along the railroad would be billed in the Hammond Company name when that company sold the goods. If Perkins sold the goods it would be billed out in Perkins' name. Perkins transacted considerable business with the defendant company; sold them goods as his individual property. Witness never had any understanding with the Hammond Company about overs—no written contract. He was in Chicago talking to the head of the concern, and the subject of shrinkage came up, and the manager told witness that he would be satisfied to receive the weights they shipped Perkins, and in any case where it would happen to be one-half of 1 per cent. less than they shipped Perkins it would be all right; and he said, "If anything else occurs, you know how to take care of it, I guess." Witness assumed that he meant if the meat ran over witness was supposed to take it and he did. Witness would accumulate stock of his own in this way with "overs." When witness considered the market right he would instruct his employee to weigh up one or two thousand pounds of meat, and put it over on witness' side of the warehouse, and go to his book and charge it to Bertig Bros., at the best market price on that day, and pay the money on that invoice and remit it to Chicago, and report the sale as having been made to Bertig Bros. Witness transacted the business in that way because appellant company would not allow witness to bill anything to himself. The bills that were billed in that way were never presented to Bertig Bros.—were not intended to be. Witness paid the company the market price for the stuff he got.

On cross-examination witness stated, among other things, that the contract under which he was employed by the appellant reflected his authority and the same had not been changed. Only the manager of plaintiff said, "Occasionally there are 'overs,' and if there are 'overs' you know what to do with them;" and witness took it for granted that witness might appropriate the "overs" to his own use. The meat that was sold to the defendant belonged to the Hammond Company. The defendant wanted bacon extras. Witness did not have it, but did have dry salt extras, and he told his employee to take the dry salt extras out of his pile and take and put them in place of the bacon extras, and take the bacon extras and deliver them to the defendant company; that was the only claim witness had to the meat sold the defendant. The Hammond Company was never advised about the transaction and was never paid for it. The meat was delivered to the defendant in the original packages as received from the Hammond Company. Witness was a merchandise broker and a manufacturer's agent. He

handled meat and lard for the appellant, and also bought from the Hammond Company and sold it on his own hook. Witness also handled oil and gasoline, and sold it as the agent of the company who owned it. Witness had no authority to buy from the Hammond Company in his own name. Appellant had no information, so far as witness knew, that witness was handling appellant's goods in his own name, or that he was handling the goods of any one else in his own name. When appellant's auditors would come to check up witness, whatever witness owned himself he would put out to one side of the house, out of the way, and take some lard and pack it around in various places, and hauled some to the oil house so that appellant's auditor could not discover it.

Another witness, an agent in the employ of Perkins since July 6, 1906, testified that any time the auditor came to audit the books and discovered any extra stock he would be told that that was sold and didn't belong to the stock. After the contract between Perkins and the appellant was executed, on July 10, 1917, up to May 7, 1918, if Perkins was engaged in any other business of any kind except representing the plaintiff and an oil company, it was so slight that witness could not remember it. Witness sometimes made collections for Perkins, including oil and other things. If the company had any knowledge of any of the transactions witness did not know it. These transactions detailed by the witness did not appear on the record. The witness further testified: "Mr. Taylor told us to sell one kind of meat and bill it out as another kind. It would be sold as the company's meat."

Witness Taylor testified that he had been working for the appellant company about 15 years. He visited Paragould at irregular intervals of about six weeks; had appellant's business at Paragould under his immediate control as inspector. He did not discover that Perkins was buying goods on his own account or selling them. During all the time he never found any meat or products in Perkins' house that Perkins claimed as his own. He had no information that Perkins was selling appellant's goods in appellant's name and collecting for them in his own name. He had no information that Perkins was billing out goods and not delivering them. The company had no information of any of these things so far as witness knew. Witness was familiar with Perkins' books, and in examining the books and the business nothing ever occurred nor did witness ever discover anything irregular. Witness never made a complete audit of Perkins' books. If there were any discrepancies he checked them up.

The court gave instructions correctly defining the issues and interpreting the contract between the appellant and Perkins, and told the jury, among other things, that the undisputed evidence showed that the title to the meat in question was in the appellant, and that the possession and sale of it by Perkins as his own would not give the appellee good title to it. The court also told the jury that if the appellee knew that Perkins was the agent or broker of the appellant when it bought the meat from him, that he was acting as such in the sale of the meat, they should find for the appellant. The court further instructed the jury as follows:

"But if you find from the evidence in the case that the plaintiff, by its manner and course of conduct and dealings with its agent, Perkins, and through him with the public, and plaintiff, by its own voluntary acts or consent, gave to, or knowingly permitted, said Perkins to sell its goods as his own; and if you further find from the evidence that the said Perkins sold the meat in question to the defendant company in accordance with the custom of the trade and usual course of business as conducted by Perkins, or others engaged in that line of business at Paragould, and known to plaintiff company; and if you further find from the evidence that the defendant company, acting in good faith, and in ignorance of the fact that plaintiff owned the meat, and in the exercise of such care as an ordinarily prudent person would use under like circumstances, bought the meat in question, believing it to be the property of said Perkins—then you will find for the defendant, but unless you do so find then you will find for the plaintiff."

The appellant duly excepted to the ruling of the court in giving this instruction No. 6. The verdict and judgment were in favor of the appellee. The appellant seeks to reverse the judgment, and concedes that the only question is as to whether or not the court erred in giving instruction No. 6.

On the first trial the issue was submitted on the theory that the undisputed evidence showed that Perkins was the factor of the appellant. This court held on the former trial that the trial court erred in instructing the jury that Perkins was the factor of the appellant. On the last trial, as shown by the present record, the court avoided that error, and the cause was submitted upon the theory that, although Perkins was the broker or agent of the appellant for the purpose of selling its meat products at Paragould, yet if the appellant by its conduct knowingly permitted Perkins to sell its goods, claiming them as his own, in pursuance of a custom or course of dealing which he had established at Paragould of which appellant had knowledge, and that the appellee, in good faith and in the exercise of ordinary care, purchased the meat from Perkins believing it to be his property, that the verdict should be in favor of the appellee.

The testimony speaks for itself, and we are convinced that it is sufficient to have warranted the court in presenting the cause to the jury upon the theory which the court did in its instruction No. 6. The testimony is voluminous, and it could serve no useful purpose to discuss it in detail. After a careful consideration of it, we have reached the conclusion that it cannot be said as a matter of law that there was no testimony to warrant the instruction and to justify the verdict. The case, on the facts as developed at the last trial, is ruled by the principle announced by this court in Rogers v. Scott, 128 Ark. 600, 603, 194 S. W. 689, 690, as follows:

"The general rule is that no man can get a title to personal property from a person who himself has no title to it. There are, however, certain exceptions to the general rule. One of these exceptions is that a bona fide purchaser will be protected where the owner has conferred upon the seller the apparent right of property as owner or for disposal as his agent."

See, also, Andrews v. Cox, 42 Ark. 473, 478, 48 Am. Rep. 68; Meyer Bannerman & Co. v. Stone & Co., 46 Ark. 210, 214, 55 Am. Rep. 577; Jetton v. Tobey, 62 Ark. 84, 34 S. W. 531; Jarvis v. Pague, 137 Ark. 475–484, 208 S. W. 601.

The instruction of the court was in conformity with the doctrine announced in the above cases, and there was testimony to warrant the court in giving it.

The judgment is therefore affirmed.

PARKER et al. v. MITCHELL. (No. 38.)

(Supreme Court of Arkansas. June 6, 1921. Rehearing Denied June 27, 1921.)

Mortgages ☞38(1)—Absolute deed held intended as such, and not as mortgage.

Finding that vendor's deed to third person who discharged purchasers' indebtedness to vendor under a land contract was intended as an absolute deed, and not as a mortgage to secure repayment of amount so paid by purchasers to third person, *held* not contrary to weight of the evidence.

Appeal from Conway Chancery Court; Jordan Sellers, Chancellor.

Suit by J. W. Parker and another against E. E. Mitchell, in which defendant filed a counterclaim. Decree dismissing plaintiffs' bill and rendering judgment for defendant upon cross-bill, and plaintiffs appeal. Affirmed.

Edward Gordon, of Morrillton, for appellants.

Sellers & Sellers, of Morrillton, and J. C. & Wm. J. Clark, of Conway, for appellee.

HUMPHREYS, J. Appellants instituted suit against appellee in the chancery court of Conway county to have a warranty deed, of date October 5, 1912, from T. A. Dowdle to appellee, conveying the north half of the northwest quarter, section 28, township 7 north, range 16 west, declared to be a mortgage, and for $505.42, alleged to have been overpaid on the indebtedness secured by the mortgage in fact, though deed in form.

Appellee answered, denying the warranty deed was a mortgage in fact, or that any amount was due appellants for money overpaid on the alleged indebtedness secured by the alleged mortgage in fact, stating that the amount of $505.42 was paid to appellee by appellants as rent for the lands aforesaid, and also filed a counterclaim against each appellant on account of alleged advances to each and secured by chattel mortgages, for which appellee asked judgment and foreclosure.

The cause was submitted to the court upon the pleadings and evidence, upon which a decree rendered dismissing appellants' bill for want of equity, and judgments and foreclosures rendered upon the cross-bill of appellee, from which is this appeal.

The abstract of the record prepared by appellants covers 149 pages of printed matter; so it is apparent that a statement of the evidence and analysis thereof would extend the opinion to impractical length. We must content ourselves, therefore, with a general statement of the substance of the evidence for and against the issues involved.

To establish that the warranty deed was intended as a mortgage to secure the indebtedness of $227.88, and that the open account was incorrect, appellants testified that on the 17th day of February, 1908, they purchased the 80-acre tract from T. A. Dowdle for $700, for which they executed notes; that T. A. Dowdle executed a title bond to them for the land, which was left with him; that on the 10th day of October, 1912, they had reduced the land notes to $214.28 and their book account to $13.60; that prior to that time their brother Tom had been fined $50 for carrying a pistol, and was in jail; that they contracted with appellee to secure him with the land for procuring the release of their brother and the payment of the balance due T. A. Dowdle; that, pursuant to the contract, appellee paid T. A. Dowdle $214.28, and by their direction Mr. Dowdle executed a warranty deed for said land to secure him; that he procured the release of Tom, but the money advanced for that purpose was repaid by him; that they paid appellee $100 each for the land debt for the years 1913, 1914, 1915, 1916, and 1917; that they had paid additional amounts on their open account which had been secured by chattel mortgages on their crops and stock; that the land was worth $10 or $15 an acre at the time it was conveyed to

appellee. Appellants introduced other witnesses who corroborated them as to the value of the land. Appellants also testified that they did not get certain items charged in the account.

T. A. Dowdle testified that his understanding from appellants, in the absence of appellee, was that he should execute the deed to appellee as security for paying his indebtedness.

Appellee testified that he refused, when approached by appellants, to pay the land out and take it as security; that, after several appeals, in which they stated they would lose the land anyway, he purchased it outright for the amount they owed T. A. Dowdle on the land and open account and the procurement of the release of their brother from jail, with the further understanding that he had the privilege of collecting from Tom such sum as he might expend in procuring his release; that he paid T. A. Dowdle $227.88 and obtained a warranty deed from Dowdle to the land; that he paid out something to procure Tom's release, which Tom afterwards refunded; that, after he procured the deed to the land, appellants attorned to him rent in the sum of $100 each per annum until this suit was instituted; that immediately after procuring the deed he built a house and dug a well upon the land, the cost of which, together with other improvements later made, amounted to about $400; that he assessed it in his own name, and has continuously paid the taxes thereon; that, subsequent to the purchase of the land, appellants secured him by chattel mortgages upon their crops and stock from year to year for supplies, and that at the time of the trial G. W. Parker was indebted to him for supplies in the sum of $922.94, after allowing all just credits, and J. W. Parker in the sum of $321, after allowing all just credits; that the amounts paid T. A. Dowdle and to secure Tom's release were never charged to appellants on his books; that it was his purpose, when appellants paid their open accounts, to sell the land to them, but that he never in any way bound himself to resell it to them; that they applied to him several times to buy the land, but he refused to sell it to them as long as they were indebted to him on open account; that he afterwards purchased an 80-acre tract adjoining the land in question for $300; that the land was worth about what he paid for it. Appellants introduced other witnesses who testified that the land was worth $250 or $300 on or about October, 1912. Appellee testified to the correctness of the open account. His books were introduced and confirmed his statements that the amounts paid to Dowdle and for the release of Tom were not included in the account, and also confirmed his statement as to the correctness of the account.

Jim Vorpe and J. J. Hill each testified that

they heard appellants say the land belonged to appellee. Appellants denied making such statement to Vorpe and Hill.

Wilson Gibson, a clerk in appellee's store, testified that appellants applied on several occasions to appellee to buy the land from him, but that appellee refused to consider the matter until they had paid for the supplies advanced to them.

From this summary of the evidence, it will be observed that it is in sharp conflict. the testimony of appellants being corroborated by the single circumstance of inadequacy of price, for we do not regard the testimony of T. A. Dowdle as competent to establish a contract between appellants and appellee with reference to the purpose of the deed; while the evidence of appellee is corroborated by that of the disinterested witnesses, Jim Vorpe and J. J. Hill, to the effect that appellants admitted appellee to be the owner of the land, by Wilson Gibson, who heard appellants try to buy the land back from appellee, and by appellee's books.

It cannot be said, in this condition of the testimony, that the finding of the chancellor was contrary to the weight of the evidence.

No error appearing, the decree is affirmed.

RUSSELL v. BARNHART MERCANTILE CO. (No. 47.)

(Supreme Court of Arkansas. June 13, 1921.)

1. Sales ⟷173—Seller sued for breach held not to have waived buyer's breach by failure to order delivery within time specified.

Where buyer suing for breach of contract failed to order shipment within the specified 60 days upon net cash terms, and seller subsequently set aside and stored the goods, insisting that buyer take them, *held*, that the seller had waived none of its rights under the contract as to the buyer's breach by failing to order the goods shipped.

2. Garnishment ⟷250—Allowance of interest to defendant on all money garnished held proper.

A judgment allowing defendant 6 per cent. interest on the total sum of money impounded by garnishment was proper.

Appeal from Circuit Court, Jefferson County; W. B. Sorrells, Judge.

Suit by E. D. Russell against the Barnhart Mercantile Company for breach of contract. Instructed verdict for the defendant, and the plaintiff appeals. Affirmed.

Rowell & Alexander, of Pine Bluff, for appellant.

Crawford & Hooker, of Pine Bluff, for appellee.

SMITH, J. Appellant is a merchandise broker engaged in business in the city of Pine Bluff. Appellee is a corporation engaged in the business of selling edible nuts, with places of business in Petersburg, Va., and St. Louis, Mo.

Through the St. Louis office, on July 7, 1919, appellant ordered 600 sacks of fancy hand-picked peanuts, and this order was evidenced by a written sales contract. In this contract the following provisions appear:

"Time of shipment, buyer's option within sixty days.

"Terms of sale, net cash. SD B-L attached f. o. b. Petersburg, Va.

"Quantity	Grade and Description	Price
600	Sax Magnolia Fancies	11."

Indorsed on face:

"Shipment in 60 days as wanted."

It was further provided that—

"All contracts subject to rules and regulations of the National Peanut Cleaners' & Shellers' Association."

It is not disputed that appellant failed, although frequently requested, to order shipment of peanuts within the 60 days from the date of the contract. An extended correspondence in regard to the peanuts occurred, and a number of telegrams were exchanged. On September 29, 1919, appellee wrote appellant the following letter:

"We weighed up on the 27th inst. the 600 bags of Magnolias we had booked for you and stored these goods on our second floor, also rendering you an invoice covering this purchase. We must have shipping instructions on these goods before Nov. 1st, as we will need our room for new crop after this date. It will be necessary for us to charge you 3c per bag per month storage on these 600 bags to comply with rules of the association. We shall expect for you to remit us covering this purchase within ten days from the date of invoice. This will comply with the terms of purchase."

It appears to be undisputed that in weighing up and invoicing the peanuts, and in charging the price thereof to appellant's account, appellee was acting within its rights under the rules and regulations of the National Peanut Cleaners' & Shellers' Association. Later appellee drew on appellant, with invoices attached, for the price of the peanuts, but the draft was not protected and was returned unpaid. Appellant appears at all times to have admitted his obligation to accept and pay for the peanuts. He had difficulty in disposing of them without sustaining a loss, and he asked indulgence in the way of furnishing shipping orders for the peanuts, although appellee continued to insist on these directions being given. There was correspondence, by letter and by telegram, in regard to a proposed resale of the peanuts for appellant's account, but the parties were unable to agree on the price at which they might be resold.

As the time for the new crop of peanuts to move came on appellee became more insistent in its demand for payment of the purchase price of the peanuts, and several letters of a peremptory character were sent, in which appellant was advised that, if remittance was not made forthwith, the peanuts would be sold for appellant's account at the best price obtainable. During all this time the quotations on peanuts were under the sales price; yet appellant at all times professed his intention to comply with his contract.

On October 25, 1919, appellant sent the following shipping instructions to appellee:

"Ship to ourselves c–o Jno. H. Poston Warehouse, Inc., at Memphis, Tenn., via rail. Terms: Draft through Bank of Commerce & Trust Co., Memphis, Tenn. Mail invoice to us at Pine Bluff, Ark., 300 Sx Magnolia peanuts, 11c and storage. Remarks: Examine carefully for worms or webs before shipping."

In response to this telegram appellee wired appellant as follows:

"Letter received; will not make shipment Memphis car fancies until you remit us covering our invoice September twenty-seventh; also storage and insurance; terms were net cash ten days from date of invoice; account been standing thirty days; wire immediately if you are sending New York exchange or not."

On October 29th appellant sent the following telegram:

"We decline to remit for peanuts. Ship both cars to Memphis, include storage and insurance in drafts. Mr. Russell was absent from office yesterday."

On October 30th appellee sent the following telegram:

"Telegram received; we decline to make shipment until you pay our invoice and charges; will sell goods immediately best price possible."

On the same day appellant wired as follows:

"Replying we renew demand for shipment; if you sell peanuts you will do so at your own peril."

To this telegram the following reply was received:

"Telegram recd.; we demand cash before making shipment; ultimatum."

Thereafter several telegrams and letters passed between the parties, and appellant offered to file a bond for $1,000 to insure prompt payment of draft covering invoices and all charges, but appellee continued to refuse to ship until receipt of exchange for the full amount of the invoices and charges.

In the meantime the price of peanuts commenced to advance, and appellant brought suit for breach of contract and prayed judgment for the difference between the contract price and the market quotations of the peanuts. There was a trial before a jury, which terminated in an instructed verdict for appellee, from which is this appeal.

[1] Appellant admits that he did not comply with the contract by furnishing shipping directions within 60 days, but he says this breach was waived when appellee weighed up and stored away the peanuts for his account, that this act of appellee operated as a complete transfer of the title to the peanuts, and that thereafter appellee should have shipped them in accordance with his directions. Appellant further contends that invoicing and storing the peanuts was a mere extension of time in which shipment might be ordered, and that he had the right to order shipment made pursuant to the terms of the original contract, to wit, with draft attached to the bill of lading issued by the railroad over which shipment had been ordered made.

We think the court properly directed a verdict in this case. The undisputed testimony shows that appellee waived none of its rights under the contract; that it at all times offered to perform and insisted on performance.

Under the contract and rules of the National Peanut Cleaners' & Shellers' Association it was appellant's duty to furnish shipping directions within 60 days from the date of the contract, and if this was not done appellee had the right to invoice and store away the peanuts for the purchaser's account and to demand payment within 10 days after invoicing the peanuts to the purchaser. Appellant failed to furnish shipping directions, or to honor draft with invoice attached. He was therefore in default and had no right to demand shipment after the 60 days under the terms which were available for 60 days or until peanuts had been stored and invoiced. In other words, appellant attempted on October 25th to avail himself of a right which his contract required him to exercise within 60 days after July 7, 1919, or before the peanuts had been invoiced or stored. Appellee was guilty of no waiver which gave appellant this right, and the verdict was therefore properly directed in appellee's favor.

[2] Appellant prayed judgment in his complaint for $1,130.31 with 6 per cent. interest from the date of the filing of the complaint until paid, and for a writ of garnishment against the Hammett Grocery Company and C. M. Ferguson & Son to impound any funds in their hands belonging to appellee.

The garnishees, C. M. Ferguson & Son and the Hammett Grocery Company, filed answers stating that they had in their hands and possession the sums of $649.44 and $949.32, respectively. The court gave judgment for interest at 6 per cent. on the amount of money in the hands of the garnishees, to wit, $1,598.76, from the date of the garnishments until paid.

Appellant insists, upon the authority of the case of Brown v. Yukon National Bank, 138 Ark. 210, 209 S. W. 734, that it was error to render judgment against appellant for interest on the total amount in the garnishees' hands; the amount sued for and the costs being the basis for computing the interest. In the case cited the facts were that the sum garnished bore no fair proportion to the sum sued for. The sum sued for was $210, and the sum garnished was $2,303.50. The costs in the case amounted to only $20. After a recitation of these facts we held that interest should have been computed only on the $230, the amount of the debt and costs.

Here, however, neither garnishee owed the amount claimed by appellant. It required the sum due both to equal the sum sued for, and we think no error was committed in rendering judgment for interest on the total sum impounded.

CRANOR v. JENKINS. (No. 42.)

(Supreme Court of Arkansas. June 18, 1921.)

Animals ⊂⟂50(2)—Fencing district operative without fence around it, where bounded by other districts.

    Under Crawford & Moses' Dig. §§ 4657, 4684, providing penalty for permitting stock to run at large within fencing districts created under section 4655 et seq., and section 4686, authorizing impounding of stock running at large, the construction of a fence around a fencing district is required only to the extent essential to protection of the district from the intrusion of stock running at large, and where there are other adjoining districts in which the running at large of stock is prohibited, the construction of a fence is not required, whether such districts have been organised under the general law or by special acts.

    Wood and Humphreys, JJ., dissenting.

Appeal from Circuit Court, St. Francis County; J. M. Jackson, Judge.

Action between Jim Cranor and N. B. Jenkins involving the right to impound two mules belonging to plaintiff, and from a judgment for defendant, plaintiff appeals. Affirmed.

J. W. Morrow, of Forrest City, for appellant.

Mann & Mann, of Forrest City, for appellee.

McCULLOCH, C. J. This case involved the right of appellee to impound certain live stock—two mules, the property of appellant —found running at large within the bounds of a fencing district in St. Francis county,

formed by order of the county court pursuant to the general statutes on that subject. Crawford & Moses' Digest, § 4655 et seq.

Appellant and appellee are both residents and owners of property situated within the boundaries of said district. The original statute authorizing the organization of fencing districts and prescribing the form of proceedings in regard to such districts was enacted by the General Assembly of 1891, but has been subsequently amended in several particulars. The original and amendatory statutes are cited in the notes to the sections of the digest referred to.

Section 4684 of Crawford & Moses' Digest was enacted as a part of the original statute (1891), and reads as follows:

"After any fencing district has been inclosed by a good and lawful fence, it shall be unlawful for any person who is the owner, or who has control of any kind of stock, to let the same run at large in said district, and any person violating the provisions of this section shall be deemed guilty of a misdemeanor, and, upon conviction, shall be fined in any sum not less than one nor more than fifty dollars, and, in addition to the above fine, shall be liable for double the amount of any damages that any person may sustain by reason of said stock running at large in said district, to be recovered by action before any court having competent jurisdiction. Provided, this section shall not prohibit any person from fencing his or her lands, or any part thereof, separately, and pasturing the same."

Section 4657 of Crawford & Moses' Digest was an amendment to the general statute enacted by the General Assembly of 1901, and reads as follows:

"It shall be unlawful for any person owning or having control of stock that have been restrained from running at large to knowingly permit such stock to run at large within the territory comprising such fencing district and any person violating the provisions of this act shall be deemed guilty of a misdemeanor, and, upon conviction thereof shall be fined not less than ten dollars nor more than twenty-five dollars."

It is unnecessary to a decision of the present case for us to determine whether and to what extent, if any, these two sections are conflicting, or whether the former was to any extent repealed by the latter.

In the case of Hill v. Gibson, 107 Ark. 130, 154 S. W. 203, we recognized the force of that part of section 4684 which provides that it shall be unlawful to permit stock to run at large after "any fencing district has been inclosed by a good and lawful fence." The statute, as originally enacted and as it stands in force to-day, provides, in substance, that the county court may create such districts upon the application of two-thirds of the landowners in the territory to be affected, and that a fencing board shall be appointed by the county court, whose duties are to "form plans for the building of a good and lawful fence and all necessary gates to inclose and protect said district," to procure estimates of the cost of such fence, and to levy assessments on property in the district to pay for the construction of the fence. In section 4671 it is provided that the cost of keeping the fence in repair from year to year shall be paid in the same manner as the original cost of construction of the fence.

Section 4686, which was an amendment to the statute enacted by the General Assembly of 1897, expressly provides that any person finding stock running at large in a fencing district may impound the stock and, after notice, cause the same to be sold.

The district within which the stock of appellant was impounded is bounded on the south by a fencing district created by a special statute enacted by the General Assembly of 1919. Acts of 1919, p. 308. It is bounded on the east by the Crittenden county line; that county being organized into a fencing district by a special statute enacted by the General Assembly of 1913. Acts 1913, p. 183. It is bounded on the north and west by another fencing district in St. Francis county, created under the general statutes, the same as this district. There was no fence built around this district, it being bounded on all sides by other districts, and the sole question presented in the briefs for our consideration is whether or not the impounding of stock is authorized by the statute until after the fence has been built on the boundaries of the district so as to completely inclose it.

It is contended that the district does not become operative until the fence is built in accordance with the provisions of the statute, and that the statute means that under all circumstances there must be a lawful fence around the boundaries of the district, except in case of a navigable river, which is expressly declared by the statute to be a sufficient barrier. On the other hand, it is contended by counsel for appellee that the statute should be interpreted to mean that the construction of a fence is required only to the extent that it is essential to the protection of the district from the intrusion of stock running at large, and that where there are other adjoining districts in which the running at large of stock is prohibited the construction of a fence is not required. Our conclusion is that the contention of appellee is correct, and that under a fair interpretation of the statute it is only meant to require the construction of a fence where necessary to constitute a barrier against the intrusion of stock from the outside. The lawmakers did not intend to require something that was wholly unnecessary for the protection of the owners of property in the district. Prohibition against permitting stock to run at large permits the farmers in the district to raise crops without inclosing their lands with fences, and the lawmakers meant to protect them by requiring sufficient barriers around the outer bounds of the district so as to prevent the incoming of stock. But where there are other adjoining districts in which the running at large of stock is prohibited, there is no need of such protection.

The special acts referred to, which created the district in St. Francis county bounding this district on the south and which created the district in Crittenden county, contained no requirements for the building of fences, but each of the statutes prohibited the running at large of stock in the respective territories, and this constituted a legislative determination in each instance that such prohibition and the penalties prescribed for the violation thereof constituted sufficient protection to the farmers who cultivate lands in those localities. This being true, we cannot assume that the lawmakers meant to require, under the general statutes, the building of a fence to keep out stock from another district where the running at large of stock is expressly prohibited. This, we think, is a more reasonable view of the statute, and is undoubtedly the one which works out the best results. Of course, we must declare the law as we find it, but we consider the reasonableness of a requirement in order to determine the scope and extent which the Legislature meant to give it.

This view of the law affirms the judgment of the circuit court, and it is so ordered.

WOOD and HUMPHREYS, JJ., dissent.

———

FRAUENTHAL v. MORTON. (No. 41.)

(Supreme Court of Arkansas. June 13, 1921.)

1. Animals ⬤⇒44—Owner of uninclosed land with open well liable for injury to stock, though dug by another.

Liability under Crawford & Moses' Dig. §§ 375, 376, for twice the value of any stock injured by an uncovered well on uninclosed land, is incurred by permitting a well dug by a former owner to remain uncovered.

2. Animals ⬤⇒44—Absolute liability imposed on owner of open well injuring stock.

Liability under Crawford & Moses' Dig. §§ 375, 376, for injury to stock by an uncovered well on uninclosed land is imposed without reference to the question of negligence, and the fact that a well is used as a source of water supply does not relieve the owner from liability if left uncovered.

3. Animals ⬤⇒44—Evidence held to show liability for drowning of horse in well.

In an action under Crawford & Moses' Dig. §§ 375, 376, for double the value of a horse drowned in an open well on uninclosed land, evidence held sufficient to sustain a verdict for plaintiff.

4. **Animals ☞44—Liability for injury to stock by open well not dependent on actual possession of land.**

Liability under Crawford & Moses' Dig. §§ 375, 376, for injury to stock by an uncovered well on uninclosed land, does not depend upon actual possession of the land by the owner; constructive possession following ownership.

5. **Judgment ☞256(6)—Judgment for twice amount of jury's verdict, under statute allowing double damages, proper.**

In an action under Crawford & Moses' Dig. §§ 375, 376, to recover twice the value of a horse drowned in an open well upon uninclosed land, the court did not err in rendering judgment for $150, where the verdict of the jury, under an instruction to find the market value of the horse, was for $75.

6. **Animals ☞44—Complaint held to warrant recovery of double damages for drowning of horse.**

In an action under Crawford & Moses' Dig. §§ 375, 376, for double the value of a horse drowned in an open well on uninclosed land, complaint amended so as to ask for double damages *held* to state facts making out a case for the recovery of double damages; there being little dispute that the horse was worth the sum fixed by the jury.

Appeal from Circuit Court, Cleburne County; J. M. Shinn, Judge.

Action by Harrod Morton against Clarence Frauenthal. Judgment for plaintiff, and defendant appeals. Affirmed.

M. E. Vinson, of Heber Springs, for appellant.

Geo. W. Reed and Lawrence Neill Reed, both of Heber Springs, for appellee.

McCULLOCH, C. J. Appellant, who was the defendant below, owns by inheritance from his father an uninclosed vacant lot in the town of Heber Springs on which is situated an exposed and uncovered well, according to the testimony, into which appellee's horse fell and was drowned. This is an action to recover double the value of the horse, under the statute which reads as follows:

"It shall be unlawful for any corporation, company, individual person, or association of persons to leave any shaft, well, or other opening uncovered on any uninclosed land. Every corporation, company, individual person, or association of persons who shall dig any such shaft, well, or other opening, whether for the purpose of mining or other purpose, shall be required to securely inclose the same, or cover and keep covered with strong and sufficient covering." Crawford & Moses Digest, § 375.

The next section of the statute prescribes a penalty for violation of the preceding section and liability to the owner of the injured stock for the recovery of twice the appraised value thereof.

There is a conflict in the testimony as to whether the excavation was originally a spring of water, but there is testimony tending to show that it was originally a flowing spring at all seasons of the year, and there was also testimony to the effect that it was what was called a "wet weather spring," i. e., water flowing during the rainy seasons. At any rate, the testimony is positive to the effect that during the year 1914 or 1915 a man named Brockman, by permission of appellant's father who then owned the lot in question, dug a well at the place in question to afford water for use at a hotel which he was operating a few blocks away. The well was dug about 20 feet deep, and being on a hillside it was walled up to the full height on the upper side and to the level of the ground on the lower side. Some of the witnesses say that it was above the ground on the lower side, and the testimony shows that an opening was left on the lower side so that stock could approach and drink out of the well and so that water could be conveniently dipped out. Originally, Brockman pumped water from the well with a gasoline engine, but the engine was removed long before appellee's horse was drowned and the well was left in the condition described above without any protection. Brockman abandoned the use of the well, but it was, according to the testimony, used for watering stock running out on the commons and was also used at times by persons for drinking purposes.

When appellant inherited the property, it was in the condition described, and on a day in the month of August, 1919, appellee's horse, which was allowed to run at large on the commons, went to the well to drink and fell into the well and was drowned. None of the witnesses in the case saw the horse fall in, but one of them saw it a few minutes after it fell, and it was still alive. He and a companion endeavored to rescue the horse, but were unable to do so. After appellee was notified, he and several other men finally dragged the horse out, then dead, by means of a rope and pulley suspended immediately over the well so that the horse could be pulled straight out and then swung over. Circumstances indicated that the horse approached the well on the side of the opening and while reaching in for water fell into the well. The water was, according to the testimony, about on a level with the ground, and the horse was found with his head and front feet in the water with his hips on the outside of the well. There was evidence tending to show that the well was at least 8 or 10 feet deep at the time the horse was drowned and was 20 feet deep when originally dug.

[1-3] The principal contention here is that the evidence is not sufficient to sustain the verdict, but we think there is sufficient evidence to establish a state of facts which would constitute liability under the terms of

the statute cited above. We decided in the case of American Building & Loan Ass'n v. State, 226 S. W. 1056, that liability is not dependent upon the fact that the person or corporation against whom liability is sought to be imposed dug the well, but that liability is incurred by permitting a well dug by another to remain uncovered. It is also observed from a perusal of the statute that it is made unlawful to leave a well, shaft, or other opening uncovered on unenclosed land, and that liability is imposed without reference to the question of negligence. In other words, the statute itself describes the circumstances under which liability is imposed, and it is not a question for the determination of a trial jury whether or not those facts constitute negligence. The statute obviously applies only to artificial excavations, but the testimony in the present case is sufficient to show that this is an artificial well dug on the land and that it was left exposed in a condition which might endanger ranging live stock. The fact that the well 'was being used as a source of water supply does not relieve the owner from liability if he permitted it to remain uncovered and exposed on unenclosed land, for that is the very circumstance upon which the statute expressly declares liability. Our conclusion is that there was evidence sufficient to sustain the verdict.

[4] It is further contended that the court erred in giving an instruction which ignored the question whether or not appellant was in actual possession of the property, it being contended that liability depended upon actual possession. Such is not the effect of the statute, which declares liability against all persons and corporations who "leave any shaft, well, or other opening uncovered on any unenclosed land." It is undisputed that appellant was the owner of the lot at the time the horse was drowned in the well, and it is unimportant to consider what overt acts of ownership were exercised. The lot was vacant and unoccupied and constructive possession follows the true ownership. There is nothing in the present case to show that there was any adverse claimant to the property or that any other person was asserting ownership or possession.

[5] The court instructed the jury that in the event of a finding for the plaintiff the damages should be assessed at the market value of the horse at the time it was killed. The jury returned a verdict in favor of appellee assessing damages in the sum of $75, and the court rendered judgment against appellant on this verdict for $150, twice the amount of damages assessed by the jury. It is contended that the verdict was general, assessing the full amount of the damages to which appellee was entitled, and that the court erred in rendering judgment for double damages. Hallum v. Dickinson, 47

Ark. 120, 14 S. W. 477. The orderly procedure in a trial of the issues under a statute of this kind is to instruct the jury as to the law in regard to double damages and permit the jury to make a finding of the full amount to be recovered. However, in the present case there was an instruction, given without objection, telling the jury to find the market value of the horse, and it is obvious that the jury did not intend by the verdict to find twice the value of the horse. This being true, it was not improper for the court to double the damages in rendering judgment on the verdict. Under the statute there is no discretion with the court or jury about allowing double damages. We think there was no error in this ruling of the court.

[6] Lastly, it is contended that the complaint did not state facts making out a case for the recovery of double damages. We think, however, that the allegations of the complaint constitute a sufficient statement of facts to warrant a recovery under the statute, and appellee was permitted during the progress of the trial to amend the complaint so as to ask for double damages. The assessment of damages is within the testimony. While there was some conflict as to the value of the horse, there is scarcely any dispute that it was worth the sum fixed by the jury in the award of damages. The testimony of appellee and some of his witnesses would, if accepted by the jury, have justified a finding for a much larger sum.

Judgment affirmed.

SATTERWHITE v. STATE. (No. 40.)

(Supreme Court of Arkansas. June 13, 1921.)

Criminal law ⟐⟩905—"Bill of review" defined and held not to lie to obtain a new trial in a criminal case after expiration of term at which conviction was had.

The only statutory method of review afforded in criminal cases in Arkansas is a writ of error or appeal, or a writ of error coram nobis, and hence a "bill of review" or in the nature of a bill of review, which is a proceeding peculiar to courts of equity at common law, will not lie to procure a new trial after conviction in a criminal case on the ground that the prosecuting witness, on whose testimony the conviction was based, had recanted her testimony by affidavit after the expiration of the term at which judgment of conviction was rendered.

[Ed. Note.—For other definitions, see Words and Phrases, First and Second Series, Bill of Review.]

Appeal from Circuit Court, Clark County; George R. Haynie, Judge.

E. E. Satterwhite was convicted of rape. Two years thereafter he filed a petition for new trial denominated a bill of review. Petition denied, and he appeals. Affirmed.

J. S. Utley, Atty. Gen., and Elbert Godwin and W. T. Hammock, Asst. Attys. Gen., for the State.

McCULLOCH, C. J. Appellant was indicted by the grand jury of Clark county for the crime of rape, and was tried and convicted on a day of the March term, 1919, and sentenced to the state penitentiary for life. He filed in the circuit court of Clark county, on February 1, 1921, a petition denominated as a bill of review setting forth his conviction aforesaid, and alleged, in substance, that within 30 days after his conviction and incarceration in the state penitentiary the prosecuting witness in the case, Edna Satterwhite, on whose testimony the state had procured a conviction, recanted and made an affidavit to the effect that her testimony against appellant accusing him of having raped her was false. It was further alleged in the petition that appellant filed a motion for a new trial in the Clark county circuit court immediately after his conviction, and that before the adjournment of the term the court overruled said motion. The prayer of the petition was that a new trial be granted on account of the change in the testimony of the prosecuting witness. The court denied this petition, and an appeal has been prosecuted to this court.

A bill of review or in the nature of a bill of review is a pleading which originated at common law, and the remedy afforded under it was one confined exclusively to courts of equity. The proceeding must be instituted in a court of equity and in the same court which rendered the decree sought to be reviewed. 10 Ruling Case Law, p. 567; note to Brewer v. Bowman, 20 Am. Dec. 158. The only statutory method of review afforded in criminal cases in this state is on a writ of error or appeal or on a writ of error coram nobis, an original proceeding in the trial court. Howard v. State, 58 Ark. 229, 24 S. W. 8; Beard v. State, 79 Ark. 296, 95 S. W. 995, 97 S. W. 667, 9 Ann. Cas. 409. Courts of equity have no jurisdiction to interfere with criminal proceedings. State v. Williams, 97 Ark. 243, 133 S. W. 1017; Ferguson v. Martineau, 115 Ark. 317, 171 S. W. 472, Ann. Cas. 1916E, 421. There is no provision for a motion for new trial in criminal cases on account of newly discovered evidence after the expiration of the term at which the judgment of conviction was rendered. Howard v. State, supra; Thomas v. State, 136 Ark. 290, 206 S. W. 435. The circuit court was therefore correct in denying the petition of appellant. Affirmed.

CARTER v. STEWART et al.   (No. 46.)

(Supreme Court of Arkansas.   June 13, 1921.)

1. Adverse possession ⬅104—Presumption of grant from state may be drawn from 50 years' possession and payment of taxes.

Possession of state lands for 50 years with payment of taxes thereon during the entire period is sufficient to sustain a presumption of fact drawn by the chancellor that the state had made a grant to the land, since, it would not have been listed for taxation nor taxes originally paid thereon unless the title had passed from the state.

2. Adverse possession ⬅104—Failure of state records to show grant of lands does not rebut presumption of grant.

The fact that the state land records do not show that any grant was ever made of the lands in controversy is merely negative evidence, and does not defeat the presumption of a grant from 50 years' possession of the land and payment of all taxes thereon.

3. Adverse possession ⬅22—Pasturing and cutting timber from swamp land held actual possession.

Where defendants and their predecessors had been in actual possession of a 40-acre tract of land adjoining the 40 acres in controversy and claiming the entire 80-acre tract as their homestead, though all the improvements were on the 40-acre tract not in controversy, the use of the disputed tract, which was swamp land, for pasturing cattle and the cutting of timber therefrom for firewood as needed during the entire time of possession, is actual possession of the tract in controversy.

4. Adverse possession ⬅100(1)—Possession of portion under deed is constructive possession of all included in description.

The actual possession of a portion of a tract of land by the grantees in the deed gives the grantees constructive possession of all the tract included in the description in the deed.

5. Adverse possession ⬅101—Constructive possession to limits of grant applies against state claim.

The exception to the rule that possession of part under a deed is constructive possession of all in a case where the deed covers separate tracts owned by different owners is limited to cases where the different owners are different private individuals, and does not apply where the tract not owned by the grantor was claimed by the state.

6. Adverse possession ⬅104—Presumption of state grant from possession and payment of taxes is not estoppel of state by unauthorized act of tax officers.

The presumption of fact of a state grant drawn from 50 years' possession of the land and payment of all taxes assessed thereon is not an estoppel of the state based on the unauthorized act of its tax officer in listing the land for taxation, since the state can, by rebutting the presumption, recover the land regardless of such unauthorized act.

McCulloch, C. J., and Smith, J., dissenting.

Appeal from Phillips Chancery Court; A. L. Hutchins, Chancellor.

Ejectment by Edna W. Carter against Oscar Stewart and another, in which the defendants asserted title to the land in themselves and had the case transferred to equity. From a decree dismissing the complaint for want of equity, plaintiff appeals. Affirmed.

Edna W. Carter instituted an action of ejectment in the circuit court against Oscar Stewart and Mary Jeter Stewart to recover 40 acres of land situated in Phillips county, Ark. She alleged that the land was granted by the United States to the state of Arkansas on August 14, 1858, under an act of Congress commonly known as the Swamp Land Grant. She further alleged that she obtained a patent to said land from the Commissioner of State Lands on the 6th day of June, 1917, and under it she has title to said lands and is entitled to the possession of the same.

The defendants asserted title to the land in themselves and moved to transfer the case to equity, which was done.

On the 26th day of April, 1873, S. D. Thomas conveyed, by warranty deed to Benjamin Jeter, 80 acres of land in Phillips county, Ark. The deed conveyed the 40 acres in controversy and another 40-acre tract adjoining it. The deed of S. D. Thomas and wife to Benjamin Jeter is dated April 26, 1873, and was acknowledged on the same day. It was duly filed for record in the clerk's office on the 1st day of August, 1873. The consideration recited in the deed is the sum of $600, the receipt of which is acknowledged.

J. R. Fielder was a witness for the defendants. According to his testimony S. D. Thomas was his stepfather. He did not know how Thomas acquired title to the land in question, but stated that he was satisfied he thought he had a title to it, or he would never have executed a deed to Jeter to the land. The land was then situated in Monroe county, and some years ago many of the deed records of that county for that time were burned in a fire. The defendants are both negroes and are husband and wife. Gertha Jeter Stewart is the daughter of Ben Jeter. Ben Jeter lived on the land and paid the taxes on it until he died. Since that time Gertha Jeter Stewart has lived on the land and paid the taxes on it. Witness helped Thomas to clear some of the land about three years before he sold it to Jeter. Mr. Thomas is now dead, and witness does not know where his old land papers are. Thomas commenced clearing the place for a home. Between 25 and 30 acres are now cleared, but the cleared land is not on the tract in controversy.

According to the testimony of Gertha Jeter Stewart, she was the only heir at law of her father. Her father commenced to pay taxes on the land in 1874 and paid taxes continually until he died. She was residing with her father when he died and continued to reside on the land with her mother until she died in 1912. They continued to pay taxes on the land until 1912. Since that time the witness has paid the taxes on the land; in other words, the Jeters have paid the taxes on the land since they bought it down to the time the case was heard in the chancery court on September 25, 1920. The cleared land and the dwelling house is on the 40-acre tract adjoining the 40 acres in controversy. The Jeters built a six-room house and cleared and cultivated between 25 and 30 acres of land on the 40 acres adjoining the 40 acres in controversy. Since they obtained the deed from Thomas, they have regarded the 80-acre tract embraced in the deed as their homestead. They have continuously cut firewood from the 40 acres in controversy and have used it for a pasture. It is low, swampy ground and none of it has been put into cultivation. The Jeters have been cutting timber ever since they have been on the land, and they have cut off all the oak and hickory timber so that there is no timber on the land except some gum timber. The record shows that Gertha Jeter Stewart is 59 years old, and that she is erroneously sued as Mary Jeter Stewart. J. R. Fielder is somewhat older.

A clerk in the State Land Office testified that he had examined the records kept in the State Land Office carefully, and that the records do not show any conveyance of the land to any one prior to the deed that was made to Edna W. Carter on June 6, 1917. The original patent of the United States to the state of Arkansas for said lands is shown by the records of the State Land Office. It is dated Aug. 14, 1858.

The chancellor found the issues in favor of the defendants, and a decree was entered of record dismissing the complaint of the plaintiff for want of equity. To reverse that decree the plaintiff has duly prosecuted this appeal.

A. D. Whitehead, of Helena, and E. L. Carter, of Little Rock, for appellant.
R. B. Campbell, of Helena, and W. H. Pemberton, of Little Rock, for appellees.

HART, J. (after stating the facts as above). [1] The principal question raised by the appeal in this case is whether 50 years' peaceable and uninterrupted possession of the land in controversy in the defendants and those under whom they claim, together with the payment of taxes during all that time, affords sufficient ground to presume a grant from the state to the lands in question. The chancellor held under the facts and circumstances adduced in evidence that he had the right to presume and find that a patent had been formerly issued by the state to the land in question under the authority of Carter v.

Goodson, 114 Ark. 62, 169 S. W. 806, and State v. Taylor, 135 Ark. 232, 205 S. W. 104. See, also, Wallace v. Hill, 135 Ark. 353, 205 S. W. 699.

In the case of Carter v. Goodson, supra, the court held that, where appellee and her grantors had held possession of land for 50 years, improving the same and paying taxes thereon, a finding by the court that a grant of the land had been made by the state to appellee's grantors was justified. The court further held that the presumption of a grant from continued and uninterrupted possession is one of fact for the court or jury trying the case.

It is claimed that the facts in the case at bar do not bring it within the principles decided in that case. It is pointed out by counsel that the notations or marks on the state land records in that case tended to show that the land had been sold by the state, while no such inference can be drawn from the state land records in the present case. For instance, the letter "S" was written on the original plat in the Land Office, and it was shown that it was the practice to place the letter "S" there when the state had sold the land. The establishment of that fact or circumstance, however, was not controlling in that case. This is shown by the decision of the court and the authorities cited in the subsequent case of State v. Taylor, supra. In that case the court clearly recognized that, where the possession of land has continued uninterrupted for a great length of time, a presumption arises as against the state and claimants under it that a grant from the state has duly accompanied the first possession, and consequently avoids any subsequent patent. It was there settled that a patent for land in cases of peaceable and uninterrupted possession of many years, together with the payment of taxes, may be presumed to have been formerly issued. We there pointed out from the decisions of other states that the courts have been constantly in the habit of presuming grants from the state upon the uninterrupted and peaceable possession of the lands for many years. The presumption springs from a lapse of time, the probable loss of evidence, and motives of public policy in settling titles and quieting possession.

Under its sovereign power, a state imposes the burden upon all its citizens to pay taxes on the property owned by them for the purpose of supporting the government. It is the duty of the officers of the state to place the lands of the state on the tax books for that purpose as soon as the state has parted with its title to them. Hence, where the state has for a long time demanded and collected taxes on property, and the property owner has acquiesced therein by paying the taxes, there arises a presumption that there was a legal liability to pay the taxes, and this furnishes a strong circumstance from which a court may infer a grant from the state. Of course from the very nature of the thing the person or persons paying the taxes must be in the uninterrupted and continued possession of the land in order to warrant the court in finding a grant from the state. In such cases the possession of the adverse claimants could have had a legal inception, and the doctrine of presumption of a grant from the state under such circumstances is recognized in many cases.

In such cases the fact of the claimant not producing the patent may have been owing to the general practice of the country at the time to take a conveyance of land without requiring all previous title deeds, or the failure to record deeds. Indeed, where a large grant of land from the state has been divided between the children of the grantee, the original patent must remain in the hands of only one of them, and might have been lost without the fault of the others.

The facts in the present case show that Thomas commenced to clear the 80 acres of land which he subsequently conveyed to Jeter in about 1870. According to the testimony of his son-in-law, he intended to make it his home. He conveyed the land to Jeter in 1873. At the time Thomas conveyed the land to Jeter, it was situated in Monroe county, but was subsequently annexed to Phillips county, where it is now situated. Thomas is dead, and the deed records of Monroe county for the year in which Thomas conveyed to Jeter have been burned. Jeter is also dead. He left surviving him his widow and one child, who continued to reside on the land until the widow died. The daughter then continued to reside on the land, until the present time. The Jeters commenced to pay taxes on the land from the time Thomas executed the deed to Ben Jeter in 1873, until the case was heard in September, 1920, in the chancery court. Of course, if Thomas and Jeter had lived, or if the deed records in Monroe county had not been destroyed, evidence might have been produced to show a grant from the state to Thomas.

[2] The fact that the state land records do not show such a grant does not repel or overcome, as a matter of law, the presumption of a grant. Such omission may be regarded as negative testimony only.

[3] But it is insisted that there has been no possession by the Jeters of the land in question. It is true that the house and cleared land are all on the adjoining 40 acres which was also embraced in the deed from Thomas to Ben Jeter, but the evidence shows that Thomas intended to have the whole 80 acres for his homestead, and that the Jeters did claim the whole 80 acres as their homestead. The evidence shows that the 40-acre tract in controversy is low, marshy land, and for that reason was not cleared and put into cultivation. During all these years however the Jeters have cut their firewood from it and have used it to pasture their cattle. In

fact, they have cut all the valuable oak and hickory timber off of it, and there is no timber left on it now except a small quantity of gum. These acts were not of a fitful and disconnected character, but they were continued and uninterrupted for nearly 50 years. Therefore the chancellor was justified in holding that they held such actual possession of the 40-acre tract in controversy as was practical under the circumstances. -

[4] Moreover, it is well settled that, where the grantee under a deed by one without record title goes into actual possession of part of the land described in the deed, his possession gives him constructive possession of the remainder.

[5] It is claimed, however, that the facts in this case bring it under the exception to that well-known rule as declared in St. L., I. M. & S. R. Co. v. Moore, 83 Ark. 377, 103 S. W. 1136, 119 Am. St. Rep. 142, and other cases of like character. In that case the court said that, where one takes possession of one of two adjoining tracts of land under a deed, conveying both tracts to him, if the actual titles to the two tracts are in different persons, his actual possession of one tract will not give him constructive possession of the other so as to oust the owner of that tract. The reason is that the possession of one tract would be no notice to the owner of the other tract that his land was claimed adversely. The court said further that, if the law were otherwise, one, by buying a small tract and taking a deed conveying adjacent unimproved lands, might by taking possession of the small tract become constructively in the possession of all of the land within the calls of his deed without any visible act to notify the owners of such adverse claim.

In the application of the exception to the present case, counsel point to the fact that the legal title to one of the 40-acre tracts was in Thomas, and that the legal title to the 40-acre tract in controversy was in the state at the time Thomas conveyed both tracts to Jeter. Now the state is the source of all land titles in this state, and the general rule announced above would illy serve its purpose and would really be worth nothing, if the exception could be applied to cases like the present one. The exception to the rule is applied in cases where different individuals claim and hold the legal title to the lands. We hold that it has no application when the facts are like those in the present case.

[6] Finally it is again contended that the rule laid down overturns the well-settled rule that the state in its sovereign capacity is not estopped to assert a claim to its own property by the unauthorized acts of its officers. Hence it is claimed that the act of the officers in placing the land on the tax books was unauthorized, and the state is not estopped by such unauthorized act. That principle, however, has no place under the facts as disclosed by the record. If the plaintiff had introduced evidence tending to oppose or repel the presumption of a grant from the state arising from the peaceable and uninterrupted possession of the Jeters and Thomas under whom they claimed for over 50 years, then it could not be said that the state, or its subsequent grantee, would be estopped from claiming title to the land by reason of the said officers placing the land on the tax books. But, as has already been pointed out, the plaintiff has introduced no testimony tending to rebut the presumption of a grant except the fact that the records of the State Land Office do not show such a grant. We have already seen that this does not, as a matter of law, overcome the presumption of a grant as found by the chancellor. Consequently the estoppel of the state from the unauthorized acts of its officers does not arise in the case. If the finding of the chancellor was correct, the state had already granted the land to Thomas and the land was rightfully placed on the tax books.

It is true, as said in Oaksmith v. Johnston, 92 U. S. 343, 23 L. Ed. 682, that in this country there can seldom be occasion to invoke the doctrine of presumption of a grant from the government or the state except in case of ancient possessions. But it is equally true that, where the facts justify it, this rule of presumption is a safe one, and has a salutary effect; and the doctrine serves a reasonable and necessary purpose.

It follows that the decree must be affirmed.

McCULLOCH, C. J., and SMITH, J., dissent.

FT. SMITH LIGHT & TRACTION CO. et al. v. WILLIAMS et al. (No. 43.)

(Supreme Court of Arkansas. June 13, 1921.)

1. **Bridges ⧪=5—Act creating district valid.**

Acts 1909, No. 119, creating the Ft. Smith and Van Buren bridge district, is valid.

2. **Bridges ⧪=33—Right to exact tolls for privilege of crossing public bridge must be conferred by statute.**

The right to exact tolls of the public for the privilege of crossing a public bridge must be conferred by statute or it does not exist.

3. **Bridges ⧪=33—Contract requiring street railroad to pay bridge district for right of way money which it was authorized to receive from passengers for transportation over bridge valid.**

In view of Acts 1909, No. 119, creating the Ft. Smith and Van Buren bridge district, as amended by Acts 1913, No. 233, contract between the bridge district and the Ft. Smith Light & Traction Company, operating a street railroad, requiring the traction company to pay the money which it was authorized to receive from passengers for transportation over the bridge to the district in payment for the concession or right of way granted by the district to the traction company, the bridge district agreeing to collect and receive such money as such payment, *held* valid.

Appeal from Sebastian Chancery Court; J. V. Bourland, Chancellor.

Action by Virgil Williams and another against the Ft. Smith Light & Traction Company and another. From decree for plaintiffs, defendants appeal. Decree reversed, and bill dismissed.

Hill & Fitzhugh and James B. McDonough, all of Ft. Smith, for appellants.

Webb Covington, of Ft. Smith, for appellees.

WOOD, J. This action was brought by the appellees, residents and real property owners of the Ft. Smith and Van Buren bridge district (hereafter called bridge district), against the bridge district and the Ft. Smith Light & Traction Company (hereafter called traction company). The traction company is an Arkansas corporation engaged in the operation of a street railway in and between the cities of Ft. Smith and Van Buren. The cars of the traction company run upon and over the bridge of the bridge district which spans the Arkansas river between the cities of Ft. Smith and Van Buren. The appellees alleged that the bridge district was requiring of them and other owners of real property in the bridge district to pay a bridge fare or toll of 1¼ cents for each ticket purchased or 5 cents per passenger cash fare if no ticket had been purchased; that the traction company permitted the agents of the bridge district to collect the fares; that no charge was made against any person for crossing the bridge except those who were passengers of the traction company; that appellees and other real property owners of the bridge district were taxed for the construction and maintenance of the bridge, and this bridge fare against them was discriminatory and illegal because other passengers of the traction company who were not owners of real property in the bridge district were allowed to cross over the bridge on the traction company's cars upon the payment of the same fare or toll as that paid by the appellees and other real property owners in the bridge district. The appellees further alleged that the bridge district was not collecting from the traction company any sum whatever for the use of the bridge; that all sums realized by the bridge district from the bridge fares collected from passengers on the cars of the traction company crossing the bridge were paid by the appellees and other passengers of the traction company and not by the traction company; that the bridge had therefore been

converted by the bridge district into a toll bridge contrary to the provisions of the act creating (Laws 1909, No. 119) the bridge district.

The appellees instituted the action for the benefit of themselves and all others similarly situated, and prayed that the bridge district and the traction company be restrained from charging and collecting the bridge fares mentioned.

The bridge district and the traction company answered separately setting up substantially that the act creating the bridge district, and Act 233 of the Acts of 1913 amending the same, authorized the bridge district to grant a right of way over the bridge upon such terms as might be provided by contract between the bridge district and the public utility, which contract was required to be submitted to the electors of the bridge district through referendum; that a contract was entered into by the bridge district and the traction company which was duly submitted to the legal voters through referendum as provided by the act and was ratified and approved by them; that the bridge district and the traction company were complying with the terms of that contract, and they set up the contract as a justification for the charges of which the appellees complain and as a complete defense to their action. The contract was made an exhibit and attached to the answers and was proved and introduced in evidence.

The contract is too long to set forth in hæc verba. It is in sections, and we will abbreviate and state in substance such of its provisions as we deem necessary.

In the first section the bridge district, for the considerations thereinafter named, grants to the traction company the right to use the free bridge and its approaches for the term thereinafter mentioned for the transportation of its passengers. This section specifically sets forth the things that the traction company is authorized to do in order to enable it to operate its passenger cars across and over the bridge and its approaches. It also specifically sets forth the things which the traction company is not authorized to do, confirming what had already been done by the traction company under a former contract and reserving in the bridge district the right to supervise and approve such improvements as the traction company should make in the future.

In the second section it is expressly agreed that in consideration of the execution and performance of all of the terms of the present contract, any and all claims of the bridge district growing out of the use of the bridge and its approaches by the traction company prior to the execution of the present contract are waived. If the contract is not performed, then the bridge district does not relinquish its claim for rentals under former contract.

fact,
hick
timl
of g
disc
tin
Th
hol
of
pr

tl
r
l

Section 12 the traction company to pay $50 per month toward bridge fare collectors if the cars the bridge are operated by two men, per month if the cars are operated by one man.

The thirteenth section makes the company responsible to the bridge for any damage it may do to the bridge approaches.

By section 14 the bridge district shall charge all other public utilities the toll or rental as the law requires for the use of the bridge.

Section 15 prescribes the period of the contract.

Section 16 makes it the duty of the bridge to keep the books and accounts with reference to the bridge tickets and the cash fares collected, and exempts the traction company from responsibility for any act of the acts of the collectors or bookkeepers, who, under the terms of the contract, are the agents of the bridge district.

One of the appellees lived in Ft. Smith and the other in Van Buren. Their res

he effect that each paid the ... ny 7 cents as passenger fare ... ion over its lines in the cities ... nd Van Buren, and an addi- ... 1¼ cents each to the bridge ... he free bridge while on the ... t ticket is used, or 5 cents cash ... ket. They own real property ... district, and each pays annual- ... $1.35 as a bridge tax. In buy- ... rom the traction company from ... Van Buren, they each had to ... s if they used a bridge ticket, ... without a bridge ticket. The ... are collected at each end of the ... ollectors who get on the cars at ... ve ends, ride across, and take up ... t the other end of the bridge. ... s testimony to the effect that the ... of the traction company on the ... nothing to do with the collection ... ge fares.

reen testified that he was the gen- ger of the traction company; that ... on company had a regular tariff of ... each passenger on cars between the ... s. This schedule of fares is on file ... e Corporation Commission as re- ... y law. His testimony and the sched- ... v that the fares were as above in- ... and that children under 12 years ... were charged 4 cents. Green testi- ... t the 7 cents covered the transporta- ... arges from any point in Van Buren to ... n avenue in Ft. Smith with free trans- ... vileges. In other words, a man gets ... car at the smelter in Van Buren and ... cents and can transfer to any point ... the city limits of Ft. Smith. An ad- ... al fare of 5 cents is collected from each ... nger crossing the bridge for a cash fare. ... traction company did not charge any ... than was set forth in its standard pub- ... chedule. This schedule was introduced ... vidence by the appellees, and it showed ... the fares were as above indicated.

here is a provision in the schedule under title of "Bridge Contract" as follows:

Under contract as entered into with the Smith and Van Buren bridge district, bridge lectors selected and employed by the bridge trict board the cars at or near the approach the bridge and collect from each passenger ossing the free bridge between Ft. Smith and an Buren five cents in cash or one bridge cket, and the money thus collected from the assengers is retained by the bridge district."

There was testimony on behalf of the ap- pellees to the effect that the deputy sheriff, who was employed by the bridge district to clean and repair the bridge, sometimes in cases of necessity assisted the collectors in the collection of fares.

The assistant secretary of the collector of taxes testified that he was the custodian of the records in the collector's office and kept all contracts with public utilities using the

bridge. There was no contract with any public utility other than the traction com- pany. The district made charges against per- sons regardless of the kind of transportation for crossing the bridge. It charged taxicabs and other concerns that carried passengers for pay.

It was admitted that the contract in evi- dence had been ratified by the legal voters of the bridge district under the referendum provided by special act. Upon the above is- sues and facts, the court decreed:

"That the aforesaid contract is ultra vires and void; that the taking of said fares by the district is contrary to law. Therefore, the said Ft. Smith and Van Buren district, its com- missioners, agents, employees, and representa- tives are perpetually enjoined from taking, re- ceiving, or attempting to take or offer to re- ceive said fares under said contract."

From that decree is this appeal.

[1] The bridge district was created under Act 119 of the Acts of 1909, p. 325. The act is valid. Shibley v. Ft. Smith and Van Bu- ren Bridge District, 96 Ark. 410, 132 S. W. 444; Nakdimen v. Fort Smith & Van Buren Bridge District, 115 Ark. 194, 172 S. W. 272, section 2 of the act provides in part as fol- lows:

"The Commission [of the bridge district] shall have the power to grant a right of way over said bridge to any public utility upon such terms as the Commission shall determine; provided, however, that the concessions which may be granted to public utilities shall not interfere with the reasonable use of such bridge as a public highway."

Section 39 of the act is in part as follows:

"The bridge district herein created shall have the power * * * to receive rents from the concessions heretofore authorized from the public utilities, for the purposes of con- struction, repair or maintenance of the public improvement herein contemplated."

Section 2 of the act was amended by the Legislature of 1913, Act 223 of the Acts of 1913, p. 1001, so as to read in part as follows:

"The Commission shall have the power to grant a right of way over said bridge to any public utility upon such terms as the Com- mission shall determine; provided, however, that the concessions which may be granted to public utilities shall not interfere with the reasonable use of such bridge as a public highway. Provided further, when the Commis- sion and the public utility shall agree upon a right of way or concession over the bridge to be enjoyed by any public utility, a contract setting forth fully the terms thereof shall be signed by the Commission and the public utility subject to a referendum thereon."

There are further provisions in the amend- atory act providing for carrying the referen- dum into effect, and the amendatory act also provides:

"That no exclusive privileges shall be granted under this section or any other provision of this act to any such public utility."

In Nakdimen v. Ft. Smith & Van Buren Bridge District, supra, construing section 2 of the original act, we said:

"We hold that the commissioners, under section 2 of the act, could only receive money for the grant of the right of way to the street car company, and the word 'terms' has reference to the time and amount of money paid, but that a discretion was left to the commissioners as to the amount of money to be charged therefor and the times of the payment thereof."

Learned counsel for appellees has made a vigorous attack upon the contract under review, the gist of his contention being that under the contract, as he construes it, the bridge district has granted to the traction company a right of way over the bridge for which the bridge district "forces the traveling public to pay tribute and designates the money thus received rental paid by the company." To support his contention counsel relies mainly upon the case of Perrine v. Chesapeake & Delaware Canal Co., 9 How. 172, 13 L. Ed. 92. In that case the canal company was granted a charter by Maryland, Delaware, and Pennsylvania to cut and maintain a canal connecting the Chesapeake and Delaware bays. The charter gave the company the right to collect tolls on certain articles on vessels carrying commodities, enumerating the articles and the tolls thereon. Empty boats or vessels were required to pay $4 "except an empty boat or vessel returning whose load has already paid the tolls fixed, in which case she shall pass toll free." The eleventh section of the charter provided:

"The said canal and works to be erected thereon by virtue of this act, when completed, shall forever thereafter be esteemed and taken to be navigable as a public highway, free for the transportation of all goods, commodities, or produce whatsoever, on payment of the toll imposed by this act, and no tax whatsoever for the use of the water of the said canal, or the works thereon erected, shall at any time hereafter be imposed by all or either of the said states."

Perrine proposed to install a line of passenger boats through the canal, and the company required him to pay a toll of $1 for each passenger. Perrine resisted the payment of this toll, and the Supreme Court of the United States held that the company had no right under its charter to demand toll from passengers who passed through the canal, or from vessels on account of the passengers on board; that the company could only exercise the powers conferred upon it by its charter.

Counsel also relies upon the case of Reed v. Hanger, 20 Ark. 625. In that case the county court granted a charter to erect a certain toll bridge which provided "that the bridge should ever remain free and open to the citizens of the county." It was held that the charter should be construed so as to give the citizens of the county the free use of the bridge whether they crossed on foot or otherwise, and also for the free passage of any means of transportation employed by them in their lawful business.

As already observed, counsel for the appellees, as a basis for the application of the doctrine of the above cases, assumes that the contract under consideration requires the traveling public generally, and not the traction company, to pay the bridge district for the right of way over the free bridge exercised by the traction company. This assumption which the counsel takes as his premise and the argument based thereon are plausible, but the premise is unsound, and his argument, however forceful, necessarily leads to an erroneous conclusion. Therefore it occurs to us that the doctrine of the above cases is not applicable to the contract under consideration when correctly construed.

We shall not undertake to analyze and comment upon the various provisions of the contract. It evidenced an agreement by which the bridge district is to receive a certain sum of money from the traction company for the right granted the latter to run its cars for the transportation of passengers over the bridge. The original act expressly authorized the bridge district to charge the traction company for its right of way over the bridge. Nakdimen v. Fort Smith & Van Buren Bridge District, supra. By the same token the traction company having thus acquired the right of way over the bridge could exercise it with all of its privileges, one of which was to charge passengers who used its facilities. The amount charged the traction company by the district is a definite and fixed sum ascertained and measured by the number of passengers which the traction company transports in its cars over the bridge and the amount which the traction company charges each passenger for such transportation. The traction company is a common carrier and had a right to charge those whom it transported on its cars across the bridge according to the tariff of rates filed with the Corporation Commission. Act 571 of the Acts of 1919, p. 411, §§ 5, 6, and 7. See Helena Water Co. v. Helena, 140 Ark. 597, 216 S. W. 26. The money derived from this source through the sale and use of tickets, and by the payment and collection of the cash fares in the absence of tickets, was primarily the property of the traction company and not of the bridge district. It became the property of the bridge district only because under the terms of the contract the traction company agreed to let the bridge district collect and use it in payment for the right of way privilege granted the traction company by the bridge district, and because the bridge district agreed to accept it as such.

It is not contended by the appellees, and could not be successfully contended under the issues herein joined, that the traction company did not have the right to charge those whom it transported over the bridge on its cars a fare of 1¼ cents where tickets were used, or a cash fare of 5 cents without tickets, as specified in its schedule of fares. As a common carrier, it could not be compelled to furnish the public its facilities of transportation over its line across the bridge without compensation. The only authority under the law authorized to determine whether these rates are just and reasonable has approved them. See section 6, Act of 1919, supra.

There is no provision in the original act creating the bridge district nor in the amendatory act authorizing the commissioners of the bridge district to charge the general public for the privilege of crossing the bridge. On the contrary, the power conferred upon the bridge district is "to construct and maintain a free public highway."

[2] It is well established by our own decisions and the authorities generally that the right to exact tolls of the public for the privilege of crossing a public bridge must be conferred by statute or it does not exist. Altheimer v. Plum Bayou Levee District, 79 Ark. 234, 95 S. W. 140; Nakdimen v. Fort Smith & Van Buren Bridge District, supra; and other cases cited in brief for appellees.

[3] Therefore, if the appellees are correct in the assumption that by the terms of this contract the general public and not the traction company is required to pay the bridge district for the right of way which the traction company has over the bridge, then the contract is ultra vires and void. But, on the other hand, the original and amendatory acts confer upon the bridge district the authority to grant the traction company a right of way upon terms to be fully set forth in a contract between the bridge district and the traction company. Therefore, if the contract requires the traction company to pay the money, which it is authorized to receive from passengers, to the bridge district in payment for the concession or right of way granted by it to the traction company, and if the bridge district agrees to collect and receive this money as such payment, then the contract is valid. We are convinced that the latter is the only correct interpretation of the contract in the light of the decision of this court in Nakdimen v. Bridge District, supra, and the amendatory act of 1913, supra.

The decree is therefore reversed, and the complaint is dismissed for want of equity.

HUMPHREYS, J., not participating.

SCHOOL DISTRICT OF NEWPORT v. J. R. HOLDEN LAND & LUMBER CO.
(No. 48.)

(Supreme Court of Arkansas.   June 13, 1921.)

1. **Deeds** ⟨⟩155—Restrictions on estate presumed not to be conditions subsequent.

Restrictions in a deed on the estate granted are presumed not to constitute a condition subsequent, which are not favored in law and which must clearly be shown by the words of the deed.

2. **Lost instruments** ⟨⟩23(1)—Burden is on grantors to show lost deed contained condition subsequent.

In a suit to quiet title where plaintiff claimed by a lost deed from defendants, the burden was on defendants to show that the deed, which they admitted they executed, contained a condition subsequent as claimed by them.

3. **Lost instruments** ⟨⟩23(3)—Evidence held not to sustain chancellor's finding that lost deed contained condition subsequent.

In a suit to quiet title, the finding of the chancellor, that the deed from defendants to plaintiff which had been lost contained a condition subsequent requiring the maintenance of a school for white children on the premises conveyed, held contrary to the preponderance of the evidence, consisting of oral testimony and the resolution accepting the offer to make the deed, which stated the condition to be the erection of a school building on the premises.

Appeal from Jackson Chancery Court; Lyman F. Reeder, Chancellor.

Suit to quiet title by the School District of Newport against the J. R. Holden Land & Lumber Company. From a decree vesting the title in the School District on condition subsequent that the property be used for a school for white children, both parties appeal. Reversed and remanded, with directions to enter a decree quieting the title in the district.

Boyce & Mack, of Newport, for appellant.
Gustave Jones, of Newport, for appellee.

SMITH, J. Appellant school district brought this suit to quiet its title to a certain block in the city of Newport. It alleged it was in possession of the block, and was occupying it for school purposes; one of the public school buildings being located thereon. It was alleged that a deed to the land had been executed, and thereafter appellant entered into the possession of the block and built an expensive and valuable school building thereon; that this deed had never been delivered and had never been recorded.

The answer admitted the execution of the deed and alleged that the deed had been delivered. The answer further alleged that the block was donated to the appellant school district, and that the deed contained a condition subsequent to the following effect:

Upon the condition that said district erect a brick school building and maintain a public school on said premises, to be equipped and have the same facilities and the same length of term as was conducted by said district in the main city of Newport, and that said block was conveyed with the condition that said premises should be so used, and that upon failure to build, maintain, and construct such school the land should revert to the grantor.

There is no question about the execution of the deed. The question is what its terms and conditions were, and there is irreconcilable conflict in the testimony of a number of witnesses. These witnesses testified about a transaction then about 14 years old, and much of this conflict can be ascribed to infirmities of memory.

On behalf of appellant district, the following persons testified: S. R. Phillips, Tom J. Gregg, T. P. Umsted, H. O. Walker, E. L. Boyce, P. H. Van Dyke, A. L. Best, J. F. Parish, R. F. Drummond, W. T. Parish, and Charles Myer. The witnesses on behalf of appellee were: W. D. McLain, Gustave Jones, and J. R. Holden.

The land in question was owned by McLain and Holden. It was a part of an addition to the town of Newport which had just been platted as an addition, and it is quite obvious that they were anxious to have a schoolhouse built in this addition. They executed a deed for the land on April 26, 1906, to the McLain & Holden Land & Lumber Company, a corporation, whose stock was owned almost entirely by themselves. The name of this corporation was later changed to J. R. Holden Land & Lumber Company. Shortly after the execution of this deed to the corporation by Holden and McLain, the corporation executed the deed in question to the school district. The deed was executed on behalf of the corporation by Holden as president and McLain as secretary.

The minutes of the meeting of the school board held on January 27, 1906, were read in evidence. At this meeting the following resolution was adopted:

"Whereas, said W. D. McLain and J. R. Holden propose to donate to the Newport special school district of Newport, Arkansas, said block designated No. eighteen, provided said district construct and supply a school building thereon, therefore, be it resolved that said offer of W. D. McLain and J. R. Holden be and the same is hereby accepted upon the conditions of said offer. Resolved further that the building committee of the board of directors of said special school district be and it is hereby designated to provide for and construct and supply a school building upon said black designated eighteen on said quarter section.

"On roll call, voted, J. M. Jones, 'Yes,' C. West, 'Yes,' R. F. Drummond, 'Yes,' Charles Myer, 'Yes,' W. R. Thompson, 'Yes,' and Gustave Jones 'Yes.' Carried."

The roll call shows that all of the directors present voted for the resolution, and included in this number was Mr. Gustave Jones. The minutes of the school board further recite that McLain was present at this meeting and presented a petition enlarging the boundaries of the school district.

Thus it appears that two of the three witnesses for appellee were present when the resolution was adopted. At a later meeting of the board held on February 24th, McLain was employed to assist in the construction of the school building.

According to the testimony of McLain, Holden, and Jones, the deed contained the condition subsequent that the property should revert to the grantors if the grantee ceased to maintain a white school on the block conveyed.

It is quite clear that the gentlemen who so testified have that recollection of the transaction, and Mr. Jones testified that he was the only lawyer on the school board and that he was for that reason requested to write the deed, and that he wrote it, and that it recited an agreement on the part of the district to put up a schoolhouse and maintain a school there for white people for an equal length of time and with equal facilities with reference to teachers and equipment as the Walnut Street school—this latter being the principal school in Newport—and that the deed recited that the lot was to be used for school purposes only, and when it ceased so to be used was to revert to the grantors.

It was the purpose of the district to conduct a white school on the land conveyed, and that purpose has since been followed. But it is a different matter to say that the deed incorporated a recital of that purpose as a condition subsequent.

The only writing on the subject offered in evidence is the resolution of the board set out above. This resolution was prepared and adopted at a meeting attended by both McLain and Jones. It purports to set out the condition on which the donation was to be made. The donation had not then been made. It had been proposed, and one of the men who proposed it was present when the board determined whether the donation would be accepted. The resolution of acceptance recited the condition upon which the donation was proposed, and that recital is that the district should construct and supply a school building thereon. This condition was met, and whatever may have been the idea of any of the participating parties as to the subsequent use the district would make of the land, we think the testimony does not show that there was written into the deed any condition not contained in the resolution of acceptance.

The deed was not produced, and the testimony is conflicting as to its loss. A strong affirmative showing on the part of the district was made that the deed was never delivered. It is also insisted on behalf of the district that the deed was shown to have been in the hands of McLain after the controversy arose over its recitals. It is fair to McLain to say, however, that, while he made statements about the deed, leaving the impression that he knew where the deed was, he furnished the explanation that his statement had been made under a misapprehension of the facts; it being his impression that the deed had been found by the secretary of the school board among the papers belonging to the district, when it had not been so found. There was also testimony to the effect that Holden, one of the parties who executed the deed, had made admissions in regard to its provisions which were in conflict with his contention and testimony at the trial.

[1] If the deed itself was before us for construction, there would be a presumption that the restrictions of the estate granted did not constitute a condition subsequent. In the case of Bain v. Parker, 77 Ark. 170, 90 S. W. 1001, the court said:

"Conditions subsequent that defeat the estate conveyed by the deed are not favored in law. The words of the deed must clearly show a condition subsequent or the courts will take it that none was intended; and when the terms of the grant will admit of any other reasonable interpretation, they will not be held to create an estate on condition. Now, if we treat the deed as containing the words referred to, there are still no words of condition in the deed, and no words indicating that the estate should be forfeited if the road was not completed at the date named. These words then import nothing more than a covenant which, upon the acceptance of the deed by the grantee, became binding upon him, and for the breach of which the grantor may recover damages suffered thereby, but the deed remains valid"—citing cases.

[2] So, here, we think it fair to say that the execution of the deed being admitted, the burden is upon the grantors to show that it contained a condition subsequent.

In addition to the testimony set out above, the district makes the most unequivocal showing that the deed was not to contain a condition subsequent and that the terms of the donation were met when the schoolhouse was built.

The gentlemen named as having testified on behalf of the district were the directors thereof, either at the time of the donation or succeeded others in office, and all gave testimony tending strongly to support the district's contention.

Myer, who voted for the resolution accepting the donation, testified that no conditions were discussed other than that the land was donated to the school district to be used for school purposes and to erect a schoolhouse on. The minutes of the school board show that this witness was unusually attentive to his duties and that he rarely missed a meeting of the board. He testified that no deed was ever delivered to the board. Mr. Drummond, who also voted for the donation resolution at the meeting of the school board, testified that the only condition he remembers anything about was that the land was to be donated to the school district and the board was to erect a building on it.

The court entered a decree divesting the title out of the corporation and vesting it in the school district "so long, and only so long, as the same is used for school purposes, and for white children only." It was also ordered that each party pay half of the costs, and both parties have appealed.

[3] Without setting out in further detail the testimony of the various witnesses, we announce our conclusion to be that the finding of the chancellor is contrary to the preponderance of the evidence, and that the only condition of the donation was that the school district should construct and supply a schoolhouse, and that if this was a condition, instead of a covenant, it was a condition precedent, which was performed when the district erected the schoolhouse, and that the title to the land immediately vested in the district upon the happening of that event.

The decree of the court below is therefore reversed, and the cause will be remanded, with directions to enter a decree quieting the title of the school district in accordance with this opinion.

FORRESTER et al. v. LOCKE et al.
(No. 50.)

(Supreme Court of Arkansas. June 13, 1921.)

1. Sales ⟐288(5)—Action for breach of warranty of quality maintainable after acceptance of part when there was no opportunity for inspection.

Where cotton sold with a warranty of quality was shipped to the buyer under a bill of lading attached to the draft for purchase price, and the buyer therefore had no opportunity to inspect the cotton until after payment of the freight and contract price, the acceptance of a part of the cotton did not bar an action for breach of warranty as to the balance of the cotton.

2. Corporations ⟐674—Evidence held to make a question for jury as to foreign corporation doing business without filing articles of incorporation.

In an action on a contract for the sale of cotton, evidence held to make a question for the jury as to whether S. B. L. & Co., to whom the cotton was sold, was a foreign corporation doing business in the state, without filing its articles of incorporation as required by Acts 1907, No. 313, or whether the members of the corporation were doing business in Arkansas as partners.

3. Commerce ☞46—Purchase of cotton by foreign corporation for shipment to itself within the state not interstate transaction.

Where an Oklahoma corporation maintained a branch office at Ft. Smith, Ark., a purchase of cotton within the state for shipment to it at Ft. Smith, the drafts for the purchase price being paid through Ft. Smith banks, and then sent to the home office in Oklahoma for final payment, was not an interstate transaction as respected the necessity for filing the corporation's articles of incorporation.

4. Appeal and error ☞172(1)—Plaintiff bound by allegations and evidence showing they were doing business within the state.

Where plaintiffs suing as partners alleged that the partnership was doing business in the state, and no issue was made in the trial court as to the particular transaction being an interstate one, and there was no evidence changing the nature of the allegations in the complaint, plaintiffs were bound by the allegations of the complaint and the evidence in their support.

5. Corporations ☞667½—Action on contract of a foreign corporation cannot be maintained by members of partnership of same name.

If a purchase of cotton was made by a foreign corporation not authorized to do business in the state, a suit for breach of warranty cannot be brought by the individuals composing a partnership of the same name without making the corporation a party, whether the transaction was an interstate one or not.

6. Evidence ☞317(2)—Testimony that third person said company was a partnership held hearsay.

The testimony of the manager of a company's branch office that the vice president and secretary told him the company was a partnership at the time the contract in question was entered into was hearsay and inadmissible.

7. Evidence ☞318(6) — Testimony based on book entries, showing account between party and third person, not admissible when witness did not keep books.

In an action by a buyer of cotton for breach of warranty of quality, testimony as to the sale by the buyer of the defective cotton and the expenses incurred in such sale, based on the buyer's books which were not kept by the witness and related to the account between the buyer and the persons to whom the cotton was sold by it, and not to transactions between plaintiffs and defendant, was inadmissible.

8. Customs and usages ☞14—Custom of seller in selling cotton inadmissible when there was a contract.

On the issue whether the parties to a sale of cotton agreed that it should contain no "bollies" or "dogs," the seller's testimony as to his custom to sell his cotton in lots "hog round" was properly excluded, where it was admitted by both parties that there was a contract, as the contract, and not the custom, must control.

9. Sales ☞442(3)—Measure of damages for breach of warranty of quality stated.

The measure of damages for breach of a seller's warranty of the quality of cotton was

the difference between its market value at the time it was discovered that the cotton was of inferior quality and the contract price, and not the difference between the contract price and the amount for which the inferior cotton was sold several months after its receipt by the buyer.

Appeal from Circuit Court, Sebastian County; John Brizzolara, Judge.

Action by S. B. Locke and others against Chas. E. Forrester and others. From a judgment for plaintiffs, defendants appeal. Reversed and remanded.

Jas. B. McDonough, of Ft. Smith, for appellants.

Hill & Fitzhugh, of Ft. Smith, for appellees.

HUMPHREYS, J. This is a suit by appellees against appellants, in the circuit court of Sebastian county, Ft. Smith district, for damages on an alleged implied warranty as to the quality of 44 bales of cotton, included in a purchase and sale of 188 bales of cotton. It was alleged, in substance, that appellees, an Oklahoma partnership, maintained an office in Ft. Smith, Ark., for the transaction of a general cotton business in Arkansas, and, during the cotton season of 1919 purchased 188 bales of merchantable cotton, according to custom, for delivery at Ft. Smith, at an agreed price of 36 cents per pound; that there were 44 bales of unmerchantable or "bollie" cotton included in the shipments, which occasioned a total loss of $4,883.91 to appellees.

Appellants interposed two defenses; the first being that appellees were not a partnership, but a foreign corporation engaged in the business of buying and selling cotton in the state of Arkansas, in violation of Act No. 313 of the Acts of 1907 of said state, and the second being that the cotton was sold and purchased without regard to grade, at an average price of 36 cents for the entire lot, including the "bollie" cotton.

The cause was submitted upon the pleadings, exhibits thereto, the evidence, and instructions of the court, which resulted in a verdict and judgment against appellants in the sum of $3,846.53, from which an appeal has been duly prosecuted to this court.

The facts revealed by the record, in so far as necessary to determine the vital questions on this appeal, are, in substance, as follows: S. B. Locke & Co., an Oklahoma corporation composed of S. B. Locke, J. M. Locke, and J. C. Fahnestock, was organized on May 29, 1913, for the purpose of conducting a general cotton business, with its main office at Muskogee, Okl., and a branch office at Ft. Smith. W. R. Locke, an uncle of J. M. Locke, was manager for the organization, and H. B. Hunt, bookkeeper of the branch office at Ft. Smith, after 1917, and have been retained in those positions and paid for their services from the Muskogee office with checks of S. B. Locke & Co. Neither W. R. Locke nor H. B. Hunt filed the articles of incorporation in the office of the Secretary of the State, as required by law before commencing business, or during the time the corporation continued business in Arkansas. J. M. Locke, the vice president and secretary of the corporation, also testified that he did not file the articles of said incorporation in this state. W. R. Locke testified that S. B. Locke was president, J. M. Locke, vice president and treasurer, and W. P. Cowen, secretary of the corporation. When first asked whether S. B. Locke & Co. was a corporation or partnership, he stated that it was a partnership for about two years before he bought the cotton in question from appellants. He was then shown the articles of incorporation, and stated that it was a corporation in Oklahoma, but a partnership in Arkansas. Being interrogated further upon this point, he made the following answers:

"Q. Then you do not know whether you were dealing as a corporation or a partnership? A. I know what I have done.
"Q. That is all you know about it? A. That is all.
"Q. Then you did not know of your own knowledge whether you were dealing as a partnership or as a corporation? A. No, sir; I did not know. I just knew I was buying cotton."

Later, and on cross-examination, over the objection and exception of appellants, W. R. Locke stated that J. M. Locke told him S. B. Locke & Co. became a partnership about two years before the cotton in question was bought.

J. M. Locke testified that, on October 10, 1918, the corporation became dormant, and the business was conducted by S. B. Locke & Co. as a partnership, being composed of S. B. Locke, J. M. Locke, and W. P. Cowen. He produced an authenticated certificate of the partnership, appearing on the register of the district clerk in Muskogee, which is as follows:

"This is to certify that the partnership of S. B. Locke & Co. doing business in the city of Muskogee, Muskogee county, Okl., is composed of S. B. Locke, J. M. Locke, and W. P. Cowen, and that each of said partner's post office and residence is Muskogee, Muskogee county, Oklahoma.
"Dated this 10th day of September, 1919.
"S. B. Locke & Co.
"By S. B. Locke,
"J. M. Locke,
"W. P. Cowen."

The certificate was filed with the register October 16, 1919. He further testified that the cotton business in the branch office at Ft. Smith was conducted by the partnership of S. B. Locke & Co., and that the money invested was the money of said partner-ship, and that the drafts drawn for the cotton in question were paid by the partnership, and denied that any of the business conducted since the 10th day of October, 1918, in Arkansas, was conducted by the corporation of S. B. Locke & Co. Letter heads and other exhibits introduced each carried the name of S. B. Locke & Co., and also the individual names of S. B. Locke, J. M. Locke, and W. P. Cowen.

The contract for the sale and purchase of the cotton in question was made on December 13, 1919, between W. R. Locke, representing S. B. Locke & Co. and Charles E. Forrester, representing himself and the other appellants. The contract was oral.

W. R. Locke testified that, as the representative of S. B. Locke & Co., he purchased from Charles E. Forrester, representing himself and others, 188 bales of merchantable cotton, situated at Waldron, Ark., to be shipped and delivered to his company at Ft. Smith, Ark.; that it was agreed the cotton should contain no "bollies" or "dogs"; "bollies" being descriptive of cotton taken by machinery from the bolls before they opened, and "dogs" descriptive of cotton which had fallen on the ground and been damaged in the field.

Charles E. Forrester testified that, representing himself and others, he sold to W. R. Locke, as the representative of S. B. Locke & Co., the entire lot of 188 bales of cotton, "hog round," delivery f. o. b. Waldron after it had been inspected by —— Heard, the representative of S. B. Locke & Co.

The cotton was billed out in several shipments, and the bills of lading, bearing the word "hog," were attached to drafts and mailed to S. B. Locke & Co. at Ft. Smith, Ark. The drafts were approved in the Ft. Smith office, and paid through the Ft. Smith banks, and then sent through the Muskogee banks to S. B. Locke & Co. at Muskogee, who made final payment. The entire 188 bales arrived in Ft. Smith at the same time, early in January, 1920. The freight was paid, and, according to the evidence of appellees, upon examination it was discovered that there were 44 bales of "bollies" contained in the shipments. Appellees disposed of 144 bales of the shipment, and, in the latter part of January offered to return the 44 bales of "bollies" to Charles E. Forrester, upon repayment of the purchase price of 36 cents per pound. Forrester refused to accept the "bollies" and return the purchase price. Appellees disposed of the "bollies" in June at 16 cents a pound, deducted all expenses for handling same from the amount, and instituted this suit against appellants for the difference between the net amount received for the "bollies" and the contract price of 36 cents per pound paid for it.

In the course of trial, appellants offered to prove that, during the cotton season of 1919,

Charles E. Forrester's custom was to sell his cotton in lots, "hog round," and the court, over the objection of appellants, refused to admit evidence of that character.

J. M. Locke was permitted to testify in relation to the damages, over the objection and exception of appellants, to the sale of the "bollies" by his office in his absence, and to the items of expense attached to the handling of same, from a statement made by him from the books of S. B. Locke & Co., in the Muskogee office, without showing that the books were properly kept or that the books were kept by him.

[1] Appellants' first contention is that appellees cannot recover because the undisputed evidence shows that, after the cotton was examined in Ft. Smith and the discovery made that the shipments contained 44 bales of "bollies," it accepted 144 bales of the cotton, which, on account of the indivisibility of the contract, constituted an acceptance of the entire lot of cotton. We cannot agree with the learned counsel for appellants in this contention, because, under appellees' version of the contract, payment of freight and the contract price of the cotton was to be made before an opportunity was given to inspect it. After paying the freight and the purchase price of the cotton and receiving same, the only remedy available to appellees was to sue for damage on account of the inferiority of any or all the cotton upon the implied warranty that it all should be merchantable, and under appellees' version of the contract no opportunity was given them to inspect and elect before receiving same.

[2] Appellants' next contention is that the court erred in refusing to submit the question of whether S. B. Locke & Co. was a foreign corporation at the time the contract was entered into for the purchase of the cotton with appellants, without first having filed its articles of incorporation in the office of the Secretary of State, in the manner required by Act No. 313 of the Acts of 1907 of the General Assembly of the state of Arkansas. Appellants requested the court in two instructions, Nos. 2 and 3, to submit this question to the jury. Appellee specifically objected to the instructions on the ground that the undisputed testimony showed that appellees were not a corporation, but were a partnership at the time they entered into the contract in question. The court refused to give either of these instructions, and, in effect, by so refusing, took that issue of fact from the jury. The evidence of appellants tended to show that, after the organization of the corporation in Oklahoma, it opened an office in Ft. Smith, and transacted a general cotton business for a number of years in violation of the Arkansas laws; that up to and including the time the contract in question was made there had been no change in the management of the business; that the manager ＿＿d bookkeeper were paid in the same man-

ner for their services during the entire ＿＿ with checks issued in the Oklahoma ＿＿ by S. B. Locke & Co. The manager, W. ＿ Locke, first testified that S. B. Locke & ＿ were a partnership, and afterwards that ＿ was a corporation in Oklahoma and a par＿ nership in Arkansas. Later he testified th＿ he did not know whether it was doing bus＿ ness in Arkansas as a corporation or as ＿ partnership. No change was made after ＿ organization of the corporation in Oklah＿ in the letter heads. They did not indic＿ whether S. B. Locke & Co. was a corpora＿ or a partnership. The offices were maint＿ ed throughout in the same place. J. M. Lo＿ testified that the corporation became dorm＿ and was supplanted by a partnership on ＿ 10th day of October, 1918. The certific＿ evidencing the partnership was dated Se＿ tember 10, 1919, sworn to September 16, 19＿ and filed in the office of the district clerk ＿ October 16, 1919. The certificate on its ＿ showed that S. B. Locke & Co. were do＿ business as a partnership in the city of Mu＿ kogee. There is nothing in the face of it ＿ indicate that the partnership assumed con＿ trol of the corporation's business outside ＿ that city. In fact, the only evidence in t＿ record to the effect that S. B. Locke & Co. ＿ Ft. Smith, was conducting its business ＿ a partnership was that of J. M. Locke, wh＿ is an appellee and a plaintiff in this acti＿ and he did not make any explanation w＿ the corporation became dormant, and, wit＿ out dissolution, permitted its activities to ＿ prosecuted by a partnership composed ＿ practically the same parties composing ＿ corporation. In addition, it appeared tha＿ the Lockes who composed the corporatio＿ were related. W. R. Locke was an uncle ＿ J. M. Locke, and S. B. Locke, the latter＿ son. It is true that J. M. Locke swore pos＿ tively that the business at Ft. Smith was ＿ partnership business at the time the con＿ tract was made; but, not only was he an ＿ terested party, but his evidence is in effe＿ disputed by that of W. R. Locke, as well ＿ by other facts and circumstances heretof＿ referred to. In this state of the record, ＿ cannot be said that the undisputed eviden＿ showed that S. B. Locke & Co. was a par＿ nership at the time it purchased the cott＿ in question. Skillern v. Baker, 82 Ark. ＿ 100 S. W. 764, 118 Am. St. Rep. 52, 12 A＿ Cas. 243; Briggs v. Collins, 113 Ark. 19＿ 167 S. W. 1114, L. R. A. 1915A, 686; Poins＿ Lbr. & Mfg. Co. v. Traxler, 118 Ark. 12＿ 175 S. W. 522; Yazoo & Miss. V. Rd. Co. ＿ Altman, 124 Ark. 490, 187 S. W. 656; Fur＿ & Thomas v. Dewberry, 136 Ark. 135, 20＿ S. W. 129.

[3-5] Appellees insist, however, that, eve＿ though appellee was a foreign corporatio＿ when it entered into the contract in que＿ tion, it pertained to an interstate transacti＿ If this contention be correct, then any forei＿ corporation may open an office in this stat＿

purchase its goods out of the state for shipment into the state, and sell its commodities
for shipments to points out of the state, and
in that way evade the statutes of the state,
requiring foreign corporations doing business
in this state to file their articles of incorporation with the Secretary of State. We
cannot subscribe to that doctrine. Again, it
is alleged in the complaint in this case that
S. B. Locke & Co. was doing business in this
state. No issue was made in the trial court
that this particular business was an interstate transaction. There is no evidence in
the record changing the nature of that allegation in the complaint. We think appellees are bound by the allegations of the complaint and the evidence adduced in support
thereof. Moreover, a complete answer to appellees' position is that this suit was brought
by them as individuals composing a partnership, and the corporation was not made a
party by them.

[6] Appellants also insist that the court
erred in permitting W. R. Locke to give hearsay testimony to the effect that S. B. Locke
& Co. was a partnership at the time the
contract in question was entered into. He
was permitted to say that J. M. Locke had
so informed him. We think the evidence
clearly hearsay and inadmissible.

[7] Appellants also insist that the court
erred in permitting J. M. Locke to testify to
the sale of the "bollies" when not present,
from the records made on the books in the
Muskogee office, and to testify what expenses
were incurred in the sale thereof, from a
statement he made up by reference to the
books. The record does not show that the
books were kept by J. M. Locke, or that the
book account related to transactions between
J. M. Locke and appellants. The book entries
from which the statement was made related
to an account between S. B. Locke & Co. and
third parties to whom the "bollies" were sold.
We think this evidence inadmissible.

[8] Appellants also contend that the court
erred in excluding evidence to the effect that
Charles E. Forrester's custom was to sell
his cotton in lots "hog round." It is admitted
by both appellants and appellees that there
was a contract with reference to the sale and
purchase of this cotton. The contract, and
not the custom, must control. The court did
not err in excluding that character of evidence.

[9] Appellants' last insistence is that the
measure of damages laid down by the court
was incorrect. The measure of damages
adopted by the court permitted the jury to
deduct the net amount received by appellees
for the 44 bales of "bollies" from the contract
price of 36 cents per pound. The evidence
shows the "bollies" were received in the early
part of January, and not sold by appellees
until the month of June following. The correct measure of damages was the difference
between the market value of the "bollies"
at the time it was discovered that the shipment contained this inferior cotton and the
contract price. No evidence was introduced
to meet this rule.

For the errors indicated, the judgment is
reversed, and the cause remanded for a new
trial.

CLEMENTS et al. v. ROBERTS, Governor, et al.

(Supreme Court of Tennessee. June 20, 1921.)

1. **Courts 248—Case involving validity of joint resolution of Legislature held within jurisdiction of Supreme Court.**

Under Acts 1907, c. 82, creating the Court of Civil Appeals and reserving to the Supreme Court jurisdiction of cases involving the constitutionality of a state statute, a suit to enjoin the Governor and other state officers from certifying the adoption and ratification of a proposed amendment to the federal Constitution, on the ground that the joint resolution ratifying it was contrary to the state Constitution, was within the jurisdiction of the Supreme Court and not of the Court of Civil Appeals, in view of Const. art. 8, § 18, recognizing the power of the Legislature to pass joint resolutions.

2. **Constitutional law 52, 79—Jurisdiction of Supreme Court cannot be interfered with by other branches of state government.**

The Supreme Court takes its rank from the Constitution, and it and its jurisdiction cannot be interfered with by the other branches of the government.

On petition for rehearing. Petition denied.

For former opinion, see 230 S. W. 30.

E. J. Smith, Thos. H. Malone, Norman Farrell, and Thos. G. Watkins, all of Nashville, for complainants.

The Attorney General, for defendants.

HALL, J. This cause is now before us on complainants' petition to rehear.

[1] It is insisted by complainants that this court was without jurisdiction to hear and determine the cause; that the jurisdiction is in the Court of Civil Appeals. This insistence is based on the fact that the cause is not either a contested election suit, an ejectment suit, or an equity suit seeking a money decree for more than $1,000. Neither is it a suit involving state revenue, or the constitutionality of a state statute; that by the statute creating the Court of Civil Appeals (chapter 82, Acts of 1907) that court is expressly given jurisdiction of all cases other than those above noted, and in all cases in which appellate jurisdiction is conferred upon the Court of Civil Appeals by said act, appeals and appeals in the nature of writs of error from the lower court shall be taken directly to said court; and said court, or any judge, is vested with exclusive power to award and issue writs of error, certiorari, and supersedeas in such cases, returnable to said Court of Civil Appeals.

The very gravamen of complainants' bill is that the Legislature violated article 2, section 32, of our state Constitution in passing said joint resolution ratifying the Nineteenth Amendment to the Constitution of the United States. This was the predicate of complainants' bill, and was the ground on which complainants sought an injunction restraining the Governor and his codefendants from certifying the action of the Legislature on said joint resolution to the Secretary of State of the United States. The question presented, then, is: Does this court have jurisdiction of all cases involving constitutional questions, or only those involving the constitutionality of a state statute?

The state Constitution expressly recognizes the power of the Legislature to pass joint resolutions. By section 18 of article 3 of our Constitution it is provided as follows:

"Every joint resolution or order (except on questions of adjournment) shall likewise be presented to the Governor for his signature, and before it shall take effect shall receive his signature, and on being disapproved by him shall, in like manner, be returned with his objections; and the same, before it shall take effect, shall be repassed by a majority of all the members elected to both houses, in the manner and according to the rules prescribed in case of a bill."

It will thus be seen that the state Constitution prescribes the manner in which joint resolutions must be passed and dealt with by the Legislature and Governor. While it is true that the statute creating the Court of Civil Appeals only expressly reserves to this court exclusive appellate jurisdiction of cases involving the constitutionality of state statutes, we do not think the Legislature intended to deprive this court of its appellate jurisdiction of any case involving a constitutional question, and that this is true, regardless of whether such question involves the validity of a statute or a joint resolution passed by the Legislature, and that no such construction should be given chapter 82, Acts of 1907. We think it was the intention of the Legislature to withhold jurisdiction of all constitutional questions from the Court of Civil Appeals. That court is not a constitutional court, but is a creature of statute only; while the Supreme Court was created and established by the Constitution and vested with its jurisdiction, and is the highest judicial tribunal in the state.

[2] As was said in Railroad v. Byrne, 119 Tenn. 320, 104 S. W. 460, it takes its rank from the Constitution, and it and its jurisdiction cannot be interfered with by the other branches of the government. Its adjudications are final and conclusive upon all questions determined by it, save those reserved to the federal courts, which may be reviewed by the Supreme Court of the United States. Miller v. Conlee, 5 Sneed, 432; Dodds v. Duncan, 12 Lea, 731; State v. Gannaway, 16 Lea, 124.

In Railroad v. Byrne, supra, this court, speaking through Mr. Justice Shields, said:

"The establishment of the court [Supreme Court] and vesting it with appellate jurisdiction only is an implied declaration that it shall possess some revisory jurisdiction and powers, and that some right of appeal to it must exist. This inviolable jurisdiction, and the right to invoke it, undoubtedly extends to cases involving questions of law of great public importance; but no definite statement of it can be outlined, and each case must be determined with regard to the questions involved as it arises. The General Assembly may, by the establishment of courts of intermediate appellate jurisdiction or other appropriate legislation, limit and restrict the right of litigants to resort to it, and regulate the mode of doing so, but not so as to unreasonably interfere with or embarrass its ultimate revisory powers; and it is always for this court to decide when its constitutional jurisdiction is encroached upon. It has exercised this power since it was first established. Miller v. Conlee, supra; State v. Bank, supra; Chestnut v. McBride, 6 Baxt. 95; Newman v. Scott County Justices, 1 Heisk. 787; Ward v. Thomas, 2 Cold. 565; Hundhausen v. Marine Fire Insurance Co., 5 Heisk. 704; McElwee v. McElwee, 97 Tenn. 657, 37 S. W. 560; Chattanooga v. Keith, 115 Tenn. 589, 94 S. W. 62."

In that case the court further said:

"The right of direct resort to this court by appeal, appeal in nature of a writ of error, and writ of error to review judgments of trial courts was provided for by appropriate legislation when it was first established; and, notwithstanding many attempts have been made to limit and restrict this right, it has never been done, unless it is by the act of 1907 amending that creating the Court of Chancery Appeals. The statutes establishing the court of referees, the arbitration court, and the Court of Chancery Appeals, all courts of intermediate appellate jurisdiction, did not limit this right. Those courts had no direct revisory jurisdiction. All proceedings in error were taken directly to this court in the usual way, and it assigned such cases as it deemed proper to those for decision.

"These are matters that must be taken into consideration in construing and passing upon the validity and effect of all statutes which in any manner affect the jurisdiction of this court and the right to invoke it, under the well-settled rules that all statutes must be construed in connection with all others constituting the system of which they are a part, and that those which limit the jurisdiction of an established court, or confer it upon another court, are to be construed strictly, so as not to interfere with the exercise of that jurisdiction by the former court, unless the legislative intent that that be done affirmatively appears."

In Campbell County v. Wright, 127 Tenn. 6, 151 S. W. 412, this court said:

"Under section 7 of chapter 82 of the Acts of 1907, supra, it is clear that the jurisdiction of constitutional questions is withheld from the Court of Civil Appeals. It is true that this particular subject is not repeated in the sentence of that section which confers jurisdiction upon the Court of Civil Appeals of cases coming from the circuit courts of the state; but there could have been no reason why that court was denied jurisdiction of this class of subjects in cases coming from the chancery court, if it was to exercise such jurisdiction in cases appealed to it from the circuit court. We are of the opinion that, under a true construction of section 7, it was intended by the Legislature to withhold entirely from the Court of Civil Appeals jurisdiction of constitutional questions. Railroad v. Byrne, 119 Tenn. 278, 325–329, 104 S. W. 460."

The other questions presented by the petition to rehear were fully considered and determined in this court's written opinion filed on a previous day of the present term, and we are satisfied with the conclusions reached.

The petition to rehear is denied.

H. D. WATTS CO. v. HAUK, Revenue Agent, et al.

(Supreme Court of Tennessee. June 10, 1921.)

1. Corporations ⬅648—Levying privilege tax on foreign construction companies restrictive.

Acts 1915, c. 101, § 4, providing that each foreign construction company, with its chief office outside the state, operating or doing business in the state, directly or by agent, or by subletting contracts, shall pay a privilege tax of $150 per annum, is restrictive, and applies only to such companies engaged in the business of constructing bridges or other structures of a public nature, and does not include companies not falling within such class.

2. Statutes ⬅245—Statutes will not be extended by implication.

Statutes levying taxes or duties on citizens will not be extended by implication beyond the clear import of the language used, nor will their operation be enlarged so as to embrace matters or persons not specifically named or pointed out, but all questions of doubt arising on their construction will be resolved against the government and in favor of the citizen.

Appeal from Chancery Court, Hamilton County; W. B. Garvin, Chancellor.

Suit by the H. D. Watts Company against O. S. Hauk, Revenue Agent, and others. From decree for plaintiff, defendants appeal. Affirmed.

Miller & Miller, of Chattanooga, for H. D. Watts Co.

D. B. Vance, of Chattanooga, and Charles L. Cornelius, of Nashville, for Hauk and others.

HALL, J. This cause involves the liability of complainant for the privilege tax imposed on foreign construction companies by section 4 of chapter 101 of the Acts of 1915, which provides as follows:

"Sec. 4. Be it further enacted, that each vocation, occupation, and business hereinafter named in this section is hereby declared to be a privilege, and the rate of taxation on such privilege shall be as hereinafter fixed, which privilege shall be paid to the county court clerk as provided by law for the collection of revenue. * * *

"Each foreign construction company with its chief office outside of this state, operating or doing business in this state, directly or by agent, or by any subletting contract, each, per annum, in each county $150.00.

"Each domestic construction company and each foreign construction company, having its chief office in this state [doing business in this state], each, per annum, in each county $25.00.

"The above tax shall be paid by persons, firms, or corporations engaged in the business of constructing bridges, waterworks, railroads, street paving construction work, or other structures of a public nature."

It appears by stipulation that complainant is a foreign construction corporation with its situs in the state of Maryland, and has never been at any time engaged in the business of constructing bridges, waterworks, railroads, street paving, or other structures of a public nature, and that it has done no work in Tennessee, or taken any contract therein other than the erection of an office building for the Volunteer State Life Insurance Company, in the city of Chattanooga.

The defendants were proceeding to enforce the collection of the privilege tax of $150 imposed by the statute from complainant by a distress warrant, when they were enjoined from doing so by the present action instituted in the chancery court of Hamilton county.

On final hearing the chancellor decreed that complainant was not liable for the privilege tax, the collection of which had previously been enjoined, and said injunction was made perpetual.

From this decree defendants appealed to this court, and have assigned the action of the chancellor for error.

[1] We are of the opinion that there is no error in the decree of the chancellor. We think the act is restrictive, and applies only to construction companies engaged in the business of constructing bridges, waterworks, street paving, or other structures of a public nature. We do not think its provisions can be broadened by construction so as to include construction companies not falling within this class; and, it being stipulated that the complainant is not of the class named in said act, we are of the opinion that it cannot be held liable for the tax imposed by it. We think the first two clauses of the act are in-

tended as a statement simply of the tax itself, while the last clause is a statement of the persons, firms, or corporations liable for the tax.

[2] It is a well-settled rule of interpretation in this state that statutes levying taxes or duties upon citizens will not be extended by implication beyond the clear import of the language used, nor will their operation be enlarged so as to embrace matters or persons not specifically named or pointed out. All questions of doubt arising upon the construction of the statute will be resolved against the government and in favor of the citizen, because burdens are not to be imposed beyond what the statute expressly imports. Plow Co. v. Hays, 125 Tenn. 155, 140 S. W. 1068; English v. Crenshaw, 120 Tenn. 531, 110 S. W. 210, 17 L. R. A. (N. S.) 753, 127 Am. St. Rep. 1025; Memphis v. Bing, 94 Tenn. 644, 30 S. W. 745; Crenshaw v. Moore, 124 Tenn. 528, 137 S. W. 924, 34 L. R. A. (N. S.) 1161, Ann. Cas. 1913A, 165; Pryor v. Marion County, 140 Tenn. 399, 204 S. W. 1152, L. R. A. 1918F, 820.

The decree is affirmed, with costs.

ATHENS HOSIERY MILLS et al. v.
THOMASON, Comptroller.

(Supreme Court of Tennessee. June 18, 1921.)

1. Statutes ⬅181(1), 205—Legislative intent must be ascertained and given effect, and in doing so act must be considered as a whole.

It is the duty of the court, in the interpretation of statutes, to ascertain and give effect to the legislative intent, and in order to arrive at this purpose the court must consider the act as a whole.

2. Statutes ⬅107(1)—All sections of Factory Inspection Act held germane to subject.

The body of Acts 1919, c. 110, known as the Bureau of Workshop and Factory Inspection Act, does not contain two subjects, and does not violate Const. art. 2, § 17, although the act is both civil and criminal in its nature.

3. Inspection ⬅2—Factory Inspection Act provision for inspection fees held not violative of constitutional rule of uniformity in taxation.

Legislature had right to require the payment of reasonable inspection fees for the purpose of providing a fund for defraying the cost of maintaining the bureau under Acts 1919, c. 110, known as the Bureau of Workshop and Factory Inspection Act, and such act does not violate the uniformity of taxation requirement of Const. art. 2, § 28, merely because a surplus remains after the payment of all expenses.

4. Master and servant ⬅12—Factory Inspection Act constitutional.

Acts 1919, c. 110, known as the Bureau of Workshop and Factory Inspection Act, is not unconstitutional.

⬅For other cases see same topic and KEY-NUMBER in all Key-Numbered Digests and Indexes

Appeal from Chancery Court, Davidson County; Jas. B. Newman, Chancellor.

Suit by the Athens Hosiery Mills and others against John B. Thomason, Comptroller, etc. Decree for defendant, and complainants appeal. Affirmed.

Dan E. McGugin and Jno. M. Cate, both of Nashville, for Athens Hosiery Mills.

Frank M. Thompson, of Chattanooga, and W. H. Swiggart, Jr., of Nashville, for Thomason.

McKINNEY, J. This suit involves the constitutionality of chapter 110 of the Acts of 1919, known as the Bureau of Workshop and Factory Inspection Act.

It is insisted by the complainants that the act violates article 2, § 17, of the Constitution, which provides that—

"No bill shall become a law which embraces more than one subject, that subject to be expressed in the title."

Both the title and the body of the act are lengthy, and we will not here copy them in full.

The substance of the title might be said to be an act creating a bureau of workshop and factory inspection, appointing officers to manage same, and defining their duties. It is not necessary that those duties be set forth in detail in the caption.

Section 1 creates a bureau of workshop and factory inspection under the control of the chief mine inspector, with its office in the mining department.

Sections 2, 3, and 4 provide for a chief inspector, four deputy inspectors, a clerk, and stenographer, divides the state into districts, and provides that each inspector shall be assigned to a certain district.

Section 5 is as follows:

"Be it further enacted, that each deputy inspector of workshops and factories assigned to a district for the inspection of workshops and factories therein shall carefully inspect the sanitary conditions, systems of sewerage, situation and condition of water closets, systems of heating, lighting and ventilating rooms where persons are employed at labor, and means of exit in case of fire or other disasters within, or connected with, such workshops and factories. They shall examine the belting, shafting, gearing, elevators, drains and machinery in and about such workshops and factories, and see that they are not so located as to be dangerous to employees when engaged in their ordinary duties, and as far as practicable, securely guarded; that they shall see that each vat, pan, or structure, filled with molten lead or hot liquor is surrounded by proper safeguards for preventing accident or injury to persons employed at or near them. For the purpose of inspection or examination required of them by law, the chief inspector of workshops and factories, and each deputy inspector, at reasonable hours may enter any workshop or factory in the state."

Section 6 provides:

"That the inspector shall make an accurate record of all examinations and inspections of the workshops and factories inspected by each, showing the date inspected, the condition in which such workshops or factories are found, the extent to which laws relating thereto are observed or violated, the progress made in the improvement of the workshops and factories, and the conditions to insure the preservation of life and health by the provisions of this act and other laws, the enforcement of which are under the direction of the bureau of workshops and factory inspection," etc.

Section 7 authorizes the inspectors to administer oaths, etc.

Section 8 is as follows:

"Be it further enacted, that the term 'workshops and factories' as used in this act, shall include the following: Manufacturing, mills, mechanical, electrical, mercantile, art, and laundering establishments, printing, telegraph, and telephone offices; department stores, or any kind of establishment wherein labor is employed or machinery used."

Sections 9 to 16, inclusive, it is insisted, add new subjects to the act; hence we copy them in full, as follows:

"Sec. 9. Be it further enacted, that every factory, workshop, association, or other establishment in which five or more persons are employed shall be so ventilated while work is carried on therein that the air shall not become so exhausted as to become injurious to the health of the persons employed therein, and shall also be so ventilated as to render harmless, as far as practicable, all gases, vapors, dust or other impurities generated in the course of the manufacturing process or handicraft carried on therein.

"Sec. 10. Be it further enacted, that every factory, workshop, association, or other establishment where a work or process is carried on by which dust, filaments or injurious gases are produced or generated, that are liable to be inhaled by persons employed therein, the person, firm, or corporation by whose authority the said work or process is carried on shall cause to be provided and used in said workshop, factory association or establishment, exhaust fans, conveyors, receptacles, or blowers with pipes and hoods extending therefrom to each machine, contrivance or apparatus by which dust, filaments, or injurious gases are produced or generated; or provide other mechanical means to be maintained for the purpose of carrying off or receiving and collecting such dust, filament, devitalized air, or other impurities as may be detrimental to the health of those in, about, or in connection with such place as herein mentioned. Provided, that if natural ventilation sufficient to exclude the harmful elements above enumerated be provided, the requirement of this section shall have been complied with by such firm, corporation, association or other establishment as herein mentioned. Said fans, blowers, pipes and hoods shall be properly fitted and adjusted and of power and dimensions sufficient to effectually prevent the dust, filaments, or injurious gases produced, or generated by said machines, contrivances, or apparati from escaping into the atmosphere of the room or rooms of said factory, workshop or other establishment, where persons are employed.

"Sec. 11. Be it further enacted, that not less than two hundred and fifty (250) cubic feet of air space shall be provided for each employee or operative at work in a room or place within the meaning of this act between the hours of six o'clock in the morning, and the hours of six o'clock in the evening, and not less than four hundred (400) cubic feet of air space for each person so employed between the hours of six o'clock in the evening and six o'clock in the morning.

"Sec. 12. Be it further enacted, that in places of amusement wherein five or more employees are engaged in duties that appertain thereto, the owners, managers, proprietors or other persons in charge, shall provide that such places shall be well ventilated and that adequate and sufficient fire protection shall be maintained and that all exit doors of such amusement places shall be opened outward, wherein in addition to the said five employees fifty or more patrons might be congregated.

"Sec. 13. Be it further enacted, that no person shall hire, employ, or contract with another to manufacture, alter, repair or finish any article in any room, apartment, or tenement, unless said room, apartment or tenement, shall be well lighted and ventilated and shall contain at least five hundred (500) cubic feet of air space for every person working therein. Provided, that where children under the age of sixteen years live in such room, apartment, or tenement, they shall not engage in any work above specified without first obtaining a permit so to do from the bureau of workshop and factory inspection.

"Sec. 14. Be it further enacted, that the chief or deputies of the bureau of workshop and factory inspection shall have authority to ascertain the average weekly wages of all employees other than officers, and that the failure or refusal on the part of any manager, owner, foreman or other person in charge of any industry under inspection or investigation to furnish such information or answer any question pertaining to any inspection or investigation, shall constitute a violation of this act, and said manager, owner, foreman or other person found guilty thereof shall be punished as provided for herein.

"Sec. 15. Be it further enacted, that any owner, manager, foreman, or other person who may refuse, fail or neglect to comply with the orders issued by said chief or deputies shall be guilty of a misdemeanor and upon conviction thereof shall be punished by a fine of not less than fifty ($50.00) dollars, nor more than one hundred ($100.00) dollars, and in addition thereto a fine of five ($5.00) dollars for each day after the time limit elapsed until said order is carried out acceptably to said bureau chief or said deputies.

"Any fine thus imposed shall through the county court be paid to the state treasurer and be credited to the bureau of workshop and factory inspection, and shall be used in paying the incidental expenses of said bureau.

"Sec. 16. Be it further enacted, that no person shall remove or make ineffective any safeguard around or attached to any machinery, vats, pans or apparatus, except for the purpose of making repairs thereon, and all safeguards so removed shall be replaced promptly. Provided, when the machine or any part thereof is found to be in dangerous condition a notice shall be attached thereto, and such notice shall not be removed until the machinery is made safe, and the required safeguards are provided, and in the meantime such unguarded or dangerous machinery shall not be in use."

Section 17 is as follows:

"Be it further enacted, that every person, firm or corporation operating a factory, workshop or other establishment, required to be inspected under the provisions of this act, where there is installed and used machinery, or mechanical devices or apparatus, the use and operation of which are calculated to be hazardous in any degree, shall pay to the comptroller of the state of Tennessee for the use of the state, an inspection fee for each inspection made by the chief inspector of workshops or factories or any of his deputies according to the following schedule:

Industries employing not less than 5 nor more than 9 persons	$ 5 00
Industries employing not less than 10 nor more than 24 persons	7 50
Industries employing not less than 25 nor more than 49 persons	15 00
Industries employing not less than 50 nor more than 99 persons	25 00
Industries employing not less than 100 nor more than 249 persons	35 00
Industries employing not less than 250 nor more than 499 persons	50 00
Industries employing not less than 500 nor more than 999 persons	75 00
Industries employing more than 1,000 persons	100 00"

Section 18 provides that not more than one inspection shall be paid for during any one year.

Section 19 fixes the salaries of the inspectors.

It is unnecessary to refer to the other sections.

[1] It is the duty of the court, in the interpretation of statutes, to ascertain and give effect to the legislative intent, and in order to arrive at this purpose the court must consider the act as a whole.

The title to the act in question cannot be said to be in any sense restrictive, but is broad and comprehensive, creating a new department with officers to conduct it and referring to the body of the act for their powers and duties.

Taking the act as a whole, it is apparent that the Legislature had in mind the creation of a bureau of workshop and factory inspection for the purpose of regulating such institutions as fall within its purview, looking to the preservation of the life and health of those employed therein.

With this object in view said bureau was charged with the duty of seeing that the premises of such establishments are kept in a sanitary condition; that a proper sewerage system is maintained; that the rooms in which the work is carried on are properly heated, lighted, and ventilated; that proper exits in case of fire or other disasters are provided; that the machinery is not so located as to be dangerous to employees when engaged in their ordinary duties; that certain safeguards are provided for the prevention of accidents, etc.

All of the foregoing provisions are contained in section 5, and undeniably tend to preserve the life and health of the employees. The sections complained of are, in the main, amplifications of section 5. Section 9 provides for proper ventilation to avoid injury to health.

It is only necessary to read the other sections complained of to see that they fall within the same category.

As previously stated, the purpose of the entire act was the preservation of the life and health of the large body of our citizens who work in such institutions, and in order to effectuate that intention the department of workshop and factory inspection was created, with the power to inspect and regulate such institutions.

[2] None of the sections complained of are in any sense foreign to or incongruous with the subject of the act, but every provision is germane to the subject. All of the requirements of the act, whether incumbent upon the officers or the employers, are related and have a common purpose, viz., the preservation of the life and health of the employees of the designated institutions.

All of the provisions of the act tend to the same end. They are consistent parts of one general scheme. Although the act is both civil and criminal in its nature, yet the subject of legislation is single, and it is not therefore invalid. State v. Yardley, 95 Tenn. 557, 32 S. W. 481, 34 L. R. A. 656.

We are therefore of the opinion that the body of the act does not contain two subjects, as insisted by the complainants, and hence same does not violate article 2, § 17, of the Constitution.

[3] It is next insisted that the chancellor erred in not holding that said act is unconstitutional on the grounds that an inspection fee which is many times the cost of the inspection and therefore excessive, and which is paid into the state treasury and provides revenue for general state purposes, renders the act void, in that it is in contravention of section 28 of article 2 of the Constitution of Tennessee, as to uniformity in taxation.

Article 2 of section 28 of the Constitution is as follows:

"All property shall be taxed according to its value, that value to be ascertained in such manner as the Legislature shall direct, so that taxes shall be equal and uniform throughout the state. No one species of property from which a tax may be collected shall be taxed higher than any other species of property of the same value."

This contention is based upon the allegations of the bill that an inspector for this bureau spent less than two hours in going over and inspecting complainants' plant, and left after making one or two minor recommendations for safeguarding the employees in the plant, and that thereafter the comptroller demanded of complainants a fee of $50, under said act, for said inspection. The fee demanded is not in contravention of the constitutional provision invoked.

The act in question is a police regulation, enacted for the preservation of the life and health of those working in the establishments enumerated therein. The Legislature had the right to require the payment of reasonable fees for the purpose of providing a fund for defraying the costs of maintaining the bureau. The fact that a surplus remains after the payment of all expenses will not affect the validity of the act.

The opinion of this court in Rhinehart v. State, 121 Tenn. 420, 117 S. W. 508, 17 Ann. Cas. 254, is decisive of this contention, and we make reference thereto for a full discussion of this question.

The complainants undertake to differentiate that case from this one upon the statement in the opinion to the effect that the insurance companies would be benefited by the enforcement of the act involved. Conceding that to be a determinative fact, it can be stated with equal confidence that the institutions affected by the act in question will be benefited by its enforcement. It will avoid accidents and delays, will insure better attendance and greater efficiency on the part of employees, and, having a modern plant, from the standpoint of safety and health, will make it easier to secure labor.

[4] Upon the whole, we find no constitutional objection to the act. The chancellor held the act to be constitutional, and his decree will be affirmed, with costs.

MOUNTAIN WATER CO. v. MAY.

(Court of Appeals of Kentucky.   June 14, 1921.)

Waters and water courses ⚖=201—Extension denied consumer under circumstances of hardship to company.

Ordinarily a consumer may compel a water company to extend its mains to any part of the city where its franchise requires it to operate, but the right is not absolute, and may be denied where the demand is wholly unreasonable in view of the hardships and disastrous consequences which would follow, as where the company's income is consumed in the operation and maintenance of its plant, its franchise expires in about two years, and it has no funds on hand with which to make the extension.

Appeal from Circuit Court, Pike County.

Suit by L. J. May against the Mountain Water Company. From judgment granting plaintiff a mandatory injunction, defendant appeals. Judgment reversed, and cause remanded, with directions to enter judgment in conformity with the opinion.

Auxier, Harman & Francis, of Pikeville, for appellant.

Picklesimer & Steele and Willis Staton, all of Pikeville, for appellee.

CLAY, C. On the application of L. J. May, a resident of Pikeville, a mandatory injunction was granted compelling the Mountain Water Company to extend its pipe line from its main line along High street to a point opposite May's residence, for the purpose of affording him the necessary water connection. The company appeals.

The facts are as follows:

The Mountain Water Company is operating its waterworks system in Pikeville, a city of the fourth class, under a franchise which became effective August 29, 1908, and expires February 28, 1923. After providing that the water pipes should be placed in the center of the streets, alleys, and public highways, the franchise contract provides as follows:

"Sec. 5. Said water works and sewerage system shall be for the use of inhabitants generally, and no street or locality shall be deprived of, nor discriminated against, in the use thereof."

High street was not opened up until the year 1914, and there are only three or four residences on the street. To reach the May premises it will be necessary for the company to extend its main for a distance of 725 feet, and the expense will amount to about $3,500. If the relief be granted in this case, the residents on other streets are preparing to make similar demands, and to meet these demands the cost of material alone will be about $16,000. When the extensions are made, the income therefrom will be wholly insufficient to pay the interest on the expenditure, to say nothing of the cost of maintenance. Furthermore, the company has an outstanding indebtedness of $7,500. It pays no dividends, and its entire income is consumed in the operation and maintenance of its plant. It has no funds on hand with which to make the extensions, and, in view of the fact that its franchise expires in 1923, it is unable to borrow the money. If compelled to make the extensions, the company will be thrown into bankruptcy, and will be unable to furnish fire protection for the city, or to continue the service to those who are now using its water.

This is not a case where a public service commission has the power to determine when and upon what terms a water company shall extend its mains for the purpose of meeting the demands of the inhabitants of the municipality. Nor is it a case where the city itself, if engaged in furnishing water to its inhabitants, and therefore exercises a governmental discretion with which the courts will not interfere. Moore v. City Council of Harrodsburg, 105 S. W. 926, 32 Ky. Law Rep. 395; Browne v. Bentonville, 94 Ark. 80, 126 S. W. 93; Linck v. Litchfield, 31 Ill. App. 118; Lawrence v. Richards, 111 Me. 95, 88 Atl. 92, 47 L. R. A. (N. S.) 654. On the contrary, it is a case where an independent corporation exercises a franchise under a contract providing in substance that the waterworks shall be for the use of the inhabitants generally, and that no street or locality shall be deprived of or discriminated against in the use thereof. Under this contract it is the duty of the water company, as new streets are opened within the limits of the city as they existed when the franchise was granted, and residences are built thereon, to extend its mains so as to furnish the occupants of such residences with water. Ordinarily, a mandamus or mandatory injunction will lie at the instance of a consumer to compel a water company to extend its mains to any part of the city where its franchise requires it to operate. Topeka v. Topeka Water Co., 58 Kan. 349, 49 Pac. 79; West Hartford v. Board of Water Com'rs, 68 Conn. 323, 36 Atl. 786; Bothwell v. Consumers' Co., 13 Idaho, 568, 92 Pac. 533, 24 L. R. A. (N. S.) 485; Hatch v. Consumers' Co., 17 Idaho, 204, 104 Pac. 670, 40 L. R. A. (N. S.) 263.

The right to such relief, however, is not absolute, and the relief may be denied where the demand is wholly unreasonable, in view of the peculiar hardships and disastrous consequences that would follow. Doubtless the mere fact that the income from the extended service would not compensate the company for the cost of the extension would furnish no cause for refusing to compel the service required by the contract, if its income were otherwise sufficient, and the rights of the public would not be injuriously affected, but the circumstances here presented do not stop there. The franchise expires in about two years. The company's income is consumed in the operation and maintenance of the plant. It has no funds on hand with which to make the extension, and is unable to borrow the money. If compelled to make the extension, the company will be thrown into bankruptcy, and will be unable to furnish fire protection for the city, or to continue the service to those who are using its water. It is clear, therefore, that the rights of the public at large would be injuriously affected if the relief prayed for should be granted. In our opinion, the case is one where the rights of the few should give way to the rights of the many, and, in the circumstances, a mandatory injunction will not lie to compel the company to make the extension. Public Service Commission v. Brooklyn, etc., Water Co., 122 Md. 612, 90 Atl. 89.

Judgment reversed, and cause remanded, with directions to enter judgment in conformity with this opinion.

LOUISVILLE GAS & ELECTRIC CO. et al. v. CITY OF LOUISVILLE.

(Court of Appeals of Kentucky. March 25, 1921. Rehearing Denied June 24, 1921.)

1. Limitation of actions ⬤=95(1)—Cause of action on gas company construction bond accrued when insufficiency of construction discovered.

In action by city against a company furnishing natural gas to the city and its inhabitants and against the surety on the bond of the gas company, held that, while the bond was a temporary bond intended to guarantee the faithful performance of the contract to construct a pipe line and equipment as called for in the gas company's franchise contract, yet, if such construction was not done within the year limited by the contract so as to conform to the franchise contract, so that, by such failure to perform, the supply of gas was insufficient or the pressure too low, recovery could be had by the city, even several years after the year for such construction, if the failure to perform the contract was not sooner discovered.

2. Gas ⬤=9—Gas company's franchise and construction bond construed.

Under a gas company's franchise contract, obligating it to construct or cause to be constructed a pipe line or lines of size to carry 12,000,000 cubic feet of gas per day from the most available source of supply in the state of West Virginia to the city giving the franchise, and to complete the line and begin to furnish gas within a year, and a bond guaranteeing such completion held that, where the

work was promptly begun and completed, if completed at all, within less than the year stipulated, there could be no recovery by the city on the bond unless the bond was breached by the gas company's failure to carry the pipe line to and connect it with the then most available source of supply of natural gas in the state of West Virginia, or by its failure to equip the pipe line with such machinery as was reasonably necessary to drive 12,000,000 cubic feet of gas in cold and unfavorable weather through the pipes to the city.

3. Gas ⬤=9—Gas company's franchise and construction bond construed.

Under a franchise contract and bond requiring a gas company to build or cause to be built a pipe line of certain capacity from the most available source of supply of natural gas in the state of West Virginia to the city to be supplied, held, that the gas company was not required itself to build or own the pipe line, but was required to have only such ownership or control over the line for the life of the franchise as to insure a compliance with its terms, and the bond would not be breached if the entire line were constructed or owned by another if the gas company had such control over it as would enable it to carry out its franchise obligation.

4. Gas ⬤=9—In city's suit on gas company's construction bond, answer held to state good defense.

In action by city on gas company's construction bond, the answer alleging the furnishing of a continuous pipe line to supply natural gas, and equipping the line with machinery to drive gas through it in cold and unfavorable weather, held not demurrable.

5. Damages ⬤=79(1)—Gas company's construction bond held to provide liquidated damages, not a penalty.

A gas company's construction bond for $250,000 held to provide liquidated damages and not a penalty, in view of the impossibility of ascertaining the loss or damage which would be sustained by the city from a failure of the gas company to construct adequate facilities for delivering the gas contracted for by its franchise contract.

Appeal from Circuit Court, Jefferson County, Common Pleas Branch, Fourth Division.

Action by the City of Louisville against the Louisville Gas & Electric Company and the National Surety Company. From judgment for plaintiff, defendants appeal. Reversed.

Alex. P. Humphrey and Matt O'Doherty, both of Louisville, and Cummins, Rolmer, Flynn & McKenna, of Chicago, Ill., for appellants.

Jos. S. Lawton, of Louisville, for appellee.

SAMPSON, J. This cause was instituted by the city of Louisville against the Louisville Gas & Electric Company and the National Surety Company to recover $250,000, on a bond executed by the gas company to the city under section 6 of a franchise granted by the city to the gas company, by the terms of which franchise it was provided that the gas company "shall in 40 days after the acceptance of the bid of grantee execute a bond to the city of Louisville with good and sufficient surety, to be approved by said city, in the sum of $250,000, conditioned upon the carrying out of the provisions of this section of this ordinance as to the beginning, continuance, and completion of the laying of said pipe line and beginning to furnish natural gas thereby." This ordinance was approved by the city, March 29, 1913, and created a franchise or privilege of acquiring, laying, maintaining, and operating in the streets, avenues, alleys, and public ways of the city of Louisville a system of mains, pipes, and appliances for the distribution and sale of natural gas, manufactured gas, and mixed gas, and providing for the sale of said franchise. The first section of the franchise reads:

"1. There is hereby created the franchise or privilege of acquiring, laying, maintaining and operating in the streets, avenues, alleys and public ways of the city of Louisville, Kentucky, a system of mains, pipes, fixtures and appliances for the distribution and sale of natural gas, manufactured gas and mixed gas for heating and lighting and other purposes."

The third section says:

"The grantee shall have the right, privilege, permission, authority, and franchise, subject to the provisions hereof and to all powers reserved to said city, to acquire, lay, construct, maintain and operate a system of mains and pipes, in, along, through and under the streets, avenues, alleys, and public ways within the corporate boundaries of the city of Louisville as they now exist or may hereafter be extended and on and under the bridges and viaducts owned and controlled by said city for distributing and selling natural, manufactured and mixed gas."

The sixth provision of the franchise reads as follows:

"Said grantee, his successors or assigns, shall within sixty (60) days after the acceptance of this ordinance begin and continue to lay a main line or lines of pipe or cause the same to be done from the most available source of supply of natural gas in the state of West Virginia to the city of Louisville, which said main line or lines shall consist of continuous piping and be a piping capable of withstanding a pressure of three hundred and fifty (350) pounds per square inch and be of a size having a capacity for supplying twelve million (12,000,000) cubic feet of gas per day to said city and provided with all necessary equipment to supply the capacity aforesaid, and said grantee shall complete said line or lines of pipe within one year from the passage and acceptance of this ordinance, unless prevented from so doing by the delays of bona fide litigation or by other cause or causes beyond the control of the grantee. And said grantee shall immediately thereafter commence to supply natural gas to consumer up to the capacity aforesaid, provided

that if the work herein authorized be delayed by injunction, bona fide litigation or by other cause or causes beyond the control of the grantee such delay or delays shall not be considered in estimating the time within which such work shall be commenced and complete and natural gas supplied. Said supply of twelve million (12,000,000) cubic feet per day shall not be reduced by reason of any connections being made with said pipe line being made between the city of Louisville and the source of supply. And said grantee, his successors or assigns shall in forty (40) days after the acceptance of the bid of grantee execute a bond to the city of Louisville with good and sufficient surety, to be approved by said city in the sum of two hundred and fifty thousand ($250,000) dollars conditioned upon the carrying out of the provisions of this section of this ordinance as to the beginning, continuance and completion of the laying of said pipe line and beginning to furnish natural gas thereby and upon said conditions being fulfilled said bond shall terminate and sureties be released, and said bond shall be given as additional security to the bond provided for in section 7."

This section of the franchise is the one under which this action was instituted, but sections 7 and 8, which we here copy, will aid in the consideration of the questions involved:

"Sec. 7. The grantee shall, within forty (40) days after the acceptance of the bid of grantee execute a bond to the city of Louisville, with good and sufficient sureties to be approved by the city, in the sum of fifty thousand ($50,000) dollars, conditioned upon the faithful performance and discharge of all the obligations imposed upon the grantee by this ordinance, including the obligations imposed by section 6 hereof, and conditioned that the grantee shall restore the sidewalks and pavements and all public ways to the original condition and maintain the same as provided in section 4, and shall save the city harmless from all loss and damage which may be done to its public ways or other property, or to persons or property of individuals by the conduct of the grantee's business, or arising out of the uses and privileges herein granted. Said bond shall be renewed from time to time as and when required by the city of Louisville. Said bond shall further be conditioned that the grantee shall defend all suits and pay all judgments against the city of Louisville and hold the city free from all liability arising out of the construction, maintenance, or operation of the grantee's mains, conduits, or other apparatus in the public ways of the city of Louisville.

"8. The quality of natural gas, or natural and manufactured gas to be furnished shall be adequate and proper for the uses and purposes herein named and shall not be less than seven hundred (700) British thermal units to the cubic feet as furnished at the point of consumption, and the pressure at no time shall be less than three ounces nor more than twelve ounces to the square inch at the point of consumption, and these facts shall be ascertained by the gas inspector provided for in section 9 hereof, and in case the quality of gas furnished shall in any month for an aggregate period of seventy-two hours fall below said

:andard of seven hundred (700) British ther-
ial units to the cubic foot at the point of con-
umption then the bills for that month of all
onsumers shall be reduced directly in the proportion that the average number of British
hermal units furnished below said standard
luring any such period of seventy-two hours,
or any period said gas falls below said standard
ibove said period of seventy-two, shall bear
:o the standard of seven hundred (700) British
thermal units established herein, and if the
pressure at the point of consumption shall in
any month for an aggregate period of seventy-
two hours fall below said standard herein fixed,
then all bills of consumers for gas furnished
during said month shall be discounted 10 per
cent. from the net price or rate provided, and
if said time that such natural gas falls below
such standard in such month exceeds seventy-
two hours then said bills shall be discounted
an additional 10 per cent. for each additional
seventy-two hours or portion thereof."

Certain provisions of section 12 of the ordinance are relied upon by appellant gas company and others, and we here copy so much
of section 12 as is pertinent to the issues:

"12. The object of the franchise 'hereby
created is to make available for the people of
Louisville natural gas at a rate commensurate
with the cost of natural gas to the people of
other cities similarly situated and below the
cost of manufactured gas, and said grantee
shall take all reasonable precaution and measures necessary to furnish natural gas hereunder, during the life of this franchise, but in
event said grantee shall, through no fault of
his own, be unable to supply natural gas in sufficient quantities to meet the demand for same,
and it shall become necessary to use a material
quantity of manufactured gas, the grantee shall
give written notice thereof to the mayor, the
board of public works, and the general council
and thereupon the board of public works shall,
by experts employed by it, make a thorough
investigation of all the facts relating to the
inability of the grantee to supply natural gas
and also of all the facts bearing on the reasonableness of rates for natural gas mixed
with manufactured gas, or for manufactured
gas, and in making said investigation said
board or said experts shall have the right to
examine the plant, business, books and records
of said grantee and said board of public works
shall, after a full hearing of the grantee, find
whether or not said grantee's claim that he is
unable to supply natural gas is well founded,
and shall report said finding to the general
council and also report all the facts which it
has ascertained by said investigation, and the
general council shall after considering said report and taking into consideration all the conditions surrounding the furnishing of said natural gas mixed with manufactured gas, or manufactured gas fix reasonable rates to be charged therefor in the event it shall find that said
grantee is unable to furnish natural gas in sufficient quantities as required by the franchise."

In executing the bond required under section 6, above quoted, the National Surety
Company became surety and co-obligor of the
gas company, and is therefore made a party

defendant. This bond for $250,000 is the
one sued on, and reads as follows:

"Know all men by these presents that the
undersigned, Louisville Gas & Electric Company, a corporation organized under the laws
of the state of Kentucky (hereinafter called
the Gas & Electric Company), as principal,
and National Surety Company, a corporation
organized under the laws of the state of New
York, as surety, parties of the first part, and
the city of Louisville (hereinafter called the
city), party of the second part, witnesses that
the said first parties are held and bound unto
the city in the full sum of two hundred and
fifty thousand ($250,000) dollars, payment
whereof well and truly to be made, the said
first parties do hereby bind themselves, their
successors and assigns, firmly by these presents, as witness the hands and seals of the
first parties hereunto affixed this July 8, 1913.

"The condition of the above obligation is such
that, whereas the city, by an ordinance approved March 29, 1913, created and provided for
the sale of a franchise or privilege of acquiring,
laying, maintaining, and operating in the
streets, avenues, alleys, and public ways of
the city of Louisville, Kentucky, a system of
mains, pipes, and appliances for the distribution and the sale of natural gas, manufactured
gas, and mixed gas, and the sale of said franchise as therein provided was thereafter duly
made, and the Louisville Gas Company became the bidder at said sale, and its bid was
accepted by the general council of the city of
Louisville, and payment was made by the
Louisville Gas Company of the purchase price
of said franchise, and since that date the
Louisville Gas Company has by agreement of
consolidation with sundry other companies,
formed the Gas & Electric Company, one of
the parties of the first part, and by said agreement of consolidation said franchise has passed
to said Gas & Electric Company:

"Now, if the Gas & Electric Company shall
carry out the provisions of section 6 of said
ordinance as to the beginning, continuance, and
completion of the laying of the pipe line therein described and the beginning to furnish natural gas thereby, the said pipe line to be a main
line or lines of continuous piping from the most
available source of supply of natural gas in
the state of West Virginia to the city of Louisville and capable of withstanding a pressure
of three hundred and fifty (350) pounds per
square inch and to be of a size having a capacity for supplying twelve million (12,000,000)
cubic feet of gas per day to said city, and provided with all necessary equipment to supply
the capacity aforesaid, then this obligation
shall be void; otherwise in full force and
virtue."

The petition admits that the gas company
within 60 days after it acquired the franchise
in July, 1913, commenced to put down a 12-
inch line of pipe from Louisville to Inez, Ky.,
a distance of about 180 miles, which reaches
within about 4 miles of the West Virginia
border, but it avers that the gas company did
not lay down a line of pipe in accordance
with section 6 of said franchise and the terms
of the bond sued on.

The alleged breaches of the bond are briefly the following:

(1) The defendant never laid a main or any line or lines of pipe, or caused the same to be done, from the most available source of supply of natural gas in the state of West Virginia to the city of Louisville.

(2) That the line laid down by defendant company did not and does not constitute a continuous piping provided with all necessary or sufficient equipment required to supply a capacity of 12,000,000 cubic feet of gas per day to said city, and it is further alleged that defendant did not immediately after the completion of said line commence to supply natural gas to consumers in the city of Louisville up to 12,000,000 cubic feet of natural gas per day, and never has supplied 12,000,000 cubic feet of natural gas to its consumers in said city, although its consumers and customers in said city have often demanded said amount of gas for their use.

(3) That defendant made connection with other pipe lines between the source of supply in West Virginia and the city of Louisville, and thus reduced its ability to supply 12,000,000 cubic feet of gas per day, as per its contract and bond.

(4) That defendant knew and had full opportunity to know when it laid down its pipe line that it was connecting with a field of supply of natural gas in West Virginia which was deficient and inadequate as a source of supply to enable it to perform and carry out its obligations and the obligations of said bond.

(5) That the defendant company never owned and does not now own any gas fields or wells, pipe lines, or equipments in West Virginia for producing and supplying natural gas, but is merely transmitting and distributing gas which it purchased under a contract from the United Fuel Gas Company, a corporation operating in West Virginia.

(6) That by the terms of the contract which the defendant gas company made with the United Fuel Gas Company of West Virginia to which the city of Louisville was not a party, it is provided that the city of Louisville shall only have the surplus supply of gas which the United Fuel Gas Company may have or acquire from its several sources after it has supplied certain other consumers, as follows: (a) The quantities of natural gas then deliverable to the Columbia Gas and Electric Company; (b) the quantities of natural gas necessary to supply at any and all times to the distributing company in the town of Portsmouth, Ohio; (c) such quantities not exceeding the capacity of an 18-inch pipe line as United Company shall then be delivering to the United Fuel Company; (d) such quantities not exceeding the capacity of an 18-inch pipe line as United Company shall then be delivering to the Hope Natural Gas Company; (e) such quantities not exceeding the capacity of a 10-inch pipe line as United Company shall then be delivering to the Central Kentucky Natural Gas Company.

The petition further alleges that the line of pipe from Louisville to Inez, Ky., was connected at the latter point with a 16-inch pipe line belonging to the United Fuel Supply Company, and with a 10-inch pipe line running to Lexington and other Central Kentucky cities and towns, and this 16-inch line of the United Company was intended to supply gas to both the 12-inch Louisville line and the 10-inch Lexington and Central Kentucky lines, but this 10-inch Lexington and Central Kentucky line had a prior contract with the United Fuel Gas Company for a large supply of gas, and this quantity, according to the contract referred to, was required for supply to Lexington and other Central Kentucky towns before the city of Louisville was entitled to take any part of the gas carried in the 16-inch pipe line from West Virginia to Inez, Ky., and was further reduced by other pipe lines carrying gas to other consumers which consumers had priority rights in the gas over the city of Louisville.

The original answer of the defendant gas company is in five paragraphs, the first of which is a traverse with reservations and admissions. For instance, the first paragraph denies that "it did not lay down said pipe line in accordance with section 6 of said franchise and in accordance with said bond; * * * denies that said defendant has not fulfilled the conditions of said bond and said section 6 of said franchise, or that it has violated said conditions, or any of them, or that it has never at any time carried out the provision of said section 6 of said franchise, or the provisions of said bond in any of the particulars in the petition named," but it admits that "it is true that the Louisville Gas & Electric Company has never owned nor does it now own any gas fields, gas wells, or equipments in West Virginia for producing or supplying natural gas," but they deny that said defendant is merely a transmitting or distributing company. The answer further says:

"It is true that the defendant gets its supply of natural gas from West Virginia under a contract with the United Fuel Gas Company, a copy of which is filed with the petition. Defendant says it is true that the Louisville pipe line is connected at Inez, Ky., with a 16-inch pipe line belonging to the United Fuel Gas Company, and not with the Fuel Supply Company named in the petition."

It is also alleged that a 10-inch pipe line running to Lexington, Ky., had theretofore been connected at Inez with said 16-inch pipe line, but they deny that said connection was made at the same point or place that the Louisville line was connected. They say it is true that the said 16-inch pipe line of the United Fuel Gas Company runs from Inez into the state of Kentucky, and to a point in West Virginia called Kermit, and at said point connected with other mains and pipe lines of the United Fuel Gas Company running to various gas fields in West Virginia.

The traverse also admits that small quantities of gas have been sold by the gas company from its line between its source of supply and the city of Louisville, and it admits that it furnished an inferior grade of natural gas from Meade county, Ky., to its customers in Louisville. There are other admissions in the first paragraph of the answer.

The second and third paragraphs of the answer plead in bar of the maintenance of the present action two other actions by the city of Louisville against the Louisville Gas & Electric Company, but these two paragraphs have been abandoned by the defendant and need not further be noticed.

The fourth paragraph of the answer pleads an estoppel. In fact, a large part of the allegations of this paragraph read like a counterclaim, for it is averred that the gas company very generously bid in the franchise and paid $25,000 for it, and then put in a pipe line with a capacity of 14,000,000 cubic feet of gas per day, whereas they were only required to put in one of a capacity to carry 12,000,000 cubic feet; that said pipe line was of a strength to resist a pressure of 400 pounds per square inch, when the contract only required them to put in a pipe of the strength of 350 pounds to the square inch; that the gas company had a year from July 1, 1913, in which to complete its line and begin to furnish gas to the city of Louisville, but it made many sacrifices in order to sooner complete the line and to begin to furnish gas at an earlier date, and thus saved to the inhabitants of Louisville at least $100,000, which they would have paid for artificial gas in excess of the price paid for the natural gas. It also avers that it sustained certain losses by reason of its hurried construction of the pipe line.

It then avers that, while it did allow certain landowners along the line of its pipe from whom the company had to obtain a right of way, the privilege of tapping its main line and thus obtain a supply of gas suited to their needs, it insists that the quantity thus taken was and is negligible and would not in any event exceed 2 per cent. of the total supply of gas carried by the pipe. It next avers that the contract which it made with the United Fuel Company of West Virginia, whereby the latter company was to furnish the gas to be carried to and sold in Louisville, was necessarily made subject to the contracts made by the United Fuel Gas Company with other

231 S.W.—58

concerns previous to the date of the contract made for the Louisville supply, and was the best contract obtainable at that time, and was subject to the priority rights of all the older contracts for gas supplying Cincinnati, Cleveland, Columbus, Portsmouth, and other cities, and it avers that this contract was made by it with the knowledge and consent of the city of Louisville, that the city of Louisville knew of the capacity and availability of the said gas field at the time it entered into the contract with the gas company, and further that the said city knew of the purpose and intention of the gas company to enter into said contract with the United Fuel Company of West Virginia, and it pleads and relies upon these facts as an estoppel against the city and its right to recover because the pipe line constructed by the gas company did not reach the most available source of supply of natural gas in the state of West Virginia, and as an estoppel to the city to complain of the nature and character of contract which the gas company made with the United Gas Company of West Virginia.

The fifth paragraph of the answer sets forth section 12 of the ordinance and prints in black letters that part thereof which says that the grantee (the gas company) "shall take all reasonable precaution and measures necessary to furnish natural gas" to the city of Louisville. It then avers that the winter of 1917–18 was unusually cold, and that up to that time it had supplied the city of Louisville with ample gas, sometimes a greater quantity than 12,000,000 cubic feet per day, and owing to the extreme weather during the winter 1917–18, and the further fact that coal was high and the factories in the cities of Columbus, Portsmouth, Toledo, Cincinnati, and other cities used gas instead of coal in their work on war orders for the United States government, the supply of natural gas from the West Virginia field was depleted, and the gas company was unable to supply, for only a few days, the demands for the city of Louisville under its contract in accordance with its charter provisions. It further says that, while its line was of sufficient capacity and thoroughly equipped with all appliances necessary to supply the city of Louisville with 12,000,000 cubic feet of gas per day when this extreme weather in the winter of 1917–18 came on, it found for the first time that it needed compressors to force the gas through the pipe lines to the city, and that it immediately called upon the United Fuel Gas Company of West Virginia to provide and install compressors for the purpose, and that the said United Gas Company did immediately place an order with a competent and responsible manufacturing establishment for new and additional gas-compressing machines which it contracted to have installed in operation at a given date;

that the manufacturers entered upon the performance of the contract to make and install the compressing machinery, but before said contract was or could be complied with the War Department of the United States government, acting under and in pursuance of the powers vested in it by the Constitution and laws of the United States, issued a priority order to the said manufacturer by which it was compelled to suspend the further execution of the said contract with the said United Fuel Gas Company and to execute instead certain other orders for the United States government given priority thereto, and the gas company pleads and relies upon its inability, owing to the government priority order, to get said compressors, as a defense to the claim of the city in this action.

The fourth paragraph of the answer was amended, but the amendment only set out with greater particularity the facts upon which the gas company relied as an estoppel in the original answer.

A general demurrer was filed to the answer as amended, and in sustaining this general demurrer the court delivered an exhaustive and able opinion, covering more than 40 printed pages in the record.

A second amended answer was then filed by the gas company to which a general demurrer was also sustained by the court, and another opinion delivered dealing in large part with the same questions discussed in his first opinion.

A third amended answer was then filed and a general demurrer was interposed' to the answer as amended for the third time and again sustained, and an opinion delivered by the learned circuit judge.

The city then moved the court for a judgment on the pleadings, to which the defendant gas company objected, and the motion being submitted, and the gas company declining to further plead, its objection to the submission on the motion for a judgment on the pleading was overruled, and the motion sustained, whereupon it was adjudged by the court that the plaintiff, city of Louisville, recover of the defendants, Louisville Gas & Electric Company and the National Surety Company, the sum of $250,000, with interest, etc. From this judgment the gas company and surety company appeal.

The appellants make the following contentions:

(1) The trial court construed the ordinance as requiring the gas company not only to begin to furnish 12,000,000 feet of gas per day as demanded, within one year after the purchase of the franchise, but that there was a continuing contract to furnish this quantity during the whole 20 years of the franchise.

(2) That this obligation upon the part of the gas company was included in and secured by the terms of the bond sued on.

(3) That the following language in section 6:

"Said supply of twelve million (12,000,000) cubic feet per day shall not be reduced by reason of any connections with said pipe line being made between the city of Louisville and the source of supply"

—was a hard and fast inhibition against the gas company's making such connections, and not an inhibition limited to such a connection as would reduce the amount of gas that should be furnished the city below 12,000,000 feet of gas per day.

(4) That this inhibition against the making of such connections was included within the terms of the bond.

(5) That, although the gas company did complete its pipe line in strict conformity to the terms of section 6, and did begin to furnish gas to the extent of 12,000,000 feet a day as demanded, within a year subsequent to its purchase of the franchise, and continued so to do down to December, 1917 (except for 40 hours in February, 1917), yet its failure to furnish the 12,000,000 feet of gas per day during the winter of 1917–18, connected with the character of contract which it made with the United Fuel Gas Company of West Virginia, constituted a breach of section 6 of the franchise ordinance, and of the terms of the bond.

The brief of appellant then argues the same contentions as follows:

(1) So far as concerns an obligation on the part of the gas company to furnish the 12,000.000 feet of gas per day during the life of the franchise, we have this to say: That we have been utterly unable to find any language in any part of this franchise ordinance that requires this, and have applied in vain to the court and counsel to point out any such language. The most that can be said is that under section 12 of the ordinance it is provided as follows:

"The object of the franchise hereby created is to make available for the people of Louisville natural gas, at a rate commensurate with the cost of natural gas to the people of other cities similarly situated, and below the cost of manufactured gas, and said grantee shall take all reasonable precautions and measures necessary to furnish natural gas hereunder during the life of this franchise."

This section goes on to provide that, if the gas company finds that through no fault of its own it is unable to supply natural gas in sufficient quantities to meet the demand for the same, it shall give a certain notice to the board of public works of the city of Louisville of that fact.

(2) There is absolutely no language whatsoever in the bond imposing any such obligation. On the contrary, the bond speaks

of "beginning to furnish natural gas thereby," viz. by the completion of the pipe line, and says nothing whatever in reference to any obligation to continue to furnish the gas during the currency of the franchise.

(3) and (4) There is absolutely nothing contained in the language of the bond to the effect that the gas company will not make connections with its line for the purpose of supplying other people or other communities with gas through its pipe line. However this clause in regard to making connections shall be construed, whether as an absolute inhibition of making any connection, or simply an inhibition against making a connection, which will prevent the proper supply to the city of Louisville, there is absolutely nothing in the terms of the bond that concerns this matter in one way or the other. And just here we may suggest this: Suppose five years after this pipe line had been laid the gas company had made such a connection could it possibly be said that this involved a breach of this particular bond?

(5) Again we must consider, in this solution of this case, whether a failure of gas supply four years and more after the completion of the pipe line can be taken as a breach of the bond sued on.

In determining the question now before the court, it must be always carefully kept in mind that by the terms of section 6 of the ordinance the bond therein provided for was expressly declared to be a temporary bond; that is to say, the conclusion of section 6 provides:

"And upon said conditions being fulfilled said bond shall terminate and said sureties be released."

To the foregoing arguments the appellee city says:

(1) That the basic reasons for violations of the bond were the limitations placed in appellant's contract with United Company and agreed to by appellant before appellant completed its line, together with the connections to its line whereby a supply of 12,000,000 cubic feet to Louisville was reduced, which contract and connections vested said United Company with the right and power from the very beginning to shut off the gas to Louisville whenever the contingencies referred to in said contract between United Company and appellant might arise. Said contract rendered appellant company powerless to control the supply of gas necessary to fulfill its franchise obligations covered by this bond.

(2) Appellant, within a year from the acceptance of this franchise, made and has continued to rely on a contract with another corporation to supply the gas which appellant company agreed to furnish to the city, and has by that contract placed it in the power of said other corporation to at

any time during the continuance of the defendant's franchise withhold any part or completely shut off the supply of gas necessary to fulfill the obligations of its franchise. A present capacity, power, and means to fulfill its franchise obligation were never possessed by the appellant within one year after the acceptance of the franchise. Appellant gas company did not lay down a main line or cause the same to be done to the most available source of supply of natural gas from the state of West Virginia to the city, and did not provide said line with all necessary equipment to supply a capacity of 12,000,000 cubic feet, and appellant company made connections with its pipe line whereby the supply of 12,000,000 cubic feet per day was reduced.

(4) The plea of impossibility of performance is not tenable in this action, because the conditions which appellant gas company now offers as an excuse for nonperformance of the obligations of this bond were made effective solely by its voluntary and unauthorized acts. If it had not entered into such a contract with the United Company, putting Louisville in such a subordinate position, and had not made such connections with its line reducing the supply, contrary to the very letter and spirit of this bond, none of the conditions now offered as its excuse could have in any way affected Louisville's supply.

The question is: Does the answer of the gas company, as a whole, present a defense to the action of the city? As all of the material allegations of the petition were either controverted or avoided by what we regard as a sufficient affirmative pleading, we think it does.

[1] While the bond sued on is a temporary bond intended to guarantee the faithful performance of the construction contract, yet, if the pipe line was not constructed within the year so as to conform to the franchise contract, and by reason of the failure of the gas company to keep and perform the terms of the contract guaranteed by the bond the supply of gas was insufficient or the pressure too low, a recovery may be had by the city, even at this time, if the failure to perform the contract was not sooner discovered.

[2] This litigation only calls for a correct construction and interpretation of the franchise ordinance, especially section 6 thereof, and the bond sued on. The parties do not agree about the meaning of these two instruments. It was the object of the city of Louisville in granting the franchise to obtain, if possible, for its citizens an adequate and regular supply of natural gas at reasonable rates. The gas company desired to and it did obtain practically the exclusive right to engage in the business of distributing and selling gas in the city of Louisville, out of which it expected a profit. So in dealing the parties finally entered into an agreement which is evidenced by the ordinance contract.

The storm center of this controversy is around section 6 of the contract, which required the gas company not only to do certain construction work and other things, but to give a bond in the sum of $250,000 for the faithful performance of this undertaking.

The gas company agreed to begin, or cause to be begun, within 60 days from the acceptance of the ordinance, the building of a pipe line or lines of a size and capacity to reasonably carry 12,000,000 cubic feet of gas per day from the most available source of supply of natural gas in the state of West Virginia to the city of Louisville, and to prosecute said work diligently and complete said pipe line and begin to furnish gas thereby within one year from said date. The line or lines were to be a continuous piping—not broken—from source to consumption, capable of withstanding a pressure of 350 pounds per square inch, and provided with all necessary equipment to supply 12,000,000 cubic feet of gas per day to the city of Louisville. It was further agreed that the gas company should immediately upon the completion of the line aforesaid commence to supply natural gas to consumers in said city up to 12,000,000 cubic feet per day, but there is no provision in the bond guaranteeing the gas company to continue to supply said quantity of gas to said city, except that the gas company by the contract was not to make or allow any connections to be made with its main pipe line between the source of supply and the said city which would reduce the supply of gas to said city below 12,000,000 cubic feet per day. Undoubtedly the contracting parties contemplated and intended to and did contract for a supply of natural gas of not less than 12,000,000 cubic feet per day, when required.

The conditions of the bond are not as broad as the contract, for the bond only undertakes to guarantee the commencement of the work within 60 days, the prosecution of the work with reasonable diligence, and the completion thereof within one year from the acceptance of the franchise and the immediate beginning to furnish gas thereby up to the capacity of the line or lines, 12,000,000 cubic feet. It does not mention the 3-ounce gas pressure required at the point of consumption by section 7 of the ordinance, nor the prohibition against connections by consumers with the main pipe line between the source of supply and the city of Louisville.

As work on the pipe line was promptly commenced, prosecuted with diligence, and completed, if completed at all, within less than the time given in the contract and bond, there can be no recovery by the city in this action unless the bond was breached by the failure of the gas company to carry the pipe line to and connect it with the then most available source of supply of natural gas in the state of West Virginia, or failed to equip the pipe line with such machinery in the nature of compressors or forcing fans as were reasonably necessary to drive 12,000,000 cubic feet of gas in cold and unfavorable weather through the pipe from the gas fields to the city of Louisville. If the gas company failed in either of these particulars, it and its surety are liable on the bond.

The petition avers a want of performance on the part of the gas company in both these particulars, as well as many others. The answer traverses part of the material averments of the petition, and pleads affirmatively in avoidance of the others. In answer to the allegations of the petition that the pipe line was not constructed by the gas company to the most available source of supply of natural gas in the state of West Virginia, the answer says:

"It [gas company] immediately proceeded to acquire and did acquire rights of way for the pipe line, in the said ordinance referred to, from the city of Louisville to the West Virginia line, a distance of almost 200 miles, and that it immediately and at great expense and outlay, proceeded thereafter to construct a pipe line, and did construct said pipe line, consisting of continuous piping, from the most available source of supply of natural gas in the state of West Virginia to the city of Louisville. Defendants say that said pipe line at Inez, a point within about 4 miles of the West Virginia line, connected with the 16-inch pipe line of the United Fuel Gas Company, which extended from said point to Kermit, in West Virginia, and to the West Virginia gas fields, with which said 16-inch pipe line was connected with various mains and pipes. Defendants say that said pipe line was constructed and laid in the most approved manner, and that it was an iron pipe 12 inches in diameter, capable of withstanding a pressure of 400 pounds to the square inch, instead of 350 pounds to the square inch, as in said franchise ordinance called for, and having a capacity for supplying over 14,000,000 cubic feet of gas per day, instead of the 12,000,000 cubic feet of gas per day provided for in the said franchise ordinance, and was provided with all the necessary equipments to supply the capacity aforesaid. * * *

"Defendants say that the West Virginia gas field with which the defendant Louisville Gas & Electric Company's said pipe line was connected, as herein set out, had at the time an output capacity of natural gas available for said defendant under its contract with the United Fuel Gas Company, in the petition set out, greatly in excess of the requirements of said defendant under its contract with the plaintiff, and was able to furnish to said defendant and to said pipe line much more than 12,000,000 cubic feet of natural gas per day, having a heating capacity far in excess of 700 British thermal units to the cubic foot, and that from the time it made the said connection and began to furnish gas on March 12, 1914, until December 10, 1917, excepting only for a period of about 40 hours in February, 1917, said defendant was ready and able to furnish 12,000,000 cubic feet of gas per day to the city of Louisville, and did furnish far in excess of said amount of gas per day to said city on several days during said period and whenever demanded.

"Defendants say that the United Fuel Gas Company, with which company the contract for natural gas for the city of Louisville was secured, as in the petition set out, and a copy of which is filed with the petition, is one of the largest and most responsible natural gas companies in the state of West Virginia, if not the largest, as defendants believe it is, and that the contract made with it, as aforesaid, was the best contract for natural gas then obtainable or that could be secured; that the cities of Cincinnati, Cleveland, Toledo, Columbus, and the town of Portsmouth, Ohio, in the petition referred to, obtain their gas supply under similar contracts by or through the United Fuel Gas Company, or its subsidiaries; that all such contracts made by the said company and others in like business for furnishing gas to cities or towns are made subject to contracts theretofore made. The contract of the United Fuel Gas Company with the defendant Louisville Gas & Electric Company for furnishing gas was necessarily made subject to contracts theretofore entered into by it to furnish gas to other cities in the said contract mentioned which had earlier contracts with the said company, which entitled them to such priority, just as the contract of the said Fuel Gas Company with said defendant has and is given priority over other contracts for natural gas made by it with other cities since the date of said contract with said defendant."

[3] Neither the contract or bond required the gas company itself to build or own the pipe line, but it guaranteed only the building of such a line or causing it to be built, and was required to have only such ownership or control over the line for the life of the franchise as to insure a compliance with its terms. If the entire line had been constructed by another, or if owned by another, there is no breach of the bond unless the gas company has no such control over the line as will enable it to carry out its franchise contract.

[4] In this view the answer presented a good defense in so far as the petition relies upon a failure to construct a continuous pipe line. But if upon the trial it is shown that the pipe line does not reach and connect with the then most available source of supply of natural gas in the state of West Virginia, or that the line is either owned or controlled by the gas company in such way as not to enable it to carry out its franchise contract, the city may recover.

It is common knowledge that gas will not flow as freely in cold weather as it does in warm, and the colder the weather the less the flow of gas. These facts were in the possession of the gas company at the time of the acceptance of the ordinance. It was its duty, therefore, to anticipate that when cold weather came the gas in its pipes would not flow as freely as in warm weather, and in very cold weather it would be worse, and to provide the pipe line with such compressors or forcing fans as would drive the gas

through the pipe lines from the source of supply in West Virginia to the city of Louisville in the coldest weather and worse conditions that could reasonably have been expected to occur in the region where the pipe line lays. If the gas company failed to perform this duty, and as a result thereof the gas supply and pressure in the city of Louisville fell below that for which the contract calls, the pipe line was not constructed or completed according to the contract and bond within one year from the date of the acceptance of the franchise, and the gas company is liable on its bond.

[5] The affirmative paragraphs of the answer of the gas company show that the line was equipped with all necessary machinery to force the gas through the pipe line in all but unusually cold weather, which the gas company could not have reasonably anticipated and did not, or have cause to expect along or on the line of its pipe. This answer was therefore good, and the demurrer should have been overruled as to it. Whether it can sustain these averments by evidence remains to be seen. Undoubtedly the bond sued on must be treated as liquidated damages, and not as a penalty. It would be well-nigh, if not absolutely, impossible to ascertain the amount of loss or damage sustained by the city through the failure of the gas company to comply with the terms of section 6 of the ordinance, if it did fail. Our rule is to hold the sum named in the bond liquidated damages where the loss resulting from the breach of the agreement would be very uncertain and evidence of this amount very difficult to obtain, and the fair import of the agreement is that the amount of money named in the bond was specified and agreed upon by the parties to save expense and avoid the difficulty of proving the actual damage, and is not out of proportion to the actual damage sustained. Commonwealth v. Ginn & Co., 111 Ky. 110, 63 S. W. 467, 23 Ky. Law Rep. 521; American Book Co. v. Wells, 83 S. W. 622, 26 Ky. Law Rep. 1159; Gropp v. Perkins, 148 Ky. 183, 146 S. W. 389; United States v. Steel Co., 205 U. S. 105, 27 Sup. Ct. 450, 51 L. Ed. 731; Sun Publishing Co. v. Moore, 183 U. S. 642, 22 Sup. Ct. 240, 46 L. Ed. 366; Fiscal Court v. Public Service Co., 181 Ky. 245, 204 S. W. 77; Scott's Adm'r v. City of Mayfield, 153 Ky. 278, 155 S. W. 376.

About the same time this action was commenced another suit was begun by the city on the $50,000 bond for which provision is made in section 7 of the city ordinance, copied above, which suit proceeded to judgment much as this one, the city being adjudged the full penalty of that bond, from which judgment an appeal was also prosecuted to this court. That judgment was, by an opinion of this court this day delivered, reversed upon the ground that the city, as an entity, had and can maintain no action for the damage, if any, sustained by individual gas users, but such action can only be prosecuted by the individual or consumer suffering the loss or damage of which complaint is made. See Louisville Gas & Electric Co. v. City of Louisville, 231 S. W. 918.

For the reasons indicated, the judgment is reversed for proceedings consistent with this opinion.

Judgment reversed.

QUIN, J., not sitting.

LOUISVILLE GAS & ELECTRIC CO. et al. v. CITY OF LOUISVILLE.

(Court of Appeals of Kentucky. March 25, 1921. Rehearing Denied June 24, 1921.)

Gas ⬅13(1)—City cannot sue on gas company's bond for damages sustained by individual gas users.

Under a gas company's bond for the use and benefit of the inhabitants of the city granting the gas company its franchise, who were users of gas under the franchise contract, they were each entitled to maintain an action on the bond for violation of the contract resulting in injury to them, but the city could not sue on the bond for damages sustained by the individual gas users, and is not a necessary party to such a suit, not being the real party in interest.

Appeal from Circuit Court, Jefferson County, Common Pleas Branch, Second Division.

Action by the City of Louisville against the Louisville Gas & Electric Company and the National Surety Company. From judgment for plaintiff, defendants appeal. Reversed, with directions.

A. P. Humphrey and Matt O'Doherty, both of Louisville, and Cummins, Rolmer, Flynn, & McKenna, of Chicago, Ill., for appellants. Jos. S. Lawton, of Louisville, for appellee.

SAMPSON, J. The city of Louisville in March, 1913, granted to the Louisville Gas & Electric Company a franchise or privilege to lay, maintain and operate in the streets, avenues, alleys, and public roadways in the city of Louisville a system of mains, pipes, and appliances for the distribution and sale of natural gas, manufactured gas, and mixed gas. By that franchise the gas company was vested with the right and privilege, permission, and authority, subject to the provisions of the ordinance and all powers reserved to said city, to acquire, lay, construct, maintain, and operate a system of mains and pipes in, along, through, and under the streets, avenues, alleys, and public ways within the corporate boundaries of the city of Louisville as they now exist or may hereafter be extended and on and under the bridges and viaducts

owned and controlled by said city, for distributing and selling natural, manufactured, and mixed gas.

The franchise also provides in section 4 that—

"All pavements and sidewalks shall be taken up and all excavations in said streets, avenues, boulevards, sidewalks, lanes, highways, alleys, and public ways shall be made only with the written permission of the Board of Public Works and under the supervision of said board. * * *"

As this litigation largely gathers around sections 6 and 7 of the franchise, we copy these sections in full:

"Sec. 6. Said grantee, his successors or assigns, shall within sixty (60) days after the acceptance of this ordinance begin and continue to lay a main line or lines of pipe or cause the same to be done from the most available source of supply of natural gas in the state of West Virginia to the city of Louisville, which said main line or lines shall consist of continuous piping and be a piping capable of withstanding a pressure of three hundred and fifty (350) pounds per square inch and be of a size having a capacity for supplying twelve million (12,000,000) cubic feet of gas per day to said city and provided with all necessary equipment to supply the capacity aforesaid, and said grantee shall complete said line or lines of pipe within one year from the passage and acceptance of this ordinance, unless prevented from so doing by the delays of bona fide litigation or by other cause or causes beyond the control of the grantee. And said grantee shall immediately thereafter commence to supply natural gas to consumer up to the capacity aforesaid, provided that, if the work herein authorized be delayed by injunction, bona fide litigation or by other cause or causes beyond the control of the grantee such delays or delays shall not be considered in estimating the time within which such work shall be commenced and completed and natural gas supplied. Said supply of twelve million (12,000,000) cubic feet per day shall not be reduced by reason of any connections with said pipe line being made between the city of Louisville and the source of supply. And said grantee, his successors or assigns, shall in forty (40) days after the acceptance of the bid of grantee execute a bond to the city of Louisville with good and sufficient surety, to be approved by said city in the sum of two hundred and fifty thousand ($250,000) dollars, conditioned upon the carrying out of the provisions of the section of this ordinance as to the beginning, continuance and completion of the laying of said pipe line and beginning to furnish natural gas thereby and upon said conditions being fulfilled said bond shall terminate and sureties be released, and said bond shall be given as additional security to the bond provided for in section 7.

"Sec. 7. The grantee shall within forty (40) days after the acceptance of the bid of grantee, execute a bond to the city of Louisville, with good and sufficient sureties to be approved by the city, in the sum of fifty thousand ($50,000) dollars, conditioned upon the faithful performance and discharge of all the obligations imposed upon the grantee by this ordinance, including the obligations imposed by section 6 hereof, and conditioned that the grantee shall restore the sidewalks and pavements and all public ways to the original condition and maintain the same as provided in section 4 and shall save the city harmless from all loss and damage which may be done to its public ways or other property, or to persons or property of individuals by the conduct of the grantee's business, or arising out of the uses and privileges herein granted. Said bond shall be renewed from time to time as and when required by the city of Louisville. Said bond shall further be conditioned that the grantee shall defend all suits and all judgments against the city of Louisville and hold the city free from all liability arising out of the construction, maintenance, or operation of the grantee's mains, conduits, or other apparatus in the public ways of the city of Louisville."

Under the foregoing sections of the ordinance the gas company executed the two bonds specified, one for $250,000 under section 6 of the ordinance, and the other for $50,000 under section 7 of the ordinance, and on each of the said undertakings the National Surety Company became and is the surety.

This suit was commenced in March, 1918, by the city of Louisville against the Louisville Gas & Electric Company and the National Surety Company to recover $50,000 on the obligation executed by the gas company under section 7, above quoted. The bond sued on is in words and figures as follows:

"Know all men by these presents that the undersigned, Louisville Gas & Electric Company, a corporation organized under the laws of the state of Kentucky (hereinafter called the Gas & Electric Company), as principal, and National Surety Company, a corporation organized under the laws of the state of New York, as surety, parties of the first part, and city of Louisville (hereinafter called the city), of the second part, witnesses that the said parties are held and bound unto the city in the full sum of fifty thousand ($50,000) dollars, payment whereof well and truly to be made the said first parties do hereby bind themselves, their successors and assigns, firmly by these presents, as witness the hands and seals of the first parties hereunto affixed this July 8, 1913.

"The condition of the above obligation is such that, whereas the city, by an ordinance approved March 29, 1913, created and provided for the sale of a franchise or privilege of acquiring, laying, maintaining, and operating in the streets, avenues, alleys, and public ways of the city of Louisville, Kentucky, a system of mains, pipes, and appliances for the distribution and sale of natural gas, manufactured gas, and mixed gas, and the sale of said franchise as herein provided was thereafter duly made, and the Louisville Gas Company became the bidder at said sale, and its bid was accepted by the general council of the city of Louisville, and payment was made by the Louisville

Gas Company of the purchase price of said franchise, and since that date the Louisville Gas Company has, by agreement of consolidation with sundry other companies, formed the Gas & Electric Company, one of the parties of the first part, and by said agreement of consolidation said franchise has passed to said Gas & Electric Company:

"Now, if the said Gas & Electric Company shall faithfully perform and discharge all the obligations imposed upon the grantee by said ordinance, including the obligations imposed by section 6 thereof, and shall restore the sidewalks and pavements and all public ways to their original condition, and shall maintain the same as provided in section 4 thereof, and shall save the city harmless from all loss and damage which may be done to its public ways or other property, or to persons, or to property of individuals, by the conduct of the business of the Gas & Electric Company as defined by said ordinance, or arising out of the uses and privileges therein granted, and shall defend all suits and pay all judgments against the city of Louisville, and hold the city free from all liability arising out of the construction, maintenance, or operation of said Gas & Electric Company's mains, conduits, or other apparatus in the public ways of the city of Louisville, then this obligation shall be void; otherwise in full force and virtue."

After a motion by the gas company and others to strike out certain parts of the petition had been passed upon and an opinion delivered by the court the defendants filed answer. The city then entered a motion to make the fourth paragraph of the answer more specific and a further motion to strike certain words and phrases from the answer. The city also filed a general demurrer to the second, third, fourth, and fifth paragraphs of the answer, all of which after hearing were sustained. The gas company and its surety then filed an amended answer, to which general demurrer was interposed by the city, and again sustained. The gas company and the surety company then filed an amended answer and counterclaim, to which a general demurrer was filed by the city, and the court again, after careful consideration of the questions involved, delivered a written opinion sustaining the demurrer. Thereupon the gas company and its surety declined to further plead, but asked for a separation of the conclusions of law and fact, which latter motion the court sustained and rendered a judgment against the gas company and the surety company for $50,000 on the bond, and made a separate finding of the facts and the law applicable thereto.

The gas company and its surety then filed motion and grounds for a new trial, in which it set forth the following reasons:

(1) Because the court's findings of fact herein do not sustain the judgment.

(2) Because the evidence heard does not sustain the findings of fact by the court or any of them.

(3) Because the court's finding of fact that

there was an agreement upon the part of the Louisville Gas Company to furnish 12,-000,000 cubic feet of gas per day when required is not sustained by the evidence.

(4) Because the court's finding that the defendant gas company agreed that the pressure at no time should fall below three ounces to the square inch is not sustained by the evidence and is contrary to the evidence.

(5) Because the court's findings of fact and the judgment of the court are contrary to the law and contrary to the evidence, and are not sustained by sufficient evidence.

(6) Because the court erred in sustaining plaintiff's motion for judgment.

(7) Because the court erred in overruling the motion of the defendants and each of them for judgment in their favor, made at the conclusion of the evidence.

(8) Because the court erred in admitting over the objection of the defendants incompetent evidence as shown by the stenographer's report of the trial.

(9) Because the court erred in excluding competent evidence offered by the defendants as shown by the said stenographer's report.

(10) Because the judgment of the court is contrary to the law and contrary to the evidence.

This motion was overruled, and the gas company and its surety appeal to this court. It urges several grounds for a reversal of the judgment, among them: (1) The finding of the court that the gas consumers were damaged in the sum of $50,000 is not supported by any evidence; (2) the city, having elected to sue in equity for specific performance, is bound by its election and cannot maintain this action; (3) error in holding that the contractual ordinance sued on in this case must be treated as a statute, and not as a contract; (4) error in holding insufficient the plea of defendants based on the action of the War Department of the United States government which rendered the gas company's obligation to furnish 12,000,000 cubic feet of gas every day impossible of performance; (5) the trial court erred in holding that the $50,000 named in the bond is liquidated damages; (6) the city had no right of action to recover damages for loss sustained by individual gas consumers; (7) as the franchise provided for liquidated damages other than that stipulated in the bond, no other damages are recoverable.

Of these several grounds urged by appellants for a reversal of the judgment it will only be necessary for us to consider the right of the city as an entity to maintain this action on the bond to recover damages which it is admitted were sustained, if at all, by individual gas consumers, inhabitants of the city, and not by the municipality; for, if the city of Louisville has not stated a cause of action in its petition or is not entitled to maintain this action, the judgment

must be reversed, with directions to dismiss the petition, and, as we have reached this conclusion, it will therefore be wholly unnecessary to consider any of the other grounds urged in brief of counsel for appellants. Very little of appellee's brief is devoted to a discussion of these questions, but reliance is had upon the written opinions of Circuit Judges Gordon and Ray, which are set out at length in the record. These opinions are rested chiefly upon the text of Dillon on Municipal Corporations, § 1231; Scott's Adm'r v. City of Mayfield, 153 Ky. 280, 155 S. W. 376; L. & N. R. R. Co. v. City of Shelbyville, 179 Ky. 132, 200 S. W. 334. In discussing this question Judge Gordon in his written opinion says:

"It is further urged upon the court that the city has lost nothing, has sustained no actual damage, and therefore cannot recover. This contention seems to be fully answered in Scott's Adm'r v. City of Mayfield, 153 Ky. 280, 155 S. W. 376."

We cannot agree with the learned circuit judge that the question under consideration is settled adversely to the gas company by the authorities cited. The bond sued on was executed for the use and benefit of the several inhabitants of the city of Louisville who were users of gas under the contract made by the city with the gas company, and they were each entitled to maintain an action upon the bond for any violation of the contract which resulted in a legal injury to them. This is the well-established rule in Kentucky. The courts of only one other state, North Carolina, adhered to this doctrine. Gorrell v. Water Supply Co., 124 N. C. 328, 32 S. E. 720, 46 L. R. A. 513, 70 Am. St. Rep. 598; Jones v. Durham Water Co., 135 N. C. 553, 47 S. E. 615. But, notwithstanding this, we consider it the soundest upon reason and calculated to afford more adequate relief then the rule adopted by the courts of the majority of the states.

As far back as December, 1889, this court in the case of Paducah Lumber Co. v. Paducah Water Supply Co., 89 Ky. 340, 12 S. W. 554, 13 S. W. 249, 7 L. R. A. 77, 25 Am. St. Rep. 536, held that a bond of the general nature of the one sued on in this case was for the use and benefit of the inhabitants of the city, and that an individual for whose benefit the bond was evidently made could sue thereon in his own name, though the engagement be not directly to or with him, and that section 18 of the Civil Code, which by express terms provides that every action must be prosecuted in the name of the real party in interest, has application to such cases as this. If the city had suffered a wrong as an entity by the failure of the gas company to keep and perform the conditions of the contract, it could, of course, maintain an action on the bond, but it is not the contention in this case that the city has suffered a wrong in its municipal capacity, but only that its inhabitants, individual members of the society who make up the city, have suffered an injury through the failure of the gas company to comply with the terms of the ordinance. The city therefore had and has no cause of action and could not and cannot maintain this suit, but each individual gas user who suffered a legal wrong through the failure of the gas company to keep and perform the terms of the contract has and may maintain an action on the bond for the injury suffered. Repeatedly this court has held that an inhabitant of a city may maintain in his own name an action on the contract or bond of a water company to recover for a loss resulting from a failure or refusal of the water company to keep and perform the conditions of the contract or bond without joining the city in whose name the contract is made as party defendant. Paducah Lumber Co. v. Paducah Water Supply Co., supra; Graves v. Ligon, 112 Ky. 775, 66 S. W. 725, 23 Ky. Law Rep. 2149; Lexington, etc., v. Oots, 119 Ky. 598, 84 S. W. 774, 86 S. W. 684, 27 Ky. Law Rep. 233, 797; Kenton Water Co. v. Glenn, 141 Ky. 529, 133 S. W. 573; Tobin v. Frankfort Water Co., 158 Ky. 349, 164 S. W. 956; Owensboro Water Co. v. Duncan Adm'x, 32 S. W. 478, 17 Ky. Law Rep. 755; Georgetown Water Co. v. Neale, 137 Ky. 197, 125 S. W. 298. To the same effect are the following cases: Gorrell v. Water Supply Co., 124 N. C. 328, 32 S. E. 720, 46 L. R. A. 513; Jones v. Durham Water Co., 135 N. C. 553, 47 S. E. 615; Woodbury v. Tampa Waterworks Co., 57 Fla. 243, 49 South. 556, 21 L. R. A. (N. S.) 1034.

The bond under consideration is a continu-

ing obligation, and the city may require it to be renewed from time to time in order to fully protect itself and its inhabitants. Under the rule adopted by this court many years ago, the city is not a necessary party to an action by an individual to recover on the bond for loss suffered through a violation of its terms. But this does not mean that the city may not in a proper case maintain an action upon the bond also. The lower court in its finding of fact does not point out a single instance in which the city has suffered a loss or wrong as an entity, but only that the city has suffered through loss to its individual inhabitants in varying importance. Under our rule allowing the real party in interest only to maintain an action, it would appear wholly unnecessary for the city to be made a party, either plaintiff or defendant, for the real party at interest is the individual gas user, who has suffered through the failure of the gas company to comply with the terms of the ordinance; such person is the real party in interest and in possession of all the facts; the bond was made for his use and benefit. We can think of no reason why he should not be permitted to maintain the action in his own name, nor can we conceive of any reason why the city of Louisville as an entity should be permitted to maintain this action when it is not the real party in interest and has suffered no appreciable damage as a municipality.

Having reached this conclusion, it is unnecessary for us to discuss the other questions made in brief of counsel.

The judgment is reversed, with directions to dismiss the petition.

QUIN, J., not sitting.

HINES et al. v. FELKINS et al. (No. 21792.)

(Supreme Court of Missouri, Division No. 1. April 9, 1921. Rehearing Denied June 6, 1921.)

1. Taxation ⟨⟩734(7)—That allegation as to defendant's nonresidence followed prayer of petition and original signature of plaintiff's attorney did not affect validity of deed.

That the allegation as to nonresidence of defendant in a tax suit in which the defendant was served by publication followed the prayer of the petition and the original signature of plaintiff's attorney was not such an irregularity as to affect the validity of title under deed pursuant to the proceedings.

2. Evidence ⟨⟩413—Parol evidence inadmissible to attack record in tax suit.

In suit to foreclose a deed of trust, in which one of the defendants claimed to be an innocent purchaser as successor in interest of tax sale purchaser, parol testimony was inadmissible to show that an allegation appearing in the record of the tax suit proceedings as a part of the petition in such suit was added to petition after it had been filed and the summons issued without an order of court; such testimony constituting an attack upon the record by parol evidence.

3. Taxation ⟨⟩648—Judgment valid on its face not subject to collateral attack.

Judgment in tax suit valid on its face was not subject to attack in action to foreclose deed of trust in which the defendant claimed title as successor in interest of tax sale purchaser.

Appeal from Circuit Court, Texas County; L. B. Woodside, Judge.

Suit by Florence O. Hines and another against Ed Felkins and others. Decree for defendants, and plaintiffs appeal. Affirmed.

This is a suit in equity to reform and foreclose a deed of trust on certain land in Texas county, Mo.

The petition is in two counts. The first count alleges that on March 18, 1911, defendants Ed Felkins and Millie Felkins, his wife, executed and delivered to plaintiff Florence O. Hines, their promissory note for $200, payable in one year, bearing interest from date at the rate of 8 per cent. per annum, and agreed to secure the same by a deed of trust on the south half of the northeast quarter of section 15, township 28, range 9 west, in Texas county, Mo.; that on the same day said defendants executed and delivered to plaintiff a deed of trust purporting to secure the said note, but that through a mistake of the scrivener who drew the deed the land conveyed was described as the south half of the southeast quarter of said section 15, instead of the south half of the northeast quarter thereof; that defendant Marion Edwards claims some interest in the property

intended to have been conveyed, the nature of which is unknown to plaintiffs, but which interest, if any, plaintiffs desire to have determined. The count closes with a prayer for reformation of the deed of trust. The second count sets up the deed of trust as sought to be reformed, alleges that the principal amount of the note secured thereby, with interest thereon from March 18, 1917, is due, and prays a foreclosure thereunder. Plaintiff Kirby Lamar is trustee under the deed of trust in suit.

Defendant Marion Edwards answered, denying generally the allegations of the petition, and pleading that he is the owner of the south half of the northeast quarter of section 15 aforesaid, being an innocent purchaser for value, and that he is in possession thereof.

Defendants Ed Felkins and Millie Felkins, who were nonresidents, were duly served with summons, but made default.

At the opening of the trial of the case it was agreed that defendant Ed Felkins is the common source of title to the land involved.

The direct evidence for plaintiffs not being material to the question here presented, we shall forego adverting thereto.

To sustain the issues for defendant Edwards, there were introduced in evidence the following deeds, to wit: Sheriff's Deed Record Book 61, page 452, showing sheriff's deed under special execution for delinquent taxes, dated November 15, 1917, reciting judgment of the circuit court on August 25, 1917, against Ed Felkins and in favor of the state of Missouri, at the relation of Jake F. McKinney, collector, conveying the south half of the northeast quarter of section 15 to E. L. Pollard and F. J. McGrath for a consideration of $86; special warranty deed dated December 3, 1917, from E. L. Pollard and wife and Frank J. McGrath and wife to F. R. Ellis, conveying the same land, for a recited consideration of $1,000 general warranty deed dated January 29, 1918, from F. R. Ellis and wife to Jesse and George Hamilton, husband and wife, conveying the same land, for a recited consideration of $1,000; general warranty deed dated May 17, 1918, from Jesse and George Hamilton to Marion Edwards, conveying the same land, for a recited consideration of $400.

Defendant Edwards testified that he bought the land in question from George Hamilton, paying $400 cash therefor, for which he exhibited a receipt, and that he is living thereon; that before he paid the purchase money he examined an abstract of title which was exhibited to him; that he knew nothing about Mrs. Hines claiming a lien or holding a mortgage on the land until he was served with summons as defendant herein. The abstract of title referred to was introduced in evidence and shows the chain of title offered in evidence, but does not show the deed of trust to plaintiff Hines.

For plaintiffs, in rebuttal, there was read in evidence the petition filed May 30, 1917, in the tax suit brought by the state at the relation of Jake L. McKinney, Collector, against defendant Ed Felkins, being the same suit under which Pollard and McGrath (remote grantors of defendant Edwards) acquired title at the delinquent tax sale held under execution issued therein. Said petition, being in the main printed, is in usual form for tax suits, but contains no allegation in the body thereof as to nonresidence of the defendant Felkins. At the close the petition is signed "John H. Sanks, Plaintiff's Attorney." Below this signature, in handwriting, occurs the following allegation:

"Plaintiff further states that the defendant Ed Felkins is a nonresident of the state of Missouri and cannot be served with the ordinary process of law in this state.
"John H. Sanks, Atty. for Plff."

The above allegation is not verified by affidavit.

For plaintiffs, in rebuttal, there was also introduced in evidence the summons in the above-mentioned tax suit, dated May 31, 1917, and the return of the sheriff thereon, as follows:

"Executed the within writ in the county of Texas and state of Missouri on the 20th day of August, 1917, by making diligent search for the within-named defendant, Ed Felkins, and failing to find him in my said county."

There was also introduced in evidence, for plaintiff, the following: Order of Publication Record N, page 178, showing an order of publication in the said tax suit, in usual form, purporting to be made by the clerk in vacation, upon an allegation of nonresidence contained in the petition; certified copy of said order of publication, directed to the Cabool Enterprise-Press, and attested by the clerk of the court under date of June 8, 1917; proof of publication of the said order in the Cabool Enterprise-Press for a sufficient length of time (the date of the order of publication does not appear upon the record entry thereof nor upon the printed copy); Tax Judgment Record T, page 125, in usual form, showing judgment against defendant Ed Felkins, but reciting service upon him by publication only.

Mr. John H. Sanks testified for plaintiff as follows:

"My profession is attorney at law. On May 30, 1917, I was attorney for the collector of Texas county for the purpose of bringing actions on delinquent taxes. I filed that suit of State ex rel. Collector v. Ed Felkins.

"Q. I show you the petition in this tax suit and call your attention to the allegation of nonresidence of the defendant at the bottom or at the end of the petition and ask you if that was in the petition at the time the petition was originally filed? A. Well, I'll state how it was, I filed this suit and originally ordered a summons for Texas county, and then I went down in the clerk's office—now I don't know how long this was filed—and the clerk said to me that this man, Felkins, was a nonresident of the state of Missouri, and didn't live here, and we had better have a statement of nonresidence, and I sat down and wrote it, and I don't know how long it had been since it was filed, but it was some time after and that allegation wasn't verified. I didn't swear to it."

Respondents in an additional abstract of the record state that—

"When appellant offered evidence tending to impeach the verity of the record of the tax suit and to show that the allegation of nonresidence was not in the petition when it was originally filed, the defendant offered the following objection, which was overruled:
"'By Mr. Lamar: We object for the further reason there are no allegations in the pleadings in this case that there are any errors in the records of this court, and it is a conclusive presumption that the records of this court are correct, and they cannot be attacked, nor shown to be wrong without being attacked in a suit in equity to change and reform the records, and for the further reason the plaintiffs are absolutely bound by the petition and records as they are, and nothing is admissible under the pleadings in this case to change the records and show that it ought to be different from what it is at this time.'"

The court rendered a judgment and decree that the plaintiffs "take nothing by this action, and that the defendant Marion Edwards be discharged with his costs." From this judgment plaintiffs appeal.

Barton & Impey, of Houston, for appellants.

Lamar & Lamar, of Houston, for respondents.

ELDER, J. (after stating the facts as above). While appellants in their briefs deal with various phases of the issue presented, they ultimately rest their case upon one contention. They insist that defendant Edwards acquired no title by mesne conveyances under the tax suit brought against defendant Ed Felkins by reason of the fact that the allegation of nonresidence, appearing at the conclusion of the petition therein, was written without an order of court, after the petition had been filed and summons issued. Learned counsel for plaintiffs argue in substance that this allegation is not a part of the petition, that the order of publication based thereon was a nullity, and that accordingly the court was without jurisdiction to render judgment against defendant Felkins, the common source of title. In their reply brief counsel say:

"In its last analysis, there is but one question in this case: Is the allegation of nonresidence, written after the suit had been filed and summons issued, in vacation, and without an order of the court, a part of the petition? If this question be answered in the affirmative, the judgment should be sustained; but if in the negative it ought to be reversed."

Accepting this statement as indicative of appellant's final insistence, we proceed.

[1-3] Standing alone, the record in the tax suit brought by the collector against defendant Felkins discloses no irregularity sufficient to void the judgment rendered therein. True, the allegation as to nonresidence, which follows the prayer of the petition and the original signature of plaintiff's attorney, does not conform to good pleading, but it is not an informality sufficient to exclude it as one of the allegations of the petition. The allegation was in the nature of an amendment to the petition, and, the same being resubscribed under the amendment, the amendment became a part of the petition. Nicodemus v. Simons, 121 Ind. 564, 23 N. E. 521. As urged by plaintiffs, however, the testimony of Mr. Sanks, attorney for plaintiff in the said tax suit, was to the effect that the amendment was made by him at the suggestion of the clerk, after the petition had been filed. But, be that as it may, such testimony amounted to an attack upon the record by parol evidence, and should not have been admitted. Davidson v. Real Estate & Inv. Co., 226 Mo. loc. cit. 29, 125 S. W. 1143, 136 Am. St. Rep. 615; Milan v. Pemberton, 12 Mo. 599; Mobley v. Nave, 67 Mo. 546; Freeman v. Thompson, 53 Mo. 183; Dennison v. County of St. Louis, 33 Mo. 168; Cook v. Penrod, 111 Mo. App. 128, 85 S. W. 676. Accordingly, disregarding such testimony, as we must, we find that an allegation of the nonresidence of defendant Felkins appears on the face of the petition; that an order of publication was properly made by the clerk in vacation; that proof of publication of such order was submitted to the court; and that pursuant thereto judgment was rendered against Felkins. Under the decisions of this court it follows that that judgment cannot be collaterally attacked, as here attempted. McDermott v. Gray, 198 Mo. 266, 95 S. W. 431; Vincent v. Means, 184 Mo. 327, 82 S. W. 96; Tooker v. Leake, 146 Mo. loc. cit. 429, 430, 48 S. W. 638; Payne v. Lott, 90 Mo. 676, 3 S. W. 402; Schmidt v. Niemeyer, 100 Mo. 207, 13 S. W. 405; Kane v. McCown, 55 Mo. 181; Brawley v. Ranney, 67 Mo. 280. Hence, the judgment being regular on its face, and the sale thereunder being unquestioned, such sale was sufficient to convey title to the purchasers thereat. Stevenson v. Black, 168 Mo. 549. 68 S. W. 909; Wellshear v. Kelley, 69 Mo. 343; Jones v. Driskill, 94 Mo. 190, 7 S. W. 111; Allen v. McCabe, 93 Mo. 138, 6 S. W. 62. We therefore rule the point against appellants.

The error in the admission of evidence tending to vitiate the proceedings in the tax suit not being prejudicial to appellants, and a review of the entire record having served to convince us that the judgment was correct, we hereby affirm the same.

All concur.

DRAKOPULOS v. BIDDLE et al.
(No. 21760.)

(Supreme Court of Missouri, Division No. 2. May 26, 1921. Motion for Rehearing Denied June 23, 1921.)

1. **Limitation of actions ⟷127(6)—Amendment substituting widow for administrator in action for wrongful death held not a departure.**

In action for wrongful death by decedent's administrator, under Gen. St. Kan. 1909, § 6014 (Code Civ. Proc. § 419), an amended petition, filed after a new suit would have been barred by limitations, by the decedent's widow as substituted plaintiff, under section 6015 (section 420), held not barred as a new cause of action; the cause of action and the beneficiaries of recovery—the widow and children —being the same, and the amendment being permissible under Rev. St. 1919, § 1274.

2. **Death ⟷27—Recovery by widow bars suit by administrator.**

A recovery for wrongful death by decedent's administrator, being for the benefit of decedent's widow and children, would bar their subsequent suit, and a recovery by them in the name of the widow would bar a suit by the administrator for their benefit.

3. **Dismissal and nonsuit ⟷58(1)—Dismissal of action on striking out amended petition for wrongful death held reversible as abuse of discretion.**

While refusing or permitting amendments is largely discretionary, striking out, in action for wrongful death, an amended petition by widow substituted as plaintiff for decedent's administrator, on ground of departure, and dismissing the action, held error, where limitations barred a new suit.

Appeal from Circuit Court, Jackson County; Daniel E. Bird, Judge.

Action by Sotero Drakopulos against W. B. Biddle and others, receivers of the St. Louis & San Francisco Railroad Company. From judgment of dismissal, plaintiff appeals. Reversed and remanded, with directions.

C. W. Prince, E. A. Harris, and Jas. N. Beery, all of Kansas City, for appellant. W. F. Evans, of St. Louis, and Guthrie, Conrad & Durham and Hale Houts, all of Kansas City, for respondents.

DAVID E. BLAIR, J. The action is for damages for the wrongful death of Gust Drakopulos, the husband of plaintiff. The original petition was filed August 7, 1915.

The fourth amended petition, filed December 3, 1918, ran in the name of Samuel B. Strother, administrator of the estate of Gust Drakopulos, deceased. It alleges that plaintiff therein was the "duly appointed administrator," etc. Certain allegations relating to the appointment of the receivers for the St. Louis & San Francisco Railroad Company, foreclosure sale of its property, and purchase thereof by defendant St. Louis and San Francisco Railway Company are made. Said petition then averred the facts relative to the death of Gust Drakopulos in the state of Kansas on April 26, 1915, and that the same was caused by the negligence of defendants; that deceased left surviving him a widow, Sotero Drakopulos, and three minor children therein named, all dependent upon him; that plaintiff has been given a right of action for said death by the laws of Kansas; and sets out section 6014 of chapter 95, art. 18, of the General Statutes of Kansas for 1909 (Code Civ. Proc. § 419), as follows:

"Action for Death by Wrongful Act; Limitations; Damages. When the death of one is caused by the wrongful act or omission of another, the personal representatives of the former may maintain an action therefor against the latter, if the former might have maintained an action had he lived, against the latter for injury for the same act or omission. The action must be commenced within two years. The damages cannot exceed ten thousand dollars, and must inure to the exclusive benefit of the widow and children, if any, or next of kin, to be distributed in the same manner as personal property of the deceased."

The prayer of said fourth amended petition is as follows:

"Wherefore, plaintiff, for and in behalf of said widow and children, asks judgment against defendants for the sum of ten thousand ($10,-000.00) dollars together with his costs herein incurred and expended."

On February 12, 1919, the widow, Sotero Drakopulos, present plaintiff, applied for leave to be substituted as party plaintiff and to adopt the pleadings and proceedings in said cause. On March 4, 1919, and over the objection and exception of defendants, she was permitted to be substituted as plaintiff, and on that date filed a fifth amended petition, in which she alleged that on and prior to April 26, 1915, she was the wife of Gust Drakopulos, and sets out the names of her three children and that she and said children were residents of the kingdom of Greece and were dependent upon said Gust Drakopulos. The fifth amended petition in other particulars is substantially in the same words as the fourth amended petition, except that it sets out in full section 6015 of the General Statutes of Kansas for 1909, chapter 95, art. 18 (Code Civ. Proc. § 420), as follows:

"Sec. 6015. *When Action may be Brought by Widow or Next of Kin.* That in all cases where the residence of the party whose death has been or hereafter shall be caused as set forth in the next preceding section is or has been at the time of his death in any other state or territory, or when, being a resident of this state, no personal representative is or has been appointed, the action provided in said section may be brought by the widow, or where there is no widow, by the next of kin of such deceased."

There is also a slight difference in the two petitions caused by the use of appropriate words to make the fifth amended petition applicable to plaintiff as widow of deceased, instead of applicable to the plaintiff named in the fourth amended petition as administrator of deceased. The prayer of the fifth amended petition is as follows:

"Wherefore, plaintiff, for and in behalf of herself and said minor children, asks judgment against defendants in the sum of ten thousand ($10,000.00) dollars, together with her costs herein incurred and expended."

On March 17, 1919, defendants filed their motion to strike out plaintiff's fifth amended petition, and said motion was sustained by the trial court, to which action plaintiff duly excepted, and judgment of dismissal with costs was entered against plaintiff. The appeal is from the order of the trial court striking out such fifth amended petition and dismissing the cause. The propriety of such action is the sole question before us.

[1] As appears from defendants' motion to strike out the fifth amended petition, the theory of defendants is that such amended petition is a departure from the cause of action stated in the fourth amended and prior petitions, because a new plaintiff is substituted, who is a stranger to the original cause of action and to the plaintiff therein, and because the fifth amended petition is based upon a statute different from the one which is the basis of the claim of the fourth amended petition, and because entirely different proof will be required in the two petitions, and because a judgment upon one petition would be no bar to the cause of action stated in the other.

We do not think there is any merit in the contention that plaintiff is a stranger to the original cause of action. It is expressly alleged in the fourth amended petition that Sotero Drakopulos is the widow of deceased, and the names of the minor children are set out therein, and that such administrator prays judgment for and in behalf of said widow and children.

Nor is it true that the fifth amended petition is based on a statute different from the one pleaded in the fourth amended petition. Both petitions plead section 6014, and both are based thereon. The fifth amended petition pleads section 6015 in addition. Section 6015° merely provides when the widow may maintain the action provided for in section 6014. Section 6015 adds nothing to the liability of defendants in any way.

The only difference in the proof required is that in the fourth amended petition such proof should show deceased was a resident of Kansas and the appointment of a competent administrator; while in the fifth amended petition the proof should show either that deceased was not a resident of Kansas, or, if a resident, that no personal representative is or has been appointed. Additional proof of section 6015 as a law of Kansas is required in the fifth amended petition. Proof of the existence of the widow and children is necessary in both petitions. The subject of the action, the cause of action, the grounds of negligence, and the measure of damages are the same in both petitions. The damages sought to be recovered are for the benefit of the widow and children in both petitions, and the proceeds recovered on a judgment under either petition are required by the law of Kansas to be distributed in the same manner.

[2] Nor are we able to agree that a recovery on the fifth amended petition would not be a complete bar to the action by the administrator, or vice versa. If the fourth amended petition properly alleges the appointment of a competent administrator, and the proof showed that fact and the administrator obtained a judgment thereon, such judgment would bar recovery upon the fifth amended petition, since a recovery by the administrator suing merely in a representative capacity would be for the benefit of the widow and children. Under section 6014 the administrator acts as a trustee for the widow and children, and not for the estate of the deceased. The damages recovered could not be subjected to the debts of the deceased. A recovery by him for them would bar their subsequent suit. A recovery by them in the name of the widow would bar a suit by the administrator for their benefit. 23 Cyc. 1245; Landis v. Hamilton, 77 Mo. 554; Davidson v. Real Estate & Investment Co., 249 Mo. loc. cit. 502, 155 S. W. 1; Cooley v. Warren, 53 Mo. loc. cit. 169.

It is true the amended petition requires somewhat different proof from the fourth amended petition, but not substantially different proof. If the test of departure be that the proof required is different in any respect, then every amendment would be a departure. We think section 1274, R. S. Mo. 1919, is sufficiently broad to cover the amendment here in question. It provides for an amendment by adding or striking out the name of a party, and even provides for amendment after the proof has been made in order to conform the pleadings to the proof, where such amendment does not substantially change the claim or defense. This is the consideration which should guide the courts. If the amendment does not substantially change the claim or defense, there is no departure.

The subject of the action here is the right of Gust Drakopulos to immunity from injury by the negligent acts of defendants. The cause of action is the alleged violation of that right by defendants. The object of the action is the recovery of damages for such violation to inure to the exclusive benefit of the widow and children. These are the substantial elements of the claim. Whether the action is brought by the administrator or the widow is a mere detail of procedure. The only concern of defendants as to parties plaintiff is that whoever prosecutes the action shall be competent to maintain it in such a way as to bar any other action for the same injury. Defendants' rights in this regard are amply safeguarded, and the amendment did not injuriously affect the substantial rights of the defendants.

Support for these views is found in Vaughan v. Railroad, 177 Mo. App. 155, 164 S. W. 144, in which case the Kansas City Court of Appeals held that it was error to enter judgment after verdict in favor of the administratrix, who was added as plaintiff after verdict, without the fact of her appointment as administratrix having been submitted as an issue for trial by the jury. On page 171 the court held that the trial court properly permitted the substitution, but should then have sustained a motion for a new trial instead of permitting the administratrix to adopt the judgment and previous proceedings, and remanded the cause for new trial with the administratrix as a party plaintiff. The action in that case was under the federal Employers' Liability Act (U. S. Comp. St. §§ 8657–8665), wherein the administratrix was the proper party plaintiff. The ruling in that case was approved by the same court in Dungan v. Railroad, 178 Mo. App. 164, 165 S. W. 1116. We are further fortified in the view we take of the amendment in this case by the opinion of Mr. Justice Pitney, of the United States Supreme Court, in M., K. & T. Ry. Co. v. Wulf, 226 U. S. 570, 33 Sup. Ct. 135, 57 L. Ed. 355, Ann. Cas. 1914B, 134. In that case the action had been instituted by the mother of the deceased as his sole heir, and subsequently she was appointed administratrix and was made a party plaintiff. The action in that case was under the federal Employers' Liability Act, where the action could only be maintained by the personal representative of the deceased. The substitution was approved, and it was ruled that the substitution did not change the cause of action.

Defendants cite the case of Broyles v. Eversmeyer, 262 Mo. 384, 171 S. W. 334, as supporting their contention. It is difficult to understand how that case is authority for defendants' position. This court, speaking through Graves, J., held proper an amend-

ment correcting a mistake in the description
of a tract of land. Section 1848, R. S. 1909
(now section 1274, R. S. 1919), was there
invoked as authority for the amendment.
That same statute provides for adding or
striking out the name of a party and for
amendment of the pleadings, even after the
proof has been made, in order to conform
pleading to proof, where such amendment
does not change substantially the claim or
defense. Defendants also cite Garber v. Mo.
Pac. Ry. Co., 210 S. W. 377. The question
there was the propriety of the action of the
trial court in striking out the third count of
the third amended petition as a departure.
The first and second counts of said amended petition were based on Missouri statutes
and the third count on the federal Employers' Liability Act. As no exceptions were
saved to the action of the trial court in
striking out such third count, it was held
that the question was not properly raised for
review and the propriety of the amendment
was not before this court, and that even if
the question had been properly saved, as
neither the original nor any other petition
prior to the third amended petition was incorporated in the record, the court was in no
position to determine the propriety of the
amendment. The question of departure was
not determined.

In Bank v. Thompson, 223 S. W. 734, relied on by defendants, the original petition
counted on a demand note and the amended
petition upon an agreement under which the
note set out in the original petition had been
given to secure the payment of other notes.
The two petitions were based on different
subject-matters and required quite different
evidence to support them. None of the other
cases on the question of departure cited by
defendant give us any additional light.

[3] No reason except the alleged departure
appears in the record before us to justify
the court's action in striking out the fifth
amended petition. It is true that the permitting of amendments is largely within the
sound discretion of the trial court. The court
having exercised its discretion in plaintiff's
favor and having permitted the substitution
of the widow as party plaintiff, we are justified in assuming that it would not have
stricken out the pleading except for the supposed departure. We are satisfied that was
not a sufficient reason. We regard the exercise of the court's power as unwise and unsound, where its action finally closed the door
to relief in plaintiff's face. The statute of
limitations is a complete bar to the prosecution of a new suit.

From what has been said it is apparent
that the court erred in striking out plaintiff's
fifth amended petition and dismissing the
cause and entering judgment against plaintiff for costs.

The judgment of the trial court must be
reversed and the cause remanded, with directions to the trial court to set aside its order
of dismissal of the cause and to reinstate
plaintiff's fifth amended petition and to proceed with the cause in conformity to law. It
is so ordered.

All concur.

STATE v. McDONALD. (No. 22639.)

(Supreme Court of Missouri, Division No. 2.
May 26, 1921. Motion for Rehearing
Denied June 23, 1921.)

1. **Homicide ⟠⇒255(3)—Evidence held sufficient to sustain verdict of manslaughter.**

In a prosecution for second degree mur-
der, evidence *held* sufficient to sustain the jury's
finding of guilty of manslaughter in the third
degree.

2. **Criminal law ⟠⇒1144(12)—Exclusion of contract, giving rise to quarrel leading to killing,
presumed proper, though no ground of objection stated.**

In a prosecution for murder resulting from
a quarrel as to the terms of a contract between defendant and deceased, and the Supreme Court is not advised of the contents of
the exhibit, it will be presumed the court did
not err in excluding the contract as an exhibit,
though defendant's objection, alleging no
ground, was invalid.

3. **Criminal law ⟠⇒706—Statement of state's
counsel that he did not want to introduce exhibit over defendant's objections not improper.**

In a prosecution for murder, a statement
by the state's counsel that he did not want to
introduce, over defendant's objections, a contract between defendant and deceased, concerning the terms of which a quarrel had arisen
resulting in the homicide, was not improper,
and afforded no ground for reversal as having
been uttered, not in good faith, but to create a
false impression against defendant.

4. **Criminal law ⟠⇒1037(1)—No error in intimation of guilt in prosecutor's statements,
where no objection to impeaching questions.**

In a prosecution for second degree murder, where no objection was made to questions asked of defendant's witness on cross-examination as to whether defendant had been
convicted of assault and battery and for disturbing the peace, and no adverse rulings were
made, a statement by the state's counsel on
cross-examination of another witness, inferring
defendant's guilt because such witness had not
been placed on the stand at the preliminary,
was not reversible error; there being nothing
for review.

5. **Criminal law ⟠⇒695(4)—Objection to question on ground not asked in good faith, not
on ground of incompetency, properly overruled.**

In a prosecution for murder, where defendant's only objection to questions as to wheth-

er defendant had committed other crimes was on the ground, not that the testimony was incompetent, but that the question objected to was not asked in good faith, the objection was properly overruled.

6. Criminal law ⏘⇒693—Objection to question, after answer, on sole ground not asked in good faith, properly overruled.

In a prosecution for murder defendant's objection to a question as to whether the witness had not heard of defendant being convicted for disturbing religious worship, on the ground it was not asked in good faith, was properly overruled, not having been made until after the witness answered, and no objection having been made to its form.

7. Witnesses ⏘⇒274(2)—Character witness may be questioned as to rumors concerning defendant's misconduct.

A character witness may be interrogated as to whether he has heard rumors concerning defendant's illegal proceedings which might affect his reputation for peace and quietude.

Appeal from Circuit Court, Texas County; L. B. Woodside, Judge.

James McDonald was convicted of manslaughter in the third degree, and he appeals. Affirmed.

On August 16, 1920, an information was filed in the circuit court of Texas county, Mo., by the prosecuting attorney of said county, charging defendant McDonald with murder in the second degree for the killing of Henry Stephens, in said county, on July 20, 1920, with a mowing machine cycle bar, etc. Defendant entered a plea of not guilty, and the trial commenced before a jury on November 11, 1920.

The evidence on the part of the state is substantially as follows: On July 20, 1920, in Texas county, Mo., the appellant assaulted Henry Stephens with a mowing machine cycle bar, inflicting a mortal wound upon the left side of his head, from which he died at Springfield, Mo., on July 23, 1920. The controversy was caused by a difference between appellant and deceased over the division of some hay which appellant was saving on the farm of deceased. Appellant and a man by the name of Jim Miller had come to the home of the deceased just after noon on July 20th, and were grinding the cycle when the deceased came to where they were, and asked appellant how much hay he had cut. Appellant told him that he had hauled four loads to his home and two to the deceased's home. The deceased contended that he was to have half of the hay, and appellant claimed he was only to have one-third. They quarreled about the matter, and in the quarrel they referred to a written contract, and the deceased told appellant finally to leave the hay in the field if he could not bring him half of it as he had agreed to do. They argued for some time about their agreement, and finally deceased said to appellant, "You have been trying to make trouble between me and my neighbors," and appellant said, "You are a liar, and whoever told you that is a d—— l—— and a s—— of a b——." In the conversation, appellant raised his hand several times towards the deceased, and one time the deceased said, "You take your hand down," and then the appellant struck the deceased, and he toppled over a little bit, and then he struck him again with the cycle. Deceased did not have any knife in his hand, and did not make any effort to strike appellant. After the deceased was taken in the house his knife fell out of his pocket. It was closed. Jim Miller, the deceased's wife, daughter, and son were present when the difficulty occurred. After the lick on the deceased's head he was never conscious so that he could talk.

The testimony for the defense was substantially as follows: Appellant and Jim Miller were at the home of the deceased, grinding a cycle for a mower. Miller was turning the grindstone, and appellant was grinding the cycle, when Stephens walked up and asked how appellant was getting along hauling hay. They got into a quarrel as to how much of the hay each was to receive. Appellant told Stephens to get his contract and read it, and whatever it said each was to receive, he would abide by that. Deceased then told appellant that he had run around over the country, and talked to his neighbors and caused trouble, and appellant said that was a d—— lie, and anybody who told him that was a d—— lying s—— of a b——, and that he would face anybody in that statement. Deceased had his knife in his hand, and put it up on his breast and said: "You have run over the wrong man. G—— d—— you. I'll kill you if I don't get half of that hay!" Appellant told him to get his contract and read it, and he said: "G—— d—— the contract. I'll kill you or have half of the hay" and deceased made a pass at him with his knife and cut within two inches of the jugular vein, and cut his shirt on the right side. Appellant pushed him back and deceased started towards him again, and appellant hit him again on the head and he fell to the ground. Appellant testified that he tried to persuade the deceased that they should not have any trouble, and they both cursed each other; that the deceased struck the appellant with a knife, and cut his shirt and suspenders; that appellant shoved him back, and deceased started towards him again, trying to cut him, and that appellant struck him with the cycle while appellant remained sitting aside the grindstone frame. Appellant thought he was hitting him with the side of the cycle. He struck him to keep him from cutting him with his knife. Deceased cut appellant once in the hand, and after appellant struck deceased, deceased's daughter came up, and was hitting and scratching appellant, and Jim Miller took hold of her and told her to stop. Appellant did not strike deceased but one lick. Several witnesses testified that the general reputation of appellant for being a peaceable, law-abiding citizen was good.

On November 12, 1920, the jury returned into court the following verdict:

"We, the jury, find the defendant guilty of manslaughter in the third degree, but can't agree on the punishment.
"[Signed] C. C. Tuttle, Foreman."

The court on the same day fixed the punishment of defendant at imprisonment in the penitentiary for a term of two years. Defendant in due time filed his motion for a new trial, which was overruled and the cause duly appealed by him to this court.

Barton & Impey, of Houston, for appellant.

Jesse W. Barrett, Atty. Gen., and Robt. J. Smith and R. W. Otto, Asst. Attys. Gen., for the State.

RAILEY, C. (after stating the facts as above). [1] 1. We have carefully read the evidence set out in the transcript, and have likewise read and considered the respective briefs on file in the case. The indictment is in proper form, and in our opinion the instructions are fair to the defendant, and properly declared all the law that was necessary for the consideration of the jury in passing upon the merits of the case. The record contains abundant substantial evidence sustaining the finding of the jury. Unless reversible error was committed by the court, during the progress of the trial, it will be our plain duty to affirm the judgment.

[2, 3] 2. The first assignment of error found in appellant's brief is couched in the following language:

"(1) The court erred in overruling defendant's objection to questions asked, not in good faith to obtain testimony, but to create a false impression against defendant."

Under appellant's "points and authorities," we are not referred to any place, in either the transcript or briefs, where the above matter complained of can be found. Neither does the argument in defendant's brief point out any part of the record which can be definitely located as containing the matters complained of in above assignment. It is not inappropriate, while passing, in view of the foregoing, to suggest that the brief on file in behalf of appellant is of little practical benefit to the court, as we are required to grope in the dark and dig out of the record the few alleged errors complained of under said assignment.

231 S.W.—59

One of the supposed errors will doubtless be found on page 5 of appellant's statement, which reads as follows:

"Just before the close of the state's evidence, the following occurred:
"By Mr. Hiett: I now want to offer in evidence the contract which was identified by the witness, Mrs. Stephens, and is marked Exhibits A and A2.
"By Mr. Barton: I object to the introduction of that contract in evidence.
"By the Court: The objection is sustained.
"By Mr. Hiett: Well, I don't want to introduce it in evidence over their objections.
"By Mr. Barton: I object to Mr. Hiett making that statement.
"By the Court: The court ruled it out; as far as the state's testimony is concerned, it is inadmissible."

We are not advised as to the contents of said exhibits, and, in the absence of evidence to the contrary, presume the court committed no error in excluding same, although defendant's ground of objection above stated was invalid as a legal objection, and amounted to nothing. The court, however, sustained the objection. Counsel for the state was guilty of no impropriety in making the statement attributed to him. The above complaint is devoid of merit, affords no ground for reversing the case, and is absolutely trivial in its nature.

[4] On pages 5 and 6 of defendant's statement, the following occurs:

"In the cross-examination of Miller, an assertion is plainly implied that Miller had not told Fitzgerald and Fugate what he said he had. Fugate was a state witness indorsed on the information, but was not called, and there was no evidence contradicting Miller on this point.
"In the cross-examination of Miller, an inference of guilt is plainly sought from the fact Miller was not put upon the stand at the preliminary. This was accentuated when the special prosecutor plainly intimated that the reason this witness was not placed on the stand at the preliminary was because defendant's counsel did not believe what the witness said.
"On cross-examination of defendant's character witness, Sam Martin, from Webster county, the following occurred:
"Q. (by Mr. Hiett). Did you ever hear of him being convicted over there, for assault and battery? A. No, sir.
"Q. Did you ever hear of him being convicted for making an assault upon a fellow by the name of Tom Smith? A. No, sir; I didn't.
"Q. Did you ever hear about him being convicted for disturbing the peace of a church there close to where you lived? A. For disturbing the peace?
"Q. Yes. A. No, sir; well, if I did, I have no remembrance of it.
"Q. You don't know whether anything like that occurred or not? A. No, sir."

We have before us the transcript on file, and find upon actual inspection that not a single objection was made by defendant to the admission or exclusion of any evidence whatever, on either pages 79, 80, 81, 82, or 83 of the transcript, and yet we are blandly asked to reverse this case on account of above statement of counsel. There was no objection made by appellant's counsel, nor was any adverse ruling made against defendant. There was nothing for review on the face of the record. The foregoing assignment is devoid of even the slightest merit.

[5-7] 3. The second assignment of error reads as follows:

"(2)· The court erred in refusing to rebuke counsel for the state for attempting, by questions not asked in good faith, to create an impression on the minds of the jury that defendant had committed several other crimes."

On pages 7 and 8 of defendant's brief, we find the following:

"The cross-examination of defendant's character witness, W. B. Burk, from Webster county, is as follows:

"Q. (by Mr. Hiett). Do you know where there is a schoolhouse, close to you, called the Carrice schoolhouse? A. I don't know the place; it ain't in that country.

"Q. Is there a school house out there, by that name, close to Fordland? A. What?

"Q. There is a schoolhouse, by that name, close to Fordland, isn't there? A. No, sir; I don't know it by that name.

"Q. You don't know it by that name? A. No, sir.

"Q. Didn't you hear of the defendant being convicted for disturbing religious worship at a schoolhouse somewhere there close to you? A. What?

"Q. Didn't you hear of the defendant being convicted of disturbing religious worship, at a schoolhouse there close to you? A. No, sir.

"By Mr. Barton: I want to object to this question on the ground that it is not asked in good faith, and I ask the court to rebuke the attorney for the state for asking a question which is not intended to elicit facts, but to cast suspicion only.

"By the Court: The court is unable to determine whether the question is asked in good faith or not; the question should not be asked by the attorney unless asked in good faith for the purpose of eliciting information, but the court, not being able to determine that it was not so asked, overrules the objection, and declines to rebuke counsel for the state for asking the question. (To which action of the court in overruling said objection and declining to rebuke counsel for the state the defendant, in open court, by counsel, objected and excepted at the time.)

"By Mr. Hiett: Q. You never heard about him being convicted for common assault? A. No, sir.

"Q. Or pleading guilty to common assault? A. No, sir.

"Q. Do you know what he left there for? A. What?

"Q. Do you know what he left there for? A. No, sir; I don't.

"Q. That is all."

It will be observed that only one objection was made by defendant's counsel to the above examination, and that too was in respect to a question which had been asked and answered. Furthermore, the objection was not made as to the incompetency of the testimony sought to be elicited, but the court was asked to sustain said objection on the ground that the above question was not asked in good faith by counsel for the state. The court very properly overruled the objection made to the single question after it had been answered. Aside from the foregoing, as there was no objection made to the form of the question, the court could not well sustain said objection, because it came too late, and because we have heretofore held that where a character witness is on the stand he may be interrogated as to whether he has heard rumors afloat concerning defendant's alleged illegal proceedings which might affect his reputation for peace and quietude. State v. Hulbert, 228 S. W. loc. cit. 501; State v. Smith, 250 Mo. loc. cit. 277, 157 S. W. 307; State v. Beckner, 194 Mo. loc. cit. 208, 91 S. W. 892, 3 L. R. A. (N. S.) 535; State v. Parker, 172 Mo. loc. cit. 206, 207, 72 S. W. 650; State v. Crow, 107 Mo. loc. cit. 345, 17 S. W. 745.

4. We have carefully considered all the questions presented herein, and find no valid grounds for reversing the case. The defendant was convicted upon substantial evidence, after a fair and impartial trial, upon a record free from error. The judgment of the trial court is accordingly affirmed.

WHITE and MOZLEY, CC., concur.

PER CURIAM. The foregoing opinion of RAILEY, C., is hereby adopted as the opinion of the court.

All concur.

NATIONAL REFRIGERATOR CO. v. SOUTHWEST MISSOURI LIGHT CO. (No. 21817.)

(Supreme Court of Missouri, Division No. 1. April 9, 1921. Motion for Rehearing Denied June 6, 1921.)

1. Appeal and error ⚫⚙643(5)—Omission of record to show that motion for new trial and bill of exceptions filed cured by failure to object in time.

Rule No. 13 of the Supreme Court, as amended December 31, 1920 (228 S. W. viii), cures the defect that the record proper, as shown by the abstract of the record, fails to show that motion for new trial and bill of exceptions were filed, where respondent failed to serve motion containing objections to the sufficiency of the abstract on appellant within 15 days after appellant had served the abstract.

2. Courts ⚷78—Rule of court cannot repeal provisions of statute.

A rule of court cannot repeal the provisions of a statute regarding any matter.

3. Commerce ⚷8(1)—No state can interfere with interstate commerce into Missouri.

Under the interstate commerce clause of the federal Constitution, no state can interfere with, lay a burden upon, or prohibit, the transportation of interstate commerce into Missouri; it being wholly immaterial where the contract effecting interstate commerce is made.

4. Courts ⚷97(5)—Decisions of federal courts as to interstate commerce controlling.

The ultimate or final disposition of all questions regarding interstate commerce rests with the federal courts.

5. Corporations ⚷642(6)—Company contracting to install ice-making plant engaged in local operation and required to take out license.

A foreign corporation which contracted with a Missouri corporation to install a 25-ton daily capacity ice-making plant, being required to undertake construction work in the state, hire labor, etc., though the ice-making machinery was purchased in other states and shipped into Missouri, was engaged in a local operation and was within Rev. St. 1909, §§ 3027-3040, requiring a foreign corporation to take out license in the state before doing business therein; no question of interstate commerce being involved.

Appeal from Circuit Court, Jasper County; Grant Emerson, Judge.

Action by the National Refrigerator Company against the Southwest Missouri Light Company. From judgment for defendant, plaintiff appeals. Affirmed.

This case was brought by the plaintiff, in the circuit court of Jasper county, against the defendant, to recover the sum of $12,-890.41, balance alleged to be due it under a written contract to furnish the material and install at Joplin, Mo., a certain ice plant described in the petition.

Judgment was for the defendant, and plaintiff appealed the cause to this court.

The contract (omitting formal parts) is as follows:

We propose to furnish and erect at Joplin, Missouri, in complete running order and condition, and of the best material and workmanship, one ice-making plant of 25 tons capacity daily, as per specifications to be submitted, for the sum of twenty-two thousand four hundred and thirty-six ($22,436) dollars, payments to be made as follows:

Six thousand ($6,000) dollars on arrival of machines in Joplin, Missouri.

Six thousand four hundred and thirty-six ($6,436) dollars when machines are installed and ready to start, less freight charges, and erecting expenses advanced by you.

Ten thousand ($10,000) dollars or balance in two notes of $5,000 each payable in one and two years with interest at the rate of 6 per cent. per annum. These notes to be executed by light company or their successors, or both, and in the event of the organization of a stock or incorporated company for the purpose of acquiring ownership in the said machines and apparatus, then the notes to be executed by the company, and secured by the entire issue of its capital stock.

The notes mentioned in the contract were never executed; hence the suit was for the balance due under the contract.

The sufficiency of the pleadings are not questioned, so we will put them aside, except to say that the answer, among other things, charges that the plaintiff was a foreign corporation organized and doing business under the laws of Colorado and had never taken out a license to do business in this state as required by the statutes hereof. The reply, among other things, stated that the contract matter involved interstate commerce, and was therefore not governed by the laws of this state.

When the cause was called for trial the following stipulation was entered in by and between counsel for the respective parties (formal parts omitted):

Whereas, there are several issues involved in the trial of this cause, some of which will require the examination and determination of long and complicated accounts and transactions; and,

Whereas, one of the issues is presented by the second court of the last amended answer and the denial thereof contained in the plaintiff's reply thereto, said issue being in substance the right of the plaintiff to have and maintain its suit and recover because of the alleged fact that it was and is a corporation under the laws of Colorado and had failed to comply with the laws of Missouri; said second count of the last amended answer and that portion of the reply referring thereto are hereby referred to and made a part hereof for a more definite statement of such issue; and,

Whereas, the determination of such issue may or may not make unnecessary the trial of the further issues in the case:

It is, therefore, agreed and stipulated that there shall first be tried to the court (a jury being waived thereon) the issue aforesaid, presented by the second count of defendant's last amended answer and that portion of reply relating thereto, that the parties shall from time to time during the present term of court submit their evidence on such issue unto the end that all the evidence must be submitted during said term of court and the matter finally submitted to the court for determination. That upon hearing and considering the matter aforesaid, the court shall determine and announce his finding on such issue. If such finding be for the defendant, thereupon final judgment shall be rendered in this cause in favor of the defendant and against the plaintiff, from which plaintiff may appeal. If such finding be for the plaintiff, the defendant shall thereupon file its counterclaim in the cause and the remaining issues, other than that above stipulated, shall remain for trial and be heard and determined by the court, no judgment to be rendered until determination of all the issues by the court, whereupon the defendant appeals.

The following admission was also made at the trial in open court:

Mr. Spencer: It is admitted that on the date of the making of the contract sued on, to wit, January 7, 1902, the plaintiff was and has ever since been a corporation organized for business purposes under the laws of the state of Colorado, and that said plaintiff has never complied with the laws of this state, Missouri, and obtained a license authorizing it to transact business within this state and that it never had or maintained a public office or place in this state for the transaction of business where legal service might be obtained upon it and where the books were kept required by the Missouri statute, and that the plaintiff never took any steps to procure a license or authority to transact business in this state.

Mr. Dewey: This further thought: Whether this business as a whole is a transaction which would be made void by the statutes of Missouri or whether it would come under the exceptions which are allowed by interstate commerce. In other words, the point we are working on to-day is whether this was a transaction or contract of interstate commerce.

In order to maintain the issues on its part plaintiff introduced the following evidence:

E. J. Ulrich, sworn as a witness on behalf of plaintiff, testified substantially as follows:

He first received a letter from the manager of the defendant by Mr. Geo. Myers, of Joplin, Mo., at Colorado Springs in September, 1901, regarding the installation of an ice plant. The letter was as follows (formal parts omitted):

"Mr. E. T. Skinkle, of Chicago, advises that you are going to be in Chicago some time next week. If it is possible for you to do so, please come via Kansas City, as I am very anxious to talk with you in regard to installation of one or two ice plants. In fact, I want to arrange my affairs so I can visit the ice plants which you now have in operation at an early date.

"Please advise me by early mail, if possible, when you will reach Kansas City, so I will be sure to be at home."

Later I met the gentleman in Chicago and entered into a contract to install an ice plant at their works near Joplin. This was in January, 1902. In pursuance of that contract we drew the plans, installed foundations for the machinery, and ordered the machinery and equipment for the plant. We put it in a building furnished us by the defendant which was already built and on the ground at Grand Falls, near Joplin, Mo. We bought a large part of the machinery from the York Manufacturing Company, some from a Chicago firm, some from the Liner Company, of Denver, and some we manufactured. We were interested in a factory in Chicago which made smaller plants, but this was too large for them to handle entirely; hence the

purchases made from other sources. The machinery and parts were all shipped to our order at Grand Falls in Newton county, Mo., and installed under our supervision. We paid the freight on it all, and the defendant later refunded it to us. The business of the plaintiff is building ice and cold storage plants and installing refrigerating machinery. What we mean by installation is this: We put in cement foundations for the machines which necessitated the hiring of carpenters, mixers, masons, the purchase of some rough lumber to make the forms, a certain amount of cement, and other matter, used in such construction. Into these foundations the templates were set with the proper bolts for attaching the machinery and making it solid. The machinery was then taken from the car, placed on the foundations previously prepared, put onto bolts in same, and made fast. These were the compressors. Then the tanks which came in sheets of steel were riveted together in one, two, or four battery arrangement as the case might be. Then the freezing coils and other coils are anchored, and lastly the cans were put in place. These cans, by the way, were bought by the York people from a can manufacturing company in the east. People specialize. Some make cans; some, ammonia compressors, etc. We purchased, in making up the parts of this plant, where we could get the best material. All of that material is assembled and put into working condition and connection is made with the power. In this case we had to connect up to the main line of shafting of the Southwest Missouri Light Company which had already been installed by them in this power plant. We bought very little stuff locally, as we had brought practically everything with us that would be necessary, except perhaps a bolt or nut, such which we happened to be short of. In doing all this you can see we would need some pipe fitters, some pipe men, trench diggers, a few machinists, and a carpenter here and there, all working under our skilled erecting engineers. There were some changes in plans and suggestions which took additional time in the installation and, moreover, the installation of an additional part of this plant by the Southwest Light Company, for which we, at their request, furnished the plans and advice—all gratuitously, however. We bought very little pipe for our installation work, though there was a good deal used by the Southwest Company. In the installation of the storage house just mentioned, it took very little cement for the foundations, as there were but two machines and of a size not to require much.

Our relations with the York people have always been very close. They have a western manager in Chicago with whom I had a conference as soon as I had made the contract with the Southwest Company. We, the western manager and I, got on the train about the 9th or 10th of January, 1902, and went to York, Pa., and there drew the plans for the installation of the plant. It was at that time that he entered into an agreement to furnish and install for us a part of the machinery. This to be done under our supervision.

The foregoing was all the testimony introduced by the plaintiff. In order to maintain the issues on its part, the defendant introduced the following evidence:

Mr. George Myers testified for the defendant that he was an official of the defendant company at the time of the installation of the ice plant by the plaintiff; being a director and general manager; that he signed the contract for the purchase of the ice plant covered by the issues in this suit; that he thought the same was signed in Kansas City, Mo.; that the plaintiff after signing the contract did install the ice-making machines in connection with all the piping needed, also installed all of the cans and other apparatus that was intended to be furnished up to a certain stage for the purpose of carrying out the contract, which work was done at Grand Falls near Joplin, after the stuff reached the land; that they were there several months doing the work, and the force of men varied; that they were men employed by and working for and paid by the plaintiff; that after the plant was installed they had trouble in making "merchantable ice," and representatives of the plaintiff stayed there working over the plant some months; that the experimental period came after six or eight months; that Mr. Weare Parsons was the superintendent who had the work in charge. He further testified that "Exhibit A" offered in evidence by plaintiff was the one signed by him; that when they found they could not make merchantable ice plaintiff "packed up their truck and got out."

Mr. Weare Parsons testified for defendant substantially as follows:

That at the time of the installation of the ice plant he was working for the defendant; that he was the superintendent of defendant's interests during the time; that plaintiff purchased a lot of material locally such as was used in the installation of the work, the material being lumber, hardware, pipe fittings, and incidental material which was necessary for the work; that they shipped in the ammonia compressor with the condenser and air compressor together with the general line of material required; that after its arrival there the plaintiff employed all the common labor necessary and purchased quite a large amount of material locally to use in the erection and installation of the equipment; that the time consumed in the installation lasted from the 1st of June till the 1st of November; that they had a force of workmen of from 4 to 15 as the work from time to time required; that these men performed their duties under the supervision of the National Refrigerator Company; that the character of the material purchased locally was such as would be required to install their work under like conditions, "in other words, such as was necessary to comply with their contract,"; that the York Manufacturing Company had a contract with the National to install, and did install, the ammonia compressor and condenser for them, and that the rest of the installation was by the plaintiff under the supervision of a Mr. Fox; that certain laterals were in wrong and had to be rearranged, a filter installed, and a tweedale system of purification put in that took time and did not work well; that the changing of the laterals and air lines took about two weeks; that the first turnover was made about the 1st of July and the changes and readjustment and water troubles ran through the rest of the period named.

And this substantially was all the evidence introduced by defendant bearing on the point at issue.

As before stated, the findings of the court and the judgment thereof were for the defendant, and the plaintiff duly appealed the cause to this court.

E. K. Robinett, of Tulsa, Okl., and Dewey & Foulke, of Joplin, for appellant.

C. O. Spencer and A. E. Spencer, both of Joplin, for respondent.

WOODSON, P. J. (after stating the facts as above). [1] I. There are some preliminary questions to be disposed of before we approach the case upon its merits. First, it is insisted by counsel for respondent that there is nothing but the record proper before the court for consideration, for the reasons that the record proper, as shown by the abstract of the record, fails to show that the motion for a new trial and the bill of exceptions were ever filed.

Upon an inspection of the abstract we find that this insistence is true, but we are of the opinion that said omissions are cured by virtue of the amendment of Rule No. 13 of this court, adopted December 31, 1920, (228 S. W. viii), which amendment reads as follows:

"If in any case any matter which should properly be set forth in the abstract as a part of the record proper, shall appear in the abstract as a part of the bill of exceptions, or vice versa, such matter shall be considered and treated as if set forth in its proper place, and all objections on account thereof shall be deemed waived, unless the other party shall, within fifteen days after the service of such abstract upon him, specify such objection and the reasons therefor in writing and serve the same upon the opposing party or his counsel; and in the event such objection be so made, the other party may within ten days, from the service of such written objection, upon him or his counsel, correct his abstract so as to obviate such objection, if under the facts as shown by the record proper or the bill of exceptions in the trial court, such correction can truthfully be made."

While this amendment is not quite as clear in meaning as it might have been drawn, yet the spirit and meaning can scarcely be misunderstood, when its purpose is considered. It provides that—

"If in any case any matter which should properly be set forth in the abstract as a part of the record proper, shall appear in the abstract as a part of the bill of exceptions, or vice versa, such matter shall be considered and treated as if set forth in its proper place, and all objections on account thereof shall be deemed waived, unless the other party shall, within fifteen days after the service of such abstract upon him, specify such objection and the reasons therefor in writing and serve the same upon the opposing party or his counsel," etc.

[2]·In reading this rule some three matters are left in doubt: (1) Whether or not the motion mentioned may be made in print as well as in writing. We think the clear meaning of the rule is that the objections to the abstract cannot be made orally, but must be made in writing or its equivalent in purpose, in print. (2) Whether or not the objection mentioned in the rule must be contained in a separate motion from the opposite party's brief. From a casual reading of the rule one might be impressed with the idea that the objections should be contained in a separate motion from the brief, but when we come to consider the purpose of the motion that purpose will be served just as well if contained in the brief as if in a separate motion. (3) The most serious objection to the rule is that it does not clearly specify what matters can and cannot be cured by the rule. Of course, the law must be followed regardless of the rule; in other words, the rule cannot repeal the provisions of the statute regarding any matter. For instance, the statutes specify what matters shall be preserved by the record proper, and what matters must be preserved by bill of exceptions, which statutes must be complied with regardless of the rule. If a matter required by the statute to be preserved in the record proper should, as a matter of fact, be preserved in the bill of exceptions only, or vice versa, that error would not be cured by the rule, and the opposite party could by his motion call the attention of the court to the fact that the matter was not in fact properly preserved in the proper legal container. The purpose of the rule is to correct errors of counsel in the preparation of their abstracts of record, where by inadvertence or oversight, they abstract a matter which was properly preserved in the proper place, but erroneously causes the abstract to show that it was not preserved in the proper place, but in an improper place.

With these preliminary observations regarding the meaning of the rule, we are of the opinion counsel for respondent are not in a position to take advantage of the rule, though their objections seem to be well grounded, for the reason that they failed to serve their motion containing their objections to the sufficiency of the abstract upon the appellant within 15 days after the appellant had served the abstract upon them, as required by said rule. The files of this court show that respondent was served with a copy of the abstract on December 10, 1920, and that respondent's motion was served upon counsel for appellant on January 5, 1921, 25 days after the service was had upon counsel for respondent, 10 days too late, according to said rule, to be available.

We therefore hold that counsel for the respondent waived the objections mentioned to the sufficiency of the abstract, and we must disregard the errors suggested in respondent's motion.

II. While counsel for appellant discuss numerous legal propositions in their brief, the ruling of the court upon but one of them is assigned as error, and under the rules of this court, we will ignore all the others.

The error assigned is stated by counsel in the following language:

The court erred in finding the issues for the defendant, Southwest Missouri Light Company, and that the contract sued upon, together with the performance of same, was within the purview of sections 3027–3040 of the Revised Statutes of Missouri 1909, relating to the licensing of foreign corporations in said state, because the contract and the evidence adduced regarding the performance of same shows that the whole transaction was interstate commerce and comprised within the meaning of the words "commerce among the several states" as used in the federal Constitution, article 1, § 8, and that the said transaction was not subject to state regulation and was not within the purview of the statutes of the state of Missouri pertaining to foreign corporations.

Before taking up the discussion of the error assigned, it may be well to notice certain rules at law involved in this case that have been so firmly established by the state and federal decisions they may be considered as elementary.

[3] (1) Under the interstate commerce clause of the Constitution of the United States, no state can interfere with, lay burdens upon, or prohibit the transportation of interstate commerce into this state.

(2) It is wholly immaterial where the contract is made effecting interstate commerce, and it will be enforced if otherwise valid.

[4] (3) And the ultimate or final disposi-

tion of all questions regarding interstate commerce rests with the federal courts.

In support of the assignment of error made by counsel for appellant, we are cited to numerous cases, and especially the case of York Manufacturing Co. v. Colley et al., 247 U. S. 21, 38 Sup. Ct. 430, 62 L. Ed. 963, 11 A. L. R. 611.

The facts of that case are thus stated by the court:

"The York Manufacturing Company, a Pennsylvania corporation, sued for the amount due upon a contract for the purchase of ice manufacturing machinery and to foreclose a lien upon the same. By answer the defendants alleged that the plaintiff was a foreign corporation, that it maintained an office and transacted business in Texas without having obtained a permit therefor and was hence under Texas statutes not authorized to prosecute the suit in the courts of the state, and a dismissal was prayed. In reply the plaintiff averred that the contract sued on was interstate commerce and that the state statute if held to apply was repugnant to the commerce clause of the Constitution of the United States. At the trial it was shown without dispute that the contract covered an ice plant guaranteed to produce three tons of ice a day, consisting of gas compression pumps, a compressor, ammonia condensers, freezing tank and cans, evaporating coils, a brine agitator and other machinery and accessories including apparatus for utilizing exhaust steam for making distilled water for filling ice cans. These parts of machinery, it was provided, were to be shipped from Pennsylvania to the point of delivery in Texas and were there to be erected and connected. This work, it was stipulated, was to be done under the supervision of an engineer to be sent by the York Manufacturing Company for whose services a fixed per diem charge of $6 was to be paid by the purchasers and who should have the assistance of mechanics furnished by the purchasers, the supervision to include not only the erection but the submitting of the machinery to a practical test in operation before the obligation to finally receive it would arise. It was, moreover, undisputed that these provisions were carried out, that about three weeks were consumed in erecting the machinery and about a week in practically testing it, when after a demonstration of its successful operation it was accepted by the purchasers.

"The trial court, not doubting that the contract of sale was interstate commerce, nevertheless concluding that the stipulation as to supervision by an engineer to be sent by the seller was intrastate commerce and wholly separable from the interstate transaction, held that the seller by carrying out that provision had engaged in local business in the state and as the permit required by the state statutes had not been secured, gave effect to the statutes and dismissed the suit. The case is here to review the action of the court below sustaining such conclusion, its judgment being that of the court of last resort of the state in consequence of the refusal of the Supreme Court of the state to allow a writ of error."

In disposing of that case the court held that the provision of the contract as to the services of the expert was germane to the transaction as an interstate contract and did not involve the doing of local business subjecting the appellant to regulations of the statute of Texas concerning foreign corporations. In the discussion of the case the court used this language:

"The only possible question open therefore is, was the particular provision of the contract for the service of an engineer to assemble and erect the machinery in question at the point of destination and to practically test its efficiency before complete delivery relevant and appropriate to the interstate sale of the machinery? When the controversy is thus brought in last analysis to this issue there would seem to be no room for any but an affirmative answer. Generically this must be unless it can be said that an agreement to direct the assembling and supervision of machinery whose intrinsic value largely depends upon its being united and made operative as a whole is not appropriate to its sale. The consequence of such a ruling if made in this case would be particularly emphasized by a consideration of the functions of the machinery composing the plant which was sold, of its complexity, of the necessity of its aggregation and unison with mechanical skill and precision in order that the result of the contract of sale—the ice plant purchased—might come into existence. In its essential principle therefore the case is governed by Caldwell v. North Carolina, 187 U. S. 622; Rearick v. Pennsylvania, 203 U. S. 507; and Dozier v. Alabama, 218 U. S. 124. In fact those cases were relied upon in the Waycross Case as supporting the contention that a mere agreement for the erection of lightning rods in a contract made concerning the shipment of such rods in interstate commerce caused the act of erection to be itself interstate commerce. But the basis upon which the cases were held to be not apposite, that is the local characteristic of the work of putting up lightning rods, not only demonstrates beyond doubt the mistake concerning the ruling as to the Waycross Case which was below committed, but serves unerringly to establish the soundness of the distinction by which the particular question before us is brought within the reach of interstate commerce.

"Of course we are concerned only with the case before us, that is, with a contract inherently relating to and intrinsically dealing with the thing sold, the machinery and all its parts constituting the ice plant. This view must be borne in mind in order to make it clear that what is here said does not concern the subject passed on in General Railway Signal Co. v. Virginia, 246 U. S. 500, since in that case the work required to be done by the contract over and above its inherent and intrinsic relation to the subject-matter of the interstate commerce contract involved the performance of duties over which the state had a right to exercise control because of their inherent intrastate character."

There is no use of considering any more of the cases cited by counsel for appellant, for the reason that if the facts of the case at bar are substantially the same as they were in the York Case, supra, then this judgment must be reversed and cause remanded for new trial, for the reason the York Case is the latest and controlling case upon that question. But in our opinion the facts in the case at bar are so materially different from those in the York Case, it is not controlling here; and we will now try to point out the differentiations between the two cases.

By referring to the contract sued on in this case, it will be seen that there is no provision that the appellant bound itself to furnish an expert to assemble and construct the ice plant at Joplin, Mo., as was the fact in the York Case. Moreover, in the case at bar the uncontradicted evidence shows that in constructing the plant appellant purchased a lot of material locally such as was used in the installation of the work, the material consisting of lumber, hardware, pipe fittings, and incidental materials which were necessary for the work; that appellant employed all the common labor necessary, consisting of a force of men numbering from 4 to 15, for a period of several months; plaintiff also purchased locally considerable quantities of cement for the foundations upon which the ice plant was to rest. And it would seem that it was the intention of the parties that the labor and material above mentioned was to be employed and purchased locally, for the next to the last clause of the contract sued on provides that "six thousand four hundred and thirty-six ($6,436) dollars (shall be paid) when machines are installed and ready to start, less freight charges and erection expenses advanced by you," meaning the respondent.

In our opinion the facts just mentioned clearly distinguish this case from the York Case, supra, and bring it squarely within the ruling of the Supreme Court of the United States in the case of General Railway Signal Co. v. Commonwealth of Virginia, 246 U. S. 500, 38 Sup. Ct. 360, 62 L. Ed. 854. The facts of that case are thus stated by the court:

"Just what did the defendant do in Virginia? It employed there about 20 men—11 signal engineers and experienced men and 9 laborers—for possibly four or five months altogether. They erected iron signal masts about two miles apart and fitted on them alternating current induction motors, signal arms, gears, relays and housings, transformers, line arresters, etc. To reach the rails they dug short, shallow trenches, to an aggregate amount of not over 1,600 feet in a hundred miles. The Southern Railway Company furnished and put up the necessary wooden poles and wires. The defendant's men applied the last coat of paint to the signal apparatus, the first coats having been applied at the factory.

"The defendant did these things in Virginia only because it could not do them in New York, and it had no desire or intention to establish its business in Virginia. Because of the nature of the defendant's products it was a complicated, tedious job to install them ready for use, [and] the defendant was in Virginia for that purpose and no other. It was merely completing a sale to the Southern Railway Company, and it did no business and had no relations with the citizens of Virginia except for hiring a few laborers.

"In short, the defendant was doing in the state isolated acts incidental to its manufacturing and selling business conducted in New York. These acts completed, it might or might never again have so much as one employee in the state. To force such a casual, occasional entrant to secure a license to do business, continuously to maintain an office, to pay a license tax of $1,000 and an annual registration tax, would be, we respectfully submit, the height of injustice. The very language of the statutes regulating foreign corporations doing business in the state is manifestly ill chosen to achieve such a result.

"This court early decided that single transactions in a state by a foreign corporation, even in the conduct of its ordinary business, did not constitute 'doing business.' Cooper Mfg. Co. v. Ferguson, 113 U. S. 727.

"Of course, the whole subject of 'doing business' is interwoven with the effect of the commerce clause of the Constitution and many decisions assign one ground or the other apparently without much discrimination. More accurately speaking, however, if a foreign corporation is not doing business, there is no need to discuss the commerce clause, while if it is doing business, it may still be relieved from compliance with state statutes if its business be interstate."

The holding of the court in that case is well stated in the syllabus of the case:

"A foreign corporation, for lump sums, made and performed contracts to furnish complete automatic railway signal systems in Virginia, in the performance of which the materials, supplies, machinery, devices and equipment were brought from without, but their installation as structures permanently attached to the soil required employment of local labor, digging of ditches, construction of concrete foundations, and painting. Held, that local business was involved, separate and distinct from interstate commerce, and subject to the licensing power of the state. Browning v. Waycross, 233 U. S. 16.

"The Virginia law imposing a fee for the privilege of doing local business of $1,000 on foreign corporations with capital over $1,000,000 and not exceeding $10,000,000 (Acts 1910 c. 53, § 38a), upheld, as not arbitrary or unreasonable under all the circumstances, though the case is on the border line."

Another case very similar to this one is that of Browning v. Waycross, 233 U. S. 17, 34 Sup. Ct. 578, 58 L. Ed. 828. The facts of that case as stated by the court are as follows:

"The plaintiff in error was charged in a municipal court with violating an ordinance which imposed an annual occupation tax of $25 upon lightning rod agents or dealers engaged in putting up or erecting lightning rods within the corporate limits' of the city of Waycross. Although admitting that he had carried on the business, he pleaded not guilty and defended upon the ground that he had done so as the agent of a St. Louis corporation on whose behalf he had solicited orders for the sale of lightning rods; had received the rods when shipped on such orders from St. Louis and had erected them for the corporation, the price paid for the rods to the corporation including the duty to erect them without further charge. This it was asserted constituted the carrying on of interstate commerce which the city could not tax without violating the Constitution of the United States. Although the facts alleged were established without dispute, there was a conviction and sentence, and the same result followed from a trial de novo in the superior court of Ware county where the case was carried by certiorari. On error to the Court of Appeals that judgment was affirmed, the court stating its reasons for doing so in a careful and discriminating opinion reviewing and adversely passing upon the defense under the Constitution of the United States (11 Ga. App. 46). From that judgment this writ of error is prosecuted because of the constitutional question and because under the law of Georgia the Court of Appeals had final authority to conclude the issue."

In affirming the decision of the state court, the Supreme Court of the United States said:

"We are of the opinion that the court below was right in holding that the business of erecting lightning rods under the circumstances disclosed was within the regulating power of the state and not the subject of interstate commerce for the following reasons: (a) Because the affixing of lightning rods to houses, was the carrying on of a business of a strictly local character, peculiarly within the exclusive control of state authority. (b) Because, besides, such business was wholly separate from interstate commerce, involved no question of the delivery of property shipped in interstate commerce or of the right to complete an interstate commerce transaction, but concerned merely the doing of a local act after interstate commerce had completely terminated. It is true, that it was shown that the contract under which the rods were shipped bound the seller, at his own expense, to attach the rods to the houses of the persons who ordered rods, but it was not within the power of the parties by the form of their contract to convert what was exclusively a local business, subject to state control, into an interstate commerce business protected by the commerce clause. It is manifest that if the right here asserted were recognized or the power to accomplish by contract what is here claimed, were to be upheld, all lines of demarkation between national and state authority would become obliterated, since it would necessarily follow that every kind or form of material shipped from one state to the other and intended to be used after delivery in the construction of buildings or in the making of improvements in any form would or could be made interstate commerce."

In the case of State ex rel. v. Arthur Greenfield, Inc., 205 S. W. 619, regarding a similar contention, this language was used:

"Clearly the defendant is not engaged in interstate commerce, but in razing and improving buildings and general construction, and in building fireproof ceilings, partitions, elevators, and dumb-waiter shafts, etc. In the very nature of things the business of the company engaged in such constructions must of necessity be fixed and local where the work is done. It might as well be contended that a farmer is engaged in interstate commerce because he imports his seed and machinery used on the farm from another state as to say that the defendant is engaged in interstate commerce because it imported some or all the materials it used in the construction of the concrete work mentioned in the record.

"Such shipments are purely incidental to the real business of the company; in the very next contract it obtains it may not be necessary to import a pound of material from another state. This defendant is not engaged in purchasing and shipping cement and lumber from one state to another for commercial purposes, but is engaged in the construction of building elevators, dumb-waiter shafts, etc., throughout the country, in which various kinds of materials are used, some of which may or may not be imported from a state different from the one in which the work is being done. That the defendant is not engaged in interstate commerce is too plain for further argument."

The question may be well shown by one of Mr. Benjamin's illustrations as the distinction between the sale of an article of merchandise and a contract for material furnished and work and labor performed. [5] In discussing the statute of fraud he said, in substance, that if a person agrees to purchase a suit of clothing at a price in excess of that provided for by the statute, without the contract was evidenced by writing, signed, etc., the contract of sale would be void in the absence of such writing, but, upon the other hand, if a person should go into a tailor shop and order a suit of clothing to be made for him out of a designated piece of cloth, even though the price should exceed the statutory amount, then the contract would be valid and binding, because the contract was for material to be furnished and work and labor to be performed—the former being purely a contract of sale of a completed manufactured article, while the latter would be contract to manufacture the article for the person designated—and. I suppose the former contract would not be valid even though the merchant should agree with the purchaser to make certain alterations of the suit in conformity to the wishes of the purchaser before it was to be delivered to him, but in the latter case no completed article exists and therefore it could not be sold as an article of commerce. It impresses me that the same is true of the case at bar: Had the contract been that the appellant sold to the respondent a completed ice-making machine of 25 tons capacity daily, with nothing more save perhaps some minor article necessary to have made the delivery complete, the contract of sale would undoubtedly. have been good, but that was not this contract; this contract bound the appellant to sell the ice-making machine to respondent, and in addition thereto, to furnish the material and labor which was necessary to erect the plant upon which the machine was to be erected, which required the furnishing of a considerable amount of material and much labor. The doing of the two latter things brings the case at bar within our statutes which requires a foreign corporation to take out a license in this state before it can do business herein. This I understand to be the ruling of the Supreme Court of the United States in Railway Signal Co. v. Commonwealth of Virginia, supra, and Browning v. Waycross, supra, and we note the same difference in the case of State ex rel. Arthur Greenfield Co., supra.

There are many other cases of like import which are as follows: General Railway Signal Co. v. Commonwealth of Virginia, 246 U. S. 500, 38 Sup. Ct. 360, 62 L. Ed. 854; Browning v. Waycross, 233 U. S. 16, 34 Sup. Ct. 578, 58 L. Ed. 828; City of St. Louis v. Parker-Washington Co., 271 Mo. 229–242, 196 S. W. 767–770; Wichita F. & S, Co. v. Yale, 194 Mo. App. 60, 184 S. W. at 121; Buffalo Refrigerating Mach. Co. v. Penn. H. & P. Co., 178 Fed. 696, 102 C. C. A. 196; St. Louis Exp. Met. F. P. Co. v. Beilharz (Tex. Civ. App.) 88 S. W. 512; S. R. Smythe Co. v. Ft. Worth G. & S. Co., 105 Tex. 8, 142 S. W. 1157; Ft. Worth G. & S. Co. v. Smythe, 61 Tex. Civ. App. 888, 128 S. W. 1186; Buhler v. E. T. Burrowes Co. (Tex. Civ. App.) 171 S. W. 791; General Railway Signal Co. v. Commonwealth, 118 Va. 301, 87 S. E. 598; Hastings Indus. Co. v. Moran, 143 Mich. 679, 107 N. W. 706; Imperial Curtain Co. v. Jacobs, 163 Mich. 72, 127 N. W. 772; American Amusement Co. v. E. Lake Chutes Co., 174 Ala. 526, 56 South. 961; Muller Mfg. Co. v. Dothan Banks, 176 Ala. 229, 57 South. 762; Nickerson v. Warren City Tank Co. (D. C.) 223 Fed. 843.

If we correctly understand the rulings of the Supreme Court of the United States, and of the various states of the Union regarding this question, the judgment of the circuit court should be affirmed; and it is so ordered.

All concur.

RICHARDSON v. KANSAS CITY RYS. CO.
(No. 21487.)

(Supreme Court of Missouri, Division No. 1.
April 9, 1921. Rehearing Denied
June 6, 1921.)

1. **Appeal and error ⬤══922—Court's finding as to qualification of juror presumed correct on appeal.**

A question concerning juror's qualification is to be tried by the court, and not by the ju-

ror, but, if the court has tried it, the ruling comes to the Supreme Court accompanied by a presumption of correctness which is overthrown only when the record shows the ruling was clearly against the evidence.

2. **Jury ⬤══97(1)—Challenge for cause on account of juror's prejudice held properly overruled.**

In a personal injury action against a street railway company, it was not error to overrule a challenge for cause against a juror who stated that he did not think the city "got a square deal on the franchise proposition" four years before; no prejudice on the juror's part appearing.

3. **Jury ⬤══149—That juror's wife was injured during trial as a passenger on defendant's lines held no ground for discharge of jury.**

In a personal injury action against a street railway company, it was not error to refuse to discharge the jury because one of the jurors had become disqualified during the trial on a bald showing that the juror's wife during the course of the trial and before verdict was injured in some way while riding as a passenger on defendant's line; such showing being insufficient to justify an inference of hostility toward defendant.

4. **Jury ⬤══149—Defendant claiming prejudice of juror because of injury to juror's wife during trial has burden of proof.**

In a personal injury action against a street railway company, where defendant predicated error upon court's refusal to discharge the jury on a showing that the wife of one of the jurors had been injured as a passenger on defendant's lines during the trial, it was essential that defendant show that it had so injured the juror's wife that prejudice on his part against defendant resulted of such character that verdict was invalidated thereby.

5. **Damages ⬤══158(4)—Petition alleging impairment of mental faculties held to justify evidence of loss of memory.**

In an action for personal injuries against a street railway company, an allegation that plaintiff received injuries resulting in the "impairment of her mental faculties" *held* sufficient to justify evidence that she was affected with loss of memory.

6. **Trial ⬤══251(8)—Where particular negligence pleaded, instructions must submit nothing outside of specific charges.**

Since an allegation of general negligence is restricted by specifications of particular negligence, instructions in such case must submit nothing outside of the specific charges.

7. **Street railroads ⬤══118(4)—Instructions held to fairly submit specific charges of negligence in striking motortruck.**

In an action for injuries to a passenger in a motortruck standing on the track when struck by defendant's street car, specifications of negligence in failing to keep the car under control following a general charge *held* a specific, and not a mere general, charge of negligence, and to be fairly submitted by instructions requiring findings that the car was negligently operated, managed, or controlled, and that the motorman negligently ran the car against the truck when he saw or in the exercise of ordinary care could have seen it on the track.

8. Street railroads ⟷118(11)—Instruction held to negative defense that motortruck backed into street car.

In an action for injuries to a passenger riding in a motortruck struck by defendant's street car, an instruction requiring a finding that the truck was standing still on the track ahead of the car *held* not insufficient as failing to negative the defense that the truck was backed into the car.

9. Street railroads ⟷118(15) — Instruction held not objectionable as omitting to require findings of motortruck passenger's obliviousness of danger and knowledge thereof by street car operatives.

In an action for injuries to a passenger in a motortruck standing on the track when struck by defendant's street car, an instruction which submitted the case on common-law negligence and conjunctively required a finding pertinent to the humanitarian doctrine *held* not defective as omitting to require findings that plaintiff was oblivious of danger, and that defendant's employés saw or could have seen that to be her condition.

10. Trial ⟷260(1)—Requested instructions already covered properly refused.

It is not error to refuse to give a requested instruction where the subject-matter is covered by other instructions given.

11. Damages ⟷132(5)—$12,000 held excessive for injuries to woman struck by street car.

$12,000 *held* excessive by $2,000 where 25-year old, strong and healthy woman, weighing about 140 pounds, was injured in a collision with a street car resulting in displacement of the kidneys and retroversion of the uterus; her eyesight and memory also being affected.

Appeal from Circuit Court, Jackson County; O. A. Lucas, Judge.

Action by Virginia A. Richardson against the Kansas City Railways Company. Judgment for plaintiff, and defendant appeals. Affirmed on condition.

R. J. Higgins and Mont T. Prewitt, both of Kansas City, for appellant.

Harry G. Kyle and Horace G. Pope, both of Kansas City, for respondent.

JAMES T. BLAIR, J. Respondent recovered judgment for damages for injuries she alleges she received when a truck in which she was seated was brought into collision with one of appellant's cars, and this appeal followed.

On July 4, 1916, a picnic party of 18 young men and women of Kansas City were on their way to Fairmount Park. They were being conveyed in a motortruck, and had proceeded to a point on Washington Park boulevard a short distance east of Cambridge avenue, when they reached the tracks of the St. Louis & San Francisco Railway Company, which there cross the avenue about at right angles. The evidence tended to show that a long freight train was then passing over the crossing. The truck was stopped upon appellant's east-bound track a few feet west of the crossing and stood there facing east toward the passing train for three or four minutes. One of appellant's cars approached from the west at a speed of 12 or 15 miles an hour. When the motorman was more than 400 feet distant from the truck he saw it upon the track upon which his car was proceeding. The back of the truck was toward the street car, and respondent was seated with her back toward the car. The track was almost level and was dry, and the car could have been stopped within a distance of 30 or 40 feet. There was a safety stop for east-bound cars, near the place where the truck was standing and between it and the point from which the motorman first saw it. The motorman sounded no signal or warning, did not check his car at all, but ran it at undiminished speed past the safety stop and against the truck, and thereby seriously injured respondent. There was a verdict for $20,000. The trial court required a remittitur of $8,000, and judgment was entered for $12,000. Appellant contends the court erred: (1) In refusing to sustain a challenge for cause to Juror Hogue; (2) in refusing to discharge the jury because Juror Barker, appellant contends, became disqualified during the trial; (3) in admitting evidence concerning respondent's mental condition; (4) in giving and refusing instructions; and (5) in permitting judgment for an excessive sum.

I. On the voir dire examinations of the panel George Hogue, in answer to a question of appellant's counsel, stated he did not think the "city got a square deal" on the "franchise proposition." The reference was to a transaction in 1914 between the city and appellant which concerned appellant's franchise. Hogue said he had no prejudice against appellant at the time of the trial in June, 1918; that he could not say he had a prejudice against appellant, but still thought the city did not "get a square deal" in 1914. In answer to questions he said, in effect, that his view of the franchise transaction would have nothing to do with his attitude toward appellant in this case, that he "would take the evidence," and that the question concerning appellant's contract rights for operation would not have anything to do with a claim for injuries inflicted in the operation of the road. Counsel argue Hogue admitted he had an existing prejudice against the company. Into the questions he propounded counsel quite skillfully wove implications and assumptions of such a prejudice. The juror avoided these as best he could, and his answers show he did not intend to adopt them. He distinguished between a "prejudice" and his opinion concerning the matter of the 1914 franchise. His whole examination shows he was not satisfied with that agreement, but, properly understood, shows no more.

[1, 2] It is true that the question concerning a juror's qualification is to be tried by the court, and not by the juror (Theobald v. Transit Co., 191 Mo. loc. cit. 417, 90 S. W. 354), but it is also true that after the court has tried it the ruling comes here accompanied by a presumption of correctness which is overthrown only when the record shows the ruling was clearly against the evidence. Theobald v. Transit Co., supra, and cases cited. The record does not convict the juror of prejudice. He, in effect, denied the assumption by counsel that he entertained such a feeling. The character of the matter with respect to which the juror did not approve appellant's course was not, in its nature, so far as the record shows, such as to prove prejudice in 1918 and disprove the juror's denial of prejudice. Hogue was apparently candid with court and counsel. He recognized the irrelevancy of the franchise question to the issue in this case. He thought it "had nothing to do with it" and that the evidence should govern. He said the evidence would govern him. We do not think the record shows the trial court erred in overruling the challenge for cause.

II. The case went to trial on June 5, 1918. The taking of evidence was finished during the afternoon of Monday, June 10, 1918. The instructions were then given, and the arguments followed. Thereafter, but at some time on June 10th, a unanimous verdict was returned. In support of its motion for new trial appellant filed the affidavit of one of its claim agents in which it was stated that on June 8, 1918, the wife of one of the jurors, George R. Barker, was injured while riding with her husband as a passenger on one of appellant's cars. Appellant also filed the affidavit of Meyers in which Meyers stated that on June 14, 1918, he presented to Barker for his signature a form of affidavit; that in this form it was set out that Barker was a foreman of the jury in this case, and that Barker and his wife were on one of appellant's cars on the evening of June 8, 1918, and Mrs. Barker was injured while riding as a passenger thereon. It was also set out in this form that Barker was present when his wife was injured, and that it "caused him to be sore and peeved under the circumstances," and that a claim for the injury to Mrs. Barker had then (June 14th) been made. Meyers, in his affidavit, stated that Barker refused to sign the paper he presented to him, but "admitted the truth of the unsigned affidavit." Respondent filed Barker's affidavit.

In it he stated that some one representing appellant presented a form of affidavit for his signature, but that he refused to sign it because it was not true in all respects; denied that he admitted to Meyers the truth of all the statements in the form he refused to sign; admitted his wife received an injury to one of her arms while he and she were passengers on one of appellant's cars on June 8, 1918, but stated that neither he nor his wife had made claim against appellant, though claim agents of appellant had called and endeavored to settle; denied that he became "sore and peeved" against appellant; and "affiant further states that said accident to his wife did not prejudice him against said defendant * * * in the trial of this cause, and that said accident to his wife had no effect whatever on his deliberations as a juror in the cause or on his verdict so given in favor of plaintiff in said cause, and that he now has no prejudice against defendant by reason thereof, and that said accident had no bearing whatever on his verdict in the above cause, but that said verdict was given by affiant because he believed it true and just."

[3, 4] Though the injury to Mrs. Barker, whatever it was, occurred on the evening of June 8, 1918, and the verdict was not returned until nearly 48 hours later, no motion to discharge the jury was made before verdict. The ruling on the point will not be put on that ground, however. With Barker's affidavit on file no additional evidence, documentary or other, was offered to show that either he or Mrs. Barker had made any claim against the company. From this and the affidavits and the date of the order overruling the motion for new trial it appears, therefore, that at least as late as July 13, 1918, neither Barker nor his wife had attached enough importance to Mrs. Barker's injury to have made claim for damages. That fact is of no great consequence, but it is not improper to mention it. The significant thing is that at no time did appellant inform the trial court of the character of Mrs. Barker's injury. It may well be that there are injuries the nature of which is such that a feeling of hostility toward the person or agency which inflicted them would be fairly inferable. We do not think that a bald showing that Mrs. Barker was injured in some way "while riding as a passenger" discloses enough to justify such an inference of hostility toward appellant. Besides the failure to show whether the injury was a serious one or a mere scratch, there was also a failure to show appellant's fault or responsibility. It is quite possible for one "riding as a passenger" to receive an injury for which the carrier is in no wise responsible. It was incumbent upon appellant, upon this ground of its motion, to convince the trial court that the incident upon which it relied so disqualified Barker that a verdict in

which he participated ought not to stand. It was essential that appellant show that appellant had so injured Barker's wife that prejudice on his part against appellant resulted of such character that the verdict was invalidated thereby. Appellant did not even admit responsibility. Perhaps it had in mind the doctrine of res ipsa loquitur. We are of the opinion that the circumstances called for a frank exposition of the facts, and that the guarded, careful, and successful effort to avoid acceptance of responsibility for·Mrs. Barker's injury, while perhaps commendable as protective of appellant's rights as against Mrs. Barker, falls short of showing the facts necessary to sustain this ground of the motion for new trial. The showing made does not convict the trial court of error in its ruling.

[5] III. Complaint is made that respondent's testimony that her injury caused her to be affected with loss of memory was not within the pleadings. The petition alleged the injury respondent received resulted in "the impairment of her mental faculties." Besides this no exception was taken to the action of the trial court in connection with appellant's motion to strike out the testimony.

IV. Complaint is made of the principal instruction given at respondent's instance. It is said: (1) That the charge of negligence in the petition is specific, and that the instruction did not confine respondent's right to recover to the specific negligence charged; and (2) the instruction did not "take into consideration" the defense that the injury was the result of the truck backing into the car.

[6, 7] 1. The petition first charged that the injury to respondent was caused by the negligence of defendant. This general allegation was followed by numerous specifications of negligent things alleged to have been done. One specification was that appellant's employés "failed and neglected to run and operate said car in a manner that said car would be under such control that it would not be run into and against said automobile when they saw, or by the exercise of reasonable care could have seen, said automobile truck ahead of said car on said track and street." There was evidence tending to support this allegation. It is a specification of negligence and was pleaded as such. The instruction required the jury, before finding for respondent, to find: (1) That she was seated in an automobile truck (2) over which she had no control and (3) which was standing still upon appellant's track ahead of the car, and (4) that respondent was in danger of being struck if the car did not stop and continued on its course; (5) that said street car was so negligently operated, managed, or controlled by the motorman that it was negligently caused to be run into and strike the

truck; (6) that the motorman negligently ran the car against the truck when he saw or in the exercise of ordinary care could have seen the truck on the track ahead of the car, and by the exercise of ordinary care could have stopped the car and have avoided striking the truck. These various findings were all required before a verdict for respondent was authorized by the instruction. The motorman was offered by appellant and testified he saw the car when he was more than 400 feet distant from the truck. It is true that instructions must be within the pleadings; that an allegation of general negligence is restricted by specifications of particular negligence; and that instructions, in such a case, must submit nothing outside the specific charges. In this case among the specifications of negligence which follow the general charge is that already quoted. That this allegation was in itself specific, and not a mere general charge of negligence, is shown by the decisions cited by respondent. Davidson v. Transit Co., 211 Mo. loc. cit. 361, 109 S. W. 583; Beier v. Transit Co., 197 Mo. loc. cit. 232, 283, 94 S. W. 876; Thompson v. Livery Co., 214 Mo. loc. cit. 490, et seq., 113 S. W. 1128. This allegation was fairly submitted to the jury by the assailed instruction.

[8] 2. There was no plea of contributory negligence. There is no claim there was any evidence of it. Nevertheless the instruction required the jury to find, before finding for respondent, that she "at the said time and place acted as a reasonably prudent person would have· acted under the same or similar circumstances for her own safety." The instruction further required the jury to find, before finding for respondent, that "at the time and place in question plaintiff was seated in the automobile truck in question, and that said truck was standing still on the track ahead of the street car," etc. That finding, if made, negatived the defense that the truck backed into the car, and the instruction did not authorize a verdict for respondent until that finding was made by the jury. If the jury found the car was not standing still, it was not authorized by the instruction to find for respondent at all. The objection is not well taken. Further, that there could be no doubt in the jury's mind, it was instructed, at appellant's instance, that if the truck backed into the car too late for the motorman to discover the consequent peril, the verdict should be for appellant. Respondent's instruction was even broader in this respect than was that asked by appellant. The instruction is not open to the objection made.

[9] 3. It is said the instruction omitted to require findings that respondent was oblivious of her danger, and that appellant's employés saw or could have seen that to be her condition. If such a finding is required on facts like those in this case in a submission

on the humanitarian doctrine, still the instruction is not vulnerable to the criticism. It submitted the case on common-law negligence. It conjunctively required a finding pertinent to the humanitarian doctrine, but this was merely one requirement more than was necessary.

[10] 4. The refusal of one instruction asked by appellant with respect to the burden of proof is justified by the fact that other instructions given at appellant's instance covered this feature.

[11] V. The verdict was for $20,000. The trial court required respondent to remit $8,000, and then rendered judgment for $12,000. It is insisted this sum is excessive. The evidence showed that at the time respondent was hurt she was 25 years old. She was "strong, healthy, and rosy." Her weight was 140 pounds. She had never been sick except an occasional "cold" or the like. Her hearing had at a time three or four years previous been slightly affected, probably from her service five or more years before in a rural telephone exchange, but this had yielded to treatment and no longer troubled her. All the organs of her body functioned normally. She lived with her mother and had been employed in stores and shops in Kansas City for about four years. She was steadily employed and lost no time by reason of any physical ailment. She was hurt on July 4, 1916. The truck in which she was sitting was struck heavily by the street car and she was thrown from her seat and rendered unconscious. Emergency treatment was given her. Her back, hip, and leg suffered bruises and abrasions of considerable severity and extent, and it was evident she had received a very severe shock. One of her kidneys was displaced to such an extent that it had four or five inches too much movement. In the course of two years this was reduced to about three inches. The uterus was retroverted so that the cervix pressed against the bladder and the body against the rectum. The ovaries were inflamed and painful. The testimony was that the effect of the displacement of the kidney was to interfere with the regularity and efficiency of its performance of its functions and to cause pain. The abnormal position of the uterus was said to result in irritation of the bladder and tend to affect control of urine, and that its position would be painful. The evidence was that respondent suffered pain much of the time; that she was unable to sleep regularly; that she was very nervous; poor appetite; suffered from frequent headaches; that she was afflicted with constipation and was drowsy; that her hearing and eyesight were somewhat affected, and she had suffered some impairment of her memory; that her mental powers had been somewhat affected; her weight at the time of the trial was 102

pounds, and she was no longer healthy in appearance, but had become thin, haggard, and sallow and appeared to have grown disproportionately older. She was kept at home in Kansas City until August 10, 1916, when she was taken to her brother's home at California. There she remained in bed continuously for two and one half or three months. During the next eight months she was able to sit up part of the time, but was confined to her bed a great deal. In November, 1917, she returned to Kansas City. She attempted to work at two or three places, but worked only a relatively short time. The evidence indicates that an operation may correct the position of the displaced organs. Unless so corrected, the conditions due to their displacement are permanent.

After a consideration of the facts and of the cases cited the court is of the opinion that the judgment is still excessive. It should be reduced to $10,000. Therefore, if respondent will within ten days remit the sum of $2,000, the judgment will stand affirmed, as of the date of its original entry, for $10,000; otherwise the judgment will be reversed, and the cause remanded.

All concur.

CITY WATER CO. v. CITY OF SEDALIA.
(No. 22530.)

(Supreme Court of Missouri, Division No. 2. May 26, 1921. Motion for Rehearing Denied June 23, 1921.)

1. Waters and water courses ⟳200(2)—Contract of city with water company not abrogated by increase of rates authorized by Public Service Commission.

Where a city contracted with a water company for the rental of fire hydrants at a stipulated sum per year, and thereafter the Public Service Commission made an order finding that the rates did not afford a reasonable return on the investment, a subsequent increase did not abrogate the contract; the latter, as modified by the Commission, being binding on both parties, and a contract between a city and a public utility being subject to modification by the paramount power of the state.

2. Waters and water courses ⟳203(12)—City's offer to allow water company to discontinue certain hydrants not reviewable on appeal, where no action taken before Public Service Commission.

Where a hearing before a Public Service Commission, a city, in response to a water company's request for permission to discontinue its fire hydrant service because of the city's refusal to pay increased rentals as authorized by the Commission, offered to allow the company to eliminate certain hydrants, the question of the elimination of such hydrants was not before the court on appeal; no action having been taken on the offer.

⟳For other cases see same topic and KEY-NUMBER in all Key-Numbered Digests and Indexes

3. Waters and water courses ⊕=203(12)—
Question as to effect of increase in rental of fire hydrants on city's indebtedness not considered where not pleaded.

· In an action by a water company against a city for increased rentals of fire hydrants authorized by the Public Service Commission, the question as to whether the action of the Commission would result in increasing the city's indebtedness to a sum in excess of the revenues provided will not be considered on appeal, when raised for the first time in the motion for new trial, instead of in defendants' answer.

4. Waters and water courses ⊕=203(12)—
Water company suing for increased rentals authorized by Public Service Commission need not prove requirements of law complied with.

In an action by a water company against a city for increased rentals of fire hydrants authorized by the Public Service Commission, where the answer admitted the execution of the company's contract with the city, but pleaded that it had been abrogated by the Commission's action in increasing the rentals without the city's consent, the company was not required to prove that the requirements of the law had been complied with; such issue not having been made.

5. Costs ⊕=260(4)—City's appeal from judgment for recovery of increased hydrant rentals by water company not vexatious.

Though the questions raised on an appeal by a city from a judgment allowing a water company to recover increased rentals for fire hydrants as authorized by the Public Service Commission without the consent of the city were res judicata, the appeal was not therefore vexatious nor for delay, so as to justify a penalty.

Appeal from Circuit Court, Pettis County; H. B. Shain, Judge.

Action by the City Water Company of Sedalia against the City of Sedalia. Judgment for plaintiff, and defendant appeals. Affirmed.

Wilkerson & Barnett and R. S. Robertson, all of Sedalia, for appellant.

J. H. Bothwell and Montgomery & Rucker, all of Sedalia, for respondent.

HIGBEE, P. J. The petition alleges, in substance, that the plaintiff is a corporation engaged in furnishing water to the city of Sedalia, a city of the third class, and its inhabitants; that on August 6, 1906, said city adopted an ordinance by which it was provided that the Sedalia Water Company, its successors and assigns, should supply water to said city and its inhabitants and, among other things, should install and maintain all necessary machinery, apparatus, reservoirs, basins, water mains, pipe lines, etc., and said city agreed to rent 198 fire hydrants as then located on the pipe system of said water company, and such additional fire hydrants as

said city might order to be installed for the term of said contract, at an annual rental of $30 for each fire hydrant, payable in semiannual installments on February 1 and August 1 of each year, and that said ordinance was accepted by said water company on August 29, 1906; that plaintiff became the successor of said water company and owner and operator of the waterworks system thereof; that on October 29, 1914, plaintiff applied to the Public Service Commission for an increase of its rates for water service; that defendant intervened, and that such proceedings were had that on April 3, 1916, said Commission made an order finding that the rates and charges aforesaid did not afford a reasonable return on plaintiff's investment and plaintiff filed a new schedule increasing the rental of fire hydrants to $45 per hydrant, which was approved and became effective August 1, 1916; that thereafter, on like proceedings, the rate was increased to $55 per hydrant, effective January 1, 1920; that after August 29, 1906, on the order of the city, 46 additional fire hydrants were installed; that in the years 1916 and 1917 seven additional fire hydrants were installed on the order of the defendant.

The petition, in separate counts, pleads the semiannual installments severally accruing; that defendant paid thereon at the rate of $30 per year for each hydrant, and in each count plaintiff prayed judgment for the unpaid balance, with interest.

The answer admits the various allegations of the petition, and pleads that the orders of the Commission increasing the rentals of the hydrants abrogated the contract and that until a new contract was made defendant was liable only for such fire hydrants as it might use at the original contract price. It further avers that on December 16, 1918, at a hearing before the Commission, plaintiff asked permission to discontinue fire hydrant service to the city because of its refusal to pay the increased rentals, and that at said hearing the defendant insisted that said original contract was in full force, but if the Commission or plaintiff did not wish to continue to operate under said contract, the city had been and was then paying for 87 designated hydrants for which it had no use and which it was willing for plaintiff to eliminate and discontinue. It also averred that plaintiff waived its contract with the city when it made application for a change of rates, and that defendant is only liable to plaintiff for hydrants actually ordered and used after the orders of the Commission increasing the rates were made.

The reply denied all the allegations of the answer, and averred that the orders of the Commission changing the rates for fire hydrant rentals had only the effect of modifying the contract, and that said modified contract is still binding and obligatory upon the parties.

On the trial before the court without a jury, the plaintiff read in evidence an itemized statement of the rentals according to the increased rates as they severally became due, credited with payments at the original contract rates, showing the balances claimed to be due on each installment, with the accrued interest. The defendant read in evidence the report of the Commission on its investigation and valuation of plaintiff's property and its order approving the schedule of increased rates for the rental of the fire hydrants and the list of the 87 hydrants filed with the Commission which might be eliminated. This was all the evidence. There were no instructions asked or given. The finding and judgment were for the plaintiff for the sums claimed in the several counts of the petition, with interest. Motion for new trial having been overruled, the defendant appealed.

Appellant assigns as error: (1) That the court erred in holding that the Commission had power to make or modify a contract on behalf of the city; (2) that the court erred in not holding that the burden of proof was on the plaintiff to show that the contract was not for an expenditure in excess of the income and revenue of the city in any year provided for such year, within the meaning of section 12 of article 10 of the Constitution; (3) because there was no evidence that the expenditure and indebtedness provided for under the contract under the increased rates was not to an amount exceeding, in any year, the income and revenue provided for such year; (4) because the court erred in holding that the Commission had power to so modify the contract as to make it necessary for the city to fund its indebtedness and to provide taxation therefor in contravention of sections 1 and 10 of article 10 of the Constitution; (5) because, if any liability was shown, it was on a quantum meruit and not on a contract; and (6) because the judgment appropriates the city revenue without any act of the city or city council, contrary to the provisions of section 9227, R. S. 1919.

When the new schedules of rates were approved by the Commission, the city, by statutory certiorari, took the matter to the circuit court of Cole county for review, where the reasonableness of the rates fixed by the Commission was approved. On appeal to this court the judgment was affirmed. State ex rel. City of Sedalia v. Pub. Serv. Com., 275 Mo. 201, 204 S. W. 497. The case was then taken on writ of error to the federal Supreme Court (251 U. S. 547, 40 Sup. Ct. 342, 64 L. Ed. 408), where the writ was dismissed for want of jurisdiction upon the authority of Pawhuska v. Pawhuska Oil & Gas Co., 250 U. S. 394, 39 Sup. Ct. 526, 63 L. Ed. 1054.

[1] 1. The very questions raised on this record were thoroughly considered by Judge Graves in State ex rel. Sedalia v. Pub. Serv. Com., supra, in an elaborate opinion concurred in by all the members of Division 1. At the top of page 206 of 275 Mo., at page 47 of 204 S. W., it is said:

"Under the facts of the record, the reasonableness of the rates fixed by the Public Service Commission cannot be seriously questioned. This leaves the single question as to whether or not the Public Service Commission had the lawful right to fix the rate, so far as the city is concerned, in excess of the ordinance rate. Such is the case when cleared of all driftwood."

Referring to the Public Service Commission Act of 1913, the learned opinion quotes from State ex inf. v. Kansas City Gas Co., 254 Mo. loc. cit. 534, 163 S. W. 857:

"That act is an elaborate law bottomed in the police power. It evidences a public policy hammered out on the anvil of public discussion. It apparently recognizes certain generally accepted economic principles and conditions, to wit, that a public utility (like gas, water, or service, etc.), is in its nature a monopoly; that competition is inadequate to protect the public, and, if it exists, is likely to become an economic waste; that state regulation takes the place of and stands for competition; that such regulation, to command respect from patron or utility owner, must be in the name of the overlord, the state, and to be effective must possess the power of intelligent visitation and the plenary supervision of every business feature to be finally (however invisibly) reflected in rates and quality of service. It recognizes that every expenditure, every devotion, every share of stock or bond or note issued as surety is finally reflected in rates and quality of service to the public, as does the moisture which arises in the atmosphere finally descend in rain upon the just and unjust willy-nilly."

The opinion concludes:

"It is, however, clear that under our section 5 of article 12 of the Constitution of 1875 (a section not theretofore found in our Constitution) the Legislature itself cannot abridge the police power of the state. Nor can it authorize a municipal corporation to make a contract abridging or limiting such police power. So that if, as we have held, the fixing of rates for public service is an exercise of the police power, then under other rulings cited above the Public Service Commission had a right to fix reasonable rates irrespective of the alleged contract. The great weight of authority so holds. Cases from a great number of states will be found in the briefs for the Public Service Commission. These discuss the question from different angles, but reach the same conclusion. We have preferred to rest the ruling in this case upon what this court has previously ruled, which rulings have been in the light of our own peculiar constitutional provision. Under it the sovereign police power of the state is preserved intact, irrespective of contracts with reference to rates for public service. Under it no contract as to rates will stand as against the order of the Public Ser-

:e Commission for reasonable rates, whether uch reasonable rates be lower or higher than he contract rate. Under the Constitution and he Public Service Commission Act, the Public Service Commission (supervised by the courts is to the reasonableness of rates) is exercising he police power of the state by its delegated authority from the Legislature. Its rates herefore constitutionally and legally supersede ny and all contract rates. Other theories of :ase law need not be noted."

In Pawhuska v. Pawhuska Oil Co., supra, the city granted a franchise to the oil company which provided that it should have its pipe lines in the streets and that it should furnish the city and its inhabitants with gas at flat or meter rates at the option of the consumers, and that the rates should not be in excess of fixed standards. Under the act of 1913 it was provided that the Corporate Commission of the state shall have general supervision over all public utilities, with power to fix and establish rates, and to prescribe rules, requirements, and regulations affecting their service. The Commission, after a hearing, made an order which recites that the evidence disclosed that the franchise rates had become inadequate and unremunerative, and that supplying gas at flat rates was productive of wasteful use. The order abrogates all flat rates, increases the meter rates, and requires that the gas be sold through meters to be supplied and installed at the company's expense. On appeal by the city, the Supreme Court of the state affirmed the order. 64 Okl. 214, 166 Pac. 1058. A writ of error was issued by the federal Supreme Court to review this judgment.

In the course of his opinion, Mr. Justice Van Devanter quoted from the opinion in New Orleans v. New Orleans Waterworks Co., 142 U. S. 79, 12 Sup. Ct. 142, 35 L. Ed. 943, as follows:

"In this case the city has no more right to claim an immunity for its contract with the waterworks company, than it would have had if such contract had been made directly with the state. The state, having authorized such contract, might revoke or modify it at its pleasure."

In Woodburn v. Pub. Serv. Com., 82 Or. 114, 161 Pac. 391, L. R. A. 1917C, 98 Ann. Cas. 1917E, 906, it is said:

"When Woodburn granted the franchise to the telephone company, the city exercised its municipal right to contract, and it may be assumed that the franchise was valid and binding upon both parties until such time as the state chose to speak; but the city entered into the contract subject to the reserved right of the state to employ its police power and compel a change of rates, and when the state did speak, the municipal power gave way to the sovereign power of the state."

See Salt Lake City v. Utah Light & T. Co., 52 Utah, 210, 173 Pac. 556, 3 A. L. R. 715.

2. The rule thus established is that every contract between cities of this state and a public utility is always subject to modification by the paramount power of the state, and when a change is so made it is binding upon the city; the change having been made by the state as the representative of the city. Hence it follows that the contention that the increase in the rates of the hydrant rentals abrogated the contract is untenable. The contract, as modified by the Commission, is binding and obligatory upon both parties until such time as the Commission may determine to reopen the case.

[2] 3. The defendant offered in evidence a list of 87 fire hydrants which it claimed should be eliminated. No action was taken by the city, the water company, or the Commission on this offer. Hence the matter is not before us.

[3] 4. The other assignments of error are not here for consideration on this record. They were not pleaded in the defendant's answer. They were first raised in the motion for new trial. It may be that the action of the Commission in raising the annual rental of the fire hydrants from $30 to $55 each would result in increasing the indebtedness of the city in one or more years to a sum in excess of the revenue provided for such years. If that be true, the natural and appropriate place to raise such a constitutional question was in the defendant's answer, and not in the motion for new trial.

[4] 5. The answer admitted the execution of the contract sued upon, that is, that it was legally executed, but pleaded that it had been abrogated by the action of the Commission in increasing the rental rates without the consent of the city. That was the sole defense. The rule announced in Thornburg v. School District, 175 Mo. 12, 75 S. W. 81, has no application. The action in that case was upon certain bonds which plaintiff alleged had been issued by the school district. The answer admitted that the bonds were issued by the persons then holding the position of directors of the district, but averred that their issue was not authorized by an election as required by law, and that the aggregate amount of the bonds so issued exceeded 5 per centum of the value of the taxable property of the district; consequently the bonds were invalid. On the issue so tendered by the answer, it was held that the burden was on the plaintiff to prove that the requirements of the law had been complied with in the issue of the bonds. It is obvious that the rule invoked has no application to this case. Plaintiff was not required to offer evidence on an issue not made by the pleadings.

[5] 6. The questions raised on this appeal were res adjudicata, but that the appeal was therefore vexatious and for delay is a non sequitur. Cases are not wanting in which

this court has been set right on a second appeal in the same case. Bagnell Timber Co. v. Railway, 242 Mo. 11, 145 S. W. 469, overruling Id., 180 Mo. 420, 79 S. W. 1130; Hamilton v. Marks, 63 Mo. 167, overruling Id., 52 Mo. 78, 14 Am. Rep. 391; Murphy v. Barron, 228 S. W. 492.

We are not persuaded that this appeal was for vexation or delay, or that the taxpayers of the city of Sedalia should be penalized as for a vexatious appeal.

The judgment is affirmed.

All concur, except DAVID E. BLAIR, J., not sitting.

ROSE v. BIDDLE et al. (No. 21988.)

(Supreme Court of Missouri, Division No. 1. Dec. 30, 1920. Motion to Modify Opinion Denied April 9, 1921. Motion to Reconsider Motion to Modify Opinion Denied June 6, 1921.)

Municipal corporations ⬅821(19)—Proof that proximate cause of injury to pedestrian falling into uncovered cellarway was violation of ordinance as alleged held insufficient to go to jury.

In an action for personal injuries sustained by a pedestrian in falling into an uncovered cellarway or coalhole in the sidewalk in front of defendant's premises, proof that the cause of the injury was the fact that the cover had been removed *held* insufficient to go to the jury on the allegation that the injury was caused by violation of a city ordinance in construction of the cellarway.

Appeal from St. Louis Circuit Court; Karl Kimmel, Judge.

Action by Mary Rose against Louisa Biddle and others for personal injuries. Judgment for plaintiff, and defendants appeal. Reversed and rendered.

This suit was brought in the circuit court of the city of St. Louis by the plaintiff against the defendants Louisa Biddle and Katherine Biddle Barrette and the Gunn Fruit Company to recover damages for injuries sustained by her through the alleged negligence of the defendants in failing to cover and to keep in safe condition a coalhole, or cellarway, in the sidewalk on Carr street near Third, in the city of St. Louis, provided for by section 1213 of Ordinance No. 22902 of the Revised Code of St. Louis for the year 1907. The judgment of the circuit court for the plaintiff was for the sum of $10,000. In due time and proper form the cause was duly appealed to this court.

It does not seem that the ordinance mentioned is preserved in the record, but the petition alleges:

"That said ordinance provides that any opening in a paved sidewalk leading into an area or vault beneath or into a cellar shall be fitted with a wood or iron cover or grating set in flagging even with the surface of the sidewalk, and said cover or grating shall have no lock, hinge, nor any fastening projecting above the sidewalk, and shall be secured in such manner as to prevent accident to any one passing over it."

Then follows a provision prescribing the penalty for those who violate the ordinance.

In the absence of objections, we assume the petition correctly pleads the ordinance. The uncontradicted evidence shows that the covering of the cellarway was not constructed in conformity to the provisions of said ordinance, but that the hole or opening in the sidewalk was some five feet by seven, and that at the time of the injury, and for many years previous, it was usually covered by a lid or gate of the same size, resting upon an elevated base extending some inches above the surface of the sidewalk, thereby forming a dangerous obstruction in the sidewalk; but the evidence further shows that one of the servants and employees of the Gunn Fruit Company, or some other person unknown, not connected with any of the defendants, removed from said cellarway said lid or gate, and leaned it up against the building occupied by said fruit company, and that on that account, and that account only, the plaintiff in passing along Carr street at that point stepped into the cellarway and was injured in consequence thereof. There is no pretense that she stumbled over the obstruction and thereby was thrown or fell into said cellarway.

The building into which the cellarway led was owned by the appellants, Biddle and Barrette, and was occupied by the Gunn Fruit Company. The suit was dismissed as to the fruit company, and the judgment was rendered against the appellants only.

At the close of the plaintiff's evidence and again at the close of all the evidence in the case, counsel for defendants asked an instruction in the nature of a demurrer, telling the jury that their verdict must be for the defendants; both of which were by the court overruled, and appellants excepted.

Counsel for appellants also requested the court to instruct the jury as follows:

"The court also instructs the jury that, even though from the evidence the jury may find that the covering over the areaway leading into the cellar of the premises mentioned in evidence from the street was not such a covering as was required by the ordinance of the city of St. Louis read in evidence, yet if the jury also believe that the injuries sustained by the plaintiff, if any, resulted, not because said covering to said areaway failed to conform to the city ordinance, but solely because said covering was left open by the lessee, or some representative of the lessee in possession of the premises, or some other person other than the defendants Louisa Biddle and Katherine Biddle Barrette, then the jury will find in favor of the defendants Louisa Biddle and Katherine Biddle Barrette."

This instruction, as requested, was by the court refused, to which action of the court the appellants duly excepted. The court then of its own motion modified the instruction requested by appellants and gave the same to the jury, in said modified form, over the objections of the appellants. Said modified instruction is as follows:

"If the jury find and believe from the evidence that a wood or iron cover or grating was provided by defendants, as required by ordinance, for the cellar hole mentioned in the evidence, at the time of or before leasing and turning over the possession of the premises mentioned in the evidence to their tenant, the Gunn Fruit Company, or at any time before the accident, and that the injuries sustained by the plaintiff, if any, resulted, 'not because said covering was left open by the lessee, or some representative of the lessee in possession of the premises, or some other person other than the defendants Louisa Biddle and Katherine Biddle Barrette, then the jury will find in favor of the defendants."

George W. Lubke and George W. Lubke, Jr., both of St. Louis, for appellants.

Frank A. Habig, of St. Louis, for respondent.

WOODSON, P. J. (after stating the facts as above). Counsel for appellants insist that the court erred in refusing the demurrers to the evidence, also in failing to give the instruction asked by them in behalf of the appellants, and in modifying said instruction and giving it in the modified form; this upon the reason stated that "the plaintiff was injured, not by reason of any defect in the cover provided, but because the cover provided was not in place; had the cover been in place the plaintiff could not have stepped into the opening," and consequently would not have been injured. In other words, the negligence of the appellants in not causing the covering to the cellarway to conform to the provisions of the ordinance pleaded was not the proximate cause of the injury, but the proximate cause thereof was the negligence of some servant of the fruit company, or of some unknown person, in leaving the gate to the cellarway open, into which cellarway the plaintiff stepped. As before stated, there is no pretense that the appellants had anything to do with leaving the gate open.

In this view of the case we are of the opinion that the court should have given the demurrers to the evidence, and after having submitted the case to the jury the court should have given the instruction as asked by the appellants, and should not have modified it, or given it in modified form. The authorities are all one way upon this proposition, and they deny the plaintiff's right to a recovery under such a state of facts. King v. Wabash R. R. Co., 211 Mo. 1, 109 S. W. 671; Schmidt v. Transit Co., 140 Mo. App. 182, 120 S. W. 96.

It would be useless to cite other authorities, because the principle is elementary and fundamental that the negligence complained of must have been the proximate cause of the injury, and this record is absolutely barren of all evidence tending to show that fact.

For the reasons stated, the judgment is reversed, and judgment entered here for the appellants.

All concur.

PHILLIPS v. TRAVELERS' INS. CO. OF HARTFORD, CONN. (No. 21700.)

(Supreme Court of Missouri, Division No. 2. May 26, 1921. Motion for Rehearing Denied June 23, 1921.)

1. **Insurance ⏿⏿646(6)—Burden on plaintiff to prove death caused accidentally.**

In an action on an accident insurance policy, the burden is on plaintiff to show that the insured received bodily injuries, effected directly and independently of all other causes through external, violent, and accidental means, causing his death.

2. **Insurance ⏿⏿646(6)—Improper to build on inference of fall from fact of bruise inference that such fall was result of accident rather than disease, and that such fall proximately caused insured's death.**

Where one insured under an accident policy was in a diseased condition, and cerebral hemorrhage took place immediately prior to his death, it was not proper to build upon the inference of a fall from the fact of a bruise the further inferences that such fall was the result of accident rather than disease, and that such fall was the proximate cause of insured's death.

3. **Evidence ⏿⏿54—Inference cannot be built on inference to establish fact.**

Inference cannot be built upon inference to establish a fact necessary to be proven.

4. **Insurance ⏿⏿665(5)—Evidence held to show as clearly that insured's fall caused by disease as by accident.**

Circumstances attending an insured's fall down a stairway did not prove his death the result of accident, where the advanced stage of the sclerotic condition of his arteries, evidence of cerebral hemorrhage causing death, and lack of evidence of any external violence causing injury to skull or brain covering argued as strongly that his fall was caused by disease.

5. **Insurance ⏿⏿668(11)—No issue for jury as to insured's death being caused by accidental fall.**

In a suit on an accident insurance policy, where there was no substantial evidence to establish that insured fell, that such fall was accidental, and that it or the efforts to avert it caused his death, there was no issue for the jury,

Appeal from St. Louis Circuit Court; Moses Hartmann, Judge.

Suit by Miriam H Phillips against the Travelers' Insurance Company of Hartford, Conn., a corporation. Judgment for plaintiff, and defendant appeals. Reversed.

Jones, Hocker, Sullivan & Angert, of St. Louis, for appellant.

Fordyce, Holliday & White, of St. Louis (John S. Lord, of Chicago, Ill., and Wilbur B. Jones, of St. Louis, of counsel), for respondent.

DAVID E. BLAIR, J. This is a suit by the beneficiary on a policy of accident insurance. It is admitted that said policy insured Milton C. Phillips, therein and herein referred to as the "insured," against bodily injuries effected directly and independently of all other causes, through external, violent, and accidental means, and that in case of death the principal sum, with accrued accumulations, amounted to $7,500, was in full force and effect at insured's death and was payable to plaintiff, the respondent here, if she is entitled to recover under the terms thereof. The death of said insured occurred at Chicago, Ill., on August 2, 1916. The policy was issued to insured in 1904 while he was a resident of the state of Wisconsin. He moved to Chicago about 1913, and consent of defendant to such removal was evidenced by a rider attached to said policy of insurance. Plaintiff is the daughter of insured, and was a resident of Ohio at the time the case was tried.

Insured was a man about 60 years of age at the time of his death. He had been engaged in the practice of law in Wisconsin, and had moved to Chicago to engage in business with his sons in that city. For some reason, stated by some of the witnesses to be on account of failing health, insured had been taking a vacation during the summer months of 1916, and had largely given up active office work, and had taken up outdoor exercises, including golf.

There is some evidence that his blood pressure had become high. On the evening before his death he visited friends in Chicago, a Mr. and Mrs. Vaughan, had dined with them, and afterwards remained an hour or two, visiting and chatting with them. The Vaughans lived in a third story apartment, and insured had climbed two flights of stairs to reach their apartment. About 8:30 he started to leave, and the Vaughans bade him good-night at the top of the stairs leading to their apartment. Mrs. Vaughan suggested to her husband, after insured had started away, that he get his hat and go with him. She then out on the porch, and, failing to observe insured go out on the street below, became alarmed, and followed her husband down the sta leading up to their apartment. At the foot the same and on a landing she found her h band bending over the insured, and sa: d beside him on a step, and directed her h to summon assistance. The only word: en by insured, as shown by the test were "my eye, my side; don't you try me." He then lapsed into apparent sciousness. Mr. Vaughan testified tha found insured on his knees on the land holding the doorknob and trying to raise self in that way, with his hat and newspa on the floor. He was carried up stairs to apartment of the Vaughans, and phys attempted to treat him there. His sons w also summoned, and soon thereafter he v removed to the hospital, where he died ab four hours after he was stricken. Some f the witnesses testified to a slight bruise abrasion on the forehead of the insured the region of his right eye.

A post mortem examination on the body the insured was made by a Dr. Reinha coroner's physician for Cook county. The post mortem extended only to opening skull and examining the brain. It showed injury to the skull or to the brain, but did veal a severe hemorrhage in the brain. The body was then shipped to Wisconsin for bi al, where it was exhumed about 26 days la An autopsy was performed thereon by Wells, of Chicago. The testimony of the d tors performing and attending this autop tended to show the presence of arterioscl sis in an advanced stage, enlargement of muscles of the heart, and chronic Bright's ease, and that there was no evidence of jury to the skull or the membranes cover the surface of the brain or the brain its Dr. Wells testified that he looked for an v served no bruise on the forehead.

The trial below resulted in a verdict f plaintiff in the sum of $8,568.75, that representing the face of the policy, with mitted accumulations and interest from tember 30, 1916. After unsuccessful m for a new trial, the defendant appealed.

The above constitutes only a general o line of the facts. Such further facts as necessary to a complete understanding of issues involved in the case will be more extensively in their proper place n opinion.

A number of assignments of error are by appellant and urged as ground for rev of the judgment below. We will only cor er the demurrer at the close of plaintiff evidence and at the close of all the eviden since our conclusion thereon disposes of case.

A careful study of the evidence offered plaintiff in the light of the decisions of this state has convinced us that the plaintiff fered no substantial evidence authorizing s mission of the case to the jury, and plaintiff's evidence was not helped out by evidence offered by the defendant.

Many pages of the record are filled with testimony tending to show that insured appeared to be in ordinarily good health during the few weeks preceding his death, as well as before that time, and that he was active and able to work, played golf, and climbed two flights of stairs frequently without apparent difficulty or distress and that there was nothing in his appearance or actions to indicate that he was not in good health for a man of his age. Evidence to the contrary appears by defendant's witnesses, and some of the plaintiff's witnesses threw doubt about his good health to a certain extent. There was ample evidence from these lay witnesses that he appeared reasonably vigorous and healthy.

However, the uncontradicted testimony of the physicians who held or witnessed the two autopsies (part of whom were called as witnesses by plaintiff) is to the effect that insured was not a healthy or vigorous man. With one voice these physicians agreed to the presence in his body of seriously diseased conditions. It is certain he was suffering from chronic Bright's disease and arteriosclerosis in an advanced stage, with corresponding enlargement of the heart muscles. It is also shown beyond question that death was caused by cerebral hemorrhage. In spite of the testimony touching the appearance of insured given by lay witnesses, there can be no doubt that he was a victim of at least two deadly maladies.

[1] The vital question for decision by the jury was whether the insured's death was caused by accident or was the result of disease. The burden was on plaintiff to show that insured received bodily injuries effected directly and independently of all other causes through external, violent, and accidental means, which caused his death. There can be little doubt in this case that if an accidental fall of insured be conceded, it was not of such a nature as to cause his death independently of the diseased condition. Appellant contends that, under such a situation plaintiff cannot recover under the law of Illinois, which appellant claims is controlling. But we pass that issue without discussing or deciding it here, although it presents an interesting question for examination and determination,

[2] There were no eyewitnesses, or at least none testified, to the events which transpired from the time insured bade the Vaughans good-night at the top of the stairs until he was found by Mr. Vaughan on his knees on the landing, apparently trying to raise himself by the doorknob. No sound of fall, outcry, or other noise was heard by any witness. Part of the witnesses testified to the presence of a bruise or abrasion on insured's forehead, and there is sufficient evidence on that point to justify a finding by the jury that such

bruise did exist. When Mrs. Vaughan reached the scene he complained of his eye and his side, and so far as was shown these were the last words that he uttered.

From the presence of the bruise on his forehead the jury was doubtless authorized to infer a fall. Such was not a necessary conclusion, however, for the reason that the bruise was of such a superficial character that it might have been caused by insured bumping or rubbing his head against the door in attempting to pull himself up, or possibly by a fall in attempting to raise himself from the floor.

But from the inference of the fall drawn from the presence of the bruise it does not necessarily follow that such fall was accidental rather than the result of the hemorrhage of the arteries of the brain. The physical condition of the insured was such that his fall could just as well have been caused by cerebral hemorrhage, conceding that such fall occurred. With the positive and uncontradicted evidence of the diseased condition of insured, and that an actual cerebral hemorrhage took place, it is not proper to build upon the inference of a fall from the fact of a bruise the further inference that such fall was the result of accident rather than disease. The fall can be as readily attributed to disease as to accident from the evidence before us, and it devolves on plaintiff to show that it was due to accident.

Furthermore, if the jury be permitted to indulge the inference of a fall and the further inference that such fall was accidental, yet must an additional step by inference be taken, and that is that such fall was the proximate cause of death of the insured. There is evidence that a fall might have caused a rupture of an artery of the brain and brought about the cerebral hemorrhage. None of the physicians undertake to testify as a fact that the hemorrhage was produced by the fall. They simply say that it might have been so produced. No evidence of injury to the outer covering of the skull or to the skull itself, or to the dura mater or to the membranes covering the brain, or to the brain itself, was found by the physicians. It is in evidence that a jar, not sufficient to injure these parts, could still be heavy enough to rupture a blood vessel in the brain of one in the condition of insured, or that the effort expended by him in attempting to avert a fall might produce the same result. But the conclusion cannot be avoided that a finding that such fall caused the death is, after all, an inference.

[3] The courts of this state have many times declared that inference cannot be builded upon inference to establish a fact necessary to be proven in a case on trial. Hamilton v. Kansas City Southern Railway Co., 250 Mo. 714, loc. cit. 722, 157 S. W. 622; Swearingen v. Wabash Railroad, 221 Mo. 644, loc. cit. 659, 120 S. W. 773; Yarnell v. Kan-

sas City, etc., Railroad, 113 Mo. 570, loc. cit. 579, 21 S. W. 1, 18 L. R. A. 599; Glick v. Kansas City, Ft. Scott & Memphis Ry. Co., 57 Mo. App. 97, loc. cit. 105. The above are negligence cases. The rule applies to any sort of case where a definite and ultimate fact must be found as a basis of recovery. It has frequently been applied in suits on accident policies, as, for example, Wright v. United Commercial Travelers, 188 Mo. App. 457, 174 S. W. 833; Atherton v. Railway Mail Ass'n (App.) 221 S. W. 752. Further citation of authority is useless. We find no contrary authority on the proposition that inference cannot be piled on inference to prove a fact.

[4] Plaintiff cited a number of cases where there were no witnesses to the accidental character of the injury, but in all such cases, so far as we understand them, the fundamental fact of injury or fall was clearly shown by direct proof or the strongest kind of circumstances. In Fetter v. Fidelity & Casualty Co., 174 Mo. 256, 73 S. W. 592, 61 L. R. A. 459, 97 Am. St. Rep. 560, there was no question that insured fell against a table. The issue was whether that fall or his diseased condition caused his death. In Goodes v. United Commercial Travelers, 174 Mo. App. 330, 156 S. W. 995, a stool slipped, and caused insured to fall. Such fall was heard by his wife. Blood flowed from his nose and ears immediately. In MacDonald v. Railway, 219 Mo. 468, 118 S. W. 78, 16 Ann. Cas. 810, the question at issue was whether the death of the deceased was due to accident or disease. The accidental injury was clearly shown. It was due to the wreck of a grip car. In Greenlee v. Kansas City Casualty Co., 192 Mo. App. 303, 182 S. W. 138, deceased rose from his bed and went into the bathroom, and his wife heard him fall and groan, and he stated he slipped and fell. It was not necessary in that case to infer the fall, and that it was due to accident rather than the disease of meningitis with which deceased was afflicted. In Lamoreux v. Ill. Commercial Men's Ass'n, 212 Ill. App. 263, the marks on the body, the position of the body with reference to the automobile, and other facts, showed circumstantially, but well-nigh conclusively, that deceased was cranking his automobile, and while doing so was struck by the crank in attempting to start the engine. The jury was authorized to find as a fact that the mark on the body was caused by the crank. Numerous other causes on this point are cited by plaintiff, but nothing can be accomplished by discussing them further.

Counsel say in their brief that—

"There is direct proof of the fall and its effect. The inference of the accidental character of the fall is properly based upon all of the circumstances preceding, accompanying, and following Mr. Phillips' fall on the stairway. The accidental character of the fall is proved by circumstantial evidence, as it is necessary to prove many facts in the trial of cases where direct evidence is not available. Proof by circumstantial evidence is not mere presumption."

We are unable to agree with plaintiff that there is direct proof of the fall. There is no proof whatever on this point, except the evidence of the bruise on insured's forehead. Complaint as to the eye and side does not exclude the hemorrhage as the cause of the fall. It is true that "proof by circumstantial evidence is not mere presumption." But that would only be true where such circumstances clearly pointed to the accidental character of the fall, and tended to exclude the theory that it resulted from a stroke of apoplexy. The advanced stage of the sclerotic condition of insured's arteries, the undisputed evidence of cerebral hemorrhage causing death, the positive proof that there was not the slightest evidence of external violence causing any injury to skull or brain covering, argues just as strongly, to say the least, that insured's fall, if he did fall, was caused by disease, as that it was caused by accident. That such fall was caused by accident is speculation. It certainly is nothing more than mere inference.

[5] It appears that there was no substantial evidence to establish the essential facts that there was a fall, that such fall was accidental, and that such fall, or the efforts to avert the same, caused the insured's death. The proof having failed at this point, there was no issue of fact to submit to the jury, and the defendant's demurrer to the evidence should have been sustained.

Let the judgment of the trial court be reversed.

All concur.

TIEDE v. TIEDE et al. (No. 21805.)

(Supreme Court of Missouri, Division No. 1. April 9, 1921. Rehearing Denied June 6, 1921.)

1. Lost instruments ⚖=23(3)—Evidence held to sustain finding against claim under alleged lost deed.

In a suit to determine title to land wherein plaintiff claimed to be the owner under deed from his father, which deed was kept in his father's safe for plaintiff's use, evidence held to sustain a finding for defendant.

2. Lost instruments ⚖=23(3)—Evidence insufficient to show execution and delivery of alleged lost deed.

In a suit to determine title, wherein plaintiff alleged that deeds to the land from his father had been placed in the hands of a custodian, evidence held insufficient to show execution and delivery of such deeds.

3. Witnesses ⟨⟩141—Plaintiff's attorney held properly refused permission to testify as custodian of deeds executed by decedent.

In a suit to determine title to land under claim of deeds from plaintiff's deceased father, alleged to have been placed in the hands of a custodian, it was not error to refuse to permit a custodian to testify fully in the case, where it appeared he was plaintiff's attorney.

4. Appeal and error ⟨⟩1056(3)—Refusal to permit plaintiff's attorney to testify held harmless error.

In action based on alleged lost deed error in refusing to permit plaintiff's attorney to testify as to his custodianship of deeds of plaintiff's father to plaintiff if erroneous *held* harmless, his testimony being without probative force.

5. Lost instruments ⟨⟩23(3)—Evidence insufficient to warrant recovery on alleged lost deed.

In a suit to determine title to land under a claim of deed from plaintiff's father, plaintiff's evidence *held* not so clear, cogent, and convincing regarding the execution and delivery of the deeds as to warrant the court in setting aside a deed to another party, which was regular upon its face.

Appeal from Circuit Court, Lawrence County; Charles L. Henson, Judge.

Suit by Martin Tiede against Edwin Tiede and others. Decree for defendants, and plaintiff appeals. Affirmed.

This suit was instituted in the circuit court of Lawrence county to ascertain and determine title of 100 acres of land situated in said county, under section 2535, R. S. 1909, by the plaintiff against the defendants. The decree of the court was for the defendants, and the plaintiff duly appealed the cause to this court.

Counsel for neither appellant nor respondents have properly complied with rule No. 15 (169 S. W. ix) of this court, requiring statements of the case, etc. Both have made statements, but they are so imperfect and confusing that we can scarcely get head or tail of the case therefrom, and were it not for the fact that we regret to dispose of a case, except upon its merits, we would be justified to dismiss the appeal for failure to comply with said rule. But under the circumstances we feel as though we should go to the abstract of the record and gather therefrom the facts, which should constitute the statement of the case.

The plaintiff and the defendants, the seven brothers of the former, constitute the parties to this suit. Originally there were other persons made parties to the suit, but in the course of the trial they dropped out, and as they are not material parties to this action, we will in the future ignore them.

The substantial facts of the case as we gather them, are as follows:

O. M. Youngblood was the common source of title, who, according to appellant's testimony, on March 20, 1907, by general warranty deed, conveyed the land to Emma Tiede, the mother of the appellant and respondents. The appellant claims that his mother by deed conveyed the land in question to him, which was not recorded, but delivered by the grantor to appellant's father for his use and benefit. The date and kind of deed this was are not shown by the evidence, nor when it was so delivered. Subsequently thereto, appellant's mother executed a second deed, purporting to convey the same land to his father, which deed was duly recorded, which it is contended conveyed the legal title to the land to the father, but, in fact, in trust for the use and benefit of the appellant, and that thereafter the father by deed conveyed said land to the appellant, and placed it in the hands of Oscar B. Elam for the appellant, which was not placed on record. Subsequently to the execution of the last deed mentioned the father executed another deed, which was recorded, and purported to convey this land to Henry Tiede, one of the respondents. The respondent Edwin Tiede claims to have acquired the title to the land through mesne conveyances from Henry Tiede.

The petition charged that appellant's said deeds were lost, destroyed, or stolen, and that respondents took the land with notice of those facts, but the evidence tending to prove the truth of those charges is very weak and unsatisfactory, as will appear more fully later on.

Appellant's evidence tended to show that Emma Tiede, the appellant's mother, made the statement that soon after she acquired title to the land she by deed conveyed the same to appellant, and the deed was placed in his father's safe for the use of the appellant; that at this time the father of appellant was worth between $75,000 and $100,000, and that he had made a partial distribution of his estate among his various children; that the father made statements to the effect that appellant was the owner of the land, and that said statements extended over a period of six or seven years next before the death of the mother, and for a year after her death; also that the respondents knew of those declarations of their father regarding the title to the land.

One of the respondents, Charles Tiede, testified for appellant to the effect that John Tiede, the father of the appellant, and respondents, told him that Edwin Tiede had stolen from his mother, Emma Tiede, the deed made by the father conveying the land to appellant, and that later Emma Tiede "admitted" to witness the theft of the deed.

Over the objection of counsel for appellant, the court admitted in evidence the will of

John Tiede; which ruling is assigned as error. The appellant was not permitted to testify as to the delivery of the deed to him, made by his mother, and the depositing of the same in his father's safe, nor that he saw the deed and examined it while it was in his father's safe; nor was appellant permitted to show by his testimony that the deed was delivered to her for him. All of those rulings of the court are assigned as error.

Appellant also offered to show by Oscar Elam that he had certain conversations with John Tiede regarding the theft of the deed, but the court excluded the testimony because it appeared upon his preliminary examination that he was the attorney for John Tiede, and the statements were confidential communications. This evidence and the offer of proof is too long to state here, but will be further noticed later on.

Appellant's evidence also tended to show that Edwin Tiede went to live with his father soon after the death of his mother; that he, while there, learned the combination of his father's safe and became to some extent the manager of his father's business. The record is silent as to the facts and circumstances inducing Emma Tiede to execute the deed mentioned to her husband, John Tiede, and as to the consideration, if any, she received for the deed. It also tended to show that the deed from Henry Tiede to Edwin Tiede was without consideration.

The evidence tended to show that this land was worth about $10,000, and that the rental value of the land was $5 per acre per annum. The record is silent as to what consideration, if any, Stiner paid Henry Tiede, for the land, or what Annie Tiede paid Stiner therefor. The evidence also tended to show that Edwin Tiede paid Henry about $2,050 for the land, and assumed the incumbrances that existed upon the land, which was between $1,000 and $3,000, the exact amount not made clear by the evidence.

The respondents' evidence tended to show that:

Emma Tiede was the wife of John Tiede. She was also the mother of plaintiff, Martin Tiede, and of the defendants. On March 30, 1908, Emma Tiede conveyed the land to John Tiede, her husband, by general warranty deed. She died in January, 1914. On January 13, 1916, John Tiede conveyed the land to the defendant Henry Tiede by general warranty deed. The deed was delivered and recorded, as was also the deed made by Emma Tiede.

John Tiede died on July 1, 1916. July 5, 1916, Henry Tiede, by general warranty deed, conveyed the land to one Stiner, who on the next day, July 6, 1916, conveyed it to Mrs. Annie Tiede. On August 28, 1917, Annie Tiede, by general warranty deed, conveyed the land to Edwin Tiede, and Edwin Tiede is claiming under this deed. After acquiring title, Annie Tiede borrowed some money on the land, secured the payment of same by deed of trust, and this indebtedness was unpaid at the time of the trial.

John Tiede made two wills, which are in evidence. The first of these is dated August 16, 1915, and the other—this one being his last will, which was admitted to probate—was dated January 16, 1916. It will be noted that the date of this last will is just three days after the date of the deed to Henry Tiede. This is significant, for the reason that Oscar B. Elam, attorney for plaintiff, in his examination as to his qualification as a witness, testifies that he wrote the last will, and that at the time of the preparation of it he spent a day and a night with Mr. Tiede, and that they discussed fully and freely all Mr. Tiede's business affairs, and particularly the disposition that he had made of his property.

In the first-mentioned will, abstracted on pages 15 and 16 of respondent's additional abstract of the record, he gives the farm in controversy to his son, Henry, one of the defendants. This, as will be noted, was some time prior to the date of the deed in which the land is conveyed to Henry. In the same will, he mentions the fact that he has already given his son Martin, the plaintiff, a farm of 80 acres in Christian county.

In his last will, as abstracted on pages 14 and 15 of respondent's additional abstract of the record, he assigns reasons why he does not give Martin a larger share of his estate. In this will, he recites the making of the deed to Henry, the defendant, by which the land in controversy is given to him. This will was the one made just three days after the execution of the deed, and is the one admitted to probate.

Plaintiff's claim rests upon the allegation that at some indefinite date Emma Tiede deeded the land to Martin Tiede, plaintiff, and delivered the deed to John Tiede, her husband for Martin. His petition also counts upon another alleged deed, supposed to have been made by John Tiede to Martin, and delivered to Oscar B. Elam to be held by him until after the grantor's death, and then delivered to plaintiff. No witness is produced who ever saw either of these deeds. No one pretends to know who wrote either of them. No notary public testified that he took the acknowledgment to any such deed or deeds. One witness testified that John Tiede said he had given the boys their farms, and that the deeds were in Charley Purdy's bank, and that when he was dead the boys could go there and get them. Mr. Charley Purdy was not called as a witness, nor was any reason shown why he was not called.

Oscar B. Elam, attorney for plaintiff, offered himself as a witness, and a question arose as to his competency, and the court required him to state what he intended to testify to, and heard it as an offer. This was done after the court had ruled that Elam was not incompetent for all purposes. In the offer made, not a word is said about the delivery to him of any deed made by John Tiede. We think that the witness would have been incompetent to testify to such matters, but this court has before it his offer, and in that offer no mention is made of the delivery to either deed upon which they seek to base their claim of title.

The only witness who testifies to any fact that would tend to establish the allegations of the petition that the deed alleged to have been made by John Tiede to Martin, the plaintiff, was Charlie Tiede. After testifying in the afternoon, he was excused and another witness examined, and then court adjourned for supper. After supper he was recalled, and on being re-examined by Mr. Elam he says that his father said:

"I took them down there to my lawyer, Oscar B. Elam, for safe-keeping, and furthermore to be delivered after my death correctly."

What deeds he is referring to in this alleged conversation is shown by his prior examination as shown on pages 34 and 35, questions 74 to 79. His testimony there is to the effect that his father in that conversation did not say what boys he referred to, nor what deeds he referred to, nor what land they conveyed, nor what kind of deeds they were. And this is the nearest plaintiff comes to getting the deed in controversy in this lawsuit into the hands of Mr. Elam to be delivered after the death of John Tiede.

This same witness, Charlie Tiede, on June 6, 1916, wrote a letter to Henry Tiede, offering to give $4,000 for the farm. On the same day his father, John Tiede, also wrote, advising Henry to sell to Charlie. These letters are in evidence. They are shown on pages 9 and 10 of our additional abstract on the record. It will be noted that these letters are written less than a month prior to the death of John Tiede. Charlie was at that time on very friendly terms with his father, and his father was at that time about to accompany him to his home in Kansas, where he died.

After hearing all the evidence, and after listening to the arguments, the court found the issues in favor of the defendants, both on plaintiff's cause of action as stated in his petition, and on defendants' cross-petition for affirmative relief, and entered judgment that plaintiff had no interest in the land, and that the defendant Edwin Tiede was the owner thereof.

Appellant makes 14 "points upon which appellant will insist in the argument," and 35 "points and authorities."

Oscar B. Elam, of Springfield, for appellant. Albert C. Hayward and Alfred Page, both of Springfield, for respondents.

WOODSON, P. J. (after stating the facts as above). [1] I. As before stated, counsel have not complied with rule No. 15, regarding the statements, briefs, etc., required to be made and prepared by them, and for that reason we will choose our own manner as to the disposition of the case, as we did in the preparation of the statement of the case, and will therefore ignore the 49 points presented by counsel for appellant for the reversal of the judgment. We are of the opinion that the finding of the trial court was amply supported by the evidence in the case, and are unable to see how it could have found otherwise under the evidence.

[2] II. We are also of the opinion that the evidence was wholly insufficient to show the execution or delivery of either of the two deeds mentioned in appellant's petition. Mr. Elam, who was supposed to be the custodian of the deeds, or at least one of them, nowhere testified, or offered to testify, that ne even saw the deed or deeds. They appear to be of the will-o'-the-wisp character; now you see them, now you don't.

[3, 4] III. Under the evidence produced on the preliminary examination of Mr. Elam's qualification as a witness, we think the trial court properly refused to permit him to testify fully in the case, but that ruling, if erroneous, seems not to have worked injury to appellant, because he does not pretend to have ever seen the deeds or that he ever had possession of them. Therefore his evidence was practically without probative force.

[5] IV. The testimony of appellant was not clear, cogent, or convincing regarding the execution and delivery of the deeds mentioned, which all the authorities require must be, before the court is warranted in setting aside a deed regular upon its face.

V. We have not so far noticed the character of appellant's evidence, which was wholly parole, consisting entirely of alleged declarations made by Emma and John Tiede. All such evidence should be received with great caution, and it has little, if any, weight when standing alone, uncorroborated by more substantial evidence. Finding no error in the record, the judgment is affirmed.

ELDER, J., concurs in result.
JAMES T. BLAIR, J., concurs in separate opinion, in which GRAVES, J., concurs.

JAMES T. BLAIR, J. (concurring). An examination of the record and briefs convinces me that the correct result is reached in the majority opinion in this case. The same examination convinces me that the statements of counsel in their briefs are not fairly open to the sweeping criticism made of them. In view of the fact that this criticism is to go into the reports and to the bar, and of the fact that I consider the statements to be in fair compliance with the rule, I believe it to be just to counsel to say that I very respectfully refrain from concurrence in that part of the opinion, but concur in the result reached.

GRAVES, J., concurs.

———

WILLIAMS v. KANSAS CITY TERMINAL RY. CO. et al. (No. 21491.)

(Supreme Court of Missouri, in Banc. May 24, 1921.)

1. **Courts ⚍488(1)—Though cause was transferred by Court of Appeals on ground bill of exceptions was not properly authenticated, corrected abstract may be filed.**

Where the judges of the Court of Appeals disagreed as to whether what purported to be a bill of exceptions in appellee's abstract of the record was properly authenticated, and the case was transferred to the Supreme Court, the Supreme Court has jurisdiction just as if the case had come by appeal from the nisi prius court, and the appellants may within due time file a corrected abstract, thus eliminating all questions of the insufficiency of the original.

2. **Carriers ⚍286(4)—Ordinary care required of carrier as to steps in station.**

Notwithstanding the high standard of care required of a carrier as to passengers during the course of their transportation and when entering or leaving the vehicle, the carrier is under no greater duty to maintain its station building than is the owner of buildings used for ordinary business purposes, and so a railroad company owes only duty of ordinary care to maintain steps in station, giving access to trains in a reasonably safe condition.

3. **Carriers ⚍286(4) — Railroad company, which equipped station steps with safety tread, not responsible for accidents to passengers.**

Where a defendant equipped steps in a station giving access to trains with safety tread, which was supposed to afford a firm footing even though wet, a passenger, who slipped on a step which had become wet presumably from the wet or muddy shoes and dripping umbrellas of the preceding passengers, cannot recover from defendant; it having exercised ordinary care.

James T. Blair, J., dissenting.

Appeal from Circuit Court, Jackson County; Clarence A. Burney, Judge.

Action by Viola L. Williams against the Kansas City Terminal Railway Company and another. From a judgment for plaintiff, defendants appeal, the case being affirmed and certified by the Kansas City Court of Appeals to the Supreme Court (223 S. W. 132). Judgment reversed.

Warner, Dean, Langworthy, Thomson & Williams, S. W. Sawyer, and John H. Lathrop, all of Kansas City, for appellants.

John T. Mathis and McVey & Freet, all of Kansas City, for respondent.

RAGLAND, C. Plaintiff sues to recover for injuries received from a fall on a stairway leading from the waiting room, in the Union Station at Kansas City, down to a platform from which passengers enter trains.

Plaintiff was at the time a passenger, and was on her way to a train. Her action is based on the alleged negligence of defendants in permitting the stairway at the time to be in an unsafe and dangerous condition. The petition charges the negligence in the following language:

"By reason of the negligence and carelessness of said defendants, their agents and servants, in maintaining said steps and stairway * * * in a slippery, dangerous, and defective condition, plaintiff slipped on said steps and stairway and fell against the banister and steps of said stairway, thereby injuring said plaintiff, as more particularly set out herein; that said defendants by the exercise of ordinary care knew, or could have known, of the dangerous and slippery condition of said steps."

One of the defendants answered with a general denial and a plea of contributory negligence; the other, with a general denial only.

From express and implied admissions, the following facts appeared on the trial: The Union Station at Kansas City is so constructed that there are no entrances from the street on the track level. The only way for passengers to get to the trains is to come into the station from the street, pass through a large lobby, thence into the main waiting room, and from thence down one of a number of stairways leading to the platforms on the train level. From the street entrance into the station to the place where plaintiff fell is from 300 to 400 feet. The stairways are not in continuous use; each serves as a means of ingress and egress only for passengers going to and coming from certain trains; hence, as to any one of them, there may be long intervals of nonuse. They are so inclosed as not to be exposed to the weather; and the train platforms are also under roof. The stairway on which plaintiff fell was constructed of concrete and iron. There were two landings; the flight from the second one to the bottom was 14 steps. The width of the stairway was not shown, nor were the dimensions of the steps. It appears, however, that there was a banister on each side, and the steps were equipped with a safety tread. The tread was a corrugated steel and lead plate, which covered the entire surface of the step. The ridges, which extended lengthwise the plate paralleling the steps, consisted of steel channels filled with lead, the lead coming up to or a little above the sides of the channels. The lead, it was said, had an adhesive quality, which is not affected by the lead becoming wet.

According to plaintiff's testimony, she went to the Union Station in the afternoon of December 31, 1916, to take a Burlington train for Palmyra, Mo., due to leave at 6:20 p. m. She procured a ticket, went to the waiting room, sat down, and waited for the gate to be opened. There was a crowd at the gate through which she would have to pass to go to her train. After about five minutes the gate was opened, and the crowd began to go through. When she got to the gate an usher took her suit case and told her to follow him. She was carrying a baby, an umbrella, and handbag. As she was starting down the last flight of steps her right foot slipped. Just as she put her weight on her right foot, in taking a step, it slipped sideways to the left along and parallel with the step. In trying to regain her equilibrium, she caught her left foot, pulling the heel off of the shoe and fell, on her back and side, about four steps. The fall caused her painful injuries. The step on which her foot slipped was wet; practically all of the steps were wet. In her language:

"They were wet, and you could see the tracks of people, mud tracks I think, you could see the tracks plain, and they were wet."

It was a drizzly, rainy day, had been raining all day. Her own testimony was all the evidence offered by plaintiff with reference to the condition of the steps. For defendants the station master and his assistant both testified that the steps were neither wet nor muddy.

At the close of the plaintiff's case in chief, and again when all the evidence was in, each of the defendants asked a peremptory instruction, directing a verdict in its behalf. These were refused. At the instance of the plaintiff the jury were instructed that, if they found that the step on which plaintiff slipped was wet and slippery, and thereby rendered unsafe for persons walking thereon, that such condition caused plaintiff to fall and sustain injury, and that defendants knew of said condition, or by the exercise of a high degree of care could have known of the same, in time to have removed it and made the step safe before plaintiff fell, they should return a verdict for her. They were further instructed, in effect, that plaintiff was a passenger, and that the defendants owed passengers the highest practicable degree of care of a very prudent person engaged in like business to prevent injury to such passengers while upon the premises and under the care of defendants.

The jury found for plaintiff, assessing her damages at $400, and judgment was rendered accordingly. Defendants appealed to the Kansas City Court of Appeals. The decision of that court on the appeal was deemed by one of the judges to be in conflict with deci-

sions of this court, and the cause was transferred here in conformity with the constitutional mandate.

That the trial court should have directed a verdict in their favor is the principal contention of appellants.

[1] 1. The judges of the Court of Appeals disagreed as to whether what purported to be the bill of exceptions in appellants' abstract of the record, filed in that court, was properly authenticated. The majority opinion held that it was not and on the record proper affirmed the judgment of the trial court. 223 S. W. 132. After the cause was transferred, appellants in due time filed in this court an abstract of the record, which wholly eliminates the question that vexed the members of the Court of Appeals. Our ruling on the questions presented by the record now before us can have no bearing upon the conflict of decision, thought to have arisen, which was the basis of the order transferring the case. Our jurisdiction, however, is not dependent upon the existence of a conflict of decision. The certification by the Court of Appeals, on the ground, within the time, and in the manner specified by the Constitution, confers upon us the jurisdiction to hear and determine the cause, just as if it had come to us by appeal from the nisi prius court. And appellants were within their rights in filing an abstract of the record here, just as though the case had reached our docket "by ordinary appellate process." Epstein v. Railroad, 250 Mo. 1, 17, 156 S. W. 699, 703 (48 L. R. A. [N. S.] 394, Ann. Cas. 1915A, 423); Bussiere's Adm'r v. Sayman, 257 Mo. 303, 307, 165 S. W. 796; Hayes v. Sheffield, 221 S. W. 705, 706.

2. Neither appellant suggests that, if it be held that there was negligence as charged in the petition, it is any less culpable than its codefendant. They make a common defense. We shall accordingly consider the question of their liability as though each owed the plaintiff the same duty with respect to the maintenance of the stairway on which she fell.

To determine whether defendants were negligent as charged, it is necessary to consider: First, what the duty was that they owed the plaintiff with reference to the stairway in question; and, second, whether they failed to perform that duty.

[2] (1) At the time she received the injury of which she complains, plaintiff was a passenger, and as such under the care and protection of the defendants. The trial court held, and so instructed the jury, that the defendants owed her the highest practicable degree of care of a very prudent person engaged in like business to prevent injury to her while upon their premises. We think the court was in error. The degree of care bound to be exercised by carriers, as well as by all other persons, is one commensurate with the dangers incident to the enterprise in which they are engaged. Accordingly, a high standard of care is required of the carrier as to

passengers during the course of their transportation, and when they are entering or leaving the vehicle of carriage. This is so because the safety and lives of the passengers rest entirely in the carrier's hands, the passengers having no control whatever over the dangerous instrumentalities employed in their transportation. But there is no reason why the carrier, generally speaking, should be held to a higher degree of care in maintaining its station buildings than that to which the owner of buildings used for ordinary business purposes is held. Station buildings in themselves neither require the employment of dangerous agencies nor possess unusual elements of danger. Persons using the stairway in question could not by any chance have come into contact with the dangerous instrumentalities made use of by defendants in their business as carriers; such persons were not subject to any greater danger than is commonly encountered in going down the steps of the ordinary public building. There can be no valid reason, therefore, for holding that the defendants owed plaintiff any higher duty than that of exercising ordinary care to maintain the steps in a reasonably safe condition. Joyce v. Railroad, 219 Mo. 344, 372, 118 S. W. 21; 4 Elliott on Railroads (2d Ed.) § 1590.

[3] (2) The petition alleges that the step on which plaintiff fell was unsafe because it was "slippery." She offered no evidence tending to show that the slipperiness arose from the material of which the step was constructed, or from the manner in which it was constructed, or from its having become worn or out of repair. All the evidence she introduced as to the condition of the step was her testimony that the step was wet, that she could see the tracks of people—mud tracks, she thought—but she could see them plainly, and they were wet. The question submitted to the jury, at her instance, with reference to the step, was whether it was "wet and slippery." It is not her contention that she stepped on a piece of mud and slipped, but that she slipped because the step was wet.

There was no direct evidence as to what caused the step to be wet or as to whether defendants had any knowledge of such condition prior to plaintiff's fall. And no evidence at all as to how long the step had been wet. The stairway was inclosed and under roof; hence not exposed to the weather. It had been raining all day, and the inference is that the water on the step came from the wet footwear and dripping raincoats and umbrellas of persons who had gone down the stairway before the plaintiff. If the steps became wet in this manner, they must have done so many times before under like circumstances, and their condition at the time of plaintiff's fall must therefore reasonably have been anticipated by defendants' agents. But, even so, what is it that it was incumbent upon them to do? Respondent's counsel suggest

that they should have used a mop or sand. Had plaintiff been the first to go down the steps after the gate was opened she would no doubt have found them dry, but at least a part of the crowd immediately preceded her. The only way defendants could have made the steps dry by the use of mops for all of their passengers would have been to have admitted but one at a time through the gate, and then followed him all the way down, mopping the steps after him. The use of sand would have made the stairway unsightly, and it is not at all certain that it would have been any more efficacious in preventing plaintiff from slipping than the safety tread. But whether it would or not is not decisive of the question under consideration. Defendants were not insurers against all hazard arising from the use of the steps; they were not bound to make them absolutely safe. By equipping them with a safety tread of standard construction, defendant did all, under the circumstances shown by the evidence, that the exercise of ordinary care required, in order to make the steps reasonably safe from the danger of slipping upon them. We hold as a matter of law that plaintiff failed to make a case entitling her to go to the jury. The judgment of the trial court is reversed.

SMALL, C., concurs.

BROWN, C., not sitting.

In Banc.

All concur, except JAMES T. BLAIR, J., who dissents because he thinks the cause should be remanded.

LACKEY v. UNITED RYS. CO. (No. 21691.)

(Supreme Court of Missouri, Division No. 2. May 26, 1921.)

1. Street railroads ⟜98(7)—Pedestrian going in front of street car negligent.

A pedestrian about to go upon a street railroad track owes a duty to himself to look and listen, and, if he goes upon the track in front of an approaching car when the exercise of ordinary care would prevent injury, he cannot recover for such injury.

2. Street railroads ⟜112(3)—Presumption of care inapplicable where facts appear.

The rule that one injured or killed in going upon a track in front of an approaching street car is presumed to have exercised ordinary care, in the absence of evidence to the contrary, is inapplicable where the facts appear as to how the collision happened.

3. Street railroads ⟜98(12)—Contributory negligence of pedestrian jumping on fender held not shown.

Evidence that a pedestrian at a crossing who was seen to step off the sidewalk and walk slowly across looking down was next seen on the second of the two parallel tracks not more than 20 feet in front of an approaching street car which was exceeding the speed limit, and failed to make the required stop at the intersection, and that, being confused on the sudden discovery of the car, he started back and then jumped for the fender to save himself, *held* not to show conclusively that he was guilty of contributory negligence.

4. Street railroads ⊂⇒98(7) — Pedestrian crossing tracks may assume car will run within speed limit and stop at intersection.

A pedestrian crossing street car tracks at an intersection has a right to assume that an approaching car is traveling within the speed limit, and that it will stop at the intersection as the statute requires, and he may act on that assumption unless he has knowledge to the contrary.

5. Street railroads ⊂⇒93(4) — Motorman may assume pedestrian will not step in front of car.

A motorman, if he sees a pedestrian approaching the track, has a right to assume, until a different intention is apparent, that he will use due care for himself, and will not step in front of the car.

6. Street railroads ⊂⇒103(2) — Motorman not negligent in failing to observe last chance rule until pedestrian is in danger.

A motorman is not negligent in failing to observe the last chance rule at any particular period until a pedestrian crossing the track is in danger or apparently going into danger.

7. Trial ⊂⇒252(9) — Error to submit question whether car could have been stopped in time to avoid hitting pedestrian where no evidence as to when he stepped onto track.

It is error to submit the question as to whether a street car injuring a pedestrian could have been stopped or checked sufficiently to avoid injuring him, in the absence of a showing that at some particular time before the immediate contact he was going into danger and was oblivious of his peril, so that the motorman could have seen him in time to act.

8. Death ⊂⇒78 — Entire recovery penal.

Under Rev. St. 1919, § 4217, allowing a recovery of not less than $2,000 nor more than $10,000 for death from injuries by cars, there is no error in permitting a recovery for the full amount, though there is no pleading or proof of pecuniary loss; the statute being penal as to the entire amount recoverable.

9. Death ⊂⇒57 — Aggravating circumstances increasing penal recovery must be pleaded.

The rule of pleading, under Rev. St. 1919, § 1220, that every fact constituting a cause of action be stated, applies to the penal recovery for death under section 4217, requiring the jury to exercise discretion in fixing the amount, and aggravating circumstances increasing the recovery are not admissible in evidence unless pleaded, although plaintiff alleges she was the wife of deceased.

10. Negligence ⊂⇒140 — Form of instruction on proximate cause of injury.

Negligence not being actionable unless it produces an injury, an instruction authorizing recovery must require a finding that the negligence complained of was the proximate cause of the injury, and, where the jury is required to find facts from which the necessary inference follows that the negligence was the cause of the injury, it is sufficient.

11. Street railroads ⊂⇒118(16) — Instruction held erroneous as not requiring finding of proximate cause of injury.

In an action for the death of a pedestrian struck by a street car, an instruction that, if the car was being run at a speed greater than 15 miles an hour, and the deceased was exercising ordinary care for his own safety, defendant would be liable, was erroneous as not requiring a finding of specific and definite facts, from which an inference necessarily followed that the negligence was the cause of the injury.

12. Trial ⊂⇒228(1) — Instruction in alternative held erroneous.

An instruction authorizing a verdict for plaintiff on account of the excessive speed of the car and also under the humanitarian rule *held* erroneous as in the alternative.

13. Street railroads ⊂⇒111(2) — Vigilant watch ordinance not pleaded held inadmissible.

In an action for the death of a pedestrian struck by a street car, the admission of the vigilant watch ordinance (Rev. Code City of St. Louis, § 2380) was error; it not having been pleaded as a ground of recovery.

14. Street railroads ⊂⇒111(2) — Stop ordinance, though not pleaded, held admissible to rebut evidence of contributory negligence.

In an action for the death of a pedestrian struck by a street car, ordinance (Rev. Code City of St. Louis, § 2386) requiring cars to stop on the near side of the street on signal was admissible, though not pleaded, to rebut defendant's evidence of contributory negligence.

Higbee, P. J., dissenting in part.

Appeal from St. Louis Circuit Court; J. Hugo Grimm, Judge.

Action by Ruby Lackey against the United Railways Company of St. Louis. Judgment for plaintiff, and defendant appeals. Reversed and remanded.

Charles W. Bates, T. E. Francis, and Albert D. Nortoni, all of St. Louis, for appellant. W. H. Douglass, of St. Louis, for respondent.

WHITE, C. The appeal in this case is from a judgment in favor of the plaintiff, recovered on account of the death of the plaintiff's husband, John W. Lackey, caused by the alleged negligence of the defendant.

Lackey, while a pedestrian on the street, was struck and killed by a street car of the defendant July 23, 1918. At that time the defendant operated two parallel street railway tracks, called the Hodiamont tracks, along its private right of way across Plymouth avenue. Plymouth avenue at the point of intersection ran east and west and was 45 feet wide. The right of way was about 22 feet wide. The street car tracks at that point were each 5 feet wide with a space of 4½ feet between them. Along that space was a ditch 3½ feet wide and 18 inches deep. North-bound cars ran on the east track, and south-bound cars ran on the west track. A drug store stood at the northwest corner of Plymouth avenue and the right of way. A granitoid walk or landing was on the east side of the drug store where passengers boarded and alighted from cars running south. This sidewalk was about 40 feet long, and at the front was against the drug store and extended 8 feet 4 inches toward the track, with a space of 20 inches between the edge of the walk and the west rail of the west track. On the southeast corner of Plymouth avenue and the right of way was likewise a granitoid walk 3½ or 4 feet wide, extending along the track southward from Plymouth avenue about 75 feet, where cars going north regularly discharged and received passengers. The following sketch shows approximately the position of the street, the car tracks, and surrounding objects:

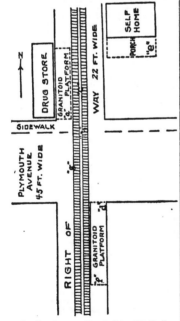

On the day mentioned John W. Lackey, husband of the plaintiff, was seen on the walk alongside the drug store. He was seen to step down from the walk into the 20-inch space between that and the west rail of the south-bound track, or upon that rail. This was at a point 8 or 10 feet north of the north line of Plymouth avenue. He was not seen any more by any witness who testified until the instant before he was struck by a car running north on the east track; he was then at a point where the sidewalk crosses that track, about 20 feet from where he was first seen.

Three witnesses for the plaintiff testified to seeing the incidents preceding and at the moment of the collision. Two of these witnesses, Hadley and Cahill, were diagonally across the street at the southeast corner of Plymouth and the right of way on the granitoid walk where passengers were received upon cars running north; the third was Katie Self, sitting on the east end of her porch on the north side of Plymouth avenue and east of the track. Referring to the plat which we have made for convenience, "a" represents the point where Lackey was seen to step down off the walk by the drug store at a point 8 or 10 feet north of the north line of Plymouth avenue; "b" is the point on the north-bound track where he was struck; his body was found at point "c" between the two tracks about 25 feet north of where he was struck; "d" is the point where two witnesses, Don Hadley and John Cahill, were standing when Hadley saw Lackey step off the walk at point "a"; "e" is the point on the porch of the house east of the track where Katie Self was sitting and saw the collision; "f" is the point where Hadley was at the moment of collision; "g" is the point where Cahill was at the instant of collision.

The only person who saw Lackey at the point "a" was Hadley. He was then at point "d," talking to Cahill, and waiting for a car to go north. The moment he saw Lackey step down from the sidewalk at point "a," witness looked south and saw a car coming from that direction about 150 feet away. He signaled that car to stop for him, turned, and walked rapidly south along the granitoid walk about 20 feet, and didn't see Lackey any more until after he was struck. The car did not stop at his signal, but passed on, struck Lackey, and stopped with the rear end of the car about 35 feet north of Plymouth avenue. Lackey at that time was lying between the two tracks in the ditch, about 30 feet north of Plymouth avenue. The car was running at a very high rate of speed about 30 or 35 miles an hour. Cars going north on that track usually stop with the rear end about 40 feet south of Plymouth avenue and the front end about at the property line. Witness expected the car to stop at that point. It was about 8:30 in the evening of July 23d, and light enough for anybody to see. The car coming from the south could have been seen at a considerable distance by any one looking. The witness was cross-examined at length. He repeated several times that at the time he saw Lackey the latter was in the act of stepping off the sidewalk alongside the drug store 8 or 10 feet north of the sidewalk on Plymouth avenue. He said Lackey was walking slowly, looking down to see where to put his feet. At the point where he was Lackey could not conveniently have crossed the ditch between the tracks, but would have had to walk south 8 or 10 feet to the sidewalk on Plymouth avenue and cross the tracks on that sidewalk.

John Cahill testified that he intended to board a south-bound car which regularly would stop at the granitoid walk beside the drug store. He stopped at the point "d" on the southeast corner for a few minutes, talking with Mr. Hadley. It was his intention then to cross diagonally to the corner where he should take the next car going south. He did not see Lackey at that time. He saw the car Hadley intended to take coming from the south, about 150 feet away, and started to run diagonally across ahead of it. He crossed the north-bound track and had got about to the middle of Plymouth avenue on the south-bound track when he saw the car coming north was not going to stop for Hadley. His testimony then continued as follows:

"Q. Now, when you started from the southeast corner across there, how far was the car south of you then that Mr. Hadley wanted to get on, do you know? A. About 150 feet.

"Q. Did you see the car any more after that? A. Not until I got in the middle of the south-bound track; then I heard him ringing the gong, and I turned around, and I seen he was going to pass Mr. Hadley up. I looked back and seen Mr. Hadley standing there; he was waving the paper for him to stop the car; I seen him ringing the bell and kept ringing, and I seen he was going to pass him up, and I stood in the middle of the south-bound track, and as he got in the middle of Plymouth avenue he started to ring the bell again; and I seen Mr. Lackey about the middle of the car track. He started to step back. He seen he was too late, and he jumped up in the air, like to jump on the fender to save himself, and the car struck him and knocked him in the middle of the ditch. He landed on his feet, his face turned south. His head hit the car track, and his head lay on the car tracks, and the rear guard on the hind trucks struck his face and knocked him in the ditch. * * *

"Q. Now, where were you then? A. Standing in the middle of the south-bound track.

"Q. Where were you in Plymouth avenue, to the north side or in the middle, or to the south side? A. Right in the middle of Plymouth."

The witness testified that the car was running at a very high rate of speed, about 35 or 40 miles an hour; that the bell of the car was ringing when it arrived about 50 feet south of Plymouth avenue, and the motorman commenced ringing again loudly about the time he reached the middle of Plymouth avenue. He rang the bell hard and "hollered 'Look out!'" He said, further, that the car did not make much noise running on the right of way because it was not on a granitoid

foundation. On cross-examination he said he would judge that Lackey jumped about 18 inches or 2 feet high; jumped like for the fender and grabbed the car so as to save himself; that he never saw Lackey until Lackey was on the north-bound track, when the front end of the car was within 15 or 20 feet of him.

Mrs. Katie Self testified that she lived on the north side of Plymouth avenue, east of the tracks; that her house stood back 50 feet from Plymouth avenue, that the west side of the house was only about 3½ feet east of the track. She sat on the east end of her porch reading. She was suddenly attracted by the violent ringing of the bell of the street car. Street cars passed that way every four minutes through the day, ringing bells and making noises, and she usually paid no attention to the noise they made, but the ringing of the bell was so violent and unusual that she looked up, and this is the way she described the collision:

"Q. What did you see when you looked up? A. When I looked up when the bell was ringing I saw a man crossing the track. He was on the last track east—that is, the north-bound car track—and when I looked up the car was just about five feet from him, and he went to step forward and became confused and jumped in the air as if to let something go under him, as if he was going to be struck, and while he was in midair the car struck him.

"Q. Where was he at that time with reference to the crossing on Plymouth avenue; was he on the regular crossing? A. He was on the right of way for going back and forth.

"Q. Where people walk across? A. Yes, sir.

"Q. Which side of Plymouth, north or south? A. On the north side. He was going east.

"Q. Did you see the car after it stopped? A. Yes, sir.

"Q. Where was it with reference to the north side of Plymouth avenue? A. From where it hit him?

"Q. Yes. A. It was about 50 or 55 feet, the back end of the car, from where it hit him.

"Q. After the car stopped did it stand stationary, or did it move or back up? A. I couldn't say; I didn't see it.

"Q. Where was the man at that time? A. He was between about 25 feet from where he was hit from the crossing; it threw him 25 feet.

"Q. I believe he was laying between the tracks you say? A. Yes, sir; there is a little ditch between the two tracks."

The witness judged that the car was going at the rate of 30 miles an hour.

Another witness, Mrs. Mary Grace, lived further east on Plymouth avenue. She testified to the unusual clamor and ringing of the bell, the screaming of the people, and that the car was going at 30 or 35 miles an hour.

No witness put the speed of the car at less than 30 miles an hour.

An ex-motorman, who was familiar with the operation of the cars of the 600 series, of which the car in question was one, swore that under the conditions shown such a car traveling at 15 miles an hour could be stopped within 40 or 45 feet, and a car traveling 30 miles an hour in from 115 to 120 feet. He said those cars could not be run faster than 30 miles an hour unless going down grade; that the appliances used for stopping cars could be applied instantaneously, "right now," in a fraction of a second. Witness also figured the speed per second of a car going 30 miles per hour is 44 feet; at 35 miles an hour a car travels 51 feet per second; and at 40 miles an hour 60 feet.

The plaintiff introduced and read Revised Code of the City of St. Louis, § 2381, prohibiting street cars from being propelled at a greater rate of speed than 15 miles an hour in parts of St. Louis, including the place where Lackey was killed. Plaintiff also introduced section No. 2386 of the Revised Code, requiring cars going southward to stop on the north side of the intersection of streets, and those going northward to stop on the south side of the intersection of streets, when signaled or motioned to by any one standing on the appropriate corners desiring to board such cars. They also introduced section 2380 of the vigilant watch ordinance, providing that each "motorman, gripman, driver or any other person in charge of each car shall keep vigilant watch for all vehicles and persons on foot, especially children, either on the track or moving towards it, and on the first appearance of danger to such persons or vehicles the car shall be stopped in the shortest time and space possible."

All of these ordinances and regulations were objected to by the defendant, and exceptions saved to their introduction.

The case was submitted to the jury on two specifications of negligence set up in the petition: First, that the car which caused the accident was running in excess of the speed limit of fifteen miles an hour; and, second, the failure of the motorman in charge of the car to stop the car or check its speed after he saw, or by the exercise of ordinary care could have seen, Lackey in time to have done so.

Defendant introduced no evidence, but demurred to plaintiff's evidence, which demurrer was overruled, and a verdict for $10,000 in favor of plaintiff resulted. The evidence is set out at some length because one main assignment of error is to the action of the court in overruling the demurrer to the evidence.

[1] I. It is conceded that the defendant was negligent in operating at an excessive rate of speed the car which caused the death. It is argued that the demurrer should have been sustained because the evidence conclusively showed Lackey's own negligence contributed to the fatal injury. Appellant relies upon the rule, established in many cases, that one who is about to go upon a railroad track

or a street railway track owes a duty to himself to look and to listen; he must have a care for his own safety. If he goes upon the track in front of an approaching car when the exercise of ordinary care would prevent injury, he cannot recover for the injury caused by collision with such car. Keele v. Railroad, 258 Mo. loc. cit. 80, 167 S. W. 433; Rollinson v. Railroad, 252 Mo. loc. cit. 542, 543, 160 S. W. 994; Gubernick v. United Railways Co., 217 S. W. loc. cit. 85; Schmidt v. Railroad, 191 Mo. loc. cit. 229, 90 S. W. 136, 3 L. R. A. (N. S.) 196; Laun v. Railroad, 216 Mo. loc. cit. 578, 116 S. W. 553.

[2] The rule that one injured or killed under such circumstances is presumed to have been in the exercise of ordinary care, in the absence of evidence to the contrary, is conceded by the appellant. McKenzie v. United Rys., 216 Mo. loc. cit. 22, 115 S. W. 13. But it is urged that it has no application here, because, appellant asserts, the facts in relation to the incident all are clearly shown. When the facts appear as to how such a collision happened, there is no room for a presumption. Burge v. Railroad, 244 Mo. loc. cit. 94, 148 S. W. 925; Tetwiler v. Railroad, 242 Mo. loc. cit. 194, 145 S. W. 780; Higgins v. St. L. & Sub. Ry. Co., 197 Mo. loc. cit. 317, 95 S. W. 863. Many other cases of like import are cited.

[3, 4] To say that one injured under such circumstances is presumed to be exercising ordinary care is but another way of saying contributory negligence is an affirmative defense and must be proven in order to be available to the defendant. Since the defendant introduced no evidence, we must examine the facts to see whether the plaintiff's own evidence shows conclusively that Lackey was negligent. It will be noted that from the time he stepped off the walk by the drug store until he was on the track immediately in front of the car which struck him he was not seen by anybody who testified. The distance between those two points may be approximately determined from the figures given. Starting at that point he had to go 8 or 10 feet to the sidewalk on Plymouth avenue, then across the west track 5 feet, and the space of 4½ feet between the tracks, and go on to the east track, a total distance of about 20 feet. That would have been his most probable course. He might have reached the point by going diagonally across from where he first stepped off the walk, but in that case he would have crossed the ditch between the two tracks, 3½ feet wide and 18 inches deep. He certainly was not negligent in anything he was seen to do at the time he stepped off the walk. He was walking slowly, looking down, as the witness stated, to see where to put his foot. Nothing in his attitude indicated lack of care.

When he was next seen he was on the track, 5, 15, or 20 feet, according to the different witnesses, in front of the approaching car. He seemed to discover the car about the time the witnesses saw him, and, from the testimony, was confused by the sudden discovery of the car so close. The mere instant's hesitation was fatal to him. He first appeared to start back and then jumped upward to save himself by jumping on the fender. His action indicates such excitement and confusion as for the moment to deprive him of quick and rational action. It is possible, with the car 15 or 20 feet from him, that he might have jumped to one side and escaped, but he certainly was not negligent in failing to do that, in the confusion of the moment. On that proposition the authorities are unanimous. Some men are slower than others to think. The ordinary individual, in sudden emergency, is incapable of instant action. To save himself then required instant action, which he seemed unable to take in the right direction. No one knows how he got on the track. It cannot be presumed that he intentionally walked on the track in front of the approaching car which he saw, or readily could have seen. He may have stumbled on the track accidentally.

Other circumstances also must be taken into consideration; circumstances which do not appear in cases relied upon by appellant as showing contributory negligence on the part of one who voluntarily steps in front of an approaching car or train. The car was running at the rate of 30 miles or more an hour—twice as fast as the speed limit permitted. If Lackey saw the car 150 feet away when he started across the right of way, he had a right, in the absence of any notice or knowledge to the contrary, to assume that it was traveling within the speed limit. Powers v. Transit Co., 202 Mo. loc. cit. 280, 100 S. W. 655; Harrington v. Dunham, 273 Mo. 414, loc. cit. 423, 202 S. W. 1066; Moon v. St. Louis Transit Co., 237 Mo. loc. cit. 430 et seq., 141 S. W. 870, Ann. Cas. 1913A, 183; Eckhard v. St. Louis Transit Co., 190 Mo. 593, loc. cit. 617, 89 S. W. 602; Riska v. Union Depot R. R. Co., 180 Mo. loc. cit. 191, 79 S. W. 445; Strauchon v. Met. Street Ry. Co., 232 Mo. 587, loc. cit. 600, 601, 135 S. W. 14. He might very well misjudge the speed of the car seeing it as it came head on. It has been said by this court to be a matter of common knowledge that one seeing a running car at an acute angle—for instance, from the front—is not nearly so well able to judge of its speed as one viewing it from the side. Strauchon v. Met. St. Ry. Co., 232 Mo. loc. cit. 599, 135 S. W. 14. Furthermore, it was the duty of the motorman of the approaching car to stop on the south side of Plymouth avenue, because it was a regular stop, and he was signaled to stop by Hadley, who sought passage. If Lackey saw the car approaching, as appellant asks us to assume, he might as well assume that he saw Hadley's signal to the car to stop. The cases in the last

231 S.W.—61

group cited discuss the assumptions upon which one approaching a track may rely under varying conditions. Lackey had a right to assume that the approaching car was running within the speed limit, and that it would stop on the other side of the street, and to act upon the assumption, unless he knew to the contrary. In either case he could have crossed in safety, and was not negligent in attempting to do so. Appellant cites the case of State ex rel. Peters v. Reynolds, 214 S. W. 121, recently determined by this court, in which one crossing a railroad track was killed, and was not seen from the time he started to cross the track a little distance away until after he was hit. It was held by this court, approving the ruling of the St. Louis Court of Appeals that the plaintiff was negligent as a matter of law, because if he had looked he must plainly have seen the approaching train, and he was negligent if he failed to look. Other cases might be cited where recovery has been denied on account of contributory negligence, although the party injured or killed was not seen for a brief interval between the fatal collision and where he was previously at some point of safety. In all of these cases the right to assume the approaching train or car was running at a given speed, or would stop, is entirely absent. This court, in case of State ex rel. Peters v. Reynolds, supra, said (loc. cit. 123), in distinguishing the cases where such assumption was allowed:

"In all those cases some specific violation of duty or of a custom by defendant company is considered, and it is held that a pedestrian may presume and act upon the presumption that there will be no such violation, but that the usual and regular, or prescribed, method will be followed. Also in each of such cases there was an absence of actual knowledge of the failure of duty; that is, the pedestrian who acted upon such presumption either could not see or hear the approaching train, or was in such position that he would likely misjudge its rate of speed."

The court then points out that the facts in that case did not show the deceased had reason to believe that the train would run at a rate of speed less than that at which it was running.

The facts in this case come clearly within the exception noted here. Here Lackey did have reason to believe the car would run at a particular rate of speed. He did have reason, if he saw the car at all, to believe that it would stop. He had a right to rely upon the observation by defendant of a duty which its regulation and the city ordinances required it to perform.

Several witnesses swore to the loud ringing of the bell without placing the distance of the car at the time. There is substantial evidence to show that the bell rang by the time it got within 50 feet of Plymouth avenue, and only rang again, very violently, about the time the front end of the car reached the middle of Plymouth avenue. That violent ringing must have occurred about the time Lackey discovered the car and became too confused to jump off the track. If he saw the car when it was 150 feet south of Plymouth avenue, it was then in the neighborhood of 200 feet from him. If it was going at 15 miles an hour, or 22 feet per second, he would have had at least six seconds in which to cross the track ahead of it. He could easily have done that at an ordinary walk. There is no view of the evidence which would authorize a conclusion of law that he was so negligent as to bar recovery.

[5-7] II. The case was submitted both on the negligence of defendant in running its car at an excessive rate of speed and on the last chance doctrine. Appellant is correct in its argument that the motorman, even if he saw Lackey approaching the track, had a right to assume until a different intention was apparent that he would use due care for himself and would not step in front of the car. The absence of evidence considered in the previous paragraph to show Lackey was not necessarily negligent applies to the question considered here. There is no evidence whatever as to when or how Lackey stepped into the dangerous position, or indicated an intention to do so. The motorman was not negligent in failing to observe the last chance rule at any particular period until Lackey was in danger, or apparently going into danger. The evidence showed the car, at the rate it was running, could not have been stopped in less than 115 or 120 feet. In order to permit the submission of the question as to whether it could have been stopped or checked sufficiently to avoid injuring Lackey, it would have been necessary to show that at some particular time before the immediate contact he was going into danger and was oblivious of his peril, so that the motorman could have seen him in time to act. Knapp v. Dunham (App.) 195 S. W. 1062; Rubick v. Sandler, (App.) 219 S. W. loc. cit. 406; Schmidt v. Railroad, 191 Mo. 215, 90 S. W. 136, 8 L. R. A. (N. S.) 196; Keele v. Railroad, 258 Mo. loc. cit. 79, 167 S. W. 433. It might be inferred from the fact that the bell began to ring violently at the middle of Plymouth avenue that the motorman at that time discovered him in a position of peril, or in the act of going upon the track; but there is no evidence that he might have discovered such peril sooner because there is no evidence that Lackey was in peril sooner than that. Then it was too late to stop the car or even sensibly check its speed. It was therefore error for the trial court to submit to the jury the issue whether the car might have stopped in time to avoid injury after the discovery of or the opportunity to discover Lackey's peril.

[8] III. Appellant claims that the statute under which this suit was brought (section 4217, R. S. 1919) is penal so far as $2,000 of the recovery provided is concerned, and compensative as to the remainder of recovery up to $10,000, and, since the petition alleged no facts showing pecuniary loss, recovery should have been limited to $2,000.

In the well-considered case of Grier v. Kansas City Electric Railway Co. (No. 21100) 228 S. W. 454, the court in banc at the present term held that the section is penal as to the entire amount recoverable, and allowed a verdict under the section for $10,000 to stand, though there was no pleading or proof of pecuniary loss. There was no error in permitting recovery for the full amount.

[9] Another question arising in this connection is whether evidence of pecuniary loss to the widow by reason of her husband's death, in an action under that section, is admissible if not pleaded. Evidence was admitted, over defendant's objection, to show the earning capacity of Lackey and his life expectancy.

The amount awarded in such an action, between the limits of $2,000 and $10,000, is "in the discretion of the jury." Of course, the jury must have facts upon which to base an estimate fixing the amount of penalty to be imposed. It is held in the Grier Case that evidence showing circumstances of aggravation and pecuniary loss may be admitted for the purpose of furnishing the jury such information, although the jury has authority to award the full amount without such evidence.

The cases construing the compensatory sections 4218 and 4219, in regard to the admissibility of such evidence, throw little or no light on the question. Johnson v. Mining Co., 171 Mo. App. 134, 156 S. W. 33; Rollinson v. Lusk, 203 Mo. App. 31, 217 S. W. 328, loc. cit. 332; Smelser v. Railroad, 262 Mo. 25, loc. cit. 42, 170 S. W. 1124.

There is no reason why in a suit under a penal statute the ordinary rules of pleading should not apply as well as under a compensatory statute, including the rule that every fact constituting a cause of action should be stated. Section 1220, R. S. 1919; Pier v. Heinrichoffen, 52 Mo. loc. cit. 336. That means not only facts necessary to a recovery, but facts affecting the amount of recovery. Evidence of special damages cannot be admitted to enhance a verdict unless pleaded. For like reason, where the jury is required to exercise discretion in fixing the amount of a penalty, they should consider the evidence which would affect the result, as held in the Grier Case. In order to meet such evidence, the defendant has a right to be apprised by the pleading that it will be offered. Unless the petition states facts in general terms from which the aggravating circumstances that would increase the penalty may necessarily be inferred, such circumstances should be pleaded, just as special damages must be pleaded in a suit for compensation. It is suggested in some of the cases cited above that an allegation that plaintiff was the wife of deceased is a sufficient averment of pecuniary loss, because the law requires him to furnish her support. But it by no means follows, as a necessary inference, because the law requires a man to support his wife, that he does support her; very often it is quite the contrary, and the death of the husband may be to the widow a large pecuniary gain.

From the holding in the Grier Case that such evidence is admissible for the purpose of giving the jury facts upon which to fix the amount of the penalty to be imposed, it is a reasonable conclusion that such facts should be pleaded.

[10, 11] IV. Appellant assigns error to the giving of instruction No. 1 on behalf of the plaintiff because it does not require a finding by the jury that the alleged negligence of the defendant was the proximate cause of the injury. The first part of the instruction, after requiring a finding as to the facts in relation to the collision and the death, and the ordinance limiting the speed of the car, proceeds:

"If you further find from the evidence that at the time the deceased was struck by the car it was being run at a speed greater than 15 miles an hour, and the deceased was exercising ordinary care for his own safety, then the defendant would be liable in this action, and your verdict should be for the plaintiff."

No other negligence is required to be found in the instruction, and nothing appears except the above-quoted passage, as to the effect of such negligence. Negligence is not actionable unless it produces an injury. In such cases it is always necessary to prove that the negligence complained of is the proximate cause of the injury which results. An instruction authorizing recovery in such case must require such a finding. King v. Railroad, 143 Mo. App. 279, loc. cit. 297, 127 S. W. 400; Battles v. Railways Co., 178 Mo. App. loc. cit. 614, 161 S. W. 614; Tranbarger v. Railroad, 250 Mo. loc. cit. 58, 156 S. W. 694. Where the jury is required to find facts from which a necessary inference follows that the negligence found was the cause of the injury, it is sufficient. State ex rel. v. Ellison, 208 S. W. 443 (Supreme Court in banc); Sutter v. Metropolitan Street Railway Co., 208 S. W. 851 (Kansas City Court of Appeals).

The instruction in this case, however, does not require a finding of specific and definite facts from which an inference necessarily

follows that the negligence, if found, was the cause of the injury, nor was there any other curative instruction given in the case. It was entirely possible for the jury to find that the defendant was negligently exceeding the speed limit, that Lackey was exercising due care for his own safety, and yet find that the negligence of the defendant was not the cause of the death; it might have been purely accidental.

[12] The instruction is erroneous also for another reason. It is in the alternative, and in addition to the part quoted above authorizes a verdict for plaintiff, not only on account of the excessive speed, but also under the humanitarian rule. It was error to submit the latter alternative, as we have seen above.

[13] V. The vigilant watch ordinance was admitted in evidence over the objection and exception of defendant. It was not pleaded in the petition as a ground of recovery, and its admission was error. Weisberg v. Boatmen's Bank, 280 Mo. 199, 217 S. W. 85; Peterson v. United Rys. Co., 270 Mo. loc. cit. 74, 192 S. W. 938; State ex rel. Oddie v. Sherman, 42 Mo. 210; Keane v. Klausman, 21 Mo. App. 485. Under some circumstances its admission may be harmless, though not pleaded, because it is declaratory of the common law, but, since the case is to be retried, we need not discuss that distinction.

[14] VI. The plaintiff introduced an ordinance which provided that cars should stop on the near side of the street, and that it should be the duty of the motorman, or other servant running the car, to bring the car to a full stop at the corner of the street as provided, whenever signaled or motioned to by any person standing on such corner desiring to board such car. This was objected to by the appellant and error assigned to the action of the court in admitting it. The ordinance was admissible, though not pleaded. The defendant's answer pleaded contributory negligence, and defendant attempted to show it in cross-examination of plaintiff's witnesses. It was then entirely competent for the plaintiff to prove any fact which would rebut evidence indicating such negligence. It was proper to show that the motorman was in duty bound to stop his car on the other side of the street. The ordinance was admissible for that reason.

For the reasons mentioned, the judgment is reversed, and the cause remanded.

RAILEY and MOZLEY, CC., concur.

PER CURIAM. The foregoing opinion by WHITE, C., is adopted as the opinion of the court.

All the Judges concur; HIGBEE. P. J., in reversing, but thinks case should not be remanded; dissents as to remanding.

WATSON v. HARDWICK et al.   (No. 18765.)

(Supreme Court of Missouri, in Banc.
May 24, 1921.)

1. **Deeds 💭129(4)—Beneficiary of trust held to have only life estate in land.**

A deed conveying land to one in trust for the benefit of another during his natural life, upon his death to become vested in his natural heirs, conveys to the beneficiary of the trust only a life estate, under Rev. St 1909, § 2874.

2. **Trusts 💭61(3), 147(1)—Trustee held not empowered to convert trust into life estate in beneficiary; beneficiary could not transfer interest.**

A deed of land to one in trust for another for his lifetime, upon the death of the beneficiary to become vested in his natural heirs, *held,* to require possession, control, and management to remain in the trustee, and trustee could not remove the trust from her shoulders by converting it into a life estate for the beneficiary, or by leasing it to the beneficiary for life, and the beneficiary could not transfer his interest.

3. **Judgment 💭743(2)—Judgment held not to estop trustee from obtaining possession.**

Where trustee holding land for the benefit of another for life attempted to convey to beneficiary a life estate, which she did not have the power to do, and suit was brought by transferees of the beneficiary, and the trustee refused to take any part in the suit, stating that she wished to be relieved of the responsibilities of the trust, she was not estopped from later suing for possession, by a judgment which declared that she had the legal title, but no right to interfere with the transferees of the beneficiary, in view of the statute of uses (Rev. St. 1909, § 2867); the possession and control of the property being indispensable to the execution of the trust.

4. **Trusts 💭167—Court had authority to remove trustee.**

In an action by a trustee to obtain possession and control of trust real estate, court had power at the instance of the defendants to ask for the removal of the plaintiff as trustee and to appoint another in her place.

5. **Trusts 💭131—Legal title not supported for purpose of transmission alone under statute of uses.**

Legal title cannot, as against the statute of uses, be supported for the purpose of transmission alone.

6. **Trusts 💭58—Donor cannot change effect of deed.**

Grantor in a deed conveying land to another in trust for a third person for life, remainder to natural heirs of beneficiary, cannot by a subsequent act change the effect of his deed.

7. **Trusts 💭147(1)—Held that beneficiary for life could assign rents and profits.**

Beneficiary of a trust for life, remainder going to natural heirs, could assign the right to annual distribution of net rents and profits conferred upon him by the deed creating the

trust, although he could not convey any interest in the land, under Rev. St. 1909, § 2867.

Appeal from Circuit Court, Carroll County; Frank P. Divelbiss, Judge.

Action by Gertie Watson, trustee for William A. Whiteley, against W. H. Hardwick and others. Judgment for plaintiff, and defendants appeal. Affirmed in part, and reversed in part, and remanded, with directions.

Preston Forsee, S. P. Forsee, and M. M. Bogie, all of Kansas City, for appellants. S. J. & G. C. Jones, of Carrollton, for respondent.

BROWN, C. This suit involves the title and possession of about 200 acres of land in Carroll county. The petition contains two counts, the first ejectment, and the second to try title under the provisions of section 2535, R. S. 1909. No question is raised upon the pleadings.

The common source of title is Abner Whiteley. In making a distribution of lands by warranty deed dated April 4, 1895, he conveyed these lands to Gertie Watson. It recited the consideration as "the natural relation existing between grandparent and grandchildren and the sum of one dollar," described the grantee as "trustee and in trust for William Whiteley for and during his natural life," and stated the "conditions" of the trust as follows:

"Said trustee to pay the taxes, necessary expenses and repairs in and about said * * * tract of land and premises, and then the net proceeds arising from the use of said land to be paid annually by said trustee to said William Whiteley for his own use and benefit, and upon his death the said * * * described tract of land to become vested in fee simple in the heirs of said William Whiteley."

William was Gertie's brother, and both were grandchildren of the grantor. Their father, Bennett Whiteley, was dead. Abner died in 1908 or 1909, and during the pendency in this court of a suit about this land to which we shall presently have occasion to refer.

October 15, 1895, Gertie signed a writing reciting that William was "desirous of managing and controlling the land, and using and renting the same," and concluding as follows:

"Now, therefore, I, the undersigned, as such trustee, hereby authorize and empower the said William Whiteley to take charge and control of said lands, and to rent, manage and control the same."

In 1904 she made him a lease for life of the same land.

On October 9, 1897, William quitclaimed the land to John W. Penland, and on March

27, 1906, Penland quitclaimed an undivided half of the same land to Frank Atwood. On April 1, 1910, Penland and Atwood quitclaimed the same land to M. T. Forsee, the wife of Samuel P. Forsee, and on a date not fixed in the abstract she quitclaimed it to the Convention City Investment Company. This grantee is a corporation of which the Forsees, husband and wife, own two-thirds of the capital stock, and Samuel P. Forsee is its president. On November 11, 1907, William A. Whiteley conveyed an undivided one-half of the same land by warranty deed to said corporation, and on February 23, 1909, by deed in like form, conveyed all his interest to that company.

In 1906 Penland and Atwood instituted suit against William Whiteley, Dollie A. Whiteley, Gertie Watson, and Ralph Muir to quiet the title to these lands under the statute then in force. Mrs. Watson refused to employ attorneys, or otherwise to have anything to do with the defense of this suit, saying, in substance, that she had had trouble enough with the transaction; that she had removed her residence to Kansas City, and only desired to be discharged and relieved from the trust. She so informed Mr. S. P. Forsee, who afterwards, by arrangement, as he says, with Abner Whiteley, then living, defended for her, as well as for William Whiteley and the other defendants.

The cause was tried, and on January 13, 1907, resulted in the following judgment:

"The court finds that under the conveyances read in evidence the plaintiffs have acquired the life estate of William A. Whiteley in and to the lands in controversy.

"That plaintiffs are entitled to the rents and profits of said land during the life of said William Whiteley, less taxes, repairs, and necessary expenses; that the agreements, assignments, and conveyances purporting to convey the interest of the trustee to William Whiteley were and are not effective to extinguish the trust in Gertie Watson created by the deed of Abner Whiteley, nor to merge the title in William Whiteley; and the court finds, ascertains, determines, adjudges, and decrees the title to said land as follows: The legal title to said land is vested in Gertie Watson as trustee; that the title in remainder is vested in the heirs of William Whiteley, and that the right to possession, rents, and profits, less necessary expenses, repairs, and taxes, is vested in plaintiffs, John W. Penland and Frank E. Atwood, equal owners thereof; that neither Ralph Muir nor Dollie A. Whiteley have any right, title, interest, or estate whatsoever in or to the lands aforesaid, nor to the possession, rents, issues, and profits thereof; that, in accordance with the finding of the court aforesaid, title is hereby ascertained, determined, adjudged, defined, and decreed.

"It is further ordered that the deed dated November 12, 1908, and recorded in Book 168, page 191, office of the recorder of deeds within and for Carroll county, Mo., from William Whiteley to Ralph Muir, be, and the same is hereby, set aside, annulled, and for naught held.

It is further ordered that a certain lease, dated November 26, 1904, executed by Gertie Watson, trustee, filed for record December 12, 1904, and recorded in Book 171, at page 573, office of the recorder of deeds aforesaid, together with the assignments thereof by William Whiteley to Dollie A. Whiteley, be, and the same is hereby, annulled, set aside, and for naught held.

"It is further ordered, adjudged, and decreed that defendants, and each of them, be forever estopped, debarred, and precluded from setting up or asserting any title in and to the aforesaid real estate inconsistent with the finding and judgment of this court as aforesaid. It is further ordered and adjudged that plaintiffs have and recover of defendants herein their costs in this behalf taxed at the sum of $———, and that they have thereof execution."

An appeal was taken by defendants in that case to this court, where, at the April term 1910, Mrs. Forsee having previously acquired all the title adjudged to Penland, it was affirmed upon the following stipulation:

"John W. Penland et al., Plaintiffs, v. William A. Whiteley et al., Defendants. No. 14128. It is hereby stipulated that the judgment of the circuit court of Carroll county, Mo., in the above-styled cause may be in all things affirmed. Lozier, Morris & Atwood, Attorneys for Plaintiffs. S. P. Forsee, Attorney for Defendants."

Although the appellants in their abstract expressly admit the sufficiency of the pleadings to present the issues, reference to them may be of assistance in arriving at a clearer understanding of this judgment.

The petition counts: (1) In ejectment upon the right of the plaintiff to possession under the deed from Abner Whiteley; and (2) for a declaration and restoration of her rights and duties as trustee under the same deed.

The answer of S. P. Forsee, Hardwick, and the Convention City Investment Company pleads: (1) A general denial; (2) the judgment in the Penland case in bar or estoppel as the case may be; (3) title and possession of the investment company, through Penland and Atwood, of the life interest of William Whiteley; (4) violation of duty by the trustee, her nonresidence and unfitness for the office of trustee, with a prayer for her removal and the appointment of another as trustee to hold the legal title in her stead.

Hughes and Whitsett answered, claiming an interest under a contract or "stipulation" dated January 16, 1912, between all the defendants in this suit except Hardwick, settling and defining their several interests in the claims by them respectively under William Whiteley. Mrs. Watson was not a party to it. Mrs. Forsee answered, disclaiming any and all interest in the controversy.

S. P. Forsee and the Convention City Investment Company replied to the claim of Hughes and Whitsett by general denial and plea of failure to perform the contract mentioned in their answer.

The circuit court, upon the evidence, rendered its judgment, from which this appeal is taken by the defendants except Hughes and Whitsett. The judgment is as follows:

"Now on this 23d day of April, 1914, it being the ninth day of the April term, 1914, of the circuit court of Carroll county, Mo., this cause coming on for final determination, a jury being waived, and the issues being submitted to the court, the court having heard the evidence and being fully advised in the premises, doth find with reference to the first count of plaintiff's petition herein that the defendants are guilty of the trespass and ejectment in plaintiff's petition alleged, and that plaintiff hath sustained damages by reason of the ejectment in the sum of $1, and that the monthly value of the lands in the petition described is the sum of $15.

"It is therefore considered by the court that the plaintiff recover of the defendants the possession of the lands in the petition described, situated and being in Carroll county, Mo., as follows, to wit: [Here follows description]— $1 for her damages, and also for the sum of $15, the monthly value of said premises until the plaintiff be restored to the possession of the said lands and tenements.

"And the court doth further order that an execution issue to restore to the said plaintiff the possession of the said tenements aforesaid and for the damages and monthly value aforesaid.

"On the second count of plaintiff's petition the court doth ascertain, adjudge, and define the title, estate, and interest of the parties, severally, in and to the following described real estate, situated and being in Carroll county, Mo., [being the premises described in plaintiff's first amended petition herein], as follows, to wit: That Gertie Watson, trustee for William A. Whiteley, plaintiff herein, has and holds the legal title to said premises in trust for and during the natural lifetime of William A. Whiteley, with full power and authority to control, lease, and rent the same and to collect and receive the rents, issues, and profits therefrom, and to pay out of said rents, issues, and profits the taxes which may be levied and assessed against said land, also necessary expenses and repairs on said premises, and then pay the net proceeds arising from the leasing and renting of said land annually to the said William A. Whiteley, his grantees and assigns, for and during the natural lifetime of the said William A. Whiteley.

"That M. T. Forsee, S. P. Forsee, and the Convention City Investment Company are the owners of an undivided one-half interest in the life estate of the said William A. Whiteley, and during the lifetime of the said William A. Whiteley are entitled to receive from said trustee, or her successor, one-half of the net rents and profits of said land, less taxes, necessary expenses, and the keeping of said premises in repair.

"That Roland Hughes and George P. Whitsett are jointly the owners of an undivided one-fourth interest of the life estate of the said William A. Whiteley, subject to the payment to ... n City Investment Company of the sum of $1,350, and are entitled to receive jointly from said trustee or her successor during the natural lifetime of the said William A. Whiteley one-fourth of the rents, issues and profits of said real estate, less the taxes, necessary expenses and keeping said premises in repair.

"That William A. Whiteley, subject to the payment of the Convention City Investment Company the sum of $1,350, is entitled to have and receive from said trustee, or her successor, for and during his natural lifetime, one-fourth of the rents and profits of said land, after the paying of taxes, necessary expenses, and keeping said premises in repair.

"The court finds that on account of the fact that said Gertie Watson is a married woman and resides in Kansas City, Mo., and her place of residence being so far removed from said land that she is not a suitable person to act as trustee and discharge the duties of said trust, wherefore it is ordered and adjudged that said Gertie Watson be removed as trustee, and that George E. Magee, a citizen and resident of Carroll county, Mo., whom the court finds to be a suitable person, be, and he is hereby, appointed trustee, and is invested with the legal title to said land, and he and his successor or successors shall have and hold the legal title thereto, and he or they are hereby given full power and authority to control said land, lease and rent the same, collect and receive the rents, issues, and profits therefrom, and out of said rents, issues, and profits shall pay: First, all taxes which are or which may hereafter be legally levied and assessed against said land; second, shall pay all necessary expenses incident to said land and to the keeping of said premises in reasonable repair; and, third, shall pay the remainder of said rents and profits to the said M. T. Forsee, Samuel P. Forsee, the Convention City Investment Company, Roland Hughes, George P. Whitsett, and William A. Whiteley, as their interests have been ascertained and declared by this judgment.

"The court further finds that said M. T. Forsee, Samuel Forsee, and the Convention City Investment Company did for the years 1911, 1912, and 1913 have charge of said land and did lease and rent the same, and have collected and received the rents and profits, and have failed and neglected to pay the taxes which have accrued for said years, which taxes are now delinquent and unpaid.

"The court further finds that for said years 1911, 1912, and 1913 that said Gertie Watson was entitled to have, collect, and receive the rents and profits, and that it was her duty to pay the taxes which for said years were levied and assessed against said land, including the special tax relating to drainage district No. 3 of Carroll county, Mo., but that by reason of the said M. T. Forsee, Samuel P. Forsee, and the Convention City Investment Company taking charge of said land and collecting said rents, she was prevented from doing so.

"Wherefore it is ordered, adjudged, and decreed that plaintiff herein have and recover of the said M. T. Forsee, Samuel P. Forsee, and the Convention City Investment Company the sum of $180 which sum shall be paid to the said George H. Magee, hereinbefore appointed trustee in the place and stead of said Gertie

Watson, and out of said sum the said George H. Magee, shall pay all state, county, and township taxes which are delinquent against said land, and shall also pay that portion of the special tax of drainage district No. 3 which is properly levied against the life estate of said William A. Whiteley as ascertained and defined by the judgment and decree, the amount of which special tax the court finds that said life estate is liable to pay is $————.

"It is further ordered and decreed that for the current year 1914 that said George H. Magee as such trustee is entitled to and shall collect and receive the rents and profits and shall appropriate and pay the same out as herein provided.

"It is further ordered and adjudged that said George H. Magee, as such trustee, shall have and is hereby given full power and authority to execute all necessary leases for said premises, including the year 1914.

"It is further ordered that said George Magee enter into a bond in the sum of $500, payable to the said M. T. Forsee, Samuel P. Forsee, the Convention City Investment Company, Roland Hughes, George P. Whitsett, and William Whiteley, conditioned that he, the said George H. Magee, will faithfully discharge his duties as such trustee and account for all moneys which may come into his hands as such trustee and as provided in this decree.

"It is further ordered and adjudged that writ of restitution issue in favor of the said George H. Magee for said lands.

"It is further ordered and adjudged that the costs of this suit be taxed against the defendants."

[1] 1. The ultimate question in this case is whether or not the deed from Abner Whiteley to Gertie Watson, as trustee, which we have set out substantially in the foregoing statement, gave William Whiteley, as against her, a vendible interest, including the right of possession, in the land described. In saying this we are not forgetful of the position taken by appellants that this very question has been already adjudicated by this court between these same parties in Penland and others against Whiteley and Watson, by the judgment we have also set out in the statement. If this be true, it only means that the effect of the deed in that respect has been established by the estoppel of the Penland judgment.

The deed conveys the land to Mrs. Watson, the grantor's granddaughter, in trust for the benefit of her brother William during his natural life, and upon his death to become vested in his natural heirs. It is unnecessary that we should speculate about the meaning of these words "natural heirs" as used in this particular instrument. The statute by which we long ago abolished the ancient rule laid down in Shelley's case (R. S. 1909, § 2874) is as follows:

"Where a remainder shall be limited to the heirs, or heirs of the body, of a person to whom a life estate in the same premises shall be given, the persons who, on the termination of the life estate, shall be the heir or heirs of the body of such tenant for life shall be entitled to take as purchasers in fee simple, by virtue of the remainder so limited in them."

That this statute not only applies to estates tail as they existed at common law, but also to estates in fee simple created by the general words of inheritance used in this deed, is apparent from its words and was expressly recognized by this court in Tesson v. Newman, 62 Mo. 198, in which that construction was directly involved. It is therefore admitted by all the parties to this suit that the equitable estate vested in William Whiteley by this deed is only a life estate, and that those designated in the deed as his "heirs" will at his death take as purchasers from the grantor under the deed. For this reason it becomes necessary to determine the nature, purpose, and extent of the legal title vested in the trustee by the terms of the deed as a measure of the equity of the life tenant, bearing in mind the question whether that equity entitles him to the possession of the land. This we must gather from the intention of the grantor expressed by the terms of his deed.

[2] 2. That Abner Whiteley, out of his own absolute property had the right to provide for his descendants in any lawful way and according to the dictates of his own judgment as to their capacity, needs, and deserts, is not questioned. In doing this he might invest them with such estates in the property devoted to that purpose as he might think best. Of these he might give them the untrammeled management and control, or appoint trustees for that purpose, and in taking the latter course in this case it is evident that he desired not only to preserve the land intact for transmission to the remaindermen indicated in the deed, but to provide safeguards to secure the immediate object of his bounty against his own improvidence. For this purpose he thought best, instead of conveying the life estate directly to William, to convey it to a trustee who should manage and control it, and each year, after paying the expense of keeping it in productive condition, pay the net income of that year to the beneficiary. It may be that he believed that at first this income might be small, but that the land would ultimately increase in value and productiveness so as to afford ample provision for his grandson in his old age and become a valuable inheritance to his heirs. Were it our duty to question his judgment, there is much in this record which indicates that it was sound, but the land was his, and it is for us to give effect to the disposition he made by this deed so far as we lawfully may.

We are satisfied that it gave William Whiteley no possessory interest in the land. On the contrary, the execution of the trust which it created necessarily required that its possession, control, and management should remain in the trustee for the purpose of keeping it in repair, paying taxes and other necessary expenses, and realizing an annual income for the beneficiary, and for those purposes all necessary discretion was lodged in her alone. While she might, perhaps, lease the same land to him, his possession would be her possession under the deed, and she alone responsible for the application of the proceeds. The deed gave her no power to shake the trust from her shoulders by converting it into a life estate in the beneficiary. His occupation could only be under her title and subject to the execution of the trust, one of the evident objects of which was the withholding from him of any vendible interest in the land itself.

The Carroll circuit court in Penland and Atwood against William Whiteley and Mrs. Watson took a different view of the legal effect of this deed, and defendants pleaded that judgment as an estoppel in this case. They make no argument as to its propriety, but rely upon it as a conclusive adjudication between themselves and this plaintiff of the meaning and effect of the deed, and we will therefore refer to the exact question then adjudicated, as well as its effect upon the rights of these parties.

[3] 3. These defendants claim a possessory estate of freehold through the plaintiffs in that case. This plaintiff claims the same estate as trustee under the deed from Abner Whiteley, the common source of title. In the former suit the plaintiffs claimed, as is shown by the judgment we have copied in our statement, by two titles; (1) Through a lease or transfer of the legal life estate by this plaintiff to Whiteley, and a conveyance from him to Penland of the same estate; and (2) by conveyance from William Whiteley of his own interest acquired under the deed from Abner Whiteley to this plaintiff.

The trial court held that Penland acquired nothing from this plaintiff, and "that the agreements, assignments, and conveyances purporting to convey the interest of the trustee to William Whiteley were and are not effective to extinguish the trust in Gertie Watson created by the deed of Abner Whiteley, nor to merge the title in William Whiteley," and that the legal title was then still vested in Gertie Watson as trustee with remainder to the heirs of William Whiteley, and expressly "annulled, set aside, and for naught held" the instrument or lease from the trustee to William through which those plaintiffs were claiming. It also held "that the right to possession, rents, and profits, less necessary expenses, repairs, and taxes, is vested in plaintiffs, John W. Penland and Frank E. Atwood, equal owners thereof." In other words, it expressly adjudged that the legal title to the land was then vested in this plaintiff as trustee, that such leases, assignments, and conveyances as she had attempted to make were utterly null and void, and that by the deed from Abner to Gertie the freehold had been vested in William with all the powers and duties which that deed purported to give the trustee, who is now here as plaintiff attempting to assert those same powers. The judgment, reduced to its lowest terms, appoints Penland and Atwood trustees under the deed of Abner and enjoins the plaintiff from doing anything in execution of her powers under the deed.

The record does not show that Gertie Watson was served with process in the Penland case or that she appeared otherwise than by the joint answer filed by Mr. Forsee as attorney for both defendants. He testifies that he was not her attorney, and never had any dealing whatever with her in the matter, and that she refused to have anything to do with the case. He signed for her the stipulation for affirmance by this court after his wife had acquired the interest of Penland and Atwood. That judgment, in its application to the trustee, is, like a bird without wings, anomalous. It determines that under the terms of her trust she had no power to transfer the possession and use of the land to her beneficiary, and sets aside and cancels all instruments by which she had attempted to do so. It also determines that the right to possession and use passed to Penland by his deed from the beneficiary. It squeezed from the trust all its active features, which depended upon the right of the trustee to the possession of the premises, so that the use was executed by the act of its creation under the provisions of section 4589 of the Revised Statutes of 1899 now section 2867 of the revision of 1909. Carter v. Long, 181 Mo. 701, 710, 81 S. W. 162; Ottomeyer v. Pritchett, 178 Mo. loc. cit. 166, 77 S. W. 62.

On the other hand, the court expressly kills this finding by holding that she is still seized of the legal title to the freehold as trustee. This is the foundation on which the present suit stands. As we said of the petition in O'Brien v. Transit Co., 212 Mo. loc. cit. 66, 110 S. W. 705, 15 Ann. Cas. 86, the Penland judgment is, on its face, a felo de se. The legal title could not, under the statute, exist without the support of the use, which it followed into whosoever hands it might fall. This follows from the fact that the statute of uses applies expressly to estates for life as well as in fee. This is the theory on which the Penland suit was instituted. The petition states that the plaintiffs were the owners of the land. The court adjudged that the defendant trustee was the owner in trust of the life estate, and she has instituted this suit to secure the adjudication of the court as to her title, rights, and duties with respect to the subject of her trust. She charges that the possession and control of the property indispensable to its execution is withheld from her by the defendants or some of them; that it is being wasted and neglected; that taxes have remained unpaid for some of which suit is already pending; and that the defendants have collected the rents and profits and appropriated them to their own use. That these things endanger the rights of remaindermen yet undetermined and perhaps nonexistent is evident, and that her trust as defined in the deed which created it has some reference to their protection is equally evident. She does not, with respect to the title reserved to her in the Penland-Atwood judgment, stand in the relation of a beneficiary, but of a fiduciary.

[4] The court has held at the instance of these defendants, who asked her removal, she ought not to be continued as trustee, and has also at defendants' instance appointed another in her place. She has not appealed from this order, which is clearly authorized by the statute, and the defendants are estopped, by the prayer of their answer to that effect, to now question that authority. The court has appointed George H. Magee trustee in her place, with full power and authority to execute the trust according to the terms of the deed. This has the effect, under the circumstances stated, to substitute him to the rights of respondent in this appeal.

[5] 4. We have already said in the preceding paragraphs: (1) That the deed from Abner Whiteley to Gertie Watson vested in her the legal title for the life of William with remainder in fee to his heirs; (2) that her title was in trust for the benefit of William during his life, and to preserve the property intact for transmission to those who should be ascertained by his death to be his heirs; (3) that this necessarily involved the active duty on her part of leasing the land, collecting the rents, expending so much as necessary in repairs, and the payment of taxes and other charges upon the title; (4) that these fiduciary functions necessarily included the actual possession and control of the land; and (5) that this right of possession was and is, with its incidents enumerated in the deed, necessary to sustain the legal title of the trustee, which would otherwise become vested in the beneficiary by the operation of the statute of uses.

In addition to what we have already said on the last of these points, we will add that the legal title cannot, as against the statute of uses, be supported for the purpose of transmission alone, because that is the very office of the statute. In this case the active duty of preserving the property from dilapidation by repairs and from sacrifice by sale for delinquent taxes was implied by the judgment.

[6] 5. Turning now from the interpretation of the terms of the Penland judgment, we will notice its effect in view of all the circumstances disclosed in the record.

The plaintiff insists that she was not served with process in that case and did not appear. No service is shown. Her appearance depends upon the authority of Mr. Forsee to act as her attorney. He testifies that she did not employ him nor did he have any dealing with her. Whatever he did was by direction of Abner, the donor of the trust, who could not, in this manner, change the effect of his deed. Ottomeyer v. Pritchett, supra. The defendants say that this want of original authority makes no difference; that she cannot avail herself of it in this collateral proceeding. It is from this standpoint that we will approach the question.

The Penland-Atwood cause resulted in the judgment in evidence, and was appealed to this court by Mr. Forsee, whose wife then acquired the title of Penland and Atwood for the corporation of which he was president and stockholder. He then signed the stipulation for the affirmance of the judgment, which he now claims devested his client of her title. He states in his testimony that the consideration paid by the corporation for the interest of William Whiteley consisted of sums previously advanced to him from time to time on the credit of this land, and $500 to Penland and Atwood. The consideration upon which their title rested is not explained.

From these facts, as well as from the complexion of this entire case as depicted in the record, the trial court was abundantly authorized to find, and probably did find, that the transaction was the culmination of a plan by which the name of this plaintiff was used to strip all semblance of restraint and limitation from the mere usufruct of William, so that he might turn it into ready money for himself, and profit for those who might make the coveted advancements. When the plan was ripe for her attorney, in that most sacred of fiduciary capacities, and without authority or notice to her of his interest, stipulated for judgment against her and in favor of himself and his associates in interest whom he represented. If anything passed from her to her lawyer, or to the corporation which he represented in the transaction adverse to her, it was, under the circumstances shown, charged with a trust in her favor coextensive with her right and duty as trustee under the deed from Abner. His duty as her attorney imposed this trust. Her right to the possession, use, and management of the property in the performance of her duties as trustee under the deed remains unimpaired.

We have already held in the preceding paragraphs that the plaintiff, Gertie Watson, has, under her deed from Abner Whiteley, at all times since the execution of said deed, and up to the time of her removal by this judgment, been entitled to the possession, management, and control of, and to collect the rents and profits realized from, the land in question, and that by the terms of this judgment Magee succeeds to all those rights and interests in the same fiduciary capacity. The abstract of the record now before us is so imperfect that it is difficult to ascertain who are here complaining of this judgment. Hardwick claims nothing in his pleading, nor does his name appear in the judgment. Hughes and Whitsett do not appeal, nor do they file any brief or make any appearance in this court, although the judgment in their favor is attacked by the real appellant, the Convention City Investment Company, on the ground, apparently well taken, that they never had any interest whatever in this particular land. Neither of the defendants Forsee claim any interest in the land otherwise than through the corporation. The issues are therefore narrowed to a contest between the trustee and the corporation over the right of possession and control of the land and the collection and application of its rents and profits, and a contest between 'the corporation and Hughes and Whitsett as to the right, as assignees of Whiteley, to receive one-fourth of the annual rents and profits. There is also a difference between the corporation and the trustee as to the duty of the latter with reference to the payment of the "drainage tax" levied upon the property. This seems to have been an afterthought, for the facts necessary to such an adjustment are not incorporated in the record. Neither the age of the equitable life tenant nor the amount and distribution of the tax is suggested. It involves the protection of persons who can only be ascertained at the death of William and improvements, the extent and character of which are not explained. Reyburn v. Wallace, 93 Mo. 326, 3 S. W. 482.

[7] The questions determined by the trial court may be stated as follows: (1) That the trustee appointed by the deed is, and at all times has been, entitled to possession, and its recovery in this suit; (2) that the right to the annual distribution of the net rents and profits conferred by the deed upon William A. Whiteley is assignable and should be paid to his assignee. Upon these two propositions we are entirely in accord with the trial court. It goes further, however, and determines that the right to one-fourth of the amount to be included in this distribution is vested in Hughes and Whitsett by virtue of a certain contract or stipulation in evidence. The corporation disputes this, and says that it is entitled, as assignee of Whiteley, to the same interest. Its appeal entitles it to be heard in this court upon that question, and we hold that neither the contract before us nor the testimony of Mr. Hughes, which was evidently a fair statement of the facts as far as it goes, indicates that they acquired, or intended to acquire, any interest of William Whiteley in the rents or profits of this particular land.

The judgment preserves to William Whiteley a one-fourth interest in the use of the land. He filed a verified answer in this case in which he states that he has sold all his interest in the property in question to Forsee and the corporation, and asks that judgment be rendered for them accordingly. There is nothing in the case which suggests the propriety of preserving to him any part of the usufruct in this land against his will formally expressed upon the record. The only question raised by this appeal with respect to the validity of his disposition, involves his right, by any such disposition, to transfer his interest in the annual profits before they accrue. The trial court sustained this right, and we have already expressed our concurrence in that view. The plaintiff also acquiesces by failure to appeal.

We are satisfied from the tenor of the deed which created this trust that the grantor intended not only to protect, as well as he could, his grandson from his own improvidence, but also to provide restraints by which it should be transmitted safely and without waste or deterioration to the remaindermen. His wisdom in guarding both the title and possession has strongly impressed us, and we can see no reason why the trust he created for that purpose should not be administered under the eye of a court of equitable jurisdiction. The petition in the Penland-Atwood case was founded upon a claim of title in fee simple, and the controversy over taxes appearing in this record suggests that the danger hanging over the transmission of the remainder has not disappeared. We agree with the trial court that the intention of the grantor requires that the trust be continued.

For the reasons we have stated, the judgment of the circuit court for Carroll county is affirmed in so far as it gives possession of the land in question to the trustee appointed by that court, and damages for its withholding, assessed the value of the monthly rents and profits, and gives costs to the plaintiff. In other respects it is reversed, and the cause remanded, with directions to so amend the judgment as to distribute the net profit arising from the management and operation of the property in accordance with the views herein expressed, and with permission, in its discretion, to allow the amendment of the answer of Hughes and Whitsett upon their application, and to permit the presentation of further evidence upon that issue. That court may also, in its discretion, and having in view the intention of Abner Whiteley as expressed in his deed, receive further evidence respecting the drainage taxes referred to in the judgment and modify the same in that respect if and as conformity to law may require it. The costs of this appeal will be paid by the party which incurred them, and reimbursed by the trustee out of funds which may come to his hands in execution of the trust.

RAGLAND and SMALL, CC., concur.

PER CURIAM. The foregoing opinion of Brown, C., is adopted as the opinion of the court.

All concur; D. E. BLAIR, J., in result.

MASON v. MASON et al. '(No. 21843.)

(Supreme Court of Missouri, Division No. 1. March 5, 1921. Motion to Transfer to Court in Banc Denied June 6, 1921.)

1. Deeds ⟜194(5)—In action to cancel for want of delivery burden is on person denying full execution.

Where a deed fully executed, but not recorded, was in the possession of the grantee at the grantor's death, and was immediately filed for record, it is prima facie valid and operative, and the burden of proof is on one attacking the instrument on the theory that it was not completed by delivery. (Per Woodson, P. J., and Elder, J.)

2. Deeds ⟜194(5)—Presumption of delivery.

Where a duly executed deed was in the possession of the grantee at the grantor's death, and was immediately filed for record, the presumption of delivery can be overturned only by strong evidence. (Per Woodson, P. J., and Elder, J.)

3. Deeds ⟜194(1)—The law presumes much more in favor of delivery in case of voluntary settlement.

In case of a voluntary settlement between near relatives the law presumes much more in favor of delivery than in ordinary cases of bargain and sale between strangers. (Per Woodson, P. J., and Elder, J.)

4. Deeds ⟜194(5)—Evidence held insufficient to rebut presumption of delivery.

In an action to cancel on the ground of want of delivery a deed found in the possession of a grantee and recorded immediately after the grantor's death, the presumption of delivery *held* not rebutted. (Per Woodson, P. J., and Elder, J.)

5. Witnesses ⟜202—Attorney is competent to testify to direction for delivery of deed.

Where an attorney prepared a deed in favor of the grantor's daughter-in-law, and as notary public took the acknowledgment, etc., he is competent to testify to the grantor's direction to deliver the deed to the daughter, for such communication, being made to the attorney acting merely in the capacity of notary public or scrivener, is not privileged as would be a communication between attorney and client relating to a disclosure of facts, etc. (Per Woodson, P. J., and Elder, J.)

6. Witnesses ⟜168—Survivor is competent to. contradict alleged admissions made after death of original party.

The survivor of a transaction with a deceased party is competent to contradict alleged admissions claimed to have been made after the death of the original party to the transaction. (Per Woodson, P. J., and Elder, J.)

7. Witnesses ⟜177—Where plaintiff testifies to admission, defendant may testify in opposition.

Where a son of decedent who stood in the shoes of a subsequent grantee seeking to avoid a prior conveyance attacked a deed by his father to defendant, asserting nondelivery, and testified to an alleged admission by defendant, defendant's incompetency was waived, and she may testify in opposition. (Per Woodson, P. J., and Elder, J.)

Appeal from Circuit Court; Livingston County; Arch B. Davis, Judge.

Suit by John T. Mason against Charlotte A. Mason, J. R. Mason, and others. From a judgment for defendants, plaintiff appeals. Affirmed.

Sutton & Huston, of Troy, and Frank Sheetz, of Chillicothe, for appellant.

Collet & Son, of Salisbury, for respondents.

BROWN, C. Suit instituted in Chariton circuit court December 31, 1917, at Salisbury. The petition is in two counts, and states that the plaintiff and defendant James R. Mason are the only children and heirs at law of one Peter Mason, who died in said county April 28, 1913, seized in fee of the land in controversy, described as the south half of the northwest quarter of section 24, township 23, range 17 in said county, the title to which then and thereby vested in them by descent as tenants in common; that soon after the death of their father there was filed in the office of the recorder of deeds of said county a warranty deed purporting to convey the said 18 acres of land to the defendant Charlotte A. Mason, the wife of J. R. Mason, to have and hold during her life with remainder in fee to three of her children, Artie May Carter, James J. Mason, and Ada S. Spratt; that said deed was signed and acknowledged December 9, 1910, but was never delivered to the grantees or either of them during the life of the grantor.

The prayer for relief asks for cancellation of the undelivered deed, for a determination of the title as between all the parties, including Rush Mason, who is alleged to make some unknown claim, and for possession, which is alleged to have been held by the grantee Charlotte continuously since the death of Peter Mason.

The substantive facts are that at the date of his death Peter Mason had owned and been in possession of a farm of 160 acres, consisting of the northwest quarter of said section 24, on which his children were born and raised. His residence, which is described as "the new house," with its messuages, was situated on the south half, upon a road running along the south side of the farm. It was something over three miles from the city of Salisbury. His wife had been dead for a number of years before the narrative of the transaction complained of begins, and he had leased his farm to different tenants, reserving a room in which he lived and kept his belongings, and when there boarded with his tenants. He sometimes stayed at the home of the defendants in Salisbury, where he had been continuously during about six months preceding his death.

On the same date and at the same time and place of the writing and acknowledgment of this deed the grantor made a will. Both instruments were written by Mr. Fred Lamb of Salisbury, an attorney at law employed by him for the purpose. The will appointed Judge Lamb executor and devised to the plaintiff and his daughter Cora Ella the north half of his farm to be held by them as follows: The undivided two-thirds to John T. Mason and the undivided one-third to Cora. He bequeathed $20 to his son James and the remainder of his personalty, which the testimony shows to have amounted to about $500, to his grandson Rush.

The testimony shows that he was dissatisfied with his son James for the reason that he did not think he had treated his wife as well as he should.

The delivery of the deed to Charlotte is the only question in issue. The evidence is simple, its force and effect depending principally upon the competency of witnesses, and can be better treated in the body of the opinion.

[1-3] 1. The sole object of this suit is the judicial cancellation of the deed from Peter Mason to the defendant Charlotte A. Mason on the ground that its execution was never completed by delivery. After the death of the grantor it was in the possession of the grantee, fully executed and acknowledged, and upon its face entitled to record, and was by her immediately filed for record in the proper office and recorded. Under these circumstances it is prima facie valid and operative, and the burden is upon any one denying its full execution to establish that denial by proof. Pitts v. Sheriff, 108 Mo. 110, loc. cit. 115, 18 S. W. 1071; McFarland v. Brown, 193 S. W. 800, loc. cit. 806; Scott v. Scott, 95 Mo. 300, 8 S. W. 161; Crutcher v. Stewart, 204 S. W. 18, loc. cit. 20; Tyler v. Hall, 106 Mo. 313, 17 S. W. 319, 27 Am. St. Rep. 337; 1 Devlin on Deeds (3d Ed.) § 294. This presumption is so strong that only strong evidence can overturn it. Devlin on Deeds, supra.

"The law presumes much more in favor of a delivery in cases of voluntary settlements in favor of a wife, child, or near relative than it does in ordinary cases of bargain and sale between strangers. Hamilton v. Armstrong, 120 Mo. 597; Crowder v. Searcy, 103 Mo. 97." Rumsey v. Otis, 133 Mo. loc. cit. 95, 34 S. W. 553.

In that case this court quoted with evident approval from Cannon v. Cannon, 26 N. J. Eq. 316, as follows:

"To make delivery of a deed, it is not necessary it should actually be handed over to the grantee, or to another person for him. It may be effected by words without acts, or • • • by both acts and words. Indeed, it may be made though the deed remains in the custody of the grantor."

The curious may find many cases cited in those to which we have already referred sustaining and elaborating their doctrine and holding that "the delivery itself is only intended to evidence the purpose of the grantor to give effect to the instrument." Acting upon this judicial suggestion, we will, before proceeding to notice the testimony of witnesses introduced by plaintiff to sustain the burden assumed by his pleading, refer to the circumstances of the transaction for such suggestions as they contain of the intention of the grantor to perfect this deed at the time of the writing.

[4] Judge Lamb, a lawyer of prominence, had aided the grantor with such legal advice as was required by the situation, and we not only may, but must, presume that, both together, they knew the law applicable to the business in which they were engaged. Judge Lamb was present at the signing of the deed, still acting, we will presume, in the capacity of legal advisor, and also in the further official capacity of notary public to perform the acts necessary to give publicity to the deed whenever such publicity should be desired by the grantee. The writing, signing, and sealing of the certificate was a public and official act, done by a public officer in the presence of witnesses who were especially called to aid in furnishing the evidence which might at some time become necessary to prove its execution.

The grantor, the chief actor in the ceremony of publicity, was sick and evidently thinking and acting in contemplation of his own dissolution. He had in mind the disposition of his entire estate to the minutest item. He also had in mind the protection of his daughter-in-law, the mother of his four grandchildren, suggested by what he considered the unjust treatment of her husband, the father of the same grandchildren. He had only the two immediate descendants, this plaintiff and the husband of the grantee, who has died during the progress of this litigation. The plaintiff lived in Chicago, had not often visited his father, and, as he tells us in his testimony, while he was present at his bedside when he died, he felt such interest in the disposition of his property that he made special inquiry of this grantee as to its disposition at the time of the mortuary services.

At the meeting to which we have referred this deed,' by which the half of the farm on which was situated the home was given to his daughter-in-law for life with remainder to three of her children, was executed. At the same time a will was executed giving the other half of the farm to this plaintiff and his daughter and the whole amount of personal property which might be and was left at his death to the remaining grandchild. Neither the husband and father of the grantees in the deed nor the grandson who was left out of it is here complaining. The disposition was evidently equitable, the deed and will were interdependent, and it was necessary that the deed should be delivered in the lifetime of the grantor to make the general plan effective. If only the will should be operative at the time of his death, the disposition which the grantor intended would entirely fail, and be replaced by the disposition sought in this case, which would make this plaintiff the highly favored beneficiary. The law presumes that the testator knew this and that he was also well advised is not questioned.

This deed was not recorded, and we are asked to consider this fact as controlling evidence that it was not delivered. In considering this question the court must necessarily place itself in the position of this old man, who was, as the evidence shows, lying in bed in the room at the time of its execution without expectation of final recovery. He wanted peace, and his daughter-in-law, who evidently returned his affection and confidence, not only desired to assist him, but wanted peace herself. Nothing is more natural than that in the interest of peace and quiet and comfort a promise should have been requested and made that this deed would not be placed upon the public records until the will should take effect, so that both might come to the knowledge of this plaintiff in connection with each other. This court has no right to stigmatize such an arrangement if it was made. It was the right of the parties and the one thing about which we have to inquire is whether this deed was actually delivered.

2. To rebut the presumption of delivery arising from the possession, we are referred to the testimony of the plaintiff in his own behalf, to the effect that after the burial of his father and after the deed had been filed for record he had a conversation with the grantee, at her house, in the presence of his uncle Ben Mason, in which the uncle took part, asked her to tell plaintiff how it was,

and that she said that she and her father (referring to the grantor) had an understanding about the deed; that they both knew where it was, and if she died first her father was to get the deed and destroy it, and if he died first she was to get the deed and record it, and that she had sent it away that morning; that she then looked at him and cried and asked if he thought she had done anything wrong. Fred Schmitt, one of the witnesses to the deed, testified that, when the deed and will were executed and handed to Judge Lamb, he asked what should be done with them, and the grantor said, "Keep them until we see further."

[5] It is not necessary to determine what effect it would have had did his testimony stand uncontradicted. It might well be said that the remark related by Schmitt had no tendency whatever to prove that further directions were not given as was evidently contemplated by the grantor. It is, however, met or supplemented by the testimony of Judge Lamb that the grantor told him to deliver it to the grantee, and that he did so either on that day or the next. It could not have been done at the moment, because the execution of the papers occurred at the farm, while the grantee resided in Salisbury, several miles away. We will consider, therefore, the contention of plaintiff that this direction was a privileged communication which the latter should not have been permitted to disclose. This, for two equally conclusive reasons, is not a correct statement of the law in its application to this case: First, whatever was said and done was not confidential in its character. Two witnesses, unconnected with the subject-matter or parties in any other capacity, were present and heard or might have heard all that was said. It was not a disclosure of fact, but was simply a direction which might have been given with equal propriety to either or all of them. Thornton in his recent excellent and elaborate treatise on Attorneys at Law says the rule in this respect is as follows:

"In order that the rule or its reason shall apply, it is inherently necessary that the communication made by the client to the attorney, or to his clerk, should be confidential; therefore, if the client chooses to make his communication in the presence of third persons, it ceases to be confidential, and is not entitled to the protection afforded by the rule." Section 117.

He cites many cases in support of this proposition, the justice and soundness of which is clearly illustrated by the circumstances of this case, in which the fact to be proven is the direction given in the presence of three persons, one of whom happened to be a lawyer aiding in the preparation and execution of the instrument, while the others are laymen there for the same purpose. That two of them are competent witnesses to prove that the other disobeyed the direction of the party to the suit, while the mouth of the accused one is closed, seems to violate the fundamental principles of our statute relating to the competency of witnesses and the principles of justice upon which it is founded. Second, the witness did not sustain the relation of attorney to the grantor in the transaction in question. He was acting with reference to the execution and delivery of this deed in the capacity of scrivener and notary public. In section 114 of the treatise to which we have already referred the learned author says:

"An attorney who is professionally employed to prepare a legal document or other writing for his client, and who afterwards witnesses its execution, may be compelled not only to prove the execution of such instrument, but also to testify whether it was antedated, whether it has been altered since its execution, whether it was actually delivered, and to give evidence of any other fact, in connection with the execution of the instrument which does not involve a disclosure of the client's confidences."

This was held by the Supreme Court of Pennsylvania in Turner v. Warren, 160 Pa. 336, 28 Atl. 781, a case strikingly similar to this. In Bank v. Mersereau, 3 Barb. Ch. (N. Y.) 528, 49 Am. Dec. 189, Chancellor Walworth, in the same connection, drew with great clearness the distinction between confidential communications from client to attorney and those acts performed by the attorney in the execution and delivery of deeds. The delivery of the deed was the matter in issue. It is generally held that communications are not privileged where they are made to an attorney acting merely in the capacity of a notary public, or conveyancer, or scrivener, or attorney in fact, or agent or as a friend. Id. § 107.

The rule is founded upon a public policy which discourages the disclosure of any fact upon which an attorney at law is required to act or base an opinion in protecting the rights of a client. In this case there is no disclosure of fact involved. The matter to which the proof goes is a simple direction for the manual delivery of an instrument in the preparation of which an attorney at law happened to be employed as scrivener and notary public. If he gave legal advice with reference to the preparation of the deed founded upon disclosures made to him by his client, such disclosures are privileged.

We think the attorney was perfectly competent as a witness to prove the direction of the grantor to hand this deed to the grantee.

On the trial the plaintiff testified that the day after the funeral of his father, Uncle Ben Mason, Charlotte, and he were standing in the door of Charlotte's residence in Salisbury, when he said:

" 'When I come back from Keytesville tomorrow I will stop by and tell you about the papers,' and Uncle Ben spoke up and said, 'Why don't you tell him how it is?' and Charlotte looked up at me and said, 'I have the south 80.' I said, 'How did you get the south 80?' She said 'By deed.' I said, 'Where is your deed?' and she said, 'I sent it away this morning to be recorded.' I said, 'Why didn't you have it recorded sooner?' And she said her and Father had an understanding about the deed; that they both knew where it was and if she died first Father was to get the deed and destroy it, and if he died first then she was to get the deed and record it, and she said she had sent it away that morning, and then she looked at me and commenced to cry and said, 'Do you think I have done anything wrong?' I said, 'I am not here to make any accusations against anybody nor to pass upon matters as to whether they are right at all.' "

Uncle Ben, after stating that the morning after the burial Charlotte had given him this deed to take to Judge Lamb with her directions to have it put on record, testified as to this same conversation:

"I heard a conversation between John T. Mason and Charlotte A. Mason on the porch after I returned from delivering the deed to be recorded; but I do not know that the conversation was about the deed. All that I do know was that they were talking, and some time during the conversation Charlotte A. Mason broke down and cried."

.[6] Charlotte, the grantee, testified in her own behalf against the objection of the plaintiff that she did not make the statements in relation to the understanding between herself and her father-in-law charged in the testimony of plaintiff. The admission of this evidence is assigned and strenuously urged as error by plaintiff.

This contention involves the assertion that, when one of the original parties to a transaction in issue and on trial is dead, any one claiming under or through the deceased may establish his case by his own testimony to admissions made to him after the death of his predecessor in title, and that the mouth of his adversary is closed by the statute to deny such admissions. The elasticity of his own conscience would measure the possibilities of his case.

This same question was before this court in banc in Weiermueller v. Scullin, 203 Mo. 466, 101 S. W. 1088, in which, after a thorough examination, both upon principle and authority, we expressly overruled the case of Curd v. Brown, 148 Mo. 95, 49 S. W. 990, and decided that the principle of the statute depriving the surviving party to the transaction in issue of the right to testify does not apply to transactions which occur after the death of the original party, and therefore leaves the survivor fully competent to contradict testimony of admissions alleged to have been made by him after such decease. This has continued to be the law as administered in this court. Elsea v. Smith, 273 Mo. 396, 202 S. W. 1071.

Another phase of this question deserves at least passing notice. For that purpose we will presume, for the moment, that the proviso in question disqualifies the surviving party to the transaction to testify to matters which have transpired between himself and the successor of the deceased party since the death of the latter.

[7] The action in this case is for the cancellation of this deed. The cause alleged is nondelivery by the deceased to his grantee. The parties to that transaction were the deceased, on one side, and Charlotte Mason, his grantee, on the other. The suit is an attack by the plaintiff upon the conveyance of his father; in other words, he seeks to "break" his father's deed and to take the land himself contrary to his father's disposition. He stands in the shoes of a subsequent grantee seeking to avoid a prior conveyance.

This court, in Hach v. Rollins, 158 Mo. 182, 59 S. W. 232, had before it this same question. A widow sued her stepchildren for dower in land conveyed to them by her husband before his marriage to her. We held that she was not a competent witness under the statute here cited in a proceeding by her against the children after the husband's death to annul his deed to them. If this be a correct statement of the law, and the disqualification imposed by this statute extends to matters transpiring after the death of the original party, the plaintiff would be disqualified in this case and his voluntary testimony of the admission of the grantee to himself would invite contradiction and waive all objection to her testimony for that purpose.

Nor do we think that there is anything in the statement attributed to Mrs. Mason which supports the theory that the deed had not been delivered to the grantee by Judge Lamb in compliance with the direction of the grantor at the time of its execution. In that case the title passed at the instant of such delivery, and no understanding as to its disposition thereafter less definite than a conveyance could revest the title in the grantor.

Seeing no reversible error in the record, the judgment of the circuit court for Livingston county is affirmed.

RAGLAND and SMALL, CO., concur.

PER CURIAM. The foregoing opinion of BROWN, C., is adopted as the opinion of the court.

All concur; JAMES T. BLAIR and GRAVES, JJ., in result.

LARRICK et al. v. HEATHMAN et ux.
(Nos. 22005, 22006.)

(Supreme Court of Missouri, Division No. 1. April 9, 1921. Rehearing Denied June 6, 1921.)

1. Trusts ⟁88—Parol testimony admissible to establish resulting trust in wife's favor, notwithstanding deed taken by husband and wife as tenants by the entirety.

In action by wife's heirs against surviving husband to enforce a resulting trust, on theory that the wife's money was used to purchase the land, parol evidence was admissible to establish the trust, though the deed to the land was taken by the husband and wife as tenants by the entirety.

2. Trusts ⟁89(5)—Plaintiff, seeking to establish resulting trust as against face of a deed, had burden of proving trust by strong evidence.

Wife's heirs, suing surviving husband to enforce resulting trust in land which had been conveyed to husband and wife as tenants by the entirety, on theory that land had been purchased with wife's money, had burden of overturning such deed by evidence of such strength as to leave no doubt as to the trust.

3. Trusts ⟁88—Presumption trust arises from one party paying consideration may be rebutted by testimony as well as by deed.

The presumption of a trust arising from the fact of one party paying all or a part of the money may be rebutted by the testimony as well as by the deed.

4. Trusts ⟁366(2)—Wife's heirs could enforce resulting trust on land purchased with wife's money, if wife herself could have done so.

The wife's right to enforce a resulting trust in land purchased with wife's money, but conveyed to husband and wife as tenants by the entirety descends to her heirs.

5. Appeal and error ⟁1009(1)—Supreme Court can weigh evidence in equitable action.

In an action in equity, the Supreme Court on appeal can weigh the evidence and exclude irrelevant evidence from consideration.

6. Trusts ⟁81(2)—Wife, who buys land jointly with husband with request that land be conveyed to them as tenants by the entirety, cannot claim resulting trust.

Where both husband and wife contributed toward payment of purchase price of land, and where they jointly directed the vendor to make the deed, so that the survivor would get the land, and where the vendor, pursuant to such joint request, conveyed land to them as tenants by the entirety, neither the wife nor her heirs could thereafter claim a resulting trust in the land, on theory that the land was purchased in part with wife's money, notwithstanding Rev. St. 1909, § 8309, prohibiting husband from disposing of wife's personal property without written authority from wife, since the wife acted for herself in purchase of such land and was not represented by her husband.

Appeal from Circuit Court, Shelby County; V. L. Drain, Judge.

Action by Mary A. Larrick and others against Frederick G. Heathman and wife. From the judgment rendered, both plaintiffs and defendants appeal. Reversed and remanded, with directions to enter judgment for defendants.

R. G. Maupin and Harry J. Libby, both of Shelbina, for appellants.

Enoch M. O'Bryen, of Shelbyville, and J. S. Arnote, of McAlester, Okl., for respondents.

GRAVES, J. Action to have declared a resulting trust in and to 80 acres of land in Shelby county, Mo. Mary A. Larrick is the mother, and James A. Larrick and Mattie L. Byers are the brother and sister, of Fannie B. Heathman, who died childless and intestate April 26, 1916, in Shelby county, Mo. These are the plaintiffs who seek to enforce a resulting trust, on the theory that the money of Fannie B. Heathman was used in the purchase of the land involved. Defendant Frederick G. Heathman is the former husband of the deceased, Fannie B. Heathman, and the defendant Addie Heathman is his present wife.

The land in question was bought in 1901 from one Homer Dale, and the deed taken in the names of "Fred G. Heathman and Fannie B. Heathman, husband and wife." They lived upon the land to the date of Fannie B. Heathman's death. Fannie B. Heathman (the wife) received from the real estate of her father's estate the sum of $1,572, and there is but little doubt that this money went into the land in question, which land cost $2,200. The difference was paid by the husband, Frederick G., who, after getting the deed as aforesaid, put valuable improvements thereon, aggregating some $2,400 or more. It is shown that Fannie B. had but little other property of her own. It included two horses, two cows, and $100 cash, which likewise came from her father's estate. The $1,572 came from the sale of the father's land.

After hearing all the testimony, the trial court decreed a resulting trust in favor of plaintiffs in said land, as follows:

"Wherefore it is ordered, adjudged, and decreed by the court that the defendant Frederick G. Heathman took and held the title to 1575/2200 of said land in trust for the said Fannie B. Heathman, and that 625/2200 thereof was taken and held in his own right, and is now so held by him; that upon the death of the said Fannie B. Heathman as aforesaid one-half of the 1575/2200 of said land descended to Frederick G. Heathman as her surviving husband and one-half thereof to the plaintiffs, Mary A. Larrick, James A. Larrick, and Mattie L. Byers, each being seized of and entitled to an equal share in the said one-half of 1575/2200 of said land, and said lands so held by said Frederick G. Heathman are here-

by impressed with a trust in favor of said plaintiffs in accordance with the findings herein. It is further adjudged and decreed that the plaintiffs recover nothing for rents from said Frederick G. Heathman, and that said defendant Frederick G. Heathman recover nothing for improvements placed upon said land, and that the costs of this action be taxed against defendant, and that execution issue therefor."

From such judgment, by both sides an appeal is taken. The vital question is the real character of the deed from Dale. Of this, and the pertinent facts in the opinion.

[1-3] I. Upon its face the deed from Dale created an estate by the entirety. If we were confined to that, the end of this case would be in sight. But a resulting trust may be shown by parol proof, and in the face of the deed, if the quantum of proof appears. The burden of proof is upon plaintiffs in this case, if they are allowed to overturn the deed. Joerger v. Joerger, 193 Mo. loc. cit. 139, 91 S. W. 918, 5 Ann. Cas. 534; Morford v. Stephens, 178 S. W. loc. cit. 441. And such proof must be of a strength that will leave no doubt as to the trust. Morford v. Stephens, supra; Ferguson v. Robinson, 258 Mo. loc. cit. 133, 167 S. W. 447. The intention of the parties at the time the deed was made is a material element in determining the question of trust or no trust; that is to say, the presumption of a trust arising from the fact of one party paying all or a part of the money may be rebutted by the testimony, as well as by the deed. The deed itself may be contradicted, so as to show a resulting trust, if the facts in evidence warrant. The question of the proof required may be gathered from the cases, supra. So in this case it but remains to measure the proof made by plaintiffs by the rule established by these cases as to quantum of proof. Many other cases might be cited, but these will suffice to illustrate the rule.

II. It would be jockeying with facts to suggest that $1,572 of Fannie G. Heathman's did not go into the land. It is clear that Fred G. Heathman put in the remainder. Whether or not he got any portion of this from Fannie's share in the personal estate of her father is not definitely shown by the evidence. It appears that Heathman was a man of limited means at his marriage a few years before this transaction, and the improvements placed upon the farm were no doubt from accumulations made after the purchase of the farm. When the farm was purchased in 1901, Fannie had not yet received her part from the sale of the father's real estate, and the first $500 payment on the farm was made by the husband. But, before the delivery of the deed in 1902, she had received the $1,572, and as indicated it is clear that this money went into the land. Had the husband taken full title to the land in his own name, under these facts, without more, a resulting trust might have to be declared as to the interest represented by the money of the wife. Moss v. Ardrey, 260 Mo. loc. cit. 604, 169 S. W. 6. So, too, it might be said that, had the husband caused the deed creating an estate by the entirety to be made without the knowledge or consent of the wife (after placing her money in as a part of the purchase money), then a like situation might result. Moss v. Ardrey, supra, and the cases therein cited and reviewed; Johnston v. Johnston, 173 Mo. loc. cit. 118, 73 S. W. 202, 61 L. R. A. 166, 96 Am. St. Rep. 486.

Our cases cover the time before, as well as the time after, the Married Woman's Act of 1889. This case, upon the facts, would come clearly under the law existing after the passage of the several Married Woman's Acts. It arose at a time when, under ordinary circumstances, the wife could even contract with her husband. It arose at a time when section 8309, R. S. 1909, formerly section 4340, R. S. 1899, was in full force and effect. Under this statute we have ruled that, when the money of the wife is invested in lands (either as full or partial consideration therefor) without the written assent of her husband, a resulting trust arose in favor of the wife (and, of course, in favor of her heirs) to the extent of the money so invested. Whether or not this construction should have been given to the peculiarly worded proviso in said section we need not now discuss. It had been so long so ruled that in Moss v. Ardrey, 260 Mo. loc. cit. 604 et. seq., 169 S. W. 6, supra, the writer took it as settled. What our views might have been, had we been dealing with it as an original proposition, is immaterial. So that, inasmuch as no written assent of the wife appears for the use of the wife's money here, this case upon this theory would fall within the line of cases cited in the Moss Case, supra. And this is the contention of the respondents.

[4] III. But grant it that it requires the written consent of the wife for the husband to possess himself of his wife's personal property, and further grant it that his agency for the wife must have this same written assent, yet on the facts in this case do the plaintiffs have an interest in these lands? Of course, if Heathman and wife were not tenants by the entirety, they did have an interest. In other words, if Mrs. Fannie Heathman could enforce a resulting trust, the plaintiffs, her sole heirs, could do the same; and in the discussion of this, the real question in this case, we shall leave out of consideration the right of the wife to contract with her husband. We shall not consider the question as to whether or not the husband and wife could have agreed to each put money in the land, and have made a deed which would create an estate by the entirety. Personally we think that, after the Married Woman's Acts, such a contract could have been made, and that the establishment of that contract would show the intent of the

231 S.W.—62

parties, and destroy the theory of a resulting trust.

[5] But, as said, we do not pass on this question, and, as this is an action in equity, we can, so far as the evidence is concerned, separate the wheat from the chaff upon vital issues, and exclude the irrelevant evidence from consideration here. This land was bought before Fannie Heathman got her $1,572 from her father's estate. It is fair to assume from the evidence that she intended to put her money into this land when she got it. The land of the father was sold in October, 1901, and the deed from Hale was made in November 1901, but not delivered until January, 1902. The greater part of the consideration for the deed was paid upon its delivery, which was after the wife got her $1,572 for the interest she had in her father's land. So run the facts as to payments.

The foregoing, however, are not all of the facts. The land purchased belonged to a young man, who was in the West at the time. His father was his agent for the sale of the land. Marion Dale, the father of Homer Dale, and the agent of Homer Dale, was a witness in the case. The importance of the witness is evidenced by the heated contest of counsel in the course of the examination of the witness. The witness was a very old man, and vigorously cross-examined; but, when his testimony is read from beginning to end, it is fairly stated in an excerpt therefrom, thus:

"A. (by witness). Will I be permitted to tell what the conversation was between Mr. Heathman and his wife and me? Q. Yes, sir. A. We talked the matter over about the deed, and they both said they had money to put in the land, and they wanted it fixed so if one died that the other would get it, and I suggested that they have a joint deed drawn, and they both agreed to it, and Mrs. Heathman said, 'Go ahead and have it drawn that way;' that was the way she wanted it; and me and Mr. Heathman went to Clarence that evening and had it drawn that way."

[6] The witness had previously testified that Mr. and Mrs. Heathman had examined the farm, and had thereafter come to see him as to the price, and on the same day had agreed to buy it. A few days afterward he went to their then home, on the old Larrick place, and asked them about how they wanted the deed to be made. From his testimony it clearly appears that the deed was made just as the purchasers desired it to be made. To my mind it is quite clear that husband and wife had previously agreed to this course, but this matter we leave out of consideration. The testimony of Marion Dale makes it clear that the husband and wife were buying this property; that both were putting money into it; that they wanted it fixed so that the survivor would get it all; that they directed the seller, through his agent, so to make the deed; that the seller did make the deed in pursuance to a joint

request and direction of the purchasers. If these be the facts, and we are satisfied that they are, then we do not have an agency of the husband for the wife, nor do we have a contract between husband and wife, for consideration. We simply have a contract between buyers and seller. Mrs. Heathman was as much a buyer as was her husband, and the two buyers, as between them and the seller, had the right to direct the devolution of title. In this situation it would be immaterial as to who checked out the funds. Mrs. Heathman was investing her own funds, and all parties so understood it. As a party to the contract of purchase, she had a right to agree upon the form of conveyance, and when the seller made to her the conveyance which she desired, both she and her heirs are precluded from questioning the character of such conveyance. It is clear to us that the intent of the two purchasers of the land involved was to create an estate by the entirety, and that they so contracted with the seller. In a case like this the intent is a vital matter. This evidence tends to show that Fannie was investing her own money, and not that her husband had gotten possession of it without her written consent, and was using it for his own benefit. That question—i. e., the use of the wife's money without her written assent—is not really in this case. Here we have husband and wife purchasing a farm (each putting money therein), and in the course of their contract of purchase directing the form of conveyance that they desired. These facts corroborate the deed, rather than tending to establish a resulting trust.

Had Mrs. Heathman made the purchase of the farm herself, and invested her own money therein to the full extent of the consideration, there would be no question that she, as the purchaser, could have had the deed made in the present form, and it would bind her. Haguewood v. Britain, 273 Mo. 89, 199 S. W. 950. The mere fact that the two were purchasers and jointly directed the form of the deed, cannot change the situation. The Haguewood Case, supra, controls this case. We conclude that the record fails to establish a resulting trust, and the judgment nisi is reversed, and the cause remanded, with directions to enter judgment for defendants.

All concur.

JACKMAN v. ST. LOUIS & H. RY. CO.
(No. 22106.)

(Supreme Court of Missouri, Division No. 2. May 26, 1921. Rehearing Denied June 23, 1921.)

1. Appeal and error ⟺995—Weight of evidence held not within the province of the Supreme Court.

In an appeal from a judgment for plaintiff in an action for personal injuries, it is not within the province of the Supreme Court to pass on the weight of the evidence.

2. Appeal and error ⟺1002—It is the province of the jury to pass on conflicting evidence.

In a passenger's action for personal injuries, where a large number of witnesses were examined on each side, and testified to conflicting facts, it was the peculiar province of the jury to pass upon the facts, determine the extent of plaintiff's injuries, and fix her compensation therefor.

3. Damages ⟺132(6)—Verdict for $12,000 for injury to knee held not unwarranted or excessive.

Where there was evidence of a swollen and inflamed condition of plaintiff's knee, which several physicians testified might have been caused by an injury which she received on plaintiff's train, and which was permanent and painful in its nature, and required the wearing of appliances to keep the joint from moving, the verdict for $12,000 held not unwarranted or excessive.

4. Continuance ⟺35—Testimony admitted by party at a former trial to avoid a continuance held properly excluded.

Under Rev. St. 1919, § 1390, relative to admissions to prevent a continuance, testimony contained in an application for a continuance, which at a former trial plaintiff, in order to avoid a continuance, admitted would be given as stated in the motion, was not admissible in a subsequent trial, especially where it was merely cumulative.

5. Continuance ⟺35—Statute held not to apply to testimony in motion made at former trial.

Where defendant asked for a continuance to obtain the testimony of certain witnesses, and plaintiff, to avoid a continuance, admitted that the witnesses would testify as stated in the motion, section 5401, Rev. St. 1919, providing that competent evidence preserved in a bill of exceptions may be used as if preserved in a deposition, does not cover the admission of such testimony at a subsequent trial of the same cause.

Appeal from Circuit Court, St. Louis County; G. A. Wurdeman, Judge.

Action by Mary Jackman against the St. Louis & Hannibal Railway Company. Judgment for plaintiff, and defendant appeals.

See, also, 206 S. W. 244, and 187 S. W. 786.

This action was brought by respondent in the circuit court of Lincoln county, Mo., on February 21, 1913. In the amended petition, upon which the cause was tried, plaintiff sought to recover $15,000 for personal injuries received by her while a passenger on defendant's train in above county on August 29, 1912. General negligence is charged in said petition, and the answer is a general denial.

The case was originally tried in Lincoln

county, Mo., in 1913. Plaintiff obtained a verdict and judgment for $7,500, and defendant appealed the cause to the St. Louis Court of Appeals, where it was reversed and remanded on July 5, 1916. It will be found reported in 187 S. W. at pages 786 and following. On account of the admission of the testimony of Dr. Pendleton at above trial, and the remarks of Judge Woolfolk concerning counsel, the cause was remanded to the Lincoln county circuit court for a new trial. Thereupon a change of venue was granted defendant, and the cause was sent to St. Louis county, where it was tried before Judge Wurdeman and a jury, in which plaintiff recovered a verdict for $15,000. The trial court reduced said amount to $8,000, and plaintiff then remitted $500 additional, so as to reduce the amount of recovery to $7,500. Defendant again appealed to the St. Louis Court of Appeals, where the case was reversed and remanded on November 6, 1918, and will be found reported in 206 S. W. at pages 244 and following. It was reversed and remanded the second time, on account of improper remarks made by Mr. Creech, counsel for plaintiff, during the argument of the case before the jury. The case was again tried before Judge Wurdeman and a jury at the September term, 1919, of the St. Louis county circuit court. A verdict was returned in favor of plaintiff for $12,000, and judgment entered thereon in due form.

The evidence discloses that plaintiff, who was 63 years of age at the last trial, having attended the county fair at Troy, in Lincoln county, Mo., was returning home to Silex, in said county, on the evening of August 29, 1912, as a passenger for hire, on defendant's train. She occupied a seat with her daughter on the left side of the aisle near the rear of the car. She was next to the window, and her daughter next to the aisle. All the coaches were crowded, the seats full, the aisles packed, with people sitting on the arms of the seats, etc. The train was behind time, and traveling at a high rate of speed. When nearing Davis, the crowded car in which the plaintiff was riding suddenly commenced jerking, bumping, lurching, tilting, etc. It and the other coaches left the rails and were running along on the ties. The front wheels of plaintiff's coach finally got off on the ground over the end of the ties. Passengers were thrown to and fro, against the windows, seats, and sides of the cars. There was great excitement and confusion; frightened women were screaming, etc. When near Davis, the train stopped with a sudden jerk, throwing passengers forward. Plaintiff's daughter was thrown forward, and on regaining her seat found that plaintiff had fallen down between the seats with her knees cramped. She lifted her mother back into the seat, and assisted her down the steps in leaving the car. An emergency train was made up, and plaintiff was carried back to Silex in the baggage car.

The defendant stood upon its general denial, but made no attempt to show what caused said coaches to leave the track.

Plaintiff claims to have been seriously and permanently injured under the circumstances aforesaid.

Appellant in its brief insists that the verdict of the jury is grossly excessive; that the jurors were actuated by passion, prejudice, or sympathy in returning so large a verdict, and we are asked to reverse and remand the cause by reason thereof.

Other errors are complained of, relating to the exclusion of the testimony of certain witnesses given at the former trial, and in regard to the alleged improper and prejudicial examination of certain physicians called as plaintiff's witnesses. In order to avoid repetition, we will consider the foregoing matters in the opinion.

Defendant, in due time, filed its motion for a new trial, which was overruled, and the cause duly appealed to this court.

Sutton & Huston, of Troy, Fauntleroy, Cullen & Hay, of St. Louis, and Hostetter & Haley, of Bowling Green, for appellant.

Creech, Penn & Palmer, of Troy, A. E. L. Gardiner, of Clayton, Frank Howell, of Troy, and Henry S. Caulfield, of St. Louis, for respondent.

RAILEY, C. (after stating the facts as above). I. Under appellant's assignments of error, we find the following:

"(1) The verdict is so grossly excessive and is indicative of such passion and prejudice on the part of the jury that the vice cannot be cured by remittitur ordered in this court; but the cure can only be properly effected by a reversal of the judgment."

[1] The printed abstract of record in this cause covers 400 pages of printed matter. More than 350 pages of said abstract, relate solely to the questions of injury and damages. Said record embraces the testimony of more than 40 witnesses, and at least 35 of these testified in respect to the extent of plaintiff's injuries, etc. We have carefully read all the evidence, as well as the briefs of counsel upon each side. It is not the province of this court to pass upon the weight of the evidence, and we shall not attempt to do so. It is clear from the undisputed facts that plaintiff on August 29, 1912, was a passenger upon defendant's train, and that the latter, or a portion of same, left the rails and threw the plaintiff between the seats of the car in which she was riding.

Plaintiff introduced substantial evidence tending to show that she received an injury at the time of the accident, although no physician was called to see her until about the 21st of October, 1912. She was about 56 years of age at the date of the accident, and had been in good health prior to that date. Both plaintiff and her daughter, as well as other witnesses, testified that after the accident her right knee was swollen and inflamed; that liniments and home remedies were used to reduce the swelling, and that from December 3, 1912, until the last trial in September, 1919, during a period of nearly 7 years, plaintiff's right knee had been swollen and inflamed; that during most of said time, her limb was in plaster or her knee covered with splints; that during said period she had been a constant sufferer, and at the trial was in practically no better condition; that she had been suffering during said period with inflammation of the tissues in and around her right knee joint; that said condition was termed by the medical profession "arthritis"; that it could have been caused by an injury and was not the result of rheumatism.

The defendant sought by a large number of witnesses to discredit plaintiff and her injuries, by introducing in evidence her statements, her appearance and apparent condition from time to time, as well as the testimony of certain doctors, including the family physician, tending to show that her injuries were mostly imaginary, or greatly exaggerated. Defendant likewise contends that if plaintiff was suffering as she alleges, it was from rheumatism, and not from the effect of any injury sustained in the accident.

On the other hand, plaintiff introduced a number of lay witnesses, whose testimony tends to support her contention as to her injuries, and in addition thereto, produced before the jury the evidence of Drs. Charles H. Riggs, Eugene Barrymore, G. C. Eggers, Harvey S. McKay, William Thomas Coughlin, and Fred Bailey.

These six reputable physicians examined plaintiff between August, 1912, and September, 1919, at different times. Some of them had her under treatment for months at a time. The testimony of Dr. Riggs tends to show that he had known plaintiff for about twenty-five years; that he commenced treating her about the 17th of December, 1912; that her right knee was sore at that time, and was larger than her left; that he had her go to bed and keep her limb quiet; that he gave her local treatment for about eight or ten months. Dr. Barrymore testified, in substance, that he commenced treating plaintiff about June, 1914; that he examined her at that time, and found symptoms of ailment; that her right knee was swollen; that she had increased temperature of that part of her body, which looked red and was tender; that, in his opinion, she was then suffering with "arthritis," which means an inflammation of the tissues in and around the joint; that the condition in which he found her knee might have been produced by an injury; that about the 1st of July, 1914,

he put her right limb at rest by fixing it in a plaster cast; that he kept it in that condition for about two months; that the swelling had subsided when he took the plaster off; that after about two weeks the swelling returned; that he then put on an ordinary board splint to keep the joint surfaces from rubbing each other; that he treated plaintiff during three years; that, in his opinion, her injury is permanent; that she would have to keep on wearing appliances to keep the kneejoint from moving, irritating, and inflaming the surfaces; that she would never be relieved, unless by an operation.

Without quoting the testimony further, the above-named physicians, with one accord, found plaintiff's right knee swollen and inflamed when they examined it at different times during said seven years. They gave it as their respective opinions that her condition might have been produced by an injury; that she was suffering with "arthritis" of the kneejoint; that, in their opinion, her condition is not produced by rheumatism; that her injury is permanent and painful.

[2, 3] The record indicates that the case was fairly and carefully tried by the court and jury; that nothing occurred during the progress of the trial which was calculated to arouse the passion, prejudice, or sympathy of the jury. The latter was confronted with a sharp conflict as to the testimony relating to plaintiff's injury and the extent of same. It is manifest from the record that the jurors believed the witnesses for plaintiff in preference to those produced by defendant. It was the peculiar province of the jury to pass upon the facts, determine the extent of respondent's injuries, and to fix her compensation therefor. Upon a careful consideration of all the evidence, we are of the opinion that the verdict of the jury for $12,000, under the circumstances of the case, should not be disturbed as either unwarranted or excessive.

The foregoing contention of appellant is accordingly overruled.

[4] 2. It is alleged that:

"The court erred in excluding the testimony or depositions or statements of three witnesses for defendant, viz.: Mary O. Teague, Missouri H. Hudson, and Mrs. William Schrader as preserved in the bill of exceptions at the former trial at Clayton, Mo., in the circuit court of St. Louis county."

It appears from the record that at the second trial at Clayton, Mo., in 1917, defendant asked for a continuance of the cause, in order that it might obtain the testimony of the three witnesses above named, to be used at the trial. Plaintiff, to obviate a continuance of the cause, admitted that, if said witnesses were personally present at the trial, they would testify in behalf of defendant, as stated in the application for a continuance. Defendant thereupon availed itself of the testimony of said witnesses as above indicated. Their evidence, as contained in the application for a continuance, was incorporated in the bill of exceptions filed in the second trial, and is set out in the abstract of record herein.

It is not claimed that an application for a continuance was filed at the last trial, nor is it claimed that plaintiff had any opportunity to cross-examine said witnesses before the second trial. The testimony of said witnesses, as set out in the abstract of record herein, is merely cumulative. It appears from the record that more than a dozen witnesses testified in behalf of defendant to substantially the same facts set out as the testimony of said absent witnesses. But, even if said testimony had not been simply cumulative, we are of the opinion that the trial court committed no error in excluding same. Section 1390, R. S. 1919; Section 5401, R. S. 1919; Padgitt v. Moll and Citizen's Ry. Co., 159 Mo. loc. cit. 154, 155, 60 S. W. 121, 52 L. R. A. 854, 81 Am. St. Rep. 347; Ely-Walker D. G. Co. v. Mansur, 87 Mo. App. loc. cit. 114, 115.

[5] Section 5401, supra, provides for the admission of competent evidence under the circumstances detailed therein, but does not cover the question presented here.

It is unnecessary to prolong this branch of the discussion, for our Supreme Court in banc, in the Padgitt Case, supra, at pages 153 and 154 of 159 Mo., at page 124 of 60 S. W. (52 L. R. A. 854, 81 Am. St. Rep. 347), has conclusively settled this question adversely to appellant's contention as follows:

"Ordinarily a party is entitled to have his adversary produce his witnesses in court, to the end that they may be seen and cross-examined, and the waiving of that right is often no trivial matter. Besides, an affidavit drawn by a skillful lawyer is apt to be very much to the point and is very forceful as evidence. The law will allow it only because the emergency demands it, and the opposite party agrees to it only to avoid delay.

"But in this instance, after the plaintiff made the admission which would authorize the affidavit to be read, the court of its own motion postponed the trial for a month and four days. The affidavit stated on its face that the witness resided in St. Louis, and could be produced at the next term; yet, when more than a month was afforded the defendant before the trial would be called, no effort was shown to have been made to produce him, but the court suffered the affidavit to be read. The emergency under which the law would have allowed the affidavit to be read had passed, and the consideration which induced the plaintiff to make the admission had failed. This was a very material witness, professing to have seen the accident, and whose evidence professed to cover every point of the defense. The affidavit said of this witness that there was no other person whose evidence 'could have been procured at this term of said court by whom he or it (affiant or defendant) can prove or fully prove the same facts.' And the record shows that that was so.

"The admission of a party under such circumstances to obtain a present trial does not stand for all time, but ceases when the emergency ceases. If it should be held to be binding a month later, there is no reason why it should not be so held six months later. A month is as long notice as is ordinarily given of the setting of a cause for new trial: certainly it is long enough to obtain the service of process for witnesses residing in the city, or to take their depositions if they are nonresidents, or at all events it is long enough to ascertain whether or not the evidence is attainable. The court erred in allowing the affidavit to be read over the plaintiff's objection."

Judge Goode, in Ely-Walker D. G. Co. v. Mansur, 87 Mo. App. loc. cit. 114, 115, reiterates the same doctrine announced by Judge Valliant in the Padgitt Case above quoted.

The above contention of appellant is without merit and overruled.

3. Defendant's third assignment of error reads as follows:

"The trial court erred in permitting counsel for the plaintiff to conduct an improper and prejudicial examination of certain physicians called by plaintiff as witnesses."

We are then referred to the argument of defendant, at pages 22 and following of its brief, where the matters complained of are set out, in respect to the testimony of plaintiff's doctors admitted at the trial, over the objections of defendant.

As heretofore stated, we have carefully read all of the abstract of record and the respective briefs of counsel. We were thoroughly familiar with the authorities cited by appellant at page 24 of its brief, in respect to foregoing matter, but have again gone over same in considering this case, and find nothing therein which would warrant us in reversing and remanding the cause. We are of the opinion that the record is remarkably free from error, and that no testimony was given by either of said physicians of which appellant can have any legal ground of complaint.

4. The plaintiff herein was injured on the 29th day of August, 1912. She has been compelled to litigate her rights as a passenger on defendant's train, through two different circuit courts, twice in the St. Louis Court of Appeals, and finally in this court. She was forced by defendant to go from her own home to another judicial circuit, to assert her rights. Upon a careful consideration of the case from every viewpoint, we find no valid grounds for reversing and remanding the cause.

The judgment below is accordingly affirmed.

WHITE and MOZLEY, CC., concur.

PER CURIAM. The foregoing opinion of RAILEY, C., is hereby adopted as the opinion of the court. All concur.

STATE ex rel. FEINSTEIN v. HARTMANN, Judge, et al. (No. 22572.)

(Supreme Court of Missouri. In Banc. May 24, 1921.)

1. Elections ⟨=⟩329—Restrictions in Constitution on use of ballots, etc., as evidence, held not to deny circuit judge power to issue subpœna for production of ballots; "elections."

The term "elections," as used in the Constitution of the state, does not include elections held merely to nominate candidates for office, and restrictions on the use of ballots, etc., as evidence and in evidence do not, by reason only of their presence in the Constitution, in any way tend to deny to a judge of the circuit court power to issue a subpœna duces tecum to require ballots at primary election to be produced before a grand jury.

[Ed. Note.—For other definitions, see Words and Phrases, First and Second Series, Election.]

2. Elections ⟨=⟩120—Constitutional provision incorporated in primary law by reference.

Const. art. 8, § 3, relating to ballots, was incorporated in the Primary Law of 1907 by reference, and became a part of such act itself, and as effective in all respects as if it had been written in at length.

3. Statutes ⟨=⟩149—Legislature has power to eliminate provisions incorporated by reference, including a constitutional provision.

The Legislature has as much power to eliminate from a statute provisions incorporated therein by reference as it has to repeal any other part of a law it has enacted, and the fact that a provision incorporated by reference is a provision of the state Constitution gives it no added force.

4. Elections ⟨=⟩329—Statute held not to permit circuit judge to issue subpœna for production of primary election ballot boxes, etc.

Rev. St. 1919, § 5403, does not permit judge of circuit court to issue subpœna duces tecum requiring production in evidence before the grand jury of the ballot boxes and contents thereof, tally sheets, poll books, and the official returns and statements made by the judges and clerks of a primary election, such section repealing by implication any antagonistic features of section 4853, including provisions of Const. art. 8, § 3, made a part thereof by reference.

5. Elections ⟨=⟩311—Legislature had power to deny grand jury right to use primary election ballots.

The Legislature had the power to enact Rev. St. 1919, § 5403, providing that grand jury could not use primary election ballots.

6. Prohibition ⟨=⟩28—Supreme Court has no authority to amend subpœna duces tecum in prohibition proceeding.

In a proceeding in the Supreme Court to prohibit circuit judge from enforcing a subpœna duces tecum, requiring the production before the grand jury of ballots of primary election, the only matter before the Supreme Court is the question of the power of the cir-

cuit judge to enforce the particular subpœna as issued, and it cannot consider a suggestion that circuit judge does not actually intend to enforce the subpœna according to its terms but only so far as may be lawful under the statutes, it not being open to the Supreme Court to amend the subpœna.

7. Constitutional law ⟨=⟩70(3)—Courts must apply law as people have made it.

When the General Assembly enacts a valid law, the Supreme Court, whatever may be the views of its members as individual citizens upon a question of policy involved, must submit to the decision of the majority, and apply the law as the people have made it.

Higbee and David E. Blair, JJ., dissenting.

Application by the State of Missouri, on the relation of H. S. Feinstein, for a writ of prohibition to Moses Hartman, Judge of the Circuit Court of the City of St. Louis, Division No. 2, and another, from enforcing a subpœna duces tecum. Preliminary rule made absolute.

Abbott, Fauntleroy, Cullen & Edwards, of St. Louis, for relator.

Curlee & Hay and Edward A. Feehan, all of St. Louis, for respondents.

JAMES T. BLAIR, J. Relator seeks to prohibit respondent, a judge of the circuit court of the city of St. Louis, from enforcing a subpœna duces tecum he had previously issued which is directed to the members of the board of election commissioners of the city of St. Louis, and which, formal parts omitted, reads thus:

"You are hereby commanded that, setting aside all manner of excuse and delay, you be and appear before our grand inquest room, 215 Municipal Courts Building, in the city of St. Louis, on the fifteenth day of November, 1920, at 2 o'clock p. m., then and there to testify, and the truth to speak, in a certain cause pending before the grand jury, wherein the state of Missouri is plaintiff, and you are further commanded to bring with you, and then and there produce in evidence the ballot boxes and contents thereof, tally sheets, poll books and the official returns and statements made by the judges and clerks of election to the board of election commissioners used and made in connection with the primary election held in the city of St. Louis, Mo., on the 3rd day of August, 1920, in the following precincts of the following wards: Second of the first; fourth of the fifth; sixteenth of the twelfth; eighteenth of the fifteenth; fifth of the seventeenth; twelfth of the seventeenth; tenth of the twenty-fifth; twenty-fourth of the twenty-seventh. And this you shall in no wise omit. And the person or officer serving this writ is commanded to have the same at the time and place aforesaid, certifying thereon his return."

In view of some suggestions which concern the scope of admissions made, it is deemed advisable to set out the pleadings in the case. These are brief, and make the issues so clear

⟨=⟩For other cases see same topic and KEY-NUMBER in all Key-Numbered Digests and Indexes

that they constitute a sufficient statement of the case. The application for the writ, caption and signatures omitted, is as follows:

"The state of Missouri comes now and brings this action at the relation and to the use of H. S. Feinstein, as relator, and thereupon shows to the honorable the Supreme Court of Missouri, that the respondent, the Honorable Moses Hartmann, is, and at all the times hereinafter mentioned was, one of the judges of the Eighth judicial circuit of Missouri, presiding in division No. 12 of the circuit court of the city of St. Louis, Mo.; that prior to the occurrence of the matters and things hereinafter complained of there was pending in the said division of the said circuit court an investigation before the grand jury for the purpose of having indictments preferred against certain judges and clerks of election who served as such at the primary election held in the city of St. Louis on August 3, 1920; that while said matters were being investigated then and there the circuit attorney of the city of St. Louis, and as such appearing for the state of Missouri, filed in the said division of said court a petition in writing, addressed to the respondent herein as circuit judge presiding in said division, praying the issuance of a writ of subpœna duces tecum directed to the chairman, secretary, and members of the board of election commissioners, commanding them to appear in said division of said court before the grand jury, and bring with them for inspection and use as evidence therein certain ballot boxes, ballots, poll books, returns and certificates used in the said primary election held in the said city of St. Louis in the month of August, 1920; that thereafter, to wit, on the 13th day of November, 1920, the respondent, having duly considered the same, gave judgment sustaining the said application, and thereupon caused to be entered upon the record of said division of said circuit court an order directing that such subpœna duces tecum should be issued, and on said 13th day of November, 1920, did issue a duces tecum, a copy of which is hereto attached, marked 'Exhibit A,' and that the said respondent is threatening and is about to enforce the said order and compel compliance therewith, although he is wholly without jurisdiction, power, or authority so to do, and will carry out his said threat and enforce his said order, unless restrained by the order of this court to the great and irreparable prejudice and injury of the said relator. That the said order of the said respondent is wholly beyond his jurisdiction to make or enforce, and is coram non judice, and null and void, because it is in direct violation of the provisions of section 3 of article 8 of the Constitution of the state of Missouri, and of the statutes of the state of Missouri, and in conflict with the prior and controlling decision and opinion of this court.

"Relator says subpœna duces tecum has been duly served upon the aforesaid parties. The said members of the board of election commissioners of the said city of St. Louis and said officers will obey the said order, and will produce and exhibit the ballots, poll books, and other election records, as required by said order, unless the same be set aside and the enforcement thereof arrested as hereinafter prayed. That for the reasons aforesaid the said ballots are not competent evidence on behalf of the state of Missouri before said grand jury or in the prosecution of any indictment that may be returned.

"Your relator states that he is a qualified voter of the city of St. Louis, and has been such at all times mentioned herein; that he was one of the judges at the primary election held in the city of St. Louis on the 3d day of August, 1920; that he resides in precinct 16, ward 25, and that he cast his vote at said primary election in said ward 25 and precinct 16. Respondent, as the judge of the circuit court, made an order directing that the ballot box and key to the same, used at the aforesaid election in said precinct and ward, on the date aforesaid, and the contents thereof, to wit, ballots cast at said primary election, the poll books, and tally sheets, and all the records made by said election officers, be produced and delivered before the grand jury with the view and for the purpose of having the ballots cast at said primary election on said date examined and used in evidence, and said ballots made public; that the purpose for which this evidence is required is to establish the correctness or falsity of the count and return made by the election officers of the ballots cast at said primary election in said precinct and ward, and that the same is sought for this purpose, and no other. It is desired by the state to produce and offer in evidence the ballots found in said box, and to use all the said records in evidence, and thereby ascertain and make public how relator and other electors voted.

"And the said petitioner further states that the proceedings instituted and followed as aforesaid are a direct encroachment upon the authority and jurisdiction of this court, and are in contempt of this honorable court, its authority, and dignity; and under the Constitution and the laws it is made the care of this court that the said circuit court, as well as all other inferior courts, keep within the bounds and limits of the several jurisdictions prescribed to them by the laws of the state.

"Wherefore, the relator prays this court to issue its order directed to the respondent herein commanding him to show cause on a certain day, to be fixed therein, why he should not be absolutely prohibited from enforcing the aforesaid order by any means whatsoever, and from compelling or further attempting to compel the production, or exhibition, or other use of the said ballots or election records mentioned in said order and in said application for the writ of subpœna duces tecum before said grand jury, and enjoining him in the meantime and until the final disposition of this cause to refrain from enforcing or attempting to enforce his said order in any manner and to any extent whatsoever."

Attached to this was a copy of the subpœna duces tecum in question, which has been set out. Upon the filing of this application, after notice, a preliminary rule was issued as prayed. Respondents appeared and filed a return, which, caption and signatures omitted, reads thus:

"Now come Moses Hartmann, judge, and Lawrence McDaniel, circuit attorney, respondents herein, and for their joint and separate return to the order to show cause heretofore issued herein state that at and prior to the times mentioned in relator's petition herein, the October term, 1920, grand jury in and for the city of St. Louis, Mo., was in session, having been duly impaneled and sworn, and had entered upon the discharge of its duties; that in the course of its deliberations the said grand jury was investigating frauds committed in the city of St. Louis at the primary election held on August 3, 1920, and had before it evidence tending to show that the judges and clerks of election in the several voting precincts of said city, and in particular in the sixteenth precinct of the twenty-fifth ward, had been guilty of fraud in the count and tally of the votes and ballots cast at said election, and of making a false return of said votes and ballots; and said grand jury, being desirous of establishing the correctness or falsity of the count and return made by the said election officers, and of voting indictments against election officers guilty of violations of law, if such violations were found, requested the production before them of the ballot boxes and other records mentioned in the subpœna duces tecum hereinafter described.

"That, pursuant to said request of said grand jury, respondent McDaniel, circuit attorney, and as such legal adviser of said grand jury, caused to be prepared and presented to respondent Hartmann, judge, a petition for a subpœna duces tecum to be directed to the board of election commissioners of the city of St. Louis, commanding the members of said board to appear before said grand jury and to bring with them the ballot boxes and contents thereof, tally sheets, poll books, and the official returns and statements made by the judges and clerks of election in certain precincts mentioned in said subpœna, including the sixteenth precinct of the twenty-fifth ward of the city of St. Louis.

"That thereafter, on the 13th day of November, 1920, respondent Hartmann, judge, caused to be issued, and there was issued by the clerk of said circuit court, a subpœna duces tecum, commanding said board of election commissioners to appear before said grand jury and bring with them the ballot boxes and contents thereof, tally sheets, poll books, and the official returns and statements made by the judges and clerks of election in the precincts mentioned in said subpœna, including the sixteenth precinct of the twenty-fifth ward of the city of St. Louis.

"Respondents admit that, as alleged in relator's petition herein, 'the purpose for which this evidence is required is to establish the correctness or falsity of the count and return made by the election officers of the ballots cast at said primary election in said precinct and ward, and that the same is sought for this purpose and no other.'

"Respondents deny that the respondent Hartmann, judge, was or is without jurisdiction, power, or authority to compel compliance with said subpœna, and deny that the order of said Hartmann, judge, causing said subpœna to issue, was or is beyond his jurisdiction, or coram non judice, or null, or void, or in violation of section 3 of article 8 of the Constitution of Missouri, or in violation of the statutes of the state of Missouri; and deny that the said or-

der was or is in conflict with prior controlling decisions and opinions of this court.

"Respondents admit that said subpœna was duly served upon the said board of election commissioners, and that the members of said board were and are willing to obey said subpœna.

"Respondents deny that the said ballots are not competent evidence on behalf of the state of Missouri before said grand jury, and deny that they are not competent evidence in the prosecution of indictments returned as a result of a true count of said ballots.

"Respondents admit that relator is and was a qualified voter of the city of St. Louis, and that he was one of the judges of election in the sixteenth precinct of the twenty-fifth ward at the primary election held on August 3, 1920; admit that respondent resides in said sixteenth precinct of said twenty-fifth ward, and that he cast his vote therein at said primary election.

"Respondents deny that said subpœna duces tecum was issued for the purpose of making public any ballot cast at said primary election, or for the purpose of making public how relator or any other elector voted.

"Respondents deny that the proceedings instituted and followed as aforesaid were or are an encroachment upon the authority or jurisdiction of this court, and deny that the same were or are in contempt of this court or of its authority or dignity.

"And for their further return to the order to show cause herein, respondents say that said subpœna duces tecum was prayed for and ordered to issue pursuant to the statutes of the state of Missouri in such case made and provided, and especially section 6347, Rev. Stat. Mo. 1909, and pursuant to controlling decisions and orders of this court, namely, Gantt v. Brown, 238 Mo. 560 [142 S. W. 422]; State ex rel. v. Coburn, 260 Mo. 177 [168 S. W. 956]; State ex rel. v. Thurman, 268 Mo. 537 [187 S. W. 1190]; and State ex rel. Ralph v. Kinsey, Judge, where an order was made denying a preliminary rule to prohibit the opening of ballot boxes used in a general election.

"Respondents further state that in the investigation of election matters by said grand jury, as aforesaid, there was no violation of any alleged right of secrecy, or other constitutional right of any voter; that in the count of ballots by said grand jury, and in the indictments voted and returned against election officers (in precincts other than the sixteenth precinct of the twenty-fifth ward, where no examination or count of ballots was had because of the pendency of this proceeding), the ballots were not compared with the poll books, and it was not disclosed how any voter voted; and respondents say that in praying for and in issuing said subpœna duces tecum it was not the intention of respondents, or either of them, to ascertain or disclose how any voter voted, nor was it necessary, nor is it necessary, that such information be had or disclosed either in the finding of indictments or in the trials which may ensue; that said grand jury did not in fact, and did not intend to, use the said ballots and poll books in such a manner as to disclose any information that would tend toward showing who voted any ballot, and that in all respects the said ballots and other records were used, and intended to be used, in full compliance with both the letter and the spirit of the safeguards prescribed by section 6347, Rev. Stat. of Mo. 1909, and by the Constitution and laws of this state, and by the decisions of its courts construing same.

"Respondents further state that, since the making of the order heretofore issued herein, respondents have refrained from action in the premises, and stand ready to comply with any further orders made by this court.

"Wherefore, having made full return to the order to show cause, respondents pray that the provisional rule in prohibition heretofore issued herein be dissolved, and that respondents go hence with their costs."

Thereupon relator filed his motion for judgment making the preliminary rule absolute. The case was briefed and argued in January. Upon consideration, in due course, several opinions were prepared. The diversity among these was of such character that it necessitated a reassignment of the case.

The question for solution is whether the circuit court has jurisdiction to enforce a subpœna duces tecum which requires the election commissioners of the city of St. Louis to produce in evidence before the grand jury "the ballot boxes and contents thereof, tally sheets, poll books, and the official returns and statements made by the judges and clerks of election to the board of election commissioners used and made in connection with the primary election held in the city of St. Louis, Mo., on the 3d day of August, 1920," in designated precincts, including that in which relator is a qualified voter and judge of election, and in which he cast his ballot.

[1] I. The term "elections," as used in the Constitution of the state, does not include within its meaning elections held merely to nominate candidates for office. As a necessary consequence the provisions of the Constitution which govern elections do not, of their own force, and by virtue of their presence in the Constitution, have any application to primary elections, or any question concerning them. This is established by previous decisions in which the reasons for the ruling are amply and convincingly set forth. It is unnecessary to repeat them in this case. They can be found in State ex rel. v. Taylor, 220 Mo. loc. cit. 630, 631, 119 S. W. 373; State ex rel. v. Coburn, 260 Mo. loc. cit. 190, 168 S. W. 956, and cases cited. The soundness of this ruling is not seriously questioned in this case, as we understand counsel. One result of this ruling is that the constitutional restrictions upon the use of the ballots, etc., as evidence and in evidence, whatever those restrictions are, do not, by reason only of their presence in the Constitution of the state, in any way tend to deny to respondent the power he is now attempting to exert by means of the subpœna duces tecum he has issued.

[2] II. Since the constitutional provisions which govern elections apply as such only to elections in which persons are chosen "for office by vote, and nowhere in the sense of nominating a candidate for office by a political party" (State ex rel. v. Taylor, supra), and since the Legislature is free to enact primary election laws, unrestricted by the mentioned provisions of the Constitution, and may include in or exclude from such primary election laws such otherwise valid restrictions and safeguards as it wills to include or exclude, it follows that the primary law itself must furnish the solution of the question presented for decision.

III. When the Legislature, in the process of enacting the Primary Law of 1907 (Laws 1907, p. 263), came to the matter of providing regulatory, restrictive, and penal provisions, it incorporated in the act a section which this court has held (State ex rel. v. Taylor, supra; State v. Peyton, 234 Mo. loc. cit. 522 et seq., 137 S. W. 979, Ann. Cas. 1912D, 154) incorporated in the primary election law, by reference, the several provisions, statutory and constitutional, of the laws of the state applicable to elections of officers, and made them all, with exceptions immaterial in this case, parts of the primary act itself, and as effective in all respects as they would have been had they been written at length into that act and formally set out and enacted as such without reference to their existence as parts of the laws governing elections of officers. The reasons for this conclusion will be found in the cases cited above, in which the opinions were written by Gantt, J., and Ferriss, J., respectively.

IV. In applying the principle stated in the preceding paragraph, it was held in State ex rel. v. Taylor, supra, that section 3 of article 8 of the Constitution was incorporated, by reference, in the primary law; that the result of this was equivalent to writing into the primary law as a part of it the very words of that section, and that the restrictive effect of this with respect to primary elections was exactly the same as the effect of the same section upon those elections to which it applied by virtue of its existence as a part of the Constitution. At the time of the decision in the case referred to there was, neither in the language of the primary law itself, nor in any act or provision incorporated therein by reference, anything which conflicted with section 3 of article 8, or diminished its force, as an incorporated part of the primary act. In the Taylor Case, therefore, section 3 of article 8, considered as a part of the primary act by incorporation by reference, was given its full force as a part of the act, and was given the same construction as was then given it when sought to be applied to matters arising out of elections to which the section applied of its own force as a part of the Constitution, i. e., elections to office.

[3] V. Since section 3 of article 8 of the Constitution does not, as a constitutional provision, apply to primary elections, and since its provisions are applicable solely because they have been made a part of the primary law by the act of the Legislature, they are applicable merely as a part of the primary law, and because they were made so by the Legislature. The Legislature put them into the primary law, and what the Legislature could do in this respect it could also undo. It has as much power to eliminate from a statute provisions incorporated therein by reference as it has to repeal any other part of a law it has enacted. The fact that a provision which the Legislature incorporates by reference in a law it is enacting is a provision in the state Constitution gives it no added force in the statute into which it is drawn by reference. By that process it becomes a part of the statute, and nothing more. As a part of the statute it may be left by the Legislature as first brought into that statute, or its effect may be limited, or it may be entirely eliminated from the statute by the Legislature. It is subject, as a part of the statute, to repeal, either direct or by implication. To repeat and repeat again, it is, and is to be considered by the courts and to be treated by the Legislature as, a part of the statute, and may be dealt with as such.

[4] VI. In 1909, the Legislature (Laws 1909, p. 501) amended the chapter on evidence as it then stood (chapter 25, R. S. 1899), by adding thereto a section which it designated as "section 3150a," which is now section 5403, R. S. 1919, and reads as follows:

"The legal custodians of the ballots or ballot boxes may be summoned before grand jurors, or before any court of record of the state, and compelled to open the ballot boxes and disclose the ballots in investigations and trials: Provided, that the ballots in no way be used or any information disclosed that would tend toward showing who voted any ballot."

This section is general in terms, and was not directly added to the primary act, but is drawn into that act by reference by virtue of section 4853, R. S. 1919, just as the constitutional restrictions upon the use of the ballots were drawn into the same act by the same section and its predecessor, section 32 of the act of 1907, as is held in State ex rel. v. Taylor, supra, and State v. Peyton, supra. The effect of this section 5403, R. S. 1919, upon the use of ballots used in elections which are such in the constitutional sense need not be discussed. Of course, no constitutional safeguard or restriction respecting such elections could be repealed or changed by any act of the Legislature. With respect to primary elections, however, the provisions of section 3 of article 8 have no force or application as constitutional provisions, as already pointed out. They only apply in so far as they are made a part of the primary

election statute by reference, i. e., have force only as parts of the statute itself. It follows that the constitutional provisions incorporated in the primary law by reference are stricken from that law by section 5403, in so far as they are so repugnant thereto that they are within the rule concerning repeals by implication.

VII. It seems to be contended that, since section 5403 struck from the primary law existing provisions repugnant to that section, whether written bodily into the law or incorporated by reference, and since (so it is argued) the terms of section 3 of article 8 of the Constitution are repugnant to section 5403, therefore they are expunged from the primary law by virtue of that repugnancy and therefore the contemplated action of respondent becomes legal and proper.

[5] One question to which this contention brings us is whether section 5403 permits to be done what respondent is seeking to do. That section, set out in the preceding paragraph, permits the ballots used in a primary election to be brought before a grand jury and "disclosed" in an investigation before that tribunal; but it is in terms—

"provided, that the ballots in no way be used or any information disclosed that would tend toward showing who voted any ballot."

Whatever authority this section gives, with respect to the use of ballots and ballot boxes, the court was empowered to employ. The section is controlling so far as concerns matters within its scope. Whether the primary act as it previously stood was more or less liberal in its provisions, with respect to the use of ballots as evidence, makes no difference in so far as such more or less liberal provisions are repealed by section 5403. To that extent they are eliminated. Does this section permit to be done what the subpoena duces tecum commands? That subpoena commands the election commissioners to appear before the grand jury and "produce in evidence the ballot boxes and contents thereof, tally sheets, poll books, and the official returns and statements made by the judges and clerks of election," etc. The purpose of this is to direct the election commissioners to bring to the grand jury room and turn over to the grand jury all the things mentioned in the subpoena duces tecum. The effect of this will be to put into the hands of the grand jury the full means of determining exactly how every voter in the designated precincts voted in the primary election. That this is true is self-evident and was so held in the case of Gantt v. Brown, 238 Mo. 560, 142 S. W. 422. Though that case dealt with an election contest only, yet this particular holding is as applicable to a grand jury proceeding as to an election contest. While in Gantt v. Brown, supra, it was held that the ballots and poll books might be used in evidence in a contested election case and the lots compared with the lists of voters, in per circumstances, nothing was decided h respect to grand jury proceedings, since question of that kind was in that case, 1 the decision depends upon an express vision in the Constitution that in election itests, under proper safeguards, such a nparison may be made. But no such proion with respect to any proceeding apars in section 5403, R. S. 1919, which govis primary elections, which are creatures the statute, and not of the Constitution, all agree. On the contrary, that section plicitly provides that ballots shall "in no ty be used or any information disclosed at would tend toward showing who voted y ballot." How is it possible to deny that put the ballots, poll book, and lists in the inds of the grand jury and thereby necesrily to furnish that body every means of termining how every voter voted. (Gantt v. rown, supra) is to violate this express statory command that the ballots shall not be "used" as to "tend toward showing who ited any ballot?"

The language of the proviso is plain and nambiguous. The language of the subœna is no less so. That the command of ae subpœna is violative of the prohibition f the statute seems to us to be so clear as o be indisputable. In view of this express rohibition we hold the court had no authorty to enforce the subpœna it issued. The ases cited from other states which, it is rgued, hold that the use of ballots in grand ury proceedings (or on trials) does not violate the secrecy of the ballots do not involve my such provision as that found in the proriso in section 5403, R. S. 1919. The Legislature had power to enact that proviso. It exercised that power, and the policy or impolicy of that enactment is not a question this court has any constitutional authority or jurisdiction to decide.

VIII. It is urged that we re-examine the construction previously given section 3 of article 8 of the Constitution, and also urged that the construction given that section in Gantt v. Brown, supra, authorized the issuance and authorizes the enforcement of the subpœna in question. Except as already discussed, neither of these questions could throw any light upon the issue in this case. Whatever may be the correct answer to either contention, in so far as elections of officers are concerned, any construction of section 3 of article 8 which brings the provisions of that section into repugnance and conflict with section 5403, R. S. 1919, immediately results in the eradication from the primary law, by the very fact of such conflict, and exactly to the extent of such repugnance, the incorporation therein, by reference, of the provisions of section 3 of article 8. The discussion, therefore, of these questions would be entirely irrelevant. The able argu-

ment advanced will be pertinent when a question shall arise concerning the use before grand juries of ballots, etc., used in elections which are such in the constitutional sense.

IX. In preceding paragraphs we have considered some questions as if it were assumed that the correctness of the doctrine of State ex rel. v. Taylor, supra, with reference to the incorporation of section 3 of article 8 of the Constitution into the primary law by reference, is conceded. In this case it makes no difference whether that doctrine is sound or unsound. If it now be assumed to be incorrect, then it results that the constitutional provisions referred to were never drawn into the primary act. That does not affect the applicability of section 5403, R. S. 1919, to the facts of this case. That section is general in its terms. It establishes a rule respecting the use of ballots as evidence in all cases in which it constitutionally can be applied, excepting those taken out of its influence by some other controlling statute. There is no constitutional obstacle to its application to primary elections and ballots cast therein, and there is no other statute which narrows its scope when applied to such ballots. In so far as other sections of the statute previously passed conflict with and are repugnant to it, they are repealed by reason of that repugnance. It is not suggested that any later enactment has restricted its force or application. It is, therefore, as applicable in this case on the theory that the mentioned ruling in the Taylor Case is incorrect as it is on the theory that the ruling is a correct one. Therefore any discussion of the question whether the Taylor Case is right or wrong in the particular mentioned would contribute nothing to the solution of the question presented on this record.

X. In State ex rel. v. Kinsey (No. 18035) a writ was refused, without opinion. The application was for a writ of prohibition against Judge Kinsey to prevent enforcement of a subpœna duces tecum he had ordered issued to require the election commissioners to bring into court upon the trial of a charge that relators had made a fraudulent return as judges and clerks in a general election in a designated precinct in the city of St. Louis, the ballot boxes, poll books, etc., used at that election in the precinct named. The application stated that these things were sought—

"to establish the correctness or falsity of the count and return made by defendants in said precinct, and that the same are sought for this purpose, and no other, and that the ballots hereby sought to be brought into court will in no way be used, nor any information disclosed, that would tend towards showing who voted any ballot."

The court thereupon entered an order for the issuance of a subpœna duces tecum, which contained, among other things, the following:

"And you and each of you are hereby still further commanded not to open said paper ballot boxes or envelopes containing the ballots cast and counted at said election in said precinct of said ward, except in open court on the trial of said cause, and in the presence of the judge presiding at said trial, and the jury sitting in the cause, and when so opened you shall not display or otherwise make known any part of any ballot contained in said paper ballot boxes or envelopes, except the face of such ballot, concealing the number on the back thereof, nor shall you copy or permit anyone else to copy the number on the back of any such ballot, or compare, or permit any other person to compare the number on the back of any such ballot with the corresponding number in the poll books or lists of voters used at said election in said precinct of said ward; nor shall you display or make known, or allow any person to examine the poll books or lists of voters used at said election in said precinct of said ward, except the parts thereof containing a statement of the judges and clerks of elections certifying the result thereof."

In addition to this, made a part of the subpœna itself, Judge Kinsey made the following additional order:

"And it is still further ordered by the court that, upon the trial of this cause, neither the jurors, nor the attorneys for the state or the defendants, nor the official stenographer of this court, nor any party to this cause, nor any witness in the cause, nor any other person, shall look at, examine, or copy any number appearing on the back of any ballot taken from the paper ballot boxes or envelopes referred to above and offered in evidence, nor shall any of the persons enumerated above compare the number on the back of such ballot with the poll books brought into court under the aforesaid subpœna duces tecum, nor shall any of the persons enumerated above examine or take notes from said poll books except only that part thereof containing the statements of the result of said election in said precinct of said ward, which are signed by the judges of said election, under penalty of being adjudged in contempt of court.   W. M. Kinsey, Judge."

In that case the subpœna was ordered for the purpose of bringing the designated documents into court before the judge; it was ordered in a prosecution under the law governing elections which are such in a constitutional sense; it was conditioned, both in the application and in the order itself, very differently from the subpœna in this case; and it was not governed by the primary election law nor governed by section 5403, R. S. 1919, in so far as that section conflicts with section 8 of article 8 of the Constitution, if it does. The constitutional provision was dominant in that case. With respect to elections of officers, to which it applies as a constitutional provision, it ought not be affected by any statute the Legislature might enact. With respect to primary elections, to which it does not apply as a constitutional provision, it may be inapplicable or inapplicable as the Legislature may ordain, as has more than once been pointed out in this opinion. The ruling in State ex rel. v. Kinsey, whether right or wrong, has no application to this case.

[8] XI. It is suggested that respondent does not actually intend to enforce the subpœna according to its terms, but only so far as may be lawful when section 5403 is considered; that it is not intended that it shall be disclosed how any voter voted. What respondent may now have in mind is not of great consequence in solving the question whether he had authority to issue the subpœna he issued in this case. So far as intent is concerned, the language of the subpœna would seem to be conclusive in this proceeding. Further, he is not bringing the ballots, etc., before himself as judge, where it may be he might control their use, but orders them to be produced in evidence before a grand jury in its inquest room. In the commissioners must do in obedience to the subpœna if the writ applied for in this case is denied. It is not open to this court to amend this subpœna in order to delay this proceeding, which is instituted, not to prevent respondent from issuing such lawful subpœna as he may, but to prohibit him from enforcing one which is beyond his power to issue or enforce if the controlling statute is not to be disregarded. It is not a question of contemplated acts in part within and in part without a court's jurisdiction. It is a question of the power of the court to enforce this particular subpœna, as issued.

In this connection respondent cites State ex rel. v. Thurman, 268 Mo. loc. cit. 546, 187 S. W. 1190, in support of his contention. We do not think that decision applicable. The order attacked in that case was made by Judge Thurman in a local option election contest. It was not a contest for which the Constitution provided. It was a statutory proceeding. Judge Thurman's order required the mayor and city officials of Mount to preserve and produce for use in evidence the ballots, poll books, etc., used in the election being contested. Relator invoked section 3 of article 8 of the Constitution, and contended the order was violative of that section. The opinion shows issues were made in the contest proceeding such as to justify the use in evidence in that proceeding of the ballots, poll books, etc., used in the local option election, even if section of article 8 was applicable. The opinion does not discuss the question whether section 6567, R. S. 1919 (then section 7242, R.

S. 1909, as amended by Laws 1913, p. 388), adopted the provisions of section 3 of article 8 of the Constitution, in all respects, as a part of the machinery for use in local option election contests. It disposed of the contention without denying the sub silentio assumption of relator that this was true. The opinion shows that the rule in Gantt v. Brown, supra, if applied to the election there in question, would warrant the use of the ballots, poll books, etc., in evidence under the issues made. In other words, there was a lawful use which the court might make of them in that case, even if section 3 of article 8 was incorporated, by reference, in the local option election contest law.

It also appears from the opinion that the attacked order contained no hint of any intention to use the ballots, poll books, etc., otherwise than in the manner which, on the assumption that section 3 of article 8 was incorporated in the local option law, was permitted to be done. In the face of all these things this court was, in effect, asked to assume that Judge Thurman, after lawfully bringing the ballots into his court for a lawful purpose, would put them to an unlawful use. Nothing that had been done, attempted, written, or said justified even a suspicion of any such design. It is needless to say that this court did not make the assumption relator in that case asked it to make. That case furnishes no support for respondent's present contention. In the instant case the subpœna shows on its face that the thing ordered to be done is directly violative of the express command of a controlling statute.

[7] XII. The briefs urge that the secrecy of the ballot is not of an importance equal to that of purity of elections and prevention of fraud. The argument is ably and eloquently pressed upon the court. If it be conceded counsel are right, and what they say is true, nevertheless that question is not one which can by any possibility be reached in this case. When the people, through their General Assembly, speak their will by enacting a valid law, this court, whatever may be the views of its members as individual citizens, upon a question of policy involved, must submit to the decision of the majority, and apply the law as the people have made it. The controlling statute in this case is so clear as to exclude all dispute as to its meaning. It denies to respondent the power he is seeking to exert. The preliminary rule is therefore made absolute.

WALKER, C. J., and GRAVES and ELDER, JJ., concur.
WOODSON, J., concurs in the result.
HIGBEE and DAVID E. BLAIR, JJ., dissent.

ST. LOUIS MALLEABLE CASTING CO. v. GEORGE G. PRENDERGAST CONST. CO. (No. 21710.)

(Supreme Court of Missouri, Division No. 1. April 9, 1921. Motion for Rehearing and Motion to Transfer to Court in Banc Denied June 6, 1921.)

1. Municipal corporations ⟨⟩485(5)—Tax bill issued for sewer prima facie evidence of validity.

A tax bill issued against property for construction of a sewer was prima facie evidence of its validity.

2. Municipal corporations ⟨⟩513(7)—Evidence held sufficient to support validity of sewer tax bill.

In suit to cancel and set aside a tax bill against plaintiff's property for the construction of a sewer, evidence held to support the validity of the bill, and not to tend to overturn it.

3. Municipal corporations ⟨⟩450(4)—No notice of establishment of taxing sewer district necessary.

No notice to property owners of the establishment of a taxing sewer district was necessary.

4. Municipal corporations ⟨⟩321(1)—Action of authorities in establishment of sewer district conclusive in absence of fraud

The action of the municipal authorities in the establishment of a sewer district in the absence of fraud is conclusive, and not subject to review by the courts.

5. Municipal corporations ⟨⟩488, 489(7)—Property owner's complaint of fraud on part of sewer contractor too late after work completed.

A complaint of fraud on the part of a contractor to construct a sewer for a taxing sewer district comes too late from a property owner suing to cancel and set aside a tax bill after the work has been completed.

6. Municipal corporations ⟨⟩321(1)—City authorities judges of dimensions of sewers.

The municipal authorities of the city of St. Louis are the sole judges of the dimensions of contemplated sewers.

7. Municipal corporations ⟨⟩488, 489(4)—Acquiescence with knowledge of sewer improvement, especially when accompanied by acceptance of benefits, estops owner.

Silent acquiescence with knowledge of the improvement, especially when accompanied by acceptance of its benefits, estops a property owner from denying the validity of a tax bill issued against his property for construction of a sewer.

Appeal from St. Louis Circuit Court; Wilson A. Taylor, Judge.

Suit by the St. Louis Malleable Casting Company against the George G. Prendergast

Construction Company. From judgment dismissing the bill, plaintiff appeals. Affirmed.

The plaintiff brought this suit in the circuit court of the city of St. Louis against the defendant to cancel and set aside a certain tax bill issued against the property of the former for the construction of Baden sewer district No. 2, amounting to $9,168.86. The trial resulted in a judgment for the defendant, and the plaintiff duly appealed the cause to this court. The petition charged substantially the following facts:

The petition of the plaintiff alleged:

That the board of aldermen of the city of St. Louis, upon the recommendation of the board of public service of the city, adopted an ordinance, approved March 22, 1915, establishing a sewer district to be known as "Baden sewer district No. 2," which ordinance is set out in full in the petition. That thereafter the board of aldermen enacted another ordinance, prepared and recommended by the board of public service for the construction of the sewer in said district, which ordinance was approved July 21, 1915, and under which the board of public service was authorized and directed to let a contract for the construction work. The ordinance further provided for the acceptance by the city of St. Louis of sewers conveyed to the city by the St. Louis Terminal Railway Company by deeds, and that part of the sewers so conveyed should be incorporated in the system to be constructed under authority of the ordinance. The ordinance further provided that, when the sewers were fully completed, the board of public service should cause the entire cost and expense thereof to be computed, and should levy and assess such cost and expense as a special tax, in accordance with the requirements of the charter of the city, and cause to be issued a special tax bill against each lot or parcel of ground liable, in the manner provided by the charter. That the defendant was awarded the contract for the construction of the sewer, and that on December 22, 1916, the city of St. Louis issued and delivered to the defendant special tax bills for the aggregate amount of $65,744.67, being the entire cost for the construction of said sewer, as calculated by the board of public service and as agreed upon in the contract between the city and the defendant, amongst which bills was one issued against the property of plaintiff for $9,168.86. That plaintiff is the owner in fee of the tract of land described in said tax bill, against which said tax bill was issued, which tract contains approximately 320,210 square feet.

That the said assessment and charge in said tax bill is excessive, unlawful, and void, for the reason that the said taxing district established by ordinance as aforesaid does not include large areas of land which were in the drainage area of said sewer, and which properties stand in the same relative position as plaintiff's with respect to the said sewer, and derive, and are so situated as to be capable of deriving, the same amount of benefit from said sewer as the property of plaintiff. That a large tract of land immediately north of plaintiff's property, hereinafter referred to as the "Kuhs" property, and containing approximately the same area as plaintiff's property, and which property is so situated with respect to the said sewer as to receive as great or greater benefit therefrom than the said property of plaintiff, was omitted from the said taxing district and exempted from taxation for any portion of the cost of the construction of said sewer. That a large tract of land fronting on the west side of Broadway and belonging to the Calvary Cemetery Association, and which property consists of a number of acres, and is in the natural drainage district of said sewer, which property is in the same relative position with respect to said sewer as the property of plaintiff, and derives as great benefit therefrom, was also omitted from said taxing district and exempted from the payment of any portion of the cost of said sewer. That by reason of the omission and exemption of the said large tracts of land from their just share of the said tax to pay the cost of construction of said sewer an unreasonable and excessive proportion of the said tax has been assessed against the said property of plaintiff.

That the ordinances aforesaid, the provisions of the charter of the city of St. Louis purporting to authorize the board of aldermen to establish a sewer district designating lands of private owners to be specially taxed to pay the entire cost of said sewer, violate the fourteenth article of the amendments to the Constitution of the United States, in that they determine that said lands within the district prescribed by said ordinances would be benefited by said sewer and should be and were especially assessed therefor, as well as the apportionment of said taxes between the several lots or parcels of land and their respective owners within said district, without any hearing being accorded to the owners of said lands upon such determination, thereby denying plaintiff due process of law; that by the establishment of said sewer district and the imposition of said entire cost of the said district sewer upon the property therein, as ordained by the ordinance aforesaid, and by the exclusion of the land as aforesaid from the taxation of the cost of said sewer, although such lands so excluded will be drained by said sewer and share equally with the property of plaintiff and other properties in said defined district in the benefits resulting from the construction of sewer, plaintiff has been denied due process of law, the equal protection of the law guaranteed to plaintiff by the said fourteenth article of the amendments to the Constitution of the United States.

That the establishment of said sewer district and the levying of said tax by the ordinance aforesaid was and is arbitrary, unjust, oppressive, and fraudulent, and by the said board of public service known to be so at the time of its recommendation of said ordinance to said board of aldermen, and that the said board of public service then knew that the aforesaid additional parcels of land would be drained by the said sewer and derive all of the benefits and advantages therefrom which every other property within the said defined sewer district can or will derive therefrom, and notwithstanding which the ordinances so recommended by the said board of public service to said board of aldermen and by the latter enacted imposed the whole cost of said sewer upon the lots within the said sewer district as defined by the said ordinance, and no part of said cost upon such additional lands. That the said board of public service in recommending to the board of aldermen the said ordinance establishing the said district acted oppressively, arbitrarily, and fraudulently in this:

That prior to the establishment of the said sewer district, for the construction of said sewer district sewer, plaintiff had, under permit of the then board of public improvements of said city, the predecessor of said board of public service, constructed a sewer system upon its said land, which private system was laid upon plaintiff's said property, along a private right of way, to a public sewer known as "Baden public sewer," with which sewer said private sewer of plaintiff was connected. That plaintiff had constructed the said sewer under permit as aforesaid at great cost and expense, and said sewer was adequate for taking care of the sewage and surface water from plaintiff's said land. That plaintiff's said property has no dwelling buildings upon it, the only buildings erected upon its said land being foundry, factory, and office buildings occupied and used by it for the transaction of its business. That the tract of land hereinabove mentioned as the "Kuhs" property, and which has been excluded from said taxing district as aforesaid, is and has been improved for a number of years by a large number of tenement and flat buildings occupied by more than 40 families. That prior to the establishment of said taxing district for the construction of said district sewer a short line of private sewer, for carrying off foul water, had been laid in said "Kuhs" property and was connected with plaintiff's private sewer above mentioned, and the sewage from said "Kuhs" property thus drained through said private sewer into said Baden public sewer. That in the planning of said district sewer it was pro-

vided for the laying of a line of said sewer along and upon a strip 7½ feet in width, being the western 7½ feet of said "Kuhs" property, extending southwardly from the south line of Christian avenue, and it was further provided in said plan for the laying of a line of said district sewer upon and along a strip being the western 10 feet in width of plaintiff's property hereinabove described and extending southwardly from the south line of Antelope street to the north line of Thatcher avenue, a distance of 495 feet, more or less.

That the city of St. Louis obtained from the plaintiff, without any consideration moving to plaintiff therefor, a deed conveying the easement of right of way for said district sewer along and upon the said strip 10 feet in width. That said city also obtained a conveyance from the owners of the said "Kuhs" property for the easement or right of way for said district sewer in said strip 7½ feet in width. That the deeds for the said sewer right of way recite a nominal consideration of $1. That, notwithstanding the deed to the sewer right of way along said Kuhs property purported to be a conveyance in consideration of $1, the sewer commissioner of the city of St. Louis, who is also a member of the board of public service, did, without authority and unlawfully, promise the owners of said Kuhs property that because of the making of said deed to said right of way the taxing district for the said Baden district sewer No. 2 should be so laid out and said district so constructed that said Kuhs property, although receiving all of the benefits from said district sewer, and being with respect to said sewer precisely in the same position as plaintiff's property, should be left out of said taxing district and exempted from the payment of any portion of the cost for the construction of said sewer. That the value of the sewer right of way upon said strip of the Kuhs property was trifling as compared with the proportion of the cost of said sewer properly and equitably taxable against said property. That the said sewer commissioner, in planning and laying out the taxing district for said district sewer, acted arbitrarily with a view of favoring the owners of the said Kuhs property, and did so plan said district as to leave out of said taxing district all of the said Kuhs property except a strip being the western 7 feet 6 inches in width and a strip 50 feet in width off the eastern part of said land, extending from the center line of Baden public sewer to the southern boundary line of said Kuhs property. That the said two strips of said Kuhs property were left in the taxing district for the fraudulent purpose of permitting the connection of said Kuhs property with said district sewer, owing to the fact that the said strips are immediately adjacent to the pipes of said district sewer, thus making it possible for the remainder of said Kuhs tract, eliminated from said taxing district as aforesaid, to obtain all the benefits and advantages of said district sewer.

That the said sewer commissioner did report to the said board of public improvements and to the committee of said board having under consideration the establishment of said district his said unlawful arrangement with the owners of said Kuhs property to so define said district as to eliminate substantially all of said Kuhs property, and did fully inform the other members of said board, and of the said committee of said board, that the said proposed elimination of said property from the taxing district was probably unlawful and might invalidate the tax bills issued for the construction of said sewer. That notwithstanding the said report of said sewer commissioner, and notwithstanding the members of said board of public improvements did fully understand that the plan for said taxing district as submitted by the sewer commissioner was unjust, inequitable, and invalid, the said board of public improvements, as a committee of the whole, did arbitrarily, fraudulently, and oppressively, and in a spirit of favoritism towards the owners of said Kuhs property, recommend the establishment of said taxing district with the elimination of substantially all of said Kuhs property as aforesaid and the said board of public improvements did then, at the regular meeting of said board, adopt the recommendation of the committee of the whole of said board, and did prepare and recommend to the board of·aldermen of the said city of St. Louis the ordinance establishing said taxing district, arbitrarily and fraudulently leaving out of the taxing district as defined in the ordinance so recommended to the board of aldermen the said Kuhs property, with the exception of the two small strips hereinbefore specified. That the board of aldermen of said city of St. Louis did, without any hearing being accorded the property owners in said proposed taxing district, and without any independent investigation of the facts, but acting solely upon the recommendation of said board of public service as hereinbefore set forth, enact the said ordinances as aforesaid.

Similar allegations were made regarding another tract of land, to wit, the Calvary Cemetery Association, containing 23 acres, and similarly situated. The petition further charged that:

Plaintiff's property is improved by its office and foundry buildings, and the Kuhs property is improved with a number of two-story brick flat and residence buildings, housing approximately 100 families.

In 1903 plaintiff obtained from Kuhs a deed for a sewer right of way along the eastern part of the Kuhs tract, extending from the northeast corner of plaintiff's property to Gingrass creek. Plaintiff at about the same time, under permit from the city of St. Louis, constructed a private 12 inch sewer running from its property over the right of way acquired from Kuhs. This sewer emptied into Gingrass creek. Subsequently, in 1907, under permit from the city, plaintiff replaced the 12-inch sewer by a 24-inch sewer. This private sewer not only carried off the foul water, but also the surface water, from plaintiff's premises, and the evidence is undisputed that this private system of plaintiff was and would continue to be entirely adequate for the plaintiff's property. .

The Kuhs property also has a private sewer system. Under permit from the city there was laid along the eastern part of the Kuhs property a 15-inch sewer paralleling the plaintiff's sewer. The records of the sewer department do not show that a permit was ever granted to Kuhs to lay any other private pipe.

Several years before the district sewer in question was built a public or main sewer, known as Baden public sewer, was constructed in the bed of Gingrass creek. The plaintiff's 24-inch pipe and the 15-inch Kuhs pipe were both connected with the public sewer, and both of these private sewers are still in use. Mr. E. L. Kuhs, for defendant, testified that there were two other pipes upon the Kuhs property, which also formerly emptied into Gingrass creek, and are not connected with Baden public sewer, but the records of the sewer department do not ,show those connections.

Under charter of the City of St. Louis, art. XXII, § 8, before the board of public service shall recommend an ordinance for the construction of a sewer to be paid by special assessments, the board of aldermen, on recommendation of the board of public service, shall establish or shall have established a sewer district or joint sewer district against the property in which it is proposed to assess benefits. The charter establishes an arbitrary rule for the assessment of all property within the district, so established, according to area. The board of aldermen has no power under the charter to amend such an ordinance emanating from the board of public service, but must either adopt the ordinance as recommended or reject it. The charter makes no provision for notice to the property owners nor for a hearing before the board of public service or the board of aldermen upon the question of benefits; that is, upon the question of what property shall be included within the benefit district, and there was not, according to the testimony, any such notice or hearing in the matter of the establishing of the taxing district for Baden district sewer No. 2.

The matter of the establishment of this

taxing district was pending before the board of public improvements for a considerable period of time before the bill defining the district was recommended by the board to the board of aldermen. According to the testimony, the matter was up for consideration before the board of public improvements, sitting as a committee of the whole, on November 18, 1913. According to the stenographer's transcript of the proceedings before the board on that date, Mr. J. L. Hornsby, as attorney for the Calvary Cemetery, appeared and presented a request that the property of the cemetery association be excluded from the taxing district and thus exempted from contributing anything to the cost of the sewer.

Mr. Hornsby stated to the board that Mr. Moreno, then sewer commissioner, had told him that 23 acres of the cemetery property sloped towards Broadway, and that the surface water would necessarily drain into the proposed sewer, and that Mr. Moreno estimated that the cemetery association's share of the cost of the proposed district sewer would be about $12,000. In the discussion before the board on that occasion Mr. Moreno said:

"I understand the attitude of Mr. Hornsby, and I think it is not unreasonable. At the same time we have to consider this, if we cut out that 22 acres and assess the entire cost of those sewers against this district that is populated, some of the property owners may contest the tax bills, as it is evident that the sewers do have to be made 20 per cent. larger than they otherwise would have to be built to take care of that property outside of the district, and I am afraid we might not be able to get a contractor to bid on the work."

And again, in the course of the same discussion, in answer to a question of one of the other commissioners as to whether there had ever been a case of exemption of that sort, Mr. Moreno replied:

"I don't recall any since I have been here. We try to lay the districts out so they will be on a basis perfectly fair to all the property owners within the district, and for that reason we could not very well exclude territory of this kind."

Mr. Kinsey, the president of the board, expressed a similar view. He said:

"The statement of the sewer commissioner, in case your cemetery was exempt, that is to say, in such an event, if the district was laid out as to exclude the cemetery, the city would have to pay the portion ordinarily assessed against the cemetery, and in that way, in imposing upon the property owners in the district that additional burden, it makes it difficult to exclude this cemetery in the present case."

Mr. Moreno thereupon suggested:

"The only thing I see we can do is to move the line over arbitrarily a portion of the dis-
231 S.W.—63

tance, if the board thought that could be done. Still that is establishing a precedent that might get us into trouble later."

To which Mr. Talbert, another commissioner, replied:

"It seems to me you would have to follow the physical fact or lay yourselves open to future trouble."

The question of the elimination of the Kuhs property from the taxing district came before the board sitting as a committee of the whole, at a meeting held February 6, 1914. At this meeting Mr. Moreno, sewer commissioner, called attention to the fact that the Kuhs property had been left out of the plan for the district submitted by him. He stated in explanation that the property was not subdivided and was drained by two private sewers connecting with the public sewer. Then he continued:

"Another thing, in order to properly drain the district, we are compelled to have a right of way from Kuhs' property in which to lay some of our sewers. He gave that right of way with the understanding that if we accepted it and laid out the district that his property would be left out, on the ground that he had started it and it did not drain through any of the district sewers. If we decide to put his property in the district, we will have to give him back his right of way and enter condemnation proceedings to acquire it. In order that these people may have relief, we have to go ahead with the district and include this property in Calvary Cemetery, regardless of their protests, and it is an open question as to whether or not we should leave this other out or put it in. * * * It occurs to me that if we do leave this property out some of these other gentlemen who own vacant property might contest the tax bills."

On May 8, 1914, the question of the elimination of Calvary Cemetery and the Kuhs property again came up for consideration by the board. Mr. Hooke, who had succeeded Mr. Moreno as sewer commissioner, brought up the matter. He reported that something like 23 acres in Calvary Cemetery drained through the territory, and that he had estimated that the cemetery should pay something like $12,000 as its proportion of the cost of the sewer. He recommended that, if the cemetery association could take care of its own drainage, he thought it would be fair to leave them out of the district, and that then the size of the district sewer could be cut. He also estimated that the private drain which the cemetery association would have to construct would probably cost $4,500. As to the Kuhs property, being asked by Commissioner Wall as to what he had done regarding that, he answered:

"Nothing, for two reasons. The first is he gave us all of those rights of way (I was sitting in there with the sewer commissioner myself) on condition that his sewers that were in there would be accepted, and, if his sewers are accepted, there is no reason why we should put him in the district. * * * I do not see anything wrong with it, especially in view of the fact if we don't do that we must pass an ordinance and give him back those rights of way which were obtained under a misrepresentation."

The records of the board do not show that there was any further discussion of the matter by the board. The only subsequent record entry in connection with the establishment of the sewer district is the entry of November 17, 1914, in the proceedings of the board, that an ordinance establishing the taxing district was recommended to the board of aldermen.

Prior to the time when the question of the extent of the taxing district was brought by the sewer commissioner before the board sitting as a committee of the whole, the sewer commissioner had obtained a deed to a right of way 7½ feet wide and approximately 247 feet in length off the western side of the Kuhs property. The deed is dated May 9, 1913, and recites a nominal consideration of $1. This is the right of way deed referred to by the sewer commissioner in the discussion of the question of the exclusion of the Kuhs property from the sewer taxing district. The testimony shows that no money consideration moved from the city to the Kuhs Realty Company for this easement.

The plaintiff had also given the city a right of way for this district sewer, of a width of 10 feet, and along the entire western line of its property a distance of 495 feet. There was no actual consideration of whatever kind for this conveyance. The deed was made about the same time as the Kuhs deed.

The ordinance for the establishment of the district, as recommended by the board of public service, was passed by the board of aldermen, the ordinance being approved by the mayor on March 22, 1915. The district laid out by the ordinance does not include any part of Calvary Cemetery and excludes all of the Kuhs property except a strip of 7½ feet in width off the entire west line and a strip 50 feet in width off the east side extending from the southern boundary line of the Kuhs property to the public sewer, a distance of approximately 230 feet. 247.04 feet of the strip 7 feet 6 inches wide embraces the sewer right of way deeded by the Kuhs Company to the city, but the remainder of the 7½-foot strip included in the district, and having a length of approximately 215 feet, although not given for or used as a right of way for the district sewer, is yet included in the district.

According to the testimony of Mr. Doods, engineer and surveyor, a witness for the plaintiff, the area of Calvary Cemetery within the natural drainage district is 23 and a fraction acres, and the area of the Kuhs property within the natural drainage area, and not included in the taxing district, is 317,398 square feet. As shown by the plat of the taxing district, and as testified to by Mr. Osthaus, the special tax assessor, the total area of the district as laid out is 2,296,039 square feet. Adding that to the area of the portion of Calvary Cemetery and the area of the Kuhs property, within the natural drainage district 3,634,919 square feet so that only 63.17 per cent. of the area of the natural drainage district has been included in the taxing district.

The size of the district sewer is greater than is necessary for the draining of the area taxed. This was testified to by Mr. Doods, witness for the plaintiff, who stated that the sewers in the district were larger than it is customary to build sewers for the draining of territory of the extent included in the taxing district and similarly situated with respect to the fall of the land. It is true that Mr. Horner, the city engineer, testified that the sewers in the district were no larger than were reasonably necessary for the needs of the territory included in the taxing district, but he admitted on cross-examination that, in calculating the sizes of the sewers, the highest percentages of the various factors entering into the calculation were used. He further admitted upon cross-examination that the plans for the construction of the sewers, including the sizes of the pipes, had been prepared before the discussion as to the size of the taxing district by the board of public improvements, and that no change in the sizes of the sewers in the district was made after the board determined to exclude Calvary Cemetery and the Kuhs property. In this connection we call attention to the statement of Mr. Moreno at the meeting of the board held on November 18, 1913:

"It is evident that the sewers do have to be made 20 per cent. larger than they otherwise would have to be built to take care of that property outside of the district."

The plans, according to Mr. Horner, were not changed after that meeting, and it is evident that the sewers, as constructed, are therefore 20 per cent. larger than the requirements of the territory taxed called for.

Mr. Hornsby, attorney for the Calvary Cemetery, and who testified in behalf of defendant, stated that the cemetery property had been left out of the taxing district by the board of public improvements in consideration of the agreement of the cemetery association to construct a drain along the Broadway front of the cemetery property of sufficient size to take care of the surface water from that portion of the cemetery within the natural drainage area of the district, the private drain to be connected with Baden public sewer. The drain along Broadway, from Calvary avenue to the center gate of the cemetery, was to be an open concrete ditch, and from there northwardly an underground pipe. It was Mr. Hornsby's recollection that this arrangement between the cemetery association and the city officials was evidenced by letters.

Notwithstanding the contract between the cemetery association and the city, the cemetery association did not begin the construction of this private drain until October, 1916, at which time the district sewer was practically completed, and did not finish the construction of the private sewer until March, 1917.

Mr. Horner, city engineer, who testified in behalf of defendant, stated the chief consideration for the leaving out of the Kuhs property was the fact that it had a private system which, with proper inlets, would be sufficient to take care of both the foul and surface water of the Kuhs land. The testimony of Mr. Hooke, sewer commissioner, was to the same effect. Mr. Horner admitted that the inlets which the sewer commissioner directed should be made for the purpose of taking care of the surface water of the Kuhs property, as a condition to the accepting of the private system as a part of the sewer system of the city, have not yet been made. Mr. Kuhs, also a witness for the defendant, likewise admitted that fact, but stated that he was making preparations for having the inlets constructed. Both Mr. Moreno and Mr. Hooke stated that they had no independent recollection of the negotiations with Mr. Kuhs, and therefore could neither confirm nor deny the correctness of their representations to the board of public improvements at the meetings held on February 6 and May 8, 1914, that the deed for the right-of-way for the district sewer from the Kuhs Realty Company had been given on condition that the Kuhs property would not be included in the taxing district, and that, if the Kuhs property were included in the taxing district, the right of way deed would have to be returned and condemnation proceedings instituted.

None of the members of the board of public improvements who testified, nor Mr. Horner, the chief engineer, could give any satisfactory explanation of why the Kuhs property was left out of the taxing district while the property of the plaintiff, which admittedly had an adequate private system, which is still draining directly into the Baden public sewer, was included. It was suggested by one of these witnesses for defendant that there was some difference between the two parcels of land, in that the Kuhs property immediately adjoined the public sewer, but when it was pointed out to this witness that the plaintiff had a right of way extending from its property to the public sewer, which right of way had been deeded to it by Kuhs, and that therefore plaintiff's property, to that extent, also abutted upon the public sew-

er, it was admitted that this was no substantial ground for differentiating between the two properties in the matter of the taxation for the building of the district sewer. In this connection we call the court's attention to the fact that the plaintiff's private sewer system, built under permits from the city, cost, according to the evidence, in excess of $4,500.

The court took the case under advisement, and on December 30, 1918, at the December term, 1918, entered a finding and judgment for defendant and dismissed plaintiff's bill.

The defendant's evidence tended to show: The sewer, for proportionate part of cost of which appellant's ground was assessed, had been fully completed when this suit was brought, and appellant had connected its said premises with this sewer and was in actual enjoyment of the benefits thereof. The evidence fails to show any act of commission or omission on the part of the contractor. The appellant does not question the utility of the sewer. Yet, without offering to pay any part of its cost, appellant comes into a court of equity and asks that the entire assessment against its property be canceled.

The charter of the city of St. Louis required the establishment by ordinance, on recommendation of the board of public service, of a taxing district preliminary to the adoption of an ordinance providing for construction of sewers within the district, and also required a public hearing, on notice, as a condition precedent to such recommendation. Prior to tentatively laying out this sewer district, members of the board of public service visited the locality in person and went over the ground. In addition to this, this board had before it information of the local conditions gathered by its assistants, and, as one of the members expressed it in his testimony, was mindful of its duty to include in the assessment district all the property that would be benefited by the sewer.

The testimony shows that two tracts of ground within the same natural basin in which this district sewer was laid, were omitted from this sewer district.

One of these tracts, about 23 acres, is a portion of Calvary cemetery. A representative of the cemetery association appeared before the board of public improvements, then existing under the old charter of the city of St. Louis, and being the predecessor of the board of public service, at a discussion of the then proposed sewer and taxing district therefor, and suggested that, since the cemetery had no foul water to drain, it might with propriety be left out of the district. At this meeting some talk was had about the cemetery constructing open drains that would carry the storm water from its ground into a nearby public sewer. The cemetery property was omitted from the sewer district; and afterwards the said proposed open drains were constructed by the cemetery association entirely at its own expense, with the result that nothing from the cemetery enters the district sewer.

The other of said two tracts omitted from the district was a portion of the "Kuhs" property, as it is called throughout the case, improved with dwelling houses accommodating about 100 families and all of which was perfectly drained by a private sewer emptying into an adjoining public sewer.

Appellant's ground, all within the present sewer district and less in area than either of the portions of the cemetery or Kuhs tracts omitted from the district, was at the time of fixing the sewer district occupied as a manufacturing plant, consisting of foundry, warehouse, and office buildings, It had a private sewer system connecting with the public sewer some distance away from it; but appellant was one of the petitioners for this district sewer, and as soon as possible connected its plant with it for purposes of additional drainage.

The cemetery association, Kuhs, and appellant all had at times prior to the fixing of the present sewer district given the city rights of way for sewer purposes.

The members of the board of public service, which recommended the present district, testifying in this case, all denied any bargain whereby portions of the cemetery or Kuhs properties were to be, or were, omitted from this taxing district. And the following facts were also established by such testimony, viz.: In the judgment of the board of public service the portions of the cemetery and Kuhs properties omitted from such district were both adequately drained at private expense into the public sewer and were not benefited by the district sewer; and appellant's property was not adequately drained by its private sewer system connected with the public sewer and was benefited by the district sewer, which it immediately made use of. That the dimensions of district sewer were not originally designed to drain any portion of the cemetery or Kuhs properties, and that the district sewer as designed and laid was exactly adapted to the present district according to the best expert opinion on the subject.

After the evidence was all in and the cause was under advisement, the defendant (respondent here) petitioned the court for leave to amend its answer. The answer, as it stood, was a general denial, and defendant sought to amend by adding thereto a plea of estoppel based on allegations to conform to the evidence to the effect that the plaintiff (appellant here), prior to the letting of the contract, knew that the city of St. Louis was about to let a contract for construction of the sewer in question and was familiar with the beginning and progress of the work of constructing said sewer, and knew that its (appellant's) said ground would be thereby benefited and

assessed therefor, and knew the extent of such assessment, and applied for permission to, and did, connect its premises therewith, but gave no notice that it would contest payment of its special tax bill, and silently stood by and permitted the work to be done and received the benefits thereof, and that plaintiff, by petitioning for said sewer, encouraged the city to form said sewer district and caused sewers to be constructed therein.

The trial court found in favor of defendant, without ruling on its said petition for leave to amend its answer.

Muench, Walther & Muench, of St. Louis, for appellant.

Rodgers & Koerner, of St. Louis, for respondent.

WOODSON, P. J. (after stating the facts as above). I. The plaintiff makes a very plausible case by the allegations of its petition, but it is not supported by either the evidence in the case or the finding of the trial court.

[1, 2] The tax bill sued on was prima facie evidence of its validity; and the testimony in the case was ample to support its validity, and not tending to overturn it.

[3] II. It is insisted that the establishment of the taxing sewer district is a nullity because no notice was given of that fact to the property owners.

No such notice was necessary, as decided by this court and the Supreme Court of the United States. Speaking upon that point, this court, in the case of Meier v. City of St. Louis, 180 Mo. 391, loc. cit. 409, 79 S. W. 955, loc. cit. 957, used this language:

"As to the contention that the special assessments amount to a taking of plaintiff's property without due process of law, it may be said that no notice is required by the Constitution to be given property owners respecting those matters which the Legislature itself determines, or delegates to the municipal authorities. [Spencer v. Merchant, 125 U. S. 345; Williams v. Eggleston, 170 U. S. 304; St. Louis v. Rankin, 96 Mo. 497.] Publication of notice to the property owners, and opportunity to be heard before the tribunal upon which is devolved the duty of ascertaining facts and acting therein in the special assessment procedure, satisfies the constitutional requirement, and is due process of law as to those matters to be passed upon by such tribunal.

"We think section 14 of article 6 of the amended charter of St. Louis complies with this requirement.

"When the taxing district has been fixed by valid legislation and when the apportionment of the cost of the improvement upon the property in the district has been so fixed, the owner of the property in the district cannot be heard to contend in the court that his property was not in fact benefited, or to the amount assessed in accordance with such apportionment. [Pryor v. Construction Co., 170 Mo. 439.]

"The charter of St. Louis adopted by a vote

of its people in obedience to an express grant by the Constitution of the state has, with respect to municipal matters, including special assessments for local improvements, all the force and effect of an act of the Legislature. [City of St. Louis v. Fischer, 167 Mo. 654; Pryor v. Construction Co., 170 Mo. 439; St. Louis v. Gleason, 15 Mo. App. 25; Id. v. Id., 96 Mo. 33; Kansas City v. Oil Co., 140 Mo. 468.]"

To the same effect are the following cases: Heman v. Allen, 156 Mo. 534, loc. cit. 551, 57 S. W. 559; Heman v. Schulte, 166 Mo. 409, loc. cit. 417, 66 S. W. 163; Embree v. K. C. Road District, 240 U. S. 242, loc. cit. 250, 36 Sup. Ct. 317, 60 L. Ed. 624.

Moreover, the interested parties were given due notice of the meeting of the board of public service where all were given full opportunity to be heard as to, and complain of, any matter which might make it inequitable · to construct the sewer as projected in the district established.

[4] III. This court has repeatedly held that the action of the municipal authorities in the establishment of a sewer district in the absence of fraud is conclusive, and not subject to review by the courts. Heman v. Allen, 156 Mo. 534, 57 S. W. 559; McGhee v. Walsh, 249 Mo. 266, 155 S. W. 445.

[5] IV. This record contains no evidence whatever of fraud, much less any evidence connecting the contractor with fraud. A complaint of fraud comes too late after the work is completed. Jennings Heights Land & Imp. Co. v. City of St. Louis et al., 257 Mo. 291, 165 S. W. 741; Bank v. Woesten, 147 Mo. 467, 48 S. W. 939, 48 L. R. A. 279.

[6] And we have also held that the municipal authorities of the city of St. Louis are the sole judges of the dimensions of contemplated sewers. Heman v. Allen, 156 Mo. 534, 57 S. W. 559.

[7] V. Silent acquiescence with knowledge of the improvement, especially when accompanied by acceptance of its benefits, estops the property owner from denying validity of the tax bill. Paving Co. v. Flemming, 251 Mo. 210, 158 S. W. 4; Heman v. Ring, 85 Mo. App. 231; Walsh v. Bank, 139 Mo. App. 641, 123 S. W. 1001; Smith v. Carlow, 114 Mich. 67, 72 N. W. 22; Fitzhugh v. City of Bay City, 109 Mich. 581, 67 N. W. 904; Atkinson v. Newton, 169 Mass. 240, 47 N. E. 1029; Board of Commissioners v. Plotner, 149 Ind. 116, 48 N. E. 635; Patterson et al. v. Baumer, 43 Iowa, 477; Wright v. Davidson, 181 U. S. 371, loc. cit. 377, 21 Sup. Ct. 616, 45 L. Ed. 900; Gibson v. Owens, 115 Mo. 258, 21 S. W. 1107.

Counsel present other questions for determination, but those we have decided fully dispose of the case, and therefore it is not necessary to notice the remaining points made,

Finding no error in the record, the judgment is affirmed.

All concur.

MORRISON et al. v. HESS et al. (No. 21698.)

(Supreme Court of Missouri, in Banc.
May 24, 1921.)

1. Appeal and error ⬟781(4)—Investigation on merits required, though restrictions sought to be enforced have lapsed.

In suit by property owners to enjoin defendants from constructing a dwelling house in violation of restrictions in the deed under which defendants claim, though the Supreme Court could not issue or direct the lower court to issue a restraining order enjoining defendants, the restrictions having terminated, nevertheless, where plaintiffs have incurred liability on an injunction bond for damages, and become responsible for the costs of the litigation should the judgment below adverse to them be affirmed or the appeal dismissed, they still have an interest in the result of the litigation, and investigation on the merits is required.

2. Appeal and error ⬟488(1)—Appeal from merits in injunction suit suspended action on motion to assess damages.

In an injunction suit, an appeal from the merits suspended action on the motion to assess damages until the case is disposed of in the Supreme Court.

3. Covenants ⬟51(2)—Six double buildings held violative of restriction against construction of more than one dwelling on 50-foot front.

Six double buildings sought to be constructed on a lot having a frontage of 125 feet and a depth of 155 feet held to violate restriction in deed reciting that not more than one dwelling house might be constructed on a 50-foot front of the lot.

Woodson, J., dissenting.

Appeal from St. Louis Circuit Court; Victor H. Falkenhainer, Judge.

Suit by Robert W. Morrison and others against Herman Hess and others. From decree for defendants dismissing the bill, plaintiffs appeal. Decree reversed, and cause remanded, with directions to enter decree for plaintiffs, with damages and costs.

This action was commenced in the circuit court of the city of St. Louis, Mo., on October 8, 1916, by the above-mentioned plaintiffs, who are residents and owners of homes in city block 4864 of the city of St. Louis, Mo., to enjoin said defendants from constructing, upon a portion of said block 4864, a three-story apartment house, containing 36 separate and distinct apartments, in violation of the restrictions in the deed under which said defendants claim title, which recites that not more than one dwelling house may be constructed on the 50-foot front of said lot.

The defendants answered, partially admitting the allegations of petition, denying other averments therein, and pleading, by way of waiver and abandonment, that the above restriction was no longer in force. The reply is a general denial of the new matter contained in the answer.

The evidence shows that Selah Chamberlain, a resident of Ohio, was the owner of city block 4864, in St. Louis, Mo., bounded on the south by Maple avenue, running east and west, and by Chamberlain avenue on the north, also running east and west; that prior to May 31, 1887, said Chamberlain and wife sold all of the property in said block 4864 to various persons; and that each and every deed made by him contained the same covenants and restrictions as are recited in the deed to defendant Hess. On May 31, 1887, said Selah Chamberlain, who was then the owner of five or six tracts of land lying in the vicinity of said block 4864, filed a plat in the recorder's office, laying off said last-described tracts of land into lots and blocks, and designating the same as Chamberlain Park. The latter entirely surrounded block 4864 supra, except on the south.

It was stipulated and agreed at the trial:

"That all of the plaintiffs and the defendants own property in city block No. 4864 and hold title to their said property by and through deeds from Selah Chamberlain, and that all of the deeds through which all of the plaintiffs and all of the defendants held title contained the same covenants and restrictions as those contained in the deed from Selah Chamberlain and wife to Josiah A. Parker, * * * and that all of the property in city block No. 4864 is subject to the same restrictions, and is held under a common source of title, namely, Selah Chamberlain, and that all of the property in city block No. 4864, had been sold by said Selah Chamberlain prior to May 31, 1887."

The deed from Chamberlain and wife to Josiah A. Parker aforesaid is dated February 19, 1887, and, among other things, contains the following:

"The foregoing conveyance and grant is hereby declared to be subject to and limited by the following exceptions, reservations, conditions, and reversion: That neither said grantee nor any one claiming by, through, or under him prior to the last day of December, A. D. 1920: I. Shall construct or allow to be constructed on the premises above described any dwelling house less than two stories in height. II. Shall construct or allow to be constructed more than one such dwelling on each 50-foot front of said lot. III. Shall construct or allow to be constructed thereon any dwelling to cost less than $4,000 in cash, nor locate or erect such dwelling nearer than 30 feet to the line of the street on which such dwelling fronts. IV. Shall construct or allow to be constructed any stable, shed, or outhouse nearer to any public driveway than 100 feet. V. Shall construct or allow to be constructed or erected, or to exist, any nuisance, or

any livery stable or manufacturing establishment of any kind on said premises. VI. Shall construct or allow to be constructed, used, or occupied, any grocery store, barroom, or business place for the bargain and sale of any kind of merchandise on said premises."

It is conceded that defendant Hess, about 60 days before the trial below, bought from defendant Schwenker the following described property, to wit:

"A lot in Chamberlain Park in block No. 4864 of the city of St. Louis, having a front of 125 feet on the north line of Maple avenue, by a depth northwardly between parallel lines of 155 feet to a line, bounded on the west by a line 130 feet east of the east line of Clara avenue."

It is admitted that the above deed to Hess contains the same covenants, restrictions, etc., as are recited in the deed from Chamberlain to Parker aforesaid. It is also undisputed that defendant Hess knew of the above restrictions when he was negotiating for said property, and when he received his deed therefor.

It appears from the evidence that all of the property in said block 4864, except about 200 feet which was vacant, had been improved, before defendant Hess purchased his property, with high-class residences, owned by the plaintiffs; that each of said houses was used as a single family dwelling house, was more than two stories in height, and each cost from $10,000 to $15,000; that each house occupied 50 feet or more of ground, fronting on either Chamberlain avenue or Maple avenue; that all of said houses were built and used in accordance with the covenants and restrictions contained in the Parker deed supra. It does not appear from the evidence that buildings of any kind were ever constructed in said block 4864, other than single private dwelling houses.

Plaintiffs offered in evidence a copy of the plans for the construction of the proposed building of defendant Hess, which is marked Exhibit C, and, in order to avoid repetition, will be considered in the opinion with such matters as may be deemed of importance.

On April 7, 1919, the court below entered a decree in favor of defendants against all of the plaintiffs and dismissed the bill of latter. Plaintiffs, in due time, filed their motion for a new trial, which was overruled, and the cause duly appealed by them to this court.

S. T. G. Smith, of St. Louis, for appellants.

Frank X. Heimenz and H. A. & C. R. Hamilton, of St. Louis, for respondents.

RAILEY, C. (after stating the facts as above). [1] 1. Upon the issuing of a temporary restraining order by the trial court in this case, plaintiffs were required to, and did, give a $5,000 injunction bond. On November 29, 1916, the restraining order aforesaid was dissolved by the court, and the temporary injunction denied. On December 2, 1916, defendants filed herein a motion to assess the damages on the bond aforesaid. The restrictions in the deed to defendant Hess terminated on December 31, 1920. While this court could not issue,. or direct the lower court to issue, a restraining order enjoining defendants from constructing said building on block 4864 aforesaid, by reason of the termination of said restrictions, yet, as plaintiffs have incurred liability on said bond for damages, and have become responsible for the costs of this litigation, should the judgment below be affirmed, or the appeal dismissed, they, as well as the public, still have an interest in the result of the litigation, which requires at our hands an investigation of the merits. Civic League v. City of St. Louis, 223 S. W. loc. cit. 892, 893, and cases cited; Stegmann v. Weeke, 279 Mo. 131, 214 S. W. loc. cit. 135, 136; State ex rel. Bayha v. Philips, 97 Mo. 331, 10 S. W. 855, 3 L. R. A. 476; Long v. Charles A. Kaufman Co., 129 La. 430, 56 South. 357; Froemke et al. v. Parker et al., 39 N. D. 628, 169 N. W. 80; Peters v. Fisher, 50 Mich. 331 (15 N. W. 496); Southern Pac. Co. v. Int. Com. Commission, 219 U. S. 433, 31 Sup. Ct. 288, 55 L. Ed. 283; So. Pac. Term. Co. v. Int. Com. Commission, 219 U. S. 498, 31 Sup. Ct. 279, 55 L. Ed. 310; People ex rel. Spire v. General Committee of Republican Party, etc., 25 App. Div. 339, 49 N. Y. Supp. 723; Russell v. Crook County Court, 75 Or. 168, 145 Pac. 653, 146 Pac. 806.

[2] (a) The appeal from the merits suspended action on the motion to assess damages until the case is disposed of here. Cohn v. Lehman, 93 Mo. 584, 6 S. W. 267; J. & W. Ry. Co. v. Railroad Co., 135 Mo. loc. cit. 554, 555, 37 S. W. 540; State ex rel. v. Gates, 143 Mo. loc. cit. 68, 44 S. W. 739; Reed v. Bright, 232 Mo. loc. cit. 415, 134 S. W. 653; Brown v. Simpson, 201 S. W. loc. cit. 899, 900.

2. It is contended by respondents that the covenants and restrictions aforesaid are in derogation of the right of unrestricted use of property, and should not be extended by implication, or to include anything not plainly prohibited. We are cited, in support of this contention, to Zinn v. Sidler, 268 Mo. 689, 187 S. W. 1172, L. R. A. 1917A, 455; Kitchen v. Hawley, 150 Mo. App. 503, 131 S. W. 142; Pank v. Eaton, 115 Mo. App. 176, 89 S. W. 586; and Hartman v. Wells, 257 Ill. 167, 100 N. E. 500, Ann. Cas. 1914A, 901. On the other hand, appellants contend that the courts should give effect to the plain intention of the parties imposing restrictions on land, and not seek ingenious subtleties of interpretation by which to avoid the same. In support of this contention we are cited to Zinn v. Sidler, 268 Mo. 680, 187 S. W. 1172, L. R. A. 1917A, 455; Reed v. Hazard, 187 Mo. App. 547, 174 S. W. 111; Noel v. Hill, 158 Mo. App. 426,

138 S. W. 364; Sanders v. Dixon, 114 Mo. App. 229, 89 S. W. 577. Keeping in mind the contention of both parties supra, is there anything in the foregoing covenants and restrictions which precludes the defendant from building an apartment on his lot, provided it is constructed as other dwelling houses were required to be built, under the covenants and restrictions aforesaid?

It is possible that if the attention of the parties had been called thereto, in devising the plan for selling lots in block 4864, they might have excluded apartments therefrom, but they did not do so, and hence we conclude that, under the covenants and restrictions before us, the defendant had the right to construct a single building in the nature of a flat or apartment, subject to the same limitations as would apply to an ordinary dwelling house; that is to say, only one such dwelling should be permitted on each 50-foot front of the lot, subject to the other covenants and restrictions aforesaid. We are therefore of the opinion that the building of an apartment, within itself, would not be violative of the covenants and restrictions aforesaid, if constructed as above indicated.

(a) By parity of reasoning, we do not find anything in said covenants and restrictions which precludes the plural use of a single dwelling house or single apartment.

3. The real question, however, in this case, is not whether a single apartment built on the same terms and subject to the same restrictions as an ordinary dwelling house would violate the covenants and restrictions aforesaid, but whether the structure contemplated by defendant Hess was to include more than one dwelling on each 50-foot front of said lot. Mr. Hess bought 125 feet frontage on Maple avenue. Under the covenants and restrictions in his deed, he could only have constructed thereon two ordinary dwelling houses, as not more than one could be built on each 50-foot frontage of his lot. This does not mean that the covenants and restrictions aforesaid authorized him to build one dwelling house on each 50-foot front of his lot, and another of the same character on the same lot in the rear of the former building; that is to say, if his lot contained a 50-foot frontage on Maple avenue, and extended back to the alley, a depth of 155 feet, he could only build on the entire lot a single dwelling house or apartment. This proposition, to our mind, is too plain for argument. We are thus brought face to face with the main question in the case, to wit, whether the plan for the Hess apartment calls for more than one dwelling house on each 50-foot frontage of his lot.

4. It is undisputed that the plan for foregoing structure called for six double buildings, with an outside entrance into each of said double buildings; that after passing through each of the outside entrances aforesaid, into a hall inside of each double build-

ing, there was to be placed a separate door, leading from said hall into each of the buildings constituting said double building. In each of the single buildings constituting the double building the plan called for an apartment, composed of a living room, dining room, kitchen, bathroom, and another room. In other words, there was to be constructed on this lot of 125-foot frontage and 155 feet in depth six double buildings, with six outside entrances respectively, or the equivalent of twelve single buildings, with each containing, on the ground floor, a living room, dining room, bathroom, and another room, each to be used by separate families as a separate dwelling, without any connection whatever with each other, except through the general entrances aforesaid. The plan called for two of said double buildings to front on Maple avenue, and the remaining four double buildings were to open on a court in the rear of said 155 feet in depth by 125 feet in frontage. It further appears from said plan and the evidence that the masonry walls of said structure, between each of said double buildings, were to extend from the ground to the first floor of the respective ground floor buildings, and that 13-inch brick walls were to be constructed on the respective tops of said masonry walls, extending through the top of the building and 8 or 10 inches above the top of same.

Passing, for the present, the question as to whether each of said twelve ground floor buildings, composing the six double buildings aforesaid, constitute twelve separate and distinct dwelling houses, on a lot 125 feet by 155 feet, we are still confronted with the undisputed fact that said plan calls for the construction of at least six double buildings, two fronting on Maple avenue and four opening into the court in the rear, with six separate solid walls between the respective double buildings, with six separate outside entrances, one opening into each double building, without any intercommunication between said double buildings, and all six of same to be used as a dwelling place for 36 separate and distinct families.

[3] We held, under the facts of this case, that the six double buildings could not be legally constructed on the Hess lot with a frontage of 125 feet and a depth of 155 feet. We are of the opinion that no well-considered case can be found announcing a contrary view. The Belin and Darr Cases, relied on by defendants, do not authorize the construction of such an apartment as that called for by the foregoing plans.

5. The latter, as shown by plaintiffs' Exhibit C, provides that two of the double buildings heretofore mentioned were to front on Maple avenue, with a granitoid passway between them, leading through the court in the rear of said 155 feet. Each of the two double buildings on Maple avenue was to have an outside entrance leading into a hall, and from the latter separate doors were to be constructed opening into each of the single buildings composing said group of double buildings. If each of the buildings composing the double buildings on Maple avenue be considered a separate dwelling house, then we would have four separate dwelling houses, to be constructed on a frontage of 125 feet on Maple avenue, in the face of restriction II, supra, which provides that not more than one such dwelling house shall be constructed on each 50-foot front of said lot.

Respondents mainly rely upon the ruling in Belin v. Tyrel Investment Co., 273 Mo. 257, 200 S. W. 1059, L. R. A. 1918C, 869, and Morrison v. Darr, 201 S. W. 1147, in support of their contention that there was only a single dwelling house to be constructed on Maple avenue instead of four separate and distinct dwelling houses.

Judge Goode, in Sanders v. Dixon, 114 Mo. App. loc. cit. 253, 89 S. W. 585, very forcefully and clearly stated the law in respect to this matter as follows:

"In St. Louis and all other large cities, there are numerous dwelling houses built together in solid rows. Such structures often have continuous outside walls and foundations, but inside partition walls. They are always spoken of and regarded as different residences or dwellings; and sometimes they cover an entire block. It would be preposterous to call them one dwelling. Unquestionably a building of that kind was prohibited by the covenant in Dixon's deed; that is, putting more than one dwelling of the kind on a single lot. If it was not, what is the restriction worth? It might hinder the building of two detached residences, but two or three semidetached residences would be lawful; that is to say, houses having continuous outside walls and constituting more than one dwelling on a lot. We think such a structure is no less obnoxious to the covenant because designed for use as flats by different families.

"Defendants' counsel lay much stress on the division wall of Dixon's flats being a fire wall put in to comply with certain municipal regulations, and not a party wall. The city ordinances are not before us, but we do not regard the point as material. It is no party wall in the legal sense, because both houses belong to one owner. It hardly would be claimed that the houses are one dwelling if two men owned them. Are they any the less plural dwellings because owned by one man? A brick wall 13 inches thick, resting on a foundation 18 inches thick, entirely separating the two halves of a building 45 feet wide, each half of which is prepared for a home or homes, is, for all practical purposes, a partition wall between two dwellings, if not a party wall. It is as much a partition wall as the dividing wall between residences built in a solid row, each of two or more stories, but all the stories designed for the use of a single family. Our opinion is that the only ambiguity in the covenant is as to whether or not it prohibits one house planned for plural use as a dwelling. It certainly prohibits two houses planned for separate dwellings and divided by a partition wall which bisects the lot; and this is enough to sustain the plaintiffs' case against the continued use of Dixon's houses as now arranged."

The law, as declared by Judge Goode, supra, meets with our approval, and is directly applicable to the case before us. In our opinion, the conclusion reached by the court in Bolin v. Tyrel Investment Co., 273 Mo. 257, 200 S. W. 1059, L. R. A. 1918C, 869, and Morrison v. Darr, 201 S. W. 1147, is unsupported by either reason or authority in respect to above matter, and should be overruled.

6. In the Bolin Case, supra, the authorities relied upon by respondents are cited and discussed, while these relied on by appellants are fully considered and reviewed by Judge Goode, in Sanders v. Dixon, 114 Mo. App. 229, 89 S. W. 577. We have preferred to consider this case, and discuss the questions presented, along common sense lines, based upon sound reason, rather than upon the technical definitions of lexicographers, lawwriters of similar import, etc. We are clearly of the opinion that the structure which defendant Hess contemplated building on the lot contained in block 4864 aforesaid, if constructed as planned, would be violative of the covenants and restrictions contained in the deed under which he claims title. We are further satisfied that the principles of law announced in the Bolin and Darr Cases, in respect to foregoing matters, are not in accord with our views as to what the law ought to be under the circumstances of this case, and should not be followed. In view of the foregoing, we are of the opinion that the case should be certified to the court en banc.

7. Appellants have not sought to recover any damages by reason of the acts complained of in petition, and as the restrictions aforesaid terminated on the last day of December, 1920, we cannot issue an injunction to restrain the completion of said structure.

We therefore simply reverse and remand the cause, with directions to the trial court to set aside its former orders and judgments, and to enter a new decree defining the issues in favor of plaintiffs, and entering judgment in their behalf for nominal damages and for costs.

WHITE and MOZLEY, C. C., concur.

PER CURIAM. The foregoing opinion of RAILEY, C., is hereby adopted as the opinion of the court.

All concur, JAMES T. BLAIR, J., in paragraphs 3, 4, 5, 6, & 7, and result; except WOODSON, J., who dissents.

STATE v. HALL. (No. 22672.)

(Supreme Court of Missouri, Division No. 2. May 26, 1921. Motion for Rehearing Denied June 28, 1921.)

1. Criminal law ⬥⇒628(7)—Failure to indorse names of state's witnesses on indictment not ground for exclusion of testimony of defendant not prejudiced.

In a prosecution for murder, where a list of the state's witnesses was handed to defendant's counsel several days before the trial, and all lived near and had been subpœnaed long before, the state's failure to indorse their names on the information did not warrant exclusion of their testimony; defendant not being prejudiced.

2. Criminal law ⬥⇒1151—Refusal of continuance not disturbed where trial court did not abuse discretion.

On application for a continuance of a murder case on the ground defendant had been unable to find what certain state's witnesses, whose names were not indorsed on the information, would swear to, though their names were handed him several days before trial, it was for the trial court to determine whether defendant was prejudiced by failure to ascertain sooner who the witnesses were, and its ruling will not be disturbed where there is nothing to indicate that it abused its discretion.

3. Homicide ⬥⇒166(8)—Evidence of trouble between accused and wife involving deceased, admissible.

In a prosecution for murder, evidence that defendant had had trouble with his wife, from whom he was divorced, involving the name of the deceased as causing the separation, was admissible; threats of defendant against deceased having been sworn to in connection therewith.

4. Criminal law ⬥⇒1043(2)—Objections to evidence not stating specific ground not reviewable.

Objections to evidence which do not apprise the court of the specific ground thereof will not be reviewed.

5. Criminal law ⬥⇒1169(2) — Admission of hearsay testimony held harmless, in view of other testimony to same effect.

In a prosecution for murder, where it was shown that deceased's brother had a gun which was kept near defendant lived, the admission of testimony of a witness that the brother had told him the gun was his was harmless, though hearsay.

6. Criminal law ⬥⇒395—Articles found in search of defendant's house during his absence admissible.

In a prosecution for murder, evidence that boots with blood stains on them were found where defendant lived, also parts of a jumper which had been thrown into the stove and burned, was admissible, though search of the premises was made during defendant's absence; his presence not affecting the identity of the property or its significance as evidence.

7. Homicide ⊄═170, 174(6)—Evidence as to tracks and that accused wore clothing or possessed weapon similar to that used in commission of offense admissible.

It is always permissible, in proving homicide, to show tracks leading to and from the scene of the crime similar to those made by defendant, the probable identity of garments worn and weapons used by the murderer with those of defendant, and blood stains on garments which the evidence indicates were his, and it is not necessary to prove conclusively that the articles were his property; evidence tending to show that he wore such clothing or possessed a weapon similar to that used being sufficient to admit them in evidence for what they are worth.

8. Homicide ⊄═174(6)—Evidence as to identity of burned jumper found on defendant's premises with one worn by murderer admissible.

In a prosecution for murder, where defendant produced a jumper which he claimed he was wearing on the day of the murder, but the state's evidence showed that it had not been worn since it was washed, and could hardly have been worn that day, and no other jumper of defendant was accounted for, except the fragments of one found in a stove on his premises, there was no error in permitting evidence as to the identity of the latter with the one worn by the murderer.

9. Homicide ⊄═228(2), 253(2)—Circumstantial evidence held sufficient to prove corpus delicti and to convict of first degree murder.

Evidence, though circumstantial, *held* sufficient to sustain a verdict of guilty of first degree murder; the corpus delicti having been proven by the finding of deceased's body under circumstances indicating he had met death by a murderer's weapon.

Appeal from Circuit Court, Pemiscot County; Sterling H. McCarty, Judge.

Floyd Hall was convicted of first degree murder, and he appeals. Affirmed.

B. A. McKay, of Caruthersville, for appellant.

Jesse W. Barrett, Atty. Gen., and R. W. Otto and Robt. J. Smith, Asst. Attys. Gen., for the State.

WHITE, C. The appellant, on a trial in the circuit court of Pemiscot county, the 28th day of July, 1920, was convicted of murder in the first degree and his punishment assessed at imprisonment for life in the state penitentiary. He was charged with having killed one John White on the —— day of November, 1919. On one Friday in November, 1919, Floyd Hall, John White, and several other men and women were employed by one Rushing to pick cotton in a field which the evidence tends to show was about a quarter of a mile from the town of Cooter. In the afternoon of that day Floyd Hall and John White weighed in their cotton, and the defendant started for home. White, how-

ever, returned to the cotton field saying he wanted to make up his 200 pounds, after which he would go to a cornfield near and get some corn for his horses. He left the cotton field about sundown and started in the direction of the cornfield, which was separated from the cotton field by a hay patch and a swamp thicket. He was not afterwards seen alive except by his murderer. Next morning, Saturday, neighbors became apprehensive that something had happened to him; they instituted a search, and his body was found in the swamp thicket near the cornfield. He had 12 bullet holes in different parts of his body, apparently fired from both the front and the rear. The bullets were 22 caliber and fitted a 22 Winchester special rifle. Two gashes were found on his head, caused by a blow from some blunt instrument. There were indications of a struggle around the place where the body was found; the body had been dragged a short distance into the grass as if to hide it. All the surrounding circumstances indicated that the deceased had been murdered, probably the night before. A cotton sack and hat were found near the body.

The circumstances which tend to connect Hall with the crime are as follows: He was at work in the cotton field Saturday morning when the body was discovered and the crowd gathered around it, but he did not go with the others to where the body was; he immediately quit picking cotton and went away towards home. The tracks of gum boots, about No. 8, nearly new, were found around where the body was found, and those tracks led by a circuitous route toward the home of Hall's sister, Mrs. Alloyd, where Hall lived. A drainage ditch, called the "big ditch," ran through or near the swampy tract, and there was a bridge across the ditch in the direction of Cooter. Following the tracks along the ditch the witness found a 22-caliber Winchester special under some old stumps which had been thrown out of a field. The gun was empty. It was shown that Martin Hall, brother of defendant, possessed a 22 Winchester special which one or two witnesses had seen and one had borrowed; the brother and defendant lived at the same place. Red gum boots which could have made the tracks mentioned were found after the arrest of the defendant at the place where he was living, and blood was on one of the boots. The officer who went to arrest the defendant found him on the porch. Defendant immediately went into the house and the officer followed him through three rooms and got him at the back door. The officer told him he was charged with killing John White, and "he never uttered a word; just picked up a dipper of water and drank the dipper of water."

About 4 o'clock in the afternoon of the day

White disappeared the defendant was seen by two or three witnesses coming from the direction of Cooter. He had a rifle in his hands, had on a pair of dark pants, a jumper, and a pair of boots. The gun was similar to the gun introduced in evidence which had been found near the place of the homicide. The defendant at that time was going in the direction of the bridge which was near the scene of the crime. A search of the house where he lived revealed remnants of a jumper found in the ashes in a sheet iron stove, where it had been thrown and burned with the exception of a piece of a sleeve and a button, which were rescued and produced at the trial. No explanation was offered by defendant regarding the boots or the remnants of the jumper.

The former wife of the defendant testified that she was divorced from him in April, 1917, and about a year later the defendant sued White for alienation of his wife's affections. In a conversation in 1918, between Mrs. Hall and her former husband, he charged her with intention of marrying Mr. White, saying that he would get even with him. Other threats against White were shown to have been made by the defendant between the time of his separation from his wife and the homicide.

The defendant introduced evidence tending to show an alibi. Several persons swore to having seen him in and about the town of Cooter at different times during the afternoon of the day on which he was charged with having committed the murder. The defendant himself testified, accounting for his whereabouts during the afternoon and evening of that day. Dan Hall, brother of the defendant, testified and produced in evidence a gun, a 22 Winchester special, which he said was his brother Martin's gun. It was like the gun found near the body of the slain man, except that the latter was bent. He said that the gun which he produced had long been in the possession of his brother Martin. On cross-examination of this witness the state endeavored to show that he had bought the gun he produced at the trial since the homicide. The witness showed some confusion when questioned about his failure to produce the gun when search was being made.

The state, in contradiction of the testimony of Dan Hall, showed that he had failed to produce Martin's gun when it was first searched for at the house where his sister lived.

[1] I. The appellant has presented no brief nor assignment of errors here. The record shows that on Monday, July 26, 1920, counsel for the state asked leave of court to indorse the names of certain witnesses on the information. The defendant filed no motion to quash the information for failure to contain the indorsement of such witnesses, but contented himself with objecting to the indorsement of the names. The objection was overruled and the ruling is assigned as error in the motion for new trial. The witnesses lived around Cooter, 20 miles from the place of the trial. Some of them had been subpœnaed long previously, and the complete list had been handed to defendant's counsel Friday, the 23d, before. The failure to indorse the names of all witnesses for the state on an indictment for a felony charge will not warrant the exclusion of the testimony of such witnesses, unless it appears that the defendant is prejudiced in some way in the conduct of his trial by the ruling. State v. Stegner, 276 Mo. loc. cit. 438, 207 S. W. 826; State v. Wilson, 223 Mo. loc. cit. 187, 122 S. W. 671. The trial court apparently discovered no such prejudicial result to the defendant, and this court finds no error in the ruling.

[2] II. After objection to the indorsement of the names of the witnesses was overruled, appellant filed an application for continuance, setting up that while he had been given a list of the witnesses on Friday, the 23d, such witnesses lived 20 miles from the scene of the homicide, and the defendant had been unable to find what such witnesses would swear to, although he had made an effort to do so, and he was therefore unprepared to meet the testimony of such witnesses. About a dozen witnesses were included in the list. Some of them already had been subpœnaed. From an examination of the record we find that only three of the witnesses mentioned in the list, not previously subpœnaed, testified in the case; the others were not called. Upon examination of their testimony it appears they lived in or near Cooter; it was not shown there was any difficulty in communication between that place and the county seat. The trial proceeded on the 27th, four days after the list was handed to the defendant. It was for the trial court to determine from the facts before him whether the defendant was prejudiced by failure to ascertain sooner who those witnesses were. This court will not disturb the ruling in that respect, because nothing appears which indicates that the trial court abused its discretion in refusing to grant the continuance. State v. Webster, 152 Mo. loc. cit. 90, 53 S. W. 423; State v. Cain, 247 Mo. loc. cit. 705, 153 S. W. 1039.

[3] III. It was shown by the testimony that the defendnat had been divorced from his wife; that he had trouble with her, which she said, involved the name of the deceased as causing the separation. This was objected to, and error is assigned to its admission. Some threats of the defendant were sworn to in connection with that matter. The evidence was admissible. State v. Keller, 263 Mo. loc. cit. 558, 559, 174 S. W. 67.

[4] IV. Objection was made to several items of evidence offered by the state and errors assigned in the motion for new trial. Several of these objections were that the

evidence was "wholly immaterial," or, "We object to that," or, "We object; no light on this matter." It has often been ruled that objections of that character, without apprising the trial court of the specific ground of objection, will not be reviewed in this court. State ex rel. v. Diemer, 255 Mo. loc. cit. 346–351, 164 S. W. 517; Heinbach v. Heinbach, 274 Mo. loc. cit. 315, 202 S. W. 1123.

[5] A witness was permitted to state that Martin Hall told him the gun, a 22 Winchester rifle, which the evidence indicated was at the place where Martin Hall and Floyd Hall lived, was Martin Hall's gun. This was objected to because hearsay. It had been otherwise shown that Martin Hall had a gun which the evidence tends to show was kept at the place where his sister, Mrs. Alloyd, and the defendant lived, so that the defendant was not harmed by the introduction of the testimony.

[6, 7] The evidence offered to show that red gum boots with blood stains on them were found at the place where defendant lived, and parts of a jumper which had been thrown into the stove and burned, of which one sleeve, one piece of sleeve, and a button were saved and produced at the trial, was all objected to because search of the premises was made when the defendant was not present— an objection of no importance because his presence would not affect one way or the other the identity of the property or its significance as evidence. As to the jumper, it was further objected that it was not identified as the jumper the defendant had on. It is always permissible, in making out a case of homicide, to show tracks leading to and from the scene of the crime similar to those made by defendant, the probable identity of garments worn and weapons used by the murderer with those of defendant, and blood stains on garments which the evidence indicates were his. State v. Barrington, 198 Mo. 110, 95 S. W. 235; State v. Jeffries, 210 Mo. loc. cit. 324, 325, 109 S. W. 614, 14 Ann. Cas. 524; State v. Prunty, 276 Mo. loc. cit. 375, 208 S. W. 91; 8 R. C. L. p. 181; 2 Wharton on Criminal Evidence, §§ 518c, 518e, and 778. It is not necessary to prove conclusively that the article of clothing or weapons connected with the crime were the property of the defendant. If the evidence tends to show the accused wore articles of clothing or possessed a weapon similar to those which the evidence indicates were associated with the crime, it is sufficient to admit them in evidence for what they are worth. State v. Barrington, 198 Mo. loc. cit. 110, 111, 95 S. W. 235; State v. Rasco, 239 Mo. loc. cit. 578, 579, 144 S. W. 449; State v. Reeves, 195 S. W. loc. cit. 1027.

[8] When the sheriff went to arrest him, the defendant produced a jumper which he claimed he was wearing that day, but the state's evidence showed that the jumper produced had not been worn since it was washed, and could hardly have been the jumper worn that day; no other jumper of the defendant was accounted for except the fragments found in the stove. There was no error in permitting the evidence.

[9] V. It was alleged by the defendant in his motion for new trial that the state failed to make out a case of first degree murder on circumstantial evidence. The corpus delicti was clearly proven. The dead man was found under circumstances which indicated most clearly that he had met his death by a murderous weapon in the hands of some person. State v. Cox, 264 Mo. loc. cit. 413, 175 S. W. 50; State v. Young, 237 Mo. loc. cit. 177, 140 S. W. 873; State v. Schyhart, 199 S. W. loc. cit. 211. While all the evidence to connect the defendant with the commission of the crime was purely circumstantial, there are many cases in the books where serious crimes were charged and the conviction sustained upon circumstantial evidence no more cogent or clear in connecting the defendant with the crime than the evidence in this case. State v. Concelia, 250 Mo. loc. cit. 421–424, 157 S. W. 778; State v. Barrington, 198 Mo. 110, 95 S. W. 235; State v. Cox, 264 Mo. 408, 175 S. W. 50; State v. Schyhart, 199 S. W. loc. cit. 212. In this case there was evidence tending to show a motive in the enmity engendered on account of the separation of the defendant from his wife. Threats of defendant against the deceased were shown. The circumstances of his appearance in the neighborhood, going toward the scene of the crime just before it was committed, wearing gum boots and a jumper and carrying a rifle similar to the one found, and the finding of the burnt jumper and the boots with blood on them at the place where the defendant lived, the boots similar to those which must have made the tracks of the murderer; the similarity of the gun used in the commission of the crime to the one defendant carried and the one to which he had access at home; the defendant's demeanor when the body was found and when he was arrested; the entire absence of any other explanation of how White met his death; all form a strong chain of circumstances.

Reluctant as courts are to convict of so grave a crime as murder on circumstantial evidence, we are not prepared to say that the evidence was insufficient to sustain the verdict of guilty, or to justify the trial court in allowing such verdict to stand.

The judgment accordingly is affirmed.

RAILEY and MOZLEY, CC., concur.

PER CURIAM. The foregoing opinion by WHITE, C., is adopted as the opinion of the court.

All concur.

ABNERTHY v. SCHEMBRA et al. (No. 2817.)

(Springfield Court of Appeals. Missouri. May 3, 1921. Rehearing Denied June 20, 1921.)

1. Tender ⟂19(2)—Tender of nominal damages admission of breach of bond.

In an action on an appeal bond, defendant's tender of nominal damages admitted a breach, so that the only question was whether the bond covered the items sued for.

2. Appeal and error ⟂1234(1)—Sureties on appeal bond liable only for elements of damage covered by its terms.

The sureties on an appeal bond are liable only for the elements of damages that are clearly covered by its terms.

3. Appeal and error ⟂1234(7)—In action on appeal bond in unlawful detainer suit interest held not recoverable.

Where, in an unlawful detainer suit in which no damages or rents were assessed, the defendant against whom judgment was rendered in both justice and circuit courts gave a bond conditioned that he should appeal with due diligence, and should pay all rents and profits, damages, and costs that might be adjudged against him, plaintiff in the unlawful detainer suit, the obligee of the bond, cannot, the appeal having been dismissed by defendant, recover as damages interest which he forgave because his purchaser was kept out of possession.

Appeal from Circuit Court, Lawrence County; C. L. Henson, Judge.

Action by B. T. Abnerthy against Joseph Schembra and others. From a judgment for defendants, plaintiff appealed. Affirmed.

D. S. Mayhew, of Monett, for appellant. Carr McNatt, of Aurora, and W. Cloud, of Pierce City, for respondents.

COX, P. J. Action on appeal bond executed by respondents. Appellants brought an unlawful detainer suit against respondent Schembra before a justice of the peace in Lawrence county, in which judgment went for plaintiff for possession of the land sued for, but no damages or rents were assessed. The defendant Schembra appealed to the circuit court, where the plaintiff again recovered judgment for possession of the land, but no damages or rents were assessed. From this judgment the defendant appealed to this court, and he and his sureties executed the appeal bond sued on in this case. Later that appeal was voluntarily dismissed and all costs paid. This suit was then instituted.

The bond sued on in this case contained the following conditions:

"Now, therefore, if the said Joseph Schembra, appellant, shall prosecute his appeal with due diligence and effect in said appellate court and without delay, neither commit nor suffer

to be committed waste on the premises whereof restitution is adjudged, and shall pay all rents and profits, damages, and costs that may be adjudged against him, and shall perform such judgment as shall be given by the said appellate court in the premises and such judgment as the said appellate court shall direct the circuit court of Lawrence county, Mo., aforesaid, to give, and in case the judgment first aforesaid of the last-named court, or any part thereof, shall, by the Springfield Court of Appeals aforesaid, or any appellate court to which this cause may be removed, be affirmed, if, then, the said appellant shall comply with and perform the same so far as it may be affirmed, and shall pay all damages and costs which may be awarded against the said appellant by the said appellate court, then this obligation shall be null and void; otherwise it shall remain in full force and effect."

The defendant Schembra was a tenant of plaintiff on the land in question and, as the court found, held over after the termination of his lease. Plaintiff sold the land and was required to bring the unlawful detainer suit to get possession so he could deliver it to the purchaser. This was in July or August, and the purchaser wanted possession so he could sow wheat on the land; but, as he did not get it immediately, the deed and $1,000 of the purchase money were placed in escrow to await the delivery of the possession. Possession was not secured until after the dismissal of the appeal in the Court of Appeals the following March. By reason of this delay, the plaintiff waived the collection of $437.50, the interest which accrued during the time plaintiff and the purchaser were kept out of possession of the land after the judgment in plaintiff's favor in the justice court.

In this case the plaintiff alleged as a breach of the bond the failure of defendant Schembra to prosecute his appeal with diligence and effect, and asked damages on account of being kept out of possession of the land by the appeal of defendant and thereby losing the growing of a wheat crop. During the trial he was given leave to amend by adding a demand for the $437.50, interest on the purchase price which he claimed he had been required to release in order to consummate the sale of his land.

The defendant tendered $1 and all costs accrued up to the time of the filing of the answer as nominal damages, but denied liability for any greater sum. The trial was had before the court, who found for defendant, and plaintiff appealed to this court.

[1, 2] The defendant, by tendering nominal damages, admitted a breach of the bond, and the only question involved here is whether or not the appeal bond covered the items sued for. We do not think that it does. It is familiar law that, in a case of this kind on condition broken, the sureties on the bond are only liable for such elements of damage as

are clearly covered by its terms. Tittman v. Green, 108 Mo. 22, 18 S. W. 885.

[3] Provision in this bond which it is contended authorizes recovery for the character of damages sued for in this case is the obligation on the part of Schembra, the principal in the bond, to "pay all rents and profits, damages, and costs that may be adjudged against him." That language evidently means rents and profits and damages and costs that might be adjudged against him in the action then pending and in which the appeal bond was given. "Damages that may be adjudged against him" could not, by any reasonable construction, be held to mean damages that might accrue but which were not considered and not adjudged in the case then pending.

In the case pending, and in which the bond in suit was given, no damages or rents had been assessed in either the justice or circuit courts, and none were thereafter assessed in the Court of Appeals. The case of Bernecker v. Miller, 44 Mo. 126, was a case similar to this, with one very important exception. In that case the value of the rents had been assessed at the trial in the justice court, and the Supreme Court there held that the bond covered the rents that accrued up to the time that restitution was made. In the instant case the damage claimed is not the value of rents, but damages of a special nature arising out of the fact that plaintiff was kept out of possession by the appeal and lost the opportunity to sow wheat on the land and lost interest on the purchase price of the land because he could not deliver possession to a party to whom the land had been sold.

In Hastings v. Hennessey, 58 Mo. App. 205, the value of rents was assessed in the justice court, and it was there held that the appeal bond given on appeal from the circuit court to the Court of Appeals covered these rents up to the time of restitution. Without any reference to these cases, the Supreme Court, in Bauer v. Cabanne, 105 Mo. 110, 16 S. W. 521, held that a bond with terms similar to the one in this case did not cover damages and rents assessed in the justice court, and there said that if the respondent wished to have these items included in the bond he should have seen to it that the bond provided for "the damages, rents, profits, and costs that are or may be adjudged against defendant," and since such rents and damages were not nominated in the bond they were not covered by it and could not be recovered in an action on the bond. That case on the facts was a much stronger case for plaintiff than the facts in this case made for appellant here. The case of Dorriss v. Carter, 67 Mo. 544, was a suit on an injunction bond. The injunction was dissolved, but no damages assessed at the time of dissolution. An action was then brought on the injunction bond, and it was

there held, in effect, that damages, to be recoverable on the bond, must have been assessed at or after the dissolution of the injunction and in the injunction suit, but could not be ascertained and assessed in the first instance in a suit on the injunction bond.

Whether or not an appeal bond could be so written as to cover such items as are sought to be recovered in this case it is not necessary for us to determine, but we are clearly of the opinion that the bond sued on in this case does not cover them.

The judgment is affirmed.

FARRINGTON and BRADLEY, JJ., concur.

STEVENS v. KANSAS CITY LIGHT & POWER CO. et al. (No. 14058.)

(Kansas City Court of Appeals. Missouri. June 18, 1921.)

Judgment ⬟342(1)—Judgment in violation of stipulation may be set aside after expiration of term.

While, ordinarily, a judgment cannot be set aside after expiration of the term at which it was rendered, yet, where a judgment dismissing an action pursuant to a stipulation between the parties assessed costs against defendant, though there was no such provision, it may be set aside after expiration of the term at which it was rendered, pursuant to Rev. St. 1919, § 1552; the lack of power to render such judgment appearing on the face of the record.

Appeal from Circuit Court, Jackson County; Daniel E. Bird, Judge.

"Not to be officially published."

Action by Lulu May Stevens against the Kansas City Light & Power Company and others. On stipulation for dismissal judgment for costs was rendered in favor of plaintiff, and thereafter the same was vacated, judgment for defendants being entered, and plaintiff appeals. Judgment affirmed.

C. W. Prince, E. C. Hamilton, E. A. Harris, and James N. Berry, all of Kansas City, for appellant.

John H. Lucas, William C. Lucas, and Ludwick Graves, all of Kansas City, for respondents.

TRIMBLE, P. J. Plaintiff brought suit to recover damages for the wrongful death of her husband through the alleged negligence of the defendant. While it was pending said suit was compromised, and the parties, on the 1st of February, 1919, entered into a stipulation reciting that—

"The above-entitled cause is hereby dismissed by the plaintiff, with prejudice to the institution of any further action against the defendant or the presentation of any claim arising out of or from the matter complained of in the petition filed herein."

On the 21st day of February, 1919, it being a part of the January, 1919, term of court, the plaintiff presented said stipulation to the court, and thereupon an entry was made wherein the dismissal by plaintiff was recited, and it was—

"Further ordered and adjudged by the court that the same [said suit] be and the same is hereby dismissed, *and that plaintiff have and recover of and from the defendants all costs herein incurred, and let execution issue therefor.*"

On the 15th of April, 1919, it being a part of the March term of that year, defendant filed a motion to set aside said judgment for the reason that—

The stipulation "did not provide for any judgment of costs against the defendant company, and that the entry of judgment in relation thereto is erroneous and void, for the reason that the court was without authority to render a judgment against* this defendant under the terms and conditions of said stipulation."

Thereafter the court sustained said motion, and the former judgment was vacated and another judgment was entered in accordance with the stipulation, reciting that plaintiff filed a stipulation for a dismissal of the cause, and of all claim arising out of the matter therein, with prejudice to the institution of any further action, and that "the said cause is hereby dismissed, with prejudice to the institution of any further action or action(s) upon the part of the plaintiff against the defendant company."

It will be observed that the second judgment is in effect the same as the former, except that the judgment as to costs, /which we have italicized, was eliminated.

Plaintiff appealed from this action sustaining said motion and vacating the former judgment as to costs. Her contention is that the term at which said former judgment was rendered had gone by, and that therefore the court could not set it aside on motion, and cites Sowers v. Ingram, 74 Mo. 193, in support of her contention. The case is not applicable here. In that case the plaintiff had brought suit for $500, but the defendant had a set-off and plaintiff recovered only $1, and the statute provided that where the plaintiff recovered an amount below the jurisdiction of the court the costs should . be adjudged against him, unless the court found that plaintiff, when he brought the suit, had reasonable grounds to believe that he was justly entitled to recover an amount within the jurisdiction of the court. The judgment rendered gave plaintiff a judgment for the costs. At the next term the court set aside the judgment and rendered another to the same effect, including therein, however, the

finding that plaintiff had reasonable grounds to believe he was entitled to recover an amount within the jurisdiction of the court. The first judgment was conclusive of the fact that the court so found, and the court at a subsequent term had no power to inquire into or disturb the finality of the judgment in that regard. In that case the court had power to render the judgment for costs which it did render, if it found a certain fact, and as it rendered such judgment it is presumed that such fact was found, and, indeed, the judgment was conclusive of that matter.

But the situation in the case at bar is wholly different. Here, under the terms of the stipulation wherein plaintiff dismissed the suit, there was nothing on which the court could render a judgment against defendant for costs, and the lack of power to render such a judgment appeared upon the face of the record. There is no question but that, as a rule, the power of the court to set aside a judgment is limited to the term at which it is rendered. But such rule is not without its limitations and exceptions. It can be done on motion filed after the term, but within three years, where there is irregularity or want of jurisdiction in the rendering of the judgment sought to be set aside, and such is apparent upon the face of the record. Section 1552, R. S. 1919; Clowser v. Noland, 72 Mo. App. 217; Reed Bros. v. Nicholson, 93 Mo. App. 29; Cross v. Gould, 131 Mo. App. 585, 110 S. W. 672. A judgment in certain instances can also be set aside on motion in the nature of a writ of error coram nobis, but we need not go into that in this case.

The judgment is affirmed.

The other Judges concur.

BOTHMANN v. METROPOLITAN LIFE INS. CO. (No. 17242.)

(St. Louis Court of Appeals. Missouri.
May 3, 1921. Rehearing Denied
June 7, 1921.)

1. Insurance ⬉367(1) — Provision for paid-up insurance held unconditional.

Where a life policy provided that upon lapse after payment of three full years' premiums the owner, "provided there be no indebtedness hereon," upon request should be entitled either to the cash surrender value, to have the insurance continued for the original amount as term insurance, or continued for a reduced amount as paid-up insurance, and that, if the owner should not within three months from default exercise the first two options, the insurance should be continued for a reduced amount of paid-up insurance, and that "any indebtedness to the company under this policy" should reduce the amount of paid-up insurance, the provision for paid-up insurance was unconditional within Rev. St. 1919, § 6154, so that the nonforfeiture law (Rev. St. 1909, §§ 6946-6949) did not apply to continue the policy for the full amount as term insurance on failure to pay the seventh annual premium, where there had been no designation of option, and on insured's death thereafter recovery could be had only for the amount of paid-up insurance, notwithstanding there was sufficient reserve to have purchased term insurance for the full amount up to the time of death; for the provision that indebtedness to the company would reduce the amount of paid-up insurance negatived the idea that the right to paid-up insurance was conditioned on there being no indebtedness against the policy.

2. Insurance ⊂═146(3)—Ambiguous provision should be construed in favor of insured.

Ambiguous provisions in life policies will be construed in favor of the insured, but, before the rule can be applied, the ambiguity must be located.

3. Insurance ⊂═146(3)—Where provisions of policy are plain, the court can indulge in no forced construction.

Where the provisions of a life policy are plain, the court can indulge in no forced construction to cast a liability on the insurer which it has not assumed.

4. Costs ⊂═42(3)—Tender to stop running of costs must be deposited in court.

Though defendant tendered to plaintiff the amount which she was entitled to recover, yet, where the tender was not kept good by deposit in court after commencement of the action, costs cannot under Rev. St. 1919, §§ 1711, 1712, be assessed against plaintiff.

5. Interest ⊂═50—Tender stops running of interest.

Where defendant tendered to plaintiff the full amount which she was entitled to recover, but it was refused, and action was brought, such tender had, under Rev. St. 1919, § 1712, the effect of preventing the running of interest.

Appeal from St. Louis Circuit Court; John W. Calhoun, Judge.

"Not to be officially published."

Action by Emma Bothmann against the Metropolitan Life Insurance Company. From a judgment for plaintiff for an alleged insufficient amount, she appeals. Reversed and remanded, with directions.

James J. O'Donohoe, of St. Louis, for appellant.

Fordyce, Holliday & White, of St. Louis, for respondent.

BIGGS, C. This action upon a life insurance policy by the beneficiary, Emma Bothmann, formerly wife, but now widow, of the insured William Bothmann, resulted in a judgment in favor of plaintiff for an alleged insufficient amount, from which she prosecutes an appeal.

We deduce from the record the following facts, which are not disputed:

Defendant, a life insurance company, organized under the laws of the state of York, and doing business in Missouri, to William Bothmann on the 30th of July, 1912, a policy of insurance in the of $1,000, in consideration of the payment of an annual premium of $15.19 due on the day of July in each year. Six annual premiums were paid on the policy, the last the 30th day of July, 1917. The premium due on July 30, 1918, was not paid, nor any premiums thereafter paid on the policy. Emma Bothmann, plaintiff, was the wife of the insured and the beneficiary of the policy. William Bothmann the insured, died about December 3, 1918.

On July 30, 1918, the date of the default, the policy had acquired a reserve or value under the Combined Experience Table of Mortality at 4 per cent. per annum of $60. In addition said policy was entitled to a dividend of $2.97, which dividend had a reserve value of 87 cents, which gave to the policy a total reserve or net value of $43.47, three-fourths of said reserve amounts to a sum of $32.60, which latter sum used as net single premium for temporary insurance under the nonforfeiture laws of Missouri would purchase temporary extended insurance for the full amount, plus dividend additions, for 4 years and 164 days from the date of the lapse, or, if applied to the purchase of paid-up insurance according to the Combined Experience Table of Mortality with 4 per cent. interest, would secure a paid-up value of $112.86. The values guaranteed by the policy are founded on the American Experience Table of Mortality at 3½ per cent. interest, which gives a greater reserve or net value than calculated under the nonforfeiture statutes, which uses the rate of 4 per cent. per annum.

At the date of the lapse, July 30, 1918, the policy under its terms had a cash value of $35, and was then entitled to a dividend of $2.97, making a total value of $37.97, which applied to the purchase of paid-up insurance according to the tables at 3½ per cent. interest, secured a paid-up value of $112.97 which was also greater than the paid-up insurance provided for by the nonforfeiture statutes.

It was further conceded that the policy was never surrendered to the defendant at its home office within three months from July 30, 1918, for cash surrender value for endorsement for term insurance or paid-up insurance, as provided under the head of "Options on Surrender or Lapse" in said policy. And it was admitted upon the death of William Bothmann the defendant tendered plaintiff the sum of $112.97, which tender was refused.

No question arises over the due notice or plaintiff's claim or over the question of proofs of death.

It appeared that prior to the institution of the suit plaintiff had demanded of defendant payment of the full sum of the policy (less forborne premium and interest thereon), and defendant disclaimed liability under said policy beyond the sum of $112.97, the sum tendered.

The only question involved in the case is stated by the plaintiff's counsel thus: Does the policy contain a provision "for the unconditional commutation of the policy for nonforfeitable paid-up insurance" within the meaning of section 6949, R. S. 1909, now section 6154, R. S. Mo. 1919? Or, as stated by defendant's counsel: There is but one question in the case, namely: Is the plaintiff entitled to have the nonforfeiture law of Missouri, being sections 6946-6949, R. S. Mo. 1909, applied to this policy and to have the same declared carried in extended insurance beyond the date of the death of the insured, or does the policy contain such a provision for unconditional commutation for nonforfeitable paid-up insurance that it is removed from the operation of the nonforfeiture law and the liability of the company limited under the policy to the payment of said paid-up insurance?

[1] As heretofore shown, it was admitted that, if the nonforfeiture statutes apply to the policy, there was sufficient reserve value to carry the same in extended insurance beyond the date of the death of William Bothmann. And it was further admitted that the value of the paid-up insurance offered by the company under the policy is greater than that provided for in the nonforfeiture law.

Section 6949, R. S. 1909, now section 6154, R. S. 1919, provides that the preceding sections (nonforfeiture statutes) shall not be applicable in the event the policy shall contain a provision for an unconditional surrender value at least equal to the net single premium, for the temporary insurance provided for in said sections, or for the unconditional commutation of the policy for nonforfeitable paid-up insurance, etc.

The question presented involves a construction of the policy in suit, the material parts of which are these:

"*Options on Surrender or Lapse.*—Upon failure to pay any premium or any part thereof when due, this policy, except as otherwise provided herein, shall immediately lapse. If however, the lapse occur after three full years' premiums shall have been paid, the owner hereof, *provided there be no indebtedness hereon,* shall, *upon written request* filed with the company at its home office, together with the *presentation of this policy* for legal surrender or for indorsement within three months from the due date of premium in default, be entitled to one of the following options (italics ours):

"First. A cash surrender value, etc. * * *
"Second. To have the insurance continued in force for its original amount as term insurance from due date of premium in default.
"Third. To have the insurance continued for

231 S.W.—64

a reduced amount of nonparticipating paid-up endowment insurance, * * * which paid-up insurance shall have an increasing cash surrender value equal to the full reserve at the date of the surrender, or a loan value up to the limit of the cash surrender value, etc. * * * *"

Immediately following the foregoing provisions is this paragraph:

"*If the owner shall not, within three months from due date of premium in default, surrender this policy to the company at its home office for a cash surrender value or for indorsement for term insurance, or for paid-up insurance as provided in the above options, the insurance shall be continued for a reduced amount of paid-up insurance as provided in the third option.*" (Italics ours.)

Then follows a provision that the values of the options shall be the entire reserve according to the American Experience Mortality Table with interest at 3½ per cent.

Then follows a provision that:

"Any indebtedness to the company under this policy will be deducted from the cash value; and such indebtedness will also reduce the amount of paid-up insurance or the amount continued as term insurance and any pure endowment payable at the end of the endowment term, in such proportion as the indebtedness bears to the cash value at due date of premium in default."

If William Bothmann, the insured, at the time he defaulted in the payment of his premium on the 30th day of July, 1919, was invested under the terms of the policy with an unconditional right to have a paid-up policy, the net value of which was equal to that provided by the nonforfeiture statutes, then the judgment of the lower court was correct in holding that his beneficiary was only entitled to recover the sum of $112.97, the amount tendered her as paid-up insurance under the policy, and which it is conceded was greater than the amount provided for in the statutes. If the terms of such policy did not give to the assured at the time of default the right unconditionally to have such paid-up insurance, then the judgment below is erroneous, and the nonforfeiture statutes apply to the policy, and in that event it is conceded plaintiff is entitled to recover the full amount of the policy under said statutes less the forborne premium with interest thereon.

The first paragraph under the heading "Options on Surrender or Lapse," standing alone, would indicate that before the insured could have the benefit of any of the options it must appear that there was no indebtedness to the company; that insured should file written request with the company within three months after default before being entitled to one of the options and should also present the policy. And, if this were all, the insured's rights to paid-up insurance on default would be conditional. Whittaker v. Ins. Co., 133 Mo. App. 664, loc. cit. 670, 114 S. W. 53; Paschedag v. Ins. Co., 155 Mo. App. 185, loc.

cit. 196, 134 S. W. 102; McLeod v. Ins. Co., 190 Mo. App. 653, 176 S. W. 234.

However, it is elemental that the contract must be construed as a whole, and not by considering one provision alone. Immediately following the provision for the options appears the following stipulation:

"If the owner shall not, within three months from due date of premium in default, surrender this policy to the company at its home office for a cash surrender value or for indorsement for term insurance or for paid-up insurance, as provided in the above options, *the insurance shall be continued for a reduced amount of paid-up insurance as provided in the third option.*" (Italics ours.)

By the use of the word "if" plaintiff's counsel would construe this provision to mean that the insured could have the benefit of paid-up insurance only in the event he within three months from default surrendered his policy to the company for indorsement for term insurance or paid-up insurance, etc. If such was a fair construction, the right of insured would be clearly conditional. The paragraph in our judgment clearly means that, unless the owner shall within three months exercise his right to have the benefit of one of the options provided, he shall continue to have the benefit of that third which is paid-up insurance. Under such a stipulation insured's right to paid-up insurance is not conditional because he has it in any event from the time of default in premium payment. He may reject that right and choose another by taking certain steps. If he fails within the time, his right to paid-up insurance continues, and that right is, we think, without any condition.

Suppose the reserve on the policy was insufficient to carry the policy in extended insurance for the full amount until the owner's death, and suppose at the time of the default in the premium payment there was a loan on the policy in an amount not equal to the reserve, and plaintiff had sued, claiming the right to recover paid-up insurance under the third option; we would construe the policy, as this court did the policy in Stark v. Ins. Co., 176 Mo. App. 574, 159 S. W. 758, to mean that the insured was in any event entitled to such paid-up insurance as the reserve less the amount of the loan would purchase under the terms of the policy.

The specific provision that any indebtedness to the company under the policy will be deducted from the cash value; and such indebtedness will also reduce the amount of paid-up insurance or the amount continued as term insurance, and any pure endowment payable at the end of the endowment term, etc., clearly negatives the idea that the right to paid-up insurance was conditioned on there being no indebtedness against the policy.

As was stated by this court in the Stark Case, supra, in construing a provision somewhat similar:

"To adopt the construction contended for by appellant [Insurance Company] would mean that, although many premiums have been paid on such a policy, nevertheless, in case of default, no right to paid-up insurance exists if the insured is indebted to the company in any amount, however small. Had it been the insurer's intention to thus forfeit all right to paid-up insurance it would have been easy indeed to employ language to clearly and unequivocally express that intention. It is not so expressed in the contract before us, and an insurer will seek in vain to have the courts apply to such a contract as this, a construction that would lead to such absurd consequences."

Plaintiff's counsel cite a number of Missouri authorities, but we do not think they are controlling here. For instance in the case of Cravens v. Ins. Co., 148 Mo. 583, 50 S. W. 519, 53 L. R. A. 305, 71 Am. St. Rep. 628, it was held that the policy provisions for paid-up insurance after the lapse for nonpayment of premiums were conditional, as the policy required the owner to surrender it and demand paid-up insurance within six months from the date of lapse. Unless such surrender was made the owner would fail to obtain paid-up insurance.

Likewise in the case of Smith v. Ins. Co., 173 Mo. 329, 72 S. W. 935, the provision was declared to be conditional, in that a certain value was payable only on condition that it be applied for within three months from the default in the payment of premium.

And in McLeod v. Ins. Co., 190 Mo. App. 653, 176 S. W. 234, relied on by plaintiff, the policy provided that after default the owner could not have the benefit of the surrender value at once, but only at the subsequent anniversary of the issue of the policy. Therefore it was held that this provision made it a conditional right to have such surrender value in that its payment was postponed until a subsequent anniversary of the issue of the policy. In that case the policy further provided that the owner would only be entitled to the benefits provided he made surrender of his policy within three months.

Also the policy in the case of Paschedag v. Ins. Co., 155 Mo. App. 185, 134 S. W. 102, differed from the policy in the present case, in that in the Paschedag Case the policy required surrender and release of the policy within six months from the date of default as a condition precedent to obtaining a paid-up policy.

And the case of Whittaker v. Ins. Co., 133 Mo. App. 664, 114 S. W. 53, referred to by plaintiff's counsel, is distinguishable from this case in that the policy in the Whittaker Case providing for automatic paid-up insurance stipulated that such right would not accrue to the owner in the event there was an unpaid loan on the policy thus rendering the right conditional. The policy in the Whittaker Case did not contain a provision like the policy in the instant case which gives to the owner the right to have paid-up insurance in any event, and which also provides for any indebtedness to the company to be deducted from the amount due under the policy.

We have been cited to no case and have found none where provisions like those in the present policy have been construed, but the following cases may be referred to as throwing some light on the construction given to the policy herein; Stark v. Insurance Co., supra; Price v. Ins. Co., 48 Mo. App. 281; Fahle v. Ins. Co., 155 Mo. App. 15, 134 S. W. 60.

[2, 3] We recognize the rule of decision well established that ambiguous provisions in policies of insurance will be construed in favor of the insured. Before that rule can be applied the ambiguity must be located, and that we have been unable to do in the instant case. Another rule is equally well established that, where the provisions of the policy are plain, the court can indulge in no forced construction of the contract to cast a liability upon the company which it has not assumed.

The provisions of the policy admit of but one meaning, namely, that upon the default in the payment of the premium the policy by its terms automatically gives to the assured an unconditional right to paid-up insurance. In view of the foregoing and of the fact that it is stipulated that the paid-up insurance provided for in the policy is equal to that provided by the nonforfeiture statute, it follows that the terms of the policy met the requirements of section 6949, R. S. 1909 (section 6154, R. S. 1919), in that the policy contains a provision "for the unconditional commutation of the policy for nonforfeitable paid-up insurance," and therefore section 6946 (section 6151, R. S. 1919), the nonforfeiture law, is inapplicable.

[4] The action of the court in giving a judgment for plaintiff for the guaranteed value stipulated in the policy was correct, but the court was unauthorized to assess the costs of the case against the plaintiff in view of the fact that the defendant offered to deposit in court for the benefit of plaintiff the amount it admitted due on the policy. While it is stipulated that a tender of the amount was made to the plaintiff before suit, such tender in order to stop the running of costs must be kept good by a deposit in court; otherwise the court is not justified in assessing the costs against the plaintiff. Sections 1711, 1712, R. S. 1919; Wolff v. Ins. Co., 223 S. W. 810 (St. Louis Court of Appeals); Landis v. Saxton, 89 Mo. 375, 1 S. W. 359.

[5] For the error noted in assessing the costs against the plaintiff, the judgment will be reversed, and the cause remanded, with directions to enter judgment in favor of plaintiff for the sum of $112.97 and costs,

but without interest, inasmuch as it is admitted that the defendant tendered the above amount to the plaintiff upon the death of William Bothmann, which tender had the effect of preventing the running of interest. Section 1712, R. S. 1919.

PER CURIAM. The foregoing opinion of BIGGS, C., is adopted as the opinion of the court.

The judgment of the circuit court is accordingly reversed, and the cause remanded, with directions as recommended by the Commissioner.

ALLEN, P. J., and BECKER, J., concur. DAUES, J., not sitting.

———

JOHNSTON v. BROWN BROS. IRON & METAL CO. (No. 14065.)

(Kansas City Court of Appeals. Missouri. June 18, 1921.)

1. Replevin ⟸70—Burden on plaintiff to show he was entitled to possession.

The burden is on plaintiff in a replevin action to show that at the time the action was instituted he was entitled to possession of the property, the burden not being on defendant to show title, as plaintiff must recover on the strength of his own title.

2. Chattel mortgages ⟸152—Purchaser of automobile from one without title could not assert invalidity of mortgage.

A purchaser of an automobile from a third party who had no title to convey acquired no interest under which it could assert the invalidity of a chattel mortgage thereon merely because such mortgage was unrecorded.

3. Property ⟸9—Possession of personalty prima facie proof of ownership.

Possession of personal property is prima facie proof of ownership and presumptive evidence that the possession is rightful.

Appeal from Circuit Court, Jackson County; Allen B. Southern, Judge.

Action by Joseph N. Johnston against the Brown Bros. Iron & Metal Company, a corporation. From judgment for plaintiff, defendant appeals. Affirmed.

Achtenberg & Rosenberg, of Kansas City, for appellant.

T. A. Witten, of Kansas City, for respondent.

TRIMBLE, P. J. This was an action, originating in the justice court, to replevin an automobile. Upon a judgment being rendered for plaintiff assessing the value of the automobile at $300, the defendant appealed to the circuit court, where a jury was waived, and the case was tried by the court. Judgment was rendered for plaintiff that he was entitled to the possession of the automobile, assessing the value thereof at $250, and that defendant return the automobile to plaintiff or pay him the assessed value thereof, at the latter's election. No declarations of law or findings of fact were asked or given. '

It appears that plaintiff sold the automobile to one Leslie B. Walters on the 22d day of May, 1919, and he gave a chattel mortgage thereon to plaintiff for the purchase price. The defendant is a dealer in junk, and on May 26, 1919, four days after plaintiff's chattel mortgage was given, defendant got possession of the car. The evidence is not as full and clear as it might be as to the circumstances under which defendant got it. All that it shows is that the car was "out on the Paseo," but "not in a running condition; it had to be towed in" to defendant's yard or place of business; and that late in the afternoon of May 26, 1919, one Roy Walters, in the office of defendant, made a bill of sale for the car to defendant, and received a check for $42.50.

The next morning plaintiff, having heard of the transaction, went to defendant's office, notified them that he held a chattel mortgage on the car, and demanded it, but was refused possession. Defendant bought the car for junk, which means that they would wreck it or take it apart and sell the material for junk. Defendant's evidence was not very definite as to the condition the car was in, save that it was not in a running condition, that for junk purposes it was worth around $50, and that after wrecking it and converting it into junk it would be worth around $70. Plaintiff's evidence is that when it was seized under the replevin writ the car looked all right and would run well, except that the pin in the cranking shaft where the crank would be put on would slip out, and then the motor could not be made to turn over; that as an automobile it was worth in the neighborhood of $300 and at least $250.

Immediately upon being notified by plaintiff of his chattel mortgage, defendant notified the bank to stop payment on the check and when it reached the bank in regular course of business, the bank refused payment, writing across the face of the check "payment refused." Defendant also endeavored to find the man, Roy Walters, to whom they had given the check, but was unable to find him as he had left town. Defendant did not know him, had never seen him before, and made no investigation as to his title to the car when they took the bill of sale and gave him the check, though they said their custom was to do so where the car was in too good a condition to be junked.

On May 29, 1919, plaintiff brought this replevin action and seized the car, but defendant gave a redelivery bond and kept it. After the service of the writ upon defendant, it notified the bank that it could pay the check, the defendant's reason for doing so being that the correspondent bank to whom Roy Walters had presented the check had paid the cash on it at the time or before the drawee bank was notified.

The plaintiff had not yet recorded his chattel mortgage when the defendant obtained possession of the automobile. And defendant's contention is that, under section 2256, R. S. 1919, which provides that an unrecorded chattel mortgage shall not "be valid against any other person than the parties thereto" unless possession be delivered to the mortgagee, the plaintiff has no interest in or title to the property sufficient to give him a right to possession. The trouble with this contention is that, under the record in this case, and the inferences to be drawn from the evidence, the defendant did not purchase the car from any one having any interest in or title to the car. As said in Elliott v. Washington, 137 Mo. App. 526, 529, 119 S. W. 42, 43:

"The statute, though broad in its language, does not deprive a mortgagee of personal property who has failed to record his mortgage or take possession of the property of every right under his instrument, no matter what the circumstances are or who is asserting a hostile claim. This defendant bought from Mrs. Delaney, who had no title' of her own to sell, and no power to sell her husband's. Defendant as the purchaser of such a title, or rather of no title, is in no better position to attack the mortgage because it was not recorded, or possession of the property given to the mortgagee, than Delaney himself would be in."

In Landis v. McDonald, 88 Mo. App. 335, 339, it is said:

"Broad as this statutory phrase, 'any other person,' is, it does not apply to strangers; and one claiming the mortgage to be void must have some right to, or claim upon, the mortgaged property."

[1, 2] It is true, in a replevin action, the burden is on plaintiff to show that at the time the action was instituted he was entitled to the possession of the property, and the burden is not on the defendant to show title. Plaintiff must recover on the strength of his own title. Leete v. State Bank of St. Louis, 141 Mo. 584, 42 S. W. 927. But in this case, unless the mortgage was invalid as to defendant because unrecorded, plaintiff had a right to the possession of the automobile to prevent the destruction of his security which would have been accomplished by its being junked. Defendant obtained no right or interest in the car, yet it asserted an ownership over it, refused to deliver possession thereof, and was on the point of junking it, and was thereby guilty of a conversion. 11 C. J. 592.

The evidence in the case is sufficient to support the reasonable inference that Roy Walters had no title to convey to defendant, and, as the latter acquired no interest therein, it was not in a position to assert the invalidity of the chattel mortgage merely because it was not recorded.

[3] It is also true that the possession of personal property is prima facie proof of ownership and presumptive evidence that possession is rightful, but there is no evidence that Roy Walters ever had possession of said car; and, as heretofore stated, the inferences arising from the evidence disclosed in the record support the conclusion, evidently reached by the trial court, that, if he ever had possession of the car, it was wrongful and without basis of ownership or title, and that defendant had nothing but the bare possession of a car which was worth from $250 to $300, for which they gave a total stranger $42.50 to give a bill of sale.

The judgment is affirmed.

All concur.

SPENCER v. BUSH. (No. 14012.)

(Kansas City Court of Appeals. Missouri. May 28, 1921. Rehearing Denied June 13, 1921.)

1. Contracts ⟐322(3)—Evidence held sufficient to show contract complied with.

In an action for breach of a contract to accept and pay for quarry waste, evidence *held* sufficient to show that the plaintiff did "make every effort to deliver material containing as large a percentage of stone as may be possible," as provided by the contract.

2. Damages ⟐124(1)—Damages for failure to accept delivery of balance of materials contracted for stated.

Where a railroad company, in violation of a contract for the delivery to it on its cars at plaintiff's quarry of a quantity of quarry waste, after receiving and paying for a part, refused to accept the rest, and the evidence showed that plaintiff's expense in attempting to carry out his part of the contract was as great as if defendant had furnished the cars on which to load the undelivered materials within the time specified, he could recover the contract price of the amount undelivered with interest.

Appeal from Circuit Court, Jackson County; B. F. Deatherage, Special Judge.

"Not to be officially published."

Action by W. M. Spencer against B. F. Bush, receiver of the Missouri Pacific Railway Company. Judgment for plaintiff, and defendant appeals. Affirmed.

Edw. J. White, of St. Louis, and Thos. Hackney and L. A. Welch, both of Kansas City, for appellant.

Cleary & Barnett, of Kansas City, for respondent.

BLAND, J. This is an action for damages for breach of contract. Plaintiff recovered a verdict and judgment in the sum of $600.90, and defendant has appealed.

The facts show that between November 20 and December 4, 1916, plaintiff and defendant entered into a contract wherein plaintiff was to furnish defendant 5,000 cubic yards of quarry waste, consisting of waste spalls and clay, at 20 cents per cubic yard, f. o. b. defendant's cars near Independence, Mo. Plaintiff was to "make every effort to deliver to us (defendant) material containing as large a percentage of stone as may be possible." Plaintiff was to deliver between 600 and 800 cubic yards of material per day. Defendant was securing the material to make a levee on the Kaw river at the James Street Bridge in Kansas City, Kan. Thirty-two cars of varying sizes were loaded at plaintiff's quarry on December 9, 11, 13, and 16, 1916. These cars contained 1,266 cubic yards of material, for which defendant paid plaintiff, at the contract price, $253.20. Defendant contended that the material which plaintiff was shipping was not of the quality to be furnished under the contract, claiming that it was mostly clay and that, it contained practically no stone, and that it was therefore not suitable for defendant's needs. Defendant refused to take any more of the material and had his engineer on December 13, 1916, notify plaintiff to that effect. However, 5 cars were sent on December 16th by the defendant for loading. These cars are included in the 32 cars above mentioned. Recovery was had at the contract price for the difference between the material taken and that agreed to be taken.

[1] Defendant's first point is that its demurrer to the evidence should have been sustained for the reason that the evidence shows that plaintiff did not "make every effort to deliver * * * material containing as large a percentage of stone as may be possible," as provided by the agreement; that plaintiff admitted that the contract was violated in that respect. On cross-examination of plaintiff the following question was asked and answer given:

"Q. It would have been possible for you to put in those piles down there, wouldn't it, with a higher per cent. of spalls than what you did put in? A. If I had spent enough money to put a track in there, which would have amounted to twice the amount of the contract, I could have done it."

Defendant's engineer, who viewed plaintiff's rock quarry before the contract was entered into, stated that it was understood that the material was to be furnished from piles of waste at the east end of the quarry, which was 1,200 or 1,300 feet in length. Plaintiff's evidence contradicts this and tends to show that it was understood that it was to be furnished from the face of the quarry about the center part thereof. He testified, as did his manager, Carter, that it was not possible to deliver to defendant out of the waste material of the quarry material of a greater percentage of rock or spalls than the material actually delivered.

Plaintiff insists that his testimony quoted supra does not contradict his testimony and that of Carter just mentioned, for the reason that the question quoted supra is double-barreled; the first part of the question being whether it was possible for plaintiff to have furnished the material from the piles of waste at the end of the quarry, and the second part, whether such piles consisted of a higher per cent. of spalls than the material furnished. Plaintiff contends that his answer related to the first part of the question as to his ability to have furnished the material from the piles. However, it is not necessary for us to decide whether this part of plaintiff's testimony was or was not as defendant contends, for the reason that there was ample testimony that the material furnished contained as large a percentage of stone as was possible to have been furnished from plaintiff's quarry, which under his contract he was required to furnish, and if there was any conflict in the testimony, it was for the jury to say which of plaintiff's two statements they were to believe. Bond v. Rd., 110 Mo. App. 131, 84 S. W. 124; Bobbitt v. Rd., 169 Mo. App. 424, 153 S. W. 70.

[2] It is next insisted that the court erred in refusing to give defendant's instruction limiting plaintiff's recovery to nominal damages and in giving plaintiff's instruction No. 2, which reads as follows:

"You are instructed that, if your verdict be in favor of the plaintiff and against the defendant, and if from the evidence in this case you further believe that the plaintiff had expended for the purpose of performing said contract all sums necessary to deliver in ordinary course 5,000 cubic yards of said material, then you may fix the amount of plaintiff's recovery at such figure as from the evidence in the case you believe to have been the amount of 5,000 cubic yards remaining undelivered on said contract at the rate of 20 cents per cubic yard, not to exceed in all, however, the sum of $740. And on such sum as you so find, if any, you may add interest at the rate of 6 per cent. per annum from the date of filing this suit, April 17, 1917."

In this connection it is contended plaintiff's measure of damages was the difference between the contract price and what it would cost plaintiff to load the remaining cars of waste, the undelivered waste being of no value; that plaintiff's testimony failed to show what it would cost to load the remaining cars; and that, consequently, recovery should have been limited to nominal damages only.

The evidence shows that plaintiff's primary business was that of operating a rock crusher in connection with his quarry. In order to fulfill his contract with defendant in regard to the waste, it was necessary for him to use the machinery that was in use in operating the rock crusher. It also became necessary for plaintiff to construct a special chute for dumping the material into defendant's cars. This chute had been entirely constructed and was torn out after the work was done. Another matter of expense in fulfilling the contract was the coal required in keeping plaintiff's dragline engine, which operated the dragline or steam shovel that lifted the material from the face of the quarry, and two dinkey engines, which hauled the dump cars used in the quarry, steamed up. The evidence shows that these engines were kept steamed up until the 16th of December or for a sufficient period of time to deliver the 5,000 cubic yards of material at the rate of 800 cubic yards per day. The other item of expense was the labor required for the doing of the work. The evidence shows that all the labor necessary for this purpose was kept on hand in readiness to do the work at plaintiff's expense, and that the other quarry operations were held up for the entire period that the work was being done. The entire organization was held in readiness exclusively to serve the purposes of the contract. Plaintiff was not able to make use of these agencies with effectiveness on account of defendant's not supplying the cars at the rate specified in the agreement.

Had the defendant fully and finally terminated the contract on December 13th, there might arise a question as to whether plaintiff had a right to keep his organization in readiness and his men on hand, paying them for additional time; for, under such circumstances, it would have been necessary for plaintiff to have minimized his loss and to have used his organization for some other purpose if possible. However, the evidence shows that defendant did not terminate the contract on December 13, for the reason that it furnished cars to be loaded on the 16th.

From what we have said plaintiff's expense in attempting to carry out his part of the contract was as great as if defendant had furnished the cars and performed the contract on his part, and there was no error in the refusal of defendant's instruction and the giving of plaintiff's instruction No. 2.

The judgment is affirmed.

All concur.

GUESS et al. v. RUSSELL BROS. CLOTH-ING CO. (No. 13575.)

(Kansas City Court of Appeals.   Missouri.
June 13, 1921.)

1. **Evidence ⟺442(6)—Sales ⟺81(3)—Parol evidence to vary contract provision for shipment "as soon as possible" is inadmissible.**

Where a written contract of sale, which was complete and not obscure, provided for shipment "as soon as possible," the determination of the meaning of the phrase "as soon as possible" was for the court, and it required the shipment to be made within a reasonable time under the circumstances, so that parol evidence tending to show an agreement for shipment in any other than a reasonable time under the circumstances was incompetent, as tending to vary the terms of the writing.

[Ed. Note.—For other definitions, see Words and Phrases, First and Second Series, As Soon as Possible.]

2. **Corporations ⟺46—Variance in corporate buyer's name signed to contract does not invalidate.**

The fact that the corporation buyer's name, as signed to the contract by its secretary, for the purpose of binding the buyer to the contract, differed from its true name, does not relieve it of obligation on the contract, since a party may bind himself in contract by a name other than his correct name.

3. **Evidence ⟺441(9)—Written contract held not entered into in performance of oral agreement, so as to make admissible evidence of oral agreement.**

Where a merchant and salesman entered into an agreement for the purchase by the merchant of a talking machine on certain terms, and thereafter the salesman filled out an order blank which was signed by the merchant, the written contract was not one entered into in performance of the previous oral agreement, within the rule permitting parol evidence of a previous agreement performed by a written contract.

4. **Evidence ⟺400(3)—In absence of fraud, representations inducing written contract are inadmissible.**

In the absence of fraud or mistake, parol evidence of representations made by an agent to a buyer to induce the buyer to purchase the goods, on which representations the buyer relied in signing the written contract, are not admissible to vary the terms of the contract.

5. **Evidence ⟺434(11)—Facts held not to show contract was procured by "fraud," justifying admission of parol evidence.**

Where there was no evidence that the seller's agent knew the representation which he made that the machine sold was on the floor of the seller's house was false, there is no showing of fraud in the procurement of the contract, justifying admission of parol evidence, since "fraud" means omissions or concealments which involve a breach of legal or equitable duty, trust, or confidence, justly reposed, and which are injurious to another, by

which an undue advantage is taken of the other.

[Ed. Note.—For other definitions, see Words and Phrases, First and Second Series, Fraud.]

Appeal from Circuit Court, Johnson County; Ewing Cockrell, Judge.

"Not to be officially published."

Action by Buford H. Guess and others against the Russell Bros. Clothing Company. Judgment for defendant in the circuit court on appeal from a justice of the peace, and the plaintiffs appeal. Reversed and remanded for new trial.

E. C. Littlefield, of Knobnoster, and Nick M. Bradley, of Warrensburg, for appellants.

James A. Kemper, of Independence, for respondent.

ARNOLD, J. This is a suit for the recovery of the purchase price of a talking machine sold defendant by plaintiffs. The cause originally was tried without contest in a justice court, the judgment being for plaintiffs in the sum of $117.50, and defendant appealed to the circuit court. There the case was tried to a jury and resulted in a verdict for defendants. Plaintiffs appeal.

The testimony shows that on September 29, 1917, one T. H. Campbell, a sales agent of plaintiffs, entered the store of defendant, at Warrensburg, Mo., and sought to sell to defendant a certain Universal talking machine, 5,000 keys, 3,000 envelopes, 1,000 circulars, 6 records, and 1 movie slide, with exclusive rights in Warrensburg; the whole being a scheme to induce people to trade with defendant company, and embraced the plan of giving to each purchaser at the store of defendant one key for each $1 worth of merchandise purchased. One only of the 5,000 keys would open the lock of the talking machine. After explanation of the plan, an agreement to purchase was entered into between plaintiffs and the defendant concern. Defendant's object in making the purchase lay in its desire to stimulate the holiday trade and to award the talking machine to the party holding the proper key at Christmas. It was shown that, as a part of said agreement to purchase plaintiffs, through their agent, represented that the machine was "on the floor" in plaintiffs' place of business in Cedar Rapids, Iowa, and would be shipped "at once, or as soon as possible."

The testimony further shows that plaintiffs' agent was desirous of catching a train due in five minutes, that he filled out an order blank inserting therein the articles above enumerated, and that he stated to Mr. Russell that he had included in the order the facts upon which an agreement had been reached, and he asked defendant's representative to sign at once, so he could catch his train, and this was done.

The order thus signed is as follows:

"New England Factories Company, Representatives of New England Factories, Cedar Rapids, Iowa, 9—27—1917. Please ship as soon as possible to Russell Bros. Town, Warrensburg. State, Mo. Ship via M. P. Terms —2 per cent., 10—30—60—90. Agreement: We make no charge for advertising matter or display racks. No verbal agreements recognized. [Here follows list of articles as above enumerated.] Exclusive rights in Warrensburg. Machines guaranteed one year. Machine 50″ high $117.50. Russell Bros. Quality Clothes Shop, Warrensburg, Mo. $1.00 plan not on accounts."

"Responsibility of shipper ceases when goods are delivered to transportation company in good condition at point of shipment. This order is not subject to countermand. All bills payable at Cedar Rapids, Iowa. This Universal talking machine is sold with the understanding that it is to be run on the key contest plan, and the executive committee is to award the machine. Salesman, T. H. Campbell. Purchaser, Russell Bros. Sept. 29, 1917."

The testimony further shows that said machine was not at Cedar Rapids, Iowa, but was shipped from Rockford, Ill., on October 29, 1917, and not received by defendant until about Thanksgiving Day, 1917, too late for the purpose desired; that the other articles named in the order were shipped from Cedar Rapids and received in due season, but were held unopened awaiting the arrival of the machine. On arrival of the machine the whole was shipped back to plaintiff at Cedar Rapids, freight prepaid. Defendant refused to receive the articles because of alleged covenant broken by plaintiffs in the prompt shipment of the machine.

The jury was instructed that if they found and believed from the evidence that the contract was partly written and partly verbal, and that plaintiffs' agent represented that the machine was on the floor of the factory at Cedar Rapids, and that it would be shipped immediately, or as soon as possible, and that the contract was dependent upon this agreement, and that it was not shipped immediately, or as soon as possible, from Cedar Rapids, their verdict should be for the defendant.

[1] The written agreement was complete and not obscure, and any verbal evidence tending to contradict or vary its terms was inadmissible, and the court's instruction was erroneous. The determination of the meaning of the words "as soon as possible" was for the court. The weight of authority on this point is to the effect that the meaning of such words, when used in a contract for the shipment of goods, requires that the shipment be made within a reasonable time under the circumstances. Rhodes v. Cleveland Rolling-Mill Co. (C. C.) 17 Fed. 426, 431; Tufts v. Morris, 87 Mo. App. 98. Testimony tending

to show that the goods were to be any other than a reasonable time in circumstances was not admissible to vary the terms of the writing. Inc: Hair Co. v. Walmsley, 32 Mo. App. 12 son v. Carson, 69 Mo. 550; Frissell v. 13 Mo. App. 331. It is, however, ex: to show whether or not the goods wen ally shipped within a reasonable time.

[2] Defendant insists that because th tract was signed by "Russell Bros. Clothing Shop" the same cannot be L be a contract of defendant "Russel Clothing Company." This contention: tenable in the face of the fact that he ant's secretary, who transacted all .. business, testified that he signed the cont for defendant. The rule of law is wait tled that a party may bind himself b tract by another than his true and name. The intent controls. Sports Transfer Co., 104 Mo. 531, 548, 15 S. W. 12 L. R. A. 714, 24 Am. St. Rep. 351; Bar v. Tucker, 104 Mass. 336, 6 Am. Rep. 3t

[3] The facts in this case do not br within the rule as enunciated in 4 Page Contracts, p. 3800, to the effect the written contract is entered into as the formance of an oral contract, evidence: existence and terms of such oral contract admissible.

[4] Defendant contends that—

"Representations made by an agent: third person for the purpose of indenc said person to purchase goods, and c the third party relied and acted, are he upon the principal, and such representation be shown by parol for the purpose of sum the contract thereby induced, even the g. said contract expressly provides that it a statements shall bind the principal"

—and cites Wright v. McPike, 70 Mo. Cole Bros. v. Wiedmair, 19 Mo. App. 31 Insurance Co. v. Owens, 81 Mo. App. 30

This statement of the law was overruled: Crim v. Crim, 162 Mo. 544, 63 S. W. 49. L. R. A. 502, 85 Am. St. Rep. 521, opinion Marshall, J.:

"But it is an invariable rule of law that: the absence of fraud or mistake, parol evidence is not admissible to contradict or vary a written contract. The written contract is conclusively presumed to merge all prior negotiations and to express the final agreement of the parties. To permit a party when seed a written contract to admit that he signed it to deny that it expresses the agreement intended or to allow him to admit that he signed it be did not read it or know its stipulations, may absolutely destroy the value of all contracts and negotiable instruments."

This opinion has become the settled law the state on this point. Spelman v. Bailway 187 Mo. App. 125, 172 S. W. 1163; Cubard v. McKnight, 180 Mo. App. 623, 163 S. W. S.

[5] Defendant urges that the contract

procured by fraud and that defendant did not understand that it was signing the contract that actually was signed.

"Fraud as a generic term, especially as the word is used in courts of equity, properly includes all acts, omissions, and concealments which involve a breach of legal or equitable duty, trust, or confidence, justly reposed, and are injurious to another, by which an undue and unconscious advantage is taken of another." 20 Cyc. 8 B.

This suit having been instituted before a justice of the peace, no formal pleadings were required. The only guiding information for the court as to defendant's position consisted in the statement of defendant's counsel from which it was determinable that it based its defense, at least in part, on deceit. The secretary of defendant testified that he obligated his company to pay for the machine as per the terms of the verbal statements of plaintiffs' agent. In the statement of defendant's counsel the chief complaint is that the machine was not shipped immediately, and that it was not "on the floor of the house at Cedar Rapids" at the time the order was signed. There is no charge that plaintiffs' agent knew the machine was not at Cedar Rapids as stated.

A careful perusal of the record fails to convince us that there was fraud in the procurement of the contract. Defendant's secretary, who conducted the negotiations on behalf of defendant, was a man of affairs, presumably capable of understanding a simple contract such as the one at issue, and if he signed the same without reading it he may not now be allowed to complain.

Under the law as above enunciated and the facts in this case, the admission of parol evidence tending to contradict, add to, or vary the terms of the written contract was error.

The judgment, accordingly, is reversed, and the cause remanded for a new trial.

All concur.

RAINEY v. REORGANIZED CHURCH OF JESUS CHRIST OF THE LATTER DAY SAINTS. (No. 16536.)

(St. Louis Court of Appeals. Missouri. May 3, 1921.)

Justices of the peace ⟸160(3)—Notice of appeal held sufficient.

Under Rev. St. 1919, § 2905, not requiring any particular form of notice of appeal from a justice court, in suit before a justice of the peace originally instituted under the style of "Eugene Rainey, Plaintiff, v. Reorganized Church of Jesus Christ of the Latter Day Saints, a Corporation, and Thomas J. Elliott, Defendants," wherein the justice found in favor of plaintiff as against defendant corporation and dismissed the case as to the individual defendant, notice of appeal to the circuit court from the judgment rendered by the justice entitling the case as "Eugene Rainey, Plaintiff, v. Reorganized Church of Jesus Christ of the Latter Day Saints, Defendant," was sufficient despite its omission to name the individual defendant and to characterize the named defendant as a corporation.

Appeal from St. Louis Circuit Court; Vital W. Garesche, Judge.

Suit by Eugene Rainey against the Reorganized Church of Jesus Christ of the Latter Day Saints, a corporation. From judgment for plaintiff, defendant appeals. Reversed, and cause remanded.

Walter Diehm, of St. Louis, for appellant. Thomas L. Anderson, of St. Louis, for respondent.

BECKER, J. Plaintiff below, in a suit on a contract, obtained judgment on March 1, 1918, for $500 against the defendant before a justice of the peace. An appeal was taken to the circuit court, where the judgment was affirmed for alleged insufficiency of notice of appeal. Defendant in due course brings this appeal.

The transcript of the record filed by the justice of the peace in the circuit court shows that the style of the suit as originally instituted before the justice was, "Eugene Rainey, Plaintiff, v. Reorganized Church of Jesus Christ of the Latter Day Saints, a Corporation, and Thomas J. Elliott, Defendants," and that the justice, after hearing the case, found in favor of plaintiff as against the defendant corporation (appellant here) in the sum of $500 and costs, and dismissed the case as to the other defendant, Thomas J. Elliott.

The sole question for our determination under this record is whether a sufficient notice of appeal from the judgment rendered by the justice of the peace was served. The notice of appeal in question is as follows:

"Before James P. Miles, Esq., Justice of the Peace, 6th District, City of St. Louis, Mo.

"Eugene Rainey, Plaintiff, v. Reorganized Church of Jesus Christ of the Latter Day Saints, Defendant.

"To Eugene Rainey or Thomas L. Anderson, His Attorney:

"You are hereby notified that the undersigned has taken an appeal to the circuit court of the city of St. Louis, Mo., from the merits of the judgment of the justice rendered in the above-entitled cause.

"Dated March 7, 1918.

"[Signed] Reorganized Church of Jesus Christ of the Latter Day Saints,

"By Walter Diehm, Its Attorney.

"Received a copy of the within notice this 11th day of March, 1918.

"[Signed] Thos. L. Anderson."

It is argued that the style of the case as set up in the notice of appeal omits the name of Thomas J. Elliott as one of the defendants, and also omits the word "corporation" after the other defendant, and that, since the notice fails to mention the amount of the judgment or the date upon which it was rendered, the notice of appeal does not comply with the requirements of the statute.

Upon the authority of the recent case of Davenport Vinegar & Pickling Works v. Shelley, 280 Mo. 398, 217 S. W. 267, we must rule this contention of learned counsel for respondent against him.

The learned trial judge, in passing upon plaintiff's motion to affirm the judgment, had before him and followed the case of Davenport Vinegar & Pickling Works v. Snelley, 196 S. W. 1085, an opinion by this court, which case, however, was certified to the Supreme Court as being in conflict with other decisions of this court and of the Springfield Court of Appeals. In the majority opinion of this court a notice of appeal from a judgment rendered by a justice of the peace was held to be insufficient, but our Supreme Court in its opinion (280 Mo. 393, 217 S. W. 267) held contra. This latter opinion of the Supreme Court was not before the learned trial judge at the time this motion to affirm the judgment was before him.

In that case our Supreme Court, in the course of its opinion, in adverting to the theretofore strict construction of the statute providing for notice of appeal from judgments rendered before a justice of the peace, ruled that—

"The decision of the several Courts of Appeals so strictly construing the statute appear to claim support in the ancient case in this court of Tiffin v. Millington, 3 Mo. 419. * * * There is nothing in that case to justify the strict requirements which have appeared in later decisions."

It is to be noted that section 2905, Revised Statutes of Missouri 1919 (section 7582, Revised Statutes of Missouri 1909), does not require any particular form of notice of appeal from a justice court, and, as was said in Munroe v. Herrington, 99 Mo. App. loc. cit. 298, 73 S. W. 222:

"The purpose of the statute * * * is to apprise the successful party of the fact that an appeal has been taken. The statute prescribes no specific form of notice and we think that a notice is good if it sufficiently describes the judgment appealed from to reasonably identify it, and informs the successful party that his adversary has appealed. Such a notice would be a substantial compliance with the statute and would meet the demands of justice; the law requires nothing more."

After an examination of the notice in discussion we are satisfied, in light of all circumstances in the case, that despite errors complained of, it sufficiently notified the plaintiff below that the defendant taken an appeal therein to the circuit in the case in which judgment had been rendered before the justice, and that the plaintiff's motion in the circuit court to affirm the judgment of the justice for failure to sufficient notice under the statute should have been overruled.

In arriving at this conclusion we bear in mind that it is not claimed that there is any other suit pending between the same parties, nor that the attorney upon whom the notice was served, had not been the attorney for plaintiff in said suit when before the justice. The same attorney filed the motion to affirm in the circuit court which motion is based, not on the ground that no notice of appeal in the cause has been given, but on the ground that no proper and sufficient notice had been served upon plaintiff, as required by statute. In said motion the same error complained of in defendant's notice of appeal appears, namely, that the caption thereof omitted the name "Thomas J. Elliott" as one of the defendants. This omission of the name, under the facts in this case, we hold is immaterial, since the justice had dismissed plaintiff's case both as against the said defendant, Elliott, and we hold the same view with reference to the omission of the word "corporation" after the name of the other defendant. See Teasdale & Co. v. American Fruit Produce Co., 120 Mo. App. 584, 97 S. W. 655.

It cannot be doubted but that plaintiff was fully informed by the notice itself that it was served as and for a notice of appeal in the case in which the attorney filed the said motion to affirm. Nowhere in the brief or argument before us by learned counsel for respondent was it suggested that the notice of appeal, by reason of the various insufficiencies complained of, failed to fully inform the plaintiff of the fact that defendant below had in point of fact taken an appeal in the said particular case, but the sole argument is based upon the bare technicality that the said notice, in the several ways pointed out, did not comply strictly with the requirements of the statute.

In light of what we have said above the judgment of the circuit court in sustaining plaintiff's motion to affirm the judgment should be, and the same is hereby, reversed and the cause remanded.

ALLEN, P. J., concurs.

WOLF v. MARPLES. (No. 14981.)

(St. Louis Court of Appeals. Missouri. June 7, 1921.)

Justices of the peace ⟜160(3)—Notice of appeal held sufficient.

Notice of an appeal from a judgment of a justice of the peace reading, "John H. Wolf, Plaintiff, v. Mrs. Sophie S. ~~Wolf~~ Marples Defendant," further omitting to state the amount of the judgment, *held* sufficient, under Rev. St. 1919, § 2905.

Appeal from St. Louis Circuit Court; William M. Kinsey, Judge.

"Not to be officially published."

Action by John H. Wolf against Sophie S. Marples. From judgment dismissing the case, plaintiff appeals. Affirmed.

Hugh D. McCorkle, of St. Louis, and Nat Steiner, for appellant.

Paul Bakewell, Jr., and Wm. R. Schneider, both of St. Louis, for respondent.

BECKER, J. Plaintiff below in a suit on an account stated obtained on October 5, 1914, a judgment for $250 against the defendant before a justice of the peace. On appeal to the circuit court the plaintiff filed a motion to affirm the judgment of the justice on account of the insufficiency of notice of appeal. This motion was overruled, and the plaintiff elected to stand on his motion to affirm and declined to plead further, whereupon the case was dismissed by the court for want of prosecution. Plaintiff in due course appeals.

The sole question for our determination, under this record, is whether a sufficient notice of appeal from the judgment rendered by the justice of the peace was served. The notice of appeal in question is as follows:

"Before James P. Miles, Justice of the Peace within and for the Sixth District of the City of St. Louis, State of Missouri.

John H. Wolf, Plaintiff, v. Mrs. Sophie S. ~~Wolf,~~ Marples, Defendant.

"To the Above-Named Plaintiff, John H. Wolff, or His Attorney:

"Take notice, that an appeal has been taken from the judgment of the justice in the above-styled cause, rendered on the 5th day of October, 1914, in favor of the plaintiff and against the defendant. Said appeal was taken on the 15th day of October, 1914, and is addressed to the circuit court of the city of St. Louis, state of Missouri, and is returnable to the December, 1914, term thereof.

"Mrs. Sophie S. Marples,
"By Paul Bakewell, Jr., Her Attorney.

"Received copy hereof this 13th day of November ~~October~~ 1914.

"Nat Steiner."

Appellant seriously argues that, since in the notice of appeal in the style of the suit the defendant's name appears as Mrs. Sophie S. *Wolf*, instead of Mrs. Sophie S. *Marples*, and since the amount of the judgment is not stated therein, the notice does not conform to the statute.

Upon authority of the recent case of Davenport Vinegar & Pickling Works v. Shelley, 217 S. W. 267, we must rule this contention of learned counsel for respondent against it. See, also, Rainey v. Reorganized Church of Jesus Christ of the Latter Day Saints, 231 S. W. 1017, a recent case of this court in which we have expressed ourselves fully upon this subject.

We are satisfied that the notice before us, in light of all the circumstances in the case, and despite the errors complained of therein, sufficiently notified plaintiff below that the defendant had taken an appeal therein to the circuit court in the case in which judgment had been rendered before the justice, and that the plaintiff's motion in the circuit court to affirm the judgment of the justice for failure to give sufficient notice under the statute was properly overruled.

It is not contended that there was any other suit or suits pending between the same parties, and it appears from the record that the attorney upon whom the notice was served had been the attorney for the plaintiff when the suit was tried before the justice. The fact that the name of the defendant in the style of the case in the notice of appeal was given as Sophie S. *Wolf* instead of Sophie S. *Marples* could not have deceived the plaintiff, in that the said notice was signed in the name of Mrs. Sophie S. *Marples* by Paul Bakewell, Jr., her attorney; nor can we hold that the omission from the notice of the amount of the judgment is sufficient to declare the notice insufficient.

While it is to be regretted that counsel inadvertently at times serve notices of appeal which contain inaccuracies and omissions, yet, since section 2905, R. S. No. 1919 (section 7582, R. S. Mo. 1909), does not require any particular form of notice of appeal from a justice court, a notice should be held good "if it sufficiently describes the judgment appealed from to reasonably identify it, and informs the successful party that his adversary has appealed. Such a notice would be a substantial compliance with the statute, and would meet the demands of justice. The law requires nothing more." Munroe v. Herrington, 99 Mo. App. loc. cit. 293, 73 S. W. 221.

In light of what we have stated above, the judgment should be, and the same is hereby, affirmed.

ALLEN, P. J., and DAUES, J., concur.

BIBB v. GRADY.   (No. 16628.)

(St. Louis Court of Appeals. Missouri. May 3, 1921. Rehearing Denied June 7, 1921.)

1. **Municipal corporations** ⬤**706(6)—Evidence held insufficient to warrant submission of negligence to the jury.**

In an action for death of a pedestrian run down by defendant's automobile on a city street, evidence *held* to fail to show causal connection between any negligent act of defendant and the death of deceased, and demurrer to evidence should have been sustained.

2. **Negligence** ⬤**83—Humanitarian rule stated.**

The humanitarian rule does not obtain unless there is evidence to show that the defendant could have averted the injury after he saw, or by the exercise of ordinary care could have seen, the person injured either in or about to come into a position of danger.

3. **Appeal and error** ⬤**1001(1)—Verdicts founded on conjecture not sustained.**

Verdicts founded on surmise and conjecture, unsupported by any evidence, cannot be allowed to stand.

4. **Municipal corporations** ⬤**706(5)—Evidence held to fail to bring case within humanitarian rule.**

In action for damages for death of pedestrian struck by defendant's automobile on a city street, evidence *held* to fail to bring the case within the humanitarian rule.

5. **Evidence** ⬤**471(23) —Answer of witness as to speed of automobile held mere conclusion.**

Answer of witness that automobile was going fast was merely a conclusion of the witness, having no probative force, where no fact was stated upon which to base it.

6. **Municipal corporations** ⬤**706(3)—Excessive speed raises no presumption that death of pedestrian was caused thereby.**

Excessive speed of automobile killing pedestrian alone raises no presumption of law that the death of deceased was caused by such excessive speed.

7. **Appeal and error** ⬤**1177(7)—Judgment need not be reversed outright.**

On appeal from a judgment awarding damages for death of a pedestrian on city street, where there was no evidence showing any causal connection between alleged excessive speed of the automobile and death of deceased, *held*, that the judgment should not be reversed outright, but should be reversed and remanded.

Appeal from St. Louis Circuit Court; Franklin Ferris, Judge.

"Not to be officially published."

Action by Joseph W. Bibb, administrator of the estate of Grace H. Bibb, deceased, against Robert F. Grady. Judgment for plaintiff, and defendant appeals. Reversed and remanded.

Jourdan, Rassieur & Pierce, of St. Louis, for appellant.

J. D. Johnson and Frank A. Habig, both of St. Louis, for respondent.

BRUERE, C. This action was instituted in the circuit court of the city of St. Louis, Mo., by the plaintiff, as administrator of the estate of Grace H. Bibb, deceased, to recover damages for the death of the deceased, alleged to have been negligently killed by defendant's automobile, while deceased was walking across Belt avenue, near the intersection with Cabanne avenue, in the city of St. Louis, Mo. At a trial a jury awarded plaintiff a verdict of $3,000. From a judgment on that verdict defendant appeals.

The negligence as charged in the petition is:

"That defendant negligently operated and ran an automobile on and along Belt avenue, southwardly towards and at and near its intersection with Cabanne avenue, in a manner and at a speed dangerous to the life and limb of persons traveling over, upon, or across said Belt avenue; that said Grace H. Bibb was then and there walking across said Belt avenue in a southerly direction from the east to the west side thereof and north of, and at and near said intersection with Cabanne avenue, with her back towards said automobile, and in sight of the defendant therein; and that while the defendant was so operating and running said automobile, as aforesaid, he negligently operated and ran the same against and over the said Grace H. Bibb, and inflicted upon her bodily injuries, which then and there caused her death."

The answer is a general denial, coupled with a plea of contributory negligence.

The facts disclosed by the evidence are:

The accident occurred on the evening of October 15, 1915, at about 7:30 o'clock on Belt avenue, near the intersection of Cabanne avenue, in the city of St. Louis, Mo. Belt avenue runs north and south.

The deceased, at the time of her death, was about 23 years old. She lived about half a block from the corner of Belt avenue and the Suburban street car tracks. The Suburban street car line runs east and west, on a private right of way, and crosses Belt avenue 219 feet north of Cabanne avenue. The width of Belt avenue is not disclosed in the evidence. A private driveway runs into Belt avenue on the east side thereof. This driveway is some distance south of the Suburban tracks; the exact distance is not given in the testimony. An apartment is located on the west side of Belt avenue near Cabanne avenue. The south end of the apartment is about 50 feet north of Cabanne avenue. There is a down spout, mentioned in the evidence, which is located on the east wall of the apartment opposite a telephone pole located in the west curb line of Belt avenue. The Chamberlain Apartment is located on the northwest corner of Vernon and Belt avenue, north of the Suburban tracks and 123 feet distant therefrom. Belt avenue at the Suburban tracks at the time of the accident was well lighted, but at the corner of Belt and Cabanne avenue it was dark.

No witness testified to seeing the automobile strike the deceased. Two witnesses testified regarding the occurrence. They were Lulu Perkins and Mrs. F. C. George.

Lulu Perkins testified:

Direct Examination.

"I was standing at the northeast corner of Belt and Cabanne; but I don't know where she was killed. I was coming, on October 15, 1915, from 5459, delivering some clothes. I had four boxes of clothes and I delivered one at 5459 to Mrs. Anderson—I was coming out of the house—I was trying to make it to 5531 Chamberlain before they went to the supper table; I discovered my boxes were untied and I stopped at the corner to tie the boxes up; while stooping over I noticed a lady coming from the east side of the street walking south to me, and I was just stooping in such a position that I thought I had better straighten up because it was dark, so I wouldn't frighten her; in the meantime I had my pocketbook in this hand and I had a present that one of the ladies gave me, and when I stood up I recognized the automobile coming and I heard a bump with a 'squeechy' noise and I jumped around and wondered if that lady—so I ran and kind of said to myself—so I came back and fixed up my boxes, walked straight across to the path that leads across the street on Cabanne and Belt that goes west, and when I went to walk across Miss Bibb was lying in the middle of the street; I walked to her feet and—Mr. Grady came too out of his machine, took the body, and put one hand under one arm and one hand under the other and dragged the body out of the street and laid it on the west sidewalk on the west— That was all I seen; I didn't see the machine when it hit her. I do not know what that 'squeechy' noise was. I do not know where it came from. I just heard the noise and it made me recognize that something had happened before I heard that bump. I saw the automobile coming. I cannot tell at what speed it was coming. It was going fast, but I don't know the rates—I don't know the rates of the speed. I didn't see the automobile stop; when I saw it it had already stopped. It was standing right on Belt avenue and kind of a little curved to the Cabanne and Belt avenue corner, towards the curb, where the curb turned around west, so that the front wheels of the automobile were standing on Cabanne and the back wheels on Belt avenue, kind of turned, just a little curve like."

Cross-Examination.

"When I heard the bump and the 'squeechy' noise, I was standing kind of cater-cornered, and as soon as I heard that I turned around. When I did that the automobile had stopped. I was busily engaged with my bundles that had come untied and I was leaning down, stooped down."

Redirect Examination.

"I was at the corner of Cabanne and Belt. The body was lying when I got there kind of cater-cornered in the middle of the street. It was not near the apartment; it was in the middle of the street—kind of in the middle of the street."

Mrs. F. C. George testified:

Direct Examination.

"I am now living on Belt and Vernon, the Chamberlain Apartments. I remember the night that this young lady was killed, October 15, 1915. I was standing in my window, the farthest window in the apartment; there is a bay window there; I stood in the extreme west one, waiting for my husband, who generally arrives at half past 6; I don't remember whether it was the last one, but it was over on the left side, and he being late I was a little anxious and was watching each car as it came, because supper was long past done and I wanted to get it on the table in time, and watching each west-bound car as it stopped, and, as I say, I was watching—as I was watching I saw a young lady alight and pass in front of the car, walk to the driveway, and passed down the driveway into Belt avenue; with this I heard a thud, and seen these things; previous to that I saw the machine, the back of the machine waiting for the car to pass, and knew that it had passed; with hearing the thud I rushed out of my front door; this made me think that something had happened; so I knew something had happened— I distinctly saw the young lady step off the driveway. She got off a west-bound car. She walked around in front of the car. I saw her clearly. She was going —she first walked south—on Belt avenue, to the driveway, and stepped off of the driveway in the street on the east side; I refer to the driveway that is in that short half block between the track and Cabanne. My apartment is a half block north of Suburban tracks, a short half of a block, because it is not really a half block, just about. This driveway is a few feet south of the Suburban tracks; how far I couldn't state positively; I never measured it. The driveway leads into the street on Belt avenue. I saw the deceased step off the driveway into the street. The distance where I last saw her step into the street—the distance from that point to where I was is a half block. I was at the corner of Vernon avenue. I had no difficulty in seeing the young lady walking down south on Belt avenue to the point where she left the sidewalk and went into the street. There was nothing there to obstruct my view. The light was sufficient where this young lady was walking for me to see her at that distance. After I heard the thud I went down to the scene of the accident. I saw the back of the machine waiting prior to the time I heard this thud. It was on the north side of the tracks going south. It had stopped. I saw a street car stopping to let people off, going west. I couldn't say positively if that car had proceeded or whether it was standing there at the time the automobile was standing there. I saw the automobile start up, I couldn't say positively that I saw it continue on south on Belt avenue; I was conscious that it moved. I don't know how fast it was going. After I saw this young lady step off into the street and heard this thud, I could not state what time had elapsed between the time she stepped off and the thud."

Mrs. Mary Slattery testified that she was waiting for a street car at the corner of the Suburban tracks and Belt avenue when she observed an automobile when it went across the tracks going south; that she could not tell whether it was going slow or fast; that while standing there she heard of the accident and immediately went to the scene of the accident and saw the body of deceased lying on the grass parking way in front of the south end of the apartment near Cabanne avenue; that she picked up a hat and a bracelet and saw that some leaves had been dragged. Her testimony regarding the hat, bracelet, and leaves is as follows:

"I picked up the hat about 48 feet from where the body was; the way I walked, I mean. I picked up the hat about 48 feet back near the middle of the street. I picked up a bracelet about 6 or 8 feet away from the hat and the leaves, south of the hat and between the hat and the body. I observed the leaves had been dragged; I noticed the blood in the middle of the street near the hat. The bracelet was between the body and the hat; I should say about middle I guess—midway between the body and the hat. Between the body and the parking place I saw dragging of leaves where something had been pushed aside; just the leaves to the parking is all I saw. It extended from the middle of the street to the parking, just across the street. I did not observe any blood in the street even with the body, on account of the leaves I guess. It is over 100 feet from the Suburban tracks to where I found the hat. I found the hat besides this pipe (indicating on photograph) opposite that down pipe. You see a pipe right by this pole (indicating). That driveway is just a very short distance south of the Suburban track. It is about as far as to the table from here (indicating).

"Mr. Kelley: From you to the table?

"The witness: Or to the railing; I guess to the railing (indicating). To the railing, that's about 30 feet.

"The witness: I don't know. At the place where I found the hat and bracelet and saw the body, the leaves were dragged there; the leaves dragging where the leaves had been brushed aside in the street. They started at the hat, where I found the hat, it continues about to—about the front of the apartment where the body was."

Charles Hussmann testified that he went to the scene after the accident and saw the body of the deceased on the grass plat between the sidewalk and the street; that he noticed that there was quite a good deal of blood opposite to where the body was, directly across from the body.

Dr. Floyd Stewart testified that a Peerless automobile going at the rate of 20 miles per hour could be stopped within its length, and going at the rate of 30 miles or 35 miles per hour could be stopped within twice its

length; that the length of the Peerless car he owned was about 15 feet in length. The defendant admitted that the automobile driven by him was a 1913 model Peerless.

The above was all the evidence introduced bearing upon the facts of the occurrence. At the close of plaintiff's case the defendant offered a peremptory instruction in the nature of a demurrer to the evidence, which the court refused to give. The defendant stood on his demurrer and offered no testimony.

The court submitted the cause to the jury on the humanitarian or last chance doctrine. Counsel for appellant insist that the demurrer to the evidence should have been given.

[1] Considering the evidence in the light most favorable to plaintiff, and admitting as true every fact and inference that may be reasonably deduced from the evidence, we are forced to the conclusion that the lower court should have given the demurrer to the evidence.

The evidence, as detailed above, fails to show a causal connection between the act of negligence charged and the death of deceased; it wholly fails to show that the negligence charged was the proximate cause of the accident. The proximate cause of the accident is left entirely to surmise and conjecture, unsupported by any evidence.

The case was submitted to the jury on the last clear chance or humanitarian doctrine. There was no evidence to bring the case within this doctrine.

[2] The humanitarian rule does not obtain unless there is evidence to show that the defendant could have averted the injury after he saw, or by the exercise of ordinary care could have seen, the person injured either in or about to come into a position of danger. "In order to recover under it it devolves upon the plaintiff to prove that after a perilous situation arose the defendant, by the exercise of ordinary care, could have averted the injury to the person injured and failed to do so."

The difficulty about plaintiff's case, as submitted to the jury, is that it fails to show how far away the automobile was when the deceased entered or was about to enter the danger zone, and within what distance the automobile could have been stopped. Absent these necessary facts, no one can intelligently determine whether defendant was negligent or not, or whether he could have stopped the automobile in time to have averted striking deceased. At what point of time the plaintiff was either in or about to enter the danger zone, and how long a time elapsed thereafter until she was struck, is left entirely to conjecture.

[3] Verdicts founded on surmise and conjecture, unsupported by any evidence, cannot be allowed to stand.

[4] The evidence failed to bring the case within the humanitarian rule. Warner v. St. L. & M. R. Ry. Co., 178 Mo. 125, 77 S. W. 67;

Chappell v. United Railways Co., 174 Mo. App. 132, 156 S. W. 819; Dey v. United Railways Co., 140 Mo. App. 461, 120 S. W. 134; Zurfluh v. People's Ry. Co., 46 Mo. App. 636; Paul v. Railroad, 152 Mo. App. 577, 134 S. W. 3; Wilkerson v. Railroad, 140 Mo. App. 306, 124 S. W. 543; Keele v. Railroad, 258 Mo. 62, 167 S. W. 433; Riggs v. Kansas City Rys. Co., 220 S. W. 698; Spiro v. St. Louis Transit Co., 102 Mo. App. loc. cit. 262, 76 S. W. 684; Fleming v. Railroad, 263 Mo. 180, 172 S. W. 355.

Respondent contends that the petition pleads and the evidence shows that the defendant negligently ran and operated his automobile upon a public highway at a rate of speed that was dangerous to the life and limb of persons traveling thereupon, and that this was the proximate cause of the death of deceased.

The only witness who testified concerning the speed of the car was Lulu Perkins. She testified as follows:

"Q. Can you tell at what speed it was coming? A. No, sir; no, sir.
"Q. Could you tell whether it was coming slow or fast? (This was objected to on the ground that the witness had not qualified. Objection was overruled.) A. It was going fast, but I don't know the rates—I don't know the rates of the speed. (Defendant's counsel moved to strike this out, but the court let it stand.)

[5] The answer was merely a conclusion of the witness; no fact was stated upon which to base her conclusion. It therefore has no probative force.

The other evidence in the case regarding the speed of the automobile was the testimony of Mary Slattery. She testified that she found a hat and bracelet. The identity of the hat or bracelet was not proven. It is argued that this evidence warrants the presumption that the deceased was struck where the hat or bracelet was found and that the automobile was traveling at an excessive speed.

[6] It is unnecessary to comment on the evidence regarding the speed of the automobile, other than to say that the excessive speed of the automobile alone raises no presumption of law that the death of the deceased was caused by such excessive speed. Battles v. United Rys. Co., 178 Mo. App. 596, 161 S. W. 614; Schmidt v. St. Louis Transit Co., 140 Mo. App. loc. cit. 187, 120 S. W. 96; Kelley v. Railroad, 75 Mo. 138; King v. Wabash R. R. Co., 211 Mo. loc. cit. 18, 14, 109 S. W. 671; Bluedorn v. Mo. Pac. Ry. Co., 121 Mo. 258, 25 S. W. 943; Lillian Winkler v. United Rys. Co., 229 S. W. 229 (St. Louis Court of Appeals), and cases cited therein (not yet [officially] reported).

The deceased might have put herself so suddenly in a place of danger that the accident could not have been avoided even if the automobile had been running slow. There was no evidence showing any causal connection between the alleged excessive speed of the automobile and the death of the deceased.

[7] We think the judgment in this case should not be reversed outright, but should be reversed and remanded; for such order we have ample authority. Riggs v. Kansas City Ry. Co., 220 S. W. 698; Rutledge v. Mo. Pac. Ry. Co., 123 Mo. loc. cit. 140, 24 S. W. 1053, 27 S. W. 827; Finnegan v. Mo. Pac. Ry. Co., 244 Mo. 608, 149 S. W. 612; Chandler v. Railroad, 251 Mo. loc. cit. 608, 158 S. W. 35.

In view of the above and foregoing the Commissioner recommends that the judgment be reversed and the cause remanded.

PER CURIAM. The opinion of BRUERE, C., is adopted as the opinion of the court.

The judgment of the circuit court of the city of St. Louis is accordingly reversed, and the cause remanded.

ALLEN, P. J., and BECKER, J., concur. DAUES, J., not sitting.

JACKELS et al. v. KANSAS CITY RYS. CO.
(No. 14040.)

(Kansas City Court of Appeals. Missouri. June 13, 1921.)

1. Street railroads ⟐117(28) — Automobile driver's contributory negligence question of fact.

In a suit for injury to an automobile in a collision at an intersection, evidence for plaintiffs, whose driver relied on the motorman's observance of the safety stop, held not to show contributory negligence as a matter of law.

2. Trial ⟐251(8)—Instruction on general negligence in failing to stop street car held outside pleadings.

Where the petition in a suit for injury in a collision was based on a failure to stop a street car at a crossing because the brakes were out of order, and that was the sole trouble according to plaintiffs' evidence, it was error to submit the case on general negligence in failing to stop.

3. Street railroads ⟐118(1)—Instruction as to street car's safety stop held within pleadings.

In a suit for injury claimed to have been caused by failure to stop a street car in time to avoid a collision at a crossing because the brakes were out of order, a reference, in an instruction submitting the negligence in issue, to a safety stop at the point in question and a custom of cars to stop there, was not erroneous as submitting a ground of recovery as being the failure to observe a custom, but was proper as submitting a situation to explain why the car was expected to stop and should have stopped there, as was alleged in the petition.

4. Damages ⚖=69—Interest not allowable in action ex delicto.

Interest is not allowable in action ex delicto.

5. Damages ⚖=217—Instruction as to measure of damages for injury to automobile held not sufficiently clear.

In a suit for injury to an automobile, an instruction to assess the damages on finding for plaintiffs at such sum as would "reimburse plaintiffs for the damages sustained," and that in computing same the jury could consider the expense of repairs and loss on being compelled to sell the car at a reduced price on account of the damage, was not sufficiently clear, where, as applied to the evidence, it meant the difference between the price at which plaintiffs held the car before the injury and the price they had to take because it was a repaired car, instead of meaning plaintiffs' recovery, as would have been preferable, by the difference between the automobile's market value immediately before and immediately after the injury, or the amount reasonably necessary to repair plus the difference between the reasonable value before and after the injury.

6. Evidence ⚖=123(12)—Admission by street car motorman after collision that his brakes did not work held not admissible as res gestæ.

The admission by a street car motorman after a collision that the "brakes did not work" was not a part of the res gestæ, and so was not admissible in a suit for resulting injury to automobile; and the fact that it was already in evidence that the brakes did not work, and that, as he applied them and the car did not stop, the jury "could have inferred" that the brakes did not work, did not justify introduction of such admission.

Appeal from Circuit Court, Jackson County; Daniel E. Bird, Judge.

"Not to be officially published."

Action by Charles F. Jackels and others against the Kansas City Railways Company in justice court. From a judgment for plaintiffs on appeal to the circuit court, defendant appeals. Reversed and remanded for a new trial.

R. J. Higgins, of Kansas City, Kan., and Chas. N. Sadler, Louis R. Weiss, and E. E. Ball, all of Kansas City, Mo., for appellant. George D. McIlrath and McIlrath & Gregory, all of Kansas City, Mo., for respondents.

TRIMBLE, P. J. This action, originating in a justice's court, was brought to recover damages for injury to an automobile, caused by a street car colliding therewith. It was, on appeal to the circuit court, tried de novo, and plaintiffs recovered judgment in the sum of $174.06, from which defendant appealed to this court.

The automobile was being "demonstrated" to a prospective purchaser, and was being driven west along Brush Creek boulevard and was approaching its intersection with Rockhill road, in Kansas City, Mo., when a southbound street car on said Rockhill road approached the same intersection. North of the north side of the intersection the street railway track was a "safety stop" at which all cars came to a standstill before proceeding across the boulevard. The driver of the automobile knew of this safety stop and that cars stopped there, and though he saw the car coming, as he approached the crossing, he thought the car would stop at the safety stop; but this time it did not do so, but came steadily on, striking the automobile as it got on the track and injuring it.

The case having originated in the justice court, there was no other pleading save a petition, which, after setting forth the situation at the said intersection, alleged that the driver of the automobile saw the street car at a point 30 feet or more north of the intersection, and knowing of the safety stop and observing the motorman applied the brakes to come to a stop there, the automobile driver started on across the tracks ahead of said street car, "having his said automobile under full control at all times and driving the same at a rate of speed of about 5 miles an hour; that through the gross carelessness, negligence, and unskillfulness of defendant's agent and employé in charge of said street car, or through the gross carelessness, negligence, and unskillfulness of defendant company in not having the brakes on said street car in good working order and condition, said street car failed to come to a stop at said intersection and failed to make the safety stop expected and required of it," etc.

[1] A number of errors are charged to have been committed, any one of which would be sufficient to call for a reversal and remanding of the case. However, the claim that the plaintiffs' own evidence shows contributory negligence so conclusively as to bar their recovery as a matter of law is one that should be disposed of first, for if that be true the other alleged errors need not be noticed.

The evidence of the driver of the automobile is that when he was at a point 40 to 50 feet east of the crossing he saw the car about the same distance north of the street he was in; that the safety stop was 20 feet or a little further north of the crossing or boulevard; that he knew of the safety stop and when the car was still north of the safety stop he saw and heard the motorman apply his brakes and saw the car slow down as if it were going to stop, whereupon he went forward at a speed he did not know how fast, and when he got within range of being struck by the car it was 5 or 6 feet from him, and his own car stopped right on the track and was struck. The claim that the driver's evidence discloses that he was conclusively guilty of contributory negligence is on the theory that the driver, knowing of the safety stop, merely relied on the motorman's observing his duty to stop there, and hence went on heedless of whether he did or not. Doubtless, if the driver did only that, then he was negligent. Clark v. Chicago, etc., R. Co., 127 Mo. 197, 213, 29 S. W. 1013. But he did more than that. He took care to ascertain that the motorman was going to stop, and, as the car slowed up, he had reason to believe that the safety stop was being observed. It is true, he said, "Yes, sir," to a long question, which included in it the idea that he saw the car moving from the time he first observed it until the collision. In other words, the contention apparently is that after the driver saw the car did not stop he nevertheless went on into danger. But the evidence does not conclusively disclose where the driver was when he realized, or should have done so, that the car was coming on to the crossing, or, in other words, the evidence does not conclusively disclose negligence in the driver at that time or at the time he started to go across the tracks. Hence, even if the judgment must be reversed for reasons hereinafter given, it should not be done outright and without remanding the cause.

[2, 3] As heretofore stated, the petition charges that—

"Through the gross carelessness, negligence, and unskillfulness of defendant's agent and employee in charge of said street car, or through the gross carelessness, negligence, and unskillfulness of defendant company in not having the brakes on said street car in good working order and condition, said street car failed to come to a stop," etc.

It makes little difference whether this is an attempt to charge general negligence against the company in not having its brakes in proper order, or whether the negligence charged against both motorman and defendant company is specified in the failure to have the brakes in working order. For, according to plaintiffs' evidence, the trouble was that the brakes were not working properly, for the motorman used them and endeavored to stop the car. Yet, notwithstanding this, the instruction submitted plaintiffs' case on general negligence, viz.:

"If the jury find and believe that such failure to stop said car, if any, was the result of negligence on the part of the defendant, its agents, servants, or employees in charge thereof," etc.

This was error. Feldewerth v. Wabash R. Co., 181 Mo. App. 630, 640, 641, 164 S. W. 711, and cases cited. The references in the instruction to the safety stop and of the custom of cars to stop there before entering upon the boulevard were not to submit a ground of recovery as being the failure to observe a custom, but merely to submit to the jury the surrounding situation, which would explain why

231 S.W.—65

the car was expected to stop, and should have stopped, there. These matters were alleged in the petition, so that it was not outside the pleadings to submit those facts regarding the situation, if they were not conceded in the evidence.

[4] Plaintiffs' intruction on the measure of damages was erroneous. It allowed interest on the amount of damages found from July 7, 1917. In actions ex delicto interest is not allowable. Gerst v. City of St. Louis, 185 Mo. 191, 211, 84 S. W. 34, 105 Am. St. Rep. 580; Humphreys v. St. Louis, etc., R. Co., 191 Mo. App. 710, 723, 178 S. W. 233; Jordan v. Chicago, etc., R. Co., 226 S. W. 1023. Besides, if interest were allowable, it is not clear why it should begin from the above-named date.

[5] The instruction on the measure of damages was not clear, as it should have been. It told the jury that if they found for plaintiffs they would assess the damages at such sum as would reimburse plaintiffs for the damages sustained, and in computing same they could take into consideration the expense of repairing the car and also the loss sustained in being compelled to sell the car at a reduced price on account of the damage. As applied to the evidence introduced on this subject, this meant the difference between the price at which plaintiffs were holding the car before the injury and the price they had to take because of the fact that it was a repaired car. If the instruction would be understood to mean that the measure of plaintiffs' damages was the expense of repairing it plus the difference between the reasonable market value of the car immediately before the accident and its reasonable value after it was repaired, it would not be far wrong. There might, however, be considerable difference between the price at which plaintiffs were holding the automobile and its reasonable market value. The instruction would have been clearer and free from all uncertainty had it told the jury that, if they found for plaintiffs, they were entitled to recover either the difference in the reasonable market value of the automobile immediately before and immediately after the injury, or that they were entitled to recover the amount reasonably necessary to repair and preserve the car plus the difference between the reasonable value of the car immediately before it was injured and its reasonable value after it was repaired.

[6] The admission of the motorman, made after the accident occurred, that his "brakes did not work," was not a part of the res gestæ, and was therefore not admissible. Ruschenberg v. Southern, etc., Co., 161 Mo. 70, 80, 61 S. W. 626; Redmon v. Metropolitan St. Ry. Co., 185 Mo. 1, 12, 84 S. W. 26, 105 Am. St. Rep. 558. The fact that it was already in evidence that the brakes did not work, and that, as the motorman applied the brakes and

the car did not stop the jury "could have inferred" that the brakes did not work, does not justify the introduction in evidence of the motorman's admission or declaration.

The judgment is reversed and the cause is remanded for a new trial.

All concur.

WHITESIDE v. COURT OF HONOR.
(No. 16347.)

(St. Louis Court of Appeals. Missouri. June 7, 1921.)

1. **Appeal and error ⟐⟐926(8)—In the absence of certificate it will be presumed a proper case for reading the deposition was disclosed.**

Under Rev. St. 1919, § 5467, declaring that the facts which would authorize the reading of depositions may be established by the testimony of the opposing witness or the certificate of the officer taking the same, it will be presumed on appeal, where the certificate was not preserved in the record, that it disclosed a proper case for reading the deposition.

2. **Evidence ⟐⟐215(1)—Proofs of death furnished by beneficiary admissible as admissions.**

Proofs of death furnished by beneficiary to the insurer in accordance with the stipulations of the policy are admissible in evidence against such beneficiary as admissions, although the admissions may be explained.

3. **Coroners ⟐⟐22—Coroner's verdict not admissible in civil case to show cause of death.**

It is the ordinary rule that a coroner's verdict is not admissible in a civil case to show the cause of death of the insured.

4. **Evidence ⟐⟐215(1)—Proceedings before coroner and report of district court to insurer admissible as admissions when joined by beneficiary to proof of death.**

In an action on a fraternal benefit certificate, where it appeared that the beneficiary joined to the proofs of death the report of the proceedings before the coroner as well, as the report of a district court to the insurer, such reports were admissible as admissions on the part of the beneficiary subject to explanation by her.

5. **Witnesses ⟐⟐219(3)—Privilege of attorney removed by client's testimony as to transaction.**

Where beneficiary volunteered testimony as to conversations with defendant's attorney concerning her claim on fraternal benefit certificate, the attorney may give his version in contradiction; the bar of privilege being removed, and it being immaterial that the attorney stated he testified in impeachment.

6. **Trial ⟐⟐253(10)—Requested instruction on presumption as to suicide properly refused where there was evidence pro and con.**

While suicide is not presumed and cannot be found as a matter of law, when the evidence is only circumstantial, unless such circumstances exclude every reasonable hypothesis, yet it

---

is improper to so state to the jury, when there is evidence both for and against suicide, for the question is one for the jury under all the facts and circumstances. Hence the refusal of an instruction that, in determining whether a member of a fraternal benefit association committed suicide, unless the facts were so clear and indisputable as to exclude every other reasonable hypothesis other than that the member committed suicide, the jury should find that death resulted from some other cause, was not error.

Appeal from St. Louis Circuit Court; Samuel Rosenfeld, Judge.

"Not to be officially published."

Action by Mae G. Whiteside against Court of Honor, a corporation. From a judgment for plaintiff for only a sum admitted to be due, plaintiff appeals. Affirmed.

Theodore C. Eggers and Harmon J. Bliss, both of St. Louis, for appellant.

W. Paul Mobley, of St. Louis, for respondent.

BECKER, J. This case was originally argued and submitted in December, 1920, and an opinion of the court, written by Reynolds, P. J., was filed therein in January, 1921. A motion for rehearing was sustained, the case reargued and resubmitted in April, 1921. The following opinion in the case is the same as the opinion written originally by Judge Reynolds, with the exception of paragraph I, which relates to the question of the admission in evidence of the deposition of Helen A. Hughes, and paragraph V, which relates to the trial court's refusal to give instruction numbered 3, requested by plaintiff.

This is an action on a benefit certificate issued to John L. Whiteside, in favor of Mae G. Whiteside, his wife, by defendant, a corporation organized as a fraternal benefit insurance company under the laws of the state of Illinois, and authorized to do business as such in this state at the date of the issue of the certificate of membership. Alleging the death of the member, plaintiff prays for judgment in the amount of the benefit certificate, $2,000, together with $200 as damages for vexatious refusal to pay, and $200 for attorney's fees.

The answer, after admitting the issue of the certificate and that it was payable, subject to the terms thereof, to Mae G. Whiteside, plaintiff, then the wife of the insured, and admitting that on December 1, 1915, John L. Whiteside, while a member in good standing of the defendant order, died, and that proofs of death had been furnished and payment demanded and refused, and admitting that it was incorporated by virtue of the laws of the state of Missouri and authorized to do business in this state as a fraternal benefit society, sets up, among other provisions in the certificate, this:

⟐⟐For other cases see same topic and KEY-NUMBER in all Key-Numbered Digests and Indexes

"I understand and agree that if I commit suicide, whether sane or insane, voluntary or involuntary, there shall be payable to the beneficiaries entitled thereto, an amount equal to five (5) per cent. per annum of the face of the certificate for each year I shall have been continuously a member of the society, and after twenty years membership the certificate shall be payable in full."

A section of the Constitution of the order to the same effect is also pleaded and, averring that Whiteside had committed suicide by shooting himself in the head with a revolver, and that at the time of his death he had been a member of the order for a period of only 4 months and 29 days, it is set up that, according to the terms of the benefit certificate and the provisions of the Constitution, plaintiff is entitled to receive from defendant the sum of only $41.39, which, it is averred, was tendered to plaintiff in lawful money and tender refused; and averring payment of the same into court, together with legal interest from December 1, 1915, amounting to the sum of 86 cents, and costs of court in the sum of $16.80, a total of $59.05, for the benefit of plaintiff, defendant prays judgment dismissing the cause with its costs. To this a reply denying the new matter was filed.

At a trial before the court and a jury there was a verdict for plaintiff in the sum of 59.05, judgment following, from which, after interposing a motion for new trial and excepting to that being overruled, plaintiff has duly appealed.

It is not necessary to set out the evidence further than to say that the member died from the effects of gunshot wound in his head; that a revolver was found near him, one shell exploded, he lying in or on a bed. Whether it was a case of suicide or accident was the issue on which the case, under the evidence, went to the jury.

The errors assigned are to the admission in evidence of a deposition given by one Helen A. Hughes, it being claimed that statutory grounds for using the same were not shown. It is further assigned for error that the trial court erroneously admitted in evidence proceedings before the coroner at the inquest held on the body of Whiteside, and in admitting the report of the "District Court" to Court of Honor, same being hearsay. Third, that the trial court erred in admitting in evidence the testimony of respondent's counsel as to statements made by plaintiff, such counsel having stated that he sought by such testimony to impeach the credibility of appellant, and, having failed to lay the foundation for impeachment by proper interrogation by him of plaintiff, the testimony was inadmissible. Fourth, that the trial court erred in admitting in evidence the testimony of one Jennie B. Sommers upon her recall to the witness stand, respondent's counsel having stated that he sought by such testimony

to impeach the credibility of appellant, and having failed to lay the foundation for impeachment by proper interrogation by him of appellant. Fifth, that the trial court erred in admitting in evidence the testimony of respondent's counsel as to the statements made at his office by appellant while consulting him as to her claim against respondent society, such communications being privileged by reason of the relation of attorney and client, thus created and existing between such counsel and appellant. Sixth, that the court erred in refusing to give instruction No. 3, offered by plaintiff (appellant). And, finally, that the court erred in refusing to grant plaintiff a new trial, the reason, as it is alleged, that the evidence does not support the verdict of the jury.

[1] I. The point is urged that the learned trial court erred in admitting in evidence the deposition of Helen A. Hughes, read in evidence on behalf of the defendant below, because the statutory grounds for reading same at the trial were not shown. An examination of the record discloses that the certificate of the officer who took the deposition is omitted from the record. Under our statute (section 5467 R. S. of Mo. 1919 [section 6411 R. S. of Mo. 1909]), relating to "when depositions may be read," it is provided:

"The facts which would authorize the reading of the deposition may be established by the testimony of the opposing witness or *the certificate of the officer taking the same.* * * *" (Italics ours.)

It has been repeatedly held that where the certificate of the officer taking the deposition is not preserved in the record, the presumption will be indulged that the certificate discloses a proper case for reading the deposition. Sullivan v. Railway Co., 97 Mo. 113, 10 S. W. 852; Klages v. Mueller, 166 Mo. App. 540, loc. cit. 543, 149 S. W. 327; Toberman, Mackey & Co. v. Gidley, 187 S. W. 593, loc. cit. 594; Sheets v. Regnier, 221 S. W. 417, loc. cit. 418.

It follows that in light of the statute and the authority of the cases cited supra we must rule this point against appellant.

[2-4] II. Touching the second alleged error in admitting in evidence the proceedings before the coroner and the report of the "District Court" to the Court of Honor, all of which, as it is claimed, were inadmissible as hearsay, the learned counsel for the appellant cite two cases only, that of Kane v. Supreme Tent, Knights of the World, 113 Mo. App. 104, 87 S. W. 547, cited as Kane v. Lodge, and Ætna Life Ins. Co. v. Milward, 118 Ky. 716, 82 S. W. 364, 68 L. R. A. 285, 4 Ann. Cas. 1092. Each of these decisions relate only to the admission in evidence of the proceedings before the coroner and his verdict or finding.

In Kane v. Supreme Tent, Knights of Maccabees of the World, supra, our court said:

"Considering the loose and unsatisfactory manner in which these post mortems are often held, we think the verdict of the coroner's jury would, in most instances, be as likely to lead the triers of the fact away from the truth as toward it. It seems to us that they ought to be classed rather as hearsay than as the result of a judicial investigation, and for this reason rejected as evidence in civil cases."

That is practically the holding of the Courts of Appeals of Kentucky, on a very elaborate examination of the question, in the case above cited.

In Queatham v. Modern Woodmen of America, 148 Mo. App. 33, 127 S. W. 651, it is stated that—

As a general rule "proofs of death furnished by a beneficiary to the insurer in accordance with the stipulations of the policy are admissible in evidence against such beneficiaries as admissions by him of the truth of the statements therein contained. Although there is strong reason for the rule where the statement is made directly by the beneficiary, it is subject to the qualification that the beneficiary will not be estopped by erroneous statements in the notice of proofs of death under all circumstances. In other words, succinctly stated, in proper cases, admissions contained in such proofs may be explained on the trial. They are only prima facie that the facts stated are true" (citing many authorities).

This rule, that the beneficiary sending in proofs is not conclusively bound by admissions contained therein, and that they are prima facie evidence of admission against interest, has been frequently followed in other cases, as see Castens v. Supreme Lodge, etc., 190 Mo. App. 57, 175 S. W. 264, where at page 66 it is said, referring to the proofs furnished by the beneficiary:

"Such proof is conclusive, too, on the party furnishing it, touching the fact of suicide unless contradicted or properly explained as by showing some mistake or misapprehension or something otherwise calculated to relieve against it."

A like holding was also made in Stephens v. Metropolitan Life Ins. Co., 190 Mo. App. 673, loc. cit. 680, 176 S. W. 253. See, also, Bruck v. Ins. Co., 194 Mo. App. 529, loc. cit. 538, 185 S. W. 753, and many other cases, the last being Williams et al. v. Modern Woodmen of Amer., not yet officially reported, but see 221 S. W. 414.

Holding that the rule did not apply in that case, and referring to the effect of the hearing before a coroner and his verdict, our court, in the Queatham Case, supra (148 Mo. App. loc. cit. 49, 127 S. W. 655) said:

"We believe, therefore, while such verdict is competent to be received in evidence as a part of the proof that the death of the insured occurred, it is not even prima facie competent as tending to prove the cause of such death and this is true when it is introduced by either party."

Several cases are cited in support of this, although there are many authorities to the contrary. The modern, certainly the American rule, is that proceedings before a coroner and the verdict of himself or the jury are not ordinarily competent in civil cases. In Sullivan v. Seattle Elec. Co., 51 Wash. 71, commencing at page 72 (97 Pac. 1109, 1110, 130 Am. St. Rep. 10), it is said, considering the challenge as to the competency of the report of the coroner:

"It was formerly held that the record of the coroner's inquest on a dead body was competent, but not conclusive, evidence of the cause of death in all civil actions, because it was the result of an inquiry made under competent public authority to ascertain matters of public interest and concern. 1 Greenleaf, § 556. This rule still prevails in a few jurisdictions, but the great weight of modern authority is against it."

A multitude of cases are cited by the court in support of this proposition, and the court concludes (51 Wash. loc. cit. 73, 97 Pac. 1110, 130 Am. St. Rep. 10):

"The rule excluding such records prevails indiscriminately in actions on insurance policies and in actions to recover damages for death by a wrongful act, as will appear from an examination of the cases cited."

In Re Estate of Bertha M. Dolbeer, 149 Cal. 227, loc. cit. 246, 86 Pac. 695, loc. cit. 704, 9 Ann. Cas. 795, the Supreme Court of California held that the action of the trial court in excluding the verdict of the coroner's inquest on the bodies of two of the parties whose interests were involved was correct, the court saying:

"It has been expressly decided in this state that a verdict of a coroner's jury is not admissible in such a case as this."

That case was a contest over a will, but the same rule applies here.

It does not appear in any of these cases last cited from other states, or in the Kane or Ætna Life Ins. Company cases, supra, that the claimant had accompanied her proof of loss with the proceedings before the coroner or his finding.

We do not find in the rules of the defendant order or in the certificate itself any requirement that the verdict of the coroner, if an inquest is held, be furnished as part of the proofs of death. There is evidence in the case, however, tending to show that the plaintiff here had accompanied her proofs of death, both with the proceedings before the coroner and the verdict of the coroner's jury, as well as by other documents. She offered evidence in explanation or denial of these as her act.

As we have seen, when the claimant, as it is said, accompanies her proof of loss with the proceedings before the coroner, such statement by her with the accompanying papers are competent and receivable in evidence as admissions by her, subject always to her right to either qualify them, explain them, or show a matter of fact she had not trans- them with her proofs of loss. That rule stated in our own courts, as will seen by the cases cited above. It is also cognized as the rule in other jurisdictions. Thus, in Krogh v. Modern Brotherhood, 153 Wis. 397, 141 N. W. 276, 45 L. R. A. (N. S.) 104, it appeared that the certificate of insurance required that if a coroner's inquest was held, a copy of the verdict of the coroner's jury, properly certified, should be furnished by the claimant as a part of the proofs of death, but this was not done; no certificate having been furnished by the plaintiff in the case. Instead of that, however, it appeared that such a copy was attached to a notification of the death of Krogh, made to defendant by its agent, as required by its by-laws, and this was the copy which was sought to be introduced in evidence, and which the trial court rejected. Plaintiff herself, it appeared, had had nothing to do with furnishing the certificate. Under these circumstances the Supreme Court of Wisconsin (153 Wis. loc. cit. 402, 141 N. W. 278, 45 L. R. A. [N. S.] 404) said:

"Had it been a part of the proofs of death furnished by her it would have been competent as an admission against interest, which, while not conclusive, would have been prima facie evidence against her [citing cases]. But where the coroner's verdict is furnished by the company's agents the rule does not apply. Nothing they do without the knowledge or consent of the plaintiff or beneficiaries can be received as admissions against them, and the verdict of the coroner's jury was properly excluded" [citing cases].

Examining the abstract in this case, it is very difficult to say how these proceedings before the coroner, as well as the proceedings before the council and the report of the "district court" to the Court of Honor got into the record. At all events, it appears that the proceedings before the coroner and before the "district court" were attached to the proofs of death, which purported to have been forwarded to the supreme officer of the defendant order. If that is the case, then we hold that these matters were properly admitted in evidence, subject, as before said, to the right of the plaintiff to make such explanation in regard to them as she was able to do. This disposes of the second point made by learned counsel for the appellant, and we hold it against them, and, as the record appears before us, these were properly admitted.

[5] III. Touching the third point made, that the statements of the attorney for defendant as to conversations between himself and plaintiff in his office, concerning this claim, were not admissible because the proper ground had not been laid for impeachment, and because privileged, we hold the point against appellant. This also applies to the fifth assignment. While it is true that de- fendant's attorney stated that he offered this as impeachment of appellant, when we examine the testimony itself it is not of the nature of an impeachment, but is contradictory of a statement which had been voluntarily made by the plaintiff herself in her cross-examination as to what had occurred between herself and that attorney. By this testimony, which came in without objection and was volunteered by plaintiff herself, the door was open for the attorney to give his version of what had occurred between them. Plaintiff had herself removed the bar of secrecy, and, while not in the line of impeachment, the testimony of the attorney was properly admissible in contradiction of the plaintiff, and was not privileged.

IV. As to the fourth point made as to the admission in evidence of the testimony of the witness Jennie S. Sommers upon her recall to the witness stand, we are not able to find any justification for this claim, nor do we find that any objection was made to that evidence.

[6] V. Error is assigned on the refusal of the trial court to give instruction numbered 3, requested by plaintiff. This instruction reads as follows:

"The court instructs the jury that, in determining whether John L. Whiteside did or did not commit suicide, unless the facts are so clear and indisputable as to exclude every other reasonable hypothesis other than that the said Whiteside committed suicide, then you must find that his death resulted from some cause other than suicide."

In the recent case of Prentiss v. Illinois Life Ins. Co., 225 S. W. 695 (loc. cit. 701) an instruction of like character was under consideration, and the court held:

"While it is true that suicide is not presumed, and cannot be found, as a matter of law, when the evidence is wholly circumstantial, unless such circumstances exclude every reasonable hypothesis except suicide, yet it is improper in an instruction to so state to the jury when there is evidence both for and against suicide. Brunswick v. Standard Acc. Ins. Co., 278 Mo. 154, 213 S. W. loc. cit. 50, 7 A. L. R. 1213; Kane v. Lodge, 113 Mo. App. loc. cit. 118, 119, 87 S. W. 547. In the case at bar, there was the strongest sort of evidence showing that the assured committed suicide, and in the face of such evidence all presumptions disappear, and it is for the jury to determine, under all the facts and circumstances in the case, whether the assured did commit suicide, and on this proposition the burden of proof was upon the defendant insurance company. In civil cases, even where the cause of action or defense is based upon a criminal charge a preponderance of the evidence is sufficient, although the evidence is all circumstantial. It need not be proved beyond a reasonable doubt, or, what is the same thing, exclude every other reasonable hypothesis. State ex rel. v. Ellison, 268 Mo. 239, 187 S. W. 23; Edwards v. Knapp Co., 97 Mo. 432, 10 S. W. 54; Smith v. Burrus, 106 Mo. 101, 16 S. W. 881, 13 L. R. A. 59, 27

Am. St. Rep. 329; Marshall v. Ins. Co., 43 Mo. 586."

On authority of the Prentiss Case, supra, we must rule that there was no error in the refusal of this instruction as drafted.

It follows from what we have stated above that there is no error in the record effecting the merits of the case, and, the judgment being for the right party it should be, and the same is hereby, ordered affirmed.

ALLEN, P. J., concurs.
DAUES, J., not sitting.

LARSON et al. v. SHOCKLEY et al.　(No. 2632.)

(Springfield Court of Appeals. Missouri.　May 3, 1921.　Rehearing Denied June 20, 1921.)

1. Appeal and error ⚖⇒543—Appliant seeking remand because lost notes of evidence prevent transcript and bill of exceptions is not entitled to retrial as of right and must be without fault.

An application for remand of a cause, appealed on the ground that the stenographer's notes of the evidence had been lost, rendering it impossible to secure the transcript and file bill of exceptions, is not a case where the appellant can demand a retrial as a matter of right, but is one in which the appellate court in the exercise of a wise discretion may grant or refuse the relief asked, and appellant to be entitled to such relief must be free from fault and must have exercised proper diligence.

2. Appeal and error ⚖⇒543—Facts held to show that appellant seeking retrial because of lost stenographer's notes was not without fault.

On appellant's motion for retrial because of lost stenographer's notes held, from facts in the record, that appellants had failed to sustain the burden of proving that they had been diligent and free from fault in not securing transcript of the evidence.

Appeal from Circuit Court, Taney County; Fred Stewart, Judge.

Action by H. A. Larson and another against Edwin M. Shockley and others. From a judgment therein plaintiffs appeal and apply for a remand for new trial because of lost stenographer's notes preventing securing a transcript and filing a bill of exceptions. Application refused, and appeal dismissed.

M. R. Lively, of Webb City, for appellants.
Lewis Luster, of Springfield, for respondents.

COX, P. J. This case was tried in the circuit court of Taney county and involved a receivership. At the April, 1918, term of the Taney county circuit court, the receiver made his final report which was modified to some extent and approved and certain allowances made and certain sums taxed against appellants. We assume that a motion for new trial was filed at that term and the cause continued on the motion for the appeal was granted in April, 1919. At the October, 1919, term of this court, respondents filed a motion to affirm the judgment for failure of appellants to comply with the rules of this court. This motion was overruled and the case continued to the March term, 1920. At that time, appellants secured a continuance to the October term, 1920, and at that term secured another continuance to this term. At this term, appellants filed an application to have the cause remanded for a new trial on the ground that the stenographer's notes of the evidence had been lost and it was therefore impossible for him to secure a transcript of the evidence and file bill of exceptions in the case. Respondents resist this application and insist that the appeal should be dismissed and this litigation ended.

[1] Appellants show by affidavit that while this receivership was pending evidence was taken by three different stenographers; that attorney for appellants soon after taking the appeal filed with the court reporter that took the last oral evidence an order for a bill of exceptions and complete transcript of the evidence in said cause. They also filed the affidavits of two of the stenographers, one made on the 15th of November, 1920, stating that she had been requested by attorney for appellants to make a transcript of the evidence taken by her but that her notes could not be found and she had not prepared the transcript for that reason. When this request was made, or when she discovered that her notes were misplaced, is not stated. The affidavit of the other stenographer was made on the 7th day of December, 1920, and stated in substance the same thing. This affidavit did not show when the request for a transcript had been made nor when he discovered that his notes were misplaced. Respondents have filed a letter received from one of these stenographers dated August 25, 1920, stating that she had not received an order for a transcript at that time and that she was then unable to locate her notes. Also, a letter from one of the stenographers, Oscar Sanders, who took part of the testimony, addressed to attorney for respondent and dated August 30, 1920, in which he stated that he resigned as stenographer and was inducted into the United States Army in December, 1917, and spent practically all of 1918 and 1919 in France; that while acting as stenographer he took testimony in this case in 1917, and while in France he had correspondence with appel-

lants' attorney in regard to another case tried in Taney county and had made a transcript for him in that case while in France, but that this case was not mentioned to him; that he left his notes in the vault of the circuit clerk at Ava, Douglas county, Mo.; and that if they are still there, he could secure them and make a transcript of the evidence taken by him.

We do not think the showing made entitles appellants to a reversal and new trial. This is not a case in which an appellant can demand a retrial as a matter of right, but is one in which the appellate court in the exercise of a wise discretion may grant or refuse the relief asked, and it is conceded that to entitle an appellant to such relief, he must be free from fault and must have exercised proper diligence. The principle involved and the rule by which appellate courts are guided in cases of this character are well stated by Judge Trimble, speaking for the Kansas City Court of Appeals in the case of Stevens et al. v. Chapin, 227 S. W. 874, loc. cit. 876, as follows:

"The right of appeal is a creature of the statute, and since there is no statute providing for a new trial because the stenographer's notes are destroyed, the right to have a cause remanded on this ground must, in a large degree, depend upon the circumstances of each case. And the question whether appellant is to be granted relief on such ground should be determined upon principles analogous to equitable doctrines rather than the strict rules of law. Appellant is not asking for something to which he is entitled as a matter of strict, absolute, legal right but for that which the court, in the exercise of inherent extraordinary powers, will grant to prevent a possible injustice being done to one who is himself wholly without fault or blame. In every case which we have examined, this freedom from fault or blame on the part of one seeking such relief is a necessary prerequisite to the granting of the relief sought"—citing cases.

Further it is stated:

"Not only must an appellant in such case be free from actual fault or negligence, but he must also show that he exercised due diligence and was free from laches."

[2] The burden is on appellants to show that they have been diligent and are free from default. Here there is no evidence of any showing that any effort was ever made to get a transcript of the testimony taken by Mr. Sanders. True, appellants state that they ordered a full transcript from the stenographer who took the last oral testimony, but they did not even inquire whether that stenographer had possession of the notes of the other stenographers or could procure them, or if procured, that they could be transcribed by him. There is no evidence showing when the stenographer's notes were first discovered to have been misplaced or

that any effort had ever been made to prepare a bill of exceptions without them. It also seems to us that proper diligence would have required appellants to have learned whether or not a transcript of the evidence could have been secured long before they knew, or claim they did learn, that fact. We do not feel that under the showing made here we ought to grant the relief asked.

The application to remand this case for new trial will be refused, and appellants' appeal dismissed.

FARRINGTON and BRADLEY, JJ., concur.

RUEMMELI-DAWLEY MFG. CO. v. MAY DEPARTMENT STORES CO.
(No. 16066.)

(St. Louis Court of Appeals. Missouri.
May 3, 1921.)

1. Work and labor ⬩13—Plaintiff suing upon quantum meruit bound by terms of special contract.

Where plaintiff has introduced a special contract in support of his action upon quantum meruit for services rendered, his claim being based upon "extras" not part of the general contract, he is bound by the terms of the contract reciting conditions under which extra labors were to be performed.

2. Contracts ⬩346(9)—Defendant always at liberty under general denial to overthrow contract asserted.

Defendant under a general denial is always at liberty to disprove and overthrow a contract asserted against him by proving that it was materially different from the one so asserted, but can introduce no evidence of new matter to avoid the legal effect or operation of allegations of fact in the complaint.

3. Work and labor ⬩27(4)—Defendant held entitled to prove that extras sued for were not authorized in writing.

Where plaintiff, suing in quantum meruit for extras furnished, introduced the contract in evidence to make out its case, and the contract specifically provided that no "extra payment" would be allowed for "extras" unless same were authorized in writing and the price agreed upon in advance, defendant was entitled under a general denial to show that no written order was ever given for any of the extra work or materials sought to be recovered for.

Appeal from St. Louis Circuit Court; Rhodes E. Cave, Judge.

"Not to be officially published."

Action by the Ruemmeli-Dawley Manufacturing Company against the May Department Stores Company. Judgment for defendant, and plaintiff appeals. Affirmed.

⬩For other cases see same topic and KEY-NUMBER in all Key-Numbered Digests and Indexes

Nagel & Kirby, of St. Louis, for appellant. Nathan Frank and Richard A. Jones, both of St. Louis, for respondent.

BECKER, J. Plaintiff was one of the contractors engaged in the preparation of the premises leased by the defendant in the Railway Exchange Building in St. Louis. The part of this work which plaintiff was to perform, namely, that of constructing and installing a refrigerating plant and the work connected therewith, was covered by a written contract between plaintiff and defendant executed prior to the doing of the work.

Under the five counts of its petition plaintiff seeks to recover upon quantum meruit for labor and material claimed to have been furnished upon and in connection with this work. The defendant's answer to each of the counts was a general denial.

The case was tried to the court without the intervention of a jury. At the trial, as part of its case in chief, plaintiff offered, and there was received in evidence the said written contract between plaintiff and defendant, and plaintiff sought to establish that the various items upon which it based its claim were "extras," and not contemplated to be furnished as a part of the general contract. This contract as introduced in evidence, as to the method by which anything for which extra compensation was to be claimed, required as a condition precedent thereto that—

"Any modification of plans and specifications deemed advisable by the owner, before or during the construction of the work, shall be estimated upon at the time by the contractor, and, if satisfactory to the owner, he will order work done at the prices agreed upon in writing; otherwise extra work shall not be allowed, and the contractor will not be allowed extra payment for same."

During the progress of the trial the defendant was permitted, over objection of the plaintiff, to introduce testimony to the effect that no written orders had been given for any of the items mentioned in plaintiff's petition.

No declarations of law were asked for or given, and the court made no finding of facts. The court found for defendant on each of the counts in plaintiff's petition, and plaintiff appealed.

Plaintiff below, appellant here, assigns as error the ruling of the court which permitted defendant to introduce testimony to the effect that no written orders were given for the work sued on in the several counts in plaintiff's petition, and in the overruling of plaintiff's objection to such testimony on the ground that the only basis for any such evidence was to be found in the written contract between plaintiff and defendant, and that this contract should have been specially pleaded by the defendant in its answer had it intended to rely upon its provisions.

"* * * It is very true that, where work is done or services performed under a special contract, and the plaintiff has fully performed the contract on his part, and nothing remains but a duty on the part of the defendant to pay the price agreed on, the plaintiff is not in such case bound to sue on the written contract, but may use the common counts in assumpsit, but still, when the contract is produced on the trial, the plaintiff will be required to prove that he has performed the contract on his part, and that by virtue of the provisions of the contract the defendant is required to pay the price agreed on; if any fact necessary to create a liability on the part of defendant to pay is wanting, the plaintiff cannot recover." Stout v. St. Louis Tribune Co., 52 Mo. 342, loc. cit. 347; Ingram v. Ashmore, 12 Mo. 574; Mansur v. Botts, 80 Mo. 651; Redman v. Adams, 165 Mo. 60, 65 S. W. 300; Williams v. Chicago Ry. Co., 112 Mo. 463, 20 S. W. 631, 34 Am. St. Rep. 408.

And it has frequently been held in such cases, however, that the contract between the parties may be "used as an instrument of proof." Neenan v. Donoghue, 50 Mo. 493. See, also, Stockman v. Allen, 160 Mo. App. 229, 142 S. W. 744; American Surety Co. v. Const. Co., 182 Mo. App. 667, loc. cit. 674, 166 S. W. 333.

"Though in form this is a suit for money had and received, and not one on a special contract, nevertheless, a special contract having been established, the rights of the parties were to be determined in accordance with it. Fox v. Car Co., 16 Mo. App. 122; Mansur v. Botts, 80 Mo. 651, 656." Beagles v. Robertson, 135 Mo. App. 306, loc. cit. 324, 115 S. W. 1042.

And in the case of Williams v. Chicago Ry. Co., 112 Mo. 463, 20 S. W. 631, 34 Am. St. Rep. 403, wherein plaintiff sued on the common count indebitatus assumpsit as for a quantum meruit on the question as to what effect the contract in evidence should be given, the court said:

"Having held that plaintiffs under the allegations in their petition could show the amount and value of their labor not exceeding the contract price, the question necessarily arises: What effect is to be given the contract in such a case? We answer that the contract must still control."

[1] Thus it would seem, under the authorities, that where plaintiff, as in this case, has introduced a special contract in support of his action upon quantum meruit for services rendered, he is bound by the terms of the contract. Here plaintiff, however, has clearly failed to prove that it has complied with the contract introduced in evidence by it, with regard to the provision which requires that any and all work in the way of "extras" must be authorized in writing and the amount to be charged therefor specifically agreed to; otherwise "extra work shall not be allowed and the contractor will not be allowed extra payments for same."

[2] In this connection it must be remembered that defendant, under a general denial is always at liberty to disprove and overthrow the contract asserted against him by proving that it was materially different from he one so asserted." Wilkerson v. Farnham, 52 Mo. 672, loc. cit. 679. And so defendant here, under its general denial, could introduce as evidence anything which tended directly to controvert the material allegations of fact in the complaint, but could introduce no evidence of new matter to avoid the legal effect or operation of such facts. A general denial goes to the facts alleged, and not to the liability arising from those facts.

[3] Under defendant's theory of the case plaintiff never had a cause of action for either or any of the counts sued on, and therefore was entitled, under its plea of general denial, to show any matter which tended to prove that plaintiff at no time had a cause of action. Therefore, since the contract itself, which plaintiff introduced in evidence to make out its case, specifically provided that no "extra payments" will be allowed for "extras" unless same are authorized in writing and the price agreed upon in advance, the defendant was clearly entitled to show that no written order was ever given for any of the "extra" work or materials sought to be recovered for in the several counts of plaintiff's petition.

As to appellant's argument that respondent waived this provision of the contract, it is sufficient to say that plaintiff did not make out such a case of waiver as to make it a question of law for the court, but it was clearly a question of fact for the court, sitting as a jury, and under the evidence the court, sitting as a jury, in rendering a general finding for the defendant decided this point against plaintiff.

No declarations of law were asked for or given, and the court made no special finding of facts. Finding no error in the record prejudicial to plaintiff's rights, and the record showing substantial testimony, if believed, to support the finding of the learned trial judge, we order the judgment affirmed.

ALLEN, P. J., concurs.

NEAL v. CROWSON. (No. 13816.)

(Kansas City Court of Appeals. Missouri.
June 13, 1921.)

1. Evidence ⬤=18—That jack has no value, except for breeding purposes, matter of common knowledge.

It is a matter of common knowledge among farmers and breeders that a jack has no value except for breeding purposes.

2. Sales ⬤=273(1)—Law implied warranty that jacks were reasonably fit for breeding purposes.

In the sale of jacks, the law implied a warranty that they were reasonably fit for the purpose for which sold, namely, that of breeding, and if they fell short of the warranty the buyer's note was without consideration.

3. Sales ⬤=445(1)—Whether there was warranty of jacks sold a jury question.

In suit on a note given for the price of jacks sold for breeding purposes, the question of whether there was a warranty of fitness for such purpose, either express or implied, was for the jury.

4. Appeal and error ⬤=1033(2)—Variance between pleading and proof in action on note given for price of jacks harmless.

In suit on a note given for the purchase price of jacks, in alleging an implied warranty of their fitness for breeding purposes and proving an express warranty, defendant buyer assumed more of a burden than the law required, and such variance between the pleadings and proof was not prejudicial to plaintiff, the purchaser of the note.

5. Sales ⬤=126(3)—Notice of rescission of purchase price of jacks given within time after permitting seller to attempt to demonstrate their utility.

Where jacks were sold for breeding purposes, and turned out to be slow workers, and the seller and the buyer co-operated in an attempt to make them work, notice given by the buyer to the seller of rescission after thus having given the seller opportunity to demonstrate the usefulness of the jacks was given within due time.

6. Trial ⬤=295(1)—Instruction must be construed with others.

An instruction not purporting to cover defendant's entire case must be construed with all of the instructions.

7. Sales ⬤=109—Instruction that seller could not rescind in part proper.

In suit on a note given for the purchase price of jacks, defendant maker claiming breach of warranty of their fitness for breeding purposes, an instruction that the seller could not rescind part of the contract of sale without rescinding all, and that if he took back one jack he must accept back both of them, etc., was in conformity with law, leaving the jury to determine whether there was a contract to rescind and to predicate their verdict on such finding.

Appeal from Circuit Court, Callaway County; David H. Harris, Judge.

"Not to be officially published."

Action by M. T. Neal against Harold Crowson. From a judgment for defendant, plaintiff appeals. Affirmed.

Irwin & Haley, of Jefferson City, for appellant.

N. T. Cave and W. B. Whitlow, both of Fulton, for respondent.

⬤=For other cases see same topic and KEY-NUMBER in all Key-Numbered Digests and Indexes

ARNOLD, J. This is a suit on a promissory note by the assignee thereof against the maker. On April 2, 1917, defendant purchased of one Grove R. Selby a one-half interest in two jacks, and in payment thereof gave his promissory note of that date in the sum of $400, payable in one year, at 7 per cent. interest per annum, compounded annually. After maturity the note was sold to plaintiff herein, and payment thereof was refused by defendant. The petition describes the said note and alleges demand and refusal of defendant to pay.

The answer admits the execution of the note as pleaded in the petition, and as further answer states that at the time the note was given the payee knew that defendant was purchasing said jacks for breeding purposes only, and knew that the only use and value of said jacks would be for breeding, and that defendant, relying on the knowledge of said Grove R. Selby as being true, and being deceived thereby, gave his note as above described. The answer further alleges that in truth and in fact the said jacks were not reasonably fit for breeding purposes, and that upon discovering said fact defendant tendered said jacks back to said Grove R. Selby, and rescinded the contract to purchase; that defendant kept said jacks at the request of Selby until the summer of 1918, at which time Selby agreed to rescind the contract, and took back one of said jacks, and has since retained him, and stated that he would take the other as soon as he had a suitable place to confine him. The answer further alleges that said note was purchased by plaintiff after maturity and not for value.

The reply is, first, a general denial, and especially denies warranty and that the jacks were not reasonably fit for breeding purposes, rescindment and agreement to rescind, and alleges that, for valuable consideration of a reduced price of the jacks, defendant waived guaranty, and pleads estoppel of defendant's right to claim warranty and rescission, and that there was an agreement that the jacks be divided between defendant and Selby.

The cause was tried to a jury, and resulted in a verdict for defendant. Plaintiff appeals, and makes six assignments of error.

First, plaintiff contends that the answer pleaded an implied warranty and that defendant's evidence, if it showed anything, showed an express warranty, and that there is a fatal variance between the pleading and the proof. Defendant's answer pleads an implied warranty in the following language:

"But defendant states that at the time said contract of purchase was made the said Grove R. Selby knew that the defendant was purchasing a one-half interest in said jacks for breeding purposes only, and knew that the only use and value of said jacks would be for breeding, and that this defendant, relying upon the knowledge of said Grove R. Selby as to the purpose for which jacks are used as being true, and being deceived thereby, was induced to purchase said jacks from said Grove R. Selby, and gave his said note as above described in payment thereof."

—thus pleading an implied warranty. In his testimony defendant stated:

"The morning the trade was made Mr. Selby told me how the jacks worked, and told me he would guarantee them to work that way."

This tends to prove an express warranty.

[1, 2] It is a matter of common knowledge among farmers and breeders that a jack has no value except for breeding purposes, and it is so alleged in defendant's answer and proved by the evidence. By the sale of the jacks by Selby to defendant the law implied a warranty that the jacks were reasonably fit for the purpose for which sold, and if they fell short of this warranty defendant's obligation was without consideration. Aultman, Miller & Co. v. Hunter, 82 Mo. App. 632.

[3, 4] The question of whether there was a warranty, either express or implied, was for the jury. In alleging an implied warranty, and proving an express warranty, which defendant evidently did to the satisfaction of the jury, he assumed more of a burden than the law required. We cannot say that plaintiff was in any way prejudiced by the variance between the pleadings in answer and the proof.

[5] As further assignment of error plaintiff insists that one seeking to rescind must do so immediately upon discovering the property to be not as warranted and represented. This court held in Window Co. v. Cornice Co., 181 Mo. App. loc. cit. 325, 168 S. W. 907 (opinion by Johnson, J.):

"The rule is well settled that upon the discovery of the fraud by the defrauded party, he is put to his election either to stand upon the contract or to rescind it. Taylor v. Short, 107 Mo. loc. cit. 392; Meinershagen v. Taylor, 169 Mo. App. 22. When a party seeks to rescind a contract he must do so unequivocally and in a reasonable time (Shultz v. Christman, 6 Mo. App. 338), and unreasonable delay, especially when accompanied by acts in recognition of the contract will condone the fraud and operate as an election to stand upon the contract (Harma v. Wolf, 114 Mo. App. 387). To put the defrauded party to his election it is not required 'that the full features of the given fraud should be known to him. * * * The right to rescind a contract must be exercised so soon as any one of the events which give rise to the right happens or is known to the person entitled to it.' Taylor v. Short, supra."

In applying this rule to the case at bar in the light of the testimony, we must conclude that the fact that the jacks were slow workers was discussed between defendant and Selby immediately on the arrival of the season for the use of the jacks, and that defendant on occasions called Selby in regard to the matter, and that the latter went to defendant's house to aid in an attempt to make the jacks work. The effort was mutual between defendant and Selby to secure the desired results. Thus having given the seller opportunity to demonstrate the usefulness of the jacks, the testimony tends to show that notice to rescind then was given.

The testimony further tends to show that the seller insisted that the jacks were not properly handled (and he so testified) and further that they were held by the buyer at the seller's request. This testimony, however, was not sufficient to convince the jury that the jacks were as warranted. We hold that notice to rescind was given within due time.

Plaintiff's third assignment of error relates to instructions 2 and 3 for defendant, and he argues that they contain abstract propositions of law, and that the court should have instructed the jury how such should be applied to the facts in the case, because there was no evidence in the record upon which to base an instruction on implied warranty. This contention is refuted by our discussion of point 1, and need not be further discussed here. There was substantial proof to support the instruction. Selby testified on cross-examination:

"These jacks were sold for breeding purposes, and I know of no other use to which they can be put, and they have no value other than for breeding purposes."

In assignment of error numbered 4, plaintiff argues that under the state of the evidence in this case, the fourth instruction given for defendant was error and prejudicial to plaintiff "because it was a direct comment upon the evidence, and because it assumes that said jacks were not reasonably fit for breeding purposes," a disputed fact, and "for the reasons, respondent's instruction numbered 6 is erroneous."

[6, 7] The instruction complained of does not purport to cover the defendant's entire case; it must be construed together with all of the instructions. We fail to discover any conflict between instructions 4 and 4A, given on behalf of plaintiff, and the instruction complained of. The complaint of plaintiff directed against instruction numbered 5, for defendant, is that it was error for the court to declare the law to be that it is incumbent upon one of the parties to do a thing that is inconsistent with the subsequent agreement, if, after entering into a contract, the parties thereto may mutually agree to rescind, and agree upon the terms of a new contract whereby defendant was to retain one of the jacks and Selby the other. The instruction informs the jury that—

"Selby could not rescind a part of the contract of sale without rescinding all; * * * if you believe and find from the evidence that defendant and Grove R. Selby agreed at any time that the sale of the jacks should be rescinded, and that in pursuance of such agreement Grove R. Selby accepted and took back the young jack mentioned in the evidence, then he must accept both of said jacks," etc.

The instruction clearly is in conformity with the law. It leaves the jury to determine whether there was a contract to rescind, and to predicate their verdict upon that finding. It covered a necessary element in defendant's case and clearly defined it.

Instruction numbered 4, for plaintiff, properly defines plaintiff's position in the matter of rescindment, and the two, taken together, are not in conflict.

We fail to find any prejudicial error in case. The verdict is for the right party, and the judgment is affirmed.

All concur.

HAY et al. v. BANKERS' LIFE CO.
(No. 15865.)

(St. Louis Court of Appeals. Missouri.
June 7, 1921.)

1. Insurance ⬦623(1)—Ground of defense may be waived.

The defense that action was not brought on an insurance certificate within the one-year period limited may be waived by the insurer.

2. Insurance ⬦615—Insistence upon one of several known grounds of defense may constitute waiver of others.

Insistence by the insurer upon one of several known grounds of defense may constitute a waiver of others.

3. Appeal and error ⬦842(1) — Waiver becomes question of law where facts are admitted.

While the question whether there has been a waiver is generally one of fact, and the sufficiency of the evidence relating thereto is for the jury, yet where the facts and circumstances relating to the subject are admitted or clearly established, waiver becomes a question of law.

4. Appeal and error ⬦842(8)—Construction of written instruments, as letters, is for the court.

The interpretation of letters and their legal effect is for the court, being a question of law.

5. Insurance ⬦623(4)—Insurer held to have waived as matter of law the right to resist recovery on the ground that action was not brought within a year.

Where an insurance certificate required action to be brought within a year after death, and insurer, which had denied liability on the theory that an assessment had not been paid, considerably after the expiration of a year, at the demand of the beneficiary's attorney, furnished blanks for proofs of death, stating, in a letter written by its general counsel, that the deceased was not a member of the insurer at the time of his death because of failure to pay assessment, such letter was a waiver of the defense of limitations.

6. Insurance ⟹360(3)—Member not entitled to have assessment paid out of so-called guaranty fund.

Where an assessment company required members to make a deposit in the guaranty fund, *held*, in view of the provisions that in case of lapse, the sum paid should go into the reserve fund, and other by-laws showing that the insurer conducted its business solely on the assessment plan, a member was not entitled to have an assessment paid out of the guaranty fund.

7. Insurance ⟹646(4)—Insurer has burden of sustaining defense of forfeiture for nonpayment of assessment.

A life insurer bears the burden of establishing the defense of forfeiture for nonpayment of an assessment.

8. Insurance ⟹646(3)—Beneficiary has burden of showing member was in good standing at time of death.

In an action on a benefit certificate, beneficiary has the burden of showing that the deceased member was in good standing at the time of his death.

9. Insurance ⟹646(3)—Certificate is proof of good standing at time of issuance, and such good standing will be presumed to continue.

Certificate of membership in a life association doing an assessment business is proof of good standing at the time of issuance of the certificate, and such good standing will be presumed to have continued until the contrary is shown; consequently, in an action by a beneficiary when the certificate is put in evidence, the burden is upon the association to show that at the time of death the member had lost his good standing.

10. Insurance ⟹646(4)—Burden of proving nonpayment of assessment continues on insurer throughout trial.

Where, under the pleadings, the insurer had the burden of proving nonpayment of assessment, such burden continued on the insurer throughout the trial.

11. Appeal and error ⟹994(3)—Evidence of nonpayment of assessments held for trial court.

In an action on an insurance certificate, where the evidence as to nonpayment of assessments was only circumstantial, the question is for the trial judge sitting as a jury to determine the credibility, weight, and sufficiency of the evidence offered.

Appeal from Circuit Court, Clark County; N. M. Pettingill, Judge.

Action by Eleanor R. Hay and others against the Bankers' Life Company. From a judgment for defendant, plaintiffs appeal. Reversed and remanded, with directions.

H. Collins Hay, of St. Louis, J. A. Whiteside, of Kahoka, Stone, Gamble, McDermott & Webb, of Kansas City, and O. S. Callihan, of Kahoka, for appellants.

B. L. Gridley, of Kahoka, and R. B. Alberson, of Des Moines, Iowa, for respondent.

BECKER, J. This is a suit on two certificates of membership issued by the Bankers' Life Association of Des Moines, Iowa, on March 22, 1898, to Nathaniel Hay, of Springfield, Ill., for $2,000 each, and a guaranty deposit of $42 on each certificate. The case was tried to the court without a jury, and resulted in a judgment for the defendant on each of the counts. Plaintiffs in due course appeal.

The petition is in two counts, and judgment was asked for $2,042 and interest on each count. The answer pleads forfeiture of both of said certificates, for the reason that assessment due in January, 1915, designated as call No. 127, had not been paid; and further pleads that this action is barred by the limitation clause in the certificates, which provided that no action shall be brought or sustained upon or under the certificate, unless suit is commenced within one year after the day of the death of the member. The reply denies the affirmative allegations in the answer, and pleads the statute of Illinois, extending the time within which action might be brought on the certificates sued on to within three years after the death of Nathaniel Hay, and pleading that defendant waived the limitation clause in the certificates by furnishing blanks for formal proof of death in December, 1916, denying liability, at the time, for the sole and only reason that said Nathaniel Hay was not a member of said company at the time of his death because of his failure to pay the January call. Plaintiffs introduced in evidence both of said certificates, and the change of beneficiaries thereon, making plaintiffs the beneficiaries, and proved that plaintiffs were the children and heirs of said Nathaniel Hay.

The uncontradicted proof showed that Nathaniel Hay died at Urbana, Ill., on February 9, 1915; that the defendant was notified of his death on February 9, 1915, by telegram sent by plaintiff H. C. Hay, and was asked for instructions as to how to present claim for the amount due under the certificates. The telegram was answered on February 15, by letter, acknowledging receipt of telegram, and stating that the company was holding the claim for advice of payment of January call; that it had been unable to find any credit for it, and inquiring as to whether it had been paid, and, if so, when and how. Deceased's son answered by letter on February 17, stating that he was reasonably cer-

tain that the January call had been paid,
but he was unable to find receipt, and inquiring when he might expect action by the company and as to how proof of death and claim
for money should be made. This was answered by the company on February 19, by
letter stating:

"Up to this time we have been unable to find
any credit showing payment of January call,
and unless you find some evidence that the
same was paid, on or before February 1st,
we fear that lapse has occurred, in which
event it would not be necessary to forward
blank for execution, as there would be no liability on the part of the company."

On February 16th an agent of the company
at Springfield, Ill., wrote said son that the
company was holding blank proof of death, as
they had not yet received the January call.
In October, 1916, plaintiffs employed counsel
to bring suit on the claim under these certificates of membership. No blanks having
been furnished plaintiffs to make formal
proof of death, such proof had not been made,
and counsel, desiring to make formal proof
of death, wrote the company the following
letter:

"October 30, 1916.
"Bankers Life Association, Des Moines, Iowa
—Dear Sirs: I have for collection claim of
Eleanor R. Hay, Howard R. Hay and Henry
Collins Hay, as beneficiaries under certificates
of membership numbers 70594 and 70595, issued by your company to Nathaniel Hay,
March 22, 1898, amounting to $2,042 each,
making a total of $4,084, together with six per
cent. interest from date that you first denied
liability under these certificates. Nathaniel
Hay died in February, I think on the 9th day,
1915. I see from the correspondence turned
over to me with the certificates that formal
proof of death has not been made for the reason that you denied liability and declined to
send blanks on which to make the proof. I
will file suit on this claim for the $4,084 and
interest, without you prefer to settle the claim
without suit, and I ask that you kindly send me
blanks on which to make the formal proof.
"After we have made the formal proof of
death you may pay the claim or contest the
question of your liability in court, as you may
prefer. Please send me the blanks and let us
get the matter going one way or the other.
"Yours truly,   J. A. Whiteside."

In answer to this letter the company sent
the blanks with the following letter:

"December 29, 1916.
"J. A. Whiteside, Hiller Building, Kahoka,
Missouri—Dear Sir: In response to your favor
of December 21, 1916, with reference to certificates Nos. 70594 and 70595, issued to Nathaniel Hay, March 22, 1898, I am sending you
herewith our form of blank for proof of death
of Mr. Hay, but with the express understanding, which is indorsed thereon, that the company does not request that the same be furnished or that any expense, time or trouble
be incurred in connection therewith; because
as stated in our letter to Mrs. Hay of May 21,
1915, Mr. Hay was not a member of this

company at the time of his death, because of
his failure to pay the January, 1915, call.
His was assessment contracts, and the failure
to pay the several assessments quarterly within a month after the same was made terminated membership, as you will see by the certificates, which I presume you have. We will
also send a copy of the by-laws and articles of
incorporation if desired.
"Yours very truly,   I. M. Earle,
"Vice President and General Counsel."

Formal proof of death was made by plaintiffs at some expense and work, and all under
the direction of counsel for plaintiffs at Kahoka, Mo., the witnesses and parties who
made the affidavits being at Springfield,
Champaign, and Urbana, Ill., and Grand
Junction, Colo. Having waited a reasonable
time after mailing formal proof of death to
the company, counsel filed suit on the claim
on January 31, 1917. The court, sitting as a
jury, found all issues of fact in favor of
plaintiffs; that call No. 127 was paid, and
that Nathaniel Hay died February 9, 1915,
and was a member of the Bankers' Life Association in good standing when he died; but
held that the limitation clause in the certificate applied and that plaintiffs' cause of action was barred by said limitations clause in
the certificates, and for that reason rendered
judgment against the plaintiffs.

[1, 2] I. We first direct our attention to the
question as to whether the defendant, under
the record in this case, can be held as a matter of law to have waived the clause in the
certificates which requires suit thereon to be
commenced within one year after the death
of the insured. Even though the limitations
clause in the certificates was valid, a point
which we need not here decide, it may be
waived, and insistence upon one of several
known grounds of defense may constitute a
waiver of the others. Home Life Ins. Co. v.
Pierce, 75 Ill. 426; Moore v. Nat. Acc. Sec.,
38 Wash. 31, 80 Pac. 171; Hansell-Elcock Co.
v. Frankfort, etc., Acc. Co., 177 Ill. App. 500;
Covenant Mut. Life Ass'n v. Baughman, 73
Ill. App. 544; Shearlock v. Mut. Life Ins. Co.,
193 Mo. App. 430, 182 S. W. 89; Dolan v.
Royal Neighbors, 123 Mo. App. 147, 100 S. W.
498. See, also, Thompson v. Traders' Ins.
Co., 169 Mo. 12, 68 S. W. 889.

[3-5] While the question whether there
has been a waiver is generally a question of
fact, and the sufficiency of the evidence relating thereto is for the jury, yet where the
facts and circumstances relating to the subject are admitted or clearly established, the
waiver becomes a question of law. 27 R. C.
L. 912. So since in this case the question of
the waiver is dependent upon the legal effect
of the letter of plaintiffs' attorney of October
30, 1916, to the defendant company, which
the defendant company admits it received,
and the letter of December 29, 1916, written
by the defendant to the attorney for plaintiffs, which letter was signed by the vice

president and general counsel of the defendant company, and which defendant admits that it sent, the question of the construction of these letters does not present an issue of fact. Their interpretation and legal effect, like that of a contract, is not for the jury, nor the judge sitting as a jury, but is a question of law. Union Service Co. v. Drug Co., .148 Mo. App. 327, loc. cit. 337, 128 S W. 7; Mounty v. Neighbors' Implement & Vehicle Co., 195 Mo. App. 21, 189 S. W. 614.

The letter of October 30, 1916, written by the plaintiffs' attorney to the defendant company, sets out in detail that the writer held for collection plaintiffs' claim on two certificates issued by defendant, giving their numbers, date of issuance, amount of each, and to whom issued, and states the total amount of the claim with interest from the date of the denial of liability on the part of the company, and *specifically sets out the day, month, and year of the insured's death*, and further notifies the defendant therein that—

"*I will file suit on this claim for the $4,084 and interest, without you prefer to settle the claim without suit. * * * (Italics ours.)*

Thus it clearly appeared from the date of plaintiffs' letter and the date of the death of the insured, as stated therein, that a period of over 18 months had elapsed since the date of the death of the insured, yet the vice president and general counsel of the defendant company, in his letter of December 29, 1916, in answer thereto (in which he inclosed forms of proof of death) specifically stated that the reason why the company did "not request that proofs of death' be furnished, or that any expense, time, or trouble be incurred in connection therewith," was "because, as stated in our letter to Mrs. Hay, of May 21, 1915, Mr. Hay was not a member in this company at the time of his death, because of his failure to pay the January, 1915, call." But no mention was made therein of the fact that the company would endeavor to invoke the provision. contained in the certificates, that suit thereon must be filed within one year from the date of the death of the insured. It is not contended that the defendant, at the time it sent said letter, was not conversant with the limitation provision in the certificates issued by it, nor that it was not aware of the fact that more than one year had elapsed since the death of the insured.

It will be noted that upon the hearing of the case the learned trial judge found against the defendant upon the sole ground which defendant sets out in the letter as its cause for disclaiming liability, and, defendant, in its letter, not having mentioned the fact that it would seek to rely upon the provision limiting the filing of a cause of action to within a period of one year, after plaintiffs had gone to the expense of engaging counsel, preparing proofs of death, and filing suit, in the belief that the only objection that the defendant made to the payment of the certificates was that the January, 1915, assessment, No. 127, had not been paid, should be held to have waived whatever right it may have had to set up the said limitation clause as a bar to plaintiffs' right to bring their action. We therefore hold that the learned trial judge erred in holding that there was no evidence proving or tending to prove a waiver of the provisions of said certificates limiting the time in which suit should be brought, and rule, as a matter of law, that the defendant company waived said limitation provision.in said certificates.

[8] II. When we turn to the conclusion arrived at by the learned trial judge, sitting as a jury, that the insured was entitled to have his assessment paid out of the so-called "guaranty fund," we are compelled to hold that the learned trial court made an error of law.

By article 10 of the articles of incorporation in evidence, it is provided that the funds of the defendant association shall be kept separate and distinct upon the books thereof, and as to the "guaranty fund" it is provided:

"The guaranty fund, the benefit fund, the reserve fund, and the contingent fund, and such other funds as the board of directors may hereafter establish.

"Section 2. The guaranty fund shall consist of the deposits pledged by each member of the association for the payment of assessments and the said deposit required of each member shall consist of the sum of one dollar for each year of the age of the member at the date of application, counted at his nearest birthday, and may consist of cash, or a note at 4 per cent. interest, payable on such terms as the board of directors may prescribe, and the said board shall have the power to declare a certificate of membership void and of no effect upon defalcation of payment for any note executed for said deposit."

According to the undisputed testimony in the present case, each member of the association on becoming such, paid to the association a sum equal to $1 for each year of his age for each $2,000 certificate, which was placed in the guaranty fund. If he dies a member in good standing, the sum is paid to his beneficiary in addition to the amount of the certificate. If the member lapses, the sum so paid goes to the reserve fund, for use in paying death losses when they exceed 1 per cent. of the insurance in force. In making the assessments on the various members quarterly, an estimate was made in advance of the amount, which would be required for the payment of death losses on the certificates for the ensuing quarter, basing the estimate upon the experience of the company during the previous year in combination with the American Experience Table of Mortality, and the expected losses for the ensuing quarter were calculated from these bases. The amount necessary to pay the call No. 127, of

January, 1915, being in excess of 1 per cent. of the insurance carried under the certificates, under the provisions of the articles of incorporation and by-laws set forth, the remainder necessary for the payment of death losses over and above the 1 per cent. was taken from the reserve fund. Then each member was directly assessed in a sum sufficient to pay the death losses, based upon the amount paid by him to the guaranty fund and not in excess of 1 per cent. of the insurance of the respondent company on the assessment plan in force. This procedure was in strict conformity with the articles of incorporation, the by-laws of the company, and the provisions of the entire contract between the member and the company.

On the record before us we can come to no other conclusion than that the defendant company conducts its business solely on the assessment plan. All that it furnishes its members is temporary insurance covering the time for which the member has paid his assessments. There is no reserve value to its certificates of membership which can carry them beyond the period for which the particular assessment has been levied and paid. This question we had before us and discussed so thoroughly in the case of Smoot v. Bankers' Life Ass'n, 138 Mo. App. 438, 120 S. W. 719, that it is unnecessary for us to discuss the question at length. The Kansas City Court of Appeals came to the same conclusion in the case of McCoy v. Bankers' Life Ass'n, 134 Mo. App. 35, 114 S. W. 551, in which case it was distinctly held that certificates such as we have before us here were issued on the assessment plan, and were not life insurance, and that such certificates are forfeitable for failure to meet the calls and assessments made upon them. It is seriously contended, however, that such a ruling on our part is in conflict with what has been said by our court in Purdy v. Bankers' Life Ass'n, 101 Mo. App. 91, 74 S. W. 486.

Our court held in the Purdy Case, on the evidence then before us, that this guaranty fund was subject to the application of the payment of assessments. In the light of the facts in evidence in the case at bar, we do not think that the decision of our court in the Purdy Case is to be followed. It is said by Judge Goode in that case that no oral proof was made concerning the practice in the collection of assessments to pay benefits, and that we can only know about the mode in which the benefits were paid from the articles and the by-laws; and, referring to the case of Mee v. Bankers Life Ass'n of Minnesota, 69 Minn. 210, 72 N. W. 74, Judge Goode said that the facts before him in the Purdy Case were entirely different, as shown by the evidence, from those in the Mee Case; more correctly, that what appeared in evidence in the Mee Case did not appear in evidence in the Purdy Case. In the case at bar, how-

ever, we have a detailed statement of the whole plan and mode of carrying on operations by the defendant company and they are identical with those reported in the Mee Case, so that we are compelled to say that the Purdy Case is no authority in the case at bar.

The character of this guaranty fund has been before the courts of other states, and they have uniformly held that it is not available for the purpose of paying assessments. See Hoover v. Bankers' Life Ass'n, 155 Iowa, 322, 136 N. W. 117; Mulherin v. Bankers' Life Ass'n, 163 Iowa, 740, loc. cit. 744, 144 N. W. 1000; Brown v. Bankers' Life Ass'n, 136 N. E. 508; Bond v. Bankers' Life Ass'n, 90 Kan. 215, 133 Pac. 854; Mee v. Bankers' Life Co., 69 Minn. 210, 72 N. W. 74. The nature and character of this guaranty fund and the manner in which the business of the company is carried on are so fully set out in the case of Bond v. Bankers' Life Co., supra, and here in evidence, that we do not think it necessary to repeat it here. We are of the opinion, and so hold, that the learned trial court committed an error of law in looking to the guaranty fund for the payment of this assessment.

III. According to the finding of facts made by the trial judge at the request of the defendant, the assessment due in January, 1915, known as call No. 127, on the two certificates here sued on, was paid in cash.

[7-9] Whatever may be the law in other states, the principle is well settled in Missouri that the defendant bears the burden of proof to sustain a defense of forfeiture for nonpayment of an assessment.

And, "while the burden was upon the plaintiff, in an action of this kind, to show that the deceased member was in such good standing at the time of his death (Seibert v. Chosen Friends, 23 Mo. App. 268, 275), yet the certificate is proof of good standing at the time when it was issued, and such good standing will be presumed to have continued until the contrary is made to appear. It follows that, in such an action, when the certificate is put in evidence, the burden is upon the defendant to show that, at the time of his death, the member had lost his good standing." Mulroy v. Knights of Honor, 28 Mo. App. 463, loc. cit. 467.

See, also, Keeton v. Nat. Union, 178 Mo. App. 301, loc. cit. 308, 165 S. W. 1107; Bange v. Supreme Council, 179 Mo. App. 21, 161 S. W. 652; Watkins v. Amer. Yeomen, 188 Mo. App. 626, 176 S. W. 516; Williams v. Modern Woodmen of Amer., 221 S. W. 414, loc. cit. 416.

[10] It is admitted here that the defendant's answer in the case admitted all the facts necessary to make plaintiffs' prima facie case, and, the defendant alleging the affirmative defense of nonpayment to relieve itself of liability on these certificates, the burden of proof as to that issue was placed

upon the defendant by the pleadings, and remained there throughout the trial of the case. Swift & Co. v. Mutter, 115 Ill. App. 374; Home Ben. Ass'n v. Sargent, 142 U. S. 691, 12 Sup. Ct. 332, 35 L. Ed. 1160; Stokes v. Stokes, 155 N. Y. 581, 50 N. E. 342.

[11] The defendant's evidence on the question of the nonpayment of the assessment No. 127 consists of the testimony of witnesses. It is all circumstantial, and its essential parts rest entirely on parol; and, even if such evidence were uncontradicted, the question must be submitted to the trial judge, sitting as a jury, to determine the credibility, weight, and sufficiency of the testimony offered. Gannon v. Laclede Gas Light Co., 145 Mo. 502, 46 S. W. 968, 47 S. W. 907; St. Louis Union Trust Co. v. Hill, 223 S. W. 434; Lafferty v. Kan. City Casualty Co. (Sup.) 229 S. W. 750.

It follows from what we have stated herein that, had the learned trial judge correctly applied the law to the facts as found by him, sitting as a jury, judgment in favor of plaintiffs would have resulted. It is therefore ordered that the judgment herein be reversed, and the cause remanded, with directions to the trial court to enter judgment in favor of appellants.

ALLEN, P. J., concurs.
DAUES, J., not sitting.

━━━━━

O'CONNELL v. KANSAS CITY.   (No. 14082.)

(Kansas City Court of Appeals. Missouri. June 13, 1921.)

1. Pleading ⟷34(6)—Petition upheld on objection to evidence if any cause of action is stated though imperfectly.

An attack on the petition by objection to evidence for insufficiency of the petition is not looked upon with favor, and the petition will be given a liberal construction and upheld if it states any cause of action whatever, though it be defectively stated.

2. Pleading ⟷34(6)—On objection to any evidence petition not insufficient if fact not expressly stated is necessarily implied.

On objection to the introduction of any evidence for insufficiency of the petition, the allegations of the petition must be construed in their most favorable light to plaintiff, and, if the existence of an elemental fact is not expressly stated, but follows as a necessary implication from the facts alleged, the petition should not be adjudged insufficient.

3. Pleading ⟷433(8)—Petition in action for injuries held sufficient after verdict as against objection that city's notice of defect was not alleged; "maintain."

In an action for injuries, a petition alleging that on the date of the injury and for a

long time prior thereto a sidewalk or footbridge was maintained by defendant city in a dangerous, unsafe, and insecure condition was sufficient after verdict as against the objection that it did not allege that the city had actual or constructive knowledge of the defect in the sidewalk as to "maintain" a defect means to keep up, preserve, or continue the defective condition, and suggests some active participation in the matter of continuing the condition.

[Ed. Note.—For other definitions, see Words and Phrases, First and Second Series, Maintain.]

4. Appeal and error ⟷231(5)—General objection to exhibition of injury to jury held insufficient.

The words "I object" were not a sufficient objection to plaintiff's exhibition of her injured wrist to the jury to raise any point on appeal.

5. Appeal and error ⟷1060(1)—Judgment not reversed for argument improper on question of damages when counsel was not arguing question of damages.

Though in an action for injuries it is improper to argue that the jury should assess plaintiff's damages in accordance with what they would take for a similar injury to themselves and to persist in such argument after a ruling has been made, the judgment will not be reversed because plaintiff's counsel asked the jury to put themselves in plaintiff's place, where there is nothing in the record to show that he was at the time arguing the question of damages.

6. Damages ⟷132(7)—Verdict for $1,725 for injuries to leg and wrist held not excessive.

Where a girl 15 or 16 years old, earning $15.40 a week, was so painfully injured by stepping through a hole in a bridge with her left leg, causing her to fall and strike her left hand and wrist, that she fainted and was in bed for six weeks, and, after returning to work, was unable to do work requiring her to stand and had a permanent injury of the wrist, necessitating a tight bandage when working and causing a knot on the wrist, a verdict of $1,725 held not excessive.

Appeal from Circuit Court, Jackson County; T. J. Seehorn, Judge.

Action by Della O'Connell by her next friend, James J. Shepard, against Kansas City. From a judgment for plaintiff, defendant appeals. Affirmed.

E. M. Harber and Francis M. Hayward, both of Kansas City, for appellant.
Rogers & Yates, of Kansas City, for respondent.

BLAND, J. This is a suit for damages for personal injuries. Plaintiff recovered a verdict and judgment in the sum of $1,725, and defendant has appealed.

The facts show that on August 12, 1919, plaintiff, a girl 15 or 16 years of age, was injured while walking in the nighttime over the sidewalk portion of a bridge across Turkey creek. This bridge was maintained by the

Mo.)   O'CONNELL v. KANSAS CITY   1041

(231 S.W.)

defendant as a highway at Thirtieth street and Southwest boulevard in Kansas City, Mo. Plaintiff's left foot and left limb went through a hole in the bridge to a point in the region of her knee, causing her to fall and to strike her left hand and wrist.

The petition charges that defendant—

" * * * maintains and operates public streets, sidewalks, and highways within the said Kansas City, and particularly at and near Thirtieth street and Southwest boulevard, at which place the defendant maintains and operates a sidewalk or footbridge across Turkey creek.

"Plaintiff states that the said sidewalk or footbridge was on the 12th day of August, 1919, and for a long time prior thereto, maintained by the defendant for the purpose of permitting pedestrians to walk upon and travel over the same in a dangerous, unsafe, and insecure condition, which said sidewalk or footbridge was not reasonably safe for persons while traveling over the same in ordinary modes.

"Plaintiff states that on said date and at about the hour of 11 p. m., while she was walking along over and upon said sidewalk or footbridge and without any knowledge of the dangerous, unsafe, and insecure condition thereof, she stepped into a hole in the sidewalk or footbridge and then and there, by reason of the aforesaid dangerous, unsafe, and insecure condition, plaintiff was caused to fall, whereby she was seriously and permanently injured and crippled."

Defendant insists that "the court erred in not sustaining defendant's objection to the introduction of any evidence because plaintiff's petition stated no cause of action whatever, and in overruling defendant's motion in arrest of judgment." In support of this contention defendant urges that there is no allegation in the petition of negligence on the part of defendant, "no allegation that the city had either actual or constructive knowledge of a defect in the sidewalk from which negligence could have been inferred." There was no demurrer to the petition, but defendant answered.

[1, 2] An attack upon the petition such as was made in the trial court is not looked upon with favor. Under the circumstances we are required to give a liberal construction to the petition, and, if it states any cause of action whatever, we must hold it good, although the cause of action may be defectively stated. Peters v. Kansas City Rys. Co., 204 Mo. App. 197, 224 S. W. 25, 27. And we must construe the allegations of the petition in their most favorable light to the plaintiff, and if the existence of an elemental fact is not expressly stated, but may be said to follow as a necessary implication from the facts alleged, the petition should not be adjudged insufficient to support a verdict. Wilson v. St. Joseph, 139 Mo. App. 557, 561, 123 S. W. 504; Hurst v. City of Ashgrove, 96 Mo. 168, 172, 9 S. W. 631; Chance v. City of St. Joseph, 195 Mo. App. 1, 5, 190 S. W. 24.

231 S.W.—66

[3] The petition alleges that "said sidewalk or footbridge was on the 12th day of August, 1919, and for a long time prior thereto, maintained by the defendant * * * in a dangerous, unsafe, and insecure condition."

"The word 'maintain' does not mean to provide or construct, but means to keep up; to keep from change; to preserve (Worcest. Dict.); to hold or keep in any particular state or condition; to keep up (Webst. Dict.).

"In Moon v. Durden, 2 Exch. 21, it was said: The verb "to maintain," * * * signifies to support what has already been brought into existence.' "

Verdin v. City of St. Louis, 131 Mo. 26, 87, 33 S. W. 480, 494; Barber Asphalt Paving Co. v. Hezel, 155 Mo. 391, 399, 56 S. W. 449, 451 (48 L. R. A. 285).

"The word 'maintain,' used as a verb, does not mean to provide or construct, but, as defined by lexicographers, means to keep up, to keep from change, to preserve. Worcester's Dictionary. To hold or keep in any particular state or condition, to keep up. Webster's Dictionary.

"In the case of Moon v. Durden, 2 Exchequer R. 21, it was said: The verb "to maintain," in pleading, has a distinct technical signification. It signifies to support what has already been brought into existence.' "

Louisville, New Albany & Chicago Ry. Co. v. Godman, 104 Ind. 490, 492, 4 N. E. 163, 164; Kendrick & Roberts v. Warren Bros. Co., 110 Md. 47, 72, 72 Atl. 461.

"Webster's Dictionary, which has become in effect a law book on questions of construction, defines the word 'maintain' as follows: To hold, preserve, or keep in any particular state or condition; to sustain; not to suffer to fail or decline.' " Brenn v. City of Troy, 60 Barb. (N. Y.) 417, 421; Benson v. Mayor, etc., of N. Y., 10 Barb. (N. Y.) 223, 236; Kovachoff v. St. Johns Lumber Co., 61 Or. 174, 180, 121 Pac. 801.

The petition in this case alleges that the city "maintained" the sidewalk in a dangerous, unsafe, insecure, and not reasonably safe condition. From the foregoing definitions of the word "maintain" it is apparent that to maintain a defect means something more than mere notice or even knowledge of the defect. It means keeping up, preserving, or continuing the defective condition, and suggests some active participation in the matter of continuing the condition. So we think that the fact that the city had notice of the defect in the sidewalk may be said to follow as a necessary implication from the facts alleged in the petition, and the petition is good after verdict under the circumstances present in this case.

[4] During the trial the following occurred:

"Q. Just come over here, please, and let the jury see it.

"Mr. Hayward: I object to that, your honor.

"Mr. Rogers: I offer to exhibit the injury on the wrist to the jury.

"The Court: Proceed. (To which ruling and action of the court the defendant by its counsel then and there duly excepted.)

"Q. Just let the gentlemen see it. (Plaintiff here steps down to the jury, and walks up and down before the jury, and the jury examines and feels of plaintiff's wrist.)"

It is insisted that the court erred "in permitting the jury to feel of plaintiff's wrist, thereby exciting the sympathy of the jury in plaintiff's behalf, and increasing the size of the verdict, which was excessive." We think that defendant is in no position to raise any point in reference to this occurrence for the reason that it did not make any valid objection. The words "I object" have often been held to be no objection whatever. State v. Lewis, 264 Mo. 420, 429, 175 S. W. 60; State v. Tatman, 264 Mo. 357, 370, 175 S. W. 69; Breen v. United Rys. Co. of St. Louis (Sup.) 204 S. W. 521, 522, and cases therein cited.

[5] It is last insisted that the verdict is excessive and that the size of it may have been increased by improper remarks of plaintiff's counsel in his final argument to the jury. The argument objected to is as follows:

"Mr. Rogers: * * * Put yourself in her place—
"Mr. Hayward (interrupting): I object to that, your honor, and ask that the jury be instructed to disregard it.
"The Court: Let that be withdrawn; and the jury is instructed to disregard it.
"Mr. Rogers: Put yourself in this little girl's shoes—
"Mr. Hayward (interrupting): I object again, to that form of argument; and I ask that the jury be instructed to disregard it.
"The Court: Yes; the jury will disregard it."

It has been held that it is improper to argue to the jury that they should assess plaintiff's damages in accordance with what they would take for a similar injury to themselves; that after a ruling is once made counsel should not persist in making the same improper argument over and over again. There is nothing in the matter preserved in the record to show that plaintiff's counsel was arguing to the jury the matter of plaintiff's injuries at the time the above words complained of in the argument were uttered. In fact, there is nothing in the argument preserved to indicate in what connection the jury were asked to put themselves in place of plaintiff. If an appellant desires to raise a point in connection with his opponent's argument to the jury, he should abstract enough of the argument for us to know exactly what it was and then point out pre-

cisely what the misconduct of his opponent consisted of. Defendant's argument to the jury made prior to that of plaintiff's counsel is not free from objection. In an ingenious way defendant's counsel drew the attention of the jury to the fact that, if some of them were taxpayers, they would be called upon to help pay any judgment returned against defendant.

[6] The evidence shows that plaintiff's injury was so painful that it caused her to faint at the time it was received, and that she was taken home in an automobile. She remained in bed for six weeks, suffering pain in her knee, back, and wrist. At the time of her injury she was employed in a packing house "putting slugs on cans." She was unable to go back to work for a period of eight weeks, and when she finally returned she was unable to do the same work for the reason that it required her to stand, so she was put to work in the labeling room, where she could sit down. She was earning $15.40 per week, which amount was lost for a period of eight weeks.

The trial was about ten months after the injury, and at that time plaintiff still had some swelling in her knee. At times her knee pained her, and if she walked a great distance it caused her to limp. However, from the admission of plaintiff in regard to being able to attend dances and to dance, we conclude that she had to a great degree recovered from the injury to her limb at the time of the trial. However, the evidence shows that at the time of the trial she had a knot on her wrist due to an injured tendon. This knot was described as "a nodule on the inner side of her wrist." This was an involvement of the little bursa, "which is one of the extensors of the muscles, that the muscles terminate in." This knot was "quite visible" at the time of the trial. This bursa was "ruptured out of its sheath and projects out a little." When working it was necessary for plaintiff to keep a tight bandage around her wrist. The medical testimony was that the injury to the wrist was permanent, that she would be able to perform ordinary work with that hand, but that the "wrist will be sore whenever she lifts anything of any weight at all." That it would be sore whenever plaintiff attempted to do heavy work; her wrist "will be weaker" than normal. In view of the evidence, we do not think the verdict is excessive.

The judgment is affirmed.

All concur.

ROAD DIST. NO. 41, HENRY TP., VERNON COUNTY, v. JACKSON.　(No. 13784.)

(Kansas City Court of Appeals. Missouri. June 13, 1921.)

1. Associations ⟐⟐20(2)—Voluntary and unincorporated association cannot sue.

An unincorporated voluntary association cannot as such sue or be sued.

2. Highways ⟐⟐150—Full compliance with statute so as to warrant recovery of poll tax shown.

In an action by a road district of a township, evidence *held* to show that there was sufficient compliance with Rev. St. 1909, §§ 11751, 11756, 11765, 11766, and section 11758, as modified by Laws 1913, p. 746, to warrant recovery of a poll tax.

3. Highways ⟐⟐150—Defect in warning notice insufficient to prevent recovery of poll tax.

Under Rev. St. 1909, § 11758, recovery of poll tax cannot be defeated because of defect of warning in notice.

4. Costs ⟐⟐42(1)—In action for poll tax tender held insufficient because not including accrued costs.

Where after commencement of an action on behalf of a road district to collect a poll tax defendant deposited to the credit of a justice of the peace without notice to him a sum less than the amount of the taxes and without accrued costs, such tender was not sufficient under Rev. St. 1909, § 7453, relating to liability for costs, because not including the accrued costs and for the further reason that it was not in sufficient amount and tendered to the wrong party.

5. Highways ⟐⟐150—Road district may sue to recover poll taxes.

A road district of a township in a county operating under that form of organization created pursuant to Rev. St. 1899, § 10321, as amended by Laws 1903, p. 272, is a political entity capable of suing and being sued, and so may recover poll taxes from one in arrears.

Appeal from Circuit Court, Bates County; C. A. Calvird, Judge.

Action by Road District No. 41, Henry Township, Vernon County, against Wallie Jackson, begun in the justice court, and appealed by defendant to circuit court. From a judgment for plaintiff in circuit court, defendant appeals. Affirmed.

J. B. Journey, of Nevada, Mo., and Thos. W. Silvers, of Butler, for appellant.

Homer M. Poage, Pros. Atty., of Nevada, Mo., for respondent.

ARNOLD, J. This suit to recover poll tax assessed against defendant for the year 1915, in the sum of $3.60, was instituted in the court of a justice of the peace by filing a plaintiff's return, as follows:

"Plaintiff's Return. Before W. H. Johnson, J. P. Road District No. 41, Henry Township, Vernon County, Missouri, Plaintiff, v. Wallie Jackson, Defendant.

"Plaintiff by her representative and supervisor, J. J. Lovell, states that she is a road district duly organized under the laws of the state of Missouri; that Wallie Jackson, the defendant, is a citizen of district No. 41, and that a poll tax of $3.60 was lawfully assessed against said defendant for the year 1915; that said defendant was duly notified to work out said poll tax or pay same in cash; that defendant failed and refused to work out said poll tax or pay the same in cash.

"Wherefore said plaintiff asks judgment for the sum of three and 60/100 dollars for her debt, together with costs of suit.

　　　　　　　"Road District No. 41.
　　　　　　　　"By J. J. Lovell.
"Filed October 8, 1915."

Summons was issued thereon on December 1, 1915. A change of venue was taken from the court of W. H. Johnson, justice of the peace, to the court of Miles Downey, justice of the peace of Henry township, Vernon county, Mo., and on December 8, 1915, the cause was tried in said court to a jury, resulting in a verdict for plaintiff in the sum of $3.60. Thereupon an appeal was taken to the circuit court of Vernon county December 20, 1915.

The answer of defendant filed in the circuit court alleges: (1) That plaintiff is neither an individual nor a corporation, has no legal entity and is not entitled to maintain this suit; (2) that prior to the institution of this suit defendant elected to pay said poll tax in work and labor, and was refused the privilege of working it out, and that he deposited the amount of said tax in the Stotesbury State Bank to the credit of and for the benefit of plaintiff; (3) denies each and every other allegation contained in plaintiff's petition.

The cause was continued from term to term until February 15, 1919, when a change of venue was taken to the circuit court of Bates county, Mo., where the cause was tried to the court without the aid of a jury, and on June 16, 1920, the court found for plaintiff in the sum sued for. Defendant appeals.

The testimony shows that Vernon county had been operating under the township organization law since 1900; and at the regular meeting of the township board of Henry county in April, 1909, by authority of section 10321, Rev. Stat. 1899, as amended by Session Laws 1903, p. 272, said township was divided into three road districts, and that part of said township in which defendant resided in 1914 and 1915 was designated as road district No. 41. Prior to the regular April, 1915, meeting, of the township board, the road overseer filed with the township clerk a list of poll tax payers of which defendant was one. At said meeting of the board a poll tax of $3.60 was levied against each name upon the said list for the year

1915. From said list the township clerk made up a list of poll tax payers so required to pay, of which defendant was one, and delivered said list to the road overseer.

The testimony further shows that on August 31, 1915, the road overseer served a warning notice on defendant to appear the next day for work on a road in said district about a half mile from the farm owned by defendant, or to pay his poll tax in cash; that defendant refused to work in obedience to the notice and refused to pay the amount in cash, saying that he preferred to work near his home, so that he would receive the benefit of his labor.

[1] Defendant first complains that the road district is neither an individual nor a public, private, or municipal corporation, and therefore cannot sue, and cites numerous decisions, including Express Co. v. Railway Co., 126 Mo. App. 471, 103 S. W. 583. In that case the court held that an unincorporated company cannot sue in the name of its trustees; that a trustee of an express trust can sue only in his own name.

In Pickett v. Walsh, 192 Mass. 572, 78 N. E. 753, 6 L. R. A. (N. S.) 1067, 116 Am. St. Rep. 272, 7 Ann. Cas. 638, it is held that an unincorporated labor union cannot be made party to a suit, as such. Nelson v. Railway Relief Department, 147 N. C. 103, 60 S. E. 724, holds that an unincorporated voluntary association cannot, as such, sue or be sued. Also in Knox v. Greenfield's Estate, 7 Ga. App. 305, 66 S. E. 805, the same ruling is upheld to the effect that an estate so designated and unincorporated is not a real party defendant. In Buck Stove & Range Co. v. Vickers, 80 Kan. 29, 101 Pac. 668, the court held that the corporation, having been dissolved, cannot maintain a suit.

[2] We conclude that these holdings are based on sound law, but do not apply to the case at bar. It remains for us to determine whether or not the Legislature delegated to the township board the power to form road districts, as township subdivisions, with power to sue for poll tax. Section 11756, Rev. Stat. Mo. 1909, is as follows:

"It shall be the duty of the road overseer to keep the roads in his district in as good repair as the funds at his command will permit. He shall keep a full and correct record of all moneys received and disbursed, and also shall keep an inventory of all tools, machinery and other property belonging to the district. It shall be the duty of each overseer, during the month of March, to prepare a list, alphabetically arranged, of all able-bodied male citizens of his district between the ages of twenty-one and fifty years who reside in his district, and he shall file said list with the township clerk of his township on or before the first day of April following, and the board of directors shall not approve the final settlement of any overseer nor pay to him any money that may be owing to him upon such settlement, on account of services or otherwise, nor allow him any credit therefor, until said list shall have been prepared and filed by such overseer in accordance herewith." Laws 1909, p. 870.

There is no contention on the part of defendant that Vernon county was not legally organized into townships, and that the townships were not legally divided into road districts. It is contended, however, that the assessment in question was not made as the statute directs, and it is to that point we shall direct our attention.

Section 11751, Rev. Stat. 1909, provides that the township board shall divide the township into convenient road districts, and appoint a road overseer. This was done in the instant case. Section 11756 defines the duties of road overseer, including the preparation by him of a list alphabetically arranged of able-bodied males in his district between the ages of 21 and 50, and directs the filing of the same with the township clerk. This also is shown to have been done in the case at bar. Section 11757 directs the township clerk in the preparation of a copy of the list directed in section 11756, and directs that the same shall be furnished to the road overseer.

Section 11758 (Laws 1913, p. 746) directs the levy of the poll tax at the regular April meeting in each year, in a sum not less than $3, and not more than $6, on each individual, and specifies that persons subject to such poll tax shall have the right in their option, to pay the same in money or labor within their respective road districts.

The sections following the one last named specify the forms of notices and receipts, the manner in which such poll taxpayers shall be warned, and the disposition of the funds; also where and when the men shall be worked, defining exemptions, and that the roads shall be worked whenever necessary.

Section 11765 directs the road overseer to file a list of delinquents, as declared by the act, before a justice of the peace of the county for suit not later than the 10th day of October each year, in the name of the road district; and section 11766 directs that the prosecuting attorney, or his deputies, shall appear in said suit, in behalf of the road district.

The testimony in this case tends to show that all the necessary things required to be done, under the sections above enumerated, were done in this case.

Defendant further complains that no properly certified tax bill ever was filed herein. The trial court held contra, and, as the record shows, correctly so, and we shall not disturb that finding.

[3] Defendant's contention that there were defects in the warning notice in this case, in that it was not served in due time, is met by the provisions of section 11758, Rev. Stat. 1909, which specifically provide "that no poll taxpayer shall be exempt from the payment

of the poll tax or any part of the same assessed against him on account of any mistake or defect in the warning notice * * * served upon him."

[4] Defendant further claims a tender, but the testimony tends to show that no sufficient tender was made, because such tender did not include the amount of the accrued costs. Section 7453, Rev. Stat. 1909. The deposit in the bank of $3.50 to the credit of the justice of the peace, without notice to him, was not a good tender because tendered to the wrong party, and not in sufficient amount.

[5] We hold that the plaintiff in this case is a statutory subdivision of the county of Vernon and township of Henry, a political entity, made so by statute duly enacted, and that it is capable of suing and being sued.

Plaintiff's motion to dismiss the appeal because of the failure of defendant to file an abstract of record within the time specified in rule 15 of this court (169 S. W. xiii) needs not now be considered. There is no reversible error shown by the record; the judgment is for the right party and should be affirmed.

It is so ordered.

All concur.

CONWAY v. FLAUGH et al.   (No. 14004.)

(Kansas City Court of Appeals. Missouri.
May 23, 1921. Rehearing Denied
June 13, 1921.)

1. Pledges ⇐⇒24—Pledgee of note to secure a forged note held to have no right thereto.

Where plaintiff's agent, who held a note payable to plaintiff, forged her name to a note for a less amount, and without any indorsement, forged or otherwise, deposited the valid note as collateral, the pledgee had no legal excuse for refusing to return the instrument pledged as collateral; the exception in regard to negotiable instruments not prevailing since the note bore no indorsement whatsoever.

2. Bailment ⇐⇒7—Possession of bailee deemed in subordination to the right of the bailor.

The possession of a bailee, in absence of some statutory provision to the contrary, is deemed in subordination to the rights of the bailor, no matter how long continued, provided there is no assertion of the adverse right.

3. Adverse possession ⇐⇒64—Pledgee not entitled to defeat replevin action on ground of limitation of action.

Where plaintiff deposited a note for $1,200 with an agent who collected interest, and he forged her name to a note for $500, and without any indorsement, forged or otherwise, deposited the $1,200 note with defendants as collateral for the forged instrument, defendants' retention of the $1,200 note for more than five years does not bar plaintiff's replevin action, for, as pledgee, defendants' rights in the note were subordinate to those of plaintiff, and, being merely bailee, who did not assert any

adverse title, their continued possession would not, under R. S. 1919, § 1317, bar plaintiff's right.

Appeal from Circuit Court, Jackson County; Daniel E. Bird, Judge.

"Not to be officially published."

Action by Josephine Conway against C. L. Flaugh and another. From a judgment for plaintiff, defendants appeal. Affirmed.

Stubenrauch & Hartz, of Kansas City, for appellants.

Burke & Kimpton and A. F. Smith, all of Kansas City, for respondent.

TRIMBLE, P. J.   This is an action in replevin to recover possession of a note for $1,200 dated September 15, 1910, due five years after date, payable to plaintiff with 6 per cent. interest, signed by Walter E. and Katie M. La Barriere, and secured by a deed of trust on certain realty purchased of plaintiff by the makers of said note. Plaintiff was a nonresident of the state, and left the note with Frank J. O'Loughlin, who was the real estate agent making the sale. O'Loughlin regularly remitted to plaintiff the interest on the note until some years later, when he absconded and became a fugitive from justice.

On January 20, 1913, O'Loughlin forged plaintiff's name to a note for $500, due one year after date, payable to the defendant Thornhill, and which pledged the $1,200 note on the La Barrieres as collateral security. The said $1,200 note was turned over to Thornhill by O'Loughlin without any indorsement being placed thereon. O'Loughlin regularly paid Thornhill the interest on said $500 note to and including the year 1917. Thornhill did not foreclose the pledge for nonpayment of the $500 note, but held the same as theretofore, and at the time of plaintiff's suit herein the $1,200 note sought to be recovered was in the hands of the defendant Flaugh as Thornhill's agent.

About the first of the year 1919 plaintiff discovered that something was wrong with O'Loughlin, and, upon coming to Kansas City and investigating, she found that O'Loughlin had absconded, that her name had been forged to the $500 note, and her $1,200 note on the La Barrieres had been pledged to Thornhill. She, thereupon, on February 25, 1919, brought this replevin suit to recover possession of the note.

Thornhill set up that he was entitled to the possession of the note as collateral security and until the $500 note was paid, and that plaintiff's rights were inferior and subject to his rights. Flaugh's original answer showed that he was in possession of the note sued for as Thornhill's agent, and was willing to deposit it in court to abide the result of the suit. His amended answer set up that the note was held as collateral for the payment of the $500 note, and that the former was charged with a lien thereon in favor of Thornhill to the extent of the indebtedness represented by the latter note; and both defendants set up the five-year statute of limitations. Section 1317, R. S. 1919.

The jury found for plaintiff, awarding her the possession of the note and one cent damages for its detention. The defendants thereupon appealed.

O'Loughlin had no authority to sign plaintiff's name to any note nor to pledge any of her property. There is no question but that O'Loughlin forged the $500 note and deceived Thornhill, and there is no charge nor claim of moral wrong upon the part of Thornhill. Appellants' brief concedes, "There is no dispute as to the facts in this case."

[1] The sole contention is that plaintiff is barred by the statute of limitations, and in reality the contention amounts to this: That since plaintiff did not discover that her name had been forged to the $500 note, and that her $1,200 note had been wrongfully turned over to Thornhill, and on that account did not bring her suit within five years, defendants are entitled to hold her note, and out of it enforce the payment of the $500 note. But, as O'Loughlin forged the latter and had no authority to pledge plaintiff's note, defendants have no claim upon or title to the $1,200 note as against her, and have no legal excuse for refusing to return it to her. 31 Cyc. 795; Rumpf v. Barto, 10 Wash. 382, 38 Pac. 1129; 35 Cyc. 362; Wilson v. Crocket, 43 Mo. 216, 217, 218, 97 Am. Dec. 389; Walsh Tie, etc., Co. v. Chester, etc., R. Co., 184 Mo. App. 26, 29, 167 S. W. 614. The exception in regard to negotiable instruments cannot prevail or arise here, since the note bore no indorsement, either genuine or forged. 8 C. J. 388; Patterson v. Carr, 61 Mo. 439; sections 817 and'835, R. S. 1919; Carter v. Butler, 264 Mo. 306, 323, 174 S. W. 399, Ann. Cas. 1917A, 483; Weber v. Orten, 91 Mo. 677, 4 S. W. 271; Bishop v. Chase, 156 Mo. 158, 170, 56 S. W. 1080, 79 Am. St. Rep. 515.

[2, 3] Plaintiff did not know until shortly before she brought suit that defendants even had possession of her note, much less that they were claiming any right to hold it. To enable them to successfully invoke the statute of limitation, their possession must be adverse. Smoot v. Wathen, 8 Mo. 522; 2 C. J. 285. Even if the $500 note had been genuine and the pledge of the $1,200 note authorized, the possession of the defendants could not be said to be adverse to the plaintiff, for the pledgee would hold only a special property in the note pledged, while the general property would remain in the pledgor. 31 Cyc. 808. And default in the payment of the note for which the other is pledged would not vest the entire property in the pledgee, but would only give him power to dispose of the thing pledged in accordance with the terms of the pledge, and, if he fail. to do so that, the general property would continue to remain in the pledgor. Sec... Trust Co. v. Edwards, 90 N. J. Law, 538, 562, 101 Atl. 384, L. R. A. 1917F, 273. D... possession of a bailee, in the absence of some special statutory provision to the contrary, is deemed to be in subordination to the right of the bailor, no matter how long continued the possession, without the assertion of some adverse right, may be. 2 C. J. 286. No mere retention of possession by a bailee, however long continued, will ... a change in ownership, and the statute will not begin to run in the bailee's favor until he asserts some adverse claim in respect to the bailment by which he acquired possession of it. Edgar v. Parsell, 184 Mich. 522, 151 W. 714, Ann. Cas. 1917A, 1160. So that in any event can defendants successfully claim to have had adverse possession of the note in suit. Taylor v. Wilkins, 22 Ga. App. 723, 8. E. 101. But, as the $500 note was forged and O'Loughlin had no authority whatever to deliver to Thornhill the note in suit, plaintiff is under no obligation whatever to pay the former in order to get possession of the latter.

The judgment is affirmed.

All concur.

KEITH v. KANSAS CITY RYS. CO.
(No. 14038.)

(Kansas City Court of Appeals. Missouri. May 23, 1921. Rehearing Denied June 13, 1921.)

1. Evidence ⚖️528(1) — Physicians' opinion that accident could have caused plaintiff's injury held proper.

In action against a street railway company for personal injuries, physicians' testimony that the accident as described could have caused the injuries suffered by plaintiff held proper, the rule being that expert testimony that the injury "might, could, or would" result from a supposed occurrence is equivalent to testifying that the occurrence was sufficient to cause the injury.

2. Appeal and error ⚖️1058(1)—Exclusion of evidence later admitted not reversible error.

The exclusion of testimony later admitted is not reversible error.

3. Carriers ⚖️320(26)—Demurrer to evidence on ground that passenger's manner of injury was against physical facts held properly overruled.

In woman passenger's action against street railway company for injuries from being injured when seized by her right hand by the conductor as she was thrown by sudden start of the car, evidence held not such as to justify demurrer to the evidence on the ground that the accident as described was a physical impossibility.

4. Appeal and error ⚖=994(2)—Inconsistency in testimony not reviewable.

Any inconsistency in plaintiff's testimony in a personal injury case *held* for the jury, and not for the court of appeals.

5. Appeal and error ⚖=1003—Verdict on plaintiff's uncorroborated testimony, although opposed by three witnesses for defendant, not contrary to weight of evidence.

In personal injury case, that plaintiff's uncorroborated testimony was contradicted in part by the testimony of three witnesses for defendant *held* not to warrant setting aside verdict for plaintiff as contrary to the weight of the evidence.

Appeal from Circuit Court, Jackson County; Allen C. Southern, Judge.

"Not to be officially published."

Action by Sarah B. Keith against the Kansas City Railways Company. From judgment for plaintiff, defendant appeals. Affirmed.

Chas. N. Sadler, John E. Connors, and Ed. O. Hyde, all of Kansas City, for appellant. William E. Byers and Lloyd R. Fraker, both of Kansas City, for respondent.

BLAND, J. This is an action for damages for personal injuries. Plaintiff recovered a verdict and judgment in the sum of $1,500, and defendant has appealed.

The facts show that about noon of January 13, 1916, plaintiff was a passenger upon an east-bound Thirty-First street car in Kansas City, Mo., being operated by Robert Dunham and Ford Harvey, receivers of the Metropolitan Street Railway Company, defendant's predecessors. Defendant has assumed all liability for the negligent acts of said receivers, their agents, and servants. Intending to alight at Benton boulevard, plaintiff signaled the motorman by pressing a button shortly after leaving the first street west of the boulevard. The car stopped at the boulevard. Plaintiff arose from her seat and walked back. On reaching the rear vestibule the conductor opened the door for her. Plaintiff stepped down upon the step, and just as she was ready to step off to the street the car started and, as she testified—

"It just started like lightning. I was holding on with this left hand, and the conductor seen it was about to throw me to the pavement, just like that, and he grabbed me by this arm, and he stood on the step and held to the car, and he dragged me and kept hollering for the motorman to stop."

When the car started she was facing south, she had put her left hand on the handrail and had stepped down, and was holding to the rail. The starting of the car broke her hold on the handrail, and caused her to swerve out, the conductor grabbing her right hand as her left hand was "breaking loose." "I was just swerving." The car ran about a block with the conductor holding to her hand and her left side dragging along the street, the conductor shouting to the motorman to "stop," "stop," during all of this time. When the car started she fell with her head toward the front of the car and her feet in the opposite direction, her left side dragging on the icy street. She testified that when the car stopped "The conductor picked me up and knocked the snow off of me, and held me up." On cross-examination she testified that after the car stopped, "I stepped off."

[1] Complaint is made that the court erred in permitting plaintiff's witnesses, Drs. Ruble and Sanders, to state their conclusions that plaintiff's condition at the time of the trial was caused by the accident. Plaintiff's counsel submitted to Dr. Ruble, plaintiff's attending physician, a suppositive state of facts wherein it was assumed that plaintiff had met with an accident such as the occurrence shown by the facts in evidence. At the conclusion of the statement of the hypothecated case counsel asked the doctor:

"I now want your expert opinion as to whether or not the accident might have caused this hernia you speak of" (the testimony being that plaintiff was suffering from a traumatic hernia as the result of the fall).

The doctor answered:

"That accident could very easily have caused it. Not the one she had on the ice. (It appearing that plaintiff had fallen on the ice about a year before the injury sued for.) Falling on the right side would put the intestines over the other way."

Objection was made by defendant's counsel, and the court said, "Yes; just answer the question." The doctor then stated, "It could very easily have caused the hernia." Dr. Sanders, who was called by Dr. Ruble to operate upon plaintiff for a traumatic hernia, was asked a hypothetical question reciting facts similar to those contained in the question asked Dr. Ruble. The question asked Dr. Sanders concluded with the words "whether or not this hernia could have been caused by this accident," the answer being, "I believe it could have been." Another similar hypothetical question was asked Dr. Sanders as to whether the accident might have caused "these headaches, this nervousness, and this sleeplessness," to which he answered, "I would say nervousness and sleeplessness could have been caused by such an accident." Neither the hypothetical questions nor the answers were improper as invading the province of the jury. The physicians did not pass upon the ultimate fact. The words "might, could, or would" were the proper ones to be used by counsel

---

⚖=For other cases see same topic and KEY-NUMBER in all Key-Numbered Digests and Indexes

and the physicians. Taylor v. Ry. Co., 185 Mo. 239, 246, 84 S. W. 873; State v. Hyde, 234 Mo. 200, 253, 136 S. W. 316, Ann. Cas. 1912D, 191; Moore v. Mo. Pac. Ry. Co., 164 Mo. App. 34, 147 S. W. 488; Eidson v. Metropolitan St. R. Co., 209 S. W. 575. Both counsel and the physicians were careful to use these words in reference to the asking and answering of these questions.

This case is unlike the case of Holtzen v. Railroad, 159 Mo. App. 370, 140 S. W. 767. In that case Dr. Haynes was asked, "What would be the probable effect of that sort of a shock on the nervous system?" The doctor answered, "Well, I believe it would produce an irreparable shock to the nervous system." This question and answer were held erroneous, the court saying (159 Mo. App. 375, 140 S. W. 769):

"He was not asked to what cause he would attribute the condition of the plaintiff, but what condition the injury would produce. We know of no rule that would justify such a course of examination. The object in such cases is not to show by expert witnesses a condition, but to account for such; that is, to ascertain the cause that produced a condition."

There was no attempt in the case at bar to show by expert testimony a condition, but the effort made was to ascertain the cause that produced plaintiff's condition or to account for her condition. It is insisted—

"that the only proper question to propound to an expert witness under such circumstances is whether a fall like the one described in any case is sufficient to cause such an injury, and not whether it did do it or might do it."

Asking a physician whether the injury "might, could, or would" result from the occurrence is equivalent to asking him whether the supposed occurrence was sufficient to cause the injury.

[2] It is insisted that the court erred in refusing to admit certain testimony of defendant's witness, Dr. Van Stavera. By this witness defendant sought to show that, at the time plaintiff slipped and fell on the ice previous to her reception of the injury sued for, she had an accident insurance policy in the Bankers' Accident Insurance Company, and that she was examined by this doctor on behalf of the insurance company. After sustaining plaintiff's motion to strike out Dr. Van Stavera's testimony that plaintiff was sent to him by the Bankers' Accident Insurance Company to be examined, the court permitted defendant to put plaintiff on the stand, and asked her whether she had a policy in the Bankers' Accident Insurance Company at the time she slipped on the ice, and she testified that she did. Dr. Van Stavera was then put on the stand, and he testified that he examined plaintiff, who had a policy in said company. The matter was fully gone into. So it is apparent there is no reversible error, if any at all, in connection

with the rulings of the court in reference to the testimony of Dr. Van Stavera.

It is insisted that the court erred in refusing to admit certain testimony of defendant's witness Dr. Pearce, to the effect that, if the intestines were pushed through the walls of the abdomen by a blow, in the process the intestines would be torn in two. The doctor had already testified that the intestines were very soft and delicate. After the court struck out the testimony of the doctor that a blow upon the body could not cause the intestines to push through the muscles of the abdomen without breaking them, counsel for defendant asked this question "Tell the jury whether or not these muscles are laid on that fascia in such a way that the intestines could push through between them." The doctor answered "It could not." He was further permitted to testify that a person who had suffered a hernia from falling in the manner claimed by plaintiff could not have walked the distance that plaintiff testified she walked after the accident. He was also permitted to testify that there is a sac accompanying all hernias that come on gradually, but that in traumatic hernia, where the contents of the abdomen are forced through the muscles, there might not be a sac. If there was no sac, he would call it a rupture of the abdomen, but that it would not be an ordinary hernia, it would be a bursted abdomen, but technically it would be called a hernia. He was permitted to testify that in a traumatic hernia, where the intestines were driven through "those muscles," "we always find the bowels torn in two. That would be a direct traumatic hernia from violence." So the doctor was finally permitted to answer fully as to whether the intestines would be torn in two where they were pushed through the walls of the abdomen by a sudden fall.

[3] It is next insisted that the court erred in refusing to give defendant's instruction in the nature of a demurrer to the evidence. In this connection it is insisted that the way plaintiff claimed that she was injured is against common experience and observation and the physical facts. It is argued that, if the car was going east, and plaintiff was alighting therefrom with her face to the south, and her handhold was broken from the rail when the car started with a sudden jerk—

"How could the conductor grab her by the right hand? And if he did not grab her, how could she fall with her head to the front of the car and her feet to the rear, as she testified? She testifies, 'I was not holding to anything when he grabbed me.'"

It is insisted that, if she was holding onto the rail with her left hand that her right hand would be so far away from the conductor who was opening the door for her that it would have been a physical impossibility for him to grab her by the right wrist.

She testified that the conductor opened the door to permit her to alight; that after the car started with a jerk the conductor saw that it was going to throw her to the pavement, and he then grabbed her by the arm. Where he was at this time is not clearly shown in the evidence, but she testified that the conductor was standing "close enough to grab me by this arm." "He stood on the step and held to the car." We are unable to see how plaintiff's claim is impossible in this regard. She did testify that she was not holding to anything when the conductor grabbed her, that "he grabbed me just as I was breaking loose." There is an inference from plaintiff's evidence that, when the conductor felt the car give a sudden jerk, or at an instant thereafter, he made a grab for plaintiff, anticipating that she might be thrown from the car, and caught her by the right arm just as her hold on the handrail was being broken loose. There is nothing in the contention that plaintiff's testimony that she fell with her head toward the front of the car and her feet toward the vestibule and was dragged on her left side, is against the physical facts under the evidence. Holland v. Metropolitan St. R. Co., 157 Mo. App. 476, 481, 137 S. W. 995; Middleton v. St. Joseph Ry., Light, H. & P. Co., 196 Mo. App. 258, 195 S. W. 527; Benjamin v. Metropolitan St. Ry. Co., 245 Mo. 598, 151 S. W. 91.

[4] In connection with defendant's contention in relation to the demurrer to the evidence, it is pointed out that plaintiff first testified that when the car stopped "the conductor picked me up and knocked the snow off of me," and that after he picked her up "I stood there; the car must have been three or four blocks away before I tried to walk. I was not hardly at myself." And that on cross-examination she testified that after she had been dragged a block the conductor let her off the car, and that "I stepped off." It is contended that plaintiff's testimony is inconsistent. Plaintiff at no time fell entirely to the pavement, but the conductor at all times had hold of her arm, holding her up as much as possible. When she testified the conductor picked her up she may have meant that he pulled her up on to the step or platform, and then brushed the snow off of her, and when she testified that she stepped off the car after it stopped, it might have been that she stepped off the car unassisted after the conductor had "picked her up," or assisted her to the step or platform. However, if there is any inconsistency in plaintiff's testimony, it was a matter for the jury, and not for this court. Bond v. Railroad, 110 Mo. App. 131, 84 S. W. 124; Bobbitt v. Unit-

ed Rys. Co. of St. Louis, 169 Mo. App. 424, 153 S. W. 70.

[5] It is insisted that the weight of the evidence is such as to authorize this court to set aside the verdict. This point is based upon the fact that plaintiff had no witness to corroborate her testimony as to how the accident happened, and the claim that defendant had three, a passenger, the motorman, and the conductor who testified contrary to plaintiff's testimony. It is doubtful from the passenger's testimony whether she was on this particular car as she did not remember of any accident happening. But the conductor testified that an accident did happen; that he was standing inside of the railing of the rear vestibule; that plaintiff safely alighted from the car while it was standing still; that she took two steps, slipped, and fell upon the icy street. The motorman stated that he made but one stop at the place where plaintiff claims she was attempting to alight; that he waited for the signal for him to proceed, and, not getting it, he went to the door and looked out, and saw the conductor talking to a lady at the rear of the car; that the car started up leaving the lady standing on the street. It is evident there is nothing involved except the mere weight of the evidence, which was for the jury and trial court. Terry v. K. C. Rys. Co., 228 S. W. 885; State ex rel. v. Ellison, 268 Mo. 239, 255, 187 S. W. 23; Harmon v. Irwin, 219 S. W. 392; Robertson v. Kochtitzky, 217 S. W. 543; Abernathy v. Mo. Pac. Ry. Co., 217 S. W. 568.

The judgment is affirmed.

All concur.

THOMPSON v. BUSINESS MEN'S ACC. ASS'N OF AMERICA. (No. 2848.)

(Springfield Court of Appeals, Missouri. May 8, 1921. Rehearing Denied June 20, 1921.)

1. Evidence ⟂265(18) — Admissions against interest preclude recovery in absence of contradictory or explanatory evidence.

An admission against interest precludes recovery in the absence of evidence to contradict or explain it.

2. Insurance ⟂646(7)—No presumption against suicide where facts appear.

A beneficiary cannot recover on an accident insurance policy on the presumption against suicide where the facts appear from which the issue whether assured's death was caused by accident or suicide may be determined.

3. Insurance ⟂668(12)—Evidence contradicting admission of suicide held sufficient to carry to jury question whether death accidental.

In a suit on an accident insurance policy, evidence contradicting plaintiff's admission in a former petition that the insured committed suicide held sufficient to take to the jury the question whether his death was caused by accident or suicide.

4. Insurance ⟨⟩665(6)—Evidence held sufficient to justify jury in finding plaintiff mistaken in conclusion assured committed suicide.

In a suit on an accident insurance policy, where no one saw or could have seen how insured's death was caused, and plaintiff and her attorney had no actual knowledge of the cause, any evidence showing that plaintiff and her attorney were mistaken in drawing a conclusion, embodied in an earlier pleading, that the insured committed suicide, will justify the jury in finding that his death was not so caused.

5. Trial ⟨⟩219—Instruction burden of proof on plaintiff by preponderance of evidence erroneous in absence of definition of terms.

It is not error to refuse instructions that the burden of proof is on plaintiff by a preponderance of the credible testimony, in the absence of definition of the terms "burden of proof" and "preponderance of evidence."

6. Appeal and error ⟨⟩1001(1)—Verdict not disturbed where sufficient evidence exists to sustain it.

In a suit on an accident insurance policy, where the jury was instructed that it must find insured's death was accidental and, if he committed suicide, to find for defendant, the verdict will not be disturbed, where there was evidence tending to prove either.

Appeal from Circuit Court, Howell County; E. P. Dorris, Judge.

Suit by Susan E. Rollins Thompson against the Business Men's Accident Association of America. Judgment for plaintiff, and defendant appeals. Affirmed.

Solon T. Gilmore and A. I. Beach, both of Kansas City, and R. S. Hogan, of West Plains, for appellant.

Stephen C. Rogers, of St. Louis, and John C. Dyott, of Willow Springs, for respondent.

FARRINGTON, J. This is a suit on an accident insurance policy in which plaintiff recovered judgment in the trial court for the full amount of the policy together with interest.

Appellant complains of error in that the trial court refused an instruction in the nature of a demurrer to the evidence, and refused two instructions on the burden of proof and the admission of some evidence offered by the plaintiff.

The suit was originally filed in the circuit court of Howell county on a policy of accident insurance issued by the appellant on the life of Elisha M. Rollins. The respondent, since the death of Elisha M. Rollins, has married and is now Susan E. Rollins Thompson. At a former trial the plaintiff recovered a judgment, and an appeal was taken to the Supreme Court, and will be found reported in the case of Susan E. Rollins v. Busi-

ness Men's Accident Ins. Co., 213 S. W. 52. In that opinion it was held that that court had no jurisdiction of the appeal, and it was transferred to this court. The opinion disposing of the appeal in this court will be found reported in 220 S. W. 1022, where we reversed the judgment and remanded the cause for the reasons therein stated. The case went back to the circuit court of Howell county, where the plaintiff amended her petition, charging that Rollins was accidentally killed from the discharge of a single-barrel shotgun, causing the top of his head to be severed. To this petition, being the third amended petition, the defendant filed an answer denying that Rollins' death was the result of an accident and specifically pleading that he committed suicide. On this, the last trial, the plaintiff again recovered a judgment for the full amount with interest, and it is this judgment which is the subject of this appeal.

In order that the facts may be fully understood, we find from the record that in the first petition filed in this cause of action the plaintiff merely alleged that Rollins was accidentally injured and killed by the top of his head being severed. A demurrer to this petition was sustained and an amendment to same was made by the plaintiff alleging that he was killed by the discharge of a shotgun, and that the same was fired or discharged by the said Elisha M. Rollins with intent to commit suicide. The defendant again demurred, but the same was overruled, whereupon it filed an answer in the nature of a general denial and pleaded the suicide statute as unconstitutional. After this was filed the plaintiff then filed a second amended petition in which she alleged "that the gun was fired or discharged either by the said Elisha M. Rollins with intent to commit suicide or that it was accidentally or inadvertently discharged by said deceased, or some other person, the means, the fact, and the real cause being unknown to the plaintiff, it being one or the other, exactly which she is unable to state," and it was on this petition that the case was disposed of in this court in 220 S. W. 1022.

On the last trial, which was merely on an allegation of the plaintiff that the discharge of the gun was accidental, and a denial of same coupled with a plea of suicide by the defendant, the plaintiff introduced testimony to the effect that on the morning of the 5th day of April, 1915, Rollins was found in his store in the city of Willow Springs, Mo., lying with his back on the floor in the rear end of the store, dead with a shotgun lying by his side which had been discharged, and the top of his head practically torn off, and a part of his brains were found on the ceiling of the store. When found he was lying on his back with one foot up over the second rung of a ladder which was standing against a case in the store. It is shown that the deceased kept his gun on top of this case, and that to take it down from the top of this case would require one to step on the ladder to the second or third rung. It was further shown by plaintiff's evidence that the hammer of the gun was so that if it received a jar it would cause the gun to go off.

It appears that the deceased had sold his stock of goods or traded it for a farm, and that he was preparing to leave Willow Springs, but he had not yet made a delivery to the purchaser. On the morning of his death he left home about the same time as usual, in good spirits; that he went to the store, swept the sidewalk, and there had a conversation with a neighbor, which indicated that he was in good spirits and expected to pack up and leave. He had loaned the gun some time before, but it had been returned to him unloaded and had been placed upon the case against which the ladder was resting, at the foot of which he was found, as before described. A few days prior to his death he had purchased some cartridges for this gun. It is shown that he was in good health, in the prime of life, and that he had no financial difficulties or family relations which would tend to make him dissatisfied with life. One witness who viewed his body before it was taken from the ladder said that the top of the ladder was a little to one side, "as though when he fell the top slipped." This constitutes the facts as shown by plaintiff surrounding the death of her former husband.

The defendant, to sustain its plea of suicide, introduced in evidence the amended petition which had been originally filed in the case by the plaintiff in which it was specifically alleged that the deceased discharged the gun with intent to commit suicide. It further introduced the testimony of one of plaintiff's attorneys who stated that he filed this amended petition alleging suicide, did so after a thorough investigation, and decided that he had committed suicide. All of the evidence in the case shows that the plaintiff did not see the deceased when he was killed, and that the last time she saw him was at the home in the morning before he left for the store, and there is no testimony offered other than has been set out which would tend to prove that the death was the result of an accident or the result of an intentional suicide. There is no claim that the deceased was insane; hence that feature of the accident is out of the case, and there is, of course, no contention that the death was a natural one, the sole issue being whether the deceased died from an accidental cause or means or from a voluntary, intentional, sane act on his part.

[1] Appellant contends that the solemn declaration in plaintiff's amended petition which it introduced in evidence bars a recovery on her part, it being a direct admission against interest that the deceased committed suicide, and for that reason there could be no recovery under an accident policy under the decisions in this state, and that she is likewise bound by the admission of her attorney that after investigation he had concluded that it was suicide and filed her petition, and that such admission against interest is a complete bar to the plaintiff's cause of action unless she brings forward some evidence to show that she was mistaken in making the admission, or some evidence which would contradict the effect of such admission against interest. In this connection we are cited particularly to the cases of Castens v. Supreme Lodge Knights and Ladies of Honor, 190 Mo. App. 57, 175 S. W. 264; Stephens v. Metropolitan Life Ins. Co., 190 Mo. App. 674, 176 S. W. 253. These cases clearly hold that an admission against interest which would bar a recovery will preclude a recovery in the absence of something offered which would contradict or explain such admission. It is held in these two authorities, and in others, such as Andrus v. Business Men's Association, 223 S. W. 70, that admissions contained in abandoned pleadings offered in evidence are not conclusive, but are to be weighed by the jury like other admissions. This, of course, has reference to a case where there is some evidence offered which does tend to contradict or explain the damaging admission. In the Stephens and Castens Cases, it being found that there was no evidence tending to contradict or explain, the plaintiff is and must be concluded from recovery by such admission. But we do not think that the evidence in this case fails to contradict the declaration in the amended petition nor the testimony of her attorney above referred to.

[2, 3] We agree with the appellant that in a case such as this, where the facts appear from which the issue of accident or suicide might be determined, then all presumptions, such as the love of living, and against suicide, are out of the case, and that a plaintiff will not be entitled to recover and bolster up the case on such presumption where the facts of the tragedy are introduced in evidence. If there is any evidence which tends to contradict the admission made, then the question is one for the jury to determine the ultimate fact of accident or suicide. In this case, being stripped as it is of the presumption which prevails against a suicide, because evidence of the death and the facts surrounding the death are submitted to the jury together with the admission, from which they must conclude the fact, we think there is evidence sufficient to carry the question to the jury to determine on the manner of his death; that is, there is evidence before the jury which tends to contradict the

fact that the deceased met his death as a result of suicide. This being true, then the jury must weigh that evidence as against the plaintiff's admission, and their determination after such weighing is final.

[4] The evidence which we hold is competent to draw a reasonable inference of accidental death in this case is that the deceased was in good health; he had no family troubles; he had no financial troubles; he gave evidence shortly prior to his death of what he intended his future actions to be; he was found at the foot of a ladder which he would naturally use to take the gun down from off the case in the store. That he was on this ladder when the gun was discharged is evident from the fact that one of his feet, when he was found dead, was up over the second rung of the ladder about where he would be standing in taking the gun down, and the ladder, evidenced by its position, as testified to by one of the witnesses, had slipped from its original position. Aside from the natural instinct of self-preservation and revulsion to suicide, and without considering them in the least, one could very readily and reasonably conclude, without entering into the field of conjecture, that the deceased met his death as a result of an accidental discharge of the gun while on the ladder getting it down from the top of the case. It required but little evidence to make this a jury question. In other words, any evidence which had gone or goes into the case tending to contradict the admission against interest is sufficient to open up the question for a determination by the jury. For instance, in the case of Clarkston v. Met. Life Insurance Company, 190 Mo. App. 624, 176 S. W. 437, where there was an admission made in the proofs of death which, without contradiction, would have barred a recovery, was overcome by the introduction in evidence by the plaintiff of the report of defendant's medical examiner, which tended to contradict the admission in the proofs of death, and was held sufficient to take the question to the jury. See Remfry v. Insurance Co., 196 S. W. 775; Bruck v. John Hancock Insurance Co., 194 Mo. App. 529, 185 S. W. 753, loc. cit. 758.

In the case at bar, where the only evidence of suicide was a declaration in a petition, and evidence of the attorney drawing that petition, and where it is shown uncontradictedly in the evidence that there was no one who saw or could have seen how death was caused, and that those mak- such declaration had no actual knowledge the cause of the death, and that such de laration, which is an admission, must n sarily be based upon a conclusion of pleader, any evidence which tended to sh that the pleader or party making such mission was mistaken in drawing such c clusion will justify a jury in such find:

We therefore hold that the court prop overruled defendant's instruction in the ture of a demurrer.

[5, 6] Appellant further contends that t court erred in refusing to give instruct 1 and 2. These instructions were on burden of proof; they tell the jury that burden is upon the plaintiff by a preponderance of the credible testimony, etc. Suct structions, nor any others which were g or asked, undertook to define the term bur of proof or preponderance of evidence. has been held in a number of cases in t state that absence of such an explanation connection with such instructions will be tify the trial court in refusing them. that he will not be convicted of error for refusing them. Berger v. Storage & Co., 136 Mo. App. loc. cit. 43, 116 S. W. Cramer v. Nelson, 128 Mo. App. loc. cit. 3 399, 107 S. W. 450. The plaintiff's instr tion in this case put the issue squarely to t jury requiring it to find that the decease death was the result of an accident, a went further and told the jury that, if the believed from the evidence that he comm ted suicide, the verdict must be for the d fendant. This was the square issue of h fought out in this case. There was evide tending to establish either the theory of t plaintiff that it was accidental or defends that it was suicide. The jury has made determination from competent and sufficient proof, and its verdict will not be disturbe The error as to the admissibility of inco petent testimony has been considered, an we have concluded that it was not prejud cial to a fair trial of the case.

The jury rendered a verdict for the f amount of the policy, which was $5,000, t gether with interest, which in all amount to $6,495.

There being no error shown, such judg ment will be affirmed.

COX, P. J., and BRADLEY, J., concur.

**JOHN O'BRIEN BOILER WORKS CO. v.
THIRD NAT. BANK OF ST. LOUIS
et al. (No. 14729.)**

(St. Louis Court of Appeals. Missouri.
March 8, 1921. Rehearing Denied
June 7, 1921.)

1. **Corporations** ⟐⟐426(11)—**Corporation held
to have ratified by its president an agreement
of its sales manager as to deposit of a
check.**

Where corporation's sales manager agreed
with a customer as to the deposit of a check to
be held until engineers pronounced a smokestack satisfactory, and its president, though objecting, stated he would agree to the arrangement, that constituted a ratification.

2. **Estoppel** ⟐⟐61—**Plaintiff contractor not entitled to rely on acceptance as estopping defendant from questioning sufficiency of smokestack.**

Plaintiff installed boilers and other appliances at a state hospital, but the stack, which
was guaranteed for five years, was constructed by a subcontractor, which gave a surety
bond. The engineer representing the hospital
accepted the stack, and on the faith of such
acceptance plaintiff paid the subcontractor the
price of the stack, and the Legislature made
appropriations for plaintiff's payment. Thereafter the board of managers of the hospital
questioned the construction and material of
the stack, and withheld payment. To procure payment, plaintiff agreed to deposit with
the board of managers a certified check to be
held until the stack was pronounced satisfactory by the engineer for the hospital and another. *Held*, that notwithstanding the original
acceptance may have estopped the board from
questioning the sufficiency of the stack, yet, as
plaintiff was protected by bond given by its
subcontractor, and there could be no final acceptance of the stack until the expiration of
five years, plaintiff, having entered into the new
arrangement with the board of managers of
the hospital, cannot successfully contend that
they were estopped from questioning the sufficiency of the stack.

Appeal from St. Louis Circuit Court; Wilson A. Taylor, Judge.

"Not to be officially published."

Action by the John O'Brien Boiler Works
Company against the Third National Bank
of St. Louis, in which the Board of Managers
of State Hospital No. 1, at Fulton, were permitted to intervene. From a judgment in favor of the intervening defendants, plaintiff
appeals. The cause was transferred from
the Court of Appeals to the Supreme Court,
and by the latter tribunal retransferred (222
S. W. 788). Affirmed.

Leahy, Saunders & Barth, of St. Louis, for
appellant.

Irwin & Haley, of Jefferson City, for respondents.

BIGGS, C. The purpose of this suit is to
require the Third National Bank to deliver
to plaintiff a certain cashier's check for
$2,800, which was deposited with it as trus-
tee under certain alleged terms and conditions. An injunction was asked to prevent
any disposition of the check pending the litigation.

The board of managers of the State Hospital No. 1 at Fulton was granted permission
to intervene in the suit as a party defendant,
and to set up its claims of ownership in the
check. The defendant bank disclaimed any
rights therein, asserting that it was a mere
stakeholder, and upon its request was permitted to deposit the check in the registry
of the court to abide its order and judgment.
Thereafter the suit resolved itself into the
question as to whether the plaintiff or the
board of managers of the hospital is entitled
to the check and its proceeds.

Upon a trial the issue thus presented was
decided in favor of the board of managers of
the hospital, and by judgment and order of
the court the check was decreed to belong to
it. After the usual steps, plaintiff appealed
the cause to this court, where on July 17,
1917, the cause was ordered transferred to
the Supreme Court as being a cause not within our jurisdiction. Thereafter, on July 4,
1920, the Supreme Court held that under the
law the power rested in this court to determine the correctness of the judgment rendered in the trial court, and retransferred the
case here (John O'Brien Boiler Works Co. v.
Third National Bank et al., 222 S. W. 788).

On July 14, 1910, plaintiff and said board
entered into a contract, by which plaintiff
agreed to install certain boilers and equipment in the State Hospital at Fulton. A
part of said equipment was a concrete smokestack, the erection of which was sublet by
the plaintiff to M. W. Kellogg Company of
New York.

As averred by plaintiff, after the work was
done, a question arose in reference to the efficiency of the smokestack, and whether or
not it complied with the terms of the contract; that thereupon, in order to adjust the
matter, the plaintiff caused to be deposited
in trust with the said bank a cashier's check
for $2,800, payable to the order of the treas-
urer of the board of managers of the State
Hospital; that said check, dated June 15,
1911, was so deposited, subject to the terms
and conditions of an agreement between the
plaintiff and the board of managers, which
provided that plaintiff should select an engineer, and the board an engineer, to investigate said stack and determine its conformity to specifications, and, if not conforming,
the check should be held until plaintiff should
make the stack conform; that if the engineers
should disagree, a third engineer should be
selected by the two, and a report signed by

a majority of the three should be final; that should the engineers hold that the stack was built in compliance with the specifications, then the bank should deliver the $2,800 check to plaintiff. This sum of $2,800 represented the cost of the smokestack.

It is further averred that the check was placed in the hands of Reubel & Wells, engineers, who were agents and representatives of the State Hospital, and that Reubel & Wells deposited said check with said bank; that thereafter the said hospital repudiated the terms of said trust agreement, and that therefore the said trust has failed, and that said bank had refused to surrender said check to plaintiff, and that it therefore was the property of plaintiff.

Thereafter, as stated, the Board of managers were permitted to file an intervening petition in the nature of a cross-bill, setting up their rights and claims to the check. By this pleading, after admitting the deposit of said check and the existence of a controversy with reference to said smokestack, it denied that the said check was deposited under the terms of the trust as set up in plaintiff's petition.

The cross-bill then averred the making of the contract with plaintiff for the sum of $27,149, being the entire contract price for the work under the contract of June 14, 1910, and further that said work was to be done, including the smokestack, in accordance with certain plans and specifications, and that said work was to be carried on under the supervision, and when completed was subject to acceptance upon the approval of Reubel & Wells Consulting Engineers Company; that because the said smokestack was not made and constructed in accordance with said plans and specifications the said board refused to pay plaintiff the contract price, namely, $27,149, or any part thereof; that thereafter, on June 13, 1911, plaintiff and the board entered into an agreement, whereby it was agreed that the plaintiff should deposit with the treasurer of State Hospital No. 1 a certified check for the sum of $2,800, to be held in escrow until E. Reubel of the firm of Reubel & Wells, and the Engineering Department of the University of Missouri had agreed that said smokestack was constructed in a satisfactory manner, and that thereupon and in consideration of said agreement and the depositing of said check by the plaintiff as security for the faithful performance of said contract of July 14, 1910, the board of managers agreed to and did pay over to the said plaintiff the entire sum of $27,149, being the whole contract price for all of said work; that said check, dated June 15, 1911, was given by plaintiff in accordance with said agreement so entered into on June 13, 1911, and not otherwise; that in compliance with said agreement the said check was obtained for the said sum of $2,800, payable as stated in the agreement, and that the said check

was delivered to the defendant for the purpose of indemnifying the hospital because of defective workmanship and material used in said smokestack; that following the delivery of said check to the defendant the said defendant, in consideration thereof, paid to the plaintiff the sum of $27,149, which included the agreed sum of $2,800 for the construction of the smokestack, and that said check was thereafter deposited in the Third National Bank at the instance and for the use and benefit of the hospital.

It is then averred in said cross-bill that the said smokestack was not in accordance with the plans and specifications and was deficient and defective, both in workmanship and composition of material, and that by reason thereof it will be necessary to tear down said smokestack and erect a new one in place thereof, to the damage of the hospital in the sum of $2,800; that the said smokestack has not been accepted or pronounced satisfactory by Mr. Reubel and the Engineering Department of the University of Missouri, or by either of them, but that both have condemned the said chimney as being defective both in workmanship and material, and not in accordance with the plans and specifications; that the plaintiff, prior to June 13, 1911, knew that said smokestack was defective and would not be accepted and paid for by defendant, and that the plaintiff made and delivered said check as a guaranty for the construction of said smokestack in accordance with the agreement; that prior to March 18, 1912, when plaintiff demanded said check from the bank, plaintiff knew that the said referees, nominated and appointed by the agreement of June 13, 1911, had refused to agree that said smokestack was satisfactory and constructed according to contract, and that a reasonable time has elapsed since said referees have condemned said smokestack, and plaintiff, though often requested, has failed and refused to reconstruct said chimney, or place same in a satisfactory condition, so as to comply with the terms of the contract, and become acceptable to the referees appointed by the agreement of June 13, 1911.

It is prayed in the cross-bill that the Third National Bank be declared the holder of the check to the use and benefit of the said board of managers, subject to the demand of the treasurer of the board, and that the defendant have judgment against the plaintiff in the sum of $2,800, and for general relief. By reply the plaintiff set up that the defendant was precluded and estopped from relying upon the alleged inefficiency of the stack, for the reason that prior to the date when said cashier's check for $2,800 was placed in trust by the plaintiff herein, the defendants, through their representatives, Reubel & Wells, did, on the 14th of January, 1911, accept the stack and direct plaintiff to pay the subcontractor in accordance with the contract; that, relying thereon, plaintiff did, on January 16, 1911, make payment to Kellogg Company for the erection of said smokestack.

Plaintiff's counsel argue two propositions, which they contend were wrongfully solved against plaintiff by the lower court, namely: First, whether the terms of the trust as alleged in plaintiff's petition controlled the disposition of the check; and, second, whether the board of managers is estopped and precluded from raising the question of the efficiency of the smokestack. The court nisi ruled that the terms of the trust were not as alleged by plaintiff, but the disposition of the check was controlled by the agreement set up in defendants' cross-bill, and that the board was not estopped or precluded from questioning the efficiency of the stack.

[1] I. As to the terms of the trust: The contract between the parties provided that before final payment was made plaintiff should furnish to the purchaser a surety bond to protect it under a guaranty of concrete stack, which bond should be in the sum of $3,000 and for a term of five years from the date of the completion of the contract. The contractor by the terms of the contract guaranteed the stack for a period of five years, agreeing to keep same in repair, provided said repairs were necessary by reason of defects in workmanship, material, or design.

After the completion of the work, and after the Legislature of 1911 made a deficiency appropriation to cover the cost of the work in the sum of $27,150, but before any sum was paid to the plaintiff, a controversy arose concerning the smokestack. On May 9, 1911, the president of the board by letter notified the plaintiff that the stack was cracked through, and that the composition was soft and apparently rotten, as though there were very little cement and plenty of sand used in its construction; that before the money was paid to plaintiff the matter would have to be investigated, and at the time notified plaintiff of the coming meeting of the board to be held on the second Tuesday of June following. Thereafter, at the June meeting of the board, Mr. William Miller sales manager of plaintiff company, appeared, representing the plaintiff. This meeting took place on June 13th. All prior negotiations between the parties had been conducted by Mr. Miller as representative of the plaintiff company, and at the meeting of the board on this day, after a full discussion and with the approval of Mr. Miller, the board passed the following resolution:

"That the hospital pay to the John O'Brien Boiler Works Company the amount of their contract for installing boilers and equipment, provided the above company deposits certified check payable to the treasurer of State Hospital No. 1, said check to be drawn for an amount equal to the cost of the concrete stack; the certified check to be held in escrow until Mr. Reubel, of the firm of Reubel & Wells Constructing Engineers Company, and the Engineering Department of the University of Missouri have agreed that the stack is satisfactory."

In view of this arrangement the bond referred to in the contract, which guaranteed the stack, was not given by the plaintiff, and thereafter, and within a day or two, when Mr. Reubel, the engineer, and Mr. Miller returned to St. Louis from Fulton, the plaintiff company left with Mr. Reubel, as the representative of the board, a certified check for $2,800. Thereupon, as had been previously arranged, Mr. Reubel wired the board to the effect that he had the certified check for $2,800, and thereupon the board paid to the plaintiff company the full contract price of $27,149.

After the return of Mr. Miller to St. Louis, the president of the plaintiff company, Mr. McKeown, took up the matter on behalf of his company, and visited Mr. Reubel's office, and left with him a certified check for $2,800, payable to the treasurer of the hospital. As to what transpired between Mr. Reubel and Mr. McKeown there is a conflict of testimony. Mr. McKeown claims that there a new and different arrangement was made in reference to the disposition of the check, and terms under which it should be deposited in escrow were agreed upon, which were substantially as embodied in the plaintiff's petition. According to Mr. Reubel, he did not pretend to make any new agreement on behalf of the board, but that the check was deposited under the terms of the resolution passed by the board at Fulton on June 13th. It appears, however, that a change of the agreement was discussed between Mr. McKeown and Mr. Reubel, and that Mr. Reubel afterwards sent to the president of the board a form of a written agreement, embodying the terms on which the check should be deposited as proposed by Mr. McKeown, and agreed with Mr. McKeown to use his best efforts to have the board adopt that agreement. However, at the time the check was left with Mr. Reubel, he immediately wired the board, and they thereupon sent check for the full contract price to the plaintiff company. Thereafter this new agreement as suggested by Mr. McKeown was sent to the president of the board, who forwarded it to the secretary, but as far as the record discloses no subsequent action was taken in the matter by the board of managers. Even though Mr. Reubel had made that new agreement with Mr. McKeown in reference to the disposition of the check, it appears from the record that such agreement would have been without authority from the board, as Mr. Reubel had no authority to make such a new contract, and his only duty in the matter was to receive the check and telegraph the board of such fact. The terms of the trust agreement had already been concluded at Fulton a few days prior thereto by the board and by Mr. Miller, representing the plaintiff company.

It is contended by the plaintiff that Mr. Miller, being a sales manager, had no authority to make the agreement referred to, and bind plaintiff thereto. However that may be, a number of the members of the board testified that thereafter at the July meeting of the board at Mexico, Mr. McKeown, president of plaintiff company, was present, and while he objected to the agreement and stated that he would not have made it, he stated he would stand by the arrangement as made by Mr. Miller. Whether or not Miller had actual authority, it is unnecessary to determine, in view of the fact that there was ample evidence in the record to sustain a finding that Mr. McKeown, president of the plaintiff company, ratified the contract as made by Mr. Miller on behalf of the plaintiff company. In addition to this, the plaintiff company deposited the check with Mr. Reubel for the board, and thereby secured from the board payment for the full contract price of the work, $27,149. The board had a right to withhold this payment, in the event the work was not done according to the contract as was contended by them at the time. They released this money to the plaintiff by reason of the contract made at Fulton on June 13th. The terms of that contract were afterwards carried out by the board, and Mr. Reubel and the Engineering Department of the State University condemned the smokestack, and the same was not afterwards repaired or put in condition by the plaintiff company. The evidence was sufficient to warrant a finding by the lower court that the check was deposited under the terms of the resolution adopted by the board, and not under the terms and conditions as alleged in plaintiff's petition, and, the conditions of the said resolution as adopted by the board not having been complied with, the check was properly decreed to belong to the board of managers.

[2] II. As to the question of estoppel. Shortly after the work was completed, and after the Legislature convened at Jefferson City in 1911, the board held a meeting at Jefferson City. It was the purpose of the parties at the time to obtain from the Legislature an appropriation to cover the work, as the plaintiff had taken the contract realizing that there was no money appropriated to pay for same. On January 14, 1911, Reubel & Wells wrote the following letter to the plaintiff:

"St. Louis, January 14, 1911.

"John O'Brien Boiler Works Co., St. Louis— Gentlemen: Re Stack at State Hospital No. 1. The writer examined the stack at Fulton last Wednesday, and while the work on this stack is not as neat and smooth as it should be, the writer believes the stack is first-class in every other way. The man in charge evidently did not use the care that he should in shifting his molds and, of course, the defects in some places impair the looks of the stack. However, we have no hesitancy in accepting the stack, and you may, therefore, pay the contractor according to the contract.

"Very truly yours,
"Reubel & Wells C. H. Co."

The contract between the parties contained the following provision:

"Should any questions arise relating to the acceptance of work done or equipment furnished, or regarding settlements of account, such questions shall be referred to the engineers, whose decision shall be binding upon both parties."

The firm of Reubel & Wells were the engineers named in the contract.

Plaintiff asserts by reason of this acceptance and by reason of the fact that they have, on the faith thereof, paid to the subcontractor Kellogg Company the price of the stack, therefore the board is now estopped and precluded from asserting that the said smokestack was not in compliance with the contract or according to plans and specifications. Defendants contend that this letter was written at a time when they did not know the condition of the stack, and that it was given by the engineers for the purpose of allowing plaintiff to show same to the state auditor in order to get the appropriation, and there is evidence in the record to this effect. However that may be, thereafter a dispute arose as to the efficiency of the stack, and the board withheld payment of the entire contract price until some arrangement was made in reference to the matter. Thereafter, in view of the dispute, plaintiff and the board entered into the contract as embodied in the resolution at the meeting of the board of June 13, 1911. If the defendant was precluded from questioning the efficiency of the stack by reason of the letter of acceptance of its engineers referred to, plaintiff at that time should have so asserted, and not entered into the agreement referred to. Certainly plaintiff was obligated to give the surety bond guaranteeing the stack for a period of five years, which it did not do, and which provision of the contract the board waived by reason of the fact that the plaintiff entered into the contract of June 13, 1911, and deposited its certified check in escrow under the terms thereof.

In view of the provisions of the contract there could be no final approval of this stack within five years, as it was guaranteed for that length of time under the express provisions of the contract, and formal approval thereof following the completion of the work would not prevent the board from thereafter raising the question as to its efficiency.

And even though plaintiff company on the faith of the formal acceptance by the engineer had paid the subcontractor for the stack, it appeared from the evidence that it was protected by a $3,000 surety bond given by the Kellogg Company to the plaintiff company, which guaranteed the stack.

In view of the record before us, we think the cause was properly decided, and that the judgment should be affirmed.

PER CURIAM. The foregoing opinion of BIGGS, C., is adopted as the opinion of the court.

The judgment of the circuit court is accordingly affirmed.

ALLEN and BECKER, JJ., concur.
REYNOLDS, P. J., not sitting.

STATE v. GARDNER. (No. 2897.)

(Springfield Court of Appeals. Missouri. May 3, 1921. Rehearing Denied June 20, 1921.)

1. Indictment and information ⟜161(3)—Amendment after jurors had qualified but before they have been sworn to try issues discretionary with court.

Amendment of information after jury had been qualified, but before they had been sworn to try the issues, was discretionary with the court.

2. Criminal law ⟜1032(1)—Amendment of information not ground for reversal in absence of affidavit of surprise or application for continuance.

Amendment of information after jurors had qualified, but before they had been sworn to try the issues, held not ground for reversal where there was no affidavit of surprise or application for continuance on account of the amendment, since in such case it did not appear that appellant had been prejudiced thereby.

3. Physicians and surgeons ⟜6(10)—State not required to prove defendant, charged with practicing without a license, had not obtained license.

In prosecution for practicing medicine in violation of Rev. St. 1919, § 7334, the state was not required to prove that the defendant had not obtained a license from the state board of health, the issuance of such a license being a matter of defense.

4. Criminal law ⟜872½—Verdict must be clear and unambiguous.

The verdict must be clear and unambiguous and must show that all 12 jurors agreed on finding the same thing.

5. Criminal law ⟜881(1)—Verdict must describe all necessary elements of the offense.

The verdict in a criminal case must describe all the elements of the offense which it was necessary for the state to prove to warrant a verdict of guilty.

6. Physicians and surgeons ⟜6(11)—Verdict finding chiropractor guilty of practicing medicine without a license held not defective.

In prosecution of a chiropractor for practicing medicine without a license in violation of Rev. St. 1919, § 7334, making "any person practicing medicine or surgery in the state and any person attempting to treat the sick or others afflicted with bodily or mental infirmities * * * without a license from the state board of health * * * guilty of a misdemeanor," verdict finding the defendant guilty as charged "by attempting to treat the sick or those afflicted with bodily infirmities by manipulating adjustments or massages" held not defective as against contention that the use of the disjunctive "or" made it indefinite as to the acts the jury found the defendant had committed.

Appeal from Circuit Court, Howell County; E. P. Dorris, Judge.

C. G. Gardner was convicted of practicing medicine without a license, and he appeals. Affirmed.

M. E. Morrow, of West Plains, and Collins & Holladay, of Springfield, for appellant.

B. L. Rinehart and W. N. Evans, both of West Plains, for the State.

COX, P. J. Defendant was prosecuted upon information filed by the prosecuting attorney under section 7334, Rev. Stat. 1919, which is levelled against persons practicing medicine without license. Defendant was convicted, and has appealed.

The portion of the statute involved here is as follows:

"Any person practising medicine or surgery in this state and any person attempting to treat the sick or others afflicted with bodily or mental infirmities * * * without a license from the State Board of Health * * * shall be deemed guilty of a misdemeanor."

The information charged that defendant did—

"willfully, unlawfully, and wrongfully practice medicine and surgery and did attempt to treat the sick and others afflicted with bodily infirmities without then and there having a license from the State Board of Health."

Instruction No. 1 for the state told the jury that if they found from the evidence that the defendant "did unlawfully practice medicine and surgery or did attempt to treat the sick or others afflicted with bodily or mental infirmities by manipulating, adjusting, or massaging the muscles or the spinal column or nerves of the body" without having a license from the State Board of Health, they should find the defendant guilty. In instruction No. 5, the jury were told that the state was not required to prove that the defendant did not have a license from the State Board of Health as that was a matter of defense. The information was clearly good. State v. Grossman, 214 Mo. 233, loc. cit. 242, 113 S. W. 1074.

[1, 2] Error is assigned based on the charge that the information was amended after the jury had been impaneled and sworn to try the issues. We find by an examination of the transcript on file here that the amendment was made after the jury had been qualified, but before they were sworn to try the issues. This was permissible in the discretion of the court, and, since no affidavit of surprise or application for continuance was filed on account of the amendment, it does not appear from the record here that defendant's rights were in any way prejudiced by the amendment.

[3] It is contended that the state failed to make a case because it was not proven that defendant did not have a license from the State Board of Health, and that the court erred in giving instruction No. 5 which told the jury that the state was not required to make such proof. This question has been settled in this state against appellant's contention. State v. Lipscomb, 52 Mo. 32; State v. Edwards, 60 Mo. 490; State v. Meek, 70 Mo. 355, 358, 35 Am. Rep. 427; State v. Hathaway, 115 Mo. 36, 44, 21 S. W. 1081; State v. Miller, 182 Mo. 370, 390, 81 S. W. 867; State v. De Groat, 259 Mo. 364, 375, 376, 168 S. W. 702; State v. Stephens, 70 Mo. App. 554, 556; State v. Schatt, 128 Mo. App. 622, 634, 107 S. W. 10; State v. Hellscher, 150 Mo. App. 230, 238, 129 S. W. 1035; State v. Zehnder, 182 Mo. App. 176, 180, 168 S. W. 660.

[4-6] It is finally contended that the verdict will not support the judgment because it is indefinite and uncertain. The part of the verdict objected to is as follows:

"We, the jury, find the defendant C. G. Gardner guilty on the first count as charged by attempting to treat the sick or those afflicted with bodily infirmities by manipulating, adjustments, or massages. * * *"

The contention is that the use of the disjunctive "or" in the verdict annuls it, because it cannot be certainly determined just what acts the jury found the defendant had committed. We agree that a verdict must be clear and unambiguous, and must show that all 12 of the jurors agreed on finding the same thing. It is also true that when a jury returns a special verdict in a criminal case the verdict must describe all the elements of the offense, but we take it that this means all the elements which it was necessary for the state to prove to warrant a verdict of guilty. The information in this case charged the defendant with attempting to treat the sick and others afflicted with bodily and mental infirmities without setting out the manner of treatment.

The evidence shows that defendant was what is known as a chiropractor. He kept an office in West Plains, and followed the usual practice of that class of supposed healers in treating those who came to him for treatment. They proceed on the theory that all human ailments are caused by a dislocation of some part of the spinal column, no matter what the ailment may be, and the only safe road to relief lies in resetting the dislocated parts, and thereby removing the cause of the trouble. In this case, one party treated said he did not know what was the matter. He signed up a card to take 24 treatments for $27. Another one had a sluggish liver and nervousness. Another had appendicitis, and took 25 or 30 treatments at $1.25 each. Whether or not it required all these treatments in order to get the bones in the spinal column all back in their proper places does not appear, but one thing is clear; the patients all received the same treatment, and in each case the purpose was to put in proper position the bones of the spinal column. This process was described as "adjustments," "manipulations," and "massages," and these terms of necessity all referred to the same thing, to wit, the replacement of the bones of the spinal column. What the jury found was that defendant had performed that service for the various witnesses who testified, and the defendant, who was plying his trade in open violation of the law, knew exactly of what he was convicted by the jury. The terms "sick," and those afflicted with "bodily infirmities," are not intended to designate two classes of persons, but the use of those terms in the statute and in the information and instructions in this case is simply the use of words to include all persons that have or think they have any ailments of any kind.

We do not think the verdict in this case uncertain or open to the objections made against it.

Judgment affirmed.

FARRINGTON and BRADLEY, JJ., concur.

STETINA v. BERGSTEIN.   (No. 15953.)

(St. Louis Court of Appeals. Missouri.
June 7, 1921.)

1. **Evidence ⊕=376(6)—Witness familiar with books of account properly permitted to state totals shown thereby when offered for inspection, though not made by her.**

For the purpose of showing the total earnings of plaintiff during a period of five years which she claimed to have turned over to her grandmother, defendant's intestate, her employer's bookkeeper, who was familiar with the employer's books and knew that the entries therein were correct, though they were not made by her, was properly permitted to state the total amounts which her inspection of the books showed had been earned by plaintiff; the books themselves being in court and offered for inspection by defendant's counsel.

2. **Appeal and error ⊕=231(5)—General objection to evidence held not sufficiently specific upon which to predicate exception.**

A general objection to the testimony of a witness concerning the total amount of plaintiff's earnings, as shown by her employer's books, was not sufficiently specific upon which to predicate an exception to the admission of the testimony.

3. **Appeal and error ⊕=1068(4)—In view of verdict, instruction on trial of claim held not cause for reversal because not telling the jury to deduct conceded amount.**

Where a claim against the estate of a decedent for an amount advanced to decedent, claimant's grandmother, showed a credit of $700, but the evidence showed that nothing was expended by the grandmother for claimant other than for clothing and board, and that the total amount was less than $700, and that decedent had received $1,687.67, but the verdict was for only $700, an instruction to deduct the amount expended by the grandmother for board and clothing, instead of the amount of the admitted credit, was not erroneous.

Appeal from St. Louis Circuit Court; Victor H. Falkenhainer, Judge.

"Not to be officially published."

Suit by Lillian Stetina against Charles Bergstein, administrator of Kathrine Zacek, deceased. From a judgment for plaintiff, defendant appeals. Judgment was reversed by the Court of Appeals (204 Mo. App. 366, 221 S. W. 420), but the record was quashed by the Supreme Court on certiorari (227 S. W. 47). Judgment affirmed.

Pierre A. Vogel, of St. Louis, for appellant. Harry G. Finley and Earl M. Pirkey, both of St. Louis, for respondent.

BECKER, J. The record of this court in this case (204 Mo. App. 366, 221 S. W. 420) was quashed by way of certiorari (227 S. W. 47) and is now before us for final disposition in light of the said Supreme Court decision.

The suit originated as a claim filed in the probate court against the estate of Kathrine Zacek, deceased, which is as follows:

"St. Louis, Mo., May 23, 1916.

Charles Bergstein. Administrator of the Estate of Kathrine Zacek, Deceased, to Lillian Stetina, Formerly Lillian Rezney, Dr.

To money loaned and advanced Kathrine Zacek under a continuous open account on various sums and amounts at various times between November 1, 1909, and July 6, 1915	$1,900 00
Credits.	
By money repaid by said Kathrine Zacek in various sums and amounts at various times between November 1, 1909, and July 6, 1915	700 00
Balance due	$1,200 00

Plaintiff's parents having died, she went to live with her grandmother, Kathrine Zacek, in 1901. When plaintiff, in 1909, was fourteen years of age, she started to work. Plaintiff's evidence tended to show that as she received her earnings she turned them over to her said grandmother, who, after providing the plaintiff with food, clothing, and shelter, was to account to plaintiff for any balance left in her hands. This arrangement continued until the plaintiff became of age and for about two years thereafter, at which time the said grandmother died.

In the probate court plaintiff's claim was allowed in the sum of $1,000, whereupon an appeal was taken to the circuit court, where the case was tried de novo to the court and a jury, resulting in a judgment in favor of the plaintiff on her claim in the sum of $700. The administrator in due course appeals.

[1] It is assigned as error that the court permitted the plaintiff, over proper objection, to introduce certain evidence.

It appears that the plaintiff, for a period of over five years (1910 to 1915), worked for the Brown Shoe Company; that plaintiff sought to show by one of her witnesses, Mrs. Gatzer (who had been a bookkeeper at the Brown Shoe Company all the time that plaintiff worked for the said company), the total amount earned by the plaintiff while in the employ of the said company. Mrs. Gatzer testified that she made out the weekly payroll sheets, and that all of the amounts contained therein were then entered in the books of the company. The witness further testified as to the correctness of the entries in said books of the company, which books were in court and offered for the inspection of counsel for defendant by plaintiff's attorney. The witness testified that she was familiar with the books of the Brown Shoe Company, that she had seen them made up, and that they were correct. She then testified that she had made an examination of the books to ascertain the total amount which according to the books had been earned by plaintiff during the five-year period of time when she worked for the Brown Shoe Company. The defendant objected "to this method of introducing the total," which objection was overruled and the witness permitted to testify that the total amount earned by plaintiff while in the employ of said company was $1,687.65. This action of the trial court in overruling defendant's objection is assigned as error.

It is apparent, from a reading of this record, that an introduction of each entry in the books in question, relative to plaintiff's payroll account with the Brown Shoe Company while she was in its employ, covering a period of five years, would have necessitated an examination of over 250 entries.

As was succinctly stated in Masonic Mut. Ben. Soc. v. Lackland, 97 Mo. 137, 10 S. W. 895, 10 Am. St. Rep. 298:

"There is no rule in the law of evidence better settled than that, where the evidence is the result of voluminous facts, or of the inspection of many books and papers, the examination of which cannot conveniently take place in court, or where a witness has inspected the accounts of the parties, though not allowed to give evidence of their particular contents, he will be allowed to speak of the general balance or result of such examination, and such statement is not hearsay. 1 Greenl. Ev. (14th Ed.) § 93, and cases cited. The case of Ritchey v. Kinney, 46 Mo. 298, does not militate against this view.

"Besides, the exhibit or tabulated statement, this being the result of the examination made by the accountant, and from which he testified as memoranda, when offered in evidence, was only objected to in a general way as incompetent, etc. Such an objection was worthless because not specific. Margrave v. Ausmuss, 51 Mo. 561."

In light of the fact that the proving of the amount earned by plaintiff at the Brown Shoe Company would have required an examination of so large a number of book entries, coupled with the fact that the books were in court available to counsel for defense for the purpose of examining them and for use in cross-examining the witness, and the fact that the witness was a bookkeeper for the said Brown Shoe Company, conversant with the books themselves, though the entries therein had not been made by her, yet she knew that the entries therein were correct, we are of the opinion, and so hold, that the learned trial court properly permitted the witness to testify as to the total amount which her inspection of the books themselves had been earned by plaintiff while in the employ of the said Brown Shoe Company.

[2] We note in this connection that the objection which was made on the part of the defendant was but a general one and was not in itself sufficiently specific to have predicated the saving of an exception to the ruling of the court thereon.

[3] II. Appellant contends that instructions numbered 1 and 2, given at the request of the plaintiff, are erroneous in that the court failed in each of said instructions to instruct the jury to allow appellant at least a credit of $700, which respondent in her statement admitted was to be deducted from the amount turned over to the said Kathrine Zacek, but permitted the jury to deduct the amount "expended by said Kathrine Zacek in the purchasing of clothing for plaintiff and a reasonable amount retained by said Kathrine Zacek in payment of plaintiff's board." This point is clearly without substantial merit.

● The evidence showed that nothing was expended other than for clothing and board, and according to the testimony the total amount thus expended was even less than the $700 allowed on the part of the plaintiff in her claim as a credit. The jury found the issues for plaintiff, and the evidence shows that deceased had received $1,687.65, while the verdict was but for $700, showing that the jury allowed credits of $987.65, considerably over the $700 which plaintiff conceded the estate was entitled to. We therefore rule this point against appellant.

From a reading of the entire record we are satisfied that the judgment is for the right party, and, finding no error in the record affecting the merits of the case, the judgment should be and is hereby ordered affirmed.

ALLEN, P. J., concurs.
DAUES, J., not sitting.

SLACK v. WHITNEY. (No. 13788.)

(Kansas City Court of Appeals. Missouri. June 13, 1921.)

1. Justices of the peace ⬅➡93—Answer held to state proper "counterclaim."

In an action instituted before a justice of the peace on an account for threshing and other items, a so-called "answer, set-off, and counterclaim" for damages from delay in doing the threshing and for labor performed was a proper counterclaim, under Rev. St. 1919, § 2887, providing that a "counterclaim" may be a cause of action arising out of the contract or transaction set forth, or any other cause of action arising on contract, as set-off and recoupment are embraced in the term "counterclaim."

[Ed. Note.—For other definitions, see Words and Phrases, First and Second Series, Counterclaim.]

2. Justices of the peace ⬅➡90—Pleadings considered as setting out details.

Though no formal pleadings are required in a justice court, where both parties did plead more or less in detail, the pleadings may be considered as setting out in reasonable detail both sides of the controversy.

Justices of the peace ⬥179—Verdict on appeal held sufficient without itemizing finding on counterclaim.

In a suit instituted in the justice court, where defendant filed an "answer, set-off, and counterclaim" for damages for delay in threshing and for labor, a verdict in the circuit court inding for plaintiff at a specified sum and for lefendant in a specified sum "on his counterlaim" was sufficient, without a special finding on each item of the counterclaim; all being embraced in the verdict under the term "counterlaim."

4. Set-off and counterclaim ⬥29(1)—"Transaction" defined.

As used in Rev. St. 1919, § 1233, providing that a counterclaim may be a cause of action arising out of the contract or transaction set forth in the petition, the "transaction" includes all the facts and circumstances out of which the injury complained of arose.

[Ed. Note.—For other definitions, see Words and Phrases, First and Second Series, Transaction.]

5. Trial ⬥330(1)—Single verdict sufficient when causes of action united in one count.

To secure a separate finding on each cause of action pleaded as a counterclaim, they should be set out in separate counts, and when united in one count and the cause tried on all a single verdict is sufficient.

6. Contracts ⬥322(2)—Evidence held admissible as showing contingency on which performance depended.

In an action for the value of threshing, in which defendant counterclaimed for damages from delay in doing the threshing, where plaintiff's testimony was that the threshing was dependent upon various contingencies, evidence of the workable condition of plaintiff's engine was admissible as evidence of such contingency.

Appeal from Circuit Court, Henry County; C. A. Calvird, Judge.

"Not to be officially published."

Action by James Slack against E. V. Whitney, brought in the justice court and appealed to the circuit court. From a judgment for plaintiff, defendant appeals. Affirmed.

Poague & Son, of Clinton, for appellant.
Ross E. Feaster, of Windsor, for respondent.

ARNOLD, J. This is a suit on account. Plaintiff and defendant were farmers residing in Springfield township, Henry county, Mo., and were neighbors. Plaintiff owned and operated a threshing machine. The suit was instituted in the court of a justice of the peace and resulted in a verdict by that court to the effect that neither side should prevail, and that each should pay one-half the costs, and from the judgment plaintiff appealed to the circuit court of Henry county. The cause was tried to a jury and resulted in a verdict for plaintiff in the sum of $40.28, and for defendant in the sum of

$11 on his counterclaim. Defendant appeals.

The testimony shows that in the fall of 1917 plaintiff and defendant entered into a verbal contract whereby plaintiff was to thresh defendant's oats and cane, the specific terms of which contract are more or less indefinite and in dispute; there was no definite time when the threshing was to be done, but it was fairly well determined that it should be done when plaintiff "rigged up" his engine to fill his (plaintiff's) silo. It appears this was done in February, 1918, but the engine developed leaky flues, and for that reason the threshing could not be done by plaintiff at that time. The testimony further shows that late in the fall or winter of 1917 plaintiff asked defendant if he was ready to have the threshing done, and defendant replied that his cane was not yet ready, but that on various occasions after that defendant asked plaintiff to do the threshing for him.

Plaintiff bases his action on a statement of account, including items of hay, $14; oats, $34; interest on indebtedness, $2.30; half day in securing justice of the peace, 75 cents; half day to file suit before justice of the peace, 75 cents; trip to market for oats, $2; and loss of one day at trial, $1.50; total, $55.30.

The answer was denominated "Answer, set-off, and counterclaim," pleaded as one count, and included the following items:

Damages to oats	$122.64
Damages to cane	116.00
Labor performed	11.00

The answer, set-off, and counterclaim acknowledges indebtedness of defendant to plaintiff for oats $35.28, and for hay purchased of defendant $5, or a total credit of $40.28.

The testimony further shows that the grain of defendant was not threshed until July, 1918, having stood in stack since 1917, and was greatly damaged. Defendant bases his contention upon the grounds that plaintiff breached his contract to thresh the grain. Plaintiff asserts that he was unable to thresh the grain because (1) defendant was not ready when called upon, and (2) that his engine developed leaky flues which he was unable to replace.

Defendant's chief complaint is directed to the verdict of the jury, and he argues that it did not find as to all the issues set out in defendant's "answer and counterclaim."

[1, 2] There is no reason for the contention that defendant had not the right to urge a counterclaim. And it may be further thoroughly understood that no formal pleadings are required in a justice court. But inasmuch as both parties to the instant suit did plead more or less in detail in the justice court, the pleadings may be considered as setting out in reasonable detail both sides of the controversy. The answer of defendant,

called his "Answer, set-off, and counter-claim," as stated above, comes clearly within the provisions of section 1233, Rev. Stat. 1919, and defendant had the right so to plead. Set-off and recoupment are embraced in the term "counterclaim." Gordon v. Bruner, 49 Mo. 570; Emery v. Railroad Co., 77 Mo. 339; Caldwell v. Ryan, 210 Mo. loc,. cit. 23, 108 S. W. 533, 46 L. R. A. (N. S.) 494, 124 Am. St. Rep. 717, 14 Ann. Cas. 314.

[3, 4] The verdict, which was signed by ten of the jurors, is as follows:

"We, the jury, find for plaintiff in the sum of $40.28, and we find for defendant on his counterclaim in the sum of $11, leaving a balance in favor of plaintiff in the sum of $29.28, for which he is entitled to judgment."

The jury were not required to make a special finding on each item of the counterclaim. All of defendant's items included in his answer were embraced in the verdict under the term "counterclaim." The word "transaction," as used in the statute (section 1233, supra), includes all the facts and circumstances out of which the injury complained of arose. Ritchie v. Hayward, 71 Mo. 560; Graham Paper Co. v. Newspaper Ass'n, 193 S. W. 1006.

[5] The law frowns upon a multiplicity of lawsuits and encourages the determination of all differences between parties in one action where it is possible to combine the causes of action existing at the institution of the suit. It is very evident this was done in the case at bar, and the verdict is responsive to all the issues involved. No special finding, therefore, was necessary on the question of damages; the same having been included in the counterclaim in one count. To have secured a separate finding on each cause of action, each should have been set out in a separate count, which was not done in this case. 18 Cyc. 118; Casey v. Transit Co., 205 Mo. 721, 103 S. W. 1146. The rule of law is fundamental and well established that where several causes of action are united in one count, the cause tried on all, and a single verdict returned in favor of plaintiff, where all of the causes pleaded are good and all supported by evidence, the verdict is good.

[6] Finally, defendant complains that the trial court erred in admitting evidence on behalf of plaintiff as to the condition of plaintiff's engine. Doubtless this testimony was admitted on the theory that the contract was indefinite and its terms in dispute. Such evidence clearly was admissible upon plaintiff's testimony that the threshing of defendant's grain was dependent upon various contingencies. The workable condition of the engine may be conceded to be a contingency. At best it was a question for the jury. In our opinion the evidence complained of was properly admitted.

This court is loath to interfere with the verdict of a jury which heard the evidence, saw the witnesses, and were in a position to judge of their credibility and the weight to be given their testimony. We fail to find any reversible error. The verdict was for the right party, and the judgment should be affirmed.

It is so ordered.

All concur.

STATE v. BLOCKER. (No. 16596.)

(St. Louis Court of Appeals. Missouri. May 3, 1921.)

Receiving stolen goods ⚖=9(2)—Instruction held erroneous, as permitting mere negligence to take place of guilty knowledge.

It was error in a prosecution for receiving stolen property to instruct the jury that, "by the term 'knowing' that the property was stolen is not meant absolute personal and certain knowledge on the part of the defendants that the property mentioned in the information had been stolen, but such knowledge and information in their possession at the time they received the same, if you believe they did receive it, as would put a reasonably prudent man, exercising ordinary caution, on his guard," etc., since it plainly permitted mere negligence to take the place of guilty knowledge in determining the criminal liability of the defendants.

Appeal from St. Louis Circuit Court; Charles B. Davis, Judge.

"Not to be officially published."

Earl F. Blocker was convicted of receiving stolen property, and appeals. Reversed and remanded.

Arthur E. Simpson, of St. Louis, for appellant.

Lawrence McDaniel, of St. Louis, for the State.

BIGGS, C. In an information filed by the circuit attorney of the city of St. Louis, defendant and another were jointly charged with burglary in the second degree, larceny, and receiving stolen property. Upon a trial before a jury, the defendant was adjudged guilty of receiving stolen property of less than $30 in value, and his punishment assessed at imprisonment in the city jail for a period of one year. From this conviction defendant appeals, contending that the court committed error in giving to the jury the following instruction:

"Fourth. By the term 'knowing' that the property was stolen is not meant absolute personal and certain knowledge on the part of the defendants that the property mentioned in the information had been stolen, but such knowledge and information in their possession at the time they received the same, if you believe they did receive it, as would put a reasonably pru-

ent man, exercising ordinary caution, on his
uard, and would cause such a man exercising
uch caution and under circumstances which
ou believe defendants received the property,
o believe and be satisfied that the property
iad been stolen.

"The mere naked fact of the possession of
iaid property by the defendants raises no pre-
iumption that the defendants knew that said
iroperty had been stolen by another."

The giving of this identical instruction has
been several times condemned by the Supreme Court and held to be reversible error.
State v. Ebbeller, 222 S. W. 396 (not yet officially reported); State v. Cavanagh, 225 S.
W. 678 (not yet officially reported); State
v. Fleischmann, 228 S. W. 461 (not yet officially reported).

The reasons assigned for holding the instruction erroneous are fully set forth by
the Supreme Court in the Ebbeller Case, and
it will be unnecessary to do more than to
refer to that decision. The instruction plainly permits mere negligence to take the place
of guilty knowledge in determining the criminal liability of the defendant.

It follows that the judgment should be reversed and the cause remanded.

PER CURIAM. The foregoing opinion of
BIGGS, C., is adopted as the opinion of the
court.

The judgment of the circuit court is accordingly reversed, and the cause remanded.

ALLEN and BECKER, JJ., concur.
DAUES, J., not sitting.

——————

BARKWELL v. CARLISLE. (No. 14075.)

(Kansas City Court of Appeals. Missouri.
June 13, 1921.)

Appeal and error ⟝82(3) — No appeal lies
from order vacating final default.

No appeal lies from an order vacating a
final default judgment.

Appeal from Circuit Court, Jackson County; O. A. Lucas, Judge.

"Not to be officially published."

Suit by George W. Barkwell against
Charles D. Carlisle. From order vacating
final default judgment, plaintiff appeals. Appeal dismissed.

Russell E. Holloway, of Columbia, and E.
M. Tipton and John C. Grover, both of Kansas City, for appellant.

H. H. McCluer and Omar E. Robinson,
both of Kansas City, for respondent.

TRIMBLE, P. J. Plaintiff brought suit
in the circuit court of Jackson county, Mo.,
on an account for hay alleged to have been
sold and delivered to defendant. The petition was filed and summons issued on July
21, 1920, and was personally served on the
defendant on July 22, 1920, returnable to
the September term, 1920, beginning on the
second Monday thereof, September 13th.

Defendant failed to appear and answer or
plead, and on the 17th day of said term, to
wit, on October 1, 1920, plaintiff appeared,
the default was noted, and the case was "submitted to the court upon the pleadings, and
the court, after hearing the evidence" for
plaintiff, rendered judgment for him in the
sum of $2,020.92.

Thereafter defendant's notice was called
to the fact that he was in default, and
that a default judgment had been rendered
against him, and within four statutory days
after the rendition of said judgment, and at
the same term, he filed a motion to set aside
the same, supported by affidavit as to the
error and mistake through which his attorney failed to get the notification to file the
necessary pleadings and take care of the
case and as to the defendant having a
meritorious defense.

Plaintiff filed no counter affidavit and
made no attempt to controvert the facts set
up by defendant as showing he was not guilty
of a lack of diligence in answering the
suit. The court, at the November, 1920,
term, sustained said motion; and plaintiff
has appealed.

We need not go into the able and exhaustive briefs filed by counsel in support of their
respective contentions inasmuch as no appeal lies from an order vacating a final
default judgment. Bussiere's Adm'r v. Sayman, 257 Mo. 303, 165 S. W. 796.

This appeal is therefore dismissed.

The other Judges concur.

——————

JACKSON v. QUARRY REALTY CO.   (No.
16677.)

(St. Louis Court of Appeals. Missouri. June
21, 1921. Rehearing Denied June
29, 1921.)

1. Negligence ⟝136(15)—Dumpkeeper's care
in directing driver held for jury.

In an action for damages resulting from the
fall of plaintiff's wagon and team into a quarry
pit where he had gone to dump refuse, evidence
held to warrant submission of the question
whether plaintiff drove along a roadway as directed by defendant's servant.

2. Negligence ⟝32(1)—Landowner owes to
invitee duty to keep premises reasonably safe
and to warn of concealed dangers.

An owner of a quarry pit who permitted
others for consideration to dump refuse therein owes to those who come on the premises
in response to his invitation the duty to keep
the premises in a reasonably safe condition
and to give warning of latent or concealed
perils.

3. Negligence ⚖️136(26)—Contributory negligence in using dump roadway held for jury.

The fact that a roadway along the edge of a quarry pit used by wagons hauling refuse to be dumped into the pit was composed of ashes and rubbish does not as a matter of law so obviously indicate danger as to warrant a directed verdict for defendant in an action to recover damages suffered by plaintiff when the roadway gave way under his team and wagon and precipitated him into the quarry.

4. Trial ⚖️296(9)—Instruction requiring finding plaintiff was on "the" roadway held not erroneous in view of other parts of instruction.

In an action for damages occasioned by plaintiff's wagon falling into a quarry pit into which he was attempting to dump refuse, where the evidence showed plaintiff at the time was driving along a roadway made of ashes and refuse, and not on the hard rock roadway, an instruction requiring a finding that plaintiff was on "the" roadway instead of on "a" roadway is not erroneous, since the word "the," while sometimes sufficient as a definite article to particularize the meaning of the noun after it in such a manner as to be of substantial consequence, could not be given in that instruction the effect of indicating the rock roadway, where other parts of the instruction indicated that the roadway on which plaintiff was driving at the time was intended.

[Ed. Note.—For other definitions, see Words and Phrases, First and Second Series, The.]

Appeal from St. Louis Circuit Court; George H. Shields, Judge.

"Not to be officially published."

Action by George J. Jackson against the Quarry Realty Company. Judgment for plaintiff, and defendant appeals. Affirmed.

Rodgers & Koerner, of St. Louis, for appellant.

Hall & Dame, of St. Louis, for respondent.

DAUES, J. This is an action for damages brought by plaintiff for the loss of a team of horses and wagon and for personal injuries alleged to have been sustained on June 6, 1918, while hauling a load of ashes to the edge of a quarry maintained as a dump by defendant near Ashland avenue in the city of St. Louis. The embankment of the quarry gave way, precipitating the team and wagon 40 feet below into very deep water, where same sank. Plaintiff himself fell to the water's edge of the quarry, where he caught hold of a tuft of weeds and rescued himself.

The petition alleges that defendant operated a dump at this abandoned quarry on charge at 25 cents a load; that plaintiff at the direction of one Ed Jones, employed by defendant as dumpkeeper, was directed to take the wagonload of rubbish upon and along the roadway maintained along the edge of the quarry. It is alleged that defendant negligently failed to prepare and maintain such roadway in a reasonably safe condition, and that it was built and largely consisted of ashes, dirt, and refuse, and that, because of the insecure foundation at the point where plaintiff was invited to dump, the horses and wagon and the plaintiff fell into the pit with the embankment, resulting in personal injuries to plaintiff and the loss of his property.

The answer is a general denial. The judgment was for the plaintiff in the sum of $500. Defendant appeals.

The suit was started against the Heman Construction Company, a corporation. During the course of the trial, by consent of the parties, the Quarry Realty Company, a corporation, was substituted as the defendant, and the case proceeded to judgment against this corporation.

The evidence tended to show that there was a roadway at the south side of the quarry. Plaintiff himself and four witnesses for him described the roadway to be covered with ashes and rubbish, but there is a sharp conflict on this point. August Heman, president of the defendant company, and two other witnesses testified that this roadway from which plaintiff is alleged to have fallen was a hard rock road and was not covered with refuse and ashes. Plaintiff maintained that he drove the way and to the point indicated by the dumpkeeper, Jones, while Jones testified that he directed plaintiff to drive east, and not west, and that, though forbidden to do so, plaintiff drove upon the hard rock road and there unskillfully attempted to turn his wagon and was thereby precipitated into the quarry.

Witness Holloway, who was at the dumping ground at the time and witnessed the accident, testified that he, too, was at that time directed by the dumpkeeper to go over the same route plaintiff took, and that he, too, drove west on the south side of the quarry, and that he heard Jones direct plaintiff where to drive, and that plaintiff drove in that direction.

It appears that it had rained a few days before the accident, and that plaintiff had not been at the dump for several days prior to the disaster, and plaintiff testified that he did not know of the unsafe condition of the road until he felt the ashes and rubbish on the roadway give way under his wagon. It is not questioned that the team and wagon fell into the deep water and became totally lost, and that plaintiff himself fell 40 feet or more over this almost perpendicular precipice, and only miraculously saved his life.

[1] Appellant makes the charge that there was no evidence adduced to show negligence of the defendant, and that therefore the peremptory instruction that plaintiff was not entitled to recover should have been given. In this connection it is said that the tes-

timony of defendant's witnesses showed that
there was a rock road along the south side
of the quarry over which plaintiff was directed to drive, and that he was on such rock
road and made an improper turn which
caused the accident. And defendant, says,
therefore, that, if plaintiff was on the soft
dump road, as claimed by him, then he was
not on a roadway in the sense treated by the
pleadings and instructions, and, further, that
the danger of this soft road sliding into the
quarry was as obvious to the plaintiff as it
was to the defendant.

As to whether the evidence shows that
plaintiff was on the rock road, we might
briefly refer to plaintiff's testimony. Plaintiff, on direct examination, testified:

"Q. Then, when you get to the dump, which
way do you go? A. Well, I turned west; at
least I did this time; you turn east or west,
and I turned this time west because Jones said,
'Drive in west and drive in close,' which I did.
"Q. Now, this roadway which you mention,
on which side of the dump was it? A. South
side.
"Q. Which way did the roadway extend? A.
East and west along the dump.
"Q. On the south side of the dump? A. Yes,
sir."

On cross-examination plaintiff testified:

"Q. Was there anything in the roadway to
indicate to you the proper place to drive or
where people had been driving along there?
A. Well, there were tracks there where they
had been driving along. I did not go clear out
where they was. This seemed like this was
safe, a safe place to drive. Until I felt that
jerk it seemed safe.
"Q. You did not go to the regular place, did
you? A. That is where I had been going all
the time, right along where the people had
been driving; I notice that plainly; the trench
I drove right in that trench.
"Q. Now, isn't it a fact, George, that you
were dumping at the wrong place? A. No;
right at the regular place where everybody
dumped; right where you are supposed to
dump.
"Q. Did you see any rock road at all on these
quarry premises? A. I was not searching for
the premises; I was dumping where the rest
dumped.
"Q. Did you see any rock road at all from
your wagon where you were driving just before you got hurt on this trip? A. No, sir;
it was ashes and rubbish and cans.
"Q. You mean to say the rock road was covered up to a depth of four feet? A. Yes, sir;
with ashes and rubbish, and so forth."

Again:

"Q. Did he [Jones] stop working at the wagon and tell you where to drive? A. He just
told me, he says, 'Just drive up here; you drive
up here.'
"Q. Where? A. West; right ahead of Holloway.
"Q. He said, 'Drive right in here; you are using your right'? A. He said, 'Drive right in
here (indicating), right in along over there.'

"Q. Did he use the word 'west'? A. He did
not say 'west,' but that is what it meant.
"Q. Now, most of the dumping was done east
of where Holloway was located? A. No, sir.
"Q. As soon as Jones saw you, he said drive
right down here to the west, did he, Mr. Jackson? A. He said, Jackson, drive right on
down there; that is west.'
"Q. Now, what did he say? A. He told me,
come right in, drive right ahead of this man
here."

Witness Holloway, seemingly disinterested,
testified that he was present, heard Jones
direct plaintiff to drive in, and that plaintiff
drove in as directed, and that he was directed to follow and did follow plaintiff on same
road where accident occurred.

Benjamin Jones testified that he was accustomed to use this quarry for dumping
purposes, and that he was at this point June
4th, two days prior to this accident, and that
he was also directed by the dumpkeeper to
drive west along the south side of the quarry,
and that he then observed that the road at
that point was not solid, that it had rained,
and that the road was covered with "rubbish
and stuff." There was other testimony to
like effect.

We have set out sufficient of the testimony
to show that there is substantial evidence
in the case tending to prove that the plaintiff drove over a road or path along the edge
of the quarry as directed by the defendant's
agent.

[2] It is the uncontroverted law of this
state that, where the owner of land invites
customers upon his property for the purpose
of trade, he owes such customers or patrons
the duty of ordinary care to keep the premises so used in a reasonably safe condition,
and, if the premises are not in a reasonably
safe condition, then it becomes the duty of
the proprietor to warn such invitee of such
dangers which are known to the occupant and
unknown to the invitee. O'Donnell v. Patton,
117 Mo. 13, 22 S. W. 903; Woods v. Railroad
Co., 192 Mo. App. 165, 179 S. W. 727; Brock
v. St. Louis Transit Co., 107 Mo. App. loc.
cit. 116, 81 S. W. 219; Shaw v. Goldman,
116 Mo. App. 332, 92 S. W. 165.

In Ruling Case Law, vol. 20, p. 51, the rule
is stated thus:

"The authorities are entirely agreed upon the
proposition that an owner or occupant of lands
or buildings who directly or by implication invites or induces others to go thereon or therein owes to such persons a duty to have his
premises in a reasonably safe condition and to
give warning of latent or concealed perils"—
citing Bennett v. Louisville & N. R. Co., 102
U. S. 577, 26 L. Ed. 235, and many other
cases.

[3] But appellant says the defendant is not
liable to an invitee for injuries which were
caused by a known or obvious danger. This
explains the persistence of defendant at the

trial in pressing the inquiry of plaintiff as to whether this was or was not a rock road upon which he was driving at the time the accident occurred. Plaintiff steadfastly maintained, as above set out, that it was a soft, refuse-made road upon which he was driving and which slid into the quarry.

The evidence showed that the defendant operated, maintained, and controlled this dumping place, and built and extended the road and dump from day to day and knew its character and condition. The employés of defendant were in constant charge of the place in carrying on this dumping business. The evidence shows that plaintiff's only purpose there was to dump refuse. He had not been on the ground for several days prior to the disaster, during which time it had rained and ashes and refuse had become washed over the road, or track, used for such hauling. There is evidence that he was directed by defendant's employé to haul to that exact point. There was, in our judgment, substantial evidence before the jury from which a reasonable inference could be drawn that defendant knew, or in the exercise of ordinary care should have known, of the soft and insecure condition of the bank and of the danger of same sliding into the quarry.

While the evidence shows that plaintiff had been on the dump before and had hauled some of the refuse thrown there, he was there upon the invitation of the occupant, and then only to drive as indicated by the dumpkeeper and unload; he was not charged with a greater concern in the condition of the road, or path, on the dump than to exercise ordinary care for his safety, and there is no showing that he knew of the dangerous condition of the road, and we cannot say as a matter of law that same was so obviously dangerous as to warn plaintiff of the danger.

Appellant relies upon the authority of the O'Donnell Case, supra, that plaintiff was himself negligent and should not recover. The O'Donnell Case does not, in our judgment, bear the analogy claimed for it. In that case, plaintiff went to a sawmill to haul shavings which were piled about 40 feet high. In securing his load plaintiff undermined the pile in such a way that same became topheavy and fell upon him. This does not meet the present state of facts before us. In our case the defendant not only invited plaintiff to come as a customer, but had upon the ground a representative who expressly directed plaintiff where and how to go to dump

the ashes, and in following such orders he was hurt and lost his property. Like observation is made of the other cases cited.

[4] Appellant argues that plaintiff's testimony showed that he was not at the time of the accident on a "roadway," that is, not on the rock road, and that therefore the instruction given on behalf of plaintiff which requires a finding that plaintiff was on "the roadway" instead of "a roadway" is error because it expressly tells the jury that there was a roadway and leaving it to the jury to find only that this roadway extended to the edge of the pit.

It is true that a finespun distinction may be drawn between "a roadway" and "the roadway," as used in the instruction, but the word "the," while sometimes sufficient as a definite article to particularize the meaning of the noun after it in such a manner as to be of substantial consequence, cannot be held here to vitiate this instruction. This instruction does not assume that defendant owned and maintained such road, which is clearly shown by the following portion of said instruction, which required the jury to find "that said roadway extended and ran by the side and edge of the quarry pit, and that said pit was deep and was partly filled with water, and further find that defendant failed to prepare and maintain said roadway in a reasonably safe condition," etc.

It must be borne in mind that it is not contended here that this road was a public street or highway, but a roadway, or track, or path, maintained by the defendant for teams to haul over to dump into this quarry, and the law imposes the duty of the defendant to use ordinary care to see that this road, or track, by whatever name, was not dangerous to those using same for such dumping purposes.

The instruction, we think, is sufficient. It required the jury to find, together with the other necessary elements, that defendant was guilty of the negligence described in the petition, and also that at the time of plaintiff's injury he was exercising ordinary care for his own sake and for the safety of his team.

We think the case was fairly tried and the verdict well supported by the evidence. The verdict of $500 was not excessive for this property loss and personal injury.

We find no prejudicial error in the case. Accordingly the judgment is affirmed.

ALLEN, P. J., and BECKER, J., concur.

FRANKLIN BANK v. MEINECKE.
(No. 16634.)

(St. Louis Court of Appeals. Missouri.
May 3, 1921.)

Pledges ⊂⊐56(7)—Pledgee purchasing collateral at sale held entitled to benefit of lien on mortgage in real estate.

Where collateral pledged to secure a note consisted of a note and deed of trust securing it upon real estate, and by the contract of pledge pledgee was authorized to bid at a sale of the pledged collateral, pledgee, upon a sale thereof, at which he became the purchaser, was entitled to the benefit of the lien of the mortgage on the real estate for the collection of the original debt.

Appeal from St. Louis Circuit Court; Victor H. Falkenhainer, Judge.

"Not to be officially published."

Action by the Franklin Bank against Louis Meinecke. Judgment for plaintiff, and defendant appeals. Affirmed.

John A. Blevins, of St. Louis, for appellant.
Jourdan, Rassieur & Pierce, of St. Louis, for respondent.

ALLEN, P. J. This is an action upon a note for the sum of $21,000, executed by the defendant on May 10, 1916, payable to the order of plaintiff, on demand, or, if no earlier demand be made, then on November 10, 1916, bearing interest at the rate of 6 per cent. per annum until maturity, and 8 per cent. per annum thereafter.

The petition pleads the execution and delivery of the note, and alleges that on March 14, 1917, the note being then due and unpaid, plaintiff caused to be sold certain collateral described in the note, and through the sale thereof defendant became entitled to a credit of $9,972.66, leaving a balance due on the note of $11,746, for which sum, together with interest at the rate of 8 per cent. per annum from and after March 14, 1917, judgment is prayed.

The answer admits the execution of the note, and avers that the collateral mentioned in the petition and pledged by plaintiff to secure the payment of the note consisted of a principal note for the sum of $21,000, payable three years after date, and six semi-annual interest notes, each for the sum of $630, together with a deed of trust, securing said notes, upon certain real estate described in the answer, consisting of a lot of ground having a frontage of 90 feet 2¾ inches on the north line of Chestnut street, beginning at a point 85 feet west of the west line of Eighteenth street in the city of St. Louis; said notes and deed of trust having been executed by defendant and his wife on November 10, 1915. And it is alleged that the real estate covered by said deed of trust is of

the reasonable value of $50,000, and that said notes and deed of trust are of the full value of the face thereof, with interest, aggregating $22,000.

The answer then alleges that plaintiff bought in the last-mentioned notes and deed of trust at the sale mentioned in the petition, at less than one-half of the value thereof, and holds the same, claiming to be the owner thereof, and claiming that defendant is liable to plaintiff thereon in the sum of $22,000, in addition to the amount claimed in the petition; that the sale of said "collateral notes" and deed of trust, and the purchase thereof by plaintiff at such sale for the sum mentioned in the petition, is "inadequate, inequitable, and unconscionable, and a fraud upon the rights of the defendant, and should be disregarded and set aside by the court, and the plaintiff held as trustee and required to account to defendant for the full value of said notes and deed of trust."

The answer concludes with a prayer that the plaintiff be required to account to the defendant for the full value of said collateral notes, and that the defendant have judgment against the plaintiff in the sum of $900, the alleged value of such notes and deed of trust in excess of the amount due on the note in suit, and for general equitable relief.

The reply denies generally the allegations of the answer. By its reply plaintiff then proceeds to make two offers. First, plaintiff tendered a deed to defendant to the said real estate, upon condition that defendant pay the amount due plaintiff as principal and interest on the note sued upon, aggregating, it is said, $24,729.72, exclusive of protest fees, the costs and expenses of the sale of the collateral, and the costs or expenses of the foreclosure sale under the deed of trust, and also exclusive of the sum of $1,695.82 alleged by plaintiff to have been expended by it in the payment of taxes upon said real estate; plaintiff waiving its right to reimbursement for such expenditures. And it is alleged that plaintiff, as evidence of its good faith in the premises, filed therewith in court its quitclaim deed to said property, to be delivered to defendant on the payment by him of the sum mentioned.

As an alternative offer, plaintiff, by its reply, offered to deed the real estate to defendant, free and clear of all liens and claims, and free of any costs and charges arising out of the sales mentioned, upon the payment to plaintiff by defendant of the sum of $20,000, such sum to be credited on the note in suit, and plaintiff to take judgment for the balance remaining due thereon.

At the trial plaintiff introduced the note in evidence. The indorsements thereon show that the interest had been paid to September 30, 1916; that by a sale of the collateral defendant had been credited, on March 14, 1917, with the sum of $10,000, less a charge of $27.-

34 for advertising, making a net credit of $9,972.66. The contract of pledge contained in the note was read in evidence. It recited a pledge of the collateral mentioned above, and authorized a sale thereof by plaintiff, upon defendant's failure to pay the note in suit, at either public or private sale, with or without advertisements, and with or without notice to defendant, and authorized plaintiff to purchase such collateral at any such sale. Plaintiff thereupon rested.

The defendant introduced in evidence the pledged collateral, namely, the principal note for $21,000, the interest notes, and the deed of trust mentioned in the answer. It was admitted that at the sale of the collateral plaintiff became the purchaser thereof, at the price of $10,000; that thereafter, by foreclosure sale under the deed of trust, plaintiff became the purchaser of said real estate for the sum of $16,000. No testimony was offered by defendant tending to show any illegality or irregularity in respect to the sale of the collateral, which was shown to have been made at the courthouse door after publication of notice thereof. And at the trial, defendant, through his counsel, expressly admitted that there was no question as to the validity of the sale under the deed of trust.

Three witnesses other than defendant were called to testify as to the value of the real estate mentioned, all being real estate dealers. One of these, Frank Obear, testified that, in his opinion, the real estate was worth about $300 per front foot on March 14, 1917. Another witness, one Schollmeyer, testified that he had "always figured" that this property was worth from $300 to $350 per front foot. Another witness, one Loewenstein, testified that the property was worth from $400 to $500 per front foot when the defendant acquired it; and that at the time of the trial it was worth from $300 to $350 per foot.

Defendant testified that, in his opinion, the real estate was worth, on March 14, 1917, $400 per front foot, or a total of $36,000. In rebuttal, five real estate dealers were called as witnesses by plaintiff. The values placed by these witnesses upon the real estate as of March 14, 1917, ranged from $200, or less, to $250 per front foot. It was shown that the property was assessed for taxation at $16,000. Plaintiff, in open court, tendered to defendant a deed to the real estate upon the conditions named in the first offer in plaintiff's reply. And plaintiff also offered to convey the property to defendant in accordance with the terms of the second offer in its reply.

The trial court rendered judgment in favor of plaintiff in the sum of $6,237.06, with interest from March 14, 1917, at 8 per cent. per annum, totaling $7,179.54; defendant's prayer for cross-relief being denied.

The judgment on its face does not show the manner in which the court arrived at the amount thereof; but it is obvious that the court disregarded entirely the sale of the collateral, and intended to give defendant credit for the amount at which the real estate was bought in by plaintiff at the foreclosure sale, to wit, $16,000, less costs and expenses and the amount paid by plaintiff for taxes due on the real estate to the date of such sale. It appears, in fact, that the court—evidently through an error of computation—allowed the defendant more than was due him as a credit upon this theory; but this is not a matter involved on this appeal.

As to the first point made in appellant's brief, namely, that the court should have disregarded the purchase by plaintiff of the collateral notes and deed of trust for $10,000, because the price was inadequate, inequitable, and unconscionable, we need only say that the court did, in fact, disregard that transaction altogether.

It is argued for defendant (appellant here) that plaintiff, by the purchase of the collateral, became a trustee for defendant, and should therefore be required to respond to defendant for the full value of the collateral pledged. But this argument is obviously unsound, in the circumstances of the case. By the contract of pledge plaintiff was authorized to bid at the sale of the pledged collateral. And when, upon due notice, a sale thereof was duly made, and plaintiff became the purchaser at such sale, the effect thereof was to give plaintiff the benefit of the lien of the mortgage on the real estate for the collection of the original debt. Dibert v. D'Arcy, 248 Mo. 617, 154 S. W. 1116. The case differs much, however, from that of Dibert v. D'Arcy, supra. In that case the contract of pledge gave no authority to the pledgee to purchase at the foreclosure sale, and, in fact, the bank's attorney, by the direction of the president of the bank, took possession of the collateral and caused it to be sold on a stock exchange, the object of the proceeding being, as said by the Supreme Court, not to sell the collateral, but to get possession of it.

In the instant case no duty owing by plaintiff to defendant appears to have been violated. Plaintiff was entitled to bid in the real estate at the foreclosure sale, as it did; and defendant has received credit for the net sale price thereof, and more. And upon no theory do we perceive how any equitable relief may be awarded defendant on its answer upon the theory that plaintiff has speculated in the collateral and profited thereby. Plaintiff acquired the real estate at the price of $16,000. While there is opinion evidence tending to show that the property was then of great value, the evidence makes it clear that no value could be placed thereupon that was not in a very considerable degree speculative and uncertain. And it is by no means certain that plaintiff will ever be able to profit by its acquisition of such real estate.

Indeed, the theory upon which the answer

proceeds is that the plaintiff bought the collateral, at the sale thereof, at a price, to wit, $10,000, that was so far inadequate as to be inequitable and unconscionable, and a fraud upon the rights of the defendant. But, as we have seen, the price paid by defendant for such collateral is no longer a matter of consequence in the case.

Obviously defendant has been offered every opportunity to protect himself against the sacrifice of his property, in any degree consistent with the rights of plaintiff in the premises. And we think that the defendant has no just ground to complain of the result below.

It follows that the judgment should be affirmed, and it is so ordered.

BECKER, J., concurs.
DAUES, J., not sitting.

JONES v. MUNROE. (No. 16256.)

(St. Louis Court of Appeals. Missouri.
June 7, 1921.)

1. **Executors and administrators** ⚹⚹⚹221(5)—**Evidence held insufficient to sustain verdict for services for collecting rents for deceased.**

Evidence that the customary compensation for services was 10 per cent. of the amount collected and that the rent of the house belonging to deceased was $10 per month, but without evidence as to the amount of the rent collected by claimant, is insufficient to sustain a verdict authorizing recovery by him for services in collecting the rents.

2. **Appeal and error** ⚹⚹⚹1033(4)—**Limitation of actions** ⚹⚹⚹182(2)—**Defense of limitations must be raised by pleading; error favorable to appellant not reviewable.**

The bar of the statute of limitations is an affirmative defense which must be raised by answer, or, if it appears on the face of the complaint, by motion to dismiss or demurrer, so that an instruction submitting to jury the question whether the plaintiff's account was a running account which could not be affected by the statute, was favorable to the defendant who had not raised the defense of the statute by any pleading.

3. **Appeal and error** ⚹⚹⚹795(2)—**Motion to dismiss must point out deficiency of abstract relied upon.**

A motion to dismiss the appeal on the ground that the abstract is insufficient will be overruled, where the motion does not state wherein the abstract was insufficient and is not accompanied by an additional abstract showing that fact, in view of Court of Appeals rule 12 (169 S. W. xvi).

Appeal from Circuit Court, Jefferson County; E. M. Deering, Judge.

"Not to be officially published."

Claim by W. T. Jones against Robert B. Munroe, executor of the estate of Veronica Schmidt, deceased. From a judgment for plaintiff in the circuit court, defendant appeals. Judgment reversed, with directions to enter for less amount if plaintiff remit a portion thereof, otherwise reversed and remanded for new trial.

E. C. Edgar, of De Soto, for appellant.
Clyde Williams, of Hillsboro, and H. B. Irwin, of De Soto, for respondent.

BIGGS, C. Originating in the probate court, where plaintiff had judgment, this cause came by appeal to the circuit court. Upon a trial there before a jury, plaintiff had a verdict for $534.17. Judgment being rendered for this sum, defendant estate has brought the cause here for review.

The following account forms the basis of the action:

Demand Sued Upon

The Estate of Veronica Schmidt, Deceased, to Walter T. Jones, Dr.

1916.	Dolls.
Oct. 15, 1914, to cash	$ 10 00
Jan. 28, 1915, to cash	60 00
Dec. 18, 1915, to cash	10 00
Jan. 20, 1916, to cash	15 00
To services as agent for her property, collecting rents, repairing property, carpenter work and material for sidewalks and houses, etc., from 1895 to Feb. 10, 1916, and personal services	500 00
Nov. 24, 1907, paid C. F. Stroupe for deceased	65 00
	$660 00

There was evidence tending to prove that plaintiff performed services for the deceased, Veronica Schmidt, in collecting rents from her property and in looking after repairs; also, that plaintiff paid repair and supply bills for the deceased and also certain sums to her in cash to be applied on notes of plaintiff held by Mrs. Schmidt, but which were not credited on the notes. Such services extended over a period of about 18 years. The evidence was sufficient to justify the jury in finding for plaintiff as to the first four items of the account and also as to the last item in the amount claimed, namely, $160, being the aggregate of the five items.

[1] As to the main item of $500, there was evidence sufficient to warrant a finding that plaintiff paid out for the deceased labor and material bills for the repair of her property to the extent of $72.42. As to the remainder of the item, being a claim for services in collecting rents, the customary charge was shown to be 10 per cent. of the amount collected; but the evidence wholly fails to show the amount of rents collected. While claimant's daughter when testifying in rebuttal stated that the rent of the Veronica Schmidt house was $10 per month, it is nowhere shown what amount was collected by plain-

tiff or from what property, and such matter is left entirely to conjecture and speculation. The evidence is insufficient to warrant a finding on account of that part of the item.

Giving to the evidence the benefit of every reasonable inference that may be drawn therefrom in favor of plaintiff, it may be said that the proof was sufficient to sustain the first four items of the account aggregating $95, the last item of $65, and the remaining item to the extent of $72.42; the latter being material bills paid out by plaintiff for the account of the deceased.

It results that plaintiff's evidence would justify a judgment for $232.42, and that the judgment appealed from for the sum of $534.-17 is excessive in the sum of $301.75.

[2] Defendant asserts that the five-year statute of limitations bars all items of the account which matured more than five years prior to the death of Mrs. Schmidt. The statute was not pleaded, and it is elemental that the defense is an affirmative one and must be raised either by answer or by demurrer or motion to dismiss where it appears upon the face of the pleading that the claim is barred. Notwithstanding a failure on the part of defendant to properly raise the defense, the court by an instruction to the jury submitted the question of fact as to whether the account sued on was a running account and told the jury that all items which accrued five years or more prior to the death of Mrs. Schmidt, and which were based upon a separate contract and were not done under the same and continuing contract, were barred by the statute of limitations, and for all of such items plaintiff could not recover. Defendant was treated with more liberality than it deserved in view of its failure to plead the statute of limitations.

The evidence was sufficient to warrant the jury in finding that the claim was a running and open account within the meaning of the law. Ring v. Jamison, 66 Mo. 424–428; Chadwick v. Chadwick, 115 Mo. 518–586, 22 S. W. 481; Sidway v. Land & Stock Co., 187 Mo. 649, 86 S. W. 150; Roberts v. Neale, 134 Mo. App. 612–616, 114 S. W. 1120.

[3] Plaintiff has filed a motion to dismiss the appeal on the ground that defendant's abstract is insufficient, but does not state wherein the same is insufficient, nor does he file an additional abstract showing wherein the defendant's abstract is incomplete. See Rule 12 of this court (169 S. W. xvi). The motion will be overruled.

The judgment is without sufficient basis of support to the extent of the sum of $801.-75. Provided the plaintiff will within 10 days remit the said sum of $301.75, the judgment should be reversed, and the cause remanded, with directions to enter judgment for plaintiff for the sum of $232.42; other-

wise the judgment should be reversed, and the cause remanded for a new trial.

PER CURIAM. The foregoing opinion of BIGGS, C., is adopted as the opinion of the court.

The judgment of the circuit court is accordingly reversed, and the cause remanded as recommended by the commissioner.

ALLEN, P. J., and BECKER, J., concur. DAUES, J., not sitting.

STATE v. ANDERSON et al.   (No. 16621.

(St. Louis Court of Appeals. Missouri. June 7, 1921.)

1. Criminal law ⇔1130(4)—Assignments of error considered in absence of brief.

Where there were assignments of error made in motions for new trial and in arrest of judgment, it is the duty of the appellate court to examine the record, having such assignments in view, although no briefs have been filed.

2. Trespass ⇔87—Information held to sufficiently charge tampering with another's motor vehicle.

An information that the defendants "did willfully and unlawfully take, use, operate, drive and tamper with a certain motor vehicle, to wit, an automobile, the property of V., without the permission of said V., the owner of said automobile, so to do, contrary to the form of the statute," etc., was sufficient in form to charge an offense under Motor Vehicles Act, § 9, subd. 6.

3. Trespass ⇔88—Evidence held to sustain conviction of tampering with automobile.

In a prosecution under Motor Vehicles Act, § 9, subd. 6 for taking, driving, and tampering with an automobile, evidence held to warrant a conviction.

Appeal from St. Louis Court of Criminal Correction.

"Not to be officially published."

John Anderson and another were convicted of a violation of the Motor Vehicles Act, and appeal. Affirmed.

John Neu, Jr., of St. Louis, for appellants. Howard Sidener, of St. Louis, for the State.

ALLEN, P. J. [1] The defendants were convicted of violating section 9, subd. 6, of the "Motor Vehicles" Act of 1917 (Laws 1917, p. 411) and their punishment assessed at confinement in the workhouse of the city of St. Louis for a period of two years, and they appeal. No briefs have been filed in this court.

but we have carefully examined the record, is is our duty to do, having in view the assignments of error made in the motions for new trial and in arrest of judgment.

[2] The information charges that the defendants, in the city of St. Louis, on July 21, 1918, "did willfully and unlawfully take, use, operate, drive and tamper with a certain motor vehicle, to wit, an automobile, the property of Valentine Trovato, without the permission of said Valentine Trovato, the owner of said automobile, so to do, contrary to the form of the statute," etc. This information is obviously sufficient in form to charge an offense under the statute, supra.

[3] The evidence amply warrants the conviction. The evidence for the state tends to show that the automobile in question was left by the owner in front of his place of residence, in the city of St. Louis, from which place it was taken by some person or persons about noon on July 21, 1918; that later that day the defendants and a third man were seen riding in the automobile in another part of the city, when a wheel came off of the automobile; that upon the approach of a police officer the three men abandoned the automobile, and one of them succeeded in escaping. The defendants were arrested, but denied at the time that they had been in the automobile, as they did at the trial below.

We perceive no reversible error in the record, and it follows that the judgment should be affirmed. It is so ordered.

BECKER and DAUES, JJ., concur.

CONSOLIDATED GARAGE CO. v. CHAMBERS. (No. 3340.)

(Supreme Court of Texas. June 22, 1921.)

I. Chattel mortgages ⊂⇒217—Foreign chattel mortgage valid against good-faith purchaser in state to which property removed in absence of statute or settled law or policy of forum.

A chattel mortgage duly executed and recorded under the laws of the state where it is executed and the property located is valid as against purchasers in good faith in another state to which the property is removed by the mortgagor unless that state has enacted some statute to the contrary or unless the transaction contravenes the settled law or policy of the forum.

2. Sales ⊂⇒451—Foreign unrecorded conditional sale contract held not effective to retain title to automobile in seller as against innocent purchaser.

Where plaintiff in California sold an automobile to defendant under an unrecorded conditional sales contract whereby plaintiff retained title, and defendant took the car to Texas, and there sold it to a good-faith purchaser for value, held, that such purchaser acquired title as against plaintiff in view of Vernon's Sayles' Ann. Civ. St. 1914, arts. 5654 and 5655, making unrecorded mortgages void as against innocent purchasers.

Error to Court of Civil Appeals of Eighth Supreme Judicial District.

Sequestration proceedings by the Consolidated Garage Company against F. H. Nichols, in which Ray Chambers filed a claimant's oath and bond. Judgment for plaintiff was reversed on claimant's appeal (210 S. W. 565), and plaintiff brings error. Affirmed.

Louis Oneal, of San Jose, Cal., and Beall, Kemp & Nagle and H. Potash, all of El Paso, for plaintiff in error.

Hudspeth & Harper, of El Paso, and Judkins & Perkins, for defendant in error.

PIERSON, J. For the material facts of the case we quote the following statement from the opinion of the Court of Civil Appeals:

"The Consolidated Garage Company is incorporated under the laws of California with its principal place of business in San Jose, Santa Clara county, Cal. Appellant, Chambers, is a resident of El Paso county, Tex. On July 6, 1917, appellee owned and was in possession of a certain automobile of the value of $1,700. On the date mentioned appellee and F. H. Nichols at San Jose, Cal., entered into a written contract by the terms whereof Nichols agreed to purchase the car from the company for the sum of $1,670.00, $600 being paid in cash, and the

balance to be paid in monthly installments of $90 each; the deferred payments to bear interest from date. Nichols agreed not to sell or dispose of the automobile, nor take the same out of the state of California, nor permit the same to be removed from his possession, attached, levied upon, nor create any liens against same. Nichols was to pay all taxes against the property. The contract provided that title should remain in the company until all payments were made and all of the conditions contained in the contract fully complied with, and that upon the performance of all of said conditions and terms by Nichols the company would execute to him a bill of sale to the property. The contract was to be performed wholly within the state of California. The automobile was removed from Santa Clara county, Cal., by Nichols without the knowledge or consent of the company and without any negligence on the latter's part. The company used due diligence to collect the amount due upon the contract and exercised due diligence in trying to locate the car after it had been taken from San Jose and the state of California. The car was finally located in El Paso, Tex., where it had been brought by Nichols, and immediately upon ascertaining its location the company brought suit in the district court of El Paso county against Nichols and sequestered the car. The contract was not filed for record in California, nor in any county in Texas. The car was purchased in El Paso county by Chambers from Nichols for a valuable consideration and without notice of any defect in Nichols' title.

"When the car was sequestered in the suit against Nichols, Chambers filed a claimant's oath and bond and possession was surrendered to him. Under the laws of California the contract between the company and Nichols was a conditional sale, and title to the automobile did not pass from the company to Nichols, and under the laws of California it was not necessary to file or register the contract, and under the laws of that state any subsequent purchaser from Nichols paying a valuable consideration without notice would not get any better title than Nichols had. The contract under the laws of that state being not a bond, but a conditional sale, the title remained in the company. The amount due by Nichols under the contract is $1,060, with interest.

"The trial court's conclusion of law was that Chambers in his purchase of the automobile from Nichols acquired no greater title than Nichols had; that the contract between the company and Nichols was a conditional sale, and, Nichols having defaulted, the company became entitled to the possession of the automobile. Judgment was rendered against Chambers and the sureties upon his bond for the value of the automobile, with interest."

The Court of Civil Appeals reversed and rendered the case in favor of Ray Chambers, defendant in error.

Article 5654, Vernon's Sayles' Texas Civil Statutes 1914, provides:

"All reservation of the title to or property in chattels, as security for the purchase money thereof, shall be held to be chattel mortgages, and shall, when possession is delivered to the vendee, be void as to creditors and bona fide purchasers, unless such reservations be in writing and registered as required of chattel mortgages."

Article 5655 provides:

"Every chattel mortgage * * * which shall not be accompanied by an immediate delivery and be followed by an actual and continued change of possession of the property mortgaged * * * shall be absolutely void as against the creditors of the mortgagor or person making same, and as against subsequent purchasers * * * in good faith, unless such instrument, or a true copy thereof, shall be forthwith deposited with and filed in the office of the county clerk of the county where the property shall then be situated, or if the mortgagor or person making the same be a resident of this state, then, of the county of which he shall at that time be a resident."

It is clear that under our statutes the contract of sale as set out above, if between parties residents of this state, and concerning property within this state, would be a mortgage and subject to our registration laws. It is equally clear that under the same state of facts an innocent purchaser for value would take good title.

Defendant in error insists, inasmuch as the contract of sale set out herein, under the laws of California, is a conditional sale and the title remained in plaintiff in error, that Nichols acquired no title under the contract, and therefore conveyed none to defendant in error, and that therefore this state under the rule of comity between states should give full force and effect to the reservation of title in plaintiff in error and award him a recovery under same according to the laws of California.

Huddy on Automobiles (5th Ed.) § 885, says:

"In some states conditional contracts of sale are not sustained as against third persons innocently purchasing the property from the vendee. The validity of a sale to a third person is generally determined by the law of the place of the sale; and hence, where such sale is in a state which refuses to recognize the validity of conditional sales, the title of the third person will be good, though the original conditional contract was made in a state where it was valid."

[1] It seems to be the general rule that a chattel mortgage duly executed and recorded according to the laws of the state where same is executed and the property is located will be held valid and effective as against purchasers in good faith in another state to which the property is removed by the mortgagor, unless that state has enacted some statute to the contrary or unless the trans-

231 S.W.—68

action contravenes the settled law or policy of the forum. Corpus Juris, vol. 11, p. 424.

Chief Justice Marshall, in Harrison v. Sterry, 5 Cranch, 289, 3 L. Ed. 104, distinguishes between the *validity* of a contract creating a lien and the *priority* of the lien over the rights of the third person as follows:

"The law of the place where a contract is made is, generally speaking, the law of the contract; i. e., it is the law by which the contract is expounded. But the right of priority forms no part of the contract. * * * It is extrinsic, and is rather a personal privilege dependent on the law of the place where the property lies, and where the court sits which is to decide the cause."

The Supreme Court of Tennessee, in the case of Snyder v. Yates, 112 Tenn. 309, 79 S. W. 796, 64 L. R. A. 353, 105 Am. St. Rep. 941, said:

"When parties to a foreign contract are impleaded in the courts of this state, this court will expound and enforce the contract according to the laws of the country where it was made, if such laws are properly pleaded and proven; but it will not, in a question of priority, set aside its own statutes and rules to the prejudice of its own citizens."

We think it is well settled that a contract is to be interpreted according to the lex loci contractus, but that the status of the personal property is to be governed by the lex loci rei.

This court in the case of Crosby v. Huston, 1 Tex. 208, in an opinion by Chief Justice Hemphill, in which the question here was an issue, used the following language:

"The rule that the nature, validity, or invalidity, the obligation, and interpretation of this deed of trust should properly be determined by the laws of Mississippi, is not to be extended to the defeat of our own laws, or any rights growing out of them after the property was found within their jurisdiction."

It further said:

"But, whatever may have been the effect of registration in Mississippi, it cannot be extended beyond the territorial limits of the state. The operation of such a municipal regulation is local, and cannot affect property in a foreign jurisdiction."

The rule announced in Crosby v. Huston by Chief Justice Hemphill is in accord with our statutes on this subject as announced above, which declare the policy of this state to be to protect the innocent purchaser for value without notice against the undisclosed or secret reservations of title, whether the same was contracted within this state or without. This is the correct and just rule.

Under the common law the mortgagee took and retained possession of the chattel until the mortgagor should pay the debt for which it was given and thereby repossess himself of it. There could be no injury to an innocent purchaser for value, because the party claiming reservation of title or lien upon the property had possession of it. For commercial convenience the rule was extended under our system of registration, and a purchaser of chattels was chargeable with notice of the reservation of title or lien upon the property if same was registered in accordance with the provisions of the law of the forum. In the absence of such registration and in the absence of notice or knowledge of the prior claim, the innocent purchaser was protected.

By the statutory law of this state a reservation of the title in chattels commonly known as a conditional sale is expressly declared to be a mortgage and subject to all the requirements of law relating to mortgages. Also the policy of this state is expressed by our statutes (articles 5654 and 5655, Vernon's Sayles' Texas Civil Statutes) that a mortgage of chattels, including conditional sales, is void as against third persons innocently purchasing the property for value, unless it is duly registered as provided therein.

[2] Plaintiff in error insists that it is a hard rule to deprive him of his reservation of title or lien upon the property without any negligence on his part. Also it is a hard rule to deprive an innocent purchaser for value of the property when he has been at no fault. The difference between them is this: While it works a hardship upon the mortgagee, yet he trusts the property to the possession of the mortgagor, and thereby puts it within the power of the mortgagor to dispose of the property to one who has no notice of his claim. The mortgagee takes the risk incident to such possession, and, while he has done no wrong and may not be negligent in regard to trying to protect his rights in the property, yet he makes it possible for a third person to be defrauded if it should be held that the rights of the third person are subject to his prior claim, of which said purchaser has no knowledge or notice.

An innocent purchaser for value has no means of protection /whatever against a private or secret unregistered reservation of title in chattels, whether made in this state or out of it.

We think these principles are fundamentally correct and conduce to less injustice than the contrary doctrine, and are clearly in consonance with our statutes and the settled policy of our state.

The judgment of the Court of Civil Appeals is affirmed.

WILSON v. GIRAUD.   (No. 3007.)

(Supreme Court of Texas. June 1, 1921.)

I. Evidence ⟺429—Oral, evidence showing inconsistencies held not inadmissible as contradicting field notes.

In proceedings involving boundaries, oral evidence is admissible as against the objection that it contradicts the written field notes where it tends to show that the calls in the field notes are inconsistent, and to show which call is true and which is false.

2. Boundaries ⟺37(1)—Evidence held to show that land was part of certain surveys as located on the ground.

In a proceeding to determine boundaries where surveys, as indicated by the field notes, were conflicting, held that evidence conclusively showed that the land in controversy was part of certain surveys as they were actually located on the ground in 1874.

3. Boundaries ⟺10—Reasonable construction of field notes harmonizing terms of patent will be adopted.

A reasonable construction of field notes which harmonizes all the terms of the patent will be adopted.

4. Boundaries ⟺6(1)—When all calls cannot be followed, as few should be disregarded as possible.

In determining boundaries, when all the calls cannot be followed, as few should be disregarded as possible.

5. Public lands ⟺176(2)—Descriptive matter inserted by mistake should be rejected.

In an ambiguous grant, such matters of description as clearly appear to have been inserted by mistake should be rejected.

Certified Questions from Court of Civil Appeals of First Supreme Judicial District.

Proceeding between J. W. Wilson and E. A. Giraud. Judgment for the latter was reversed by the Court of Civil Appeals, a rehearing granted, and questions certified. Questions answered.

E. P. & Otis K. Hamblen, of Houston, for appellant.

Baker, Botts, Parker & Garwood, of Houston, for appellee.

Certified Questions.

GREENWOOD, J. The certificate of the honorable Court of Civil Appeals is as follows:

"To the Honorable Supreme Court:

"By an opinion filed by us in this case on the 10th day of November, 1916, a certified copy of which accompanies this certificate, we reversed the judgment of the trial court in favor of appellee Giraud, and rendered judgment for appellant Wilson.

"On the 25th day of November, 1916, appellee filed his motion for rehearing, which was, by a majority of this court, refused, Mr. Chief Justice Pleasants dissenting.

"Entertaining doubts as to the correctness of our opinion since the order refusing the motion for rehearing was entered, we have, on our own motion, set aside the order refusing the motion, and the cause is now pending before this court on motion for rehearing. Inasmuch as we now entertain doubts as to the correctness of our original opinion, we deem it advisable to certify to your honors, under article 1619, Vernon's Sayles' Civil Statutes, the questions hereinafter set out, upon the following statement of facts:

"On the 10th day of August, 1824, the Wm. Bloodgood league of land in Harris county was surveyed and located. Beginning at its northeast corner it runs south 9½° east 5,000 varas, to a post and mound in the prairie for its southeast corner; thence south 80½° west, at 3,000 varas timber, at 3,500 varas Cedar bayou, at 5,000 varas to a post in prairie for its southwest corner; thence north 9½° west 5,000 varas to a post from which an elm marked 'W. B.' bears north 50° west 1 vara, a water oak marked 'W. B.' bears south 25° west 6 varas, for its northwest corner; thence north 80½° east 5,000 varas, to place of beginning.

"Thereafter a group of surveys were made which call for connection with the lines of the Wm. Bloodgood as follows:

"The George Ellis league was surveyed and located by surveyor George M. Patrick on the 17th day of August, 1835. By its locative field notes it begins at a stake and mound on the west bank of Cedar bayou, on the north line of the Bloodgood league, to run thence with Bloodgood's north line south 80½° west 950 varas to Bloodgood's northwest corner; thence with Bloodgood's west line south 9½° east 560 varas prairie, 3,400 varas a stake and mound on Bloodgood's west line in prairie for its southeast corner; thence south 80½° west 4,827 varas to a stake and mound in prairie for its southwest corner; thence north 9½° west 5,000 varas to a stake in prairie for its northwest corner; thence north 80½° east 4,777 varas, a stake on the west bank of Cedar bayou for its northwest corner; thence down said bayou with its meanders to place of beginning.

"The Benjamin Barrow survey was surveyed and located by George M. Patrick, the same surveyor who located the George Ellis in 1835, and in the same year. By its locative field notes it is described as follows:

"'Beginning at a stake on the west bank of Cedar bayou and on the south line of a league of land granted to William Bloodgood, from which a pine 10 inches diameter bears north 70° east distant 8.5 varas, and an elm 8 inches in diameter bears south 60° east distant 4 varas; thence with said Bloodgood's line south 80° 30' west 4,000 varas stake and mound in prairie for N. W. corner; thence south 9° 30' west 1,490 varas, set stake and raised mound in prairie for S. W. corner; thence north 80° east 4,230 varas to the bank of said Cedar bayou, corners on three small pin oaks from which another pin oak 8 inches in diameter bears south 35° west distant 5.5 varas, and a pine 30 inches diameter bears north 11° west distant 10.4 varas; thence up

said Cedar bayou with its meanders to the place of beginning.'

"On the 23d day of December, 1874, J. J. Gillespie surveyed and located for Ashbel Smith a tract of land which was thereafter patented to him. By its locative field notes it is described as follows:

"'Beginning at a stake on the north line of B. Barrow's ¼ league survey 1,500 varas from Cedar bayou in prairie; thence north 9½° west 1,600 varas with the west line of the Wm. Bloodgood league to stake in prairie, the S. E. corner of George Ellis league; thence south 80½° west with the south line of George Ellis 1,471 varas to a stake in prairie; thence south 9½° east 1,600 varas to a stake in said Barrow's north line; thence north 80½° east 1,471 varas with Barrow's line to the beginning.'

"On the 23d day of December, 1874, J. J. Gillespie surveyed and located for Ashbel Smith, assignee of William Ritchie, a tract of land, which was thereafter patented to Ashbel Smith on the 13th day of December, 1877. By its locative field notes it is described as follows:

"'Beginning at a stake in the north line of Benjamin Barrow's ¼-league survey; being 2,971 varas from Cedar bayou; thence north 9½° west along the western boundary of Ashbel Smith's survey 1,600 varas to a stake in prairie in the south line of George Ellis league; thence south 80½° west along said south line of Ellis league 1,256 varas to a stake in said line in the prairie; thence south 9½° east 1,600 varas to a stake in H. F. Gillett's north line 227 varas from Barrow's N. W. corner and the N. E. corner of said Gillett's survey; thence north 80½° east along said Gillett's and Barrow's north lines to place of beginning, 1,256 varas, containing 356 acres.'

"On the —— day of September, 1886, J. J. Gillespie, who surveyed and located the two Ashbel Smith surveys in 1874, surveyed and located the Martha Mings survey, which is described as follows:

"'Beginning at the most southerly S. E. corner of land grant of Geo. Ellis, stake corner in prairie; thence north 9½° west 3,400 varas to corner in prairie, in inner southeast corner of said Ellis; thence north 80½° east 550 varas to corner in prairie on northwest corner of Wm. Bloodgood's league survey; thence south 9½° east 4,093 varas, the northeast corner of survey in name of A. Smith on Bloodgood's west line; thence south 80½° west 2,512 varas to corner in prairie, Wm. Ritchie's north line; thence north 9½° west 693 varas to corner in prairie south line of said George Ellis; thence north 80½° east 1,963 varas to the beginning.'

"For a better understanding of the location of these several surveys and their relation one to the other, your honors are referred to maps A and B in certified copy of our original opinion, which accompanies this certificate.

"Appellee made application for the purchase of the Mings survey on November 8, 1907, and on November 21, 1907, the application was approved and the land sold him by the commissioner of the land office in accordance with the statute regulating the sale of public lands.

"Appellant has title to 575 acres of land off of the north ends of the Smith and Ritchie surveys. This 575 acres is described as follows in the deed under which appellant acquired title:

" 'Beginning 7 varas from the northeast corner of the Ashbel Smith survey, patent No. 288, vol. 29, on the west side of the county road, on the south line of the George Ellis league; thence south 9½° east 1,193 varas along the west side of said road to the northeast corner of 400 acres conveyed by Ruby to Porter; thence south 80½° west 2,770 varas to said Porter's northwest corner on the west line of the said Ritchie survey; thence north 9½° west 1,193 varas to the northwest corner of the said Ritchie survey, on the south line of the George Ellis league; thence north 80½° east 2,770 varas to the place of beginning.'

"It is apparent from the field notes of appellant's land that his boundaries conflict with the Mings survey owned by appellee, if the north lines of the Smith and Ritchie surveys, as actually located on the ground, are identical with the south line of the George Ellis survey, as the calls in the field notes of the Smith and Ritchie before set out indicate. The true location of the Smith and Ritchie surveys depends upon the true location of the north line of the Benjamin Barrow survey.

"S. J. Sjolander, witness for appellee, testified that he moved into the neighborhood where the Benjamin Barrow survey is located in 1871 (36 years after the Barrow was located); that he had lived there ever since, a period of 43 years; that he is acquainted with the north boundary line of the Barrow survey; that he lived on the Wm. Bloodgood league, perhaps 700, 800 or 1,000 yards, something like that, from the Barrow north boundary line; that the north line of the Barrow survey was fenced by Rosamond, Milam & Bro., in about 1878 or 1879, something like that; that before that fence was constructed he had seen and known and was familiar with the north boundary line of the Barrow survey; that he cut wood on both sides of the line, and always tried to avoid cutting line trees. He further testified:

" 'I knew Mr. J. J. Gillespie, a surveyor, many years ago. The north line of the Benjamin Barrow survey was always considered to start at a little gully down on the bayou, right opposite the Armstrong survey in Chambers county; there is where they always got their line down there, and I remember when Mr. Gillespie was there surveying that he run across certain lines there to get that line, and when he struck this place, always considered that was the line. There were some elm trees, as near as I can remember, on the bank of the gully, right on the bank of the gully almost, that had surveying marks on it; if I remember right, it was cuts and a cross on this little elm, and further out, through the timber, there was small pine trees, some scattering trees, and you could see the hacks along there, and that is what we were guided by in wood chopping.

" 'I know Mr. P. G. Omohundro. I have seen him in that vicinity, saw him there a couple of months ago, doing some surveying down there. I did not point out to him any marks or lines of any surveys of land; I found him on the line of the Benjamin Barrow tract, lower end of it, on the north line; this line upon which Omohundro was at the time I saw him is the north

line of the Benjamin Barrow survey about which I have been testifying. It was the line I spoke of as having been marked through the timber there, and known by reputation in that neighborhood as the north line of the Benjamin Barrow, where the fence is placed to-day. I spoke about Mr. J. J. Gillespie being out there doing some surveying, and that I left him on the bayou; Mr. Omohundro was virtually in the same place that Mr. Gillespie was at the time I saw Mr. Gillespie.'

"Mr. Omohundro testified: 'I went to that point (the northwest corner of the Armstrong survey), and picked up my work at that point on the bank of Cedar bayou, on the west side of it on the line which, produced west, would be a prolongation of the Armstrong, and I measured that distance and ran that line which has the correct bearing as given in the Benjamin Barrow notes, south 80½° west; all these latter surveys ran at that, apparently. Mr. Sjolander was with me at the time, and I asked him if he recognized that as the Barrow line, and he said he knew it was, and measurements as made from there are as shown on this map here as the north line of the Benjamin Barrow.'

"This witness further testified: 'With reference to the northwest corner of the Bloodgood, I found the original oak and the original elm called for at that point represented on the map in red; that corner, I would like to get my notes on that, so as to be exact, I went to the accepted northwest corner of the Bloodgood league from which an old oak marked X bears south 40½° west 12½ varas, and ran north 58¾° west 115½ varas; the reason I ran on a different course, I had already found the corner, and it is indicated here by the red circle; at that point there was an elm 19 inches in diameter, with very old marks, bears north 50° west 1 vara, and an old water oak 26 inches in diameter, with evidence of W. B. marked on it, bears south 25° west 6 varas; this elm is broken off, and a snag stands five feet from the ground, and the oak is also broken off, and stands 7½ feet high.'

"It was also shown that many years ago the then owner of the Ritchie survey sold a small tract of land out of the southern portion thereof, describing it as beginning on the north line of the Barrow, and that the purchaser, in fencing this tract, recognized the line described by the witnesses Sjolander and Omohundro as the north line of the Barrow.

"There is no testimony showing any marked line along the south line or extending west from the S. W. corner of the Bloodgood, and no testimony showing the bearing trees from the beginning corner of the Barrow in the south line of the Bloodgood as called for in Barrow field notes. The line described by the witnesses Sjolander and Omohundro as the north line of the Barrow is 702 varas south of the south line of the Bloodgood.

"Upon these facts we respectfully certify for your determination the following questions:

"First. Was the testimony of the witnesses Sjolander and Omohundro tending to show that the true north boundary line of the Barrow survey was not tied to, and did not run for a distance with, the Bloodgood south boundary line, as called for in the field notes by which it was located, but that, as a fact, it is located 702 varas south of Bloodgood's south boundary line, admissible over the objection that it contradicted the written field notes of the survey? "Second. Was the evidence above set out sufficient to sustain the finding of the jury that the 575 acres of land in controversy was not in conflict with the Smith and Ritchie surveys as those surveys were actually located upon the ground in 1874?"

The following are the maps referred to in the certificate:

as running south 80° 30″ west from a stake for beginning corner, which was described as follows: First, as being at the point of intersection of the west bank of Cedar bayou with the south line of the league granted to William Bloodgood; and second, as being at a point from which a pine 10 inches in diameter bears north 70° east at a distance of 8.5 varas, and from which an elm 8 inches in

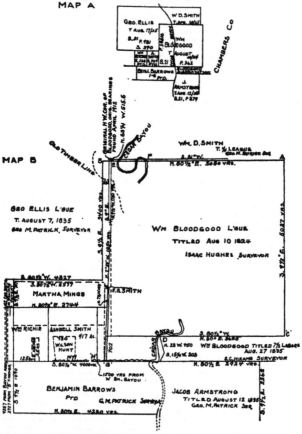

MAP A

MAP B

[1] We answer that the testimony of the witnesses Sjolander and Omohundro was admissible over the objection that said testimony contradicted the written field notes of the Barrow survey. The written field notes identified the north boundary line of the Barrow

diameter bears south 60° east at a distance of 4 varas.

The testimony of Sjolander and Omohundro tended to show that the elm tree called for in the field notes was not at a distance of 4 varas, on a course south 60° east, from where the west bank of Cedar bayou intersected the south line of the William Bloodgood league, but instead that it was at almost the point of intersection of the west bank of Cedar bayou with the south line of the William Bloodgood 7½ labors. The points of intersection of the west bank of the bayou with the south line of the Bloodgood league and with the south line of the Bloodgood 7½ labors were 702 varas apart, and hence the testimony objected to tended to show that the calls in the field notes were inconsistent.

Once testimony is adduced to establish an inconsistency in field notes, parol evidence which throws light upon which call is true and which call is false is admissible. The purpose of admitting the parol evidence is not to override that which is written, but to properly interpret it. Where it is impossible to give effect to all that is written, effect will be given to that which may be found to be true.

The testimony as to the marked line on a course south 80½° west from the intersection of the bayou with the south line of the Bloodgood 7½-labor survey, and as to the recognition of that line, and as to the absence of marks along the designated course from the intersection of the bayou with the south line of the Bloodgood league, was all admissible on the inquiry as to what part of the description in the Barrow field notes was true and what part was false.

In Duren v. Presberry, 25 Tex. 517, a call for bearing trees was held to control as against a call for the corner of an adjacent survey, where no such bearing trees were found at the corner of the adjacent survey, and no marked line led therefrom, and where a marked line, running on the specified course, and the bearing trees, which were called for, were found 1,000 varas to the north. In delivering the court's opinion, Chief Justice Wheeler said:

"We know of no rule for the construction of grants which would give a controlling influence to a call for the corner of a survey over a call for bearing trees and marked lines, which are found upon the ground to correspond with the calls. * * * What distinguishes this case from Anderson v. Stamps, 19 Tex., is that there are calls in the patent which correspond with objects found upon the ground. The correspondence of the bearing trees with the calls in the grant, and the marked line running to the second corner of the survey, render it reasonably certain, we think, that the point where these objects are found is the true beginning corner of the survey, and that the call for the southwest corner of the Brooks Williams league, is a mistake."

[2] While the evidence was sufficient to support the finding that the true north line of the Barrow was 702 varas south of the south line of the Bloodgood league yet the evidence was conclusive that the land in controversy was a part of the Smith and Ritchie surveys as located upon the ground in 1874.

[3] Apart from course and distance, the field notes identify the land patented to Smith by reference to the north line of the B. Barrow survey, the west line of the Wm. Bloodgood league, the S. E. corner of the George Ellis league, and the south line of the George Ellis league. To construe the call for the north line of the B. Barrow survey as a call for that line at a distance of 702 varas south of the south line of the William Bloodgood league is to make the call repugnant to every call in the Smith patent, except the calls for course and distance. By construing the call for the north line of the B. Barrow survey as a call for that line as it was at the time designated on the official maps, and as the Barrow field notes pointed to its location by the call to run with the south line of the Bloodgood league, is to prevent any repugnancy between the calls of the Smith patent. The latter construction is reasonable, and, since it harmonizes all the terms of the patent, it must be adopted under the general rule for the interpretation of written instruments.

[4] If, however, it were impossible to reasonably so interpret the patent as to prevent the disregard of any of the calls, we would still have no hesitancy in rejecting the call for the Barrow north line. In determining boundaries, when all the calls cannot be followed, as few should be disregarded as possible. Hill v. Smith, 6 Tex. Civ. App. 312, 25 S. W. 1083. Therefore, if we had to disregard either the call for the Barrow north line or the calls for the Bloodgood west line, the Ellis southeast corner, and the Ellis south line, the call for the Barrow north line would be disregarded.

[5] The call for the Barrow north line if repugnant to the other calls, would be the call to be ignored, under the rule which rejects such matters of description in an ambiguous grant, as clearly appear to have been inserted by mistake, and which gives controlling effect to such matters as seem certain and "most consistent with the intention to be derived from the entire description." Hubert v. Bartlett, 9 Tex. 104; Finberg v. Gilbert, 104 Tex. 547, 141 S. W. 82; Lilly v. Blum, 70 Tex. 712, 6 S. W. 279; Harrell v. Morris, 5 S. W. 626, 627.

There is no substantial difference in the Ritchie and Smith field notes, in so far as concerns the application of the principles we have announced. If the Smith survey extends to the south line of the Ellis league, no one questions that the Ritchie does also.

We answer to the second question that the land in controversy was conclusively shown to be a part of the Smith and Ritchie surveys, and included in the patents to Ashbel Smith, and that the testimony of Sjolander and Omohundro did not warrant a contrary finding.

PARR et al. v. CHITTIM.   (No. 247–3446.)

(Commission of Appeals of Texas, Section B. June 22, 1921.)

Dismissal and Nonsuit ⟺60(1)—Judgment of dismissal only one proper, where plaintiff failed to appear at trial.

Where, the case being regularly called for trial on the day on which it had been set by agreement, neither plaintiff nor her counsel appeared, but made default, sending no explanation to the court, and trial was had and evidence heard, the court instructing a verdict for defendants, who had filed no cross-action or prayer for affirmative relief, such action was error; under the circumstances, the only proper judgment would have been one dismissing the case for want of prosecution without prejudice.

Error to Court of Civil Appeals of Fourth Supreme Judicial District.

Action by Annie E. Chittim against G. A. Parr and others. To review a judgment for defendants, plaintiff brought error to the Court of Civil Appeals, which reversed and rendered judgment dismissing the cause for want of prosecution (216 S. W. 635), and defendants bring error. Judgment of the Court of Civil Appeals affirmed.

Hicks, Hicks, Dickson & Bobbitt, of San Antonio, James B. Wells, of Brownsville, and C. C. Forry, of Alice, for plaintiffs in error.

Dougherty & Dougherty, of Beeville, and G. O. Robinson, of El Paso, for defendant in error.

POWELL, J. On December 8, 1905, in the district court of Bexar county, Tex., the estate of J. M. Chittim recovered judgment against A. Parr for $60,115.30, with interest from the date thereof at the rate of 6 per cent. per annum and all costs of court. Said judgment was kept alive by issuance of various executions from time to time, which were returned "nulla bona." An abstract of said judgment was duly recorded in the office of the county clerk of Duval county, Tex., on December 18, 1905, and March 3, 1916. The filing, recording, and indexing of said judgment became a lien on such real estate as A. Parr then owned or might thereafter acquire in Duval county, Tex. On August 1, 1916, G. A. Parr acquired by deed some 12,728 acres of land situated in Duval county, Tex.

On March 23, 1917, Mrs. Annie E. Chittim, representing the estate of her deceased hus-

band, J. M. Chittim, filed suit in the district court of Duval county, Tex., alleging that A. Parr had furnished to G. A. Parr the money for the purchase of said 12,728 acres of land; that, while the deed was taken in the name of G. A. Parr, it was really for the benefit of A. Parr; that the latter and G. A. Parr conspired together to take this deed as they did, in the name of G. A. Parr, in order that the property might be placed beyond the reach of the creditors of A. Parr, and especially the Chittim obligation. The plaintiff asked for a foreclosure of her judgment lien on said 12,728 acres of land.

Each of said defendants denied all the allegations of plaintiff's petition, generally and specially. G. A. Parr alleged he bought the property in good faith, as his own and with his own money. Neither defendant filed any cross-action or prayer for affirmative relief.

On May 22, 1917, the cause was continued for service. On December 3, 1917, the case was set down by agreement for December 18, 1917, when it was finally continued for that term of court by consent without prejudice. On May 21, 1918, in term time, the case was placed on the jury docket and set by agreement for May 30, 1918.

We shall refer to the parties hereafter as they were known in the trial court, as plaintiff and defendants. On May 30, 1918, the defendants, accompanied by their counsel and witnesses, appeared in court. But, the case being regularly called for trial on the very day for which it had been set by agreement, neither the plaintiff nor her counsel appeared, but wholly made default, nor did they send any word of explanation to the court of their failure to appear. The case being called, the defendants announced ready for trial. A jury was had, and when the evidence was all in the trial court, upon request, instructed a verdict for the defendants, which was accordingly returned. Judgment was so entered.

In due course thereafter plaintiff sued out a writ of error to the Court of Civil Appeals at San Antonio, alleging that under the circumstances of this case the only judgment the trial court was authorized to enter was one dismissing the case for want of prosecution. The Court of Civil Appeals adopted that view and reversed the judgment of the trial court, rendering judgment dismissing the case for want of prosecution without prejudice. See 216 S. W. 638. The case is now before the Supreme Court, which granted defendants' application for writ of error.

We have carefully reviewed the authorities relied upon by the Court of Civil Appeals in this case, as well as others we have found, and have reached the conclusion that that court correctly disposed of this case. In the case of Burger v. Young, 78 Tex. 656,

15 S. W. 107, Judge Henry announces the rule as follows:

"The refusal of plaintiff's attorney to read his pleadings or to offer any evidence was in effect an abandonment of the prosecution of his cause. It was as much so as an entire failure to appear would have been. In that state of the case the only order that the court could have properly made was one dismissing his cause for want of prosecution as to the defendants who appeared. For the error of the court in rendering judgment upon the merits in favor of such defendants, instead of dismissing the cause as to them for want of prosecution, the judgment is reversed and the cause is remanded."

The decision by Judge Henry has been followed by the Supreme Court in the cases of Browning v. Pumphrey, 81 Tex. 163, 16 S. W. 870, and Harris v. Schlinke, 95 Tex. 88, 65 S. W. 172. It seems clear to us that, under a rule of the Supreme Court which has long obtained in this state, the only proper judgment the trial court could have entered was one dismissing the case for want of prosecution.

Not only would we not feel disposed to recommend a modification of the former holdings of our Supreme Court, but we think the rule they announce is in reason the better one. Where a defendant asks no affirmative relief, he is really in no position to demand a trial because of the plaintiff's failure to appear and prosecute his action. In fact, he is in court simply in response to the plaintiff's action. If the plaintiff then refuses to prosecute his action, the defendant can justly have no further concern with the proceeding. If the action is treated as abandoned and dismissed by the trial court, it would seem that the defendant is accorded full relief. Where the latter asks no affirmative relief himself, we find it difficult to see how he is entitled to ask anything more than a dismissal of the plaintiff's cause.

It follows, from what has been said, that we are of the opinion that the judgment of the Court of Civil Appeals should be affirmed; and we so recommend.

PHILLIPS, C. J. The judgment recommended in the report of the Commission of Appeal is adopted, and will be entered as the judgment of the Supreme Court.

PARIS TRANSIT CO. v. FATH.
(No. 248-3447.)

(Commission of Appeals of Texas, Section A. June 22, 1921.)

1. Street railroads ⬥⇒90(4)—Motorman should use ordinary care to avoid collision.

The motorman of a street car, after discovering the peril of the driver of a horse and buggy on the track, is required only to exercise that degree of care which a person of ordinary prudence would use under the same or similar circumstances, by the use of all the means at his command consistent with the safety of the car and its passengers, to avoid the injury, and is not under absolute duty, after discovering the peril, to stop the car by the use of all the means at his command consistent with the safety of car and passengers.

2. Street railroads ⬥⇒117(11)—Motorman's negligence jury question.

In suit against a street railroad for injuries to plaintiff buggy driver struck by a car, it is for the jury to determine what measure of diligence is necessary on the part of the motorman to constitute the required care on his part to avoid injury to plaintiff after discovering his peril.

3. Trial ⬥⇒194(17)—Court should have left jury free to decide whether motorman exercised requisite care.

In suit against a street railroad for injuries to plaintiff buggy driver struck by a car, the trial court should not have instructed the jury under the circumstances that it was the duty of the motorman to have done any particular thing to avoid the injury after discovering plaintiff's peril, but should have left the jury free to decide whether he exercised the requisite care to avert injury to plaintiff after discovering him.

Error to Court of Civil Appeals of Fifth Supreme Judicial District.

Action by C. F. Fath against the Paris Transit Company. From judgment for plaintiff, defendant appealed to the Court of Civil Appeals, which affirmed (216 S. W. 482), and defendant brings error. Judgments of the Court of Civil Appeals and of the trial court reversed, and cause remanded for new trial.

Templeton, Beall, Williams & Callaway, of Dallas, for plaintiff in error.

John White and Marcus M. Parks, both of Dallas, for defendant in error.

SPENCER, J. Defendant in error, C. F. Fath, sued plaintiff in error, Paris Traction Company, a corporation, and recovered judgment against it for the alleged negligent injury of defendant in error, after having discovered him upon its track in a position of peril. Upon appeal the judgment was affirmed. 216 S. W. 482.

The facts proven by defendant in error in support of the judgment are that, while defendant in error was crossing plaintiff in error's street car track at the intersection of Washington Avenue in Paris, Tex., in a horse-drawn vehicle, the horse became ungovernable, and that plaintiff in error's motorman, in charge of one of its motorcars, saw defendant in error's perilous condition when 225 feet distant from the street intersection, and in ample time to have stopped the car, but that he made no attempt to do so, and as a result of which struck the buggy, which was upon the street car track, throwing defendant in error therefrom, and injuring him.

Plaintiff in error's motorman testified that he saw defendant in error and the horse and buggy upon the track when 100 feet or more distant, but made no effort to stop the car; that when within 40 or 50 feet of defendant in error—at which time the buggy had cleared the track by two or three feet—he wound the slack in his brake in order to be prepared to stop the car. He also testified that the front end of the car passed the horse and buggy in safety, and that the horse backed into the car.

Upon the issue of discovered peril, the court charged the jury as follows:

"If you find and believe from the evidence in this case that the balking, fright, or ungovernable disposition of the horse driven by the plaintiff or his companion on the occasion of the accident in question placed the plaintiff upon the defendant's track in a buggy and in a position of peril from the approach of the defendant's street car to the place of the accident; and if you further find and believe from the evidence that the defendant's motorman, as he approached the place of the accident in charge of defendant's car, actually discovered the peril of the plaintiff in time to have stopped the car and have avoided the accident by the use of all the means at the motorman's command, consistent with the safety of the car and its passengers; and that said motorman, after discovering such peril of the plaintiff, if you find he did discover the same, failed to stop said car, and that such failure, if any, to stop the said car proximately resulted in any injury or damage to the plaintiff. * * *"

[1, 2] The charge quoted makes it the absolute duty of the motorman, after discovering the perilous situation of defendant in error, to stop the car by the use of all the means at his command consistent with the safety of the car and its passengers. This was error. The motorman was only required, after discovering defendant in error's peril, to exercise that degree of care which a person of ordinary prudence would have used under the same or similar circumstances by the use of all the means at his command consistent with the safety of the car and its passengers to avoid the injury. That degree of care is all that any one owes to another, except when special relations exist. The degree of diligence constituting this care may, and often does, vary in the different instances. The degree of diligence to be used must be in proportion to the danger. It is for the jury, however, to determine what measure of diligence is necessary in a given case to constitute the required care. M., K. & T. Railway Co. of Texas v. Reynolds, 103 Tex. 31, 122 S. W. 531.

[3] The charge under consideration utterly ignores this standard of care, by imposing upon the motorman the absolute duty to stop the car without regard to whether, in the exercise of the degree of care which the law requires, it was incumbent upon him to do so. The court thus invaded the province of the jury, and determined for them a question which they should have determined. The court should not, under the circumstances, have instructed the jury that it was the duty of the motorman to have done any particular thing to avoid the injury, but should have left the jury free to decide whether he exercised the requisite care to avert injuring the defendant in error after discovering him.

As pointed out by Judge Williams in Railway v. Reynolds, supra, some charges reviewed by the Supreme Court requiring the doing of particular things have been held unobjectionable because the instruction complained of exacted no more than the doing of that which obviously was necessary in the particular instance, or about which there was no dispute as to what should have been done under certain circumstances; but the holding based upon such a state of facts is not authority for holding the charge here complained of unobjectionable. It cannot be said that the evidence was undisputed that the motorman should have stopped the car, nor can it be said that obviously it was his duty, as a matter of law, to have stopped the same. He testified:

"I never set my brakes. I didn't set my brakes ahead of time because I had a clear track. I did say that I discovered the unruly condition of the horse when I was 100 feet from the place of the accident. It is like I told you, when I got within 40 or 50 feet of the buggy, it had cleared the track. My contention is that the back end of the buggy ran into me, and that I never ran into the buggy with my car."

Under the evidence, the court should have left it to the jury to determine whether the motorman, in the exercise of due care, by the use of all the means at his command commensurate with the safety of the car and its passengers, exercised that degree of diligence which a person of ordinary prudence would have exercised to avert injuring the defendant in error.

We recommend, therefore, that the judgment of the Court of Civil Appeals and of the district court be reversed, and the cause remanded to the district court for a new trial.

PHILLIPS, C. J. The judgment recommended in the report of the Commission of Appeals is adopted, and will be entered as the judgment of the Supreme Court.

We approve the holding of the Commission of Appeals on the question discussed in its opinion.

BRISCOE v. BRIGHT'S ADM'R.
(No. 181-3214.)

(Commission of Appeals of Texas, Section B. June 15, 1921.)

1. Specific performance ⟞⟞117—Variance between pleading and evidence held not material.

Where plaintiff, an attorney, alleged a verbal agreement on the part of deceased to cancel certain notes in consideration of "legal services theretofore and thereafter to be rendered" by plaintiff, and the evidence showed such promise if plaintiff would continue to do decedent's work as he had done, as long as decedent lived, there was no material variance between the allegations and the proof.

2. Contracts ⟞⟞346(10)—Rule as to variance stated.

Where, eliminating every allegation not substantially supported by evidence, and eliminating all proof not fairly alleged, there is left sufficient evidence of a contract which meets the requirements of law, it cannot be said there is not sufficient evidence to support a judgment for the plaintiff on the issue as to whether the contract was made as alleged.

3. Appeal and error ⟞⟞930(1) — Evidence viewed most strongly in support of judgment.

Treating the question as to the sufficiency of the proof to clearly and satisfactorily establish the contract as one of law, only, the evidence must be viewed most strongly in support of the trial court's judgment in favor of the contract.

4. Appeal and error ⟞⟞994(2)—Credibility of witnesses not question within province of Commission of Appeals.

That the witnesses may not have been disinterested or may have made conflicting statements, or that their credibility may have been attacked, are matters solely within the province of the jury subject to revision by the trial judge and Court of Civil Appeals, and are not matters with which it is the province of the Commission of Appeals to deal on appeal from the Court of Civil Appeals.

5. Specific performance ⟞⟞121(1) — When proof of terms of oral contract sufficient stated.

It is only essential that the terms of an oral contract with a decedent to cancel notes in consideration of services be shown by evidence sufficiently clear for the court to determine what those terms were, without resorting to inference or conjecture.

6. Appeal and error ⟞⟞1083(6)—Reversal and rendition of judgment by Court of Civil Appeals held ruling on law and not on facts.

Where the Court of Civil Appeals on appeal from a judgment for plaintiff rendered judgment for defendant and did not exercise its province to determine the facts and order another trial because of its difference with the jury on the facts, its ruling is one purely upon the question of law whether there be any evidence under the required quantum of proof which will support the jury's finding.

7. Specific performance ⟞⟞121(4)—Evidence held sufficient to support finding.

In suit for specific performance of an oral contract by payee, since deceased, to cancel notes in consideration of legal services, evidence *held* sufficiently clear, strong, cogent, satisfactory, and convincing to support the jury's finding that such a contract was made.

8. Appeal and error ⟞⟞842(7)—Facts held not to warrant holding, as a matter of law, that contract was procured by undue influence.

Where the issue of undue influence by an attorney in procuring a contract with a client was not submitted to the jury, and no request for submission was made, and deceased was in full possession of his faculties and was competent to make a contract, and there was evidence to support a finding that he voluntarily made it, it could not be held by Court of Civil Appeals as a matter of law that the contract was procured by undue influence and was therefore nudum pactum.

Error to Court of Civil Appeals of Fourth Supreme Judicial District.

Action by John T. Briscoe against the administrator of the estate of J. M. Bright, deceased, and cross-action by the defendant. Judgment of the Court of Civil Appeals (202 S. W. 183) reversing the trial court's judgment for the plaintiff, and plaintiff brings error. Judgment of the Court of Civil Appeals reversed, and that of the district court affirmed.

C. C. Harris, of San Antonio, De Montel & Fly, of Hondo, and Hertzberg, Kercheville & Thomson, of San Antonio, for plaintiff in error.

J. F. Carl, of San Antonio, for defendant in error.

McCLENDON, P. J. This action was brought by John T. Briscoe against the administrator of the estate of J. M. Bright, deceased, to cancel certain notes which plaintiff had executed in favor of the deceased during his lifetime, upon the ground that the deceased had made a verbal contract with plaintiff to the effect that if the latter would attend to the business of deceased for the rest of his life, as he had theretofore done, deceased would cancel all notes owing to him by plaintiff at the time of his death. Defendant by way of cross-action sought judgment against plaintiff upon the notes. The case was tried twice, each of which trials was by jury and upon one special issue only—whether the contract was made as alleged—and upon each trial judgment was rendered for the plaintiff upon favorable answer to that issue. Appeal from the first judgment resulted in its reversal and a remand of the cause for further trial upon the holding, among others, that the evidence was not of sufficient certainty and clearness to support recovery. 193 S. W. 156. On the last appeal the Court of Civil Appeals, upon like holding as to the sufficiency of the evidence, reversed the trial court's judgment and rendered judgment that plaintiff take nothing and that defendant recover upon his cross-action. 202 S. W. 183.

The cause was presented in the Court of Civil Appeals upon 16 assignments of error, 10 of which were sustained by that court, and the remaining 6 overruled. The latter need no mention for the reason that they are not brought before the Supreme Court for review by any assignment or cross-assignment of error. The 10 assignments sustained by the Court of Civil Appeals, eliminating duplications, may be grouped under the three following holdings of that court:

(1) That there was a variance between the contract declared upon and the contract proved.

(2) That the evidence was not of that clear, strong, cogent, satisfactory, and convincing character required to support a judgment in cases of this character.

(3) That the relation of plaintiff to deceased being that of attorney to client, and therefore confidential and fiduciary, and deceased being aged and infirm, the contract was unfair, unreasonable, and procured by undue influence, which rendered it nudum pactum.

We will state only sufficient of the pleadings and evidence to make clear our conclusions upon these holdings.

Plaintiff alleged that, beginning with the year 1907, when he began practicing law, and up to the 28th day of April, 1914, he had attended to all of deceased's business, during which time he had received no compensation for his services. That on the date last named—

"the said J. M. Bright orally agreed and contracted * * * with this plaintiff that in consideration of the plaintiff having rendered legal services to him in the past, and in consideration of all legal services to be rendered by the plaintiff to him in the future and during the life of said J. M. Bright, that he, the said J. M. Bright, would pay the plaintiff for same by cancelling all notes and indebtedness owing by plaintiff to said J. M. Bright at the time of the death of said J. M. Bright."

The notes sought to be canceled were specifically described in the petition.

It was shown that at the time of making the alleged contract deceased was very old and infirm. He had no family of his own, and all his heirs-at-law lived in another state. Plaintiff had transacted all of deceased's business for a number of years and continued to do so up to the time of his death, which occurred some eight or more months after the alleged contract was made. There was no evidence that deceased ever paid plaintiff anything for any service rendered. The witnesses who testified in support of plaintiff's allegations were Mrs. Adelia Ray and her husband, A. L. Ray, Mrs. O. G. Newcomb, John H. Snyder and J. C. Stroud. Mrs. Ray had been housekeeper and nurse for deceased for about seven years prior to his death. She married A. L. Ray about two years before deceased's death, and they both lived with deceased during those two years. Mrs. Newcomb had also been a housekeeper for deceased. Mrs. Ray gave the following testimony:

"As to what conversation I heard between Mr. Bright, before his death, and Mr. Briscoe, with reference to the contract between them, for Mr. Briscoe to continue doing his business, in 1914, on May 28th, Mr. Briscoe came up tuere to pay some interest on his notes, and he said, 'John, I hate to take this from you, but I have to live, but if you will just continue to pay interest as long as I live, why at my death the notes will be canceled, you will owe me nothing,' and Mr. Briscoe said, 'All right, I will do the work for you.' Which he did, as long as he lived."

"As to whether he said anything in that conversation about Mr. (Briscoe) continuing to attend to his business as long as he lived, he did; Mr. Bright said, 'If you will continue to attend to my business, as you have done, as long as I live, at my death you will owe me nothing and the notes will be canceled at my death,' and Mr. Briscoe said, 'All right, Mr. Bright, I will do the work for you as I have done.'

"Mr. Bright told me before he died that if he never lived to make a will, he wanted me to testify after his death that Mr. Briscoe would not owe him anything, that the notes would all be canceled and Mr. Briscoe would not owe him anything.

"Mr. Bright did not say anything about who would testify to establish my claim; he didn't tell me who would do that.

"As to what Mr. Bright's exact words were on that occasion to Mr. Briscoe, I don't remember. Mr. Briscoe came to pay the interest on his notes, and he said, 'John, I hate to take this from you, but I have to live, but if you will continue to do my work for me, as you have done, as long as I live, at my death the notes will be canceled and you owe me nothing,' and Mr. Briscoe said, 'All right, I will,' Mr. Briscoe said, 'All right, Mr. Bright, I will do the work for you, attend to your business for you, as I have done, as long as you live.' Mr. Bright said, 'The notes will be canceled and you will owe me nothing at my death.' I am sure that he said that he would cancel those notes."

The following is from the testimony of Mr. Ray:

"As to having a conversation myself with Mr. Bright with reference to an understanding between Mr. Bright and Mr. Briscoe, I did. Mr. Briscoe had been up there, I think it was in May, 1914; I don't know what day of the month it was. He had been up there to pay some interest on some notes, and Mr. Bright had a conversation with Mr. Briscoe in the presence of my wife, and that evening, that night after supper, we were out on the front porch, sitting out there, and he went over the matter. He told me what he had told Mr. Briscoe. He said that he wanted Mr. Briscoe to continue attending to his business, and he wanted him to pay interest on those notes as long as he lived and that at his death the notes would be canceled. These were notes that were due by Mr. John T. Briscoe to Mr. J. M. Bright. This conversation occurred at Mr. Bright's house after supper, out on the front porch."

Mrs. Newcomb testified:

"As to when I saw Mr. Briscoe pay Mr. Bright some interest on some notes, that was in December, before Mr. Bright died, which was in March.

"As to what conversation took place between them at that time, when he took the money, Mr. Bright said, 'I hate to take it, but I have to live.' That is what he said. He told me that he hated to take the money from John, as he always called him, but, of course, he had to live. He said John was a good fellow, and I don't know what all he didn't say, like that; he went on praising him like that, how he had helped him."

Snyder testified:

"I knew Mr. J. M. Bright during his lifetime. I also know Mr. John T. Briscoe. Mr. Bright died in March, 1915. I was living there at the time of his death.

"As to whether I ever visited Mr. Bright at his home before his death, I went there in 1914, and brought him some plums. When I went there he said, 'Get down and come here, I want to talk to you.' Then I stopped and talked a while and said, 'Mr. Bright,' I said, 'You are getting old to attend to your business.' 'Well,' he said, 'I have turned it over to John T. Briscoe, turned it over to him. He will attend to my business as long as I live here. I made a contract with him.' That is so. Mr. Bright said, 'I will pay him well for it after my death.' That is what he said. That was the first of June, 1914."

Stroud testified to a conversation with deceased in which the latter said:

"'John don't owe me nothing on the lots,' and he said, 'When I go down to my grave, John Briscoe's debts go down in the grave with me; but he won't owe me nothing when I am dead.'"

[1, 2] We do not think the evidence of the contract proved was materially variant from that alleged. The only respect in which a variance is claimed which in our opinion deserves mention is that with reference to the character of services which constituted the consideration for the promise to cancel plaintiff's notes. Those services as alleged were "legal services theretofore and thereafter to be rendered," whereas, the language of deceased testified to was, "if you will continue to do my work for me, as you have done, as long as I live," and, "If you will continue to attend to my business, as you have done." The Court of Civil Appeals, in sustaining the contention that there

was a fatal variance between the allegations and proof, say:

"The only attention given by Mr. Briscoe to Mr. Bright's business, shown by the record, is that disclosed by the general statement that Mr. Briscoe stepped into the shoes of Mr. Bright, from which it may be inferred that Mr. Briscoe managed the estate generally, and incidentally borrowed money and bought land from Mr. Bright for which he executed promissory notes."

Accepting this general statement as substantially correct, still the record does not necessarily present a case of variance. Deceased's property consisted largely, if not entirely, in lands, in the handling of which the services of an attorney were essential. Whether all the services performed by plaintiff fell strictly within the designation of legal services, we think is not material. No assignment of error was made predicated upon objection to this testimony upon the ground of variance. The contract being verbal, it was not essential that it be proved in the exact language alleged. It was only necessary to allege a valid contract sufficiently clear in its terms to enable the court to determine what those terms were, and that the contract proved be of like clearness. In other words, eliminating every allegation not substantially supported by evidence and eliminating all proof not fairly alleged, if there be left sufficient evidence of a contract which meets the requirements of a contract which meets the requirements of the law, then the objection of variance between the allegations and the proof, arising, as it does, upon the sufficiency of the evidence to support the judgment, should be overruled.

[3, 4] The sufficiency of proof to meet the requirement that it should clearly and satisfactorily establish a contract which the courts can enforce is presented here only as a question of law. Conceding for the purposes of this case that the contract sought to be enforced falls within the rule requiring that its terms be proved clearly and satisfactorily and treating the question as one of law only, the evidence must be viewed most strongly in support of the trial court's judgment. The fact that the witnesses who testified may not have been disinterested, or may have made conflicting statements, or that their credibility may have been attacked, are matters with which it is not our province to deal. As we understand the rule contended for, it is not violated by objections to the evidence of this character. It only requires that the terms of the contract essential to recovery be supported by evidence sufficiently clear for the court to determine what those terms were without resorting to inference or conjecture. In this, as in every other class of cases that we now recall, the credibility of the witnesses and the weight to be given to their testimony are questions solely within the province of

the jury, subject, however, to be revised by the trial judge and the Court of Civil Appeals. The latter court might have reviewed the facts, set aside the verdict of the jury, and remanded the cause for further trial; but that court has not "sought to exercise its province in determining the facts and ordering the case remanded for another trial because of its difference with the jury on the facts," but has rendered judgment for defendant. Its ruling is therefore one purely upon a question of law—whether there be any evidence under the quantum of proof required which will support the jury's finding. Tweed v. Telegraph Co., 107 Tex. 255, 166 S. W. 696, 177 S. W. 957.

[7] We think the testimony of Mrs. Ray concerning the conversations which took place in her hearing between plaintiff and deceased was sufficiently clear and certain to meet the requirements of the rule invoked. She was not disqualified by law from testifying, and whatever doubt might be cast upon her testimony addressed itself to the jury as affecting her credibility. The testimony of witnesses whose testimony has been quoted were corroborative of Mrs. Ray, and the jury may have regarded the surrounding circumstances as affording further corroboration. The issue submitted to the jury, and answered by them in the affirmative, was:

"Did J. M. Bright, deceased, on May 28, 1914, in consideration of legal services rendered to said Bright prior to said time and in consideration of such services to be rendered to said Bright down to the time of his death by plaintiff, Jno. T. Briscoe, enter into and make an oral agreement with the said John T. Briscoe wherein the said Bright agreed that he would pay the said Briscoe for such legal services by canceling all notes and indebtedness owing by the said Briscoe to the said Bright at the time of his, the said Bright's decease?"

Our conclusion is that there was sufficient evidence under the rule contended for to support the finding embodied in that issue.

[8] With regard to the finding of the Court of Civil Appeals to the effect that the contract was procured by undue influence and was therefore nudum pactum, we think it only necessary to state that this issue was not submitted to the jury and no request for its submission was made. While it is true that plaintiff occupied toward deceased the relation of attorney, and this fact might require that the transaction be examined with more than ordinary scrutiny, nevertheless, the evidence does not present a case in which it could be held as a matter of law that the contract was unfair, that the deceased was overreached, or that undue influence or pressure was brought to bear upon him. So far as the record shows, deceased was in full possession of all his faculties and was entirely competent to make the contract. The

evidence will support a finding that he voluntarily made the contract without the exertion of any influence or persuasion. In fact, the evidence supports the inference that the deceased was anxious to make the contract in order that he might have the full benefit of the interest and income from his property during his life and not be required to pay his obligation to the plaintiff until his death.

We conclude that the judgment of the Court of Civil Appeals should be reversed and that of the district court affirmed.

PHILLIPS, C. J. The judgment recommended in the report of the Commission of Appeals is adopted, and will be entered as the judgment of the Supreme Court.

AMERICAN EXPRESS CO. et al. v. CHANDLER. (No. 243-3436.)

(Commission of Appeals of Texas, Section A. June 15, 1921.)

1. Master and servant ⊜301(1)—Railroad and express company liable for negligence of joint employee.

Where an express messenger handled baggage as well as express matter, and was paid by the express company, which, however, charged part of his remuneration against the railroad company, and would have discharged him at that company's request, both the express company and the railroad company are liable to an employee of the railroad company for injury caused by the negligence of the messenger in throwing a trunk out of a car, regardless of whether it was baggage or express.

2. Master and servant ⊜301(1)—Railroad not liable for negligence of express company's sole employee assisting joint employee.

Where express messengers who were in fact joint employees of the express company and the railroad company were assisted by a sole employee of the express company at a time when a trunk was thrown out of a car and injured an employee of the railroad company, an instruction allowing recovery against the railroad company though the trunk was thrown by the assistant, who was solely an employee of the express company, was improper.

3. Trial ⊜29(2)—Statement by court that he saw no benefit in so much medical testimony improper as comment on evidence.

In a personal injury action, a statement by the court that he saw no benefit in so much medical testimony offered by defendant held incompetent, as a comment on the evidence, in violation of Rev. St. art. 1971.

4. Appeal and error ⊜1046(5)—Comment by judge on weight of evidence held prejudicial.

In a personal injury action, where a medical witness testified to facts directly contradictory of plaintiff's case, a remark by the trial judge that he did not think so much medical testimony was beneficial, coupled with the further remark when defendant took bill of exceptions to call another doctor. and that he would give a second bill of exceptions, was prejudicial error, the remarks being a comment on the weight of the evidence, in violation of Rev. Laws, art. 1971 (Const. art. 1, § 15), notwithstanding in the charge the trial court admitted his error and withdrew the statement, for such remarks may well have influenced the jury.

Error to Court of Civil Appeals of Sixth Supreme Judicial District.

Action by Emmett L. Chandler against the American Express Company and another. On appeal by defendants, a judgment for plaintiff was affirmed by the Court of Civil Appeals (215 S. W. 364), and defendants bring error. Judgments of Court of Civil Appeals and of district court reversed, and cause remanded.

Smith, Robertson & Robertson and Chas. C. Huff, all of Dallas, and Dinsmore, McMahon & Dinsmore, of Greenville, for plaintiffs in error.

B. Q. Evans, of Greenville, and W. A. Shields, of Eastland, for defendant in error.

SPENCER, J. Defendant in error, Emmett Chandler, instituted this suit and recovered a joint and several judgment against plaintiffs in error, the American Express Company and the Missouri, Kansas & Texas Railway Company, of Texas, in the sum of $15,000, for personal injuries alleged to have been sustained by him. Upon appeal, the Court of Civil Appeals affirmed the judgment. 215 S. W. 364.

The facts briefly are that Chandler was employed as telegraph operator for the railway company at Winsboro. His duties also required him to assist in handling the baggage received and forwarded. His version of how the alleged injuries occurred is that, in returning from the east door of the combination baggage and express car, where it was his duty to deliver a pouch of mail, while passing the west door of the car a heavy trunk was thrown from the door, causing the injuries. At the east door baggage was loaded and unloaded, while express was handled from the west door. It was no part of his duties to assist with the express. It does not appear whether the trunk, which defendant in error testified struck him, was express or baggage. The railway company contends that if it was express matter it is not liable, while the express company, insists that it is not liable if the trunk was baggage.

[1] Upon the issue of joint liability, the uncontroverted evidence is that in May, 1915, the month in which the injury is alleged to have occurred, there was one man in charge of the baggage and express on the train, designated as a joint baggageman and express messenger, who performed duties for both companies. The express company paid his salary, and billed upon the railway company for 50 per cent. of it. The express company employed him, and had the power to discharge him. The express company would also have discharged him upon the request of the railway company.

Under these circumstances, if the joint employee negligently threw the trunk which it is alleged injured defendant in error, it is our opinion that both the express and the railway company are jointly and severally liable for the injury, regardless of whether the trunk was baggage or express. Moore v. Sou. Ry. Co., 165 N. C. 439, 81 S. E. 603, 51 L. R. A. (N. S.) 866.

[2] Ben Harper and Joe D. Adams were joint employees of plaintiffs in error. There is evidence in the record to the effect that Roy Thompson, an employee of the express company, was in the car on the occasion when it is claimed the trunk was thrown therefrom, assisting the joint employee with the loading and unloading of the express. The court charged the jury as follows:

"If you believe from the evidence that, on or about the time and at the place alleged in plaintiff's petition, while in the performance of his duties, plaintiff, Emmett L. Chandler, was passing a baggage or express truck of defendant, lined up by the side of a baggage and express car of the defendants, and that at the time plaintiff was passing said truck Ben Harper, Joe D. Adams, or his assistant, the joint agent or agents of the defendants, were attempting to unload a trunk from said car; and if you believe that the said agent or agents unloading said trunk, if it was being unloaded, knew that plaintiff was passing said truck, or in the exercise of ordinary care, as defined herein, should and would have known that plaintiff or some other person was likely to be so passing at said time; and if you believe from the evidence that at said time the said joint agent or agents of defendants negligently and carelessly and without warning to plaintiff so threw or unloaded said trunk from said car in such manner that it was caused to be and was propelled onto and over said truck and onto and against plaintiff, and thereby injuring plaintiff in any or all the ways alleged in his petition; and if you believe in so unloading said trunk, if it was so unloaded, the agent or agents of defendants were guilty of negligence as defined in paragraph 1 hereof, and that such negligence, if any, was the proximate cause of plaintiff's injuries, if any, then you will find for the plaintiff, unless you should find for defendants under subsequent paragraphs of this charge."

The court erred in authorizing a recovery against the railway company in the event the jury found the trunk was thrown by an assistant of Harper or Adams. Thompson was the only person mentioned in the record as being an assistant, and the uncontroverted evidence is that he was an employee of the express company solely, and in no sense an employee of the railway company. If, therefore, the jury should find that Thompson, acting alone, negligently threw the trunk that caused the alleged injury, the express company, and not the railway company, would be responsible therefor.

[3, 4] Plaintiffs in error assign error to certain remarks of the trial court made in the presence of the jury during the progress of the trial. The evidence of defendant in error tended to show that his injuries consisted in part of an impacted fracture of the socket of the hip bone. Plaintiffs in error introduced Dr. McBride as a witness, who testified in effect that such impacted fracture could not have resulted in the manner which defendant in error testified that his injuries were received. In other important particulars, he contradicted the testimony of the defendant in error. While upon the stand giving this testimony, he received an emergency call to attend a patient. Defendant in error's counsel stated to the court that they would waive cross-examination of the witness, but plaintiffs in error desired to continue their examination, stating that it would take much longer than five minutes to complete the examination. Following this remark by plaintiffs in error's counsel, the following remarks were made:

The Court: "They seem to be bent on using you, Doctor, and keeping you as long as they can. I will excuse you."

To which counsel for defendants replied: "I think the court is a little unkind to state we are bent on keeping him. I don't think that is correct."

To which the court replied: "In using so much time on these doctors I get tired of it; I don't know how you are; I don't think it is beneficial to have so much medical testimony."

To which counsel for defendants took a bill of exception, stating: "We except to the remarks of the court."

To which the court replied: "I will give you two of them; call another doctor, and let's have another one."

"At the close of the testimony of Dr. E. F. Wright, who followed next after Dr. A. D. McBride, the court made the following remarks: 'Before we go I want to make this statement to the jury: Upon second thought I conclude that I was in error about making a remark about the continuation of the testimony of Dr. McBride or any other of the doctors in a case of this kind; where the issue or question is a matter of injury, the parties have a right to introduce such doctors as they may desire, especially in a case like this, where there are a good many phases of the question. I don't desire any time to make an expression that would have any bearing one way or the other upon the facts of the case; therefore, I make that statement, because I recognize this is a case where testimony of that character is perfectly admissible.'"

That it was error for the court to make the comment that it did cannot be questioned. The trial court recognized that an error had been made, and undertook to correct it.

The only question presented therefore, is, Was the error cured by the instruction given?

In jury trials, our statute prohibits the trial judge from charging or commenting upon the weight of evidence. Article 1971. The right of trial by jury is a fundamental one guaranteed by the Bill of Rights. Const. art. 1, § 15. It was to protect this right that the statute was designed and enacted. The original statute, prohibiting comment by the trial court upon the weight of the evidence, was enacted by the first Legislature assembled under the first Constitution of Texas. Acts May 13, 1846, p. 390, § 99. It was not passed to strengthen the fundamental law, because it needed no added strength, but it was enacted in pursuance of and as an admonition to heed that law. A failure to obey the statute violates the Constitution. Not every comment by the court upon the weight of the evidence is reversible error. If the comment is upon the weight of evidence concerning a material issue, and is such as will probably influence the jury in its decision, such comment will operate to reverse the judgment.

The testimony of Dr. McBride struck at the very vitals of defendants in error's case. From the remarks of the court to the effect that he did not think so much medical testimony was beneficial, the jury may have concluded that the trial court excused the witness because the testimony was not beneficial. This may have impressed the jury that the trial court thought the testimony worthless. The court aggravated the error, when counsel excepted to the remarks, by stating that he would give them two bills of exceptions—to call another witness and get another bill. This last remark is susceptible of the construction, and may have conveyed to the minds of the jury, that the court did not think the testimony beneficial, and that he would give defendant in error a bill of exceptions instead of the testimony.

In view of what was said, it is impossible to determine the full extent of the prejudicial effect the comment may have had upon the minds of the jury, and we do not think that the error was cured by the court's subsequent comment that he did not want to influence the jury in the premises. It is true the court informed the jury that the testimony was perfectly admissible, but this did not suffice to cure the error. He had stated that he did not think so much medical testimony was beneficial. The testimony could have been admissible, and yet not beneficial. The gravamen of the error was in saying in the jury's presence that the testimony was not beneficial.

To determine whether the error has been cured by instructions withdrawing the comment is always one of serious import, and is made to depend upon the facts in each particular case. If a court may comment upon the weight of the evidence and thereafter withdraw such comment, the very purpose of the law may be circumvented, and the statute and Constitution rendered of no force and effect; and unless it can be said that in all probability the error was primarily harmless, or rendered so by the withdrawal of the comment, a reversal of the judgment will follow.

Defendant in error cites Sabine & E. T. Ry. Co. v. Brousard, 75 Tex. 597, 12 S. W. 1126, as sustaining their position that the remarks of the court was harmless error. The court in that case concluded that the remarks of the court were harmless when considered in connection with the evidence upon which the court commented. We cannot, in view of the evidence in the case at bar, reach this conclusion that the error was harmless.

We recommend, therefore, that the judgments of the Courts of Civil Appeals and of the district court be reversed, and the cause remanded for a new trial.

PHILLIPS, C. J. The judgment recommended in the report of the Commission of Appeals is adopted, and will be entered as the judgment of the Supreme Court.

We approve the holding of the Commission of Appeals on the questions discussed in its opinion.

PRAIRIE OIL & GAS CO. et al. v. STATE.
(No. 237–3424.)

(Commission of Appeals of Texas, Section B. June 15, 1921.)

1. Judgment ⟜702—Judgment in suits against persons licensed by the state to explore for oil not binding against the state.

Where the state was not a party to actions against those to whom it was given permits under Acts Reg. Sess. 35th Leg. (1917) c. 83 (Vernon's Ann. Civ. St. Supp. 1918, arts. 5904–5904w), to explore for oil on lands claimed to belong to the state, judgments rendered in suits against such licensees will not, under Rev. St. art. 5432, be binding against the state; hence a suit by the state to enjoin defendants, who had sued the licensees from drilling on the land involved, will not be dismissed on the theory that the state was bound by the judgment in previous suit.

2. Mines and minerals ⟜48—Oil is not subject of property except while in actual occupancy.

Petroleum oil, like water, is not subject of property except while in actual occupancy, and a grant of either water or oil is not a grant of the soil, or of anything for which ejectment will lie.

3. Mines and minerals ⟜52—Landowner will not be enjoined from drilling on his own property on the theory that it would draw oil from adjacent lands.

Where defendant, who asserted rights in oil lands claimed by the state, secured a tem-

porary injunction restraining licensees from proceeding with operation, the state is not entitled to a temporary injunction restraining defendant from drilling wells on the lines between its own lands and those in controversy on the theory such wells would drain oil from under the lands in controversy, but the state should seek relief from the court's granting the first injunction, for, while oil belongs to the owner of the lands, and is part thereof, yet, when it escapes and comes into the control of another, the title of the first person is gone.

Error to Court of Civil Appeals of Third Supreme Judicial District.

Suit by the State of Texas against the Prairie Oil & Gas Company and others. An order granting temporary injunction was modified and affirmed by the Court of Civil Appeals (214 S. W. 363), and defendants bring error. Modified.

W. J. Oxford, of Fort Worth, Chandler & Pannell, of Stephenville, Vinson, Elkins & Wood, of Houston, and Brooks, Hart & Woodward, of Austin, for appellants.

C. M. Cureton, Atty. Gen., and W. J. Townsend, W. A. Keeling, and W. F. Schenck, Asst. Attys. Gen., for the State.

KITTRELL, J. The facts out of which the litigation in this case arose are, so far as it is necessary to set them forth, as follows:

1. The state issued a permit to one Hodges and another permit to one Collett to explore for oil and gas on certain small areas of land within carefully defined boundaries, in Eastland county, which land the state claimed to be parts of the vacant and unappropriated public domain. The permits were issued pursuant to the provisions of chapter 83 of the Acts of the Regular Session of the Thirty-Fifth Legislature (Vernon's Ann. Civ. St. Supp. 1918, arts. 5904–5904w).

2. The permittees went on the land, and Collett or his assignee, the Gulf Production Company, developed oil, and Hodges or his assignees penetrated nearly to the oil sands.

3. In October, 1918, plaintiffs in error here filed two suits in the district court of Eastland county in the ordinary form of trespass to try title, one of which was against Hodges and his assignees, and one against the Gulf Production Company, assignee of Collett.

4. In the first-named case an injunction was issued restraining the defendants from drilling on the land described in the permit issued to Hodges, and the defendants in that case appealed to the Court of Civil Appeals at El Paso, where the appeal was pending when the state filed its action in the instant case in the district court of Travis county. An injunction was refused in the second case, but it stands for trial on the merits in the district court of Eastland county.

5. On January 29, 1919, the state of Texas filed in the district court of Travis county its

action against the plaintiffs in the two suits in Eastland county, alleging that it was the owner of the legal and equitable title to the land in Eastland county on which it had issued the permits above referred to, and on which its permittees were drilling for oil, and set up the filing of the two suits against its permittees as above set forth, and alleged that injunction had issued against one of its permittees, while the plaintiffs in the Eastland county suits were drilling on their land adjoining that of the state, and that unless restrained they would draw out all the oil under the state's land; and that the state was not a party to the suits in Eastland county, and had not given her consent to be sued therein, and could not be bound by any judgment rendered in these suits; but that its title was clouded thereby, and it would suffer irreparable injury if the defendants were permitted to continue drilling for oil on their own land, while the state's permittees were restrained from drilling on land covered by the state's permit.

6. On an ex parte hearing, and without notice to defendants in the instant case, the district court of Travis county issued its injunction restraining defendants (plaintiffs in error here) both from drilling on their own land and from prosecuting the two suits brought by them in Eastland county.

7. The Court of Civil Appeals for the Third District held the state was not, under the terms and provisions of article 5432, Revised Statutes, a party to the suits in Eastland county, and could not be bound by any judgment rendered therein, and reversed the judgment of the district court in so far as it enjoined the prosecution of the Eastland county suits, but affirmed the judgment of that court in so far as it enjoined the defendants (plaintiffs in error here) from drilling on their own land adjoining the land on which the state had issued permits to Hodges and Collett.

The contention of appellants in the Court of Civil Appeals (plaintiffs in error here) was that the state had to all intents and purposes sold the land, and that the permits issued, taken in connection with the provisions of article 5432, had the effect to make the state a party to the Eastland county suits, and that it would be concluded by any judgment rendered therein because it had by the terms of article 5432 authorized suit against it in Eastland county; hence the suits in Eastland county and the suit filed in Travis county (out of which this appeal arose) were between the same parties with reference to the same subject-matter, and seeking the same relief; therefore the district court of Eastland county, a court of equal and co-ordinate constitutional jurisdiction with that of Travis county, having first obtained jurisdiction, had the right to hold and exercise the same without interference on the

231 S.W.—69

part of any other court of the same jurisdiction.

The Court of Civil Appeals overruled the above-summarized contention, and held that the case is not "within the purview" of article 5432, by which we understand is meant that the state is not, by virtue of that article, a party to the suits in Eastland county to the extent that it will be bound by any decree rendered therein. Article 5432, or at least that part of the same which was construed by the Court of Civil Appeals, reads as follows:

"When any land, lying between older surveys, is held by the Commissioner of the General Land Office to be unsurveyed or vacant land appropriated to the public school fund by the Act of February 23, 1900, and is sold as such under the provisions of this chapter, and thereafter any suit arises between the owner or owners of such older surveys, and the purchaser from the state or his vendees, any final judgment rendered in such suit shall be deemed and held conclusive as to the existence or nonexistence of such vacancy; provided, if in any suit judgment is obtained through collusion or fraud against the state, the same may be set aside and vacated at the suit of the state any time within five years thereafter."

In order that the concrete question presented may be clearly understood, we will set forth the propositions stated by plaintiffs in their application for the writ:

First. The suits in the district court of Eastland county and the suit in the district court of Travis county are in reality between the same parties, with reference to the same matter, and seeking the same relief.

Second. The state has authorized the institution against it of the suits pending in the district court of Eastland county, Tex.

The above propositions are stated under its first assignment of error. The following proposition is stated under the third and fourth assignments of error.

"The court erred in enjoining the appellants from drilling wells on their own land along the line of the land claimed by the state and from taking oil from the wells so drilled on their own land, because the state of Texas does not own the oil beneath the land in dispute, even if it owns said land, until it shall have reduced such oil to possession, and the appellants have a right to drill upon their own land and to take from the well so drilled oil and gas, even though by so doing they draw same from under the land claimed and owned by the state."

The state, defendant in error, states the following counter proposition to all the above propositions of plaintiffs in error, since, as it alleges, all of them embrace the same question of law:

"The suits described pending in the district court of Eastland county were between different parties, and not between parties to this suit; the state was not a party defendant or plaintiff in the suits in Eastland county, and the district court of Eastland county in neither of said cases attempted to, nor could, obtain jurisdiction of the state of Texas without consent of the Legislature, which has not been granted; that the subject-matter of the suits in Eastland county was not, and could not be, the state's title to the lands described in said suits, nor the lands described in this proceeding, and no judgment or decree rendered in either of said suits could conclude or be binding upon the state, the plaintiff in this action; therefore the district court of Eastland county never acquired jurisdiction over the subject-matter of this action, nor over the parties to this suit, and the district court of Travis county in this action alone has jurisdiction of the parties and subject-matter of the suit, and alone is capable of rendering a decree binding alike on all parties claiming an interest in the lands in controversy."

It is obvious that the propositions and counter propositions above quoted present clear-cut, acute, interesting, and important questions. We will address ourselves first to the first and second propositions of plaintiffs in error, and whether these propositions are sound depends upon the construction of article 5432, Revised Statutes.

It is evident that the state claims that the land upon which it had issued permits was vacant and unappropriated public domain, while the actions brought by the plaintiffs in the Eastland county suits (plaintiffs in error here) are based on the assertion that they own the land; hence it is not vacant.

The inevitable conclusion to be drawn from such a state of facts is that a question of boundary is involved, and that it is sought to determine the question by actions of trespass to try title; indeed, the state, in its petition in the instant case, states in connection with its allegations as to the land on which Hodges was issued a permit that "the real and fundamental matter in controversy in this suit is the title of this plaintiff to the lands herein described, and the lands embraced in this petition"; and, as to the land on which a permit was issued to Collett, it alleges "that in determining the issues in said case it will be necessary for the court to determine the title to the land described in said petition."

In paragraph IV of its petition the state alleges that the land—

"is chiefly valuable as a mineral property, and for the development of oil and gas, and petroleum oil and gas is being produced in large quantities in the immediate vicinity of said lands."

[1] The argument of plaintiffs in error upon the construction of article 5432 is very ingenious and persuasive, but we are of the opinion that the Court of Civil Appeals correctly determined the question. It is clear that the state has not "sold" the land, but has only granted a permit to certain parties to explore it for oil and gas, and, if certain results be obtained, by operation of the stat-ute the permit will eventuate into a lease of indefinite duration, yet the state has issued no patent or other muniment of title to the fee in the land.

The language of the statute is "is sold," not "is leased." As Chief Justice Key very aptly says:

"The statute is, by its own terms, limited to judgments rendered in suits between the owners of older surveys and *purchasers* [italics ours] from the state."

A "lessee" or "permittee" cannot be said to be in legal meaning a "purchaser."

The plaintiffs in the actions in Eastland county asserted that they owned title to land which the state claimed to own, and the title to which it had in nowise parted with. In other words, it had not "sold"; therefore it was not a party to these actions, because its permittees were sued for land as to which they had only a permissive right for a certain purpose. The recital in the state's petition that the land is "chiefly valuable for the minerals and oil and gas" conveys the implication that it had yet other value, separate and apart from the substance under the surface, the right to explore for which it had for a consideration granted to its permittees. The permit with the accompanying right to lease in event of development of oil or gas conclusively implies that it retained the title to the land itself.

[2] The language of Mr. Gould in his work on Waters (2d Ed.) § 291, quoted by Justice White in Ohio Oil Co. v. Indiana, 177 U. S. 190, 20 Sup. Ct. 576, 44 L. Ed. 729, which case is hereinafter cited, is very apposite in this connection:

"Petroleum, oil, * * * like water, * * * is not the subject of property, except while in actual occupancy, and a grant of either water or oil is not a grant of the soil or of anything for which ejectment will lie."

The state is not in a legal sense a party to these actions; therefore, cannot be bound by any judgment entered therein; therefore had the right to assert its title in another action, as the suits in Eastland county and the instant case are not between the same parties, and we know of no law requiring the state to intervene in any action in which the right of its permittees or lessees are involved. Though it might have elected to intervene, it could not be made a party without its own consent.

[3] We come next to consideration of the proposition of plaintiffs in error stated under their third and four assignments, to the effect that the district court erred in enjoining plaintiffs in the suits in Eastland county (defendants in the court below in this action) in drilling for oil on their own land, and that the Court of Civil Appeals erred in affirming such judgment. The question has never been directly before a Texas appellate court so far as our examination of authorities has

revealed, except in the case of Hermann v. Thomas (Civ. App.) 143 S. W. 195. It was held in that case· that Hermann could not be prevented from drilling for oil on his own land lying south of and adjoining land to which both he and Thomas claimed title. That, if the result of Hermann drilling on his own land would be that it would draw oil from under the land which Thomas claimed to own, that fact gave Thomas no right of action against Hermann.

In the case of H. & T. C. Ry. Co. v. East, 98 Tex. 146, 81 S. W. 279, 66 L. R. A. 738, 107 Am. St. Rep. 620, 4 Ann. Cas. 827, it was held that the railroad company had the right to bore a well on its own property and use the water for its own purposes, and the fact that the operation of the well decreased, or even exhausted, the water in the well of East gave East no right of action for damages.

In Brown v. Spilman, 155 U. S. 665, 15 Sup. Ct. 245, 39 L. Ed. 304, it is said:

"Petroleum gas and oil are substances of a peculiar character. * * * They belong to the owner of the land, and are part of it, so long as they are on it or in it, or subject to his control, but when they escape and go into other land, or come under another's control, the title of the former owner is gone. If an adjoining owner drills his land and taps a deposit of oil or gas, extending under his neighbor's field, so that it comes into his well, it becomes his property."

In the case of Hague v. Wheeler, 157 Pa. 324, 27 Atl. 714, 22 L. R. A. 141, 37 Am. St. Rep. 736, it is held that the owner of a gas well bored on his own land who did not utilize the gas could not be enjoined, at the suit of another landowner who had a gas well on his land, on the ground that the escape of gas was an injury to the latter. In Jones v. Forest Oil Co., 194 Pa. 379, 44 Atl. 1074, 48 L. R. A. 748, it is held that a landowner could not be enjoined from using a gas pump to increase the flow of gas in his well, on the ground that oil would be drawn from under plaintiff's land.

Neither party to the record has cited the case of Texas Co. v. Daugherty et al., 107 Tex. 226, 176 S. W. 717, L. R. A. 1917F, 989, in which the nature and extent of property rights in oil and gas is ably and exhaustively discussed by Chief Justice Phillips, but we have carefully examined that case, and the conclusion we have reached is intended to be, and we believe is, in entire harmony with the holding therein.

If we correctly construe the holding in that case, it is that the conveyance of "all the oil, gas, coal, and other minerals in and under" land with the right to enter and mine for same, with the habendum clause, and with the recital that the instrument was not intended as a mere franchise, but as a conveyance of the property, but conditioning the conveyance upon the commencement of operation within a certain time, operated to convey a defeasible title in fee to the oil and gas, which was taxable as an interest in the land against the grantee. While, as is said in that case—

"The conveyance of [oil and gas] in place, with a right to the use of the land for their extraction from the earth which may prove, under the instrument, of unlimited duration, creates a freehold interest in the land itself."

Yet it does not appear to us to follow that a landowner can be legally prevented from drilling on his own land lest he draw oil from under adjoining land, since it is the fugitive character of oil which qualifies the title to it, and puts upon the owner of the soil the risk of its flowing from under or being drawn from under the land before he can or has reduced it to possession, and consequent absolute ownership. We are of the opinion that the injunction preventing the plaintiffs in error from drilling on their own land was improperly issued.

It is urged that the permittees of the state are enjoined from drilling on the land claimed to be owned by the state; but it must be assumed that before injunction issued the bond required by statute for the protection of the defendants in the suit in Eastland county was given. If it was not, and the rights of the state, if any it has, are imperiled, it can invoke the equitable powers of the district court of Eastland county for its protection. It will not be contended that, if no action had been instituted by the plaintiffs in the Eastland county cases, the state or its permittees could have enjoined them from drilling on their own lands, and the rule of law has not been changed, because the Eastland county plaintiffs claim that land occupied by the state's permittees is not vacant, but is their land, and have in pursuance of that claim taken legal action to recover the property, and invoked the equitable power of the district court of Eastland county to prevent injury to their rights.

We recommend that the judgment of the Court of Civil Appeals, in so far as it reversed the judgment of the district court enjoining the prosecution of the Eastland county suits, be affirmed, and that, in so far as it affirmed the judgment of the district court enjoining the plaintiffs in error from drilling on their land, it be reversed, and that judgment be here rendered dissolving the injunction.

PHILLIPS, C. J. The judgment recommended in the report of the Commission of Appeals is adopted, and will be entered as the judgment of the Supreme Court.

SCHELLER et al. v. GROESBECK et al.
(No. 242–3435.)

(Commission of Appeals of Texas, Section B. June 15, 1921.)

1. **Deeds ⊜⇒93—Cardinal ruling of construction is to ascertain parties' intent.**

The cardinal rule for construction of a written instrument as a deed is to arrive at the intention of the parties.

2. **Deeds ⊜⇒97—All parts should be given effect, if possible.**

All parts of deeds should be given effect, if possible.

3. **Deeds ⊜⇒111—General description yields to particular description.**

Where a particular description in a deed is followed by a general description, the latter yields, but, where it is possible, the real intention must be gathered from whole description, including the general as well as special.

4. **Deeds ⊜⇒112(1) — All instruments in a chain of title when referred to will be read into deeds.**

All instruments in a chain of title when referred to in a deed will be read into it.

5. **Evidence ⊜⇒461(3)—Where deed is clear, parol evidence is inadmissible to show intention.**

Where the description in a deed is plain, clear, and unambiguous, parol evidence is inadmissible to show that it was intended by the parties to convey land not described.

6. **Deeds ⊜⇒112(1)—Conveyance of league of land held not to embrace labor.**

Where the grantor owned a league of land lying in Jasper county and labor of land lying in Liberty county, though it was supposed that they both lay in the latter county, a deed reciting a sale of a league of land lying in county of Liberty which referred to previous conveyances wherein the league and labor were referred to as the league and C. survey did not, though the grantee later attempted to convey both parcels of land, include the labor, on the theory that such conveyance by the grantee, coupled with the fact that that grantor did not thereafter assert any right to the labor, shqwed an intention to pass both parcels.

Error to Court of Civil Appeals of Ninth Supreme Judicial District.

Action by J. N. Groesbeck and others against L. Scheller and others, in which George M. Coale was impleaded, and Katherine Wolf subsequently was made a defendant. A judgment for plaintiffs against Scheller and Wolf and in favor of the named defendants against defendant Coale on his covenant of warranty was affirmed by the Court of Civil Appeals (215 S. W. 353), and defendant Scheller and others bring error. Judgments of district court and Court of Civil Appeals reversed, and judgment rendered for defendants.

W. R. Blain and Oswald S. Parker, both of Beaumont, for plaintiffs in error.

E. B. Pickett, Jr., of Liberty, for defendants in error.

KITTRELL, J. The sole question to be determined in this case is whether a deed executed January 30, 1842, by John H. Walton to Lent M. Hitchcock, Jr., for "a league of land, the said league of land being the same that was granted to," etc., operated so as to convey a "labor" of land surveyed coincident with the survey of the league, incorporated in the same Mexican grant, and both believed to have been in the same county (Liberty), and both so described and dealt with, though, as was subsequently developed, the league is in fact in Jasper county.

The chain of title begins with a grant (the original of which was offered in evidence) made to Salvador Castillo November 6, 1835, in which the land conveyed is described as "lying 1½ miles south of the road leading from the town of Liberty to the village of Beaumont, about 12 miles from Liberty," and then a description is given by the beginning corner and the other corners of a survey 1,-000 varas square "thus forming one labor of land," then immediately following, with the interposition only of a comma, is the language, "completed afterwards the survey of one league of land for the same Salvador Castillo, which league of land is situated near the Neches river 10 miles from Grant's Bluff," then follows complete field notes of a survey 5,000 varas square, or one league.

By a regular chain of conveyances (not necessary to be set forth in detail), beginning with a deed from Castillo to John K. Allen of date August 27, 1836, and ending with a conveyance to John H. Walton of date January 26, 1842, there being exclusive of the original grant six conveyances, the title to the league and the labor passed into John H. Walton.

The description in all the conveyances was practically the same except that in the sixth instrument in the chain part of the description is "known as the Castillo league." By that deed the league and labor was conveyed to John H. Walton and William Turner.

In the next or seventh instrument by which William Turner conveyed his undivided half of "one league and labor" to John H. Walton part of the description is, "known as the Castillo survey." In each conveyance reference is made back to the preceding conveyances and to the record thereof in Liberty county for more particular description. The deed from John H. Walton to Hitchcock bears date January 28, 1842, and the description therein is as follows:

"A league of land lying and being in the county of Liberty in said republic, the said league of land being the same that was granted to Salvador Castillo by the state of Coahuila and Texas."

Then is given the name of the commissioner by whom "title of possession" was executed, then follows a detailed list in consecutive order of all prior conveyances, all of which were referred to "for the boundaries and a fuller description of said land."

On August 2, 1845, Hitchcock made a deed to John D. Groesbeck, ancestor of defendants in error, describing the land conveyed thereby as "one league and labor of land lying and being in the county of Liberty, republic aforesaid," etc., then follows substantially the same description as in preceding deeds, except that the detailed list of preceding conveyances contains that of Walton to Hitchcock, and the reference back to all preceding deeds is made, as was done in preceding conveyances.

If the deed from Walton to Hitchcock conveyed the labor, then by the deed of date August 2, 1845, made by Hitchcock complete title to the "league and labor passed into John D. Groesbeck, and later by inheritance into defendants in error, as to whose heirship no question is raised. The litigation between the parties to the record arose in the following way: Acting evidently upon the belief that according to the record John H. Walton had never conveyed the labor, his heirs, through an agent and attorney in fact, conveyed the labor to George M. Coale on October 22, 1903, for a consideration of $885, which was paid by Coale, according to the terms of the deed to him.

On the same day that Coale bought (October 22, 1903) he conveyed the labor to plaintiff in error L. Scheller for a consideration of $1,150 partly in cash and partly on credit, and Scheller paid in full, and received a release of the lien. When Scheller bought he had the title to the labor examined by competent attorneys, and had no notice of any adverse claim, since no person was occupying the land, and he went on it before he bought it, and a year after he bought it he put a house on it.

On March 6, 1916, defendants in error instituted suit for title and possession of the labor against Scheller, who impleaded Coale as his warrantor. The trial court rendered judgment in favor of plaintiffs for the land against Scheller, and awarded Scheller judgment over against Coale, his warrantor. The Court of Civil Appeals of the Ninth District affirmed that judgment (215 S. W. 353).

As we have stated in the opening paragraph of this opinion, the single and concrete question to be determined is: Did the labor pass by the deed from Walton to Hitchcock? If it did, then defendants in error were and are entitled to the judgment recovered, and the affirmance of that judgment was correct. If the title to the labor did not pass by the deed from Walton to Hitchcock,

the judgment recovered and affirmed was erroneous.

We have examined every case cited by both parties and have found no material conflict of authorities. The counsel do not materially disagree as to the rules of law, but differ as to their application to the facts.

[1-4] That in the construction of written instruments the cardinal rule to be followed is to arrive at the intention of the parties and that all parts of a deed shall be given effect if possible, and where there is a particular description followed by general description the latter shall yield, though where it is possible the real intent must be gathered from the whole description, including the general, as well as the special, and that all instruments in a chain of title when referred to in a deed will be read into it, are all rules of law so familiar that citation of authorities is unnecessary.

[5] It is equally well settled that, where the description in a deed is plain, clear, and unambiguous, parol evidence is inadmissible to show that it was intended by the parties to convey land not described in the deed.

In Davis v. George, 104 Tex. 108, 134 S. W. 326, 328, appellees contended that they were entitled to introduce parol proof to show that, where a deed called to begin at the northeast corner of a certain tract, the grantor meant the southeast corner. If their contention had prevailed, 10 acres on the south instead of 10 acres on the north would have been held to pass by the deed.

Answering a certified question, Justice Williams said:

"Parol evidence, whether brought by parties or strangers, cannot make it [a deed] convey land which it does not purport to convey, nor prevent it from conveying that which it clearly purports to convey."

"It is too well settled to admit of doubt that such a deed cannot be collaterally attacked by the parties to it, or their privies, by evidence tending to show an intention different from that which its language unmistakably expresses. * * * If it were admitted that Grimwell intended to convey the lower 10 acres, * * * that intention could not effect such conveyance nor prevent the deed, unless corrected in some proper way, from standing as the legal conveyance of the land described in it. A contrary decision would virtually repeal the statutes regulating the conveyance of lands."

The following earlier cases were followed in Davis v. George: Farley v. Deslonde, 69 Tex. 461, 6 S. W. 786; Watts v. Howard, 77 Tex. 88, 13 S. W. 966—and the holding in Davis v. George has never been departed from, but is cited as controlling authority in the case of Browne v. Gorman, 208 S. W. 387, in which case writ of error was denied.

[6] In that case it was held that, where the grantor owned survey No. 425, but described by his deed adjoining survey No. 426 located by virtue of the same certificate,

which latter survey he did not own, parol testimony was inadmissible to show that No. 425 was meant to be conveyed.

It is manifest that both the league and labor passed by all the conveyances down to and including the last made to John H. Walton; and it is equally as clear that Walton conveyed only a league of land, the said land being the same league, etc.

It will be observed that the land is not referred to as the "Castillo survey" or the "Castillo league," nor does the deed purport to convey all the land owned by him in Liberty county, or all the land described in the deeds from Castillo to Allen, or all the land described in the subsequent deeds, but the description is limited to a league that was granted to Castillo, etc. As was said in Schaffer v. Heidenheimer, 43 Tex. 'Civ. App. 366, 96 S. W. 61, in which appellants made practically the same contention as defendants in error make here, "It was the same land, but not all of it."

The only language in the deed from Walton to Hitchcock by which any particular land can be identified as the subject of the conveyance is that which describes the land conveyed as a league of land in Liberty county, being the league granted by Coahuila and Texas to Salvador Castillo, with additional reference to previous deeds by which it had been conveyed.

This being true, that deed could not be interpreted as conveying land other than the league referred to. There is no ambiguity in the deed itself, nor does any ambiguity arise when the deed is applied to the subject-matter of the conveyance. There is, therefore, no room for construction or for the admission of explanatory parol testimony.

The fact that the grantee of Walton afterwards conveyed more land than he acquired under the deed from his grantor could not have the effect of divesting out of the latter title to land which he had not conveyed.

Much stress is laid by defendants in error on the reference back for description. When we go back, as we must, to the original grant, we find the labor first specifically described as "a labor" and find next, in like manner, the "league" described.

In Powers v. Minor, 87 Tex. 83, 26 S. W. 1071, it was said concerning the terms "headright" and "bounty" "the difference is well understood in this state," so we can say here that the term "league" and the term "labor" are well understood in Texas, and when conveyance of a "league" in clear unambiguous terms is made by careful description, limiting the conveyance to a "league," the instrument cannot be held to convey a separately surveyed and described labor. When the description was of a league conveyed by certain preceding deeds, the description of the "league" as found in the grant was read into the deed from Walton

to Hitchcock, and the general reference back to preceding conveyances did not extend the effect of the deed beyond the limits of the "league." The reference back must be held to apply to the "league" as described in the original grant.

In the case of Cullers v. Platt, 81 Tex. 258, 16 S. W. 1003, there was a particular description by metes and bounds, followed by a general description, "being all of said survey except 140 acres," etc. Appellant claimed that his grantor received title to the strip of land in controversy under the general description, and the extent of the land conveyed was not limited by the particular description, but his contention was overruled. It is said in the opinion:

"Where a grantor conveys specially by metes and bounds, so there can be no controversy about what land is included and really conveyed, a general description as of all of a certain tract conveyed to him by another person, or, as in this case, all of a survey except a tract belonging to another person, cannot control, for there is a specific and particular description about which there can be no mistake and no necessity for invoking the aid of the general description. * * *

"A general description may be looked to in aid of a particular description that is defective or doubtful, but not to * * * override a particular description about which there can be no doubt. There can be no doubt what land was conveyed, whatever he may have intended to convey."' 81 Tex. 264, 16 S. W. 1005.

All the authorities, both from text-books and from the Texas Reports, cited by counsel for defendants in error, are applicable to cases where it is permissible to prove intention of parties in making a deed. Necessity for such proof exists only where the terms of the deed are not clear, and proof outside the deed is therefore necessary to identify the subject of the conveyance. They have no application where the deed is clear and unambiguous in its terms, as is the deed under consideration in the instant case.

It is earnestly contended that the intention of Walton and the belief of Hitchcock is shown by the fact that Walton never after he made the deed asserted any right to the land, and that Hitchcock conveyed the league and labor, which shows that they interpreted the instrument as conveying the labor, and much stress is laid on the fact that defendants in error were in possession of all the original title papers.

Undoubtedly those facts are very persuasive in indicating Walton's intention, and the belief of Hitchcock and Groesbeck, but neither the intention of the one nor the belief of the others can change the legal meaning of plain language, or be perpetuated as notice by record.

It is said in Farley v. Deslonde, supra, that the vendees in the chain of deeds in the absence of any knowledge of mistake in description, if there was any, had the right to rely on the description contained in the deeds through which they claimed. So it can be said here that those claiming under the Walton heirs relied upon the advice of competent counsel as to the meaning and effect of the deed from Walton to Hitchcock, and neither the intention of Walton nor the belief of Hitchcock can change its meaning or effect. What Walton did, not what he intended to do, must control the situation. If this were not true, the effect would be, as Justice Williams says in Davis v. George, supra, "to virtually repeal the statutes regulating the conveyance of lands."

The following further language quoted from the opinion in the same case is most apposite in this connection:

"If the agreement between Grimmell and Kinkler, of their intention, as a mere fact, apart from the question as to the legal effect of the deed, were important to any inquiry in the case, the deed would not be the exclusive evidence of such agreement or intention; but when the question is, what land did the deed convey? its legal effect between the parties is the very test invoked, and it must therefore answer the inquiry by its own terms, since no land was conveyed except by it, and it conveys no land except that which by its terms it undertook to convey."

In Yarbrough v. Clarkson, 155 S. W. 955, it is said:

"The description in the deed being definite and certain, it was not permissible to show by parol that other land than that described was intended to be conveyed. Davis v. George [supra]. It is only in a suit to correct a deed on the ground of fraud or mutual mistake that its terms can be varied or contradicted by parol evidence."

It appears to us to be very significant that, though every conveyance in the chain of title down to Walton specified distinctly a "league and labor," yet he not only in clear unambiguous language specified a league of land, but added "the said league of land being the same," etc.

It is also significant that, while every instrument in the chain of title down to the deed from Hitchcock to Groesbeck was recorded in Jasper county in November, 1856, that deed was not filed for record in Liberty county until January, 1877, though the labor lies in that county.

In Culler v. Platt, supra, it is said:

"Purinton did not convey the land to Collins, and consequently the latter did not convey it to * * * Cullers" (appellant).

So in this case it must be said that Walton never conveyed the labor to Hitchcock; therefore Hitchcock could not have conveyed it, and did not convey it to Groesbeck. This being true, defendants in error had no title to it.

We therefore recommend that the judgment of the district court and Court of Civil Appeals be reversed, and judgment be here rendered for plaintiffs in error.

PHILLIPS, C. J. The judgment recommended in the report of the Commission of Appeals is adopted and will be entered as the judgment of the Supreme Court.

JACKSON v. STATE. (No. 6338.)

(Court of Criminal Appeals of Texas. June 8, 1921.)

Banks and banking ⊜21—Debtor held not guilty of issuing check intended to circulate as money.

Where debtor gave creditor a check without sufficient funds in the bank, went to the bank the following morning to make a deposit to meet the check, but on hearing that the check had been turned over to officers, took the money directly to the creditor and paid him, instead of depositing it in the bank, he was not guilty of issuing a check intended to circulate as money, in violation of Pen. Code 1911, art 514, in the absence of evidence that check war issued to creditor for any other purpose than to pay debt.

Appeal from County Court, Harrison County; W. H. Strength, Judge.

L. A. Jackson was convicted of unlawfully issuing a check intended to circulate as money, and he appeals. Reversed, and prosecution ordered dismissed.

W. B. Lea, of Marshall, for appellant.
R. H. Hamilton, Asst. Atty. Gen., for the State.

HAWKINS, J. The record in this case presents a novel situation, to say the least. Appellant was prosecuted and convicted under an information as follows:

"Now comes F. M. Scott, county attorney of Harrison county, Texas, upon affidavit of Ellis Johnson, hereto attached and made a part hereof, and in behalf of said state presents in the county court of Harrison county, Texas, at the September term, 1920, of said court, that L. A. Jackson, on or about the 18th day of October, 1920, in the county of Harrison and state of Texas, and before the making and filing of this information, did then and there, in the county and state aforesaid, unlawfully issue a check intended to circulate as money, the same being as follows to wit:

" 'Marshall, Tex. Oct. 18, 1920.

" 'The Marshall National Bank (88–46) of Marshall, Texas: Pay to A. A. Gorrell or order bearer $2.57 Two and 57/100 dollars.

" 'L. A. Jackson.'

—against the peace and dignity of the State.
" 'F. M. Scott,
"County Attorney, Harrison County, Texas."

Appellant was convicted and fined $10.

The prosecution in this case seems to have proceeded under article 514 (868) P. C., which is as follows:

."If any person within this state shall issue any bill, promissory note, check or other paper * * * to circulate as money, he shall be fined not less than $10, nor more than $50 for each bill, promissory note, check or other paper so issued."

The undisputed evidence shows that on October 18, 1920, appellant owed the mercantile establishment of A. A. Gorrell in the city of Marshall an account amounting to $2.57. He gave the check in question in payment of the account. Gorrell claimed that appellant told him he had the money in the bank to cover the check. Appellant claimed that he told him he did not know whether he had sufficient funds to cover the check or not, but that he would make a deposit the next morning sufficient to cover it. The check was presented to the bank, and payment refused, because there were not sufficient funds. Appellant claims to have gone to the bank the next morning to make the deposit, but found the check had been turned over to the officers, and instead of making the deposit took the money and paid Gorrell. This is practically all the evidence in the case.

There is not one line of testimony in the record which would indicate that the check was issued by Jackson for any other purpose than checks are ordinarily issued, to wit, to pay a debt, and on what theory the prosecution proceeded, under the statute in question, to charge him with issuing a check with the intention that it should circulate as money, is more than we have been able to ascertain from the record.

The judgment of the trial court is reversed, and the prosecution ordered dismissed, so far as this information is concerned.

SMITH v. STATE. (No. 6331.)

(Court of Criminal Appeals of Texas. June 8, 1921.)

Criminal law ⟐1094—Judgment affirmed, in absence of bill of exceptions or statement of fact.

A conviction will be affirmed, where there appears in the record neither bill of exceptions nor statement of facts, and the indictment and the charge are in conformity with the law.

Appeal from Criminal District Court, Dallas County; C. A. Pippen, Judge.

Bill Smith was convicted of theft, and appeals. Affirmed.

R. H. Hamilton, Asst. Atty. Gen., for the State.

LATTIMORE, J. Appellant was convicted in the criminal district court of Dallas county of the offense of theft, and his punishment fixed at confinement in the state penitentiary for a term of five years.

There appears in the record neither bills of exceptions nor statement of facts. We have examined the indictment and the charge of the court, and, finding same in conformity with the law, the judgment of the lower court will be affirmed.

VOGEL v. STATE. (No. 6330.)

(Court of Criminal Appeals of Texas. June 8, 1921.)

Criminal law ⟐1159(2) — Judgment not reversed for insufficiency of evidence, unless against great weight of testimony.

Court of Criminal Appeals will not reverse a case because of insufficiency of testimony, unless it appears that the judgment is without support, or is so manifestly against the great weight of the testimony as to make probable the fact of a verdict resulting from prejudice.

Appeal from Guadalupe County Court; J. B. Williams, Judge.

Oscar Vogel was convicted of killing a cow with intent to injure its owner, and he appeals. Affirmed.

Dibrell & Mosheim, of Seguin, for appellant.

R. H. Hamilton, Asst. Atty. Gen., for the State.

LATTIMORE, J. Appellant was convicted in the county court of Guadalupe county of the offense of killing a cow with intent to injure the owner, and his punishment fixed at a fine of $10.

No bill of exceptions appears in the record, either as to the charge of the lower court, or any other matter that occurred during the trial. The only contention made in this court is that the evidence does not support the verdict. We have carefully examined the statement of facts, and conclude therefrom that, while the appellant and his wife testified to some actions on the part of the animal killed by him from which the jury might have concluded there was some reason for him to take the life of said cow, there is also evidence in the record sustaining the state's contention that the cow in question was gentle, and that appellant's act in killing her was not the result of any need or desire to protect his life or his property, but was the result of willfulness.

In order to justify us in reversing a case

because of the insufficiency of the testimony, it must appear to us that the judgment is without support, or is so manifestly against the great weight of the testimony as to make probable the fact of a verdict resulting from prejudice. We are not able to come to any such conclusion concerning this case, and the judgment will be affirmed.

GAINES v. STATE. (No. 6283.)

(Court of Criminal Appeals of Texas. June 8, 1921.)

Criminal law ⏘1131(5)—Appeal dismissed, where defendant has escaped from custody.

Where defendant escapes pending his appeal from conviction for murder, and does not return to custody, the appeal will be dismissed, under Code Cr. Proc. 1911, art. 912.

Appeal from District Court, Stephens County; W. R. Ely, Judge.

Harry Gaines was convicted of murder, and he appeals. Appeal dismissed.

R. H. Hamilton, Asst. Atty. Gen., for the State.

MORROW, P. J. Conviction is for murder; punishment fixed at confinement in the penitentiary for a period of five years.

Charging that the appellant has made his escape, and has not returned to custody, the Assistant Attorney General moves that the appeal be dismissed. Accompanying the motion are affidavits of the sheriff of Stephens county, in which the fact charged is made to appear.

In accord with the statute (article 912 of the Code of Criminal Procedure), the appeal is dismissed.

HARDY v. STATE. (No. 6324.)

(Court of Criminal Appeals of Texas. June 8, 1921.)

1. Criminal law ⏘631(7)—Motion to quash service of purported copy of jurors properly denied.

Where the state exhausted a challenge in each instance of variance between the name of the juror as shown on the original venire and the officer's return and copy, and where no service was shown on the juror drawn, defendant waived his right to have such juror attached and brought in, defendant is not entitled to have quashed the service on him of a purported copy of the jurors summoned on account of variance between the return and copy.

2. Criminal law ⏘597(3)—Denial of a continuance on the ground of absent witness not error where result would not have been changed.

In a prosecution for robbery, where the state contended that defendant and other negroes broke into a boarding car, robbing Mexicans therein, the denial of a continuance because of the absence of a witness who would testify that a few minutes before the trouble arose he saw several Mexicans and negroes gambling, and shortly thereafter he heard a commotion, *held* not error, as such evidence, if admitted, would not have resulted in a more favorable verdict for defendant, it being entirely possible gambling preceded the robbery.

3. Criminal law ⏘365(2)—Evidence of previous robbery admissible where part of same transaction.

Where as part of the same transaction two Mexicans in a boarding car were assaulted and robbed, and one of them escaped to an adjacent car containing more Mexicans, which was later robbed, evidence in prosecution for the latter robbery that one of the two Mexicans in a bloody and bruised condition came to second car was admissible, being part of a continuous transaction in which defendant and his companions were acting together.

4. Criminal law ⏘423(3)—Evidence that one victim was struck with a wrench admissible, regardless of whether defendant or confederate struck blow.

In a prosecution for robbery, testimony that one of the victims was struck with a wrench was admissible without showing whether defendant or one of his confederates struck the blow, for the act of one was the act of all.

5. Criminal law ⏘365(1)—Evidence that defendant was pointing a pistol at a witness while his companion took witness' money admissible in prosecution for another robbery.

In a prosecution for robbery, testimony that defendant pointed a pistol at a witness while a companion took the witness' money. is admissible, over objection that it was a new and distinct offense, for it was res gestæ, being part of the general transaction.

6. Criminal law ⏘684—Common-law rules as to rebuttal evidence do not apply in criminal cases.

The common-law rule does not apply in criminal cases; therefore, in a prosecution for robbery, where some of the victims testified in chief, defendant cannot complain that after closing his case the others testified, on the theory that such testimony was not rebuttal under Vernon's Ann. Code Cr. Proc. 1916, art. 717, prescribing the order of trial.

7. Criminal law ⏘829(4)—Refusal of charge substantially covered was not error.

Refusal of a requested charge covering defendant's claim that he did not participate in the robbery was not error, being substantially covered by a charge that, if defendant was engaged in gambling at the place of the robbery, and a dispute arose, and subsequently some other person committed the crime, in which defendant did not participate, he would not be guilty.

⏘For other cases see same topic and KEY-NUMBER in all Key-Numbered Digests and Indexes

Appeal from District Court, Titus County; R. T. Wilkinson, Judge.

Sam Hardy was convicted of robbery, and he appeals. Affirmed.

I. N. Williams and J. A. Ward, both of Mt. Pleasant, for appellant.

R. H. Hamilton, Asst. Atty. Gen., for the State.

HAWKINS, J. Conviction was for robbery. Punishment was assessed at 12 years in the penitentiary.

[1] Appellant filed a motion to quash the service on him of the purported copy of the jurors summoned to try the case, because the officer's return showed O. M. *Shurtliff*, O. T. *Fishback*, E. F. *Stenson*, and W. Porter, to have been summoned, and in the purported copy served on him W. Porter's name was omitted, and the other names appeared as O. M. *Shutliff*, O. F. *Fishback*, and E. T. *Stenson*. The court overruled the motion. The bill of exception presenting this matter bears the following explanation from the trial judge:

"In each instance where was a variance in the name as shown on the original venire and the officer's return and copy, the state exhausted a challenge, and where no service was shown on the juror drawn defendant waived his right to have the juror attached and brought in."

There was no error in the court's action in the particular complained of. The variance was no ground for quashing the service or the panel. It seems in this case, the state having assumed the burden of challenging such jurors, no possible injury could result. Mitchell v. State, 36 Tex. Cr. R. 278, 33 S. W. 367, 36 S. W. 456; Hudson v. State, 28 Tex. App. 323, 13 S. W. 388; Thompson v. State, 19 Tex. App. 593; Melton v. State, 71 Tex. Cr. R. 130, 158 S. W. 550.

[2] An application for continuance on account of the absence of Olin Robertson was overruled, and appellant assigns error. The diligence was sufficient. The facts which appellant shows he expected to prove by this witness—

"is that on the night of the alleged offense, and a few minutes before the trouble arose the said witness was near the car, and saw several Mexicans and negroes in the car, and they were gambling; that shortly thereafter the witness heard a commotion at the said car where he had seen the parties, and at once the lights went out and he heard holloaing and saw several persons run from the said car, where it is claimed by the state the robbery took place. That he was near to the said car and did not hear any noise like a person beating or knocking on the car."

The evidence in the record shows that on the night of the alleged robbery Nicholas Hernandez and five other Mexicans were occupying a boarding car, and two other Mexicans were in another boarding car about two car lengths away. That after the Mexicans had retired for the night appellant and his companions first went to the car occupied by the two, gained entrance to the car, made an assault on one, and the other one escaped. The wounded Mexican went to the car where the six were, and was taken in. Appellant and his confederates proceeded to that car, battered the door down, gained entrance, and assaulted the Mexicans, and robbed Hernandez and others. Three or four of the Mexicans were considerably beaten and bruised. No marks of injury were visible on any of the negroes. The testimony showed from the officers and others that the side door of the car was broken practically to splinters from blows from the outside. Appellant testified that he and his companions were gambling with the Mexicans, and that a dispute and fight arose over the game, and denied in toto the robbery.

We had occasion, in the recent case of Clowers v. State, 228 S. W. 226, to review some of the authorities relative to applications for continuances. After quoting from several cases announcing the general rules, it was said:

"If the witness Jaggears had been present in court and had testified to all the facts which appellant claims he would have sworn to, we do not believe a verdict more favorable to the appellant would have resulted."

This statement seems to be peculiarly applicable here. The Mexicans all denied that any gambling was going on. That was only an incidental question. If the fact that all parties had been gambling was established it would not disprove a subsequent robbery charge. The application states that the witness would testify that he heard a "commotion" at the car. There is no question that a commotion of a very serious character occurred during the progress of the alleged robbery, attended by considerable noise, and the discharge of a pistol, either during the time, or immediately preceding it. We cannot bring ourselves to believe that any injury was done appellant by the action of the court in overruling the application for continuance, or, in view of the entire record, hold any error was committed therein.

[3] Appellant complains because the state was permitted to prove what occurred at the car where the two Mexicans were, and that one of them, in a bloody and bruised condition, came to the car where the six were. The evidence shows it to have been a continuous transaction from the time of the attack on the first car until the robbery was effected. One of the parties in the car where the six were was awakened by the beating on the other car, and roused his companions. Appellant and his companions were acting together, and it was immaterial which one com-

mitted the various assaults on the different Mexicans. It was a joint enterprise, in which all were participating.

[4] Hernandez was permitted to testify over appellant's objection that one of the negroes hit him in the head with a track wrench, which still had blood on it at the time of the trial, the objection being that it had not been shown that appellant struck him. It was immaterial whether it was appellant or some of his confederates who struck the blow. The act of one was the act of all, and properly provable against whichever one was on trial.

[5] The witness Chaves was permitted to testify over objection that he saw appellant at the car where the robbery is claimed to have occurred, and that appellant was pointing a pistol at witness while some one else took his money. The objection offered was that it was a new and different offense than the one for which accused was on trial. What has been said heretofore applies equally to this assignment. It was all one and the same transaction. The development of the case disclosed the acts of the various participants, and although it may have shown the robbery of more than one party, it was res gestæ, and proper and permissible to prove all that appellant and his confederates did during the entire affair. Burnett v. State, 83 Tex. Cr. R. 97, 201 S. W. 409.

[6] In making out its case in chief, the state used two of the Mexicans who were present, at the time of the alleged robbery. After appellant rested his case, the state then put on the other Mexicans who were present, over the objection that it was not in rebuttal. The testimony of all these witnesses was pertinent to the issues under investigation, and there is no merit in the objection that it was not in rebuttal. The common-law rule does not apply in this state in criminal cases. Article 717, Vernon's C. C. P., and note on page 398.

[7] Appellant requested the following special charge:

"You are instructed in this case that, if you find from the evidence that the defendant and others went to the camp of Nicholas Hernandez for the purpose of gambling with the Mexicans in the said camp, and did gamble with the said Mexicans, and that while so engaged in gambling a dispute arose between the Mexicans and negroes, and a fight ensued, and the Mexicans were beat up, and Nicholas Hernandez was assaulted; and that the defendant then ran off and did not rob the said Nicholas Hernandez,

and did not aid others in robbing him, then you will find the defendant not guilty.

"And if you have a reasonable doubt as to whether the difficulty arose over a gamble game, and as to whether the defendant robbed the said Nicholas Hernandez, then you will find the defendant not guilty."

Error was assigned because of the failure of the court to give the charge requested. When we look to the main charge of the court, we find the following:

"You are further instructed that if you believe from the evidence that this defendant, together with others, charged in the indictment, is alleged to have occurred, and that they went there for the purpose of engaging in a gambling game, and that afterwards the defendant with such other persons and the Mexicans got into a dispute, and that afterwards some other person, other than the defendant, made an assault and robbed Nicholas Hernandez, if you find beyond a reasonable doubt that he was robbed, the defendant would not be guilty, unless you further find from the evidence beyond a reasonable doubt that the defendant was present at the time, and knowing the unlawful intent of such other person, if any, aided by acts or encouraged by words or gestures such other person who was actually engaged in the unlawful act, if any, and that such other person, with defendant, acted together in the commission of the offense, and such act was in pursuance of a common intent, and in pursuance of a previously formed design, in which the minds of all united and concurred."

Appellant's defense was that he did not participate in the robbery of Hernandez, if he was robbed. The issue as to whether the parties had been engaged in a gambling transaction prior to the robbery was only a collateral matter. We find the court telling the jury that, if appellant, together with others, went to the place where the robbery is alleged to have occurred for the purpose of engaging in a gambling transaction, and that a dispute arose, and that afterwards some other person besides the appellant robbed Hernandez, that appellant could not be found guilty, unless he in some way participated in the robbery. This substantially presents to the jury the same issue incorporated in the special charge requested and it was not necessary for the court to practically repeat an instruction which had substantially been given to the jury.

Finding no error in the record, the judgment is affirmed.

ALLRED et al. v. STATE. (No. 6285.)

(Court of Criminal Appeals of Texas. May 25, 1921.)

Appeal from Garza County Court; H. G. Smith, Judge.

S. F. Allred and J. N. Atkinson were convicted of the theft of cotton seed, and they appeal. Affirmed.

R. H. Hamilton, Asst. Atty. Gen., for the State.

HAWKINS, J. Conviction was for the theft of cotton seed of less than $50 in value. Punishment was assessed at a fine of $100 and 15 days in jail against each appellant.

The proceedings upon the trial appear to be regular. No fundamental error is apparent from the record, and, in the absence of a statement of facts and bills of exceptions, the judgment of the trial court will be affirmed.

FRAZIER v. STATE. (No. 6307.)

(Court of Criminal Appeals of Texas. June 1, 1921.)

Appeal from Criminal District Court, Dallas County; Chas. A. Pippen, Judge.

Lucius Frazier was convicted of assault to rape, and appeals. Affirmed.

C. M. Cureton, Atty. Gen., and C. L. Stone, Asst. Atty. Gen., for the State.

MORROW, P. J. Conviction is for the offense of assault to rape; punishment fixed at confinement in the penitentiary for five years.

The record reveals that the appellant was tried upon an indictment regularly presented and sufficient in form and substance. No bills of exceptions are presented; no statement of facts is before us. We have discovered no fundamental errors.

The judgment is affirmed.

DAVIS v. STATE. (No. 6267.)

(Court of Criminal Appeals of Texas. June 1, 1921.)

Appeal from District Court, Kaufman County; Joel R. Bond, Judge.

Henry Davis was convicted of aggravated assault, and he appeals. Appeal dismissed.

Wynne & Wynne, of Kaufman, for appellant. R. H. Hamilton, Asst. Atty. Gen., for the State.

LATTIMORE, J. Appellant was convicted in the district court of Kaufman county of aggravated assault, under an indictment charging him with maiming, and his punishment fixed at a fine of $25 and confinement in the county jail for 30 days.

There is before us a request on behalf of appellant for the dismissal of the appeal of this case, which request is hereby granted, and the appeal is accordingly dismissed.

Ex parte FOSTER. (No. 5928.)

(Court of Criminal Appeals of Texas. March 23, 1921. Rehearing Denied June 15, 1921.)

Original application by Clarence Foster for habeas corpus. Relief denied, and relator remanded.

Sid Crumpton, of Texarkana, for appellant. Alvin M. Owsley, Asst. Atty. Gen., for the State.

HAWKINS, J. This is an original application for habeas corpus, seeking release of relator from the State Juvenile Training School at Gatesville, where he was confined by virtue of judgment and sentence of the district court of Bowie county, finding him to be a delinquent and incorrigible child. The writ was issued, bail granted, and the matter is now before us on its merits.

This is a companion case to that of Morris Gordon, 228 S. W. 1095, and the same questions are presented in both cases. They are identical in that respect; but the original Gordon Case is before us on appeal, together with habeas corpus proceedings, and the Clarence Foster Case was not appealed, but is only presented on habeas corpus proceeding.

Relator contends that he should be released from custody because he says: (1) "The law defining delinquent and incorrigible children is so incongruous and unintelligible in its terms as to render it of such doubtful construction that it cannot be understood and is therefore unenforceable." (2) "The provisions of the law in reference to the trial and commitment of delinquent children violates the fundamental rights of the accused to a trial by jury, and of being heard by counsel."

If the foregoing contentions are correct, of course, relator is entitled to the relief sought; but they have all been decided against his contention. It would be useless to repeat what has been said heretofore in Re Morris Gordon, 228 S. W. 1095, a companion case, this day decided, both on motion for rehearing and original habeas corpus proceedings. See cases cited in those opinions.

The other questions presented are identical with the ones raised and discussed in the case just referred to. It constitutes a collateral attack on the judgment, there being no appeal in the instant case, and might be disposed of under the authority of the case of Ex parte Davis, 85 Tex. Cr. R. 218, 211 S. W. 456. But all matters presented have been disposed of in the Gordon Case, to which reference is made.

The relief prayed for is denied, and relator is remanded to the custody of the superintendent of the Juvenile Training School at Gatesville, Tex.

WESTERN INDEMNITY CO. v. LEONARD.
(No. 689.)

(Court of Civil Appeals of Texas. Beaumont.
May 26, 1921. Rehearing Denied
June 8, 1921.)

1. **Master and servant** ⟫348—Compensation
Act liberally construed.

To effectuate the purpose of the Workmen's Compensation Act (Vernon's Ann. Civ.
St. Supp. 1918, arts. 5246—1 to 5246—91), to
provide means for speedy adjustment of industrial accidents, and to insure compensation,
its provisions should be liberally construed in
favor of those claiming compensation.

2. **Master and servant** ⟫375(2)—Injury to
employé boarding train to return home held
in "course of employment," within Compensation Act.

Where a shipbuilding company operated
under a contract with the federal government,
on a cost plus profits basis, and the company's
expenses in furnishing railroad transportation
to its employés were part of the cost, and an
employé, after leaving the train at the place of
work and while he was on the railroad right
of way, started to return to the train on seeing
a signal that there would be no work that day,
and was injured in jumping across a ditch between him and the train, the injury occurred
in the course of the employment, within Workmen's Compensation Act, pt. 4, § 1 (Vernon's
Ann. Civ. St. Supp. 1918, art. 5246—82), so as
to be compensable, though he occupied the relation of passenger to the federal administration of railroads as carrier; there being an
election of remedies under part 2, § 6a (article 5246—47), of the act, if the circumstances
created a liability against the carrier.

[Ed Note.—For other definitions, see Words
and Phrases, First and Second Series, Course
of Employment.]

Appeal from District Court, Harris County; Ewing Boyd, Judge.

Proceeding by Effie V. Leonard under the
Workmen's Compensation Act against the
Western Indemnity Company to recover for
the death of her husband, an employé of
the Universal Shipbuilding Company. From
a judgment of the district court, sustaining
an award of the Industrial Accident Board,
the Indemnity Company appeals. Affirmed,
with directions.

Andrews, Streetman, Logue & Mobley, W.
L. Cook, and E. J. Fountain, Jr., all of Houston, for appellant.

Atkinson & Atkinson, of Houston, for appellee.

WALKER, J. This appeal is from a judgment of one of the district courts of Harris
county, sustaining an award made by the
Industrial Accident Board, under the Texas
Workmen's Compensation Act, allowing Mrs.
Effie V. Leonard, appellee, compensation
against the appellant for the death of her

husband, James Leonard. On the 29th day
of October, 1918, the date of his injury,
James Leonard lived in the city of Houston,
and was an employé of the Universal Shipbuilding Company, and had been for many
months previous thereto. It was agreed:

"It is also agreed that due to the fact that
the plant of the Universal Shipbuilding Company was several miles distant from the city of
Houston, and also to the fact that transportation facilities to such plant were limited, and
due to the lack of housing facilities, and to the
fact that at the time and place there was a
scarcity of skilled and experienced labor, it
became necessary to provide transportation
for the employés of Universal Shipbuilding
Company engaged in the work of shipbuilding
at its plant in question, and said transportation was in fact provided for said employés
to carry them from the Southern Pacific
(Grand Central) Station, in the city of Houston, to said ship building plant, and from said
plant on the return trip to said station. At
the time of the injuries sustained by said James
Leonard, above mentioned, and for a considerable period prior thereto, the transportation
of the employés to and from their work was
without cost to said employés, the same being
carried forward into the transportation cost
paid, in addition to the daily wage became and
was a part of the contract of employment between the employés, including the said James
Leonard and the said Universal Shipbuilding
Company. The train upon which said employés
were carried to and from their work was operated on a certain fixed schedule, and was not
a train exclusively for such employés, but employés of other industries were carried to and
from their work thereon, and at the same
charge per man. In the case, however, of the
shipbuilding employés at the time of the injuries to James Leonard, and for some time prior
thereto, the commutation tickets used for the
purpose were furnished to its employés by the
Universal Shipbuilding Company at its shipyard, said tickets being regularly issued by the
Federal Railroad Administration, and being
paid for to said Railroad Administration by
Universal Shipbuilding Company in accordance
with the arrangements theretofore made to relieve the employés of the cost of said transportation. The ships were being built by said
Universal Shipbuilding Company on a basis of
cost plus a percentage computed thereupon as
profit, and the additional expense of transporting the men to and from their work was
under authority of the Emergency Fleet Corporation, acting for the United States government, included as a part of the cost of building
the ships. The trains upon which the employés
in question rode, and the tracks upon which
they were operated, were in no sense under
the control of the Universal Shipbuilding Company, but were under the control of, and operated by, the United States Federal Administration of Railroads, and each and every employé who rode upon such train or trains
thereby became a passenger and occupied the
relation of passenger to the Federal Administration of Railroads as carrier."

This arrangement for the payment of the
transportation, as set forth in the above

agreement, was made by the Universal Shipbuilding Company under authority given by the Emergency Fleet Corporation, and as shown by the agreement, the cost of this transportation was carried into the cost of the ships, and the shipbuilding company was allowed the same percentage of profit on the cost of this transportation as on the other items of expense incurred in building ships. In other words, every time James Leonard rode to and from the ship plant, he was making money for his employer. This transportation was allowed the employés of shipyards by virtue of the Macy award, and in connection with this award it was agreed:

"It is further agreed that such award was adopted by and put into effect at once by said Universal Shipbuilding Company, and that the same was effective until after November 11, 1918, and that the said James Leonard and the other employés of said Universal Shipbuilding Company would have been compelled, had it not been for such free transportation to and from such shipyards, to spend regularly more than 10 cents a day in coming to and from their work at such shipyards, and that the transportation actually furnished was furnished to the employés of said shipyards by reason of the facts above set forth, and by reason of the contract and agreement between such Universal Shipbuilding Company and its employés, and by reason of the Macy award above set forth."

The following agreement was made as to the immediate circumstances under which James Leonard was injured:

"It is further agreed that on or about said October 29, 1918, the said James Leonard boarded said train at Houston, Tex., for the purpose of proceeding to the plant of said shipbuilding company, which was several miles distant, and performing his daily duties at such plant; that in due course said train reached the plant of said shipbuilding company, and the said James Leonard, together with several hundreds of the other employés of said shipbuilding company, got off said train and started toward the entrance gate of said shipbuilding company, in order to begin the daily work; that after leaving said train, and before the reaching of said entrance gate, but while yet on the railroad right of way, the said James Leonard and other employés with and around him were notified by said shipbuilding company by means of a signal used for that purpose that no work would be performed on that day, which signal was given by reason of the fact that at that time it was raining; that the said James Leonard immediately turned around and started back to said train, and in order to board said train, in order to return to Houston, Tex., jumped across a ditch between him and said train; and that in so doing the said James Leonard received the injuries from which he subsequently died.

"It is also agreed that before said injuries above set forth the said James Leonard was a strong, healthy, able-bodied man, but that in jumping said ditch in order to get on board said train, the same James Leonard suffered a rupture of the small intestines, from which peritonitis developed, and that by reason of said injuries and said peritonitis the said James Leonard died in Houston, Tex., on or about the 9th day of November, 1918, and that the death of said James Leonard was due directly and proximately to the injuries received by him as aforesaid."

On these facts, appellant assigns error against the judgment of the court on the ground that "the deceased, James Leonard, did not sustain an injury in the course of his employment, as that term is defined" in the Texas Workmen's Compensation Act. Part 4, § 1, of this act (Vernon's Ann. Civ. St. Supp. 1918, art. 5246–82), is as follows:

"The term 'injury sustained in the course of employment,' as used in this act, shall not include:

"1. An injury caused by the act of God, unless the employé is at the time engaged in the performance of duties that subject him to a greater hazard from the act of God responsible for the injury than ordinarily applies to the general public.

"2. An injury caused by an act of a third person intended to injure the employé because of reasons personal to him and not directed against him as an employé, or because of his employment.

"3. An injury received while in a state of intoxication.

"4. An injury caused by the employé's willful intention and attempt to injure himself, or to unlawfully injure some other person, but shall include all injuries of every kind and character having to do with and originating in the work, business, trade or profession of the employer received by an employé while engaged in or about the furtherance of the affairs or business of his employer whether upon the employer's premises or elsewhere."

[1, 2] The purpose of this act is to provide a means for speedy adjustment of industrial accidents, and to insure compensation to those injured within its terms. To effectuate that purpose its provisions should be liberally construed in favor of those claiming compensation. We believe this claim for compensation comes within the meaning of the quoted section of this act. The employés of the Universal Shipbuilding Company lived in the city of Houston, and it was necessary to transport them from the city to the plant, and in addition to their daily wages these employés were entitled to this transportation. It was as much a part of the contract as the compensation for the labor performed; it being agreed that—

"In addition to the daily wages [the transportation] became and was a part of the contract of employment between the employés, including the said James Leonard and the said Universal Shipbuilding Company."

Leonard's employer selected the means of such transportation, bought the ticket, and delivered it to him. While neither the train nor the track were under the control of the employer, it was the means—we might say agent—of the employer in transporting its employés from their homes to their place of work. This transportation was "incidental to" Leonard's employment—was a part of the contract, and in fact a part of his compensation. It was said in Donovan's Case, 217 Mass. 76, 78, 104 N. E. 431, Ann. Cas. 1915C, 778, 779:

"The finding of the Industrial Accident Board that Donovan's transportation was 'incidental to his employment' fairly means, in the connection in which it was used, that it was one of the incidents of his employment, that it was an accessory, collateral, or subsidiary part of his contract of employment, something added to the principal part of that contract as a minor, but none the less a real feature or detail of the contract."

Leonard was on his way to his work, traveling in the usual way over the route selected by his employer, and as directed by his employer. While not on his employer's premises, he was in obedience to the orders of his employer, and was injured in the course of his obedience to such orders. The duties of his employment did not end at the gates of the plant, for the employer had contracted to carry him back to the city, and the cost of such transportation was not an overhead expense, to be taken care of in the price charged for the finished product, but was itself a direct source of revenue and profit. It seems to us that the rule announced in Donovan's Case, supra, is applicable to the facts of this case, to wit:

"There have been several decisions in England as to when and how far an employé can be said to have been in the employ of his master, while traveling to and from his work in a vehicle, or means of conveyance provided by the latter, and how far injuries received in such a conveyance can be said to have arisen out of and in the course of the employment. Many of these decisions have been cited and discussed by Professor Bohlen in 25 Harvard L. Review, 401 et seq. From his discussion and the cases referred to by him, and from the later decisions of the English courts, the rule has been established, as we consider in accordance with sound reason, that the employer's liability in such cases depends upon whether the conveyance has been provided by him, after the real beginning of the employment, in compliance with one of the implied or express terms of the contract of employment, for the mere use of the employés, and is one which the employés are required, or as a matter of right are permitted, to use by virtue of that contract."

Peculiarly so in this case, because of the profit and advantage accruing to the employer through such transportation. We conclude that Leonard's injury did originate in his work, and was received in the course of his employment, and, at the time of receiving such injury, that he was engaged in the furtherance of his master's business. The fact that he did not work that day, and that appellant received no premium for his services on that day, are not controlling. Leonard was at the place of his employment, under the terms of his contract. Being there under these circumstances, the relation of employer and employé existed, within the meaning of the Workmen's Compensation Act. Appellant did not contract with the shipbuilding company to pay compensation to employés only on the days they worked, but "while engaged in or about the furtherance of the affairs or business of their employer."

In support of its assignment, appellant cites the Dinkins Case, 211 S. W. 949, an opinion by this court, in which writ of error was denied by the Supreme Court, and Rausch v. Standard Shipbuilding Corporation, 111 Misc. Rep. 450, 181 N. Y. Supp. 513. The Dinkins Case is so different from this case on its facts that we do not consider it in point. The Rausch Case is somewhat similar on its facts, but it does not appear from the statement of the case that the defendant was receiving a profit on the cost of transportation; also it appeared from the statement of the case that the transportation "in no wise figured in the pay or wages of the plaintiff's intestate." Here, as we have seen, it was expressly agreed that the cost of this transportation was "a part of the contract of employment."

As appears from the agreed statement of facts, the trains upon which James Leonard rode, and the tracks on which these trains were operated, were not under the control of the Universal Shipbuilding Company, but were under the control and operated by the United States Federal Administration of Railroads, and Leonard, while riding on such train, was a passenger and occupied the relation of passenger to the Federal Administration of Railroads, as carrier. We do not believe that this fact took Leonard from under the protection of the Workmen's Compensation Act. Had he been injured under circumstances creating a liability against the Railroad Administration, the appellee would have had an election of remedies. It would not have defeated the right to compensation. Workmen's Compensation Act, part 2, § 6a (article 5246—47).

Appellant's fourth assignment of error is:

"The trial court erred, to the prejudice of the plaintiff in error, in decreeing any amount of compensation to the defendants beyond that which had matured upon the basis of weekly payments to the date of judgment."

The proposition is:

"Since the accrued compensation at the time of the trial amounted to $990, the decreeing of $1,027.62, as due on the date of the judgment, was error."

We find the following notation in pencil writing under this proposition:

"This question will be withdrawn by consent of counsel, as per agreement on trial of the case."

The judgment of the trial court in decreeing successive executions for the collection of the compensation as it matures is sustained by U. S. Fidelity & Guaranty Co. v. Davis, 212 S. W. 242.

Believing that this case was correctly tried, the judgment of the trial court is affirmed. This order is made, however, without prejudice to the rights of appellant to reopen the case, should conditions arise which, under the Workmen's Compensation Act, would terminate appellee's right to receive compensation. In making this order, it is our purpose to decree that the interest of appellees in this recovery shall be held by them under the restrictions and privileges provided by the Workmen's Compensation Act.

WILCOX v. CRAWFORD. (No. 1221.)

(Court of Civil Appeals of Texas. El Paso. May 26, 1921.)

1. Trial ⬥➝390—Court may refuse to make and file findings and conclusions before entry of judgment, in view of statute.

Since Vernon's Sayles' Ann. Civ. St. 1914, art. 2075, provides that the judge shall have 10 days after adjournment in which to prepare his findings of fact and conclusions of law, it is not error for the court to decline to make and file his findings before entry of judgment.

2. Mines and minerals ⬥➝74—Buyer of interest in lease under executory contract held entitled to recover amount paid as for failure of consideration.

Where the buyer within the time provided for in his executory contract, for the purchase of an interest in an oil, gas, and mineral lease, approved the title and tendered the balance of the consideration and demanded a deed, but the seller was unable to perform, for the reason that his option contract to purchase from the record owner, which he assigned to the buyer, had expired. The buyer was entitled to recover the amount paid as for failure of consideration.

3. Payment ⬥➝73(4)—Evidence of payment of check held sufficient.

Where plaintiff executed and delivered to defendant a check for $500, which was indorsed by defendant and marked "paid" by a bank, there was sufficient evidence to sustain a finding of payment of the $500.

4. Mines and minerals ⬥➝74—Where seller of interest in lease fails to perform, purchaser entitled to interest on an advance payment recovered.

Where purchaser of an interest in oil, gas, and mineral lease recovered from the seller a sum paid in advance to the seller for the interest, which the seller could not convey, the purchaser was also entitled to interest on such sum from the date of its payment.

Appeal from Eastland County Court, at Law; R. L. Rust, Judge.

Action by Frank Crawford against J. T. Wilcox. Judgment for plaintiff and defendant appeals from the judgment, and from an order denying a new trial. Affirmed.

Harry E. Pratt, of Eastland, for appellant. Carl P. Springer, of Eastland, for appellee.

PER CURIAM. Frank Crawford brought this suit against J. T. Wilcox to recover of him the sum of $500, alleged to have been paid by him to Wilcox as a part consideration for an oil, gas, and mineral interest in certain lands described, said interest alleged to be equal to five acres of royalty undivided in the lands described. The suit is based upon the following contract:

"The State of Texas, County of Eastland.

"J. T. Wilcox has agreed to sell and Frank Crawford has agreed to buy the oil, gas and other minerals subject to an oil and gas lease on same in favor of Caldwell Oil Co., as follows:

"Acreage: 5 full acres of royalty therein.

"Land: The S. ½ of Sec. 458, S. P. Ry. Co. the N. W. ¼ of Sec. 36, Block 4, H. & T. C. Ry. Co. the N. ¾ of N. E. ¼ Sec. 36, Bl. 4, H. & T. C. Ry. Co.

"Consideration: $1,500.00 as follows: $500.-00 paid upon approval of title this day by check on the City National Bank of Eastland to be $1,000.00 additional sixty days from date hereof, with no interest on same. Upon payment of said $1,000 and delivery of said $500.00 check above on or before August 10, 1919, said royalty deed, also in escrow with a copy of this contract shall be delivered to Crawford.

"Abstract: to be furnished for examination, and Crawford has full ten days in which to have same examined. This deal to be closed only in event that title to said land is good and merchantable in W. H. Green, in the opinion of attorneys for Crawford who are to be exclusive judges of said title. If title proves defective and is not made merchantable, said $500.00 check to be returned to Crawford. If title is good and merchantable, and Crawford fails and refuses to pay said additional sum of $1,000.00 as herein stipulated, then said $500.00 to be paid Wilcox as liquidated damages herein.

Date: June 10, 1919.

"J. T. Wilcox,
"Frank Crawford.

"Witness:
"V. T. Seaberry."

Crawford alleged that at the time of the making of the above contract he paid to Wilcox the $500 called for in the contract, and that it was fully understood and agreed by the parties to the contract that in case Wilcox should for any reason fail or refuse to deliver a proper conveyance of the property Wilcox should return to him the $500 paid. He alleged his ability and willingness to discharge his part of the contract, and so notified Wilcox, but that Wilcox refused to comply with the terms of the contract, and refused to make proper conveyance of the property, and refused to return to him the $500 paid. Appellant answered by general demurrer and general denial. The case was tried without a jury, and the court rendered judgment for Crawford for $500, with interest.

Wilcox filed a motion for a new trial, which the court overruled to which ruling Wilcox excepted and gave notice of appeal. Appellant, upon the commencement of the trial on the 14th day of June, 1919, requested the court to make findings of fact before the entry of the court's judgment, which request the court refused to comply with, stating that he would make such findings after judgment, but not before.

The court made and filed findings of fact and conclusions of law. Briefly stated, the court found that the above contract was made and entered into by appellant and appellee; that said contract, together with a deed to said royalty, were placed in the First State Bank of Eastland, to be held in escrow; that on June 10, 1919, Crawford delivered to Wilcox, through V. T. Seaberry, his check on the City National Bank for $500; that Wilcox executed an assignment of his interest in said royalty to Crawford and that said assignment was placed with said contract and royalty deed and held in escrow by the First State Bank of Eastland; that prior to the 60-day period called for in the contract Crawford duly tendered his check for $1,000 to both the bank and Wilcox, and demanded the royalty deed; that said Bank refused to deliver any of the papers held by it; that at no time has appellant delivered said royalty deed to appellee; that appellee's check on the City National Bank for $500 was duly indorsed by appellant and marked paid by the bank.

[1] There is no merit in the second assignment complaining of the refusal and failure of the court to make and file his findings of fact and conclusions of law prior to the entry of judgment. Article 2075, V.S., provides that the judge shall have 10 days after the adjournment at which the cause may be tried in such court in which to prepare his findings of fact and conclusions of law. The Legislature of this state has fixed the time within which the trial court in this state must make and file the findings of fact, and the courts have no power to require trial courts to perform that service earlier than the time fixed by the Legislature.

[2] The first assignment claims reversible error in entering judgment for appellee on the ground that there was no evidence to sustain the judgment, the evidence showing that appellee had paid appellant $500 for the execution of the assignment of appellant's interest, as called for in the above contract;

231 S.W.—70

the assignment having been executed on June 27, 1919.

The assignment of the interest by appellant to appellee referred to, reads:

"For and in consideration of the sum of $500.00 cash in hand paid me by Frank Crawford, the receipt whereof is hereby acknowledged, I, J. T. Wilcox, hereby assign and transfer my interest in the attached contract of sale in said five acres of royalty as described in said contract and royalty deed from W. H. Green and wife, so that said Crawford may pay the additional sum of $1,000.00 to be credited W. H. Green, and take up said contract, and be delivered said deed."

The assignment was signed by Wilcox and duly acknowledged. Crawford made tender of the $1,000, but the escrow holder of the royalty deed from Green and wife to Wilcox, under instruction from Green, refused to deliver to Crawford the Green royalty deed. Thereupon Crawford demanded of Wilcox the return to him of the $500 paid. This Wilcox refused to do. Wilcox's contention is that, having assigned his royalty interest to Crawford under the assignment contract, and Crawford, having appellant's interest in the five-acre royalty he had a right to compel Green and wife to convey, and therefore appellant had no right of recovery for the $500.

The interest Wilcox had is expressed in an executory contract with W. H. Green, Sr., and wife, of date April 7, 1919. In which Green and wife, for a consideration of $1 paid, and an additional $1,000 to be paid upon the acceptance of title, agreed to deliver a royalty deed to the undivided five-acre interest in 172 acres of land described. The royalty deed was executed by Green and wife and placed in escrow in the escrow bank, with the direction to the bank to deliver the deed to Wilcox upon the payment of the $1,000. Wilcox was to have 10 days in which to have his attorneys pass upon the title as certified by the abstractors of title when the $1,000 was to be paid to Green or paid to the escrow bank for Green. The title was passed upon by Wilcox on July 27, 1919, and was satisfactory, but the $1,000 was not tendered or paid to Green or the escrow bank until about the 10th day of August 1919. On July 21, 1919, Green wrote the bank to the effect that Wilcox's time within which he was to sell the property was up, and, if he had not then paid the $1,000, not to deliver the deed.

We have concluded that on the 10th day of August, 1919, Green having declared the option to Wilcox forfeited for the failure to pay the $1,000, Wilcox had no interest to convey, and that his assignment to Crawford was without consideration. The trial court was not in error in rendering the judgment, as claimed in the first assignment.

[3] The evidence is sufficient to sustain the court's finding that the $500 had been

paid by Crawford to Wilcox, as complained of in the third and fourth assignments.

The evidence is sufficient to sustain the court's finding, as complained of in the fifth assignment, that Crawford tendered payment of the $1,000 both to Wilcox and the escrow bank, and demanded the delivery of the escrow deed.

[4] There is no merit in the sixth assignment complaining of the court's conclusion of law that Crawford was entitled to recover of Wilcox the $500 paid, with interest from the date of its payment. Crawford had received no interest or title to the property sought to be conveyed to him under the assignment by Wilcox.

Finding no reversible error, the case is affirmed.

CONCHO CAMP, NO. 66, W. O. W., v. CITY OF SAN ANGELO. (No. 5722.)

(Court of Civil Appeals of Texas. Austin. May 25, 1921.)

1. **Taxation ⊆⇒241(3)—Voluntary association not exempt in view of use of lodge room and first story of building by others.**

A benevolent association whose lodge room was not only rented to other charitable institutions, but the first story of whose building was rented for commercial purposes, was not entitled to exemption from taxation on its property under Vernon's Sayles' Ann. Civ. St. 1914, art. 7507, prescribing what property shall be exempt from taxation, in view of Const. art. 8, § 2, conferring power on the Legislature to pass laws exempting institutions of purely public charity.

2. **Taxation ⊆⇒241(3)—Local camp of benevolent association not entitled to exemption in view of its life insurance feature; "purely public charity."**

Local camp of voluntary benevolent order *held* not entitled to exemption from taxation, under Vernon's Sayles' Ann. Civ. St. 1914, art. 7507, on account of its issuing insurance policies to its members, so that it was not an institution purely for public charity within the constitutional authorization of the Legislature to make exemptions. Const. art. 8, § 2.

[Ed. Note.—For other definitions, see Words and Phrases, First and Second Series, Purely Public Charity.]

3. **Municipal corporations ⊆⇒962—Levies to pay for funding bonds and to pay off judgment on street improvement bonds not limitation on power of city to levy taxes for street improvements to extent of 15 cents per $100.**

In view of Vernon's Sayles' Ann. Civ. St. 1914, arts. 882, 924–926, and 937, levies made by the city of San Angelo to pay off funding bonds issued in 1903, and to obtain funds to pay off a judgment obtained against the city on street improvement bonds issued in 1899, *held* not to have constituted any limitation on the power of the city to levy taxes for street improvements to the extent of 15 cents on the $100.

4. **Municipal corporations ⊆⇒926, 951—Provision to pay interest on and create sinking fund for high school bonds in year of dating proper though they were not sold until next year.**

Where certain high school bonds issued by a city were to bear interest from May 1, 1914, it was proper that provision should be made to pay interest and create a sinking fund for the year 1914, as well as all subsequent years, though the bonds were not sold and in such sense not issued until June, 1915.

Appeal from District Court, Tom Green County; J. W. Timmins, Judge.

Suit by the City of San Angelo against Concho Camp, No. 66, Woodmen of the World. From judgment for plaintiff, defendant appeals. Affirmed.

Hill, Lee & Hill, of San Angelo, for appellant.

Jos. Spence, Jr., of San Angelo, for appellee.

KEY, C. J. Appellee brought this suit against appellant to recover taxes alleged to be due for the years 1909 to 1914, inclusive, on appellant's lot and lodge building in the city of San Angelo. Appellant defended upon the ground, first, that the property was exempt from taxation under the Constitution and laws of Texas; and, second, that, if not so exempt, some of the taxes sought to be recovered were illegal, because appellee had no power to levy and collect them. The case was submitted to the court without a jury, upon an agreed statement of facts, and judgment was rendered for appellee; and appellant has brought the case to this court and insists that the judgment should be reversed.

The case has been held under submission longer than usual, awaiting the decision of the Supreme Court in City of Houston v. Scottish Rite Benevolent Association et al., 230 S. W. 978, which case has been recently decided by that court.

Under the first and second assignments of error, appellant contends that the property is exempt from taxation. As pertinent to that question, we copy from appellant's brief the following statement:

"Appellee, in the years for which it seeks to recover taxes, was a municipal corporation, created and existing under the general laws of Texas. The plaintiff's first amended petition upon which the case was tried was in the usual form, and alleged that the appellant was a voluntary benevolent association owning the real estate described therein which was held for it by its trustees. Appellant, besides its demurrers, filed a general denial and a special answer in which it denied liability for the taxes, its said special answer being as follows:

" 'For further and special answers herein, defendant denies that its said property in plaintiff's petition described was, for the years therein mentioned and alleged, subject to taxation by plaintiff, but it avers that the same was, under the Constitution and laws of Texas, exempt from taxation in this, that defendant was the owner of said lot and had erected thereon a two-story brick building, the upper story being used by defendant as a place for holding its meetings, and renting to other societies the use thereof for their meetings, and the lower or ground floor thereof was rented for a store; that said building was not used by defendant with a view of profit, and that all of the rents arising therefrom were appropriated by defendant solely to pay its current lodge expenses, and for the benefit of its sick and disabled members and their families, and for the burial of its members and their families, and for the maintenance of its members when unable to provide for themselves, besides other benevolent and charitable purposes often done and performed by it. Defendant avers that it is a local camp at San Angelo of what is known as the Woodmen of the World; that as such local camp it dispenses aid to its members and others in sickness or distress or death without regard to poverty or riches of the recipient; that its funds, property, and assets are placed and bound to relieve and minister to the relief of its members when in want, sickness, and distress, and to educate and maintain the orphans of its deceased members; that the sources of its income and means of raising money with which to discharge its benevolent and charitable purposes is raised by monthly dues upon its members and the rental from said building, all of which is appropriated and used for the purposes aforesaid, that by reason of the facts the defendant is, within the meaning of the Constitution and laws of Texas, a public charity, engaged in a purely charitable work, and as such its property, money, and assets are exempt from taxation, and this it is ready to verify.'

"The admitted facts show that appellant is a local subordinate camp of the Sovereign Camp of the Woodmen of the World; that said Sovereign Camp of the Woodmen of the World is a fraternal, beneficiary, benevolent society, organized and existing under the name of the Sovereign Camp of the Woodmen of the World, with head office at Omaha, Neb., the object of the society being to combine its members into a secret, fraternal, beneficiary and benevolent society; to comfort the sick, and cheer the unfortunate by attention and ministrations in time of sorrow and distress; to promote fraternal love and unity; to create a fund out of which, on the death of a member, a sum not exceeding $3,000 may be paid to the beneficiary named by the deceased member, and to erect a monument at his grave, such fund for the payment of the death losses to the beneficiary, and the erection of a monument to the deceased member, being raised by advance assessments against each member taking insurance therein, based upon his age at nearest birthday at date of his admission as a member, according to a specified table prescribed by said Sovereign Camp according to the amount of insurance taken.

"The appellant is a local camp of said society at San Angelo, Tex., and under the jurisdiction of the Sovereign Camp having its head office at Omaha, Neb., and collects from each beneficiary member the advanced assessments under benefit certificates which may be issued to him, and remits the same to the Sovereign Camp at Omaha, Neb.

"The appellant, for the years 1909 to 1914, inclusive, owned the west 25 feet of lot No. 7, block 13, in the city of San Angelo, upon which it had a two-story brick building erected, the second story of which is used as a lodge room for the purpose of holding the meetings of the local society, and is also used by other societies, who pay rent to appellant for such use; the ground floor of said building is used by appellant for rental purposes, and during the years mentioned was rented and occupied as a store, monthly rentals being paid by the tenant to appellant.

"The title to said property is held and vested in appellant, and the Sovereign Camp has no title or interest in said lot and building, and none of the rents or revenues therefrom go to or constitute any fund to the Sovereign Camp having its head office at Omaha, Neb., and no part thereof is used for the payment of death losses and monument purposes.

"Appellant levies and collects from its members monthly dues of 35 cents per month, which, together with rents received by defendant from said building, constitute a fund under the control, use, and disposition of appellant, over which the Sovereign Camp of Omaha, Neb., has no control whatever; that said monthly dues and rents aforesaid are appropriated by appellant solely to sustain it and to pay its current expenses, and for the benefit of the sick and disabled members, and their families, and the burial of the same, and for the maintenance of members when unable to provide for themselves, and the fund so arising from said rentals and monthly dues are bound by the laws of the society to relieve, aid and minister to the relief of its members when in want, sickness and distress, and to maintain the orphans of its deceased members. If defendant did not receive the rents from said building, it would have to increase its monthly dues in order to meet the expenses incident to dispensing aid to its members and others in sickness and distress, and to provide for its helpless and dependent members an aid in the education and maintenance of the orphans of its deceased members.

"That, in addition to dispensing aid to its own members, it also dispenses, out of said fund arising from said dues and rentals, aid and assistance to members of other local camps coming to San Angelo in search of health, and for other purposes, and contributes out of said fund to other charitable purposes such as the Galveston sufferers, and other similar calamities, the aid and assistance, however, to members of other local camps and sufferers, being voluntary on the part of the camp, and not obligatory."

It is contended on behalf of appellant that its property comes clearly within the scope of article 7507, Vernon's Sayles' Ann. Civ. St.

1914, prescribing what property shall be exempt from taxation. But, if that contention be conceded, it must be held that the statute is in conflict with article 8 of the Constitution which regulates the subject of exemptions from taxation. That article makes no specific exemption of anything except $250 worth of household and kitchen furniture; but the second section confers power upon the Legislature to pass laws, exempting, among other things—

"All buildings used exclusively and owned by persons * * * for school purposes (and the necessary furniture of all schools), and institutions of purely public charity; and all laws exempting property from taxation, other than the property above mentioned, shall be void."

[1] In the City of Houston v. Scottish Rite Benevolent Association, above referred to, the Supreme Court seems to have modified the rule announced in Morris v. Masons, 68 Tex. 701, 5 S. W. 519, upon the question of what constitutes a purely public charity within the purview of the Constitution. It was there held that, in order to obtain the benefit of the exemption, the property must not only be an institution for purely public charity, but must also be used exclusively by the owner; and that it does not satisfy that constitutional requirement, because the use by others was permitted by the owner to obtain revenues to be devoted entirely to the owner's work of purely public charity. The court said:

"The actual, direct use must be exclusive on the part of such an institution as is favored by the constitutional provision."

And because in that case the owner of the property had permitted others to use a portion of it, it was held that the property was not exempt from taxation. That ruling applies to this case, because appellant's lodge room was not only rented to other charitable institutions, but the first story of the building was rented for commercial purposes.

[2] We also hold that in this case appellant is not entitled to the exemption, because of the fact that it issues insurance policies to its members; and therefore it is not an institution purely for public charity. Counsel for appellee have incorporated in their brief an able opinion prepared by Attorney General C. M. Cureton, and we copy therefrom and adopt the following:

"We now come down to the question as to whether or not fraternal beneficiary associations are institutions of 'purely public charity.'

"Section 1 of chapter 113, General Laws of the Thirty-Third Legislature (Vernon's Sayles' Ann. Civ. St. 1914, art. 4827), being our fraternal beneficiary act, by which title we will hereafter refer to it in this opinion, declares:

" 'Any corporation, society, order or voluntary association, without capital stock organized and carried solely for the mutual benefit of its members and their beneficiaries, and not for profit, and having a lodge system with ritualistic form of work and representative form of government, and which shall make provision for the payment of benefits in accordance with section 5 hereof, is hereby declared to be a fraternal benefit society.'

"Section 5 of the act (article 4831) sets forth the benefits which institutions of this character may provide for in their certificates, and provides in substance that every such society transacting business under this act shall provide for the payment of death benefits, and may provide for the payment of benefits in the case of temporary or permanent physical disability, either as the result of disease, accident, or old age. It likewise provides for qualified policy loans and the granting to members with paid-up insurance policies protection and withdrawal equities, somewhat after the manner of old line insurance companies.

"Section 8 (article 4834) provides that every certificate issued by such societies shall specify the amount of benefit provided thereby and the charter or articles of incorporation, constitution, by-laws, etc., shall be a part of the certificate and agreement between the association and its policy holders.

"Section 6 (article 4832) declares to whom the benefits may be payable, and limits the benefits to wife, husband, relative by blood to the fourth degree, father-in-law, mother-in-law, son-in-law, daughter-in-law, stepfather, stepmother, stepchildren, children by legal adoption, or to a person or persons dependent upon a member, etc.

"Other sections of the act govern the investment and distribution of the funds of the society, which may be only used in the manner set forth and for the purposes provided in the law.

"Institutions of this character are plainly insurance companies and not in any sense of the words 'benevolent and charitable institutions.' This has been expressly decided by the Supreme Court of this state in the case of Farmer v. State, 69 Tex. 561 [7 S. W. 220]. In that case a corporation known as the Masonic Mutual Benevolent Association announced in its charter that its purpose was to provide for its members during life and for their families after death. To accomplish this a contract was made with each member who joined the society that, for a sum of money paid, and for designated installments of money to be paid afterwards, the association would, after the member's death, pay to the designated beneficiaries a sum graduated in amount according to the length of time the member lived after he became a member. An examination by a physician was required of each member, and membersip was forfeited for nonpayment of assessments. The Supreme Court, as suggested, held that the contract had all the elements of a life insurance policy, and that, though it had been entered into for a benevolent purpose, yet the corporation could not legally exist unless incorporated in accordance with the laws of the state regulating the incorporation of insurance companies, and that it could not be chartered under the statutes of this state, providing for the incorporation of benevolent associations. In that case the court, speaking through Chief Justice Willie, said:

" 'This contract has all the features of a life insurance policy. It is a contract by which one party for a consideration promises to make a certain payment of money upon the death of the other; and it is well settled that, whatever may be the terms of payment of the consideration by the assured, or the mode of estimating or securing payment of the insurance money, it is still a contract of insurance, no matter by what name it may be called. Comm. v. Weatherbee, 105 Mass. 149; State v. Farmer's Benevolent Ass'n, 18 Neb. 281 [25 N. W. 81].

" 'It is in effect the ordinary contract made by insurance companies with the assured, differing from it in no important respect. The terms of payment are somewhat different, the amount being greater or less, accordingly as the member lives long or dies early; still it is a payment to be made at his death. The assured cannot be forced by suit to pay future premiums; but he loses his membership if he defaults in this respect. It is a common provision in insurance policies, that, if the assured fails to perform some of the conditions of his contract, that his policy may be canceled, and the premiums paid shall, in that event, become forfeited to the company. The provision that membership may be forfeited for nonpayment of assessments is in effect the same thing, for the assessments serve the purposes of premiums in an ordinary life policy. The examination which precedes admission into membership is the same as that which occurs before the issuance of a policy, and is intended to secure the society against fraud or imposition; to prevent an unsound person from becoming insured, and to reduce its risks of loss, or increase its chances of profit.

" 'It matters not that the member was entitled to benefits in case of sickness. Insurance can be effected upon the health as well as the life of an individual. These benefits, too, are incidental to the main object of the institution, and the certificates issued by it are none the less policies of insurance, though the insured derive sums of money from the contract other than those for which he has specially bargained.

" 'We are of opinion, therefore, that the appellants constituted an insurance company within the spirit and true meaning of that term, and not an association conducted in the interest of benevolence, as contemplated by title 20 of our Revised Statutes. This question has been frequently before the courts of other states, and, so far as we can ascertain, has been universally decided in accordance with the opinion above expressed.

" 'In Bolten v. Bolten, 78 Me. 299, the subject underwent thorough investigation, and an institution with purposes similar to the present was held a mutual life insurance company. In State v. Lietehelt, 32 N. W. 787, the Supreme Court of Minnesota held a company formed by unmarried men, with the purpose of endowing the wife of each member upon marriage with a sum of money equal to the then number of members not to be a benevolent association. The members paid a quid pro quo, and did not receive their money as an act of benevolence on the the part of their fellow members.

" 'In State v. Tex. Benevolent Association, supra, a society with a constitution like the present was held an insurance company, within the meaning of a statute similar to our own.

" 'The benefits received are not gratuitous. They are due to the members on account of the money he pays into the society. It takes the risk of his continued existence and good health. If it be benevolence to pay our money under such circumstances then every mutual life insurance company is acting in a benevolent manner towards the family of an insured member when it pays the policy it has issued them for a money consideration. It matters not what name the association may assume. The law looks to the real objects of the body and not to the name indicative of benevolence which it may have assumed.

" 'These views will be found supported by the following authorities in addition to those already cited: May on Ins., § 550; State v. Citizens' Ass'n, 6 Mo. App. 163; State v. Merchants,' etc., Ass'n, 72 Mo. 146; People v. Wilson, 46 N. Y. 477; State v. Standard Life Ass'n, 38 Ohio, 281.' 69 Tex. 566, 567 [7 S. W. 222, 223].

"This case would seem to settle the question that a fraternal beneficiary association is not a charitable or benevolent association, much less could it be considered an institution of 'purely public charity.' The rule is laid down in 37 Cyc. 931, as follows:

" 'In some states it is considered that fraternal associations, such as the Masonic order, and the Odd Fellows, are to be classed as "charitable" or "benevolent" institutions on account of their philanthropies, and therefore entitled to hold their property exempt from taxes; while a contrary doctrine is that the fact of their relief work being confined to members of the order and their families removes them from the class of public charities, so that they are not entitled to exemption. In some cases, it is held that the question depends upon whether the exemption granted is in terms restricted to institutions of "purely public charity" or applies generally to "charitable institutions." Where the principal object of a fraternal order is to provide for the payment of sick benefits to members and special payment to the next of kin or designated beneficiaries of deceased members out of funds raised by dues and assessments, it is not a charitable organization, but in the nature of an insurance company, and its property is not exempt.'

"The last phrase quoted is supported by a long line of authorities, cited by the authority from which we have quoted, and by others which we have collated. Those cited in support of the text are shown in 37 Cyc. p. 932, note 27, as follows: Illinois—Supreme Lodge M. A. F. O. v. Effingham County Bd. of Review, 223 Ill. 54, 79 N. E. 23 [7 Ann. Cas. 38]; State Council of Catholic Knights v. Effingham Co. Bd. of Review, 198 Ill. 441, 64 N. E. 1104. Kansas—National Council K. & L. S. v. Phillips, 63 Kan. 799, 66 Pac. 1011. Massachusetts —Young Men's Protestant, etc., Soc. v. Fall River, 160 Mass. 409, 36 N. E. 57. Mississippi —Ridgeley Lodge No. 23 I. O. O. F. v. Redus, 78 Miss. 352, 29 South. 163. Nebraska—Royal Highlanders v. State, 77 Neb. 18, 108 N. W. 183, 7 L. R. A. (N. S.) 380. New York— Matter of Jones, 1 Con. 125, 2 N. Y. Supp.

671. South Dakota—Masonic Aid Association v. Taylor, 2 S. D. 324, 50 N. W. 93. England —In re Linen, etc., Drapers', etc., Inst., 58 L. T. Rep. N. S. 949.

"In addition to the authorities just cited, we also direct your attention to the following: State Council O. K. of I. v. Board of Review [198 Ill. 441] 64 N. E. 1104; Royal Highlanders v. State [77 Neb. 18, 108 N. W. 183] 7 L. R. A. (N. S.) 380; Desty on Taxation, vol. 1, p. 114; City of Newport v. Masonic Temple Association, 108 Ky. 333, 56 S. W. 405, 49 L. R. A. 252; Widows' & Orphans' Home v. Bosworth [112 Ky. 200] 65 S. W. 591; Philadelphia v. Masonic Home [160 Pa. 572, 28 Atl. 954] 23 L. R. A. 545 [40 Am. St. Rep. 736]; National Council, etc., v. Phillips [63 Kan. 799] 66 Pac. 1011; Fitterer v. Crawford [157 Mo. 51, 57 S. W. 532] 50 L. R. A. 193.

"In the case of Royal Highlanders v. Nebraska, cited above, it was held by the Supreme Court of that state that a fraternal beneficiary association conducted for the mutual benefit of its members and for the purpose of providing a fund by the payment of stated dues and fees by such members, and providing for the payment of a special amount on the death of each member to a beneficiary named by him, was not a charitable association, and that its property was not exempt from taxation under the laws of the state exempting property used exclusively for charitable purposes.

"The annotator annotating this case for the L. R. A. system, in his note states: The general rule established by the decisions is in accord with the Royal Highlanders v. State, holding that fraternal benefit societies, not organized for profit or gain, but purely for the purpose of paying indemnity upon the death of their members, for an agreed compensation, are, in effect, life insurance companies, and not charitable or benevolent institutions, within the meaning of statutory provisions exempting the property of such institutions from taxation.'

"He cites a number of cases in support of the conclusion stated in his note, and gives a brief analysis of each case. Among the cases cited are the following: National Council K. & L. of S. v. Phillips [63 Kan. 799] 66 Pac. 1011–1014; State Council O. K. v. Effingham County [198 Ill. 441] 64 N. E. 1104; Supreme Lodge M. A. F. O. v. Effingham Co. [223 Ill. 54] 79 N. E. 23; Jones' Estate [1 Con. 125] 2 N. Y. Supp. 671; Young Men's Benevolent Society v. Fall River [160 Mass. 409] 36 N. E. 57."

For both of the reasons stated, we hold that the property was not exempt from taxation.

Under several assignments of error it is contended that the city of San Angelo exceeded the constitutional limitation of 15 cents on the $100 for streets, roads, and bridges, when it levied certain taxes for each of the years here involved for the purpose of paying interest and providing a sinking fund for certain funding bonds, issued for the purpose of paying off a former debt; and concerning that matter we copy this statement from appellee's brief:

"The city of San Angelo, in the years 19__ to 1914, both inclusive, had a population of more than 10,000 inhabitants. Said city assumed charge of its public schools in 19__ and has continued such control ever since. "Prior to the year 1903 the city was incorporated under the general laws of Texas, and on the 1st day of May, 1889, issued $10,0__ street improvement bonds under the laws authorizing same to be done. Thereafter incorporation was dissolved by vote of the people, and remained so until again incorporated in 1903, and immediately after incorporation, and during the year 1903, the city of San Angelo passed an ordinance authorizing the funding of the old city of San Angelo street improvement bonds, said ordinance providing for the issuance of said funding bonds, and the creation of a sinking fund to pay said bonds, which said bonds were afterwards issued in payment of the indebtedness of the city incurred under the former incorporation, the bonds called in the ordinance 'funding bonds of the city of San Angelo,' and are commonly known as 'the Shapleigh bonds,' he being the owner of the indebtedness for which said bonds were issued in payment, and plaintiff in the judgment rendered in favor of August F. Shapleigh against the city of San Angelo in the Circuit Court of the United States, rendered on the 6th day of November, 1899. The tax levies made by the city for the years 19__ to 1914, inclusive, are as follows:

For 1909:
For general purposes..... ___
For streets, roads, and bridges..... ___
For permanent improvements..... ___
For maintenance of public free schools..... ___
For interest and sinking fund for street improvement bonds (being the Shapleigh bonds)..... ___
For interest and sinking fund for schoolhouse bonds..... ___
For interest and sinking fund on ward school bonds of 1906..... ___
For interest and sinking fund on ward school bond No. 2 of 1909..... ___

Total..... ___

For 1910:
For general purposes..... ___
For streets, roads, and bridges..... ___
For permanent improvements..... ___
For public free schools..... ___
For interest and sinking fund for street improvement funding bonds (these being the Shapleigh bonds)..... ___
For redemption of schoolhouse bonds..... ___
For redemption of ward school bonds of 1906..... ___
For redemption of ward school bonds No. 2 of 1909..... ___
For redemption of fire station bonds..... ___

Total..... ___

For 1911:
For general purposes..... ___
For streets, roads, and bridges..... ___
For redemption of $20,000.00 City of San Angelo street improvement bonds, theretofore levied out of the road and bridge fund..... ___
For permanent improvements..... ___
For free schools..... ___
For interest and sinking fund for street improvement funding bonds (these being the Shapleigh bonds)..... ___
Schoolhouse bonds..... ___
For ward school bonds of 1906..... ___
Wor ward school bonds No. 2 of 1906..... ___
For fire station bonds..... ___

Total..... ___

For 1912:
'or general purposes .... .50
'or streets, roads, and bridges .... .05
'or interest and sinking fund for redemption
 of $20,000 street improvement bonds of 1911
 out of road and bridge fund .... .08
'or redemption of $50,000 street and bridge
 bonds of 1912, heretofore levied out of road
 and bridge fund .... .07
'or permanent improvements .... .08
'or maintenance of public free schools in
 said city .... .50
'or interest and sinking fund for street improvement funding bonds (these being the
 Shapleigh bonds) .... .03
'or schoolhouse bonds .... .04
'or ward school bonds of 1908 .... .04
'or ward school bonds No. 2 of 1909 .... .04
'or fire station bonds .... .02
   Total $1.46
For 1913:
'or general purposes .... .50
'or streets, roads, and bridges .... .08½
'or redemption of $20,000 street improvement
 bonds of 1911 out of road and bridge fund... .03
'or interest and sinking fund for $50,000 street
 and bridge bonds of 1912 out of road and
 bridge fund .... .04½
'or public free schools .... .50
'or interest and sinking fund for street improvement funding bonds (these being the
 Shapleigh bonds) .... .03
'or schoolhouse bonds .... .03
'or ward school bonds of 1908 .... .03
'or ward school bonds No. 2 of 1909 .... .03
'or fire station bonds .... .01½
   Total $1.40
For 1914:
'or general purposes .... .65
'or park purposes .... .05
'or road and bridge fund proper .... .05
'or redemption of $20,000 street improvement
 bonds of 1911 out of road and bridge fund.. .01½
'or redemption of $50,000 street and bridge
 bonds of 1912 out of road and bridge fund... .04½
'or redemption of $15,000 street and bridge
 bonds No. 2 of 1914 out of bridge fund ..... .04
'or permanent improvement fund proper .... .04½
'or interest and sinking fund for redemption
 of city of San Angelo street improvement
 funding bonds (these being the Shapleigh
 bonds) .... .03
or schoolhouse bonds .... .01
or ward school bonds of 1908 .... .02½
or ward school bonds No. 2 of 1909 .... .02½
or fire station bonds .... .00½
or $80,000 high school bonds of 1914 .... .10
or public free schools .... .50
   Total $1.40

[3] We do not concur in appellant's contention that the levies made for the purpose f paying off funding bonds that were issued 1 1903, for the purpose of obtaining funds) pay off the judgment which had been obtained against the city on street improvement onds, issued in 1889, constituted any limitaon upon the power of the city to levy taxes)r street improvements to the extent of 15 ents on the $100. Suit had been brought pon the bonds referred to, and judgment obtained against the city of San Angelo, and hat judgment constituted a valid charge gainst all the property within the city limits ubject to taxation. In our opinion, the city f San Angelo had the power to issue bonds)r the purpose of obtaining funds to discharge that judgment, and the bonds so is-

sued and the provision made for their payment did not in any wise limit the power of that municipality to levy and collect 15 cents on the $100 for street improvements. Vernon's Sayles' Civil Statutes of 1914, arts. 882, 924, 925, 926, and 937.

[4] At an election held March 25, 1914, and an ordinance passed in pursuance thereof April 6, 1914, an issuance of $80,000 high school bonds was authorized to be dated May 1, 1914, and bear interest from that date at 5 per cent. per annum, payable semiannually. On March 22, 1915, the city, having offered the bonds for sale, accepted the bid of the First National Bank of San Angelo to purchase the same at par, accrued interest, and premium of $150, subject to the approval by the Attorney General, registration by the comptroller, and waiving of the right to purchase by the State Board of Education, and the bank was required to have the bonds printed. The bonds were approved by the Attorney General, and registered by the comptroller June 3, 1915; the State Board of Education waived its right to purchase June 4, 1915, and on June 10, 1915, the bonds were delivered to the bank, and the purchase money paid to the city. The first year's interest on the bonds, when paid to the city, was by it paid over to the school board, which used the same. Appellant's property for 1914 was assessed at $2,500, and on September 8, 1914, the city made a levy of 10 cents on the $100 valuation for the interest and sinking fund on said bonds. The bonds were dated May 1, 1914, and bore interest from that date. Inasmuch as the bonds were not in fact issued and sold until after the expiration of the year 1914, appellant contends that the levy and collection of taxes for that year is illegal, and in support of that contention cites Nalle v. City of Austin, 42 S. W. 780, and Petty v. McReynolds, 157 S. W. 180.

In the Nalle. Case the question referred to was not decided on appeal. It seems that the trial court had ruled in favor of Nalle upon a somewhat similar question, but had rendered a judgment against him for a certain amount, and he appealed. The ruling referred to being in his favor, of course he did not complain of it on appeal; nor does it appear that there was any cross assignment complaining of it. While it is true that it is stated in one place that this court adopted the trial court's findings of fact and conclusions of law, in concluding the opinion, Chief Justice Fisher said:

"We do not care to discuss the various questions raised by the assignments of error, as, in our opinion, the conclusions of the court below were correct on all the points presented. We find no error in the judgment, and it is affirmed."

Thus, it will be seen that this court limited its decision to the complaints made by Nalle, and these complaints did not include the question under consideration. In refusing an application for a writ of error in that case, the Supreme Court wrote an opinion, but not upon that question. See Nalle v. City of Austin, 91 Tex. 424, 44 S. W. 66. In fact, that question was not presented on appeal in either court.

In the case of Petty v. McReynolds, referred to above, the facts are not analogous, and it was there held that where, after the levy of a tax, the purpose for which it was levied was abandoned, and the commissioners' court, without authority, attempted to transfer the tax to a fund for another purpose, such action upon the part of the commissioners' court was illegal, and could be restrained.

So it is not made to appear that any appellate court has rendered a decision sustaining appellant's contention, and it does not appeal to us as being sound. According to the terms of the contract of sale, the bonds in question in this case were to bear interest from May 1, 1914, and therefore it seems that it was just and proper that provision should have been made, as it was, to pay interest and create a sinking fund for that year as well as all subsequent years. The fact that the bonds were not sold, and in that sense not issued until June, 1915, in our judgment, ought not to require a decision on this point in appellant's favor. In fact, the bonds were sold, and the city of San Angelo obtained and applied to the use of its free schools the money for which they were sold. This being the case, it is nothing but fair and right that all the property subject to taxation within the city of San Angelo should be required to contribute to the fund required to pay interest and a sinking fund from the date of the bonds to the time of their maturity. To hold otherwise might result in much inconvenience and confusion, if it did not frustrate the purpose of the law. Before such bonds can be disposed of, they must be submitted to the Attorney General, and approved by him; also the school board has the preferential right to purchase them; and therefore it is important, if not absolutely necessary, that they should be dated and signed by the proper officers of the municipalities issuing same, before submitting them to the Attorney General and state school board; and, necessarily, a considerable time may elapse before the approval of the Attorney General and the waiver of the school board to purchase can be obtained; and, no matter whether the bonds bear date prior to the time they are actually signed, or subsequent to that time, they may not be ready for actual manual delivery to the purchaser until after the time they bear date, and during the next calendar year.

In this case it is not shown nor claimed that there was any unreasonable delay in disposing of the bonds; and therefore, and for the other reasons given, we overrule appellant's contention, and hold that it is liable for the amount levied to pay interest and create a sinking fund on school bonds from the year 1914.

No reversible error has been shown, and the judgment is affirmed.

Affirmed.

PULLMAN CO. v. BULLOCK.   (No. 683.)

(Court of Civil Appeals of Texas. Beaumont. May 9, 1921. Rehearing Denied May 25, 1921.)

1. **Carriers ⟺413(1)—Sleeping car company not insurer of effects of passengers, but must use reasonable care to see they are not stolen.**

A sleeping car company is not an insurer of personal effects belonging to a passenger, but only required to use reasonable diligence or care in seeing that property of passengers is not purloined or stolen.

2. **Carriers ⟺417—Mere loss of passenger's personal effects insufficient to establish negligence of the company.**

The loss alone of personal effects of a passenger while occupying a berth of a sleeping car is not sufficient on which to base a finding of negligence against the company.

3. **Carriers ⟺417—Evidence held to authorize jury's conclusion that porter stole passenger's diamond.**

In a passenger's action against a sleeping car company for the loss of a diamond stickpin, evidence held sufficient to authorize a reasonable deduction or conclusion by the jury that the defendant's porter was guilty of the theft of plaintiff's diamond stud.

4. **Carriers ⟺413(2)—If porter steals diamond left under pillow, carrier is liable.**

If a porter steals a passenger's diamond left under his pillow, the carrier, in contemplation of law, is guilty of negligence, and liable for its value.

5. **Carriers ⟺417—Passenger going to washroom and leaving diamond under pillow held not contributorily negligent as matter of law.**

A passenger going from his berth to the washroom and leaving his diamond under his pillow was not guilty of contributory negligence as a matter of law.

Appeal from Harris County Court; George D. Sears, Judge.

Suit by C. M. Bullock against the Pullman Company. Verdict and judgment for plaintiff, and the defendant appeals. Affirmed.

Andrews, Streetman, Logue & Mobley, and E. J. Fountain, Jr., all of Houston, for appellant.

Meek & Kahn, of Houston, for appellee.

HIGHTOWER, C. J. This suit was filed by the appellee, C. M. Bullock, in the county court, at law, of Harris county, against appellant, to recover the value of a diamond stud which the appellee alleged was stolen from him in consequence of negligence on the part of appellant, while appellee occupied a berth on one of appellant's sleeping cars, and the trial resulted in a verdict and judgment in favor of appellee for $247.50, from which judgment this appeal is prosecuted.

Appellee alleged, substantially, that he boarded one of appellant's Pullman cars between 8 and 9 o'clock one night, at Dallas, Tex., for the purpose of being transported to Knoxville, in the state of Tennessee; that he did not retire for the night until some time between 9 and 10 o'clock, at which time he went to his berth, and at the time wore a diamond stud in his necktie, which he removed on retiring, and placed the same again in the tie, pinning it through a cardboard, so that it would firmly be held in the tie, and, after doing this, placed the tie containing the diamond stud, thus fastened, under his pillow on the berth, and between the pillow and the slip in which it was incased; that during the night some time the diamond stud pen was stolen from the pillow, and that this was because of a negligent failure on the part of appellant to keep a proper and reasonable watch for the protection of his property, etc., and further, he alleged, substantially, that he believed that appellant's porter was the person who stole his diamond.

The case was tried with a jury, and in answer to a special issue it was found that appellant was guilty of negligence, as claimed, which resulted in the theft and loss of appellee's diamond, judgment following accordingly.

The first assignment of error complains of the refusal of the trial court to give a peremptory instruction in favor of appellant. There are several propositions under this assignment, the principal ones being that there was no evidence whatever showing or tending to show that appellant was guilty of negligence, as claimed, or even that appellee's diamond was stolen at all.

The only evidence offered upon the trial of this case was that of the appellee himself. He testified, substantially, that, upon retiring, between 9 and 10 o'clock, he took off his tie and took the diamond therefrom, and again placed the diamond in the tie, pinning the same through a pasteboard, just as he had alleged in his petition, and then placed the tie, with the diamond in it, under his pillow, as before stated. He further testified that he was accompanied on the journey from Dallas to Knoxville by his sister, who occupied a berth right under his; that after retiring he was not disturbed in his slumbers at any time during the night, and, so far as he knew, no person was at or near his berth, other than his sister, who, as we have just stated, occupied a berth right under his.

He further testified that the next morning, about 8 o'clock, he arose from the berth and went immediately to the washroom in the car, and after being there a few moments, not exceeding three or four minutes, it occurred to him that he had left his diamond stud in his tie under his pillow, and he immediately went back to his berth to get the diamond, and that, when he returned to his berth, he found appellant's porter at the berth, taking off and replacing the linen, etc., and saw that the pillow under which he had placed his tie containing the diamond had been removed; that he immediately told the porter that he had left his diamond in his tie under his pillow, to which the porter replied that he had removed the pillow, and that it was back in the pillow room, and that the case had been removed from it, but that he saw no diamond about the pillow, and knew nothing about the diamond.

Appellee further testified that he found his tie on the berth, where the porter was standing when he returned to the berth, as before stated, but was never able to find his diamond stud. He immediately reported the loss to appellant's conductor, and that gentleman and the porter stated to appellee that they would make investigation, and search for the diamond, etc., and try to locate it. Appellee further testified that he heard nothing else from appellant's conductor about the diamond, and that if either of them made any effort to locate it, he knew nothing about it. Neither the conductor nor the porter was placed on the witness stand.

[1] It is correctly contended by counsel for appellant, in the brief, that a sleeping car company is not an insurer of passengers on one of its cars, but is only required to use reasonable diligence or care in seeing that such effects belonging to passengers are not purloined or stolen while occupying berths in their cars. This, in effect, was the holding of the Supreme Court of this state, speaking through Justice Stayton, in the case of Pullman Co. v. Pollock, 69 Tex. 120, 5 S. W. 814, 5 Am. St. Rep. 31, and the rule there announced has been followed and reiterated wherever the point afterwards arose in this state. Pullman Co. v. Arents, 28 Tex. Civ. App. 71, 66 S. W. 329; Pullman Co. v. Matthews, 74 Tex. 654, 12 S. W. 744, 15 Am. St. Rep. 878; Stevenson v. Pullman Co., 26 S. W. 112; Belden v. Pullman Co., 43 S. W. 22.

[2] It is also correctly contended by appellant, under this assignment, that the loss alone of personal effects of a passenger while occupying a berth of a sleeping car company is not sufficient upon which to base a finding of negligence against the company. Pullman Co. v. Hatch, 30 Tex. Civ. App. 308, 70 S. W. 771; Pullman Company v. Arents, supra.

[3, 4] While admitting, however, the cor-

rectness of the legal propositions contended for, we hold in this case that the evidence of the appellee, which we have substantially stated above, was sufficient, if given credence by the jury, to authorize a reasonable deduction or conclusion by the jury that appellant's porter was guilty of the theft of appellee's diamond stud. And if the porter did steal appellant's diamond, then, in contemplation of law, appellant was guilty of negligence, and liable to appellee for the value of his diamond. We do not deem it necessary to discuss the point further.

[5] There is nothing in appellant's contention that appellee was guilty of contributory negligence, as a matter of law, in going from his berth to the washroom, leaving his diamond under his pillow.

Other assignments raised have been considered, but we find nothing in them, and the judgment will be affirmed.

MITCHELL v. SMITH. (No. 8553.)

(Court of Civil Appeals of Texas. Dallas. June 4, 1921.)

1. **Brokers ⚖➡82(4)—A petition being for commissions on express contract, no recovery on any other basis.**

The petition being on an express contract to pay a certain commission for effecting sale on stipulated terms, recovery cannot be had on any basis other than such contract.

2. **Appeal and error ⚖➡1011(1) — Finding of facts on conflicting evidence conclusive.**

The evidence having been conflicting, the judgment is conclusive as to the facts of making and breach of contract.

Appeal from Dallas County Court; T. A. Work, Judge.

Action by W. S. Mitchell against J. H. Smith. Judgment for defendant, and plaintiff appeals. Affirmed.

R. H. Capers and Lee R. Stroud, both of Dallas, for appellant.

Ross M. Scott, of Dallas, for appellee.

HAMILTON, J. Appellant sued appellee for a broker's commission, alleged to have accrued by reason of appellant finding a purchaser for a certain lot in Dallas listed with him, as agent, for sale, and which, it was alleged, appellee sold to the purchaser discovered by appellant, who was the procuring cause of the sale made.

[1] The suit was upon an alleged express contract to pay a commission of 5 per cent. for effecting sale upon certain stipulated terms, and the allegations are insufficient to support a recovery upon any basis other than the alleged contract.

[2] The proof was conflicting upon the issue of whether or not the contract was made and violated as alleged. The judgment of the court resolved this issue of fact against appellant.

The judgment upon the facts is conclusive of the issue, and we are not authorized to disturb it in the absence of some harmful error of procedure. No such error is disclosed by the record or pointed out in appellant's brief.

Accordingly, the judgment of the court below is affirmed.

PAYNE, Agent, v. WALLIS. (No. 702.)

(Court of Civil Appeals of Texas. Beaumont. June 1, 1921.)

1. **Railroads ⚖➡5½, New, vol. 6A Key-No. Series—Federal Director General liable for injuries from defective crossing.**

Where the Director General of Railroads, after taking charge of a railroad, continued to maintain and operate trains over a crossing without in any way attempting to remedy the defective and dangerous conditions surrounding it, he was responsible for negligence in maintaining such condition, though the crossing was constructed long before he took charge.

2. **Appeal and error ⚖➡1010(1)—Finding that failure to ring bell was cause of collision held not to be disturbed.**

A finding that the failure to ring the bell as a train approached a crossing was the proximate cause of a collision with an automobile cannot be disturbed, though there was a brakeman on the end of the car colliding with the automobile to give warning to persons approaching where the evidence showed that the crossing was in such a deep cut, and the view thereof was so obstructed by an embankment that it was doubtful whether the driver of the automobile could have been seen by the brakeman in time to prevent the collision.

3. **Railroads ⚖➡350(22) — Automobile driver going 12 miles an hour, though view was obstructed, held not negligent as a matter of law.**

It was not contributory negligence as a matter of law to approach a railroad crossing in an automobile at a speed of 12 miles an hour, though the view of approaching trains was greatly obstructed, and the automobile driver was familiar with the crossing, where he knew that trains were not operated over the crossing more than once a day, and sometimes not oftener than once a week, and he testified that he was looking and listening for trains.

Appeal from District Court, Milam County; W. G. Gillis, Judge.

Action by R. C. Wallis against John Barton Payne, Agent, and another. From a judgment for plaintiff, defendant Payne appeals. Affirmed.

Chambers & Wallace, of Cameron, for appellant.

E. A. Camp, of Rockdale, for appellee.

HIGHTOWER, C. J. The appellee, Wallis, filed this suit in one of the justice courts f Milam county against James A. Baker, in is capacity as receiver of the International : Great Northern Railway Company, and the)irector General of Railways, praying a recovery for damages to a Ford automobile in he sum of $150. It was alleged that the .utomobile was damaged in a collision with ne of appellant's trains at a point where one if appellant's spur tracks crosses over a pub ic highway. Negligence was predicated on mproper construction and maintenance of appellant's crossing over the highway, and also upon the negligent operation of the train at the time of the collision, in that the air brakes of the train were not connected; that a proper lookout was not kept; that the bell on the engine was not ringing, nor was the whistle blown at the time the train was approaching the crossing.

The appellant answered by general demurrer and general denial, and contributory negligence on the part of appellee.

Judgment was rendered in favor of appellee for $150, and on appeal to the county court on trial de novo judgment was rendered by the trial judge without a jury for the same amount. The trial judge filed the following findings of fact:

"I find that at the time alleged in plaintiff's petition the I. & G. N. Railroad ran through Milam county, and from Rockdale to and through Milano, Tex.; that a public road known as the Rockdale and Milano public road ran parallel with and adjacent to said railroad right of way; that at a point about 2 miles east of Rockdale was what was known as the International coal mine, located some distance north of said railroad; that a spur or switch track ran from the main line of the railroad northeast across said public road to said mine; and that the location of the railroad, public road, and switch, and their relative locations and conditions, had been the same for a long period of time, and were well known to both plaintiff and defendant.

"I find that the main line track to the east of the point where said switch leaves the main line of railroad track is in a considerable cut, and gradually goes out of the cut to the west, and that said switch leaves the main track on the westward side, but in such cut, and that said switch at the point where it crosses the public road is in a cut some 2 or 3 feet below the natural lay of the land at this point, and that the natural lay of the land along the dirt road and the railroad from said switch and switch point eastward is considerably down grade; that the dirt moved in making the excavation for the switch and the main line of the railroad was piled up on the right of way along the main line track, and in the apex of the angle made by the intersection of the switch track and the main line track, and that on account of the main line track and switch track being in the cut below the natural lay of the land, and on account of the dirt being piled as above found, and on account of the up grade going westward on the public road, that one approaching such switch on the east along the public road, could not see coal cars at and along said road crossing until such person was within 15 to 30 feet of the crossing and until such person had reached a point near the down grade in the road approaching the switch.

"I find that at the time of the accident the road was wet and slippery; that the plaintiff was traveling said public road, and approached said switch crossing from the east, traveling about 12 miles per hour, in a Ford automobile; that at the time the defendant's employés were switching some empty coal cars from the main line towards said coal mine; that the engine was near the point where the switch leaves the main line, either on the main line or just entering the switch, and was pushing five empty coal cars over said switch towards said road crossing, and that the train was moving about 8 miles per hour; that the air brakes on the cars were unconnected with the locomotive; that the bell was not ringing, and that the plaintiff did not see such cars until he was within about 15 feet of the switch crossing; that plaintiff immediately applied his emergency brakes, and the brakeman, who was on the front car, immediately signaled the engineer to stop the train; that after the plaintiff and defendant's employés each discovered the other, all parties did all they could to prevent the collision; that after plaintiff discovered the cars, on account of the down grade approaching the switch, and the wet, slippery condition of the road, the plaintiff was unable to stop the automobile before getting on the switch, and the defendant's employés were unable to stop the train before the front car had passed the road crossing; and that said front car collided with plaintiff's automobile, damaging the same to the amount of $150."

The court further found that appellant was guilty of negligence in failing to ring the bell on the locomotive as it approached the crossing where the collision occurred, and that it was also guilty of negligence in the construction and maintenance of the crossing over the public road, and that such negligence became and was the proximate cause of the collision which resulted in the damage to appellee's automobile, and further found as a fact that appellee was not guilty of contributory negligence as claimed by appellant.

Appellant, by proper assignments, has challenged each finding made by the trial court.

Upon examination of the evidence found in the record, we have concluded that the evidence was abundantly sufficient to warrant the finding made by the trial judge that as the train approached the crossing where the collision occurred the bell on the engine was not ringing, and that the court was justified in his conclusion that a failure to have the bell ringing at the time constituted negligence, and that such negligence was a proximate cause of the collision. We are also of the opinion that the evidence was abundantly sufficient to warrant the finding of the trial court that the manner in which the crossing over this public road was constructed and maintained constituted negligence, and that it also was a proximate cause of the collision.

[1] With reference to the contention of appellant that the undisputed evidence showed that the crossing was constructed long prior to the time appellant took charge of the railroad, and that therefore, appellant, in his capacity as Director General of Railroads under the government, could not be held liable for such negligent construction, cannot be sustained, for the reason that it is undisputed that the Director General did continue to maintain and operate trains over such crossing without in any way attempting to remedy the defective and dangerous conditions surrounding the same, and therefore for negligence in maintaining such condition he must be held responsible. While appellant makes this contention, no authorities are cited in its support, and we think that the assignment must be overruled.

[2] It is further contended by appellant that the failure to have the bell on the engine ringing as the coal train approached the crossing, if negligence, was not a proximate cause of the collision wth appellee's automobile, for the reason, as contended by appellant, that there was a brakeman on the end of the car which collided with the automobile to give warning to persons approaching the crossing on the highway, and that the brakeman was just as effectual for this purpose as would have been the ringing of a bell on the engine. Appellant, in making this contention, loses sight of the fact that the undisputed evidence showed that this train, while approaching the crossing, was in such a deep cut and the view thereof so obstructed by dirt that had been thrown up, constituting an embankment, that it is doubtful whether appellee, while approaching the crossing, could have been seen by the brakeman in time for him to have warned appellee and prevented the collision; whereas it is very probable that, if the engine bell had been kept ringing, appellee might have heard it in time to have saved himself from the collision, whether he saw the train or brakeman thereon or not. The record is not in such shape as to permit us to disturb the finding of the trial court on this point, and the assignment is overruled.

[3] The contention made by appellant that the evidence showed that appellee was guilty of contributory negligence as a matter of law is overruled. This contention is based upon the fact that the evidence shows that appellee was thoroughly familiar with conditions surrounding this crossing, and that, notwithstanding his knowledge of such conditions, he approached the same at the rate of speed of 12 miles per hour, and that an ordinarily prudent person, under said circumstances and with said knowledge, would not have

approached the crossing at such a high rate of speed; and appellant further contends that the undisputed evidence showed that appellee used no care in approaching this crossing to ascertain whether a train might be approaching at that time, and that under all these facts appellee was guilty of contributory negligence as a matter of law.

The appellee testified, positively, that while approaching the crossing at the time of the collision he did look and listen for any train that might be approaching the crossing, and that he neither saw nor heard any train until he was within a distance of between 15 and 30 feet of the crossing, and that then he was unable to stop his car in time to prevent the collision. Unquestionably the undisputed evidence shows that the view to an approaching train to this crossing by one on the public highway was greatly obstructed, and that, while appellee was familiar with this situation, he also knew, as is shown by the undisputed evidence, that not more than once a day was a train operated over this crossing, and sometimes not oftener than once a week, and in view of the fact, as testified to by him, that he was both looking and listening for the approach of a train to the crossing at the time, we would not be warranted in holding that he was guilty of negligence which proximately contributed to the collision as a matter of law, simply because his Ford car was going at a rate of speed of 12 miles an hour. In this connection counsel for appellant cite several authorities, which we have given careful consideration, but, without discussing them, we find that they would not be authority for holding that appellee, in this connection, was guilty of contributory negligence as a matter of law.

Among the cases cited is that of Railway Co. v. Edwards, 100 Tex. 22, 93 S. W. 106. We have many times had occasion to refer to the decision in the Edwards Case, and are convinced that the conclusion there reached and the rule there announced is sound, notwithstanding the fact that the Supreme Court of this state, in several cases of more recent date, has, in our opinion, held contrary to the rule there announced. In such decisions, however, no mention was made by the court of the Edwards Case, and, so far as we know, it has never been expressly overruled. The rule announced in the Edwards Case was, substantially, that where it was admitted or shown without contradiction by the evidence that a person approaching a railroad crossing, a place of inherent danger, without using any care, such as by looking or listening, for the approach of a train to the crossing, and where it was shown that there was no obstruction to the view of an approaching train to the crossing, such person so approaching the crossing would be guilty of contributory negligence as a matter of law. We understand that to be the holding in the Edwards Case, and many other cases prior thereto, by the Supreme Court of this state, and, when a situation of that sort comes before this court, we will follow the holding in the Edwards Case until the Supreme Court of this state shall have expressly overruled it. But the rule announced in the Edwards Case cannot be invoked here, for the reason, as we have shown, that the evidence shows conclusively that the view to the approaching train, which collided with appellee's automobile, was seriously obstructed, and also because the evidence was sufficient to warrant a finding by the trial judge that appellee used proper care, by both looking and listening for an approaching train, at the time he was approaching the crossing, but that he was unable to see the train by reason of such obstructions, and was unable to hear it, because no signal of its approach was given.

This disposes, in effect, of all assignments of error, and they are overruled, and the judgment will be affirmed.

———

SMITH et al. v. FLEMING et ux.
(No. 1214.)

(Court of Civil Appeals of Texas. El Paso.
June 23, 1921.)

Appeal from District Court, Eastland County; E. A. Hill, Judge.

Motion for leave to file motion for rehearing. Motion overruled.

For former opinion, see 231 S. W. 136.

Scott, Brelsford & Smith, of Cisco, for appellant.

W. O. Morton, of Breckenridge, and Burkett, Anderson & Orr, of Eastland, for appellee.

HARPER, C. J. Appellees file an application for leave to file a motion for rehearing of the judgment in favor of appellants Smith and Dorsey. Our opinion and judgment, reversing and rendering the judgment of the lower court, were filed and entered of record on the 12th day of May, A. D. 1921. The 15 days thereafter within which motions for rehearing are permitted to be filed expired on the 27th day of May, 1921. No motion for rehearing was presented for filing in this case in said period. On June 6, 1921, appellees filed their application to be permitted to file a motion for rehearing in said cause beyond the time allowed by statute.

The reasons given for the failure to file the motion for a rehearing within the time prescribed by statute furnished no excuse for this failure, and the excuses presented are insufficient to relieve the appellees of the operation of the statute.

Motion for leave to file motion for a rehearing is overruled. Sams v. Creager, 85 Tex. 497, 22 S. W. 399; Anderson v. First Nat. Bank, 191 S. W. 842 (12).

———

WHITNEY HARDWARE CO. v. McMAHAN
et al. (No. 7769.)

(Court of Civil Appeals of Texas. Dallas.
March 31, 1917. Rehearing Denied
June 18, 1921.)

1. Husband and wife ⬅146 — Husband contracting for his wife with her tenant for repairs not liable to tenant for negligent performance.

A husband merely contracting as agent of his wife, the landlord, with her tenant for repair of her building, neither concealing his agency nor agreeing to be bound individually, is not liable to the tenant for injury to his goods through negligent performance of the work.

2. Husband and wife ⬅213 — Wife liable for negligent performance of her contract with her tenant for repairs.

Under Vernon's Sayles' Ann. Civ. St. 1914, arts. 4621, 4622, 4624, giving to a wife the sole management and control of her separate property, including rents therefrom, except that the husband must join in disposition or incumbrance of real estate, she is liable for negligent performance through her agents of her contract with her tenant for repairs, whereby his goods are injured.

3. Husband and wife ⬅213 — Husband must be joined in action against wife for her negligent performance of contract.

The husband must be joined in action against a married woman for negligent performance of her contract with the tenant of her separate property for repairs thereof, whereby the tenant's goods were injured.

Appeal from District Court, Hill County; Horton B. Porter, Judge.

Action by the Whitney Hardware Company against E. K. McMahan and others. From judgment of dismissal, plaintiff appeals. Reversed and remanded.

For Supreme Court's answer to certified questions, see 231 S. W. 694.

Wear & Frazier, of Hillsboro, for appellant.

R. M. Vaughan, of Hillsboro, for appellees.

RAINEY, C. J. Appellant instituted this suit to recover from appellees the sum of $2,500 for damages to its stock of merchandise in repairing the roof of a building, the separate property of Mrs. McMahan, and occupied by appellant as a tenant.

The appellees interposed a general demurrer, which was sustained by the court, and appellant refusing to amend its petition judgment was entered dismissing the case, from which judgment this appeal is taken.

The petition of appellant, omitting formal parts and the exhibit, is as follows:

"Now comes the plaintiff, Whitney Hardware Company, a corporation, leave of the court first having been had and obtained, and makes and files this, its second amended original petition in lieu of all other pleadings heretofore filed by it, and for such amendment pleads as follows:

" 'That it complains of E. K. McMahan and wife, Effie McMahan, who reside in Matagorda county, Tex., and Waul McMahan, who resides in Hill county, Tex., defendants, and for cause of action represents the following facts: That the plaintiff is a corporation organized and existing under and by virtue of the laws of the state of Texas, and as such, is engaged in the hardware business in the town of Whitney, Hill county, Tex., where it has and maintains its principal office and place of business; that it has been engaged in such business since the time and long before the happening of the matters and things hereinafter complained of; that during the year 1915 it occupied a building in the town of Whitney, which belonged to and was the separate property and estate of Mrs. Effie McMahan; that it carried its main stock of hardware, including shelf hardware and generally such things as a first class hardware store usually keeps in stock for sale to the general public; that during the time it occupied said building it rented the same from the said Mrs. Effie McMahan, her husband, and the defendant Waul McMahan, agreeing to pay them a rental of $100 per month therefor; that said building became in very bad state of repair and it became impractical for plaintiff to continue as a tenant in said building with its said stock of hardware which aggregated the sum of $15,000 in value, unless it could procure certain repairs to said building.

" 'That it communicated these facts to the defendants and each of them, as a result of which the defendants each agreed, acting for themselves individually and as the agent of one another, to repair said building and to generally put it in a good tenantable state; that in consideration for said agreement on the part of said defendants to so repair said building and relying and acting thereon the plaintiff did continue to occupy same believing that it would be repaired in time as the defendants had promised.

" 'Plaintiff further represents that the defendants did make one or more ineffectual attempts to repair said building and some time about in July, 1915, or the first of August of that year, with the knowledge and consent and acquiescence of each of the other defendants hereinabove named and as their duly constituted agent, the defendant Waul McMahan did begin and undertake to have said building repaired; that plaintiff was not in any wise acquainted with the undertaking of said Waul McMahan and the defendants at the time; neither were they acquainted with the full purpose of what they intended to do. Plaintiff does represent, however, that the defendants negligently failed to properly repair said building and plaintiff further states that the defendants, instead of repairing said building, greatly impaired the roof in that they tore off a part of the covering and roof and the flash-ing and caused the same to become more open and in a greater state of bad repair than it formerly was. All of which was unknown to the plaintiff at the time. As plaintiff is informed and believes and therefore charges the fact to be, the defendants tore off a portion of said roof without having on hand sufficient material of the right kind and character to put the same back either in a good state of repair or in as good condition as it was when they attempted to repair the same; that while it was in such condition there came a very heavy rain, which poured through the roof, the cracks and the holes and wet the stock of goods, which plaintiff at that time had in said building and greatly damaged the salability of said goods and generally rendered them in an unsalable condition, detracting from their market value at least 50 per cent. and greatly damaging all of the fixtures which plaintiff had in said building; that the plaintiff's said stock of goods and fixtures, as a result of the misconduct and negligence on the part of the defendants hereinabove complained of and their failure to repair the roof in the manner agreed by them and on account of the great rain which came at the time, as above alleged, its said stock of goods was damaged at least in the sum of $2,500.

" 'In this connection, plaintiff further shows to the court that it is impossible for it to include each and every item of its said stock of goods which were so damaged and injured as aforesaid, but that it has attached to this petition "Exhibit A," here referred to and made a part hereof, which is a partial list of its goods, fixtures, wares, and merchandise so damaged at such time and place by the negligence and failure on the part of the defendants as above alleged, which said list of items was made by the plaintiff, its agents and employés, at the time and just after the damage and injury herein complained of; that each and every item of which it made a list at said time has noted the amount of injury received and damage done to said respective items by the rain mentioned and on account of the negligence of the defendants and their failure to comply with their agreement to repair said building; that a more detailed statement cannot be made by plaintiff, neither can more detailed information be given with respect to the various items of goods damaged nor the amount or character of the damage suffered by each respective item than is here shown.

" 'Plaintiff further shows, however, that the defendants' failure to comply with their agreement to repair the roof of said building and their negligence in making ineffectual and bad repairs was the direct and proximate cause of their injury and that said agreement was made by each and all of the defendants, and that the agreement and undertaking of said E. K. McMahan and the said Waul McMahan was ratified by the said Mrs. Effie McMahan and was agreed to by her. In this connection plaintiff further shows that the defendant Mrs. Effie McMahan has intrusted the management of all of her business to her husband, E. K. McMahan, and her brother-in-law, Waul McMahan, including their authority to repair, at her expense and for her, the building in question.

" 'Whereupon, premises considered, defendants having each answered herein, plaintiff prays that upon final trial it have judgment against them collectively and severally for the sum of $2,500, and for any other relief, general and special, in law or in equity, to which it may show itself entitled.'"

[1] In our opinion the petition states a good cause of action against Effie McMahan and husband, E. K. McMahan, but fails to show any liability on the part of Waul McMahan, who is alleged to be agent in the transaction. There is nothing showing that he owned any interest in the building or that he was benefited in what was done, nor did he agree to be bound individually. Whitney v. Wyman, 101 U. S. 392, 25 L. Ed. 1050. He did not conceal his agency or do anything that would make him primarily liable in the transaction.

[2] The question of liability of the wife is raised by appellee. By the act of the Legislature of 1913, amending articles 4621–4624 (Vernon's Sayles') R. S. 1911, a change was made as to the control and management of the wife's separate property, in that the wife is given "the sole management, control and disposition of her separate property, both real and personal," except in the disposition or incumbrance of real estate, in which event the husband must join. Said act, 1913, now article 4622, Vernon's Sayles' R. S. 1914, further provides that—

"The personal earnings of the wife, the rents from the wife's real estate, the interest on bonds and notes belonging to her and dividends on stocks owned by her shall be under the control, management and disposition of the wife alone."

By these articles the rents from the separate estate of the wife and other income became subject to her management and control. Before the passage of said act, 1913, it was the community property of herself and husband and was under his control and management. Now does the act of 1913 make her right to contract broader than it was under the old law? We think so, at least, as to the subject of her personal earnings, rents of her real estate, interest on notes and bonds belonging to her, and dividends on stock owned by her. This view is supported, we think, by article 4624, R. S., as amended by act 1913 (Vernon's Sayles' Ann. Civ. St. 1914, art. 4624), which reads:

"Neither the separate property of the husband nor the community property other than the personal earnings of the wife, and the income, rents and revenues from her separate property shall be subject to the payments of debts contracted by the wife, except those contracted for necessaries furnished her or her children, provided, the wife shall never be the joint maker of a note or a surety on any bond or obligation of another without the joinder of her husband with her in making such contract."

The caption of the act of 1913, concerning marital rights of the husband and wife, states it is for the purpose of "defining separate and community property of the husband and wife, conferring upon the wife the power to make contracts, authorizing suits on such contracts," etc., and in the later clause, section 2, of the act, it states:

"The fact that the present law denies to married women the right to manage their separate property, and to make contracts is unjust to a large number of citizens of this state creates an emergency and an imperative public necessity that the constitutional rule requiring bills to be read on three several days be suspended, and it is hereby suspended."

From these and the body of the act giving her the sole management, control, and disposition of her separate property, both real and personal, except with the disposition and incumbrance of real estate, etc., and divesting the husband of the control of her separate property, as formerly existed, it is evident that the Legislature intended to empower her to contract with reference to rents, etc., from her separate property and making it subject to debts and liabilities incurred by her.

[3] The allegations show that injury to the property of plaintiff occurred in attempting to improve and repair her separate property by her husband and Waul McMahan, who were acting as her agents, which was agreed to and ratified by her. It was necessary to join her husband in a suit against her, and as to them it was error to sustain a general demurrer to the petition.

The judgment is reversed, and the cause remanded.

On Motion for Rehearing.

TALBOT, J. On April 13, 1917, the appellees filed a motion for a rehearing in this case. Pending this motion we certified the controlling question involved to the Supreme Court of Texas for adjudication. On May 25, 1921, that question was answered by the Supreme Court in accord with the decision of this court.

The motion for rehearing is therefore overruled.

INDEX-DIGEST

THIS IS A KEY-NUMBER INDEX

It Supplements the Decennial Digests, the Key-Number Series and
Prior Reporter Volume Index-Digests

ABATEMENT AND REVIVAL.

III. DEFECTS AND OBJECTIONS AS TO PARTIES AND PROCEEDINGS.

⊕40 (Tex.Com.App.) Refusal to submit to examination after loss does not avoid policy, but only suspends right of recovery until examination, and hence is pleadable in abatement, not in bar.—Humphrey v. National Fire Ins. Co. of Hartford, Conn., 750.

Plea of failure to submit to examination, being in abatement, waived if not made at proper time.—Id.

VI. WAIVER OF GROUNDS OF ABATEMENT AND TIME AND MANNER OF PLEADING IN GENERAL.

⊕85 (Tex.Com.App.) Plea of failure to submit to examination, being in abatement, waived if no special ruling asked thereon before trial on merits.—Humphrey v. National Fire Ins. Co. of Hartford, Conn., 750.

ACCOUNT STATED.

⊕6(1) (Ark.) Letter by buyer, setting forth premature shipment and that goods would not be immediately inspected, held not acquiescence and account stated.—Brin Bros. v. Lyon Bros., 560.

ACKNOWLEDGMENT.

I. NATURE AND NECESSITY.

⊕5 (Ky.) Acknowledgment unnecessary to make instrument binding on parties and privies with notice.—Riddle v. Jones, 503.

ACTION.

See Abatement and Revival; Dismissal and Nonsuit.

II. NATURE AND FORM.

⊕27(3) (Mo.App.) Consignee may sue on common-law liability.—McNeill v. Wabash Ry. Co., 649.

III. JOINDER, SPLITTING, CONSOLIDATION, AND SEVERANCE.

⊕48(1) (Tex.Com.App.) Rule against multifariousness not applied where the causes of action grow out of the same transaction.—Hudmon v. Foster, 346.

⊕48(3) (Tex.Civ.App.) Causes of action for excessive freight and demurrage charges and damages for shortage of coal properly joined.—Payne v. White House Lumber Co., 417.

ADJOINING LANDOWNERS.

See Boundaries.

ADMINISTRATION.

See Executors and Administrators.

231 S.W.—71

ADMIRALTY.

See Shipping.

ADVERSE POSSESSION.

I. NATURE AND REQUISITES.

(B) Actual Possession.

⊕22 (Ark.) Pasturing and cutting timber from swamp land held actual possession.—Carter v. Stewart, 887.

(E) Duration and Continuity of Possession.

⊕47 (Tex.Com.App.) Owner's entry on land to cut timber broke continuity of adverse claimant's possession except as to land inclosed by claimant.—Evans v. Houston Oil Co. of Texas, 731.

⊕50 (Tex.Com.App.) Purchase of other land three-quarters of a mile distant from land occupied did not preclude purchaser from obtaining title to land occupied by adverse possession.—Evans v. Houston Oil Co. of Texas, 731.

(F) Hostile Character of Possession.

⊕60(2) (Tex.Com.App.) Possession with owner's permission not adverse possession.—Evans v. Houston Oil Co. of Texas, 731.

⊕64 (Mo.App.) Pledgee not entitled to defeat replevin action on ground of limitation of action.—Conway v. Flaugh, 1045.

⊕71(1) (Tex.Civ.App.) Conveyance of interest held to support plea of five years' limitation as a deed and not quitclaim.—Brownfield v. Brabson, 491.

⊕80(2) (Tex.Civ.App.) Deed must contain sufficient description to support plea of five years' limitation.—Brownfield v. Brabson, 491.

⊕82 (Tex.Civ.App.) Five-year statute begins to run from registration of deed.—Brownfield v. Brabson, 491.

(G) Payment of Taxes.

⊕90 (Tex.Civ.App.) Title may be acquired to undivided interest in land.—Brownfield v. Brabson, 491.

Taxes must be paid under proper description.—Id.

⊕93 (Tex.Civ.App.) Payment of taxes for five years held sufficient.—Brownfield v. Brabson, 491.

⊕94 (Tex.Com.App.) Taxes must be paid before becoming delinquent under five-year statute of limitations.—Houston Oil Co. of Texas v. Jordan, 320.

⊕94 (Tex.Civ.App.) Payment of taxes after delinquency insufficient.—Brownfield v. Brabson, 491.

II. OPERATION AND EFFECT.

(A) Extent of Possession.

⊕100(1) (Ark.) Possession of portion under deed is constructive possession of all included in description.—Carter v. Stewart, 887.

☌101 (Ark.) Constructive possession to limits of grant applies against state claim.—Carter v. Stewart, 887.

(B) Title or Right Acquired.

☌104 (Ark.) Presumption of grant from state may be drawn from 50 years' possession and payment of taxes.—Carter v. Stewart, 887.

Failure of state records to show grant of lands does not rebut presumption of grant.—Id.

Presumption of state grant from possession and payment of taxes is not estoppel of state by unauthorized act of tax officers.—Id.

III. PLEADING, EVIDENCE, TRIAL, AND REVIEW.

☌115(1) (Tex.Com.App.) Whether plaintiff's possession of land was adverse held for jury.—Evans v. Houston Oil Co. of Texas, 731.

☌115(1) (Tex. Civ. App.) Whether party claiming under five-year statute paid taxes properly held for jury.—Brownfield v. Brabson, 491.

AGENCY.

See Principal and Agent.

ANIMALS.

See Carriers, ☌212-230.

☌44 (Ark.) Owner of uninclosed land with open well liable for injury to stock, though dug by another.—Frauenthal v. Morton, 884.

Absolute liability imposed on owner of open well injuring stock.—Id.

Evidence held to show liability for drowning of horse in well.—Id.

Liability for injury to stock by open well not dependent on actual possession of land.—Id.

Complaint held to warrant recovery of double damages for drowning of horse.—Id.

☌50(2) (Ark.) Fencing district operative without fence around it, where bounded by other districts.—Cranor v. Jenkins, 883.

ANTI-TRUST LAWS.

See Monopolies, ☌17-21.

APPEAL AND ERROR.

See Courts, ☌231-247; Criminal Law, ☌1025-1192.

For review of rulings in particular actions or proceedings, see also the various specific topics.

I. NATURE AND FORM OF REMEDY.

☌2 (Tex.Civ.App.) Statute giving right of appeal from order on plea of privilege not unconstitutional.—Hill v. Brady, 145.

III. DECISIONS REVIEWABLE.

(D) Finality of Determination.

☌66 (Tex.Civ.App.) No appeal except from final judgment.—Taylor v. Masterson, 856.

☌78(3) (Tex.Civ.App.) Order sustaining demurrer to pleas held not a final appealable judgment.—Taylor v. Masterson, 856.

☌80(1) (Tex.Civ.App.) No order or decree not precluding further litigation is a "final judgment."—Taylor v. Masterson, 856.

Judgment for plaintiff disposes of defendant's plea in reconvention or cross-action and is appealable.—Id.

☌82(3) (Mo.App.) No appeal lies from order vacating final default.—Barkwell v. Carlisle, 1063.

IV. RIGHT OF REVIEW.

(B) Estoppel, Waiver, or Agreements Affecting Right.

☌162(1) (Ky.) Acceptance of voluntary satisfaction of juugment does not bar appeal, when judgment not for full amount sought.—Clay v. Thomas, 512.

V. PRESENTATION AND RESERVATION IN LOWER COURT OF GROUNDS OF REVIEW.

(A) Issues and Questions in Lower Court.

☌172(1) (Ark.) An issue of account stated, not presented in trial court, cannot be presented on appeal.—Brin Bros. v. Lyon Bros., 560.

☌172(1)(Ark.) Plaintiff bound by allegations and evidence showing they were doing business within the state.—Forrester v. Locke, 897.

☌172(1) (Mo.App.) Contention not pleaded cannot be raised.—Insurance Agency Co. v. Blossom, 636.

☌172(1) (Tex.Com.App.) Claim as to time of acquisition of property asserted to be community cannot be made for first time on appeal.—Roberson v. Hughes, 734.

☌173(6) (Mo.App.) Defense of statute of frauds held waived.—Heath v. Beck, 657.

(B) Objections and Motions, and Rulings Thereon.

☌207 (Tex.Civ.App.) Improper remarks of counsel available on appeal notwithstanding failure to object.—Home Life & Accident Co. v. Jordan, 802.

☌215(1) (Tex.Com.App.) Instruction as to false representation held correct on appeal, in absence of objection thereto.—Waggoner v. Zundelowitz, 721.

☌216(1) (Ky.) Appellant cannot complain of failure to give instruction not offered.—Frankfort Elevator Coal Co. v. Williamson, 241.

☌218(2) (Tex.Civ.App.) Failure to submit issue not available on appeal, in absence of request.—Jemison v. Estes, 797.

☌231(5) (Mo.App.) General objection to exhibition of injury to jury held insufficient.—O'Connell v. Kansas City, 1040.

☌231(5) (Mo.App.) General objection to evidence held not sufficiently specific upon which to predicate exception.—Stetina v. Bergstein, 1059.

☌231(9) (Ark.) Errors in verbiage of instruction not reviewed, unless specifically pointed out.—Texarkana & Ft. Smith Ry. Co. v. Adcock, 866.

☌232(2) (Mo.App.) Objections to evidence, not made below, not considered.—Baldwin v. Kansas City Rys. Co., 280.

☌238(3) (Mo.) In the absence of motion for arrest of judgment, nothing but record proper can be considered.—State ex rel. Dolman v. Dickey, 582.

(C) Exceptions.

☌260(2) (Ark.) Exclusion of evidence not excepted to cannot be reviewed.—Sanderson v. Marconi, 554.

☌263(3) (Tex.Civ.App.) Refusal of requested charge not fundamental error reviewable in absence of exception.—Priddy v. Childers, 172.

☌265(1) (Tex.Com.App.) On exception to judgment, exceptions need not to be taken to findings of court.—Temple Hill Development Co. v. Lindholm, 321.

(D) Motions for New Trial.

☌281(1) (Mo.) In the absence of motion for new trial, nothing but record proper can be considered.—State ex rel. Dolman v. Dickey, 582.

☌282 (Tex.Civ.App.) In case tried to court, motion for new trial not necessary.—Canter v. Canter, 706.

☌300 (Ark.) Judgment affirmed where appellant failed to file motion for new trial with prayer for appeal within 30 days after decision.—Spivey v. Spivey, 559.

☌301 (Ark.) Defendant cannot raise for first time on appeal question of excessive verdict.—Battle v. Draper, 869.

☌301 (Ky.) Sufficiency of evidence to sustain verdict not reviewable without motion for new trial on that ground.—National Council Knights and Ladies of Security v. Dean, 29.

🗝=301 (Ky.) Matters not assigned as ground for new trial cannot be reviewed.—Commonwealth Power Ry. & Light Co. v. Vaught, 247.

🗝=302(5) (Ky.) Objection that verdict is contrary to law does not raise error in giving and refusing instructions.—Grove Lodge No. 274, I. O. O. F., v. Fidelity Phenix Ins. Co., 215.

VI. PARTIES.

🗝=327(10) (Ky.) All creditors not necessary parties to appeal.—Hamer v. Boreing, 497.

VII. REQUISITES AND PROCEEDINGS FOR TRANSFER OF CAUSE.

(D) Writ of Error, Citation, or Notice.

🗝=396 (Tex.Civ.App.) Exception in notice of appeal not necessary for appeal from temporary injunction.—Blaylock v. Slocomb, 864.

Exception and notice of appeal necessary to perfect appeal from final judgment perpetuating injunction.—Id.

(E) Entry, Docketing, and Appearance.

🗝=434 (Mo.) Appeal from judgment forfeiting recognizance in criminal prosecution dismissed where no appearance made.—State v. Carroll, 565.

🗝=434 (Tex.Civ.App.) Execution of agreement by defendant in error operated as appearance in Court of Civil Appeals.—Indemnity Co. of America v. Mahaffey, 861.

IX. SUPERSEDEAS OR STAY OF PROCEEDINGS.

🗝=488(1) (Mo.) Appeal from merits in injunction suit suspended action on motion to assess damages.—Morrison v. Hess, 997.

X. RECORD AND PROCEEDINGS NOT IN RECORD.

(A) Matters to be Shown by Record.

🗝=494 (Mo.App.) When certified copy of decree on one count not filed, it is not reviewable.—Heath v. Beck, 657.

(B) Scope and Contents of Record.

🗝=516 (Ky.) Argument objected to must be made part of bill of exceptions.—Louisville Woolen Mills v. Kindgen, 202.

🗝=543 (Mo.App.) Appellant seeking remand because lost notes of evidence prevent transcript and bill of exceptions is not entitled to retrial as of right and must be without fault.—Larson v. Shockley, 1030.

Facts held to show that appellant seeking retrial because of lost stenographer's notes was not without fault.—Id.

(C) Necessity of Bill of Exceptions, Case, or Statement of Facts.

🗝=544(1) (Tex.Civ.App.) Court cannot consider propriety of giving charge, in absence of statement of facts.—Jemison v. Estes, 797.

Court will not pass on whether issues were fully submitted, in absence of statement of facts.—Id.

(E) Abstracts of Record.

🗝=581(3) (Mo.App.) Abstract held insufficient, as not complying with court rule.—Poshek v. Marceline Coal & Mining Co., 70.

🗝=586(1) (Mo.App.) "Abstract" of record, containing nothing but copy of petition and answer, held insufficient.—Poshek v. Marceline Coal & Mining Co., 70.

(F) Making, Form, and Requisites of Transcript or Return.

🗝=596 (Tenn.) Appellees' counsel should direct insertion of portion of record material to his clients.—State v. Colored Tennessee Industrial School, 544.

(I) Defects, Objections, Amendment, and Correction.

🗝=643(5) (Mo.) Omission of record to show that motion for new trial and bill of exceptions filed cured by failure to object in time.—National Refrigerator Co. v. Southwest Missouri Light Co., 980.

(K) Questions Presented for Review.

🗝=672 (Tex.Com.App.) Jurisdiction of Court of Civil Appeals limited to errors assigned and error of law apparent on face of record.—Roberson v. Hughes, 734.

Holding of court based upon finding of fact not error of law apparent on face of record.—Id.

🗝=688(2) (Ky.) Record held not to show denial of right to make proper argument.—Louisville Woolen Mills v. Kindgen, 202.

Party must show nature of argument which he claims he was prohibited from making.—Id.

🗝=704(1) (Tex.Civ.App.) No review of refusal of special issue without record showing issues submitted.—Holden v. Evans, 146.

(L) Matters Not Apparent of Record.

🗝=714(5) (Ky.) Court can consider undenied statement in brief in connection with silence of record.—Louisville Woolen Mills v. Kindgen, 202.

XI. ASSIGNMENT OF ERRORS.

🗝=719(1) (Mo.) Appeal from judgment forfeiting recognizance in criminal prosecution dismissed where no errors assigned.—State v. Carroll, 565.

🗝=719(1) (Tex. Com. App.) Jurisdiction of Court of Civil Appeals limited to errors assigned and error of law apparent on face of record.—Roberson v. Hughes, 734.

🗝=722(1) (Tex.Com.App.) Appellant may either adopt assignments in motion for new trial or independent assignments.—Temple Hill Development Co. v. Lindholm, 321.

🗝=722(1) (Tex.Com.App.) Appellant not restricted to assignments in motion for new trial.—Harlan v. Acme Sanitary Flooring Co., 348.

🗝=722(1) (Tex.Civ.App.) Copies of findings of fact designated as assignments of error held not such.—Busbee v. Busbee, 441.

🗝=724(1) (Tex.Com.App.) Statute as to sufficiency of assignment of error liberally construed.—Morrison v. Neely, 728.

🗝=725(2) (Tex.Civ.App.) Assignments of error complaining of overruling of exceptions held insufficient for consideration.—Holden v. Evans, 146.

🗝=730(1) (Tex.Civ.App.) Requested charge held not in fact a charge requiring consideration under general assignment of error.—Priddy v. Childers, 172.

🗝=731(1) (Tex.Civ.App.) Assignment of error to verdict held too general to be considered.—Priddy v. Childers, 172.

🗝=731(5) (Tex.Civ.App.) Assignment of error to sufficiency of evidence held too general to be considered.—Priddy v. Childers, 172.

🗝=742(1) (Tex. Civ.App.) Reference necessary in brief to transcript in connection with statements made under assignments.—Western Union Telegraph Co. v. Brett, 449.

🗝=742(1) (Tex.Civ.App.) Statement under assignment as to contributory negligence should be full and fair.—Baker v. Hodges, 844.

🗝=742(2) (Tex.Civ.App.) Jurisdictional question considered though not germane to assignment.—Erwin v. Erwin, 834.

🗝=742(3) (Tex.Civ.App.) Assignments of error complaining of overruling of exceptions without showing made as to action taken in exception held insufficient for consideration.—Holden v. Evans, 146.

🗝=742(5) (Tex.Civ.App.) Assignment of error insufficient as a proposition held too general for consideration.—Holden v. Evans, 146.

🗝=742(5) (Tex.Civ.App.) Proposition held not to cure defect in too general assignment.—Priddy v. Childers, 172.

⚫═742(6) (Tex.Clv.App.) Assignment of error to verdict should be followed by proposition.—Priddy v. Childers, 172.

Assignment of error to sufficiency of evidence to sustain verdict, should be followed by proposition.—Id.

⚫═743(I) (Tex.Clv.App.) Assignments of error complaining of overruling of exceptions without record reference being given *held* insufficient for consideration.—Holden v. Evans, 146.

⚫═744 (Tex.Clv.App.) In case tried to court, assignments of error must be filed before appeal.—Canter v. Canter, 796.

⚫═745 (Tex.Clv.App.) Assignments of error may be considered though not filed below.—Busbee v. Busbee, 441.

⚫═747(2) (Tex.Clv.App.) Inconsistency of conclusions not considered when only one party has assigned error.—Hull v. Guaranty State Bank of Carthage, 810.

⚫═750(4) (Tex.Com.App.) Assignments of error *held* to attack sufficiency of evidence to sustain findings of fact.—Morrison v. Neely, 728.

⚫═753(2) (Tex.Clv.App.) Judgment affirmed in absence of assignments of error and fundamental error.—Busbee v. Busbee, 441.

XII. BRIEFS.

⚫═757(I) (Mo.App.) Statement of the case *held* sufficient.—Hartweg v. Kansas City Rys. Co., 269.

⚫═759 (Mo.App.) Brief need not contain separate assignments of error.—Lange v. Midwest Motor Securities Co., 272.

⚫═766 (Mo.App.) Appeal dismissed for violation of statute and court rule requiring a clear and concise statement of the case.—Hartweg v. Kansas City Rys. Co., 269.

⚫═773(2) (Mo.) Appeal from judgment forfeiting recognizance in criminal prosecution dismissed where no briefs filed.—State v. Carroll, 565.

⚫═773(4) (Tex.Clv.App.) Case not briefed affirmed in absence of fundamental error.—Barefield v. Allen, 170.

XIII. DISMISSAL, WITHDRAWAL, OR ABANDONMENT.

⚫═781(4) (Mo.) Investigation on merits required, though restrictions sought to be enforced have lapsed.—Morrison v. Hess, 997.

⚫═781(6) (Tex. Com.App.) Case dismissed where issues have become merely academic.—Moore v. American Lumber Co., 318.

⚫═795(2) (Mo.App.) Motion to dismiss must point out deficiency of abstract relied upon.—Jones v. Munroe, 1069.

XVI. REVIEW.

(A) Scope and Extent in General.

⚫═842(I) (Mo.App.) Waiver becomes question of law where facts are admitted.—Hay v. Bankers' Life Co., 1035.

⚫═842(7) (Tex.Com.App.) Facts *held* not to warrant holding, as a matter of law, that contract was procured by undue influence.—Briscoe v. Bright's Adm'r, 1082.

⚫═842(8) (Mo.App.) Construction of written instruments, as letters, is for the court.—Hay v. Banker's Life Co., 1035.

⚫═843(2) (Mo.App.) Assignment of excessiveness of verdict need not be noticed where reversed on other grounds.—Noah v. L. B. Price Mercantile Co., 300.

⚫═846(3) (Mo.App.) Judgment affirmed if sustainable on any theory when no declarations of law asked or given.—Heath v. Beck, 657.

⚫═854(I) (Tex.Clv.App.) Court must affirm judgment of lower court if any ground to support it.—Denton v. Kansas City Life Ins. Co., 436.

⚫═854(2) (Ky.) Correct judgment not reversed for erroneous reason.—Louisville Woolen Mills v. Kindgen, 202.

(B) Interlocutory, Collateral, and Supplementary Proceedings and Questions.

⚫═870(3) (Tex.Clv.App.) Defendant waived right to review action of trial court on plea of privilege when he failed to appeal from order.—Hill v. Brady, 145.

(C) Parties Entitled to Allege Error.

⚫═882(12) (Mo.App.) Defendant's requested instruction on burden of proof *held* not to adopt plaintiff's instruction.—Fidelity & Casualty Co. of New York v. Kansas City Rys. Co., 277.

⚫═882(12) (Mo.App.) No complaint of error in instruction adopted by complainant.—Vogelsang v. Board of Education of City of Cape Girardeau, 645.

⚫═882(12) (Tex.Com.App.) Error in placing burden of proof *held* not invited.—First Nat. Bank v. Todd, 322.

(D) Amendments, Additional Proofs, and Trial of Cause Anew.

⚫═894(2) (Tenn.) Evidence not presumed to sustain finding, when not before the court in equity.—State v. Colored Tennessee Industrial School, 544.

(E) Presumptions.

⚫═901 (Ark.) Refusal of instructions not error in absence of showing that they were not covered by other instructions given.—Taylor v. Walker, 550.

⚫═907(3) (Tenn.) Evidence presumed to sustain finding, when not before the court at law.—State v. Colored Tennessee Industrial School, 544.

⚫═922 (Mo.) Court's finding as to qualification of juror presumed correct on appeal.—Richardson v. Kansas City Rys. Co., 988.

⚫═926(I) (Tex.Clv.App.) Where court admitted evidence on issue after sustaining exception, and petition not amended, it is presumed court changed mind.—Payne v. White House Lumber Co., 417.

⚫═926(8) (Mo.App.) In the absence of certificate it will be presumed a proper case for reading the deposition was disclosed.—Whiteside v. Court of Honor, 1026.

⚫═927(3) (Mo.App.) Cause considered most favorably to appellant on appeal from nonsuit.—Elms v. Mutual Benefit Life Ins. Co., 653.

⚫═927(5) (Mo.App.) In reviewing denial of demurrer to evidence. only evidence supporting verdict can be considered.—Evans v. Clapp, 79.

In reviewing denial of demurrer to evidence, plaintiff entitled to every reasonable inference.—Id.

⚫═928(5) (Ky.) Omission in instruction presumed to have been cured by other instructions.—National Council Knights and Ladies of Security v. Dean, 29.

⚫═930(I) (Tex.Com.App.) Evidence viewed most strongly in support of judgment.—Briscoe v. Bright's Adm'r, 1082.

⚫═930(I) (Tex.Clv.App.) Everything sustained by testimony deemed found in support of judgment.—Maier v. Langerhans, 145.

⚫═930(3) (Tex.Com.App.) In absence of objection, it will be presumed that special issues conform to pleadings and evidence.—Baker v. Shafter, 349.

⚫═931(I) (Tex.Com.App.) No presumption evidence sufficient to support judgment by court without jury, where agreed statement of facts contains all the evidence.—Garza v. City of San Antonio, 697.

⚫═931(I) (Tex.Clv.App.) Viewed in aspect most favorable to appellee.—Anderson v. Smith, 142.

(F) Discretion of Lower Court.

⚫═957(I) (Tex.Clv.App.) Discretion in setting aside of judgments cannot be arbitrarily exercised.—Hubb-Diggs Co. v. Mitchell, 425.

⚫═959(I) (Ky.) Discretion of court in refusing amendments not disturbed unless abused.—Foxwell v. Justice, 509.

⊕══966(1) (Mo.App.) Granting continuance is within the sound discretion of the trial court subject to review.—Noah v. L. B. Price Mercantile Co., 300.

⊕══966(1) (Tex.Civ.App.) Where application for continuance shows failure to use means for procuring testimony, it is addressed to the court's discretion not disturbed on appeal.—Short v. Walters, 161.

⊕══981 (Mo.App.) The granting of new trial for newly discovered evidence rests largely in discretion of trial court.—Gerth v. Christy, 639.

Appellate court will interfere with denial of new trial on the ground of newly discovered evidence only in clear case.—Id.

(G) Questions of Fact, Verdicts, and Findings.

⊕══987(1) (Tex.Com.App.) Duty of court of Civil Appeals to set aside judgment for insufficiency of evidence to sustain verdict.—Wisdom v. Chicago, R. I. & G. Ry. Co., 344.

⊕══989 (Tex.Civ.App.) On question of sufficiency of evidence, only evidence supporting verdict considered.—W. T. Rawleigh Co. v. Smith, 799.

⊕══994(2) (Mo.App.) Inconsistency in testimony not reviewable.—Keith v. Kansas City Rys. Co., 1046.

⊕══994(2) (Tex.Com.App.) Credibility of plaintiff as witness for the jury.—Texas & N. O. R. Co. v. Gericke, 745.

⊕══994(2) (Tex.Com.App.) Credibility of witnesses not question within province of Commission of Appeals.—Briscoe v. Bright's Adm'r, 1082.

⊕══994(3) (Mo.App.) Evidence of nonpayment of assessments held for trial court.—Hay v. Bankers' Life Co., 1035.

⊕══994(3) (Tex.Com.App.) Evidence to discredit testimony, not considered on appeal, where any evidence of sufficient probative force to support court's finding.—Roberson v. Hughes, 734.

⊕══995 (Mo.) Weight of evidence held not within the province of the Supreme Court.—Jackman v. St. Louis & H. Ry. Co., 978.

⊕══997(2) (Mo.App.) Overruling demurrer to evidence sustained, unless no evidence to support verdict.—Evans v. Clapp, 79.

⊕══1001(1) (Ky.) Finding supported by evidence of probative value not disturbed.—John R. Coppin Co. v. Richards, 229.

⊕══1001(1) (Mo.App.) Verdicts founded on conjecture not sustained.—Bibb v. Grady, 1020.

⊕══1001(1) (Mo.App.) Verdict not disturbed where sufficient evidence exists to sustain it.—Thompson v. Business Men's Acc. Ass'n of America, 1049.

⊕══1001(2) (Ky.) That the appellate court might have found differently immaterial.—City of Newport v. Schmit, 54.

⊕══1002 (Mo.) It is the province of the jury to pass on conflicting evidence.—Jackman v. St. Louis & H. Ry. Co., 978.

⊕══1002 (Tenn.) Finding of jury on disputed questions of fact binding on Supreme Court.—Hines v. Partridge, 16.

⊕══1002 (Tex.Com.App.) Verdict on conflicting evidence not disturbed.—Waggoner v. Zundelowitz, 721.

⊕══1003 (Ky.) Verdict unsupported by evidence cannot be allowed to stand.—Hines v. Wilson's Adm'x, 23.

⊕══1003 (Ky.) Verdict not disturbed unless clearly against weight of evidence.—Frankfort Elevator Coal Co. v. Williamson, 241.

⊕══1003 (Mo.App.) Verdict on plaintiff's uncorroborated testimony, although opposed by three witnesses for defendant, not contrary to weight of evidence.—Keith v. Kansas City Rys. Co., 1046.

⊕══1005(4) (Mo.) Order, granting new trial on ground that verdict is against weight of evidence, reversed.—Borack v. Mosler Safe Co., 823.

⊕══1005(4) (Mo.App.) Denial of motion for new trial based on evidence not disturbed.—Buehler v. Waggener Paint & Glass Co., 283.

⊕══1008(1) (Tex.Com.App.) Findings by court are not conclusive on appeal, where a statement of facts appears in the record.—Temple Hill Development Co. v. Lindholm, 321.

⊕══1009(1) (Mo.) Supreme Court can weigh evidence in equitable action.—Larrick v. Heathman, 975.

⊕══1010(1) (Mo.App.) Finding of fact not interfered with when supported by substantial evidence.—Williams v. John T. Hesser Coal Co., 680.

⊕══1010(1) (Tex.Civ.App.) Finding that failure to ring bell was cause of collision held not to be disturbed.—Payne v. Wallis, 1114.

⊕══1011(1) (Ky.) Determination of trial court as to amount of trustee's land sold with trust property not disturbed where evidence conflicting.—Clay v. Thomas, 512.

⊕══1011(1) (Tex.Civ.App.) Trial judge's finding on issue of fact not disturbed.—Hull v. Guaranty State Bank of Carthage, 810.

⊕══1011(1) (Tex.Civ.App.) Finding of facts on conflicting evidence conclusive.—Mitchell v. Smith, 1114.

(H) Harmless Error.

⊕══1033(2) (Mo.App.) Variance between pleading and proof in action on note given for price of jacks harmless.—Neal v. Crowson, 1033.

⊕══1033(4) (Mo.App.) Error favorable to appellant not reviewable.—Jones v. Munroe, 1069.

⊕══1033(5) (Ky.) Defendant cannot complain of instruction placing undue burden on plaintiff.—Krieger v. Standard Printing Co., 27.

⊕══1033(5) (Mo.App.) Defendant cannot complain of an instruction unduly favorable to it.—Evans v. Clapp, 79.

⊕══1033(5) (Mo.App.) Appellant cannot complain of favorable instruction.—Hartweg v. Kansas City Rys. Co., 269.

⊕══1033(5) (Mo.App.) Defendants cannot complain of instruction placing undue burden on plaintiff.—Orr v. Russell, 275.

⊕══1033(5) (Tex.Com.App.) Instruction that plaintiff, suing to rescind, must have discovered falsity of all representations before waiver established, held harmless.—Waggoner v. Zundelowitz, 721.

⊕══1040(3) (Tex.Com.App.) Erroneous sustaining of exceptions on ground of multifariousness not harmless.—Hudmon v. Foster, 346.

⊕══1040(10) (Tex.Civ.App.) Overruling of exception to allegations held harmless in view of judgment.—Home Life & Accident Co. v. Jordan, 802.

⊕══1042(1) (Tex.Civ.App.) Error in striking petition harmless where it does not appear it was amendable.—Wilmarth v. Reagan, 445.

⊕══1046(5) (Tex. Com. App.) Comment by judge on weight of evidence held prejudicial.—American Express Co. v. Chandler, 1085.

⊕══1050(1) (Ky.) Erroneous admission of evidence as to disease in personal injury action prejudicial if size of verdict might be attributed thereto.—Cincinnati, N. O. & T. P. R. Co. v. Owsley, 210.

⊕══1050(1) (Tex.Civ.App.) Evidence harmless where same testimony given without objection.—Great Southern Oil & Refining Ass'n v. Cooper, 157.

⊕══1050(1) (Tex.Civ.App.) Error in admission of evidence rendered harmless by reception of other like evidence.—City of Dallas v. Maxwell, 429.

⊕══1051(1) (Tex.Civ.App.) Evidence harmless where fact otherwise shown.—Great Southern Oil & Refining Ass'n v. Cooper, 157.

⊕══1051(2) (Ky.) Erroneous acceptance of finding by Compensation Board sustained by undisputed evidence is harmless.—Louisville Woolen Mills v. Kindgen, 202.

⟸1051(2) (Tex.Civ.App.) Admission of evidence harmless where uncontradicted evidence established same fact.—Kurz v. Solis, 424.

⟸1056(2) (Tex.Civ.App.) Error in exclusion of testimony immaterial.—Great Southern Oil & Refining Ass'n v. Cooper, 157.

⟸1056(3) (Mo.) Refusal to permit plaintiff's attorney to testify *held* harmless error.—Tiede v. Tiede, 950.

⟸1058(1) (Mo.App.) Exclusion of evidence later admitted not reversible error.—Keith v. Kansas City Rys. Co., 1046.

⟸1060(1) (Ky.) New trial should be granted for prejudicial denial of right to be heard in person and by counsel.—Louisville Woolen Mills v. Kindgen, 202.

⟸1060(1) (Mo.App.) Judgment not reversed for argument improper on question of damages when counsel was not arguing question of damages.—O'Connell v. Kansas City, 1040.

⟸1062(1) (Tex.Civ.App.) Error in submission of whether brokers were procuring cause immaterial, in view of finding that broker had no contract with owner.—Jemison v. Estes, 797.

⟸1064(1) (Mo.App.) Instruction *held* reversible error.—Forrester v. Walsh Fire Clay Products Co., 668.

⟸1064(1) (Tex.Com.App.) Argumentative charge on ordinary care of deceased *held* prejudicial.—Missouri, K. & T. Ry. Co. of Texas v. Merchant, 327.

⟸1066 (Mo.App.) Instruction allowing jury to assume fact unsupported by evidence reversible error.—Hunter v. American Brake Co., 659.

⟸1066 (Tex.Civ.App.) Reversible error to submit issue without evidence to support it.—Smith v. Fleming, 136.

⟸1067 (Tex.Com.App.) Failure to instruct that party suing to rescind must have had knowledge before he could waive fraud *held* not prejudicial.—Waggoner v. Zundelowitz, 721.

⟸1068(3) (Tex.Com.App.) No reversal for erroneous instruction, where judgment was the only one proper under the evidence.—Pullman Co. v. Gulf, C. & S. F. Ry. Co., 741.

⟸1068(4) (Mo.App.) Instruction omitting requirement that damages for delay in payment of loss insured against must be limited to 10 per cent. cured by verdict.—North v. National Life & Accident Ins. Co. of Nashville, Tenn., 665.

⟸1068(4) (Mo.App.) In view of verdict, instruction on trial of claim *held* not cause for reversal because not telling the jury to deduct conceded amount.—Stetina v. Bergstein, 1059.

⟸1071(6) (Tex.Civ.App.) Failure to embrace undisputed facts in findings harmless.—Davis v. Campbell-Root Lumber Co., 167.

(J) Decisions of Intermediate Courts.

⟸1082(2) (Tex.) Supreme Court is without jurisdiction of assignments of error not passed upon by Court of Civil Appeals.—Mills v. Mills, 697.

⟸1082(2) (Tex.Com.App.) Holding of intermediate court not questioned by petition for error is not reviewable.—Pullman Co. v. Gulf, C. & S. F. Ry. Co., 741.

⟸1083(6) (Tex.Com.App.) Reversal and rendition of judgment by Court of Civil Appeals *held* ruling on law and not on facts.—Briscoe v. Bright's Adm'r, 1082.

⟸1094(1) (Tex.Com.App.) Court of Civil Appeals has exclusive jurisdiction over questions of fact.—Haynes v. Western Union Telegraph Co., 361.

⟸1094(1) (Tex.Com.App.) Sufficiency of evidence to support judgment exclusively a question for the Court of Civil Appeals.—Morrison v. Neely, 728.

⟸1094(2) (Tex.) Findings of trial court and Court of Civil Appeals upon questions of fact are conclusive on Supreme Court.—Kenedy Pasture Co. v. State, 683.

⟸1094(2) (Tex.Com.App.) Finding of usury approved by Court of Appeals not reviewed.

—Farmers' & Merchants' State Bank of Ballinger v. Cameron, 738.

⟸1094(5) (Tex.Com.App.) Supreme Court bound by finding of Court of Civil Appeals on conflicting evidence.—Rea v. Luse, 310.

⟸1094(5) (Tex.Com.App.) Supreme Court bound by Court of Civil Appeals' holding as to insufficiency of evidence to sustain verdict.—Wisdom v. Chicago, R. I. & G. Ry. Co., 344.

(K) Subsequent Appeals.

⟸1096(1) (Mo.) Propriety of former judgment not reviewable.—State ex rel. Dolman v. Dickey, 582.

⟸1097(1) (Mo.) Party by appealing from judgment in his own behalf cannot obtain review of former adverse ruling of appellate court in same cause.—State ex rel. Dolman v. Dickey, 582.

XVII. DETERMINATION AND DISPOSITION OF CAUSE.

(A) Decision in General.

⟸1108 (Tex.Com.App.) Rights under stipulations in deeds made subsequent to application for writ of error cannot be determined.—Moore v. American Lumber Co., 318.

⟸1114 (Tex.) Judgment remanding to district court modified to one remanding to Court of Civil Appeals which failed to pass on certain assignments.—Mills v. Mills, 697.

⟸1114 (Tex.Com.App.) Findings by court not passed on by Court of Appeals should be remanded for it to pass on.—Temple Hill Development Co. v. Lindholm, 321.

⟸1114 (Tex.Com.App.) Where Court of Civil Appeals had not passed on questions over which the Supreme Court has no jurisdiction, the case must be remanded.—Clark v. Texas Co.-Op. Inv. Co., 381.

(B) Affirmance.

⟸1140(2) (Mo.App.) Excessive recovery remediable by remittitur.—Mayfield v. George O. Richardson Machinery Co., 288.

⟸1140(3) (Mo.App.) Where verdict for damages is excessive and the amount of excess admitted, it may be remitted.—Clayton v. Kansas City Rys. Co., 68.

(D) Reversal.

⟸1170(3) (Mo.App.) Defects in pleading disregarded on appeal, where substantial rights not affected.—Orr v. Russell, 275.

⟸1170(7) (Mo.App.) Admission of evidence *held* not reversible error in view of verdict which could be corrected by remittitur.—Mayfield v. George O. Richardson Machinery Co., 288.

⟸1170(7) (Tex.Civ.App.) Erroneous admission of evidence harmless in view of other evidence.—Hartford Life Ins. Co. v. Patterson, 814.

⟸1175(5) (Tex.Com.App.) Court of Civil Appeals not authorized to render judgment in reversal for insufficiency of evidence.—Wisdom v. Chicago, R. I. & G. Ry. Co., 344.

⟸1177(7) (Mo.App.) Judgment need not be reversed outright.—Bibb v. Grady, 1020.

⟸1177(8) (Tex.Civ.App.) Judgment not rendered on verdict on ambiguous issue.—Pickrell v. Imperial Petroleum Co., 412.

⟸1178(8) (Tex.Civ.App.) Court, where jurisdictional amount exceeded only by inadvertence, will remand for amendment.—Gulf, C. & S. F. Ry. Co. v. Hamrick, 166.

⟸1180(3) (Ky.) Reversal of judgment in creditor's suit *held* to bar relief to general creditor not party to appeal.—Hamner v. Boreing, 497.

(F) Mandate and Proceedings in Lower Court.

⟸1195(1) (Tex.Civ.App.) After affirmance by Supreme Court, opinion of Court of Civil

Appeals stands as law of case.—Kanaman v. Gahagan, 797.
☞1201(1) (Mo.) Petition deemed amended in case of remand for trial on particular issue.—State ex rel Dolman v. Dickey, 582.
☞1213 (Tex.Com.App.) Judgment on former appeal not conclusive where pleadings and facts differ.—Roberts v. Armstrong, 371.

XVIII. LIABILITIES ON BONDS AND UNDERTAKINGS.

☞1234(1) (Mo.) Sureties on appeal bond liable only for elements of damage covered by its terms.—Abnerthy v. Schembra, 1005.
☞1234(7) (Mo.) In action on appeal bond in unlawful detainer suit interest *held* not recoverable.—Abnerthy v. Schembra, 1005.

ARGUMENT OF COUNSEL.

See Criminal Law, ☞706-729; Trial, ☞114-132.

ARREST.

II. ON CRIMINAL CHARGES.

☞63(4) (Ky.) Officers *held* to have sufficient ground for believing felony committed to justify arrest without warrant.—Turner v. Commonwealth, 519.

ARREST OF JUDGMENT.

See Criminal Law, ☞970.

ARSON.

☞22 (Mo.) An indictment not defective because not stating owner of the building containing goods burned.—State v. Ritter, 606.

ASSAULT AND BATTERY.

See Homicide.

II. CRIMINAL RESPONSIBILITY.

(A) Offenses.

☞54 (Tex.Cr.App.) Automobile law *held* to add to law of aggravated assault.—Worley v. State, 391.

(B) Prosecution and Punishment.

☞75 (Tex.Cr.App.) Indictment for assault with intent to commit another offense need not give elements of offense intended to be committed.—Jones v. State, 122.

ASSESSMENT.

See Highways, ☞142; Municipal Corporations, ☞439-513; Taxation, ☞380.

ASSIGNMENTS.

IV. ACTIONS.

☞120 (Tex.Civ.App.) Buyer of notes pending suit thereon can prosecute suit in name of seller.—Pickrell v. Imperial Petroleum Co., 412.

ASSIGNMENTS FOR BENEFIT OF CREDITORS.

V. RIGHTS AND REMEDIES OF CREDITORS.

(A) In Aid of Assignment.

☞295(5) (Ky.) All creditors not necessary parties to suit.—Hammer v. Boreing, 497.

ASSOCIATIONS.

☞20(2) (Mo.App.) Voluntary and unincorporated association cannot sue.—Road Dist. No. 41, Henry Tp., Vernon County, v. Jackson, 1043.

ASSUMPSIT, ACTION OF.

See Work and Labor.

ASSUMPTION OF RISK.

See Master and Servant, ☞204-226.

ATTACHMENT.

See Garnishment.

ATTORNEY AND CLIENT.

See Trial, ☞114-132.

IV. COMPENSATION AND LIEN OF ATTORNEY.

(B) Lien.

☞182(3) (Ark.) Lien at common law was on evidence in hands of attorney, and not on debt itself.—Cosby v. Hurst, 194.
☞192(2) (Ark.) Lien at common law was on evidence in hands of attorney, and not on debt itself, and complaint must show possession of evidence of indebtedness.—Cosby v. Hurst, 194.

BAIL.

II. IN CRIMINAL PROSECUTIONS.

☞82 (Mo.) Proceedings by scire facias to forfeit bail *held*, in form and effect, a civil case.—State v. Carroll, 565.

BAILMENT.

See Pledges.
☞7 (Mo.App.) Possession of bailee deemed in subordination to the right of the bailor.—Conway v. Flaugh, 1045.
☞12 (Tenn.) Care to be exercised by bailee.—Pennington v. Farmers' & Merchants' Bank, 545.

BANKRUPTCY.

See Assignments for Benefit of Creditors.

BANKS AND BANKING.

I. CONTROL AND REGULATION IN GENERAL.

☞21 (Tex.Cr.App.) Debtor *held* not guilty of issuing check intended to circulate as money.—Jackson v. State, 1095.

II. BANKING CORPORATIONS AND ASSOCIATIONS.

(D) Officers and Agents.

☞54(3) (Ky.) Cashier liable for negligence in making loans, though authorized.—Dennis v. First State Bank, 538.

III. FUNCTIONS AND DEALINGS.

(B) Representation of Bank by Officers and Agents.

☞106 (Tex.Civ.App.) Bank not liable for president's failure to deposit money as agreed individually.—Hull v. Guaranty State Bank of Carthage, 810.
☞118(2) (Tenn.) Cashier not presumed to have communicated knowledge to bank when interest antagonistic.—People's Bank of Springfield v. True, 541.

(C) Deposits.

☞121 (Ark.) Bank, receiving deposits after hours cannot escape liability for deposit.—Farmers' Bank & Trust Co. v. Boshears, 10.
☞149 (Ark.) Bank drawing cashier's check on which payee's indorsement was forged entitled to recover from other bank which paid on such indorsement.—Farmers' Bank & Trust Co. v. Farmers' State Bank of Brookport, 7.
☞153 (Tenn.) Bank *held* to become bailee of bond and not only box in which kept.—Pennington v. Farmers' & Merchants' Bank, 545.
☞154(7) (Tenn.) Usage and custom as affecting care exacted of bailee.—Pennington v. Farmers' & Merchants' Bank, 545.
☞154(8) (Ark.) Evidence *held* to warrant inference customer was diligent in protesting failure of bank to show deposit on statement rendered.—Farmers' Bank & Trust Co. v. Boshears, 10.
Evidence *held* to warrant finding deposit made.—Id.

⬅154(9) (Ark.) Whether objection by customer to statement not showing deposit made within reasonable time a jury question.—Farmers' Bank & Trust Co. v. Boshears, 10.

⬅154(9) (Tenn.) Whether proper care was exercised as to bond deposited held for jury.—Pennington v. Farmers' & Merchants' Bank, 545.

(H) Actions.

⬅228 (Tex.Civ.App.) Evidence held to make issue of fact as to whether president was acting for bank.—Hull v. Guaranty State Bank of Carthage, 810.

IV. NATIONAL BANKS.

⬅233 (Tex.Com.App.) Federal statutes control on any point with reference to national banks, including organization and issuance of stock.—Citizens' Nat. Bank of Stamford v. Stevenson, 364.

⬅242 (Tex.Com.App.) Facts held to constitute a payment of money for stock.—Citizens' Nat. Bank of Stamford v. Stevenson, 364.

⬅260(2) (Tex.Com.App.) One national bank may lend, taking a note secured by stock of another such bank.—Citizens' Nat. Bank of Stamford v. Stevenson, 364.

BILLS AND NOTES.

I. REQUISITES AND VALIDITY.

(C) Execution and Delivery.

⬅56 (Tex.Civ.App.) Notes not void because maker did not affix revenue stamps.—State Nat. Bank of Texarkana v. Potter, 828.

V. RIGHTS AND LIABILITIES ON INDORSEMENT OR TRANSFER.

(D) Bona Fide Purchasers.

⬅342 (Tex.Civ.App.) Lack of cancellation of revenue stamps on transfer to holder in due course not a circumstance of suspicion.—State Nat. Bank of Texarkana v. Potter, 828.

⬅343 (Tenn.) Grantee giving note by way of restitution liable to purchaser having knowledge of fraudulent transaction.—People's Bank of Springfield v. True, 541.

⬅358 (Mo.) Holder of notes as collateral for pre-existing debt not innocent purchaser.—Thomas v. Goodrum, 571.

⬅359 (Mo.App.) Indorsee of note for which maker received nothing held a "holder in due course" for value.—Swift & Co. v. McFarland, 65.

⬅370 (Tex.Civ.App.) Want or failure of consideration not defense against holder in due course.—State Nat. Bank of Texarkana v. Potter, 828.

VIII. ACTIONS.

⬅452(1) (Tex.Com.App.) Failure of creditor to notify debtor that debt had not been paid not negligence.—Shaw v. First State Bank of Abilene, 325.

⬅497(2) (Mo.App.) Burden on defendant to show purchaser before maturity not holder in due course.—Swift & Co. v. McFarland, 65.

⬅497(3) (Mo.App.) Indorsement and delivery of note raises presumption of transfer for value.—Swift & Co. v. McFarland, 65.

⬅497(5) (Mo.) Burden on holder to prove that he or person under whom he claims acquired title as holder in "due course."—Thomas v. Goodrum, 571.

⬅497(5) (Mo.App.) Where instrument was obtained through fraud, plaintiff has burden of showing he was a "holder in due course."—Ensign v. Crandall, 675.

⬅503 (Tex.Civ.App.) Evidence by defendant to show that third person owned interest in note sued on admissible on issue of no consideration.—Rawlings v. Ediger, 163.

⬅537(6) (Mo.App.) Plaintiff making prima facie showing that he was a holder in due course is entitled to directed verdict unless the showing is controverted.—Ensign v. Crandall, 675.

Evidence held insufficient to carry to the jury the issue as to whether plaintiff was a bona fide holder.—Id.

BOUNDARIES.

I. DESCRIPTION.

⬅3(1) (Tex.) When all calls cannot be followed, as few should be disregarded as possible.—Wilson v. Giraud, 1074.

⬅3(3) (Ark.) Course and distance yield to fixed monuments.—Meyer v. Board of Imp. Paving Dist. No. 3, 12.

⬅3(3) (Ky.) Natural object held to control over courses and distances.—Scott v. Thacker Coal Mining Co., 498.

⬅10 (Tex.) Reasonable construction of field notes harmonizing terms of patent will be adopted.—Wilson v. Giraud, 1074.

II. EVIDENCE, ASCERTAINMENT, AND ESTABLISHMENT.

⬅37(1) (Tex.) Evidence held to show that land was part of certain surveys as located on the ground.—Wilson v. Giraud, 1074.

⬅56 (Ky.) Whether tree was in an alley and ordered removed by town authorities held for jury.—Bardin v. Commonwealth, 208.

BRIDGES.

I. ESTABLISHMENT, CONSTRUCTION, AND MAINTENANCE.

⬅5 (Ark.) Act creating district valid.—Ft. Smith Light & Traction Co. v. Williams, 890.

II. REGULATION AND USE FOR TRAVEL.

⬅33 (Ark.) Right to exact tolls for privilege of crossing public bridge must be conferred by statute.—Ft. Smith Light & Traction Co. v. Williams, 890.

Contract requiring street railroad to pay bridge district for right of way money which it was authorized to receive from passengers for transportation over bridge valid.—Id.

BRIEFS.

See Appeal and Error, ⬅757–773.

BROKERS.

IV. COMPENSATION AND LIEN.

⬅63(1) (Ark.) Owners preventing sale cannot set up their refusal to deed as ground of defense to claim for commission.—Vaughan v. Odell & Kleiner, 562.

⬅66 (Tex.Civ.App.) Fact that assistance was required in selling land no bar to compensation under agreement to divide commissions.—Quinn v. Quinn, 442.

One who first pointed out a farm for sale after listed entitled to agreed part of commission, though before listed broker called purchaser's attention thereto.—Id.

Ordinary rules governing rights of real estate agents held not to apply to commissions as between brokers.—Id.

V. ACTIONS FOR COMPENSATION.

⬅82(4) (Tex.Civ.App.) A petition being for commissions on express contract, no recovery on any other basis.—Mitchell v. Smith, 1114.

⬅85(1) (Tex.Civ.App.) Whether broker who procured exchange praised property immaterial.—Maier v. Langerhans, 145.

Whether plaintiff broker put forth effort to get abstract of title immaterial.—Id.

⬅86(1) (Ark.) Finding for broker in suit for procuring purchaser to whom owners refused to sell warranted.—Vaughan v. Odell & Kleiner, 562.

⬅88(2) (Mo.App.) Whether defendant employed plaintiff to effect an exchange held for the jury.—Gerth v. Christy, 639.

⬅88(4) (Ark.) In suit for procuring purchaser to whom owners refused to sell, direction of verdict for defendants held error.—Vaughan v. Odell & Kleiner, 562.

VI. RIGHTS, POWERS, AND LIABILITIES AS TO THIRD PERSONS.

⚖106 (Ark.) Evidence *held* to warrant instruction that, if plaintiff packing company permitted its broker to sell meat as his own, defendant purchaser was not liable.—G. H. Hammond Co. v. Joseph Mercantile Co., 875.

⚖106 (Tex.Civ.App.) In action against agent to recover earnest money deposited, principal was necessary and proper party defendant, and there was no error in rendering judgment against both.—Ballew & Huston v. Blakeny, 495.

BURGLARY.

II. PROSECUTION AND PUNISHMENT.

⚖28(6) (Ky.) No variance where indictment charged breaking into store of corporation, and evidence showed owner was partnership.—Lowery v. Commonwealth, 234.

⚖41(1) (Ark.) In a prosecution for burglary evidence *held* sufficient to sustain conviction. —Townsend v. State, 1.

CANCELLATION OF INSTRUMENTS.

II. PROCEEDINGS AND RELIEF.

⚖37(4) (Tex.Civ.App.) Pleading readiness to repay, if required, *held* not a tender.—Fisher v. Gulf Production Co., 450.

CARRIERS.

I. CONTROL AND REGULATION OF COMMON CARRIERS.

(A) In General.

⚖12(2) (Tex.) Commission's order dividing through rate on shipment of terminal carrier's coal over its own and initial carrier's lines *held* valid.—Texas-Mexican Ry. Co. v. Rio Grande & E. P. Ry. Co., 308.

Terminal carrier not entitled to switching charges on its coal billed for through shipment, but stopped at intermediate point without notice to initial carrier.—Id.

II. CARRIAGE OF GOODS.

(D) Transportation and Delivery by Carrier.

⚖88 (Tex.Civ.App.) Carrier relieved of liability for shipment on delivery to purchaser's agent.—Fort Worth Elevators Co. v. Keel & Son, 481.

(E) Delay in Transportation or Delivery.

⚖100(1) (Tex.Civ.App.) Though cars were bunched owing to washouts, carrier, though without fault, not entitled to demurrage for free time allowed shipper in such case.—Payne v. White House Lumber Co., 417.

(F) Loss of or Injury to Goods.

⚖134 (Tex.Civ.App.) Evidence *held* to support judgment for shortage in coal delivered, though there was probable chance of loss or error in ascertaining weight thereof.—Payne v. White House Lumber Co., 417.

⚖134 (Tex.Civ.App.) Evidence *held* to show proximate cause of loss of wheat due to act of God.—Fort Worth Elevators Co. v. Keel & Son, 481.

⚖135 (Tex.Civ.App.) Where no objection to bills showing weight of car of coal delivered to consignee, no error in allowing amount stated therein.—Payne v. White House Lumber Co., 417.

(I) Connecting Carriers.

⚖177(4) (Tex.Com.App.) Connecting carrier issuing bill of lading for shipment *held* liable for damages, though it did not have possession. —Missouri, K. & T. Ry. Co. of Texas v. Plano Milling Co., 100.

III. CARRIAGE OF LIVE STOCK.

⚖212 (Mo.App.) Delivery of sheep to same consignee at wrong yards *held* not to exonerate carrier.—McNeill v. Wabash Ry. Co., 649.

⚖229(5) (Mo.App.) An award of $2,125 for misdelivery of 218 breeding ewes which, as a result, were sold for slaughter, *held* not excessive.—McNeill v. Wabash Ry. Co., 649.

⚖230(1) (Mo.App.) Waiver of right of action for misdelivery by acceptance of proceeds from sale of breeding ewes *held* for jury.— McNeill v. Wabash Ry. Co., 649.

IV. CARRIAGE OF PASSENGERS.

(D) Personal Injuries.

⚖283(2) (Tex.Com.App.) Conductor not negligent in temporarily blocking aisle.—Steed v. Gulf, C. & S. F. Ry. Co., 714.

⚖286(4) (Mo.) Ordinary care required of carrier as to steps in station.—Williams v. Kansas City Terminal Ry. Co., 954.

Railroad company, which equipped station steps with safety tread, not responsible for accidents to passengers.—Id.

⚖287(5) (Mo.App.) However long a stop may be, street car must not be started without looking to situation of passengers boarding same.—Baldwin v. Kansas City Rys. Co., 280.

⚖303(1) (Tex.Com.App.) Degree of care railroad owes alighting passenger stated.—Wisdom v. Chicago, R. I. & G. Ry. Co., 344.

⚖303(4) (Ark.) Carrier must allow passenger reasonable opportunity to alight.—Texarkana & Ft. Smith Ry. Co. v. Adcock, 866.

⚖303(5) (Mo.App.) Employés required to ascertain whether passengers are alighting before starting street car.—Hartweg v. Kansas City Rys. Co., 269.

⚖303(8) (Tex.Com.App.) Railroad required to furnish safe steps, or aid passenger in alighting.—Wisdom v. Chicago, R. I. & G. Ry. Co., 344.

Required to assist alighting passenger where need of assistance is apparent.—Id.

⚖305(1) (Tex.Com.App.) Conductor's temporary blocking of aisle not proximate cause of woman passenger's falling while waiting for him to let her pass.—Steed v. Gulf, C. & S. F. Ry. Co., 714.

⚖315(1) (Mo.App.) Testimony that car started with jerk admissible in action for premature starting.—Hartweg v. Kansas City Rys. Co., 269.

⚖318(10) (Mo.App.) Evidence *held* to show car started before passenger had reasonable time to alight.—Hartweg v. Kansas City Rys. Co., 269.

⚖320(25) (Tex.Com.App.) Whether alighting passenger should have been assisted is a question for the jury.—Wisdom v. Chicago, R. I. & G. Ry. Co., 344.

⚖320(26) (Mo.App.) Demurrer to evidence on ground that passenger's manner of injury was against physical facts *held* properly overruled.—Keith v. Kansas City Rys. Co., 1046.

(H) Palace Cars and Sleeping Cars.

⚖413(1) (Tex.Civ.App.) Sleeping car company not insurer of effects of passengers, but must use reasonable care to see they are not stolen.—Pullman Co. v. Bullock, 1112.

⚖413(2) (Tex.Civ.App.) If porter steals diamond left under pillow, carrier is liable.— Pullman Co. v. Bullock, 1112.

⚖417 (Tex.Civ.App.) Mere loss of passenger's personal effects insufficient to establish negligence of the company.—Pullman Co. v. Bullock, 1112.

Evidence *held* insufficient to justify conclusion that porter stole passenger's diamond.—Id.

Passenger going to washroom and leaving diamond under pillow *held* not contributorily negligent as matter of law.—Id.

CHAMPERTY AND MAINTENANCE.

⚖5(8) (Tex.Civ.App.) Violation of law by attorney does not prevent suitor's recovery.— Kurz v. Solis, 424.

CHANCERY.

See Equity.

CHATTEL MORTGAGES.

III. CONSTRUCTION AND OPERATION.

(D) Lien and Priority.

⋘⟹138(1) (Tex.Civ.App.) Superior to mechanic's lien for repairs.—Dallas County State Bank v. Crismon, 857.

⋘⟹139 (Tex.Com.App.) "Subsequent mortgagees in good faith" against whom mortgage, unless filed as required, is void, defined.—First Nat. Bank v. Todd, 322.

Extension of note sufficient consideration as against prior unfiled mortgage.—Id.

⋘⟹152 (Mo.App.) Purchaser of automobile from one without title could not assert invalidity of mortgage.—Johnston v. Brown Bros. Iron & Metal Co., 1011.

⋘⟹157(2) (Tex.Com.App.) Holder of prior unfiled mortgage claiming superiority held to have burden of proof as to good faith of subsequent mortgagee.—First Nat. Bank v. Todd, 322.

IV. RIGHTS AND LIABILITIES OF PARTIES.

⋘⟹162 (Mo.App.) Seizure of automobile by mortgagee after default not conversion.—Lange v. Midwest Motor Securities Co., 272.

Acceptance of overdue previous installments not a waiver of future defaults.—Id.

VII. REMOVAL OR TRANSFER OF PROPERTY BY MORTGAGOR.

(A) Rights and Liabilities of Parties.

⋘⟹217 (Tex.) Foreign chattel mortgage valid against good-faith purchaser in state to which property removed in absence of statute or settled law or policy of forum.—Consolidated Garage Co. v. Chambers, 1072.

CHILDREN.

See Infants.

CITIES.

See Municipal Corporations.

CLERKS OF COURTS.

⋘⟹26 (Ky.) Motor Vehicle Act of 1920 impliedly prohibits commission for collecting licenses.—Lewis v. James, 526.

Authority in Motor Vehicle Act to deduct fees "under this act" does not authorize deduction of commission allowed by other statute.—Id.

General statute allowing commissions on licenses collected not read into Motor Vehicle Act.—Id.

Statute giving fees for specific acts in addition to commissions does not indicate intention to allow commission on motor vehicle licenses.—Id.

Statute authorizing commission on moneys other than licenses does not authorize commission on motor vehicle licenses.—Id.

COMMERCE.

I. POWER TO REGULATE IN GENERAL.

⋘⟹8(1) (Mo.) No state can interfere with interstate commerce into Missouri.—National Refrigerator Co. v. Southwest Missouri Light Co., 980.

II. SUBJECTS OF REGULATION.

⋘⟹33 (Tex.Com.App.) Shipment held interstate.—Missouri, K. & T. Ry. Co. of Texas v. Plano Milling Co., 100.

⋘⟹46 (Ark.) Purchase of cotton by foreign corporation for shipment to itself within the state not interstate transaction.—Forrester v. Locke, 897.

IV. INTERSTATE COMMERCE COMMISSION.

⋘⟹89 (Tex.Civ.App.) District Court has jurisdiction of suit to recover demurrage and excess freight charges made in violation of Interstate Commerce Commission rule.—Payne v. White House Lumber Co., 417.

COMMERCIAL PAPER.

See Bills and Notes.

COMMUNITY PROPERTY.

See Husband and Wife, ⋘⟹254–268.

CONDEMNATION.

See Eminent Domain.

CONDITIONAL SALES.

See Sales, ⋘⟹451.

CONSTITUTIONAL LAW.

For validity of statutes relating to particular subjects, see also the various specific topics.

Subject and title of act, see Statutes, ⋘⟹107–117.

II. CONSTRUCTION, OPERATION, AND ENFORCEMENT OF CONSTITUTIONAL PROVISIONS.

⋘⟹35 (Ky.) Provisions of Constitution mandatory.—Commonwealth v. Bowman, 35.

III. DISTRIBUTION OF GOVERNMENTAL POWERS AND FUNCTIONS.

(A) Legislative Powers and Delegation Thereof.

⋘⟹52 (Tenn.) Jurisdiction of Supreme Court cannot be interfered with by other branches of state government.—Clements v. Roberts, 902.

(B) Judicial Powers and Functions.

⋘⟹70(3) (Mo.) Courts must apply law as people have made it.—State ex rel. Feinstein v. Hartman, 982.

⋘⟹70(3) (Tex.Com.App.) Courts not concerned with wisdom of legislative enactment.—Texas Employers' Ins. Ass'n v. Bondreau, 756.

(C) Executive Powers and Functions.

⋘⟹79 (Tenn.) Jurisdiction of Supreme Court cannot be interfered with by other branches of state government.—Clements v. Roberts, 902.

XI. DUE PROCESS OF LAW.

⋘⟹276 (Tex. Civ. App.) Statutory provision that change in plan of construction shall not affect liability on contractor's bond held unconstitutional.—Southern Surety Co. v. Nalle & Co., 402.

⋘⟹276 (Tex.Civ.App.) Statute relating to contractor's bond held void as interference with the right to contract.—Cobb v. J. W. Allen & Bro., 829.

CONTINUANCE.

See Criminal Law, ⋘⟹589–608.

⋘⟹7 (Mo.App.) Granting continuance is within the sound discretion of the trial court.—Noah v. L. B. Price Mercantile Co., 300.

⋘⟹24 (Ark.) Will not be granted merely to obtain cumulative testimony.—Texarkana & Ft. Smith Ry. Co. v. Adcock, 866.

⋘⟹26(1) (Tex.Civ.App.) Where application for continuance shows failure to use means for procuring testimony, it is addressed to the court's discretion.—Short v. Walters, 161.

⋘⟹26(11) (Tex.Civ.App.) Where no commission was issued, although adversary party waived its issuance, there was not due diligence.—Short v. Walters, 161.

⋘⟹31 (Mo.App.) Defendant held not negligent in failing to procure testimony of court stenographer on surprise by testimony differing from former testimony.—Noah v. L. B. Price Mercantile Co., 300.

Facts shown by application *held* to entitle defendant to continuance.—Id.

←35 (Mo.) Testimony admitted by party at a former trial to avoid a continuance *held* properly excluded.—Jackman v. St. Louis & H. Ry. Co., 978.

Statute *held* not to apply to testimony in motion made at former trial.—Id.

←46(5) (Tex.Civ.App.) Application addressed to discretion of court should show applicant expected to procure testimony by next court term.—Short v. Walters, 161.

←54 (Mo.App.) Where plaintiff consented to oral application and waived motion, affidavit, and oath, application containing essential elements *held* sufficient.—Noah v. L. B. Price Mercantile Co., 300.

CONTRACTS.

See Assignments; Bills and Notes; Champerty and Maintenance; Covenants; Frauds, Statute of; Indemnity; Novation; Sales; Specific Performance; Stipulations; Vendor and Purchaser.

I. REQUISITES AND VALIDITY.

(A) Nature and Essentials in General.

←9(1) (Tex.Civ.App.) Uncertainty immaterial after performance.—Elmendorf v. Mulliken, 164.

←10(1) (Ark.) Contract of purchaser from mortgagor to bid in land on foreclosure sale did not lack mutuality.—Battle v. Draper, 869.

(B) Parties, Proposals, and Acceptance.

←28(3) (Ky.) Evidence insufficient to show that plaintiff had contract with defendant development company to drill oil well.—Irvine Development Co. v. Clark, 589.

(E) Validity of Assent.

←92 (Ark.) Whether a party had mental capacity determined by facts of particular case. —Hawkins v. Randolph, 556.

←94(8) (Ark.) Will not be set aside for mere inadequacy of construction.—Hawkins v. Randolph, 556.

←96 (Ark.) Between persons in fiduciary relationship closely scrutinized.—Hawkins v. Randolph, 556.

(F) Legality of Object and of Consideration.

←125 (Ky.) Against public policy for officer to agree to accept less than fixed salary.— Town of Nortonville v. Woodward, 224.

II. CONSTRUCTION AND OPERATION.

(A) General Rules of Construction.

←152 (Tex.Civ.App.) Words to be taken in common sense.—Great Southern Oil & Refining Ass'n v. Cooper, 157.

←171(1) (Mo.) Rule as to severability of items stated; "severable contract."—State ex rel. Dolman v. Dickey, 582.

←176(1) (Ark.) Court construes written contract and declares terms and meaning where it is not ambiguous.—Battle v. Draper, 869.

(C) Subject-Matter.

←202(2) (Mo.App.) Contract in restraint of trade strictly construed.—State ex rel. Youngman v. Calhoun, 647.

V. PERFORMANCE OR BREACH.

←322(2) (Mo.App.) Evidence *held* admissible as showing contingency on which performance depended.—Slack v. Whitney, 1060.

←322(3) (Mo.App.) Evidence *held* sufficient to show contract complied with.—Spencer v. Bush, 1013.

VI. ACTIONS FOR BREACH.

←346(9) (Mo.App.) Defendant always at liberty under general denial to overthrow contract asserted.—Ruemmeli-Dawley Mfg. Co. v. May Department Stores Co., 1031.

←346(10) (Tex.Com.App.) Rule as to variance stated.—Briscoe v. Bright's Adm'r, 1082.

CONVERSION.

See Trover and Conversion.

←16(5) (Mo.App.) Discretionary power of sale not exercised does not work a conversion. —In re Dwyer's Estate, 672.

CORONERS.

←22 (Mo.App.) Coroner's verdict not admissible in civil case to show cause of death.— Whiteside v. Court of Honor, 1026.

CORPORATIONS.

See Banks and Banking; Carriers; Gas; Municipal Corporations; Railroads; Street Railroads; Telegraphs and Telephones.

III. CORPORATE NAME, SEAL, DOMICILE, BY-LAWS, AND RECORDS.

←46 (Mo.App.) Variance in corporate buyer's name signed to contract does not invalidate. —Guess v. Russell Bros. Clothing Co., 1015.

←50 (Ky.) Lessee corporation's surrender of charter and doing of business under old name *held* not to warrant refusal to extend as to other tenants.—Kozy Theater Co. v. Love, 249.

IV. CAPITAL, STOCK, AND DIVIDENDS.

(A) Nature and Amount of Capital and Shares.

←65 (Mo.App.) Though property of corporation a trust fund for payment of debts, shares of stock fully paid for are not such a fund.— Insurance Agency Co. v. Blossom, 636.

(D) Transfer of Shares.

←111 (Mo.App.) Officer and director had right to sell shares *held*.—Insurance Agency Co. v. Blossom, 636.

V. MEMBERS AND STOCKHOLDERS.

(A) Rights and Liabilities as to Corporation.

←174 (Mo.App.) Purchaser of stock required merely right in management and interest in property after payment of debts.—Insurance Agency Co. v. Blossom, 636.

VI. OFFICERS AND AGENTS.

(B) Authority and Functions.

←298(1) (Ky.) Informal acts of directors of corporation binding where authorized by by-laws or custom.—Kozy Theater Co. v. Love, 249.

(D) Liability for Corporate Debts and Acts.

←333 (Mo.App.) Judgment creditor could hold officer of company who received assets in reorganization.—Insurance Agency Co. v. Blossom, 636.

VII. CORPORATE POWERS AND LIABILITIES.

(A) Extent and Exercise of Powers in General.

←382 (Tex.Com.App.) Note *held* not in violation of prohibition of use of corporation's funds for other than legitimate object of its creation.—Richardson v. Bermuda Land & Live Stock Co., 337.

(B) Representation of Corporation by Officers and Agents.

←426(11) (Mo.App.) Corporation *held* to have ratified by its president an agr* its sales manager as to deposit of a check.—John O'Brien Boiler Works Co. v. Third Nat. Bank, 1053.

(D) Contracts and Indebtedness.

&=464 (Tex.Com.App.) Note *held* not within prohibition of creation of indebtedness by corporation.—Richardson v. Bermuda Land & Live Stock Co., 337.

(F) Civil Actions.

&=503(3) (Tex.Civ.App.) Defendant corporation not entitled to change where acts complained of were performed in county of suit.—First Nat. Bank v. Childs, 807.
&=514(1) (Ky.) Plea denying existence of corporation plea of nul tiel corporation.—Stange v. Price, 532.
Pleading of nul tiel corporation is in abatement, and, if sustained, additional parties may be ordered.—Id.

XI. DISSOLUTION AND FORFEITURE OF FRANCHISE.

&=603 (Mo.App.) Sale of stock did not cause dissolution.—Insurance Agency Co. v. Blossom, 636.
&=613(1) (Tenn.) Intervener *held* not entitled to question authority to bring suit to dissolve.—State v. Colored Tennessee Industrial School, 544.

XII. FOREIGN CORPORATIONS.

&=642(6) (Mo.) Company contracting to install ice-making plant engaged in local operation and required to take out license.—National Refrigerator Co. v. Southwest Missouri Light Co., 930.
&=648 (Tenn.) Levying privilege tax on foreign construction companies restrictive.—H. D. Watts Co. v. Hauk, 908.
&=667½ (Ark.) Action on contract of a foreign corporation cannot be maintained by members of partnership of same name.—Forrester v. Locke, 897.
&=674 (Ark.) Evidence *held* to make a question for jury as to foreign corporation doing business without filing articles of incorporation.—Forrester v. Locke, 897.

COSTS.

I. NATURE, GROUNDS, AND EXTENT OF RIGHT IN GENERAL.

&=42(1) (Mo.App.) In action for poll tax tender *held* insufficient because not including accrued costs.—Road Dist. No. 41, Henry Tp., Vernon County v. Jackson, 1043.
&=42(3) (Mo.App.) Tender to stop running of costs must be deposited in court.—Bothmann v. Metropolitan Life Ins. Co., 1007.

VII. ON APPEAL OR ERROR, AND ON NEW TRIAL OR MOTION THEREFOR.

&=260(4) (Mo.) City's appeal from judgment for recovery of increased hydrant rentals by water company not vexatious.—City Water Co. v. City of Sedalia, 942.

COUNTERCLAIM.

See Set-Off and Counterclaim.

COUNTIES.

III. PROPERTY, CONTRACTS, AND LIABILITIES.

(B) Contracts.

&=114 (Ky.) County clerk may make binding contract for printing ballots.—Krieger v. Standard Printing Co., 27.
&=116 (Ky.) County clerk may contract for ballots without competitive bidding.—Krieger v. Standard Printing Co., 27.
&=125 (Ky.) Where contract is unenforceable, but services and work are accepted by agency empowered to contract therefor, re-

covery may be had on quantum meruit.—Krieger v. Standard Printing Co., 27.
&=129 (Ky.) Verdict in favor of printer against fiscal court not contrary to instructions.—Krieger v. Standard Printing Co., 27.

COURTS.

See Clerks of Courts; Justices of the Peace; Prohibition.

II. ESTABLISHMENT, ORGANIZATION, AND PROCEDURE IN GENERAL.

(C) Rules of Court and Conduct of Business.

&=78 (Mo.) Rule of court cannot repeal provisions of statute.—National Refrigerator Co. v. Southwest Missouri Light Co., 930.

(D) Rules of Decision, Adjudications, Opinions, and Records.

&=97(5) (Mo.) Decisions of federal courts as to interstate commerce controlling.—National Refrigerator Co. v. Southwest Missouri Light Co., 930.

IV. COURTS OF LIMITED OR INFERIOR JURISDICTION.

&=169(3) (Tex.Civ.App.) Total of items comprises amount in controversy in county court.—Gulf, C. & S. F. Ry. Co. v. Hamrick, 166.
&=183 (Ark.) County court *held* without jurisdiction to restrain unlawful acts under void district organization.—Wilson v. Mattix, 197.

VI. COURTS OF APPELLATE JURISDICTION.

(B) Courts of Particular States.

&=231(6) (Mo.App.) Where constitutional question is raised, Supreme Court alone has jurisdiction.—California Special Road Dist. v. Bueker, 71.
&=231(23) (Mo.) Constitutional question must be raised at earliest practical opportunity, in order to give Supreme Court jurisdiction.—Lavelle v. Metropolitan Life Ins. Co., 616.
' Supreme Court has no jurisdiction, where constitutional question injected into case by exception to ruling excluding depositions.—Id.
&=231(40) (Mo.) Appeal from judgment for profits and rents of which widow been deprived *held* not within jurisdiction of Supreme Court.—Jenkins v. Jenkins, 581.
&=246 (Tenn.) Case involving validity of joint resolution of Legislature *held* within jurisdiction of Supreme Court.—Clements v. Roberts, 902.
&=247(10) (Tex.) Court of appeals' judgment as to boundary respected, where whole case does not depend upon boundary controversies.—Kenedy Pasture Co. v. State, 683.

VIII. CONCURRENT AND CONFLICTING JURISDICTION, AND COMITY.

(A) Courts of Same State, and Transfer of Causes.

&=487(1) (Mo.) Where no constitutional question is presented and less than jurisdictional amount is involved, Supreme Court must transfer case to Court of Appeals.—Lavelle v. Metropolitan Life Ins. Co., 616.
&=488(1) (Mo.) Though cause was transferred by Court of Appeals on ground bill of exceptions was not properly authenticated, corrected abstract may be filed.—Williams v. Kansas City Terminal Ry. Co., 954.

COVENANTS.

II. CONSTRUCTION AND OPERATION.

(B) Covenants of Title.

&=39 (Ky.) Deed with warranty cannot be defeated by extrinsic facts as to prior sale of mineral or knowledge of grantee.—Foxwell v. Justice, 509.

(C) Covenants as to Use of Real Property.

☞51(2) (Mo.) Six double buildings *held* violative of restriction against construction of more than one dwelling on 50-foot front.—Morrison v. Hess, 997.

III. PERFORMANCE OR BREACH.

☞101 (Ky.) Title which must prevail over other title *held* "paramount" and "superior."—Isaacs v. Maupin, 49.

☞102(1) (Ky.) Eviction not condition to right of action for breach of warranty in favor of one who could not acquire possession.—Foxwell v. Justice, 509.

☞102(2) (Ky.) Grantee failing to obtain possession in ejectment suit may sue his covenantor as though evicted.—Isaacs v. Maupin, 49.

IV. ACTIONS FOR BREACH.

☞121(2) (Ky.) Purchaser suing for possession without calling on covenantors, if unsuccessful, may show judgment to show eviction, but must prove adversary's paramount title.—Isaacs v. Maupin, 49.

☞130(3) (Ky.) Purchaser compromising with grantee's heirs can recover from them only the damages for breach of covenant.—Isaacs v. Maupin, 49.

☞131 (Tex.Com.App.) Interest not allowable on damages from breach of covenant from date of accrual of cause of action to the judgment.—Morriss v. Hesse, 317.

CRIMINAL LAW.

See Arson; Assault and Battery, ☞54–75; Bail, ☞82; Burglary; Extradition; Homicide; Indictment and Information; Larceny; Perjury; Rape, ☞20–57; Receiving Stolen Goods; Trespass, ☞87, 88.

II. CAPACITY TO COMMIT AND RESPONSIBILITY FOR CRIME.

☞49 (Ark.) When delusional insanity constitutes a defense.—Woodall v. State, 186.

VII. FORMER JEOPARDY.

☞195(2) (Tex.Cr.App.) Where defendant fires at one and wounds another, state may charge assault on both or either, but judgment in one case bars prosecution in other.—Jones v. State, 122.

☞200(4) (Tex.Cr.App.) Conviction of unlawful sale of liquor will not preclude conviction of unlawful possession.—Chandler v. State, 108.

☞200(4) (Tex.Cr.App.) Conviction of unlawful sale of liquor will not preclude conviction of having possession.—Chandler v. State, 109.

IX. ARRAIGNMENT AND PLEAS, AND NOLLE PROSEQUI OR DISCONTINUANCE.

☞273 (Mo.) Plea of guilty confesses only truth of fact stated in information, not guilt of violation of statute against offense charged.—State v. Pearson, 595.

X. EVIDENCE.

(A) Judicial Notice, Presumptions, and Burden of Proof.

☞308 (Ky.) Accused entitled to every reasonable doubt in favor of presumption of innocence.—Bardin v. Commonwealth, 208.

☞318 (Tex.Cr.App.) Inference unfavorable to accused cannot be drawn from absence of testimony available to the state.—Davis v. State, 784.

(B) Facts in Issue and Relevant to Issues, and Res Gestæ.

☞351(2) (Tex.Cr.App.) Offer of bribe to arresting officer to release accused *held* inadmissible.—Stanchel v. State, 120.

☞363 (Tex.Cr.App.) Evidence of finding of weapon at place of crime admissible as part of res gestæ.—Flores v. State, 786.

☞365(1) (Tex.Cr.App.) Evidence that defendant was pointing a pistol at a witness while his companion took witness' money admissible in prosecution for another robbery.—Hardy v. State, 1097.

☞365(2) (Tex.Cr.App.) Evidence of previous robbery admissible where part of same transaction.—Hardy v. State, 1097.

☞368(1) (Mo.) Act of defendant's brother in shooting at prosecuting witness' son admissible as res gestæ.—State v. Cruts, 602.

☞368(1) (Tex.Cr.App.) Statements as to ownership of grain by those hauling it *held* res gestæ.—Davis v. State, 784.

(C) Other Offenses, and Character of Accused.

☞369(11) (Mo.) Evidence of statement by defendant as to his previous connection with incendiary fires admissible.—State v. Ritter, 606.

☞369(15) (Tex.Cr.App.) That accused had automatic pistol at time of arrest the night after robbery not admissible where accused not charged with use of firearms.—Stanchel v. State, 120.

☞371(7) (Mo.) Testimony as to statements made by defendant as to his connection with other incendiary fires admissible.—State v. Ritter, 606.

☞371(8) (Tex.Cr.App.) That accused had automatic pistol at time of arrest the night after robbery not admissible where it did not shed light on intent.—Stanchel v. State, 120.

☞372(1) (Tex.Cr.App.) That accused had automatic pistol at time of arrest the night after robbery not admissible where not bearing on showing system.—Stanchel v. State, 120.

(D) Materiality and Competency in General.

☞394 (Ky.) Arresting officer may search person of prisoner and use evidence thus obtained.—Turner v. Commonwealth, 519.

☞394 (Tex.Cr.App.) Illicit liquor equipment admissible, though discovered by officers without search warrant.—Thielepape v. State, 769.

☞395 (Mo.) Articles found in search of defendant's house during his absence admissible.—State v. Hall, 1001.

(E) Best and Secondary and Demonstrative Evidence.

☞404(3) (Tex.Cr.App.) Jugs found in defendant's possession admissible to show preparation of container for liquor when made.—Thielepape v. State, 769.

Jugs found in defendant's possession admissible on charge of having equipment in possession.—Id.

☞404(4) (Tex.Cr.App.) Exhibition to jury of articles found on scene of robbery not erroneous.—Williams v. State, 110.

(F) Admissions, Declarations, and Hearsay.

☞406(1) (Mo.) Testimony of police chief, as to defendant's admissions in his presence, admissible.—State v. Lee, 619.

☞406(1) (Tex.Cr.App.) Oral statement of accused, leading to finding of pistol with which offense committed, admissible.—Patterson v. State, 763.

☞406(3) (Mo.) Written admissions, not obtained by promises or threats, admissible.—State v. Lee, 619.

☞406(5) (Tex.Cr.App.) Oral statement of accused, leading to finding of pistol with which offense committed, admissible.—Williams v. State, 110.

☞406(7) (Tex.Cr.App.) Statement of defendant bootlegger to sheriff admissible to show intent.—Rainey v. State, 118.

☞407(2) (Ark.) Conversation between mother of prosecutrix in rape case inadmissible as admission by defendant's silence.—Robinson v. State, 2.

⟐==409 (Tex.Cr.App.) Accused may prove exculpatory statements made in connection with inculpatory statements proved by state.—Williams v. State, 110.

Accused may testify as to acts and declarations explanatory of admission, though not part of res gestæ.—Id.

Accused may introduce in evidence statement explanatory of statement used to incriminate him, though latter claimed exculpatory.—Id.

⟐==419, 420(1) (Tex.Cr.App.) Evidence *held* inadmissible, as hearsay.—Byrd v. State, 399.

⟐==419, 420(11) (Ark.) Conversation between mother of prosecutrix in rape case inadmissible as hearsay.—Robinson v. State, 2.

(G) Acts and Declarations of Conspirators and Codefendants.

⟐==422(1) (Tex.Cr.App.) When preparation of, or weapons found on, conspirators may be shown stated.—Flores v. State, 786.

⟐==423(3) (Tex.Cr.App.) Evidence that one victim was struck with a wrench admissible, regardless of whether defendant or confederate struck blow.—Hardy v. State, 1097.

⟐==426 (Tex.Cr.App.) No error in rejection of testimony of one indicted for participation in same offense as to exculpatory statements by him similar to those of defendant.—Patterson v. State, 763.

(I) Opinion Evidence.

⟐==448(8) (Tex.Cr.App.) Testimony as to condition of scene of killing inadmissible as conclusion.—Lewis v. State, 113.

⟐==449(1) (Tex.Cr.App.) Question of identity of liquor in bottle and in jugs did not involve expert testimony.—Thielepape v. State, 769.

⟐==450 (Ark.) Testimony of witness as to what certain fact indicated properly excluded.—George v. State, 9.

⟐==451(1) (Tex.Cr.App.) Opinion that smoke on defendant's barn looked like fresh smoke admissible as shorthand rendering of facts.—Thielepape v. State, 769.

⟐==459 (Tex.Cr.App.) Testimony of witnesses that defendant had whisky admissible.—Rainey v. State, 118.

Testimony of witness that bottles contained homemade whisky admissible.—Id.

⟐==465 (Ark.) Exclusion of opinion as to defendant's sanity by witness who had not detailed facts proper.—Woodall v. State, 186.

⟐==465 (Ark.) Sheriff can give opinion of defendant's sanity, based on observation of defendant while in custody.—Roberts v. State, 759.

(J) Testimony of Accomplices and Codefendants.

⟐==507(1) (Tex.Cr.App.) A purchaser of liquor is an "accomplice."—Chandler v. State, 105.

⟐==507(1) (Tex.Cr.App.) Purchaser of liquor will be deemed an "accomplice" if prosecution is for unlawful possession.—Chandler v. State, 107.

For evidential purposes, an accomplice is any one connected with the offense.—Id.

⟐==507(1) (Tex.Cr.App.) Purchaser of liquor is accomplice.—Chandler v. State, 108 (two cases), 109.

⟐==507(5) (Tex.Cr.App.) Purchaser of stolen goods is an accomplice.—Chandler v. State, 107.

⟐==507(7) (Tex.Cr.App.) Prosecutrix in an incest case *held* to be an accomplice.—McClure v. State, 774.

⟐==510 (Tex.Cr.App.) Testimony of accomplice is alone insufficient to sustain conviction.—Chandler v. State, 108.

⟐==510 (Tex.Cr.App.) Testimony of accomplice must be corroborated.—Chandler v. State, 109.

⟐==511(1) (Tex.Cr.App.) Evidence corroborative of accomplice *held* sufficient.—Hunt v. State, 775.

⟐==511(5) (Tex.Cr.App.) Testimony of prosecutrix, an accomplice, *held* not sufficiently corroborated.—McClure v. State, 774.

⟐==511(6) (Ark.) Evidence of defendant's possession of property offered for sale *held* sufficient to corroborate accomplice witnesses.—Townsend v. State, 1.

(L) Evidence at Preliminary Examination or at Former Trial.

⟐==539(2) (Tex.Cr.App.) Voluntary testimony by defendant in own behalf can be used against him on subsequent trial, or in different case.—Roberts v. State, 759.

XI. TIME OF TRIAL AND CONTINUANCE.

⟐==589(2) (Ky.) Denial of continuance because defendant physically and mentally unable to prepare defense not abuse of discretion.—Turner v. Commonwealth, 519.

⟐==593 (Ark.) Denial of continuance for absence of employed counsel except for sickness or unavoidable casualty discretionary.—Brickey v. State, 549.

⟐==594(1) (Tex.Cr.App.) Court *held* not within its discretion in overruling application for continuance for absence of witness.—Roberts v. State, 762.

⟐==594(1) (Tex.Cr.App.) Continuance erroneously denied where impossible to secure attendance of absent witnesses.—Giles v. State, 765.

⟐==595(4) (Tex.Cr.App.) Evidence of absent witnesses *held* so material as to make refusal of continuance error.—Byrd v. State, 399.

⟐==596(1) (Tex.Cr.App.) Rule as to cumulative testimony not strictly applied to first applications for continuance.—Byrd v. State, 399.

⟐==596(3) (Ark.) Overruling of motion for continuance based only on impeaching evidence, discretionary.—Brickey v. State, 549.

⟐==597(1) (Tex.Cr.App.) Testimony of absent witness *held* not shown to be of controlling importance.—Roberts v. State, 759.

⟐==597(1) (Tex.Cr.App.) On first application for continuance state cannot contest truth of testimony of absent witness.—Giles v. State, 765.

⟐==597(3) (Tex.Cr.App.) Denial of continuance for absence of witnesses whose testimony would establish no defense not erroneous.—Thielepape v. State, 769.

⟐==597(3) (Tex.Cr.App.) Denial of a continuance on the ground of absent witness not error where result would not have been changed.—Hardy v. State, 1097.

⟐==598(2) (Tex.Cr.App.) Showing of diligence *held* sufficient to justify continuance for absence of witnesses.—Byrd v. State, 399.

Showing of diligence *held* insufficient to justify continuance for absence of witnesses.—Id.

⟐==598(5) (Tex.Cr.App.) Defendant *held* not entitled to continuance because of lack of diligence in securing witness.—Boaz v. State, 790.

Defendant not entitled to continuance for absent witness where not diligent in discovering witness' whereabouts.—Id.

⟐==598(8) (Tex.Cr.App.) Failure to issue compulsory process to compel attendance of witness defeats right to continuance.—Roberts v. State, 759.

⟐==598(9) (Tex.Cr.App.) Issuance of subpœna for witness in another case is not sufficient diligence to require continuance.—Roberts v. State, 759.

⟐==608 (Ark.) Overruling of motion for continuance, not verified, discretionary.—Brickey v. State, 549.

⟐==608 (Tex.Cr.App.) On hearing application for continuance, court need not accept telegram stating presence of witness could not be obtained.—Roberts v. State, 759.

XII. TRIAL.

(A) Preliminary Proceedings.

⟐==625 (Ky.) Refusal to postpone trial for investigation of defendant's sanity *held* not error.—Turner v. Commonwealth, 519.

⊕═628(6) (Mo.) Permitting witnesses to testify, although not indorsed on information, *held* not error.—State v. Howard, 255.

⊕═628(7) (Mo.) Admission of testimony of witnesses whose names were not indorsed on indictment *held* not error.—State v. Lee, 619.

⊕═628(7) (Mo.) Failure to indorse names of state's witnesses on indictment not ground for exclusion of testimony of defendant not prejudiced.—State v. Hall, 1001.

⊕═631 (7) (Tex.Cr.App.) Motion to quash service of purported copy of jurors properly denied.—Hardy v. State, 1097.

⊕═632 (Tex.Cr.App.) For transfer to juvenile docket, defendant has burden of showing age.—Flores v. State, 786.

(B) Course and Conduct of Trial in General.

⊕═633(2) (Tex.Cr.App.) The statute requiring the reading of the indictment *held* mandatory.—Theriot v. State, 777.

⊕═641(1) (Ark.) Right to be heard by counsel not denied defendant, to whom continuance refused for absence of counsel.—Brickey v. State, 549.

⊕═655(1) (Mo.) Remarks of judge to jury not reversible error, in view of instructions, and where rights of accused not prejudiced.—Patterson v. State, 763.

(C) Reception of Evidence.

⊕═663 (Tex.Cr.App.) Equipment taken from defendant properly allowed to remain in court-room.—Thielepape v. State, 769.

⊕═673(2) (Tex.Cr.App.) Special charge *held* to cure error.—Shields v. State, 779.

⊕═684 (Tex.Cr.App.) Common-law rules as to rebuttal evidence do not apply in criminal cases.—Hardy v. State, 1097.

(D) Objections to Evidence, Motions to Strike Out, and Exceptions.

⊕═693 (Mo.) Objection to question, after answer, on sole ground not asked in good faith, properly overruled.—State v. McDonald, 927.

⊕═695(4) (Mo.) Objection to question on ground not asked in good faith, not on ground of incompetency, properly overruled.—State v. McDonald, 927.

⊕═695(6) (Ky.) Objection to evidence as a whole unavailing, where part is competent.—Lowery v. Commonwealth, 234.

⊕═696(2) (Tex.Cr.App.) Answer of witness in liquor prosecution *held* to have required motion to strike rather than objection.—Rainey v. State, 118.

⊕═696(5) (Mo.) Error to refuse to strike out evidence, though question was not objected to.—State v. Edelen, 585.

⊕═696(8) (Tex.Cr.App.) Evidence equivalent to that admitted without objection not rejected.—Flores v. State, 786.

(E) Arguments and Conduct of Counsel.

⊕═706 (Ky.) Laying foundation for impeachment of witness without introducing impeaching statement *held* improper.—Jones v. Commonwealth, 31.

Action of prosecuting attorney in insisting upon introduction of testimony knowing it to be incompetent *held* improper.—Id.

⊕═706 (Mo.) Statement of state's counsel that he did not want to introduce exhibit over defendant's objections not improper.—State v. McDonald, 927.

⊕═713 (Mo.) Arguments of prosecuting attorney referred to and based on evidence legitimate.—State v. McBride, 592.

⊕═713 (Mo.) Prosecuting attorney's statement that defendant was charged with raping a white woman not objectionable though indictment did not charge prosecutrix was white.—State v. Lee, 619.

⊕═720(9) (Tex.Cr.App.) Argument of prosecuting attorney based on immaterial testimony *held* improper.—Theriot v. State, 777.

⊕═721½(2) (Tex.Cr.App.) Statements in argument as to why defendant's witness was not put on stand *held* harmful error in absence of evidence justifying same.—Stanchel v. State, 120.

⊕═723(3) (Mo.) Argument of prosecuting attorney referring to prevalence of particular crime, etc., not error.—State v. McBride, 592.

⊕═729 (Tex.Cr.App.) Inaccurate statement in argument of crime of which defendant had been convicted harmless.—Flores v. State, 786.

(F) Province of Court and Jury in General.

⊕═736(1) (Ky.) Whether certain persons were accomplices of defendant *held* for the jury on conflicting evidence.—Commonwealth v. Milburn, 502.

⊕═740 (Ark.) Whether defendant was afflicted with mental disease question for jury, but whether mental disease rendered him irresponsible is an issue of law.—Woodall v. State, 186.

⊕═741(1) (Ky.) Weight of evidence for jury.—Bardin v. Commonwealth, 208.

⊕═742(1) (Ky.) Jury sole judge of credibility of witnesses.—Bardin v. Commonwealth, 208.

⊕═749 (Tenn.) Jury must fix sentence of one under 18 years of age.—Haynes v. State, 543.

⊕═755½ (Mo.) Instruction commenting on portion of testimony properly refused.—State v. Cruts, 602.

⊕═762(5) (Tex.Cr.App.) Instruction against verdict by lot not erroneous, as conveying impression court was of opinion defendant would be convicted.—Lewis v. State, 113.

(G) Necessity, Requisites, and Sufficiency of Instructions.

⊕═776(1) (Mo.) Evidence *held* to warrant instruction on good character.—State v. Baird, 625.

Meaning of words "whenever necessary," within statute requiring instruction on good character.—Id.

⊕═778(11) (Mo.) Instruction on flight, though not submitting defendant's explanation, not reversible error.—State v. Likens, 578.

⊕═780(2) (Tex.Cr.App.) Charge on accomplice testimony necessary.—Chandler v. State, 105.

⊕═789(3) (Tex.Cr.App.) Instruction erroneous as omitting element of conviction of jury beyond reasonable doubt.—Lewis v. State, 113.

⊕═789(12) (Ark.) Instruction defining reasonable doubt as one on which person would be willing to act in everyday walks of life erroneous.—Robinson v. State, 2.

⊕═805(1) (Ark.) Separate instructions on different phases of cases not prejudicial, where both correct.—George v. State, 9.

⊕═811(2) (Mo.) Instruction that jury should consider physical strength of prosecutrix and defendant *held* reversible error as a palpable comment on a portion of state's evidence.—State v. Edelen, 585.

⊕═814(17) (Ark.) Refusal of instruction on circumstantial evidence where such evidence is not alone relied on *held* proper.—Trotter v. State, 177.

⊕═814(17) (Mo.) When instruction on circumstantial evidence is necessary.—State v. Baird, 625.

Failure to instruct on circumstantial evidence *held* not error.—Id.

⊕═814(20) (Ky.) Instruction to convict of petit larceny properly refused, where evidence showed market value of stolen property more than $20.—Commonwealth v. Milburn, 502.

⊕═822(1) (Mo.) Instructions construed together.—State v. Caldwell, 613.

⊕═823(5) (Mo.) Failure to define words "just cause or excuse" *held* not to render instruction objectionable in view of definition of "malice."—State v. Caldwell, 613.

☞823(6) (Mo.) Instruction *held* not objectionable for failure to charge on self-defense in view of other instructions.—State v. Caldwell, 613.

(H) Requests for Instructions.

☞829(1) (Mo.) Requested instructions covered by others given properly refused.—State v. Howard, 255.

☞829(1) (Mo.) Instructions need not be repeated on request.—State v. Cruts, 602.

☞829(4) (Tex.Cr.App.) Refusal of charge substantially covered was not error.—Hardy v. State, 1097.

☞829(5) (Tex.Cr.App.) Instruction that defendant could arm himself in anticipation of attack by deceased not required where jury instructed on self-defense against apparent danger.—Boaz v. State, 790.

Failure to repeat instruction that defendant could use any means at his command to protect himself, and was not bound to retreat, was not error.—Id.

Refusal to charge jury to view facts as they appeared to defendant at time of killing was not error where jury was instructed on self-defense from apparent danger.—Id.

☞829(14) (Tex.Cr.App.) Instruction in prosecution for carrying pistol covered proper portion of requested charge.—Dodaro v. State, 394.

☞829(18) (Tex.Cr.App.) Refusal to charge upon matters covered by another charge not error.—Boaz v. State, 790.

(I) Objections to Instructions or Refusal Thereof, and Exceptions.

☞844(1) (Ark.) General objection to instruction defining involuntary manslaughter *held* sufficient.—Trotter v. State, 177.

☞844(2) (Ark.) General objection reaches inherent defect, as improper definition of reasonable doubt.—Robinson v. State, 2.

(J) Custody, Conduct, and Deliberations of Jury.

☞854(3) (Tex.Cr.App.) Conviction reversed where jurors separated.—Dibbles v. State, 768.

☞854(6) (Tex.Cr.App.) Permitting juror to go home for an hour because of sickness in his family erroneous.—Garner v. State, 389.

☞855(4) (Mo.) Court did not abuse its discretion in refusing to discharge jury for misconduct of prosecutrix.—State v. Hightower, 566.

☞858(3) (Tex.Cr.App.) Jury would have had right to take equipment with them during deliberations.—Thielepape v. State, 769.

(K) Verdict.

☞872½ (Mo.App.) Verdict must be clear and unambiguous.—State v. Gardner, 1057.

☞875(3) (Mo.) Verdict under indictment finding defendant guilty as charged in information not error.—State v. McBride, 592.

☞881(1) (Mo.App.) Verdict must describe all necessary elements of the offense.—State v. Gardner, 1057.

XIII. MOTIONS FOR NEW TRIAL AND IN ARREST.

☞905 (Ark.) "Bill of review" defined and *held* not to lie to obtain a new trial in a criminal case after expiration of term at which conviction was had.—Satterwhite v. State, 886.

☞913(3) (Tex.Cr.App.) Absence of complete diligence in securing absent testimony does not necessarily justify denial of new trial.—Giles v. State, 765.

☞939(1) (Tex.Cr.App.) No sufficient reason shown why so called newly discovered evidence should not have been ascertained by counsel.—Flores v. State, 786.

☞939(2) (Tex.Cr.App.) Defendant not entitled to new trial for absent witness where not

diligent in discovering witness' whereabouts.—Boaz v. State, 790.

☞941(2) (Tex.Cr.App.) Refusal of new trial for cumulative evidence *held* not abuse of discretion.—Boaz v. State, 790.

☞970(7) (Tex.Cr.App.) Information for theft failing to use word "fraudulently" subject to motion in arrest.—Phillips v. State, 400.

XIV. JUDGMENT, SENTENCE, AND FINAL COMMITMENT.

☞977(3) (Ark.) Defendant, who did not object, waived time specified for pronouncing sentence.—Brickey v. State, 549.

XV. APPEAL AND ERROR, AND CERTIORARI.

(A) Form of Remedy, Jurisdiction, and Right of Review.

☞1025 (Tex.Cr.App.) Jurisdiction on appeal defeated by defendant's escape and failure to return.—Campbell v. State, 105.

(B) Presentation and Reservation in Lower Court of Grounds of Review.

☞1032(1) (Mo.App.) Amendment of information not ground for reversal in absence of affidavit of surprise or application for continuance.—State v. Gardner, 1057.

☞1032(4) (Tex.Cr.App.) Information for theft failing to use word "fraudulently" subject to objection on appeal.—Phillips v. State, 400.

☞1037(1) (Mo.) No error in intimation of guilt in prosecutor's statements, where no objection to impeaching questions.—State v. McDonald, 927.

☞1037(2) (Tex.Cr.App.) Argument of state's counsel in prosecution of bootlegger not reversible error, in absence of request for corrective instruction.—Rainey v. State, 118.

☞1038(1) (Tex.Cr.App.) Objection to instruction not made at time of trial will not be considered.—Boaz v. State, 790.

☞1038(3) (Mo.) Defendant not requesting instructions cannot complain of those given which properly declared the law.—State v. Wilson, 596.

☞1038(3) (Mo.) Instructions sufficient, in absence of a showing that defendant requested others.—State v. Lee, 619.

☞1043(2) (Mo.) Objections to evidence not stating specific ground not reviewable.—State v. Hall, 1001.

☞1044 (Mo.) Defendant could not complain of testimony of witnesses whose names were not indorsed on indictment, in absence of motion to quash indictment or motion for continuance.—State v. Lee, 619.

☞1056(1) (Ky.) Failure to except to oral instruction estopped defendant from objecting on appeal.—Bardin v. Commonwealth, 208.

☞1056(1) (Mo.) Instructions sufficient in absence of exception as to failure to give others.—State v. Lee, 619.

☞1056(1) (Tex.Cr.App.) Failure to charge as to accomplices *held* not reversible error.—Byrd v. State, 399.

(C) Proceedings for Transfer of Cause, and Effect Thereof.

☞1081 (Tex.Cr.App.) Notice of appeal essential to jurisdiction.—Jones v. State, 122.

(D) Record and Proceedings Not in Record.

☞1090(1) (Tex.Cr.App.) In absence of statement of facts, bills of exceptions, or fundamental error apparent, judgment affirmed.—Franklin v. State, 392.

☞1090(8) (Tex.Cr.App.) Judgment cannot be overturned for admission of hearsay testimony in absence of bill of exceptions to it.—Crisp v. State, 392.

☞1090(12) (Tex.Cr.App.) Matters relating to conduct of jury not supported by bill of exceptions not considered.—Shields v. State, 779.

⚫═1090(13) (Tex.Cr.App.) Matters relating to argument of counsel not supported by bill of exceptions not considered.—Shields v. State, 779.

⚫═1091(1) (Tex.Cr.App.) Bills of exception not complying with rule may not be considered.—Crisp v. State, 892.

Compliance with statute relative to bills of exception necessary.—Id.

⚫═1091(4) (Tex.Cr.App.) Bill of exceptions to admission of evidence *held* not to comply with rule, and incomplete.—Crisp v. State, 392.

⚫═1091(5) (Tex.Cr.App.) Where excluded evidence relevant and material, bill of exceptions need not so state.—Williams v. State, 110.

⚫═1091(10) (Tex.Cr.App.) Bill of exceptions to admission of evidence must show meritorious ground of objections.—Rainey v. State, 118.

⚫═1094 (Tex.Cr.App.) Judgment affirmed, in absence of bill of exceptions or statement of fact.—Smith v. State, 1096.

⚫═1097(1) (Tex.Cr.App.) Single statement of facts accompanying three separate records, etc., objectionable.—Thielepape v. State, 769.

⚫═1101 (Tex.Cr.App.) Where there is but one statement for two cases tried simultaneously, court will consider record not containing statement as being before it without same.—Patterson v. State, 763.

⚫═1109(3) (Tex.Cr.App.) Appeal dismissed in absence of compliance with law.—Ray v. State, 396.

⚫═1120(3) (Tex.Cr.App.) Exclusion of evidence not reviewable, where matter excluded is not shown by bill of exceptions.—Williams v. State, 110.

(E) Assignment of Errors and Briefs.

⚫═1130(2) (Ky.) Blanket objection to overruling objections to evidence insufficient.— Lowery v. Commonwealth, 234.

⚫═1130(4) (Mo.App.) Assignments of error considered in absence of brief.—State v. Anderson, 1070.

(F) Dismissal, Hearing, and Rehearing.

⚫═1131(5) (Tex.Cr.App.) Appeal dismissed, where defendant has escaped from custody.— Gaines v. State, 1097.

(G) Review.

⚫═1134(3) (Mo.) Defects in information may be remedied on new trial after reversal for other reasons.—State v. Edelen, 585.

No decision on qualification of jurors where new trial granted.—Id.

⚫═1134(3) (Mo.) Where a conviction is reversed, other questions not likely to arise on retrial need not be considered.—State v. Rongey, 609.

⚫═1134(4) (Ky.) Court cannot reverse order granting new trial in felony case.—Commonwealth v. Milburn, 502.

⚫═1137(5) (Mo.) The state, having produced evidence as to defendant's character, could not complain that his character was not in issue.— State v. Baird, 625.

⚫═1144(12) (Mo.) Exclusion of contract, giving rise to quarrel leading to killing, presumed proper, though no ground of objection stated.— State v. McDonald, 927.

⚫═1144(17) (Ark.) Presumption sentence pronounced in due time according to statute.— Brickey v. State, 549.

⚫═1151 (Mo.) Refusal of continuance not disturbed where trial court did not abuse discretion.—State v. Hall, 1001.

⚫═1159(2) (Mo.) Not province of Supreme Court to pass upon weight of evidence.—State v. Wilson, 596.

⚫═1159(2) (Mo.) Verdict, supported by substantial evidence, not disturbed.—State v. Caldwell, 613.

231 S.W.—72

⚫═1159(2) (Tex.Cr.App.) Judgment not reversed for insufficiency of evidence, unless against great weight of testimony.—Vogel v. State, 1096.

⚫═1160 (Ky.) New trial will not be granted unless verdict is palpably and flagrantly against the weight of the evidence.—Cloninger v. Commonwealth, 535.

⚫═1166½(6) (Tex.Cr.App.) Reversible error for court to stand aside accepted juror.—McGowen v. State, 763.

⚫═1166½(12) (Tex.Cr.App.) Remarks of judge to jury not reversible error in view of instructions, and where rights of accused not prejudiced.—Williams v. State, 110.

⚫═1169(1) (Mo.) Question asked defendant on cross-examination as to acts of third person not harmful.—State v. Bloomer, 568.

⚫═1169(1) (Tex.Cr.App.) Testimony *held* not prejudicial as conveying impression defendant engaged in selling liquor found in possession.— Rainey v. State, 118.

⚫═1169(2) (Mo.) Admission of hearsay testimony *held* harmless, in view of other testimony to same effect.—State v. Hall, 1001.

⚫═1169(12) (Ark.) Conversation between mother of prosecutrix in rape case inadmissible, not effecting an admission by silence.—Robinson v. State, 2.

⚫═1170(2) (Tex.Cr.App.) Error in exclusion of evidence of no weight where same testimony given by state's witness.—Patterson v. State, 763.

⚫═1170½(1) (Tex.Cr.App.) Question *held* not harmful to defendant.—Rainey v. State, 118.

⚫═1170½(5) (Mo.) Cross-examination of defendant charged with murder in no event harmless.—State v. Likens, 578.

⚫═1170½(6) (Tex.Cr.App.) Question as to whether accused had been charged with robbery at former time not reversible error where court refused to permit answer and instructed jury not to consider question.—Patterson v. State, 763.

⚫═1171(1) (Mo.) State's dramatic attempt to browbeat defendant witness by presenting questions on matters not covered by main examination *held* to require reversal.—State v. Edelen, 585.

⚫═1171(6) (Ky.) Remark of counsel on motion prior to trial not prejudicial when no juror shown to have been present.—Turner v. Commonwealth, 519.

⚫═1172(1) (Mo.) Number and prolixity of instructions do not warrant reversal.—State v. Ritter, 606.

⚫═1172(6) (Ark.) Erroneous instruction allowing conviction for manufacture of intoxicating liquor under indictment charging manufacture of spirits harmless.—Robertson v. State, 865.

⚫═1172(6) (Tex.Cr.App.) No reversal for a charge unless harm might have resulted.— Flores v. State, 786.

(H) Determination and Disposition of Cause.

⚫═1186(1) (Tex.Cr.App.) Cause not reversed unless wrong may be righted on another trial. —Shields v. State, 779.

⚫═1186(4) (Ky.) Misconduct of counsel *held* ground for reversal.—Jones v. Commonwealth, 31.

⚫═1189 (Ky.) Newly discovered evidence *held* ground for reversal and new trial.—Jones v. Commonwealth, 31.

XVII. PUNISHMENT AND PREVENTION OF CRIME.

⚫═1213 (Ky.) Habitual criminal act does not inflict cruel punishment contrary to Constitution.—Turner v. Commonwealth, 519.

CROPS.

⊂═5 (Tex.Com.App.) Crops pass under deed unless severed, but are personal property.—Roberts v. Armstrong, 371.

CUSTOMS AND USAGES.

⊂═14 (Ark.) Custom of seller in selling cotton inadmissible when there was a contract.—Forrester v. Locke, 597.

⊂═19(3) (Tex.Civ.App.) Evidence insufficient to show custom that seller might require buyer to deal with other party direct.—Tecumseh Oil & Cotton Co. v. Gresham, 468.

DAMAGES.

III. GROUNDS AND SUBJECTS OF COMPENSATORY DAMAGES.

(A) Direct or Remote, Contingent, or Prospective Consequences or Losses.

⊂═22 (Mo.App.) Damages for breach of contract should compensate for actual loss naturally and proximately resulting.—Mayfield v. George O. Richardson Machinery Co., 288.

⊂═50 (Mo.App.) Mental anguish and physical pain are proper elements of damage.—Evans v. Clapp, 79.

(B) Aggravation, Mitigation, and Reduction of Loss.

⊂═62(2) (Tex.Civ.App.) Only ordinary care required in treatment of injuries.—Baker v. Hodges, 844.

⊂═65 (Tex.Civ.App.) Action construed as one for misappropriation of funds in which plaintiff was estopped to claim more than damage actually suffered.—Stonewall v. McGown, 850.

(C) Interest, Costs, and Expenses of Litigation.

⊂═69 (Mo.App.) Interest not allowable in action ex delicto.—Jackels v. Kansas City Rys. Co., 1023.

IV. LIQUIDATED DAMAGES AND PENALTIES.

⊂═79(1) (Ky.) Gas company's construction bond held to provide liquidated damages, not a penalty.—Louisville Gas & Electric Co. v. City of Louisville, 909.

VI. MEASURE OF DAMAGES.

(A) Injuries to the Person.

⊂═99 (Mo.App.) Husband entitled to damages for loss of wife's society and services, without direct proof of value thereof.—Baldwin v. Kansas City Rys. Co., 280.

(C) Breach of Contract.

⊂═124(1) (Mo.App.) Damages for failure to accept delivery of balance of materials contracted for stated.—Spencer v. Bush, 1013.

VII. INADEQUATE AND EXCESSIVE DAMAGES.

⊂═130(2) (Tex.Civ.App.) Verdict for $3,500 for injuries to shoulder and other injuries not excessive.—Baker v. Hodges, 844.

⊂═131(1) (Ky.) $1,500, for being bumped around in buggy struck by freight cars without visible injuries, held excessive.—Cincinnati, N. O. & T. P. R. Co. v. Owsley, 210.

⊂═132(1) (Ky.) Award of $2,500 damages held not excessive for injury to hand, testicles, etc.—Commonwealth Power, Ry. & Light Co. v. Vaught, 247.

⊂═132(1) (Tex.Civ.App.) $10,000 for severe physical injuries and disfigurement of married woman not excessive.—City of Dallas v. Maxwell, 429.

⊂═132(2) (Mo.App.) Award of $1,000 in favor of girl whose kneecap was dislocated and prob-

ably permanently affected held not excessive.—Thomas v. City of St. Joseph, 63.

⊂═132(3) (Mo.App.) Verdict for $5,000 for injury causing acute meningitis of brain and resulting inability to work steadily held not excessive.—Buehler v. Waggener Paint & Glass Co., 283.

⊂═132(5) (Mo.) $12,000 held excessive for injuries to woman struck by street car.—Richardson v. Kansas City Rys. Co., 938.

⊂═132(6) (Mo.) Verdict for $12,000 for injury to knee held not unwarranted or excessive.—Jackman v. St. Louis & H. Ry. Co., 978.

⊂═132(7) (Ky.) $5,000 award to injured woman not excessive.—City of Newport v. Schmit, 54.

⊂═132(7) (Mo.App.) Verdict for $1,725 for injuries to leg and wrist held not excessive.—O'Connell v. Kansas City, 1040.

⊂═132(12) (Ky.) $10,000 for loss of right arm of 15 year old boy held not excessive.—Louisville Woolen Mills v. Kindgen, 202.

⊂═133 (Mo.App.) $5,000 for injuries rendering plaintiff's wife an invalid held not excessive.—Baldwin v. Kansas City Rys. Co., 280.

⊂═140 (Mo.App.) Verdict for sales agent in action for wrongful discharge held not excessive.—Williams v. John T. Hesser Coal Co., 680.

VIII. PLEADING, EVIDENCE, AND ASSESSMENT.

(A) Pleading.

⊂═158(3) (Mo.App.) Injury to woman's pelvic organs and consequences thereof sufficiently pleaded.—Baldwin v. Kansas City Rys. Co., 280.

Loss of wife's sexual ability admissible under general pleading of loss of consortium.—Id.

Testimony of wife's fainting spells held admissible.—Id.

⊂═158(3) (Tex.Civ.App.) Testimony of jitney bus passenger and physician as to injuries admissible.—City of Dallas v. Maxwell, 429.

⊂═158(4) (Mo.) Petition alleging impairment of mental faculties held to justify evidence of loss of memory.—Richardson v. Kansas City Rys. Co., 938.

⊂═160 (Tex.Civ.App.) Allegation that plaintiff was "obliged" to pay held to sustain admission of evidence of reasonableness of doctor's charges; "compelled."—Texas Electric Ry. v. Jones, 823.

⊂═161 (Mo.App.) Physical pain and mental anguish may be recovered, though not stated.—Evans v. Clapp, 79.

(C) Proceedings for Assessment.

⊂═216(1) (Mo.App.) Instruction not objectionable as tending to improper recovery.—Evans v. Clapp, 79.

⊂═216(2) (Mo.App.) Instruction should not allow recovery for injuries complained of.—Forrester v. Walsh Fire Clay Products Co., 668.

⊂═216(8) (Ky.) Instruction as to permanent impairment of earning power erroneous, in absence of evidence as to permanency of injuries.—Cincinnati, N. O. & T. P. R. Co. v. Owsley, 210.

⊂═216(8) (Mo.App.) No error in instruction as to damages for impairment of earning capacity after injured employee reached 21.—Buehler v. Waggener Paint & Glass Co., 283.

⊂═216(8) (Tex.Civ.App.) Evidence held to support a charge on loss of time and diminished earning capacity.—Texas Electric Ry. v. Jones, 823.

⊂═216(10) (Mo.App.) Instruction not objectionable as allowing recovery for mental anguish unaccompanied by injury.—Evans v. Clapp, 79.

⊂═217 (Mo.App.) Instruction as to measure of damages for injury to automobile held not sufficiently clear.—Jackels v. Kansas City Rys. Co., 1023.

DEATH.

II. ACTIONS FOR CAUSING DEATH.

(A) Right of Action and Defenses.

∞24 (Tenn.) Beneficiary not prejudiced by contributory negligence of cobeneficiary.—Hines v. Partridge, 16.

∞27. (Mo.) Recovery by widow bars suit by administrator.—Drakopulos v. Biddle, 924.

∞33 (Tex.Civ.App.) Joint tort-feasors liable.—Anderson v. Smith, 142.

Father *held* liable as "joint tort-feasor" with son who shot deceased.—Id.

(D) Pleading and Evidence.

∞57 (Mo.) Aggravating circumstances increasing penal recovery must be pleaded.—Lackey v. United Rys. Co., 956.

∞58(1) (Tenn.) Burden of proving contributory negligence on defendant.—Hines v. Partridge, 16.

∞67 (Tex.Civ.App.) Evidence of deceased fireman's chance of promotion admissible.—Lancaster v. Allen, 148.

∞75 (Tex.Civ.App.) Evidence *held* to show concerted killing.—Anderson v. Smith, 142.

(E) Damages, Forfeiture, or Fine.

∞78 (Mo.) Entire recovery penal.—Lackey v. United Rys. Co., 956.

∞99(4) (Tenn.) $10,000 not excessive for death of wife.—Hines v. Partridge, 16.

(F) Trial, Judgment, and Review.

∞104(6) (Tenn.) Instruction on damages for death of wife *held* not prejudicial error.—Hines v. Partridge, 16.

DEDICATION.

I. NATURE AND REQUISITES.

∞31 (Ky.) Acceptance necessary to make road a public highway.—Wilson v. Pioneer Coal Co., 37.

∞35(3) (Ky.) Accepted by public user and official action.—Wilson v. Pioneer Coal Co., 37.

∞41 (Ky.) Dedication presumed from public use.—Wilson v. Pioneer Coal Co., 37.

∞44 (Ky.) Evidence insufficient to show dedication for burial purposes.—Wilson v. Pioneer Coal Co., 37.

DEEDS.

See Mortgages.

I. REQUISITES AND VALIDITY.

(B) Form and Contents of Instruments.

∞38(1) (Ky.) Deeds *held* to have covered tract involved in action to quiet title.—Wilson v. Pioneer Coal Co., 37.

∞38(1) (Tex.Civ.App.) Description is certain which can be made certain.—Pope v. Witherspoon, 837.

III. CONSTRUCTION AND OPERATION.

(A) General Rules of Construction.

∞93 (Tex.Com.App.) Cardinal ruling of construction is to ascertain parties' intent.—Scheller v. Groesbeck, 1092.

∞97 (Tex.Com.App.) All parts should be given effect, if possible.—Scheller v. Groesbeck, 1092.

(B) Property Conveyed.

∞111 (Tex.Com.App.) General description yields to particular description.—Scheller v. Groesbeck, 1092.

∞112(1) (Tex.Com.App.) All instruments in a chain of title when referred to will be read into deeds.—Scheller v. Groesbeck, 1092.

Conveyance of league of land *held* not to embrace labor.—Id.

(C) Estates and Interests Created.

∞121 (Tex.Civ.App.) Quitclaim deed conveys no more than present interest of grantor.—Gulf Production Co. v. State, 124.

∞129(4) (Mo.) Beneficiary of trust *held* to have only life estate in land.—Watson v. Hardwick. 964.

∞134 (Ky.) Difference between "limitation" and "condition."—Eastham v. Eastham, 221.

Held to convey an estate upon limitation and not upon condition.—Id.

∞134 (Ky.) Conveyance to grantee so long as she remains the wife or unmarried widow of grantor limits the estate and is not a condition for defeating it.—Jones v. Black, 512.

(E) Conditions and Restrictions.

∞147 (Ky.) When conditions are void.—Eastham v. Eastham, 221.

∞151 (Ky.) Grantee takes estate freed of void condition.—Eastham v. Eastham, 221.

∞155 (Ark.) Restrictions on estate presumed not to be conditions subsequent.—School District of Newport v. J. R. Holden Land & Lumber Co., 895.

∞156 (Tex.Com.App.) Right of re-entry after condition subsequent broken not assignable at common law.—Perry v. Smith, 340.

Right of re-entry after condition subsequent broken assignable.—Id.

∞166 (Tex.Com.App.) Consent to placing mechanic's lien upon property *held* not waiver of condition in deed.—Perry v. Smith, 340.

IV. PLEADING AND EVIDENCE.

∞194(1) (Mo.) The law presumes much more in favor of delivery in case of voluntary settlement.—Mason v. Mason, 971.

∞194(5) (Mo.) In action to cancel for want of delivery burden is on person denying full execution.—Mason v. Mason, 971.

Presumption of delivery.—Id.

Evidence *held* insufficient to rebut presumption of delivery.—Id.

DEPOSITARIES.

∞10 (Ky.) Commonwealth can recover from depository only balance above payments from defaulter's surety.—Commonwealth v. Farmers' Bank of Kentucky, 25.

∞13 (Ky.) Surety of defaulting employee *held* real party in interest to suit in name of commonwealth.—Commonwealth v. Farmers' Bank of Kentucky, 25.

DEPOSITIONS.

∞98 (Mo.App.) Deposition used by plaintiff in former trial admissible to contradict plaintiff's contentions, although witness is within jurisdiction.—Noah v. L. B. Price Mercantile Co., 300.

DESCENT AND DISTRIBUTION.

See Executors and Administrators; Wills.

II. PERSONS ENTITLED AND THEIR RESPECTIVE SHARES.

(A) Heirs and Next of Kin.

∞47(1) (Mo.App.) Pretermitted heir *held* to take by descent and not by purchase.—In re Dwyer's Estate, 672.

III. RIGHTS AND LIABILITIES OF HEIRS AND DISTRIBUTEES.

(C) Debts of Intestate and Incumbrances on Property.

∞126 (Ky.) Purchaser may recover from vendor's heirs for failure of title, where they have inherited property sufficient to cover loss.—Isaacs v. Maupin, 49.

∞129 (Ky.) Heir or gratuitous grantee is bound by unacknowledged conveyance, though having no notice.—Riddle v. Jones, 508.

DISMISSAL AND NONSUIT.

See Appeal and Error, ⚓781–795.

I. VOLUNTARY.

⚓5 (Tex.Civ.App.) Plaintiff may dismiss as to defendant whose plea for change is about to be allowed.—First Nat. Bank v. Childs, 807.

II. INVOLUNTARY.

⚓58(1) (Mo.) Dismissal of action on striking out amended petition for wrongful death *held* reversible as abuse of discretion.—Drakopulos v. Biddle, 924.
⚓60(1) (Tex.Com.App.) Judgment of dismissal only one proper, where plaintiff failed to appear at trial.—Parr v. Chittim, 1079.

DIVORCE.

⚓27(3) (Tex.Civ.App.) Physical violence not indispensable to show cruelty.—Erwin v. Erwin, 834.
⚓27(18) (Ky.) Testimony as to numerous quarrels not sufficient to establish cruel and inhuman treatment.—McKee v. McKee, 213.
⚓27(18) (Tex.Civ.App.) Husband's mistreatment of wife *held* to entitle her to divorce.—Erwin v. Erwin, 834.
⚓29 (Ark.) Remedy of divorce for indignities only for unavoidable evils.—Poe v. Poe, 198.
Cruelty of wife to stepchildren in absence of husband not ground.—Id.
⚓36 (Ky.) Separation not "abandonment" and does not authorize divorce until after five years.—Shockey v. Shockey, 508.

III. DEFENSES.

⚓55 (Tex.Civ.App.) Cruelty must not approach mutuality.—Wiedner v. Wiedner, 448.

IV. JURISDICTION, PROCEEDINGS, AND RELIEF.

(C) Pleading.

⚓93(1) (Ky.) Petition *held* to sufficiently allege abandonment, but not cruelty.—Shockey v. Shockey, 508.
⚓93(3) (Tex.Civ.App.) Petition alleging cruelty, etc., *held* sufficient.—Erwin v. Erwin, 834.
⚓108 (Ky.) Evidence of cruelty without allegation thereof does not authorize decree.—Shockey v. Shockey, 508.
⚓108 (Tex.Civ.App.) Evidence that husband cursed wife and another in her presence *held* admissible under petition.—Erwin v. Erwin, 834.

(D) Evidence.

⚓124 (Tex.Civ.App.) Court must be satisfied that divorce should be granted.—Erwin v. Erwin, 834.
⚓127(2) (Tex.Civ.App.) Court not required to accept uncontradicted testimony of party in divorce action.—Wiedner v. Wiedner, 448.
⚓130 (Ky.) Evidence *held* to establish wife's right to an absolute divorce for cruel and inhuman treatment.—McKee v. McKee, 213.
Right to inflict corporal punishment on other spouse in self-defense must be clearly established.—Id.
⚓130 (Tex.Civ.App.) Evidence *held* not to show husband's cruelty.—Hubbard v. Hubbard, 160.
⚓132 (Mo.App.) Evidence *held* insufficient to establish plaintiffs' right to divorce on the ground of indignities.—Van Horn v. Van Horn, 634.

V. ALIMONY, ALLOWANCES, AND DISPOSITION OF PROPERTY.

⚓201 (Ky.) Court had jurisdiction on appeal of question of alimony, where defendant entered appearance pending appeal.—McKee v. McKee, 213.
⚓223 (Tex.Civ.App.) Awarding of attorney's fee discretionary with trial court.—Wilson v. Wilson, 880.

Refusal to award wife attorney's fee *held* not abuse of discretion.—Id.
⚓227(2) (Ky.) Wife *held* entitled to $25 attorney's fee.—McKee v. McKee, 213.
⚓235 (Mo.App.) Alimony largely discretionary.—Kinney v. Kinney, 267.
⚓240(5) (Ky.) Wife *held* entitled to $25 allowance.—McKee v. McKee, 213.
⚓240(5) (Mo.App.) Award of $80 per month to wife, with custody of child, where husband has remarried and is earning about $125 per month, *held* not excessive.—Kinney v. Kinney, 267.
⚓245(2) (Mo.App.) Wife's securing allowance for child's support may be considered as ground for reducing her alimony.—Kinney v. Kinney, 267.
⚓282 (Mo.App.) Defendant, not objecting below that petition failed to ask alimony, waived the defect.—Kinney v. Kinney, 267.
⚓286 (Ark.) Allowance of alimony will not be disturbed except for changed conditions.—Poe v. Poe, 198.

VI. CUSTODY AND SUPPORT OF CHILDREN.

⚓308 (Ky.) Wife *held* entitled to $15 allowance for child.—McKee v. McKee, 213.

VII. OPERATION AND EFFECT OF DIVORCE, AND RIGHTS OF DIVORCED PERSONS.

⚓324 (Tex.) Father's liability to maintain child not lost by divorce decree awarding custody to mother without provision for support.—Gully v. Gully, 97.

DOCKS.

See Wharves.

DRAINS.

I. ESTABLISHMENT AND MAINTENANCE.

⚓16 (Ark.) County court *held* not to have authority to dissolve drainage district.—Wilson v. Mattix, 197.

DRAMSHOPS.

See Intoxicating Liquors.

DUE PROCESS OF LAW.

See Constitutional Law, ⚓276.

EASEMENTS.

I. CREATION, EXISTENCE, AND TERMINATION.

⚓3(2) (Ky.) Presumed to be appurtenant and not in gross.—Riddle v. Jones, 503.
Passway *held* to be appurtenant and not in gross.—Id.
⚓12(3) (Ky.) Indefiniteness of road description is cured by passway established on ground.—Riddle v. Jones, 503.
⚓22 (Ky.) Heir of gratuitous grantee is bound by unacknowledged conveyance, though having no notice.—Riddle v. Jones, 503.
⚓24 (Ky.) Exchange of roads establishes sufficient consideration for grant of each easement.—Riddle v. Jones, 503.
⚓36(3) (Ky.) Conveyance *held* to show signature to grant of easement was genuine.—Riddle v. Jones, 503.
Evidence *held* not to show undue influence in obtaining conveyance of easement.—Id.

II. EXTENT OF RIGHT, USE, AND OBSTRUCTION.

⚓53 (Ky.) Conveyance *held* quitclaim deed.—Riddle v. Jones, 503.

EJECTMENT.

I. RIGHT OF ACTION AND DEFENSES.

⚓12 (Ky.) Party in actual possession has superior title to one unable to prove complete paper title from commonwealth.—Isaacs v. Maupin, 49.

ELECTION OF REMEDIES.

⟵1 (Tex.Com.App.) Valid available remedies essential.—Poe v. Continental Oil & Cotton Co., 717.

⟵7(1) (Ky.) Appearance before tribunal chosen by adversary whose jurisdiction is contested is not election.—Louisville Woolen Mills v. Kindgen, 202.

⟵7(1) (Tex.Civ.App.) Institution of proceeding not a conclusive election.—Hartford Life Ins. Co. v. Patterson, 814.

⟵12 (Ky.) Adoption of erroneous remedy is not election against proper remedy.—Louisville Woolen Mills v. Kindgen, 202.

⟵12 (Tex.Civ.App.) One does not have two remedies to elect between where there is valid defense to one of them.—Hartford Life Ins. Co. v. Patterson, 814.

ELECTIONS.

VI. NOMINATIONS AND PRIMARY ELECTIONS.

⟵120 (Mo.) Constitutional provision incorporated in primary law by reference.—State ex rel. Feinstein v. Hartmann, 982.

XI. VIOLATIONS OF ELECTION LAWS.

⟵311 (Mo.) Legislature had power to deny grand jury right to use primary election ballots.—State ex rel. Feinstein v. Hartmann, 982.
⟵326(2) (Mo.) Information failed to charge illegal voting in violation of statute.—State v. Pearson, 595.
⟵329 (Mo.) Restrictions in Constitution on use of ballots, etc., as evidence held not to deny circuit judge power to issue subpoena for production of ballots; "elections."—State ex rel. Feinstein v. Hartmann, 982.
Statute held not to permit circuit judge to issue subpoena for production of primary election ballot boxes, etc.—Id.

EMINENT DOMAIN.

II. COMPENSATION.

(B) Taking or Injuring Property as Ground for Compensation.

⟵101(1) (Tex.Civ.App.) Damages to abutting property from elevating highway recoverable.—Dallas County v. Barr, 453.

(C) Measure and Amount.

⟵141(3) (Tex.Civ.App.) Measure of damages difference in value before and after injury.—Dallas County v. Barr, 453.
⟵145(1) (Ark.) "Just compensation" in benefits received where public use for which land taken enhances value of remainder.—Gregg v. Sanders, 190.
Rule of damages reduced by benefits not applicable to case of improvement district constructing improvement paid for by special assessment.—Id.
⟵148 (Tex.Civ.App.) Interest from injury allowable as part of damages.—Dallas County v. Barr, 453.

IV. REMEDIES OF OWNERS OF PROPERTY.

⟵280 (Tex.Civ.App.) Right of abutting owner to damages from elevating highway not affected by prior deed from his grantor for highway.—Dallas County v. Barr, 453.
⟵285 (Tex.Civ.App.) County liable for damage from its elevating highway.—Dallas County v. Barr, 453.
⟵300 (Tex.Civ.App.) Finding of damages held supported by evidence.—Dallas County v. Barr, 453.

EQUITY.

See Cancellation of Instruments; Conversion; Injunction; Partition; Quieting Title; Reformation of Instruments; Specific Performance; Subrogation; Trusts.

I. JURISDICTION, PRINCIPLES, AND MAXIMS.

(B) Remedy at Law and Multiplicity of Suits.

⟵48 (Ark.) Sole basis of suit to recover money is inadequacy of legal remedy.—Cosby v. Hurst, 194.

IV. PLEADING.

(A) Original Bill.

⟵136 (Ark.) Formal statement of no adequate remedy at law ineffective.—Cosby v. Hurst, 194.

ERROR, WRIT OF.

See Appeal and Error.

ESCROWS.

⟵1 (Tex.Com.App.) Valid contract of sale necessary to make deposit of deed a genuine "escrow."—Simpson v. Green, 375.
⟵1 (Tex.Civ.App.) Defined and held to have no application to money placed with another to be applied as directed by owner.—Stonewall v. McGown, 850.
⟵8(2) (Tex.Com.App.) Deposit of deed sufficient to meet statute of frauds held an irrevocable escrow.—Simpson v. Green, 375.

ESTATES.

See Descent and Distribution; Executors and Administrators; Life Estates; Remainders; Wills.

ESTOPPEL.

III. EQUITABLE ESTOPPEL.

(A) Nature and Essentials in General.

⟵59 (Ark.) One preventing the doing of a thing cannot benefit by the nonperformance.—Vaughan v. Odell & Kleiner, 562.
⟵61 (Mo.App.) Plaintiff contractor not entitled to rely on acceptance as estopping defendant from questioning sufficiency of smokestack.—John O'Brien Boiler Works Co. v. Third Nat. Bank, 1053.
⟵62(2) (Mo.) State bound by a position assumed.—State v. Baird, 625.

(B) Grounds of Estoppel.

⟵68(1) (Mo.) Parties bound to positions assumed.—State v. Baird, 625.
⟵88(1) (Tex.Com.App.) Effort to compromise not estoppel to assertion of rights in court.—Poe v. Continental Oil & Cotton Co., 717.
⟵92(2) (Ky.) Lessor accenting payment of rent held not estopped to claim forgery.—Curry v. Hinton, 217.

(E) Pleading, Evidence, Trial, and Review.

⟵119 (Mo.App.) Where reasonable minds can differ, question of waiver is for jury.—McNeill v. Wabash Ry. Co., 649.

EVIDENCE.

See Criminal Law, ⟵308–539; Depositions; Witnesses.
For evidence as to particular facts or issues or in particular actions or proceedings, see also the various specific topics.
For review of rulings relating to evidence, see Appeal and Error.
Reception at trial, see Criminal Law, ⟵663–673; Trial, ⟵105.

I. JUDICIAL NOTICE.

⟵10(3) (Mo.App.) No judicial notice of city streets.—Fidelity & Casualty Co. of New York v. Kansas City Rys. Co., 277.
⟵13 (Tex.Com.App.) Maturity of crops matter of common knowledge.—Roberts v. Armstrong, 371.
⟵18 (Mo.App.) That jack has no value, except for breeding purposes, matter of common knowledge.—Neal v. Crowson, 1033.

⌐⇒20(2) (Tex.Com.App.) That banks daily make loans secured by stock of other banks is matter of common knowledge.—Citizens' Nat. Bank of Stamford v. Stevenson, 364.

⌐⇒23(1) (Mo.App.) Judicial notice of cessation of control by federal government of telegraph companies taken.—Taylor v. Western Union Telegraph Co., 78.

⌐⇒34 (Mo.App.) Judicial notice of acts of Congress taken.—Taylor v. Western Union Telegraph Co., 78.

⌐⇒44 (Tex.Civ.App.) Judicial notice that Director General of Railroads was succeeded by Agent of President.—Payne v. White House Lumber Co., 417.

⌐⇒46 (Mo.App.) Judicial notice of acts of Congress and proclamations of President thereunder taken.—Taylor v. Western Union Telegraph Co., 78.

⌐⇒48 (Ky.) Judicial notice taken of regular meetings of board of council of town.—Town of Nortonville v. Woodward, 224.

II. PRESUMPTIONS.

⌐⇒54 (Mo.) Inference cannot be built on inference to establish fact.—Phillips v. Travelers' Ins. Co. of Hartford, Conn., 947.

⌐⇒65 (Tex.Com.App.) Testator presumed to have known that in absence of will his children would inherit equally.—Haupt v. Michaelis, 706.

⌐⇒67(1) (Ky.) Presumption is that possession of deed to wife continued in husband.—Petty's Heirs v. Petty, 52.

⌐⇒69 (Tex.Com.App.) Pledgee presumed to follow law as to manner of sale in absence of evidence.—Haynes v. Western Union Telegraph Co., 361.

⌐⇒78 (Ky.) Defendant's failure to produce deed executed by him and in his possession held strong evidence against him.—Petty's Heirs v. Petty, 52.

⌐⇒80(1) (Tex.Com.App.) It is presumed that laws of foreign state are like those of forum.—Pendleton v. Hare, 334.

⌐⇒83(3) (Tex.Civ.App.) State lands presumed to have been appraised and notice given.—Gulf Production Co· v. State, 124.

⌐⇒87 (Tex.Civ.App.) Presumption of conveyance one of fact and not of law.—Brownfield v. Brabson, 491.

IV. RELEVANCY, MATERIALITY, AND COMPETENCY IN GENERAL.

(B) Res Gestæ.

⌐⇒123(12) (Mo.App.) Admission by street car motorman after collision that his brakes did not work held not admissible as res gestæ.—Jackels v. Kansas City Rys. Co., 1023.

(C) Similar Facts and Transactions.

⌐⇒135(1) (Tex.Civ.App.) No' error in refusing evidence of other fraudulent transactions.—Smith v. Fleming, 136.

V. BEST AND SECONDARY EVIDENCE.

⌐⇒175 (Ky.) Oral testimony inadmissible to show action of city council.—Town of Nortonville v. Woodward, 224.

VII. ADMISSIONS.

(A) Nature, Form, and Incidents in General.

⌐⇒215(1) (Mo.App.) Proofs of death furnished by beneficiary admissible as admissions.—Whiteside v. Court of Honor, 1026.

Proceedings before coroner and report of district court to insurer admissible as admissions when joined by beneficiary to proof of death.—Id.

(C) By Grantors, Former Owners, or Privies.

⌐⇒236(2) (Tex.Com.App.) Notes executed by deceased husband after death of first wife admissible as admission of community debt.—Roberson v. Hughes, 734.

(D) By Agents or Other Representatives

⌐⇒242(2) (Tex.Civ.App.) Statement of agent of limited authority not part of res gestæ, hearsay.—Southern Surety Co. v. Nalle & Co., 402.

⌐⇒244(8) (Tex.Civ.App.) Testimony by surety company's agent held competent as admission, as against objection that it was hearsay.—Southern Surety Co. v. Nalle & Co., 402.

(E) Proof and Effect.

⌐⇒265(18) (Mo.App.) Admissions against interest preclude recovery in absence of contradictory or explanatory evidence.—Thornton v. Business Men's Acc. Ass'n of America, 1077.

VIII. DECLARATIONS.

(A) Nature, Form, and Incidents in General.

⌐⇒271(18) (Tex.Civ.App.) Instrument signed by plaintiff held properly admitted when offered by plaintiff.—Peacock v. Aug. A. Busch & Co., 447.

⌐⇒271(19) (Tex.Civ.App.) Letters written by plaintiff not admissible in his behalf.—Hartford Life Ins. Co. v. Patterson, 814.

IX. HEARSAY.

⌐⇒317(2) (Ark.) Testimony that third person said company was a partnership held hearsay.—Forrester v. Locke, 897.

⌐⇒318(6) (Ark.) Testimony based on book entries, showing account between party and third person, not admissible when witness did not keep books.—Forrester v. Locke, 897.

X. DOCUMENTARY EVIDENCE.

(C) Private Writings and Publications.

⌐⇒353(9) (Tex.Civ.App.) Instrument signed only by party offering it held admissible.—Peacock v. Aug. A. Busch & Co., 447.

(D) Production, Authentication, and Effect.

⌐⇒376(1) (Tex.Civ.App.) Testimony of witnesses as to weight of cars of coal admissible along with original scale tickets showing weights of cars and coal in pounds.—Payne v. White House Lumber Co., 417.

⌐⇒376(6) (Mo.App.) Witness familiar with books of account properly permitted to state totals shown thereby when offered for inspection, though not made by her.—Stetina v. Bergstein, 1059.

⌐⇒383(7) (Tex.Com.App.) Evidence held sufficient to support finding tract of land purchased on credit, despite recital in deed of cash consideration.—Roberson v. Hughes, 734.

XI. PAROL OR EXTRINSIC EVIDENCE AFFECTING WRITINGS.

(A) Contradicting, Varying, or Adding to Terms of Written Instrument.

⌐⇒390(1) (Tex.Com.App.) Parol evidence inadmissible to show covenant against incumbrances did not include tenant's occupancy.—Morriss v. Hesse, 317.

⌐⇒400(3) (Mo.App.) In absence of fraud representations inducing written contract are inadmissible.—Guess v. Russell Bros. Clothing Co., 1015.

⌐⇒413 (Mo.) Parol evidence inadmissible to attack record in tax suit.—Hines v. Felkins, 922.

⌐⇒427 (Mo.App.) Oral agreement by vendor to open street does not vary written contract and deed.—Heath v. Beck, 657.

(B) Invalidating Written Instrument.

⌐⇒429 (Tex.) Oral evidence showing inconsistencies held not inadmissible as contradicting field notes.—Wilson v. Giraud, 1074.

⌐⇒433(6) (Mo.App.) Consignee may show that written contract did not express destination.—McNeill v. Wabash Ry. Co., 649.

←434(6) (Tex.Civ.App.) Testimony *held* not to vary written instrument.—Smith v. Fleming, 136.

←434(11) (Mo.App.) Facts *held* not to show contract was procured by "fraud," justifying admission of parol evidence.—Guess v. Russell Bros. Clothing Co., 1015.

←437 (Tex.Civ.App.) Communications subsequent to contract *held* admissible and to render contract violative of statute.—W. T. Rawleigh Co. v. Smith, 799.

(C) Separate or Subsequent Oral Agreement.

←441(9) (Ark.) Warranty cannot be ingrafted by parol upon complete unambiguous sales contract.—Federal Truck & Motors Co. v. Tompkins, 553.

←441(9) (Mo.App.) Written contract *held* not entered into in performance of oral agreement, so as to make admissible evidence of oral agreement.—Guess v. Russell Bros. Clothing Co., 1015.

←442(6) (Mo.App.) Parol evidence to vary contract provision for shipment "as soon as possible" is inadmissible.—Guess v. Russell Bros. Clothing Co., 1015.

(D) Construction or Application of Language of Written Instrument.

←450(5) (Tex.Civ.App.) Contract *held* not ambiguous to admit parol evidence.—Great Southern Oil & Refining Ass'n v. Cooper, 157.

←450(8) (Mo.App.) Parol evidence admissible to elucidate indefinite warranty.—Mayfield v. George O. Richardson Machinery Co., 288.

←456 (Mo.App.) Parol evidence inadmissible to show the meaning of a word which is not ambiguous.—State ex rel. Youngman v. Calhoun, 647.

←461(1) (Tex.Civ.App.) Parol evidence inadmissible to show intent of parties to unambiguous written contract.—Great Southern Oil & Refining Ass'n v. Cooper, 157.

←461(3) (Tex.Civ.App.) Where deed is clear, parol evidence is inadmissible to show intention.—Scheller v. Groesbeck, 1092.

XII. OPINION EVIDENCE.

(A) Conclusions and Opinions of Witnesses in General.

←471(2) (Tex.Civ.App.) Irrelevant conclusion properly rejected.—Maier v. Langerhans, 145.

←471(23) (Mo.App.) Answer of witness as to speed of automobile *held* mere conclusion.—Bibb v. Grady, 1020.

←471(25) (Tex.Civ.App.) Testimony of secretary he performed duties not a conclusion.—Great Southern Oil & Refining Ass'n v. Cooper, 157.

←474½ (Ky.) Neither agency nor extent can be established by opinion evidence.—Irvine Development Co. v. Clark, 539.

←481(1) (Mo.App.) Whether surgeon's decision to operate was negligence should be determined from testimony of experts.—Gottschall v. Geiger, 87.

←489 (Tex.Civ.App.) Testimony as to what constituted market value admissible where witness testified he knew the market value.—Payne v. White House Lumber Co., 417.

(B) Subjects of Expert Testimony.

←509 (Mo.App.) Expert physicians could give opinions as to wife's injuries.—Baldwin v. Kansas City Rys. Co., 280.

←528(1) (Mo.App.) Physicians' opinion that accident could have caused plaintiff's injury *held* proper.—Keith v. Kansas City Rys. Co., 1046.

(D) Examination of Experts.

←554 (Ky.) Physician's testimony as to a certain disease inadmissible, in absence of

showing that plaintiff had such disease.—Cincinnati, N. O. & T. P. R. Co. v. Owsley, 210.

(F) Effect of Opinion Evidence.

←571(7) (Tex.Civ.App.) Jury are not bound by opinion based on disputed facts.—Pickrell v. Imperial Petroleum Co., 412.

Jury are not bound by opinion of interested witness.—Id.

←571(9) (Tex.Com.App.) Conductor's opinion on hypothetical case *held* incompetent.—Steed v. Gulf, C. & S. F. Ry. Co., 714.

XIII. EVIDENCE AT FORMER TRIAL OR IN OTHER PROCEEDING.

←575 (Tex.Civ.App.) Testimony at former trial inadmissible unless witness absent or dead.—Kurz v. Solis, 424.

XIV. WEIGHT AND SUFFICIENCY.

←589 (Mo.App.) Alighting passenger's testimony as to how she fell on premature starting of car *held* not contrary to physical laws.—Hartweg v. Kansas City Rys. Co., 269.

←598(1) (Ark.) Mere number of witnesses does not establish weight of evidence.—Texarkana & Ft. Smith Ry. Co. v. Adcock, 866.

EXCEPTIONS, BILL OF.

See Appeal and Error, ←544.

EXECUTIVE POWER.

See Constitutional Law, ←79.

EXECUTORS AND ADMINISTRATORS.

See Descent and Distribution; Wills.

IV. COLLECTION AND MANAGEMENT OF ESTATE.

(A) In General.

←111(1) (Tex.Com.App.) Reasonable attorney's fees are expenses of administration.—Pendleton v. Hare, 334.

←111(3) (Tex.Com.App.) In contracting with attorney for services in probate of will, executor acts in representative capacity.—Pendleton v. Hare, 334.

Executor may bind estate for reasonable attorney's fees in connection with probate of will.—Id.

(B) Real Property and Interests Therein.

←150 (Tex.Civ.App.) Executors not authorized to grant oil and gas lease.—Smith v. Womack, 840.

VI. ALLOWANCE AND PAYMENT OF CLAIMS.

(A) Liabilities of Estate.

←221(5) (Mo.App.) Evidence *held* insufficient to sustain verdict for services for collecting rents for deceased.—Jones v. Munroe, 1069.

XI. ACCOUNTING AND SETTLEMENT.

(D) Compensation.

←495(1) (Mo.App.) Executors *held* not entitled to commissions on property not included within the power of sale in the will.—In re Dwyer's Estate, 672.

Executors not entitled to commissions on value of land as personalty.—Id.

XII. FOREIGN AND ANCILLARY ADMINISTRATION.

←521 (Tex.Civ.App.) Attorney's services in will contest in other state may be charged against estate in Texas in hands of ancillary administrator.—Pendleton v. Hare, 334.

EXEMPTIONS.

See Homestead; Taxation, ←241.

EXTRADITION.

II. INTERSTATE.

⊂⇒34 (Tex.Cr.App.) Requisition paper must be accompanied by certified copy of affidavit or indictment.—Ex parte Gradington, 781.

FACTORS.

See Brokers.

FIXTURES.

⊂⇒14 (Ark.) Machinery parts added under agreement for removal on expiration of lease did not become part of realty.—Taylor v. Walker, 550.

FOREIGN CORPORATIONS.

See Corporations, ⊂⇒642–674.

FORMER JEOPARDY.

See Criminal Law, ⊂⇒195–200.

FRAUD.

See Frauds, Statute of; Fraudulent Conveyances.

I. DECEPTION CONSTITUTING FRAUD, AND LIABILITY THEREFOR.

⊂⇒13(3) (Tex.Com.App.) Belief of party misrepresenting fact unimportant.—Graves v. Haynes, 383.

⊂⇒20 (Tex.Com.App.) Reliance on representations as to diseased cattle affecting right to recover damages.—Graves v. Haynes, 383.

⊂⇒22(1) (Tex.Com.App.) Duty to investigate truth of representation as to diseased cattle. —Graves v. Haynes, 383.

II. ACTIONS.

(B) Parties and Pleading.

⊂⇒41 (Tex.Com.App.) Vendor's complaint *held* to state cause of action for deceit.—Rea v. Luse, 310.

(D) Damages.

⊂⇒59(3) (Tex.Com.App.) Measure of damages stated.—Rea v. Luse, 310.

FRAUDS, STATUTE OF.

III. PROMISES TO ANSWER FOR DEBT, DEFAULT OR MISCARRIAGE OF ANOTHER.

⊂⇒33(2) (Tex.Civ.App.) Where purpose of promisor is to subserve own purpose, promise not within statute.—Great Southern Oil & Refining Ass'n v. Cooper, 157.

Promise of members of association made for own benefit to pay salary of secretary not within statute.—Id.

VI. REAL PROPERTY AND ESTATES AND INTERESTS THEREIN.

⊂⇒58(2) (Ky.) Verbal consent to extension not objectionable on the ground that it was within the statute of frauds.—Kozy Theater Co. v. Love, 249.

VIII. REQUISITES AND SUFFICIENCY OF WRITING.

⊂⇒103(1) (Tex.Com.App.) Deed deposited in escrow *held* not insufficient as memorandum.— Simpson v. Green, 375.

⊂⇒108(4) (Tex.Com.App.) Consideration need not be expressed in writing.—Simpson v. Green, 375.

Recital of consideration of deed in escrow *held* sufficient to meet requirements of statute. —Id.

⊂⇒116(5) (Ark.) Authority of seller's agent to contract with purchaser that latter should bid in land on foreclosure not required to be in writing.—Battle v. Draper, 869.

IX. OPERATION AND EFFECT OF STATUTE.

⊂⇒125(1) (Mo.App.) Does not render contract void but is rule of evidence.—Heath v. Beck, 657.

⊂⇒125(1) (Tex.Com.App.) Statute does not declare parol sale of land void, but merely provides means of resistance.—Simpson v. Green, 375.

⊂⇒127 (Tex.Com.App.) Decree enforces prior oral contract reduced to writing and not memorandum.—Simpson v. Green, 375.

⊂⇒144 (Mo.App.) Defense *held* waived.— Heath v. Beck, 657.

FRAUDULENT CONVEYANCES.

I. TRANSFERS AND TRANSACTIONS INVALID.

(D) Indebtedness, Insolvency, and Intent of Grantor.

⊂⇒58 (Tex.Civ.App.) Intent to defraud not necessary.—Davis v. Campbell-Root Lumber Co., 167.

(E) Consideration.

⊂⇒76(1) (Tex.Civ.App.) $20 consideration *held* nominal.—Davis v. Campbell-Root Lumber Co., 167.

III. REMEDIES OF CREDITORS AND PURCHASERS.

(A) Persons Entitled to Assert Invalidity.

⊂⇒220 (Tex.Civ.App.) Immaterial that creditor's note was secured by chattel mortgage in action to set aside conveyance of land.—Davis v. Campbell-Root Lumber Co., 167.

GARNISHMENT.

XI. WRONGFUL GARNISHMENT.

⊂⇒250 (Ark.) Allowance of interest to defendant on all money garnished *held* proper.— Russell v. Barnhart Mercantile Co., 881.

GAS.

⊂⇒9 (Ky.) Gas company's franchise and construction bond construed.—Louisville Gas & Electric Co. v. City of Louisville, 909.

Gas company's franchise and construction bond construed.—Id.

In city's suit on gas company's construction bond, answer *held* to state good defense.—Id.

⊂⇒13(1) (Ky.) City cannot sue on gas company's bond for damages sustained by individual gas users.—Louisville Gas & Electric Co. v. City of Louisville, 918.

GOOD WILL.

⊂⇒6(4) (Mo.App.) Contract for sale of a physicians' practice construed in respect to restriction on sellers as to continuing practice.—State ex rel. Youngman v. Calhoun, 647.

GUARANTY.

See Indemnity.

HABEAS CORPUS.

II. JURISDICTION, PROCEEDINGS, AND RELIEF.

⊂⇒85(1) (Tex.Com.App.) Third person may defeat habeas corpus by father to regain custody of child by showing it is not to the benefit of the child.—Dunn v. Jackson, 351.

⊂⇒85(2) (Tex.Cr.App.) Burden *held* on relator to show that warrant of extradition was not based on proper affidavit.—Ex parte Gradington, 781.

⊂⇒99(1) (Tex.Com.App.) Parent is natural guardian of his children, as respecting right to habeas corpus.—Dunn v. Jackson, 351.

Father, though suitable, is not entitled to custody of child at all events.—Id.

⊂⇒99(3) (Tex.Com.App.) Interests of child prevail in proceedings for custody.—Dunn v. Jackson, 351.

⚖99(6) (Tex.Com.App.) Wishes of child of sufficient age to judge for itself should be considered in habeas corpus proceedings.—Dunn v. Jackson, 351.

⚖107 (Tex.Cr.App.) Where jury fixed punishment of applicant at less than capital, court erred in denying bail.—Ex parte Cates, 396.

⚖113(9) (Tex.Cr.App.) Court without jurisdiction where no notice of appeal in transcript.—Ex parte Cates, 396.

HARMLESS ERROR.

See Appeal and Error, ⚖1063–1071; Criminal Law, ⚖1166½–1172.

HIGHWAYS.

See Bridges.

III. CONSTRUCTION, IMPROVEMENT, AND REPAIR.

⚖103 (Tex.Civ.App.) Change of route for construction of county road not an abuse of "discretion," warranting judicial interference therewith.—Board of Permanent Road Com'rs of Hunt County v. Johnson, 859.

IV. TAXES, ASSESSMENTS, AND WORK ON HIGHWAYS.

⚖142 (Ark.) Statute held not to authorize circuit court to set aside whole assessment of benefits.—Road Improvement Dist. No. 9 of Sevier County v. Bennett, 552.

⚖150 (Mo.App.) Full compliance with statute so as to warrant recovery of poll tax shown.—Road Dist. No. 41, Henry Tp., Vernon County, v. Jackson, 1043.

Defect in warning notice insufficient to prevent recovery of poll tax.—Id.

Road district may sue to recover poll taxes.—Id.

HOLIDAYS.

See Sunday.

HOMESTEAD.

I. NATURE, ACQUISITION, AND EXTENT.

(C) Acquisition and Establishment.

⚖37 (Tex.Com.App.) Homestead interest of tenants in common not confined to land actually inclosed by them.—Massillon Engine & Thresher Co. v. Barrow, 368.

Inclosure of part of tract by tenants in common does not limit their homestead to inclosed part where remainder is wild land.—Id.

(D) Property Constituting Homestead.

⚖84 (Tex.Com.App.) Tenants in common held to have impressed tract with homestead character.—Massillon Engine & Thresher Co. v. Barrow, 368.

Tenants in common may impress land with homestead.—Id.

⚖89 (Tex.Com.App.) Both widow and remainderman cannot have homestead in same land.—Massillon Engine & Thresher Co. v. Barrow, 368.

II. TRANSFER OR INCUMBRANCE.

⚖122 (Tex.Civ.App.) Wife's right to homestead ceases on acquiring a new one, and husband's deed estops him.—Fisher v. Gulf Production Co., 450.

⚖123 (Tex.Civ.App.) Acceptance of money held ratification of transaction barring action for misrepresentations.—Fisher v. Gulf Production Co., 450.

⚖128 (Tex.Com.App.) Purchaser held estopped to deny validity of mortgage lien on ground that property constituted homestead.—Rice-Stix Dry Goods Co. v. First Nat. Bank, 386.

III. RIGHTS OF SURVIVING HUSBAND, WIFE, CHILDREN, OR HEIRS.

⚖134 (Mo.) Title to homestead vested in heirs of decedent free from payment of debts

contracted after it was acquired.—In re Boward's Estate, 600.

⚖135 (Mo.) Rights of parties must be determined by law in force at time of homestead owner's death.—In re Boward's Estate, 600.

⚖142(1) (Tex.Civ.App.) Decedent's homestead may be set over to minor daughter living with decedent's divorced wife.—Scripture v. Scripture, 826.

Father legally bound for child's support after divorce giving custody to wife so that such minor may have homestead set apart.—Id.

⚖150(1) (Tex.Civ.App.) Divorced wife as guardian of their minor child could apply to have deceased husband's homestead set apart for use of child.—Scripture v. Scripture, 826.

HOMICIDE.

II. MURDER.

⚖8 (Tex.Cr.App.) Automobile law held not to change law of homicide.—Worley v. State, 391.

⚖11 (Ky.) Guilt of murder requires malice aforethought or predetermination to kill without lawful reason existing at the time.—Cloninger v. Commonwealth, 535.

Circumstances establishing malice stated.—Id.

⚖27 (Ark.) Rule as to insanity as constituting defense stated.—Woodall v. State, 186.

III. MANSLAUGHTER.

⚖49 (Tex.Cr.App.) Epithet "son of a bitch" does not support a charge on manslaughter.—Lewis v. State, 113.

IV. ASSAULT WITH INTENT TO KILL.

⚖89(2) (Tex.Cr.App.) Fact shot fired at one with intent to murder him wounded another no excuse.—Jones v. State, 122.

⚖90 (Mo.) Instruction authorising a conviction for assault with intent to kill where defendant simply used fists is error.—State v. Rongey, 609.

V. EXCUSABLE OR JUSTIFIABLE HOMICIDE.

⚖112(5) (Mo.) Doctrine of self-defense not available, where defendant brought on difficulty.—State v. Caldwell, 613.

⚖116(1) (Tex.Cr.App.) Defendant had right to act on appearances in own defense.—Lewis v. State, 113.

⚖119 (Mo.) One who is struck by another's fist is not entitled to resort to use of deadly weapon in self-defense.—State v. Caldwell, 613.

⚖122 (Ark.) Illicit relations between deceased and defendant's wife no justification.—Fisher v. State, 181.

VI. INDICTMENT AND INFORMATION.

⚖127 (Mo.) Information for murder held sufficient.—State v. Wilson, 596.

⚖134 (Tex.Cr.App.) Indictment for negligent homicide by use of automobile must charge all essential elements of offense.—Worley v. State, 391.

Indictment for negligent homicide by use of automobile held insufficient.—Id.

⚖142(10) (Tex.Cr.App.) Under charge of assault to murder one, proof of intent to murder another is admissible.—Jones v. State, 122.

VII. EVIDENCE.

(A) Presumptions and Burden of Proof.

⚖145 (Mo.) One who uses deadly weapon on another's body is presumed to know that result is likely death.—State v. Caldwell, 613.

Intent inferred from assault with deadly weapon.—Id.

⚖151(2) (Tex.Cr.App.) Presumption and burden of proof as to mental derangement stated.—Roberts v. State, 759.

(B) Admissibility in General.

⬥158(2) (Ky.) Testimony as to defendant's threat *held* too remote.—Jones v. Commonwealth, 31.

⬥158(3) (Ky.) Testimony as to defendant's threat *held* too indefinite.—Jones v. Commonwealth, 31.

⬥163(2) (Ark.) Good character of deceased admissible only after defendant has attacked character.—Fisher v. State, 181.

Evidence deceased had borrowed a pistol when visiting defendant's wife *held* not to make evidence of good character admissible.—Id.

⬥166(8) (Mo.) Evidence of trouble between accused and wife involving deceased, admissible.—State v. Hall, 1001.

⬥170 (Mo.) Evidence as to tracks and that accused wore clothing similar to that used in commission of offense admissible.—State v. Hall, 1001.

⬥174(6) (Mo.) Evidence that accused possessed weapon similar to that used in commission of offense admissible.—State v. Hall, 1001.

Evidence as to identity of burned jumper found on defendant's premises with one worn by murderer admissible.—Id.

⬥179 (Tex.Cr.App.) Testimony as to defendant's demeanor when arrested competent on issue of insanity.—Roberts v. State, 759.

⬥188(5) (Ark.) General reputation, but not personal opinion of witness as to deceased's character, admissible.—Trotter v. State, 177.

⬥190(7) (Ky.) Uncommunicated threats admissible.—Jones v. Commonwealth, 31.

(E) Weight and Sufficiency.

⬥228(2) (Mo.) Circumstantial evidence *held* sufficient to prove corpus delicti.—State v. Hall, 1001.

⬥231 (Ky.) Malice may be shown by threats or by circumstances.—Cloninger v. Commonwealth, 535.

⬥234(1) (Tex.Cr.App.) Evidence *held* to show presence of accused accounted for in manner consistent with innocence.—Giles v. State, 765.

⬥244(1) (Mo.) Doctrine that one assaulted may act upon appearances *held* inapplicable under the evidence.—State v. Caldwell, 613.

Evidence *held* insufficient to show self-defense.—Id.

⬥253(2) (Mo.) Circumstantial evidence *held* sufficient to convict of first degree murder.—State v. Hall, 1001.

⬥254 (Mo.) Evidence sustaining conviction of murder in second degree.—State v. Howard, 255.

⬥254 (Mo.) Conviction of murder in the second degree sustained.—State v. Likens, 578.

⬥254 (Mo.) Evidence sufficient to support conviction for killing in hold-up.—State v. Wilson, 596.

⬥255(3) (Mo.) Evidence *held* sufficient to sustain verdict of manslaughter.—State v. McDonald, 927.

VIII. TRIAL.

(A) Conduct in General.

⬥261 (Tex.Cr.App.) Dead bodies not exhumed for examination unless justice demands.—Shields v. State, 779.

Exhumation of body *held* not imperatively demanded.—Id.

(B) Questions for Jury.

⬥270 (Ark.) Whether defendant was insane at time of killing *held* for jury.—Woodall v. State, 186.

⬥281 (Tex.Cr.App.) Evidence *held* sufficient for submission of issue of participation.—Flores v. State, 786.

(C) Instructions.

⬥292(4) (Mo.) An instruction as to striking with a pair of heavy shoes *held* reversible error where not justified by evidence.—State v. Rongey, 609.

Assumption in instruction without supporting evidence that defendant was wearing heavy shoes was error.—Id.

Instruction assuming without evidence that defendant assaulted another with a weapon is erroneous.—Id.

Instruction as to deadly weapon *held* erroneous in the absence of evidence.—Id.

⬥297 (Mo.) Every fact which would justify must be submitted.—State v. Nelson, 590.

⬥300(2) (Tex.Cr.App.) Instruction on appearance of danger to defendant erroneous.—Lewis v. State, 113.

⬥300(2) (Tex.Cr.App.) Charge relative to threats *held* not subject to criticism.—Shields v. State, 779.

⬥300(3) (Mo.) Instruction on provoking difficulty *held* not misleading.—State v. Caldwell, 613.

⬥300(7) (Tex.Cr.App.) Failure to instruct that defendant could continue to shoot as long as danger from deceased continued, as viewed from defendant's standpoint, *held* not error.—Boaz v. State, 790.

⬥300(8) (Ark.) Instruction accused could not plead self-defense, if aggressor, *held* not abstract.—George v. State, 9.

⬥300(12) (Mo.) Failure to charge on self-defense against attack by companions of deceased *held* error.—State v. Nelson, 590.

⬥301 (Mo.) Instruction as to defendant's right to shoot in defense of brother unnecessary.—State v. Cruts, 602.

⬥308(1) (Tex.Cr.App.) Elements of offense of murder stated; may be embraced in charge.—Lewis v. State, 113.

⬥309(1) (Ark.) Court's mistake in use of term "voluntary manslaughter" instead of "involuntary manslaughter" in instruction *held* error.—Trotter v. State, 177.

⬥309(1) (Tex.Cr.App.) Proper charge on manslaughter outlined.—Lewis v. State, 113.

⬥309(1) (Tex.Cr.App.) Converse of state's charge on provoking difficulty should have been submitted.—Garner v. State, 389.

⬥309(2) (Mo.) Evidence *held* to justify charge of manslaughter.—State v. Nelson, 590.

⬥309(2) (Tex.Cr.App.) Issue of manslaughter becomes pertinent, where it is claimed killing resulted from fight.—Lewis v. State, 113.

⬥309(4) (Tex.Cr.App.) Charge on manslaughter proper where there is evidence from which jury may deduce finding.—Lewis v. State, 113.

⬥309(4) (Tex.Cr.App.) Evidence of previous difficulties and of fear and excitement on the part of accused *held* to require submission of the issue of manslaughter.—Theriot v. State, 777.

⬥309(5) (Mo.) Instruction on manslaughter in fourth degree properly refused.—State v. Likens, 578.

⬥309(6) (Tex.Cr.App.) Special charge on manslaughter, requested by defendant, incorrect.—Lewis v. State, 113.

⬥309(6) (Tex.Cr.App.) Charge on provoking difficulty *held* appropriate.—Garner v. State, 389.

⬥310(3) (Mo.) No error in refusing to instruct as to grade of assault not involving intent to kill.—State v. Cruts, 602.

(D) Verdict.

⬥312 (Mo.) Verdict of guilty of murder in the second degree sufficient.—State v. Likens, 578.

IX. NEW TRIAL.

⬥319 (Tex.Cr.App.) No error in overruling motion for new trial, where testimony of absent witness is contradictory.—Jones v. State, 122.

New trial for newly discovered evidence properly denied, where defendant knew of same before trial.—Id.

X. APPEAL AND ERROR.

⚖═325 (Tex.Cr.App.) Failure to charge on law of homicide in defense of one's person after threats *held* not reversible error.—Bean v. State, 776.

⚖═332(2) (Ky.) Verdict of guilty *held* not result of passion or prejudice, and not palpably or flagrantly against the evidence.—Cloninger v. Commonwealth, 535.

⚖═338(4) (Ky.) Withdrawal of testimony from jury before submission of case cured error in introduction.—Jones v. Commonwealth, 31.

⚖═340(4) (Tex.Cr.App.) Errors in charge as to murder immaterial, where conviction was for manslaughter.—Shields v. State, 779.

⚖═346 (Ark.) Appellate court on appeal from conviction for voluntary manslaughter may affirm conviction of involuntary manslaughter. —Trotter v. State, 177.

XI. SENTENCE AND PUNISHMENT.

⚖═354 (Tex.Cr.App.) Finding relative to death penalty that defendant was not under 17 supported by evidence.—Flores v. State, 786.

HUSBAND AND WIFE.

See Divorce.

IV. DISABILITIES AND PRIVILEGES OF COVERTURE.

(E) Torts.

⚖═102 (Tex.) Married woman liable for tort in connection with removal of roof on her building.—Whitney Hardware Co. v. McMahan, 694.

Wife liable for tort, though connected with contract.—Id.

Wife, as well as husband, liable for wife's torts.—Id.

V. WIFE'S SEPARATE ESTATE.

(B) Rights and Liabilities of Husband.

⚖═146 (Tex.Civ.App.) Husband contracting for his wife with her tenant for repairs not liable to tenant for negligent performance.—Whitney Hardware Co. v. McMahan, 1117.

(C) Liabilities and Charges.

⚖═152 (Tex.) Act granting married woman power to manage and control separate estate carried with it power to contract with her tenant for repairs.—Whitney Hardware Co. v. McMahan, 694.

VI. ACTIONS.

⚖═209(2) (Ark.) Under Texas statute wife may maintain in her own name action for personal injuries, damages therefor not being community property.—Texarkana & Ft. Smith Ry. Co. v. Adcock, 866.

⚖═209(3) (Mo.App.) In case of injury to married woman two causes of action arise, one to the wife for pain and suffering, and the other to the husband for his marital injury.—Alexander v. Kansas City Rys. Co., 66.

⚖═209(3) (Mo.App.) Husband entitled to damages for loss of wife's society and services, without direct proof of value thereof.—Baldwin v. Kansas City Rys. Co., 280.

Husband entitled to damages for loss of "consortium."—Id.

⚖═213 (Tex.) Feme covert liable for breach of contract and negligence in management and control of her separate estate.—Whitney Hardware Co. v. McMahan, 694.

⚖═213 (Tex.Civ.App.) Wife liable for negligent performance of her contract with her tenant for repairs.—Whitney Hardware Co. v. McMahan, 1117.

Husband must be joined in action against wife for her negligent performance of contract. —Id.

VII. COMMUNITY PROPERTY.

⚖═254 (Tex.Civ.App.) Property acquired from rents and revenues of wife's separate property

constituted community.—Davis v. Campbell-Root Lumber Co., 167.

⚖═268(2) (Tex.Civ.App.) Partition did not affect community property as against creditor. —Davis v. Campbell-Root Lumber Co., 167.

IMPROVEMENTS.

See Municipal Corporations, ⚖═321–513.

INDEMNITY.

⚖═11 (Tex.Civ.App.) There is no right of action on an indemnity contract until the indemnitee has suffered loss.—St. Paul Fire & Marine Ins. Co. v. Charlton, 862.

⚖═16 (Ark.) Evidence *held* to sustain judgment in favor of indemnitor against bondsmen who compromised liability.—Sanderson v. Marconi, 554.

INDICTMENT AND INFORMATION.

See Homicide, ⚖═127–142.

III. FORMAL REQUISITES OF INDICTMENT.

⚖═30 (Mo.) Indictment for larceny not insufficient as to return by grand jury, etc.—State v. McBride, 592.

V. REQUISITES AND SUFFICIENCY OF ACCUSATION.

⚖═110(5) (Ky.) Indictment for abortion need not follow language of statute.—Commonwealth v. Allen, 41.

⚖═110(7) (Mo.) For arson sufficient if in language of statute.—State v. Ritter, 606.

⚖═110(18) (Mo.) Information for grand larceny in language of statute *held* sufficient.— State v. Bloomer, 568.

⚖═110(22) (Ky.) Charge of offense in language of statute sufficient.—Commonwealth v. Louisville & N. R. Co., 236.

⚖═110(31) (Tex.Cr.App.) Indictment for possessing intoxicants sufficient, though not using expression "had in his possession."—Rainey v. State, 118.

VI. JOINDER OF PARTIES, OFFENSES, AND COUNTS, DUPLICITY, AND ELECTION.

⚖═125(16) (Ky.) Indictment charging railroad with failure to provide waiting room not duplicitous or demurrable.—Commonwealth v. Louisville & N. R. Co., 236.

Charge of two offenses relative to waiting room renders indictment bad for duplicity. —Id.

⚖═125(44) (Tex.Cr.App.) Indictment may charge murder of two or more by same act in single count.—Jones v. State, 122.

VII. MOTION TO QUASH OR DISMISS, AND DEMURRER.

⚖═137(1) (Tex.Cr.App.) Information not subject to quashal because misdesignating court. —Dodaro v. State, 394.

VIII. AMENDMENT.

⚖═161(3) (Mo.App.) Amendment after jurors had qualified but before they have been sworn to try issues discretionary with court. —State v. Gardner, 1057.

IX. ISSUES, PROOF, AND VARIANCE.

⚖═171 (Ky.) Material variance defined.— Lowery v. Commonwealth, 234.

⚖═174 (Tex.Cr.App.) Principal offender may be convicted under indictment charging him directly with offense.—Jones v. State, 122.

XI. WAIVER OF DEFECTS AND OBJECTIONS, AND AIDER BY VERDICT.

⚖═193 (Mo.) Irregularity in indictment for larceny cured by statute of jeofails.—State v. McBride, 592.

INFANTS.

III. PROPERTY AND CONVEYANCES.

⊚⇒29 (Ky.) Retention of land in which proceeds of sale invested only estops infant to attack validity of sale.—Beale v. Stroud, 522.

⊚⇒41 (Ky.) Purchaser at sale of land has no remedy for loss of land where there is no express warranty and no representations.—Beale v. Stroud, 522.

⊚⇒42 (Ky.) Warranty of title in commissioner's deed not binding on infant.—Beale v. Stroud, 522.

VII. ACTIONS.

⊚⇒98 (Ky.) Conveyance of land with warranty presumed unauthorized when petition does not allege authority.—Beale v. Stroud, 522.

INJUNCTION.

II. SUBJECTS OF PROTECTION AND RELIEF.

(E) Public Officers and Boards and Municipalities.

⊚⇒74 (Tex.Civ.App.) Courts cannot invade discretion to correct mistakes of judgment.—Board of Permanent Road Com'rs of Hunt County v. Johnson, 859.

INSOLVENCY.

See Assignments for Benefit of Creditors.

INSPECTION.

⊚⇒2 (Tenn.) Factory Inspection Act provision for inspection fees held not violative of constitutional rule of uniformity in taxation.—Athens Hosiery Mills v. Thomason, 904.

INSTRUCTIONS.

See Criminal Law, ⊚⇒755½–844; Trial, ⊚⇒186–296.

INSURANCE.

III. INSURANCE AGENTS AND BROKERS.

(A) Agency for Insurer.

⊚⇒84(4) (Tex.Civ.App.) Insurer's agreement with agent as to renewal held not to supplant prior agreement.—Hartford Life Ins. Co. v. Patterson, 814.

⊚⇒92 (Ky.) Evidence held not to show agency for defendant insurer.—Grove Lodge No. 274, I. O. O. F., v. Fidelity Phenix Ins. Co., 215.

V. THE CONTRACT IN GENERAL.

(A) Nature, Requisites, and Validity.

⊚⇒133(1) (Tex.Civ.App.) Life insurance policy provision that, if insured die within six months, only one-half of amount will be paid, contravenes statute prohibiting settlement for less than face of policy.—American Nat. Ins. Co. v. Dixon, 165.

⊚⇒136(2) (Tex.Civ.App.) Manual delivery of policy unnecessary, where issued and mailed to agent for delivery.—Denton v. Kansas City Life Ins. Co., 436.

⊚⇒136(4) (Tex.Civ.App.) Delivery of policy during applicant's good health is condition precedent to liability.—Denton v. Kansas City Life Ins. Co., 436.

Policy delivery not unconditional where agent directed to ascertain applicant's health before delivery.—Id.

Where application provided that the policy should be void unless delivered to assured while in good health there was not an unconditional acceptance of the risk.—Id.

Implied delivery by placing in mails held not binding, where insurer had no knowledge of subsequent illness of insured.—Id.

Applicant taken with influenza not in "good health" within policy condition of delivery during applicant's good health.—Id.

(B) Construction and Operation.

⊚⇒146(3) (Mo.App.) Plain forfeiture clause will be enforced.—Elms v. Mutual Benefit Life Ins. Co., 653.

⊚⇒146(3) (Mo. App.) Ambiguous provision should be construed in favor of insured.—Bothmann v. Metropolitan Life Ins. Co., 1007.

Where provisions of policy are plain, the court can indulge in no forced construction.—Id.

VIII. CANCELLATION, SURRENDER, ABANDONMENT, OR RESCISSION OF POLICY.

⊚⇒232 (Mo.App.) No cancellation of policy where agents promised to cancel but neglected to do so before loss.—Clark v. Fidelity-Phenix Fire Ins. Co. of New York, 74.

IX. AVOIDANCE OF POLICY FOR MISREPRESENTATION, FRAUD, OR BREACH OF WARRANTY OR CONDITION.

(C) Matters Relating to Person Insured.

⊚⇒300 (Mo.App.) Voluntary application of reserve of paid-up insurance does not waive forfeiture.—Elms v. Mutual Benefit Life Ins. Co., 653.

X. FORFEITURE OF POLICY FOR BREACH OF PROMISSORY WARRANTY, COVENANT, OR CONDITION SUBSEQUENT.

(A) Grounds in General.

⊚⇒308 (Tex.Com.App.) Anti-technicality statute not applicable to breaches which could in no event contribute to loss.—Humphrey v. National Fire Ins. Co. of Hartford, Conn., 750.

(E) Nonpayment of Premiums or Assessments.

⊚⇒349(1) (Mo.App.) Policy held to provide for forfeiture for nonpayment of premium.—Elms v. Mutual Benefit Life Ins. Co., 653.

⊚⇒349(4) (Mo.App.) Provision for deduction for indebtedness held not to apply where policy was forfeited.—Elms v. Mutual Benefit Life Ins. Co., 653.

⊚⇒360(3) (Mo.App.) Reserve under policy held forfeited for nonpayment of premiums.—Elms v. Mutual Benefit Life Ins. Co., 653.

In absence of statute forfeited reserve is property of company.—Id.

⊚⇒360(3) (Mo.App.) Policy not forfeited for nonpayment of premiums when insured was entitled to sick benefits sufficient to pay premiums.—North v. National Life & Accident Ins. Co. of Nashville, Tenn., 66.

Specific order from insured to apply sick benefits in payment of premiums not necessary.—Id.

⊚⇒360(3) (Mo.App.) Member not entitled to have assessment paid out of so-called guaranty fund.—Hay v. Bankers' Life Co., 1085.

⊚⇒361 (Ark.) Insured's direction to bank authorized to collect premiums to pay premium and charge to insured's account held sufficient payment.—Illinois Bankers' Life Ass'n v. Dowdy, 183.

⊚⇒367(1) (Mo.App.) Provision for paid-up insurance held unconditional.—Bothmann v. Metropolitan Life Ins. Co., 1007.

⊚⇒368(1) (Mo.App.) Clause giving right to paid-up insurance not inconsistent with forfeiture clause.—Elms v. Mutual Benefit Life Ins. Co., 653.

XI. ESTOPPEL, WAIVER, OR AGREEMENTS AFFECTING RIGHT TO AVOID OR FORFEIT POLICY.

⊚⇒388(3) (Mo.App.) Where insured procured other insurance in belief induced by agents of company that policy was canceled, company estopped to assert defense.—Clark v. Fidelity-Phenix Fire Ins. Co. of New York, 74.

XII. RISKS AND CAUSES OF LOSS.

(E) Accident and Health Insurance.

⚖466 (Mo.App.) Disease resulting from accidental injury within accident policy.—Anderson v. Mutual Benefit Health & Accident Ass'n, 75.

XIII. EXTENT OF LOSS AND LIABILITY OF INSURER.

(C) Guaranty and Indemnity Insurance.

⚖514 (Tex.Civ.App.) On loss of bonds in mail, insured bank had right of action against insurer under indemnity policy, transferable to plaintiff.—St. Paul Fire & Marine Ins. Co. v. Charlton, 862.

(E) Accident and Health Insurance.

⚖525 (Mo.App.) Where insured could not lie in bed because of bad heart, he was "confined to bed" within policy.—North v. National Life & Accident Ins. Co. of Nashville, Tenn., 665.

XIV. NOTICE AND PROOF OF LOSS.

⚖548 (Tex.Com.App.) Anti-technicality statute not applicable to breaches such as breach of provision for examination after loss.—Humphrey v. National Fire Ins. Co. of Hartford, Conn., 750.

Policy requirement of examination of insured after loss held a material condition.—Id.

Requirement that insured submit to examination must be reasonably enforced.—Id.

Insured has right to have attorney present at examination after loss.—Id.

Insured, failing to submit to examination after loss on reasonable notice, may do so later. —Id.

XVI. RIGHT TO PROCEEDS.

⚖585(1) (Mo.App.) Deceased's husband held entitled to sue on industrial insurance policy for sick benefits, though not administrator.—North v. National Life & Accident Ins. Co. of Nashville, Tenn., 665.

XVIII. ACTIONS ON POLICIES.

⚖615 (Mo.App.) Insistence upon one of several known grounds of defense may constitute waiver of others.—Hay v. Bankers' Life Co., 1035.

⚖615 (Tex.Com.App.) Refusal to submit to examination after loss does not avoid policy, but only suspends right of recovery until examination.—Humphrey v. National Fire Ins. Co. of Hartford, Conn., 750.

⚖623(1) (Mo.App.) Ground of defense may be waived.—Hay v. Bankers' Life Co., 1035.

⚖623(4) (Mo.App.) Insurer held to have waived as matter of law the right to resist recovery on the ground that action was not brought within a year.—Hay v. Bankers' Life Co., 1035.

⚖637 (Tex.Civ.App.) Automobile purchaser's petition seeking to recover on fire and theft policy on car demurrable in not showing assignment of policy to him.—Indemnity Co. of America v. Mahaffey, 861.

⚖640(2) (Tex.Com.App.) Insurer can defend on ground of insured's failure to submit to examination only if pleading and proving that the time and place of examination were reasonable. --Humphrey v. National Fire Ins. Co. of Hartford, Conn., 750.

⚖646(3) (Mo.App.) Beneficiary has burden of showing member was in good standing at time of death.—Hay v. Bankers' Life Co., 1035.

Certificate is proof of good standing at time of issuance, and such good standing will be presumed to continue.—Id.

⚖646(4) (Mo.App.) Insurer has burden of sustaining defense of forfeiture for nonpayment of assessment.—Hay v. Bankers' Life Co., 1035.

Burden of proving nonpayment of assessment continues on insurer throughout trial.—Id.

⚖646(6) (Mo.) Burden on plaintiff to prove death caused accidentally.—Phillips v. Travelers' Ins. Co. of Hartford, Conn., 947.

Improper to build on inference of fall from fact of bruise inference that such fall was result of accident rather than disease, and that such fall proximately caused insured's death. —Id.

⚖646(7) (Mo.App.) No presumption against suicide where facts appear.—Thompson v. Business Men's Acc. Ass'n of America, 1049.

⚖651(2) (Tex.Civ.App.) Letter from company, instructing local agent to ascertain whether insured in good health before delivering policy, held competent.—Denton v. Kansas City Life Ins. Co., 436.

⚖665(3) (Tex.Com.App.) Evidence held to support jury finding that time and place fixed for examination were unreasonable.—Humphrey v. National Fire Ins. Co. of Hartford, Conn., 750.

⚖665(5) (Mo.) Evidence held to show as clearly that insured's fall caused by disease as by accident.—Phillips v. Travelers' Ins. Co. of Hartford, Conn., 947.

⚖665(6) (Mo.App.) Evidence held sufficient to justify jury in finding plaintiff mistaken in conclusion assured committed suicide.—Thompson v. Business Men's Acc. Ass'n of America, 1049.

⚖668(1) (Mo.App.) Evidence adjuster canceled policy and threatened to sue insured held to raise question of vexatious refusal to pay. —Anderson v. Mutual Benefit Health & Accident Ass'n, 75.

⚖668(11) (Mo.) No issue for jury as to insured's death being caused by accidental fall.— Phillips v. Travelers' Ins. Co. of Hartford, Conn., 947.

⚖668(11) (Mo.App.) Evidence held sufficient to take to the jury the question whether disease resulted from accidental injury.—Anderson v. Mutual Benefit Health & Accident Ass'n, 75.

⚖668(12) (Mo.App.) Evidence contradicting admission of suicide held sufficient to carry to jury question whether death accidental.— Thompson v. Business Men's Acc. Ass'n of America, 1049.

⚖668(14) (Mo.App.) Fraud by agent in securing release from insured is question for jury. —Anderson v. Mutual Benefit Health & Accident Ass'n, 75.

⚖669(10) (Mo.App.) Instruction on accidental injury as proximate cause of disease held correct.—Anderson v. Mutual Benefit Health & Accident Ass'n, 75.

INTEREST.

See Usury.

III. TIME AND COMPUTATION.

⚖50 (Mo.App.) Tender stops running of interest.—Bothmann v. Metropolitan Life Ins. Co., 1007.

INTOXICATING LIQUORS.

VI. OFFENSES.

⚖137 (Tex.Cr.App.) Defendant who used equipment already on premises guilty of having it in possession.—Thielepape v. State, 769.

⚖168 (Tex.Cr.App.) One who advised purchaser as to procuring liquor is not a principal. —Chandler v. State, 105.

VIII. CRIMINAL PROSECUTIONS.

⚖233(2) (Ark.) Testimony concerning finding of whisky near defendant's home admissible.—Robertson v. State, 865.

⚖233(2) (Tex.Cr.App.) Testimony that defendant had whisky in possession like that in jugs in his barn admissible.—Thielepape v. State, 769.

⚖236(6½) (Tex.Cr.App.) Evidence insufficient to sustain a conviction of unlawful possession.—Chandler v. State, 108.

⚖236(6½) (Tex.Cr.App.) Evidence held to sustain conviction of having liquor in possession.—Thielepape v. State, 773 (second case).

§⇒236(19) (Ark.) Evidence *held* sufficient to show defendant manufactured liquor.—Robertson v. State, 865.

§⇒236(19) (Tex.Cr.App.) Evidence held sufficient to sustain conviction of having illicit equipment in possession.—Thielepape v. State, 760.

§⇒236(19) (Tex.Cr.App.) Evidence *held* to sustain conviction of illicit manufacture.—Thielepape v. State, 773 (first case).

JEOPARDY.

See Criminal Law, §⇒195-200.

JUDGES.

See Justices of the Peace.

JUDGMENT.

For judgments in particular actions or proceedings, see also the various specific topics.
For review of judgments, see Appeal and Error.

IV. BY DEFAULT.

(B) Opening or Setting Aside Default.

§⇒139 (Tex.Civ.App.) Discretion in setting aside of judgments cannot be arbitrarily exercised.—Hubb-Diggs Co. v. Mitchell, 425.

§⇒143(3) (Tex. Civ. App.) Default entered against corporation set aside, where neither officers nor attorneys of corporation had actual knowledge of service of citation until after judgments.—Hubb-Diggs Co. v. Mitchell, 425.

§⇒145(4) (Tex.Civ.App.) Answer to petition alleging illegal contract *held* to present a meritorious defense on motion to set aside default.—Hubb-Diggs Co. v. Mitchell, 425.

VI. ON TRIAL OF ISSUES.

(B) Parties.

§⇒238 (Tex.Civ.App.) Recovery authorised against one under allegation that two parties to contract made promise.—Priddy v. Childers, 172.

(C) Conformity to Process, Pleadings, Proofs, and Verdict or Findings.

§⇒251(1) (Tex.Com.App.) Judgment must conform to issues pleaded.—Baker v. Shafter, 349.

§⇒256(2) (Tex.Com.App.) Courts may not ignore findings and pass judgment.—Baker v. Shafter, 349.

§⇒256(2) (Tex.Civ.App.) Judgment erroneous as not conforming to special findings.—Pickrell v. Imperial Petroleum Co., 412.

§⇒256(6) (Ark.) Judgment for twice amount of jury's verdict, under statute allowing double damages, proper.—Frauenthal v. Morton, 884.

VIII. AMENDMENT, CORRECTION, AND REVIEW IN SAME COURT.

§⇒333 (Tex.Com.App.) Answer to motion for correction of judgment entry could raise issue as to fraud in rendition of judgment.—Waggoner v. Knight, 357.
Answer to motion for correction of judgment entry *held* to raise issue as to fraud in its rendition.—Id.

IX. OPENING OR VACATING.

§⇒342(1) (Mo.App.) Judgment in violation of stipulation may be set aside after expiration of term.—Stevens v. Kansas City Light & Power Co., 1006.

§⇒342(2) (Mo.App.) Judgment making allowance to widower as separate property could not be set aside after term.—In re Schill's Estate, 641.

XII. CONSTRUCTION AND OPERATION IN GENERAL.

§⇒525 (Tex.Com.App.) Recital as to rights of codefendants as claimed in their answer *held*

not adjudication between them.—Laidack-Palmer, 362.

XIV. CONCLUSIVENESS OF ADJUDICATION.

(B) Persons Concluded.

§⇒702 (Tex.Com.App.) Judgment in suit against persons licensed by the state to explore for oil not binding against the state.—Prairie Oil & Gas Co. v. State, 1068.

(C) Matters Concluded.

§⇒741 (Tex. Com. App.) In proceedings motion to correct judgment entry, where answer to motion alleged invalidity, order of res judicata as to validity of judgment, the issue was not expressly decided.—Waggoner v. Knight, 357.

§⇒743(2) (Mo.) Judgment *held* not to estop trustee from obtaining possession.—Watson v. Hardwick, 964.

(D) Judgments in Particular Classes of Actions and Proceedings.

§⇒747(5) (Ky.) Judgment in suit to quiet title between parties to action for waste *held* bar to assertion of title by defendant.—Adams v. Bates, 238.

JUDICIAL POWER.

See Constitutional Law, §⇒70.

JUDICIAL SALES.

§⇒52 (Ky.) No implied warranty of title and doctrine of caveat emptor applies.—Beale v. Stroud, 522.
Purchaser will be relieved before confirmation but not afterwards if he will acquire no title.—Id.

JURY.

See Criminal Law, §⇒854-858.

II. RIGHT TO TRIAL BY JURY.

§⇒28(17) (Mo.) Where defendant in suit in equity to cancel notes set up counterclaim at law, plaintiff could not claim trial by jury.—Thomas v. Goodrum, 571.

§⇒34(3) (Ky.) Court not empowered to direct verdict against defendant whose plea is not guilty.—Bardin v. Commonwealth, 208.

IV. SUMMONING, ATTENDANCE, DISCHARGE, AND COMPENSATION.

§⇒72(3) (Ky.) Denial of motion that sheriff in summoning extra jurors be instructed to make no distinction between men and women not error.—Turner v. Commonwealth, 519.

V. COMPETENCY OF JURORS, CHALLENGES, AND OBJECTIONS.

§⇒97(1) (Mo.) Challenge for cause on account of juror's prejudice *held* properly overruled.—Richardson v. Kansas City Rys. Co., 938.

§⇒109 (Tex.Cr.App.) Court may not of own motion set aside juror.—McGowen v. State, 763.

§⇒110(3) (Tex.Cr.App.) Accused may waive challenge of juror not householder or freeholder.—McGowen v. State, 763.

VI. IMPANELING FOR TRIAL AND OATH.

§⇒149 (Mo.) That juror's wife was injured during trial as a passenger on defendant's line *held* no ground for discharge of jury.—Richardson v. Kansas City Rys. Co., 938.
Defendant claiming prejudice of juror because of injury to juror's wife during trial has burden of proof.—Id.

JUSTICES OF THE PEACE.

III. CIVIL JURISDICTION AND AUTHORITY.

§⇒44(3) (Mo.) Jurisdiction in tort action determined by demand.—Peter Hauptmann Tobacco Co. v. Unverferth, 628.

IV. PROCEDURE IN CIVIL CASES.

⟹90 (Mo.App.) Pleadings considered as setting out details.—Slack v. Whitney, 1060.
⟹93 (Mo.App.) Answer *held* to state proper counterclaim.—Slack v. Whitney, 1060.

V. REVIEW OF PROCEEDINGS.

(A) Appeal and Error.

⟹160(3) (Mo.App.) Notice of appeal *held* sufficient.—Rainey v. Reorganized Church of Jesus Christ of the Latter Day Saints, 1017; Tolf v. Marples, 1019.
⟹161(3) (Mo.) Appeal from default judgment in justice court an appearance.—Peter Hauptmann Tobacco Co. v. Unverferth, 628.
⟹179 (Mo.App.) Verdict on appeal *held* sufficient without itemizing finding on counterclaim.—Slack v. Whitney, 1060.

LANDLORD AND TENANT.

I. CREATION AND EXISTENCE OF THE RELATION.

⟹1 (Mo.App.) Relation may arise from privity of contract or privity of estate.—Geyer v. Denham, 61.

III. LANDLORD'S TITLE AND REVERSION.

(B) Estoppel of Tenant.

⟸61 (Ark.) Tenant cannot dispute title of landlord.—Lewis v. Harper, 874.
⟸65 (Ark.) Tenant cannot dispute title of purchaser from landlord.—Lewis v. Harper, 874.
⟸66(2) (Tex.Civ.App.) Landlord *held* not charged with notice of change of possession from tenants at will to their former agent.—Lobit v. Dolen, 831.
⟸66(3) (Tex.Civ.App.) Agent of tenants at will *held* charged with notice of landlord's rights.—Lobit v. Dolen, 831.
Agent of tenants at will *held* to stand in employer's shoes, and not entitled to claim adversely until landlords had notice.—Id.

IV. TERMS FOR YEARS.

(C) Extensions, Renewals, and Options to Purchase or Sell.

⟸83(1) (Ky.) Privilege to "renew" or extend not identical, but construction depends on intention.—Kozy Theater Co. v. Love, 249.
⟸84 (Ky.) Surrender by one lessee of corporate charter *held* not to invalidate an extension.—Kozy Theater Co. v. Love, 249.
⟸85½ (Ky.) Though provision be deemed one for renewal, lessor cannot evict lessee who tendered new lease.—Kozy Theater Co. v. Love, 249.
Assignees of reversion take lease as construed by the parties.—Id.
⟸86(2) (Ky.) Notice of desire to continue lease given by only two of the several lessees *held* binding.—Kozy Theater Co. v. Love, 249.

(D) Termination.

⟸111 (Ark.) Relation ceases upon disavowal of landlord's title.—Lewis v. Harper, 874.

VII. PREMISES AND ENJOYMENT AND USE THEREOF.

(E) Injuries from Dangerous or Defective Condition.

⟸169(11) (Ky.) Responsibility for injury to contractor's workman by elevator *held* for jury.—John R. Coppin Co. v. Richards, 229.

VIII. RENT AND ADVANCES.

(A) Rights and Liabilities.

⟸208(2) (Mo.App.) Lessee's assignee liable for rent regardless of his actual entry.—Geyer v. Denham, 61.
⟸208(4) (Mo.App.) Lessee's assignee, who reassigned lease to lessee, liable for rent for period subsequent to reassignment.—Geyer v. Denham, 61.

IX. RE-ENTRY AND RECOVERY OF POSSESSION BY LANDLORD.

⟸290(2) (Mo.) Lessee who holds over with knowledge that lease cannot be renewed guilty of unlawful detainer.—Bonfils v. Martin's Food Service Co., 60.

X. RENTING ON SHARES.

⟸326(1) (Ark.) Rent agreement *held* not to include volunteer hay crop, but only cultivated grains.—Porter v. Vail, 3.

LARCENY.

See Receiving Stolen Goods.

I. OFFENSES AND RESPONSIBILITY THEREFOR.

⟸7 (Tex.Cr.App.) Defendant not guilty if he took timber from barn of which he had control; "owner."—Fleischman v. State, 397.

II. PROSECUTION AND PUNISHMENT.

(A) Indictment and Information.

⟸29 (Tex.Cr.App.) Information for theft *held* not to have used words equivalent to "fraudulently."—Phillips v. State, 400.

(B) Evidence.

⟸41 (Tex.Cr.App.) State required to prove that automobile found in defendant's possession was that claimed to have been stolen.—Hunt v. State, 775.
⟸43 (Mo.) Question asked defendant on cross-examination as to acts of third person not erroneous.—State v. Bloomer, 568.
⟸43 (Tex.Cr.App.) Evidence of amount paid and price per bushel is admissible to show quantity of wheat.—Davis v. State, 784.
⟸55 (Ark.) In a prosecution for larceny, evidence *held* sufficient to sustain conviction.—Townsend v. State, 1.
⟸55 (Tex.Cr.App.) Circumstances *held* not sufficient to overcome presumption of innocence.—Lemon v. State, 388.
⟸55 (Tex.Cr.App.) Evidence *held* not to sustain conviction for theft of wheat.—Davis v. State, 784.
⟸57 (Mo.) Evidence *held* to warrant finding that defendant attempted to convert hogs with knowledge of prosecutor's ownership.—State v. Bloomer, 568.
⟸62(2) (Tex.Cr.App.) Want of consent not inferred from other circumstances, where owner, though a witness, did not testify with reference thereto.—Hunt v. State, 775.
⟸64(1) (Tex.Cr.App.) Evidence of possession *held* not to justify inference of guilt.—Lemon v. State, 388.
⟸65 (Tex.Cr.App.) Evidence *held* sufficient to sustain conviction of theft of seed cotton.—Crisp v. State, 392.

(C) Trial and Review.

⟸68(1) (Ky.) Evidence *held* to make question for jury.—Turner v. Commonwealth, 519.
⟸75(2) (Mo.) Instruction not erroneous because not in terms requiring finding that taking was felonious and without owner's consent.—State v. Bloomer, 568.
⟸77(2) (Mo.) Instruction in relation to recent possession of stolen property sustained by evidence.—State v. McBride, 592.

LEASE.

See Landlord and Tenant.

LEGISLATIVE POWER.

See Constitutional Law, ⟸52.

LEVEES AND FLOOD CONTROL.

⟸5 (Tex.Civ.App.) Existence of district could be questioned only by state.—Wilmarth v. Reagan, 445.

⬥═6 (Tex.Civ.App.) Levee improvement district lawfully created in so far as commissioner's court concerned.—Wilmarth v. Reagan, 445.

⬥═7 (Tex.Civ.App.) Court of Civil Appeals must treat as concluded questions of boundaries of district, etc.—Wilmarth v. Reagan, 445.

⬥═11 (Tex.Civ.App.) Plaintiffs held not entitled to maintain suit in so far as it was to annul report of commissioners of appraisement. —Wilmarth v. Reagan, 445.

⬥═34 (Tex.Civ.App.) Bond election not invalid because held by manager alone.—Wilmarth v. Reagan, 445.

LIBEL AND SLANDER.

II. PRIVILEGED COMMUNICATIONS AND MALICE THEREIN.

⬥═41 (Tex.Civ.App.) No recovery in case of qualified privilege unless malice present.—Foley Bros. Dry Goods Co. v. McClain, 459.

⬥═45(2) (Tex.Civ.App.) Statement of store manager relative to theft by employé held qualifiedly privileged.—Foley Bros. Dry Goods Co. v. McClain, 459.

IV. ACTIONS.

(B) Parties, Preliminary Proceedings, and Pleading.

⬥═89(1) (Tex.Civ.App.) Petition held to state cause of action, though not alleging special damages.—Foley Bros. Dry Goods Co. v. McClain, 459.

(C) Evidence.

⬥═101(4) (Tex.Civ.App.) Plaintiff has burden in case of qualified privilege to show statement was actuated by malice.—Foley Bros. Dry Goods Co. v. McClain, 459.

⬥═112(2) (Tex.Civ.App.) Evidence insufficient to justify finding of malice in making charge of theft.—Foley Bros. Dry Goods Co. v. McClain, 459.

LICENSES.

See Mechanics' Liens.

I. FOR OCCUPATIONS AND PRIVILEGES.

⬥═14(1) (Ky.) Motor Vehicle Act of 1920 was intended to embrace all statutory law on subject.—Lewis v. James, 526.

LIENS.

See Attorney and Client. ⬥═182–192; Vendor and Purchaser, ⬥═257–274.

⬥═7 (Tex.Com.App.) Purchaser, who accepted notes in part payment on strength of recitals as to security for notes, entitled to equitable lien.—Rea v. Luse, 310.

LIFE ESTATES.

⬥═28 (Ky.) Petition held to state cause of action for voluntary waste.—Adams v. Bates, 238.

LIMITATION OF ACTIONS.

See Adverse Possession.

I. STATUTES OF LIMITATION.

(B) Limitations Applicable to Particular Actions.

⬥═28(1) (Tex.Com.App.) Action for fraudulently inducing plaintiff to subscribe for stock construed as one for rescission not governed by the two-year statute.—Clark v. Texas Co-Op. Inv. Co., 381.

II. COMPUTATION OF PERIOD OF LIMITATION.

(F) Ignorance, Mistake, Trust, Fraud, and Concealment of Cause of Action.

⬥═95(1) (Ky.) Cause of action on gas company construction bond accrued when insufficiency of construction discovered.—Louisville Gas & Electric Co. v. City of Louisville, 909.

(H) Commencement of Action or Other Proceeding.

⬥═127(6) (Mo.) Amendment substituting widow for administrator in action for wrongful death held not a departure.—Drakopulos v. Biddle, 924.

V. PLEADING, EVIDENCE, TRIAL, AND REVIEW.

⬥═177(2) (Ky.) Plaintiff need not allege facts showing action not barred by statute.—Adams v. Bates, 238.

⬥═182(2) (Mo.App.) Defense of limitations must be raised by pleading.—Jones v. Munroe, 1069.

⬥═187 (Ky.) Infancy must be pleaded to bar running of statute.—Adams v. Bates, 238.

LIQUOR SELLING.

See Intoxicating Liquors.

LOST INSTRUMENTS.

⬥═8(1) (Tex.Civ.App.) Possession not indispensable prerequisite to presumption of existence of deed.—Brownfield v. Brabson, 491.

⬥═8(3) (Tex.Civ.App.) Execution of quitclaim deed for consideration does not show acquiescence of heirs in presumed deed.—Brownfield v. Brabson, 491.

⬥═23(1) (Ark.) Burden is on grantors to show lost deed contained condition subsequent. —School District of Newport v. J. R. Holden Land & Lumber Co., 895.

⬥═23(3) (Ark.) Evidence held not to sustain chancellor's finding that lost deed contained condition subsequent.—School District of Newport v. J. R. Holden Land & Lumber Co., 895.

⬥═23(3) (Mo.) Evidence held to sustain finding against claim under alleged lost deed.— Tiede v. Tiede, 950.

Evidence insufficient to show execution and delivery of alleged lost deed.—Id.

Evidence insufficient to warrant recovery on alleged lost deed.—Id.

MANSLAUGHTER.

See Homicide.

MARRIAGE.

See Divorce; Husband and Wife.

MASTER AND SERVANT.

I. THE RELATION.

(A) Creation and Existence.

⬥═8(2) (Mo.App.) Employment for another year presumed from continuance in service.— Williams v. John T. Hesser Coal Co., 680.

(B) Statutory Regulation.

⬥═12 (Tenn.) Factory Inspection Act constitutional.—Athens Hosiery Mills v. Thomason, 904.

(C) Termination and Discharge.

⬥═40(3) (Mo.App.) Evidence held to show wrongful discharge.—Williams v. John T. Hesser Coal Co., 680.

⬥═43 (Mo.App.) Cause of discharge question of fact.—Williams v. John T. Hesser Coal Co., 680.

III. MASTER'S LIABILITY FOR INJURIES TO SERVANT.

(A) Nature and Extent in General.

⬥═95 (Ky.) Infant held unlawfully employed. —Louisville Woolen Mills v. Kindgen, 202.

(B) Tools, Machinery, Appliances, and Places for Work.

⬥═101, 102(2) (Mo.App.) Master not an insurer of safety.—Yarbrough v. Hammond Packing Co., 72.

⟲191, 102(8) (Mo.App.) Ordinary care to furnish reasonably safe place *held* limit of duty.—Forrester v. Walsh Fire Clay Products Co., 668.

(F) Risks Assumed by Servant.

⟲204(1) (Tex.Com.App.) Assumption of risk defense under federal act.—Texas & N. O. R. Co. v. Gericke, 745.

⟲217(13) (Tex.Com.App.) Risk of unsafe place assumed by servant having knowledge of danger.—Texas & N. O. R. Co, v. Gericke, 745.

⟲217(16) (Tex.Com.App.) Risk of failure to give warning of vehicles not assumed by bridge painter on scaffold known to be too low.—Texas & N. O. R. Co. v. Gericke, 745.

⟲218(7) (Ky.) Assumption of risk not defense to recovery by illegally employed infant.—Louisville Woolen Mills v. Kindgen, 202.

⟲219(5) (Ark.) Risk of unloading logs *held* assumed.—T A. Thomas & Sons v. Wolfe, 195.

⟲226(1) (Tex.Com.App.) Risk of master's negligence not assumed.—Texas & N. O. R. Co. v. Gericke, 745.

(G) Contributory Negligence of Servant.

⟲228(1) (Ky.) Contributory negligence not defense to recovery by illegally employed infant.—Louisville Woolen Mills v. Kindgen, 202.

(H) Actions.

⟲280 (Tex.Com.App.) Evidence *held* to show bridge painter on scaffold did not assume risk.—Texas & N. O. R. Co. v. Gericke, 745.

⟲285(2) (Mo.App.) Evidence of cause of escape of illuminating gas *held* to demand a peremptory instruction.—Yarbrough v. Hammond Packing Co., 72.

⟲286(12) (Tex.Civ.App.) Railroad's negligence in violating federal rule as to safety of locomotive wheel *held* for jury.—Lancaster v. Allen, 148.

⟲286(40) (Tex. Civ. App.) Negligence in warning of danger of using defective fuses in exploding dynamite *held* for jury.—Dool v. City of Waco, 176.

⟲288(5) (Tex.Com.App.) Assumption of risk question for jury.—Texas & N. O. R. Co. v. Gericke, 745.

⟲289(15) (Mo.App.) Contributory negligence in stepping on loose board *held* for jury.—Forrester v. Walsh Fire Clay Products Co., 668.

⟲297(4) (Tex. Civ. App.) Special findings *held* to show railroad's negligence under federal safety rules as to locomotive trucks.—Lancaster v. Allen, 148.

IV. LIABILITIES FOR INJURIES TO THIRD PERSONS.

(A) Acts or Omissions of Servant.

⟲301(1) (Tex.Com.App.) Railroad and express company liable for negligence of joint employee.—American Express Co. v. Chandler, 1085.

Railroad not liable for negligence of express company's sole employee assisting joint employee.—Id.

(C) Actions.

⟲330(1) (Mo.App.) Presumption of liability raised by proof of ownership of automobile negligently driven by employé.—Fidelity & Casualty Co. of New York v. Kansas City Rys. Co., 277.

⟲330(1) (Tex.Civ.App.) Burden is on person injured to show servant acted within scope of employment.—City Service Co. v. Brown, 140.

Automobile driver presumed acting within scope of employment.—Id.

⟲330(3) (Tex. Civ. App.) Evidence insufficient to show driver of automobile acted within scope of employment.—City Service Co. v. Brown, 140.

231 S.W.—73

⟲332(2) (Mo.App.) Automobile owner's responsibility for chauffeur's negligence *held* for jury.—Fidelity & Casualty Co. of New York v. Kansas City Rys. Co., 277.

Chauffeur's departure from scope of employment for jury.—Id.

VI. WORKMEN'S COMPENSATION ACTS.

(A) Nature and Grounds of Master's Liability.

⟲348 (Tex.Civ.App.) Compensation Act liberally construed.—Western Indemnity Co. v. Leonard, 1101.

⟲358 (Ky.) Involuntary appearance before Compensation Board *held* not to estop prosecution of common-law action by infant unlawfully employed.—Louisville Woolen Mills v. Kindgen, 202.

Court's acceptance of finding of Compensation Board that infant was unlawfully employed *held* error.—Id.

Infant unlawfully employed *held* not estopped from prosecution of common-law action by reliance on finding of Compensation Board.—Id.

⟲358 (Tex.Com.App.) Common-law remedy in lieu of compensation available to employee without statutory notice.—Poe v. Continental Oil & Cotton Co., 717.

Common-law remedy not waived by making compensation claim after limitation.—Id.

Application for compensation not waiver of want of notice to employee.—Id.

Reservation before compensation board *held* to prevent implied waiver of common-law remedy.—Id.

⟲367 (Tex.Civ.App.) Traveling salesman *held* "employé" within Compensation Act, and not an "independent contractor."—U. S. Fidelity & Guaranty Co. of Baltimore, Md. v. Lowry, 818.

⟲375(2) (Tex.Civ.App.) Injury to employé boarding train to return home *held* in "course of employment," within Compensation Act.—Western Indemnity Co. v. Leonard, 1101.

(B) Compensation.

⟲386(1) (Tex.Com.App.) Compensation for death arises out of contractual relation and is in lieu of damages.—Texas Employers' Ins. Ass'n v. Boudreaux, 756.

⟲386(5) (Tex.Com.App.) Statutes of descent looked to in apportioning compensation among dependents.—Texas Employers' Ins. Ass'n v. Boudreaux, 756.

Compensation for death distributed as community property.—Id.

⟲388 (Tex.Com.App.) Compensation for death payable directly to dependents.—Texas Employers' Ins. Ass'n v. Boudreaux, 756.

(C) Proceedings.

⟲396 (Tex.Civ.App.) Compensation claim *held* within district court's jurisdiction.—Home Life & Accident Co. v. Jordan, 802.

⟲397 (Tex.Com.App.) Compensation Board not a court.—Poe v. Continental Oil & Cotton Co., 717.

⟲401 (Tex.Civ.App.) Compensation claimant's petition for doctor's bills *held* insufficient.—Home Life & Accident Co. v. Jordan, 802.

⟲418(5) (Tex.Civ.App.) Admission of compensation award in evidence *held* not reversible error.—U. S. Fidelity & Guaranty Co. of Baltimore, Md., v. Lowry, 818.

⟲418(6) (Tex.Com.App.) Court's findings on question of lump sum compensation reviewable.—Texas Employers' Ins. Ass'n v. Boudreaux, 756.

MECHANICS' LIENS.

VIII. INDEMNITY AGAINST LIENS.

⟲313 (Tex.Civ.App.) Statute relating to contractor's bond *held* void as interference

with the right to contract.—Cobb v. J. W. Allen & Bro., 829.
➡315 (Tex.Civ.App.) Contractor's bond *held* not available to materialmen.—Cobb v. J. W. Allen & Bro., 829.

MINES AND MINERALS.

II. TITLE, CONVEYANCES, AND CONTRACTS.

(A) Rights and Remedies of Owners.

➡48 (Tex.Com.App.) Oil is not subject of property except while in actual occupancy.—Prairie Oil & Gas Co. v. State, 1088.
➡52 (Tex.Com.App.) Landowner will not be enjoined from drilling on his own property on the theory that it would draw oil from adjacent lands.—Prairie Oil & Gas Co. v. State, 1088.

(B) Conveyances in General.

➡55(2) (Ky.) "Exception" of lease in conveyance of oil and gas in land does not show ownership of lease by grantor.—Arnett v. Elkhorn Coal Corporation, 219.
➡55(4) (Ky.) One in possession of surface under separated title holds mineral as trustee for owner.—Foxwell v. Justice, 509.

(C) Leases, Licenses, and Contracts.

➡58 (Tex. Civ. App.) Fraudulent statement as to term ground for avoiding lease.—Smith v. Fleming, 136.
Lessor estopped to deny validity of lease fraudulently obtained.—Id.
➡59 (Ky.) Evidence *held* to sustain finding that leases were executed for three, instead of five, years.—Curry v. Hinton, 217.
➡59 (Tex. Civ. App.) Issue submitted *held* without basis in pleading in suit to cancel lease.—Smith v. Fleming, 136.
➡73 (Tex.Civ.App.) Oil and gas lease conveys interest in the land.—Smith v. Womack, 840.
➡74 (Ky.) Where lease for three years was altered, so as to call for five-year term, innocent purchasers could only hold for three.—Curry v. Hinton, 217.
➡74 (Tex.Com.App.) In suit to rescind transfer of interest in lease instruction for defendants *held* not error, if misrepresentations were all as to facts.—Waggoner v. Zundelowitz, 721.
A false statement, claimed to obtain a transfer of interest in lease, *held* a statement of fact.—Id.
Waiver of fraud affecting rescission of transfer of interest in lease not dependent on knowledge that transferee knew representations were false.—Id.
Falsity of an opinion representation to obtain option on interest in lease *held* not material as affecting right to rescind.—Id.
Fraud in obtaining option on interest in lease waived by transfer after notice of misrepresentations as to nearby well.—Id.
Charge as to waiver of fraud by signing transfer properly refused for failing to submit sufficiency of knowledge of fraud.—Id.
In suit to rescind transfer of interest in lease, charge as to waiver of fraud *held* erroneous as to necessity of knowledge of bad faith.—Id.
Fraud in obtaining option on interest in lease may be waived by executing final assignment if assignor only knows material facts.—Id.
➡74 (Tex.Civ.App.) Purchaser of lease ratifying contract by suing for deceit is liable for interest on purchase-money notes.—Pickrell v. Imperial Petroleum Co., 412.
Vendor *held* entitled to attorney's fee on purchase-money notes notwithstanding fraud in sale of lease.—Id.
➡74 (Tex.Civ.App.) Where the title to be conveyed would be doubtful, specific performance of contract to purchase oil and gas lease will not be granted.—Smith v. Womack, 840.

➡74 (Tex.Civ.App.) Buyer of interest in lease under executory contract *held* entitled to recover amount paid as for failure of consideration.—Wilcox v. Crawford, 1104.
Where seller of interest in lease fails to perform, purchaser entitled to interest on an advance payment recovered.—Id.

MINORS.

See Infants.

MONEY PAID.

➡8 (Tex.Civ.App.) Complaint to recover money expended *held* to show consideration.—Elmendorf v. Mulliken, 164.

MONOPOLIES.

II. TRUSTS AND OTHER COMBINATIONS IN RESTRAINT OF TRADE.

➡17(1) (Tex.Civ.App.) Contract *held* to fix price in violation of anti-trust laws.—Hubb-Diggs Co. v. Mitchell, 425.
➡17(1) (Tex.Civ.App.) Communications subsequent to contract fixing resale prices *held* admissible and to render contract violative of statute.—W. T. Rawleigh Co. v. Smith, 799.
➡21 (Tex.Civ.App.) Province of court stated.—W. T. Rawleigh Co. v. Smith, 799.

MORTGAGES.

See Chattel Mortgages.

I. REQUISITES AND VALIDITY.

(A) Nature and Essentials of Conveyances as Security.

➡32(1) (Tex.Civ.App.) Deed absolute on its face may be shown to be a mortgage.—Young v. Blain, 851.
➡32(2) (Tex.Civ.App.) For deed absolute on its face to be *held* a mortgage, it must have been so intended by the parties.—Young v. Blain, 851.
➡32(5) (Tex.Com.App.) Whether deed is mortgage depends on extinguishment of debt.—Holmes v. Tennant, 313.
➡36 (Tex.Civ.App.) Party asserting that deed absolute on its face is a mortgage has burden of proof.—Young v. Blain, 851.
➡38(1) (Ark.) Absolute deed *held* intended as such, and not as mortgage.—Parker v. Mitchell, 879.
➡39 (Tex.Com.App.) Whether conveyance a mortgage or conditional sale *held* question of fact.—Holmes v. Tennant, 313.
➡39 (Tex.Civ.App.) Evidence insufficient to carry to jury whether deed absolute on its face was a mortgage.—Young v. Blain, 851.

III. CONSTRUCTION AND OPERATION.

(C) Property Mortgaged, and Estates of Parties Therein.

➡137 (Tex.Com.App.) Mortgagor remains owner of land.—Holmes v. Tennant, 313.

VI. TRANSFER OF PROPERTY MORTGAGED OR OF EQUITY OF REDEMPTION.

➡282(4) (Tex.Com.App.) Proceeding against mortgaged property before action against its purchaser necessary.—Farmers' & Merchants' State Bank of Ballinger v. Cameron, 738.

VII. PAYMENT OR PERFORMANCE OF CONDITION, RELEASE, AND SATISFACTION.

➡319(3) (Ark.) Evidence showing release by 80 year old mortgagee invalid for want of mental capacity.—Hawkins v. Randolph, 556.

IX. FORECLOSURE BY EXERCISE OF POWER OF SALE.

➡372(4) (Tex.Com.App.) Owner cannot sever crops or rents by reservation on foreclosure sale.—Roberts v. Armstrong, 371.

XI. REDEMPTION.

⊄═596, 597 (Tex.Com.App.) Mortgagee *held* not entitled to invoke defense of stale demand.—Holmes v. Tenant, 313.

MUNICIPAL CORPORATIONS.

See Counties; Schools and School Districts; Street Railroads.

IV. PROCEEDINGS OF COUNCIL OR OTHER GOVERNING BODY.

(B) Ordinances and By-Laws in General.

⊄═111(1) (Tenn.) Ordinance requiring flagman at crossing not void for failing to prescribe penalties.—Hines v. Partridge, 16.

⊄═111(2) (Ky.) Ordinance must have enacting clause.—Town of Nortonville v. Woodward, 224.

V. OFFICERS, AGENTS, AND EMPLOYÉS.

(B) Municipal Departments and Officers Thereof.

⊄═183(1) (Ky.) Filling vacancy of marshal *held* "appointment," and not "election."—Town of Nortonville v. Woodward, 224.

⊄═183(4) (Ky.) De facto marshal not entitled to salary.—Town of Nortonville v. Woodward, 224.

IX. PUBLIC IMPROVEMENTS.

(B) Preliminary Proceedings and Ordinances or Resolutions.

⊄═321(1) (Mo.) Action of authorities in establishment of sewer district conclusive in absence of fraud.—St. Louis Malleable Casting Co. v. George G. Prendergast Const. Co., 989.

City authorities judges of dimensions of sewers.—Id.

⊄═323(3) (Ark.) Demurrer to answer in action attacking organization of improvement districts *held* properly overruled.—Johnson v. Hamlen, 6.

(E) Assessments for Benefits, and Special Taxes.

⊄═439 (Ark.) That betterments assessed equal to the estimated cost of improvement no ground for objection.—Meyer v. Board of Imp. Paving Dist. No. 3, 12.

⊄═440 (Ark.) That property in improvement district abutted on streets already paved should be considered.—Meyer v. Board of Imp. Paving Dist. No. 3, 12.

Construction of improvements by owners should be considered by commissioners of improvement districts.—Id.

⊄═450(2) (Ark.) Mistake in description of boundaries of improvement district in notice *held* unimportant.—Johnson v. Hamlen, 6.

⊄═450(2) (Ark.) Boundaries of improvement district sufficient.—Meyer v. Board of Imp. Paving Dist. No. 3, 12.

⊄═450(4) (Mo.) No notice of establishment of taxing sewer district necessary.—St. Louis Malleable Casting Co. v. George G. Prendergast Const. Co., 989.

⊄═463 (Ark.) Assessment for street improvements open to attack as exceeding 20 per cent. limit.—Meyer v. Board of Imp. Paving Dist. No. 3, 12.

⊄═484(3) (Ark.) Testimony that separate improvements could be constructed as one will not overcome presumption in favor of legality of separate districts.—Meyer v. Board of Imp. Paving Dist. No. 3, 12.

⊄═485(5) (Mo.) Tax bill issued for sewer prima facie evidence of validity.—St. Louis Malleable Casting Co. v. George G. Prendergast Const. Co., 989.

⊄═488, 489(1) (Ark.) Property owners may estop themselves to attack validity of improvement districts.—Meyer v. Board of Imp. Paving Dist. No. 3, 12.

⊄═488, 489(3) (Ark.) Signing of petition for improvement district does not estop petitioners from attacking ordinances on the ground that they exceeded the law.—Meyer v. Board of Imp. Paving Dist. No. 3, 12.

⊄═488, 489(4) (Mo.) Acquiescence with knowledge of sewer improvement, especially when accompanied by acceptance of benefits, estops owner.—St. Louis Malleable Casting Co. v. George G. Prendergast Const. Co., 989.

⊄═488, 489(7) (Mo.) Property owner's complaint of fraud on part of sewer contractor too late after work completed.—St. Louis Malleable Casting Co. v. George G. Prendergast Const. Co., 989.

⊄═513(5) (Ark.) After expiration of time to question validity of improvement assessments, third persons cannot be made parties.—Meyer v. Board of Imp. Paving Dist. No. 3, 12.

⊄═513(7) (Mo.) Evidence *held* sufficient to support validity of sewer tax bill.—St. Louis Malleable Casting Co. v. George G. Prendergast Const. Co., 989.

XI. USE AND REGULATION OF PUBLIC PLACES, PROPERTY, AND WORKS.

(A) Streets and Other Public Ways.

⊄═678 (Ky.) Trustees could order removal of tree in alley.—Bardin v. Commonwealth, 208.

⊄═705(4) (Mo.) Negligence per se to violate ordinance relating to manner of turning at intersections.—Borack v. Mosler Safe Co., 623.

⊄═705(11) (Mo.) Violation of traffic ordinance to be actionable, must be proximate cause of injury.—Borack v. Mosler Safe Co., 623.

Cutting corner in violation of city ordinance *held* not proximate cause of death.—Id.

⊄═706(3) (Mo.App.) Excessive speed raises no presumption that death of pedestrian was caused thereby.—Bibb v. Grady, 1020.

⊄═706(5) (Mo.App.) Evidence *held* to fail to bring case within humanitarian rule.—Bibb v. Grady, 1020.

⊄═706(6) (Mo.App.) Evidence *held* insufficient to warrant submission of negligence to the jury.—Bibb v. Grady, 1020.

⊄═706(8) (Mo.App.) Instruction making operation of automobile at excessive rate of speed in violation of ordinance negligence *held* not supported by evidence.—Fidelity & Casualty Co. of New York v. Kansas City Rys. Co., 277.

XII. TORTS.

(A) Exercise of Governmental and Corporate Powers in General.

⊄═733(1) (Tex.Com.App.) In hauling sand and adjusting damages for injuries to one therein engaged, the city acts in its proprietary capacity.—Cawthorn v. City of Houston, 701.

⊄═741(1) (Tex.Com.App.) Charter requiring injured party to give 90 days' notice to mayor and council before beginning suit upheld.—Cawthorn v. City of Houston, 701.

Charter provision requiring notice within 90 days after injury applies to one injured while hauling sand for city.—Id.

Requirement of notice of injury applies to city employees.—Id.

⊄═741(3) (Tex.Com.App.) Mayor and council may waive strict compliance with provision requiring notice of personal injury before bringing suit.—Cawthorn v. City of Houston, 701.

A commissioner as agent for commissioners and mayor may waive strict compliance with charter provision.—Id.

City *held* estopped by conduct of its officers from requiring strict compliance with charter provision.—Id.

⊄═742(4) (Tex.Com.App.) Requirement of 90 days' notice of injury to mayor and council must be alleged if applicable, unless waived, or the city estopped.—Cawthorn v. City of Houston, 701.

⊄═742(6) (Tex.Com.App.) Whether city commissioner waived strict compliance with charter provision for notice of personal injury **and** a jury question.—Cawthorn v. City of Houston, 701.

(C) Defects or Obstructions in Streets and Other Public Ways.

⏀764(3) (Ky.) Municipality liable for failure to maintain entire width sidewalks in reasonably safe condition if sufficient time has elapsed to give notice.—City of Newport v. Schmit, 54.

⏀771 (Ky.) Municipality not guarantor of safety of pedestrians, and not liable for slippery sidewalk caused by rain.—City of Newport v. Schmit, 54.

⏀796 (Tex.Civ.App.) City under duty to erect barriers at necessary points on streets. —City of Dallas v. Maxwell, 429.

Whether ravine into which jitney bus plunged private or municipal property immaterial.—Id.

⏀800(5) (Tex.Civ.App.) City not relieved from liability to jitney bus passenger injured through its negligence and that of driver.— City of Dallas v. Maxwell, 429.

⏀808(1) (Ky.) Subsequent owner or lessee liable for injuries resulting from defective sidewalks which amounted to nuisance.—City of Newport v. Schmit, 54.

Occupant not liable for defects in sidewalks which he did not create.—Id.

Abutting owner who imposes "servitude" on sidewalk is liable if he allows it to become a nuisance and dangerous.—Id.

Subsequent owner or lessee not liable for nuisance by predecessor until request for abatement.—Id.

⏀808(3) (Ky.) One opening doorway in sidewalk is negligent, if he fails to guard the opening.—Commonwealth Power Ry. & Light Co. v. Vaught, 247.

⏀808(4) (Ky.) Occupant not liable for failure to repair sidewalk.—City of Newport v. Schmit, 54.

⏀809(1) (Ky.) Both creator and maintainer of a nuisance liable.—City of Newport v. Schmit, 54.

⏀812(2) (Mo.App.) Notice to city condition precedent to maintaining action for injuries from defective streets or sidewalks.—Thomas v. City of St. Joseph, 63.

⏀817(1) (Ky.) Consent of municipality to replacing sidewalk with tiles inferable.—City of Newport v. Schmit, 54.

⏀819(4) (Tex.Civ.App.) Evidence *held* sufficient to sustain finding city's negligence was proximate cause of jitney bus passenger's injury.—City of Dallas v. Maxwell, 429.

⏀819(7) (Tex.Civ.App.) Evidence *held* to sustain finding jitney bus passenger did not appreciate dangers of use of street.—City of Dallas v. Maxwell, 429.

⏀821(6) (Ky.) Whether a tiled portion of sidewalk laid by an abutting owner was unsafe question for the jury.—City of Newport v. Schmit, 54.

⏀821(17) (Ky.) Whether defendant's servants, who opened doorway in pavement, took precautions to warn travelers, question for the jury.—Commonwealth Power Ry. & Light Co. v. Vaught, 247.

⏀821(19) (Mo.) Proof that proximate cause of injury to pedestrian falling into uncovered cellarway was violation of ordinance as alleged *held* insufficient to go to jury.—Rose v. Biddle, 946.

⏀822(1) (Mo.App.) Instruction that fact of fall was no evidence of negligence improper.— Walker v. City of St. Joseph, 65.

XIII. FISCAL MANAGEMENT, PUBLIC DEBT, SECURITIES, AND TAXATION.

(C) Bonds and Other Securities, and Sinking Funds.

⏀926 (Tex.Civ.App.) Provision to pay interest on high school bonds in year of dating proper though they were not sold until next year.—Concho Camp, No. 66, W. O. W., v. City of San Angelo, 1106.

⏀951 (Tex.Civ.App.) Provision to create sinking fund for high school bonds in year of dating proper though they were not sold until next year.—Concho Camp, No. 66, W. O. W., v. City of San Angelo, 1106.

(D) Taxes and Other Revenue, and Application Thereof.

⏀962 (Tex.Civ.App.) Levies to pay for funding bonds and to pay off judgment on street improvement bonds not limitation on power of city to levy taxes for street improvements to extent of 15 cents per $100.—Concho Camp, No. 66, W. O. W., v. City of San Angelo, 1106.

MURDER.

See Homicide.

NAMES.

⏀10 (Ky.) Contract executed by one doing business under assumed name is voidable only. —Kozy Theater Co. v. Love, 249.

NATIONAL BANKS.

See Banks and Banking, ⏀233–260.

NAVIGABLE WATERS.

See Wharves.

NEGLIGENCE.

See Master and Servant, ⏀95–332; Municipal Corporations, ⏀733–822; Railroads, ⏀307–400; Street Railroads, ⏀90–118.

I. ACTS OR OMISSIONS CONSTITUTING NEGLIGENCE.

(C) Condition and Use of Land, Buildings, and Other Structures.

⏀32(1) (Ky.) Reasonable care required as to customer.—Bridgford v. Stewart Dry Goods Co., 22.

⏀32(1) (Mo.App.) Landowner owes to invitee duty to keep premises reasonably safe and to warn of concealed dangers.—Jackson v. Quarry Realty Co., 1063.

⏀48 (Mo.App.) Care required as to invitee using wall as passway.—Hunter v. American Brake Co., 659.

⏀51 (Ky.) Shopkeeper may allow customers on wet floor.—Bridgford v. Stewart Dry Goods Co., 22.

⏀52 (Ky.) Warning of starting of elevator required.—John R. Coppin Co. v. Richards, 229.

II. PROXIMATE CAUSE OF INJURY.

⏀56(3) (Tex.Com.App.) Law of proximate cause applicable to violations of statutory and common-law duty.—San Antonio & A. P. Ry. Co. v. Behne, 354.

⏀59 (Tex.Com.App.) Foreseeableness of injury as "natural and probable result" element of proximate cause.—San Antonio & A. P. Ry. Co. v. Behne, 354.

⏀59 (Tex.Com.App.) One liable only for injury reasonably anticipated.—Steed v. Gulf, C. & S. F. Ry. Co., 714.

III. CONTRIBUTORY NEGLIGENCE.

(A) Persons Injured in General.

⏀65 (Ky.) Risk of injury by elevator not assumed by contractor's workman.—John R. Coppin Co. v. Richards, 229.

⏀66(2) (Ky.) Customer knowingly going on wet floor assumes risk.—Bridgford v. Stewart Dry Goods Co., 22.

⏀67 (Ky.) Electrician in elevator shaft *held* not guilty of contributory negligence.—John R. Coppin Co. v. Richards, 229.

⏀83 (Mo.App.) Humanitarian rule stated.— Bibb v. Grady, 1020.

⏀83 (Tex.Com.App.) Doctrine of "discovered peril" stated.—Baker v. Shafter, 349.

IV. ACTIONS.

(A) Right of Action, Parties, Preliminary Proceedings, and Pleading.

⊂══117 (Mo.App.) Contributory negligence must be pleaded.—Baldwin v. Kansas City Rys. Co., 280.

⊂══119(1) (Mo.) Proof of all acts alleged unnecessary.—Hartweg v. Kansas City Rys. Co., 269.

⊂══119(1) (Mo.App.) Specific charge must be established.—Yarbrough v. Hammond Packing Co., 72.

Proof of one of specific acts charged sufficient. —Id.

⊂══119(6) (Tex.Com.App.) Discovered peril must be pleaded.—Baker v. Shafter, 349.

(B) Evidence.

⊂══134(2) (Ky.) May be proven by circumstantial evidence.—John R. Coppin Co. v. Richards, 229.

⊂══134(10) (Ky.) Degree of proof required.— John R. Coppin Co. v. Richards, 229.

⊂══134(10) (Mo.App.) Evidence that an injury resulted from one of two causes insufficient.—Hunter v. American Brake Co., 659.

(C) Trial, Judgment, and Review.

⊂══136(9) (Ky.) Contributory negligence for jury.—Cincinnati, N. O. & T. P. R. Co. v. Owsley, 210.

⊂══136(15) (Mo.App.) Dumpkeeper's care in directing driver *held* for jury.—Jackson v. Quarry Realty Co., 1063.

⊂══136(22) (Mo.App.) As to switchman stumbling on coal left on passway in building *held* question for jury.—Hunter v. American Brake Co., 659.

⊂══136(26) (Mo.App.) Contributory negligence in using dump roadway *held* for jury.—Jackson v. Quarry Realty Co., 1063.

⊂══136(26) (Tenn.) Contributory negligence question for jury.—Hines v. Partridge, 16.

⊂══136(27) (Ky.) Contributory negligence of person injured by falling coal pile *held* for jury. —Frankfort Elevator Coal Co. v. Williamson, 241.

⊂══138(1) (Mo.App.) Instruction objectionable in not requiring finding of negligence.— Hunter v. American Brake Co., 659.

⊂══139(1) (Mo.App.) Instruction defining "ordinary care" *held* correct.—Buehler v. Waggener Paint & Glass Co., 283.

⊂══139(2) (Mo.App.) Instruction *held* erroneous, as imposing absolute liability for invitee's injury.—Hunter v. American Brake Co., 659.

⊂══140 (Mo.) Form of instruction on proximate cause of injury.—Lackey v. United Rys. Co., 956.

NEGOTIABLE INSTRUMENTS.

See Bills and Notes.

NEW TRIAL.

See Criminal Law, ⊂══905–941.

II. GROUNDS.

(H) Newly Discovered Evidence.

⊂══99 (Mo.App.) The granting of new trial for newly discovered evidence rests largely in discretion of trial court.—Gerth v. Christy, 639.

⊂══102(9) (Mo.App.) Denial of new trial on ground of newly discovered evidence not an abuse of discretion, though witness was not friendly with movant.—Gerth v. Christy, 639.

III. PROCEEDINGS TO PROCURE NEW TRIAL.

⊂══163(2) (Mo.App.) Sustaining motion on one ground overrules other grounds.—Buehler v. Waggener Paint & Glass Co., 283.

NONSUIT.

See Dismissal and Nonsuit.

NOTES.

See Bills and Notes.

NOVATION.

⊂══7 (Tex.Civ.App.) Seller could not substitute other party in its place.—Tecumseh Oil & Cotton Co. v. Gresham, 468.

NUISANCE.

I. PRIVATE NUISANCES.

(D) Actions for Damages.

⊂══42 (Ky.) Subsequent owner or lessee not liable for nuisance by predecessor until request for abatement.—City of Newport v. Schmit, 54.

II. PUBLIC NUISANCES.

(B) Rights and Remedies of Private Persons.

⊂══76 (Ky.) That subsequent owner or lessee not liable for nuisance by predecessor until request for abatement not applicable to public nuisance.—City of Newport v. Schmit, 54.

OFFICERS.

See Clerks of Courts; Coroners; Justices of the Peace; Receivers.

III. RIGHTS, POWERS, DUTIES, AND LIABILITIES.

⊂══94 (Ky.) Neither state nor county is liable to officers in absence of legal obligation.— Lewis v. James, 526.

⊂══99 (Ky.) Legislature can add to duties without providing additional compensation.— Lewis v. James, 526.

⊂══100(1) (Ky.) Requirement of services without compensation does not violate provision against change of compensation unless existing laws authorize compensation.—Lewis v. James, 526.

⊂══100(2) (Ky.) Prohibition against change of salaries applies only to salaried officers.— Lewis v. James, 526.

PARENT AND CHILD.

See Infants.

PARTIES.

For parties on appeal and review of rulings as to parties, see Appeal and Error.

For parties to particular proceedings or instruments, see also the various specific topics.

V. DEFECTS, OBJECTIONS, AND AMENDMENT.

⊂══94(2) (Ky.) Mere mistake or misnomer in plaintiff's name pleadable in abatement only. —Stange v. Price, 532.

⊂══95(5) (Ky.) Amended petition setting up that plaintiff which sued a corporation was in fact a partnership permissible.—Stange v. Price, 532.

PARTITION.

II. ACTIONS FOR PARTITION.

(B) Proceedings and Relief.

⊂══96 (Ky.) Court or commissioner cannot give warranty unless authorized by parties.— Beale v. Stroud, 522.

⊂══116(1) (Ky.) Implied warranty of title does not run to alienees.—Beale v. Stroud, 522.

Purchaser of coparcener's share at judicial sale not entitled to benefits of implied warranty of title.—Id.

Parties not presumed to have assumed obligations not implied by law.—Id.

Parties do not acquire new title.—Id.

PARTNERSHIP.

II. THE FIRM, ITS NAME, POWERS, AND PROPERTY.

⊂══64 (Ky.) That corporate lessee transacted business in name of its president will not warrant refusal of extension of lease.—Kozy Theater Co. v. Love, 249.

PAYMENT.

See Subrogation; Tender.

I. REQUISITES AND SUFFICIENCY.

⚫—33 (Mo.App.) Check not only insufficient, but also conditional, not operative as payment.—Lange v. Midwest Motor Securities Co., 272.

IV. PLEADING, EVIDENCE, TRIAL, AND REVIEW.

⚫—73(4) (Tex.Civ.App.) Evidence of payment of check *held* sufficient.—Wilcox v. Crawford, 1104.

PENSIONS.

⚫—2 (Ark.) "Pension" defined.—Hawkins v. Randolph, 556.

PERJURY.

I. OFFENSES AND RESPONSIBILITY THEREFOR.

⚫—13 (Ark.) Defendant who induced his wife to make false affidavit cannot be guilty of "perjury," offense being "subornation of perjury."—Thomas v. State, 200.

Where defendant induced his wife to swear to false affidavit, he is not guilty of subornation of perjury unless she knew of the falsity.—Id.

PHYSICIANS AND SURGEONS.

⚫—6(10) (Mo.App.) State not required to prove defendant, charged with practicing without a license, had not obtained license.—State v. Gardner, 1057.

⚫—6(11) (Mo.App.) Verdict finding chiropractor guilty of practicing medicine without a license *held* not defective.—State v. Gardner, 1057.

⚫—14(4) (Mo.App.) Degree of care required by physicians using X-ray machines stated.—Evans v. Clapp, 79.

⚫—15 (Mo.App.) Where X-ray was used merely for diagnosis and patient was burned, physician cannot defeat recovery on the ground of honest mistake in treatment.—Evans v. Clapp, 79.

In action for X-ray burns, the rules governing the liability of physicians and surgeons are applicable.—Id.

⚫—15 (Mo.App.) Physician's mistake in diagnosis, to be actionable, must have been negligent.—Gottschall v. Geiger, 87.

Negligence in advising an operation must be determined in light of conditions existing before operation.—Id.

⚫—18(7) (Mo.App.) That X-ray examinations do not, when carefully used, produce burns, might be considered on question of care.—Evans v. Clapp, 79.

⚫—18(8) (Mo.App.) Evidence *held* to warrant finding that plaintiff was burned by defendant's negligent use of X-ray machine.—Evans v. Clapp, 79.

⚫—18(9) (Mo.App.) Whether physician was negligent in advising unnecessary operation *held* for jury.—Gottschall v. Geiger, 87.

⚫—18(10) (Mo.App.) Instruction on the care required of a physician not erroneous.—Evans v. Clapp, 79.

PLEADING.

See Equity, ⚫—136.

For pleadings in particular actions or proceedings, see also the various specific topics.

For review of rulings relating to pleadings, see Appeal and Error.

I. FORM AND ALLEGATIONS IN GENERAL.

⚫—8(16) (Tex.Civ.App.) Allegations of undue influence *held* mere conclusions.—Ater v. Moore, 457.

⚫—34(6) (Mo.App.) Petition upheld on objection to evidence if any cause of action is stated though imperfectly.—O'Connell v. Kansas City, 1040.

On objection to any evidence petition not insufficient if fact not expressly stated is necessarily implied.—Id.

⚫—36(3) (Tex.Civ.App.) Evidence in support of plea in confession and avoidance admissible despite defendant's admission.—Rawlings v. Ediger, 163.

II. DECLARATION, COMPLAINT, PETITION, OR STATEMENT.

⚫—54 (Mo.App.) Each separate count must be a complete statement of cause of action.—Orr v. Russell, 275.

III. PLEA OR ANSWER, CROSS-COMPLAINT, AND AFFIDAVIT OF DEFENSE.

(B) Dilatory Pleas and Matter in Abatement.

⚫—106(1) (Ky.) Plea in abatement does not deny right of action, and must give better writ.—Stange v. Price, 532.

⚫—111 (Ky.) Pleading of nul tiel corporation is in abatement, and, if sustained, additional parties may be ordered.—Stange v. Price, 532.

After plea of nul tiel corporation sustained, defendant entitled to dismissal in absence of tendered amendment.—Id.

⚫—111 (Tex.Com.App.) Sustaining plea in abatement effective only as a dismissal of premature action.—Humphrey v. National Fire Ins. Co. of Hartford, Conn., 750.

⚫—111 (Tex.Civ.App.) Plea of privilege prima facie proof of right to transfer.—Sinton State Bank v. Tyler Commercial College, 170.

⚫—111 (Tex.Civ.App.) Controverting plea of privilege need not set out facts required by statute where they are alleged in the petition.—First Nat. Bank v. Childs, 807.

Not proper to express opinion on matters going to the merits in hearing upon change of venue.—Id.

On plea of privilege, it is sufficient for plaintiff to plead a cause of action, and prove that it arose in whole or in part in county where suit was brought.—Id.

Prima facie right to change of venue under plea of privilege overcome by evidence.—Id.

V. DEMURRER OR EXCEPTION.

⚫—214(1) (Tex.Civ.App.) Facts alleged in petition admitted by general demurrer.—Hubb-Diggs Co. v. Mitchell, 425.

⚫—214(1) (Tex.Civ.App.) Allegations of fact taken as true on demurrer.—Home Life & Accident Co. v. Jordan, 802.

⚫—216(1) (Ky.) On demurrer to petition only petition and exhibits filed with it can be considered.—Arnett v. Elkhorn Coal Corporation, 219.

VI. AMENDED AND SUPPLEMENTAL PLEADINGS AND REPLEADER.

⚫—229 (Ky.) Amended pleadings must be in furtherance of justice and not substantially change claim or defense.—Foxwell v. Justice, 509.

⚫—236(3) (Tex.Civ.App.) Permitting plaintiff to file trial amendment discretionary with court.—Holden v. Evans, 146.

⚫—236(7) (Ky.) Refusal to file amended answer changing issues, etc., not abuse of discretion.—Foxwell v. Justice, 509.

⚫—237(8) (Ky.) Court may refuse to file offered amendment if it appears to change issue.—Foxwell v. Justice, 509.

⚫—238(3) (Ky.) Offered amendment should be supported by affidavit.—Foxwell v. Justice, 509.

⚫—248(4) (Tex.Civ.App.) Plaintiff could amend petition by asserting remedy on contract inconsistent with that first pleaded, that contract had been repudiated.—Hartford Life Ins. Co. v. Patterson, 814.

⟦⟧252(2) (Mo.App.) Though plaintiff elected to go to trial on the second count, the first count of the petition did not become an abandoned pleading.—Orr v. Russell, 275.

XIII. DEFECTS AND OBJECTIONS, WAIVER, AND AIDER BY VERDICT OR JUDGMENT.

⟦⟧406(5) (Mo.App.) Defective reference from one count to another waived by failure to object.—Orr v. Russell, 275.

⟦⟧411 (Mo.) Objection to counterclaim in suit to cancel notes waived by failure to demur.—Thomas v. Goodrum, 571.

⟦⟧433(3) (Tex.Com.App.) Pleadings not specially excepted to *held* to support judgment on finding cotton was not compressed in workmanlike manner.—Elder, Dempster & Co. v. Weld-Neville Cotton Co., 102.

⟦⟧433(8) (Mo.App.) Petition in action for injuries *held* sufficient after verdict as against objection that city's notice of defect was not alleged; "maintain."—O'Connell v. Kansas City, 1040.

PLEDGES.

⟦⟧24 (Mo.App.) Pledgee of note to secure a forged note *held* to have no right thereto.—Conway v. Flaugh, 1045.

⟦⟧56(1) (Tex.Com.App.) Collateral to be sold at public auction after advertisement and notice to pledgor in absence of agreement to contrary.—Haynes v. Western Union Telegraph Co., 361.

⟦⟧56(7) (Mo.App.) Pledgee purchasing collateral at sale *held* entitled to benefit of lien on mortgage in real estate.—Franklin Bank v. Meinecke, 1067.

PRACTICE.

For practice in particular actions and proceedings, see the various specific topics.

PRESCRIPTION.

See Adverse Possession; Limitation of Actions.

PRINCIPAL AND AGENT.

See Attorney and Client; Brokers.

I. THE RELATION.

(A) Creation and Existence.

⟦⟧21 (Ky.) Agency may be shown by agent's testimony.—Grove Lodge No. 274, I. O. O. F., v. Fidelity Phenix Ins. Co., 215.

II. MUTUAL RIGHTS, DUTIES, AND LIABILITIES.

(A) Execution of Agency.

⟦⟧70 (Tex.Com.App.) Same person may be appointed agent for collection and payment by different parties.—Shaw v. First State Bank of Abilene, 325.

III. RIGHTS AND LIABILITIES AS TO THIRD PERSONS.

(A) Powers of Agent.

⟦⟧92(2) (Tex.Com.App.) Payment of note is complete when funds have reached hands of agent authorized to receive it.—Shaw v. First State Bank of Abilene, 325.

⟦⟧103(9) (Ark.) Owner of land authorizing agent to sell, bound by terms of contract made by him.—Battle v. Draper, 869.

⟦⟧103(11) (Ky.) Agent to sell land authorized to sell for cash, and principal not bound by other sale, in absence of ratification.—Barriger v. Bryan, 506.

⟦⟧124(3) (Tex.Com.App.) Whether representative of loan company was agent of holder of vendor's lien note authorized to receive payment of the note *held* for the jury.—Shaw v. First State Bank of Abilene, 325.

PRINCIPAL AND SURETY.

See Indemnity.

III. DISCHARGE OF SURETY.

⟦⟧100(4) (Tex.Civ.App.) Test stated as to whether modifications affect liability under contractor's bond reserving right to modify.—Southern Surety Co. v. Nalle & Co., 402.

Change from three-story to four-story building may release surety under contractor's bond reserving right to "alter or modify plans and specifications."—Id.

⟦⟧128(1) (Tex.Civ.App.) Change in plans ratified by surety will not release him.—Southern Surety Co. v. Nalle & Co., 402.

IV. REMEDIES OF CREDITORS.

⟦⟧161 (Tex.Civ.App.) Evidence sustaining finding that surety had received additional compensation on account of alterations in plans.—Southern Surety Co. v. Nalle & Co., 402.

PROHIBITION.

I. NATURE AND GROUNDS.

⟦⟧5(3) (Mo.) Application for, *held* a collateral attack on order for sale of property by receiver.—State ex rel. Missouri Motor Bus Co. v. Davis, 570.

⟦⟧10(2) (Mo.App.) Want of jurisdiction *held* to appear as a matter of law on the face of a judgment awarding an injunction so that prohibition would lie.—State ex rel. Youngman v. Calhoun, 647.

II. JURISDICTION, PROCEEDINGS, AND RELIEF.

⟦⟧28 (Mo.) Question of malice in writing letter cannot be considered by Supreme Court on application for prohibition.—State ex rel. Tune v. Falkenhainer, 257.

⟦⟧28 (Mo.) Supreme Court has no authority to amend subpœna duces tecum in prohibition proceeding.—State ex rel. Feinstein v. Hartman, 982.

PROMISSORY NOTES.

See Bills and Notes.

PROPERTY.

⟦⟧9 (Mo.App.) Possession of personalty prima facie proof of ownership.—Johnston v. Brown Bros. Iron & Metal Co., 1011.

PUBLIC IMPROVEMENTS.

See Municipal Corporations, ⟦⟧821–513.

PUBLIC LANDS.

III. DISPOSAL OF LANDS OF THE STATES.

⟦⟧173(4) (Tex.Civ.App.) Evidence *held* to prove land appraised at figure at which it was sold.—Gulf Production Co., State, 124.

⟦⟧173(22) (Tex.Civ.App.) Purchaser's right to reinstatement on same terms as original purchase not affected by Land Commissioner's subsequent reclassification of land.—Gulf Production Co. v. State, 124.

Forfeitures not favored.—Id.

Purchaser after forfeiture of previous sale, who voluntarily abandoned land, had no intervening rights barring reinstatment of original purchaser.—Id.

Right to reinstatement not affected by fact that cancellation of abandoned sale to third person had not been formally entered on Land Office books.—Id.

Quitclaim deed, executed after forfeiture, entitled grantee to reinstatement under statute.—Id.

Right to reinstatement not affected by false representations to Land Commissioner.—Id.

⟦⟧176(2) (Tex.) Descriptive matter inserted by mistake should be rejected.—Wilson v. Giraud, 1074.

V. SPANISH, MEXICAN, FRENCH, AND RUSSIAN GRANTS.

☞=198 (Tex.) Treaty of Guadalupe Hidalgo does not protect Mexican land grants not in existence when the treaty was signed.—Kenedy Pasture Co. v. State, 683.

☞=199 (Tex.) A nation may not grant title to land to which it has no title.—Kenedy Pasture Co. v. State, 683.

Power of Mexican government to grant land in territory ceded to this country ended with signing of treaty.—Id.

☞=203 (Tex.) Appropriation void on its face does not give character of "titled land" or "land equitably owned" within constitutional provision.—Kenedy Pasture Co. v. State, 683.

☞=209 (Tex.) Abandonment of grant must be shown by unequivocal act evidencing intention, and mere failure to assert right is insufficient.—Kenedy Pasture Co. v. State, 683.

Parties, allowing rights to slumber 70 years in buried records in foreign country with no possession, held not entitled to establish claim against innocent purchasers.—Id.

☞=210 (Tex.) Copies of original letters, shown to be genuine and found in Mexican archives, held admissible to show equitable title.—Kenedy Pasture Co. v. State, 683.

Parties buying from state held innocent purchasers as against record of invalid Mexican grant.—Id.

Parties purchasing from the state not required to search Mexican records of ancient towns. —Id.

☞=223(1) (Tex.) Party having paid for land and had it surveyed prior to 1836 acquired inchoate and equitable title protected by treaty. —Kenedy Pasture Co. v. State, 683.

Claimants under Mexican grant cannot complain of judgment for innocent purchasers whom they did not reimburse.—Id.

PUBLIC SERVICE CORPORATIONS.

See Carriers; Gas; Railroads; Street Railroads; Telegraphs and Telephones.

QUANTUM MERUIT.

See Work and Labor.

QUIETING TITLE.

I. RIGHT OF ACTION AND DEFENSES.

☞=10(4) (Ky.) Title by adverse possession supports action.—Wilson v. Pioneer Coal Co., 37.

II. PROCEEDINGS AND RELIEF.

☞=34(1) (Ky.) Petition claiming ownership and possession of land and setting forth matter of adverse claims is sufficient.—Arnett v. Elkhorn Coal Corporation, 219.

☞=35(2) (Ky.) Petition showing defendant claimed under plaintiff's grantor without showing date of plaintiff's deed is insufficient.—Arnett v. Elkhorn Coal Corporation, 219.

☞=44(4) (Ky.) Evidence held to warrant finding of delivery of deed by defendant husband to first wife, plaintiff's ancestor, etc.—Petty's Heirs v. Petty, 52.

QUO WARRANTO.

I. NATURE AND GROUNDS.

☞=8 (Tex.Civ.App.) Existence of levee district could be questioned only by state in quo warranto proceeding.—Wilmarth v. Reagan, 445.

RAILROADS.

See Street Railroads.

I. CONTROL AND REGULATION IN GENERAL.

☞=5½ [New, vol. 6A Key-No. Series]
(Tex.Civ.App.) Judgment fixing lien against properties of dismissed defendant owning road under federal control erroneous.— Gulf, C. & S. F. Ry. Co. v. Hamrick, 166.

☞=5½ [New, vol. 6A Key-No. Series]
(Tex.Civ.App.) Substitution of federal agent under Transportation Act.—Payne v. White House Lumber Co., 417.

☞=5½ [New, vol. 6A Key-No. Series]
(Tex.Civ.App.) Federal Director General liable for injuries from defective crossing. —Payne v. Wallis, 1114.

VI. CONSTRUCTION, MAINTENANCE, AND EQUIPMENT.

☞=113(10) (Tex.Com.App.) Insufficient drainage held not proximate cause of drowning in flood.—San Antonio & A. P. Ry. Co. v. Behne, 354.

X. OPERATION.

(B) Statutory, Municipal, and Official Regulations.

☞=226 (Ky.) Waiting room, which is dark, stuffy, too small, or dirty, not "suitable waiting room."—Commonwealth v. Louisville & N. R. Co., 236.

☞=236 (Tenn.) Ordinance limiting speed to 4 miles per hour not unreasonable.—Hines v. Partridge, 16.

☞=255(8) (Ky.) Indictment charging railroad with failure to provide waiting room not duplicitous or demurrable.—Commonwealth v. Louisville & N. R. Co., 236.

Indictment for failure to provide suitable waiting room should not couple word "public" with "passengers."—Id.

(F) Accidents at Crossings.

☞=307(4) (Tex.Civ.App.) Flagman only required at unusually dangerous crossings.—Baker v. Hodges, 844.

☞=308 (Tex.Civ.App.) Violation of ordinance requiring flagman negligence.—Baker v. Hodges, 844.

☞=312(4) (Mo.App.) Lookout required.—Ruenzi v. Payne, 294.

☞=313 (Mo.App.) Omission of statutory signal prima facie negligence.—Ruenzi v. Payne, 294.

☞=316(4) (Mo.App.) Speed of 50 miles an hour common-law negligence.—Ruenzi v. Payne, 294.

☞=316(4) (Tex.Civ.App.) Speed ordinance immaterial where speed was negligent.—Baker v. Hodges, 844.

☞=317 (Mo.App.) Violation of speed ordinance held negligence.—Ruenzi v. Payne, 294.

☞=324(1) (Mo.App.) Care required of pedestrian.—Ruenzi v. Payne, 294.

☞=324(3) (Tenn.) Automobilist's violation of statute does not affect right to recover damages.—Hines v. Partridge, 16.

☞=327(5) (Mo.App.) Failure to look both ways for trains held negligence.—Ruenzi v. Payne, 294.

☞=337(1) (Tex.Civ.App.) Failure to have flagman at obstructed crossing held proximate cause of injury.—Baker v. Hodges, 844.

☞=338 (Mo.App.) Contributory negligence no defense under humanitarian rule.—Ruenzi v. Payne, 294.

Discovered peril doctrine applied.—Id.

☞=345(1) (Tex.Com.App.) Issue of discovered peril held not raised by pleading.—Baker v. Shafter, 349.

☞=346(5) (Tex.Com.App.) Burden of showing contributory negligence on defendant.—Missouri, K. & T. Ry. Co. of Texas v. Merchant, 327.

☞=348(6) (Tex.Com.App.) Jury may consider evidence most favorable to plaintiff.—Missouri, K. & T. Ry. Co. of Texas v. Merchant, 327.

☞=348(8) (Tex.Com.App.) Driver of auto struck held not conclusively shown to have seen train in time.—Missouri, K. & T. Ry. Co. of Texas v. Merchant, 327.

☞=350(5) (Tenn.) Negligent in backing train over crossing without flagman held for jury.— Hines v. Partridge, 16.

⟞350(5) (Tex.Civ.App.) Negligence in maintaining flagman question of fact.—Baker v. Hodges, 844.

Negligence of conductor failing to station flagman at crossing *held* question of fact.—Id.

⟞350(11) (Tenn.) Negligence in backing train at unlawful speed over crossing *held* for jury.—Hines v. Partridge, 16.

⟞350(11) (Tex.Civ.App.) Negligent speed *held* question of fact.—Hines v. Partridge, 16.

⟞350(13) (Tenn.) Automobilist's negligence *held* for jury.—Hines v. Partridge, 16.

⟞350(16) (Tex.Com.App.) Failure to look and listen not conclusive of contributory negligence.—Missouri, K. & T. Ry. Co. of Texas v. Merchant, 327.

⟞350(22) (Tex.Civ.App.) Automobile driver going 12 miles an hour, though view was obstructed, *held* not negligent as a matter of law.—Payne v. Wallis, 1114.

⟞350(25) (Mo. App.) Contributory negligence of pedestrian with obstructed view *held* for jury.—Ruenzi v. Payne, 294.

⟞350(33) (Mo.App.) Negligence under humanitarian rule *held* for jury.—Ruenzi v. Payne, 294.

(G) Injuries to Persons on or near Tracks.

⟞355(2) (Ky.) Joint right in passway.—Cincinnati, N. O. & T. P. R. Co. v. Owsley, 210.

⟞356(1) (Ky.) Habitual use of tracks determines right to go thereon.—Hines v. Wilson's Adm'x, 23.

⟞356(3) (Ky.) Trespassers becoming licensees by user.—Cincinnati, N. O. & T. P. R. Co. v. Owsley, 210.

⟞369(3) (Ky.) Lookout and signals required where tracks are used by public.—Hines v. Wilson's Adm'x, 23.

⟞377 (Ky.) Injury to pedestrian who steps directly in front of train not actionable.—Hines v. Wilson's Adm'x, 23.

⟞400(2) (Ky.) License to use tracks *held* question for jury.—Hines v. Wilson's Adm'x, 23.

⟞400(12) (Ky.) Contributory negligence of buggy driver on mill track *held* for jury.—Cincinnati, N. O. & T. P. R. Co. v. Owsley, 210.

⟞400(14) (Ky.) Negligence under last clear chance doctrine *held* for jury.—Cincinnati, N. O. & T. P. R. Co. v. Owsley, 210.

RAPE.

II. PROSECUTION AND PUNISHMENT.

(A) Indictment and Information.

⟞20 (Mo.) Indictment *held* sufficient.—State v. Lee, 619.

(B) Evidence.

⟞52(4) (Mo.) Evidence *held* to establish the age of prosecutrix at less than 15 years.—State v. Hightower, 566.

(C) Trial and Review.

⟞57(1) (Mo.) Evidence *held* to make out a case for the jury.—State v. Hightower, 566.

REAL ACTIONS.

See Ejectment; Partition; Quieting Title; Trespass to Try Title.

RECEIVERS.

IV. MANAGEMENT AND DISPOSITION OF PROPERTY.

(A) Administration in General.

⟞90 (Tex.Civ.App.) Need not carry out executory contract, but estate is liable for breach.—Tecumseh Oil & Cotton Co. v. Gresham, 468.

(D) Sale and Conveyance or Redelivery of Property.

⟞131 (Mo.) Court may order sale of property in hands of receiver before final judgment, where necessary to preserve interests of

parties.—State ex rel. Missouri Motor Bus Co. v. Davis, 570.

RECEIVING STOLEN GOODS.

⟞3 (Mo.) Knowledge of information leading reasonably prudent man to believe property to be stolen not sufficient guilty knowledge.—State v. Henderson, 596.

⟞8(3) (Tex.Cr.App.) Evidence of possession *held* not to justify inference of guilt.—Lemon v. State, 388.

⟞9(2) (Mo.App.) Instruction *held* erroneous, as permitting mere negligence to take place of guilty knowledge.—State v. Blocker, 1062.

RECORDS.

See Appeal and Error, ⟞494–714; Criminal Law, ⟞1090–1120.

REFORMATION OF INSTRUMENTS.

II. PROCEEDINGS AND RELIEF.

⟞45(4) (Ark.) Evidence *held* to support decree of reformation.—Harton v. Durham, 193.

REMAINDERS.

⟞17(2) (Ky.) Action for waste committed by grantee of estate for life of grantor need not be delayed until after grantor's death.—Adams v. Bates, 238.

⟞17(3) (Ky.) Statute begins to run against owners of remainder in fee after life estate from time of commission of waste by grantee of such estate.—Adams v. Bates, 238.

REPLEVIN.

IV. PLEADING AND EVIDENCE.

⟞70 (Mo.App.) Burden on plaintiff to show he was entitled to possession.—Johnston v. Brown Bros. Iron & Metal Co., 1011.

VI. TRIAL, JUDGMENT, ENFORCEMENT OF JUDGMENT, AND REVIEW.

⟞96 (Ark.) Rendition of verdict in solido not ground for reversal.—Taylor v. Walker, 550.

Statute providing for fixing value of each article not jurisdictional.—Id.

REVENUE.

See Taxation.

REVIEW.

See Appeal and Error.

RISKS.

See Master and Servant, ⟞204–226.

ROADS.

See Highways.

SALES.

See Judicial Sales; Taxation, ⟞615–648; Vendor and Purchaser.

II. CONSTRUCTION OF CONTRACT.

⟞77(2) (Ark.) Buyer of automobile *held* not obligated to pay costs of transporting car to city of purchase.—Berger v. Jonesboro Motor Co., 4.

⟞81(3) (Mo.App.) Parol evidence to vary contract provision for shipment "as soon as possible" is inadmissible.—Guess v. Russell Bros. Clothing Co., 1015.

III. MODIFICATION OR RESCISSION OF CONTRACT.

(B) Rescission by Seller.

⟞109 (Mo.App.) Instruction that seller could not rescind in part proper.—Neal v. Crowson, 1033.

(C) Rescission by Buyer.

⟞126(3) (Mo.App.) Notice of rescission of purchase price of jacks given within time after permitting seller to attempt to demonstrate their utility.—Neal v. Crowson, 1033.

IV. PERFORMANCE OF CONTRACT.

(C) Delivery and Acceptance of Goods.

⚙️168(2) (Ark.) Seller estopped from contending that buyer was bound to inspect within reasonable time after receiving shipment.—Brin Bros. v. Lyon Bros., 560.

⚙️173 (Ark.) Seller sued for breach *held* not to have waived buyer's breach by failure to order delivery within time specified.—Russell v. Barnhart Mercantile Co., 881.

⚙️173 (Tex.Civ.App.) Receiver of buyer company *held* to have furnished cars for shipment, though cars belonged to other.—Tecumseh Oil & Cotton Co. v. Gresham, 468.

⚙️175 (Tex.Civ.App.) Purchaser could not cancel items of order and then sue for nondelivery.—Solomon v. Schwartz Bros. & Co., 174.

⚙️181(11) (Tex.Civ.App.) Evidence insufficient to show buyer refused to pay for car of oil on demand.—Tecumseh Oil & Cotton Co. v. Gresham, 468.

⚙️181(13) (Ky.) Evidence *held* to show that consignee sold wheat for shipper, and not as its own.—Early & Daniel Co. v. C. S. Evans & Co., 226.

(D) Payment of Price.

⚙️191 (Tex.Civ.App.) Payee, who accepted notes by selling them, bound to ship machinery.—State Nat. Bank of Texarkana v. Potter, 828.

V. OPERATION AND EFFECT.

(A) Transfer of Title as Between Parties.

⚙️200(2) (Tex.Civ.App.) Where wheat shipped consigned to shipper's order, title passes on the payment of draft attached to bill of lading and delivery of the bill of lading, though weighing at destination necessary.—Fort Worth Elevators Co. v. Keel & Son, 481.

⚙️201(1) (Ky.) Possession must be delivered before title passes.—People's Sav. Bank & Trust Co. v. Klempner Bros., 244.

⚙️201(4) (Ky.) Whether possession of carrier possession of consignee buyer question of shipper's intention.—People's Sav. Bank & Trust Co. v. Klempner Bros., 244.

Evidence conclusive that debtor consignor did not intend title or possession of goods to vest in creditor consignee.—Id.

⚙️218½ (Ky.) Possession of carrier presumptively possession of consignee.—People's Sav. Bank & Trust Co. v. Klempner Bros., 244.

VI. WARRANTIES.

⚙️273(1) (Mo.App.) Law implied warranty that jacks were reasonably fit for breeding purposes.—Neal v. Crowson, 1033.

⚙️288(5) (Ark.) Action for breach of warranty of quality maintainable after acceptance of part when there was no opportunity for inspection.—Forrester v. Locke, 897.

VIII. REMEDIES OF BUYER.

(A) Recovery of Price.

⚙️390 (Tex.Com.App.) Defrauded buyer may stand by contract and recover damages, or he may rescind.—Clark v. Texas Co-op. Inv. Co., 381.

(C) Actions for Breach of Contract.

⚙️418(12) (Tex.Civ.App.) Buyer which resold entitled to recover for seller's failure to deliver.—Tecumseh Oil & Cotton Co. v. Gresham, 468.

(D) Actions and Counterclaims for Breach of Warranty.

⚙️426 (Mo.App.) Under contract providing for return and rescission on failure of warranty as exclusive remedy, seller, by refusing to accept return, becomes liable for the usual damages for breach of warranty.—Mayfield v. George O. Richardson Machinery Co., 288.

An exclusive remedy for breach of warranty must be clearly expressed.—Id.

⚙️437(2) (Mo.App.) Interest not allowable on buyer's recovery for seller's breach unless asked in pleadings.—Mayfield v. George O. Richardson Machinery Co., 288.

⚙️442(3) (Ark.) Measure of damages for breach of warranty of quality stated.—Forrester v. Locke, 897.

⚙️442(5) (Mo.App.) On breach of warranty of tractor, purchaser entitled to recover loss of season's use of land.—Mayfield v. George O. Richardson Machinery Co., 288.

⚙️442(6, 7) (Mo.App.) On breach of warranty of tractor, expense in endeavoring to make machine work *held* recoverable.—Mayfield v. George O. Richardson Machinery Co., 288.

⚙️442(16) (Mo.App.) Purchaser on breach of warranty *held* entitled to recover not only freight money, but also amount he was compelled to pay on notes given for the goods.—Mayfield v. George O. Richardson Machinery Co., 288.

⚙️445(1) (Mo.App.) Whether there was warranty of jacks sold a jury question.—Neal v. Crowson, 1033.

IX. CONDITIONAL SALES.

⚙️451 (Tex.) Foreign unrecorded conditional sale contract *held* not effective to retain title to automobile in seller as against innocent purchaser.—Consolidated Garage Co. v. Chambers, 1072.

SCHOOLS AND SCHOOL DISTRICTS.

II. PUBLIC SCHOOLS.

(D) District Property, Contracts, and Liabilities.

⚙️84 (Mo.App.) Clause in construction contract relating to insurance *held* not to include derrick.—Vogelsang v. Board of Education of City of Cape Girardeau, 645.

(E) District Debt, Securities, and Taxation.

⚙️101 (Mo.) Repairing and furnishing not the "erection of buildings," for which annual tax rate may be exceeded.—Harrington v. Hopkins, 263.

⚙️103(2) (Tex.Com.App.) Trustees of school district *held* not to have right to call election for levy of maintenance tax.—Millhollon v. Stanton Independent School Dist., 332.

SENTENCE.

See Criminal Law, ⚙️977.

SEPARATE PROPERTY.

See Husband and Wife, ⚙️146-152.

SET-OFF AND COUNTERCLAIM.

II. SUBJECT-MATTER.

⚙️29(1) (Mo.App.) "Transaction" defined.—Slack v. Whitney, 1060.

SEWERS.

See Drains.

SHIPPING.

See Wharves.

VII. CARRIAGE OF GOODS.

⚙️108 (Tex.Com.App.) Finding against general custom fixing density of cotton *held* not to conflict with finding of density after proper baling.—Elder, Dempster & Co. v. Weld-Neville Cotton Co., 102.

Contract for shipment of compressed cotton implies it is to be compressed in workmanlike manner.—Id.

Provisions relating to standard cotton *held* applicable to high density cotton, except as to weight.—Id.

Proof additional cargo was available unnecessary to recovery for shipment of cotton not properly compressed.—Id.

SLANDER.

See Libel and Slander.

SPECIFIC PERFORMANCE.

I. NATURE AND GROUNDS OF REMEDY IN GENERAL.

⋙16 (Tex.Com.App.) All circumstances must be taken into consideration in determining whether remedy inequitable.—Simpson v. Green, 375.

IV. PROCEEDINGS AND RELIEF.

⋙117 (Tex.Com.App.) Variance between pleading and evidence *held* not material.—Briscoe v. Bright's Adm'r, 1082.

⋙121(1) (Tex.Com.App.) When proof of terms of oral contract sufficient stated.—Briscoe v. Bright's Adm'r, 1082.

⋙121(3) (Tex.Com.App.) Evidence insufficient to show that enforcement for contract of sale would be inequitable.—Simpson v. Green, 375.

⋙121(4) (Tex.Com.App.) Evidence *held* sufficient to support finding.—Briscoe v. Bright's Adm'r, 1082.

STATUTE OF FRAUDS.

See Frauds, Statute of.

STATUTE OF LIMITATIONS.

See Limitation of Actions.

STATUTES.

For statutes relating to particular subjects, see the various specific topics.

III. SUBJECTS AND TITLES OF ACTS.

⋙107(1) (Tenn.) All sections of Factory Inspection Act *held* germane to subject.—Athens Hosiery Mills v. Thomason, 904.

⋙117(8) (Tex.Civ.App.) Amendatory statute making natural person liable for death caused by agent, invalid.—Anderson v. Smith, 142.

IV. AMENDMENT, REVISION, AND CODIFICATION.

⋙141(1) (Ky.) Amendatory act as to carrying concealed weapons, invalid because not setting out any of amended act.—Commonwealth v. Bowman, 35.

V. REPEAL, SUSPENSION, EXPIRATION, AND REVIVAL.

⋙149 (Mo.) Legislature has power to eliminate provisions incorporated by reference, including a constitutional provision.—State ex rel. Feinstein v. Hartman, 982.

VI. CONSTRUCTION AND OPERATION.

(A) General Rules of Construction.

⋙181(1) (Ark.) Primary object in construction to ascertain intention of Legislature from language used.—Howell v. Lamberson, 872.

⋙181(1) (Tenn.) Legislative intent must be ascertained and given effect.—Athens Hosiery Mills v. Thomason, 904.

⋙195 (Tex.Com.App.) Expression of one thing excludes another.—Millhollon v. Stanton Independent School Dist., 332.

⋙205 (Tenn.) Legislative intent must be ascertained and given effect, and in doing so act must be considered as a whole.—Athens Hosiery Mills v. Thomason, 904.

⋙225 (Ky.) Previous motor vehicle acts can be considered in ascertaining intention in subsequent act.—Lewis v. James, 526.

(B) Particular Classes of Statutes.

⋙239 (Tex.Com.App.) Laws depriving citizens of rights strictly construed.—Poe v. Continental Oil & Cotton Co., 717.

⋙245 (Tenn.) Statutes will not be extended by implication.—H. D. Watts Co. v. Hauk, 908.

STATUTES CONSTRUED.

STIPULATIONS.

⟐⟐14(12) (Tex.Civ.App.) Costs improperly charged in judgment against bank under stipulation.—Ballew & Huston v. Blakeny, 495.

STREET RAILROADS.

II. REGULATION AND OPERATION.

⟐⟐90(4) (Tex.Com.App.) Motorman should use ordinary care to avoid collision.—Paris Transit Co. v. Fath, 1080.

⟐⟐93(4) (Mo.) Motorman may assume pedestrian will not step in front of car.—Lackey v. United Rys. Co., 956.

⟐⟐98(7) (Mo.) Pedestrians going in front of street car negligent.—Lackey v. United Rys. Co., 956.

Pedestrian crossing tracks may assume car will run within speed limit and stop at intersection.—Id.

⟐⟐98(12) (Mo.) Contributory negligence of pedestrian jumping on fender *held* not shown. —Lackey v. United Rys. Co., 956.

⟐⟐103(2) (Mo.) Motorman not negligent in failing to observe last chance rule until pedestrian is in danger.—Lackey v. United Rys. Co., 956.

⟐⟐111(2) (Mo.) Vigilant watch ordinance not pleaded *held* inadmissible.—Lackey v. United Rys. Co., 956.

Stop ordinance though not pleaded, *held* admissible to rebut evidence of contributory negligence.—Id.

⟐⟐112(3) (Mo.) Presumption of care inapplicable where facts appear.—Lackey v. United Rys. Co., 956.

⟐⟐117(11) (Tex.Com.App.) Motorman's negligence jury question.—Paris Transit Co. v. Fath, 1080.

⟐⟐117(27) (Mo.App.) Motortruck driver *held* not negligent as a matter of law in not clearing track.—Clayton v. Kansas City Rys. Co., 68.

⟐⟐117(28) (Mo.App.) Automobile driver's contributory negligence question of fact.— Jackals v. Kansas City Rys. Co., 1023.

⟐⟐117(29) (Mo.App.) Driving on track without looking back *held* not contributory negligence as matter of law.—Clayton v. Kansas City Rys. Co., 68.

⟐⟐118(1) (Mo.App.) Instruction as to street car's safety stop *held* within pleadings.—Jackels v. Kansas City Rys. Co., 1023.

⟐⟐118(4) (Mo.) Instructions *held* to fairly submit specific charges of negligence in striking motortruck.—Richardson v. Kansas City Rys. Co., 938.

⟐⟐118(11) (Mo.) Instruction *held* to negative defense that motortruck backed into street car. —Richardson v. Kansas City Rys. Co., 938.

⟐⟐118(15) (Mo.) Instruction *held* not objectionable as omitting to require findings of motortruck passenger's obliviousness of danger and knowledge thereof by street car operatives. —Richardson v. Kansas City Rys. Co., 938.

⟐⟐118(16) (Mo.) Instruction *held* erroneous as not requiring finding of proximate cause of injury.—Lackey v. United Rys. Co., 956.

SUBROGATION.

⟐⟐14(2) (Tex.Civ.App.) Subsequent incumbrancer *held* not entitled to subrogation against purchaser of one of several tracts.— Pope v. Witherspoon, 837.

SUNDAY.

⟐⟐30(3) (Mo.App.) Notice of injury sufficient, though received by mayor on Sunday.— Thomas v. City of St. Joseph, 63.

SURETYSHIP.

See Principal and Surety.

TAXATION.

See Highways, ⟐⟐142-150.

III. LIABILITY OF PERSONS AND PROPERTY.

(B) Corporations and Corporate Stock and Property.

⟐⟐117 (Ark.) Local corporations owning property are subject to franchise tax as "doing business," though they merely leased coal lands.—Arkansas Anthracite Coal Co. v. State, 184.

(D) Exemptions.

⟐⟐241(3) (Tex.Civ.App.) Voluntary association not exempt in view of use of lodge room and first story of building by others.—Concho Camp, No. 66, W. O. W., v. City of San Angelo, 1106.

Local camp of benevolent association not entitled to exemption in view of its life insurance feature; "purely public charity."—Id.

V. LEVY AND ASSESSMENT.

(D) Mode of Assessment of Corporate Stock, Property, or Receipts.

⟐⟐380 (Ark.) Stock of foreign corporation not taxable where not of value exceeding value of other property assessed in state.—State v. Eagle Lumber Co., 180.

VII. PAYMENT AND REFUNDING OR RECOVERY OF TAX PAID.

⟐⟐515 (Ark.) Taxpayer may pay one tax while refusing to pay other taxes on his land.— Howell v. Lamberson, 872.

VIII. COLLECTION AND ENFORCEMENT AGAINST PERSONS OR PERSONAL PROPERTY.

(A) Collectors and Proceedings for Collection in General.

⟐⟐561 (Ark.) Collector not liable for failure to collect tax or omission to advise taxpayer, where he made proper effort; "fail" and "omit to advise" implying neglect or omission.—Howell v. Lamberson, 872.

Collector cannot refuse to accept payment of general taxes because taxpayer refused to pay drainage tax also.—Id.

IX. SALE OF LAND FOR NONPAYMENT OF TAX.

⟐⟐615 (Tex.Com.App.) In suit to recover delinquent taxes all legal requirements must be strictly complied with.—Garza v. City of San Antonio, 697.

⟐⟐620 (Tex.Com.App.) Delinquent taxes on tract assessed to husband cannot be enforced against part of the tract assessed in name of wife for part of period.—Garza v. City of San Antonio, 697.

⟐⟐643 (Tex.Com.App.) To foreclose lien for delinquent taxes must allege and prove nonpayment.—Garza v. City of San Antonio, 697.

⟐⟐644 (Tex.Com.App.) Assessment roll not proof of nonpayment of taxes.—Garza v. City of San Antonio, 697.

Delinquent tax rolls are prima facie evidence of nonpayment of taxes.—Id.

⟐⟐647 (Tex.Com.App.) Description of land ordered to be sold for taxes *held* insufficient.— Garza v. City of San Antonio, 697.

⟱848 (Mo.) Judgment valid on its face not subject to collateral attack.—Hines v. Felkins, 922.

XI. TAX TITLES.

(A) Title and Rights of Purchaser at Tax Sale.

⟱734(7) (Mo.) That allegation as to defendant's nonresidence followed prayer of petition and original signature of plaintiff's attorney did not affect validity of deed.—Hines v. Felkins, 922.

TELEGRAPHS AND TELEPHONES.

II. REGULATION AND OPERATION.

⟱26¾ [New, vol. 7A Key-No. Series] (Mo.App.) Not liable for delay during federal control.—Taylor v. Western Union Telegraph Co., 78.

TENDER.

⟱19(2) (Mo.) Tender of nominal damages admission of breach of bond.—Abnerthy v. Schembra, 1005.

TORTS.

See Fraud, ⟱13–59; Libel and Slander, ⟱41–112; Municipal Corporations, ⟱733–822; Negligence, ⟱32–140; Nuisance, ⟱42–76; Trover and Conversion.

⟱22 (Tex.Civ.App.) Joint tort-feasors jointly and severally liable.—Anderson v. Smith, 142. "Joint tort-feasors" defined.—Id.

TRESPASS.

III. CRIMINAL RESPONSIBILITY.

⟱87 (Mo.App.) Information *held* to sufficiently charge tampering with another's motor vehicle.—State v. Anderson, 1070.
⟱88 (Mo.App.) Evidence *held* to sustain conviction of tampering with automobile.—State v. Anderson, 1070.

TRESPASS TO TRY TITLE.

I. RIGHT OF ACTION AND DEFENSES.

⟱11 (Tex.Civ.App.) Plaintiff need prove title only from common source.—Pope v. Witherspoon, 837.

II. PROCEEDINGS.

⟱35(1) (Tex.Civ.App.) Plaintiff confined to proof of title specially pleaded.—Brownfield v. Brabson, 491.
Title by limitations not permissible under general allegations.—Id.
Presumption of execution of deed asserted under general allegation.—Id.
⟱35(2) (Tex.Civ.App.) Equitable right cannot be relied on under plea of not guilty.—Pope v. Witherspoon, 837.
⟱41(2) (Tex.Civ.App.) Descriptions in deeds *held* sufficient to show parties deraigned title from common source.—Pope v. Witherspoon, 837.

TRIAL.

See Continuance; Costs; Criminal Law, ⟱625–881; Jury; New Trial; Venue.
For trial of particular actions or proceedings, see also the various specific topics.
For review of rulings at trial, see Appeal and Error.

III. COURSE AND CONDUCT OF TRIAL IN GENERAL.

⟱29(2) (Tex.Com.App.) Statement by court that he saw no benefit in so much medical testimony improper as comment on evidence.—American Express Co. v. Chandler, 1085.

IV. RECEPTION OF EVIDENCE.

(C) Objections, Motions to Strike Out, and Exceptions.

⟱105(2) (Tex.Civ.App.) Hearsay testimony not objected to is evidence.—Southern Surety Co. v. Nalle & Co., 402.

Failure to object to evidence of inferior grade a waiver of best evidence.—Id.

V. ARGUMENTS AND CONDUCT OF COUNSEL.

⟱114 (Tex.Civ.App.) Counsel in argument may state how much plaintiff should recover. —City of Dallas v. Maxwell, 429.
⟱118 (Ky.) Counsel cannot argue to jury against adverse rulings of the court.—Louisville Woolen Mills v. Kindgen, 202.
⟱122 (Ky.) Comment on defendant's failure to call one of physicians appointed to examine plaintiff proper.—Commonwealth Power Ry. & Light Co. v. Vaught, 247.
⟱125(4) (Tex.Civ.App.) Remarks of counsel in argument to jury *held* to inflame jurors' minds against defendant.—Home Life & Accident Co. v. Jordan, 802.
⟱132 (Tex.Civ.App.) Opening statement of plaintiff's counsel informing jury as to effect of finding not reversible error where withdrawn.—City of Dallas v. Maxwell, 429.

VI. TAKING CASE OR QUESTION FROM JURY.

(A) Questions of Law or of Fact in General.

⟱139(1) (Mo.) Demurrer to plaintiff's evidence properly overruled if there is any substantial evidence to support cause of action.—Burton v. Holman, 630.
⟱139(3) (Tex.Civ.App.) Peremptory instruction properly denied where evidence sufficient as to one of two defendants.—Priddy v. Childers, 172.
⟱141 (Tex.Com.App.) Charge submitting undisputed question, properly refused.—Pullman Co. v. Gulf, C. & S. F. Ry. Co., 741.
⟱143 (Tenn.) No direction of verdict where material evidence conflicting.—Hines v. Partridge, 16.
⟱143 (Tex.Civ.App.) In case of disputed facts issue should be submitted to jury.—Young v. Blain, 851.

(B) Demurrer to Evidence.

⟱155 (Mo.App.) Defendant's demurrer to evidence admits truth of plaintiff's evidence for purposes of motion only.—Grams v. Novinger, 265.
⟱156(3) (Mo.) Plaintiff given benefit of legitimate inference on defendant's demurrer to the evidence.—Burton v. Holman, 630.
⟱156(3) (Mo.App.) In passing on a demurrer the evidence should be viewed most favorably to plaintiff.—Hunter v. American Brake Co., 659.

(D) Direction of Verdict.

⟱177 (Ark.) Where each party requested peremptory instruction, the court may decide the issue.—Sanderson v. Marconi, 554.
⟱178 (Tenn.) On motion for directed verdict for defendant, view of evidence most favorable to plaintiff to be taken.—Hines v. Partridge, 10.
⟱181 (Tex.Com.App.) Statute requiring objection to charge before submission to jury not applicable to peremptory instruction.—Harlan v. Acme Sanitary Flooring Co., 348.

VII. INSTRUCTIONS TO JURY.

(A) Province of Court and Jury in General.

⟱186 (Mo.) Instruction *held* properly refused as a comment on a part of evidence.—Burton v. Holman, 630.
⟱191(11) (Mo.App.) Instruction on measure of damages *held* not to assume defendant's negligence.—Hartweg v. Kansas City Rys. Co., 269.
⟱192 (Mo.App.) No error in instruction assuming undisputed fact that defendant's employee was acting within scope of his employment.—Buehler v. Waggener Paint & Glass Co., 283.

⟜194(11) (Tex.Com.App.) Charge on fraudulent representations *held* erroneous as on weight of the evidence.—Waggoner v. Zundelowitz, 721.

⟜194(16) (Mo.App.) Instruction that fact of fall was no evidence of negligence improper.—Walker v. City of St. Joseph, 65.

⟜194(17) (Tex.Com.App.) Court should have left jury free to decide whether motorman exercised requisite care.—Paris Transit Co. v. Fath, 1080.

(B) Necessity and Subject-Matter.

⟜219 (Mo.App.) Instruction need not define meaning of "society, assistance, and domestic services," where evidence indicates their meaning.—Baldwin v. Kansas City Rys. Co., 280.

⟜219 (Mo.App.) Instruction burden of proof on plaintiff by preponderance of evidence erroneous in absence of definition of terms.—Thompson v. Business Men's Acc. Ass'n of America, 1049.

(C) Form, Requisites, and Sufficiency.

⟜228(1) (Mo.) Instruction in alternative *held* erroneous.—Lackey v. United Rys. Co., 956.

⟜228(3) (Mo.App.) Instruction *held* error as giving probable understanding that plaintiff had right to be where he was when struck and injured.—Noah v. L. B. Price Mercantile Co., 300.

⟜233(3) (Mo.App.) Instruction referring to jury to petition for date of plaintiff's injury *held* not error.—Buehler v. Waggener Paint & Glass Co., 283.

⟜235(1) (Ark.) Words emphasizing the fact that the jury is the sole judge of weight of evidence improper.—Texarkana & Ft. Smith Ry. Co. v. Adcock, 866.

⟜240 (Tex.Com.App.) Charge on ordinary care of deceased *held* argumentative.—Missouri, K. & T. Ry. Co. of Texas v. Merchant, 327.

(D) Applicability to Pleadings and Evidence.

⟜251(1) (Mo.App.) Instruction must not be broader than the pleadings.—Forrester v. Walsh Fire Clay Products Co., 668.

⟜251(8) (Mo.) Where particular negligence pleaded, instructions must submit nothing outside of specific charges.—Richardson v. Kansas City Rys. Co., 938.

⟜251(8) (Mo.App.) Instruction should be limited to the defect complained of.—Forrester v. Walsh Fire Clay Products Co., 668.

⟜251(8) (Mo.App.) Instruction on general negligence in failing to stop street car *held* outside pleadings.—Jackels v. Kansas City Rys. Co., 1023.

⟜252(9) (Mo.) Error to submit question whether car could have been stopped in time to avoid hitting pedestrian when no evidence as to when he stepped onto track.—Lackey v. United Rys. Co., 956.

⟜252(9) (Mo.App.) Instruction on contributory negligence *held* contrary to the evidence.—Ruenzi v. Payne, 294.

⟜252(11) (Mo.App.) Instruction *held* broader than evidence in allowing recovery if loose board was placed on runway by foreman or agent.—Forrester v. Walsh Fire Clay Products Co., 668.

⟜253(10) (Mo.App.) Requested instruction on presumption as to suicide properly refused where there was evidence pro and con.—Whiteside v. Court of Honor, 1026.

(E) Requests or Prayers.

⟜255(1) (Tex.Civ.App.) Charge that jurors were exclusive judges of facts must be requested.—Jemison v. Estes, 797.

⟜255(3) (Tex.Civ.App.) Failure to instruct on burden of proof not error, in absence of request therefor.—Holden v. Evans, 146.

⟜256(13) (Mo.App.) More limited instruction, if desired, must be asked for.—Baldwin v. Kansas City Rys. Co., 280.

⟜260(1) Requested instructions already covered properly refused.

—(Ark.) Texarkana & Ft. Smith Ry. Co. v. Adcock, 866;

(Ky.) Frankfort Elevator Coal Co. v. Williamson, 241;

(Mo.) Richardson v. Kansas City Rys. Co., 938.

⟜260(9) (Tex.Civ.App.) Refusal of charge not erroneous where matter covered by general charge.—Elmendorf v. Mulliken, 164.

⟜261 (Tex.Com.App.) Requested instruction not technically correct *held* to require correct instruction.—Graves v. Haynes, 388.

⟜261 (Tex.Com.App.) Special charge properly refused, unless correct in all its parts.—Waggoner v. Zundelowitz, 721.

⟜261 (Tex.Com.App.) No error to refuse a charge in part incorrect.—Pullman Co. v. Gulf, C. & S. F. Ry. Co., 741.

(F) Objections and Exceptions.

⟜278 (Ark.) Specific objection to instruction necessary.—Texarkana & Ft. Smith Ry. Co. v. Adcock, 866.

(G) Construction and Operation.

⟜295(1) (Mo.App.) Instruction must be construed with others.—Neal v. Crowson, 1033.

⟜296(1) (Mo.App.) Omission, in instruction to plaintiff purporting to cover entire case, not cured by defendant's instructions.—Alexander v. Kansas City Rys. Co., 66.

⟜296(2) (Tex.Civ.App.) Instruction on assumed risk *held* not to ignore negligence and contributory negligence, in view of other instructions.—Texas Electric Ry. v. Jones, 823.

⟜296(3) (Mo.App.) Error in instruction not reversible in view of other instructions.—Noah v. L. B. Price Mercantile Co., 300.

⟜296(9) (Mo.App.) Instruction requiring finding plaintiff was on "the roadway" *held* not erroneous in view of other parts of instruction.—Jackson v. Quarry Realty Co., 1063.

IX. VERDICT.

(A) General Verdict.

⟜330(1) (Mo.App.) Single verdict sufficient when causes of action united in one count.—Slack v. Whitney, 1060.

⟜337 (Ky.) Judgment reversed where jury disregards instructions, whether right or wrong.—Krieger v. Standard Printing Co., 27.

(B) Special Interrogatories and Findings.

⟜351(5) (Tex.Civ.App.) Refusal of requested special issue *held* proper, in view of special issue submitted.—Holden v. Evans, 146.

⟜352(1) (Tex.Civ.App.) Special issue of railroad's violation of federal rule as to safety of locomotive wheel *held* proper.—Lancaster v. Allen, 148.

⟜352(1) (Tex.Civ.App.) Special issues *held* not objectionable as invading province of jury.—Priddy v. Childers, 172.

⟜352(4) (Tex.Civ.App.) Issue must be supported by evidence to be submitted.—Jemison v. Estes, 797.

⟜365(1) (Tex.Civ.App.) Verdict must be construed in light of circumstances.—Pickrell v. Imperial Petroleum Co., 412.

Special answer *held* to find value of entire lease not merely of interest in controversy.—Id.

X. TRIAL BY COURT.

(A) Hearing and Determination of Cause.

⟜382 (Mo.) Court sitting without jury may give mandatory instruction only when it could do so were the trial by jury.—Grams v. Novinger, 265.

⟜383 (Mo.) Defendant's demurrer to evidence admits truth of plaintiff's evidence for purposes of motion only.—Grams v. Novinger, 265.

(B). Findings of Fact and Conclusions of Law.

⟜390 (Tex.Civ.App.) Court may refuse to make and file findings and conclusions before entry of judgment, in view of statute.—Wilcox v. Crawford, 1104.

⟜404(1) (Tex.Com.App.) Findings should be given construction which supports judgment.—Elder, Dempster & Co. v. Weld-Neville Cotton Co., 102.

XI. WAIVER AND CORRECTION OF IRREGULARITIES AND ERRORS.

⟜418 (Mo.) Defendants, by presenting own evidence, waived overruling of demurrer to plaintiff's evidence.—Burton v. Holman, 630.

TROVER AND CONVERSION.

II. ACTIONS.

(E) Trial, Judgment, and Review.

⟜66 (Mo.) Embezzlement held question for jury.—Peter Hauptmann Tobacco Co. v. Unverferth, 628.

TRUST DEEDS.

See Mortgages.

TRUSTS.

See Monopolies, ⟜17–21.

I. CREATION, EXISTENCE, AND VALIDITY.

(A) Express Trusts.

⟜13 (Tex.Com.App.) Rule requiring payment of part of consideration for land not applicable in cases of express trust.—Holmes v. Tennant, 313.

⟜58 (Mo.) Donor cannot change effect of deed.—Watson v. Hardwick, 964.

⟜61(3) (Mo.) Trustee held not empowered to convert trust into life estate in beneficiary.—Watson v. Hardwick, 964.

(B) Resulting Trusts.

⟜81(2) (Mo.) Wife, who buys land jointly with husband with request that land be conveyed to them as tenants by the entirety, cannot claim resulting trust.—Larrick v. Heathman, 975.

⟜88 (Mo.) Parol testimony admissible to establish resulting trust in wife's favor, notwithstanding deed taken by husband and wife as tenants by the entirety.—Larrick v. Heathman, 975.

Presumption trust arises from one party paying consideration may be rebutted by testimony as well as by deed.—Id.

⟜89(5) (Mo.) Plaintiff, seeking to establish resulting trust as against face of a deed, had burden of proving trust by strong evidence.—Larrick v. Heathman, 975.

II. CONSTRUCTION AND OPERATION.

(B) Estate or Interest of Trustee and of Cestui Que Trust.

⟜131 (Mo.) Legal title not supported for purpose of transmission alone under statute of uses.—Watson v. Hardwick, 964.

⟜147(1) (Mo.) Beneficiary could not transfer interest.—Watson v. Hardwick, 964.

Held that beneficiary for life could assign rents and profits.—Id.

III. APPOINTMENT, QUALIFICATION, AND TENURE OF TRUSTEE.

⟜167 (Mo.) Court had authority to remove trustee.—Watson v. Hardwick, 964.

V. EXECUTION OF TRUST BY TRUSTEE OR BY COURT.

⟜283(2) (Ky.) Trustees accounting for profits on resale of property purchased from

beneficiaries entitled to discount on purchase-money notes, on distribution of proceeds.—Clay v. Thomas, 512.

Trustees on distribution of proceeds of resale of trust property purchased from beneficiaries may deduct reasonable amount expended for services of employee in caring for land until disposed of.—Id.

Trustees, on distribution of proceeds of resale of trust property purchased from beneficiaries may retain interest on expenses incurred before sale.—Id.

Trustees on distribution of proceeds of resale of trust property cannot deduct for depreciation of property not included in sale.—Id.

Trustees, on distribution among heirs of proceeds of resale of part of trust property, may recover losses by operation of mill, which was not resold.—Id.

Trustees, on distribution of proceeds of resale of trust property purchased from beneficiaries, not entitled to credit for taxes paid on proceeds belonging to other heirs.—Id.

Trustees, on distribution of proceeds of resale of trust property, not entitled to credit for enhanced value of property by reason of general warranty deed executed by them.—Id.

Heirs, by accepting benefits of sale of trust property by trustees, estopped to assert liability of each trustee for entire amount of judgment, contrary to provisions of deed.—Id.

VI. ACCOUNTING AND COMPENSATION OF TRUSTEE.

⟜317 (Ky.) Trustees not entitled to allowance for making sale in addition to that allowed by terms of will.—Clay v. Thomas, 512.

VII. ESTABLISHMENT AND ENFORCEMENT OF TRUST.

(C) Actions.

⟜366(2) (Mo.) Wife's heirs could enforce resulting trust on land purchased with wife's money, if wife herself could have done so.—Larrick v. Heathman, 975.

USURY.

II. PENALTIES AND FORFEITURES.

⟜137 (Tex.Com.App.) Held paid and received by purchase under deed of trust, allowing recovery of penalty.—Farmers' & Merchants' State Bank of Ballinger v. Cameron, 738.

VENDOR AND PURCHASER.

I. REQUISITES AND VALIDITY OF CONTRACT.

⟜18(½) (Tex.Com.App.) Optionee did not acquire title by option contract.—Roberts v. Armstrong, 371.

⟜37(4) (Mo.) Representations inducing purchase of land held statements of fact not expressions of opinion.—Thomas v. Goodrum, 571.

Excessive purchase price may be element of fraud.—Id.

⟜45 (Mo.) Representations as to value held not fraudulent as matter of law.—Thomas v. Goodrum, 571.

II. CONSTRUCTION AND OPERATION OF CONTRACT.

⟜70 (Ark.) Contract by purchaser to bid in land on foreclosure sale held construable to mean he must bid amount due mortgagee.—Battle v. Draper, 869.

IV. PERFORMANCE OF CONTRACT.

(A) Title and Estate of Vendor.

⟜143 (Mo.App.) Purchasers taking possession without receiving abstract held to waive

s being furnished within specified time.—
rams v. Novinger, 265.

V. RIGHTS AND LIABILITIES OF PARTIES.

(A) As to Each Other.

⭫196 (Tex.Com.App.) Owner entitled to
ents and crops until title defeated by exer-
ise of option.—Roberts v. Armstrong, 371.
 Option contract gave optionor right to re-
erve crops and rents.—Id.

(C) Bona Fide Purchasers.

⭫240 (Tex.Civ.App.) Innocent purchase must
)e pleaded.—Kurz v. Soliz, 424.

VI. REMEDIES OF VENDOR.

(A) Lien and Recovery of Land.

⭫257 (Tex.Civ.App.) Lienholder does not acquire title without foreclosure.—Pope v. Witherspoon, 837.
⭫259 (Tex.Com.App.) Vendor *held* not entitled to vendor's lien on other land to
secure payment of third person's notes transferred to vendor in part payment of purchase
price.—Rea v. Luse, 310.
⭫274(1) (Tex.Com.App.) Delivery of vendor's lien note to representative, together with
the release, *held* not negligence on the part of
the holder.—Shaw v. First State Bank of
Abilene, 325.

VII. REMEDIES OF PURCHASER.

(B) Actions for Breach of Contract.

⭫343(1) (Mo.App.) Purchaser entitled to recover for breach of vendor's oral agreement to
plat land so as to give outlet.—Heath v. Beck,
657.
⭫351(8) (Ky.) Purchaser not entitled to
damages for loss of bargain on inability of vendor, who acted in good faith, to convey good
title.—Crenshaw v. Williams, 45.
 Vendor's failure to disclose condition of title
to purchaser *held* not fraud entitling purchaser
to damages for loss of bargain.—Id.

VENUE.

I. NATURE OR SUBJECT OF ACTION.

⭫4 (Ark.) Action for personal injuries is
transitory.—Texarkana & Ft. Smith Ry. Co. v.
Adcock, 866.
⭫7 (Tex.Civ.App.) Proof of plaintiff *held* not
to show case within exceptions to venue statute.—Sinton State Bank v. Tyler Commercial
College, 170.
⭫7 (Tex.Civ.App.) Action for breach of
written contract properly brought in county in
which it was performable.—Landa v. F. S. Ainsa Co., 175.
⭫8 (Tex.Civ.App.) Injury alleged *held* a
"trespass" within statute.—First Nat. Bank v.
Childs, 807.
⭫16½ (Tex.Civ.App.) Cause of action properly joined with another regardless of whether venue was properly laid in county in which
action on other cause of action was properly
brought.—Landa v. F. S. Ainsa Co., 175.
⭫17 (Tex.Com.App.) Statute as to where
suit to enjoin execution shall be brought one
of venue, and so waivable.—Martin v. Kieschnick, 330.
 Claim of privilege not waived by following
general demurrer in the same answer.—Id.
 Claim of privilege waived by invoking action
on general demurrer and acquiescing in action
thereon.—Id.

VERDICT.

See Criminal Law, ⭫872½–881; Trial, ⭫
830-865.

231 S.W.—74

WATERS AND WATER COURSES.

See Drains.

IX. PUBLIC WATER SUPPLY.

(A) Domestic and Municipal Purposes.

⭫200(2) (Mo.) Contract of city with water
company not abrogated by increase of rates
authorized by Public Service Commission.—
City Water Co. v. City of Sedalia, 942.
⭫201 (Ky.) Extension denied consumer under circumstances of hardship to company.—
Mountain Water Co. v. May, 908.
⭫203(12) (Mo.) City's offer to allow water
company to discontinue certain hydrants not
reviewable on appeal, where no action taken
before Public Service Commission.—City Water Co. v. City of Sedalia, 942.
 Question as to effect of increase in rental of
fire hydrants on city's indebtedness not considered where not pleaded.—Id.
 Water company suing for increased rentals
authorized by Public Service Commission need
not prove requirements of law complied with.
—Id.

WEAPONS.

⭫17(3) (Tex.Cr.App.) Evidence defendant
placed pistol against side of witness, and what
he said, admissible.—Dodaro v. State, 394.
⭫17(5) (Tex.Cr.App.) Whether defendant
was a traveler at time of carrying a pistol *held*
for the jury.—Witt v. State, 395.
⭫17(6) (Tex.Cr.App.) Court did not err in
refusing to instruct where issue not raised.—
Dodaro v. State, 394.

WHARVES.

⭫20(1) (Tex.Civ.App.) Removal of wheat by
wharf company to place where destroyed *held*
remote and not proximate cause of loss.—Fort
Worth Elevators Co. v. Keel & Son, 481.
 Wharf company *held* not obligated to raise
tracks above level of flood waters of previous
storms to prevent injury to wheat delivered to
it.—Id.
 Removal of wheat by wharf company to escape floods *held* not actionable negligence.—Id.
⭫20(7) (Tex.Civ.App.) Evidence *held* to
show proximate cause of loss of wheat due to
act of God.—Fort Worth Elevators Co. v. Keel
& Son, 481.
 Evidence sustaining finding that loss from
storm could not have been prevented by defendant.—Id.

WILLS.

See Descent and Distribution; Executors and
Administrators.

II. TESTAMENTARY CAPACITY.

⭫52(1) (Mo.App.) Burden on proponents as
to issue of sanity.—Carroll v. Murphy, 642.

IV. REQUISITES AND VALIDITY.

(F) Mistake, Undue Influence, and Fraud.

⭫153 (Tex.Civ.App.) Advice given by third
party not fraud on part of beneficiary.—Ater
v. Moore, 457.
⭫155(3) (Tex.Civ.App.) Not undue influence for wife to plead with testator.—Ater v.
Moore, 457.
⭫163(2) (Mo.) Undue influence presumed on
showing of confidential relationship between
testatrix and beneficiary.—Burton v. Holman,
630.

(G) Revocation and Revival.

⭫167 (Tex.Civ.App.) Not revoked by mere
expression of desire on part of testator.—Ater
v. Moore, 457.
⭫177 (Tex.Civ.App.) Not changed by expression of desire and unintentional deception.
—Ater v. Moore, 457.

V. PROBATE, ESTABLISHMENT, AND ANNULMENT.

(G) Petitions, Objections, and Pleadings.

☞277 (Tex.Civ.App.) Facts to be pleaded in will contest.—Ater v. Moore, 457.

(I) Hearing or Trial.

☞324(2) (Mo.App.) Issue of insanity for jury on substantial evidence.—Carroll v. Murphy, 642.

Evidence *held* to make prima facie case of testatrix's mental capacity.—Id.

☞324(3) (Mo.) Whether will making testatrix's physician and confidential adviser a beneficiary was procured by undue influence *held* for jury.—Burton v. Holman, 630.

☞327 (Mo.App.) Courts may peremptorily instruct on lack of capacity if evidence permits.—Carroll v. Murphy, 642.

(K) Review.

☞384 (Tex.Civ.App.) Sustaining of an exception to part of answer *held* harmless if error.—Ater v. Moore, 457.

☞400 (Mo.) Instructions *held* not ground for reversal as against contention that jury might have been misled into considering mental capacity an issue.—Burton v. Holman, 630.

VI. CONSTRUCTION.

(A) General Rules.

☞439 (Ky.) Intention controls other rules of construction.—Hill v. Bridges, 30.

☞439 (Tex.Com.App.) Intention of testator must control.—Haupt v. Michaelis, 706.

☞439 (Tex.Com.App.) Cardinal rule of construction is to ascertain intention.—Gilliam v. Mahon, 712.

☞439 (Tex.Civ.App.) Intention not to be conjectured.—Barmore v. Darragh, 472.

☞441 (Tex.Com.App.) Law at time of execution of grandchild *held* precatory.—Barmore v. Darragh, 472.

☞447 (Tex.Com.App.) Construction consistent with lawful intention adopted.—Barmore v. Darragh, 472.

☞457 (Tex.Civ.App.) To effectuate intention, words may be given other than technical import.—Barmore v. Darragh, 472.

☞460 (Tex.Com.App.) Words or sentences may be transposed to show testator's intent.—Haupt v. Michaelis, 706.

☞467 (Tex.Civ.App.) Direction for education of grandchild *held* precatory.—Barmore v. Darragh, 472.

☞470 (Tex.Com.App.) Intent of testator must be arrived at by considering entire will.—Haupt v. Michaelis, 706.

☞470 (Tex.Civ.App.) All provisions looked to in ascertaining testator's intention.—Barmore v. Darragh, 472.

☞488 (Tex.Com.App.) Parol evidence inadmissible where will is free from doubt.—Haupt v. Michaelis, 706.

Evidence of surrounding circumstances not admissible to contradict expressed intention.—Id.

Extrinsic evidence admissible where intent of testator ambiguous.—Id.

(B) Designation of Devisees, and Legatees and Their Respective Shares.

☞495 (Tex.Civ.App.) Clause *held* to give remainder to children of devisee of life estate.—Barmore v. Darragh, 472.

☞506(4) (Tex.Civ.App.) "Heirs of his body"; "issue of his own body"; "inherit"; "take"; defined.—Barmore v. Darragh, 472.

☞535 (Tex.Com.App.) Holographic will construed to exclude one of testator's children.—Haupt v. Michaelis, 706.

(C) Survivorship, Representation, and Substitution.

☞538 (Tex.Civ.App.) Devise over on death of another is presumed to refer to death before testator's death.—Barmore v. Darragh, 472.

☞545(3) (Tex.Civ.App.) Devise over on devisee's death effective only on devisee's predeceasing testator.—Barmore v. Darragh, 472.

Devise *held* to give life estate; "in case"; "without heirs of his body."—Id.

☞545(4) (Ky.) Limitation over on death of child *held* to relate to death in the lifetime of the life tenant.—Hill v. Bridges, 30.

(E) Nature of Estates and Interests Created.

☞601(1) (Tex.Com.App.) Provision giving fee to wife *held* not cut down by subsequent ambiguous provision.—Gilliam v. Mahon, 712.

☞601(1) (Tex.Civ.App.) Statute does not prohibit subsequent provision from limiting absolute estate previously given.—Barmore v. Darragh, 472.

Clause following absolute devise *held* to give devisee life estate with remainder to surviving children.—Id.

☞608(1) (Tex.Civ.App.) Rule in Shelley's Case *held* inapplicable.—Barmore v. Darragh, 472.

(G) Conditions and Restrictions.

☞649 (Tex.Civ.App.) Clause restricting giving away of estate received under will *held* void.—Barmore v. Darragh, 472.

☞658 (Tex.Civ.App.) Devise *held* to vest fee on condition subsequent.—Adams v. Henry, 152.

☞665 (Tex.Civ.App.) Right of devisee not affected by his statement before testatrix's death nor by subsequent belief of one entitled to benefit under condition of will.—Adams v. Henry, 152.

Word "refuse" in condition of will cannot be construed as "fail."—Id.

WITNESSES.

See Depositions; Evidence.

I. ATTENDANCE, PRODUCTION OF DOCUMENTS, AND COMPENSATION.

☞16 (Mo.) Circuit court had inherent power to issue subpœna duces tecum to secretary of board of complaint of city.—State ex rel. Tune v. Falkenhainer, 257.

II. COMPETENCY.

(A) Capacity and Qualifications in General.

☞52(1, 2) (Mo.App.) Husband competent witness in wife's lawsuit only where made so by statute.—Gottschall v. Geiger, 87.

☞53(4) (Tex.Cr.App.) Where defendant proved by his wife that she occupied room with deceased at hotel, it was proper for state to develop from her that no criminal conduct took place.—Boaz v. State, 790.

☞56(3) (Mo.App.) Husband's testimony *held* incompetent in wife's action against physician for malpractice.—Gottschall v. Geiger, 87.

☞60(2) (Ky.) Abandonment is matter of proof, and wife is not competent witness.—Shockey v. Shockey, 508.

☞61(1) (Ky.) Wife may testify to abortion on her.—Commonwealth v. Allen, 41.

(C) Testimony of Parties or Persons Interested, for or against Representatives, Survivors, or Successors in Title or Interest of Persons Deceased or Incompetent.

☞140(19) (Ky.) Conveyance *held* quitclaim deed so that grantor had no interest which disqualified him as witness.—Riddle v. Jones, 503.

☞141 (Mo.) Plaintiff's attorney *held* properly refused permission to testify as custodian of deeds executed by decedent.—Tiede v. Tiede, 950.

☞150(2) (Tex.Civ.App.) Fraudulent declarations of lessee since deceased *held* admissible in action against assignees to cancel lease.—Smith v. Fleming, 136.

⊂⇒168 (Mo.) Survivor is competent to contradict alleged admissions made after death of original party.—Mason v. Mason, 971.

⊂⇒177 (Mo.) Where plaintiff testifies to admission, defendant may testify in opposition.—Mason v. Mason, 971.

(D) Confidential Relations and Privileged Communications.

⊂⇒202 (Mo.) Attorney is competent to testify to direction for delivery of deed.—Mason v. Mason, 971.

⊂⇒203 (Ark.) Prosecuting attorney can testify to communications made to him officially.—Fisher v. State, 181.

⊂⇒219(3) (Mo.App.) Privilege of attorney removed by client's testimony as to transaction.—Whiteside v. Court of Honor, 1026.

III. EXAMINATION.
(A) Taking Testimony in General.

⊂⇒240(4) (Tex.Cr.App.) Question *held* not leading.—Rainey v. State, 118.

⊂⇒252 (Tex.Civ.App.) Plaster cast of wheel *held* sufficiently identified to be used as basis of measurement.—Lancaster v. Allen, 148.

⊂⇒255(7) (Tex.Civ.App.) Testimony from records made by witness was admissible, though records themselves were exhibits and witness had no independent recollection of facts.—Payne v. White House Lumber Co., 417.

Testimony from original sheets made by witness admissible, though book in which same kept not offered in evidence.—Id.

Testimony as to weight of cars of coal weighed and entered in books by witness at time of unloading admissible, where witness' superior testified as to correctness of entries.—Id.

(B) Cross-Examination and Re-examination.

⊂⇒269(1) (Mo.) Cross-examination of defendant relative to same matters inquired about in chief *held* not error.—State v. Howard, 255.

⊂⇒270(3) (Mo.) Facts improperly brought out on cross-examination may be rebutted.—State v. Ritter, 606.

⊂⇒274(2) (Mo.) Character witness may be questioned as to rumors concerning defendant's misconduct.—State v. McDonald, 927.

⊂⇒277(2) (Mo.) Cross-examination of defendant showing for what length of time he had carried pistol, proper.—State v. Likens, 578.

⊂⇒277(4) (Mo.) Cross-examination of defendant charged with murder not erroneous.—State v. Likens, 577.

⊂⇒278 (Mo.) Exclusion of answers by witness to question, whether she expected in making statement not to be prosecuted, *held* not error.—State v. Ritter, 606.

IV. CREDIBILITY, IMPEACHMENT, CONTRADICTION, AND CORROBORATION.
(B) Character and Conduct of Witness.

⊂⇒337(2) (Mo.) Defendant may be impeached by evidence as to his veracity and morality, but not as to his character as a quarrelsome citizen.—State v. Baird, 625.

⊂⇒345(2) (Tex.Civ.App.) Witness cannot be impeached by inquiry as to particular crimes.—Young v. Blain, 851.

⊂⇒350 (Mo.) Defendant subject to cross-examination to prove prior convictions.—State v. McBride, 592.

⊂⇒360 (Mo.) State entitled to rebut showing that witness kept house of ill fame.—State v. Ritter, 606.

Evidence of good character inadmissible.—Id.

(C) Interest and Bias of Witness.

⊂⇒370(1) (Mo.) Evidence of bias of witness against codefendant inadmissible where severance was granted.—State v. Ritter, 606.

(D) Inconsistent Statements by Witness.

⊂⇒383 (Tex.Cr.App.) Cannot be impeached as to an immaterial matter.—Theriot v. State, 777.

WORDS AND PHRASES.

"Abandonment."—Shockey v. Shockey (Ky.) 568.

"Abstract."—Poshek v. Marceline Coal & Mining Co. (Mo. App.) 70.

"Accomplice."—Chandler v. State (Tex. Cr. App.) 106, 107, 108.

"Alter or modify the plans and specifications."—Southern Surety Co. v. Nalle & Co. (Tex. Civ. App.) 402.

"Appointment."—Town of Nortonville v. Woodward (Ky.) 224.

"As soon as possible."—Guess v. Russell Bros. Clothing Co. (Mo. App.) 1015.

"Bill of review."—Satterwhite v. State (Ark.) 886.

"Compelled."—Texas Electric Ry. v. Jones (Tex. Civ. App.) 823.

"Condition."—Eastham v. Eastham (Ky.) 221.

"Confined to bed."—North v. National Life & Accident Ins. Co. of Nashville, Tenn. (Mo. App.) 665.

"Consortium."—Baldwin v. Kansas City Rys. Co. (Mo. App.) 280.

"Counterclaim."—Slack v. Whitney (Mo. App.) 1060.

"Course of employment."—Western Indemnity Co. v. Lenard (Tex. Civ. App.) 1101.

"Discovered peril."—Baker v. Shafter (Tex. Com. App.) 349.

"Discretion."—Board of Permanent Road Com'rs of Hunt County v. Johnson (Tex. Civ. App.) 859.

"Doing business."—Arkansas Anthracite Coal Co. v. State (Ark.) 184.

"Due course."—Thomas v. Goodrum (Mo.) 571.

"Election."—Town of Nortonville v. Woodward (Ky.) 224; State ex rel. Feinstein v. Hartmann (Mo.) 982.

"Employé."—U. S. Fidelity & Guaranty Co. of Baltimore, Md., v. Lowry (Tex. Civ. App.) 818.

"Erection of buildings."—Harrington v. Hopkins (Mo.) 263.

"Escrow."—Simpson v. Green (Tex. Com. App.) 375; Stonewall v. McGown (Tex. Civ. App.) 850.

"Exception."—Arnett v. Elkhorn Coal Corporation (Ky.) 219.

"Fall."—Howell v. Lamberson (Ark.) 872.

"Final judgment."—Taylor v. Masterson (Tex. Civ. App.) 856.

"Fraud."—Guess v. Russell Bros. Clothing Co. (Mo. App.) 1015.

"Good cause."—Denton v. Kansas City Life Ins. Co. (Tex. Civ. App.) 436.

"Heirs of his body."—Barmore v. Darragh (Tex. Civ. App.) 472.

"Holder in due course."—Swift & Co. v. McFarland (Mo. App.) 65; Ensign v. Crandall (Mo. App.) 675.

"In case."—Barmore v. Darragh (Tex. Civ. App.) 472.

"Independent contractor."—U. S. Fidelity & Guaranty Co. of Baltimore, Md., v. Lowry (Tex. Civ. App.) 818.

"Inherit."—Barmore v. Darragh (Tex. Civ. App.) 472.

"Issue of his own body."—Barmore v. Darragh (Tex. Civ. App.) 472.

"Joint tort-feasors."—Anderson v. Smith (Tex. Civ. App.) 142.

"Just cause or excuse."—State v. Caldwell (Mo.) 613.

"Just compensation."—Gregg v. Sanders (Ark.) 190.

"Land equitably owned."—Kenedy Pasture Co. v. State (Tex.) 683.

"Limitation."—Eastham v. Eastham (Ky.) 221.

"Maintain."—O'Connell v. Kansas City (Mo. App.) 1040.

"Malice."—State v. Caldwell (Mo.) 613.

"Natural and probable result."—San Antonio & A. P. Ry. Co. v. Behne (Tex. Com. App.) 354.

"Neglected child."—Gully v. Gully (Tex.) 97.

"Obliged."—Texas Electric Ry. v. Jones (Tex. Civ. App.) 823.

"Omit to advise."—Howell v. Lamberson (Ark.) 872.

"Owner."—Fleischman v. State (Tex. Cr. App.) 397.

"Paramount title."—Isaacs v. Maupin (Ky.) 49.

"Pension."—Hawkins v. Randolph (Ark.) 556.

"Perjury."—Thomas v. State (Ark.) 200.

"Purely public charity."—Concho Camp, No. 66, W. O. W., v. City of San Angelo (Tex. Civ. App.) 1106.

"Renew."—Kozy Theater Co. v. Love (Ky.) 249.

"Severable contract."—State ex rel. Dolman v. Dickey (Mo.) 581.

"Society, assistance, and domestic services."—Baldwin v. Kansas City Rys. Co. (Mo. App.) 280.

"Subornation of perjury."—Thomas v. State (Ark.) 200.

"Subsequent mortgagees in good faith."—First Nat. Bank v. Todd (Tex. Com. App.) 322.

"Suitable waiting room."—Commonwealth v. Louisville & N. R. Co. (Ky.) 236.

"Superior title."—Isaacs v. Maupin (Ky.) 49.

"Take."—Barmore v. Darragh (Tex. Civ. App.) 472.

"The."—Jackson v. Quarry Realty Co. (Mo. App.) 1063.

"Titled land."—Kenedy Pasture Co. v. State (Tex.) 683.

"Transaction."—Slack v. Whitney (Mo. App.) 1060.

"Trespass."—First Nat. Bank v. Childs (Tex. Civ. App.) 807.

"Without heirs of his body."—Barmore v. Darragh (Tex. Civ. App.) 472.

WORK AND LABOR.

⛛13 (Mo.App.) Plaintiff suing upon quantum meruit bound by terms of special contract.—Ruemmeli-Dawley Mfg. Co. v. May Department Stores Co., 1031.

⛛27(4) (Mo.App.) Defendant *held* entitled to prove that extras sued for were not authorized in writing.—Ruemmeli-Dawley Mfg. Co. v. May Department Stores Co., 1031.

WORKMEN'S COMPENSATION ACTS.

See Master and Servant, ⛛348–418.

WRIT OF ERROR.

See Appeal and Error.

WRITS.

See Garnishment; Habeas Corpus; Injunction; Prohibition; Quo Warranto; Replevin.

TABLES OF SOUTHWESTERN CASES

IN

STATE REPORTS

VOL. 191, KENTUCKY REPORTS

Ky. Rep.	S.W. Rep.		Ky. Rep.	S.W. Rep.		Ky. Rep.	S.W. Rep.		Ky. Rep.	S.W. Rep.		Ky. Rep.	S.W. Rep.		Ky. Rep.	S.W. Rep.		Ky. Rep.	S.W. Rep.	
Pg.	Vol.	Pg.	Pg.	Vol.	Pg.	Pg.	Vol.	Pg.	Pg.	Vol.	Pg.	Pg.	Vol.	Pg.	Pg.	Vol.	Pg.	Pg.	Vol.	Pg.
1	229	51	103	229	112	226	229	1033	331	230	307	465	230	934	595	231	249	717	231	502
9	228	1027	106	229	135	231	230	37	337	230	300	470	230	959	605	231	244	730	231	229
10	228	1028	114	229	80	234	229	1043	346	230	304	477	230	910	612	231	52	730	231	234
12	228	1032	121	229	128	238	230	50	351	230	942	485	231	31	617	231	221	734	231	532
17	228	1028	124	229	379	242	229	1029	364	230	293	498	230	924	622	231	29	741	231	506
20	228	1035	128	229	372	246	229	1086	368	230	295	503	230	921	624	231	41	744	231	539
22	228	1030	133	229	99	253	229	1041	370	230	542	508	230	929	634	231	236	749	231	509
28	229	80	138	229	122	256	229	1021	376	230	532	515	230	932	639	231	30	755	231	532
32	228	1025	147	229	84	258	229	1089	380	230	296	518	230	917	641	231	247	763	231	502
37	228	1036	157	229	114	263	230	57	385	230	540	521	230	947	647	231	35	769	231	536
42	229	79	162	229	127	270	230	38	389	230	539	527	231	49	661	231	208	782	231	498
45	229	130	165	229	94	276	230	61	392	230	963	533	230	918	657	231	234	789	231	915
58	229	74	175	229	75	284	230	706	401	230	529	538	230	960	661	231	221	797	231	908
61	229	130	183	229	88	288	230	51	408	231	37	543	231	23	668	231	215	817	232	40
67	229	48	186	229	50	290	230	291	416	230	534	547	231	25	669	231	213	825	231	519
71	229	145	188	229	72	295	230	52	418	230	535	552	231	27	674	231	241	831	231	512
72	229	109	191	229	369	299	230	41	428	230	536	557	231	22	681	231	217	833	231	497
75	229	132	198	229	1032	306	230	56	428	230	904	569	231	45	685	231	512	837	231	538
81	229	109	202	229	377	309	230	64	433	230	545	568	231	302	699	231	226	839	231	508
82	229	82	207	220	374	312	230	43	437	230	914	581	230	961	706	231	219	841	231	535
85	229	101	213	229	707	316	230	310	443	230	936	585	231	54	710	231	238	846	232	63
92	229	104	219	230	44	325	230	293	456	230	906									

VOL. 191, KENTUCKY REPORTS

VOL. 282, MISSOURI REPORTS

Mo. Rep. Pg.	S. W. Rep. Vol.	Mo. Rep. Pg.	S. W. Rep. Vol.	Mo. Rep. Pg.	S. W. Rep. Vol.	Mo. Rep. Pg.	S. W. Rep. Vol.	Mo. Rep. Pg.	S. W. Rep. Vol.	Mo. Rep. Pg.	S. W. Rep. Vol.	Mo. Rep. Pg.	S. W. Rep. Vol.
1	220 1	108	221 31	204	220 950	412	221 1066	463	222 462	564	222 443	660	222 783
19	221 34	118	221 1	213	221 721	435	221 708	471	222 403	580	222 650	663	222 763
36	220 959	133	220 920	236	221 712	436	222 766	497	222 412	599	222 755	670	222 788
51	221 10	163	220 839	261	221 728	438	222 389	521	222 795	610	222 1018	672	222 427
75	220 675	180	221 51	292	221 70	446	221 705	534	222 143	632	222 783	680	232 442
82	221 353	198	221 358	304	221 95	458	222 384	559	222 114	649	222 759	685	223 45
101	220 880												

VOL. 282, MISSOURI REPORTS

VOL. 205, MISSOURI APPEAL REPORTS

VOL. 205, MISSOURI APPEAL REPORTS

9 780260 818652